P9-DOG-217

The Design Encyclopedia

Mel Byars

The Design Encyclopedia

Foreword by Terence Riley
The Museum of Modern Art

Laurence King Publishing, London
The Museum of Modern Art, New York

Copublished in 2004 by Laurence King Publishing Ltd
71 Great Russell Street
London WC1B 3BP
United Kingdom
Tel: + 44 20 7430 8850
Fax: + 44 20 7430 8880
e-mail: enquiries@laurenceking.co.uk
www.laurenceking.co.uk

And by The Museum of Modern Art, New York
11 W. 53rd Street, New York, New York 10019
www.moma.org

Laurence King Publishing Limited and MoMA would like to thank the institutions and individuals who have kindly provided photographic materials for use in this book as identified in the captions. Every effort has been made to contact copyright holders, but should there be any errors or omissions we would be pleased to insert the appropriate acknowledgment in any subsequent edition of this publication.

ISBN 0 87070 012 x

Design concept by Angus Hyland
Designed by Mel Byars
Cover designed by Amanda Washburn

Printed in Hong Kong

Foreword: The User's Guide to the Universe of Design—A Grand Obsession

The history of encyclopedias, as we know them, really begins in the 18th century with the 1751–72 *Encyclopédie, ou Dictionnaire raisonné des sciences, des arts et des métiers, par une société de gens de lettres* (systematic encyclopedia or dictionary of the sciences, arts, and trades, by a group of writers), published under Denis Diderot's direction. While the term 'encyclopedia' was derived from a pre-existing Greek phrase meaning 'general education,' Diderot's 28-volume treatise on human affairs was unprecedented. In the words of the historian John H. Lienhard, 'The *Dictionnaire*, as it was called, laid bare the workings of the known world in a way no one had ever tried to do... [It] nurtured revolution both by including the trades along with the arts and sciences, and by recognizing the intimate link between technology and culture.'

Diderot's desire to make the knowledge of the world accessible to all was indeed a bold step. Even so, the mid-18th century might have been the last point in time when it might be imagined that it was possible to classify the entirety of science, the arts and technology. The coming Industrial Revolution would make the *Encyclopédie*, despite Diderot's intentions, a lavish and irreplaceable look backward on a bygone world.

The fate of Diderot's attempt to capture all of human knowledge in print prefigures Marshall McLuhan's observation: 'We look at the past through a rear-view mirror. We march backwards into the future.' Yet, in McLuhan's view of the world, if encyclopedias can only fully capture the past like a rearview mirror, it begs the question: What would it be like to drive without one? Indeed, since Diderot's time, encyclopedists have grappled with this conundrum and undertaken their works with the full and somewhat heroic awareness that they will never be complete but are projects in constant stages of informational change.

Mel Byars's *The Encyclopedia of Design*, like Diderot's *Encyclopédie*, began as a project to provide the information that forges the essential links between technology and culture to whoever seeks it. Even so, it engages a vast scale of design conception and production that has operated on an unprecedented scale over the last 130 years, in ways that Diderot could not have imagined. It attempts to document fully the leading as well as the less-well-known protagonists of an era that had hoped to leave history behind.

A journalist and an anthropologist by training and a former collector of modern design by avocation, Byars naturally brought a sense of rigor to his research and writing on design topics. What was not available to him or anyone else, however, was a single reference volume on modern design. Existing compendia did not satisfy his criteria for research: 'I wanted to bring a standard of scholarship to the discipline of design that has already been established for fine art. I was being continuously disappointed by books—particularly pre-1970s publications—that identified the dates of objects as being of the "1950s," for example, instead of specifically "1958," or "mid-1920s" instead of "1924."'

Byars began working on the project in 1989. And, after devoting some hours to it—between four and 20 a day over a four-year period, he recalls—the first edition was published by Laurence King in 1994.

Yet, it was not Byars's academic credentials or his expertise in the field that ultimately herded the book into print. He recollects: 'Regardless of what I did or did not know about the whole history of the world of design (more of the latter than the former, I admit), it was probably my obsessive nature that brought the book to completion. Initially, I was afraid that I might abandon the project. Some colleagues warned me that it would become a monster and consume me. However, my profound interest in design, which I ponder continuously, fueled the tome's completion as the first edition. For the second edition, far more difficult than the first, I was merely naive in the beginning, like an innocent child.'

Now, Diderot had the luxury of believing he could describe the entire universe, while Byars knew from the outset it would be difficult enough to describe even the particular galaxy known as Design. How to even begin, how to set the contours of this corner of the cosmos? Byars's parameters look something like this: Originally, his intention was to use the year 1900 as a place to begin and interpose functionality as a turning point twixt the traditional notion of the decorative arts and the modern conception of design. Realizing that certain key figures would be omitted by this formula—William Morris, for example, who died in 1896—Byars gradually let his topic define itself: 'The encyclopedia begins more or less with the pursuit of Functionalism, Rationalism, modernism, the Industrial Revolution, a shift from country to city life, socialism, a new way of looking at living and wanting to live, and myriad other factors and new ideas.'

While endlessly arguable, the principal outline of the book was nuanced by further judgments. Architects are mentioned, but principally those whose work has embraced the environment, that is, not just structures but interiors and objects. While the inclusion of fashion and/or graphics might seem to some logical—especially graphics—Byars felt it was more important to retain the goal of a single volume. Reflecting a peculiar mix of objectivity and subjectivity, which such projects entail, Byars also made a conscious decision to limit the size of the entries of the best-known designers—especially those whose lives and work have been commonly documented elsewhere. This was done so that as much space as possible could be retained for those designers whose lives and work are not well known and for whom few other reference books exist.

While he originally did not anticipate a second edition, Byars came to understand what physicists know: The universe is constantly expanding. The longstanding relationship of the publisher Laurence King with Michael Maegraith, MoMA's publisher, complemented Byars's connections with MoMA's Department of Architecture and Design. MoMA Curator Paola Antonelli had actually done some research for the original *Encyclopedia* before she joined the museum, and Harriet Bee, MoMA's Editorial Director, frequently turned to Byars for expert editing and reviews of design topics. (For example, an essay I wrote with Ed Eigen on MoMA's Good Design program benefited enormously from Byars's expertise.)

Close readers will note some changes in this new edition. Unsurprisingly, it is larger—832 versus 612 pages—even though the type size is slightly smaller in the new edition. The first edition had 100 black-and-white images; the current edition has 700 images in color. Two-thirds of them come from MoMA's recent project to document extensively its collection in a high-resolution digital format.

There are also a number of changes in content as well. All the references to jewelry designers and firms were deleted to keep the book to one volume, even as significant automobile designers were added (reflecting MoMA's longtime interest in and expanding collection of automotive design). The previously mentioned mix of the objective and the subjective came into play as well. In Byars's words: 'I deleted what I consider to be not particularly important entries in the first edition, even though "important" is problematic and personal. And I expanded many of the original undernourished entries as well as I could, calling on information, some obscure or elusive, which I was able to discover.'

Readers familiar with the first edition will also note a change in the 'style.' Every publishing house develops, over the years, a distinctive voice. The current volume reflects a hybrid voice of the museum and the publisher, orchestrated by the editorial staff at MoMA with the collaboration of Robert Shore and Nell Webb at Laurence King Publishing. It is intended to be lighter and easier to read. And to make a last reference to the objective/subjective: MoMA's curatorial staff (Paola Antonelli, Peter Reed, Bevin Cline, Tina di Carlo, Christian Larsen, and I) reviewed endless entries and provided additional information and editorial comment. Chrisy Ledakis also worked closely with Byars on the unexpectedly subjective art of dating design objects. (For example, the date of a design and that of its production are often different.)

In addition to our personal and professional connections, The Museum of Modern Art's interest in participating in Byars's work-in-progress is an obvious one. Founded 75 years ago this year, the museum's breadth of interest in architecture, product design, graphics, typography, and fabrics is well matched by the scope of this publication. In 1929, no museum was systematically collecting or exhibiting the work of the architects and designers represented here, and, consequently, the sources of information about their production are few and, even less so, attempt to present the scholar with a single-volume resource for essential information. Even the museum's own archives—including the archives of the designers themselves—yield less complete information than is required by scholars today. In its early years before World War II, MoMA was, like the architects and designers whose work it exhibited, more focused on the modern utopia, which was believed to be in the making, than centered on providing historians with the evidence of its production.

While its founding mission was to promote contemporary architecture and design, The Museum of Modern Art has found that, after 75 years, it has unavoidably acquired an additional mission: to provide a rearview mirror on modernism's past. Even though this new role will not supplant the museum's restless interest in the contemporary world, it is not nostalgic to think that interest in the 20th century will only grow in the 21st. Like the influence the Renaissance exerted over the 16th century and beyond, the 20th century remains, in so many aspects, the headwaters of architecture and design today.

Even as it documents past achievements, *The Design Encyclopedia* also contains valuable knowledge for the creation of contemporary culture. In this sense, it is an essential tool for thoughtfully moving forward and a rearview mirror on what Lewis Mumford called 'the usable past.'

Terence Riley
The Philip Johnson Chief Curator
Department of Architecture and Design
The Museum of Modern Art
New York

Introduction

Fine-art history has existed as a scholarly discipline for over two centuries. As a result, there is a well-established canon of major artists and movements, and there are innumerable sources for almost any kind of information you might wish to know about them. Design history, by way of contrast, is a recent academic endeavor, and published works on design are far less comprehensive and precise in their coverage.

The Design Encyclopedia attempts pay the same acute attention to design that fine-art history publications have to their subject matter. That is, the dates, titles, and other information here are as full, precise, and accurate as possible. The entries cover a period of time from the last third of the 19th century to the present, concerning the design of furniture, lighting, ceramics, glassware, metalware, fabrics, objects in a range of other materials, and mechanical, electrical, and electronic appliances, as well as automobiles, some inventions, and toys.

Even though this book is about design, the use of the word 'design' is problematic, especially in English. 'Design' has come to have both abstract and concrete meanings. However, the context here is a concrete, specific one: the design of an object that has a function. This general definition separates design from fine art. The arguable distinction is not always absolute, and there are gray areas where craft and the decorative arts merge with industrial design.

There are separate entries in the book for these categories of people, groups, institutions, and adjunct subjects:

- designers and craftspeople
- design studios, consortiums, and partnerships
- noteworthy manufacturers or editors of products
- significant historical periods and styles
- materials

There are also entries for major automobile designers and entrepreneurs, though not for individual automobile manufacturers. To qualify for inclusion, architects must have been active, to some degree, in design as a distinct practice. Graphic, fashion, and jewelry designers are not given space here, unless, like architects, their work has included industrial design or similar. All of the excluded categories of designers have been well documented in other specialized publications.

Th entries are self-contained, and training information, bibliographies, exhibition participation, and prize receipts accompany each separate entry. As such, there are no back-of-the-book general lists and appendices. A kind of 'index' is provided by cross-references at the ends of some entries or by one-line entries, such as 'Atelier Martine > See Poiret, Paul.'

The information is an amalgamation of data gathered from a vast number of sources, as the bibliographies reveal. While Internet sites proved valuable, some of them, which are listed in the bibliographies, may unfortunately disappear in time. This will not occur, of course, with the hardcopy publications cited. In any entry for which there is no bibliography, the information for the entry may have been acquired directly from a designer or manufacturer.

The varying lengths of the entries do not imply significance. The information to provide longer entries, in some instances, was not available within the time constraints of the volume's preparation. And the absence of a designer's year of birth or death means that the date was unobtainable.

Proper names with prepositions or articles have been alphabetized under the first letter of that preposition or article. As such, the entries for Georges de Feure can be found in 'D' under 'de Feure,' for Theo van Doesburg in 'V' under 'van Doesburg,' etc. The exception to this is 'The,' where it prefixes the name of a firm or an institution in English. Thus, the entry for The Hall China Company can be found in 'H' under 'Hall China Company, The.' However, it is best to look for an entry under the preposition and, if absent, under the family name, or vice versa.

In the captions—'Vase. 1995,' for example—the date given is the date of the design as we know it. If there is another date in parentheses following the name of the manufacturer, this is the date, also as known, of the manufacture of a particular example in the Permanent Collection of The Museum of Modern Art. This date may also mean that the object was designed before manufacture began.

Concerning those who contributed to the *Encyclopedia*'s realization, Steven Kroeter provided the initial impetus, and Michael Maegraith and Terence Riley of The Museum of Modern Art and Laurence King of Laurence King Publishing subsequently embraced the project.

An undertaking of this magnitude can only be brought to fruition with a great deal of expert editorial assistance. Therefore, those who helped must be acknowledged and include Harriet Bee and Matilde McQuaid of The Museum of Modern Art, and Jo Lightfoot, Robert Shore, and Nell Webb of Laurence King Publishing.

The specialists who assisted with the verification and/or the provision of information were Cinzia Anguissola d'Altoé, Brice d'Antras, Britta Bommert and the Galerie Ulrich Fiedler in Cologne, Guillemette Delaporte, Leena Ervamaa, Andrea Jóhannsdóttir, Milena Lamarová, Nina Lobanov-Rostovsky, Mikko Mansikka, Elisenda Rasero i Rebull and the Barcelona Centre de Disseny (BCD); Stefania Riccini, Mike Roemer, Jan Romsaas, and Alice Unander-Scharin. There are also those at The Museum of Modern Art, whom Terence Riley cites in his Introduction. And many others provided a range of information—from a birth or death year to an appreciable amount of data. I offer my sincerest thanks to all.

Not to be forgotten are the seven advisors of the first edition of the *Encyclopedia*: Arlette Barré-Despond, Stuart Durant, Milena Lamarová, David Revere McFadden, Gillian Naylor, Penny Sparke, and Josef Straßer. And Professor Durant was also an instigator of the first edition.

The *Encyclopedia* contains 700 full-color images, most of which are drawn from the collection of The Museum of Modern Art. The others were generously donated by Askan Quittenbaum of the Quittenbaum Kunstauktionen in Munich and Hamburg. Those not credited in the captions were provided by the designers or the manufacturers.

The book was prepared by me on premises in Paris generously provided by the baron and baronne Kirgener de Planta.

Responsibility for inclusions, exclusions, errors, and oversights is mine alone and not that of any others who made direct or indirect contributions.

Mel Byars
Paris

A

AEG: Peter Behrens. Fan (no. GB1) (detail). c. 1908. MoMA.

Aalto, Aino (b. Aino Marsio 1894–1949)

Finnish architect and designer; active Finland; wife of Alvar Aalto.

Training Teknillinen korkeakoulu, Helsinki.
Biography 1924, Aino Marsio worked in the office of Alvar Aalto before they were married; collaborated with him and ran the drawing office until her death. At first, she experimented on bentwood furniture by boiling pieces of birch in a saucepan in the rear of a local furniture store. On her own, she also designed interiors and glassware, including the 1932 Bölgeblick water set (pitcher and drinking glasses), the oldest design still in production at today's iittala oy ab (now written in lowercase), produced 1933–50s by Karhula-Iittala and revived in the 1970s. 1935 with Alvar Aalto, Nils-Gustaf Hahl, and Maire Gullichsen, she founded Artek for direct sales of Alvar's designs in Finland and elsewhere. Aino and Hahl ran the business together, until Hahn died in World War II. From that time, Aino was assisted by interior designer Maija Heikinheimo. The Artek-affiliated firm Artek-Pascoe operated a shop in New York and distributed Aalto furniture in the US.
Exhibitions/citations Second prize (Bölgeblick water set), 1932 design competition, sponsored by Karhula-Iittala glassworks; gold medal, 1936 (6th) Triennale di Milano. With Alvar, designed the Aalto Flower four-piece vase for exhibition at 1939–40 *New York World's Fair: The World of Tomorrow*. The Aaltos' glassware was the subject of a 1988 exhibition, Finland (catalog below).
Bibliography Cat., David Revere McFadden (ed.), *Scandinavian Modern Design 1880–1980*, New York: Abrams, 1982. *Villa Mairea, 1937–1939, Norrmark: Arkitekterna Aino och Alvar Aalto*, Finland: Martinpaino, 1982. Cat., Satu Grönstrand et al., *Alvar ja Aino Aalto lasin muotoilijoina: Näyttely Iittalan lasimuseossa*, Sävypaino: Iittala-Nuutajärvi Oy/Iittalan Lasi, 1988.
> See Artek.

Aalto, Hugo Alvar Henrik (1898–1976)

Finnish architect, town planner, and designer of furniture, lighting, textiles, and glass; born Kuortane, near Jyväskylä; husband of Aino Marsio and 'Elissa' Elsa Kaisa Mäkiniemi.

Training 1916–21 under Armas Lindgren and Lars Sonck, architecture, Teknillinen korkeakoulu, Helsinki.
Biography After his schooling, Aalto traveled widely in central Europe, Scandinavia, and Italy; probably participated in planning the 1923 Gothenburg fair; except for minor previous works, was professionally active from the 1922 *Industrial Exhibition* in Tampere; 1923, began an architecture practice in Jyväskylä; was active 1927–33 in Turku and 1933–76 in Helsinki. 1924, he married Aino Marsio; 1924–49, collaborated with her until her death. His 1929 exhibition (with Erik Bryggman) celebrating 700th anniversary of Turku represented the first complete, public, modern structure in Scandinavia. Widely published examples of his International Style architecture include 1927–35 Viipuri Library and 1929–33 Tuberculosis Sanatorium at Paimio. An active and important designer of goods for the Wohnbedarf store, Zürich, an entire bentwood furniture collection was included in the *New Wooden Furniture: Aalto, Wohnbedarf* (1934) sales catalog, designed by Herbert Bayer. c. 1934, he furnished the new Corso theater, Zürich; designed some laminated plywood chairs that were influenced by the Bauhaus and not accidentally cantilevered like the bent-steel chairs of Marcel Breuer, Mies van der Rohe, and Mart Stam, some of which he purchased in 1928 for his own Finnish apartment. Aalto's designs in turn were influential in Britain and the US, inspiring others like Jack Pritchard of Isokon. Aalto's 1930 Paimio (or Scroll) chair's seat/back, exclusive of the frame, was made from a single undulating plywood sheet for 1929–33 Paimio Tuberculosis Sanatorium. Dubbed the first 'soft' chair in wood, it was manufactured initially by Huonekalu-ja Rakennustyötehdas (Turku, Finland), subsequently by Artek. Many wooden Aalto chair designs followed. 1933, he collaborated with Otto Korhonen on developing a technique for bending solid wood, resulting in the L-, Y-, and X-leg furniture; considered this solution to bentwood technology his single most important contribution to furniture design, calling it 'the little sister of the architectonic column.' 1933, he met the wealthy Maire Gullichsen and her industrialist husband, Harry, and Aalto and wife Aino with art historian Nils-Gustaf Hahl and Maire Gullichsen established Artek, one of the first modern home-furnishings shops in Helsinki. Gullichsen commissioned Aalto to design 1936–38 Sunila Cellulose Factory, its workers' housing, and the Gullichsens' residence (1938–39 Villa Mairea). 1933, Finmar Limited was established in London as importer and distributor of Aalto's furniture and furnishings. Aalto designed glass for Karhula-Iittala in asymmetrical shapes and curves, of which his Savoy (or Aalto) vase is the best known. 1936, Karhula-Iittala announced a design competition to find items to exhibit at 1937 *Exposition Internationale des Arts et Techniques dans la Vie Moderne*, Paris. First-prize winner was Aalto's 1936 Eskimoerindens Skinnbuxa (later named Savoy, the vase shape having been said, among numerous other theories, to reflect the riparian shorelines of Aalto's homeland but was initially named after Eskimo pants). He designed the Finnish Pavilion (having won the competition for it) at 1937 Paris *Exposition* (receiving frst and second prizes with A. Ervi and V. Rewell); also won the Finish Pavilion competition for 1939–40 *New York World's Fair: The World of Tomorrow* (first, second, and third prizes). Though a practitioner of the International Style, calling on ferrocement and stucco extensively, Aalto often called on

Aino Aalto. Tumbler. 1932. Pressed glass, h. 3 3/8 x dia. 3" (7.6 x 8.6 cm). Mfr.: Karhula-Iittala glassworks, Finland. Greta Daniel Fund. MoMA.

exposed brick. ceramic tile, wood, and copper; advocated employing natural materials and organic forms, promoting a humanistic tradition in architecture and design. 1929, he became a member, Congrès Internationaux d'Architecture Moderne (CIAM), which, along with Sigfried Giedion's nod of approval, gave Aalto prominence in the international avant-garde community; 1940–49, was professor, College of Architecture, Massachusetts Institute of Technology (MIT), Cambridge, Mass.; 1952, married 'Elissa' Elsa Kaisa Mäkiniemi (1922–1994), who had qualified as an architect in 1949; 1952–76, collaborated with her. After Aalto's death in Helsinki, she finished some of his incomplete work.

Work Aside from an extensive architectural body of work, his equally wide range of designs, many still in production through Artek, include: 1929–30 611 side chair and 606 (Paimio) table; 1931–32 41 (Paimio) armchair, 44 armchair, and 915 table; 1932–33 402 armchair; 1933 60 stool and 4/905 table; 1933–35 217 cabinet, 80 L-leg table range, and 63, 65, 66, and 68 side chairs; 1935–36 109 clothes rack and 400 armchair; 1935–37 615 side chair; 1936–37 tea trolley (no. 98 and other versions); 1936–37 43 chaise longue; 1937 39 chaise longue; 1937/1954 A330 hanging lamp; 1938–39 406 armchair; 1940–45 153A/153B benches; 1946–47 46 armchair and Y805 Y-leg glass/ wood tables; 1953–54 A622A sconce and A331 hanging lamp; 1954 X-leg stool and tables; 1959 A810 floor lamp; 1965 616 baby's highchair. Iittala continues to produce numerous glassware pieces.

Exhibitions/citations Work subject of 1984 *Alvar Aalto: Furniture and Glass* and 1998 *Alvar Aalto: Between Humanism and Materialism*, both The Museum of Modern Art, New York; 1986 *Aalto Interiors*, Alvar Aalto-museo, Jyväskylä; 1988 exhibition of glass, Iittalan lasitehtaan Museossa, Sävypaino, Finland (catalogs below). Other work at a large number of exhibitions and one-person shows, including those recognizing Aalto's 1998 birth centenary. 1947, honorary doctoral degree, Princeton University; 1947, elected Honorary Royal Designer for Industry, UK; 1955–68, honorary member, Akademie der Künste, Berlin; 1957, member, Academy of Finland; 1957, Royal Gold Medal of Architecture, Britain; 1968, gold medal, Royal Institute of British Architects.

Bibliography *Alvar Aalto: Architecture and Furniture*, New York: The Museum of Modern Design, 1938. Leonardo Mosso, *L'opera di Alvar Aalto: Alvar Aalto, I: 1922–62*, Zürich, 1963; *Alvar Aalto, II: 1963–70*, Zürich, 1971; *Alvar Aalto, III: Projekte und letzte Zeichnungen*, Zürich, 1978. Cat., J. Stewart Johnson, *Alvar Aalto: Furniture and Glass*, New York: The Museum of Modern Art, 1984. Göran Schildt, *Alvar Aalto: The Early Years*, New York: Rizzoli, 1984. *Alvar Aalto Furniture—Museum of Finnish Architecture—Finnish Society of Crafts and Design*, Cambridge, Mass.: MIT, 1985. Cat., Göran Schildt, *Aalto Interiors 1923–1970*, Jyväskylä: Alvar Aalto-museo, 1986. Göran Schildt (ed.), *Alvar Aalto: The Decisive Years*, New York: Rizzoli, 1986. Satu Grönstrand, *Alvar ja Aino Aalto lasin muotoilijoina = Alvar and Aino Aalto as Glass Designers*, Sävypaino: Iittalan lasitehtaan Museossa, 1988; 1996 rev. ed. *Alvar Aalto: The Mature Years*, New York: Rizzoli, 1991. Göran Schildt, *Alvar Aalto: The Complete Catalogue of Architecture, Design and Art*, London: Academy, 1994. Göran Schildt (ed.), *Alvar Aalto in His Own Words*, New York: Rizzoli, 1998. Cat., Peter Reed (ed.), *Alvar Aalto: Between Humanism and Materialism*, New York: The Museum of Modern Art, 1998. Pirkko Tuukkanen (ed.), *Alvar Aalto Designer*, Vammala: Alvar Aalto Foundation, Alvar Aalto Museum, 2002. Paola Antonelli (ed.), *Objects of Design: The Museum of Modern Art*, New York: The Museum of Modern Art, 2003: 130.

> See Aalto, Aino; Artek.

Aalto, 'Elissa' Elsa Kaisa Mäkiniemi (1922–1994)

> See Aalto, Hugo Alvar Henrik.

Aarnio, Eero (1932–)

Finnish interior and industrial designer.

Training 1954–57, Taideteollinen korkeakoulu, Helsinki.

Biography 1962, Aarnio opened his own office Niittykumpu in Tontunmäki, Finland, working as an industrial and interior designer,

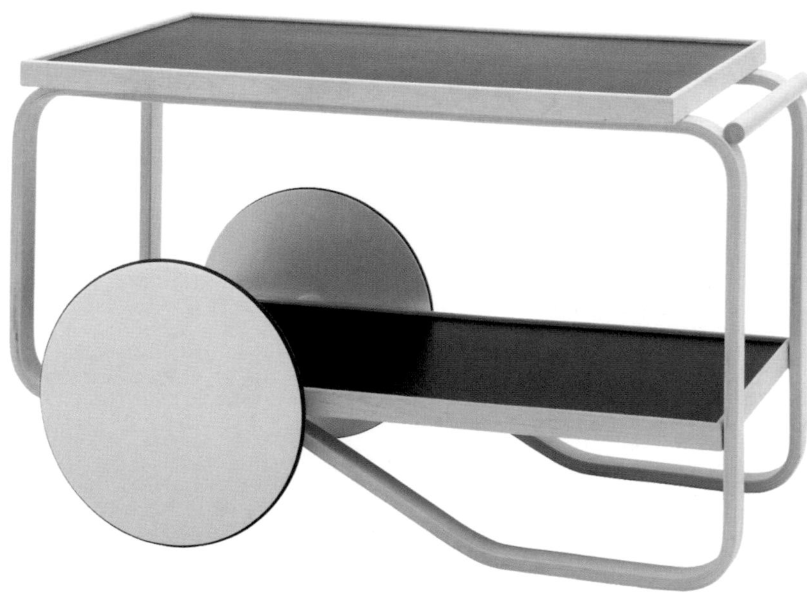

Hugo Alvar Henrik Aalto. Tea trolley (no. 98). 1936-37. Linoleum, birch, lacquer, and rubber, 22 x 35 1/2 x 18" (55.9 x 90.2 x 45.7 cm). Mfr.: Huonekalu-ja Rakennustyötehdas, Finland. Marshall Cogan Purchase Fund. MoMA.

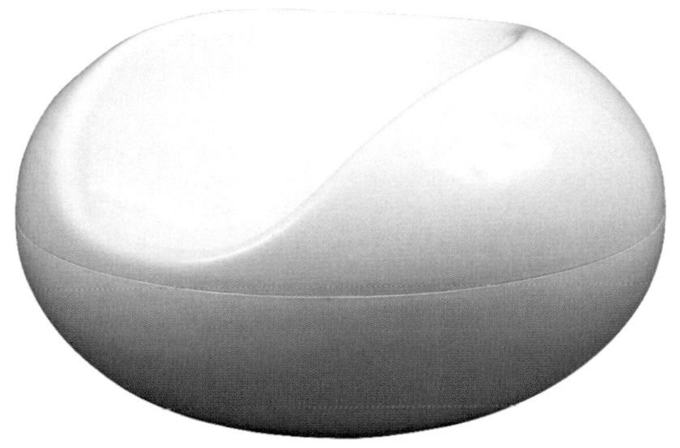

Eero Aarnio. Gyro chair. 1968. Two-part molded fiberglass shell, 21 x 36 3/4 x 36 3/4" (53.3 x 93.3 x 93.3 cm), seat h. 12" (30.5 cm). Mfr.: Asko, Finland. Joy E. Feinberg Fund and Friends of the Department Fund. MoMA.

specializing in furniture design in synthetic materials; is best known outside Finland for his chair designs; 1960, began designing in plastics, executing two of the best-known designs of the decade: womb-like 1962 Ball (or Globe) fiberglass chair (produced from 1965) with built-in telephone or stereo speakers, and 1968 Gyro (or Pastille or Pistil) fiberglass chair, both by Asko in Lahti, Finland. Others by Asko were 1954–60 Mushroom can stool (his first, which he also wove himself, from 1960 in rattan and from 1998 in fiberglass), 1968 Bubble (or Bing Bong) clear-acrylic suspended seat, 1970 Imperial armchair/sofa /table, 1971 Tomato chair, 1973 Pony (or Mustang) children's chair/ stool; all were later reissued by Adelta. Other designs include 1965 objects (tableware, scoop, bottle opener, ashtray) by OKO bank, 1966 Cognac (or V.S.O.P.) chair and Kanttarelli tables, 1968 Serpentine sofa, 1979 Avec chair, 1991 Copacabana table, 1992 Screw tables, 1994 Delfin armchair, 1994 Parabel table, 1996 door handles (by Valli & Valli), 1998 Formula chair (a return to plastics). In his later works, he also used more traditional materials, including 1982 Viking dining table/chairs by Polardesign.
Exhibitions/citations Work included in numerous exhibitions and fairs; Gyro chair first shown at 1968 Internationale Möbelmesse, Cologne. First prize, 1964 Scandinavian Park Furniture Competition; 1968 award (Gyro chair), American Institute of Decorators (AID).
Bibliography Cat., *Les assises du siège contemporain*, Paris: Musée des Arts Décoratifs, 1968. Cat., *Modern Chairs 1918–1970*, London: Lund Humphries, 1971. Eileene Harrison Beer, *Scandinavian Design: Objects of a Life Style*, New York: Farrar, Straus & Giroux, 1975. Charlotte and Peter Fiell, *Modern Furniture Classics Since 1945*, London: Thames & Hudson, 1991.

Abdi (b. Abdi Abd el-Kader 1955–)

Algerian designer; born Algiers; active Paris.

Training École Nationale des Beaux-Arts, Algiers; École Nationale Supérieure des Arts Décoratifs, Paris.
Biography Abdi was professor, École Nationale des Beaux-Arts, Algiers, where he established his own studio, designing furniture collections, including for the French Embassy; was briefly artistic director, Forum Design, Korea; furniture clients have included Artistes et Modèles, Paris. His 1980 Buffet Saha sideboard sponsored by VIA (French furniture association) was produced by Benoteau, 1999 cooking/couscous-preparation set by Alessi, 1999 Goutte vase by Cinna, Hana sideboard and bookcase by Costantino, Jouvence mirror by Glas, 2001 Tour de Babel shelving by Lemarchand, 2001 Tool Box articulating low/high table by Cinna, 2002 Bolo articulating coffee table by Ligne Roset. 1982–91, he taught in Algiers and, subsequently, at École Nationale Supérieure des Arts Décoratifs, Paris, where he lives; claims his cultural influences are the Casbah and craftspeople of Algiers, marrying them with Western technology.
Exhibitions/citations Work exhibited in Paris (catalogs below). 1981 and 1992 Appel Permanent grants, VIA.
Bibliography Cat., *Les années VIA*, Paris: Musée des Arts Décoratifs, 1990. 'Les designers du soleil,' *Maison française décoration internationale*, June 1992. Cat., Sophie Tasma Anargyros et al., *L'école française: les créateurs de meubles du 20ème siècle*, Paris: Industries Françaises de l'Ameublement, 2000.

Åberg, Gunhild (1939–)

Danish ceramicist.

Training 1959–64, Kunsthåndværkerskolen, Copenhagen.
Biography 1964 with Jane Reumert and Beate Andersen, Åberg formed the workshop Strandstræde Keramik, Copenhagen; executed designs for Royal Copenhagen Porcelain Manufactory and for Dansk Designs.
Exhibitions 1982 in New York (catalog below); 1992 *Scandinavian Festival of Art*, Barbican Centre, London; 1997 *Images of Denmark*, Ghana; 1999 Nordisk Keramik Triennial, Stockholm, Gothenberg, and Berlin; 2002 *From the Kilns of Denmark*, American Craft Museum, New York.
Bibliography Cat., David Revere McFadden (ed.), *Scandinavian Modern Design 1880–1980*, New York: Abrams, 1982.

Aberg, Margareta (1929–)

Swedish designer; born Stockholm; wife of Rolf Aberg.

Training Interior architecture and furniture design, Konstfackskolan, Stockholm.
Biography 1956 with her husband, Aberg opened her own architecture studio, specializing in interior architecture; designed hospitals, hotels, and schools including the Bracke Osterjard Hospital, Gothenburg, for handicapped children; c. 1986, designed Salabim cupboard by Swedfun, Sweden.
Bibliography Robert A.M. Stern (ed.), *The International Design Yearbook*, New York: Abbeville, 1985–86.

Abraham, Jeanine (1929–)

French furniture designer; wife of Dirk Jan Rol.

Training École Nationale Supérieure des Beaux-Arts; Centre d'Art et de Techniques (today École Camondo); both Paris.
Biography 1950s, Abraham was active in furniture design; collaborated with René-Jean Caillette and Jacques Dumond in a studio, where she met her husband-to-be, Dutch architect and designer Rol, with whom she collaborated in their own firm, Abraham & Rol, designing furniture by Meubles TV and the decoration of Les Huchers Minvielle wood factory and stores. According to Rol, he worked on the technical aspects, and Abraham more on 'inventive' ideas. Their materials of choice included wood, aluminum, and rattan. c. 1955 chair with steel-rod frame and plywood back and seat is her best-known work.
Bibliography Pascal Renous, *Portraits de créateurs*, Paris: H. Vial, 1969. Yolande Amic, *Intérieurs: le mobilier français 1945–1965*, Paris: Regard/VIA, 1983. Cat., Sophie Tasma Anargyros et al., *L'école française: les créateurs de meubles du 20ème siècle*, Paris: Industries Françaises de l'Ameublement, 2000. Patrick Favardin, *Les décorateurs des années 50*, Paris: Norma, 2002: 170.

Abramovitz, Gerald (1928–)

British industrial designer; born South Africa; from 1970 active the US.

Training 1949–51, architecture, University of Pretoria, South Africa; 1952–54, design, Royal College of Art, London.
Biography Abramovitz specialized in seating, including 1961 furniture by Knoll and 1966–67 furniture by Hille; designed children's play equipment, prefabricated housing parts, and kitchen appliances, and designed award-winning lighting (see below) by Best and Lloyd.
Citations Second prize (1963 armchair, based on example for Knoll), 1963 international furniture design competition sponsored by *The Daily Mirror*; 1966 Design Centre Award (1961–63 Cantilever desk lamp).
Bibliography 'Design Centre Awards 1966: Cantilever Desk Lamp,' *Design*, no. 209, May 1966: 40–41. Cat., Kathryn B. Hiesinger and George H. Marcus III (eds.), *Design Since 1945*, Philadelphia: Philadelphia Museum of Art, 1984.

Acerbis

Italian furniture manufacturer; located Seriate, Bergamo.

History 1870, Acerbis was founded by cabinetmaker Benvenuto Acerbis as a carpenter's shop. His grandson Lodovico Acerbis (Albino, Bergamo, 1939–), a student of business and economics, Università degli Studi, Milan, joined the firm in 1963 and is now president. He designed his first piece of furniture in 1956—a miniature table and chairs—and his 1992 Granducale furniture collection was an homage to Kazimir Malevich. The firm became known for its case

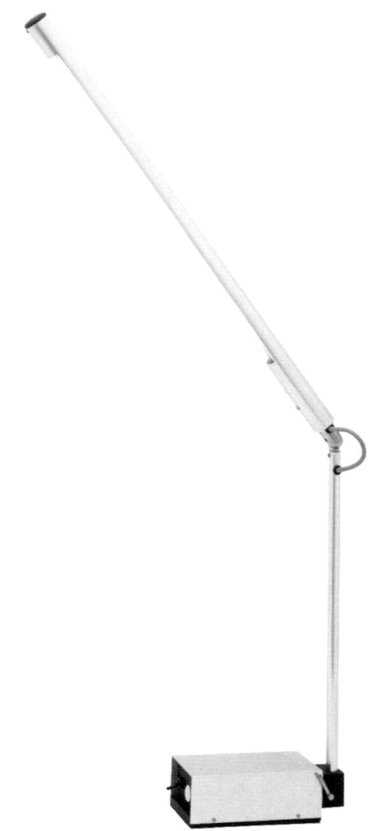

Gerald Abramovitz. Cantilever desk lamp (no. 41555 Mark 2). 1961–63. Aluminum and steel, 20 x 27 1/2 x 3 5/8" (50.8 x 69.8 x 9.2 cm). Mfr.: Best & Lloyd, UK. Greta Daniel Design Fund. MoMA.

goods. Designers have included Mario Bellini, Gianfranco Frattini, Giotto Stoppino, and Nanda Vigo.
Citations 1979 Premio Compasso d'Oro (Sheraton furniture by L. Acerbis and Stoppino); and others.
Bibliography 'Milan à l'heure du design,' *Maison et jardin*, Apr. 1992: 124. Michele De Lucchi (ed.), *The International Design Yearbook*, London: Laurence King, 2001.

Acking, Carl-Axel (1910–2001)

Swedish architect and furniture designer.

Training 1930–39, Kungliga Tekniska Högskolan, Stockholm.
Biography 1930s, Acking worked as architect Gunnar Asplund's assistant; 1939, set up his own studio. He taught, 1943–76 Tekniska Skolan/ Konstfackskolan; and Tekniska Högskolan in Lund. Acking was architect of Swedish Embassy, Tokyo, architect in charge of cathedral in Lund, and interior designer of North Star Line ships; 1944, designed laminated bentwood chair by Avenska Möbelfabrikerna and telephone book for Swedish telephone commission; 1949, furnishings for Hotel Malmen, Stockholm; with others, 1955 *H 55* exhibition, Hälsingborg. Other furniture was produced by the Kooperativa Förbundet, Stockholm; Nordiska Kompaniet, Stockholm; Svenska Möbelfabrikerna, Bodafors. Work also included designs for wallpaper, textiles, and lighting.
Exhibitions/citations Work shown at 1936 (6th) Triennale di Milano; 1937 *Exposition Internationale des Arts et Techniques dans la Vie Moderne*, Paris; 1939–40 *New York World's Fair: The World of Tomorrow*; 1956 *Lunning Prize Winners Exhibition*, New York; 1986 *The Lunning Prize Exhibition*, Nationalmuseum, Stockholm. 1952 Lunning Prize.
Bibliography Cat., David Revere McFadden (ed.), *Scandinavian Modern Design 1880–1980*, New York: Abrams, 1982. Cat., *The Lunning Prize*, Stockholm: Nationalmuseum, 1986.

Adamovich, Mikhail Mikhailovich (1884–1947)

Russian porcelain designer.

Training To 1907, Stroganov School of Applied Art, Moscow.
Biography 1907–09, Adamovich traveled to Italy; 1910s, was a decorative painter in Moscow and St. Petersburg; 1912–13, was commissioned by the Greek government to design a mosaic for King George I's tomb; 1918–19 and 1921, was a designer at State Porcelain Factory, Petrograd (today St. Petersburg), and, 1924–33, at the Volkhov and the Dulevo ceramic factories.
Bibliography Cat., *Kunst und Revolution: Russische und Sowjetische Kunst 1910–1932*, Vienna: Österreichisches Museum für angewandte Kunst, 1988.

Adams, John (1882–1953)

British ceramicist and designer; active London, Durban, and Poole; husband of Truda Carter (b. Gertrude Sharpe).

Training Hanley School of Art; 1908, Royal College of Art, London.
Biography Adams spent his early years in Stoke-on-Trent; 1895–c. 1902, worked in Bernard Moore's studio, which specialized in the production of plain and painted ceramics, using reduction-fired glazes; married Gertrude Sharpe, fellow student at Royal College of Art; 1912–14, was head, School of Art, Durban Technical College, South Africa; 1921–50 with Cyril Carter and Harold Stabler, set up the firm Carter, Stabler and Adams in Poole (Dorset, England), where Adams designed almost all the shapes for its decorative and domestic ware, including 1936 Streamline tableware; experimented with and produced high-temperature, crackle-finish, and other glazes.
Bibliography Cat., *Thirties: British Art and Design Before the War*, London: Arts Council of Great Britain/Hayward Gallery, 1979.

Adamson, Jerry (1937–)
> See Dudas, Frank.

Adie Brothers

British silversmiths.

History 1879, the firm was founded in Birmingham; 1930s, produced modern silver designs by Harold Stabler and Fernand Pire, one of its best-known, Stabler's 1935 tea set, featuring smooth, rectangular forms, rectangular wooden handles, flat, rectangular, hinged lids, and semicircular disk finials.
Bibliography Annelies Krekel-Aalberse, *Art Nouveau and Art Déco Silver*, New York: Abrams, 1989.

Adler, Allan (1916–2002)

American metalworker; active Los Angeles; son-in-law of silversmith Porter Blanchard.

Biography Adler's cutlery patterns included Capistrano, Chinese Key, Fiddle, Modern Georgian, Round End, Starlit, Sunset, Swedish Modern. A mid-1940s Paul Revere-inspired tea service sold at Sotheby's at end of 1990s for over $1 million (£650,000). His work lacked ornamentation; some may have been designed for the Reed & Barton silversmithy. Adler—still active into the 21st century—purportedly worked ten-hour days in a Los Angeles workshop with seven assistants; was one of the few who continued to produce pieces

Allan Adler. Bowl. 1960s. Sterling silver, 3 x 6 13/16" (7.5 x 17.4 cm). Mfr.: the designer, US. Courtesy Quittenbaum Kunstauktionen, Munich.

entirely by hand. Some critics claim that Adler had become, just before his death, the last living professional silversmith and spoon-maker still pursuing the philosophy of the Arts and Crafts movement. Owing to his workshop's location, clients included a number of movie stars. He created the American Film Institute's Silver Star statuette and gold Oscar Memento (not the Oscar itself) presented to winners of awards of the Academy of Motion Picture Arts and Sciences.
Bibliography Robert Summers, 'Allan Adler: Modern Silver Master, Part I,' *Silver Magazine* 30, 1998: 32–42; Robert Summers, 'Allan Adler: Modern Silver Master, Part II,' *Silver Magazine* 31, 1999: 24–29.

Adler, Friedrich (1878–c. 1942)

German sculptor and designer; born Laupheim; son of a confectioner; active Munich and Hamburg.

Training Debschitz-Schule (aka Lehr- und Versuchs-Ateliers für angewandte und freie Kunst), Munich.
Biography 1904–07, Adler taught at Debschitz-Schule, a private art school for applied-arts and crafts training; 1907–1910 and 1918–33, at Kunstgewerbeschule, Hamburg; 1910–13, was director of a master class in Nuremberg; designed silver by P. Bruckmann & Söhne, Heilbronn. Work included jewelry, utensils, furniture, metalware, ceramics, stucco work, glass etching, and textiles. 1918, he returned to Hamburg after serving in World War I and resumed his teaching there; developed industrial-production methods based on batik techniques for the firm he founded in 1926, called ATEHA (Adler-Textildruckgesellschaft Hamburg); designed for metalsmiths O.G.F. Schmitt, Nuremberg; went from the Jugendstil style to abstract and, later, tectonic decorations. 1933, Adler was dismissed from the Hamburg school; 1936, was urged by Walter Gropius to emigrate to the US and did not; 1942, was deported to the Auschwitz concentration camp, where he died in an unknown year.
Exhibitions 1902 *Esposizione Internazionale d'Arte Decorativa Moderna* (created entrance to Württemberg group), Turin; 1914 *Werkbund-Ausstellung* (designed the synagogue), Cologne. Subject of 1994 exhibition, Münchner Stadtmuseum, and traveling (catalog below).
Bibliography Hans Vollmer, *Allgemeines Lexikon der bildenden Künstler*, Leipzig: Seemann, 1953. Giovanni Fanelli et al., *Il tessuto moderno: designo, modo, architettura, 1890–1940*, Florence: Laterza, 1976: 166. Annelies Krekel-Aalberse, *Art Nouveau and Art Déco Silver*, New York: Abrams, 1989. Cat., Brigitte Leonhardt, *Friedrich Adler: zwischen Jugendstil und Art Déco*, Stuttgart: Arnoldsche, 1994.

Adler, Rose (1892–1969)

French decorative and bookbinding designer; born and active Paris.

Training 1917–25 under Andrée Langrand, École de l'Union Centrale des Arts Décoratifs, Paris, and, from 1923, under Henri Nouilhac.
Biography 1923, when Adler was a student exhibitioner at Pavillon de Marsan of the Louvre, couturier Jacques Doucet bought three of her bindings, and she worked for him until his 1929 death. Occasionally, she executed furniture for Doucet and others. A table commissioned by Doucet is today housed in Virginia Museum of Fine Arts, Richmond, Va., US. She produced small table-top accessories, including picture frames; worked in glass, metalized calfskin, reptile skin, and precious stones, in a style called *rythmes géométriques*; was greatly influenced by Pierre Legrain, whom she had met through Doucet and with whom she worked from 1923, incorporating abstract patterns and unusual materials; 1931, became a member, Union des Artistes Modernes (UAM), showing her bindings and picture frames at its exhibitions. Her bindings—mostly non-figurative and geometric with overlapping lettering—included those for books *Calligrammes*, *Le Paysan de Paris*, *Mon beau souci*, and *A.O. Barnabooth*. She created a wide range of objects, including jewelry, toiletry items, furniture, and clothing; when Doucet died, concentrated on work for private book collectors, libraries, and institutions, including the Bibliothèque Nationale, Fondation Littéraire Jacques Doucet, Victoria and Albert Museum, and New York Public Library; 1947, became a member, Société de la Reliure Moderne, showing at its exhibitions.
Exhibitions 1924–29, work shown independently at Salons of Société des Artistes Décorateurs; 1931 *Exposition Internationale du Livre*, Paris; 1934, events with Chareau-Cournault-Garnier group; 1937 *Exposition Internationale des Arts et Techniques dans la Vie Moderne*, Paris; 1939 *Golden Gate International Exposition*, San Francisco; 1939–40 *New York World's Fair: The World of Tomorrow*. Bindings in Paris: 1949 (1st) *Formes Utiles* and 1956–57 (1st) Triennale Française d'Art Contemporain, both Pavillon de Marsan.
Bibliography Rose Adler, *Reliures*, Paris: Charles Moreau, 1929. Georges Blaizot, *Masterpieces of French Modern Bindings*, New York: Services Culturels Français, 1947: 125. Yvonne Brunhammer, *The Nineteen-Twenties Style*, London: Hamlyn, 1969. Pierre Kjellberg, *Art déco: les maîtres du mobilier, le décor des paquebots*, Paris: Amateur, 1986. Arlette Barré-Despond, *UAM*, Paris: Regard, 1986. Cat., *Les années UAM 1929–1958*, Paris: Musée des Arts Décoratifs, 1988: 144.

Adnet, Jacques (1900–1984)

French architect and decorator; born Chatillon-Coligny; active Paris; twin brother of Jean Adnet.

Training With twin brother Jean, École Nationale Supérieure des Arts Décoratifs, Paris.
Biography Adnet worked for Henri Rapin and Tony Selmersheim and, 1920–22, for Maurice Dufrêne; designed accessories in metal and glass and executed sturdy modern furniture designs, mixing them with traditional pieces, much like Jean-Michel Frank; used a logical, clear, refined approach, often collaborating with twin brother Jean; from 1922, worked in the decorating studio La Maîtrise of department store Les Galeries Lafayette, Paris; designed the *salle commune* of 1927 oceanliner *Île-de-France*; 1928–59, was director of design at Süe et Mare's Compagnie des Arts Français (CAF); 1930s, often incorporated metal and glass into his furniture; applied a philosophy of stark Functionalism to all of his ensembles, including chromed tubular-metal dressing tables, mobile drinks cabinets, and furniture in exotic woods; designed furniture suites for Franck Jay Gould's townhouse, Alice Cocéa's apartment, French president Vincent Auriol's office in the residence at Château de Rambouillet, oceanliners of Ferdinand de Lesseps; 1959, left CAF; from 1970, director, École Nationale Supérieure des Arts Décoratifs, Paris. Designed inventive, severely geometric, kinetic lighting, with few concessions to ornamentation, showing contemporary *machinisme*'s influence. A 1929 table lamp with four lighted tubes forming a square, cantilevered from a marble base, was reproduced by Lumen Center 1988–91 and subsequently by Pentalux.
Exhibitions/citations Work shown at annual Salons through studio affiliations including La Maîtrise and Saddier et Fils to 1928, when he took over CAF furniture at both foreign and French stands at 1925 *Exposition Internationale des Arts Décoratifs et Industriels Modernes*, Paris. Grand prize for architecture of St. Gobain pavilion (with René Coulon), 1937 *Exposition Internationale des Arts et Techniques dans la Vie Moderne*, Paris.
Bibliography Alastair Duncan, *Art Nouveau and Art Déco Lighting*, New York: Simon & Schuster, 1978: 144. Pierre Kjellberg, *Art déco: les maîtres du mobilier, le décor des paquebots*, Paris: Amateur, 1986: 27–29. Bruno Foucart and Jean-Louis Gaillemin, *Les décorateurs des années 40*, Paris: Norma, 1998. Cat., Sophie Tasma Anargyros et al., *L'école française: les créateurs de meubles du 20ème siècle*, Paris: Industries Françaises de l'Ameublement, 2000. Patrick Favardin, *Les décorateurs des années 50*, Paris: Norma, 2002: 18.

Adnet, Jean (1900–1995)

French designer; active Paris; twin brother of Jacques Adnet.

Training With twin brother Jacques, École Nationale Supérieure des Arts Décoratifs, Paris.
Biography Jean and Jacques Adnet collborated under the name 'JJAdnet' and then worked independently. During his brother's tenure in the La Maîtrise decorating department of Les Galeries Lafayette, Paris, Jean worked in the window-display department there. 1928, when Jacques departed, Jean became the store's artistic manager.
Bibliography Cat., Sophie Tasma Anargyros et al., *L'école française: les créateurs de meubles du 20ème siècle*, Paris: Industries Françaises de l'Ameublement, 2000.

ADSA + partners

French design group.

History 1985, ADSA was founded by Marc Lebailly (president) and Maïa Wodzislawska (vice-president); included designers Gil Adamy, Pierre Paulin, Dominique Pierzo, and Roger Tallon. Their work exhibited a variety of approaches to the problems of industrial design in heavy industry, transportation (for example, Tallon and his TGV high-speed train), and domestic and office furniture for banks, museums, cultural institutions, and others. Paulin's inexpensive 1980 Dangari outdoor chair in polypropylene (reminiscent of early Thonet silhouettes in bentwood) by Stamp was an aesthetically superior version of plastic stacking designs that became ubiquitous in the 1990s.

AEG: Peter Behrens. Fan (no. GB1). c. 1908. Painted cast iron and brass, 11 1/4 x 10 3/4 x 6" (28.6 x 27.3 x 15.3 cm). Mfr.: Allgemeine Elektrizitäts Gesellschaft (AEG), Germany. Melva Bucksbaum Purchase Fund. MoMA.

Bibliography Robert A.M. Stern (ed.), *The International Design Yearbook*, New York: Abbeville, 1985/1986.

Aebi, Aurel (1966–)
> See Atelier Oï.

AEG (Allgemeine Elektrizitäts Gesellschaft)
German electrical manufacturer; located Berlin.

History 1883, Emil Rathenau (1838–1915) founded AEG to produce electrical products. In Berlin, Franz Schwechten designed the 1889 AEG factory on Ackerstrasse and monumental 1896 portal on the Brunnenstrasse, and Alfred Messel the late-1890s administration building on the Friedrich-Karl-Ufer. Otto Eckmann designed AEG's catalogs and advertising literature for 1900 *Exposition Universelle*, Paris. 1907, Peter Behrens was appointed artistic director. (Though credit for the appointment is generally given to Rathenau, Behrens said that the initiator was Paul Jordan, the director of the Holbaek factories.) Behrens's AEG turbine factory in Berlin is considered a pioneering example of modern architecture, although, even before the Behrens appointment, the firm was noted for the high technical qualities of its products. Behrens established an 'intimate union' between the process and style of mass-produced goods and 'artistic and creative work' designed to foster 'a general improvement in public taste.' Today an industrial giant, AEG is still noted for its high design standards.
Bibliography Karl Wilhelm, *Die AEG*, Berlin, 1931. Ernst Schulin, *Walter Rathenau—Gesamtausgabe*, Munich and Heidelberg, 1977. Tilman Buddensieg et al., *Industrie-Kultur, Peter Behrens und die AEG, 1907–1914*, Berlin: Mann, 1979. S. Anderson, 'Modern Architecture and Industry: Peter Behrens, the AEG, and Industrial Design,' *Oppositions*, no. 21, summer 1980: 78–93. Paola Antonelli (ed.), *Objects of Design: The Museum of Modern Art*, New York: The Museum of Modern Art, 2003: 220–21.

Aesthetic Movement
European and American style.

History Based in Great Britain in the second half of the 19th century, the Aesthetic Movement was never formally organized. Its exponents sought to rid themselves of the rigidness of Victorian design in favor of freer expression in the fine and decorative arts. Some historians describe it as proto-modern and include it within the Arts and Crafts movement led by William Morris, the neo-Queen Anne architecture of E.W. Godwin and Norman Shaw, the Pre-Raphaelite art led by Dante Gabriel Rossetti and Edward Burne-Jones, the *japonisant* painting of James Abbott McNeill Whistler and Aubrey Beardsley, and the work of writers including Oscar Wilde. Philosophically, the movement owed much to the doctrine of 'art for art's sake,' a phrase coined by Walter Pater in 1868. In practical terms the eclecticism of the 1862 *International Exhibition on Industry and Art*, London, was influential. Christopher Dresser's *The Art of Decorative Design* (London, 1862) might be thought of as the first of the Aesthetic Movement pattern books. The movement's designers included William Burges, Walter Crane, Lewis Day, Christopher Dresser, E.W. Godwin, Thomas Jekyll, A.H. Mackmurdo, Norman Shaw, and Bruce Talbert. And its influence spread to Europe, contributing to Art Nouveau and the Wiener Sezession, and to the US, influencing Gustav Stickley, Louis Comfort Tiffany, and manufacturers such as the Herter Brothers.
Exhibitions An aspect of the movement was the subject of 1986 exhibition; subject of 2000 exhibition, Toronto (catalog below).
Bibliography Elizabeth Aslin, *The Aesthetic Movement: Prelude to Art Nouveau*, London: Elek, 1969. Cat., Robin Spencer et al., *The Aesthetic Movement and the Cult of Japan*, London: The Fine Art Society, 1972. Mark Girouard, *Sweetness and Light: The 'Queen Anne' Movement, 1860–1900*, Oxford, 1977. Cat., Doreen Bolger Burke et al., *In Pursuit of Beauty: Americans and the Aesthetic Movement*, New York: The Metropolitan Museum of Art/Rizzoli, 1986. Cat., Dennis T. Lanigan and Douglas E. Schoenherr, *A Dream of the Past: Pre-Raphaelite and Aesthetic Movement...*, Toronto: Art Centre, University of Toronto, 2000.

Agitprop
Soviet Union propagandist art.

History Agitprop—a shortening of Agitpropbyuro, the Communist Party's bureau for agitation and propaganda—was emphatically focused on contemporary Russia, although artists incorporated themes and images from the past. Agitprop was the state-sponsored propagandist art in the Soviet Union in the years following the 1917 Communist Revolution. Traditional distinctions between different art forms were blurred in the search for a revolutionary artistic synthesis. Since art had long been thought to be a 'teacher of life' by Russians, it appeared to be appropriate to use the propagandistic functions of art at a time of social change. Agitprop forms had to be produced with little advance notice, in large quantities, and from inexpensive materials. 1918, Lenin presented a program, called 'monumental propaganda,' which became the basis for official art during the revolutionary era. Agitprop's influence could be seen in Imperial/State/Lomonosov porcelain, where, 1918–22, there was a collision between the old and the new, represented notably in the work of Mikhail Adamovitch, Zinaida Kobyletskaia, and Maria Lebedeva. Credited with much of the Agitprop porcelain of the period, Sergei Chekhonin executed elegantly painted pieces with colorful slogans on ceramic blanks originally intended for pre-revolutionary service, applying the same slogans, illustrations, and quotations as those reproduced on posters, Agit-reliefs, and festival decorations. 1918, Natan Al'tman designed Futurist Agit-decorations for buildings and monuments in the Uritskii Square in Petrograd (now St. Petersburg) for the Revolution's first anniversary. 1919–20, Vasilii Ermilov was involved in the design of various Agitprop projects, including Agit-posters, interiors of clubs, trains, and steamships, and others painted Agit-décor on the carriages of touring railroad caravans, in an effort to stimulate popular support for the Revolution. Architecture included 1918–19 *Monument to Liberty* (destroyed) by architect D. Osipov and sculptor Nikolai Andreev; 1920–25 *Monument to Marx* (unrealized) by sculptor S. Alyoshin and other sculptors and architects Alekandr and Viktor Vesnin; 1919 *Bakunin Monument* (unrealized) and 1920 *Labor Liberated* by Boris Korolyov; and a relief portrait of Robespierre by Sarra Levedeva. Even though construction was halted, Vladimir Tatlin's renowned 1918 *Monument to the Third International* was a typically grandiose architectonic Agitprop statement. Other notable Agitprop practitioners were Gustav Klutsis, Nikolai Kolli, and El Lissitzky.
Bibliography Cat., *Kunst und Revolution: Russische und Sowjetische Kunst 1910–1932*, Vienna: Österreichisches Museum für angewandte Kunst, 1988. Nina Lobanov-Rostovsky, *Revolutionary Ceramics*, London: Studio Vista, 1990. S.O. Khan-Magomedov, *Vhutemas: Moscou*, Paris: Regard, 1990.

Agnoli, 'Tito' Juan Bautista (1931–)
Italian-Peruvian designer and teacher; active Lurgo d'Erba, Como.

Training Under Romantic Expressionist painter Mario Sironi, in painting; to 1959, Politecnico, Milan.
Biography Agnoli was born to a family in Cadore, Italy, that emigrated to Peru. He returned to study and work in Italy; 1950s–60s, taught,

Cesare Correnti Art Institute, Lissone, and concurrently was an assistant to Gio Ponti and Giancarlo De Carli in the Facoltà di Architettura, Politecnico, Milan; designed furniture (example, 843 table by Montina) and lighting (examples, lamps by O luce); from 1960, designed primarily for furniture clients, preferring to work on clients' premises in collaboration with their technicians and executives. Clients have included Arflex, Cinova, Citterio, Data International, Disegno Due, Lema, La Linea, Mateograssi, Molteni, Montina, Pierantonio Bonacina, Poltrona Frau, Schiffini, Tandem Vefer, Ycami, and Zanotta.
Citations 1954, 1955, 1956, and 1967 Premio Compasso d'Oro; gold medal, 1986 NeoCon, Chicago.
Bibliography Cat., Hans Wichmann, *Italien Design 1945 bis heute*, Munich: Die Neue Sammlung, 1988. Flavio Conti, *I progettisti italiani, Tito Agnoll*, Milan: Rima, 1988. *Modo*, no. 148, Mar. Apr. 1993.

Ahlmann, Lis (1894–1979)

Danish textile designer.

Biography A pioneer in textile design, Ahlmann shifted to commercial production in 1950s; 1953, became artistic consultant at C. Olesen of Copenhagen, where she collaborated with Børge Mogensen on furnishing and upholstery weaves, using harmonizing colors and interchangeable patterns; became known for her muted colors in plaids and stripes; wove on simple power looms based on hand-loom methods; eventually, through Mogensen's intervention, began weaving bolder colorations on more sophisticated machinery.
Exhibitions Work included in 1960 exhibition organized by Danish Society of Arts and Crafts and Industrial Design, United States of America; 1983–84, Philadelphia Museum of Art (catalogs below).
Bibliography Bent Salicath and Arne Karlsen (eds.), *Modern Danish Textiles*, Copenhagen: Danish Society of Arts and Crafts and Industrial Design, 1959: 12–15. Arne Karlsen, *Made in Denmark*, Copenhagen: Danish Society of Arts and Crafts and Industrial Design, 1959: 72–79, 122–23. Cat., *The Arts of Denmark: Viking to Modern*, Copenhagen: Landsforeningen Dansk Kunsthaandværk, 1960. Arne Karlsen, *Furniture Designed by Børge Mogensen*, Copenhagen: Christian Ejlers, 1968. Thomas Mogensen, *Lis Ahlmann Tekstiler*, Copenhagen, 1974. Cat., Kathryn B. Hiesinger and George H. Marcus III (eds.), *Design Since 1945*, Philadelphia: Philadelphia Museum of Art, 1983.

Aicher, Otl (1922–1991)

German graphic and industrial designer; born Ulm.

Training 1946–47, sculpture, Akademie der bildenden Künste, Munich.
Biography 1948, Aicher established a graphic-design studio in his hometown of Ulm, 1967 in Munich, and 1972 in Rotis, Allgäu. 1949, he became a founding member of Hochschule für Gestaltung, Ulm; 1954–65, taught in its communications department; 1962–64, was rector of the school. 1958, he was a guest lecturer at Yale University and, 1959, in Rio de Janeiro; developed corporate-identity programs for Braun, Dresdner Bank, Erco lighting, Frankfurt airport, Lufthansa, Severin & Siedler publishers, and ZDF; worked at Braun with Fritz Eichler, Hans Gugelot, and Dieter Rams; 1967–72, was in charge of visuals for the Munich Olympiad; 1984, founded Institut für Analoge Studien in Rotis; 1968–87, wrote numerous books on design and drawing.
Bibliography Otl Aicher, *Innenseiten des Kriegs*, Frankfurt: S. Fischer, 1985. H. Lindinger (ed.), *Hochschule für Gestaltung—Ulm*, Berlin, 1987.

Aida, Yüsuke (1931–)

Japanese ceramics and industrial designer.

Training Town planning, Chiba University; under Ken Miyanohara, in ceramics.
Biography 1961–64 in the US, Aida was chief designer at Bennington Potters, Vermont, where he executed its 1961 Classic range of industrially produced tableware, still in production; returned to Japan and reverted to studio pottery; executed large ceramic wall panels for Tourist Hotel in Nagoya and 1970s Ina building in Osaka; 1972–74, was director of the Japanese Designer Craftsman Association and, from 1976, director of its successor, Japan Craft Design Association.
Bibliography Cat., *Contemporary Vessels: How to Pour*, Tokyo: Crafts Gallery, National Museum of Modern Art, 1982. Cat., Kathryn B. Hiesinger and George H. Marcus III (eds.), *Design Since 1945*, Philadelphia: Philadelphia Museum of Art, 1983.

Airborne

French furniture manufacturer; located Mérignac.

History Airborne was established in 1950s; became well known for its production of AA (or Butterfly) steel-and-canvas chair replica, from 1950s, of the 1938 original by Ferrari Hardoy, Bonet, and Kurchan (still in production); 1965 Djinn seating range (featured in the film *2001: A Space Odyssey*, 1969) by Pascal Mourgue; 1969 Albatros chair by Danielle Quarante; 1990 Biscuter chair by Javier Mariscal. The firm continues trading, introducing more recent designs; is now a part of Steelcase France group.
Bibliography Patrick Favardin, *Les décorateurs des années 50*, Paris: Norma, 2002: 286. www.airborne.fr.
> See Ferrari Hardoy, Jorge.

Airstream Trailer Co.
> See Wally Byam.

Aisslinger, Werner (1964–)

German designer; born Nördlingen.

Training 1987–93 under 'Nick' Hans Roericht, Hochschule der Künste, Berlin.
Biography 1989, Aisslinger worked at Ron Arad's One Off studio and was an assistant to Jasper Morrison, both London; 1989–90, worked in the office of designer Andreas Brandolini, Berlin; 1991–92, in the studio of Michele De Lucchi, Milan; 1993, set up his own studio, Berlin; 1995, taught design, Hochschule der Künste, Berlin; 1997, taught, Design Institute, Lahti, Finland; from 1998, was professor, product and interior design, Hochschule für Gestaltung, Karlsruhe. 1992, he designed ticket check-in counters for Lufthansa Design Center; video-conferencing system for Wilkhahn at 1993 Designers' Saturday fair, Düsseldorf; 1994 Endless Shelf by Porro, Italy; 1995–97 e-shop system by e-plus mobile-radio store chain; 1996 Juli home/office chair by Cappellini; 1997 modular shop-in-shop component system for e-plus; automatic tellers for NCZ Cash Automation; 1998 Mercedes Benz's MB-Communications Center, Frankfurt; 1999 Soft Cell gel furniture by Zanotta.

Werner Aisslinger. Juli armchair. 1996. Integral polyurethane foam and steel, 29 1/2 x 25 x 21 5/8" (75 x 63.5 x 54.9 cm). Mfr.: Cappellini, Italy. Gift of the mfr. MoMA.

Exhibitions/citations 1990 *Kombination*, Ost-West-Design, Berlin; 1995 and 1997 *Design Time Bremen*, Neues Museum, Weserburg; 1999 *Smart-China: 10 Europäische Designer*, Galerie Arosa 2000, Frankfurt; 1998 BIO 16 industrial-design biennial, Ljubljana; 1999 *Identity Crisis*, Glasgow; 1999 *Soft Cell*, Galeria La Poste, Milan; 2000 exhibition (with Volker Albus), Galerie Fiedler, Cologne. 1992 Design Plus prize, Ambiente fair, Frankfurt; 1994 Red Dot award, Design Zentrum Nordrhein Westfalen, Essen; 1994 first prize, Wogg Design Competition, Zürich; 1995 Premio Compasso d'Oro; 1996 Bundespreis Produktdesign (for Endless Shelf), Rat für Formgebung (German design council), Frankfurt.
Bibliography Michele De Lucchi (ed.), *The International Design Yearbook*, London: Laurence King, 2001.

AJS Aérolande

French designer and architect group.

Biography 1960s, the group was active in Paris and named 'A' for Jean Aubert, 'J' for Jean-Paul Jungman, 'S' for Antoine Stinco. 1968, they designed the first inflatable armchair in PVC, produced by Quasar Khahn's firm.

Akaba

Spanish furniture firm; located San Sebastián.

History 1986, Akaba was established by Txema García Amiano, who had previously worked at Enea. Amiano, who is critical of conservatism, set out to take risks, and produced 1986 Frenesi stool designed by Ramón Benedito. Akaba's first piece by Javier Mariscal and Pepe Cortés was 1986 Trampolín stool. Mariscal's subsequent work for the firm has included 1986 M.O.R. Sillón sofa.
Citations 1997 Delta d'Oro, ADI/FAD (industrial-design/decorative arts associations); 2000 National Design Prize (for Amiano's business career); both Spain.
Bibliography Guy Julier, *New Spanish Design*, London: Thames & Hudson, 1991.

Alavoine, L.

French interior decorators; located Paris and New York.

History Late 19th century, Alavoine prided itself on being able to produce decorations in any of the historicist styles popular at the time, including Tudor, Pompeiian, Georgian, and Turkish. Armand Rateau was director 1905–14. 1920, the firm opened studios and offices at 712 Fifth Avenue, New York, with its façade by Lalique. Employing Jules Bouy 1924–27, it was especially celebrated from 1920s to early 1970s for its Louis-revival interiors and dramatic flair. The firm ceased trading 1972–73 in France and the US.
Exhibitions Its overwrought Marie Antoinette room was shown at 1893 *World's Columbian Exposition*, Chicago, and published in *The Decorator and Furnisher*, New York, Nov. 1893. A room from the apartment of the Worgelt family in Manhattan, New York, designed and furnished by the firm, has been on permanent display, Brooklyn Museum of Art, Brooklyn, N.Y.
Bibliography Jessica Rutherford, *Art Nouveau, Art Déco and the Thirties: The Furniture Collections at Brighton Museum*, Brighton: The Royal Pavilion, Art Gallery and Museums, 1983: 40. Pierre Kjellberg, *Art déco: les maîtres du mobilier, le décor des paquebots*, Paris: Amateur, 1986. Stephen Calloway, *Twentieth-Century Decoration*, New York: Rizzoli, 1988: 27, 39.

Alberhill Pottery

American ceramics manufactory; located Alberhill, Cal.

History The Alberhill-Corona district in the western part of Riverside County, Cal., was one of the three most important clay-producing areas in California. 1912, James H. Hill, president of Alberhill Coal and Clay, hired Alexander Robertson to experiment with Alberhill clays and, thus, to establish the Alberhill Pottery. (Robertson left Halcycon Art Pottery in Halcycon, Cal., to accept the position.) 1912–14, Robertson threw finely crafted art pottery in primarily unglazed models. The colors of his bisque vases ranged from a very light pink color and white to red terracotta. Alberhill's output was small and exclusively the work of Robertson.
Citations Gold medal (to Robertson for his Alberhill Pottery work), 1915 *Panama-Pacific International Exposition*, San Francisco.
Bibliography Andersen et al., *California Design 1910*, Salt Lake City: Peregrine Smith, 1980 (reprint of 1974 edition).

Alberius, Olle (1926–)

Swedish glassmaker.

Training 1952–56, Konstfackskolan, Stockholm.
Biography 1957–63, Alberius worked for Syco in Strömstad; 1963–71, Rörstrands Porslinsfabriker in Lidköping; from 1971, for Orrefors Glasbruk, designing glassware and studio pieces in a return to the modern forms of an earlier time.
Exhibitions/citations Work subject of numerous exhibitions, beginning 1968 at the Artium in Gothenburg. Received numerous prizes.
Bibliography Ann Marie Herlitz Gezelius, *Orrefors: A Swedish Glassplant*, Stockholm, 1984. Frederick Cooke, *Glass: Twentieth-Century Design*, New York: Dutton, 1986: 86.

Albers, Anni (b. Annelise Fleischmann 1899–1994)

German textile designer, artist, and teacher; born Berlin; active Germany and US; wife of Josef Albers.

Training 1916–19 under Martin Brandenburg, in Berlin; 1919–20, Kunstgewerbeschule, Hamburg; 1922–30 under Georg Muche, Gunta Stölzl, and Paul Klee, Bauhaus, Weimar and Dessau.
Biography 1928/29–31, she taught textile design at the Bauhaus, Dessau; 1925, married Josef Albers; was the first to experiment with weaving cellophane; 1930–33, worked independently in Dessau and Berlin; 1933 with Josef, emigrated to the US helped by Edward M.M. Warburg and Abby Aldrich Rockefeller on the instigation of Alfred H. Barr Jr., director, The Museum of Modern Art, New York, and on a non-quota visa guaranteed by Philip Johnson and Warburg; 1933–49, became a professor of art, Black Mountain College, N.C., and, concurrently, a freelance textile designer; 1949, moved with Josef to New Haven, Conn.; was active in both handweaving and machine production. Her designs sometimes reflected the geometry of her husband's paintings. From 1959 for more than 25 years, she designed textiles by Knoll and, from 1978, for Sunar; became known for her collection of Pre-Columbian Mexican miniatures. She died in Orange, Connecticut.
Exhibitions/citations 1999–2000 one-person exhibition, recognizing her centenary birth year, sponsored by the Solomon R. Guggenheim Foundation, touring Venice, Paris, and New York. 2000, subject of the

Anni Albers. Wall hanging. 1927. Cotton and silk, 58 1/4 x 47 3/4" (147.9 x 121.3 cm). Mfr.: Workshop of Gunta Stölzl, Zürich. Gift of the designer in memory of Greta Daniel. MoMA.

Josef Albers. Tea glass with saucer and stirrer. 1925. Heat-resistant glass, chrome-plated steel, ebony, and porcelain, cup 2 x 5 1/2 x 3 1/2" (5.1 x 14 x 8.9 cm), saucer dia. 4 1/8" (10.5 cm), stirrer l. 4 1/4 x w. 7/16" (10.8 x 1.1 cm). Mfr: Bauhaus Metal Workshop, Weimar, Germany. Gift of the designer. MoMA.

first comprehensive exhibition, The Jewish Museum (former mansion of Edward M.M. Warburg), New York. 1961 gold medal for craftsmanship, American Institute of Architects (AIA).
Bibliography Anni Albers, *Anni Albers: Pictorial Weavings*, Cambridge, Mass.: MIT, 1959. Anni Albers, *On Designing*, Middletown, Conn.: Wesleyan University, 1962/1971. Anni Albers, *On Weaving*, Middletown, Conn., 1965. Cat., *Anni und Josef Albers. Eine Retrospektive*, Munich: Villa Stuck/Josef Albers Museum Bottrop, 1989. Cat., Nicholas Fox Weber and Pandora Tabatabai Asbaghi, *Anni Albers*, New York: Guggenheim Museum, 1999. Paola Antonelli (ed.), *Objects of Design: The Museum of Modern Art*, New York: The Museum of Modern Art, 2003: 77.

Albers, Josef (1888–1976)

German painter, designer, theoretician, and teacher; born Bottrop, Westphalia; active Germany and the US; husband of Anni Albers.

Training 1905–20, in art in Buren, Berlin, Essen, and Munich; 1920–23, Bauhaus, Weimar.
Biography As a young man, Albers was a primary-school teacher in Bottrop, studied in Berlin, and subsequently received certification to teach art. And, during this time, he began to consider himself an artist; 1920 at age 32, enrolled at the Bauhaus school in Weimar and, 1923, began teaching there, becoming a master in 1925; 1923, taught the Bauhaus's preliminary course in form (with Lázsló Moholy-Nagy) on which many design schools today base their courses; while at the Bauhaus, designed the innovative 1923 vitrine and mirror in chrome and clear and opaque glass items, 1925 glass-and-metal tableware, and, 1927, some furniture models. 1925, he married Anni Fleischmann, whom he had met at the Bauhaus; 1933, when the Nazis closed the Bauhaus in Berlin, was among the first of the Bauhaus teachers to emigrate to the US, with Anni—assisted through the financial support of Edward M.M. Warburg and Abby Aldrich Rockefeller on the instigation of Alfred H. Barr Jr., director, The Museum of Modern Art, New York, and on a non-quota visa guaranteed by Philip Johnson and Warburg; 1933–49, taught at Black Mountain College, an avant-garde school in N.C., and. subsequently. at Harvard University, Cambridge, Mass.; 1950–60, was professor and chairperson of the design department, Yale University, New Haven, Conn. He is best known today for his color theories and minimalist color-interactive art, particularly in the *Homage to the Square* series of paintings and the book *Interaction of Color*. (Yale University, 1963/1971; CD-ROM edition, 1994). 1983, the Josef Albers Museum was established at his birthplace, Bottrop, in a building designed by Bernhard Küppers. Albers died in Orange, Connecticut.
Exhibitions Living room installed at 1931 Berlin *Deutsche Bauhausstellung* and included in 1932 *Modern Architecture—International Exhibition*, The Museum of Modern Art, New York. Work subject of 1991 exhibition organized by Art Services International and traveling; 1994 exhibition organized by Peggy Guggenheim Collection, Venice, and Josef Albers Foundation, Orange, Conn. (catalogs below).
Bibliography Manfred Luck, *Josef Albers Bibliographie*, Bottrop: Stadt Bottrop, 1983. Cat., *Josef Albers*, New York: Guggenheim Museum, 1988. Cat., *Anni und Josef Albers. Eine Retrospektive*, Munich: Villa Stuck/Josef Albers Museum Bottrop, 1989. Kelly Feeney, *Josef Albers: Works on Paper*, Alexandria, Va.: Art Services International, 1991. Cat., Josef Albers, *Josef Albers: Glass, Color, Light*, New York: Guggenheim Museum, 1994.

Alberti, Maurizio (1953–)

Italian designer; born Milan.

Training To 1970, Liceo Artistico di Brera; subsequently, architecture, Politecnico; both Milan.
Biography Alberti worked as a graphic designer in various studios; 1975, with Giuseppe Bossi, Pierangelo Marucco, Francesco Roggero, and Bruno Rossio, founded studio Original Designers 6R5 in Milan. Clients have included Bassetti, Griso-Jover, Lanerossi, Sasatex, and Taif in Italy, and Griffine Marechal and Le Roi in France. 6R5 designed tapestry murals by Printeco and wallpaper by a French firm.
Bibliography *ADI Annual 1976*, Milan: Associazione per il Disegno Industriale, 1976.

Albertus, Gundorph (1887–1970)

Danish silversmith; brother of Vilhelm Albertus.

Training Sculpture, Det Kongelige Danske Kunstakademi, Copenhagon.
Biography Albertus, a brother-in-law of Georg Jensen, joined the Jensen Sølvsmedie in Copenhagen in 1911 as a chaser and, 1926–54, was assistant director there, where he designed Mitra, the company's first mass-produced stainless-steel cutlery and 1930 Cactus pattern, still in production.
Exhibitions/citations Work shown at Salon d'Automne, Paris; participated in numerous worldwide exhibitions. Gold medal, 1925 *Exposition Internationale des Arts Décoratifs et Industriels Modernes*; diploma of honor, 1937 *Exposition In-ternationale des Arts et Techniques dans la Vie Moderne*; both Paris.
Bibliography Cat., *Georg Jensen Silversmithy: 77 Artists, 75 Years*, Washington, D.C.: Smithsonian, 1980.

Albini, Franco (1905–1977)

Italian architect, city planner, and interior, exhibition, furniture, and consumer-products designer; born Robbiate (CO); father of Marco Albini.

Training To 1929, architecture, Politecnico, Milan.
Biography Albini was active in Gio Ponti's studio long before graduating in architecture; 1930, left after meeting Edoardo Persico, who appeared to be more truly Rationalist, and, with Renato Camus and Giancarlo Palanti, set up his own studio in Milan; for a 1933 competition, designed a prototype transparent radio, housed between two sheets of Perspex; in the prewar years, was a member of Rationalist groups, working in Milan and culturally supported by the journal *Casabella-continuità*, of which he was editor 1945–46. His 1940s and 1950s furniture clearly reveals his Rationalist leanings in its logical form and manufacturing process. His tension-wire suspension shelving has been widely published. Through *Casabella-continuità*, he expressed his theories and his interest in novelty, uniqueness, mass production, and commonplace construction materials; 1949–64, he taught, Istituto Universitario di Architettura, Venice; 1954–55, Facoltà di Architettura, Turin; and, 1963–77, architectural composition, Politecnico, Milan. 1951, Franca Helg joined Albini's studio, which became Studio di Architettura Franco Albini e Franca Helg; accompanied him in his lecturing. This was a highly active period of activity for them in interior design, architecture, town planning, and design. They codesigned furniture from the beginning of their association. Albini was the first architect-designer to work for Cassina furniture firm; became a member, Congrès Internationaux d'Architecture Moderne (CIAM), Istituto Nationale di Urbanistica (INU), Accademia di San Luca, Istituto Scientifico of the Consiglio Nazionale delle Ricerche (CNR) for Museography, and Associazione per il Disegno Industriale (ADI). 1962, Antonio Piva joined Albini's studio; 1965, his son Marco Albini joined the firm that became known, after Albini's death, as Marco Albini, Franca Helg, Antonio Piva, Architetti.
Work 1957 La Rinascente department store in Rome and 1962 Milan subway interior; Tensistructure bookshelves, transparent radio, and a chair for Cassina. Furniture in wood and metal included 1938–39 desk by Knoll/Gavina (produced from 1949), 1950 Margherita and Gala wicker armchairs by Bonacina, 1952 Fiorenza chair by Arflex, 1951 Luisa armchair and 1956 PS16 rocking chair by Poggi, 1968 lighting system (with Helg and Piva) by Sirrah. 1950–68, Poggi furniture company produced only Albini's designs. Other designs were produced by FontanaArte, San Lorenzo, and Siemens.

Franco Albini. Luisa Armchair. 1951. Wood and fabric, 30 5/16 x 22 1/16 x 22 7/16" (77 x 56 x 57 cm). Mfr.: Poggi, Italy (1955). Gift of the mfr. MoMA.

Exhibitions/citations As early as 1930, participated in the 3rd Esposizione Biennale delle Arti Decorative e Industriali Moderne, Monza, as a Rationalist practitioner; in the Triennali di Milano. Work subject of 1981 exhibition, Rotonda della Bosana, Milan; 1989–91 *Franco Albini and His Studio: Architecture and Design 1930–1988* touring the US (catalog below). 1955, 1964 (with others), 1989 (with others), Premio Compasso d'Oro; 1958, Premio Olivetti in Architecture; 1963, Premio IN-Arch Lazio; 1971, Biscione d'Oro. 1971, elected Honorary Royal Designer for Industry, UK, and honorary member, American Institute of Architects (AIA).
Bibliography Paolo Fossati, *Il design in Italia*, Turin: Einaudi, 1972. Cat., Franca Helg et al., *Franco Albini: architettura e design 1930–1970*, Florence: Centro Di, 1979. Andrea Branzi and Michele De Lucchi, *Design italiano degli anni '50*, Milan: Ricerche Design Editrice, 1985. Stephen Lee, *Franco Albini and His Studio: Marco Albini, Franca Helg, Antonio Piva: Architecture and Design 1934–77*, New York: Princeton Architectural Press, 1990. Antonio Piva and Vittorio Prina, *Franco Albini, 1905–1977*, Milan: Electa, 1998.

Albini, Marco (1940–)
Italian architect-designer; born Milan; son of Franco Albini.

Training To 1965, architecture, Politecnico, Milan.
Biography 1965, Albini joined his father's architecture studio in Milan; was a member, managers' board of documentation center, IN/ARCH, 1969–72, was in charge of industrial design course at the art school in Venice and, 1971–73, at Istituto Universitario di Architettura, Venice; from 1980, was a researcher, Politecnico, Milan, where, 1981–84, was in charge of architecture file and projects section, documentation center; participated in numerous conferences in Italy and abroad.
Bibliography Fumio Shimizu and Studio Matteo Thun (eds.), *The Italian Design: Descendants of Leonardo da Vinci*, Tokyo: Graphic-sha, 1987.

Albinson, Donald (1915–)
American furniture designer.

Training In Sweden; Cranbrook Academy of Art, Bloomfield Hills, Mich.; Yale University, New Haven, Conn.
Biography Albinson collaborated with Charles Eames and George Nelson at Herman Miller Furniture Company, Zeeland, Mich. In Eames's office in Venice, Cal., Albinson created the fiberglass shell, encouraged by Eames and often incorrectly credited solely to Charles and Ray Eames; was instrumental in sculptor Harry Bertoia's joining the Eames design studio in California; 1964–71, was head of the design department at Knoll in New York. The 1965 Albinson stacking chair by Knoll is similar to British designer Robin Day's highly popular 1963 Mark II (or Polyprop) chair by Hille, although Albinson's may be more sophisticated. After Knoll, Albinson became a consultant designer to Westinghouse on office seating and furniture systems.
Exhibitions/citations Chairs shown at 1968 Paris and 1971 London exhibitions (catalogs below). 1967 award, American Institute of Architects (AIA); 1967 award, American Institute of Decorators (AID).
Bibliography Cat., *Les assises du siège contemporain*, Paris: Musée des Arts Décoratifs, 1968. Cat., *Modern Chairs 1918–1970*, London: Lund Humphries, 1971.

Alchimia, Studio
Italian design cooperative; located Milan.

History 1976, the Alchimia Studio was founded by Alessandro Guerriero. It was a proto-Memphis design group that examined mass culture and communication rather than the technological aspects of design; makes and sells rather than merely intellectualizes about innovative design. The neo-modern group researches the essential environmental and psychological ideas behind objects, striving toward a new theory of romantic design. At its core is an eclecticism that allows for the development of real objects that marry poetic design concepts with skilled craft manufacture. Members are known for recycling or transforming existing images, particularly famous works of art, as a form of commentary on the process of mass replication. Its membership came from late-1960s radical groups; has included Donatella Biffi, Pier Carlo Bontempi, Stefano Casciani, Carla Ceccariglia, Rina Corti, Walter Garro, Bruno Gregori, Giorgio Gregori, Adriana Guerriero, Rainer Hegele, Jeremy King, Yumiko Kobajashi, Ewa Kulakowska, Mauro Panzeri, and Patrizia Scarzella. The Milan design establishment was shocked by the use of kitsch and popular-culture images as metaphor, when Alchimia's 1979 Bau.Haus Uno and 1980 Bau.Haus Due collections included recycled and repainted second-hand furniture. The particularly provocative 1981 Mobile Infinito brought Alchimia to international notice. 1984, the Zabro furniture-production firm was established to unite the 'New Craft' and industry. The group was placed in charge of the art direction of the 1985 *Japanese Avant-Garde in the Future* festival, Genoa. Alchimia has produced objects by Andrea Belloni, Lapo Binazzi, Andrea Branzi, Riccardo Dalisi, Trix and Robert Haussmann, Michele De Lucchi, Alessandro Mendini, Paola Navone, Daniela Puppa, Franco Raggi, Ettore Sottsass, and others. Still active, Alchimia designs furniture/furnishings, stage sets, seminars, interiors, clothes, and paintings, and produces videos, music, architecture, and publications.
Exhibitions/citations Work shown in its own gallery. Bau.Haus Uno and Bau.Haus Due were shown at 1979 (16th) Triennale di Milano.

The Aluminum Cooking Utensil Co. Wear-Ever rotary food press. 1932. Aluminum, steel, and wood, pestle l. 10 3/4 x dia. 1 3/4" (4.4 x 27.3 cm), sieve and frame assembled h. 9 x dia. 11 3/8" (28.9 x 22.9 cm). Mfr.: The Aluminum Cooking Utensil Co., US. Gift of Lewis & Conger. MoMA.

Exhibitions have included 1978 *Room of the Century*, Palazzo dei Diamanti, Ferrara; 1980 *Forum Design, Design Phenomene*, Linz; 1980 *Eulogy to the Banal*, Biennale di Venezia, Venice; 1981 *Manual Room*, Gallery of Modern Art, Bologna; 1981 *Hermaphrodite Architecture*, Contemporary Art Pavilion, Milan; 1982 *House of Juliet*, Gallery of Modern Art, Verona; 1983 *House of the Newlyweds*, Triennale di Milano, Milan; 1985 *Never-Ending Furniture*, Museum of Modern Art, Tokyo and Kyoto; 1987 *La Chambre Fin-de-Siècle*, Centre Georges Pompidou, Paris; 1987 Documenta 8, Museo Universale, Kassel; 1992 *Città Alchimia*, Erfurt. Group received 1981 Premio Compasso d'Oro (one citation with Mendini; one for design research).
Bibliography Studio Alchimia, *Bauhaus collection 1980–1981*, Milan: Alchimia Editore, 1980. Pier Carlo Bontempi and Giorgio Gregori (designers, editors), *Alchimia*, Milan: Idea, 1985. Guia Sambonet, *Alchimia 1977–78*, Turin: Allemandi, 1986. Stefano Casciani, *Disegni Alchimia 1982–87*, Turin: Allemandi, 1986. Kazuko Sato, *Alchimia: italienisches Design der Gegenwart*, Berlin: Taco, 1988.
> See Guerriero, Alessandro; Mendini, Alessandro.

Alcoa (Aluminum Company of America); The Aluminum Cooking Utensil Co.; Kensington; Wear-Ever

American manufacturer of raw aluminum and aluminum products and domestic-ware divisions.

History 1888, the Pittsburgh Reduction Company in New Kensington, Pa., was founded by scientist Charles Martin Hall (1863–1914); 1907, was renamed Aluminum Company of America. By 1929, ALCOA, as an acronym, was in popular use with a logo designed as a 'Norman' shield, redesigned 1955 by Harley Earl Associates (the automobile designer) of Detroit, again redesigned 1963 by Saul Bass of Los Angeles. 1999, the firm's corporate name was offically changed to Alcoa Inc. with a slightly updated logo by Arnold Saks of New York. Early on, Alcoa was the only American company making raw aluminum. Even so, Alcoa recognized the need to persuade manufacturers of household goods to use the metal and, thus, 1901, decided to enter the cookware market and, 1903, established the subsidiary The Aluminum Cooking Utensil Co. to make no-nonsense, functional kitchen utensils under the Wear-Ever brand name. 1934, another Alcoa brand, Kensington, was introduced, with decorative accessories designed by Lurelle Guild and made of a special alloy, said to resist staining and tarnishing. 1956–60, Alcoa promoted ideas for aluminum's future domestic use through the Forecast Program and commissioned 22 well-known designers, including Jay Doblin, Charles and Ray Eames, Alexander Girard, and Isamu Noguchi.
Bibliography Trade cat., *Wear-Ever Aluminum Specialties*, New Kensington, Pa.: Aluminum Cooking Utensil Co., c. 1927. Charles C. Carr, *Alcoa: An American Experience*, New York: Rinehart, 1952. Paula Ockner and Leslie A. Piña, *Art Deco Aluminum: Kensington*, Atglen, Pa.: Schiffer, 1997. George David Smith, *From Monopoly to Competition: The Transformation of Alcoa, 1888–1986*, Cambridge: Cambridge University Press, 1988. Cat., Sarah Nichols et al., *Aluminum by Design*, New York: Abrams, 2000. Douglas McCombs, 'Aluminum Tomorrow,' *Echoes*, no. 36, May 2001.
> See aluminum; also Reynolds, Richard S.

Alemagna, Renata (1948–)

Italian furniture designer; born and active Milan.

Biography From 1975, Alemagna was professionally active; designed furniture for clients, including De Gioanni, Face Standard, Gnecchi, Parolini, Pavus, and Pozzi Figli di Cesare & Eugenio.
Bibliography *ADI Annual 1976*, Milan: Associazione per il Disegno Industriale, 1976.

Alessandri, Marc (1932–)

French environmental architect and designer; born Paris.

Training École Supérieure Nationale des Beaux-Arts, Paris.
Biography 1967, Alessandri set up his own architecture office, L'Abaque in Paris; designed numerous hotels and office interiors in France, Belium, Spain, and Africa. His 1969 3000 ergonomic chair range was produced by Airborne. 1970–76, he was president, Interior Architects Union; 1977–79, president, Société des Artistes Décorateurs; 1979, became a founding member, VIA (French furniture association); from 1988, was a freelance designer and associated with Asymétrie in Paris and, 1987–92, designed Interface Cosmos office-furniture system by Mobilier International, Hémisphères series by Airborne, and for Décade and Paros.
Citations 1982, Lauréat du Concours de Mobilier de Bureau (produced by Knoll-France) sponsored by APCI.

Alessi

Italian domestic metal-products manufacturer; located Crusinallo, Verbania.

History 1921, Alessi was founded by Giovanni Alessi. Its earliest products were coffee sets and trays. The firm was known as F.A.O. (Fratelli Alessi Omegna) 1921–47, Alfra (Alessi Fratelli) 1947–68, and Ceselleria Alessi 1968–70. From 1929, Alessi has specialized in bar-counter and domestic tableware items, including bread baskets, teapots, egg cups, condiment sets, and cheese dishes. 1932, under Carlo Alessi (Gravellona Toce, 1916–), the firm began to focus on the appearance of its wares. (His most significant project was 1945 Bombé coffee and tea set, discontinued 1972 and re-entered into production 1980.) From 1935, more attention was being paid to its industrial techniques in an attempt to abandon its slow, craft-based approach. From 1945, Carlo was the firm's general manager; shortly afterward, began commissioning consultant designers. 1950, with large US orders, mass production was begun. By 1991, the 1950s cocktail shaker (no. 870) designed by Luigi Massoni had sold 1.5 million pieces. Carlo became president and brother Ettore Alessi vice-president. Producing numbered and signed pieces by international architects and designers, including Ettore Sottsass, the firm gained popularity in the 1970s. Its first cult object was 1978 espresso coffee pot designed by Richard Sapper. The 1983 Tea and Coffee Piazza project initiated by Carlo Alessi's son Alberto (1946–), described as an attempt to create 'architecture in miniatures,' commissioned 11 architects: Óscar Tusquets Blanca, Michael Graves, Hans Hollein, Charles Jencks, Richard Meier, Alessandro Mendini, Paolo Portoghesi, Aldo Rossi, Stanley Tigerman, Robert Venturi, and Kasumasa Yamashita. Each set was made in a limited edition of 99 in silver (plus three artists' proofs in other metals); only Tusquets Blanca's service was also available in silver-plated brass. The tremendous success of the venture prompted a wave of architect-designed goods from Alessi and other manufacturers. 1991, designs by women on the theme of serving and offering began to be produced as part of a project coordinated by the Alessi Study Center in Milan, set up 1990 and directed by Laura Polinoro. From 1982, the Officina Alessi division produced

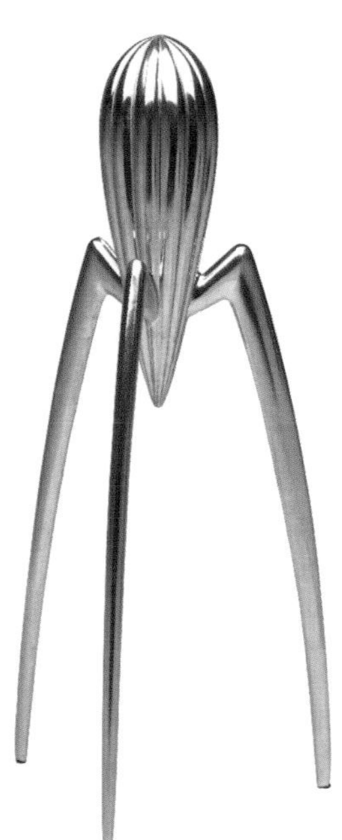

Alessi: Philippe Starck. Juicy Salif lemon squeezer. 1990. PTFE-treated pressure cast aluminum and polyamide, h. 11 1/2 x dia. 5" (12.7 x 29.2 cm). Mfr.: Officina Alessi (1991). David Whitney Collection, Gift of David Whitney. MoMA.

limited editions of metalwares; 1988, Alessi acquired a wooden-products factory (Battista Piazza), and the Twergi range of wooden tabletop items and kitchen utensils was launched; 1990, Alessi's ceramic line Tendentse was introduced. 1,200 products were advertised in Alessi's 1991 catalog. Alberto Alessi's Casa della Felicità on the Lago d'Orta was created as a laboratory and domicile; it was designed by Alessandro and Francesco Mendini and the Atelier Alchimia (Giorgio Gregori), with a tower by Aldo Rossi, and Falvio Albanese and Alberto Gozzi were consultants on the wine cellar. 1992, Alessi acquired the rights to 1950s–60s (and some 1980s) Enzo Mari designs from Danese. 1994 Alessofono was an attempt to redesign the saxophone; A highly successful enterprise, Alessi continues to produce the work of well-known and little-known designers as well as historical reproductions of metalware by Christopher Dresser, Josef Hoffmann, the Bauhaus, and others; 1998, established the Alessi Museum in its Crusinallo headquarters.
Work Large inventory of products have included cocktail shaker (no. 870) by Luigi Massoni; 1978 espresso coffee set by Richard Sapper; kettles by Michael Graves and Aldo Rossi; Falstaf cookware by Alessandro Mendini; 1990 Juicy Salif lemon squeezer, 1991 Hot Bertaa kettle, and 1991 Max le Chinois colander, all by Philippe Starck; Leina fireplace poker and calipers by Pep Bonet; coffee mills (from Twergi division) by Riccardo Dalisi and Milton Glaser; 1992 100 Vases by 100 Designers series; 1993 teapot by Frank Gehry; 1993 plastics, 2001 cutlery and glasses, and 2002 porcelain by Guido Venturini; 1997 Dauphine calculator by George Sowden; a wide range of products by Stefano Giovannoni from 1993, including 2002 Il Bagno Alessi (produced with Inda, Laufen, and Oras); 2000 bowl by Francesca Amfitheatrof; and a large number of others.
Exhibitions/citations Products subject of *Paesaggio Casalingo: La Produzione Alessi nell'Industria dei Casalinghi dal 1921 al 1980*, originating at the 1979 (16th) Triennale di Milano (catalog below), and 1990 *Alessi/Mendini: dix ans de collaboration*, Centre Georges Pompidou, Paris. Product designs by women coordinated by the Alessi Study Center were first shown at 1991 Salone del Mobile, Milan. 1996, Kho Liang le Prize (for Philips Alessi household products), Netherlands. To Carlo Alessi: first prize (export activities) from Chamber of Commerce and Industry, Novara Prefecture; Gold Mercury from European Commerce Committee; Premio Marazza (human relationships in the workplace).
Bibliography Cat., Alessandro Mendini, *Paesaggio Casalingo: la produzione Alessi nell'industria dei casalinghi dal 1921 al 1980*, Milan: Editoriale Domus, 1979. Patrizia Scarzella, *Tea and Coffee Piazza: 11 servizi da tè e caffè*, Crusinallo: Alessi, 1983. Fumio Shimizu and Studio Matteo Thun (eds.), *The Italian Design: Descendants of Leonardo da Vinci*, Tokyo: Graphic-sha, 1987. F.A. Lita Talarico, 'Alessi SpA,' *Graphis*, no. 272, Mar.–Apr. 1991: 61–77. Alberto Alessi, *The Dream Factory: Alessi Since 1921,* Milan: Electa/Elemond, and Crusinallo: Alessi/F.A.O., 2000. Raffaella Poletti (ed.), *Vedi alla voce: bagno*, Milan/Crusinallo: Electa/Alessi, 2002. Mel Byars, *Design in Steel*, London: Laurence King, 2002.

Alias
> See Forcolini, Carlo.

Alix, Charlotte (1897–1987)
French furniture designer.

Biography 1925–27, Alix worked for the baron de Rothschild; encouraged by her friend Gaston Roussel, the director of the Laboratoires Roussel, Paris, she pursued the study of new materials and forms and, with his support, designed pieces produced by artisans in the Faubourg Saint-Antoine furnituremaking area of Paris; from 1928, worked with Louis Sognot in the design office Bureau International des Arts Français. Their first major commission was the 1929 Laboratoires Roussel, for which they designed furniture in bent-metal tubing and glass. They also designed offices of *La semaine à Paris* newspaper (archiect, Robert Mallet-Stevens), Polo de Bagatelle bar, and interior of graphic artist Jean Carlu's residence, Paris. 1929, Alix became a member, Union des Artistes Modernes (UAM); to 1952, remained a member, Salon d'Automne.
Exhibitions Work with Sognot was regularly shown at Salons of the time, particularly the Salon d'Automne, Paris; as members of UAM, at its 1930s exhibitions, Paris.
Bibliography Raymond Cogniat, 'Louis Sognot et Charlotte Alix,' *Art et décoration*, vol. 59, July–Dec. 1930. Arlette Barré-Despond, *UAM*, Paris: Regard, 1986: 506–09. Pierre Kjellberg, *Art déco: les maîtres du mobilier, le décor des paquebots*, Paris: Amateur, 1986.
> See Sognot, Louis.

Allard, Gunilla (1957–)
Swedish film-set and furniture designer.

Training 1983–88, Konstfackskolan, Stockholm; 1985, guest student, Institute of Visual Communication, Det Kongelige Danske Kunstakademi, Copenhagen
Biography Initially, she was a set designer for Swedish films, including property manager on Ingmar Bergman's *Fanny and Alexander* (1982); from 1993, designed furniture, including 1994–99 Cinema seating and table, 1997 Chicago modular seating, 1999 Cosmos stacking chair and Chicago I and Z trolleys, 2002 Saturn table; all by Lammhults.
Citations 1990 Dagens Nyheter's Designer; 1991, 1992, 1996, 1999 Utmärkt Svensk Form (outstanding Swedish-design citation); 1995 and 2000 Design Prize Swedish Design; 1996 Georg Jensen prize; 2000 Bruno Mathsson prize.
Bibliography Michele De Lucchi (ed.), *The International Design Yearbook*, London: Laurence King, 2001.

Allen, David (1916–)
American interior designer; born Ames, Iowa; active New York.

Training 1934–36, Brown University, Providence, R.I.; 1939, Kungliga Tekniska Högskolan, Stockholm; 1940, architecture, Yale University, New Haven, Conn.; after World War II, interned at Skidmore, Owings and Merrill (SOM), New York; 1946–47, returned to Yale.
Biography 1947, Allen settled in New York and worked at Knoll Planning Unit as an interior designer and briefly at Raymond Loewy's industrial design office; subsequently, through architects Harrison and Abramovitz, designing furnishings for General Assembly Building, United Nations, New York. 1950, he was hired by architect Gordon Bunschaft at SOM architecture firm as an interior designer, with the penthouse offices of 1954 Manufacturers Hanover Trust Building, New York, as his first important assignment. To late 1980s, a large number of Allen-designed or -supervised interiors followed. 1965, he became associate partner and senior interior designer, SOM; 1985, went into semi-retirement. Designed furniture produced by Bernhardt, GF, Hickory Business Furniture, Steelcase, and Stow & Davis, including 1983 Andover chair range by Stendig; most was originally designed for site-specific use in SOM architecture commissions.
Citations Elected to Hall of Fame, *Interiors* magazine.
Bibliography Maeve Slavin, *David Allen*, New York: Rizzoli, 1990.

Allen, 'Harry' Harold (1964–)
American designer; born Plainfield, N.J.

Training 1992, master's degree in industrial design, Pratt Institute, Brooklyn, N.Y.
Biography Early on, Allen worked for Prescriptive Cosmetics; 1993, opened Harry Allen & Associates, New York, to design interiors, furniture, products, lighting, graphics, and exhibitions for clients, including Benza, Dom Pérignon, IKEA, Donna Karan, George Kovacs, MAC Cosmetics, and Magis; became known for his design of the Moss design store, New York. Also designed Sony Plaza and North Face Store, Chicago; Dragon Fly Selects jewelry store, Taiwan; new offices of *Metropolis* magazine and of Guggenheim Museum, both New York.
Exhibitions/citations Work included in 1995 *Mutant Materials* and 2002 *U.S. Design* traveling exhibition (catalogs below). 2000 Young Designer Award, Brooklyn Museum of Art, New York.
Bibliography Cat., Paola Antonelli, *Mutant Materials in Contemporary Design*, New York: The Museum of Modern Art/Abrams, 1995. Wang Hanbai, *Design Focus: Harry Allen*, Beijing: China Youth, 2001. Michele De Lucchi (ed.), *The International Design Yearbook*, London: Laurence King, 2001. Cat., R. Craig Miller (intro.), *U.S. Design: 1975–2000*, Munich: Prestel, 2002.

Alons, 'Cor' Cornelius Louis (1892–1967)
Dutch interior architect and industrial designer; born Groningen.

Training 1913–17, drawing and painting department, Academie van Beeldende Kunsten, The Hague.
Biography 1917–21 under architect Hendrik Wouda, Alons worked as a draftsperson in the modern-interior-art department, H. Pander & Sons, The Hague; 1919–20, taught an evening furniture-drawing class, Patrimonium, The Hague; 1919, became member of Vakgroep voor Drukkunst, Bindkunst en Leerbewerking (VANK); 1921–23, worked

as a designer at painted- and stained-glass window firm G. van Geldermalsen, Rotterdam; 1922, a designer at furniture firm LOV; 1923, traveled in France, Germany, and Hungary; designed stained-glass windows for the Baarns Lyceum; settled in The Hague; became an independent interior architect and member of Haagsche Kunstkring; 1923–27, designed pottery by NV De Duinvoet; was a prolific interior designer who collaborated with prominent Dutch architects; 1928, designed cutlery for Emailleerfabriek 'De IJsel'; 1928–36, was active in own design office and showroom in his own residence in The Hague; 1929–57, taught furniture construction, Academie van Beeldende Kunsten, The Hague, and, 1934, founded its interior-arts course; 1932–33, designed textiles by Van den Bergh's firm in Oss; 1933, designed store front of decorative-arts shop De Kerhuil in Haarlem; 1935–40, tubular-steel furniture by Oostwoud Fabrieken in Kraneker; stained-glass windows and bar of 1938 oceanliner *New Amsterdam*; 1942, was imprisoned by the Germans and returned to the Netherlands; designed 1948 wooden furniture by C. den Boer and 1954 metal and glass furniture.
Exhibitions/citations Work included in 1920 *Modern Interior Art* (stained-glass windows and decorative panels) organized by LOV in Oosterbeek; 1925 *Exposition Internationale des Arts Décoratifs et Industriels Modernes*, Paris; 1927, one-person exhibition, The Hague; designed PTT pavilion, Jaarbeurs fair, Utrecht; 1932 VANK exhibition (showing chrome-plated steel furniture by Ph. Dekker), Rotterdam; designed exhibition for 250th anniversary of Academie van Beeldende Kunsten, Pulchri Studio, The Hague; Dutch pavilion, 1937 *Exposition Internationale des Arts et Techniques dans la Vie Moderne,* Paris. 1962, elected honorary member of GKf.
Bibliography R.J. Risseeuw, 'Binnenhuiskunst: een vraaggesprek met den binnenhuisarchitect Cor Alons,' in *Op den Uitkijk, tijdschrift voor het Christelijk gezin*, no. 5, 1929. P.J. Risseeuw, 'In gesprek met Cor Alons,' in *Omtmoeting: Letterkundig en Algemeen Cultureel Maandblad*, no. 5, 1951: 4–5, 151–61. Marg van der Burgh, *Cor Alons: Binnenhuisarchitect en industrieel ontwerper 1892–1967*, Rotterdam: 010, 1988.

Alpico
> See Pillivuyt.

Alring, Leif (1936–)

Danish furniture designer.

Training Kunsthåndværkerskolen, Copenhagen.
Biography Alring, a qualified cabinetmaker, has designed carpets, furniture, and industrial goods; written regularly in the Danish press on technical matters; and lectured widely in Scandinavia on plastics and their application to design. 1964, he experimented with plastics in an attempt to form a one-piece chair, realized as the Series 261 expanded-polystyrene model. Several of his designs were manufactured under license by firms in Japan and elsewhere.
Citations Prizes in numerous competitions, including 1966 annual prize, Danish Cabinetmakers' Society, and 1971 Bundespreis Produktdesign, Rat für Formgebung (German design council), Frankfurt.
Bibliography Cat., Milena Lamarová, *Design a Plastické Hmoty*, Prague: Uměleckoprůmyslové Muzeum, 1972.

Altherr, Jeanette (1965–)
> See Liévore, Alberto.

Al'tman, Natan Isaevich (1889–1970)

Russian painter, sculptor, set designer, and propagandist; born Vinnitza (now Ukraine).

Training 1901–07 under Kostandi and Ladyzhensky, painting and sculpture, Odessa Art School; 1910–12, Mariia Vasil'eva's Free Russian Academy, Paris.
Biography Early 1910s, Al'tman became interested in Cubism; 1912–17, contributed to the satirical magazine *Riab* (ripple) in St. Petersburg; was active in the avant-garde art group Union of Youth; 1918, became a professor at SVOMAS, a member of IZO Narkompros, and designed agitprop decorations in the Uritskii Square, Petrograd (now Palace Square, St. Petersburg) to celebrate the first anniversary of the October Revolution. Although on the verge of collapse, the Soviet government provided him with 50,000 ft (15,240 m) of canvas for his Futurist designs hung on the Winter Palace walls and General Staff Arch and the Aleksandr Column, which was turned into a Futurist sculpture. 1919, Al'tman became a leading member of Komfut (Communist Futurism); 1921, published an album of Lenin drawings and designed the set for Vladimir Maiakovskii's play *Misteriya ili buff mystery or bouffe* (1918; first performed 1921) and, early 1920s, designed ceramics; 1929–35, lived in Paris; 1936, returned to Russia; 1936, settled in Leningrad (now St. Petersburg); was active as portrait, still-life, and landscape painter, sculptor, and set designer; died in Leningrad.
Exhibitions 1910s–20s, showed paintings, sculpture, and designs in many avant-garde exhibitions in Moscow, Petrograd, Berlin, Venice, and Paris, some supporting the cause of Russo-Jewish artists. Work subject of 1968 exhibition, Leningrad.
Bibliography Waldemar George and Il'ia Ehrenburg, monograph on Al'tman in Yiddish, Paris, 1933. M. Etkind, *Natan Altman*, Moscow, 1971. V. Petrov, 'O vystavke N.I. Altmana,' in D. Chebanova (ed.), *V.N. Petrov: Ocherki i issledovaniia*, Moscow, 1978: 250–54. Cat., Stephanie Barron and Maurice Tuchman, *The Avant-Garde in Russia, 1919–1930: New Perspectives*, Cambridge, Mass: MIT, 1980. Nina Lobanov-Rostovsky, *Revolutionary Ceramics*, London: Studio Vista, 1990. Cat., *The Great Utopia: The Russian and Soviet Avant-Garde, 1915–1932*, New York: Guggenheim Museum, 1992.

aluminum (aka aluminium)

Silver-colored metal extracted from bauxite ore.

History 1808, Humphrey Davy (1778–1829) of the UK established that aluminum existed and named it so. However, it was later (1821) that French chemist P. Berthier (1782–1861) discovered a hard, red substance that contained 52% aluminum oxide near Les Baux, France, and thus named it bauxite, which is today's most commonly extracted aluminum ore. 1827, Freidrich Wohler (1800–1882) of Germany was able to produce aluminum powder through a chemical reaction. However, aluminum first captured public attention in the mid-19th century when it began to be used in jewelry and, at the time, was more highly valued than gold or diamonds. An electrolytic process, invented 1886 by Charles Martin Hall (1863–1914) of the US, contributed to costs being appreciably decreased. Some US production companies, like the Pittsburgh Reduction Company (established 1888, renamed Aluminum Company of America and now Alcoa), were established, and aluminum eventually became readily available and was dubbed 'a new material for a new century.' Because it is light in weight, brilliant, and strong, aluminum is often used in the manufacture of aircraft and in household utensils, cookware, and other domestic objects, including furniture. In Vienna, Otto Wagner specified aluminum for 1894 Der Anker shop façade and 1906 furniture by Thonet

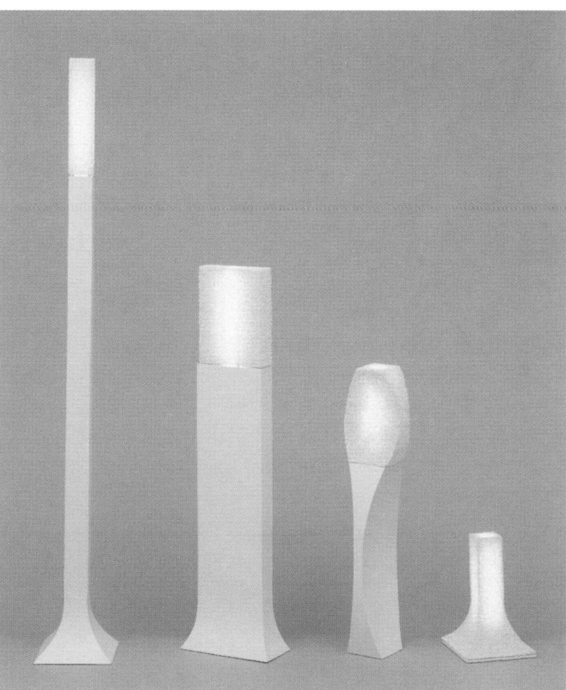

Harold Allen. Lighting fixtures. 1994. Ceramic, tower 1 68 1/4 x 8 3/4 x 8 3/4" (173.4 x 22.2 x 22.2 cm), tower 2 44 1/4 x 11 3/4 x 5 3/4" (112.4 x 29.8 x 14.6 cm), twist 33 x 8 1/2 x 4 1/2" (83.8 x 21.6 x 11.4 cm), table lamp 13 1/2 x 8 1/2 x 8 1/2" (34.3 x 21.6 x 21.6 cm). Mfr.: Harry Allen and Associates, US. Gift of the mfr. MoMA.

Aluminum: Aluminum Company of America. Outboard propeller. Pre-1934. Aluminum, dia. 9" (22.8 cm), blade l. 3 1/2" (8.9 cm). Mfr.: Aluminum Company of America, US. Gift of the mfr. MoMA.

installed in the Österreichische Postsparkasse (postal savings bank, extant today). Interior architect Fritz August Breuhaus de Groot, collaborating with Ludwig Dürr (the chief constructor at Luftschiffbau-Zeppelin) used aluminum extensively in the layout and fittings (including a Blüthner grand piano) of 1936 *Hindenburg* (LZ 129) dirigible. 1930 in Los Angeles, American manufacturer/designer Warren McArthur patented the use of aluminum in furniture. 1930s, it was incorporated into furniture by Donald Deskey and Gerrit Rietveld, and wholly used in Hans Coray's 1938 Landi outdoor chair at 1939 *Schweizerische Landesaustellung* (Swiss national exhibition), Zürich. Alcoa promoted the use of aluminum in domestic accessories and functional household goods, from cookware to vases, including the 1944 Navy chair, initially for use on oceancraft, by Emeco (with the US Navy), still in production. Ernest Race in Britain reprocessed World War II aluminum surplus for his 1945 BA chair and other models. The drawbacks of the metal include surface corrosion as chalky oxidation (unless anodized) and a tendency to become scratched. Brightly colored domestic aluminum ware for the kitchen, particularly popular in the 1950s, included tumblers and water pitchers.
Exhibitions 2000 *Aluminum by Design*, organized by Carnegie Museum of Art, Pittsburgh, Pa., and traveling (catalog below).
Bibliography Roy A. Hunt, *The Aluminum Pioneers*, New York: Newcomen Society, 1951. *The ABC's of Aluminum: From Raw Material to Application*, Louisville, Ky.: Reynolds Metal, 1955. Rosamond McPherson Young, *Made of Aluminum: A Life of Charles Martin Hall*, New York: David McKay, 1965. Cat., *Aluminium: das Metall der Moderne*, Cologne: Kölnisches Stadtmuseum, 1991. Paula Ockner and Leslie A. Piña, *Art Deco Aluminum: Kensington*, Atglen, Pa.: Schiffer, 1997. Cat., Sarah Nichols et al., *Aluminum by Design*, New York: Abrams, 2000.
> See Alcoa; Emeco.

Alves de Souza, Flavia (1969–)

Brazilian designer; born Niterol, Rio de Janeiro; active Brazil and Italy.

Training To 1992, Universidade Federal de Minas Gerais, Belo Horizonte, Brazil; 1992, school of jewelry design; 1994, Politecnico, Milan.
Biography c. 1993, she began designing jewelry; from 1994, worked in the design studios of Iosa Ghini, Anna Gill, and Bonini Spicciolato, all Milan; subsequently, with Marco Zanini, worked at Sottsass Associati, Milan; also, as a freelance, has designed silverware by Pampaloni, silk-screened glass vases by Egizia, stainless-steel wares by Brognoli, decorations by Muraoka, china by Rosenthal, and 2001 Pororoga chaise longue/ottoman by Edra.
Exhibitions/citations Participated in 1992 *Nel Segno dell'Angelo*, Galleria Bianca Pilat, Milan; *Contenitorio*, 1995 (19th) Triennale di Milano; 1998 Lorenz competition of children's toy designs, Germany; 1999 *Tanto di Coppola*, Palazzo Intelligente Foundation, Palermo. Award, 2001 Continental (1992 electrical appliances), Brazil.

Alviar, Christopher (1961–)

Filipino industrial designer; born Manila.

Training To 1986, industrial design, University of Washington, Seattle.
Biography Alviar settled in the US; designed through various firms as a freelancer, including O'Brien International and Walter Dorwin Teague, before joining Ziba in 1987; subsequently, was a senior industrial designer at Microsoft, where he designed and developed several hardware products; has also taught, University of Washington, Washington state; is a consultant on design promotion, policies, and strategies, United Nations Development Program (UNDP) and Philippine Department of Trade & Industry.
Citations 1985 and 1986 Merit Awards, Industrial Designers Society of America (IDSA); 1988, another IDSA award (for electronic transparency-system work); others
Bibliography Albrecht Bangert and Karl Michael Armer, *80s Style: Designs of the Decade*, New York: Abbeville, 1990: 226.

Alvin

American silversmithy.

History 1886, Alvin Manufacturing was founded in Irvington, N.J., by William H. Jamouneau, president until his 1898 retirement. 1895, name changed to Alvin-Beiderhase; moved from New Jersey to Sag Harbor, Long Island, N.Y.; 1897, purchased by Joseph Fahys and Co. and operated as a branch of the firm c. 1898–1910; 1919, changed name to Alvin Silver, becoming makers of sterling-silver cutlery, hollow-ware, dresserware, silver-deposits ware, and plated-silver cutlery. 1928, was purchased by Gorham and moved to Providence, R.I.
Bibliography Dorothy R. Rainwater, *Encyclopedia of American Silver Manufacturers*, New York: Crown, 1979. Annelies Krekel-Aalberse, *Art Nouveau and Art Déco Silver*, New York: Abrams, 1989.

Ambasz, Emilio (1943-)

Argentine architect and designer, born Resistencia, Chaco; active US, Europe, and Asia.

Training 1966, bachelor's degree in architecture; 1967, master's degree in architecture, Princeton University, N.J., US.
Biography 1966–67, Ambasz was visiting professor, Hochschule für Gestaltung, Ulm, Germany; has lectured and written widely; 1968, cofounded Institute of Architecture and Urban Studies, New York; 1969, Philippe Freneau Professor of Architecture, Princeton University; 1969–76, was curator of design, The Museum of Modern Art, New York, directing and installing numerous exhibits, including 1972 *Italy: The New Domestic Landscape*, 1974 *The Architecture of Luis Barragan*, and 1976 *The Taxi Project: Realistic Solutions for Today* and wrote the catalogs. 1981–85, Ambasz was two-term president, Architectural League of New York; 1976, established building and industrial-design practice Emilio Ambasz & Associates, New York; has designed award-winning 'green buildings,' as a precursor of the movement, in Europe, Japan, and the US, including The Fukuoka Across Building, Japan; Mycal Cultural and Sports Center, Japan; Conservatory of San Antonio Botanical Center, Texas; The Venice-Mestre Hospital, Italy; Nuova Concordia large hotel and residential complex, Italy; Glory Museum, Taiwan; ENI Office Headquarters, Italy; Monuments Towers office building, US; The Museo de Arte Moderno, Buenos Aires, Argentina. He has patented a large number of industrial and mechanical designs; invented the first automatic ergonomic office-seating system (1974–75 Vertebra by Castelli); from 1978, has been chief designer, Cummins Diesel Engine Corp.; designed 1984 Logotec and 1985 Oseris track lighting by Erco Leuchten, 1985 Agamennone floor lamp by Artemide, 1995 Brief office chair by Poltrona Frau; 1998 Visor stacking chair by Knoll; 1998 X & Y stacking chair by Interstuhl; 1989 Qualis office chair by Tecno; 1998 Saturno urban lighting by ILVA; 2000 portable desktop computer by IBM. In addition to The Museum of Modern Art catalogs, he wrote *The Poetics of the Pragmatic* (1989) and *Inventions: The Reality of the Ideal* (1995) and edited *The International Design Yearbook* (1992).
Exhibitions/citations Work subject of exhibitions, Axis Design and Architecture Gallery, Tokyo, 1985; Halle Sude, The Institute of Contemporary Art, Geneva, 1986 and 1987; Centre d'Art Contemporain, Bordeaux, 1987. Retrospectives: 1989 *Emilio Ambasz: Architecture*, The Museum of Modern Art, New York; 1989–93 *Emilio Ambasz: Architecture, Exhibition, Industrial and Graphic Design*, traveling US, Canada, Japan, and Mexico; third venue at Triennale di Milano. Represented US, 1976 Biennale di Venezia; 1983 Annual Award and Special Commendation (for BBL bank), *Interiors* magazine; first prize and gold medal

and 1986 Architectural Projects Award (for 1992 Universal Exhibition master plan), American Institute of Architects (AIA), New York; grand prize, 1987 International Interior Design Award; 1986 IDEA award, Industrial Designers Society of America (IDSA); 1976, 1980, and 1987 *Progressive Architecture* awards; 1988 Award for Excellence in Commerical Design, The National Glass Association Award; 1990 Quaternario Award (for technological achievement); 1997 Vitruvius Award, Museo Nacional de Bellas Artes, Buenos Aires; 2000 AIA/*Business Week* Architecture Award (for Prefectural and International Hall, Fukuoka, Japan) and 2001 first prize in environmental architecture (for same building), Japanese Institute of Architects. Citations for industrial design: 1976 Gold Prize (for Vertebra chair), Institute of Business Designers (IBD); 1977 and 1979 Premio SMAU Industrial Design, Salone della Machina e Attrezzature per l'Ufficio, Milan; 1981 (for Vertebra), 1991 (for Qualis chair), and 2000 (for Saturno lighting) Premio Compasso d'Oro; Jury Special award for contributions to design, 1984 BIO 10 industrial-design biennial, Ljubljana; 1985 (for N14 diesel engine) and 1980 (for Logotec) Annual Design Review, *I.D.* magazine; 1980, 1983, 1986, 1987, and 1988 Design Excellence Awards and 1987, 1992, and 2000 ID Designer's Choice Awards, Industrial Designers' Society of America (IDSA); 2000 Gold Award, IDSA/*Business Week* magazine.
Bibliography Mario Bellini et al., *Emilio Ambasz: The Poetics of the Pragmatic—Architecture, Exhibit, Industrial, and Graphic Design*, New York: Rizzoli, 1989. Peter Buchanan et al., *Emilio Ambasz, Inventions: The Reality of the Ideal*, New York: 1992. Mel Byars, *On/Off: New Electronic Products*, New York: Universe, 2001. Terence Riley (intro.), *Emilio Ambasz: Natural Architecture, Artificial Design*, Milan: Electa, 2002. Michael Sorkin et al., *Analyzing Ambasz*, New York: Monacelli Press, 2004. Fulvio Irace, *Emilio Ambasz: Arcadia Tecnologica*, Milan: Skira, 2004.

American Designers Gallery

American artists' group.

History 1928, American Designers Gallery was formed in New York to foster the professional status of designers and promote high aesthetic values in the modern decorative arts. Its headquarters were located at the gallery of interior designer and decorator Paul Frankl. Members included Donald Deskey, Wolfgang and Pola Hoffmann, Ruth Reeves, Joseph Urban, Henry Varum Poor, others.
Exhibitions Work subject of 1928 (1st) exhibition (15 designers in ten complete rooms and some displays), Chase National Bank building; 1929 (2nd) exhibition; both New York.
Bibliography Karen Davies, *At Home in Manhattan*, New Haven, Conn.: Yale, 1983. Mel Byars (intro.), 'What Makes American Design American?,' in R.L. Leonard and C.A. Glassgold (eds.), *Modern American Design, by the American Union of Decorative Artists and Craftsmen*, New York: 1930; Acanthus, 1992 reprint.

Emilio Ambasz and Giancarlo Piretti. Vertebra operational chair. 1975. Injected molded thermoplastic, die-cast aluminum, and fabric upholstery, 30 3/4 x 19 x 23 3/8" (78.1 x 48.2 x 59.4 cm), seat h. 18" (45.7 cm). Mfr.: Anonima Castelli, Italy. Gift of Open Ark B.V. MoMA.

American Encaustic Tiling

American ceramics firm; located Zanesville, Ohio.

History 1875, American Encaustic Tiling (incorporated 1878) was founded by F.H. Hall with backing by Benedict Fischer and G.R. Lansing; was one of the firms in the US quick to take advantage of varicolored local clays; was in the forefront of tile manufacturing for more than 50 years; by 1880s, had a salesroom in New York. The factory made glazed tiles from 1880, relief tiles from 1881, and white wall tiles from 1895. The large number of commissions for encaustic tiles for 1870s buildings included the State Capitol, Albany, N.Y., as well as tiles for the Holland Tunnel, New York. c. 1891 on tiles, it produced the illustrations of Walter Crane (from *The Baby's Own Aesop* of 1887) and, 1890s, William Morris patterns. Herman Mueller, a sculptor trained in Munich and Nuremberg, designed draped classical figures in pastoral scenes. Karl Langenbeck experimented with new glazes and Parian wares at the factory. 1894, they both left American Encaustic and formed Mosaic Tile, Zanesville. 1935, the firm closed.
Bibliography Doreen Bolger Burke et al., *In Pursuit of Beauty: Americans and the Aesthetic Movement*, New York: The Metropolitan Museum of Art/Rizzoli, 1986.
> See Mueller, Herman Carl.

American Union of Decorative Artists and Craftsmen (AUDAC)

American artists' group.

History 1928, AUDAC was formed in New York through an informal initial meeting of a group of designers, who included Donald Deskey, Frederick Kiesler, Lee Simonson, and Kem Weber, and headed by Paul Frankl, with the intention of promoting modern decorative art; is considered to have been officially formed in 1930 when the first of its only two exhibitions was mounted; grew to include more than 100 members active in design, photography, and architecture, including Margaret Bourke-White, William Lescaze, Gilbert Rhode, Joseph Urban, and Frank Lloyd Wright; c. 1932, was discontinued.
Exhibitions Members' work subject of exhibitions, Grand Central Palace, 1930, and Brooklyn Museum of Art, 1931; both New York.
Bibliography Karen Davies, *At Home in Manhattan*, New Haven, Conn.: Yale, 1983. Mel Byars (intro.), 'What Makes American Design American?' in R.L. Leonard and C.A. Glassgold (eds.), *Modern American Design, by the American Union of Decorative Artists and Craftsmen*, New York: 1930; Acanthus, 1992 reprint.

Ammotzbøll, Anne (1934–)

Danish textile designer.

Training Finn Juhl School of Interior Design; Mulle Høyrup's experimental school for textile printing, Kokkedal.
Biography She designed children's clothing sold through her own shop and leather goods by Form & Farve in Copenhagen. In metalware, she began working with Andreas Mikkelsen in 1970 and with Georg Jensen Sølvsmedie in Copenhagen from 1978.
Bibliography Cat., *Georg Jensen Silversmithy: 77 Artists, 75 Years*, Washington, D.C.: Smithsonian, 1980.

Amstelhoek

Dutch ceramics workshop; located Amsterdam.

History 1897, Willem Hoeker founded the Amstelhoek workshop to produce modern ceramics, metalwork, and furniture. 1899, Jan Eisenlöffel, who had worked as a draftsperson in Hoeker's firm, became artistic director of the metalworking section. Handmade objects—simple with sparse geometric ornamentation—were decorated with enameled and pierced squares and rectangles. From 1903, spun pieces had concentric circles around the rim, reminiscent of Wiener Werkstätte products. Amstelhoek produced a 97-piece dinner service

for the City Council of Amsterdam, to celebrate Queen Wilhelmina's 1901 marriage. However, Eisenlöffel was not acknowledged for his Amstelhoek designs shown at the 1900 Paris *Exhibition* and 1902 Turin *Esposizione* and soon left the firm; was succeeded by J. Blinxma. 1903, Amstelhoek's metalworking section was closed.
Exhibitions/citations Awards at 1900 *Exposition Universelle*, Paris, and 1902 *Esposizione Internazionale d'Arte Decorativa Moderna*, Turin.
Bibliography Annelies Krekel-Aalberse, *Art Nouveau and Art Déco Silver*, New York: Abrams, 1989: 176.

Andersen, Gunnar Aagaard (1919–1982)
Danish architect and designer; active Copenhagen.

Training 1936–39, Skolen for Kunsthåndværk, Copenhagen; 1939, Konstakademiet, Stockholm; 1940–46, Det Kongelige Danske Kunstakademi, Copenhagen.
Biography 1951, Andersen began to design furniture; 1951–75, worked for magazine *Mobilia*; was also active as a fine artist. His 1952 chair sketch for a cantilevered model and 1953 prototype made from chicken wire and newspaper clearly presaged Verner Panton's 1960 plastic chair of a cantilevered configuration, although the Panton version is generally acknowledged as being the first of its kind. From 1972, Andersen was a professor, Kunstakademiet; 1973–74, was vice-president, Akademiet; designed furniture by Fritz Hansen, Jensen Kjær, and Rud. Rasmussen.
Exhibitions/citations Work first shown at 1939 *Kunstnernes Efterårsudstilling*, and worldwide thereafter. H.O. Stoltenberg and Bindesbøll prizes and Danmarks Nationalbank Jubilee Foundation.
Bibliography Cat., *Der Kragstuhl*, Stuhlmuseum Burg Beverungen, Berlin: Alexander, 1986: 118–19, 130. Frederik Sieck, *Nutidig Dansk Møbeldesign – en kortfattet illustreret beskrivelse*, Copenhagen: Bondo Gravesen, 1990.

Andersen, Hans Munck (1943–)
Danish ceramicist.

Training 1968, Kunsthåndværkerskolen; 1972–73, Kunstakademiets Arkitektskole; both Copenhagen.
Biography 1968–71, Andersen was a designer for the Royal Copenhagen Porcelain Manufactory; 1973, set up a workshop at Rø on Bornholm Island.
Exhibitions Work included in numerous venues. Subject of 1971 and 1976 venues at the Royal Copenhagen Porcelain Manufactory.
Bibliography Cat., David Revere McFadden (ed.), *Scandinavian Modern Design 1880–1980*, New York: Abrams, 1982: 262.

Andersen, Ib Just (1884–1943)
Danish silversmith; active Copenhagen.

Training Under Mogens Ballin and Peter Hertz.

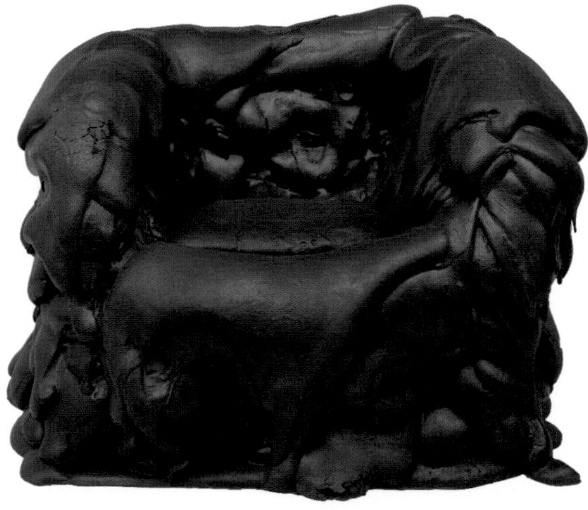

Gunnar Aagaard Andersen. Armchair. 1964. Poured polyurethane, 29 1/2 x 44 1/4 x 35 1/4" (74.9 x 112.4 x 89.5 cm). Mfr.: Dansk Polyether Industri, Denmark. Gift of the designer. MoMA.

Biography Andersen was originally a painter and sculptor; 1918, established his own company Just Andersen Pewter; produced designs by Georg Jensen Sølvsmedie in Copenhagen. His wife, Alba Lykke, was a pupil of Jensen.
Bibliography Cat., *Georg Jensen Silversmithy: 77 Artists, 75 Years*, Washington, D.C.: Smithsonian, 1980. Annelies Krekel-Aalberse, *Art Nouveau and Art Déco Silver*, New York: Abrams, 1989.

Andersen, Knud Holst (1935–)
Danish designer.

Training In silversmithing in Denmark; 1961–64, Tokyo National University of Fine Arts and Music; 1975, Royal College of Art, London.
Biography From 1973, Andersen was associated with Georg Jensen Sølvsmedie in Copenhagen.
Exhibitions/citations Silver and bronze hollow-ware included in exhibitions in Denmark, Sweden, Germany, and France. 1973 Artist/Craftsman of the Year, Danish Society of Arts and Crafts.
Bibliography Cat., *Georg Jensen Silversmithy: 77 Artists, 75 Years*, Washington, D.C.: Smithsonian, 1980.

Andersen, Rigmor (1903–1995)
Danish furniture designer.

Training Architecture, Det Kongelige Danske Kunstakademi, Copenhagen; 1944, in its furniture school.
Biography 1929–39, she worked with Kaare Klint; from 1944, taught, Det Kongelige Danske Kunstakademi; collaborated with Annelise Bjørner on 1968 Margrethe cutlery pattern by Georg Jensen Sølvesmedie.
Exhibitions/citations Work shown at 1933, 1942 *Dansk Kunsthåndværk*, Nationalmuseum, Stockholm, and 1980 Smithsonian exhibition (catalog below). Knut V. Englehardt memorial prize. Various awards (with Bjørner), including 1968 Eckersberg Medal (for Margrethe cutlery), 1968 C.F. Hansen prize, 1968 Zacharias Jacobsen prize.
Bibliography Cat., *Georg Jensen Silversmithy: 77 Artists, 75 Years*, Washington, D.C.: Smithsonian, 1980. Frederik Sieck, *Nutidig Dansk Møbeldesign – en kortfattet illustreret beskrivelse*, Copenhagen: Bondo Gravesen, 1990.

Andersen, Steffen (1936–)
Danish designer.

Training 1956–58, Guldsmedehoejskolen, Copenhagen.
Biography 1959–60, Andersen designed at Georg Jensen Sølvsmedie in London; 1961–71, in its design department in Copenhagen; 1971–75, in its advertising department; from 1975, in its hollow-ware department.
Exhibitions Work in 1980 Smithsonian exhibition (catalog below).
Bibliography Cat., *Georg Jensen Silversmithy: 77 Artists, 75 Years*, Washington, D.C.: Smithsonian, 1980.

Anderson, Mark Roy (1964–)
American industrial designer; born Newburyport, Mass.

Training 1987, bachelor's degree in fine art, Rhode Island School of Design, Providence, R.I.; 1991, master's degree in architecture, Syracuse (N.Y.) University.
Biography 1982–87, Anderson was a part-time cabinetmaker at Shaker Tree (handmade reproduction Shaker furniture), West Stockbridge, Mass.; 1988–89, designer at Lerner Associates interiors, architecture, and planning, Providence; 1991, settled in Milan, Italy, where, 1991–94, was project architect/designer, Studio di Architettura Luca Scacchetti; 1995–96, was an independent consultant; 1997, established Mark Anderson Design in Milan for architecture and design; from 1995, has taught at institutions in Barcelona, Ferrara, and Ravenna; from 1995, has been professor of furniture design, Scuola di Design, Istituto Europeo di Design, Milan; from 1998, has designed domestic and commercial interiors. Clients have included Moretti Arredamenti and Alfaline (furniture), Simed (machinery and artistic direction/communications consultancy), Whirlpool Europe (product graphics).
Exhibitions/citations From 1996, work included in a number of venues. Special mention for best new product (1999 Khan [Kublai] by Roncoroni), Young and Design '99, Salone del Mobile, Milan.
Bibliography Mel Byars, *50 Lights...*, Hove: RotoVision, 1996. 'Places of Design: A Project, a Collection in Wood,' *L'industria del*

mobile, Jan. 2003: 124–27. 'The High-wood Project,' *Domus*, no. 818, Sept. 1999: 64–69.

Anderson, Olle (1939–)

Swedish architect and designer; active Gothenburg.

Training In architecture and interior design.
Biography Anderson has taught, University of Gothenburg, and in the UK, Denmark, Norway, Finland, Brazil, Estonia, Italy, and South Africa; is a member, Inredningsarkitekt (SIR) and Föreningen Svenska Industridesigner (SID). Wide-ranging work in architecture and design has encompassed textiles, glass, and furniture, including 1997 Q range of chairs and tables by Offecct that called on automobile-industry technology for comfort, and a contract-furniture range by Klaessons; founded and organized six Wood Workshops (1992–2000); has written several books, including *Käbba Lyssna Lykta Smaka* (feel, listen, smell, taste), *Rum och Ljus* (rooms and light), and *Alla vägar bär till bo* (all roads lead home). He became artistic and managing director, White Design studio, Gothenburg; senior partner, White Architects; board member, International Federation of Interior Architects/Designers, and chairperson from Sept. 2001.
Exhibitions/citations 2000 *Olle Anderson formgivare: möbler, lampor, textil och glas*, Kalmar Konstmuseum, Kalmar, Sweden. 19 times, Utmärkt Svensk Form (outstanding Swedish-design citation); first prize (for Nordic lighting), 1994 Hemma Belysning competition; first prize for 1994 Nya tunnel system under Stockholm.
Bibliography Mailis Stensman, *Olle Anderson Formgivare*, Stockholm: Arena, 1999.

Anderson, Winslow (1917–)

American ceramicist and glassware designer; born Massachusetts

Training To 1946, New York State College of Ceramics, Alfred, N.Y.
Biography 1946, Anderson joined Blenko Glass in Milton, W. Va.; designed simple silhouettes blown by others, working closely with the factory craftspeople; 1953–79, worked at Lenox China in Trenton, N.J., first as designer and, subsequently, as the design director.
Citations 1952 *Good Design* exhibition/award (Blenko's bent-necked decanter, an accidental form arrived at by overheating), The Museum of Modern Art, New York, and Chicago Merchandise Mart.
Bibliography Don Wallance, *Shaping America's Products*, New York: Reinhold, 1956: 82, 105, 115–17. Cat., Kathryn B. Hiesinger and George H. Marcus III (eds.), *Design Since 1945*, Philadelphia: Philadelphia Museum of Art, 1983. Eason Eige and Rick Wilson, *Blenko Glass 1930–1953*, Marietta, Ohio: Antique Publications, 1987.

Anderssen, Torbjørn (1976–)
> See Norway Says.

Andersson, John (1900–1969)

Swedish ceramicist.

Biography Andersson designed ceramics by Andersson & Johansson (today Höganäs), for which he executed 1955 Old Höganäs ceramic ovenproof tableware, produced in traditional earthenware in olive-green, mustard-yellow, and manganese-brown associated with Höganäs's production since last half of 19th century. c. 1969, the firm abandoned earthenware for nonporous ware.
Bibliography Erik Zahle (ed.), *A Treasury of Scandinavian Design*, New York: Golden Press, 1961: 268, no. 295. Cat., Kathryn B. Hiesinger and George H. Marcus III (eds.), *Design Since 1945*, Philadelphia: Philadelphia Museum of Art, 1983.

André, Émile (1871–1933)

French architect and furniture designer; born Nancy.

Biography André was a founding member and the most notable architect of École de Nancy; advocated a union of the arts, designing furniture to coordinate with houses he built; showed architectural studies and photographs of his houses, apartment buildings, and stores. His most distinguished architecture is 1903 house at 92 and 92 bis, quai Claude-le-Lorrain, and 1903 house at 34, rue du Sergent-Blandan, both Nancy. His sons Jacques and Michel took over the family business and collaborated with Jean Prouvé and others.
Bibliography Yvonne Brunhammer et al., *Art Nouveau Belgium, France*, Houston: Rice University, 1976.

Henning Andreasen. Folle 26 stapler. 1977. Stainless steel, hardened steel, and iron, 1 3/4 x 6 x 1 1/2" (4.5 x 15.2 x 3.8 cm). Mfr.: Folmer Christensen, Denmark. Gift of the designer. MoMA.

Andreasen, Henning (1923–)

Danish designer.

Biography Andreasen designed 1980 DA 80 telephone, which became a major export item for GNT-Automatic, its Danish manufacturer, and was accepted as standard equipment in Ireland where telephone users wanted a push-button phone. Also designed the 1977 Folle 26 stapler and 1978 sound-level indicator.
Citations Den Danske Designpris (for DA-80 phone).

Andresen, Marius (1971–)
> See K8 industriedesign.

Angelini, Edgardo (1959–)
> See Design Group Italia.

Angelini, Lamberto

Italian vehicle designer.

Training In mechanical engineering.
Biography 1979–80, Angelini worked at Volkswagen Style Center in Wolfsburg, Germany, originally sketching the Passat 88; 1980, founded Angelini Design in Bologna; has designed automobiles, motorbikes, and boats for clients, including BMW, Ducati, Ferretti Craft, KTM, and Motobecane. Other work: polyurethane TV remote-control unit and other household items by Meliconi, suitcases by Roncato, a bicycle frame (four pressed sheet-metal modules) by Bianchi, remote-controlled lawnmower by Goldoni, vase (to keep plants alive for 12 months) by Fito, fork-lift trucks by Cesab, a no-license-required car with an aluminum wire frame by Grecav, and a new car by a manufacturer in the Middle East. Angelini is a member, Italian Experimental Group (IEG).
Citations 1991 Premio Compasso d'Oro (lawnmower by Goldoni).
Bibliography Michele De Lucchi (ed.), *The International Design Yearbook*, London: Laurence King, 2001.

Angénieux

French firm.

History 1935, Angénieux was founded by Pierre Angénieux in Saint-Héand, Saint-Étienne; 1945, produced the Rétrofocus lens that was the decisive step toward the single-lens reflex camera. From 1964, NASA has used Angénieux lenses. 1985, the firm produced DEM 180F2-3 APO zoom lens with automatic focusing from 71" (180 cm) to infinity, based on the Angénieux patent called Differential Element Movement (DEM).
Bibliography Agnès Lévitte and Margo Rouard, *100 objets quotidiens made in France*, Paris: APCI/Syros-Alternatives, 1987.

Ängman, Jacob (1876–1942)

Swedish architect and furniture and silver designer; active Stockholm.

Training 1893 and 1896–1903, Kungliga Tekniska Högskolan, Stockholm; 1903–04, in Germany.
Biography 1896–98, Ängman worked at the Otto Meyer Bronze Casters works; 1899, for C.G. Hallberg bronze foundry in Stockholm; for a few months under Henry van de Velde at Theodore Müller's works in Weimar; 1903–04, with metal sculptor Otto Bommer in Berlin. 1904–07, he managed the engraving, casting, and metalwork department of Elmquist in Stockholm; 1907–42, worked at Guldsmedsaktiebolaget

(GAB) in Stockholm, where he became the artistic director; 1919–20, worked with architect Gunnar Asplund on St. Peter's Church, Malmö. His simple forms appeared contemporary, though his silver pieces were traditional.
Exhibitions Silver for GAB shown for the first time abroad at 1925 *Exposition Internationale des Arts Décoratifs et Industriels Modernes*, Paris. Work included in 1927 exhibition of Danish wares, The Metropolitan Museum of Art, New York, and subject of 1942 exhibition, Nationalmuseum, Stockholm (catalog below).
Bibliography Cat., *Jacob Ängmans silver: en minnesutställning*, Stockholm: Nationalmuseum, 1942. Åke Stavenow, *Silversmeden Jacob Ängman 1876–1942*, Stockholm: Nordisk Rotogravyr, 1955. Cat., David Revere McFadden (ed.), *Scandinavian Modern Design 1880–1980*, New York: Abrams, 1982. Annelies Krekel-Aalberse, *Art Nouveau and Art Déco Silver*, New York: Abrams, 1989.

Anguissola d'Altoè, Cinzia (1959–)
Italian architect and interior designer; born Bologna; active Milan; wife of architect Luca Scacchetti.

Training To 1986 architecture, Politecnico, Milan.
Biography Concurrent with her universities studies, Anguissola traveled widely, including in Spain, Australia, and Africa; subsequently, was active as a freelance fabric designer for firms such as Chicco, Ratti, and Mantero; 1990–96, worked in the studio of Manolo De Giorgi and as coorganizer of a number of significant Italian-design exhibitions in Paris, Chicago, and Milan; has written on design and participated in landmark books on the subjects; 1996, set up her own studio in Milan; 1994–98, taught furniture design, Istituto Europeo di Design (IED), and, from 2002, Istituto Superiore Architettura e Design (ISAD), both in Milan. Design work has included ceramic vases and façade tiles by Terre Blu and by Manor, wooden furniture by Roncoroni Frau and by Faber Mobili, wash basins by Arcadia, other furniture, and interior design. She supervised the reissue of Guglielmo Ulrich's classic products and furniture by Pizzitutti and by Matteograssi; with her husband Scacchetti, has participated in several international architecture competitions and, for her own clients, been active as an architect on new structures, installations, and restorations.
Exhibitions 1980s, during university studies and as a painter, one-person exhibitions, Paris and Hanover. Participated in a number of design projects, Abitare il Tempo fair, Verona.

Annink, Ed (1956–)
Dutch interior, furniture, product, and exhibition designer; born The Hague.

Training In jewelry, furniture, and product design.
Biography 1985, Annink established Ontwerpwerk in The Hague, a studio for the design of products, graphics, and interiors; has been highly active in seminars/conferences. Designs include Brothers V chopping boards by Driade/D'House and products by Anthologie Quartett, Authentics, Droog Design/DMD, O'Neill, and Vitra.
Exhibitions Work included in 1996 *Contemporary Design from the Netherlands*, The Museum of Modern Art, New York.
Bibliography Lucy Bullivant, 'Bellezza quotidiana,' *Interni*, no. 507, Dec. 2000: 166–69. Ingo Maurer (ed.), *The International Design Yearbook*, London: Laurence King, 2000: 149. Ed van Hinte et al., *Ed Annink, Designer*, Rotterdam: 010, 2001.

Annoni, Franco (1924–)
Italian architect and designer; born and active Milan.

Training To 1954, architecture, Politecnico; from 1956, Albo; both Milan.
Biography An industrial and exhibition designer, Annoni has designed exhibitions and industrial products for clients, including Ampaglas, Madular, Mauri, Reguitti, Stylresine, and Velca; as a specialist in plastics, designed a motorcycle helmet by Kartell and furniture by Sole.
Bibliography *ADI Annual 1976*, Milan: Associazione per il Disegno Industriale, 1976.

Anthologie Quartett
German manufacturer.

History 1983, Anthologie Quartett was founded as a four-part (or 'quartet') group of architecture, design, art, and fashion galleries in Hanover, which showed work by Bellefast, Bořek Šípek, Ettore Sottsass, Matteo Thun, and Daniel Weil; 1987, separated from the Anthologie Quartett consortium to become a separate entity, retaining the same name and relocating to Schloss Hünnefeld/Bad Essen. 1980s, the group issued primarily furniture and lighting designed by more than 50 Europeans; 1988, established Design...Connections to offer services in research, art direction, exposition design, and public relations; 1989, established Best Friends jewelry collection; 1990, established Mus'ign for exhibitions; 1997, added work by Garouste & Bonetti, Bohuslav Horák, Alessandro Mendini, George Nelson, and others; 1998, established Gartenreich garden-furniture brand; 2000, pursued an architectural program.
Exhibitions Showed first collection at 1984 Internationale Möbelmesse, Cologne, and 1984 Salone del Mobile, Milan.

Anti-Design: Gruppo DAM (Designer Associati Milano), Alberto Colombi, Ezio Didone, and Studio Gruppo 14. Libro chair. 1970. Polyurethane foam, vinyl, and steel, 37 1/2 x 32 1/2 x 48" (95.3 x 82.6 x 121.9 cm). Mfr.: Modernariato-Gruppo Industriale Busnelli, Italy. Clarissa Bronfman Purchase Fund. MoMA.

Anti-Design (or Radical-Design)
Italian design movement.

History Anti-Design, characterized by idealism and irony, aligned itself with the European student unrest of late 1960s and early 1970s and was inspired by Ettore Sottsass's 1966 furniture exhibition in Milan. With some members deciding that Florence's industrial and cultural traditions were a handicap, they dispersed to Milan, Rome, and Turin. Rather than creating products, Anti-Design was a self-critical philosophy, typified by deliberate bad taste. Writing, photography, and idealized architectural projects replaced objects as a means of communicating ideas. The exponents related art to design politics and protested against limitations to political, social, and creative freedom; were interested in ecology, expressing themselves through the use of natural materials. Influenced by Claes Oldenburg's soft sculptures, the movement's manifestations appeared in Gruppo DAM's/others 1970 Libro chair, Gatti/Paolini/Teodoro's 1969 Sacco pellet-filled seat, and De Pas/Lomazzo/D'Urbino's 1970 Joe seat. The movement declared (translated from the Italian): 'The designer... is no longer the artist who helps us to make our homes beautiful, because they will never be beautiful, but is the individual who moves on a dialectical... and on a

Arabia. Ashtray. Unknown date. Glazed porcelain, h. 1 1/4 x dia. 3 1/4" (3.2 x 8.3 cm). Mfr.: Arabia, Finland. Gift of the Chase Manhattan Bank. MoMA.

Ron Arad. FPE (Fantastic, Plastic, Elastic) chair. 1997. Aluminum and polypropylene plastic, 31 1/4 x 17 x 22" (79.4 x 43.2 x 55.9 cm). Mfr.: Kartell, Italy. Gift of the mfr. MoMA.

formal plane and stimulates behavioral patterns... to contribute to a full awareness—the sole premise required for a new equilibrium of values and... the recovery of man himself.'

Bibliography Almerico de Angelis, 'Anti-Design,' in Franco Raggi, 'Radical Story,' *Casabella*, no. 382, 1973: 39. Cat., *Michele De Lucchi, A Friendly Image for the Electronic Age: Designs for Memphis, Alchimia, Olivetti, Girmi*, The Hague: Komplement, 1985. Penny Sparke, *Design in Italy, 1870 to the Present*, New York: Abbeville, 1988.

APCI (Agence pour la Promotion de la Création Industrielle)

French government institution.

History 1983, APCI was founded to support industrial and graphic design as they relate to the human environment; published books and catalogs; participated (in conjunction with the Ministère de la Culture, France, from which it receives funding) in sponsoring French and international competitions, including 1982 Concours de Mobilier de Bureau (won by Norbert Scibilla, Serge Guillet, and Clen Associates), 1985 Concours pour les Arts de la Table (won by Guy Boucher and Société Deshoulières), 1992 Concours Mobilier Hospitalier (won by Sylvain Dubuisson and Corona). Rules dictate that each competition must be associated with an established manufacturer which undertakes to produce the winning design.

Apple Computer

> See Jobs, Steven P.

Arabia

Finnish ceramics firm; located Helsinki.

History 1873, Arabia was established as a subsidiary of Swedish firm Röstrand Pottery; produced undecorated, glazed stoneware table and kitchen ware at first; later bone china. The models and molds were in Sweden, and Rörstrand had a controlling interest to 1916. From 1895, Thure Öberg, its first permanent designer, designed and painted distinctive vases. Jac Ahrenberg also worked there. 1922, the factory was updated and began production of modern houseware forms; early 1920s, employed several young artists, including Friedl Holzer-Kjellberg and Greta-Lisa Jäderholm-Snellman, and decorators Svea Granlund and Olga Osol. Swedish artist Tyra Lundgren had a studio at Arabia, where the world's largest tunnel kiln for firing household wares was built in 1929. 1930s, Kurt Ekholm founded the art department within the firm and commenced the design of modern tableware. Artists included Birger Kaipiainen, Toini Muona, Michael Schilkin, and Aune Siimes. 1944, Kaj Franck began working at Arabia, and, to 1978, served as the art director, succeeding Ekholm. Potters including Toini Muona and Kyllikki Salmenhaara had a works studio there. 1947, Arabia, which had helped establish Scandinavian modern design, became a part of the Wärtsilä conglomerate. Designers Kaarina Aho joined the firm in 1946 and Ulla Procopé in 1948. Its wares included 1948 heat-proof earthenware cooking and tablewares (produced from 1953); 1957 Liekki or Ruska ware; and 1960 wares designed by Procopé. From 1960s, Wärtsilä made its utility-ware designers anonymous. Today the Arabia brand is under iittala oy ab.

Exhibitions/citations Wares included in 1878 *Exposition Universelle*, Paris; 1951 (9th) Triennale di Milano. Gold medal, 1882 Moscow fair; silver medals, 1893 hygiene exhibition and medical congress in St. Petersburg; gold medal, 1900 *Exposition Universelle*, Paris; grand prize, 1929–30 *Exposición Internacional de Barcelona*, Spain; diploma of honor for an entire collection, 1933 (5th) Triennale di Milano.

Bibliography Pirkko Aro, *Arabia Design*, Helsinki: Otava, 1958. Leena Maunula, 'A Hundred Years of Arabia Dishes... Since 1874,' *Ceramics and Glass*, Helsinki: Arabia, 1973. C. Marjut Kumela et al., *Arabia*, Helsinki: Uudenmaan Kirjapaino: 1987. Jennifer Hawkins Opie, *Scandinavia: Ceramics and Glass in the Twentieth Century*, New York: Rizzoli, 1989.

Arad, Ron (1951–)

Israeli designer; born Tel Aviv; active London.

Training 1971–73, Jerusalem Academy of Art; 1974–79 under Peter Cook and Bernard Tschumi, Architectural Association, London.

Biography Arad worked with Cook at Architectural Association in London on a design competition entry for a museum in Aachen. 1980, Arad joined Povey and Groves. (The high-tech Kee Klamp assembly system, incorrectly attributed to Arad, was actually a 1979 concept by Povey and Groves, according to Povey.) 1981 with Caroline Thorman, Arad set up the design firm One Off in London, with the logo designed by Neville Brody. Early on, Arad developed artistic/cultural interests outside architecture and became interested in the non-rhetorical use of materials. Best-known early piece is 1981 Rover chair (followed by double-seat couch version) made from salvaged seats of Rover Model 2000 automobiles; these were necessarily individual pieces, since there was a dwindling supply of 1960s seats. Arad designed/made lighting, including Aerial light inspired by the post-apocalypse *Mad Max* movies, but later moved from scavenging to new materials; his late-1980s Rocking chair represented a more custom-made, refined approach. 1980s, Arad designed fashion shops and offices in Milan and elsewhere. The One Off workshop attracted collaborators, including John Mills, Simon Scott, and Danny Lane. Arad designed monumental and sculptural sheet-metal furniture by Sawaya & Moroni and Zeev Aram, and, 1990, for the Robin Wight house in London. Mass-produced design work includes 1987 Well Tempered chair and 1989 Schizo wooden chair and 1998 FPE chair by Vitra; 1990 Big Easy Red seating by Moroso; 1993 This Mortal Coil and Bookworm bookcases by Driade (1994 Bookworm version by Kartell); 1996 Cler étagère by Fiam; 1997 Fantastic Plastic Elastic chair, 1998 Infinity wine rack, and 1999 Konx glass table by Fiam, 2000 H-Shelving by Kartell; 2000 Not Made by Hand; Not Made in China vases, lamps, and bowls formed by stereolithography; 2002 door handle by Valli & Valli. Architecture and interior schemes range from 1988–94 opera house foyer in Tel Aviv to 1998 Alan Journo clothing store in Milan, and 1999 *Winning—The Design of Sport* exhibition, Glasgow. In London: 1993–95 Belgo Noord bar; 1995 Belgo Centraal restaurant; 2000 Windwand mast, Canary Wharf; and 2001 Selfridges Technology Hall. 1994, established Ron Arad Associates for architecture and design in London and a production unit in Como, Italy; 1994–97, was professor, Hochschule, Vienna; from 1997, Royal College of Art. Became a British citizen; was editor, *The International Design Yearbook* (1994).

Exhibitions/citations Work included in large number of exhibitions from 1986 *Intellectual Interiors* (with Philippe Starck, Rei Kawakubo, Shiro Kuramata), Tokyo; and subject of others from 1990 *Ron Arad: Recent Works*, Museum of Art, Tel Aviv, to 2000 *Before and After Now*, Victoria and Albert Museum, London. 1994 creator of the year, Salon du Meuble, Paris; 1999 Design Plus prize, Ambiente fair, Frankfurt; 1999 Internationaler Designpreis Baden-Württemberg, Design Center Stuttgart; 2001 cowinner, Perrier-Jouet design award; 2001 Primavera international award for design, Barcelona; 2001 Gio

Ponti International Design Award, Design Council and Denver (Colorado) Art Museum; 2001 Oribe Art and Design Award, Japan.
Bibliography Deyan Sudjic, *Ron Arad, Restless Furniture*, New York: Rizzoli, 1989. Alexander von Vegesack, *Ron Arad*, Weil am Rhein: Vitra, 1990. Ettore Sottsass and Cedric Price (intros.), *Ron Arad Associates: One Off Three*, London: Artemis Architectural Publications, 1993. Raymond Guidot and Olivier Boissière, *Ron Arad*, Paris: Dis Voir, 1997. Volker Arbus, *Design Classics: Bookworm*, Frankfurt: Form, 1997. Deyan Sudjic, *Ron Arad*, London: Laurence King, 1999.

Arai, Junichi (1932–)

Japanese textile designer and manufacturer; born Kiryu, Gumma.

Biography From 1950, Arai has been active in the textile industry; has developed new manufacturing processes; 1984, cofounded Nuno Corporation in Tokyo for the manufacturing and retail sale of innovative functional fabrics; specialized in deeply textured, sculptural fabrications, incorporating celluloid, aluminum tape, metallic filament, silk, and/or polyester; shifted to technological experimentation, maximizing the potential of punched-card computer-controlled jacquard looms; created fabrics from yarns of different shrinkage rates and under extreme heat; lacerated film into complex weavings; heat-fixed synthetic fibers. Clients have included Issey Miyake and Comme des Garçons. 1987, closed his firm Anthologie; has taught, Otsuka Textile Design Institute, Tokyo.
Exhibitions/citations Work included in 1999 exhibition, New York and St. Louis (catalog below). Subject of 1993 *Hand and Technology* exhibition, Pacific Design Center, Los Angeles. 1987, elected Honorary Royal Designer of Industry, UK.
Bibliography Albrecht Bangert and Karl Michael Armer, *80s Style: Designs of the Decade*, New York: Abbeville, 1990. Cat., Cara McCarty and Matilda McQuaid, *Structure and Surface: Contemporary Japanese Textiles*, New York: Abrams/The Museum of Modern Art, 1999.

Arbeitsgruppe 4

Austrian art and architecture group.

History Late 1950s, Arbeitsgruppe was founded by Wilhelm Holzbauer (1930–), Friedrich Kurrent (1931–), and Johannes Spalt (1920–) in Vienna. Its furniture incorporated severe modular elements in various bright colors and right-angle planes for the Musikhaus 3/4 elements.
Bibliography Günther Feuerstein, *Vienna—Present and Past: Arts and Crafts—Applied Art—Design*, Vienna: Jugend und Volk, 1976: 61.

Junichi Arai. Crinkled sheer fabric. c. 1995. Polyester and nylon, 240 x 32" (609.6 x 81.3 cm). Mfr.: Junichi Arai, Japan. Gift of the designer. MoMA.

Arbén, Love (1962–)

Swedish furniture designer and interior architect.

Training To 1978, interior architecture/furniture design, Konstfackskolan, Stockholm.
Biography 1985, Arbén established his own architecture office and, 1988, Arkimedes' Architects Office; from 1994, was professor of interior architecture at the renamed Konstfack. Work by Lammhults includes 1993 Folix easy chair, 1995 Folini table, 1997 Bank bench, 2001 Sunday sofa/easy chair, Friday sofa/easy chair, Saturday table, and Monday armchair.
Citations From 1983, several Utmärkt Svensk Form (outstanding Swedish-design citations), 1984 and 1989 Forum Närmiljö prize, 1991 Forsnäs Design prize, and others.

Arbus, André (1903–1969)

French architect and decorator; born Toulouse.

Training École des Beaux-Arts, Toulouse.
Biography Arbus was active in the cabinetmaking workshop of his father and grandfather in Toulouse; 1925, became active in Salons of the Société des Artistes Décorateurs and the Salon d'Automne; designed the first-class smoking lounges on 1927 oceanliner *Île-de-France*; 1930, set up the shop Époque in Paris to show his work; 1932, established a cabinetmaking shop in Paris, making furniture for a number of clients, in the refined, rigorous approaches of Jules Leleu, Émile-Jacques Ruhlmann, and Süe et Mare; designed furniture with elegant lines and volumes reflective of a kind of mannerism. His 1928 satin-finished lacquer chairs shown at 1932 Salon of Société des Artistes Décorateurs had Louis XV legs. The influence of Ledoux's neoclassical forms was also evident, yet Arbus's lines were pure, lacked ornament, and gave the appearance of fragility. He compared the joints in his pieces to the joints of a human hand. Arbus was antithetical to Le Corbusier; called on exotic and rare materials in his furniture; sometimes incorporated the applied painting of Marc Saint-Saëns; after 1935, set up the decoration department Les Beaux Métiers in the Palais de la Nouveauté department store in Paris. 1945, Le Mobilier National commissioned a desk design for US Ambassador W.H. Harriman. Architecture, important to Arbus, included 1937 Ministère de l'Agricole building in Paris and, after World War II, the Médici Room of the Château de Rambouillet, the townhouse of Aimé Maeght on the Parc Monceau in Paris, and oceanliners, including 1922 *Bretagne*, 1927 *La Provence*, and 1961 *France* (the smoking room in the first-class section). He also drew up plans for Crau, built 1942; Planier in Marseille, built 1950; and the new bridge in Martigues, built 1962.
Exhibitions/citations Furniture was shown at Salons of Société des Artistes Décorateurs and Salons d'Automne; 1925 *Exposition Internationale des Arts Décoratifs et Industriels Modernes*, Paris, 1937 *Exposition Internationale des Arts et Techniques dans la Vie Moderne*, Paris (a suite and interior design for the Maison d'une Famille Française); 1939–40 *New York World's Fair: The World of Tomorrow* (in charge of French section). Received 1935 Blumenthal prize.
Bibliography Yolande Amic, *Mobilier français 1945–1964*, Paris: Regard, 1983. Pierre Kjellberg, *Art déco: les maîtres du mobilier, le décor des paquebots*, Paris: Amateur, 1986. Yvonne Brunhammer with Marie-Laure Perrin, *André Arbus: architecte-décorateur des années 40*, Paris: Norma, 1996.

Archeworks
> See Tigerman, Stanley.

Archizoom Associati

Italian design studio; located Florence; active 1966–74.

History 1966, Archizoom Associati was founded in Florence by architects Andrea Branzi, Gilberto Corretti, Paolo Deganello, and Massimo Morozzi to specialize in product and architectural design and urban planning; 1968, industrial designers Dario and Lucia Bartolini joined. Archizoom was dedicated to applying Anti-Design ideas to furniture design, realized in a number of visionary environments and fantasy furniture models. The group attempted to move Italian design away from consumerism and high style and argued against tradition, familiarity, and comfort, as well as the 'anti-humanism of modernism.' (The contemporary Superstudio took a similar approach.) The undulating Superonda, Archizoom's version of the standard polyurethane foam sofa, was highly graphic and assertive for its time. The group described its Safari sofa as 'an imperial piece within the sordidness of your own home, a beautiful piece that you simply don't deserve. Clear

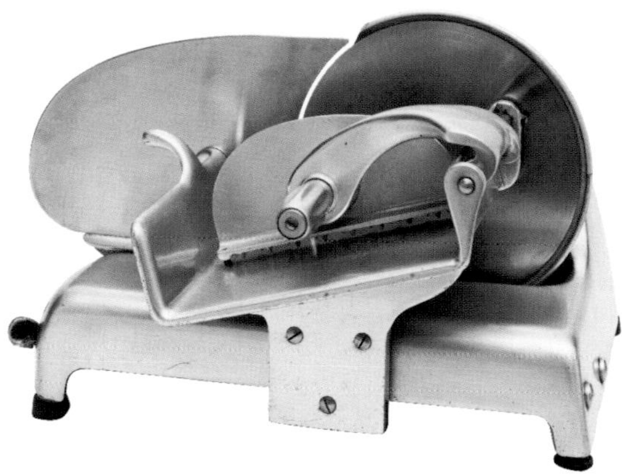

Egmont Arens and Theodore C. Brookhart (1898–1942). Streamliner meat slicer (no. 410). c. 1940. Aluminum, steel, and rubber, 13 x 20 1/4 x 17" (33 x 51.4 x 43.2 cm). Mfr.: Hobart Manufacturing, US. Gift of Eric Brill in memory of Abbie Hoffman. MoMA.

out your lounges! Clear out your own lives!' Its 1969 Mies chair, produced by Poltronova with a rubber membrane across a chromium frame, was particularly daring and starkly simple. Though an homage to Ludwig Mies van der Rohe, it was an essentially ironic example of 'counter-design.' The group's 1973 AEO chair (credited to Deganello), produced by Cassina, was likewise radical, and the 1967 Presagio di Rose bed tested conventional notions of good taste. The Archizoom archive is in Archives of Communication, Institute of Art History, University of Parma. Archizoom produced two films (*Vestirsi è facile* and *Come è fatto il capotto di Gogol*) based on the theme of clothing and dressing shortly before disbanding in 1974.
Exhibitions With Superstudio, organized *Superarchitettura* exhibition, Pistoia 1966 and Modena 1967; 1967 *Dream Beds*; and numerous others in Milan, Modena, Turin, London, and Rotterdam, including 1970 *No-Stop City* (radical-architecture exhibition). Work included in *Radicals: Architettura e Design 1960–75*, 1996 (6th) Mostra Internazionale di Archittettura, Venice.
Bibliography Cat., *Modern Chairs 1918–1970*, London: Lund Humphries, 1971. *Italy: The New Domestic Landscape*, New York: The Museum of Modern Art, 1972. 'Allestimento come informazione,' *Ottagono*, no. 34, Sept. 1974: 82–83. Andrea Branzi, *La casa calda: esperienze del nuovo disegno italiano*, Milan: Idea, 1982. Cat., Hans Wichmann, *Italien Design 1945 bis heute*, Munich: Die Neue Sammlung, 1988. Jonathan M. Woodham, *Twentieth-Century Ornament*, New York: Rizzoli, 1990: 264–65.

Aregall Fusté, Josep (1957–)

Spanish interior and product designer; born Barcelona

Training Design, Escola de Desseny i Art (Eina), Barcelona.
Biography 1976–83, Aregall collaborated with Pepe Cortés in a design studio in Barcelona, where he established his own studio in 1983. Design work has included a diverse number of office, store, and residential interiors and lighting by Metalarte. Teaches at Eina, Barcelona.
Bibliography Jeremy Myerson and Jennifer Hudson (eds.), *International Lighting Design*, London: Laurence King, 1996.

Arens, Egmont (1888–1966)

American industrial designer and theoretician; husband of Camiller David.

Training University of New Mexico; University of Chicago.
Biography 1916, Arens was sports editor on the *Tribune-Citizen* newspaper of Albuquerque, N.M.; 1917, settled in New York, managing his own Washington Square bookstore; 1918–27, published newspapers under the name Flying Stag Press; 1922–23, was art editor of *Vanity Fair*; with an interest in art, 1925–27, was managing editor of magazines *Creative Arts* and, for a time, of *Playboy* (the first American magazine specializing in modern art—not the Hefner publication of today); 1929, became advertising director, Calkin & Holden advertising agency, New York, where he established an industrial-styling department in 1935, for what he termed 'consumer engineering'; was influential on others through his 1930s writings, which emphasized a relationship of design to marketing. He believed in 'obsolescence as a positive force,' a resource to be used to drive the market forward (in his book, with Roy Sheldon, *Consumer Engineering: A New Technique in Prosperity*, 1932). One of his best-known designs is c. 1940 Streamliner electric meat slicer, with Theodore C. Brookhart (1898–1942) by Hobart Manufacturing, produced 1944–85; others are 1937 KitchenAid K electric kitchen mixer on a stand (one of three, virtually unchanged today), world's first coffee grinder (1938 KitchenAid A-9, reproduced today as an updated replica), coffee-filter packaging by A&P grocery stores, ink bottle by Higgens, and Philip Morris trademark. 1944, Arens was cofounder (with 15 others) and first secretary of Society of Industrial Designers (SID), predecessor of today's Industrial Designers of America (IDSA). Some sources claim 1889 as Arens's birth year.
Exhibitions *Good Life*'s main exhibit, Consumers Building, 1939–40 *New York World's Fair: The World of Tomorrow*. Meat slicer in 2000–02 *American Modern* touring exhibition, organized by American Federation of the Arts; and in 2000–03 *Aluminum by Design* touring exhibition, organized by Carnegie Art Museum, Pittsburgh (catalogs below).
Bibliography Arthur J. Pulos, *American Design Ethic: A History of Industrial Design*, Cambridge, Mass.: MIT, 1983. Stuart Ewen, 'Waste a Lot, Want a Lot: Our All-Consuming Quest for Style' in *All-Consuming Images: The Politics of Style in Contemporary Culture*, New York: Basic Books, 1988. Cat., Sarah Nichols et al., *Aluminum by Design*, New York: Abrams, 2000. Cat., J. Stewart Johnson, *American Modern, 1925–1940*, New York: Abrams, 2000.

Arequipa Pottery

American ceramics factory; located Fairfax, Cal.

History 1911, Frederick H. Rhead became a ceramicist and instructor at Arequipa Sanatorium in Fairfax, Cal., founded by doctor Philip King Brown, and at the onset of the Arequipa Pottery's founding. The Sanatorium's tuberculosis patients, made ill by the ash-filled air caused by 1907 San Francisco earthquake, produced the pottery. Like other potters, Rhead used California clays. He had earlier worked at Weller Pottery in Zanesville, Ohio; called on many of its decorative techniques at Arequipa, including the squeeze-bag method of decoration; 1913, left Arequipa, and was succeeded by Albert Solon, who greatly expanded its output. 1916, F.H. Wilde succeeded Solon; introduced new glazes and attempted to shift Arequipa's production from artware to handmade tiles, particularly of the Spanish type. 1918, the pottery and, 1957, the Sanatorium closed.
Exhibitions Wares included in 1915 *Panama-Pacific International Exposition*, San Francisco. Arequipa work subject of 2000–01 exhibit, Oakland Museum of California (catalog below).
Bibliography Paul Evans, in Timothy J. Andersen et al., *California Design 1910*, Salt Lake City: Peregrine Smith, 1980: 66–67. Cat., Suzanne Baizerman and John Toki, *Fired by Ideals: Arequipa Pottery and the Arts and Crafts Movement*, Oakland: Oakland Musum of California, 2000.
> See Rhead, Frederick H.

Arflex

Italian furniture manufacturer; located Limbiate.

History 1948, Pirelli rubber company opened a new division, Arflex, to design seating with foam-rubber upholstery; employed Marco Zanuso Sr. to explore the use of rubber in furniture and manufacture; 1950, established Arflex as a legitimate entity to produce furniture. Zanuso designed 1951 Lady chair with rubber webbing and foam-rubber padding, and 1954 Martingala lounge chair and Sleep-O-Matic sofa-bed. Franco Albini designed 1952 Fiorenza cross-legged armchair. Other Arflex freelance designers have included Tito Agnoli, Carlo Bartoli, Lodovico Belgiojoso, Francesco Berarducci, Cini Boeri, Maurizio Calzavara, Erberto Carboni, Cesare Casati, Antonio A. Colombo, Joe Colombo, Marcello Cuneo, Giancarlo De Carlo, E. Gentili, Martin Grierson, Laura Griziotti, Roberto Lucci, Mario Maioli, Mario Marenco, L. Martellani, Roberto Menghi, Piero Menichetti, Giulio Minoletti, M. Napolitano, Herbert Ohl, Carlo Pagani, Enrico Perressutti, Gustavo Pulitzer, Ernesto N. Rogers, Alberto Rosselli, Carlo Santi, Pierluigi Spadolini, Carla Venosta, and Guido Zimmerman. 1953, Alberto Burzio joined the firm; subsequently, became the general director and, 1966–71, was the committee director.
Bibliography *ADI Annual 1976*, Milan: Associazione per il Disegno Industriale, 1976. *Arflex 1951–1981*, Milan: Arflex, 1981. Cat., Leslie

Jackson, *The New Look: Design in the Fifties*, New York: Thames & Hudson, 1991: 126–27.

Argy-Rousseau, Gabriel (b. Joseph-Gabriel Rousseau 1885–1953)
French glassware designer; born Meslay-le-Vidame, Beauce.

Training École Breguet; 1902–06, École de Sèvres.
Biography At Sèvres, he was a fellow pupil of Jean Cros, son of Henri Cros, who developed the *pâte-de-verre* technique; from 1909, produced enameled scent bottles; 1913, married Marianne Argyriadès and began signing his name Gabriel Argy-Rousseau, adopting the first four letters of her name to acknowledge her moral support; 1921, became a partner of G.G. Moser-Millot, who financed his atelier; made pieces in opaque *pâte-de-verre* and translucent *pâte-de-cristal* in animal, human, and abstract decorative motifs; 1928, produced crystal sculptures based on H. Bourraire drawings and bowls, plates, medallions, pendants, and bonbonnières, and c. 1930 Tanagra figurines in clear crystal (with Bourraire).
Exhibitions Showed work first in 1914; participated in annual Salons of Société des Artistes Français from 1919, Salon d'Automne from 1920, and Société des Artistes Décorateurs from 1920. At 1925 *Exposition Internationale des Arts Décoratifs et Industriels Modernes*, Paris, work was included in the Grand Palais and French Embassy; was a member of the exposition's jury for glass.
Bibliography R. and L. Grover, *Carved and Decorated European Art Glass*, Rutland, Vt.: Tuttle, 1970: 69. H. Hilschenz, *Das Glas des Jugendstils*, Munich, 1972: 148–51. Duret Robert, *Connaissance des arts*, no. 287, Jan. 1976: 79–84. Janine Block-Dermant, and preface and catalogue raisonné by Yves Delaborde, *G. Argy-Rousseau: Glassware as Art*, London: Thames & Hudson, 1991.

Arietti, Fabienne (1956–)
French furniture designer.

Training École des Arts Appliqués et des Métiers d'Art, Paris.
Biography With Dominique Maraval, Arietti designed wall decorations, posters, and interiors for stores and hotels; 1986, began collaborating with Thierry Husson. Arietti and Husson designed 1986 Babylone chair sponsored by VIA (French furniture association) and produced by their own Édition AH!. A suite based on the Babylone motif was installed in offices of the Ministère de la Culture and of the Assemblée Nationale, Paris. 1987, Arietti & Husson was established to sell through Édition AH!, including folding pieces and those in 'brutal' materials like unfinished steel and rough concrete.
Citations Young creators' prize for contemporary furniture (with Husson), 1987 Salon du Meuble, Paris.
Bibliography *Les carnets du design*, Paris: Mad-Cap Productions/APCI, 1986. Cat., *Les années VIA*, Paris: Musée des Arts Décoratifs, 1990.
> See Husson, Thierry.

Gabriel Argy-Rousseau. Statuette of armored knight. c. 1929. Colorless *pâte-de-verre* with light and dark amber veins, h. 5 3/16" (13.1 cm). Mfr.: the designer, France. Courtesy Quittenbaum Kunstauktionen, Munich.

Armstrong, John (1893–1973)
British painter, designer, and ceramicist.

Training 1912–13, law, Oxford University; 1913–24, St. John's Wood School of Art, London.
Biography 1931, Armstrong executed designs for the ballet *Façade*; 1932–52, designed posters for Shell and costumes for Alexander Korda-produced films *The Private Life of Henry VIII* (1933), *The Scarlet Pimpernel* (1935), *Rembrandt* (1935), *Things to Come* (1935), and *I, Claudius* (1937); 1933, became a member of artists' group Unit One and painted eight mural panels for Shell-Mex House, London; 1933–34, created theater designs for the Old Vic/Sadler's Wells; 1934 Chevaux ceramic dinnerware by A.J. Wilkinson in Burslem; under Clarice Cliff's direction, designed 1934 tableware in the Bizarreware range by A.J. Wilkinson, Royal Staffordshire Pottery; 1940–44, was active as an official war artist.
Exhibitions Work subject of one-person exhibition, Leicester Gallery, London. Included in 1934 Unit One show, Mayor Gallery, Liverpool; 1934 *Modern Art for the Table* (his A.J. Wilkinson ceramics), Harrods department store, London.
Bibliography Cat., *Thirties: British Art and Design Before the War*, London: Arts Council of Great Britain/Hayward Gallery, 1979.

Arnal, Charlotte (1951–)
> See Fevre, Francis.

Arnal, François (1924–); Atelier A
French painter; born La Valette (Var).

Biography 1969, Arnal, an Abstract Expressionist, founded Atelier A in Paris to produce furniture and objects designed by artists; issued more than 200 designs by 46 artists, such as Enrico Baj, Mark Brusse, César, Peter Klasen, Piotr Kowalski, Annette Messager, Pierre Restany, Jean-Michel Sanejouand, Hervé Télémaque, Bernar Venet, and Arnal himself. Some of the best-known work includes 1967 Luminescent Stones floor lamps by André Cazenave, Drum armchair and 1972 Demi-Violin neon light by Arman, 1970 Fesses thermoformed-plastic armchair by Roy Adzak and Z metal-rod side chair and stool. 1975, Atelier A closed.
Exhibitions Large number of Arnal's own one-person shows. Atelier A subject of 2003 exhibition, VIA gallery, Paris (catalog below).
Bibliography Gilles de Bure, *Le mobilier français 1965–1979*, Paris: Regard/VIA, 1983. Cat., Françoise Jollant Kneebone and Chloé Braunstein, *L'Atelier A, la rencontre de l'art et de l'objet*, Paris: Norma, 2003.

Arnaldi, Gianluigi (1938–)
Italian industrial designer; born Asmara, Eritrea.

Biography From 1955, Arnaldi worked in the design department of Olivetti, designing P203 calculating machine and Lexikon 83DL typewriter; 1973, set up own design studio in Milan; became a consultant to lighting manufacturer Arteluce; early 1980s, began collaborating with Luigi Gaetani; designed Daisy lamp by PAF (with Gaetani). Other clients have included Poltronova and the Design Centre.
Bibliography *ADI Annual 1976*, Milan: Associazione per il Disegno Industriale, 1976.

Arndt, Alfred (1896–1976)
German architect and industrial designer; born Elbing.

Training 1921–26, Bauhaus, Weimar and Dessau.
Biography 1926, Arndt practiced architecture in Thüringen; 1929–32, was in charge of the Bauhaus's interior-design department and the furniture and the wall-painting workshops; designed furniture, including a cantilever chair; 1933 when the Bauhaus closed, set up again as an architect, working in Probstzella and in Jena; 1948, fled Soviet-controlled East Germany to Darmstadt in West Germany, where he was active as a painter and architect. Died in Darmstadt.
Bibliography Cat., *Alfred Arndt, Maler und Architekt*, Darmstadt: Bauhaus-Archiv, 1968. Hans M. Wingler, *The Bauhaus*, Cambridge, Mass.: MIT, 1969. Lionel Richard, *Encyclopédie du Bauhaus*, Paris:

Somogy, 1985: 148. Cat., *Der Kragstuhl*, Stuhlmuseum Burg Beverungen, Berlin: Alexander, 1986: 118–19, 130.

Arnodin, Maïmé (1916–2003); Denise Fayolle (1923–1995); MAFIA

French designers and entrepreneurs; agency.

Training Arnodin: engineering, École Centrale des Arts et Manufactures, Paris. Fayolle: engineering.
Biography 1951–57, Arnodin was a journalist and managed fashion paper *Jardin des modes*; 1958–60, sales manager and advertising director, Au Printemps department store, Paris; 1961–67, ran her own *bureau de style* and promotion agency; 1968–88, with her companion Denise Fayolle, operated Maïmé Arnodin Fayolle International Associées (MAFIA), an advertising agency/product-design office. (1953, Fayolle, formerly the editor of magazine *Vogue beauté*, had become director of style, press relations, and publicity of the Prisunic 'five-and-dime' chain in France and, with Arnodin and Andrée Putman, developed the *style Prisu* for Prisunic's own productions developed by them.) Through MAFIA, Fayolle and Arnodin became active in styling, design, products, packaging, production, public relations, promotion, and film and TV production; originally specialized in fashion and textiles; conceived as well as promoted MAFIA's own products. Their first big success was Yves Saint Laurent's Opium scent, for which they wrote the slogan 'For the addict.' They promoted the fashion and furniture of young designers, through mail order, including Azzedine Alaïa, Issey Miyake, and Philippe Starck, none well known at the time. Subsequently, they established Nouvelle Organisation Maïmé and Denise (NOMAD), a communications agency, and continued to contribute to the public's design consciousness, particularly in France.
Bibliography Arlette Barré-Despond (ed.), *Dictionnaire international des arts appliqués et du design*, Paris: Regard, 1996: 373.

Arnold, Eisenmöbelfabrik L. und C.
> See Stendal, L. & C.

Aroldi, Danilo (1925–); Corrado Aroldi (1936–)

Italian designers; born Casalmaggiore; brothers.

Biography 1960, the Aroldi brothers opened their own studio in Milan; were members of Associazione per il Disegno Industriale (ADI); designed 1968 Periscopio articulated table lamp by Stilnovo and 1975 Pala table lamp by Luci; became best known for lighting and kitchens by Campi e Calegari, Delta, Pabis, Tonon, and Zetamobili.
Bibliography *ADI Annual 1976*, Milan: Associazione per il Disegno Industriale, 1976. Cat., *Lumière, je pense à vous*, Paris: Centre Georges Pompidou, 1985. Cat., Hans Wichmann, *Italien Design 1945 bis heute*, Munich: Die Neue Sammlung, 1988.

Aromaa, Arni (1975–)

Finnish industrial designer.

Training Product and strategic design, Taideteollinen korkeakoulu, Helsinki.
Biography Aromaa established Design Agency Pentagon in Helsinki. His best-known design may be Bytepak interlocking covers for floppy/Zip disks and CD-ROMs.
Exhibitions/citations Smart Bath (an 'intelligent' bathroom developed with Sauli Suomela) was introduced at 1998 Design Forum Finland, Helsinki. Participated in numerous exhibitions and fairs. Received 1997 Pro Finlandia Design citation and 1998 prize of Industrie Forum Design (iF) (both for Bytepak), Hanover.
Bibliography Mel Byars, *On/Off: New Electronic Products*, New York: Universe, 2001.

Arribas, Alfredo (1954–)

Spanish architect, interior, and product designer; born and active Barcelona.

Training 1977, Escola Técnica Superior d'Arquitectura de Barcelona (ETSAB).
Biography Arribas is active in his firm Alfredo Arribas Arquitectos Asociados; became known in Spain for the interiors of 1987 Velvet Bar and 1990 Torres de Ávila, both Barcelona, and has also received commissions from foreign clients; has designed buildings in Spain,

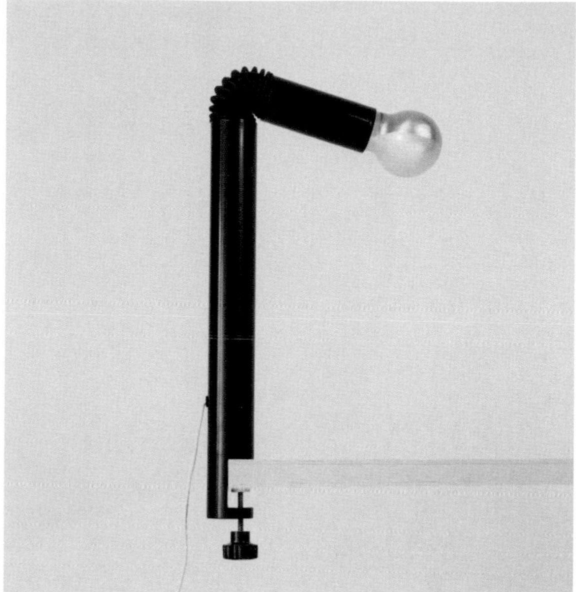

Danilo Aroldi and Corrado Aroldi. Periscopio adjustable table lamp. 1968. Lacquered metal and rubber, h. 18 1/2 x w. 4" (47 x 10.2 cm). Mfr.: Stilnovo, Italy. Gift of the mfr. MoMA.

Japan, China, Germany, France, Belgium, and Italy, including stages and structures for the opening and closing ceremonies of the 1992 Barcelona Olympiad, and products, including 1992 Zenio ashtray by Bd Ediciones de Diseño.
Citations 1987 Premi FAD d'Interiorisme (for best interiors).
Bibliography Georg C. Bertsch and Óscar Tusquets, *Alfredo Arribas: Architecture and Design 1986–1992*, Berlin: Wasmuth, 1994. Helmut Seemann and Enric Miralles, *Alfredo Arribas: Architecture and Design 1986–1992*, Berlin: Wasmuth, 1996. Ignasi de Solà-Morales, *Alfredo Arribas Works 1992–1998*, New York: Princeton Architectural Press, 1998.

Arström, Folke (1907–97)

Swedish metalworker.

Training Kungliga Tekniska Högskolan, Stockholm.
Biography 1934, Arström opened his own design studio in Stockholm; 1940, became head designer of Gense. For the metalware firm, he designed c. 1946 Thebe range of cutlery in stainless steel to counter the public's resistance to the material; 1955–56 Focus de Luxe

Folke Arström. Cutlery. c. 1946. Stainless steel, longest (dinner knife) l. 8 1/4" (21 cm), shortest (teaspoon) l. 6" (15.2 cm). Mfr.: Gense, Sweden. Gift of the Education Department. MoMA.

Art Nouveau: Hector Guimard. Settee. 1897. Carved mahogany and tooled leather, 36 1/2 x 67 1/2 x 21" (92.7 x 171.4 x 53.3 cm). Greta Daniel Design Fund. MoMA.

cutlery, particularly popular in the US; 1950–51 Facette cutlery; and other tableware.
Bibliography Graham Hughes, *Modern Silver Throughout the World*, New York: Crown, 1967: nos. 59, 61. Jay Doblin, *One Hundred Great Product Designs*, New York: Van Nostrand Reinhold, 1970: no. 79. Cat., Kathryn B. Hiesinger and George H. Marcus III (eds.), *Design Since 1945*, Philadelphia: Philadelphia Museum of Art, 1983.

Art Déco

International style of decorative art, design, and architecture.

History The term 'Art Déco' was conjured in 1960s from the name of 1925 *Exposition Internationale des Arts Décoratifs et Industriels Modernes*, Paris. Other terms for the style, particularly contemporary ones, have included Art Moderne, Jazz Moderne, and Déco or the Déco style. Couturier Paul Poiret showed dress designs in the 1908 portfolio *Les robes de Paul Poiret racontées par Paul Iribe* and the 1911 *Les choses de Paul Poiret vues par Georges Lepape*. These publications presaged Art Déco, a style that first appeared in interiors, furniture, furnishings, and architecture in France and rapidly became popular worldwide. Partly traditional and partly avant-garde, Art Déco amalgamated influences from various movements, including Dada's machine aesthetic, Surrealism's use of the subconscious, Cubism's and Fauvism's geometry and bold colors, machine forms of Futurism, Constructivism, Vorticism, the Wiener Werkstätte, and the Münchner Werkbund. The French leaders of Cubist Art Déco architecture were Le Corbusier and Robert Mallet-Stevens. The more formal, traditionally oriented and luxurious aspects of the French movement were seen in Pierre Patout's Pavillon du Collectionneur at the 1925 exposition. Originally planned for 1915, this event was one of the most influential ever in the international applied arts, including fashion, fabrics, interior decoration, furniture design, and architecture. (The US and Germany were absent.) An idealistic approach to the style was expressed in Pierre Chareau and Bernard Bijvoet's 1928–32 Maison de Verre, Paris. The influence of Expressionism was seen in Bernhard Hoetger's 1929 Paula Modersohn-Becker house, Bremen. The influence of Frank Lloyd Wright's block-like structures appeared in the brick buildings of the School of Amsterdam, exemplified by Pieter Kramer's 1926 Bijenkorf department store in The Hague and the work of the De Stijl exponents. Expressed through color and ornamentation in the US, the Art Déco style was realized in structures, including William van Alen's 1928–30 Chrysler building and Raymond Hood's 1930 McGraw-Hill building, both New York. Expressed as the International Style, William Lescaze and George Howe designed 1929–32 Philadelphia Savings Fund Society building in Philadelphia. Cubist forms were expressed by Wells Coates's 1933 Lawn Road flats, London, and Guiseppe Terragni's 1928 apartment house, Como. The claim that Art Déco was essentially Cubism tamed is supported by 1930s kitsch domestic products. Even though largely rejecting abstract art, the middle classes of the 1920s and 1930s purchased Cubist-inspired wallpaper and linoleum in colors that originated in the hyper-tinted palette of the Ballets Russes. Art Déco interiors paraphrased African art (in the furniture of Pierre Legrain), Egyptian temples and furniture (in George Coles's 1929 Carlton Cinema, Upton Park, Essex, England), animal-fantasy themes (Armand-Albert Rateau's 1912 Jeanne Lanvin apartment, Paris), Native American wares, Babylonian ziggurats, Mexican forms (in the silverware of Jean Puiforcat), and Pre-Columbian architecture (in the Mayan forms of Wright's 1920 Hollyhock House, Hollywood, Cal., and, in New York, Edward Sibbert's 1935 Kress building and Starrett and Van Vleck's 1930 Bloomingdale's store). Jacques-Émile Ruhlmann's designs were derived from Louis XV and Louis Philippe styles, and Süe et Mare's furniture was neo-baroque.
Exhibitions The seminal event that gave the style its current name—1966 *Art déco: les années 25: collections du Musée des Arts Décoratifs*, Musée des Arts Décoratifs, Paris. Subject of 2003 *Art Deco, 1910–1939*, London (catalog below).
Bibliography Cat., Yvonne Brunhammer, *Art déco: les années 25: collections du Musée des Arts Décoratifs*, Paris: Musée des Arts Décoratifs, 1966. Cat., François Mathey, *Les années '25': Art Déco/Bauhaus/Stijl/Esprit Nouveau*, Paris: Musée des Arts Décoratifs, 1966. Bevis Hillier, *Art Déco*, Minneapolis: Minneapolis Institute of Arts, 1971. Cervin Robinson and Rosemaire Haag Bletter, *Skyscraper Style*, New York: Oxford, 1975. Bevis Hillier, *The Style of the Century, 1900–1980*, New York: Dutton, 1983. Robert Heide and John Gilman, *Popular Art Déco: Depression Era Style and Design*, New York: Abbeville, 1991. Cat., Charlotte Benton et al. (eds.), *Art Deco, 1910–1939*, London: Victoria and Albert Museum, 2003.

Art Nouveau

Movement of design and architecture.

History Idiosyncratic yet romantic, the Art Nouveau style was a reaction to the academic classicism espoused by the École des Beaux-Arts, Paris. Its exponents wished to created a modern aesthetic to suit the modern world and chose to amalgamate the fine and plastic arts into a whole, or *Gesamtkunstwerk* (total work of art). They had an intense interest in the organic, whose physical aspects were derived from nature and the female body and expressed as plant-like forms such as tendrils, sinuous and whiplash curves, lavish and undulating shapes. Claiming to be anti-historicist, in truth the style owed much to the studies of ornamentation of earlier periods; a foretaste of Art Nouveau may be found in Eugène-Emmanuel Viollet-le-Duc's curvilinear 1860s–70s metalwork and in his brilliant coloring for the stenciled side chapels of Notre Dame, Paris. *Japonisme* became an integral aspect of Art Nouveau, heightened by a profusion of Japanese prints and wares at 1867 *Exposition Universelle* in Paris. The style first appeared in the decorative arts (interior design, furniture, ceramics, metalware, etc.), and into architecture in the 1890s. 'Art Nouveau' (or

'new art') was coined first by contemporary critics in Belgium and then by Siegfried Bing in 1895 to name his gallery/shop, L'Art Nouveau, in Paris. The approach appeared fully realized at 1900 *Exposition Universelle* in Paris, where, among numerous other examples, Bing's L'Art Nouveau pavilion featured interiors by Edouard Colonna, George de Feure, and Eugène Gaillard. Significant in the propagation of the movement—and generally important in the dissemination of visual ideas in the 19th century—were periodicals such as *Art et décoration* in France, *Kunst und Dekoration* in Germany, *Ver Sacrum* in Austria, and, to a lesser extent, *The Studio* in the UK. From c. 1880 to 1914 beginning of World War I, the Art Nouveau movement had centers throughout Europe—in Paris and Nancy, Darmstadt and Munich, Brussels, Glasgow, Barcelona, Vienna, Prague, and Budapest, and, to a lesser degree, in the US. Was also called by a number of names: Modern Style in Britain, Jugendstil (from Munich journal *Jugend*) in Germany, Paling Style (based on Victor Horta's work), Coup de Fouet (whiplash), and Style des Vingt (after the Belgian artists' group Les Vingt headed by Octave Maus) in Belgium, Stile Liberty (after Liberty's in London) or Stile Floreale in Italy, Modernismo in Catalonia, Style Guimard (after Guimard, the designer of many Paris Métro station entrances) in France, Style Nouille (noodle style), and Style 1900. The decorative arts first expressed the style in the 1880s designs of Arthur H. Mackmurdo and Henry van de Velde, glassware of Émile Gallé, textiles of William Morris, and furniture of Gustave Serrurier-Bovy. Architecture followed, notably Victor Horta's 1892–93 Tassel house, Brussels, and August Endell's 1897–98 Elvira photographic studio, Munich. Also: Paul Hankar's 1893–1900 houses, Brussels; Guimard's 1897–98 Castel Béranger, Paris; Horta's 1896–99 Maison du Peuple and 1895–1900 Hôtel Solvay, Brussels; Kromhout's, Sluyterman's, and Wolf's structures, the Netherlands; Henry van de Velde's 1900–02 Museum Folkwang and its interiors, Hagen, Germany; Antonin Balsanek and Osvald Polivka's 1903–12 U Obecni Dum (the municipal house), Prague; Antoni Gaudí's 1905–10 Casa Milá, Barcelona; and Otto Wagner's 1897 Karlsplatz Stadtbahn station, Vienna.
Bibliography Victor-Marie-Charles Ruprich-Robert, *Flore ornementale: essai sur la composition de l'ornement...*, Paris: Dunod, 1866, 1876 2nd ed. Ernst Haeckel, *Kunstformen der Natur*, Leipzig/Vienna: Bibliographischen Instituts, 1899–1904. Fritz Schmalenbach, *Jugendstil: ein Beitrag zu Theorie und Geschichte der Flächenkunst*, Würzburg: K. Triltsch, 1935. Stephan Tschudi-Madsen, *Sources of Art Nouveau*, Oslo: Aschehoug, 1956. Helmut Seling (ed.), *Jugendstil: Der Weg ins 20. Jahrhundert*, Heidelberg/Munich: Keysersche, 1959. Peter Selz and Mildred Constantine (eds.), *Art Nouveau: Art and Design at the Turn of the Century*, New York: The Museum of Modern Art, 1959. Italo Cremona, *Il tempo dell'Art Nouveau...*, Florence: Vallecchi, 1964. Maurice Rheims, André Breton (intro.), *L'art 1900, ou le style Jules Verne*, Paris: Arts et Métiers Graphiques, 1965. Valentino Brosio, *Lo Stile Liberty in Italia*, Milan: A. Vallardi, 1967. Eleonora Bairiti et al., *L'Italia Liberty: arredamento e arti decorativi*, Milan: Görlich, 1973. Frank Russell (ed.), *Art Nouveau Architecture*, London: Academy, 1983. Jean-Paul Bouillon, *Art Nouveau 1980–1914*, New York: Rizzoli, 1985. François Loyer (ed.), *L'École de Nancy, 1889–1909: Art nouveau et industries d'art*, Paris: Réunion des Musées Nationaux, 1999. Peter Greenhalgh et al., *The Art Nouveau 1890–1914*, London: Victoria and Albert Museum, 2000.

Artek
Finnish furniture and interior-design company.

History 1935, Artek was established by Aino and Alvar Aalto, Maire Gullichsen, and art historian Nils-Gustaf Hahl as a center for modern design, art, and architecture in Helsinki. The shop, first at Fabianinkatu 31 in Helsinki, opened 1936. The main objective was to market and sell Alvar Aalto's furniture in Finland and abroad. Aino Aalto ran the enterprise with Hahl until his death in World War II and, subsequently, was assisted by interior designer Maija Heikinheimo. Aalto's furniture was distributed in the UK by Finmar and in the US by Artek-Pascoe. Under Aino's leadership, Artek's design studio also took care of the interior design of Alvar Aalto's main projects. Artek designers have always actively participated in the development of Aalto's furniture, lamps, and textiles. More recently, the Artek collection has included designs by Vesa Danski, Brita Flander, Bertel Gardberg, Juha Leiviskä, Pirkko Stenros, Jörn Utzon, and by the current design director, Ben af Schultén. Artek and Artek's Art & Technology division are now owned by Provenus of Sweden, becoming 'Art & Technology by Proventus.'
Bibliography Sales cat., *Artek*, Helsinki: Artek, 1982. Cat., J. Stewart Johnson, *Alvar Aalto: Furniture and Glass*, New York: The Museum of Modern Art, 1984. Juhani Pallasmaa (ed.), *Alvar Aalto Furniture*, Cambridge, Mass: MIT, 1985. Cat., *Alvar Aalto: Furniture 1929–1939*, London: Haslam & Whiteway, 1987.
> See Aalto, Aino; Aalto, Hugo Alvar Henrik.

Artelano
French furniture firm; located Paris.

History 1972, Artelano was established by Annick and Samuel Coriat for the marketing of furniture, including sofas, chairs, tables, bookcases, and complementary pieces, in honed-down clean forms. Its stable of commissioned designers includes Atelier Eoos, Emmanuel Dietrich, Olivier Gagnère, Piero Lissoni, Pascal Mourgue, Christophe Pillet, Patricia Urquiola, and Marco Zanuso Jr.

Artěl
Czech cooperative and art studio; located Prague.

History Active from 1908, Artěl was founded by members of the young Czech avant-garde: Jaroslav Benda, Vratislav H. Brunner, Aloie Dyk, Pavel Janák, Helena Johnová, Jan Konůpek, Marie Teinitzerová, and Otakar Vondráčk. Its manifesto declared it was 'against industrial stereotypes and surrogates.... [We wish] to improve the sense of art and good taste in everyday life... from minor decorative objects to textiles, ceramics, furniture, bookbinding, and fashion.' The organization also commissioned young designers and Cubist architects, who worked in different studios and factories; 1911–14, was thus influenced by Cubism; published its work in magazine *Umĕleckyměsíčník* (artistic monthly); designed 1922 interiors of Hotel Hviezdoslav in Štrbské Pleso (Slovakia), for which Vlastislav Hofman, Jaromír Krejčar, Ladislav Machoň, Otakar Novotný, and Rudolf Stockar designed furniture, textiles, and wall paintings; 1934, was unable to withstand the Great Depression and closed.
Exhibitions Work shown at 1923 (1st) *Esposizione Biennale delle Arti Decorative e Industriali Moderne*, Monza; 1928 *Contemporary Culture*, Brno; and others.
Bibliography Alena Adlerová, *České užité umění 1918–1938*, Prague: Odeon, 1983.

Arteluce
Italian lighting manufacturer.

History 1939, Gino Sarfatti founded Arteluce, at first producing lamps and lighting designed by himself; later commissioned others, including Cini Boeri, Livio Castiglioni, Ezio Didone, Gianfranco Fratini, and Vittoriano Vigano. The small firm achieved international renown in 1950s and has continued to produce imaginative lighting, including 1980 Jill halogen floor lamp and 1983 Donald by King and Miranda (with G. Arnaldi). From 1974, Arteluce has been a part of Flos as Flos-Arteluce.

Arteluce. Table lamp (no. 594). 1962. Painted steel, 4 1/2 x 4 1/2 x 4 1/2" (11.4 x 11.4 x 11.4 cm). Mfr.: Arteluce, Italy. Greta Daniel Design Fund. MoMA.

Bibliography Alfonso Grassi and Anty Pansera, *Atlante del design italiano 1940–1980*, Milan: Fabbri, 1980.
> See Flos.

Artemide
> See Gismondi, Ernesto.

Artificers' Guild
British silversmiths; located London.

History Neil Dawson learned enameling from Alexander Fisher; 1901, established the Artificers' Guild in London. His wife enameled most of its objects. 1903, the operation encountered financial difficulties and was taken over by Montague Fordham, who, previously the director of Birmingham Guild of Handicraft, transferred the activities of the Artificers' Guild to the Montague Fordham Gallery in London; 1900, bought the premises at Maddox Street that was known to 1906 as 'Montague Fordham, House Furnisher, Jeweller and Metalworker' and, 1906–11, as 'The Artificers' Guild (late Montague Fordham) Art Metal-workers.' Edward Spencer, a former assistant to Dawson, succeeded Dawson as the principal designer, combining silver with numerous other materials, including ivory, shagreen, coconut, mother-of-pearl, and wood. John Paul Cooper's and Henry Wilson's works were sold at the Guild. 1942, it closed.
Bibliography Charlotte Gere, *American and European Jewelry 1830–1914*, New York: Crown, 1975. Annelies Krekel-Aalberse, *Art Nouveau and Art Déco Silver*, New York: Abrams, 1989.

Artifort
Dutch furniture manufacturer; located Maastricht.

History For over a century, Artifort has been active in the production of domestic and office furniture; produces chairs, settees, and tables; has commissioned freelance designers, including Kho Liang Ie and Pierre Paulin; first used plastics in Paulin's 1965 Chair 582 in tensioned rubber and Latex foam and in his 1965–66 Armchair 303 in polyester fiberglass; also produced Paulin's 1953 Chair 157 in polyester, ABS, and elastomers, and his 1967 F577 chair. Mid-1960s, Paulin designed a succession of sculptural furniture forms, in elasticized fabric, such as his ribbon-like 1965 Chair 582. Since 1962, British designer Geoffrey Harcourt has designed more than 20 seating models, including 1971 Armchair 976 in polyester fiberglass and undulating 1973 Cleopatra sofa. Since 1979, Gijs Bakker has designed for the firm. More recent seating includes Spirit Stack stacking chair by Hajime Oonishi (for Houtoku, the Japanese licensee of Artifort products, and installed at Schiphol Airport, Amsterdam), Prof. armchair by Wolfgang C.R. Mezger, Nina and Hanna chairs by René Holten, and What's Up chaise/sofa and 2001 Apollo pedestal chair by Patrick Norguet.

Artifort: Pierre Paulin. Mushroom armchair (no. 560). 1959. Fabric, padding, and metal-armature frame, h. 25 3/16" (64 cm). Mfr.: Artifort, the Netherlands. Courtesy Quittenbaum Kunstauktionen, Munich.

Exhibitions/citations Chair 582 by Paulin shown at 1965 Jaarbeurs fair, Utrecht, and Salon du Meuble, Paris. Work exhibited in numerous other exhibitions. 1969 Interior Design International award, UK.
Bibliography Cat., *Les assises du siège contemporain*, Paris: Musée des Arts Décoratifs, 1968. Cat., *Modern Chairs 1918–1970*, London: Lund Humphries, 1971. Cat., Milena Lamarová, *Design a Plastické Hmoty*, Prague: Uměleckoprůmyslové Muzeum, 1972: 136.

Arts and Crafts Exhibition Society
> See Art-Workers' Guild.

Arts and Crafts movement (American)
Style and theory in interior furnishings and architecture.

History The Arts and Crafts movement in the US, lasting c. 1875–1910s, was more a mood than a definite style and is sometimes regarded merely as a precursor of modern design. With its utopian ideals, the movement was a call for the reform of the way people lived and the way they produced art. The images of Native Americans captured in the misty, romantic photography of Edward Curtis, Edward Steichen, and Alfred Stieglitz—supposedly ennobling, though, to revisionist historians, appearing demeaningly synthetic—reflected the ideas and intentions of the movement, which included some of America's greatest artists, who produced works markedly different in form, subject matter, and themes from those created in Britain and the rest of Europe. The finest exponents of the style included Charles and Henry Greene in California. The American Arts and Crafts interpretation was popularized by publications such as Elbert Hubbard's *Little Journeys* series and his journal *The Philistine*, Gustav Stickley's *The Craftsman*, and Adelaide Robineau's *Keramic Studio*. The movement's success was due in part to inexpensive wares, particularly those of the Stickleys, available to middle-class Americans, even by mail order. The use of the machine proved far less contentious in the US than in Britain, though for many American exponents the movement was folksy and associated with gardening, stenciling, quilting, and a general rejection of European classicism. Frank Lloyd Wright, Japanese-style printmaker Arthur Wesley Dow, and others sought new ways of creating art and images to rival the best that Europe could produce. Art was to be placed in domestic settings and made usable, rather than enshrined. Some Americans thought that there could never be a break with Europe and held on to European traditions through the American Renaissance movement, which proposed that the foundation of American art should be the importation or reproduction of 18th-century furniture, Old Master paintings, French châteaux, and Continental *objets d'art*. Exponents of this position included Edith Wharton, John La Farge, Isabella Stewart Gardner, and Charles F. McKim. The American Renaissance and its after-effects in the 1920s–30s had a distinct American flavor while retaining its links with Europe. Popular taste at about the time of World War I, which favored a more traditional and less severe style, brought an end to America's first exposure to modern design.
Exhibitions The movement was subject of 1976 *The Arts and Crafts Movement in America, 1876–1916*, Princeton University Art Museum, and numerous other important subsequent exhibitions (catalogs below).
Bibliography Gillian Naylor, *The Arts and Crafts Movement...*, London: Studio Vista, 1971. Cat., Robert Judson Clark (ed.), *The Arts and Crafts Movement in America, 1876–1916*, Princeton, N.J.: Princeton University, 1976. David M. Cathers, *Furniture of the American Arts and Crafts Movement*, New York: The New American Library, 1981. Cat., Wendy Kaplan (ed.), *'The Art That Is Life': The Arts and Crafts Movement in America, 1875–1920*, Boston: Museum of Fine Arts, 1987. Cat., Leslie Greene Bowman, *American Arts and Crafts: Virtue in Design*, Los Angeles: Los Angeles County Museum of Art, 1990.

Arts and Crafts movement (British)
Style and theory in the decorative arts and architecture.

History The Arts and Crafts movement was a reaction against the proliferation, from the mid-19th century, of poorly designed, cheap, machine-made goods. The movement's leading figure, architect and social reformer William Morris (1834–1896), was inspired by the writings of A.W.N. Pugin and above all John Ruskin, who celebrated the dignity of the craftsman/artisan. Morris led the practical revival of handcrafting, and his 1859 Red House at Bexley Heath, Kent, designed by Philip Webb, was the symbolic beginning of the movement. The Red House, in a simplified Gothic Revival style, was offered as an epitome of good taste in contrast to the pretensions of contemporary

design. 1861, extending his influence, Morris set up a group of architects and painters in the firm of Morris, Marshall, and Faulkner. 1862, Webb and Morris began designing wallpaper together to encourage collaboration. Morris's company, based on Henry Cole's Art Manufacturers, produced tapestries, fabrics, wallpaper, and stained glass. Though ostensibly for the middle class, Morris's goods, with their handmade mode of production based on medieval models, proved expensive and exclusive. A Socialist, Morris wrote *News from Nowhere* (1891), a utopian novel. Influential groups that grew out of Morris's ideas included the Century Guild of Arts, founded 1882 by Arthur Heygate Mackmurdo and his friends, and St. George's Art Society, founded 1883 by William Richard Lethaby, Edward S. Prior, and others. 1884, the latter organization became the Art-Workers' Guild, from which the Arts and Crafts Exhibition Society was formed in 1888. Walter Crane, who was admantly against machine production and allied with the historicist aesthetic of the Pre-Raphaelites, was the Society's first president. C.R. Ashbee, Lethaby, Edwin Lutyens, Prior, C.F.A. Voysey, and George Walton exhibited at the Society's events; Charles Rennie Mackintosh and the Glasgow School were excluded because of their tolerance of machine work. The 1888 founding of Ashbee's Guild and School of Handicraft was a landmark in the movement. Ashbee, who was no longer able to shun the machine and had publicly decided to use it as an ally, adopted industrial-design methods. The Arts and Crafts exponents were especially interested in house design. Site-specific furniture and furnishings were instrumental in the creation of the house as a total work of art, or *Gesamkunstwerk*. Ebenezer Howard's book *Tomorrow: A Peaceful Path to Social Reform* (1898; later retitled *Garden Cities of Tomorrow*) initiated the Garden City movement, which grew out of the theories espoused by the Domestic Revival. The efforts of these crusaders resulted in a widespread rejection of 19th-century historicism and in an interest in high standards of taste augmented by machine production. Hermann Muthesius, who worked in England for a time, argued for the amalgamation of art, industry, and the machine in the Deutscher Werkbund. The Arts and Crafts movement prepared the way for both the Art Nouveau style (through its philosophy of design and ornamentation) and the modern movement (through its rigorous discussions of design and architecture). Although the influence of the Arts and Crafts movement was far-reaching and exceptionally long-lived, its study has tended to be neglected due to a preoccupation with modern design, the International Style, and anti-ornamentation; yet Walter Gropius, Adolf Loos, Muthesius, Henry van de Velde, and other modern-movement pioneers acknowledged a debt to the British idea of an environment that served and expressed human needs.
Bibliography C.R. Ashbee, *Craftsman in Competitive Industry*, London: Essex House, 1908. Nikolaus Pevsner, *The Sources of Modern Architecture and Design*, London: Thames & Hudson, 1968. Gillian Naylor, *The Arts and Crafts Movement...*, London: Studio Vista, 1971. Peter Davey, *The Arts and Crafts Movement in Architecture*, London: Architectural Press, 1980. Gillian Naylor, *The Arts and Crafts Movement*, London: Trefoil, 1990.

Art-Workers' Guild

British craftsmen's fraternity; located London.

History 1884, Art-Workers' Guild was founded by members of St. George's Art Society, a group of architects and artists who were pupils and assistants of architect Richard Norman Shaw. Its founding members were Gerald Horsley, W.R. Lethaby, Mervyn Macartney, Ernest Newton, and Edward S. Prior. Another group, The Fifteen, led by Lewis F. Day and Walter Crane, joined the group early on. All the leading members of the Craft Revival movement became members, including C.R. Ashbee, Basil Champneys, Roger Fry, Edwin Lutyens, A.H. Mackmurdo, William Morris, Beresford Pite, Shaw, Harrison Townsend, C.F.A. Voysey, and George Walton. The Art-Workers' Guild provided a meeting place for lectures and discussions. 1888, the Arts and Crafts Exhibition Society, an extension of Guild activities, was established. The Guild (extant today) and the Exhibition Society contributed to the longevity of the crafts movement in England.
Exhibitions Guild venues were held in 1888, 1889, and 1890, with quality beginning to decline after the 1890 edition; thereafter they were held every third year until the beginning of World War I.
Bibliography *The Art and Work of the Art Workers' Guild*, London: National Book League, 1975. Isabelle Anscombe and Charlotte Gere, *Arts and Crafts in Britain and America*, New York: Rizzoli, 1978. Cat., *Architects of the Art Workers' Guild 1884–1984*, London: Heinz Gallery/RIBA, 1984.

Arzberg, Porzellanfabrik

German porcelain manufacturer.

History 1887, an industrial area and a factory for the production of porcelain was established in Arzberg, Bavaria; 1928, was named the Porzellanfabrik Arzberg; became known for its simple Functionalist tableware, exemplified by 1931 Model 1382 porcelain dinnerware designed by Hermann Gretsch, in both plain white and with a thin red line. The service was used by the SS in the Nazi period. Arzberg's designers have included Heinrich Löffelhardt, Hans Theo Baumann, Lutz Rabold, and Matteo Thun-Hohenstein.
Bibliography Karl H. Bröhan, *Kunst der 20er und 30er Jahre*, vol. 3, Berlin: Bröhan Sammlung, 1985. Cat., Wilhelm Siemen (ed.), *100 Jahre Porzellanfabrik Arzberg. 1887–1987*, Hohenberg a. d. Eger: Museum der Deutschen Porzellanindustrie, 1987.

Asbjørnsen, Svein (1943–)

Norwegian interior architect and furniture designer.

Training To 1967, Statens Håndverks og Kunstindustriskole, Oslo.
Biography Asbjørnsen was an interior designer at NIL; 1970, with Jan Lade, established the studio Møre Design in Norway. Their 1970 Ecco chair was produced by L.K. Hjelle Møbelfabrikk. Asbjørnsen established his firm Sap Design; has been granted a number of patents; designed for SAS, British Airways, and furniture firms in Norway, Italy, and Japan; is active in acoustics and screening technology; from 1981, has designed for Håg of Røros, Norway, including c. 1986 Split Returner lounge chair, Signét seating range, and Air chair.
Citations 1971 design prize (Ecco chair group), Norska Designrådet (ND, Norwegian design council); first prize (People Are Different furniture), 1976 Nordic Furniture Competition; first prize (with Lade, Split furniture group), 1981 Nordic Furniture Competition; others.
Bibliography Robert A.M. Stern (ed.), *The International Design Yearbook*, New York: Abbeville, 1985–86. Fredrik Wildhagen, *Norge i Form*, Oslo: Stenersen, 1988.

Åse, Arne (1940–)

Norwegian ceramicist; active Oslo.

Training 1965, Kunsthåndverksskole, Bergen.
Biography From 1965, Åse taught, Statens Håndverks-og Kunstindustriskole, Oslo, where he was head of its ceramic department 1975–86; 1965, set up his own workshop, producing stoneware and porcelain; 1986–87, was professor, ceramics department, Kunsthåndverksskole, Bergen; designed Wien, Ring, and Quadrat ceramics by Gabbianelli in Cerrione, Italy.
Bibliography Cat., David Revere McFadden (ed.), *Scandinavian Modern Design 1880–1980*, New York: Abrams, 1982. Fredrik Wildhagen, *Norge i Form*, Oslo: Stenersen, 1988: 174. Jennifer Hawkins Opie, *Scandinavia: Ceramics and Glass in the Twentieth Century*, New York: Rizzoli, 1989.

Ashbee, Charles Robert (1863–1942)

British furniture, furnishings, and jewelry designer; born Isleworth.

Training Cambridge University and under architect G.F. Bodley.
Biography Ashbee became a designer, writer, and major force in the Arts and Crafts movement; was strongly influenced by John Ruskin's and William Morris's idealized anti-industrialism; 1888, founded the Guild and School of Handicraft at Toynbee Hall, London, the school where he lived and for which he designed metalwork and furniture in a light Morris style; 1890, moved the Guild and School to Essex House in Mile End, London; 1898, translated and published Benvenuto Cellini's *Treatises*; 1902, moved the Guild's workshops again, to the idyllic setting of Chipping Campden in the Cotswolds, where the School of Arts and Crafts was active 1904–14; designed most of the Guild's work, although some pieces were designed by Hugh Seebohm. The Guild's two retail shops in London were a financial burden to Guild activities. 1907, a catalog was issued that offered silverwork and jewelry at inexpensive prices. 1908, the Guild, unable to compete with commercial ventures such as Liberty's, went into liquidation. Some of the craftsmen continued to work independently. Ashbee played a part in a movement involved in issues ranging from the conservation of historic buildings to early town planning. He was strongly influenced by the designs of Liberty's jewelry and silverwork and the Wiener Sezession; published *Modern English Silverwork* (1909); 1910, met Frank Lloyd Wright in Chicago, with whose work and phi-

Charles Robert Ashbee. Loop-handled dish. 1901. Silver and lapis lazuli, 2 11/16 x 7 13/16 x 4 3/8" (6.8 x 19.8 x 11.1 cm). Mfr.: Guild of Handicraft, UK. Estée and Joseph Lauder Design Fund. MoMA.

losophy he was impressed; wrote the introduction to Wright's 1911 photographic portfolio *Ausgeführte Bauten*. Ashbee lectured in the US; was a prolific designer, building structures in Budapest and Sicily and notable riverside houses in Chelsea, designing simple sturdy furniture, and creating jewelry in a complicated Art Nouveau style (a term he would have rejected). His silverwork consisted of both traditional and original vessels with dramatic, disproportionate, sweeping thin handles. 1898, after Morris's death and the demise of his Kelmscott Press, Ashbee founded the Essex House Press, printing books by hand. 1915–19, he gave up his practice and became a professor of English at Cairo University; 1919–23, worked on restoring Jerusalem.
Exhibitions From 1888, he showed with the Arts and Crafts Exhibition Society and in Wiener Sezession exhibitions. Work subject of 1981 Cheltenham exhibition (catalog below).
Bibliography C.R. Ashbee, *A Book of Cottages and Little Houses*, London: Batsford, 1906. Alistair Service, *Edwardian Architecture: A Handbook*, London: Thames & Hudson, 1978. Cat., Fiona MacCarthy, *The Simple Life: C.R. Ashbee in the Cotswolds*, Berkeley: University of California, 1981. Cat., Alan Crawford, *C.R. Ashbee and the Guild of Handicraft*, Cheltenham: Cheltenham Art Gallery and Museum, 1981.
> See Guild of Handicraft.

Sergio Asti. 18" TV set (no. TVC 3). 1973. Plastic body, 15 3/4 x 19 5/8 x 18 3/16" (40 x 49.8 x 46.2 cm). Mfr.: Brionvega, Italy. Gift of the mfr. MoMA.

Ashley, Laura (b. Laura Mountney 1925–1985)

Welsh fashion and fabric designer and entrepreneur; born Merthyr Tydfil, Wales.

Biography 1953, Ashley began making screen-printed linen tea-towels in her attic in London for herself and her friends; encouraged by her husband, Bernard Ashley, set up textile printing firm Ashley-Mountney, active 1954–68 (1954–56 in Pimlico, London; 1956–61 in Kent; 1961–68 in Machynlleth, Wales), and Laura Ashley, active from 1968, adapting 19th-century printed cotton fabrics for her dress designs. Her clothing line began with the 1961 cotton-drill apron. Setting up shops worldwide, she transformed her hobby into a large enterprise, producing women's and children's wear and promoting a nostalgic vision of a rural idyll that struck a chord with urban middle-class Britons in the 1960s–70s. She became the leading exponent of the 'cottagey' style associated with rural British design and chintz fabric; diversified into coordinated furnishing fabrics, wallpaper, and paint. Late 1980s, her firm began producing furniture in a similar historicist mode; by 1991, had 475 stores in 15 countries, selling 25,000 products, including paint, perfume, furniture, women's clothing, and the floral chintz for which it was best known. On Ashley's 1985 death, her son Nick Ashley became head of the firm.
Bibliography Iain Gale and Susan Irvine, *Laura Ashley Style*, New York: Harmony, 1987. Jonathan M. Woodham, *Twentieth-Century Ornament*, New York: Rizzoli, 1990: 242–43, 271. Anne Sebba, *Laura Ashley: A Life by Design*, London: Weidenfeld & Nicolson, 1990. Hugh Sebag-Montefiore, *Laura Ashley: The Struggle for Flower Power*, London: The Observer, 1992.

Asikainen, Teppo (1968–)
> See Snowcrash.

Asplund, Erik Gunnar (1885–1940)

Swedish architect and designer; active Stockholm.

Training 1905–09, Kungliga Tekniska Högskolan, Stockholm, and privately under Begsten, Tengbom, Westman, and Österberg.
Biography Initially, Asplund sought to paint; 1909, set up his own architecture office in Stockholm, designing primarily small houses and entering many competitions, winning 1912 and 1913 ones for schools (one of which was later built); 1912–13, was assistant lecturer in Stockholm and, 1917–18, special instructor in ornamental art; 1917–20, was editor of journal *Teknisk Tidskrift Arkitektur*; 1911–30, designed architecture and furniture in a neoclassical style, then fashionable in Sweden; garnered some attention as a result of his designs for room settings at the 1917 exhibition at Liljevalchs Art Gallery in Stockholm; 1920, visited the US to research public libraries for Stockholm city council; designed furniture for the Nordiska Kompaniet store, for Stockholm City Hall, and for his own 1924–27 Stockholm City Library. Production of his 1925 Senna chair and other models was revived in 1980s by Cassina. He was the creative force, as the chief architect, behind 1930 *Stockholmsutställningen* exposition organized by the Svenska Slöjdföreningen (the equivalent of the Deutscher Werkbund) under its director Gregor Paulsson. Originally planned as a local event, it became an international exposition of the modern movement; Asplund's Paradiset restaurant was considered by many to be the best building at the exposition. Asplund's exhibition buildings intro-

duced Sweden to the International Style and the social ideals of the Svenska Slöjdföreningen. 1931–40, he was professor of architecture, Kungliga Konsthögskolan, Stockholm; was identified with modern design but was no radical and often produced simplified neoclassical forms that incorporated decorative details and color influenced by the Scandinavian neoclassical and romantic revival. Realized an appreciable body of architectural work.
Exhibitions/citations Exhibited at 1917 *Home* exhibition (room settings), Liljevalchs Art Gallery, Stockholm, and at 1925 *Exposition Internationale des Arts Décoratifs et Industriels Modernes*, Paris. Work subject of 1988 exhibition, London (catalog below). 1913 first prize in architectural competition (extension to the Law Courts in Gothenburg; realized in 1937 after some controversy over façade style) and 1914 international competition (layout of the Stockholm South Cemetery, with Sigurd Lewerentz).
Bibliography Erik Gunnar Asplund et al., *Acceptera*, Stockholm: Bokförlagsaktiebolaget Tiden, 1931. Bruno Zevi, *Erik Gunnar Asplund*, Milan: Il Balcone, 1948. Gustav Holmdahl, Sven Ivar Lind, and Kjell Odeen (eds.), *Gunnar Asplund, Architect 1885–1940*, Stockholm: Tidskriften Byggmästaren, 1943. E. de Maré, *Gunnar Asplund: A Great Modern Architect*, London, 1955. Stuart Wrede, *The Architecture of Erik Gunnar Asplund*, Cambridge, Mass.: MIT, 1980. *Eric Gunnar Asplund: mobili e oggetti*, Milan: Electa, 1985. Cat., *Gunnar Asplund 1885–1940: The Dilemma of Classicism*, London: Architectural Association, 1988.

Asti, Sergio (1926–)
Italian architect and designer; born and active Milan.

Training To 1953, architecture, Politecnico, Milan.
Biography 1953, Asti set up his own studio in Milan; 1956, became a founding member of Associazione per il Disegno Industriale (ADI); designed furniture, lighting, glassware, wood products, ceramics, electrical appliances, interiors, stores, and exhibitions; lectured widely. His designs included 1956 kitchen system by Boffi and soda syphon by Saccab, 1970 folding chair by Zanotta. 1953, he began experimenting in plastics and, 1957–58, executed acrylic-resin lamp models by Kartell; stainless-steel cutlery by ICM; 1969–72 architectonic range of vases by Knoll; 1973 18" TV set (no. TVC 3) and other appliances by Brionvega; 1975 ski boots; 1976 Boca cutlery by Lauffer; 1979 and 1981–82 cookware by Corning France. His 1972 Dada tableware, reflective of Josef Hoffmann motifs, was produced by Ceramica Revelli in an 'anti-craft' matt white-and-black ceramic. Asti was active in glass design for Salviati & C. 1961–66, 1982–83, 1989; for Vetreria Vistosi 1968; for Venini 1968–74; for Arnolfo di Cambio 1970s; for Seguso Vetri d'Arte 1986–88; for Barovier e Toso 1988.
Exhibitions/citations Work shown extensively, including at events of Triennale di Milano; 1968 (2nd) Eurodomus, Turin; 1959, 1963, 1971 exhibitions, The Museum of Modern Art, New York; and numerous venues in Brussels, Copenhagen, London, Paris, Philadelphia, Prague, Stockholm, Tokyo, and Venice. Silver medal (for soda syphon by Saccab) and gold medals at 1957 (11th) Triennale di Milano; 1955, 1956, 1959, 1962, and 1970, individually and with others, Premio Compasso d'Oro; and numerous other citations.
Bibliography Agnoldomenico Pica, *Forme nuove in Italia*, Milan: Bestetti, 1962. 'Sergio Asti, tradition, recherches et dynamisme,' *L'œil*, no. 190, Oct. 1970: 60–67. 'Sergio Asti,' *Interiors*, Nov. 1970: 120-21. 'Le design italien: Sergio Asti,' *L'œil*, Jan.–Feb. 1976: 66–71. *ADI Annual 1976*, Milan: Associazione per il Disegno Industriale, 1976. 'Piccoli progetti ere ecologiche,' *Modo*, no. 54, Nov. 1982: 46–48. Vittorio Gregotti and Ettore Sottsass, *The World of Sergio Asti*, Kyoto: International Craft Center, 1983. Cat., Kathryn B. Hiesinger and George H. Marcus III (eds.), *Design Since 1945*, Philadelphia: Philadelphia Museum of Art, 1983. Cat., Hans Wichmann, *Italien Design 1945 bis heute*, Munich: Die Neue Sammlung, 1988. K. Sato, *Vivere il tempo: design italiano*, Tokyo: Mita, 1995.

Astori, Antonia (1940–)
Italian designer; born Melzo, Milan; sister of Enrico Astori.

Training 1956–59, Liceo Artistico, Milan; 1960–65, interior architecture and design, Athenaeum, Lausanne.
Biography 1968–82, Astori designed in the Studio Lambda, within Driade, the firm she and brother Enrico Astori and his wife founded, where work included single pieces, furniture groups, and systems that were instrumental in forming Driade's design reputation; pursued a style said to be derived from De Stijl, particularly the paintings of Piet Mondrian and designs of Gerrit Rietveld. Her first system was 1968 Driade 1. Her best-known furniture ranges include 1973 Oikos, 1973 Kaos, and 1998 Fuoko. With Enzo Mari, designed the Bri system and various shops in Brussels, London, and Paris. 1983, with Fiorella Gussoni as her technician, Astori established her own design studio in Milan; collaborated on projects with Marithé and François Barband in Brussels, Milan, and Paris; continues to design for Driade, including interior layouts of Dadriade stores in Milan, Berlin, Tokyo, Rome.
Citations 1979 and 1981 Premio Compasso d'Oro; others.
Bibliography Fumio Shimizu and Studio Matteo Thun (eds.), *The Italian Design: Descendants of Leonardo da Vinci*, Tokyo: Graphic-sha, 1987. *Mobili italiani 1961–1991: le varie età dei linguaggi*, Milan: Cosmit, 1992. Fulvio Irace, *Driadebook: un quarto di secolo in progetto*, Skira, 1995; Corte Madera, Cal.: Gingko, 1995. Cristina Morozzi and Silvio San Pietro, *Contemporary Italian Furniture*, Milan: L'Archivolto, 1996. Benedetto Gravagnuolo, *Antonia Astori*, Naples: Lan.

Astuguevieille, Christian (1946–)
French designer; born and active Paris.

Biography Astuguevieille has been a teacher, including, 1975–82, in the children's workshop of Centre Georges Pompidou, Paris; has an interest in and extensive knowledge of materials; designed jewelry for couturiers and was artistic director first of Rochas and then of Nina Ricci. From 1980, he created furniture and objects incorporating textile and wood fibers. His best-known work involves antique or old furniture, which he wraps in rope and then paints, such as 1992 Racines side tables and 1995 Strates range of furniture, including tables and seating.
Exhibitions Work first shown at Galerie Yves Gastou, Paris, 1989; subsequently at Galerie Vivienne, Paris, and venues in Brussels, Chicago, Tokyo, and elsewhere.
Bibliography Cat., Sophie Tasma Anargyros et al., *L'école française: les créateurs de meubles du 20ème siècle*, Paris: Industries Françaises de l'Ameublement, 2000.

Asymétrie
French design cooperative.

History 1984, Asymétrie was established by furniture designer and interior architect Bernard Fric (1944–). For each area in which the cooperative specializes, one or two designers work independently or together within disciplines, including graphics, architecture, lighting, and scenic design. From 1988, Marc Alessandri was a freelance designer to Asymétrie.
Exhibitions Work subject of *La Fureur de Lire*, sponsored by Ministère de la Culture at Musée Louis Vuitton, Asnières, France.

Asymptote
American architecture and design studio; active Milan and New York.

History Asymptote's principals are Hani Rashid and Lise Anne Couture. Its founder, Rashid (Cairo, Egypt, 1958–), received a bachelor's degree in architecture, Carlton University, Ottawa, 1983; master's degree in architecture, Cranbrook Academy of Art, Bloomfield, Mich., 1985; from 1989, was professor, Graduate School of Architecture, Columbia University, New York. 1986, Couture (US, 1959–) received master's degree in architecture, Yale University, New Haven, Conn.; has taught at a number of institutions, including, from 1990, as professor, Department of Architecture, Parsons School of Design, New York. 1988, Rashid established Asymptote in Milan, Italy; 1988 with Couture, formed a partnership and moved Asymptote to New York. 1989, Asymptote's first significant commission was its controversial 'Steel Cloud' proposal for the Los Angeles Gateway. Rashid and Couture published monographs *Architecture at the Interval* (New York: Rizzoli, 1995) and *Asymptote Flux* (London: Phaidon, 2002); built 1996 Univers Theater, Århus, Denmark; 1999 Flux 1.0, San Francisco; 1999, first large-capacity virtual environment for New York Stock Exchange and its Advanced Training Floor Operations Center; forthcoming Technology Culture Museum, New York; 2002 Hydrapier (now Haarlemmermeerpavillon, for the Floriade show), Hoofddorp, the Netherlands. Designed 2002 A3 office-furniture system by Knoll.
Exhibitions/citations Work subject of 2003–04 *Approach the Future: The Asymptote Experience*, Netherlands Architecture Institute (NAi), Rotterdam. Showed Flux 3.0 at 2002 Documenta 11, Kassel, Germany; with Greg Lynn, Rashid received several awards and represented the US at American Pavilion, 2000 Biennale di Venezia. 1996 Danish Building of the Year (Univers Theater), Danish Society of Architects; Forty Under Forty architecture prize; Emerging Voices prize,

Asymptote. A3 office furniture system. 2002. Steel, UV-cured tensile-mesh screens, powder-coated wood, and injection-molded plastic; 69 x 108" (175.5 x 273.3 cm). Mfr.: Knoll International, US.

Architectural League of New York; artists-in-residence (Rashid and Couture), CCAC Cap Street project, San Francisco.

Atelier A
> See Arnal, François.

Atelier Martine
> See Poiret, Paul.

Atelier Oï
Swiss architect and design partnership.

History Aurel Aebi (1966–), Armand Louis (1966–), and Patrick Reymond (1962–) design under the name Atelier Oï for clients, including Belux, Hidden, IKEA, Swatch, Woog, and 2002 Expo Schweiz; have lectured at the École Cantonale d'Art de Lausanne (ECAL) and abroad.

Atelier Vorsprung
> See Frank, Beat.

Athelia
French design studio.

History 1928, Athelia was opened as the design workshop of Les Trois-Quartiers department store, Paris; was managed by architect Robert Bloch; employed a group of designers who produced sober classical furniture and interiors, in some cases discreetly incorporating metal and consistently paying great attention to detail. 1930s, Paul Delpuech succeeded Bloch as the Athelia director.
Bibliography Pierre Kjellberg, *Art déco: les maîtres du mobilier, le décor des paquebots*, Paris: Amateur, 1986: 32.

Atika
Czech design group; located Prague.

History 1987, Atika was formed and aligned with the Anti-Design orientation of Alchimia, Archizoom, and Memphis in Italy. One goal was to support the postmodern style, seeking an outlet for experimentation and new means of expression. Its language of symbolic signs referred to nature, society, and urban destruction. Before the fall of the so-called Iron Curtain in Czechoslovakia, Néotù gallery in Paris had somewhat helped the Atika group to reach an international audience. Designers worked mostly with wood, metal, and leather in a wide range of colors. Describing themselves as 'angry young designers,' members included Bohuslav Horák, Vít Cimbura, Jaroslav Susta Jr., and Jiří Javurek. Its best-known was Jiří Pelcl. Its exponents focused on a broader cultural context than on certain concerns about manufacturing or economic situations found in Western industrialized countries. 1992, Atika was dissolved.
Bibliography Albrecht Bangert and Karl Michael Armer, *80s Style: Designs of the Decade*, New York: Abbeville, 1990. Cat., *Object Contra Design Atika*, Moravská Galerie v Brne, Prague: Forum Praha, 1992.

Atlason, Hlynur Vagn (1974–)
Icelandic product designer; born Reykjavik.

Training To 1994, Kvennaskolinn, Reykjavik; 2001, fine arts, Parsons School of Design, New York.
Biography 1999–2001, Atlason worked as designer and on product and furniture development at Boym Partners, New York; 2000–02, was a guest critic, Parsons School of Design, New York, and Rhode Island School of Design, Providence; from 2002, was a principal of G2 studio, New York, for clients including Absolut Vodka and Dunhill; 1999–2000, designed prototype furniture by DIA for Bloomingdale's department store, New York; developed stereo-system concepts by Aiwa; 2000 prototype furniture for US market by Leana Kain; 2001 products for Totem shop, New York; and 2002 PS clock by IKEA.
Exhibitions Work shown at 2001 *Public Life, Private Realm*, Parsons School of Design; 2001 and 2002 *In Transit 1 & 2*, Terminal store, New York; 2002 *Make Room*, Salone Satellite, Salone del Mobile, Milan.

Auböck, Carl (1924–)
Austrian architect and designer; born Vienna.

Training To 1949, Technische Universität, Vienna; 1952, Massachusetts Institute of Technology (MIT), Cambridge, Mass.
Biography Auböck designed furniture and ceramics by the firm in Vienna founded by his father and still active, creating designs in wood and metal, and occasionally leather and textiles too, which blended Scandinavian and Viennese styles. Independently, he designed many scientific instruments, houses, exhibitions, churches, and commercial buildings; interested in ergonomics and with a crafts orientation, he also designed machinery, packaging, and sporting goods. He taught at the Hochschule für angewandte Kunst, Vienna. Auböck also designed 1957 2060 cutlery service by Neuzeughammer-Ambosswerk,

1963 microscope by Optische Werke C. Reichert, glassware and enamel cooking ware by Culinar, chairs for serial production, ski boots with improved fastenings, brightly colored ski wear, and ceramic and metal tableware, including 1990 oven-to-table ware.
Exhibitions Work subject of 1997 exhibition, Historisches Museum der Stadt Wien, Vienna (catalog below).
Bibliography Jocelyn de Noblet, *Design: introduction à l'histoire de l'évolution...*, Paris: Stock-Chêne, 1974. Carl Auböck, 'Design für Überfluss, Design für Not,' in Helmuth Gsöllpointner et al., *Design ist unsichtbar*, Vienna: Löcker, 1981: 573–80. Cat., Kathryn B. Hiesinger and George H. Marcus III (eds.), *Design Since 1945*, Philadelphia: Philadelphia Museum of Art, 1983. Cat., *Carl Auböck 1900–1957: Maler und Designer*, Vienna: Museen der Stadt Wien, 1997.

Aucoc, Maison
French silversmiths; located Paris.

History 1821, the firm was established by Casimir Aucoc; 1854, was succeeded by his son Louis Aucoc as director, who soon added jewelry to the inventory, although it was considered a sideline to 1900. 1876, René Lalique was apprenticed to Louis Aucoc. When André Aucoc took over as director, he concentrated on the reproduction of the work of famous 18th- and 19th-century silversmiths. 1900, the firm produced works by Édouard Becker.
Exhibitions Work included in 1902 *Comité Français des Expositions à l'Étranger* (silverwares), St. Petersburg; 1925 *Exposition Internationale des Arts Décoratifs et Industriels Modernes*, Paris; 1930 *Décor de la Table*, Musée Galliéra, Paris.
Bibliography Charlotte Gere, *American and European Jewelry 1830–1914*, New York: Crown, 1975. Annelies Krekel-Aalberse, *Art Nouveau and Art Déco Silver*, New York: Abrams, 1989.

AUDAC
> See American Union of Decorative Artists and Craftsmen.

Audsley, George Ashdown (1838–1925); William James Audsley
British architects and authors; born Elgin; active Liverpool; brothers.

Biography 1856, the Audsley brothers set up an architectural practice in Liverpool. Their ornamental work was derived from that of Christopher Dresser. They published the books *The Sermon on the Mount* (1861), printed chromolithographically in the manner of Owen Jones's *Grammar of Ornament* (1856); *Outlines of Ornament in the Leading Styles* (1881); and *The Practical Decorator and Ornamentalist* (1892). George Audsley published *The Art of Chromolithography* (1883).
Bibliography Stuart Durant, *Ornament from the Industrial Revolution to Today*, Woodstock, N.Y.: Overlook, 1986: 45, 320.

Aulenti, Gae (b. Gaetana Aulenti 1927–)
Italian architect and designer; born Palazzolo dello Stella, near Udine; active Milan.

Training To 1953, architecture, Politecnico, Milan.
Biography 1955–61, Aulenti was a member of Movimento Studi per l'Architettura (MSA); 1955–65, trained under Ernesto N. Rogers's architecture group and, concurrently, under editor Rogers, was a member of the editorial department of journal *Casabella-continuità*; 1956, established her own practice; 1960–62, assisted Giuseppe Samonà (1898–1983) in the 'Composizione Architettonica' course, Istituto Universitario di Architettura, Venice; 1960, became a member, Associazione per il Disegno Industriale (ADI), of which she was vice-president 1966–69; 1964–69, taught, Politecnico, Milan; from 1974, was an executive committee member of *Lotus International*; served on the editorial boards of *Lotus*'s several architectural periodicals. Late 1950s, she became known as an exponent of the controversial Neo-Liberty style, illustrated by her 1961 Sgarsul bentwood rocking chair by Poltronova; from 1964, designed lighting by Artemide, Candle, Francesconi, Kartell, Martinelli Luce, Stilnovo, and, from 1985, iGuzzini Illuminazine; designed showrooms for Olivetti in Paris 1967 and Buenos Aires 1968, for Knoll in Boston 1968 and in New York 1970, and for Fiat in Brussels, Turin, and Zürich 1970–71. Her architecture and industrial-design office is located in Milan, where she created stage designs from 1975 for operas with theater director Ronconi (1933–) for his Laboratorio di Luca Ronconi in Prato, including *L'Anitra Selvatica* in Genoa, and *Wozzeck* at La Scala, Milan. 1976–79, she collaborated on research with members of the Laboratorio di Progettazione Teatrale in Prato; designed 1980–86 architectural interiors, Musée d'Orsay, Paris; 1985 Palazzo Grassi, Venice; 1982–85 Musée d'Art Moderne at and 1999 renovation of Centre Georges Pompidou, Paris; 1985 Museu Nacional d'Art de Catalunya, Barcelona; Italian Pavilion, *Expo '92*, Seville; 1999 Scuderie Papali (Papal stables); 1997–2003 Asian Art Museum, San Francisco. 1995–96, was president, Accademia di Belle Arti di Brera, Milan.
Work Her designs have included 1963 Pipistrello telescoping table lamp and 1968 Ruspa articulated metal lamp by Martinelli Luce, 1964 April folding chair by Zanotta, 1965 Jumbo coffee table and 1975 furniture collection by Knoll, 1972 Mezzo Pileo table lamp and 1975 Alcindo blown-glass table lamp and Patroclo table lamp by Artemide, 1973 Faretti lighting range by Zanotta, 1978 Otto A and 1982 Tre A handles by Fusital, 1980 coffee service by Cleto Munari, 1980 Tavolo con Ruote (table) by FontanaArte, 1983 Cardine sawhorse-table by Zanotta and 1984 706 Appia table series by Zanotta, and 1986 0086 sofa by Maxalto. 1975 Patroclo table lamp reissued in Modern Classic series by Artemide. Numerous other clients.
Exhibitions/citations Work shown worldwide, including one-person exhibitions. Participated in numerous Triennali di Milano, receiving an award for her design of the Italian pavilion at its 1964 (13th) session.

Gae Aulenti. Tavolo con Ruote (no. 2652). 1980. Glass and rubber, h. 11 1/4 x w. 27 1/2 x l. 54 5/8" (28.6 x 69.9 x 138.7 cm). Mfr.: FontanaArte, Italy. Gift of Donn Golden. MoMA.

Masayo Ave. Cool cushion. 2000. Polyester foam and tulle, two sizes 16 1/2" (42cm) square, or 12 1/2" (32cm) square. Mfr.: prototype by Atrox.

La Scatola Armonica was shown at 1985 Triennale di Milano. 1967, elected honorary member, American Society of Interior Designers (ASID), US; silver medal (Faretti range of lighting by Stilnovo), 1973 (15th) Triennale di Milano; 1977 award, Design Center Stuttgart; 1987, appointed Chevalier of the Légion d'Honneur, France; 1990, elected honorary fellow, American Institute of Architects (AIA), US; 1991 Praemium Imperiale for architecture, Tokyo; 2001, honorary doctor of fine arts, Rhode Island School of Design, Providence, US.
Bibliography *Gae Aulenti*, Milan: Electa, 1979. P.-A. Croset, 'Aménagement intérieur del Museo d'Orsay,' *Casabella* 46, no. 482, 1982: 48–61. P.-A. Croset and S. Milesi, 'Gae Aulenti, Piero Castiglioni, Italo Rota: il nuovo allestimento del Museo Nazionale d'Arte Moderna nel Centre Georges Pompidou,' *Casabella* 49, no. 515, 1985: 54–59. Lamia Doumato, *Gae Aulenti*, Monticello, Ill.: Vance Biographies, 1987. Jean Jenger et al., *Gae Aulenti e il Museo d'Orsay*, Milan: Electa, 1987. Juli Capella and Quim Larrea, *Design by Architects in the 1980s*, New York: Rizzoli, 1988. Margherita Petranzan, *Gae Aulenti*, Milan: Rizzoli, 1996; New York: Rizzoli, 1997. Herbert Muschamp, 'Designing for a World That's Already Filled,' *The New York Times*, 30 May 1999. Jesse Hamlin, 'Ascending into Light and a World of Art,' *San Francisco Chronicle*, 10 Mar. 2002.

Aurdal, Synnöve Anker (1908–2000)
Norwegian textile designer; born and active Kristiania (now Oslo).

Biography Aurdal was an exponent of the Norwegian weaving tradition and active from early 1940s; became known for her individualism and monumental compositions; said that her work was a visual expression of the amalgamation of colors, rhythms, music, and words; adopted the Norwegian landscape as a source of inspiration in her abstract patterns; 1960s, began experimenting with new materials and techniques, although she retained wool as a medium for its special color characteristics.
Exhibitions Represented Norway at 1982 Biennale di Venezia.
Bibliography Cat., David Revere McFadden (ed.), *Scandinavian Modern Design 1880–1980*, New York: Abrams, 1982: 262. Cat., Anne Wichstrflm, *Rooms with a View: Women's Art in Norway 1880–1990*, Oslo: The Royal Ministry of Foreign Affairs, 1990: 32.

Authentics
German design manufacturer; located Baden-Württemberg.

History 1981, Authentics was established by Hansjerg Maier-Aichen (1940–) as a trademark of artipresent GmbH, his family's firm; hired Christophe Radl to design the corporate logo; from 1989, using translucent polypropylene, specialized in the serial production of household goods such as kitchen utensils. In fact, Authentics may have single-handedly been responsible for popularizing small, colorfu, translucent polypropylene goods. The firm's simple forms and relatively reasonable prices quickly gained attention for its products in the design press. Maier-Aichen, with experience in both marketing and design, hired primarily European cutting-edge freelance designers to conceive the firm's products, although he contributed to some himself and employed two staff designers. Matthew Hilton's 1997 Wait chair marked the first step toward producing furniture; Sebastian Bergne's stool was introduced the same year. The Wait chair (made in Italy) as well as other products, some in glass, were produced, under the control of Authentics, by various manufacturers. The one-piece Hilton stacking chair recognized the need for an inexpensive ($45/£27.50) model of this form. Others designers included Karl-Axel Andersson, Ed Annink, Masayo Ave, Fabio Bortolani, the Boyms, Matali Crasset, Konstantin Grcic, Alfredo Häberli/Christophe Marchand, and Vogt + Weizenegger. However, the good idea behind Authentics attracted plagiarists who produced cheap imitations; the result—lawsuits. 2000, a gallery/shop was established in Berlin. Jan. 2001, the firm was sold to Flötotto in Gütersloh, which has retained the name 'Authentics.' However, the spirit of the former firm may not be transferable according to Maier-Aichen, who served as the artistic director to the end of 2001.
> See Maier-Aichen, Hansjerg.

Avant-Première
> See Rhinn, Eric.

Ave, Masayo (1962–)
Japanese architect and designer; born Tokyo.

Training 1983–87, architecture, engineering department, Hosei University, Tokyo; 1990, industrial design, Domus Academy, Milan.
Biography 1985–89, Ave worked at the architecture office of Ichiro Ebihara (1905–1990), Tokyo; 1990, settled in Milan, where, 1991, she worked at design studio of Dante Donegani and, 1993, established her own studio; 1996–97, was artist-in-residence, Academie Schloss Solitude, Stuttgart; from 1996, has designed architecture, furniture, lighting, textiles, packaging, and products for clients, including Authentics and Casio; became known for her use of open-cell foam in lighting and furnishings, exemplified by 1998 Genesi-Stella lamp range by Antonangeli Illuminazione; 2000, introduced her own collection MasayoAve Creation; artistic research for Du Pont Corian from 2001; has designed for Colobostile from 2001 and for C-Lection by De Jager Product from 2003. She organized international design workshop 'Sound of Material,' École des Beaux-Arts, Saint-Étienne, France.
Exhibitions/citations From 1992, work subject of or shown at a large number of exhibitions in Europe and Japan, including 2000 Biennale Internationale du Design, Saint-Étienne. First prize, 1987 Loof Top design competition, Tokyo; one of top three entries, 1991 Napoleon Bullukian textile competition, Lyon.
Bibliography *The International Design Yearbook*, London: Laurence King, 1997. 'Portrait: Masayo Ave,' *Annabelle Creation*, Oct. 2000. 'Five New Ideas of Design: Masayo Ave,' *Domus*, no. 832, Dec. 2000. Virginio Briatore, 'Japan Made in Italy,' *Interni*, no. 513, July–Aug. 2001.

Avril, Jean-Louis (1935–)
French designer; born Saint-Nazaire; active Paris.

Training To 1955, École Nationale Supérieure des Beaux-Arts, Paris.
Biography From 1964, Avril worked in the studio Perret-Hervé-Albert and, from 1967, assisted Édouard Albert, Paris; 1967, purportedly was the first to use lacquered cardboard, or *celloderme*, in the design of a range (by the firm Marty 1967) of case goods, chairs, storage units, tables, and other pieces for children; from 1970, taught history of modern architecture at École d'Architecture de Paris-la-Villette and designed interiors; 1980s, explored furniture in steel and aluminum.
Exhibitions Cardboard furniture shown in *Universal and International Exhibition (Expo '67)*, Montréal; 1968 (14th) Triennale di Milano; 1968 *Les Assises du Siège Contemporain*, Musée des Arts Décoratifs, Paris.
Bibliography Gilles de Bure, *Le mobilier français 1965–1979*, Paris: Regard, 1983: 30–32. Arlette Barré-Despond (ed.), *Dictionnaire international des arts appliqués et du design*, Paris: Regard, 1996.

Awashima, Masakichi (1914–1979)
Japanese glassware designer.

Training Design, Japan Art School, Tokyo.
Biography 1935–46, Awashima worked for craftsperson Kozo Kagami, who had studied glassmaking in Germany; 1946–50, was director of the industrial-art department, Hoya glass factory; 1950, established Awashima Glass Design Research Institute, developing mold-blown techniques for mass production; 1954, patented his process for *shizuku* (dripping water) textured glassware and, 1956, applied the process to practical use with the establishment of Awashima Glass Company. The *shizuku* glassware, mass produced in metal molds, manifested the irregular forms of glass made in traditional ceramic molds.

Citations 1956 Inventor's Prize, Invention Society of Japan.
Bibliography Dorothy Blair, *A History of Glass in Japan*, New York: Kodansha, 1973. Cat., *Modern Japanese Glass*, Tokyo: The National Museum of Modern Art, 1982: nos. 127–31. Cat., Kathryn B. Hiesinger and George H. Marcus III (eds.), *Design Since 1945*, Philadelphia: Philadelphia Museum of Art, 1983.

Awatsuji, Hiroshi (1929–1995)

Japanese textile and graphic designer; born Kyoto.

Training To 1950, Municipal College of Fine Arts, Kyoto.
Biography From 1950, Awatsuji worked as a textile designer for Kanebo; c. 1955, set up his own studio. His mid-1960s bold and colorful printed textiles broke with traditional Japanese designs. From 1964, he collaborated with the Fujie textile company; 1971–72, designed furnishing fabrics on commission for Tokyo Hotels, Ginza, and, 1982, tapestries for IBM, Japan. His 1982 'art screens' in the form of roller screens were drawn from popular advertising images.
Bibliography 'New Print Textile Designed by Hiroshi Awatsuji,' *Japan Interior Design*, no. 252, Mar. 1980: 82–85. Chihaya Nakagawa, ' "Art Screen" by Hiroshi Awatsuji,' *Japan Interior Design*, no. 280, July 1982: 73–77. Cat., Kathryn B. Hiesinger and George H. Marcus III (eds.), *Design Since 1945*, Philadelphia: Philadelphia Museum of Art, 1983. Albrecht Bangert and Karl Michael Armer, *80s Style: Designs of the Decade*, New York: Abbeville, 1990.

Axelsson, Åke (1932–)

Swedish furniture and interior designer; born Urshult, Småland.

Training 1947–51, Visby Stads Verkstadsskola, Gotland; 1952–57, Konstfackskolan, Stockholm.
Biography 1951–52, Axelsson was active in a woodwork shop, Munich; 1957–59, worked in the office of architect Gösta Åberg and, 1959–61, of architect Peter Celsing; 1961–67 with interior designer Erik Karlström, was a partner in an architecture firm; 1967, established own architecture studio and prototype workshop in Vaxholm; 1970–79, taught, Konstfackskolan, Stockholm; has designed interiors and furniture, including a large number of chairs by Gärsnäs Möbel of Sweden and 2001 Baltic chair for Baltic Centre for Contemporary Art (opened 2002), UK.
Exhibitions/citations Work included in 2002 *Strictly Swedish: An Exhibition of Contemporary Design*, Scandinavia House, New York. 1963 Pro-Beech Competition award; 1967 Red Beech Prize; 1968 Swedish Furniture Industry Design Association prize; 1978 Nordic Design prize; 1989 designer prize of *Vi* magazine; 1985, 1988, 1992, 1993 Utmärkt Svensk Form (excellent Swedish design); 1994 Prince Eugene Medal; 1995 Bruno Mathsson Prize; 1995, named Professor by Swedish government; others.

Axelsson, Lena (1972–)

Norwegian furniture designer; born Skein; active Oslo.

Training 1988–90, Frogner og Ekelig Videregående Skole, Norway; 1992–93, fashion design, Grenland Folkehøyskole, Norway; 1994–96, IPA 'Adelina Mariotti,' Rome; 1996–99, bachelor's degree in furniture design, Loughborough University, UK; 2000, design, Domus Academy, Milan.
Biography 1990–92, Axelsson worked at SAS Royal Viking Hotel, Stockholm; 1998, Seprini Design and Architecture Studio, Milan; 1999, BOA (Barber Osgerby Associates) architecture/design studio, London.
Exhibitions/citations Work included in 1998 exhibition (chaise longue), Gard Gallery, Rome; from 2000–02 *Generation X: Young Nordic Design*, traveling the world; 2000 *New Designers* (Wind table), Business Design Centre, London; 2000 Salone del Mobile (1999 Wind chair), Milan. Finalist, 1998 Memorial Seat Competition, Loughborough University; 1999 Wedgwood non-ceramics award (Wind chair); 2000 Scheiblers Legat, prize for young artists, Norway; 2000 cover competition, *Domus* journal.

Axén, Gunila (1941–); 10-Gruppen

Swedish textile designer.

Biography From 1971, Axén executed patterns for printed fabrics produced by Kooperativa Förbundet, Stockholm; was a member of 10-Gruppen (or 10 Swedish Designers), founded 1970 by Axén, Britt-Marie Christoffersson, Carl-Johan De Geer, Susanne Grundell, Lotta Hagerman, Birgitta Hahn, Tom Hedqvist, Ingela Håkansson, Tage Möller, and Inez Svensson. The consortium designed graphics (from 1971), textiles (from 1972, including by IKEA 1978), wallpaper (by Duro from 1979); remains active.
Bibliography Monica Boman, *Design Art: Schwedische Alltagsform zwischen Kunst und Industri*, Munich: Elefanten, 1988. Jan Brunius, *Svenska textilier 1890-1990*, Lund: Signum, 1995. Kerstin Wickman, *10-gruppen—Mönstertryck*, Stockholm: Raster, 2001

Azambourg, François (1963–)

French furniture designer.

Training 1982–83, École des Beaux-Arts, Caen; 1986, industrial design and, 1987, technical-school teaching, École Nationale Supérieure des Arts Appliqués et des Métiers d'Art, Paris.
Biography Azambourg's designs include: 1986–1990 furniture for La Chausseria shoe-store chain and Sylvie Hessel boutique in Paris; 1987–1990 furniture for Madison record-store chain; 1990 furniture for Gastinne-Renette armory and boutique in Paris; 1991 L'Aiglon boutique, Paris; 1992 Fromentine crêpe shop, Limoges, and public furniture for the town of Maisons-Alfort; 1994 archeological exposition in Henin-Beaumont; 1997 exhibition at Musée-Galerie de la Seita (gallery of tobacco history), Paris; 1998, plywood/foam-sandwich (a material he patented) in seating; 1998–99, developed new materials for Hermès, Louis Vuitton, and Mandarina Duck, and a saxophone by Sel-mer; 1999 Poufeuil natural-rubber stool and Pack self-inflating (polyurethane-foam-making) side chair; 1999 furniture by Cappellini, Chainey, and Domeau & Perez; 2000 3D Textile lamp and other lighting by Light, Ligne Roset, and Dacryl; 2000–01 lighting by Certex, Dubar Warneton, and Tissavel; 2001–02 graphic design for Cebal; restaurant and lighting of *Lille 2004* event; and furniture for Plank by Sentou. Teaching positions: 1993–94, micro-technology, Lycée Branly, Créteil; 1993–94, product design and, 1995, packaging, Institut Supérieur de Communication et Publicité, Paris; 1995–2003, furniture design, École Boulle, Paris; 2000–03, product design, École Camondo, Paris.
Exhibitions/citations Work included in a number of exhibitions. 1985 laureate, 'Moving' competition, Musée des Arts Décoratifs, Paris; 1988 laureate, Fondation de France; 1993 laureate, Fondation de la Vocation; 1994 laureate, Matériaux d'Avenir pour l'Ameublement competition, Centre Technique du Bois et de l'Ameublement (CTBA), France; 1998, 1999, 2000, 2001, 2002 Appel Permanent grants, VIA (French furniture association); 1999 Creator of the Year and 2000 Prix Qualité de la Recherche, International Press Jury, Salon du Meuble, Paris; 2001 and 2002 Top Plastique prize (2002 Yvette optic-fiber lamp), Syndicat des Producteurs de Matières Plastiques, France; Prix Fibre d'Or.
Bibliography Philippe Tretiack, 'François Azambourg,' *Intramuros*, no. 88, Apr.–May 2000. Michele De Lucchi (ed.), *The International Design Yearbook*, London: Laurence King, 2001.

Azumi, Shin (1965–)

Japanese designer; born Kobe; active London, UK; husband of Tomoko Azumi.

Training To 1989, product design, Kyoto City University of Art, Japan; to 1994, industrial design, Royal College of Art, London.
Biography 1989–92, Shin Azumi worked in the Personal Computer Department, NEC Designer Centre Co., Ltd., Japan; settled in London after studying there. From 1995 with wife Tomoko Azumi, has been active in their design studio, London; initially, produced their own-design furniture; subsequently, designed furniture, interior accessories, tableware, and architecture for others, including products by Authentics, Matmos, Toa, and Wire Works, and furniture by Abode, Biegel, E&Y Tokyo, Habitat, Hitch Mylius, Isokon Plus, Keen, Lapalma, Meshman, Purves & Purves, others. They were directors and art directors for the Vital Theatre dance company at 1993 Edinburgh Festival.
Exhibitions/citations Work shown in numerous exhibitions, including 1999 *British Design at the Château de Bosmelet*, Auffay, France; 1999–2000 *Lost & Found* touring exhibition; 2001 *Design Now*, Design Museum, London; 2001 *Home Sweet Home*, Kulturhuset, Stockholm; 2002 *Simplicity and Surprise*, British Council Window Gallery, Prague. 1989 grand prize, Seki Cutlery Design Competition, Japan; 1991 (PC Engine DUO) and 1992 (Bungo Mini 5 Si personal word processor) G-Mark Good Design award, Japanese Industrial Design Promotion Organization (JIDPO).

Bibliography Alexander Payne, *Ideas = Book: Azumi*, London: Black Dog, 1999. Michele De Lucchi (ed.), *The International Design Yearbook*, London: Laurence King, 2001. Mel Byars, *Design in Steel*, London: Laurence King, 2002.
> See Azumi, Tomoko.

Azumi, Tomoko (b. Tomoko Nakajima 1966–)
Japanese designer; born Hiroshima; active London, UK; wife of Shin Azumi.

Training 1989, environmental design, Kyoto City University of Art, Japan; 1995, furniture design, Royal College of Art, London.
Biography 1989–90, Tomoko Azumi worked at Kazuhiro Ishii Architect and Associates, Japan; 1990–92, in design department, Toda Corporation, Japan; from 1995 with husband Shin, in own studio, London.
Citations 1993 ABSA/Arthur Andersen trophy, UK; 1995 FX/HNB furniture award, *New Designers* exhibition, UK.
> See Azumi, Shin.

Azzabi, Karim (1957–)
Italian designer; born Milan.

Training To 1987, industrial design; to 1990, architecture; both Milan.
Biography Azzabi began designing for various clients and, 1994, established his own studio, Design Network, Milan. Work has included 1991 Floating Matilda lamp by Oceano Oltreluce, 1992 Floating Matilda inflated armchair by Edra, 1993 Brondi telephone by Balena, and numerous others. Participated in 1991 Neolite multipurpose material project at Domus Academy Research Center and is active in seminars.
Exhibitions 1991 'Neolite' multipurpose material (a 100% heterogeneous recycled plastic, developed with several others at the Domus Research Center, Milan), manufactured by Montedipe/RPE (now Consortium Replastic, Italy), in 1995 *Mutant Materials* traveling exhibition (catalog below). Participated in 1996 Absolut Glass Design International.
Bibliography Cat., Paola Antonelli, *Mutant Materials in Contemporary Design*, New York: The Museum of Modern Art/Abrams, 1995.

Azzolini, Paola (1966–); Paola Tinuper (1967–)
Italian designers. Azzolini: born Verona; Tinuper: born Lecco.

Training Both: to 1992, architecture, Politecnico, Milan.
Biographies As architects, they specialize in research into and design with innovative materials and technology; 1991–92 in collaboration with Stone Italiana and Breton, developed a composite-marble material and, with Mandarina Duck, new techniques in luggage manufacture. From 1992, they have been consultants, in collaboration with Esperanza Nuñez Castain, specializing in the material, surface, color, finish, and texture development of industrial products and architecture for firms such as Arclinea (kitchen furniture); Knoll, Castelli, Lamm, and Unifor (office furniture); and Poltrona Frau (contract furniture). From 1994, they have been active in the design of products and interiors; 1996, established Paola Azzolini e Paola Tinuper Architetti working for clients, including Belli e Forti, Bertolaso, Biesse, Ciacci, Epson, Fiat, Fila Sport, Habitat Italiana, L'Inglesina Baby, Martex, Mobilmetal, Pugi RG, Rimadesio, Sacmi Group, Softline, Steelcase, Vittorio Bonacina, Whirlpool Europe, and others. They teach at Istituto Europeo di Design, Milan.
Citations 1998 Compasso d'Oro (Pulsar washing machine by Sacmi).

Karim Azzabi. Floating Mathilda lounge chair (no. 74). 1992. Inflated PVC, metal frame, flexible belts, painted wood, and padded foam, 31 1/8 x 54 5/16 x 30 11/16" (79 x 138 x 78cm). Mfr.: Edra, Italy. Courtesy Quittenbaum Kunstauktionen, Munich.

Shin and Tomoko Azumi. Stool/table. c. 1998. Maple and steel, h. 16 7/8 x 13 3/4 x 12 5/8" (43 x 35 x 32cm). Mfr.: Azumi, U.K.

B

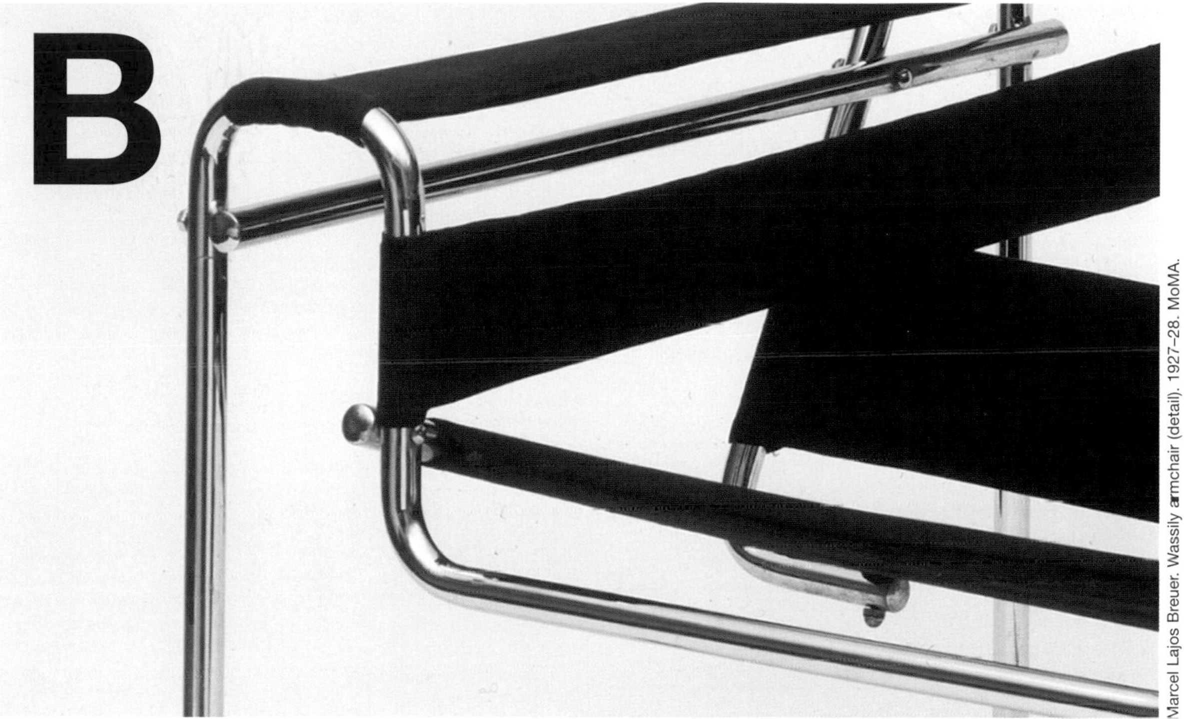

Marcel Lajos Breuer. Wassily armchair (detail). 1927–28. MoMA.

B2
French design collaboration.

History 1980s, Bruno Borrione and Bruno Lefèvbre founded studio B2 (a name derived from the two Brunos); took an approach said to be 'from the school of Starck,' or reflecting Philippe Starck's early simplicity. Their work has also been compared to the furniture designs of Friso Kramer and Arne Jacobsen. Of note is their 1987 table and side chair made of logs and some prototype projects financed by VIA (French furniture association).
Citations 1987 Appel Permanent grant (chair in tree trunk and steel), VIA.
Bibliography Christine Colin, *Design d'aujourd'hui*, Paris: Flammarion, 1988. Suzanne Tise, 'Innovators at the Museum,' *Vogue Décoration*, no. 26, June–July 1990: 48.

Babled, Emmanuel (1967–)
French designer.

Training Istituto Europeo di Disegno, Milan.
Biography For several years, Babled worked with Prospero Rasulo and Gianni Veneziano in Studio Oxido, Milan; from early 1990s, has been active in Milan and Venice, working freelance for furniture, accessories and lighting clients, including Fine Factory, Steel, Casprini, Waterford Wedgwood, Kundalini, and Rosenthal; from 1995, independently produced ceramics and Murano glass vases (some working with master glass blower Livio Serna for pieces by Idée, Tokyo, and by various kilns. Designed 2001 Hypnos bowl models and cups in crystal with a Corian base by Baccarat.
Bibliography Michele De Lucchi (ed.), *The International Design Yearbook*, London: Laurence King, 2001.

Baccarat
French glassware manufacturer; located Metz, Meurthe-et-Moselle.

History 1764, a glass factory (later known as Baccarat) was founded by Bishop Montmorency-Laval of Metz, with the permission of King Louis XV, in the village of Baccarat in Lorraine. During the early years, Antoine Renaut ran the factory. 1806, the company was bought by Lippman-Lippmann, a merchant from Verdun, who was joined by Duroux in 1808. 1816, d'Artiques, owner of the crystal factory of Vonèche in Belgium, bought the factory and was exempted from tariffs by King Louis XVIII on condition that the factory produced at least 500 tons of crystal annually. 1817, the company produced its first pieces from raw crystal. Known for its opaline glassware, paperweights, and engraved rock crystal in the 19th century, the factory became the Verrerie de Vonèche à Baccarat; 1841, the Compagnie des Cristalleries de Baccarat; and 1843, by royal decree, the Compagnie des Verreries et Cristalleries de Baccarat. By the early 20th century, Baccarat had distinguished patrons: Czar Nicholas II, the Shah of Iran, and other sovereigns purchased its wares. During World War I, Baccarat was closed down by the Germans and, 1920, resumed production to full capacity. 1925–37, Georges Chevalier produced modern models, often with geometric silhouettes. After World War II, the firm produced both traditional wares and contemporary pieces. 1949, it opened a branch store in New York. American designer/teacher Van Day Truex collaborated with the firm as a designer for a time, creating its 1973 Dyonisos decanter. The firm used other outside designers; 1970, sculptor Robert Rigot began with the firm; 1972, Czech designer Yan Zoritchak began. Roberto Sambonet designed vases. 1982, Thomas Bastide became design director; created hundreds of designs. 2001, Baccarat produced Ettore Sottsass's first product in crystal, the Anu bowl (black and clear), and Emmanuel Babled's Hypnos bowl in crystal with a Corian base. Société du Louvre began developing a luxury-goods industry sector by investing in the Compagnie des Cristalleries de Baccarat, of which it took a majority holding in 1992. 2003, Baccarat exhibition space, designed by Philippe Starck, was installed in the former mansion of the vicomte/vicomtesse de Noailles, place des États-Unis, Paris.
Exhibitions/citations Numerous awards, first at 1823 *Exposition Nationale* and showed engraved crystal inspired by rock crystal and in the *japonisant* taste at 1878 *Exposition Universelle*, both Paris.
Bibliography Cat., *Verriers français contemporains: art et industrie*, Paris: Musée des Arts Décoratifs, 1982. Jean-Louis Curtis, *Baccarat*, Paris: Regard, 1991; New York: Abrams, 1992. Dany Sautot, *Baccarat: Une histoire: 1764–*, Baccarat: Éditions Baccarat, 1993.

Bach, Alfons (1904–1999)
German industrial designer; husband of interior designer Anita Stewart Bach.

Training Schule Reimann, Berlin; later in Italy.
Biography Bach emigrated to US; had clients including Heywood Wakefield (furniture), Bigelow-Sanford (carpets), General Electric (electrical appliances); was president, Industrial Designers Society of America; member, International Institute of Arts and Letters; national president, FIDSA. The Alfons Bach Archive is housed at Cooper-Hewitt National Design Museum, New York.
Exhibitions/citations 1934, 1936, and 1938, work shown at The Metropolitan Museum of Art, New York; Philadelphia Arts Center;

Compagnie des Cristalleries de Baccarat. Magnum champagne glass (no. 15881). 1950. Crystal, h. 6" x dia. 4 5/16" (11 x 15.2 cm). Mfr.: Compagnie des Cristalleries de Baccarat, France. Gift of Baccarat & Porthault, Inc. MoMA.

Newark Museum of Art. Subject of one-person exhibitions of paintings at Babcock Gallery, New York, 1948, and Stamford (Conn.) Museum, 1954. Silver medal, Industrial Designers Institute (IDI).
Bibliiography James D. Beebee, 'Alfons Bach,' master's degree dissertation, New York: Bard Graduate Center, 2000.

Bach, Oscar Bruno (1884–1957)

German metalsmith.

Training Art, Royal Art Academy, Berlin.
Biography 1914, Bach emigrated to the US; received commissions from Christ Church at Cranbrook Academy, Mich., and Riverside Church and Temple Emanuel, both New York; was active until the beginning of World War II.
Citations 1928 medal of honor (for doors of The Toledo [Ohio] Museum of Art), Architectural League of New York.

Bach, Richard Franz (1887–1968)

American museum curator and writer.

Biography 1918, Bach became associate curator in industrial arts, The Metropolitan Museum of Art, New York; was influenced by John Cotton Dana (a pioneer in the trend to make museums more responsive to consumers, manufacturers, and retailers, and the head of the Newark Museum Association). From 1921, Bach organized the Metropolitan Museum's pioneering annual design exhibitions; from late 1920s, became active in the selection of the American Federation of Arts' International Exhibitions of Contemporary Industrial Arts; 1930–32, was editor of *Magazine of Art*. With design-exhibition activities disrupted by World War II, 1941–49 Bach was dean of the museum's Department of Education and Extension; 1952, left the museum.

Båck, Göran (1923–)

Finnish ceramicist.

Training 1957–58, Höhr-Grenhausen, Germany.
Biography From 1948–86, worked at Arabia.
Bibliography Jennifer Hawkins Opie, *Scandinavia: Ceramics & Glass in the Twentieth Century*, New York: Rizzoli, 1989.

Backström, Monica (1939–)

Swedish glassware designer; born Stockholm.

Training Advertising and industrial design, Konstfackskolan and Tekniska Skolan, Stockholm.
Biography 1965, she became a glassware designer for Boda. Her glass pieces have often incorporated metal, in the form of threads, nails, and small flakes. She has sometimes applied enamel decoration to a silvered surface and executed large glass decorations for commercial and public buildings and Swedish oceanliners.
Bibliography Lennart Lindkvist (ed.), *Design in Sweden*, Stockholm: Svenska Institutet, 1977: 16–18. Geoffrey Beard, *International Modern Glass*, London, 1976: 112, 139, 329. Cat., Kathryn B. Hiesinger and George H. Marcus III (eds.), *Design Since 1945*, Philadelphia: Philadelphia Museum of Art, 1983. Jennifer Hawkins Opie, *Scandinavia: Ceramics and Glass in the Twentieth Century*, New York: Rizzoli, 1989.

Bäckström, Olaf (1922–2001)

Finnish engineer and industrial designer.

Training In electrical engineering.
Biography Bäckström spent the first 11 years of his career as an engineer; 1954, turned to woodcarving and designing; created wooden household articles at first and, from c. 1960, cutlery; 1958–80, was an industrial designer at Fiskars, Helsinki, where his initial project was a melamine tableware collection. 1961–67, he worked on his best-known project, the popular 1967 O-Series orange-handled general-purpose scissors (produced from 1967) and pinking shears, both by Fiskars, which have been recognized as ergonomic innovations. Though production models had ABS-plastic handles, the prototype was carved by Bäckström in wood. For a time, Fiskars produced the scissors for Wilkinson Sword and sold licenses worldwide.
Exhibitions/citations Work included in 1958 *Formes Scandinaves*, Musée des Arts Décoratifs, Paris, and 1961 *Finlandia*, Zürich/Amsterdam/London. Silver medal (for wooden domestic wares), 1957 (11th) edition and silver medal (for camping cutlery) at its 1960 (12th) edition of Triennale di Milano.
Bibliography *Design*, 13 Mar. 1952: 8. Cat., David Revere McFadden (ed.), *Scandinavian Modern Design 1880–1980*, New York: Abrams, 1982: 262. Cat., Kathryn B. Hiesinger and George H. Marcus III (eds.), *Design Since 1945*, Philadelphia: Philadelphia Museum of Art, 1983. Cherie Fehrman and Kenneth Fehrman, *Postwar Interior Design, 1945–1960*, New York: Van Nostrand Reinhold, 1987. Mel Byars with Arlette Barré-Despond, *100 Designs/100 Years: A Celebration of the 20th Century*, Hove: RotoVision, 1999: 138–39.

Bacon, Francis (1909–1992)

Irish painter and designer; born Dublin; active London.

Biography 1925, Bacon moved to London; 1926–27, lived in Berlin and Paris; from 1929, had rugs woven to his designs and, the same year, began painting; 1930, exhibition (see below) achieves modest notice; 1933, participated in a group exhibition; 1934, established the Transition Gallery, London, which failed 1937. The grotesque nature of his paintings, his open homosexuality, heavy drinking, and dubious acquaintances made him a figure of some notoriety. His highly disordered studio-home became legendary. With links to Surrealism, Picasso, and German Expressionism, he is best known for his images of screaming popes, contorted portraiture, and dismembered carcasses.
Exhibitions Earliest venues: 1930, showed own-design carpets and furniture in his studio; 1945, exhibited *Three Studies for Figures at the Base of a Crucifixion* at Lefevre Gallery, London. Work included 1954 Biennale di Venezia. Subject of 1971 exhibition at Grand Palais, Paris, and, 1975, The Metropolitan Museum of Art, New York; latter subsequently traveled.
Bibliography 'The 1930 Look in British Decoration,' *The Studio*, Aug. 1930. Cat., *Thirties: British Art and Design Before the War*, London: Arts Council of Great Britain/Hayward Gallery, 1979. Obituary, Michael Kimmelman, 'Francis Bacon, 82, Artist of the Macabre, Dies,' *The New York Times*, 29 Apr. 1992: A1, D25.

Bacon, Francis H. (1856–1940)

American furniture and interior designer; active Boston; brother of architect Henry Bacon.

Training To 1877, Massachusetts Institute of Technology (MIT), Cambridge, Mass.
Biography 1878–79, Bacon traveled in Europe; worked briefly as a draftsperson in the offices of architects McKim, Mead and Bigelow, New York, and of architect and decorator Prentis Treadwell, Albany, N.Y.; was a designer at furniture producer Herter Brothers, the firm commissioned to furnish the William H. Vanderbilt House, New York; 1881–83, worked on excavations at Assos (Turkey) for the Archaeological Institute of America; worked in the office of architect H.H. Richardson, Boston, before joining furniture firm A.H. Davenport, Boston, as its principal designer and, 1885–1908, a vice-president, and where he translated hand-crafted furniture and furnishings models into machine-produced wares; may have been responsible for introducing the Colonial Revival style of Davenport furniture designed by H.H. Richardson and probably designed some of the furniture for the 1886 John Jacob Glessner House in Chicago credited to Richardson; when Albert H. Davenport died in 1906, attempted without suc-

cess to buy the company; from 1908, managed his own business.
Exhibitions Work included in 1986–87 Metropolitan Museum exhibition (catalog below).
Bibliography Anne Farnam, 'A.H. Davenport and Company, Boston Furniture Makers,' *Antiques*, no. 109, May 1976: 1048–55. Cat., Doreen Bolger Burke et al., *In Pursuit of Beauty: Americans and the Aesthetic Movement*, New York: The Metropolitan Museum of Art/Rizzoli, 1986.

Bader, Matthias (1970–)

German designer.

Training In toolmaking; to 1997, Fachhochschule, Kaiserlauten.
Biography Bader worked for Hartz and for Hermès and designed showrooms for Villeroy & Boch worldwide; 1999, established his own studio and, from 2000, was a partner of Andrea Winkler in Karlsruhe active in store design and planning.
Bibliography Michele De Lucchi (ed.), *The International Design Yearbook*, London: Laurence King, 2001.

Badovici, Jean (1893–1956)

Hungarian architect; born Budapest; active France.

Training 1917–19 under Julien Guadet and Jean-Baptiste Paulin, École des Beaux-Arts; École Spéciale d'Architecture; both Paris.
Biography c. 1918 when Badovici met architect/designer Eileen Gray in Paris, he was penniless, studying for an architecture degree, working at odd jobs in the evening, and living with Greek journalist Christian Zervos. He introduced Gray to the most important architects of the time and encouraged her to pursue architecture herself; was editor of avant-garde journal *L'architecture vivante*, which he and Zervos persuaded Albert Morancé to publish, during 1922–33 in 21 issues, including one devoted to Frank Lloyd Wright in 1926, and for *Wendingen*; with Gray, visited numerous architecture exhibitions in Europe, including 1927 *Deutscher Werkbund-Ausstellung*, Stuttgart, and 1931 *Deutsche Bauausstellung*, Berlin. 1927–29, Gray outfitted her own house (assisted by Badovici), named 'E 1027,' at Roquebrune, Cap Martin, on the Côte d'Azur. (E 1027 represents 'E' for Eileen, '10' for 10th alphabet letter 'J' for Jean, '2' for 2nd letter 'B' for Badovici, '7' for 7th letter for Gray.) Clean and sparse, every area was multi-functional with collapsible furniture, including some in tubular steel, glass, plate glass, and painted wood. 1931, Gray designed Badovici's apartment in Paris, where her furniture and rugs were installed; the metal tables, stools, and chairs were produced by Alixia of Paris. Badovici disliked Gray's shop Jean Désert and refused to bring potential clients there. 1932, she turned over 'E 1027' to Badovici and built the house 'Castellar' in the Alpes-Maritimes, occupying it alone. 1929, he and Gray traveled to Peru, and Badovici attended 1933 Congrès Internationaux d'Architecture Moderne (CIAM) in Athens, where the Athens Charter was drafted. 1934, they traveled to Mexico and to New York, where they visited 1934 *Machine Art* exhibition, The Museum of Modern Art, New York, and architect/designer Frederick Kiesler. After World War II, Badovici became Adjunct Chief Architect of Reconstruction (with chief architect André Lurcat) for Maubeuge and Solesmes (France); 1955, joined Union des Artistes Modernes (UAM) but had little work. Gray began working on the reconstruction of the house 'Maubeuge' for Badovici and gave up her studio, where some of her furnishings were still installed. Badovici renovated old houses in Vézelay, adding modern architectural elements such as metallic beams and large bay windows. Le Corbusier and wife Yvonne were often guests in Vézelay and in Roquebrune. However, Le Corbusier, Gray, and Badovici later became estranged, 1950, Le Corbusier bought land in Cap Martin near Gray's property in Roquebrune, on which he later built a very small prefabricated house. Badovici spent most of the summer months with Gray in Roquebrune, where she lived with Louise Dany, but Gray found his womanizing, heavy drinking, and friends tedious. After Badovici's death, Le Corbusier arranged for Madame Schelbert to buy 'E 1027.' Originally Schelbert wanted to destroy the Gray furniture but kept the property, including the furniture, intact, until her death.
Exhibitions Images of Badovici's flat by Eileen Gray shown 1931 (2nd) UAM exhibition, Galerie Georges Petit, Paris. Work subject of 1956 exhibition sponsored by UAM, Pavillon Marsan, Paris.
Bibliography Jean Badovici, *Intérieurs français*, Paris: Albert Morancé, 1925. Jean Badovici, *La maison d'aujourd'hui: maisons individuelles*, 1st series, Paris: Albert Morancé, 1925. Florence Camard, *Ruhlmann*, Paris: Regard, 1983. Arlette Barré-Despond, *UAM*, Paris: Regard, 1986. Peter Adam, *Eileen Gray, Architect/Designer*, New York: Abrams, 1987. Philippe Garner, *Eileen Gray: Design and Architecture, 1878–1976*, Cologne: Taschen, 1993.

Olaf Bäckström. O-Series scissors. 1967. ABS polymer and stainless steel, h. 8 1/2 x w. 2 3/4" (21.6 x 7 cm). Mfr.: Fiskars, Finland. Greta Daniel Fund. MoMA.

Baekeland, Leo Hendrik (1863–1944); Bakelite

Belgian chemist and entrepreneur; born Ghent. Material.

Training University of Ghent.
Biography 1889, Baekeland settled in the US; invented Velox photographic paper, whose rights he sold in 1899 to George Eastman for $1 million; 1904, began his search for a synthetic substitute for shellac; 1907, patented the first all-artificial plastic, which he named Bakelite, after himself; 1909, introduced Bakelite at a chemical conference and established General Bakelite Corp.; 1916, began commerical production of the substance in Yonkers, N.Y. Bakelite is produced by combining phenol (a coal-tar product) with a solution of formaldehyde. Unlike earlier plastics, such as celluloid, Bakelite must be formed in a mold by high heat, and once hardened cannot be reformed. Its production created the plastics compression-molding industry; was often used in casings for electronic items, including radios in dark colors in Britain; was popular in brightly colored costume jewelry and radios in US; made it possible to create three-dimensional curves; due to its brittleness, fell from popularity, although the term mistakenly continues to be used generically for other hard plastics.
Exhibitions 1981 venue, Rotterdam (catalog below).
Bibliography John Kimberly Mumford, *The Story of Bakelite*, New York: Stillson, 1924. T.J. Fielding, *History of Bakelite Limited*, London: Bakelite, c. 1945. Cat., *Bakeliet: techniek, vormgeving, gebruik*, Rotterdam: Museum Boymans-van Beuningen, 1981. Rob Perrée (ed.), *Bakelite: The Material of a Thousand Uses: Based on the Becht Collection*, Rome: Leonardo-De Luca, 1991; Amsterdam: Cadre, 1996.

Baeyens, Marie-Christine (1936–)
> See Smout-Baeyens, Marie-Christine.

BAG

Swiss electronics and lighting manufacturer; located Turgi.

History 1889, Egloff & Co. was founded in Turgi to produce primarily domestic products in metal, including candlesticks and oil lanterns. 1900, when electricity was becoming popular, the firm opened another facility on the Limmat river and registered both operations as Leuchtenfabrik Egloff & Co. It started to specialize in lamp manufacture, primarily in aluminum and bronze; 1909, was organized as Schweizerische Bronzewarenfabrik AG and, subsequently, shortened to Bronzewarenfabrik AG (BAG). At the end of World War II, with the introduction of its fluorescent fixtures, the firm also began making magnetic booster units. Early 1930s, BAG produced a table lamp by Karl Trabert, under license from Schanzenbach of Frankfurt am Main.

1967, began making igniters through its electronics division. When the firm's business was discontinued in 1998, the electronics division became BAG Turgi Electronics AG, an independent company, which continues today with operations also in Hong Kong, China, and Germany.
> See Trabert, Karl.

Bagge, Éric Anthony (1890–1978)
French architect and interior decorator; born Antony, near Paris.

Biography Bagge designed furniture, wallpaper, fabrics, accessories, and silver. His furniture was produced in precious woods with geometric motifs (inspired by Cubist art) in ivory marquetry; 1929, was in charge of the design of the new exhibition space, Musée Galliéra, Paris. (The museum's 1879–94 building by Paul-René-Léon Ginain was formerly the home of Marie Brignole-Sale, the duchesse de Galliéra.) Bagge was a member of the Groupe des Architectes Modernes and of the French exhibitions committee of the Société d'Encouragement à l'Art et l'Industrie; from 1922, designed furniture for La Maîtrise decorating department of Galeries Lafayette department store, Paris, and for Paris furniture firms including Saddier Frères, Mercier Frères, and Dennery. He designed the grand suite of 1927 oceanliner *Île-de-France*; 1925–29, was artistic director, Palais du Marbre, Paris, the modern furniture store; late 1920s, designed a collection of fabrics and rugs using geometric motifs and both vivid and somber colors by Lucien Bouix, and elegant wallpapers by Desfossés and by Karth. 1930, he opened his own shop, where he sold his own-design furniture, furnishings, and lighting. As an architect, his work included townhouses, stores, Church of Saint-Jacques in Montrouge, and pavilions at 1937 Paris *Exposition*; became director of the École Practique de Dessin de la Chambre Syndicale de la Bijouterie Joaillerie Orfèvrerie.
Exhibitions Participated in Salons of Société des Artistes Français from its beginning, editions of Salon d'Automne from 1919, Salons of Société des Artistes Décorateurs, and Salons of Union Centrale des Arts Décoratifs. At 1925 *Exposition Internationale des Arts Décoratifs et Industriels Modernes*, Paris, he designed the Hall of Jewelry in the Grand Palais, including other stands and the bedroom and bath of the 'French Ambassador' suite and other rooms in exhibitions for Les Gobelins and Beauvais.
Bibliography Victor Arwas, *Art Déco*, New York: Abrams, 1980. Sylvie Raulet, *Bijoux art déco*, Paris: Regard, 1984. Pierre Cabanne, *Encyclopédie art déco*, Paris: Somogy, 1986: 117. Pierre Kjellberg, *Art déco: les maîtres du mobilier, le décor des paquebots*, Paris: Amateur, 1986.

Baggs, Arthur Eugene (1886–1947)
> See Marblehead Pottery.

Baguès Frères
French designers; located Paris.

History The Baguès brothers had outlets in Brussels, London, and New York, with its main shop in Paris, where it sold lighting (particularly Louis XIV and Empire styles), *objets d'art*, and ironwork; favored the use of glass crystal beads, like those found in its lamp for clothing designer Jeanne Lanvin, and topaz and amethyst stones; produced four large reflecting vases for the lounge of 1931 oceanliner *L'Atlantique* and, for the Crane showroom, Paris, by Charles Knight (with Jacques-Émile Ruhlmann), and various accessories.
Exhibitions Widely published pine-cone chandelier with five overlapping rows of seed pods in chromed metal bordered by crystal pearls was shown at Pavillon de l'Elegance of 1925 *Exposition Internationale des Arts Décoratifs et Industriels Modernes*, Paris. Participated in 1934 Salon de la Lumière, Paris, and 1937 *Exposition Internationale des Arts et Techniques dans la Vie Moderne,* Paris.
Bibliography Alastair Duncan, *Art Nouveau and Art Déco Lighting*, New York: Simon & Schuster, 1978: 161–62.

Bahner, Franz
German silversmiths; located Düsseldorf.

History 1895, the firm was founded and specialized in silver cutlery; commissioned designs from Peter Behrens in c. 1905, Henry van de Velde in 1905, Gerhard Duve in c. 1930, and Emil Lettré in the late 1930s. 1960s, the firm closed.
Bibliography Annelies Krekel-Aalberse, *Art Nouveau and Art Déco Silver*, New York: Abrams, 1989. Karl H. Bröhan (ed.), *Metallkunst*, Berlin: Bröhan-Museum, 1990: 2–11.

Bahnsen, Uwe (1930–)
German automobile designer.

Training Freie Akademie der Künste, Hamburg.
Biography Bahnsen joined Ford motor company in Germany as a young designer and, 1976, was appointed vice-president of design there. He was effective in turning the concentration by Ford of Europe from engineering to design. His appreciable two contributions have favorably been called typically European by critics. One of them is the German-built 1960 Ford Taunus, nicknamed 'bathtub,' with oval headlamps and a rounded body. The other is the 1982 Ford Sierra, an early, successful attempt to generate wide public interest in aerodynamic design. The models expressed Ford's courageous, if intermittent, policy of innovation. Bahnsen worked in his own German-based studio.
Bibliography Penny Sparke, *A Century of Car Design*, London: Mitchell Beazley, 2002.

Baholyodhin, 'Ou' Nopadon (1966–)
Thai furniture, object, and interior designer; active London.

Training Furniture design, Kingston University, UK; others.
Biography 1997, Baholyodhin established Ou-B Designs, London, initially for the design of simple furniture, eventually adding textiles, ceramics, and tabletop objects; has created designs and settings for Kenzo, Joseph, Donna Karan. His client rostrum is extensive. From 2002, creative director, Jim Thompson silk producers, Thailand.
Exhibitions/citations Garnered attention with 11 other Thai designers at 2000 (2nd) Biennale Internationale du Design, Saint-Étienne, France. Prize for excellence, Meji International Design Competition, Best New Products, 1995 Formex, Stockholm; New Designer award, 1997 International Furniture Fair (ICFF), New York.
Bibliography Ou Baholyodhin, *Living with Zen*, London: DPD, 2000. Ou Baholyodhin and Erez Yardeni, *Being with Flowers*, London: DPD, 2001. www.ou-b.com.

Baier, Fred (1949–)
British furniture designer; born Kingston-upon-Hull; active UK.

Training To 1971, furniture, Birmingham Polytechnic; to 1975, Royal College of Art, London.
Biography A craft revivalist, Baier designed the anti-craft 1989 Roll Top Drop Leaf Transforming Robot Desk, a brightly colored object almost unrecognizable as a piece of furniture and based on 1950s Japanese science-fiction fantasies and images from the film *Forbidden Planet* (1956). 1976–78, he taught at Wendell Castle School, New York; 1979–82, at Brighton Polytechnic, England; 1982, at Royal College of Art, London.
Exhibitions/citations Work shown at 1989 *British Design: New Traditions*, Museum Boymans-van Beuningen, Rotterdam; 1990 exhibition, Crafts Council, London. 1976 award, Advisory Committee, Crafts Council, London.
Bibliography Frederique Huygen, *British Design: Image and Identity*, London: Thames & Hudson, 1989. Jonathan M. Woodham, *Twentieth-Century Ornament*, New York: Rizzoli, 1990. Charlotte Fiell and Peter Fiell, *Modern Furniture Classics Since 1945*, London: Thames & Hudson, 1991.

Bailey Banks & Biddle
American silversmiths and retailers.

History 1832, the firm Bailey & Kitchen Co. was established by Joseph Trowbridge Bailey Sr. (1835–1892) and Andrew B. Kitchen in Philadelphia, Pa. When Kitchen retired in 1846, J.T. Bailey Sr. was joined by Jeremiah Robbins, James Gallagher, and Bailey's brother Eli Wescott Bailey to reorganize as Bailey & Co. 1878, Joseph T. Bailey, George W. Banks (of J.E. Caldwell & Co.), and Samuel Biddle (of Robbins, Clark & Biddle) formed the partnership Bailey Banks & Biddle. 1903, the firm was commissioned to replicate the die of the Great Seal of the US (eagle on one side and pyramid-and-eye on the other), engraved in hardened steel by Max Zeitier but not until 1986 was the Bailey Banks & Biddle design declared the official and final version; 1927, produced Distinguished Flying Cross medal, awarded to Charles Lindbergh; 1932, produced first of 40,000 Purple Heart medals awarded to World War I soldiers wounded in action; 1961, was amalgamated into the Zale Corporation. The firm remains active in Philadelphia.

Bibliography Charlotte Gere, *American and European Jewelry 1830–1914*, New York: Crown, 1975: 149. Dorothy T. Rainwater, *Encyclopedia of American Silver Manufacturers*, New York: Crown, 1979.

Baillie Scott, Mackay Hugh (1865–1945)

British architect and interior designer; born Ramsgate.

Training School of Art, Douglas, Isle of Man.
Biography At the Isle of Man school, one of his teachers was Archibald Knox, with whom he designed stained glass and ironwork. On a visit to London, Baillie Scott decided to become an architect; 1886–89, was apprenticed to Bath city architect Charles E. Davis; c. 1886, returned to settled on the Isle of Man. Following Arts and Crafts ideals, most of his houses used traditional materials and forms. Showing some Art Nouveau motifs, his work was influenced by Ernest George and C.F.A. Voysey. Baillie Scott became known in Germany and Austria following his designs for the 1898 palace and furniture at Darmstadt for Grand Duke Louis IV of Hesse-Darmstadt; the furniture was made by C.R. Ashbee's Guild of Handicrafts. Because exponents of the European avant-garde idolized the English gentlemen and their art, interest in Baillie Scott's picturesque ruralist style in flexibly planned interiors spread throughout Germany. His drawings for the competition 'Haus eines Kunstfreundes' (house of an art lover), sponsored by magazine *Innen-Dekoration*, spread Baillie Scott's fame further; the series editor was the influential Hermann Muthesius, the anglophile who encouraged German taste for the Arts and Crafts style. Favorable publicity followed in *Kunst und Kunsthandwerk* (1901 and onward), in *Deutsche Kunst und Dekoration* (1903 and onward), and in *House Beautiful* (1904) in America. His practice extended to Switzerland, Poland, Russia, Italy, Poland, and the US. His reputation reached Romania, where he did work for Queen Marie for her forest eyrie Le Nid. 1903, he moved to Bedford (England) and built a pair of cottages at the 1905 Letchworth exhibition; 1914, planned a garden city for Kharkov (Ukraine). *The Studio Yearbook of Decorative Art*, before its switch to modern design in 1929, favored Baillie Scott's work. Strongly opposed to the modern, he was greatly assisted by A. Edgar Beresford, his partner 1905–14 and resumed 1919; moved his practice from Bedford to London in c. 1914, continuing to build small country houses. The practice flourished; 1935, Baillie Scott turned to painting; 1939, retired; died in Brighton.
Exhibitions Work shown with Mackintosh, 1902 exhibition of British decorative art, Hungary.
Bibliography Emil Hochdanz, *Baillie Scott, London: Haus eines Kunstfreundes*, Darmstadt: Alex. Koch, c. 1902. M.H. Baillie Scott, *Houses and Gardens*, London: George Newnes, 1906 (London: Architecture Illustrated, 1933; Woodbridge, Suffolk: Antique Collectors' Club, 1995). M.H. Baillie Scott, Raymond Unwin et al., *Town Planning and Modern Architecture in the Hampstead Garden Suburb*, London: T.F. Unwin, 1909. M.H. Baillie Scott et al., *Garden Suburbs, Town Planning and Modern Architecture*, London, T.F. Unwin, 1910. James D. Kornwulf, *M.H. Baillie Scott and the Arts and Crafts Movement: Pioneers of Modern Design*, Baltimore: Johns Hopkins University, 1972. Katharina Medici Mall, *Das Landhaus Waldbühl von M.H. Baillie Scott: Ein Gesamtkunstwerk zwischen Neugotik und Jugendstil*, Bern, 1979. Diane Haigh, *Baillie Scott: The Artistic House*, London: Lanham, 1995. Gregory John Slater, *Mackay Hugh Baillie Scott: An Architectural History*, Amulree, 1995. Diane Haigh, *Baillie Scott: The Artistic House*, London: Academy, 1995.

Bakelite.
> See Baekeland, Leo Henrik.

Bakker, Gijs (1942–)

Dutch sculptor and jewelry, furniture, lighting designer; born Amersfoort.

Training 1958–62, gold- and silversmithing, Instituut voor Kunstnijverheidsonderwijs, Amsterdam; 1962–63, Konstfackskolan, Stockholm.
Biography 1963–66, Bakker worked as a designer at Van Kempen en Begeer in Zeist; 1966 with wife Emmy van Leersum, set up a studio in Utrecht and became a leader in contemporary jewelry design and designed other products for Polaroid and Rosenthal. From mid-1960s, they produced collars and bracelets in aluminum in their Atelier voor Sieraden, Utrecht; 1970s, extended their craft into art, performance, and sculpture. 1971–78, Bakker taught, Academie voor Beeldende Kunsten, Arnhem; from 1979, became a freelance designer for firms such as Bussum, Artifort, and Van Kempen en Begeer; from 1972, has designed furniture, including 1974 Strip chair, 1979 Finger chair, 1986 plywood-framed chair, and a number of product designs, including 1973 Paraplu (umbrella) table lamp by Artimeta of Haarlem. Mid-1980s, Bakker's massive jewelry pieces were composed of color photographs encased in plexiglas. 1985–87, he taught industrial design, Technische Hogeschool, Delft; from 1987, has taught, Akademie voor Industriële Vormgeving, Eindhoven; became a partner, design studio BRS/Premsela/Vonk, Amsterdam; 1993 with Renny Ramakers, founded Droog Design and DMD (Droog's production entity); 1996 with Marijke Vallanzasca, established the 'Chi ha paura...?' foundation. Recent Bakker clients have included Flos, Levi's, Mandarina Duck, and Salviati.
Exhibitions/citations 1965, first jewelry exhibition organized by Riekje Swart. Work included in 1996 *Contemporary Design from the Netherlands*, The Museum of Modern Art, New York; and subject of 1974 exhibition, Kunsthistorisch Instituut, Groningen. Received 1965 (2nd) Van den Rijn-prijs voor Beeldhouwers; 1968 Gouden en Zilveren Medaille Jablonec; 1983 architecture prize, foundation De Fantasie, Almere; 1988 Françoise van den Bosch prize (jewelry design); 1995 Prins Bernhard Fonds Prijs voor Toegepaste Kunsten en Bouwkunst; 1996 Ra award.
Bibliography Cat., Gert Staal, *Gijs Bakker, vormgever: Solo voor een solist*, 's-Gravenhage: SDU, 1989. Ida van Zijl, *Droog Design, 1991 – 1996*, Utrecht: Centraal Museum, 1997. Renny Ramkers and Gijs Bakker (eds.), *Droog Design: Spirit of the Nineties*, Rotterdam: 010 Publishers, 1998. Ida van Zijl, *Gijs Bakker, Objects to Use*, Rotterdam: 010, 2000.
> See Droog Design.

Bakst, Léon (aka Léon Rozenberg; b. Lev Samuïlovitch Bakst 1866–1924)

Russian theater designer and illustrator; born Grodno, Belarusse; active Russia, France, and the US.

Training Under Chistyakov and Venig, Academy of Art, St. Petersburg; in Jean-Léon Gérome's studio and at Académie Julian, both Paris; 1893–99, under A. Edelfelt, Paris.
Biography 1890s, Bakst traveled in France, Germany, Belgium, Spain, and Italy; 1891–97, was a regular participant in exhibitions of Association of Russian Artists; illustrated several books; from 1910s, designed for the theater and was a graphic designer and illustrator of works published in journals; painted portraits of Alexandre Benois (1898) and V.V. Rozanov (1901). Other work included portraits and decorative designs for the Symbolist journal *Zolotoe runo* (the golden fleece) and a portrait of Serge Diaghilev. 1899, Bakst was one of the main organizers and founders of V Mir Iskusstva (the world of art) group and its journal; 1906–09, taught at Y. Zvantseva's School for Painting and Drawing, St. Petersburg; from 1909 in Paris, introduced vibrant colors and oriental patterns into his sets and costumes for Diaghilev's Les Ballets Russes, including for *Carnaval* (1910, music by Schumann), *Schéhérazade* (1910, by Rimski-Korsakov), *L'oiseau de feu* (1910, by

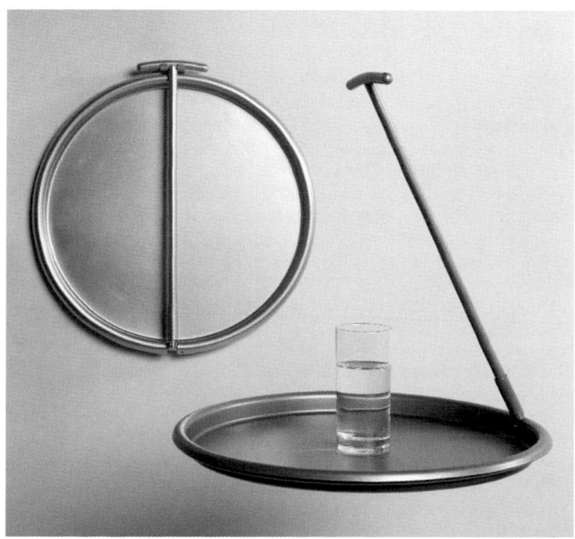

Gijs Bakker. Balance tray. c. 2000. Steel; h. 1 1/8 x dia. 16 1/8" (3 x 41 cm). Mfr.: Meccano, the Netherlands.

Stravinskii), *Spectre de la rose* (1911, by Weber), *Narcisse* (1911, by N. Tcherepnine), and *Prélude à l'après-midi d'un faune* (1894, by Debussy, performed by Les Ballets Russes 1911); from 1914, was one of the leading stage, costume, and set designers not only for Diaghilev's Les Ballets Russes but also for the Paris Opéra, Ida Rubinstein's company, and others; was instrumental in transforming French and other Western concepts of interior design, particularly encouraging the use of bright color schemes. Living for a time in the US, designed stage sets and stenciled mosaic-like patterns based on Russian folk art for the transformation of the gymnasium into a private theater at John and Alice Garrett's 'Evergreen' residence in Baltimore, Md.; late 1980s, the theater was restored. Some of his printed patterns on silk for a New York firm were based on Zuñi and Hopi designs. He died in Paris.
Exhibitions Work subject of venues in Jerusalem 1992 and Stockholm 1993 (catalogs below).
Bibliography Cat., Victor Beyer, *Les Ballets Russes de S. de Diaghilev*, Strasbourg, 1969. Hélène A. Borisova and Gregory Sterine, *Art nouveau russe*, Paris: Regard, 1987. Cat., *Kunst und Revolution: Russische und Sowjetische Kunst 1910–1932*, Vienna: Österreichisches Museum für angewandte Kunst, 1988. Cat. Eva Sznajderman, *On Stage: The Art of Léon Bakst, Theatre Design and Other Work*, Jerusalem: Israel Museum, 1992. Cat., *Leon Bakst: sensualismens triumf*, Stockholm: Dansmuseet, 1993. Charles Spencer, *Leon Bakst and the Ballets Russes*, London : Academy, rev. ed. 1995.

Balderacchi, Paola (1944–)
Italian designer; born Milan.

Training 1965–69, history of modern art, Università degli Studi, Milan.
Biography From 1967, Balderacchi has designed wooden furniture in small serial production for Tupa, including 1989 Aalto, 1990 Gravità, 1992 Spina Quadra, and 1996 Camera d'Aria beds, and 1996 Bambooring bookshelves.
Exhibitions Work included in 1992 *Art of Living—Discovery of Italy*, New York; 1994 *Ecodesign Europe*, Bruxelles; 1996 *RI-USI*, Triennale di Milano; 1999 *Pluriexistenzen*, Dusseldorf.
Biobliography Mel Byars, *50 Beds...*, Hove: RotoVision, 2000.

Baldessari, Luciano (1896–1982)
Italian designer; born Rovereto (then Hapsburg Empire).

Training To 1922, Politecnico, Milan.
Biography As a young man, Baldessari participated with Futurist artist Fortunato Depero; 1920s, at the beginning of his career, designed stage sets and was a painter. His widely published 1929 Luminator Torchère lamp was one of the few Rationalist designs for furniture or lighting put into production in Italy. The lamp that presaged later 'light sculptures' was inspired by German experimental work and intended to be an abstraction of an 'illuminated mannequin' with the curved tubular steel representing arms. Baldessari, as an architect, was one of the least predictable exponents of Italian Rationalism. His architecture included 1929–32 De Angeli Frua Press building (with Luigi Figini and Gino Pollini), Milan; 1930 Craja bar, Piazza P. Ferrari, Milan; 1932–33 Cima chocolate factory (with Gio Ponti), Milan; Vesta pavilion, 1933 (5th) Triennale di Milano; 1951, 1952, 1953, 1954 International Trade Fair installations.
Exhibitions 1929 Luminator Torchère was designed for the Barnocchi stand at 1929–30 *Exposición Internacional de Barcelona*, Spain. Work subject of 1985 exhibition, Trento and Milan (catalog below).
Bibliography Guilia Veronesi, *Luciano Baldessari Architetto*, Trento: Collana di Artisti Trentini, 1957. Cat., *Luciano Baldessari*, Trento: Museo Provincale d'Arte, 1985. *Baldessari: progetti e scenografie*, Milan: Electa, 1982. Penny Sparke, *Design in Italy, 1870 to the Present*, New York: Abbeville, 1988. Richard A. Etlin, *Modernism in Italian Architecture, 1890–1940*, Cambridge, Mass.: MIT, 1991.

Baldwin, Benjamin James (1913–1993)
American interior decorator; born Baltimore; active New York.

Training 1931–35, architecture, Princeton University; 1935–36 under Hans Hofmann, painting, New York and Provincetown, Mass.; 1936–38, architecture, Princeton University; 1938–39 under Eliel Saarinen, Cranbrook Academy of Art, Bloomfield Hills, Mich.
Biography 1939–40, Baldwin worked with Eliel and Eero Saarinen; 1941–45, was partner of Harry Weese in Kenilworth, Ill.; 1945–46, worked at architecture firm Skidmore, Owings and Merrill, Chicago, where he was in charge of the interior design of 1947 Terrace Plaza Hotel, Cincinnati, among others; 1947, set up his own interior-design studio, designing residences in Chicago, New York, and Sarasota, Fla.; c. 1948–56, was partner of William Machado. He practiced in Montgomery, Ala., 1948–55; in Chicago 1956–63; in New York 1963–73. His work was simple and minimal. He worked with architects Edward Larrabee Barnes, I.M. Pei, and Louis Kahn on the interiors of their buildings; from 1973, practiced in East Hampton, N.Y., and Sarasota, Fla.
Exhibitions/citations Awards (with Harry Weese), 1940 *Organic Design in Home Furnishings* competition/exhibition, The Museum of Modern Art, New York. 1985, elected charter member, Hall of Fame, *Interior Design* magazine.
Bibliography Robert Judson Clark et al., *The Cranbrook Vision*, New York: Abrams/The Metropolitan Museum of Art, 1983. *Benjamin Baldwin: Autobiography in Design*, New York: Norton, 1995.

Baldwin, Billy (1903–1984)
American interior decorator; born Baltimore; active New York.

Training Princeton University, N.J..
Biography Baldwin was already an interior decorator in Baltimore when Ruby Ross Wood invited him to join her decorating practice in New York in 1935. Accepted into the ranks of the city's powerful design figures, Baldwin's associates included Elsie de Wolfe. He lived in one of the townhouses on Sutton Place whose façades interior decorator Dorothy Draper had painted black. 1950, when Wood died, Baldwin became a partner of Edward Martin, designing residential interiors. His work depended heavily on the use of English and French antiques, detailing, and a highly tasteful style. He became known for glossy brown walls and fabrics in cotton. The décor of the apartment of songwriter Cole Porter with its tubular-brass bookcases was widely published. Having set up his own business, his clients in the world of New York high society commissioned him to design their city apartments, country houses, and summer retreats. His work, combining antiques with modern elements, was highly regarded by the American interior-design press of the time.
Bibliography *Billy Baldwin Decorates*, New York: Holt, Rinehart and Winston, 1972. *Billy Baldwin Remembers*, New York: Harcourt Brace Jovanovich, 1974. Billy Baldwin with Michael Gardine, *Billy Baldwin, An Autobiography*, Boston: Little, Brown, 1985. Stephen Calloway, *Twentieth-Century Decoration*, New York: Rizzoli, 1988. John Esten and Rose Bennett Gilbert, *Manhattan Style*, Boston: Little, Brown,

Benjamin James Baldwin. Primitive Forms printed fabric. 1950. Linen, 53 x 34 1/4" (134.6 x 87 cm). Mfr.: Design Unit New York, US. Given anonymously. MoMA.

1990. Mark Hampton, *Legendary Decorators of the Twentieth Century*, New York: Doubleday, 1992.

Baleri, Enrico (1942–)
Italian designer and entrepreneur; born Albino.

Training Architecture, Politecnico, Milan, not graduating.
Biography Baleri was a founder of design companies Pluri in 1968 and Alias in 1979; was artistic director at Alias to 1983, when he set up Baleri Italia, producing the works of Philippe Starck, Alessandro Mendini, Hans Hollein, and others, including himself; designed 1979 Coloforte table system by Knoll and 1983 Pauline mirror by Baleri Italia; 1986, founded Studio Baleri & Associati.
Bibliography Albrecht Bangert and Karl Michael Armer, *80s Style: Designs of the Decade*, New York: Abbeville, 1990: 227. *Modo*, no. 148, Mar.–Apr. 1993: 116.

Ball, Douglas (1935–)
Canadian industrial designer; born Peterborough, Ontario.

Training To 1958, industrial design, Ontario College of Art, Toronto.
Biography After a short time in Europe, Ball worked at Sunshine Office Equipment (division of Massey-Ferguson Industries), Waterloo, Ontario, from 1964, was associated with the firm for almost three decades; by late 1960s, developed open-office systems for the firm (which became Sunar Industries); subsequently, set up his own industrial-design studio in Montréal; from 1979, was director of design at Sunar (having been sold to Hauserman in 1978 and, later, segments of the firm to others, including Haworth). His design work for Sunar has been extensive and has included office-furniture/seating systems, 1969 S System steel desk, and 1978 Race open-office system. Considered to be Canada's most significant, successful industrial designer, his other designs include 1991 folding-table range and 2001 Lucy chair by Vecta, 2000 Fly Away seating by Arconas, and transportation aids for the physically disadvantaged.
Citations 1993, fellow, Canadian Industrial Design; two gold awards (for chairs by Arconas and Vecta), 2000 NeoCon, Chicago.
Bibliography Cat., *Seduced and Abandoned: Modern Furniture Designers in Canada, the First Fifty Years*, Toronto: The Art Gallery at Harbourfront, 1986: 23. Rachel Gotlieb and Cora Golden, *Design in Canada Since 1945: Fifty Years from Teakettles to Task Chairs*, Toronto: Knopf Canada, 2001.

Balla, Giacomo (1871–1958)
Italian artist and designer; born Turin.

Training 1891 briefly, Accademia Albertina di Belle Arti, and Liceo Artistico; c. 1892, Università degli Studi; all Turin.
Biography 1895, Balla moved to Rome and was active for several years as an illustrator, caricaturist, and portrait painter. His first painting was *Lampada—Studio di luce* (street light—study of light [aka *Arc Lamp]*, dated 1909 but painted 1910–11, in the collection of The Museum of Modern Art, New York, and inspired by Filippo Tomasso Marinetti's *Uccidiamo it chiaro di luna!* [let us kill the moonlight!, 1909]). Balla taught painting to Gino Severini and Umberto Boccioni; 1910, became a Futurist, signing the *Manifesto of Futurist Painters* and the *Technical Manifesto of Futurist Painting*, by which time he was already well known. He was influenced by the pointillism of Giuseppe Pellizza da Volpedo and Giovanni Segantini, the initimism of Eugène Carrière, and the French Impressionists and Post-Impressionists; 1912, traveled to Düsseldorf, where designed the Löwenstein house (later destroyed); 1913 or 1914, returned to complete its furnishings and decoration, using the motif of bichromal, iridescent 'compenetrations.' In a dramatic 1913 gesture, he placed all of his paintings up for auction, declaring, 'Balla is dead. Here the works of the late Balla are on sale.' He designed Futurist clothing, arguing in his *Futurist Manifesto on Menswear* (1914) for practical clothing that would be 'dynamic,' 'strong-willed,' and 'violent'; fought for a complete break with the past, expressed in his manifesto on interior decoration in his c. 1918 Futurist House in Rome, where his colorful painted and cut-out furniture was installed; designed the interior of Futurist-style 1921 Bal Tik-Tak dance-hall; and many pieces of furniture, ceramics, and lighting in a highly developed abstract mode, and 1917 sets for Les Ballets Russes' *Fireworks* ballet (music by Stravinskii); end of 1930s, broke from Futurism. He died in Rome.
Exhibitions Showed six large painted wall hangings (with Fortunato Depero and Enrico Prampolini) at 1925 *Exposition Internationale des Arts Décoratifs et Industriels Modernes*, Paris.

Enrico Baleri. Lunella stool. 1999. Polyurethane, 9 7/8 x dia. 22 7/8" (25 x 58 cm). Mfr.: Baleri Italia, Italy.

Bibliography Maurizio Fagiolo Dell'Arco, *Balla, the Futurist*, New York: Rizzoli, 1988. Pontus Hulten (organizer), *Futurism and Futurisms*, Milan: Fabbri, 1986. Enrico Crispolti, *Il futurismo e la moda: Balla e gli altri*, Venice: Marsilio, 986. Fabio Benzi, *Balla*, Florence: Giunti, 2000.

Ballets Russes
> See Diaghilev, Sergei Pavlovich.

Ballin, Mogens (1871–1914)
Danish painter and metalworker; active Copenhagen.

Biography Ballin's workshop made copper and pewter as well as silver objects. 1900s–10s in the workshop, Ballin produced his own silver designs and those of assistants Gudmund Hentze and Peter Hertz. Ballin-made hollow-ware often bore the initials or signature of the designer. Georg Jensen worked for Ballin before setting up his own silversmithy, and Ballin's and Thorwald Bindesbøll's influences appeared in Jensen's work. After 1901, Jensen produced his first jewelry designs for the Ballin firm. Ballin allowed Jensen to exhibit under his own name. After Ballin's death, Hertz took over the management of the workshop.
Bibliography Annelies Krekel-Aalberse, *Art Nouveau and Art Déco Silver*, New York: Abrams, 1989.

ballpoint pen
> See BIC; Marcel Bich.

Balsamo Stella, Guido (1882–1941)
Glass designer; born Torino.

Biography c. 1918, Balsamo Stella was a freelance designer of glass for Artisti Barovier; by 1923, was operating his own glass-engraving workshop in the Giudecca quarter of Venice. 1925, the firm merged with Studio Ars et Labor Industrie Riunite (S.A.L.I.R.), a mirror-engraving and painting firm that used other firms' blanks and at which, to 1929, Stella was the artistic director. 1929–33, he was head of the Accademia di Bella Arti, Villa Reale, Monza; from 1933, taught in Venice; died in Asolo, Italy.
Exhibitions 1924, 1928, 1930 Biennale di Venezia and others.

Balzer, Gerd (1909–1986)
German typographer, architect, and designer; born Rostock.

Training 1929–33, Bauhaus, Dessau.
Biography Balzer produced the 1929 precursor of the adjustable architect's lamp designed by Czech designer Josef Pohl. A similar lamp was produced by Körting und Mathieson as part of its Kandem range. 1932, Balzer and Pohl were assigned the chore of organizing

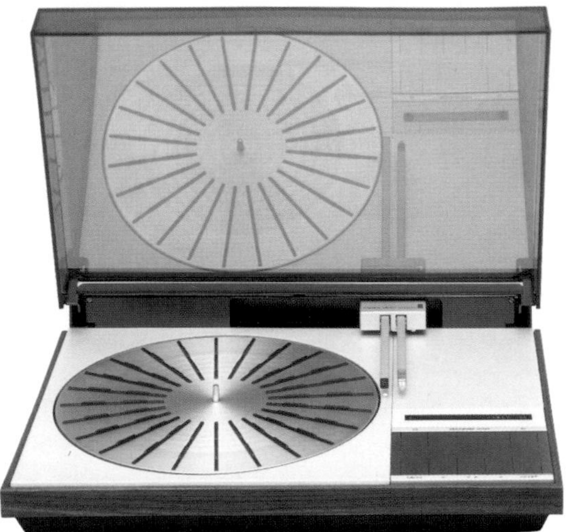

Bang & Olufsen: Jacob Jensen. Beogram 4000 record player. 1972. Rosewood, aluminum, stainless steel, and plastic, 3 3/4 x 14 1/2 x 19" (9.5 x 36.8 x 48.2 cm). Mfr.: Bang & Olufsen, Denmark. Gift of the mfr. MoMA.

Bauhaus students' work, which resulted in a conference and a furniture-design competition. After the Bauhaus, he worked in the offices of several architects and, from 1933, for an architect in Rostock and, after World War II, one in Hanover.
Bibliography Lionel Richard, *Encyclopédie du Bauhaus*, Paris: Somogy, 1985: 179. Cat., *The Bauhaus: Masters and Students*, New York: Barry Friedman, 1988. Cat., *Die Metallwerkstatt am Bauhaus*, Berlin: Bauhaus-Archiv, 1992: 132, 122, 314, 315.

Ban, Shigeru (1957–)
Japanese architect and designer; born Tokyo.

Training 1977–80, Southern California Institute of Architecture, Los Angeles; 1980–82, School of Architecture, The Cooper Union for the Advancement of Science and Art, New York (with a sabbatical working for Isozaki), graduating 1984.
Biography 1982–83, Ban worked in the office of Arata Isozaki, New York; after 1984 graduation from the Cooper Union, returned to Japan to design a house for his mother (now his office and mother's studio); 1985, founded his own firm in Tokyo; from 1996, taught architecture, Nihon University, Tokyo; became known for his imaginative use of paper in architecture and furniture. In his words, his paper-tube furniture/furnishings 'can be recycled to make more tubes.... I am interested in weak materials.' His use of paper tubes in architecture questioned permanent vs. temporary shelter. 1994, he installed pillars and chairs made of cardboard (calling it 'used wood') in Issey Miyake gallery, Tokyo, and other structures. In the aftermath of the 1995 earthquake in Kobe, Japan, Ban used donated 34-ply paper tubes to build a community hall and houses for refugees. Architecture has included 1990 Odawara pavilion, Kanagawa; 1992 housing at Shakujii-Park, Nerima, Tokyo; 1995 Paper House, Lake Yamanaka; 1995, Paper Church; 'Standard Type 1' ephemeral structures, such as United Nations High Commissioner for Refugees (UNHCR) Paper Refugee Shelter, incorporating plastic sheets and paper tubing; 1997, Wall-less House; apartments in Honegi Forest; Square Grids House—Steel Furniture Structure, Kanagawa; 2000 paper-tube structure on Canal de Bourgogne, Pouilly-en-Auxois, France; specializes in ecologically friendly buildings; from 1995, was a consultant to UNHCR; 1995, established Voluntary Architects' Network (VAN).
Exhibitions/citations Numerous Ban-designed installations include 1985, 1989, 1993 *Emilio Ambasz* exhibitions; 1986 *Alvar Aalto* show, Axis Gallery, Tokyo; 1994 *GA Japan League*, GA Gallery, Tokyo; 1994 *Architecture of the Year*, Metropolitan Hall, Tokyo. Work subject of 1999 *Works in Progess*, Gallery Ma, Tokyo. Designed (with Frei Otto) recyclable Japanese pavilion, *Expo 2000*, Hanover. Received 1995 Minichi design prize; 1996 Yoshioka prize, Shinkenchiku Jutaku Tokusyu; 1996 Kansai Architects prize, Japanese Institute of Architects (JIA); 1997 Best Young Architect of the Year, JIA.

Bandobranski, Niklas (1977–)
Swedish industrial designer; born Stockholm.

Training 1997–98, interior design, Accademia Italiana, Florence; 1998–2000, industrial design, Istituto Europeo di Design, Milan.
Biography 2001, Bandobranski worked on a cordless-phone design in the studio of George Sowden in Milan; 2001, returned to Sweden and set up his own industrial-design firm, Branski; designed/produced 2001 Finger Tip Table sold by Klara store, Stockholm.
Exhibitions 2002 SaloneSatellite, Salone del Mobile, Milan.

Banfi, Gianluigi (1910–1945)
> See BBPR.

Bang, Arne (1901–1983)
Danish potter; brother of Jacob E. Bang.

Training In schools and an apprenticeship, Copenhagen.
Biography 1926–30, Bang was active in a pottery studio with Carl Halier; from 1932, threw pots independently and also contributed to Ipsen Ceramics in 1930s; married elements of the Bauhaus with neo-classical concepts in rich, textured glazes influential on Scandinavians of 1960s–70s.
Exhibitions Work shown at 1929–30 *Exposición Internacional de Barcelona*, Spain; 1937 Paris. Subject of 1932 exhibition, Den Permanente, Copenhagen. Regularly awarded prizes in Scandinavia and Europe.

Bang, Jacob E. (1899–1965)
Danish sculptor, architect, and industrial designer; brother of Arne Bang.

Training 1916–21, sculpture, Det Kongelige Danske Kunstakademi, Copenhagen.
Biography 1925–42, Bang worked at Holmegård Glasværk, where he was the artistic director, pursuing modern forms, from 1928 (replaced by Per Lütken in 1942); 1942–57, worked in own studio

Beata Bär, Gerhard Bär, and Hartmut Knell. Zeitdokumente chair. 1996. Recycled plastics and printed paper, 29 3/4 x 16 3/4 x 17 1/2" (75.5 x 42.5 x 44.5 cm). Mfr.: Bär + Knell, Germany. Courtesy Quittenbaum Kunstauktionen, Munich.

with clients, including Nymølle faïence factory, Pan Aluminium, and F. Hingelberg Sølvsmedie; from 1957, was artistic director, Kastrup Glasværk, which merged with Holmegård in 1965.
Exhibitions Work included in editions of Triennale di Milano; 1954–57 *Design in Scandinavia*, touring the US; 1956–59 *Neue Form aus Dänemark*, Germany; 1958 *Formes Scandinaves*, Musée des Arts Décoratifs, Paris; 1960–61 *The Arts of Denmark*, touring the US.
Bibliography Jacob E. Bang, 'Lidt om Glasset i Hjemmet,' in Sigvard Bernadotte and Johannes Lehm-Laursen (eds.), *Moderne dansk boligkunst*, vol. 1, Odense: Skandinavisk Bogforlag, 1946: 255–60. Erik Lassen and Mogens Schlüter, *Dansk Glas: 1925–1975*, Copenhagen: Nyt Nordisk, 1975: 21–31, 37–40. Cat., David Revere McFadden (ed.), *Scandinavian Modern Design 1880–1980*, New York: Abrams, 1982. Cat., Kathryn B. Hiesinger and George H. Marcus III (eds.), *Design Since 1945*, Philadelphia: Philadelphia Museum of Art, 1983.

Bang Design

Australian design studio.

History 1989, college classmates Bryan Marshall and David Granger formed the Bang Design Pty Ltd. partnership and established a studio/workshop in Balmain, Australia (where two additional members are on staff). Their furniture by Anibou includes Jump, Piggly Wiggly, Quick, and Quick & Arms upholstered lounge seating, and Radius shelving. For 2000 Sydney Summer Olympiad, Bang designed the lane and distance markers for events, such as the javelin, and carved-wood message sticks given to Olympic delegates. Projects have included Bar Ristretto café (interior), Central Synagogue (pew seating), Source Four Ninety design center, and Watermark Restaurant (interior).
Citations 2001 Design Mark (for Talon chair); furniture category (for Plus seating), 2001 Australian Design award.
Bibliography www.users.bigpond.com/bang_design.

Bang & Olufsen

Danish domestic electronic equipment manufacturer; located Stuer, Jutland.

History 1925, engineers Peter Boas Bang (1900–1957) and Svend Andreas Grøn Olufsen (1897–1949) set up a workshop in the attic in the house on the Olufsen family estate; began with a modest production of radios; 1928, built a small factory in Stuer, Jutland, that could be converted into a school if the manufacturing business failed; 1929, were producing technologically innovative equipment, including a radio with push-button tuning and the first mass-produced 5-valve radio; 1930, produced their first radio-gramophone; were from the beginning concerned with sophisticated technology aligned with visual elegance. Previously housed in historicist cabinet work, the new 1935 Huperbo 5 RG Steel was the firm's first truly modern-design radio cabinet, based on the 1927–28 B3 tubular-steel chair by Marcel Breuer and possibly encouraged by the negative criticism of B&O's cabinetry by Danish designer Ole Wanscher; early 1960s when transistors replaced valves, offered an elegant and novel slim radio. Architect Henning Moldenhawer's cabinet design of 1964 Beomaster 900 transitorized radio, which broke with B&O's traditional face designs, was a success throughout Europe and set a standard for B&O. The innovative 1965 pick-up arm by E. Rorbæk Madsen was incorporated into the Beogram 3000 turntable. Acton Bjørn designed 1966 Beolit 500 radio with its natural wood face and single row of black control buttons. Jacob Jensen designed 1969 Beogram 1200 component hi-fi group, 1972 Beogram 4000 (the first electronic turntable with two separate arms), 1979 Beocenter 7002 unit, 1980 Beogram 8000 phonograph, MX5000 television, and VX5000 videocassette recorder. Late 1970s, a complete overhaul of the firm's low-watt products was made when the Japanese became competitors. The originality of B&O lies in its close collaboration with its designers and in its focus on good design, both aligned from the first stages of product development with marketing and manufacturing. B&O's designers have also included Ib Fabiansen, Lone Lindinger-Loewy, Gideon Loewy, Eric Madsen, David Lewis, and Steve McGugan.
Exhibitions/citations Work subject of 1978 Bang & Olufsen exhibition (39 pieces), The Museum of Modern Art, New York, and 1979 exhibitions at Israel Museum, Jerusalem; Musée des Arts Décoratifs, Paris, 1990; 2000 *Vision & Legend*, Dansk Design Center, Copenhagen. Grand prize, 1937 *Exposition Internationale des Arts et Techniques dans la Vie Moderne,* Paris; 1962–98 Industrie Forum Design (iF); 1965–94 Dansk ID Prize; 1974, 1975, 1977 SIM; 1984–98 Danish IG graphic-design award; 1978 award, Industrial Designers Society of America (IDSA); 1985 Osaka design award; 1985–98 G-Mark Good Design award, Japanese Industrial Design Promotion Organization (JIDPO).
Bibliography Cat., Chantal Bizot, *Bang & Olufsen, design et technologie*, Paris: Musée des Arts Décoratifs, 1990. Jens Bang, *Bang & Olufsen: Fra vision til legende = From Vision to Legend*, Denmark: Vidsyn, 2000.

Bani, Marina (1962–)

Italian architect and consultant; born Vedano al Lambro, Milan.

Training To 1988, architecture, Università degli Studi, Milan.
Biography 1975–90, Bani worked at the Zanotta furniture company on new-product development; subsequently, was a consultant on research and engineering to some of the main Italian furniture/furnishings firms; from 1994 as an architect, has been a partner of Marco Penati and Patrizia Scarzella in studio Sigla, Milan.
> See Scarzella, Patrizia.

Bär + Knell; Beata Bär (1962–); Gerhard Bär (1959–); Harmut Knell (1966–)

German design partnership.

Training The Bärs: interior architecture. Knell: carpentry; subsequently, Fachakademie für Gestaltung, Regensburg.
Biography Because the three young designers were offended by public garbage but interested in the colorful material collected by Dual System from German households and firms that was only occasionally being reprocessed as dull-brown drain pipes, flowerpots, and park benches that simulated wood, they set out in 1992 to use the refuse more creatively and colorfully as 'mass-produced one-offs,' essentially an oxymoron. Drawing on influences from Nouveau Realisme and Pop Art, Bär + Knell, as the studio-partnership has become known, has designed and made furniture from posters, for example, by adding epoxy and retaining the lithographic messages and vivid images. In addition to furniture, work included ComeBack lamps and Multicolor ring binders.
Exhibitions/citations Work included in 1995 *Plastics 2000: Visions in Recycled Plastic* touring exhibition, sponsored by Deutsche Gesellschaft für Kunststoff-Recycling, Cologne; frequent installations at Salone del Mobile, Milan; 2000 *World's Fair*, Hanover; *Design World 2000*, Konstindustrimuseet, Helsinki; 2000 *Made in Germany*, Kunsthaus Rhenania, Cologne; others. Received 1986 Franz Vogt prize (for studio/partnership work).
Bibliography Cat., *Design—Made in Germany*, Cologne: Kunsthaus Rhenania Köln, 2000: 199, no. 108. Auction cat., *Modernes Design Kunsthandwerk nach 1945*, Munich: Quittenbaum, 4 Dec. 2001.

Barbaglia, Mario (1950–)

Italian architect and designer; born Milan.

Training Architecture, Milan.
Biography 1975 with Marco Colombo (Milan 1952–), Barbaglia began as an architect with activities in domestic and industrial design; from 1984, specialized in industrial design, beginning with commissions from Studio PAF, including 1984–85 Dove table lamp (with Colombo), now by Nemo Italianaluce. Barbaglia also designed lamps by Italianaluce (before its acquisition by Nemo, as well as more recent Arcturus sconce by Nemo) and fixtures by Antonangeli, such as 2000 Gondola table lamp.
Bibliography Cat., Hans Wichmann (ed.), *Italien Design 1945 bis heute*, Munich: Die Neue Sammlung, 1988. Giuliana Gramigna and Paola Biondi, *Il design in Italia dell'arredamento domestico*, Turin: Allemandi, 1999.

Barbe, Pierre (1900–)

French architect and designer; born Paris.

Training 1919–28, École des Beaux-Arts, Paris.
Biography 1929, Barbe became a founding member, Union des Artistes Modernes (UAM), secretary 1932–33, and participant in its group exhibitions to 1935; with Le Corbusier, was a UAM delegate to 1929 (2nd) Frankfurt and 1930 (3rd) Brussels meetings of Congrès Internationaux d'Architecture Moderne (CIAM). To 1933, Barbe was a member, Comité International pour la Résolution des Problèmes de l'Architecture Contemporaine (CIRPAC); to 1937, of the French section of CIAM. He designed numerous pieces of furniture in simple,

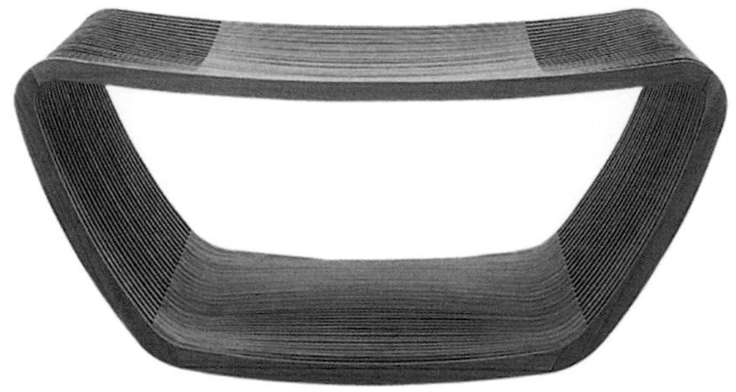

Barber Osgerby Associates (Edward Barber and Jay Osgerby). Hula stool/table. 2000. Teak heartwood, h. 13 3/8 x w. 15 3/4 x d. 29 1/2" (34 x 40 x 75 cm). Mfr.: Cappellini, Italy.

sleek forms, including plate-glass tables and bent tubular-steel seating; several post offices; 1926–39 Compagnie du Nord thermoelectric plant; 1929 Mimerel house ('La Pacifique') in Sanary-sur-Mer; 1929 interiors of Madame Dubonnet's domicile, Paris; 1931 furniture for the vicomtesse de Noailles; 1930–34 Lambiotte townhouse in Neuilly.
Exhibitions/citations Work shown at 1928 Salon of Société des Artistes Décorateurs. Silver medal, 1925 *Exposition Internationale des Arts Décoratifs et Industriels Modernes*, Paris; gold medal (for 1930 townhouse, Neuilly), 1936 (6th) Triennale di Milano.
Bibliography Waldemar George, 'Meubles français: les meubles de Pierre Barbe,' *L'amour de l'art*, Feb. 1934. Arlette Barré-Despond, *UAM*, Paris: Regard, 1983. Jean-Baptiste Minnaert, *Pierre Barbe, architecte*, Paris: Université de Paris, 1987. Cat., *Les années UAM 1929–1958*, Paris: Musée des Arts Décoratifs, 1988: 146–47. Jean-Baptiste Minnaert, *Pierre Barbe: architectures*. Liège: Mardaga, 1991.

Barbedienne, Ferdinand (1810–1892)

French bronze manufacturer; son of a farmer; born Saint-Martin-de-Fresnay.

Training 1822, apprenticeship at a paper maker, Paris.
Biography By 1834, Barbedienne was a modest farmer; then made his fortune in the production of wallpaper; 1838, came in contact with mechanic Achille Collas (1795–1859), who invented machinery for making small-scale bronze objects. 1839, Barbedienne and Collas set up a bronze factory (Collas & Barbedienne, 63, rue de Lancry, Paris), eventually employing 300 artists and workers who created a number of statues, at first reduced versions of famous Greek and Roman works, in a small scale that encouraged their decorative use in domestic interiors. Barbedienne worked with sculptors and interior designers to realize an appreciable amount of bronzes; 1865–85, was president, Réunion des Fabricants en Bronze. 1870s, enamelist André-Fernand Thesmar apprenticed in the factory. Some of Barbedienne's most renowned pieces include the casting of Antoine-Louis Barye's animals, 125 models of which he purchase in a 1876 sale. His nephew Gustave Leblanc-Barbedienne succeeded him and added the production of monumental works, many as reproductions of famous historical sculptures, and of trophies for, as examples, gymnastic and shooting clubs and tournaments. He set up agencies to sell in the UK, the US, and Germany; purchased the estates of Auguste Rodin and Emmanuel Fremiet. As La Maison Leblanc-Barbedienne et Cie, it was active from 1892 to 1952 or 1955. Ferdinand is buried in Cimetière Père Lachaise, Chemin Mont-Louis, with a bronze tomb sculpture by Henri Chapu (1833–1991).
Citations Numerous medals (to the factory) at international exhibitions, including 1862 International Exhibition, London; 1886 Jean Goujon Gold Medal (to Barbedienne himself), Société d'Encouragement pour l'Industrie Nationale.
Bibliography G. Vapereau, *Dictionnaire universel des contemporains*, Paris: Hachette, 1858: 101-102. www.groveart.com. www.archivesnationales.culture.gouv.fr.

Barber Osgerby Associates

British designers.

Training Barber and Osgerby: Royal College of Art, London.
Biography Edward Barber (1969–) and Jay Osgerby (1969–), who met at the Royal College of Art, established Barber Osgerby Associates design office, London, in 1996; soon achieved recognition designing for clients, including Asplund, Dornbracht, Gorgeous Productions, Isikon Plus, Levi Strauss, Magis, Offecct, Paul Smith, Razorfish, and Trevor Sorbie International. Were commissioned by Cappellini to design a 1999 furniture collection and, 2001, by Sotheby's to participate in a project for new products for South African communities to make and export. Recent commissions have been the design of Soho Brewery Company (brewery/restaurant), interior of a pharmacy; and the Trevor Sorbie flagship hair salon; all London.
Exhibitions/citations 2002 exhibition of Sotheby's South African project. Best New Designer, 1998 International Contemporary Furniture Fair (ICFF), New York; Best Piece of Furniture design award (for Hula stool), 2000 FX/*Blueprint* magazine, UK; Judges' Prize (for Home table), 2001 *Homes & Gardens* magazine Design Award, UK.
Bibliography Michele De Lucchi (ed.), *The International Design Yearbook*, London: Laurence King, 2001.

Barber, Wendy (1944–)

British painter, ceramicist, and textile designer.

Training In Sussex; 1960–65, Slade School of Fine Art, London.
Biography 1981 with John Hinchcliffe, Barber established a small studio in Charlton Marshall, Dorset, designing and producing their own textiles and ceramics. From 1983, they were active in a formal partnership with Poole Pottery and with Saville Pottery, both Staffordshire; 1991, closed their studio and moved to France; 1996, returned to Dorset, and Barber painted again and designed scarves. Their designs are retailed through Liberty's and other UK stores.
Exhibitions 1983, spongeware and hand-painted wares exhibited at Salisbury Arts Centre; curated 1991 *A Contemporary Tradition*, Russell-Cotes Art Gallery and Museum, Bornemouth. With others, exhibition in Brampton (catalog below).
Bibliography Robert A.M. Stern (ed.), *The International Design Yearbook*, New York: Abbeville, 1985/1986. Cat., *Wendy Barber, Doug Cocker, Barbara Gray*, Brampton, Cumbria: LYC Museum & Art Gallery, 1982.

Barbera, Larry (1950–)

American industrial designer.

Training To 1973, Ohio State University.
Biography From 1973, Barbera worked at design firm Richard-Smith; subsequently, settled in California and became a designer at Hewlett-Packard; from 1987, was a designer at Apple Computer, Cupertino, Cal., where he worked on 1988 Columbo tower-model concept and 1989 Macintosh IIsi (both with Mike Nuttall), and 1990 Macintosh Color Classic (with Daniele Del Iuliis); oversaw 1991 Hook and 1993–94 Bongo projects and 1994–95 printer-and-display-project design by Apple's IDg (Industrial Design Group); after eight years at Apple (longer than any other designer), departed 1995 and joined Design Edge studio in Austin, Tex.
Bibliography Paul Kunkel, *Apple Design: The World of the Apple Industrial Design Group*, New York: Graphis, 1997.

Barbieri, Raul (1946–)

Italian architect and industrial designer; born and active Milan.

Training To 1972, degree in architecture, Politecnico, Milan.
Biography 1970–73, Barbieri worked in the Olivetti design studio, directed by Ettore Sottsass; with Giorgio Marianelli, opened Raul Barbieri e Giorgio Marianelli Architetti studio, Milan, collaborating on architecture and industrial design; from 1989, has been working independently in his own studio in Milan on a number of products, including those by Rexite (tabletop and office wares) and Tronconi (lighting). By Ycami, he designed 1992 *Mago* and 2001 *Dinner Two* folding serving trolleys and 2001 *Kursaal* revolving wall shelving. Other clients have included Cidue, Magis, Mobilvetta, Villa, and Zuchetti; has collaborated with design schools such as ENSCI, Paris, and Istituto Europeo di Design, Milan and, from 1999, with Associazione per il Disegno Industriale (ADI), coordinating the Designer Department.
Exhibitions/citations Project for an area of terraced houses in Milan presented at Compasso d'Oro/ADI architecture and design exhibition, London. Individually and with Marianelli: 1984 Premio SMAU Industrial Design, Salone della Machina e Attrezzature per l'Uffizio, Milan; 1987 and 1989 Forum Design, Milan; 1988 and 1989 Design for Europe, Intérieur '88, Courtrai; 1988 BIO 12 industrial-design biennial (two citations), Ljubljana; 1989, 1992 Design Plus, Ambiente fair, Frankfurt; 1989, 1991 (two citations), 1994 (two citations), and 1999 Premio Compasso d'Oro; 1992 Industrie Forum Design (iF), Hanover; 1992

ADI Tecnhotel (two citations); 1993 Neste Forma Finlandia; 1994, 1995, and 2001 awards, Tendence fair, Frankfurt; 1998 and 2001 Good Design award, Chicago Athenaeum; 2000 Design Index, ADI; 2001 Best of Show (two citations), NeoCon, Chicago.
Bibliography Cristina Morozzi and Silvio San Pietro, *Contemporary Italian Furniture*, Milan: L'Archivolto, 1996. Silvio San Pietro, *Nuovi negozi a Milano*, Milan: L'Archivolto, 1998. Mel Byars, *50 Products...*, Hove: RotoVision, 1998. Giuliana Gramigna and Paola Biondi, *Il design in Italia dell'arredamento domestico*, Turin: Allemandi, 1999. Cat., Paolo Antonelli, *Workspheres: Design and Contemporary Work Styles*, New York: The Museum of Modern Art, 2001.

Barbieri, Roberto (1942–)
Italian designer; born Milan.

Training To 1969, architecture, Politecnico, Milan.
Biography From 1969 with architect Marco De Carli, Barbieri has been active in product and graphic design and architecture; has designed for furniture makers, including B&B Italia, and, from 1994, for Zanotta. Zanotta chairs include 1994 Petra, 1995 Medea, 1996 Eletta, 1996 Orione, and 1998 Lia.
Exhibitions Architectural and decorative schemes in 1970 *Living Space for 1970s Homes*, staged by Lissone Furniture Body and School of Architecture. Work included in 1975 *Living Space in Public Buildings*, (15th) Triennale di Milano; 1979 *Italienische Möbel Design 1950/80* (Cartiglia bed), Kölnisches Stadt Museum, Cologne.

Barbini, Alfredo (1912–)
Italian glass manufacturer; born and active Murano.

Training From age ten, Abate Zanetti (design school at Murano glass museum).
Biography The family of Barbini's father descended from an early-15th-century glass-bead maker. His mother's family, the Fugas, were glassblowers. 1925, Alfredo began his own career as a glassblower at Società Anonima Industrie Artistiche Riunite Ferro Toso (S.A.L.I.R.); 1929, became a master glassblower at Cristalleria di Venezia e Murano; 1932, worked in a glass workshop in Milan but soon returned to Murano as master glassblower with the new firm Zecchin & Martinuzzi Vetri Artistici e Mosaici; 1936, was briefly at Seguso Vetri d'Arte but, 1936–44, was a partner and master glassblower at Società Anonima Vetri Artistici Murano (SAVAM); 1945, received a grant to study with Napoleone Martinuzzi; 1947, was briefly a partner at Vetreria Vistosi; 1947–50, was owner, designer, and master glassblower at Gino Cenedese & C., for which he created a number of modeled sculptures, including works in the Acquario series; 1950, founded Vetreria Alfredo Barbini, reorganized 1983 as Alfredo Barbini S.r.l. 1969–71, also designed on a freelance basis for Gral-Glashütte, Germany; by 2000, was still active.
Exhibitions/citations Showed work independently at 1948 and 1950 Biennale di Venezia. 1955 Croce de Cavaliere al Merito, Italian government.
Bibliography Cat., *Venini and Murano Renaissance: Italian Art Glass of the 1940s and 50s*, New York: Fifty/50, 1984. Marc Heiremans, *Art Glass from Murano 1910–1970*, Stuttgart: Arnoldsche, 1993.

Barillet, Louis (1880–1948)
French stained-glass designer.

Biography 1920s–30s, Barillet received commissions from modern architects, including Robert Mallet-Stevens; 1920–45, was active in a partnership with Jacques Le Chevallier in Paris, and they were known for their geometrical approach and realized vigorous Cubist and modern forms in clear and colored glass. With Le Chevallier, Barillet designed and produced the glass decoration for the windows of 1928–29 offices of the periodical *La semaine à Paris* (architect, Mallet-Stevens), using motifs portraying days of the week; other commissions with Le Chevallier included 1935 Capucins de Blois church; designed stained-glass windows for the stairwells and large bay windows in buildings on the rue Mallet-Stevens, Auteuil; 1930, became a member, Union des Artistes Modernes (Union des Artistes Modernes), at whose venues he exhibited until 1937; from 1945, was partner of Théodore Hansen. Barillet's 1932 Paris studio on square Vergennes was designed by Mallet-Stevens.
Bibliography Robert Mallet-Stevens, 'Les vitraux de Barillet,' in *Les arts de la maison*, Paris: Albert Morancé, 1926. Arlette Barré-Despond, *UAM*, Paris: Regard, 1986. Jean-François Pinchon (ed.), *Robert Mallet-Stevens, architecture, mobilier, décoration*, Paris: Sers, 1986; Cambridge, Mass.: MIT, 1990 (English ed.). Cat., *Les années UAM 1929–1958*, Paris: Musée des Arts Décoratifs, 1988: 148.

Barker, Frederick
British glassware designer and engraver.

Training Hornsey School of Art; Holloway Polytechnic.
Biography At the London Sand-Blast Decorative Glass Works, Barker treated the door panels designed by Raymond McGrath and painted by Jan Juta for RIBA building; designed for oceanliners *Queen Mary* and *Queen Elizabeth* in 1934, 1936, and 1938, and for 1935 *Orion* and 1937 *Orcades*; 1930s–80s, was an engraver at T.W. Ide, London, and associate member, British Society of Master Glass Painters.
Bibliography Cat., *Thirties: British Art and Design Before the War*, London: Arts Council of Great Britain/Hayward Gallery, 1979.

Barlach, Ernst (1870–1938)
German sculptor, graphic artist, and ceramicist.

Biography Barlach began an association with Richard Mutz on the 1902 commemorative plaque for 25th anniversary of the Hamburg museum; to 1904, modeled and relief-decorated ceramics in the Mutz workshop; from 1904, taught, Fachschule für Keramik, Höhr-Grenzhausen; 1905–10, in Berlin developed his own style of expression, a form of social and ethical realism; 1906, returned from a trip to Russia and began producing sculptures for white porcelain and redware by Meissen, on the theme of suffering peasants; wrote *Keramik: Stoff und Form* (1908).
Bibliography Cat., W. Scheffler (ed.), *Werke um 1900*, Berlin: Kunstgewerbemuseum, 1966. K. Reutti, *Mutz-Keramik*, Hamburg: Ernst-Barlach-Hauses, 1966. Elisabeth Cameron, *Encyclopedia of Pottery and Porcelain*, London: Faber & Faber, 1986: 36.

Barman, Christian (1898–1980)
British writer and designer.

Training Architecture, Liverpool University.
Biography 1925, Barman became the editor of *Architects' Journal* and, 1927, joint editor with H. de C. Hastings of both *Architects' Journal* and *Architectural Review*; 1930s, was a product designer; was commissioned by HMV to design 1934–36 electric iron and electric fan with innovative streamlined housing; 1935–41, succeeded G.W. Duncan as publicity officer (with Frank Pick) of London Passenger Transport Board in charge of visual public presentations; 1941–45, was assistant director of postwar building program of Ministry of Works; 1947–62, managed the Railway Design Panel; 1947-63, was chief publicity officer of British Transport Commission; wrote numerous books on architecture; 1949–50, was president of Society of Industrial Artists.
Citations 1948, elected Royal Designer for Industry, UK; 1963, Order of the British Empire (OBE).
Bibliography Michael Farr, *Design in British Industry: A Mid-Century Survey*, London: Cambridge, 1955: 59. Cat., *Thirties: British Art and Design Before the War*, London: Arts Council of Great Britain/Hayward Gallery, 1979. Fiona MacCarthy and Patrick Nuttgens, *An Eye for Industry*, London: Lund Humphries, 1986: 26, 81.

Barnack, Oscar (1879–1936)
German engineer and amateur photographer; active Wetzlar.

Biography c. 1911–13, Barnack created the first Leica 35mm camera, a small metal version that used standard perforated movie film. (Earlier 35mm cameras were unwieldy models that took a large number of pictures per roll of perforated cine film.) 1918, after several alterations and a delay due to World War I, E. Leitz, a manufacturer of high-quality optical instruments and Barnack's employer, put his camera into production. The Leica A, based on the UR and made by Leitz Wetzlar in Germany, had features that included controls on the top of the body and a film winder on the right side. Convenient, practical, and attractive, it established 35mm photography as a new standard for picture making, thus completely revolutionizing photography. Camera design was to remain essentially unchanged until the digital camera was invented. A small quantity of the next model (1923–24 Pilot) was sold, but it was not a prototype. The 1925 Model A and 1926 Model B followed. The name 'Leica' came from 'Lei' in 'Leitz' and 'ca' in 'camera', although 'camera' in German is *Kamera*.
Bibliography *The Camera*, London: Design Museum, 1989. Mel

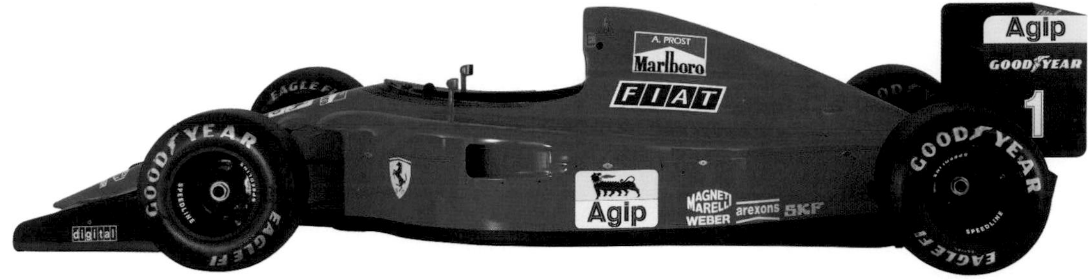

John Barnard and Ferrari. Formula 1 racing car (641/2). 1990. Honeycomb composite with carbon fibers, Kevlar, and other materials, 40 1/2 x 84 x 174 1/2" (102.9 x 213.4 x 448.3 cm). Mfr.: Ferrari, Italy. Gift of the mfr. MoMA.

Byars with Arlette Barré-Despond, *100 Designs/100 Years: A Celebration of the 20th Century*, Hove: RotoVision, 1999: 36–37.

Barnard, Jane (1902–)
British silversmith; active London.

Training Central School of Arts and Crafts, London.
Biography 1920s–30s, she designed silver for her father's firm, Edward Barnard and Sons, London; produced smooth, round silhouettes embellished with blue enamel lines and edges. R.M.Y. Gleadowe also designed for the firm.
Bibliography Annelies Krekel-Aalberse, *Art Nouveau and Art Déco Silver*, New York: Abrams, 1989.

Barnard, John (1946–)
British automobile/motorcyle designer.

Training Watford College of Technology, London.
Biography Barnard worked for a time for GEC as the designer of lightbulb-manufacturing machinery; from 1968, was a junior designer at Lola, where he began working on Formula V and Super V projects and designed Lola's T 260 Can Am car and its T 280 and T 290 sportscars; from 1975 at McLaren, designed M 16 Indycar, Formula 1 M 23, and Formula 5000 M 25, and garnered favorable attention for his c. 1987 McLaren MP 4/1, the first all-composite monocoque Formula 1 model, possibly contributing to McLaren's 1980s dominance in the Formula 1 arena. Barnard developed Formula 1's first semi-automatic gearbox, and the first car (1998 Arrows A 19 Formula 1 model) with a carbon-composite gearbox. 1987, he was hired by Ferrari, paid $2 million, and provided with his own design center (Ferrari Technical Office) in the UK; soon after, worked at Benetton, set up Benetton Advanced Research Group in Godalming, and designed the B 191; 1997, bought FDD from Ferrari and established B3 Technologies while concurrently (1999) serving as technical consultant to Prost; 2003, became technical director of Kenny Roberts's motocycle-racing team in Banbury, Oxfordshire, responsible for all engineering and technical developments, including 2003 four-stroke Proton KR V-5 grand-prix-racing motorcycle.
Bibliography Paola Antonelli (ed.), *Objects of Design: The Museum of Modern Art*, New York: The Museum of Modern Art, 2003: 174–75.

Barnard, Bishop and Barnards
British manufacturer of iron and brass; located Norwich, Norfolk.

History 1826, Charles Barnard (1804–1871) established a foundry in Norwich; 1846, joined forces with John Bishop. 1859, the firm became known as Barnard, Bishop and Barnards, reflecting the inclusion of Barnard's sons Charles the younger and Godfrey; produced innovative agricultural and domestic products, including 1838 self-rolling mangle, a so-called noiseless lawn mower, hot-water heating systems, and kitchen ranges. Charles Barnard the elder developed the machine-made wire netting, commonly known as chicken wire, in production to this day. 1851, moving to a new site, the Barnards began production of ornamental iron work. Barnard's chief craftsperson Frank Ames and Norwich architect Thomas Jeckyll collaborated on the Norwich Gates, well received at the 1862 London exhibition (see below) and made as 1863 wedding gift of the Gentlemen of Norfolk and Norwich to the Prince of Wales and Princess Alexandra, still standing today at Sandringham. The zenith of Barnard's production was Jeckyll's 40-ton two-story pavilion, first shown at 1876 Philadelphia exhibition and purchased by Norwich City Council in 1888. Jeckyll also designed cast-iron furniture and brass and cast-iron fireplace surrounds and grates. In addition, Barnard's produced utilitarian metalwork, including manhole covers.
Exhibitions/citations Work included in 1851 *Great Exhibition of the Works of Industry of All Nations* (wrought-iron hinge and door knocker), London; *International Exhibition of 1862*, London (Norwich Gates), 1876 *Centennial Exposition*, Philadelphia (pavilion by Jeckyll), 1878 *Exposition Universelle*, Paris, and in expositions until 1888. Gold medal (slow-combustion stove), 1878 *Exposition Universelle*, Paris.
Bibliography Doreen Bolger Burke et al., *In Pursuit of Beauty: Americans and the Aesthetic Movement*, New York: The Metropolitan Museum of Art/Rizzoli, 1986: 402.

Barnes, James F.
> See Reinecke, Jean Otis.

Barnes, Jhane (1954–)
American textile and clothing designer; born Maryland; active New York and Japan.

Training From 1972, Fashion Institute of Technology, New York.
Biography 1976, Barnes first began as a professional designer/manufacturer with $5,000, borrowed from a school professor to make 1,000 pairs of pants; from 1978, designed men's clothing for clients such as Paul Simon, Elton John, and John Lennon; 1979, trained with master tailor Eddie DeRusso; became internationally known for her clothing designs for men and women; from 1983, designed furnishing fabrics for Knoll; 1995, first contract-furniture textitle range, for Bernhardt; 1997, carpet tiles, for Collins & Aikman; 1998 with Bernhardt, founded Jhane Barnes Textiles; by 2000, had established independent stores in US.
Citations 1980 and 1984 Coty American Fashion Critics award for menswear (to the first woman); 1981 citation, Council of Fashion Designers, US; 1981 and 1982 menswear awards, Cutty Sark; 1990 gold award (textiles by Knoll), American Society of Interior Designers (ASID); 1994 gold award (textiles by Knoll), Resources Council, US; 1995 (textiles by Knoll) and 1995 and 1996 (Bernhardt furniture fabrics), Best of NeoCon, Chicago; 1996 (products by Knoll and Bernhardt) and 1997 (carpet tiles by Collins & Aikman) Good Design award, Chicago Athenaeum; and others.
Bibliography Timothy J. Ward, 'A 60s House Meets '90s Dreams,' *Metropolitan Home*, Sept.–Oct. 1993: 72–74. www.jhanebarnes.com.

Barnsley, Ernest (1863–1926); Sidney Barnsley (1865–1926)
British architects, furniture designers, and craftsmen; brothers.

Biographies Edward Barnsley worked with Gothic Revival architect J.D. Sedding and for a time with Norman Shaw; 1895 with brother Sidney Barnsley and Ernest Gimson, set up a workshop in Pinbury, Gloucestershire. They specialized in vernacular forms and called on traditional materials; 1902, established the Cotswold School in Sapperton, Gloucestershire, designing and making simple hand-made furniture. 1926–37, production was continued by Peter van der Waals, who had worked in the shop since 1901, in his shop in Chalford, Gloucestershire.
Bibliography William Lethaby et al., *Ernest Gimson, His Life and Work*, Stratford-upon-Avon: Shakespeare Head; London: Benn, 1924; New York: Garland, 1978. Mary Comino, *Gimson and the Barnsleys:*

'Wonderful Furniture of a Commonplace Kind,' London, Evans Bros., 1980.
> See Barnsley, Edward.

Barnsley, Edward (1900–1987)

British furniture maker and designer; born Pinbury, Gloucestershire; active Froxfield, Hampshire; son of Sidney Barnsley.

Training 1919, apprenticeship under Geoffrey Lupton at Froxfield.
Biography 1923, Barnsley took over Lupton's furniture workshop, where he worked until his retirement; designed historicist furniture that was based on the practice of his father and Ernest Gimson and that followed 18th-century and some Arts and Crafts models; 1930s, collaborated with Francis Troup on furniture; 1937, succeeded Peter van der Waals as design adviser to Loughborough Training College; from 1945, was furniture design consultant, Rural Industries Bureau; was a member of Art-Workers' Guild.
Exhibitions Work subject of 1981 venue, London and Bath; 1985 venue, Stockport Memorial Gallery (catalogs below).
Bibliography Cat., *Edward Barnsley: Sixty Years of Furniture Design and Cabinet Making*, London: Fine Art Society, 1982. Cat., *Fitness for Purpose and Pleasure in Use: Furniture from the Edward Barnsley Workshop 1922 to the Present Day*, Stockport: Stockport Metropolitan Borough Leisure Services Division, 1985. Annette Carruthers, *Edward Barnsley and His Workshop: Arts and Crafts in the Twentieth Century*, Wendlebury, Oxon: White Cockade, 1992.

Barovier, Angelo (1927–)

Italian glassware designer; active Murano; son of Ercole Barovier.

Biography Angelo Barovier came from a line of Venetian glassmakers dating back to the 13th century; worked with his father and produced vessels in elongated forms in *vetro a fili*, the technique of incorporating colored glass rods into bubbled and colored glass to form stripes; created glass sculptures in which constantly changing internal effects were produced by the characteristics of pattern and light.

Barovier, Fratelli (aka Barovier e Toso); Ercole Barovier (1889–1974)

Italian glassware designer; active Murano; father of Angelo Barovier; son of Benvenuto Barovier.

Biography 1878, Benedetto, Benvenuto, and Giuseppe Barovier established a factory known as Fratelli Barovier to make beads and vessels in historicist 16th-century styles. 1936, under the management of Ercole Barovier, son of Benvenuto, the firm became Barovier e Toso, under which name it operates today. (Founded in 1295, Barovier e Toso has been cited by *The Guinness Book of World Records* as being the oldest extant firm in the world.) Ercole's son Angelo Barovier, painter and glass designer, began at the firm in late 1950s; with Piero Toso, assumed management of the firm. 1919, Ercole Barovier established Artisti Barovier and, subsequently, Barovier e C.; was effective, like Paolo Venini and Giacomo Cappelin, in reviving Murano glassmaking in 1920s; served as chief designer, artist, and chemist and created more than 25,000 different models of decorative and functional pieces; formulated new color compounds and developed new techniques for textural surface effects and *vetro gemmato* (stony surface), *vetro barbarico* (applied rough surface), *vetro parabolico* (patchwork surface), and others; used subtle colors and open textures; with son Angelo Barovier, produced vases and bottles in elongated forms in *vetro a fili* (glass with lines), for which colored glass rods were embedded into colored, bubbled glass to form a stripe effect; created glass sculptures in which constantly changing internal effects were produced by the characteristics of pattern and light. Early 1930s, Ercole developed the *vetro rugiada* (glass with a dew effect) technique, in which small air bubbles create controlled texturing. Some historians have suggested that Ercole's contribution to Venetian glass may have been greater than Paolo Venini's.
Exhibitions/citations Participated in 1930 (17th) Biennale di Venezia; 1902 *Esposizione Biennale delle Arti Decorative e Industriali Moderne*, Turin. Work subject of 1994–95 venue, Verona (catalog below). 1956 (Millefili 21689 vase) Premio Compasso d'Oro.
Bibliography Cat., Hans Wichmann, *Italien Design 1945 bis heute*, Munich: Die Neue Sammlung, 1988. Attilia Dorigato, *Ercole Barovier, 1889–1974, vetrario muranese*, Venice: Marsilio, 1989. Marina Barovier (ed.), *Art of the Barovier: Glassmakers in Murano, 1866–1972*, Venice: Arsenale, 1993. Cat., *Luci e trasparenze: vetri storici di Ercole Barovier, 1889–1974*, Verona: Fondazioni Museo Miniscalchi-Erizzo, 1994.
> See Barovier, Angelo.

Ercole Barovier. Vase. 1935–36. Mouth-blown glass with brown spotting and gold flecks as *autonno gemmato* effect, h. 8 7/16" (21.5 cm). Mfr.: Barovier e Toso, Italy. Courtesy Quittenbaum Kunstauktionen, Munich.

Barrau, Gérard (1945–)

French industrial designer; active Paris.

Training École Nationale Supérieure des Arts Décoratifs, Paris.
Biography Barrau was active in his own design office, Architral; designed 1979 electrical switches by Legrand and specialized in chain-store layouts, including 30 stores for FNAC (domestic hi-fi and electronic equipment) and 12 shops for Darty (electric appliances). He also developed the design of stores for Grand Optical (quick-service eyeglasses) and designed furniture for the retail shops of Lacoste (clothing).
Bibliography Francois Mathey, *Au bonheur des formes, le design français 1945 à 1992*, Paris: Regard, 1993: 83, 171–325.

Barrault, Jean-Louis (1938–)

French industrial designer; active Paris.

Training École Nationale Supérieure des Arts Decoratifs; atelier Le Corbusier-Wogensky; both Paris.
Biography After schooling, Barrault became a designer at Raymond Loewy's Compagnie de l'Esthétique Industrielle (CEI), Paris; subsequently, was product director of the Harold Barnett group; 1963, set up his own design office. His industrial-product designs included 1968 Méhari automobile (first all-plastic integrated body in France) by Citroën (produced to 1987), 1977 corporate-identity program of Zodiac boats, 1972 4012 coffee machine and 1982 679 mini-stove and 1986 microwave oven by Moulinex, 1988 Futura casserole pot by Le Creuset; 1989 new generation of telephones by Mercelec, and 1989 radiators by Airelec; from 1986, was president, Union Française des Designers Industriels (UFDI); from 1995, was president, chamber of commerce of Haut-de-Seine, and vice-president, chamber of commerce and Industries of Paris.
Citations 1983 (Moulinex mini-oven) and 1985 (Shell oil can) Oscars, *La Nouvelle Economiste* magazine.

Barray, Jean-Paul (1930–)

French industrial designer and painter; born Saint-Étienne; active Paris.

Training École des Beaux-Arts, Lyon.
Biography In Paris, Barray worked in the offices of Le Corbusier-Wogensky, Édouard Albert, ALIA, Henri de Truchis, Jean Prouvé, and, subsequently, the Conservatoire National des Arts et Métiers. 1967, he opened his own office in Paris; was a consultant designer to Bureau d'Études Technès, Maison Créa, and Daum; designed 1970 Penta Chair (with Kim Moltzer) in a thin zinc-plated frame with a canvas seat, first mass produced in 1970 by Wilhelm Bofinger, and other

furniture by the firm from 1968. He taught, École Nationale Supérieure des Arts Décoratifs and ENCI (Les Ateliers), both Paris.
Exhibitions/citations Work shown at 1968 (14th) Triennale di Milano, and also 1968 Musée des Arts Décoratifs (catalog below), 1970 Internationale Möbelmesse, Cologne, and 1971 Whitechapel Gallery, London (catalog below).
Bibliography Cat., *Les assises du siège contemporain*, Paris: Musée des Arts Décoratifs, 1968. Cat., *Modern Chairs 1918–1970*, London: Lund Humphries, 1971. Arlette Barré-Despond (ed.), *Dictionnaire international des arts appliqués et du design*, Paris: Regard, 1996.

Barrese, Antonio (1945–)

Italian graphic designer; born and active Milan.

Biography 1964, Barrese began his professional career; was on the staff of MID Design 1964–70, and Gruppo Professionale PRO (aka Studio PRO); 1980, set up his own studio; designed 1977–78 Spazio bus (with I. Hosoe, A. Locatelli, R. Salmiraghi, and A. Torricelli) by Iveco Orlandi.
Bibliography Alfonso Grassi and Anty Pansera, *Atlante del design italiano 1940/1980*, Milan: Fabbri, 1980. Cat., Hans Wichmann (ed.), *Italien Design 1945 bis heute*, Munich: Die Neue Sammlung, 1988.
> See Studio PRO.

Barret, Maurice (1905–1985)

French interior architect; born Besançon.

Training Initially in medicine, which he abandoned to enter École Nationale Supérieure des Arts Décoratifs, Paris.
Biography 1930, Barret established his own architecture studio; was influenced by the architecture of Le Corbusier and interiors of Francis Jourdain; 1934, became a member, Union des Artistes Modernes (UAM); 1933–50s, wrote on environments and rational furnishings in the review *Le décor d'aujourd'hui* and on the subject of school architecture and furniture in the journal *L'architecture d'aujourd'hui*; 1937, built and designed all the furniture for a house in Villefranche-sur-Mer.
Exhibitions Work shown at 1926 Salon d'Automne; from 1934, Salon des Arts Ménagers; 1936 Salon de l'Habitation (bedroom-studio). Participated in competitions for school furniture design for Office Technique pour l'Utilisation de l'Acier (OTUA).
Bibliography Maurice Barret, 'Retour des USA,' *Mobilier et décoration*, no. 4, 1956. Maurice Barret, 'Humanisme et architecture, l'avenir de la maison familiale,' *Le décor d'aujourd'hui*, no. 39, 1947. Cat., *Les années UAM 1929–1958*, Paris: Musée des Arts Décoratifs, 1988. Arlette Barré-Despond (ed.), *Dictionnaire international des arts appliqués et du design*, Paris: Regard, 1996.

Barron, Phyllis (1890–1964)

British textile designer; active London and Painswick, Gloucestershire.

Training Drawing and painting, Slade School of Fine Art, London.
Biography Early on, Barron collected 19th-century French print-block textiles and began experimenting with textile printing and block cutting using 19th-century methods; printed textiles in her studio in Hampstead, London; from early 1920s, collaborated with Dorothy Larcher in Barron and Larcher. 1930, they moved to Painswick, Gloucestershire, and printed dressmaking textiles and furnishing fabrics using both new and historic French blocks, rejecting aniline dyes; developed vegetable-dye solutions and revived discharge-printing techniques; were best known for fabrics that displayed bold monochromatic prints for furnishings in unbleached cottons and linens; sold through Footprints, London. In the first half of 20th century, Barron and Enid Marx were the foremost exponents of the hand-blocked print in England, executing commissions including soft furnishings for Duke of Westminster's yacht *The Flying Cloud* and the Senior Common Room, Girton College, Cambridge.
Bibliography *Phyllis Barron and Dorothy Larcher: Handblock Printed Textiles*, Bath: Crafts Study Centre, 1978. Cat., *Thirties: British Art and Design Before the War*, London: Arts Council of Great Britain/ Hayward Gallery, 1979.

Bartels, Heiko (1947–)

German industrial designer.

Biography Bartels designed kitchen and camping equipment, automobiles, and motorcycles and, from 1977, lighting and interiors; 1982 with designers Fischer, Hullmann, and Hüskes, set up the Kunstflug design group to produce their own lighting.
Bibliography Albrecht Bangert and Karl Michael Armer, *80s Style: Designs of the Decade*, New York: Abbeville, 1990.

Bartlmae, Kerstin (1941–)

Swedish industrial and furniture designer; born Stockholm; active Ulm (Germany) and Varese (Italy).

Training 1956–57, ceramics, and at Konstfackskolan, Stockholm; 1957, business school, Rapallo, Italy; 1958, art college, Florence; 1962, Hochschule für Gestaltung, Ulm.
Biography 1961, she was an industrial ceramicist at Schwedische Form, Stockholm, and Rörstrand porcelain factory, Lidköping; 1965–66, worked in a design office, Milan; 1968–69 under Prof. Lindinger, worked at Institut für Produktgestaltung, Ulm; 1969, set up her own design office; 1970–80, was guest lecturer on product design, State Institute for Architecture and Town Planning, Antwerp, and, 1983, guest lecturer, Fachhochschule für Druck (graphic arts college), Stuttgart; from 1987, worked in her own design office in Varese, Italy, and was a guest lecturer on packaging design, graphic design department, Istituto Europeo di Design, Milan; wrote on design and packaging and was a jury member for various design competitions. Designs included 1969–70 1140 plastic wall scales by Soehnle Waagen; 1978 TK-matic 9725 and 9725 L fine drawing pencils, the first with an automatic lead feed; 1984–85 Rolo seating by Fröscher Sitform; and 1986 Lobby seating by Casa Möbel-Werke. Works independently and with Volker Bartlmae, for other clients such as Mauser, Becker, and Brunner.
Bibliography Cat., Design Center Stuttgart, *Women in Design: Careers and Life Histories Since 1900*, Stuttgart: Haus der Wirtschaft, 1989: 64–67.

Bartoli, Carlo (1931–)

Italian architect, interior designer, and teacher; born and active Milan and Monza.

Training 1951–57, Politecnico, Milan.
Biography 1959–68, Bartoli collaborated with architects Luciano Baldessari and Annig Sarian; from 1960, has been active in his own office for architecture, furniture, and industrial design, Milan, and, from 1981, Monza; 1967–70, was an instructor of planning, Corso Superiore di Disegno Industriale, Florence; 1966, became interested in plastic materials used for housing; by Arflex, designed 1966 Gaia chair in fiberglass and 1969 Bicia armchair by Kartel; 1970 4875 side chair. Other clients have included Antonangeli, Arc Linea, Colombo Design, Con & Con, Faver, Gonfalonieri, Kristalia, Laurameroni Design Collection, Lualdi, Multipla, Oscam, Rossi di Albizzate, Tisettanta, and UCG Confalonieri. 1988–90, he taught, Istituto Superiore delle Industrie Artistiche (ISIA), Rome. 1990s chair designs by Segis proved highly successful, both in sales and citations. From 1999, Bartoli Design has included staff members Albertina Amadeo, Anna Bartoli, Carlo Bartoli, Paolo Bartoli, Paolo Crecenti, and Giulio Ripamonti, working collaboratively and independently for international clients.
Citations 1995 Breeze armchair: 1996 Design Distinction Award, Annual Design Review, *I.D.* magazine; 1996 Red Dot award, Design Zentrum Nordrhein Westfalen, Essen; 1996 Apex Product Design Award, IIDA; 1998 Industrie Forum Design (iF), Hanover.
Bibliography Cat., *Modern Chairs 1918–1970*, London: Lund Humphries, 1971. Cat., Milena Lamarová, *Design a Plastické Hmoty*, Prague: Uměleckoprůmyslové Muzeum, 1972. *ADI Annual 1976*, Milan: Associazione per il Disegno Industriale, 1976. Alfonso Grassi and Anty Pansera, *Atlante del design italiano 1940/1980*, Milan: Fabbri, 1980. 'Allora questo italian style?,' *Modo*, May 1981. 'Intervista a Carlo Bartoli,' *Ufficio Stile*, Jan. 1983. Cat., Hans Wichmann, *Italien Design 1945 bis heute*, Munich: Die Neue Sammlung, 1988. *I progettisti—Carlo Bartoli*, Milan: Rima, 1988. 'Carlo Bartoli—Il prodotto? Un progetto infinito...,' *DDN*, Jan. 1993. 'Carlo Bartoli—Monza,' *md*, July 2001.

Bartolini, Dario (1943–)

Italian industrial designer; born Trieste.

Training 1972, degree in architecture.
Biography 1967–73, Bartolini and his wife Lucia (1942–) were members of Archizoom Associati, Florence, which was founded 1966. 1967–70, Dario designed interactive machines and installations with sound and light sensors; 1973-96, performed research in clothing design and was a consultant in the clothing and fiber industries; 1973–79 and 1987–89, designed and produced children's books;

1976–87, designed educational tools, solar machines, maps for territorial orientation, books, and computer software for bibliographic research; has been active as a painter and sculptor.
Exhibitions A number of venues, from 1968 *Centro di Cospirazione Eclettica* at the Triennale di Milano to 1999 installation at Thames Wharf, London.
Bibliography Cat., *Modern Chairs 1918–1970*, London: Lund Humphries, 1971. *ADI Annual 1976*, Milan: Associazione per il Disegno Industriale, 1976.

Barwig, Franz (1868–1931)
Austrian sculptor.

Training 1888–97, sculpture, Kunstgewerbeschule, Vienna.
Biography Barwig worked in bronze and wood and won numerous public commissions; though not himself a designer, had a great influence on designers in Vienna; following his suicide, was honored with a memorial service by exponents of the Wiener Sezession.
Bibliography Hans Vollmer, *Allgemeines Lexikon der Bildenden Künstler*, vol. I, Leipzig: Seemann, 1953: 124. Auction catalog, Christie's New York, 9 Dec. 1989.

Basile, Ernesto (1857–1932)
Italian designer; born Palermo.

Training Università degli Studi, Palermo.
Biography 1881, Basile settled in Rome; 1892, became professor, Università degli Studi, Palermo; from 1893, taught, Università degli Studi, Rome; designed 1883–84 Parliament Building, Rome, and 1899 Villino Florio, Palermo; subsequently, developed a style that combined his own neo-Norman approach with a highly refined version of Art Nouveau, expressed in his 1903 Villino Basile, Palermo. Later on, classical traits appeared, as in 1920–25 Istituto Provinciale Antitubercolare and 1925 Albergo Diurno, both Palermo; this approach was in opposition to 1920s Italian Rationalist architecture. Active in the prevailing Stile Floreale, he designed highly ornate, carved furniture by Ducrot in Sicily.
Bibliography Salvatore Caronia Roberti, *Ernesto Basile e cinquant' anni di architettura in Sicilia*, Palermo: Ciuni, 1935. *Ernesto Basile, Studi e schizzi*, Turin: Crudo, 1911. *Mobili e arredi di Ernesto Basile: nella produzione Ducrot*, Palermo: Novecento, 1980. Cat., Paolo Portoghesi et al., *Ernesto Basile architetto*, Venice: Biennale di Venezia, 1980. Anna Maria Ingria et al., *Ernesto Basile e il liberty a Palermo*, Palermo: Herbita, 1987. Cat., Gabriel P. Weisberg (ed.), *Stile Floreale: The Cult of Nature in Italian Design*, Miami: The Wolfsonian Foundation, 1988.

Basseches, Stuart (1960–)
American designer

Training Graduate studies, Yale University, New Haven, Conn.
Biography Basseches, an architect, and wife Judith Hudson (US, 1959–), a graphic designer and also a Yale graduate, met at Yale. They established firm BiProduct, San Francisco, and designed modular lighting and furniture, including 1999 I-Beam table of anodized aluminum.
Exhibitions/citations 2000–03 *Aluminum by Design* touring exhibition, organized by Carnegie Art Museum, Pittsburgh. 1999 Good Design award, Chicago Athenaeum; 1999 IDSA/*Business Week* award (with Turett Collaborative Architects); 1999 50 Books/50 Covers of AIGA (American Institute of Graphic Art); 2000 Colbert Grant for Emerging Artists.
Bibliography Cat., Sarah Nichols et al., *Aluminum by Design*, New York: Abrams, 2000.

Bastard, Georges (1881–1939)
French wax tablet maker and designer; born Anderville, Oise.

Training École Nationale Supérieure des Arts Décoratifs, Paris.
Biography Member of a family of wax tablet makers active from the 17th century in Paris, Bastard was director of École des Arts Décoratifs, Limoges, to 1938; 1938, became director of Manufacture Nationale de Céramique, Sèvres; from 1930, was a member of Union des Artistes Modernes (UAM); collaborated with Jacques-Émile Ruhlmann and Pierre-Paul Montagnac; created precious small boxes, ceramics, and glass.
Exhibitions Work included in Salons of the Société Nationale des Beaux-Arts; editions of Salon d'Automne from 1910–12; 1933 and 1934 editions of Salon des Tuileries; 1925 *Exposition Internationale des Arts Décoratifs et Industriels Modernes*, Paris; from 1930, UAM's first three exhibitions. Subject of 1950 exhibition, Musée des Arts Décoratifs, Paris; 1959 exhibition, Lisbon (catalog below).
Bibliography Gabrielle Rosenthal, 'Georges Bastard,' *L'amour de l'art*, no. 12, Dec. 1927. Cat., *Obras de Georges Bastard*, Lisbon: Musée National d'Art Antique, 1959. Victor Arwas, *Art Déco*, New York: Abrams, 1980. Sylvie Raulet, *Bijoux art déco*, Paris: Regard, 1984. Arlette Barré-Despond, *UAM*, Paris: Regard, 1986. Cat., *Les années UAM 1929–1958*, Paris: Musée des Arts Décoratifs, 1988.

Bastide, Thomas (1954–)
French glassware designer; born Biarritz.

Training École Supérieure d'Arts Graphiques, Penninghen, and École des Métiers d'Art, both France; industrial design, Pilchuck Glass School, Stanwood, Wash., US.
Biography Batide's mother was a Swedish painter and stylist who worked at the Haviland porcelain factory. He worked at CEI, the design office of Raymond Loewy and there contributed (without credit) to 1965 Elna Lotus sewing machine by Tavaro and other products; 1981–99, worked at Baccarat, where he became director of design in 1983 and created hundreds of designs in crystal, including 1986 Triangle drinking glass, 1993 Océanic vase, 1993 Modern Time bowl, 1996 and 1997 Empriente high and low tables, 1999 Texture of the Sky vase, 1999 Cubes cocktail shaker and drinking glass, and 1999 Spirale vase. He designed some furniture, but never serially produced.
Bibliography *Les carnets du design*, Paris: Mad Cap Productions/APCI, 1986: 51. Jean-Louis Curtis, *Baccarat*, Paris: Regard, 1991. www.via.asso.fr.

Bataille & Ibens
> See Ibens, Paul.

Batchelder, Ernest Allen (1875–1957)
American ceramicist; born Nashua, N.H.; active Pasadena, Cal.

Training To 1899, Massachusetts Normal Art School (today Massachusetts College of Art), Boston.
Biography 1902–09, Batchelder was director of art and taught design theory and the manual arts, Throop Polytechnic Institute; also held summer classes at the Handicraft Guild Summer Schools in Minneapolis. Influenced by the design theory of Harvard University professor Denman W. Ross, Batchelder wrote *The Principles of Design* (1904) and *Design in Theory and Practice* (1910); 1905, traveled to centers of the Arts and Crafts movement in Europe; 1909, established a pottery for tile making on his own property in Pasadena, Cal.; 1916, moved Batchelder Tiles to Los Angeles, where conveyor belts took sand-pressed tiles into large kilns; in the early years, designed most of the hand-molded tiles himself. His work was almost entirely in brown with blue glaze rubbed into and around reliefs of vines, peacocks and other animals, flowers, and Viking ships, and with depictions of the California landscape. 1930s, the firm closed, and Batchelder later occupied a small shop in Pasadena, where he produced delicate slip-cast pottery.
Bibliography Paul Evans in Timothy J. Andersen et al., *California Design 1910*, Salt Lake City: Peregrine Smith, 1980: 75.

Battersby, George Martin (1914–1982)
British collector, illustrator, and writer.

Training Architecture, Regent Street Polytechnic; 1934–35, Royal Academy of Dramatic Arts; both London.
Biography Late 1920s, Battersby was a junior draftsperson in studios of decorators Gill and Reigate, London; worked briefly at Liberty's, London; designed a 1938 production of *Hamlet* at the Old Vic and sets for other productions; worked at the couture house of Bunny Rogers; by the end of World War II, had become a collector of Art Nouveau; from late 1940s to 1951, was assistant set designer to Cecil Beaton; 1948–51 with Philip Dyer, worked on backgrounds for Beaton's photographs for Modess sanitary-napkin advertisements; became active as an independent set designer; designed interiors and painted murals for private clients, including 1959 murals for Carlyle Hotel, New York, and 1964 murals for First National Bank of Wisconsin; designed interior schemes of Ken Russell's 1965 BBC TV film on Claude Debussy; from mid-1960s, operated Sphinx Studio with partner Paul Watson, whose suicide ended the business; designed

Helmut Bätzner. Chair and stool (no. BA 1171). 1966. Plastic, chair: 29 1/8 x 20 7/8 x 20" (74 x 52 x 53.5 cm), stool 15 x 20 1/2 x 18 7/8 (38 x 52 x 48 cm). Mfr.: Bofinger Production, Germany. Courtesy Quittenbaum Kunstauktionen, Munich.

many exhibitions for Brighton Museum, including 1969 *The Jazz Age* and 1971 *Follies and Fantasies*; 1978, sold his entire collection, except for minor gifts, to Brighton Museum; is best known for his books *The Decorative Twenties* (1966), *Art Nouveau* (1969), *The Decorative Thirties* (1969), *Art Déco Fashion* (1974), and *Trompe l'Œil* (1974).
Exhibitions/citations Work subject of 1948 exhibition at Brook Street Gallery, London; 1956 exhibition at Sagittarius Gallery, New York; numerous subsequent exhibitions including at Ebury Gallery, London, 1982. Became known as collector and connoisseur with 1964 *Art Nouveau, The Collection of Martin Battersby* exhibition, Brighton Museum. Award (for 1974 *Intermezzo* opera production design), *Evening Standard* newspaper, London.
Bibliography 'Sleight of Eye,' *Vogue*, 15 Feb. 1960. John Marley, 'Martin Battersby,' *The Decorative Arts Society Journal*, no. 7, 1983. Jessica Rutherford, *Art Nouveau, Art Déco and the Thirties: The Furniture Collections at Brighton Museum*, Brighton: The Royal Pavilion, Art Gallery and Museums, 1983: 4. Philippe Garner, 'Martin Battersby: A Biography,' *The Decorative Twenties*, New York: Whitney, 1988 (2nd ed.).

Bätzner, Helmut (1928–)
German architect and designer; born Nagold.

Training In Stuttgart.
Biography 1960, Bätzner opened his own office in Karlsruhe; designed 1966 BA 1171 chair in molded fiberglass, the first single one-piece plastic chair suitable for mass production, by Wilhelm Bofinger to 1984 (1995, reentered into producion by Menzolit-Werke/Albert Schmidt Menzolit-Werke/Albert Schmidt). He designed 1951–56 Konzerthaus Liederhalle (with Adolf Abel and Hermann Kiess), Stuttgart, and 1970–75 Badisches Staatstheater (Baden state theater), Karlsruhe.
Exhibitions/citations BA 1171 introduced at 1966 Internationale Möbelmesse, Cologne (reintroduced at 1995 edition of the Möbelmesse); included in 1966 *Vijftig Jaar Zitten*, Stedelijk Museum, Amsterdam; 1968 *Les assises du siège contemporain*, Musée des Arts Décoratifs, Paris. Received 1966 Studio Rosenthal Prize, and awards for IBM office building, Berlin, for 1960 Cologne University Library, and for 1963 Karlsruhe Theater.
Bibliography Cat., *Modern Chairs 1918–1970*, London: Lund Humphries, 1971. Michael Erlhoff (ed.), *Designed in Germany Since 1949*, Munich: Prestel, 1990. Klaus-Jürgen Sembach et al., *Möbeldesign des 20. jahrhunderts*, Cologne: Taschen, 1993. Auction cat., *Modernes Design Kunsthandwerk nach 1945*, Munich: Quittenbaum, 4 Dec. 2001, lot 37; 1 June 2002, lot 58.

François Bauchet. Meridienne fireside chair. 1997. Wood and fabric, h. 20 7/8 x 43 1/4 x 23 5/8" (53 x 110 x 60 cm). Mfr.: Néotù, France.

Bauchet, François (1948–)
French sculptor and furniture designer; born Montluçon; active Saint-Étienne.

Training École des Beaux-Arts, Saint-Étienne.
Biography Bauchet has taught, École des Beaux-Arts, Saint-Étienne, where his pupils included Eric Jourdan. His furniture designs and sculpture are influenced by American Minimalism and show a preference for metal, resin, plywood, and color-stained wood surfaces. Initial designs (early 1980s) were for tables. He designed 1988 interiors commissioned by Fondation Cartier pour l'Art Contemporain. Bauchet's Minimalism is exemplified in his 1982 C'est Aussi une Chaise and 1987 Table Carrée and undulating plastic forms in his 1987 Chaise Liliplon, 1988 Tabouret Foundation, 1989 Cabinet, and his 1997 furniture collection, all edited by Néotù. Other work: 1990 Vallauris tea/coffee set by Artcodif, 1996 public benches, trash bins, and signage for the Château Azay-le-Rideau, 2002 Yang modular sofa by Cinna, 2001 HL polyester shelving edited by Kréo, 2002 Résonance dinnerware by Haviland, 1999 Collection Vallauris tea-and-coffee service in Vallauris, and 2001 Yang settee by Cinna. Supported by the French Ministère de la Culture, participated in a furniture workshop of Centre International de Recherche sur le Verre (CIRVA) for the French department of La Réunion (1992 Collection Tropicale) and in 1995 Collection Brésil.
Exhibitions/citations Work included in numerous exhibitions, including at Octobre des Arts, Centre d'Art Plastique, Villefranche-sur-Saône; Gallery Arterieur, Berlin; 1987 Documenta 8, Kassel; Musée d'Aix-les-Bains. Work subject of 1988 exhibition, Centre d'Art Contemporain de Vassivière, near Limoges, and at Galerie Néotù, Kréo, and Musée des Arts Décoratifs (catalog below), all Paris. 1982 Appel Permanent grant (lacquered chairs), VIA (French furniture

association); Creator of the Year, 2002 Salon du Meuble, Paris.
Bibliography Jacques Beauffet and Hubert Besacier, *François Bauchet formes adressées*, Paris: Á Priori, 1987. Pierre Staudenmeyer, *Desco*, Milan: Zeus, 1987. Cat., *François Bauchet designer*, Limoges: Centre d'Art Contemporain, 1988. Elisabeth Vedrenne, 'François Bauchet,' *Beaux Arts*, Mar. 1989. Enzo Biffi Gentili, *François Bauchet à Vallauris*, Nice: Gardette, 1999. Pierre Bonnaval and Claire Fayolle, *François Bauchet*, Paris: Dis Voir, 2000. Cat., Constance Rubini, *François Bauchet, mobilier et objets 1980–2000*, Paris: Musée des Arts Décoratifs, 2000. Sophie Tasma Anargyros, 'Portrait: François Bauchet,' *Intramuros*, no. 75, Aug.–Sept. 2000. Constance Rubini, *Les cinq sens autour de la table*, Nice: Gardette, 2002.

Baudisch-Wittke, Gudrun (b. Gudrun Baudisch 1906–1982)

Austrian ceramicist; born Pöls.

Training 1922–26 under Hans Adametz, ceramics, Österreichische Bundeslehranstalt für das Baufach und Kunstgewerbe, Graz; and under Josef Hoffmann and Michael Powolny, Kunstgewerbeschule, Vienna.
Biography 1926–30, Baudisch-Wittke was a member of the ceramics workshop (established 1914) of the Wiener Werkstätte; designed the three-dimensional binding (with 'Vally' Wieselthier) of the volume that celebrated the 25th anniversary of the Werkstätte (*Die Wiener Werkstätte, 1903–1928: Modernes Kunstgewerbe und sein Weg* (Vienna: Krystall, 1929); 1930, became active in her own workshop with Mario von Pontoni; worked with others on the Austrian pavilion at 1935 *Exposition Universelle et Internationale de Bruxelles*. 1936, she moved to Berlin and, 1945, to Hallstatt, Austria, where she established the Hallstatt Keramik workshop in 1946; produced numerous stucco ceilings for churches and other buildings.
Bibliography Otto Wutzel and Gudrun Baudisch, *Keramik von der Wiener Werkstätte bis zur Keramik Hallstadt*, Linz, 1980. Waltraud Neuwirth, *Die Keramik der Wiener Werkstätte*, Vienna: Selbstverlag, 1981. *Wiener Werkstätte: Glas, Keramik, Holz, Leder, Metall: aus den beständen des Österreichischen Museums für angewandte Kunst, Wien*, Vienna : Österreichisches Museum für angewandte Kunst, 1990. Cat., *Expressive Keramik der Wiener Werkstätte 1917–1930*, Munich: Bayerische Vereinsbank, 1992: 126–27.

Bauhaus Metal Workshop. Table lamp. 1928. Aluminum and nickel-plated brass, h. 16 x base dia. 6 1/4" (40.6 x 15.9 cm), shade dia. 10 1/2" (26.7 cm). Mfr.: Bauhaus Metal Workshop, Germany. Gift of Anna Moellen-hoff. MoMA.

Bauer, Karl Johann (1877–1914)

German designer and teacher; active Munich.

Training Debschitz-Schule (Lehr- und Versuchs-Atelier für Angewandte und freie Kunst), Munich.
Biography From 1904. Bauer taught at the Debschitz-Schule, where Marga Jess was his pupil.
Exhibitions Participated in 1914 *Deutscher Werkbund-Ausstellung*, Cologne.
Bibliography Annelies Krekel-Aalberse, *Art Nouveau and Art Déco Silver*, New York: Abrams, 1989.

Bauer, Leopold (1872–1938)

Austrian architect, artisan, and technical writer; born Jägerndorf, Silesia (now Krnov, Czech Republic).

Training 1893 under Carl Hasenauer and 1894–96 under Otto Wagner, Akademie der bildenden Künste, Vienna,.
Biography Bauer was a founding member of the Siebenerklub and one of the first members of the Wiener Sezession (1897); 1902, was an editor of art journal *Ver Sacrum*; 1913–19, succeed Wagner as a professor, Akademie der bildenden Künste, Vienna. As a decorative artist, primarily in the 1910s, designed carpets and glass (including by Lötz); worked mainly in Vienna, Silesia, and Moravia. Buildings included 1904–08 hunting lodge, Jägerndorf; 1922–25 National Bank and British-Austrian Bank, Vienna; 1927–28 Weinstein department store, Troppau; 1932–38 St. Hedwig's Church, Troppau; hotel, Graefenberg, Silesia; and Catholic church, Bielitz. He wrote *Gesund wohnen und freudig arbeiten* (1919); died in Vienna.
Exhibitions 1900–05, designed of the décor and fittings of a number of rooms at annual exhibitions of Wiener Sezession.
Bibliography Hans Vollmer, *Allgemeines Lexikon der Bildenden Künstler*, Leipzig: Seemann, 1953. F. Fellner von Feldegg, *Leopold Bauer: der Künstler und sein Werk*, Vienna.

Bauer, Lisa (1920–)

Swedish glassware designer and graphic artist.

Training 1937–42, Konstindustriskolan, Gothenburg, and Konstfackskolan, Stockholm.
Biography From 1969, she was a freelance designer for Kosta Boda glassworks, specializing in engraved designs for glass forms by Sigurd Persson.
Bibliography Cat., David Revere McFadden (ed.), *Scandinavian Modern Design 1880–1980*, New York: Abrams, 1982.

Bauer, Pascal (1959–)

French furniture designer; born Madagscar.

Training École Nationale Supérieure des Arts Décoratifs, Paris.
Biography Bauer has designed furniture, accessories, exhibitions, and shop interiors and has been favorably compared to Jean Prouvé for his Minimalism and interest in new techniques and materials. Work includes the human-figure-high 1998 CD Roll, which has the appearance of a large fan, by Ycami.
Citations 1987 and 1989 Presse au Moving; 1996 Critique International, Salon du Meuble, Paris.
Bibliography Cat., Sophie Tasma Anargyros et al., *L'école française: les créateurs de meubles du 20ème siècle*, Paris: Industries Françaises de l'Ameublement, 2000.

Bauhaus

German architecture, art, and design school; located Weimar 1919–25, Dessau 1925–32, and temporarily Berlin-Steglitz Oct. 1932–Apr. 1933; directors Walter Gropius 1919–28, Hannes Meyer 1928–30, and Ludwig Mies van der Rohe 1930–33.

History 1919, the Staatliches Bauhaus in Weimar was founded by the architect Walter Gropius. Gropius had taken over the Kunstgewerbeschule, founded by Henry van de Velde, and the Hochschule für bildende Kunst to improve standards of craftsmanship in the town. The Bauhaus's first manifesto (1919), whose cover showed a woodcut by Lyonel Feininger, proclaimed the unity of the arts through craftsmanship, stating in German, 'Architects, painters, and sculptors, we must all return to the crafts!' To achieve this aim, Gropius organized a study program whose basic structure ultimately became adopted by numerous colleges of design worldwide after World War II. A preliminary or basic course, taken by all students, introduced

Bauhaus: Theodor Bogler. Teapot. 1923. Metallic-glazed earthenware with raffia, overall h. 7 5/8 x w. 8 1/8" (19.4 x 20.6 cm). Mfr.: Bauhaus Pottery Workshop, Germany. Estée and Joseph Lauder Design Fund. MoMA.

them to a range of crafts and skills and to color, perception, materials, and form. Students then studied in specialized workshops; in Weimar, there were workshops for metalwork, cabinetmaking, glass painting, weaving, and ceramics. Gropius devised a system of dual control in the workshops, with an artist as a *Formmeister* (master of form) and a craftsperson as a *Lehrmeister* (master of craft). Studies in color, perception, and form continued in challenging courses taught by Vasilii Kandinsky and Paul Klee, who attracted aspiring artists to the school. In the early period of the Bauhaus in Weimar, Johannes Itten, head of preliminary courses and an associate in the metalworking and glass-painting workshops, was the most influential personality. His teaching, which aimed to 'release the forces of the soul,' was related to the Romantic Idealism of German Expressionism and was in opposition to Gropius's pragmatic aim of establishing links with commerce and industry; Itten left in 1923. Other influences on the Bauhaus included Russian Constructivism and Dutch De Stijl. 1923, Hungarian Constructivist László Moholy-Nagy ran the metal workshop and, with former student Josef Albers, the preliminary course. Moholy-Nagy was in sympathy with Gropius's Bauhaus credo, 'Art and Technology: a new unity,' the idea manifested in the Weimar exhibition of 1923 that included the show house Am Horn designed by Georg Muche and furnished by workshop students. Although the exhibition was successful and international recognition for the school had grown, the Weimar authorities demanded that it be closed for political and financial reasons. Moving to the industrial city Dessau, the Bauhaus incorporated the local trade school, and a new 1925–26 building complex was designed by Gropius. He reorganized the workshops along 'type-forms' or typical types for industrial production. Moholy-Nagy and Albers jointly continued to run the preliminary course. Moholy-Nagy was in charge of the metal workshop and Muche of the weaving workshops to 1927, when Gunta Stölzl took over. Other former students were in charge of other workshops, including Marcel Breuer of furniture, Herbert Bayer of printing, and Hinnerk Scheper of wall painting. 1926–31, the school's own journal *Bauhaus* published a series of books. The ceramics workshop remained in Weimar, where Otto Bartning replaced Gropius as the director. Distinguished Bauhaus students included Marianne Brandt, Gyula Pap, and Wilhelm Wagenfeld in metalworking; Anni Albers, Otti Berger, and Margaret Leichner in weaving; Alfred Arndt in furniture; and Joost Schmidt in typography. A Functionalist aesthetic was established at this time along with the production of furniture, textiles, lighting, and graphics, some examples of which have become icons of the modern movement. In Weimar and Dessau, the Bauhaus experimental theater was under the direction of Oscar Schlemmer from 1921; Klee and Kandinsky were staff members to 1931 and 1933, respectively. 1927, an architecture department was set up and headed by architect Hannes Meyer. 1928, Gropius left the Bauhaus; 1930, his successor, radical Swiss architect Hannes Meyer, was summarily dismissed because of his left-wing convictions. Mies van der Rohe was put in charge and, with partner Lilly Reich, attempted to establish a new apolitical program focusing on *Bau und Ausbau* (building and development). 1932, the Nazis, already in control of the Dessau city council, closed the school. Re-established in Berlin-Steglitz, the school operated from a former telephone factory for a further six months before finally closing in 1933 due to Gestapo and other pressures. Many of its staff emigrated to the US, including Gropius, Breuer, Mies van der Rohe, Hilberseimer, Moholy-Nagy, and Josef Albers.

Exhibitions The Bauhaus (1919–28) subject of 1938 exhibition, The Museum of Modern Art, New York. 50th anniversary observed by 1968 *50 Jahre Bauhaus* touring exhibition (catalog below); numerous others.

Bibliography *Staatliches Bauhaus Weimar 1919–23*, Munich and Weimar: Bauhaus, 1923. Walter Gropius, *Idee und Aufbau des Staatlichen Bauhauses*, Munich and Weimar: Bauhaus, 1923. Walter Gropius, *The New Architecture and the Bauhaus*, New York: The Museum of Modern Art, 1936. Herbert Bayer and Walter and Ilse Gropius (eds.), *Bauhaus 1919–1928*, New York: The Museum of Modern Art, 1938. Cat., Wulf Herzogenrath (ed.), *50 Jahre Bauhaus*, Stuttgart: Württembergischer Kunstverein; London: Royal Academy of Arts; 1968. Hans M. Wingler, *The Bauhaus: Weimar Dessau Berlin Chicago*, Cambridge, Mass., MIT, 1969. Marcel Franciscono, *Walter Gropius and the Creation of the Bauhaus in Weimar*, Urbana: University of Illinois, 1971. Lionel Richard, *Encyclopédie du Bauhaus*, Paris: Somogy, 1985. Cat., *The Bauhaus: Masters and Students*, New York: Barry Friedman 1988. Cat., *Experiment Bauhaus*, Berlin: Bauhaus Dessau, 1988. Magdalena Droste, *Bauhaus*, Cologne: Taschen, 1990. Eckhard Neumann, *Bauhaus and Bauhaus People*, London: Chapman & Hall, 1993.

Baumann, Hans Theo (1924–)

Swiss ceramicist and glassware designer; active Germany.

Training In Dresden and Basel.

Biography Baumann was among Germany's leading postwar designers of ceramics and glassware; 1955, opened his own studio and designed ceramics for Rosenthal, Thomas, Arzberg, and Schönwald and glassware for Süßmuth, Rosenthal, Thomas, Gral, Rheinkristall, and Daum; also furniture, lighting, and textiles, frequently incorporating his characteristic circular motifs. Work includes1971 Brasilia coffee and tea services by Arzberg (similar to Hermann Gretsch's 1931 pattern, also by Arzberg). Other porcelain dinnerware: 1970 Form 3000, 1972 Delta, and 1972 Donau by Arzberg; 1958 Berlin by Rosenthal; and 1971 Rastergeschirr 2298 by Schönwald.

Exhibitions Work subject of 1979–80 venue, Cologne (catalog below).

Bibliography Cat., *Hans Theo Baumann Design*, Cologne: Kunstgewerbemuseum, 1979. Cat., Kathryn B. Hiesinger and George H. Marcus III (eds.), *Design Since 1945*, Philadelphia: Philadelphia Museum of Art, 1983. Cherie Fehrman and Kenneth Fehrman, *Postwar Interior Design, 1945–1960*, New York: Van Nostrand Reinhold, 1987.

Bawden, Edward (1903–1989)

British painter, illustrator, and graphic designer.

Training From 1919, Cambridge School of Art; 1922–25, Royal College of Art, London, under Paul Nash.

Biography Bawden became a member of artists' group Seven and Five Society; 1928–29, collaborated with Eric Ravilious on murals for Morley College (destroyed during World War II and repainted by Bawden in 1958); designed advertising for clients, including Westminster Bank and Shell-Mex, and booklets for Fortnum and Mason; illustrated books for publishers such as Faber & Faber, Nonesuch Press, and Kynoch Press; designed borders, endpapers, and wallpapers by Cole, posters (often reproduced by linoleum-cut printing) for London Passenger Transport Board, textiles for the Orient Steam Navigation, and decorated earthenware by Wedgwood. Commissions included murals for Hull University, Pilkington, British Petroleum, oceanliners, and the VIP lounge of the British pavilion at 1967 *Universal and International Exhibition (Expo '67)*, Montréal. His tile decorations were installed on London Underground's Victoria Line.

Bibliography Douglas Percy Bliss, *Edward Bawden*, Godalming: Pendower, 1979. Cat., *Thirties: British Art and Design Before the War*, London: Arts Council of Great Britain/Hayward Gallery, 1979.

Baxter, Geoffrey (1922-)

British glassware designer.

Training Guildford School of Art; from 1951, Royal College of Art, London.

Biography 1954, Baxter was hired by William Wilson to work at James Powell & Sons (Whitefriars) Ltd., known as Whitefriars Glass Ltd. from 1963, where he created a wide range of utility and ornamental glass designs; introduced innovative forms of molded glass based on themes from nature, including tree-bark and seashells.

B&B Italia: Gaetano Pesce. Up 1 chair. 1969. Injected polyurethane and stretch fabric, 26 3/8 x 39 3/8 x 39 3/8" (67 x 100 x 100 cm). Mfr.: B&B Italia, Italy. Gift of Atelier International. MoMA.

Bibliography Frederick Cooke, *Glass: Twentieth-Century Design*, New York: Dutton, 1986: 75. Wendy Evans et al., *Whitefriars Glass: James Powell & Sons of London*, London: Museum of London, 1995. Lesley Jackson (ed.), *Whitefriars Glass: The Art of James Powell & Sons*, Shepton Beauchamp: Richard Dennis Publications, 1996.

Bayer

German chemical manufacturer; headquarters Leverkusen.

History 1863, a small dye plant was established by Friedrich Bayer and Johann Friedrich Weskott in Wuppertal-Barmen. Since then, the firm has had a long history as an innovative chemical manufacturer, including the launch of aspirin in 1899. 1925, the enterprise became part of I.G. Farbenindustrie, a large chemical conglomerate which was broken up at the end of World War II; 1951–72, was known as Farbenfabriken Bayer; from 1971, as simply Bayer AG with plants worldwide today. Bayer was accused of collaborating in new-drug experimentation (purportedly supervised by Dr. Joseph Mengele) on people held by the Nazis during World War II in concentration camps. According to Bayer, the firm did not exist as an entity 1925–51. Even so, Bayer and several other large German companies active in the war era agreed to pay $5,200,000 to compensate concentration-camp survivors. The Bayer corporation has sponsored a number of high-design exhibitions and promotions. They have included *Visiona* exhibitions at the Möbelmesse in Cologne: 1st and 2nd editions (1968 and 1970) for which Verner Panton and 3rd edition (1972) for which Joe Colombo and Olivier Mourgue created some unusual interiors.

Citations Design of the Decade (1990s) silver, (1997 Microlet blood fingertip sampler), IDSA/*Business Week* magazine; numerous others.
Bibliography Cat., Milena Lamarová, *Design a Plastické Hmoty*, Prague: Uměleckoprůmyslové Muzeum, 1972: 38. BBC News, 18 Feb. 1999.

Bazzicalupo, Leopoldo Matteo (1966–)

Italian designer; born Parma.

Training 1984, scientific studies, Parma; 1985–91, industrial design, Faculty of Architecture, Politecnico, Milan.
Biography 1992, Bazzicalupo worked as architect in offices of Iemmi & Fabbri, Parma; 1999 with Raffaella Mangiarotti, established the studio Deepdesign, Milan. Their work has included products, electrical appliances, packaging, and exhibition stands for Alessi, Giorgetti, Piaggio, Barilla, Whirlpool Europe, Panasonic, Kraft Italia, Imetec, Castelli Haworth, Glaxo Smith Kline, Espresso Italian, Coca-Cola Italia, Ycami, Flou, Cassina, and Giorgetti.
> See Mangiarotti, Raffaella.

B&B Italia

Italian furniture manufacturer; located Novedrate (CO)

History 1953, Piero Ambrogio Busnelli and his brother Franco set up Fratelli Busnelli fu Giuseppe. Substituting polyurethane for latex rubber (discovered through the forming of toy ducks by Interplastic of London), Piero conceived the idea for cold molding furniture forms; 1966, wishing to experiment further, left the family firm and took ten employees to Plestem, a small plastics firm; set up a workshop in Meda, where designers included Paolo Caliari and Gianfranco Frattini; from the beginning, produced furniture in plastics or foam; 1966, in partnership with Cesare Cassina, established C&B Italia, using new assembly-line methods executed by workers who were purposefully inexperienced in furniture production; initial designers included Vico Magistretti, Mario Bellini, and Tobia Scarpa. Its first furniture was 1966 flower-pot holder designed by Caliari, 1966 Quattro Gatti table by Bellini, 1966 Amanta armchair in Fiberlite by Bellini, 1966 Coronado by Scarpa, and Serenza divan-bed by Busnelli. It produced Gaetano Pesce's 1969 Up seating range of furniture in polyurethane and nylon jersey and Scarpa's 1971 Bonanza armchair in Duraplum and leather. 1973, Busnelli bought out Cassina's share and changed the firm's name to B&B Italia. 1975, the firm bought wooden-chair manufacturer Maspero and established Compagnia delle Filippine to produce rattan furniture; 1981, the Office Furniture Division and Contract Division were established. Today, the firm claims to produce 80% of polyurethane chairs worldwide. Other freelance designers have included Carlo Bimbi, Jeffrey Bernett, Antonio Citterio, Gianfranco Ferré, Nilo Gioacchini, Studio Kairos, Paolo Nava, Paolo Piva, Richard Sapper, Afra Scarpa, Kazuhide Takahama, and Marco Zanuso.
Exhibitions/citations From 1968, C&B's work shown at Salone del Mobile, Milan; 1970 (3rd) and 1972 (4th) Eurodomus, and other fairs and exhibitions. International Design prize (Bellini's *Quattro Gatti* tables); four Premio Compasso d'Oro.
Bibliography Cat., Milena Lamarová, *Design a Plastické Hmoty*,

Hans Theo Baumann. Glasses (no. 20/200). 1966. Glass, shortest (whisky tumbler, middle) h. 3 1/2 x dia. 3" (8.9 x 7.6 cm), tallest (beer/water glass, far right) h. 6 3/8 x 2 5/8" (16.2 x 6.7 cm). Mfr.: Thomas, division of Rosenthal, Germany. Gift of Rosenthal China, Inc. MoMA.

BBPR (Gian Luigi Banfi, Lodovico Barbiano di Belgiojoso, Enrico Peressutti, and Ernesto N. Rogers). **Arco desk system. 1960. Painted sheet steel and plastic, desk 30 11/16 x 55 1/8 x 27 1/2" (78 x 140 x 70 cm), typewriter table-extension 27 1/4 x 34 5/8 x 11 13/16" (69 x 88 x 30cm). Mfr.: Ing. C. Olivetti & C., Italy. Courtesy Quittenbaum Kunstauktionen, Munich.**

Prague: Umĕleckoprůmyslové Muzeum, 1972: 172, 174. Mario Mastropietro and Roland Gorla, *Un'industria per il design: la ricerca, i designers, l'immagine B&B Italia = An Industry for Design: The Research, Designers and Corporate Image of B&B Italia*, Milan: Lybra Immagine, 1986/1999.

BBB Emmebonacina

Italian furniture company; located Meda.

History c. early 1950s, BBB Emmebonacina was founded to produce modern furniture; was one of the first to conduct research on the use of newly developed mid-century materials and advanced technologies in the production of seating and furnishings; also explored the use of plastics (including polyurethane) in tandem with accomplished designers, who have included Achille Castignioni, Paolo Ferrari, De Pas/D'Urbino/Lomazzi, Italo Lupi, Carlo Santi, Giorgi Decursu, Laura Griziotti, Gianmarco Blini, Thomas Mittermair, and Massimo Colombo.
Bibliography www.bbbemmebonacina.com.

BBPR

Italian architectural, town planning, and design group.

History 1932, BBPR was founded by Gianluigi Banfi (1910–1945), Lodovico Barbiano di Belgiojoso (1909–), Enrico Peressutti (1908–1976), and Ernesto N. Rogers (1909–1969). The firm began its activities in town planning (for the Valle d'Aosta 1936–37 and tourist plan for Isola d'Elba 1936), architecture (1933 Villa Morpurgo in Opicina-Trieste and 1934 Ferrario house in Milan), and interior design (1933 [5th] Triennale pavilion, 1933 Marietti apartment, 1936 [6th] Triennale conference hall). It was a member of Congrès Internationaux d'Architecture Moderne (CIAM) from 1935. During World War II, Rogers was interned in Switzerland, teaching architecture (Alberto Rosselli a student of his); Banfi died in the Mauthausen concentration camp. BBPR, retaining its full name, continued after the war. 1955–63, Belgiojoso taught, Istituto di Architettura, Venice. 1950–62, Peressutti taught design in England and the US. Rogers taught, Facoltà di Architettura, Politecnico, Milan; 1946–47, Peressutti was co-editor (with Zanuso) of *Domus*; 1954–65, editor of journal *Casabella*; and a writer. The group continued, taking in Aberico Bardiano as a member. Criticized after World War II for its rejection of the modern movement, the group had always shown an awareness of historicist elements. Its other architecture included 1937–38 Sanatorium in Legnano and 1940 Monastery of San Simpliciano (with E. Radice Rossati), 1946 memorial to concentration camp victims (Belgiojoso, Peressutti, and Rogers), 1950 INA-Casa quarter (with Franco Albini and Gianni Albricci) in the Cesate area, 1950–51 (completed 1958) Torre Velasca skyscraper, 1954–56 restoration and layout of the museums of the Castello Sforzesco, 1954–58 Torre Velasca, 1958–59 Immobiliare Cagisa office building in the Piazza Meda, and 1969 offices of Chase Manhattan Bank, all in Milan. Its design work included 1950 electric clock by Solaroli, 1955 TV set by CGE Electric, 1956 Spazio and 1960 Arco metal office-furniture systems by Olivetti, and 1954–64 furniture by Arflex, including the 1954 Elettra suite. Belgiojoso, Peressutti, and Rogers designed glassware by Venini, including lighting c. 1955.
Exhibitions/citations Work subject of 1982 *BBPR a Milano* exhibition, Milan. 1954 (Elettra seating by Arflex) and 1962 (Spazio office furniture by Olivetti) Premio Compasso d'Oro.
Bibliography Enzo Pacù, 'Continuità e coerenze dei BBPR,' *Zodiac*, no. 4, 1959: 82–115. E. Bonfanti and M. Porta, *Città, museo e architettura: il gruppo BBPR nella cultura architettonica italiana 1932–1970*, Florence: Vallecchi, 1973. Alfonso Grassi and Anty Pansera, *Atlante del design italiano 1940/1980*, Milan: Fabbri, 1980. Andrea Branzi and Michele De Lucchi, *Design italiano degli anni '50*, Milan: Ricerche Design, 1985. Antonio Piva (ed.), *BBPR a Milano*, Milan: Electa 1982. Cat., *Lumière je pense à vous*, Paris: Centre Georges Pompidou, 1985.
> See Peressutti, Enrico.

Bd Ediciones de Diseño

Spanish furniture and furnishings manufacturer; located Barcelona.

History 1972, Studio PER members Óscar Tusquet Blanca, Lluís Clotet, Pep Bonet, Cristian Cirici, Xavier Carulla, and Mireia Riera with others founded Bd Ediciones de Diseño. The firm produced many of Tusquets's furniture and product designs and those of others considered too risky by other Spanish manufacturers at the time. The initials 'Bd' represent *Bocaccio Design*, referring to entertainment tycoon and host of the 'gauche divine' Oriol Regás, the firm's chief banker, whose various companies were named 'Bocaccio.' Bd Ediciones de Diseño began as a retail sales showroom for furniture designed by Studio PER members and for reproductions of pieces by Alvar Aalto, Antoni Gaudí, Eileen Gray, Josef Hoffmann, Josep M. Jujol, Adolf Loos, Charles Rennie Mackintosh, and Giuseppe Terragni. Lectures and exhibitions were organized in the retail space and a public library set up to foster contemporary design in Barcelona. The firm is housed in Lluís Domènech i Montaner's 1898 Casa Thomas. Its own products, edited by Bd rather than self manufactured, have included 1973 Florero Shiva pink-penis ceramic vase by Ettore Sottsass, 1976/1992 Carrito Versátil carts (with Clotet) and 1985/1989 Bib Luz Libro book-shaped table lamp by Tusquets Blanca, 1981/1983 Taburete Dúplex

stool by Javier Mariscal (with Pepe Cortés), 1983 Araña lamp by Cortés and Mariscal, 1986 Lámpara TMC/TMC lamp (1956 design) by Miguel Milá, 1987 Sillón Coqueta chair by Pete Sans, and, more recently, 1993 Ebro and Pólux hanging lamps by Clotet, 1996 Luz Skyline lamp by Manuel Romagosa, and 2000 Serie Axes group of stantion, umbrella stand, lectern by Ferran Estela (second years indicating reintroduction dates). The firm remains active.
Citations Numerous awards, including 1989 National Design Prize, Spain; 1990 European Community Design Prize.
Bibliography Guy Julier, *New Spanish Design*, New York: Rizzoli, 1991.

Beam, J. Wade (1944–)
American designer.

Training School of Architecture, Clemson University, Clemson, S.C.
Biography Beam held key positions in sales and marketing, product research and development, and manufacturing for firms including Dunbar, Wrightline, and OSI; from 1973, was active in his own furniture-design and manufacturing firm in conjunction with an architecture and interior-design practice; became director of sales and marketing, Brueton Industries; designed the Bearing console, Reflections mirror, Fushion table, and 1991 Cristal table produced by Brueton.
Citations Three International Product Design awards, American Society of Interior Designers (ASID); two Roscoe Awards, Resources Council, Inc.; silver Production Design award, Institute of Business Designers (IBD); Product Design award, Corporate Design and Realty.

Beaton, Cecil Walter Hardy (1904–1980)
British photographer, interior designer, and stage designer.

Training From 1922, Cambridge University.
Biography To 1945, the house Beaton occupied at Ashcombe, Wiltshire, near friend Edith Olivier, was decorated with limited funds using ornate baroque furniture; the walls of the 'Circus Bedroom' were painted by visiting artist friends, including Rex Whistler and Oliver Messel, in a kind of surrealistic overstatement. He published *The Book of Beauty* (1930) and his memoirs in *Scrapbook* (1937); most of 1930s, worked in France and the US as photographer for Condé Nast, publishers of *Vogue* and *Vanity Fair*; 1939–45, was a war photographer for the British Ministry of Information, working in Africa and India. 1950s, Beaton's house in Broadchalke, Wiltshire, was decorated by Felix Harbord, who used rich and grand furnishings, including wine velvet and leopard skin. In his later years, Beaton rented for a short time each year a suite at the St. Regis Hotel, New York, which he decorated with *Vogue's* publishing the results. He designed the sets and costumes for films *Gigi* (1959) and *My Fair Lady* (1965), winning Academy awards. An active set designer, he was assisted from late 1940s by Martin Battersby and others.
Citations 1957, appointed Commander of the British Empire; 1960, elected Chevalier of Légion d'Honneur, France.
Bibliography Cat., *Thirties: British Art and Design Before the War*, London: Arts Council of Great Britain/Hayward Gallery, 1979. Hugo Vickers, *Cecil Beaton: A Biography*, New York: Donald I. Fine, 1987. Hugo Vickers, *Cecil Beaton: The Authorized Biography*, London: Weidenfeld & Nicolson, 1985. Stephen Calloway, *Twentieth-Century Decoration*, New York: Rizzoli, 1988.

Beaurin, Vincent (1960–)
French furniture designer; born Vervins.

Training To 1979, École Boulle, Paris.
Biography Beaurin worked with Shiro Kuramata on the Ego collection; is active as an interior designer, including of the Homme Bleu restaurant, Paris, and a product designer. His unusual Noli Me Tangere stool, which called on the use of new materials, was sponsored by VIA (French furniture association).
Exhibitions/citations Work shown at Comme des Garçons (sponsored by VIA), Tokyo, and Artists Space, New York. 1979, first prize, Société d'Encouragement aux Métiers d'Art (SEMA), Paris.
Bibliography Cat., Sophie Tasma Anargyros et al., *L'école française: les créateurs de meubles du 20ème siècle*, Paris: Industries Françaises de l'Ameublement, 2000.

beautiful room, the
> See Krásná Jizba Družstevní Práce.

Beaux-Arts
Style of architecture.

History The Beaux-Arts style was an architecture on a grand scale. The name is derived from the École Nationale des Beaux-Arts, Paris, where historical and eclectic ideas were taught during the 19th century and into the 20th century and whose students went on to spread the style widely and prolifically. The influence of Beaux-Arts design can be seen through Eastern and Western Europe and was expressed in America particularly during the early 19th century. Even though many had studied at the Paris school (still extant), exponents of the modern movement came to consider it decadent and retrograde.

Becchi, Alessandro (1946–)
Italian architect and designer; born and active Florence.

Training To 1966, Istituto Statale d'Arte, Florence.
Biography Active professionally from 1969, Becchi founded Metaform industrial-design studio in Florence; collaborated with Graziano Giovannetti with some furniture produced by Giovannetti Collezioni; executed a series of sofas in 1970s, restating the standard convertible sofa; designed the frameless, soft-pad 1971 Anfibio sofabed by his own firm. Clients have included Emerson, B&B Italia, Art Museum in Jerusalem, Arflex, Universities of Illinois and of Texas.

Alessandro Becchi. Anfibio convertible couch. 1971. Leather-covered polyurethane, closed 25 1/2 x 73 x 38 1/2" (64.8 x 185.4 x 97.8 cm). Mfr.: Giovannetti, Italy. Gift of the mfr. and ICF, Inc. MoMA.

Exhibitions/citations Participated in 1975 *Desegno Italiano +* exhibition, São Paulo. 1979 Premio Compasso d'Oro (Anfibio sofabed).
Bibliography 'The Anfibio Collection,' *Industrial Design*, vol. 19, Apr. 1972: 28–29. *ADI Annual 1976*, Milan: Associazione per il Disegno Industriale, 1976. *Moderne Klassiker, Möbel, die Geschichte machen*, Hamburg: Gruner + Jahr, 1982: 119. Cat., Kathryn B. Hiesinger and George H. Marcus III (eds.), *Design Since 1945*, Philadelphia: Philadelphia Museum of Art, 1983. Cat., Hans Wichmann (ed.), *Italien Design 1945 bis heute*, Munich: Die Neue Sammlung, 1988.

Bécheau, Vincent (1955–); Marie-Laure Bourgeois (1955–)

French design collaborators; active Saint-Avit. Bécheau: born Périgueux. Bourgeois: born Paris.

Training Bourgeois: architecture, Unité Pédogogique (UP6), Paris, 1981.
Biographies The designers are known for their manipulation of new material (known as 'third type') in furniture design and call on sophisticated combinations of woods with kitsch, colorful corrugated plastic sheets, and high-tech substances with traditional materials. 1982, two Bécheau/Bourgeois prototypes were sponsored for production by VIA (French furniture association). 1984, they designed the office of the Conseiller Artistique of Bordeaux; had a permanent installation realized at Galerie Eric Fabre, Paris; opened a design office in Lille. 1986, they designed offices of the ADDC in Périgueux; 1987, reception hall of Font de Gaume les Elysées in Paris; and reception hall of FRAC Aquitaine in Dax.
Exhibitions Work first shown at Galerie Ocheb et Nitro, Bordeaux, 1983, and in exhibitions, including French Cultural Center, Belgrade, 1983; Musée des Arts Décoratifs, Bordeaux, 1983; École des Beaux-Arts, Dunkerque, 1985. Work subject of exhibitions at Galerie Néotù, Paris; *Made in France*, Nantes and Bordeaux, and Galerie Brice d'Antras, Berlin, 1986; Galerie BDX, Bordeaux, 1988. Shiro Kuramata included the designers' work in his 1988 *In-Spiration* lighting exhibition for Yamagiwa, Tokyo. 1983, winners, *Progressive Architecture* magazine competition, Chicago; 1986 Folies Siffait competition, Nantes.
Bibliography Christian Schlater, *Les années 80*, Paris: Flammarion, 1983. Sophie Anargyros, *Intérieurs 80*, Paris: Regard, 1983. *SD* journal, Tokyo, 1983. Sophie Anargyros, *Le style des années 80: architecture, décorations, design*, Paris: Rivages, 1986. *Wohnen von Sinnen*, Cologne: Dumont, 1986. Brochure, Christine Colin, *Vincent Bécheau, Marie-Laure Bourgeois, 1982 mobilier 1987*, 1987.

Bedin, Martine (1957–)

French designer; born Bordeaux.

Training From 1974, architecture, Unité Pédogogique (UP6), Paris; 1978, in Florence.
Biography 1978, she met Adolfo Natalini in Italy and worked with the Superstudio group, Florence; discovered Radical Architecture; 1979, built a small house for 1979 (16th) Triennale di Milano; 1980, met Ettore Sottsass and, 1981, joined a group of designers, who, instigated by Sottsass, founded the Memphis group; to 1988 through Memphis, designed a number of lighting fixtures, including 1981 Super multiple-lights on wheels, 1981 Splendid lamp, 1982 Lodge bookcase, 1984 Charleston, 1985 Olympia lamp, 1985 Daisy, and also 1985 Cucumber ceramic vase, 1986 Paris chair, and 1987 Charlotte sideboard. Other clients have included Veha (handbags and cases), Sedap (lighting), Jacob Delafon (faucets), Sasaki (glassware and metalwork), Algorithme (metalwork), Acme (jewelry), Martell (handbags), Bd Ediciones de Diseño (carpet), Koch & Lowy (clocks), Hélène Darroze restaurant in Paris (logo), Negalit (lighting), buses for city of Nîmes, Vuitton (luggage), others. 1980–81, Bedin was a correspondent for French journal *Architecture interieur crée*; 1982, set up her own studio in Milan; from 1983, taught, École Camondo, Paris; 1986, was artistic director of domestic-interiors department of Daniel Hechter; 1990, designed layout of bookstore of Caisse Nationale des Monuments Historiques (Hôtel de Sully), Paris; 1991 with Piotr Serakowski and Mathilde Brétillot, founded La Manufacture Familiale, near Bordeaux, to produce furniture, mostly in wood, including 1995 lamps, low table, wardrobe, pedestal. She taught, École des Beaux-Arts, Bordeaux; returned to Milan to work in the studio of Michele De Lucchi; 2000, founded the association Les Escarpolettes Réinventées.
Exhibitions/citations Memphis work shown with the group at its 1981 (1st) exhibition, Salone del Mobile, Milan. Work included in numerous subsequent venues such as 2001–02 *Memphis Remembered*, Design Museum, London. Subject of 2003 exhibition, Bordeaux (catalog below). Award, 1983 office-lighting competition (for Gédéon lamp), Ministère de la Culture, France; 1991 Carte Blanche production support, VIA (French furniture association), 1993. named Chevalier de l'Ordre des Arts et des Lettres, Ministère de la Culture et Francophonie.
Bibliography Cat., *Lumière je pense à vous*, Paris: Centre Georges Pompidou, 1985. 'Martine Bedin,' *Intramuros*, no. 8, 1986. Cat., *Design français 1960–1990: trois décennies*, Paris: APCI/Centre Georges Pompidou, 1988. Cat., Design Center Stuttgart, *Women in Design: Careers and Life Histories Since 1900*, Stuttgart: Haus der Wirtschaft, 1989. François Mathey, *Au bonheur des formes, le design français 1945 à 1992*, Paris: Regard, 1992. Cat., *Martine Bedin: prova d'autore, meubles et objets 1981-2003*, Bordeaux: Musée des Arts Décoratifs de Bordeaux, France, 2003.

Alexander Begge. Stacking chair (no. 2004/2005). 1976. Plastic, 30 3/8 x 20 7/8 x 20 1/2" (77.2 x 53 x 52 cm). Mfr.: Casala Werke, Germany. Courtesy Quittenbaum Kunstauktionen, Munich.

Beef

French designers.

History Beef is a design studio established by Simon Clark (1972–) and Sébastien Dragon (1970–), who initially worked in the studio of Philippe Starck for less than a year. Clark says: 'In our profession, breaking the rules is the driving force behind innovation, which is more than image, font or composition. Innovation is the way in which such elements question conformity and validity.' As graphic designers, they designed the 1999 exhibition catalog of Jasper Morrison/Marc Newson/Michael Young, Ireland; and for products, collaborate with Adrien Haas.
Bibliography Pascale Cassgnau and Christophe Pillet, *Beef, Brétillot/Valette, Matali Crasset, Patrick Jouin, Jean-Marie Massaud: petits enfants de Starck?*, Paris: Dis Voir, 2000.

Beese, Hedda (1944–)

German product designer; born Guhrau; active London.

Training 1965–68, Pädagogische Hochschule, Berlin; 1973–76, Central School of Arts and Crafts, London.
Biography 1968, she settled in London; 1976, became active in industrial design; 1976–87, was joint manager of design studio Moggridge Associates, London; from 1976, member of the board of directors, Design Developments, London; returned to Germany and, 1987, set up Moggridge's Design Drei division in Hanover. She has lectured at Central School of Arts and Crafts and Royal College of Art, both London; Newcastle Polytechnic; and DZ Design Center,

Bilboa, 1987. She became a member, 1983, of Chartered Society of Designers and Fellow of Royal Society of Arts, London, and, 1988, of Verband Deutscher Industrie-Designer. Designs include 1985 microwave by Hoover, 1985 SL 48 solar lantern by BP Solar International, 1986 Venturer telephone by Alcatel Bell, and 1987 laboratory filter by Anotec Separations.
Citations 1982 Design Council award (STC wide-area radiopager), London; 1988 Design Innovation award (SL 48 solar lantern), Haus Industrieform, Essen, Germany; Best of Category Consumer Products, 1988 citation, Annual Design Review, *I.D.* magazine; 1993 (phone by Bosse Telekomsysteme) and three 1997 citations (telephones by Deutsche Telekom), Industrie Forum Design (iF), Hanover.
Bibliography Liz McQuiston, *Women in Design: A Contemporary View*, New York: Rizzoli, 1988: 10. Cat., Design Center Stuttgart, *Women in Design: Careers and Life Histories Since 1900*, Stuttgart: Haus der Wirtschaft, 1989: 72–77. Albrecht Bangert and Karl Michael Armer, *80s Style: Designs of the Decade*, New York: Abbeville, 1990.

Beese, Lotte (1903–1968)
> See Stam, 'Mart.'

Begeer
Dutch silversmiths; located Utrecht.

History 1868, C.J. Begeer founded the eponymous firm; c. 1885, the firm's first modern designs began to appear, for which Cornelis L.J. Begeer, who joined the family firm 1888, was responsible. He left 1904 to set up his own workshop, Stichtsche Zilverfabriek. At the turn of the century, C.J. Begeer sold silver from the Wolfers factory in Brussels, which made both modern and classic patterns. Cornelis's half-brother Carel J.A. Begeer set up his own workshop in the family firm's premises and produced the silver designs of Jan Eisenloeffel. The most important exponent of the geometrical style in the Netherlands, he signed a contract with Begeer 1904 to put his designs into production. Even though his wares attracted much attention at exhibitions they were not commercially successful. A.F. Gips designed for the firm. The silver H.P. Berlage designed for the Kröller-Müllers was made by Begeer. 1919, the firm merged with former competitor J.M. van Kempen and jeweler J. Vos, becoming Van Kempen, Begeer en Vos. The merger greatly diminished artistic development, until the new company was reorganized 1925 under the name Zilverfabriek Voorschoten with Begeer as director. He met Christa Ehrlich at the 1927 *Europäisches Kunstgewerbe* exhibition, Leipzig, where she supervised the Austrian pavilion designed by Josef Hoffmann. Begeer persuaded Ehrlich to come to the Netherlands; there she produced outstanding designs in a modern style.
Bibliography Cat., *Mensen en zilver: Bijna twee eeuwen werken voor Van Kempen en Begeer, 1975–1976*, Rotterdam: Museum Boymans-van Beuningen, c. 1975. Annelies Krekel-Aalberse, *Art Nouveau and Art Déco Silver*, New York: Abrams, 1989.
> See Van Kempen en Begeer.

Begeer, Carel J.A. (1883–1956)
Dutch silversmith; active Utrecht.

Training In Hanau.
Biography 1904, Carel Begeer set up his own workshop on the premises of the family firm, C.J. Begeer, producing the silver designs of Jan Eisenloeffel and other leading artists. Also 1904, he took over the artistic direction of the firm from his half-brother Cornelis L.J. Begeer, who left the firm to set up his own workshop. Most of the wares of Carel were stamped with his own and the factory's mark. Begeer taught a drawing class, where Gerrit Rietveld rendered some medal designs. While Carel Begeer was at the firm, it sold silver by Georg Jensen, Josef Hoffmann, and Adolf von Mayrhofer, among others. Begeer, also a silversmith, experimented on his own. Influenced by German silversmiths such as Ernst Riegel, Begeer's work called on less and less decoration. 1919, the merger of competitor van Kempen and C.J. Begeer with the jeweler J. Vos further dampened artistic development. Carel became director of the merged and reorganized firms; 1925, renamed Zilverfabriek Voorschoten.
Bibliography Carl J.A. Beeger, *Inteiding ete de Geschiedenis der Nederlandische Edelsmeedkunst*, 1919. Cat., *Industry and Design in the Netherlands, 1850–1950*, Amsterdam: Stedelijk Museum, 1985. Annelies Krekel-Aalberse, *Art Nouveau and Art Déco Silver*, New York: Abrams, 1989.

Begeer, Cornelis L.J. (1868–)
Dutch silversmith; active Utrecht.

Training Königliche Preussische Zeichenakademie, Hanau.
Biography Cornelis Begeer was largely responsible for the appearance of the first modern designs at C.J. Begeer, which he had joined 1888. He visited 1893 *World's Columbian Exposition*, Chicago; returned to the Netherlands with new ideas and executed designs inspired by nature, some of which were scarcely distinguishable from those of the Wolfers firm of Brussels, whose wares his family firm C.J. Begeer sold. 1904, he left to set up his own workshop Stichtsche Zilverfabriek, producing mostly smaller objects. Half-brother Carel J.A. Begeer succeeded him as artistic director at C.J. Begeer.
Exhibitions Work included in 1900 *Exposition Universelle*, Paris.
Bibliography Cat., *Industry and Design in the Netherlands, 1850–1950*, Amsterdam: Stedelijk Museum, 1985. Annelies Krekel-Aalberse, *Art Nouveau and Art Déco Silver*, New York: Abrams, 1989.

Begge, Alexander (1941–)
German designer; born Lodz.

Training Carpentry, 1962–67, interior architecture, Werkkunstschule, Düsseldorf; 1977–79, ceramics studio, Höhr-Grenzhausen.
Biography 1969–74, Begge worked for Casala Werke in Lauenau; c. 1979, established own workshop for architectural ceramics; has become best known for his seating by Casala, including the one-piece molded-plastic 1970 Casalino, 1970 Casalino I (child's chair), and 1976 2004/2005 model.
Bibliography Cat., *1960–73, L'Utopie du Tout Plastique*, Brussels: Fondation pour l'Architecure, 1994: 65. Auction cat., *Modernes Design Kunsthandwerk nach 1945*, Munich: Quittenbaum, 1 June 2002: 23.

Behár, Yves (1967–)
Swiss designer; born Lausanne.

Training 1988–91, Art Center College of Design Europe, Montreux, Switzerland, and Art Center College of Design, Pasadena, California
Biography Behár worked at frogdesign and Lunar Design, both Cal.; 1999, established fuseproject in San Francisco; has developed technology and designs for clothing, cosmetics, sports, furniture, packaging, and environments for clients, including Birkenstock, MINI, Nike, Nissan, Peoplepc, Philou, Puig, Herman Miller, Hewlett-Packard, Microsoft, and Alcatel. From 1995, he taught, Art Center College of Design, Pasadena.
Exhibitions/citations Work included in 2000 National Design Triennial and 2002 *Skin: Surface, Substance, and Design*, Cooper-Hewitt National Design Museum, New York. Eleven IDSA/*Business Week* awards; three Industrial Designers' Society of America (IDSA) awards; eleven Good Design awards, Chicago Athenaeum; eight citations and two Best of Category, Annual Design Review, *I.D.* magazine; 1996 Industrie Forum Design (iF), Hanover; 1996 Premio SMAU Industrial Design, Salone della Machina e Attrezzature per l'Uffizio, Milan; 2001, fuseproject ranked one of top-ten international design firms by *Business Week* magazine.

Yves Béhar. Lush Lily tray (one in a series). c. 1998. Cast aluminum, 1 1/8 x d. 5 1/2 x l. 13" (3 x 14 x 33 cm). Mfr.: Lush Lily, US.

Bibliography Wang Hanbai, *Design Focus: Yves Behár*, Beijing: China Youth, 2001. Cat., Ellen Lupton et al., *Skin: Surface, Substance, and Design*, New York: Princeton Architectural Press, 2001. www.fuseproject.com.
> See Lunar Design.

Behrens, Peter (1868–1940)

German graphic artist, architect, and designer; born Hamburg.

Training 1886–88, Gewerbeschule, Hamburg; 1888–91, painting, Kunstschule, Karlsruhe, and under various painters.
Biography 1893, Behrens joined the avant-garde group associated with the Münchner Sezession; 1896, traveled in Italy; 1898, studied industrial mass production; 1897, following the lead of the Wiener Werkstätte, with Hermann Obrist, Bruno Paul, Bernhard Pankok, and Richard Riemerschmid, founded Vereinigte Werkstätten für Kunst im Handwerk (united workshops for art in hand-work), aiming to sell everyday objects designed by modern artists. Inspired by Japanese woodcut prints, he worked at the Werkstätten as a painter and graphic designer. Early Jugendstil designs were replaced by a Cubist and Rationalist style that can be seen in his designs for the house in the Darmstadt artists' colony of 1901 and for the pavilion of decorative arts at 1902 *Esposizione Internazionale d'Arte Decorativa Moderna*, Turin. 1899, Grand Duke Louis IV of Hesse-Darmstadt had invited Behrens to design and direct the production of goods at the art colony of Darmstadt. His first building was his 1901 house at Darmstadt, where he had an opportunity to employ his abilities as architect and designer of furniture, glass, ceramics, silver, and jewelry; in Darmstadt, designed silver cutlery in the Wiener Sezession style made by M.J. Rückert and a desk set by Martin Mayer. Ornamentation disappeared on his silverwork, especially that produced by Franz Bahner, Düsseldorf. Other silverwares were made by Bruckmann und Söhne, Heilbronn. Leaving the artists' colony, he lived in Düsseldorf, where he was director of the Kunstgewerbeschule 1903–07; (with Hermann Muthesius and others) founded the Deutscher Werkbund (German work association). From 1907 on the invitation of Walter Rathenau, the managing director of Allgemeine Elektrizitäts Gesellschaft (AEG), Behrens began to work in Berlin on the corporate identity of the giant German industrial combine, for which he created the architecture, graphics, kettles, electric fans, and clocks. This was a landmark event due to its being the first time any firm, particularly a large one, had hired and developed an alliance with an artist to advise on all facets of industrial design. Behrens also designed the seminal 1908–09 AEG's Turbinenfabrik (turbine factory) and several other buildings for AEG. Some porcelain designs were produced by Manufaktur Mehlem Gebrüder Bauscher, Weiden, Bonn, and glass designs by Rheinische Glashütten, Köln-Ehrenfeld. For a time in 1910, Le Corbusier (1910–11), Gropius (1907–10), and Mies van der Rohe (1908–11) were working side by side in Behrens's office. 1910s, Behrens designed linoleum patterns for Delmenhorster Linoleum Fabrik, an early member of the Werkbund; from 1922, was director of both schools of architecture at Akademie der bildenden Künste, Vienna, and, from 1936, Preussische Akademie der Künste, Berlin; 1923–25, designed the house New Ways, Northampton, UK; 1932, collaborated with Ferdinand Wilm and others to form Gesellschaft für Goldschmiedekunst (society for goldsmiths' work). Behrens played a significant role in Jugenstil's transition to Industrial classicism and, thus, the development of German modernism. Oddly, at the end of his career, he returned to historicist forms. He died in Berlin.
Work Architecture included 1901 Behrens's own house (with every component, from the structure to the cutlery), Darmstadt; 1905–07 Obenauer House, Saarbrücken; 1908–10 Cuno and Schroeder houses, Eppenhausen, near Hagen; 1908–09 turbine factory, 1910 high-tension plant, and 1910–11 small-motors factory of AEG, Berlin; 1910–11 district of apartments for AEG workers, Henningsdorf, near Berlin; 1911–12 Mannesmann offices, Düsseldorf; 1911–12 German Embassy, St. Petersburg; 1911–20 offices of Continental Rubber, Hanover; 1920–25 technical administration building, Hoechst Dyeworks, Frankfurt; 1920–25 IG Farben office, Frankfurt.
Exhibitions 1901 Behrens's own house was built for the first exhibition at Darmstadt. Participated in 1910 *Exposition Universelle et Internationale*, Brussels. Work subject of 1980 exhibition, Nationalmuseum, Nürnberg; 1990, Fachbereich Architektur and Fachbereich Design of the Fachhochschule, Düsseldorf; and 1992, Oldenberger Kunstvereins, Oldenburg.
Bibliography Fritz Hoeber, *Peter Behrens*, Munich, 1913. Paul Joseph Cremers, *Peter Behrens, Sein Werk von 1909 bis zur Gegenwart*, Essen, 1928. K.M. Grimme, *Peter Behrens und seine Wiener akademische Meisterschule*, Vienna, 1930. *Peter Behrens (1868–1940)*, Pfalzgalerie Kaiserslautern, 1966–67. Hans-Joachim Kadatz, *Peter Behrens: Architekt, Maler, Grafiker und Formgestalter, 1868–1940*, Leipzig: E.A. Seemann, 1977. Tilman Buddensieg et al., *Industriekultur, Peter Behrens und die AEG, 1907–1914*, Cambridge, Mass.: MIT, 1979. Stanford Anderson, 'Modern Architecture and Industry: Peter Behrens, the AEG, and Industrial Design,' *Oppositions*, no. 21, Summer 1980: 78–93. Cat., *Peter Behrens und Nürnberg*, Nuremberg: Germanisches Nationalmuseum, 1980. Alan Windsor, *Peter Behrens, Architect and Designer, 1869–1940*, London, 1981. Annelies Krekel-Aalberse, *Art Nouveau and Art Déco Silver*, New York: Abrams, 1989. Kurt Asche, *Peter Behrens und die Oldenburger Ausstellung 1905: Entwürfe, Bauten, Gebrauchsgraphik*, Berlin: Mann, 1992. Stanford Anderson, *Peter Behrens and a New Architecture for the Twentieth Century*, Cambridge, Mass.: MIT, 2002. Paola Antonelli (ed.), *Objects of Design: The Museum of Modern Art*, New York: The Museum of Modern Art, 2003: 220–21.

Peter Behrens. Electric Kettle. 1909. Nickel-plated brass and rattan, 9 x 8 3/4 x 6 1/4" (22.9 x 22.2 x 15.9 cm). Mfr.: Allgemeine Elektrizitäts Gesellschaft (AEG), Germany. Gift of Manfred Ludewig. MoMA.

Bel Geddes, Norman
> See Geddes, Norman Bel.

Belgiojoso, Lodovico Barbiano di (1909–)

Italian designer; born and active Milan.

Training Politecnico, Milan.
Biography 1928, Belgiojoso joined the Fascist Party; 1932, began his professional career with the founding of the architecture design firm BBPR, Milan; 1955–63, taught, Istituto Universitario di Architettura, Venice, and, from 1963, Politecnico, Milan; with others at BBPR, was active as an architect and designed 1956 Spazio and 1960 Arco metal office-furniture systems by Olivetti, as well as other products.
Bibliography Alfonso Grassi and Anty Pansera, *Atlante del design italiano 1940/1980*, Milan: Fabbri, 1980. Andrea Branzi and Michele De Lucchi, *Design italiano degli Anni '50*, Milan: Ricerche Design, 1985. Vittorio Magnago Lampugnani, *Encyclopedia of 20th-Century Architecture*, New York: Abrams, 1986: 37–38, 41. Richard A. Etlin, *Modernism in Italian Architecture, 1890–1940*, Cambridge, Mass.: MIT, 1991: 641.
> See BBPR.

Bell, Cressida (1958–)

British textile designer; born Newcastle-upon-Tyne; active London; granddaughter of Vanessa Bell.

Training To 1984, fashion design, St. Martin's School of Art, London, and textile design, Royal College of Art, London.
Biography 1984, Bell set up her own studio, designing and hand-printing textiles; produced dress and furnishing fabrics; has designed interiors and decorated furniture; became a member, Independent Designers Federation, London.

Bibliography Albrecht Bangert and Karl Michael Armer, *80s Style: Designs of the Decade*, New York: Abbeville, 1990.

Bell, Vanessa (b. Vanessa Stephen 1879–1961)

British painter, muralist, and interior designer; sister of Virginia Woolf.

Training 1901–04, Royal Academy Painting School, London, and Slade School of Art, London.
Biography 1913–19 with Clive Grant, she was a co-director of Roger Fry's Omega Workshops, where she painted furniture and screens and executed interior schemes, rugs, tableware, and printed textiles in a painterly style; with Duncan Grant of Omega Workshops, executed interior-decoration schemes for others and for her house Charleston, near Firle, Sussex; designed embroideries executed by herself, Mary Hogarth, and Grant's mother Bartle Grant. 1920s and 1930s, Bell and Grant realized commissions, including 1926 decorations of the Bell house, London; Mrs. St. John Hutchinson's house, London; and houses of Lady Dorothy Wellesley and Kenneth Clark. She lived with Grant at Charleston, where John Maynard Keynes wrote *The Economic Consequences of the Peace*. Bell and Grant also designed fabrics screened onto cotton, linen, and a satin-finished cotton-rayon. 1932, Bell designed printed fabrics by Allan Walton; 1933–34, decorated ceramic tableware by E. Brain; book covers for Hogarth Press; and, 1934, tableware by A.J. Wilkinson, under Clarice Cliff's direction. 1940–43, Bell painted murals for Berwick Church, Sussex; became a member, AIA.
Exhibitions Her paintings were included in 1912 second Post-Impressionist exhibition, London, and subject of 1937 exhibition, Lefevre Galleries, London; numerous others.
Bibliography Cat., *Thirties: British Art and Design Before the War*, London: Arts Council of Great Britain/Hayward Gallery, 1979. *British Art and Design, 1900–1960*, London: Victoria and Albert Museum, 1983. Frances Spalding, *Vanessa Bell*, London: Weidenfeld & Nicolson, 1983. Richard Shone, *Bloomsbury Portraits: Vanessa Bell, Duncan Grant, and Their Circle*, London: Phaidon, 1993. Sales cat., *The Decorations and Designs of Duncan Grant and Vanessa Bell*, London: Bloomsbury Workshop, 2001.

Bellefroid, Guillaume Marie Edmond (1893–1971)

Dutch designer; born Maastricht.

Training From 1907, painting, Zondagsschool voor Decoratieve Kunsten, Maastricht; 1910–12, painting, École Saint Luc.
Biography Due to financial problems, G.M.E. Bellefroid returned to Masstricht in 1912 and assumed an office job; 1920s, developed an interest in ceramics; 1929–46, designed crystal and ceramics at De Sphinx, including pottery models and decoration, and also c. 1939 Stramino drinking glass set by Kristalunie. He became an aesthetic consultant and designer to Mosa porcelain factory of Maastricht, where he realized a number of services and wares, including 1954 Noblesse porcelain coffee set; was also known to have painted, based on his early training. He died in Maastricht.
Exhibitions Work included 2002–03 *From Cuypers to Dibbets: 100 Years of Art in Limburg*, Bonnefanten Museum, Maastricht.
> See De Sphinx.

Bellery-Desfontaines, Henri (1867–1909)

French furniture designer; born Paris.

Biography An eclectic artist, Bellery-Desfontaines was an illustrator, decorator, and designer of rugs, fabrics, bank notes, graphics, and posters; showing a predilection for the Middle Ages, designed a church in Cruse (France) based on the principles of Eugène-Emmanuel Viollet-le-Duc. Toward the end of his career, he developed a simple approach to his furniture design that was solidly architectonic, in a style between Le Style 1900 and Art Déco.
Bibliography Pierre Kjellberg, *Art déco: les maîtres du mobilier, le décor des paquebots*, Paris: Amateur, 1986.

Belling, Charles (1884–1965)

British stove manufacturer; born Bodmin, Cornwall; active Enfield, Middlesex.

Training Apprenticeship in electrical engineering at Crompton & Co., Chelmsford.
Biography After his apprenticeship, Belling worked for Ediswan in Chelmsford; 1912, founded an electric-heater factory on Lancaster Road in Enfield; 1913, acquired additional space on Derby Road, Edmonton. The range of products included electric water heaters (1913), first domestic electric stove (1919), immersion heaters (1920). 1924, he opened a purpose-built factory; 1929, began producing the Baby Belling stove, as it was best known; early 1930s, was the first manufacturer in Britain of white vitreous-enamel electric stoves. 1992, the firm ceased trading but, subsequently, was transformed as Belling Appliances in South Yorkshire as a division of Glen Dimplex Cooking.
Bibliography *Issue 4*, London: Design Museum, Autumn 1990. www.belling.co.uk.

Bellini, Carlo (1960–)

Italian architect and designer; born Perugia; active Milan.

Training Architecture, Università degli Studi, Milan; engineering, Università degli Studi, Perugia.
Biography With Marco Ferreri, Bellini designed the widely published 1986 Eddy lamp by Luxo Italiana.
Citations Winner, 1984 Concorso di Design Regione Toscana.
Bibliography Albrecht Bangert and Karl Michael Armer, *80s Style: Designs of the Decade*, New York: Abbeville, 1990: 94, 227.

Bellini, Claudio (1963–)

Italian designer; son of Mario Bellini.

Training To 1990, architecture and industrial design, Politecnico, Milan.
Biography 1987–96, Claudio Bellini worked in architecture/design office Mario Bellini Associates, participating with his father on projects, including the new Milan fair, Tokyo Design Center, Villa Erba Conference Center in Cernobbio, Extra Dry office furniture by Marcatrè, Eclipse spotlight system by Erco, glass vase collection by Venini, and leather chairs by Cassina. In addition to products with Mario, work has included 1986 2000 ITI ceiling lamp by Artemide, 2000 DS-460 leather sofa collection by De Sede, and 2000 Op Lá sofa by Hans Kaufeld. 1997, founded Atelier Bellini to design for Vitra, Heller, Artemide, Fiat, Venini, Driade, Rosenthal, Guzzini, Fritz Hansen, and others.
Citations Including 2000 Red Dot award, Design Zentrum Nordrhein Westfalen, Essen; 2001 American Furniture award, *Home* magazine. With Mario Bellini: Best of Category, 2001 Annual Design Review, *I.D.* magazine; mentioned, 2001 Premio Compasso d'Oro; gold prize, 2001 G-Mark Good Design award, Japanese Industrial Design Promotion Organization (JIDPO). With John Bennett: 2000 Good Design award, Chicago Athenaeum; Editor's Choice, 2001 NeoCon, Chicago; 2001 citation, Premio Compasso d'Oro.
Bibliography Michele De Lucchi (ed.), *The International Design Yearbook*, London: Laurence King, 2001. Mel Byars, *Design in Steel*, London: Laurence King, 2002.

Bellini, Dario (1937–)

Italian industrial designer; brother of Mario Bellini.

Biography With Mario Bellini, Dario worked on a number of designs in the Bellini studio in Milan, including 1970 Totem hi-fi unit with detachable speakers by Brionvega (from 1972) and 1974 stereo tape deck by Nippon Gakki Co. for Yamaha.
Bibliography Jonathan M. Woodham, *Twentieth-Century Ornament*, New York: Rizzoli, 1990: 258–59. Mel Byars with Arlette Barré-Despond, *100 Designs/100 Years: A Celebration of the 20th Century*, Hove: RotoVision, 1999: 160–61.

Bellini, Mario (1935–)

Italian industrial designer; born and active Milan.

Training To 1959, architecture, Politecnico, Milan.
Biography 1959–62, Bellini worked for La Rinascente department store; 1962–65, was a professor of industrial design, Instituto Superiore del Disegno Industriale, Venice; 1962, opened his own office in Milan; became a prolific designer for B&B Italia, Cassina, Pedretti, C&B, Poltrona Frau, Poggi, Bras, Bacci, Marcatré, Rosenthal, and numerous others; a consultant designer to Olivetti from 1965, also to Yamaha, Brionvega, Irradio, Minerva, Ideal Standard, and Vitra; designed lighting by Artemide, Flos, and Erco, as well as office machinery, furniture, kitchen systems, modular office furniture, TVs and hi-fis, soda dispensers, automobiles by Renault. 1981, he established the magazine *Album*; 1982–83, was professor of industrial design, Hochschule für angewandte Kunst, Vienna;

Hans Bellmann. Einpunkt side chair. 1951–52. Chromium-plated steel tubing, painted bent plywood, and one screw, 31 7/8 x 16 3/4 x 15 3/8" (81 x 42.5 x 39 cm). Mfr.: Horgen-Glarus Möbelfabrik, Switzerland. Courtesy Quittenbaum Kunstauktionen, Munich.

1983–85, of new residential models, Domus Academy, Milan; 1986–91, was editor of *Domus*; became a member, Associazione per il Disegno Industriale (ADI), and, 1969–71, its vice-president. He has lectured at numerous European and American universities, and became a member, Scientific Council of the Design Division of 1983 (17th) Triennale di Milano. Work has included 1965 Chair 932 in leather-covered, injection-molded foam polyurethane, 1977–82 Il Colonnato marble table, 1977 Cab chair, 1982 Victoria sofa, 1982 La Loggia table, all by Cassina, 1972 Divisumma 18 calculator by Olivetti, 1974 cassette deck by Yamaha, 1970 Totem audio unit by Brionvega, 1978 Corium 1 leather-covered steel chair by Matteo Grassi, 1974 Area 50 lighting range, 1985–86 ETP 55 portable electric typewriters by Olivetti, 1985 Eclipse spotlight series by Erco, and 1985 bracelet by Cleto Munari. More recent work includes 1998 Bellini chair by Heller, 1999 Tavollini table/stool, 2000 Vol au Vent armchair (a softer version of the 1978 Cab), and 2000 kettle (with son Claudio) by Barazzoni for Cherry Terrace. 1996, with son Claudio, transferred product and furniture design to new firm Atelier Bellini; 2002, founded Bellini Studios.
Exhibitions/citations Work included in exhibitions in the US, Canada, Argentina, Brazil, England, France, Germany, Belgium, Italy, the Netherlands, and Russia, including 1972 *Italy: The New Domestic Landscape* (showing his Kar-a-Sutra mobile environment), The Museum of Modern Art, New York, where his work was the subject of a 1987 exhibition (catalog below). Awards include 28 citations (individually and with others) from 1962 of Premio Compasso d'Oro; gold medal, 1968 BIO industrial-design biennial, Ljubljana; 1973 Bolaffi design award; 1977 and 1979 Delta d'Oro, ADI/FAD (industrial-design/decorative-arts association), Spain; 1985 Made in Germany award; 1991, fellow of Bezalel award, Bezalel Academy of Art and Design, Israel; 1992 gold medal, Chartered Society of Designers, UK; 1992 Kasumigaseki prize (for Yokohama Business Park), Japan; 1992 elected Royal Designer for Industry, UK; 1992, first prize, Japanese Society of Commercial Space Designers; 1998 Pinnacle (for the Natuzzi Americas headquarters), US. 1998 Good Design Award, Chicago Athenaeum; 1999 award, IDSA/*Business Week* magazine; numerous others.
Bibliography 'Mario Bellini per la Olivetti,' *Domus*, no. 494, Jan. 1971: 32–42. *ADI Annual 1976*, Milan: Associazione per il Disegno Industriale, 1976. Cat., *Design Process Olivetti 1908–1978*, Los Angeles: Frederick S. Wight Art Gallery (University of California), 1979: 255–56. 'Talking with Four Men Who Are Shaping Italian Design,' *Industrial Design*, vol. 28, Sept.–Oct. 1981: 30–35. Cat., Kathryn B. Hiesinger and George H. Marcus III (eds.), *Design Since 1945*, Philadelphia: Philadelphia Museum of Art, 1983. Cat., Cara McCarty, *Mario Bellini Designer*, New York: Museum of Modern Art, 1987. Penny Sparke, *Design in Italy, 1870 to the Present*, New York: Abbeville, 1988. Ermanno Ranzani, *Mario Bellini: Architecture 1984–1995*, Basel: Birkhäuser, 1996. Paola Antonelli (ed.), *Objects of Design: The Museum of Modern Art*, New York: The Museum of Modern Art, 2003: 227–28, 237.

Bellmann, Hans (1911–1990)

Swiss designer; born Turgi.

Training 1927–30, construction drafting; 1931–33 under Ludwig Mies van der Rohe, Bauhaus, Dessau and Berlin.
Biography From 1934, Bellman worked in the office of Ludwig Mies van der Rohe; 1934–46, in various architecture offices in Zürich, Lugano, and Gebensdorf/Aargau; 1946, established his own studio in Zürich, designing furniture for the Wohnbedarf store, standardized furniture for social housing, 1948 tripod table and 1950 tripod demountable table imported by Knoll to the US and made in Switzerland, 1951–52 Einpunkt side chair by Horgen-Glarus, his best known and reentered into production today, and 1954 GA side chair in bentwood and tubular steel by Horgen Glarus, and furniture (1954–56 Sitwell side chair) by Strässle Söhne of Kirchberg. 1948–54, he taught, Kunstgewerbeschule, Zürich; 1958–62, interior architecture, Allgemeine Gewerbeschule, Basel; and, 1964–65 in the US, lectured at University of Washington, Seattle, and Harvard University, Cambridge, Mass.
Bibliography Josef Kremerskothen, *Möbel die Geschichte machen: Moderne Klassiker*, Hamburg: Gruner + Jahr, 1998. Lotte Schilder-Bär and Norbert Wild, *Designland Schweiz Gebrauchsgüterkultur im 20. Jahrhundert*, Zürich: Pro Helvetia, 2001.

Belotti, Giandomenico (1922–)

Italian architect and designer; born Bergamo; active Milan.

Training From 1938 under Marino Marini, sculpture, Monza; Liceo Artistico di Brera and Politecnico, both Milan; Instituto Universitario di Architettura, Venice.
Biography Belotti was profoundly influenced by architect Franco

Giandomenico Belotti. Spaghetti side chair. 1980. Steel frame and PVC winding, 32 3/4 x 15 7/8 x 20 1/8" (83.2 x 40.3 x 51.1 cm), seat h. 18 1/4" (46.4 cm). Mfr.: Alias, Italy. Gift of ICF, Inc. MoMA.

Niels Sylvester Bendtsen. Ribbon chair. 1975. Tubular steel, cotton canvas, and polyester fill, 27 1/2 x 28 x 28" (69.9 x 71.1 x 71.1 cm). Mfr.: Kebe Møbler, Denmark. Friends of the Department Fund. MoMA.

Marescotti; designed residential, industrial, and public buildings for public institutions and private firms; was an urban planner and industrial designer, who became known for creating furniture based on earlier 20th-century models, including chairs entitled Omaggio a Chareau and Omaggio a Rietveld made by Alias. He and Vico Magistretti were Alias's first designers. His work for Alias included 1979 Odessa chair (nicknamed the Spaghetti chair) and Pardi table, 1980 Kiev and Spaghetti armchairs, 1981 Spaghetti armrests, Tavolino and Tadini bookshelves, 1982 Decimo bed and 'Outdoor Collection' of chairs, chaises, and cart, 1984 Tavolo Outdoor, Paludis chair, Alterego wall cabinet, Tavolo Forcolini, Carelli cart series, Twist folding chair, Omaggio a Man Ray chair, and Omaggio a Theo Van Doesburg chair, 1985 Omaggio a Chareau chair, Fratus table, Ventura shelving, Wiener Collection, Tower coat rack, and Paludis stool, 1986 Spaghetti Gemini chair, Paludis Gemini chair, Orsi bed, Iaia sofa, and Tavolo Restaurant, 1987 Trois Étoiles chair, Domestica chair, Four Balls tables, and Consolle, and 1988 Hoffmann, Moser, and Wagner casegoods range.
Bibliography Robert A.M. Stern (ed.), *The International Design Yearbook*, New York: Abbeville, 1985/1986.

Benbassa, Efi (1963–)
Israeli designer and teacher; active Jerusalem.

Training 1985–88, fine art, City of London Polytechnic, UK; 1991–92, department of art, Bezalel Academy of Art and Design, Jerusalem; 1991–93, Rammat Hasharon Fine Arts Institute, Israel.
Biography 1993, Benbassi was active in textile applications, New York; 1994, established own design studio, Jerusalem; has designed and also produced lighting and furniture, served a group of clients, and become known for work in unusual forms, particularly chairs in fantastical, insect-like shapes; 1996–2001, lecturer, department of design, Ascola School of Design, Tel Aviv; 1998–2000, lectured, department of architecture, Wizo College of Design, Haifa.
Exhibitions From 1995, work shown in a number of venues in Israel.

Bendtsen, Niels Sylvester (1943–)
Danish architect and furniture designer; born Copenhagen.

Biography 1952, Bendtsen emigrated with his family from Denmark to Moose Jaw, Saskatchewan, Canada; learned cabinetmaking from his father; from 1963, sequentially opened two Danet stores, West Vancouver, Canada, and, 1972, sold them; spent 12 years as a freelance designer in Copenhagen, where he designed 1975 Ribbon chair; from 1977, collaborated with Nina Koppel and designed furniture by Kebe, N. Eilersen, Ljungvist, and others; with a partner, reacquired the Danet store and soon changed the name to Inform, Vancouver, and eventually bought out the partner; from 1999, has managed the store (that also sells wares by others) and a manufacturing facility with wife Nancy; 2000, established another branch of Inform, Seattle, Wash., US. Bendtsen-designed products (made by his 2-B firm) include 1994 Partu modular cabinet system, Neo seating system from 1996, 1997 Cube table, 1999 Index shelving, and, for Starbuck coffee shops, 1985 Aura stool that was depicted on a Canadian postage stamp acknowledging industrial design.
Exhibitions Work shown in Cologne, 1975; in Paris, 1976; at Nordiska Galleriet, Stockholm, 1977; Illums Bolighus, 1977; Design Research store, New York.
Bibliography Frederik Sieck, *Nutidig Dansk Møbeldesign – en kortfattet illustreret beskrivelse*, Copenhagen: Bondo Gravesen, 1990. Adele Weder, 'The Bendtsen Empire,' *Azure*, May–June 2002: 74–79. www.bensen.ca.

Bénédictus, Édouard (1878–1930)
French painter, decorative designer, and scientist; born and active Paris.

Biography Benedictus designed fabrics and published a portfolio of abstract Art Moderne patterns used in decoration; regularly designed for textile firms Tassinari et Châtel and for Brunet et Meunié; designed rugs and carpets; 1911, developed Triplex safety glass and, during World War I, continued his research as a scientist.
Exhibitions/citations Work shown at Salons of the Société des Artistes français, and in first important exhibition of La Matrise at 1922 Salon d'Automne. Various awards at 1899, 1902, 1907, and 1909 Salons of the Société des Artistes Français; was appointed Chevalier and Officier of Légion d'Honnour.
Bibliography Victor Arwas, *Art Déco*, New York: Abrams, 1980. Stuart Durant, *Ornament from the Industrial Revolution to Today*, Woodstock, N.Y.: Overlook, 1986.

Benedito Graells, Ramón (1945–)
Spanish industrial designer; born Barcelona.

Training Universitat de Barcelona; 1974-87, Elisara (Escola Superior de Disseny), Barcelona.
Biography From 1973, Benedito has been active as a designer and also taught at Elisara and, subsequently, Eina (Escola de Desseny i Art), Barcelona; specializes in the design of electronic and data-processing equipment, technical and scientific instruments, machines and tools, lighting, household goods, fixture and construction equipment, packaging, and furniture. Clients have included Amat, Akaba, Balay, Carlsberg, Cía. Roca Radiadores, Contenur, Diagnòstic Grífols, Disform, Faema, Fermax Electrónica, Font Vella, Generalitat de Catalunya, Grupté, Henkel Ibérica, Escofet, Indo, Industrias JBC, Magnum, Mobba, Niessen, Otto, Pinti, Policad, Rank Xerox, Sanyo, Taurus, Uralita, Vibia, Vieta, and Vilagrasa. 1983 with Lluís Morillas and Josep Puig, he founded Transatlàntic, an experimental design group; was a consultant to Korean Institute of Industrial Design and Packaging (KIIDP); 1979–82, was a member of the board, Asociación de Diseñores Profesionales (ADP); 1987–89, chairperson of executive board, ADI/FAD (promotion of industrial design/decorative arts); 1987–90, member of executive council, FAD; 1990-2000, member of board of trustees, BCD Barcelona Centre Disseny (Barcelona design center); has lectured worldwide.
Exhibitions/citations Work included in numerous international exhibitions. 1992 National Design Prize, Spain.
Bibliography Patrizia Scarzella, 'Barcelona Portraits,' *Domus*, no. 669, Feb. 1986. Georg C. Bertsch, *form*, no. 124/88, 1988. *Product Design 5*, New York: PBC, 1992. www.beneditodesign.com.

Benktzon, Maria (1946–)
> See Ergonomi Design Gruppen.

Bennett, Garry Knox (1934–)
American furniture craftsperson; born Alameda, Cal.; active California.

Training Painting and sculpture, California College of Arts and Craft, Oakland; self-taught in woodworking.
Biography Bennett was originally a sculptor; 1960s, founded a metal-plating business; early 1970s, built clocks and expanded to include furniture; became known for his exuberant and unconventional crafts furniture that ranged from large cabinets and tables to clocks and lamps. He also designed tabletop accessories; uses a bandsaw, drill press, and milling machines to create unusual organic forms; was influenced by Japanese crafts, especially wooden com-

partmented *tansu* chests; incorporates humor into his work; 1980s, pioneered the use and marriage of unconventional materials like plywood and aluminum with brass and plastics, as in ColorCore project by Formica.
Exhibitions 1997 *100 Lamps*, Peter Joseph Gallery, New York; 2001 retrospective of his work, Oakland Museum of California and American Craft Museum (catalog below).
Bibliography Cat., Ursula Ilse-Neuman (ed.), *Made in Oakland: The Furniture of Garry Knox Bennett*, New York: American Craft Museum, 2000.

Bennett Jr., John (1840–1907)

British ceramicist; active New York.

Training At Staffordshire potteries, UK.
Biography John Sparkes, head of Lambeth School of Art, London, recommended Bennett to Henry Doulton, who hired him to set up a faïence department where he taught underglazing techniques to Doulton artisans. His work became known as 'Bennett ware.' 1877, encouraged by his success at 1876 Philadelphia exhibition, he left for New York; by 1879, had set up a studio. His pieces were sold at Tiffany & Co. and Davis Collamore, both New York, and at Abram French, Boston. His motifs included flowers, grasses, apple, hawthorn and dogwood blossoms, peonies, roses, and asters in mustard yellow, lapis lazuli, Persian red, violet, and olive green with umber and gray shading. Bennett's work showed influences from British designers, including William Morris, and from Persian ceramics. 1878–79, Bennett was head of ceramics-painting classes at newly formed Society of Decorative Art, New York. Amateur ceramicists worldwide came to study his techniques.
Exhibitions Pieces included in Doulton stand at 1876 *Centennial Exposition*, Philadelphia. Work shown frequently, particularly in New York and Cincinnati.
Bibliography Edmund Grosse, *Sir Henry Doulton: The Man of Business as a Man of Imagination*, London, 1970: 87. Doreen Bolger Burke et al., *In Pursuit of Beauty: Americans and the Aesthetic Movement*, New York: The Metropolitan Museum of Art/Rizzoli, 1986: 402–03.

Bennett, Ward (1917–2003)

American artist, sculptor, and textile, jewelry, industrial, and interior designer; active New York and Paris.

Training Under sculptor Constantin Brancusi, Paris; under painter Hans Hoffman and sculptor Louise Nevelson, New York.
Biography From 1930 at age 13, Bennett worked as a dress designer, sketch artist, and store-window dresser; 1947, began as an interior designer with the penthouse of Harry Jason. His interior design work included corporate offices, banks, and residences in New York, London, Venice, Rome, and Neptuno (Italy). He became best known for his industrial products such as furniture, textiles, and jewelry; 1970s and 1980s, created more than 100 furniture designs by Brickel. His 1985 Double Helix stainless-steel cutlery and late-1980s Sengai crystal range were produced by Sasaki and 1990 22-piece furniture collection by Geiger International, to respond to the trend to smaller executive offices.
Bibliography Robert A.M. Stern (ed.), *The International Design Yearbook*, New York: Abbeville, 1985/1986. 'Celebrating Design Innovation,' *Designers West*, Apr. 1991: 30.

Benney, Gerald (1930–)

British silversmith; born Hull.

Training Brighton College of Art; Royal College of Art, London.
Biography 1955, Benney set up his own workshop; 1957–70, was a consultant to Viners for mass produced metalware; 1963, began his work for Reading Corporation's collection of civic-plate patterns; from 1970, created a range of Beenham enamels; 1974–83, was professor of silversmithing, Royal College of Art.

Benois, Alexandre (aka Aleksandr Nikolaevitch Benua) (1870–1960)

Russian artist, illustrator, and set designer; active St. Petersburg and Paris.

Training Imperial Academy of Arts, St. Petersburg; 1890–94, University of St. Petersburg.
Biography Benois ran the art journal and organization *V Mir*

Ward Bennett. Double Helix cutlery. 1985. Stainless steel, longest (knife) l. 9 1/8 x w. 1/2" (23.2 x 1.3 cm), shortest (teaspoon) l. 6 1/2 x w. 1 1/8" (16.5 x 2.8 cm). Mfr.: Sasaki Glass Co, Japan. Zaidee Dufallo Fund. MoMA.

Iskusstva (the world of art); illustrated books, including Pushkin's poem *The Bronze Horseman* (written 1833); created theater sets such as for Wagner's opera *Twilight of the Gods* (1902), his own collaboration with Igor Stravinskii, *Petroushka* (1911–57), Molière's *Le mariage forcé*, Pushkin's *The Feast at the Time of the Plague* (1914). Benois rendered watercolors and gouaches with landscape and architectural subjects. His prolific critical writings on art were influential in Russia at the beginning of the 20th century. 1926, he settled in Paris, where he died.
Bibliography Cat., Peter Lieven, *Alexandre Benois*, London: Arthur Tooth & Sons, 1937. Cat., *Alexandre Benois, 1870–1960: Drawings for the Ballet*, London: Hazlitt, Gooden & Fox, 1980. Hélène A. Borisova and Gregory Sterine, *Art nouveau russe*, Paris: Regard, 1987.

Benson, William Arthur Smith (1854–1924)

British designer, metalworker, and architect; born and active London.

Training 1874–78, classics and philosophy, Oxford University; 1877–80, apprenticeship under Basil Champneys.
Biography Benson met Edward Burne-Jones in 1877 and William Morris in 1878; encouraged by the latter, set up his own workshop in 1880 and began producing metalwork, to become the leading designer of Arts and Crafts metalwork, specializing in brass and copper; unlike Morris, was not averse to mechanical production and designed exclusively for it, including coat stands, firescreens, chafing dishes, music stands, and electroplated kettles. Benson's innovative designs included vacuum flasks and lighting. The only internationally recognized British lighting designer of his time, he showed models throughout Europe, especially at Siegfried Bing's shop L'Art Nouveau, Paris; in his sales catalogs, offered lighting models for each area of the house; 1880s, designed furniture for Art Nouveau cabinetmakers J.S. Henry, incorporating exotic-wood inlays and elaborate metal fittings; designed metal fireplaces and grates for Falkirk and for Coalbrookdale iron firms; set up a factory and, 1887, a London shop; assumed the directorship of Morris and Co. on William Morris's 1896 death. When Benson retired, the business closed. 1884, he became a founding member of the Art-Workers' Guild; 1888, Arts and Crafts Exhibition Society; 1915, Design and Industries Association; and published *Elements of Handicraft and Design* (1893), *Rudiments of Handicraft* (1919), and *Drawing, Its History and Uses* (1925).
Exhibitions Work shown at Manchester Arts and Crafts Exhibition, 1895; Hirschwald Gallery, Berlin, 1899; Ashmolean Museum, Oxford, 1919.

Bibliography Alastair Duncan, *Art Nouveau and Art Déco Lighting*, New York: Simon & Schuster, 1978: 65. Cat., *W.A.S. Benson 1854–1924*, London: Haslam and Whiteway, 1981. *British Art and Design, 1900–1960*, London: Victoria and Albert Museum, 1983.

Benza
> See Pellone, Giovanni.

Bepler, Emma (1864–1947)
American woodworker; active Cincinnati.

Training 1881–84, drawing and decorative design, University of Cincinnati School of Design; 1886–87 and 1891–92 under Benn Pitman, wood carving, Art Academy, Cincinnati, and, 1893–94, under William Fry
Biography As a secondary figure in the art movement in Cincinnati, her woodcarvings were strongly influenced by teachers Pitman and Fry, who both emphasized the application of wood carvings to domestic interiors. 1906–47, a member, Cincinnati Women's Art Club.
Exhibitions/citations Regularly showed drawings and painted textiles in annual exhibitions of University of Cincinnati School of Design. Prize (china painting), 1904 *Louisiana Purchase Exposition*, St. Louis.
Bibliography Doreen Bolger Burke et al., *In Pursuit of Beauty: Americans and the Aesthetic Movement*, New York: The Metropolitan Museum of Art/Rizzoli, 1986: 403. 'Woman Woodcarver, Artist, Dies at Eighty-Three,' *Cincinnati Times-Star*, 23 Feb. 1947. Anita J. Ellis, 'Cincinnati Art Furniture,' *Antiques*, no. 121, Apr. 1982: 930–41.

Beran, Gustav Josef (1912–)
Austrian designer, painter, and silversmith; active Zeist (Netherlands).

Training 1928–33 under Josef Hoffmann and Eugen Mayer, Kunstgewerbeschule, Vienna.
Biography Settling in the Netherlands, Beran was a designer for its largest silverware producer, Gerritsen en Van Kempen, 1934–41 and its artistic director 1948–77.
Exhibitions Representing Gerritsen en Van Kempen, work shown at 1937 *Exposition Internationale des Arts et Techniques dans la Vie Moderne,* Paris. Subject of 1982 exhibition, Galerie Mara, Fribourg, Switzerland (catalog below).
Bibliography *Gold und Silber, Uhren und Schmuck*, no. 1, Jan. 1963: 30–31. Cat., *Gustav Beran: Miniatures and Design*, Fribourg: Galerie Mara, 1982. Cat., Kathryn B. Hiesinger and George H. Marcus III (eds.), *Design Since 1945*, Philadelphia: Philadelphia Museum of Art, 1983. Annelies Krekel-Aalberse, *Art Nouveau and Art Déco Silver*, New York: Abrams, 1989.

Berchicci, Guglielmo (1957–)
Italian designer; born and active Milan.

Training 1979–84, architecture, Politecnico, Milan.
Biography 1986, Berchicci established his own studio in Milan; has specialized in lighting and, 1987, began calling on the use of a refuse material—particles of broken display windows. This resulted in the Geko and Random lamps, distributed by Dilmos. Other work has included 1991 Glugluglu aluminum lamp by Lumi, 1992–93 jewelry from recycled metal and glass, 1997 Loto and 1998 Voga tables by Kundalini, 1998 hi-fi unit and CD holder by Around, 1998 Orbital and 2000 Tsonga mirrors and 1998 Flowers table by Glas, 2000 Mir and 2001 Spacebug lamps by Valenti, 2001 Jetsons chair by Giovannetti, and 2002 Zoe chair and Fuse lamp by Slide. His best-known work may be 1996 ETA (Extra Terrestrial Angel) fiberglass floor lamp by Kundalini.
Exhibitions 1992 project with Atelier Mendini, *Nuovo Bel Design*, Triennale di Milano, Milan. Work included in *Italian Design Furniture*, touring Zürich, Milan, Cologne, London, and New York; 2000 *50 Anni di Design Italiano e Tedesco*, Kunsthalle Museum, Bonn; 2000 *Essere Benessere*, Triennale di Milano; 2000 *100 Forme della Luce: Italia 1945–2000*, Triennale di Milano.
Bibliography Nally Bellati, *New Italian Design*, New York: Rizzoli, 1990. Mel Byars, *50 Lights: Innovations in Design and Materials*, Hove: RotoVision, 1997. Giuliana Gramigna and Paola Biondi, *Il design in Italia dell'arredamento domestico*, Turin: Allemandi, 1999. Almerico de Angelis, *Design, the Italian Way*, Milan: Editoriale Modo, 2001. Silvana Annichiarico, *1945–2000 il design in Italia*, Rome: Gangemi Editore, 2001.

Henri Bergé. Arbousiers vase. 1920s. Pâte-de-verre with melted powder pigments, h. 3 1/8" (8 cm). Mfr.: Schneider/Amalric Walter, France. Courtesy Quittenbaum Kunstauktionen, Munich.

Berg, Franco Alberto (1948–)
German designer; active Hanover.

Training To 1978, Hochschule für Bildende Künste, Brunswick.
Biography 1979, Berg set up the Berg Design Studio for product development in Brunswick; later moved to Hanover; worked on consumer goods. His 1984–85 Argon, Radon, and Exnon light sculptures were produced by Berg Licht und Objekt.
Bibliography Robert A.M. Stern (ed.), *The International Design Yearbook*, New York: Abbeville, 1985/1986. Albrecht Bangert and Karl Michael Armer, *80s Style: Designs of the Decade*, New York: Abbeville, 1990: 105, 227.

Bergé, Henri (1870–1937)
French sculptor, painter, and glass and graphic designer; born Diarville.

Biography c. 1897–1914, Bergé was artistic director at Daum glassworks, Nancy; forwarded Daum toward a floral and landscape style. His drawings, studies, and objects were in a botanical or *animalier* manner, always with a scientific precision that revealed his interests in the public gardens near the Daum factory. After 1908, Bergé made models for Almaric Walter's *pâte-de-verre* sculptures. He was active in graphic design, including of menus, posters, and advertising; in stained glass; and as an artist of canvases with flower motifs and landscapes; was a member of the Comité Directeur, École de Nancy; concurrent with his artistic activities, directed the workshop of drawing and modeling within the Daum firm, and taught, École Professionnelle de l'Esta. He died in Nancy.
Bibliography Yvonne Brunhammer et al., *Art Nouveau Belgium, France*, Houston: Rice University, 1976, biblio. Noël Daum: *One Hundred Years of Glass and Crystal*, Washington, D.C.: Daum and Smithsonian, 1978. Cat., *Peinture et Art Nouveau: l'École de Nancy*, Paris: Réunion des Musées Nationaux, 1999.

Berger, Arthur (1892–1981)
Austrian metalworker; active Vienna and Moscow.

Training 1911–15 under Josef Hoffmann, Kunstgewerbeschule, Vienna.
Biography Berger designed silver for the Wiener Werkstätte and, 1920–36, sets for more than 30 films; 1936–81, lived in Moscow.
Bibliography Werner J. Schweiger, *Wiener Werkstätte*, Vienna: Christian Brandstaetter, 1980. Annelies Krekel-Aalberse, *Art Nouveau and Art Déco Silver*, New York: Abrams, 1989.

Berger, Otti (1898–1944)
Croatian designer; born Zmajavac; active Dessau, Berlin, England, Prague, and Croatia.

Training 1921–26, Akademija Likovnih Umjetnosti (academy of fine arts), Zagreb; 1927–30 under Gunta Stölzl, Bauhaus, Dessau; 1929, in Sweden.
Biography 1931, she became the temporary head of the weaving department, Bauhaus, Dessau, replacing Anni Albers; 1932, continued there under Lilly Reich; 1933, set up her own workshop and lab-

Susi Berger-Wyss and Ueli Berger. Soft chair. 1967. Vinyl-covered polyester foam, 27 1/4 x 24 1/4 x 36" (69.2 x 61.6 x 91.5 cm). Mfr.: Victoria-Werke, Switzerland. Gift of the mfr. MoMA.

oratory in Berlin; collaborated with Gunta Stölzl and worked for various commercial firms in Germany, England, the Netherlands, and Czechoslovakia; 1933, became a design consultant to Wohnbedarf store of Zürich, which commissioned her to design textiles and wallcoverings for the Corso cinema and restaurant in Zürich (completed 1934). 1934, Wohnbedarf showed and sold her textiles and Alvaräs wooden furniture. 1935, she designed curtain materials for De Ploeg in Bergeyk (the Netherlands); settled in England and designed textiles by Helios of Bolton; refused a visa to US, went to Prague and then to Croatia; died in the Nazi concentration camp at Auschwitz/Birkenau.
Exhibitions Carpet of c. 1930 shown at 1938 *Bauhaus 1919–1928* exhibition, The Museum of Modern Art, New York.
Bibliography Cat., Barbara von Lucadou, 'Otti Berger—Stoffe für die Zukunft,' in *Wechselwirkungen. Ungarische Avantgarde in der Weimarer Republik*, Kassel, 1986: 301. Cat., *The Bauhaus: Masters and Students*, New York: Barry Friedman, 1988. Friederike Mehlau-Wiebking et al., *Schweizer Typenmöbel 1925–35, Sigfried Giedion und die Wohnbedarf AG*, Zürich: gta, 1989. Cat., Hans Wichmann (ed.), *Von Morris bis Memphis. Textilien der Neuen Sammlung. Ende 19. bis Ende 20. Jahrhundert*, Basel: Birkhäuser, 1990: 120, 168, 439.

Berger-Wyss, Susi (b. Susi Wyss 1937–); Ueli Berger (1937–)

Swiss artists and designers. Both: born Bern; active Ersigen.

Training Susi Wyss: to 1958, graphic art.
Biography 1962, they married; have worked together and individually. Susi Berger-Wyss has been active as a consultant in architecture and designer of furniture, and Ueli Berger primarily as a sculptor. They designed a chest of drawers with the appearance of stacked boxes, by Röthlisberger Kollektion; 1989–96 Ring project, Musée des Transports, Lucerne; 1995 Hommage à Dieter Roth, St. Andreasplatz, Basel; 2002 House in a Tree electrical sculpture, boulevard des Philosophes, Geneva; others.
Exhibitions Numerous venues.

Hagbard Elis Bergh. Charm tumbler.. c. 1942. Mouth-blown crystal, h. 3 x dia. 2 3/8" (7.6 x 6 cm). Mfr.: Kosta Glasbruk, Sweden. Gift of D. Stanley Corcoran, Inc. MoMA.

Bergh, Hagbard Elis (1881–1954)

Swedish metalworker and glassware designer; active Stockholm.

Training 1897–99, Kungliga Konsthögskolan, Stockholm; 1899–1902, Konstfack, Stockholm; 1905–06, architecture, Munich.
Biography 1906–16, Bergh worked at Arv, Böhlmarks, and Pukeberg; 1916–21, was director and artistic consultant at Herman Bermans Konstgiuteri metalworks, Stockholm; 1921–29, designed simple, sober silver objects for C.G. Hallbergs Guldsmedsaktiebolag intended for mass production. (Other Hallbergs designers of the time were Hakon Ahlberg, Sylvia Stave, and Edvin Ollers.) Bergh is mainly known for his 1929–50 designs by Kosta Boda glassworks, where he was artistic director from 1929; 1950–54, a freelance designer. Work included architecture, lighting, and gold jewelry.
Bibliography Cat., David Revere McFadden (ed.), *Scandinavian Modern Design 1880–1980*, New York: Abrams, 1982. Sales cat., *The Kosta Boda Book of Glass*, 1986: 5. Jennifer Hawkins Opie, *Scandinavia: Ceramics and Glass in the Twentieth Century*, New York: Rizzoli, 1989. Annelies Krekel-Aalberse, *Art Nouveau and Art Déco Silver*, New York: Abrams, 1989.

Berghof, Norbert (1949–)

German architect and designer.

Training Architecture, Technische Universität, Darmstadt.
Biography 1981 with Michael A. Landes and Wolfgang Rang, Berghof set up an architectural partnership. Work has included architecture, interior renovation, graphic design, and furniture. By Draenert Studio: the monumental 1985–86 F1 Frankfurter Schrank writing desk and 1986–87 FIII Frankfurter Stuhl armchair and other furniture; by Rasch: wallpaper in the 1992 Zeitwände series. Berghof established a partnership with Reiner Haller; from 1992, taught, Fachhochschule, Detmold. With Landes and Rang, participated in Frankfurt architecture: 1988 Landes-zentralbank Hessen (with Albrecht Jourdan Müller), 1991 public housing at Rottweiler Platz, and Römer urban-train station.
Citations 1987, elected to Bund Deutscher Architekten (BDA).
Bibliography Charles Jencks et al., *Architectural Design*, Nov.–Dec. 1988 Albrecht Bangert and Karl Michael Armer, *80s Style: Designs of the Decade*, New York: Abbeville, 1990.
> See Landes, Michael A.; Rang, Wolfgang.

Bergne, Sebastian (1966–)

British industrial designer; active London and Bologna.

Training Industrial design, Central School of Art and Design; to 1990, Royal College of Art; both London.
Biography Bergne worked in Hong Kong and Milan; 1990, established 'Bergne: design for manufacturer,' London; has designed products and offered product development for numerous firms. Work has included 1991 clip-on lamp reflector and 1993 Tower of Babel bookmark by Radius, 1994 Ring soap and peg and 1997 Leg Over stacking stool by Authentics, 1995 Emergency disposable cufflinks by Bergne:dfm, 1995 Mr. Mause coathanger by Driade/d-house, 1998 Torso lamp by Proto design, 1999 Ixix folding table by Vitra, and 2000 Kult breakfast service by WMF. Other clients: Cappellini and O luce. Is a visiting tutor, Central St. Martin's College of Art and Design, and London Institute; lecturer, Royal College of Art; all London.
Exhibitions Work included in 1995 *Mutant Materials*, New York and traveling (catalog below).
Bibliography *The International Design Yearbook*, London: Laurence King, 1999, 2000, and 2001. Cat., Paola Antonelli, *Mutant Materials in Contemporary Design*, New York: The Museum of Modern Art/Abrams, 1995. Michele De Lucchi (ed.), *The International Design Yearbook*, London: Laurence King, 2001. Mel Byars, *Design in Steel*, London: Laurence King, 2002.

Bergner, 'Léna' Helene (aka 'Léna' Meyer 1906–1981)

German textile designer; born Coburg; active Germany, Russia, Mexico, and Switzerland; wife of Hannes Meyer.

Training 1926–30, Bauhaus, Dessau.
Biography She took over the direction of the Bauhaus dyeing workshop; produced fabric, carpets, and wallpaper; 1931, became direc-

tor of the Ostpreussische Handweberei in Königsberg (today Kaliningrad, Russia); with husband Meyer and a group of Bauhaus students, emigrated to the USSR, where her work was influenced by Russian avant-garde painters, including Liubov' Popova and Alexandra Exter; from 1939, lived in Mexico and, from 1949, in Lugano, Switzerland.
Exhibitions c. 1930 carpet shown at 1938 *Bauhaus 1919–1928*, The Museum of Modern Art, New York.
Bibliography Cat., *Der Kragstuhl*, Stuhlmuseum Burg Beverungen, Berlin: Alexander, 1986: 134. Cat., Gunta Stölzl (ed.), *Weberei am Bauhaus und aus eigener Werkstatt*, Berlin: Bauhaus-Archiv, 1987: 159. Cat., *The Bauhaus: Masters and Students*, New York: Barry Friedman, 1988.

Bergslien, Gro (b. Gro Sommerfeldt 1940–)
Norwegian textile and glassware designer.

Training 1957–60, Statens Håndverks -og Kunstindustriskole, Oslo; 1960, weaving at Dannebrog Weavers and Material Printers, Amsterdam; 1964, attended State School for teachers of drawing and woodwork; 1971, Royal College of Art, London.
Biography 1961, she was a textile designer at Plus in Fredrikstad and, from 1964, a glassware designer at Hadelands Glassverk, where her work presaged the studio glass movement and for which she designed freeblown, color-inclusion pieces; from c. 1964, was a part-time designer of enamels at David-Andersen in Oslo.
Bibliography Cat., David Revere McFadden (ed.), *Scandinavian Modern Design 1880–1980*, New York: Abrams, 1982. Jennifer Hawkins Opie, *Scandinavia: Ceramics and Glass in the Twentieth Century*, New York: Rizzoli, 1989. Leslie Jackson, *20th Century Factory Glass*, London: Octopus, 2000.

Berlage, Hendrik Petrus (1856–1934)
Dutch architect, theorist, and designer; born Amsterdam; active The Hague and Amsterdam.

Training Briefly, Rijksakademie van Beeldende Kunsten, Amsterdam; 1875–78 under Gottfried Semper, Bauschule, Eidgenössische Technische Hochschule, Zürich.
Biography 1889, Berlage set up his own architecture practice in Amsterdam. His historicism strongly influenced the development of Dutch Expressionism, particularly through his 1903 Stock Exchange building, Amsterdam, for which he designed furniture and many fittings. His attraction to the Romanesque was revealed in his wide, unbroken wall surfaces and semi-circular arches, similar to features of the work of H.H. Richardson, Louis Sullivan, and Frank Lloyd Wright in the US. Of a high technical quality, much of his furniture was bulky and made in the Amsterdam workshop Het Binnenhuis. One of the first to abandon historicism, he encouraged others through his writings to seek logical construction techniques and high standards of workmanship, calling it 'an honest awareness of the problems of architecture'; even considered it architecturally dishonest to plaster a wall. 1912, Berlage was instrumental in introducing Wright's work to Dutch and Swiss architects, proselytized Wright's theories. After his 1911 visit to Austria, he settled in The Hague; published *Een drietal lezingen in Amerika gehouden*, containing three lectures held in the United States (Rotterdam: Brusse, 1913); designed silver for Mr. and Mrs. Kröller-Müller, produced by C.J. Begeer, Utrecht, and by W. Voet, Haarlem, and austere, simple stained-glass vessels by Pantin and by Baccarat; 1923–29 and 1931, worked at Leerdam Glassworks, where Andries Copier was his apprentice, and designed c. 1924 canary-yellow pressed-glass service there; admired Ludwig Mies van der Rohe and Gerrit Rietveld; 1928, attended Congrès Internationaux d'Architecture Moderne (CIAM) but did not join due to its modernism being in opposition to his own, more traditional expression; 1928–30, designed wallpaper by Rath & Doodeheefver. Architecture included 1899–1900 Diamond-Workers' House, Amsterdam; 1897–1903 Stock Exchange, Amsterdam; 1912–13 Jahrhunderthalle, Breslau (now Wroclaw, Poland); and 1914 Holland House, London.
Citations Winner, 1897 Stock Exchange competition, Amsterdam.
Bibliography Hendrik Petrus Berlage, *Gedanken über den Stil in der Baukunst*, Leipzig, 1905. Hendrik Petrus Berlage, *Grundlagen und Entwicklung der Architektur*, Berlin and Rotterdam, 1908. Hendrik Petrus Berlage, *Studies over Bouwkunst, Stijl en Samenleving*, Rotterdam, 1910. Jan Gratama, *Dr. H.P. Berlage Bouwmeester*, Amsterdam, 1925. 'H.P. Berlage,' *Bouwkundig Weekblad Architectura*, no. 51 (special commemorative issue), 1934. Reyner Banham, *Theory and Design in the First Machine Age*, London, 1960. Pieter Singelenberg, *H.P. Berlage*, Amsterdam, 1969. Cat., *Industrie U Vormgeving in Nederland 1850–1950*, Amsterdam: Stedelijk Museum, 1985. Annelies Krekel-Aalberse, *Art Nouveau and Art Déco Silver*, New York: Abrams, 1989.

Sebastian Bergne. Hanging lamp (no. T13). c. 1998. Ceramic, h. 8 5/8 x w. 4 3/8" (22 x 11 cm). Mfr.: Authentics, artipresent, Germany.

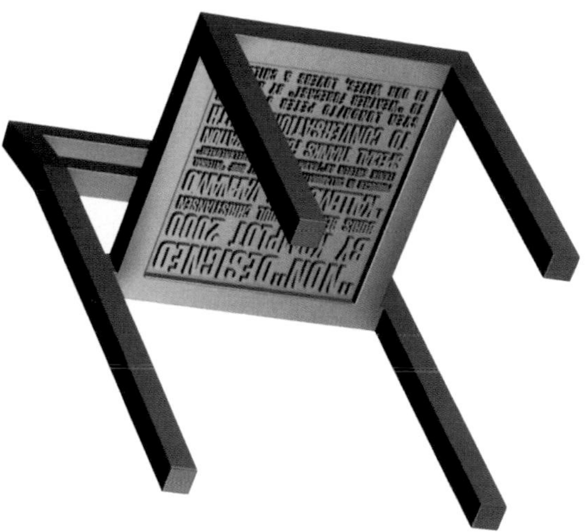

Boris Berlin and Poul Christiansen (Komplot Design). Non chair (underview). 2000. PUR rubber, h. 30 x w. 17 3/8" (76 x 44 cm) x d. 16 1/8" (41cm). Mfr.: Källemo, Sweden.

Berlin, Boris (1951–)
Russian designer; born Leningrad (now St. Petersburg).

Training To 1975, Institute of Applied Arts and Design, Leningrad.
Biography 1975, Berlin worked at Vinte in Leningrad and, concurrently, as a freelance designer of a wide range of products and graphics; 1993, settled in Denmark and established an eponymous firm working for Penta Design (computerized work place of Danish Post and Telegraph Office); 1987, established Komplot Design with Poul Christiansen, primarily active in industrial, graphic, and furniture design, including a number of chairs and tables by Klaesson. Other clients have included System B8 Møbler, Bent Krogh, fritzsons, Møremøbler, Tendo, and Källermo. Berlin is a member, Foreningen Danske Designere (association of Danish designers).
Citations With Christiansen at Komplot, a number of awards, including Konstfond (Danish art fund); first prize, Institute of Business Designers (IBD); 2002 Furniture of the Year, *Sköna Hem* magazine.

Jeffrey Bernett. Metropolitan armchair. 2002. Nickel-plated or graphic metal, aluminum, and fabric, h. 28 3/4 x w. 33 1/8 x d. 32 5/8" (73 x 84 x 83 cm). Mfr.: B&B Italia, Italy.

Berlinetta

German design studio; located Berlin.

History 1984, the Berlinetta design office was established by John Hirschberg (Eldoret, Kenya, 1949–), Inge Sommer (Paderborn, Germany, 1955–), Susanne Neubohn (Kiruna, Sweden, 1960–), and possibly Christof Walther. To 1991, they were active in furniture design, town planning, and environmental issues.
Exhibitions/citations Work subject of 1987 exhibition *Berlinetta—Möbel 84–86*, Cologne. 1983, second prize (Kitchens competition), Design Plus, Ambiente fair, Frankfurt.
Bibliography Cat., Design Center Stuttgart, *Women in Design: Careers and Life Histories Since 1900*, Stuttgart: Haus der Wirtschaft, 1989: 78–80. Georg C. Bertsch, Euro-Design-Guide, Munich: Wilhelm Heyne, 1991.
> See Neubohn, Susanne; Sommer, Inge.

Bernadotte, Count Sigvard (1907–2002)

Swedish metal, furniture, textile, bookbinding, and theatre set designer; son of King Gustavus VI of Sweden.

Training To 1929, Kungliga Konsthögskolan, Stockholm.
Biography 1930, Bernadotte joined the Georg Jensen Sølvsmedie; was the first designer in the Jensen workshop to break with the traditional naturalistic 'Jensen style,' preferred a more modern, austere approach that was severe, smooth, and often had horizontal, vertical, or diagonal linear decoration, influenced by Johan Rohde. The best-known of his work for Jensen is the 1939 Bernadotte silver cutlery pattern; other work included jugs, bowls, and candlesticks. He served as a director at Jensen; 1949 with Dutch architect Acton Bjørn, opened a design studio in Copenhagen, expanding later to Stockholm and New York; as an industrial designer with Bjørn, designed other silver, furniture, textiles, plastics, camping, and heavy-machinery designs; 1964, set up his own independent design studio; from 1967, was a director, consulting firm Allied Industrial Designers, London.
Bibliography Sigvard Bernadotte (ed.), *Moderne dansk boligkunst*, Odense: Skandinavisk Bogforlag, 1946. Gotthard Johansson and Christian Ditlev Reventlow, *Sigvard Bernadotte sølvarbejder: 1930–1955*, Copenhagen: Georg Jensen, 1955. 'Designs from Abroad,' *Industrial Design*, vol. 4, Feb. 1956: 76–79. Cat., *Georg Jensen Silversmithy: 77 Artists, 75 Years*, Washington, D.C.: Smithsonian, 1980: nos. 11–14. Jens Bernsen, *Design: The Problem Comes First*, Copenhagen: Dansk Design Center, 1992: 68–71. Cat., David Revere McFadden (ed.), *Scandinavian Modern Design 1880–1980*, New York: Abrams, 1982. Cat., Kathryn B. Hiesinger and George H. Marcus III (eds.), *Design Since 1945*, Philadelphia: Philadelphia Museum of Art, 1983.

Bernal Rosell, Gemma (1949–)

Spanish industrial designer; born Barcelona.

Training Philosophy, Universitat de Barcelona; industrial design, Eina (Escola de Desseny i Art), Barcelona.
Biography With Ramon Isern and Beth Galí, Bernal set up a small studio in Barcelona, designing toys, sound amplifiers, and other products; from 1971, was manager of the design department of a metal construction firm; 1973, began working once more with Isern, with whom Bernal established the studio Bernal-Isern in 1983, designing furniture, packaging, stationery products, and bathroom fixtures for clients, including Andreu, Blauet, Concepta, Dytecma, Enea, Est, Miquelrius, Montseny, Nova Norma, Roca Henkel, and Vilagrasa; designed 1984 Eclipse table by Disform, 1986 Biblos shelving system by Grupo T, 1988 Gala armchair by Sellex. 1998 with David Ramos and Jordi Bassols, she founded Gemma Bernal & Associats in Barcelona; is a member, Asociación de Diseñadores Profesionales (ADP).
Citations 1969 Delta d'Oro, ADI / FAD (industrial-design/decorative-arts associations). Three first prizes, National Furniture Design Competition, Feria Internacional de Mueble de Valéncia; all Spain.
Bibliography Cat., Design Center Stuttgart, *Women in Design: Careers and Life Histories Since 1900*, Stuttgart: Haus der Wirtschaft, 1989: 306–09.

Bernard, Oliver Percy (1881–1939)

British architect and designer; active Manchester, London, and Boston.

Biography Bernard began his career working with a Manchester theater, where he became a scenery painter; 1901–05, worked with scenery designer Walter Hann in London; 1905, traveled to US with Thomas Ryan as a theatrical decorator; became a resident technician at Boston Opera House; returned to England after World War I and worked as a scenery designer and later chief architect for J. Lyon; designed sets for Drury Lane productions and interiors for theaters and cinemas; designed the decorations for 1924 *Empire Exhibition*, Wembley; was technical director for the British pavilion, 1925 *Exposition Internationale des Arts Décoratifs et Industriels Modernes*, Paris; has become known for his steel furniture by Pel (consultant designer there 1931–33), which was fashionable, inexpensive, and comparable with 1920s German models; also designed for Pel's rival Cox; was attracted to new materials like steel and glass, which he incorporated to great effect in commissions, including 1929–30 Strand Palace Hotel, London, which may have been his earliest use of metal furniture; he placed two Thonet tubular-steel chairs in the foyer. Interior design included 1930 Cumberland Hotel, Regent Palace Hotel, 1932 Marble Arch Corner House, Oxford Street Corner House, and other Lyons restaurants; offices and shops for Bakelite; and the Vickers Supermarine aviation works in Southampton.
Bibliography Cat., *Exhibition, architectural and stage decoration by Oliver P. Bernard*, London: attributed to Abbey Gallery, 1926. Cat., Dennis Sharp et al., *Pel and Tubular Steel Furniture of the Thirties*, London: Architectural Association, 1977. Cat., *Thirties: British Art and Design Before the War*, London: Arts Council of Great Britain/ Hayward Gallery, 1979. Barbie Campbell-Cole and Tim Benton (eds.), *Tubular Steel Furniture*, London: The Art Book Company, 1979: 53.

Bernardaud, Porcelaines
French ceramics firm; located Limoges.

History 1863, the firm was founded by Pierre Guerry, who was joined by brother-in-law Rémy Delinières in 1868. 1895, Léonard Bernardaud became an associate and, 1900, head of the firm. The firm is managed today by Pierre Bernardaud and sons Michel and Frédéric; produces fine porcelain dinnerware, having expanded into jewelry, furniture, and lighting that employ fine porcelain. Since 1940s, special editions have included Les Anémones pattern by Bernard Buffet, Le Coq and Les Roses patterns by Theo Van Dongen, and a vase by Raymond Crevel. Raymond Loewy's 1967 dinnerware, commissioned by Pierre Bernardaud, was the first ever contemporary-design service to be made of Limoges porcelain. Other subsequent designers: Marie-Christine Dorner, Roy Lichtenstein, George Segal, Cindy Sherman, Jean Tinguely, Joseph Kosuth, and César, and others, and more recently Mathilde Bretillot, Olivier Gagnère, Marina Karella, Richard Peduzzi, and Ettore Sottsass. In summer 2002, Bernardaud Manufacture in Limoges presented a group of contemporary ceramics produced by the Manufacture Nationale de Porcelaine, Sèvres
Exhibition/citation Silver medal (for a square plate), 1889 *Exposition Universelle*, Paris.

Bernardi, Bernardo (1921–1985)
Croatian furniture and interior designer and theoretician; born on the island of Koršula; active Zagreb.

Training 1948, master's degree in architecture, Fakulteta Architekture, Sveučilište, Zagreb.
Biography 1951, Bernardi cofounded interdisciplinary group EXAT 51; 1964, cofounded SIO (Studio za Industrijsko Oblikovanje, or studio for industrial design); from early 1950s, worked as a freelance architect and product designer. His theoretical ideas were influential in the post-World War II renewal of urban life in Croatia, when it was within Yugoslavia. In the rancorous post-war debate on the role of art in crafts and/or industrial production, he argued strongly that machinery could be the means for developing a standard to nurture everyday lifestyle and considered industrial design as a path toward a more democratic social paradigm. Designed 1952 standard school furniture, 1961 furniture and interior of the Open University of Workers in Zagreb, and interior of Zagreb airport. Late 1970s, designed hotel and office furniture by Tvin, the furniture manufacturer in Virovitica, Croatia; wrote numerous articles and papers on interior and furniture design. Died on the island of Brač, Croatia.
Exhibitions Work included in 1955 (1st) and 1959 (2nd) Triennial of Zagreb and 1957 (11th) Triennale di Milano. Furniture examples housed in Muzej za Umjetnost i Obrt (museum of arts and craft), Zagreb.
Bibliography Stane Bernik, *Bernardo Bernardi*, Zagreb: Grafički zavod Hrvatske, 1992. Fedja Vukic, *A Century of Croatian Design*, Zagreb: Meandar, 1998.

Bernaux, Émile (1883–1997)
French sculptor and furniture designer; born Paris.

Biography From 1909, Bernaux produced furniture with highly carved human, floral, and fruit motifs.
Exhibitions/citations Work shown regularly at Salons of Société des Artistes Décorateurs 1911–29, an active member to end of 1940s. Designed a dining room (with architect Alfred Levard) at 1925 *Exposition Internationale des Arts Décoratifs et Industriel Modernes*, Paris. Elected Chevalier of the Légion d'Honneur.
Bibliography Maurice Dufrêne, *Emsembles mobiliers, Exposition internationale 1925*, Paris: Charles Moreau, 1925: 76. Pierre Kjellberg, *Art déco: les maîtres du mobilier, le décor des paquebots*, Paris: Amateur, 1986.

Bernett, Jeffrey (1964–)
American designer; born Champaign, Ill.

Training 1984–88, business, Northwestern University, Evanston, Ill.; 1988–89, business, University of Minnesota, Saint Paul/Minneapolis; 1993–94, furniture design, Parnham College, Dorset, UK.
Biography 1995, Bernett set up 'studio B,' New York. His design work has included 1997 furniture collection designed and produced by Bernett for Troy, a New York retail shop; 1998 Progetto Oggetto collection (with others), 1999 Monza chair, 2000 Monza light, 2001 Urban table by Cappellini; 1999, 2000, and 2001 object collections by Ligne Roset; 2000 Tulip chair, 2001 Landscape chaise longue, Metropolitan range, and others by B&B Italia; 2000, retail-store furniture and fixtures for Michael Kors; 2000 in-flight airplane seating for Northwest Airlines; 2001 Box sink by Boffi; 2001 Murano-glass collection by Covo; 2001 Academy storage, 2001 Freelance seating, 2001 Collectable object group by Hidden; wristwatch by Brand. The 2001 minimalist chaise longue by B&B Italia was widely published.
Exhibitions/citations At International Contemporary Furniture Fair (ICFF), New York: 1996 Best of Show/Editors' Award; 2000 Best of Show, *Wallpaper* magazine website; Best of Show/Editors' Award (with Dune). Best of Show (glass by Covo), 2000 Tokyo Designer Block. Designer of the Year (younger generation category), 2000 Internationale Möbelmesse, Cologne.
Bibliography *Ottagano*, Aug.–Sept. 2000. Sophie Tasma Anargyros, 'Le charm discret de Jeffrey Bernett,' *Intramuros*, no. 96, Aug.-Sept., 2001: 50–53. *Vogue* (Germany), Apr. 2001. *Wohnrevue*, June 2001. 'King Size: Guide for the Salone,' *Interni*, Apr. 2001. Mel Byars, *50 Beds...*, Hove: RotoVision, 2000. Michele De Lucchi (ed.), *The International Design Yearbook*, London: Laurence King, 2001. Mel Byars, *Design in Steel*, London: Laurence King, 2002.

Bernini Mobili e Arredamenti
Italian furniture manufacturer; located Ceriano Laghetto (MI).

History First decades of the 20th century, Bernini was founded to produce furniture primarily in wood; 1964, first employed plastics but remained focused on wood production. Its designers have included Gio Ponti, Rodolfo Benetto, Giotto Stoppino, Fabio Lenci, Gianfranco Frattini, and Silvio Coppola (Bernini's art director). It produced Piergiacomo and Achille Castiglioni's 1940 Sanluca armchair and 1963 Rampa wheeled container, the latter arguably the forerunner of 1980 Radical Design. Also produced Joe Colombo's 1963–64 Combi-Center mobile unit, S. Coppola and T. Kita's 1970 Chair 622 in covered polyurethane for auditoria, Carlo Scarpa's 1974 Zibaldone bookcase, Lenci's 230–232 table-chair-tray set, Benetto's 1971 Quattroquarti 700 flexible units in ABS, and Gianfranco Frattini's Screen 835.
Bibliography Cat., Milena Lamarová, *Design a Plastické Hmoty*, Prague: Umĕleckoprůmyslové Muzeum, 1972: 172. www.bernini.it.

Bernstein, Harvey (1941–)
American designer.

Training 1969, degree, Pratt Institute, Brooklyn, N.Y.
Biography Bernstein established Bernstein Design Associates, New York, for the design of interiors, products, graphics, and exhibitions; has been chairperson, Industrial Designers Society of America (IDSA), New York chapter; taught, Parsons School of Design, New York, and at Pratt Institute, Brooklyn, N.Y.; lectured in Norway, Sweden, England, Japan, and the US.
Citations Numerous awards, including 1997 Gold Award (with others, for desk accessories by Zeco), IDSA.

Bernstrand, Thomas (1965–)
Swedish funiture designer; born Stockholm.

Training 1994–99, Konstfackskolan, Stockholm; 1999, Danmarks Designskole, Copenhagen.
Biography Through his firm Bernstrand & Co. in Stockholm, Bernstrand has designed for clients CBI Design, IKEA (1999 Flop chair and chaise), Soderbergs Møbler (2001 Boxer armchair), Nola Industrier (2002 GreNoLi outdoor bench), do + Droog Design (1997 'do Swing' light), and for his own production (1997 Wembley three-tier sofa versions and 1998 Paperrecyclecarrier).
Exhibition/citations Work widely and frequently shown, including in 2000–02 *Generation X: Young Nordic Design*, traveling the world. 1998 Young Swedish Design Award.
Bibliography Mel Byars, *Design in Steel,* London: Laurence King, 2000. Michele De Luchi (ed.), *International Design Yearbook*, London: Laurence King, 2001.

Bernt (aka Bernt Petersen 1937–)
Danish designer.

Training To 1960, Kunsthåndværkerskolen; to 1973, Skolen for Brugskunst (formerly Kunsthåndværkerog Kunstindustriskolen); both Copenhagen.
Biography 1960–63, Bernt worked with Hans J. Wegner; 1963, set up his own studio and designed furniture, some by by Wørts'

Marc Berthier. Tykho soft radio. 1997, Synthetic rubber and other materials, 5 1/2 x 5 1/2 x 1 5/8" (14 x 14 x 4.1 cm). Mfr.: Lexon, France. Gift of the mfr. MoMA.

Møbelsnedkeri, Odense Stole-og Møbelfabrik, and Søren Willadsens, as well as CH 71 and CH 72 plywood chairs by Carl Hansen. He executed commissions, including for 1972 Olympiad, Munich; taught and exhibited widely; 1978, was a lecturer, Det Kongelige Danske Kunstakademi, Copenhagen.
Bibliography Robert A.M. Stern (ed.), *The International Design Yearbook*, New York: Abbeville, 1985/1986. Frederik Sieck, *Nutidig Dansk Møbeldesign – en kortfattet illustreret beskrivelse*, Copenhagen: Bondo Gravesen, 1990.

Berreux, Fabrice (1964–)

French designer; born Boulogne-Billancourt.

Training To 1986, École Nationale Supérieure des Beaux-Arts, Dijon.
Biography From 1986, Berreux has been active in interior architecture; 1987 with Pascal Oriol and Bruno Moretti, founded '18 août' (reformed as 'dix heurs dix' in 1991), which designed, made, and marketed objects, accessories, and lighting that called on inspiration from art movements such as Pop Art and Land Art. 1990, at 'dix heurs dix,' his work included Saint-Cloud solid-wood chair by Meubles d'Argenta. He has taught in France; recently, has collaborated with other designers on lighting.
Bibliography Cat., Sophie Tasma Anargyros et al., *L'école française: les créateurs de meubles du 20ème siècle*, Paris: Industries Françaises de l'Ameublement, 2000. Michele De Lucchi (ed.), *The International Design Yearbook*, London: Laurence King, 2001.

Berry, Albert (d. 1949)

American metalworker.

Biography In the 1899 exhibition catalog of The Society of Arts and Crafts, Boston, Berry is listed as a silverware designer, Rhode Island School of Design, Providence; subsequently, lived in Alaska and, from 1918, in Seattle, Wash., where he set up Albert Berry's Craft Shop; produced imaginative hand-wrought designs such as lamps, incorporating various natural materials, including mica, shells, and even fossilized walrus tusks, into copper. French Art Nouveau and German Jugendstil styles were reflected in his work. In addition to its own wares, Berry's shop stocked native-American baskets and textiles.
Exhibitions Work shown at 1899 exhibition, The Society of Arts and Crafts, Boston.
Bibliography Cat., *From Architecture to Object*, New York: Hirschl and Adler, 1989.

Berthet, Jean-Louis (1940–)

French furniture designer; born Grenoble.

Training Interior design, École Nationale Supérieure des Arts Décoratifs, Paris.
Biography 1967 after training, Berthet set up a research and design company in Paris, then in Avignon, followed by New York in 1986; 1974–77, was president, Société des Artistes Décorateurs; in addition to interiors of numerous private apartments, offices, and corporate headquarters in France and abroad, designed 1987 Maestro sofa and other furniture primarily in wood and metal, such as Deck Nomade mobile table by Haworth and others by Airborne and by Mobilier International; has collaborated with Yves Pochy, Jean Crumière, and Gérard Sammut.
Bibliography Louis Bériot, *Berthet-Pochy architectes d'intérieur*, Paris: EPA, 1990.

Berthier, Elise

French industrial designer; daughter of Marc Berthier.

Biography In Paris: Berthier worked in the Bercat Studio; and in her father's group, Eliumstudio, and, from 1998, has been a partner of studio Design Plan. Work for clients in France and Japan has included Ric Rac coffee set, 2001 Soap radio, Diabolo FM radio, Diabolo Messenger digital message recorder and Ric Rac dinnerware, chess game by Lexon; Néo vacum cleaner by Rowenta.
Exhibitions Work included in *Design d'Elle*, Galerie VIA (French furniture association), Paris.

Berthier, Marc (1935–)

French designer; born Compiègne.

Training To 1967, École Nationale Supérieure des Arts Décoratifs, Paris.
Biography 1967, Berthier set up a design studio at department store Les Galeries Lafayette, Paris, where he organized two late-1960s exhibitions: *Domus, Formes Italiennes* and *L'Univers des Jeunes*. 1976, Berthier began designing for Japanese and Italian manufacturers and for them and others designed 1973 Twentytube children's furniture collection in lacquered tubes and linen, 1979 Pliaviva folding-furniture series (with Alain Chauvel) by Magis, lighting by Holight, furniture by Knoll, 1985 Kyoto tea service in sanded melamine and silver-plated metal by Cité Future, 1967–68 Ozoo 600 polyester-and-fiberglass furniture for Les Galeries Lafayette (reprised as 1970 Ozoo 700 by Roche-Bobois). He works with his-own-organized Eliumstudio group (whose members include Frédéric Lintz, daughter Elise Berthier, Pierre Garner, Gilles Caillet, Nieves Contreras), and independently, on products, systems, packaging, corporate identities, advertising. Products by Lexon: 1997 Tykho soft radio, 1998 flashlight, 2000 Tykho fan, 2000 folding chair, others), Magis (1985 office chairs, 1986 shelving, 1998 coat rack, 1998 knock-down chair, others. Berthier teaches, ENSCI (Les Ateliers), Paris.
Exhibitions/citations Work shown at numerous Salons du Meuble, Paris. Won 1975 school-furniture competition (with Daniel Pigeon), sponsored by Centre de Création Industrielle (CCI); various awards and production supports from VIA (French furniture association), Paris.
Bibliography Gilles de Bure, *Le mobilier français 1965–1979*, Paris: Regard/VIA, 1983. *Les carnets du design*, Paris: Mad-Cap Productions /APCI, 1986: 19. Francois Mathey, *Au bonheur des formes, design français, 1945–1992*, Paris: Regard, 1992. Yvonne Brunhammer and Marie-Laure Perrin, *Le mobilier francais 1960–1998*, Paris: Massin, 1998. Michele De Lucchi (ed.), *The International Design Yearbook*, London: Laurence King, 2001.

Berti, Enzo (1950–)

Italian designer; born Venice.

Training To 1973 under Alberto Viani, Accademia delle Belle Arti; 1975, industrial-design advanced course, Istituto Universitario di Architettura; both Venice.
Biography Working in a range of materials from the late 1970s, Berti has designed kitchens by Aiko and Arc-Linea, lamps by VeArt (Artemide), contract seating and seating systems by Bros's, The Night Zone interior-design system by Cadel, quilted seating systems by Cinova and by Ferlea, interior-design systems by Frighetto and by Interlübke; contract seating by Lapalma, home-cleaning products by Libman, domestic plastic home furnishings by Magis, contract seating by Montina, office system by Ultom, wood products by Lago, and a number of other longtime clients.
Citations Several awards, including 1991 product design, Institute of Business Designers (IBD), US.
Bibliography Claudia Neumann, *Design Lexikon Italien*, Cologne: DuMont, 1999. Cristina Morozzi, *Mobili italiani contemporanei*, Milan: L'Archivolto, 1996. Giuliana Gramigna and Paola Biondi, *Il design in Italia dell'arredamento domestico*, Turin: Allemandi, 2000.

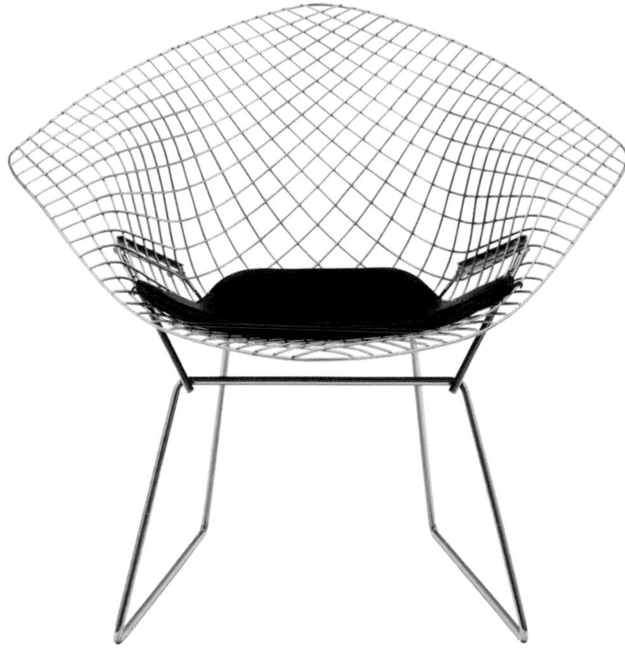

Harry Bertoia. Diamond chair. 1952. Steel rod and Naugahyde seat pad, overall h. 30 x w. 21 1/2" (76.2 x 54.6 cm). Mfr.: Knoll International, US. Purchase Fund. MoMA.

Bertoia, Harry (b. Arieto Bertoia 1915–1978)

Italian sculptor, printmaker, and jewelry and furniture designer; born San Lorenzo (UD); active US.

Training 1932–36, Cass Technical High School, Detroit, Mich.; 1936, School of Arts and Crafts, Detroit; 1937–39 under Eliel Saarinen, Cranbrook Academy of Art, Bloomfield, Mich.
Biography 1930, Bertoia settled in the US; 1939–43, taught jewelry and metalworking at Cranbrook Academy of Art in the metal workshop he set up there; produced jewelry and utilitarian metal objects; 1943–46, worked with Charles and Ray Eames at the Eameses's Evans Products, Venice, Cal., including on molded-plywood technology and airplane and medical equipment for the war effort through the Evans firm; and through the Eameses' Plyform Products Company, Venice, Cal. Eames used Bertoia's pioneering metal-basketwork seat design without acknowledging its source, and Bertoia left the Eameses's workshop in 1950 to become a designer for Knoll. Using the metal-wire basketwork technique, Bertoia designed his famous Diamond Chair range for Knoll, which put it into production 1952–53. The range includes a pivoting lounge chair, small lounge chair, lounge chair with a back extension and footstool, side chair for adults and two sizes for children. From mid-1950s, he was mainly active as a sculptor, producing metal pieces that moved with the wind, sometimes configured to produce percussive sounds. Eero Saarinen often used Bertoia's sculpture prominently in his buildings, including at the chapel of 1953–55 MIT building, Cambridge, Mass., and 1958–63 Dulles International Airport, Chantilly, Va. Bertoia archive is housed in the Vitra Design Museum, Weil am Rhine.
Exhibitions/citations Work subject of 1975–76 venue, Allentown, Pa. (catalog below) 1955 Fine Arts Medal; 1956 Craftsmanship Medal; 1957 Graham Foundation Grant for European travel; 1963 Fine Arts Medal, American Institute of Architects (AIA), Pennsylvania chapter; 1973 gold medal, AIA.
Bibliography Cat., *Les assises du siège contemporain*, Paris: Musée des Arts Décoratifs, 1968. June Kompass Nelson, *Harry Bertoia, Sculptor*, Detroit: Wayne State University, 1970. Cat., *Harry Bertoia: An Exhibition of His Sculpture and Graphics*, Allentown, Pa.,: Allentown Art Museum, 1975. Eric Larrabee and Massimo Vignelli, *Knoll Design*, New York: Abrams, 1981: 66–71. Cat., *Modern Chairs 1918–1970*, London: Lund Humphries, 1971. Cat., *Knoll au Louvre*, Paris: Musée des Arts Décoratifs, 1972. Muriel Emanuel et al. (eds.), *Contemporary Artists*, New York: St Martin's, 1983: 84–95. Charlotte and Peter Fiell, *Modern Furniture Classics Since 1945*, London: Thames & Hudson, 1991.

Bertoldi, Giorgio (1940–)

Italian designer; born and active Venice.

Biography Bertoldi designed glassware by Vistosi, 1963–64 lamp by Tre Vi, public furniture by Malvestic, 1968 and 1972 kitchen systems by Noalex and by Mobilgas, office schemes and modular domestic storage systems by Longato Arredamenti; was member, Associazione per il Disegno (ADI).
Exhibitions Participated 1963 Triennale del Corso Superiore di Disegno Industriale, Venice.
Bibliography *ADI Annual 1976*, Milan: Associazione per il Disegno Industriale, 1976.

Bertolini, Patrizia (1962–)

Italian industrial designer; born and active Bolzano.

Training 1989, on a scholarship in product design, Istituto Europeo di Design (IED), Milan; 1991, degree in industrial design, Istituto Superiore per le Industrie Artistiche (ISIA), Rome.
Biography 1994, Bertolini and Christof Burtscher (Schruns, Austria, 1964–2001) established Burtscher & Bertolini Design, first in Vienna then in Bolzano. They worked as interior and knock-down wood-furniture designers by Horm, Malofancon, Triangolo, and others. (To 1989, Burtscher studied product design on a scholarship, Istituto Europeo di Design [IED], Milan.
Citations 1992 1st prize (for urban color concept), Sichtbank, Dornbirn; 1997 and 1998 1st prize (Slim bookcase by Atelier and Bilove bed by Malofancon), 1999 selection, Young & Design, Milan; 1999 selection (for Twist folding bed by Horm), Young & Design, Milan; 2000 ADI index and 2001 Compasso d'Oro (for Sottiletto bed by Horm).
Bibliography Carlo Vannicola, *La qualità del dormire*, Milan: Rima Editrice, 1997. Mel Byars, *50 Beds...*, Hove: RotoVision, 2000.

Bertone, Nuccio (1914–1997)

Italian automobile designer.

Training In business accounting.
Biography Early 1950s, Bertone became the manager of the firm his father Giuseppe Bertone (1884–1972) founded in 1912 as a traditional coachbuilder in Turin, Italy, which between the World Wars worked with Alfa Romeo on a number of bodies, including 1934 Tipo 6C 2300. 1930, Nuccio became head of the firm and continued the firm's management strategy but was not himself a designer. He had the ability to recognized talented young designers, offered them complete free-

dom to pursue new and innovative concepts, and credited their work; over a period of time, had employed Marc Deschamps, Marcello Gandini, Giorgetto Giugiaro (Fiat 850 Spider), Franco Scaglione (Alfa Romeo Giulietta Sprint, resulting in the Bertone firm's entry into mass production), and others who contributed their individuality to the firm, resulting in a number of cutting-edge designs that became influential in car design and ranging from important series-production cars to exotic sports models. The fecund 15-year partnership with Marcello Gandini realized 1966 Lamborghini Miura, 1968 Lamborghini Espada, 1970 Alfa Romeo Montréal, 1971 Lamborghini Urraco, 1972 Lamborghini Countach, 1972 Maserati Khamsin, 1973 Fiat X1/9, 1973 Ferrari 308 GT4, and 1974 Lancia Stratos. 1980s–90s, the Bertone firm manufactured Fiat X1/9 and designed 1982 Citroën BX, 1989 Citroën XM, 1993 Citroën Xantia, and then assembled 1993 Opel Astra and 1994 Fiat Punto cabriolet. Of its old clients, only Citroën remains today, but produced 1999 BMW C1 scooter, 1999 Opel Astra coupé, and 2000 Opel Astra cabriolet.
Citations 1979, Cavaliere del Lavoro (to Giuseppe Bertone for his contribution to Italian industrial development), Italian Republic Committee.
Bibliography Luciano Greggio, *Bertone*, Milan: Giorgio Nada, 1992. Giancarlo Perini, *Bertone Design Machine*, Milan: Automobilia, 1998. Luciano Greggio, *Bertone: 90 Years, 1912–2002*, Milan: Giorgio Nada, 2002. Penny Sparke, *A Century of Car Design*, London: Mitchell Beazley, 2002.

Bertoni, Flaminio (1903–1964)

Italian automobile designer; born Masnago (Como region, now Varese borough); active in France.

Training 1918, diploma, technical school 'Francesco Daverio,' Varese; from 1919 under Giuseppe Talamoni, drawing and carving; in workshops of sculptors Lodovico Pogliaghi and Enrico Butti.
Biography With Pogliaghi and Butti, Bertoni designed the World War I memorial in Varese; 1918, was an apprentice joiner, Carrozzeria Macchi carriage-body works, and, from 1922, a draftsperson there; 1923, was discovered by French technicians and invited to and left for Paris; 1924, returned to the Macchi factory and, concurrently, was active in his own studio in Varese; 1929, left Macchi and began working for clients Carrozzeria Varesina and Carrozzeria Baroffio, near Varese; 1931, closed his two workshops and again moved to Paris, working for Citroën from 1932; in only one night, designed legendary 1934 Citroën Traction Avant in plasticine (first time in history for a car-design idea to be realized in a medium other than on paper); 1935 under Citroën chairperson Pierre-Jules Boulanger (Sin-le-Noble 1885–near Clermont-Ferrand 1950), began work on the T.P.V. (Très Petite Voiture, later known as the 2CV); 1940 due to Italy's role in World War II, was arrested and to be deported by the French government but this was thwarted by the German occupation of Paris; all the while and throughout his lifetime, continued as a sculptor; 1941, returned to Citroën; 1944 on the liberation of Paris, was arrested again for purported German collaboration but freed; 1945, took up work again on the T.P.V. and V.D.G. (a replacement for the Traction Avant); 1946, returned to Varese; 1950, returned to Paris and designed 1955 Citroën DS19 (claimed by some historians to be his masterpiece and one of the best-ever car designs). His last design was 1961 Citroën Ami 6 with an upwardly-slanting rear window. He died in Paris. 1999, the Associazione Internazionale Flaminio Bertoni was founded in Varese.
Exhibitions Particated in three 1930 venues: *Exhibition of San Pedrino*, Varese; *Esposizione Sociale*, Accademia di Bella Arti, Milan; first *Mostra degli Animali nell'Arte*, Rome. Other exhibitions (many for his fine art), with awards, including 1948 (7th) (Citroën 2CV introduction) and 1955 (Citroën DS19 introduction) Salon de l'Automobile Paris, and Triennale di Milano (DS19). 2003 *When Flaminio Drove to France: Flaminio Bertoni's Designs for Citroën*, Design Museum, London. From 1928, member, Accademia di Bella Arti, Milan; 1961, assigned Chevalier of the Ordre des Arts et des Lettres, France.
Bibliography Fabien Sabates et Leonardo Bertoni, *Bertoni: 30 ans de style Citroën*, Boulogne Billancourt, ETAI, 1998. Leonardo Bertoni, *Flaminio Bertoni—la vita, il genio e le opere*, Milan: Macchioni Editore, 2002.

Fulvio Bianconi. Fazzoletto vase. 1949. Glass, h. 10 1/4" (26 cm). Mfr.: Venini, Italy. Gift of R. H. Macy & Co., New York. MoMA.

Bertoni, Maurizio (1946–)

Italian designer; born Milan.

Training Accademia di Belle Arti di Brera, Milan; 1967, Hochschule für Gestaltung, Ulm.
Biography Bertoni worked in Peter Raacke Design Studio, Frankfurt, designing paper furniture, packaging, and domestic goods; from 1978, designed lighting by Castaldi Illuminazione and by Firmen-Images.
Bibliography Cat., Hans Wichmann (ed.), *Design Italien 1945 bis heute*, Munich: Die Neue Sammlung, 1988.

Best, Robert Dudley (1892–1984)

British lighting designer and manufacturer of lighting fittings and architectural metalwork.

Training Meisterschulerin Kunstakademie, Dusseldorf; interior-design atelier, Paris.
Biography Best worked in a studio in Paris; 1925, became managing director of the family lighting business Best and Lloyd (founded 1840) in Smethwick, UK; was introduced to modern design through the work of Walter Gropius and 1925 *Exposition Internationale des Arts Décoratifs et Industriels Modernes*, Paris; while on a trip to Zürich, was influenced by Christian Dell's 1929 Typ K table lamp that Best described as 'frankly mechanistic in appearance'; modified the model (essentially a plagiarization of Dell's) for the British market, resulting in 1930 Bestlite lamp, with some collaboration with Serge Chemayeff. The lamp was reentered into production in various permutations from early 1990s. Best became an early member of the Design and Industries Association (formed 1915). Active before and after World War II, the Best and Lloyd firm was known for its inexpensive lighting fixtures with high-design standards.
Exhibitions Bestlite table lamp included in 1979–80 *Thirties* exhibition, Hayward Gallery, London (catalog below).
Bibliography Cat., *Thirties: British Art and Design Before the War*, London: Arts Council of Great Britain/Hayward Gallery, 1979.

Bettonica, Franco (1927–)
> See OPI, Studio.

Bevilacqua, Carlotta De
> See De Bevilacqua, Carlotta.

Béwé (b. Bruno Weill)
> See Thonet Frères.

Bey, Jurgen (1965–)

Dutch designer.

Training 1984–89, environmental department, Akademie voor Industriële Vormgeving (now Design Academy), Eindhoven.
Biography Bey worked with designer Jan Konings. They designed for the Droog Design group, including a paper bookcase, and, 2000, a sundial in Amersfoort, their last collaboration, for bed manufacturer Auping. Individual work for Droog: 1999 Kokon chair/table and chair/

lamp sheathed in plastic film; 1999 Broken Family dinner service of handleless cups and cracked plates; 2002 Tree Trunk Bench old-chair backrests cast in bronze on a natural tree trunk; 1999 Healing Series I chairs with shortened leg replaced by a stack of magazines or books (the missing leg made into a toy automobile); and Healing Series II table-and-heater combination. The Healing Series became 2000 'do add,' a range of products by, or a department of, Droog. Currently only rarely collaborates; teaches, Akademie voor Industriële Vormgeving, Eindhoven. Other work: movable video screens at the Valéncia Biennale; a disintegrating bench for Amersfoort town; garden designs at Het Princessehof Museum, Leeuwarden; interior design of Wedding Room, City Hall, Utrecht; seating at Rietveld Pavilion, Centraal Museum, Utrecht; tactile interior architecture for an institute for the blind (with Hella Jongerius); 1999 shop-window concept with LCD monitors for Levi Straus and Droog Design; 1999 Lightshade Shade hanging lamp by Moooi.
Exhibitions/citations Work included in 1996 *Contemporary Design from the Netherlands*, The Museum of Modern Art, New York; *Design World 2000*, Konstindustrimuseet, Helsinki. 2003 Lensvelt de Architect Interieurprijs (LAI), the Netherlands.
Bibliography Renny Ramkers and Gijs Bakker (eds.), *Droog Design: Spirit of the Nineties*, Rotterdam: 010, 1998. Michele De Lucchi (ed.), *The International Design Yearbook*, London: Laurence King, 2001.
> See Droog Design.

Bézard, Aristide-Calixte (1876–1916)
French ceramicist.

Biography c. 1902 with Émile Mousseux, Bézard founded a faïence factory in Marlotte and made earthenware with barbotine decoration and flambé stoneware. Bézard died in World War I. 1933, Mousseux closed the factory.
Bibliography Yvonne Brunhammer et al., *Art Nouveau Belgium, France*, Houston: Rice University, 1976, biblio.

Bialetti, Alfonso (1888–1970); Bialetti Industrie
Italian entrepreneur and manufacturer.

Biography 1930 in Omegna, Italy, Alfonso Bialetti (the maternal grandfather of Alberto Alessi) invented the Moka Express, which marked a departure in coffeemaker design. In cast aluminum, it was made according to new industrial techniques being adopted in Italy and purportedly based on an American top-loading washing machine that spouts water through a center tube and over the top of the clothing. At first, the Bialetti pot was handmade. The first model, in a rather squat form, was quite different from the final, more refined 1933 version which remains unchanged today and currently can be found in 90% of Italian households and about 300 million homes worldwide. To distinguish it from others, a caricature of Bialetti's mustachioed likeness is applied to a facet on the pot, which is now also available electrified and in other versions, including colored. The firm has expanded into kitchen cookware.
Bibliography Penny Sparke, *Design in Italy, 1870 to the Present*, New York: Abbeville, 1988. Mel Byars with Arlette Barré-Despond, *100 Designs/100 Years: A Celebration of the 20th Century*, Hove: RotoVision; Paris: Amateur; 1999. Mel Byars, 'To Be Continued,' *Metropolitan Home*, Nov.–Dec. 1999: 80 f. www.bialetti.it.

Bianconi, Fulvio (1915–1996)
Italian illustrator, graphic and glass designer; born Padova; active Murano.

Training Design and drawing, Accademi di Belle Arti; Liceo Scientifico; both Venice.
Biography 1939, Bianconi settled in Milan and worked for Motta; became known primarily for his mid-century glass designs produced in Murano, where he went in 1945 to learn glassmaking techniques and began designing glass almost exclusively by Venini, like 1949 Fazzoletto (handkerchief) vases and practical objects produced by the 1950 *vetro pezzato* process. Graphics clients included publishers Mondari and Garzanti; recording firms HMV, Pathé, and Columbia; and Teatro Olimpico, Fiat, and Pirelli.
Bibliography A. Gatto, *Disegni di Bianconi*, Milan: Garzanti, 1959. Cat., Hans Wichmann (ed.), *Italien Design 1945 bis heute,* Munich: Die Neue Sammlung, 1988. Franco Deboni, *Venini Glass*, Turin: Allemandi, 1989. Rossana Bossaglia, *I vetri di Fulvio Bianconi*, Turin: Allemandi, 1993.

BIC; Marcel Bich (1914–1994)
Italian manufacturer/entrepreneur; born Turin.

History The ballpoint pen may have been originally invented by John J. Loud of Massachuetts, US, patented in 1888 by him in an intricate version. Other equally complicated and leaky interpretations followed. Hungarian typographer Lászlo József Biró (with chemist-brother Georg Biró and technician Imre Gellért) married the best features of the early models and patented their version in France in 1938 and applied for a fresh patent in Argentina in 1943. Biró variously sold the rights to others and eventually to the Italian baron Marcel Bich, who had been the production manager of a French ink manufacturer. 1945 with partner Édouard Buffard, Bich occupied a factory near Paris to make fountain pen parts and mechanical lead pencils; 1950, introduced his version of the ballpoint pen in Europe, calling it BIC, a shortened, more memorable version of his family name and also the name of his firm; 1956, set up operations in Brazil and introduced M10 Clic retractable ballpoint pen. (However, the successful 1954 Jotter retractable version by Don Doman and others had been introduced by Parker Pen Company of Janesville, Wisc., US.) 1958–60, BIC bought Waterman Pen Company, Seymour, Conn., and began BIC pen distribution/production worldwide; 1965, reached for sales in Japan. From 1972, BIC has been publicly traded on the Bourse (Paris stock exchange); diversified, developing 1973 BIC Lighter with an adjustable flame, 1975 one-piece inexpensive BIC Shaver, 1985 BIC Mini lighter. 1973, bought DIM glue (sold to Sara Lee in 1987) and, 1979, Guy Laroche fashion house, which later became a financial liability; 1981, set up BIC Sport for production of sailboards (becoming no. 1 worldwide); 1992, bought Wite-Out Products and introduced Softfeel Ball Pen; 1997, bought Tipp-Ex correction products and Sheaffer writing Instruments; from 1998, has actively developed a number of new products including SureStart child-resistant lighter. Today, more than 21 million pieces of the c. 1950 BIC Crystal ballpoint pen are sold worldwide annually. The firm's boat *France* participated in 1970, 1974, 1977, and 1980 America's Cup yacht races. Marcel Bich died in Neuilly-sur-Seine, France, having turned over the firm to his two sons in 1993.
Bibliography www.bicworld.com.
> Biró, László József.

Bidasoa, Porcelanas del
Spanish porcelain manufacturer; located Irún, Guipúzcoa.

History From its 1934 founding, Porcelanas del Bidasoa has worked with industrial designers and artists, including Jean Michel Cornu, Salvador Dalí, Gerard Gulotta, Raymond Loewy, André Ricard, Agatha Ruiz de la Prada, Pedro Torrent-Peret, and Óscar Tusquets Blanca; produced Javier Mariscal's 1988 Florero jar and Andrés Nagel's 1988 Plata Azul Verde tableware.
Bibliography Guy Julier, *New Spanish Design*, New York: Rizzoli, 1991.

Biecher, Christian (1963–)
French architect and designer; born Selestat.

Training 1981–83, Unité Pédagogique d'Architecture, Strasbourg; 1984–89 under Henri Ciriani, École d'Architecture de Paris-Belleville.
Biography 1986–92, Biecher was an assistant to architect Bernard Tschumi, Paris and New York; 1992, settled in Paris, where he established Christian Biecher & Associés (CBA) for art, architecture, and interior and graphic design in 1997. Products have included 1994 600 Système chairs by Addform, 1996 Yvon chair by Sazaby, 1998 Trois-roses crystal vase by Baccarat, 1999 Grigri range of domestic furniture by H.A. Deux, 1999 Slide office furniture by Aridi, 2000 Strip leather chair by Poltrona Frau, and, 2001, glass lamps by De Majo, furniture edited by Néotù, and nylon backpack by Pantone Universe. Architecture includes 1994 Bibliothèque Départmentale d'Aude, Carcassone; 1999 60-bed clinic and building, Hôpital Charlon, Hènin-Beaumont; 2000 interior and furniture, Issey Miyake office, Tokyo; 2000 interior, Yvon art gallery, Paris; 2001 Tur building and offices (with D'Urban Inc.), Tokyo. 1990–97, he was assistant professor, Graduate School of Architecture, Planning and Preservation, Columbia University, New York; 1997, guest professor, product design department, Bauhaus, Weimar; 1999–2000, guest professor, École Spéciale d'Architecture (ESA), Paris.
Citations 1999 Carte Blanche production support, VIA (French furniture association).
Bibliography Joël Cariou, *Maisons d'architectes*, Paris: Alternatives,

Bieffeplast: Joe Colombo. Boby 3 portable storage system. 1970. Injection-molded ABS polymer, 29 x 16 x 16 7/8" (73.7 x 40.7 x 42.8 cm). Mfr.: Bieffeplast, Italy. Gift of Inter/Graph. MoMA.

1997. Sophie Tasma-Anargyros, 'Christian Biecher, éclectique et attentif,' *Intramuros*, no. 80, Dec. 1998. Anne Bony, *Les années 90*, Paris: Regard, 2000. Lionel Blaisse, 'La ligne de démarcation de Christian Biecher,' *ArchiCréé*, Jan. 2001. Béatrice Brasseur, 'Christian Biecher sous une bonne étoile,' *L'express*, no. 2586, Jan. 2001. Prosper Keating, 'The Light Fantastique in Interiors,' *New York*, Apr. 2001. *Mel Byars, On/Off: New Electronic Products*, New York: Universe, 2001: 129.

Bieffeplast

Italian furniture manufacturer; located Caselle di Selvazzano (PD).

History 1960, Bieffeplast was established; has become best known for 1970 Boby articulating plastic portable storage systems by Joe Colombo. Other furniture has included 1975 Amico articulating table by Terence Conran, 1982 Attic table by Ettore Sottsass, 1970 Omstack chair and 1984 Grafitti shelving system by Rodney Kinsman, 1984 Tux chair and table by Haigh and Haigh, 1984–1986 Sguish lamp versions and 1986 Trasparia sconce by Fabio Di Bartolomei, 1986 Stillight lamp series by Matteo Thun, 1986 Abate side chair by Michele De Lucchi, 1987 Angel chair by Terri Pecora, and 1989 Alfa armchair by Anna Anselmi; others.
Citations 1984 Progressive Architecture International Conceptual Furniture Competition (Tux chair and table).
Bibliography www.bieffeplast.it.

Bigas, Ramón (1941–)

Spanish designer; born Barcelona.

Training Universitat de Barcelona.
Biography Bigas founded the ZUT collective, which organized 1968 *Homenaje a Martín Luthero King exhibition*, Museo de Arte Contemporáneo; 1958, became active as a designer of domestic objects, including by Módulo Muebles and Contacto, and, at the time, wrote about various designers, including Rietveld, Balla, and Green and Abbot; was a cofounder of Programa group, Grup Barcelona, and diseño 73; 1981, founded Sociate Designers, which realized more than 1,000 projects; 1992, designed Olympic Flame for Olympic Games and trains for the Spanish railway; 1994 with Miquel de Moragas and Claret Serrahima; 1995, established his own office Ramón Bigas Disseny, remodeling the ground floor of Gaudí's La Pedrera in 1996, and designing 1975-2000 Ramón chair by Santa & Cole and 2000 signage of the province of Barcelona; 1994–2001, was president, FAD (decorative-arts association).
Bibliography Cat., *Diseño industrial España*, Madrid: Museo Nacional de Arte Reina Sofía, 1989.

Bigaux, Louis

French architect and interior designer; born Lessay.

Biography c. 1900, Bigaux developed new concepts of form and decoration for interior decoration; gathered around himself a group of young disciples, who contributed to his projects. His studio handled every aspect of the decorative arts, including painting, design, sculpture, and carpentry.
Exhibitions At 1900 *Exposition Universelle*, Paris, showed a luxurious interior, using the products of manufacturers who commissioned him to update their designs, in a pavilion that included bronzes by Eugène Baguès, wallpaper by Isidore Leroy, ceramics by Alexandre Bigot, furniture and paneling by Le Coeur, and marbles by Poincet.
Bibliography Yvonne Brunhammer et al., *Art Nouveau Belgium, France*, Houston: Rice University, 1976.

Bigot, Alexandre (1862–1927)

French ceramicist; born Mer, Loir-et-Cher.

Biography Bigot discovered the stoneware and porcelain pieces of the Far East at 1889 *Exposition Universelle*, Paris; produced flambé stoneware and architectural products such as bricks, tiles, decorative panels, and other items; specialized in tile friezes, producing the designs of Guimard, Van de Velde, Roche, Jouve, Sauvage, Majorelle, de Baudot, Formigé, Lavirotte, and, for the Samaritaine department store, Frantz Jourdain; 1897, sold work (sometimes with bronze mounts designed by Edward Colonna) at Siegfrid Bing's shop L'Art Nouveau, Paris; executed the ceramics for Lavirotte's building, and the vestibule of Guimard's Castel Béranger, both Paris. Bigot's catalog showed stoves and bathtubs. 1914, his shop closed.
Exhibitions/citations 1894, first pieces (simple forms with yellow, green, and brown matt glazes) and later work included in editions of Salon d'Automne. First prize (for his animal frieze, based on designs of Paul Jouve, installed at the exposition's monumental gateway, architect René Binet),1900 *Exposition Universelle*, Paris.
Bibliography Yvonne Brunhammer et al., *Art Nouveau Belgium, France*, Houston: Rice University, 1976, biblio.

Bijvoët, Bernard (1889–1979)

Dutch architect; born Amsterdam; active Netherlands and France.

Biography 1916, Bijvoët and Johannes Duiker became partners in an architecture practice in Amsterdam. They designed 1926–28 Zonnestraal Sanatorium, Hilversum, known for its extensive use of glass and projecting terraced roofs. Meeting Pierre Chareau in Paris 1919, Bijvoët left the Amsterdam practice in 1925; collaborated with Chareau on 1928–32 Maison de Verre (home/office of Dr. Jean Dalsace), 31, rue Saint-Guillaume, Paris; 1935, returned to Amsterdam to carry out Duiker's work after his death; 1937–40, worked with Eugène Beaudoin and Marcel Lods in France; to 1970, practiced on his own in the Netherlands.
Bibliography Johannes Duiker, *Hoogbouw*, Rotterdam, 1930. T. Boga (ed.), *B. Bijvoet & J. Duiker 1890–1935*, Zürich. R. Vickery, 'Bijvoet and Duiker,' *AA Quarterly*, vol. 2, no. 1, 1970: 4–10. 'Duiker 1' and 'Duiker 2' in *Forum*, Nov. 1971 and Jan. 1972. Vittorio Magnago Lampugnani (ed.), *Encyclopedia of 20th-Century Architecture*, New York: Abrams, 1986: 85.

Bilibin, Ivan Yakovlevich (1876-1942)

Russian painter, theater designer, and illustrator, born St. Petersburg; husband of Alexandra Shchekotikhina-Pototskaia.

Training 1895–98, school of Society for the Encouragement of the Arts, and, concurrently, law, St. Petersburg University; 1898, briefly, Azbé School, Munich; 1898–1900, Princess Tenisheva's Art School, St. Petersburg; 1900–04 under Ilya Repin, as an external student, Academy of Fine Arts, St. Petersburg.
Biography Folk art, with which Bilibin was fascinated, was a major theme of his early work.1902–04, he travelled on ethnographic expeditions to the north of Russia; 1901–10, produced colorful illustrations for folk stories; 1907 to the 1917 Revolution, taught, the school of Society for the Encouragement of the Arts; was also an active theater designer; 1914–18, provided illustrations for the periodical *New Satirikon*; 1915, painted murals for Kazan Railroad Station, Moscow; 1917–20, left Petrograd to live in the Crimea but staying until his participation in 1919 (1st) *State Free Exhibition of Artworks*. 1920, he emigrated first to Cairo then moved to Alexandria, Egypt; 1925, moved

to Paris with ceramics artist Alexandra Shchekotikhina-Pototskaia, whom he later married in Alexandria. 1936, he returned to the Soviet Union with her and her son (his stepson); 1936–42, was professor, Graphic Art Studio, Academy of Fine Arts, Leningrad; illustrated books for Goslitizdat publishers; died of hunger in Siege of Leningrad.
Exhibitions 1900–17, exhibited with V Mir Iskusstva (the world of art) and with Union of Russian Artists. Diaghilev included his work in his exhibition of Russian art, 1906 Salon d'Automne, Paris. Work subject of 1952 exhibition in Leningrad.
Bibliography S.V. Golynets, *Ivan Bilibin*, Leningrad: Aurora, 1981. A. Kamensky, *The World of Art Movement,* Leningrad: Aurora, 1991. John Milner, *A Dictionary of Russian & Soviet Artists*, Woodbridge, Suffolk: Antique Collectors' Club,1993.

Bill, Max (1908–1994)

Swiss industrial designer, sculptor, painter, architect, teacher, and writer; born Winterthur; active Zürich.

Training 1924–27, silversmithing, Kunstgewerbeschule, Zürich; 1927–29, Bauhaus, Dessau.
Biography 1929, Bill moved to Zürich and became active as an architect, painter, graphic designer, and, from 1932, sculptor; from 1936, a publicist; and, from 1944, a product designer. He was one of the architects of the Schweizerischer Werkbund's (SWB's) 1930–32 Neubühl estate, near Zürich, a model for the modern style; designed the letterhead, advertisements, flyers, invitation cards of Wohnbedarf store, Zürich, and 1931 logo for its first branch store; 1930, set up his architecture practice; 1930–62, was a member, SWB; 1932–36, member of artists' group Abstraction-Création, Paris. He joined joined the Allianz (an association of modern Swiss artists) in 1937, Congrès Internationaux d'Architecture Moderne (CIAM) in 1939, Union des Artistes Modernes (UAM) in 1939, Institut d'Esthétique in 1953, Deutscher Werkbund in 1956, Bund Schweizer Architekten in 1959. From 1944, he was active as an industrial designer in Zürich; was responsible for Bundespreis *Die gute Industrieform* exhibitions, Frankfurt; was a co-founder of Hochschule für Gestaltung, Ulm, where, 1951–56, he was rector and head of its architecture and 'Produktform' departments and, as a teacher, espoused Bauhaus theories and principles. The Ulm approach (as it became known) profoundly influenced postwar German designers and design, including Hans Gugelot and Dieter Rams. His best-known structure is the 1953–55 building of Hochschule für Gestaltung, Ulm. Pursuing functionalism, Bill's work was based on an amalgamation of mathematical laws with aesthetic standards. 1956, he invited Tomás Maldonado to succeed him as director of the Ulm school; 1957, set up his own studio in Zürich, where he became a painter and sculptor; 1961–64, was chief architect of the Educating and Creating pavilion, 1964 *Schweizerische Landesausstellung (Expo '64)*, Lausanne; 1964, an honorary member of the American Institute of Architects; 1967–71, member of the Swiss parliament; 1967–74, professor of environmental design at the Staatliche Hochschule für bildende Künste, Hamburg. His product designs included 1950 three-legged plywood chair by Horgen-Glarus, 1954 stacking chair, 1957 wall clock, and lighting, including the 1951 Sun table-model health-lamp (no. IV-5) by Novelectric, Zürich.
Exhibitions/citations Industrial-design work included in numerous exhibitions, and subject of 1974 one-person touring exhibition, originating at Albright-Knox Art Gallery, Buffalo, N.Y. Prix d'honneur (Swiss pavilion), 1936 (6th) Triennale di Milano; 1949 Kandinsky prize, Paris; 1951 first prize, Biennale, São Paulo; 1956 Premio Compasso d'Oro; 1966 gold medal, Italian Chamber of Deputies, Verucchio; 1968 art prize, City of Zürich.
Bibliography Max Bill, *Die gute Form*, Bern and Zürich, 1949. Max Bill, *Form: A Balance Sheet of Mid-Twentieth Century Trends in Design*, Basel, 1952. Max Bill, 'The Bauhaus Idea: From Weimar to Ulm,' *The Architects' Year Book*, no. 5, 1953: 29–32. Tomás Maldonado, *Max Bill*, Buenos Aires, 1955; Stuttgart, 1956. Margit Staber, *Max Bill*, London, 1964. Margit Staber, *Max Bill*, St. Gallen, 1971. Cat., *Max Bill*, Buffalo: Buffalo Fine Arts Academy and Albright-Knox Art Gallery, 1974. Eduard Hüttinger, *Max Bill*, Zürich: Abc, 1977; New York: Rizzoli, 1978. Cat., Kathryn B. Hiesinger and George H., Marcus III (eds.), *Design Since 1945*, Philadelphia: Philadelphia Museum of Art, 1983. Friederike Mehlau-Wiebking et al., *Schweizer Typenmöbel 1925–35, Sigfried Giedion und die Wohnbedarf AG*, Zürich: gta, 1989.

Max Bill. Sun table-model health-lamp (no. IV-5). 1951. Enameled metal, extended h. 22 1/2 x base dia. 5 3/4" (57.2 x 14.6 cm). Mfr.: Novelectric, Zürich. Gift of the mfr. MoMA.

Billinghurst, A. Noel
> See Graydon-Stannus, A.N.

Biloxi Art Pottery
> See Ohr, George Edgar.

Bimbi, Carlo (1944–)

Italian designer; born Volterra; active Florence.

Training To 1968, Istituto Superiore delle Industrie Artistiche (ISIA), Florence.
Biography 1960, Bimbi settled in Milan; 1968–69, worked at Studio Nizzoli Associati, Milan; 1970 with Nilo Gioacchini and Gianni Ferrara, founded Gruppo Internotredici, where they executed industrial design for various clients, including machinery, domestic environmental units, and furniture; organized 1984 *Volterra, cercase l'alabastro* exhibition. Clients have included Arketipo, B&B Italia, Ciatti, Guzzini, Metalmobile, and Zucchetti Rubinetterie.
Exhibitions/citations Designed 1,076 sq. ft. (100 m^2) apartment for magazine *Rassegna* at 1971 (9th) Mostra Selettiva del Mobile, Cantù. First prizes, 1968 (8th), 1969 (9th), and 1970 (10th) Concorso Internazionale del Mobile, Trieste; first and second prizes (for plastic furniture in Abet-Print laminates), Concorso Nazionale, Pesaro; first prize (for alabaster objects), 1972 exhibition, Volterra.
Bibliography *ADI Annual 1976*, Milan: Associazione per il Disegno Industriale, 1976. *Modo*, no. 148, Mar.–Apr. 1993: 116. Carlo Bimbi, *Designer: diario di lavoro (1970–1995)*, Florence: Alinea, 1995.

Binazzi, Lapo (1943–)

Italian designer; born and active Florence.

Biography 1967 in Florence, Binazzi was instrumental in the formation of design group UFO and part of the original group that established Architettura Radicale; 1968 with UFO, created large-scale objects located in unlikely areas of Florence, known as Transient Urbans; 1969, was active as an interior designer for various shops; wrote for journals, including *Domus* and *Modo*, and produced videos and films. His first architectural work was the 1971 house in Castel Rigone. 1975, he founded an architecture and design studio in Florence, designing a number of lighting models, ceramics by Eschanbach Porzellanen and silverware by Pampaloni.
Exhibitions From 1968 with UFO, participated in exhibitions in Italy and abroad. His work subject of a 1981 one-person exhibition at Alchimia in Florence.
Bibliography Andrea Branzi, *La casa calda: esperienze del nuovo disegno italiano*, Milan: Idea, 1982. *Modo*, no. 148, Mar.–Apr. 1993: 116.

Bindesbøll, Thorvald (1846–1908)

Danish designer of furniture, ceramics, metalwork, and textiles; active Copenhagen; son of architect M. G. Bindesbøll.

Training 1861–76, architecture, Kunstakademiet; chemistry, Polyteknisk Læreanstalt, Copenhagen
Biography From early childhood, Bindesbøll designed embroidery for his sisters; from 1872, was active in architecture, decorative and monumental commissions, furniture design, embroidery, and book illustration; worked for J. Walmann Pottery in Utterslev; 1891–1902, for Københavns Lervarefabrik ceramics factory; from c. 1898, for Mogens Ballin and A. Michelsen. He combined influences of William Morris and oriental art; derived some of his patterns from clouds and seaweed. His first silver designs—simple forms with strong abstract decoration—date from 1899. Bindesbøll was highly accomplished and his work diversified; from 1890s, was the most important designer of ceramics, furniture, and textiles in Denmark; had a profound influence on an entire generation of young Danish designers There were many contemporary imitators of his work, including Fr. Hegel (who began working at A. Michelsen in 1906), Molger Kyster of Kolding, and Georg Jensen (in his early work). Museet på Koldinghus in Kolding holds the largest collection of his work, a major part donated by goldsmith Holger Kyster of Kolding when Kyster died in 1944. Bindesbøll literally worked up to the day of his death, with pen in hand. The Thorvald Bindesbøll Award was established by the Akademirådet, Denmark.
Exhibitions Work subject of 1982, 1996, 1997 exhibitions, Copenhagen and Kolding (catalogs below) Grand prizes for a number of works, 1900 *Exposition Universelle*, Paris.
Bibliography Karl J.V. Madsen, *Thorvald Bindesbøll*, Copenhagen: Det Danske Kunstindustrimuseum/Fischers, 1943. Svend Hammershøi, *Thorvald Bindesbøll in Memoriam, 1846–1946*, Copenhagen: Fischer, 1946. Cat., Charlotte Christensen (ed.), *Thorvald Bindesbøll, arkitektur, keramik, formgivning*, Copenhagen: Kunstforeningen, 1982. Cat., *Thorvald Bindesbøll: en dansk pioner*, Copenhagen: Danske Kunstindustrimuseum, 1996. Cat., Poul Dedenroth-Schou, *Thorvald Bindesbøll og sølvsmedene = Thorvald Bindesbøll und die Silberschmiede = Thorvald Bindesbøll and the Silversmiths*, Kolding: Museet på Koldinghus, 1997.

Binet, René (1866–1911)

French architect and designer; active Paris.

Training To 1892, École Nationale Supérieure des Beaux-Arts, Paris.
Biography Late 1890s, Binet designed jewelry and silverware; was best known for his entrance to 1900 *Exposition Universelle*, Paris; 1905, designed sections of Au Printemps department store, Paris, including fittings; wrote *Esquisses décoration* (Paris: Librairie Centrale des Beaux-Arts, 1903).
Bibliography Bernard Marrey, *Les grands magasins*, Paris: Picard, 1979: 263. René Julian, *Histoire de l'architecture moderne*, Paris: Sers, 1984. Stuart Durant, *Ornament from the Industrial Revolution to Today*, Woodstock, N.Y.: Overlook, 1986.

Binfaré, Francesco (1939–)

Italian designer; born Milan.

Training Under his father, Carlo.
Biography 1960, Binfaré began working for Cassina, first as a new-technologies researcher, then as the assistant of director Cesare Cassina on new products and the development of prototypes; 1969–76, was director, Centro Cassina, and supervised the creation of what have become classics, such as 1969 Up 5 seating by Gaetano Pesce and 1973 AEO chair by Paolo Deganello; 1980, established Centro Design e Comunicazione for project development at Cassina and Venini; is considered to have been the midwife for some of Cassina's most important furniture, such as 1980 Wink by Toshiyuki Kita, 1980 Tramonto à New York canapé and 1987 Feltri armchair by Gaetano Pesce, and 1982 Torso chair by Deganello; 1991, left Cassina. Binfaré himself designed 1993 L'Homme et la Femme matching-sofa unit, 1994 H/F Tangeri sofa, 1996 Angels sofa/seating system, 2002 Damier adjustable sofa, all by Edra; and 1994 Girotonda armchair and 1995 Grand'angolo sofa by Adele C. His 2001 Diamond Sofa (or Flap) garnered attention due to its unusual articulated backrests, glittering fabric incorporating 750,000 Swarovski crystals, and high price. Binfaré paints and considers himself an artist working for the design industry.
Bibliography Michele De Lucchi (ed.), *The International Design Yearbook*, London: Laurence King, 2001.

Bing, Marcel (1875–1920)

French designer; born Paris; son of Siegfried Bing.

Training École du Louvre, Paris.
Biography Bing designed bronze sculpture and jewelry for his father's shop L'Art Nouveau, Paris; on his father's 1905 death, took control of the business and moved it from 22, rue de Provence, to 10, rue Saint-Georges, dealing in oriental and medieval antiques.
Exhibitions Showed jewelry at 1901 Salon of Société Nationale des Beaux-Arts, Paris.
Bibliography Yvonne Brunhammer et al., *Art Nouveau Belgium, France*, Houston: Rice University, 1976, biblio.

Bing, Siegfried (1838–1905)

French writer and entrepreneur; born Hamburg; active Paris.

Training Before 1870–71 Franco-Prussian War, in ceramics decoration, ceramics factory, Paris.
Biography His forename is 'Siegfried' not 'Samuel.' After working in a ceramics factory, Bing opened a warehouse in 1877 to sell Japanese art in Paris; became a friend of Louis Comfort Tiffany, whose glassware he sold from the 1895 opening of Bing's gallery/shop L'Art Nouveau at 22, rue de Provence, Paris—an enterprise for which he is best known and was extended to ateliers and workshop. Bing also sold glass also by Emile Gallé, René Lalique, and Karl Köpping. (The term 'Art Nouveau' partially originated from the name of Bing's shop; however, was earlier coined by Belgian contemporary critic.) Particularly in the early years of Art Nouveau, he was the most imporant promoter of the movement; from 1888, was editor of journal *Le Japon artistique*, a highly influential publication. Designer/decorator Alexandre Charpentier, designer/writer Eugène Gaillard, and ceramicist Auguste Delaherche also designed for Bing's enterprise, as well as Edouard Colonna and Georges de Feure. Pierre Bonnard's stained-glass designs were made by Tiffany for the shop. Bing wrote the books *Le japon artistique: documents d'art et d'industrie* (Paris: Japon Artistique, 1888–91), and *La culture artistique en Amérique* (Paris, 1896), the latter based on his visit to 1893 *World's Columbian Exposition*, Chicago, and a publication commissioned by the French government in 1894. 1887, John Getz opened a branch of Bing's firm in New York.
Exhibitions Bing's L'Art Nouveau pavilion (with interiors by Colonna, de Feure, and Gaillard), 1900 *Exposition Universelle*, Paris; 1986 exhibition, organized by Smithsonian Institution Traveling Exhibition Service, touring the US.
Bibliography Julius Meier-Graefe, 'L'Art Nouveau: die Salons,' *Das Atelier*, no. 6, 15 Mar. 1896. Cat., Gabriel P. Weisberg (ed.), *Art Nouveau Bing: Paris Style 1900*, New York: Abrams, 1986. Annelies Krekel-Aalberse, *Art Nouveau and Art Déco Silver*, New York: Abrams, 1989. Nancy J. Troy, *Modernism and the Decorative Arts in France: Art Nouveau to Le Corbusier*, New Haven: Yale, 1991. Jacob Baal-Teshuva, *Louis Comfort Tiffany*, Cologne: Taschen, 2001.

Bing & Grøndahl Porcelænsfabrik

Danish ceramics manufacturer.

History 19 April 1853, Meyer Herman Bing and Jacob Herman Bing, paper and art dealers, and artist Frederik Vilhelm Grøndahl (formerly of Den Kongelige Porcelænsfabrik, or Royal Copenhagen Porcelain Factory) set up a factory. By 1880, J.H. Bing's two sons Ludvig and Harald had joined the firm, with Ludvig as general manager and Harald in charge of technical developments. 1885, Harald appointed Pietro Krohn artistic director, serving 1885–97, followed by sculptor/painter J.F. Willumsen, serving 1897–1900. Krohn oversaw the production of 1888 Heron dinner service, designed in a proto-Art Nouveau style. 1895, Harald Bing introduced the first Christmas plate, since then a tradition. Some artists of the day worked for both Bing & Grøndahl and Royal Copenhagen porcelain factories. The latter became known for its figurines of women and children, based on models by Ingeborg Plockross-Irminger, and also for the work of Jean Gauguin, son of Paul Gauguin. 1920s and 1930s, designers included Knud Kyhn, Axel Salto, Kai Nielsen, Ebbe Sadolin, Hans Tegner, and Kay Bojesen. After World War II, a new factory for dinnerware was built in Valby (Denmark) with the original plant specializing in artware. The factory's designers later included Finn Juhl. 1987, the firm was bought by Royal Copenhagen.

Bibliography *Porcelænsfabrikkon Bing & Grøndahl 1853–1928*, Copenhagen, 1928. Cat., *Porzellan-Kunst: Sammlung Karl H. Bröhan*, Berlin, 1969. Erik Larssen, *En københavnsk porcelænsfabriks historie: Bing & Grondahl 1853–1978*, Copenhagen, 1978. Jennifer Hawkins Opie, *Scandinavia: Ceramics and Glass in the Twentieth Century*, New York: Rizzoli, 1989.
> See Krohn, Pietro.

Binns, Charles Fergus (1857–1934)

British ceramicist and teacher; born Worcester.

Biography Early on, Binns worked at Royal Porcelain Works in Worcester, where his father was the director, but boldly changed the direction of his career, when, 1897, he became the principal, Trenton (New Jersey) Technical School of Science and Art, and superintendent of its sponsor, Ceramic Art Company (later named Lenox China Company). He became the first director, New York School of Clay-working and Ceramics, Alfred (N.Y.) University, where he was highly influential, melding aesthetics with technology rather than, as at other institutions, solely emphasizing ceramic engineering. Binns's own specialty was high-fired stoneware, influenced by early Chinese pottery. He became known primarily for creating the notion of the 'studio potter' in the US and for his writings, some before he arrived in America and including *Ceramic Technology* (1897) and *The Potter's Craft* (1922). Despite his knowledge of clay processes, he did not learn to use the potter's wheel until his tenure at Alfred University, where he remained until his death. The American Ceramics Society established an award in Binns's name.
Bibliography Margaret Carney, *Charles Fergus Binns: The Father of American Studio Ceramics* (including a catalogue raisonné), New York: Hudson Hills and International Museum of Ceramic Art, 1998.

Birmingham Guild of Handicraft

British metal workshop; located Birmingham.

History 1890, the Birmingham Guild of Handicraft was established to produce 'handmade articles superior in beauty of design and soundness of workmanship to those made by machinery'; became known for works in precious and base metals. Montague Fordham served as the first director. 1895 when Fordham was joined by other directors, the Guild became a limited company and expanded with architect/silversmith Arthur S. Dixon and C. Napier-Clavering as the chief designers. 1903, Fordham left to take over the Artificers' Guild. 1910, the Birmingham Guild was amalgamated with Gittins Craftsmen, also of Birmingham. Specializing in high-quality hand-made jewelry and other metalwork, its chief jewelry designer was H.R. Fowler. Production of jewelry at the Guild probably began with the Gittins merger. Despite its motto 'by hammer and hand,' members used machinery, including the lathe, in some production; produced simple wares rather than luxury goods like those of the Guild of Handicraft in London; made silverwares that showed simple, honest forms, often incorporating semi-precious cabochon-finished stones.
Bibliography Charlotte Gere, *American and European Jewelry 1830–1914*, New York: Crown, 1975. Cat., Alan Crawford (ed.), *By Hammer and Hand: The Arts and Crafts Movement in Birmingham*, Birmingham: Birmingham Museum and Art Gallery, 1984. Annelies Krekel-Aalberse, *Art Nouveau and Art Déco Silver*, New York: Abrams, 1989.

Biró, László József (1899–1985)

Hungarian of many endeavors; born Budapest.

Training Medical School, Budapest, but did not graduate.
Biography 1921–38, Biró was a journalist, sculptor, painter, art critic, stockbroker, hypnotizer, race-car driver, car salesman, and an inventor; as a journalist, was frequently irritated by the faults of fountain pens and, thus (with brother György Biró, an industrial chemist in the workshops of Goy & Kovalszky), sought a pen that did not dry up or leak. They developed a fast-drying ink—like that used in printing—that could feed a writing ball at the tip of a pen through capillary action, finding an appropriate ballbearing from a Swedish firm. (From 1880s, various people had unsuccessfully attempted to create a workable example of this device.) 1939, fearing the Nazis, Biró emigrated to Paris and, 1940, to Argentina, continuing his pen experimentations independently; 1938, had patented the device in Paris and, 1943, in Argentina. From 1945, his ballpoint pens were sold in large numbers to the public and marketed in Argentina under the name Eterpen. The pen was first manufactured in Britain by the Miles-Martin Pen company for World War II pilots, who used it to mark maps and charts at high altitudes, where traditional pens leaked and froze; in fact, a ballpoint pen is often generically called a Biro by the British. Finally, 1948, Biró sold the patent to Parker Pen Company, US, and possibly to others. Subsequently, the pen was introduced to an international consumer market through Marcel Bich, who used a clear acrylic plastic for the housing and a tungsten-carbide ball and established the BIC company in France. Assuming the patent, Bich first produced a disposable model, 1958 Bic Crystal. Biró's other accomplishments included the invention of the automatic automobile gearshift. 1932 with engineer/friend Rigó, he rode from Budapest to Berlin (more than 625 miles/1000 km) on a motorcycle with a sealed gearshift, the patent to which General Motors bought in order to kill competition. Biró died in Buenos Aires, Argentina, where Argentine Inventors' Day is celebrated on his birthday, 29 September.
Bibliography Stuart L. Schneider, *The Incredible Ball Point Pen: A Comprehensive History and Price Guide*, Atglen, Pa.: Schiffer, 1998.

Birsel, Ayse (1964–)

Turkish industrial designer; born Izmir (formerly Smyrna); active New York.

Training 1981–85, Orta Doğu Teknik Üniversitesi (ODTÜ, aka Middle East Technical University/METU), Ankara; under Bruce Hannah, Rowena Reed, and Peter Barna, on a Fullbright scholarship, Pratt Institute, Brooklyn, N.Y.
Biography Birsel established Olive 1:1 design studio, New York. Work has included 1995 bidet/toilet combination by Toto; 1997, began work on Resolve office system and, subsequently, RED Rocket desk by Herman Miller. Other clients have included Authentics, Dansk International, Gilford, Knoll, and Vitra.
Citations 1990 (for Water Room) and 1996 awards, Annual Design Review, *I.D.* magazine; 1994 award (for furniture), VIA (French furniture association). For Zoe Washlet: 1995 Good Design award, Chicago Athenaeum; 1996 Industrial Design Excellence award. 1999 Overall Best of Competition award and Most Innovative award (for Resolve), NeoCon, Chicago; Young Designer award, 2001 *Brooklyn Museum of Art/Modernism Show*.

Bissell, Brad (1957–)

American industrial design; born San Jose, Cal..

Training University of California, Los Angeles; Rhode Island School of Design, Providence.
Biography From 1983, Bissell was a designer at Apple Computer, Cupertino, Cal., and soon after joined Helmut Esslinger's frogdesign staff which assumed the industrial design of Apple's products; for Apple, designed a unrealized version of the SnowWhite project, the AppleTalk connector family, and, with Stephen Peart, the Vertical LaserWriter concept; 1986, left frogdesign to join Stephen Peart at Vent Design and, as a commissioned designer there, collaborated on the 1987 Apple Goldilocks concepts; 1993 for Apple, designed Rebound and Transformer, subsequently transfigured into Jay Meschter's Bongo version.
Bibliography Paul Kunkel, *Apple Design: The World of the Apple Industrial Design Group*, New York: Graphis, 1997.

Bitsch, Hans-Ullrich (1946–)

German architect and interior and industrial designer; born Essen; active Düsseldorf.

Training 1964–68, architecture and interior architecture, Hochschule des Saarlandes; 1970–71, industrial design in Chicago.
Biography Bitsch taught in Washington, D.C., in 1969, in Chicago 1969–72, and Hochschule in Düsseldorf from 1972. 1977–82, he worked as an architect/designer in the US and Europe; has been president, Bund Deutscher Innenarchitekten (BDIA); established his own architecture/design office in Düsseldorf; 1983, was president, Weltkongresses der internationalen Föderation der Innenarchitekten, Hamburg. His clients have included West Deutscher Rundfunk (WDR), Vorwerk (1988–89 confetti-patterned carpet in *Dialog* carpet collection), and Kuch+Co contract furniture (from 1980).
Exhibitions/citations Work shown extensively. A number of awards.
Bibliography Albrecht Bangert and Karl Michael Armer, *80s Style: Designs of the Decade*, New York: Abbeville, 1990: 191, 227.

Bjørn, Acton (1910–1992)
Danish architect and industrial designer.

Training 1932–33, Det Kongelige Danske Kunstakademi, Copenhagen.
Biography 1933–34 with Ivar Bentsen and Jørgen Berg, Bjørn participated in the construction of the housing complex Blidah in Hellerup; during World War II, became an industrial designer; 1949 with Sigvard Bernadotte, founded Scandinavia's first industrial-design firm, Bernadotte & Bjørn, where, among others, Jacob Jensen and Jan Trägårdh were trained. The firm's clients and products were numerous, including for metalwork, ceramics, industrial machinery, and office equipment. The best-known work from this period is the 1950 Margrethe bowl (named for Danish Queen Margrethe II and designed by Jensen) by Rosti. 1966–90, Bjørn headed the design firm on his own; became known for user-friendly designs of everyday tools, like kitchen equipment, calculators, and packaging. Bjørn's 1965 Beolit 500 transistor radio by Bang & Olufsen was favorably acknowledged.
Citations 1966 Dansk ID Prize (Beolit 500 radio).
Bibliography 'Designs from Abroad,' *Industrial Design*, vol. 4, Feb. 1956: 76–79. 'Acton Bjørn,' *Industrial Design*, vol. 14, Oct. 1967: 50–51. Jens Bernsen, *Design: The Problem Comes First*, Copenhagen, 1982. Cat., Kathryn B. Hiesinger and George H. Marcus III (eds.), *Design Since 1945*, Philadelphia: Philadelphia Museum of Art, 1983. Jens Bang, *Bang & Olufsen: Fra vision til legende/From Vision to Legend*, Denmark: Vidsyn, 2000.

Blenko Glass Co. Pitcher (no. 3750 L). c. 1937. Glass, h. 5 1/2" (14 cm). Mfr.: Blenko Glass Co., US. Gift of the mfr. MoMA.

Bjørner, Annelise (1932–)
Danish furniture and metalwork designer.

Training To 1957, architecture and industrial design, Det Kongelige Danske Kunstakademi, Copenhagen.
Biography She worked with architects Arne Karlsen, Mogens Koch, and Vilhelm Wohlert; collaborated with Rigmor Andersen on 1968 Margrethe cutlery pattern by Georg Jensen Sølvsmedie; designed furniture by Karl Andersson and furniture for 1972 Olympiad, Munich.
Citations Various awards (with Andersen), including 1968 Eckersberg Medal (for Margrethe cutlery), 1968 C.F. Hansen prize, 1968 Zacharias Jacobsen prize.
Bibliography Cat., *Georg Jensen Silversmithy: 77 Artists, 75 Years*, Washington, D.C.: Smithsonian, 1980. Frederik Sieck, *Nutidig Dansk Møbeldesign – en kortfattet illustreret beskrivelse*, Copenhagen: Bondo Gravesen, 1990.

Björquist, Karin (1927–)
Swedish ceramicist.

Training 1945–50, Konstfackskolan and Tekniska Skolan, Stockholm, under Edgar Böckman.
Biography From 1950, Björquist was an assistant to Wilhelm Kåge at Gustavsberg ceramics factory, where she was a designer from 1950 and artistic director 1980–88; on Kåge's 1961 death, took over his studio.
Exhibitions/citations Work included in 1982 and 1986 exhibitions, New York and Stockholm (catalogs below). Gold medal, 1954 (10th) Triennale di Milano; 1963 Lunning Prize.
Bibliography Cat., David Revere McFadden (ed.), *Scandinavian Modern Design 1880–1980*, New York: Abrams, 1982. Cat., *The Lunning Prize*, Stockholm: Nationalmuseum, 1986: 138–41. Jennifer Hawkins Opie, *Scandinavia: Ceramics and Glass in the Twentieth Century*, New York: Rizzoli, 1989.

Black, Misha (1910–1977)
Azerbaijani industrial and exhibition designer; born Baku; active Britain.

Biography 1929, Black became an architect and designer in London, when he designed the Kardomah coffee shops in London and Manchester; 1933–39, was in partnership with Milner Gray in the Industrial Design Partnership, the first multi-skilled design group in England; designed radios and TV sets by E.K. Cole's Ekco firm, including the traditionally rendered 1938 UAW 78 cabinet radio in exotic veneer; became an active member of the anti-war Artists' International Association; 1938, became secretary of the Modern Architecture Research Group (MARS); 1940–45, was an exhibition designer for the Ministry of Information; 1943 with Milner Gray, established the Design Research Unit (DRU); 1945 with Gray, established Design Research Group (DRG); was chief exhibition designer of 1946 *Britain Can Make It* exhibition, Victoria and Albert Museum, London; designed the cars and stations of London Underground's Victoria Line, and interiors of London buses; specialized in corporate design, also designed interiors, furnishings, and engineering products; 1959–75, professor of industrial design, Royal College of Art, London, and pioneered design education and was an effective good-design propagandist.
Citations Large number of honors and public and professional appointments, including Royal Designer for Industry, UK, 1957; and knighthood, 1972.
Bibliography *The Black Papers on Design: Selected Writings of the Late Sir Misha Black*, Oxford: Pergamon, 1983. Avril Black, *Misha Black*, London: The Design Council, 1984. Fiona MacCarthy and Patrick Nuttgens, *An Eye for Industry*, London: Lund Humphries, 1986.

Blackband, William Thomas (1885–1949)
British metalworker; active Birmingham.

Training Vittoria Street School for Jewellers and Silversmiths, Birmingham; Central School of Arts and Crafts, London.
Biography Blackband designed civic regalia and church plate in soft-finished historicist styles and 1934–35 cup to commemorate the Silver Jubilee of King George V; was a teacher at Vittoria Street School and, 1924–46, succeeded Arthur Gaskin its headmaster.
Bibliography Cat., *Thirties: British Art and Design Before the War*, London: Arts Council of Great Britain/Hayward Gallery, 1979. Annelies Krekel-Aalberse, *Art Nouveau and Art Déco Silver*, New York: Abrams, 1989.

Blackman, Leo (1956–)
American architect and industrial designer; born and active New York.

Training To 1981, architecture, Columbia University, New York.
Biography Blackman designed lighting and furniture, including the *Quahog* lamp (with Lance Chantry), and c. 1992 Waste Not rocking chair and Want Not table in a recycled plastic by Yemm and Hart Green Materials of Marquand, Mo.—and architecture, such as 2003 addition to Village Community School, New York.
Exhibitions Work included in gallery and museum exhibitions.
Bibliography Albrecht Bangert and Karl Michael Armer, *80s Style: Designs of the Decade*, New York: Abbeville, 1990: 227.

Blaess, Steven (1970–)
Australian designer.

Biography Blaess has become known for his conceptual interiors, architecture, furniture and product designs, design development, and detailing. He designed the 2000 Summer Olympiad torch, Sydney; 1999 products by Alessi; 2001 Meditation-Pod seat by Edra; 2001 lighting by Nemo Italianaluce; and products by other European and international companies; has been active as a nightclub interior designer for establishments such as the Tantra club, Sydney, and the Crown Casino and the Goodbar, Melbourne; calls on assistance from 3-D CAD designers in Melbourne.

Blaich, Robert (1931–)

American industrial designer.

Training Architecture, Syracuse (N.Y.) University.
Biography 1980–92, Blaich was design director, Philips's Concern Industrial Design Centre (CIDC), the Netherlands, where he supervised 200 designers in 22 countries and asserted that the design of any product or communication should primarily satisfy the customers. He conceived products as 'statements about the image of the company'; at one time, guided Charles Eames and George Nelson at Herman Miller furniture company, US; 1992, founded Blaich Associates (after leaving Philips) in Aspen, Colo.; is chairperson of Teague Design; teaches/lectures, various institutions; is author of *Product Design and Corporate Strategy: Managing the Connection for Competitive Advantage* (with Janet Blaich, 1993) and *New and Notable Product Design* (1991 and 1995); a member of board of advisors, College of Visual and Performing Arts, Syracuse University.
Citations 1990 honorary doctoral degree, Syracuse University; 1992, World Design Medal, Industrial Designers Society of America (IDSA)
Bibliography Arlene Hirst, *American Home*, Apr. 1990: 129. www.design.philips.com.
> See Philips.

Blaisdell, George G. (1895–1978)

American inventor.

Biography The Zippo cigarette lighter, arguably one of the best products ever made, was developed by Blaisdell in Bradford, Pa., where the Zippo factory is still active today. According to lore, he developed his own version of a windproof lighter from an unattractive Austrian version he had seen at a cocktail party. The name Blaisdell gave his interpretation was a play on the word 'zipper.' The Zippo débuted in 1932 and was patented in 1936. Over the years, the design and size have been slightly altered. By the end of the 20th century, more than 300 million examples had been sold.
Bibliography A.M. Van Weert, *The Legend of the Lighter*, Abbeville, 1995. David Poore, *Zippo: The Great American Lighter*, Atglen, Pa.: Schiffer, 1997. Mel Byars with Arlette Barré-Despond, *100 Designs/100 Years: A Celebration of the 20th Century*, Hove: RotoVision, 1999: 76–77. Avi R. Baer and Alexander Neumark, *Zippo: An American Legend*, London: Apple, 1999. Tobias Kuhn, *Design Classics: The Zippo by George G. Blaisdell*, Frankfurt: form, 1999.

Blanchard, Porter George (1886–1973)

American silversmith; born Littleton, Mass.

Training Under his father, silversmith George Porter Blanchard.
Biography Blanchard became a member, Society of Arts and Crafts, Boston, and Detroit Society of Arts and Crafts; before 1923, moved to Burbank, Cal., and produced Colonial Revival silverwork; 1924, cofounded Arts and Crafts Society of Southern California; established a firm under his own name, producing historicist-design silver, including hand-hammered cutlery and handspun hollow-ware—sold by him directly to customers and also in stores.
Bibliography Charles Venable, *Silver in America, 1840–1940: A Century of Splendor*, Dallas, Tex.: Dallas Museum of Art, 1994: 267.

Blank and Cables
> See Craven, Walter.

Blau, Luigi (1945–)

Austrian teacher, architect, and designer.

Training 1966–73 under Ernst A. Plischke, Akademie der bildenden Künste, Vienna.
Biography 1974–78, Blau was a teaching assistant, Hochschule für angewandte Kunst, Vienna; 1984–91, taught, Institut für Werkerziehung der Akademie der bildenden Künste, Vienna; specializes in architecture and the design of furniture, interiors, and exhibitions.

Blenko, William John (1854–1926); Blenko Glass Company

British glassmaker; born Bethnal Green; active in the UK and the US. Glass manufacturer.

Training At age 10, in a bottle factory, London; French and chemistry, night school.
Biography 1890, Blenko introduced Norman slab-type stained glass for a church in Norfolk, UK; 1893, settled in Kokomo, Ind., but, 1905, returned to England when his business failed. 1909, Blenko settled again in the US at Point Marion, Pa., moving 1911 to Clarks-burg, W. Va., near fine sand deposits. 1913, he was forced to close his doors for the third time; developed a method of molding glass, assisted by son Walter Blenko; 1919, may have accepted a prestigious position working at Louis Tiffany's glassworks, Long Island, N.Y.; 1921 in Milton, W. Va., set up Eureka Art Glass (essentially in a shack, his 4th attempt, at age 67 to set up his own glass company, which became Blenko Glass Company 1930, financially assisted by sons Walter and William); 1921, his son William Henry Blenko joined the firm and helped produce blown sheet glass for use as stained-glass window material; recognized the need for utilitarian ware; his son's wife Marion Hunt, daughter of Pittsburgh stained-glass artists, ran the office. Orders began to come in: Blenko's stained glass was used in Liverpool's Anglican cathedral, England; Chartres Cathedral, France; St. John the Divine and St. Patrick's Cathedrals, New York; chapel of the Air Force Academy, Colorado; American Memorial Chapel, Meuse-Argonne, France. 1926, a decision was made to produce decorative and utilitarian glassware, first for the Carbonnes store, Boston, which had been importing goods from Italy and Sweden. Swedish-American glassworkers and brothers Louis Miller and Axel Muller (who never Americanized his name) were hired. 1932, R.H. Macy & Co. department store in New York began selling Blenko glassware and, by 1935, major stores throughout the US carried Blenko ware. 1936, the firm received authorization to reproduce the glassware of Colonial Williamsburg, the restored British colony in Virginia. 1938 Water Bottle is still in production. 1946, a new plant was built. 1946-52, Winslow Anderson was Blenko's design director and first trained designer. Makers of inexpensive glassware, Blenko produced free-blown forms in inventive modern designs in bright colors that reflected America's prosperity; made tall ribbed bottles, which took advantage of the plasticity of the molten medium, but the drooping necks were often accidental. 1955, Blenko was first American company to produce *dalle de verre* (slab glass). Design directors: Wayne Husted (Hudson, N.Y., 1927–) from 1952, Joel Philip Myers (1934–) from 1963 (later leaving to become a studio artist in Bloomington, Ill., later Ording, Denmark), John Nickerson from 1971, Don Shepherd 1976, Hank Adams from 1988, Chris Gibbons in 1994, Matt Carter from 1995–2002. Shephard designed the Leaf dish and Honey Bear (with a sugar additive). By 1987, Blenko had five staff designers. Its molds are carved from cherrywood without blueprints. Max Harder created the Oriental Tangerine graded-color vase. From 2003, designers were former design directors Wayne Husted, John Nickerson, and Hank Adams. From 1996, Richard Deakin Blenko has directed the firm.
Exhibitions Wares included in 1933–34 *A Century of Progress International Exhibition*, Chicago; Bent Decanter by Anderson at 1952 Good Design exhibition/award, The Museum of Modern Art, New York, and Chicago Merchandise Mart. Subject of 2001 *Blenko: American Art Glass 1940–1980*, 20th-Century Gallery, New York; Winslow Anderson subject of 1999 exhibition, Huntington Museum of Art, Hungtington, W. Va.
Bibliography Eason Eige and Rick Wilson, *Blenko Glass 1930–1953*, Marielta, Ohio: Antique Publications, 1987. Leslie Piña (preface), *Blenko Glass: 1962–1971 Catalogs*, Atglen, Pa.: Schiffer, 2000. Leslie Piña and Ramon Piña, *Blenko: Fifties and Sixties Glass*, Atglen, Pa.: Schiffer, 2000. Leslie Piña, *Blenko Catalogs Then and Now: 1959–1961, 1984–2001*, Atglen, Pa.: Schiffer, 2002. www.blenkoglass.com.

Blet, Thierry (1954–)

French industrial designer; born Saint-Cloud.

Training École Camondo, Paris.
Biography 1987 with Catherine Le Teo (Paris, 1957–), Blet formed architecture/interior design studio Elixir. (Le Teo also studied at École Camondo, and her own work has been inspired by the design and colors of *haute couture*.) They designed a prize-winning picnic-tableware set and furniture such as Apia tandem seating and Huit range of seating and tables by Haworth France. Blet designed 1991 Titiana table lamp.
Citations Picnic tableware recognized in 1986 competition sponsored by APCI (Agence pour la Promotion de la Création Industrielle) and UGAP (Union des Groupements d'Achats Publics).
Bibliography *Les carnets du design*, Paris: Mad-Cap Productions/APCI, 1986: 87.

Blickensderfer, George Canfield (1850–1917)

American engineer; born Erie, Pa.; active Stamford, Conn.

Biography After study in a secondary school in Erie, Pa., Blickensderfer began working in dry-goods stores; 1892, invented a new kind of typewriter 20 years after the first practical model had been introduced; 1889, founded The Blickensderfer Manufacturing Company and became an early pioneer in the development of the single-element typewriter, including his 1894 Featherweight Blick model in aluminum. His machines were far ahead of their time, presaging IBM's 'golf ball'-element Selectric electric typewriter by 70 years. The typewheel of the Blick spun into place when a key was pressed, trajecting it down to the platen and, in its course, brushing past the ink roller. It accommodated different type styles and sorts for foreign languages. This revolving-type machine became the world's best seller, and the company grew into one of the world's largest typewriter manufacturers. Blickensderfer also developed the first electric typewriter, 1902 Blickensderfer Electric (with a single 'golf ball' element; 104 volts AC, 60 cycles), only one example of which is known to still exist, at British Typewriter Museum, Bournemouth. Purportedly his no. 8 typewriter was one of the first and said to be the best portable model invented. However, when World War I eliminated his large export trade to Europe, he invented a belt-loading bullet dispenser for machine guns, and orders from the French government kept his firm afloat financially. Three years after Blickensderfer's death, the firm was taken over by L.R. Roberts Typewriter Company.
Exhibitions The Blick introduced at 1893 *World's Columbian Exposition*, Chicago; c. 1894 aluminum Featherweight Blick included in *Aluminum by Design* traveling exhibition from 2000, organized by Carnegie Art Museum, Pittsburgh.
Bibliography *The Daily Advocate*, triennial industrial edition, Stamford, Conn., 24 June 1909: 16. Cat., Sarah Nichols et al., *Aluminum by Design*, New York: Abrams, 2000. www.stamfordhistory.org.

Block Hellum, Charlotte (1911–)

German ceramicist, metalworker, and enamelist; born Görlitz; active Germany and Oslo.

Training Kunstgewerbeschule, Dresden, and pottery, Kunstgewerbeschule, Berlin.
Biography 1937, she settled in Oslo, where she set up her own workshop in 1946; from 1960s, became a specialist in enamelwork; called on traditional Norwegian motifs from nature.
Exhibitions 14 one-person venues 1959–91; 2001 *Charlotte Block Hellum: Emaillekunst*, Städtische Sammlungen für Geschichte und Kultur, Görlitz; 2002 *Charlotte Block Hellum: Emalje*, Blomqvist Kunsthandel, Oslo.
Bibliography Cat., David Revere McFadden (ed.), *Scandinavian Modern Design 1880–1980*, New York: Abrams, 1982. Helene Brekke, *Barokk Minimalist*, Oslo: Hand to Mouth, 2002.

Blomberg, Hugo (1897–1994)

Swedish teletechnician.

Training Electrical engineering, Kungliga Tekniska Högskolan, Stockholm.
Biography 1929, Blomberg joined Ericsson as head of its technical department; later became chief engineer and head of development; 1940–54 with Ralph Lysell (1907–) conceived the Ericofon (aka Cobra) telephone set as a prototype, patented 1941, but in an unattractive form. However, Thames and the Ericsson design group were responsible for the design and construction of the sleek 1954 version (developed from 1949–54). The telephone was distinctive for its one-piece construction; it had fewer components and was lighter than earlier models.
Bibliography Hugo Blomberg, 'The Ericofon—The New Telephone Set,' *Ericsson Review*, vol. 33, no. 4, 1956: 99–109. Cat., Kathryn B. Hiesinger and George H. Marcus III (eds.), *Design Since 1945*, Philadelphia: Philadelphia Museum of Art, 1983.
> See Ericsson, Telefonaktiebolaget L.M. Lysell, Ralph.

Blomsted, Pauli (1900–35)

Finnish architect and designer.

Training In architecture.
Biography Blomsted was active in Funkis, a Finnish Functionalist group and counterpart to the German Bauhaus, although less doctrinaire. His architecture includes a bank in Kotka. In his furniture designs, he married natural materials such as wood with metal tubing; was rediscovered by Kenneth Smith in the early 1980s through archival material at Cranbrook Academy of Art, Bloomfield, Mich., where Blomsted taught in 1930s; designed 1930s seating, desks, and tables that have been reissued by Smith's firm Arkitektura, from late 1980s.

Blount, Godfrey (1859–1937)

British artist and craftsperson.

Training Cambridge University; Slade School of Fine Art, London.
Biography 1896, Blount founded Haslemere Peasant Industries, producers of textiles and simple furniture; subsequently, established the Peasant Arts Society; wrote *Arbor Vitae: A Book on the Nature and Development of Imaginative Design for the Use of Teachers, Handicraftsmen & Others* (London: Dent, 1899), an early primer of the Arts and Crafts movement. Other writings include *For Our Country's Sake: An Essay on the Return to the Land and the Revival of Country Life and Crafts* and *The Rustic Renaissance*.
Bibliography Stuart Durant, *Ornament from the Industrial Revolution to Today*, Woodstock, N.Y.: Overlook, 1986: 214, 233, 320–21.

Blu Dot

American design studio and marketing firm.

History 1996, Blu Dot was founded in Minneapolis, Minn., by John Christakos (Oneida, N.Y., 1964–), Charles Lazor (Morristown, N.J., 1964–), and Maurice Blanks (Midland, Tex., 1965–). The studio/firm began as a loose collaboration among these three college friends trained in architecture and art, offering over 40 models of lower-priced, high-design furniture/furnishings, including its 1997 2d:3d customer-self-folding metal collection, 2000 FeltUp chair, and items by Target.
Citations Numerous national and international awards, including 2000 Best in Category, Annual Design Review, *I.D.* magazine; 2000 Good Design award, Chicago Athenaeum; 2002 National Design Award, Cooper-Hewitt National Design Museum, New York.
Bibliography Dennis Cass, 'Blu Dot Special,' *Midwest Home & Garden*, Feb.–Mar. 1999. Alexandra Lange, 'Blu Dot's Big Plans,' *Metropolis*, Nov. 2000. Marisa Bartolucci et al., *American Contemporary Furniture*, New York: Universe, 2000. Mel Byars, *Design in Steel*, London: Laurence King, 2002. www.bludot.com.

Bluitgen, Ib (1921–)

Danish metalworker.

Training Georg Jensen Sølvsmedie; 1945–48, Det Kongelige Danske Kunstakademie; both Copenhagen.
Biography 1948–61, Bluitgen worked in Jensen's design department; later, set up his own workshop, producing hollow-ware and jewelry.
Exhibitions Work shown at 1980 Smithsonian exhibition (catalog below).
Bibliography Cat., *Georg Jensen Silversmithy: 77 Artists, 75 Years*, Washington, D.C.: Smithsonian, 1980.

Blümel, Otto (1881–1973)

German architect, furniture designer, and painter; born Augsburg.

Training Architecture, Technische Universität; painting, Debschitz-Schule (Lehr- und Versuchs-Ateliers für angewandte und freie Kunst); both Munich.
Biography 1907–14, Blümel was head of the design department, Vereinigte Werkstätten für Kunst im Handwerk, Munich, and art master there 1916–20 and designed furniture; 1920–49, was director, Partenkirchner Schnitzschule; 1925, established the Heimatmuseum, while at the Museumsverein Werdenfels; wrote extensively.
Citations Order of the Verdienstkreuz am Bande, Germany.

Blumer, Riccardo (1959–)

Italian designer; born Bergamo.

Training Architecture, Politecnico, Milan.
Biography 1989, Blumer established a studio in Morosolo (VA); is primarily an architect and designed two towers (his first commission) in the industrial quarter, near Milan, and furniture by Alias, including 1999 Ilvolo table with inner-polyurethane injections, realized through the same process called on for building glider wings.
Citations 1998 Premio Compasso d'Oro, and Design Preis Schweiz (both for 1996 Lalegerra chair, weighing only 9 lbs./4 kg, by Alias).
Bibliography Michele De Lucchi (ed.), *The International Design Year-*

book, London: Laurence King, 2001. *Spoon: 100 Designers, 10 Curators, 10 Design Classics*, London: Phaidon, 2002.

Boberg, Anna Katarina (1864–1935)

Swedish ceramicist and glassware and textile designer; active Stockholm; wife of Ferdinand Boberg.

Biography 1900–02, she designed ceramics for Rörstrand in Lidköping and multi-colored art glass by the Reijmyre glassworks; was a textile designer for Handarbetets Vänner.
Bibliography Cat., David Revere McFadden (ed.), *Scandinavian Modern Design 1880–1980*, New York: Abrams, 1982.

Boberg, Ferdinand (1860–1946)

Swedish architect and designer; active Stockholm; husband of Anna Katarina Boberg.

Biography Boberg designed glass, ceramics, and textiles; became known for his furniture designs for the Swedish royal family; was one of the few designers to produce modern silver in Sweden c. 1900; used pine branches as decoration for his silverworks by C.G. Hallberg in Stockholm.
Exhibitions Swedish royal family's furniture shown at Swedish pavilion, 1900 *Exposition Universelle*, Paris.
Bibliography Annelies Krekel-Aalberse, *Art Nouveau and Art Déco Silver*, New York: Abrams, 1989.

Bobergs Fajansfabrik (aka Bo fajans)

Swedish ceramics firm; located Gefle (now Gävle).

History 1874, a factory for ceramic utilitarian wares was founded by Erik Boberg as a small-size family company that made pottery. ranging from jam pots to unique objects; 1910, was enlarged to include art and decorative wares. 1925, Maggie Wiborn became the first female potter to work at the plant. 1930, production included work by Ewald Dahlskog. 1931, John Boberg and Gösta Boberg assumed management of the company, which effloresced until 1940s. 1946–50, a new electric tunnel oven replaced the former round wood-burning one. 1967, was bought by Steninge Keramik; c. 1978–80, closed.
Exhibitions Maggie Wiborn's work subject of 2000 exhibition; Bobergs subject of an exhibition; both Länsmuseet Gävleborg, Gävle.
Bibliography Jennifer Hawkins Opie, *Scandinavia: Ceramics and Glass in the Twentieth Century*, New York: Rizzoli, 1989.

Bobrovniczky, Bert T. (1940–)

Hungarian industrial designer; born Budapest; active Toronto.

Training To 1968, Magyar Iparművészeti Egyetem (MIE, university of applied arts), Budapest.
Biography 1975, Bobrovniczky opened b & b design associates, a design office, Toronto, Canada; from 1979, was a professor, packing and graphic design, School of Media Studies, Humber College, Toronto; designed 1972 communication system for Oshawa Police Headquarters in Oshawa, Canada, that was the first time human engineering and environmental aspects of communication were applied to police work; was research director, 1974 Interdesign Ontario, the first in the western hemisphere to study design for small communities; was president, Association of Canadian Industrial Designers (ACID).
Exhibitions/citations 1970 Best Commercial and Industrial Product of 1970 (telephone power-system pole), National Design Show; 1971 Best of Show, EEDFE award (street furniture/fitting group), National Design Show; 1981 and 1984 Product of Excellence award, Design Canada Awards, sponsored by National Design Council, Design Canada, and Department of Industry, Trade and Commerce; Canadian representative, 'Worldesign,' International Council of Societies of Industrial Designers (ICSID), Washington, 1985, and New York, 1988; Ontario representative, 1985 'Ontario-Design,' London; 1986 'The Creative Spark,' Royal Canadian Academy of Arts, Toronto; 1993 Best in Show, Certificate of Merit, *The Financial Post* Design Effectiveness Award, sponsored by the Ministry of Economic Development and Trade, Ontario.
Bibliography Douglas Cleminshaw, *Design in Plastics: Successful Product Design in Plastics*, Gloucester, Mass.: Rockport, 1989.

Boch, Anna (1848–1936)

Belgian ceramicist; daughter of director of Boch ceramics factory.

Biography 1886, Boch, a painter, became a member of Les Vingts (founded in Belgium 1883 and succeeded by La Libre Esthétique 1894). She persuaded A.W. Finch to work at the Kéramis factory (the Boch ceramic branch in La Louvière, Belgium); decorated some ceramics there herself; designed Die Kugel dinner service using a single, spherical modular unit by Villeroy & Boch.
Bibliography Yvonne Brunhammer et al., *Art Nouveau Belgium*, France, Houston: Institute for the Arts, Rice University, 1976.

Boch Frères
> See Villeroy & Boch.

Boch, Helen von (1938–)

German ceramics designer; member of Boch family of ceramic and glassware producers.

Biography Boch designed 1968–69 Bomba stainless-steel cutlery (with Frederigo Fabbrini), 1973 Sphere stoneware, and 1973 Bomba melamine-plastic dinner services by Villeroy & Boch, whose pieces were designed to fit together into one transportable unit.
Bibliography 'Design in Action: Inner Beauty,' *Industrial Design*, vol. 18, May 1971: 34. Sylvia Katz, *Plastics: Designs and Materials*, London: Studio Vista, 1978: 71–72. Cat., Kathryn B. Hiesinger and George H. Marcus III (eds.), *Design Since 1945*, Philadelphia: Philadelphia Museum of Art, 1983.

Boda
> See Kosta Boda.

BodaNova–Höganäs Keramik
> See Höganäs Keramik.

Bodin, Jean-François (1946–)

French architect and designer; born Paris.

Training École des Langues Orientales; École des Monuments Historiques; both Paris.
Biography With Andrée Putman, Bodin cofounded Ecart International furniture/design firm, Paris, which he left in 1988; began independently designing, renovating, and restructuring a number of museums, including the Matisse in Nice, Art Moderne de la Ville in Paris, Beaux-Arts in Cambrai, and, late 1990s, the library and exhibition spaces of Centre Georges Pompidou. His 1999 table for the Bibliothèque Publique d'Information was produced by Tecno.
Bibliography Cat., Sophie Tasma Anargyros et al., *L'école française: les créateurs de meubles du 20ème siècle*, Paris: Industries Françaises de l'Ameublement, 2000.

Bodum

Danish tabletop/dinnerware manufacturer; located Langaa and Hørsholm.

History 1944, Bodum was founded by Peter Bodum; is managed today by son Jørgen Bodum and continues as a 100% family-owned firm; initially imported glassware from Eastern Europe to sell in Denmark. 1958, its first product, the Santos vacuum coffeemaker, was designed exclusively for the company by Kaas Klæson and is still in production. 1974, the Presto coffeemaker was introduced as Bodum's Chambord trademarked device; however, the so-called French press was developed 1933 by a little-known Italian named Calimani. The Presto was the first collaborative design by Jørgen Bodum and Carsten Jørgensen. 1986 in London, first Bodum retail store was opened to become the flagship store with other outlets following, in Paris, Porto, Copenhagen, Lisbon, Zürich, Lucerne. By 1996, Bodum was employing 400 people; today, is divided into nine sales entities, two production companies, and the design studio Pi Design AB in Switzerland.
Bibliography www.bodum.com.

Boehm, Michael (1944–)

German glassware and ceramics designer; born Merseburg.

Training 1959–62, Glasfachschule, Hadamar; 1962–66, Hochschule für Bildende Künste, Kassel.
Biography 1966, Boehm joined Rosenthal. His limited-edition Reticelli range illustrated his interest in Italian glass through the incorporation of cotton-twist threads in the molten glass for an effect similar to that in 17th-century Venetian vessels. Rosenthal stemware includes two-color Sunflower and 1976 Papyrus ranges. Boehm collaborated with

Cini Boeri Mariani. Suitcase. 1966. Injection-molded ABS polymer, aluminum frame, and nylon wheels, 24 7/8 x 17 x 7 7/8" (63.2 x 43.2 x 20 cm). Mfr.: Società Franzi, Italy. Gift of the designer. MoMA.

Claus Josef Riedel on the Calyx range, whose faint mold lines became a design feature.
Bibliography Frederick Cooke, *Glass: Twentieth-Century Design*, New York: Dutton, 1986: 86. Cat., Kathryn B. Hiesinger and George H. Marcus III (eds.), *Design Since 1945*, Philadelphia: Philadelphia Museum of Art, 1983. *Mit Kunst leben*, Selb: Rosenthal: 52–53.

Boeri Mariani, Cini (1924–)

Italian designer; born and active Milan.

Training To 1950, architecture, Politecnico, Milan.
Biography 1952–63, Boeri worked as an interior and furniture designer in the studio of Marco Zanuso, Milan; 1963, set up her own studio, specializing in civil and interior architecture and industrial design; 1979, formed Cini Boeri Associati in Milan; early 1970s, collaborated with Laura Griziotti on designs for Arflex. Her interior architecture was sparsely furnished; her furniture was multi-functional and expandable, often combining standardized fittings. She lectured and wrote widely; 1966, began experimenting in plastics, her first designs being a 1966 set of luggage made of injection-molded ABS by Società Franzi. 1970–71 Serpentone foam-rubber seating system (with Laura Griziotti) by Arflex offered an Anti-Design attitude. 1975–85, she designed showrooms for Knoll International in Los Angeles, Stuttgart, Paris, Milan, Foligno, and New York; 1983 series of prefabricated single-family houses for Misawa Company, Tokyo. Other clients have included Artemide, Fiam Italia, and Rosenthal; designed lighting for Stilnovo, Arflex, and, in mid-1980s, Venini; 1980–83, taught architecture, planning, industrial design, and interior design at Politecnico, Milan, and at universities and colleges in Spain, Brazil, and the US, including the University of California at Berkeley; wrote *The Human Dimensions of the House* (with F. Angeli, 1980) and 'La dimensione del domestico' (with with Marisa Bertoldini) in *La casa tra techniche e sogno* (1988). Other work by Arflex: 1968 Cubetto mobile storage unit, 1980 doubleface bookshelf, 1983 Pacific sofa and loveseat, 1983 Malibu table (which shows her conservative approach), and 1986 Past modular sofa. By Knoll: 1970 Luario glass-chrome cantilevered table, 1977 Gradual System sofa system. Other work: hardware fixtures by Fusital from 1981, 1981 Rever door by Tre Più, 1984 Chiara lighting by Venini, and 1986 Brontes lighting fixture by Artemide. By Fiam Italia: 1987 Voyeur screen and, her best-known piece, all-glass one-piece 1987 Ghost chair (with Tomu Katayagi). Was a member of the organizing committee, 1979 (16th) Triennale di Milano.
Exhibitions/citations Collaborated on design of and showed furniture in Arflex stand, 1965 (13th), Triennale di Milano; subsequently, and at a vast number of other exhibitions. First prize, 1966 Piastrella d'Oro Cedit, ADI competition, Milan; diploma of collaboration, 1968 (14th) Triennale di Milano; 1970 mention and 1979 gold (1972 Strips seating by Arflex) Premio Compasso d'Oro; 1978 and 1984 Roscoe award, New York; mention and gold medal (1981 Rever door), 1984 BIO 10 industrial-design biennial, Ljubljana; 1984 Design 85 award, Design Center Stuttgart; 1985 German Selection award.
Bibliography Cat., *Italy: The New Italian Landscape*, New York: The Museum of Modern Art, 1972. Alfonso Grassi and Anty Pansera, *Atlante del design italiano 1940/1980*, Milan: Fabbri, 1980. Cat., Kathryn B. Hiesinger and George H. Marcus III (eds.), *Design Since 1945*, Philadelphia: Philadelphia Museum of Art, 1983. Cat., Design Center Stuttgart, *Women in Design: Careers and Life Histories Since 1900*, Stuttgart: Haus der Wirtschaft, 1989.

Bögel, Ulrike (1954–)

German designer; born Blaubeuren, Ulm.

Training 1974–79, product design, Fachhochschule für Gestaltung, Schwäbisch-Gmünd; 1979, Centro Internazionale della Ceramica, Rome.
Biography 1982, Bögel set up her own design office for work in glass, porcelain, ceramics, plastic, and metal; became a member, Verband Deutscher Industrie-Designer (VDID). Work included the curvaceous 1980 Tondo drinking glass by Hutschenreuther, 1984 Teaworld ceramic tea service by Porzellanfabrik Arzberg, and 1989 Club Cuisine kitchen-utensil range in ABS plastic by Buchsteiner.
Bibliography Cat., Design Center Stuttgart, *Women in Design: Careers and Life Histories Since 1900*, Stuttgart: Haus der Wirtschaft, 1989: 84–87.

Bogler, Theodor (1897–1968)

German ceramicist; born Hofgeismar.

Training From 1919, Bauhaus, Weimar; Universität München.
Biography 1923–24 with Otto Lindig, Bogler shared supervision of the Production Workshop, Dornburg, near Weimar, the ceramics annex of the Bauhaus; designed 1923 six-part porcelain mocha set and kitchen storage jars that became the first Bauhaus products to be produced industrially (closely succeeded by Otto Lindig's 1925 plain-white porcelain coffee pots). 1925, his commercial work by the Velten factory, lasting a little over a year, resulted in numerous designs. 1927, Bogler became a Benedictine monk; 1934–38, occasionally collaborated with the HB-Werkstätten für Keramik/Hedwig Bollhagen, Marwitz, and, 1936–68, with Staatliche Majolika-Manufaktur, Karlsruhe. 1939–48, he was the abbot of the monastery in Maria Laach, Germany, and worked on the production of numerous catalogs, books, and religious objects; died in the monastery.
Exhibition Earthenware kitchen containers (first Bauhaus industrial production), by Velten-Vordamm ceramic factory, shown at 1923 Bauhaus Exhibition.
Bibliography Theodor Bogler, *Maria Laach...*, Munich: Schnell & Steiner, 1953. Cat., *50 Jahre Bauhaus*, Stuttgart, 1968. Lionel Richard, *Encyclopédie du Bauhaus*, Paris: Somogy, 1985: 149. Cat., *The Bauhaus: Masters and Students*, New York: Barry Friedman, 1988. Cat., *Keramik und Bauhaus*, Berlin: Bauhaus-Archiv, 1989.

Bogoslovskaia, Olga Vasil'evna (1905–)

Russian textile designer.

Training To 1929, art school, Mstera village, Ivanovo province.
Biography She worked as a textile designer in the Krasnaïa Talka textile mill in Ivanovo province, and, 1931–33, in the Sosnevskii United textile mill in Ivanovo.
Exhibitions Participated in several Soviet exhibitions abroad.
Bibliography Cat., *Kunst und Revolution: Russische und Sowjetische Kunst 1910–1932*, Vienna: Österreichisches Museum für angewandte Kunst, 1988.

Bohuš, Peter (1963–)

Slovakian designer; born Považská Bystrica.

Training 1979–83, furniture and interior design, Technical College of Woodworking, Spišská Nová Ves; 1986–92, architecture, Vysoká Škola Výtvarných Umení (academy of fine arts and design), Bratislava; 1991 under Jaume Beach and Gabriel Mora, Wiener Architekturseminar, Barcelona.
Biography 1994, Bohuš set up his own studio Bohuš Peter–Design in Bratislava; organized production programs of and designed for three

furniture firms. Furniture has included 1996 Reno armchair and settee, 1997 Sergio seating system by Domark in Žilina, 1998 Knut II seating range and 2000 Dora swivel armchair by Krupec in Sučany, 1999 JDG semi-armchair by Dovičn in Martin, and other models. He designed the interiors of Stadthotel Viechtach in Germany in 1994 and advertising agency Publicis Knut–Mobilár in 1998. Architecture has included 1995 lookout tower of the dam in Žilina and 1997 headquarters of TS Motory in Martin. From 1997, a member of fine artists' group Modré Hrušky.
Exhibitions/citations Work shown at 1998, 1999, 2000 *Design Forum* exhibitions, Bratislava. 1997 Slovakian National Prize for Design (Reno, Nora, and Hugo upholstered armchairs).

Boiceau, Ernest (1881–1950)

Swiss designer; active Paris.

Training Drawing, painting, and architecture, École des Beaux-Arts, Paris.
Biography Boiceau became known for his tapestries and embroideries; 1918, opened a shop in Paris, where he sold furnishing textiles and embroidery; from 1926, decorated and furnished numerous apartments and townhouses in Switzerland, France, and the US. Commissions included those for Cécile Sorel, Paris; Louise de Vilmorin, Varrières-le-Buisson; Jérôme and Jean Tharaud, Versailles; Hôtel de Wendel and couture house of Worth, both Paris.
Exhibitions Work shown at 1928 and 1929 editions of Salon d'Automne and subject of 1982 exhibition, Galerie Eric Philippe, Paris.
Bibliography Pierre Kjellberg, *Art déco: les maîtres du mobilier, le décor des paquebots*, Paris: Amateur, 1986.

Boileau, Louis-Hippolyte (1878–1948)

French architect and designer.

Biography Late 1920s, Boileau designed the tea room of Au Bon Marché department store and restaurant Prunier-Traktir (with Léon Carrière), Paris, on the façade of which he used shades of green mosaic in a circular pattern. (Louis-Charles Boileau, who succeeded Alexandre Laplanche, designed the 1869 Au Bon Marché building.)
Exhibition Participated in 1925 *Exposition Internationale des Arts Décoratifs et Industriels Modernes*, Paris.
Bibliography *Restaurants, dancing, cafés, bars*, Paris: Charles Moreau, no. 45–46, 1929. Paul Chemetov et al., *Banlieue*, Paris: Bordas, 1989.

Boin-Taburet

French silversmiths; located Paris.

History c. 1857, the firm was founded; sold the silver designs produced by Christopher Dresser in last quarter of 19th century and a great deal of Art Déco ware at least to 1930s, when the firm was considered one of the distinguished silversmiths, in a league with Puiforcat, Tétard, Queille, Christofle, and Hénin.
Exhibitions Work shown at exhibitions 1881–1937, including 1881 *Exposition Internationale*, Paris; 1902 *Comité Français des Expositions à l'Étranger*, St. Petersburg.

Theodor Bogler. Pot and saucer. 1925. Glazed faience, h. 4 3/4" (12 cm). Mfr.: Steingutfabriken, Germany. Courtesy Quittenbaum Kunstauktionen, Munich.

Bibliography Annelies Krekel-Aalberse, *Art Nouveau and Art Déco Silver*, New York: Abrams, 1989.

Boissel, Eric (1947–)

French designer and entrepreneur; born Caen.

Training 1966–70, architecture, École Nationale Supérieure des Arts et Industries, Strasbourg.
Biography With his parents when young, Boissel traveled in Turkey, Austria, Egypt, and Germany; 1970–73, worked for various architectural firms in Strasbourg; 1973, developed a solar-powered heater at Faculty of Agriculture, Ankara Üniversitesi (taken over by Çukurova Üniversitesi in 1973), Adana, Turkey; 1976, designed a solar house; 1978, established a frame joinery firm; 1989–90, designed/developed an innovative post-and-beam-construction system for sawing wood before drying; 1993–98, designed various houses, agricultural hangars, and furniture, including own-made/marketed C1 reclining chair and Philibert armchair; 1998, opened his own restaurant Les Manins; designed 1999 Takerkart house and 2000 C2 chair and stool.
Exhibitions 1998 installation, Tranche de l'Art, Embrun.

Boisselier, Philippe (1942–)

French designer and interior architect.

Training Sculpture, École Boulle; École Nationale Supérieure des Arts Décoratifs; both Paris.
Biography 1971, Boisselier set up his own studio as an interior architect. He designed, at the invitation of Denise Fayolle, a modular room design for and 1982 furniture collection by 3 Suisses mail-order firm; furnishings for IBM in 1983; office of Jean-Claude Decaux in Plaisir (Yvelines) in 1984; locale of the Société Auxiliaire d'Entreprises in 1987; stand of magazine *Intramuros* at 1988 Salon du Meuble, Paris; furniture by Unifor; exhibitions and spaces of museums, including various commerical areas of the Château de Versailles 1991–92; cabin of the Concorde for Air France in 1993; dozens of houses and apartments. from 1980, Boisselier was a professor, École Camondo, Paris, and its director 1989–92; 1995, succeeded Eric Jourdan as head of design, École Nationale Supérieure des Beaux-Arts, Paris.
Bibliography Arlette Barré-Despond (ed.), *Dictionnaire international des arts appliqués et du design*, Paris: Regard, 1996.

Boissevain, Antoinette (1898–1973)

Dutch painter, lighting designer and retailer; born The Hague; active London.

Training From 1918, painting, Central School of Arts and Crafts, London.
Biography 1918, Boissevain settled in London; 1924, took over the management of Merchant Adventurers, importers of china and glass from Europe, which, from 1930, imported Wilhelm Gispen's Giso lighting range, first used on a contract for a yacht club (designed by Joseph Emberton) in Burnham-on-Crouch. Merchant Adventurers began producing lighting of its own design as well as Gispen's lighting under license. Architectural commissions for its fixtures included Shell-Mex House, Savoy Hotel, Harrods, and Bush House, all London. Boissevain and her husband were members, Design and Industries Association (DIA).
Bibliography Cat., *Thirties: British Art and Design Before the War*, London: Arts Council of Great Britain/Hayward Gallery, 1979.

Bojesen, Kay (1886–1958)

Danish silversmith, ceramicist, and woodenware designer; active Copenhagen.

Training 1907–10 under Jensen, Georg Jensen Sølvesmedie, Copenhagen; 1911, Royal Craft School of Precious Metals, Württemberg.
Biography Bojesen worked in Copenhagen and Paris; subsequently, 1913, set up his own workshop in Copenhagen; broke from Jensen's style in c. 1930; pursued simple, undecorated forms that emphasized their mechanical production; became a pioneer in the Danish modern style; 1930s, produced the designs of painters Lauritz Larsen and Svend Johansen and architects G.B. Petersen and Magnus Stephensen; 1930–31, was an art consultant to Bing & Grøndahl Porcelænsfabrik; designed stainless-steel tablewares by Universal Steel and, in Sweden, by Motala Verkstad; in an effort to promote modern design, instigated the establishment of a permanent center for Danish crafts and mass-produced products, resulting in the 1931 opening in Copen-

hagen of Den Permanente, one of the first design exhibition spaces in Europe; became known for his toy designs; 1952, was appointed silversmith to the King of Denmark.
Exhibitions/citations Work shown at 1925 *Exposition Internationale des Arts Décoratifs et Industriels Modernes*, Paris, and numerous other smaller venues, particularly exhibitions specializing in Scandinavian design. Work subject of 1938 exhibition, Det Danske Kunstindustrimuseum, Copenhagen.
Bibliography Edgar Kaufman Jr., 'Kay Bojesen: Tableware to Toys,' *Interiors*, no. 112, Feb. 1953. Mary Lyon, 'Master Plays Wide Field,' *Craft Horizons*, vol. 13, July 1953. Pierre Lübecker, *Applied Art by Kay Bojesen*, Copenhagen: National Association of Danish Handicraft, 1955. 'Kay Bojesen,' *Design Quarterly*, no. 39, 1957: 2–5. Erik Zahle (ed.), *A Treasury of Scandinavian Design*, New York: Golden Press, 1961. Cat., David Revere McFadden (ed.), *Scandinavian Modern Design 1880–1980*, New York: Abrams, 1982. Cat., Kathryn B. Hiesinger and George H. Marcus III (eds.), *Design Since 1945*, Philadelphia: Philadelphia Museum of Art, 1983. Annelies Krekel-Aalberse, *Art Nouveau and Art Déco Silver*, New York: Abrams, 1989.

Bolek, Hans (1890–1978)
Austrian architect, painter, and designer; active Vienna.

Training Under Josef Hoffmann, Kunstgewerbeschule, Vienna
Biography Bolek designed silver by Eduard Friedmann, Alfred Pollak, and Oskar Dietrich.
Bibliography Annelies Krekel-Aalberse, *Art Nouveau and Art Déco Silver*, New York: Abrams, 1989.

Bolidista, Movimento
Italian design movement.

History Amalgamating retro-1950s and streamline styling, Bolidista was established in Bologna in 1986 by a group of young architects and designers. They claimed, among a number of assertions, 'that ideology is a useless and harmful brake..., that a Bolidist does not die for a cause...,' and uses institutions as working instruments and the planet as a field of action. The much of its manifesto was lighthearted. Members were Maurizio Castelvetro, Giovanni Tommaso Garattoni, Guido Venturini, Stefano Giovannoni, Anna Perico, Fabrizio Galli, 'Rocky' Roberto Semprini, Pierangelo Caramia, Daniele Cariani, Dante Donegani, Ernesto Spicciolato, Bepi Maggiori, Giusi Mastro, Massimo Iosa Ghini, Maurizio Corrado. Examples of their approach can be seen in Caramia's 1987 Arcadia Swing glass and aluminum table by XO and jewelry by Directory King Kong (Venturini and Giovannoni).

Bollani, Eros (1947–)
Italian industrial designer; born Covo, Bologna; active Modena.

Biography 1974, Bollani began his professional career. His Italian clients included G3 Ferrari electrical appliances, Caggiati Claudio bath and kitchen accessories, Laminart Pannelli, Simonini motor division of cross-country motorcycles, and Rampinelli REG Accessori for bicycles and motorcycles.
Bibliography *ADI Annual 1976*, Milan: Associazione per il Disegno Industriale, 1976.

Boltenstern, Erich (1896–1991)
Austrian architect and interior designer; born Vienna.

Training 1918–22, Technische Hochschule, Vienna; 1922–28 under Hans Poelzig, Preussiche Akademie der Künste, Berlin; under Siegfried Theiss and Hans Jaksch in Vienna.
Biography 1928–34, Boltenstern was an assistant under Oskar Strnad at Kunstgewerbeschule, Vienna; 1930, began as an independent architect; was associated with the Wiener Werkstätte; from 1946, taught, Technische Hochschule, Vienna.
Bibliography Günther Feuerstein, *Vienna—Present and Past: Arts and Crafts—Applied Art—Design*, Vienna: Jugend und Volk, 1976: 49, 61, 80. Astrid Gmeiner and Gottfried Pirhofer, *Der Österreichische Werkbund*, Salzburg/Vienna: Residenz, 1985: 223–24.

Bolz, Anne (1958–)
German designer; born Mömlingen.

Training From 1980, product design, Hochschule für Gestaltung, Offenbach am Main.
Biography To 1986, Bolz worked at Mathias Hoffmann Furniture Design office, Tübingen; from 1986, as an independent consultant designer of furniture; 1988, became product coordinator at Eugen Schmidt in Darmstadt.
Citations 1987 Bayrischer Staatspreis für Nachwuchsdesigner (Bavarian state prize for promising designers).
Bibliography Cat., *Bayerischen Staatspreis für Nachwuchsdesigner 1987*, Munich: Die Neue Sammlung, 1987: 28. Cat., Design Center Stuttgart, *Women in Design: Careers and Life Histories Since 1900*, Stuttgart: Haus der Wirtschaft, 1989: 88.

Bolze, Franz (1902–1974)
German silversmith; active Bremen.

Biography 1926–76, Bolze worked as a silversmith in Bremen; 1920s–30s, was one of many independent silversmiths working in prosperous North Germany; produced designs by sculptor Bernhard Hötger, including 1927–28 mocha service.
Bibliography Annelies Krekel-Aalberse, *Art Nouveau and Art Déco Silver*, New York: Abrams, 1989.

Boman, Carl-Johan (1883–1969)
Finnish interior designer.

Training 1906, Königliches Institut für angewandte Künste, Berlin.
Biography 1906–11, Boman was director of the drafting office of Boman in Helsinki and, 1919–55, general director there; 1955–59, was active in his own studio. The simplicity of his work can be seen in 1962 Boman I chair with a folding seat by Schauman in Helsinki.
Exhibitions/citations Work shown in exhibitions, including 1908 exposition, St. Petersburg; 1925 *Art and Design*, Monza; 1929–30 *Exposición Internacional de Barcelona*, Spain; and in Brussels and Paris in 1952. 1951 (9th) gold medal and 1954 (10th) diploma of honor, Triennale di Milano; 1951 silver medal, Concours International d'Invention, Paris.

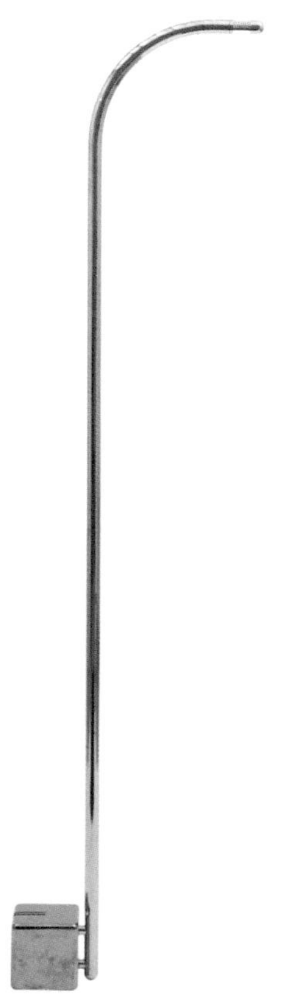

Claus Bonderup and Torsten Thorup. Floor lamp. 1978. Chrome-plated metal, 66 1/2 x 17 3/8 x 4 3/4" (168.9 x 44.2 x 12 cm). Mfr.: Focus Belysning, Denmark. Gift of the designer. MoMA.

Bibliography Cat., *Modern Chairs 1918–1970*, London: Lund Humphries, 1971.

Bon Marché, Le
> See Pomone.

Bonacina, Pierantonio
Italian furniture manufacturer.

Biography 1889, the company was established in Lurago d'Erba, Brianza, and became particularly adept in the production of goods in wicker, rush, rattan, and other plant materials which are beautiful, robust and versatile; eventually applied modern techniques and combined wood, metals, and plastics to the production of high-design furniture, some having become classics. Most notable work may be Franco Albini's 1950 Margherita wicker armchair. Other commissioned designers have included Marco Agnoli, Mary Bloch, Joe Colombo, D'Urbino/Lomazzi, Nanna Ditzel, Gio Ponti, Fabiano Trabucchi, and Marco Zanuso Sr. 1966, Mario Bonacina (1947–) began his professional career at the family firm, where he became the artistic director.
Bibliography *ADI Annual 1976*, Milan: Associazione per il Disegno Industriale, 1976. Cat., Leslie Jackson, *The New Look: Design in the Fifties*, New York: Thames & Hudson, 1991: 126.

Bonaldo
Italian furniture company; located Villanova.

History 1936, the mother firm was founded. 1950s, Bonaldo was established as part of the Bonaldo Casa group; specialized in furniture accessories at first; 1970s, began producing sofas and, today, tables, chairs, and accessories. 1980s, Led&Co was added to the group to produce cash-and-carry design products for young customers. Bonaldo exports 68% of its goods to Germany, Switzerland, Austria, and the Netherlands; eventually became a group of three companies (Bonaldo, Styling, and Led&Co.) with four factories and 180 employees; commissioned designers include Studio Archirivolto, J. Hoffmann, K.L. Heitlinger, A. Weber, T. Müller, and S. Heiliger; seating has included 2000 Adagio reclining armchair by Denis Santachiara and 2001 stool by Massimo Iosa Ghini.
Citations 1996 prize and 1998 first prize, Young & Design.

Bonderup, Claus (1943–)
Danish architect, urban planner, and designer; born Ålborg; husband of painter Anne Just.

Training 1965–69 under Henning Larsen, architecture and planning, Det Kongelige Danske Kunstakademi, Copenhagen.
Biography Bonderup designed lighting fixtures by Focus Belysning in Holte, some with Torsten Thorup, with whom he collaborated from 1968; others by Fox Design and, with Thorup, 1967 Semi hanging lamp by Fogh & Mørup; 1969–70, worked in the office of architect Henning Larsen in Copenhagen; 1970–71, collaborated with architect Sergio Bernardes in Rio de Janeiro; 1971–73, worked with architects Vischer und Weber, Basel; is professor of architecture, Institut for Arkitektur & Design, Ålborg Universitet, Ålborg.
Exhibitions/citations Beach house was shown at 1979 *Transformations of Modern Architecture*, The Museum of Modern Art, New York. 1982 Eckersberg Medal.
Bibliography Cat., David Revere McFadden (ed.), *Scandinavian Modern Design 1880–1980*, New York: Abrams, 1982.

Bongard, Hermann (1921–1988)
Norwegian graphic artist and glassware designer.

Training 1938–41 under Sverre Pettersen and Per Krogh, lithography and design, Statens Håndværks -og Kunstindustriskole, Oslo.
Biography 1947–55, Bongard designed crystal and glassware by Hadelands Glassverk under Sverre Pettersen and working alongside Willy Johansson. His glassware in imaginative silhouettes with engraved decoration included 1954 Ambassador for Norwegian embassies. When he left Hadelands, he was somewhat replaced in 1956 by Severin Brørby, previously an engraver at the factory from 1948. From 1955, Bongard was a multi-talented consultant designer of glass, ceramics, textiles, silver, and architectural decorations; 1957–63, was advisor to Figgjo Fajanse ceramics works in Stavanger; from mid-1960s, specialized in graphic design, for which he became best known; 1966–68, was chief design advisor to J. W. Cappelens publishing firm; from 1968, taught, graphic-design department, Statens Håndværks-og Kunstindustriskole, Oslo.
Exhibitions/citations Work included in 1983 and 1986 exhibitions, Philadelphia and Stockholm (catalogs below). Gold and silver medals, 1954 (10th) Triennale di Milano; 1957 Lunning Prize.
Bibliography 'Thirty-four Lunning Prize-Winners,' *Mobilia*, no. 146, Sept. 1967. *Tegneren Hermann Bongard*, Oslo: Kunstindustrimusset, 1971. Cat., Kathryn B. Hiesinger and George H. Marcus III (eds.), *Design Since 1945*, Philadelphia: Philadelphia Museum of Art, 1983. Cat., *The Lunning Prize*, Stockholm: Nationalmuseum, 1986. Fredrik Wildhagen, *Norge i Form*, Oslo: Stenersen, 1988: 127. Jennifer Hawkins Opie, *Scandinavia: Ceramics and Glass in the Twentieth Century*, New York: Rizzoli, 1989. Leslie Jackson, *20th Century Factory Glass*, London: Octopus, 2000.

Bonebakker en Zoon
Dutch silversmiths; located Amsterdam.

History 1853, Bonebakker was founded as a silver workshop, headed by P. Pieterse and known for its high-quality, handmade work. It commissioned others (including D.L. Bennewitz and T.G. Bentveld) to make its silverwares; 1862, began employing craftspeople and apprentices; by 1898, had 38 foreign suppliers even though its most important clients were domestic. 1888–93, Frans Zwollo Sr. was an apprentice to his father at Bonebakker en Zoon, after which he produced chased coins for the firm. From 1896, when he set up his own business, Bonebakker was his most important client, for which he created rococo and neoclassical designs. The sculptor L.F. Edema van der Tuuk supplied the firm with drawings. Bonebakker imitated styles and plagiarized the designs of competitors, including models of Jan Eisenloeffel originally by Van Kempen and of Christopher Dresser; sold silverwares made by Wolfers Frères in Brussels; 1910s–20s, produced wares with the pliant ornamentation of the Dutch Expressionist school of architecture in Amsterdam. 1952, the factory closed though the shop still exists.
Bibliography Cat., *Industry and Design in the Netherlands 1850–1950*, Amsterdam: Stedelijk Museum, 1985. Annelies Krekel-Aalberse, *Art Nouveau and Art Déco Silver*, New York: Abrams, 1989.

Boner, Jörg (1968–)
> See N2.

Bonet, Pep (1941–)
Spanish designer; born and active Barcelona.

Training 1965, Escola Tècnica Superior d'Arquitectura de Barcelona (ETSAB).
Biography 1963–65, Bonet worked in the office of architect José Antonio Coderch; 1964 with Cristián Cirici, Óscar Tusquets Blanca, and Lluís Clotet Ballús, formed Studio PER, and, after 1972, the group founded (also with Mireia Riera) Bd Ediciones de Diseño and began to design furniture and building components. 1969–71 and 1995–99, Bonet taught product design, Escola de Disseny i Art (Eina); 1975–78, was professor of design, Escola Tècnica Superior d'Arquitectura de Barcelona, and, 1981, at Washington University, St. Louis, Mo. Work by Bd Ediciones de Diseño and others has included 1975 Mesa Sevilla table and Sevilla chair (with Cirici and Riera), 1980 Galán de Baño towel rack, 1984 Mantis armchair by Levesta, 1986 chain-holder barrier and Albor bookcase, 1993 Alba bookcase, 1994 Serie Tiptic mirror series (some discontinued and reissued).
Citations 1969, 1971–72, and 1987 Premi FAD d'Interiorisme Award; 1978–79 Premi FAD de Restauración; 1967, 1976, 1990 and 1991 Delta d'Oro and 1986 Delta de Plata, ADI/FAD (industrial-designer and descorative-arts associations).
Bibliography Robert A.M. Stern (ed.), *The International Design Yearbook*, New York: Abbeville, 1985/1986. Juli Capella and Quim Larrea, *Design by Architects in the 1980s*, New York: Rizzoli, 1988.

Bonet Castellana, Antoni (1913–1989)
> See Ferrari-Hardoy, Jorge.

Bonetti, Alfredo (1938–)
Italian designer; born Erba; active Milan.

Biography 1966, Bonetti began his professional career. His clients have included Tecno, Gallotti e Radice, Riva foundry, and Fede Cheti.
Bibliography *ADI Annual 1976*, Milan: Associazione per il Disegno Industriale, 1976.

Bonetti, Massimo (1949–)
> See Kairos, Studio.

Bonetti, Mattia (1953–)
Italian furniture designer; born Lugano; active Paris.

Training Centro Scolastico per l'Industria Artistica, Italy.
Biography Bonetti worked as a color consultant to Rhône-Poulenc in Paris; was a stylist with Marie Berani; collaborated with designer Andrée Putman; c. 1977, began collaborating with Elisabeth Garouste.
Exhibitions Photography was shown at Galerie Samia Saoumia, Paris; showed furniture and objects with Garouste et Jansen, Paris.
> See Garouste, Elizabeth.

Bonetto, Marco (1962–)
Italian designer; born Milan; son of Rodolfo Bonetto.

Biography 1983, Bonetto began as an assistant in his father Rodolfo Bonetto's studio, then became manager of the design affairs; from 1986, has been a member, Associazione per il Disegno Industriale (ADI); from 1989, president, Bonetto Design, and, 1994, president, Bonetto Design Center, Monte Carlo, Principality of Monaco; from 1997, has been a member, Società d'Ergonomia Italiana (SEI); from 1998, lecturer, industrial-design department, Politecnico, Milan; 2001, president, committee of Premio SMAU Industrial Design, Salone della Machina e Attrezzature per l'Uffizio (SMAU),, Milan. Design work has included 1986 public telephone by Telecom Italia, 1987 console by TAC-NMR Elscint, 1988 refrigerator by Zanussi, 1989 ski boots by Nordica, 1994 advanced automobile interior for Fiat, 1996 coffee machine by Rancilio, 1998 videophone by Bpt, 2000 vacuum cleaner by Rega, 2000 lamps by Valenti, 2001 advanced automobile interior for Fiat 199, 2001 advanced-design scooter by Piaggio, and others. His articles have been published in newspaper *Sole 24 Ore* and magazines *Design* and *Ottagono*.
Exhibitions/citations Curated 1992 *Rodolfo Bonetto, Thirty Years of Design* and 1998 *40ennale Bonetto Design*. 1992, established Targa Rodolfo Bonetto Prize of SMAU Industrial Design, Milan.

Bonetto, Rodolfo (1929–1991)
Italian furniture and industrial designer; active Milan.

Biography Bonetto began his design career at the Pininfarina automobile body design firm; 1958, founded his own studio; has been a member, Associazione per il Disegno Industriale (ADI), and its advisory committee and, 1963 and 1969, was a member, ADI's guidance council of International Council of Societies of Industrial Design (ICSID); participated in numerous other professional organizations; from 1974, a member, committee on scientific education, Istituto Superiore per le Industrie Artistiche, Rome. In ICSID, he was a delegate at 1972 event of ADI at Beda (Brussels), member of the executive board 1971 and 1973, vice-president 1973 and 1976, and president from 1981–83. 1961–65, he taught, product-design department, Hochschule für Gestaltung, Ulm; 1971–73, taught, Istituto Superiore Disegno Industriale, Rome. He has designed more than 400 products for clients, including Driade, Brionvega, Valextra, and Bilumen. While manifesting the austere Functionalism of the Ulm school, his work exhibits humor and irony, illustrated by his 1971 Boomerang polyfoam chair and colorful 1969 Quattro Quarti sectional table (produced 1970–78) by Bernini. Known for his use of plastic molding, his 1970 Fiat 132 molded interior is notable. Work has included included 1962 sewing machine by Borletti, 1963 Sfericlock and timer by Veglia Borletti, 1966 soda dispenser by BRAS, 1968 espresso machine by Gaggia, 1969 canister radio by Autovox, 1970 television (with Naoki Matsunaga) by Voxson, 1977 air conditioner by Sime, 1971 auto parts by Shell, heavy industrial machinery (with Matsunaga) by Olivetti, and 1983 Ala table lamps by Fratelli Guzzini.
Exhibitions/citations Work in numerous exhibitions. Premio Compasso d'Oro: 1964 (Sfericlock alarm clock) and 1967 (Auctor office machine by Olivetti); 1964, 1967 (three citations), 1970, 1979 (nine citations with others), 1981 (five citations, individually and with others), 1984, 1989 (three citations), 1991 (nine citations).
Bibliography 'Rodolfo Bonetto, designer italiano,' *Domus*, no. 446, Jan. 1967: 43–50. Cat., *Italy: The New Domestic Landscape*, New York: The Museum of Modern Art, 1972: 28, 33, 49, 71–72. Cat., *Design Process Olivetti*, Los Angeles: Frederick S. Wight Art Gallery (University of California), 1979: 256. Cat., Kathryn B. Hiesinger and George H. Marcus III (eds.), *Design Since 1945*, Philadelphia: Philadelphia Museum of Art, 1983. Vittorio Gregotti, *Il disegno del profotto industriale 1860–1980*, Milan: Electa, 1986. Gianni Pettena, *Rodolfo Bonetto—trent'anni di design*, Milan: Idea Books, 1992.

Bonfante, Egidio (1922–)
Italian architect and designer; born Treviso.

Training Accademia di Belle Arti di Brera; architecture, Politecnico; both Milan.
Biography Bonfante was editor of magazines *Posizione* (1942–43), *Numero* and *Il Ventaglio* (1946); was co-editor of *A. Arredamento* (1946), *Comunità* (1946–70), *Urbanistica* (1946–67); from 1948, worked for Olivetti as a graphic designer; designed exhibitions, showrooms, exhibition catalogs, and advertising; was highly active as a painter.
Exhibitions Work subject of 1984 exhibition, traveling worldwide; 1999 venue, Ferrara (catalog below); 2003 *Le Fantasie e le Geometrie di Egidio Bonfante Dentro e Fuori Olivetti*, Villetta Casana, Ivrea.
Bibliography Cat., *Design Process Olivetti 1908–1978*, Los Angeles: Frederick S. Wight Art Gallery (University of California), 1979: 375. Cat., Hans Wichmann (ed.), *Italien Design 1945 bis heute*, Munich: Die Neue Sammlung, 1988. Cat., *Egidio Bonfante*, Ferrara: Palazzo Massari, 1999.

Bonfanti, Lorenzo (1949–)
Italian industrial designer; born Brivio.

Biography 1968, Bonfanti began his career in the planning office of Delchi; subsequently, became an independent designer; 1977 with Gianni Arduini and Gianfranco Salvemini, set up a design studio, serving clients including Carrier and Gelman Elow Famak.
Citations 1984 Premio Compasso d'Oro (FB 33 water purifier by Folletto).
Bibliography Cat., Hans Wichmann (ed.), *Italien Design 1945 bis heute*, Munich: Die Neue Sammlung, 1988.

Bonfanti, Renata (1929–)
Italian textile designer; born Bassano del Grappa; active Mussolente.

Biography 1955, Bonfanti began her professional career in textile design and established her own studio/production firm.
Citations 1956, 1960, 1962, 1979, 1989 Premio Compasso d'Oro; 1961 first prize, Concorso del Cotone; 1998 1st prize (for Terra d'Ombra carpet), Internationaler Südtiroler Handwerkspreis.
Bibliography *ADI Annual 1976*, Milan: Associazione per il Disegno Industriale, 1976. Cat., Cinzia Anguissola d'Altoé, 'Tessuti e Rivertimenti,' in *'45–'63 un museo del disegno industriale in Italia*, Milan: Abitare Segesta, 1995.

Bonfils, Robert (1886–1971)
French bookbinder, painter, and designer; born Paris.

Training From 1903, École Germain-Pilon; from 1906, École Nationale Supérieure des Beaux-Arts; both Paris.
Biography Bonfils worked for Henri Hamm (Bordeaux 1871–Paris 1961), architect, furniture designer, and artist. Bonfils's work included paintings, bookbindings, ceramics (by Sèvres), silks (by Bianchini-Frérier), wallpaper, layouts for interior design, tea room of the Au Printemps department store, Paris, painting its walls with images of the seasons. From 1919, he was professor of design, École Supérieure Estienne, Paris.
Exhibitions Work shown at Salons d'Automne 1909–1938, Salons des Tuileries to 1938, and Salons of Société des Artistes Décorateurs from 1910. Showed first bookbinding (*Clara d'Ellebeuse*) at 1913 Salon in Paris. Was an organizer of 1925 *Exposition Internationale des Arts Décoratifs et Industriels Modernes*, Paris, where he exhibited in nine categories and designed a poster and the catalog cover. Participated in 1937 *Exposition Internationale des Arts et Techniques dans la Vie Moderne,* Paris; 1939–40 *New York World's Fair: The World of Tomorrow*; 1958 *Exposition Universelle et Internationale de Bruxelles* (*Expo '58*).
Bibliography Léon Deshairs, 'Robert Bonfils,' *Art et décoration*, Feb. 1929. Robert Burnand, 'Robert Bonfils: peintre, Illustrateur, et relieur,' *Byblis*, Summer 1929. Yvanhoe Rambosson, 'Les reliures de Robert Bonfils,' *Mobilier et décoration*, Feb. 1932. '5 Relieurs,' *Mobilier et décoration*, Apr. 1935. Thérèse Charpentier, *L'École de Nancy et la reliure d'art*, Paris, 1960. Roger Devauchelle, *La reliure en France de ses origines à nos jours*, vol. 3, Paris, 1961. Victor Arwas, *Art Déco*, New York: Abrams, 1980. Alastair Duncan and Georges de Bartha, *Art Nouveau and Art Déco Bookbinding*, New York: Abrams, 1989.

Bonnot, Jacques (1950–)
> See Totem.

Rodolfo Bonetto with Naoki Matsunaga. TV set (no. 2406). 1970. Metal, plastic, and glass, 19¾ x 24⅜ x 15⅜" (50 x 62 x 39 cm). Mfr.: Voxson, Italy. Courtesy Quittenbaum Kunstauktionen, Munich.

Bontempi, Piercarlo (1954–)
Italian architect; born Fornovo Taro.

Training Facoltà of Architettura, Università degli Studi, Florence.
Biography Bontempi was an assistant to Adolfo Natalini, who also taught at the university in Florence; 1980, joined Studio Alchimia; executed designs by Alessi; from 1980, specialized in architecture.
Bibliography Piercarlo Bontempi and Giorgio Gregori, *Alchimia*, The Hague: Copi Den Haag, 1985. Kazuko Sato, *Alchimia*, Berlin: Taco, 1988.

Bonvallet, Lucien (1861–1919)
French designer.

Training École Nationale Supérieure des Arts Décoratifs, Paris; under Georges Lechevallier-Chevignard, director of Sèvres porcelain works.
Biography Bonvallet designed fabrics, lace, and furniture; from 1885, specialized in metal; became a master of copperware; designed mountings by Ernest Cardeilhac for ceramics and glass by designers, including Pierre Dalpayrat and Émile Gallé.
Bibliography Yvonne Brunhammer et al., *Art Nouveau Belgium, France*, Houston: Rice University, 1976, biblio.

Bookprinter, Anna Marie (1862–1950)
> See Valentien, Anna Marie.

Boonzaauer, Karel (1948–)
Dutch designer.

Training Hogeschool voor de Kunsten, Utrecht.
Biography For ten years, Boonzaauer worked for furniture manufacturer Pastoe; from 1979, was in a partnership with Pierre Mazairac; through their studio, specialized in product development and interior architecture. Their MB armchair of c. 1986 was produced by Metaform in the Netherlands.
Bibliography Robert A.M. Stern (ed.), *The International Design Yearbook*, New York: Abbeville, 1985/1986.

Boote, T. and R.
British ceramics manufacturer; located Burslem, Staffordshire.

History 1842, T. and R. Boote was founded in Burslem; first produced encaustic tiles by the plastic-clay method; 1863 collaborating with Boulton and Worthington, patented the pressed-dust method, an inexpensive process that made encaustic tiles more widely available; produced Parian ware. By the last quarter of 19th century, along with Minton and Maw, Boote became one of the largest producers of decorative tiles in Britain; 1880s, applied the illustrations of Walter Crane to a number of its tiles; at the end of 19th century, made encaustic and transfer-printed tiles and also numerous majolica tiles in Art Nouveau motifs. Its large white utilitarian tiles were used for public works, including in 1892–97 Blackwall Tunnel under the river Thames.
Exhibitions Parian copy of the Portland Vase was shown at 1851 *Great Exhibition of Works of Industry of All Nations*, London
Bibliography Michael Messenger, 'Revival of a Medieval Technique: Encaustic Tiles in the Nineteenth Century,' *Country Life*, no. 163, Jan. 26, 1978. Jill and Brian Austwick, *The Decorated Tile: An Illustrated History of English Tile-making and Design*, London: Pitman House, 1980. Doreen Bolger Burke et al., *In Pursuit of Beauty: Americans and the Aesthetic Movement*, New York: The Metropolitan Museum of Art/Rizzoli, 1986.

Booth, Charles (1844–1893)
British stained-glass designer; born Liverpool; active New York, Orange, N.J., and London.

Biography 1870s, Booth had a workshop in New York; 1880, returned to England and took over the stained glass workshop of George Edward Cook in London but retained the New York branch of his business. The workshops in England and America continued to operate after his death, to c. 1905. Incorporating some modern Gothic motifs, his style was based on the geometric plant forms of Christopher Dresser and was typical of 1870s Anglo-Japanese aesthetic. A number of his stained-glass windows were published, including those in the Jefferson Market Courthouse (architect, Stamford White) and Calvary Church, both New York.
Exhibitions Work included in 1986–87 Metropolitan Museum of Art exhibition (catalog below).
Bibliography Charles Booth, *Hints on Church and Domestic Windows, Plain and Decorated*, Orange, N.J., 1876. Martin Harrison, *Victorian Stained Glass*, London, 1980. James L. Sturm, *Stained Glass from Medieval Times to the Present: Treasures to Be Seen in New York*, New York: Dutton, 1982. Cat., Doreen Bolger Burke et al., *In Pursuit of Beauty: Americans and the Aesthetic Movement*, New York: The Metro politan Museum of Art/Rizzoli, 1986.

Booty Jr., Donald (1956–)
American designer.

Training Illinois Institute of Technology, Chicago.
Biography 1988, Booty established Booty Design Associates in Scottsdale, Ariz.; designs electronic equipment, housewares, lighting, and industrial products such as 1986 Double Plus calculator by Zelco.
Bibliography Cat., R. Craig Miller (intro.), *U.S. Design: 1975–2000*, Munich: Prestel, 2002.

Borden
> See Corning.

Bordier, Primerose (1929–1995)
French textile designer; born and active Paris.

Training Atelier Charpentier, Paris.
Biography 1949–54, she worked as a textile designer; 1954–57, as a stylist at Cosserat; 1958–60, with the Boussac textile factory; 1958–60, at Au Printemps department store, Paris; 1962, set up her own textile design studio Couleurs Dessins Modèles (CDM); designed tableware and houseware by Descamps.
Citations Chevalier of the Légion d'Honneur.

Borg, Olli (1921–79)
Finnish interior and furniture designer.

Training Taideteollinen korkeakoulu, Helsinki.
Biography 1947–50, Borg was an interior designer for Te-Ma; 1950–54, for Viljo Rewell; 1954–57, for Askon Tehtaat, Lahti. He set up his own studio; 1956, was head of industrial-design department, Taideteollinen korkeakoulu.
Exhibitions Work shown at 1954 (10th) Triennale di Milano.
Bibliography Cat., David Revere McFadden (ed.), *Scandinavian Modern Design 1880–1980*, New York: Abrams, 1982.

Borgersen, Tore (1966–)
> See Norway Says.

Borrelli, Corrado (1947–)
Italian industrial and graphic designer; born Trento; active Milan.

Training Corso Superiore di Disegno Industriale, Florence.
Biography From 1969 in Milan, Borrelli worked in the studio of Marcello Nizzoli and, 1971–73, in the studio of Giorgio Decursu. Subsequently,

Borrelli became a consultant designer of graphics, electronics, and furniture for clients, including Vittorio Bonacina (Carlotta bamboo chair) in Lurago d'Erba, Green Star Motor Oil in Bresso in Milan, and Reprorex in Milan; from 1974, was an industrial designer at Sogetel, where he designed the no. 1475 television by AEG Telefunken.
Bibliography *ADI Annual 1976*, Milan: Associazione per il Disegno Industriale, 1976.

Borsani, Osvaldo (1911–1985)

Italian furniture designer and architect; born Varedo, Italy; twin brother of Fulgenzio Borsani.

Training To 1937, architecture, Politecnico, Milan.
Biography Borsani joined the Atelier Varedo, his father's workshop in Varedo; designed for A. and G. Pomodoro, Fontana, Sussu, Crippa, and Fabbri and executed 1946 wall-mounted bookshelf system; was fastidious abut his furniture designs and, thus, 1953 with twin brother Fulgenzio Borsani, established their own furniture company Tecno out of Atelier Varedo facilities and the subsequently established small firm Arredamento Borsani. Tecno's products have been derived from technological research rather than superficial styling. Borsani has become best known for his 1955 articulated chaise longue (no. P40) and its mate, the 1954 sofa version (no. D70), both 'machines for sitting,' purportedly by Tecno literature to assume 486 positions. c. 1950, also collaborated with Piero Fornasetti and Lucio Fontana on Novecento-style furniture. The firm continues with commissioned designs by others.
Exhibitions/citations Participated in the Casa Minima project (with architects Cairoli and G.B. Varisco) at 1933 (5th) Triennale di Milano; showed T95 desk at 1940 (7th) Triennale di Milano. 1954 (D70 chair) Premio Compasso d'Oro.
Bibliography Cat., *Modern Chairs 1918–1970*, London: Lund Humphries, 1971. Charlotte and Peter Fiell, *Modern Furniture Classics Since 1945*, London: Thames & Hudson, 1991. 'Fulgenzio Borsani,' *Ottagono*, no. 105, Dec. 1992. Giuliana Gramigna and Fulvio Irace, *Osvaldo Borsani*, Rome: De Luca, 1992. www.tecnospa.com.
> See Tecno.

Osvaldo Borsani. Armchair (no. P40). 1955. Wool, polyurethane foam, and steel, from minimum h. 24 1/8 x d. 28 1/4" (61.3 x 71.8 cm) to maximum h. of 41 3/8 x d. 70 x w. 26 3/8" (105.1 x 177.8 x 67 cm). Mfr.: Tecno, Italy. Gift of the mfr. MoMA.

Bortnyik, 'Sándor' Alexander (1893–1976)

Hungarian artist, designer, and writer; born Marosvásárhely (now Tirgu Mures, Romania).

Training Fine art, Budapest.
Biography 1918–22, Bortnyik was active in avant-garde artistic circles; worked with Lajos Kassák on the revue *Ma*, to which Bortnyik contributed illustrations and geometric lino prints and was a member of a group surrounding *Ma*; began as a poster designer with one of his first successes, the 1915 Unicum poster, which remained in print for decades; participated in the Russian Revolution and the Budapest Commune; 1920, settled in Vienna; 1921, began to produce abstract architectonic Constructivist works at the same time as Kassák but, 1922, broke his association with Kassák; 1924, settled in Weimar but was not connected with the Bauhaus; 1925, returned to Hungary, where he worked as an advertising graphic designer, theater designer, journalist, and painter in a Cubo-Constructivist or Cubo-Futurist style; 1928–38, was active in a studio he named the Hungarian Bauhaus; after World War II, became a teacher, school of industrial design, Budapest, and, subsequently, at another applied-arts institution. He died in Budapest.
Bibliography Lionel Richard, *Encyclopédie du Bauhaus*, Paris: Somogy, 1985.

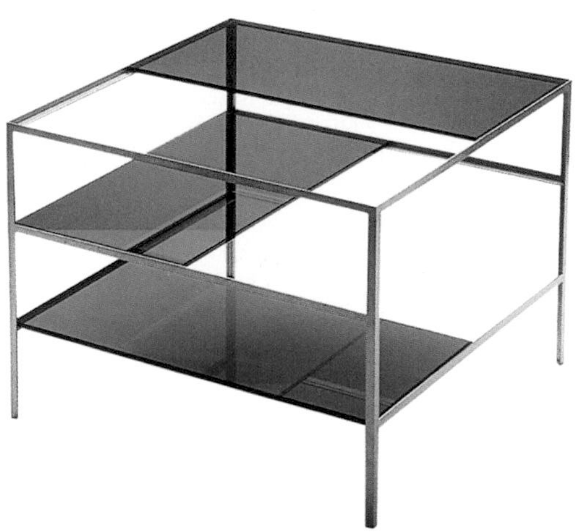

Fabio Bortolani and Emilio Nanni. Table. c. 1998. Aluminum and glass; h. 20 7/8 x w. and d. 27 1/2" (53 x 70 cm). Mfr.: Tonelli, Italy.

Bortolani, Fabio (1957–)

Italian designer; born Modena.

Training Architecture, Università degli Studi, Florence; 1987–88, architecture office of C. Leonardi and F. Stagi, Modena.
Biography 1990, Bortolani began working as an industrial designer, with a studio in Spilamberto, designing furniture, furnishings, and products for clients, including Agape, Alessi, Authentics, Cappellini, Driade, Magis, Wireworks, and Virtually Design.
Exhibitions/citations Work included in 2000 *Daytools* and 2001 *Clandestino*, both Spazio Opos, Milan; 2000 *Usa e Getta*, Inter Nos, Milan; 2000 *Aperto Vetro*, Museo Correr, Venice. Top Ten prize, Salone Internazionale della Sedia (Promodedia), Udine; 1991–96 Selection Opos, Milan; Design Plus prize, 1997 Ambiente fair, Frankfurt; projects sponsored by VIA (French furniture association).
Bibliography Claudia Neumann, *Design Lexikon Italien*, Cologne: DuMont, 1999. *Aperto vetro*, Milan: Electa, 2000. *Opos 1991/2001*, Milan: Abitare Segesta, 2000. Mel Byars, *Design in Steel*, London: Laurence King, 2002.

Bosch, Stephan (1945–)

Dutch architect; born Nijmegen; active Milan.

Training Koninklijke Academie van Beeldende Kunsten, The Hague.
Biography Bosch participated in research concerning the Cuban Construction Center under architect W.P. Graatsma; 1960, was a sculptor and traveled in Africa and the US, before turning to the design of objects and interiors; 1971, settled in Milan and was a consultant to Braun; designed numerous exhibition stands and shop interiors; from 1975, concentrated on the production of heavy machinery.
Bibliography *ADI Annual 1976*, Milan: Associazione per il Disegno Industriale, 1976.

Bose, Amar G. (1929–)

American electronics entrepreneur and inventor; active Massachusetts.

Biography From 1956, Bose taught electrical engineering, Massachusetts Institute of Technology (MIT), Cambridge, Mass.; 1964 with Sherwin Greenblatt, founded the Bose Corporation, Farmingham, Mass., to manufacture loudspeakers because he concluded that speakers with high technical specifications did not provide the experience of a live musical performance. His work in speaker design and psychoacoustics resulted in important new design concepts. He developed the 1968 Model 901 Direct/Reflecting speaker system, his first model, with a Saarinen-like pedestal; subsequently, developed Wave radio, Acoustic Wave music systems, Acoustimass speaker and Auditioner audio-demonstrator technologies, and other innovations.
Citations 2001 and 2003 (Lifestyle 50, and 3.2.1 home-entertainment centers) Red Dot awards, and 2002 Red Dot Best of the Best (QuietComfort earphones), Design Zentrum Nordrhein Westfalen, Essen.
Bibliography Barbara Mayer, 'Who's Got the Button,' *Elle Decor*, Nov. 1990: 162.

Bossanyi, Ervin (1891–1975)

Hungarian painter, sculptor, and stained-glass designer and maker; active Britain.

Biography 1934, Bossanyi settled in Britain; designed stained glass for 1934 Senate House of London University, 1935 *Beaux-Arts Exhibition*, 1938 Uxbridge Underground Station, Victoria and Albert Museum, and 1938–41 Tate Gallery, all London. Other commissions included stained glass for Canterbury Cathedral, the church at Port Sunlight, Anglican cathedral in Washington, D.C., Michaelhouse School Chapel in Durban (South Africa), and York Minster. He was considered a radical exponent of stained glass.
Bibliography Cat., *Thirties: British Art and Design Before the War*, London: Arts Council of Great Britain/Hayward Gallery, 1979.

Bossi, Giuseppe (1951–)

Italian textile and graphic designer; born and active Milan.

Training Architecture, Milan.
Biography 1973, Bossi began working with Designers 6R5 studio, producing designs for textiles and ceramics; 1975 with Pierangelo Marucco, Francesco Roggero, Maurizio Alberti, and Bruno Rossio, cofounded Original Designers 6R5 studio in Milan. The group designed textiles by Lanerossi, Sasatex, Taif, and Bassetti, and tapestry producers Printeco and Sirpi, in Italy; Griso and Jover in Spain; Le Roi, Griffine, Marechal, and wallpaper printers in France.
Bibliography *ADI Annual 1976*, Milan: Associazione per il Disegno Industriale, 1976.

Botta, Mario (1943–)

Swiss architect and designer; born Mendrisio, Ticino; active Lugano.

Training 1958–61, technical drafting; 1961–64, Liceo Artistico, Milan; 1964–69, Istituto Universitario di Architettura, Venice.
Biography Before his architectural studies, he built 1961–63 clergy house in Genestretta, showing his early interest in geometrical forms and an emphasis on craftsmanship; 1958–61, was an apprentice building draftsperson in the studio of architects Tita Carloni and Luigi Camenisch in Lugano; 1950s, was influenced by the organic architecture espoused by Bruno Zevi in Italy; 1965, did practical work on a hospital project in Le Corbusier's studio in Paris, and in Guillermo Jullian de la Fuente and José Oubrerie's studio in Venice. Botta's 1960s houses reflected the influence of Le Corbusier. 1969, he met architect Louis Kahn in Venice; participated on the project for the new Palazzo dei Congressi Laurea all'UIA in Venice; 1969, set up his own studio in Lugano, where he designed private, industrial, and public buildings in Switzerland; from 1969, was visiting professor and member of institutions and organizations in Europe and the US; 1976, visiting professor, École Polytechnique Fédérale, Lausanne, and, from 1983, professor there. Large number of buildings range from 1961–63 clergy house at Genestretta to 1997 Museum Jean Tinguely in Basel and 2000 San Francisco Museum of Modern Art. Furniture designs by Alias include 1982 Prima side chair, 1982 Seconda armchair, 1983 Terzo table, 1984 Quarta chair, 1985 Quinta armchair, 1985 Sesta armchair, 1985 Sesto King and Queen chairs, 1986 Tesi table, and 1987 Latonda armchair. His 1985–86 Shogun lighting range and 1987 Melan-os table lamp were produced by Artemide.
Bibliography Italo Rota (ed.), *Mario Botta: Architetture e progetti negli anni '70*, Milan, 1979. *Mario Botta: Bâtiments et projets, 1978–1982*, Paris, 1982. Futagawa Yukio (ed.), *Architect Mario Botta*, New York: Rizzoli, 1984. Stuart Wrede, *Mario Botta*, New York: The Museum of Modern Art, 1986. Francesco Dal Co (ed.), *Mario Botta, Architecture, 1960–1985*, New York: Rizzoli, 1987. Dieter Hezel (ed.), *Architekten, Mario Botta* (bibliography), Stuttgart: IRB, 1995. Emilio Pizzi (ed.), *Mario Botta: The Complete Works*, Milan: F. Motta, 1993; Zürich: Artemis, 1998.

Bottoni, Piero (1903–1973)

Italian architect and designer.

Biography A Rationalist architect, Bottoni designed the maid's room and bath of the Casa Elettrica (architects of which were fellow Gruppo Sette members Luigi Figini and Gino Pollini) for Montedison at 1930 (4th) Exposition at Monza. It was the first truly public expression of modern architecture in Italy and the prominently featured kitchen was influenced by German and American models. 1930–33, Bottoni collaborated on interiors with Giuseppe Terragni; was a member, Movimento Italiano per l'Architettura Razionale (MIAR); 1933, editor, journal *Quadrante*. Bottoni designed a housing development (with Enrico Griffini) at 1933 (5th) Triennale di Milano. Bottoni's 1930s Lira plated tubular-steel chair with its prominent vertical wire splats was produced by Thonet and, 1980s, revived by Zanotta; its tension wires suspended the seat on the frame in a technically and aesthetically sophisticated, if busy, manner.
Exhibitions Participated in 1928–31 Rational architecture exhibition, Rome; 1930 (4th) *Esposizione Biennale delle Arti Decorative e Industriali Moderne*, Monza; 1936 (6th) and 1947 (8th) Triennali di Milano.
Bibliography Barbie Campbell-Cole and Tim Benton (eds.), *Tubular Steel Furniture*, London: Art Book Company, 1979: 47. Stefano Casciani, *Mobili come architettura*, Milan: Arcadia, 1984: 160. Penny Sparke, *Design in Italy, 1870 to the Present*, New York: Abbeville, 1988. Cat., Hans Wichmann (ed.), *Italien Design 1945 bis heute*, Munich: Die Neue Sammlung, 1988. Giancarlo Consonni et al. (eds.), *Piero Bottoni: opera completa*, Milan: Fabbri, 1990.

Mario Botta. Seconda armchair. 1982. Steel and polyurethane, 28 1/4 x 20 1/2 x 22 5/8" (71.8 x 52 x 57.5 cm), seat h. 18 1/4" (46.4 cm). Mfr.: Alias, Italy. Gift of ICF, Inc. MoMA.

Boucher, Guy (1935–1992)
French designer.

Training Under Jean Prouvé, engineering, Conservatoire National des Arts et Métiers, Paris.
Biography Boucher was involved with advanced technology as well as artistic projects, including a technical project for Télémécanique; also designed 1968 SAFTBP12 dinnerware by Duralex-Saint-Gobain, 1983 Service Antares drinking glasses by Daum, and first one-piece pocket lamp (1971), by Mazda.
Citations 1986 competition sponsored by APCI (Agence pour la Promotion de la Création Industrielle).
Bibliography *Les carnets du design*, Paris: Mad-Cap Productions/APCI, 1986: 50. François Mathey, *Au bonheur des formes, design français 1945–1992*, Paris: Regard, 1992: 123, 339.

Bouchet, Léon-Émile (1880–1940)
French decorator, furniture designer, and teacher; born Cannes; active Paris.

Training Furniture making at Carpezza and Carlhian, Paris.
Biography From 1898, Bouchet designed furniture by notable firms, including Bec and Le Confortable, and fabric by Bianchini-Férier; worked in a conservative Art Nouveau style inspired by Louis XVI models; during World War I, was in charge of the camouflage service; subsequently, adopted a modern approach, again based on 18th- and 19th-century models; from 1913, taught, École Boulle, Paris; c. 1926, became artistic director, G.E. et J. Dennery, Paris; worked with Epéaux and Soubrier; designed domestic interiors, offices, stores, and a suite on 1931 oceanliner *L'Atlantique*.
Exhibitions Work shown at all Salons of Société des Artistes Décorateurs—his most notable presentation was the Bureau d'un Homme d'Affaires at 1929 edition; Salon d'Automne; 1925 *Exposition Internationale des Arts Décoratifs et Industriels Modernes*; 1929 *Exposition de la Décoration Française Contemporaine*; all Paris.
Bibliography *Ensembles mobiliers*, vol. 2, Paris: Charles Moreau, 1937. Pierre Kjellberg, *Art déco: les maîtres du mobilier, le décor des paquebots*, Paris: Amateur, 1986.

Bouguennec, Pierre
French designer; born Brittany.

Training In cabinetmaking, New York.
Biography 1987, Bouguennec moved to New York and began a practice as an architect; 1989, set up Boum Design, a studio where he designs furniture, lighting, and interiors, including modular spaces; is also a member of Samba Inc. Plug In lamp was produced by Ligne Roset and a range of inflatable furniture was self-produced.
Exhibitions/citations Work included in 2000 *The American Design Challenge* and 2001 *New Design New York*, Totem gallery, New York. Two awards (for Plug In lamp), 1999 Salon du Meuble, Paris.
Biobliography Mel Byars, *50 Beds...*, Hove: RotoVision, 2000. Michele De Lucchi (ed.), *The International Design Yearbook*, London: Laurence King, 2001.

Bouilhet, Henri (1931–1999)
French architect and designer.

Training In architecture.
Biography An heir of the Christofle metalware family, Bouilhet worked on the interior architecture of Centre Georges Pompidou with Renzo Piano and Richard Rogers and designed new factory of Christofle; joined brothers Albert and Marc in management of Christofle enterprise; was influenced by the Bauhaus in his designs; designed c. 1970 Géométrie tea service and other metalware by Christofle, where he became the artistic director. Not to be mistaken for his heir Henri Bouilhet, who took over Christofle on the death of his uncle Charles Christofle (1905–1963).
> See Christofle.

Bouisson, Michel
> See Fourniture.

Boulestin, X. Marcel (1878–1943)
French chef and interior decorator; active London.

Biography Boulestin worked in Paris with novelist Colette and her husband Willy. Encouraged by friends including Max Beerbohm, Boulestin came to England 1906 to pursue a literary career; 1911, founded the shop Décoration Moderne, Elizabeth Street, London, one of the first small avant-garde decorator showrooms there; stocked furniture and furnishings from Paris, including complete range by Paul Poiret's Atelier Martine. Clients included Lady Curzon, the baronne d'Erlanger, and Syrie Wellcome. When the fashion for exotic wares declined after World War I, Boulestin turned to the production of painted 'java paper' (silk glued to paper) lampshades. 1921, Décoration Moderne closed. Collaborating with friend Jean-Émile Laboureur, Boulestin became a renowned restaurateur, hiring architect Clough Williams-Ellis and decorator Allan Walton for the 1925 Restaurant Français and 1927 Restaurant Boulestin. André Groult supervised the latter, where circus-theme panels by Marie Laurencin and Laboureur and curtains by Raoul Dufy were installed. Boulestin wrote *Simple French Cooking for English Homes* (1923) and others, popularizing French cuisine in Britain.
Bibliography X.M. Boulestin, *Ease and Endurance*, London, 1948. William Gaunt, *The Studio*, 1928. Stephen Calloway, *Twentieth-Century Decoration*, New York: Rizzoli, 1988: 63–64, 109, 137, 167.

Boulle, École
> See École Boulle.

Bourgeois, Édouard-Joseph (aka Djo-Bourgeois; Georges Djo-Bourgeois 1898–1937)
French architect and interior and furniture designer; born Bezons; active Paris; husband of Elise Bourgeois.

Training To 1922 under Robert Mallet-Stevens, École Spéciale d'Architecture, Paris.
Biography Early 1920s, Djo-Bourgeois worked alongside Étienne Kohlmann and Maurice Matet at the Studium-Louvre decorating studio of Les Grands Magasins du Louvre department store, for which he designed furniture and interiors. His architectural training spurred his interest in the spatial arrangement of movable furniture. His furniture designs and interiors were geometric, austere, right-angled, and enlivened by the bright colors in the curtains and rugs designed by his wife Elise Bourgeois and by Hélène Henry. He was attracted to innovative materials, including Terazolith composition rubber, as well as traditional lacquer for furniture. From 1926, he used metal in his furniture, particularly aluminum with wood, and nickel-plated steel tubing. His interests included the design of kitchens and children's rooms. He renovated the apartment of the princess Faucigny-Lucinge in an old mansion on Île Saint-Louis, Paris, an example of his archi-

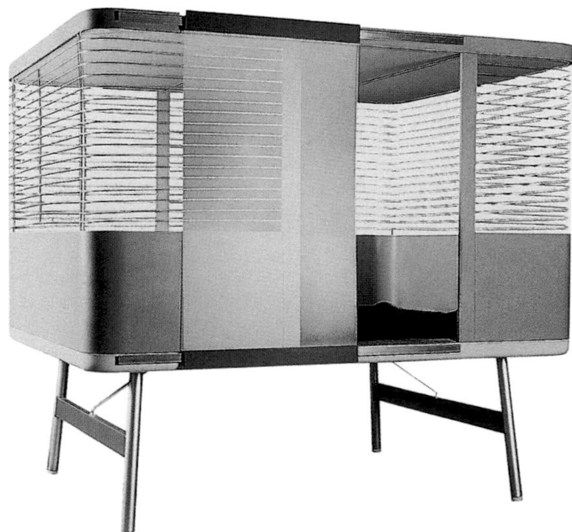

Ronan Bouroullec and Erwan Bouroullec. Lit Clos. 1997 (design and prototype, produced from 2000). Steel, plywood, aluminum, metacrylate, cellulose, and fabric; h. 29 1/2–127 1/2 x 94 1/2 x 78 3/4" (75–324 x 240 x 200 cm). Mfr.: Cappellini, Italy.

tectural work, which also included private homes and apartment buildings with some domestic architecture in the south of France such as the Lahy house in Saint-Clair. 1925, his personal style was illustrated fully formed in the interiors (with others) of 1924–33 villa of the vicomte and vicomtesse de Noailles in Hyères. 1929, he established a studio at 25, rue Vaneau, Paris, the same year he designed a dining-room suite in aluminum for a townhouse in Paris and, hence, executed the interiors for a number of apartments and shops; 1920s, designed for the Metz store in Amsterdam; has been attributed with having designed accessories for Desny in Paris. Despite the modern approach of his work and closeness with Robert Mallet-Stevens, he did not join Union des Artistes Modernes (UAM).
Exhibitions Work first shown at 1922 Salon d'Automne; regularly at Salons of Société des Artistes Décorateurs (SAD) from 1923. Designed office-library of Studium Louvre pavilion at 1925 *Exposition Internationale des Arts Décoratifs et Industriels Modernes*, Paris. Appartement d'un Yachtman sur la Côte d'Azur (completed posthumously by friends and colleagues) was shown at SAD pavilion, 1937 *Exposition Internationale des Arts et Techniques dans la Vie Moderne,* Paris.
Bibliography Léon Deshairs, *Modern French Decorative Art: A Collection of Examples of Modern French Decoration*, Paris: Albert Lévy, c. 1925–30. A.H. Martinie, 'Djo-Bourgeois architecte et décorateur,' *Art et décoration*, 1981. Pierre Kjellberg, *Art déco: les maîtres du mobilier, le décor des paquebots*, Paris: Amateur, 1986. Hubert Damisch, *Villa Noailles*, Paris: Marval, 1997. François Carassan et al., *Villa de Noailles*, Paris: Plume, 2001. François Carassan et al., *Villa de Noailles*, Paris: Plume, 2001.

Bourgeois, Elise (d. 1986)
French fabric designer; wife of Édouard-Joseph Bourgeois.

Biography Bourgeois's printed curtain material, fabrics, and rugs were included in the interior architecture of husband Édouard-Joseph Bourgeois (Djo-Bourgeois). Her designs were bold, brightly colored, and geometric. She died in Oran, France.

Bourgeois, Marie-Laure (1955–)
> See Bécheau, Vincent.

Bourne, Agnes (1944–)
American furniture designer; active San Francisco.

Biography From 1970s, she designed retail displays, theater sets, historical restorations, remodeling, and interiors; was an interior designer and manager of a shop, San Francisco; taught design at California College of Arts and Crafts; was co-author of a series of books on decorating. Her furniture designs included the Chevy Chaise, Ham and Eggs suite of tables and cubes, and the Tao chair. 1990s, she became known for her generous philanthropic activities.
Bibliography Ylanda Gault, 'The New American Entrepreneurs,' *Metropolis*, May 1991: 65–66, 68.

Bouroullec, Ronan (1971–); Erwan Bouroullec (1976–)
French designers; born Quimper; active Paris; brothers.

Training Ronan: 1991, industrial design, École des Arts Appliqués et Professions Artistiques; 1995, École Nationale Supérieure des Arts Décoratifs; both Paris. Erwan: to 1995, École National Supérieure des Arts Décoratifs; to 1999, visual arts, École Nationale d'Art, Cergy (near Paris).
Biography 1996, Ronan designed a group of vases by Evans and Wong. Erwan began working with his brother while at the Cergy school of art, inaugurating the association with a jewelry collection by Smack. 2000, together they designed Aio ceramic dinnerware by Habitat, sponges by Authentics, the Métropole display at the Salon du Meuble, Paris, and, subsequently, furniture and furnishings for others including Cappelini, Boffi, Authentics, Ligne Roset, Sommer, La Monnaie de Paris, Smak Iceland, and Evans and Wong; Corian furniture, Du Pont invitational exhibition, 2001 Salone del Mobile, Milan; highly publicized 1997 elevated-bedroom prototype (later by Cappellini), VIA (French furniture association) stand, 2001 Salon du Meuble, Paris; achieved recognition rather quickly.
Exhibitions/citations Participated in international exhibitions in France and other countries. Work subject of 2002 *Ronan and Erwan Bouroullec: The Fabulous Bouroullec Boys*, Design Museum, London. Citations in France and abroad, including 1997 FIACRE grant (to Ronan for Gigogne vase group by Cappellini); 1997 Carte Blanche production support, VIA; Grand Prix de la Critique et de la Presse, Salon du Meuble, Paris; Grand Prix de la Création de la Ville de Paris.
Bibliography Cat., Sophie Tasma Anargyros et al., *L'école française: les créateurs de meubles du 20ème siècle*, Paris: Industries Françaises de l'Ameublement, 2000.

Bouval, Maurice (1863–1916)
French metalworker; born Toulouse.

Training Under Alexandre Falguière.
Biography Bouval made lamps and small bronze objects; often gilded his work and incorporated idealized Art Nouveau interpretations of the female form into utilitarian designs as well as nymphs, water lilies, poppies, and lotuses; adapted traditional sculpture into letter openers, inkwells, *garnitures de cheminée*, and other accessories. His bronzes were cast at the foundries of Colin, of Jollet, and of Thiebaut Frères. Work included the Ophelia bust, The Secret statuette, Dream and Obsession candelabra, and c. 1900 Weeping Girl vase, and lighting fixtures (sconces, table lamps, candelabra, and candlesticks), some in *bronze doré*.
Exhibitions Work shown regularly at Salons of Société des Artistes Français, first as a sculptor and then as a designer in the decorative-arts section, where his Tristesse bronze candlestick was shown at the 1897 edition. Pair of gilt-bronze flambeaux (produced by La Maison Goldscheider) was included in Goldscheider's exhibit at 1900 *Exposition Universelle*, Paris.
Bibliography Yvonne Brunhammer et al., *Art Nouveau Belgium, France*, Houston: Rice University, 1976, biblio. Alastair Duncan, *Art Nouveau and Art Déco Lighting*, New York: Simon & Schuster, 1978.

Bouvier, Pierre (1964–)
> See Meyer, Philippe.

Bouy, Jules (1872–1937)
French metalsmith; active Belgium and US.

Training Under Edgar Brandt, metalworking, Paris.
Biography Bouy directed an interior-decoration firm in Belgium; 1913, settled in New York; 1924–27, was associated with L. Alavoine, the Parisian decorating firm with an office in Manhattan; concurrently, was head of Ferrobrandt, New York, which produced his own designs and sold the metalwork of Edgar Brandt and historicist French furniture; by 1928, had set up his own firm, with fashionable clients including Agnes Miles Carpenter and Lillie P. Bliss.
Bibliography *American Art Annual*, 1930: 511. *The New York Times*, 29 June 1937: 22. Karen Davies, *At Home in Manhattan: Modern Decorative Arts, 1925 to the Depression*, New Haven: Yale, 1983.

Boven, Gert (1957–)
Dutch lighting designer.

Training Akademie voor Industriële Vormgeving, Eindhoven.
Biography 1984–88, Boven was an associate designer at Neonis Design and Styling; 1988, joined Lumiance Design Team.
Citations 1984 Kho Liang le Encouragement award.

Bowerman Jr., 'Bill' William Jay (1911–1999)
American entrepreneur; born Portland, Ore.

Training To 1934, runner and football player, University of Oregon; accepted by a medical school.
Biography Rejecting medical school, Bowerman was active from 1934 as the track/football coach, Medford High School, Medford, Oregon; from 1949, was the track coach, University of Oregon, becoming renowned for his commanding presence and dogged determination, even handcrafting the runners' shoes; 1962 with former runner Phil Knight whom Bowerman coached, established the Blue Ribbon Sports company and sold Tiger running shoes, imported from a Japanese manufacturer. 1971, they developed lightweight athletic shoes that featured greater traction than standard running shoes, a form that had changed little since the 1917 introduction of Keds 'sneakers'; 1972, established the Nike company/brand (named for the winged Greek goddess of victory) in Braverman, Ore. The 1970s interest by the public in physical fitness and running, particularly in America, ensured its initial success. Famous athletes like Michael Jordan were generously paid endorsers, and the now highly recognizable 'Swoosh' trademark (designed by Caroline Davidson in 1971 for $35/£14.50) and the much-later-coined 'Just Do It' slogan (by Dan Wieden in 1988 of

advertising agency Wieden + Kennedy, Portland, Oregon) were introduced. However, a glue that Bowerman had used to make experimental footwear contained hexane, whose fumes caused permanent damage to his neurological system, causing him to limp and wear a leg brace; nevertheless, coached the US men's track team, 1972 Munich Olympiad. Nike headquarters are in Portland.
Citations 1981 National Track and Field Hall of Fame, US (to Bowerman but rejected due to his college coach Bill Hayward's never having been chosen).
Bibliography Obituary, 'Bill Bowerman, 88, Nike Co-Founder, Dies,' *The New York Times*, 27 Dec. 1999: A20. Tom Vanderbilt, *The Sneaker Book...*, New York: The New Press, 1998. Cat., R. Craig Miller (intro.), *U.S. Design: 1975–2000*, Munich: Prestel, 2002.

Bowlen, Nord (1909–)
> See Lunt Silversmiths.

Box Design
Design studio; located Stockholm.

History 1986, Box Design was established by Ann Morsing and Beban Nord. Morsing studied in San Francisco and at Konstfackskolan, Stockholm, and, subsequently, worked at IKEA and at Matell Arkitekter. Nord studied at Konstfackskolan and woodworking in Stockholm and, subsequently, worked at the joinery of the Royal Palace, Stockholm, and at Svenka Rum Arkitekter. Initially, they designed offices and shops and, subsequently, furniture of their own design and produced furniture by Lloyd Schwan and architect Johannes Norlander.
Exhibitions Work shown many times, Scandinavia and Italy.
Bibliography Michele De Lucchi (ed.), *The International Design Yearbook*, London: Laurence King, 2001.

Boyer, Michel (1935–)
French architect and designer; born and active Paris.

Training École Nationale Supérieure des Arts Décoratifs, Paris.
Biography 1973, Boyer established his own design studio in Paris; 1976, designed Boudin chaise with a tubular-steel base and Osaka, Québec, Montréal, and Brasilia office chairs by Airborne, and 1977 furniture by Strafor; specialized in interior design such as of French embassies in Washington and Brasilia. Other work included public furniture for a number of offices located in La Défense, near Paris; interiors of houses and palaces in the Middle East; 1980s–90s furniture in small editions. 1992, he was president, Société des Artistes Décorateurs.
Citations 1978 René Gabriel prize.
Bibliography Gilles de Bure, *Le mobilier français 1965–1979*, Paris: Regard/VIA, 1983. François Mathey, *Au bonheur des formes, le design français 1945–1992*, Paris: Regard, 1992. Arlette Barré-Despond (ed.), *Dictionnaire international des arts appliqués et du design*, Paris: Regard, 1996.

Boym, Constantin (b. Konstantin Boit 1955–); Laurene Leon Boym (1964–)
Furniture, product, interior, and exhibition designers; husband and wife. Constantin: born Moscow; Laurene: born New York.

Training Constantin Boym: to 1978, Architectural Institute, Moscow; to 1984, Domus Academy, Milan. Laurene Boym: School of Visual Arts, and design, Pratt Institute, Brooklyn; both New York.
Biography 1981, Constantin Boym settled in the US and worked for several architectural firms in Boston, including Graham Gund Associates; 1984–86, collaborated with Matteo Thun in Milan on the design of furniture, objects, interiors, and conceptual architecture; 1985–86, worked with Alessandro Mendini on Alberto Alessi's villa; 1986, returned to New York and set up his own studio; 1995, was joined in the studio by wife Laurene Leon Boym. 1993, she was designer-in-residence at Cooper-Hewitt National Design Museum, New York. He has become known for his Souvenirs for the End of the Century, a special take on miniatures of historical monuments and buildings. Together and separately have designed products and furniture for clients, including Acerbis, Alessi, Benza, Brickel, Detail, Droog/DMD, Elika, Formica, and Sasaki. The Boyms' work is deeply rooted in the meaning and history of objects rather than solely focused on new forms and materials. His activities have also included interior and exhibition design and writing for magazines *Domus*, *Modo*, *Ufficiostile*, *Axis*, *FP*, *Interiors*, *I.D.*, *House and Garden*, and *Metropolis*. From 1986, he taught design at Parsons School of

Constantin Boym. Taxicab chair (prototype). 2001. Steel and wooden balls; h. 36 x w. 16 x d. 18" (91.4 x 40.6 x 45.7 cm). Mfr.: Boym Partners, US.

Design, New York, and, 1994–2001, she also taught there.
Citations 1988 and 1990 Annual Design Review (range of clocks), *I.D.* magazine; first prize (for a writing instrument), 1989 design competition, Industrial Designers Society of America (IDSA).
Bibliography Konstantin Boit, *Novyi russkii dizain*/Constantin Boym, *New Russian Design*, New York: Rizzoli, 1992. Mel Byars, *50 Chairs...*, Hove: RotoVision, 1996. Mel Byars, *Design in Steel*, London: Laurence King, 2002. Constantin Boym et al., *Curious Boym: Design Works*, New York: Princeton Architectural Press, 2002.

Boyton, Charles (1885–1958)
British silversmith; active London.

Biography Initially, Boyton worked at his family's firm; from 1930s, made contemporary objects; 1934, set up his own workshop for modern silver. His work appeared to be influenced by the work of the Georg Jensen Sølvsmedie, including a cutlery set resembling Harald Nielsen's 1927 Pyramid pattern by Jensen.
Bibliography Annelies Krekel-Aalberse, *Art Nouveau and Art Déco Silver*, New York: Abrams, 1989.

Braakman, Cees (1917–95)
Dutch designer.

Biography Cees Braakman's father, cabinetmaker D.L. Braakman, had been the manager and head draftsperson of Dutch furniture firm UMS, and from him he learned the trade. After the destruction caused by World War II, Cees Braakman initiated the reorganization of UMS Pastoe (which merged in 1955), having worked for UMS since 1934 and, 1945–78, was the manager and head of design there. 1947, he visited the US to study manufacturing methods at 12 companies, including Herman Miller Furniture Company; returned to Netherlands and, having seen Charles and Ray Eames's work, experimented with bent plywood and created Pastoe's first modern furniture, including c. 1948 EE 02 desk and c. 1952 BB 04 wooden secretary/bookcase; developed several lines of furniture and a new approach to the firm's corporate identity and catalog design; created a new naming system for furniture with informal titles like Eric, instead of less-friendly codes like EE 02; encouraged graphic designer Harry Sierman to create visually interesting 'books,' rather than catalogs; 1955–1960s, focused on modular cabinets, including those to be self-assembled by customers such as 1960s U+N Series.
> See UMS.

Bracquemond, Félix-Henri (1833–1914)

French artist, etcher, ceramicist, and engraver; born Paris.

Biography Bracquemond became involved in executing woodcuts, having been influenced by Katsusika Hokusai, whose discovery in the West heralded *japonisme* in France. Bracquemond's interest in ceramics began in early 1860s, when he decorated large earthenware plates by Joseph-Theodore Deck. Bracquemond left the Sèvres porcelain factory and joined Charles Haviland's firm, where he was artistic director of its new studio to 1881 (1875, had invited Ernest Chaplet to join the studio) and created designs for use on ceramics; subsequently, returned to engraving and began to write art criticism and to organize exhibitions; became a founding member, Société Nationale des Beaux-Arts; attempted interior design at about the turn of the century, collaborating with Alexandre Charpentier and Jules Chéret on a billiard room for the baron Vitta's domicile; designed enameled jewelry by Alexandre Riquet, bookbindings by Marius-Michel, and vases by Émile Muller.
Exhibitions The baron Vitta's billiard room shown at 1902 Salon of Société Nationale des Beaux-Arts, Paris.
Bibliography Yvonne Brunhammer et al., *Art Nouveau Belgium, France*, Houston: Rice University, 1976.

Braden, Norah (1901–)

British potter; active Brighton.

Training 1919–21, Central School of Arts and Crafts; from 1921, Royal College of Art; both London.
Biography 1925–28, Braden worked with Bernard Leach in St. Ives; met Katherine Pleydell-Bouverie, at whose pottery in Coleshill, Wiltshire, Braden worked 1928–36 and where they produced a variety of ceramics with wood- and plant-ash glazes. Much of their finest work was produced in 1930s. Braden destroyed much of her small output; c. 1939, began teaching, Brighton Art School, and discontinued her work as a potter.
Bibliography Cat., *Thirties: British Art and Design Before the War*, London: Arts Council of Great Britain/Hayward Gallery, 1979. Frederick Cooke, *Glass: Twentieth-Century Design*, New York: Dutton, 1986.

Bragdon, William Victor (d. 1959)

American ceramic engineer; active Berkeley, Cali.

Training To 1908, Alfred (N.Y.) University.
Biography From 1908, Bragdon taught, University of Chicago, and, under Taxile Doat, University City Porcelain Works, Miss.; 1915, settled in Berkeley, Cal., and taught, California School of Arts and Crafts there; 1916 with Chauncey R. Thomas, established California Faïence, producing art tiles and pottery to 1930s. Subsequently, the pottery facilities were used by local artists and amateur decorators.
Bibliography Paul Evans in Timothy J. Andersen et al., *California Design 1910*, Salt Lake City: Peregrine Smith, 1980.

Braham, Philip
> See Steelchrome.

Brambilla, Giorgio (1951–)

Italian designer; born Desio, Milan; active Milan.

Training Industrial design, Scola Politecnica di Design (SPD), Milan.
Biography From 1974, Brambilla collaborated with Lorenzo Tosi, Fabio Stojan, and Anna Castelli in studio Gruppo in Milan. They studied solar-energy applications in housing for Montedison's office of accident prevention. With Castelli, Brambilla developed lightweight cardboard playground equipment.
Bibliography *ADI Annual 1976*, Milan: Associazione per il Disegno Industriale, 1976.

Brandi, Ulrike (1957–)

German lighting designer; born Göttingen.

Training From 1976, literature, Universität Hamburg; 1984–88 under Dieter Rams, Achim Czemper, and Peter Raacke, industrial design, Hochschule der Bildenden Künste, Hamburg.
Biography 1986, Brandi became an independent consultant designer and lighting designer, establishing Ulrike Brandi Licht in Hamburg. Associates include Christoph Geissmar-Brandi, Christof Fielstette, Jörn Hustedt, Beatrice Seidt, and Heike Siemers. The consortium offers advice/consultation on the lighting of interior/exterior spaces. They handle all project phases, specializing in interdisciplinary planning; designed

Cees Braakman. Desk (no. EE 02). c. 1948. Oak and laminated wood, h. 29 1/8 x 49 1/2 x 24" (74 x 125.7 x 61.5 cm). Mfr.: UMS Pastoe, the Netherlands. Courtesy Quittenbaum Kunstauktionen, Munich.

1987 solar-powered light by Erco Leuchten and Mannesmann-DEMAG. Other commissions: Munich airport and new Mercedes-Benz museum.
Citations To Brandi: Design Plus prize (bedside table), 1985 Ambiente fair, Frankfurt; 1985 Design Bourse (chair design), Haus Industrieform Essen; 1986 Wilkhahn firm competition (chair design); 1986 Bauwelt competition (drawing instrument), Büro für das Existenzminimum; 1987 Design zur Zeit competition (timepiece), Museum für Kunst und Gewerbe, Hamburg; 1988 competition, Österreichisches Institut für Formgebung, Vienna.
Bibliography *Frauen im Design: Berufsbilder und Lebenswege seit 1900*, Stuttgart: Design Center, 1989. *Jahrbuch für Licht und Architektur 1993*, Berlin: Ernst & Sohn, 1994, 1995. Anja Lösel, '*Licht-Designer: Effekte mit Beleuchtung*,' *Stern Extra—Bauen und Wohnen*, no. 17, 2000: 150–58.

Brandolini, Andreas (1951–)

German designer; born Taucha, near Leipzig.

Training 1973–79, architecture, Technische Universität, Berlin.
Biography 1979–81, Brandolini worked as an industrial designer; lectured in industrial design, Hochschule der Künste, Berlin, Architectural Association, London, and Hochschule für Gestaltung, Offenbach.1981–85, he was a partner of Block-Brandolini-Rolfes Architects, Berlin; 1982–86 with Joachim B. Stanitzek, was active in experimental studio 'Bellefast–workshop for experimental design,' Berlin (Bellefast being a play on German words meaning 'instant beauty'). Bellefast work included 1984 Hommage à Yuri Gagarin lighting fixture and 1984 Frühlingserwachen coat rack. 1986–93, Brandolini was active in his own studio Brandolini Büro für Gestaltung, Berlin. Designed 1986 Bonanza limited-production table. Teaching activities include: 1981– 89, lecturer in industrial design, Hochschule der Künste, Berlin; 1984, visiting professor, Hochschule für Gestaltung, Offenbach; 1984–85, visiting professor, Royal College of Art and Architectural Association, both London; 1984–85, workshop, Technischen Universität Graz; 1989, workshop, MAC, São Paulo; 1990–91, workshop, Sommer-Akademie Graz, with Utilism International, a firm he founded with Axel Kufus and Jasper Morrison; from 1989, full-time professor of design, Hochschule der Bildenden Künste, Saarbrücken, Germany. 1993, he settled in Petit Réderching, France, with a studio in Saarbrücken, Germany; from 1998, has been director, Centre International d'Art Verrier, Meisenthal, France.
Exhibitions Work shown in numerous exhibitions of new design in German cities (including 1987 *Documenta 8*, Kassel) and in Milan, London, Paris, Vienna, Toronto, New York, Los Angeles, Singapore, Tokyo, Riga, St. Petersburg, and São Paolo (1987 19th Bienal Internacional).
Bibliography Christian Borngraeber, *Prototypen: Avantgarde Design uit/aus Berlin*, Rotterdam: 010 Publishers, 1986. Albrecht Bangert and Karl Michael Armer, *80s Style: Designs of the Decade*, New York: Abbeville, 1990. *Ottagono*, no. 100, 1991: 1.

Brandt, Åsa (1940–)

Swedish glassware designer.

Training 1962–67, Konstfackskolan and Tekniska Skolan, Stockholm; 1967, Gerrit Rietveld Academie, Amsterdam; Royal College of Art, London.

Edgar Brandt. Table lamp. 1920s. Patinated bronze and glass (flashed *verre-de-jade* with powder and gold-foil inclusions), h. 19 5/8 x 13" (50 x 33 cm). Mfr.: Daum Frères, France. Courtesy Quittenbaum Kunstauktionen, Munich.

Biography 1968, Brandt set up her own workshop in Torshälla; with Ulla Forsell and Eva Ullberg, established cooperative studio Freeblowers; became one of the pioneers of studio glass in Europe and a member, Konsthantverkarna, Stockholm, Sweden's oldest and largest collective for handcrafts. Notable work installed in Arlanda Airport, Stockholm, and Kitayama Children's Daycare Center, Tokyo.
Exhibitions Work included in 2002 *Female Artists: Svenska Glasakademin Sweden*, ART O NIVO gallery, Brugge, Belgium. Subject of one-person exhibitions at Länsmuseet Varberg, 1980; Konsthantverkarna in Stockholm, 1972, 1978, and 1981.
Bibliography Cat., David Revere McFadden (ed.), *Scandinavian Modern Design 1880–1980*, New York: Abrams, 1982.

Brandt, Edgar-William (1880–1960)

French metalworker and designer; born Paris.

Training École Professionnelle, Vierzon (Seine-et-Marne).
Biography From c. 1905 in a partnership, Brandt executed lighting fixtures that incorporated glass by Daum with his own bronze. The partnership lasted into 1930s. He established his own workshop in Auteuil, and, 1919, on the site of his father's old ironworks, where he installed the newest equipment. Henri Favier designed the showroom, called La Maison d'un Ferronnier. Inspired by the Art Nouveau style, Brandt's metalwork was applied to dark, colorful, and even ornate ensembles that lent a sense of dimension and space. Known for his wrought-iron work, Brandt gilded, silvered, and polished metals, marrying them with bronze and marble; designed the Tombeau du Soldat Inconnu at the Arc de Triomphe, Paris, and the Armistice Monument in Rethondes. After 1925, his work became more geometric. 1926, he moved his offices, gallery, and atelier to Paris; designed interiors, including those of apartments, offices, public spaces, and oceanliners; 1925, opened a branch of his wrought-iron business in New York, called Ferrobrandt and managed by Jules Bouy, and a branch for a time in London; 1926, was commissioned to decorate the Cheney Stores, New York.
Exhibitions/citations Work shown at Salons of Société des Artistes Français from 1900, Salon d'Automne from 1900, Salon des Beaux-Arts 1900–14, Salons of Société des Artistes Décorateurs from 1910, and most of the international exhibitions. At 1925 *Exposition Internationale des Arts Décoratifs et Industriels Modernes*, Paris, his wrought-iron metalwork was an essential part of many stands (including with Favier and Ventre, and for the gates of the Porte d'Honneur and for the Hôtel du Collectionneur of Jacques-Émile Ruhlmann). Awarded numerous citations.
Bibliography Salon catalogs, Société des Artistes Décorateurs, 1910, 1911, 1919–22, 1924, 1926. Salon catalogs, Société des Artistes Français, 1919–20. Salon catalogs, Salon d'Automne, 1920–24, 1926, 1934. Guillaume Janneau, *Le luminaire et les moyens d'éclairages nouveaux*, Paris: Charles Moreau, 1st, 2nd, and 3rd series, [n.d.]. Cat., Bevis Hillier (ed.), *The World of Art Déco*, New York: Dutton, 1971: figs. 358–61. Cat., *Decorative Arts 1925 Style*, New York: Didier Aaron, 1979. Katherine Morrison McClinton, 'Edgar Brandt Art Déco Ironworker,' *The Connoisseur*, Sept. 1979: 8–14. Victor Arwas, *Art Déco*, New York: Abrams, 1980. Joan Kahr, *Edgar Brandt: Master of Art Déco Ironwork*, New York: Abrams, 1999.

Brandt, Marianne (1893–1983)

German painter, designer, and metalworker; born Chemnitz; active Weimar, Chemnitz, Dresden, and Berlin.

Training 1911–17, painting, Akademie der bildenden Künste, Weimar; 1923–29, metalworking, Bauhaus, Weimar and Dessau.
Biography 1917, Brandt set up her own studio; with Wilhelm Wagenfeld, became the best-known pupil of the Bauhaus metalwork studio, directed by László Moholy-Nagy, whose Constructivist geometric forms inspired her and whose influence turned her from an Arts and Crafts metalworker in 1924 into an industrial designer of lamps in 1925. Brandt's designs for domestic products were based on uncompromising geometric principles. She designed 1928 Kandem nightlight (with 'Hin' Hinrich Bredensieck) as a class project. At the Bauhaus, her colleagues included Christian Dell and Hans Pryzembel. 1928–32, succeeding Moholy-Nagy, she was head of the Bauhaus metal workshop; 1929, briefly worked in the office of Walter Gropius in Berlin; 1928–29, designed a series of Kandem lamps by Körting & Mathiesen in Leipzig; became a consultant designer for various firms and a teacher; 1930–33, worked on various designs at Ruppelwerk metalworking factory in Gotha, including a distinctive red-painted metal inkwell; from 1933, was unemployed, returning to Chemnitz (then Karl-Marx-Stadt) and taking up painting; attempted to sell a license to the Wohnbedarf store in Zürich for the production of her bowls, ashtrays, dining utensils, and an egg cooker; 1949–51, taught in Dresden and, 1951–54, worked at the Institut für Industrieformgestaltung, Berlin; briefly, was a freelance industrial designer before, back again in Chemnitz, devoting herself to painting and sculpture. Some of her designs are still produced, notably 1930s tea set's inclusion in Tea and Coffee Piazza project by Alessi from 1983, the year she died in Kirchberg, Sachsen. Her 1920s ceiling lamps, ashtrays, and a teapot are now being reproduced by Tecnolumen in Bremen.
Bibliography Walther Scheidig, *Crafts of the Weimar Bauhaus...*, London: Studio Vista, 1967. Stephan Waetzold and Verena Haas, *Tendenzen der zwanziger Jahre*, 15, Berlin: Europäische Kunstausstellung, 1977. Officina Alessi, *Tea and Coffee Piazza: 11 Servizi da tè e caffè...*, Milan: Crusinallo, 1983. F. Whitford, *Bauhaus*, London, 1984. Eckhard Neumann (ed.), *Bauhaus und Bauhäusler*, Cologne, 1985. Cat., *The Bauhaus: Masters and Students*, New York:

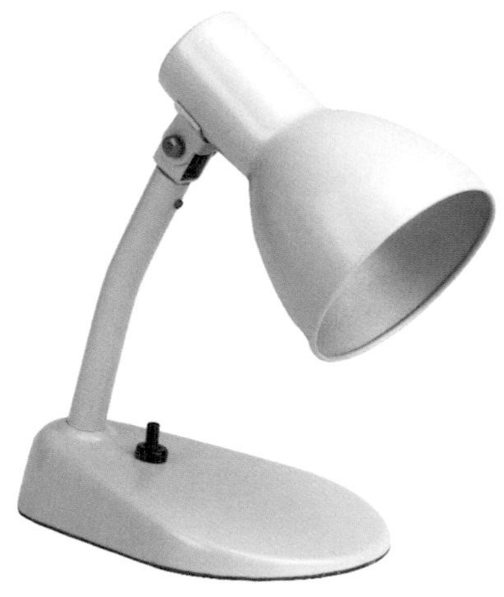

Marianne Brandt and 'Hin' Hinrich Bredendieck. Kandem bedside table lamp (no. 702). 1928. Lacquered steel, h. 9 1/4" (23.5 cm), base w. 7 1/4" (18.4 cm). Mfr.: Körtig & Matthiesen, Germany. Phyllis B. Lambert Fund. MoMA.

Barry Freidman, 1988. Cat., *Die Metallwerkstatt am Bauhaus*, Berlin: Bauhaus-Archiv, 1992. Hans Brockhage and Reinhold Lindner, *Marianne Brandt: 'Hab ich je an kunst gedacht,'* Chemnitz: Chemnitzer Verlag, 2001. Paola Antonelli (ed.), *Objects of Design: The Museum of Modern Art*, New York: The Museum of Modern Art, 2003: 74–75.

Brangwyn, Frank (1867–1956)

British artist and designer; born Bruges, Belgium; active London.

Biography From 1882, through his friendship with Arthur H. Mackmurdo, Brangwyn worked as a draftsperson and designed tapestries for William Morris; 1885, rented a studio and showed his work for the first time at the Royal Academy; 1895, executed murals for the entrance of and a frieze in Siegfried Bing's shop L'Art Nouveau, Paris; 1900, designed a bedroom for E.J. Davies with the furniture produced by Norman and Stacey, London. His designs, including furniture, textiles, and ceramics, illustrate his considerable knowledge of historical sources. The coromandel-like doors on his own print cabinet, published in 1914 *Studio Year Book of Decorative Art*, reflect Far Eastern influences and are close to his contemporary painting style. After the 1914 murals for San Francisco *Exposition*, many commissions followed in the US. c. 1927, he designed tableware by Doulton; painted 1928–32 *British Empire* panels for the House of Lords (rejected in 1930 but installed in 1934 in the Guildhall in Swansea); 1930, designed two chenille carpets by James Templeton and hand-knotted Donegals by Alexander Morton; 1932, painted a mural at Rockefeller Center, New York, where other muralists included Diego Rivera and Jose Maria Sert; 1933, designed the new façade of the Rowley Gallery, London, using carved wood panels depicting craftsmen at work over Portland stone. 1936, the Brangwyn Museum was opened in Bruges, Belgium. On the walls of Skinners' Hall, London, he painted his 1937 *Education* and *Charity*. His work was revived following his 1952 Royal Academy of Arts exhibition, the first devoted to a living academician.
Exhibitions/citations 1885, work first shown at the Royal Academy of Arts, London. Painting *Buccaneers* shown at 1893 Paris Salon. Painted murals at 1914 *Panama-Pacific International Exposition*, San Francisco. Designed British exhibits at 1905 and 1907 Biennale di Venezia. Work subject of 1967 centenary exhibition, National Museum of Wales, Cardiff, and a large number of others. 1941, was knighted.
Bibliography Walter Shaw Sparrow, *Frank Brangwyn and His Work*, London: Kegan Paul, French & Trubner, 1910. Herbert Furst, *The Decorative Art of Frank Brangwyn*, London: Bodley Head, 1924. Cat., Frank Brangwyn Centenary, Cardiff: National Museum of Wales, c. 1967. Rodney Brangwyn, *Brangwyn*, London: William Kimber, 1978. Cat., *The Art of Frank Brangwyn*, Brighton: Brighton Polytechnic and Fine Art Society, 1980. Jessica Rutherford, *Art Nouveau, Art Déco and the Thirties: The Furniture Collections at Brighton Museum*, Brighton: The Royal Pavilion, Art Gallery and Museums, 1983: 50, 55.

Branzi, Andrea (1938–)

Italian designer; born Florence; active Milan.

Training To 1966, architecture and design, Florence.
Biography Branzi is known for his theoretical furniture; 1966 with Paolo Deganello and others, founded Archizoom Associati, the avant-garde group in Florence that brought the 1960s irony of Anti-Design to furniture design; participated in the Consulenti Design Milano (CDM) design studio, with whom he published the two-volume *Decorattivo 1* and *2* on environmental décor; 1973, set up his studio in Milan; early 1980s, participated with proto-Memphis group, Studio Alchimia, which explored metaphysical aspects of design; 1972–75, wrote on avant-garde architecture in *Casabella*; 1983–87, was managing editor of *Mode* and, for a time, president of magazine *Domus*; with Michele De Lucchi, organized 1977 *Il Design Italiano degli Anni 50*, the first major retrospective exhibition of Italian postwar design, at Naviglio, Milan, and co-wrote the catalog; 1982–83, was professor, Istituto del Disegno Industriale, the architecture department of Università degli Studi, Palermo; was visiting professor and lecturer at universities and schools in Italy, the Netherlands, France, Japan, Argentina, Brazil, and the US; from 1983, was educational director, Domus Academy, Milan. His attempt to establish a new relationship between man and his possessions is the subject of his book *Domestic Animals: The Neoprimitive Style* (with Nicoletta Branzi, 1987), in which he suggests that it is valid to think of a sofa or a light fixture as a household pet. His other books have included *The Colors of Energy* (1975), *Pre-Synthetic Colors* (1976), *Environmental Colors* (1977), *Good and the Metropolis, La casa calda: esperienze del nuovo disegno italiano* (1982), *Learning from Milan: Design and the Second Modernity* (1988), *Neues europäisches Design* (edited with François Burkhardt, 1991), *Television at the Crossroads* (with Alessandro Mendini and Stefano Marzano, 1995).

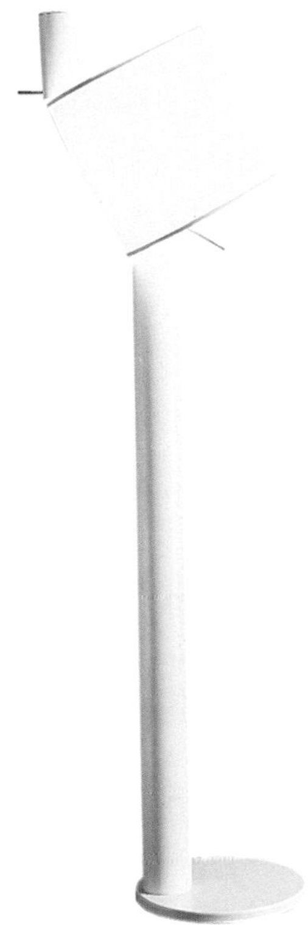

Andreas Branzi. Quirino floor lamp. c. 1998. Lacquered metal and fabric; h. 71 1/4" (181 cm). Mfr.: Artemide, Italy.

Work By Memphis, work included 1982 Gritti bookcase, Century divan, and silver sauce boat, 1983 Beach chaise longue, 1985 Magnolia bookcase, 1987 Andrea chaise longue, and 1988 Foglia electro-luminescent wall lamp. Other designs have included 1982 Labrador silver sauce dish by Rossi e Arcandi, 1985 Animali Domestici range of seating by Zabro, 1986 Berlino sofa by Zanotta, 1986 Frande Tapetto Ibrido range of tables by Zabro, and 1989 Iudola bench by Zanotta.
Exhibitions/citations Participated in 1968 (14th), 1979 (16th), and 1983 (17th) Triennali di Milano, was general coordinator of its 15th edition, and in 1976, 1978, and 1980 Biennali di Venezia. Participated in Memphis's first (1981) exhibition, during Salone del Mobile, Milan. 1979 (with others) and 1987 (Berlino sofa and chair by Zanotta) Premio Com-passo d'Oro. Early 1980s, participated in the exhibitions of Studio Alchimia. Work included in number other group exhibitions. Work sub-ject of exhibitions at The Museum of Modern Art, New York; Lijbanam Centrum, Rotterdam; CAYC, Buenos Aires; Musée Saint Pierre, Lyon; Palazzo dei Diamanti, Ferrara; and elsewhere; and included in numerous group exhibitions.
Bibliography Penny Sparke, *Ettore Sottsass Jnr*, London: Design Council, 1982. 'Andrea Branzi,' *Intramuros*, no. 18, May – June 1988. Germano Celant, *Andrea Branzi: The Complete Works*, New York: Rizzoli, 1992. François Burkhardt and Cristina Morozzi, *Andrea Branzi*, Paris: Dis Voir, 1997.

Brateau, Jules-Paul (1844–1923)

French metalworker and jewelry designer; born Bourges.

Training Under sculptor August Nadaud, École Nationale Supérieure des Arts Décoratifs, Paris; and under H.-S. Boudoncle.
Biography Brateau became the primary designer at Boucheron and at Bapst et Falize, both Paris; collaborated with enameler Paul Grandhomme; end of 19th century, contributed to the resurgence of French

Braun. Aromatic KMM 1 coffee grinder. 1965. Plastics, 7 1/2 x 5 3/4 x 3 1/4" (19 x 14.6 x 8.2 cm). Mfr.: Braun, Germany. Gift of the mfr. MoMA.

interest in the art of pewter, a material he called on to make attractive and inexpensive objects; inspired by the work of Dammouse, designed delicate pieces in *pâte-de-verre* c. 1910–12.
Exhibitions Jewelry and pewter work shown at 1889 and 1900 editions of *Exposition Universelle*, Paris.
Bibliography Yvonne Brunhammer et al., *Art Nouveau Belgium, France*, Houston: Rice University, 1976, biblio.

Brauckman, Cornelius (c. 1866–c. 1954)
> See Grand Feu Art Pottery.

Brauer, Arik (Erich) (1929–)

Austrian painter, printmaker, stage designer, and singer; born Vienna.

Training 1945–51 under Albert Paris Gütersloh, Akademie der bildenden Künste, Vienna.
Biography With Ernest Fuchs, Rudolf Hausner, Wolfgang Hutter, and Anton Lehmden, developed a style known as Fantastic Realism; 1950, earned a living as a folk singer; from 1958, was an artist in Paris; from 1964, lived in Vienna and in artists' village Ein Hod, Israel. Early paintings were strongly influenced by Pieter Bruegel I, then Hieronymus Bosch, expressed through an anecdotal style and, from 1955, by Persian and Indian miniatures; designed furniture that combined fine art and utility, and stage sets; became a successful folk singer.
Exhibitions Works shown with the Art-Club at Zedlitzhalle, Vienna.
Bibliography Günther Feuerstein, *Vienna—Present and Past: Arts and Crafts—Applied Art—Design*, Vienna: Jugend und Volk, 1976. Arik Brauer, *Werkverzeichnis*, Dortmund: Harenberg, 1984.

Braun

German manufacturer; located Frankfurt.

History 1921, engineer W. Max Braun (East Prussia 1890–1951) set up a workshop in Frankfurt for the production of drive-belt connectors and scientific equipment; 1923, began producing plastic components for radios and record-players and, 1929, entire radio sets, the first radio/speaker combination, becoming the largest German radio manufacturer. 1933, Braun AG was established; c. 1949, began to develop whole products, including flashlights and electric shavers. On Max Braun's 1951 death, his sons Artur (1925–) and Erwin (1921–1992) assumed management of the firm. Artur Braun embarked on a new design program, emphasizing function and design, and hired Fritz Eichler, who worked with the teaching staff of the Hochschule für Gestaltung, Ulm. Eichler revised the entire Braun line, beginning with radios. The collaborative designs of Dieter Rams, Hans Gugelot, and Otl Aicher of the Ulm school manifested austere, unadorned forms. 1955, Rams joined the staff at Braun and, 1961, became its chief designer. Braun's 1956 Phonosuper SK4 record player by Gugelot and Rams was the first of its products to speak the new design language. The Braun team produced geometrically proportioned, unadorned electronic products in white and gray cases punctuated with Swiss-style graphics. The influential Braun-Ulm design philosophy was carried through to every facet of the firm's activities, including the logo, advertising, and packaging. However, its products sometimes looked better than they performed; 1961 HT1 Toaster by Reinhold Weiss was not tall enough to toast the top section of a slice of bread. 1967, The Gillette Company of Boston, Mass., acquired the firm, resulting in wide global distribution but the loss of its distinction.
Exhibitions/citations Work (1955 Phonosuper SK4 record player) was first shown at 1955 Düsseldorf exhibition; subsequent work shown at numerous design exhibitions and competitions. Work subject of 1990–91 exhibition, Hamburg (catalog below). A number of awards, including award (for 'for exceptional achievements in phonographs') at 1937 *Exposition Internationale des Arts et Techniques dans la Vie Moderne,* Paris; British Interplas; 1998 Red Dot award of Design Zentrum Nordrhein Westfalen, Essen.
Bibliography Francois Burkhardt and Inez Franksen, *Dieter Rams &*, Berlin: Gerhardt, 1980. Cat., *Mehr oder Weniger: Braun-Design im Vergleich*, Hamburg: Museum für Kunst und Gewerbe, 1990. Jo Klatt and Günter Staeffler, *Braun + Design*, Hamburg, 1995. Cat., Hans Wichmann (ed.), *Mut zum Aufbruch: Erwin Braun, 1921–1992*, Munich: Prestel, 1998. www.braun.com.

Braun, Jürgen W. (1938–); FSB

German business and design manager; born Berlin. FSB located Brakel.

Training Jurisprudence, Bonn and Paris; for a time, Düsseldorf.
Biography For five years after his university studies, Braun worked in business management at Daimler-Benz in Stuttgart; subsequently, managed a ball-bearing distribution agency importing products from the Far East; 1981–c. 2003, was managing director, doorhandle manufacturer FSB (founded 1881 by Franz Schneider as a hardware firm in Iserlohn, Germany and, 1909, was moved to Brakel, where it is today; initials 'FSB' represent 'Franze Schneider Brakel.') In the post-World War II period, began using lightweight metals and incorporating curvaceous forms. The firm's logo by Otl Aicher was modeled on a doorhandle design by philosopher Ludwig Wittgenstein. Braun reorganized the firm as a successful medium-sized enterprise with high design standards. Beginning with Aicher, Braun has commissioned a number of renowned designers; has based the design principles of the firm on mathematical interpretations of beauty or 'the dynamic golden-growth spiral' (expressed in *Die Natur der Schönheit: Zur Dynamik der schönen Formen* [Insel, 1992] by Friedrich Cramer and Wolfgang Kampfer). Braun was a member, German Design Council, and Internationales Design Zentrum Berlin; retired c. 2001.
Citations To FSB: 1993 Design Management Prize, Nordrhein Westfalen, Esseu; 1994 Deutschen Umweltpreis (federal German environmental prize), Deutsche Bundesstiftung Umwelt (DBU, federal German foundation for the environment).

Braun-Feldweg, Wilhelm (b. Wilhelm Braun 1908–1998)

German designer; born Ulm.

Training 1922, steel engraving; art school, Stuttgart; 1935, art history, Tübingen and Stuttgart.
Biography From 1950, Braun became active as a designer and, in time, created a wide range of products from lighting (1958 Tokio) and cutlery (1965 Annette by Carl Prinz) to door handles (1952 Erno 127); was attracted to glass and designed a number of utilitarian pieces, including 1954 Marina bowls by Hirschberg and 1959 Tasso set. He also designed 1953 550L 35mm transparency projector by Kindermann. While he might be favorably compared to Wilhelm Wagenfeld due to their common nationality, his quest for simplicity, and an interest in glass, Braun-Feldweg was additionally a prolific writer and theoretician. His book on metal and design is highly regarded. Known as an obsessive, he frequently made up to 20 maquettes for a single design; late 1950s, became the newly created chairperson of industrial design, Hochschule der Künste, Berlin; is little known due to his morality, which dictated that all designers remain anonymous. Books include *Schmiedeeisen und Leichtmetall am Bau Kunstschmiede- und*

Schlosserarbeiten (Ravensburg: Maier, 1952), *Normen und Formen industrieller Produktion* (Ravensburg: Maier, 1954), *Industrial Design heute, Ümwelt aus der Fabrik* (Rowohlt: Reinbek, vols. 254–55, 1966), *Metall: Werkformen und Arbeitswesen...* (Ravensburg: Maier, 1950 (also in English eds.).
Bibliography Siegfried Gronert (ed.), *Form und Industrie: Wilhelm Braun-Feldweg*, Frankfurt, 1998. Siegfried Gronert (ed.), *184 Seiten, 160 Abbildungen. Die Havanna, Die Havanna—Pendelleuchten von Wilhelm Braun-Feldweg*, Frankfurt: form, 2001. Marion Godau and Bernd Polster, *Design Directory Germany*, London: Pavilion, 2000.

Braunstein, Claude (1940–)

French industrial designer; born and active Paris.

Training École des Arts Appliqués; subsequently, Cours Supérieur d'Esthétique Industrielle; both Paris.
Biography From 1961, Braunstein worked at Roger Tallon's agency Technès, Paris; 1964–70, was director of product design, IBM; 1970–72 with others, established Institut de l'Environment, Paris; 1972–84, worked at Ministère de la Culture, responsible for the establishment of the departments of design and environment in France's art schools, and, concurrently, professor, École des Beaux-Arts in Marseille and Bourges, ENSCI (Les Ateliers) in Paris, and others and consultant at public-relations firm Signis (a founding member and associato); 1985 with Clément Rousseau, cofounded Plan Créatif/Crabtree Hall industrial-design firm, Paris, active there to 1994. In 1995, he established agency BB&A for product and interior design, corporate-ID development, publishing, and multimedia for clients such as Rosières, EDF, Société Générale, Crédit Agricole, others.

Brazier-Jones, Mark (1956–)

New Zealand designer; born Auckland; active England.

Biography Mid-1960s, Brazier-Jones settled in Sandon, Buntingford, Hertfordshire, UK; in London, became an ad hoc member of 1980s neo-Baroque movement, which was associated with architects, artists, journalists, antiques dealers, and designers, including Tom Dixon and André Dubreuil. The designers worked primarily in forged metal, and their work came to be called Creative Salvage due to its realization through the use of blow torches, angle grinders, welders, and hammers. Brazier-Jones's celebrity clients have included Madonna, Sylvester Stallone, Mick Jagger, Yasmin Le Bon, Elton John. Clocks became one of his specialties, but best-known works are 1990 Whale Tail limited-production side chair in cast aluminum and an upholstered seat, and Dolphin (similar to the Whale Tail) and winged Angel side chairs. He designed 2001 bar of the Lucorum café in Barnsley, UK. His zoomorphic metal furniture often incorporates wings, hoofs, claws, tentacles.
Exhibitions 1984 Creative Salvage collective exhibition (with Dixon and Brazier-Jones), London.

Bredendieck, 'Hin' Hinrich Bredendieck (1904–)

German lighting and furniture designer; born Aurich, East Friesland.

Training Kunstgewerbeschule, Stuttgart and Hamburg.
Biography From 1927, Bredendieck worked in the Bauhaus workshop, Dessau, designing furniture and, with Marianne Brandt, lamps, including 1928 Kandem table fixture; 1930–31, worked in Herbert Bayer and László Molholy-Nagy's studio in Berlin and, 1932–33, for lighting manufacturer BAG, Turgi (Switzerland); lived in Oldenburg (Germany) and designed fabrics for furniture; with Sigfried Giedion, designed lamps, including the c. 1932 indi lamp; 1935–37, was a furniture designer in Oldenburg. He settled in Chicago: 1937, became director of the basic design and metalworking workshops, New Bauhaus; from 1939, was as an independent designer; 1945–52, taught product design, Institute of Design (successor of New Bauhaus); 1949–54, was head of Lerner-Bredendieck Designs. In Atlanta, Ga.: 1952–73, was associate partner and active in the industrial-design department, Institute of Technology, becoming its head.
Exhibitions Bredendieck and Giedion's indi lamp was shown at 1932 *Lichtausstellung*, Kunstgewerbe Museum, Zürich.
Bibliography Lionel Richard, *Encyclopédie du Bauhaus*, Paris: Somogy, 1985: 182. *New Bauhaus*, Berlin: Bauhaus-Archiv, 1987. Friederike Mehlau-Wiebking et al., *Schweizer Typenmöbel 1925–35, Sigfried Giedion und die Wohnbedarf AG*, Zürich: gta, 1989. Cat., *Die Metallwerkstatt am Bauhaus*, Berlin: Bauhaus-Archiv, 1992.

Breger, Carl-Arne (1923–)

Swedish industrial designer; active Malmö; husband of Bibi Breger.

Training 1943–48, Konstfackskolan, Stockholm.
Biography 1953–57, Breger worked at Gustavsberg porcelain factory, designing tableware, sanitary fittings, and plastics, including the widely published 1959 square plastic bucket. 1957–59, he was chief designer of Bernadotte & Bjørn studio in Stockholm; from 1959 with his wife, was active in a studio with offices in Stockholm, Malmö, and Rome, where he designed the Diavox telephone by Ellemtel and 1976 new Ericofon telephone (to recognize L.M. Ericsson Co.'s 100th anniversary).
Citations Best plastic product for 1950–60 decade (for square bucket), Swedish Plastic Association; 1975 Bundespreis Produktdesign (for handsaw), Rat für Formgebung (German Design Council), Frankfurt.
Bibliography *Gustavsberg 150 år*, Stockholm, 1975. Carl-Arne Breger, 'The Story Behind a Design,' *Tele*, no. 2, 1979: 12–15. Cat., Kathryn B. Hiesinger and George H. Marcus III (eds.), *Design Since 1945*, Philadelphia: Philadelphia Museum of Art, 1983.

Breidfjord, Leifur (1945–)

Icelandic stained-glass and textile designer.

Training 1962–66, Icelandic College of Art; 1966–68, Edinburgh (UK) College of Art; 1973 and 1975 under Patrick Reyntiens, Burleighfield House, England.
Biography Breidfjord has been a flat- and stained-glass designer, installed in more than 50 public buildings and, with wife Sigridur Johannsdottir, a textile designer.
Exhibitions/citations Work included in numerous venues. First prize (with architect Gudmundur Jonsson), Icelandic pavilion, *Expo 92*, Seville.
Bibliography Cat., David Revere McFadden (ed.), *Scandinavian Modern Design 1880–1980*, New York: Abrams, 1982.

Bremer Silberwarenfabrik

German silversmiths; located Bremen.

History 1905, Bremer Silberwarenfabrik was founded; specialized in silver cutlery; 1981, closed.
Bibliography Annelies Krekel-Aalberse, *Art Nouveau and Art Déco Silver*, New York: Abrams, 1989.

Bremer Werkstätte für Kunstgewerbliche Silberarbeiten

German silversmiths; located Bremen.

History 1920, the Bremen workshop for industrial design in silver was founded; produced items such as candelabra and bowls. Its designers included Wilhelm Schulze.
Bibliography Annelies Krekel-Aalberse, *Art Nouveau and Art Déco Silver*, New York: Abrams, 1989.

Bremers, Peter (1957–)

Dutch artist and designer; born Maastricht.

Training 1976–80, sculpture, Université des Beaux Arts, Maastricht; a number of others, including under Willelm Heesen at Atelier 'Hot Glass,' Acquoy.
Biography Bremers was first active as a sculptor; subsequently, executed furniture, including 1986–87 table lamp produced in Corian synthetic marble by Galerie Néotù in Paris, a wrist-watch design by Lincoln in Switzerland, and, foremost, as a glass designer. From 1990, taught at institutions in the Netherlands and, 1998, was a designer at Leerdam.
Exhibitions Work shown at Galerie Néotú; Interieur design biennial, Courtrai, Belgium; and in Marseilles, Berlin, and Arnhem.
Bibliography Philippe Starck (ed.), *The International Design Yearbook*, New York: Abbeville, 1990. Albrecht Bangert and Karl Michael Armer, *80s Style: Designs of the Decade*, New York: Abbeville, 1990. Sophie Anargyros, *Le style des années 80: architecture, décorations, design*, Paris: Rivages, 1986.

Bresler, F.H.

American furniture manufacturer, print dealer, and art importer.

History 1900, the F.H. Bresler Company in Milwaukee (which succeeded F.H. Durbin) was incorporated by Frank H. Bresler, a business

associate of George Mann Niedecken. A furniture maker, print dealer, and art importer, Bresler specialized in American Arts and Crafts products, Chinese ceramics, and Japanese prints; helped Niedecken realize his first interior-design commissions; invested in the firm of Niedecken-Waldbridge, established 1907 and which, 1907–10, supervised the production of Frank Lloyd Wright furniture made by F.H. Bresler. The firm produced some of Wright's famous spindle-back chairs, including those for 1908 Robert W. Evans house, Chicago and continues today, specializing in custom framing.
Bibliography David A. Hanks, *The Decorative Designs of Frank Lloyd Wright*, New York: Dutton, 1979. Cat., Anne Yaffe Phillips (ed.), *From Architecture to Object*, New York: Hirschl and Adler, 1989.

Breuer, Marcel Lajos (1902–1981)

Hungarian architect and industrial designer; born Pécs.

Training 1920, Akademie der bildenden Künste, Vienna; 1920–24, Bauhaus, Weimar.
Biography 1920, Breuer went to Vienna, intending to become a painter and sculptor; dissatisfied with the Akademie der bildenden Künste, enrolled at the Bauhaus in Weimar and became one of its best-known students; following a period in Paris, returned in 1925 to the Bauhaus, Dessau, as director of its carpentry workshop, to 1928; 1928–31, practiced architecture and design in Berlin; 1932–33, traveled throughout Europe and worked in Zürich. His first chair (1922) was named the Lattenstuhl by Breuer and based on his anatomical research; it was built in wood with fabric upholstery of horsehair fabric woven in the Bauhaus weaving workshop, and the design imitated Gerrit Rietveld's early furniture. 1923, when the chair was shown (illustrated in *Bauhausbücher 7)*, the enthusiastic reaction encouraged Breuer to continue research on seating models. Rietveld included Breuer's furniture at the Bauhaus exhibition in the Netherlands, but by then the De Stijl influence was already strong among Bauhaus designers. The design of Breuer's tubular-steel 1925 Wassily armchair (originally named the Club and later B3) is related to Breuer's first chair design. He claimed to have bought his first bicycle in 1925 and, thus, was so impressed by the lightness and strength of the frame that he visualized using tubular steel in furniture. The first experimental tubular-steel chair was the club-type Wassily armchair that he described in 1927 as 'my most extreme work, both in its outward appearance and in its use of materials; it is the least artistic, the most logical, the least "cosy," and the most mechanical'; it was named Wassily because of Vasilii Kandinsky's admiration of it. In the Bauhaus building in Dessau, Breuer's designs were used in the canteen (his stool) and in the assembly hall (his folding-and-linking auditorium chairs), all produced in tubular steel by the aircraft plant of Hugo Junkers in Dessau. One of the first designs to go into production independently of the Bauhaus was the B32 side chair, manufactured first by Standardmöbel 1927 (by Thonet from c. 1928); is closely related to his Bauhaus designs, particularly his 1926 chairs for the Bauhaus auditorium. 1926, about 500 pieces were made and, 1927, 1,000–1,500 pieces. From 1929, the Wassily chair was also produced by Standardmöbel Lengyel. 1928, the firm Anton Lorenz in Berlin took over production, to become the first manufacturer to produce tubular-steel furniture on a commercial scale. Second half of 1920s, it was used in Gropius's many interiors, including Gropius's own apartment. The 1928 B64 chair was renamed Cesca (after Breuer's daughter Francesca) by furniture manufacturer Dino Gavina, who reentered it into production from 1950 in his Foligno (Italy) factory, and through Knoll Associates, which purchased Gavina, from 1968. Breuer's 1927 B4 folding chair in tubular steel was fitted with an industrial belting fabric (Eisengarn or 'iron yarn'), employed on lathe machinery, for the seat and the back, as was all his early chairs. 1928, he established an architecture practice in Berlin; designed 1931 cantilever sofa and reclining chair on wheels. Resulting from a 1933 entry in International Bureau for Applications of Aluminum, he designed 1932–33 aluminum furniture, some of whose frames were innovatively bent from a single thick sheet of aluminum—produced by EMBRU-Werke AG (as well as other Breuer furniture) in Switzerland and by others. 1932, he completed his first building, the Harnischmacher house in Wiesbaden; 1935, moved to Britain, where, 1935–37, he was in an architecture practice with F.R.S. Yorke and designed bent-plywood furniture for Isokon, including 1935–36 Long Chair chaise longue, 1936 Short Chair, 1936 armchair and sofa, 1936 side chairs, and 1936 nest of tables; with Yorke, designed houses at Angmering-on-Sea (West Sussex), Bristol, Eton, Berkshire, and Lee on the Solent (Hampshire), and the competition project 'A Garden City of the Future'; 1937, settled in the US where, 1937–46, he was a professor of architecture at Harvard University, Cambridge, Mass.; 1937–41, collaborated with Walter Gropius in Massachusetts. His students included Florence Knoll, Philip Johnson, Edward Larrabee Barnes, Eliot Noyes, Paul Rudolph, and John Johansen. 1946, Breuer gave up teaching and settled in New York, when his interest shifted from furniture design to architecture, establishing Marcel Breuer Associates and executed numerous architecture commissions. Some of his buildings were in reinforced concrete imprinted with wooden mold marks, illustrated by 1963–66 Whitney Museum of American Art, New York. He often incorporated local stone into his architecture, exemplied by a photograph of stones as wallpaper in the reception area of the New York office.

Marcel Lajos Breuer. Wassily armchair. 1927–28. Chrome-plated tubular steel and canvas, 28 1/4 x 30 3/4 x 28 (71.8 x 78.1 x 71.1 cm). Mfr.: Standardmöbel Lengyel, Germany. Gift of Hebert Bayer. MoMA.

Architecture Buildings included 1932 Wohnbedarf furniture shop, Zürich; 1935–36 multiple housing (with A. and E. Roth) in the Doldertal, Zürich; his own 1947 house, New Canaan, Conn.; 1953–58 Unesco Headquarters (with Pier Luigi Nervi and Bernard Louis Zehrfuss), Paris; 1953–61 buildings at St. John's Abbey and the University in Collegeville, Minn.; 1956–61 campus at University Heights, New York; 1960–60 IBM Research Center, La Gaude, France; 1963–66 Whitney Museum of American Art, New York; 1967–77 IBM buildings, Boca Raton, Fla.; and 1970 Cleveland (Ohio) Museum of Art.
Exhibitions Tubular-steel furniture by Standardmöbel included in Gropius's prefabricated house at 1927 *Weissenhofsiedlung*, Stuttgart; aluminum furniture included in 2000–03 *Aluminum by Design,* touring the US. Work subject of 1948 touring exhibition, organized by The Museum of Modern Art, New York, where his House in the Museum Garden was installed in 1949 and where his work was subject of 1981 *Marcel Breuer Furniture and Interiors*. Also: 1972–73 exhibition, The Metropolitan Museum of Art, New York; 1974, CCI/Centre Georges Pompidou, Paris; 2002 centennial exhibition, Archives of American Art, New York; 2003–04 exhibition, Vitra Design Museum, Weil am Rhein.
Bibliography Marcel Breuer, 'Metallmöbel,' in W. Gräff, *Innenräume*, Stuttgart, 1928: 133–34. Peter Blake, *Marcel Breuer: Architect and Designer*, New York: An Architectural Record Book with The Museum of Modern Art, 1949. Peter Blake (ed.), *Sun and Shadow: The Philosophy of an Architect*, London, New York, and Toronto, 1956. Giulo Carlo Argan, *Marcel Breuer, disegno industriale e architettura*, Milan, 1957. Cat., Richard G. Stein (ed.), *A View of Marcel Breuer*, New York: The Metropolitan Museum of Art, 1972. Cat., Christopher Wilk, *Marcel Breuer Furniture and Interiors*, New York: The Museum of Modern Art, 1981. Sonja Güntha (intro.), *Thonet Tubular Steel Furniture Card Catalogue*, Weil am Rhein: Vitra Design Publications, 1989. Otakar Máčel, 'Avant-garde Design and the Law-Litigation over the Cantilever Chair,' *Journal of Design History*, vol. 3, nos. 2 and 3, 1990: 125. Magdalena Droste and Manfred Ludewig, *Marcel Breuer, Bauhaus-Archiv*, Cologne:

Taschen, 1992. Robert F. Gatje, *Marcel Breuer: A Memoir*, New York: Monacelli, 2000. Paola Antonelli (ed.), *Objects of Design: The Museum of Modern Art*, New York: The Museum of Modern Art, 2003: 84–87.
> See Lorenz, Anton.

Breuhaus de Groot, Fritz-August (1883–1960)

German architect and designer; born Solingen; active Düsseldorf.

Training Technische Hochschule, Stuttgart and Darmstadt, and Kunstgewerbeschule, Düsseldorf.
Biography Breuhaus worked for Peter Behrens, his fellow student in Düsseldorf; 1920 with others, designed for Nymphenburger Porzellan-Manufaktur; after 1927, designed metalwork and silver by Württembergische Metallwarenfabrik (WMF). Hildegard Risch, a pupil of Karl Müller and collaborator of Eva Mascher-Elsässer, worked under Breuhaus. Late 1920s, some of Breuhaus's tubular-steel chairs were produced by Thonet. From 1932, he taught in Berlin. Breuhaus (as interior architect) and artist Otto Arpke (1886–1943) collaborated with Ludwig Dürr (the chief constructor at the Luftschiffbau-Zeppelin airship factory) on the layout and decoration of 1936–37 *Hindenburg* (no. LZ 129) dirigible. Breuhaus made extensive use of aluminum, including for a Blüthner grand piano, in the airship. He also designed for trains and oceanliners, and his work included ceramics, wallpaper, and bookbindings.
Bibliography Barbie Campbell-Cole and Tim Benton (eds.), *Tubular Steel Furniture*, London: The Art Book Company, 1979. Annelies Krekel-Aalberse, *Art Nouveau and Art Déco Silver*, New York: Abrams, 1989. J. Gordon Vaeth, 'Zeppelin Decor: The Graf Zeppelin and the Hindenburg,' *Journal of Decorative and Propaganda Art*, no. 15, Winter / Spring 1990: 53. Cat., *Metallkunst*, Berlin: Bröhan Museum, 1990: 585–86.
> See Zeppelin.

Brewster, Anthony (1794–1838)
> See Shaker furniture.

Brindeau de Jarny, Paul

French designer; active Paris; brother of painter Edward de Jarny.

Biography Brindeau de Jarny produced a wide range of domestic metalwork, including keys and key escutcheons, door handles, *portemanteaux*, and numerous lighting fixtures; was an associate of metalworkers Edward Brandt and Édouard Schenck. Purportedly none of his unsigned, or crudely signed, output has been identified. His Art Nouveau designs included themes from nature, such as chandeliers and table lamps with motifs of ivy, camellias, dandelions, mimosa, vines, and trees. He patented a twisted metal chain that supported his chandeliers.
Exhibitions Work shown at Paris Salons for over 30 years, almost annually into 1930s, including at 1901 Salon of Société Nationale des Beaux-Arts, Salon d'Automne from 1909–30, and Société des Artistes Décorateurs from 1904.
Bibliography Alastair Duncan, *Art Nouveau and Art Déco Lighting*, New York: Simon & Schuster, 1978: 75. Salon catalogs, Salon d'Automne, 1903, 1905–09, 1922–23. Salon catalogs, Salon des Beaux-Arts, 1908–10, 1921. Salon catalogs, Société des Artistes Décorateurs, 1904, 1914, 1924.

Brion, Giuseppe (1909–1968); Brionvega

Italian manufacturer of sound equipment and televisions; located Milan.

History Brion worked at Phonola and at Radiomarelli; 1945 with engineer Pajetta, founded electronics-components firm B.P.M. on the via Pordenone in Milan; 1950–51, reorganized the firm as Vega P.P. Radio to comply with American business standards and initially specialized in radio sets; 1952, added TV sets, forming Vega Radio-Televisione, and, 1954, produced the first TV set completely built in Italy. Subsequently, the firm was directed by his son Ennio Brion with the designs of 1950s models, in wood, by Giovanni Sacchi. From early 1960s, the firm began production of what were to be recognized as distinctive, award-winning models, like 1961 TS 207 radio by Rodolfo Bonetto and 1962 Orion 23 TV by Franco Albini/Franca Helg. 1962, Marco Zanuso Sr. and Richard Sapper began a highly fruitful collaboration with the firm with the introduction of the Doney 14 TV, coinciding with the birth of Italy's first network TV company, RAI. The 1963 TS 502 1° folding radio with two hinged compartments, by Marco Zanuso and Richard Sapper, (reissued as 1977 TS 505) was a highly original concept. Zanuso-Sapper also designed 1966 Algol 11 transistorized portable TV with an angled

Brionvega: Marco Zanuso Sr. and Richard Sapper. Radio (no. TS 502). 1963. ABS polymer and aluminum casing, overall 5 1/4 x 8 5/8 x 5 1/4" (13.3 x 21.9 x 13.3 cm). Mfr.: Brionvega, Italy. Gift of the mfr. MoMA.

screen, 1969 ST 201 1° 12 (aka Black, essentially a black box), and 1971 Fd 1101 transistor radio. Achille Giacomo Castiglioni designed 1965 RR 126 radio-phonograph, and Ettoro Sottsas 1980 Memphis 1 TV (in an Abet Laminati case). 1992, Brionvega was acquired by Gruppo Sèleco. 1997, Industrie Formenti, the largest producer of color TVs in Italy, bought Sèleco and subsidiaries Brionvega and Tamberg for $14.25 million/13 million euros/25.25 billion lira (1997 rate equivalencies), forming Gruppo Formentí Sèleco and producing the Séleleco and Brionvega brands. From 2001, new Brionvega models have been dominated by reinterpretations of the brand's former œuvre, like 1992 Cuboglass 15 color TV (a Mario Bellini redesign of 1969 ST 201 by Sèleco and again as 2001 Cuboglass by Formenti). Other 2001 models included Algol 11 color TV and TS 522 folding radio (formerly TS 502 and then TS 505).
Exhibitions/citations Included in Italian Pavilions, 1967 *Universal and International Exhibition (Expo '67)*, Montréal, and 1970 *Japan World Exposition (Expo '70)*, Osaka; 2001 *1951–2001 Made in Italy?*, Triennale di Milano. 1970 (six citations), 1979, 1981, 1984 Premio Compasso d'Oro; grand prize, 1964 (13th) Triennale di Milano. Other citations: gold medals, 1964 BIO 1 (Algol TV) and 1966 BIO 2 (TS502 radio) industrial-design biennials, Ljubljana; 1969 Bundespreis Die Gute Form (TS502), West Germany; special prize (TXS1000 hi-fi and AX3500 amplifier), SIM76 competition.
Bibliography Andrea Rosetti, *Il design di Brionvega*, Milan: Spazio '900, 2001. www.brionvega.it.

Brno Devětsil

Czech literary, art, and design group.

History 1923–27, the Brno Devětsil group was active in Brno. Its members included Bĕdrich Václavek, Zdenĕk Rossmann, Jan Markalous, poet František Halas, and art-critic Artuš Černík.
Bibliography *Devětsil: The Czech Avant-Garde Art, Architecture and Design of the 1920s and 1930s*, Oxford; Museum of Modern Art, London: Design Museum, 1990.
> See Devětsil.

Brocard, Philippe-Joseph (1831–96)

French restaurateur, collector, and enameler.

Biography Brocard was influenced by the enameled decorations of the mosque lamps he saw at the Cluny Museum, Paris; painted designs in gold and enamel on white or lightly tinted glass. At first, he merely copied Egyptian and Persian lamps, vases, and bowls. Other influences on his work included Gallo-Roman, German, and Italian Renaissance glasswares. As its best exponent, he revived enameled glass in France. Brocard may have introduced Émile Gallé to the art of enameled glass, while Gallé in turn introduced Brocard to naturalism. c. 1880, Brocard began using mistletoe, satinpod, and cornflower motifs; from 1884 with his son, produced glass with enameled decoration of gold, silver, platinum, and copper, signed 'Brocard et fils.'
Exhibitions Copies of Islamic models were included in 1867 and 1878 editions of *Exposition Universelle*, Paris.

Bibliography Yvonne Brunhammer et al., *Art Nouveau Belgium, France*, Houston: Rice University, 1976, biblio. Cat., *Verriers français contemporains: art et industrie*, Paris: Musée des Arts Décoratifs, 1982.

Brodovitch, Alexey (1898–1971)

Russian graphics artist and designer.

Biography Brodovitch began his career in Paris; 1930, emigrated to the US; became significantly influential on a whole generation of American graphic designers and photographers; for 15 years, was art director of *Harper's Bazaar*; exposed Americans to the European avant-garde by commissioning European artists/photographers such as Cartier-Bresson, Cassandre, Dalí, and Man Ray; became the first designer to teach design as a profession, in classes at his own Design Laboratory and at The New School, both New York, where some of his students went on to become accomplished and famous; was known to have designed furniture. Brodovitch archive is housed in Wallace Library, Rochester (N.Y.) Institute of Technology. Annual Alexey Brodovitch Prize is awarded to a 2nd-year graphic-design student for outstanding freelance work, Yale University, New Haven, Conn.
Exhibitions Participated in 1948 *International Competition for Low-Cost Furniture Design*, The Museum of Modern Art, New York. Work subject of 1972 exhibitions, Philadelphia College of Art with Smithsonian Institution, and 1982 Grand Palais exhibition (catalogs below); 1998 *Alexey Brodovitch: La photographie mise en page*, Maison Européenne de la Photographie, Paris.
Bibliography Edwin Denby (text) and Alexey Brodovitch (photos), *Ballet*, New York: J.J. Augustin, 1945. Cat., George R. Bunder (ed.), *Alexey Brodovitch and His Influence*, Philadelphia: Philadelphia College of Art/Smithsonian Institution,1972. Cat., Philippe Soupault, *Alexey Brodovitch* (Grand Palais), Paris: Ministère de la Culture, 1982. Andy Grundberg, *Brodovitch*, New York: Abrams, 1989. Gabriel Bauret and Alexey Brodovitch, *Alexey Brodovitch Portfolio*, Paris: Assouline, 1998. Kerry William Purcell, *Alexey Brodovitch*, New York: Phaidon, 2002.

Brodt, Helen Tanner (1838–1908)

American teacher, painter, and ceramics decorator; born Elmira, N.Y.; active Oakland and Berkeley, Cal.

Biography 1863, she settled in Red Bluff, Cal., where she taught; by 1867, had moved to the San Francisco area, where she taught in an Oakland public school, managing the art program 1872–87; painter Arthur F. Matthews was her student. She opened a studio in Oakland; by 1881, was interested in china painting, evidenced by her Oriental Fantasy porcelain plate. The remainder of her career is unknown. Much of her work was lost in the 1906 San Francisco earthquake.
Exhibitions/citations Award (for china painting), 1884–85 *World's Industrial and Cotton Centennial Exposition*, New Orleans. Showed paintings at exhibitions of Mechanics Institute, San Francisco; a portrait, 1893 *World's Columbian Exposition*, Chicago; other work, 1986–87 *In Pursuit of Beauty*, New York (catalog below).
Bibliography Cat., Phil Kovinick, 'Helen Tanner Brodt,' in *The Woman Artist in the American West, 1860–1960*, Fullerton, Cal.: Muckenthaler Cultural Center, 1976: 13. Chris Petteys, 'Brodt, Helen Tanner,' in *Dictionary of Women Artists: An International Dictionary of Women Artists Born Before 1900*, Boston: G.K. Hall, 1985: 97. Cat., Doreen Bolger Burke et al., *In Pursuit of Beauty: Americans and the Aesthetic Movement*, New York: The Metropolitan Museum of Art/Rizzoli, 1986: 405.

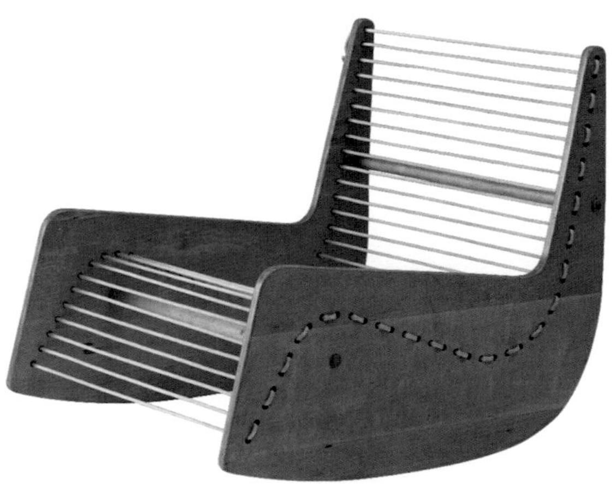

Alexey Brodovitch. Floor chair (no. 1211-C). c. 1950. Plywood, wood dowels, and plastic-covered cord, 23 3/4 x 23 1/2 x 28" (60.3 x 59.7 x 71.1 cm). Gift of the designer. MoMA.

Bromberg, Paul (1893–1949)

Dutch interior architect and theoretician; born Amsterdam.

Biography From 1908–09, Bromberg was active in Berlin; 1913, established an interior-architecture office in Amsterdam; 1913–18, designed and produced furniture; 1918, became head of modern-decorative-arts and interior-design departments, Metz & Co., Amsterdam, and designed several interiors and furniture for the firm 1918–24; 1921, redecorated the Metz store; from 1924, worked as an interior architect in modern interiors department, Pander & Zoon, The Hague and Amsterdam, designing furniture and interiors of model houses and showrooms; 1927 with H.A. van Anrooy, decorated the interior of a villa. 1930, he also decorated a villa in Antwerp and a house in Rotterdam; model house for 1931 Klein Zwitserland project (architect, D. Roosenburg), The Hague; 1931 model rooms of Pander's new building, The Hague; and houses in Rotterdam, Overschie, and Scheveningen (The Hague). 1931–37, he designed a chair for the Rotterdam section of Vakgroep voor Drukkunst, Bindkunst en Leerbewerking (VANK) exhibition; 1940–45, lived in the US; 1945, returned to Amsterdam and set up a consultation office.
Exhibitions Work included in 1918 *Tentoonstelling van Ambachts-, Nijverheids- en Volkskunst*, Rotterdam; 1919 exhibitions in Haarlem and at Stedelijk Museum, Amsterdam; 1923 Salon d'Automne, Paris; 1923 industrial-design exhibition (with Penaat), Kunstkring, Rotterdam; interiors at 1927 *Moderne Interieurs*, Stedelijk Museum. For Metz store: organized 1919 Netherlands touring exhibition of Metz's endeavors; 1934, Stedelijk Museum; stand, 1939–40 *New York World's Fair: The World of Tomorrow*. Organized VANK exhibitions at the Stedelijk Museum, Amsterdam. Designed 1928 *Hedendaagsche Huisinrichting* (contemporary house decoration) exhibition (with Arnold Pijpers and Leo Visser) in Enschede. At Jaarbeurs fair in Utrecht, designed VANK pavilion in 1932, Dutch Department of Economics stand in 1937, and De Eland stand in 1938.
Bibliography C. Brandes, 'Beschouwingen over binnenhuisarchitectuur en het werk van Paul Bromberg,' *Levende Kunst*, 1918: 137–46. 'Inleiding tot de binnenhuiskunst van Paul Bromberg,' *Kunst in Arnhem*, no. 1, 1919: 7, 73–81. H.G. Cannegieter, 'Paul Bromberg,' *Morks Magazijn*, no. 39, 1937: 280–94. Cat., *Industrie u Vormgeving in Nederland 1850–1950*, Amsterdam: Stedelijk Museum, 1985. Monique Teunissen, *Paul Bromberg: Binnenhuisarchitect en publicist 1893/1949*, Rotterdam: 010, 1988.

Brookes and Adams

British plastics manufacturer; located Birmingham

History 1927, Brookes and Adams introduced a plastic (a substance called Bandalasta Ware) for the first time into lamps and lighting fixtures. Marketed as 'both artistic and useful,' the shades and bases were molded from Bettle powders developed in Britain, which made it possible to create colorful forms that, in the case of the Bandalasta lamps, created a warm glow. 1950s–60s, the firm produced plastic tableware and storage containers designed by Ronald Brookes.
Bibliography Jeremy Myerson and Sylvia Katz, *Conran Design Guides: Lamps and Lighting*, London: Conran Octopus, 1990: 29.

Brookhart, Theodore (1898–1942)

American designer.

Biography Brookhart is best known for 1940 Streamliner meat slicer (with Egmont C. Arens), produced by Hobart Manufacturing 1944–85.
Exhibitions Meat slicer included in 2000–03 *Aluminum by Design* touring exhibition, organized by Carnegie Art Museum, Pittsburgh, and *American Modern*, The Metropolitan Museum of Art, New York (catalogs below).
Bibliography Cat., Sarah Nichols et al., *Aluminum by Design*, New York: Abrams, 2000. Cat., J. Stewart Johnson, *American Modern, 1925–1940...*, New York: Abrams, 2000.

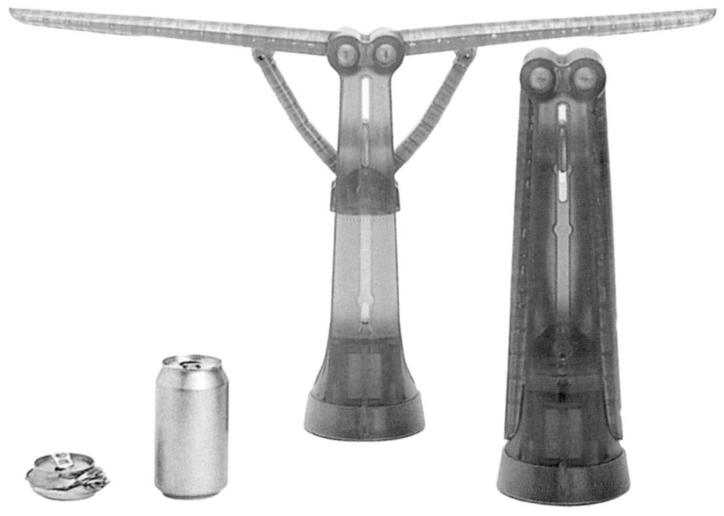

Julian Brown. Cricket plastic-bottle compactor. 1997. Polypropylene and steel, h. 29 1/8 x dia. 6 1/2" (74 x 16.5 cm). Mfr.: Rexite, Italy.

Brouwer Jr., Theophilus Anthony (1864–1932)

American ceramicist.

Biography 1894, Brouwer opened a small workshop known as Middle Lane Pottery in East Hampton, Long Island, N.Y., where he worked alone in throwing, turning, molding, and developing glaze technology; created distinctive luster and lusterless glazes. Characterized by surface iridescence and multiple color effects, his five vibrant and rich iridescent, metallic or crystalline glazes were Fire Painting, Iridescent Fire Painting, Kid Surface, Sea-Grass Fire Painting, Gold-Leaf Underglaze. Brouwer, who was also a painter, woodcarver, plaster modelmaker, and metalworker, built a new pottery, active from 1904 and known as Brouwer Pottery in East Hampton, Long Island, where he perfected his Flame Painting glaze that combined his five earlier glazes; c. 1911, discontinued his ceramic work but continued to lecture and to sell his wares; made several large statuesque figures which adorn the grounds of Casa Basso Restaurant, Westhampton, and other nearby locations on eastern Long Island. Brouwer Pottery (aka Middle Lane Pottery) in East Hampton continued after his death and, 1946, closed.
Bibliography 'Theophilus Anthony Brouwer, Jr., A Twentieth Century Long Island Artist,' *AAP Journal*, vol. 1, no. 2, Mar.–Apr. 1985. Edwin Atlee Barber, *Marks of American Potters*, Philadelphia: Patterson and White, 1904: 86. *American Art Pottery*, New York: Cooper-Hewitt Museum, 1987: 72.

Brown, Barbara (1932–)

British textile and fashion designer.

Training 1953–56, Canterbury College of Art; Royal College of Art, London.
Biography She designed a range of printed furnishing fabrics by Heal's in bold Op-Art patterns of black and white, neutral, and narrow-ranged colors; taught, Royal College of Art; was a consultant designer to clients in Britain, France, Italy, Germany, and the US.
Citations 1968 and 1970 awards (for the range by Heal's), Council of Industrial Design, London.
Bibliography Cat., *Brown/Craven/Dodd: 3 Textile Designers*, Manchester: Whitworth Art Gallery, 1965: 6–10. 'Furnishing Fabrics: Heal's Chevron, Complex and Extension,' *Design*, no. 233, May 1968: 42-43. Cat., Kathryn B. Hiesinger and George H. Marcus III (eds.), *Design Since 1945*, Philadelphia: Philadelphia Museum of Art, 1983.

Brown, Eleanor McMillen (b. Eleanor Stockstrom 1890–1990)

American interior decorator; born St. Louis, Mo.

Training Under William Odom, New York School of Fine and Applied Arts, and its successor, Parsons School of Design, New York.
Biography She began decorating in the office of Elsie Cobb Wilson; mid-1920s, established her own studio, McMillen, and developed the so-called McMillen Method of record-keeping. Clients included the Winthrop, Aldrich, Rockefeller, and Lorillard families. No matter her conservative clientele, she was not afraid of making strong statements in her decorative schemes; late 1920s, decorated the New York house of Mr. and Mrs. Henry Parish II. (Mrs. Parish, aka Sister Parish, later also became an interior decorator.) Brown was a trustee of Parsons School of Design and almost exclusively hired Parsons graduates. 1926, she hired Grace Fakes and, late 1930s, Marian 'Tad' Morgan. Her firm became a training ground for young designers, including Nathalie Davenport, Mark Hampton, Kevin McNamara, and Albert Hadley. Her firm is still active, managed by Betty Sherrill.
Bibliography Mark Hampton, *House and Garden*, May 1990: 145–49, 214. Mark Hampton, *Legendary Decorators of the Twentieth Century*, New York: Doubleday, 1992.

Brown, F. Gregory (1887–1948)

British commercial artist and textile designer.

Training 1903, art metalworking.
Biography Brown turned from metalworking to illustration. As a commercial artist, his first important contact was from *TP's Weekly* and *TP's Magazine*. 1915, Brown became a founding member of Design and Industries Association. From 1920, Brown's textile work, including his roller-printed 1931 Leaping Deer with Hillocks and Trees, was produced by William Foxton. His fabric designs, printed in black (a 1920s predilection), were published in Design and Industries Association's yearbook *Design in Modern Industry*. His graphic-design clients included the London and North East, the Southern, and the Great Western Railways; Mac Fisheries; Derry and Toms; Cadbury; Odhams Press; and Bobby's department store.
Exhibitions/citations Work shown at Royal Academy, London, 1908. Gold medal (for a linen fabric by Foxton), 1925 *Exposition Internationale des Arts Décoratifs et Industriels Modernes*, Paris; 1983 *British Art and Design*, London (catalog below).
Bibliography Cat., *Thirties: British Art and Design Before the War*, London: Arts Council of Great Britain/Hayward Gallery, 1979. Cat., *British Art and Design, 1900–1960*, London: Victoria and Albert Museum, 1983. Jonathan M. Woodham, *Twentieth-Century Ornament*, New York: Rizzoli, 1990. Valerie Mendes, *The Victoria and Albert Museum's Textile Collection, British Textiles from 1900 to 1937*, London: Victoria and Albert Museum, 1992.

Brown, Julian (1955–)

British industrial designer; born Northampton.

Training Royal College of Art, London.
Biography Brown worked in Porsche Design, Austria, responsible for the Studio eyeglasses and other products; 1990, established StudioBrown in London; has designed for a number of firms, including Rexite, which has produced a number of his award-winning products such as 1996 Attila can compactor, 1997 Cricket plastic-bottle compactor, 1998 Hannibal tape dispenser. Other clients are Sony (TV set),

Frighetto (sofas), and Bauknecht (appliances).
Citations 1996 (for Attila) and 1998 (for Hannibal) Good Design award, Chicago Athenaeum; Best Product (for Isis stapler), 1999 International Gift Fair, New York; 1998 Best of Category award, Product Design (for Hannibal), Annual Design Review, *I.D.* magazine; 2002 Premio Dedalo Minosse, Milan; others
Bibliography Richard Sapper (ed.), *The International Design Yearbook*, London: Laurence King, 1999. Mel Byars, *50 Products...*, Hove: RotoVision, 2000.

Brown, Tim (1962-)
British industrial designer.

Training Newcastle-upon-Tyne Polytechnic, and to 1985, Royal College of Art, London.
Biography From 1987, Brown worked at Moggridge Associates, London, where he designed office equipment and computer systems. Other designs have included fax machines by Dancall in Sweden.
Citations Bursary award (office-equipment designs), Royal Society of Arts, London.
Bibliography Albrecht Bangert and Karl Michael Armer, *80s Style: Designs of the Decade*, New York: Abbeville, 1990.

Brørby, Severin (1932–2001)
Norwegian glassware designer.

Training Statens Håndverks- og Kunstindustriskole, Oslo.
Biography From 1948, Brørby worked as a glass engraver at Hadelands Glassverk in Jevnaker and, from 1956, was a designer there. His work included bulky everyday tableware and sculpture that featured colorful optical effects.
Bibliography Cat., David Revere McFadden (ed.), *Scandinavian Modern Design 1880–1980*, New York: Abrams, 1982. Fredrik Wildhagen, *Norge i Form*, Oslo: Stenersen, 1988. Leslie Jackson, *20th Century Factory Glass*, London: Octopus, 2000.

Bruckmann & Söhne
German silversmiths; located Heilbronn.

History 1805, Bruckmann & Söhne was founded; trained its own designers, silversmiths, chasers, and engravers; was the first of German silversmiths to introduce a steam engine in the 19th century, when it became that country's biggest silver factory. One of its founders, Peter Bruckmann (1867–1937), first president of the Deutscher Werkbund, produced the silver designs of leading German artists. Designers in 1910s included Fritz Schmoll von Eisenwerth, while a teacher at the Debschitz-Schule; Hans Christiansen (cutlery pattern with abstract ornament); and Emanuel Josef Margold (1913 silverwork). 1923, Peter Bruckmann was succeeded by his son Dietrich, who had trained under Adolf von Mayrhofer at the Kunstgewerbeschule in Munich. 1924–27, Erna Zarges-Dürr was the first woman to work in its silversmiths' department. Greta Schröder and Paula Strauss produced silver designs there later. 1973, the firm closed.
Exhibitions Wares included in 1910 *Exposition Universelle et Internationale*, Brussels, by freelance artists Friedrich Adler, Franz Böres, Friedrich Felger, Paul Haustein, Otto Rieth, Karl Wahl, and Bernhard Wenig, and staff designers Adolf Amberg, Hélène Brandt, Josef Lock, Karl Stock, and Karl Zeller.
Bibliography *Die Goldschmiedekunst*, 1911: 18–26. Annelies Krekel-Aalberse, *Art Nouveau and Art Déco Silver*, New York: Abrams, 1989. Cat., *Metallkunst*, Berlin: Bröhan Museum, 1990.

Robert Brunner. Mindset personal computer. 1983. Injection-molded ABS polymer casing, keyboard 2 x 16 x 6 7/8" (5 x 40.7 x 17.5 cm), stacked system unit and expansion unit: 5 3/4 x 16 5/16 x 12 1/2" (14.6 x 41.5 x 31.8 cm). Mfr.: Mindset Corporation, US. Gift of the mfr. MoMA.

Brüel, Axel (1900–1977)
Danish ceramicist.

Biography 1928–56, Brüel produced ceramics in his own workshop; 1956, became artistic consultant to a porcelain manufacturer in Denmark; used newly developed materials and techniques in his work, including heat-resistant cookware. The absence of handles on his 1957 Thermodan coffee service was practical, thanks to its double-wall design.
Exhibitions Thermodan was shown at 1957 (11th) Triennale di Milano.
Bibliography Arne Karlsen, *Made in Denmark*, New York: Reinhold, 1960. Cat., Kathryn B. Hiesinger and George H. Marcus III (eds.), *Design Since 1945*, Philadelphia: Philadelphia Museum of Art, 1983.

Brummer, Arttu (1891–1951)
Finnish interior architect, designer, and theorist.

Biography 1913, Brummer set up his own interior-design studio; 1919–51, taught general composition, furniture design, heraldic design, and form theory at Taideteollinen korkeakoulu, Helsinki, where, 1944–51, he was the art director and mentored the generation of designers who included Ilmari Tapiovaara, Antti Nurmesniemi, and Vuokko Nurmesniemi. 1915–51, Brummer wrote a large number of articles; was editor of Finnish design journal *Domus* (published only 1930–1933); designed for the Riihimäen glassworks, including 1945 Finlandia vase; became chairperson of TKO (Finnish association of industrial designers)/Ornamo (Finnish association of designers), which posthumously established the Arttu Brummer award, and a member of its administrative board, and of the board of Suomen Käsityön Ystävien (friends of Finnish handicraft).
Citations First prize, 1932 glass competition sponsored by Karhula; diploma of honor, 1937 *Exposition Internationale des Arts et Techniques dans la Vie Moderne,* Paris.
Bibliography Marianne Aav (ed.), *Arttu Brummer: taideteollisuuden tulisielu*, Helsinki, University of Art and Design, 1991. Ilkka Huovio, 'Näkijä ja tekijä: Arttu!,' *Bulletin of the University of Art and Design*, March 1991.

Brummer, Eva (1901-)
Finnish textile designer; born Tampere.

Training 1925, Taideteolli, Helsinki.
Biography 1929, Brummer set up her own studio with the intention of reviving traditional Finnish 'rya' (or *ryijy*), a thick hand-knotted textile; at first, incorporated bright-colored, later more subdued, yarns into an unevenly cut pile, creating a relief; was associated throughout her career with Suomen Käsityön Ystävien (friends of Finnish handicraft).
Citations 1951 (9th) grand prize, 1954 (10th) diploma of honor, and 1957 (11th) gold medal at Triennali di Milano; others.
Bibliography Oili Mäki (ed.), *Finnish Designers of Today*, Helsinki:Söderström, 1954. Erik Zahle (ed.), *A Treasury of Scandinavian Design*, New York: Golden Press, 1961. Anja Louhio, *Modern Finnish Rugs*, Helsinki, 1975. Cat., Kathryn B. Hiesinger and George H. Marcus III (eds.), *Design Since 1945*, Philadelphia: Philadelphia Museum of Art, 1983. Leena Svinhufvud, 'A Trailblazer in the Art of Textiles,' *Form Function Finland*, Feb. 2001.

Bruni, Tat'iana Georgievna (1902-)
Russian stage designer.

Training 1918–20, School of the Association for the Encouragement of the Arts, Petrograd (now St. Petersburg); 1920–26 under O. Braz and N. Radlov, VKhUTEIN, Petrograd/Leningrad.
Biography 1923, she designed her first stage sets, later Giuseppe Verdi's *La Traviata* (1944 production, directed by Ilya Shlepyanov).
Exhibitions From 1927, work shown in various venues.
Bibliography G.M. Levitin, *Tatiana Georgievna Bruni*, Leningrad: Izd-

vo 'Khudozhnik RSFSR,' 1986. Cat., *The Great Utopia: The Russian and Soviet Avant-Garde, 1915–1932*, New York: Guggenheim Museum, 1992. Cat., *Polifonia: From Malevich to Tatiana Bruni 1910–1930, Theatre Designs of Russian Avant-Gard*, Milan: Electa, 1998.

Brunner, Robert (1958–)

American industrial design; born San Jose, Cal.

Training To 1981, industrial design, San Jose State University.
Biography Brunner first worked at design studios GVO and Interform; 1985, cofounded Lunar Design and, to 1989 with Ken Wood, produced a number of concepts that culminated in 1989 Apple Macintosh LC computer casing (with Ray Riley); 1990, became director of Apple's IDg (Industrial Design Group) and designed the first (1990) of the Jaguar project concepts and managed and codesigned (with Gavin Ivester) the 1990–91 PowerBook; provided the aesthetic language for the Espresso project; hired Daniele De Iuliis, Tim Parsey, Masamichi Udagawa, and Jonathan Ive, thus establishing Apple's design as cutting edge. From 1992, he developed the curved-front Spartacus (Twentieth Anniversary Macintosh), introduced in 1996. Soon after, he left Apple and joined the Pentagram studio office in San Francisco.
Citations Under Brunner's management, Apple received more design awards than any other American corporation.
Bibliography Paul Kunkel, *Apple Design: The World of the Apple Industrial Design Group*, New York: Graphis, 1997.

Brunner, Vratislav Hugo (1886–1928)

Czech designer and teacher, born Prague.

Training 1903–06 under V. Bukovac and M. Priner, Akademie Výtvarných Umení (academy of fine arts), Prague; in Munich.
Biography 1908, Brunner became a member, Mánes Association of Plastic Artists; 1908, became a cofounder, Artěl Cooperative, where he was principally a designer of toys, painted gingerbreads, souvenirs, painted glass, and other items; 1911, left Mánes and became an executive of newly formed Group of Plastic Artists; 1912, studied in Leipzig, resigned from the Group of Plastic Artists and returned to Mánes; from 1919, was professor, Vysoká Škola Umělecko-průmyslová (VŠUP, academy of arts, architecture, and design), Prague, where, 1928, he became the rector; was active as a book designer for Books by Good Authors (the imprint of Kamila Neumannova), for K.H. Hilar, and particularly for Aventinum; was also an illustrator for magazines. He died in Lomnice, near Jilové.
Exhibitions/Citations Work included in various venues of Czech Cubism and art (catalogs below). Grand prize and gold medal (book designs), 1925 *Exposition Internationale des Arts Décoratifs et Industriels Modernes*, Paris.
Bibliography Alexander von Vegesack et al., *Czech Cubism: Architecture, Furniture, and Decorative Arts, 1910–1925*, New York: Princeton Architectural Press, 1992. Cat., *Prague, 1900–1938: capitale secrète des avants-gardes*, Dijon: Musée des Beaux-Arts, 1997.

Brustand, Tore Vinje (1976–)
> See Permafrost Designstudio.

Bryere, Joseph O.A. (1860–1941)

American furniture designer and maker, camp builder, carpenter, and tourist guide; born Québec.

Biography c. 1880, Bryere first visited Raquette Lake, N.Y., and later settled there; 1883–86, was employed by Charles Durant as a carpenter and caretaker at Camp Fairview; 1886–90, worked at the camp of the Stott family on Bluff Point; later 1880s, began building Brightside-on-Raquette hotel, Raquette Lake; in addition to being a carpenter, camp builder, and tourist guide, was a furniture designer and maker in a rough-hewn style known today as Adirondack, after the Adirondack Park, upper New York State.
Bibliography Craig Gilborn, *Adirondack Furniture and the Rustic Tradition*, New York: Abrams, 1987: 318.

Bryk, Rut (1916–1999)

Finnish ceramicist and graphic and textile designer; wife of Tapio Wirkkala.

Training 1939, graphic design, Taideteollinen korkeakoulu, Helsinki.
Biography 1942, she worked at the Arabia pottery in Helsinki; from 1959, was a freelance ceramics designer for Rosenthal in Selb; from 1960s, worked at Vaasa Cotton Company.
Exhibitions/citations Work included in 1951 (9th), 1954 (10th), 1957 (11th), and 1960 (12th) Triennali di Milano; 1954–57 *Design in Scandinavia*, touring the US. 1951, grand prize, and 1954, diploma of honor, Triennali de Milano. 1968 Pro Finlandia prize; 1980, first Finnish woman to receive order of Commandeur of the l'Ordre des Arts et des Lettres, from Ministère de la Culture et de la Communication, France.
Bibliography Cat., David Revere McFadden (ed.), *Scandinavian Modern Design 1880–1980*, New York: Abrams, 1982. Jennifer Hawkins Opie, *Scandinavia: Ceramics and Glass in the Twentieth Century*, New York: Rizzoli, 1989.

Buatta, Mario (1936–)

American interior designer; active New York.

Biography With an office in New York, Buatta (with Mark Hampton) designed the interiors of Blair House, Washington, D.C., America's government guest-house for visiting dignitaries. With décors that evoked 19th-century English interiors with their extensive use of flowered coated fabrics, he was dubbed the 'Prince of Chintz,' which referred to his elegant English cottagey-style interiors that frequently include chintz fabrics. His 1990 furniture collection was made by John Widdicomb and products by other clients for mass-production goods such as Fabriyaz (fabric), Revman Industries (bed linens), Thimbelina (needlepoint), Imperial-Sterlin (wallpaper), Aromatique (home fragrance), Sunweave/Vera Division (table linens), Frederick Cooper (lighting), Shyam Ahuja and Tianjin-Philadelphia Carpet (carpets), and Framed Picture Enterprise (artwork).
Bibliography Marlene Elizabeth Heck, *Blair House, the President's Guest House/Interior Decorators Mario Buatta and Mark Hampton*, Charlottesville, Va.: Thomasson-Grant, 1989.

Bûcheron, Le
> See Sylve, Le.

Bücking, Peter (aka Peer Bücking 1906–1940)

German designer.

Training 1928, Bauhaus, Dessau.
Biography His 1928 wood chair produced at the Bauhaus furniture workshop, Dessau, had innovative L-shaped legs. The chair, often attributed to Hannes Meyer, was an attempt to create lightness with strength; was inexpensive, resilient, and easy to carry; represents one of the first uses of plywood construction at the Bauhaus.
Bibliography Cat., *The Bauhaus: Masters and Students*, New York: Barry Friedman, 1988.

Buckland, Wilfred

American film set designer.

Biography Buckland, hired by Cecil B. De Mille, and working for him 1914–1927, was the first stage designer to work in films, having been prior employed by David Belasco, a New York theater producer. Buckland's glamorous bathroom set in De Mille's *Male and Female* (1919) featured Charles Ray's cut-glass bathtub for actress Gloria Swanson and was publicized as having cost $75,000. De Mille called Buckland 'the first man of a recognized ability to forsake the theater for the motion picture, and to him are attributed the first consistent and well-designed motion picture sets. He brought to the screen a knowledge of mood and a dramatic quality which until then had been totally lacking.' Others of his film sets include those for *The Deuce of Spades* (1922), *Adam's Rib* (1923), *Icebound* (1924), *Almost Human* (1927), and *The Forbidden Woman* (1927).
Bibliography Howard Mandelbaum and Eric Myers, *Screen Deco: A Celebration of High Style in Hollywood*, New York: St. Martin's, 1985.

Budimirov, Bogdan (1928–)

Yugoslavian architect and designer; born Izbište, Yugoslavia (now Croatia); active in Zagreb.

Training 1949–55, architecture, Sveucilište u Zagrebu, Croatia.
Biography Budimirov was naturalized as a Croatian; late 1950s, collaborated with a number of architecture teams; early 1960s, worked for Jugomont in Zagreb, a firm specializing in prefabricated constructions; from late 1970s, has been a freelance architect and designer. His design work has included a 1958 prototype chair with an elastic seat (with Berislav Jurinjak), 1961–62 prefabricated construction system (with Željko Solar and Dragutin Stilinovič) by Jugomont, 1964 pre-

Peer Bücking. Side chair. 1928. Stained wood, 29 1/2 x 16 1/2 x 21" (75 x 41.9 x 53.3 cm), seat h. 18 1/2" (47 cm). Mfr.: Bauhaus, Dessau, Germany. Edward Larrabee Barnes Purchase Fund. MoMA.

fabricated single-housing unit (with Vladimir Robotič, Zlatko Šokalj, and Željko Solar) by Spačva in Vinkovci, Croatia.
Exhibitions/citations Work included in several exhibitions, including 1997 *Stoljeće hrvatskog dizajna* [a century of Croatian design], Museum and Gallery Centre, Zagreb. 1982 prize (folding drawing-table prototype), Industrie Forum Design (iF), Hanover.
Bibliography Fedja Vukic, *A Century of Croatian Design*, Zagreb: Meandar, 1998.

Budlong, Robert Davol (1902–1955)

American industrial designer.

Biography Budlong managed a large industrial design studio; was commissioned by Zenith Radio Corp.'s founder Eugene F. McDonald, to design most of the radio casings produced by Zenith, Budlong's most important client. 1937 Zephyr radio range with horizontal louvres was his first significant design in a range that, by 1939, was calling on the use of Bakelite. Budlong assisted Zenith to achieve a high level of design for its radio casings and, thus, sales prominence.
Bibliography Harold Cones and John Bryant, 'The Car Salesman and the Accordion Designer: Contributions of Eugene F. McDonald and Robert Davol Budlong to Radio,' *Journal of Radio Studies*, vol. 8, no. 1, summer 2001: 143–59. Harold Cones et al., *Zenith Radio*, 2 vols., Atglen, Pa.: Schiffer 2003.
> See McDonald Jr., Eugene F.

Buehner, Frederic (1908–1971)

German designer.

Training Under Bruno Paul, Vereinigte Staatsschulen für freie und angewandte Kunst (Kunstgewerbeschule), Berlin-Charlottenburg, concurrently with 'Kem' Weber and Walter von Nessen as fellow students.
Biography 1929, Buehner emigrated to the United States; 1933, registered Buenilum as an aluminum trademark (in the image of a castle) under which, from 1933, he designed and made domestic handwrought accessories such as 1930s cocktail shaker, 1950 three-tier compote, and more historicist pieces under the manufacturer name Buenilum-Wanner Co. 1969, ceased production due to terminal illness.
Bibliography 'An Introduction: Aluminum Decorative Arts,' *The Echoes Report*, spring 1996.

Buehrig, Gordon Miller (1904–1990)

American automobile engineer and stylist; born Mason City, Ill.

Training Bradley College, Peoria, Ill.
Biography 1924, Buehrig first worked in the auto industry as an apprentice at Gotfredson Body Company, Wayne, Mich.; 1925–29, at Dietrich, Packard, General Motors, and Stutz; 1929, was chief body designer at Duesenberg, America's most prestigious auto firm, and, late 1920s–early 1930s, designed its Shreve Archer Judkins coupé, Judkins Victoria coupé, Beverly Berline, Derham Tourster, Torpedo Phaeton, and many other models, including Arlington (or The Twenty Grand) and the renowned 'Duesenbird' radiator ornament; 1930, altered a new Ford to create his first truly Buehrig body design; designed less expensive 1933 Baby Duesenberg. 1934, he was hired by Harold Ames to redesign the new range (produced 1935) by Auburn Automobile Company and the popular 1934–35 Auburn 851 and 852 Speedster; was chief engineer at Cord, where his legendary 1935–37 coffin-nose Cord 810 and 812 called on the Baby's concepts; left Auburn, worked for the Budd Company, and, subsequently, transferred to Studebaker; privately designed the unsuccessful Tasco, from which the removable T-tops for the Thunderbird and Corvette were later adapted by others; 1949–65 in retirement, was active at Ford Motor Company where he designed 1951 Victoria coupé, 1952 all-metal Ranchwagon station wagon, and 1956 Lincoln Continental Mark II; for five years, taught a plastics course, Art Center College of Design, Los Angeles.
Citations Cord 810 introduced at 1935 Auto Salon, New York. Buehrig was 1989 inductee, The Automotive Hall of Fame, Dearborn, Mich., US; is recognized by Gordon Buehrig Day Celebration, Mason City, Ill.
Bibliography Gordon M. Buehrig with William S. Jackson, *Rolling Sculpture: A Designer and His Work*, Newfoundland, N.J.: Haessner, 1975.

Buffa, Paolo (1903–1970)

Italian furniture designer and craftsperson.

Biography Like Carlo De Carli and Carlo Mollino, Buffa was considered a craft furniture maker; however, is the least known of the trio; worked primarily in Cantù, Italy, and offered a bridge between the crafts industry there and the rest of the world through venues such as the 1930s–50s Triennali di Milano; reinterpreted traditional furniture; also designed buildings, domestic and naval interiors, and commercial products; briefly designed for Cassina.
Exhibitions/citations Work subject of 2001–02 exhibit, Galleria del Design e dell'Arredamento, CLAC, Cantù. 1954 (two citations) and 1955 Premio Compasso d'Oro, all for products by Radaelli.
Bibliography 'Paolo Buffa furniture,' *Abitare*, no. 413, Jan. 2002: 25.

Bugatti, Carlo (1856–1940)

Italian designer and maker of furniture; born and active Milan; father of Rembrandt Bugatti and Ettore Bugatti; grandfather of Jean Bugatti.

Training Accademia di Belle Arti di Brera, Milan.
Biography Bugatti worked most of his life in Milan; was active in several fields but is best known as designer and maker of bizarre furnishings; later denied that he studied at the Brera Academy in an attempt, some suggest, to present himself as self-taught; 1880, designed his earliest-known furniture for the marriage of his sister Luiga to Austro-Italian painter Giovanni Segantini (1858–1899). Bugatti's proto-Futurist 1880s furniture shows influences from the fashionable Moorish and *japonisant* styles of the day. Breaking with traditional concepts of furniture, his often-asymmetrical work was covered with parchment (sometimes painted), leather, metal inlays, beaten-copper plaques, *passementerie*, and exposed tacks. 1890s, Bugatti turned from picturesque asymmetry to more balanced geometrical shapes, culminating in his most notable achievement, the extravagant Snail Room installed with its site-specific furniture, including parchment-covered Cobra side chairs, at the 1902 Turin exposition, in which he combined rich inlaid and veneered woods, pewter and other metals, gilded and colored vellum, and formalized designs of birds, insects, and flowers. 1900, he supplied furniture for the Khedive's palace, Istanbul; designed c. 1901 room in the house of Cyril Flowers (the first Lord Battersea) in London. The Flowers room was something of a rarity, being a complete private ensemble and décor treatment. 1904, Bugatti sold his furniture business to the De Becchi firm in Milan and moved to Paris, where his last design work included silverware. The silver was cast and chased by the craftsmen of A.A. Hébrard, Paris, where he also exhibited. He devoted most of his time to painting in Paris. Bugatti's sons were successful in their own right, Rembrandt Bugatti (1884–

1916) as an *animalier* sculptor and Ettore (1881–1947) as painter and automobile designer. Carlo Bugatti's work was rediscovered in late 1960s and 1970s by show-business personalities wishing to furnish their residences eccentrically, although his furnishings have less impact out of their original context.
Exhibitions/citations Furniture shown at 1888 Italian Exhibition, Earl's Court, London; 1898 Turin exhibition; 1900 *Exposition Universelle*, Paris; 1902 *Esposizione Biennale delle Arti Decorative e Industriali Moderne* (Snail Room, first prize), Turin. Paintings and some furniture at 1907 Salon des Peintres Divisionistes, Paris. Work subject of 1976 exhibition, Emporio Floreale, Rome, and 1983 exhibition, Hamburg. 1902 *Esposizione Internazionale d'Arte Decorativa Moderna*, Turin.
Bibliography V. Rossi-Sacchetti, *Rembrandt Bugatti, Sculpteur, Carlo Bugatti et son Art*, Paris: De Vaugirard, 1907. L'Ebé Bugatti, *The Bugatti Story*, London, 1967. Simon Jervis, 'Carlo Bugatti,' *Arte Illustrata*, no. 3, 1970: 80–87. Cat., P. Spadini and M.P. Maino, *Carlo Bu-gatti, i mobili scultura*, Rome: Emporio Floreale, 1976. Philippe Garner et al., *The Amazing Bugattis*, London: Design Council, 1979. Philippe De Jean, *Carlo—Rembrandt— Ettore—Jean Bugatti*, Paris: Regard, 1981. Cat., *Die Bugatti*, Hamburg: Museum für Kunst und Gewerbe, 1983.

Bugatti, Ettore Isidoro Arco (1881–1947); Jean Bugatti (1909–1939)
Italian automobile entrepreneurs and designers.

Biographies Ettore Bugatti built his first car in 1901, then the first serious small car by anyone in 1910, and thence others in a factory in Molsheim, Alsace, from 1918, when he became a French citizen. His models were made not only in series but also with parts used in other Bugatti models, a innovative procedure. His 1924–31 Bugatti Type 35 (produced for 3 Aug. 1924 Grand Prix in Lyon) became the world's most important racing car, with over 1,000 first-place victories. Purportedly, 353 examples were built. He failed to move from his successful light cars to the luxury market, exemplified by his exotic and expensive models and badly performing 16-cylinder racers. The huge 1926 (11.0-liter) Bugatti 'La Royale' Type 41 was a commercial failure; six were produced, and three sold at a 1930 price three times that of a Rolls-Royce. 1936, he left Alsace for Paris and placed his son Jean Bugatti, a third generation member of the artistic family, in charge of the factory. Jean became a renowned automobile pioneer in his own right; designed attractive automobile models that augmented his father's technical innovations; became well known for the design of 1936 Bugatti Atlantic with its emphatic aerodynamic form and distinctive coach-building features—still considered a landmark sports car—some historians say the most flamboyant ever.
Bibliography J.P. Mutschler, *L'odysée de la première Bugatti*, Molsheim: Société d'Histoire et d'Archéologie, 1970. Philippe Garner et al., *The Amazing Bugattis*, London: Design Council, 1979. Philippe De Jean, *Carlo—Rembrandt—Ettore—Jean Bugatti*, Paris: Regard, 1981.

Robert Budlong. The Pacemaker table radio. 1948. Plastic and metal casing, $6\frac{7}{8} \times 12\frac{1}{4} \times 6\frac{3}{4}$" (17.5 x 31.1 x 17.1 cm). Mfr.: Zenith Radio Corporation, US. Gift of the mfr. MoMA.

Bulo
Belgian furniture manufacturer; located Mechelen.

History 1963, the original firm was established by Walter Busschop in Antwerp; subsequently, has expanded to a large factory in nearby Mechelen; began as a maker of a mobile file-cabinet system and grew into a major European producer of office furniture, when the name Bulo was coined; 1970, began promoting a 'total look' for offices; 1980, set up its own design department; developed 1989 Buloflex desk systems of interchangeable parts and 1992 Bulosafe keyless cabinets; introduced 1996 Carte Blanche range, subsequently designed by freelancers Jean Nouvel, Annabelle d'Huart, bOb van Reeth (1943–), and fashion designers Dirk Bikkembergs (1959–) and Ann Demeulemeester (1959–); 1998 Pub & Club all-purpose chair by the Bulo staff de-signers; 1999 Schraag tessel table by Maarten van Severen; 1999 Spine table by Evelyne Merkx; 2001 Mat furniture by Dirk Bikkembergs.
Bibliography www.bulo.be.

Bülow-Hübe, Torun Vivianna (1927–)
Swedish jewelry designer.

Training Konstfackskolan, Stockholm.
Biography 1951–56, she worked in her own studio in Stockholm, concentrating on jewelry in wood; 1951, was commissioned by Orrefors to design silver jewelry; from 1967, designed for the Georg Jensen Sølvsmedie, for which she produced prototypes for jewelry and watches in gold, silver, and stainless steel; designed porcelain and ceramics by Hutschenreuther and glassware by Glashütte Löhnberg; 1969–77, collaborated with Argentine sculptor Rainer Gualterio Anz; 1978, moved to Jakarta and became a diversified designer of a wide range of products, including kitchen utensils, textiles, baskets, lamps, and office equipment.
Exhibitions/citations Work included in 1980 and 1986 exhibitions, Stockholm, and touring the US; 1996–97 group show, Röhsska Museet, Gothenberg. Silver medal, 1954 (10th), and gold medal, 1960 (12th), Triennali di Milano; 1960 Lunning Prize; 1965 Swedish State's Grand Prize for Artists; 1983 Honorary Smith, Association of Contemporary Swedish Silversmiths, Stockholm.
Bibliography Cat., *Georg Jensen Silversmithy: 77 Artists, 75 Years*, Washington, D.C.: Smithsonian, 1980. Cat., *The Lunning Prize*, Stockholm: Nationalmuseum, 1986. Cat., *Torun Vivianna Bülow-Hübe, Ingrid Dessau, Signe Persson-Melin: klassiker i svensk formgivning*, Gothenberg: Röhsska Museet, 1996.

Bunnell, Harry C.
American furniture designer and maker.

Biography Bunnell has become known for the design of a legendary outdoor chair that features a raked back and seat and wide, horizontal arms. 1905, he patented the model, composed of 11 pieces of wood, that has long since become generically known as the Adirondack chair (in Canada, as the Muskoka chair, named for the cottage area in Ontario). However, Bunnell called his the Westport chair; also produced at least four other variants to 1930 in a shop behind his house in Westport, N.Y. Yet, according to Adirondack Museum of New York State, he purloined the design from an original 1900 board-back chair design by Thomas Lee, the owner of Westport Mountain Spring. Lee was someone Bunnell knew and from whom Bunnell borrowed a constructed example from which to copy.
Bibliography Coy L. Ludwig, *The Arts and Crafts Movement in New York State 1890s–1920s*, Hamilton, N.Y.: Gallery Association of New York State, 1983: 31. Craig Gilborn, *Adirondack Furniture and the Rustic Tradition*, New York: Abrams, 1987.

Buquet, Édouard-Wilfrid
French lighting designer.

Biography Little is known of Busquet or his 1927 articulated lamp. In fact, he may have been completely unknown until Eric Philippe investigated him in the 1970s and discovered the patent documentation and, thus, the lamp's attribution. For a time, the lamp was also manufactured by Hauskley & Sons Ltd., London, and today by Tecnolumen, Bremen. Soon after its appearance on the 'Desk of a Technician' by Lucien Rollin at a Paris Salon, the lamp became one of the most practical and popular lighting fixtures of the period; was used by architects and interior designers, including Marcel Breuer, Louis Sognot, Maurice Barret, Joubert and Petit, Lucien Rollin, Suzanne Guiguichon, Marcel Coard, and Jean Sedlak. The lamp, also made as a wall-mounted model, was widely published in French periodicals

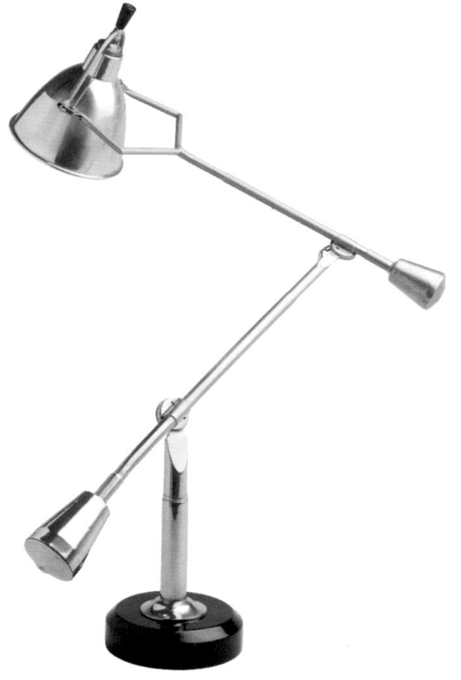

Edouard-Wilfrid Buquet. Desk lamp. 1927. Nickel-plated brass, aluminum, and lacquered wood, h. 36 x base dia. 5 7/8" (91.5 x 15 cm). Mfr.: Edouard-Wilfred Buquet, France. D.S. and R.H. Gottesman Foundation. MoMA.

during 1938–39 without crediting the designer. Buquet's lamps were handmade to different specifications and are frequently confused with the 1932 Anglepoise by British automobile designer George Carwardine and the 1937 Luxo by Norwegian designer Jacob Jacobsen. Unlike the others, the Busquet's arm with the bulb diffuser at one end and a weight at the other is balanced to 'occupy all positions and orientations in space without exception, because the arm can inscribe complete circles around each of its joints,' as the patent information states.
Bibliography Alastair Duncan, *Art Nouveau and Art Déco Lighting*, New York: Simon & Schuster, 1978. Cat., Aaron Lederfajn and Xavier Lenormand, *Le Louvre des Antiquaires présente: 1930 quand le meuble devient sculpture*, Paris, 1986. Mel Byars with Arletee Barré-Despond, *100 Designs/100 Years...*, Hove: RotoVision, 1999: 66–67.
> See Carwardine, George.

Burckhardt, Ernst F. (1900–1958)

Swiss architect; born Zürich; active Zürich and Britain; husband of Elsa Burckhardt-Blum.

Training 1920–24, architecture, London.
Biography 1922–24, he was active as set designer, designing theater sets for two productions at University of London. His writings on theater architecture were numerous. 1920, worked as a volunteer in architecture office Gebrüder Pfister, Zürich; 1925, set up an architecture practice, Zürich; 1931, was head of Krater cabaret and designed the first interiors for Wohnbedarf department store, both Zürich; 1934, designed the renovation of Corso theater, Zürich; 1937, wrote for *Neue Zürcher Zeitung* newspaper; 1944, began contributing to journal *Plan*, of which he was editor, 1946–52. His buildings included 1950 Zürcher Volkstheater and 1956 university theater, Durban. He designed exhibition buildings for 1939 *Schweizerische Landesaustellung* (Swiss national exhibition), Zürich, and 1940 (7th) Triennale di Milano.
Exhibitions/citations Work included in a Zürich exhibition (catalog below). 1957 (with his wife) honored for work in city of Zürich.
Bibliography *Schweizerische Bauzeitung*, 1958/42: 633ff; 49: 745ff. *Künstler-Lexikon der Schweiz, XX. Jahrhundert, Frauenfeld*, 1963–67, vol. 1. Cat., *Um 1930 in Zürich*, Kunstgewerbemuseum der Stadt Zürich, 1977. Friederike Mehlau-Wiebking et al., *Schweizer Typenmöbel 1925–35, Sigfried Giedion und die Wohnbedarf AG*, Zürich: gta, 1989.

Burdick, Bruce (1933–)

American designer; born Los Angeles; active near San Francisco.

Training University of Southern California and Art Center College, both Los Angeles.
Biography In his second year at Art Center College, Burdick worked in the office of Charles Eames, Venice, Cal.; after Art Center, worked for designers John Follis and Herb Rosenthal; 1970, set up his own design office, The Burdick Group. He has pioneered the use of computers in exhibitions on economics and nutrition (at Museum of Science and Industry, Chicago); participated in development/design of environmental education centers, an oceanography museum, and the concept of Institute of Automotive Science and History; often designs with his wife and partner, Susan Burdick (1952–). He has designed a number of products for Herman Miller; the first was the Burdick Group System (an open-office configuration) and included the Burdick Group Table with an articulated top, also offered by Herman Miller for the Home and widely published because of its unusual nature, particular with a glass top. Work included a range of exhibition designs such as 1991 Dow Plastic Recycling Exhibit and other environments; 1995 Philips Competence Centre, Eindhoven, Netherlands; 1996 Rock & Roll Hall of Fame, Cleveland, Ohio; 1998 garden, Samsung Electronics, Seoul; and 1999 Crayola café and store.
Citations 1980 award, Institute of Business Designers (IBD), US, and 1980 award, Industrial Designers Society of America (IDSA) (both for Burdick Group System); Best of 1981 for Industrial Design, *Time* magazine; 1997 IDSA/*Business Week* magazine award (Indoor/Outdoor chair by Itoki, Japan); winner, information-graphics category, American Institute of Graphic Design (AIGA); others.
Bibliography www.burdickgroup.com.

Bureaux, Stéphane (1963–)

French industrial designer; born Nancy.

Training 1986–89, ENSCI (Les Ateliers), Paris.
Biography 1989, he established Agence Stéphane Bureaux Design, Paris. Work has included 1989–95 Quick meat grill, Spresso coffeemaker, and other electrical appliances by SEB; 1993 passenger seating for Pullman car of Wagons-Lits; 1995 stationary, cordless, and multi-system phones by Alcatel; 1995 linens by Couzon; 1995–2001 vacuum cleaner, hair dryer, coffeemaker, and other electrical appliances by Triangle Partners; toys by Pinpon; 2000 new cake for Patisserie Stef; and wheelchair for Fédération Française des Handicapés. From 1992, professor of design, École Supérieure des Arts Décoratifs (ESAD), Reims.
Exhibitions/citations Work included in 1993 *Design, Miroir du Siècle*, Grand Palais, Paris; 2000 Biennale Internationale de Design, Saint-Étienne; 2001 *Tapis et Feutre*, Musée du Feutre, Mouzon. 2002 Salon du Meuble, Paris. 1988 laureate (for halogen lamp), Les Galeries Lafayette, Paris; selection (for urban cycle), 1990 Du Pont de Némours competition; 1995 laureate (for 5-euro piece), 1995 European-wide competition for design of euro; laureate and top eight (for eyeglass frames), 1997 and 1998 Jeunes Créateurs, À Vous de Voir competition; laureate (for urban backpack, or rucksack), 2001 Le Sac competition; 2001 Appel Permanent grant and 2001 Carte Blanche production support (for Chair-i), VIA (French furniture association); Appel Permanent grant (for Biomorphe lamp), VIA.
Bibliography Tucker Viemeister (ed.), *Product Design 6*, Glen Cove, N.Y.: PBC, 1994. Robert Blaich (ed.), *New and Notable Product Design 2*, Gloucester, Mass.: Rockport, 1995. *Panorama Design France*, Paris: APCI, 1996, 1999, 2001 eds. 'Design Report,' *Zu Schön zum Fressen*, Apr. 2000.

Burges, William (1827–81)

British architect, antiquary, and designer; born London

Training 1844-49, under architect Edward Blore.
Biography 1849, Burges joined the office of architect Matthew Digby Wyatt; was a friend of the Pre-Raphaelite painters and became one of the most important Gothic Revival architects of the mid-19th century. His work was based on a scholarly knowledge of 13th-century French Gothic, but his interest in the arts of non-industrial cultures and his use of opium may also have contributed to his style. The house he built for himself in London, the design for St. Finbar's Cathedral in Cork, and commissions from Lord Bute (the Cardiff Castle restoration, Castell Coch, and marriage jewelry) reflected his wide interests in Gothic and French Renaissance architecture, antique metalwork and jewelry, archeology, and Indian and Japanese art. As early as 1858,

he designed painted architectonic furniture with complex motifs, an example showing his pet dogs; later designed stained glass, metalwork, ceramics, textiles. His article 'Antique Jewellery and its Revival,' *Gentleman's Magazine and Historical Review* (1862), showed his interest in Fortunato Piò Castellani's research into antique techniques. His only non-Gothic jewelry was an Etruscan-style necklace and earrings. He designed metalwork, and possibly jewelry, for Hardman and Co.; 1870–74, produced designs for wallpapers for Jeffrey and Co., some reaching US, including in late-1870s the George Peabody Wetmore mansion, Newport, R.I.; was one of first in Britain to collect Japanese prints, after seeing the 1862 London exhibition of them. Mid-1870s, his medievalism put him outside the architectural mainstream. His architecture included two winning designs, for Lille Cathedral (1855, unrealized) and Crimea Memorial Church, Constantinople (now Istanbul, 1856, unrealized); 1863 cathedral, St. Finbar, Cork, Ireland; 1865 restoration, Cardiff Castle; 1874 commission to design part of Trinity College, Hartford, Conn.; 1875 Castell Coch, Glamorganshire, Wales; and his own 1875–81 London residence, Tower House in Melbury Road, Kensington.
Exhibitions Furniture included in Medieval Court, *International Exhibition of 1862*, London; *In Pursuit of Beauty*, exhibition, New York (catalog below).
Bibliography William Burges, *Art Applied to Industry*, Oxford and London, 1865. Charlotte Gere, *American and European Jewelry 1830–1914*, New York: Crown, 1975. J. Mordaunt Crook, *William Burges and the High Victorian Dream*, Chicago and London, 1981. Cat., Doreen Bolger Burke et al., *In Pursuit of Beauty: Americans and the Aesthetic Movement,* New York: The Metropolitan Museum of Art/Rizzoli, 1986.

Burkhalter, Jean (1895–1982)

French furniture designer, painter, decorator, and ceramicist; born Auxerre.

Training 1916–19, École Nationale Supérieure des Arts Décoratifs, Paris.
Biography Burkhalter first learned gold- and silvercarving, weaving, and tapestry and, subsequently, designed some furniture for the Primavera decorating studio of Au Printemps department store, Paris. His furniture in metal and bent-metal tubing was sometimes painted and sometimes nickel plated; rendered furniture designs and prototypes for Primavera decorating studio of Au Printemps department store, Paris; collaborated frequently with Pierre Chareau and Robert Mallet-Stevens; employed new materials, including painted and chromed tubular steel, enameled sheet metal, and Bakelite, in his furniture; designed ceramics for the Manufacture Nationale de Sèvres, silver accessories for Hénin, rugs and fabrics for Boutique Pierre Chareau, furniture for Maison de Verre (architects, Pierre Chareau and Bernard Bijvöet); 1929, was a founding member, UAM (Union des Artistes Modernes), exhibiting at its events to 1937; 1920s–1930s, designed for Metz, Amsterdam; collaborated with Jan and brother-in-law Joël Martel on 1932 monument to Claude Debussy; from 1935, director, École Municipale des Arts Décoratifs, Auxerre, and, 1946, of École des Arts Décoratifs, Limoges, but, from 1937, was primarily a painter. Some furniture was marketed by Les Fleurs de Nice and Primavera. He died in Avallon.
Exhibitions/citations From 1919, showed rugs, fabrics, enameled metal and goldwork, posters, bibelots, and tubular-steel furniture at Salons des Artistes Décorateurs. Was designer of a dining room and domestic items and member of judging jury, 1925 *Exposition Internationale des Arts Décoratifs et Industriels Modernes*, Paris; with Joël and Jan Martel, designed the fountain of the exposition's commissariat of tourism. To 1937, showed at UAM's expositions, including ceramics and glassware in UAM pavilion, 1937 *Exposition Internationale des Arts et Techniques dans la Vie Moderne,* Paris. Grand prize, 1925 Paris *Exposition*; 1924 Prix Blumenthal.
Bibliography Léon Moussinac, 'Jean Burkhalter,' *Art et décoration*, vol. 57, 1930. Cat., Yvonne Brunhammer, *Le cinquantenaire de l'exposition de 1925*, Paris: Musée des Arts Décoratifs, 1976. Arlette Barré-Despond, *UAM*, Paris: Regard, 1986. Pierre Kjellberg, *Art déco: les maîtres du mobilier, le décor des paquebots*, Paris: Amateur, 1986. Cat., *Les années UAM 1929–1958,* Paris: Musée des Arts Décoratifs, 1988. *Jean Burkhalter (1895–1982)*, La Ferté-sous-Jouarre: G.E.D.A., 2000.

Stephen Burks. Screen/room divider. c. 1998. Sheet aluminum and steel rods, each module 63 x 9" (60 x 23cm). Mfr.: Readymade, US.

Burkhardt, Linde (b. Friedlinde Burkhardt; 1937–)

German artist and designer; born Singen.

Training In Zürich, Berlin, and Hamburg.
Biography Living and working in Germany, France, and Italy, Burkhardt has designed carpets and objects; is an architect and design critic; teaches, organizes exhibitions, and paints, considering herself to be primarily an artist; has an abiding interest in how objects and places influence people; develops public-space environments at Urbane Design, Hamburg, a group she cofounded. Her design work includes the exploration of sculptural forms and inclusion of lettering, signs, and symbols, and emotionally provocative colors. Has designed carpets by Toulemonde-Bochart, 1987; Driade/Follies, 1987; and Vorwerk, 1988. Her ceramics collections have been produced by DriadeStore, 1995 (Snow White dinnerware, shape by Antonia Astori, decoration by Linde Burkhardt), and, by Alessi, 2001 (*In Due* steel/ceramics collection of vases, bowls, plates, and centerpieces).
Exhibitions Explored the theme of play at 1972 Documenta 5, Kassel.
Bibliography Cat., Linde Burkhardt (ed.), *Kindertagesstätten*, Berlin: Internationalen Design-Zentrums, 1976. Cat., Linde Burkhardt (ed.), *...und wie wohnst du?*, Berlin: Internationales Design-Zentrum, 1980. Linde Burkhardt, *Abitare con i bambini*, Milan: Emme, 1982.

Burks, Stephen (1969–)

American industrial designer; born Chicago; active New York.

Training 1987–92, product design, Institute of Design, Illinois Institute of Technology, Chicago; 1992–94, architecture, Graduate School of Architecture, Columbia University, New York.
Biography 1997, Burks established design/production studio Readymade Projects, New York. Wide range of work includes 1993 Woman and Kerouac limited-edition screen prints by Idée; 1999, establishment of *Independent Design Guide* to off-site events during International Contemporary Furniture Fair (ICFF), New York; 1999 Hall Hanger by Die Imaginaire Manufaktur (DIM); 1999 Utility beach towel by Möve; Display shelving system by Cappellini; 2000 Hanger lamp by Sputnik; 2000 E.S.S., Elements Shelving System by Pure Design; 2000 Some Assembly Required by Readymade; 2000 Pixel Print doormat and rug by Nedia Enterprises; 2001 Serving Vases PO-001-3 in Cappellini's Progetto Oggetto collection; Crown and Sample limited-edition glass by Covo; Found collection by Readymade (shown at Zero, New York); coordinator of *Interni* magazine's *NY Inside/Out Guide* to ICFF events in New York; contributor of 'Suffix' article to *Surface* magazine; redesign of Triple Five Soul flagship stores, New York and Tokyo, and

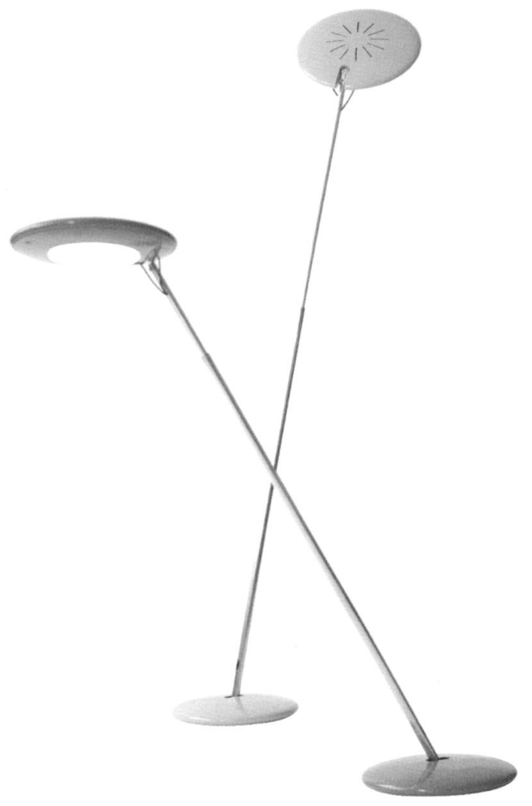

büro für form (Benjamin Hopf and Constantin Wortmann). Lollipop floor lamp. c. 2002. Aluminum, h. 35 3/8"–59 x w. 7 7/8 x l. 7 7/8"–39 3/8" (90–150 x 20 x 20–100 cm). Mfr.: büro für form, Germany.

Homewear collection shown in the former; Relative picture frame by Pure Design. 1998, guest-designer workshop host, Biennale Internationale du Design, Saint-Étienne, France; 1998, guest lecturer, Anders Beckman School of Design, Stockholm.
Exhibitions/citations Work shown at 1997 Salone del Mobile (Room Service collection), Milan; 1998 International Contemporary Furniture Fair (ICFF) (furnishings collection), New York; 1999 exhibition, Néotù Gallery, New York. 1991 Best of Concepts award, Annual Design Review, *I.D.* magazine.
Bibliography Jasper Morrison (ed.), *The International Design Yearbook*, London: Laurence King, 1999. Mel Byars, *Design in Steel*, London: Laurence King, 2002.

Burne-Jones, Edward (1833–1898)
British artist and designer; born Birmingham

Training From 1848, evening classes, Birmingham School of Design; to 1856, divinity, Oxford University.
Biography With friend William Morris, whom he met at Oxford, Burne-Jones discovered art, architecture, poetry, and the writings of John Ruskin and Thomas Carlyle; 1856, studied painting under Dante Gabriel Rossetti; from 1856, shared a house with Morris until the 1859 Morris–Jane Burden marriage; 1859 with Philip Webb and Morris, designed much of the furniture for Morris's Red House, Bexley Heath, Kent, whose architect was Webb; 1861, became a partner with Webb, Rossetti, and Ford Madox Brown in the firm Marshall, Faulkner and Company. The firm's early commissions for stained-glass windows were designed by Marshall, Rossetti, Brown, Webb, Morris, and Burne-Jones. Morris taught embroidery to Burne-Jones's wife Georgiana, who later took charge of the firm's embroidery workshop. By mid-1870s, the firm was in financial trouble; Morris bought out his fellow partners and reorganized as Morris and Company. Burne-Jones continued to work for Morris, designing figurative tapestries produced by the firm; 1883, was commissioned by John Ruskin to execute designs for Whitelands College cross medal. Burne-Jones's jewelry sketches showed delicate bird and leaf designs. The jewelry he designed for his wife and daughter was produced by Child and Child or by Giuliano, both London.
Exhibitions Work included in 1986 *In Pursuit of Beauty*, New York (catalog below).
Bibliography Georgina Burne-Jones, *Memorials of Edward Burne-Jones*, London: Macmillan, 1904. Martin Harrison and Bill Walters, *Burne-Jones*, London: Barrie & Jenkins, 1973. Penelope Fitzgerald, *Edward Burne-Jones: A Biography*, London: Michael Joseph, 1975. Charlotte Gere, *American and European Jewelry 1830–1914*, New York: Crown, 1975. Cat., Doreen Bolger Burke et al., *In Pursuit of Beauty: Americans and the Aesthetic Movement*, New York: The Metropolitan Museum of Art/Rizzoli, 1986.

büro für form
German design studio.

Training Both: 1993–98, industrial design, Akademie der bildenden Künste, Munich.
Biographies Benjamin Hopf (Hamburg, 1971–) worked in the design department of Siemens, and Constantin Worthmann (Munich; 1970–) at Ingo Maurer, Munich. Subsequently, 1998, they established their own studio, büro für form, in Munich, for the design of interiors, furniture, and lighting. Work has included 1999 Flapflap suspended lamp by Next, 1999 Il Crollo chair by Kundalini, 1999 Telemodul control unit by H+P, 2000 Oby Light 1 and 2000 Flight chair by Habitat, as well as corporate identity/graphics for Next Home Collection and for Fingermax. Others have been 1999 portable, rechargeable, squeeze-for-on/off Dicke Trude lamp, that brought wide attention to the designers, and 2003 Valeri chair by Ycami.
Exhibitions/citations Work subject of 2000 *Urban Gravity* and 2001 *Charlie's Angels*, SaloneSatellite, Salone del Mobile, Milan; 2000 *Lightandlounge* and 2001 *Liquid Light* exhibitions, Passagen, Internationale Möbelmesse, Cologne. 1997 innovation award, Sonderpreis; 1997 Hoesch design award, Passagen, Internationale Möbelmesse, Cologne; 1998 Nachlux, Internationale Möbelmesse, Cologne; 1998 Designale (third prize), Munich; 1999 Designpreis Neunkirchen (second prize); 1999 Bonaldo design contest (third prize); 2000 Best of Category, SMI (Swiss international furniture fair); 2000 Best Lamp, Design For Europe; 2000 award (for GbR children's finger brush by Fingermax), Industrie Forum Design (iF), Hanover; 2001 citation, *form* magazine.

Burri, Werner (1898–1972)
Swiss ceramicist; born Bern.

Training 1921–25, Bauhaus, Weimar.
Biography 1926–31, Burri was head of design, ceramics firm Velten-Vordamm; 1932–33, worked in the workshop of Marcel Novarrez, Geneva, and, 1933–40, occasionally with HB-Werkstätten, Hedwig Bollhagen, Marwitz (Germany); 1941–63, taught, Keramische Fachschule, Bern.
Bibliography Cat., *The Bauhaus: Masters and Students*, New York: Barry Friedman, 1988. Cat., *Keramik und Bauhaus*, Berlin: Bauhaus-Archiv, 1989: 262.

Burton, Scott (1939–1989)
American sculptor; born Greensboro, Ala.; active New York.

Training 1957–59, painting, Leon Berkowitz, Washington, D.C., and Hans Hofmann, Provincetown, Mass.; 1962, Columbia University, New York; 1963, New York University.
Biography Both literate and artistic, Burton was for a time a staff member of magazine *Art in America*; was considered a fine artist; produced sculpture that was indistinguishable from furniture in a variety of materials (stone, wood, metal, plastic); created 1972–75 Bronze Chair (a cast-bronze of a real Queen Anne-style chair), his first work, and numerous other art furniture pieces, including 1976 Lawn Chair (an Adirondack-type chair), his first original chair design. Died of Aids.
Exhibitions Work shown first as a performance, 1971 *Eighteen Pieces*, Finch College, New York, with vast number of subsequent international museum and gallery exhibitions.
Bibliography Charles F. Stuckey, *Scott Burton Chairs*, Cleveland: Cleveland Art Center, Fort Worth: Forth Worth Art Museum, 1983. Brenda Richardson, *Scott Burton*, Baltimore: Baltimore Museum of Art, 1986. Jiří Svestka (ed.), *Scott Burton*, Düsseldorf: Kunstverein für die Rheinlande und Westfalen, 1989.

Burtscher, Christof (1964–2001)
> See Bertolini, Patrizia.

Burylin, Sergei Petrovich (1876–1942)

Russian designer.

Biography From 1893, Burylin worked at Voznesenskii Textile Mill, Ivanovo-Vosnesensk; to 1930, was a designer at the N. Zhiderev factory in Ivanovo-Vosnesensk and a textile designer for various textile mills. His widely published 1930 Tractor cotton fabric was printed in Ivanovo-Vosnesensk. According to wife Valentina, 'For him the world was three things—the military, science, and our family.'
Exhibitions Work was included in exhibitions in Vienna, 1988, and New York, 1992 (catalogs below).
Bibliography Cat., *Kunst und Revolution: Russische und Sowjetische Kunst 1910–1932*, Vienna: Österreichisches Museum für angewandte Kunst, 1988. Jonathan M. Woodham, *Twentieth-Century Ornament*, New York: Rizzoli, 1990: 119. Cat., *The Great Utopia: The Russian and Soviet Avant-Garde, 1915–1932*, New York: Guggenheim Museum, 1992.

Burzio, Alberto
> See Arflex.

Buscher, Alma
> See Siedhoff-Buscher, Alma.

Bush, Robin (1921–1982)

Canadian designer; born Vancouver; active Toronto.

Training 1940s, architecture by correspondence, School of Art, Vancouver.
Biography 1950 with Earle Morrison, Bush took over Standard Furniture Plant, Victoria, British Columbia, and received a major commssion for metal-frame furniture for public spaces of Kitimat, British Co lumbia, a new town founded by Alcan corporation, and other contracts; established Robin Bush Design Associates, Toronto, whose 1963 Lollipop tandem-seating system in steel was produced by Canadian Office and School Furniture, Preston, Ontario, for the Lester B. Pearson International Airport, Toronto. 1960s, the firm's employees included Douglas Ball and Thomas Lamb. Bush turned to exhibition design; 1972–75, was director, School of Arts and Crafts, Sheridan College; drowned in Vancouver while taking photographs.
Bibliography Cat., *Seduced and Abandoned: Modern Furniture Designers in Canada, the First Fifty Years*, Toronto: The Art Gallery at Harbourfront, 1986. Rachel Gotlieb and Cora Golden, *Design in Canada Since 1945: Fifty Years from Teakettles to Task Chairs*, Toronto: Knopf Canada, 2001.

Busnelli: Gruppo G14 (Gianfranco Facchetti, Umberto Orsoni, Gianni Pareschi, Giuseppe Pensotti, and Roberto Ubaldi). Fiocco Lounge chair. 1970. Steel-tube frame and stretch fabric, 42 3/4 x 28 7/8 x 46 1/2" (108.6 x 73.3 x 118.1 cm). Mfr.: Gruppo Industriale Busnelli, Italy. Gift of the mfr. MoMA.

Bush-Brown, Lydia (1887–)

American textile artist; born Florence, Italy.

Training Pratt Institute, Brooklyn, New York.
Biography Middle Eastern crafts influenced her work. She called on images of trees (a favorite), abstract figures, animals, and natural forms to fabricate her wallhangings called 'silk murals.'
Bibliography 'Modernistic Wall Hangings,' *Good Furniture Magazine*, Aug. 1928: 108. Karen Davies, *At Home in Manhattan: Modern Decorative Arts, 1925 to the Depression*, New Haven: Yale, 1983: 43.

Busnelli, Gruppo Industriale

Italian furniture manufacturer; located Misinto.

History 1968, the firm was established by Giuseppe Busnelli to produc upholstered furniture; 1969, began using plastics; made the Zen table and Non-Stop seat; has produced orthodox designs as well as those such as the unusual 1970 Fiocco lounge chair by Gruppo G14 (Gianfranco Facchetti, Umberto Orsony, Gianni Pareschi, Giuseppe Pensotti, and Roberto Ubaldi) and 1970 Libro chair by Gruppo DAM in the shape of a book. Currrent and past designers have included those in the Busnelli Study and Research Centre as well as commissioned designers: Archstudio (Augusto Mandelli and Walter Selva), Gigi Capriolo, Tarcisio Colzani, Adalberto Dal Lago, Sergio Giobbi/Alessandro Mazzoni, Mario Mazzer, Ugo La Pietra, Gianluigi Landoni, Pietro Laviani, Libiarch goup, Franco Poli, Paolo Rizzatto, Alberto Salvati, Ambrogio Tresoldi, others. From c. 1984 for a time, La Pietra was artistic director.
Exhibitions/citations Work included in numerous exhibitions and awards, including 1987 Premio Compasso d'Oro (for models by La Pietra, Salvati, and Tresoldi).
Bibliography Cat., Milena Lamarová, *Design a Plastické Hmoty*, Prague: Uměleckoprůmyslové Muzeum, 1972. Anty Pansera and Mario Abis, *La Fabbrica Verticale: Il Gruppo Industriale Busnelli*, Milan: Electa, 1998. www.busnelli.com.
> See B&B Italia.

Busse, Rido (1934–)

German industrial designer; active Elchingen.

Training To 1959, Hochschule für Gestaltung, Ulm.
Biography 1959, Busse established Busse Design Ulm in Elchingen; has since designed more than 2,000 products and served more than 300 clients, with his first complete product development in 1963; founded Plagiarius e.V., a not-for-profit organization to counter product-design theft and the bequeathing of 'awards' to plagiarists; 1978, established the triennial Busse Longlife Design Award for recognition of products in the marketplace for more than eight years. Longtime clients include Carl Zeiss and Britax Römer Kindersicherheit (10 years); Hiti Corporation and Vega (15 years); Andreas Stihl, Moeller, and Laesko (30 years). And others: Krups, Rotpunkt, Henckels, Osram, and Dahle. Busse was a member, Verband Deutscher Industrie Designer (VDI), 1980–84; chairperson of design committee, Deutschen Industrie- und Handelskammertages (DIHK), 1994; initiator, advisor, and permanent juror, Staatspreis für Nachwuchsdesigner (state prize for young designers), Bayerischen Ministeriums für Wirtschaft und Verkehr; honorary professor, Kunsthochschule, Berlin-Weißensee; chairperson, Museum Plagiarius, Berlin, from 2001. With partner Joy A. Busse, founded Busse Design USA, 1997.
Citations Numerous prizes.
Bibliography Hugh Eakin, 'Double Trouble,' *Metropolis*, June 2002. www.busse-design-ulm.de.

Buthaud, René (1886–1987)

French ceramicist; born Saintes.

Training École des Beaux-Arts, Bordeaux; painting and gravure, Paris.
Biography Buthaud is considered by many to have been the finest ceramicist of the Art Moderne period; 1918, encouraged by Jean Dupas and Roger Bissière, became a ceramicist; 1923, set up ceramics factory known as Primavera, Sainte-Radegonde; developed a technique for a cracked-glaze surface; returned to Bordeaux and set up his own workshop. Maison Rouard in Paris was his primary sales outlet. He worked mostly in stoneware and faïence; treated his ceramic surfaces as canvas; his most important commissions, 1937, were for four monumental vases for Bordeaux Parc des Sports, designed by Jacques d'Welles, and bas-reliefs of the Four Seasons for Bouscat town hall. In later years, he drew and painted on mirror-glass.
Exhibitions/citations Work shown in numerous exhibitions, including,

from 1911, Salons of Société des Artistes Français; 1920–29, Salons d'Automne; from 1920, Salons of Société des Artistes Décorateurs; 1925 *Exposition Internationale des Arts Décoratifs et Industriels Modernes*, Paris; 1928 exhibition, The Metropolitan Museum of Art, New York. 1928–61, work shown regularly, Galerie Rouard, Paris. Work subject of 1976 exhibition, Musée des Arts Décoratifs, Bordeaux; 1981, Michel Fortin Gallery, New York. Grand prize, 1914 Prix de Rome (for gravure work).
Bibliography Cat., *Céramiques de René Buthaud*, Bordeaux: Musée des Arts Décoratifs, 1976. Cat., *Rene Buthaud: Collection of the Artist*, New York: Michel Fortin Gallery, 1981. Jacques Sargos (interview), Jacqueline du Pasquier and Valérie de Raigniac (lexicon), *René Buthaud*, Bordeaux: Horizon Chimérique, 1987. Pierre Cruège with Anne Lajoix, *René Buthaud 1886–1986*, Paris: Amateur, 1996.

Buti, Remo (1938–)
Italian designer; born and active Florence.

Training Architecture, Università degli Studi, Florence.
Biography Late 1960s, Buti was active in avant-garde architectural movement in Italy; 1973, cofounded Global Tools; in Florence, worked in a studio where he designed furniture, ceramics, lamps, and jewelry for clients including Mark Cross, Takashemaya, Targetti; lectured on interior architecture and decoration, Università degli Studi, Florence; worked for communities of Florence, Prato, and Livorno, and Centro Moda di Firenze and Bancadi Toscana; with Andrea Branzi, entered competition for partial restoration of Castel di Sangro; c. 1986, designed Stars lighting range and Iris uplighter for Targetti Sankey.
Exhibitions/citations Projects were shown at 1968 (14th), 1979 (16th), 1983 (17th) Triennali di Milano; 1978 Biennale di Venezia. Won 1980 design competition (furnishing fabrics), sponsored by *Jardin de mode* magazine; with others, won Construction et Humanism competition, Cannes. Work included in *Radicals: architettura e design 1960–75*, 1996 (6th) *Mostra Internazionale di Archittettura*, Venice.
Bibliography Robert A.M. Stern (ed.), *The International Design Yearbook*, New York: Abbeville, 1985/1986. Andrea Branzi, *La casa calda: esperienze del nuovo disegno italiano*, Milan: Idea, 1982. *Modo*, no. 148, Mar.–Apr. 1993: 117.

Butler, Nick (1942–)
British industrial designer.

Training Leeds College of Art; Royal College of Art, London.
Biography Butler worked under the guidance of Eliot Noyes on an IBM fellowship; 1967, became a founding partner of BIB Design Consultants, where he designed radar and navigational devices by Racal Decca; 1969–83, designed medical products by Ohmeda, pens and watches by Dunhill , British Telecom's Tribune telephone, earth-moving equipment by JCB, Agenda electronic diary, and cameras by Minolta; was interested in combining product aesthetics with function and practical engineering principles; 1986, designed range of TV sets by Ferguson.
Citations 1985 Best European Camera award (for Minolta 7000 camera); other awards, including for 1980-84 flashlight product line by Duracell.
Bibliography Fiona MacCarthy and Patrick Nuttgens, *An Eye for Industry*, London: Lund Humphries, 1986.

Butter
American design studio.

History Lindsey Adams Andelman (1968–) and David Weeks (1968–) studied industrial design and painting, respectively, and both at Rhode Island School of Design, Providence. Andelman worked at Resolute, a lighting firm in Seattle, and, 1998, returned to New York to work at Weeks's already-established David Weeks Lighting. They began self-production of 1999 Lunette clip-on lamp and other products under the Butter label (established 2000). Butter Editions also produces work by commissioned artists and designers, such as the Eames busts by Charlie Becker. Clients have included Pure Design.
Citations 1999 recognition, Annual Design Review, *I.D.* magazine; award, *Blueprint* magazine; Editor's Award for Best Lighting, 2001 International Contemporary Furniture Fair (ICFF), New York.
Bibliography Interview by Jenny Schnetzer, *I.D.*, June 2002. www.butter-ny.com.

Butterfield, Lindsay Philip (1869–1948)
British designer of textiles and wallpapers.

Training South Kensington National Art Training School, London.
Biography Like C.F.A. Voysey, 1890s, Butterfield became a freelance designer, creating textile designs for Alexander Morton, including 1899 Squill and c. 1901 Tudor patterns. 1880s and 1900s, his subtly colored, flowing designs were made into woven wool-and-cotton reversible fabric (or doublecloth). 1892, he worked at the same address as Harrison Townsend; from 1902, had an exclusive arrangement to design tapestries for Morton, but also designed linens for G. & P. Baker, textiles and wallpaper for Liberty's, wallpaper for Essex and Co. and for Sanderson; in *Floral Forms in Historic Designs* (1922), showed 18 plates of objects from Victoria and Albert Museum, London, and designs by William Morris and Voysey. Also sold designs to G & P. Baker, Warner & Sons, Thomas Wardle, Turnbull & Stockdale, Newman, Smith & Neuman, and David Barbour; taught at several art schools; was a founder member of Society of Designers.
Bibliography *British Art and Design, 1900–1960*, London: Victoria and Albert Museum, 1983. Simon Jervis, *The Penguin Dictionary of Design and Designers*, London: Penguin, 1984.

Buxton, Sam (1972–); Mathias Bengtsson (1971–)
Buxton: British designer; born London. Bengtsson: Danish designer; born Copenhagen.

Training Buxton: furniture design, Middlesex University. Both: to 1999 under Ron Arad, Royal College of Art, London.
Biographies 1997, Bengtsson and Buxton met at the Royal College of Art; 1999, founded design firm At The Third Stroke, London, together with Stuart Lawson and Tim Derhang, to explore new ways of living and working through environments, products, and furniture for clients, including Habitat, Kenzo, Keen, and Eurolounge. Technologically advanced work includes 1999 Timepiece clock by Buxton, 1999 Slice three-dimensional chair by Bengtsson created by stacking more than 250 laser-cut layers of plywood into a chair that can vary in shape and size, 2000 Fold Out Man stainless-steel business card, 2001 MAC modular aluminum chair, and 2001 H-Bottle bottle rack.
Exhibitions/citations Group work shown at Memphis Gallery, Milan; Institute of Contemporary Arts, London; 2001 *Design Now—London*, Design Museum, London. 1999 design-business award, Deutsche Bank.

Byam, Wally (1896–1962); Airstream Trailer Co.
American inventor and designer.

Biography Late 1920s, Byam was a magazine publisher when he printed an article on the building of trailers (or caravans) written by another; to correct errors in it, wrote an article of his own and began selling instructional construction guides; 1932, opened a factory in Jackson Center, Ohio, to build trailers made of plywood; 1934, coined the name 'Airstream' for a mobile home in the popular streamline styling of the time, as seen in Chrysler's 1934 Airflow automobile; 1936, Byam's Airstream Trailer Co. introduced the first aircraft-style all-aluminum Clipper mobile home (probably a reference to Igor Sikorsky's early 1930s Clipper airships), with a puffy but sleek aluminum-clad silhouette like a loaf of bread; with the shortage of aluminum for civilian uses during World War II, closed his shop, reopening in 1948. (After the war, Americans took to the road in large numbers in Airstreams, and the Wally Byam Caravan Club was formed in 1955.) 1946, Curtis-Wright and Airstream jointly produced a new model but broke the relationship within months. June 1949, Curtis-Wright sold the trailer business to Silver Streak, which continued into the 1950s as a separate company. Other more recent Airstream models have included the Bambi and Safari. Now a cult object, the Airstream is still being manufactured by Airstream Inc., a division of Thor Industries, Jackson, Ohio. One or two of the original 1932–36 Airstreams are known to exist.
Bibliography Robert Landau and James Phillippi, *Airstream*, Salt Lake City: G.M. Smith, 1984. Bryan Burkhart and David Hunt, *Airstream: The History of the Land Yacht*, San Francisco: Chronicle, 2000. www.airstream.net.

Bye, Bjørn (1971–)
> See K8 industriedesign.

Mata i Crasse:. Artican wastepaper basket (detail). 1999. MoMA.

Caccia Dominioni, Luigi (1913–)
Italian architect and designer; born Milan.

Training 1931–36, architecture, Politecnico, Milan.
Biography 1938–40 with brothers Livio Castiglioni and Pier Giacomo Castiglioni, Caccia Dominioni collaborated in a studio in Milan (see Livio Castiglioni concerning work of the period). 1939–45, Caccia Dominioni was somewhat inactive due to the war and political situation in Italy; 1938–46, collaborated with Pier Giacomo Castiglioni and brother Livio; 1943–45, was an intern in Switzerland and worked as an advertising illustrator; 1947, set up his own practice for architecture and design (thereafter, active without interruption in Milan, and, 1975–82, in Monaco). 1947 with Corrado Corradi Dell'Acqua and Ignazio Gardella, he cofounded the legendary design firm/store Azucena, Milan; became known for his eclecticism; sought to recover the representational value of the image in his architecture, like others in Italy in late 1950s; designed interiors and restaurants; was an industrial designer with work including ceramic tiles for Cooperativa Ceramica. Since his 1968 Maniglia Saint Roman door handle by Olivari, Caccia Dominioni has designed no products for firms other than Azucena, for which he is still active. Architecture included 1947–49 house, Piazza Sant'Ambrogio; 1954–55 villa and 1965 residential and office building, both Milan; 1957–60 Istituto della Beata Vergine Addolorata; 1965–66 Vanoni library, Morbegno; 1972–73 residences, Campo da Golf, Monticello; 1975 Résidence du Parc Saint-Roman, Monaco; participated in competitions (city center of Morbegno and schools of Vimercate, 1958–59); residential buildings, Monaco, Monticello Brianza, and, with Vico Magistretti, Milano San Felice. Town planning included that for Milan, 1975–84.
Exhibitions/citations Work shown in numerous exhibitions, including in Munich (catalog below). Participated in Triennali di Milano. Premio Compasso d'Oro in 1947 (apartment in QT8 project), 1960 (T 12 Palini wooden school chair, with P. and A. Castiglioni), 1984 (Super by Lualdi), and 1991 (Caccia cutlery with L. and P. Castiglioni by Alessi).
Bibliography G. Polin, 'Un architetto milanese tra regionalismo e sperimentazione: Luigi Caccia Dominioni,' *Casabella* 46, no. 508, 1984: 40–51. M.A. Crippa, *Luigi Caccia Dominioni. Flussi, spazi e architettura*, Turin: Universale di Architettura, 1996. Cat., Fuivio Irace and Paola Marini, *Case e cose da Abitare—stile di Caccia Dominioni,* Venice: Marsiglio, 2002. S. Bernasconi and M. De Min, *Tipologie abitative di Luigi Caccia Dominioni*,
> See Castiglioni, Livio; Castiglioni, Pier Giacomo and Achille Castiglioni.

Cachet, Carel Adolph Lion (1864–1945)
> See Lion Cachet, Carel Adolph.

Cadestin, Michel (1942–)
> See Ragot, Christian.

Cadovius, Poul (1911–)
Danish furniture designer.

Biography 1945, Cadovius established furniture manufacturer Royal Systems, which produced shelving/storage systems. Cadovius, initially working with six employees, successfully promoted himself as a modern designer of the 1960 Abstracta exhibition-display and construction system and other work for Cado Center, Cadomus, France & Søn (a spin off of Royal Systems), Euroart, Barcelona, and La Boutique Danoise, Paris.
Citations Silver medal, 1957 (11th) Triennale di Milano; gold medal, 1961 (10th) International Investors' Fair, Brussels; and numerous other awards.
Bibliography Frederik Sieck, *Nutidig Dansk Møbeldesign – en kortfattet illustreret beskrivelse*, Copenhagen: Bondo Gravesen, 1990.

CAF
> See Compagnie des Arts Français.

Cagani, Fabien (1961–)
> See Delo Lindo.

Caillères, Jean-Pierre (1941–)
French architect and designer; born Paris.

Training Architecture and town planning, École Nationale Supérieure des Beaux-Arts, Paris.
Biography Caillères began as an architect and town planner but turned to interior and furniture design; 1979, set up his own studio Papyrus, specializing in the design of office, shop, and hotel interiors and furniture; designed 1979 Eventail rotating coffee table by Cinna, 1984 faïence dinner services Dorique and Angles by Gien, 1983 Equerre armchair edited by his own Papyrus firm, 1989 Genius chair range by Sigebene, microwave-oven-proof dishes by Pillivuyt; and shops for Ercuis, Saint-Hilaire, Haviland, and for Chromex.
Exhibitions/citations Participated in VIA (French furniture association) exhibition, Paris (catalog below). Won 1983 competition (1980 table

Luigi Caccia Dominioni. Stamp box. c. 1954, Brass and glass, overall h. 1 x dia. 2 13/16" (2.5 x 7.1 cm). Mfr.: Azucena, Italy. Gift of Philip Johnson. MoMA.

by Papyrus), organized by VIA and Bloomingdale's; 1983 Appel Permanent grant (Basculator table), VIA.
Bibliography Cat., *Les années VIA: 1980–1990*, Paris: Musée des Arts Décoratifs, 1990. Mel Byars, *50 Tables: Innovations in Design and Materials*, Hove: RotoVision, 1997. Cat., Sophie Tasma Anargyros et al., *L'école française: les créateurs de meubles du 20ème siècle*, Paris: Industries Françaises de l'Ameublement, 2000.

Caillette, René-Jean (1919–)

French furniture and interior designer; born Fay-aux-Loges.

Training École des Arts Appliqués, Paris.
Biography 1948, Caillette became associated with Roger Landault and other young designers who formed a group in Paris; also worked with Marcel Gascoin and Michel Mortier and collaborated with Jacques in a studio where Jeanine Abraham and her husband-to-be, Dutch architect Dirk Jan Rol, worked. Caillette studied serially produced furniture; 1950s–60s, was active in designing wooden and rattan furniture, later in MDF. Probably his best work is the 1957 Diamant molded plywood side chair edited by Steiner, which appears more like plastic than wood.
Exhibitions/citations Work shown regularly at Salons des Arts Ménagers and Salons of the Sociéte des Artistes Décorateurs, Paris. 1952 René Gabriel prize; silver medal, 1957 (11th) Triennale di Milano; grand prize, 1958 *Exposition Universelle et Internationale de Bruxelles* (*Expo '58*); gold medal, 1962 exposition, Munich; 1982 Appel Spécifique award (Primevère chair by Collomb, and Trèfle folding chair in lacquered steel tubing and Formica), sponsored by VIA (French furniture association).
Bibliography Pascal Renous, *Portraits de créateurs*, Paris: H. Vial, 1969. Yolande Amic, *Intérieurs: le mobilier français, 1945–1964*, Paris: Regard/VIA, 1983: 82. Cat., H. Besacier and X. Laboulbenne, (ed.), *MDF: des créateurs pour un matériau*, Jouy-en-Josas: Fondation Cartier pour l'Art Contemporain, 1988. Cat., *Les années VIA 1980–1990*, Paris: Musée des Arts Décoratifs, 1990. Cat., Sophie Tasma Anargyros et al., *L'école française: les créateurs de meubles du 20ème siècle*, Paris: Industries Françaises de l'Ameublement, 2000. Patrick Favardin, *Les décorateurs des années 50*, Paris: Norma, 2002:

Calatrava, Santiago (1951–)

Spanish architect, engineer, and furniture designer; born Valencia.

Training 1969–74, Escuela Técnica Superior de Arquitectura, Valencia; in Paris; civil engineering, Eidgenössische Technische Hochschule (ETH), Zürich.
Biography Calatrava taught at ETH in Zürich for three years; subsequently, opened his own architecture and engineering office; executed 1986 furniture designs, including 1986–87 Espada DS-150 leather-and-metal chaise longue by De Sede, Switzerland, and 1990 Montjuic floor lamp for Artemide; was the architect of bridges in Spain, factory sheds in Germany, and train stations in Switzerland; with architects Bruno Reichlin and Fabio Reinhart, was active in an architecture office in Switzerland; became known for his distinctive and dramatic bone-like structures.
Exhibitions/citations Participated in 1983 (17th) Triennale di Milano; was general coordinator of 1980 Biennale di Venezia. Work subject of exhibitions in Zürich, 1991; Valencia, 1986 and 1993; and New York, 1993 (catalog below). 1987 Premi FAD d'Arquitectura Award (for best Barcelona building); 1991 City of Zürich Award (for Stadelhofen Railway Station); 1999 Príncipe de Asturias Award for the Arts.
Bibliography Albrecht Bangert and Karl Michael Armer, *80s Style: Designs of the Decade*, New York: Abbeville, 1990: 62–63, 228. Matilda McQuaid, *Santiago Calatrava: Structure and Expression*, New York: The Museum of Modern Art, 1993. Dennis Sharp (ed.), *Santiago Calatrava*, London and New York: E. & F.N. Spon, 1994. Sergio Polano, *Santiago Calatrava: Complete Works*, Corte Madera, Ca.: Gingko, 1996.

Caldas, José Zanine (1919–2001)
> See Zanine, José Caldas

California Faience

American ceramics manufactory; located Berkeley, California.

History 1916, William V. Bragdon and Chauncey R. Thomas set up a collaboration to produce pottery in Berkeley, Cal., originally known as Thomas and Bragdon; 1922, pottery was named The Tile Shop. Tiles and art-pottery operation may have been named California Faience before 1924, when the firm took over the name. Dirk van Erp's hammered copperwares were applied with glazes by California Faience.

Poul Cadovious. Royal wall-mounted shelving system with desk unit. 1944. Painted steel, solid wood, and teak veneer, 80 11/16 x 46 1/4 x 11 5/8" (205 x 117.5 x 29.5 cm). Mfr.: Royal Systems, the Netherlands. Courtesy Quittenbaum Kunstauktionen, Munich.

Bragdon's and Thomas's production was mostly cast. Thomas was responsible for the technical aspects of pottery, including mold making; was in charge of the development of primarily matt glazes, though some were high-gloss. 1930, art-pottery production ended, although some c. 1932 pieces were shown at the Chicago fair. c. 1932, Bragdon bought out Thomas; early 1950s, sold the manufactory to other parties.
Exhibitions Pottery of c. 1932 shown at 1933–34 *A Century of Progress International Exhibition*, Chicago; also in Oakland and New York (catalogs below).
Bibliography Waldemar F. Dietrich, *The Clay Resources and the Ceramic Industry of California, Bulletin 99*, Sacramento: California State Mining Bureau, 1928. Paul Evans in Timothy J. Andersen et al., *California Design 1910*, Salt Lake City: Peregrine Smith, 1980: 73–74. Hazel V. Bray, *The Potter's Art in California, 1885–1955*, Oakland, Cal.: Oakland Museum, 1980. *American Art Pottery*, New York: Cooper-Hewitt Museum, 1987: 130.

Calka, Maurice (1921–1999)

French sculptor, architect, urban planner, and designer; active Paris.

Training In sculpture.
Biography Calka was primarily a sculptor who came to priminance with the monumental stone lion, *Lion of Judea*, commissioned 1955 by Haile Selassie, Emperor of Ethiopia, for Addis Ababa. Some claim that it was a symbol of Africa's entry into the modern period. Calka rendered a number of other bronze animal sculptures and marble portraits during a long career; was somewhat active in architecture and urban planning and an indefatigable researcher; taught, École Nationale Supérieur des Beaux-Arts, Paris; worked in the atelier at 1 bis, rue Raffet, Paris, for about 50 years. In design circles, he has become known for 1969 Boomerang desk in fiberglass of a biomorphic form with four drawers and an attached seat, by Leleu-Deshay.
Citations 1950 Premier Grand Prix de Rome.

Cammas, Fabienne (1961–)

French furniture designer.

Training École Nationale Supérieure des Arts Décoratifs, Paris; engineering, INSA, Lyon.
Biography Cammas turned from industrial design to become a teacher at Domus Academy, Milan; designed 1988 table with a circular moveable area, by Giogetti, and tableware by Alessi.
Citations First prize (with Luc Jozancy and Jean-Yves Maurel), 1986 picnic-tableware design competition, sponsored by APCI (Agence pour la Promotion de la Création Industrielle) and UGAP (Union des Groupements d'Achats Publics).
Bibliography *Les carnets du design*, Paris: Mad-Cap Productions/APCI, 1986: 86.

Campana, Humberto (1953–); Fernando Campana (1961–)

Brazilian designers; Huberto: born Rio Claro; Fernando: born Brotas; brothers.

Training Humberto: 1972–77, law, Universidade de São Paulo. Fernando: 1979–84, architecture, Universidade de São Paulo.
Biographies The brothers are partners in an industrial-design practice. 1998, they taught industrial design, Fundação Armando Alvares Penteado, São Paulo; 1999–2000, taught, Museu Brasileiro de Escultura, São Paulo; from 1996, have lectured or participated in conferences and workshops worldwide. At first they designed a number of prototypes, which were serially produced; and some unique widely published work has included 1997 Estela lamp by O luce, 1993 Vermella and 2001 Anemona chairs and 2002 Boa sofa by Edra, 2000 Bambu and Plastic lamp by FontanaArte, 2001 inflating table by The Museum of Modern Art, 2001 jewelry collection by H. Stern, 2001 Bambu metal chair by Hidden, 2001 pen collection by Acme, 2001 furniture for L'Est Parisienne bar, Paris, and, subsequently, more recent work by Edra, by Alessi, and by others.
Exhibitions/citations Work first exhibited in group venues, from 1989, and the subject of a number of exhibitions from 1989 *Desconfortáveis*, A Arquitetura da Luz, São Paulo. 1992 Aquisição award, Museu de Arte Brasileira, Fundação Armando Alvares Penteado, São Paulo; first prize (design category), 1996 (21st) Salão de Arte, Ribeirão Preto, Brazil; first prize (residential furniture), 1997 ABIMÓVEL (Associação Brasileira de Industria de Móveis/Brazilian furniture-industry association), São Paulo; 1999 George Nelson Design award, *Interiors* magazine, US.
Bibliography Mel Byars, *50 Chairs...*, Hove: RotoVision, 1996. Mel Byars, *50 Tables...*, Hove: RotoVision, 1997. Mel Byars, *50 Lights...*, Hove: RotoVision, 1997. Mel Byars, *50 Products...*, Hove: RotoVision, 1998. Mel Byars (ed.), *Tropical Modern: The Designs of Fernando and Humberto Campana*, New York: Acanthus, 1998. Paola Antonelli (ed.), *Objects of Design: The Museum of Modern Art*, New York: The Museum of Modern Art, 2003: 278. Ignacio de Loyola Brando et al., *Campanas*, São Paulo: Bookmark, 2003.

Campbell, Critz (1967–)

American designer; born West Point, Miss.

Training 1986–87, Mississippi State University, Starkville; 1987–80, fine arts, Art Institute of Chicago; 1991, Arco Centro de Communicao Visual, Lisbon, Spain; 1994–96, Penland School of Crafts, Penland, N.C.; 1997–99, Parnham College, Beaminster, UK.
Biography Campbell has designed a number of furniture pieces.
Exhibitions/citations Work shown at 1999 *New Designers*, London; 2000 *Future Furniture*, sponsored by *Interior Design* magazine, Chicago; 2000 *Chicago Design Show*; 2001 and 2002 International Contemporary Furniture Fair (ICFF), New York; 2003 National Design Triennial, Cooper-Hewitt National Design Museum, New York. 1996 artist fellowship grant, NEA and Mississippi Arts Council.

Campbell, Louise (1970–)

Danish furniture designer; born and active Copenhagen

Training 1992, furniture design and innovation, London College of Furniture; to 1995 under fashion designer Sonja Nuttall, Kunsthåndværkskolen, Copenhagen.
Biography Campbell worked in a studio in Jakarta, Indonesia; 1996, established her own studio in Copenhagen. Work has included the design of 1998 Butterfly café in Glastrup Center and various furniture pieces, including the 1995 single-sheet corrugated cardboard table and chair; 1995 ensemble in snow by the canal in Nyhavn. 2002, became a member of the board, Danish Design Center; designed a chair for Crown Prince Frederik and other furniture and lamps by Bahnsen Collection, Erik Jørgensens Møbelfabrik, Interstop, and others. 1999, Campbell, Sebastian Holmbäck, Torben Holmbäck, and Cecilia Enevoldsen initiated *Walk the Plank*, a traveling exhibition of Danish designers' and manufacturers' work (later to be sold via the Internet), and another installment followed.
Exhibitions/citations Entry in 1994 ICI Waterlily competition shown Germany, Italy, and Spain. Work also shown at large number of venues

Fernando Campana and Humberto Campana. Vermelha chair. 1993. Steel with epoxy coating, aluminum, and cord, 31 x 29 1/8 x 22 3/4" (78.7 x 74 x 57.8 cm). Mfr.: Edra, Italy (1998). Gift of Patricia Phelps de Cisneros. MoMA.

from 1997–98 Kropsholder-reprise, Scandinavian Trade Mart, both Copenhagen, and 1999 *Walk the Plank*, Museum of Applied Arts, Copenhagen, to 1999 *H99*, Gothenburg; *Generation X: Young Nordic Design*, traveling the world from 2000; and 2003 *Walk the Plank 2*, Museum of Decorative Arts, Trapholt, traveling to Paris, Hamburg, and London. 1999 first prize, Bo Bedre 'Element 99' Design competition, Designfonden, Copenhagen; 2002 Erik Herløw Travel Grant; 2002 annual award, Dansk Designråd (Danish design council); 2003 Red Dot award, Design Zentrum Nordrhein Westfalen, Essen; others.
Bibliography Michele De Lucchi (ed.), *The International Design Yearbook*, London: Laurence King, 2001. www.louisecampbell.com.

Campi, Antonia (1921–)
Italian ceramics and industrial designer.

Biography Campi designed household objects and ceramics for clients including Ermenegildo Collini and Richard Ginori. Her scissors and poultry shears were widely published.
Exhibitions/citations Work included in Philadelphia exhibition (catalog below). 1956 (products by Collini) and 1959 (scissors) Premio Compasso d'Oro; 1964 National Industrial Design Council of Canada award (poultry shears).
Bibliography Carlo Bestetti (ed.), *Forme nuove in Italia*, Rome, 1962: 109. Cat., Kathryn B. Hiesinger and George H. Marcus III (eds.), *Design Since 1945*, Philadelphia: Philadelphia Museum of Art, 1983. Cat., Hans Wichmann (ed.), *Italien Design 1945 bis heute*, Munich: Die Neue Sammlung, 1988. Cat., *Terra e terra quattro: presenze negli anni cinquanta*, Cero: Palazzo Perab, 1989. Cat., Cinzia Anguissola and Emanuela Uboldi, 'Oggetti di piccola serie,' in *'45–'63 un museo del disegno industriale in Italia*, Milan: Abitare Segesta, 1995.

Campo, Franco
> See Graffi, Carlo.

Canal
French architecture and design collaborative.

History 1981, Canal was established by architects Daniel Rubin, Patrick Rubin, and Annie Le Bot who designed furniture for public use in museums, stores, and work areas and offices for magazines *Actuel*, 1982, and *Libération*, 1987, and Claude Montana boutiques; renovated Centre National des Lettres and building of Direction des Musées de France (DMF), 1990–92. The 1984 Frégate chair, by SERQH, was designed for Jack Lang, then French Ministère de la Culture.

Cananzi, Mario (1958–)
Italian designer; born Rimini.

Training To 1985, architecture, Università degli Studi, Florence; 1989, industrial design, Domus Academy, Milan.
Biography 1986, Canenzi established his own studio for architecture and for furniture by firms such as Vittorio Bonacina, Disform, Edra, Metals, Ollko, Masterly, Steel, Morphos, and Mimo. The 1989 Tatlin spiraling two-seater sofa (with Roberto Semprini) by Edra garnered wide press attention. After 2000, he designed for motorcycle/scooter firms, including Piaggio, Bimora, Yamaha, and KTM (having made a prototype motorcycle as his architecture-degree thesis); has been a consultant for retail-store spaces, including Fiorucci and Basile.
Citations 1992 Forum Design prize (Quadronda armchair by Vittorio Bonaccini), Salone del Mobile, Milan; 1993 Top Ten prize (Tatlin sofa), organized by du Pont International, Düsseldorf.
Bibliography Fumio Shimizu and Studio Matteo Thun (eds.), *The Italian Design: Descendants of Leonardo da Vinci*, Tokyo: Graphic-sha, 1987. Francisco Asensio Cerver, *Furniture and Lamps 9: European Masters*, Barcelona: Atrium, 1991. Mel Byars, *50 Chairs: Innovations in Design and Materials*, Hove: RotoVision, 1996.

Antonia Campi. Italicus poultry shears (no. 397). 1960. Hot-drop forged and mirror-polished stainless steel, l. 9 11/16 x w. 1 3/4" (l. 24.6 x w. 4.4 cm). Mfr.: Ermenegildo Collini, Italy. Gift of the mfr. MoMA.

Canella, Guido (1931–)
Italian architect and designer; born Bucharest; active Milan.

Training To 1959, architecture, Politecnico, Milan.
Biography 1960, Canella began his professional career, designing furniture and lighting; became a member, Associazione Disegno Industriale (ADI); taught, Istituto Universitario di Architecttura, Venice; was professor of architectural design in the architecture faculty in Milan-Bovisa; from 1990, member of the National Academy of San Luca. Editor of *Architettura e Città* series of books and of *Hinterland* and *Zodiac* architectural reviews. His main publications are *Il sistema teatrale a Milano* (Bari: Dedalo, 1966) and, with Lucio Stellario D'Angiolini, *Università, ragione, contesto, tipo* (Bari: Dedale, 1975). 1979–82, member of the executive board, 1979 (16th) Triennale di Milano.
Citations 1969 National Prize for Architecture, IN/ARCH; 1995 CICA (international committee of architecture critics) prize, Buenos Aires.
Bibliography *ADI Annual 1976*, Milan: Associazione per il Disegno Industriale, 1976. Enrico Bordogna, *Guido Canella. Architetture 1957–87*, Milan: Electa, 1987. Enrico Bordogna, *Guido Canella, opere e progetti*, Milan: Electa, 2002.

Canovas, Manuel (1935–)
French textile designer; born Paris.

Training To 1957, École Nationale Supérieure des Beaux-Arts, Paris; Scuola di Belle Arti, Rome.
Biography Canovas created fabrics influenced by 1960s American, Mexican, and Japanese designs; 1963, founded Les Tissus Manuel Canovas to produce fabrics, wallpaper, and carpets sold through offices in US, Europe, Australia, and Japan; designed a 1980s porcelain service by Puiforcat. His firm is a member of Comité Colbert. (His daughter Isabel Canovas is a textile designer known for her fashion accessories.)
Exhibitions Work subject of 1987 exhibition, Musée de la Mode, Paris.

Capey, Reco (1895–1961)
British designer; born Burslem.

Training Royal College of Art, London; in France, Italy, and Sweden.
Biography Capey designed pottery, glass, metal, textiles, and lacquerware; 1928–38 as art director of Yardley, was best known for his distinctive packaging designs; 1924–35, chief instructor in design, Royal College of Art; wrote *The Printing of Textiles* (1930); 1938–41, was president, Arts and Crafts Exhibition Society.
Exhibitions/citations Work shown in various exhibitions (catalog below). 1937, elected Honorary Royal Designer for Industry, UK.
Bibliography Cat., *Thirties: British Art and Design Before the War*, London: Arts Council of Great Britain/Hayward Gallery, 1979. Stuart Durant, *Ornament from the Industrial Revolution to Today*, Woodstock, N.Y.: Overlook, 1986: 254.

Cappelli, Sergio (1948–)
Italian designer; born and active Naples.

Training Architecture, Università degli Studi di Napoli 'Federico II.'
Biography From 1975, Cappelli has practiced architecture, and, from 1980, in partnership with Patrizia Ranzo as Cappelli & Ranzo; has designed products and furniture/furnishings by Abet Laminati, Alessi, Anthologie Quartett, Bardelli, Lapis, Stilart, Ultima Edizione, and Cappellini; 1986, lectured on design, University of Illinois, US. Projects included the BMW showrooms in Avellino, Naples, and Caserta; Fiat showrooms; and so-called urban scenery and temporary architecture for 'Summer in Naples' and 'Piedigrotta' in Naples. 1999, was the promoter of Italian Size, a design-oriented enterprise.
Exhibitions/citations Work in numerous exhibitions, including *La mo-*

Cappellini: Marc Newson. Wood chair. 1988. Wood, 24 3/8 x 32 1/4 x 39 3/4" (61.9 x 82.6 x 101 cm). Mfr: Cappellini, Italy (1998). Gift of the mfr. MoMA.

dernité ou l'esprit du temps, 1982 Biennale de Paris; 1985 *La casa del naturalista*, Centro Ellisse, Naples; 1989 *Habitat & identità*, Centro Affari e Promozioni, Arezzo; 1989 Binnen Expositieruimte, Amsterdam; 1991 *Mobili Italiani 1961–1991*, Triennale di Milano; 1996 *Il Design Italiano 1964–1990*, Triennale di Milano; 2000 Abitare il Tempo, Verona; 2001 *Italia e Giappone: design come stile di vita*, Tokyo. With Ranzo: 1986 1st prize, Atelier Nouveau competition, Seibu, Tokyo-Osaka; 1987 Premio Compasso d'Oro (Agave table by Stildomus).
Bibliography Andrea Branzi, *La casa calda: esperienze del nuovo disegno italiano*, Milan: Idea, 1982. Fumio Shimizu and Studio Matteo Thun (eds.), *The Italian Design: Descendants of Leonardo da Vinci*, Tokyo: Graphic-sha, 1987. Cristina Morozzi, *1956–1988: Trent'anni e più di design*, Milan: Idea, 1988. Cat., *Domestic Nature: S. Cappelli, P. Ranzo 1979–89*, Amsterdam: Galleria Binnen, 1989. Nally Bellati, *Nuovo design italiano*, Milan: Rizzoli, 1991. Cat., *Design, miroir du siècle*, Paris: Flammarion, 1993. Cat., *Il design italiano: 1964–1990*, Milan: Electa, 1996. *Contemporary Italian Famous Designs*, World Famous Designers and Designs Series, Shijiazhuang, China: Hebei Fine Arts, 1999.
> See Ranzo, Patrizia.

Cappellin, Giacomo (1887–1968)
> See Venini, Paolo.

Cappellini
Italian furniture manufacturer; located Arosio (CO).

History 1946, the firm was established to produce furniture through crafts methods; 1960, began to make contemporary lacquer and wood furniture, somewhat more industrially produced; 1975, expanded to include the use of a variety of other materials; 1987, established the Mondo brand/mark to include fabrications in various countries; 1992, inaugurated the 'Progetto Oggetto' home-and-office-object collection, overseen by Jasper Morrison and James Irvine; 1994, added Cappellini Collezione and Cappellini Sistemi marks to its category of wares; is currently directed by Giulio Cappellini. Using an international freelance design stable, the firm infused new life into the Italian furniture industry with Marc Newson, Shiro Kuramata, Jeffrey Bernett, Geert Koster, Ross Lovegrove, Christophe Pillet, Konstantin Grcic, Koivisto/Rune, Lloyd Schwan, Konstantin Grcic, Alfredo Häberli, and many others. Kuramata's 1970 cabinets (Furniture in Irregular Forms 1 and 2) with 18 drawers each were widely published. The firm's Italian designers have included Michele Barro, Daniela Puppa, Franco Raggi, Alberto Meda, Carlo Colombo, Catalano/Marelli, and Rodolfo Dordoni. Its extensive inventory has included Morrison's 1987 Thinking Man's Chair and 1992 Three sofa; Tom Dixon's 1985 Bird 1 lounge chair, 1991 S chair, 1989 candelsticks, and 1992 Pylon chair; Anna Gili's 1991 Tonda armchair; Marc Newson's 1988 Wood chair (from 1998 by Cappellini), 1988 Embryo chair, 1989 Orgone chaise longue, and 1993 Felt chair; Thomas Eriksson's 1992 Medicine cabinet; Dafne Koz's 1994 container; Werner Aisslinger's 1996 Juli home/office chair; Bouroullec/Bouroullec's 1997 Lit Clos bed/environment unit; Barber/Osgerby's 1999 Hula stool/table; Stephen Burks's 2000 Display shelving system and 2001 Serving Vases PO-001-3; Jeffrey Bernett's 2001 Urban table. Quite actively continuing further, its 2003 collection included Thomas Meyerhoffer's M2 chair/ottoman, Piero Lissoni's Coupé love chair, Fabio Novembre's SOS Sofa of Solitude, Bouroullec/Bouroullec's Samourai chair and some cabinets, Morrison's Simplon table, and Karim Rashid's Carim armchair. 1996, Cappellini established Units to produce kitchen equipment; 1998, to sell directly, opened boutiques in Milan, (with associates) in Vienna, New York, and São Paolo, and Paris, all part of the c. 400 showrooms displaying its furniture and 30 Mono-brand stores worldwide; 2003, introduced its cooperation with Philips to market the Paesaggi Fluidi (fluid landscapes) range of electronics from Cappellini stores. Cappellini has become known for having made a positive contribution to the contemporary-design milieu of the 1990s and turn of the century; 2003–04, became part of the Poltrona Frau Group.
Bibliography http://www.cappellini.it.

Capriolo, Gigi (1940–)
Italian designer; born and active Milan.

Biography 1967, Capriolo began her professional career designing lighting, furniture, and shelving systems for clients in Italy, including FLB, DID, Emmezeta, Gruppo Industriale Busnelli, Citterio, Fiarm, Temi, Arve, Complemento Idea, Bishop, Fian Forma Funzione, Nava, Elle, Giocarredo, Gallotti e Radice, Maya sanitary fixtures, Jobs, and Elle 2 furniture.
Bibliography *ADI Annual 1976*, Milan: Associazione per il Disegno Industriale, 1976.

Carabin, François-Rupert (1862–1932)
French furniture designer; born Alsace.

Biography Carabin carved cameos in Paris before learning woodcarving from a sculptor in 1873. One of his best-known sculptures is a 1896–97 figurine of Loïe Fuller, rendered more realistically than the Fuller images by Théodore Rivière, Raoul Larche, and Pierre Roche. A commission for a bookcase for collector Henry Montandon prompted his conclusion that furniture was not architecture but sculpture, and that decoration in furniture was both sculptural and symbolic; used caryatids repeatedly in his work and, from 1899, the female form; from 1890, made jewelry, metalwork, and ceramics with Carriès; 1914, became director of École des Arts Décoratifs, Strasbourg, where he followed German turn-of-the-century teaching methods.
Exhibitions Work shown at Salon des Indépendants from its 1884 founding.
Bibliography Yvonne Brunhammer et al., *Art Nouveau Belgium, France*, Houston: Rice University, 1976.

Carallo, Nunzia Paola (1962–)
Italian designer and journalist; born Taranto.

Training To 1989, Architecture, Università degli Studi, Florence; 1991, industrial design/design management, Domus Academy, Milan.
Biography 1983 with Giuseppe Di Somma and Vincenzo Lauriola, founded multimedia group Syntax Error; 1986, founded a cultural association specializing in videos, articles, and exhibitions; lectured 1988 (on art history) and 1990 (on Radical Architecture), Faculty of Architecture, Università degli Studi, Florence, and at Pennsylvania State University; 1991, collaborated on the book/catalog *Nuovo bel design*; designed 1992 interior of Kumabala Disco, Taranto; 1993, collaborated with studios of Aldo Cibic, Makio Hasuike, and Centro Studi Alessi; 1994–95, was project manager/industrial designer of Taipei Design Center, Milan, working for Taiwanese design firms; 1995–96, worked in Japan for two years, where she also coordinated the design department of Nichibei in Tokyo; 2000, established Palm Design group, working primarily with Asian firms; 2001, worked as a freelance designer and journalist; 2002, collaborated on product development for Fratelli Guzzini, kitchenwares/housewares manufacturer. Has designed furniture, tableware, and carpets for clients, including Marna, Moroso, Nichibei, Peter Creative, Sisal, Suncraft, Young Lin, Ultima Edizione, and Umbra.
Exhibitions 1985 Young Cultural Production of Mediterranean Europa's Biennial (with Syntax Error), Barcelona.
Bibliography Fumio Shimizu and Studio Matteo Thun (eds.), *The Italian Design: Descendants of Leonardo da Vinci*, Tokyo: Graphic-sha, 1987. *Il design delle donne*, Milan: Mondadori, 1991. Anna Gili, *Nuovo bel design*, Milan: Electa, 1992. 'Il museo da vivere,' *Modo*, no. 145, 1992. 'L'abitare futuro,' *Ottagono*, no. 102, 1992. 'Milan in City,' *Axis*, no. 52, 1994.
> See Di Somma, Giuseppe.

Caramia, Pierangelo (1957–)
Italian designer; born Cisternino; active Milan and Paris.

Training To 1984, Architecture, Università degli Studi, Florence; to 1986, Domus Academy, Milan.
Biography 1984, Caramia became active as an architect and designer; from 1986, was a member of design group ELETTRA. He associated himself with the Movimento Bolidista formed in 1986 in Bologna and typified by a retro-1950s/streamline aesthetic and claiming, among a number of assertions, 'that ideology is a useless and harmful brake.' 1987, Caramia settled in France, collaborating on several projects with Philippe Starck; realized a number of design commissions in Paris and New York; taught at the École des Beaux-Arts, Rennes. He designed 1989 Arcadia Swings table, which he compared to the Statue of Liberty, the Christ of São Paulo, and the Oscar statuette. Also designed 1990 Pigalle armchair by XO, 1991 Jet & Trevi large/small tables by Cassina, 1993 Rio salt/pepper shakers and 1993 Penguin pitcher by Alessi, 1996 humidifier by Il Coccio, 1997 Versace/Versus showroom in Paris, 1999 La Vie en Bleu rug by Sommer, 2001 Secret hall chest by Lemarchand. Other clients have included Poltrona Frau and Arredaesse.
Bibliography Fumio Shimizu and Studio Matteo Thun (eds.), *The Italian Design: Descendants of Leonardo da Vinci*, Tokyo: Graphic-sha, 1987. *Modo*, no. 148, Mar.–Apr. 1993: 117. www.via.asso.fr.

Caran d'Ache
Swiss writing-instrument manufacturer; located Thônex.

History 1924, Arnold Schweitzer (1885–1947) acquired the Ecridor Pencil Factory (founded 1915 in Geneva) and changed the name to Caran d'Ache Swiss Pencil Factory, after Emmanuel Poiré (Moscow, 1859–1909)—a French Belle Époque caricaturist and son of a Napoléonic Grande Armée officer—who signed his drawings 'Caran d'Ache,' the French romanization of 'lead pencil,' *karandash* in Russian. And a modified version of his signature is used as the firm's logo for its color products. 1929, Caran d'Ache bought the rights to the Fixpencil, the world's first mechanical pencil and named by founder Schweitzer. It had been invented and patented the same year by engineer Carlo Schmid (1894–1988) of Geneva. (Schmid, nicknamed 'The Tiger,' was an engineer at Sécheron, still a manufacturer of trains/ trams, with headquarters in Satigny, Switzerland.) The invention was adapted to high-end 1930s Ecridor model in brass and, subsequently, also in silver and gold. 1931, Caran d'Ache introduced the Prismalo, world's first water-soluble color pencil, which revolutionized drawing in color; 1952, introduced Neocolor wax-oil crayons; 1970, the 'Cd'A' logo was designed; 1974, plant/offices were moved to Thônex, near Geneva. Caran d'Ache remains Switzerland's only manufacturer of pencils and exclusive writing instruments.
Citations 1988 City of Geneva Prize for Industry.
Bibliography *Unbekannt—Vertraut: 'Anonymes' Design im Schweizer Gebrauchsgerät seit 1920*, Zürich: Museum für Gestaltung, 1987. www.carandache.ch. www.leadholder.com.

Cardeilhac; Ernest Cardeilhac (1851–1904)
French silversmiths; located Paris.

History 1804, Maison Cardeilhac was founded; 1817, registered its mark; for a number of years specialized in cutlery. The founder's grandson, Ernest Cardeilhac, who apprenticed under Harleux, added gold- and silversmithing. The firm's most important designer of the time, Lucien Bonvallet, frequently employed volutes and trefoils in his designs; c. 1900, was one of the important Paris workshops making modern silver; with restrained, naturalistic decoration, incorporated ivory, wood, and different patinas. 1927, Ernest's sons Pierre and Jacques became directors of the firm. 1944, Pierre died and Jacques alone managed the firm, which merged with Orfèvrerie Christofle 1951.
Exhibitions Ernest Cardeilhac showed his own wares and traditional designs by Bonvallet at 1900 *Exposition Universelle*, Paris. The firm's wares were shown at 1925 *Exposition Internationale des Arts Décoratifs et Industriels Modernes* and 1930 *Décor de la Table*, Musée Galliéra, both Paris. Silver medal, 1889 *Exposition Universelle*, Paris.
Bibliography Yvonne Brunhammer et al., *Art Nouveau Belgium, France*, Houston: Rice University, 1976. Annelies Krekel-Aalberse, *Art Nouveau and Art Déco Silver*, New York: Abrams, 1989: 57, 59, 63, 64, 252.

Carder, Frederick C. (1863–1963)
British glassware designer; born Brockmoor, Kingswinford, Staffordshire; active Britain and the US. Manufacturer.

Training Father's pottery; chemistry and metallurgy, Dudley Mechanics Institute, and under John Northwood, Stourbridge School of Art.
Biography 1881, encouraged by Northwood, Carder joined the glass firm Stevens and Williams in Brierly Hill, as designer in charge of applied decorations and shapes; 1902, failing to be promoted to the position of artistic director, toured glassworks in Germany and Austria and urged Stevens and Williams to update its facilities by designing new kilns; after a scouting trip to the US, during which he visited the Corning Glassworks, Corning, N.Y., concluded that American production was as deficient as that in Britain. T.G. Hawkes was a small firm (founded 1880 and located in Corning) that purchased its blanks from Corning Glassworks; its president Thomas G. Hawkes incorporated the S.W. Payne Foundry premises into his operation and established facilities to

Frederick C. Carder. Perfume bottle. Before 1933. Opaque glass, overall h. 3 1/2 x dia. 1 3/4" (8.9 x 4.5 cm). Mfr.: Steuben Glass Works, US. Joseph H. Heil Bequest. MoMA.

produce crystal and colored glass. 1903, Carder joined Hawkes and founded Steuben Glass Works, named after Steuben County, Corning, N.Y., where Carder re-created the moss agate glass developed by Northwood in late 1880s, and Stevens and Williams's other techniques and patterns; also introduced new forms and processes, including a type of iridescent glass called Aurene; initiated the production of cased (or cameo) glass, similar to late 18th-century Chinese models; retired 1933, but continued to work in his own laboratory on vases produced by the lost-wax casting process; became known as the father of modern art glass in the US.
Exhibitions/citations Work subject of 1985 and 1991 exhibitions at Rockwell Museum, Corning, N.Y., and, 1984, Museum of Fine Arts, St. Petersburg, Fla.
Bibliography Robert F. Rockwell and Jack Lanahan, *Frederick Carder and his Steuben Glass 1903–33*, West Nyack, N.Y., 1968. Paul Vickers Gardner, *The Glass of Frederick Carder*, New York: Crown, 1971. Paul Vickers Gardner, *Frederick Carder: Portrait of a Glassmaker*, Corning, N.Y.: Corning Museum of Glass/Rockwell Museum, 1985. Thomas P. Dimitroff et al., *Frederick Carder and Steuben Glass: American Classics*, Atglen, Pa.: Schiffer, 1998.
> See Steuben Glass Works.

Cardew, Michael (1901–1983)
British ceramicist.

Training 1921–23, Oxford University.
Biography 1921–22, Cardew learned to throw pottery from William Fishley Holland at the Braunton Pottery, North Devon; 1923, met Bernard Leach and Shoji Hamada at St. Ives; 1923, became Leach's first and best-known pupil; 1926, acquired a traditional pottery at Winchcombe, Gloucestershire, where he revived English slipware; 1929, moved to Wenford Bridge, Cornwall; 1942–45, taught pottery at Achimota College, Gold Coast (now Ghana); 1945–48, worked in his own pottery, Vumé-Dugamé (Lower Volta River); 1948, returned to England; 1951–52, established Pottery Training Centre, Abuja (Nigeria); to early 1980s, worked in his pottery, Wenford Bridge, Cornwall, traveled, and lectured.
Bibliography Garth Clark, *Michael Cardew*, London: Faber, 1978. Cat., *Thirties: British Art and Design Before the War*, London: Arts Council of Great Britain/Hayward Gallery, 1979.

Carr, Alwyn Charles Ellison (1872–1940)
British silversmith and enamelist; active London.

Training Sheffield School of Art.
Biography Carr met Omar Ramsden at Sheffield School of Art. After graduating, they traveled in Belgium, France, Italy, Switzerland, and Germany. 1898, Carr and Ramsden established a workshop in London, largely financed by Carr and named St. Dunstan, after the patron saint of silversmiths; worked in a style influenced by the Arts and Crafts movement. It is probable that before World War I Carr was responsible for most of the output; 1919, partnership was dissolved. 1920s, Carr continued as a designer of wrought iron and silversmith.
Bibliography Charlotte Gere, *American and European Jewelry 1830–1914*, New York: Crown, 1975. Annelies Krekel-Aalberse, *Art Nouveau and Art Déco Silver*, New York: Abrams, 1989.

Carré, Alain (1945–)
French industrial designer; active Paris.

Training École Nationale Supérieure des Arts Décoratifs, Paris.
Biography 1971–76, Carré was active in his own design office, Alain Carré Design, and was director of Pierre Cardin's design department; designed for a number of shops and restaurants, packaging, and products, including Waterman pens and watches. 1986, his agency was ranked among the top four design firms in France.
Citations 1987 silver medal (Squale prototype motorcycle by Suzuki), Société des Artistes Décorateurs, Paris.
Bibliography Cat., *Design français 1960–1990: trois décennies*, Paris, Centre Georges Pompidou/APCI, 1988. François Mathey, *Au bonheur des formes, design français 1945–1992*, Paris: Regard, 1992.

Carrier-Belleuse, Albert-Ernest (1824–1887)
French ceramicist; born Anizy-le-Château; father-in-law of Joseph Chéret.

Training École Nationale des Beaux-Arts, and École Royale Gratuite de Dessin (now ENSAD); both Paris.
Biography Carrier-Belleuse entered chaser Bauchery's studio c. 1837 and, subsequently, the workshop of goldsmith Jacques-Henri Fauconnier; was one of the first jewelers to produce neo-Renaissance designs. When Fauconnier died 1839, Carrier-Belleuse worked for his nephews, the brothers Fannière; met Péquegnot and Jules Salmson at the École des Beaux-Arts; became a freelance designer of metalwork for Barbedienne and for the porcelain factory of Michel Aaron. Following Vechte, Arnoux, and Jeannest to England, he designed for Minton, Stoke-on-Trent; taught at schools of design in Hanley and in Stoke; on Jeannest's recommendation, designed majolica and Parian wares at Minton; while sending metalwork designs to Paris, also designed for Wedgwood and for William Brownfield; returning to Paris 1855, became a successful sculptor as well as prolific designer. Clients included La Paiva 1867; the Saïd Pasha, Viceroy of Egypt, 1862; the Louvre; Christofle; Lucien Falize; Alphonse Fouquet; and Grohé. From 1876, Carrier-Belleuse revitalized the Sèvres porcelain manufactory as its artistic director, to his 1887 death at Sèvres when he was succeeded by his son-in-law Chéret.
Exhibitions Work shown at 1855 *Exposition Universelle des Produits de l'Agriculture, de l'Industrie et des Beaux-Arts*, Paris; 1862 *International Exhibition of Industry and Art*, London; 1867 *Exposition Universelle*, Paris. Had his own stand at 1863 (1st) exhibition, Union Centrale des Arts Décoratifs, Paris (which he founded with Jules Klagmann).
Bibliography Albert-Ernest Carrier-Belleuse, *Études de figures appliquées à la décoration*, Paris, 1866. Albert-Ernest Carrier-Belleuse, *Application de la figure humaine à la décoration et à l'ornementation industrielle*, Paris, 1884. Achille Segard, *Albert Carrier-Belleuse, 1824–1887*, Paris: Champion, 1928. June Ellen Hargrove, *The Life and Work of Albert Carrier-Belleuse*, New York: Garland, 1977.

Carriès, Jean (1855–1894)
French sculptor and ceramicist; born Lyon.

Biography Carriès executed his most important sculpture 1878–80 and 1888; influenced by the stoneware at the Japanese section of the 1878 *Exposition Universelle*, Paris, he moved to Saint-Amand-en-Puisaye, Nièvre, a small potters' village, to learn stoneware techniques. 1889, he showed his pottery for the first time in his Paris studio, when the Princess of Scey-Monbéliard commissioned a monumental doorway in glazed stoneware; with plans by Grasset, the project was a financial disaster for Carriès. His wares included Chinese and Japanese forms, pinched pots without handles, vases decorated with sculpture, and large pieces. He used glazes ranging from wood ash to copper base. His sculpture-ceramics were in the forms of masks, monsters, and *putti*.
Exhibitions Work shown at 1892 Salon of Société des Artistes Français.
Bibliography Yvonne Brunhammer et al., *Art Nouveau Belgium, France*, Houston: Rice University, 1976.

Carsalade
> See Rosinski, Irena.

Carter, Ronald (1926–)
British furniture designer.

Training 1949, interior design, Birmingham College of Art; furniture, Royal College of Art, London.
Biography 1952–53, Carter was a staff designer, Corning Glassworks, Corning, N.Y., before setting up his own business in London and Birmingham 1954; 1956–74, taught at School of Furniture Design, Royal College of Art; 1960–68, was a partner in Design Partners; 1968–74, was a partner in Carter Freeman Associates; 1974, set up his own practice; 1980, became a design director of Peter Miles Furniture; designed mass-production furniture for Stag, Consort, Habitat, and Peak and handmade furniture that utilized machine methods for Gordon Russell; from 1980, was in partnership with Peter Miles of Miles/Carter. Carter's commissions included furniture for the BBC, Victoria and Albert Museum, and Terminal Four at Heathrow Airport, London. The Hardwick sofa of the late 1980s was widely published in a zebra printed fabric.
Exhibitions/citations Work (1984 Liverpool bench) was shown at 1989 *British Design: New Traditions*, Museum Boymans-van Beuningen, Rotterdam, and exhibitions in San Francisco, Chicago, Cologne, Milan, Tokyo, Vienna, and Paris. 1974, elected Honorary Royal Designer for Industry, UK; honorary fellow, Royal College of Art, London.
Bibliography Robert A.M. Stern (ed.), *The International Design Yearbook*, New York: Abbeville, 1985/1986. *Decorative Arts Today*, London: Bonhams, 1992: no. 48a.

Carter, Truda (b. Gertrude Sharp; aka Gertrude Adams 1890–1958)

British ceramic designer; wife of ceramicists John Adams and Cyril Carter.

Training c. 1908–13, Royal College of Art, London.
Biography 1914–18, she taught art in Durban, South Africa; 1921, worked with husband John Adams at their own pottery, Carter, Stabler & Adams in Poole, Dorset; 1921–39, created embroidery patterns based on Tudor and Jacobean models; 1932–58 with her second husband Cyril Carter, lived at Yaffle Hill (E. Maufe, architect), Broadstone, Dorset, and designed its furnishings, decorations, and color schemes; 1948–58, was a design consultant to Carter, Stabler & Adams.
Bibliography Cat., *Thirties: British Art and Design Before the War*, London: Arts Council of Great Britain/Hayward Gallery, 1979.

Carwardine, George (1887–1947)

British automobile engineer and lighting designer; born Bath.

Training 1901, for priesthood (illness disrupted plan to become a missionary in China); 1901–05, apprenticeship, Whiting Auto Works, Bath.
Biography Carwardine worked in a number of engineering workshops in Bath, concurrently studying at home; 1912, became chargehand, Horstman Car Company, and, from 1916, works manager and chief designer there, responsible for the design of its automobiles, traveling on occasion to the Brooklands race trials; 1924, founded Cardine Accessories, Bath, and specialized in the design of suspension systems; late 1920s, closed his firm and returned to Horstman; 1931, became a freelance consulting engineer and inventor. Carwardine has become best known for the Anglepoise (or angle weight) articulated table lamp, prototyped 1931, and he patented the springs 1932 (under Cardine Accessories). Carwardine's original idea was to create a simple, efficient lighting model made from basic metal components. The springs were the equivalent of the muscles in the human arm. The design was licensed by Herbert Terry & Sons, Redditch, England (originally a hardware manufacturer, including of coiled springs), and, 1934, the firm began production of the four-spring Anglepoise 1208, and later, full-scale production with the smaller three-spring Anglepoise 1227 (patented 22 February 1934 as the 'Equipoising mechanism'). 1935, the first large order for lamps came from Birmingham Medical School. The original name Equipoise was rejected by the British Trade Marks Registry at the Patent Office on the grounds that it was an existing word; 1947, Anglepoise was registered. Made for over 50 years by Herbert Terry and discontinued, was recently re-entered into production by Tecta, thanks to the efforts of Herbert Terry heir, Ray Terry. And, subsequently, was produced by Anglepoise Ltd. in Redditch. The lamp sold well in the UK to 1937, when Norwegian lighting designer Jacob Jacobsen acquired the license, slightly redesigned it with less success, and renamed the fixture the Luxo, which was subsequently produced in Norway and is now marketed worldwide.
Bibliography Stephen Bailey, *In Good Shape: Style in Industrial Products*, London: The Design Council, 1979. John Heskett, *Industrial Design*, London: Thames & Hudson, 1980. Chris Pearce, *20th Century Design Classics*, London: Blossom, 1991. Mel Byars with Arlette Barré-Despond, *100 Designs/100 Years: A Celebration of the 20th Century*, Hove: RotoVision, 1999: 66–67. Stephen Van Dulken, *Inventing the 20th Century: 100 Inventions that Shaped the World*, New York: New York University, 2000. www.tecta.de. www.anglepoise.com.

Casas, Pablo (1979–)
> See Nó Design.

Casas Mobilplast/Muebles Casas

Spanish furniture manufacturer; located Barcelona.

History 1961, the firm was founded by Óscar Tusquets Blanca, Lluís Clotet Ballús, Pep Bonet, and Cristian Cirici as an offshoot of the furniture workshop Casas of Carles Riart; from 1961, produced non-Spanish design under licenses; 1978, began production of its own collection. Initial production was of furniture in expanded polystyrene from Norway and, 1968 through an agreement with C&B Italia, production began of furniture models in polyurethane. Firm's products included 1984 Varius polyurethane, metal, and leather armchair by Óscar Tusquets Blanca.
Citations 1987 National Design Prize, Spain.

Casati, Cesare (1936–)

Italian designer.

Biography 1965 with Emanuele Ponzio, Casati established Studio DA (Designer Associati); designed interiors of hotels, banks, and other public buildings; clients included Phoebus, Nai Ponteur, and Autovox; is best known for the brightly colored 1968 Pillola 'medicine pill' lamp (with Ponzio), that has become an archetypal symbol of the era and a statement at the time of Radical-Design. Shaped like a medicine capsule, the lamp is composed of two vacuum-formed plastic sections (a white translucent upper section and a weighted base, in primary colors, green, or white, that sits on a clear acrylic ring), manufactured by Ponteur, Italy.
Bibliography Cat., *Lumière je pense à vous*, Paris: Centre Georges Pompidou, 1985. Cat., Hans Wichmann (ed.), *Italien Design 1945 bis heute*, Munich: Die Neue Sammlung, 1988.
> See Studio DA; C. Emanuele Ponzio; Radical-Design.

Casati, Giorgio (1942–)

Italian designer; born Giussano; active Milan.

Biography From 1965 with C. Emanuele Ponzio, Casati was active as

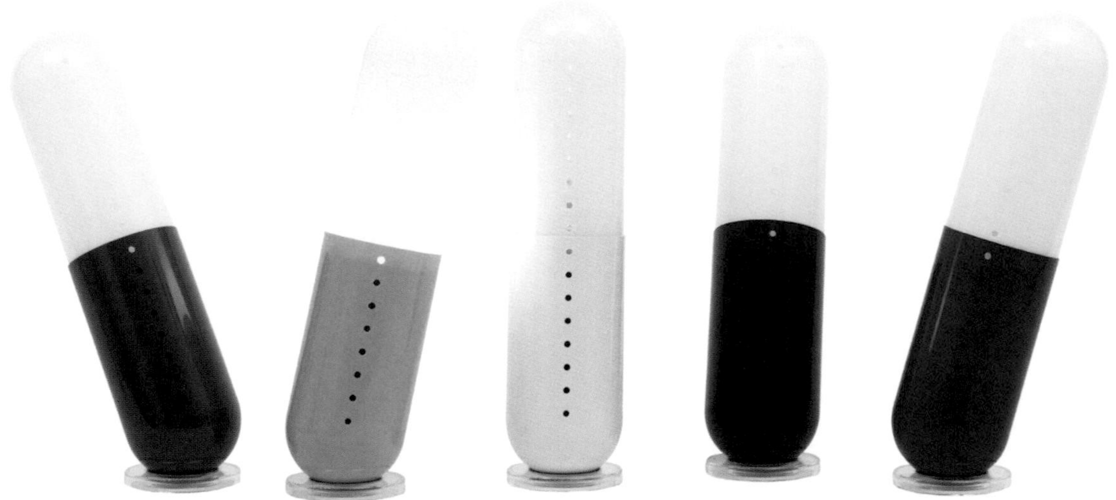

Cesare Casati and C. Emanuele Ponzio. Pillola lamps. 1968. ABS polymer and acrylic, each h. 21 3/4 x dia. 5 1/8" (55.2 x 13 cm). Mfr.: Ponteur, Italy. Celeste Bartos Purchase Fund. MoMA.

Cassina: Gaetano Pesce. Feltri chair. 1986. Wool felt and polyester resin, 50 1/8 x 55 1/8 x 28" (127.3 x 140 x 71.1 cm), seat h. 17 1/2" (44.5 cm). Mfr.: Cassina, Italy. Gift of the mfr. MoMA.

an industrial designer in Studio DA; from 1967, was coordinator and organizer of the furniture-production committee, Biennale dello Standard nell'Arredamento, Mariano; the office of economic problems in furniture production at the Mariano, Cantù, and Lissone events; and the provincial office for the promotion of exported furniture of Brianza at the Como, Cantù, and Mariano events. 1969 with Marcello De Carli, Casati proposed a school for professional design focusing on industrial furniture; 1972 with C. Conte, Leonardo Fiori, and C. Visani, developed a prefabricated system for the Edilizia Sociale e Scolastica building; from 1974, was active in textile-design education; from 1975, was a consultant on the Larco/System.
Bibliography *ADI Annual 1976*, Milan: Associazione per il Disegno Industriale, 1976.

Casciani, Stefano (1955–)

Italian architect and designer; born Rome; active Rome and Milan.

Training Architecture, Rome.
Biography Casciani produced industrial designs for Istituto Superiore di Disegno Industriale; from 1979, was associated with journal *Domus*; also wrote for *Modo* and *Raum*; from 1980, worked for Zanotta furniture company; taught architecture in Florence and Milan.
Exhibitions Participated in 1980 Biennale di Venezia and 1981 Triennale di Milano.
Bibliography Robert A.M. Stern (ed.), *The International Design Yearbook*, New York: Abbeville, 1985/1986.

Casimir (b. Casimir Reynders 1966–)

Belgian designer; born Koersel; husband of photographer Anna Leoni.

Training To 1991, industrial design, Stedelijk Hoger Instituut voor Visuelle Kommunikatie en Vormgeving, Genk, Belgium.
Biography From 1995, Casimir has worked as an independent furniture designer; from 1997, also as an architect and interior, exhibition, product, and graphic designer.
Exhibitions/citations Work shown at Intérieur 2000 biennial, Kortrijk, Belgium; 2001 Passagen section, Internationale Möbelmesse, Cologne; 2001 *Ambiance Magasin*, Abbey of Saint-André, Centre d'Art Contemporain, Meymac, France. 2001 Sporen van Kunst (to the Casimir office), Hasselt, Belgium.
Bibliography 'Casimir: Passie voor lijnen,' *Residence*, Apr. 2001: 61. 'Un style de vie globale: Een mondiale lifestyle,' *Villas*, Mar. 2001. 'Het geheim van België,' *Man*, Mar. 2001: 140–44. 'Sztuka upr szczania,' *Wnetrze*, Feb. 2001: 58–60. Mel Byars, *Design in Steel*, London: Laurence King, 2002. www.casimir.be.

Cassina (Cassina Amadeo)

Italian furniture manufacturer; located Meda (MI).

History 1927, founded by brothers Umberto Cassina (d. 1991) and Cesare Cassina (1908–1981), the Cassina Amadeo company was initially a shop for craft production. Early 1900s, the family turned from producing chairs and barrels to upholstered furniture; used outside craftspeople extensively. Its early work was principally produced for shops in Milan and large-scale middlemen; its designs were based on historicist 19th-century models. 1930s, the firm made armchairs and dining-room sets for La Rinascente department store and Mobilificio di Fogliano, both Milan; 1935, changed its name to Figli di Amadeo Cassina; 1937–39 focusing more on Rationalist models, built a new workshop; 1940, installed German and French machinery; began managing its own advertising and distribution. It belatedly moved into a modern style. Produced at first for single customer-decorators, contemporary pieces were put into limited production, although few were innovative. After World War II, Cassina expanded its production and distribution procedures; 1947–52, produced large quantities of furniture for the Italian navy; from 1950s, was an international success with a new generation of designers who thrust the firm into the forefront of modern design. There was a short collaboration with Paolo Buffa and a successful collaboration with architect-designer Franco Albini. The most fruitful design arrangement was with Gio Ponti, with whom Cesare Cassina worked from 1950 on furniture including the Distex armchair and 1951 Superleggera side chair, an international success that established Cassina's reputation and is still in production. 1960, Cassina began a relationship with Vico Magistretti; 1963, with Tobia Scarpa; from 1965, reproduced vintage modern designs under official licensing agreements, beginning with 1920s furniture of Le Corbusier, Jeanneret, and Perriand. Later reproductions included the furniture of Frank Lloyd Wright, Rietveld, Mackintosh, and others. Late 1980s, Cassina was amalgamated into Steelcase Group, and, subsequently, was sold to the Fimalac Group (with Fimalac, Alias, and Nemo Italianluce).
Bibliography Pier Carlo Santini, *Gli anni del design italiano: Ritratto di Cesare Cassina*, Milan: Electa, 1981. Penny Sparke, *Design in Italy, 1870 to the Present*, New York: Abbeville, 1988. 'La saggezza di Umberto,' *Ottagono*, no. 104, Sept. 1992: 61–64. www.cassina.it.

Castelli, Anna (1954–)
Italian designer; born and active Milan.

Training Scuola Politecnica di Disegno, Milan.
Biography From 1974, Castelli collaborated with Giorgio Brambilla, Fabio Stojan, and Lorenzo Tosi in the design studio Gruppo, Milan; with Bruno Munari and Brambilla, developed toys; while teaching at Facoltà di Architettura, Politecnico, Milan, participated in Montedison's office of accident prevention.
Bibliography *ADI Annual 1976*, Milan: Associazione per il Disegno Industriale, 1976.
> Not to be confused with Anna Castelli Ferrieri, which see.

Castelli, Clino (1944–)
Italian designer and design theorist; born Civitavecchia; active Milan.

Biography 1958, Castelli began working at Centro Stile, Fiat; from 1969, was a consultant at Olivetti with Ettore Sottsass; 1967 with Elio Fiorucci, founded Intrapresa Design; 1969, returned to Olivetti to work on its corporate-identity program and designed fabrics for Abet Print; 1973, with Andrea Branzi and Massimo Morozzi, organized Centro Design Montefibre; 1974, founded the studio CDM (now Castelli Design); 1978, established Colorterminal IVI, the first research and consulting center in Europe on color and design; 1979, cofounded Habitaco, owned by Fiat-Comind, where he became design coordinator; subsequently, worked for automobile firms and for 3M on lighting. Clients included Vitra, Herman Miller, Ermenegildo Zegna, Dartington Mills, Visconti di Modrone, Zanotta, Cassina, Sony, Canon, and Fiat.
Bibliography Andrea Branzi, *La casa calda: esperienze del nuovo disegno italiano*, Milan: Idea, 1982. *Modo*, no. 148, Mar.–Apr. 1993: 117. Clino Trini Castelli, *Transitive Design*, Milan: Electa, 1999.

Castelli, Giulio (1920–)
> See Kartell.

Castelli del Bue, Livia (1945–)
Italian industrial designer; born Rome; active Milan.

Biography 1971, Castelli del Bue began her professional career designing small domestic appliances, plastic kitchenware, and furniture. Her hair brushes were produced by Verbania. Clients in Italy have included Dal Vera, Elco, Fanini, Fain, Merlett, Mazzucchelli, Gedy, BBB Bonacina, and Chicco Arisana; others have included Domco Industries, Canada, and Meblo Jugoplastics, Yugoslavia (now Slovenia).
Bibliography *ADI Annual 1976*, Milan: Associazione per il Disegno Industriale, 1976.

Castelli Ferrieri, Anna (1918–)
Italian architect and designer; born and active Milan.

Training 1938–42, architecture, Politecnico, Milan.
Biography 1945, Ferrieri became founding member, Movimento Studi per l'Architettura, Milan; 1946–47, editor, journal *Casabella-costruzioni* and again, early 1950s, assistant editor; 1946, set up her own architecture office, Milan. From 1952, member, Istituto Nazionale di Urbanistica; 1955–60, architecture correspondent, *Architectural Design*; 1956, became a founding and honorary member, ADI, and its president 1969–71; 1959–73, partner of architect/designer Ignazio Gardella, working on public housing, town planning, and furniture design; with Gardella, designed pioneering plastic furniture for Kartell; from 1965, was active as an industrial designer; from 1966, consultant designer, Kartell, and, eventually, artistic director of its in-house design group, Centrokappa; was a plastics technology expert, designing injection-molded plastic chairs, tables, and storage systems. Her 4870 stacking armchair, which did not camouflage its crudely mixed polymer material, was influential. Architecture includes 1984–85 Parish Center, Casate, and 1983–85 Castek office building, Milan. 1984–86, was guest professor of industrial design at the Politecnico; from 1987, taught, Domus Academy, Milan; 1992, taught industrial design, RMIT Centre for Design, Melbourne; also lectured, Art Center College of Design, Pasadena, Cal. She wrote *Plastics and Design* (Milan: Arcadia, 1984) and *The Interfaces of Materials* (Milan: Domus Academy, 1991).1990 with Luca Piatti, she established ACF Officina, a young architects and designers group.
Exhibitions/citations Work shown at numerous exhibitions, beginning with 1968 *Design Italian Style*, Hallmark Gallery, New York. Triennali di Milano: two gold medals 1947 (8th) and one gold medal 1950 (9th) editions; 1968 Oscar Plast; 1969 silver medal, Österreichisches Bauzentrum, Vienna; 1972 gold medal, Mostra Internazionale Arredamento (MIA), Monza; 1972 prize, Mostra di Articoli Casalinghi e Ferramenta (MACEF), Milan; 1973 Bundespreis Produktdesign, Rat für Formgebung (German design council), Frankfurt; 1977 Premio SMAU Industrial Design, Salone della Machina e Attrezzature per l'Ufficio, Milan; 1979 Product Design award, Resources Council, US; 1954, 1970, 1979 (seven citations), 1981, 1984, 1987 (five citations), 1991, 1994 Premio Compasso d'Oro and ten special mentions in 1970, 1972, 1979, and 1984; 1981 design award, American Society of Interior Designers (ASID); gold medal, 1981 BIO 9 industrial-design biennial, Ljubljana; 1982 design award, Internationale Möbelmesse, Cologne; 1996 and 2000 Good Design awards, Chicago Athenaeum; 1998 award, Annual Design Review, *I.D.* magazine.
Bibliography Alfonso Grassi and Anty Pansera, *Atlante del design italiano 1940/1980*, Milan: Fabbri, 1980. Andrea Branzi and Michele De Lucchi, *Design italiano degli anni '50*, Milan: Ricerche Design, 1985. Fumio Shimizu and Studio Matteo Thun (eds.), *The Italian Design: Descendants of Leonardo da Vinci*, Tokyo: Graphic-sha, 1987. Cristina Morozzi, *Anna Castelli Ferrieri*, Bari: Laterza, 1993.

Castiglioni, Giorgina (1943–)
Italian designer; active Milan.

Training To 1969, architecture, Politecnico, Milan.
Biography 1971, Castiglioni began her professional career designing furniture and lighting. Clients (in Italy) included Audiomatic, Bilumen, Crien, Elle, Gufram, Kartell, Pedano, Sirrah, and Valenti; and Sirrah Iberica, Barcelona.
Citations First prize (plastic seating by Kartell), 1965 Fiera di Trieste. Participated in 1971 UCIMU competition of Associazione per il Disegno Industriale (ADI); first prize, 2001 Grandesign, Milan.
Bibliography *ADI Annual 1976*, Milan: Associazione per il Disegno Industriale, 1976.

Castiglioni, Livio (1911–1979)
Italian industrial designer; active Milan; brother of Pier Giacomo Castiglioni and Achille Castiglioni.

Training To 1936, architecture, Politecnico, Milan.
Biography 1938–40, Livio Castiglioni and brother Pier Giacomo with Luigi Caccia Dominioni were active in a studio in Milan. Their best-known work of this period includes 1938 silver and aluminum cutlery and the first (1939–40) Italian all-plastic radio (no. 547, in Bakelite) by Phonola. The cutlery, called the Caccia, has been produced by Alessi from 1990 with originally unrealized pieces added to the range. The claims of the Phonola radio's being the first-ever mass-produced plastic object in Italy and the first true, non-furniture radio are unfounded. 1940–60, Livio Castiglioni was a consultant to Phonola; 1960–64, consultant and an agent to Brionvega; from 1946, collaborator on audio-visual

Anna Castelli Ferrieri. Cabinet (no. 4970). 1967. Cycolac plastic, 9 1/16 x 15 x 15" (23 x 38 x 38 cm). Mfr.: Kartell, Italy. Courtesy Quittenbaum Kunstauktionen, Munich.

technology to Radio Televisione Italiana, Montecatini Edison, Fiat, Eni, Italsider, Osram, Eurodomus fairs, La Rinascente department store, and Olivetti; to c. 1952, had pursued lighting design, sometimes collaborating with brothers Pier Giacomo and Achille; 1956, was a cofounder of Associazione per il Disegno Industriale (ADI) and president 1959–60. His lighting work often incorporated industrial materials and new types of bulbs, including 1970 Boalum snake-like lighting (with Gianfranco Frattini) by Artemide.
Exhibitions/citations Livio designed audio-visual presentations, Italian pavilion (with Umberto Eco), 1967 *Universal and International Exhibition (Expo '67)*, Montréal; with Davide Boriani, designed the audio-visuals in the experimental section, 1970 (35th) Biennale di Venezia. Gold medal (with others), 1936 (6th) Triennale di Milano; grand prize (design) and gold medal (audio-visual environment), 1940 (7th) Triennale (introduction of the 1938 cutlery collaboration); grand prize (audio-visual environment), 1965 (13th) Triennale; 1968 gold medal for Pioneering Industrial Design. Jury member, 1954 (10th) Triennale; 1991 (for Caccia cutlery) Premio Compasso d'Oro.
Bibliography Paolo Fossati, *Il design in italia*, Turin: Einaudi, 1972. *ADI Annual 1976*, Milan: Associazione per il Disegno Industriale, 1976. Alfonso Grassi and Anty Pansera, *Atlante del design italiano 1940/1980*, Milan: Fabbri, 1980. Andrea Branzi and Michele De Lucchi (eds.), *Design italiano degli anni '50*, Milan: Ricerche Design Editrice, 1985. Daniele Baroni, *L'oggetto lampada forme e funzione...*, Milan: Electa, 1981. Cat., *Lumière je pense à vous*, Paris: Centre Georges Pompidou, 1985. Cat., Paolo Ferrari (ed.), *Castiglioni*, Milan: Electa; Paris: Centre Georges Pompidou, 1985.

Castiglioni, Pier Giacomo (1913–1968); Castiglioni, Achille (1918–2002)

Italian designers; active Milan; brothers of Livio Castiglioni.

Training To 1937 and 1944, respectively, architecture, Politecnico, Milan.
Biography 1938–40, Pier Giacomo Castiglioni and brother Livio set up a studio with Luigi Caccia Dominioni (see Livio Catiglioni for partial activities). 1945, Pier Giacomo and Achille began collaborating separately from Livio, though participating with him occasionally, and also collaborated with other designers. The Castiglioni brothers were instrumental in founding the Triennale di Milano, 1954 founding of Premio Compasso d'Oro citiation, and 1956 founding of Associazione per il Disegno Industriale (ADI); collaborated on journal *Stile Industria*; taught architecture in Milan and Turin, together and separately. Their collaboration on exhibition and product design lasted 25 years. Using industrial materials, experimental forms, and advanced technology, they also produced lighting. The brothers' notable exhibition-design work was for 1958 Radio Exhibition and 1962 Montecantini Pavilion, both at the Milan fairs. They went on to design in plastics; ceramics; glassware; appliances by Nova Radio (1956 six-valve radio), Elettrodomestici, and Brionvega; metalware by Alessi; earphones by Phoebus Alter; and furniture by Kartell, Bernini, Zanotta, and Gavina. Other clients included Knoll, Lancia, Siemens, Gilardi e Barzaghi, Fonderie Perani, SLM, S. Giorgio, B&B Italia, Poggi, Ideal Standard, Bonacina, Bacci, Rem, and OMSA. 1965–77, Achille was head of Facoltà di Architettura, Politecnico, Milan, and lectured there until his death, influencing generations of architects/designers; 1983, began working with Danese; tended to continue with the same, established stable of manufacturers. His 1982 Dry cutlery by Alessi proved popular. Continuing prolifically until his death in Milan, designed 1999 40/80 suspended-cloth lounge chair by Moroso and others.
Work Their lighting included the 1949 Tubino desk lamp by Arredoluce, 1950 Taraxacum hanging lamp by Flos, 1951 hanging lamp by Castaldi, 1954 street lamp by Pollice, and 1955 Luminator indirect light by Gilardi. Their best-known designs include 1956 Spalter vacuum cleaner by Rem, 1962 Arco lamp and 1972 Toio lamp by Flos adapted from an automobile headlight, 1957 Mezzadro seat designed with Pier Giacomo (a supported tractor seat, produced by Zanotta from 1971), 1979 Cumano folding metal tables by Zanotta. Achille's work included 1980–84 oil and vinegar flasks by Alessi; 1980 Gibigiana lamp and 1985 Grip lamp by Flos; 1982 Solone table system by Marcatré; 1983 Poltrona Imperiale chair, 1983 Rosacamuna chair, 1984 Cot bench, 1986 flagpoles, 1986 Spluga stool, and 1983 Alberto flowerpot holder by Zanotta; 1983 Paro drinking glasses by Danese; 1984 Cinque C door handle by Fusital; and 1986 Itititi bed (with Giancarlo Pozzi) by Interflex.
Exhibitions/citations Work included in 1984 *Design Since 1945*, Philadelphia Museum of Art; 1985 *Lumière Je Pense à Vous* (catalog below); 1991 *Mobili Italiani 1961–1991: Le Varie Età dei Linguaggi*, Salone del Mobile, Milan. Subject of 1984–86 touring exhibition, originating at Triennale di Milano; 1997–98 *Achille Castiglioni: Design!*, The

Achille Castiglioni, Pier Giacomo Castiglioni, and Livio Castiglioni. Mezzadro seat. 1957. Tractor seat, steel, and beech, 20 1/4 x 19 1/2 x 20 1/4" (51.4 x 49.5 x 51.4 cm). Mfr.: Zanotta, Italy (1971). Gift of the mfr. MoMA.

Museum of Modern Art, New York; others. Achille's lighting subject of 1987 exhibition, Center for the Fine Arts, Miami. The brothers participated in editions of Triennale di Milano, 1947 (8th) to 1964 (13th); Achille alone thereafter. With Livio and Pier Giacomo to their deaths, individually, and/or with others, Achille received 1955, 1957, 1960, 1962, 1964, 1967, 1979, 1981, 1984, 1987, 1989, 1991, 1994 Premio Compasso d'Oro; 1986, elected Honorary Royal Designer for Industry, UK.
Bibliography Agnoldomenico Pica, 'Piergiacomo Castiglioni,' *Domus*, no. 470, Jan. 1969: 1–2. Vittorio Gregotti, 'Ricordo di Pier Giacomo Castiglioni,' *Ottagono*, no. 12, Jan. 1969: 20–23. Paolo Fossati, *Il design in Italia*, Turin: Einaudi, 1972: 122–27, 224–33, pls. 310–54. Andrea Branzi and Michele De Lucchi, *Design italiano degli anni '50*, Milan: Ricerche Design Editrice, 1985. Alfonso Grassi and Anty Pansera, *Atlante del design italiano 1940/1980*, Milan: Fabbri, 1980: 279. Daniele Baroni, *L'oggetto lampada forme e funzione...*, Milan: Electa, 1981: 128–37, figs. 292–321. Cat., *Lumière je pense à vous*, Paris: Centre Georges Pompidou, 1985. Cat., Paolo Ferrari (ed.), *Castiglioni*, Milan: Electa/Paris: Centre Georges Pompidou. 1985. Juli Capella and Quim Larrea, *Designed by Architects in the 1980s*, New York: Rizzoli, 1988. Paola Antonelli, Steven Guarnaccia (illus.), *Achille Castiglioni*, Mantua: Corraini, 2001. Sergio Polano, *Achille Castiglioni: opera completa*, Milan: Electa/Elemond, 2001. Paola Antonelli (ed.), *Objects of Design: The Museum of Modern Art*, New York: The Museum of Modern Art, 2003: 198, 210, 252, 256.

Castle, Wendell (1932–)

American furniture designer; born Emporia, Kansas.

Training To 1961, industrial design and sculpture, University of Kansas, Lawrence, Kan.
Biography Early 1960s, Castle taught, School of American Craftsmen, Rochester, N.Y., and established a studio there; was head, woodworking department, Rochester Institute of Technology. Stylistically, his furniture can often be grouped by the different approaches he takes to the base; later designed and produced one-of-a-kind furniture in provocative forms and pioneered a technique in which he used stacked, laminated wood, carved into biomorphic chairs and other seating forms; designed the idiosyncratic *Library of Dr. Caligari* installation in the residence of furniture collector Peter Joseph, New York, who underwrote Castle's Angel Chair project. Unusual in his single-example woodcarving work, the 1969 Molar two-seater sofa was mass-produced in fiberglass. He also designed very-limited-edition plastic furniture. His whole œuvre, though difficult to place within a

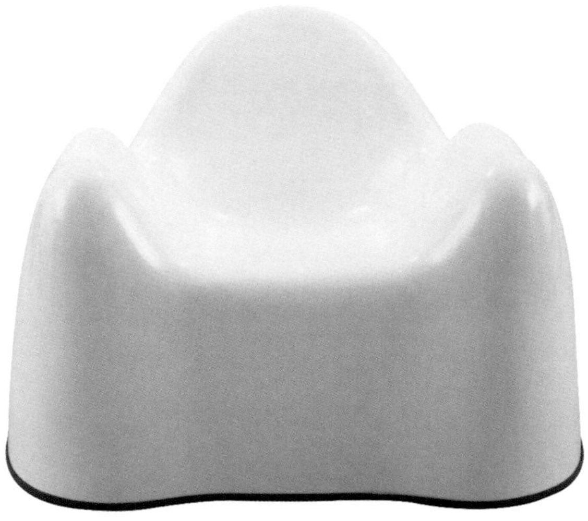

Wendell Castle. Molar chair. 1969. Glass-reinforced polyester, 25 x 37 x 31" (63.5 x 94 x 78.8 cm). Mfr.: Northern Plastics, US. Andrew Cogan Purchase Fund. MoMA.

movement, appears to have been inspired by Art Nouveau and the Arts and Crafts movement. Late 1960s, his furniture featured fiberglass-coated plastic and metal cones. Inspired by Italian Pop furniture, he designed for Beylerian and Stendig, with his small-production Molar sofa and chair a playful example by the former; was chairperson, sculpture department, State University of New York, Brockport. Of his work as a whole, he has written his goal to be the creation of a piece that 'performs some useful function in addition to, I hope, being beautiful.'
Exhibitions/citations Work subject of 1969 exhibition, Wichita, Kan. (catalog below); 1989, Detroit, Mich.; 1991 exhibition touring the US, including American Craft Museum, New York; 1991, Peter Joseph Gallery, New York, where Angel Chair project was introduced; 1994, Duxbury, Mass. (catalogs below). 1994 Visionaries of the American Craft Movement award, American Craft Museum, New York; 1997 gold medal, American Craft Council; grants, National Endowment for the Arts and the Louis Comfort Tiffany Foundation.
Bibliography Cat., *The Furniture of Wendell Castle*, Wichita: Wichita Art Museum, 1969. *Wooden Works: Five Objects by Five Contemporary Craftsmen*, Washington: Renwick Gallery, 1972. *Fine Art of a Furniture Maker: Conversations with Wendell Castle*, Rochester: Memorial at Gallery of University of Rochester, 1981. Patricia Bayer, *The Fine Art of the Furniture Maker* (conversations with Wendell Castle and Penelope Hunter-Stiebel, curator, about selected works from The Metropolitan Museum of Art), Rochester, N.Y.: Memorial Art Gallery, University of Rochester, 1981. Cat., Davira Spiro Taragin et al., *Furniture of Wendell Castle*, New York: Rizzoli with Detroit Institute of Arts, 1989. Cat., Arthur C. Danto, *Angel Chairs: New Works by Wendell Castle*, New York: Peter Joseph Gallery, 1991. Cat., *Wendell Castle: Environmental Works*, New York: The Gallery, 1993. 'Wendell Castle: miscellaneous uncataloged materials' (clippings, invitations, etc.), Washington, D.C.: National Museum of American Art/National Portrait Gallery Library Vertical Files, no. ACQ3029LB.

Caturegli, 'Beppe' Giuseppe (1957–)

Italian architect and designer; born Pisa.

Training Architecture, Università degli Studi, Florence.
Biography From 1982, Caturegli worked at Sottsass Associati, Milan; 1987 with Giovanella Formica, opened a studio in Milan and pursued architectural projects (Italy and India) and industrial design projects for Sanjo (Japan) and Max Ray; from 1993, were advisers to Computer Associates, planning its Italian branches in Milan and Rome. Caturegli designed 1984 jewelry (produced from 1985), Acme Studios.
Citations Award, New Architecture Design competition; first prize (with Formica), residential-settlement invitation competition, Italy; first prize (with Formica), 1993 Pantone European Colour Awards for Architecture.
Bibliography Fumio Shimizu and Studio Matteo Thun (eds.), *The Italian Design: Descendants of Leonardo da Vinci*, Tokyo: Graphic-sha, 1987.
> See Formica, Giovanella.

Cavaillon, Gaston

French furniture designer.

Biography Cavaillon designed the inexpensive c. 1945 510 chair of which c. 350,000 copies, produced by Mullca, were sold at less than $25 (c. 30 euros) to colleges, universities, and other institutions. Is aka the UGAP chair due to its purchase by the Union des Groupements d'Achat Publics, French purchasing agency for institutional goods.

Cavallaro, Liana (1965–)

Italian designer and goldsmith.

Training 1980, goldsmithing; 1985, languages; 1986–87, Dipartimento di Musica e Spettacolo (DAMS), Università degli Studi, Bologna; 1988, Polytecnico, Milan.
Biography From 1990, she collaborated with architect Ettore Sottsass. Her projects have included work for Philips, Alessi, Rash, Swid Powel, Venini, Twergi, Vitra, Poltronova, Interflex, and Sèvres, and domestic and office interiors and furnishings, such as for Hamano Institute, Tokyo. Was involved in organizing exhibitions such as 1990 *Ettore Sottsass Senior*, museums in Trento and Rovereto; 1990 *Energieen*, Stedelijk Museum, Amsterdam; 1991 *Abitareitalia*, Tokyo; 1992 *Rovine*, Design Gallery Milano; 1993 *Ettore Sottsass*, Cunvent de Catalunja, Barcelona, 1993 *Ettore Sottsass, Adesso Però*, Deichtorhallen Museum, Hamburg; and 1994 Ettore Sottsass exhibition, Centre Georges Pompidou, Paris.

Cavart

Italian design group.

History Active in Padova 1973–76, Cavart was founded by then-students Michele De Lucchi, Piero Brombin, Piera Paola Bortolami, Boris Premrù, and Valerio Tridenti. The name derives from *cava* (quarry). A contemporary of Global Tools and the Anti-Design movement, the group organized events in and around the quarries of Florence, which served as natural amphitheaters. At one meeting, participants designed paper shirts that they wore and, 1975, copied Pablo Picasso's *Guernica* to show in the main squares of Milan, Venice, and Padova to protest the violation of human rights, particularly in Chile; the copy created for Bologna was destroyed. 1975, about 100 architects, artists, and students attended Cavart's 'Architettura Impossibile' meeting, where utopian structures were designed in, and in some cases built in, the quarries at Monselice, near Padova. Cavart's films, happenings, performances, and contests were manifestations of the Anti-Design movement in Italy.
Bibliography 'Itinerario di Guernica,' *Casabella*, no. 406, 1975: 10–13. Cat., *Michele De Lucchi*, The Hague: Komplement, 1985.

Cazin, Jean-Charles (1841–1901)

French painter ceramicist; born Samer (Pas-de-Calais).

Training École Gratuite de Dessin, Paris; in the studio of Lecoq de Boisbaudran.
Biography Cazin is considered to have been a precursor of the ceramics-arts revival; 1863, taught, École Speciale d'Architecture, Paris; 1868, was head, Musée de Dessin and École de Dessin, Tours; 1871, worked at Fulham Pottery, London, where he made brown sandstone pottery tableware, influenced by Japanese ware; returned to Paris and turned again to painting.
Exhibitions Work shown 1882 exhibition, Union Centrale; other venues, particularly 1897 Salon of the Société Nationale des Beaux-Arts.
Bibliography Léonce Bénédite, 'J.-C. Cazin,' in *Art et décoration: revue mensuelle d'art moderne*, Paris: Emile Lévy-Librairie Centrale des Beaux-Arts, tome 2, July–Dec. 1897 Léonce Bénédite, *Jean-Charles Cazin*, Paris: Librarie de l'Art Ancien et Moderne, n.d. *Europäische Keramik, 1880–1930: Sammlung Silzer*, Darmstadt: Hessisches Landesmuseum, 1986: 77.

C&B Italia
> See B&B Italia.

CCI (Centre de Création Industrielle)

French design organization.

History 1969, CCI was founded by François Mathey, Yolande Amic, and François Barré; was modeled on London and Brussels design centers. Mathey was chief curator at Musée des Arts Décoratifs, Paris, when Barré proposed the idea of a French design center. CCI operated

an information center for business people, students, and designers, and became a department of Centre Georges Pompidou, Paris.
Exhibitions Its first exhibition (furniture by Roger Tallon, Charles Eames, Joe Colombo, and others) was 1969 *Qu'est ce que le design?* and 1971 *Le Design Français* was dedicated to young designers.

CDM (Consulenti Design Milano)

Italian design firm.

History 1973, CDM was founded by Andrea Branzi, Gianni Cutolo, Alessandro Mendini, Clino Trini Castelli, and Ettore Sottsass with the intention of handling large-scale projects, such as corporate-identity programs and landscapes, and conducting advanced research. Commissions included Leonardo da Vinci airport (landscape and corporate image), Rome; new Italian post offices (information system); Louis Vuitton (products); first center of Colorterminal (creative colorimetrics); Piaggio (color system); and 1973–77 work on Centro Design Montefibre.
Citations 1979 Premio Compasso d'Oro (Fibermatching 25-Meracion by A. Branzi, C.T. Castelli, M. Morozzi, and CIM).
Bibliography Alfonso Grassi and Anty Pansera, *Atlante del design italiano 1940/1980*, Milan: Fabbri, 1980: 295. Andrea Branzi, *La casa calda: esperienze del nuovo disegno italiano*, Milan: Idea, 1982. Cat., Hans Wichmann (ed.), *Italien Design 1945 bis heute*, Munich: Die Neue Sammlung, 1988.

Ceccariglia, Carla (1955–)

Italian designer; born Rome; active Milan.

Training Industrial Design Institute of Art, Rome.
Biography 1979–80, Ceccariglia worked with Enzo Mari and on the staff of Decòro at the Centrodomus Studio; 1981, joined Studio Alchimia; was in charge of textile design and clothing by Limonta.
Bibliography Kazuko Sato, *Alchimia*, Berlin: Taco, 1988.

CEI (Compagnie de l'Esthétique Industrielle)

French design firm.

History 1951, CEI was established by Raymond Loewy, Paris; for 25 years, produced a wide variety and large number of designs. Loewy was French, primarily active in New York, with other offices elsewhere. CEI played an important role in promoting the spread of Loewy's American-style industrial design and the culture of consumption in postwar Europe. CEI's best-known works are late-1950s cookware by Le Creuset; 1965 Elna Lotus (CEI's only sewing-machine design, with Douglas Kelley and Roger Riche [1930–]) by Tavaro; 1968 DF 2000 range of cabinets by Doubinsky Frères; and, for Air France, meal ware and interior of the first (1976) Concorde (with the meal tray produced by Christofle). 1982, CEI was taken over by five of its former employees; mainly designs industrial products.
Bibliography P. Descargues, 'Compagnie de l'Esthétique Industrielle (CEI), Raymond Loewy, Paris,' *Graphis*, vol. 22, no. 128, 1966.
> See Gautier-Delaye, Pierre; Loewy, Raymond.

CEI (Compagnie de l'Esthétique Industrielle), Douglas Kelley, and Roger Riche (1930–). Elna Lotus sewing machine. 1965. Lacquered aluminum casing, 9 1/4 x 12 1/8 x 4 7/8" (23.5 x 30.8 x 12.4 cm). Mfr.: Tavaro, Switzerland. Gift of the mfr. MoMA.

Celada, Gianni (1935–)

Italian designer; born and active Milan.

Biography 1961, Celada began his professional career; was artistic consultant, FontanaArte, and designed its 1970 Katiuscia medicine-capsule-shaped table lamp in ABS and others. Other works has included furniture, lighting, and shelving systems for clients including Saint-Gobain, Cedit, Reflex-Vastill, Lar, and Giancarlo Pozzi.
Bibliography *ADI Annual 1976*, Milan: Associazione per il Disegno Industriale, 1976.

celluloid

Plastic material.

History Celluloid nitrate was the first plastic. 1865, a patent for its commercial application was applied for. 1899, casein, a type of protein plastic, was produced in Germany and used for buttons and jewelry, thanks to its ability to hold bright colors. After World War I, cellulose acetate was developed and used for fabrics, still-picture film, motion-picture film, and, later, injection-molded toilet articles and buttons, and, as early as 1870s, artificial teeth.
Bibliography Friedrich Böckmann *Celluloid: Its Raw Material, Manufacture, Properties and Uses*, London: Scott, Greenwood & Sons, 1921 (3rd. ed.). Gustav Bonwitt, *Das Celluloid und seine Ersatzstoffe...*, Berlin: Union Deutsche, Zweigniederlassung Berlin, 1933. Robert D. Friedel, *Men, Materials and Ideas: A History of Celluloid*, Ann Arbor, Mich.: University Microfilms, 1981. Robert D. Friedel, *Pioneer Plastic: The Making and Selling of Celluloid*, Madison, Wis.: University of Wisconsin, 1983.

Cenedese, Gino (1907–1973)

Italian glass manufacturer; born Murano.

Training 1925–31, glassblowing at Maestri Vetrai Muranesi Cappellin & C., Murano.
Biography Cenedese did not continue glass blowing following his training. However, 1946 with Gino Fort, Pietro Scaramal, Angelo Tosi, and Edgardo Valmarana, he cofounded Gino Cenedese S.r.l.; directed the firm, which achieved immediate success, until his death. The firm was known as Gino Cenedese S.r.l. 1946–47, Gino Cenedese & C. 1947–50, Gino Cenedese 1950–64, Vetreria Artistica Cenedese 1964–73, and Gino Cenedese & Figlio from 1973. 1947–50, Alfredo Barbini was active there as an owner, designer, and master glassblower. The firm has developed a number of techniques, including *scavo* (rough, matt surface suggesting antiquity) and the application of minerals to surfaces. 1950s, Antonio Da Ros designed transparent sculpture; from 1965, was its chief designer. On Gino's 1973 death, the ownership passed to his son Amelio Cenedese (1946–). 1993, the firm acquired the name of former glass factory Seguso Vetri d'Arte, which had closed in 1992.
Bibliography Cat., *Venini and Murano Renaissance: Italian Art Glass of the 1940s and 50s*, New York: Fifty/50, 1984. Helmut Ricke and Eva Schmitt, *Italian Glass, Murano, Milan, 1930–1970...*, New York: Prestel, 1997.

Century Guild, The

British cooperative; located London.

History 1882, The Century Guild was formed by A.J. Mackmurdo and Selwyn Image and included Herbert P. Horne, sculptor Benjamin Creswick, stained-glass designer, enamelist, and metalworker Clement Heaton, and metalworkers George Esling and Kellock Brown. Heywood Sumner and William De Morgan were also associated with the group. Members executed decorative work of all types, much of it shown as cooperative work. The first issue of the Guild magazine, *The Hobby Horse*, printed at the Chiswick Press, appeared 1884; next issue 1886. Successful to 1888, the Guild was less productive subsequently, although members continued to work together. Among the first of the crafts guilds, it exerted a great influence on the Craft Revival movement.
Exhibitions Guild's stand at 1886 *Liverpool Exhibition* influenced interior decoration at the turn of 19th century. Music Room (furnished and designed by members), first shown at 1884 *Health Exhibition*, and with minor changes at 1887 *Inventions Exhibition*; both London.
Bibliography Isabelle Anscombe and Charlotte Gere, *Arts and Crafts in Britain and America*, New York: Rizzoli, 1978: 111.

Donald T. Chadwick and William Stumpf. Aeron office chair. 1992. Structure: Glass-reinforced polyester and die-cast aluminum, and pellicle: Hytrel polymer, polyester, and Lycra, h. 37 1/4 to 43 x w. 28 1/2 x d. 28 1/2" (94.6 to 109.2 x 72.4 x 72.4 cm). Mfr.: Herman Miller, US. Gift of the employees of Herman Miller. MoMA.

Cerri, Pierluigi (1939–)

Italian architect and industrial, graphic, and exhibition designer.

Training Architecture, Politecnico, Milan.
Biography Cerri was a partner in architecture firm Gregotti Associati; designed 1976 Biennale di Venezia, for Electa publishing company, and for Palazzo Grassi, Venice; was a designer of books and the art director of journals *Rassegna* and *Casabella*, editor of the latter, and associated with journal *Lotus International*; was responsible for graphic design series Pagina. Industrial-design clients have included B&B Italia, Fiat, IBM, Molteni, Unifor, Missoni, and Marotto. Operating as Studio Cerri & Associati, designed 1997 Lola hard-leather side chair and 2000 Donald fused-aluminum and leather folding chair by Poltrona Frau. Exhibition designs have included 1978 *Peter Behrens und die AEG*, Berlin; 1978 *Carrozzeria Italiana*, Turin and Rome; 1981 *Identité Italienne*, Centre Georges Pompidou, Paris; 1983 *Alexander Calder*, Turin; 1984 *Italian Design*, Stuttgart and Tokyo; 1984 *Venti Progetti per il Futuro del Lingotto*, Turin; and 1986 *Futurismo e Futurismi*, Venice.
Exhibitions Okuspokus armoire-vitrine shown at 1983 (17th) Triennale di Milano.
Bibliography Auction cat., *Asta di Modernariato 1900–1986*, Auction cat., *Modernariato*, Milan: Semenzato Nuova Geri, 8 Oct. 1986. Juli Capella and Quim Larrea, *Designed by Architects in the 1980s*, New York: Rizzoli, 1988.

César (aka César Baldaccini 1921–1998)

French sculptor; born Marseille; active Paris.

Training École des Beaux-Arts, Marseilles; École Nationale Supérieure, Paris.
Biography Late 1950s, César was first recognized as an artist with his assemblages of scrap from a suburban foundry and went on to compress old cars and combine other junk as sulptural compositions; 1960s, began to design in crystal, encouraged by Jacques Daum; 1970s–80s, experimented with synthetic materials; used expanding plastic-foam in his sculpture as well as in his furniture, including 1968 prototype lounge chair in expanded foam by Le Mobilier National; as a designer, is best known for 1969 César chair by Zol in carved wood in the shape of a hand; 1965, made a 6 ft. (1.85 cm) enlargement of his thumb and, subseqently, 40 ft. (12 m) version in La Défense, near Paris.
Exhibitions/citations 1954, work was first the subject of an exhibition, Paris. Represented in French pavilion, 1956 Biennale di Venezia, and 1959 Documenta 2, Kassel. Shown worldwide, including 1961 *Modern Jewellery Exhibition*, London; experimental furniture, 1962 *Antagonisme II: L'Objet* (organized by François Mathey), and 1968 *Les Assises du Siège Contemporain*, both Musée des Arts Décoratifs, Paris. César chair included 1970 Internationale Möbelmesse, Cologne, and 1970 *Modern Chairs* exhibition (catalog below). Work by Cristallerie Daum subject of exhibition (organized by F. Mathey), Musée des Arts Décoratifs, Paris.1957, first prize as foreign sculptor, Carrara.
Bibliography Cat., *Les assises du siège contemporain*, Paris: Musée des Arts Décoratifs, 1968. Cat., *Modern Chairs 1918–1970*, London: Lund Humphries, 1971. Cat., *Verriers français contemporains: Art et industrie*, Paris: Musée des Arts Décoratifs, 1982. Otto Hahn, *César*, Lausanne: Favre, 1988. Cat., *César*, Paris: Galerie Nationale du Jeu de Paume: Gallimard/Réunion des Musées Nationaux, 1997.

Chabanne; Chabanne-Brugère

French metalworkers; located Thiers.

History 1912, Chabanne was founded by François Chabanne; in the beginning, produced cutlery. 1924, the family of Brugère joined the firm, thus renamed Chabanne-Brugère. Production included the use of stainless steel from 1930, silver from 1953.

Chadwick, Donald T. (1936–)

American furniture designer; born Los Angeles.

Training 1959, industrial design, University of California, Los Angeles.
Biography Chadwick worked for architect Victor Gruen; 1964, set up his own practice, Los Angeles; 1977 with William Stumpf, established design studio Chadwick, Stumpf and Associates in Winona, Minn., and designed 1974 Chadwick Modular Seating, 1979 C-Forms office system, ergonomic 1984 Equa 1 flexing-plastic chair (over 3 million sold), 1995 Equa 2, and Equa Rocker. The best-known of their chairs is the highly successful 1992 Aeron office chair. All were by Herman Miller Furniture Company, which also produced their Arrio Freestanding Furniture (with Jack Kelley). Subsequently, Chadwick established Don Chadwick & Associates in Santa Monica, Cal.
Citations 1970, 1971, 1973, 1974 Design Excellence, *I.D.* magazine; 1977 Governor's Award, *Design Michigan* exhibition; 1980 awards (for casegoods), Institute of Business Designers (IBD), and Industrial Designers Society of America (IDSA); 1984 gold medal (for Equa 1), IBD; 1986 International Product Design award, American Society of Interior Designers (ASID); 1990 Design: Best of the Decade (for Equa 1), *Time* magazine; 1992 first-place award for seating, IBD; Design Inno-vations 95 award, Design Zentrum, Germany.
Bibliography Cat., Paola Antonelli, *Mutant Materials in Contemporary Design*, New York: The Museum of Modern Art/Abrams, 1995. Cat., R. Craig Miller (intro.), *U.S. Design: 1975–2000*, Munich: Prestel, 2002. Paola Antonelli (ed.), *Objects of Design: The Museum of Modern Art*, New York: The Museum of Modern Art, 2003: 170.

Chafik, Gasmi (1962–)

Algerian furniture designer; born Algiers; active Paris.

Training Architecture, Paris-Tolbiac University.
Biography Chafik intended to be an architect but, 1989, set up his own furniture-production firm Univers Intérieur; designed 1990 Monsieur, Madame, Mademoiselle, and Culbuto chairs and some furniture was produced through his own firm. Other designs: Simple-X chair/table and Opaline resin folding chair by Moulin Galland, Ying club chair by Hugues Chevalier, layout of Sephora store in Tokyo.
Exhibitions/citations From 1991, work shown at Salons du Meuble, Paris. 1991 citation (for Sellette Gazelle), VIA (French furniture association); 1992 Grand Prix de la Critique et de la Presse, Salon du Meuble, Paris.
Bibliography François Mathey, *Au bonheur des formes, design français 1945–1992*, Paris: Regard, 1992: 265. Cat., Sophie Tasma

Anargyros et al., *L'école française: les créateurs de meubles du 20ème siècle*, Paris: Industries Françaises de l'Ameublement, 2000. www.via.asso.fr.

Chaix, Philippe (1949–); Jean-Paul Morel (1949–)

French architects and designers.

Biography Chaix first came to prominence with the design of 1984 Zénith concert hall, Parc de La Villette, Paris, and the *Tepee* temporary exhibition there. Other exhibition designs have been of Toulouse-Lautrec, 1992, Grand Palais. Other French architecture includes archeology-museum layout, Saint-Romain-en-Gal; the Avancée wing, Renault Technocentre, Guyancourt; École Nationale des Ponts et Chaussées and École Nationale des Sciences Géographiques, Marne-la-Vallée; teepee reception space, Centre Georges Pompidou, Paris. While primarily active as architects, they founded a design workshop where they pursue experimentations in glass and new materials, and work from there has included 1991 glass Tables de Verre I and II by Sté Forma, Paris, and Tepee range (wood-multiply-cardboard table and fiber-and-cardboard chair).
Exhibitions/citations Work subject of 1995 exhibition, Galerie Plan Venise, Paris. Creators of the Year, 1996 Salon du Meuble, Paris.
Bibliography Mel Byars, *50 Tables: Innovations in Design and Materials*, Hove: RotoVision, 1997. Arlette Barré-Despond (ed.), *Dictionnaire international des arts appliqués et du design*, Paris: Regard, 1996.

Chalon, Louis (1866–1916)

French painter and designer; active Paris.

Training Under Jules Lefebre and Boulanger, painting.
Biography Chalon began his career as a painter and illustrator, illuminating Rabelais, Boccaccio, and Balzac novels; 1898, was commissioned to produce a series of *trompe-l'œil* illustrations to mimic white-and-blue porcelain; by 1900, had become an accomplished illustrator and rendered drawings for periodicals *Figaro illustré*, *L'illustration*, and *La vie parisienne*; was also active as a gem-setter, couturier, ceramicist, and sculptor. c. 1898, he began designing lamps, inkwells, vases, clocks, and furniture and, subsequently, others, including a range of bronzes, frequently cast by Louchet. Chalon's portrait busts, clocks, inkwells, a vase of the Hesperides, and a silvered-and-chased watering-can could be mistaken for the work of Théodore Rivière, Maurice Bouval, Jules Michelet, and Julien Caussé. His lighting fixtures, incorporating the popular *femme-fleur* theme, featured bronze nymphs, naiads holding torches, women with poppies, flower petals that held electric bulbs, and marble butterflies.
Exhibitions/citations From early 1880s, work shown at Salons of Société des Artistes Français. Awards, 1889 and 1900 editions, *Exposition Universelle*, Paris.
Bibliography Yvonne Brunhammer et al., *Art Nouveau Belgium, France*, Houston: Rice University, 1976. Alastair Duncan, *Art Nouveau and Art Déco Lighting*, New York: Simon & Schuster, 1978: 71.

Chambellan, René Paul (1893–1955)

American architect and sculptor; born West Hoboken, N.J.

Training To 1915, The Cooper Union for the Advancement of Science and Art, New York.
Biography Chambellan worked as an architect and architectural sculptor; became a leading figure in the Art Déco movement in New York; displayed a vigorous modern style that garnered various public and private commissions, including Criminal Courts Building, New York State Office Building, Kings County Hospital, Queen's County Hospital, North Corona Gate at 1939–40 *New York World's Fair: The World of Tomorrow*, and East Side Airlines Terminal, all New York. However, his ironwork for 1928 Chanin Building (architects, Sloan and Robertson; New York's third tallest building at the time) and Fountain Court and ceiling of RKO Center Theater, Rockefeller Center, were the most important. So fine was his metalwork that he produced the 1933 Advancement of Motor Transportation medal (General Motors's 25th anniversary), designed by Norman Bel Geddes, and made by Medallic Art Company, N.Y., and designed the 1921 Newbery medal (children's literature published in the US). With two brothers, founded a successful firm that built theaters (1931 The Majestic, 1932 The Century, and 1932 Roxy) and apartment houses.
Bibliography Jonathan M. Woodham, *Twentieth-Century Ornament*, New York: Rizzoli, 1990: 62, 108. Peter Hastings Falk, *Who Was Who in American Art*, Madison, Conn.: Sound View, 1985.

Champion, Georges (1889–1940)

French decorator and furniture designer; born Chaumont; active Paris.

Biography From 1928 Champion, a prolific furniture designer, was artistic director of Studio Gué, the decorating department of Georges et Gaston Guérin, Paris; designed furniture in severe geometric forms and simple planes in contrasting colors, influenced by De Stijl; 1930, opened Atelier 75; with Jacques Guenne, managed the journal *L'art vivant*, which published information on the work of young artists.
Exhibitions/citations Dining rooms installed at 1929 Salon of Société des Artistes Décorateurs; 1920s, at other SAD editions and Salon d'Automne editions; 1925 *Exposition Internationale des Arts Décoratifs et Industriels Modernes*, Paris. Gold medal, 1937 *Exposition Internationale des Arts et Techniques dans la Vie Moderne,* Paris.
Bibliography *Ensembles mobiliers*, vol. 2, Paris: Charles Moreau, 1937. *Ensembles mobiliers*, vol. 6, Paris: Charles Moreau, 1945: nos. 42–44. R. Moutard-Uldry, *Dictionnaire des artistes décorateurs*, Paris: Mobilier et Décoration, 1953–57, Sept.–Oct. 1954. Pierre Kjellberg, *Art déco: les maîtres du mobilier, le décor des paquebots*, Paris: Amateur, 1986: 41. *Meubles 1920–1937*, Paris: Musée d'Art Moderne, 1986.

Chan, Eric (1952–)

Chinese furniture and product designer; born Canton.

Training 1976, Hong Kong Polytechnic; 1980, Cranbrook Academy of Art, Bloomfield Hills, Mich.
Biography 1989, Chan established Ecco Design, New York; designed furniture and products by Apple Computer, Corning, Herman Miller, LG Electronics, Motorola, Oxo, Sharp, and Siemens.
Citations 1988–92, 1994, 1997–98, 2001 Annual Design Review, *I.D.* magazine; 1990 international design competition, Forma Finlandia; 1990 Design Plus prize, Ambiente fair, Frankfurt; 1994–95, 1997, 2000, and 2001 IDSA/*Business Week* awards.
Bibliography Cat., R. Craig Miller (intro.), *U.S. Design: 1975–2000*, Munich: Prestel, 2002.

Chan, Kwok Hoi (1939–1987)

Chinese architect and interior designer.

Training University of Architecture, Hong Kong.
Biography Chan executed interior-design commissions and furniture for Air India and for IBM offices in Hong Kong; 1966–68, worked in a design studio in London, contributing to interiors of 1969 oceanliner *Queen Elizabeth II*; subsequently, designed for Spectrum furniture, the Netherlands and, by Sièges Steiner: 1969 cantilevered Pussy-Cat chair in tubular steel and leather-covered thermoplastic material, Alligator lounge chair, Chromatic range, and Zen chair.
Exhibitions A chair included in 1968 venue, Paris (catalog below); Pussy-Cat chair first shown, 1969 (15th) Triennale di Milano.
Bibliography Cat., *Les assises du siège contemporain*, Paris: Musée des Arts Décoratifs, 1968. Cat., *Modern Chairs 1918–1970*, London: Lund Humphries, 1971.

Chanaux, Adolphe (1887–1965)

French designer and interior decorator; active Paris.

Training École Nationale Supérieure des Beaux-Arts, Paris.
Biography Chanaux became known for his painstakingly matched and executed veneers in parchment, vellum, ivory, straw marquetry, leather, and shagreen; late 1910s–1924 or 1925, worked for André Groult; left to work for Jacques-Émile Ruhlmann. Chanaux's chairs for Groult with applied paintings by Marie Laurencin were entered (without attribution) in a 1924 competition of chair design organized by Pierre David-Weil at the Musée des Arts Décoratifs, Paris. Certain pieces signed by Ruhlmann also have Chanaux's stamp; however, his association with Ruhlmann proved unsuccessful. For a time, he also designed for Eugène Printz. 1931, Jean-Michel Frank, searching for furnishings for his Paris apartment, met Chanaux. For a year, they collaborated in a decorating business with workshops in La Ruche. 1932, they opened a shop at 140, rue du Faubourg Saint-Honoré, Paris; sold furniture, furnishings, and lighting that they designed and made, and those designed by friends and associates such as designer Emilio Terry, metalworkers Alberto and Diego Giacometti, painter Christian Bérard. 1941, Chanaux became the artistic advisor at Guerlain, Paris.
Exhibitions Through Ruhlmann, work shown at 1925 *Exposition Internationale des Arts Décoratifs et Industriels Modernes*, Paris.
Bibliography Léopold Diego Sanchez, *Jean-Michel Frank, Adolphe Chanaux*, Paris: Regard, 1980. Pierre Kjellberg, *Art déco: les maîtres*

du mobilier, le décor des paquebots, Paris: Amateur, 1986: 42. Stephen Calloway, 'Perfectly Frank,' *House and Garden*, Feb. 1990: 180ff. François Baudot, *Jean-Michel Frank*, Paris: Assouline, 1998; New York: Universe, 1999.

Chaplet, Ernest (1835–1909)

French ceramicist; born Sèvres.

Training From 1847 at age 12, worked at Sèvres ceramics factory, while learning design, painting, and basic pottery techniques.
Biography 1857–74, Chaplet worked with Laurin, the domestic pottery manufacturer; 1871, perfected barbotine on terracotta at Bourg-la-Reine and, 1875, developed the technique in the Haviland ceramics studio in Auteuil, Paris; in a Paris studio given to him by the Havilands, began applying Japanese and natural motifs on brown stoneware, a material he discovered in Normandy in 1881. 1884, the Haviland factory at Limoges produced porcelain pieces in this style, using molds from Chaplet's workshop. 1885, he began working with the *sang-de-boeuf* glaze of Chinese origin, applying it first to stoneware and then to porcelain; 1887, began collaborating with Paul Gauguin and moved his studio to Choisy-le-Roi, where Émile Lenoble later practiced; was in touch with the avant-garde and applied its ideas to ceramics; toward the end of his life, was forced to abandon his work due to blindness.
Bibliography Yvonne Brunhammer et al., *Art Nouveau Belgium, France*, Houston: Rice University, 1976.

Chapman, Colin (1928–1982)

British automobile engineer and designer.

Biography Chapman established the small-series Lotus production car; was able to develop his radical and innovative ideas about improved automobile handling; constantly pursued technical improvements, including the first full-monocoque composition bodywork (in 1957 Lotus Elite sports coupé), 1962 aluminum-bodied Lotus 25 Formula-1 chassis, and effective independent suspension; made cars that were very lightweight.
Bibliography Jeremy Walton, *Lotus Spirit: The Complete Story*, Ramsbury, Wiltshire: Crowood, 1997. William Taylor, *Lotus—Series 2*, London: Coterie, 1998. Hugh Haskell, *Colin Chapman, Lotus Engineering: Theories, Designs and Applications*, Oxford: Osprey, 1999.

Charalambides-Divanis, Sonia (1948–)

Greek furniture designer; born Athens.

Training 1966–72, architecture, École Nationale Supérieure des Beaux-Arts, Paris; computer science, Unité Pédogogique (UP6), Paris.
Biography 1972–77, she taught at École Spéciale d'Architecture, Paris, and in the computer science and linguistics department, UP6; performed research on design methods, computers in architecture, and workplace design, at Institut de l'Environnement, Paris; 1978, set up an architecture practice in Athens; 1978–85, was a scientific collaborator at National University of Athens, where she taught from 1985. 1981, began collaborating with architect Giorgos Parmenidis, and they designed furniture and objects, including 1987 First one-piece tubular armchair and 1988 Animate birch/steel side chair, both by Tubecon.
Bibliography Cat., Design Center Stuttgart, *Women in Design: Careers and Life Histories Since 1900*, Stuttgart: Haus der Wirtschaft, 1989.

Chareau, Pierre-Paul-Constant (1883–1950)

French architect and decorator; born Bordeaux.

Biography c. 1900–14, Chareau worked for British furniture firm Waring and Gillow in Paris, before becoming an independent interior decorator and, appropriately, was strongly influenced by English architecture and decoration before 1914. His furniture was generally site-specific for the requirements of a particular ensemble. He favored mahogany, rosewood, and sycamore; 1917–18 while on leave during World War I, designed a study and bedroom set for the Paris apartment of Annie Dalsace, a friend of his wife Dollie. 1918, he set up his own office, where he designed interiors, furniture, and lighting and occasionally executed architectural commissions; is best known for Jean and Annie Dalsace's 1928–32 office-residence Maison de Verre, Paris, for which he designed the architecture and furniture with Dutch architect Bernard Bijvoët, whom he met at 1925 Paris *Exposition*, and metalsmith Louis Dalbet; with Bijvoët, designed several other buildings. The Dalsace house, that was built on an awkward stie and included exposed iron beams and glass cubes, was revolutionary in design and aesthetics and manifested Le Corbusier's notion of the house as a 'machine for living.' The glass tiles, effectively concave lenses, transformed the internal light. The innovative flooring tiles (linoleum, featuring coin shapes) were made by Pirelli, still available today. The house was on three levels, linked by sliding and revolving doors. Chareau's furniture often featured mechanisms, combined plain wrought-iron elements, and was influenced by English 18th- and 19th-century styles, including Thomas Sheraton, whose chairs were installed in Chareau's own residence. His floor and table lamps and chandeliers were produced in wrought iron with slices of glass or alabaster and occasionally with cloth shades, such as the 1926 model he designed for Mme. Jacques Errers. The 1928 Club House for Émile Bernheim in St. Tropez was his first architectural commission. c. 1930, he designed the salon in Robert Mallet-Stevens's house in Neuilly (now Paris), where his La Religieuse alabaster chandelier (first shown at 1924 Groupe des Cinq exhibition) was installed. He often used concealed lighting, as in the French pavilion, 1925 Paris *Exposition*, with a domed cornice, and 1929 reception rooms, Grand Hôtel, Tours, where illuminated ceiling tracks were featured; occasionally worked with lighting engineer André Salomon. With Mallet-Stevens, Fernand Léger, and other friends and associates, he collaborated on sets for Marcel L'Herbier's 1923 film *L'inhumaine*; was a member of Groupe des Cinq with Dominique, Pierre Legrain, Jean Puiforcat, and Raymond Templier; 1924, opened a shop next to Jeanne Bucher's art gallery, in which, alongside a few original pieces, his catalog of photographs from Thérèse Bonney's agency illustrated his exhibition stands and interiors; by 1924, had begun working with Louis Dalbet, the wrought-iron metalworker who made limited editions of Chareau's furniture models; designed furniture for 1925 Jacques Lipschitz studio-house by Le Corbusier and 1924 furniture for the Noailles villa in Hyères (architect, Mallet-Stevens); 1928, cofounded Congrès Internationaux d'Architecture Moderne (CIAM); 1929, cofounded Union des Artistes Modernes (UAM); 1931, joined the editorial board of journal *L'architecture d'aujourd'hui*. 1937, André de Heering began working in the Chareau office. The large personal collection of modern art, which Chareau owned, included the second painting sold by Piet Mondrian, purchased in 1928. 1939, he designed packing crates that soldiers overseas could convert to furniture (a commission by the French colonial administration). From 1940, Chareau lived in the US; 1941, worked for the cultural section of the French Embassy, organizing exhibitions of French art; designed 1947 Quonset-hut conversion for painter Robert Motherwell, one-room open-plan house for himself, and 1948 alterations, 'La Colline,' residence of Germaine Monteux and Nancy Laughlin; opened an office in New York, though he had few commissions. His death thwarted plans for return to Paris.
Exhibitions 1917–18 office and bedroom designs for Jean and Annie Dalsace shown at 1919 Salon d'Automne, Paris, and numerous other 1920s–30s exhibitions, including at Salons of Société des Artistes Décorateurs from 1922; office-library for French Embassy pavilion at 1925 *Exposition Internationale des Arts Décoratifs et Industriels Modernes*, Paris. 1926 and 1927, work shown with Groupe des Cinq, Galerie Barbazanges, Paris; exhibitions of Union des Artistes Modernes (UAM) from 1930; with André Salomon, on corner illumination of 1934 and 1935 editions of Salon du Luminaire; 1936 Salon d'Automne (demountable school furniture).
Bibliography *Pierre Chareau, meubles*, Paris: Moreau, 1929. René Herbst, *Un inventeur, l'architecte Pierre Chareau*, Paris, 1954. 'Pierre Chareau with Bernard Bijvoët, Maison Dalsace ("Maison de Verre"),' *Global Architecture*, Tokyo, 1977. Luciano Rubino, *Pierre Chareau & Bernard Bijvoet: dalla Francia dell'art déco verso un'architettura vera*, Rome: Kappa, 1982. Marc Vellay and Kenneth Frampton, *Pierre Chareau: architecte-meublier, 1883–1950*, Paris: Regard, 1984 (New York: Rizzoli, 1985, English ed.). Brian Brace Taylor, *Pierre Chareau: Designer and Architect*, Cologne: Taschen, 1992. *Pierre Chareau: architecte, un art intérieur*, Paris: Centre Georges Pompidou, 1993. Olivier Cinqualbre, *Pierre Chareau: la maison de verre, 1928–1933, un objet singulier*, Paris: Jean-Michel Place, 2001.

Charles

French metalworkers; located Paris.

History 1908, Ernest Charles founded bronzery Maison Ullmann, Paris. 1920, Émile-Albert Charles took over management of the firm; 1932, was joined by his brother Pierre, when the firm was named Charles Frères. It became known for its bronze lighting fixtures and sculptural lighting in historicist models. 1959, Émile-Albert was joined by sons Jean (a student of interior architecture and sculpture, École Boulle) and Jacques (interior architecture, École des Arts Appliqués). The

best-known designs included lighting fixtures Pineapple, Maize, Fir Cone, Lotus, and Medici Vases. Jacques Charles designed 1965 Ligne Inox (stainless-steel collection), and, 1971, joining the firm, Chrystiane Charles (wife of Jean Charles and student of sculpture, École Supérieure Nationale des Beaux-Arts) designed Chrystiane Charles Sculpte la Lumière collection. 1982, Laurent Charles (D.P.L.G. architect) joined the firm and created Nouvelles Sources de Lumière collection. Recent commissioned designers have included Arman, Martine Bedin, Jean-Charles de Castelbajac, Sylvain Dubuisson, Christian Duc, Didier La Mache, Jacques Pierrejean, Zebulon.
Exhibitions/citations 1978, 1981, 1984, 1991, 1992 Lampe d'Or de la Création awards (to the firm or to individuals), Salon International du Luminaire de Paris.

Charpentier, Alexandre (1856–1909)

French sculptor, medalist, designer, and decorator; born Paris.

Biography Charpentier was associated with Siegfried Bing and his gallery/shop L'Art Nouveau, Paris; 1890–1902, was actively involved in both the fine and applied arts; with Jean Dampt, Félix Aubert, Tony Selmersheim, and Etienne Moreau-Nélaton, formed Les Cinq (not Groupe des Cinq), a group renamed Les Six when Charles Plumet joined it and once again renamed L'Art dans Tout when others, like Henri Sauvage, were included. Charpentier designed furniture, interiors, metalwork, ceramics, lighting, and leather; was considered one of the best representatives of the Parisian interpretation of Art Nouveau; designed numerous interiors, including a dining room in mahogany, oak, and poplar with ceramics by Alexandre Bigot at Champrosay for Adrien Bénard, president of Société du Métropolitain, who commissioned Guimard to design the Paris Métro entrances. Charpentier collaborated with Félix-Henri Bracquemond and Jules Chéret on the billiard room in 1895–96 La Sapinière, the villa of the baron Joseph Vitta in Evian.
Exhibitions Work shown 1895, with Les Vingt, in Brussels; at 1899 Salon de La Libre Esthétique, Brussels; and the baron Vitta's billiard room at 1902 exhibition, Paris (catalog below).
Bibliography Cat., *Salon of the Société Nationale des Beaux-Arts*, Paris, 1902. Yvonne Brunhammer et al., *Art Nouveau Belgium, France*, Houston: Rice University, 1976. Arlette Barré-Despond and Suzanne Tise, *Jourdain*, Paris: Regard, 1988.

Charpentier, Marcel (1888–1966)

French furniture designer and maker; born Saint-Mandé; active Paris.

Biography Charpentier established and edited furniture and objects for his firm on the rue des Pyramides in Paris; designed simple, massive pieces, sometimes lacquered; to end of 1940s, was a member, Société des Artistes Décorateurs.
Exhibitions Bookcase (with Victor Courtray) at 1923 editon of Salon d'Automne; desk shown at 1923 Salon of Société des Artistes Décorateurs (a member to end of 1940s).
Bibliography Pierre Kjellberg, *Art déco: les maîtres du mobilier, le décor des paquebots*, Paris: Amateur, 1986/1990.

Charpin, Pierre (1962–)

French furniture designer; born Saint-Mandé (Val-de-Marne); active Ivry-sur-Seine.

Training École des Beaux-Arts, Bourges.
Biography Charpin's work was influenced by that of Ettore Sottsass and Alessandro Mendini and acknolwedged the designs of other post-World War II Italians and Le Corbusier. It has included furniture, tableware, and other products such as 1998–99 table/wall lamp edited by Kréo. He has taught, Écoles des Beaux-Arts in Bourges, Limoges, and Reims, and Istituto Europeo di Design, Turin.
Citations 1993 Appel Permanent grant and 1996 Carte Blanche production support (Camp Meeker rocking chair), VIA (French furniture association).

Chartered Society of Designers (CSD)

British design organization.

History 1930, the Society of Industrial Arts was founded by Milner Gray and others as a professional association to advance and protect the interests of its members, as a forum for the exchange of ideas, and as an organization where standards of conduct and practice could be codified. The organization played an important role in planning 1951 *Festival of Britain* exposition, London. 1950s–60s, its membership grew

Chase Brass and Copper Co. Pitcher. c. 1927–41. Copper-plated metal, h. 6 1/16 x w. 8 1/8 x dia. 6 3/16" (15.4 x 20.6 x 15.7 cm). Mfr.: Chase Brass and Copper Co., US. Gift of Edgar Kaufmann Jr. MoMA.

appreciably. 1976, it was incorporated under a Royal Charter with the Duke of Edinburgh as patron; 1987, changed its name to the Chartered Society of Designers; publishes quarterly journal *Chartered Designers*. Its c. 7,000 members are active in product, graphic, interior, fashion, and textile design, design education, and design management.
Bibliography *Issue 4*, London: Design Museum, Autumn 1990. www.csd.org.uk.

Chase, William Merritt (1849–1916)

American artist and teacher; active New York.

Training 1873–78, in Munich.
Biography In New York: 1878, Chase settled there; subsequently, taught, Art Students League; and, 1896, founded New York School of Fine and Applied Art (sometimes referred to as Chase School of Art). He became known as America's most important art teacher; encouraged a lively approach; played a part in the infusion of fresh colorations in much of the best painting in America in the early 20th century. Chase's prolific work included still lifes, portraits, landscapes, and interiors. His students included Charles Demuth, Georgia O'Keefe, and Charles R. Sheeler. 1904, Chase offered courses in interior decoration, which were eventually to make an appreciable contribution to the decorative arts and industrial design in America; however, may have had no idea of his impact. From 1904, Frank Parsons was a faculty member and the first teacher of interior-design history at the New York School of Fine and Applied Art, where Parsons was the director from 1908 to his 1930 death. 1941, the institution was renamed Parsons School of Design by then-director William Odom and, 1970, became a division of New School for Social Research (now New School University).
Bibliography Ian Chilvers, Harold Osborne, and Dennis Farr, *The Oxford Dictionary of Art*, Oxford: Oxford University Press, 1988. John Esten and Rose Bennett Gilbert, *Manhattan Style*, Boston: Little, Brown, 1990: 5.
> See Parsons, Frank Alvah; Truex, Van Day.

Chase Brass and Copper Co.

American manufacturer of plumbing supplies; located Waterbury, Conn.

History 1876 in Waterbury, Conn., August Sabin Chase and others acquired the U.S. Button Company, with Chase as the president. His son Henry Sabin Chase introduced the first brass rolling mill in Waterbury, Conn., in 1900. The Chase 'Centaur' logo appeared in an advertisement in *The Saturday Evening Post*, 6 Oct. 1928. 1929, Chase Meltalworks was purchased by Kennecott Copper Corp. and became Chase Brass & Copper Co. Rodney Chase, son of then company president, set up a design division in c. 1927 to produce domestic metal products that called on the mother firm's pre-existing industrial forms. The objects included ashtrays, cutlery, vases, lighting, and tea sets. He commissioned designers Russel Wright, Walter von Nessen, Lurelle Guild, Ruth Gerth, Albert Reimann, and artist Rockwell Kent. Reimann probably sent his designs from Berlin; the others Rodney Chase knew personally and sometimes were guests in his home.
The wholesale showroom was located in New York; the headquarters building in Waterbury was designed by Cass Gilbert. 1930s, Chase developed sophisticated advertising and marketing techniques.

1945, production of the domestic line was discontinued.
Bibliography Thomas M. Rosa, *Chase Chrome*, Stamford, Conn.: Robert Koch, 1978. Jim Linz, *Art Déco Chrome*, Atglen, Pa.: Schiffer, 1999. Donald-Brian Johnson and Leslie A. Piña, *Chase Complete: Déco Specialties of the Chase Brass & Copper Co.*, Atglen, Pa.: Schiffer, 1999. Donald-Brian Johnson and Leslie A. Piña, *1930s Lighting: Déco and Traditional by Chase*, Atglen, Pa.: Schiffer, 2000. Donald-Brian Johnson and Leslie A. Piña, *The Chase Era: 1933 and 1942 Catalogs of the Chase Brass & Copper Co.*, Atglen, Pa.: Schiffer, 2000. Leslie A. Piña, *Chase Era: 1933 and 1942 Catalogs of the Chase Brass and Copper Co.*, Atglen, Pa.: Schiffer, 2001.

Chashnik, Il'ia Grigorievich (1902–1929)

Russian artist, architect, designer, and ceramicist; born Vitebsk.

Training 1916–19 under I. Pen (Marc Chagall's teacher), Institute for Practical Art, Vitebsk (now Belorussia); 1919 briefly, VKhUTEMAS, Moscow; 1919–22 under Kazimir Malevich, Art and Industry School, Vitebsk.
Biography Chasnik collaborated with Kazimir Malevich; 1919, became a founding member of POSNOVIS (later named UNOVIS) in Vitebsk; within Malevich's group, worked closely with Vera Ermolaeva, Lazar Khidekel, Gustav Klutcis, El Lissitzky, Nikolai Suetin, and Lev Yudin; 1920 with Lazar' Khidekel', edited POSNOVIS's journal *AERO*; 1921, co-founded the journal *UNOVIS*; 1922 followed Malevich and his group The Affirmers of the New Art (whose motto was 'wear the black square as a sign of the world's economy ... and the red square as a sign of the world revolution in art') to INKhUK (institute of artistic culture), Petrograd (now St. Petersburg). There he worked on ceramic designs with Nikolai Suetin and Malevich at Lomonosov State Porcelain Factory 1922–24, with Malevich on 'arkhitektony' and 'planity' (architectural constructions), and on his own suprematist paintings. 1923, Chashnik was a researcher, Museum of Painterly Culture, which closed that year, when he designed the residential housing for Bolshevik factory, Leningrad (now St. Petersburg). From 1924, he worked at Ginchuk as assistant to Malevich on architectural models; 1925, was a research associate, Decorative Institute; 1925–26, worked with Suetin and architect Aleksandr Nikolskii; 1927, led the workshop of IZO RAM (expressive art of working youth).
Exhibitions Work shown at 1923 *Exhibition of Paintings of Petrograd Artists of All Tendencies*, Petrograd; numerous subsequent venues.
Bibliography Cat., Stephanie Barron and Maurice Tuchman, *Avant-Garde Russia, 1919–1930: New Perspectives*, Cambridge, Mass.: MIT, 1980. Cat., *Kunst und Revolution: Russische und Sowjetische Kunst 1910–1932*, Vienna: Österreichisches Museum für angewandte Kunst, 1988. Cat., *The Great Utopia: The Russian and Soviet Avant-Garde, 1915–1932*, New York: Guggenheim Museum, 1992.

Chauchet-Guilleré, Charlotte (b. Charlotte Chauchet 1878–1964)

French artist, decorator, and furniture designer; born Charleville (Ardennes); wife of René Guilleré.

Training Under genre painter Gabriel Thurner, painting.
Biography Shortly after 1904, Chauchet married René Guilleré, who, 1913, established the Primavera decorating department of Au Printemps department store, Paris, and appointed her the artistic director. She served as both decorator and administrator there, designing a range of bedroom and dining-room ensembles by Primavera; was also a painter, muralist, and ceramicist and a friend of Hector Guimard; collaborated on interiors with architect Alfred Levard; was known for her robust forms and somber colors; painted 1912 frieze *Les Treilles* (vine trellis) in the dining room of cabinetmaker Mathieu Gallerey; 1931 when Guilleré died, became director of Primavera, where she collaborated with Colette Guéden, who succeeded her 1939.
Exhibitions Early 1910s, showed painting and decorative panels; from 1904, exhibited under Primavera at Société des Artistes Décorateurs; from 1910, under her own name, regularly in the Paris Salons, including a dining room (with Marcel Guillemard) at 1922 Salon of Société des Artistes Décorateurs; furniture in 1923 exhibition of L'Art Urbain et le Mobilier; rosewood work cabinet at 1924 Salon d'Automne, and bedroom in 1925 *Exposition Internationale des Arts Décoratifs et Industriels Modernes*, Paris.
Bibliography Léon Deshairs (intro.), *Modern French Decorative Art: A Collection of Examples of Modern French Decoration*, Paris: Albert Lévy, c. 1925–30. Pierre Kjellberg, *Art déco: les maîtres du mobilier, le décor des paquebots*, Paris: Amateur, 1986: 44, 47. Maurice Dufrêne, *Ensembles mobiliers, Exposition internationale 1925*, Paris: Charles Moreau, 1925; Woodbridge, Suffolk: Antique Collectors Club 1989: 126.

Chauvel, Alain (1955–)

French designer; born Pornichet.

Training École Boulle, Paris.
Biography After schooling, Chauvel worked as an interior designer at the Marc Bethier agency, while there designing 1979 Pliaviva folding-furniture series (with Berthier) by Magis. 1980, Chauvel set up his own studio and a type of corporate group (or a G.I.E., *groupement d'intérêt économique*). The G.I.E. was composed of seven manufacturers, for which he designed wood and metal furniture, upholstered chairs, and lighting. After some time in Nîmes, he returned to Paris and established Équilibre, which produced furniture, including storage cupboards. His 1999 Feira chair (with Thibault Desombre) was produced by Soca.
Citations Creator of the year, 1986 Salon du Meuble, Paris; 1987 Carte Blanche production support, VIA (French furniture association).
Bibliography Cat., Sophie Tasma Anargyros et al., *L'école française: les créateurs de meubles du 20ème siècle*, Paris: Industries Françaises de l'Ameublement, 2000.

Cheeseman, Kenneth (1900–1964)

British architect and interior designer; active London.

Biography c. 1929–30, Cheeseman was the chief draftsperson in the office of architect Oliver P. Bernard; 1933–c. 1950, was the architect to glassmaker Pilkington; with Sigmund Pollitzer, designed late-1930s Pilkington showrooms in London and in St. Helens, Lancashire. Much of Cheeseman's architecture incorporated decorative features by Pollitzer. Work included interiors (with Pollitzer and architect T.H. Johnson), 1934 Kirk Sandall Hotel near Doncaster; 1934 showrooms in Glasgow, 1935–36 in Leeds, and 1937 in St. Helens; 1937 Glass Train stand; and 1934 British Vitrolite showroom in London.
Exhibitions His work was shown at 1938 *British Empire Exhibition*, Glasgow; 1949 *Engineering and Marine Exhibition*; 1950 *Selwyn House* exhibition; 1951 *Festival of Britain*, London.
Bibliography Cat., *Thirties: British Art and Design Before the War*, London: Arts Council of Great Britain/Hayward Gallery, 1979.

Chekerdjian, Karen (1970–)

Lebanese designer; born Beirut.

Training In film, Paris; 1997 under Massimo Morozzi and Ampelio, in design with the No Tables No Chairs project, Domus Academy, Milan.
Biography 1991–93, Chekerdjian worked at Leo Burnett-Beirut advertising agency; 1993 with two associates, founded Mind the Gap communications and graphic-design agency in Beirut; 1998, became active in product design, including furniture by Edra.
Citations Recognition in several competitions, including Casio G-Shock, Driade-Spremiagrumi, and Nava-Minerva.

Chekhonin, Sergei Vasil'evich (1878–1936)

Russian ceramicist and graphic artist; active St. Petersburg and Paris.

Training 1896–97, Art School of the Society for the Encouragement of the Arts; 1897–1900 under Il'ia Repin, painting, private art school of the Princess Maria Tenisheva; both St. Petersburg.
Biography 1904–06, Chekhonin worked in sculpture and ceramics at the Abramtsevo Ceramic Workshop of S. Mamontov, Moscow; 1905–06, contributed caricatures and cartoons to revolutionary journals; 1907, made a number of majolica panels for buildings in St. Petersburg with Piotr Vaulin at the Kikerino ceramics factory, near St. Petersburg; 1910, became member of the revived V Mir Iskusstva (the world of art) group and regularly contributed to its exhibitions to 1924; 1913–18, was a specialist consultant on artistic crafts to the Ministry of Agriculture and directed the school for decorative work on enamel at Rostov-Yaroslavkii; 1913–23 and 1925–27, artistic director, State Porcelain Factory, Petrograd/Leningrad; was credited with much of the Agitprop (or agitation-propaganda) porcelain of the period and executed brightly painted forms with colorful slogans on ceramics blanks originally intended for pre-revolutionary ware; made no new shapes for porcelain but painted many plates, cups, and saucers himself and produced hundreds of compositions, drawings, monograms, and anniversary marks for Volkhov Factory, near Novgorod, where he was artistic director 1923–24; 1928, settled in Paris, where he worked as a designer for Nikita Baliev's 'Chauve-souris' cabaret, 1929, for Les Ballets

Russes' Vera Nemtchinova, and for *Vogue* magazine; designed jewelry, porcelain, and posters.
Exhibitions/citations 1912, first prize for new typography design from Leman publishers. Work shown at 1925 *Exposition Internationale des Arts Décoratifs et Industriels Modernes*, Paris; 1910–24 with V Mir Iskusstva society in Russia; was subject of 1928 exhibition, Paris.
Bibliography Cat., *Kunst und Revolution: Russische und Sowjetische Kunst 1910–1932*, Vienna: Österreichisches Museum für angewandte Kunst, 1988. Nina Lobanov-Rostovsky, *Revolutionary Ceramics*, London: Studio Vista, 1990.

Chelsea Keramic Art Works

American pottery factory; located Chelsea, Mass.

History Descended from at least five generations of potters, the Robertson family founded Chelsea Keramic Art Works in Chelsea in 1872. James Robertson (Edinburgh 1810–1880) had learned mold-making techniques and modeling from his father, head workman at Fife Pottery in Dysart; from 1826, worked for a number of ceramics factories in Scotland and England; 1853, arrived at Roundabout (now Sayreville), N.J., US; 1853–58, worked first at James Carr ceramics factory, South Amboy, N.J., and, subsequently, at Speeler, Taylor and Bloor, Trenton, N.J.; c. 1859, moved to Boston. His son Hugh Cornwall Robertson (1845–1908) stayed behind as an apprentice at Jersey City (N.J.) Pottery. In partnership, James and Nathaniel Plympton produced crockery from yellow and white New Jersey clays. 1862, the partnership dissolved, and Robertson became manager after the firm reverted to its former owner. 1866, James's son Alexander W. Robertson (1840–1925) produced simple brownware in Chelsea, Mass., an area where a supply of fine, iron-content red clay occurred. c. 1868, brothers Hugh and Alexander Robertson began producing flower pots, ferneries, matchboxes, and other domestic accessories. 1872, James, his sons, and George W. Robertson (1840–1925) formed the Chelsea Keramic Art Works and turned production to art pottery. Hugh became the firm's primary artist. 1880, when James died, the firm was renamed James Robertson and Sons, though the pottery remained commonly known as Chelsea Keramic Art Works. James Robertson most notable accomplishment was as inventor of the first tile-pressing machine in the US. Hugh experimented with various glazes, including *bourg-la-reine*, and developed under-glaze painting with colored clays at the firm. With his brothers' departure and his father's death, Hugh ran Chelsea Keramic Art Works; 1880s, was enthusiastic about the *sang-de-boeuf* glaze on Ming vases and sought its secret, finally succeeding with the production of c. 300 pieces before the firm closed in 1889. Assets of the firm were later renamed Chelsea Pottery U.S., active 1891–95, and then Dedham Pottery, active 1896–1943, having been moved to Dedham, Mass., with blue and white crackleware (developed 1886 by Robertson) as its specialty. Hugh's son and grandson managed Dedham Pottery after Hugh's 1908 death (attributed to lead poisoning) until it closed 1943.
Exhibitions/citations Third prize (J. Robertson and Plympton's pottery), 1860 (9th) Massachusetts Charitable Mechanics Association Fair. *Sang-de-boeuf* vases shown at 1876 *Centennial Exposition*, Philadelphia. Prizes (for H. Robertson's wares), 1900 *Exposition Universelle*, Paris; 1904 *Louisiana Purchase Exposition*, St. Louis; 1915 *Panama-Pacific International Exposition*, San Francisco.
Bibliography Cat., Lloyd E. Hawes et al., *The Dedham Pottery and the Earlier Robertson's Chelsea Potteries*, Dedham, Mass.: Dedham Historical Society, 1968. *American Art Pottery*, New York: Cooper-Hewitt Museum, 1987. Doreen Bolger Burke et al., *In Pursuit of Beauty: Americans and the Aesthetic Movement*, New York: The Metropolitan Museum of Art/Rizzoli, 1987: 407–08.

Chemetov, Paul (1928–)

French architect and furniture designer; born and active Paris.

Training 1947–59 under André Lurçat, École Nationale Supérieure des Beaux-Arts, Paris.
Biography Chemetov worked with Borja Huidobro et René Allio Site; 1961, became a founding member of Agence d'Urbanisme et d'Architecture (AUA); specialized in low-cost housing in Paris suburbs, as did the agency; designed new Ministère de l'Economie des Finances building, Paris; with Jean Deroche, was commissioned to work on 1969 French Communist Party offices (architect, Oscar Niemeyer), Paris; from 1977–89, taught architecture, École Nationale des Ponts et Chaussées, and 1993–94, invitational professor, École Polytechnique Fédérale, Lausanne; individually and with others, wrote a number of books on architecture, including the Paris suburbs.
Exhibitions/citations Work included in 1990 exhibition of VIA (French furniture association), Paris (catalog below).1980 National Grand Prize for Architecture; 1987 Carte Blanche production support (two armchairs and table in wood, glass, and steel, with Borja Huidobro), VIA. Elected officer of the the orders of Légion d'Honneur, of Arts et des Lettres, and of National du Mérite.
Bibliography *Dictionnaire encyclopédie de l'architecture moderne et contemporaine*, Paris: Philippe Sers/Vilo, 1987: 75–76. Cat., *Les années VIA 1980–1990*, Paris: Musée des Arts Décoratifs, 1990. *Paul Chemetov, un architecte dans le siècle*, Paris: Moniteur, 2002.

Cheney Brothers

American textile manufacturers; located Manchester and Hartford, Conn.

History The business expertise of the family and a broad knowledge of technical processes contributed to Cheney Brothers's becoming one of the leading silk manufacturers in the US. A prosperous farmer in Manchester, Conn., had eight sons, four of whom speculatively became involved in the planting of imported Chinese mulberry trees and the silkworms that fed on them. The four brothers—Ralph (1806–1897), Ward (1813–1876), Rush (1815–1882), and Frank (1817–1904)—bought additional property in Burlington, N.J., in Georgia, and in Ohio, where they planted the trees; failed due to the 1837 depression, the high cost of labor, and the 1844 mulberry-tree blight. Based on the brothers' ownership of Mount Nebo Silk Mills in Manchester, Conn., they turned to producing silk thread commercially, by importing oriental raw silk, and became the only silk mill in the US to continue production into late 19th century. c. 1854, the name was changed to Cheney Brothers Silk Manufacturing Company and, 1873, to Cheney Brothers. During the 1861–65 Civil War, the firm produced rifles for the Union (northern) Army. 1861 and 1864 when heavy silk-import tariffs were levied, the domestic market was strengthened. By 1880, the firm led in the production of plush, velvet, printed, and jacquard silks. Candace Wheeler and her Associated Artists designed silk goods that were sophisticated and attractive. The 1875 Cheney Block (its office building complex, Hartford) was designed by architect H.H. Richardson. Early 1900s, the firm was still a leader in silk production, but, 1920s, overproduction and the advent of synthetic fabrics led to decline and bankruptcy due to the 1929 Great Depression. 1940s, demand for parachutes and other military products for the war effort boosted the firm's fortunes. 1955 saw the end of silk production in the US, and Cheney Brothers was bought by J.P. Stevens & Co. (founded 1813), which was in turn acquired by WestPoint Pepperell in 1993 to form WestPoint Stevens. (1965, Westpoint Manufacturing Company and Pepperell Manufacturing Company had prior merged to form WestPoint Pepperell.)
Bibliography H.H. Manchester, *The Story of Silk and Cheney Silks*, South Manchester, Conn., and New York: Cheney Brothers, c. 1916. Doreen Bolger Burke et al., *In Pursuit of Beauty: Americans and the Aesthetic Movement*, New York: The Metropolitan Museum of Art/Rizzoli, 1987: 408–09.

Cheong, Carmen K.M. (1970–)
> See lemongras.

Chéret, Gustave Joseph (1838–1894)

French sculptor and ceramicist; born Paris; brother of poster designer Jules Chéret (1836–1932); husband of Marie-Gabrielle, Albert-Ernest Carrier-Belleuse's daughter.

Training Under Albert-Ernest Carrier-Belleuse, in sculpture.
Biography Chéret designed models and decorations for ceramics produced by Sèvres, where Carrier-Belleuse was the artistic director of the modeling studio of which Chéret became the artistic director on Carrier-Belleuse's 1887 death. 1894, Chéret became a member, Société Nationale des Beaux-Arts, Paris; made a number of centerpieces and plates in pewter and produced designs for Orfèvrerie Christofle, Grobé, and Baccarat; designed bronzes and electrified sconces produced by Soleau, Paris. Some of his bronzes produced ten years after his death still showed his signature, suggesting that Soleau may have recast a range of bronzes from maquettes still in the foundry. He died in Paris.
Exhibitions/citations Work was first shown, at 1863 Salon, and 1889 *Exposition Universelle*, Paris. Recasts of lighting fixtures shown by Soleau at 1900 *Exposition Universelle*, Paris. Gold medal (for work by Maison Fourdinois), 1889 *Exposition Universelle*, Paris.
Bibliography Yvonne Brunhammer et al., *Art Nouveau Belgium, France*,

Houston: Rice University, 1976. Alastair Duncan, *Art Nouveau and Art Déco Lighting*, New York: Simon & Schuster, 1978: 72.

Chérif (b. Chérif Medjeber 1962–)

Algerian furniture designer; active Paris.

Training To 1984, architecture, École Nationale des Beaux-Arts, Algiers; to 1989, École Nationale Supérieure des Arts Décoratifs, Paris.
Biography In Algeria, Chérif collaborated with Fernand Pouillon on several projects, including furnishings for a hotel in Algeria; 1977, settled in Paris; was the architect of a village in Algeria and a small building in the Arbalète; designed a rattan furniture collection by Chambon and group of vases by En Attendant les Barbares. Some furniture, such as 1986 Gazelle by En Attendant les Barbares, shows influences from native cultures. Other work edited by himself includes Vague II daybed, Miami sofa, Grenada love seat and coffee table, Esméralda sofa and chair, Ginza console, and ceramics, metalwork, and lighting.
Exhibitions/citations Work shown at Galerie En Attendant les Barbares, Paris; 1991 with other North African artists, Institut du Monde Arabe, Paris; 1992 *Barcelona, Düsseldorf, Milan, Paris* exhibition of European design, Centre Georges Pompidou, Paris.
Bibliography Cat., *Les années VIA 1980–1990*, Paris: Musée des Arts Décoratifs, 1990: 187. François Mathey, *Au bonheur des formes, design français de 1945–1992*, Paris: Regard, 1992: 265. 'Les designers du soleil,' *Maison française décoration internationale*, June 1992. Mel Byars, *50 Tables...*, Hove: RotoVision, 1997. Cat., Sophie Tasma Anargyros et al., *L'école française: les créateurs de meubles du 20ème siècle*, Paris: Industries Françaises de l'Ameublement, 2000.

Chermayeff, Serge Ivan (b. Sergius Ivan Chermayeff 1900–1996)

Russian architect and designer; born Grosny (now capital of Chechnya); active Britain and US; father of graphic designer Ivan Chermayeff.

Training 1910–13, Royal Drawing Society, London; 1914–17, Harrow School; 1922–25, in Germany, Austria, France, and the Netherlands.
Biography 1910, Chermayeff settled in London, where, 1918–23, he was on the editorial staff of Amalgamated Press; 1924–27, was chief designer for decorating firm E. Williams, London; 1928–29 with Paul Follot, was joint director of Modern Art Department of Waring & Gillow, London, which he tried to reorganize in the image of a great Parisian department store; 1929, qualified as an architect; pioneered the acceptance of tubular-steel furniture in England; came to modern architecture via interior and product design in the new 1920s style. 1930–39, he was in his own architecture practice (1933–35, in an uneasy partnership with Eric Mendelsohn, producing some of the most notable buildings of the time); 1932, founded the furniture retailer Plan; worked closely with manufacturers Walter Knoll and Franz Schuster, both in Germany, from whom much of Plan's designs were derived; 1936, sold Plan; collaborated on lighting with Best and Lloyd on R.D. Best's Bestlite lamp, producing the similar Bestplan lighting; mid-1930s, pioneered modern industrial design in Britain with his Bakelite radio casings by Ekco and designed bent-metal tubular furniture by Pel; 1933, had begun an architecture practice, with a house in Rugby as his first structure. By 1935, his architecture work included extensive use of his own furnishings, including clocks, rugs, textiles, radios, and furniture. He commissioned *Recumbent Figure* sculpture (1938) by Henry Moore for the terrace of his own 1935–38 house in Bentley Wood, East Sussex; 1937–39, was a member, Modern Architectural Research Group (MARS). Chermeyeff's use of Samuely's structural engineering began a period coinciding with the British modern movement in architecture. 1939, he settled in the US and first worked as an architect and town planner, 1940–41 in San Francisco and 1942–46 in New York; 1942–46, was director of department of art, Brooklyn College, N.Y.; 1946–51, succeeded László Moholy-Nagy as president, Institute of Design, Chicago, which became a department of Armour Institute of Technology (later named Illinois Institute of Technology); 1951–52, taught at MIT; 1953–62 and 1974, professor of architecture, Harvard University, Cambridge, Mass.; 1962–71, professor, Yale University, New Haven, Conn.; 1952–57, partner of Heywood Cutting, who had taught at Chicago Institute of Design; while at Harvard, collaborated with Christopher Alexander and, at Yale, with Alexander Tzonis; during his time in the US, designed textiles, interiors, and exhibitions and painted; co-wrote the books *Community and Privacy: Toward a New Architecture of Humanism* (with Alexander, 1963) and *Shape of Community* (with Tzonis, 1971). He died in Wellfleet, Mass. His archive is housed in Avery Architectural Library, Columbia University, New York.
Exhibitions/citations Came into prominence with furnishings for 1928–29 *Exhibition of Modern Furnishings*, Waring & Gillow store, London. His Plan furniture was shown in his Weekend House installation, 1933 *British Industrial Art in Relationship to the Home* exhibition, London; 1979 London exhibition (catalog below). Work subject of 2001 *Serge Chermayeff 1900–96: The Shape of Modern Living*, Kettle's Yard, Cambridge, UK (catalog below). 1974 gold medal, Royal Canadian Institute of Architects, and fellow, Royal Institute of British Architects, UK, Royal Society of Arts, UK, American Institue of Architects (AIA).
Bibliography Cat., Dennis Sharp et al., *Pel and Tubular Steel Furniture in the Thirties*, London: Architectural Association, 1977. Cat., *Thirties: British Art and Design Before the War*, London: Arts Council of Great Britain/Hayward Gallery, 1979. Barbie Campbell-Cole and Tim Benton (eds.), *Tubular Steel Furniture*, London: The Art Book Company, 1979: 52–53. Richard Plunz (ed.), *Design and the Public Good: The Selected Writings of Serge Chermayeff, 1930–1980*, Cambridge, Mass.: MIT, 1982. Mary A. Vance, *Serge Chermayeff: A Bibliography* (microform), Monticello, Ill.: Vance Bibliographies, 1983. Alan Powers, *Serge Chermayeff, Designer, Architect, Teacher*, London: RIBA, 2001.

Cherner, Norman (1920–)

American designer; born Brooklyn, N.Y.

Training Fine-arts department, Columbia University, New York.
Biography Cherner taught at Columbia University, and 1947–49, The Museum of Modern Art, New York; work included graphic design, architecture, and interior and industrial design; specialized for a time in prefabricated housing, such as for 1948 cooperative community in Ramapo, N.Y., and designed one of the first prefabricated houses in the US (1957 'Pre-built' in Camden, Maine, later commissioned by US Department of Housing and, after international exhibition, was Cherner's home). The hour-glass-shaped 1958 walnut-veneer bent-plywood Cherner Chair® (with or without ribbon-like arms), still in production, may have been inspired by the Pretzel chair by George Nelson Associates, New York, and appeared in the movie sets of *Mighty Aphrodite* (1995) and *Toy Story 2* (1999). The Cherner Chair Company (founded in Westport, Conn., in 1999 by the sons of Norman Cherner and which owns many original Cherner drawings, sketches, and models) is today reproducing his work, including other 1950s–60s chairs as well as tables and casegoods. However, Plycraft Inc., Mass., the original producer of the chair, is concurrently continuing its manufacture. He wrote *Make Your Own Modern Furniture...* (with Frank Stork, New York: McGraw-Hill, 1951), *Make Your Own Modern Furniture* (New York: McGraw-Hill, 1953), *How to Build Children's Toys and Furniture* (New York: McGraw-Hill, 1954), *Fabricating Houses from Component Parts: How to Build a House for Less than $6,000* (New York: Reinhold, 1957).

Cherry, Wayne (1938–)

American automobile designer; born Indianapolis, Ind.

Training To 1962, Art Center College of Design, Pasadena, Cal.
Biography Cherry began as a designer at Vauxhall and developed a new image for the firm; from 1962, became active in the advanced-design studio at the British subsidiary of General Motors (GM) and, from 1974, was head of design there; 1983–91, held the same position at Opel, where he infused new life into its design program; 1991, returned to the US to work at GM's headquarters, Detroit, Mich., and, 1992, became the fifth person to be the vice-president of GM Design, responsible for global design; subsequently resurrected some of the old design essences of GM, including concept cars for its separate American brands. 2004, he retired, succeeded by Ed Welburn (1951–).
Bibliography Arlette Barré-Despond (ed.), *Dictionnaire international des arts appliqués et du design*, Paris: Regard, 1996: 122. Penny Sparke, *A Century of Car Design*, London: Mitchell Beazley, 2002.

Chessa, Paolo Antonio (1922–)

Italian architect and furniture, interior, and exhibition designer; born Milan; active Pescara.

Training To 1945, architecture, Milan.
Biography From 1945, Chessa has been a freelance architect and designer in Milan, executing a number of small commissions; late 1940s–early 1950s, turned to furniture design; became best known for Butterfly chair in lacquered plywood components; subsequently, began designing furniture in plastics for serial production. His 1955 ideas for kitchen furniture were later taken up by others. 1945–47, he was editor of journal *Domus*; from 1945, contributed to numerous other magazines and journals; was an instructor, Politecnico, Milan.

Architecture included Youth Hostel in the Park, Milan; Teatro Carlo Felice, Genoa; General Roca Hydro-Electric Centre, Rio Negro, Argentina; Chiavari Housing Block, Genoa; residential center, Montréal; three cooperative centers, Pakistan; Ethioplast building, Addis Ababa; and numerous industrial buildings.
Bibliography Gustav Hassenpflug, *Stahlmöbel*, Düsseldorf, 1960. Pier Carlo Santini and Guiseppi Luigi Marini, *Catalogo Bolaffi dell'architettura italiana 1963–1966*, Turin: Bolaffi Arte, 1966. Anty Pansera, *Storia e cronaca della Triennale*, Milan: Longanesi, 1978.

Cheti, Fede (1905–1978)
Italian textile designer; active Milan.

Biography 1930, Cheti established her own firm in Milan; was discovered and encourage by Gio Ponti and her work became known outside Italy 1930s–40s and in the US in 1938. Her oversized motifs, printed and painted chintzes, and velvet and silk fabrics were popular. She also designed fabrics for Ponti and Giorgio de Chirico in Italy and for René Gruau and Raoul Dufy in France.
Exhibitions/citations Work shown at 1930 (4th) Biennale di Monza; 1933 (5th) Triennale di Milano; 1971 Milan exhibition (catalog below); and subsequent venues. First prize (art fabrics), 1950 Biennale di Venezia.
Bibliography Cat., *Milano 70/70: un secolo d'arte*, Milan: Museo Poldi Pezzoli, vol. 2, 1971: 195. Maria Vittoria Alfonsi, *Donne al vertice*, Milan, 1975: 41–43. Cat., Kathryn B. Hiesinger and George H. Marcus III (eds.), *Design Since 1945*, Philadelphia: Philadelphia Museum of Art, 1983. Cat., Pinuccia Magnesi (ed.), *Tessuti d'autore degli anni cinquanta*, Turin: Avigdor: 1987. Cinzia Anguissola, 'Tessuti e rivestimenti,' in *'45–'63 un museo del disegno industriale in Italia*, Milan: Abitare Segesta, 1995.

Cheuret, Albert (1884–1966)
French sculptor and designer; born Paris.

Training Under Perrin and Philippe-Joseph-Henri Lemaire, in sculpture.
Biography Cheuret designed bronze and alabaster lighting fixtures in abstract and naturalistic forms and table top objects, clocks, and sculptures of birds.
Exhibitions From 1907, work shown regularly at Salons of Société des Artistes Français. Designed and executed the decoration of a shop (with lighting and bronzes) at 1925 *Exposition Internationale des Arts Décoratifs et Industriels Modernes*, Paris.
Bibliography Victor Arwas, *Art Déco*, New York: Abrams, 1980. Pierre Kjellberg, *Art déco: les maîtres du mobilier, le décor des paquebots*, Paris: Amateur, 1986: 47.

Chevalier, Georges (1894–1987)
French designer; born Vitry-sur-Seine.

Training Decorative arts, fine art, and architecture.
Biography Chevalier worked with Maurice Dufrêne and Léon Bakst; with the latter, studied interior decoration and scenography; brought his interpretation of Cubism and Orientalism to his glass work by Baccarat, where he worked from 1916, designing crystal table wares, vases, decanters, and Baccarat's first purely decorative pieces, such as crystal animals. Many of Chevalier's pieces are still being made, including 1937 Panthère, 1947 Robinet, 1949 Tête de Mâle, 1957 Aigle.
Exhibitions Work shown at 1925 *Exposition Internationale des Arts Décoratifs et Industriels Modernes*, Paris; 1937 *Exposition Internationale des Arts et Techniques dans la Vie Moderne,* Paris; 1958 *Exposition Universelle et Internationale de Bruxelles* (*Expo '58*).
Bibliography Léon Deshairs (intro.), *Modern French Decorative Art: A Collection of Examples of Modern French Decoration*, Paris: Albert Lévy, c. 1925–30. Jean-Louis Curtis, *Baccarat*, Paris: Regard, 1991.

Chevallier, Jacques Le (1896–1987)
> See Le Chevallier.

Chicago Art Silver Shop
American firm; located Chicago.

History 1912, Chicago Art Silver Shop was established at 11 East Illinois Avenue, Chicago, by Edmund Boker and Ernest Gould; 1913–17, was located at 638 Lincoln Parkway; 1918–34, known as Art Silver Shop, 17 North State Street, and renamed Art Metal Studio, which it is today. Before c. 1914, designer and chaser Boker, who worked in French and Belgian Art Nouveau styles, and producer Gould made slender vases, tea services, and pitchers. Work was in copper and bronze, often with silver overlay and floral patterns. The firm still produces some of Boker's handmade jewelry designs.
Bibliography Sharon S. Darling, *Chicago Metalsmiths: An Illustrated History*, Chicago: Chicago Historical Society, 1977.

Chiesa, Pietro (1892–1948)
Italian furniture, glassware, and lighting designer; born Milan.

Training In Grenoble and Turin; under Giovan Battista Gianotti, the painter, furniture designer, and decorator.
Biography 1921, Chiesa opened Bottega di Pietro Chiesa, Milan; 1927 with Gio Ponti, Michele Marelli, Tomaso Buzzi, Emilio Lancia, and Paolo Venini, founded Il Labirinto, which produced high-quality glassware. 1932, Ponti established FontanaArte as an artistic division of Luigi Fontana's glass firm, and FontanaArte incorporated the Bottega di Pietro Chiesa. 1933, Ponti chose Chiesa as the artistic director of FontanaArte. Chiesa designed glass and wood-and-glass furniture; had a thorough knowledge of illumination engineering; is possibly best known for 1936 Luminator (no. 0836) floor lamp produced in polished brass, one of his simpler pieces, and c. 1935 Cartoccio 'handkerchief-type' glass vase, still in production by Fontana Arte.
Exhibitions/citations Work shown 1923 (1st), 1925 (2nd), 1927 (3rd), and 1930 (4th) *Esposizione Triennale delle Arti Decorative e Industriali Moderne* (Biennale di Monza); 1924 and 1926 Biennale di Venezia; 1925 *Exposition Internationale des Arts Décoratifs et Industriels Modernes*, Paris; 1929–30 *Exposición Internacional de Barcelona*; 1985 lighting venue, Paris (catalog below).
Bibliography *Moderne Klassiker: Möbel, die Geschichte machen*, Hamburg: Gruner + Jahr, 1982: 125. Cat., *Lumière je pense à vous*, Paris: Centre Georges Pompidou, 1985. Guglielmo Ulrich, *Arredamento mobili e oggetti d'arte decorativa*, Milan: Edizioni Görlich, 1942. Irene Guttry and Maria Paola Maino, *Il mobile déco italiano*, Rome-Bari: Laterza, 1988.

Chihuly, Dale (1941–)
American glass designer; born Tacoma, Washington.

Training To 1965, University of Washington, Seattle; to 1967, University of Wisconsin, Madison, Wis.; to 1968, Rhode Island School of Design, Providence, R.I.; under Hope Foot, Warren Hill, Harvey Littleton, and Doris Breckway.
Biography Early on, Chihuly produced environmental glass and, later, major architectural installations; c. 1965, was active briefly as an architect in Seattle; 1968, became first American glassblower at the Venini factory in Murano, where his later work reflected this influence; from 1968 for four summers, taught at Haystack School, Maine; 1969–80, chairperson of glass department, Rhode Island School of Design, and artist-in-residence there from 1980; 1971, established Pilchuck Glass School in Stanwood, Wash., on the forestry-research farm of John and Anne Gould Hauberg. Work includes early-1970s Glass Forests, 1974–75 Navajo Cylinders, Pilchuck Baskets from late 1970s, Sea Forms from 1980, and Macchia groups from 1981. Losing one eye in an automobile accident and thus his depth perception, he began working with a group of artisan-craftspeople. From early 1990s, his workshop has been housed in a factory on the waterfront of Seattle. He designed 1991 sets and lighting for a production of *Pelléas et Mélisande* by the Seattle Opera Company and, subsequently, executed a large number of dynamic, imaginative commissions for public spaces, including his most ambitious (1999 Light of Jerusalem, Israel).
Exhibitions Numerous, including 2001 one-person venue, Victoria and Albert Museum, London.
Bibliography Monroe Michael, *Baskets and Cylinders: Recent Glass by Dale Chilhuly*, Washington, D.C.: Renwick Gallery, 1978. Lloyd E. Herman, *Clearly Art: Pilchuck's Glass Legacy*, Bellingham, Wash.: Whatcom Museum of Art, 1992. Donald B. Kuspit, *Chilhuly*, New York: Abrams/Portland, 1998, 2nd ed.

Chiparus, Demêtre (1886–1947)
Romanian sculptor; active Paris.

Training In Italy, and under Antonin Mercié and Jean Boucher, École des Beaux-Arts, Paris.
Biography His best-known work shows exotic dancers in carved ivory and highly worked bronze. The subject matter of these chryselephantine (Greek *chrysos* for gold; *elephantinos* referring to ivory) sculptures was taken from popular personalities of the day, including 'The Sisters' from contemporary theater characters, and from Jules Massenet's

opera *Thaïs* (1894). His early pieces on relatively simple bases were primarily cast by Etling, a 1920s–30s foundry in Paris and retailer of contemporary French domestic furnishings. Chiparus also designed a number of figures in polychrome ceramics made by Etling. Later sculptures were made in the 'LN & JL' foundry, which appears to have produced the elaborate stepped and zig-zag marble and onyx bases.
Exhibitions Work was shown at 1914–28, 1942, and 1943 Salons of Société des Artistes Français.
Bibliography Victor Arwas, *Art Déco*, New York: Abrams, 1980. Alberto Shayo, *Chiparus: Master of Art Déco*, New York: Abbeville, 1993 (1999, 2nd edition).

Chipperfield, David (1953–)
British architect and designer; born London.

Training To 1977, architecture, Architectural Association, London.
Biography Chipperfield worked for the various architecture offices of Douglas Stephen, Richard Rogers, and Norman Foster; held the Mies van der Rohe Chair, Escola Tècnica Superior d'Architectura, Barcelona; from 1982, corporate member, Royal Institute of British Architects (RIBA); 1984, established David Chipperfield Architects in London; 1984, cofounded 9H Gallery; 1988–89, design tutor, Royal College of Art, London; from 1987, has been a visiting professor at a number of international institutions. His design work has included 1998 AirFrame and 2000 AirFrame Mid Range seating system by Inter Decor, 1999, Mirror chair by B&B Italia, 2000 HM 991 and HM 992 sofas by Hitch Mylius, 2000 Abaco lighting system by FontanaArte, 2000 DCA brassware collection by Czech & Speake, 2001 Home Office furniture by Driade, 2002 DC Duemiladue door handles by Valli & Valli. However, he is primarily an architect.
Citations A number of architectural prizes, including 1993 Andreas Palladio Prize, Vicenza, and 1994 first prize, to reconstruct Neues Museum, Berlin.
Bibliography David Chipperfield, Kenneth Frampton (foreword), *David Chipperfield: Architectural Works 1990–2002*, New York: Princeton Architectural Press, 2003.

Chochol, Josef (1880–1956)
Moravian architect, furniture designer, architectural theoretician; born Písek (now Czech Republic).

Training 1889–1904, České Vysoké Učení Technické (Czech technical university), Prague; 1908–09, Akademie der bildenen Künste, Vienna, under Otto Wagner.
Biography Chochol was of the first generation of architecture pupils under Jan Kotera, who established Czech Cubism as a program, resulting in an emotionally based furniture of architecture that was a drastic break from tradition; was a member, Cubist group Skupina Výtvarných Umělcu; designed three Cubist houses in Prague-Vyšhrad; however, abandoned Cubism in 1914; by 1920s, influenced by Russian Constructivism. His purist projects in Prague included 1920–21 office block, 27 Jindřišska; Inženýrska Komora; the union house, 19 Dittrichova St.; 1924 Barikádniku Bridge (demolished); and 1928–29 apartment buildings, 1–9 U Vody St. His unrealized projects, influenced by Russian Constructivism, included a 1927 competition design for the bridge across the Nusle valley and 1927 design of the Osvobozené Divadlo theater, which copied Barchin's design for 1925 Lenin cultural house in Ivanovo-Voznesensk, Russia. From 1923 until its 1931 close, Chochol was a member, Devětsil group; designed 1930–31 house and interior, Neherovská St., Prague-Dejvice, featuring a built-in settee and bookcases in light wood and dining table and chair by the Vavrouš firm in Prague, 1934. Died in Karlovy Vary.
Exhibitions 1912–14, suite of Cubist furniture, English Circle salon, Municipal Hall, Prague; some of his purist projects 1921 exhibition of Tvrdošíjní group; work shown at 1923 Bauhaus exhibition, Weimar.
Bibliography Cat., *Devětsil: Czech Avant-Garde Art, Architecture, and Design of the 1920s and 30s*, Oxford: Museum of Modern Art, and London: Design Museum, 1990. Cat., *Prague, 1900–1938: capitale secrète des avants-gardes*, Dijon: Musée des Beaux-Arts, 1997. Mel Byars with Arlette Barré-Despond, *100 Designs/100 Years: A Celebration of the 20th Century*, Hove: RotoVision, 1999: 94–95.

Choh, Daisaku (1921–)
Japanese designer; born Manchuria.

Training Tokyo National University of Fine Arts.
Biography Choh began working at Itakura Junzo Architecture Laboratory; 1972, established his own studio for architecture and the supervision and design of furniture, mostly for houses; was influenced by French designer Charlotte Perriand, as can be seen in his low 1960 11 1/2" (29 cm) chair, a piece compatible with the Japanese lifestyle.
Citations 1964 G-Mark award (low chair), Japan.

Christensen, Kari (1938–)
Norwegian ceramicist.

Training 1961, Statens Håndverks-og Kunstindustriskole, Oslo; from 1963–65, Det Kongelige Danske Kunstakademi, Copenhagen.
Biography 1961–66, Christensen worked at Royal Copenhagen Porcelain manufactory; from 1966, was active in own workshop in Oslo; from c. 1966, taught, Statens Håndverks-og Kunstindustriskole, Oslo, and was a professor there from c. 1986.
Bibliography Cat., David Revere McFadden (ed.), *Scandinavian Modern Design 1880–1980*, New York: Abrams, 1982. Jennifer Hawkins Opie, *Scandinavia: Ceramics and Glass in the Twentieth Century*, New York: Rizzoli, 1989.

Christiansen, Hans (1866–1945)
German painter, designer, and silversmith; active Munich, Hamburg, Darmstadt, Wiesbaden, and Paris.

Training 1887/88, Kunstgewerbeschule, Munich; 1896–99, Académie Julian, Paris.
Biography 1899–1902, Christiansen was a member of the Darmstadt artists' colony; designed silver by E.L. Viëtor in Darmstadt, and Martin Mayer in Mainz; cutlery by Bruckmann & Söhne in Heilbronn; enameled boxes by Louis Kuppenheim in Pforzheim; c. 1903 porcelain by Krautheim und Aldelberg; ceramics by Waechtersbacher Steingfabrik.
Bibliography Margret Zimmermann-Degen, *Hans Christiansen, leben und werk eines jugendstilkunstlers* (vol. 1, *Einfuhrung und werkanalsye*; vol 2, *Werkverzeischnis)*, Königstein im Taunus, 1981. Annelies Krekel-Aalberse, *Art Nouveau and Art Déco Silver*, New York: Abrams, 1989.

Christiansen, Ole Kirk (1891–1958); LEGO
Danish inventor; firm located Billund.

Biography 1932, Ole Christiansen, a carpenter/joiner, established a business in Billund, Denmark, to make wooden ironing boards, stepladders, and toys. 1934, the firm adopted the name LEGO, an acronym from *LEg GOdt* (Danish for 'play well') for its toys developed by Godtfred Kirk Christiansen (1920–1995), son of the founder and who began working at the firm at age 12 and creating toys from age 17. 1947, Godtfred became managing director, and LEGO became the first Danish company to buy a plastic-injection-molding machine for toy production; by 1949, was marketing c. 200 different plastic or wooden toys, sold in Denmark, including Automatic Binding Bricks (from 1953, known as LEGO Mursten, or LEGO Bricks, and, 1954, 'LEGO' was registered as a trademark). By 1951, toys in plastics accounted for half the factory's production. After some refinement, the firm introduced 1955 LEGO System of Play (25 sets, 8 vehicles, and separate pieces in the range); 1958, developed/patented the 'stud-and-tube' connection method for greater stability and for almost infinite configurational possibilites; 1959, established the Futura department for product development; subsequently, has invented a number of other construction toys, all purporting to assist child development. LEGOs differ from the 1913 Tinkertoy and 1935 Erector Set in that they appeal to older children, and the 1998 LEGO Mindstorms (to build and program a robot from a box of 700 pieces) is intended for use by teenagers or young adults. By 1998, 189 billion LEGO elements and 11 billion LEGO Duplo bricks had been molded by the firm, which is still managed by the Christiansen family in Billund.
Bibliography *The Ultimate Lego Book: Discover the Lego Universe*, London: Dorling Kindersley, 1999. Paola Antonelli (ed.), *Objects of Design: The Museum of Modern Art*, New York: The Museum of Modern Art, 2003: 109. http://www.lego.com.

Christiansen, Poul (1947–)
Danish furniture and lighting designer; born Copenhagen.

Training To 1973, School of Architecture, Kungliga Tekniska Högskolan, Stockholm.
Biography From 1979, Christiansen was a freelance designer with clients, including Le Klint for lighting; 1977–86, worked at Ib and Jørgen Rasmussen's architecture/design studio for clients such as Kevi and Herman Miller; concurrently 1982–87, designed furniture by Sorø Stolefabrik in Denmark and Lübke and Brunner in Germany; 1987 with

Godtfred Kirk Christiansen. LEGO Building Bricks. 1954–58. ABS polymer, piece 1: 7/16 x 1 1/4 x 5/8" (1.1 x 3.2 x 1.6 cm), piece 2: 7/16 x 15/16 x 5/8" (1.1 x 2.4 x 1.6 cm), piece 3: 7/16 x 5/8 x 5/8" (1.1 x 1.6 x 1.6 cm). Mfr.: LEGO Group, Denmark. Gift of the mfr. MoMA.

Boris Berlin, established Komplot Design. Christiansen is a member, Foreningen Danske Designere (association of Danish designers).
> See Berlin, Boris.

Christofle; Charles Christofle (1805–1863)

French silversmithy; located Paris.

History 1830, Charles Christofle established his eponymous jewelry firm; 1845, opened a silver and gilt silversmithy at 56, rue de Bondy, (near place de la République), Paris; was an innovator and developed the techniques of electroplating, galvanoplasty, and other processes for which he had bought the rights in 1842 and which eventually made him renowned. Christofle used artists who were sympathetic to the process. 1852, his son Paul and nephew Henri Bouilhet took over directorship of the firm prior to his 1863 death. Bouilhet, with chief designer Ernest Reiber, produced objects of oriental inspiration, including pieces with *cloisonné* enameling and several novel processes, such as new stamping methods and galvanoplasty for mass producing large-scale architectural ornaments and statues in a single piece. Christofle was at the forefront of technology, calling on methods such as mechanical damascening and electromagnetic engraving. The term 'christofle' has come to mean silverplating. Bouilhet's last years were devoted to writing the history *Orfèvrerie française aux XVIIIe et XIXe siècles*. King Louis-Philippe, Emperor Napoleon III, and his cousin Prince Joseph-Charles patronized Christofle. Before 1890, Christofle wares were in Louis XV and XVI styles and occasionally *japonisant*. Best-known wares include 1854 large electroplated dinner service for the Tuileries commissioned by Napoleon III, coffee set 'L'union fait le succès' design by Louis Carrier-Belleuse, and two 1869 galvanized copper monumental groups on the façade of Opéra, Paris. c. 1900, the firm produced cutlery for Maxim's restaurant, in the Art Nouveau style, which began to appear in Christofle's wares in the 1890s; after World War I, becoming more adventurous, the firm began producing many models in the Style 1925, including those by Luc Lanel for 1935 ocean-liner *Normandie*. Designers included Jean-Baptiste Carpeaux, Albert and Louis Carrier-Belleuse, Émile Reiber, and Charles Rossigneux in the 19th century, and Maurice Dufrêne, André Groult, Christian Fjerdingstad, Paul Follot, Luc Lanel, Louis Süe, André Mare, Gio Ponti, Jean Cocteau, Lino Sabattini, Jean-Michel Folon, Arman, and Tapio Wirkkala in the 20th century. The 1984 Aria silver-plated cutlery became the best-selling cutlery worldwide; was produced by the Christofle research team following an open design competition with over 3,000 entries. 1986, Christofle created its first jewelry collection; is still active as an enterprise managed by descendants of Henri Bouilhet. Musée Bouilhet-Christofle is located in Saint-Denis, near Paris.
Exhibitions/citations Showed inlaid ironwood and ebony furniture with gilt bronze mounts and damascened objects in the *japonisant* style at 1878 *Exposition Universelle*, Paris. Silver in the new heavy type of plate called Gallia Metal designed by Eugène Bourgouin and *chef de l'atelier* shown at 1900 *Exposition Universelle*, Paris. Work subject of 1981 *Christofle, 150 Ans d'Orfèvrerie*, Louvre des Antiquaires, Paris; 1991 exhibition, Château de Loches, and 1992 exhibition, Musée Mandet, Rion (catalogues below); 2000 exhibition at the Christofle museum. 1851–1937, received a number of awards at exhibitions, including grand prize (coffee set, designed Louis Carrier-Belleuse) at 1880 *Exposition des Arts du Métal* organized by Union Centrale des Arts Décoratifs.
Bibliography Hugh Honour, *Goldsmiths and Silversmiths*, London, 1971. Yvonne Brunhammer et al., *Art Nouveau Belgium, France*, Houston: Rice University, 1976. Henri Bouilhet, *Christofle, 150 ans d'orfèvrerie = Christofle, Silversmiths since 1830*, Paris: Le Chêne, 1980. Annelies Krekel-Aalberse, *Art Nouveau and Art Déco Silver*, New York: Abrams, 1989. 'Christofle, 150 ans d'art et de rêve,' *Les dossiers de l'art*, no. 2, July–Aug. 1991. Cat., *Christofle, 150 ans d'orfèvrerie*, Tours: Conseil Général d'Indre et Loire, 1991. Cat., *Christofle, une certaine idée de l'orfèvrerie, 1925–92*, Clermont Ferrand, 1992.
> See Bouilhet, Henri.

Ciaramitaro, Pietro (1950–)

Italian industrial designer; born Trapani; active Modena.

Training To 1969, Istituto Tecnico B. Amico, Trapani; Istituto Superiore di Scienza dell'Automobile, Modena.
Biography 1972–74, Ciaramitaro collaborated in studio Bollani, Modena, specializing in thermoplastic, resin-based, metal-and-wood furniture and furnishings. Clients in Italy have included Electromondial (furnishings), Caggiati (ecclesiastical furnishings), Simonini Moto (motorcycles), and G3 Ferrari (domestic electrical appliances). He worked at the 1972 cycling race (with Bollani and Ottonelli) in Tokyo; 1976, joined studio Progettisti Designers Associati in Modena.
Exhibitions Two-seat sports-car design at 1970 Salon, Turin.
Bibliography *ADI Annual 1976*, Milan: Associazione per il Disegno Industriale, 1976.

Cibic, Aldo (1955–)

Italian architect and designer; born Schio; active Milan

Biography 1975–79, Cibic worked in his own studio on shop and office interior design; 1979, settled in Milan to work with Ettore Sottsass; 1980, with Sottsass, Marco Zanini, and Matteo Thun, became a partner of Sottsass Associati; became active in industrial design, restoration, furniture design, interior design, and store design (Fiorucci and Esprit); has had clients including Standard (objects and textiles), Cleto Munari (silver), Tissot (timepieces); was active at Memphis (aligned with Sottsass Associati), where he designed 1982 Belvedere console, 1985 Sophia desk, 1985 Cabbage-Pepper-Radish ceramic tea set, 1986 Rio tea cart, 1986 Buenos Aires floor lamp with Cesare Ongaro, 1987 Andy side table, 1987 Sandy bookcase, and 1987 Louis table. 1989 with Antonella Spiezio, established Cibic & Partners in Milan, for design of products, interiors, and architecture; designed 1993 Antologia furniture range by Boffi. Store designs include Selfridges, Manchester, UK; Beymen department stores, Istanbul; shop system for Esprit; Habitat stores, Italy and UK. Teaches, Royal College of Art, London, and, from 1989, Domus Academy, Milan.
Exhibitions Work shown in numerous exhibitions and subject of 1999 exhibition, LAMeC, Basilica Palladiana, Vicenza (catalog below).

Aldo Cibic. Pitcher. c. 2000. Glass, h. 13 1/2" (34.5 cm). Mfr.: Cibic & Partners, Italy.

Bibliography Fumio Shimizu and Studio Matteo Thun (eds.), *The Italian Design: Descendants of Leonardo da Vinci*, Tokyo: Graphic-sha, 1987. *Modo*, no. 148, Mar.–Apr. 1993: 118. Cat., Andrea Branzi et al., *Aldo Cibic: Designer*, Milan: Skira, 1999. Michele De Lucchi (ed.), *The International Design Yearbook*, London: Laurence King, 2001.

Cigler, Václav (1929–)

Czech glass designer; born Vsetin.

Training 1951–57 under Josef Kaplický, Akademie Výtvarných Umení (academy of fine arts); Vysokou Školu Umĕleckoprůmyslovou (academy of arts, architecture, and design); both Prague.
Biography 1957–65, Cigler was a freelance artist; 1965–79, was in charge of the studio of glass architecture, Výsoka Škola Výtvarnych Umení (academy of fine arts and design), Bratislava. Work has also included plastics but primarily cut and optic sculptural glass, lighting, jewelry, and spacial projects and compositions for architecture.
Exhibitions/citations Work shown extensively at glass exhibitions, Czechoslovakia; 1957 and 1960, Milan; 1958, São Paulo, Corning, N.Y., and Brussels; 1969, American Craft Museum, New York; 2003 *Mystéres de l'Espace* (from collection of Slovak National Gallery), Bratislava Castle, Bratislava; numerous others. Subject of large number of venues, from 1967 at Galériou Platy'z (glass, jewels), Prague, to 2002 *Václav Cigler a jeho s'kola*, Galériou Pokorná, Prague. A number of prizes.
Bibliography Cat., Milena Lamarová (ed.), *Design a Plastické Hmoty*, Prague: Umĕleckoprůmyslové Muzeum, 1972. Cat., Alena Adlerová, *Václav Cigler glasobjecten*, Rotterdam: Museum Boymans-van Beuningen, 1975.

Cimini, Tommaso (1947–); Lumina

Italian lighting designer; active Arluno.

Biography Cimini worked as a technician at Artemide lighting firm in Milan; 1975, founded Lumina in Arluno (MI) for the production of lighting, including his own-design Elle thin articulated floor lamp and the landmark fixture, 1975 Daphne. Other designers have include De Pas/D'Urbino/Lomazzi, Yaacov Kaufman, Giuseppe Linardi, Walter Monici, Paolo Salvo, Lorenzo Stano, Emanuele Ricci, others. The firm has become large with subsidiaries in Germany and Switzerland.
Bibliography Fumio Shimizu and Studio Matteo Thun (eds.), *The Italian Design: Descendants of Leonardo da Vinci*, Tokyo: Graphic-sha, 1987.

Cirici, Cristian (1941–)

Spanish architect and designer; born Barcelona.

Training To 1965, Escola Tècnica Superior d'Arquitectura de Barcelona (ETSAB).
Biography 1962–65, Cirici worked in the office of architects Frederic Correa and Alfonso Milá, Barcelona, and, 1962, office of architects James Cubitt and Partners, London; 1965 with Pep Bonet, Lluís Clotet Ballús, and Óscar Tusquets Blanca, founded the Studio PER; 1972, was a cofounder of Bd Ediciones de Diseño and, currently, its chairperson; 1975–78, Cirici taught design, Escola Tècnica Superior d'Arquitectura de Barcelona; 1981, was visiting professor, Washington University, St. Louis, Missouri, and, 1983, University of New Mexico, Albuquerque; 1974–77, was director of cultural activities, Collegi d'Arquitectes de Catalunya (Catalan architects' association); 1980–82, was chairperson, ADI/FAD (industrial-design/applied-arts associations). Work by Bd Ediciones de Diseño: 1974/1988 Silla Sevilla chair with Bonet and Riera, 1975 Mesa Sevilla table with Bonet, 1986 hardware, 1986 Armariu cabinet, and 1986 audio stand.
Citations 1966, 1969, and 1972 Premi FAD d'Interiorisme award (for best interiors); 1978–79 Premi FAD de Restauració award (for best restoration work), Spain.
Bibliography Juli Capella and Quim Larrea, *Designed by Architects in the 1980s*, New York: Rizzoli, 1988.

CIRVA (Centre International de Recherche sur le Verre et les Arts Plastiques)

French glass workshop; located Marseille.

History 1986, CIRVA (international research center of glass and the plastic arts) was established as a glass workshop in Marseille for artists, designers, and architects; unique in Europe, is neither school nor exhibition gallery but rather a laboratory with a permanent team of technicians and engineers; accommodates c. 30 artists working on the premises each year; serves as an center for professional artists working in glass and provides information on techniques, materials, and industrial processes; is directed by Françoise Guichon. Designers working there have included Marc-Camille Chaimowicz, Eric Dietman, Gaetano Pesce, Marie-Christine Dorner, Sylvain Dubuisson, Olivier Gagnère, Piotr Kowalski, Elisabeth Garouste, Mattia Bonetti, and Bořek Šípek.
Bibliography Cat., *30 vases pour le CIRVA*, Marseille: Michel Aveline/CIRVA, 1989.

Cisotti, Biagio (1955–)

Italian art director and designer; born Aradeo (LE); active Florence.

Training 1974–81, architecture, Università degli Studi, Florence.
Biography 1981–89, Cisotti was active in product development at Poltronova furniture firm in Pistoia; 1981–90, assistant teacher of architecture at the university in Florence; from 1989, has taught, Istituto Superiore per le Industrie Artistiche (ISIA), Florence; 1989–2000, was art director of Poltrona and designed the firm's 1989 Serena chair; 1991, art director of B.R.F. furniture firm in Siena; from 1997, art director of Plan in Bolzano; 1995 with Sandra Laube, established studio Cisotti Laube in Florence.
> See Laube, Sandra.

Cissarz, Johann Vincenz (1873–1942)

German architect, painter, graphic artist, silversmith, wallpaper and furniture designer; active Dresden, Darmstadt, Stuttgart, and Frankfurt.

Training Under painter Ferdinand Wilhelm Pauwels, Akademie der Künste, Dresden.
Biography Cissarz was one of the first designers at the Dresdner Werkstätten für Handwerkskunst; 1903–07, was a member of the Darmstadt artists' colony; designed silver by E.L. Viëtor in Darmstadt; From 1906, was a teacher (from 1909–1916, professor) at Lehr- und Versuchsstätten des Vereins Württembergischer Kunstfreunde, Stuttgart, and, from 1916, at Kunstgewerbeschule, Frankfurt.
Bibliography Annelies Krekel-Aalberse, *Art Nouveau and Art Déco Silver*, New York: Abrams, 1989.

Citterio, Antonio (1950–)

Italian furniture designer; born Meda; active Milan; husband of Terry Dwan.

Training 1970–75, architecture, Politecnico, Milan.
Biography 1967, Citterio began in industrial design; 1972, set up a studio with Paolo Nava in Lissone, working together to 1981 and collaborating on design and industrial strategy; 1973, began working with furniture firm B&B Italia. Clients have included Artwis, Boffi, Kartell, Flexform, Moroso, Paravicini, Rivaplast, Tisettanta, Vitra, Xilitalia. He has taught, Domus Academy, Milan. From 1987, he has collaborated with American wife Terry Dwan (1957–) and German designer Glen Oliver Löw (1959–). Dwan designed 2001 Bloomington chair by the 'Riva 1920' firm. The studio designed the partial restoration (with studio Gregotti Associati) of Pinacoteca di Brera, Milan; showrooms of B&B Italia; offices and showrooms of Vitra, Weil am Rhein (Germany) and Paris; office furniture system by Olivetti; 1992 commercial center near Milan; offices in Tokyo and, with Toshiyuki Kita, in Osaka. Work by B&B Italia: 1980 Diesis sofa by B&B Italia, 1986 Sity modular and

stand-alone seating in variety of models (with Dwan), Panca sofa, Sento Muto table, Lunga square armchair, Tonda round chair, 1981 Ialea chair and 1993 Indo, Cina, Cubis, and Oriente seating. Others include 1983 Max divan and 1985 Phil sofa by Flexform, and 1987 Enea lamp by Artemide. A large body of work for numerous clients has followed.
Exhibitions/citations Work subject of 1993 exhibition, Arc en Rêve, Centre d'Architecture, Bordeaux, France; and widely included in venues elsewhere. 1987, 1991, 1994 (individually and with Löw), and 1998. Premio Compasso d'Oro.
Bibliography Andrea Branzi, *La casa calda: esperienze del nuovo disegno italiano*, Milan: Idea, 1982. Fumio Shimizu and Studio Matteo Thun (eds.), *The Italian Design: Descendants of Leonardo da Vinci*, Tokyo: Graphic-sha, 1987. Juli Capella and Quim Larrea, *Designed by Architects in the 1980s*, New York: Rizzoli, 1988. Mel Byars with Arlette Barré-Despond, *100 Designs/100 Years: A Celebration of the 20th Century*, Hove: RotoVision, 1999. Cat. Brigitte Fitouss et al., *Antonio Citterio & Terry Dwan, Architecture & Design: 1992–1979*, Zürich: Artemis, 1993. Pippo Ciorra, *Antonio Citterio, Terry Dwan: Ten Years of Architecture and Design*, Basel/Boston: Birkhäuser, 1995.

Claesson, Mårten (1970–)

Swedish architect, teacher, and furniture and interior designer; born Lidingö; active Stockholm.

Training Konstfackskolan, Stockholm.
Biography 1993 with Eero Koivisto and Ola Rune, Claesson established Claesson Koivisto Rune Arkitektkontor in Stockholm The group gained initial recognition with the Vila Wabi, a long box-like temporary structure on Sergel square in Stockholm, intended to house a four-person family; subsequently, has designed a large number of shops, showrooms, bars, restaurants, offices, and houses, both abroad and in Sweden. Claesson is a writer and lecturer in architecture and design. The group's designs from 1999 included seating, a bathroom fixture, lighting, and accessories by Offecct, Swedese, Skandiform, Ateljé Lyktan, Cappellini, David design, Living Divani, and Boffi.
Exhibitions/citations Work subject of 2002 exhibition, Arkitekturmuseet, Stockholm. To group: 1993–1996 and 1998–2000 Utmärkt Svensk Form prize (Swedish design excellence); 1998 grand prize (for exhibition design), Formex Design Fair, Stockholm; 2000 Guldstolen ('golden chair') bi-annual award (for Sony Music headquarters, Stockholm), Association of Swedish Interior Architects (SIR); 2000 jury award, The Future of Wood in Our Homes (housing project), Bo 01 building fair, Qbkl house, Malmö. To Claesson: 1993 Scandinavia-Japan Sasakawa Foundation (with Rune); 1994 Freemason's scholarship; 1995 Forsnäs Prize (for bentwood furniture); 1996 Swedish Institute's Scandinavian-American culture exchange scholarship.
Bibliography Terence Riley et al., *Claesson Koivisto Rune*, Barcelona: Gustavo Gili: 2001.
> See Koivisto, Eero; Rune, Ola.

Antonio Citterio with Glen Oliver Löw (1959–). Mobil container system (exemplary configuration). 1994. Bulk-dyed thermoplastic polymer and steel, 38 1/2 x 19 3/8 x 18 3/4" (97.8 x 49.2 x 47.6 cm). Mfr.: Kartell, Italy. Gift of the mfr. MoMA.

Mårten Claesson, Eero Koivisto, and Ola Rune. Bowie lounge chair. c. 1998. Bent birch or oak, h. 26 3/4 x w. 28 1/8 x d. 27 1/8" (68 x 72 x 69cm). Mfr.: David design, Sweden.

Clements, Eric (1925–)

British silversmith; born Rugby.

Training Birmingham College of Art; 1949–53, Royal College of Art, London.
Biography 1954, Clements taught, School of Silversmithing and Jewellery (now part of University of Central England), Birmingham; 1954–72, was head, industrial-design department, Birmingham College of Art (from 1971, known as College of Art & Design, City of Birmingham Polytechnic); from 1972, was dean of industrial design, Wolverhampton Polytechnic; designed metalware and products—from teapots and ashtrays to ceremonial maces, highly influenced by 1950s Scandinavian modern style; was a consultant designer to Mappin and Webb of Sheffield which made his tableware and cutlery.
Exhibitions 2002 *Passion and Perfection, Eric Clements: Silver & Design 1950–1992* (1st Clements retrospective, catalog below).
Bibliography Cat., Martin Ellis (ed.) and Rebecca Holland (text), *Eric Clements: Silver & Design 1950–1992*, Birmingham: Birmingham Museum & Art Gallery, 2001.

Clemmensen, Ebbe Thejll (1917–); Karen Clemmensen (b. Karen Mundt 1917–2001)

Danish architects and furniture designers; born Copenhagen; husband and wife. Ebbe: son of architect/technical writer Mogens Clemmensen and painter Augusta Thejll. Karen: daughter of architect Holger Mundt and painter Harriet Fischer-Jørgensen.

Training Ebbe: to 1941, Det Kongelige Danske Kunstakademi, Copenhagen. Karen: 1942, Det Kongelige Danske Kunstakademi, Copenhagen; 1943–45, Stockholm; 1946, architecture, Copenhagen.
Biography Ebbe Clemmensen collaborated with Poul Holsøe and Fritz Schlegel and, from 1946, with wife Karen. From 1964, he taught at Kunstakademi. They designed furniture produced by Fritz Hansen and, as architects, 1969 LO-Skolen conference center (with Jarl Heger) in Elsinore (aka Helsingør) and 1970 Kildeskovshallen health center in Gentofle.
Citations To both: 1961 Eckersberg Medal, 1968 Træprisen, 1993 C.F. Hansen Medal.
Bibliography Frederik Sieck, *Nutidig Dansk Møbeldesign – en kortfattet illustreret beskrivelse*, Copenhagen: Bondo Gravesen, 1990.

Clendinning, Walter Max (1924–)

British interior designer and architect; born Richhill, Northern Ireland.

Training 1942–44, Belfast College of Art; 1944–50, architecture office of H. Lynch-Robinson; 1950–51, architectural design, Belfast College of Art; from 1953, Architectural Association, London.

Biography 1954–55, Clendinning worked in the architecture office of Morris in Metz, 1955–56, with architects Maxwell Fry, Jane Drew, and Denys Lasdun; 1956–60, in the architecture bureau of British Railways in an updating program of stations in Manchester and Oxford; from 1960, was a partner of Sir John Brown, A.E. Henson and Partner; 1965–85, was an independent interior designer in London; became interested in laminated wood furniture and, 1965, designed a series of colorful chairs for Liberty's made by his family's firm in Northern Ireland and 1965 Maxima modular furniture series (composed of 25 separate and differently colored wooden parts for forming 300 possible chairs, sofas, tables, or cabinets) by Race in the US. The Maxima range failed due to cost but became a cult idea and, thus, realized Clendinning as a typical representiave of the Pop culture in British furniture design. Also designed inflatable furniture range, some with plastic granules, to be variously arranged as 'futuristic' living ensembles; c. 1970, designed shops in London's Covent Garden area, including the façade of Terance Conran's restaurant on Neal Street. His own domicile (with designer Ralph Adron) was widely published.
Bibliography *Studio Dictionary of Design and Decoration*, New York: Viking, 1973: 99–100.

Cliff, Clarice (1899–1972)

British ceramic designer and painter; born Tunstall, Staffordshire.

Training Before 1916, painting in evening classes, School of Art, Tunstall, and 1924–25, evening classes, School of Art, Burslem, both in Stoke-on-Trent; 1927, sculpture, Royal College of Art, London.
Biography 1912 at age 13, Cliff began work at earthenware potter Lingard Webster near her home in Staffordshire, learning freehand painting on pottery, and, subsequently, at Hollinshead and Kirkham, Tunstall, learning lithography, while concurrently studying painting in evening classes in Tunstall; 1916–20 at Stoke-on-Trent, worked for local pottery manufacturer A.J. Wilkinson (the potter for Royal Staffordshire), where she was associated with managing director Colley Shorter, whom she married in 1941; subsequently, set up her own studio; c. 1924–27, having been given full rein by Shorter and decorating manager Jack Walker, executed hand-painted Art Déco and ad hoc patterns on old stock for Newport Pottery, one of Wilkinson's subsidiaries; 1929–35 at Newport, produced the Bizarre design range, which achieved instant success; to meet demand, hired young painters to follow her style. Fantasque and Biarritz wares followed. At Wilkinson's, under the Bizarre name from 1934, she became artistic director for ceramics designed by Paul Nash, Laura Knight, Duncan Grant, Vanessa Bell, and other well-known names 1932–34; oversaw more than 150 employees in the decorating workshop. (Knight designed her own shapes for the Circus range as well as decorated them, although finished blanks were almost always sent to the artists.) Cliff painted the motifs executed by the artists, including Graham Sutherland. To 1963, she continued to design brilliantly colored motifs and geometrically shaped pottery.
Exhibitions Bizarre ware exhibitions were held in London, throughout Britain, in Australia and New Zealand. Wilkinson's range of tableware by well-known designers under Cliff was shown at 1934 *Modern Art for the Table*, Harrods department store, London. Other work included in 1979 venue, London (catalog below).
Bibliography Cat., *Thirties: British Art and Design Before the War*, London: Arts Council of Great Britain/Hayward Gallery, 1979. Leonard Griffin and Louis K. and Susan Pear Meisel, *Clarice Cliff: The Bizarre Affair*, New York: Abrams, 1988. Irene and Gordon Hopwood, *The Shorter Connection: A.J. Wilkinson, Clarice Cliff, Crown Devon: A Family Pottery, 1874–1974*, Shepton Beauchamp, Somerset: Dennis, 1992. Leonard Griffin, *Clarice Cliff: The Art of Bizarre, A Definitive Centenary Celebration*, London: Pavilion, 1999.

Franco Clivio and Dieter Raffler (1942–). Accu 6 cordless lawn shears. 1974. Plastic casing, Xylan coated blades, and self-charging electrical cord, 4 1/4 x 11 x 3 3/4" (10.8 x 27.9 x 9.5 cm). Mfr.: Gardena, Kress & Kastner, Germany. Gift of the mfr. MoMA.

Clivio, Franco (1942–)

Swiss industrial designer; active Zürich and Ulm.

Training 1965–68 under Walter Zeischegg and others, Hochschule für Gestaltung, Ulm, Germany.
Biography Clivio became an assistant lecturer at the Ulm design school; from 1968, was product designer for Gardena of Ulm. Design clients have included Design Emscherpark International, Erco (lighting), FSB (doorhandles), Siemens (electronics), and others, including with Austrian designer Dieter Raffler (1942–). From early 1980s, Clivio has lectured in product design, Hochschule für Gestaltung und Kunst (HGKZ), Zürich; Istituto Universitario di Architettura (IUAV), Venice; and institutions in Finland, Germany, and the US.
Citations Three 1987 awards (for Schleichers products) and two 2000 awards (for Erco lighting), Industrie Forum Design (iF), Hanover; and others.

Clotet Ballús, Lluis (1941–)

Spanish architect and furniture designer; born Barcelona.

Training 1965, Escola Tècnica Superior d'Arquitectura de Barcelona (ETSAB).
Biography 1961–64, Clotet worked in offices of Frederic Correa and Alfonso Milá; 1964 with Pep Bonet, Cristian Cirici, and Óscar Tusquets Blanca, founded Studio PER; 1984 with Ignacio Paricio, established an architecture practice; all Barcelona. Work has included 1970–72 Casa Regás and the belvedere in Llofriu, Girona; 1972–78 Casa Vittoria, Pantelleria Island, Italy. Clotet was a founding partner of Bd Ediciones de Diseño, which produced some of his furniture and furnishings, including 1974 Estanteria Hialina and 1980 Estanteria Hipostila bookshelves, 1986 Zoraida series of knock-down metal tables and pedestals, and numerous other pieces. 1977–84, he was professor, Escola Tècnica Superior d'Arquitectura de Barcelona (ETSAB); from 1990s, has been working with Ignacio Paricio on buildings, including 1992 Palacio de Los Deportes, Granada; 1992 Viviendas, Summer Olympiad Village, Barcelona; 1995 swimming pool, Barcelona.
Citations 1965 and 1970–71 Premi FAD d'Interiorisme (for best interiors) , 1977–78, 1978–79, 1988, 1989 Premi FAD d'Arquitectura (for best Barcelona building), 1978–79 Premi FAD de Restauració (for best restoration work); 1990 Premi Nacional del Patrimoni Cultural, Generalitat de Catalunya; 1995–97 first prize, 4th Concurso de Arquitectura de Ladrillo.
Bibliography Juli Capella and Quim Larrea, *Designed by Architects in the 1980s*, New York: Rizzoli, 1988. Albrecht Bangert and Karl Michael Armer, *80s Style: Designs of the Decade*, New York: Abbeville, 1990.

Coard, Marcel (1889–1975)

French architect and furniture designer; active Paris.

Training Architecture, École Nationale Supérieure des Beaux-Arts, Paris.
Biography 1919, Coard began working as an interior designer and opened his own shop in Paris, where he offered antique furniture and reproductions and through which he designed classical interiors; worked for only a few clients, including couturier Jacques Doucet, for whom he designed and made furniture in simple forms; regularly used rare and unusual materials and appliqués, including shagreen, mirror-glass, mother-of-pearl, lapis lazuli, lacquer, and semi-precious stones; designed only one-of-a-kind pieces; was one of the first to cover furniture surfaces with parchment, except for Bugatti, who had used the material at the turn of the century. Like Pierre Legrain and Jean Dunand, Coard's designs were inspired by Cubist forms and West Africa and the South Pacific native art. His predilection for glass was expressed in c. 1920 interior design of a town-house near the Bois de Boulogne, Paris.
Bibliography Yvonne Brunhammer, *Le cinquantenaire de l'exposition de 1925*, Paris: Musée des Arts Décoratifs, 1976: 122. Victor Arwas, *Art Déco*, New York: Abrams, 1980. Frederick R. Brandt, *Late 19th and Early 20th Century Decorative Arts...*, Richmond, Va.: Virginia Museum of Fine Arts, 1985. Pierre Kjellberg, *Art déco: les maîtres du mobilier, le décor des paquebots*, Paris: Amateur, 1986: 47–48.

Nigel Coates. OXO modular chairs. c. 1999. Beech, foam, and plywood, 'O' model: h. 29 1/2 x l. 29 x d. 29" (75 x 73.5 x 73.5 cm); 'X' model: h. 29 1/2 x l. 31 3/8 x d. 31 1/2" (75 x 79.5 x 80 cm). Mfr.: Hitch Mylius, UK.

Coates, Nigel (1949–)

British architect and furniture designer; born Malvern, Worcestershire.

Training 1969–71, Nottingham University; 1972–74, Architectural Association, London.
Biography 1971, Coates settled in London, working in the architecture department of Lambeth Town Hall; 1985 with Doug Branson, set up Branson Coates, realizing domestic and commercial commissions for clients in Britain and Japan, some of which included the designs of restaurants in London, the restaurants and shops for clients Jasper Conran (1987 Dublin and 1989 Tokyo), Katharine Hamnett (1988 Glasgow), and Jigsaw (1988 London). He worked regularly in Japan; commissions included mixed-use development, Tokyo; 1985 Metropole club/café; Noah's Ark restaurant; and Hotel Marittimo, Otaru. From 1976, he taught, Architectural Association; was a founding member of group Narrative Architecture Today (NATO), collaborating with it on 1986 Caffè Bongo and 1986 Bohemia jazz club in Japan. To end of 1980s, his furniture was only produced in Japan. Subsequently, designed 1988 Otaru couch and chair, Lips sofa (based on Salvador Dalí original), Tongue chair, and other models by SCP (Sheridan Coakley Products), London. Recently, became best known for the British pavilion, 1998 *Esposizione Inter-nazionale (Expo '98)*, Lisbon, and Body Zone at 2000 Millennium Dome, London; is professor of architectural design, Royal College of Art.
Bibliography Rick Poynor, *Nigel Coates: The City in Motion*, New York: Rizzoli, 1989. Albrecht Bangert and Karl Michael Armer, *80s Style: Designs of the Decade*, New York: Abbeville, 1990: 228. *Contract*, July 1990: 26. *Issue 5*, Design Museum, winter 1990.

Coates, Wells Wintemute (1895–1958)

Canadian architect and designer; born Tokyo; active Britain.

Training 1913–15 and 1919–21, engineering, University of British Columbia, Vancouver; to 1924, engineering, University of London.
Biography His mother was an architecture pupil of Louis Sullivan and Frank Lloyd Wright in Chicago. 1924–27, he was a journalist, draftsperson, personal assistant, and lumberjack in Canada; 1923–26, worked with architects in London and Paris; 1929, settled in London and began working on his own, first on interiors and later on architecture and industrial design; designed shop interiors for Cresta and others; 1931 with Jack and Molly Pritchard, formed The Isokon Furniture Company, an association that produced innovative plywood furniture and Functionalist buildings; commissioned by Pritchard, introduced Britain to the International Style with his 1931–32 Lawn Road flats, Hampstead; was a member of Twentieth Century Group and of Unit One; 1933, became a founding member of the Modern Architecture Research Group (MARS); 1933–34, was in partnership with David Pleydell-Bouverie and, 1932–34, with Patrick Gwynne. The tubular-steel furniture for his own flat in Yeoman's Court, Knightsbridge, London, and 1925 Embassy Court, Brighton, was produced by Pel. From 1932, designed widely published radio casings by Ekco, the first truly modern appliance designs in Britain. Coates's 1934 AD65 circular plastic radio was also widely published and became the best-known radio in Britain. Others by Ekco include 1946 A22 radio and Princess portable radio. Though a restyled version of the cabinet was reissued after World War II, Coates completely redesigned Princess, resulting in the 1948 Princess radio in colorful plastic to look like an attaché case, with an adjustable clear handle; 1950s, produced designs for TV casings. Even though an innovative and influential architect and designer in the 1930s, producing little after World War II, he practiced in Vancouver and unsuccessfully pursued rail and ocean transportation studies and town planning while working on aircraft interiors for De Havilland and BOAC.
Work 1932–34 Isokon flats, Lawn Road, Hampstead; designs for c. 1932 'Isotype' dwellings; 1934 'Sunspan' house (with Pleydell-Bouverie); furniture for Isokon from 1931; 1931–32 studios, control rooms, and effects suites, and 1935 studios for the BBC (with Raymond McGrath and Serge Chermayeff), Broadcasting House, London, and Newcastle; 1934 Embassy Court flats, Brighton; Ekco radio and radiogram housings, including 1934 Cole AD65 radio in brown phenolic; 1934 heater for Lawn Road penthouse of Pritchard; Flexunit furniture of c. 1936 by P.E. Gane; Thermovent heater; 1937–39 flats, Palace Gate, London; Commander and Mrs. Gwynne's 1937–39 'The Homewood' residence (with Patrick Gwynne), Esher; steel furniture produced by Pel; shops and showrooms for Crysede, Silks Ltd., and Cresta Silks; Telekinema for 1951 *Festival of Britain*, London; Wingsail catamaran; various one-off furniture models; and many unrealized projects and entries for design competitions (including flats, with Denys Lasdun, for *News Chronicle* Schools Competition).
Exhibitions/citations Participated in 1951 *Festival of Britain* exposition, London. Work subject of 1979 traveling exhibition, beginning at Museum of Modern Art, Oxford (catalog below). Elected fellow, Royal Institute of British Architects (RIBA) in 1938; 1944, Honorary Royal Designer for Industry, UK, in 1944.
Bibliography Wells Coates, 'The Conditions for an Architecture for Today,' *Architectural Association Journal*, Apr. 1938. J.M. Richards, 'Wells Coates 1893–1958,' *Architectural Review*, vol. 124, Dec. 1958: 357–60. 'Wells Coates 1895–1958: An Address to the 1957 Graduation Banquet, School of Architecture, University of British Columbia,' *Journal of the Royal Architectural Institute of Canada*, vol. 36, June 1959: 205–11. Cat., Dennis Sharp et al., *Pel and Tubular Steel Furniture in the Thirties*, London: Architectural Association, 1977. Sherban

Cantacuzino, *Wells Coates: A Monograph*, London: Gordon Fraser, 1978. Cat., *Wells Coates, Architect and Designer*, Oxford: Oxford Polytechnic, 1979. Cat., *Thirties: British Art and Design Before the War*, London: Arts Council of Great Britain/Hayward Gallery, 1980. Cat., Kathryn B. Hiesinger and George H. Marcus III (eds.), *Design Since 1945*, Philadelphia: Philadelphia Museum of Art, 1983.

Coca-Cola
> See Samuelson, Alexander.

Cocteau, Jean-Maurice-Clément-Eugène (1889–1963)

French poet, novelist, playwright, actor, cinematographer, sculptor, draftsperson, and decorative designer; born Maisons-Laffitte; active Paris.

Biography Cocteau dramatically parlayed himself into becoming internationally well known for his avant-garde intellectual pursuits; was a friend of leading artists, including Amedeo Modigliani; persuaded Pablo Picasso to collaborate with Les Ballets Russes on *Parade* (1917); though associated with Cubism and Surrealism, was himself of no school; was a prolific draftsperson, drawing on every imaginable medium and surface, and a poet and called his work 'graphic poetry'; with musicians Darius Milhaud and Jean Wiener, introduced jazz to France in the café Le Bœuf sur le Toît, Paris, where intellectuals of the time met; was active in theater design with Sergei Diaghilev and composers Igor Stravinskii and Eric Satie and as a filmmaker, including his adaptation of *La belle et la bête* (1946) and three films on the role of the artist: *Le Sang d'un poète* (1930), *Orphée* (1950), and *Testament d'Orphée* (1960). Cocteau's nightclub in Paris was known as the Grand Écart. Active as a novelist (such as *Les enfants terribles*, 1923) and playwright (such as an adaptation of *Antigone*, 1928), he also produced a great number of paintings and drawings, including a large body of homosexual erotica; practiced pottery 1957–63, working with Marie-Madeleine and Phillipe Madeline-Jolly; 1960, gave friend François Hugo drawings and models from which a series of jewels was produced. Cocteau designed idiosyncratic ceramics and other jewelry, and silverware for Christofle. Credit to Cocteau for having designed Cartier's 1923 Trinity three-band ring, based on a much older concept, may be fallacious.
Bibliography *Dictionnaire de l'art moderne et contemporain*, Paris: Hazan, 1992.

CODIFA (Comité de Développement des Industries Françaises de l'Ameublement)

French trade association.

History 1971, CODIFA was established to represent the interests of the French furniture industry; promotes research, innovation, and modernization of manufacturing processes; assisted in the 1979 creation of VIA (Valorisation de l'Innovation dans l'Ameublement), a French furniture association, and in VIA's public relations and promotion of new French furniture.
> See VIA.

Codman Jr., Ogden (1863–1951)

American interior designer and architect; active New York.

Biography In contrast to prevailing cluttered Edwardian interiors, Codman introduced white paint, flowered fabrics, and airy rooms; with Edith Wharton, wrote the influential book *The Decoration of Houses* (1897). Codman's most important commission came in the winter of 1893 from Alice and Cornelius Vanderbilt II. The Breakers of 1895, as the Vanderbilt house in Newport, Rhode Island, became known, had Richard Morris Hunt as its architect. J. Allard, Parisian decorators, were assigned the first-floor reception areas. Codman's rooms, which inspired generations of designers, were light and informally elegant, with simple fabrics and cream-colored furniture and the first of many variations on neoclassical themes. c. 1903, he and Mrs. Wharton designed her house on Park Avenue, New York. He borrowed freely from 18th-century French, English, and American styles; preferred small rooms to grand ones, paneling to wallpaper, painted furniture to stained, and symmetry to asymmetry. He was hired by Elsie de Wolfe to help her design at the beginning of her career, though, like Wharton, she kept his collaboration a secret. Codman's work included the Lloyd Bryce Colonial Revival mansion, Roslyn, N.Y., and Bayard Thayer house (now Hampshire House restaurant), Boston. His masterpiece is considered to be 1929–31 La Leopolda, a large palazzo in Villefranche-

Luigi Colani. Zocker child's desk/seat. 1971–72. Polyethylene, 25 1/2 x 21 1/16 x 24 3/8" (64.8 x 53.5 x 62 cm). Mfr.: Top System, Germany. Courtesy Quittenbaum Kunstauktionen, Munich.

sur-Mer, France, which he had built for himself; later rented to the Duke and Duchess of Windsor. Codman compiled a 36,000-entry index to French châteaux.
Bibliography Edith Wharton and Ogden Codman Jr., *The Decoration of Houses*, New York: Scribners, 1897. Cat., Pauline C. Metcalf (ed.), *Ogden Codman and the Decoration of Houses*, New York: National Academy of Design, 1988. Stephen Calloway, *Twentieth-Century Decoration*, New York: Rizzoli, 1988: 61–62, 80–81. Mitchell Owens, 'Let the Sunshine in,' *Elle Decor*, May 1990: 28, 32.

Cogliati, Paolo (1963–)

Italian designer; born Milan.

Training To 1998, architecture, Politecnico, Milan.
Biography From 1989–95, Cogliati mainly worked as a freelance architect; 1992–95, was active as a furniture designer and, from 1996, particularly through Totem, which he founded as a producer of knockdown furniture; 1997–2001, founded and was president of Materia Utile, an ecological furniture consortium of four companies; 1998, was a guest lecturer on bioarchitecture, ELEA, Milan, and, 2000, INBAR, Milan, and Facoltà di Architettura, Università degli Studi 'La Sapienza,' Rome; 2000 in collaboration with 'La Sapienza' and other institutions, participated in a project to determine the criteria for furniture used in agritourism structures; 2002, was a member, committee for the definition of an Italian standard for ecological furniture, with Associazione Nazionale Architettura Biologica (ANAB), Isituto Certificazione Etica e Ambientale (ICEA), Forest Stewardship Council (FSC), and 'La Sapienza.' His clients for furniture and lighting have included Effebi, Fun Life, Ony-Ki, and Riva.
Exhibitions 2001 *Carrefour de la création* (1998 Canoa bed with Luigi Barba, by Totem), Centre Georges Pompidou, Paris.
Bibliography Mel Byars, *50 Beds...*, Hove: RotoVision, 2000.

Colani, Luigi (b. Lutz Colani 1928–)

German/Italian designer; born Berlin to a Swiss father.

Training From 1946, sculpture and painting, Hochschule für bildende Künste, Berlin; 1949–52, in aerodynamics; subsequently, at the Sorbonne, Paris.
Biography 1952–53, Colani worked at the Douglas aircraft factory in California and was active in research on new materials and high-speed technology; 1954, went to Paris and then returned to Berlin; 1957, changed his forename to Luigi; 1968, organized a design team Rheda, Westphalia, Germany, to specialize in the use of plastics in furniture and automobiles. His widely published 1970 Drop porcelain dinner service by Rosenthal included a teapot with the handle near the center of gravity to facilitate pouring, footed cups to prevent liquid from collecting in the saucer, and thin-walled porcelain to minimize heat loss. 1972, he moved to Harkotten Castle in Fuchtorf/Sassenberg, Germany, and teaches experimental design, sponsored by automobile

and aircraft companies and NASA space authorities; 1973, founded Colani Design Center in Japan; designed 1985 Robot Theater in Tokyo, in the shape of an open mussel; 1986, founded Colani Design Center in Bern and 1988, opened branches in Toulouse and Bremen; 1988, was named honorary professor, Universität Bremen; designed 1995 Bio City, intended for Changming island, China; 1995, taught, University of Tongji; 1996–97, was active in Siro, Japan, and designed pianos, TV sets, eye glasses, jewelry, office furniture, tools, wallpaper, decorative furniture. Over a period of time, other work has included a 1969 plastic pedestal armchair attributed to manufacturer Lusch, 1971–72 Der Colani one-piece polyethlene chair by Top System, 1977 Plycor side chair in fiberglass, 1981 tea service by Melitta, various 1980s cameras by Canon, 1981 No. 1 and 1986 441/432 writing instruments by Pelikan.
Citations 1972 Bundespreis Produktdesign (for Drop service), Rat für Formgebung (German design council).
Bibliography Luigi Colani, *For a Brighter Tomorrow*, Tokyo: San ei Shobo, 1981. Tommaso Trini, 'Il design post-diluviano di Luigi Colani,' *Domus*, no. 636, Feb. 1983: 48–49. Cat., Kathryn B. Hiesinger and George H. Marcus III (eds.), *Design Since 1945*, Philadelphia: Philadelphia Museum of Art, 1983. *Luigi Colani: Design 1*, Zofingen: Inova, 1986. Peter Dunas (ed.), *Luigi Colani und die organisch—dynamische form seit dem Jugendstil*, Munich: Prestel, 1993/1997. Philippe Pernodet and Bruce Mehly, *Luigi Colani*, Paris: Dis Voir, 2000.

Cole, Eric Kirkham (1901–1965); Ekco Radio Company
British domestic electronics industrialist.

History 1921, Ekco Radio (named for Eric Kirkham COle) was founded by Eric Kirkham Cole in Southend-on-Sea, Essex; first produced radio casings in wooden, resembling conventional historist furniture pieces; 1930s, was the first radio manufacturer in Britain to set up a plastics molding plant (Ekco Mouldings), although early Bakelite cabinets were unsatisfactory and sold badly. Plastic models included 1930 Ekco 313 and 1932 M25 radio receivers. Based on patterns for traditional wooden cabinets, they were unappealing. However, Cole commissioned designers including Serge Chermayeff and Wells Coates to design a new line of radio casings, notable were Coates's inventive geometric and widely published plastic casings for the firm in the early 1930s; his stylish 1934 Ekco AD65 radio was Cole's first break with the 'furniture style' tradition and became the most popular wireless cabinet of the period in Britain, with its chrome grille, circular silhouette, and prominent dials. Ekco cabinets were produced in conservative finishes (black, brown, and walnut) compared to some contemporary American sets in brightly colored plastics.
Exhibitions Coates's concentric plastic-and-chrome 1946 A22 model was shown at 1946 *Britain Can Make It* exhibition, Victoria and Albert Museum, London.
Bibliography Penny Sparke, *Introduction to Design and Culture in the Twentieth Century*, London: Allen and Unwin, 1986. *The Radio*, London: Design Museum, 1989.
> See Coates, Wells Wintemute.

Colefax, Sibyl (b. Sibyl Halsey c. 1875–1950)
British collector and interior designer; active London.

Biography She entertained guests at Onslow Square and Argyll House; rivaled hostesses Lady Oxford, Lady Asquith, Lady Cunard, and Lady Ottoline Morrell; when her husband Arthur Colefax died in 1936, continued to entertain on a small scale at her home on Lord North Street, London; from 1922, cultivated the artists of the Bloomsbury circle, who treated her with some disdain. 1936, Virginia Woolf read the paper 'Am I a Snob?' at the Memoir Club, mocking Colefax's social pretensions, though they remained friends. By 1933, Colefax had begun working as an interior decorator; 1938, setting up Colefax and Co.; with codirector John Fowler, designed highly detailed interiors in unconventional colors. Colefax was one of the 'lady decorators' in London between the wars, 'helping' with the decoration of wealthy friends' houses. John Fowler, a decorator of some prominence, had, before his partnership with Colefax, been active in his own shop on King's Road, London, near the residences of Lady Colefax and Syrie Maugham. Both had courted him to join their firms.
Bibliography Cecil Beaton, *The Glass of Fashion*, London, 1954. J. Schulkind (ed.), *Moments of Being*, London, 1976. Alan and Veronica Palmer, *Who's Who in Bloomsbury*, New York: St. Martin's, 1987. Stephen Calloway, *Twentieth-Century Decoration*, New York: Rizzoli, 1988: 139, 141, 216, pl. 326. Chester Jones, *Colefax & Fowler: The Best in English Interior Decoration*, London: Barrie & Jenkins, 1989. Mark Hampton, *The Legendary Decorators of the Twentieth Century*, New York: Doubleday, 1992. Robert Banks-Pye, *Inspirational Interiors*, London: Ryland, Peters & Small, 1997.

Colenbrander, Theodorus A.C. (1841–1930)
Dutch architect and ceramicist; born Doesburg.

Training Possibly, first lessons in architectural drawing in Doesburg.
Biography Colenbrander moved to Arnhem, worked with L.H. Eberson (later principal architect to King Willem III), and won architectural competitions, including 1867 town hall in Amsterdam; designed a number of country houses in Arnhem and, subsequently, became the draftsperson at the Ministry of War in The Hague; 1884–89, was artistic advisor to and designer at Rozenburg, an art pottery in The Hague; became an interior designer to artists and wealthy clients; at the end of the 19th century, designed carpets; from 1895, was designer and advisor to the carpet factory at Amersfoort and later at Deventer; shortly before World War I, returned to ceramics at Zuid-Holland at Gouda but left due to artistic differences. 1917, ceramics factory RAM was established in Arnhem, founded by banker Charles Engelberts and art dealer Henri van Lerven, with the first vases produced in 1921. Over a ten-year period, Colenbrander designed some 700 different motifs at RAM for over 60 new vase, plate, and bowl models. 1924–26, several thousand pieces of his were made. Except for one visit to Paris, he never left the Netherlands.
Bibliography Cat., *Industry and Design in the Netherlands, 1850–1950*, Amsterdam: Stedelijk Museum, 1985.

Coles, Peter (1954–1985)
> See Dumas, Rena.

Collas, Achille (1795–1859)
> See Barbedienne, Ferdinand.

Coll-Part, Rashdar (1964–)
French designer.

Biography Wishing to be an enigma, he uses the Coll-Part pseudonym and provides a possibly incorrect year of his birth; makes lighting and furniture, calling on reprocessed and old materials such as in the 1997 Xmas Tree (a piled collection of traditional lamps designed by others), a chandelier (made of dangling wine bottles), and a table (with legs composed of stacked cooking pots). He presents his biography thus: 'Sketchy training. Disappointing experiences. A great desire for any old collaboration on anything. Activities in other fields of creation or in teaching: fewer and fewer. Publications/bibliography: All that is either useless or vain. Personal cultural references: BEPC [French junior-high-school diploma].'
Bibliography Mel Byars, *50 Tables: Innovations in Design and Materials*, Hove: RotoVision, 1997. www.via.asso.fr.

Collin, Vincent (1963–)
French designer; active Paris.

Training Auto-didact.
Biography 1991, Collin met French decorator Olivier Gagnère, with whom he established a partnership and began making Gagnère's vases, lamps, and furniture; subsequently, established Éditions Limitée shop and manufacturing facility in Paris and began to design and make, or have made, his own vases, lamps, and furniture, both in small series and customized, in steel, bronze, ceramics, and wood.
Bibliography www.via.asso.fr.

Collinson and Lock
British furniture manufacturer; located London.

History 1870, Frank G. Collinson and George James Lock formed a firm to produce and market so-called art furniture. Illustrated by J. Moyr Smith, its first catalog, *Sketches of Artistic Furniture* (1871), included designs by Smith and architect Thomas Edward Collcutt. Its stenciled, turned, and incised furniture included cabinets, sideboards, tables, chairs, wardrobes, and dressing tables. E.W. Godwin designed some of Collinson's furniture, including the 1873 Lucretia cabinet painted by Pre-Raphaelite artist Charles Fairfax Murray. The firm's commissions included furnishings for G.E. Street's Law Courts, London, 1874–82, and the Savoy Theatre, 1881; during the 1870s, promoted ebonized furniture and Japanese lacquerwork, which it helped popu-

Gino Colombini. Covered pail (no. KS 1146). 1954. Polyethylene and metal, overall h. 10 1/2 x dia. 11" (26.7 x 27.9 cm). Mfr.: Kartell, Italy (1970). Gift of Philip Johnson. MoMA.

larize in the US. Some of the birds and female figures on its ebonized furniture were painted by Albert Moore. 1885, sculptor Stephen Webb joined the firm as chief designer and took his inspiration from French and Italian furniture. Seeking commissions from wealthy clients, the firm moved to Oxford Street in London in c. 1885; 1897 when George Lock withdrew his capital to set up his own business, was bought by Gillow and Company.
Exhibitions Collcutt's furniture shown at 1878 *Exposition Universelle*, Paris, and 1876 *Centennial Exposition*, Philadelphia. Other models (including ebonized furniture painted by Albert Moore) shown at 1871 (2nd) and 1873 (3rd) editions of *Annual International Exhibition*, London.
Bibliography Julian Kinchin, 'Collinson and Lock,' *Connoisseur*, no. 201, May 1979: 46–53. Doreen Bolger Burke et al., *In Pursuit of Beauty: Americans and the Aesthetic Movement*, New York: The Metropolitan Museum of Art/Rizzoli, 1987: 412.

Colombi, Alberto (1941–)

Italian designer; born and active Milan.

Training To 1965, Politecnico, Milan.
Biography 1965, Colombi began his professional career; designed furniture, accessories, and interiors; worked with Gruppo DAM (Designer Associati Milano), including participation in the conception of 1970 Libro chair produced by Gruppo Industriale Busnelli.
Citations First prize (Gruppo DAM fabric designs by Arredamento) at 1969 (1st) Concorso Internazionale Arve Bayer; first prize (plastic-laminate designs, with architect P. Guzzetti) at 1973 (3rd) Concorso Mia Abet Print; and first prize (furnishings by Driade and by Kartell for Casa Vacanza Mini Appartamenti) at open competition, 1974 Fiera Internazionale, Genoa.
Bibliography *ADI Annual*, Milan: Associazione per il Disegno Industriale, 1976.
> See Anti-Design.

Colombini, Gino (1915–)

Italian industrial designer; born Milan.

Biography 1933–52, Colombini worked in the studio of architect Franco Albini, where he designed furniture and commercial and domestic architecture; 1949–61, headed the Kartell Samco technical department in Binasco; was a pioneer in high-quality plastic furniture manufactured in Italy. His interest in subtlety and precision was manifested in plastic items ranging from tureens and colanders to lemon squeezers and buckets, including a 1955 vertical-ribbed garbage can (re-entered into production by Kartell).
Citations Premio Compasso d'Oro (all but one for products by Kartell) in 1954, 1955, 1956 (three citations), 1957 (three citations, one for a product by Verbinia), 1959 (four citations), and 1960 (three citations).
Bibliography Gillo Dorfles, *Il disegno industriale e la sua estetica*, Bologna, 1963: figs. 113, 136, 138. Cat., *Design & Design*, Florence: Centro Di, 1979: 44, 60, 69, 74. Augusto Morello, *Plastic and Design = Plastiche e design*, Milan: Arcadia, 1988. Jeremy Myerson and Sylvia Katz, *Conran Design Guides: Tableware*, London: Conran Octopus, 1990: 38–39, 72–73. Cat., *Kartell Museo*, Milan: Fondazione Museo Kartell, 1999. Marie-Laure, *La donation Kartell: un environnement plastique 1949–2000*, Paris: Centre Georges Pompidou, 2000.

Colombo, Carlo (1967–)

Italian designer; active Carimate (CO).

Biography From 1993, Colombo has been primarily active as a designer and consultant; however, from 1995, also executed design commissions of offices and residences; taught packaging and is assistant chairperson of interior architecture, Facoltà di Architettura, Politecnico, Milan; has participated in industrial-design conferences in Israel, Greece, and Portugal. Furniture/furnishings clients have included Agape, Cappellini, Vittorio Bonacina, Ycami, Obumex, Poliform, Varenna, and Units.
Exhibitions Work shown at 1993 *Design, Miroir du Siècle* (Ligabue table by Vittorio Bonacina), Grand Palais, Paris; 1995 exhibition (Archimede bed by Cappellini), Neues Museum Weserburg Bremen; 1996 exhibition (Zigozago carpet by Cappellini), Museum für angewandte Kunst, Cologne.

Colombo, 'Joe' Cesare (1930–1971)

Italian painter, sculptor, and designer; born Milan.

Training To 1949, Accademia di Belle Arti di Brera, and 1950–54, Politecnico; both Milan.
Biography 1951–55, Colombo was principally an avant-garde painter and sculptor; joined the Movimento Nucleare (founded 1951 by Enrico Baj and Sergio Dangelo) and Movimento Arte Concreta (MAC); 1953, showed art at the jazz club Santa Tecla in Milan, for which he designed a ceiling. His first architecture work was a 1956 condominium building. From 1959, he managed the family electrical-equipment business; 1962, opened his own design office in Milan. His first commissions include 1961 Impronta armchair, 1962 Acrilica lamp by O luce, 1963 Mini-kitchen by Boffi, and 1964 Corsair air-conditioning unit by Rheem-Safim. His range of objects included furniture, pottery, lighting, and electrical appliances. Among Italian designers of the 1955–65 decade, he is notable for his development of an elegant Functionalist furniture aesthetic. The 1963 Combi-Center, 1963 Elda armchair, 1965 Spider lamp, and 1969 Tube chair exemplify his approach. Clients included Bernini, Candy, Comfort, Elco, Sormani, Stilnovo, O luce, and Italora. His 1965–67 stacking chair (no. 4867, or Universale), produced by Kartell in injection-molded polypropylene, was an unsuccessful attempt to create a single-component chair. Work also includes 1968 Poker card table by Zanotta, 1970 air conditioner by Candy, and, still in production by Bieffeplast, 1969 Boby portable storage system in ABS polymer. Designed Associazione per il Desegno (ADI) pavilion, 1968 (2nd) Eurodomus, Turin, and a futuristic environment at 1972 *Visiona 3* (sponsored by Bayer at the Möbelmesse in Cologne), with adjunct installations by Verner Panton and Olivier Mourgue.
Exhibitions/citations Fine art was shown with Movimento Nucleare group at 1952 exhibition, Amici della Francia; 1952 *Arte Organica Disintegrismo Macchinismo Arte Totale*, Saletta dell'Elicotero; 1953 exhibition, Galerie Saint Laurent, Brussels; 1954 exhibitions (with Baj), Ca' Giustinian, Venice and Verviers; three open-air rest areas with benches and 'television shrines,' where TV sets appeared as miniature theaters, 1954 (10th) Triennale di Milano. His designs appeared in a large number of exhibitions, including the Triennali di Milano (from 1954 onward), 1967 Salone del Mobile, Milan (1965–6 Chair 4860), and 1972 *Italy: The New Domestic Landscape* (prototype, with Ignazia Favata, of Total Furnishing Unit and of Uniblock furniture habitats), The Museum of Modern Art, New York (catalog below). Work subject of 1984 venue, Musée d'Art Moderne, Villeneuve d'Ascq, France; 1966, Design Research store, New York; 1995, Galleria d'Arte Moderna e Contemporanea, Bergamo. Received 1964 (13th), Triennale di Milano (three medals); 1963 National Institute of Architecture IN/Arch award (1963 Hotel Continental interiors, Sardinia); 1967 and 1968 ADI awards, US; 1967, 1970 (four citations), and posthumously 1981 and 1991 Premio Compasso d'Oro.
Bibliography 'Una nuova concezione dell'arredamento: Joe Cesare Colombo,' *Lotus*, vol. 3, 1966–67: 176–95. M. Pia Valota, 'Joe C.

Colombo,' *Casabella* 35, no. 358, 1971: 46–48. Cat., *Milano 70/70: un secolo d'arte, dal 1946 al 1970*, vol. 3, Milan: Museo Poldi Pezzoli, 1972. Cat., Emilio Ambasz, *Italy: The New Domestic Landscape*, New York: The Museum of Modern Art, 1972. Alfonso Grassi and Anty Pansera, *Atlante del design italiano 1940/1980*, Milan: Fabbri, 1980. Cat., Kathryn B. Hiesinger and George H. Marcus III (eds.), *Design Since 1945*, Philadelphia: Philadelphia Museum of Art, 1983. Ignazia Favata, *Joe Colombo, Designer 1930–1971*, Milan: Idea, 1988. Cat., Vittorio Fagone (ed.), *I Colombo: Joe Colombo 1930–1971/Gianni Colombo 1937–1993*, Milan: Mazzotta, 1995. Paola Antonelli (ed.), *Objects of Design: The Museum of Modern Art*, New York: The Museum of Modern Art, 2003: 159, 162, 253–54, 261, 264.

Colombo, Marco (1952–)
> See Barbaglia, Mario.

Colombo Ari, Antonio (1946–)

Italian designer; born and active Meda.

Biography 1967, Colombo Ari began his professional career; designed ceramics, glassware, and furniture in wood, metal, and glass. Clients have included Arflex (1970 research on seating, 1971 Twin table, and 1974 Tuli table), Manifattura Isa (optical research in color and design), Selenova (research in lighting and furniture), Saint-Gobain (marketing of crystal), Airborne (1975 Sofone furniture collection), Giancarlo Pozzi (furniture), Ceramiche Mauri, and IKS.
Bibliography *ADI Annual 1976*, Milan: Associazione per il Disegno Industriale, 1976.

Colonna, Edward (b. Edouard Klönne 1862–1948)

German designer and decorator; born near Cologne.

Training 1877–81, architecture in Brussels.
Biography 1882, Colonna moved to New York and worked for Associated Artists, a group of interior decorators headed by Louis Comfort Tiffany; participated in the interior design for real estate businessman Ogden Goelet and shipping magnate Charles Flint; 1884–85, worked for architect Bruce Price; 1885 with Price's assistance, settled in Dayton, Ohio, and worked for Barney and Smith Manufacturing Company, where he designed railroad cars; while there, wrote the book *Essay on Broom-Corn* (1887), showing Art Nouveau work, and designed furniture and *objets d'art*. The book presaged the work of Belgian artists, including Victor Horta and Henry van de Velde, and showed work resembling that of Chicago architect Louis Sullivan. He also published *Materiae Signa, Alchemistic Signs of Various Materials in Common Usage* (1888); was active in Cincinnati, Ohio, as well as Dayton; after a brief stay in Canada in 1888, became an architect in Montréal, primarily of railroad stations; 1893, moved to Paris, where, 1898–1903, he worked for Siegfried Bing's gallery/shop L'Art Nouveau, designing jewelry, furniture, fabrics, porcelain table services, and vases; with Georges de Feure and Eugène Gaillard, installed Bing's pavilion at 1900 *Exposition Universelle*, Paris; after Bing's store closed, went to Toronto in c. 1903, where he was an antiques dealer and interior designer for about five years; from 1913, was based in New York again. Although his designs began to reflect fashionable French Art Déco geometry, his 1920s work lacked the distinctive originality of that of the turn of the century. 1923, he left the US and settled in Nice, France.
Exhibitions Work shown in Bing's pavilion at 1900 *Exhibition Universelle*, Paris. Subject of 1983–84 exhibition, Dayton, Montréal, and Washington, D.C. (catalog below).
Bibliography Charlotte Gere, *American and European Jewelry 1830–1914*, New York: Crown, 1975: 107–68. Yvonne Brunhammer et al., *Art Nouveau Belgium, France*, Houston: Rice University, 1976. Cat., Martin Eidelberg (ed.), *Edward Colonna*, Dayton, Ohio: The Dayton Art Institute, 1983. Annelies Krekel-Aalberse, *Art Nouveau and Art Déco Silver*, New York: Abrams, 1989.

'Joe' Cesare Colombo. Stacking side chair (no. 4867, or Universale). 1965–67. Polypropylene and rubber, 29 x 16 1/2 x 18 1/2" (73.7 x 41.9 x 47 cm), seat h. 16 15/16" (43 cm). Mfr.: Kartell, Italy. Gift of the mfr. MoMA.

Colotte, Aristide (1885–1959)

French glassware designer; born Baccarat.

Training École du Dessin, Cristallerie de Baccarat.
Biography From 1919, Colotte worked as an engraver at Corbin; c. 1920, began producing vessels and animal and human forms (including the head of Christ c. 1928) by cutting solid blocks of crystal into geometric and figurative motifs; c. 1925, became a molder at Cristallerie de Nancy, a rival of Daum, and produced several pieces signed with his name; with the aid of Henri Bossut, produced acid-engraved work for Magasins Réunis; 1926, established his own engraving workshop in Nancy known as Maison d'Art, where he specialized in custom work and Art Déco jewelery. 1939, the Bossut–Colotte collaboration was interrupted by World War II, in which Bossut died. Colotte's work included *pâte-de-verre* and engraving on metal.
Exhibitions/citations Work shown at editions of Salon d'Automne and Société des Artistes Décorateurs. Received Meilleur Ouvrier de France medal (for metal engravings), 1925 *Exposition Internationale des Arts Décoratifs et Industriels Modernes*, Paris.
Bibliography Cat., *Verriers français contemporains: art et industrie*, Paris: Musée des Arts Décoratifs, 1982. *Sammlung Bröhan Kunst der 20er und 30er Jahre*, vol. 3, Berlin, 1985: 99. Janine Bloch-Dermant, *Le verre en France: d'Émile Gallé à nos jours*, Paris: Amateur, 1986. Jean-Louis Curtis, *Baccarat*, Paris: Regard, 1992.

Colucci, Claudio (1965–); CCD

Italian designer; born Locarno, Switzerland; active Paris.

Training 1983–83, decorative arts, Geneva; 1988–91, ENSCI (Les Ateliers), Paris; 1990, exchange student, Kingston Polytechnic (now Kingston University), London.
Biography 1990, Colucci was an assistant at Ron Arad's One Off studio in London; 1992, a trainee at Branson & Coates Architecture in London; 1992, a designer at Pascal Mourgue's studio in Paris; 1992, cofounded Radi Designers in Paris; 1995 under Philippe Starck, was a designer in the Tim Tom department of Thomson multimédia; 1998, established a branch of Radi Designers in Tokyo; 1998 with Philippe Starck, designed/supervised 'Philippe Starck for 7/Eleven [stores],' Tokyo; 2000, left Radi Designers and set up Claudio Colucci Design (CCD), Tokyo and Paris; 2001, introduced his own brand, Supreme Love by Claudio Colucci. Products range from 2001 Elecom wares in Japan) and 2001 wok by Suze Wan in Paris to 1995–97 furniture by Idée in Tokyo, 2000 furniture (including *Duo & Solo* convertible chair and sofa) by Habitat in the UK and a wide range of furniture by Sentou in Paris. From 1999, he designed a number of store interiors and window displays and graphics in Japan and France.
Exhibitions/citations Include 1991 Salon des Artistes Décorateurs, Grand Palais, Paris; 1996 *Design Français: L'Art du Mobilier 1986/1996* (with Radi Designers), Centre Culturel, Boulogne-Billancourt; 1999 *New Generation of Designers* (with Radi Designers), Hamburg; 2001 *Japan Design Nouvelle Generation*, Galerie VIA (French furniture association),

Paris; 2001 *Sputnik*, Salone del Mobile, Milan. Creators of the year (with Radi Designers group), 2000 Salon du Meuble, Paris; 2000 VIA and Du Pont Appel Permanent grant (for a lamp); winner, 2000 'Marche' project, Daikanyama, Tokyo.
Bibliography Arlette Barré-Despond (ed.), *Dictionnaire international des arts appliqués et du design*, Paris: Regard, 1996. *Fonction et fiction, les villages*, Paris: Pierre Mardaga, 1996. Mel Byars, *50 Products: Innovations in Design and Materials*, Hove: RotoVision, 1998. Cat., *Radi Designers, réalité fabriquée, Fondation Cartier pour l'Art Contemporain*, Paris: Act Sud, 1999.
> See Radi Designers.

Colwell, David (1944–)
British industrial designer.

Training Royal College of Art, London.
Biography 1968, Colwell opened his own design office in London; was a consultant to ICI Plastics. His range of objects has included lighting and chairs such as 1968 Contour chair by 4's Company in London, from a molded acrylic sheet.
Exhibitions Contour chair was first shown at 1968 *Prospex* exhibition sponsored by ICI, Royal College of Art, London; subsequently, at 1968 *Décor International*, and 1970 *Modern Chairs 1918–1970*, Whitechapel Gallery, both London.
Bibliography Cat., *Modern Chairs 1918–1970*, London: Lund Humphries, 1971.

Côme, Christophe (1965–)
French designer; born Paris.

Training In hotel management; subsequently, in moulding, chasing, and bronze casting.
Biography From 1994, Côme has designed in bronze for consoles, pedestal tables, candle holders; then in rougher, more rustic forms that married glass to steel. His 1999 optical multi-glassball cabinet was edited by Néotù in Paris.
Bibliography Cat., Sophie Tasma Anargyros et al., *L'école française: les créateurs de meubles du 20ème siècle*, Paris: Industries Françaises de l'Ameublement, 2000.

Cometti, Giacomo (1863–1938)
Italian sculptor, craftsperson, and designer.

Biography Cometti turned from sculpture to the applied arts; by the 1902 Turin *Esposizione*, had established a successful workshop. Although he practiced in the prevailing Stile Floreale, his work is considered simple and geometric, showing German influence.
Citations Honorable mention, 1900 *Exposition Universelle*, Paris; diploma of honor, 1902 *Esposizione Internazionale d'Arte Decorativa Moderna*, Turin.
Bibliography Cat., Gabriel P. Weisberg (ed.), *Stile Floreale: The Cult of Nature in Italian Design*, Miami: The Wolfsonian Foundation, 1988.

Comité Colbert
French commercial association of manufacturers and merchants of luxury goods.

History Comité Colbert was established by Jean-Baptiste Colbert (1619–1683), statesman and financier under Louis XIV, to encourage high standards in domestic luxury goods. The association today is composed of a large number of French luxury-goods firms, such as Louis Vuitton, Baccarat, Daum, Hermès, Puiforcat, and S.T. Dupont, including most couturiers and even the hotels Crillon and Ritz. 1954, there were 12 firms comprising the group; by 2002, there were 64. Associate members include Air France and the Château de Versailles. Comité Colbert awards prizes, such as Les Espoirs de la Création (young designers' awards) and sponsors events to promote the work of young designers active in the luxury industries of France; developed a program to fight against piracy; surveys and reports on the economic climate of the luxury-goods business; supports educational projects and cooperates with the French departments of the Ministère de l'Education Nationale and the Ministère de la Culture et de la Communication.

Comma
American design partnership.

History David Khouri (Reedley, Cal., 1960–) moved from California to New York, where he received a masters degree in architecture and in historical preservation, Columbia University; subsequently, designed retail stores and showrooms while at Bohn Associates. 1987, Roberto Guzman (Los Angeles, 1962–) received a master's degree in archiecture, Columbia University; worked in architectural offices, including of Kohn Pederson Fox and of Peter Marino Associates; was active designing theater sets and assistant art director of 1999 Summer Olympiad, Atlanta, and 1997 Grammy Awards (Broadway-theater citations). 1998. Khouri and Guzman formed Comma design studio, New York.
Exhibitions Khouri and Guzman's first collection of furniture, 1998 International Contemporary Furniture Fair, New York.
Bibliography Jasper Morrison (ed.), *The International Design Yearbook*, London: Laurence King, 1999.

Compagnie des Arts Français (CAF)
French decorating firm, furniture maker, and shop; located Paris.

History 1919, Compagnie des Arts Français was founded by Louis Süe and André Mare at 116, rue du Faubourg Saint-Honoré as the successor to L'Atelier Français, which Süe and Mare had established in 1910 on the rue de Courcelles. 1928, Jacques Adnet took over management of the firm. For furniture, light woods were used, including sycamore and lemonwood, in simple shapes and a classic modern style. CAF collaborated with painters, sculptors, and metalsmiths, including Jean Lurçat and Jean Auricoste. Gilbert Poillerat and Richard Desvallières produced forged ironwork for the firm. CAF, a kind of artisans' collective, was active to 1959.
Exhibitions Work by Süe and Mare included in Pavillon Fontaine and Musée d'Art Contemporain at 1925 *Exposition Internationale des Arts Décoratifs et Industriels Modernes*, Paris, along with works of Jaulmes, Richard Desvallières, Paul Véra, Bernard Boutet de Monvel, Segonzac, Boussingault, André E. Marty, and Marinot.
Bibliography Yvonne Brunhammer, *Le cinquantenaire de l'exposition de 1925*, Paris: Musée des Arts Décoratifs, 1976. Pierre Cabanne, *Encyclopédie art déco*, Paris: Somogy, 1986: 183. Pierre Kjellberg, *Art déco: les maîtres du mobilier, le décor des paquebots*, Paris: Amateur, 1986: 48.

Conran, Terence (1931–)
British interior decorator, designer, and entrepreneur; born Esher, Surrey; active London.

Training 1946–48, Bryanston School, Dorset; 1948–50 under Eduardo Paolozzi, textile design, Central School of Arts and Crafts, London.
Biography From c. 1950, Conran worked for the Rayon Centre in London, and, 1951–52, was an interior designer at architects Dennis Lennon and Partners, where he designed his first furniture; 1952, founded own furniture-making business, selling primarily to the contract market, soon expanding the company to Thetford, Norfolk; 1953, visited France for the first time and, subsequently, opened his first restaurant (Soup Kitchen in London); late 1950s, was a freelance designer; 1955 with John Stephenson, founded the Conran Design Group,

Conran Associates and Martin Roberts (1943–). Input 14 ice bucket. 1973. ABS polymer, overall 6 3/4 x dia. 7" (17.1 x 17.8 cm). Mfr.: Crayonne, UK (1977). Gift of Conran's. MoMA.

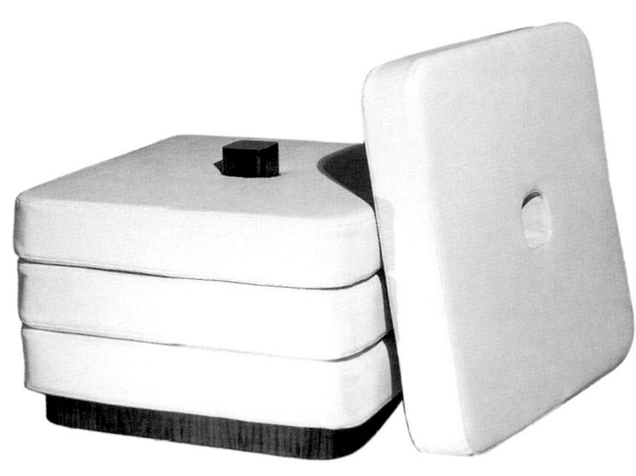

Comma: David Khouri. TV Time stacking cushions. c. 1998. Foam, vinyl, MDF, and veneer, h. 18 x w. 23 x d. 23" (46 x 59 x 59 cm). Mfr.: Comma, US.

which grew to become one of largest consultancies in Europe, as Conran Associates; was best known for his Habitat stores (the first of which opened at 77 Fulham Road, London, in 1964, to sell low-priced furniture and furnishings in a contemporary style). 1968, CDG merged with stationers Ryman, becoming Ryman Conran. 1970, Conran bought back Habitat; 1971, opened first Conran Shop, in Fulham Road, London; 1980, founded the Conran Roche architects and town-planning firm, which would design the Design Museum and Michelin Building renovation, both London, and others; 1982, acquired Mothercare and, 1983 through the Habitat/Mothercare group, Heal's furniture store and Richard Shops womenswear chain; also 1983, British Home Stores was added to these holdings to form the Storehouse Group with c. 1,000 retail outlets. 1983, Habitat/Mothercare, with Octopus Books, founded publisher Conran Octopus (later sold to Reed International). 1985 with Sean Sutcliffe, Conran founded Benchmark Woodworking to produce furniture for his restaurants and Conran Shop retail sales. 1986, Habitat/Mothercare merged with British Home Stores to form Storehouse plc, with Conran as chairperson and chief executive. 1982–86, the Conran Foundation funded the Boilerhouse Project, which showed and promoted good design in a basement space in the Victoria and Albert Museum, London; 1989, supported the establishment of the Design Museum, Butlers Wharf, London, first directed by Stephen Bayley. Late 1980s, Conran acquired the Michelin building, London, from which he managed his activities, and, as architect, Conran designed a hotel in Butlers Wharf. 1989, he resigned as chief executive and, 1990, as chair of Storehouse and, also 1990, bought back The Conran Shop from Storehouse and CDG from French communications group RSCG (now Euro RSCG Partners); 1990, became joint president of RSCG's international design division; 1992, resigned again and a year hence continued to manage and open a number of restaurants and Conran Shops worldwide; wrote *The House Book* (London: Mitchell Beazley, 1979), a best-selling guide to home design, the first of his numerous 'style' books, and others followed.
Restaurants In London: opened Soup Kitchen (his first), Chandos Place, 1953; The Orrery, King's Road, 1954; Neal Street Restaurant, Covent Garden (now operated by brother-in-law Antonio Carluccio), 1971; Bibendum (in renovated Michelin Building), Fulham Road, 1987; Blue Print Café (in Design Museum), Butlers Wharf, 1989; Le Pont de la Tour, Butlers Wharf, 1991; Cantina del Ponte, Butlers Wharf, 1992; Quaglino's restaurant and Butlers Wharf Chop House, 1993; Mezzo, Soho, 1995; Bluebird (and shop), Zinc Bar & Grill, and Orrery, 1997. Elsewhere, from 1993: Sartoria, Coq d'Argent, and Alcazar, all Paris, 1998; Guastavino's, New York, 2000.
Citations Knighthood in 1983 Queen's New Year Honours, UK; 1989 President award (outstanding contribution to British design), British Design & Art Direction (D&AD); 2000 Art/Modernism Design award for lifetime achievement, Brooklyn Museum of Art, New York.
Bibliography Barty Phillips, *Conran and the Habitat Story*, London: Weidenfeld & Nicolson, 1984. Elizabeth Wilhide, *Terence Conran: Design and the Quality of Life*, London: Thames & Hudson, 1999.

Consolidated Lamp and Glass Company
American manufacturer; located Coraopolis, Pennsylvania.

History 1893, Fostoria Shade and Lamp Company was almalgamated with Wallace and McAffee Company to form Consolidated Lamp and Glass Company in Fostoria, Ohio. The factory burned downed and was moved to Coraopolis, Penn., in 1895. It first produced glass lighting fixtures and diffusers and, subsequently, began making art-glass works at the turn of 19th century. Nicholas Kopp designed some tableware. 1925, glass designer Reuben Haley left U.S. Glass Company and established his own design company in space rented from Consolidated; was influenced by a touring exhibition of 400 objects, including by René Lalique, that had been shown at 1925 *Exposition Internationale des Arts Décoratifs et Industriels Modernes*, Paris. He persuaded Consolidated to produce glass to his designs, direct copies of Art Moderne glassware in the manner of Lalique, including the Aras, Love Birds, Perruches, and Bird of Paradise vases. However, Haley's 1928–32 Ruba Rombic range of 37 items (patented and introduced in 1928 and far more original in concept) was highly successful. The pattern's name was derived from the name of its designer ReUBen HAley and the angular form of a rhomboid. The concept showed influences from European, and particularly Czech, Cubism. The line was advertised in an unprecedented 7-page layout (1928) in a gift-shop magazine. But the original range was discontinued, when Consolidated closed in 1932. And, on Haley's 1933 death, his son Kenneth (also a glass designer) transferred the molds, whose rights were owned by Reuben Haley, to Phoenix Glass Company (founded 1880, Monaca, Penn.), where the *martelé* designs were produced as the Phoenix Reuben-Line from 1933. When Consolidated reopened in 1936, it took back the molds and renewed production. Even so, Phoenix continued its production as the renamed Sculptured glass line, which was also marketed by Howard G. Selden as the Selden glass line. Together with lighting fixtures and bases, Consolidated continued to make the Haley vases, some as lamp bases, to 1963. Sinclair Glass in Indiana obtained some original Haley *martelé* molds and made vases in milk glass and plain crystal to 1960s. Westclair division of Sinclair also made some examples in the late 1980s, some very much like Consolidated's *martelé* models. Fenton Art Glass made their own mold of Consolidated's Dogwood vase, sold as reproductions in 1984 with the Fenton logo on the bases.
Bibliography William Heacock, 'Phoenix/Consolidated Copies and Look-Alikes,' in *Collecting Glass*, vol. 2, Marietta, Ohio: Antique Publications, 1986: 29–40. Jack D Wilson, *Phoenix & Consolidated Art Glass 1926–1980*, Marietta, Ohio: Antique Publications, 1989. Kathy Kelly, 'An Identity Crisis: Phoenix or Consolidated,' in *Glass Collectors Digest*, vol. III, no. 2, Aug.-Sept. 1989: 78–82. Carolus Hartmann, *Glasmarken Lexikon 1600–1945, Europa und Nordamerika*, Stuttgart: Arnoldsche, 1998: 549, 756.
> See Haley, Reuben.

Constructivism
Russian movement in architecture, fine art, and design.

History The stylistic development of the Russian avant-garde up to the time of Kazimir Malevich's suprematist compositions and Vladimir Tatlin's constructions paralleled the development of modernism in Western Europe. 1920, the advent of Constructivism was signaled by two manifestos: *The Program of the Group of Constructivists* by Alexei Gan, Aleksandr Rodchenko, and Varvara Stepanova, and others, and *A Realistic Manifesto* by Antoine Pevsner and Naum Gabo. Constructivism had separate aspects: Agitprop (or agitation-propaganda), expressed through revolutionary forms of street art and exhibitions, and building construction, expressed in a variety of ways from machine forms to biomorphic structures, including interlocking living units and access elements, such as ramps and elevators. The further inclusion of elements outside the architectural norm (such as radio aerials, film making equipment, and sky-signs) alienated the architect Nikolai Ladovskii (founder of formalist group Asnova [new association of architects] in 1923), El Lissitzky (an important link between Constructivism and the European avant-garde), and Dutch neoplasticist leader Theo van Doesburg. Vladimir Tatlin's 1918 model for *Monument to the Third International* was a manifestation of the success of modern technology, inspired by the Eiffel Tower, Paris, and influenced by Alexei Kruchenykh's 1923 Futurist opera, *Pobeda nad Solntsem* (victory over the sun). The project was criticized by Gabo as being neither functional architecture nor pure art, but both. Although never built, Tatlin's maquette was influential in turning numerous artists from fine art to industrial design. Several artist-designers wished to become known as

'productivists' rather than Constructivists, including Tatlin, Liubov' Popova, Rodchenko, Gan, and Stepanova. Much of Constructivism in Russia was not oriented toward production but rather a re-creation of traditional Russian agrarian (but non-folkloric) forms as expressed by Konstantin Mel'nikov in his Makhorka pavilion at the 1923 *All-Russia Agricultural and Craft Exhibition*; 1923 Sucharev Market, Moscow; and Russian pavilion at the 1925 *Exposition Internationale des Arts Décoratifs et Industriels Modernes*, Paris. Russian Constructivist architecture was pursued through two basic themes: utopian socialist town planning (expressed by N.A. Miliutin's model for a 'six-banded' linear city) and the new 'social condensers' (expressed by the workers' clubs and the communal housing prototypes of Moisei Ginzburg's 1929 Narkomfin housing block in Moscow). Factions of the Constructivist movement were widely divergent; the Asmova group's gestalt theories were incompatible with the Functionalist-oriented Association of Contemporary Architects (OCA), the group founded by Aleksandr Vesnin in 1925. Constructivists were closer to European Functionalists, while Rationalists were more romantic, attempting to bring novelty to every project. In an effort to form a new architectural expression appropriate to the 1917 Revolution, Vesnin was one of the first to create the architectural language of constructivism, a prime example being his 1923 project Leningradskaia Pravda building in Moscow, which manifested the aesthetic of constructivism in a unified whole, including signage, loudspeakers, elevator interiors, and advertising. Due to the essential underlying social theories of Russian Constructivism, its buildings were realized primarily through public works, including factories, workers' clubs, offices, department stores, plants, hospitals, and hydroelectric installations, such as Viktor Vesnin's massive 1932 Dneprostroi Dam. Late 1920s, the influence of constructivism began to be seen in structures by Walter Gropius and Hannes Meyer in Germany, Johannes Duiker, Johannes Brinkman, Cornelius van der Vlugt, and Mart Stam in the Netherlands, and in buildings in Czechoslovakia, Sweden, France, Switzerland, Britain, and the US. Aspects of international Constructivism appeared in Pierre Chareau and Bernard Bijvoët's 1928–32 Mai-son de Verre in Paris, and even Richard Rogers's early-1960s studies.
Bibliography Anatole Kopp, *Ville et révolution*, Paris: Anthropos, 1967. Vieri Quilici, *L'architettura del costruttivismo*, Bari: Laterza, 1969. El Lissitzky, *Russia: An Architecture for World Revolution*, Cambridge, Mass.: MIT, 1970. O.A. Shvidkovsky, *Building in the USSR, 1917–1932*, New York: Praeger, 1971. Kenneth Frampton in Vittorio Magnago Lampugnani (ed.), *Encyclopedia of 20th-Century Architecture*, New York: Abrams, 1986: 73–74. Jaroslav Andel et al., *Art into Life: Russian Constructivism 1914–1932*, New York: Rizzoli, 1990. S.O. Khan-Magomedov, *Vhutemas: Moscou, 1920–1930*, Paris: Regard, 1990. Cat., *The Great Utopia: The Russian and Soviet Avant-Garde, 1915–1932*, New York: Guggenheim Museum, 1992.

Conti, Flavio (1943–)

Italian architect and designer; born Legnago, Verona; active Milan.

Training To 1968, architecture, Politecnico, Milan.
Biography 1969, Conti began his professional career; from 1969, was a subeditor at journal *Arredamento-Interni*; 1971–76, managed his own magazine; from 1973, was professor, Politecnico, Milan; worked out of his own studio in Milan where he designed furniture, primarily knock-down models and in wood, for clients including Arcum, Former, Pedanoshop, Poggenpohl Italia, and Rosi Riparato. From 2000, chairman, Istituto Italiano dei Castelli (IIC).
Bibliography *ADI Annual 1976*, Milan: Associazione per il Disegno Industriale, 1976.

Coop Himmelb(l)au

Austrian architecture partnership; located Vienna.

History 1968, Wolf Dieter Prix (Vienna 1942–), Helmut Swiczinsky (Poznan 1944–), and Rainer Michael Holzer founded Coop Himmelb(l)au. The group was influenced by Haus-Rucker-Co and Hans Hollein and, at first, interested in pneumatic-space buildings; offered alternatives to standard concepts of town planning at its 1976 'Wiener Supersomer,' with a 'cloud windowshade.' Its design work has included 1974 mobile kitchen elements by Ewe-Küchen and 1988 Vodöl chair by Vitra. An early proponent of Deconstructivism before the term was coined, its so-called 'demonstration objects' (interiors, sketches, and projects) included 1977 Reiss Bar in Vienna; HUMANIC-Filialen (branches) in Mistelbach 1979 and Vienna 1980, illustrating deformation; 1980 Flammenflügel (flamewing) in Graz; and 1981 Roter Engel (red angel) music bar, Vienna. Its architecture included the 1995 new wing of the Akademie der bildenden Künste, Munich, and a number of buildings outside Austria (such as 1992 Deutsches Hygienemuseum and 1993–98 Ufa-Kinozentrum, both Dresden).
Exhibitions/citations Work included in *Radicals: Architettura e Design 1960–75*, 1996 (6th) Mostra Internazionale di Archittettura, Venice; 1988 venue, The Museum of Modern Art, New York. Subject of 1993 venue, Paris (catalogs below). Received 1992 Erich Schelling Prize, 1999 Großer Österreichischer Staatspreis für Architektur, and others.
Bibliography *Coop Himmelblau, Architektur muß brennen*, Graz, 1980. Cat., Philip Johnson and Mark Wigley, *Deconstructivist Architecture*, New York: The Museum of Modern Art, 1988. S.S. Richardson, *Coop Himmelblau: Wolf Prix and Helmut Swiczinsky: A Bibliography*, Monticello, Ill.: Vance Bibliographies; 1989. Albrecht Bangert and Karl Michael Armer, *80s Style: Designs of the Decade*, New York: Abbeville, 1990. *Coop Himmelblau: 6 Projects for 4 Cities*, Darmstadt: Jürgen Häusser. 1990. Cat., *Coop Himmelblau, construire le ciel*, Paris: Centre Georges Pompidou, 1992. Frank Werner, *Coop Himmelblau*, Basel: Birkhäuser, 2000.
> See Swiczinsky, Helmut; Prix, Wolf Dieter.

Cooper, John Paul (1869–1933)

British architect, silversmith, and jeweler; active London, Birmingham, and Westerham, Surrey.

Training From 1887 under architect J.D. Sedding; 1891 under Henry Wilson, architecture and metalworking.
Biography 1897, Cooper began silversmithing, specializing in combinations with unusual materials, especially shagreen, which he began using in 1903, before other British Arts-and-Crafts practitioners or Clément Mère in Paris. From turn of 19th century, Cooper's work was frequently published in reviews *The Studio* and *Art Journal*. He set up a workshop in his house in Westerham, which he designed; from 1906, combined silver and copper in a Japanese metalworking technique. Strongly architectural in form, his work is often indistinguishable from Henry Wilson's; 1904–07, was head, metalworking department, Birmingham Central School, where Robert Catterson-Smith was director, and where he was succeeded by his son Francis Cooper; after 1907, was active solely in silversmithing.
Bibliography *The Studio*, June 1900: 48. Charlotte Gere, *American and European Jewelry 1830–1914*, New York: Crown, 1975. Annelies Krekel-Aalberse, *Art Nouveau and Art Déco Silver*, New York: Abrams, 1989. N. Natasha Kuzmanovic, *John Paul Cooper: Designer and Craftsman of the Arts & Crafts Movement*, Stroud: Sutton, 1999.

Cooper, 'Susie' Susan Vera (1902–1995)

British ceramicist; born Staffordshire; active Burslem.

Training 1918–22 under Gordon M. Forsyth, Burslem School of Art, .
Biography Starting her career in dress design, she took Gordon M. Forsyth's suggestion to pursue pottery; 1922–29, worked for decorating firm A.E. Gray as a decorator of ceramics, becoming the company's chief designer and the first woman in the Staffordshire potteries to be acknowledged as a designer with her name stamped on her wares; 1929, set up Susie Cooper Pottery in a factory rented from Doulton; 1931, moved to Crown Works in Burslem, where she remained for more than 50 years; bought blanks but also designed her own shapes, both produced by various firms, until she made an arrangement with Wood and Sons to produce her wares; at first painted designs by hand; by 1933, used a lithographic-transfer process, and employed over 40 painters. 1935, her first major commission came from John Lewis; others followed, from Peter Jones, Harrods, Waring and Gillow, Selfridges, and Heal's. She designed c. 1933 Curlew shapes and c. 1935 Kestrel shapes and 1937–38 inflight dinnerware for Imperial Airways. She became known for her elegant and utilitarian shapes and was a major innovator in domestic ceramics throughout 1930s and after; produced bone china at Jason Works in Longton, which she acquired in 1950, renaming it Susie Cooper China. Bone china came to be her main product, and, by early 1960s, earthenware production virtually ended. 1961, she merged with R.H. & S.L. Plant (aka Tuscan Works), and was in turn acquired by Wedgwood, where she remained as a senior designer and director to 1972. A prominent potter for six decades, her wares received acclaim in Britain and abroad. 1972, her husband Cecil Barker died; 1986, she retired to the Isle of Man but produced new work in 1992 to celebrate her 90th birthday. Patterns have been digitalized on the internet by the Wedgwood Museum, Stoke-on-Trent.
Exhibitions/citations Kestrel shapes were shown with other work at British Pavilion, 1937 *Exposition Internationale des Arts et Techniques*

dans la Vie Moderne, Paris. Designed stand and produced tableware for Royal Pavilion and Royal Society of Arts, 1951 *Festival of Britain* exposition, London. Work subject of 1978 Sanderson exhibition, London (catalog below); 1987 exhibition, Victoria and Albert Museum, London; 1989 exhibition, Ipswich Museums and Galleries; 1999, Croydon Museum; 2002 centenary exhibition, The Wedgwood Museum. 1938, elected fellow, Royal Institute of British Architects (RIBA); 1940, Honorary Royal Designer for Industry, UK; 1978, Order of the British Empire (OBE).
Bibliography Cat., *Susie Cooper: Elegance and Utility*, Barlaston: Wedgwood, 1978. Cat., *Thirties: British Art and Design Before the War*, London: Arts Council of Great Britain/Hayward Gallery, 1979. Adrian Woodhouse, *Susie Cooper*, Matlock: Trilby, 1992. Bryn Youds, *Susie Cooper: An Elegant Affair*, New York: Thames & Hudson, 1996. Andrew Casey and Ann Eatwell (eds.), *Susie Cooper*, Woodbridge, Suffolk: Antique Collectors' Club, 2002.

Copeland, Steve (1955–)
Canadian designer; born Toronto.

Training To 1978, product and systems design, Ontario College of Art, Toronto.
Biography Copeland began his career designing laboratory and office furniture; late 1970s, designed and developed cookware and computer casings; 1980–85, was design supervisor, Cooper Canada Ltd., where, with others, developed Cooper hockey, golf, motocross, sports bags, ice hockey equipment, including award-winning helmets and faceguards; 1985, designer/consultant/developer of award-winning sporting goods, toys, hardware, and wheelchairs by numerous manufacturers; 1987, founded Paradox Design, where he is president; is a specialist in computer-aided design and three-dimensional surface and solid modeling; has taught industrial design, Humber College, Toronto, and Fanshawe College, London; is long-standing member, Association of Canadian Industrial Designers, where he has assisted in the establishment of safety standards for helmets and protective gear; senior member, Society of Plastics Engineers.

Coper, Hans (1920–1981)
British ceramicist; born Chemnitz, Germany.

Training Textile engineering.
Biography 1939, Coper settled in Britain; 1946, discovered pottery in the London Albion Mews Pottery of Lucie Rie, with whom he shared a studio to 1958. He was influenced by oriental techniques and models and developed a distinctive style of his own; 1959, moved to Digswell, Hertfordshire. 1962, his candlesticks were installed in Coventry Cathedral. He admired the work of sculptors Alberto Giacometti and Constantin Brancusi, Cycladic statuary, and primitive art; played a role in renewing ceramic art in England through his teaching efforts at Camberwell School of Arts and Crafts 1961–69; 1966, moved to London, where he taught, Royal College of Art, 1966–75.
Exhibitions/citations From first (1950) at Berkeley Galleries, London, work shown worldwide in association with Rie, including at 1955 exhibition, Röhsska Konstslöjdmuseet, Gothenburg; 1957 exhibition, University of Minnesota, Minneapolis; 1967 exhibition, Museum Boymans-van Beuningen, Rotterdam; 1972 exhibition, Museum für Kunst und Gewerbe, Hamburg. He and Rie were co-subjects of 1997 Barbican Art Gallery exhibition, London (catalog below). Work included independently at 1951 *Festival of Britain*, London; 1953 *Engelse Ceramiek*, Stedelijk Museum, Amsterdam; 1954 (10th) Triennale di Milano; 1959 Ceramics International, Syracuse, New York; 1969 exhibition (with Peter Collingwood), Victoria and Albert Museum, London; 1972 *International Ceramics*, Victoria and Albert Museum, London. Coper's work subject of 1956 exhibition (first one-person show) at Bonnier's in New York; 1958 exhibition at Primavera, London; 1965 exhibition, Berkeley Galleries; 1980 retrospective, Hetjens-Museum, Düsseldorf; and 1983–84 exhibitions, Sainsbury Centre, University of East Anglia, Norwich; Museum Boymans-van Beuningen; and Serpentine Gallery, London. Gold medal, 1954 (10th) Triennale di Milano.
Bibliography Cat., *Nine Potters*, London: Fischer Fine Arts, 1986: 8–15. Tony Birks, *Hans Coper*, Marston Magna, Somerset: Marston House, 1983, rev. ed. 1991. Cat., Conrad Bodman, Margot Coatts, and Nicky Shearman (eds.), *Lucie Rie & Hans Coper: Potters in Parallel*, London: Herbert/Barbican Art Gallery, 1997.

Hans Coper. Vase. c. 1960. Stoneware, h. 7 3/4 x dia. 7" (19.7 x 17.8 cm). Mfr.: Hans Coper, UK. Given anonymously. MoMA.

Copier, Andries Dirk (1901–1991)
Dutch glassware designer; active Leerdam.

Training From 1914 under Hendrikus Petrus Berlage, Glasfabriek Leerdam, Netherlands.
Biography His talent was recognized by Leerdam's general manager P.M. Cochius and, thus, was sent to typographical school in Utrecht as preparation for designing advertising materials for Leerdam. However, he was adept at glass. 1927, Copier was appointed the general artistic director of the Glasfabriek Leerdam. His 1928 Unica series (with glassblower Gerrit Vroegh), as one-of-a-kind glassware, was in continuous production to after World War II and, along with pieces produced by colleagues, brought distinction to Leerdam, which merged in mid-1930s with Vereenigde to form Vereenigde Leerdam Glasfabriek. Copier's Srica range of table glass was artistically and commercially successful. From 1922, he designed glassware for himself; influenced by De Stijl from the late 1920s, executed severe, unadorned forms, including 1947 Primula pressed-glass tableware range and other designs in tumblers, pitchers, and stemware; from the beginning, was interested in Functionalist mass-produced glass appropriate to the modern movement. Other work included 1958 Gourmet set of glasses. 1971, he left Leerdam; 1977 with glass blower Piet van Klei, worked on Unica again at De Oude Horn in Hessen, near Leerdam; 1980, experimented with etched and colored decorations and fluid forms in Murano and in the studio of Ann Wärff in Sweden; visited the glass workshop in Spruce Pine, N.C., US, where he worked with Harvey Littleton and Gary Beecham.
Exhibitions/citations Work subject of first large-scale exhibition at 1927 *Weissenhofsiedlung*, Stuttgart; 1963 Rotterdam exhibition (catalog below); and 1982 and 1990 exhibitions, The Hague (catalog below). Received silver medal (for Smeerwortel set of glasses), 1925 *Exposition Internationale des Arts Décoratifs et Industriels Modernes*, Paris.
Bibliography Cat., *A.D. Copier, Glas*, Rotterdam: Museum Boymans-van Beuningen, 1963. Geoffrey Beard, *International Modern Glass*, London, 1976. Cat., *A.D. Copier*, The Hague: Gemeentemuseum, 1982, 1990. D.U. Kuyken-Schneider, 'The Old Man—Andries Dirk Copier,' *Neues Glas*, Feb. 1982: 102–03. Reino Liefkes, 'Master of Pure Form,' *Dutch Heights*, no. 1, Winter 1986–1987: 8–41. Reino Liefkes, *A.D. Copier: Glass Designer, Glass Artist*, Zwolle/Amsterdam : Waanders/Foundation Prins Bernhard Cultuurfonds, 2nd ed. 2002.

Coppola, Silvio (1920–1986)
Italian architect, designer, graphic artist, and teacher; active Milan.

Training Architecture, Politecnico, Milan.
Biography From 1947, Coppola was active as a graphic designer; 1960, began working in plastics, designing folding toys, book shelves, and various furniture pieces; was the architect of buildings, including a department store, Baghdad, and structures at the city university, Zaïre; was artistic director of Bernini; also designed for Bernini (furniture, including Gru seat made from a single bent metal tube), Cilsa (tiles),

Tigamma (home furnishings), and Tessitura di Mompiano (textiles); was consultant designer to numerous other Italian and foreign firms, including Bayer Italia, Montecatini, Monteshell, Cinzano, and Laminati Plastici; from 1967 with Bruno Munari, Franco Grignani, Cofalonieri, Pino Tovaglia, and Mario Bellini, participated in the group called Exhibition Design; from 1975, was professor of design, Accademia di Belle Arti in Carrara; became a member, ADI, Architetti di Genoa, Alliance Graphique Internationale (AGI), and American Institute of Graphic Art (AIGA).
Citations Include 1962 Palma d'Oro, 1966 and 1968 Rizzoli Prize, 1968 Oscar Imballaggio, and 1967 Colonna Antonina.
Bibliography Cat., Milena Lamarová, *Design a Plastické Hmoty*, Prague: Umĕleckoprůmyslové Muzeum, 1972: 106. *ADI Annual 1976*, Milan: Associazione per il Disegno Industriale, 1976. *Moderne Klassiker: Möbel, die Geschichte machen*, Hamburg: Gruner + Jahr, 1982: 39.

Coppolo, Giuseppe (1958–)

Italian designer; born Caserta.

Training To 1983, architecture, Università degli Studi, Naples.
Biography From 1983, Coppolo was active in didactic and research activities in various aspects of architecture; 1988, carried out research in the Certificat d'Études Approfondies en Architecture Domestique programs of the architecture departments of École d'Architecture (in Paris-Villemin and in Versailles) and École d'Architecture de Normandie (Rouen). 1980s, he was active in the design of interiors and exhibition stands and research on domestic living; 1992, set up a ceramics laboratory in Caserta, conducting experiments with materials and calling on designs by architects and designers such as Cinzia Anguissola, Franco Poli, Daniela Puppa, Franco Raggi, Prospero Rasulo, Denis Santachiara, Luca Scacchetti, Sigla Studio, and Coppolo himself, and producing a 1940-design vase collection by Guglielmo Ulrich. Coppolo has written for *Interni*, *Elle Decor*, *Casa Amica*, *Bravacasa*, *Interior Digest*, *D-Repubblica*. 1992, his doctoral degree resulted in the essay 'Architettura surrealista: squisito cadavere' (Palermo: Facoltà di Architettura, Università degli Studi, 1991). From 2002, he has taught, Facoltà di Architettura, Università degli Studi di Napoli 'Federico II.'
Exhibitions Work included in 1994 *Piccolo Mercato*, Mendini studio, Milan; 1994 *Marry X-mart*, Glas, Milan; 1996 *Passaggi di Senso*, Abitare il Tempo fair, Verona; 1998 *Souvenir di Napoli*, Palazzo Reale, Naples; 1999 *International Room of Art*, Ferrara; 2002 *Artigiani per New York*, Ravello and New York (catalog below).
Bibliography 'Le dernier café, le Café Belvédère,' in Gérard-Georges Lemaire, *Les cafés littéraires*, Paris: Henri Veyrier, Paris 1987. Cat., *Craftspeople for New York*, Naples: Alter Studio, 2002. Giuseppe Rago, 'Giuseppe Coppola: Una sontuosa contaminazione,' *Casa Mia Decor*, no. 85, May 2003.

Coray, Hans (1906–1991)

Swiss designer and artist; born Wald.

Training To 1929, University of Zürich.
Biography 1930, Coray designed his first furniture; became best known for 1938 Landi-Stuhl, a chair commissioned by Hans Fischli for use at 1939 *Schweizerische Landesaustellung* (Swiss national exhibition), Zürich. To 1980s, the chair was made solely by Swiss cookware manufacturer P. und W. Blattmann Wädenswil Metallwaren- und Aluminiumwarenfabrik, modified in 1962. From 1970, was produced by Zanotta as the Spartana no. 2070 model. It weighs 6.4 lbs (2.9 kg.) and is water resistant. Late 1940s, Coray designed furniture for the Wohnbedarf store, Zürich, including tables and other aluminum chairs; first half of 1950s, designed various chairs, including upholstered, wire, and aluminum models; was also a painter/sculptor. He died in Zürich.
Exhibitions Subject of 1986 Zürich exhibition (catalog below).
Bibliography Cat., *Hans Coray—Künstler und Entwerfer*, Zürich: Museum für Gestaltung, 1986. 'Hans Coray, 1906–1991,' *Abitare*, no. 306, 1992: 122. Paola Antonelli (ed.), *Objects of Design: The Museum of Modern Art*, New York: The Museum of Modern Art, 2003: 153.

Cordero, Toni (1937–)

Italian product and furniture designer; born Lanzo.

Training In architecture, Turin.
Biography 1962, Cordero opened a design studio in Turin. Architecture clients have included Banco Mediceo del Filarete, Blumarine, Fiat, Kenzo, Olivetti, and Turin's Museo Biscaretti (automobile museum). Has designed furniture and products by Acerbis, Artemide, Driade, and Sawaya & Moroni.
Bibliography Michele De Lucchi (ed.), *The International Design Yearbook*, London: Laurence King, 2001.

Corette, Sylvia (1960–)

French designer.

Training École Camondo, Paris.
Biography She has been active in the design of the interiors of hotels, bars, and apartments; worked at Sleeping Concept company on commissions for the city of Paris and, subsequently, designed a collection of furniture by Protis.
Citations 1989 Roxane Princesse des Djins chair in aluminum and crushed velour was sponsored by VIA (French furniture association).
Bibliography Cat., *Les années VIA*, Paris: Musée des Arts Décoratifs, 1990.

Corian®

Proprietary material.

History 1969, E.I. du Pont de Nemours developed Corian first as a non-porous surface material for countertops, sinks, and other building uses; eventually, perceived it as being more like stone than laminate. It resists stains, scratches, and burns and can be invisibly fused in sections. Du Pont subsequently promoted it as a material for high design, possibly based on a similar, earlier marketing technique by Formica. Calling on the material in part, Marc Newson has designed chairs by B&B Italia, installed in the restaurant of Lever House, New York; the Bouroullec brothers for the Apok concept for the Issey Miyake boutique, Paris; Masayo Ave and Joseph Licciardi for bath fixture for Dorbracht; and others for restaurant and stores of Giorgio Armani and Prada, Milan.
Exhibitions Du Pont has held a number of invitational design competitions to promote Corian's use for other than flat surfaces, including 2000 *Exercises in Another Material* (by Sottsass Associati), Museum of Contemporary Art, Chicago; 2001 *Sottsass for Corian* (furniture/sculpture) and *Cappellini for Corian* (furniture by Bouroullec brothers, Jasper Morrison, Alfredo Häberli, Giorgetti Scolari, Kevin Walz), Salone del Mobile, Milan.

Hans Coray. Landi Chair. 1938. Bent and pressed aluminum, and rubber, 30 1/2 x 21 1/4 x 22 1/8" (77.5 x 54 x 56.2 cm). Mfr.: P. und W. Blattmann Metallwaren- und Aluminiumwarenfabrik, Switzerland. Gift of Gabrielle and Michael Boyd. MoMA.

Corning Glass Works
American glass manufacturer; located Corning, N.Y.

History 1868, Brooklyn Flint Glass company moved to Corning, N.Y., and changed the name to Corning Glass Works. 1918, it acquired Steuben Glass Works (founded 1903 by Frederick Carder), which became a division. Today employs 40,000 people worldwide and about 8,000 in Corning, N.Y., 80% of the total population. Pyrex, Corning's proprietary borosilicate (heat-resistant) glass developed in late 1800s by others, was introduced in 1915 but not patented until 1926. 1924–51, Corning produced electrical-insulators, including the largest example ever made; 1935, joined with Owens-Illinois to develop fiberglass (patented by Corning researchers Dale Kleist and Jack Thomas as 'Fiberglas'). 1936, the companies formed the entity Owens-Corning Fiberglas. 1934–36, based on the proposal of astronomer George Ellery Hale (1868–1938), Corning cast the 200-inch mirror for the telecope on Mt. Palomar, Cal. Other inventions include: 1949 lightweight television tubes, 1961 heat-resistant glass for space travel, 1964 Photogray eye-sunglass lenses, 1966 glass-ceramic cooktops, 1970 optical-fiber technology, 1972 Celcor ceramic substrates, 1990 commercial multi-wavelength amplifiers, 1998 LEAF optical fiber, 2000 MetroCor™ optical fiber, 2000 EAGLE2000 glass substrates, 2000 microarrays for gene analysis. Also developed CorningWare (aka Corelle), a dense glass product that is more like a ceramic, for use as cook- and dinnerware. 1988, Corning purchased Revere Ware, which became a brand in its Corning Consumer Products group, along with Corelle, CorningWare, and Pyrex. 1998, Corning Consumer Products subsidiary was sold to Borden, which formed its own subsidiary, World Kitchen, with the acquisition. 1999, World Kitchen in turn bought the EKCO Group and, subsequently that year, General Housewares, which owned the Oxo, Chicago Cutlery, and other brands. Ultimately, the World Kitchen brands have comprised Oxo, Ekco, Corrélle, Pyrex, Revere, Olfa, Regent Sheffield, Magnalite, Chicago Cutlery, Bakers Secret, and Visions.
Exhibitions/citations Corning operated a live exhibit at Glass Pavilion, 1893 *World's Columbian Exposition*, Chicago, where 130 craftspeople cut and blew Steuben glass. To Corning: Design of the Decade (1990s) bronze award (Glass Innovation Center by Ralph Applebaum Associates), IDSA/*Business Week* magazine; numerous others.
> See Carder, Frederick C.; Steuben Glass Works; Revere Copper and Brass.

Corning Glass Works. Frying Pan. c. 1942. Borosilicate glass and steel, overall h. 2 3/4 x l. 12 1/2 x dia. 7" (7 x 31.8 x 17.8 cm). Mfr.: Corning Glass Works, US. Purchase. MoMA.

Coronado, Hector (1938–)
Mexican designer.

Biography Coronado specializes in the use of wood; focuses on bending, particular for pressure-laminated wood; is commissioned primarily by US firms; designed 2002 series of stools, bowls, trays, magazine racks, waste baskets, and children's furniture by Benetec of Los Angeles. In plastics and metal: Spice and BX series office chairs by Scope Seating Technologies in Elkhart, Ind.; office chairs by SitOnIt in Cypress, Cal.

Corretti, Gilberto (1941–)
Italian designer; born and active Florence.

Training To 1966, architecture.
Biography 1966 with Andrea Branzi, Paolo Deganello, Massimo Morozzi, and Dario and Lucia Bartolini, Coretti cofounded design studio Archizoom Associati in Florence. Archizoom's radical, Anti-Design 1974 AEO chair was produced by Cassina and Arc 02 by Marcatré. Corretti was active as an industrial and graphic designer, and research consultant on industrial products; from 1985, taught at Istituto Superiore per le Industrie Artistiche (ISIA), Rome and Florence. Design clients have included Adica Pongo, Cassina, Cidue, Emme Edizioni, Marcatré, Mobel Racing, Planula, and Prénatal.
Bibliography *ADI Annual 1976*, Milan: Associazione per il Disegno Industriale, 1976. *Modo*, no. 148, Mar.–Apr. 1993: 119.

Cortés, Pepe (1946–)
Spanish furniture, interior, and furnishing designer; born and active Barcelona.

Training Eina (Escola de Desseny i Art), Barcelona.
Biography Active from early 1970s, Cortés founded Grupo Abierto de Diseño (open group of design), an association of diverse design professionals, which designed the record store Werner and offices of Poliglas. 1980s, Cortes designed the interiors of Azulete restaurant, offices of Puerto Autónomo in Barcelona, Daniel Hechter showroom, warehouse and offices of Tejidos Sivila, and the furniture series Muebles 'Muy Formales' (with Javier Mariscal). 1990s, he designed offices of Consorcio de la Zona Franca in Barcelona, Tascón shoe store, premises of Optica 2000, and other commissions, including exhibitions and public spaces. His work has included a large amount of furniture and lighting, many with Mariscal, by Bd Ediciones de Diseño (such as 1975 Olvidada lamp by Cortés individually and 1983 Araña table lamp with Mariscal) and others: Memphis (for its first collection of 1981), Akaba (1986–87 Trampolin chair and 1986 M.O.R. Sillon sofa), Amat, Grupo T, Artespaña, Signes, Punt Mobles, and Technal.
Citations 1976, 1986, and 1987 selections, FAD (decorative-arts association);1984, 1986 and 1988 selections, ADI/FAD; 1983 Premi FAD d'Interiorisme (best interiors) for Azulete restaurant.
Bibliography *The International Design Yearbook*, London: Thames & Hudson, 1987 and 1990. Albrecht Bangert and Karl Michael Armer, *80s Style: Designs of the Decade*, New York: Abbeville, 1990: 40, 116, 228. Juli Capella and Quim Larrea, *Nuevo diseño español*, Barcelona: Gili, 1991. Mihail Modoveanu, *Barcelona: arquitecturas de la exuberancia*, Barcelona: Lunwerg, 1996. *Casa Residentia: Wohnarchtektur und Interieurs Spanien*, Cologne: Könemann, 2001.

Hector Coronado. K armchair with writing wing. 1978. Laminated beech, foam cushions, and fabric upholstery, overall 29 1/2 x 22 1/4 x 22 3/8" (74.9 x 56.5 x 56.8 cm), seat h. 18 1/4" (46.4 cm). Mfr.: O.C. Sedie Internazionale, US. Gift of the designer. MoMA.

Cortesi, Angelo (1938–)

Italian industrial designer; born Asola; active Milan.

Biography 1966, Cortesi began his professional career; 1968 with Carlo Ronchi and Patrizia Pataccini, set up Studio GPI; became a specialist in public areas and their equipment. Clients included DID (furniture and furnishing), Mostek (Digitalclock mini-computer), Plan (lighting), First (upholstered seating), Parker (writing pen), Video International (television camera, mini-computer, and microphone), Seibu, Kartell, Tecno, and Mitsukoshi. He was artistic director of glass-furniture manufacturer Fiam, Tavullia; from 1973, was a member of the organizing committee of Associazione per il Disegno Industriale (ADI) and its president 1985–89.
Citations 1981 (two citations) and 1984 (Alitalia's corporate image and agency design, with others) Premio Compasso d'Oro; gold medal, 1981 BIO 9 industrial design biennial, Ljubljana.
Bibliography *ADI Annual 1976*, Milan: Associazione per il Disegno Industriale, 1976. Alfonso Grassi and Anty Pansera, *Atlante del design italiano 1940/1980*, Milan: Fabbri, 1980: 296. Fumio Shimizu and Studio Matteo Thun (eds.), *The Italian Design: Descendants of Leonardo da Vinci*, Tokyo: Graphic-sha, 1987. Cat., Hans Wichmann (ed.), *Italien Design 1945 bis heute*, Munich: Die Neue Sammlung, 1988. *Modo*, no. 148, Mar.–Apr. 1993: 118.

Costard, Philippe (1960–)

French industrial designer; born Lyon.

Training To 1983, École Nationale Supérieure des Arts Décoratifs, Paris.
Biography 1983, Costard established the agency Synergie-Design; is interested in technological and marketing issues associated with mass-produced goods; used computer-aided technology in design of 1985 Sillage cutlery, 1986 Pédalo pedalcraft, 1990 Piki children's games (with Centre Georges Pompidou), 1991–94 redesign of kitchen appliances in Thirode, 1994 farm tractors by Hardi Evrard, 1995 Groom door springs, 1995 microwave oven by Be Incorporated, 1996 graphics and ID for paint containers by La Seigneurie, 1996 packaging and kitchen gadgets by Vital. From 1985, has taught, ENSCI (Les Ateliers), Paris; from 1990, Institut Supérieure de Design Industriel, Valenciennes.
Exhibitions/citations Bronze medal for design (for Sillage cutlery), 1985 Salon of Société des Artistes Décorateurs; Janus de l'Industrie and Janus de Design Industriel, Institut Français de Design Industriel; 1985 Prix de la Création, Salon Bijorhca.
Bibliography Arlette Barré-Despond (ed.), *Dictionnaire international des arts appliqués et du design*, Paris: Regard, 1996.

Cottier, Daniel (1838–1891)

British stained-glass designer, decorator, and art dealer; born Glasgow; active Glasgow, Edinburgh, London, New York, Sydney, and Melbourne.

Training Early 1850s under David Kier, in stained glass, Glasgow.
Biography Cottier attended lectures of, and worked for, John Ruskin and Ford Madox Brown in London; by 1862, had returned to Scotland, working for stained-glass producers Field and Allen; was one of the first to design stained glass that diverged from the Gothic Revival style of the day; 1864 with Andrew Wells (also formerly with Field and Allen), set up workshop at 40 George Street in Edinburgh; 1864–68, designed windows for the Cathedral of Saint Machar in Aberdeen; with architects William Leiper and Alexander Thomson, collaborated on painted decorations of Dowanhill Church and United Presbyterian Church, Queen's Parish, both Glasgow; 1869, set up 'Cottier and Company, Art Furniture Makers, Glass and Tile Painters' in London, of which Scottish architects John McKean Brydon, William Wallace, and Bruce J. Talbert were briefly partners. Cottier's staff designed the Colearn House in Auchterarder, Tayside (that included Talbert's dining room and its furniture, fireplace, and sideboard and Cottier's allegorical stained-glass windows). 1873, Cottier opened a branch at 144 Fifth Avenue, New York, where furniture, Venetian glass, oriental rugs, fabrics, faïence, lacquerwork, and bronzes were sold. He designed furniture in Anglo-Japanese and Queen Anne styles; was one of the first to produce Aesthetic Movement stained glass in the US, where his earliest-known commission was the 1878 window in the Green Memorial Alcove of New York Society Library, of which Léon Marcotte was the decorator; produced stained-glass windows for H.H. Richardson's Trinity Church in Boston; Calvary Church (Gramercy Park), Church of the Incarnation, First Presbyterian Church (Brooklyn), Grace Church (Brooklyn), all in New York; St. John's Church in Canadaigua, N.Y.; private residences; and structures at Yale and Harvard Universities. 1873 with John Lamb Lyon, Cottier opened a branch in Sydney, Australia, and later Melbourne.
Exhibitions Stained-glass window (by Field and Allen) was shown at 1864 *Exhibition of Stained Glass and Mosaics*, Victoria and Albert Museum, London.
Bibliography *The New York Times* (obituary), 8 Apr. 1891: 5. 'The Late Daniel Cottier,' *Journal of Decorative Art and British Decorator*, no. 22, May 1902: 145. Mark Girouard, *Sweetness and Light: The Queen Anne Movement, 1860–1900*, Oxford: Clarendon, 1977: 210–12, 241. Michael Donnelly, *Glasgow Stained Glass: A Preliminary Study*, Glasgow: Glasgow Museums and Art Galleries, 1981. James L. Sturm, *Stained Glass from Medieval Times to the Present: Treasures to Be Seen in New York*, New York: Dutton, 1982. Doreen Bolger Burke et al., *In Pursuit of Beauty: Americans and the Aesthetic Movement*, New York: The Metropolitan Museum of Art/Rizzoli, 1987: 415.

Cottis, Jennifer (1946–)

British industrial designer; born London.

Training 1963–65, industrial design, Ealing Technical College; 1965–68, industrial design, Central School of Art and Design, London.
Biography 1968–70, she was a staff designer at Parnals in Bristol, designing cookers, tumble dryers, and other electrical appliances; 1977–81, was a freelance consultant designer; 1981–83, worked for Herman Miller in Bath, designing and supervising the installation of materials, handling systems for clients in Europe, including Philips, Data General, and Digital Equipment; 1983, became a member, Chartered Society of Designers; from 1983, was freelance consultant designer again; 1984–87, was a member, selection committee for domestic equipment, Design Centre ; 1985–88, was a 'product group' member, Chartered Society of Designers; from 1986, a part-time lecturer in design and technology, Goldsmiths College, London. Work has included 1987 Neco System 4 Digital DC-motor controller by Normand Electrical, 1987 Emerson uninterruptible power supply unit by Emerson Electric Industrial Controls, and 1987–88 Multi-In-Feed parcel sorting machine for the Royal Post Research Centre.
Citations 1984, elected fellow, Royal Society of Arts.
Bibliography Cat., Design Center Stuttgart, *Women in Design: Careers and Life Histories Since 1900*, Stuttgart: Haus der Wirtschaft, 1989: 264–67.

Coughlan, John
> See Waterford Crystal.

Coulon, René-André (1908–1997)

French furniture designer.

Training To 1937, architecture.
Biography With Jacques Adnet, Coulon incorporated tempered glass into his pieces, some of which were produced by Hagnauer, Vienna; designed furniture for rooms by Adnet for Saint-Gobain; 1944, became a member, Union des Artistes Modernes (UAM); is best known for 1937 tempered-glass radiator by Saint-Gobain and for a 1938 glass chair; was instrumental in establishing Saint-Gobain Institute of Iron and Steel Research and its laboratory; 1955, was associated with Ionel Schien and Yves Magnant.
Exhibitions At 1937 *Exposition Internationale des Arts et Techniques dans la Vie Moderne:* participated in Saint-Gobain pavilion (which Coulon designed with Jacques Adnet, and in which Coulon's glass radiator and furniture were shown), in Hygiène pavilion (collaborated with Robert Mallet-Stevens on its design), and in UAM pavilion (a collection of glass furniture). Participated in editions of Salon des Arts Ménagers. All Paris.
Bibliography Jean Favier, 'Le Pavillon de Saint-Gobain,' *La construction moderne*, no. 4, 24 Oct. 1937. Cat., *Verriers français contemporains: Art et industrie*, Paris: Musée des Arts Décoratifs, 1982. Cat., Aaron Lederfajn and Xavier Lenormand (eds.), *Le Louvre des Antiquaires présente: 1930 quand le meuble devient sculpture*, Paris, 1986. Cat., *Les années UAM 1929–1958*, Paris: Musée des Arts Décoratifs, 1988. Arlette Barré-Despond (ed.), *Dictionnaire international des arts appliqués et du design*, Paris: Regard, 1996

Council for Art and Industry

British-government research committee on art and industry.

History 1932, the Board of Trade under Lord Gorell (based on 1932 Non-Parliamentary Papers of the Board of Trade) set up The Gorell Committee on Art and Industry (sometimes called British Committee

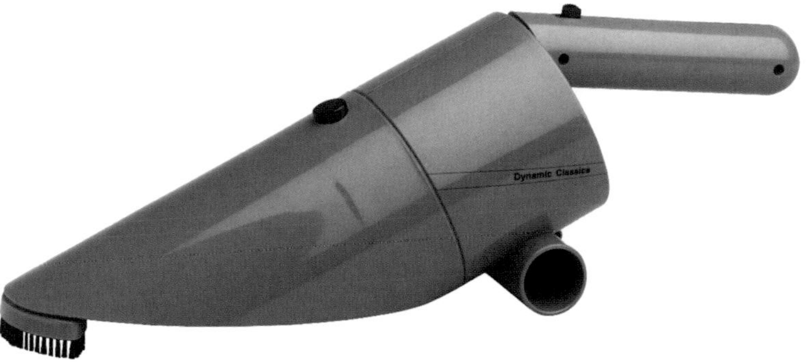

Michael Alan Cousins and John Lonczak (1954–), Morison S. Cousins + Associates. Vacuum cleaner. 1981. ABS polymer, 5 x 15 x 3 7/8" (12.7 x 38.1 x 9.8 cm). Mfr.: Dynamic Classics, US. Gift of the mfr. MoMA.

on Art and Industry), composed of artists, craftspeople, architects, critics, the director of the Victoria and Albert Museum of London, and the chairperson of the British Institute of Industrial Art. Initial members included Roger Fry, A.E. Gray, C.H. St. John Hornby, Sir Hubert Llewellyn Smith, Sir Eric Maclagan, Howard Robertson, Harry Trethowan, E.W. Tristram, and Clough Williams-Ellis. The group was asked to study the state of production and exhibition of everyday domestic goods. The committee's report, published in 1932, presented a survey of the collaboration of art and industry in Britain during 1754–1914 and the educational requirements. It recommended further investigation into the relationship between art and industry, and a permanent exhibition on industrial art in London to tour the UK. 1933 following the Gorell Committee recommendations, the British Board of Trade set up the Council for Art and Industry, with members from the industrial, commercial, artistic, and design communities, and critics. 1934 under Frank Pick, the council began to study the training and employment of designers in the pottery, textile, jewelry, metalsmithing, and other industries and published the 'Report by the Council for Art and Industry: Design and the Designer in Industry' (1937); sponsored/mounted exhibitions (including those at and with the Victoria and Albert Museum), and studied art education in primary schools and adult visual education; in an effort to educate the general consumer, mounted exhibitions promoting inexpensive, well-designed products, including 1937 *The Working Class Home*; was responsible for the organization and selection of entries in the British exhibition at 1937 *Exposition Internationale des Arts et Techniques dans la Vie Moderne*, Paris.
Bibliography Cat., *Thirties: British Art and Design Before the War*, London: Arts Council of Great Britain/Hayward Gallery, 1979.

Counot-Blandin, Pierre (1911–2001)
French furniture designer and manufacturer.

Biography 1930, Counot-Blandin set up a workshop; produced furniture for oceanliners 1935 *Normandie* and for Le Mobilier National, copies of which are still produced, also by his own still-extant Pierre Counot-Blandin firm in Liffol-Le-Grand, France, which today reproduces 1920s–20s furniture by Ruhlmann and others.

Courrèges, André (1923–)
French couturier; active Paris.

Training 1945, École Supérieure du Vêtement, Paris; École des Ponts-et-Chaussées; 1948–59 under Cristobal Balenciaga; both Paris.
Biography 1950, Courrège began his career as a cutter for Cristobal Balenciaga; 1965, had his first fashion show, featuring Futurist-looking clothing, mini-skirts, and trousers in white and pastel shades; 1967, set up own workshop; 1987, opened an architecture and design office.
Bibliography Ruth Lynam, *Couture: An Illustrated History...*, New York: Doubleday, 1972. Cat., *Design français, 1960–1990: trois décennies*, Paris: Pompidou/APCI, 1988. Katherine Betts, 'Courrèges: Back to the Future,' *Women's Wear Daily*, 22 Jan. 1981.

Courtaulds
British textile firm; located Braintree, Essex, and surrounding areas.

History 1816, Samuel Courtauld 3rd (1793–1881) managed the Bocking silk mill; became principal founder of Courtaulds Ltd., which was incorporated in 1913 and became known for its production of crepe. It pioneered rayon made by the viscose process, 1959 with ICI, began producing their brand of nylon, called Bri-Nylon; by 1940, as part of the ICI conglomerate, was one of the largest textile firms worldwide; 1950s, took over Lancashire Cotton Corporation and Fine Spinners' and Doublers' Association; 1963, took over Edinburgh Weavers. 1992, Courtaulds became separate from ICI and thus a competitor of ICI. 1999, Dutch corporation Asko Nobel Fibres took over Courtauds to form Acordis.
Bibliography Valerie Mendes, *The Victoria and Albert Museum's Textile Collection, British Textiles from 1900 to 1937*, London: Victoria and Albert Museum, 1992.

Cousins, Morison Stuart (1934–2001); Michael Alan Cousins (1938–)
American industrial designers; born Brooklyn, N.Y.; brothers.

Training Morison Cousins: to 1955, Pratt Institute, Brooklyn.
Biography Morison Cousins worked on truck design for International Harvester and, subsequently for two years, served in the army; from 1963, was a partner with Michael Cousins in Morrison S. Cousins + Associates studio in New York and, individually and with others, designed hair dryers, telephones, and other products for firms such as AtariTel, General Electric, and Heller. Their 1970 Dixie Cup dispenser by American Can Company sold more than 100 million examples during two decades. From 1990, Morison Cousins was vice-president of design at Tupperware Corporation, Orlando, Fla., and brought a more up-to-date style to the firm's primarily plastic food containers; was a member, Industrial Designers Society of America (IDSA). To c. 2000, Michael Cousins continued the studio in New York and became independent.
Exhibitions/citations Morison Cousins's Tupperware designs subject of 1997 exhibit, Moss shop, New York. 1984 Rome Prize, American Academy, Rome; 1999 Good Design award (1996–98 T.2 Mixer by Tupperware), Chicago Athenaeum.
Bibliography Douglas Martin, 'Morison S. Cousins, Revamped Tupperware's Look with Flair, Dies at 66', *The New York Times*, 18 Feb. 2001. Obituary, *Sidney Morning Herald*, 24 Feb. 2001: 41. Mel Byars and Laetitia Wolff, 'Tupperware: Is the Party Over?,' *Graphis*, no 337, Jan.–Feb. 2002: 88–95.

Coutellerie à Thiers, La
French cutlery industry; located Thiers.

History 1272, a group of master cutlerysmiths established themselves in Thiers, now the center for such activities in France. From 14th century, cutlery made in Thiers was exported to Spain and the Netherlands. By 1596, more than 170 workers were active in the area; the number grew to 700 by 1615. Cutlery activities attracted other industries. Using the resources of the Durolle river, on which the town is situated, electricity and gas motors aided the production of hand-forged, molded, and polished knives. Today in Thiers the workshops still produce cutlery along with surgical tools and vessels in stainless steel.

Couture, Lise Anne (1959–)
> See Asymptote.

Matali Crasset. Artican wastepaper basket. 1999. Plastic and metal, h. 24 x dia. 16 1/2" (61 x 41.9 cm). Mfr.: Sas/OO, France. Gift of the designer. MoMA.

Cowan, R. Guy (1884–1957); Cowan Pottery Studio

American ceramics designer and entrepreneur; born East Liverpool, Ohio. Factory.

History c. 1912, Cowan, who had studied under Charles Fergus Binns at New York College of Clayworking and Ceramics, Alfred (N.Y.) University, set up a kiln; 1913, incorporated it as Cleveland Pottery and Tiles Company; after World War I, opened the operation as as Cowan Pottery Studio in Lakewood, Ohio, and, 1920, moved to Rocky River, Ohio; 1927, began small-scale production of the work of ceramicists, including Russell B. Aitken, Thelma Frazier, Arthur E. Baggs, Waylande Gregory, and Viktor Schreckengost. The firm made both commercial and art pottery. 1913, Richard O. Hummel (c. 1899–c. 1976) joined the pottery, later becoming a chemist; glazed the work of other ceramicists and produced his own innovative, decorated forms, although never considered himself a ceramic artist. The Great Depression caused the closing of the pottery in Dec. 1931. From 1932, Cowan worked as a research engineer, Ferro Enamel company, Cleveland; moved to Syracuse, N.Y., where he became artistic director, Onondaga Pottery Company; played an important role in the organization of Ceramic Nationals competition, Syracuse Museum of Fine Arts. He died in Syracuse.
Exhibitions/citations Work included in 1920–30s annual exhibitions of industrial art, The Metropolitan Museum of Art, New York; 1927 *Exposition of Art in Trade at Macy's*, R.H. Macy department store, New York; 1928 *Exposition of Art in Industry at Macy's*. First prize, 1917 Annual Exhibition of Applied Art, Art Institute of Chicago; 1924 Logan Medal for Beauty in Design (limited production work), Art Institute of Chicago.
Bibliography Karen Davies, *At Home in Manhattan: Modern Decorative Arts, 1925 to the Depression*, New Haven: Yale, 1983: 51. Janet Kardon (ed.), *Craft in the Machine Age 1920–1945*, New York: Abrams, 1995.

Cox and Company

British furniture manufacturer; located Watford.

History Rowland Wilton Cox was general manager of Rotax Accessories, manufacturers of components for automobiles in London and Birmingham until it was bought by Joseph Lucas in 1926. 1927, Cox bought back the Birmingham plant. At the same time, he also bought car-window and car-hood (bonnet) manufacturers. The staff moved to new premises in South London. From 1929 when sales of automotive products declined, Cox pioneered the production in Britain of tubular-metal car seats and folding seats and tables for the garden. 1930, sales manager Harry Taylor tried unsuccessfully to obtain rights to make Thonet tubular-steel furniture in England; Cox began producing a range of its own tubular-steel furniture to designs adapted from Thonet models. 1931, Bobby's department store in Bournemouth placed an order with Cox for 5,000 chairs and 2,500 tables for 'Dreamland' at Margate. Cox produced tubular-steel frames, designed by Richter, for Bath Cabinet Makers; 1931–32, manufactured the furniture that Raymond McGrath and Serge Chermayeff had designed for the new BBC studios in Broadcasting House, London. 1933 after Oliver Bernard left Cox's competitor Pel, Cox produced Bernard-design chairs for the Lyon's Corner Houses and 1933 winter garden of Cumberland Hotel in London. 1934, Cox was involved in legal action with Pel over the production of the RP6 stacking chair, the rights to which Pel had purchased from Austrian designer Bruno Pollock in 1934; hence, Cox agreed to pay Pel a royalty. Cox's domestic-furniture designs were never as sophisticated as Pel's, and it never hired a professional designer; its models were designed by Cox himself or adapted by his technical staff from the designs of other manufacturers. 1935, Cox's first contract for fold-up auditorium seating came from the Royal Institute of British Architects' London headquarters at Portland Place. 1936, Cox moved to Watford; 1939, supplied aircraft assemblies and parts to Hawker Aircraft and to Vickers; to 1945, produced war materials, including aircraft-engine mountings, gun turrets, and tanks.
Bibliography Cat., Dennis Sharp et al., *Pel and Tubular Steel Furniture of the Thirties*, London: Architectural Association, 1977. Barbie Campbell-Cole and Tim Benton (eds.), *Tubular Steel Furniture*, London: The Art Book Company, 1979: 53.

Crabeth, Vennootschap

Dutch glassmaker; active The Hague.

Biography Crabeth, of a family of stained-glass artisans, executed Theo van Doesburg's work, including Composition IV triptych stained-glass window for Jan Wils's own 1917 townhouse in Alkmaar and Compositions II and V for 1918–1931 Villa Allegonda (architect, J.J.P. Oud, with Menso Onnes and van Doesburg) in Katwijk aan Zees.
Bibliography Evert van Straaten, *Theo van Doesburg, Painter and Architect*, The Hague: SDU, 1988. Jonathan M. Woodham, *Twentieth-Century Ornament*, New York: Rizzoli, 1990: 111.

Crane, Walter (1845–1915)

British designer, artist, and writer; born Liverpool; son of portrait painter Thomas Crane (1808–59).

Training 1859–62 under William J. Linton, in woodcarving, London.
Biography By 1863, Crane had begun his long collaboration with publisher and printer Edmund Evans (1826–1906); from 1860s, designed and illustrated books; 1870s, was influenced by Japanese art and the work of Edward Burne-Jones, Botticelli, and William Blake. His books were popular; *The Baby's Opera: A Book of Old Rhymes with New Dresses* (1877) sold over 40,000 copies. In original and pirated editions, his books were available in the US. American Encaustic Tiling Company, Zanesville, Ohio, produced transfer-printed tiles from illustrations in *The Baby's Own Æsop* (1887). Also in the US, Helen Metcalf adapted his 1865–66 illustrations for her drawings for *Jack and the Beanstalk* (1874). Crane designed tiles by Maw, vases by Wedgwood, wallpapers by Jeffrey & Co. (from 1874), a tapestry by Morris and Company, textiles by Wardle (1880s), carpets by Templeton's of Glasgow, and embroideries by Royal School of Art Needlework; collaborated with William Morris and Thomas Jeckyll on the decoration of collector Alexander A. Ionides's house in London; early 1870s, revived the art of decorative plasterwork; 1884, cofounded the Art-Workers' Guild, serving as master 1888–89; a socialist from c. 1885, was a founder-member and president of Arts and Crafts Exhibition Society from its formation in 1888 to 1912 (excluding 1893–96); 1891–92, visited the US and designed stained glass for Catharine Lorillard Wolfe house in Newport, R.I., and a church in Newark, N.J.; designed two books by Houghton, Mifflin in Boston; and painted murals for Women's Christian Temperance Building in Chicago. His work became influenced by graphic designers in the US, including Will Bradley, Howard Pyle, and Edwin Austin Abbey. From 1890s, Crane was director of design, Manchester School of Art, and briefly taught art, Reading College; wrote numerous books on the decorative arts. One of the most versatile decorative artists of late 19th century, his greatest contribution was in graphic art; 1898, became principal, Royal College of Art, London. By late 1890s, he was already well known in Europe. 1895, his late work was on display at Siegfried Bing's gallery/shop L'Art Nouveau in Paris. An honorary member of the Wiener Sezession, he designed the 1898 cover of its review *Jugend*. His style heralded

continental Art Nouveau, which he adversely criticized. His books and illustrations disseminated the Arts and Crafts style.
Exhibitions/citations Work subject of 1891–96 exhibition, Fine Art Society, London, traveling to Chicago, St. Louis, Boston, Philadelphia, and Brooklyn. Work shown in Budapest in 1900; in Vienna in 1902; 1902 *Esposizione Internazionale d'Arte Decorativa Moderna*, Turin. A prize (for wallpapers by Jeffrey), 1876 *Centennial Exposition* (embroidered screen with peacocks and portières for Royal School of Art Needlework), Philadelphia; 1905 gold medal from Royal Society of Arts.
Bibliography P.G. Konody, *The Art of Walter Crane*, London, 1902. Russell Sturgis, 'English Decoration and Walter Crane,' *Architectural Record*, no. 12, Dec. 1902: 685–91. *Royal Institute of British Architects Journal*, 3rd series 22, 1914–15: 240, 277, 280. *The New York Times*, obituary, 16 Mar. 1915: 11. Gertrude C.E. Massé, *A Bibliography of First Editions of Books Illustrated by Walter Crane*, London: Chelsea, 1923. Isobel Spencer, *Walter Crane*, London: Studio Vista, 1975. Doreen Bolger Burke et al., *In Pursuit of Beauty: Americans and the Aesthetic Movement*, New York: The Metropolitan Museum of Art/ Rizzoli, 1987: 417. David E. Gerard, *Walter Crane and the Rhetoric of Art*, London: Nine Elms, 1999.

Crasset, Matali (1965–)
French designer; born Chalons-en-Champagne; active Paris.

Training École Nationale Supérieure de Création Industrielle (Les Ateliers), Paris.
Biography 1990, Crasset worked as a designer in the studio of Raul Barbieri in Italy, on products by Rexite and by Magis; 1992, of Denis Santachiara in Italy, on furniture and objects by Moroso, Bross, Domodinamica, and others; 1993–97, of Philippe Starck, in France, responsible for Tim Thom products by Thomson multimédia; 1998, established her own studio in Paris and has designed products and furniture by Authentics, Domeau & Pérès, Lexon, Möve, Dornbracht, and others. Work has included 1995 Don O radio/cassette player and 1998 Icipari radio by Thomson multimédia, 1997 Capriccio di Ugo chair by Modular, 2001 Omni crystal (three glasses and carafe) by Saint-Louis, 2000 standard public-bar tumbler for Origina, 2001 Metafloor collection (three 'furniture-carpets') by Sam Laïk, 2002 Sunic perfume by Dragoco in Paris, 2002 glassware by Ajeto in the Czech Republic; and 2003 'hi-Hotel' in Nice. From 1994, she has taught and participated in a number of seminars and workshops at institutions and venues in Amsterdam, Bordeaux, Compiègne, Copenhagen, Lausanne, Paris, Reims, among others.
Exhibitions/citations Participated in 1992 *Identità e Differenza* (her 'Domestic Trilogy' presentation) at Triennale di Milano. Work included in a number of exhibitions; subject of 2002 *Casaderme* project, Pitti Immagine Uomo no. 61, Florence; 2002 *Matali Crasset for Dornbracht: Update*, Galerie Ulrich Fiedler, Cologne; 2002 *Sunic* (installation and perfume), Nadine Gandy Gallery, Prague; 2002 *Matali Crasset: Un Pas de Côté*, mu.dac (Musée de Design et d'Arts Appliqués Contemporains), Lausanne (catalog below). A number of national and international grants and awards, from 1991 first prize (for leather handbag for Louis Vuitton), Comité Colbert.
Bibliography Pascale Cassagnau and Christophe Pillet, *Beef, Brétillot/Valette, Matali Crasset, Patrick Jouin, Jean-Marie Massaud: petits enfants de Starck?*, Paris: Dis Voir, 2000. Mel Byars, *50 Beds...*, Hove: RotoVision, 2000. Cat., *Matali Crasset, un pas de côté (1991–2002)*, Lausanne: Musée de Design et d'Arts Appliqués Contemporains, 2002. Gareth Williams (preface), *Matali Crasset*, Paris: Pyramyd, 2003.

Craven, Shirley (1934–)
British textile designer.

Training 1955–58, painting, sculpture, and textile design, Kingston-upon-Hull and Royal College of Art, London.
Biography From 1960 as a consultant designer, she designed printed fabrics by Hull Traders, where she was director from 1963. 1972, the firm closed, and she returned to painting and teaching.
Citations Awards from Council of Industrial Design (for fabrics by Hull Traders, including 1961 Le Bosquet, 1964 Division, Sixty-Three, and Shape, and 1968 Simple Solar and Five).
Bibliography Cat., *Brown/Craven/Dodd: 3 Textile Designers*, Manchester: Whitworth Art Gallery, 1965: 6–10. Ken Baynes, *Industrial Design and the Community*, London, 1967: 57–59. 'Furnishing Fabrics: Hull Traders' Simple Solar, Five,' *Design*, no. 233, May 1968: 30–31. Cat., Kathryn B. Hiesinger and George H. Marcus III (eds.), *Design Since 1945*, Philadelphia: Philadelphia Museum of Art, 1983.

Craven, Walter (1971–)
American designer; born Boston, Mass.

Biography 1996, Craven established Blank and Cables for the design of products and furniture, in San Francisco; has an in-house workshop for production; 1999, introduced its first furniture collection in San Francisco and New York. Widely published furniture designs include Camel and Box chairs, Baño table, and Pillow Boxes cabinet/table. Has served clients such as Banana Republic, Chroma Copy, Conger Design, The Gap, Gary Hutton Design, Levi-Strauss, Orlando-Diaz Ascuy (interior designer), Pottery Barn, and Warner Brothers.
Exhibitions Work shown at editions of International Contemporary Furniture Fair (ICFF), New York; SaloneSatellite, Salone del Mobile, Milan; Museum of Modern Art, San Francisco.
Bibliography www.blankandcables.com.

Craver, Margaret Withers (1907–1991)
American silversmith; born Kansas City, Miss.; active Boston.

Training Art School, University of Kansas City, Missouri; under Wilson Weir of Tiffany, New York; Stone Associates, Gardner, Mass.; tool making under Leonard Heinrich, armor conservator of The Metropolitan Museum of Art, New York; Atelier Borgila of Baron Erik Fleming.
Biography Craver was one of the few women silversmiths to achieve international recognition; 1940s–50s in her workshop, revived hand-wrought silver hollow-ware. Her first major work in hollow-ware was a 1936 silver and ebony teapot, made under the direction of ecclesiastical metalworker Arthur Nevill Kirk, Detroit. Craver's work combined full, organic shapes with the influence of Art Moderne. 1930s, began her studies in metalsmithing, although the craft had long suffered from inadequate training due to the introduction of mechanized silver production in the 19th century. After her studies in Europe, she returned to the US in 1938 and set up a workshop producing hollow-ware, sometimes decorated with enamel; later worked at precious-metal refinery Handy and Harmon to develop a program for rehabilitating veterans returning from World War II; while there, also developed a training program for design teachers. Most veteran US craftspeople working today in silversmithing were either trained at or learned from Craver's silversmithing conferences sponsored by Handy and Harmon, from which she resigned in 1953. Craver revived the lost *enresille* enameling technique and concentrated on jewelry at the end of her career.
Exhibitions Work shown at numerous exhibitions, including 1970 *Objects USA* and 1987 *The Eloquent Object*.
Bibliography Annelies Krekel-Aalberse, *Art Nouveau and Art Déco Silver*, New York: Abrams, 1989. Jeannine Falino, 'MFS Boston acquires Craver Silver Teapot,' *Antiques and the Arts Weekly*, 16 Feb. 1990.

Creadesign
> See Kähönen, Hannu.

Crémaillère, La
French furnishings store and maker; located Paris.

History 1923, André Champetier de Ribes and Jacques Delore established La Crémaillère shop at 148, avenue Malakoff, Paris, where they sold ceramics, glassware, silver, and various furnishings for domestic interiors. The design department was managed by Charles Goetz and Jacques Krauss. 1930, André Renou joined the firm and became president and director general in 1941, and, 1933, Jean-Pierre Génisset joined the firm. Their collaboration, on work signed 'Renou et Génisset,' continued to 1965. Renou's wife selected unusual objects for the firm. 1937, the shop moved to 5, boulevard des Malesherbes, and, 1967, to 74, boulevard des Malesherbes. Thérèse Bentz was one of its designers of tables and lamps, and Germaine Montereau of fabrics, including table linen.
Bibliography Yolande Amic, *Intérieurs: le mobilier français 1945–1964*, Paris: Regard/VIA, 1983: 44–45. Pierre Kjellberg, *Art déco: les maîtres du mobilier, le décor des paquebots*, Paris: Amateur, 1986/1990. Arlette Barré-Despond, *UAM*, Paris: Regard, 1986.
> See Renou, André

Cret, Paul Philippe (1876–1945)
French architect and designer; born Lyon.

Training École des Beaux-Arts, Lyons; to 1903 under Pascal, École des Beaux-Arts, Paris.
Biography 1890, Cret worked in his uncle's architecture office in Lyon; 1903, was invited to teach, University of Pennsylvania, Philadelphia,

US, where he espoused the Beaux-Arts style initially, and remained at the university to 1937. His architecture included 1907–10 Pan American Union Building (with Albert Kelsey), Washington, D.C.; 1922 Detroit Institute of Arts; 1922 Delaware River Bridge (today, Benjamin Franklin Bridge), Philadelphia; 1929 Folger Shakespeare Library, Washington, D.C.; and 1932 Federal Reserve Bank, Washington, D.C. He worked in collaboration with others, and turned to a streamline approach with his design of 1941 Empire State Express Train of New York Central Railroad and 1941 California Zephyr Train. His archive is housed in the Fine Arts Library, University of Pennsylvania, Philadelphia.
Exhibitions/citations He designed a number of room settings for and was the director of the East Gallery of the 1935 *Contemporary American Industrial Art, 1934*, The Metropolitan Museum of Art, New York. Drawings subject of 1983 exhibition, Texas (catalog below). Philadelphia (Bok) award.
Bibliography Theo B. White (ed.), *Paul Philippe Cret: Architect and Teacher*, Philadelphia: Art Alliance, 1973. Cat., Carol McMichael, *Paul Cret at Texas: Architectural Drawing and the Image of the University in the 1930s*, Austin, Tex.: Archer M. Huntington Art Gallery, University of Texas, 1983. R. Craig Miller, *Modern Design 1890–1990*, New York: Abrams, 1990, notes.

Crevel, René (1900–1935)

French writer, painter, and jewelry designer; born Rouen.

Biography Crevel belonged to the Surrealist group; was preoccupied in his writings with death and solitude; worked as a jewelry designer with Gérard Sandoz and assisted with the furniture for Sandoz's shop and apartment, rue Royale, Paris; painted portraits and bucolic and marine scenes, decorated panels, and designed wallpaper.
Exhibitions Work shown at editions of Salon d'Automne and Salons of Société des Artistes Décorateurs. Participated (with Paul Follot) in 1925 *Exposition Internationale des Arts Décoratifs et Industriels Modernes*, Paris, and with others showed textiles, tapestries, and *toiles* in Une Ambassade Française pavilion there.
Bibliography Yvonne Brunhammer, *Le cinquantenaire de l'exposition de 1925*, Paris: Musée des Arts Décoratifs, 1976: 122.

Crhak, Frantisek (1926–)

Czech teacher and industrial designer.

Training 1946–50, architecture, České Vysoké Učení Technické (Czech technical university), Prague.
Biography From 1953, Crhak was a professor, Vystudoval Střední Uměleckoprůmyslové Škole (secondary school of applied arts) in Uherské Hradiště, where he taught artistic-technical subjects. With Zdenek Kovar, he moved to the workshop of Vystudoval Střední Uměleckoprůmyslové Škola (secondary school of applied arts) in Gottwaldov (formerly Zlín) and introduced training in 'artistic geometry' as a part of the basic education of students; from 1960s, designed several products by Tesla and participated in the firm's corporate ID program; developed Tesla's sport airplanes with types Z-42 and Z-43 engines; with Kovar, designed fluorescent street lamps, street-lighting stantions, and others by Elektrosvit Nove Zamky, Nove Zamky, Slovakia.

Crinion, Jonathan (1953–)

British architect and designer; active Toronto, Canada.

Training Industrial design, Carleton University, Ottawa; To 1980, Ontario College of Art, Toronto.
Biography 1981, Crinion worked with Jan Kuyper at KAN (Kuyper Adamsom Norton Ltd.), Toronto, and established KAN in California; 1984, worked independently; 1988 in London, worked in the office of architects Norman Foster and Partners (participated in work on Nomos furniture system, subway system of Bilbao, Spain, and the practice's new office in Battersea, 1983); returned to Canada and reopened his own practice, Crinion Associates, in Toronto. He and/or his staff have designed thousands of products, including gas baseboard heaters, banking systems, task lighting, and ergonomic keyboards, but is primarily known for furniture and office systems; is a member, Chartered Society of Designers (CSD), UK. Clients have included Knoll, Steelcase, Teknion, Egan Visual, Area, Keilhauer, Tecno, and Sunwood. 1990s Bebop café chair was produced by Kosk Design in Toronto. His iconic 1986 Gazelle chair appeared on a Canadian postage stamp commemorating Canadian industrial design.
Citations 1993 award, Institute of Business Designers (IBD), US; 1994 award, American Society of Interior Designers (ASID); two Best of Show, *Financial Post* Design Effectiveness Awards, Canada; Best of NeoCon several times, Chicago; 1994 International Design 40 and 1999 Best of Category, Annual Design Review, *I.D.* magazine; 1997 FX Design award; 1998, elected to Royal Canadian Academy of the Arts; 2000 Arts Award for Design and Architecture, City of Toronto.
Bibliography Rachel Gotlieb and Cora Golden, *Design in Canada Since 1945: Fifty Years from Teakettles to Task Chairs*, Toronto: Knopf Canada, 2001.

Cristalleries de Saint-Louis
> See Saint-Louis.

Cristiani, Mario (1921–)

Italian designer; born and active Milan.

Training Accademia di Belle Arte di Brera; architecture, Politecnico; both Milan.
Biography From 1957, Cristiani worked at La Rinascente department store, where he was manager of its design center, including being in charge of Settore furniture line.
Exhibitions/citations Participated in 1951 (9th), 1957 (11th), and 1960 (12th) Triennali di Milano. 1970 (T 92 table with Eugenio Gerli by Tecno) Premio Compasso d'Oro.
Bibliography *ADI Annual 1976*, Milan: Associazione per il Disegno Industriale, 1976.

Cromie, Robert (1887–1971)

British architect.

Training Architectural Association, London; under architect A.J. Wood.
Biography Cromie became the first in Britain to use tubular-steel furniture on a large public scale, in the restaurant of 1929 Capital Cinema in Epsom, Surrey; was best known for his theater and cinema designs and the house architect for the Ritz and Regal cinema chains. 1930s work included Regal cinemas in Bexley Heath, Canterbury, Godalming, Kingston-upon-Thames, Margate, and Wimbledon; Ritz cinemas in Birkenhead, Chelmsford, Huddersfield, Oxford, Southend, and Tunbridge Wells; Paris cinemas in Regent Street (1938) and Drayton Gardens, London; Gaumont Palace Cinema in Hammersmith, London; 1937 Prince of Wales Theatre in London; Plaza, Rex, and Embassy cinemas; and interiors of Oddenino's hotel in London and of nurses' training school in Hove.
Exhibitions Work shown at 1979–80 *Thirties* exhibition, Hayward Gallery, London (catalog below).
Bibliography Cat., *Thirties: British Art and Design Before the War*, London: Arts Council of Great Britain/Hayward Gallery, 1979. Barbie Campbell-Cole and Tim Benton (eds.), *Tubular Steel Furniture*, London: Art Book Company, 1979: 53.

Crompton, Rebecca (1894–1947)

British embroiderer.

Training Under Dorothy Benson, Singer Machine Workroom.
Biography She became known for her modern embroidery and was a proponent of free-machine work in tandem with hand techniques; lectured in Aberdeen, Dundee, Edinburgh, and Glasgow for the Needlework Development Scheme, established 1934 in Scotland; was an examiner and inspector of embroidery and women's crafts, UK Board of Education, and an examiner in embroidery, Advanced Section, Lancashire and Cheshire Institute; contributed to books *Modern Needlecraft* 1932 (edited by Davide C. Minter), *Modern Design in Embroidery* (1936), and *A Plea for Freedom* (1936); was among the leading 1930s British embroiderers, along with Mary Hogarth, Kathleen Mann, and Molly Booke
Exhibitions Work shown at 1932 *Modern Embroidery*, sponsored by British Institute of Industrial Art, Victoria and Albert Museum, London; 1938 *Needlework Through the Ages*; 1979–80 *Thirties* exhibition, Hayward Gallery, London (catalog below).
Bibliography Cat., *Thirties: British Art and Design Before the War*, London: Arts Council of Great Britain/Hayward Gallery, 1979.

Cros, César-Isidore-Henri (1840–1907)

French ceramicist, sculptor, and glass designer; born Narbonne.

Training Under François Jouffroy, Antoine Étex, and Suzanne Valadon, École Nationale des Beaux-Arts, Paris.
Biography Cros is credited with rediscovering the secret of making *pâte-de-verre*, a technique originally perfected by ancient Egyptians;

first experimented with wax and turned to *pâte-de-verre* after a long period of research; and realized through powdered glass, mixed into a paste with flux and colored with metallic oxides; bonded the glass in molds at sufficiently high temperature for it to melt, but without sections of different colors running together; made mainly bas-reliefs and medals, with some masks, portraits, vases, and goblets; was active in research in an atelier at the Manufacture Nationale de Sèvres.
Exhibitions/citations Work first shown, at 1864 Salon in Paris. Gold medal (bas-relief *L'Histoire du Feu*), 1900 *Exposition Universelle*, Paris.
Bibliography Yvonne Brunhammer et al., *Art Nouveau Belgium, France*, Houston: Rice University, 1976. Cat., *Verriers français contemporains: art et industrie*, Paris: Musée des Arts Décoratifs, 1982.

Crosbie, Nick (1971–)
> See Inflate.

Cumini, Carlo (1953–)
Italian designer; born Gemona del Friuli (UD).

Training To 1974, Istituto Tecnico Statale per Geometri 'G.G. Marinoni,' Udine.
Biography From 1974, Cumini worked for his family's firm Horm as a salesperson and furniture designer, becoming the main designer, principally for wood items and systems. From 1991, he has also designed for others, including Luc-e and Nuova Auras, and collaborated with designers Alberto Freschi and Carlo Biancolini.
Bibliography Michele De Lucchi (ed.), *The International Design Yearbook*, London: Laurence King, 2001.

Cumming, Rose (1887–1968)
American interior decorator; born Australia; active New York.

Biography 1917, Cumming arrived in New York. Frank Crowninshield, editor of *Vanity Fair*, suggested that she become a decorator; she is said to have inquired, 'What is it?' Cumming worked briefly at Au Quatrième, the decorating studio of Wanamaker's department store, New York; subsequently, opened a shop of her own on Madison Avenue, and became one of the first in America to import chintzes and silks from London and Paris. The distinctive windows of the shop were noticed by the public and the press. Her house on East 53rd Street was fitted with theatrical mirrors and a great many black candles. The drawing room, shown in 1946 photographs, featured Louis XV sofas and chairs with tattered original upholstery and walls covered with antique Chinese wallpaper; the furniture frames were white or natural wood. The house was neither heated in winter nor artificially cooled in summer. Her tinted violet hair was a personal trademark. In the design of clients' interiors, she included silver-foil wrapping paper applied to walls, smoked mirrors, and full curtains in chintz fabrics vividly colored to her specifications. Her firm continues today, selling fabrics, furnishings, and furniture, after Cumming's taste and unchanged since their introduction in 1920s–40s, including her La Fenice tête-à-tête and renowned Cheeta velvet.
Bibliography Mark Hampton, *House and Garden*, May 1990: 145–49, 214. John Esten and Rose Bennett Gilbert, *Manhattan Style*, Boston: Little, Brown, 1990: 8. Mark Hampton, *Legendary Decorators of the Twentieth Century*, New York: Doubleday, 1992.

Cuneo, Marcello (1933–)
Italian designer; born Cagliari; active Peschiera Borromeo.

Training Politecnico, Milan.
Biography 1959, Cuneo began his professional career; 1962–70, collaborated with Gio Ponti; 1971, set up his own design studio; was designer for the minister of Islamabad, Pakistan, and for De Bijenkorf, Eindhoven. His clients in Italy included Ampaglas (plastic accessories), Arflex (seating), Assioma, Gabbianelli (ceramics), La Linea (furniture in wood), Mobel Italia (seating in metal), and Valenti (lighting). He worked as consultant on prefabrication for Sculponia and for FEAL; became known for his lighting fixtures.
Exhibitions/citations Work included in 1972 *Italy: The New Domestic Landscape*, The Museum of Modern Art, New York. First prize (for Longobardo lighting fixture), 1967 Internazionale Andrea Palladio, Venice; 1978 Bundespreis Produktdesign (for desk chair by Comforto), Rat für Formgebung (German design council), Frankfurt.
Bibliography *ADI Annual 1976*, Milan: Associazione per il Disegno Industriale, 1976. Alfonso Grassi and Anty Pansera, *Atlante del design italiano 1940/1980*, Milan: Fabbri, 1980: 297. *Modo*, no. 148, Mar.–Apr. 1993: 118.

Curro Claret, Martí (1968–)
Spanish designer; born and active Barcelona.

Training 1987–92, industrial design, Elisava (Escola Superior de Disseny), Barcelona; 1993–95, industrial design, Central St. Martin's College of Art and Design, London.
Biography 1988, Curro Claret worked as a graphic design at studio B&R; 1993–99, collaborated with studio HTT Arquitectes; from 1996, has been active as a freelance designer for Dou Deu, Camper, Barcelona Tecnologia, Concha Blanc, Cha-Cha, Massimo Dutti, Helix Equipaments, FAD (decorative-arts association), and private clients; from 1998, has taught in various design schools; writes on design for journals.
Exhibitions Work included in 1993 Espace Jeunes Créateurs, *Design, Miroir du Siècle*, Grand Palais, Paris; 1998 (1st) and 2000 (2nd) Biennale Internationale du Design, Saint-Etienne, France; 1999 *Italia–Europa* (young designers), Abitare il Tempo fair, Verona; 1999, 2001, and 2002 young designers exhibition, Opos, Milan.
Bibliography Mel Byars, *50 Products...*, Hove: RotoVision, 1998. Ramón Prat, *Barcelona+*, Barcelona: Actar, 2001.

Custer, Walter (1909–1992)
Swiss architect; born Rapperswil; born Rapperswil; active Zürich.

Training Under Otto Rudolf Salvisberg, architecture, Eidgenössische Technische Hochschule (ETH), Zürich; 1931–32 under Hans Poelzig, Technische Hochschule, Berlin-Charlottenburg; 1935, received a diploma from the ETH.
Biography While still at technical school in Zürich, Custer was hired to direct the technical activities of the Wohnbedarf department store in Zürich; there he met Alvar Aalto and worked on Aalto's furniture prototypes until they were put into industrial production; 1934, traveled through the Netherlands and Britain, looking for the appropriate hinge for Wohnbedarf's 'incombi' model. Alvar and Aino Aalto invited him to their studio in Helsinki, where he worked on the competition design for the national post office building, Helsinki. After the granting of his 1935 diploma from the ETH, he worked in the office of German architect Werner M. Moser (later named Haefeli, Steiger und Moser); 1940–48, worked at the Central Studienbüro der Arbeitsgemeinschaft für Landesplanung and at the Büro für Regionalplanung, Kantonalem Hochbauamt Zürich der Orts-, Regional- und Landesplanung; 1948–51, traveled in Ceylon (now Sri Lanka), Nepal, and India, working on Swiss government development projects; 1951, worked in Calcutta with Moser; from 1958, taught in the architecture department, Eidgenössische Technische Hochschule in Zürich, where he died.
Bibliography Huber et al. (eds.), *Urbanisationsprobleme in der Ersten und in der Dritten Welt: Festschrift für Walter Custer*, Zürich: ETH, 1979. Friederike Mehlau-Wiebking et al., *Schweizer Typenmöbel 1925–35, Sigfried Giedion und die Wohnbedarf AG*, Zürich: gta, 1989.

Cuttoli, Marie (1879–1973)
Entrepreneur; active Paris and North Africa.

Biography 1926, Cuttoli established the Myrbor shop and gallery in Paris, where she had woven and sold the carpets/tapestries of Jean Lurcat, Le Corbusier, Fernand Léger, and others, some of which were made in Marrakesh; contributed significantly to reviving the art of tapestry; as early as 1922, reproduced Jean Lurçat's 'Le Cirque' painting series as five tapestries; 1925–30, significantly updated the production technique of tapestries by using punch cards to transform the art of Picasso, Braque, and Rouault into cloth; 1929, commissioned architect Ernö Goldfinger to design the Paris shopfront and furniture, and the Marrakesh factory (neither was realized). André Lurçat subsequently designed the shop. She later occupied the 1929 apartment that Goldfinger had designed for interior-decorator De Verac. 1932, first showed Alexander Calder's mobiles. Early 1930s, Picasso, Miró, and Braque tapestries, developed by Marie Cuttoli, were exhibited side by side with the paintings that had inspired them; the tapestries frequently sold for more than the paintings. Le Corbusier's first tapestries, of c. 1936, were produced by Cuttoli's workshop in Aubusson; 1930s, occupied a house in Antibes and hosted Picasso and others.
Exhibitions Work shown in the Myrbor stand, 1925 *Exposition Internationale des Arts Décoratifs et Industriels Modernes*, Paris; and included in 2000 *Meister des 20. Jahrhunderts*, Kunst Haus, Vienna, and 2001 *Lurçat, les années 20*, Atelier Musée Lurçat, Saint-Laurent-Les-Tours, France.
Bibliography *Les tapisseries de Le Corbusier*, Geneva and Paris, 1975. Cat., James Dunnett and Gavin Stamp (eds.), *Ernö Goldfinger*, London: Architectural Association, 1983: 18. Margit Rowell (Joan Miró letter to

Gunnar Cyrén. Bowl. 1967. Glass, h. 2 x dia. 14 1/2" (5.1 x 36.8 cm). Mfr.: Orrefors, Sweden. Gift of Bonniers, Inc., New York. MoMA.

various, including Marie Cuttoli), *Les Cahiers du Musée National d'Art Moderne*, no. 43, Apr. 1993. Susan Day, *Art Deco and Modernist Carpets*, London: Thames and Hudson, 2002.

Cuzner, Bernard (1877–1956)

British silversmith and jeweler; born Warwickshire; active Birmingham.

Training Redditch School of Art; Birmingham Central School of Art; under Robert Catterson-Smith and Arthur Gaskin; 1896–1900 under R. Catterson-Smith and Arthur Gaskin, apprenticeship.
Biography Cuzner was apprentice to his watchmaker father in Warwickshire; worked for a Birmingham silver firm, while attending night-classes at Redditch School of Art; worked as an independent silversmith, designing for Liberty's c. 1900 and subsequently for Goldsmiths' and Silversmiths' Companies in London and for Elkington in Birmingham; may have worked for Birmingham Guild of Handicrafts; produced fine one-off pieces for private customers, churches, and government organizations, and simple designs for silver firms, establishing high standards for decoration and craftsmanship; 1910–42, was head of the metalwork department, Birmingham Central School of Art, where one of his pupils was Cyril James Shiner. Though his objects for Liberty's were unattributed, they were identified as his when published in *The Studio* journal and at exhibitions. He wrote *A Silversmith's Manual...* (London: N.A.G.,1935). One of his major commissions was the Torch, by the Goldsmiths' Company, for 1948 Summer Olympiad in London.
Exhibitions A reconstruction of Cuzner's workshop and a collection of his drawings for silverwork and jewelry are housed in Birmingham Museum of Science and Industry.
Bibliography Charlotte Gere, *American and European Jewelry 1830–1914*, New York: Crown, 1975. Cat., *Thirties: British Art and Design Before the War*, London: Arts Council of Great Britain/Hayward Gallery, 1979. Annelies Krekel-Aalberse, *Art Nouveau and Art Déco Silver*, New York: Abrams, 1989.

Cyrén, Gunnar (1931–)

Swedish glassware designer and metalworker; active Stockholm.

Training 1951, goldsmithing; 1951–56, gold- and silversmithing, Konstfackskolan, Stockholm; 1954, Kölner Werkschule, Cologne.
Biography 1959–70, Cyrén was a glassware designer at the Orrefors Glasbruk, where he broke with its house style of pure undecorated table and decorative wares, using the *graal* technique to produce Anti-Design forms. His 1967 Pop range of glasswares is an example. From 1970, he was a freelance designer to Dansk Design; 1975, worked independently as a silversmith and for Gävie; from 1976, concentrated on cutting, engraving, and acid-etched ornamentations. Work included cut-glass lighting, tableware, and one-of-a-kind art glass.
Citations 1956 Medal for Proficiency and Industry, Föreningen Svenska Industridesigner (SID); 1966 Lunning Prize; both Stockholm.
Bibliography 'Thirty-four Lunning Prize-Winners', *Mobilia*, no. 146, Sept. 1967. Eileene Harrison Beer, *Scandinavian Design: Objects of a Life Style*, New York: Farrar, Straus & Giroux, 1975: 98–99. Cat., David Revere McFadden (ed.), *Scandinavian Modern Design: 1880–1980*, New York: Cooper-Hewitt Museum, 1982. Cat., *Aktuel Svensk Form*, Skien: Ibsenhuset, 1982: 24–27. Cat., Kathryn B. Hiesinger and George H. Marcus III (eds.), *Design Since 1945*, Philadelphia: Philadelphia Museum of Art, 1983. Frederick Cooke, *Glass: Twentieth-Century Design*, New York: Dutton, 1986. Cat., *The Lunning Prize*, Stockholm: Nationalmuseum, 1986: 166–69. Jennifer Hawkins Opie, *Scandinavia: Ceramics and Glass in the Twentieth Century*, New York: Rizzoli, 1989.

Czech Cubism

Czech architectural movement.

History Influential architect and teacher Jan Kotěra's first generation of pupils (including Josef Chochol, Pavel Janák, and Josef Gočár) established the 1911 program of Czech Cubism, which encouraged the manipulation of plastic masses, in a reaction against the prevailing Sezession style. They sought a new aesthetic language, expressing the spiritual and psychological through a rhythmic integration of triangles, crystals, and other 'privileged forms,' extending the aesthetic and philosophical intentions of Cubist painting and sculpture into architecture and utilitarian objects. The Cubist apartment houses and villas, furniture, ceramics, and metalwork are startling even today. The architects applied three-dimensional surfaces to façades and included elements from disparate sources, such as local architectural features (late-Gothic diamond vaults), the early 18th-century baroque (or pseudo-Gothic) forms of Giovanni Santini-Aichel, French Cubist art, and the aesthetics of the *Theorie der Einfühlung* of Munich scientists Theodor Lipps and Wilhelm Worringer. 1914 saw the culmination of Czech Cubism, when architects and artists in Prague collaborated with the journal *Der Sturm* (Herwarth Walden, chief editor) in Germany, and in the building of the Czech pavilion (Otakar Novotny, architect) at 1914 *Werkbund-Ausstellung* in Cologne.
Exhibitions Subject of *Czech Cubism: Architecture and Design, 1910–1925* touring exhibition, from 1992, organized by National Technical Museum and Umĕleckoprůmyslové Muzeum, both Prague, and with the cooperation of Vitra Museum, Weil am Rhein, Germany.
Bibliography Vladimir Slapeta essay, *Czech Functionalism*, London: Architectural Association, 1987: 8. Cat., Alexander von Vegesack et al., *Czech Cubism: Architecture, Furniture, and Decorative Arts, 1910–1925*, New York: Princeton Architectural Press/Vitra Design Museum, 1992.

Czeschka, Carl Otto (1878–1960)

Austrian architect, painter, graphic designer, and designer of jewelry, embroidery, and stained glass; born Vienna; active Vienna and Hamburg.

Training 1894–99, Akademie der bildenden Künste, Vienna.
Biography 1905, Czeschka joined Josef Hoffmann at the Wiener Werkstätte; with fellow Kunstgewerbeschule graduate Eduard Josef Wimmer-Wisgrill, who joined the Wiener Werkstätte 1907, played a part in the introduction of ornamentation; Czeschka was the first to do so in silverware. From c. 1900, he was associated with the Wiener Sezession (founded 1897–98), where he designed, including metalware; 1902–07, taught, Kunstgewerbeschule, Vienna; 1907, left the Werkstätte and became professor, Kunstgewerbeschule, Hamburg, while continuing to create many designs for the Werkstätte. He died in Hamburg.
Bibliography Charlotte Gere, *American and European Jewelry 1830–1914*, New York: Crown, 1975. Werner J. Schweiger, *Wiener Werkstätte*, Vienna: Brandstaetter, 1982. Annelies Krekel-Aalberse, *Art Nouveau and Art Déco Silver*, New York: Abrams, 1989.

D

Christopher Dresser. Toast rack (detail). 1878. MoMA.

D-sign by O
> See Fevre, Francis.

Da Silva-Bruhns, Ivan (1881–1980)

Brazilian painter, rug designer, and weaver; active Aisne (France) and Paris.

Training In biology and medicine.
Biography Until 1918, Da Silva-Bruhns was active as a painter and sometime interior designer who had emigrated to France; was particularly influenced by a 1917 exhibition of Moroccan art, where knotted pile rugs were included, and thus began producing rugs in Paris in 1919, when he received a commission from Louis Majorelle. 1922, he set up a small weaving workshop and furnished small-scale watercolor patterns to weavers; used the *point noué* technique in his geometrical interpretations of Near and Far Eastern rug and textile motifs, especially those of the Berbers and other North Africans. He was commercially successful, active in small workshop in Aisne. His motifs were Cubist, geometric, or African-inspired styles and in somber colors, including brown, indigo, and black with white highlights; was an active member of Société des Artistes Décorateurs; 1925, opened a gallery on the rue de l'Odéon in Paris and, 1930, moved to 79, rue du Faubourg Saint-Honoré; produced rugs for leading contemporary decorators and furnished 1935 oceanliner *Normandie* and received rug commissions from Le Mobilier National, French embassies in Washington, Berlin, and Warsaw; League of Nations, Geneva; and, through Hermann Muthesius, the Maharajah Bahadur for his palace in Indore, India. His work was much imitated. Da Silva-Bruhns's rug production was disrupted by the outbreak of World War II, after which he returned to painting.
Exhibitions/citations His rugs were first shown at 1911 event of Salon des Indépendants; subsequently, at Salons of Société Nationale des Beaux-Arts; editions of Salons d'Automne; 1925 *Exposition Internationale des Arts Décoratifs et Industriels Modernes*, Paris; 1931 *Exposition Coloniale*, Paris; and 1931 exhibition, Curtis Moffat Gallery, London, organized by *Vogue* editor Mage Garland. Grand prize, 1925 exposition, Paris.
Exhibitions 1937 venue of modern-design rugs, The Metropolitan Museum of Art in New York, and number exhibitions of Art Déco.
Bibliography Peter Adam, *Eileen Gray, Architect/Designer*, New York: Abrams, 1987: 182. Pierre Cabanne, *Encyclopédie art déco*, Paris: Somogy, 1986: 183. Maurice Dufrêne, *Ensembles mobiliers, Exposition internationale 1925*, Paris: Charles Moreau, 1925; Woodbridge, Suffolk: Antique Collectors' Club 1989: 72. Susan Day, *Art Deco and Modernist Carpets*, London: Thames & Hudson, 2002.

Dada
> See Molteni.

Dahl, Birger (1916–1998)

Norwegian interior architect and lighting designer.

Training Statens Håndverks og Kunstindustriskole, Oslo.
Biography 1944–59, Dahl designed lighting fixtures by Sønnico Fabrikker, Oslo; was known for his aluminum lighting; was a consultant designer to Vallø wallpaper firm; from 1947, taught at Statens Håndverks-og Kunstindustriskole.
Bibliography Cat., David Revere McFadden (ed.), *Scandinavian Modern Design 1880–1980*, New York: Abrams, 1982. Fredrik Wildhagen, *Norge i Form*, Oslo: Stenersen, 1988: 146.

Dahlerup, Jørgen (1930–)

Danish metalworker.

Training Sculpture and industrial design, Det Kongelige Danske Kunstakademi, Copenhagen; silversmithing.
Biography His work included hollow-ware by Georg Jensen Sølvsmedie and religious objects.
Exhibitions Work in 1980 exhibition, Washington, D.C. (catalog below).
Bibliography Cat., *Georg Jensen Silversmithy: 77 Artists, 75 Years*, Washington, D.C.: Smithsonian, 1980.

Dahlström, Björn (1957–)

Swedish graphic artist and industrial designer; born Stockholm.

Biography Dahlström designed 1998 Compound Technology cookware by Hackman, Finland; c. 2000 BD5 easy chair, BD6 bar stool, and Soft Transport toys by cbi of Sweden; and Configuratable bench by Christian Springfieldt.
Exhibitions/citations Work subject of 2001 exhibit, Röhsska Museet, Gothenberg, Sweden. 2001 Torsten and Wanja Söderberg prize.
Bibliography Kerstin Wickman, *Björn Dahlström*, Stockholm: Arvinius, 2001.

Dair, Thomas (1954–)

American industrial designer; born Rome, N.Y.

Training To 1977, industrial design, Syracuse (N.Y.) University.
Biography Dair has designed computer and medical products and, for Richmond Engineering Company, pressure vessels, mechanical equipment and systems for various industries; 1979, was founding

Björn Dahlström. Casserole pot (in Dahlström 98 series of pots/pans). 1998. Multi-layered stainless steel, aluminum, and cast iron, h. 7 1/2 x dia 10 1/8" (20 x 26 cm). Mfr.: Hackman Designor, Finland.

partner of Smart Design (formerly Davin Stowell Association), where he became executive vice-president. The firm's clients have included Corning Glass, 3M, Knoll, Copco, Singer, Sanyei, Pottery Barn, and Kohler. Products include electrical appliances, sewing machines, and sunglasses. Dair taught product design, Parsons School of Design, New York; is a member, Industrial Designers Society of America (IDSA).
Citations Annual Design Review, *I.D.* magazine.

Dal Lago, Adalberto (1937–)

Italian architect and designer; born and active Milan.

Biography 1964–70, Dal Lago was an assistant instructor, Facoltà di Architettura, Politecnico, Milan; subsequently, chair of interior design there and then of the elements of composition. He wrote books on design and modern architecture; with architect Marco Zanuso, was commissioned by the European Council to publish a book on postwar European design; 1968–75, was director of bimonthly architecture-design journal *Rassegnamodi*; became a member, Associazione per il Disegno Industriale (ADI). Designing a range of products from plastic furniture and electronics to lighting and laminate prints, clients included Abet Laminati, Anic, Bieffeplast, Driade, Fanini Fain, Fantoni, Francesconi, Busnelli, IVM, Kartell, La Rinascente department store, Lanerossi.Linoleum, Louis de Poortere, Misura Emme, Nonwoven, Pirelli, Piriv, Reguitti, Rossiflor, Salvarani, and SIR.
Citations First prize (with others), Nazionale SIR/In Arch competition (proposal for an industrial-building firm).
Bibliography *ADI Annual 1976*, Milan: Associazione per il Disegno Industriale, 1976. *Modo*, no. 148, Mar.–Apr. 1993: 118.

Dalí, Salvador (b. Salvador Felipe Jacinto Dalí y Domenech 1904–88)

Spanish painter, sculptor, engraver, designer, book illustrator, and writer; born Figueres, Girona.

Training 1921–25, Academia de San Fernando, Madrid: suspended for unorthodox behavior; 1926, dismissed: refusal to take final examination.
Biography 1919–21, he worked as a book and magazine illustrator in Figueres; 1925–30, was an independent artist in Sitges, 1930–40, in Paris, 1940–48, in Pebble Beach, Cal., and, 1948, returned with his lifelong companion Gala to Port Lligat, Cadaqués (Spain), where he lived for the remainder of his life. In Paris, he had met fellow Spaniards Pablo Picasso, Luís Buñuel, the Surrealists, and Gala, then wife of poet Paul Éluard; 1929, became an official member of the Surrealist movement, following his 1928 film with Buñuel, *Un chien andalou*; work publicly acclaimed in his 1929 one-person exhibition, Galerie Goemans. 1930, he married Gala Éluard. When his article on Surrealist objects was published in the third issue of *Le Surréalisme au Service de la Révolution*, object-making became integral to the Surrealists' activities. 1930s, his relations with other Surrealists grew distant. Dalí was the most successful of all propagandists for Surrealism, not merely as a style of painting or writing but as a way of life. Dalí's best-known decorative design was 1934 sofa for Edward James in the shape of Mae West's lips, realized in several copies by Green and Abbott, London, and by Jean-Michael Frank, Paris; reissued in a loose Studio 65 interpretation of 1970 by Gufram and subsequently by others. It was derived from Dalí's idea that the mouth was an aesthetic form; he used it in his 1934 painting *Mae West* and 1934–35 drawing *The Birth of the Paranoiac Furniture*. Other works included 1936 lobster telephone and 1936 chair with hands for its back (both also for Edward James's residence, West Dean (England), 1938 and 1940 Steuben glass; 1957 Mollusc cutlery by François Hugo, scarves for Simpsons of New York, and Surrealist jewelry. Dalí was inspired by the writings of Sigmund Freud, including his theories of the unconscious. His *Dream of Venus* exhibition was mounted at 1939–40 *New York World's Fair: The World of Tomorrow*. He thought he could conjure a fantasy of the unconscious through a series of controlled associations; while in the US, designed the dream sequence in the Alfred Hitchcock film *Spellbound* (1945). From 1968, his glassware for Daum began with the sculpture *Fleur du mal* in *pâte-de-verre*. Later glass work included *Anti-fleur*, *Pégase*, *Poisson malbranche*, and *Désir hyperrationnel*. 1988, under different management, Daum revived production of his work, including *Venus aux trois tiroirs*, *Montre molle* (the widely published melting clock on a clothes hanger), and *Débris d'une automobile donnant naissance à un cheval aveugle mordant un téléphone*.
Exhibitions Jewelry pieces subject of 1950s touring exhibition; 1936 Hand Chair in 1970 *Modern Chairs 1918–1970*, Whitechapel Gallery, London. Work subject of 1929 exhibition, Galerie Goemans, Paris, where his work was first shown 1925; 1980 Paris retrospective (catalog below); and 1980 exhibition, Tate Gallery, London.
Bibliography Salvador Dalí, *The Secret Life of Salvador Dalí*, New York: Dial, 1942. Salvador Dalí, *Diary of a Genius*, New York: Doubleday, 1965. Cat., *Modern Chairs 1918–1970*, London: Lund Humphries, 1971. Philip Purser, *The Extraordinary World of Edward James*, London, 1978. Léopold Diego Sanchez, *Jean-Michel Frank, Adolphe Chanaux*, Paris: Regard, 1980. Cat., *Salvador Dalí rétrospective 1920–1980*, Paris: Centre Georges Pompidou, Musée National d'Art Moderne, 1980. Cat., Simon Wilson, *Salvador Dalí*, London: Tate Gallery, 1980. Muriel Emanuel et al. (eds.), *Contemporary Artists*, New York: St Martin's, 1983: 219–220. Jessica Rutherford, *Art Nouveau, Art Déco and the Thirties: The Furniture Collections at Brighton Museum*, Brighton: The Royal Pavilion, Art Gallery and Museums, 1983: 59–60. Auction cat., Christie's New York, 9 Dec. 1989. Auction cat., *Applied Arts of Twentieth Century Artists*, Christie's Geneva, 13 May 1991.

Dalisi, Riccardo (1931–)

Italian architect, designer, and artist; born Potenza; active Naples.

Training To 1957, Facoltà di Architettura, Università degli Studi, Naples.
Biography 1970s, Dalisi was identified with the ad-hoc Radical Architecture and Radical Group movements in Naples which formed the nucleus of the debates on Anti-Design; organized working groups to participate in the poorer districts of Naples; 1973, was a participant in the formation of Global Tools; subsequently (with Filippo Alison) organized Minimal Arts; 1975–2002, wrote 15 books, including *Architettura d'animazione* (Perugia, 1975) and *Gaudí, mobili e oggetti* (Milan, 1979); from 1982, has been professor, Progettazione Architettonica II and, from 2000, has been director, Scuola di Specializzazione in Disegno Industriale, both at Università degli Studi 'Federico II,' Naples; was credited with the revitalization of design research in southern Italy. Work has included 1986 Pavone chair, 1989 Mariposa bench, 1990 Metopa bed headboard by Zanotta; 1987 Caffettiera Napoletana coffee maker by Alessi; 1989 Idea table by Baleri, 1992 dinnerware by Eschenbach; 1993 furniture by Playtime; 1993 furniture by Glas; 1994 Leone armchair by Promemoria; 1995 Sfiziosa shelving by Morphos; 1995 coffee/tea sets by Cleto Munari; 1997 lamps and objects by Slamp; and others.
Exhibitions/citations Participated in several editions of Triennale di Milano and Biennale di Venezia. 1959 Arflex Domus-Premio; 1981 (research on Napolitana coffee-pot series, by Alessi), 1989 (*La caffetteria e Pulcinella* book by Alessi) and 1991 (Sister 365 and Zefiro lamps by O luce) Premio Compasso d'Oro; 1998 2nd prize (Ciabatta car), European Car Design Competition by Fiat.
Bibliography Andrea Branzi, *La casa calda: esperienze del nuovo disegno italiano*, Milan: Idea, 1982. Fumio Shimizu and Studio Matteo Thun (eds.), *The Italian Design: Descendants of Leonardo da Vinci*, Tokyo: Graphic-sha, 1987: 336. Kazuko Sato, *Alchimia*, Berlin: Taco, 1988. Albrecht Bangert and Karl Michael Armer, *80s Style: Designs of the Decade*, New York: Abbeville, 1990. Cristina Morozzi and Silvio San Pietro, *Contemporary Italian Furniture*, Milan: L'Archivolto, 1996. Franco Irace, 'Riccardo Dalisi: due Chiese in Campania,' *Abitare*, no.

347, Jan. 1996: 77–83. Franco Irace, 'Riccardo Dalisi a Napoli: una casa farfalla,' *Abitare*, no. 357, Dec. 1996: 102–09. A. Trimarco, *Sculture Rua Catalana Riccardo Dalisi*, Naples: Electa, Napoli 1997. Charlotte and Peter Fiell, *Design of the 20th Century*, Cologne: Taschen, 1999.

Dalmon, Gérard (1945–)

French furniture designer and entrepreneur; active Paris and New York.

Biography Dalmon was initially involved in the fields of chemical engineering and data processing in France; early 1980s, began designing furniture. Dalmon and Pierre Staudenmeyer established Galerie Néotù, Paris, in 1984 and New York, in 1990. Incorporating inexpensive and unusual materials, his applied art included 1985 Chaise YM, 1986 lacquered, pressed-board chair with animal hair, and 1989 Bouton de Porte and Poignée de Porte door handles, all by Néotù.
Exhibitions Work included in 1985 *Onze Lampes*, Néotù, Paris; 1985 Salon of Société des Artistes Décorateurs; 1985 *Un Tapis n'Est pas un Tableau*, Néotù; 1986 exhibitions, Galerie Théorème, Brussels; Galerie Lechanjour, Nice; Galerie Silicone, Nice; Tokyo exhibition (catalog below); 1987 in Desco at Zeus, Milan; 1987 *Cent Chaises*, Boulogne Billancourt, France; 1988 *Design Français*, Berlin decorative arts museum; Jouy-en-Josas exhibition (catalog below); VIA (French furniture association) exhibition, Netherlands; *Just Your Image* (with Alessandro Mendini, Alessandro Guerriero, and Riccardo Dalisi), 1988 Salone del Mobile, Milan.
Bibliography Sophie Anargyros, *Le style des années 80: architecture, décorations, design*, Paris: Rivages, 1986. *Design: actualités fin de siècle* (Cahiers du CCI), Paris: Centre Georges Pompidou. Cat., *Primitive Chairs*, Tokyo: Shiseido, 1986. Cat., *Médium*, Jouy-en-Josas, France: Fondation Cartier, 1988. Christine Colin, *Design d'aujourd'hui*, Paris: Flammarion, 1988.

d'Alpaos, Giuseppe (1890–1980); Mario d'Alpaos (1942–)
> See Ioso, Decio.

Dalpayrat, Pierre-Adrien (1844–1910)

French porcelain painter and ceramicist; born Limoges.

Biography 1867, Dalpayrat lived in Bordeaux and, 1867–88, in Toulouse and Monte Carlo; after a short time in Limoges, settled in Bourg-la-Reine, near Paris, in 1889, where he specialized in stoneware, developing the color known as 'Dalpayrat rouge,' a copper-red glaze; by combining this color with others, created a marbleized effect which he applied to Japanese-inspired forms of gourds and fruits and to figures and animals in high relief or sculpted shapes; collaborated with Adèle Lesbros and Voisin to produce reasonably priced stoneware; produced forms designed by Maurice Dufrêne for La Maison Moderne and by sculptors, including Constantin Meunier. Cardeilhac and others mounted several of his pieces in silver.
Exhibitions 'Dalpayrat rouge' glaze was shown at 1892 Paris Salon.
Bibliography Yvonne Brunhammer et al., *Art Nouveau Belgium, France*, Houston: Rice University, 1976.

Dalton, William Bower (1868–1965)

British watercolorist and potter; active Kent and the US.

Training Manchester School of Art; Royal College of Art, London.
Biography 1899–1919, Dalton was principal of Camberwell School of Arts and Crafts, London; during and after this time, was curator of South London Art Gallery; was a potter as well as a watercolorist and wrote three books on ceramic art; 1909, designed and built his own residence in Kent, residing there until his workshop was bombed during World War II; settled in the US, where he continued to pot and paint; 1965, returned to England.
Exhibitions 1920s–30s, his work was shown with Red Rose Guild and at Colnaghi's, London; 1935 *English Pottery Old and New*, Victoria and Albert Museum, London; 1937 *Exposition Internationale des Arts et Techniques dans la Vie Moderne,* Paris; 1979–80 *Thirties* exhibition, Hayward Gallery, London (catalog below).
Bibliography Cat., *Thirties: British Art and Design Before the War*, London: Arts Council of Great Britain/Hayward Gallery, 1979.

Dammouse, Albert-Louis (1848–1926)

French ceramicist; born Sèvres; son of sculptor and porcelain decorator Pierre-Adolphe Dammouse of Sèvres factory.

Training École Nationale Supérieure des Arts Décoratifs; under François Jouffroy, École Nationale Supérieure des Beaux-Arts; both Paris.
Biography Dammouse was interested in technical problems and became apprentice of Marc-Louis Solon and, subsequently, Solon's collaborator. Solon introduced him to *pâtes-d'application*, under-glaze slip decoration. Working in Charles Haviland's workshop in Auteuil, Dammouse designed the form for the famous soft-paste *Service aux Oiseaux* porcelain decorated with designs after Félix-Henri Bracquemond; 1892 with brother Édouard-Alexandre Dammouse, set up a studio at Sèvres, where they produced porcelain, earthenware, and stoneware in Japanese- and Chinese-inspired forms, at first monochromatic, then with painted foliage, algae, and flowers; by 1904, was a master of the material; 1897 encouraged by Ringel d'Illzach, turned to working in glass; probably influenced by Thesmar's enameled bowls, went on to develop *pâte-d'émail*, a kind of cloisonné *pâte-de-verre*. But little is known about his technique; the number of colors may have been determined by the number of firings.
Exhibitions Work included in 1869, 1874, 1878, 1889, and 1900 (*pâte-de-verre* cups, bowls, and goblets) *Expositions Universelles*, Paris. Posthumous retrospective, Musée Galliéra, Paris.
Bibliography Yvonne Brunhammer et al., *Art Nouveau Belgium, France*, Houston: Rice University, 1976. Cat., *Verriers français contemporains: Art et industrie*, Paris: Musée des Arts Décoratifs, 1982.

Dammouse, Édouard-Alexandre (1850–1903)

French ceramicist; born Paris; son of sculptor-decorator Pierre-Adolphe Dammouse of Manufacture Nationale de Sèvres factory; brother of Albert-Louis Dammouse.

Training Under Félix-Henri Bracquemond, in painting.
Biography At the Lurin factory, makers of ordinary domestic ceramics, Dammouse worked with Ernest Chaplet. When Chaplet and Dammouse's brother Albert-Louis went to Haviland's workshop in Auteuil, he followed to become a member of the group of painters there, Les Cinq (Alexandre Charpentier, Jean-Auguste Dampt, Étienne Moreau-Nélaton, Charles Plumet, Henri Sauvage), not to be confused with Le Cinq (Le Groupe des Cinq) in Paris in 1920s; worked in the Auteuil studio until its 1881 closing; 1882 with Chaplet, moved to the Haviland workshop, rue Blomet, where he decorated stoneware in naturalistic and Japanese-derived styles; 1886, when rue Blomet studio closed, set up a workshop with Albert-Louis at Sèvres, where they later produced objects in *pâte-de-verre* and thence *pâte d'émail*.
Exhibitions Work included in 1878–1900 Salons of Société des Artistes Français.
Bibliography Yvonne Brunhammer et al., *Art Nouveau Belgium, France*, Houston: Rice University, 1976.

Damon

French lighting designer and manufacturer; located Paris.

History Active 1920s–30s, Damon was established at 4, avenue Pierre-Ier-de-Serbie, Paris; became known for its particular use of glass in lighting fixtures, with designs executed in white glass to create a dazzle effect without glare. Boris Lacroix designed many lamps, incorporating engraved mirror and frosted-glass tubes for the firm. Pressed glass was dismissed as being appropriate only for architectural lighting fixtures. Damon manufactured glass enameled on the inside and frosted on the outside, creating a diffused light suitable for reading and known as *verre émaillé difussants*, held by metal mountings often of gilded or silvered bronze, chrome, or nickeled copper, and placed on black marbrite bases. Damon-commissioned designers also included Gorinthe, André Roy, André Basompierre, Jean Baignères, Georges Martin, and Daniel Stéphan Damon also sold standard lighting fixtures, illuminated vases, *bouts de table*, and other lamp types.
Bibliography Guillaume Janneau, *Le luminaire et les moyens d'éclairage nouveaux*, Paris: Charles Moreau, 2nd series, plate 5, [n.d.]. Alastair Duncan, *Art Nouveau and Art Déco Lighting*, New York: Simon & Schuster, 1978: 164–65. Cat., Aaron Lederfajn and Xavier Lenormand (eds.), *Le Louvre des Antiquaires présente: 1930 quand le meuble devient sculpture*, Paris, 1986.

Dampt, Jean-Auguste (1854–1946)

French sculptor and designer.

Biography Dampt executed furniture, interiors, goldsmiths' works, clock cases, electric lights, and jewelry in the Art Nouveau style; was a founder of Les Cinq, a group of designers and craftsmen, not to be confused with Le Cinq (Le Groupe des Cinq); was a member, artists' group L'Art dans Tout.

Danese: **Enzo Mari. Timor perpetual calendar** (French-language version here). 1966. Plastic, 6 9/16 x 4 11/16 x 3 9/16" (16.7 x 11.9 x 9 cm). Mfr.: Danese, Italy. Gift of Paola Antonelli. MoMA.

Danese
Italian domestic goods manufacturer; located Milan.

History 1955, Produzioni Danese was founded by Bruno Danese and Jacqueline Vodoz; began with the production of plastic tabletop items. Its freelance designers were Bruno Munari and Enzo Mari. Munari's work for Danese included 1957 Cubic ashtray 2000B in melamine and anodized aluminum, 1958 desk set 2002 in melamine and aluminum, and 1961 triangular lamp 2006 in blue opalescent fiberglass and anodized aluminum. Mari's work for Danese included 1966 Timor perpetual calendar 3079 (in French, English, German, and Italian versions), 1967 pencil stand, 1967 ashtray 3076, 1969 set of hemispherical bowls 3089A-D, and 1970 container 3008B. Danese also produced children's games and toys; 1992, was acquired by Steelcase-Strafor, and its design research was halted; Jan. 1993, was bought by Cassina from a holding company; late 1994, was absorbed into Alias, various merchandising arrangements having previously been made with firms like Alessi, which acquired the Enzo Mari designs. Finally, Oct. 1999, other parts of Danese were bought by Carlotta De Bevilacqua, who has given the firm a new position, while showing respect for its past achievements.
Citations 1960 (four citations), 1979, 1987, 1994 (as an Alias division) Premio Compasso d'Oro; 2002 Lifetime Achievement award (to Danese and Vodoz), *Abitare* magazine.
Bibliography Cat., Milena Lamarová (ed.), *Design a Plastické Hmoty,* Prague: Umĕleckoprůmyslové Muzeum, 1972: 178. Cat., Manolo de Giorgi, *45–63 un museo del disegno industriale in Italia*, Milan: Abitare Segesta, 1995. 'Danese,' *Modo*, no. 213, June–Aug. 2001.

Daney, Philippe (1956–)
French architect, interior architect, and set and industrial designer; born Neuilly-sur-Seine.

Training DPLG architecture (governmental diploma), France.
Biography 1986 with Pascal Bauer, Daney cofounded Tébong contemporary furniture firm, directing it to 1995; in addition to being a furniture designer, is artistic director of the Vianne glassworks and has designed a number of lamps.
Bibliography Cat., Sophie Tasma Anargyros et al., *L'école française: les créateurs de meubles du 20ème siècle*, Paris: Industries Françaises de l'Ameublement, 2000.

D'Aniello, Pierangela (1939–)
Italian architect and industrial designer.

Training Politecnico, Milan.
Biography 1966, she opened her own office in Milan; designed 1966 Trieste folding chair (with Aldo Jacober) by Alberto Bazzani. Work has included designs for furniture, tablewares, and power tools.
Citations Premio Selettiva, 1967 (18th) Corso Internazionale del Mobile, Cantù; first prize (for Trieste chair), 1969 Fiera di Trieste.
Bibliography Cat., *Modern Chairs 1918–1970*, London: Lund Humphries, 1971. Cat., Hans Wichmann, *Italien Design 1945 bis heute*, Munich: Die Neue Sammlung, 1988.

Danko, Peter (1949–)
American furniture designer; active Red Lion, Pa.

Training 1971, bachelor of arts degree in art and art history, University of Maryland, Baltimore.
Biography According to Danko, he first became aware of wooden ply-bent (or bent-plywood) objects while inspecting a tennis racket as a teenager. Subsequently, he has modeled his work, such as chairs, after the approaches of Michael Thonet, Alvar Aalto, and Charles Eames.
Exhibitions/citations From 1978 *New Handmade Furniture*, American Crafts Museum, New York, a number of group venues. 1975 National Endowment for the Arts Craftsman Fellowship; 1980 National Endowment for the Arts Design Fellowship; 1983 Certificate of Achievement (for Everychair series), Industrial Designers Society of America (IDSA); 1998 Silver Award, Best of NeoCon, Chicago.

Dansk International Designs
> See Quistgaard, Jens H.

Danski, Vesa (1969–)
Finnish designer

Biography Danski has designed products, ranging from glasswork and lighting to furniture and interior design, particularly for restaurants. His products include 1997 Galileo glassware and the attention-garnering puffy Kuukuna chair that looks like a pea pod and Object table/chairs, both by Artek. 1997 with Ilkka Koskela and Harri Koskinen, Danski established the Raket design group, with Artek as its major client.
Exhibitions/citations Work shown at numerous exhibitions and fairs,

Peter Danko. Bodyform side chair. 1980. Molded plywood with maple veneer, 31 7/8 x 21 x 21" (81 x 53.3 x 53.3 cm), seat h. 17 1/2" (44.5 cm). Mfr.: Peter Danko and Associates, US. Gift of the designer. MoMA.

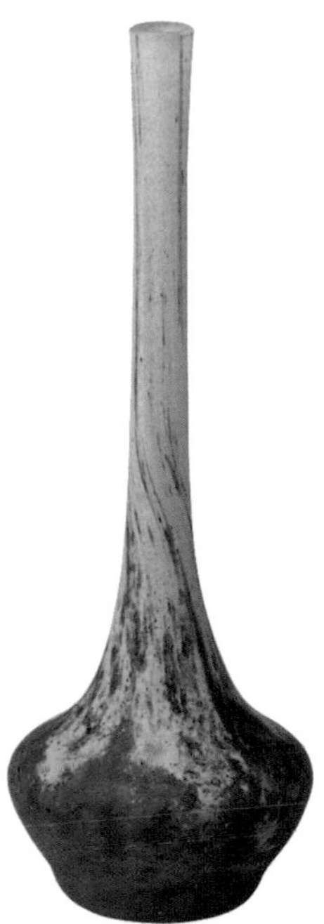

Daum Frères. Bud vase. c. 1910. Blown and painted glass, h. 6 x dia. 2" (15.2 x 5.1 cm). Mfr.: Daum Frères, France. Joseph H. Heil Bequest. MoMA.

including in Helsinki, Cologne, Milan, and Singapore, and at first exhibition of Raket, Artek showroom, Helsinki. 1996, Ten Most Beautiful Products award (chairs by Damski), *Marie Claire Maison* magazine.
Bibliography Richard Sapper (ed.), *The International Design Yearbook*, New York: Abbeville, 1998.

Darmstadt artists' colony

German artist-led crafts industry and community; located duchy of Hesse-Darmstadt.

History Ernst Ludwig was Grand Duke Louis IV of Hesse-Darmstadt, 1892–1918, the last ruler of a formerly independent state that became part of the new German Empire in 1871. He learned about the English Arts and Crafts movement from H.M. Baillie Scott, who furnished two rooms in the palace at Darmstadt; C.R. Ashbee's Guild of Handicraft, London, made the furniture. The Grand Duke saw in the movement a practical way to foster the cultural and economic well-being of the duchy, and signed three-year contracts with numerous young artists, including Peter Behrens, Rudolf Bosselt, Paul Bürck, Hans Christiansen, Ludwig Habich, Patriz Huber, and Josef Maria Olbrich, to design and direct the production of goods by these craftspeople and workshops. The results were published and promoted by Alexander Koch through his journals *Innendekoration* and *Deutsche Kunst und Dekoration*. From 1899 to the 1914 end of the venture, 23 artists worked there at various times. There were two silversmiths, Ernst Riegel and Theodor Wende, although others designed for silver. Huber, Olbrich, and Christiansen arrived in Darmstadt in 1899, Haustein in 1903, Müller in 1906, and Riegel in 1907. Margold and Wende were the last to arrive. Behrens showed his multiple talents in architecture, furniture, silver, jewelry, glass, and porcelain. He taught the four-week 'Applied Art Master Course' in Nuremberg in 1901 and 1902 and left the colony in 1903. Courses were subsequently taught by Richard Riemerschmid, Paul Haustein, and Friedrich Adler. Many of the artists who began their careers at Darmstadt went on to national and international renown.
Exhibitions Participated in 1900 *Exposition Universelle*, Paris. Organized 1901 *A Document of German Art* (room settings in specially built houses by Olbrich and Behrens), Darmstadt. Subject of 1976–77 venue, Hessischen Landesmuseum (catalog below).
Bibliography Cat., Gerhard Bott (ed.), *Kunsthandwerk um 1900: Jugendstil, art nouveau, modern style, nieuwe Kunst*, Darmstadt: Hessisches Landesmuseum, 1965. Cat., *Ein Dokument deutscher Kunst: Darmstadt 1901–1976*, Darmstadt: Hessisches Landesmuseum, 1976. Annelies Krekel-Aalberse, *Art Nouveau and Art Déco Silver*, New York: Abrams, 1989.

Darrin, 'Dutch' Howard A.

French automobile designer; active the US.

Biography Darrin settled in the US; 1922, returned to Paris, where he and 'Le Baron' Thomas Hibbard founded Hibbard & Darrin coachworks and designed/built automobile bodies for Minerva (initially) in Belgium and, by 1927, for Rolls Royce, Hispano-Suiza, Duesenberg, and Renault (including 1929 Renault Reinastella). 1931, Hibbard left the association and returned to the US to work under Harley Earl at General Motors in Detroit, Mich., and Darrin became an associate of a wealthy banker to form Fernandez & Darrin coachworks (under which Darrin designed/built 1934 Hispano Suiza K6 sedanca coupé). 1937, Darrin closed the enterprise and returned to the US, in Hollywood (or possibly Santa Monica), Cal., to design car bodies under the name 'Darrin of Paris' for a clientele that included movie stars; designed several production bodies, including 1939 Packard Victoria 120 convertible, 1941 Packard 1903 convertible coupé, and Packard Clipper; during World War II, was active in a flight-training school in Nevada, an experience in aviation that clearly influenced his work, particularly in 1953 Kaiser Darrin (with a plastic body, in limited numbers from 1954); worked at Kaiser-Fraser but departed on two occasions due to artistic differences, however remained amicable with the firm; from 1954, worked in his own southern California studio on bodies based on Kaiser's Henry J mini-car chassis and designed for Rolls-Royce in the US. By 1972, Darrin was still active.
Bibliography Penny Sparke, *A Century of Car Design*, London: Mitchell Beazley, 2002.

D'Ascanio, Corradino (1891–1981)
> See Piaggio.

Daum

French glassware designers and manufacturers; located Nancy.

Biography 1875, Jean Daum (1825–1885) settled in Nancy after a series of unsuccessful business ventures; 1878, purchased Verrerie Sainte-Catherine bottle factory in Nancy; was joined there by his sons Auguste (1853–1909) in 1879 and Antonin (1864–1930) in 1887. Antonin managed the firm from his father's 1885 death, when it became Daum Frères. At first the Daums produced rather dull table and domestic glassware. Auguste was in charge of the firm's administrative and financial activities and Antonin, trained as an engineer, the production activities. They assembled a stable of designers, artists, and artisans. The factory gradually became known for its fine glassware with cut, etched, and gilt decorations in traditional styles. From 1890 and greatly influenced by Émile Gallé, with whom the brothers were on good terms, their objects were executed in the Art Nouveau style. 1891, they opened a decoration studio directed by Eugène Damman, employing artists Émile Wirtz, Amalric Walter from 1906, Jacques Gruber 1894–97, and Henri Bergé from 1900. Two specialities emerged: *berluzes* (vases with long necks) and lamps, produced mainly from 1893 in acid-etched cameo, often finished on an engraver's wheel, with decoration inspired by nature. Daum furnished the glass for Louis Majorelle's lamps and the metalwork for their own; the same arrangement was made with Edgar Brandt from 1905 and less frequently with André Groult. 1906, Almaric Walter worked at Daum with *pâte-de-verre*. 1909, Auguste's son Paul Daum (1888–1944) assumed management of the firm, which closed during World War I and, 1918, reopened with a radical change of style. Under Paul's direction, the firm attempted to satisfy public demand for simpler designs, producing acid-etched, thick, colored glass vessels with geometric or stylized motifs. The technique required up to four acid baths for very deep etching. 1925, Paul formed a partnership with nephews Paul and Henri Daum and son-in-law Pierre Froissart. 1920s–30s, Louis Majorelle and Paul Brandt designed for the firm. Due to the effects of the 1929 Great Depression, art-glass production was dropped and replaced by glass tableware. The Générale Transatlantique Compagnie commissioned 70,000 sets of crystal tableware for its 1935 oceanliner *Normandie*, prompting research into new techniques and designs. Paul Daum, arrested in the World War II German occupation of France, escaped, fought with the French Resistance, and was killed in 1943. The firm reopened in 1946 under the management of Henri Daum (1910–) and Michel Daum (1889–1960). Various artists, including Salvador Dalí, were commissioned to design models. 1976, Pierre de Chérisey-Daum (1936–) became president of the firm, which continues to be

active today. 1986, Clotide Bacri became artistic director. Recent commissioned artists/designers have included César and Garouste & Bonnetti. Daum made Hilton McConnico's 1980s cactus-pattern *pâte-de-verre* and crystal ware, Philippe Starck's 1988 Étrangetés vase series, sculptor Eric Théret's 2001 Daïchi *pâte-de-verre* vase/lamp, and designs by André Dubreuil and c. 2003 artichote-like bowl and vase by Enzo Mari.
Exhibitions Work included in 1893 *World's Columbian Exposition*, Chicago; 1900 *Exposition Universelle*, Paris. Deeply etched glass was first shown at 1925 *Exposition Internationale des Arts Décoratifs et Industriels Modernes*, Paris. Work shown regularly at Salons in Paris, including 1921, 1926, and 1932 editions of Salon d'Automne.
Bibliography Yvonne Brunhammer et al., *Art Nouveau Belgium, France*, Houston: Rice University, 1967. R. & L. Grover, *Carved and Decorated European Art Glass*, Rutland, Vt.: Tuttle, 1970: 70–71. *Le modern style*, Paris: Baschet, 1974. J. Bloch-Dermant, *L'art du verre en France 1860–1914*, Lausanne: Denöel, 1975: 135–43. Alastair Duncan, *Art Nouveau and Art Déco Lighting*, New York: Simon & Schuster, 1978. *Éclairage de 1900 à nos jours*, Brussels: L'Écuyer, nos. 38, 72, 75, 87. Cat., *Verriers français contemporains: art et industrie*, Paris: Musée des Arts Décoratifs, 1982. Clotilde Bacri, *Daum: Masters of French Decorative Glass*, New York: Rizzoli, 1993. Leslie Jackson, *20th Century Factory Glass*, London: Octopus, 2000.

Davenport and Company, A.H.

American furniture producers and interior decorators; located Boston and East Cambridge, Mass.

History 1842, the firm began as a 'furniture and feathers' business owned by Ezra H. Brabrook. 1880, Brabrook died, and the thriving firm was purchased by Albert H. Davenport (1845–1906), who had been a bookkeeper from 1866. Davenport's cabinet shop, working department, and display of carpet, drapery, upholstery, wallpaper, and furniture were housed in a five-story building at 96–98 Washington Street, Boston. 1875–1910, Davenport was one of the most important decorating firms in the US; 1883, expanded its quarters by acquiring 108 Cambridge Street, East Cambridge, Mass., and opening a New York office; was one of the few companies capable of supplying large amounts of deluxe furniture and interior-furnishing goods to the growing number of expensive public and private buildings of the day; c. 1882, it supplied 225 pieces of furniture and draperies for Hawaiian King Kalakaua's Iolani Palace, and, 1902, furnished several rooms in architect McKim's refurbishings of The White House, Washington, D.C. Its wares were often specified by architects H.H. Richardson; Peabody and Stearns; McKim, Mead and White; and Shepley, Rutan and Coolidge. Davenport produced the dining furniture and chairs for 1886 John Jacob Glessner House, Chicago, designed by Charles Allerton Coolidge for architect H.H. Richardson. Francis H. Bacon was Davenport's principal designer, and vice-president from 1885 to 1908, when the firm was sold. 1914, Irving and Casson bought out Davenport, which evenutally closed in 1973. However, its most productive period ended in the 1930s. The name 'davenport' came to be used generically for a large upholstered sofa that can be converted to a bed, a type that was originally made by A.H. Davenport at the end of the 19th century.
Bibliography Anne Farnam, 'A.H. Davenport and Company, Boston Furniture Makers,' *Antiques*, no. 109, May 1976: 1048–55. Anne Farnam, 'H.H. Richardson and A.H. Davenport: Architecture and Furniture as Big Business in America's Gilded Age,' in Paul B. Kebabian and William C. Lipke (eds.), *Tools and Technologies: America's Wooden Age*, Burlington, Vt.: Robert Hull Fleming Museum, University of Vermont, 1979: 80–92. Doreen Bolger Burke et al., *In Pursuit of Beauty: Americans and the Aesthetic Movement*, New York: The Metropolitan Museum of Art/Rizzoli, 1986: 418.

Davey, Andy (1962–)

British industrial designer.

Training To 1987, Worthing College of Art and Royal College of Art, London.
Biography 1987, Davey began working for design consultancy Wharmby Associates, London, where he designed 1988 Taurus telephone in black ABS plastic with a rubber cord by Browns Holdings; 1990, established own design studio TKO in Tokyo.
Citations 1989 Silver Award (for Taurus telephone), Design and Art Directors Association, London.
Bibliography Jeremy Myerson and Sylvia Katz, *Conran Design Guides: Home Office*, London: Conran Octopus, 1990: 33, 73.

David, Xavier (1940–)

French designer; born Nevers; active Bologna and Paris.

Biography 1965, David began his professional career; 1969 with Gaetano Pesce and Beppe Vida, designed accessories, lighting, and inflatable seating; became a member, Associazione per il Disegno Industriale (ADI); designed David range of glass furniture by Glass Design Collection. Other clients in Italy have included Gavina, Ny Form, Mari Arreda, Expansion Design, and Malferrari, and, in France, Souplina.
Bibliography *ADI Annual 1976*, Milan: Associazione per il Disegno Industriale, 1976.

David-Andersen, Arthur (1875–1970)

Norwegian metalworker; active Oslo.

Biography 1876, the David-Andersen goldsmith workshop was founded in Oslo by David Andersen; became famous for high-quality enamel work. Arthur David-Andersen worked for the family firm. Its other designers included Harry Sørby, Johan Lund, Thorolf Holmboe, Ludvig Wittmann, and Johan Sirnes. 1891–1910, Gustav Gaudernack worked for the firm. Late 1920s, Ivar David-Andersen (1903–), who had studied at Statens Håndverks-og Kunstindustriskole, Oslo, began as a designer and, from late 1930s, worked mainly as a manager in the family firm, of which he was the director from 1952.
Bibliography Jan-Lauritz Opstad, *David-Andersen, 100 år i Norsk Gullsmedkunst*, Oslo: David-Andersen / Oslo Museum of Applied Art, 1976. Annelies Krekel-Aalberse, *Art Nouveau and Art Déco Silver*, New York: Abrams, 1989. Fredrik Wildhagen, *Norge i Form*, Oslo: Stenersen, 1988. Cat., David Revere McFadden (ed.), *Scandinavian Modern Design 1880–1980*, New York: Abrams, 1982.

David design

Swedish design manufacturer; headquarters and shop Malmö; showroom and shop Stockholm.

History 1988, David design was established by David Carlson (Malmö, 1963–) for the original design and production of domestic furniture, lighting, and accesories; at first, called on Scandinavian freelance designers. More recent stable includes a group of international designers such as Stephen Burks, Charlotte Christiansson, Mårten Claesson, Johanna Egnell, Andreas Engesvik, Monica Förster, Nina Jobs, Karin Johansson, Eero Koivisto, Olof Kolte, Jon Lindström, Erica Mörn, Tim Power, Karim Rashid, Andreas Roth, Ola Rune, Per Söderberg, Mats Theselius, and Damian Williamson.
Bibliography Mel Byars, *50 Tables...*, Hove: RotoVision, 1997. Mel Byars, *50 Lights...*, Hove: RotoVision, 1997. 'David design,' *Forum*, Feb. 2002. Lina Pihl, 'David-Design trivs bäst vid...,' *Kvällsposten*, 7 June 2002. Maria Wahlberg, 'Hur vågar ni öppna en butik i Tokyo?,' *Näringsliv*, 30 Aug. 2002.

Davis, Owen William (1838–1913)

British architect and designer.

Training Architecture under James Kellaway Colling.
Biography Davis was an assistant to architect Matthew Digby Wyatt; was known for his ability to produce designs in fabrics and wallpaper in which the repeats were successfully camouflaged; designed wallpaper by Woollams. Davis was of the school of designers who rejected medievalism. Work included furniture, carpets, and metalwork produced by major manufacturers.
Bibliography Stuart Durant, *Ornament: A Survey of Decoration Since 1830*, Woodstock, N.Y.: Overlook, 1986: 43, 322.

Dawson, Nelson Ethelred (1859–1942); Edith Dawson (b. Edith Robinson 1862–1928)

Nelson: British architect, painter, and metalworker. Edith: artist and enamelist; both active London; husband and wife.

Training Nelson: architecture in uncle's office; painting, South Kensington Schools; 1891 under Alexander Fisher, in enameling.
Biographies Dawson was more interested in painting and silversmithing than in architecture; met future wife Edith Robinson while working in an art shop in Scarborough, where her watercolors were for sale; 1891, moved to London, where he began metalworking and attended Alexander Fisher's enameling lectures; set up his own workshop, where his wife executed most of the enameling and, after 1897, probably all of it; designed the metalwork crafted by apprentices in his studio; 1901, founded the Artificers' Guild and was artistic director 1901–03; left

when it was taken over by Montague Fordham, a prosperous businessman who had previously directed Birmingham Guild of Handicraft. The Dawsons' work was frequently published in *The Studio and Art Journal*. They developed an architectonic style for silverwork that incorporated delicate enamels (often of flowers and birds); employed upward of 20 craftspeople at one time, who executed commissions and prepared for exhibitions. Nelson Dawson abandoned metalworking altogether after 1914 and turned to painting.
Exhibitions Work included in 1893 *Arts and Crafts Exhibition*; subject of 1900 exhibition (125 pieces), Fine Art Society, London.
Bibliography Charlotte Gere, *European and American Jewelry 1830–1914*, New York: Crown, 1975. Toni Lesser Wolf, 'Women Jewelers of the British Arts and Crafts Movement,' *The Journal of Decorative and Propaganda Arts*, no. 14, Fall 1989: 32–33. Annelies Krekel-Aalberse, *Art Nouveau and Art Déco Silver*, New York: Abrams, 1989.

Day, Lewis Foreman (1845–1910)

British designer, writer, and teacher; born Peckham Rye.

Biography 1870, Day, an Arts and Crafts proponent, opened his own studio; 1884, became a founding member of the Art-Workers' Guild and, 1888, the Arts and Crafts Exhibition Society; produced designs for fabrics and wallpaper; wrote his first pattern book *Instances of Accessory Art* (1880), showing a Japanese influence, and inexpensive books on ornamentation, including *The Anatomy of Pattern* (London: B.T. Batsford, 1887), *The Planning of Ornament* (also as *The Application of Ornament*, London: 1887), and *The Application of Ornament* (London: B.T. Batsford, 1888) and soon after combined as *Ornamental Design*.
Bibliography Stuart Durant, *Ornament from the Industrial Revolution to Today*, Woodstock, N.Y.: Overlook, 1986: 322.

Day, Lucienne (1917–)

British textile designer; born Surrey; wife of Robin Day.

Training 1934–37, Croydon School of Art; 1937–40, Royal College of Art, London.
Biography 1942–47, she taught at Beckenham; 1948 with husband Robin Day, opened a design studio and began designing dress and furnishing fabrics, carpets, wallpapers, and table linens; designed for Edinburgh Weavers, Cavendish, Wilton Royal Carpets, John Lewis, and Heal Fabrics (for 25 years); designed the wiry-lined Calyx pattern for 1951 *Festival of Britain* exposition, London, that has since become an archetypal 1950s image; 1957–59, designed porcelain decorations for Rosenthal; from 1978, moved toward a crafts approach while still respecting mass production and began to produce single examples of abstract wall hangings that she named 'silk mosaics'; often collaborated with her husband producing stained glass (mainly for domestic use) and textiles and wallpapers by a number of companies; wrote design textbooks.
Citations Her first award (for Calyx pattern) was from American Institute of Decorators (AID); gold medal, 1951 (9th) Triennale di Milano, and grand prize at its 1954 (10th) edition; 1950s–60s, three awards, Council of Industrial Design, UK.
Bibliography '8 British Designers,' *Design Quarterly*, no. 36, 1956: 9–10. 'Furnishing Fabrics: Heal's Chevron, Complex and Extension,' *Design*, no. 233, May 1968: 42–43. Fiona MacCarthy, *British Design Since 1880*, London, 1982: figs. 17, 165. Cat., Kathryn B. Hiesinger and George H. Marcus III (eds.), *Design Since 1945*, Philadelphia: Philadelphia Museum of Art, 1983. Stuart Durant, *Ornament from the Industrial Revolution to Today*, Woodstock, N.Y.: Overlook, 1986: 288, 291, 294–95.

Day, Robin (1915–)

British furniture designer; born High Wycombe, Buckinghamshire; husband of Lucienne Day.

Training From 1928, Technical Institute, High Wycombe; from 1931, School of Art, High Wycombe; 1933, in a furniture factory; 1934–38, Royal College of Art, London.
Biography 1945, Day became a freelance designer; 1948 with Lucienne Day, opened a design studio, often collaborating subsequently. His work was noticed by Hille at 1948 international furniture-design competition at The Museum of Modern Art, New York; the plywood cabinet at the exhibition (with Clive Latimer) was realized through a special technique which enabled its construction with only two joints. However, American firm Johnson-Carper Furniture, in reproducing the design, abandoned the original concept; the laminated wood became solid wood-and-joint construction, the tubular steel legs became separate legs, the sliding doors were hinged, and standardization and flexible interiors were eliminated. From 1949, Day was a design consultant to Hille, designing contract furniture. His 1962–63 Mark II (or Polyprop) polypropylene chair by Hille and others sold more than 12 million examples. 1962, Day became a consultant to the John Lewis department store chain. Work has included pieces in the design section of 1951 *Festival of Britain* exhibition, London, 1951 seating for Royal Festival Hall, London, interiors for the *Super VC10* and other aircraft, appliances by Pye, cutlery, carpets, and, from 1968, seating for many auditoria, including the Barbican Arts Centre, London, and 1970 seating for London Underground carriages.
Exhibitions/citations First prize (with Clive Latimer for storage furniture), 1948 *International Competition for Low Cost Furniture Design*, The Museum of Modern Art, New York; gold medal, 1951 (9th), and silver medal, 1954 (10th) Triennali di Milano; six awards, Design Council, UK. 1959, elected Honorary Royal Designer for Industry, UK.
Bibliography Edgar Kaufmann Jr., *Prize Designs for Modern Furniture*, New York: The Museum of Modern Art, 1950: 34–41. Michael Farr, *Design in British Industry: A Mid-Century Survey*, London: Cambridge, 1955. Richard Carr, 'Design Analysis: Polypropylene Chair,' *Design*, no. 194, Feb. 1965: 33–39. Sutherland Lyall, *Hille: 75 Years of British Furniture*, London, 1981. Fiona MacCarthy, *British Design since 1880*, London, 1982. Lesley Jackson, *Robin and Lucienne Day: Pioneers of Modern Design*, London: Princeton Architectural Press, 2001.

de Angelis, Almerico (1942–)

Italian writer, editor, teacher, theoretician, and designer; born Naples.

Training To 1969, architecture, Università degli Studi, Naples.
Biography 1970, Angelis founded the 'For an Eventual Architecture' movement and, 1974, four-month-long 'Che' movement; 1975 participated in the seminars of Global Tools, 1977 *Assenza/Presenza* exhibition at Galleria Comunale d'Arte Moderna in Bologna, and 1978 Biennale Architettura di Venezia; organized 1986 (1st) Forum Design; 1987 with others, cofounded Istituto Italiano del Design and, 1992 in Milan with Alessandro Mendini, the Piccola Scuola; from 1990, was artistic director, Giornate Napoletane del Design; from 1996, has been editor of journal *Modo*; from 1997, was a board member, CNAD (national council of the design organizations); has organized numerous exhibitions. 1975–80, Angelis was professor in charge of scenography, Facoltà di Architettura, Universitè degli Studi, Naples, where, 1981–97, he was chairperson of interior architecture; 1993, was director of Scuola Normale di Design at Institut Français de Naples; from 1998, chairperson of industrial design, Politecnico, Milan. Also active as a designer, his work includes 1972 Mondrian umbrella stand, 1973 Scrab paper holder, and 1974 Play ashtray by Riam; 1990 Vesuvio ceramic vase by Alissio Sarri; 1993 Maat mirror and 1994 Paesaggio 1 carpet by Glas; 1999 Fiordiloto tableware by Yalos Casa; 2002 Stati d'Animo mirror (with T. Garattoni) by Tonelli.
Bibliography Andrea Branzi, *La casa calda: esperienze del nuovo disegno italiano*, Milan: Idea, 1982. By de Angelis (partial list): *Scenografia: il disegno dell'ambiente*, Naples: Fratelli Fiorentino, 1981; *250 Faces of Our Time*, Milan: Modo, 1999; *Design: The Italian way*, Milan: Modo, 2001.

de Baan, Jacob (1961–)

Dutch industrial designer; born Spijkenisse.

Training To 1987, Gerrit Rietveld Academie, Amsterdam.
Biography To 1991 with Frans van Nieuwenborg and Martijn Wegman, Jacob de Baan worked in Amsterdam and Leyden; 1992, moved to Germany and worked at Team Buchlin Design; to 1994, with frogdesign in Altensteig, Germany, on lighting, consumer electronics, and ecological projects; 1995, returned to Amsterdam and established D4 agency with clients such as Dutch Ministry of Finance, Jumbo, NOVEM, Osram, and Philips. He is particularly adept at unusual lighting, including candle power.
Bibliography Michele De Lucchi (ed.), *The International Design Yearbook*, London: Laurence King, 2001.

de Bardyère, Georges (1883–1942)

French decorator and furniture designer; born Wassy, Haute-Marne; active Paris.

Biography By 1912, Bardyère was a decorator and furniture designer in Paris of classical furniture in a style similar to Léon Jallot's, in the early Art Déco style; was fond of vegetal forms and the use of ivory.
Exhibitions From 1919, work included in Salons of Société des Artistes

Jean-Charles de Castelbajac. On Pax Joy carpet. c. 2000. 100% wool, 67 x 94 1/2" (170 x 240 cm). Mfr.: Ligne Roset, France.

Décorateurs; from 1921, editions of Salon d'Automne.
Bibliography Pierre Kjellberg, *Art déco: les maîtres du mobilier, le décor des paquebots*, Paris: Amateur, 1986/1990.

De Barros Morais Caldas, Joaquim Manuel (1948–)

Portuguese designer; born Montalegre; active S. Stefano Roero (Italy).

Biography 1969, De Barros began his professional career; became a member, Associazione per il Disegno Industriale (ADI). Clients in Italy have included Selenova (Spot 2001 lighting system), Gufram (Dog Wood table and chairs), Ultravox (television sets), Seimart, and Coemi and, in Portugal, Plastidom, A. Campos, and EMHA.
Bibliography *ADI Annual 1976*, Milan: Associazione per il Disegno Industriale, 1976.

De Bevilacqua, Carlotta (1957–)

Italian designer and entrepeneur; active Milan.

Training 1982, architecture, Politecnico, Milan.
Biography 1983, De Bevilacqua opened her own studio for architecture and interior, exhibition, and product design; from 1986, coordinated communications of the Artemis group; 1989–93, was the artistic director of Memphis and of Alias; from 1997, was director of marketing and communication director and, from 2001, general executive manager of brand strategy, marketing, and communications of Artemis; has been active as the brand-strategy and development manager of Artemide, for which she has also designed a number of innovative lamps, including 2000 light-changing Yang, and showrooms worldwide; 1999, bought Danese and, while retaining its former associations and historical links, repositioned its design and marketing structure, commissioning designers, such as Paolo Rizzatto, Andrea Branzi, and others who are developing products based on new ideas and material. De Bevilacqua is also currently an independent architect and designer.
> See Danese.

de Boer, Antoinette (1939–)

German textile designer.

Training 1957–61 under Margret Hildebrand, Hochschule für bildender Künste, Hamburg.
Biography 1962, she became a textile designer for Stuttgarter Gardinenfabrik, where Margret Hildebrand was artistic director; from 1963, was artistic director of the firm; specializing in printed fabrics, attempted to relate fabric design to architecture and designed 1969 Zazi range, influenced by the shapes and colors of Italian design; 1973, set up her design studio.
Bibliography 'Antoinette de Boer et ses dessins de tentures aux tendances nouvelles,' *Meubles et décors*, Nov. 1969. 'Textil-Design ist keine Kunst,' *Meubles et décors*, Apr. 1976. Cat., Kathryn B. Hiesinger and George H. Marcus III (eds.), *Design Since 1945*, Philadelphia: Philadelphia Museum of Art, 1983. Cat., Hans Wichmann (ed.), *Von Morris bis Memphis, Textilien der Neuen Sammlung, Ende 19. bis Ende 20. Jahrhundert*, Basel: Birkhäuser, 1990: 225, 439.

De Carli, Carlo (1910–1999)

Italian architect and designer; born Milan.

Training 1934, architecture, Politecnico, Milan.
Biography De Carli's expressive furniture incorporated bent plywood, foam rubber, and steel rods; 1950s with Gianfranco Frattini and Ico Parisi, created ranges of furniture by Cassina. Planned and directed the Office Secion of 1940 (7th) Triennale di Milano; member of the executive committee for 1954 (10th) and 1957 (11th) editions of the Triennale and, to 1973, of the board of directors. Taught, Politecnico, Milan; promoted the cultural renewal of furniture manufacturing in his writings, particularly through the publication *Il mobile italiano*.
Citations 1954 (683 chair by Cassina) Compasso d'Oro.
Bibliography Roberto Aloi and Agnoldomenico Pica, *Mobili tipo*, Milan: Ulrico Hoepli, 1956. Penny Sparke, *Introduction to Design and Culture in the Twentieth Century*, London: Allen & Unwin, 1986. Cat., Leslie Jackson (ed.), *The New Look: Design in the Fifties*, New York: Thames & Hudson, 1991. Cat., Gianni Ottolini, *Omaggio a Carlo de Carli*, Milan: CLAP—DPA Politecnico, 1995.

de Castelbajac, Jean-Charles (1949–)

French fashion designer; born Casablanca; active Paris.

Training 1966–67, law, Faculté de Droit, Limoges.
Biography 1968 with mother Jeanne-Blanche de Castelbajac, founded 'Ko' ready-to-wear fashion firm in Limoges; from 1968, worked as a freelance fashion designer for firms, including Reynaud, Pierre d'Alby, Max Mara, Levi-Strauss, Jesus Jeans, Hilton, Ellesse, Carel shoes, Etam, Gadging, Julie Latour, Fusano, and Amaraggi; 1970 in Paris, established a line of women's clothing under his own name; has been primarily known for women's clothing designs that incorporated canvas, blankets, plastic, automobile upholstery, parachute cloth, cheesecloth, and leather; 1973 in Paris, had his first fashion show; 1975–76, set up boutiques in Paris, New York, and Tokyo; 1976, designed stage costumes for musicians Rod Stewart, Elton John, and Talking Heads; 1978, became director of Société Jean-Charles de Castelbajac in Paris; designed costumes for films including *Violette et François* (1976), *Annie Hall* (1977), *Who Killed My Husband?* (1979), and US TV series *Charlie's Angels* (1978–80); from 1979, has been active in interiors and furniture, designing 1989 'Castelbajac' furniture range by Ligne Roset, which provided 14 mix-and-match polychrome cushions on sofas, all reversing to black leather on a black-leather frame and, subsequently, others for the firm, including lighting; 1999 crystal drinking glass by Baccarat; and the classic B9 chair by Thonet, which he recolored and reupholstered. Rugs by Ligne Roset have included 1991 Stripe Dialogue, 1999 Jours d' Amour, and 1999 Valentine (which Philippe Starck has used with his own facial image imprinted on the upholstery). Has taught, Central St. Martin's School of Design, London, and Akademie der bildenden Künste, Vienna.
Bibliography 'Hot Properties,' House and Garden, May 1991: 30. Anne Lee Morgan (ed.), *Contemporary Designers*, London: Macmillan, 1984: 144. www.via.asso.fr.

de Coster, Germaine (1895–1992)

French designer and bookbinder; born Paris.

Training Under Jules Chadel, École Nationale Supérieure des Arts Décoratifs, Paris; under Yoshigiro Urishibora, in Japanese wood-engraving.
Biography From c. 1920, she was Chadel's assistant, designing book

Rudolph de Harak. Clock (no. 101). 1966. Chrome-plated metal and plastic, d. 3 1/4 x dia. 9" (8.3 x 22.9 cm). Mfr.: Rudolph de Harak Industrial Design, US. Gift of the designer. MoMA.

plates, bookbindings, and jewelry; from early 1920s to 1961, was professor of decoration and gravure, École Nationale Supérieure des Arts et Métiers, Paris; from 1934 with Hélène Dumas, collaborated on bookbindings for volumes, some including Coster's illustrations. The highly decorative designs in exotic skins and stones were executed by Coster and produced by Dumas, assisted by gilders Raymond Mondage and André Jeanne. Coster also designed interiors, theater costumes, textiles, and posters.
Exhibitions Work included in Salons of Société des Artistes Décorateurs.
Bibliography Alastair Duncan and Georges de Bartha, *Art Nouveau and Art Déco Bookbinding*, New York: Abrams, 1989: 24, 190. Roger Devauchelle, *La Reliure en France de ses origines à nos jours*, vol. 3, Paris, 1961. Henri Nicolle, 'La reliure moderne,' *Les arts français: la reliure d'art*. Cat., *Reliure française contemporaine*, New York: The Grolier Club, 1987–88.

De Distel
Dutch ceramics firm; located Amsterdam.

History 1895, De Distel (the thistle) was founded as a small ceramics firm by Jacobus Lob (1872–1942); employed artists as both designers and painters. 1897, Plateelbakkerij De Distel was established to manufacture and sell art pottery, utility ware, tiles, ceramics for special occasions, and small sculpture. At De Distel from 1895 as a painter, Cornelis de Bruin became the artistic director; designed décors on dark backgrounds in a Rosenburg style, tableaux with naturalistic pictures, tiles with Jugendstil motifs, and directed artists, who both painted and designed ceramics in similar styles. At De Distel 1898–1923, Willem van Norden was head of the decoration department. J. Eisenloeffel was a designer 1900–08; Bert Nienhuis, a designer 1900–11, also became head of the decoration department. 1910, V.H. Amstelhoek was incorporated into De Distel; 1923–24, De Distel was incorporated into Goedewaagen.
Exhibitions Wares were shown widely before World War I, including at 1904 *Louisiana Purchase Exposition*, St. Louis.
Bibliography Cat., *Industry and Design in the Netherlands 1850–1950*, Amsterdam: Stedelijk Museum, 1985.

De Driehoek, Potterie
> See E.S.K.A.F.

de Feure, Georges (b. Georges Joseph van Sluijters 1868–1928)
Dutch decorative artist, designer, painter, lithographer, and engraver; active Paris.

Training c. 1890, under Jules Chéret.
Biography Feure was a symbolist painter, watercolorist, illustrator, poster artist, and designer of Art Nouveau furniture, fabrics, stained glass, wallpaper, glassware, and ceramics; 1890, moved to Paris; designed furniture for Maison Fleury; 1900, joined Siegfried Bing's gallery/shop L'Art Nouveau, Paris, and became head of the design department; after World War I, became professor of decorative arts, École Nationale Supérieure des Beaux-Arts, Paris; when public interest in the Art Nouveau style faded, moved to England, where he became a stage designer; returned to Paris and designed carpets, stained glass, decorative frescoes, lighting, mirrors, fabrics, with tapestries produced by Manufacture Française de Tapis et Couverture, and, 1924, all the furniture for Madeleine Vionnet's sumptuous fashion house in Paris, which featured 18 changing rooms, each differently arranged.
Exhibitions Work subject of 1894 one-person exhibition (which brought him to public attention), Paris, and included in Salons of Société Nationale des Beaux-Arts from 1894; 1893 and 1894 salons of Rose-Croix; and 1896 Münchner Sezession exposition. Designed the pavilion and the furnishings (with others) in the pavilion of the shop L'Art Nouveau at 1900 *Exposition Universelle*, Paris. Designed and decorated the pavilion of Roubaix et Tourcoing at 1925 *Exposition Internationale des Arts Décoratifs et Industriels Modernes*, Paris.
Bibliography Salon catalog, Société des Beaux-Arts, 1902. E. Mannoni, *Meubles et ensembles: Style 1900*, Paris: C. Massin, 1968: 5. Yvonne Brunhammer et al., *Art Nouveau Belgium, France*, Houston: Rice University, 1976. Alastair Duncan, *Art Nouveau and Art Déco Lighting*, New York: Simon & Schuster, 1978. *Éclairage de 1900 à nos jours*, Brussels: L'Écuyer: nos. 44, 45, 47. Cat., *Europa 1900*, Paris: Musée des Beaux-Arts, 1967: no. 342. Victor Arwas, *Art Déco*, New York: Abrams, 1980.

De Genneper Molen
Dutch furniture cooperative; located Gennep.

History 1899, C.W. Steinmann founded De Genneper Molen as a sawmill and turnery on the Niers river to produce small items, including curtain fittings; c. 1917, began making furniture, which by 1924 had formed the bulk of the firm's business. By 1927, its production included small tea tables, work tables, smoking tables, small wall cabinets, coat racks, lamps, umbrella stands, and curtain fittings. Factory manager and director C.R. Steinmann was also its furniture designer. 1929, the firm contracted P.E.L. Izeren, an author and teacher in Arnhem, as a designer to at least 1938. At first symmetrical, Izeren's taut Cubist designs used woods and aluminum plymax. 1934–37, architect A.F. Schutte, as company manager, designed furniture and other items. After World War II, the firm shifted its production to wood boards and paneling, with some piano benches. 1982, it went out of business.
Bibliography Cat., *Industry and Design in the Netherlands 1850/1950*, Amsterdam: Stedelijk Museum, 1985.

de Gueltzl, Marco (1962–1991)
French sculptor and furniture and glass designer.

Training Otis Pearson School of Design, Los Angeles.
Biography Gueltzl designed chandeliers, lamps, and furniture made in glass produced by Avant-Scène. One of his last designs was 1989 large bureau and chair in sanded glass and *fer-à-béton*.

de Harak, 'Rudy' Rudolph (1924–)
American designer; born Culver City, near Los Angeles, Cal.

Training School of Industrial Arts, New York.
Biography As an adolescent, Rudolph de Harak moved with his family to New York; served in World War II, after which returned to Los Angeles, where he apprenticed in a small art services/advertising agency. Late 1940s, he was influenced by Will Burton lectures at Art Center School, Los Angeles; Gyorgy Kepes's *Language of Vision* (Chicago: Theobald, 1951); and Max Bill. With Saul Bass, Alvin Lustig, and Lou Danziger, he founded Los Angeles Society for Contemporary Designers; 1950, returned to New York, where he became promotional art director, *Seventeen* magazine; 1958, established Rudolph de Harak Incorporated; created hundreds of record covers, posters, and book jackets, including almost 350 covers for McGraw-Hill Paperbacks, using a rigid grid system and the Helvetica type font; has been a versatile designer in a number of disciplines. He designed Man, His Planet, and Space pavilion at *Universal and International Exhibition (Expo '67)*, Montreal; with Ivan Chermayeff and Tom Geismar, US Pavilion, 1970 *Japan World Exposition* (Expo '70), Osaka; with architect Kevin Roche, Egyptian Wing of The Metropolitan Museum of Art, New York; Cummins Engine Museum, Columbus, Ind.; monumental digital clock, façade, and entry of 127 John Street, New York. Taught, The Cooper Union for the Advancement of Science and Art (from 1952 and later as Frank Stanton Professor of Design there), New York, and was visiting

professor, Yale University, Alfred (N.Y.) University, Parsons School of Design, Pratt Institute, and others.
Citations Late 1940s, his first award (for an advertisement), from Los Angeles Art Directors Club; honorary doctorate of fine arts degree, School of Art, Corcoran Museum, Washington, D.C.; Gold Medal, American Institute of Graphic Design (AIGA); others.
Bibliography Steven Heller, *Rudolph de Harak: A Humanist's Modernist*, www.aiga.org, 2003.

De Iuliis, Daniele (1961–)
British industrial designer; born Bristol.

Training Central School of Art and Design, London.
Biography From 1983, De Iuliis worked at the ID Two design studio in San Francisco on Apple Computer products, including 1987 Goldilocks project concepts; from 1992, worked in the IDg (Industrial Design Group) of Apple Computer, Cupertino, Cal.; designed 1992 Macintosh Color Classic computer (with Larry Barbera) and 1992 Comet printer and collaborated on 1993–94 PowerBook 500 (BlackBird) computer, which defined the essentials of laptops: Newton 110 Charging Station (Crib) and Newton MessagePad 2000 (Q); was later in charge of Apple's business desktop products.
Citations 2002 Red Dot Best of the Best (for iPod, with others) and 2003 Red Dot award (for 12" and 17" PowerBooks, with others), Design Zentrum Nordrhein Westfalen, Essen.
Bibliography Paul Kunkel, *Apple Design: The World of the Apple Industrial Design Group*, New York: Graphis, 1997.

de Jarny, Paul Brindeau
> See Brindeau de Jarny, Paul.

de Klerk, Michel (1884–1923)
Dutch architect and designer; born Amsterdam.

Biography His 1913–19 Spaarndammerbuurt housing development in Amsterdam illustrated his eccentricity and lack of concern for function and construction. His idiosyncratic Amsterdam Arts and Crafts expressionistic work was exemplified by 1913–17 Shipping Offices. He joined the architecture practice of Hendrik Berlage and created closed and flattened forms in 1920–22 Amstellaan housing in Amsterdam South; was one of the architects of the School of Amsterdam known for expressing modern architecture through the use of brick shells (for example, in his c. 1920 Zaanstraat apartments, Amsterdam) rather than the stucco called on elsewhere in Europe. He designed furniture for 1913 Dr. J. Polenaar residence, Amsterdam; 1915 directors' offices (with lighting produced by H.J. Winkelman) of the Scheepvaarthuis; 1915 Mr. and Mrs. Polak-Krop residence (furniture produced by H.P. Mutters, The Hague), Steenwijk; 1916 't Woonhuys residence (furniture produced by Randoe), Haarlem. He was also a graphic artist.

Michele De Lucchi. Hansa vase. 1999. Mouth-blown Murano glass, h. 10 1/8 x dia. 7" (26 x 18 cm). Mfr.: Produzione Privata, Italy.

Exhibitions Living room furniture by 't Woonhuys was shown at 1925 *Exposition Internationale des Arts Décoratifs et Industriels Modernes*, Paris. Work subject of 1997 exhibition, Rotterdam (catalog below).
Bibliography Pieter Kramer, 'De Bauwwerken van Michel de Klerk,' *Wendingen*, nos. 9–10, 1924. Suzanne Frank, 'Michel de Klerk's Design for Amsterdam's Spaarndammerbuurt,' *Nederlands Kunsthistorik Jaarboek*, vol. 22, 1971: 175–213. Helen Searing, 'With Red Flags Flying: Politics and Architecture in Amsterdam,' in Henry A. Millon and Linda Nochlin (eds.), *Art and Architecture in the Service of Politics*, Cambridge, Mass.: MIT, 1978. Jonathan Woodham, *Twentieth-Century Ornament*, New York: Rizzoli, 1990: 126–27. Cat., Manfred Bock et al., *Michel de Klerk: Architect and Artist of the Amsterdam School, 1884–1923*, Rotterdam: NAi, 1997.

de La Godelinais, Renan (1908–1986)
French decorator.

Biography La Godelinais was student and collaborator of designer/maker Jacques-Émile Ruhlmann, after whose death he worked for Ruhlmann's nephew Alfred Porteneuve; 1942, became *chargé de mission* of Musée Nationale des Arts et Traditions Populaires, Paris, and, 1949, a member of the Formes Utiles of Union des Artistes Modernes (UAM); 1948, was responsible for Centre de Documentation de l'Habitation, Pavillon de Marsan, Musée du Louvre, Paris.
Bibliography Arlette Barré-Despond, *UAM*, Paris: Regard, 1986: 522.

de Lanux, 'Lise' Eyre (b. Elizabeth Eyre 1894–1996)
American artist, writer, and designer; active Paris and New York.

Training 1912, 1914–15 under George Bridgman and John C. Johansen, art, Art Students League, New York. 1919–20 in Paris: under Maurice Denis, Académie Ranson, and under Paul Sérusier, Académie Colarossi; 1920s under Constantin Brancusi, in fresco painting.
Biography 1918, she married writer Pierre Combret de Lanux (1887–1955), former secretary of writer André Gide and, subsequently, a member of French High Commission; was a painter and later designed a small amount of uncompromising furniture, some in a Cubist style, and rugs (with Evelyn Wyld, who worked with Eileen Gray). De Lanux's pieces were considered among the most sophisticated of the period, often innovatively using industrial products. She associated with André Gide, Ernest Hemingway, Henri Matisse, Picasso, and Bernard Berenson; was photographed by Man Ray, Berenice Abbott, and Arnold Genthe; 1924, left her husband to live with Evelyn Wyld, with whom she worked 1927–31, designing geometric-patterned rugs; late 1920s, began using the name Eyre de Lanux; designed a 1927 rug for the vicomte and vicomtesse de Noailles's villa in Hyères and a 1928 monumental table of sandblasted glass supported by two stacks of glass blocks; 1929, moved to La Bastide Blanche and soon after to La Bastide Caillenco and, 1932 with Wyld, opened the shop Décor in Cannes, closing a year later; designed interiors and lacquered furniture, some with assistance from Seizo Sugawara; moved to Rome. 1920s for magazines in the US, she regularly contributed 'Letters of Elizabeth' to *Town and Country* and, 1960s, short stories to *The New Yorker*. From 1961, she lived permanently in New York. Her 1905–92 papers are housed in the Smithsonian Institution's Archives of American Art.
Exhibitions De Lanux and Wyld work included in 1930 (1st) exhibition of Union des Artistes Modernes (UAM); 1931 exhibition, Curtis Moffat Gallery, London; from 1932, Salons des Artistes Décorateurs.
Bibliography Cat., Jennifer Hawkins and Marianne Hollis (eds.), *Thirties: British Art and Design Before the War*, London: Arts Council of Great Britain/Hayward Gallery, 1979. Philippe Garner, 'Introduction,' *Important 20th Century Furniture in a Philip Johnson Townhouse*, Sotheby's auction catalog, 6 May 1989. Rita Rief, 'A "Lost" Designer Is Rediscovered,' *The New York Times*, 4 May 1989. Philippe Garner, *Eileen Gray: Design and Architecture, 1878–1976*, Cologne: Taschen, 1993. http://archivesofamericanart.si.edu/findaids/lanueyre/lanueyre.htm.
> See Gray, Eileen; Wyld, Evelyn.

de Looze, Hervé (1921–1986)
Belgian architect and industrial designer; born Brussels; active Paris.

Training Under Victor Servranckx and Le Corbusier.
Biography 1946, de Looze became a member, Union des Artistes Modernes (UAM), of which he was the secretary 1949–55; member of the selection committee, *Formes Utiles* exhibitions, where he was the architect from 1951, secretary general in 1954, and president from 1969.
Exhibitions Sanitary-bathroom and heating fixtures were shown at

1956–67 (1st) Triennale d'Art Français Contemporain, Paris. Responsible for sanitary features in first (1956) all-plastic house, for Ionel Schein (designed with René Coulon) at 1956 Salon des Arts Ménagers, Paris. Designed steel-and-iron section at 1949–50 (1st) *Formes Utiles* exhibition, Pavillon de Marsan; exposition entry, 1954 *Exposition Formes Utiles* at Salon des Arts Ménagers. All Paris.
Bibliography Cat., *Les années UAM 1929–1958*, Paris: Musée des Arts Décoratifs, 1988: 218–19.

De Lucchi, Michele (1951–)

Italian architect and designer; born Ferrara; active Milan and Rome.

Training To 1974 under Adolfo Natalini, architecture, Università degli Studi, Florence.
Biography De Lucchi dabbled in new forms of art and film at the university in Florence; 1973 with Piero Brombin, Pierpaola Bortolami, B. Pastovicchio, and Valerio Tridenti, founded the group Cavart, which played a leading role in Architettura Radicale, film-making, written works, and happenings; during this time, held the seminar 'Culturally Impossible Architecture' in the Monselice marble quarry near Padova; 1975–77, taught architecture, Università degli Studi, Florence; 1978, settled in Milan and joined Centrokappa, befriended Ettore Sottsass, and worked for Studio Alchimia (1979); from 1978, assisted Sottsass in creating the first Memphis exhibition of 1981, to which he contributed some pieces (see below); 1979 with Sottsass, became a consultant designer to Olivetti on its 1979 Synthesis office-furniture line and designed Olivetti's 1982 Icarus office-furniture range (with Sottsass) and collaborated at Sottsass Associati on the interiors of over 50 Fiorucci shops throughout Europe. His focus on the use of color can be seen in 1979 prototype household appliances for Girmi and the hi-fi-equipment sketches of 1981. He described his Peter Pan armchair as a 'chromatic experiment'; has pursued a design approach that attempted to make household objects look more like toys. For Memphis's initial 1981 collection, he designed the Pacific armoire, Atlantic cabinet, Kristall side table, and Oceanic floor lamp. His most widely published Memphis piece has been 1983 First chair. Other work has included 1984 Cadetti tables and 1985 Mist table by Acerbis, 1985 Witness armchair by Massoli, 1985 rings by Cleto Munari (with Giancarlo Fassina), 1986–87 Tolomeo aluminum desk lamp (with Fassina) by Artemide; designed metal furniture by Bieffeplast and Elam and wood furniture by ADL and by T70; late 1980s, designed plastic tableware for Bodum. Other clients included Vistosi, RB Rossana, Girmi, Matau, Kumewa, Up & Up, Baldini, and FontanaArte. 1984, he set up his own studio; 1986, founded Solid, a group of young international designers, who first met as a consortium in Dec. 1985 and showed first its prototypes in Bergamo; taught, Domus Academy, Milan; Facoltà di Architettura, Palermo; and Cranbrook Academy of Art, Bloomfield Hills, Mich. From early 1990s, he has been active in his own De Lucchi Group in Milan, with a staff, including Angelo Micheli, Nicholas Bewick, James Irvine, Geert Koster, and Ferruccio Laviani and a long list of design and architecture clients who commission diverse assignments. 2000, established Ufficiale della Repubblica for services to Italian design and architecture; from 2001, chairperson of design and art, Facoltà di Architettura, Venice.
Exhibitions/citations Organized (with Andrea Branzi) 1977 *Italian Design of the Fifties* exhibition, Milan, resulting in their book *Il design italiano degli anni 50* (1979). Participated in (16th) 1979 (prototype household appliances) and (17th) 1983 Triennale di Milano. Memphis's first exhibition (Lido sofa), during 1981 Salone del Mobile, Milan; 1991 *Mobili Italiani 1961–1991: Le Varie Età dei Linguaggi* exhibition (1983 First chair by Memphis), Salone del Mobile, Milan. Work subject of 1985 *Michele De Lucchi: Eenvriendelijk gezicht voor het elktronisch rijdperk* (a friendly image for the electronic age), Ja-Vormgeving, Tilburg, Netherlands (catalog below). Numerous citations, including Premio Compasso d'Oro: 1987 (Delphos office furniture by Olivetti; 214 Rossana kitchen by RC & B), 1989 (Tolomeo lamp), 1991 (I Segmenti office accessories with Takaichi Tadao by Kartell; CD 630 bank machine with Mario Trimarchi and Paper on Paper Stick with Irvine, both by Olivetti), 1994 (Echos portable computer with Hagai Shvadron by Olivetti). 2000 award (ArtJet 10 by Olivetti), Industrie Forum Design (iF), Hanover.
Bibliography Michele De Lucchi, 'Camin Elettrico,' *Modo*, no. 10, 1978: 73. Alessandro Mendini, 'Dear Michele De Lucchi,' *Domus*, no. 617, 1981: 1. R. Sias, 'Ufficio Stile Intervista: Michele De Lucchi,' *Ufficio stile*, no. 3, 1983. Michele De Lucchi, 'La rivoluzione degli accostamenti cromatici,' *Interni*, no. 330, 1983: 16–18. Barbara Radice, *Memphis: ricerche, esperienze, risultati, fallimenti e successi del nuovo design*, Milan: 1984 (English ed.: New York: Rizzoli, 1984). Cat., *Michele De Lucchi: Eenvriendelijk gezicht voor het elktronisch rijdperk*, The Hague: Komplement, 1985. Frédérique Huygen, *Michele De Lucchi*, Antwerp: Idea Books, 1985. Sophie Anargyros, 'Michele De Lucchi,' *Intramuros*, no. 70, 1989. Sibylle Kicherer (texts) and Silvio San Pietro (ed.), *Michele De Lucchi*, Milan: L'Archivolto, 1992. Cat., Uta Brandes (ed.), *Citizen Office: Ideen und Notzien zu einer neuen Bürowelt, Andrea Branzi, Michele De Lucchi, Ettore Sottsass*, Göttingen: Steidl, 1994. Antonella Boisi, 'Il nuovo laboratorio di Michele De Lucchi,' *Interni*, Dec. 1994. Marina Kern, *Intervista a Michele De Lucchi*, Milan: CDA, 2000. Marina Kern, 'La teoria delle quattro fasi, intervista a Michele De Lucchi,' *Eda*, Jan. 2001.
> See Solid.

de Mandrot, Hélène (1867–1948)

Swiss designer and arts patron; born Geneva; active Paris and Switzerland.

Biography 1922, Mandrot established La Maison des Artistes in her medieval château, La Sarraz, north of Lake Geneva, Switzerland, to which, from 1927, she began inviting artists, scientists, writers, and others. Her intention was to create a center for the decorative and fine arts, music, and literature. She also sponsored conferences for film making, one of which was attended by Sergei Eisenstein. 1928, hosted and was a major participant in the initial planning of first Congrès Internationaux d'Architecture Moderne (CIAM) at La Sarraz; 1920s in Paris, designed rugs and collapsible furniture produced by Jean Bonino; commissioned Le Corbusier to design 1930–31 villa Le Pradet near Toulon, in stone and concrete with sculptures by Jacques Lipchitz on the terrace and lawn.
Exhibitions Rugs and furniture shown at 1929 Paris Salon d'Automne. Was in charge of the Swiss pavilion containing furniture, furnishings, rugs, and paintings at *Esposizione Biennale delle Arti Decorative e Industriali Moderne*, Monza. Efforts subject of 1999 *Hélène de Mandrot und 'La Maison des Artistes' in La Sarraz*, Kunsthaus, Zürich.
Bibliography Sigfried Giedion, *Space, Time and Architecture*, Cambridge, Mass.: Harvard, 1982: 696. Jacques Gubler, *Nationalisme et internationalisme dans l'architecture moderne de la Suisse*, Geneva: Archigraphic, 1988: 145.

de Mestral, Georges (1907–1990)

Swiss engineer.

Biography Mestral lived in the the château of Saint-Saphorin-sur-Morges. 1945, while he was walking in the Jura mountains, cocklebeurs attached themselves to the fur of his dog. Although the stories vary from source to source, he realized that the plant seeds had a maze of clinging fingers and, thus, got the idea of what was to become Velcro (or *Klettverschluss*, German for 'burr-fastener'). The two-part fastener of his invention, patented 1951 with production by Mestral himself beginning in Aubonne, Switzerland, features tiny hooks on a 'male' tape that cling to a fuzzy 'female' tape, thus holding together two elements such as the two sides of a coat opening. Available today in different strengths, it is serving myriad applications, not only on clothing and luggage but also industrially, for example in and on automobiles to attached interior panels or hold a 'bra' in place on a hood.
Bibliography Charles Panati, *Panati's Extraordinary Origins of Everyday Things*, New York: Harper & Row, 1987: 317–18. Allyn Freeman and Bob Golden, *Why Didn't I Think of That?*, New York: John Wiley, 1997: 99–103.

de Montaut, Adrienne Gorska (1899–1969)
> See Gorska de Montaut, Adrienne.

de Montaut, Pierre (1892–1947)
> See Gorska de Montaut, Adrienne.

De Morgan, William Frend (1839–1917)

British painter, ceramicist, and tilemaker; born and active London.

Training Cary's Art School, Bloomsbury; 1859, Royal Academy Schools, London.
Biography c. 1862, De Morgan began working for William Morris, designing tiles and stained glass; late 1860s, became interested in pottery and decorative tiles; 1872, began firing tiles independently in his house at 30 Cheyne Row, Chelsea, London, which were sold, as well as his mosaic designs, by Morris & Co. More than 300 tile designs of 1872–81 have been documented; they were made on blanks from Holland at Wedgwood, and the Architectural Pottery Company at Poole.

De Padova: Vico Magistretti. Trio table. c. 1998. Aluminum and MDF, h. and dia. 27 1/2" (70 cm). Mfr.: De Padova, Italy.

He produced designs for fabrics and wallpaper; 1872–81, worked in Chelsea; 1882, moved to Morris's Merton Abbey works. His most prolific period was while living in Fulham 1888–98. His Hispano-Moresque lusterware and Iznik colored pottery reflect the powerful influence of Middle Eastern art; mid-1870s, he and Morris studied Islamic fabrics and pottery at South Kensington Museum (today Victoria and Albert Museum), London. De Morgan produced decorative schemes (with Halsey Ricardo) for 12 oceanliners of the P&O line; 1898, his firm and partnership with Ricardo were dissolved. 1898–1907, he was active in a partnership with Frank Iles and the Passenger brothers; wrote the novels *Joseph Vance* (1906) and *Alice for Short* (1907), which began his late career as author.
Bibliography Robert Pinkham, *Catalogue of Pottery by William de Morgan*, London: Victoria and Albert Museum, 1973. William Gaunt and M.d.E. Clayton-Stamm, *William De Morgan: Pre-Raphaelite Ceramics*, Greenwich, Conn.: New York Graphic Society, 1971. Jon Catleugh et al., *William De Morgan Tiles*, New York: Van Nostrand Reinhold, 1983. Cat., Martin Greenwood (ed.), *The Designs of William De Morgan*, Shepton Beauchamp: Dennis & Wiltshire, 1989.

de Noailles, vicomte Charles (1891–1981); vicomtesse Marie-Laure de Noailles (1900–1970)

French socialites, tastemakers, and patrons of the arts.

Biographies The vicomte's interests centered on architecture and the decorative arts and the vicomtesse's on fine art. Their villa in Hyères—commissioned in 1924, completed in 1933, and at the time one of the most radical modern buildings in France—was built to the designs of Robert Mallet-Stevens and included his furniture and furnishings along with those of others, including Djo-Bourgeois (several bedrooms and living rooms), Pierre Chareau (a suspended bed and American-style open-air room on the roof), Gabriel Guévrékian (triangular Cubist garden), Théo van Doesburg (color scheme for a 'little flower room'), Jean-Michel Frank, and Eyre de Lanux. At the end of Guévrékian's garden was Jacques Lipchitz's *Joie de vivre* sculpture, cast by Jean Prouvé. Mallet-Stevens received the Hyères commission on the strength of his design for an aeronautics-club pavilion (with architect Paul Ruault, glassmaker Louis Barillet, and sculptor Henri Laurens) at 1922 Salon d'Automne, Paris, though he had no realized buildings. The vicomte disliked Le Corbusier's rudeness; Mies van der Rohe was not available, and the director of the Musée des Arts Décoratifs in Paris recommended Mallet-Stevens for the architecture. Composed of Cubist volumes, the house was used as a setting for Man Ray's film *Les mystères du Château du Dé* (1928), with the vicomte's guests as its actors. The Noailleses entertained the cultural and artistic élite at Hyères. Additions to the house included a covered pool, squash court, gymnasium, bedrooms, and a studio in an enclosed courtyard lit from above by a monochrome stained-glass skylight at different levels by Louis Barillet, all resulting in a 60-room complex with dramatic views of the Mediterranean Sea. Eight of the 15 guest bedrooms had porches for outdoor sleeping. Charles de Noailles commissioned a documentary film on the villa, directed by Jacques Manuel. Housed in the villa were the works of young contemporary artists, including Pablo Picasso, Christian Bérard, and Salvador Dalí, all of whom painted portraits of the vicomtesse. Abandoned for many years, the restoration of the house was begun in the late 1980s. The Noailles's 18th-century Paris townhouse—the Hôtel Bischoffsheim on the place des États Unis—contained rooms with period furniture, furnishings, and *boiseries* as well as some in contemporary styles of 1920s, including the study with vellum walls and furnishings by Jean-Michel Frank. The house fell into disrepair upon Marie-Laure's death. Many of the fittings had been stolen when it was somewhat restored in the late 1990s. 2003, it was further restored/transformed as the Cristalleries de Baccarat exhibition space, designed by Philippe Starck.
Bibliography 'Une des maison-clés pour l'histoire du goût au XXe siècle,' *Connaissance des arts*, Oct. 1964: 68–91. Cécile Briolle et al., *Rob Mallet-Stevens, la villa Noailles*, Paris: Parenthésis, 1990. Arlette Barré-Despond, *UAM*, Paris: Regard, 1986. Hubert Damisch, *Villa Noailles*, Paris: Marval, 1997. François Carassan et al., *Villa de Noailles*, Paris: Plume, 2001. Laurence Benaïm, *Marie-Laure de Noailles: la vicomtesse du bizarre*, Paris: Grasset, 2001.

De Padova

Italian furniture manufacturer; located Milan.

History 1950s, the De Padova family first began in the furniture trade by opening a store on the via Montenapoleone in Milan, selling Danish furniture exclusively imported to Italy. 1958 with the founding of International Contract Furnishings (ICF), De Padova acquired the license to produce Herman Miller furniture by designers such as Charles and Ray Eames and George Nelson; late 1960s, acquired German licenses for other designs. 1984, Maddalena De Padova discovered and introduced to Europe reproductions of the furniture of the Shakers of America. From 1985, produced its own-commissioned furniture by Achille Castiglioni, Dieter Rams, Marco Zanuso Jr., and De Pas/Lomazzi/D'Urbino; however, 80% of its beds, sofas, casegoods, seating, and tables was designed by Vico Magistretti.
Citations 2002 Lifetime-Achievement award (to Maddalena De Padova), *Abitare* magazine.

De Pas, Gionatan (1932–1991); Donato D'Urbino (1935–); Paolo Lomazzi (1936–)

Italian architects and designers; all born and active Milan.

Training De Pas and D'Urbino: to 1959 and to 1960, architecture, Politecnico, Milan. Lomazzi: 1955–60, Institut d'Architecture Atheneum, Lausanne.
Biography 1966, De Pas, D'Urbino, and Lomazzi set up a design studio in Milan, working on architecture, design, exhibitions, interior decoration, and town planning. From 1967, encouraged by the restlessness of the late 1960s, the threesome argued that a fresh design voice closer to the new general Pop culture was needed. Early on, they developed furniture ideas and prototypes with little concern for mass production. Eventually, their innovative 1967 Blow chair in inflatable clear or transparent, tinted polyvinylchloride film and 1968 Joe seat (named after Joe Di Maggio) in the form of a leather baseball glove were produced by equally young firm Zanotta. At a time when architectural inflatables were being built by others, the Blow heralded the first practical piece of pneumatic furniture and became the first inflatable Italian design object without a high price and an élitist pedigree. The solution, made possible by radio-frequency plastic-seam welding, was a distinct departure from traditional upholstered furniture. From 1970s, the designers' studio became prolific and designed interchangeable and flexible units for modular seating, storage systems, and plastic and plywood furniture by BBB Bonacina, Driade, and Palina. More main-stream furniture, furnishings, and products were produced by Alessi, Zanotta, Poltronova, Forges, Gabbianelli, Marcatré, Hamano, Ligne Roset, Stilnovo, Sirrah, and others. De Pas became a member, Associazione per il Disegno Industriale (ADI). The threesome produced 1983 TV program 'Dal cucchiaio alla città; il design italiano dal 1950 al 1980' (RAI TV). Since De Pas's 1991 death, D'Urbino and Lomazzi have continued as prolific partners; from 1999, taught, Faculty of Industrial Design, Politecnico, Milan.
Work Pas, D'Urbino, and Lomazzi: includes 1967 Blow chair, 1968 Joe seat, and 1972 multi-position lamp by Stilnova; 1972 Flap range

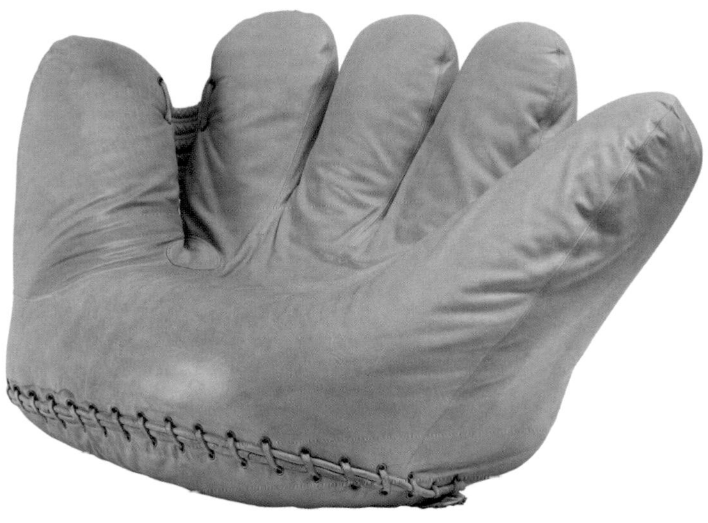

Gionatan De Pas, Paolo Lomazzi, and Donato D'Urbino. Joe sofa. 1968. Polyurethane foam and leather, 33 1/2 x 65 1/4 x 41 3/4" (85.1 x 165.7 x 106 cm). Mfr.: Poltronova, Italy (1971). Gift of the mfr. MoMA.

of modular seating, 1975 Jointed modular-pillow range of seating, and Dado & Vite (cube & screw) knock-down furniture by BBB; 1980 Grand-'Italia, 1981 Dinamo, 1982 Milano, 1983 Zona, and 1984 Wave sofas, 1983 ET table, and 1984 Palmira side chair by Zanotta; 1982 Cloche lamp by Sirrah; 1983 Sidone lamp by Artemide; 1984 Mollo bed by Cast Design; 1985 Valentina lamp by Valenti; 1985 Iago chair by Ligne Roset; 1986 Airone armchair by Poltronova; and 1986 Verbamis armchairs by Matteo Grassi. D'Urbino and Lomazzi: 1991 Octopus folding coat rack, 1992 Volare furniture, 1996 Silvergate bookcase, and 1997 Bikini chair by Zerodisegno; 1999 Gliss side and armchair by Naos; and 2000 Augh! folding trivet and 2002 Double bowls by Alessi.
Exhibitions/citations Work, particularly Blow chair, included in numerous exhibitions. 1979 (three citations), 1981, 1987 (two citations), 1989 (three citations), 1991 Premio Compasso d'Oro; award, 1977 BIO 7 industrial-design biennial, Ljubljana.
Bibliography Flavio Conti, *I progettisti italiani: De Pas D'Urbino Lomazzi*, Milan: Rima, 1989. Cat., J. De Pas, D. D'Urbino, and P. Lomazzi (eds.), 'I nuostri buoni propositi,' in *Milano 70/70: un secolo d'arte, dal 1946 al 1970*, vol. 3, Milan: Museo Poldi Pezzoli, 1972. Cat., Emilio Ambasz, *Italy: The New Domestic Landscape*, New York: The Museum of Modern Art, 1972. *New Furniture 11*, New York: Praeger, 1973. Alfonso Grassi and Anty Pansera, *Atlante del design italiano 1940/1980*, Milan: Fabbri, 1980: 299. Andrea Branzi, *La casa calda: esperienze del nuovo disegno italiano*, Milan: Idea, 1982. Fumio Shimizu and Studio Matteo Thun (eds.), *The Italian Design: Descendants of Leonardo da Vinci*, Tokyo: Graphic-sha, 1987. Juli Capella and Quim Larrea, *Designed by Architects in the 1980s*, New York: Rizzoli, 1988. Mel Byars with Arlette Barré-Despond, *100 Designs/100 Years: A Celebration of the 20th Century*, Hove: RotoVision, 1999: 146–47. Claudia Neumann, *Design Directory Italy*, London: Pavilion, 1999. Giuliana Gramigna and Paola Biondi, *Il design in Italia dell'arredamento domestico*, Turin: Allemandi, 1999. Eva Karcher and Manuela Von Perfall, *Italienisches Design*, Monaco: Heyne, 2000. Cat., *Design: The Italian Way* (*Italian Design Furniture* traveling exhibition), Milan: Modo, 2001. Paola Antonelli (ed.), *Objects of Design: The Museum of Modern Art*, New York: The Museum of Modern Art, 2003: 213, 259, 263.

De Ploeg

Dutch fabric group; located Bergeyk.

History 1923, De Ploeg was founded by W. van Malsen in Bergeyk as the Coöperatieve Productieen Verbruiksvereeniging (cooperative production association); eventually included farming and other activities appropriate to cooperative production. It was W. van Malsen's second experiment in alternative production—the first was a utopian agrarian colony established in 1919 with C. Hijner in Best, Netherlands. 1921, intending to set up a colony for the production of vegetables and household textiles, W. van Malsen had left for Bergeyk. The new association's unprofitable weaving mill was closed in 1925 and its health resort in 1928. However, De Ploeg became successful with domestic goods and inexpensive textiles; c. 1926 when trade in household textiles declined, began to sell upholstery furnishings in checked patterns woven by various other manufacturers; from c. 1928, had goods woven to its own designs. Freelance designs by some of the friends of De Ploeg's staff made possible an unusually wide product range. By 1930, De Ploeg sold its textiles to arts-and-crafts, drapery-goods, and fabric stores; 1937, ceased to be a cooperative. A new division, 't Spectrum, was set up in 1941 to make and sell arts-and-crafts products and to prevent workers being taken to Germany. After the war, 't Spectrum became independent, and De Ploeg set up its own weaving works, with power looms added in 1950. Frit Wichard became its exclusive designer at the firm, which is still active today.
Bibliography Cat., *Industry and Design in the Netherlands 1850–1950*, Amsterdam: Stedelijk Museum, 1985.

de Poorter, Christian (1946–)

French designer; active Milan.

Training Mechanical construction.
Biography 1970, Poorter worked in France on industrial aeronautics; 1971–74, was active in the studio of Rodolfo Bonetto in Milan; 1974, set up his own studio in Milan; 1973, became a member of Associazione per il Disegno Industriale (ADI) and of Consueil Supérieur d'Esthétique Industrielle (CSEI), Paris.
Citations Honorable mention, 1970 Prix Jacques Viénot competition.
Bibliography *ADI Annual 1976*, Milan: Associazione per il Disegno Industriale, 1976.

de Rijk, Vincent (1962–)

Dutch industrial designer.

Training Akademie voor Industriële Vormgeving, Eindhoven.
Biography 1987, Rijk established his own design studio; has worked on commissions for architects, including O.M.A. and Rem Koolhaas; has become best known for his experiments in the combination of materials, such as the colorful 1986 Kom BV resin/ceramic bowls (with Bart Guldemond) by Goods from 1986 (and others by Goods), but has designed furniture, including a sink; with architects MVRDV (Winy Maas [1959–], Jacob van Rijs [1964–], and Nathalie de Vries [1965–]), designed dishes for Unica series acknowledging 40th anniversary (1993) of Cor Unum Ceramics & Art in 's-Hertogenbosch; and 2002 resin fittings for Prada New York Epicenter (Rem Koolhaas, architect).
Exhibitions Work included in 1996 *Contemporary Design from the Netherlands* (resin/ceramic bowls), The Museum of Modern Art, New York; 1998–2000 Netherlands pavilion (maquettes), *World's Fair*,

Vincent de Rijk. Kom BV vase. 1986. Synthetic resin and ceramic, h. 5 x dia. 10" (12.7 x 25.4 cm). Mfr.: Goods, the Netherlands. Gift of the mfr. MoMA.

Hanover; 2002 *Easy Dutch* (ceramics and glass), Corcoran Gallery of Art, Washington, D.C.
Bibliography 'Zoveel mogelijk weglaten—over de kommen van Vincent de Rijk = Leaving as Much as Possible Out—The Bowls of Vincent de Rijk,' *Karmiek*, Apr. 2000.

De Rossi, Pucci (1947–)

Italian furniture designer and artist; born Verona; active New York and Paris.

Training Under H. Brooks Walker, in sculpture.
Biography 1971, Pucci De Rossi became active as a sculptor, using metal at first. His first furniture piece was possibly 1972 Trône armchair (no. 5). 1973, he added wood to his repertoire of materials; became known for furniture and lighting with a sense of humor; 1982 in New York, produced works in metal. His 1982 Tristan table and 1985 Bear rug were put into production by Galerie Néotù. Other furniture, many one-of-a-kind, includes 1985 Luis Luis chair, 1988 La Dernière Tentation chair, 1991 Lido Cocktail side table, 1990 Plack & Déquerres chair, Vizir console, Lancelot candelabra, 1996 Napoléon desk/chair. Objects include 1994–95 Les Inflatables experimental glass made at Centre International de Recherche sur le Verre et les Arts Plastiques (CIRVA) in Marseille.
Exhibitions Work subject of numerous exhibitions including, for the first time, at Galerie Art 3, Paris, 1973.
Bibliography Sophie Anargyros, *Intérieurs 80*, Paris: Regard, 1983. *Style 85*, Paris: Salon de la Société des Artistes Décorateurs, 1985. Sophie Anargyros, *Le style des années 80: architecture, décorations, design*, Paris: Rivages, 1986. Christine Colin, *Design aujourd'hui*, Paris: Flammarion, 1989. Cat., *Pucci De Rossi '71–'96*, Turin: Arte Fratelli Pozzo, 1996.

de Rothschild, baronne Pauline (b. Pauline Fairfax Potter 1908–1976)

American tastemaker; born Baltimore, Md.

Biography Potter has been described as having been a muse to American interior designer Billy Baldwin and was a designer of the domiciles of Elsa Schiaparelli and Hattie Carnegie. From 1954, she was second wife of vineyard proprietor Baron Philippe de Rothschild (1902–1988); became known for her highly original, eccentric room décor, more empty than not. Photographer Cecil Beaton described her approach as evoking memories of beauty rather than actually being beautiful. She lived in France, but, for a time at the end of her life, also in London.
Bibliography *Baron Philippe: The Very Candid Autobiography of Baron Philippe de Rothschild*, New York: Ballantine, 1984. Annette Tapert and Diana Edkins, *The Power of Style: The Women Who Defined the Art of Living Well*, New York: Crown, 1994. Mitchell Owens, 'Remembrance of Beauty,' *Nest*, no. 3.

de Ruijter, Linda (1953–)

Belgian industrial designer; born Antwerp.

Training 1972–77, industrial design, Nationaal Hoger Instituut Voor Bouwkunst en Stedebouw, Antwerp.
Biography From 1979, she worked with IDEA and was a designer for Laurent David leather goods. Other work has included 1986 Unibind sealing/binding machine by Peleman Saerens, 1987–88 plastic kitchenware (with IDEA) by DBP, 1988 Fluo—Ottago—1952 luggage by Laurent David.
Exhibitions Work included in 1981 *Fashion and Design* exhibition, Design Center, Brussels.
Bibliography Cat., Design Center Stuttgart, *Women in Design: Careers and Life Histories Since 1900*, Stuttgart: Haus der Wirtschaft, 1989.

De Salvo, Ross (1955–)
> See Design Group Italia.

de Santillana, Ludovico (1931–)

Italian architect, designer, teacher, and administrator; active Venice; son-in-law of Paolo Venini.

Training To 1955, Istituto Universitario di Architettura, Venice.
Biography 1959–68, Santillana taught architectural design, Istituto Universitario di Architettura, Venice; was director of Venini International to 1959, when (with wife Ginette Venini) took over the firm's management on Paolo Venini's death. 1960 Battuto range (with Tobia Scarpa) was among de Santillana's first designs for the new administration at Venini. He designed 1963 Faraono eggs and 1969 vases, bowls, and accessories designed for Pierre Cardin; from 1960s, continued the Venini tradition of producing new techniques and forms by hiring consultant designers Tobia Scarpa, Tapio Wirkkala, Toni Zuccheri, Dale Chihuly, and Richard Marquis; 1965, founded glassware manufacturers V-Linea and Ve-art, which called on traditional mouth-blowing but also semi-automatic production techniques. 1970s–80s, in addition to traditional objects, these firms were known for their architectural lighting.
Bibliography *Venini Glass*, Washington, D.C.: Smithsonian, 1981. Cat., Kathryn B. Hiesinger and George H. Marcus III (eds.), *Design Since 1945*, Philadelphia: Philadelphia Museum of Art, 1983.

de' Silva, Walter (1951–)

Italian automobile design; born Lecco (CO).

Biography c. 1971, de' Silva worked at Fiat as a designer; subsequently, at various industrial-design studios such as Rodolfo Bonetto's in Milan and the IDEA Institue and, a short time, at Trussardi; 1999, became the director of design of Seat motor company in Martorell, Spain; from 2002, has been director of design for the entire Audi group (Audi, Seat, and Lamborghini).
Exhibitions Work (including product design) subject of 2003 *Walter de' Silva 'Autoemoción Exhibition,'* Mies van der Rohe Pavilion, Barcelona.
Bibliography Ricardo P. Felicioli, *Walter de' Silva: Centro Stile Alfa Romeo*, Milan: Automobilia, 1998

De Sphinx

Dutch glass, crystal, and ceramics firm; located Maastricht.

History 1827, Petrus L. Regout set up a glass-cutting operation in Maastricht, where he was originally a dealer in glass, crystal, and ceramics; from 1836, manufactured ceramics, at first mainly inexpensive red-bodied *fayence commune*. 1840s, the firm hired skilled British potters and began producing hard, white-bodied ceramics, similar to 18th-century Wedgwood wares, that it exported worldwide. Second half of 19th century, Regout became the largest utility-ware firm in the Netherlands. 1913, at the peak of its success, the firm's 3,750 workers operated 43 kilns around the clock. Its products ranged from the

William Hendrik de Vries. Bowl. Pre-1952. Glazed pottery, h. 2 7/8 x dia. 12 7/8" (7.3 x 32.7 cm). Mfr.: Keramische Industrie Fris, the Netherlands (pre-1952). Gift of Foreign Advisory Service Corp. MoMA.

inexpensive to the highest quality, and it made every imaginable ceramic object, including music-organ knobs. 1899, the factory became known as the Kristal-, Glasen Aardewerkfabrieken De Sphinx. 1917–34, J.H. Lint was its first designer and chief modeler. When joined by pictorial artist W.J. Rozendaal (who was the chief designer 1924–29), Lint devoted himself to modeling. 1929, sculptor Ch. H.M. Vos worked for the firm and designed its sphinx figurine. G.M.E. Bellefroid designed models and decorations for De Sphinx 1929–41 and 1946, and more than 30 services in 1920s; was interested in solving the technical problems of mechanized ceramic production; introduced new designs by varying the spouts, handles, and lids, without changing the body shapes. The 1934 Maas service (with a sugar bowl with no handles) by wholesale ceramics dealer De Bijenkorf was Bellefroid's most successful design. 1946, he left De Sphinx, which thus had no designer to 1950, when Pierre Daems was hired. 1958, the firm merged with Société Céramique in Maastricht.
Bibliography Cat., *Industry and Design in the Netherlands, 1850/1950*, Amsterdam: Stedelijk Museum, 1985.

De Stijl

Dutch architecture, art, and design group and journal; active 1917–31.

History 1917, the artists' group and monthly magazine *De Stijl* (published to 1931) was founded in Leiden by Theo van Doesburg. De Stijl (the style) went on to become more a movement rather than a mere fraternity, with a utopian vision, which responded to the horrors of World War I. The quest was for a new art, one to forget the past and begin anew, one baed on a universal modern style, applicable to all the arts. Architectural and functional principles were sought to satisfy 'spiritual and physical means.' Many of the visual characteristics of the group's production were derived—through the most elemental means—from the primary-colored, matrix-arranged geometric paintings of Pieter Cornelis Mondriaan (aka Piet Mondrian). Neoplasticism (the theory and practice of De Stijl developed by Mondrian) was expressed through architecture, furniture, textiles, interior decoration, graphics, and other media, particularly abstract painting. The ideas of architects H.P. Berlage and Frank Lloyd Wright also influenced De Stijl. The group's approach to form and color in domestic interiors, tiled floors, store-front lettering, and stained-glass windows was somewhat static and limiting until van Doesburg's introduction of dynamic diagonal lines in 1924 or 1925. Van Doesburg taught briefly at the Bauhaus, Weimar; developed contacts with Constructivist El Lissitzky and László Moholy-Nagy. The 1923 exhibition, Galerie l'Effort Moderne, Paris, was the beginning of the organization's 'international phase' and produced a pronounced change in its membership, resulting in Mondrian's withdrawal 1925. From 1919 to late 1920s, De Stijl member Bart van der Leck experimented with printed textiles. The designer of the first issue of *De Stijl*, Vilmos Huszár, also applied the group's principles to interiors and textiles. One of its best-known members, Gerrit Rietveld, produced a wide range of structures and furniture, including the legendary 1918 Rood Blauwe Stoel (red blue chair) and the canonical 1924 Schröder House (with Truus Schröder-Schräder), Utrecht. One of van Doesburg's more accomplished works was 1926–28 Café l'Aubette, Strasbourg. With van Doesburg's 1931 death, De Stijl ended.
Exhibitions The group's first (1922) exhibition of architectural designs was shown in the Netherlands. A landmark event for the group, van Doesburg collaborated with Cornelis van Eesteren and Gerrit Rietveld on models and architectural drawings, 1923 De Stijl architecture exhibition, Léonce Rosenberg's Galerie l'Effort Moderne, Paris. Subject of 1982 exhibition, Walker Art Center, Minneapolis, Minn.); 1985, Institut Français d'Architecture, Paris; 1990, Fondazione Giorgio Cini, Venice; and 1997, Stadsgalerij Heerlen, Heerlen, the Netherlands.
Bibliography Hans L.C. Jaffé et al., *De Stijl: 1917–1931, Visions of Utopia*, Abbeville, 1982. Carel Blotkamp et al., *De Stijl: The Formative Years, 1917–1922*, Cambridge, Mass.: MIT, 1986 (translation of *De Beginjaren van De Stijl, 1917–1922*). Paul Overy, *De Stijl*, London: Thames & Hudson, 1991. Dieter Hezel, *De Stijl: Neuere Literatur* (bibliography), Stuttgart: IRB, 1994. Cornelis van Eesteren, *Urbanismus zwischen 'de Stijl' und C.I.A.M.*, Brunswick: Vieweg, 1999.
> See van Doesburg, Theo.

de Vries, Derk Jan (1930–)

Dutch designer; born Hilversum; active Netherlands and Milan.

Training 1950–54, Akademie voor Industriële Vormgeving, Eindhoven; 1954–58, Akademie voor Industriële Vormgeving, Amsterdam.
Biography 1954–58, de Vries worked at Hiemstra & Evenblij, Amsterdam, designing projects for schools, the theater, hospitals, and civic and military marinas; 1958, was an advisor to Technische UNI, Amsterdam, and the firm W.J. Stokvis-Reale Industria Metallurgica, Arnhem; 1960–68, designed sanitary fittings for public use; 1969, was design consultant to Meroni-Maisa in Seveso; from 1969, was design consultant to Olivetti and La Rinascente; 1975, was designer at Arspect in Bergeyk, Netherlands; from 1987, became a member of KIO (Dutch industrial design organization), of Associazione per il Disegno Industriale (ADI) in Milan, and committees of International Council of Societies of Industrial Designers (ICSID); taught, Gerrit Rietveld Akademie, Amsterdam, and AIVE, Eindhoven.
Citations Gold medal, 1969 Expo/Ct/69.
Bibliography *ADI Annual 1976*, Milan: Associazione per il Disegno Industriale, 1976. Giancarlo Iliprandi and Pierluigi Molinari (eds.), *Industrial designers italiani*, Fagagna: Magnus, 1985. Cat., Hans Wichmann, *Italien Design 1945 bis heute*, Munich: Die Neue Sammlung, 1988.

de Vries, Willem Hendrik; Keramische Industrie Fris

Dutch ceramicist and ceramics enterprise.

Biography/history 1943, Keramische Industrie Fris, an earthenware factory, was established in Gouda and, 1947, moved to Edam. (*Fris* is 'fresh' in Dutch.) De Vries was the consultant and designer and quite active at the pottery. Typical of the late 1940s–50s, his so-called studio pottery was colorful as well as black-and-white and pastel. Early production was of tea services (from 1947), followed by coffee services (from 1949–50). Initial success was realized through tight forms. Some wares were matt glazed; others had a more handcrafted appearance, such as de Vries's 1961 Cleopatra dinner service, available both plain or with dark side stripes and rims. The 1955 Symfonie service, possibly by Floris Meydam (the other important designer for Fris), is a hard-glazed service in a form much like Trude Petri's 1947 Urbino Oval service by KPM in Berlin. Other designers, E. Truyen and J. Lucassen, created the 1963 Marijke service, more free in form in contrast to de Vries's work. Nel Bruynzeel and Dick Gerrits also designed for Fris, which marked its wares 'Fris Edam Made in Holland' and 'Studio Fris Made in Holland.' The pottery was active from 1943–69.
Bibliography Anna Sterk, *Fris: N.V. Keramische Industrie Fris, Edam 1947–1969*, Leeuwarden: Museum het Princessehof, 1985. Marie-Rose Bogaers, *Made in Holland: 1945–1988 gebruikskeramiek*, 's-Hertogenbosch: Het Kruithuis, 1988.

de Wolfe, Elsie (aka Lady Mendl, b. Ella Anderson de Wolfe 1865–1950)

American interior designer; born New York; active New York, Paris, and Los Angeles.

Biography Wolfe has been dubbed the first interior decorator in America; was a trailblazer and went onto the theatrical stage at a time when the profession of actress was not socially acceptable; 1892 with long time companion 'Bessie' Elisabeth Marbury (1856–1933), a theatrical agent, moved into a small house in Irving Place, near Gramercy Park, New York. (It did not originally belong to author Washington Irving, as often incorrectly claimed.) The couple was given the nickname 'the bachelors.' Wolfe transformed the small house's dark Victorian clutter into the light colors and furnishings of the Louis XV and XVI periods; had walls and furniture painted white and installed numerous mirrors. 1904, she retired from the stage and went into the business of helping people decorate their homes; with architect Ogden Codman, worked on the structure of the Irving Place house and renovated several New York brownstones. These properties included a townhouse on East 71st Street that she bought in 1910 for a highly publicized professional experiment. She decorated the interior of The Colony Club, a women's organization, founded in 1905 by Wolfe's rich friends, using the indoor-outdoor effect of trelliswork, for the first time. A new building for the club had been erected on Madison Avenue, designed by McKim, Mead and White, and Stanford White persuaded the building committee to hire Wolfe as decorator. 1913, she decorated the private rooms of Henry Clay Frick on the second floor of his mansion on Fifth Avenue, New York. For her Villa Trianon, Versailles, France, she created rooms of pleasing style and luxury. 1926, she married British diplomat Sir Charles Mendl, becoming Lady Mendl. During World War II, they lived in a house in Beverly Hills, Cal., US, that had a primarily white décor, including a plethora of white-flower arrangements. Her book *The House in Good Taste* (1913) was ghost written by Ruby Ross Wood, who later became an independent practicing interior decorator. Wolfe's notable contributions to 20th-century decoration

Christopher C. Deam, Wilsonart International, and Inside Design. Interior of Mobile Materials Travel Trailer (caravan). 2000. Aluminum (exterior), plywood, and plastic laminates (interior), overall exterior l. 176 x h. 90 x w. 84" (447 x 226.6 x 213.4 cm) without the hitch. Mfr. of interior: Wilsonart International, US.

included trelliswork in interiors, leopard-printed velvet pillows, naïve painted furniture, chinoiserie accents, bold stripes, topiary plants, tarnished gilding, and mirrored walls.
Bibliography Elsie de Wolfe, *The House in Good Taste*, New York: The Century, 1913. Mark Hampton, *House and Garden*, May 1990: 145–49, 214. John Esten and Rose Bennett Gilbert, *Manhattan Style*, Boston: Little, Brown, 1990: 2–3. N. Campbell and C. Seebohm, *Elsie de Wolfe*, New York: Panache-Potter, 1992.

Deacon, Tom (1956–)
Canadian designer; active Toronto.

Training 1982, bachelor's degree in architecture, University of Toronto, with honors and RAIC medal.
Biography After working briefly as an architect, Deacon turned to furniture and product design; 1984, set up AREA Design to design, manufacture, and sell contract seating and tables; 1990, established his own design studio with clients, including leading Canadian and American manufacturers, such as Bernhardt, Krug, and Nienkamper; designed the Deacon chair, Junior adjustable office chair, Tom range of task seating, and other furniture by Keilhauer, and 2001 Ah polypropylene armchair by Umbra.
Citations Numerous citations, including Gold Innovative Product award (Junior chair), IIDEX (floor-covering sector), NeoCon, Chicago, and others from *Virtu* and *I.D.* magazines.

Deam, Christopher C. (1962–)
American architect and designer; born Ann Arbor, Mich.; active San Francisco.

Training To 1991, architecture, University of Notre Dame, Ind.
Biography While at the university, Deam worked in studio of Matteo Thun in Milan, Italy, 1986; in office of Frank Gehry in Venice Beach, Cal., 1986; and with Antonio Citterio in Milan, Italy, 1990. 1991, established the studio CCD in San Francisco to design architecture, furniture, interiors, and products. He designed 2000 interior of Mobile Materials Travel Trailer by Wilsonart and furniture by Herman Miller, Pure Design, Idée, Totem design store, and David Design; teaches, California College of Arts and Crafts, San Francisco.
Exhibitions/citations Work included in 1996 *Pure Form, AD/50*, San Francisco; 1996 *Not so Simple*, New York; 1997 *Design mit Zukunft*, Focke Museum, Bremen, Germany; 1997 *Eames and Beyond*, San Francisco Museum of Modern Art; *G7 Young American Furniture Designers*, Milan, 2000; and International Contemporary Furniture Fair (ICFF), New York, 1999 and 2000; 2001 *Aluminum by Design* (Bambi Airstream mobile home), Cooper-Hewitt National Design Museum, New York; 2002 *U.S. Design 1975–2000*, Denver Art Museum. Awards include 1997 Editor's Awards, 1998 Best Body of Work, and 2000 Editor's Award (for Airstream mobile home), International Contemporary Furniture Fair (ICFF), New York; 1999 George Nelson award (for furniture design), *Interior* magazine; 2000 Good Design award (for Airstream mobile home), Chicago Athenaeum; 1999 honor award, American Institute of Architects (AIA).
Bibliography *Domus*, Oct. 1987. *Tempo*, Nov. 1986. Cat., Sarah Nichols et al., *Aluminum by Design*, New York: Abrams, 2000. Cat., R. Craig Miller (intro.), *U.S. Design: 1975–2000*, Munich: Prestel, 2002. www.cdeam.com.

Dearle, John Henry (1860–1932)
British fabric designer; active London

Training In tapestry.
Biography From 1878, Dearle worked as an assistant at Morris & Co. shop on Oxford Street, London. Morris himself trained Dearle as a tapestry weaver who, by 1887, had made his first tapestry design. By 1890, Dearle became the firm's chief designer, active in woven and printed textiles, carpets, embroidery, and, of course, tapestries. After Morris's 1896 death, Dearle became the artistic director. Duncan Dearle, his son, who also worked for Morris, directed the firm until its closing 1940.
Bibliography Cat., *Arts and Crafts Textiles in Britain*, London: Fine Art Gallery, 1999.

Deboni, Franco (1950–)
Italian architect and glassware designer; born Trieste; active Venice.

Training To 1974, architecture and industrial design, Istituto Universitario di Architettura, Venice.
Biography Deboni worked for various firms in Italy and Yugoslavia; received a patent for a bookcase-component system. Clients have included Ferro & Lazzarini (glassware) and Italianline. He is best known for his lighting in glass and a mushroom-shaped table lamp in marble; became a member, Associazione per il Disegno Industriale (ADI); wrote *Venini Glass* (Turin: Allemandi, 1996 and 2002) and *Murano novecento: vetri e vetrai* (Milan: Bocca, 1996) and managed an art auction house.
Bibliography *ADI Annual 1976*, Milan: Associazione per il Disegno Industriale, 1976.

Debschitz, Wilhelm von (1871–1948); Debschitz-Schule

German artist and designer; born Görlitz.

Biography Influenced by William Morris and Walter Crane of England, von Debschitz and Hermann Obrist founded the Lehr- und Versuchs-Ateliers für angewandte und freie Kunst (aka Debschitz-Schule) in Munich in 1902. The institution was a private art school organized along new lines, offering instruction in applied arts and crafts. Rather than copying models in its foundation courses, students were encouraged to use their powers of observation. Workshops were taught by Eduard Steinicken and M.T. Wetzlar. Students included Josef Urban, Marga Jess, Gertraud von Schnellenbühel, Fritz Schmoll von Eisenwerth, Friedrich Adler, and Carl Johann Bauer. With H. Lochner, von Debschitz cofounded a workshop for the applied arts in 1906. His own work was boldly abstract. After World War I, he became head, State Handwerker- und Kunstgewerbe-schule, Hanover.
Exhibitions Debschitz-Schule students' work first shown in 1903.
Bibliography Beate Ziegert, 'The Debschitz School Munich 1902–1914,' master's-degree thesis, Syracuse, N.Y.: Syracuse University, 1985. Beate Ziegert, 'The Debschitz School Munich: 1902–1914,' *Design Issues*, vol. 3, no. 1, Spring 1986: 28–41. Katherine Bloom Hiesinger (ed. and intro.), *Art Nouveau in Munich: Masters of the Jugendstil from the Stadtmuseum, Munich...*, Philadelphia: Philadelphia Museum of Art and Prestel, 1988. Dagmar Rinker, *Die Lehr- und Versuchs-Ateliers für angewandte und freie Kunst (Debschitz-Schule), München 1902–1914*, Munich: Tuduv, 1993.

Decaux, Jean-Claude (1937–)

French manufacturer; active Paris.

Biography 1955, Decaux established the eponymous firm, JC Decaux, specializing in highway advertising; 1964, turned to urban street advertising; created a bus shelter tested in cities, including Lyon, Grenoble, and Poitiers; 1972, established Mobilier Urbain pour l'Information (MUPI) and, 1976, Point d'Information Service Animé (PISA); offered municipalities free street-information displays in exchange for rights to place his MUPI mobile units and bus shelters; diversified into information columns, panels, lighting, and public toilets; 1990, set up design agency Decaux Design, working with Philippe Starck, Jean-Michel Wilmotte, Andrée Putman, and others. JC Decaux for outdoor advertising and installations has become highly successful.

Deck, Joseph-Theodore (1823–1891)

French art potter; born Guebwiller.

Biography Leaving his job as a foreperson of a stove factory in Paris, he set up his operation as ceramicist in 1856 ; was inspired by Persian and Near Eastern ceramics, especially cobalt blue and turquoise floral patterns. The ceramics of China fostered his interest in porcelain. He was the first French ceramicist to be successful with red *flambé* glazes, incised decoration on celadon glazes, imitation jade, and underglaze enamels; was inspired by a trip to Venice and, thus, began to use gold background underglazes; also in Venice, discovered Japanese ceramics; 1887, became director of Manufacture National de Sèvres ; perfected *la grosse porcelaine*, a name he coined for vases, sculptures, and outdoor objects covered with durable transparent glazes; was concurrently active in his own studio on the boulevard Saint-Jacques in Paris and at Sèvres.
Exhibitions Plates (with applied designs by Ranvier, Glück, Anker, Bracquemond, Harpignies, Raphaël Collin, and Reiber) shown at 1878 *Exposition Universelle*; Japanese-inspired ceramics at 1880 Salon of Union Centrale des Arts Décoratifs; both Paris.
Bibliography Yvonne Brunhammer et al., *Art Nouveau Belgium, France*, Houston: Rice University, 1976.

Decœur, Émile (1876–1953)

French decorator and ceramicist; born Paris.

Training Under ceramicist Edmond Lachenal.
Biography Decœur was allowed to place his signature jointly on Lachenal's pots; was associated for a short time with Fernand Rumèbe; 1907, established his own workshop in Fontenay-aux-Roses, France, and turned from faïence to specialize in stoneware; later worked in porcelain; 1925, abandoned the Art Nouveau style, increasingly favoring a simplified approach, which evolved into absolutely plain, symmetrical forms; produced simple vases, dishes, and bowls enveloped in heavy, pale glazes of yellow, blue, green, white, and pink; 1942–48, was artistic consultant at Manufacture Nationale de Sèvres.
Bibliography Guillaume Janneau, *Émile Decœur*, Paris: La Connaissance, 1923. Yvonne Brunhammer et al., *Art Nouveau Belgium, France*, Houston: Rice University, 1976. Victor Arwas, *Art Déco*, New York: Abrams, 1980. Pierre Cabanne, *Encyclopédie art déco*, Paris: Somogy, 1986: 184.

Décoration Intérieure Moderne
> See D.I.M.

Decorchemont, François-Émile (1880–1971)

French painter, sculptor, ceramicist, and glass worker; born Conches.

Training To 1900, École Nationale Supérieure des Arts Décoratifs, Paris.
Biography 1902–03, Decorchemont was initially known for his ceramics, producing stoneware; 1903, worked with his father, sculptor Émile Decorchemont, experimenting in glass with *pâte-d'émail* and matt surfaces, influenced by Albert-Louis Dammouse; from 1903, created very thin *pâte-de-verre* pieces that were slightly translucent with matt surfaces; 1907–08, created a true *pâte-de-verre* using colored-crystal powdered glass and metallic oxides that he bought at Cristalleries de Saint-Denis; c. 1910 at Daum, developed a denser colored, yet translucent, material. 1910–20, his work was influenced by the Art Nouveau style, realized as monumental, simplified, geometric flower, fruit, and animal motifs. 1928, he adopted somber, linear motifs. From 1933 to the beginning of World War II, he was primarily active in producing leaded-glass windows for churches, including Église de Sainte-Odile in Paris.
Exhibitions His work was shown regularly at Salons of Société des Artistes Français, Salon d'Automne, and Salon des Artistes Décorateurs, and included in L'Hôtel du Collectionneur and the Rouard pavilions, 1925 *Exposition Internationale des Arts Décoratifs et Industriels Modernes*, Paris.
Bibliography 'François Decorchemont, 1880–1971,' *Nouvelles de l'Eure*, no. 42–43, Aug. 1971. Yvonne Brunhammer et al., *Art Nouveau Belgium, France*, Houston: Rice University, 1976. Victor Arwas, *Art Déco*, New York: Abrams, 1980. Cat., *Verriers français contemporains: art et industrie*, Paris: Musée des Arts Décoratifs, 1982. Cat., Aaron Lederfajn and Xavier Lenormand (eds.), *Le Louvre des Antiquaires présente: 1930 quand le meuble devient sculpture*, Paris, 1986. Pierre Cabanne, *Encyclopédie art déco*, Paris: Somogy, 1986: 185.

Decursu, Giorgio (1927–)

Italian industrial designer; born and active Milan.

Biography 1955, Decursu began his professional career; 1956–66, collaborated with Marcello Nizzoli for clients, including Olivetti, Agip, Faema, Laverda, and Olivari; 1968, was a partner in Decursu, De Pas, D'Urbino & Lomazzi studio ; from 1970, set up his own independent studio in Milan, designing a range of industrial products from furniture to heavy industrial equipment (sometimes with Junko Murase and others) by BM Biraghi, Cisa, Comev, D'Andrea, Elesa, Paso, and Poletti & Osta; became a member, Associazione per il Disegno Industriale (ADI). 1971–73, Borrelli Corrado worked in Decursu's studio.
Citations First prize, 1972 Du Pont-Dacron Fiberfill competition; 1979 (two citations), 1989 (four citations), 1991 (two citations), 1994 (two citations), 1991, 1994, 1998 (with Junko Murase) Premio Compasso d'Oro.
Bibliography *ADI Annual 1976*, Milan: Associazione per il Disegno Industriale, 1976. *Modo*, no. 148, Mar.–Apr. 1993: 117.

Dedham Pottery
> See Chelsea Keramic Art Works.

Deepdesign
> See Bazzicalupo, Leopoldo Matteo; Mangiarotti, Raffaella.

Deganello, Paolo (1940–)

Italian architect and designer; born Este; active Milan.

Training To 1966, architecture, Università degli Studi, Florence.
Biography 1963, Deganello began his professional career by collaborating on restoration of Orsammichele, Florence; 1966–74, worked in the urban-planning office of the city of Calenzano; 1966 with Andrea Branzi, Gilberto Corretti, and Massimo Morozzi, founded studio Archizoom Associati in Milan, which closed in 1974, but he was with the group to 1972, when he established his own studio in Milan. One of Archizoom works is 1969 Mies chair by Poltronova. Deganello taught

architecture, Università degli Studi, Florence, 1966; Architectural Association, London, 1971–72; 1976, Università degli Studi, Milan; was professor of design, Istituto Superiore per le Industrie Artistiche (ISIA), Rome; 1975 with Corretti, Franco Gatti, and Roberto Querci, founded Collettivo Tecnici Progettisti; 1975, founded the journal *Quaderni del Progetto*; wrote for *Casabella*, *IN*, *Rassegna*, *Domus*, *Urban Politics Problems*, *Modo*, and *Lotus*. Design clients have included Planula, Marcatré, Driade, Venini, Mega Editions (Tribu collection), Cidue, Cassina, Ycami, Mclandia, Casigliani, and Vitra. His early 1980s furniture, especially for Cassina, was associated with 1950s revival style, including 1967 Superonda banquette, 1973 AEO armchair by Cassina, and 1982 Torso armchair, sofa, and bed, for which he is best known. Product work also includes 1981 Squash sofa by Driade, 1984 Palomar coat rack by Ycami, 1985 Aurore lamp by Venini, 1985 Duala floor lamp by Ycami Collection, and 1985 Articifi table range by Cassina. Was a member, Associazione per il Disegno Industriale (ADI); 1983, designed Schöner Wohnen interior design and housewares shop in Zürich, where his Monument to the Snow was mounted on the plaza in front of the store. From 1992, taught architecture, Univerisità di Firenze; and at others worldwide. Work has been primarily in architecture, including 1993 Stefanel showroom and a second (1998) showroom/gallery, both Verona; from 1991 with others, was commissioned to connect old and new towns of Gubbio; 1994 with Barbuscia, restoration of villa and private park, Laveno (on Lake Maggiore); 1996 with Alberto Magnaghi's town-planning team, restoration of a building in Gavorrano (Grosseto). 1996–2001, wrote monthly for magazine *Casa amica*, and periodically and consistently for others.
Exhibitions Projects included in *Design by Circumstance*, Clocktower, New York. Participated in international exhibitions, competitions, and all editions from 1968 (14th) to 1995 (19th) Triennali di Milano. Work included in 1987 *Les Nouvelles Tendances*, Centre Georges Pompidou, Paris; 1987 Documenta 8, Kassel; one of five rooms built at *Abitare Italia 2000*, New York. Work subject of 1998 and 1991 exhibitions, Amsterdam and Tokyo; and, subsequently, Cantù.
Bibliography Paolo Deganello, 'Post-Modern Boulevard,' *Domus*, no. 614, Feb. 1981: 9–10. 'Colloqui di Modo: Il progetto sulle spine,' *Modo*, no. 57, Mar. 1983: 26–30. Cristina Morozzi, 'Incastro simmetrico,' *Modo*, no. 56, Jan.–Feb. 1983: 48–49. *Italianisches Mobeldesign Klassiker von 1945 bis 1985*, Munich: Bangert, 1985. Cat., *Nouvelles tendances: les avant-garde de la fin du 20ème siècle*, Paris: Centre Georges Pompidou, 1987. Andrea Branzi, 'Cose e case,' *Domus*, no. 699, Nov. 1988. Juli Capella and Quim Larrea, *Designed by Architects in the 1980s*, New York: Rizzoli, 1988. Cat., Roberto Rizzi and Alberto Colzani, *Anche gli oggetti hanno un'anima. Paolo Deganello—opere 1964–2002*, Cantù: Ycami Collection, 2002.

Deichmann, Oliver (1975–)

German designer; born Stuttgart.

Training From 1996, industrial design, Hochschule der Künste, Berlin.
Biography 1997–98, Deichmann was a member of the project group 'transiteure,' organized by 'Nick' Hans Roericht, a professor at Hochschule der Künste in Berlin, as an interdisciplinary experiment; 1998 with Blasius Osko (Danzig, 1975–), who concurrently studied with Diechmann at the Berlin art school, set up the studio 'wunschforscher' in Berlin. Their projects have included 1998–2002 Springschuh, a shoe to increase jumping by storing and releasing energy into a pneumatic 'muscle'; 2001 SushiRoller, a manual apparatus for rolling the Japanese food Maki Sushis; 2002 'top.table,' furniture concept for work spaces; 2002 Fall/Big Leaf, a large autumn leaf made of wicker.
Exhibitions 2001 Hanover Industry Fair (Springschuh shown), Hanover; 2001 Tendence fair (SushiRoller shown), Frankfurt; 2002 Salon des Artistes Décorateurs (SAD) ('top.table' shown), Carrousel du Louvre, Paris; 2002 Intérieur biennial (Fall/Big Leaf shown), Courtrai.

Del Corno, Marco (1924–)
> See Design Group Italia.

Del Guidice, Frank (1917–1993)

American industrial designer.

Biography Del Guidice worked in the Walter Dorwin Teague Associates industrial-design office, New York; with the staff, participated in the design of several commissions there, including interiors and livery of Boeing's 1946 Stratocruiser and 1958 models of 707, 727, and 747. Claims have been made that he designed the 1939 desk lamp by Polaroid (but was possibly from the hand of Teague's son Dorwin Teague Jr. as the son has asserted). 1967–72, Milton Immerman unsuccessfully managed the Teague office, when Del Guidice became president and chief executive officer and served in the positions to the end of 1970s.
Citations 1982 honorary doctorate, Pratt Institute, Brooklyn, N.Y.
Bibliography 'Frank Del Guidice,' *Innovation* (IDSA quarterly journal), vol. 2, no. 2, 1983.

Del Marie, Félix (1889–1952)

French painter and furniture designer; active Bécon-les Bruyères.

Biography Known as a painter, he was an enthusiastic promulgator of Italian Futurism as espoused in his 1913 manifesto published in *Paris-Jour*. 1922, he became a follower of Piet Mondrian and De Stijl group and, 1924, editor of journal *Vouloir*, which he turned into *Revue mensuelle d'esthétique néo-plastique*; from 1925, created interiors and furniture; designed chairs in two and three colors in the manner of Gerrit Rietveld and other models in bent tubular steel; worked in wrought iron, painted metal, and frosted and painted glass used in lighting; 1951 with André Bloc, founded Groupe Espace.
Bibliography Pierre Kjellberg, *Art déco: les maîtres du mobilier, le décor des paquebots*, Paris: Amateur, 1986/1990.

Delaherche, Auguste (1857–1940)

French ceramicist; born Beauvais.

Training École Nationale Supérieure des Arts Décoratifs, Paris.
Biography With Lechevallier-Chevignard, Delaherche helped restore the stained-glass windows of Église de Saint-Acceul in Ecouen; 1883–86, worked as a designer for religious jeweler Chartier; created his first pots in salt-glazed stoneware inspired by folk pottery, producing them under the direction of Ludovic Pilleux at L'Italienne ceramics factory, near Goincourt; 1887, bought Ernest Chaplet's workshop in the rue Blomet in Paris; 1894, moved to Armentières; abandoned modeled decoration for overflow glazes appropriate to the materials and to an unembellished form; began working in porcelain; from 1904, made only one-of-a-kind pieces, often in stoneware; with Chaplet, is recognized as one of the most important ceramicists at the turn of the century. His work developed into a formal simplicity. He introduced ceramic work into architecture by modeling panels and borders into fireplaces. Siegfried Bing showed Delaherche's work at his gallery/shop L'Art Nouveau in Paris.
Exhibitions Participated in 1887 Salon of Union Centrale des Arts Décoratifs; showed decorated stoneware in gourd-shaped vases, vases with exaggerated handles, and pear-shaped cups at 1889 *Exposition Universelle* (gold medal), Paris.
Bibliography Yvonne Brunhammer et al., *Art Nouveau Belgium, France*, Houston: Rice University, 1976.

Delaunay, Robert (1885–1941)

French painter and designer; born Paris; husband of Sonia Terk Delaunay.

Biography 1902, Delaunay began as a scenery painter; 1905, became a fine artist, at first influenced by neo-Impressionism and then Cubism; using Eugène Chevreul's theories of simultaneous contrasts of color, painted a series of canvases that were prismatically brilliant and colorful, calling them 'simultaneous paintings.' Guillaume Apollinaire called the technique Orphism in his book *Le bestiaire or cortège d'Orphée* (Paris: Deplanche, 1911). Delaunay passed through a neo-Impressionist period, during which he painted canvases, including *Solar Disk,* that presaged Futurism; some other works were more suggestive of Cubism. Delaunay's *Premier Disque* (1912) has been called the first French abstract painting. He designed film sets, such as *Le p'tit parigot* (1926, directed by René Le Somptier), with others including his wife, and for Diaghilev's Ballets Russes; was highly influential on other artists of his generation.
Exhibitions Work included in Salons des Indépendants from 1904 and at Salon des Tuilleries. His painting of a woman and the Eiffel Tower hung in Rob Mallet-Stevens's hall in the French pavilion, 1925 *Exposition Internationale des Arts Décoratifs et Industriels Modernes*, Paris.
Bibliography Victor Arwas, *Art Déco*, New York: Abrams, 1980. Pontus Hulten, *Futurism and Futurisms*, New York: Abbeville, 1986. Georges Bernier, *Robert et Sonia Delaunay: naissance de l'art abstrait*, Paris: J.-C. Lattès, 1995. Werner Spies, *Robert Delaunay: de l'impressionisme à l'abstraction, 1906–1914*, Paris: Centre Georges Pompidou, 1999.
> See Delaunay, Sonia.

Delaunay, Sonia (b. Sonia Terk 1885–1979)

Russian painter and designer; born Gradiesk (Ukraine); active Paris; wife of Robert Delaunay.

Training To 1902, St. Petersburg; 1903–04, drawing and anatomy, Karlsruhe; 1905, painting, Académie de la Palette, Paris.
Biography 1905, she settled in Paris and began designing fabrics, lampshades, wall textiles, mosaics, interior schemes, and painted an automobile in her characteristic syncopated geometric shapes; experimented with embroidery, fabric design, and printing, transforming her rhythmical patterns from the artist's canvas to fabrics; 1913, made a patchwork quilt in geometric polychrome forms for her son's crib, the first of her Robes et Gilets Simultanés; used *simultané* to indicate that a piece of clothing was to be considered as a whole and as a work of art, without focusing on its separate elements; studying color and materials, investigated (with husband Robert Delaunay and Swiss-born French writer Blaise Cendrars) the modern *simultané* movement influenced by Eugène Chevreul, including his book *De la loi du contraste simultané des couleurs, et de l'assortiment des objets colorés, considéré d'après cette loi* (Paris: Pitois-Levrault, 1839). Her collages and stenciled illustrations were published in *La prose du transsibérien et de la petite Jehanne de France* (Paris: Hommes Nouveaux, 1913) by Cendrars, who dedicated to her his so-called dress-poem 'Sur la robe elle a un corps' (On the dress she has a body), aptly summing up her theory of *simultané*. The book was 72" (200 cm) long in an accordion format, using different typographic styles and faces. 1914, she opened a fashion workshop, where she designed fabrics, shawls, and clothing for men and women; was attracted to working in ceramics after a 1915 trip to Portugal. Like her husband, she designed for Serge Diaghilev's Ballets Russes, including costumes for its 1918 revival of *Cléopâtre* (music by Anton Arensky and others). 1920, she set up residence and workshop in an apartment, boulevard des Malesherbes, Paris; 1922, designed bookstore Au Sans Pareil, Paris; 1925, published *Sonia Delaunay, ses peintures, ses objets, ses tissus simultanés, ses modes* (preface by André Lhote); closely identified with Art Déco, designed interiors, clothing, and theater and ballet sets and costumes, emphasizing bright solid colors. Her clothes were worn by writers, artists, and *beau monde* personalities. She designed fabrics for the film *Le vertige* (1926, directed by Marcel L'Herbier) and (with husband Robert) sets and costumes for the film *Le p'tit parigot* (1926, directed by René Le Sompitier). Her friends and associates included Walter Gropius, Marcel Breuer, Jean Arp, Sophie Tauber-Arp, and Erich Mendelsohn. She designed furs for Jacques Heim; 1927, arranged the conference 'L'influence de la peinture sur l'art vestimentaire' (The influence of painting on the art of clothing) at the Sorbonne, Paris. Her activities were greatly diminished from 1929 due to the Great Depression; 1930 briefly, was a member, Union des Artistes Modernes (UAM); after 1920s, concentrated on painting but continued in design, particularly of fabrics, maintaining her association with the Metz store in the Netherlands (for which she designed 1920s–1950s).
Work 1912–13 *simultané* dress-painting on live models; 1914 posters for Pirelli and Dubonnet; 1922–26 robe poems and clothing; 1925 interior decoration/fitting of Citroën 10 HP type B12 automobile (1925–27; same body style as B2); Simultanée boutique (with Jacques Heim) on pont Alexandre III at 1925 *Exposition Internationale des Arts Décoratifs et Industriels Modernes*, Paris; 1940s–1960s rhythm color paintings, graphics, and tapestries; 1959 playing cards produced 1964 by Bielefelder Spielkarte Museum; 1967 decoration of Matra B530 automobile; 1975 UNESCO poster for International Women's Year; and ceramics, including posthumous 1984 faïence dinner service by Les Faïenceries de Moustiers.
Exhibitions Work included in 1913 *Erster Deutsche Herbstsalon*, Galerie der Sturm, Berlin; 1916, Nya Konstgallerien, Stockholm; 1920, Galerie der Sturm, Berlin; 1938, Stedelijk Museum, Amsterdam; 1945 *Art concret*, Galerie Drouin, Paris; and a large number of post-war venues, including with her husband's work. Her own was subject of numerous exhibitions, including 1981 retrospective, Art Institute of Chicago, and 1985 exhibition, Musée d'Art Moderne de la Ville de Paris. Collaborated with her husband on two projects (Palais des Chemins de Fer and Palais de l'Air), 1937 *Exposition Internationale des Arts et Techniques dans la Vie Moderne*, Paris. First prize (neon-tube Zig-Zag sculpture), 1936 competition, Société d'Électricité de France.
Bibliography Sonia Delaunay, *Tapis et tissus*, Paris: Charles Moreau, 1929. Cat., Madeleine Delpierre and Henriette Vanier (eds.), *Grands couturiers parisiens 1910–1939*, Paris, 1965. Cat., Bernard Dorival (ed.), *Sonia Delaunay*, Paris, 1965. Cat., Michael Hoog (ed.), *Sonia Delaunay*, London, 1969. Cat., Jacques Damase (ed.), *Sonia Delaunay: Rhythmes et couleurs*, Paris: Hermann, 1971. Donata Devoti, *L'arte del tessuto in Europa*, Milan: Bramante, 1974. Germain Viatte (preface), *Sonia Delaunay: noirs et blancs dessins*, Paris: Jacques Damase 1978. Victor Arwas, *Art Déco*, New York: Abrams, 1980. Anne Lee Morgan (ed.), *Contemporary Designers*, London: Macmillan, 1984: 148–49. Cat., *Delaunay*, Paris: Musées/SA-MAM, 1985. Pierre Cabanne, *Encyclopédie art déco*, Paris: Somogy, 1986: 186–87. Cat., *Les années UAM 1929–1958*, Paris: Musée des Arts Décoratifs, 1988: 172–73. Jacques Damase, *Sonia Delaunay: Fashion and Fabrics*, New York: Abrams, 1991.

Christian Dell. Table Lamp. 1926. Chromed metal, h. 12 1/4 base x dia. 6 3/8" (31.1 x 16.2 cm), h. (extended) 15 7/8" (40.3 cm), shade dia. 5 1/2" (14 cm). Mfr.: Schwintzer & Gäff, Germany. Gift of Mrs. Stanley Resor. MoMA.

Delheid Frères

Belgian silversmith; located Brussels.

History Before setting up his own workshop in Amsterdam in 1897, Frans Zwollo, the first teacher of 'art metalwork' in the Netherlands, was apprenticed at Delheid. After 1925, the firm began producing modern silver designs, and, c. 1930, made a number of fine objects in which silver was combined with wood and ivory from the Belgian Congo (now Zaire). The angular forms appearing in its wares can be likened to French 1920s forms and the undulating curves to 1930s streamline styling.
Bibliography Annelies Krekel-Aalberse, *Art Nouveau and Art Déco Silver*, New York: Abrams, 1989.

Delisle

French lighting firm; located Paris.

History 1895, the eponymous firm was founded by Henry Delisle in the Hôtel de Lamoignon in Paris, and, 1935, moved to the Hôtel de Canillac on the rue du Parc Royal, where it is located today and managed by Jean-Michel Delisle. Its best-known fixtures include those for the Grand Trianon of the Palais de Versailles; Geihinkan Palace in Tokyo; Florence Goubol Theatre of San Francisco Fine Art Museum; Hotel Plaza Athenée in New York; and oceanliners 1927 *Île-de-France*, 1935 *Normandie*, and 1961 *France*. Christian Duc designed its 1987 Archéologie Future spherical lamp (with glass by Patrick Desserme and Bernard Pictet).
Citations Awards at 1895 *Exposition Universelle*, 1937 *Exposition Internationale des Arts et Techniques dans la Vie Moderne*, and variously in 1980, 1982, and 1988; all Paris.

Dell, Christian (1893–1974)

German metalworker and designer; born and active Hanau; also active Weimar and Frankfurt.

Training 1909–10 and 1920–21, Königliche Preussische Zeichenaka-

demie, Hanau; 1913 under Henry van de Velde, Kunstgewerbeschule, Weimar.
Biography 1922–25, Dell was the *Werkmeister* of the metal workshop at the Bauhaus, Weimar. He contended that a designer should not totally abandon historicist styles, and, through this declaration, he represented a shift from the original stance taken by the Wiener Werkstätte and the Dessau Bauhaus under the guidance of László Moholy-Nagy. Dell was successful in developing lighting design for mass production. Kaiser produced a wide range of his innovative lighting fixtures for the modern office and workplace, including the range of lighting called Idell (an acronym of 'IDEal' and 'DELL') that was plagiarized by Helo and another, the 1927 Type-K table lamp (presaging 1930 Bestlite) by Robert Best, UK. 1926–33, Dell was in charge of the metal workshop of Staedelschule in Frankfurt and, 1933 with the seizure of power by the Nazis, was dismissed. He died in Wiesbaden.
Exhibitions Work subject of 1995 *Idee* exhibition in Arnsberg (catalog below); 1995–96 exhibition, *Christian Dell—'Silberschmied und Gestalter,'* Museum Schloß Philippsruhe, Hanau.
Bibliography *Sammlung Katalog*, Berlin: Bauhaus-Archiv, Museum für Gestaltung, 1981, pls. 188–89. Lionel Richard, *Encyclopédie du Bauhaus*, Paris: Somogy, 1985: 150. *Experiment Bauhaus*, Berlin: Bauhaus-Archiv Museum, 1988: 126. Cat., *The Bauhaus: Masters and Students*, New York: Barry Friedman 1988. Cat., *Die Metallwerkstatt am Bauhaus*, Berlin: Bauhaus-Archiv, 1992: 192–207, 316. Cat., Peter M. Kleine and Klaus Struve, *Idee: Christian Dell: einfache, zweckmäßige Arbeitsleuchten aus Neheim*, Arnsberg: Verein zur Förderung des Museum für Licht und Beleuchtung, 1995

Delo Lindo
French design partnership; active Paris.

Training Both partners: École Nationale Supérieure des Arts Décoratifs, Paris.
Biography 1985, Fabien Cagani (Paris 1961–) and Laurent Matras (Strasbourg 1961–) established themselves as Delo Lindo ('extremely beautiful' in Spanish); worked first as interior architects, specializing in fashion boutiques and exhibitions, soon after extending into furniture and furnishings. Some critics have labeled them 'observers of the banal.' Work has included 1998 Butane chair/stool; 2000 bowls, cups, and vases in angled PVC tubing; 2000 hanging support for Galerie Valentin; Butterfly side chair and Monique polypropylene/metal and Stanislas armchairs by Soca Line; porcelain door knobs by Mérigous; Nestor coat rack, umbrella stand, and others by Ligne Roset; floor lamps, 1994 Papageno side chair, News table, and others by Cinna; and ceramics by J. Merigous Porcelain.
Exhibitions/citations Work included in 2001–03 *Mobilisation, le Design pour Réunir* (sponsored by AFAA–Association Française d'Action Artistique, French embassies, and VIA [French furniture association]), traveling South America and to Paris; 2001 *Exposition Feutre*, Musée du Feutre, Mouzon; *Nouveaux Regards*, 2001 (46th) Expofil, Paris; 2001 *Continuous Connection Part 1*, Felissimo store, New York; 2001 *Saint Etienne, le Design, une École*, Centre d'Art Contemporain, Brussels; 2001 *Céramique-Design-Industrie*, Evêché, Salle des Atlantes, Uzès; exhibition of CRAFT (fire and earth arts research center), 2002 (3rd) Ceramic Network, Limoges; 2002 *Idéales* (maquette of a small house), Villa Noailles, Hyères; and numerous others. 1992 Carte Blanche production support, VIA; 1993 Grand Prix de la Critique et de la Presse (Bingo and Butterfly side chairs by Soca Line), Salon du Meuble, Paris.
Bibliography Cat., Sophie Tasma Anargyros et al., *L'école française: les créateurs de meubles du 20ème siècle*, Paris: Industries Françaises de l'Ameublement, 2000. www.via.asso.fr.

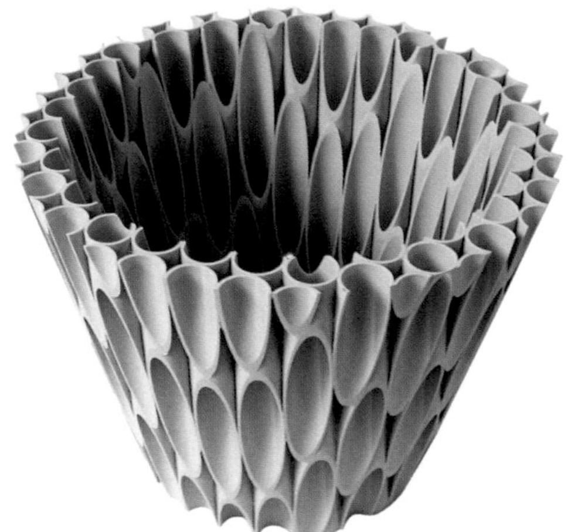

Delo Lindo (Fabien Cagani and Laurent Matras). Contenants container. 2000. PVC tubing, h. 9¾ x dia. 11¾" (25 x 30 cm). Limited production, France.

Demaria, Pierre (1896–1984)
French painter and furniture designer.

Biography Primarily a painter, Demaria designed furniture and ornate rugs in abstract geometric motifs.
Exhibitions With architect Djo-Bourgeois, collaborated on kiosks and pavilions at 1925 *Exposition Internationale des Arts Décoratifs et Industriels Modernes*, Paris.
Bibliography Pierre Kjellberg, *Art déco: les maîtres du mobilier, le décor des paquebots*, Paris: Amateur, 1986/1990.

den Boon, Wim (1912–1968)
Dutch interior architect; born Waddinxveen (Netherlands).

Training 1924–29, Hogere Handelsschool, Rotterdam; 1941–45, interior design, Academie van Beeldende Kunsten, The Hague.
Biography 1924–29, he worked as exhibition designer at Unilever; c. 1945, became a founding member with Hein Stolle and Pierre Kleykamp of Groep &; 1948 with Groep &, designed departure room of Schiphol airport in Amsterdam, and waiting room of Thomsen's harbor company; 1948–50, editor of magazine *Goed Wonen* that had its own furniture collection 'Groep &,' lectured widely in the Netherlands, and designed interiors and architecture for showcase houses; 1950 with Dora Mees and J.W. Jansen, set up the group Mens en Huis and, thus, dissolved the Groep & studio; 1950, became an interior architect in The Hague and designed upholstered and bamboo furniture by Jonkers; from 1950s, was very active in interior design, architecture, and rebuilding/reconstruction in the Netherlands; 1954, traveled to Morocco, Spain, and France to study the architecture of Le Corbusier and Gaudí; 1955, traveled to Scandinavian countries to study architecture of Alvar Aalto. The Wim den Boon archive is housed in the Gemeentemuseum in The Hague.
Exhibitions/citations Participated in Groep &'s 1947 *my home* exhibition; and (with Groep &) in 1949 Salon of Société des Artistes Décorateurs, Paris. c. 1951 *Mens en Huis* exhibition, Stedelijk Museum, Amsterdam, and Gemeentemuseum, The Hague; and 1951 *Woon Goed*, Academie van Beeldende Kunsten, The Hague.
Bibliography D. Sliedregt, 'De ivoren toren, in memoriam Wim den Boon,' *Goed Wonen*, no. 11, 1968: 7. P. Vöge and B. Westerveld, *Stoelen, Nederlandse ontwerpen 1945–1985*, Amsterdam, 1985. Peter Vöge, *Wim den Boon: Binnenhuisarchitect, 1912/1968*, Rotterdam: 010, 1989.

Denis, Maurice (1870–1943)
French artist and decorator; born Grandville.

Training Académie Julian; École Nationale Supérieure des Beaux-Arts; both Paris.
Biography Denis met Ker-Xavier Roussel and Édouard Vuillard at the Lycée Condorcet and became one of the chief exponents of Symbolism. After the meeting of Paul Sérusier and Paul Gauguin at café Brady in Paris, Denis cofounded the Nabis group in 1888 with H.-G. Ibels, Paul Ranson, Pierre Bonnard, and Sérusier. Denis became spokesperson and theoretician for the group; 1890, published his first theoretical article 'Art et critique'; painted canvases and murals (at Hotel Morozov, Moscow, and Palais de Chaillot, Paris) and illustrated books by Paul Verlaine, André Gide, and others. Denis was a devout Catholic intent on reviving religious painting. His decorative work was primarily in the form of stained glass and wallpaper. 1917, he painted frescoes in the Église de Saint-Paul, Geneva, and, 1919 with Georges Desvallières, founded the Ateliers d'Art Sacré. His writings on art can be found in his books *Théories* (1912), *Nouvelles Théories* (1922), and his 1939 history of religious art. Denis's former home near Paris, the priory of Saint-Germain-en-Laye, is today the Musée des Symbolistes et Nabis (Musée Départmental du Prieuré).

Bibliography Maurice Brillant, *Portrait de Maurice Denis*, Paris: Bloud & Gay, 1945. Yvonne Brunhammer et al., *Art Nouveau Belgium, France*, Houston: Rice University, 1976. Ivan Chilvers et al., *The Oxford Dictionary of Art*, Oxford: 1988: 140. Claire Frèsches-Thory and Antoine Terrasse, *The Nabis: Bonnard, Vuillard and Their Circle*, New York: Abrams, 1991.

Denzel, Marianne (c. 1932–1971)

Austrian industrial designer; born Vienna.

Biography Denzel designed hotel ceramics by Berndorf-Ranshofen and metalwares for Vereinigte Metallwerke Ranshofen.
Bibliography Günther Feuerstein, *Vienna—Present and Past: Arts and Crafts—Applied Art—Design*, Vienna: Jugend und Volk, 1976.

Depero, Fortunato (1892–1960)

Italian artist and furniture designer; born Fondo, Trento.

Biography 1907, Depero began painting and, thence, sculpting and writing, becoming a social realist and focusing on Symbolism; wrote the booklet *Spezzature—Impressioni—Segni e ritmi* (1913; breakings—impressions—signs and rhythms) and met the Futurists in Rome; 1925–26, was active in Paris and, 1928–30, in New York. From early 1930s, his work was more elaborate, ambitious, and dramatic. His work included the manifesto *Futurist Reconstruction of the Universe* (1915) known as 'Complessità plastica—gioco libero futurista—L'essere vivente-artificiale' (plastic complexity—free Futurist play—the living-artificial being). His architectural visions are expressed in *Padiglioni plastici futuristi* (1916) and *Vegetazione a deformazione artificiale* (1916); stage set for *Mimismagia* (1916); Les Ballets Russes's 1916–17 sets for *Nightingale* and *Zoo* (both unrealized); late-1910s wall hangings (with wife Rosetta), furniture, advertising posters, and various applied art works; 1917 'constructions' including brightly colored objects in wood and cardboard; 1921–22 interiors and furnishings for the Devil's Cabaret in Hôtel Élite et des Étrangers, Rome; exhibition of a project for the statue-building to hold Futurist theater-cabaret Polychrome Plastic Luminous Glorification of F.T. Marinetti at 1923 (1st) *Internazionale delle Arti Decorative et Industriali Moderne*, Monza; 1924 Tridentine Venice pavilion, Milan Trade Fair, with advertising stands; 1924 stand for his own Casa d'Arte Futurista; 1924 stand for Campari; 1924 comic-grotesque ballet *Anihccam of the Year 3000*; theater staging of *The New Babel* and costumes for *American Sketches*, both New York; writing of *L'impero* (1925); book pavilion at 1927 (3nd) *Internationale delle Arti Decorative et Industriali Moderne*, Monza; magazine covers of late 1920s and 1930s; renowned bolted-book *Depero Futurista* (Milan: Dinamo-Azari, 1927); advertising designs for Campari and Verzocchi; 1929 interior of Enrico e Paglieri and 1930–31 interior of Zucca restaurants, both New York; 1932 theoretical treatise, *Manifesto of Advertising Art*; as a journalist, contributions to newspapers and magazines; in Rovereto, 1932 almanac *Futurismo 1932—Anno X—F.T. Marinetti nel Trentino* and magazine *Dinamo Futurista*; unpublished 1932 free-word 'sound' book *New York—Film vissuto (*New York—a real-life film*)*; 1934 radio-poetry work *Radio Lyrics*; and one-of-a-kind furniture pieces from 1930s through 1950s.
Exhibitions 1914, at Giuseppe Sprovieri's Galleria Futurista, participating in events with Giacomo Balla, Francesco Cangiullo, and Filippo Tommaso Marinetti; to 1935, continued to show with Futurists. Work shown at 1923 (1st) *Esposizione Biennale delle Arti Decorative e Industriali Moderne*, Monza; and 1928–30 venues in New York. Work subject of 1986 and 1988–89 exhibitions, Rovereto; 1988, Capri; 1990 Sedicesimo Salone del Mobile Triveneto, Padova; 1992, Trento; 1996, Paris; 1999 *Depero Futurista*, The Wolfsonian, Miami Beach, Fla.
Bibliography Pontus Hulten (organizer), *Futurism and Futurisms*, New York: Abbeville, 1986. Cat., Maurizio Scudiero (ed.), *Depero: Casa d'Arte Futurista*, Florence: Cantini, c. 1988. Mario Universo, *Fortunato Depero e il mobile futurista*, Venice: Marsilio, 1990. Bruno Passamani, *La sala del consiglio provinciale di Trento di Fortunato Depero*, Trento: Temi, 1990. *Maurizio Scudiero, Fortunato Depero, stoffe futuriste*, Trento: Calliano, 1995.

DePree, Dirk Jan (1891–1990)

American furniture manufacturer; active Zealand, Mich.; son-in-law of Herman Miller.

Biography 1923, Dirk Jan DePree and his stepfather Herman Miller purchased the majority of the shares of Star Furniture Company and changed the name to Herman Miller Furniture Company. Before hiring Gilbert Rohde as the design director in 1931, the firm produced historicist furniture models. An enthusiastic proponent of the modern movement in Europe, Rohde persuaded DePree to produce some of his modern designs. But, the cautious DePree continued concurrently to issue historicist models. Finally embracing modernism, DePree became an enthusiastic evangelist. On Rohde's 1944 death, DePree hired George Nelson as design director. The firm became highly successful after World War II, particularly after Nelson introduced DePree to Charles Eames, who became its most prominent consultant designer. Others followed Eames, including sculptor Isamu Noguchi, textile designer Alexander Girard, and Paul László. 1950s, DePree encountered Robert Propst, a Colorado sculptor and inventor, who developed the concept of 1964 Action Office 1 (realized by the Nelson group of designers). Action Office, refined as the 1968 Action Office 2, is an open-office configuration of component desks, walls, and furniture that transformed the office environment and Herman Miller's fortunes. DePree was a highly effective salesperson but never a designer himself, who believed in 'design custodianship,' whereby all those in the firm were duty bound to support the success of a design, when it was accepted for production. He devised an arrangement for selling Herman Miller's line through representative firms that often also carried the furniture of other manufacturers, a policy changed in late 1990s. From 1950s, the firm issued an impressive, attractive amount of sales literature, some as hardbound books rather than as traditional catalogs.
Bibliography Cat., *A Modern Consciousness: D.J. DuPree, Florence Knoll*, Washington, D.C.: published for the National Collection of Fine Arts by the Smithsonian Institution Press, 1975. Ralph Caplan, *The Design of Herman Miller*, New York: Whitney, 1976. 'Celebrating Design Innovation,' *Designers West*, Apr. 1991: 34. Leslie S. Piña, *Classic Herman Miller*, Atglen, Pa.: Schiffer, 1998.
> See Herman Miller.

Derain, Gilles (1944–)

French designer; active Paris.

Biography An expert on the history of the decorative arts, Derain designed furniture, lighting, and accessories for Lumen and carpets for Géométrie Variable. His 1979 Merci Chareau Pierre (or MCP) lamp for Lumen Center sold 40,000 copies. 1980s, Derain designed jewelry for Gay Frères, Paris, combining gold and semi-precious stones; was the first French designer to be commissioned to design for Zanotta, Italy, designing its 1985 Omega metal pedestal; 1991, set up own firm to manufacture desk accessories and furnishings. From 1992, his designs were produced by Pentalux. He has since turned to pursuits other than product design.
Exhibitions Work shown at 1989 *L'Art de Vivre* exhibition, Cooper-Hewitt National Design Museum, New York (catalog below); from 1989, Salon du Meuble, Paris; from 1991, Euroluce fair, Milan.
Bibliography Cat., *L'Art de Vivre*, New York: Vendome, 1989. François Mathey, *Au bonheur des formes, design français 1945–1992*, Paris: Regard, 1992: 150, 302.

Derby Silver

American silversmiths; located Derby, Conn.

History 1873, Derby Silver began production, specializing in affordable silverplated hollow-ware. 1879, Watson John Miller, who had managed his own silverplating factory in Middletown, Conn., took control of Derby Silver. Superintendent Thomas H. Newcomb and designer and master mechanic Henry Berry assisted Miller. Derby became known for its high-quality German (or nickel) silver, silver-copper alloy, zinc, and nickel used in the plating process; produced wares in styles to satisfy the taste of the Aesthetic Movement, incorporating *japonisant* motifs, butterflies, cranes, and cattails; 1933, was purchased by International Silver.
Bibliography *Victorian Silverplated Holloware*, Princeton, N.J.: Pyne Press, 1972: 105–06, 109–56. Doreen Bolger Burke et al., *In Pursuit of Beauty: Americans and the Aesthetic Movement*, New York: The Metropolitan Museum of Art/Rizzoli, 1986: 419.

Derossi, Pietro (1933–)

Italian architect, designer, and author; born Turin.

Training To 1959, Politecnico, Turin.
Biography At the Politecnico, Derossi was an assistant to Carlo Molino. His 1960s open-plan structures were configured so that the interiors could be easily changed or rearranged, realized best by the

1968 house in the hills of Lucca (LU), designed with Riccardo Rosso and Giorgio Ceretti (Domodossola, VB, 1932–). The building expresses an approach to easy living or nomadism, a concept also being explored by others in the late 1960s. And Derossi's kindergarten and residential complexes attempted to restore order to the disorganized urban complexes prevailing prior to the 1960s. Rather than his architecture, interior design, and urban planning, Derossi has become best known for the 1971 Pratone expanded polyurethane 'seat,' designed with Rosso and Ceretti. This is especially so now that the Pratone has been re-entered into production by its original manufacturer, Gufram. The 'seat' exemplifies the approach of the Anti-Design movement in Italy at the time and in particular the work of Radical-Design consortium Gruppo Strum, which was founded in Turin in 1966 by Derossi, Ceretti, Rosso, Carla Giammarco, and Maurizio Vogliazzo. Derossi has since become active primarily as a theoretician and an architect.
Bibliography Cristina Morozzi and Silvio San Pietro, *Contemporary Italian Furniture*, Milan: L'Archivolto, 1996. Andrea Branzi, *Il design italiano 1964–1990*, Milano: Elemond, 1996. Cat., Stefano Casciani (ed.), *Design italiano nei musei del mondo 1950–1990*, Milano: Abitare Segesta, 1998. Cat., Franco Mello, Ennio Chiggio, and Stefano Casciani, *The Rock Furniture = Il design della Gufram negli anni del rock*, Turin: Castello di Rivoli. 2002. www.archinform.net.
> See Global Tools.

Design 3 Produktdesign
> See Moggeridge, Bill.

Design and Industries Association (DIA)
British industrial-design organization.

History A group of British artists and craftsmen who had attended the 1914 *Deutscher Werkbund-Ausstellung* (exhibition) in Cologne, were encouraged to persuade the UK Board of Trade to establish a similar design-reform organization in Britain. An exhibition took place and with it was published the pamphlet *Design and Industry: a proposal for the foundation of a Design and Industries Association*. Thus, 1915, the Design and Industries Association was formed to encourage private individuals, manufacturers, and retailers to insist on high standards of design in British industry; the initial membership numbered 199. The first council included James Morton, H.H. Peach, Frank Pick, and Sir Frank Warner from the industrial sector, C.G. Brewer, B.J. Fletcher, Ambrose Heal, C.H. St. John Hornsby, E.F. Jackson, W.R. Lethaby, and Harold Stabler from art and architecture. The association was allotted a section to show articles of good design from retail stores at the 1916 *Arts and Crafts Exhibition* at Burlington House in London. Its membership grew from 292 in 1916 to 602 in 1928. 1916, its small journal was begun with articles attacking poor design and inferior craftsmanship. From 1922, the association began to publish well-written and illustrated yearbooks, modeled on the Deutsche Werkbund yearbooks. It showed its members' works in the British section (organized by H.H. Peach) at the 1927 *Europäisches Kunstgewerbe* exhibition in Leipzig and in exhibits in the British provinces. From early 1930s, the organization focused on raising the quality and lowering the price of consumer goods; members W.F. Crittall, Jack Pritchard, Maxwell Fry, and John Gloag developed the DIA Plan, chaired by Frank Pick; 1932, published the periodical *Design for Industry*, renamed *Design for Today*; 1936–38, published *Trend in Design of Everyday Things*, discontinued due to lack of public interest. Indirectly encouraged by the association was 1933 *British Industrial Art in Relation to the Home* exhibition, London, sponsored by *Country Life* magazine. The Birmingham branch sponsored the 1934 *Midlands Industrial Art Exhibition*. From 1935, the organization sponsored exhibitions in large shops and department stores; goods selected by the association from the stores' stocks were displayed at events held at stores Bowman's, Harrods, Peter Jones, and Whiteleys in London, Furlong's in Woolwich, Kendall Milne in Manchester, Dunn's in Bromley, Jones's in Bristol, and Rowntree's in Scarborough. 1933 and 1934, model home exhibitions were organized. 1938, most of the DIA's activities were curtailed by the threat of war, although exhibitions dealing with housing and domestic design were sent to army camps, art galleries, and schools. DIA principles were complemented by the bases of other contemporary associations (1930 Society of Industrial Artists, 1933 Council for Art and Industry [Frank Pick, chairman], and 1944 Council of Industrial Design), so that the DIA was to a large extent replaced by its progeny; 1953, sponsored *Register Your Choice* exhibition, Charing Cross Underground station, London—60% of commuters voted for a 'contemporary' room, 40% preferred a 'reproduction' or historicist room. The DIA is still active today as a forum for discussion.
Bibliography Michael Farr, *Design in British Industry: A Mid-Century Survey*, London: Cambridge, 1955: 192–98. Cat., *Thirties: British Art and Design Before the War*, London: Arts Council of Great Britain/Hayward Gallery, 1979.

Design Central
American design studio.

History 1985, Design Central was established in Columbus, Ohio, with concurrent additional offices in San Francisco and Hollis, N.H. The principals are Rainer Teufel, Gregg Davis, and Deb Davis-Livaich. Clients include Artromick, Caterpillar, Daewoo, General Electric Europe, Mead, Nike, Rubbermaid, Siemens, Sunbeam, and Whirlpool.
Citations 1989, 1994, 1995, 1999, 2000 IDSA/*Business Week* awards; 1996 award, Industrie Forum Design (iF), Hanover; 1996, 2000, 2001 *Appliance Manufacturer* magazine awards; 2000 Gold award, American Society for the Aging.
Bibliography Cat., R. Craig Miller (intro.), *U.S. Design: 1975–2000*, Munich: Prestel, 2002.

Design Continuum
> See Zaccai, Gianfranco.

Design Exchange, The (DX)
Canadian industrial-design collection.

History 1945, The Design Exchange was established as the only institution with a mandate to preserve modern Canadian industrial-design history. With few pieces still in existence in some cases, the organization's aim was to retrieve some notable examples. For instance, some examples of 1963 Lollipop tandem-seating system by Robin Bush were rescued from the Toronto Island Airport, which was about to discard them. Aug. 1996, the DX began to actively and systematically collect examples of notable Canadian design. Since then, the collection has grown to include historical and contemporary examples of the decorative arts, furniture, graphic design, housewares, lighting, medical equipment, sporting goods, and tableware. A 1997 45-cent Canada Post stamp series acknowledged Canadian industrial design; 16 of the 22 items depicted are in the DX collection. Selected objects are on permanent display in DX's Exhibition Hall and Resource Centre in Toronto. The DX established the Design Effectiveness Awards with gold and silver categories, the only Canadian multidisciplinary citations to judge work on its commerical success, rather than its aesthetic values, which can be fickle as times change.
Bibliography www.dx.org.

Design Group Italia
Italian design cooperative studio.

History 1968, the industrial-design studio was founded by Edgardo Angelini (Pennabilli, Italy, 1959–), Ross De Salvo (Kidderminster, UK, 1955–), Sigurdur Thorsteinsson (Reykjavik, Iceland, 1965–), and Marco Del Corno (Milan, Italy, 1924–). Angelini graduated from Instituto Superiore Industrie Artistiche, Rome, 1982, and Domus Academy, Milan, 1984; De Salvo from ISSAM, Modena, 1978, and Instituto Superiore Industrie Artistiche, Rome, 1982; Thorsteinsson from Instituto Europeo Design, Milan, 1992; Del Corno from Accademia di Belle Arti di Brera, Milan. The studio's design work has included electronic equipment, recording instruments, and housewares. Projects have included the Pulsar electronic telephone by Sip, and 1994 Nos (new opening system) by CAS. Product clients: Jacuzzi, Magis, Resinart Plastics, Tupperware, and Vetta cycling components. Packaging clients: Ala Zignago, Meseta, Ponti, and Splendid. Design staff members have included Gianni Arduini, Franco Butti, Tullio Merlini, Luigia Micciantuono, Maria Gemma Piva, Paolo Rognoni, Franco Salvemini, and Ennio Saska.
Citations 1979 (three citations), 1981 (two citations), 1989, 1991 (two citations), 1994, and 1998 Premio Compasso d'Oro; 1994 (two citations), 1997, and 1999 awards, Industrie Forum Design (iF), Hanover; 1994, 1996 (four citations), and 1997 Red Dot award, Design Zentrum Nordrhein Westfalen, Essen; 1994 Design Auswhal, Stuttgart; Top Ten prize, 1994 Salone Internazionale della Sedia (Promodedia), Udine; 1998 design award, Norska Designrådet (ND, Norwegian design council); 1999 Premio INTEL Design, Milan; 1981, 1988, and 1994 (two citations), BIO 14 industrial-design biennial, Ljubljana; 1988 Janus de l'industrie, Paris; 1982 Premio SMAU Industrial Design, Salone della Machina e Attrezzature per l'Ufficio, Milan; 1994 Les

Electro, Paris; 1999 (three citations) and 2000 Design Index, ADI.
Bibliography Alfonso Grassi and Anty Pansera, *Atlante del design italiano 1940/1980*, Milan: Fabbri 1980. Cat., Hans Wichmann, *Italien Design 1945 bis heute*, Munich: Sammlung, 1988. Vittorio Gregotti, *Il disegno del prodotto industriale 1860–1980*, Milan, 1988. Anty Pansera, *Storia del disegno industriale in Italia*, Bari: Laterza, 1993. Anty Pansera, *Dizionario del design italiano*, Milan: Cantini, 1995. Andrea Branzi, *Il design italiano 1964/1990: per un museo del design italiano*, Milan: Electa with Triennale di Milan, 1996. Annamaria Scevola and Silvio San Pietro, *Il prodotto industriale italiano contemporaneo*, Milan: L'Archivolto, 1999. Giuliana Gramigna and Paola Biondi, *Il design in Italia dell'arredamento domestico*, Turin: Allemandi, 1999. Claudia Neumann, *Design Lexikon Italien*, Cologne: DuMont, 1999.

Design House Stockholm

Danish firm; located Copenhagen.

History 1992, Design House Stockholm was founded by Anders Färdig (1951–). A chain of stores was established, and a wide range of many products has been produced—from cutlery, dinnerware, and tabletop objects to seating, tables, and lighting. More than 25 people have designed for the firm, including Jan Berg, Jonas Grundell, Signe Persson-Melin, Timo Sarpaneva, Rolf Sinnemark, and Kristina Starck. Its 1995–96 Block lamp, and subsequent 2000 Mini Block lamp (both made of two solid pieces of clear glass) by Harri Koskinen has become well known. 2000, the firm was bought by Expanda Design Group, within which are also Abstracta, Atran, BCI, Eurobib, Galleri Stolen/Gärsnäs, Lammhults, Scandinavian Eyewear (Scanda), and Voice Furniture.
Bibliography www.designhousestockholm.com.

Design Logic

American design consultancy.

History David Gresham (a graduate of Cranbrook Academy of Art, Academy, Bloomfield Hills, Mich.) designed a video camera for RCA; worked for IBM. Martin Thaler (graduate of Royal College of Art, London) worked at Siemens, Munich. They both taught in the department of design, Illinois Institute of Technology (IIT), Chicago, and, 1983, founded the design consultancy Design Logic. The firm restyled the 3-D Viewer and designed toys by View-Master Ideal Group, answering machines by Dictaphone, as well as other work including conducting design research for RC computer company and Bang & Olufsen, both Denmark.
Bibliography Cat., R. Craig Miller (intro.), *U.S. Design: 1975–2000*, Munich: Prestel, 2002.

Designor
> See HackmanGroup.

Designum

Dutch tabletop-products manufacturer.

History 1980, Designum was cofounded by Paul Schudel (1951–) to produce contemporary domestic accessories designed by young and by experienced Dutch designers, including Schude himself and Ruud-Jan Kokke, Herman Hermsen, Erik-Jan Kwakkel, Dick van Hoff, Benne Premsela, Ine van der Sluis, Arnout Visser, and Ed Wilhelm. Schudel has become best known for his 1980 DK glass wall clock whose frameless, numberless face is sandblasted glass with the hands placed behind. Other designs include van der Sluis's 1986 VI plastic vase, Kokke's 1990 TC bentwood stool, Schudel 1991 AKW wall clock, Visser's 1993 FW fruit bowl on wheels, Hermsen's 1992 BF and 1993 BS letter openers, Wilhelm's 2000 EV glass vases

Designum: Paul Schudel. DK wall clock. 1980. Frosted glass and plastic, h. 2 x dia. 15" (5.1 x 38.1 cm). Mfr.: Designum, the Netherlands (1997). Gift of Ameico, Inc. MoMA.

Deskey, Donald (1894–1989)

American industrial, furniture, and interior designer; born Blue Earth, Minn.; active New York.

Training Architecture, University of California at Berkeley; painting, Art Students League, New York; School of the Art Institute of Chicago, Ill.; Académie de la Grande Chaumière, Paris.
Biography With Raymond Loewy, Norman Bel Geddes, and Henry Dreyfuss, Deskey was one of the earliest consultant designers in US; 1920, began his career as a graphic designer at an advertising agency in Chicago; was greatly influenced by his visit to 1925 *Exposition Internationale des Arts Décoratifs et Industriels Modernes*, Paris; 1926, became active as an interior designer in New York. His first commissions were modern display windows for Saks Fifth Avenue and Franklin Simon department stores. He produced hand-painted screens for Paul Frankl's gallery; designed the interiors of apartments for prominent clients, including Adam Gimbel; 1927, became an associate of Phillip Vollmer, setting up Deskey-Vollmer, a firm specializing in lighting and furnishings which was active to early 1930s. Deskey's 1927 Zigzag table lamp is particularly distinctive. 1932–33, he came to prominence as the competition-winning creator of the furniture and furnishing for Radio City Music Hall, a tour de force of glamorous American modernism with murals by Witold Gordon, paintings by Stuart Davis, and fabrics by Ruth Reeves. All of Deskey's late 1920s designs had been custom-made for wealthy clients; however, in the 1930s, he collaborated with mass manufacturers such as Widdicomb Furniture Company. One of the great modernist figures of the 1930s, his work was characterized by experimentation with new materials, including aluminum, cork, and linoleum, and his furniture incorporated Bakelite and aluminum; late 1920s, invented a stained-wood laminate called Weldtex. Deskey also designed exhibitions, products, and packaging; to c. 1970, was active in his own industrial-design firm; designed a lighting fixture, reissued in 1990s by Écart International. In the later part of his career, he specialized in packaging. The Deskey archive is housed in the Cooper-Hewitt National Design Museum in New York.
Exhibitions With Walter von Nessen, sculptor William Zorach, Paul Frankl, and others, work shown at John Cotton Dana's 1929 *Modern American Design in Metal*, Newark Museum, Newark, N.J. Dining room installed in West Gallery (Ely Jacques Kahn, director), 1935 *Contemporary American Industrial Art* exhibition, The Metropolitan Museum of Art, New York.
Bibliography Karen Davies, *At Home in Manhattan: Modern Decorative Arts, 1925 to the Depression*, New Haven: Yale, 1983. David A. Hanks and Jennifer Toher, *Donald Deskey*, New York: Dutton, 1987.

Desny, La Maison

French design firm; located Paris.

History 1927–33, La Maison Desny was active at 122, avenue des Champs-Elysées in Paris. The principals of the firm were the designers Desnet and René Mauny (or possibly Nauny), and financial backer Tricot. There was a staff designer, Louis Poulain. (Desnet and Mauny were formerly sketch artists for the circus.) The firm became known for its innovative modern lighting fixtures that incorporated glass and chrome-plated metal; also produced silverware, bath accessories, carpets, and murals. Its work was characterized by severe geometric forms and plain surfaces and influenced by Cubism. Though of a distinctly modern spirit, it often included the use of exotic woods and other expensive materials. Its furniture sometimes had aluminum components. 1931, it received commissions to design the interiors of the apartments of Georges-Henri Rivière and Pierre David-Weill and the highly sophisticated, elegant quarters of Mlle. Thurnauer. For ambient lighting, the firm produced its chromium-plated sconces, chandeliers, and floor lamps with concealed bulbs, and a range of illuminated bibelots in clear glass and in metal. For task lighting, it offered

Desny. Cocktail goblets. c. 1930. Silver, each h. 4 3/4 x dia. 3" (12.1 x 7.6 cm). Mfr: Desny, France. Philip Johnson Fund. MoMA.

'genre spot lights.' Commissioned designers included André Masson (painted panels), Alberto and Diego Giacometti (fire dogs and crystal lamp bases in the apartment of David-Weill), Jean-Michel Frank (parchment walls in the Thurnauer apartment), Djo-Bourgeois, and, with whom Desny was associated on several decorating projects, Robert Mallet-Stevens. 1933 when Desnet died, the business closed. René Mauny later opened a small chain of costume-jewelry shops called Hippocampe in Paris and Lyon, and designed some of the jewelry himself.
Bibliography Alastair Duncan, *Art Nouveau and Art Déco Lighting*, New York: Simon & Schuster, 1978. Cat., Aaron Lederfajn and Xavier Lenormand (eds.), *Le Louvre des Antiquaires présente: 1930 quand le meuble devient sculpture*, Paris, 1986. Pierre Kjellberg, *Art déco: les maîtres du mobilier, le décor des paquebots*, Paris: Amateur, 1986/1990. Alastair Duncan and Audrey Friedman, 'La Maison Desny,' *Journal of Decorative and Propaganda Arts*, Summer 1988: 86–93.

Desombre, Thibault (1958–)

French designer; born Lille; active Montpellier.

Training Cabinetmaking; École Nationale Supérieure des Arts Décoratifs, Paris.
Biography 1981, Desombre settled in Paris; designed some 1983 furniture for the Palais de l'Élysée and 1992 Camille side chair by Soca Line, 1994 Mondo sofa and chair and 1994 Finn wooden chair by Ligne Roset, which began his association with Ligne Roset and its Cinna division. 1996, left Paris for Montpellier; designed 1999 Soho sofa and Luna chair and bridge table by Cinna; has become known for furniture, primarily in wood, that reveals his crafts background, as exemplified by the Finn chair.
Exhibitions/citations Work was subject of 2002 *Thibault Desombre: en Pleines Formes Design*, Galerie VIA (French furniture association), Paris. 1989, 1990, and 1991 Appel Permanent grants and 1994 Carte Blanche production support, VIA. At Salon du Meuble editions, Paris: 1988 Creator of the Year, 1990 Critique d'Art grand prize (for Zina chair by Soca Line), 1993 Grand Prix de la Critique et de la Presse, 1994 Contemporary furniture prize (to Desombre and Soca Line).
Bibliography Cat., Sophie Tasma Anargyros et al., *L'école française: les créateurs de meubles du 20ème siècle*, Paris: Industries Françaises de l'Ameublement, 2000.

Desprès, Jean (1889–1980)

French silversmith and jeweler; born Souvigny; active Paris.

Training In jewelry in Avallon village, France; in silver- and goldsmithing, Paris; painting.
Biography An airplane pilot and aeronautical draftsperson, Desprès acquired a fascination for machinery and geometrical forms. He established his own gallery and workshop in Paris, making and selling silver, gold, and pewter objects, and jewelry in severe geometric silhouettes. However, due to his only weekly visits to the gallery, customers preferred visits to his workshop, often to inspect drawings of Desprès's work-in-progress. His work looked as if it were produced by machines rather than by hands, with quasi-technical ornamentation applied to smooth, shiny surfaces. Unlike other smiths working in leading ateliers or for independent artisans, he also made his own designs for jewelry and silver; c. 1930 with Etienne Cournault, collaborated on Surrealist jewelry forms; 1934, became director of Galerie de l'Art et de la Mode, Paris; was frequently associated with the jewelry activities of Union des Artistes Modernes (UAM). He died in Avallon, where he had a boutique in the center of the village.
Exhibitions/citations From 1929, pewter work included in Salons of Société des Artistes Décorateurs and, from 1930, at UAM exhibitions. Dressing table set was shown at 1925 *Exposition Internationale des Arts Décoratifs et Industriels Modernes*. Work shown at various international exhibitions, including editions of Salon des Indépendants and 1937 *Exposition Internationale des Arts et Techniques dans la Vie Moderne* (diploma of honor). 1935 gold medal, Aéro-Club de France. All Paris.
Bibliography Victor Arwas, *Art Déco*, New York: Abrams, 1980. Pierre Cabanne, *Encyclopédie art déco*, Paris: Somogy, 1986. Annelies Krekel-Aalberse, Art *Nouveau and Art Déco Silver*, New York: Abrams, 1989.

Despret, Georges (1862–1952)

French glass designer.

Training Université de Liège.
Biography 1884, Despret became director of Glacerie de Jeumont, a mass producer of window glass and mirrors; while working in a research studio at the Jeumont factory, rediscovered the secret of polychrome *pâte-de-verre*; reinterpreted Japanese themes freely in his work, often applying them to cups, vases, and small sculptures made in thick-walled and lumpy *pâte-de-verre* designed for mass production; used *pâte-de-verre* to imitate marble, onyx, agate, and even stoneware; 1908, founded Compagnie Réunie des Glaces et Verres Spéciaux du Nord de la France.
Exhibitions After several exhibitions, his work (with Géo Nicolet) was shown at 1900 *Exposition Universelle*, Paris.
Bibliography Yvonne Brunhammer et al., *Art Nouveau Belgium, France*, Houston: Rice University, 1976. Cat., *Verriers français contemporains: art et industrie*, Paris: Musée des Arts Décoratifs, 1982.

Dessau, Ingrid (1923–2000)

Swedish textile and industrial designer.

Training 1939–35, Kungliga Tekniska Högskolan, Stockholm.
Biography 1945–49, she worked for the Kristianstads Läns Hemslöjdsförening (handcraft society of Kristianstad County); from 1954–78, designed for Kasthalls Mattfabrik and, 1970–84, for Kinnasand. From 1953 also for others, she was a freelance designer of hand-knotted and hand-tufted carpets and of textiles installed in many public interiors; produced rya and knotted pile weaving and was perhaps more interested in the *rölakan*, and basket weave or double weave.
Exhibitions/citations Work included in 1996–97 group show, Röhsska Museet, Gothenberg (catalog below). 1955 Lunning Prize.
Bibliography Cat., *Möbler Bruno Mathsson, mattor Ingrid Dessau, tygtryck Borás Wäfveri*, Stockholm: Nationalmuseum, 1958. Cat., *Torun Vivianna Bülow-Hübe, Ingrid Dessau, Signe Persson-Melin: klassiker i svensk formgivning*, Gothenberg: Röhsska Museet, 1996.

Dessonnaz, Georges

Swiss inventor; active Fribourg.

Biography Dessonnaz designed the 1940 Gedess Minenschärfer (pencil sharpener; patented in the US in 1941). It is comprised of only four parts and has a single screw and a rotating ball-bearing finial. 1944, the firm Kuhn in Zürich bought the rights to the now legendary device and has since been the producer.

DESTA
> See Deutsche Stahlmöbel.

Desvallières, Richard (1893–1962)

French metalworker; born and active Paris.

Biography Desvallières used medieval forging techniques; rejected industrial methods; produced wrought-iron work for interiors, particularly in 1920s–30s, including those designed by Louis Süe/André Mare at Compagnie des Arts Français for their various commissions. The banister in the reception hall of the 1924–25 villa of actress Jane Renouardt at 2, avenue Buzenval, Saint-Cloud, is one such example. In his workshop, he wrought grilles, fire dogs, fire screens, tables, consoles, and étagères; made the choir stall and other ironwork for

the Église de Sainte-Agnès in Maison-Alfort.
Exhibitions Ironwork for the Cubist house of Raymond Duchamp-Villon shown at 1912 Salon d'Automne; cockerel weather vane in 1920 Salon d'Automne; numerous grilles at 1925 *Exposition Internationale des Arts Décoratifs et Industriels Modernes*. All Paris.
Bibliography Léon Deshairs (intro.), *Modern French Decorative Art: A Collection of Examples of Modern French Decoration*, Paris: Albert Lévy, c. 1925–30. Pierre Kjellberg, *Art déco: les maîtres du mobilier, le décor des paquebots*, Paris: Amateur, 1986/1990.

Deuber, Christian (1965–)
> See N2.

Deutsche Stahlmöbel (DESTA)

German manufacturer; located Berlin.

History 1929, Hungarian businessman Anton Lorenz established Deutsche Stahlmöbel to manufacture bent tubular-steel furniture, setting it up in a workshop formerly occupied by Standardmöbel at Teltowerstrasse 47–48, Berlin, which had been bought by Thonet. Lorenz won the 1929 suit filed against him by Thonet, giving DESTA sole rights to the cantilever-chair design principle. Lorenz then sold Thonet rights for resilient tubular-steel furniture. 1933, DESTA closed, although Lorenz continued using the DESTA name to 1935.
Bibliography Otakar Máčel, 'Avant-garde Design and the Law: Litigation over the Cantilever Chair,' *Journal of Design History*, vol. 3, nos. 2 and 3, 1990: 125–35.
> See tubular-steel furniture.

Deutsche Werkstätten für Handwerkskunst

German arts and crafts group.

History The story of the Deutsche Werkstätten für Handwerkskunst (German workshop for arts and crafts) began in 1898 with Karl Schmidt (Zschopau, 1873–Hellerau, 1948) and his carpentry workshop, Bau-Möbelfabrik und Fabrik kunstgewerblicher Gegenstände. He began producing simple, modern 'reform' furniture and showed it at various exhibitions around 1900. The furniture—designed by well-known 'reform' proponents (those reacting against inferior mass-production)—was a compromise between low-cost machine production (with handcrafting) and tasteful design. 1907, the workshop was combined with the efforts of the Münchner Werkstätten für Wohnungseinrichtung (Munich workshops for furnishing) and, 1910, moved to Hellerau. (1908, Schmidt was an initiator of Hellerau's becoming a garden city with housing for its workers. He had prior become familiar with the garden-city concept while in England.) Apart from the various residential complexes in Hellerau, Richard Riemerschmid designed a factory there. 1913, the enterprise was converted into a corporation and, thus, quickly became one of the most important German manufacturers of 'good design' furniture, in contrast to most mass-produced furniture by others in Germany at the time. 1927, began producing *Typenmöbel* ('type' or standardized furniture). Bruno Paul, one of the most respected designers of the time, also contributed designs. Having financial trouble due to the Great Depression, the workshop was nevertheless saved from bankruptcy in 1930 and, 1946, was expropriated by the Deutsche Werkstätten Hellerau under the pretext of Schmidt's participation being necessary in the wartime economy. Karl Schmidt, whose firm had been called Schmidt Hellerau since 1938, separated from the organization. 1950s–60s, designers included Franz Ehrlich, a former Bauhaus student and concentration-camp prisoner, and Rudolph Horn. 1992, the company became private again, no longer governmental, but furniture production greatly decreased. Since 1996, concentration has been on domestic and commercial interior design. Today, the main building at the Moritzburger houses various enterprises and, 1995, the Werksmuseum was established there.
Bibliography Hans Wickmann, *Deutsche Werkstätten und WK-Verband, 1898-1990,* Munich: Prestel, 1992.

Deutscher Werkbund

German artistic and production association.

History 1907, the Deutscher Werkbund was founded by Peter Bruckmann (also its first president), Peter Behrens, Hermann Muthesius, Josef Maria Olbrich, Fritz Schumacher, and Richard Riemerschmid. By 1909, membership had increased to 700, including Henry van de Velde, Ludwig Mies van der Rohe, Walter Gropius, and Friedrich Neumann. Members, who included architects, industrialists, craftspeople, teachers, and publicists, argued that German products must be improved technically and aesthetically in order to compete abroad. Sharing the ideals of the Arts and Crafts movement in Britain, the Werkbund sought to revive the prestige of craft skills through a collaborative effort of art and industry, and a campaign of propaganda and education. Karl Scheffer was straightforward about revealing that the Germans wished to capture the clientele of the Paris furniture makers: 'German industrial artists understand that it is not simply a question of aesthetics, but a question of life and death.... We have to create an art industry that is capable of becoming a world-wide industry' (catalog of the 1910 *Exposition Internationale*, Brussels). Some industrialists recognized the commercial advantages of producing tasteful modern goods; for example, in 1907, AEG founder Emil Rathenau hired Peter Behrens as designer of the firm's factories, corporate graphics, products (including lighting), and workers' estates. New developments illustrated in 1912–20 yearbooks of the Deutscher Werkbund included automobiles by Ernst Naumann; factories by Hans Poelzig, Behrens, and Walter Gropius; steamship interiors by Bruno Paul; railway coaches by Gropius; and furniture produced by the Deutsche Werkstätten für Handwerkskunst, Hellerau, near Dresden. The Deutscher Werkbund organized one of the most important exhibitions of industrial design of the 20th century, the 1914 *Deutscher Werkbund-Ausstellung* in Cologne. It was an impressive manifestation of the modern movement in Germany, showing Bruno Taut's Glass Pavilion, Gropius's model factory building, and Henry van de Velde's Werkbund Theater. A vigorous debate ensued among members on the relative importance of individual design and industrial standardization. Muthesius's attempt to reconcile the two opposing principles was resisted by van de Velde, supported by Taut and Gropius, all three being against any suggestion of canon or standardization. 1919, Poelzig delivered a speech in Stuttgart opposing the mass-production approach advocated by Muthesius and Naumann and reaffirming handicraft as the standard for the Werkbund. Meanwhile, Gropius, as head of the newly formed Bauhaus, suggested that humanity's needs could be best served by the machine. The Werkbund undertook a bold and unique project at *Die Wohnung* exhibition, 1927 *Weissenhofsiedlung*, Stuttgart, under the supervision of Ludwig Mies van der Rohe. Modernist architects and practitioners throughout Europe were invited to realize their ideas. Mart Stam's 1925 cantilever tubular-steel chair with leather seat and back-rest was shown; Mies's own cantilever steel chair, the Weissenhof in wicker and tubular steel, was exhibited for the first time. In the house designed by Gropius at the *Die Wohnung* exhibition at Weis-senhof, there were beds made from metal tubes by Le Corbusier and Alfred Roth that could be folded away during the day. Most of the furniture at *Die Wohnung* was by Marcel Breuer. Similar exhibitions followed in Breslau (now Wroclaw, Poland) 1929 and Vienna 1932. The Werkbund stand at 1930 (20th) Salon of Société des Artistes Décorateurs, Paris, was less than successful and, designed by Gropius with interiors and furniture by Marcel Breuer, focused on the efforts of the Bauhaus rather than the Werkbund, though the tubular-steel furniture shown created a sensation. Divided by the advent of the Third Reich, the Werkbund's conservative members, including Mies and Winfried Wendland, sought an accommodation with the Nazis; 1934, the organization discontinued its activities (without an official dissolution), although the Nazis attempted to co-opt the Werkbund's principles through the Amt Schönheit der Arbeit (office for the beauty of work). Revived in 1947, the Werkbund designed the German pavilion at 1958 *Exposition Universelle et Internationale de Bruxelles* (*Expo '58*). The buildings by Egon Eiermann and Sep Ruf, objects, and gardens by Walter Rassow demonstrated that Germany had returned to high quality in design. Never interested in the superficial aspects of mere 'good form,' the Werkbund was nevertheless dubbed by critics the Tassenwerkbund (coffee-cup Werkbund), implying that it was merely concerned with the design of trivial objects rather than with all aspects of the environment beyond the narrow parameters of industrial culture. Its early journals included *Jahrbücher des Deutschen Werkbundes* 1912–15, 1917, and 1920, and *Die Form* 1922 and 1925–34. Later efforts were documented in the journal *Werk und Zeit* from 1952.
Bibliography Karl Scheffer, Official catalog for the German pavilion of the 1910 *Exposition Internationale*, Brussels. Gordon Logie, *Furniture from Machines*, London, 1933. Cat., *Zwischen Kunst und Industrie: Der Deutscher Werkbund,* Munich: Die Neue Sammlung, 1975. Joan Campbell, *The German Werkbund, The Polity of Reform in the Applied Arts*, Princeton, N.J.: Princeton University, 1978. Lucius Burckhardt (ed.), *The Werkbund: Studies in the History and Ideology of the Deutscher Werkbund 1907–1933*, London: The Design Council, 1980. Kurt Junghanns, *Der Deutscher Werkbund: Sein erstes Jahrzehnt,*

Freda Diamond. Classic Crystal glasses. 1949. Glass, tallest h. 5 1/4 x dia. 3 3/16" (13.4 x 8.1 cm), shortest h. 3 1/2 x dia. 2 5/8" (8.9 x 6.6 cm). Mfr.: Libbey Glass Company Division, Owens-Illinois Co., US. Given anonymously. MoMA.

Berlin: Henschelverlag, 1982. *75 Jahre Deutscher Werkbund*, Frankfurt, 1983. Ot Hoffmann (ed.), *Der Deutscher Werkbund—1907, 1947, 1987...*, Berlin: Ernst & Sohn, 1987. 'Documents,' *Journal of Design History*, vol. 3, nos. 2 and 3, 1990: 167–68. Karin Kirsch, *The Weissenhofseidlung*, New York: Rizzoli, 1992.

Devesa, Sergi (1961–); Oscar Devesa (1963–)

Spanish designers; brothers; born Barcelona.

Training Both: 1980–81, design studios of Llotja Escola Superior d'Arts Plàstiques i Disseny; 1981–83, Escuela de Diseño Básico; 1983–86, Elisava (Escola Superior de Disseny); all Barcelona.
Biography 1987, the brothers set up studio D&D Design for the design of residential and office furniture/furnishings, lighting, bathroom fittings, and packaging for clients including Blauet, IBP–Supergrif (Grupo Delta), Oken, Grober, Bike-Romanes, and Metalarte. Work has included 1990 Zen all-metal table light by Metalarte and 1988 Chincheta coffee table by Disform, both widely published. They have also designed exhibitions.
Exhibitions Participated in 1988–93 *Design in Catalonia*, traveling worldwide; 1989–90 *JAL Design Review Barcelona: The Emerging Design*, traveling, first in Tokyo; 1989 (5th) D.E.A. (Design Europeo Anteprima), Milan; 1990 *Iberdiseño 90*, Gran Casino de Barcelona; 1992 selection, *Diseño de España*, Japan Industrial Design Promotion Organization (JIDPO), traveling from Tokyo; 1996 *Design and Identity: Aspects of European Design*, Louisiana Museum for Moderne Kunst, Humlebæk, Denmark; 1998 BIO 16 industrial-design biennial, Ljubljana; 1999 *Futur Compost: el Disseny de Barcelona per al Segle Vinent*, Barcelona; and others.
Bibliography *Anuari del Disseny a Catalunya*, Barcelona: BCD, 1987–93. Óscar Tusquets (ed.), *The International Design Yearbook*, London: Thames & Hudson, 1990. *European Community Design Prize*, Barcelona: BCD, 1990. Albrecht Bangert and Karl Michael Armer, *80's Style: Designs of the Decade*, New York: Abbeville, 1990. Mel Byars, *50 Tables...*, Hove: RotoVision, 1997. Mel Byars, *50 Lights...*, Hove: RotoVision, 1997.

Devětsil

Czech artists' and writers' group; active Prague.

History 1920, the Devětsil association was founded by Karel Teige; proclaimed a program of Czech Purism and Poetism with members, including Josef Chochol, Bĕdrich Rozehnal (a collaborator of French architect Auguste Perret), Josef Havlícek, and Jaromír Krejcar. Devětsil's most active members were 'The Four Purists': Jaroslav Frágner, Karel Honzík, Evžen Linhart, and Vít Obrtel. Krejcar wrote *Život II* (1922–23), his almanac of new aesthetics, which encouraged Czech artists to develop contacts in international centers of architecture, art, theater, film, music, and literature. The group's poets and writers, who included Vĕtĕzslav Nezval, Vladimír Vanícura, and Jaroslav Seifert, stressed the poetic aspects of architecture. Devětsil's journals were *DISK*, *Pásmo*, and *ReD*.
Bibliography Vladimir Šlapeta, *Czech Functionalism*, London: Architectural Association, 1987: 9. Cat., *Devětsil: The Czech Avant-Garde of the 1920s and 30s*, Oxford: Museum of Modern Art; London: Design Museum; 1990.

Di Bartolomei, Fabio (1954–)

Italian designer.

Training 1975–78, Istituto Universitario di Architettura, Venice.
Biography 1975–79, Di Bartolomei worked in the studio of architect Walter Rizzi in Udine; 1979, set up his own studio in Udine; established branches in New York and Warsaw in 1998 and Brendale, Brisbane, Australia, in 2002. Beginning with 1984–86 Sguish lamp range and 1986 Trasparia sconce, his body of design work, often incorporating glass, is large and has included furniture, furnishings, and other lamps by Tonon, Fiam, Rossi di Albizzate, Cidue, PSM, Frag, and others. More recently, designed 2001 Key West, King, and Link side chair/armchair by NFK International and 2002 Oasi, Easy, and On-Line side and armchairs by IMS. He has written the cultural column 'Design & Designer' in the architectural section of *Messaggero Veneto*, a daily newspaper.
Exhibitions/citations Work included in 1995 exhibition, The Museum of Modern Art, New York, and traveling (catalog below); 1996 *Designers of the Veneto Region*, Verona. 1991 Young and Design award, Milan; 1996 Marcello d'Olivo design award, Italy; Top Ten prize (for Shuttle chair and My Chair by PSM), 1997 and 1999 Salone Internazionale della Sedia (Promodedia), Udine.
Bibliography Cat., Paola Antonelli, *Mutant Materials in Contemporary Design*, New York: The Museum of Modern Art/Abrams, 1995.

Di Sarno, Flavio (1978–)
> See Nó Design.

Di Somma, Giuseppe (1962–)

Italian designer; born Taranto; active Florence.

Training 1976–80, Liceo Artistico Statale 'Lisippo,' Taranto; 1983–84, advertising graphics, Regione Toscana, Florence; 1980, architecture, Università degli Studi, Florence.
Biography 1983–86, Di Somma was active with the multimedia group Syntax Error, which he cofounded with Nunzia Paola Carallo and Vincenzo Lauriola, for fashion, graphic, and interior design, and performance art; 1986–88, participated with theater group Orient Express and, 1988–89, with theater group Macchine di Bosco, designing sets and videos; 1990, set up his own studio for the design of interiors, products, and graphics for clients, including Aquilonedue, Bertocci, Crunch New York, Molteni & Molteni, Nichibei, Oceano Oltreluce, and Steel; from 1993, assistant instructor, interior design, under architect R. Buti, Facoltà di Architettura of the university in Florence; from 1994, art director of Romanini shoe manufacturer; from 2001, exhibition designer for Perry Ellis America.
Bibliography Fumio Shimizu and Studio Matteo Thun (eds.), *The Italian Design: Descendants of Leonardo da Vinci*, Tokyo: Graphic-sha, 1987. Fumio Shimuzu, *Interior Design*, Tokyo: Graphic-sha, 1988.

Samuele Mazza, *Reggi-Secolo*, Milan: Idea, 1992. Samuele Mazza, *Scarperentola*, Milan: Idea, 1993. Fumio Shimizu, *Euro Design*, Tokyo: Graphic-sha, 1993. San Pietro and Paola Gallo, *Nuovi negozi a Milano 2*, Milan: L'Archivolto, 1994. L. Basso Peressut et al, *L'architettura del caffé*, Milan: Abitare Segesta, 1994. Samuele Mazza, *Imprevisto*, Milan: Idea, 1995. Samuele Mazza, *Contenitorio*, Milan: Idea, 1996.
> See Carallo, Nunzia Paola.

Diaghilev, Sergei Pavlovich (1872–1929)

Russian theatrical impresario; born Novgorod province.

Biography Diaghilev was the creator and impresario of Les Ballets Russes, which arrived in Paris 1909 and in London 1911. Diaghilev had already presented Russian bass singer Feodor Chaliapin in a season of Russian opera in Paris 1908. Important works were *Les sylphides* (1909), *L'oiseau de feu* (1910), *Le spectre de la rose* (1911), *Petroushka* (1911), *L'après-midi d'un faune* (1912), *Le sacre du printemps* (1913), *Le chanson du rossignol* (1920), *Apollo* (1928), and *Le fils prodigue* (1929). The bright colors used in the work of his set and costume designers, particularly Léon Bakst, influenced 1920s interiors. Other set and costume designers were Alexandre Benois, Henri Matisse, Pablo Picasso, Marie Laurencin, Natalia Goncharova, and Georges Braque. Diaghilev's troupe included dancers Vaslav Nijinsky, Tamara Karsavina, and Lydia Lopokova; choreographers Michel Fokine and Léonide Massine; and composers Claude Debussy, Maurice Ravel, Igor Stravinskii, and Sergei Prokofiev. After Diaghilev died in poverty, the 20-year-old company's properties were claimed by creditors, and the dancers dispersed. 1931, Colonel V. de Basil, a former Russian army officer, reunited many of Diaghilev's dancers and choreographers as Les Ballet Russes, which disbanded after his death in 1952. In Monaco, Massine and others formed Les Ballets Russes de Monte Carlo in 1937, managed by Russian banker Serge Denham, to continue the great tradition of the original Ballets Russes. At the outbreak of World War II, the troupe relocated in the US. However, a number of other splinter groups were formed before and after the war, and New York City Ballet, American Ballet Theater, and San Francisco Ballet Company are direct descendants of Diaghilev's Ballets Russes.
Bibliography Richard Buckle, *Diaghilev*, London: Weidenfeld & Nicolson, 1979. Lynn Garafola, *Diaghilev's Ballets Russes*, New York: Oxford, 1989. Militsa Pozharskaya and Tatiana Volodina, *The Art of the Ballets Russes: The Russian Seasons in Paris 1908–1929*, London: Aurum, 1990.

Diamond, Freda (1905–1998)

American glassware designer.

Training Women's Art School, The Cooper Union for the Advancement of Science and Art, New York.
Biography Diamond worked for William Baumgarten, a high-end furniture store in New York, with her first assignment to design a house for the dog of rich heiress Barbara Hutton; early 1930s for six years, worked in the furnishings department of Stern Brothers department store in New York; late 1930s, became an independent consultant designer and designed historicist furniture by Herman Miller (before its turn to modern design); 1942, was commissioned by Libbey Glass to conduct market research into consumer preferences concerning glassware, which took a year. After World War II, her first glassware went into production; subsequently, low-price glass ranging from cut-glass to crystal wine goblets and whimsical scenes that sold in the millions. To 1982, she was a consultant to Libbey. 1945, she had visited Italy through a program sponsored by Handicraft Development, a not-for-profit organization paid for by Italian Americans to rehabilitate war-torn Italy. 1950s, she became known for her inexpensive, tasteful tableware and furniture. A Diamond suggestion for production was 'theme' glassware, that is, in packaged sets supported by extensive advertising, some of which featured Diamond herself. Other Libbey work: 1949 Classic Crystal tumbler set and later more ornamental glassware. Even though advocating unadorned wares, most of her work was decorative. She was also an advisor on design and marketing to other clients; became known as an arbiter of American taste. 1954, *LIFE* magazine proclaimed that Diamond had 'probably done more to get simple, well-styled furnishings into every room of the average U.S. home than any other designer.' Her archive is housed in National Museum of American History, Smithsonian Institution, Washington, D.C.
Exhibitions Work shown at 1950 *Good Design* exhibition/award (Classic Crystal range), The Museum of Modern Art, New York, and Chicago Merchandise Mart.
Bibliography Freda Diamond, *The Story of Glass*, New York: Harcourt, Brace, 1953. 'Designer for Everybody,' *LIFE*, vol. 36, 5 Apr. 1954: 69–70. Carl U. Fauster, *Libbey Glass Since 1918: Pictorial History And Collectors Guide*, Toledo, Ohio: Len Beach, 1979. Cat., Kathryn B. Hiesinger and George H. Marcus III (eds.), *Design Since 1945*, Philadelphia: Philadelphia Museum of Art, 1983. Cherie Fehrman and Kenneth Fehrman, *Postwar Interior Design, 1945–1960*, New York: Van Nostrand Reinhold, 1987. Cat., Pat Kirkham (ed.), *Women Designers in the USA, 1900–2000: Diversity and Difference*, New York: Bard; New Haven: Yale; 2000.

Dicker-Brandeis, Friedl (1898–1944)

Austrian architect and furniture, interior, and textile designer; born Vienna.

Training 1912–14, photography and fabric design, Graphische Lehr- und Versuchsanstalt, Vienna; 1916–19, private school of Johannes Itten, Vienna; 1919–23 under Johannes Itten, Bauhaus, Weimar.
Biography 1923–26, Dicker was active with Franz Singer in their Werkstätten bildender Kunst, Berlin; 1923, she settled in Vienna and set up a first studio with Anny Moller-Wottitz and, 1924, a second studio with Martha Döberl; 1926, amalgamated her studio with Singer's in Vienna, designing houses, apartments, kindergartens, offices, textiles, interiors, and furniture; 1927 with Singer, also worked in Stuttgart for a textile firm. When the Dicker-Singer studio closed, Dicker set up her own in Vienna, 1930–31; 1934, was arrested during the Starhemberg Putsch in Vienna; 1934–38, in Prague, practiced interior architecture with Grete Bauer-Fröhlich, taught drawing, and was active as an artist and anti-fascist; 1938, turned down a visa to settle in Palestine; 1938–42, lived in Mettau (now Hronöv, Czech Republic), taught drawing, and was active as an architect, artist, and, for B. Spiegler und Söhne, textile designer; 1942–44, was imprisoned in the Theresienstadt concentration camp near Prague, where she taught children's drawing courses; 1944, died at Auschwitz-Birkenau extermination camp.
Exhibitions/citations Participated in 1927 Kunstschau, Vienna; 1929 *Ausstellung Moderner Inneneinrichtungen*, Österreichisches Museum für Kunst und Industrie, Vienna; 1938 exhibition on the 20th anniversary of Czechoslovakia's declaration of independence. Work subject of exhibitions at Royal Academy, London, 1940; with Singer, Hochschule für angewandte Kunst, Vienna, 1989–89; Musée d'Art et d'Historie du Judaïsme, Hôtel de Saint-Aignan, Paris, 2000–01. Award (for efforts in the Werkstätten with Singer), 1924 Deutsche Spitzenmesse, Berlin; gold medal and award (for textiles by Spiegler), 1938 Czechoslovakian exhibition.
Bibliography Cat., *Franz Singer/Friedl Dicker: 2X Bauhaus in Wein*, Vienna: Hochschule für angewandte Kunst, 1988. Sigrid Wortmann Weltge, *Women's Work: Textile Art from the Bauhaus*, London: Thames & Hudson, 1993. Marie-Sandrine Sgherri, 'L'œuvre brisée de Friedl Dicker-Brandeis,' *Le Figaro*, 17 Dec. 2000: 33.

Dieckmann, Erich (1896–1944)

German designer and teacher; born Kauernik/Westpreußen; active Weimar and Berlin.

Training 1921–25, Bauhaus, Weimar.
Biography After Marcel Breuer, Dieckmann was the most important furniture designer who had trained at the Bauhaus; remained in Weimar, when the Bauhaus moved to Dessau; 1925–30, was head of the joiners' workshop of Staatliche Hochschule für Handwerk- und Baukunst in Weimar, under Otto Bartning. He designed a 1925 cherrywood and cane armchair and side chair while at the Bauhaus; produced handcrafted furniture designs by Haus am Horn. He later called on the experience acquired at the Bauhaus for many chairs in wood and steel by Thonet and other firms. 1931–33, he was a master, Kunstgewerbeschule Burg Giebichenstein, Halle; died in Berlin.
Bibliography Cat., *The Bauhaus: Masters and Students*, New York: Barry Friedman, 1988. Cat., *Erich Dieckmann, Praktiker der Avantgarde, Möbelbau 1921–33*, Weil am Rheim: Vitra Design Museum, 1990.

Diederich, Wilhelm Hunt (1884–1953)

Hungarian metalworker; born Hungary; active New York.

Training Pennsylvania Academy of Fine Arts, Philadelphia; under Emmanuel Fremiet, Paris.
Biography c. 1900 with his mother, Diederich settled in the house of his grandfather/painter William Morris Hunt in Boston; 1907 with sculptor Paul Manship, traveled in Spain and alone to Africa, Rome, Berlin,

and Paris; in Paris for the next ten years, studied with *animalier* Emmanuel Fremiet; by 1910, had become known as a sculptor of animals; met Polish sculptor Elie Nadelman and Russian sculptor Alekandr Archipenko, later renewing the friendships in New York. Diederich worked in cast bronze, sheet metal, and glazed ceramics, producing sculptures, weather vanes, metal wall reliefs, crayon drawings, paper silhouettes, and woodcut prints. His furnishings included wrought-iron candelabras, candlestands, and firescreens. His stylish and light-hearted objects interpreted images of cats, dogs, roosters, stags, and horses, many produced to his designs by blacksmiths in Greenwich Village, New York. His work was characterized by elegant, thin, curvaceous lines. He also produced bronze sculptures of romping and prancing animals frozen in a moment of action, including 1913–16 *Playing Greyhounds* and 1916 *Antelope and Hound*, the former included in his second exhibition (1920). 1923 in Morocco, he developed an interest in pottery, collected local examples, and began painting and glazing his own plates and bowls; 1930s, was a Nazi sympathizer; 1937, moved to Mexico, where he remained during World War II in the company of other American artists; became well known both for his silhouettes and sculpture; 1947, was expelled from the National Institute of Arts and Letters for using its mailing envelopes to send anti-Semitic material.
Exhibitions/citations 1910s–20s, work regularly included in Salon d'Automne, Paris; 1920s, at Whitney Studio Club (precursor of Whitney Museum of American Art), New York; 1928 *International Exhibition of Ceramic Art*, The Metropolitan Museum of Art, New York. Work subject of 1917 exhibition, 'Interior Decorator's Apartment,' New York; 1920 New York exhibition (catalog below); 1991 exhibition, Whitney Museum of American Art. Gold medal (pottery), 1927 exhibition, Architectural League of New York.
Bibliography Cat., Christian Brinton (intro.), *Catalogue of the First American Exhibition of Sculpture by Hunt Diederich*, New York: Kingore Galleries, 1920. 'Diederich, W. Hunt,' in *Who's Who in American Art*, 1936–37. Cat., Susan E. Menconi (ed.), *Uncommon Spirit: Sculpture in America 1800–1940*, New York: Hirschl and Adler Galleries, 1989. Marvin D. Schwartz, 'Hunt Diederich,' *Antiques and Arts Weekly*, 9 Aug. 1991: 1, 36. Exhibition pamphlet, Richard Armstrong, *W. Hunt Diederich*, New York: Whitney Museum of American Art, 1991.

Dietrich, Oscar (1853–1940)

Austrian silversmith; active Vienna.

Biography 1881, Dietrich took over the directorship of his father's silversmithy and was also admitted to the goldsmith's trade; produced designs by leading artists, including Emanuel Josef Margold, Dagobert Peche, Franz Karl Delavilla, Milla Weltmann, and architects A.O. Holub and Hans Bolek. 1931, the firm was closed and, subsequently, was taken over for a short time by Carius.
Exhibitions/citations Firm's work shown at 1900 *Exposition Universelle*, Paris; from 1909, Österreichisches Museum für Kunst und Industrie, Vienna; from 1924 and in jubilee exhibition, Wiener Kunstgewerbeverein; 1925 *Exhibition Internationale des Arts Décoratifs et Industriels Modernes*, Paris. Firm received awards in Vienna, 1873 and 1931; Paris, 1879; Wels, 1884; Linz, 1885; gold medal, 1914 Darmstadt Artists' Colony exhibition, Vienna.
Bibliography Annelies Krekel-Aalberse, *Art Nouveau and Art Déco Silver*, New York: Abrams, 1989. Deanna F. Cera (ed.), *Jewels of Fantasy: Costume Jewelry of the 20th Century*, New York: Abrams, 1992.

Diez Blanco, Javier (1966–); José Luis Diez Blanco (1968–)

Spanish designers; born Madrid; brothers;

Training Javier: industrial design, Escuela Experimental de Diseño, Madrid. José: interior design, Escuela de Artes no. 4, Diseño de Interiores, Madrid.
Biography They established their own office, diez+diez Diseño; have designed for the Bd Ediciones de Diseño firm in Barcelona, including 1996 Vértigo carpet.

Diffloth, Émile (1856–1933)

French ceramicist; born Couleuvre.

Training École Nationale Supérieure des Arts Décoratifs, Paris.
Biography c. 1899, Diffloth worked at Kéramis, the Belgian pottery of Boch Frères in La Louvière, where he became artistic director; c. 1910 departed and joined Taxile Doat in University City, Missouri, US, where he became a ceramics instructor at the School of Ceramic Art; returned to France; was a member, Société des Artistes Français.
Exhibitions/citations Work shown at Musée Galliéra, Paris. Gold medal, 1929 Salon of Société des Artistes Français.
Bibliography Yvonne Brunhammer et al., *Art Nouveau Belgium, France*, Houston: Rice University, 1976.

Diffrient, Niels (1928–)

American industrial designer; born Star, Miss.; husband of textile designer Helena Hernmarck.

Training Aeronautical engineering, Cass Technical High School, Detroit, Mich.; Cranbrook Academy of Art, Bloomfield Hills, Mich.
Biography 1949, Diffrient worked on the design of automobiles at General Motors in Detroit; 1946–51, in the office of architect Eero Saarinen in Bloomfield Hills, Mich.; 1951–52, in the office of Walter B. Ford; 1954–55, in the office of Marco Zanuso in Milan; to 1981, in the office of Henry Dreyfuss where, 1956, he became partner; 1981, set up his own studio and designed chairs and office systems by Knoll and others. His 1984 Helena steel and leather office chair by Sunar-Hauserman exemplifies his interest in ergonomics. He designed the Jefferson chair for Sunar-Hauserman; with Alvin R. Tilley, wrote the books *Humanscale 1–2–3* (1974), *Humanscale 4–5–6* (1981), and *Humanscale 7–8–9* (1981).
Bibliography Eric Larrabee and Massimo Vignelli, *Knoll Design*, New York: Abrams 1981: 56. Ann Lee Morgan (ed.), *Contemporary Designers*, London: Macmillan, 1984. Michael Kimmelman, 'Last of the Heroes: This Man Should Redesign American Industry,' *Connoisseur*, vol. 216, Aug. 1986: 36–41.

Dillon, Jane (b. Jane Young 1943–)

British furniture and lighting designer; born Manchester; wife of Charles Dillon (Windsor, UK, 1945–1992).

Training To 1965, interior design, Manchester College of Art and Design; 1968, master of arts degree in furniture design, Royal College of Art, London.
Biography 1968–69, Jane worked at Knoll International UK and under Ettore Sottsass at Olivetti as a color consultant and graphic designer on the Synthesi 45 furniture system; 1971–72, worked at Conran in London; with her husband, was a consultant to Casas for office and domestic seating. From 1971 with her husband, was an agent in Britain for ICF of the US and Casas of Spain, thus their contacts in Spain; 1972, formed a studio-business partnership with her husband. She designed 1972–73 Cometa hanging lamp, 1975 Piramid hanging lamp (with husband) by Bd Ediciones de Diseño; 1977–78, was consultant to Habitat; 1978–79, to Wolff Olins and, 1982–85, to Habitat/Mothercare; mid-1980s with Peter Wheeler and her studio partner Floris van den Broecke, produced one-of-a-kind furniture commissions for architects; from 1968, taught at Royal College of Art, London; 1971–73, at Middlesex Polytechnic; 1973–79, at Kingston Polytechnic (now Kingston University); from 1985, at Glasgow School of Art and at Parnham Trust, Dorset. 1997, developed her own-brand products; recently has designed seating for Science Museum; has consulted to Globe Theater, both London; also a collection by W. Lusty & Sons; teaches, Royal College of Art; active with projects for Guy Mallinson Furniture and Keen Group.
Exhibitions/citations From 1980, member, exhibition juror, and award recipient, Design Council, UK; 1983 selection (Jobber chair range by Casas), ADI/FAD (associations of industrial design and decorative arts), Spain.
Bibliography Liz McQuiston, *Women in Design: A Contemporary View*, New York: Rizzoli, 1988: 36. *Actis* (Casas firm publication), Barcelona: Swindon and Bristol International, 1985. Michele De Lucchi (ed.), *The International Design Yearbook*, London: Laurence King, 2001.

D.I.M. (Décoration Intérieure Moderne)

French interior design firm and manufacturer; located Paris.

History 1914, D.I.M. was established by René Joubert and Georges Mouveau on the rue Royale, Paris. Joubert had earlier worked for decorating firm Jansen and was the prime mover in D.I.M. Having previously been involved with stage design (particularly for the Opéra de Paris), Mouveau left D.I.M. in 1922 to return to this discipline. In 1923, after a brief period in 1922 when Viénot was the co-director of D.I.M., Philippe Petit became a partner. Joubert et Petit, as it is sometimes called, carried out a wide range of commissions; designed furniture of the finest quality in the firm's workshop. Production included lighting, mirrors, furnishings, fabrics, carpets, and rugs, and they designed the

interiors of airplanes. Their metal-and-wood furniture was installed on 1931 oceanliner *L'Atlantique*. Later located at 19, place de la Madeleine, Paris, the firm then moved to 40, rue du Colisée, in 1925; by 1930, had become one of the largest studio-galleries in Paris. In addition to Joubert's and Petit's own designs, a number of others designed lamps for the firm, including Jacques Le Chevallier, Gabriel Guévrékian, Jean Prouvé, Leroy, Jean Lesage, Daniel Stéphan, and, in Murano, Paolo Venini. On Joubert's 1931 death, Petit left the firm, which continued to operate through the 1940s.
Exhibitions Boutique located on the pont Alexandre III at 1925 *Exhibition Internationale des Arts Décoratifs et Industriels Modernes*, Paris, where Joubert and Petit also designed the dining room of Une Ambassade Française pavilion. Cafeteria in New York setting shown at 1928 Salon d'Automne.
Bibliography Victor Arwas, *Art Déco*, New York: Abrams, 1980. Pierre Kjellberg, *Art déco: les maîtres du mobilier, le décor des paquebots*, Paris: Amateur, 1986/1990.
> See Joubert, René; Petit, Philippe.

D.I.M.E.A.
French decorating studio; located Paris.

History Pierre and Max Bloch established the decorating studio at 14, avenue Victor-Emmanuel III in Paris, where it was active at least in the 1920s, designing both modern and period interiors for clients, including soberly classical furniture.
Citations Work included in 1925 *Exposition Internationale des Arts Décoratifs et Industriels Modernes*, Paris.
Bibliography Pierre Kjellberg, *Art déco: les maîtres du mobilier, le décor des paquebots*, Paris: Amateur, 1986/1990.

Dinand, Pierre-François (1931-)
French designer; active Paris.

Training Architecture, École Nationale Supérieure des Beaux-Arts, Paris.
Biography Dinand has designed over 150 perfume bottle ranges, beginning with his first, the 1961 Madame Rochas container, and subsequent 1968 Calandre by Paco Rabanne; 1970 Givenchy III, Eau Sauvage by Christian Dior, and Opium by Yves Saint Laurent; 1984 Obsession by Calvin Klein; 1987–88, was commissioned by Francesco Smalto to design a bottle to celebrate Tiffany's 50th anniversary; has studios in Paris, New York, and Tokyo.

Dine, Nick (1966-)
American designer; born New York.

Training To 1987, sculpture, Rhode Island School of Design, Providence; to 1991, design, Royal College of Art, London.
Biography To 1973, Dine lived in London; 1991, established his own studio in New York, where he founded Dinersan in 1993; 1992–95, taught, Parsons School of Design, New York; has designed furniture by Idée, Pure Design, Habitat, and Dune. Interiors in New York have included 1995 Embassy bar, 1995 Take restaurant, 1997 Totem design store, Kirna Zabete flagship store, 2000 Stussy flagship store, 2001 Dune flagship store, and R Twentieth Century store; also private residences. Currently, design director, Dune furniture company, New York.
Bibliography Cat., R. Craig Miller (intro.), *U.S. Design: 1975–2000*, Munich: Prestel, 2002.

Dioptaz, Laurent (1948-)
French designer, sculptor, and film animator.

Training École Supérieure des Arts Appliqués, Paris.
Biography Dioptaz designed 1969 Isotope chair in polyurethane foam covered in nylon jersey, produced and marketed from 1970 by Zol, Paris; 1970, set up his own office in Paris.
Exhibitions Work included in 1969 Salon of Société des Artistes Décorateurs and 1970 *Terres des hommes*, Montréal. Isotope Chair introduced at 1970 *Sitzen '70*, Vienna, and included in 1970 *Modern Chairs 1918–1970*, Whitechapel Gallery, London.
Bibliography Cat., *Modern Chairs 1918–1970*, London: Lund Humphries, 1971.

Disform
Spanish furniture manufacturer; located Barcelona.

History 1969, Carlos Riera, a member of the Riera family, proprietors of the Metalarte lighting firm, set up his own firm, Disform, to produce domestic objects. 'Disform' is derived from *diseño y forma* in Spanish (design and form). Riera subcontracted component work to four metal workshops and two woodworking shops and assembled the final models in his own factory in Sant Just Desvern. The Disform inventory was exclusively contemporary, even during the 1970s economic crisis, when some Spanish manufacturers reverted to conservative models. 1977, Disform produced its first furniture. The firm began with a table-calendar by Carlos Riart and Bigas Luna, waste-paper bin by Alberto Udaeta, and seat by Cristiani, and imported clocks by Joe Colombo, Pio Manzù, and Richard Sapper from Alessi in Italy, and Jane Dillon's 1972–73 Cometa hanging light from Britain. Most of its own designs were by non-Spanish artists, including Philippe Starck, who designed 1983 Jon Lld shelving in MDF. Much of the collection was sold in kit form. Spanish designers have included Sergi Devesa, who also designed for Metalarte.
Citations 1990 European Community Design Prize.
Bibliography Guy Julier, *New Spanish Design*, London: Thames & Hudson, 1991.

Dissing, Hans (1926–1999)
Danish architect and designer.

Training To 1947, in bricklaying; 1947, building technology, Horsens Builders' School; to 1955, Kunstakademiet, Copenhagen.
Biography 1952–71, Dissing worked in the architect/design office of Arne Jacobsen; from 1971, was a partner of Otto Weitling in Dissing + Weitling architecture firm in Copenhagen. Working alone, Dissing's best-known buildings are 1971–74 Central Bank in Kuwait; 1973–76 Danish Embassy in London; and planning of 1971–75 first and second sections of Danmarks Nationalbank Jubilee Foundation. Through Dissing + Weitling, they designed 1988 culture centre in Rødovre; 1991 research laboratories for Novo Nordisk; 1992 telecommunications tower in Hanover; and 1996 Royal Veterinary and Agricultural University. The partnership became known for their 1989 Air Titanium eyeglasses by Lindgerg Optic Design.
> See Weitling, Otto.

Dittert, Karl (1915-)
Austrian gold- and silversmith and industrial designer; active Schwäbisch-Gmünd. (Germany).

Training Silversmithing, Bibus & Sohn, Mährisch-Trübau; sculpture, Akademie der Schönen Künste, Berlin; 1945–46 under Hans Warnecke, gold- and silversmithing, Fachschule für Edelmetallgewerbe, Schwäbisch-Gmünd.
Biography 1946, Dittert set up his own industrial-design studio in Schwäbisch-Gmünd, where he produced designs for a number of products, from office-furniture systems to domestic goods; from 1957, designed for Bruckmann & Söhne metalworkers in Heilbronn; became known particularly for his designs of stainless steel and silver objects, including 1960 nesting cooking set and burner by Kühn, 1966 Classica cutlery range by Felix Gloria-Werk, and 1981 food slicer by Ritter. From 1970, was director, Fachschule, Schwäbisch-Gmünd; was a member, Deutscher Werkbund; member, from its initiation, Verbandes Deutscher Industriedesigner (VDID).
Bibliography Graham Hughes, *Modern Silver Throughout the World*, New York: Crown, 1967: nos. 83–101. *Industrial Design*, vol. 28, Nov.–Dec. 1981: 23. Cat., Kathryn B. Hiesinger and George H. Marcus III (eds.), *Design Since 1945*, Philadelphia: Philadelphia Museum of Art, 1984. Cat., *Silber für die Welt*, Heilbronn: Städtische Museen, 2001.

Ditzel, Jørgen (1931–1961); Nanna Ditzel (1923-)
Danish architects and furniture, metalwork, ceramic, and textile designers. Nanna: wife of Jørgen Ditzel (1948) and Kurt Heide (1968).

Training Jørgen: to 1939, upholstery and, to 1944, other studies, Kunsthåndværkerskolen, Copenhagen. Nanna: 1945, furniture school of Det Kongelige Danske Kunstakademi, Copenhagen; 1946, Kunsthåndværkerskolen, Copenhagen.
Biography 1946 after marrying, they set up their own design studio and collaborated together to Jørgen's 1961 death; designed jewelry by A. Michelsen and by Georg Jensen and, 1954, began a long-time association with the latter; created a 1952 experimental modular-furniture system; 1952, began a cooperation with fabric firm Unika-Vaev and furniture firm Halling Koch; wrote the book *Danish Chairs* (1954). 1950s–60s, Nanna Ditzel designed simple furniture, including

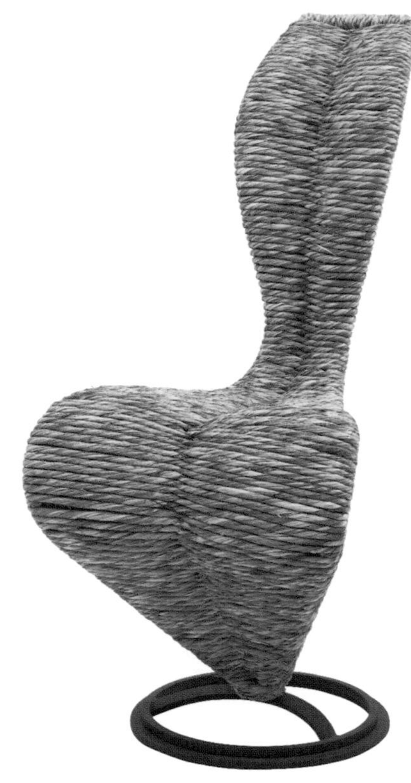

Tom Dixon. S chair. 1991. Rush and steel, 40 3/8 x 19 1/4 x 22 7/8" (102.6 x 48.9 x 58.1 cm). Mfr.: Cappellini, Italy. Gift of the mfr. MoMA.

some cane and basketwork chairs by Wengler, wooden models (including 1955 baby's high chair) by Poul Kold, upholstered seating by LCP Furniture (UK) and by Invincible Cane Furniture (UK). Den Permanente commissioned them to design 1961 *Deense Woonkunst* exhibition in Amsterdam. 1967 with Poul Henningsen, Hans Bendix, Ågård, and others, Nanna became associated with design magazine *Mobilia*; 1968, settled in Britain. From 1970, her clients included Domus Danica, Georg Jensen, Scandus, Dunflex form furniture, and Poul Kold. She produced a range of wooden tableware for Den Permanente; 1980, began a cooperation with Brdr. Krüger Traedrejeri; 1981, became chairperson, Design and Industries Association, UK; 1986, set up a studio in Copenhagen; 1988, developed a color scheme for textiles and other interior features of the Danish State Railway's new *IC3* train; designed 1989 Bench for Two and 1991 Butterfly chair by Fredericia Stølefabrik and 1990 Hallingdal textile range in 15 colors by Kvadrat.
Exhibitions/citations Their work shown at 1944 Cabinetmakers' Autumn Exhibition, Cophenhagen. Nanna Ditzel's work alone shown at 1963 one-person exhibition, New York; 1965 exhibition (with children's book authors Ågård Andersen and Egon Mathiesen), Museum of Decorative Art, Copenhagen; 1972 exhibition, Lerchenborg Castle; 1980–84 and 1986–91 Cabinetmakers' Autumn Exhibition, Copenhagen; 1991 exhibition, Èstbanen, Århus; 2003 exhibition, Maison du Danemark, Paris. The Ditzels' jewelry designs (by Michelsen and Jensen) received numerous citations, including 1950 first prize, Goldsmiths' Joint Council competition; 1950 Cabinetmakers' Guild competition; silver medals, 1951 (9th), 1954 (10th), and 1957 (11th) Triennali di Milano and gold medal at its 1960 (12th) edition; 1953 Good Design award, The Museum of Modern Art, New York; 1956 Lunning Prize. Nanna Ditzel was also awarded 1990 gold medal (for Bench for Two), International Furniture Design Competition, Asahikawa, Japan; 1996, elected Honorary Royal Designer for Industry, UK; 1998, lifelong artist's grant, Danish Ministry of Culture.
Bibliography Bent Salicath and Arne Karlsen (eds.), *Modern Danish Textiles*, Copenhagen, 1959. 'Nanna Ditzel: An Exhibition,' *Interiors*, vol. 123, Dec. 1963: 102–03. 'Thirty-four Lunning Prize-Winners,' *Mobilia*, no. 146, Sept. 1967. Cat., *Georg Jensen—Silversmiths: 77 Artists, 75 Years, 1980*: nos. 25–29. Frederik Sieck, *Nutidig Dansk Møbeldesign – en kortfattet illustreret beskrivelse*, Copenhagen: Bondo Gravesen, 1990. Cat., *The Lunning Prize*, Stockholm: Nationalmuseum, 1986. Tanker Bliver Ting, *Nanna Ditzel Design*, Allerod: Kunstindustrimuseet, 1994. Film, Nanna Ditzel's designs and working methods, produced by Danish Ministry of Education and National Center for Educational Materials, 1991. Henrik Sten Møller, *Motion and Beauty: Nanna Ditzel*, Munkeruphus: Rhodes, 1998.

Dixon, Arthur S. (1865–1940)
> See Birmingham Guild of Handicraft.

Dixon, Harry St. John (1890–1967)
American metalsmith; active San Francisco.

Training California School of Arts and Crafts, Oakland, Cal.; and training elsewhere.
Biography 1908, Dixon became an apprentice to Dirk Van Erp, working concurrently in Van Erp's establishment and other crafts shops in the San Francisco Bay area; for five years, trained in Lillian Palmer's shop; subsequently, worked in the shipyards. 1916, Van Erp left his shop in the care of his daughter and Dixon. c. 1921, Dixon opened his own shop and began stamping his pieces with a punchmark showing a man forging a bowl that had been designed by his painter/brother. Major commissions included 1920s elevator doors of San Francisco Stock Exchange Club and, his last, 48" (1.2 m) sundial in the shape of a lotus blossom for the Burbank Memorial Garden in Santa Rosa, Cal.
Bibliography Cat., Ann Yaffe Phillips, *From Architecture to Object*, New York: Hirschl and Adler, 1989. Bonnie Mattison in Timothy J. Andersen et al., *California Design 1910*, Salt Lake City: Peregrine Smith, 1980: 86.

Dixon, Tom (1959–)
British designer; born Sfax, Tunisia, to English father and French-Latvian mother; active London.

Training 1979 for six months, Chelsea School of Art, London.
Biography 1963, Dixon moved to England; 1980, worked as a graphics designer and colorist for animated films; 1983, learned welding to repair his motorcycle and, thus, began making welded furniture using scrap metal and completed his first interior-design project; 1984, welded scrap metal on stage as performance art at the Titanic Club in London, which he established, leading to an exhibition and commission; 1985, abandoned life in the night-club world and turned to manufacturing. Also 1985 with André Dubreuil, decorated Rococo Chocolats boutique and, with Dubreuil, Mark Brazier-Jones, and others, became associated with the neo-Baroque movement in London, whose designers produced metal one-of-a-kind furniture pieces and fixtures, including chandeliers (initially for the Creative Salvage collective and its 1984 exhibition). 'Creative Salvage' referred, in the case of Dixon's 1987 S chair prototype, to wrapping tire inner tubes and later straw, recalling his early interest in found materials. Other work has included 1986–87 chair made from found cast-iron pieces, 1986 organ-pipe screen of galvanized steel, welded-steel and glass table, and, by Capppellini, 1985 Bird 1 lounge chair, 1988 S chair, and 1992 Pylon chair. 1987, he set up the production workshop Dixon PID. To 1989 when his association with Cappellini was in full force, he claims to have been unaware of the potential of 'design vis-à-vis industry' because 'in the Thatcherite early eighties, England was a cultural desert.' 1989, Dixon set up Space studio to batch-produce metal furniture and to execute stage-design and retail-design project (and, 1992, Space shop on All Saints Road, Notting Hill, to see his own and others' work); 1990 to produce the Pylon series, experimented with lightweight structures as realized by 3-D wire-frame computer programs and bridge engineering. He developed a number of multifunctional furnishings sold through the firm Eurolounge, which was cofounded in 1994 (Eurolounge goods distributed by Inflate from 2001) to produce Dixon's 1997 Jack lamp and other plastic lights. Dixon designed objects and interiors for Terence Conran, Jean-Paul Gaultier, Romeo Gigli, Ralph Lauren, and Vivienne Westwood; became best known for his products by Cappellini, Driade, Moroso, and SCP. He has taught at Royal College of Art, London; Kingston Polytechnic (now Kingston University), and Plymouth University. 1998, he became head of design in the UK for Habitat store chain; 1999, the head of international design; 2001, the creative director and chose to reproduce the historic designs of Robin Day, Achille Castiglioni, Ettore Sottsass, Verner Panton, and others, and, through Habitat, has been able fullfil an ambition to make good design available to the masses. 2001, he launched the first

range of Fresh Fat Plastic products (spaghetti-like extrusions); concurrently with Habitat, directs Tom Dixon, The Company (established in 2002).
Exhibitions/citations 1984 Creative Salvage collective exhibition (with Dubreuil and Brazier-Jones), London. First (1986) one-person exhibition, One Off shop, Neale Street, London; 1988, Galerie Yves Gastou, Paris; cosubject of *The Italian Job* (Eurolounge and Inflate) exhibition, 1997 Salone del Mobile, Milan; 2001 exhibition of Fresh Fat Plastic products, Selfridges, London, and traveling to Europe, Japan, and Australia. Included in: *Design World 2000*, Konstindustrimuseet, Helsinki; 2003–04 *Somewhere Totally Else—The European Design Show*, Design Museum, London; 2004 *Brilliant* (lighting), Victoria and Albert Museum, London. 2000, elected officer of Order of the British Empire (OBE), for service to design and innovation.
Bibliography Frédérique Huygen, *British Design: Image and Identity*, London: Thames & Hudson, 1989: 133–36. Cat., *Tom Dixon*, Paris: Galerie Yves Gastou, 1989. 'Tom Dixon,' *Maison française*, July–Aug. 1989. 'Tom Dixon, l'enfant terrible de la ferraille coudée,' *Beaux arts*, no. 709, July–Aug. 1989. Albrecht Bangert and Karl Michael Armer, *80s Style: Designs of the Decade*, New York: Abbeville, 1990. Cat., *Acquisitions 1982–1990 arts décoratifs*, Paris: Fonds National d'Art Contemporain, 1991. Jennifer Kabat, 'At Home at Habitat,' *I.D.*, vol. 46, no.3, May 1999: 72-75. Tom Dixon, *Rethink*, London: Conran Octopus, 2000. Paola Antonelli (ed.), *Objects of Design: The Museum of Modern Art*, New York: The Museum of Modern Art, 2003: 145.
> See Brazier-Jones, Mark.

Dixon and Sons, James
British silversmiths; located Sheffield.

History 1806, the firm James Dixon and Sons was founded; from 1878, produced designs by Christopher Dresser and published catalogs illustrating numerous examples of his designs; later produced silver in Art Déco and Art Nouveau styles.
Bibliography Annelies Krekel-Aalberse, *Art Nouveau and Art Déco Silver*, New York: Abrams, 1989.

Djo-Bourgeois (1898–1937)
> See Bourgeois, Édouard-Joseph.

Djo-Bourgeois, Élise
> See Bourgeois, Élise.

DMD
> See Droog Design.

Doat, Taxile Maxmilien (1851–1938)
French ceramicist; born Albi; active University City, Miss.

Training Dubouché school of sculpture; under Dumont, École Nationale Supérieure des Beaux-Arts, Paris.
Biography 1877, Doat joined Manufacture Nationale de Sèvres; c. 1892, installed a kiln in his home on the rue Bagneaux, studying clays and glazes for porcelain to 1899; 1900, built a wood kiln at Sèvres; combined stoneware and porcelain in the same piece; c. 1900, applied crystalline and metallic glazes to gourd-shaped vases. His technical study 'Grand Feu Ceramics' first appeared in the journal *Keramic Studio* and in a 1905 book by Keramic Studio Publishing Co., Syracuse, N.Y., US, with a condensed version appearing in 1906 and 1907 issues of the magazine *Art et décoration*. 1909, the American Women's League invited him to build an art pottery, and Doat became director of the School of Ceramic Art, University City, Miss., with the first kiln functioning by 1910. For a time, University City was one of the most successful potteries in US. When the establishment closed in 1915, Doat returned to France.
Exhibitions Work shown at 1900 *Exposition Universelle*, Paris.
Bibliography Yvonne Brunhammer et al., *Art Nouveau Belgium, France*, Houston: Rice University, 1976.

Doblin, Jay (1920–1989)
American industrial designer and teacher.

Training 1939–42, Pratt Institute, Brooklyn, N.Y.
Biography Early 1950s, Doblin worked in the industrial-design office of Raymond Loewy in New York. Of the experience, Doblin said, 'I never got credit for anything I did at Raymond Loewy, nor did anybody else. But I didn't care.' 1964–72, Doblin was a cofounder of Unimark in Chicago; 1972, established Jay Doblin & Associates in Chicago; 1948–52, director industrial-design evening classes, Pratt Institute in Brooklyn, N.Y.; 1955–78, taught and was codirector, School of Design in Chicago. He wrote the books *Perspective: A New System for Designers* (New York: Whitney, 1956) and *One Hundred Great Product Designs* (New York: Van Nostrand Reinhold, 1970). Jay Doblin & Associates (now Doblin Group) is still active in Chicago. The annual Jay Doblin Award was established by Design Management Institute to recognize design-business literature.
Bibliography Ann Lee Morgan (ed.), *Contemporary Designers*, London: Macmillan, 1984. Penny Sparke, *Introduction to Design and Culture in the Twentieth Century*, London: Allen and Unwin, 1986. 'Jay Doblin,' *Innovation* (IDSA quarterly journal), vol. 2, no. 2, 1983.

Dobson, Frank (1886–1963)
British sculptor.

Training Painting, City and Guilds Schools, Kensington, London.
Biography 1920, Dobson joined artists' organization Group X, of which he was the only sculptor/member; 1922, joined the London Group, becoming president 1924–27; 1930, rendered ceramic reliefs for Hay's Wharf building in London; 1920s, produced resist (or batik) printed fabrics; early 1930s, designed painted composition fashion mannequins; throughout 1930s, designed silk-screened fabrics, often in abstract vegetal motifs, produced by Allan Walton Textiles and lino-printed fabrics produced by himself; designed 1935 Calix Majestatis silver-gilt cup (commissioned by Llewelyn Amos, who was the director of National Jewellers' Association), presented to King George V; 1940, became a governmental war artist; 1942, was appointed an associate of the Royal Academy and, 1953, RA; was an early member, Society of Industrial Artists (founded in 1930); 1946–53, was professor of sculpture, Royal College of Art, London.
Exhibitions 1914, work shown at Chenil Galleries, London, and, 1921, at Leicester Galleries. His fashion mannequin shown at 1933 *British Industrial Art in Relation to the Home*, Dorland Hall, London.
Bibliography Cat., *Thirties: British Art and Design Before the War*, London: Arts Council of Great Britain/Hayward Gallery, 1979. Valerie Mendes, *The Victoria and Albert Museum's Textile Collection, British Textiles from 1900 to 1937*, London: Victoria and Albert Museum, 1992.

Doesburg, Theo van
> See van Doesburg, Theo.

Dohner, Donald R. (1907–1944)
American industrial designer; born Indiana; active East Pittsburgh, Pa.

Biography Dohner was a teacher of design, Carnegie Institute of Technology; 1927–30, was consultant to Westinghouse in East Pittsburgh, Pa.; turning down offers to work at Marshall Field and Carson Pirie Scott department stores in Chicago to be empoloyed as the director of art in the engineering department of Westinghouse 1930–34, where he designed 128 products, ranging from micarta ashtrays and vacuum cleaners to mechanical water coolers, electric ranges, and diesel-electric locomotives. One of his designs was originated as a stubby-silhouetted locomotive intended as a stand at an exposition, painted to appear longer and more elegant. It sold right off the exhibit floor.
Bibliography *Fortune*, Feb. 1934: 90.

Doléac, Florence (1968–)
> See Radi Designers.

Domecq, Jean-Louis (1920–83)
French designer.

Biography Domecq designed the 1950 articulated metal lamp with wireless joints for full-circle articulation. Originally it was for his own use. His firm Jieldé, founded 1953, is an acronym based on his own initials as pronounced in French: 'gel-day.' The first brochure/advertisement for the lamp was published in 1955. The public began to call it the Standard rather than the Jieldé. 1987, the configuration was expanded to include models for various applications, on walls, tables, floors; is still in production by Jieldé SA in Saint-Priest, France.
Bibliography www.jielde.com.

Domin, André (1883–1962)
> See Dominique.

Jean-Louis Domecq. Standard table lamp. 1953. Extruded steel, sheet steel, and paint, extended l. 30 5/16" (77 cm). Mfr.: Jieldé, France. Courtesy Quittenbaum Kunstauktionen, Munich.

Domingo, Alain (1952–); Nemo

French designer; active Paris.

Training 1979, DPLG architecture (governmental diploma), France.
Biography Domingo collaborated with François Scali under the name of Nemo, the design studio they established in 1982. They became known for their furniture designs for Cité des Sciences at Parc de la Villette, Paris; produced carpets for Géométrie Variable and Élisée Éditions, graphic design for MBK and Motobécane, pasta shapes for Panzani, and packaging for Lesieur; designed furniture and furnishings for their own firm Tébong in Paris; 1982 Faizzz chair, 1983 Marini and Moreno chairs, and 1984 Mediabolo chair by Nemo Édition; 1984 print lamp by Formica; and 1985 computer monitor.
Citations Won competitions, including those sponsored by VIA (French furniture association) and Le Mobilier National, 1983; French Ministère de la Culture, 1984 (a lamp by Mégalit); public furniture, Parc de la Villette, 1985; layout and furniture, entrance hall of the offices, Caisse Nationale des Monuments Historiques et des Sites, Hôtel de Sully, Paris, 1986; with François Scali, Centre Georges Pompidou for its 10th anniversary (Génitron clock, counting down seconds to the year 2000).
Bibliography Juli Capella and Quim Larrea, *Designed by Architects in the 1980s*, New York: Rizzoli, 1988. Cat., *Design français, 1960–1990: trois décennies*, Paris: Centre Georges Pompidou/APCI, 1988. Cat., Catherine Arminjon et al., *L'Art de Vivre: Decorative Arts and Design in France 1789–1989*, New York: Vendome, 1989: 40. Cat., *Les années VIA, 1980–1990*, Paris: Musée des Arts Décoratifs, 1990. Cat., *Acquisitions 1982–1990 arts décoratifs*, Paris: Fonds National d'Art Contemporain, 1991. François Mathey, *Au bonheur des formes, design français 1945–1993*, Paris: Regard, 1992. Didier Laroque (intro.), *Nemo: Alain Domingo, François Scali*, Barcelona: Gustavo Gili, 1992.

Dominick and Haff, H.B.

American silversmiths; located New York.

History 1821, the firm of William Gale and Son was established in New York. 1868, its name was changed to Gale, North and Dominick, when Henry Blanchard Dominick joined the firm. 1867, Leroy B. Haff had begun working in its retail department. 1870, Haff became a partner, and the firm's name was changed to Gale, Dominick and Haff and located to 451 Broome Street. Eventually, the name became H.B. Dominick and Haff. From 1871, it was located on Bond Street; 1893–1904, at 860 Broadway, moving to various other addresses in 1920s. Its customers included Bailey, Banks and Biddle, the jewelry and silver store in Philadelphia. The firm became known for its high standards of craftsmanship; c. 1880, acquired the silverware tools and patterns of Adams and Shaw, a silver and silverplate manufacturer in New Jersey, where Shaw continued to oversee the plate production of Tiffany & Co. 1928, H.B. Dominick and Haff was purchased by Reed & Barton, Taunton, Mass.
Bibliography 'H.B. Dominick,' *The New York Times*, 24 Dec., 1928: 13. Doreen Bolger Burke et al., *In Pursuit of Beauty: Americans and the Aesthetic Movement*, New York: The Metropolitan Museum of Art/ Rizzoli, 1986.

Dominioni, Luigi Caccia
> See Caccia Dominioni, Luigi.

Dominique

French interior designers; located Paris.

History 1922, André Domin (1883–1962) and Marcel Genévrière (1885–1967) founded the decorating firm Dominique at 104, rue du Faubourg Saint-Honoré in Paris, whose slogan was *délivré du cauchemar de l'ancien* (deliverance from the nightmare of the ancient). (Domin had been a journalist and art critic for journals, including *Comœdia*, *Gil blas*, and *L'intransigeant*.) Their furniture was moderately priced but nevertheless elegant, in exotic woods, inlaid brass, and mother-of-pearl, with gilt bronze and applied carved motifs. c. 1925–35, they frequently incorporated shagreen into their pieces; used fabrics by Hélène Henry and Raoul Dufy produced by Bianchini-Férier. They designed and furnished Jean Puiforcat's villa in Biarritz in the so-called Parisian style of Gothic-Renaissance, and the offices of Houbigant perfume factory in Neuilly. For these projects, their furniture was produced in luxurious materials: amaranth, ebony, Brazilian rosewood, shagreen, and parchment; their door handles and silvered bronze plaques were produced by Puiforcat. 1926, they became cofounders of Groupe des Cinq with Pierre Chareau, Pierre Legrain, Jean Puiforcat, and Raymond Templier, exhibiting with the group in 1926 at Galerie Barbazanges, Paris. c. 1926, they began to design in a more rigorous Cubist manner, yet produced robust forms in the tradition of Jacques-Émile Ruhlmann. 1929, they moved the design office and store to 29, avenue Kléber in Paris, at about a time when they began incorporating metal into their work in a limited manner. From 1933, they collaborated with Compagnie Générale Transatlantique on its oceanliners, furnishing four cabins of 1935 *Normandie;* after World War II, designed some furniture for the Palais de l'Élysée. Domin was also a graphic designer of advertisements, posters, brochures, books, and periodicals. To 1970, Dominique operated under the management of Alain Domin, the elder son of André Domin.
Exhibitions Work shown at Salon d'Automne from 1922 and Salons of Société des Artistes Décorateurs. Small salon of private apartments included in Une Ambassade Française pavilion at 1925 *Exposition Internationale des Arts Décoratifs et Industriels Modernes*, Paris, and collaborated in its other sections (musical instruments, Arts de la Rue, and boutique of Maneaux Salf); also at 1935 *Exposition Universelle et Internationale de Bruxelles*.
Bibliography *Ensembles mobiliers*, Paris: Charles Moreau, no. 17, 1954. Alastair Duncan, *Art Nouveau and Art Déco Lighting*, New York: Simon & Schuster, 1978: 168. Victor Arwas, *Art Déco*, New York: Abrams, 1980. Pierre Kjellberg, *Art déco: les maîtres du mobilier, le décor des paquebots*, Paris: Amateur, 1986/1990. Patricia Bayer, *Art Deco Interiors: Decoration and Design Classics of the 1920s and 1930s*, London: Thames & Hudson, 1990.

Donald Brothers

British fabric manufacturer; located Dundee.

History 1930s, its designers included P.A. Staynes, Marion Dorn, and E. Dean. It was described as a manufacturer of 'Old Glamis fabrics' and listed its specialties as art canvas, art linens, and decorative fabrics; became known for high-quality linen upholstery fabric, as well as cotton and jute fabrications in natural colors. Its Festoon pattern, often seen on cube-form chairs by Arundell Clarke, was a bestseller. The firm was able to screenprint fabrics in a quality equal to its woven goods.
Bibliography Cat., *Thirties: British Art and Design Before the War*, London: Arts Council of Great Britain/Hayward Gallery, 1979. Valerie Mendes, *The Victoria and Albert Museum's Textile Collection, British Textiles from 1900 to 1937*, London: Victoria and Albert Museum, 1992.

Donegani, Dante (1957–)
Italian designer; born Pinzolo, Trento; active Milan.

Training To 1983, Facoltà di Architettura, Università degli Studi, Florence.
Biography 1987–90, Donegani worked on the corporate identity of Olivetti; from 1993, was director of the design master's course, Domus Academy, Milan; 1993 with Giovanni Lauda, set up design studio D&L, which has designed, among others, exhibitions, fairs, and showrooms; is active in architecture, interiors, and product design for clients such as Cavari, Edra, Isuzu, Luceplan, Memphis, Radice, and Stildomus; designed exhibition systems for Fissler, Nolan Helmets, St Pauls International, Montell, Guzzini and furniture for private houses, shops, and clients. Exhibition designs include *Michelangelo Architetto*, *Artemisia Gentileschi*, *Mondrian e De Stijl*, *Impressionists* at Washington's National Gallery of Washington, and *Piero della Francesca*.
Citations Architecture competition awards: first prize *ex aequo*, 1988 Waterfront of Manhattan, New York; first prize (with Andrea Branzi), 1987 Berlin Wall, Berlin; second prize (with Andrea Branzi), 1991 A Square with a Monument, Kejhanna, Japan.
Bibliography Philippe Starck (ed.), *The International Design Yearbook*, New York: Abbeville, 1997. Catherine McDermott, *The Product Book: D&AD*, Hove: RotoVision, 1999: 22–27. Michele De Lucchi (ed.), *The International Design Yearbook*, London: Laurence King, 2001.

Donzelli, Rinaldo (1921–)
Italian designer; born and active Mariano Comense.

Biography 1935–40, Donzelli carved furniture; 1946–50, was a painter, decorator, and scenic, advertising, and exhibition designer at RIMA Palazzo dell'Arte, Milan, including stands for tourism and manufacturers of furniture, toys, automobile bodies, radios, bicycles, and motor cycles; 1950–64, was a graphic and industrial designer at Moto Gilera; 1957–66, a staff member at Biennale dello Standard nell'Arredamento, Mariano Comense; 1965–72, a graphic and industrial designer at Moto Guzzi; from 1972, pursued research; became a member, ADI (Associazione per il Disegno Industriale).
Bibliography *ADI Annual 1976*, Milan: Associazione per il Disegno Industriale, 1976.

Dordoni, Rodolfo (1954–)
Italian consultant designer; born and active Milan.

Training To 1979, architecture, Politecnico, Milan.
Biography Dordoni was active for a time in architects' offices and began working in industrial design; 1979–89, was artistic director of Cappellini International Interiors and in charge of its corporate image and communications; from 1982, was consultant designer for several firms on pavilions, shops, and exhibition stands. His clients for furniture and lighting have included Flos, Moroso, Barovier & Toso, Bassani Ticino, Ferlea, Realizza, Cappellini, FontanaArte, Dolce & Gabbana, Molteni, Moroso, Venini, and Vistosi. He designed Musa ceiling lights by Artemide and Halloween ceiling light by Arteluce.
Bibliography Fumio Shimizu and Studio Matteo Thun (eds.), *The Italian Design: Descendants of Leonardo da Vinci*, Tokyo: Graphic-sha, 1987. *Modo*, no. 148, Mar.–Apr. 1993: 119.

Dorfles, Gillo (1910–)
Italian teacher, design activist, and theorist; born Trieste; active Milan.

Biography 1948, with Atanasio Soldati, Gianni Monnet, and Bruno Munari, Dorfles was a cofounder of artists' group Movimento Arte Concreta (MAC); 1956, became a member, Associazione per il Disegno Industriale (ADI), of which he was the promotion committee member; was a professor of aesthetics, Università degli Studi, Trieste. He was a member of the committee of 1955 industrial-design exhibition in London, of the international industrial-design stand at 1957 (11th) Triennale di Milano, of the jury at BIO industrial-design biennial in Ljubljana, of the jury at the event in Jablonec (now Czech Republic), of the 1967 (9th) Compasso d'Oro, and commissioner of the industrial stand at 1960 (12th) Triennale di Milano and participated in its congress at the 1954 (10th) edition. Participated in 1957 *Journée de l'Ésthetique Industrielle* in Paris, 1957 meeting of Congrès Internationaux d'Architecture Moderne (CIAM) in Venice, 1961–63 events at Corso Superiore di Disegno Industriale in Florence, Italian Institute in London, and Kunstgewerbemuseum in Zürich. He wrote the books *Il disegno industriale e la sua estetica* (1963), *Introduzione al disegno industriale* (1971), and numerous other titles; was one of the first to observe the kitsch in decoration and design, in his *Kitsch: An Anthology of Bad Taste* (London: Studio Vista, 1969).
Exhibitions Numerous one-person shows including: 1954 Wittenborn Gallery, New York; 1990 Galleria Editalia, Rome; 1991 Studio d'Arte Contemporanea Dabbeni, Lugano.
Bibliography *ADI Annual 1976*, Milan: Associazione per il Disegno Industriale, 1976. Letizia Tedeschi, *Gillo Dorfles. Scritti di architettura 1930–1998*, Mendrisio: Accademia di Architettura, 2000.

Dorn, Marion Victoria (1899–1964)
American fabric and carpet designer; born San Francisco; active London; wife of E. McKnight Kauffer.

Training 1914–16, Stanford University, Cal.
Biography 1921–25, Dorn worked in Paris and, 1925, settled in London with her future husband E. McKnight Kauffer; began to design and produce a variety of resist (batik) printed textiles and was commissioned to design individual soft furnishings, including one-of-a-kind batiks for interiors, such as Matisse-like patterns for curtains; was influenced by Cubist painters in Paris, which was reflected in her designs of carpets and textiles in modern abstract motifs for public places, including hotels Savoy 1933–35, Claridges 1932, and Berkeley, all London, and oceanliners such as 1934 *Queen Mary* and 1935 *Orion*. She illustrated William Beckford's book *Vathek* (Bloomsbury: Nonesuch, 1929); with Kauffer, designed carpets by Wilton Royal Carpet Factory; by mid-1930s, was the best-known carpet designer in Britain and recognized as a leading textile designer, with clients including Warner, Donald Brothers, Old Bleach Linen, and Alastair Morton's Edinburgh Weavers. Syrie Maugham installed a white carpet by Dorn in her all-white 1933 living room in London. 1934, Dorn set up a shop at 10 Lancashire Court, New Bond Street, London, and diversified into weaving; from 1940, continued her textile practice in New York but with few commissions; made scarves and any commission that came her way, no matter how small or poorly paying; from 1950s, met some success and became a consultant designer to Edward Fields custom-carpet company; was commissioned to design carpets for the diplomatic lounge of the White House, Washington, D.C.; 1962–64, was active in a studio in Tangier.
Exhibitions Work included in major decorative- and industrial-art exhibitions in 1930s, including 1931 rug exhibition, Curtis Moffat Gallery, London, organized by *Vogue* editor Madge Garland, and 1979–80 *Thirties* exhibition, Hayward Gallery, London (catalog below). Work sugject of 1996–97 *The Architect of Floors*, London and Manchester (catalog below).
Bibliography Cat., Jennifer Hawkins and Marianne Hollis (eds.), *Thirties: British Art and Design Before the War*, London: Arts Council of Great Britain/Hayward Gallery, 1979. Cat., Pat Kirkham (ed.), *Women Designers in the USA, 1900–2000: Diversity and Difference*, New York: Bard; New Haven: Yale; 2000. Christine Boydell, *The Architect of Floors: Modernism, Art and Marion Dorn Designs*, Coggeshall: Schoeser with British Architectural Library, Royal Institute of British Architects, 1996.

Dorner, Marie-Christine (1960–)
French furniture and interior designer; born Strasbourg.

Training 1979–84, École Camondo, Paris.
Biography From 1984, Dorner worked in Paris for Patrick and Daniel Rubin at Atelier d'Architecture Intérieure Canal and, to 1985, for Jean-Michel Wilmotte; 1986, settled in Tokyo, where she designed her first furniture (a 13-piece collection based on origami forms by Idée) and interiors for a Tokyo clothing boutique and a restaurant in Yokohama; 1987, designed a coffee table and armchair by Cassina and two shops and a café for Komatsu in Tokyo; 1987, returned to Paris and set up her own design office with clients, including Cassina, Scarabat, Baccarat, Bernardaud, Élisée Éditions, and Artelano; designed 1988 Asap television table by Artelano, 1988 Dede illuminated console by Scarabat, furniture for the Au Printemps department store in Paris, and tableware, graphics, and interiors for others. 1988, she designed the hotel La Villa near Saint-Germain-des-Près; 1989, furniture for the Comédie Française cafeteria in Paris, commissioned by the French Ministère de la Culture; and 1991 Dorner porcelain dinnerware by Bernardaud. She founded the design department, École Supérieure d'Art et de Design, Reims; subsequently, became a visiting tutor, Royal College of Art, London; from 1996, has lived in London. Other work includes 1990 tableware by Bernardaud; 1990 presidential stand (now reerected each year in Place de la Concorde, Paris, for 14 July military parade); 1993 'Esplanade' bus station, Nîmes, with special

urban fixtures; and 1998 products for boutique of Musée du Louvre.
Exhibitions/citations Idée furniture range shown 1987 and subsequently at Axis Gallery, Tokyo; Cassina furniture in Paris and New York. Work included in 1989 *The Most Contemporary French Furniture*, Victoria and Albert Museum, London; 1997 *Made in France*, MNAM/Georges Pompidou Centre, Paris; 1997 *Design Francais: l'Art du Mobilier 1986–1996*, Boulogne-Billancourt Cultural Center, Paris; 1998 *La Vie en Roses*, Foundation Cartier, Paris; 2000 Biennale Internationale du Design, Saint-Étienne, France. First prize (table design), 1985 design competition sponsored by Fondation des Galeries Lafayette; 1995 Grand Prix de la Ville de Paris.
Bibliography Cat. Margo Rouard Snowman, *Avant Première: The Most Contemporary French Furniture*, London: Victoria and Albert Museum, 1988. Cat., Design Center Stuttgart, *Women in Design: Careers and Life Histories Since 1900*, Stuttgart: Haus der Wirtschaft, 1989: 244–47. François Mathey, *Au bonheur des formes, design français 1945–1992*, Paris: Regard, 1992. *Who's Who in France*, Paris: Dictionnaire Lafitte, 1994–95 (26th ed.) and following.

Dottori, Arduino (1946–)

Italian industrial and graphic designer; born Cupra Montana; active Milan.

Training Istituto Statale d'Arte, Ancona; 1966–70, Corso Superiore di Disegno Industriale, Florence.
Biography 1971, Dottori began his professional career in his own studio in Milan, designing products, furniture, and interiors; concurrently, was graphic designer to a pharmaceutical firm; 1973 with industrial designers Enrico Picciani and Roberto Ingegnere, set up studio ERA. He has been primarily active in industrial design for clients including Feraboli (agricultural machinery and corporate identity), Ama (agricultural machinery), Elektrolume (electrical appliances), Torelli (corporate identity and packaging), Panunion (graphic design), Teomr (electronic control systems), and Evoluzione (an interior design program for small apartments worldwide). He became a member, Associazione per il Disegno Industriale (ADI).
Bibliography *ADI Annual 1976*, Milan: Associazione per il Disegno Industriale, 1976.

Doucet, Jacques (1853–1929)

French couturier and art collector; active Paris.

Biography 1896–1910, Doucet amassed an impressive collection of 18th-century art and furniture; 1912, had the entire collection auctioned, realizing a record 3 million francs, and turned to 19th- and 20th-century art, furniture, and furnishings; collected paintings by Cézanne, van Gogh, Monet, Sisley, Degas, and Manet; purchased Picasso's *Les demoiselles d'Avignon* in 1920 and *La charmeuse de serpents* by Henri Rousseau. He commissioned furniture and furnishings by Pierre Legrain, Eileen Gray, Rose Adler, Paul Iribe, Marcel Coard, Jean-Charles Moreux, and others; bought Gustav Miklos's sculpture, carpets, and door handles; René Lalique's glass doors, Degaine's lacquerwork and enamels, Jean Lurçat's rugs, Joseph Hecht's lacquered panels, and Étienne Cournault's decorated mirrors. He had met Miklos at 1919 Salon des Indépendants, Adler at École de l'Union Centrale des Arts Décoratifs 1923, and Lurçat at 1925 *Exposition Internationale des Arts Décoratifs et Industriels Modernes*, Paris. On the advice of André Breton, he purchased works by Francis Picabia, Joan Miró, Max Ernst, and André Masson. Architect Paul Ruaud built the 1926 *studio-moderne* annex in the courtyard of the house on the rue Saint-James in Neuilly, near Paris, that Doucet's wife owned. Doucet had an apartment at 43, avenue du Bois (now avenue Foch) in Paris; founded Doucet Bibliothèque and Institut d'Histoire de l'Art et d'Archéologie. Doucet's Art Déco collection remained intact following his 1929 death; 1972, it was auctioned at another sensational sale at Galerie Drouot in Paris.
Bibliography François Chapon, *Mystère et splendeurs de Jacques Doucet 1853–1929*, Paris: Lattès, 1984. Pierre Cabanne, *Encyclopédie art déco*, Paris: Somogy, 1986: 187–89.

Dourgnon, Jean (1901–1985)

French lighting designer and engineer.

Training To 1923, École Supérieure d'Électricité, Paris.
Biography 1928, Dourgnon began extensive research into lighting; 1930, founded lighting group Association Française de l'Éclairage, which collaborated with architects Robert Mallet-Stevens and Georges-Henri Pingusson, designers René Herbst and Pierre Chareau, and lighting engineer André Salomon; 1947, became its president and, 1930, a member, UAM (Union des Artistes Modernes).
Exhibitions Work shown with UAM group from its 1930 (1st) exhibition, presenting dramatic lighting effects at its 1932 and 1935 events; in UAM pavilion (with André Sive), 1937 *Exposition Internationale des Arts et Techniques dans la Vie Moderne*, Paris. Designed the vast vertical illuminated area (with Mallet-Stevens, and Salomon) at 1935 Salon de la Lumière. Was in charge of lighting and photographic sections at 1949 (1st) *Formes Utiles* exhibition of UAM, Pavillon de Marsan, Musée du Louvre; participated in preparation of lighting at 1953 *Formes Utiles*, Salon des Arts Ménages
Bibliography Jean Dourgnon, 'Confort, lumière et architecture,' *Cahiers du CSTB*, no. 492. Bernard Barraqué, *L'éclairagisme entre art et science, Jean Dourgnon (1901–1985)*, Institut d'Urbanisme de Paris, 1986. Arlette Barré-Despond, *UAM*, Paris: Regard, 1986. Cat., *Les années UAM 1929–1958*, Paris: Musée des Arts Décoratifs, 1988.

Dovecot Studios
> See Edinburgh Tapestry Company (Dovecot Studios).

Dózsa-Farkas, Kinga (1943–)

Hungarian industrial designer; born Budapest.

Training 1964–68, product design, Hochschule für Gestaltung, Ulm.
Biography 1968, she married Andreas Dózsa-Farkas and, from 1970, was a freelance designer in the 'dózsa-farkas' design studio in Munich. Work included 1974 Zitrosine citrus fruit press by Buchsteiner, 1976 storage shelf by Buchsteiner, 1987 'Argoflex 44' office-chair range by Albert Stoll Argoflex, 1987 parking system by Skidata Computerhandelsgesellschaft, 1988 control console system for washing installations by H. Kleindienst, and 1988 Gass-Center stove by Wamsler Herd und Ofen.
Exhibitions Traffic lights (designed as a student in Ulm) were shown at 1967 *Universal and International Exhibition (Expo '67)*, Montréal.
Bibliography Cat., Design Center Stuttgart, *Women in Design: Careers and Life Histories Since 1900*, Stuttgart: Haus der Wirtschaft, 1989: 104–09.

Drach, Ami (1963–); Dov Ganchrow (1970–)

Israeli industrial designers. Drach: born Haifa. Ganchrow: born Boston, Mass.

Training Drach: 1987–91, bachelor of design degree, department of industrial design, Bezalel Academy of Art and Design, Jerusalem. Ganchrow: 1985–87, department of product design and graphics, Hagymnasia Haivrit, Jerusalem; 1988–92, bachelor of design degree, Department of Industrial Design, Bezalel Academy.
Biography Drach: from 1994, senior lecturer, Industrial Design Department, Bezalel Academy. Ganchrow: also there, from 2000 as a lecturer. 1995, they established their own product-design practice in Tel Aviv, specializing in medical and surgical equipment, interiors, furniture, and lighting. 2001, received an Israeli patent for a pocket knife.
Exhibitions/citations Work included in large number of exhibitions, including 1993 *National Furniture '94 Exposition*, Tel Aviv; 1993 *Wooden Furniture Design Exhibition*, Brussels; 1994 *Luggage Design*, Tokyo; 1996 Asahikawa Furniture Design Fair, Hokkaido, Japan; 1997 *Cellular Phone*, Askola Gallery; 1997 *Lightbulb*, Periscope Contemporary Design Gallery, Tel Aviv; 1998 *Out of the Box* (young designers of packaging), Openspace Piano Ammezzato, Milan; 1998, 2001, 2003 *Israel Furniture Design Exposition*, Tel Aviv; 1999 *Plans for/of a Drawer*, Askola Gallery, Tel Aviv; 2000 *2000 Objects for a New Millennium*, Gallery 91, New York; 2001, 2002, 2003 *Industrious Designers*, Abitare il Tempo, Verona; 2002 *Israeli Habitat*, Dwek Gallery, Mishkenot Sha'ananim, Jerusalem; 2002 *Industrious Designers*, Frankfurt and Prague. Awards together, except where noted: 1991 Brandenburg Scholarship (Drach); 1992 Meisler Award for Outstanding Product Design (Ganchrow); 1992 Sharett Fund, America-Israel Foundation Prize (Ganchrow); 1994 work selected, Luggage Design competition, Tokyo (Drach); 1996 finalist, Asahikawa International Furniture Design Competition, Hokaido, Japan; 1996 Contemporary Design Award, competition of *National Furniture '97 Expo*, Tel Aviv.
Bibliography Giora Urian, *From the Israel Museum to the Carmel Market: Israeli Design*, Ramat-Hasaron: Urian/The Architect's Encyclopedia, 2001. Cats., Vanni Pasca and Ely Rozenberg, *Industrious Designers = Giovani designer israeliani*, Verona: Abitare il Tempo, 2001 and 2002.

Draper, Dorothy (b. Dorothy Tuckerman 1889–1969)

American interior designer; born Tuxedo Park, N.Y.

Biography After World War I, she initially became known through the renovation of her own house on Manhattan's Upper East Side in New York; also owned a house in Tuxedo Park, N.Y.; 1925, established the Architectural Clearing House, matching architects to appropriate commissions; 1929, designed Carlyle Hotel public areas, 35 East 76th Street, New York, in a so-called Roman Deco style. Her oversized, extremely bold décors appeared in the commissions that followed, including apartment buildings and department stores. She established a reputation for hotels and restaurants with her décors for 1946 Greenbriar resort, White Sulphur Springs, W. Va., and 1935–36 Hampshire House, New York, whose cabbage-rose chintz (produced by Schumacher) was a highly popular fabric, and the hotel's vibrant scarlet front doors with white frames and black exterior walls became a fashionable design appurtenance. She designed 1935 interiors of Mark Hopkins Hotel, San Francisco; late-1930s and 1940s public and private rooms of Statler Hotel chain; 1940 The Camellia House in the Drake Hotel, Chicago; 1944 interiors of Quitandinha resort, Petrópolis (near Rio de Janeiro), Brazil; and the 1954 Roman-inspired restaurant (demolished) of The Metropolitan Museum of Art, New York. Even so, not all her work was for the privileged; for example, there was the 1948 Manhattan Beach Housing Project, New York, with Thonet bentwood chairs. She became a well-known personality, appearing on her own radio program, wrote books and a regular column for *Good Housekeeping* magazine during World War II, and directed the magazine's Studio of Living. Possibly due to her towering physical height, she incorporated dark and bold colors, oversized fabric motifs, wide moldings, and large black-and-white marble floor tiles in her interior design. She pioneered the picture window, white organdy curtains, and bedspreads in chenille (French for 'caterpillar'). 1940s–50s, much of the furniture and textiles in America were designed or inspired by Draper. Manufactured fabrics included 1947 Brazilance and Scatter Floral fabrics by Schumacher and 1940s Stylized Scroll by Waverly. 1960, she sold her business, which was then managed by Carleton Varney.
Bibliography Carleton Varney, *The Draper Touch: The High Life & High Style of Dorothy Draper*, Englewood Cliffs, N.J.: Prentice-Hall, 1988. John Esten and Rose Bennett Gilbert, *Manhattan Style*, Boston: Little, Brown, 1990: 9. Mitchell Owens, 'Larger than Life,' *Elle Decor*, Sept. 1990: 54–56. Mark Hampton, *The Legendary Decorators of the Twentieth Century*, New York: Doubleday, 1992.

Draper, Elisabeth (b. Elisabeth Carrington Frank 1900–1993)

American interior designer; born and active New York.

Training In radio operation during World War I.
Biography A self-taught designer, she established the decorating firm Taylor & Low (with her sister Tiffany Taylor) in New York; 1936, set up her own decorating firm in her own name; became one of the *grandes dames* of American decorating when the discipline was dominated by women; decorated numerous country houses, city apartments, townhouses, and executive suites of banks. In New York, she also designed the somewhat-spare 1948 interiors of the apartment of Gen. and Mrs. Dwight Eisenhower (who later became a US president) at 60 Morningside Drive and the restoration of 1832 Seabury Tredwell residence (today Old Merchant's House). Commissions also included the US Embassy in Paris for Ambassador Amory Houghton.
Bibliography Suzanne Slesin, 'Elisabeth Draper, Grande Dame of Interior Design, Is Dead at 93' (obituary), *The New York Times*, 8 July 1993: D19.

Drasler, Giorgio (1962–)

Italian designer; born and active Udine.

Training To 1991, civil engineering, Università degli Studi, Udine; 1991–92, master's degree, Consorzio Universitario per gli Studi di Organizzazione Aziendale, Altavilla Vicentina, Vicenza.
Biography From 1991, Drasler worked on marketing and design management in consultancies in Udine, including Anna Lombardi Studio, Communicare, Dario Enrico Taurian studio, DesignWork, Enrico Franzolini studio, and Plus Marketing; from 1993, has been a freelance consultant for design management, art direction, and design; for eight years, taught aesthetics and product management. Design work has included 1998 bookcase, wall bracket, CD holder, table, and magazine stand by Vettori; 1998 Notturno Edilizio lamp and 1999 Bottom Shine stool produced by himself; 2000 Vista bookcase by View; 1999 chairs and 2001 table by Montina; 2001 chopping board by FattoAdArte; others.

Dreier, Hans (1885–1966)

German film set designer; born Bremen; active Germany and US.

Training Architecture, Germany.
Biography 1919–23, Dreier worked at UFA/EFA film studios in Berlin. 1923, settled in the US at the invitation of film director Ernst Lubitsch; was art director 1923–28 and head of the design department 1928–51 at Paramount film studios, Hollywood; brought the Bauhaus approach of team effort to his work there, willingly sharing screen credits with the art directors under his supervision, particularly from 1932; was the first supervising art director to search regularly for new talent at design and architecture schools; was strongly influenced by modernism, which was realized in sets for Lubitsch-directed movies, including *Monte Carlo* (1930), *One Hour with You* (1932), and *Trouble in Paradise* (1932). Bauhaus furniture from Dreier's own residence was included in *Trouble in Paradise*, a high point in 1930s film design; the nickel-plated casement clock and hanging light fixture over the dining table are distinctive. Each element in a Dreier-supervised film was fastidiously planned and coordinated; for example, the canal water in *Top Hat* (1935), with white-marble Art Déco 'Venetian' architecture above, was dyed black.
Citations Oscars (for *Frenchman's Creek* of 1944, *Samson and Delilah* of 1949, and *Sunset Boulevard* of 1950), Academy of Motion Picture Arts and Sciences, US.
Bibliography Ann Lee Morgan (ed.) *Contemporary Designers*, London: Macmillan, 1984. Howard Mandelbaum and Eric Myers, *Screen Déco: A Celebration of High Style in Hollywood*, New York: St. Martin's, 1985.

Drésa, Jacques (b. André Saglio 1869–1929)

French painter, decorator, teacher, and curator.

Biography Jacques Drésa was a painter and designed for the Paris Opéra and other theaters, and fabrics and wallpapers for André Groult at Décoration Intérieure Moderne (D.I.M.) and for others; taught, École des Beaux-Arts, Paris, and a curator at the Grand Palais, where he was an organizer of the Salon d'Automne installments and where, c. 1910, became the commissioner general of foreign exhibitions; wrote a number of books and articles on the decorative arts, including *French Furniture* (London: Newnes; New York: Scribner's Sons, 1913), *Maisons d'hommes célèbres* (Paris: Hachette, 1893), and 'Marionnettes Javanaises' in *L'illustration* (no. 105, 23 Feb. 1895: 161). Served as minister of the Beaux-Arts.
Bibliography Victor Arwas, *Art Déco*, New York: Abrams, 1980. Léon Deshairs (intro.), *Modern French Decorative Art: A Collection of Examples of Modern French Decoration*, Paris: Albert Lévy, c. 1925–30. www.archivesnationales.culture.gouv.fr.

Dresselhaus, Bill (1944–)

British industrial designer; active San Francisco.

Training 1973, product design, Stanford University, Berkeley, Cal.
Biography 1979, Dresselhaus shared studio space with Jerry Manock (head of industrial design at Apple Computer, Cupertino, Cal.), who invited him to work at Apple. Dresselhaus designed 1979–80 Lisa computer by Apple that featured a forward-thrusting display face, daring for its time and a variation later used on the Macintosh; 1983, resigned from Apple and, subsequently, was active as a freelance designer in Portland, Ore.
Bibliography Paul Kunkel, *Apple Design: The World of the Apple Industrial Design Group*, New York: Graphis, 1997.

Dresser, Christopher (1834–1904)

British botanist, metalworker, ceramicist, and glass and industrial designer; born Glasgow.

Training 1847–53, School of Design of Somerset House, London; under botanist John Lindley.
Biography Dresser is considered the first independent industrial designer, running a studio supplying designs to manufacturers. 1852, he attended Owen Jones's lectures 'On the True and False in the Decorative Arts,' a prelude to Jones's book *The Grammar of Ornament* (1856), for which Dresser illustrated ten plates that showed designs from nature; c. 1854, began to lecture on botany at School of Design;

1857, wrote the first of several articles on botany in the *Art Journal*; was appointed professor, Botany Applied to the Fine Arts, Department of Science and Art, School of Design, South Kensington, London. He failed to be assigned the chair of botany, University College, London, and, thus, turned to design, focusing on the artistic value of plant forms; 1862, wrote the book *The Art of Decorative Design*, expanded from an 1857 article and inspired by Japanese objects at 1862 London Exhibition; from mid-1860s, was an active industrial designer, independently and assisted by J. Moyr Smith and others; became associated with Wedgwood and Minton ceramics works, c. 1875 creating tile designs for Minton; from c. 1871, designed for Watcombe Pottery Company, Devon; 1879–82, was artistic director of Linthorpe Pottery, designing ceramics for the firm c. 1880; from c. 1871, designed cast-iron furniture by Coalbrookdale Ironworks and also for most of the major British carpet and textile manufacturers, including Brinton (carpets) and Warner (textiles); visited 1876 *Centennial Exposition*, Philadelphia, where he delivered three lectures recommending improvements in the American art industry; while in the US, designed wallpaper patterns and lectured at the newly established School of Industrial Design, Pennsylvania Museum; traveled to Japan, acquiring a large number of objects for Tiffany & Co., New York. In partnership with Charles Holme of Bradford from 1879, he set up the short-lived oriental warehouse Dresser and Holme in London. He wrote *Japan: Its Architecture, Art, and Art Manufactures* (1882) and *Modern Ornamentation* (1886). 1879–85, produced designs for electroplated metalware. From 1878, Hukin & Heath produced his innovative silver designs. He supplied silver designs to Thomas Johnson c. 1880; James Dixon & Sons from 1878, as well as to foreign firms, including Boin-Tabert in Paris. 1880, he established the Art Furnishers' Alliance to sell furniture and ceramics of his own design; 1884, it closed despite financial backing from Arthur Lasenby Liberty. 1883, Dresser became editor of *Furniture Gazette*, an influential periodical; designed wallpaper by Jeffrey & Co., brassware by Perry and c. 1885 glassware by James Cooper. 1889, Dresser set up a studio in Barnes, near London, where he employed ten assistants; before closing in the 1890s, it created textile and product designs. Dresser was a prolific metalworker, primarily of tea sets and table goods executed in proto-modern geometric forms. His shapes were strikingly stark and rigorous, presaging Bauhaus silhouettes. In his metalware, he used thin sheets of silver strengthened by rims or angles. In contrast, his ceramics showed his mastery of ornamentation and his sense of humor. He has become known as one who designed 'novel things in the most perfect accord with the process that is destined to translate them into being' (*The Studio*, Nov. 1898: 113). Since 1990s, a number of pieces have been reproduced, even in plastic by Alessi.

Exhibitions/citations Work subject of 1972 Fine Arts Society exhibition, London; 1981 Kunstgewerbemuseum, exhibition; 2004 Cooper-Hewitt National Design Museum, New York, and Victoria and Albert, London (catalogs below). 1860, honorary doctorate, University of Jena; 1861 fellow, Linnaean Society

Christopher Dresser. Toast rack. 1878. Silver electroplated metal, 5 1/4 x 5 1/4 x 4 1/4" (13.3 x 13.3 x 10.8 cm). Mfr.: James Dixon & Sons, UK. Mrs. John D. Rockefeller 3rd Purchase Fund. MoMA.

Bibliography Nikolaus Pevsner, 'Minor Masters of the Nineteenth Century, 9: Christopher Dresser, Industrial Designer,' *Architectural Review*, no. 81, Mar. 1937: 183–86. Cat., Stuart Durant et al., *Christopher Dresser, 1834–1904*, London: Fine Arts Society, 1972. Stuart Durant, 'Aspects of the Work of Dr. Christopher Dresser (1834–1904), Botanist, Designer, and Writer,' thesis, London: Royal College of Art, 1973. Cat., Michael Collins (ed.), *Christopher Dresser, 1834–1904*, London: Camden Arts Centre, 1979. Cat., *Christopher Dresser: Ein Viktorianischer Designer, 1834–1904*, Cologne: Kunstgewerbemuseum, 1981. Widar Halen, *Christopher Dresser*, Oxford: Phaidon/Christie's, 1990. Stuart Durant, *Christopher Dresser*, London: Academy; Berlin: Ernst & Sohn; 1993. Harry Lyons, *Christopher Dresser: People's Designer 1834–1904*, Alastair Carew-Cox, 1999. Michael Whiteway et al., *Christopher Dresser, 1834–1904*, Skira, 2002. Paola Antonelli (ed.), *Objects of Design: The Museum of Modern Art*, New York: The Museum of Modern Art, 2003: 30–31. Cat., Michael Whiteway (ed.), *The Shock of the Old: Christopher Dresser's Design Revolution*, New York/London: The Cooper Hewitt Museum/Victoria and Albert Museum, 2004.

Dreyfuss, Henry (1904–1972)

American industrial designer; born and active New York.

Training Ethical Culture School, New York.

Biography 1923, Dreyfuss became active as a stage designer, working with Norman Bel Geddes on several successful productions on Broadway; served an unsatisfactory stint as design consultant for Macy's, insisting on collaborating with the manufacturers; 1929, opened his own studio in New York, with a traditional kitchen storage-jar as one of his first commissions; subsequently, opened a second office in Pasadena, Cal.; was a founding member, Society of Industrial Designers (SID) and first president of Industrial Designers Society of America (IDSA). The large number of objects Dreyfuss designed included aircraft interiors for Lockheed, hearing aids, 1932 electric toaster by Birtman Electric Co., 1934 kitchen utensils by The Washburn Company, 1938 Big Ben alarm clock by General Time Instruments (Westclox division), Bell telephones (1930–33 Bell 300 and 1965 Trimline models), Hoover products (from 1934), RCA TV sets (from 1946), 1935 decanter/tray by American Thermos Bottle, farm vehicles for John Deere (including 1956 720 tractor), oceanliners 1951 *Constitution* and 1951 *Independence*, and New York Central Railroad's 1941 *Twentieth Century Limited* carriage (a design more glamorous than usual for Dreyfuss, including 1938 dinnerware by Buffalo China). He developed a basic system of anthropometrics for ergonomic design, the results published in a series of volumes by MIT Press and discussed in his 1955 and 1960 books (see below), the latter representing 'Joe and Josephine,' average male/female proportions/sizes manifesting his lifelong interest in the relationship of human beings to functional design. Niels Diffrient, the collaborator on Dreyfuss's books, was a member of his staff. 1968, Dreyfuss retired from his design firm but remained a consultant to Bell Laboratories, Polaroid, and others; committed suicide with his wife Doris, with whom he endowed The Memorial Study Center at the Cooper-Hewitt National Design Museum, New York, where his archive is housed.

Bibliography Henry Dreyfuss, *Designing for People*, New York: Simon & Schuster, 1955. Henry Dreyfuss, *Industrial Design: A Pictorial Accounting, 1929–57*, New York, 1957. Henry Dreyfuss, *The Measure of Man*, New York: Whitney, 1960. 'Henry Dreyfuss 1904–1972,' *Industrial Design*, vol. 20, Mar. 1973: 37–423. Russell Flinchum, *Henry Dreyfuss, Industrial Designer: The Man in the Brown Suit*, New York: Cooper-Hewitt National Design Museum/Rizzoli, 1997.

Driade

Italian furniture manufacturer; located Milan.

History 1968, Driade was founded by Enrico Astori, his sister Antonia Astori, and his wife Adelaide Acerbi, when the Astoris took over soft furnishings firm Ideal in Piacenza. Driade has produced a full range of furniture, furnishings, and ceramics designed by Antonia Astori, Gio Ponti, Rodolfo Bonetto, Alberto Dal Lago, Rocco Serini, De Pas/D'Urbino/Lomazzi, Franco Fraschini, Enzo Mari, Adelmo Rascaroli, Giotto Stoppino, Philippe Starck, and Nanda Vigo; from the outset, used plastics, primarily ABS molding and fiberglass. At first, other manufacturing entities were commissioned to produce wood-frame, steel, and polyurethane components. Driade designers rejected Bauhaus models in favor of Neo-Dada, Pop Art, Arte Povera, Conceptual Art,

Driade: Enzo Mari. Sof-Sof chair. 1971. Chromed-plated steel rods and fabric, 31 1/2 x 18 x 20 7/8" (80 x 45.7 x 53 cm). Mfr.: Driade, Italy. Gift of the mfr. MoMA.

and Earth Art. The 1968 Driade I collection, produced 1968–78, consisted of three pieces: the Cherea easychair and Mala armchair by Fraschini, and Cidonio table by Astori. Driade's 1970 Alessia chair and Febo table by Stoppino were made in fiberglass. The factory moved from Piacenza to Fossadello di Caorso in 1969, when it produced only one furniture item: the Duecavalli armchair by De Pas/D'Urbino/Lomazzi. From 1972, the firm produced the Ipercubo series of soft furnishings by De Pas/D'Urbino/Lomazzi and, subsequently, expanded its range greatly, including a line of tabletop objects and dinnerware utensils.
Products Include 1970 Melania armchair by Bonetto, 1970 Canopo, 1973 Oikos and 1980 Oikosdue systems by Astori, 1974 Ara series and Gazebo settle by the Vignellis, 1974 Makeba club chair by Dal Lago, 1978 Bris system by Astori and Mari, 1981 Demel couch and 1981 Sacher chair by Sottsass Associati, 1982 Sabrina couch by Alessandro Mendini, 1982 Backbottom seat by Deganello, and 1982 Sancarlo chair by Castiglioni. Mari designed 1971 Sof-Sof chair, 1972 Day-Night convertible sofa, 1976 Gambadilegno club chair and ottoman, 1977 Capitello table series, 1981 Vela side chair, and 1974 Fratello table. Starck's 1985 range for Driade's Adeph division was named 'Ubik' after the science-fiction novel by Philip K. Dick and comprised Sarapis stool, Mickville chair-stool, Von Vogelsang chair, Titos Apostos table, and Tippy Jackson table. Since, its inventory has included furniture, furnishings, and glass, metal, stone, and ceramic tableware and objects by Mario Bellini, Mathew Hilton, Marta Laudani/Marco Romanelli, Elliott Littmann, Ross Lovegrove, Kazuyo Sejima, Michel Sempels, George Sowden, Roderick Vos, and others.
Citations 1979, 1981, 1987, 2001 Compasso d'Oro.
Bibliography Cat., Milena Lamarová (ed.), *Design a Plastické Hmoty*, Prague: Uměleckoprůmyslové Muzeum, 1972: 52, 180. Renato De Fusco, *Il 'gioco' del design: Vent'anni di attività della Driade*, Naples: Electa, 1988.

Drocco, Guido (1942–)

Italian architect and designer; born San Benedetto Belbo; active Turin.

Training To 1974, architecture, Politecnico, Turin.
Biography 1967, Drocco began his professional career in design; from 1962, has designed architecture and furniture with the Gabetti & Isola office, with partners Roberto Gabetti (1925–) and Aimaro Isola (Aimaro d'Isola Oreglia, 1931–), Turin. Drocco has become best known for 1972 Cactus coat rack (with Franco Mello) in expanded polyurethane, by Gufram, reflective of the Radical Design movement of the time. Other Drocco design work has included a 1969 low-priced lamp, various multi functional furniture, particularly 1970 example by Arbo, 1972 Trampolino transformable table by Colli (with Mello), 1990 office furniture (with Gabetti & Isola), and 1992 Valturio general-purpose automobile; became a member, Associazione per il Disegno Industriale (ADI).
Exhibitions/citations Work included in numerous venues and Cactus coat rack included in 2002 exhibition of Gufram, Manica Lunga, Castello di Rivoli, Turin (catalog below). Participated in a number of architectural competitions. First prizes:1969 Mostra Internazionale dell'Arredamento, Monza, and 1970 Mostra Internazationale del Mobile; special jury citation, Premio Luigi Cosenza, Naples; others.
Bibliography *ADI Annual 1976*, Milan: Associazione per il Disegno Industriale, 1976. *Provokationen Design aus Italien*, Hanover: Werkbund, 1982. Fulvio Irace, 'Minima architectonica: sede municipale a Bagnolo Piemonte; architects: Roberto Gabetti & Aimaro Isola, with Guido Drocco, 1982,' *Domus*, no. 632, 1982: 2–9. *Allgemeines Künstlerlexikon*, Leipzig, E.A. Seemann, 1990. Cristina Morozzi and Silvio San Pietro, *Contemporary Italian Furniture*, Milan: L'Archivolto, 1996. Andrea Branzi, *Il design italiano 1964–1990*, Milan: Elemond, 1996. Cat., Stefano Casciani (ed.), *Design italiano nei musei del mondo 1950–1990*, Milan: Abitare Segesta, 1998. Cat., Franco Mello, Ennio Chiggio and Stefano Casciani, *The Rock Furniture = Il design della Gufram negli anni del Rock*, Turin: Castello di Rivoli, 2002.
> See Gufram.

Droog Design

Dutch designer cooperative.

History 1993, Droog Design, an ad-hoc design cooperative, was founded by jewelry designer Gijs Bakker and design critic Renny Ramakers. The managers of Droog Design have collected ideas and concepts from young designers and offer art direction to companies looking for innovative approaches to products, marketing, or sales.

Henry Dreyfuss. Trimline telephone. 1960–65. Plastic, 3 1/2 x 8 1/2 x 2 3/4" (8.9 x 21.6 x 7 cm). Mfr.: Western Electric, US. Gift of the Bell Telephone System. MoMA.

1993–96, DMD, the manufacturing arm of Droog Design, produced about 20 products. The introductory collection garnered an enthusiastic response from the press at 1993 Salone del Mobile in Milan and included 1991 Milkbottle lamp by Tejo Remy, 1991 Archimedes letter scale by Arnout Visser, 1992 85 Lamps by Rodi Graumans, 1993 Soft Vase by Hella Jongerius, and generally represented the first phase of Droog Design. The bathroom project, by various designers, was introduced in 1997, produced from 1998. Numerous products have followed by designers such as Constantin Boym, Arian Brekveld, Richard Hutten, Saar Oosterhof, and more recently Martí Guixé, and RADI Designers. (However some Droog Design projects, such as 1991 You Can't Lay Down Your Dreams chest of drawers by Tejo Remy, are produced by the designers themselves.)
Exhibitions/citations Work shown at 1993 Salone del Mobile, Milan, and Internationale Möbelmesse, Cologne; 1996 *Thresholds: Contemporary Design from The Netherlands*, The Museum of Modern Art, New York; 1998 'The Inevitable Ornament' project (B-set, Table Cloth with Bowl, Optic Glasses, and Bronto child's chair, produced from 1999), Milan; 1998, 2001, and subsequent editions of Salone del Mobile, Milan; *Droog Design in the AA*, London; 2002–03 *Conran Foundation Collection–Droog Design*, Design Museum, London. Received 1998 Incentive award (for Soft Washbowl), Amsterdam Art Foundation for Industrial Design; 2000 Kho Liang le applied-arts prize of Amsterdam Fonds voor de Kunst; 2002 selection (by Bakker and Ramakers), Conran Foundation Collection.
Bibliography Ida van Zijl, *Droog Design, 1991–1996*, Utrecht: Centraal Museum, 1997. Renny Ramakers and Gijs Bakker (eds.), *Droog Design: Spirit of the Nineties*, Rotterdam: 010 Publishers, 1998. José Teunissen et al., *Droog & Dutch Design*, Utrecht: Centraal Museum, 2000. Renny Ramakers, *Less + More: Droog Design in Context*, Rotterdam: 010 Publishers, 2002.
> See Bey, Jurgen (1965–).

Drouet, René (1899–1993)
French designer.

Training École Boulle, Paris.
Biography Drouet began working as a designer at Décoration Intérieure Mobilier (D.I.M.); subsequently at La Maîtrise decorating studio of Les Galeries Lafayette department store, Paris; 1929, set up his own studio and designed furniture in a historicist or classical form of Art Déco, calling on luxury materials and techniques, such as ebony, sycamore, leather, inlays, lacquer finishes, and winding *bronze d'oré* round wrought iron
Bibliography Cat., Sophie Tasma Anargyros et al., *L'école française: les créateurs de meubles du 20ème siècle*, Paris: Industries Françaises de l'Ameublement, 2000.

Drugman, Giovanni (1960–)
Italian architect and designer.

Training To 1987, Politecnico, Milan.
Biography Drugman worked at the studio of Umberto Riva; 1992, set up his own studio in Milan, practicing as an architect and designer; 1999, established a partnership with Michele Pizzinato. Work has included 1996 Trina deck chair and 1997 Lucignolo mirror, Bis deck chair, Pippo trolley, July chair, Pilone lamp, Constantino plate rack, all by Squadramobile; 1998 Sottile bookcase, 1998 Edi lamp, and Blocco notepad produced in partnership with Pizzinato.
Bibliography *Abitare*, Oct. 1995. *Ottagono*, nos. 119, July–Aug. 1996; no. 122, Mar.–May 1997. *Domovoi*, no. 4, 1997. *Design News*, no. 241, 1998.
> See Pizzinato, Michele.

Dryad
> See Peach, Harry Hardy.

du Chayla, Frédéric (1957–)
French designer; born Lyon.

Biography 1980–87 with Jacques Bonnot, Vincent Lemarchands, and Claire Olivès, Chayla was a member of the Totem group in Lyon; 1987–91, coparticipation with Bonnot only; from 1991, represented the group, working with architects and others, as well as individually designing in his own name; under the Totem label, has designed and made lighting, furniture, furnishings, and interiors; from 1994, taught design, École Supérieur des Beaux-Arts, Marseille; 1992–2000 with architect Rudy Ricclotti, has been a designer for the theater and of

Droog Design: Hella Jongerius. Soft Vase. 1993. Polyurethane, h. 10 x dia. 7 1/2" (25.4 x 19.1 cm). Mfr.: Droog Design, the Netherlands. Frederieke Taylor Purchase Fund. MoMA.

furniture and lighting.
> See Totem.

du Pasquier, Nathalie (1957–)
French artist and textile designer; born Bordeaux; active Milan; wife of George J. Sowden.

Biography 1980, she joined Studio Rainbow as a textile designer; 1981–88, was actively designing for the Memphis group in Milan; frequently collaborated with husband George Sowden, both for Memphis and others. They designed 1980s Progetto Decorazione silkscreen printed papers. Much of the visual excitement of early Memphis designs was due to du Pasquier's busy, vividly colored, overall patterns, inspired by her earlier travels. She designed Memphis's first fabrics, used for upholstered furniture by Sowden; set up own design office with Sowden in Milan, active in architecture projects, ceramics research, and textile studies; 1982, joined the creative staff of Fiorucci; 1985 with Sowden, designed cutlery and pocket knives, commissioned by Maison des Couteliers (a cooperative of French cutler artisans). Her work included moquettes, ceramics, and clocks (with Sowden) by Lorenz, and fashion textiles by Pink Dragon, Missoni Kids, Esprit, and NAS Oleari. 1987, she turned exclusively to painting; subsequently while continuing to paint, returned to design, with work including 1998 Fritto Misto watch by Swatch.
Work For Memphis, included 1983 Royal chaise longue, 1985 Cauliflower and Onion ceramic bowls, 1986 Madras table, 1986 Bombay side table, 1986 Bordeaux table lamp, and 1987 Denise armchair. Her Memphis textiles included 1981 Mali and Burundi, 1982 Zambia, Zaire, and Gabon, and 1983 Cerchio cotton prints, and 1983 Arizona and California rugs. Her 1988 tableware was produced by Algorithme, France.
Exhibitions Included in 1981 (1st) exhibition of Memphis, during Salone del Mobile, Milan, and subsequently. Showed her 20 patterns on paper (with Sowden), Objects for the Electronic Age collection, and Ten Modern Carpets collection by Palmisano.
Bibliography Andrea Branzi, *La casa calda: esperienze del nuovo disegno italiano*, Milan: Idea, 1982. Cat., Kathryn B. Hiesinger and George H. Marcus III (eds.), Design Since 1945, Philadelphia: Philadelphia Museum of Art, 1983. Liz McQuiston, *Women in Design: A Contemporary View*, New York: Rizzoli, 1988: 80. Barbara Radice, 'Mosaici Morbidi,' Modo, no. 54, Nov. 1982: 68.

du Plantier, Marc (1901–1975)
French painter, decorator, and furniture designer; born Madagascar.

Training École Nationale Supérieure des Beaux-Arts, Paris.
Biography He began as a fashion designer in couture houses in Paris; through commissions from the Comédie Française, designed stage

sets and, soon thereafter, interiors of private Parisian apartments and houses, including 1936 furnishings in a graphic modern style for the salon of couturier Jacques Heim. From the last half of 1930s, he became known for his elegant furniture, comparable to Jean-Michel Frank's, produced in natural materials including oak, white marble, and parchment; later showed a preference for patinated bronze and wrought iron and classical forms in precious woods but eventually turned to a spare modern style. He died in Paris.
Bibliography François Mathey, *Au bonheur des formes, design français 1945–1992*, Paris: Regard, 1992: 236. Cat., Sophie Tasma Anargyros et al., *L'école française: les créateurs de meubles du 20ème siècle*, Paris: Industries Françaises de l'Ameublement, 2000.

Dubois, Fernand (1861–1939)
Belgian sculptor and metalworker; born Renaix; brother of Paul Dubois.

Training 1877, natural sciences, Université de Bruxelles; sculpture under Charles van der Stappen.
Biography He was a medalist and modeler of silver and bronze objects and jewelry. His 1901–06 house at 80 avenue Brugmann, Brussels, was designed by his friend Victor Horta. Working in bronze, pewter, and enamels, he produced a wide range of ornaments, including fans, candelabra, medallions, plaques, and bas-reliefs; is known for the exuberant five-branched candelabra in the Horta Museum, Brussels; from 1896, taught metalworking, École Industrielle, Brussels.
Exhibitions Medals, jewelry, chandeliers, candelabra, an inkwell, and ivory figurines set in silver were shown at 1894, 1895, 1897, and 1899 Salons of La Libre Esthétique. Marriage casket in ivory and silver-bronze shown in Congo Palace at 1879 Tervueren chryselephantine sculpture exposition.
Bibliography Yvonne Brunhammer et al., *Art Nouveau Belgium, France*, Houston: Rice University, 1976. Alastair Duncan, *Art Nouveau and Art Déco Lighting*, New York: Simon & Schuster, 1978: 49. Annelies Krekel-Aalberse, *Art Nouveau and Art Déco Silver*, New York: Abrams, 1989.

Dubois, Paul (1859–)
Belgian designer; brother of Fernand Dubois.

Biography Dubois was colleague of sculptors Constantin Meunier and Victor Rousseau; created monumental sculpture and designed and produced *objets d'art,* including vases, candelabra, plaqettes, jugs, belt clasps, and paperweights; became one of the most successful of the Belgian sculptors who produced work in both monumental forms and the applied arts.
Exhibitions Small objects frequently shown in exhibitions of Les Vingt group and, subsequently, at Salons of La Libre Esthétique.
Bibliography Alastair Duncan, *Art Nouveau and Art Déco Lighting*, New York: Simon & Schuster, 1978.

Dubreuil, André (1951–)
French interior and furniture designer; born Lyon; active London.

Training Architecture in Switzerland; design, Inchbald School of Design, London.
Biography 1972–76, Dubreuil was a freelance interior designer; 1977, worked as an antiques dealer in London, and as a muralist and interior designer; 1983, began experimenting with *trompe-l'œil* effects; 1985, collaborated on the decoration of Rococo Chocolats boutique (with Tom Dixon) in London and began designing furniture; 1986, concentrated on designing and producing wrought-iron furniture, including his widely published 1987–88 Spine chair in limited quantities by Personalities, Japan, and 1988 Paris chair; 1990, produced his first glassware collection, inspired by a small Roman vase and including large glass floor lamps and wall models. His glassware was sold at Daum.
Exhibitions Work shown in London, Paris, Tokyo, New York, and Brussels.
Bibliography Albrecht Bangert and Karl Michael Armer, *80s Style: Designs of the Decade*, New York: Abbeville, 1990. Cat., *Acquisitions 1982–1990 arts décoratifs*, Paris: Fonds National d'Art Contemporain, 1991.

Dubuisson, Sylvain (1946–)
French architect-designer; born Bordeaux; active Paris.

Training Architecture, École Supérieure d'Architecture de Saint-Luc, Tournai, Belgium.
Biography Dubuisson designed interiors, furniture, exhibitions, and lighting; 1973, worked in the architecture office of Ove Arup in London; from 1980, has been an independent architect; designed 'Espace du Livre' at 1985 *Art et Industrie* exhibition, Musée National des Monuments Français; 1986 exhibitions, Cité des Sciences et de l'Industrie, Parc La Villette, Paris, and Centre Georges Pompidou, Paris; 1986, furniture for Tour Nord, Notre-Dame cathedral, and Caisse Nationale des Monuments Historiques et des Sites; 1988 furniture by Fourniture for the director's office, Musée Historique des Tissus, Lyon; 1987 Équerre d'Argent (the trophy for the grand prize in architecture) and trophy for Initiative Qualité 87 prize, Ministère de l'Industrie et de la Recherche; 1988, designed for lighting firm Yamagiwa, Tokyo, and various lamp studies for Daum;1989 extension to the exhibition, Cathédrale de Notre Dame, Paris; 1993 *Design, Miroir du Siècle* exhibition, Grand Palais, Paris; and c. 1999 bookstore and a section, from 2002, of Musée des Arts Décoratifs, Paris.
Work Includes 1982–83 Quasi una Fantasia woman's desk, 1983 Le Castelet child's desk, and 1983 Beaucoup de Bruit pour Rien table lamp, all produced by Écart for Fonds National d'Art Contemporain in 1984; 1984 Le Cœur d'Amour Épris table lamp (unique piece); 1984 Lulita desk lamp (with engineer Jean-Sébastien Dubuisson) produced by Mazda Éclairage Lita; 1985 Tetractys table lamp produced by Galerie Néotù for Fonds National d'Art Contemporain in Bordeaux; 1985 Applique A4 signage/lighting unit (with Jean-Sébastien Dubuisson) produced by Écart and installed in 1989 Mobilier National for Centre National des Arts Plastiques at the French national bicentennial exhibition; 1986 La Licorne lamp and 1986 T2/A3 disk clock (both unique pieces); 1986 73 Secondes candlesticks produced in 1989 by Creative Agent; 1987 Table Composite in carbon-steel tubing and mono-composite-epoxy film; 1987 L'Elliptique hot plate and 1987 Volcan—Un Mont ashtray produced by Algorithme for Nestor Perkal's La Collection; 1987 L'Aube et le Temp qu'Elle Dure one-piece aluminum chair sponsored by VIA (French furniture association); 1987 L'Inconscient bed by Fourniture; 1988 Lettera Amorosa vase in blown glass and metal by Lino Tagliapietra; 1988 Étagère JNF wall-shelf by Fourniture; 1989 Héraclite aluminum clock; 1989 elliptical desk for the office of Jack Lang (then the French minister of culture); 1990 L'Aiguillère Retrouvée by Algorithme; bookstore of Musée des Arts Décoratifs, Paris.
Exhibitions/citations Work included in 1985 *Onze Lampes*, Galerie Néotù, Paris; 1985 *Lumière, Je Pense à Vous*, at Centre Georges Pompidou, Paris; 1985 *Art et Industrie*, Espace du Livre, Musée des Monuments Français, Paris; 1987 exhibition, Galerie Desco, Bordeaux; 1988 BDX and *Arc-en-Rêve* exhibition, CAPC, Musée des Arts Contemporains, Bordeaux; 1988 *MDF—des Créateurs pour un Matériau*, Fondation Cartier, Jouy-en-Josas; 1988 *Tandem* at Musée de Romans, Salone del Mobile, Milan; 1988, Centre Culturel de Ribérac; and 1990 VIA exhibition (catalog below). Subject of 1989 Musée des Arts Décoratifs exhibition (catalog below); 1992 *Sylvain Dubuisson: Design and Dessin*, The Israel Museum, Jerusalem. Won 1984 competition sponsored by the APCI (Agence pour la Promotion de la Création Industrielle); 1989 Carte Blanche production support (for 1989 Jack Lang desk), VIA; Creator of the Year, 1990 Salon du Meuble, Paris.
Bibliography Sophie Anargyros, *Intérieurs: le mobilier français*, Paris: Regard/VIA, 1980: 57–64. Cat., *Lumière, je pense à vous*, Paris: Centre Georges Pompidou/Hermé, 1985. Sophie Anargyros, *Le style des années 80: architecture, décoration, design*, Paris: Rivages, 1986: 106–10. Christine Colin, *Design aujourd'hui*, Paris: Flammarion, 1988. Cat., *MDF—des créateurs pour un matériau*, Paris: Fondation Cartier, 1988. Cat., *Inspiration: éloge de la lumière*, Tokyo: Parco, 1988. Cat., Yvonne Brunhammer (ed.), *Sylvain Dubuisson: Objets et Dessins*, Paris: Musée des Arts Décoratifs, 1989. Cat., *Les années VIA*, Paris: Musée des Arts Décoratifs, 1990. Cat., *Acquisitions 1982–1990 arts décoratifs*, Paris: Fonds National d'Art Contemporain, 1991. François Mathey, *Au bonheur des formes, design français 1945–1992*, Paris: Regard, 1992. *Sylvain Dubuisson*, Paris: AFAA, 1992.

Duc, Christian (1949–)
Vietnamese designer; active Paris.

Training English literature and fine art.
Biography Duc worked as a book illustrator for an American publisher in Amsterdam; 1973–77, designed cinema and café interiors in Berlin; 1977, established Galerie DCA (Duc et Cameroux Associés) in Paris for the distribution of furniture, rugs, and interior accessories that he designed. Clients have included Toronto Museum of Modern Art (lighting with Bruynzeel), V'Soske rugs, Mobilier International, and African Queen restaurant (1988 furniture) in Paris. Other work: rugs by Elisée Éditions (from 1988), rugs by Toulemonde Bochart (from 1987), 1987 Archéologie Future spherical lamp was produced by Delisle (with glass by Patrick Desserme and Bernard Pictet), and ceramics by Faïenceries

de Gien (1988). A number of his pieces and collections were sponsored by VIA (French furniture association).
Exhibitions/citations Work included in 1989 *L'Art de Vivre* exhibition, Cooper-Hewitt National Design Museum, New York, and 1990 *Les années VIA* exhibition, Musée des Arts Décoratifs, Paris. Interior design prize, 1985 Salon of Société des Artistes Décorateurs; prize (for Archéologie Future lamp), 1987 Salon du Luminaire, Paris; Grand Prix de la Presse et de la Critique, 1989 Salon du Meuble, Paris; 1990 Grand Prix de la Création de la Ville de Paris.
Bibliography Cat., *Les années VIA*, New York: Vendome, 1989. François Mathey, *Au bonheur des formes, design français 1945–1992*, Paris: Regard, 1992. Cat., Sophie Tasma Anargyros et al., *L'école française: les créateurs de meubles du 20ème siècle*, Paris: Industries Françaises de l'Ameublement, 2000.

Ducaroy, Michel (1925–)
French designer.

Training École Nationale Supérieure des Beaux-Arts, Lyon.
Biography Born to a family of furniture designers and makers, Ducaroy was a designer at the Ligne Roset firm, for which he created numerous modular chairs and sofas, including 1973 Togo sofa and lounge chair in folded and horizontal-pleated latex foam rubber and polyester wadding (typical of the new cushion-type, rather than traditional rigid-frame-type, seating). 1998, Togo seating won a further claim to fame when installed in the lobby of the retro-decorated Standard Hotel in Los Angeles and called 'voluptuously squashy' and 'caterpillar-shaped' by *Absolute Mirabella* magazine.
Bibliography Cat., Sophie Tasma Anargyros et al., *L'école française: les créateurs de meubles du 20ème siècle*, Paris: Industries Françaises de l'Ameublement, 2000.

Ducrot, Vittorio (1867–1942)
Italian furniture manufacturer; located Palermo.

Biography Active in the first three decades of the 20th century, Ducrot produced furniture and interior designs to the specifications of Ernesto Basile.
Bibliography *Mobili e arredi di Ernesto Basile: nella produzione Ducrot*, Palermo: Novecento, 1980. Cat., Gabriel P. Weisberg, *Stile Floreale: The Cult of Nature in Italian Design*, Miami: The Wolfsonian Foundation, 1988.

Dudas, Frank; DKR
Canadian industrial designer; active Toronto.

Biography 1960, Dudas, Jan Kuypers, and Doug Rowan worked in the Product Unit within Stewart & Morrison design studio in Toronto. 1963, the three departed to form a studio that, in 1967, was known as Dudas Kuypers Rowan (DKR), with a staff of 16 and also offices in Ottawa and Montréal. Dudas designed furniture including seating for IIL International. Jerry Adamson (Cambridge, Ontario, 1937–), a graduate in industrial design from Ontario College of Art, worked with Robin Rush before he joined DKR in 1963 and became a partner in 1968. Within DKR, he designed Habitat chair. Other DKR partners were Ian Norton (small-appliance designs) and Gerald Beekenkamp (phone booths by King Products and Duraglide slide by Paris Playground Equipment). Beekenkamp's slide is safe, colorful, durable in many climates, and easy to ship to save 50% over normal cost.
Bibliography Cat., *Seduced and Abandoned: Modern Furniture Designers in Canada, the First Fifty Years*, Toronto: The Art Gallery at Harbourfront, 1986: 21. Rachel Gotlieb and Cora Golden, *Design in Canada Since 1945: Fifty Years from Teakettles to Task Chairs*, Toronto: Knopf Canada, 2001.

Dufet, Michel (1888–1985)
French interior designer and writer; born Deville-les-Rouen; active Paris.

Training Painting and architecture, École des Beaux-Arts, Paris.
Biography 1913, Dufet established the decorating studio Mobilier Artistique Moderne (MAM) at 3, avenue de l'Opéra in Paris to produce modern furniture, wallpaper, fabrics, and lighting; 1918, staged the theatrical revue *Feuillets d'art* (with Paul Claudel, André Gide, Marcel Proust, and Gabriel Fauré), which ran for two years; 1920, began a collaboration with Louis Bureau on design at MAM; 1924, sold MAM to the firm P.-A. Dumas, but Dufet continued to make furniture. 1922–24, Dufet was head of the interior-decorating firm Red Star in Rio de Janeiro; designed interiors of stores, cinemas, bars, and offices; 1924–39, worked with art critic Léandre Vaillat at the newly formed Le Sylve design studio of Le Bûcheron store, where he designed furniture and furnishings, including a desk in Canadian birch for the director of Agence Havas and 1929 ebony, zinc, and cellulose-veneered desk for Compagnie Asturienne des Mines; c. 1924, designed the first Cubist wallpapers. His commissions included children's playroom of 1927 oceanliner *Île-de-France*, 40 first-class cabins of 1935 oceanliner *Normandie*, 1950 oceanliner *Foch*, a yacht for Marcel L'Herbier. Dufet wanted to design for mass production but received little interest from manufacturers; was influenced by neo-Cubism, reflected in his furniture in exotic woods with elegant, refined lines. He designed numerous shops, theaters, offices, and public spaces; 1933, became editor-in-chief of journal *Décor d'aujourd'hui*; 1947, designed the layout for Musée Antoine Bourdelle in Paris. From 1950, was primarily active promoting the work of his father-in-law/sculptor Antoine Bourdelle.
Exhibitions Several furniture pieces in 1914 Salon of Société des Artistes Français. From 1919, MAM's work shown at Salons of Société des Artistes Décorateurs, and editions of Salon d'Automne. Designed the reception salon of Maréchal Lyautey, the commissioner general of 1931 *Exposition Coloniale*, Paris. Was architect of French pavilion at 1939–40 *New York World's Fair: The World of Tomorrow*. Participated in wallpaper pavilion (with René Gabriel) at 1937 *Exposition Internationale des Arts et Techniques dans la Vie Moderne*, Paris.
Bibliography Léon Deshairs (intro.), *Modern French Decorative Art: A Collection of Examples of Modern French Decoration*, Paris: Albert Lévy, c. 1925–30. Victor Arwas, *Art Déco*, New York: Abrams, 1980. Pierre Cabanne, *Encyclopédie art déco*, Paris: Somogy, 1986: 189–90. Pierre Kjellberg, *Art déco: les maîtres du mobilier, le décor des paquebots*, *Paris*: Amateur, 1986/1990. Auction cat., Sotheby's New York, 16 June 1989, lot nos. 372–73.

Duffner and Kimberly
American lighting manufacturer; located New York.

History Before 1906, Frank Duffner and Oliver Kimberly may have been employees at the Tiffany studios. Active c. 1906–11 at 11 West 32nd Street in New York, they produced leaded-glass floor and table lamps, chandeliers, wall brackets, electric-'candle' sconces, and electric chandeliers. 1911, the firm became Kimberly, located at 317 East 38th Street, where the Ancient Texture lamp range was made in English antique glass with painted scenes illustrating heraldry, the Crusades, and the signing of the Magna Carta.
Bibliography Alastair Duncan, *Art Nouveau and Art Déco Lighting*, New York: Simon & Schuster, 1978: 44–45.

Dufrêne, Maurice (1876–1955)
French furniture, textile, glassware, ceramic, and silverware designer; born Paris.

Training École Nationale Supérieure des Arts Décoratifs, Paris.
Biography 1899, Dufrêne became director and manager of Julius Meier-Graefe's La Maison Moderne store/enterprise in Paris, designing small silver objects such as umbrella handles; 1904, cofounded Société des Artistes Décorateurs as a reaction against the excesses of Art Nouveau, favoring the spare ornamentation of the Style 1900; by 1906, was designing in plain, solid shapes with little ornament; worked in wood, metal, glass, textiles, and leather and designed stoneware and porcelain for Pierre-Adrien Dalpayrat; 1912–23, taught, École Boulle, and, subsequently, École des Arts Appliqués, both Paris; with Claude Autant-Lara, designed the first modernist film sets (for Marcel L'Herbier's 1919 film *Le carnaval des vérités*). 1922–52, Dufrêne was creator and director of La Maîtrise design studio of Les Galeries Lafayette department store in Paris, where he designed furniture, silverware, carpets, wallpaper, ceramics, glassware, and complete interiors. His furniture pieces in refined forms were soberly decorated and inspired by 18th- and early 19th-century models. He advocated mass-production and industrial techniques; however, his modernism had traditional leanings that, even so, ranged eclectically from the interiors of the townhouse of Pierre David-Weill to the 'baroque' Art Déco apartment of Pierre Benoit and his avant-garde late-1920s designs for glass, metal, and mirrors of the casino in Challes-les-Eaux. Late 1920s, he executed commissions from Le Mobilier National for embassies and for Palais de l'Élysée in Paris.
Exhibitions Work first shown at 1902 Salon of Société des Artistes Décorateurs; from 1903, regularly at editions of Salon d'Automne and Salons of Société Nationale des Beaux-Arts. At 1925 *Exposition Internationale des Arts Décoratifs et Industriels Modernes*, Paris: designed

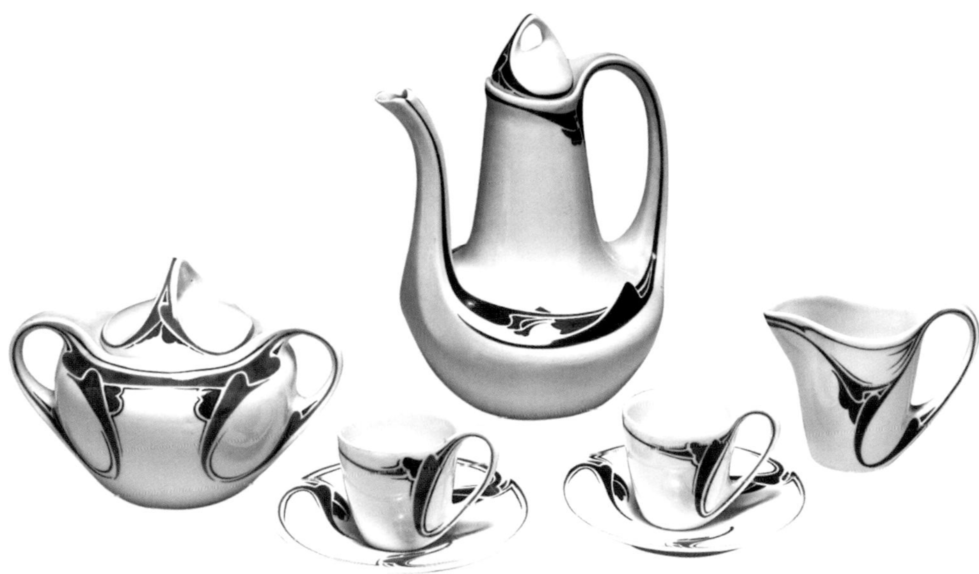

Maurice Dufrêne. Moka service. c. 1903. Glazed white porcelain, sugar bowl h. 5 1/8" (13 cm), pot h. 9 1/8" (23.3 cm), creamer h. 3 5/8" (9.2 cm), cup/saucer overall h. 2 3/8" (6 cm). Mfr.: Loui [sic] Foecy Laurioux for La Maison Moderne, Paris, France. Courtesy Quittenbaum Kunstauktionen, Munich.

luxury boutiques on the pont Alexandre III, layout and furniture for the small living room of Une Ambassade Française pavilion, and the interior of La Maîtrise pavilion.

Bibliography Yvonne Brunhammer et al., *Art Nouveau Belgium, France*, Houston: Rice University, 1976. Victor Arwas, *Art Déco*, New York: Abrams, 1980. Yvonne Brunhammer, *Art Déco Style*, London: Academy, 1983. Florence Camard, *Ruhlmann*, Paris: Regard, 1983. Pierre Kjellberg, *Art déco: les maîtres du mobilier, le décor des paquebots*, Paris: Amateur, 1986/1990. Pierre Cabanne, *Encyclopédie art déco*, Paris: Somogy, 1986: 190–91. *Restaurants, dancing, cafés, bars*, Paris: Charles Moreau, nos. 32–34, [n.d.].

Dufresne, Charles-Georges (1876–1938)

French painter and designer.

Training Sculpture and pastel, École Nationale Supérieure des Beaux-Arts, Paris.

Biography 1923, Dufresne cofounded the Salon des Tuileries; designed a set of tapestries woven at Beauvais for a furniture suite commissioned by Le Mobilier National, based on the story of Paul and Virginie.

Exhibitions/citations 1924 tapestries for a suite of furniture designed by Süe et Mare shown at 1925 *Exposition Internationale des Arts Décoratifs et Industriels Modernes*, Paris. Refused all honors and awards except the Carnegie Prize, Pittsburgh, Pa., US..

Bibliography Victor Arwas, *Art Déco*, New York: Abrams, 1980. Cat., Aaron Lederfajn and Xavier Lenormand (eds.), *Le Louvre des Antiquaires présente: 1930 quand le meuble devient sculpture*, Paris, 1986.

Dufy, Raoul (1877–1953)

French painter and decorative designer; born Le Havre.

Biography Dufy was associated for a time with the Fauve artists' group through Othon Friesz and Albert Marquet; designed letterheads for fashion designer Paul Poiret, who commissioned him in 1911 to design fabrics, and set him up in a studio; 1923–30, designed a tapestry screen and seat cover by Manufacture Nationale de Beauvais and, 1912–30, dress textiles, upholstery fabrics, and printed panels by Bianchini-Férier in Lyon. The composition of his balanced, over-all patterns is comparable to that of William Morris. His fabric by Bianchini-Férier was used by architect/designer Francis Jourdain in 1924–33 Noailles villa (achitect, Rob Mallet-Stevens), Hyères; 1930–33, designed printed silk motifs by Amalgamated Silk, Onandaga, N.Y., US. Created over 3,000 works on paper, fabric designs, and ceramics, as well as, of course, oil paintings, for which he became best known.

Exhibitions Work shown at Salons of Société des Artistes Français from 1901 and at Salons d'Automne from 1903. For Poiret's houseboats moored on the river Seine near 1925 *Exposition Internationale des Arts Décoratifs et Industriels Modernes*, Paris, he designed 14 large textile hangings: Orgues. Painted the vast 200 x 30 ft. (61 x 9 m) *La fée électricité*, said to be the world's largest picture, at Pavilion du Lumière, 1937 *Exposition Internationale des Arts et Techniques dans la Vie Moderne*, Paris. Work subject of numerous exhibitions including 1983 *Raoul Dufy, 1877–1953*, organized by Arts Council of Great Britain, London. 2003 one-person exhibition, Fondation Dina Vierny/Musée Maillol, Paris.

Bibliography Paul Poiret, *En habillant l'époque*, Paris: Bernard Grasset, 1930, 120–22. Victor Arwas, *Art Déco*, New York: Abrams, 1980. Stuart Durant, *Ornament from the Industrial Revolution to Today*, Woodstock, N.Y.: Overlook, 1986: 245, 322, passim. Dora Perez-Tibi, *Dufy*, New York: Abrams, 1989.

Duiker, Johannes (1890–1935)

Dutch architect and furniture designer; born The Hague.

Training Technische Hogeschool, Delft.

Biography 1916, Duiker and Bernard Bijvoët became partners in an architecture office in Amsterdam. 1932–35, Duiker was the editor of journal *De 8 en Opbouw*; is best known for 1926–28 Zonnestraal Sanatorium (with Bijvoët) in Hilversum, with its extensive glazing and projecting roof terraces. Other architecture included 1928–30 Open Air School, Cliostraat, Amsterdam, for which he designed metal-and-wood furniture, and Constructivist-inspired 1934 Handelsblad-Cineac Cinema in Amsterdam.

Bibliography T. Boga (ed.), *B. Bijvoët & J. Duiker 1890–1935*, Zürich, [n.d.]. Johannes Duiker, *Hoogbouw*, Rotterdam, 1930. F.R. Yerbury, *Modern Dutch Buildings*, New York: Charles Scribner's Sons, 1931. 'Zonnestraal,' *Forum*, vol. 16, no. 1, Jan. 1962. 'Bijvoët & Duiker,' *AA Quarterly*, vol. 2, no. 1, 1970: 4–10. 'Duiker 1' and 'Duiker 2,' *Forum*, Nov. 1971 and Jan. 1972. Vittorio Magnago Lampugnani (ed.), *Encyclopedia of 20th-Century Architecture*, New York: Abrams, 1986: 85.

Dulac, Edmund (1881–1953)

French illustrator and designer; born Toulouse; active England.

Biography 1912, Dulac became a naturalized British citizen; produced caricature wax figurines, including those of George Moore and Thomas Beecham; designed the Cathay Lounge of 1931 oceanliner *Empress of Britain*. Work included playing-card designs and Dutch banknotes by De la Rue, 1935 Old Plantation Chocolates package for Cadbury's, and specimens of Edward VIII coins. 1940–45, philatelic designs in-

cluded 1937 stamp for George VI's coronation, Free French issues, commemorative stamps 1951 *Festival of Britain* exposition, London, and 1953 coronation of Queen Elizabeth II. His numerous illustrated books, most published by Hodder & Stoughton in London, include *Stories from Hans Andersen* (1912), *Edmund Dulac's Book for the French Red Cross* (1915), *The Green Lacquer Pavilion* (1926), *Myths the Ancients Believed in* (1932), and *Rock Climbs Around London* (1938).
Bibliography Cat., *Thirties: British Art and Design Before the War*, London: Arts Council of Great Britain/Hayward Gallery, 1979.

Dumas, Rena (1937–)

Greek interior architect and furniture designer; born Athens; active Paris.

Training To 1961, École Nationale Supérieure des Métiers d'Art, Paris; subsequently, in Greece and the US.
Biography 1962, Dumas became a designer for Hermès, which produced her leather goods; 1964, set up her own office, designing interiors of private houses, offices, restaurants, and shops. The 1968 meeting with architect André Wogenscky led to her becoming director of Robert Anxionnat's Paris agency, working with Michel Folliasson on the project for the prefecture building in Seine-Saint-Denis. She eventually established Rena Dumas Architecture Interieure, now with an architecture staff of 25. 1983, she began designing furniture with Peter Coles (1954–1985); designed 1983 Pippa folding-furniture collection (with Coles) by Hermès. She designed furniture for Galerie Agora; interiors of branches for Saint-Louis and Hermès (as the wife of the Hermès chairperson, Jean-Louis Dumas-Hermès), including those in New York (1983), San Francisco (1987), Milan (1987), Madrid (1990), Paris (extension of Faubourg Saint-Honoré main store, 1992, and Ateliers Hermès de Pantin, 1992); 1991 Complice teapot for Hermès; 1992 Pippa II folding chair, desk, stool, screen, and campaign bed by Hermès, and a large body of architecture/interior-design work since.
Citations 1988 Carte Blanche production support (mobile, multifunctional units), VIA (French furniture association).
Bibliography Suzanne Tise, 'Innovators at the Museum,' *Vogue Décoration*, no. 26, June–July 1990: 48.

Dumoffice

Dutch design cooperative; located Amsterdam.

History 1997, Dumoffice was established by designers Wiebe Boonstra (Drachten, 1968–), Martijn Hoogendijk (Bergambacht, 1970–), and Marc van Nederpelt (Zwolle, 1970–) in Amsterdam. All are 1994 graduates of Akademie voor Industriële Vormgeving, Eindhoven. They have designed domestic objects (seating, shelving, and lighting), both under their own label, DUM, and for clients, including Belux and Hidden/sdb. Their style has been described as an amalgamation of nonconformist materials and production techniques with references from sportswear and architecture. In their words, 'We like to sample images and materials from sources other than the home environment and mix them into DUM homewear.'
Exhibitions/citations Work included in a large number of exhibitions. 1999, 2001 Rotterdam Design Award; 1999 Kho-Lliang le Encouragement Award; 2000 Red Dot award, Design Zentrum Nordrhein Westfalen, Essen.
Bibliography Michele De Lucchi (ed.), *The International Design Yearbook*, London: Laurence King, 2001.

Dumond, Jacques (1906–1988)

French designer; active Paris.

Training From 1923, École Boulle, Paris.
Biography All activities in Paris: 1929–34, Dumond worked in the studio of architect Pierre Patout; 1947, joined Union des Artistes Modernes (UAM); with Jacques Viénot, cofounded and became vice-president of Institut d'Esthétique Industrielle; from 1947, professor of furniture construction, École Nationale Supérieure des Arts Décoratifs; was director of the journal *Art présent* and of the Formes Utiles association (within the UAM) with André Hermant; designed a 1943 rattan-chair design for Société Industrielle; furniture for 1961 oceanliner *France*; worked in glass and bentwood; designed the 1958 chair considered his masterpiece, in a single sheet of plywood. He espoused the maxim 'new material + new technique = new shape.' For a time was professor of interior architecture, École Comondo.
Exhibitions Work included in 1943 Salon of Société des Artistes Décorateurs; 1949–50 *Formes Utiles* exhibitions, Pavillon de Marsan, Musée du Louvre, Paris; and 1956 (1st) Triennale d'Art Français

Dumoffice. Whoosh hanging light. 2000. Mouth-blown frosted glass and two fused 40w bulbs, h. 7 3/4 x w. 15 x d. 3" (20 x 38 x 7.5 cm). Mfr.: the designers, Germany.

Contemporain, where he showed the office with glass tables, bentwood seating, and Formica furnishings (designed with André Renou, Jean-Pierre Génisset, and André Sive).
Bibliography René Chavance, 'Confort et plaisir de yeux pour un aménagement de Jacques Dumond,' *Mobilier et décoration*, no. 6, 1953. Jacques Dumond, interview by Pascal Renous, *Portrait de décorateurs*, Paris: Vial. Arlette Barré-Despond, *UAM*, Paris: Regard, 1986: 394. Cat., *Les années UAM 1929–1958*, Paris: Musée des Arts Décoratifs, 1988. Arlette Barré-Despond (ed.), *Dictionnaire international des arts appliqués et du design*, Paris: Regard, 1996

Dunaime, Georges

French designer.

Biography Dunaime designed lighting by E. Etling, but most of his work was produced by founder and engraver Gagnon, including table lamps, torchères, and chandeliers in silver, gilt, and patinated bronze with cloth, cut glass, quartz, marble, and alabaster shades. He designed a variety of lighting for 1921 oceanliner *Paris*. 1921–27, his work was marketed through five agents.
Exhibitions/citations 1922, lighting shown at Gagneau. Work shown at stands of Gagnon, Gagneau, Bézault, and Christofle, 1925 *Exposition Internationale des Arts Décoratifs et Industriels Modernes*, Paris. First prize, 1922 competition, Union of Bronze Manufacturers; first prize (for a table lamp) and honorable mention (for a piano lamp), 1924 Great Lighting Competition, Paris.
Bibliography Alastair Duncan, *Art Nouveau and Art Déco Lighting*, New York: Simon & Schuster, 1978: 169.

Dunand, Jean (b. Jules-John Dunand 1877–1942)

Swiss sculptor, cabinetmaker, metalworker, and artisan; born Lancy, near Geneva.

Training To 1896, École des Arts Industriels, Geneva.
Biography 1897, Dunand began working in Paris with sculptor Jean Baptiste Auguste Dampt, an admirer of John Ruskin and the Arts and Crafts movement. To 1902, Dunand worked as a sculptor; studied coppersmithing in Geneva and turned to metalworking; 1903, set up a studio in Paris; 1905, exhibited his first vases in the Art Nouveau style in hammered copper, steel, tin, lead, and silver. 1909, he saw the work of Paris-based Japanese craftsmen and turned to lacquer and changed his name to Jean Dunand; c. 1913, moved from Art Nouveau to geometric forms; from 1912, learned lacquering from Japan-

cse artist Seizo Sugawara, who had also taught Eileen Gray; 1919, began producing lacquer panels, tables, chairs, and other piece work for Pierre Legrain, Eugène Printz, Jean Goulden, and Jacques-Émile Ruhlmann to incorporate into their work. His furniture designs after World War I featured straight lines and planes and were ideally suited to lacquer decoration in near-natural colors, black and red tints, or tortoiseshell effects. Dunand is credited with having invented the use of crushed eggshell in lacquer, known as *coquille d'oeuf.* 1919, he opened a workshop at 70, rue Hallé in Paris to meet the rapidly growing demand for his lacquer, metal, and cabinet goods. His infrequent collaborators included Serge Rovinski, Georges Dorinac, Henri de Varoquier, and Bieler. Dunand created monumental screens from his own designs and those by Paul Jouve, François-Louis Schmied, Jacques-Émile Ruhlmann, Eugène Printz, Gustav Miklos, and Jean Lambert-Rucki. His clients included clothing designers Madeleine Vionnet and Jeanne Lanvin, Ambassador Bertholet, Mme. Yakoupovitch, and Mme. Labourdette. For the Labourdette smoking room, he produced four large decorative murals in lacquer with sculptured relief. Other commissions included lacquered panels for oceanliners 1927 *Île-de-France*, 1931 *L'Atlantique*, and 1935 *Normandie*. Dunand and Lambert-Rucki collaborated on widely published lacquer screens and decorative pieces. Dunand also diluted lacquer to paint fabrics for scarves and dresses for Agnès and designed handbags and belt buckles for Madeleine Vionnet.
Exhibitions Work first shown (as sculptor/metalworker) at 1904 Salon of Société Nationale des Beaux-Arts in Paris. Work shown regularly at Salons of Société des Artistes Décorateurs and at 1910 *Exposition Universelle et Industrielle*, Brussels. 1921 (group exhibition with Paul Jouve, François-Louis Schmied, and Jean Goulden), first pieces of lacquered furniture, screens, and panels were shown at Galerie Georges Petit, Paris. With Ruhlmann, lacquer work in the smoking room of Une Ambassade Française pavilion and L'Hôtel du Collectionneur pavilion at 1925 *Exposition Internationale des Arts Décoratifs et Industriels Modernes*; and in 1931 *Exposition Coloniale*, both Paris. Work subject of 1973 *Jean Dunand—Jean Goulden* exhibition, Galerie du Luxembourg, Paris.
Bibliography Yvonne Brunhammer, *Jean Dunand, Jean Goulden,* Galerie du Luxembourg, Paris, 1973: biblio. Philippe Garner, 'The Lacquer Work of Eileen Gray and Jean Dunand,' *Connoisseur*, Mar. 1973: 3–11. Yvonne Brunhammer et al., *Art Nouveau Belgium, France*, Houston: Rice University, 1976. Katherine Morrison McClinton, 'Jean Dunand, Art Déco Craftsman,' *Apollo*, Sept. 1982: 177–80. Alastair Duncan and Georges de Bartha, *Art Nouveau and Art Déco Bookbinding*, New York: Abrams, 1989. Félix Marcilhac, *Jean Dunand: His Life and Work*, London: Thames & Hudson, 1991.

Dunn, Geoffrey (1909–)

British furniture retailer, manufacturer, and designer; active Bromley.

Biography In Bromley, Dunn worked in his family's retail store Dunn's of Bromley (today part of Heal's Group), where he encouraged and supported contemporary design and young designers. The store sold furniture by Marcel Breuer, Serge Chermayeff, and Alvar Aalto; fabrics by Donald Bros., Edinburgh Weavers, and Warners; ceramics by Wedgwood and Michael Cardew. Geoffrey Dunn's own simple furniture was made by Goodearl Brothers, William Barlett, Keen in High Wycombe, Stones in Banbury, and in Dunn's own workshops. 1936, he was council member, Design and Industries Association; chairperson of the design committee and an independent member, Domestic Handblown Glassware Working Party. 1938 with Crofton Gane (a retailer in Bristol known for a subdued modern style) and with manufacturer Gordon Russell, Geoffrey Dunn established the Good Furnishing Group to select good modern design work available at reasonable prices and, 1953, became its chairperson. 1946, he was a council member, Council of Industrial Design.
Citations 1974, fellow, Society of Industrial Artists; 1975 bicentenary medal, Royal Society of Art; 1976, Commander of the British Empire.
Bibliography Cat., *Thirties: British Art and Design Before the War*, London: Arts Council of Great Britain/Hayward Gallery, 1979. Jennifer Hawkins Opie, 'Geoffrey Dunn and Dunn's of Bromley: Selling a Good Design, A Lifetime of Commitment,' *Journal of the Decorative Arts Society*, no. 10.

Dupas, Jean (1882–1964)

French artist; active Paris.

Training Under Albert Besnard, École des Beaux-Arts, Bordeaux.
Biography Though awarded prizes at the Paris Salons, Dupas did not receive international fame until the 1925 Paris *Exposition*. He decorated the Église de Saint-Esprit in Paris, the silver-display room of the royal palace in Bucharest, reception rooms of the Bourse du Travail in Bordeaux, and various oceanliners, including painted-glass panels for 1935 *Normandie*. 1941, taught, Académie des Beaux-Arts; from 1942, professor, École des Beaux-Arts.
Exhibitions/citations Two panels—*Les Perruches,* mounted in the grand salon of Jacques-Émile Ruhlmann's Hôtel du Collectionneur pavilion, and *Le Vin,* in the Tour de Bordeaux on the Esplanade des Invalides—shown at 1925 *Exposition Internationale des Arts Décoratifs et Industriels Modernes*, Paris. 1910 (1st) Grand Prix de Rome; gold medal, 1921 or 1922 Salons of Société des Artistes Français; 1926, elected Chevalier of the Légion d'Honneur.
Bibliography Yvonne Brunhammer, *Le cinquantenaire de l'Exposition de 1925*, Paris: Musée des Arts Décoratifs, 1976: 127. Pierre Cabanne, *Encyclopédie art déco*, Paris: Somogy, 1986: 193.

Dupeux, Geneviève (1924–)

French textile designer; active Paris.

Biography 1958, Dupeux opened her own textile-research studio; was associated for a short time with Olivier Mourgue and Jean-Philippe Lenclos; 1971–85, taught, École Nationale Supérieure des Arts Décoratifs, Paris; 1976, established Atelier National d'Art Textile at Manufacture des Gobelins; from 1980, was a textile advisor to Renault automobiles.
Exhibitions Participated in numerous venues including Tapestry Biennial, Lausanne. Work subject of an exhibition (designed by Pierre Paulin), Centre Georges Pompidou, Paris.

Dupont, S.T. (aka Tissot-Dupont)

French accessories manufacturer; located Paris.

History 1872, the firm was founded by Simon Tissot-Dupont; to World War II, produced expensive luggage; 1940, introduced a cigarette lighter in an aluminum alloy. The lighter was inspired by an earlier solid-gold accessory designed for inclusion in an overnight bag for the Maharaja of Patiala and became the model for Dupont's legendary 1953 Briquet cigarette lighter. 1973, Dupont began producing the Montparnasse line of writing instruments; 1978, returned to luxury leather articles; from 1981, issued a line of timepieces, including pocket alarm clocks and dress and sports (1984) wrist watches; 1983, produced gold and silver jewelry created by Boucheron. Dupont was family owned to 1973, when it was sold to the Gillette group.

Dupré-Lafon, Paul (1900–1971)

French interior architect; born Marseille; active Paris.

Training École des Beaux-Arts, Marseille.
Biography 1923, Dupré-Lafon settled in Paris, where he practiced as an interior architect, working on commissions in a variety of styles; 1925, created his first furniture. Clients through 1930s included the Dreyfus family, other rich collectors, and the firm Hermès. He designed apartments, townhouses, and villas, as well as custom-made furniture and furnishings in luxury materials.
Bibliography *Ensembles mobiliers*, Paris: Charles Moreau, vol. 5, nos. 40–41; vol. 6, nos. 12–18, 1945. Cat., Aaron Lederfajn and Xavier Lenormand (eds.), *Le Louvre des Antiquaires présente: 1930 quand le meuble devient sculpture*, Paris, 1986. Pierre Kjellberg, *Art déco: les maîtres du mobilier, le décor des paquebots*, Paris: Amateur, 1989. Thierry Couvrat Desvergnes, *Dupré-Lafon: décorateur des millionaires*, Paris: Amateur, 1990. François Mathey, *Au bonheur des formes, design français 1945–1992*, Paris: Regard, 1992: 153.

Duranti, Maurizio (1949–)

Italian architect and designer; born Florence; active Milan.

Training To 1976, architecture, Genoa.
Biography Duranti was an corporate-image and product consultant for many firms; designed furniture, lamps, tableware, umbrella stands, clocks, candlesticks, and other tabletop objects in wood, iron, plastic, glass, marble, silver, porcelain, ceramics, including a range of stainless-steel kitchenware by Barazzoni and bathroom accessories by Valli & Valli; has organized and designed numerous exhibitions for firms, including Acerbis, Coca-Cola, De Vecchi, Eschenbach, Mira Lanza, Nito, Pampaloni, Pomellato, Valli & Valli, and Villeroy & Boch.
Citations Good Design awards, Chicago Athenaeum: 1996 (for Attila bottle opener by Mepra), 1997 (for Le Monachine porcelain dinnerware

by ANCAP), and 1998 (for 1997 Gitano Home Office by Gallotti & Radice).
Bibliography Daniele Baroni, *Maurizio Duranti: avventure progettuali*, Milan: Agepe Edizioni, 1991. Daniele Baroni (texts) and Silvio San Pietro (ed.), *Maurizio Duranti: disegni & design*, Milan: L'Archivolto, 1993.

D'Urbino, Donato (1935–)
> See De Pas, Gionatan.

D'Urso, Joseph Paul (1943–)

American interior designer; born Newark, N.J.

Training 1958–61, interior design, Pratt Institute, Brooklyn, N.Y.; 1965–66, interior design and architecture, Pratt Institute; 1965, Royal College of Art, London; 1966–67, Manchester College of Art and Design, UK.
Biography 1968, D'Urso founded his own eponymous design firm in New York and designed private residences, restaurants, art galleries, discothèques, and offices. Work included the 'I' complex (restaurants, art gallery, library, media room, and discothèque) in Hong Kong, Calvin Klein Menswear showrooms and offices in New York, 1980 range of seating and tables by Knoll International; showrooms of Esprit in Los Angeles. He became known for his widely published minimalist, monochromatic (white/gray/black) interiors; was the originator of 1970s High-Tech style in interior design in the US. For a time was design director (following John Hutton) of Donghia Furniture/Textiles in New York; through an office in East Hampton, N.Y., continues to be active as an interior designer.
Exhibitions/citations Work subject of exhibitions at The Museum of Modern Art, New York (Manchester school studies and projects), 1968, and Pratt Institute, 1968. 1973 Designer of the Year, Burlington Industries; best in show (Knoll table collection), 1982 Stuttgarter Messe; 1983 Bundespreis Produktdesign (table collection by Knoll), Rat für Formgebung (German design council), Frankfurt.
Bibliography Joan Kron and Suzanne Slesin, *High-Tech: The Industrial Style and Source Book for the Home* (New York: Potter, 1978). 'The New Romantic Movement,' *The New York Times Magazine*, 28 Sept. 1980. 'A Los Angeles Apartment,' *Casa Vogue*, Jan. 1981. 'Designing the Post Industrial World,' *Art News*, Feb. 1981. 'Joe D'Urso: The Mastermind of Minimalism,' *Metropolitan Home*, June 1981. Barbaralee Diamondstein (ed.), *Interior Design: The New Freedom*, New York: Rizzoli, 1982. Joe D'Urso/Designer, *Design Quarterly*, no. 124, 1984. Philippe Starck (ed.), *The International Design Yearbook*, London: Thames & Hudson, 1987. Anne Lee Morgan (ed.), *Contemporary Designers*, London: Macmillan, 1984; Detroit: St. James Press, 1997.

Dwan, Terry (1957–)
> See Citterio, Antonio.

Dynco
> See Hammarplast.

Dyson, James (1947–)

British industrial designer; born Norfolk.

Training 1965–66, drawing and painting, Byam Shaw School; 1966–70, furniture and interior design, Royal College of Art; both London.
Biography 1967–70, Dyson's design work has included New Stratford East Theatre and auditorium and seats of Roundhouse, both London; within the Conran Design Group, seating and crèche furniture design of Terminal 1, Heathrow Airport, and Peter Dominic wine shops, London and Cheltenham, 1970; designed/engineered Sea Truck for inventor Jeremy Fry. From 1970, Dyson started and managed the new marine division of Rotork in Bath, where he was director in 1973; 1974, established his own firm to develop the Ballbarrow and designed the Waterolla, a water-filled plastic garden roller; 1978, invented Trolleyball, a boat launcher with ball wheels; 1978–84, developed the bagless vacuum cleaner, building 5,127 prototypes of the Dual Cyclone model; 1983, produced final prototype vacuum cleaner, G-Force; 1982–84, was not able to acquire a licensee in the UK. From 1986, the G-Force began to sell in Japan, eventually becoming a status symbol. 1993 Dyson opened his own factory in Wiltshire, UK, but, experiencing late-1990s financial problems, moved production to the Far East; produces other vacuum cleaners and washing machines, featuring advanced technology; 1990–92, was chairperson, College of Higher Education, Bath. Subsequent vacuum-cleaner models: 1993 DC 01, 1997 DC 02 Clear, 1998 DC 03, 2000 DC 06 Motorhead, and 2000 DC 02 robot.
Exhibitions/citations G-Force included in 1987 *British Design* exhibition, Vienna; 1989 *British Design: New Traditions*, Museum Boymans-van Beuningen, Rotterdam. Award, Design Council, UK, and 1975 Duke of Edinburgh's special prize (for Sea Truck); 1977 Building Design Innovation award (for Ballbarrow); and 1991 International Design Fair prize (for G-Force), Japan.
Bibliography Jonathan M. Woodham, *Twentieth-Century Ornament*, New York: Rizzoli, 1990: 296. James Dyson, *Against the Odds* (autobiography), London: Orion, 1998. Mel Byars, *On/Off: New Electronic Products*, New York: Universe, 2001. www.dyson.co.uk.

Dysthe, Sven Ivar (1931–)

Norwegian furniture and interior designer.

Training Cabinetmaking, Royal College of Art, London.
Biography 1944–60, Dysthe was the chief designer at Sønnico Fabrikker in Oslo; designed 1960 System Dysthe shelving for the store Egil Rygh, 1964 bentwood chairs, and 1986 bent-metal furniture by Møremøbler.
Citations International Design award, American Institute of Decorators (AID).
Bibliography Fredrik Wildhagen, *Norge i Form*, Oslo: Stenersen, 1988: 153. Cat., David Revere McFadden (ed.), *Scandinavian Modern Design 1880–1980*, New York: Abrams, 1982.

Dziekiewicz, Victor I. (1951–)

Argentine designer; active Chicago.

Training Design, University of Detroit; architecture, Virginia Polytechnic Institute, and State University, Blacksburg, Va.
Biography 1980, Dziekiewicz set up DesignBridge in Chicago to combine synergistic architecture, interior design, visual communications, and product design; designed the corporate image of Brueton Industries, its Tango seating series, and Concerto series low tables; has been associate professor, School of Art, Northern Illinois University, De Kalb, Ill.
Citations Outstanding Building award, Association of American Architects; citation, Interior Architecture award, AIA; Silver Product Design award, Institute of Business Designers (IBD); Merchandising award, Sales and Marketing Council of Greater Chicago; citation, Design Excellence, *I.D.* magazine.

E

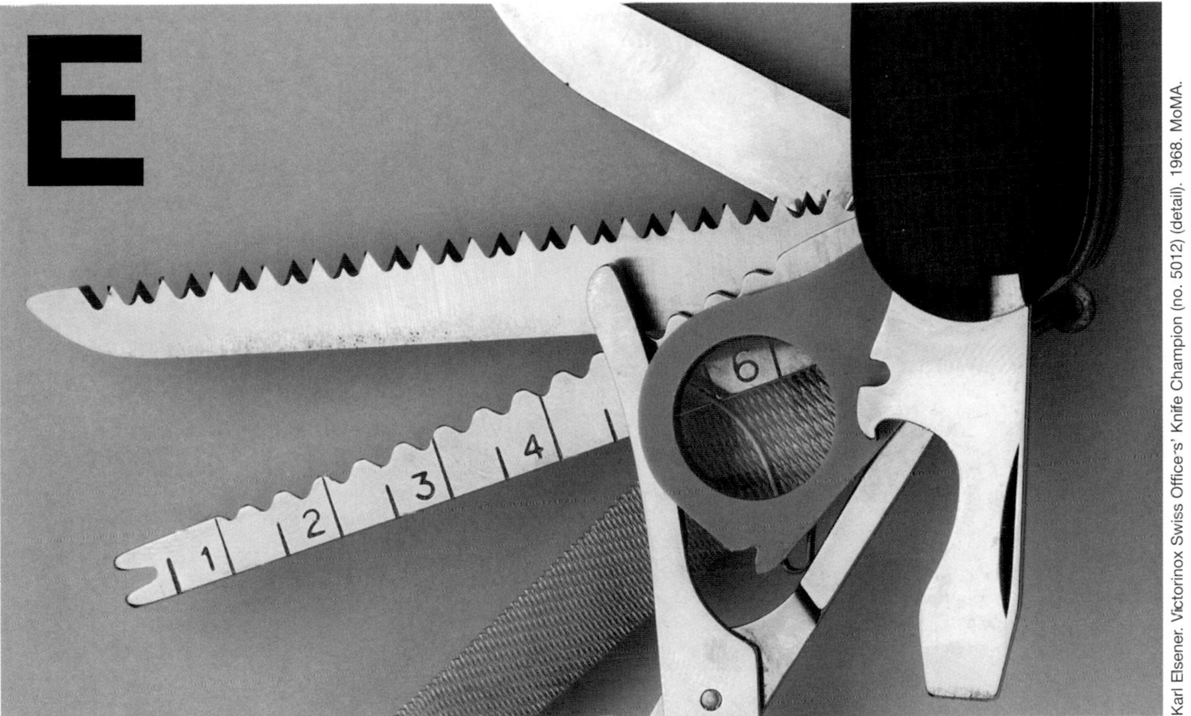

Karl Elsener. Victorinox Swiss Office's' Knife Champion (no. 5012) (detail). 1968. MoMA.

E&Y

Japanese furniture firm; located Tokyo.

History c. 1986, E&Y, or E&Y Tokyo, was founded by Yoichi Nakamuta to manufacture and sell its own cutting-edge wares, mostly furniture, as well as those manufactured by other firms. Commissioned designers have included Christophe Pillet, Jean-Marie Massaud, Richard Hutten, Alex Macdonald, Midori Miraki, Michael Sodeau, and Paul Daly. Its official magazine is *Toolpub*.
Exhibitions Regular exhibitions are mounted, particularly during Tokyo Designers Week, and sometimes include clothing and media.

Eames Jr., Charles Ormond (1907–1978)

American architect-designer; born St. Louis, Mo.; active Bloomfield Hills, Mich., and Venice, Cal.; husband of Ray Kaiser Eames.

Training 1924–26, architecture, Washington University, St. Louis; 1936, Cranbrook Academy of Art, Bloomfield Hills, Mich.
Biography Charles and Ray Eames became two of the most influential furniture designers of the 20th century, or possibly they became the primary furniture designers of the period. Eames himself was a steel-mill worker before serving as a technical draftsperson; 1925–27, worked for architecture firm Trueblood and Graf in St. Louis; 1938, was in private practice at in the partnership Gray and Eames in St. Louis; 1934, traveled and worked in Mexico; 1935, returned to private practice in the partnership Eames and Walsh in St. Louis; 1936, received a fellowship to study at Cranbrook Academy of Art, Bloomfield Hills, Mich., where he met future second wife Ray Kaiser and friend Eero Saarinen and where, 1937–40, he was head, department of experimental design under the school's director Eliel Saarinen. 1939–40, Eames worked in Eero Saarinen's office. Together they came to prominence by winning 1940 *Organic Design in Home Furnishings* competition/exhibition at The Museum of Modern Art, New York, with their most notable entry being a chair with aluminum legs whose plywood seat was formed into a multi-curved shell that presaged forms taken by plastics after World War II. A chair of theirs there was awarded a prize, but, due to wartime shortages, it could not be produced. With Saarinen, Eames designed innovative seating for Mary Seaton Room of streamline-modern styled 1940 Kleinhans Music Hall, Buffalo, N.Y. 1941, Eames and Ray Kaiser married and moved to California, where he worked in the art department of Metro-Goldwyn-Mayer movie studios. Also, from 1941, Eames and Saarinen also with Ray experimented with molded plywood and metal in their own office. The Eames furniture combined steel rods, in some models, with two-way bent plywood, a wood technique developed from the Eameses' and Saarinen's work for the US Navy 1941–42, designing a leg splint and stretcher (produced 1942–43) and a range of other plywood fittings/components. 1942–46, their office employees included John Entenza, Don Albinson, Gregory Ain, Margaret Harris, Griswald Raetze (joined in 1943 by Herbert Matter and Harry Bertoia), and others. Most went on to individual prominence. From 1944, was in partnership with his wife Ray Eames in various facilities from time to time in and around Los Angeles. 1943, they sold their manufacturing entity (Plyformed Wood Company) to Evans Manufacturing Co., and the Eames enterprise became the Molded Plywood Products Division of Evans. Thus, Evans became the first firm to mass-produce their designs. From 1946, Charles was consultant designer to the Herman Miller Furniture Co., and, from 1948, the firm distributed Eames studio designs and, subsequently, mass produced them. Late 1940s, the Eameses' use of plywood influenced Italian, German, and Scandinavian design. 1948, they (with others) designed the now classic fiberglass-shell chair with thin multiple metal rod leg supports, subsequently dubbed the 'Eiffel Tower' base. (Their designs attracted nicknames: as examles, a low elliptical coffee table became the 'Surfboard' table, and a plywood chair, the 'Potato Chip' chair.) Their fiberglass technology came from its use in wartime radar disks manufactured in the Zenith Fabricators plant near their studio. The fiberglass was tinted in the grey, orange, and red colors popular in the 1950s. Eames's interest in exhibition design and film making made him a more formidable and celebrated spokesperson for American design than his relatively modest portfolio of mass-produced furniture would warrant, and included innovative 1959 American National Exhibition, Moscow (employing a multi-screen audio-visual presentation, progressive for its time) and the film *Powers of Ten* (1968). The Eameses made over 100 short films, from one to 30 minutes, often with Elmer Bernstein's background music. 1949 in Pacific Palisades, Cal., the Eameses built their own house, a steel-frame building made with standard prefabricated parts and suggesting a Japanese influence with its open plan, lightness, and obvious geometric articulation; it has become a shrine for student designers from the world over. 1953–56, he taught, lectured, and served as a consultant, University of California, Los Angeles and Berkeley; Los Angeles public schools; University of Georgia, Athens; Yale University; California Institute of Technology, Pasadena. Work credited to Charles Eames alone should rightly be assigned to both him and his wife Ray, and, further, the studio's work in general to a number of staff members. 1989, the Eameses' daughter Lucia Demetrios sold her parents' archive of 400 pieces of furniture, prototypes, and maquettes to Vitra Design Museum, Weil am Rhein, Germany, where the studio was recreated c. 1994. Eames papers, drawings, and photos are housed in The Library of Congress, Washington, D.C. Eames died in St. Louis, Mo. The estate today is

Charles Eames and Ray Eames. Low side chair. 1946. Molded and bent birch plywood, and rubber shockmounts, 25 3/4 x 22 1/4 x 25" (65.4 x 56.5 x 63.5 cm). Mfr.: Evans Products Co., US. Gift of Eugene Eppinger. MoMA.

managed by Eames's grandson Eames Demetrios.
Work 1941 first molded plywood seat, 1942 molded plywood experiments and molded-plywood prototypes for a US Navy Department splint, 1943 production of molded plywood splints and molded plywood glider, 1945 Case Study houses #8 and #9, 1945 experimental chairs and children's plywood furniture, 1945 first production-model plywood ('potato chip') chair with plywood legs, 1945 plywood tables with wood or 'hairpin' metal-rod legs, 1946 case goods, 1946 plywood ('potato chip') chair with metal legs, 1946 FSW plywood folding screen, 1947 plywood folding tables, 1947 Jefferson Memorial competition, 1948 (first Eames) Herman Miller graphics, 1949 (first Eames) Herman Miller showroom, 1949 *An Exhibition for Modern Living* exhibition, 1950 Eames Storage Units (ESU), 1950 *Good Design* exhibition (design of), 1950 fiberglass armchairs and side chair, 1950 low table rod base, 1951 ETR elliptical ('surfboard') table, 1951 wire sofa, 1952 wire chair, 1952 House of Cards game, 1953 Hang-It-All clothes rack, 1954 Sears compact storage, 1954 Sofa Compact (foldable for shipping), 1954 stadium/public seating, 1955 stacking chair, 1956 Eames lounge chair and ottoman (no. 570/571), 1958 Aluminum Group chairs and tables, 1959 Revell toy house, 1960 Time-Life chair and stool, 1961 La Fonda chair, 1961 Eames contract storage, 1962 Tandem Sling seating, 1963 Tandem Shell seating, 1964 #3473 sofa, 1964 segmented-base table, 1968 intermediate desk chair, 1968 metal-frame leather chaise, 1970 drafting chair, 1971 molded plastic chair, 1971 two-piece secretary's chair, 1971 loose-cushion chair, 1974 IBM Newton cards, and 1984 leather-and-teak sofa.
Exhibitions/citations Work included in 1940 *Organic Designs in Home Furnishings* (first prize award), The Museum of Modern Art, New York, and 1946 and 1973 one-person exhibitions there; 1948 *International Competition for Low-Cost Furniture Design* (second prize), also The Museum of Modern Art; and a large number of subsequent Eames exhibitions. 1960, elected Honorary Royal Designer for Industry, UK.
Bibliography Don Wallance, *Shaping America's Products*, New York: Reinhold, 1956: 177–81. 'Eames Celebration,' *Architectural Design*, vol. 36, Sept. 1966. Charles Eames, *A Computer Perspective*, Cambridge, Mass.: MIT, 1973. Arthur Drexler, *Charles Eames: Furniture from the Design Collection of the Museum of Modern Art*, New York: The Museum of Modern Art, 1973. 'Nelson, Eames, Girard, Probst: The Design Process at Herman Miller,' *Design Quarterly 98/99*, 1975. Cat., Philip Morrison, *Connections: The Work of Charles and Ray Eames*, Los Angeles: Frederick S. Wight Art Gallery (UCLA), 1976. John Neuhart, Marilyn Neuhart, and Ray Eames, *Eames Design*, New York: Abrams, 1989. Pat Kirkham, *Charles and Ray Eames: Designers of the Twentieth Century*, Cambridge, Mass.: MIT, 1995. *Vitra.Eames*, Weil am Rhein, Vitra, 996. Donald Albrecht et al., *The Work of Charles and Ray Eames: A Legacy of Invention*, New York: Abrams/ Library of Congress/Vitra Design Museum, 1997. Eames Demetrios, *Eames Primer*, London: Thames & Hudson, 2001. Paola Antonelli (ed.), *Objects of Design: The Museum of Modern Art*, New York: The Museum of Modern Art, 2003: 133–34, 154–55, 191, 195, 201, 204. Films, converted to video tapes/DVDs, www.eamesoffice.com.
> See Eames, Ray.

Eames, 'Ray' Bernice Alexandra Kaiser (1912–1988)

American designer; born Sacramento, Cal.; wife of Charles Eames.

Training 1933–39, painting under Hans Hofmann, New York, and Gloucester and Provincetown, Mass.; weaving under Marianne Strengell, Cranbrook Academy of Art, Bloomingfield Hills, Mich.
Biography 1936, she became a founding member of the group American Abstract Artists; 1941, married Charles Eames with a gold wedding ring designed and made by Harry Bertoia. 1941 with Charles, settled in Southern California; 1942, produced her first plywood sculpture; 1942–48, designed covers for the magazine *Arts & Architecture* and, 1948–53, magazine advertisements for her and her husband's furniture by Herman Miller Furniture Company; from late 1940s, worked collaboratively with her husbands, and, thus, all of his work should be attributed to her also but has often not been so in the past, partly due to the efforts, or silence, of her husband himself.
Exhibitions Work (paintings) first shown, at 1937 (1st) American Abstract Artists exhibition, Riverside Museum, New York; paintings at 1944 group show, Los Angeles County Museum of Art; 2003 *Changing Her Palette: Painting by Ray Eames*, Eames Office Gallery, Santa Monica, Cal. Other work such as fabrics included in 1991 *What Modern Was*, Montréal and touring the US; 2001 *Women Designers in the USA, 1900–2000*, Bard Graduate Center, New York.
Bibliography 'Nelson, Eames, Girard, Probst: The Design Process at Herman Miller,' *Design Quarterly 98/99*, 1975. John Neuhart, Marilyn Neuhart, and Ray Eames, *Eames Design*, New York: Abrams, 1989. Cat., Martin Eidelberg (ed.), *Design 1935–1965: What Modern Was*, New York: Musée des Arts Décoratifs/Abrams, 1991. Cat., Pat Kirkham (ed.), *Women Designers in the USA, 1900–2000: Diversity and Difference*, New Haven: Bard Graduate Center and Yale, 2000. Eames Demetrios, *Changing Her Palette: Paintings by Ray Eames*, Venice: Eames Office, 2000.
> See Eames, Charles.

Earl, Harley (1893–1969)

American automobile designer.

Training Law, University of Southern California, Los Angeles; Stanford University, Berkeley, with no degree granted.
Biography 1905, 'J.W.,' Harley Earl's nickname, moved to Los Angeles and began working for the J.N. Tabor Carriage Works; 1908, opened his own small Earl Automobile Works.; from 1917, designed/ produced auto bodies, including for some Hollywood movie stars; visited 1926 Salon de l'Automobile, Paris; from 1926, worked in Art and Color Section at General Motors, Detroit, Mich., where he designed elegant forms for 1927 and 1934 LaSalle (Cadillac's new marque); was promoted to head of GM's Art and Color Section, generally thought to be the world's first purpose-oriented design studio; designed the intriguing 1938 Buick Y-Job concept car and 1952–53 (1st) Corvette with Robert McLean, Ed Cole, and Maurice Olley; went on to revolutionize car design and became well known for his flowing shapes, later influenced by aircraft tailfins which he incorporated into car design, notably prominent in 1959 Cadillac Coupe de Ville and Sedan de Ville models. Even though experts consider much of his post-1940s work to be vulgar, it nevertheless influenced car design in 1930s–60s, and possibly forever. His approach to the business of car design and the organization of the car-design studio became somewhat of a standard.
Bibliography Stephen Bayley, *Harley Earl and the Dream Machine*, London: Trefoil, 1990. Penny Sparke, *A Century of Car Design*, London: Mitchell Beazley, 2002.

Eastlake, Charles Lock (1836–1906)

British designer and writer; born Plymouth; active London.

Training Apprenticeship under architect Philip Hardwick; subsequently, Royal Academy Schools.
Biography During the 1860s, Eastlake was a journalist, writing on

furniture and decorations, beginning with the 1864 article 'The Fashion of Furniture' in *Cornhill Magazine*; 1866–71, was assistant secretary, Royal Institute of Architects, becoming its first permanent paid secretary 1871–78. Eastlake's *Hints on Household Taste in Furniture, Upholstery, and Other Details* (London: Longmans, Green, 1868) was greatly influential in the US on the Aesthetic Movement and was the first and most influential British publication on household art. The quotation from Viollet-le-Duc on its title page suggests the French theorist's influence on Eastlake. Eastlake included illustrations of furniture, wallpapers, tiles, and artifacts, influenced by medieval and early-English sources. His own solid and undecorated furniture was markedly similar to the work of Bruce J. Talbert shown in Talbert's book *Gothic Forms Applied to Furniture, Metal Work, and Decoration for Domestic Purposes* (Birmingham/London: S. Birbeck/Talbert, 1867). Few examples exist of Eastlake's furniture by Jackson and Graham and wallpapers by Jeffrey & Co. More effective as a tastemaker than a designer, he discussed principles of good taste in everyday articles and was a prolific writer, including of *A History of the Gothic Revival* (London: Longmans, 1872). He influenced American cabinetmakers, including Herter Brothers, Daniel Pabst, and A. Kimbel and J. Cabus.
Bibliography Elizabeth Aslin, *Nineteenth Century English Furniture*, New York: Yoseloff, 1962: 61. J. Mordaunt Crook (Intro.), Charles Lock Eastlake, *A History of the Gothic Revival*, Leicester and New York: Humanities, 1970 (facsimile ed.). Cat., *Eastlake-Influenced American Furniture, 1870–1890*, Yonkers, N.Y.: Hudson River Museum, 1973. Doreen Bolger Burke et al., *In Pursuit of Beauty: Americans and the Aesthetic Movement*, New York: The Metropolitan Museum of Art/Rizzoli, 1986.

Eastman, George (1854–1932); Eastman Kodak

American camera and film manufacturer; headquarters Rochester, N.Y.

History George Eastman was born in Waterville, N.Y.; worked as a junior clerk in a bank; was equally a spirited capitalist and an imaginative inventor. His first (1880) notable invention was a process for making photographic dry plates, on the basis of which he founded his manufacturing company in Rochester, N.Y. Other inventions followed: flexible film, patented 1884; the Kodak camera, 1888; his most distinctive, certainly most popular, contribution was the Brownie camera, 1900. Over time, more than 50 million Brownies were sold for $1 each and film for 10 cents a roll. (The name of the Brownie camera, which was highly popular with children, for whom it was intended, was adopted from an equally popular series of books by Palmer Cox [1840–1924] about fictional little people called Brownies.) Eastman knew the power of good marketing; from the beginning, Kodak products were promoted through advertisements, which Eastman himself wrote and published in leading newspapers and magazines of the time. 1888, he registered the name Kodak, which essentially has no meaning and was derived from nothing; Eastman said that he merely liked the letter 'k.' As early as 1897, the Kodak name appeared on an electrical sign in Trafalgar Square, London. Generally, the firm has not focused on high-industrial-design values but rather on film and equipment technology; however, Kenneth Grange designed Kodak's 1959 Brownie 44A, 1964 Brownie Vecta, 1970 Instamatic, and 1975 Pocket Instamatic. A mammoth corporation today, it has made a number of important contributions to photographic history.
Bibliography *The Home of Kodak: Facts about the World's Largest Photographic Organization/Eastman Kodak Company*, Rochester, N.Y.: Eastman Kodak, 1929. Mel Byars with Arlette Barré-Despond, *100 Designs/100 Years...*, Hove: RotoVision, 1999: 12–13. Richard S. Tedlow, *Giants of Enterprise: Seven Business Innovators and the Empires They Built*, New York: HarperBusiness, 2001. Michael Burgan et al., *Leading American Businesses: Profiles of Major American Companies and the People Who Made Them Important*, Farmington Hills, Mich.: UXL, 2003.

Easton, Louis B. (1864–1921)

American architect and furniture designer, born Half Day, Ill.; active near Chicago, Ill., and Pasadena, Cal.; brother-in-law of Elbert Hubbard.

Training In pedagogy, Bloomington Normal School, Bloomington, Ill.
Biography Easton was vice-principal and taught manual arts, Lemont High School; built furniture in oak and leather as a hobby; 1902, moved to Pasadena, Cal.; 1904, designed and built a house for his family and hung a sign outside reading 'Bungalows and Furniture'; designed about 25 houses, with a few tradespeople, in the Pasadena area. His 1906 Carl Curtis's ranch in redwood-and-batten construction was his most notable building. The structure, with its deeply overhung roof, illustrated his belief that construction materials should serve the dual purpose of creating a finished surface and structural support. The furniture was site-specific. Easton was said to have designed the house on the back of an envelope on receiving the commission; worked on its details during construction while sitting on the floor of the unfinished dwelling. Some of the furniture and the exterior of the house were finished with a wire brush. In an Arts and Crafts style, the furniture could be easily disassembled due to its post-and-peg construction. Easton designed 1911 weekend beach house, near Palos Verdes, Cal., of architect Myron Hunt, using redwood inside and out and, again, site-specific furniture, integrated fixtures, and an elaborate fireplace. 1914, Easton moved to rural Anaheim, Cal., where he remodeled an adobe house and farmed.
Exhibitions 1903 *Handicraft Exhibition* (furniture), Chicago Art Institute; 1913 Los Angeles Architectural Club exhibition (house designs).
Bibliography Timothy J. Andersen et al., *California Design 1910*, Salt Lake City: Peregrine Smith, 1980: 122–23, 127.

Eberson, John (1875–1964)

American architect and designer, born Romania.

Biography Eberson was known for his cinema interiors. One of his earliest, 1923 Majestic Theater in Houston, Texas, was a loosely re-created garden of a late-Renaissance palazzo in Italy. Through his workshop Michelangelo Studios, he was successful at producing elaborate plasterwork for his theater décors in Spanish, Moorish, Dutch, Chinese, and other styles.
Bibliography Jonathan M. Woodham, *Twentieth-Century Ornament*, New York: Rizzoli, 1990: 53–54.

Écart

French interior-design, furniture-design, and furniture-production firm; located Paris.

History 1978, Écart International was established as a furniture-production firm by designer Andrée Putman. The Écart design studio was established as a separate entity by Putman and Jean-François Bodin. The furniture-production unit issued reproductions of the designs of Eileen Gray, Robert Mallet-Stevens, Pierre Chareau, René Herbst, Michel Dufet, and others, including 1907 projection lamp by Mariano Fortuny (from 1979), as well as the contemporary designs of Patrick Naggar, Sylvain Dubuisson, Sacha Kétoff, and others. Putman began Écart's efforts by having the carpet designs of Gray woven. Écart S.A., managed by Gilles Leborgne, focuses on interior architecture and design projects, including interiors of Tache diamond merchants in Antwerp, reception areas of Total, Sofitel hotel in Paris, Hammerson building in Paris, Deutsche Bank's head office in Berlin, Sheraton Hotel at Charles de Gaulle airport, near Paris.
> See Putman, Andrée.

Eastman Kodak Company: Andrew McClare (1936–). Disc camera (no. 6000). 1980. Plastic and aluminum, 3 1/8 x 5 1/4 x 1 3/16" (8 x 13.4 x 3 cm). Mfr.: Eastman Kodak Company, US. Gift of the mfr. MoMA.

Eckhardt, Claus-Christian (1965–)

German industrial designer.

Training Industrial design, Hochschule für bildende Künste, Braunschweig.
Biography Eckhardt worked as an interior designer at Silvestrin Design in Munich; 1992–99, was in charge of the design of domestic electronic appliances and communication products in the design department, including Bosch mobile phones, at Blaupunkt in Hildesheim; from 2000, has been chief designer and head of global product design at Bosch Telecom in Frankfurt.
Citations Numerous international awards, including 2000 (for 510 mobile phone by Bosch) and 2002 (for D3 cordless phone by Tenovis) Red Dot awards, Design Zentrum Nordrhein Westfalen, Essen.
Bibliography Michele De Lucchi (ed.), *The International Design Yearbook*, London: Laurence King, 2001.

Eckhoff, Tias (1926–)

Norwegian metalworker, glass designer, and ceramicist.

Training 1947–48 under Nathalie Krebs, ceramics at Saxbo, Copenhagen; to 1949, Statens Håndverks-og Kunstindustriskole, Oslo.
Biography 1949, Eckhoff became designer at Porsgrunds Porselænsfabrik in Norway, where he was the artistic director 1952–60. His Triennale di Milano awards brought great success to Porsgrunds. From c. 1950, he designed for Georg Jensen (silver), Dansk Knivfabrik (cutlery), Halden Aluminumvarefabrik (aluminumware), and Norsk Stålpress (metalware). Remaining a consultant designer to Porsgrunds, he set up his own design studio in 1957 with clients, including Trio-Ving in Oslo, Ludtofte Design in Copenhagen, and Norsk Stålpress in Bergen; became known for the popular 1953 Cypress cutlery by Georg Jensen. The Jensen award for this pattern began his career in metalsmithing; he subsequently designed stainless-steel cutlery: Fuga and Opus by Dansk and 1961 Maya by Norsk.
Citations 1953 inter-Scandinavian design competition (for Cypress cutlery), sponsored by Georg Jensen to celebrate its 50th anniversary. Prizes at 1954 (10th) (two gold medals), 1957 (11th) (two gold medals), and 1960 (12th) (gold medal) Triennali di Milano; 1962, 1965, and 1966 emblems for Good Norwegian Design, Norska Designrådet (ND, Norwegian design council); 1953 Lunning Prize.
Bibliography Tias Eckhoff, 'Keramiske materialer i husholdningen,' *Bonytt*, vol. 15, 1955: 183–85. Alf Bøe, *Porsgrunds porselænsfabrik: bedrift of produksjon gjenom åtii år*, Oslo: Tanum, 1967. Cat., *Georg Jensen Silversmithy: 77 Artists, 75 Years*, Washington: Smithsonian, 1980. Cat., David Revere McFadden (ed.), *Scandinavian Modern Design 1880–1980*, New York: Abrams, 1982. Cat., Kathryn B. Hiesinger and George H. Marcus III (eds.), *Design Since 1945*, Philadelphia: Philadelphia Museum of Art, 1983. Cat., *The Lunning Prize*, Stockholm: Nationalmuseum, 1986. Jennifer Hawkins Opie, *Scandinavia: Ceramics and Glass in the Twentieth Century*, New York: Rizzoli, 1989. Alf Bøe and Inger Helene N. Stemshaug, *Tias Eckhoff: en pioner i norsk industridesign*, Oslo: Kunstindustrimuseet, 1998.

Eckmann, Otto (1865–1902)

German designer, printer, and painter; born Hamburg.

Training Graphics, painting, and the applied arts, Kunstgewerbeschule, Hamburg and Nuremberg; Akademie der bildenden Künste, Munich.
Biography Eckmann began as a painter; subsequently, pursued the decorative arts, influenced by the techniques and art of Japanese printmaking. 1896 and 1897, his ornaments and illustrations were published in journals *Pan* and *Die Jugend*. He was a professor, Kunstgewerbeschule, Berlin, where he specialized in the applied arts; designed furniture, rugs; ceramic tiles (by Villeroy & Boch), interiors (of the Grand Duke Louis IV of Hesse-Darmstadt), among others. Eckmann was one of the major proponents of Jugendstil.
Bibliography Yvonne Brunhammer et al., *Art Nouveau Belgium, France*, Houston: Rice University, 1976. Kathryn Bloom Hiesinger (ed.), *Art Nouveau in Munich: Masters of Jugenstil*, Munich: Prestel, 1988.

École de Nancy

French artists' group; active Nancy.

History The Alliance Provinciale des Industries d'Art (aka École de Nancy), under the leadership of Émile Gallé, was founded in Nancy in 1901. The artists in the group included the Daum brothers, Auguste Legras, Louis Majorelle, Victor Prouvé, Eugène Vallin, and d'Argental. When Gallé died, the Daum brothers headed the group.
Exhibitions First showing of group's work, at 1903 Salon of Union Centrale des Arts Décoratifs, Paris.
Bibliography Jessica Rutherford, *Art Nouveau, Art Deco and the Thirties: The Furniture Collections at Brighton Museum*, Brighton: The Royal Pavilion, Art Gallery and Museums, 1983: 14, 18. Frederick Cooke, *Glass: Twentieth-Century Design,* New York: Dutton, 1986.

Eda Glasbruk

Swedish glassworks.

History 1833, Emterud glassworks was established in the Värmland district, Sweden, by two Norwegians; 1838, went out of business; 1842, was taken over and resumed by Eda Bruksbolag, under Gustaf S. Santesson's management, and, thus, renamed Eda in 1843 and made window glass, bottles, and small flasks; 1845, began pressing glass and became the first in Sweden to mold blown glass; 1848, introduced cut glass to its range; by c. 1900, was hiring glass cutters and producing decorative wares; 1903 with other firms, formed De Svenska Kristallglasbruken (association of Swedish cyrstal manufacturers) to foster good design; 1927–33, was managed by Edvard Strömberg (1872–1946), who was previously the manager of Kosta and of Orrefors. Strömberg was to revitalize the operation, with designs by his wife Gerda Strömberg (1879–1960). 1933, the Strömbergs departed to establish their own Strömbergshyttan firm. During the next two decades, Eda was owned by several parties, until its 1953 closing.
Exhibitions 1930 *Stockholmsutställiningen* (Stockholm exhibition).
Bibliography Jennifer Hawkins Opie, *Scandinavia: Ceramics and Glass in the Twentieth Century*, New York: Rizzoli, 1989. Leslie Jackson, *20th Century Factory Glass*, London: Octopus, 2000.
> See Strömbergshyttan.

Edenfalk, Bengt (1924–)
> See Skrufs Glasbruk.

Edinburgh Tapestry Company (Dovecot Studios)

British textile firm.

History 1912, the firm was founded by the 4th Marquess of Bute. The first two master craftspeople at Dovecot Studios came from William Morris's Merton Abbey workshops. Edinburgh Tapestry is one of the few tapestry manufacturers of the past still active today; has commissioned established contemporary artists such as David Hockney. Pepsi-Cola ordered a group of 11 tapestries in motifs by American painter Frank Stella. The firm stocks yarn in more than 1,500 hues.

Edinburgh Weavers

British fabric and carpet manufacturers; located Carlisle.

History Edinburgh Weavers was the experimental unit of Sundour Fabrics and became known, like Wilton Royal Carpets, as a firm that took risks and produced knotted carpets in modern avant-garde motifs; was originally established in Edinburgh, Scotland, in 1929 and eventually merged with the main weaving factory in 1930. Alec Hunter and Theo Moorman were responsible for hand-woven prototypes. Hunter provided the groundwork for Edinburgh Weavers, which was later managed by Alastair Morton who commissioned some of the most accomplished 1930s British designers and artists. Hans Tisdall designed intriguing abstracts; Ashley Havinden, elegant curls, birds in flight, and ribbon motifs; and Marion Dorn, swirling abstractions. Artists Ben Nicholson and his wife Barbara Hepworth designed 1937 Constructivist Fabrics range. 1963, Edinburgh was taken over by Courtaulds, and, subsequently, Courtaulds by others.
Bibliography Cat., *Thirties: British Art and Design Before the War*, London: Arts Council of Great Britain/Hayward Gallery, 1979. Valerie Mendes, *The Victoria and Albert Museum's Textile Collection, British Textiles from 1900 to 1937*, London: Victoria and Albert Museum, 1992.

Edra

Italian furniture manufacturer; located Perignano, Pistoia.

History 1987, Edra began as a furniture company with the introduction of I Nuovissimi collection that included the work of some cutting-edge younger designers; claims to be a firm of the 'second industrial generation'; achieved recognition quickly, due to appreciable assistance by the press; appointed Radical Design-movement architect/designer/writer Massimo Morozzi (1941–) as artistic director, who has imbued Edra's inventory with a strong identity and made an appreciable contribution to Edra's success; aims to offer new rational and

emotive thinking in domestic furniture; may have created 21st-century icons by producing the work of highly imaginative designers; has possibly infused a new spirit into Italian design at a time when some asserted that its world leadership is waning; however, many in the stable are not Italian. Freelance designers have included Francesco Binfaré, Steven Blaess, Mario Cananzi, Karen Chekerdjian, Matali Crasset, John Denton, Häberli/Marchand, Christophe Pillet, Karim Rashid, Masanori Umeda, and Maarten Van Severen. The chairs in rope (1993–98) or plastic tubing (2001) by the Campana brothers of Brazil have garnered much attention, while some other seating and storage units designed by others are more functional. Edra also reissued Studio 65's Bocca sofa (based on the 1934 Mae West Lips version by Salvadore Dalí for Charles James), 1970–71 design originally produced by Gufram.
Bibliography www.edra.com.

EG + AV; Elisabeth Gonzo (1962–); Alessandro Vicari (1960–)

Italian design studio. Gonzo born Ravenna. Vicari born Modena.

Training Both: under Aldolfo Natalini, architecture, Università degli Studi, Florence.
Biography Gonzo and Vicari are architects, researchers, and professors; have designed tabletop objects, glassware, other products, and furniture, including a rocking chair/crib in wicker. They work and live in Ravenna, Milan, and Paris.

Egawa, Rie (1960–); Burgess Zbryk (1964–)

American designers; active Kansas City, Mo.

Training Egawa: 1983, bachelor's degree in fine art (printmaking), Pratt Institute, Brooklyn, N.Y. Zbryk: self-taught.
Biography From 1997, Egawa and Zbryk have collaborated on design objects through their studio E+Z Design; frequently work in wood but also call on the use of fiberboard and laser-cutting technology. The widely published Puzzle Screen is in metal, also in wood. Work includes lighting, cabinets, and chairs.
Exhibitions/citations Participated in numerous exhibits. Several design awards, including first prize, Idée Award; Case Da Abitare Award; James Irvine Award; Jon C. Jay Award; Emmanuel Babled Award—all for Puzzle Screen and all in 2001 Idée Design Competition group, Tokyo; a number of others.
Bibliography www.egawazbryk.com.

Egender, Karl (1897–1969)

Swiss architect and interior designer; born Burzwiller, Alsace (now France).

Training 1912–1915, apprenticeship as technical draftsman at Gebrüder Wasmer, Zürich.
Biography 1921–29, Egender and Adolf Steger were partners in an architecture practice in Zürich. 1930–39, Egender and Wilhem Müller were partners with co-worker Bruno Giacometti. Egender was active as a fine artist as well as an architect. 1927, he began his career as an interior decorator and was a member of the studio Schweizer Kollektivgruppe which furnished six apartments in Ludwig Mies van der Rohe's buildings at the *Die Wohnung* exhibition of 1927 *Weissenhofsiedlung*, Stuttgart and, 1930, designed furniture for his own apartment. His mid-1930s design of a tubular steel chair was put into production. He also designed 1938 chairs for Gübelin jewelers' shop in Geneva and a 1940 garden chair. His architecture included 1927–30 Limmathaus, Zürich; 1927–33 Gewerbeschule of the Kunstgewerbemuseum, Zürich; 1928–31 planning for the zoological garden, Zürich; 1936–38 stadium, Zürich-Oerlikon; 1937–41 Baur's Building, Colombo, Ceylon (now Sri Lanka); and the terrace restaurant and the fashion section at 1939 *Landesausstellung*, Zürich.
Bibliography *Künstler-Lexikon der Schweiz, XX. Jahrhundert*, Frauenfeld 1963–1967, vol. 1. Friederike Mehlau-Wiebking et al., *Schweizer Typenmöbel 1925–35, Sigfried Giedion und die Wohnbedarf AG*, Zürich: gta, 1989: 226–27.

Egnell, Johanna (1966–)

Swedish furniture and industrial designer; born Stockholm.

Training 1992–93, Nyckelviksskolan (art and design school); 1993–94, Basis Art School; 1995–2000, Anders Beckman School of Design; all Stockholm.
Biography 1994–98, Egnell was a production designer for Swedish television and commercials; 2000, an industrial designer for a water kettle by HVR Water purification company; from 2001, has designed products by IKEA, particularly a living-room suite in the children's PS collection. She has designed products by Room AB (bathrooms) and furniture by Söderbergs; taught, Anders Beckman School of Design. In Malmö, she was the production designer on a short film and designed the sets for a Kollo commerical (by Forsman & Bodenfors agency) and for Farfar (by DDX agency) as well as the interior of Föreningssparbankens real-estate agency and furniture produced by David Design, including She table.
Exhibitions/citations Work included in the David Design stand at international fairs, including 2001 Salone del Mobile in Milan, 2000 and 2001 Stockholm Furniture Fairs, 2001 100% Design in London. Other work included in 2000 *Ung svensk form* (young Swedish design) exhibition. Received 2000 Young Swedish Design Award; 2000 (2nd) Annual Calvin Klein Award; 2000 working scholarship, IKEA.

Ehrlich, Christa (1903–1995)

Austrian silversmith; born Croatia; active Vienna and The Hague.

Training Kunstgewerbeschule, Vienna.
Biography 1925–27, Ehrlich was an assistant in the architecture practice of Josef Hoffmann in Vienna; 1927, moved to the Netherlands and created graphics; also modern silver by Zilverfabriek Voorschoten, managed by Carel J.A. Begeer. She became one of the silver designers in the Netherlands realizing severe, modern work, although she introduced some playful minor decoration.
Exhibitions Painted ceiling-height showcases in a leaf pattern in the Austrian pavilion designed by Hoffmann and Haedtl at 1925 *Exposition Internationale des Arts Décoratifs et Industriels Modernes*, Paris. Was in charge of the construction and installation of Austrian section at 1927 *Europäisches Kunstgewerbe*, Grassi Museum, Leipzig.
Bibliography Cat., *Industry and Design in the Netherlands, 1850/1950*, Amsterdam: Stedelijk Museum, 1985: 221. Annelies Krekel-Aalberse, *Art Nouveau and Art Déco Silver*, New York: Abrams, 1989.

Ehrlich, Franz (1907–1984)

German architect, sculptor, painter, and designer; born Leipzig.

Training 1927–30 under Josef Albers, Paul Klee, Vasilii Kandinsky, and Joost Schmidt, Bauhaus, Dessau.
Biography Ehrlich became involved in the Constructivist stage productions of Oskar Schlemmer, who was a master-teacher at the Bauhaus. Ehrlich worked in the architecture office of Walter Gropius in Berlin; was active in decoration, advertising, and printing before being arrested by the Nazis for anti-fascist activities; 1936–39, was imprisoned in the concentration camp of Buchenwald, near Weimar; after the war, was active in Leipzig and Dresden in East Berlin and designed numerous exhibitions.
Bibliography Lionel Richard, *Encyclopédie du Bauhaus*, Paris: Somogy, 1985: 185. Cat., *The Bauhaus: Masters and Students*, New York: Barry Friedman, 1988.

Ehrmann, Marli (b. Marie Helene Heimann 1904–1982)

German textile designer and teacher; born Berlin; wife of Eliezer Ehrmann.

Training 1923, Kunstgewerbeschule, Berlin; 1923–27, Bauhaus, Weimar and Dessau; universities in Jena and Weimar; fabric design, Hamburg.
Biography 1926–27, she was an independent weaver at the Bauhaus after her studies there; became a teacher in Hamburg; 1933, was dismissed from a teaching position in Holstein because she was Jewish and, thence, taught at Herzl School in Berlin, where she met Eliezer Ehrmann whom she married 1938; 1938, settled in the US where, 1939–47, she was invited by László Moholy-Nagy to teach fabric design, School of Design (later Institute of Design), Chicago. Here students organized themselves as the Marli-Weavers, in existence 1947–91. She taught immigrant children at Hull House, Chicago; 1947–56, was a freelance designer. Work included curtains of Ludwig Mies van der Rohe's Lake Shore Apartments, Chicago; 1956, opened Elm Shop in Oak Park, Ill., near Chicago, selling modern design. She died in Santa Barbara, Cal.
Citations First prize, 1940–41 Organic Design in Home Furnishings Competition, The Museum of Modern Art, New York.
Bibliography Lionel Richard, *Encyclopédie du Bauhaus*, Paris: Somogy,

1985: 185. Cat., Gunta Stölzl, *Weberei am Bauhaus und ams eigener Werkstatt*, Berlin: Bauhaus-Archiv, 1987: 148.

Ehrner, Anna (1948–)

Swedish glassware designer; born Stockholm.

Biography Ehrner was a designer at the Kosta Boda glassworks, which produced her 1993 12-piece Epoque range of utility glassware. She represented a new generation of artists who worked with different methods to realize their concepts; works with an underlay method and produces bowls in mouth-blown superthin crystal; has become known for her soft color palette and purple-pinks with color flecks. Her Line clear-crystal table glass with its cut spiral pattern was a breakthrough in her œuvre.
Exhibitions Work included in venues in Stockholm, Japan, Germany, and Copenhagen.
Bibliography www.kostaboda.nu.

Ehrström, Eric O.W. (1881–1934)

Finnish metalworker.

Biography Ehrström designed and executed the metalwork for some of the buildings of the Finnish architecture firm Gesellius, Lindgren & Saarinen, including 1898–1900 Pohjola fire insurance company at Aleksanterinkatu and Mikonkatu in Helsinki; 1901–03 Hvitträsk house, Lake Hvitträsk; 1901–04 Hvittorp house; Remer house; 1902–12 Suomen Kansallismuseo (Finnish national museum); 1903–04 Pohjoismaiden Osakepankki bank in Helsinki. 1925, he was commissioned by Karhula to design engraved glass.
Bibliography Marika Mausen et al., *Eliel Saarinen: Projects 1896–1923*, Cambridge: MIT, 1990.

Eichenberger, Walter (1936–)

Italian industrial designer; born Milan; active Zug, Switzerland.

Biography 1961, Eichenberger began his professional career; from 1967, was a partner at M + E Design, Zug; was a consultant designer of utensils, textile machinery and apparatus, and precision instruments, and to manufacturers of domestic electronics; designed kitchen components by Franke; became a member, Associazione per il Disegno Industriale (ADI).
Bibliography *ADI Annual 1976*, Milan: Associazione per il Disegno Industriale, 1976.

Eichler, Fritz (1911–1991)

German teacher and designer; born Niedehorn, Luxemburg; active Ulm and Frankfurt.

Training 1931–35, art history and drama, Berlin and Munich.
Biography 1945–63, Eichler worked in theater-set design; became professor, Hochschule für Gestaltung; Ulm; 1954, was hired by Artur Braun and became program director and a Braun-board director; with Artur Braun's sons, was responsible for commissioning a series of radios and phonographs from the Hochschule für Gestaltung, Ulm, and, thus, establishing the stark Functionalist forms of the shavers, sound-equipment, and household wares that followed. Subsequently, Ulm teacher Hans Gugelot and student Dieter Rams joined the design staff of Braun in Frankfurt.
Bibliography 'Braun's Guiding Light,' *Design*, no. 180, Dec. 1963: 61. Cat., *Qu'est-ce que le design?*, Paris: Centre Georges Pompidou, 1969. Jocelyn de Noblet, *Design*, Paris: Somogy, 1974: 265–66. François Burkhardt and Inez Franksen (eds.), *Dieter Rams &*, Berlin: Gerhardt, 1980–81: 11–16. Cat., *Mehr oder weniger: Braun-Design im Vergleich*, Hamburg: Museum für Kunst und Gewerbe, 1990. Cat., Hans Wichmann, *Mut zum Aufbruch: Erwin Braun, 1921–1992*, Munich: Prestel, 1998.
> See Braun.

Eichner, Laurits Christian (1894–1967)

Danish metalsmith; born Stuer.

Training In engineering.
Biography Initially, Eichner was an engineer; subsequently, turned to metalsmithing and made objects in pewter and silver, often historicist in form and pattern, for clients including Hayden Planetarium in New York and Franklin Institute in Philadelphia. During World War II, he operated a plant that made precision instruments for the US government and, concurrently, taught, Craft Students League, New York.
Citations Gold medal, 1937 *Exposition Internationale des Arts et Techniques dans la Vie Moderne*, Paris.
Bibliography Cat., Janet Kardon (ed.), *Craft in the Machine Age 1920–1945*, New York: Abrams with American Craft Museum, 1995.

Eiermann, Charlotte (1912–)

German interior designer; born Potsdam.

Biography 1938–42, she worked in the office of architect Egon Eiermann in Berlin, whom she married; 1959–69, led the housing council of the Deutscher Werkbund in Berlin; designed the permanent exhibition *Living*; 1970–80, worked at Internationales Design-Zentrum, Berlin; 1982–84, taught, department of construction art, Hochschule der Künste, Berlin; 1979, became a member of the board of directors, Bauhaus-Archiv, Berlin.
Exhibitions Furnished model apartments at 1956–57 *Interbau* (international construction fair), Berlin.
Bibliography Cat., Design Center Stuttgart, *Women in Design: Careers and Life Histories Since 1900,* Stuttgart: Haus der Wirtschaft, 1989: 348–49.

Eiermann, Egon (1904–1970)

German architect and designer; born Neuendorf.

Training 1923–27, Technischen Hochschule, Berlin-Charlottenburg; 1925–28, master class of Hans Poelzig, Akademie der Künste, Berlin.
Biography 1928, Eiermann joined the Deutscher Werkbund; 1930–45, was an architect in Berlin and, from 1948, in Karlsruhe; 1948, designed his first furniture, by Friedrich Herr in Karlsruhe; designed ranges of tubular-steel-and-wood furniture by Wilde + Spieth and 1949–70 wovenwicker furniture by Heinrich Murmann, including 1949 E10 tube chair; 1950s glassware by Richard Süßmuth; furniture by Honeta. 1952–63, he was a member of the board, Deutscher Werkbund, Baden-Würtemberg; 1960s, served as an advisor on new buildings to the *Deutscher Bundestag* (federal daily journal) and the Upper House of the Parliament in Bonn. Eiermann's plywood chairs (1949 three-legged SE 42 and 1951 steel/wood SE 68) by Wilde + Spieth may be criticized for their unabashed plagiarism of designs by Charles and Ray Eames; his others (1952 folding SE 18 and 1958 rush-seat SE 119) were somewhat undistinguished; many models are still in production, some by by Richard Lampert in Stuttgart. He died in Baden-Baden.
Bibliography Cat., *Design im 20. Jahrhundert*, Cologne: Museum für Agnewandte Kunst, 1989. Cat., *Egon Eiermann: Die Möbel*, Karlsruhe: Badisches Landesmuseum, 1999.

Marli Ehrman. Original fabric sample (no. 13309). 1941. Cotton, 24 5/8 x 24 5/8" (62.5 x 62.5 cm) (framed). Gift of the designer. MoMA.

Eikerman, Alma (1909–1995)

American jewelry designer and metalsmith; born Kansas.

Training Liberal arts, Kansas State University, Emporia, Kans.; design, painting, and metalsmithing, University of Kansas, Lawrence, Kans.; Columbia University, New York, to 1942.
Biography From 1945, Eikerman taught general-design courses and jewelry design in Wichita, Kans., and became a jewelry designer and metalsmith; from 1947, taught at Indiana University, where she developed one of the best schools for metalworking in the US and became a key figure in the resurgence of metalsmithing in the post-World War II period. Goldsmith Karl Gustav Hansen, who was the designer director at Hans Hansen Sølvmedie in Kolding, Sweden, was her mentor in metalsmithing. She also studied under baron Erik Fleming in his Stockholm workshop. Her work was influenced by artists Vasilii Kandinsky, Claude Cézanne, Henri Matisse, Arthur Dove, Georgia O'Keefe, Stuart Davis, Charles Burchfield, Charles R. Sheeler, and Hans Hofmann.
Exhibitions/citations Work included in large number of exhibitions and subject of 1985 venue, Indiana University Art Museum. 1948 Handy and Harmon Silversmithing Award (for study at Rhode Island School of Design under Fleming); 1968 Carnegie Foundation grant (for funding her renowned workshop and which resulted in the film *Creative Silversmithing)*.
Bibliography Alma Eikerman, 'Creative Designing in Metal,' *Craft News* (Handy and Harmon), May 1952: 4–9. 'Eikerman-Wilson-Martz Exhibition Review,' *Creative Horizons*, no. 18, July–Aug 1958: 44. Cat., Constance L. Bowen, *A Tribute to Alma Eikerman: Master Craftsman*, Indiana University Art Museum, 1985.

Einarsdottir, Sigrun (1951–)

Icelandic glassware designer.

Training In Denmark.
Biography Late 1970s, she set up the first hot-glass workshop in Iceland; designed both one-of-a-kind work and production glassware decorated with fluidly rendered human figures.
Bibliography Cat., David Revere McFadden (ed.), *Scandinavian Modern Design 1880–1980*, New York: Abrams, 1982.

Einarsson, Gudmundur (1895–1963)

Icelandic ceramicist.

Training 1921–26, in Munich.
Biography Einarsson's double-walled ceramic pieces included pierced strapwork and animal figures; set up the first (1927) ceramics workshop in Iceland and became a leading figure in the development of the Icelandic ceramics tradition.
Bibliography Cat., David Revere McFadden (ed.), *Scandinavian Modern Design 1880–1980*, New York: Abrams, 1982.

Eisch, Erwin (1927–)

German glassware designer and craftsperson; born Frauenau; active Bavaria.

Training 1945–47 under his father, in glassblowing; to 1949, engraving, Glasfachschule, Zwiesel; 1949–52 under Heinrich Kirchner, Akademie der Künste, Munich.
Biography Eisch worked in hot glass; from 1960, experimented with glass as a sculptural medium; 1975, delivered an influential lecture to the Deutsche Glastechnische Gesellschaft; was a leading member of the New Wave Studio Movement of the 1960s.
Exhibitions Subject of 1960 exhibit, Stuttgart.
Bibliography Frederick Cooke, *Glass: Twentieth-Century Design*, New York: Dutton, 1986: 105. *Die Sammlung Wolfgang Kermer, Glasmuseum Frauenau*, Munich/Zürich: Schnell und Steiner, 1989: 19–27.

Eisenlöffel, Jan W. (1876–1957)

Dutch silversmith, metalworker, glass designer, and ceramicist; active Laren.

Training At the firm Hoeker en Zoon; 1898, in Russia.
Biography Eisenlöffel designed silver for a metal workshop in Amstelhoek. His wares at Hoeker en Zoon were not identified as his when shown in international exhibitions. 1902, he set up his own company with J.C. Stoffels; 1903–04, worked for De Woning, Amsterdam; until 1907, for Fabriek van Zilverwerk, Utrecht; 1908, for Vereinigte Werkstätten für Kunst im Handwerk in Munich. Begeer, who was the director of Fabriek van Zilverwerk, credited his designers, including Eisenlöffel. Riemerschmid liked Eisenlöffel's work, and his copper sets appeared in Riemerschmid's interiors. Eisenlöffel worked for a time in the workshop of Carl Peter Fabergé in St. Petersburg, Russia, where he became interested in the *champlevé*-enamel technique.
Exhibitions/citations Work in the geometrical style shown at Hoeker en Zoon stand, 1900 *Exposition Universelle*, Paris, where some of his (uncredited) wares won awards and were bought by Tiffany. Medals (for his own separately shown work and, uncredited again, at the Hoeker stand), 1902 *Esposizione Internazionale d'Arte Decorativa Moderna*, Turin. Silver objects shown at 1904 exhibition, Turin, and Hermann Hirschwald's Hohenzollern Kunstgewerbehaus, Berlin.
Bibliography Annelies Krekel-Aalberse, *Art Nouveau and Art Déco Silver*, New York: Abrams, 1989. Cat., *Metallkunst*, Berlin: Bröhan Museum, 1990: 142–53.

Egon Eiermann. SE 18 folding chair. 1953. Beech and laminated woods, 29 1/2 x 20 7/8 x 17" (75 x 53 x 43 cm). Mfr.: Wilde & Spieth, Germany. Courtesy Quittenbaum Kunstauktionen, Munich.

Eisenman, Peter (1932–)

American architect and teacher; born Newark, N.J.

Training 1955, bachelor's degree in architecture, Cornell University, Ithaca, N.Y.; 1960, master's degree in architecture, Columbia University, New York; 1963, Ph.D. degree in theory of design, Cambridge University, UK.
Biography 1957–58, Eisenman collaborated with The Architects' Collaborative (TAC), Cambridge, Mass.; taught at Harvard University, Syracuse (N.Y.) University, and Princeton University; from 1967, The Cooper Union for the Advancement of Science and Art, New York. 1967, he founded the Institute for Architecture and Urban Studies, New York, of which he was the director to 1982; was co-editor of architecture journal *Oppositions*; early 1970s, became known as one of ad-hoc New York Five group of architects, along with John Hejduk, Richard Meier, Michael Graves, and Charles Gwathmey. His work was associated with Italian Rationalism; the red staircase in his House VI could not be climbed and did not lead anywhere. Known as a Deconstructivist, he designed eccentric non-site-specific buildings until early 1980s, ceramic dinnerware in the 1980s by Swid Powell, and 1991 34-fabric range by Knoll. Eisenman archive is housed at Canadian Center for Architecture in Montréal.
Work Architecture has included 1967–68 House I (Barenholtz Pavilion), Princeton, New Jersey; 1969–70 House II (Falk house), Hardwick, Connecticut; 1969–70 House III (Miller house), Lakeville, Connecticut; 1970 House VI (Frank house), Cornwall, Connecticut; 1978 E1 Even

Jan Eisenlöffel. Pepper mill. c. 1902. Brass sheet over wood, 6 7/8 x 1 7/8 x 1 7/8" (17.5 x 4.8 x 4.8 cm). Mfr.: the designer, Amsterdam. Courtesy Quittenbaum Kunstauktionen, Munich.

Odd House; 1990 Wexner Center for the Visual Arts, Ohio State University, Columbus, Ohio.
Exhibitions Work included in various venues at The Museum of Modern Art, New York: 1967 *The New City: Architecture and Urban Renewal,* 1968 *Architecture of Museums*, and 1973 *Another Chance for Housing*. Work shown at 1970 (15th), 1985 (17th), and 1996 (19th) editions of Triennale di Milano, 1976 Biennale di Venezia, and 1978 *Assenza-Presenza* in Bologna. Work subject of 1994 exhibition, Centre Canadien d'Architecture/Canadian Centre for Architecture, Montréal (catalog below).
Bibliography Kenneth Frampton and Colin Rowe, *Five Architects: Eisenman, Graves, Gwathmey, Hejduk, Meier*, New York: Wittenborn, 1972. Peter Eisenman, *House of Cards*, New York: Oxford University Press, 1987. Cat., Carlo Guenzi, *Le affinità elettive*, Milan: Electa, 1985. Auction cat., *Asta di modernariato 1900–1986, Auction 'Modernariato,'* Milan: Semenzato Nuova Geri, 8 Oct. 1986. Cat., Jean-François Bédard and Alan Balfour, *Cities of Artificial Excavation: The Work of Peter Eisenman, 1978–1988*, New York: Rizzoli, 1994. Jeffrey Kipnis and Thomas Leeser (eds.), *Chora L Works: Jacques Derrida and Peter Eisenman*, New York: Monacelli, 1997.

EKCO Products
American manufacturer.

History 1888, EKCO Products was established in Chicago, as a producer of undistinguished kitchen tools; at the end of World War II, upgraded the design and quality of its merchandise, its own employees acting as designers. Its 1946 Flint kitchen tools were designed by manager Arthur Keating, industrial designer James Hvale (hired in 1944), and engineers Myron J. Zimmer and James Chandler. The tools were sold as a set with a metal holder in packaging designed by Richard Latham of Raymond Loewy Associates, Chicago. In the 1950s, Latham worked on marketing and product planning for EKCO's kitchen products. Others have followed, including Henning Speyer, EKCO's director of design 1993–94, who designed Syroco monoblock outdoor stacking chairs, electronic cases for various products, pediatric products such as bathtub handles and adjustable resin bathtub chairs. Subsequently, cooking pot/pan ranges have included Copperelle stainless-steel, Radiance non-stick, Endura non-stick, Eterna stainless-steel, and Resolutions non-stick, as well as handheld kitchen utensils. 1999, the firm was amalgamated with other firms into the EKCO Group (including EKCO Housewares) of Frankling Park, Ill.—a part of World Kitchen. EKCO's Woodstream subsidiary (purchased by EKCO in 1989), which produced Victor leghold animal traps and Conibear animal-body-gripping devices, discontinued production of these devices in 1998 due to legislation by the State of California and others.
Citations Good Design awards, Chicago Athenaeum: 1997 (for 1997 Extendible barbecue tools by Ancona 2) and 1999 (for 1998 Clip 'n Stay clothespins by Bruce Ancona and Louis Henry of Ancona 2).
Bibliography Eliot Noyes, 'The Shape of the Thing: Good Design in Everyday Objects,' *Consumer Reports*, Jan. 1949: 27. 'The Change at Ekco: Merchandising Bows to a Unique Planning Group,' *Industrial Design*, vol. 3, Oct. 1956: 103–05. Don Wallance, *Shaping America's Products*, New York: Reinhold, 1956: 129–31. Jay Doblin, *One Hundred Great Product Designs*, New York: Van Nostrand Reinhold, 1970: 46. Cat., Kathryn B. Hiesinger and George H. Marcus III (eds.), *Design Since 1945*, Philadelphia: Philadelphia Museum of Art, 1983.

Ekco Radio Company
> See Cole, Eric Kirkham.

Ekholm, Kurt (1907–1975)
Finnish ceramicist.

Biography 1932–48, Ekholm was the artistic director, Arabia pottery, Helsinki, where he contributed new designs. His everyday earthenware dinnerware was easy to produce and decorate. 1943, he set up the Arabia Museum; 1949–50, worked for Rörstrand in Lidköping, Sweden.
Bibliography Cat., David Revere McFadden (ed.), *Scandinavian Modern Design 1880–1980*, New York: Abrams, 1982.

Eklund, Antti-Mikael (1960–)
Finnish product and interior designer; born Turku, Finland.

Training 1988, master of science degree in architecture, Teknillinen korkeakoulu, Helsinki.
Biography 1983–84, Eklund worked in the architecture office of Reima Pietilä; from 1986, was chairperson, Daf Design Management (advertising and graphics agency), and of Animal Design Oy (marketing and sales of Animal-brand products, with the Maus can opener as its first product); 1989–90, worked on interiors at architects Kohn Pedersen Fox Conway, New York; from 1998, as a professor, department of graphic design, Taideteollinen korkeakoulu, Helsinki. Work includes products, furniture, and interiors by Animal Design, from 1989; Alessi table-top objects, from 1990; furniture design, graphics, and advertising for various clients, from 1994; interiors of Nokia and of Sonera; user-interactive digital TV by Telecom Finland.
Exhibitions/citations Work included in 1992 *Suomi muotoilee 9* (Finnish design exhibition), 1995 *Estradi* (modern-art exhibition), 1996 *Nuorten Forum* (design exhibition), 1996 *TKO 30 vuotta* (exhibition of Finnish association of industrial designers), all Helsinki; and *Expo 2000*, Hanover. Citations include 1996 Design Distinction in Environments award, Annual Design Review, *I.D.* magazine; 1997 Innovative Design from Finland, touring Asia; 1998 Tendence fair

EKCO Products Co. Vegetable peelers. c. 1944. Steel. Mfr.: Ekco Products Co., US. Purchase. MoMA.

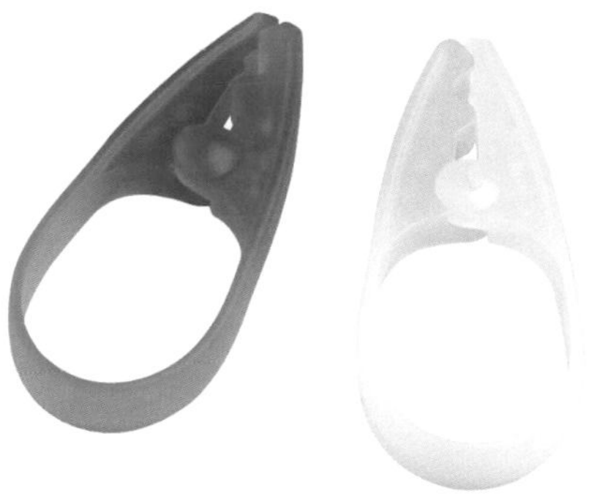

EKCO Housewares: Bruce Ancona (1956–) and Louis Henry (1971–). Clip'n Stay clothespins (two examples of other colors). 1998. Low-density polypropylene and metal spring, each 3 1/4 x 1 1/2 x 5/8" (8.3 x 3.8 x 1.6 cm). Mfr.: Ekco Housewares, US. Gift of the mfr. MoMA.

(Maus can-opener introduction), Frankfurt; 1999 and 2001 Good Design award, Chicago Athenaeum; 2001 Brands Designed in Finland, Helsinki; Form 2001, Frankfurt.
Biography Mel Byars, *Design in Steel*, London: Laurence King, 2002.

Ekström, Yngve (1913–1988); Swedese Möbler
Swedish furniture designer.

Biography 1945, Ekström and his brother Jerker Ekström founded Swedese Möbler in Vaggeryd, Sweden. Yngve directed and designed for the firm until his 1988 death, including its head office building, logo, and catalogs; also cooperated with Alvar Aalto, Arne Jacobsen, Poul Kjærholm, and Bruno Mathsson. His best-known design is 1956 Lamino lounge chair, still in production along with other models. From 1950s, he worked with Stolfabriks in Småland, designing its c. 1955 Arka armchair, Björka modular pedestal table, and other furniture; was a major participant in developing what is known today as the Scandinavian modern style. Swedese has also commissioned contemporary designers, including Bror Boije, Sophia Dahlén, James Irvine, Björn Hultén, Joel Karlsson, Komplot Design (Boris Berlin/Poul Christiansen), koncept.ab, Yuriko Takahashi, Mårten Claesson/Eero Koivisto/Ola Rune, Thomas Sandell, Skala Design (Lasse Pettersson/Lennart Notman) Michael Young, others.
Citations 1999, Lamino was designated Twentieth Century's Best Swedish Furniture Design, *Sköna Hem* magazine; a number of Excellent Swedish Design diplomas; +1 Diploma (for Brasili coffee table by Koivisto/Rune), *Forum* magazine, 2002 Stockholm Furniture Fair; Interior Innovation Award (Lamino chair), 2003 Internationale Möbelmesse, Cologne; 2003 Forsnäs Prize (for Twister stool by Takahashi), The Forsnäs-Fonden Foundation; 2003 International Design Award (for Papermaster magazine rack by Torbjørn Anderssen of Norway Says), Norska Designrådet (ND, Norwegian design council).
Bibliography Monica Boman (ed.), *Svenska møbler 1890–1990*, Kristianstad: Signum, 1991.

Elbe, Lili (1892–1961)
German fabric designer; active Weimar

Training Kunstgewerbeschule, Weimar, headed by Henry van de Velde.
Biography Elbe's fabrics were highly colored with swirling patterns, often realized by the resist (batik) method.
Bibliography Klaus-Jürgen Sembach and Birgit Schulte, *Henry van de Velde: Ein europäischer Künstler seiner Zeit*, Cologne: Wienand, 1992: 285. Auction cat., *Modernes Design Kunsthandwerk nach 1945*, Munich: Quittenbaum, 4 Dec. 2001, lot 21.

Electrolux
Swedish domestic appliance firm.

History 1901, Aktiebolaget Lux was founded in Stockholm. 1910, Elektromekaniska was founded. 1912, a relationship developed between Lux and Axel Wenner-Gren (1881–1961). 1912, the Lux 1 was introduced, as the first electrical horizontal-cylinder vacuum cleaner, whose flexible hose made it possible to clean in places other floor models could not reach. Wenner-Gren was the agent for Lux in Germany, France, and the UK and, 1915, established the sales company Svenska Elektron (later Finans AB Svetro) and the method of in-home sales. 1918, Svenska Elektron was given sole sales rights by Lux, with Wenner-Gren as the primary proprietor and the name changed to AB Elektrolux (the name's combining Elektromekaniska and Lux). 1924, the Elektrolux vacuum cleaner was successfully introduced in the US. 1930, a plant was built in the US for the production of vacuum cleaners and the first (L1) air-cooled refrigerators; and, 1936, a plant in Australia. 1930s, the firm began commissioning consultant designers, including Raymond Loewy, Carl Otto, and Lurelle Guild of the US, and Sixten Sason of Sweden. Its distinctive late-1920s shop on the boulevard des Malesherbes, Paris, was designed by architect Germain Debré. 1939, Wenner-Gren retired to the Bahamas. 1951, the first domestic clothes-washing machine and, 1956, first chest freezer were introduced. 1956, Wenner-Gren sold his share in the firm to Wallenberg Group. 1957, the firm name was changed from Elektrolux to Electrolux; 1974, became primary producer of vacuum cleaners worldwide. The corporation acquired a large number of firms in the 1970s, and further with Zanussi 1984, Zanker and Duo-Therm 1985, White Group (Westinghouse products) 1986, Lehel 1991, and others, resulting in its having become the world's largest producer of powered appliances for kitchen, cleaning and outdoor use, selling more than 55 million products ($15 billion/15 billion euros worth) in 150 countries by the year 2000. 1991, developed industrial robotic vacuum cleaner; introduced in 2001 as the Trilobite, the world's first domestic robotic vacuum cleaner (designed by Per Inese Ljunggren and Inese Ljunggren).
Bibliography Mel Byars with Arlette Barré-Despond, *100 Designs/100 Years...*, Hove: RotoVision, 1999. www.electrolux.com.

Elixir
> See Blet, Thierry.

Elkington
British silversmiths; located Birmingham.

Biography 1829, George Richard Elkington (1801–1865) became diirector of his family's firm that produced gilt objects, gold eye-glass cases, and small domestic accessories, including silver-mounted scent bottles; during 1830s with cousin Henry Elkington, patented various refinements of the electrogilding process; experimented with electroplating and, 1840, patented the first commercially successful process for electroplating silver and gold. 1841, Elkington's chief metallurgist Alexander Parkes filed for a patent for electrotyping. These patents advanced metallurgy at Elkington and had far-reaching effects in Britain and the US. Having bought up other electroplating patents, the firm had control of the industry in Britain until c. 1875. Josiah Mason, a wealthy pen manufacturer, was taken into partnership in 1842, when

Yngve Ekström. Arka armchair. c. 1955. Oak and teak, 25 3/8 x 28 3/8 x 17 7/8" (64.5 x 72 x 46.5 cm). Mfr.: Stolfabriks, Sweden. Courtesy Quittenbaum Kunstauktionen, Munich.

the firm became Elkington, Mason & Co. Since electroplating was inexpensive, Sheffield plating became obsolete. With silverplated objects as popular as sterling silver by 1860s, Elkington hired Danish consultant designer Benjamin Schlick, who designed historicist models in Greek and Roman styles, produced from 1845. c.1850, the South Kensington Museum (later Victoria and Albert Museum), London, had Elkington reproduce some of the objects in its collection. George Elkington's son Frederick joined the firm in the 1850s and, from 1865, was its director. As well as silverplated pieces, Elkington produced sterling silver and *champlevé* and *cloisonné*-enameled objects. Its Renaissance and classical motifs were the result of the influence of French designers Pierre-Émile Jeannest, who joined the firm in c. 1848, Léonard Morel-Ladeuil, who joined in 1859, and Albert Willms, another Frenchman and head of the design department from the 1860s to c. 1900. From 1865, Willms was instrumental in Elkington's introduction of *japonisant* forms and techniques. 1875–85, the firm produced objects designed by Christopher Dresser and, from 1935, modern designs by John Walker, Bernard Cuzner, Reginald Hill, and Frank Nevile. Its 20th-century production was mostly domestic plate along with hot-brass stamping and copper refining. 1954, Elkington moved to Goscote Lane in Walsall, near Birmingham; 1956, became part of the Delta Group of Companies and is today part of Delta's metal products division Elkington Mansill Booth, producing industrial stampings in non-ferrous alloys.
Exhibitions Represented Britain with silver presentation pieces at 1876 *Centennial Exposition*, Philadelphia, and at 1878 *Exposition Universelle*, Paris.
Bibliography Shirley Bury, 'Elkington's and the Japanese Style,' *Worshipful Company of Goldsmiths' Review*, 1874–75: 27–28. Shirley Bury, 'The Silver Designs of Dr. Christopher Dresser,' *Apollo*, no. 76, Dec. 1962: 766–70. Doreen Bolger Burke et al., *In Pursuit of Beauty: Americans and the Aesthetic Movement*, New York: The Metropolitan Museum of Art/Rizzoli, 1986: 424. Annelies Krekel-Aalberse, *Art Nouveau and Art Déco Silver*, New York: Abrams, 1989.

Ellin and Kitson

American architectural sculptors; located New York.

History Active from c. 1867, Ellin and Kitson produced architectural sculpture in carved wood and stone, modeled plaster, and *papier-mâché*; specialized in church decoration; was located 1887–89 at 513–519 West 21st Street, New York, and in the building at no. 511 also occupied subsequently; 1891–1900, was located at the end of West 25th Street on the Hudson River. Its principals were Britons Robert Ellin and John W. Kitson. In the late 1860s, they hired architect P.B. Wight to carve capitals for the National Academy of Design on upper Fifth Avenue; Wight was the architect of the building, completed in 1865. c. 1880–84, Ellin and Kitson furnished satinwood panels for the dining room of the Samuel J. Tilden house (the National Arts Club from 1906), Gramercy Park, New York, when Calvert Vaux supervised the remodeling of the building.
Exhibitions Jacobean-style oak sideboard shown at 1876 *Centennial Exposition*, Philadelphia.
Bibliography 'Work on Mr. Tilden's House,' *New York Daily Tribune*, 29 Jan. 1882: 12. Charles Rollinson Lamb, *The Tilden Mansion—Home of the National Arts Club*, New York, 1932: 9. Doreen Bolger Burke et al., *In Pursuit of Beauty: Americans and the Aesthetic Movement*, New York: The Metropolitan Museum of Art/Rizzoli, 1986.

Ellis, Eileen (1933–)

British textile designer.

Training 1950–52, Leicester College of Art; 1952–54, Central School of Arts and Crafts, London; 1954–57, Royal College of Art, London.
Biography 1957–59, she worked for the Ascher firm, designing printed and woven fabrics for the garment trade and Marks and Spencer; in 1960, formed Orbit Design Group; designed fabrics for BEA's Trident airplane and others in the fleet, the proscenium curtain for a theater in Birmingham, and fabrics by Alastair Morton's Edinburgh Weavers, John Lewis, Morton Sundour, and others. 1970 with Ann Bristow, she formed Weaveplan Favershankent, becoming its sole proprietor in 1975 with five designers in her stable; worked for Irish Ropes (overseeing all carpet design there), C. and J. Hirst furnishing fabrics, Vescom wallcoverings, Abbotsford Fabrics, John Orr Eire upholstery fabrics, and Jamasque fabrics.
Citation1984, elected Honorary Royal Designer for Industry, UK.
Bibliography Fiona MacCarthy and Patrick Nuttgens, *An Eye for Industry*, London: Lund Humphries, 1986.

Ellis, Harvey (1852–1904)

American architect and designer; born Rochester, N.Y.

Training West Point Military Academy, West Point, N.Y.
Biography Ellis began his career as a draftsperson under architect H.H. Richardson in Albany, N.Y.; 1879–84, practiced as an architect with his brother Charles Ellis in Rochester; subsequently, worked as a journeyman draftsperson in the Midwest; mid-1890s, returned to Rochester and designed in the manner of the British Arts and Crafts movement and, from 1903, furniture by Gustav Stickley's United Crafts Workshop in Eastwood, N.Y., and wrote for Stickley's magazine *The Craftsman*. Ellis's furniture was influenced by H.H. Richardson. During the last months of his life, he designed the houses, furniture, and wall decorations at Stickley's workshop. His inlaid furniture, expensive to produce and discontinued after 1904, was used mostly for display and speciality purposes. His late work was strongly influenced by British designers C.F.A. Voysey, Charles Rennie Mackintosh, and Hugh Baillie Scott. Ellis's wide tabletop overhangs, arched skirts, inlaid elements, and native-American and Art Nouveau motifs departed from the sober lines of typical Stickley furniture. The Mackintosh influence was expressed in his use of inlays in pewter, copper, and wood. It is not known if Ellis designed furniture for his own buildings; however, his drawings reveal an interest in the relationship between furniture design and architecture.
Exhibitions Inlaid furniture shown at 1904 *Louisiana Purchase Exposition*, St. Louis.
Bibliography Hugh M.G. Garden, 'Harvey Ellis, Designer and Draftsman,' *The Prairie School Review 5*, First/Second Quarter, 1968: 36–39. Roger G. Kennedy, 'Long Dark Corridors: Harvey Ellis,' *The Prairie School Review 5*, First/Second Quarter, 1968: 5–18. Cat., David Cathers, *Genius in the Shadows: The Furniture Designs of Harvey Ellis*, New York: Jordan-Volpe Gallery, 1981. Cat., Lisa Phillips (intro.), *Shape and Environment: Furniture by American Architects*, New York: Whitney Museum of American Art, 1982: 26. Cat., Anne Yaffe Phillips, *From Architecture to Object*, New York: Hirschl and Adler, 1989: 40–41.

Ellwood, George Montague (1875–c. 1960)

British furniture designer; born London.

Training Camden School of Art
Biography Ellwood designed for J.S. Henry in Old Street, London, a manufacturer of an extensive range of furniture in the early years of the 20th century, for Trapnell & Gane of Bristol, and for the Guild of Art Craftsmen. Ellwood's work was widely published, including in *The Studio*. He worked in a style close to continental Art Nouveau.
Exhibitions 1899–1906, designs of interiors shown at the Royal Academy of Arts, London.
Bibliography *British Art and Design 1900–1960*, London: Victoria and Albert Museum, 1983.

Elmslie, George Grant (1871–1952)

British architect; born Aberdeenshire; active US.

Biography 1884, Elmslie's family settled in Chicago, from Britain. 1885, he began working in the office of architect Lyman Silsbee, first as an errand boy and, subsequently, an apprentice; 1889 with Frank Lloyd Wright's help, joined architects Dankmar Adler and Louis Sullivan; worked alongside Wright in Silsbee's and in Sullivan's offices; in the latter's office for 20 years, executed many of Sullivan's detailed designs for organic ornamentation and may have been the author of the ornamentation often credited solely to Sullivan; designed the interiors, furnishings, and ornamental windows of Sullivan's 1907–09 Henry B. Babson house in Riverside, Ill., his last project for Sullivan. 1912–13, Elmslie made revisions on the Babson house and, c. 1924, designed some notable stained-glass windows that incorporated modern geometric motifs; 1910, joined William Gray Purcell and George Feick Jr. in their architecture office in Minnesota. 1910–13, the firm was known as Purcell, Feick and Elmslie and, 1913–22, as Purcell and Elmslie. Its commissions included numerous banks in small Midwestern towns. Like Wright and Sullivan, Elmslie and Purcell avoided obvious Beaux-Arts forms and neoclassical detailing, producing an indigenous American style; were known for their attention to integrated site-specific interiors. In a style of his own, though influenced by Sullivan, Elmslie designed furniture, stained glass, embroidery, carpets, and metalwork. A Prairie school architect, he was primarily interested in private houses; considered the house and its furnishings to be a unified entity. His use of ornamentation on furniture showed Sullivan's influence and was uncommon among Prairie School practitioners. Elmslie's furniture dates

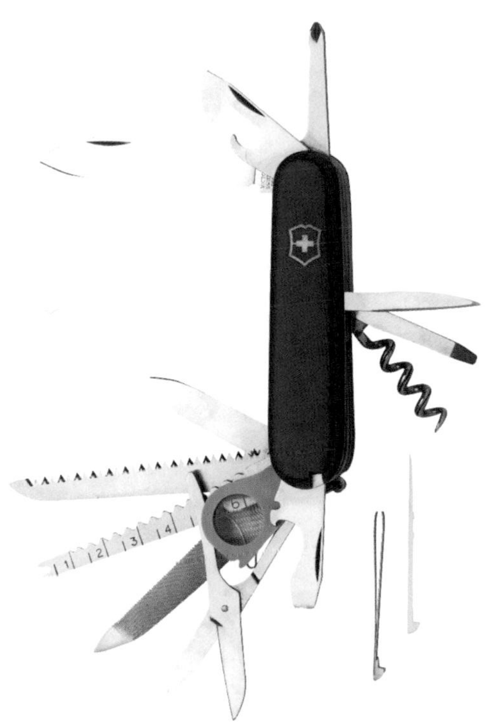

Karl Elsener. Victorinox Swiss Officers' Knife Champion (no. 5012). 1968. Plastic and stainless steel, 3 5/8 x 1 x 1 1/8" (9.2 x 2.5 x 2.9 cm). Mfr.: Victorinox, Switzerland. Gift of Golden West Merchandisers, US. MoMA.

mainly from the time of his Purcell partnership.
Exhibitions Work (with Purcell) subject of 1953 *Purcell and Elmslie: Architects, 1910–1922*, Walker Art Center, Minneapolis, Minn.
Bibliography Cat., David Gebhard, *Purcell and Elmslie: Architects, 1910–22*, Minneapolis: Walker Art Center, 1953. David Gebhard, *Drawings for Architectural Ornament, 1902–1936*, Santa Barbara, Cal.: University Art Galleries, University of California, 1968. Cat., Lisa Phillips (intro.), *Shape and Environment: Furniture by American Architects*, New York: Whitney Museum of American Art, 1982: 28. Cat., Anne Yaffe Phillips, *From Architecture to Object*, New York: Hirschl and Adler, 1989: 72.

Elsener, Karl (1860–1918)

Swiss cutler; fourth son of hatmaker Balthasar Elsener-Ott.

Training To 1884, apprentice and journeyman, France, and Tuttlingen, Germany.
Biography Elsener became a master knifemaker, specializing in surgical instruments and razor edges; after training abroad, returned to Switzerland in 1884 and set up a small workshop in Ibach (near Schwyz) and sold his knives in the hat shop of his mother; 1890 or 1891, organized the Swiss Cutlery Guild in order to develop a pocket knife for the Swiss military. At the time, the army was buying its knives from factories in Solingen, Germany. Oct. 1891, the first Swiss-made knives were delivered to the troops of the Swiss Army. The original model featured a blade, screwdriver, reamer for hole punching, and can opener. Registered 12 June 1897, Elsener developed his own version of the Officer's Knife (in addition to ones he named Student Knife, Cadet Knife, and Farmer's Knife), and Elsener's version of the Officer's Knife, or *Offiziersmesser* or officer's measurer, was immediately accepted by the troops, who bought it with their own money. However, the red model of today is not the regulation-issue Swiss army knife which was made of an alloy (dull silver and aluminum) with a large blade, reamer, can opener, small and large screwdrivers, bottle-cap lifter, and wire stripper. 1909, after the death of his mother, the firm was given her Christian name Victoria in her honor, but, with the 1921 development of stainless steel, the name was changed to Victorinox, 'inox' being the European name of stainless steel, and the cross and shield symbols were adopted. After World War II (1945–49), American soldiers became familiar with the Victorinox knife; however, because *Offiziersmesser* was too difficult for them to pronounce, they called it the Swiss Army Knife, as it has become primarily known by English speakers. The French called it the Couteau Suisse; the Germans and Austrians, the Schweizer Messer. 1951, Victorinox patented its knife-attached can opener, claiming it to be the best available. From 1976, the firm has supplied the German army with its pocket knife, in an olive-green color, not red, and with a German-eagle insignia, not the Swiss cross. Authentic Swiss Army Knives have an aluminum case; red ones are for civilians and export. The firm today makes about 120,000 knives daily in 100 Swiss Army versions and 300 others, including the largest (SwissChamp XLT) with 50 features, and has introduced a number of products that call on the 'Swiss Army' brand such as watches, luggage, and clothing and those of the R.H. Forschner cutlery division.
Exhibitions Subject of 1998 exhibition, Kunsthalle, Bern (catalog below).
Bibliography Rick Wall, *Swiss Army Knife Companion: The Improbable History of the World's Handiest Knife*, Swiss Army Knife Society, 1986. Kathryn Kane, *Swiss Army Knife Handbook: The Official History and Owner's Guide*, Oracle, Ariz.: Birdworks, 1988. Cat., Thomas Hirschhorn et al., *Swiss Army Knife*, Bern: Kunsthalle, 1998. Nick Constable, *Swiss Army Knives Companion*, Hove: Apple, 1999. Paola Antonelli (ed.), *Objects of Design: The Museum of Modern Art*, New York: The Museum of Modern Art, 2003: 63. www.victorinox.ch.

EMBRU-Werke (Eisen- und Metallbettenfabrik)

Swiss furniture manufacturer; located Rüti.

History 1904, EMBRU was established to produce steel beds; subsequently, other metal furniture was added to the inventory; 1930, began the production of furniture reflecting the so-called Neue Sachlichkeit (new reality) aesthetic, under the reorganization of Sigfried Giedion, who also designed the factory. The firm acquired licenses to produce the designs of tubular-steel furniture designed by Swiss architects, including Werner M. Moser, Max E. Haefeli, Alfred Roth, and Flora Steiger-Crawford, as well as Alvar Aalto and Marcel Breuer; from 1931, had the rights to produce Thonet models. At this time, its designer furniture was sold through the Wohnbedarf store in Zürich. Recently, the firm was reorganized as Embru-Werke, Mantel & Cie., specializing in standardized health-care, school, and office furniture; has re-entered earlier models into current production: Moser's 1930 lounge chair (no. 2) and 1931 table (no. 91), Breuer's 1934 bent-aluminium/slat-wood

EMBRU-Werke. Caruelle table/lecturn. c. 1942. Walnut veneer and brushed steel tubing, 39 15/16 x 20 1/4 x 16 5/16" (101.5 x 51.5 x 41.5 cm). Mfr.: EMBRU-Werke (under 1929 patent of Carulle, France), Switzerland. Courtesy Quittenbaum Kunstauktionen, Munich.

lounge chairs (nos. 1090 and 1096), and Wilhelm Kienzle's 1949 Spaghetti folding outdoor chairs and armchair (no. 2722) in tubular galvanized metal.
Bibliography Friederike Mehlau-Wiebking et al., *Schweizer Typenmöbel 1925–35, Sigfried Giedion und die Wohbedarf AG*, Zürich: gta, 1989: 83–84. *Über Möbel*, Rüti: Embru-Werke, Rüti, 2001.

Emeco (The Electric Machine and Equipment Co.)

Furniture manufacturer; located Hanover, Pa., US.

History 1944, Emeco was founded by tool-and-die maker Wilton C. Dinges (1916–1974), based on exhaustive experiments by the US Navy, which had begun in the 1920s, to develop chairs for use on ships/submarines. A collaboration among Navy consultants, the Alumunum Company of America (ALCOA) technicians, and Emeco resulted in an aluminum chair that would satisfy rigid criteria. Manufacture demanded new, expensive tooling and time-consuming handcrafting. Production, which began in 1944 and continues today, is realized through 77 steps, including a process that results in aluminum's molecular structure being altered to become three times harder than steel. The hand-finished, oxidized surface is impervious to almost every agent, including fire. The manufacturer claims the no. 1006 (or Navy) chair will last 150 years. Dinges managed Emeco until 1964 when he became less active due to illness. 1998, the firm was purchased by Gregg Buchbinder (1956–), who revitalized its image and products by, among other efforts, commissioning Philippe Starck to design new models, including the 2000 Hudson chair range, while continuing to make the original Navy chair and other furniture.
Bibliography Mel Byars, 'To Be Continued,' *Metropolitan Home*, Nov.-Dec. 1999: 80+. www.emeco.net.

Emmebonacina
> See BBB Emmebonacina.

En Attendant les Barbares

French design collaboration and gallery.

History Members of En Attendant les Barbares ('waiting for the barbarians' after the title of John Maxwell Coetzee's 1980 novel) included Elisabeth Garouste, Mattia Bonetti, Jean-Philippe Gleizes, jewelry designers Patrick Retif and Christian and Marie-Thérèse Migeon, fashion designer Catherine Grimaldi, interior designer Jean Neuville, and musician Eric Schmitt. Their work, associated with the 1980s Barbarist movement in France and Britain, eschewed the finesse and refinement of prevailing French design of the period. Garouste and Bonetti's was the first work (tables, lamps, and other objects), in the so-called *style barbare*, to be edited by the gallery which was located in the rue Étienne-Marcel, Paris; but today at 35, rue de Grenelle. The new generation of designers of this loosely formed association includes Arik Levy, Christian Ghion, Matilde Brétillot and Valette, Matt Sindall, Eric Jourdan, Eric Robin, Jean-Marc Gady, and others such as artists Valérie Raymond-Stempowska, Fabienne Jouvin, and T.-J. Naf. (*Waiting for the Barbarians* by Coetzee was translated into French by Sophie Mayoux in 1982, reissued by Le Seuil in 1987.)
Bibliography Pierre Staudenmeyer et al., *Elizabeth Garouste & Mattia Bonetti*, Paris: Dis Voir, 1998. Elisabeth Vedrenne, *Elizabeth Garouste & Mattia Bonetti 1981–2001*, Brussels: Ante Post, 2001. www.barbares.com.

Endell, August (1871–1925)

German architect, sculptor, and designer; born Berlin; active Munich and Breslau (now Wroclaw, Poland).

Training In philosophy, psychology, and aesthetics, Tübingen; under philosopher Theodor Lipps, in Munich.
Biography Endell was a member of the Munich group associated with Hermann Obrist, Richard Riemerschmid, Bernhard Pankok, and art journal *Jugend*; became acquainted with Lipps's ideas on empathy; in his architecture and interiors, applied restrained ornamentation to flat surfaces; was both a theorist and an architect. He began writing on aesthetics with the essay 'Um die Schönheit' (1896); 1918–25, was director of the academy in Breslau. Work included 1897–98 Photoatelier Elvira (Elvira photographic studio) in Munich, reminiscent of Obrist's work; decoration of 1901 Buntes Theater (aka Multi-Colored Theater) in Berlin; 1912 Trabrennbahn in Berlin-Mariendorf; department stores in Berlin and Breslau.
Exhibitions Elvira photographic studio subject of 1977 exhibition,

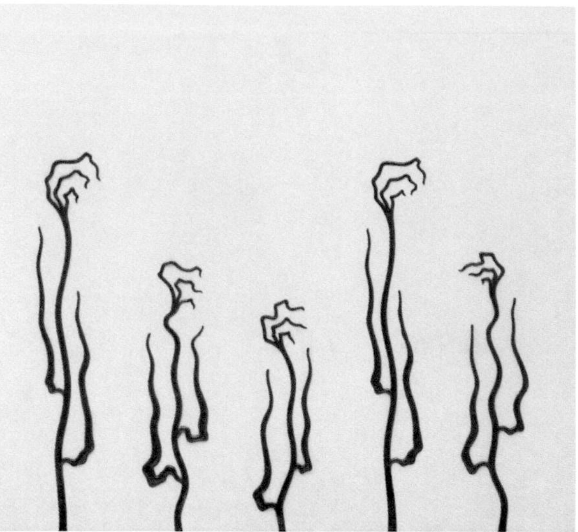

August Endell. Desk mounts. c. 1899. Wrought iron and wood, 28 1/2 x 34 x 1" (72.4 x 86.4 x 2.5 cm). Mfr.: R. Kirsch, Germany. Acquired by exchange. MoMA.

Museum Villa Stuck, Munich; 1986 exhibition, Stadtmuseum, Munich.
Bibliography Karl Scheffler, 'August Endell,' *Kunst und Künstler*, no. 5, 1907: 314–24. Karl Scheffler, 'Neue Arbeiten von August Endell,' *Kunst und Künstler,* no. 11, 1913: 350–59. Klaus-Jürgen Sembach, *August Endell: Der Architekt des Photoateliers Elvira 1871–1925*, Munich, 1977. Gabriele Bader-Griessmeyer, *Münchner Jugendstil-Textilien...*, Munich: Tuduv, 1985. Kathryn Bloom Hiesinger (ed.), *Art Nouveau in Munich: Masters of Jugenstil*, Munich: Prestel, 1988. Helge David (ed.), *Vom Sehen: über architektur, Formkunst und 'Die Schönheit der grossen Stadt'/August Endell*, Basel: Birkhäuser, 1995.

Endt, Evert (1933–)

Dutch industrial designer; active Paris.

Training 1950, in Zürich.
Biography 1958, Endt became artistic director of Raymond Loewy's Compagnie de l'Esthétique Industrielle (CEI) and its director from 1970; 1975, established Endt Fulton Partners in Paris, associated with Fulton Partners in New York; specialized in industrial design, communication, and transportation; was director, ENSCI (Les Ateliers), Paris; 1992, became a naturalized French citizen.
Bibliography Arlette Barré-Despond (ed.), *Dictionnaire international des arts appliqués et du design*, Paris: Regard, 1996.
> See CEI.

Enevoldsen, Cecilia (1970–)

Dutch designer.

Training To 1995, industrial design, Kunsthåndværkerskolen, Copenhagen.
Biography 1995, Enevoldsen established her own studio primarily for the design of furniture. She has been an advisor in the school of architecture of Det Kongelige Danske Kunstakademi, Copenhagen, and lectures at the Kunsthåndværkerskolen. 1999, Enevoldsen, Louise Campbell, Sebastian Holmbäck, and Torben Holmbäck initialed *Walk the Plank*, a traveling exhibition of Danish designers' and manufacturers' work (later to be sold via the Internet), and another installment followed in 2003.
Bibliography Michele De Lucchi (ed.), *The International Design Yearbook*, London: Laurence King, 2001.

ENFI Design

French design agency; located Paris.

History 1961, ENFI Design (Esthétique Nouvelle de la Forme Industrielle) was established by Jacques Inguenaud for the design of products, graphics, and interiors for stores, transportation, and industries; by 1987, had become a leading French group for the design of offices and corporate-identity programs, including those for banks; designed the Aramis transportation system by Matra, 1977 Écureuil public helicopter by Aérospatiale, and 1984 Minitel terminal by Alcatel.

Engberg, Gabriel (1872–1953)
Finnish textile designer.

Training Under Akseli Gallen-Kallela.
Exhibition Engberg's textiles for Suomen Käsityön Ystävien (friends of Finnish handicraft) shown at 1900 *Exposition Universelle*, Paris.
Bibliography Cat., David Revere McFadden (ed.), *Scandinavian Modern Design 1880–1980*, New York: Abrams, 1982.

Engelbart, Douglas (1925–)
American inventor; born Oregon.

Training From 1942, electrical engineering, Oregon State University, Corvallis, graduating 1948; 1955, doctoral degree in electrical engineering, University of California, Berkley.
Biography Englebart's studies in Oregon were interrupted by naval service in the Philippines during World War II, during which he read and was profoundly influenced by Vannevar Bush's 'As We May Think' (*The Atlantic Monthly*, vol. 176, no. 1, July 1945: 101–08); from 1948, worked at NASA Ames Research Center in Moffett Field, Cal.; becoming restless, began to 'envision people sitting in front of displays, "flying around" in an information space where they could formulate and organize their ideas with incredible speed and flexibility,' in his words; 1955, became assistant professor, University of California, Berkeley, and, subsequently, a reseacher, Stanford Research Institute (SRI); wrote the seminal paper 'Augmenting Human Intellect: A Conceptual Framework' (1962); 1963, set up his own laboratory Augmentation Research Center within Stanford; 1960s–70s, developed highly evolved 'windows,' hypermedia, GroupWare, and other systems, known as the 'oNLine System' (NLS), which emplopyed a new (1963) computer-monitor pointing device (aka the mouse, a term not coined until the 1980s). He invented the mouse for easier computer interaction and also an on-screen video-teleconferencing capability, groundbreaking for their time; at 1968 Fall Joint Computer Conference, San Francisco, demonstrated the mouse and the capabilities of the NLS in a 90-minute multimedia presentation with a video contact with the staff back at his laboratory, 25 miles (40 km) away from the presentation itself. In the presentation, he used a 192 kilobyte mainframe computer, considered highly primitive today. So astounding was the event, that some thought it a hoax. Thus, the NST became the second node on the US Department of Defense's Advanced Research Projects Agency Network (ARPANET), the grandparent of today's Internet system. Engelbart patented the mouse (no. 3,541,541) in 1970 as an 'X-Y position indicator for a display system.' It was subsequently called the mouse due to the cord extending like a 'tail' from the small handheld device. 1989, Engelbart established Bootstrap Institute in Freemont, Cal. (housed rent-free in mouse-maker Logitec Corp.'s facility), to continue his work, including a type of GroupWare called 'an open hyperdocument system' whose mandate is to replace paper recordkeeping entirely in the future. Engelbart has been granted more than 45 patents.
Citations 1997 Lemelson-MIT Prize of $500,000 (£305,000, equivalency at the time), the largest single prize for invention/innovation.

Engelbrecht, Moritz (Berlin (1964–)
> See Lemongras.

Eva Englund. Vase. 1978. Flashed (*graal* technique) colorless and amber glass, h. 5 1/8" (13 cm). Mfr.: Orrefors Glasbruk, Sweden. Courtesy Quittenbaum Kunstauktionen, Munich.

Engesvik, Andreas (1970–)
> See Norway Says.

Englehardt, Valdemar (1869–1915)
Danish ceramicist.

Training In chemical engineering.
Biography Englehardt succeeded Adolphe Clément in 1891 as the technical manager at Royal Copenhagen Porcelain Manufactory; was influenced by production at Manufacture Nationale de Sèvres in France and, thus, designed a series of crystalline glazes applied to Royal Copenhagen ceramic artwares. His glazes moved away from the factory's late 19th-century naturalistic painted decorations.
Bibliography Cat., David Revere McFadden (ed.), *Scandinavian Modern Design 1880–1980*, New York: Abrams, 1982.

Englinger, Gabriel (1898–1983)
French artist, decorator, and furniture designer; born Paris.

Training École Boulle, Paris.
Biography 1922–28, Englinger worked in La Maîtrise design studio of Les Galeries Lafayette department store in Paris; concurrently, was a designer and furniture maker at the Cornille firm. Various of his ensembles, including a 1928 boudoir and 1929 work cabinet and smoking stand, were produced by Studio Abran. He taught decoration in Grenoble and drawing in Voiron, where he settled after World War II; 1949–63, abandoned his other activities and taught decoration, École Régionale des Beaux-Arts, Rennes.
Exhibitions From 1921, interiors were shown (with student designers of École Boulle) at Cercle Volney. 1923, dining room shown (again with École Boulle students) at Musée Galliéra, Paris. Small room (with Suzanne Guiguichon) by La Maîtrise and his design for Salon d'Honneur for Cornille shown in City of Paris Pavilion at 1925 *Exposition Internationale des Arts Décoratifs et Industriels Modernes*, Paris. Work shown regularly at 1926–29 Salons of Société des Artistes Décorateurs; a room in the regional-industries stand in Dauphiné pavilion at 1937 *Exposition Internationale des Arts et Techniques dans la Vie Moderne*, Paris; work at 1946 and 1947 Salons d'Automne; a dining room (produced by La Maîtrise) at 1948 Salon of Société des Artistes Décorateurs.
Bibliography Pierre Kjellberg, *Art déco: les maîtres du mobilier, le décor des paquebots*, Paris: Amateur, 1986/1990.

Englund, Eva (1937–)
Swedish glassware designer and ceramicist.

Biography Englund became active as a glassware designer in 1964; worked for a time for Pukeberg glassworks; from 1974, for Orrefors and became known for her revival of the *graal* technique (a producing of flashing ornamentation within the glass), which had been developed by Edward Hald and others at Orrefors; was also a ceramicist.
Bibliography Cat., David Revere McFadden (ed.), *Scandinavian Modern Design 1880–1980*, New York: Abrams, 1982.

Engø, Bjørn (1920–1981)
Norwegian interior, furniture, and textile designer and enamelist.

Biography Engø set up a workshop in 1948 to design for production; 1955 with Karl-Edvard Korseth, designed the H-55 furniture range by Helsingborg. For others, he also designed furniture, lighting, textiles, and the domestic wares in aluminum and enameled copper for which he became best known.
Bibliography Fredrik Wildhagen, *Norge i Form*, Oslo: Stenersen, 1988: 137. Cat., David Revere McFadden (ed.), *Scandinavian Modern Design 1880–1980*, New York: Abrams, 1982.

Ennemlaghi
British design group and manufacturer.

History The group claims to be a 'virtual space,' performing research in plastics, theory, and ephemeral (but not inexpensive) objects such as 2000 Red Cube armchair and hassock in an inflated clear or a transparent red PVC with clearly visible upholstery springs, also convertible into a bed. The group also designed 2000 Twentieth Century Air, an 8" (20 cm) long pharmaceutical-glass ampoule in an edition of 10,000, containing 20th-century air, each one numbered by 2,001 different people and engraved with the date: 19 October 2000.

Ennemlaghi. Red Cube armchair. 2000. Steel and PVC, h., w., and d. 35 3/8" (90 cm). Mfr.: the designers, UK.

Bibliography Auction cat., *Design Moderne*, Paris: Salle Rossini, 22 Oct. 2001, lots 97–100.

Eoos Design

Austrian design partnership; active in Vienna.

History 1988–94, Martin Bergmann (Lienz 1963–), Gernot Bohmann (Krieglach 1968–), and Harald Gründl (Vienna 1967–) studied design concurrently at Akademie für angewandte Kunst, Vienna; 1990, began their first collaboration; 1995, founded Eoos Design studio in Vienna, which has become active in the fields of product, furniture, and architectural design. ('Eoos' is the name of one of the four sun horses in Greek mythology and represents the group's programmatic approach to design.) Work includes Net chair and Filo chair by Keilhauer, Jason sofa and 2000 Scoop chair by Walter Knoll, Derby and Coco chairs by Matteograssi, Console table and others by Artelano, Bloom sofa bed by Moroso, flagship stores of Armani and Adidas, and Euro-RSCG advertising offices in Vienna.
Exhibitions/citations Work subject of 1999 exhibit, Carla Sozzani gallery, Milan. Bronze medal (for Net chair), 2001 NeoCon, Toronto. Red Dot awards: 2001 (Good Time 421 seating range by Walter Knoll) and 2003 (for Jason Lite 1700 and Nelson 601 sofa range, both by Walter Knoll), Design Zentrum Nordrhein Westfalen, Essen. 2003 Adolf Loos Staatspreis Design (for Sweetwood chair by Montina).

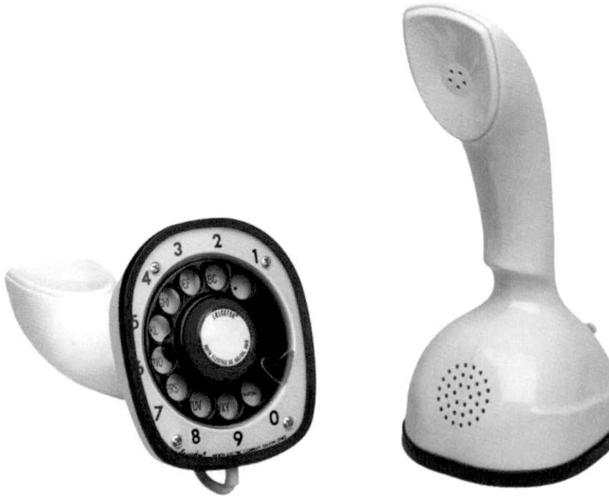

Telefonaktiebolaget L.M. Ericsson: Hugo Blomberg, Ralph Lysel, and Has Gösta Thames. Ericofon telephone. 1954. ABS plastic, rubber, and nylon housing, white: 8 1/2 x 3 7/8 x 4 3/8" (21.6 x 9.8 x 11.1 cm), yellow: 9 1/8 x 3 7/8 x 4 3/8" (23.2 x 9.8 x 11.1 cm). Mfr.: Telefonaktiebolaget L.M. Ericsson, Sweden (1954–59). Anonymous gift. MoMA.

Epply, Lorinda (1874–1951)

American ceramicist; active Cincinnati, Ohio.

Training Cincinnati Art Academy, Cincinnati, Ohio; ceramics, Columbia University, New York.
Biography 1904–48, she worked at Rookwood Pottery in Cincinnati; during the late 1920s with William Hentschel, produced some of Rookwood's most individual work; with others at the pottery, developed new glazes and forms of ornamentation.
Exhibition With Hentschel, Epply represented Rookwood at 1926–27 *American Industrial Art, Tenth Annual Exhibition of Current Manufactures Designed and Made in the United States*, The Metropolitan Museum of Art, New York.
Bibliography Herbert Peck, *The Book of Rookwood Pottery*, New York: Crown, 1968. Virginia Raymond Cummins, *Rookwood Pottery Potpourri*, Silver Spring, Md.: Cliff R. Leonard and Duke Coleman, 1980. Karen Davies, *At Home in Manhattan: Modern Decorative Arts, 1925 to the Depression*, New Haven: Yale, 1983: 40.

Epson
> See Seiko Epson.

Erector Set
> See Gilbert, A.C.

Ergonomi Design Gruppen

Swedish design research and development group; located Bromma.

History 1969, Designgruppen and Ergonomi Design were amalgamated to form Ergonomi Design Gruppen, one of Scandinavia's largest consultancies; was financed by the Swedish Work Environment Fund of the National Board for Occupational Health and Safety to pursue design research and development based on ergonometric principles; realized commissions from engineering, heavy equipment, plastics, and mechanical/technology firms. Its staff has executed designs, including cutlery, for the handicapped and elderly, and for printing and welding machinery. Two members of the group, Maria Benktzon (1946–) and Sven-Eric Juhlin (1940–), have specialized in products for handicapped people. (Benktzon studied at Konstfackskolan, Stockholm.) Other award-winning staff members have included Malin Andersson, Håkan Bergkvist, Olle Bobjer, Elisabeth Broms, Oskar Juhlin, Hans Himbert, Charlotte Störiko. Some staff members have collaborated with manufacturer's in-house designers.
Exhibitions/citations Work shown in 1982 *Aktuell Svenske Form*, Kunstindustrimuseet, Oslo, and Nationalmuseum, Stockholm. 1985 Japan Design Foundation Prize; 1987 Excellent Swedish Design; 1991 Excellent Swedish Design Prize (for feeder spoon); Design of the Decade (1990s), IDSA/*Business Week* magazine; 2001 and 2003 Red Dot Best of the Best and 1999, 2000, and 2002 Red Dot awards, Design Zentrum Nordrhein Westfalen, Essen.
Bibliography Cat., *Gustavsberg 150 ar*, Stockholm: Nationalmuseum, 1975. Cat., Monica Boman, *Aktuell Svensk Form*, Skien, Sweden: Ibsenhuset, 1982: 52–55. Cat., David Revere McFadden (ed.), *Scandinavian Modern Design 1880–1980*, New York: Abrams, 1982. Cat., Kathryn B. Hiesinger and George H. Marcus III (eds.), *Design Since 1945*, Philadelphia: Philadelphia Museum of Art, 1983.

Ericsson, Henry (1898–1933)

Finnish painter, graphic artist, and designer; active Helsinki.

Training To 1915, Taideteollinen korkeakoulu, Helsinki.
Biography Ericsson's earliest silver designs were produced by Taito, including a plain oval tea set resembling the work of Jacob Ängman of Sweden. Ericsson also designed textiles and glassware; shared a studio with Alvar Aalto for a time.
Bibliography Annelies Krekel-Aalberse, *Art Nouveau and Art Déco Silver*, New York: Abrams, 1989.

Ericsson, Telefonaktiebolaget L.M.

Swedish telephone manufacturer.

Biography 1876, Lars Magnus Ericsson (Vergebols 1846–Stockholm 1926) founded Aktiebolaget L.M. Ericsson & Co. and installed the first telephone exchange in Kiev and, 1896, in Kharkov. Telefonaktiebolaget

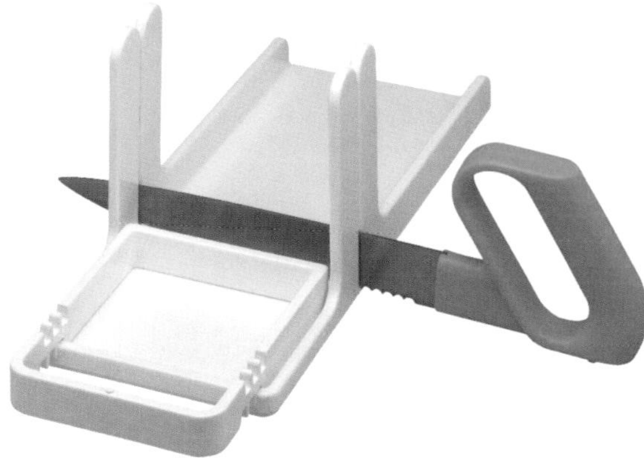

Ergonomi Design Gruppen, Sven-Eric Juhlin, and Maria Benktzon. Kitchen knife/cutting board. 1973. Stainless steel and polypropylene, knife 3 1/2 x 4 x 1" (8.9 x 10.2 x 2.5 cm); plastic, cutting board 5 1/4 x 15 1/16 x 5 3/8" (13.3 x 38.3 x 13.7 cm). Mfr.: AB Gustavsberg Fabriker, Sweden. Gift of RFSU Rehab. MoMA.

L.M. Ericsson was the first and became the largest manufacturer of telephones in Sweden; by 1900, was producing 50,000 telephone units annually. Concerning design: Norwegian sculptor/pedagogue Jean Heiberg (1884–1976) designed the iconic Bakelite telephone for the Norsk Elektrisk Bureau, a subsidiary of Ericsson whose managers decided that a new telephone model was required for the burgeoning world telephone market. The model, produced as no. DBH 1001 from 1932, was a standard worldwide for a number of years, at least to the 1950s. Concerning another innovative Ericsson model: Hugo Blomberg (1897–1994) and Ralph Lysell (1907–) conceived the Ericofon (aka Cobra) telephone model as a prototype, patented 1941, but in an unattractive form. However, Gösta Thames (1916–) and the Ericsson design group were responsible for the improved design of the models, realized as the sleek 1954 version (developed from 1949–54). (1938–81, Thames worked as deputy technical manager in the instrument-engineering department, with no formal training but an interest in shape and color.) Because there were only easily scratched and brittle acrylic and cellulose plastics available up to the 1950s, this was a hurdle that had to be overcome. With the advent in the mid-1950s of the ABS plastic, the problem was solved. From 1956, when home-use sales began, 2.5 million pieces of the Ericofon were eventually sold. The phone was modified in c. 1959, in a slightly shorter version. When American sales surged, manufacturing in the US was assigned to North Electric there in c. 1961. A push-button model with ten keys was introduced in c. 1967. Ericsson acknowledged its 100th anniversary in 1976 with an updated but unsuccessful model, the Ericofon 700, selling 30,000. 1981, Thames retired from Ericsson after 43 years; lives today in Mjölby. By the year 2000 or so, Telefonaktiebolaget L.M. Ericsson, with headquarters in Stockholm, had became the largest supplier of mobile telecommunication systems worldwide and was employing 82,000 employees in more than 140 countries. c. 2001, Ericsson introduced the first device (HBH-10 headset telephone) with Bluetooth capabilities, a wireless-reception system pioneered by Ericsson that eventually became part of the Special Interest Group (SIG), a consortium of 1,700 firms that freely share Bluetooth technology. Ericsson was also a forerunner in the development of multimedia-messaging-service (MMS) technology. 2001, Sony Ericsson Mobile Communications became an equally owned entity of the two corporations with shared capacities for the manufacture of sophisticated mobile phones, adjunct services, and development of machine-to-machine (M2M) equipment, including picture-message transmission.

Exhibitions/citations Included in numerous international exhibitions; received several awards, including 1998 Red Dot award (for GF 768 and PF 768 GSM phones by Tom Waldner of Richard Lindahl Design), Design Zentrum Nordrhein Westfalen, Essen; others.

Bibliography Hugo Blomberg, 'The Ericofon—The New Telephone Set,' *Ericsson Review*, vol. 33, no. 4, 1956: 99–109. Cat., Kathryn B. Hiesinger and George H. Marcus III (eds.), *Design Since 1945*, Philadelphia: Philadelphia Museum of Art, 1983. Mel Byars, *On/Off: New Electronic Products*, New York: Universe, 2001. Paola Antonelli (ed.), *Objects of Design: The Museum of Modern Art*, New York: The Museum of Modern Art, 2003: 198.

> See Blomberg, Hugo; Heiberg, Jean.

Eriksson, Algot (1868–1930)

Swedish ceramicist.

Training 1882–89, Kungliga Tekniska Högskolan, Stockholm, and in Denmark, Germany, and France.

Biography From 1880s to 1920, Eriksson worked at Rörstrand pottery in Lidköping, along with other ceramicists known for sumptuous wares in the Natural style popular in the late 19th and early 20th centuries; was known for his ceramics with underglaze painting and relief decoration.

Bibliography Cat., David Revere McFadden (ed.), *Scandinavian Modern Design 1880–1980*, New York: Abrams, 1982.

Eriksson, Thomas (1959–)

Swedish architect and furniture designer; born Örnsköldsvik.

Training Konstfackskolan, Stockholm.

Biography Eriksson is active in his own architectural office in Stockholm; has designed furniture by Offecct such as E-Seat and F-Seat benches, and the Hästens store (with the Hästens staff) in Köping. Other clients have included Audi, Ericsson, Kapp Ahl, Cappellini, and Absolut Vodka. For architectural credit, uses the acronym TEArk (Thomas Eriksson Arkitekter). With graphic designer Björn Kusoffsky and design strategist Göran Lagerström, Eriksson founded Stockholm Design Lab, serving as many as two dozen clients such as SAS airlines (including aircraft exterior graphics and SAS Scandinavian type font, with Agfa Monotype), Sony Ericsson (branding), and IKEA (packing).

Citations To Stockholm Design Laboratory: 1995 best product range (for PS furniture by IKEA) and 1999 Special Prize (for SAS ID program), Utmärkt Svensk Form (outstanding Swedish design); 2001 First Prize and Diploma, Core Design.

Thomas Eriksson. Medicine cabinet. 1992. Lacquered steel, 17 1/4 x 17 1/4 x 5 3/4" (43.8 x 43.8 x 14.6 cm). Mfr.: Cappellini, Italy. Gift of Murray Moss. MoMA.

Erkins, Henry

American designer.

Biography Erkins designed 1907 Murray's Roman Gardens at 228–32 West 42nd Street in New York. Its Egyptian dining room had mock-Egyptian motifs and ornamentation. Its illuminated atrium, with a mixture of classical motifs, was intended to represent a garden in ancient Pompeii. The building's entrance was redone in a design from the 18th-century Paris residence of the cardinal Rohan. Through his Erkins Studios, he sold indoor and outdoor furniture and furnishings to possibly 1930s or after; wrote the book *New York Plaisance: An Illustrated Series of New York Places of Amusement* (1908).

Bibliography Jonathan M. Woodham, *Twentieth-Century Ornament*, New York: Rizzoli, 1990: 50. Christopher Gray, 'Streetscapes: Percival/Hubert's, 230 West 42nd Street, McKim, Mead and White/Henry Erkins,' *The New York Times*, 16 June 1996.

Ermilov, Vasilii Dmitrievich (1884–1968)

Russian architect, book and set designer, interior designer, and illustrator; born Kharkov (now Ukraine).

Training 1905–09, School of Decorative Arts, Kharkov; 1910–11,

Kharkov Art School and in private studios; from 1913 under Il'ia Mashkov and Petr Konchalovski, Moscow Institute of Painting, Sculpture, and Architecture.
Biography After early contacts with Cubists and Futurists, including David Burliuk and Vladimir Maiakovskii, Ermilov explored neo-Primitivism, Suprematism, Futurism, and Cubism from c. 1913. His decorations appeared in *7 + 3* (Kharkov's Futurist album). His work for the album was influential on his later book designs and illustrations, including the first edition of Velimir Khlebnikov's *Ladomir* (1920) and journal *Avangard* (1923–30). 1918, he joined the Union 7 monumental artists' group; 1919–20, was involved in the design of various Agitprop projects including Agit-posters, interiors of clubs, and Agit-trains; 1922, was a cofounder of the Kharkov Art Technicum and lecturer at the Kharkov Art Institute; pursued architectural and theatrical design projects in late 1920s and the 1930s. Valerian Polishchuk wrote the monograph *Vasilii Ermilov: Ukrainske maliarstvo* (Kharkov, 1931).
Exhibitions With Anatolii Petritskii, designed interior of Ukrainian pavilion at 1937–38 *All-Union Agricultural Exhibition*, Moscow.
Bibliography L. Zhadova, 'Prokty V. Ermilova,' *Dekorativnoe iskusstvo*, Moscow, no. 9, 1972: 30–32. Z. Fogel, *Vasilii Ermilov*, Moscow, 1975. Cat., Stephanie Barron and Maurice Tuchman, *Avant-Garde Russia, 1919–1930: New Perspectives*, MIT, 1980. Cat., *The Great Utopia: The Russian and Soviet Avant-Garde, 1915–1932*, New York: Guggenheim Museum, 1992.

Ermolaeva, Vera Mikhailovna (1893–1938)

Russian teacher and illustrator; born Petrovskii.

Training From 1912, art school of Mikhail Bernstein; to 1917, Archeological Institute; both Petrograd.
Biography Her artistic development was marked, from the beginning, by contact with leading artistic figures of the time: Vladimir Tatlin, Mikhail Larionov, and Union of Youth members such as Pavel Filonov, Kazimir Malevich, and Mikhail Matiushin. 1918, she became a member of IZO NKP (visual arts section of the People's Commissariat for Enlightenment); 1918–19, worked for the City Museum in Petrograd; interested in folk art, wrote a paper on old shop signboards for the 1919 issue of journal *Iskusstvo kommuny* (art of the commune); illustrated children's books and met Annenkov, Lebedev, and others; up to 1920s, was influenced by the ideas of Malevich through Malevich's Suprematism and joined Malevich's group of followers; designed sets for Aleksei Kruchenykh/Mikhail Matiushin's 1920 Futurist opera *Pobeda nad solntsem* (victory over the sun); 1923, accompaned Malevich and his students, when they moved to Petrograd where she became head of color laboratory of the local branch of INKhUK (institute of artistic culture) to 1926; from mid-1920s, illustrated children's books by Aseev, Kharms, Vvedenskii, Zabolotskii, and others, including editions of Ivan Krylov's fables. Due to her brother's involvement with the Mensheviks, she was arrested and, 1934, exiled in Siberia and died there.
Exhibitions Work included in several venues of the Suprematists.
Bibliography E. Kovtun, 'Khudozhnitsa knigi Vera Mikhailovna Ermolaeva,' in D. Shmarinov (ed.), *Iskusstvo knigi*, Moscow: 'Kinga,' 1975: 68–81. John E. Bowlt, 'Malevich and His Students,' *Soviet Union*, Arizona State University, vol. 5, part 2, 1979: 256–86. Cat., E. Kovtun, 'Vera Mikhailovna Ermolaeva,' *Women Artists of the Russian Avant-Garde 1910–1930*, Cologne: Galerie Gmurzynska, 1979: 102–10. Cat., Stephanie Barron and Maurice Tuchman, *Avant-Garde Russia, 1919–1930: New Perspectives*, MIT, 1980: 146. Cat., *The Great Utopia: The Russian and Soviet Avant-Garde, 1915–1932*, New York: Guggenheim Museum, 1992.

Erté (b. Romain de Tirtoff 1892–1990)

Russian designer.

Training In St. Petersburg under Il'ia Repine; architecture in Kronstadt; in 1912, painting, Académie Julian, Paris.
Biography 'Erté' was derived from the French pronunciation of his initials, R and T. 1913, he worked for Paul Poiret in Paris as a fashion designer alongside José de Zamora; 1914–22, lived in Monte Carlo and executed cover designs and fashion illustrations; designed costumes and sets for music-hall personalities, including Mata Hari and Zizi Jeanmaire, and for other theatrical productions on Broadway such as the Ziegfeld Follies and George White's *Scandals*. His stage designs appeared in productions in Paris, London, Blackpool, Milan, Berlin, Naples, and New York. He designed clothing collections for the Henri Bendel and B. Altman stores, both New York; produced drawings for *Harper's Bazaar* in 1920, created sets and costumes for the film *Restless Sex* (1925), signed a contract with Metro-Goldwyn-Mayer movie studio, moved to Hollywood, and designed costumes and film sets for Louis B. Mayer and Cecil B. de Mille. He was known for an ostentatious style inspired by the Orient and the use of spangles, sequins, and *lamé* fabric on gowns with long trains; after 1929 New York Stock Market crash, worked for Pierre Sandini at the Bal Tabarin and the Folies Bergères in Paris, designing sets and costumes, and, concurrently, for Théâtre du Châtelet and Théâtre Marigny. He also designed for the Glyndebourne Opera. From the 1960s, his small sculptures and graphics, produced in multiple editions, were successfully sold through a New York agent, bringing him unexpected renown in his dotage.
Exhibitions Work was first shown in France, at 1926 exhibition, Hôtel Charpentier, Paris. Work subject of 1966 and 1967 exhibitions, Paris, Milan, New York, and London.
Bibliography Charles Spencer, *Erté,* New York: Potter, 1970. Yvonne Brunhammer, *Le cinquantenaire de l'exposition de 1925*, Paris: Musée des Arts Décoratifs, 1976. Victor Arwas, *Art Déco*, New York: Abrams, 1980. Erté, *My Life, My Art: An Autobiography*, New York: Dutton, 1989.

Hartmut Esslinger: frogdesign. Macintosh SE home computer. 1984. ABS polymer casing, CPU 13 1/2 x 9 3/4 x 10 3/4" (34.3 x 24.8 x 27.3 cm), keyboard 2 1/4 x 15 1/2 x 5 1/2" (5.7 x 39.4 x 14 cm), mouse 1 1/2 x 3 3/4 x 2 1/2" (3.8 x 9.5 x 6.4 cm). Mfr.: Apple Computer, US. Gift of the designer and the mfr. MoMA.

Esherick, Wharton (1887–1970)

American sculptor and furniture designer; born Philadelphia.

Training 1907–08, painting, Philadelphia School of Industrial Arts; 1909–10, Pennsylvania Academy of the Fine Arts, Philadelphia.
Biography 1919, Esherick began to produce carved wood sculpture and furniture in Paoli, Pa.; was familiar with the work of the German Expressionists and became active in avant-garde theater design. The oblique angles and triangular forms in his primarily one-of-a-kind furniture pieces were partially derived from the furniture of Frank Lloyd Wright and Cubism, although voluptuous and organic. He died in Paoli, Pa., where his former home is now a museum.
Exhibitions Work included in a 1929 exhibition, American Designers Gallery, New York.
Bibliography *The Wharton Esherick Museum: Studio and Collection*, Paoli, Pa.: Wharton Esherick Museum, 1977. Karen Davies, *At Home in Manhattan: Modern Decorative Arts, 1925 to the Depression*, New Haven: Yale, 1983: 100. Auction cat., *Contemporary Works of Art*, Sotheby's New York, 14 Mar. 1992.

E.S.K.A.F. (De Eerste Steenwijker Kunst Aardewerk Fabriek)

Dutch ceramics firm; initially located Steenwijk.

History 1919, Hillebrand Ras organized a group of residents of the village of Steenwijk to form the E.S.K.A.F. for them to produce attractive wares. German émigré A.A. Schröder was the technical director. The factory, opened 1920, was designed by Amsterdam architect G.F. La Croix. German porcelain painters and faïence painters from Gouda were hired. A large number of ceramic wares of the Amsterdam school, with an unusual plastic structure, were designed by Hildo Krop, whose father, Hendrik Krop, was a cofounder and chairperson. Other designers included W.H. van Norden, J.H. de Groot, and C. van der Sluys. J. Jongert and W. Bogtman also contributed. Van der Sluys's designs were severe and geometric. Some of E.S.K.A.F.'s wares were undecorated, and others lightly decorated. Decorations included multi-colored motifs by W.H. van Norden as well as the popular butterfly and Sonja and Fuga motifs. In 1927, the firm was bought by P. van Stam and H. Hamming, and production continued in Huizen on a cooperative basis. Only van der Sluys was retained. E.S.K.A.F. customers were mostly well-to-do with a taste for the modern. Briefly successful, the firm became bankrupt in 1934. For a time, CV Kunstaardewerkfabriek HAHO produced E.S.K.A.F. models with the cold varnish pottery method. 1935, CV HAHO was amalgamated with Potterie De Driehoek to sell new glazed goods. After World War II, the pottery was prosperous for a time and machine-made dinner sets were produced for the first time from 1951 when the factory was updated. In the 1980s, Potterie De Driehoek was the only firm manufacturing dinnerware in the Netherlands.
Bibliography Cat., *Industry and Design in the Netherlands 1850/1950*, Amsterdam: Stedlijk Museum, 1985.

Esslinger, Hartmut (1944–); frogdesign

German industrial designer; born Beuren, West Germany; active Altensteig, Germany, and Sunnyvale, Cal.

Training Electrical engineering, Technische Hochschule, Stuttgart; industrial design, Fachhochschule, Schwäbisch-Gmünd.
Biography 1969 in Altensteig, Esslinger established Esslinger Design, an industrial design consultancy whose first client was Wega Radio; susequently, designed for others including AEG, Louis Vuitton, and Sony and developed a cult following among American and European designers; became involved in the Japanese market when Wega was bought by Sony. Wega Radio's 1978 Concept 51K hi-fi by Esslinger was notable for its sleekness. 1981, Esslinger opened a second branch in Campbell, Cal., and began to work with Steven Jobs, the head of Apple Computer (with subsequent clients including AEG, AT&T, NeXT, Olympus, and other firms in California's so-called Silicon Valley), and, subsequently, established an office in Taiwan. 1982, the name Esslinger Design was changed to frogdesign ('frog' as an acronym for Federal Republic Of Germany and, presumably, also to be amusing). Esslinger had won 1982–83 SnowWhite competition of Apple Computer, which resulted in a $1-million annual contract with the firm and the design of other products typified by the Apple IIc and IIGS and 1984 Apple SE home computer, keyboard, and box-like mouse. The more-corporate second phase of the Apple models included the Macintosh II, Mac SE, 1984 LaserWriter II printer, and 1984–85 concepts leading to the 1989 Macintosh Portable. Esslinger also served as Apple's corporate design manager, but, with the departure of Jobs, Esslinger also left in early 1986. Clients in Europe have included Erco, König & Neurath (office furniture), Rosenthal, and Villeroy & Boch. Esslinger's design work incorporates Functionalist forms with colorful Postmodern influences and was a mixture of the approaches of Dieter Rams and Ettore Sottsass, with an emphasis on the former, although not purely either. The studio, with offices in Sunnyvale (Cal.), San Francisco, New York, Austin (Tex.), and Altensteig (Germany), established its own award, the 'frogjunior.'
Exhibitions/citations frogdesign work subject of 2002 exhibition, Atlanta Contemporary Art Center. Numerous citations, including recent examples: 1998 Clio award; three 2000 Design Distinction awards, *I.D.* magazine; four 2000 IDSA/*Business Week* awards.
Bibliography Uta Brandes, *Hartmut Esslinger & frogdesign*, Göttingen: Steidl, 1992. Paul Kunkel, *Apple Design: The World of the Apple Industrial Design Group*, New York: Graphis, 1997. Fay Sweet, *Frog: Form Follows Emotion (Cutting Edge)*, New York: Watson-Guptill, 1999. Mel Byars with Arlette Barré-Despond, *100 Designs/100 Years: A Celebration of the 20th Century*, Hove: RotoVision, 1999: 180–81, 186–87. Paola Antonelli (ed.), *Objects of Design: The Museum of Modern Art*, New York: The Museum of Modern Art, 2003: 227–28, 242.
> See Peart, Stephen.

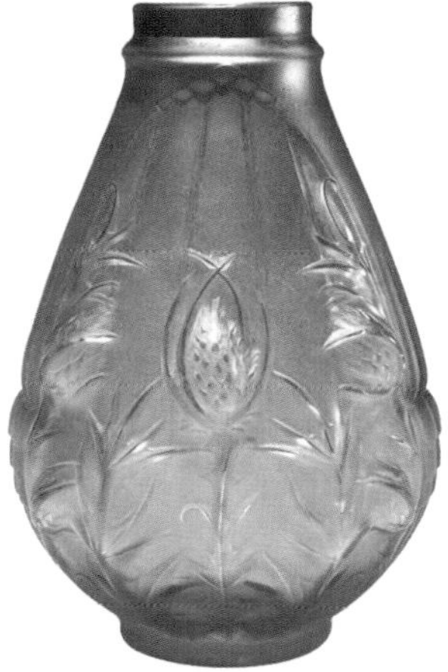

Edmond Etling. Chardons vase. 1920s. Polished and unpolished colorless pressed glass, h. 10 13/16" (27.4 cm). Mfr.: Edmond Etling, France. Courtesy Quittenbaum Kunstauktionen, Munich.

Étienne-Martin, Henri (1913–1995)

French decorator and furniture designer; active Paris and Vanves.

Training École Boulle, Paris.
Biography Étienne-Martin met metalworker Gilbert Poillerat while at the École Boulle; for three years, worked for metalworker Edgar Brandt; 1938–45, was artistic director of Les Grands Magasins du Louvre in Paris; subsequently, artistic director of Au Bon Marché department store in Paris; was influenced by the work of Louis Sognot and René Guilleré; by 1954, had set up a workshop at 6, avenue de Clamart in Vanves, near Paris; designed furniture, some by JER, Borgeaud, Soubrier, and Thevenon.
Bibliography *Ensembles mobiliers*, vol. 2, 1937; vol. 5, nos. 8–9; 1954. Paris: Charles Moreau. Pascal Renous, *Portraits de décorateurs*, Paris: H. Vial, 1969.

Etling, Edmond

French metalware and glassware merchant; located Paris.

Biography Edmond Etling established his eponymous firm in Paris, where he made and sold small metal and glass *objets d'art*, including table lamps and illuminated bibelots. His designers included Bonnet, Laplanche, Guillard, and Georges Dunaime. Though concealed lighting was popular, Etling met a demand for visible fixtures similar to Lalique's. His range included small chromium-plated metal and crystal lamps and illuminated *bouts-de-table*.
Exhibitions *Bouts-de-table* shown at 1934 (2nd) Salon de la Lumière and 1937 *Exposition Internationale des Arts et Techniques dans la Vie Moderne*, both Paris.

Bibliography Alastair Duncan, *Art Nouveau and Art Déco Lighting*, New York: Simon & Schuster, 1978. Gabriel Henriot, *Luminaire*, Paris: Charles Moreau, 1937: plates 39–40.

Eureka Company, The

American manufacturer; initially located Detroit, Mich.

History 1909, The Eureka Company was founded in Detroit; is located today in Bloomington, Ill.; by 1927, was selling its vacuum cleaners through door-to-door salespeople; at one time accounted for one-third of domestic sales of vacuum cleaners in the US; established a large research and design department; by mid 1980s, was making more than 40 models. Eureka's chief industrial designer Samuel Hohulin, with design consultant Kenneth Parker, designed Eureka's 1982 Mighty Mite compact model in a colorful plastic casing.
Bibliography Cat., Kathryn B. Hiesinger and George H. Marcus III (eds.), *Design Since 1945,* Philadelphia: Philadelphia Museum of Art, 1983. Wolf von Eckardt, 'Fashionable Is Not Enough,' *Time*, vol. 121, Jan. 3, 1983: 76–77.

Eureka Pottery

American ceramics manufacturer; located Trenton, N.J.

History 1883, the Eureka Pottery Company was established in Trenton, N.J.; reacted to the influence of the growing popularity of British brightly colored majolica shown at 1876 *Centennial Exposition*, Philadelphia, by producing two successful lines—the Bird and Fan and the Prunus and Fan. 1883–85, Eureka was located on Mead Avenue in Trenton. The first year (1883), Leon Weil and R. Weil were known to have been associated with Eureka. 1885–86, Noah W. Boch was the proprietor, and Charles Boch was a potter there. Then, 1886–87, Charles Boch was the proprietor, and the operation became known as Eureka Porcelain Works, while Noah Boch became the 'pottery superintendent.'
Bibliography M. Charles Rebert, *American Majolica, 1850–1900*, Des Moines, Iowa: Wallace-Homestead, 1981: 63, 69, 82. Doreen Bolger Burke et al., *In Pursuit of Beauty: Americans and the Aesthetic Movement*, New York: The Metropolitan Museum of Art/Rizzoli, 1986: 426.

Evanson, James (1946–)

American lighting designer.

Training Architecture, Pratt Institute, Brooklyn, N.Y., and Art Center College of Design, California.
Biography Evanson is best known for his large lighting constructions that emulate buildings and entire skylines when amassed, including, during 1985–86, Lightstruck table lamp, Hi-beam floor lamp, and Light Collection by Art et Industrie. They were produced in small editions.
Bibliography Albrecht Bangert and Karl Michael Armer, *80s Style: Designs of the Decade*, New York: Abbeville, 1990: 230.

Exner Sr., Virgil Max (1909–1973)

American automobile designer; born Ann Arbor, Mich., US; orphaned and adopted by Mormons.

Training 1926–28, University of Notre Dame, South Bend, Ind.
Biography 1929–34, Exner worked as a designer at Advertising Artist Inc., where he became attracted to automobile design through the agency's brochures for the Art Déco styling of Studebaker cars; 1933–37, was a stylist at General Motors in Detroit, Mich., in charge of the Pontiac marque but was overshadowed by the extroverted Harley Earl there. From 1937, he worked in the studio of Raymond Loewy, who moved Exner to the Studebaker automobile company in South Bend, Ind., in 1939. 1944, Loewy, another extroverted personality, fired Exner because he thought that Exner was promoting himself as the sole designer of Studebaker's 1947 model. Even so, Studebaker hired back Exner as an independent design consultant. From 1948, Exner worked at the Chrysler automobile company, where he was the highly effective director of styling from 1953. He thought of car bodies as sculpture; took a voluptuous Italian approach to styling; resisted the incorporation of Harley Earl's exaggerated Cadillac tail fins; imbued Chrysler models with a subtle elegance, resulting in a strong brand recognition; attempted to free himself of standard American glitz by consulting with Ghia, the Italian design firm. Exner's bodies include 1952 Chrysler K310, 1953 Chrysler d'Elegance (strongly Italian influenced), 1953–54 Dodge Firearrow series, 1955 De Soto Adventurer, 1956 Chrysler Dart, and 1957 Plymouth Belvedere. 1961–73 with son Virgil Jr (1933–), was active in his own design studio.
Citations 1993 Edsel B. Ford Design History Award (posthumous), Henry Ford Museum, Dearborn, Mich.
Bibliography James T. Lenzler and Ron Kowalke (eds.), *Standard Catalog of Chrysler, 1914–2000*, 2nd ed., Iola, Wis.: Krause, 2000. Dennis Adler, *Chrysler*, St. Paul, Minn.: Motorbooks International, 2000. Penny Sparke, *A Century of Car Design*, London: Mitchell Beazley, 2002.

Exter, Aleksandra (b. Aleksandra Alexandrovna Grigorovich 1882–1949)

Russian artist and textile, set, fashion, interior, and book designer; born Belestok near Kiev.

Training To 1907, Kiev Art School.
Biography Exter traveled regularly to Paris and other Western European cities; 1912, moved to St. Petersburg; continued to travel and met Russian and Western avant-gardists; became close to Benedikt Livshits and other poets, to whom she gave some of her art work; was associated with artists' group Union of Youth. Her career in the theater began with design work for Innokentii Annenskii's *Thamira Khytharedes* (the first of several commissions with producer Alexandr Tairov) at the Chamber Theater in Moscow. 1918, she set up her own studio in Kiev, where Anatolii Petritskii, Isaak Rabinovich, Nisson Shifrin, Pavel Tchelitchew, and Alexandr Tyshler were among her students; 1923, began working on sets and costumes for the film *Aelita* (1924); 1924, moved to Paris, where she produced designs for the theater, fashion, interiors, and books.
Exhibitions Participated in several Kiev venues, including David Burliuk's *Link*. Work shown at 1908 and 1909 exhibitions of St. Petersburg New Society of Artists, 1909–10 and 1911 Izdebskii Salons, 1911–12 Moscow Salon, first and last shows of the Union of Youth, 1915–16 *Tramway V* and *The Store*. c. 1924, designed decorations (with Nivinskii) for *First Agricultural and Handicraft-Industrial Exhibition*, Moscow. Work subject of 1974 exhibition, New York Public Library; 1972 exhibition, Paris (catalog below); 1991, Archivio del'900, Rovereto. Work included in 2000 exhibition, Guggenheim Museum, New York (catalog below); 2000–01 *Amazons of the Avant-Garde*, Guggenheim Museum, New York (catalog below).
Bibliography Alexandre Tairoff (preface), *Alexandra Exter*, Paris: Quatre Chemins, 1930. Cat., Andrei B. Nakov, *Alexandra Exter*, Paris: Galerie Jean Chauvelin 1972. Georgii Kovalenko, *Aleksandra Ekster: Put Khudozhnika/Khudozhnik i Vremia*, Moscow: Galart, 1993. Cat., John E. Bowlt and Matthew Drutt (eds.), *Amazons of the Avant-Garde: Alexandra Exter, Natalia Goncharova, Liubov Popova, Olga Rozanova, Varvara Stepanova, and Nadezhda Udaltsova*, Abrams: Guggenheim Museum, 1999.

Eysselinck, Gaston (1907–1953)

Belgian architect and urban planner; born Tienen; active Ghent and Ostend.

Training 1928, diploma in architecture, Koninklijke Academie, Ghent.
Biography 1927–29, Eysselinck visited the Netherlands for personal study and became familiar with the work of the Amsterdam School of architects. Of the second-generation Belgian architects whose activities began in c. 1930, Eysselinck was nevertheless one of the most socially radical and strongly convicted; from 1933, taught, Koninklijke Academie, Ghent; 1934, joined the editorial staff of magazine *La Cité*. His architecture includes his own 1930–31 house and studio in Ghent, 1933 Peeters house in Antwerp, 1953 apartment block in Ghent. In Ostend: 1945–52 postal and telephone company building (first major commission, considered his masterpiece) and 1947–53 various commissions of the Spaarzaamheid, Economie, Oostende (SEO, a cooperative association). 1945–53, he worked in Ostend. He designed some tubular-steel furniture in 1931 that he wanted to produce under the tradename Fratsta. The group included a chaise longue, stackable cantilevered chair, and serving table. Some critics consider this collection to be Belgium's most important contribution to modern metal furniture. (Examples are housed in the Museum voor Sierkunst en Vormgeving in Ghent.) He also designed built-in units for some of his buildings; died in Ostend at age 46.
Citations 1937 Van de Ven prize (for Verplanken terraced house).
Bibliography Cat., *Der Kragstuhl*, Stuhlmuseum Burg Beverungen, Berlin: Alexander, 1986: 35, 132. Cat., L. Daenens, *Buismeubelen in België: Tijdens het interbellum*, Ghent: Museum voor Sierkunst,1987. Mil De Kooning and Ronny De Meyer, *Horta and After, 25 Masters of Modern Architecture in Belgium*, Ghent: Ghent University, 2001 (2nd rev. ed.).

F

Flexform: Joe Colombo. Tube chair nesting and combinable elements (detail). 1969. MoMA.

Fabbian Illuminazione

Italian lighting company; located Castelminio di Resana (TV).

History Founded in 1961, Fabbian makes a range of suspension, table, floor, wall, and ceiling lamps; exports 65% of its production to more than 40 countries. Its commissioned designers have included Grazia Azzolin, Paolo De Lucchi, Giampiero Derai, Alessandra Baldereschi, Francesco Lucchese, Renato Montagner, Roberto Pamio, Philippe Bestenheider, Prospero Rasulo, Afra and Tobia Scarpa, and Marc Sadler.

Fabergé, Gustav (1814–1881)

Russian goldsmith and jeweler; born Pernu, Estonia; father of Peter Carl Fabergé.

Training Apprenticeship under a jeweler in St. Petersburg.
Biography Fabergé was descended from a Huguenot family; 1842, opened a jewelry shop on the fashionable Bolshaia Morskaia Street in St. Petersburg; 1860, left the business in the hands of his managing director and partner, Peter Hiskias Pendin, to 1870, when his son Peter Carl Fabergé became old enough to manage the firm.
Bibliography Charlotte Gere, *American and European Jewelry 1830–1914*, New York: Crown, 1975: 175. A. Kenneth Snowman, *Fabergé: Jeweler to Royalty*, New York: Cooper-Hewitt Museum, 1983.

Fabergé, Peter Carl (1846–1920)

Russian goldsmith and jeweler; born St. Petersburg; active St. Petersburg and Moscow; son of Gustav Fabergé.

Training In Frankfurt, and, under Peter Hiskias Pendin, goldsmith and chief assistant to his father, in St. Petersburg.
Biography 1870, Peter Carl Fabergé took over the firm his father had founded 1842; was trained both as a goldsmith and in business practices; managed the activities of more than 500 assistants, designers, modelers, gem-cutters, enamelers, and metalsmiths at the peak of the firm's appreciable success. Its St. Petersburg silversmiths included S. Wäkeva, Jan Lieberg-Nyberg, J. Nevalainen, and J.A. Rappoport. Dutch metalsmith Jan Eisenloeffel worked for a time in the workshop, where he became interested in the *champlevé*-enamel technique. 1887, a branch was opened in Moscow, where many more silver pieces were produced; the manager there of the silver department, Mikhail Tchepournoff, oversaw production in simple styles as well the Old Russian style popular in the second half of the 19th century. Fabergé produced pieces for Tiffany & Co. and Daum glass. The most famous products of the workshop were the 56 Imperial Easter eggs made from 1884. Having specialized in fashionable jewelry 1870–81, the firm received the Imperial warrant in 1884 from Czar Aleksandr III, in connection with the completion that year of the first Imperial Easter egg. Czar Nicholas II continued his father's custom of ordering an egg every year from Fabergé. However, he ordered two, one for his wife and one for his widowed mother. Each of these costly trinkets contained a miniature surprise such as a ship, palace, coach, or the like. 1883, Fabergé's younger brother Agathon joined the firm, and, thence, the firm became known for his cigarette cases, boxes, electric bells, photograph frames, desk accessories, and other *bibelots* in enamel, gold, semi-precious stones, and other luxury materials. 1884 on the suggestion of Count Stroganoff, Fabergé goldsmith Edward Kollin produced copies of 4th-century B.C. gold ornaments found in the Crimea. Working in minute detail Agathon imbued his jeweled *objets de fantaisie* with a certain preciousness. Fabergé's superb enameling technique is regarded as one of his main contributions to the decorative arts. Most of the firm's *cloisonné* enamel work on items in neo-Russian style came from the workshops of Fedor Rückert. 1900, the St. Petersburg branch moved to larger quarters, and branches were opened in 1903 in London and in 1905 in Odessa and Kiev. Workmasters operated separate workshops, some of which Fabergé provided rent free; while Fabergé himself oversaw the production of each piece and supplied the designs and materials, the workmasters hired assistants and paid their wages. Michael Perchin, Henrik Wigström, and A.W. Holmström were his chief workmasters. However, the Moscow branch, where jeweler Oskar Piehl as the co-manager, did not operate this system. Because the firm was a jeweler to the Russian Imperial court, the firm closed in 1918 after the Revolution, and the Bolsheviks seized its remaining stock. Fabergé fled to Lausanne; 1921, his sons Eugène and Alexandre founded the house in Paris under the name Fabergé et Cie.
Exhibitions/citations Showed copies of 4th-century BC Scythian gold ornaments at 1885 *International Goldsmiths' Exhibition*, Nuremberg. Work subject of exhibitions 1980, Helsinki; 1986–87, Munich; 1989–90, Imperial eggs, San Diego and Moscow; 1989, Leningrad; 1992, 150th anniversary exhibition, Catherine Palace, Tsarskoye Selo (catalog below); 1992, Genoa; 1993, touring St. Petersburg, Paris, and London; 1995, Museum für Kunst und Gewerbe, Hamburg; 1996, Queen's Gallery, London; 1998, Forbes Magazine Galleries, New York; 2000, The State Historical Museum, Moscow (catalog below), and the US. Gold medal, 1882 *Pan-Russian Exhibition*, Moscow; gold medal, 1896 *Pan-Russian Exhibition*, Nijny Novgorod. At 1900 *Exposition Universelle*, Paris, Fabergé was a juror and received the Légion d'Honneur.
Bibliography A. Kenneth Snowman, *Carl Fabergé : Goldsmith to the Imperial Court of Russia*, New York: Viking, 1979. Alexander von Solodkoff et al., *Masterpieces from the House of Fabergé*, New York: Abrams, 1984. Annelies Krekel-Aalberse, *Art Nouveau and Art Déco*

Preben Fabricius and Jörgen Kastholm. Tulip chair (no. KF6725). 1964. Steel tubing, leather, and fiberglass, 40 1/2 x 29 5/16 x 24 3/4" (103 x 74.5 x 63 cm). Mfr.: Alfred Kill, Germany. Courtesy Quittenbaum Kunstauktionen, Munich.

Silver, New York: Abrams, 1989. Larisa Piterskaya (compiler), *The Fabulous Epoch of Fabergé: St. Petersburg—Paris—Moscow*, Moscow: Nord, 1992. Irina Aleksandrovna Rodimtseva, *The Art of Fabergé*, Moscow: Kremlin State Historical and Cultural Museum-Monument, 1995. Natalia Nedoshivina et al., *The Fabergé Collection & 1000 Years of Russian Craftsmanship*, Moscow: International Museum Exhibitions, 2000. Will Lowes and Christel Ludewig McCanless, *Fabergé Eggs: A Retrospective Encyclopedia*, Lanham, Maryland: Scarecrow, 2001.

Fabiansen, Ib (1927–)

Danish architect and industrial designer.

Training Architecture, Det Kongelige Danske Kunstakademi, Copenhagen, to 1957.
Biography Fabiansen designed Illum's Bolighus store in Copenhagen; 1958, set up his own studio, becoming a consultant designer to Bang & Olufsen and designing 1962 Horizon TV set; designed commercial and domestic architecture and interiors and garden furniture and lighting for Fog & Morup.
Bibliography Cat., Chantal Bizot, *Bang & Olufsen: design et technologie*, Paris: Musée des Arts Décoratifs, 1990: 8. Jens Bang, *Bang & Olufsen: Fra vision til legende/From Vision to Legend*, Denmark: Vidsyn, 2000.

Fabricius, Preben (1931–1984)

Danish furniture and interior designer; born Odense.

Training To 1957, interior architecture, Skolen for Boligindretning, Copenhagen.
Biography 1952, Fabricius worked under Finn Juhl as a cabinetmaker and designed seating for the United Nations building in New York; 1962–70, was a partner with Jørgen Kastholm; from 1967, taught furniture design, Skolen for Boligindretning; 1968, set up his own office in Holte, where Kastholm also had an office. With Kastholm, he designed 1962 Scimitar Chair 63 (reminiscent of a tractor seat) by Ivan Schlechter and 1964 Tulip (KF6725) armchair and others by Alfred Kill. Other furniture designs were produced by Arnold Exclusiv.
Exhibitions/citations Scimitar Chair 63 was first shown, at 1963 *New Forms*, Charlottenborg Museum, Copenhagen, and included in 1966 *Vijftig Jaar Zitten*, Stedelijk Museum, Amsterdam, and 1968 *Les Assises du Siège Contemporain*, Musée des Arts Décoratifs, Paris. Received 1969 Illum Prize; 1969 Bundespreis 'Die Gute Form,' Rat für Formgebung (German design council), Frankfurt; 1969 Erster Prize.
Bibliography Cat., *Modern Chairs 1918–1970*, London: Lund Humphries, 1971. Hans Wichmann, *Industrial Design Unikate und Serienerzeugnisse*, Munich: Die Neue Sammlung, 1985. Frederik Sieck, *Nutidig Dansk Møbeldesign – en kortfattet illustreret beskrivelse*, Copenhagen: Bondo Gravesen, 1990.

Facchetti, Gianfranco (1939–)
> See Gruppo G14.

Facchini, Umberto (1935–)

Italian industrial designer; born Villafranca, Verona; active Treviso.

Biography 1962, Facchini began his professional career; designed domestic and office storage and shelving systems; collaborated on some projects with architect Paolo Bandiera; became a member, Associazione per il Disegno Industriale (ADI). Clients have included Faram furniture and Vidal Hermanos.
Bibliography *ADI Annual 1976*, Milan: Associazione per il Disegno Industriale, 1976.

Fadda, Caterina

Italian designer; born Sassari, Sardinia; active London.

Training 1995, Bachelor of arts degree, University of Westminster, London; 1997, master of arts degree, ceramics and glass, Royal College of Art, London.
Biography 1998, Fadda established her own design studio in London; designs tabletop objects produced by her own firm, such as Cellule dishwasher-safe slip-cast earthenware, as well as by international companies.
Exhibitions/citations Work included in 1995 *Ceramic Contemporaries 2*, Victoria and Albert Museum, London; 2001 *Living Britain*, Ozone Gallery, Tokyo; 2001 *Now*, Maison & Objet fair, Villepinte, France; Tendence fair, Frankfurt. 1999 Peugeot-Oxo Design Award (for Sasso light).
Bibliography www.caterinafadda.com.

Faiccia, Mario (1966–)

Italian architect and industrial designer; born Monza.

Training To 1996, in architecture; from 1999, doctoral degree in design, Politecnico, Milan.
Biography From 1987, Faiccia has been active as an interior designer and also as a industrial designer for clients, including Ferrero and Whirlpool; is also active in research at UdR PPI (product-design research unit) at the Politecnico, Milan; from 2001 with Francesco Trabucco, has been a partner of FT&A, collaboratively designing furniture and appliances by Ariete, Artsana, Canalplast, Emmegi, Foppa Perdetti, Rib, and Vortice.

Faience Manufacturing Company

American ceramics firm; located Brooklyn, N.Y.

History The Faience Manufacturing Company operated 1880–92 in the Greenpoint area of Brooklyn, New York; manufactured earthenware vases, jardinières, and baskets at first. 1884–90, British émigré Edward Lycett was artistic director and supervised at least 25 decorators; experimented with a fine grade of white porcelain; produced the metallic glazes of Persian lusterware; 1890, retired to Atlanta, Ga., to assist his son William, who had established a china-painting business there.
Bibliography Edwin AtLee Barber, *The Pottery and Porcelain of the United States...*, New York: Feingold & Lewis, 1893. Cat., Doreen Bolger Burke et al., *In Pursuit of Beauty: Americans and the Aesthetic Movement*, New York: The Metropolitan Museum of Art/Rizzoli, 1987.
> See Lycett, Edward.

Falbe, Kaare (1968–)

Danish designer; active Finland.

Training In strip and plate making; in fitting of electronics; bachelor's degree, department of furniture and tools, Danmarks Designskole, (DDS), Denmark; 1997, master's degree, department of interior architecture and furniture design, Taideteollinen korkeakoulu, Helsinki.
Biography 1997, Falbe established his own studio and, concurrently, worked for Yrjö Wiherheimo at Pekka Kojo & Yrjö Wiherheimo, Helsinki.

Falcon Products (The Falcon Collections)
> See Thonet Industries.

Falk, Tuula (1957–)

Finnish designer; active Sweden.

Biography Falk is known for her furniture designs in solid wood; however, others have included the Arena M chair in steel and plywood by Arvo Piiroinen in Finland; from 1990, served as the main designer at Rintala Meuble (founded 1970; furniture sold through outlets in Helsinki and Stockholm), for which her first design was the curved-back Sonetti chair and subsequently included desks, stool, chairs, sofas, cupboards, chests, and bookcases. Falk's work has furnished the Mäntyniemi (official residence of Finland's president) and the Smolna (Finnish council of state) in Helsinki. Other clients have included Woodnotes (upholstery textiles), Peltola (bedding), and, for furniture, Asko, Rintala Meuble (such as Aaria table in birch and paper yarn), and Puuart.
Citations 1997 furniture design award, Sisustusarkkitehdit (SIO, Finnish association of interior architects); 1998 invitation (chest by cabinetmaker Kari Hänninen), Finnish Wood and Architecture and Construction group; others.

Farina, Battista 'Pinin' (1893–1966)
> See Pininfarina, Battista.

Farina, Roberto (1949–)

Italian designer; born and active Milan.

Training To 1970, Liceo Artistico di Brera; subsequently, architecture, Politecnico; both Milan.
Biography From 1971, Farina collaborated on a number of architecture and design studies in the studio of Giorgio Decursu in Milan; subsequently, worked on industrial and furniture design in the studio of Alberto Meda, furniture in the studios of Venosta and Serini, and, from 1974, furniture and interior design independently and also with Alina Vianini; became a member, Associazione per il Disegno Industriale (ADI).
Bibliography *ADI Annual 1976*, Milan: Associazione per il Disegno Industriale, 1976.

Farquharson, 'Clyne' William (1906–1972)

British glassware designer.

Training To 1924, Birmingham School of Art.
Biography From 1924, Farquharson worked in the design department of John Walsh Walsh. However, his work in the firm's literature was not specifically identified and introduced more contemporary design. This new approach can be seen in Farquharson's Leaf, Kendal, Barry, Albany patterns (first record in the firm's Feb. 1936 advertisement in the *Pottery Gazette*). (Some historians claim his Arches pattern to be of 1935.) Regent and Glamis became available in Feb. 1937. He remained at the factory to its 1951 closing, when he was also the sales manager. Like Keith Murray and Irene Stevens, he made a major contribution to the design of British glassware in the 1930s. attempted to break away from traditional prismatic cutting by introducing more contemporary design. He moved onto Stevens and Williams, where he was its chief designer from 1951–56, when he was replaced by Tom Jones.
Exhibitions Work included in 1937 *Exposition Internationale des Arts et Techniques dans la Vie Moderne*, Paris, and at British Industries Fairs. Cosubject of 2004 *English Glass Between the Wars: Cut glass from 1930–1939 by Keith Murray & Clyne Farquharson*, Hamilton Art Gallery, Victoria, Australia
Bibliography Kenneth Farr, *Design in British Industry: A Mid-Century Survey*, London: Cambridge, 1955. Ric Reynolds, *The Glass of John Walsh Walsh 1850–1951*, Somerset: Richard Dennis, 1999: 27–28. Roger Dodsworth, *William 'Clyne' Farquharson (1906–1972): A Short Biography*, Kingswinford: Broadfield House Glass Museum, 1986.

Farrage, David

British industrial designer.

Training Industrial design, Royal College of Art, London.
Biography Ferrage worked in Ross Lovegrove's Studio X; subsequently, at Sekisui Jushi, an architectural- and urban-product manufacturer; returning to London, for FM Design; from 1996, for Smart Design in New York (with OXO as a client); subsequently, for the East Coast Design Center of Sony electronics in Park Ridge, N.J.
Citations 1997 Good Design (for 1996 Good Grips scrub brush by OXO), Chicago Athenaeum.
Bibliography Michele De Lucchi (ed.), *The International Design Yearbook*, London: Laurence King, 2001.

Fasulo, Paolo (1965–)
> See N2.

Fatřa

Czech furniture manufacturer; located Napajedla.

History 1935, Fatřa Napajedla, as a state enterpise, was originally founded as a rubber producer. From 1940 and gradually, it came to produce goods in plastics exclusively and helped to introduce plastics to a number of other firms in the country. From a single factory that produced gas masks in the beginning, the operation became the largest Czech plastics manufacturer with the widest assortment of PE and PVC. It even produces consumer goods, such as 1969 children's toys designed by Libuše Niklová in PVC in various sizes; from 1998, has been a division of AliaChem, of Prague. Still located in Napajedla, today Fatřa produces a wide range of products, including floor coverings, packaging, tablecloths, sealed clothing, films/laminates, and a number of industrial raw plastics, such as granules.
Bibliography Cat., Milena Lamarová, *Design a Plastické Hmoty*, Prague: Uměleckoprůmyslové Muzeum, 1972: 54, 84. www.fatra.cz.

Faubourg Saint-Antoine

Street and neighborhood in Paris.

History Parisian furniture manufacturers in and around the Faubourg Saint-Antoine produced pastiches and copies of classical designs, from the early 19th century. At the beginning of the 20th century, production became more original, first with the Art Nouveau style and, subsequently, Art Déco in both the 'baroque,' classically oriented forms and the unornamented modern forms. Important furniture makers active in the 1920s included Gouffé, Speich Frères, Soubrier, Beligant et Fesneau, Haentgè Frères, Marquis et Krast, Meyniel Frères, Schugt et Beaudoin, and Krieger. The studio Gué of Georges and Gaston Guérin was directed by Georges Champion. Mercier Frères opened the shop Palais du Marbre at 77, avenue des Champs-Élysées, directed by Eric Bagge. Fernand and Gaston Saddier were active in the quarter.
Bibliography Pierre Kjellberg, *Art déco: les maîtres du mobilier, le décor des paquebots*, Paris: Amateur, 1986/1990. Daniel Alcouffe et al., *Le Faubourg Saint-Antoine*, Paris: Action Artistique de la Ville de Paris, 1998.

Faure, Camille (1874–1956)

French enameler and painter.

Biography Faure began working as a fabricator of enamel street signs; collaborating with daughter Andrée Faure, produced vases in geometric designs on enameled copper; c. 1930, developed a technique for applying enamel thickly with a spatula.
Bibliography Cat., Aaron Lederfajn and Xavier Lenormand, *Le Louvre des Antiquaires présente: 1930, quand le meuble devient sculpture*, Paris, 1986.

Fauser, Herman (1874–1947)
> See Kayser, J.P.

Faux, Alfred (1931–1978(

Canadian furniture designer; born Toronto.

Training To 1957, Ryerson Institute of Technology, Toronto.
Biography Faux first began as a journeyman machinist for the Algoma Railway in Sault Ste. Marie, Ontario, and, thence, studied at Ryerson Institute. As a designer, he first worked at Robin Bush Associates and then McInstosh Design Association in Toronto; by 1965, had formed Design Collaborative studio in Toronto with graphic designers Rolf Harder, Ernst Roche, and Anthony Mann, with clients, including Clairtone Sound Corporation. The agency received a 1.3 million Canadian dollar contract for furniture to the Universtiy of Guelph; furnished Ontario Pavilion at 1967 *Universal and International Exhibition (Expo '67)*, Montréal. 1968, Faux left Design Collaborative and established Al Faux Associates. He designed a number of chairs, plywood beds, and spun-steel accessories by the firm L'Enfant and furniture for the Ryerson; is best known for his 1964 drafting table (with Thomas Lamb) produced by Norman Wade; also designed lamps by Galaxi Lighting and a 1967 bent chromium-plated tubular-steel chair. By the end of 1960s, taught, Ontario College of Art, Toronto.
Bibliography Cat., *Seduced and Abandoned: Modern Furniture*

Designers in Canada, the First Fifty Years, Toronto: The Art Gallery at Harbourfront, 1986: 23. Rachel Gotlieb and Cora Golden, *Design in Canada Since 1945: Fifty Years from Teakettles to Task Chairs*, Toronto: Knopf Canada, 2001.

Favre-Pinsard, Gisèle (b. Gisèle Favre)

French ceramicist and designer.

Biography 1935, with her father, mother, and sister, she founded Les Quatre Potiers, where tableware and fixtures for the bath and kitchen were produced; laid out the interior of the house of couturier André Courrèges in the Netherlands; from 1937 with husband Pierre Pinsard, was a member, Union des Artistes Modernes (UAM).
Bibliography Arlette Barré-Despond, *UAM*, Paris: Regard, 1986: 522.

Fayolle, Denise (1923–1995)
> See Arnodin, Maïmé.

Fazioli, Domenico (1937–)

Italian designer; active Milan.

Training To 1971, in architecture, Rome.
Biography 1960–64, Fazioli was responsible for interior-design projects for studio MIM in Rome; designed the Executive range of office furniture, Galileo range of tables and desks, Pascal shelving and storage system in wood and plastic laminate, and Compact range of chairs for auditoria and meeting rooms; 1973–76, was in charge of the corporate image of Geres in Milan, the group of companies of MIM, Siam, and Viotto, and designed new showrooms for Siam in Milan, Paris, Brussels, and Turin; became a member, Associazione per il Disegno Industriale (ADI).
Bibliography *ADI Annual 1976*, Milan: Associazione per il Disegno Industriale, 1976.

Fear, Jeffrey (1945–)

Canadian industrial designer; born Toronto.

Training Ryerson Polytechnic Institute, Toronto.
Biography Fear worked for Salmon-Hamilton Design Consultants (1969–72 partnership of Philip Salmon and Hugh Hamilton) and, subsequently, for a contract-furniture manufacturer in California. His 1971 upholstered tubular-steel chair and ottoman were produced by Kinetics Furniture in Toronto.
Bibliography Cat., *Seduced and Abandoned: Modern Furniture Designers in Canada, the First Fifty Years*, Toronto: The Art Gallery at Harbourfront, 1986: 25.

Featherston, Grant (1922–1995)

Australian designer; born Geelong, Victoria.

Biography Featherston designed 1938–39 decorative-glass panels by Oliver-Davey Glass in Melbourne and 1939–40 lighting by Newton & Gray in Melbourne; 1946–52, designed and made jewelry and invented manufacturing equipment; 1947–50, designed and made webbing and the fabric-upholstered Relaxation Chair. 1951–52, followed by numerous other accompanying models (such as 1953 B210 chair) and tables. One of his best known is the 1951 Contour (R160) chair which he patented and had manufactured by Emerson Bros. Other work; 1949 House of Tomorrow in Melbourne and street decorations for 1955 Olympic Civic Committee of the City of Melbourne. In Melbourne, he moved to 7 Davidsons Place in 1956 and to 131 Latrobe Street in 1957; was a consultant designer to numerous architects; 1963, sold his firm Featherston Interiors to Aristoc Industries; formed a partnership with his wife, resulting in a collaboration on all their work from 1966 onward; is Australia's best known furniture designer. Featherston expounded the virtues of good design; though he designed hundreds of chairs, did not consider himself to be essentially a designer of seating. According to Featherston, 'A chair should reflect the central organic theme of its existence.' Grant and Mary Featherston worked for 18 months on the design of 1969 Stem chair; also designed mid-1970s Numero VII chair by Uniroyal. Additionally, were active as a graphic and interior designers and designed textiles, ceramics, jewelry, toys, and trophies. 1947, Grant cofounded the Society of Designers for Industry (now Design Institute of Australia), with Frances Burke, Frederick Ward, R. Haughton James, and Selwyn Coffey.
Exhibitions 'Expo 67 talking chair' (commissioned by Robin Boyd, later produced as 'Expo mark II sound chair'), for 1967 *Universal and International Exhibition (Expo '67)*, Montréal. Produced furniture for Boyd's model home shown at 1949 *Modern Home Exhibition*, Exhibition Buildings, Melbourne. Furniture shown at 1952 exhibition, Stanley Coe Gallery, Melbourne. Floating chairs, storage, and work stations subject of 1960 exhibition, Argus Gallery, Melbourne.
Bibliography Cat., *Featherston Chairs*, Victoria, Australia: National Gallery of Victoria, 1988.

Featherston, Mary (b. Mary Currey; 1943–)

British designer; active Australia.

Biography 1964–66, Featherston was an interior designer at Mockridge, Stahle and Mitchell, Carlton, architects; 1966 with her husband, formed the Grant and Mary Featherston partnership; from 1966, was a consultant to numerous furniture manufacturers and, from 1973, research consultant to the Melbourne government on children's playgrounds.
Bibliography Cat., *Featherston Chairs*, Victoria, Australia: National Gallery of Victoria, 1988.
> See Featherston, Grant.

Fehér, Paul (1898–1992)

Hungarian metalsmith and designer; born Nagy-Kanizsa.

Training Royal Art Academy, Budapest.
Biography Fehér emigrated to France and, thence, to the US, where, he worked at Rose Iron Works c. 1928, frequently collaborating with its founder Martin Rose; subsequently, became head of this factory.
Exhibitions Editions of Salon des Artistes Décorateurs and Salon d'Automne, Paris; 1931 *12th Annual Exhibition of Artists and Craftsmen*, The Cleveland Museum of Art, Ohio.
Bibliography Cat., Janet Kardon (ed.), *Craft in the Machine Age 1920–1945*, New York: Abrams with American Craft Museum, 1995.

Feick Jr., George (1881–1945)

American architect and designer.

Training Cornell University, Ithaca, N.Y.
Biography At Cornell, Feick met architect William Gray Purcell, who later worked for five months in the architecture office Adler and Sullivan, Chicago; 1907 with Purcell, set up the architectural firm Purcell and Feick. 1910, George Grant Elmslie joined their firm to form Purcell, Feick and Elmslie. Feick left in 1913, and the firm became Purcell and Elmslie to 1922. The firm's commissions included numerous banks in small Midwestern towns. Like Frank Lloyd Wright, whom they met in the Louis Henri Sullivan office, and like Sullivan himself, they avoided obvious Beaux-Arts forms and neoclassical details to produce an indigenous American style, or Prairie Style. They became known for their attention to integrated site-specific interiors, furniture, and fittings, or European *Gesamtkunstwerk* (whole work of art).
Bibliography Anne Yaffe Phillips, *From Architecture to Object*, New York: Hirschl and Adler, 1989: 72.

Feildel, Jean

French decorator and furniture designer.

Biography Active from 1928, Feildel designed furniture for 1932 *Pavillon de la Chasse*, Paris.
Exhibitions Work was first shown, at 1927 Salon of Société des Artistes Décorateurs and *Exposition Générale d'Art Appliqué*, Palais Galliéra, Paris.
Bibliography Pierre Kjellberg, *Art déco: les maîtres du mobilier, le décor des paquebots*, Paris: Amateur, 1986/1990.

Feinauer, Albert (1886–1955)

German silversmith; born Kupferzell; active Weimar.

Biography Feinauer was an instructor in the silversmithing workshop of Institut für Kunstgewerbe und Kunstindustrie in Weimar, founded by Henry van de Velde in 1906. The workshop, through Feinauer, produced a number of tea sets designed by Henry van de Velde and was described by van de Velde as 'incomparable in their craftsmanship and among the best things I have designed in my life.'
Bibliography Henry van de Velde, *Geschichte meines Lebens*, Munich: Piper, 1962: 295. Annelies Krekel-Aalberse, *Art Nouveau and Art Déco Silver*, New York: Abrams, 1989.

Feiz, Khodi (1963–)

Iranian industrial designer; active Amsterdam.

Training To 1990, industrial design, Syracuse (N.Y.) University.
Biography To 1986, Feiz worked at Texas Instruments Design Center; from 1990, at Philips Design in the Netherlands, becoming the manager of and senior designer at the Advanced Design Group there; 1998 with wife/graphic designer Anneko Feiz-van Dorsen, established their own Feiz Design Studio in Amsterdam to specialize in product, furniture, graphics, and strategic design for clients, including Alessi, Bang & Olufsen, Cappellini, Declathlon, EMI Music, LEGO, LG Electronics, Loewe, Lost Boys, Nokia, and Offecct.
Exhibitions/citations Work subject of 2003 exhibition *VIVID Vormgeving*, Rotterdam. 1996 IDSA/*Business Week* award (for Philips's Vision of the Future project); 1998 award (for an espresso machine), Industrie Forum Design (iF), Hanover; finalist, 1999–2000 World Technology Award for Design.
Bibliography Michele De Lucchi (ed.), *The International Design Yearbook*, London: Laurence King, 2001.

Fellerer, Max (1889–1957)

Austrian architect and interior designer; born Linz.

Training In Linz; from 1909 under the neoclassicist Karl König, Technische Hochschule, Vienna.
Biography 1913–14, Fellerer work in the studio of Josef Hoffmann at the Kunstgewerbeschule, Vienna; after World War I, returned to Hoffmann and became his senior assistant, particularly on the creation of the Wiener Werkstätte. 1926, Fellerer began working in the studio of Clemens Holzmeister and taught with him at Akademie der bildenden Künste, Vienna. 1920s–30s, Fellerer was active in the Österreichischer Werkbund and designed two houses (1932) for the *Werkbundsiedlung* in Vienna; 1934, succeeded Hoffmann as the head of the architecture section of the Kunstgewerbeschule but was dismissed by the Nazis in 1938. From 1934, he was a partner of Eugen Wörle (Bregenz 1909–Vienna 1996); 1945, returned to the Kunstgewerbeschule, where he was appointed the president in 1946; was president of Zentralvereinigung der Architekten Österreichs from 1945–51. Vienese architecture included 1947–51 Per-Albin-Hansson Siedlung and 1955–56 alterations on the Parliament building and during this time designed furniture. Even though there was no distinctly Viennese approach to interior design after World War II, Fellerer offered some of the substance of a style, much like Otto Niedermoser, Erich Boltenstern, and Franz Schuster. Fellerer died in Vienna.
Citations Grand prize, 1937 *Exposition Internationale des Arts et Techniques dans la Vie Moderne*, Paris.
Bibliography Günther Feuerstein, *Vienna—Present and Past: Arts and Crafts—Applied Art—Design, Vienna:* Jugend und Volk, 1976.

Fennemore, Thomas Acland (1902–1959)

British pottery, wallpaper, and textile designer.

Biography 1919–26, Fennemore worked in advertising at Samson Clarke, at Peter Jones in London, and at Edgar Lawley (china and glassware) in Stoke-on-Trent. 1927–29 with others, he set up a business known as Fennemore, Haydon; 1929–31, was general manager of Paragon China; from 1932, director of pottery at Brain and Co. in Fenton, where he painted and designed china and hired artists, including Albert Rutherston, Vanessa Bell, and Duncan Grant to paint china; 1937, became the registrar of the National Register of Industrial Art Designers and founded the Central Institute of Art and Design to promote the activities of British designers during World War II; 1947, became director of exhibitions of Odhams Press; 1947–53, was consultant designer to Sanderson, J.B. Brooks, Odhams Press, Antler, Luggage, Lawley Group potteries, Bolton Leathers, and A.J. Wilkinson pottery; sold designs to Wilton Royal Carpet Factory, Heals, John Lewis, Bradford Fabrics, and Horrockses; founded and was vice-president, Society of Mural Painters.
Exhibitions Organized 1934 *Modern Art for the Table*, Harrods department store, London, where Brain and Co, A.J. Wilkinson, and Royal Staffordshire Pottery displayed the painted ceramics of artists, including Bell, Sutherland, Grant, Rutherston, Laura Knight, and Paul Nash. Work shown at 1979–80 *Thirties* exhibition, Hayward Gallery, London (catalog below).
Bibliography Cat., *Thirties: British Art and Design Before the War*, London: Arts Council of Great Britain/Hayward Gallery, 1979.

Feraud, Roger (1890–1964)
> See Géo.

Ferebee, Chris (1971–)
> See Five Twenty One Design.

Fermigier, Étienne (1932–1973)

French industrial designer, active Paris.

Training École Boulle; to 1954, École Nationale Supérieure des Arts Décoratifs; both Paris.
Biography Fermigier set up his own studio for interior architecture and industrial design; 1959 with Pierre Perrigault, established Meubles et Fonctions, a showroom and manufacturer of work by young designers Jean-Paul Barray, Michel Mortier, and Daniel Pigeon. Fermigier designed furniture by Meubles et Fonctions and Mobilier de France and seating by Airborne, Arflex, and Sentou, lighting by Disderot and Verre et Lumière; taught, École Camondo, Paris.
Citations 1967 René Gabriel Prize.
Bibliography François Mathey, *Au bonheur des formes, design français 1945–1992*, Paris: Regard, 1992: 241, 303–18.

Ferrara, Gianni (1928–)

Italian designer; born and active Florence.

Biography 1970 with Carlo Bimbi and Nilo Gioacchini, Ferrara set up the industrial design studio Gruppo Internotredici in Florence. Ferrara taught, Istituto Superiore per le Industrie Artistiche (ISIA), Florence; participated in the Urban Traffic on a Human Scale committee (at the 1975 Interdesign meeting of the International Council of Societies of Industrial Designers [ICSID] in Bruges), sponsored by Associazione per il Disegno Industriale (ADI), of which he was a member; has been active as a designer, particularly of furniture.
Exhibitions/citations Participated in Scuole di Disegno Industriale pavilion, 1967 *Universal and International Exhibition (Expo '67)*, Montréal; contributed furniture to 100 m^2 (1,075 sq. ft.) apartment, 1971 *Mostra Selettiva del Mobile*, Cantù; 1972 *Italy: The New Domestic Landscape*, The Museum of Modern Art, New York; Italian section, 1973 BIO 5 industrial-design biennial, Ljubljana; *Italia Oggi*, Gimbel's department store, Pittsburgh, Pa.; furniture, sculpture, visuals, and an alabaster project, *Volterra '73*, Italian-design pavilion, 1975 Salon d'Ameublement, Lausanne. Bayer special prize (furniture design) at 1970 (10th) Concorso Internazionale del Mobile, Trieste; first and second prizes (laminated-plastic furniture by Abet-Print), 1971 Concorso Nazionale; first prize (alabaster accesories by Volterra), 1972 Concorso Nazionale, where he was a juror.
Bibliography *ADI Annual 1976*, Milan: Associazione per il Disegno Industriale, 1976.

Ferrari Hardoy, Jorge (1914–1977); Juan Kurchan (1913–1975); Antoni Bonet Castellana (1913–1989)

Architects Ferrari Hardoy and Kurchan: born Argentina. Architect Bonet: born Barcelona.

Biography 1938, Ferrari Hardoy, Kurchan, and Bonet worked in architect Le Corbusier's office in Paris; became known for their legendary 1938 B.K.F. chair—also, over the years, variously named the Hardoy, Papillon (Mariposa or Butterfly), AA, and even, in Norway, Bat. 1938 or 1939, Kurchan and Ferrari Hardoy resettled with Bonet in Argentina where they developed a prototype of the chair based on a 19th-century version that featured a wooden folding frame (patented in 1877 by Joseph Barly Fenby in England) and that had become popular for camping and travel. The architects' B.K.F. version includes two bent-steel, rigidly welded rods, and a fabric- or leather-sling cover. From late 1930s, it has been produced at different times, under various names, by a number of manufacturers: Artek-Pascoe, US (c. 1,500 examples) from c. 1941–43; Knoll Associates, US (more than 5 million examples as no. 198) from 1945; Airborne, France, from 1947; others have included Stohr and Verax. Kurchan and Ferrari Hardoy's architecture includes 1941–42 Casa del Árbol in Buenos Aires. Principally an architect, Ferrari Hardoy initiated the EPBA (1938–39 Buenos Aires urban plan, published in 1947), with Bonet, Kurchan, Le Corbusier, Ernesto Rogers, Clorindo Testa, and others; was a member, Congrès Internationaux d'Architecture Moderne (CIAM); 1938 or 1939 with Kurchan, Bonet, and others, organized Grupo

Jorge Ferrari Hardoy, Juan Kurchan, and Antoni Bonet Castellana. B.K.F. chair. 1938. Painted wrought-iron rod and leather, overall 34 3/8 x 32 3/4 x 29 3/4" (87.3 x 83.2 x 75.6 cm). Mfr.: Artek-Pascoe, US (c. 1941–43). Edgar Kaufmann, Jr. Fund. MoMA.

Astral (based on a Catalan architectural association) which published the adjunct *Astral* journal (founded on the same day that the B.K.F. chair is created), whose manifesto was written by Kurchan, Bonet, and Ferrari Hardoy, and which was dissolved early 1940s. Ferrari Hardoy's family donated his archive to Frances Loeb Library, Harvard University, Cambridge, Mass., US, which asserts that the design date of the B.K.F. chair is 1939. Some accounts of Bonet credit him as the major author of the B.K.F. chair; after working in the Le Corbusier office and rather than returning to Spain, Bonet probably went directly to Argentina in 1939 to escape the oppressive new Franco regime in Spain and may have intended the chair to represent a denigration of Spain's dark Franco period when creativity and free expression were supressed. Strongly influenced by Le Corbusier, Bonet, known as a perfectionist, designed Argentine buildings that combined stark modernism with a tropical regionalism; had an interest in furniture design, also fostered by Le Corbusier; 1943, initiated Organización de la Vivienda Integral en la República Argentina (OVRA), an organization for integral housing; 1945–48, lived and worked in Uruguay; returned to Argentina; 1957, founded *Mirador* (viewpoint) magazine; 1950s–70s, was highly active as the architect of numerous buildings.
Exhibitions/citations 1999 symposium 'A Chair, a House, a City: On the Works of Jorge Ferrari Hardoy,' Harvard Design School, Cambridge, Mass. Based on parameters of the chair's design morphology, 2001 *NUDO* international competition/exhibition, Argentina, was created.
Bibliography Guy Julier, *New Spanish Design*, New York: Rizzoli, 1991: 23. Fernando Álvarez et al., *Antoni Bonet Castellana: 1913–1989*, Barcelona: Collegi d'Arquitectes de Catalunya, Ministeri de Foment, 1996. 'Antoni Bonet Castellana,' *Quaderns,* no. 194 (journal of Colegio de Arquitectos de Cataluña), July 1992.

Ferrer Thomàs, Mariano (1945–)

Catalan designer and entrepreneur; born and active Sant Feliu de Guíxols, Baix Empordà, Girona.

Training 1969–71, industrial design, Eina (Escola de Desseny i Art), Barcelona.
Biography 1971, Ferrer Thomàs began to design for Gris with designers Carles Riart, Bigas Luna, and J.M. Massana; 1973 with Massana and Josep Maria Tremoleda, cofounded Mobles 114, a firm for the design, production, and marketing of furniture, furnishings, and lamps; 1981, settled in Santa Cristina d'Aro. He has worked for Miscellanià MB S.L. in Barcelona, Confalonieri in Italy, town council house in Sant Feliu de Guíxols, Villa Clara and Brancós in La Bisbal de l'Empordà, Catalonia, and a number of others. Work has included 1970 Espiral coat hooks, 1979 Gira table lamp (with Tremoleda and Massana) by Mobles 114; 1982 Póllux lamp; 1983 Pinça and Pinça Plus shelf brackets, 1989 Faristeu standard lectern; 1994 Joan Bordàs street lamp; 1996 Filippo ceramic bowl; 1996 Pròleg table lectern; 1998 Lo magazine rack, 1999 Zebra table and stool by Miscellàna de Mercè Bohigas; and many others.
Exhibitions/citations Work included in 1992 *Design aus Spanien*, Cologne; 1992 Ínclit inclining shelf was selected for Sala de Amigos del Museo Reina Sofía, Madrid; 1970 and 1999 Delta d'Oro, ADI/FAD; 1982–90 BCD selections included in *Anuari del Desseny*.

Ferreri, Marco (1958–)

Italian architect and designer; born Imperia.

Training 1981, architecture, Politecnico, Milan.
Biography Ferreri worked as an architect in the studios of Angelo Mangiarotti and of Bruno Munari to 1984, when he set up his own independent office with clients, including Danese, FontanaArte, IBM, McCann Erikson, City Council of Milan, Olivetti, and Robots; with Carlo Bellini, designed 1985 Eddy lamp by Luxo Italiana. Became known for his use of innovative new materials such as die-pressed Softwood™ in 1993 Less chair and Is stool by Nemo and subsequent design work.
Exhibitions 1995 exhibition (Less chair), The Museum of Modern Art, New York, and traveling (catalog below).
Bibliography Albrecht Bangert and Karl Michael Armer, *80s Style: Designs of the Decade*, New York: Abbeville, 1990. Cat., Paola Antonelli, *Mutant Materials in Contemporary Design*, New York: The Museum of Modern Art/Abrams, 1995. Mel Byars, *50 Chairs: Innovations in Design & Materials*, Hove: RotoVision, 1996.

Ferrieri, Anna Castelli (1918–)
> See Castelli Ferrieri, Anna.

Festival Pattern Group

British design project.

History 1951, the Festival Pattern Group was established as a project by the British Council of Industrial Design to encourage manufacturers to produce decorative wares based on crystallographic structures shown at 1951 *Festival of Britain* exposition, London. In 1940s, Britain was a leader in crystallography. Brociacid, aluminum hydroxide, hemoglobin, and insulin were among the chemicals whose crystal structures influenced design attempts to unite science, industry, and art. Twenty-six diverse manufacturers participated, including Wedgwood which produced a commemorative bone china plate. Other manufacturers included Chance Brothers, Goodearl Brothers, London Typographical Designer, Spicers, and Warerite. Many of these products were displayed at the exhibition. Plates by Wedgwood in the restaurant, decorative motifs in the Dome of Discovery in snowflake and atomic patterns, and Ernest Race's Antelope chair with its 'mole-

Marco Ferreri. Is stool. 1993. Die-pressed Softwood, beech, and polyurethane foam, 17 3/4 x 15 3/4 x 13 3/4" (45.1 x 40 x 35 cm). Mfr.: Nemo, Italy. Gift of the mfr. MoMA.

cular' (ball) feet reflected the influence of the project.
Bibliography Jonathan M. Woodham, *Twentieth-Century Ornament*, New York: Rizzoli, 1990: 204, 206.

Feuerstein, Bedřich (1892–1936)

Czech architect, set designer, and essayist; born Dobrovice.

Training 1911–17, České Vysoké Učení Technické (Czech technical university), and, under Jozef Plečník, Vysoká Škola Uměleckoprůmyslová (VŠUP, academy of arts, architecture, and design); both Prague.
Biography Feuerstein was introduced to Cubism and Purism in France where he stayed with Josef Šíma 1920–21; worked in Auguste Perret's office in Paris 1924–26, and in Antonin Raymond's office in Tokyo 1926–30. His 1913–22 painting and architecture had both Cubist and classical elements. He designed 1921–22 sets in a 'structural logic' style in bright colors and Purist forms for the Národní Divadlo (national theater), Prague; the classical 1922–25 Zeměpisný Ústav building in Prague; 1922–24 crematorium in Nymburk, in the Purist style and influenced by the Pantheon in Rome. 1925, he became opposed to Karel Teige's Constructivist 'elimination of art'; Teige was a Devětsil cofounder. From 1922 to its 1931 end, Feuerstein was a member, Devětsil; 1930, returned to Czechoslovakia and was active as a set designer until his suicide in Prague.
Exhibitions Work shown in Prague (with the Tvrdosíjní group) and at 1923 Bauhaus exhibition, Weimar.
Bibliography Cat., *Devětsil: Czech Avant-Garde Art, Architecture, and Design of the 1920s and 30s*, Oxford: Museum of Modern Art, London: Design Museum, 1990. Cat., *Prague, 1900–1938: capitale secrète des avants-gardes*, Dijon: Musée des Beaux-Arts, 1997.

Feuillâtre, Eugène (1870–1916)

French artist, sculptor, and metalworker; born Dunkerque; active Paris.

Biography 1893, Feuillâtre began experimenting with complex enameling techniques on silver and platinum, becoming known as a remarkable enamelist and for perfecting a technique for enameling on platinum; worked with René Lalique originally and set up his own workshop in 1899. Specializing in *plique-à-jour* and *cloisonné* enameling, Feuillâtre produced some of the most outstanding examples of intricate Art Nou-veau metalwork. His objects in translucent enamel, with colors overlapping on engraved grounds, were particularly attractive and incorporated natural motifs, including blackberries and fish in *plique-à-jour* enamel on bowls and boxes. He also experimented with glass combined with enameled silver.
Exhibitions Work (enameled silver objects) was first shown under his own name, at 1898 Salon of Société des Artistes Français and in its 1910 Salon. Work included in 1899 Salon de La Libre Esthétique, Brussels; New Gallery, London; 1900 *Exposition Universelle*, Paris, 1902 *Esposizione Internazionale d'Arte Decorativa Moderna*, Turin.
Bibliography Charlotte Gere, *American and European Jewelry 1830–1914*, New York: Crown, 1975. Yvonne Brunhammer et al., *Art Nouveau Belgium, France*, Houston: Rice University, 1976. Annelies Krekel-Aalberse, *Art Nouveau and Art Déco Silver*, New York: Abrams, 1989.

Fevre, Francis (1960–); Charlotte Arnal (1951–)

French designers. Fevre born Troyes. Arnal born Hyères; daughter of François Arnal.

Training Fevre: 1982, diploma, École Boulle, Paris.
Biography 1992–93, Fevre was an interior architect and designer. 1969–70, Arnal designed printed textiles and, 1979–92, was director of marketing of a chain of contemporary-furniture stores. 1992, the husband/wife team established 'D-sign by O' in Paris for interior architecture, product design, and production. In addition to products for others, work under the 'O' mark has included 1992 rubber vases, 1996 Toto illuminated table, 1997 Tutu illuminated shelf, 2000 Trio wooden trivets; 2000 Zozo illuminated table-tray, 2001 Cousins containers.

Fiam Italia

Italian furniture manufacturer; located Tavullia.

History 1973, Fiam Italia was founded by Vittoro Livi, a young entrepreneur and designer, to produce furniture and furnishings that incorporated innovative bent glass and hardware and, thus, change the role of glass from simple ornamentation to an essential component. The firm has become known for its intricate one-piece glass furniture. Its art director was Angelo Cortesi and graphic designers Patrizia Pataccini and Carla Caccia. Rocco Serini was a consultant designer. Danny Lane's work for Fiam included 1988 Shell and Atlas tables. It produced Vittorio Livi's 1984 Ragno table, Cini Boeri's 1987 Ghost one-piece glass chair (with Tomu Katayanagi), Enzo Mari's 1992 table Montefeltro, Ron Arad's 1999 Knox and 2001 Marilor coffee tables, Christophe Pillet's 2001 c + c coffee table, and designs by Giugiaro Design, Makio Hasuike, Massimo Iosa Ghini, Massimo Morozzi, Hans von Klier, and others. Also Philippe Starck's 1992 Illusion table, 1999 Caadre mirror, and 1999 Gelly table range. 50% of its production is exported.
Bibliography *ADI Annual 1976*, Milan: Associazione per il Disegno Industriale, 1976. 'Milan à l'Heure du Design,' *Maison et Jardin*, April 1992: 128. http://www.fiamitalia.it.

Fiberglass

Synthetic, reinforced material.

History Fiberglass (or Fiberglas) contains glass spun in a fibrous form. An early example of the use of fiberglass, formed as a solid by being mixed with plastic polymers, was the dish for radar detection during World War II. After they had developed the molding technology for seating in their California studio Charles and Ray Eames had the Herman Miller Furniture Company, Zeeland, Mich., commission the production of the shells for their 1950 armchairs and side chairs from radar dish manufacturer Zenith Zenith Fabricators in Gardena, Cal. Herman Miller later produced the seats independently. From early 1950s, particularly in the US, fiberglass became popular in the manufacture of furniture, automobile bodies, and a large number of other products, including for fabrics.
> See Eames, Charles Ormond; Corning.

Figini, Luigi (1903–1984)

Italian architect-designer; born Milan.

Training To 1926, Politecnico, Milan.
Biography 1926, Figini became a founding member of Gruppo Sette (group seven), an association of Italian architects who initiated the Rationalist movement. Figini was a member, Movimento Italiano per l'Architettura Razionale (MIAR); from 1929, collaborated with Gino Pollini and, with Pollini, Adalberto Libera, Guido Fretti, and Piero Bottoni, designed the Casa Elettrica pavilion for Montedison company at 1930 (4th) *Esposizione Biennale delle Arti Decorative e Industriali Moderne*, Monza, with its prominently featured all-electric kitchen, based on German and American models. It was the first public expression of modern architecture in Italy. 1930–33, Figini and Pollini designed the Craja Bar in Milan, and the offices of De Angeli Frua (with Luciano Baldesari). They may be best-known for the radio-gramophone that won the 1933 design competition sponsored by the National Gramophone Co. and was subsequently put into limited production. They designed an artist's studio at 1933 (5th) Triennale di Milano; worked in the Rationalist style through 1930s, designing 1934–35 Olivetti building (built 1939–41) in Ivrea and 1935 Studio 42 portable typewriter (with 'Xanti' Schawinsky) by Olivetti. Their New Brutalism was illustrated by 1952–56 Church of the Madonna dei Poveri in Milan. After the deaths of Giuseppe Pagano and Giuseppe Terragni, Figini and Pollini became the standard-bearers of the Rationalist tradition.
Exhibitions/citations Work (with Pollini) shown at 1926 (2nd) Biennale di Monza. Designed (with Pollini and others) Casa Elettrica, 1930 Biennale di Monza. Designed (with Pollini) villa-studio for an artist (in a park), 1933 (5th) Triennale di Milano, with steel-and-wood furniture. Work was the subject of 1997 *Luigi Figini, Gino Pollini, architettura 1927–1991*, Museo di Arte Moderna e Contemporanea di Trento e Rovereto. Won (with Pollini) design competition for a writing desk sponsored by 1936 (6th) Triennale di Milano and designed the terrace setting there.
Bibliography Luigi Figini and Gino Pollini, 'Origines de l'architecture moderne en Italie,' *L'architecture d'aujourd'hui*, vol. 22, no. 41, June 1952: 5–9. Eugenio Gentili Tedeschi, *Figini e Pollini*, Milan: Il Balcone, 1959. Cesare Blasi, *Figini e Pollini*, Milan: Monumità, 1963. Luigi Figini, 'Architettura Italiana 1963,' special issue, *Edilizia moderna*, no. 82–83, 1964. J. Rykwert, 'Figini & Pollini,' *Architectural Design*, Aug. 1967: 369–78. Barbie Campbell-Cole and Tim Benton (eds.), *Tubular Steel Furniture*, London: The Art Book Company, 1979: 47. Penny Sparke, *Design in Italy, 1870 to the Present*, New York: Abbeville, 1988. Richard A. Etlin, *Modernism in Italian Architecture, 1890–1940*, Cambridge: MIT, 1991. Vittorio Savi, *Figini e Pollini: architetture, 1927–1989*, Milan: Electa, 1990. Cat. Vittorio Gregotti (ed.), *Luigi Figini, Gino Pollini: opera completa*, Milan: Electa, 1996.

Robert Fischer. Coffee service. c. 1932. Silver and ivory, pot h. 7 7/8" (20.1 cm), creamer h. 4 5/16" (11 cm), sugar bowl h. 4 3/4" (12.2 cm), tray 17 x 12" (43.3 x 30.4 cm). Mfr.: the designer, Germany. Courtesy Quittenbaum Kunstauktionen, Munich.

Filippi, Francesco (1956–)

Italian designer, sculptor, and engineer; born and active Milan.

Training To 1983, in mechanical engineering; 1989, master's degree in business administration.
Biography 1988, Filippi created EOS (Earth Object System), which he claims to be the first 'mobile furniture,' as his undulating sofa illustrates; 1993, set up Kreo to manufacture objects and has since been designing unusual interpretations of traditional products, influenced by his engineering training and personal interests, and that evoke, as is his wont, strong emotional responses. Design work has included 1993 Cutfish circular scissors by Kreo. Others: 1991 Sea Upside Down mechanical-electronic sofa in a wave shape, 1992 Girogirotondo toy for use in parks, 1994 Bollicina floating soap, 1995 Pesci knife with a retractible blade, 1996 Pro ovo a Volare bird-shaped egg slicer, 2000 Specchio di Biancaneve double-sided holographic mirror, 2001 Skycubes wooden cubic puzzle, 2001 sculpture for Bayer in Makrolon (a proprietary polycarbonate plastic), 2001 sculpture (*Tree...vira*) for Trevira in Plexicor (Trevira's proprietary synthetic yarn).
Citations A number of citations from first prize (for Sea Upside Down sofa), Europa '93, and 1993 Swiss Design Prize (for Cutfish scissors), Geneva, to Top Design selection (for Snow White's Olographic Mirror), 2000 Grandesign, Milan.
Bibliography Mel Byars, *50 Products...*, Hove: RotoVision, 1998. Mel Byars, *50 Beds...*, Hove: RotoVision, 2000. www.oniris.it; www.francescofilippi.it.

Filkor, Marian (1971–)

Slovakian designer; born Banská Bystrica; active Badín.

Training 1985–89, furniture design, secondary technical school, woodworking industry, Zvolen; 1989–95, Faculty of Wood Sciences and Technology, Department of Furniture and Wood Products, Section of Furniture Design and Wood Products, Technická Univerzita, Zvolen; 1993, Fakulta Architektúry, Slovenská Tehcnická Univerzita, Bratislava.
Biography 1997, Filkor established an office in Badín for commissions from furniture manufacturers and interior architects; 1999, began producing own products; from 2001 with others, has designed private and office interiors.
Exhibitions/citations University project on multi-functional bedding, produced by Bytterm, shown at 1997 Moddom fair, Bratislava. Work included in 1998 *Arte Eslovaca e Design*, Lisbon, Portugal; 1999 Furniture and Dwelling fair (certificate of merit and work shown in *Forum of Design* exhibition there), Nitra; Slovakian pavilion (exhibitor), 2001 *Art and Interior*, Prague. Work subject of 1998 exhibition, KFA Gallery, Bratislava. 1999 National Prize for Design.

Finch, Alfred William (1854–1930)

Belgian ceramicist; born Brussels; active Finland.

Training 1878–80, painting, École des Beaux-Arts, Brussels; ceramics at Boch Frères, La Louvière.
Biography An Impressionist painter, Finch became a founding member of artists' group Les Vingt in 1884; met James Whistler in London in 1886 and tried unsuccessfully to get him to join Les Vingt. Finch became familiar with the Arts and Crafts movement, sharing a knowledge of it with Henry van de Velde and Les Vingt members. 1888, Finch became interested in Pointillism through Georges Seurat. Les Vingt member Ann Boch introduced him to Kéramis, the Boch ceramics factory at La Louvière where he worked 1890–93. 1896, he experimented with glazed pottery in his own studio in Forges-Chimay; 1897–1902, was head of the ceramics department of the Iris factory in Porvoo, Finland; after the Iris factory closed, was head of ceramics department, Taideteollinen korkeakoulu, Helsinki, until 1930.
Bibliography Yvonne Brunhammer et al., *Art Nouveau Belgium, France*, Houston: Rice University, 1976. Cat., David Revere McFadden (ed.), *Scandinavian Modern Design 1880–1980*, New York: Abrams, 1982: 263, no. 40. Jennifer Hawkins Opie, *Scandinavia: Ceramics and Glass in the Twentieth Century*, New York: Rizzoli, 1989.

Finmar
> See Aalto, Aino; Aalto, Hugo Alvar Henrik; Artek.

Fioravanti, Leonardo (1939–)

Italian automobile designer.

Biography Fioravanti was possibly the best-known of many designers who worked in the Pininfarina studio in Turin; made an appreciable contribution to the change from front-placed to rear- or mid-placed engines; created the much emulated, especially in Detroit, Ferrari Daytona; became known for developing true aerodynamic forms and ideas for mass-produced saloons; working at Pininfarina for 24 years and departing in 1988, became the managing director and general manager of Pininfarina Studi & Ricerche; in addition to the Daytona (his favorite of all his car work), designed others by Ferrari including the Dino, 308/328 GTB, Berlinetta Boxer, and Testarossa, all still considered the most beautiful Ferraris ever; worked briefly at Fiat; 1987 in Moncalieri (near Turin), established his own studio; 1998, designed the F100 with a patented bubble-shaped windshield and hood cover, the first concept car under his own name; designed the favorably received 2001 Alfa Romeo Volta spider show car.

Firth, T. F., and Sons

British textile firm; located Brighouse and Heckmondwike.

History 1822, Edwin Firth founded the firm. It was incorporated 1889; 1936, produced Axminster, Wilton, Brussels, Velvet, and tapestry carpets at Brighouse, and seamless Axminster squares, a range of rugs, mantle cloths, and upholstery velvets at Heckmondwike.
Bibliography Valerie Mendes, *The Victoria and Albert Museum's Textile Collection, British Textiles from 1900 to 1937*, London: Victoria and Albert Museum, 1992.

Fischer, Christa (aka Craftcow; 1957–)

German industrial designer; born Würzburg; active Berlin.

Training 1977–81, interior design, Fachhochschule, Rosenheim.
Biography 1981, she settled in Berlin; 1981–86, worked in an architecture office; 1986, set up her own interior-architecture office and was active as a freelance interior and exhibition designer within the Berliner Zimmer design group, designing under the pseudonym Craftcow.
Exhibitions Work included in Berliner Zimmer stand, 1986 and 1988

Internationale Möbelmesse, Cologne; 1986 *Transit Berlin West*, Berlin. Also, 1988 *Berlin: les avant-gardes du mobilier*, Centre Georges Pompidou, and concurrently at Galerie VIA (French furniture association) and Galerie Néotù, all Paris.
Bibliography Cat., *Berlin: les avant-gardes du mobilier*, Berlin: Design Zentrum, 1988. Cat., Design Center Stuttgart, *Women in Design: Careers and Life Histories Since 1900*, Stuttgart: Haus der Wirtschaft, 1989: 112–13.

Fischer, Richard (1935–)

German industrial designer.

Training Hochschule für Gestaltung, Ulm.
Biography Fisher designed products by Braun and BASF; 1968–75, was a docent, Werkkunstschule in Offenbach, and, 1975–99, professor of product design and image function, Hochschule in Ulm; with Gerda Mikosch, wrote *Grundlagen einer Theorie der Produktsprache, 'Anzeichenfunktion,'* booklet 3 (Ulm: Hochscule für Gestaltung, 1984).
Citations Prizes for Dynavit-Trainer by Keiper of Kaiserslautern, for 35 GL and 35 LX compact cameras by Minox of Gießen, and for portable overhead projector and Mini-Laser Delta light pen by Medium of Düsseldorf. Elected professor emeritus/product design, Hochschule für Gestaltung, Ulm.

Fischer, Robert (1906–1941)

German silversmith; active Schwäbisch-Gmünd.

Training Under Wilhelm Binder, in metalworking; Staatliche Höhere Edelmetallfachschule (state school of precious metals), Schwäbisch-Gmünd.
Biography Fischer was an independent silversmith in Berlin and Leipzig to 1932, when he settled in Schwäbisch-Gmünd and became quite active for a relatively short time; from 1934, taught, Edelmetallfachschule; often combined simple silver forms with ivory elements.
Exhibitions/citations Work included in exhibitions of 1930s and 1937 *Exposition Internationale des Arts et Techniques dans la Vie Moderne*, Paris. Numerous awards.
Bibliography Annelies Krekel-Aalberse, *Art Nouveau and Art Déco Silver*, New York: Abrams, 1989. Cat., Dedo von Kerssenbrock-Krosigk and Claudia Kanowski, *Modern Art of Metalwork*, Berlin: Bröhan-Museum, 2001: no. 133.

Fischer, Uwe (1958–)

German designer.

Biography 1985 with Klaus-Achim Heine (1955–), Fischer cofounded design studio Ginbande in Frankfurt and designed highly articulated furniture by Sawaya & Moroni and others. Their widely published 1988 Tabula Rasa table-bench combination by Vitra extended from 20 to 197" (50 to 500 cm). Fischer became chairperson of industrial design, Staatlicher Akademie der bildenden Künste, Stuttgart; has designed signage, information systems, and other furniture, as well as the interior spaces of the Municipal Art Gallery in Nuremberg. Clients have included B&B Italia, Ciba-Geigy, and Rat für Formgebung (German design council) in Frankfurt.
Bibliography Albrecht Bangert and Karl Michael Armer, *80s Style: Designs of the Decade*, New York: Abbeville, 1990. Mel Byars, *50 Tables: Innovations in Design & Materials*, Hove: RotoVision, 1997.

Elsa Fischer-Treyden and Margret Hildebrand. Vase. 1966. Glazed porcelain, h. 9 1/4 x dia. 8" (23.5 x 20.3 cm). Mfr.: Porzellanfabrik Ph. Rosenthal & Co., Germany. Gift of the mfr. MoMA.

Fischer-Treyden, Elsa (1901–1995)

Russian textile, glassware, and ceramics designer; born Moscow; active Berlin.

Training 1925–32 under Wilhelm Wagenfeld, Hochschule für bildende Künste, Berlin.
Biography Mid-1920s, Fischer-Treyden moved from Russia to Berlin and worked as an independent designer while studying in Berlin; from 1953, worked for Rosenthal (including with Margret Hildebrand), designing glassware, porcelain, and stoneware such as the widely published 1969 Fuga glass stemware range. She taught, Pädagogische Hochschule (now part of Technische Universität), Berlin; was a member of the Deutscher Werkbund; even at age 90, was still active in many disciplines; was called the 'grande dame' of design; died in Selb, Germany.
Citations Received medals at 1951 (9th) and 1954 (10th) Triennali di Milano and 1969 Bundespreis 'Die Gute Form' (Fuga glassware range), Rat für Formgebung (German design council), Frankfurt.
Bibliography Cat., *Rosenthal: Hundert Jahre Porzellan*, Hanover: Kestner-Museum, 1982: 174–75, Nos. 90, 103, 111–12. Cat., Kathryn B. Hiesinger and George H. Marcus III (eds.), *Design Since 1945*, Philadelphia: Philadelphia Museum of Art, 1983.

Fisher, Alexander (1864–1936)

British metalworker and fabric designer.

Training Painting in Britain; studies in enameling, Paris.
Biography After Paris, Fisher returned to England in 1887 and set up a studio where he made jewelry and objects featuring Pre-Raphaelite-style figures; wrote and lectured on enameling; became the one to revive the so-called Limoges technique; taught briefly, Central School of Arts and Crafts, London; 1904, founded his own school in Kensington; designed embroidery patterns made by The Royal School of Art Needlework and by his wife. Work was often published in *The Studio* and *Art Journal* periodicals.
Exhibitions Work included in numerous international exhibitions, including at the Royal Academy and at the Arts and Crafts Exhibition Society; both London.
Bibliography Cat., *Arts and Crafts in Britain*, London: Fine Art Society/Francesca Galloway, no., 48, [n.d.]. Erika Speel, *Dictionary of Enamelling: History and Techniques*, Aldershot, UK: Ashgate, 1998.

Fisker, Kay (1893–1965)

Danish architect, furniture designer, and metalworker; active Copenhagen.

Training To 1920, Kunstakademiets Arkitektskole, Copenhagen.
Biography The first of a new generation of architect-designers who produced historicist silver patterns with modern leanings, he designed silver by A. Michelsen in Copenhagen in c. 1925 and furniture and book covers for others; 1936–63, was a professor, Kunstakademiets Arkitektskole.
Exhibitions/citations Work shown at 1925 *Exposition Internationale des Arts Décoratifs et Industriels Modernes*, Paris. Subject of 1934 and 1953 exhibitions, Berlin-Charlottenburg; 1939, Paris; 1950, London; 1953, Århus. 1921, gold medal in Ghent.
Bibliography Annelies Krekel-Aalberse, *Art Nouveau and Art Déco Silver*, New York: Abrams, 1989. Cat., David Revere McFadden (ed.), *Scandinavian Modern Design 1880–1980*, New York: Abrams, 1982.

Five Twenty One Design

American design firm.

History 1999, the firm was established by Laurice Parkin (Virginia Beach, Va., 1971–) and Chris Ferebee (Houston, Texas, 1966–) in New York for the design of products and furniture, including—primarily in 2000—'40 Sq. Yrds.' bench, 2000 Hive modular shelving, Hollow table, Reflector Light II, 32/30 seating unit, Joseph felt bench, Low-Tek table, and Ghost table.
Exhibitions/citations 2001 *TAG Team* (ten avant-garde designers),

Five Twenty One Design: Chris Ferebee. Joseph bench. c. 2002. Industrial wool felt, h. 16 x w. 18 x l. 24" (40.6 x 45.7 x 60.9 cm). Mfr.: Five Twenty One Design, US.

Milan, sponsored by *Surface* magazine and New York's Totem store; 2001–02 *Carrefour de la Création*, Centre Georges Pompidou, Paris. 2000 Good Design award, Chicago Athenaeum; 2001 Design Distinction Award, *I.D.* magazine.
Bibliography Karim Rashid (ed.), *The International Design Yearbook*, London: Laurence King, 2003. www.fivetwentyonedesign.com.

Fjerdingstad, Carl Christian (1891–1968)
Norwegian designer; born Kristiansand; active Blaricum (Norway), Netherlands, and Paris.

Biography Fjerdingstad worked as a designer for Orfèvrerie Christofle in Paris in 1921, and as an independent silversmith. Henry van de Velde regarded him as one of the best silversmiths of the time; he executed a 1922 tea set for van de Velde's new house in Wassenaar, the Netherlands; sometimes produced his own designs. His work combined French ornamentation with the hammered surfaces and the rounded forms of Danish silverware. He designed Christofle's famous 1933 Cygne silver-plated gravy boat and its 1933 Art Déco tea set based on the circle, and reissued in 1983.
Exhibitions Work (Christofle wares) included in 1925 *Exposition Internationale des Arts Décoratifs et Industriels Modernes*, Paris, where Christofle's display was entirely devoted to tableware.
Bibliography *Les carnets du design*, Paris: Mad-Cap Productions/ APCI, 1986: 62. Annelies Krekel-Aalberse, *Art Nouveau and Art Déco Silver*, New York: Abrams, 1989. Cat., *Metallkunst*, Berlin: Bröhan Museum, 1990.

Flatøy, Torstein (1956–)
Norwegian furniture designer.

Biography Flatøy has designed indigenously contemporary furniture, including 1985 Concorde chairs by Gustav Bahus; furniture by Møre Lenostolfabrikk; more recently, a wood furniture range by Låte Møbel.
Bibliography Fredrik Wildhagen, *Norge i Form*, Oslo: Stenersen, 1988: 203.

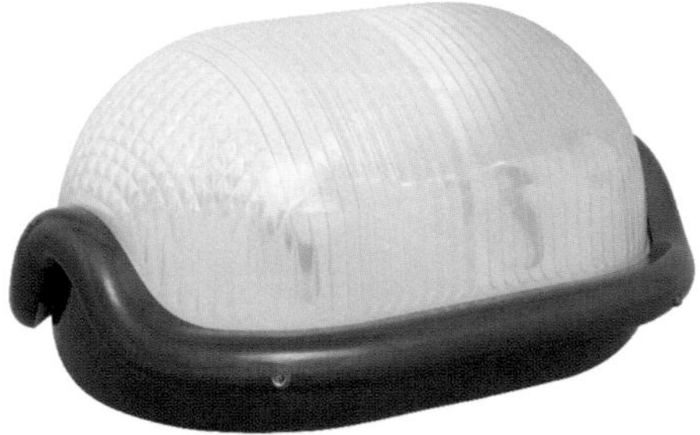
Flos: Achille Castiglioni. Noce floor lamp. 1972. High-pressure-cast shatterproof glass, and stamped metal casing with plastic molding, 8 x 10 x 13 1/2" (20.3 x 25.4 x 34.3 cm). Mfr: Flos, Italy. Gift of Atelier International, Ltd. MoMA.

Flécheux, Luc (1966–)
French designer.

Biography Flécheux has designed furniture, tableware, and theater sets. His 1986 geometric exercise for earthenware dinner plates by Siècle was based on an amphitheater.
Bibliography *Les carnets du design*, Paris: Mad-Cap Productions/ APCI, 1986: 34.

Fleming, Erik (1894–1954)
Swedish designer and silversmith; active Stockholm.

Training In Berlin and Munich.
Biography 1920, the baron Erik Fleming founded the Atelier Borgila, which became one of Sweden's leading modern silver workshops and specialized in handmade silverwares. However, the Goldsmiths' Company was engaged in the large-scale production of Fleming-designed sterling silver, silver plate, and pewter and bronze ware, and also various art goods. His 1920s designs were classical; those of the 1930s showed angular forms and stepped edges typical of Art Déco and were more architectonic. 1930s, Fleming and Wiwen Nilsson were preeminent in Swedish silver. 1932, the Swedish government commissioned Fleming to produce an 800-piece silver set as a wedding present for Prince Gustaf Adolf and Princess Sybilla. 1938–39, he taught in the US, and Margaret Craver trained and worked for some years under Fleming.
Exhibition Work subject of 1994 exhibition, Nationalmuseum, Stockholm (catalog below).
Bibliography Carl Hernmarck, *Erik Fleming och Atelier Borgila*, Stockholm: Atelier Borgila, 1955. Annelies Krekel-Aalberse, *Art Nouveau and Art Déco Silver*, New York: Abrams, 1989. Cat., Jan von Gerber, *Erik Fleming, Atelier Borgila*, Stockholm: Nationalmuseum, 1994.

Flexform
Italian furniture manufacturer; located Meda.

History Romeo, Pietro, and Agostino Galimberti founded Figli di Giovanni Galimberti for the production of lacquered and upholstered furniture. 1959, the name was changed to Flexform; the production of contemporary furniture styles began, with the 1960 opening of a new plant and showroom. 1967 when a second factory was opened, Flexform issued limited joint stock. Today, the firm is managed by the sons of the founders. Commissioned designers have included Sergio Asti, Cini Boeri, Rodolfo Bonetto, Joe Colombo, and, more recently, Paolo Nava and Antonio Citterio, and Asnago/Vender. The firm cosponsors Formula 1 and C.I.V.T. automobile races (including the Porsche Pirelli Supercup) and gymnasts Igor Cassina, Andrea Coppolino, and Jordan Jovtchev.
Bibliography www.flexform.it.

Flight, Claude (1888-1955)
British artist and decorator.

Biography Flight is best known for establishing the linocut method of printmaking; was a central figure in Grosvenor School of Modern Art (founded in 1925), where he and Edith Lawrence taught; late 1920s with Lawrence, set up a small interior design and decoration firm; received modest commissions and applied a somewhat daring taste reminiscent of the colorful designs of the Omega workshop.
Bibliography Stephen Calloway, *Twentieth-Century Decoration*, New York: Rizzoli, 1988: 163.

Flögl, Mathilde (1891–1950)
Moravian textile designer; born Brno (now Czech Republic).

Training 1909–16 under Oskar Strnad, A. Böhm, A. von Kenner, and Josef Hoffmann, Kunstgewerbeschule, Vienna.
Biography 1916–31, she was on the staff of the Wiener Werkstätte, designing textiles, clothing, fashion accessories, and lace, and contributing to the 1914–15 fashion folder *Die Mode*; produced jewelry in ivory and enamel; decorated glass for Loetz in Bohemia. She and Josef Hoffmann edited and produced the commemorative album (with a molded three-dimensional binding by 'Vally' Wieselthier and Gudrun Baudisch) that acknowledged the 25th anniversary of the workshop: *Die Wiener Werkstatte, 1903–1928: Modernes Kunstgewerbe und sein*

Flexform: Joe Colombo. Tube chair nesting and combinable elements. 1969. PVC plastic tubes, padded with polyurethane, covered in fabric. Mfr.: Flexform, Italy. Gift of the mfr. MoMA.

Weg (1929), published by Krystall-Verlag, Vienna.
Bibliography Günther Feuerstein, *Vienna—Present and Past: Arts and Crafts—Applied Art—Design*, Vienna: Jugend und Volk, 1976. Deanna F. Cera (ed.), *Jewels of Fantasy: Costume Jewelry of the 20th Century*, New York: Abrams, 1992.

Flos

Italian lighting manufacturer; located Bovezzo.

History 1959, Arturo Eisenkeil from Merano, an importer of a spray-on plastic coating produced in the US, was searching for possible applications in Itality. 1962, Eisenkeil, Dino Gavina, and Cesar Cassina established the lighting firm Flos in Merano, Italy, and began producing lighting fixtures made from this cocoon *floss*. Maria Sinoncini and Cesare Cassina were directors, followed by Sergio Gandini. Pier Giacomo Castiglioni was put in charge of design, followed by brother Achille Castiglioni and Tobia Scarpa (and soon after by wife Afra Scarpa). Flos was eventually moved to the Brescia area. Its earliest models by the Castiglionis, in the cocoon material, were 1973 Teli synthetic fabric (designed 1959), Viscontea, and Taraxacum stretched-polymer-skin hanging lights (both designed 1960), and 1962 Gatto floor lamp. 1962 Arco arching lamp by A. Castiglioni (who designed for the firm to his 2002 death) revolutionized the classical chandelier. Other designers have been Kazuhide Takahama, Mariyo Tagi with the Studio Simón, Valerio Sacchetti, and many others. 1968, the first showroom (designed by A. Castiglioni) was opened in Milan, then, 1971, others followed in Rome and Florence. 1974, bought Arteluce. 1983, Flos USA was established in Huntington Station, N.Y. The firm acknowledged its international influence with the first commissions from Philippe Starck in 1988; continued its non-Italian stable of designers with 1998 lamps, including Jasper Morrison's Glo-Ball and Konstantin Grcic's May Day and Boxer; also produced Antonio Citterio's Lastra. Grcic continued with 2000 Magnum and Hertz ceiling spots.
Bibliography Virgilio Vercelloni, *The Adventure of Design: Gavina*, New York: Rizzoli, 1987. http://www.flos.net.
> See Arteluce.

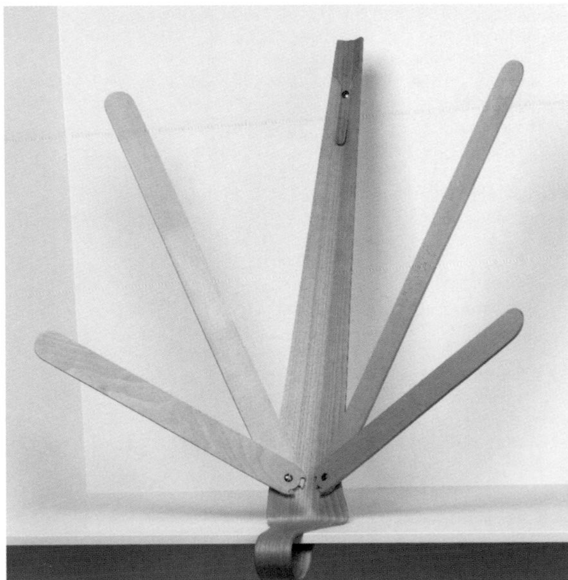

Johannes Foersom and Peter Hiort-Loerenzen. Folding newspaper holder. 1981. Laminated beechwood, 29 x 23 1/4 x 15" (73.7 x 59 x 38.1 cm). Mfr.: Hospitalsartikler, Denmark (c. 1981–88). Gift of the mfr. MoMA.

Flou

Italian furniture firm; located Meda.

History 1970, Rosario Messina established the firm Flou for bed manufacture; began production with Lodovico Magistretti's 'textile bed' in numerous configurations, still in production today. The firm has commissioned numerous designs from Magistretti, including the 1984 Ermellino bed. Other designers have been Rodolfo Dordoni, Massimo Iosa Ghini, Enzo Mari, Vittorio Prato, and studio Sigla (Marina Bani, Patrizia Scarzella, Marco Penati), and studio Opera Work in Progress (Mario Dell'Orto, Emanuela Garbin, Enrico Cattaneo).
Bibliography 'Milan à l'Heure du Design,' *Maison et Jardin*, April 1992: 127.

Flygenring, Hans (1881–1958)

Danish ceramicist.

Training 1907–22 under Johan Rohde, Det Kongelige Danske Kunstakademi, Copenhagen.
Biography 1920–2, Flygenring worked at Porsgrunds Porselænsfabrik in Porsgrunn, as the artistic director.
Bibliography Fredrik Wildhagen, *Norge i Form*, Oslo: Stenersen, 1988: 85. Jennifer Hawkins Opie, *Scandinavia: Ceramics and Glass in the Twentieth Century*, New York: Rizzoli, 1989.

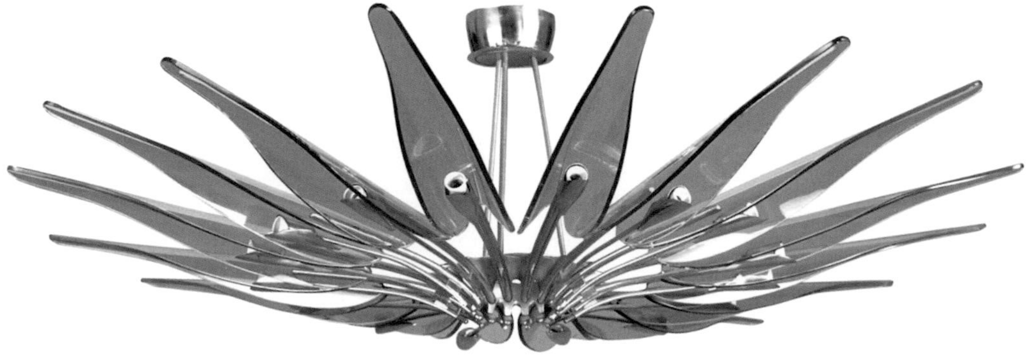

FontanaArte. Margarite ceiling lamp. 1956–57. Tinted glass and brass, h. 18 1/2" (47 cm). Mfr.: FontanaArte, Italy. Courtesy Quittenbaum Kunstauktionen, Munich.

Foersom, Johannes (1947–)

Danish furniture designer.

Training To 1969, furniture-carpentry apprentice, Gustav Gerthelsen, Copenhagen; to 1972, Kunsthåndværkskolen, Copenhagen.
Biography 1972, Foersom established his own design studio and, from 1977, was in partnership with Peter Hiort-Lorenzen; 1975, lecturer, Danmarks Designskole, Denmark; clients have included Berga Form, Erik Jørgensen Møbelfabrik, ICF, Lammhults, and Svendborgt.
Citations Most with Hiort-Lorenzen: 1970, 1972, 1977 Danish State Art's Fund; 1974, 1975 Kröyer's Memorial Award; 1980 Danmarks Nationalbank Jubilee Foundation; 1985 Annual Award, Danish Furniture manufacturers; 1992, 1994, 1995, 1999 Red Dot awards, Design Zentrum Nordrhein Westfalen, Essen; 1994 Forsnäs Prize; 1995, 1996, 1997 Bo Bedre's Design Award; 1995 Best of NeoCon, Chicago; 1998 Bruno Mathsson Award; 2000 and 2002 Excellent Swedish Form.
Bibliography www.lammhults.se.
> See Hiort-Lorenzen, Peter.

Fog, Astrid (1911–)

Danish designer.

Biography Fog designed her first jewelry collection for Georg Jensen Sølvsmedie in 1969; also designed clothing and lamps and worked with Royal Copenhagen Porcelain Manufactory and continued with Georg Jensen's.
Bibliography Cat., *Georg Jensen Silversmithy: 77 Artists, 75 Years*, Washington: Smithsonian, 1980.

Follot, Paul (1877–1941)

French decorative artist and sculptor; born Paris.

Training Under Eugène Grasset, École Normale d'Enseignement du Dessin, Paris.
Biography His early graphic design showed an interest in medieval and Pre-Raphaelite art. 1901, he joined Julius Meier-Graefe's shop La Maison Moderne in Paris, where he met Maurice Dufrêne and for which he designed bronzes, jewelry, and fabrics; was a founding member of artists' group L'Art dans Tout; 1904, began as an independent artist. He moved from abundant carved decoration influenced by English styles and the 18th-century *style tapissier* and, c. 1909–10, began to seek *des architectures calmes* (tranquil architecture) through the use of beautiful and rare materials, refined techniques, and harmonious and balanced forms in the emerging Art Déco style. Wedgwood commissioned him in 1911 to design a range of ceramics, its production delayed by World War I until 1919. He contributed to the decoration of oceanliners, including 1921 *Paris* and the *appartement de luxe* for 1935 *Normandie*; succeeded Grasset as professor of an advanced course on Parisian decorative arts; 1923, became artistic director of interior-decoration studio Pomone of Au Bon Marché department store in Paris and its director to 1928. His rugs were produced by Schenck. Early 1920s, he designed silver by Orfèvrerie Christofle and, 1925, by Lapparra. The wood carving on his furniture was executed by Laurent Malclès and by Harribey; painted wall panels and pictures by his wife Hélène Follot. 1928, he was made codirector with Serge Chermayeff of the Modern Art Department of Waring and Gillow, a British firm with a branch in Paris, which opened in 1928 with an exhibition of about 60 furnished modern interiors. He was also a teacher and theoretician; considered ornamentation an essential element of design and had no interest in the minimalism of Le Style 25; rejected mass-production art in favor of the aristocratic tradition of luxury.
Exhibitions Work was first shown at 1901 Salon of Société des Artistes Français; showed at Salons of Société des Artistes Décorateurs 1919–35, Société Nationale des Beaux-Arts, and Salon d'Automne 1920–32. Designed the Pomone display in Au Bon Marché exhibit, antechamber of Une Ambassade Française pavilion, and motifs for Maison Pleyel (including three Pleyel pianos in various pavilions), and Pavillon de Roubaix-Tourcoing, all at 1925 *Exposition Internationale des Arts Décoratifs et Industriels Modernes*, Paris.
Bibliography Guillaume Janneau, 'Notre enquête sur le mobilier moderne: Paul Follot,' *Art et décoration*, no. 40, Nov. 1921: 141–48. Léon Riotor, *Paul Follot*, Paris: La Connaissance, 1923. Guillaume Janneau, *Le luminaire et les moyens d'éclairage nouveaux*, Paris: Charles Moreau, 1st series: plates 17–18, 21, 23, 32, 44, [n.d.]. *Ensembles mobiliers*, vol. II, Paris: Charles Moreau, 1937. E. Mannoni, *Meubles et ensembles: style 1900*, Paris: C. Massin, 1968: 39. Yvonne Brunhammer et al., *Art Nouveau Belgium, France*, Houston: Rice University, 1976. Alastair Duncan, *Art Nouveau and Art Déco Lighting*, New York: Simon & Schuster, 1978. Jessica Rutherford, 'Paul Follot,' *Connoisseur*, vol. 204, June 1980: 86–91. Victor Arwas, *Art Déco*, New York: Abrams, 1980. Jessica Rutherford, *Art Nouveau, Art Deco and the Thirties: The Furniture Collections at Brighton Museum, Brighton:* The Royal Pavilion, Art Gallery and Museums, 1983: 33. Yvonne Brunhammer, *Art Déco Style*, London: Academy, 1983. Annelies Krekel-Aalberse, *Art Nouveau and Art Déco Silver*, New York: Abrams, 1989. Maurice Dufrêne, *Ensembles mobiliers, Exposition internationale 1925*, Paris: Charles Moreau, 1925; Woodbridge, Suffolk: Antique Collectors' Club, 1989: 40.

Fong, Danny Ho (1915–1992)

Chinese furniture manufacturer and designer; born Canton; active Los Angeles.

Biography 1930s, Fong settled in California; 1952 with his wife Muey Fong, founded Tropi-cal, which became a leading producer of contemporary rattan furniture and subsequently also in teak, primarily manufactured in the Philippines and Indonesia. Fong's Tropi-cal designs were noted for their lightness. His two sons, Ted and Miller, took over the family business in 1985 and soon changed the name to Fong Brothers Company, Los Angeles.
Bibliography Steve Holley, 'Tracy Fong's California Spin on Wicker,' *Elle Decor*, Aug. 1991: 24.

Fong, Tracy (1975–)

American furniture designer; active San Francisco; granddaughter of Danny Ho Fong.

Training Art Center College of Design, Pasadena, Cal.
Biography She designed 1988 SOFA (Studio of Furniture Art) collection, her first furniture, followed by a collection of chairs and occasional pieces. Other work has included a special Southeast Asian promo-

tion for Seibu department store in Tokyo and three-drawer Three-D side chair and other seating by T-Style group of Fong Brothers, where she has been the head designer.
Exhibitions SOFA shown at international merchandise event, Tokyo; next collection at international furniture event, Manila.
Bibliography Steve Holley, 'Tracy Fong's California Spin on Wicker,' *Elle Decor*, Aug. 1991: 24.

Fontaine
French interior designers; located Paris.

Biography 1920–40, Fontaine regularly commissioned consultant decorators, including Maurice Dufrêne, René Prou, André Groult, Louis Süe and André Mare, and Pierre-Paul Montagnac.
Exhibitions The Fontaine pavilion (designed by Süe and Mare) was installed at 1925 *Exposition Internationale des Arts Décoratifs et Industriels Modernes*, Paris.
Bibliography Pierre Kjellberg, *Art déco: les maîtres du mobilier, le décor des paquebots*, Paris: Amateur, 1986/1990.

FontanaArte
Italian lighting and furniture company; located Corsico, Milan.

History 1932, FontanaArte was founded by Gio Ponti as a design division of Luigi Fontana's glass firm, and incorporated the Bottega di Pietro Chiesa. 1933, Ponti appointed Chiesa the artistic director of FontanaArte, and the two of them designed a number of products, including lighting, furniture (incorporating glass), and tabletop items. 1979, a private group bought the firm, headed by Carlo Guglielmi, with Gae Aulenti as the artistic director and Pieri Luigi Cerri in charge of advertising materials and the corporate image. Piero Castiglio consulted on lighting technology. Daniela Puppa and Franco Raggi were in charge of exhibitions, showrooms, and other interiors. Gruppo FontanaArte has incorporated these brands: Fontana-Arte with glass as the main element, Candle for a young market (acquired 1993), Schopenhauer furniture (acquired 1993), Naskaloris office lighting (acquired 1996), Tecnica contract lighting fixtures (established 1996), FontanaArte Arredo furniture, and Gli Oggetti di FontanaArte tabletop products (established 1998).
Bibliography Roberto Aloi, *L'arredamento moderno*, Milan: Hoepli, 1934. Gae Aulenti et al., *FontanaArte: una storia trasparente*, Milan: Skira, 1998.
> See Chiesa, Pietro.

Forbicini, Fulvio (1952–)
Italian industrial designer; born Ravenna.

Training To 1975, in industrial design, Florence.
Biography For a time, Forbicini worked for furniture manufacturer Roche-Bobois; subsequently, opened a design studio with Fabrizio Ballardini; they designed the widely published 1988–89 Ribalta sofa produced by Arflex, a kind of day bed, its corners turned up to form six different positions.
Exhibitions Ribalta sofa shown at 1991 *Mobili Italiani 1961–1991: Le Varie Età dei Linguaggi* exhibition, Salone del Mobile, Milan.
Bibliography Albrecht Bangert and Karl Michael Armer, *80s Style: Designs of the Decade*, New York: Abbeville, 1990: 38, 230. *Mobili italiani 1961–1991: le varie età dei linguaggi*, Milan: Cosmit, 1992.

Forcolini, Carlo (1947–)
Italian designer; born Como; active Milan.

Training Liceo Artistico di Brera; painting and sculpture, Accademia di Belle Arti di Brera; both Milan.
Biography 1965, Forcolini, Frederico Pedrocchi, and Maurizio Bertoni experimented with kinetic art. 1970–74, Forcolini designed his first products, with Roberto Coizet and Piergiorgio Vianello, produced by Amar Collezioni in Milan. From 1975, his encounter with Vico Magistretti was influential on his future work as a designer. 1978, he began his activity as an independent designer, working between Milan and London; 1979 with partners, founded manufacturer Alias to produce furniture and furnishings designed by himself, Mario Botta, Giandomenico Belotti, Vico Magistretti, and Alberto Meda; 1980, began designing lighting for Artemide, including mid-1980s Polifemo lamp and 1985 Icaro wall light; 1981, founded Artemide GB in the UK as a subsidiary of Artemide Italia; 1989, became artistic director of a new firm in the Artemide Group; returned to Italy; was artistic director of Sidecar. Furniture and furnishings by Forcolini for Alias have included: 1979 Alien side chair, 1982 Aleph mirror, 1983 Buñel dressing table and Onlyou plant stand, 1984 Apocalypse Now coffee table in rustable steel with a lighting fixture in the center, 1985 Bukowsky's Holiday coat rack and Karaté small table, 1986 Signorina Chan chair, 1987 Le Voyeur clock, 1991 Ran bookshelves and Uni-X sofa. By Futura: 2002 Very. By Artemide: 1980 Alesia, 1983 Polifemo, 1984 Icaro, 1985 Circe, and 1987 Nestore lamps. By Nemo: 1997 Auriga, 1998 Hydra, 2001 Regulus-system lamps. By Cassina: 1994 Ghiro bed. By Pomellato: 1995 Dodo clocks. 1993, Forcolini founded Nemo for lighting and, 1998, Forcolini Lab as a multidisciplinary studio; was president, Associazione per il Disegno Industriale (ADI). Alias has become a division of the Fimalac Group (with Fimalac, Cassina, and Nemo Italianluce).
Exhibitions Participated in editions of the Triennale di Milano. From 1983, work shown worldwide. Participated with Melotti, Botta, and Meda in 1987 *Ways of Planning*, Villa Pignatelli Museum, Naples. Work shown at 1990 Tokyo *Creativitalia* exhibition on Italian design.
Bibliography Fumio Shimizu and Studio Matteo Thun (eds.), *The Italian Design: Descendants of Leonardo da Vinci*, Tokyo: Graphic-sha, 1987: 325. Penny Sparke, *Design in Italy*, London: Calman and King, 1988. Cat., Fulvio Irace et al., *Carlo Forcolini: immaginare le cose*, Milan: Electa, 1990. Gabriele Lueg, *Halogen—20. Jahre neues Licht*, Laupheim: Novus, 1991. Matthias Dietz and Michael Monninger, *300 Lights—Leuchten—Lampes*, Cologne: Taschen, 1993. Mel Byars, *50 Chairs...*, Hove: Rotovision, 1996.

Formes Utiles
French organization and exhibitions; located Paris.

History 1949, Formes Utiles became an independent association of Union des Artistes Modernes (UAM) through the influence of René Herbst and Charlotte Perriand and its first exhibition held at Musée des Arts Décoratifs in Paris. Its theoretician was architect André Hermant. It opened its exhibitions to foreigners; from 1951, held exhibitions organized by Salon des Arts Ménagers to present furniture, furnishings, and equipment designed for mass production. The subjects of its various exhibitions included sanitation, 1951; sanitary seating, 1952; portable and small lighting fixtures and drinking glasses, 1953; rattan chairs, cutlery, and door knobs, 1954; casseroles, children's furniture, and the first exhibition of plastic furniture, 1956; and table settings, tableware, and table cloths. Painters and sculptors were invited to all exhibitions; Alexander Calder, Le Corbusier, Fernand Léger, Joan Miró, and others participated.
Bibliography Arlette Barré-Despond, *UAM*, Paris: Regard, 1986: 105–07. Cat., *Les années UAM 1929–1958*, Paris: Musée des Arts Décoratifs, 1988: 178–79.

Formica
Proprietary plastic material.

History 1907, Herbert A. Faber and Daniel J. O'Conor met in their first year at Westinghouse in Pittsburgh. 1910, Bakelite was used at Westinghouse to impregnate heavy canvas. 1911, O'Conor became head of the process section of the research-engineering department. O'Conor produced his first laminated sheet by winding and coating

Paul Follot. Partial coffee service. 1902. Silver-plated brass with gilded interiors, sugar bowl h. 4 3/4" (12.2 cm), creamer h. 3 13/16" (9.7 cm). Mfr.: F. W. Quist, Germany. Courtesy Quittenbaum Kunstauktienen, Munich.

paper on a mandrel. The resulting uncured tube was slit and then flattened in a press and, thus, Formica, as it was subsequently named, was first manufactured in 1913, with a 1918 patent for the process assigned to Westinghouse. Because Westinghouse did not make use of the product, Faber and O'Conor left Westinghouse in 1913 and settled in Cincinnati. Lawyer and banker J.G. Tomlin bought a one-third share in their newly formed Formica Company of Cincinnati. The acronym name (FORm MICA) was coined by Faber from mica, the expensive mineral used for insulation. After a poor first year, Tomlin brought in two other partners, lawyer John L. Vest and banker David Wallace. The firm was incorporated as The Formica Insulation Company, producing only rings and tubes initially. By 1921, Formica had begun to be used as a laminate in the production of radio cabinets. By 1923, the firm was financially sound and began the successful production of gears for automobile engines. 1927, the addition of 'a lithographed wood grain' marked the beginning of the modern Formica period as decorative sheets. By 1930, Formica was both a consumer and an industrial product. Late 1940s, industrial designer Brooks Stevens worked with Formica to create Luxwood, the wood-grain laminate used on much of the furniture of the time and a replacement for its earlier unsatisfactory Realwood pattern. The 1947 license agreement with de la Rue in London opened the door for production in Europe to 1977. 1956, the firm was purchased by American Cyanamid and became its subsidiary, The Formica Company. 1950s, Raymond Loewy Associates designed patterns as well as the Formica logo; a serif type font was replaced by designer Michael Abramson in 1980 with the sans-serif Helvetica font. 1982, ColorCore solid laminate was introduced. 1985, Formica's senior managers and private investors bought the firm from American Cyanamid.
Exhibitions Formica House built at 1939–40 *New York World's Fair: The World of Tomorrow*, the kitchen of which was rebuilt for 1989 *Remembering the Future: The New York World's Fairs from 1939 to 1964*, Queens Museum, New York City. ColorCore subject of Formica-sponsored exhibitions, including 1986 *Surface and Ornament* and *Material Evidence: New Color Techniques in Handmade Furniture*, that included the work of established designers, artists, and architects, and toured the US. Formica subject of 1987 *A Material World*, National Museum of American History, Washington, D.C.
Bibliography Susan Grant Lewin (ed.), *Formica and Design: From the Counter Top to High Art*, New York: Rizzoli, 1991.

Formica, Giovanella (1957–)
Italian designer; born Florence.

Training To 1982, Facoltà di Architettura, Università degli Studi, Florence.
Biography For a year, Formica was an assistant of the planning course held by Remo Buti at the university in Florence; for six years, collaborated with Sottsass Associati in Milan; 1987 with Beppe Caturegli, opened a studio in Milan, becoming active in industrial design projects for Sanjo in Japan and Max Ray and architectural projects in Italy and India. From 1987, they periodically traveled in Africa and South India, developing a series of projects over the years there; from 1988, contributed to journal *Terrazzo*; from 1993, were advisors to Computer Associates in Milan and Rome. 1992, Formica was a visiting professor of the study course, Department of Architecture, Catholic University of Washington, D.C., organized in Italy.
Exhibitions Participated in numerous venues, including Triennale di Milano and Biennale di Venezia; 1987, exhibition of Memphis's work; 1993 *Architettura italiana contemporanea: esperienze ricerche delle nuove generazioni,* Milan, Genoa, Palermo, and Bari. With Caturegli, first prize, residential-settlement invitation competition; with Caturegli, 1993 first prize, Pantone European Colour Awards for architecture.
Bibliography Fumio Shimizu and Studio Matteo Thun (eds.), *The Italian Design: Descendants of Leonardo da Vinci*, Tokyo: Graphic-sha, 1987.
> Caturegli, 'Beppe' Giuseppe.

Formosa, Daniel (1953–)
American industrial designer.

Training Industrial design, Syracuse (N.Y.) University; ergonomics and biomechanics, New York University, New York.
Biography Formosa holds several patents in consumer products and equipment design; from 1981, was a consultant at Smart Design studio in New York. Clients have included Atomic Energy of Canada, Corning Glass sunglass products, Esselté Letraset, IBM, International Playtex infant care, Kepner-Tregoe, Merck Sharp & Dohme, Pfizer Medical, Raytheon Nuclear Diagnostics, and Singer.
Citations Three Designer's Choice Awards, *I.D.* magazine.

Fornasetti, Piero (1913–1988)
Italian artist-designer; born Milan.

Training 1930–32, Accademia di Belle Arti di Brera, Milan.
Biography After Gio Ponti saw Fornasetti's work at 1940 (7th) Triennale di Milano, Fornasetti became a student of Ponti and, subsequently, his protégé and assistant, designing the Lunari commissioned by Ponti; 1942, executed frescoes for Palazzo Bo in Padova; 1943–46, was exiled in Switzerland; collaborated with Ponti on a number of projects, replicating the 17th-century technique of applying two-dimensional images to furniture for a three-dimensional effect. The model forms were designed by Gio Ponti and decorated by Fornasetti. Fornasetti's appliqués were also used on ceramics blanks produced by Eschenbach Arzberg and Richard Ginori. Fornasetti designed 1950 interiors of the Casino in San Remo and 1952 oceanliner *Andrea Doria*; was a designer, artist, illustrator, printer, graphic designer, craftsperson, manufacturer, and business entrepreneur, whose products were sold in shops including his own Galeria dei Bibliofili, established with associates in 1970, and in his shop Themes and Variations in London, established in 1980. He received several major commissions, including the ballroom in the Time-Life building in New York. His style was an interpretation of Surrealist *trompe-l'oeil,* primarily in black-and-white, which he applied or had applied by others to almost everything—from cabinets and chairs to ceramics, even slatted window blinds and a 1984 decorated bicycle. His career spanned three-quarters of a century. Since his death, his business has continued.
Exhibitions Work included in numerous venues such as 1940 (7th) Triennale di Milano (scarves) and 1947 (8th) edition (ceramics commissioned by Ponti), 1948 Salon of Société des Artistes Décorateurs, Paris, 1950 *Italy at Work*, touring the US for a year. From the first (1944) venue in the Foyer des Étudiants in Geneva, work subject of numerous exhibitions, including 1991–92 *Fornasetti: Designer of Dreams*, Victoria and Albert Museum, London.
Bibliography Patrick Mauriès, *Fornasetti: Designer of Dreams*, London and Paris: Thames & Hudson, Boston: Little, Brown, 1991.

Forsell, Ulla (1944–)
Swedish glassware designer.

Training 1966–71, Konstfackskolan, Stockholm; 1971–73, Orrefors Bruk glass school; 1972, Gerrit Rietveld Akademie, Amsterdam.
Biography Forsell worked at Orrefors before she set up her own workshop in Stockholm in 1974. With Åsa Brandt, Eva Ullberg, and Anders Wingård, she established the workshop/studio Freeblowers.
Bibliography Cat., David Revere McFadden (ed.), *Scandinavian Modern Design 1880–1980*, New York: Abrams, 1982: 263, no. 270. Jennifer Hawkins Opie, *Scandinavia: Ceramics and Glass in the Twentieth Century*, New York: Rizzoli, 1989.

Förster, Monica (1966–)
Swedish furniture designer; born Stockholm.

Training To 1995, Anders Beckman School of Design, Stockholm; 1997, furniture and interior design, Konstfack, Stockholm.
Biography Förster calls on new technologies and materials in her designs of furniture, furnishings, and lighting; 2002, became one of the second group of member designers of Snowcrash; has also designed for Elle Interior, Magis, and Simplicitas. Her work by David Design has included 1999 Silikon lamp in molded heat-resistant silicon with the appearance of glass, 2001 Bob furniture in single-sided flame-resistant polyester, and 2001 Load rechargeable cordless lamp in rotationally molded ethylenevinylacetate (EVA, new-class polymeric-plastic material).
Exhibitions/citations Work included in *Svensk Form,* 2000 Summer Olympiad in Sydney; 2000 *Ny sydsvensk form*, Design Center, Malmö; 2000 exhibition, Centre Culturel Suèdois, Paris; 2001 *3D + Staging 3D Design*, traveling to Brussels, Dublin, and Berlin; 2001 *Spiral Garden* (Load lamp), Tokyo. 1998 and 1999 awards, Sweden Innovation Centre; 1999, 2-year grant, The Art Grants Committee, Sweden; 2000 Design Plus prize (Silikon lamp), Ambiente fair, Frankfurt.

Forstner, Leopold (1878–1936)
Austrian mosaic craftsperson; born Leonfelden.

Training Under Kolomann Moser, Kunsgewerbeschule, Vienna.
Biography 1908, Forstner established the Mosaikwerkstätte and, 1918, continued his specialty in mosaics with the establishment of the Stockerau als Edelglas-, Mosaik- und Emailwerkstätte; was active with Moser and Josef Hoffmann's Wiener Werkstätte and the Österreichi-

Piero Fornasetti and Gio Ponti. Architettura secretary. 1951. Printed wood and metal, 86¼ x 31⅞ x 15⅜" (219 x 81 x 39 cm). Mfr.: Fornasetti Atelier, Italy. Courtesy Quittenbaum Kunstauktionen, Munich.

scher Werkbund. Known for his high-quality mosaic work, Forstner contributed to Otto Wagner's 1904–1907 Kirche am Steinhof and Josef Hoffmann's 1905–1911 Palais Stoclet in Brussels and 1913 Ast house in Vienna.
Bibliography Günther Feuerstein, *Vienna—Present and Past: Arts and Crafts —Applied Art—Design*, Vienna: Jugend und Volk, 1976.

Forsyth, Gordon Mitchell (1879–1952)
British artist, designer, decorator, ceramicist, calligrapher, teacher, and writer; father of Moira Forsyth.

Training Robert Gordon's College, Grays School of Art, Aberdeen.
Biography 1902–05, Forsyth was the artistic director of Minton, Hollins and Co.; to 1915, was the artistic director of Pilkington's Royal Lancastrian Pottery in Manchester, where he specialized in lusterware, managing its pottery artists, who included Geuldys Rodgers, W.S. Mycock, and Richard Joyce. Forsyth was a fellow, British Society of Master Glass Painters; principal, Stoke-on-Trent Schools of Art; superintendent, Art Institution of the City of Stoke-on-Trent; art advisor, British Pottery Manufacturers Federation. He wrote *Art and Craft of the Potter* (London: Chapman & Hall, 1934) and *Twentieth Century Ceramics...* (London: The Studio, 1936).
Citations Received medals as a painter at exhibitions in Paris, Venice, Turin, Brussels, and in Britain.
Bibliography Cat., *Europäisches Keramik des Jugenstils*, Düsseldorf: Hetjens-Museum, 1974. Cat., *Thirties: British Art and Design Before the War*, London: Arts Council of Great Britain/Hayward Gallery, 1979. *British Art and Design, 1900–1960*, London: Victoria and Albert Museum, 1983.

Forsyth, Moira (1905–1991)
British ceramicist and stained-glass artist; daughter of Gordon Mitchell Forsyth.

Training Burslem School of Art; 1926–30 under Martin Travers, stained glass, Royal College of Art, London.
Biography She set up her own workshop in Brickhouse Street in Burslem, using a local pottery for her firing; produced stained-glass commissions for buildings for which Edward Maufe was architect, including the dome of St. Joseph's Church in Burslem and windows in Guildford Cathedral and St. Columba's Church in London; continued to produce earthenware figures; prepared 1942 report on the pottery industry for Nuffield College; 1943–46, was a research officer for southeast England, Ministry of Town and Country Planning; after World War II, rendered heraldic windows for the chapel of Eton College, the Benedictine window for Norwich Cathedral, and 1970s window for the Benedictine abbey in Fort Augustus; was a fellow and council member, Master Glass Painters.
Exhibitions 1930–32 Cello Player earthenware figure shown at 1979–80 *Thirties* exhibition, Hayward Gallery, London (catalog below).
Bibliography Cat., *Thirties: British Art and Design Before the War*, London: Arts Council of Great Britain/Hayward Gallery, 1979.

Fortuny y Madrazo, Mariano (1871–1949)
Spanish designer; born Granada; active Venice.

Training In Paris.
Biography Fortuny was a painter, engraver, sculptor, photographer, and interior, lighting, furniture, theatrical-set, and costume designer with a deep knowledge of historical textiles; collaborated with his wife Henriette on the design and printing of the now-legendary Fortuny fabrics printed in metallic inks and made into narrow-pleated silks; created a secret method for printing and embossing fabric to replicate ancient silk brocades, interpreting European Renaissance, Turkish, Indian, Chinese, Japanese, and Persian motifs. Working in a palazzo in Venice, he imported raw, undyed fabric and made his own vegetable dyes, colors, blocks, stencils, and machinery. Fortuny invented a process, patented in 1911, that used stencils made of very fine cloth, like silk. He soaked a fabric in gelatin and manually or photographically outlined the design with a chemical solution. When exposed to light, the treated area became fixed, and the other areas disappeared when washed. The method for creating the flaky, uneven appearance is still being kept a secret today. But Fortuny may have smeared pigments over a natural paste such as albumin and pressed colors (even gold and silver) into the fabric with a roller or other special tool. The process was the forerunner of modern rotary screen printing. His garment designs, including Aesthetic-style Empire-line dresses, coats, and capes, changed little from early 1900s to his death. His best-known design was the 1909 Delphos dress with a hem weighted with beads, which he patented; warp-pleated and body-sheathing, it was, according to Fortuny, properly worn with ancient Greek jewelry and sandals. It kept its pleats when tied in a knot and stored in a small box. This pleated-silk technique has been subsequently replicated by Mary MacFadden for clothing and Gretchen Bellinger for interior-design use. After Fortuny's death, interior designer Elsie McNeil (aka the countessa Gozzi) presided over the Fortuny estate, Palazzo Orfei, Venice, now the Fortuny Museum, where she attempted to guard the secrets of the fabric manufacture. His Paris shop was located at 67, rue Pierre-Charron. His large 1907 Arc lamp was reissued from 1979 by Écart International. His early so-called Chinese lights (printed silk covering a wire frame) are likewise being reproduced. Other work included 1909 Knossos scarves, and first cyclorama (for the comtesse de Béarn's private theater in Paris and its proscenium curtain). 1910s, Allgemeine Elektrizitäts Gesellschaft (AEG) installed his dome and lighting system in a number of European theaters. Late-19th- and early-20th-century stage-set designs included that for Wagner's opera *Tristan und Isolde* (La Scala, Milan, 1910).
Exhibitions Work subject of numerous exhibitions including in 1934, Galerie Hector Brame, Paris; 1935, Galleria Dedalo, Milan; 1965, Ca Pesaro, Museo d'Arte Moderna, Venice; 1980 and 1994, Biblioteca Nacional, Madrid; 1989, Centre Cultural, Fundació Caixa de Pensions, Barcelona; 1996–97, Biblioteca Nazionale Marciana, Venice; 1997, Museu Salvador Vilaseca, Barcelona; 1998–99, Carmen Thyssen-Bornemisza collection, Museo Civico Castello Ursino, Catania, and Accademia di Spagna, Rome.
Bibliography M. Zamacois, *Mariano Fortuny y Madrazo*, Milan: Galeria Dedalo, 1935. Elena Paez, *Exposición Fortuny y Marsal y Fortuny y Madrazo*, Madrid: Biblioteca Nacional, 1951. Doretta Davanzo Poli, *Seta & Oro: La collezione tessile di Mariano Fortuny*, Venice: Arsenale, 1997. Anne-Marie Deschodt, *Mariano Fortuny: un magicien de Venise*, Paris: Regard, 1979. Guillermo de Osma et al., *Mariano Fortuny (1871–1949)*, Lyon: Musée Historique des Tissus; Brighton: Brighton Museum, 1980. Cat. raisonné, Rosa Vives i Piqué, *Fortuny, Gravador: Estudi Crític i Catàleg Raonat*, Reus: Associació d'Estudis Reusencs, 1991. Guillermo de Osma, *Fortuny: The Life and Work of Mariano Fortuny*,

Kaj Franck. Kilta covered containers. 1948. Glazed earthenware, tall container h. 4 5/8 x x dia. 4 1/8" (11.7 x 10.5 cm), short container h. 2 1/4 x dia. 4 1/8" (5.7 x 10.5 cm), lids dia. 4 5/16" (11 cm). Mfr.: Arabia/Wärtsilä, Helsinki. Gift of Wärtsilä Corp. MoMA.

London: Aurum, 1994. Delphine Desyeaux, *Fortuny*, Paris: Assouline, 1998. Mel Byars, 'To Be Continued,' *Metropolitan Home*, Nov.–Dec. 1999: 80+.

Foster, Norman (1935–)

British architect and designer; born Manchester; active London.

Training To 1963, architecture and urbanism, Manchester University; architecture, Yale University, New Haven, Conn.
Biography 1963, Foster began his architecture practice; 1966, opened architecture studio Team 4 with wife Wendy Foster, Su Rogers, and Richard Rogers; with Richard Rogers, became a pioneer of high-tech design based on the development of an architectural aesthetic determined by modern technological equipment and fittings. From 1967, the firm operated as Foster Associates with ten partners, Norman and Wendy Foster, Loren Butt, Chubby S. Chhabra, Spencer de Gray, Roy Fleetwood, Birkin Haward, James Meller, Graham Phillips, and Mark Robertson. 1968–83, Foster collaborated with Buckminster Fuller and lectured in the US and Europe; was known for his neutral spaces that could be filled according to the occupants' requirements for differentiated functions. He and/or his staff designed door handles by Fusital; 1986 Nomos furniture system by Tecno (workstations and tables, originally stemming from a 1981 design for Foster's own offices, in aluminum, plastic, and steel with exposed construction); 1986 lighting system by Erco for Hong Kong and Shanghai Bank; 1988 carpets in Dialog collection by Vorwerk. Foster was vice-president, Architectural Association, London; member of the council, Royal College of Art, London; honorary member, Bund Deutscher Architekten; member, International Academy of Architecture, Sofia. Currently, Foster and Partners employs 500 people in studios in London, Berlin, and Hong Kong. Buildings have included 1971 passenger terminal and administration building, Fred Olsen Lines, London; 1975 Willis-Faber and Dumas Insurances head office, Ipswich; 1978 Sainsbury Centre for the Visual Arts, University of East Anglia, near Norwich; 1979–86 Hammersmith Centre, London; 1981–91 Stansted airport terminal, Essex; 1983 Renault distribution center, Swindon; 1985–93 Carré d'Art, Nîmes; 1986 Hong Kong and Shanghai Bank Tower, Hong Kong; 1987 Century Tower, Hong Kong; 1992–99 Reichstag headquarters, Berlin; 1997 Commerzbank headquarters, Berlin; from 2000, British Museum additions, London; 2001 Millennium Bridge and 2003 Greater London Assembly, London.
Exhibitions/citations Work shown at The Museum of Modern Art, New York; Royal Academy, London; and exhibitions including 1979 *Transformations in Modern Architecture* and 1983 *3 Skyscrapers*, both The Museum of Modern Art, New York. Nomos furniture shown at 1991 *Mobili Italiani 1961–1991: Le Varie Età dei Linguaggi*, Milan. Work subject of 1988 exhibition, Florence; 1989, Barcelona; 1991, Berlin. 1983 gold medal, Royal Institute of British Architects; 1999 Pritzker Archi-tecture Prize; 1999, knighthood.
Bibliography *Foster Associates, London*, 1979. François Chaslin et al., *Norman Foster*, Milan/Paris: Electa Moniteur, 1986. *Foster Associates and Tecno: Nomos*, Milan: Tecno, 1986. Juli Capella and Quim Larrea, *Designed by Architects in the 1980s*, New York; Rizzoli, 1988. Volker Fischer, *Bodenreform: Teppichboden von Künstlern und Architekten*, Berlin: Ernst und Sohn, 1989. David Jenkins et al., *On Foster... Foster on*, Munich/New York: Prestel, 2000. David Jenkins, *Norman Foster: Catalogue of Work*, Munich and New York: Prestel, 2001.

Fourniture

French furniture studio; located Paris.

History 1985, Michel Bouisson founded Fourniture as a furniture and interior-design studio; from 1987, edited a furniture collection in wood; produced Bureau pour une Femme and 1989 MB side chair; commissioned designers, including Marie-Christine Dorner, Rena Dumas, Olivier Gagnère, and Elizabeth Garouste/Mattia Bonetti; produced a desk by Silvain Dubuisson for the Ministère de la Culture, France, and furnishings for the boutique of Christian Lacroix by Garouste/Bonetti. 1999, Bouisson closed Fourniture and became responsible for relations among the designers, schools, and Valorisation de l'Innovations dans l'Ameublement (VIA, French furniture association), Paris.

Fowler, John (1906–1977)

British interior decorator.

Biography Fowler worked first for a printer; subsequently, was a decorator/painter at Thornton Smith in London; worked for antiques dealer and decorator Margaret Kunzer and, from 1931, was the head of her painting studio in the Peter Jones home-furnishings store; 1934, set up his own studio. 1938, he went into partnership with Sibyl Colefax; rarely invented designs but rather adopting them from 18th- and 19th-century fragments; studied draperies in decorative design books by French baroque designer Daniel Marot; during World War II, designed the interior of actor Michael Redgrave's house, in which Fowler incorporated parachute silk for the curtains; Duchess of Hamilton's blue-and-white-chintz bedroom; Queen Elizabeth II's audience room in Buckingham Palace; rooms for Lord Rothermere in Daylesford; rooms for Evangeline Bruce's London flat; and Mrs. James de Rothschild's apartment in Albany. 1946, American expatriate Mrs. Ronald Tree (later, Nancy Lancaster) bought Colefax and Fowler (Fowler himself never owning any part of the business). Fowler's most popular chintz design was, and remains, Old Rose. He used dyed tape borders as an edge to patterns such as Berkeley Sprig, now the logo of Colefax and Fowler. His chintz designs were influenced by Nancy Lancaster's fabric prints, which were deliberately faded by putting furniture in bright sunlight and dyeing the fabrics with tea. Another Fowler invention was the attachment of silk bows to the tops of picture-hanging cords at the cornice.
Bibliography Elizabeth Dickson, 'English Elegance,' *Elle Decor*, Winter 1990: 38. Mark Hampton, *The Legendary Decorators of the Twentieth Century*, New York: Doubleday, 1992. Chester Jones, *Colefax and Fowler: The Best in English Interior Design*, London: Barrie & Jenkins; Boston: Little, Brown & Company/Bullfinch Press Book, 1989.

Foxton, W.

British textile manufacturer; located London.

History 1903, William Foxton (1861–1945) established the firm of W. Foxton; produced textiles designed by artists, including Gregory Brown and Riette Sturge Moore. 1920s, the firm's goods were innovative. Foxton intended to create a collaboration of artists with industry, an

approach he promoted through the firm's advertising; was president of Wholesale Furnishing Textile Association; 1915, became a founding member, Design and Industries Association; was board member, British Institute of Industrial Art (BIIA).
Exhibitions Gregory Brown's fabrics shown at 1925 *Exposition Internationale des Arts Décoratifs et Industriels Modernes*, Paris, and reproduced in Design and Industry Association's yearbook *Design in Modern Industry*. Brown's and Moore's fabrics included in 1979–80 *Thirties* exhibition, Hayward Gallery, London (catalog below).
Bibliography Cat., *Thirties: British Art and Design Before the War*, London: Arts Council of Great Britain/Hayward Gallery, 1979. *British Art and Design, 1900–1960*, London: Victoria and Albert Museum, 1983. Valerie Mendes, *The Victoria and Albert Textile Collection, British Textiles from 1900 to 1937*, London: Victoria and Albert Museum, 1992.

Frágner, Jaroslav (1898–1967)
Czech architect and interior and furniture designer; born Prague.

Training 1917–22, České Vysoké Učení Technické (Czech technical university), Prague.
Biography 1922, Frágner established his own architecture studio in Prague; from 1923 until its 1931 close, was a member, Devětsil group; 1921–23, was active in the Puristická Čyřka group with Evžen Linhart, Karel Honzík, and Vít Obrtel, who applied strong three-dimensional ornament to bare geometric structures and espoused Czech Cubist architecture. Frágner was the first Devětsil architect to turn to the International Style, illustrated by his 1924–28 children's ward in a hospital in Mukačevo (now in Ukraine). He designed the 1927 apartment block at 30–32 Pod Kavalírkou St. in Prague; apartment blocks in Chust (now Ukraine) in c. 1929; the important 1929–30 pharmaceutical factory in Dolní Měcholupy; 1928 Esso power station in Kolín; 1929–30 family house at 408 Bezručova St. in Kolín for Václav Budil. Budil also commissioned Frágner in 1929–30 to design wooden furniture to accompany the Thonet bentwood chairs in the house. Frágner's furniture for the Budil house was simpler than his earlier models. The most notable part of the house was the kitchen, completed in 1929 and equipped with built-in cupboards and electric cooker, the first of its kind in Czechoslovakia.
Exhibitions Work included in 1923 Bauhaus exhibition, Weimar.
Bibliography Cat., *Devětsil: Czech Avant-Garde Art, Architecture, and Design of the 1920s and 30s*, Oxford: Museum of Modern Art; London: Design Museum, 1990. Cat., *Prague, 1900–1938: capitale secrète des avants-gardes*, Dijon: Musée des Beaux-Arts, 1997.

France & Søn
Danish furniture and industrial manufacturer; located Hillerød.

History France & Søn was established as one of the factories of Royal System, which had been originally founded by Poul Cadovius in 1945. Cadovius, initially working with six employees, successfully promoted himself as a modern designer. The firm produced furniture, building systems, and boats. Its designers included Cadovius himself and Steen Èstergaard, Leif Alring, and Sidse Werner. Its furniture was made mostly from wood products and upholstered.
Exhibitions Poul Cadovius received a silver medal for France & Søn furniture at 1957 (11th) Triennale di Milano and a gold medal at 1961 (10th) *International Investors' Fair*, Brussels.
Bibliography Cat., *Milena Lamarová, Design a Plastické Hmoty*, Prague: Uměleckoprůmyslové Muzeum, 1972: 54, 56, 186.

Francès, Elsa (1966–)
> See Policar, Jean-Michel.

Franck, Kaj (1911–1989)
Finnish textile and glassware designer and ceramicist; born Viipuri; active Helsinki.

Training 1929–32, furniture department, Taideteollinen korkeakoulu, Helsinki.
Biography Franck worked initially as a freelance designer; 1933–45, designed lighting and textiles. 1945–73, was a designer at Arabia pottery in Helsinki, becoming artistic director in 1950; from 1946–50, was a designer at Iittala glassworks, and from 1950–76 at Nuutajärvi-Notsjö glassworks; from 1945, was a teacher, Taideteollinen korkeakoulu, and, 1960–68, its art director. When Nuutajärvi-Notsjö merged with the Wärtsilä group in c. 1950, he produced his first glassware designs. Franck's unbreakable 1948–1975 Kilta was considered to be a revolution in everyday tableware and a classic Finnish design object. More than 25 million pieces of it were sold. Later reissued, it was chosen for the cafeteria of the Picasso Museum in Paris. 1973, Franck left Arabia; 1978, left the Wärtsilä group; from 1979, was a full-time consultant designer, sometimes working for the Wärtsilä group (Arabia, Nuutajärvi, and sanitary porcelain and enamel) division; designed 1979 Pitopöytä melamine plate and bowl range by Sarvis and 1981 Teema black or white stoneware by Arabia.
Exhibitions/citations From 1995, work included in numerous venues, and subject of small 1992 exhibition, The Museum of Modern Art, New York (brochure below) and 1992 exhibition, Taideteollisuusmuseo, Helsinki (catalog below). Prizes at 1951 (9th) (gold medal), 1954 (10th) (two diplomas of honor), and 1957 (11th) (grand prize) Triennali di Milano; 1955 Lunning Prize; 1957 Pro Finlandia; 1965 Prince Eugen Medal; 1977 Finnish State Award for Industrial Arts; 1983 granted honorary doctoral degree, Royal College of Art, London.
Bibliography Kaj Franck, 'Finland,' *Craft Horizons*, vol. 16, July 1956: 24–25. Erik Zahle (ed.), *A Treasury of Scandinavian Design*, New York: Golden Press, 1961. Kaj Frank, 'Anonymity,' *Craft Horizons*, vol. 27, Mar. 1967: 34–35. Kaj Franck, 'The Arabia Art Department,' *Ceramics and Glass*, Nos. 1–2, 1973: 47–57. *Finland: Nature, Design, Architecture*, Helsinki: Finnish Society of Crafts and Design, 1980–81: 60–66. Kaj Franck with Eeva Siltavuori, 'Constructive Thinking in Finnish Design: Our Organic Heritage,' *Form Function Finland*, no. 2, 1981: 51–57. Cat., *The Lunning Prize*, Stockholm: Nationalmuseum, 1986: 70–75. Jennifer Hawkins Opie, *Scandinavia: Ceramics and Glass in the Twentieth Century*, New York: Rizzoli, 1989. Brochure, *Kaj Franck: Designer*, New York: The Museum of Modern Art, 1992. Cat., *Kaj Franck Designer*, Helsinki: Taideteollisuusmuseo, 1992. Jarno Peltonen et al., *Kaj Franck, muotoilija, formgivare, designer*, Porvoo: Werner Soderstrom, 1997. Paola Antonelli (ed.), *Objects of Design: The Museum of Modern Art*, New York: The Museum of Modern Art, 2003.

Francken, Ruth (1924–)
Czech sculptor and sometime furniture designer; born Prague.

Training 1939-40 under Arthur Segal, in painting, Oxford, UK; 1941, painting, Art Students League, New York.
Biography 1924–37, Francken lived in Vienna; 1937–39, in Paris; 1941, emigrated to New York; 1942, was naturalized as an American citizen; 1943–49, was active as a textile designer; 1950, settled in Venice and pursued painting; 1952, moved to Paris and, 1966–78, worked there; 1977–79, taught painting, Sarah Lawrence College extension program, Paris; 1979–80, guest lecturer, University of California, Santa Barbara; from 1985, continued working in Paris. From late 1960s as a designer, created furniture in human forms, particularly 1971 Homme chair in polyurethane and stainless steel by Eric and Xiane Germain in France.
Exhibitions/citations Work included in and subject of a large number of exhibitions worldwide. 1964–65 grant, Noma Copley Foundation, New York; same years, grant, Ford Foundation/DAAD, Berlin.

Frank, Beat (1949–)
Swiss designer; active Berne.

Biography 1986, Frank and Andreas Lehmann established the Atelier Vorsprung design office in Berne. Their limited-production 1989 Sitzkreuz furniture-sculpture was created for a hotel lobby in the south of France and for an acting school. The Atelier's work spanned art and utility, a popular late-1980s orientation.
Bibliography Albrecht Bangert and Karl Michael Armer, *80s Style: Designs of the Decade*, New York: Abbeville, 1990.

Frank, Jean-Michel (1893–1941)
French interior decorator and furniture designer; born Paris; active Paris and New York; great uncle of Anne Frank.

Training In the law.
Biography The approach Frank took to his design work was greatly influenced by Eugenia Errazuriz, whom he met in the 1920s. Impressed by her quest for simplicity and perfection, he mixed modern lighting fixtures with provincial Louis XVI furniture. After World War I, he worked as a cabinetmaker in Jacques-Émile Ruhlmann's workshop in Paris; while searching for furnishings for his own apartment in the rue de Verneuil, met decorator Adolphe Chanaux, who had worked with André Groult and Jacques-Émile Ruhlmann on the 1925 *Exposition Internationale des Arts Décoratifs et Industriels Modernes*, Paris. 1927–33, Frank probably produced designs for the Desny firm; with his stable of designers, was the first to use white-leaded wood, in the 1920s;

1932 after a year of collaborating in a decorating business with workshops in La Ruche, opened the shop with Chanaux at 147, rue du Faubourg Saint-Honoré in Paris and sold pieces designed by himself and Chanaux and associates, including painter Christian Bérard, Salvador Dalí, Diego and Alberto Giacometti, de Pisis, Rodocanachi, and Emilio Terry. At first Frank's designs were hard-edged and rectilinear, indebted to Le Corbusier and Robert Mallet-Stevens. It was through Mallet-Stevens that Frank acquired the commission to decorate rooms of 1924–33 villa of vicomte and vicomtesse de Noailles, Hyères. One of the most important modern interiors of the century was Frank's 1929 decorations and furnishings for rooms in the Noailles's Hôtel Bischoffsheim residence on the place des États-Unis in Paris. The walls were covered in beige vellum, in subtle contrast to the macassar ebony furniture and a modernist carpet on an old parquet floor. The huge bronze door was trimmed in ivory. Sofas and chairs were upholstered in bleached leather and tables and screens covered in shagreen, leather, or lacquer. 'Pity the burglars got everything,' quipped Jean Cocteau, alluding to the sparseness of the furnishings. The 1930 living room in Frank's own residence showed straw applied to the ceiling and walls to suggest grained marquetry. Dark gypsum tables were placed among chairs, a 'tuxedo' sofa, and a screen covered in white leather. Frank shared with Emilio Terry an interest in the visionary 18th-century projects of Claude-Nicolas Ledoux and Étienne-Louis Boullée. Frank's work became more theatrical, and he introduced more complicated forms. By the mid-1930s, he collaborated more with the Giacomettis and commissioned their white plaster and patinated bronze decorative accessories. With them and others including Bérard, Frank created a dramatic setting for the Guerlain family with *trompe l'œil* effects. Elsa Schiaparelli commissioned Frank to decorate her rooms on the boulevard Saint-Germain. Bright chintz in the main room contrasted with black, including black porcelain plates in the dining room. Other clients included the baron de l'Epée, Philippe Berthelot, and Lucien Lelong. Frank's personality was reflected in his somber office, nicknamed 'the confessional.' He designed the so-called Parsons (or T-square) table, evolved from his lectures at Parsons School of Design in Paris. 1940, he settled in New York with backing from the interior design firm McMillen; had earlier designed 1937 interiors and furniture of Nelson A. Rockefeller's apartment in New York and rooms for M. Templeton Crocker in San Francisco. Depressed and possibly lovesick, he jumped to his death from a window of the Hotel St. Regis, after only one week in New York. His influence was wide, despite a career of a mere decade. Only one Frank project is intact today: Count Cecil and Countess Minie Pecci Blunt's 1930 three-room apartment on the third floor of a 16th-century palace, near Rome. 1986, Écart International, and later Palazzetti, began reproduction of Frank's canapé for the Noailles mansion in Paris, the precursor of the 'tuxedo' sofa, as well as production of other models.
Exhibition 1997 *Villa Noailles (Hyères)*, Hyères, France (catalog below).
Bibliography Elsa Schiaparelli, *Shocking Life*, London: New York: Dutton, 1954: 43. Van Day Truex, 'Jean-Michel Frank Remembered,' *Architectural Digest*, Sept.–Oct. 1976: 71–75, 170–71. C. Ray Smith, *Interior Design in Twentieth-Century America: A History*, New York: Harper & Row, 1987. Cécile Briolle et al., *Villa Noailles*, Paris: Parenthèses, 1990. Cat., Hubert Damisch (text) and Jacqueline Salmon (photos), *Villa Noailles (Hyères)*, Paris: Marval, 1997. Laurence Benaïm, *Marie-Laure de Noailles: la vicomtesse du bizarre*, Paris: Grasset, 2001. François Carrassan (director), *La villa Noailles: une aventure moderne*. Paris: Plume (Flammarion), 2001.

Frank, Josef (1885–1967)
Austrian architect, interior, furniture, and textile designer; born Baden; active Vienna and Stockholm.

Biography 1919–25, Frank was a professor, Kunstgewerbeschule, Vienna; 1925–34 with Oskar Wlach, founded and directed the interior-design cooperative Haus und Garten in Vienna, which produced furniture, textiles, and utensils. 1934, Frank, a modernist, settled in Sweden and became chief designer at Svenskt Tenn, where he worked until his death, designing furniture, printed fabrics, and interiors. His textile work included 1944 Vegetable Tree in bright, unusually combined colors. In his later furniture, he modified his earlier Purist ideas and included pattern and texture into his designs for furniture, lighting, and textiles; 1942–46, was a teacher, New School for Social Research, New York; wrote books including *Architectur als Symbol: Elemente deutschen neuen Bauens* (Vienna: A. Schroll, 1931) and *Accidentism* (1958); was an early proponent of the Swedish modern movement.
Exhibitions/citations Work shown at 1925 *Exposition Internationale des Arts Décoratifs et Industriels Modernes*, Paris; 1927 *Die Wohnung*, Stuttgart; 1937 *Exposition Internationale des Arts et Techniques dans la Vie Moderne*, Paris; 1939–40 *New York World's Fair: The World of Tomorrow*. Work subject of 1968 exhibition, Nationalmuseum, Stockholm; 1996, Bard Graduate Center, New York. Litteris et Artibus Medal.
Bibliography Cat., David Revere McFadden (ed.), *Scandinavian Modern Design 1880–1980*, New York; Abrams, 1982. Kristina Wängberg-Eriksson, *Pepis Flora: Josef Frank som mönsterkonstnär*, Lund: Signum, 1998. Nina Stritzler-Levine (ed.), *Josef Frank: Architect and Designer, An Alternative Vision of the Modern Home*, New Haven: Yale University, 1996. Christopher Long, *Josef Frank: Life and Work*, Chicago: University of Chicago, 2002.

Frankl, Paul Theodore (1887–1958)
Austrian designer; born Vienna; active New York and California.

Training In architecture and engineering, Vienna, Paris, Munich, and Berlin.
Biography 1914, Frankl settled in the US; mid-1920s, began designing modular bookcases-desks that have come to be called 'skyscraper' furniture. They were sold in his own gallery in New York and were one-of-a-kind pieces, never mass produced. He saw classic geometry as the key to good design. Many of Frankl's designs have little to do with the philosophy in his writings. His notable work includes c. 1927 large combined 'skyscraper' desk and bookcase and c. 1929 chrome, aluminum, and leather chair. In conjunction with the 1927 *Art in Trade* exhibition at Macy's department store in New York, he lectured on 'The Skyscraper in Decoration'; illustrated his and others' furniture and interior designs in his influential book *Form and Re-Form...* (New York: Harper, 1930) in which he documented the best of American and European designers, and in his books *New Dimensions...* (New York: Brewer & Warren, 1928) and *Space for Living...* (New York: Doubleday, Doran, 1938); spent the early part of his career in New York and the latter part in California; late 1940s, specified cork veneer in furniture by Johnson Furniture Company. Frankl used materials lavishly and his work is comparable to that of the French designers of the time, although the construction of Frankl's designs was frequently inferior to French craftsmanship and materials. He was the main force behind the formation of the American Designers' Gallery in 1928 and American Union of Decorative Artists and Craftsmen (AUDAC) in 1930, both of which had memberships consisting of the most accomplished designers, architects, and photographers in America at the time.
Exhibitions Work included in 1927 *Exposition of Art in Trade* at Macy's department store, New York; with that of Walter von Nessen, sculptor William Zorach, Donald Deskey, and others, at John Cotton Dana's 1929 *Modern American Design in Metal* exhibition, Newark Museum, Newark, N.J.
Bibliography 'American Modernist Furniture Inspired by Skyscraper Architecture,' *Good Furniture Magazine*, Sept. 1927: 119. Pierre Migennes, 'Un artiste décorateur américain: Paul Th. Frankl,' *Art et Décoration*, Jan. 1928: 49. 'Frankl, Paul T.,' *Britannica Encyclopedia of American Art*, Chicago: Britannica, 1973. Karen Davies, *At Home in Manhattan: Modern Decorative Arts, 1925 to the Depression*, New Haven: Yale, 1983. Richard Guy Wilson et al., *The Machine Age in America 1918–1941*, New York: Abrams, 1986. Mel Byars (introduction), 'What Makes American Design American?' in R.L. Leonard and C.A. Glassgold (eds.), *Modern American Design, by the American Union of Decorative Artists and Craftsmen*, New York: 1930; Acanthus, 1992 reprint.

Franzen, Ulrich (1921–)
German architect and designer; born Düsseldorf.

Training To 1942, Williams College, Williamstown, Mass.; to 1948 under Walter Gropius and Marcel Breuer, Graduate School of Design, Harvard University, Cambridge, Mass.
Biography 1950–55, Franzen worked for architects I.M. Pei and Partners and, from 1955, was principal, Ulrich Franzen and Associates; both in New York. He was primarily influenced by Mies van der Rohe's International Style and shared Mies's sense of order and precision and admiration for precious materials. Franzen's few pieces of furniture included a 1968 tractor-seat stool. (The tractor seat as a stool was originally designed by the Castiglioni brothers in 1957, produced by Zanotta from 1971.) Buildings included 1983 Champion International headquarters and 1984 Philip Morris headquarters, both New York.
Exhibitions Work included in 1982 *Shape and Environment: Furniture by American Architects*, Whitney Museum of American Art, Fairfield

County, Conn.
Bibliography Stanley Abercrombie, 'Ulrich Franzen: Architecture in Transition,' *Process Architecture*, no. 8, 1979: 11–159. Ulrich Franzen, 'Changing Design Solutions for a Changing Era,' *Architectural Record*, no. 158, Sept. 1978: 81–88. Cat., Lisa Phillips (intro.), *Shape and Environment: Furniture by American Architects*, New York: Whitney Museum of American Art, 1982: 30–31.

Fraschini, Franco (1930–)

Italian industrial designer; born and active Pavia.

Biography 1958, Fraschini began his professional career; designed irons, kitchenware, furniture, lighting, including Octans table lamp by Zonca; became a member, Associazione per il Disegno Industriale (ADI). Clients in Italy have included Driade, Indesit, Lai, Nuova Immi, Roche, and Saima.
Bibliography *ADI Annual 1976*, Milan: Associazione per il Disegno Industriale, 1976.

Fraser, Alberto (1945–)

British designer; born Glasgow; active US and Milan.

Training Rhode Island School of Design, Providence, R.I.
Biography Fraser settled in Milan. Work has included furniture, industrial design, and lighting for clients, including Arflex, Artemide, Bausch & Lomb, B&B Italia, Mont Blanc, and Wang Computer Laboratories. His 1984–85 Nastro halogen table lamp with its electrical elements housed in a colorful, malleable arm was produced by Stilnova.
Bibliography Robert A. M. Stern (ed.), *The International Design Yearbook*, New York: Abbeville, 1985/1986. Albrecht Bangert and Karl Michael Armer, *80s Style: Designs of the Decade*, New York: Abbeville, 1990: 93, 230.

Fraser, Claud Lovat (1890–1921)

British textile designer, painter, illustrator, and theater designer; born London.

Training From 1907, law; from 1911 under Walter Sickert and Sylvia Gosse, Westminster School of Art.
Biography Influenced by folk and traditional designs, Fraser was best known for his theatrical costumes and set designs, including most notably for the 1920 production of John Gay's *The Beggar's Opera*; was successful as an illustrator; 1920s, executed patterns for fabrics by William Foxton.
Bibliography Stuart Durant, *Ornament from the Industrial Revolution to Today*, Woodstock, N.Y.: Overlook, 1986: 250, 323. Valerie Mendes, *The Victoria and Albert Museum Textile Collection, British Textiles from 1900 to 1937*, London: Victoria and Albert Museum, 1992.

Fraser, June (1930–)

British graphic and industrial designer.

Training Royal College of Art, London, to 1957.
Biography 1957–80, she worked at Design Research Unit; 1980–84, was head of graphic design, John Lewis; from 1984, was head of industrial design, The Design Council; became a member, The Design Council, board of Design and Industries Association, advisory board of *Product Design Review*, Court of the Royal College of Art, The London Institute, College of Art in Bournemouth and in Poole, and International Council of Societies of Industrial Designers (ICSID).
Exhibitions/citations Work shown internationally. Numerous awards.
Bibliography Liz McQuiston, *Women in Design: A Contemporary View*, New York: Rizzoli, 1988: 44.

Frateili, Enzo (1914–)

Italian designer; born Rome; active Milan.

Biography 1955, Frateili began his professional career; 1955–60, worked at journal *Stile Industria*; 1962, was the Italian correspondent to the journal *form*. Books included *Continuità e trasformazione: una storia del design italiano, 1928–1988* (Milan: A. Greco, 1989) and *Design e civiltà della macchina* (Rome: Editalia, 1969). His paper on the theoretical and methodological aspects of problem-solving was published by the Istituto di Architettura e Urbanistica, Università degli Studi, Trieste. 1963, he led a seminar, Hochschule für Gestaltung, Ulm; 1963–65, taught a course, CSDI (now Istituto Superiore per le Industrie Artistiche [ISIA]), Venice; 1968, led a lecture-conference, CSDI, Rome; 1962–64, was a member of the guidance committee, Associazione per il Disegno Industriale (ADI); 1967, was a member of ADI's pre-selection committee, Premio Compasso d'Oro; 1970, sat on ADI's awards preparation commission; 1973, coordinator of ADI's college direction. Work included furniture and shelving systems.
Citation 1970 Premio Compasso d'Oro (for *Design e civiltà della macchina* book).
Bibliography *ADI Annual 1976*, Milan: Associazione per il Disegno Industriale, 1976. Piercarlo Crachi (ed.), *Enzo Frateili: architettura, design, tecnologia*, Milan: Skira, 2001.

Josef Frank. Side chair. Date unknown. Wood frame and leather upholstered seat, 35 1/4 x 18 3/4 x 17 3/4" (89.5 x 47.6 x 45.1 cm). Mfr.: Svenskt Tenn, Sweden. Edgar Kaufmann, Jr., Purchase Fund. MoMA.

Frattini, Gianfranco (1926–)

Italian architect and interior and industrial designer; born Padova; active Milan.

Training To 1953, architecture, Politecnico, Milan.
Biography 1948, Frattini began his professional career; 1952–54, collaborated in architecture with Gio Ponti; from 1954, worked for Cassina and, concurrently, collaborated with Gio Ponti on equipment for Triennale di Milano; set up his own studio for architecture and industrial and interior design; 1956, cofounded Associazione per il Disegno Industriale (ADI). Work has included upholstered furniture, lacquered wood, wicker, and plastics for clients Acerbis-Morphos, G.B. Bernini, C&B Italia, Citterio, Fratelli Faber, Gio Caroli, Lema, Molteni, Progetti, Ricci, and others. Designs included Model 595 Sesann armchair in leather and foam on a bent-wire frame produced by Cassina, (with Livio Castiglioni) lighting designs in the early 1970s for Artemide, including the snake-like 1971 Boalum lamp; designed for industrial plastics including late-1970s hard hats for Montecatini and 1987 Bull sofa and chair range by Cassina; from 1983, was a board member, Triennale di Milano.
Citations Gold medal and grand prize, Triennali di Milano; 1955, 1956, 1957, 1979, 1981, 1987, 1989, 1991 Premio Compasso d'Oro; honorable mention (Boalum lamp), 1973 BIO 5 industrial-design biennial, Ljubljana; Oscar Plast; prize, Mostra di Articoli Casalinghi e Ferramenta (Macef), Milan; Diamond International Award, DeBeers.
Bibliography *ADI Annual 1976*, Milan: Associazione per il Disegno Industriale, 1976. Alfonso Grassi and Anty Pansera, *Atlante del design*

Gianfranco Frattini. Pitcher. 1983. Frosted mouth-blown glass, h. 7 3/16 x w. 5 1/8" (18.2 x 13 cm). Mfr.: Progetti, Italy. Gift of the mfr. MoMA.

italiano 1940/1980, Milan: Fabbri, 1980: 178, 224, 282. Cat., Kathryn B. Hiesinger and George H. Marcus III (eds.), *Design Since 1945*, Philadelphia: Philadelphia Museum of Art, 1983. Cat., Hans Wichmann, *Italien Design 1945 bis heute*, Munich: Die Neue Sammlung, 1988.

Frau, Renzo (1880–1926); Poltrona Frau

Italian designer; born Cagliari, Sardinia. Firm located Tolentino (MC).

Biography At the beginning of the century, Frau worked as a joiner in the Italian royal household; 1912, founded Poltrona Frau furniture company, designing the legendary Poltrona armchair of same year. On Frau's 1926 death in Turin, the firm was appointed supplier to the Italian royal family; 1930s, was active in interior design to titled clients and in interior furnishings for 1931 oceanliner *Rex*. Designers have included Gae Aulenti, Marco Zanuso, and Tito Agnoli. The firm produced F.A. Porsche's 1983 Antropovarius series; has become known for its leather-covered seating, some available in 66 colors. Twenty-one different stages are needed to change a raw animal skin into a soft, durable upholstery material. The firm has outfitted automobiles (BMW, Ferrari, Lancia, Mercedes, Nissan, Pininfarina), airplanes, and other users of industrial leather seating; established a department for the production of office furniture, for which Pierluigi Frau designed 1985 Pausa leather sofa. 2001 inventory included Donald folding chair by Studio Cerri & Associati and desk accessories by Lella and Massimo Vignelli, Michele De Lucchi, and Frau's Centro Ricerca e Sviluppo. Has become Poltrona Frau Group, acquiring Cappellini, Gufram, and others.
Bibliography Decio Giulio and Riccardo Carugati, *Poltrona Frau: senza tempo nel tempo*, Milan: Electa, 2000. http://www.poltronova.it.

Fréchet, André (1875–1973); Paul Fréchet

French decorators and furniture designers; born Châlons-sur-Marne; active Paris.

Biography Working together and individually from 1906, the Fréchet brothers designed furniture produced by various firms including Jacquemin Frères in Strasbourg, E. Verot, and Charles Jeanselme. 1909–11, André was professor, École des Beaux-Arts, Nantes; 1911, settled in Paris and became director of studies, École Boulle, where he was the director 1919–34; from 1923, was editor of magazine *Mobilier et décoration*; designed for the Studium Louvre; 1935–39, taught at Académie Julian, Paris; executed numerous private commissions. Some of his students were recruited for Jacques-Émile Ruhlmann's cabinetworks. His tapestry designs were produced by Manufacture de Beauvais for various rooms in the Palais de l'Élysée in Paris.
Exhibitions Throughout the 1920s to mid-1930s, work shown at Salons of Société des Artistes Décorateurs and, sporadically, at editions of Salon d'Automne. With 72 of his students, designed the pavilion of the city of Paris (also with Pierre Lehalle and Georges Levard) and participated in pavilion of design atelier Studium of Les Grand Magasins du Louvre, both at 1925 *Exposition Internationale des Arts Décoratifs et Industriels Modernes*, Paris.
Bibliography *Ensembles mobiliers*, vol. II, Paris: Charles Moreau, 1937. Pierre Kjellberg, *Art déco: les maîtres du mobilier, le décor des paquebots*, Paris: Amateur, 1986/1990.

Frederick, William N. (1921–)

American silversmith; born Sycamore, Ill.

Training To 1941, Gallagher School of Business, Kankakee, Ill.; 1953, bachelor's degree in art and, 1959, master's degree in art, School of the Art Institute of Chicago, partially there under metalworker Daniel H. Pedersen.
Biography From 1946, Frederick was an industrial designer at the Turner Corporation, Sycamore; 1955, Frederick established his silver workshop at 1322 East 49th St., Chicago; from 1964–65, at Lake Park Street; 1965, at 1858 North Sedgwick St., where he is still active today and highly regarded.
Bibliography Sharon S. Darling with Gail Farr Casterline, *Chicago Metalsmiths*, Chicago Historical Society, 1977.

Freij, Edla (1944–)

Norwegian glassware designer and ceramicist.

Training 1966–71 under Jens von de Lippe, Statens Håndverks-og Kunstindustriskole, Oslo; 1970–73, Hochschule für angewandte Kunst, Vienna.
Biography She designed glass with cut and sandblasted motifs; from 1968, worked at Hadelands Glassverk in Jevnaker, where she was head of the product department from 1979; called on the cold-decoration techniques of sandblasting, engraving, etching, and cutting, which transformed blown glass from its anticipated norm. From 1973–c. 1976, she was active in her own studio in Vienna.
Bibliography Cat., David Revere McFadden (ed.), *Scandinavian Modern Design 1880–1980*, New York: Abrams, 1982. Jennifer Hawkins Opie, *Scandinavia: Ceramics and Glass in the Twentieth Century*, New York: Rizzoli, 1989. Leslie Jackson, *20th Century Factory Glass*, London: Octopus, 2000.

Frémiet, Emmanuel (1824–1910)

French sculptor and metalworker; active Paris; nephew of sculptor François Rude.

Training Under François Rude, sculpture.
Biography In addition to sculptural lighting, Frémiet produced animal images such as marabou storks, butterflies, pelicans, orangutans, and dragons, which appeared on the friezes, column capitals, and antechamber floors of buildings; pioneered the use of lighting in his work where a combustion-type system would not have been possible; was one of the few Art Nouveau artists whose work expressed humor.
Exhibitions Work (bronze animal group) was first shown at 1843 Salon of Société des Artistes Français, Paris.
Bibliography Cat., *Un siècle de bronzes animaliers*, Paris: Galerie P. Ambroise, 1975: 76–77. Alastair Duncan, *Art Nouveau and Art Déco Lighting*, New York: Simon & Schuster, 1978.

Frenning, Pelle (1943–)

Swedish designer and interior architect.

Training Industrial arts, Gothenburg University.
Biography Frenning worked for several interior-architecture companies, including Folke Sundberg and Lund Valentin, before joining White Architects in Gothenburg; has designed furniture.
Exhibitions/citations Work shown at several exhibitions.1980 first prize (lighting for the elderly), Swedish Lighting Association.
Bibliography Robert A. M. Stern (ed.), *The International Design Yearbook*, New York: Abbeville, 1985/1986.

Frette, Guido (1901–)

Italian architect; born Viareggio.

Exhibitions Frette and Adalberto Libera designed the furnishings for the living room, dining room, and master bedroom of Casa Elettrica (architects, fellow Gruppo Sette members Luigi Figini and Gino Pollini) for Montedison Company at 1930 (4th) *International Exposition of Decorative Arts*, Monza. In its kitchen, features of German and American models were incorporated. Casa Elettrica was the first public expression of modern architecture in Italy.
Bibliography Barbie Campbell-Cole and Tim Benton (eds.), *Tubular Steel Furniture*, London: The Art Book Company, 1979: 47.

Frey, Albert (1903–)

Swiss architect; born Zürich.

Biography For a time, Frey worked closely with Le Corbusier in Paris; 1930, settled in New York; with A. Lawrence Kocher, set up an architecture partnership and, with Kocher, designed subsistence farmsteads and 1931 Aluminaire House, a prototype in aluminum for mass production. Originally built for an exhibition, the house was relocated on the property of architect Wallace K. Harrison in Syosset, N.Y.; c. 1991, was relocated again and rebuilt by architecture students on the grounds of New York Technical College in East Islip, N.Y. 1935, Frey corresponded with Le Corbusier; moved to Palm Springs, Cal., where, until 1986, Frey designed numerous buildings suited to desert conditions, with overhanging roofs and swimming pools in living rooms; designed his own house and that of Raymond Loewy, also in Palm Springs.
Exhibitions Aluminaire House built at 1932 *Modern Architecture—International Exhibition*, The Museum of Modern Art, New York.
Bibliography Jeffrey Book, 'Statements of Style,' *Elle Decor*, Mar. 1991: 20. Joseph Rosa, *Albert Frey, Architect*, New York: Rizzoli, 1990.

Frey, Pierre (1903–1994); Patrick Frey (1947–)

French fabric designers.

Biographies Pierre Frey initially worked at the Burger fabric house and, from 1932, at the Lauer fabric house; 1935, established his own firm in Paris to produce decorative fabrics; became the first to use the designs of established artists on printed materials, unusually colorful for the time. 1955, sister firm Patifet was set up to produce contemporary fabrics. 1969, Frey's son Patrick (trained in the US) joined the firm and became director of design in 1975 and chairperson a few years later. From late 1980s, the firm has been prolific, producing more than 5,000 colorways and 30 designs yearly. From 1983, Patrick Frey's own designs and those of freelance designers and illustrators were produced under the firm names of Patrick Frey, Natccru, and contract range Margueroy. The firm has distributed the fabrics of Valentino Piu, Warner Greef, and Yves Halard; from 1987, produced upholstered furniture, decorative accessories, household fragrances, and Frey's widely published 1991 teacup-motif print. 1991, the Frey group took over Braquenié, founded in 1824 to produce fabrics, tapestries, and wallpaper, specializing in 18th- and 19th-century printed materials, including those from Jouy and Nantes, with dyeing workshops in Aubusson.
Citations Navette d'Honneur (for Pierre Frey's career accomplishments).
Bibliography 'Hot Property,' *House and Garden*, May 1991. www.pierrefrey.com.

Freyrie, Leopoldo (1958–)

Italian architect, designer, and teacher; born Milan; son of Enrico Freyrie.

Training To 1983, Politecnico, Milan.
Biography From 1982, Freyrie collaborated on architecture and design with Guido Stefanoni; 1984–86, taught, Istituto Europeo di Design, Milan; from 1987, was associated with design school Arte Design Tecnica.
Exhibitions Work included in 1983 *Light '83* and 1986 *Itinerari Manzoniani*, both Milan.
Bibliography Cat., Hans Wichmann, *Italien Design 1945 bis heute*, Munich: Die Neue Sammlung, 1988.

Friberg, Berndt (1899–1981)

Swedish ceramicist.

Training 1915–18, in throwing at Höganäsbolaget stoneware factory, and Höganäs Technical School.
Biography 1918–c. 1934, Friberg worked in workshops in Denmark and Sweden; from 1934–81, at Gustavsberg pottery, producing unique stoneware vessels in refined silhouettes and using Oriental-type glazes; from 1933–44, was a thrower for Wilhelm Kåge at Gustavsberg and was active in the studio there from 1944–81.
Exhibitions/citations Work subject of exhibitions, Nordiska Kompaniet, Stockholm, 1946, 1954, 1956, 1959, and 1964; Nationalmuseum, Stockholm, 1949; 1954 *Vi Tre*, Gothenburg and Karlstad; 1956 *Höganäs Stengods av Skånelera*, Malmö Museum, 1957; Smålands Museum, Växjö, 1958. Gold medals at 1948 (8th), 1951 (9th), and 1954 (10th) editions of Triennale di Milano; 1965 first prize, Concorso Internazionale della Ceramica d'Arte, Faenza; 1960 Gregor Paulsson trophy.
Bibliography Ulf Hård af Segerstad, *Berndt Friberg Keramiker*, Stockholm: Nordisk Rotogravyr, 1964. Cat., David Revere McFadden (ed.), *Scandinavian Modern Design 1880–1980*, New York: Abrams, 1982. Jennifer Hawkins Opie, *Scandinavia: Ceramics and Glass in the Twentieth Century*, New York: Rizzoli, 1989. George Fischler and Barrett Gould, *Scandinavian Ceramics and Glass: 1940s to 1980s*, Atglen, Pa.: Schiffer, 2000.

Fric, Bernard (1944–)
> See Asymétrie.

Fricker, Fritz (1928–)

Italian architect and designer; born Genoa; active Milan.

Biography Fricker practiced architecture in Switzerland; 1959, became a member, Associazione per il Disegno Industriale (ADI); designed building components and interiors; was a consultant to Gulf, Swissair, and Swiss-government tourist office.
Bibliography *ADI Annual 1976*, Milan: Associazione per il Disegno Industriale, 1976.

Friedell, Clemens (1872–1963)

American ceramicist; born New Orleans; active Vienna and California.

Training Unpaid apprentice to a Viennese silversmith.
Biography 1892, Friedell returned to the US and began working for a silversmith in San Antonio, Tex.; 1901–07, was employed by the Gorham company, America's largest silver factory, in Providence, R.I.; 1908, settled in Los Angeles, producing silver ashtrays for the Broadway Department Store; 1909, moved to Pasadena, Cal., and set up a workshop on the back porch of his own house; subsequently, set up shops on North Lake Avenue, on Colorado Boulevard and in the Huntington and Maryland hotels; was known for his fine craftsmanship, especially in *repoussé* work. His most notable commission was a 107-piece dining set in hand-wrought and chased sterling silver, on which he spent more than 6,000 hours and applied over 10,000 orange-blossom images. For a number of years, Friedell designed the silver cups awarded to floats in the Tournament of Roses, Pasadena.
Bibliography Bonnie Mattison in Timothy J. Andersen et al., *California Design 1910,* Salt Lake City: Peregrine Smith, 1980: 86–87.

Friedlander, Dan (1952–)
> See Gilliam, Kenneth.

Friedländer, Gebrüder

German silversmiths; located Berlin.

History 1829, Gebrüder Friedländer was founded; became a court jeweler; produced some striking silver objects after designs of c. 1900 by painter Wilhelm Lucas von Cranach.
Bibliography Annelies Krekel-Aalberse, *Art Nouveau and Art Déco Silver*, New York: Abrams, 1989.

Friedländer-Wildenhain, Marguerite (1896–1985)
> See Wildenhain, Marguerite.

Friedman, Stanley Jay (1938–)

American designer.

Training Parsons School of Design, New York.
Biography Friedman worked as an interior designer; 1970, set up his own studio in New York and has been active as the designer of a number of interiors and products, including furniture and lighting; designs total environments from the floor coverings to the architectural elements; 1971, began designing furniture by Brueton, including Satellite Table, Jena Desk and Credenza, and Athens Table and Credenza, and, subsequently, became design consultant to Brueton.
Citations Five Roscoe Awards, *Interior Design* magazine; two Product Design Awards, Institute of Business Designers (IBD); two Interior Design Awards and International Product Design Award, American Society of Interior Designers (ASID); Du Pont Award.

Friedmann, Eduard

Austrian silversmiths; located Vienna.

History 1877, the firm Eduard Friedmann was founded in Vienna; executed designs by Rudolf Karger, A.O. Holub, and Milla Weltmann, and architects Hans Bolek, Philippe Häusler, Emanuel Josef Margold, and Otto Prutscher. The firm closed in 1920.

Bibliography Annelies Krekel-Aalberse, *Art Nouveau and Art Déco Silver*, New York: Abrams, 1989.

Friend, George T.

British engraver; active London.

Biography Friend engraved the designs of R.M.Y. Gleadowe and Eric Gill; from 1929, worked for the silversmithies Edward Barnard and Wakely & Wheeler in London; taught engraving, Central School of Arts and Crafts, London.
Bibliography Annelies Krekel-Aalberse, *Art Nouveau and Art Déco Silver*, New York: Abrams, 1989.

Frink, I.P.

American lighting manufacturer; located New York.

History 1857, Isaac P. Frink established the firm in Newark, N.J., as the 'Original Inventor, Patentee, and Sole Manufacturer of the Silver-Plated and Crystal-Corrugated, Glass-Lined Reflectors.' His flat, rectangular reflector (or diffuser), working like a mirror, was attached to the outside of a building and directed sunlight into a room; light was reflected off a ceiling, creating ambient light. The invention was advantageous in dark Victorian interiors. The device was later attached to oil lamps and, subsequently, to gaslights. 1880s, Frink's reflectors were widely used in public spaces and domestic interiors. Late 1870s and 1880s, the firm added decorative lighting fixtures and chandeliers to its range; became known nationwide; 1863–1910, was located at 549–551 Pearl Street, New York; 1928, acquired the Sterling Bronze Company, manufacturers of ornamental fixtures and marine and custom lighting; moved to Long Island City, N.Y., and, 1950s, to Brooklyn, N.Y.; was known at this time as Frink Corporation, claiming to be the largest specialty-lighting company in the world; 1960, was purchased by Westinghouse; produced lighting for 1972–77 World Trade Center, New York; ceased trading in 1974.
Bibliography Denys Peter Myers, *Gaslighting in America: A Guide for Historic Preservation*, Washington: U.S. Dept. of the Interior, Heritage Conservation, and Recreation Service, Office of Archeology and Historic Preservation, Technical Preservation Services Division, 1978: 205, plate 98. Doreen Bolger Burke et al., *In Pursuit of Beauty: Americans and the Aesthetic Movement*, New York: The Metropolitan Museum of Art/ Rizzoli, 1987: 427–28.

Fris, Keramische Industrie
> See de Vries, Willem Hendrik.

Fristedt, Sven (1940–)

Swedish textile designer.

Biography From the 1960s, Fristedt designed textiles by Borås Wäfveri. His patterns were aligned with mid-1960s fine art, with sophisticated handling of repeats.
Bibliography Cat., David Revere McFadden (ed.), *Scandinavian Modern Design 1880–1980*, New York: Abrams, 1982.

frogdesign
> See Esslinger, Hartmut.

Fronek, Michal (1966–)
> See Olgoj chorchoj.

Fronzoni, A.G. (1923–2002)

Italian architect and designer; born Pistoia.

Biography From 1945, Fronzini was an architect, industrial designer, and typographer; 1965–67, was an editor at journal *Casabella*; designed 1963 attaché case by Valextra, 1964 Serie 64 furniture by Galli, 1966–67 reading room of Istituto di Storia dell'Arte, 1976 display design at Museo Walser, and 1979–80 display design at Palazzo Reale in Genoa; was consultant designer for much of Galli's production of furniture and furnishings.
Bibliography Alfonso Grassi and Anty Pansera, *Atlante del design italiano 1940/1980*, Milan: Fabbri, 1980.

Frost, Derek (1952–)

British interior designer; active London.

Training At Mary Fox Linton design firm, London.
Biography 1984, Frost set up his own design studio in London; has designed both commercial and domestic interiors and produced one-of-a-kind furniture, including 1987–88 stereo cabinet with silver doors, painted by Yumi Katayama.
Bibliography Albrecht Bangert and Karl Michael Armer, *80s Style: Designs of the Decade*, New York: Abbeville, 1990: 36, 230.

Arthur Fry and Spencer Silver (1941–). Post-it® note. c. 1977 Paper and adhesive, 2 7/8 x 2 7/8" (7.3 x 7.3 cm). Mfr.: 3M, Minnesota (mfr. from 1980). Purchase. MoMA.

Frua, Pietro (1913–1983)

Italian automobile designer; born and active Turin.

Biography 1928–30, Frua was an apprentice at Fiat; 1930–40, was first a junior designer at Stabilimenti Farina and then general manager there; shortly before World War II, was active as an independent product designer and may have contributed to what became the Vespa motor scooter. 1944, he bought a bombed-out factory building to manufacture automobiles through his Carrozzeria Pietro Frua (to 1958), where he produced late-1940s one-of-a-kind cars, including a Lacia Aprilia with a wooden body; 1957, worked with Ghia coachworks, for which he designed bodies for Maserati and 1957 Renault Floride; 1957–64, worked with Viotti coachworks and, to 1967, for others; 1958–64 and 1965–83, was active in his own design consultancy for several small clients such as Maserati, Audi, BMW, Borgward, Glas, Opel, Renault, and Volkswagen; became known for his elegant, flowing lines; as a coach builder, created the only 4-door Lamborghini (one-of-a-kind 1974 Espada Series II) and one-of-a-kind 1971–73 Rolls-Royce Phantom VI. His talent may not have been recognized during his lifetime.
Exhibitions The 1974 Lamborghini shown at 1978 (57th) Salone Internazionale dell'Automobile, Turin, and 1980 Salon International d'Automobile, Geneva.
Bibliography Detlef Lichtenstein, *Pietro Frua und seine Autos*, Bremen: Peter Kurze, 2001. Penny Sparke, *A Century of Car Design*, London: Mitchell Beazley, 2002.

Fry, Arthur (1931–)

American inventor; active Minneapolis, Minn.

Training Chemical engineering, University of Minnesota.
Biography From 1953 while still a student at the University of Minnesota, Fry began working at Minnesota Mining and Manufacturing Company (3M), where he perfected his most significant contribution, the 1980 Post-it® note (developed from 1977). Fry discovered the adhesive, on which the Post-it depends, from another 3M scientist, Dr. Spence Silver (1941–). Silver had developed a substance that would stick lightly to many surfaces while remaining tacky, even repositionable, when removed. But Silver at the time knew of no practical application for the glue. Always interested in bookmarks, Fry began using the adhesive on a portion of small pieces of paper, employing them as reminder notes for himself. However, when fellow workers discovered the invention, they wanted samples for themselves, according to the legend. Thus, the Post-it began manufacture as a 3M product from 1980 in the US and from 1981 in Europe. At first available as canary-yellow paper, other colors were later offered, and, to foster continuing sales, the basic product has been turned into various permutations of the basic idea. Yet its imitators abound.
Bibliography Mel Byars with Arlette Barré-Despond, *100 Designs/*

100 Years: A Celebration of the 20th Century, Hove: RotoVision, 1999, 172–73. Paola Antonelli (ed.), *Objects of Design: The Museum of Modern Art*, New York: The Museum of Modern Art, 2003: 121.

Fry, Henry Lindley (1807–1895); William Henry Fry (1830–1929)

British woodcarvers; active Cincinnati, Ohio; father and son.

Biography Henry Fry was a wood carver and engraver in Bath, England. His important commissions included the screen designed by George Gilbert Scott for Westminster Abbey and the decoration of the chambers of the Houses of Parliament under architects Charles Henry and A.W.N. Pugin. 1850, Fry joined his son William in New Orleans, La., US, and, 1851, moved to Cincinnati, Ohio, where he lived at 150 West Third Street from 1853. c. 1866, William Fry joined his father in Cincinnati. The Frys decorated several churches in Cincinnati, including the Church of New Jerusalem; decorated residences, including those of department store magnates John Shillito and Henry Probasco, and the State House in Columbus, Ohio; produced a dining-room table for US President Rutherford B. Hayes; decorated the Joseph Longworth residence in Rookwood during late 1850s and the Maria Longworth Nichols residence in 1868, both in Cincinnati. Influenced by William Morris and John Ruskin, the Frys added ornamentation to every possible surface. Their style incorporated Aesthetic Movement motifs of flowers and medieval and Italianate elements such as images of the Pegasus, lions' heads, paws, scrolls, and acanthus leaves, and imported Italian mosaics. They taught woodcarving privately. William taught at the Art Academy to 1926; his daughter Laura Fry was an accomplished ceramicist active at the Rookwood Pottery (see below).
Exhibitions/citations Work shown at 1876 *Centennial Exposition*, Philadelphia. W. Fry's work subject of 1910 exhibition, Saint Louis City Art Museum. W. Fry received a prize for a carved Baldwin piano shown at 1900 *Exposition Universelle*, Paris.
Bibliography Erwin O. Christensen, *Early American Wood Carving*, Cleveland and New York: Dover, 1952: 91–92 (and 1972 ed.). Anita J. Ellis, 'Cincinnati Art Furniture,' *Antiques*, no. 121, April 1982: 930–41. E. Jane Connell and Charles R. Muller, 'Ohio Furniture, 1788–1888,' *Antiques*, no. 125, Feb. 1984: 468, plate 7. Doreen Bolger Burke et al., *In Pursuit of Beauty: Americans and the Aesthetic Movement*, New York: The Metropolitan Museum of Art/Rizzoli, 1987.

Fry, Laura Anne (1857–1943)

American wood carver and ceramics decorator; born near Monticello, Ind.; active Cincinnati, Ohio; daughter of William Henry Fry.

Training 1869–76 and 1886–88 under Benn Pitman, Maria Eggers, and Thomas Noble, drawing and sculpture, University of Cincinnati School of Design (later Art Academy of Cincinnati); 1886, Art Students League, New York.
Biography In addition to the 1877–78 decoration of the Cincinnati Music Hall organ, she designed nine of its floral panels; working in the 'scratch-blue' technique, trained for a time in ceramics in Trenton, N.J.; 1881–88, designed shapes and painted pieces at Maria Longworth Nichols's Rookwood Pottery; was an instructor at the short-lived Rookwood School of Pottery Decoration; 1884, developed a technique of spraying colored slips through a mouth-blown apparatus onto moist clay, which became a standard process for creating backgrounds at Rookwood. 1889, she applied for a patent for a process that used a commercial atomizer, called the 'Fry method'; was briefly a freelancer for Rookwood; 1891, became professor of industrial art, Purdue University, West Lafayette, Ind., and founded the Lafayette Ceramic Club; 1892–94 in Steubenville, Ohio, worked for the Lonhuda Works, a Rookwood competitor, where she also used the atomizer technique. 1892–98, she was involved unsuccessfully in a lawsuit against Rookwood to bar its use of the 'Fry method'; 1894, worked in her own studio in Cincinnati; was a founder of the Porcelain League of Cincinnati; 1896, returned to Purdue University, where she taught until her 1922 retirement.
Exhibitions/citations Prize (for wood carving), 1893 *World's Columbian Exposition*, Chicago
Bibliography Herbert Peck, *The Book of Rookwood Pottery*, New York: Crown, 1968. Kenneth R. Trapp, '"To Beautify the Useful": Benn Pitman and the Women's Woodcarving Movement in Cincinnati in the Late Nineteenth Century,' in Kenneth L. Ames, *Victorian Furniture: Essays from a Victorian Society Autumn Symposium*, Philadelphia: Victorian Society in America, 1982: 173–92. Chris Petteys, 'Laura Anne Fry,' in *Dictionary of Women Artists: An International Dictionary of Women Artists Born Before 1900*, Boston: G.K. Hall, 1985: 265. Doreen Bolger Burke et al., *In Pursuit of Beauty: Americans and the Aesthetic Movement*, New York: The Metropolitan Museum of Art/Rizzoli, 1987: 429.

Fry, Roger Eliot (1866–1934)

British painter, writer, art critic, designer, and lecturer; born London.

Training 1885–88, natural sciences, Cambridge University; 1892, Académie Julian, Paris.
Biography Fry wrote articles for the *Athenaeum* and *Burlington Magazine*; published his first book, *Giovanni Bellini* (London: At the Sign of the Unicorn, 1899); 1906–10, was a curator, The Metropolitan Museum of Art, New York, and in conflict with its chairperson J.P. Morgan; 1910, met Clive and Vanessa Bell; became artistic leader of the Bloomsbury group; had affairs with Lady Ottoline Morrell and Vanessa Bell; c. 1911, produced paintings that showed Byzantine and Post-Impressionist influences; 1913, opened the Omega Workshops in an attempt to apply Post-Impressionism to the decorative arts; 1913–19, was its codirector, designing textiles, pottery, and furnishings including painted furniture. The workshop was set up to provide income for Fry's young avant-garde artist friends, including Vanessa Bell and Duncan Grant. The printed and woven fabrics, carpets, and embroideries designed and sold by Omega Workshops artisans revolutionized textile design in Britain in the early 20th century. 1919, Fry closed the workshop; in his last ten years, published eight more books on art; lectured on art at Queen's Hall in London; began to paint commissioned portraits; 1933, became Slade professor, Cambridge University, espousing unorthodox views on Greek and ethnographic art. His ashes were interred in an urn decorated by Vanessa Bell.
Exhibitions Paintings subject of 1912 exhibit, Grafton Galleries, London.
Bibliography D. Sutton (ed.), *Letters of Roger Fry*, London: Chatto & Windus, 1972. *British Art and Design, 1900–1960*, London: Victoria and Albert Museum, 1983. Alan and Veronica Palmer, *Who's Who in Bloomsbury*, New York: St. Martin's, 1987. Virginia Woolf, *Roger Fry: A Biography*, Oxford: Blackwell for Shakespeare Head Press, 1995. Clive Bell, *Roger Fry: Anecdotes for the Use of a Future Biographer, Illustrating Certain Peculiarities of the Late Roger Fry*, London: Cecil Woolf, 1997.

Frysia Workshops

Norwegian ceramics, textile, glass firm.

History c. 1970, Frysia set up a group of workshops and studios near Oslo. The facilities were later rented out to individual artisans including Ulla-Mari Brantenberg, Lisbeth Daehlin, Karen Klim, and Bent Saetrang.
Bibliography Jennifer Hawkins Opie, *Scandinavia: Ceramics and Glass in the Twentieth Century*, New York: Rizzoli, 1989.

FSB
> See Braun, Jürgen.

Fuerst, Edwin W. (1903–1988)

American designer.

Biography From 1936, Fuerst worked at Owens-Illinois Glass Company and became head of its packaging department. With Walter Dorwin Teague Sr., designed 1939 Embassy stemware for 1939–40 *New York World's Fair: The World of Tomorrow*, by Libbey. He also developed 1940–42 Modern American series, which included Embassy absent of the crest and was popular but discontinued at the beginning of World War II. He also designed a number of new tableware and art-glass pieces, some with thick walls, plain and ribbed. His architectonic wares included Monticello stemware.
Bibliography Leslie Jackson, *20th Century Factory Glass*, London: Octopus, 2000.

Fujie, Kazuko (1947–)

Japanese designer; born Toyama Prefecture.

Training To 1967, Junior College of Industrial Design, Musahino Fine Arts University.
Biography 1969, Fujie joined Miyawaki Architecture Office and Endo Planning; 1977, began as freelance designer and founded Field Shop Office; designed furniture for Maezawa Garden House in 1982, for Keio University New Library in 1982, for Toyama Airport in 1984; 1983 conference table by Dentsu in Osaka.
Bibliography Cat., *Kagu-mobilier japonais*, Tokyo: Shibaura Institute of Technology, 1985.

Fujii, Nobuhiro (1968–)
> See Sharp.

Fujimori, Taiji (1967–)
Japanese designer; born Saitama.

Training To 1991, design department, Tokyo Zokei University; subsequently, under furniture designer Teruaki Ohashi.
Biography From 1992, Fujimori worked at the Itsuko Hasegawa Atelier architectural-planning studio; 1999, established his own design studio in Tokyo, working on various projects with architects and developing new products. One of his most distinctive designs is the simple, easily transportable flat-packed table/bench set by E&Y Tokyo. He is a lecturer, Kanto-gakuin University, Yokohama, and The Special Engineering College, Kogakuin University, Tokyo.

Fujita, Jun (1951–)
Japanese glass designer.

Training 1975, philosophy of literature, Gakushuin University, Tokyo.
Exhibitions Work subject of 1984 exhibition, Takashimaya department store, Tokyo. Work included in 1984 *Glass '84 in Japan*, Tokyo; 1985 *New Glass in Japan*, Badisches Landesmuseum, Karlsruhe; 1986 *International Exhibition of Glass Craft*, Industrial Gallery of Ishikawa Prefecture, Kanazawa; 1987 *Glass '87 in Japan*, Tokyo; 1988 *Arte en Vidro*, São Paulo Art Museum; 1990 *Glass '90 in Japan*, Tokyo; 1991 (5th) Triennale of Japan Glass Art Crafts Association.
Bibliography Cat., *Glass Japan*, New York: Heller Gallery and Japan Glass Art Crafts Association, 1991: no. 2.

Fujita, Kyohei (1921–)
Japanese glass designer.

Training To 1944, Tokyo University of Arts.
Biography President, Japan Glass Art Crafts Association; member, Japan Art Academy.
Exhibitions/citations Work subject of exhibits, 1977 Kunstsammlungen der Veste, Coburg (Germany); 1988 and 1990, Heller Gallery, New York; and included in two-person 1989 exhibition (with Harvey K. Littleton), Glass Museum, Ebeltoft (Denmark). Work included in 1990 *Glass '90 in Japan*, Tokyo; 1991 (5th) Triennale of Japan Glass Art Crafts Association. 1986 invited artist *Japon des Avant Gardes*, Centre Georges Pompidou, Paris; 1986 prize, Minister of Education, *Japan Modern Decorative Arts*, Tokyo; invited artist and selection committee juror, 1988 *World Glass Now '88*, Hokkaido Museum of Modern Art, Sapporo; 1989 Imperial Prize and Award, Japan Art Academy; 1991 (5th) Triennial of Japan Glass Art Crafts Association.
Bibliography Cat., *Glass Japan*, New York: Heller Gallery and Japan Glass Art Crafts Association, 1991: no. 3.

Fukasawa, Naoto (1956–)
Japanese industrial designer; born Kofu.

Training To 1980, Product Design Division, Department of Design, Tama Art University, Tokyo.
Biography Fukasawa was chief designer at Seiko Epson Corporation, 1989, joined the staff of IDEO industrial-design studio in San Francisco; 1996, returned to Japan as director of IDEO there; has lectured, Royal College of Art, London, and Tama Art University, and, currently, teaches at Matsushita Design; 2002, established his own studio in Tokyo; designed a massage chair by inter.office, the Infobar by Sanyo, electronics within the 'au' design-development section of KDDI/Domestic Cooking Tools by Matsushita (Panasonic), and home electronics under his '±0' brand, developed with Takara. His wall-mounted CD player (designed while at IDEO, discovered by the Muji store/firm as a prototype in an exhibition, and put into production by Ryohin Keikaku) is unusual in that Muji does not publish the names of its designers.
Exhibitions/citations Work included in 2001 *Workspheres*, The Museum of Modern Art, New York, for which Personal Skies (with its view of the sky from a windowless office) and A Chair with a Soul Left Behind were created (catalog below). 1995 (for NEC product), 1998 award (for Alps Electric scanner) and 2002 gold award (for CD player by Muji), Industrie Forum Design (iF), Hanover; gold award (for CD player by Muji), *Design Week* magazine; Hanover; 2003 Mainichi Design Award; and more than 40 others in Japan, Europe, and the US.
Bibliography Michele De Lucchi (ed.), *The International Design Yearbook*, London: Laurence King, 2001. Cat., Paolo Antonelli, *Workspheres: Design and Contemporary Work Styles*, New York: The Museum of Modern Art, 2001.

Fuller, Richard Buckminster (1895–1983)
American architect and inventor; born Milton, Mass.

Training 1913–15, Harvard University; US Naval Academy, Annapolis, Maryland.
Biography While at the Naval Academy, Fuller started his 'theoretical conceptioning' and worked on the 'flying jet-stilts porpoise' transport, published in 1932; after World War I, developed a modernist principle based on getting more from less, calling it 'Dymaxion' (derived from 'DYnamic' and 'MAXImum efficiency'). The first hexagonal Dymaxion House was designed in 1927 to be mass produced, affordable, and easily transported but not built until 1947. The house design was a configuration of mechanical parts rather than a place for living; the only extant full-size example is on permanent display at Henry Ford Museum in Dearborn, Mich., US. 1932, Fuller established the Dymaxion Corporation in Connecticut. The 1932 Dymaxion Three-Wheeled Auto followed. His 1946 Wichita House in Kansas weighed only 6,000 lbs. (2700 kg), was designed to collapse, and could be fitted into a steel cylinder for easy transport. 1947, his study of structures led him to the highly publicized geodesic domes and his first major building, 1958 Union Tank Car Repair shop in Baton Rouge, La., in which spaces between the struts were filled in with panels. At the time, the Baton Rouge dome, spanning 384 ft. (117 m), was the world's largest clear-span enclosure. Fuller designed the US Pavilion at 1967 *Universal and International Exhibition (Expo '67)*, Montreal, and several similar domes for the US government that, due to the cost savings on the government's part, were used repeatedly at international exhibitions, including 1992 *Exposición Universal de Sevilla (Expo '92)*. He developed building systems that he called 'Tensegrity' structures (derived from 'TENSion intEGRITY'). Fuller was admired by the students and the press and taught occasionally at Cornell, Princeton, and Yale Universities and MIT; 1949–75, was a professor, Southern Illinois Institute of Technology, Carbondale, and a popular public speaker, especially with young audiences, and prolific writer of articles and books, including *Ideas and Integrities: A Spontaneous Autobiographical Disclosure* (Englewood Cliffs, N.J.: Prentice-Hall, 1963), *No More Secondhand God and Other Writings* (Carbondale: Southern Illinois University, 1963), *I Seem to Be a Verb* (New York: Bantam, 1970), *Critical Path* (New York: St. Martin's, 1981). A vintage Fuller geodesic dome with a canvas cover is installed at the Vitra Design Museum, Weil am Rhine, Germany.
Exhibitions/citations Work shown at Keck's Crystal House (Dymaxion Car no. 3*)*, 1933–34 *A Century of Progress International Exposition*, Chicago. Work subject of 1999 *Your Private Sky: R. Buckminster Fuller, The Art of Design Science*, Design Museum, London; Kunsthalle, Tirol; Stiftung Bauhaus, Dessau; 1999, Zeppelin-Museum, Friedrichshafen (catalog below). 1980, elected Honorary Royal Designer for Industry, UK.
Bibliography Robert W. Marks and Richard Buckminster Fuller, *The Dymaxion World of Buckminster Fuller*, Garden City, N.Y.: Doubleday, 1960. J. Michale (ed.), 'Richard Buckminster Fuller,' *Architectural Design*, special issue, July 1961. John McHale, *R. Buckminster Fuller*, New York: Braziller, 1962. James Meller (ed.), *The Buckminster Fuller Reader*, London: Cape, 1970. Donald W. Robertson, *Mind's Eye of Buckminster Fuller*, New York: Vantage, 1974. Cat., Joachim Krausse and Claude Lichtenstein (eds.), *Your Private Sky: R. Buckminster Fuller, Design als Kunst einer Wissenschaft*, Ennetbaden: Lars Müller, 1999. Thomas T.K. Zung, *Buckminster Fuller: Anthology for the New Millennium*, New York: St. Martin's, 2001.

Fulper Pottery
American pottery manufacturer; located Flemington and Trenton, N.J.

History 1814, the Samuel Hill Pottery was established in Flemington, N.J.; ultimately became the oldest pottery manufacturer in the US. 1860, Abraham Fulper, a partner at Hill, acquired the firm and, thus, became Fulper Pottery, to produced drain tiles and utilitarian earthenware and stoneware. When Fulper died, his son William Hill Fulper turned the firm's production to high-quality pottery. After extensive experimentation, Fulper released its first art pottery in 1909, under the Vasekraft brand name. It was immediately successful. Patterns, such as Famille Rose, were prestigious and expensive. By the end of the 19th century, Fulper had become a supplier of relatively inexpensive, well-made art pottery. The rarest and most highly regarded of Fulper's wide range of glazes was the crystalline with 'Copper dust' that produced unpredictable firing results. Successful through the 1920s, the Trenton

plant was expanded in 1928 but destroyed by fire in 1929. The second plant in Flemington continued, but the Vasekraft line was discontinued in 1929. 1930, J. Martin Stangl acquired the firm, continuing the art pottery line to 1935. 1955, the firm's name was changed to Stangl Pottery Company, but, 1994, Fulper was reestablished.
Exhibitions Work (crystalline glazes) shown at 1915 *Panama-Pacific International Exposition*, San Francisco. Work subject of 1979 exhibition, Jordan-Volpe Gallery, New York (catalog below).
Bibliography 'The Oldest Pottery in America,' *Art World*, no. 3, Dec. 1917: 252–54. Cat., Robert W. Blasberg with Carol L. Bohdan, *Fulper Art Pottery: An Aesthetic Appreciation, 1909–1929*, New York: Jordan-Volpe Gallery, 1979. Cat., *American Art Pottery*, New York: Cooper-Hewitt Museum, 1987: 116–17. Anne Yaffe Phillips, *From Architecture to Object*, New York: Hirschl and Adler, 1989: 60. Harvey Duke, *Stangl Pottery*, Radnor, Pa.: Wallace-Homestead, 1993.

Funakoshi, Saburo (1931–)
Japanese glassware designer.

Training To 1954, crafts, Tokyo National University of Fine Arts and Music.
Biography Funakoshi worked in the design department of Shizuoka Prefectural Industrial Institute; from 1957, was a glass designer at Hoya Crystal and became head of the Hoya design department in Musashi, where he produced designs for numerous crystal objects made by both hand and machine. Work included 1976 hand-pressed vessels with sand-blasted decorations and, by Hoya, 1978 soy-sauce bottle and 1981 capsule receptacles.
Exhibitions Work subject of a large number of venues.
Bibliography Cat., *New Glass: A Worldwide Survey*, Corning, N.Y.: Corning Museum of Glass, 1979: 255, no. 63. *Modern Japanese Glass*, Tokyo: Kokuritsu Kindia Hakubutsukan (exhibition held at Crafts Gallery, The National Museum of Modern Art, Tokyo), 1982, no. 142. Cat., *Contemporary Vessels. How to Pour*, Tokyo: Crafts Gallery, 1982: Nos. 189–90. Cat., Kathryn B. Hiesinger and George H. Marcus III (eds.), *Design Since 1945*, Philadelphia: Philadelphia Museum of Art, 1983. Cat., *Glass Japan*, New York: Heller Gallery and Japan Glass Art Crafts Association, 1991: no. 5.

Functionalism
Architectural principle.

History Functionalism is a philosophical, symbolic, social, and economic approach to architecture and design whereby form is arrived at through its intended function. It is often thought to be one of the two approaches to architecture and design in the 20th century; historicism is the other. The roots of Functionalism can be traced back to the beginning of design theory, particularly to Vitruvius, the Roman architect and engineer of the 1st century B.C. who asserted that the design of a structure should be determined by its use or function. Prominent followers of Vitruvius included, in the 18th century, Rationalists Fra Carlo Lodoli, Marc-Antoine Laugier, and Francesco Milizia and, in the 19th century, Eugène-Emmanuel Viollet-le-Duc, Henri Labrouste, and Gottfried Semper. With his motto 'form ever follows function,' American architect Louis Henri Sullivan is considered the founder of 20th-century Functionalism. Functionalism has become a label for an extremely wide variety of avant-garde architecture and design in the first half of the 20th century, including Ludwig Mies van der Rohe's classical Rationalism, Erich Mendelsohn's Expressionism, Giuseppe Terragni's unadorned, heroic structures, Frank Lloyd Wright's organic architecture, and Le Corbusier's Cubist solids. There appears to be no clear distinction between Rationalism and Functionalism, despite much debate on the subject.
Bibliography E.R. de Zurko, *Origins of Functionalist Theory*, New York: Columbia University, 1957. Reyner Banham, *Theory and Design in the First Machine Age*, London: Architectural Press, 1960. Julius Posener, *Anfänge des Funktionalismus: Von Arts and Crafts zum Deutscher Werkbund*, Berlin: Ullstein, 1964. Peter Blake and Vittorio Magnago Lampugnani in Vittorio Magnago Lampugnani, *Encyclopedia of 20th-Century Architecture*, New York: Abrams, 1986: 112–13. Martin Pawley, *Theory and Design in the Second Machine Age*, Oxford: Basil Blackwell, 1990.

Fundarò, Anna Maria (1936–1999)
Italian industrial designer and architect; born Alcamo; active Palermo.

Training To 1960, in Palermo.
Biography 1959, Fundarò began her professional career; collaborated with Franco Santapà, Alfonso Porrello, and Antonio Martorana; directed the Istituto di Disegno Industriale; headed the *Annuario Design Sicilia* (annual review of design) and journal *Quarderni*; became a member, Associazione per il Disegno Industriale (ADI). From 1977, she was a professor of industrial design, Faculty of Architecture, Palermo; from 1981, director, Istituto di Disegno Industriale; from 1990 to her death, director, Scuola di Specializzazine in Disegno Industriale. Paticipated in a number of public-space designs, most realized in the last year of her life. Her work was widely published.
Bibliography *ADI Annual 1976*, Milan: Associazione per il Disegno Industriale, 1976. *Modo*, no. 148, March–April 1993: 120. 'Design in Palermo,' *Abitare*, no. 320, 1993. 'Design in Sicilia,' *Interni*, no. 4, 1994. 'Il design in Sicilia: ipotesi e storia,' *Nuove Effemeridi,* no. 31 (monographic issues), 1995. Giuseppe Damiani, *Almeyda tre achitetture tra cronaca e storia,* Palermo: Flaccovio, 1999.

Furness, Frank (1839–1912)
American architect; born Philadelphia.

Training Drafting in the office of architect John Fraser.
Biography 1859–61, Furness worked in the office of architect Richard Morris Hunt and, 1867–71, with architect John Fraser; 1871–75, practiced architecture with anglophile George W. Hewitt, through whom Furness was influenced by British botanical ornamentation, especially as executed by Owen Jones and Christopher Dresser; designed 1876 Pennsylvania Academy of Fine Arts (with Hewitt), Philadelphia, although the Furness-Hewitt partnership was dissolved in 1875. Completed in time for 1876 *Centennial Exhibition*, Philadelphia, the designs for the Philadelphia Academy of Art showed metalwork influenced by Dresser and by French architecture. Louis Henri Sullivan studied under Furness in 1873. A contemporary of H.H. Richardson, Furness designed churches, railroads, and libraries in the Gothic style; his buildings were heavily decorated. The earliest preserved examples of his highly architectonic furniture include the chairs for 1869–71 Rodef Shalom Synagogue in Philadelphia. The 1881–95 period included numerous railroad stations and suburban houses. His masterwork of this period is 1888–91 library of University of Pennsylvania (today called the Furness Building after his brother Horace Howard Furness). From 1895, he designed a number of large-scale commercial and small buildings. His posthumous reputation was low, until the 1970s revival of an interest in his work.
Exhibitions Work subject of 1973 exhibition, Pennsylvania. Furniture included in 1982 exhibition, Whitney Museum of American Art, Fairfield County, Conn. (catalog below).
Bibliography Cat., James F. O'Gorman, *The Architecture of Frank Furness*, Philadelphia: Philadelphia Museum of Art, 1973. Cat., Lisa Phillips (intro.), *Shape and Environment: Furniture by American Architects*, New York: Whitney Museum of American Art, 1982: 32–33. Cat., David A. Hanks and Donald Peirce, *The Virginia Carroll Crawford Collection: American Decorative Arts, 1825–1919*, Atlanta: High Museum of Art, 1983: 78–87. Doreen Bolger Burke et al., *In Pursuit of Beauty: Americans and the Aesthetic Movement*, New York: The Metropolitan Museum of Art/Rizzoli, 1986. George E. Thomas et al., *Frank Furness: The Complete Works*, New York: Princeton Architectural Press, 1991. Edward R. Bosley, *University of Pennsylvania Library: Frank Furness*, London: Phaidon, 1996. Michael J. Lewis, *Frank Furness: Architecture and the Violent Mind*, New York: Norton, 2001.

Furniture Shop, The
American store and workshop; located San Francisco.

History By 1910, Arthur and Lucia Mathews were at the pinnacle of their success in representing the arts community in San Francisco and were identified with the California Decorative Style of the 1890s–1920s. They established The Furniture Shop in San Francisco, where they and their staff of craftspeople were prolific producers of frames, paintings, furniture, fixtures, and accessories in the Arts and Crafts tradition of integrating whole environments, or European *Gesamtkunstwerk*. 1906–20, The Furniture Shop benefited from the rebuilding of San Francisco after the 1906 earthquake and fire. John Zeile was a partner, financial backer, and business manager of the enterprise. Thomas McGlyn oversaw the execution of the shop's work from Arthur Mathews's sketches to the final pieces, managing 30 to 50 carpenters, cabinetmakers, wood carvers, and finishers, although fewer were there on a regular basis. They produced domestic and public pieces, including large suites of furniture and fixtures, and custom murals to the work intended for the Mathews's own use. The limited-production and contract furnishings were the more conservative in design. The Mathews's

work is distinguishable from the simplier Craftsman-style furniture of the Stickleys and the furnishings of the Greenes. Lucia Mathews was fastidious in her decoration applied to smaller pieces; her picture frames were considered works of art.
Bibliography Harvey L. Jones in Timothy J. Andersen et al., *California Design 1910*, Salt Lake City: Peregrine Smith, 1980: 88–93.

Furuta, Toshikazu (1947–)

Japanese glass designer.

Biography Work subject of 1990 exhibition, Kyoto. Work shown in 1988 *International Exhibition of Glass Craft*, Industrial Gallery of Ishikawa Prefecture, Kanazawa; 1990 *Glass '90 in Japan*, Tokyo; 1991 (5th) Triennale of Japan Glass Art Crafts Association.
Bibliography Cat., *Glass Japan*, New York: Heller Gallery and Japan Glass Art Crafts Association, 1991: no. 6.

fuseproject
> See Behár, Yves.

Fusi, Renata (1954–)

Italian designer; born Milan.

Training 1968–73, Liceo Scientifico Leonardo da Vinci; 1973–79, Facoltà di Architettura, Politecnico; both Milan.
Biography All activities in Milan: 1982–84, Fusi worked in the studio of Perry King and Santiago Miranda; 1980–88, was a consultant to and designer for Cappellini and also designed the Artu lamp by Vistosi; 1988 with Silvana Mollica and Paolo Zanotto, established Fusi Mollica Zanotto Architetti Associati. Their design work has included interior architecture of 1987 boutique and 1988 showroom of Maurizio Baldassri in Milan and 1990 Bluemarine boutique in Bari, also 1989–91 hiking shoes and mountain-climbing equipment by Asolo Sport, 1991–93 plastic tabletop items by Arredoplast, 1998 Town and Country hiking-shoe collection by Aku, 2000 modular eyeglass by Zero Industry, a number of exhibitions and fair stands for Cappellini, Cidue, Esper, Solomon, Tomasoni Topsail; others.
Exhibitions/citations *Natural-Mente* (with Studio Cortesi Design), 1991 (18th) Triennale di Milano; others. 1991 Premio Compasso d'Oro; 1996 Annual Design Review, *I.D.* magazine.
> See Mollica, Silvana; Zanotto, Paolo.

Futurism

Artistic movement.

History Futurism expressed a radical rejection of the past, glorification of the machine, pleasure in the transient, and enthusiasm for speed. This combination of ideas was first realized in poet Filippo Tommaso Marinetti's manifesto 'Le futurisme' (published in *Le Figaro* newspaper, Paris: 20 Feb. 1909) and in 'Technical Manifesto of Futurist Painting' (11 April 1910), signed by Carlo Carrà, Luigi Russolo, Giacomo Balla, Gino Severini, and Umberto Boccioni 1910. The Futurists used neo-Impressionist color techniques that Severini and Boccioni had acquired from Balla. By the time of 1912 Futurist exhibition at Galerie Bernheim Jeune in Paris, followers of the movement had adopted Cubist techniques for depicting speed; as Marinetti declared in *Le Figaro*, 'The splendor of the world has been enriched with a new form of beauty—the beauty of speed.' Influential written works by Antonio Sant'Elia followed in 1914 with his 'Manifesto of Futuristic Architecture' in the library journal *Lacerba* and in his catalog introduction that year for *Group of New Trends* exhibition in Milan. However, Sant'Elia left no constructed architectural works. Virgilio Marchi contributed his 'Manifesto of Futurist Architecture—Dynamic, a State of Mind, Dramatic' (1920), in which he described architecture as 'habitable sculpture' and a 'machine for living in.' Futurism, as an effective movement, lasted little beyond Boccioni's 1916 death and/or the 1918 end of World War I. It had considerable influence in Russia, where the movement included Mikhael Fedorovich Larionov, Natalia Goncharova, and Kazimir Malevich. 1911, the Ego-Futurists were the first Russian art group to use the term 'Futurism.' Futurism had some influence on the Dadaists in France (*dada*, French for 'hobby horse') and on Vorticism in Britain. Marcel Duchamp and Robert Delaunay in France were also, but differently, indebted to the movement.
Exhibitions Subject of 1986 *Futurismo e Futurismi* exhibition, Palazzo Grassi, Venice, and 1992 *Futurism 1909–44*, Hokkaido Museum of Art, Sapporo.
Bibliography Antonio Sant'Elia, 'L'architettura futurista,' *Lacerba*, 1 Aug. 1914. D. Gambillo and T. Fiori, *Archivi del futurismo*, Rome: De Luca, 1958–62. Michael Kirby, *Futurist Performance*, New York: Dutton, 1971. Umbro Apollonio, *Futurismo*, Milan: Mazzotta, 1970. Caroline Tisdall and Angelo Bozzolla, *Futurism*, London: Oxford, 1978. Pontus Hulten (organizer), *Futurism and Futurisms*, New York: Abbeville, 1986. John J. Whites, *Literary Futurism: Aspects of the First Avant-Garde*, New York: Oxford, 1990. Filippo Tommaso Marinetti, *Let's Murder the Moonshine: Selected Writings*, Los Angeles: Sun & Moon Classics, 1991.

G

Edward William Godwin. Table (detail). c. 1875. MoMA.

GAB
> See Guldsmedsaktiebolaget.

Gabetti, Roberto (1925–)
> See Drocco, Guido.

Gabriel, René (1890–1950)

French decorator and furniture designer; born Maisons-Alfort; active Paris.

Biography A follower of Francis Jourdain, Gabriel designed wallpaper, fabric, rugs, porcelain (particularly for the Manufacture Nationale de Sèvres), and theater sets (including those in 1927 for Louis Jouvet and his *Léopold le bien-aimé*). Some of his furniture was produced by Kurtz. From 1923, his limited-production furniture became very simple and, c. 1935, was produced in modular combinations of various elements, known as Éléments RG. Subsequently, he designed bent-metal tubular seating and structures; 1920, established the small wallpaper store Au Sansonnet on the rue de Solférino, Paris, and designed papers printed by Papiers Peints de France et Nobilis; 1934, established Ateliers d'Art in Neuilly. He was active in architecture and interior design; 1947, became president, Société des Artistes Décorateurs; continued the limited production of furniture in the style of Francis Jourdain; to 1946, taught, École des Arts Appliqués, and, from 1946, was director, École Nationale Supérieure des Arts Décoratifs, both Paris; participated in the establishment of René Gabriel Prize.
Exhibitions From 1919, work shown at Salon d'Automne and at Salons of Société des Artistes Décorateurs; 1925 *Exposition Internationale des Arts Décoratifs et Industriels Modernes* (girl's bedroom with a rug by Émile Gaudissart and lighting by Jean Perzel), Paris; pavilion of Société des Artistes Décorateurs, 1937 *Exposition Internationale des Arts et Techniques dans la Vie Moderne*. All Paris.
Bibliography *Ensembles mobiliers*, vol. 2, Paris: Charles Moreau, 1937; vol. 6, nos. 19–23, 1945. René Chavanie, 'René Gabriel ou la continuité dans la recherche,' *Mobilier et décoration*, V, 1949: 15–25. Arlette Barré-Despond (ed.), *Dictionnaire international des arts appliqués et du design*, Paris: Regard, 1996. Patrick Favardin, *Les décorateurs des années 50*, Paris: Norma, 2002: 90.

Gabrielsen, Bent (1928–)

Danish metalworker.

Training 1950–53, Danish College of Jewelry, Silversmithing and Commercial Design.
Biography 1953–56, Gabrielsen designed for Hans Hansen in Kolding and, subsequently, for Georg Jensen Sølvesmedie in Copenhagen. Special work included the communion silver and altarpieces of Brændkjær Church in Kolding. 1969, he set up his own workshop.
Exhibitions/citations Work shown at 1956–59 *Neue Form aus Dänemark*, Germany; 1960–61 *The Arts of Denmark* touring the US; 1964 *Modern Scandinavian Jewelry*, New York; 1967 *Lunning Prize Winners*; Den Permanente in Copenhagen; 1968 *Two Centuries of Danish Design*, London; 1969 *Modern Danish Design*, Moscow; 1973, 1976, and 1979 *Jewelry Arts Exhibition*, Tokyo. Gold medal, 1960 (12th) Triennale di Milano; 1964 Lunning Prize.
Bibliography Cat., *Georg Jensen Silversmithy: 77 Artists, 75 Years*, Washington: Smithsonian, 1980. Cat., David Revere McFadden (ed.), *Scandinavian Modern Design 1880–1980*, New York: Abrams, 1982.

Gady, Jean-Marc (1971–)

French designer; born Charenton-le-Pont; active Paris.

Training 1992–97, interior and environmental design, L'École Bleue, Paris.
Biography From 1992, Gady worked for short periods in advertising agencies Publicis Étoile and McCann Erickson in Paris on various advertising accounts and Specimen on promotional films. His products include 1998–99 Angelus and Punch-Light (silicon-coated bulb) lamps, Submarine blown-Pyrex vase, and Air Cup vessel by Ligne Roset; Season light/vase/shelf and Spirit desk by WU gallery; 1999 Moods multi-position chaise; Simple side chair and Nest lounge chair by Liv'it; La Chose porcelain ashtray by G2; lighting by En Attendant les Barbares.
Exhibitions/citations From 1996, work included in a number of venues. Received 1997, 1998, and 2000 Appel Permanent grants, VIA (French furniture association.)
Bibliography Mel Byars, *50 Beds...*, Hove: RotoVision, 2000.

Gaetani, Luigi (1948–)

Italian designer and technician.

Training Industrial technology in province of Alessandria.
Biography At Olivetti, Gaetani worked first in the numerical-control division and, subsequently, technical industrial-design service; was active in developing the engineering design of calculators and other office machines; 1974, worked on color studies at Centro Design Montefibre; from 1978–84, in the studio of Makio Hasuike on the design of Ariston products and a wide range of others; 1979 with Gianluigi Arnaldi, was active in the AD (Agenzia di Design), which became Arnaldi & Gaetani Associati 1989.
Bibliography *Modo*, no. 148, Mar.–Apr. 1993: 120.

Gafforio, Luca (1956–)

Italian architect-designer.

Training Architecture, Istituto Universitario di Architettura, Venice; master's degree in fashion design, Domus Academy, Milan.
Biography 1989, Gafforio cofounded studios Onami Design, consultant for consumer products to a large number of clients, and Surface Digital Design, specialists in CAD-oriented design; has taught design, Politecnico, Milan; collaborated with the European Community, Korean and Taiwanese governments, and the industrial districs of Fukul and Figu, Japan.
Citations 2001 Special prize (X-901 motocycle helmet by Nolan), Premio Compasso d'Oro.
Bibliography Cat., Hans Wichmann, *Italien Design 1945 bis heute*, Munich: Die Neue Sammlung, 1988.

Gaggia, Achille (1895–1961)

Italian inventor; active Milan.

Biography Gaggia worked originally as a bartender in Milan; was dissatisfied with coffee made by steam-driven machine and, thus, experimented on new models in his attic; devised a piston to force water through coffee grounds at high pressure which in turn produced a better-tasting coffee brew with a foamy head; 1937–38, installed his first machines in Milan coffee shops. 1944, he patented a process to produce espresso without the use of steam; 1947, founded Brevetti Gaggia to manufacture his machines with the Classico as the first, operated by gas or electricity; subsequently, produced the world's first domestic electric espresso coffeemaker, the 1952–54 Gilda, named after the 1946 eponymous film featuring Rita Hayworth.
Bibliography Jeremy Myerson and Sylvia Katz, *Conran Design Guides: Kitchenware*, London: Conran Octopus, 1990: 16, 61, 73–74.

Gagnère, Olivier (1952–)

French designer.

Training In economics and law, Paris.
Biography 1980s, Gagnère worked with the Memphis group in Milan. In his own studio, one of his first works was the abstract-form 1984 Verseuse teapot, using industrial materials. His ceramic tea service was produced by Martine Haddad and other work by Écart International. He designed a number of ceramics produced in Vallauris; dinnerware and vases by Bernardaud and its tea rooms in Paris and New York (from 1992) and showrooms; objects by Édition Limitée (a firm of which he is a partner) in Paris; glass in Murano, Italy; glassware and lighting by Cristal Saint-Louis (from 1995); furniture by Artelano; furniture and lighting for Café Marly (interior designer, Yves-Germain Taralon) in Turgot Pavillon of the Louvre; numerous objects in stone, wood, textiles, and metal; and a large body of work in a wide range of traditional materials.
Exhibitions/citations From 1983 at Salons of Société des Artistes Décorateurs, Paris; numerous other venues such as 1986 *New European Design*, Centre Shisheido, Tokyo; 1987 *Le Virtu della Mano*, Verona; 1990 *Métamorphose du Verre*, Strasbourg; 1997 *Made in France 1947–1997*, Centre Georges Pompidou, Paris; 2000 *Absolut Ego* with 16 other designers, Musée des Arts Décoratifs, Paris. Numerous one-person exhibitions, ranging from 1981 at Galerie Détails, Paris, and 1990 *Gagnère–Kuroda*, Galerie Egelund, Ostergade, Denmark, to 2001 *Oliver Gagnère, Designer Français* retrospective, Musée Mandet, Riom, France; 2003 full retrospective *'L'Or avec le Fer,' Le Savoir-Faire d'Olivier Gagnère* full retrospective, Passage de Retz, Paris. 1983 Appel Permanent grant and 1990 Carte Blanche production support, both VIA (French furniture association); Creator of the Year, 1998 Maison & Objet fair, Villepinte, France.
Bibliography François Mathey, *Au bonheur des formes, design français 1945–1992*, Paris: Regard, 1992. Cat., Enzo Biffi Gentili, *Il disegno ceramico: Gagnère, Laudani, Romanelli, Székely*, Milan: Electa, 1999. Marie-Josée Linou, *Olivier Gagnère, designer français*, Paris: Samogy éditions d'art, 2001. www.via.asso.fr

Gaillard, Eugène (1862–1933)

French designer and writer; brother of jeweler Lucien Gaillard.

Biography Gaillard was associated with Siegfried Bing's gallery/shop L'Art Nouveau in Paris; with Georges de Feure participated in activities of the group L'Art Nouveau; is best known for his refined moldings; 1900–14, designed simple, elegant furniture; felt that decoration, even though inspired by nature, should be 'unreal... so that it might be completely natural without evoking any precise form from the animal or vegetable kingdoms.' He wrote the book *À propos du mobilier* (1906).
Exhibitions Showed work at Salons of Société des Artistes Décorateurs, also a founding member; 1900 *Exposition Universelle* (created Bing's stand of six fully decorated rooms, with de Feure and Edward Colonna, and bedroom and dining room), Paris.
Bibliography Yvonne Brunhammer et al., *Art Nouveau Belgium, France*, Houston: Rice University, 1976. Pierre Kjellberg, *Art déco: les maîtres du mobilier, le décor des paquebots*, Paris: Amateur, 1986: 78. Peter van Dam, *Eugène Gaillard: meublier (1862–1933)*, The Hague: Peter van Dam, 1986.

GAKhN (state academy of artistic sciences)

Russian learning institution.

History Active 1921–30, RAKhN (Russian [state] academy of artistic sciences) was the successor to the Museums of Artistic Culture in Moscow and Petrograd/Leningrad and and one of the most important groups organized for interdisciplinary research of the early Soviet period; was founded in Moscow partially with the help of Vasillii Kandinsky and composed of departments of physiomathematics, physiopsychology, philosophy, and sociology; later changed to GAKhN, within which a cinema museum was created in the 1920s; 1932, was disbanded.
Bibliography Cat., *Kunst und Revolution: Russische und Sowjetische Kunst 1910–1932*, Vienna: Österreichisches Museum für angewandte Kunst, 1988. Cat., *The Great Utopia: The Russian and Soviet Avant-Garde, 1915–1932*, New York: Guggenheim Museum, 1992.

Galaaen, Konrad (1923–)

Norwegian ceramicist.

Training 1943–47, painting and ceramics, Statens Håndverks-og Kunstindustriskole, Oslo.
Biography From 1947, Galaaen designed serially produced ceramics and art pieces for Porsgrund and established the Studio Galaaen there; received numerous commissions from others for architectural ceramics and tiles.
Bibliography Fredrik Wildhagen, *Norge i Form*, Oslo: Stenersen, 1988: 87. Jennifer Hawkins Opie, *Scandinavia: Ceramics and Glass in the Twentieth Century*, New York: Rizzoli, 1989.

Gale, Thomas C. (1943–)

American automobile designer; born Flint, Mich.

Training Bachelor's degree in mechanical engineering and master's in business administration, Michigan State University, Lansing.
Biography After the university, from 1967, Gale became a body engineer at Chrysler Corporation, Detroit, Mich.; subsequently there, a designer of car and truck interiors, then of exteriors, then active in product planning; late 1980s through 1990s, managed some of the influential designers of automobile bodies at Chrysler, whose heritage he respected and where, due to his enthusiasm for hot-rods, he developed some of the 1990s more radical, exotic, and advanced approaches; had initial success with 1984 minivans; 1985, became vice-president of Chrysler design and, 1991, supervisor of the minivan platform group and, 1993, director of the vehicle-development program. These positions were rare for a designer in a big auto firm; Gale rose to a higher corporate position than any other recent car designer. He incorporated early car-design elements with bold and new idiosyncratic, distinctly American features; masterminded Dodge's 1992 Viper, 1991 Neon Mk1 and 2, 1993 Intrepid Mk1, 1994 Ram pickup truck, and Intrepid; 1993 Plymouth Prowler; and 2001 Chrysler PT Cruiser and Chrysler Cirrus (with a 'cab-forward' configuration to offer a 'cabin room'). The new bodies under his supervision appreciably helped the financially troubled Chrysler firm but certainly excited consumers with bodies plagiarized by competitors. 31 Jan. 2001, Gale relinquished his position as vice-president of product development and design and general manager of passenger-car operations at Chrysler to Trevor Creed, senior vice-president of design, and Richard Schaum, executive vice-president of product development. Gale became a consultant to the new amalgamation, DaimlerChrysler.
Bibliography *50 Years of Chrysler's Hottest Cars*, New York: Random House Value, 1999. Matt DeLorenzo and John Lamm, *Chrysler PT Cruiser*, Osceola, Wis.: Motor Books International, 2000. Jim McCraw, 'He Put a New Face on Chrysler,' *The New York Times*, 9 Feb. 2001: F1. Penny Sparke, *A Century of Car Design*, London: Mitchell Beazley, 2002. Matt Stone, *The Viper*, Saint Paul, Minn.: Motor Books International, 2003.

Gallé, Émile (1846–1904)

French designer and glassmaker; born and active Nancy.

Training In painting and design under artists in Nancy; 1862, botany, Université de Nancy, under naturalist Dominique-Alexandre Godron; 1865–66, philosophy and mineralogy in Weimar and Atelier für Architektur und Kunstgewerbe in Weimar; 1866–67, apprenticeship in glassmaking at Burgun und Schverer in Meisenthal, Germany.
Biography Gallé learned the ceramics and glass crafts in his father Charles Gallé's workshop in Saint-Clément. His father also operated a store in Nancy for the sale of ceramics and glassware, some of which the father designed, finished, and decorated, and acquired partial proprietorship of a pottery near Saint-Clément. Émile Gallé himself cut and enameled glassware and painted faïence; 1862–72, traveled, worked with his father, studied, and served in the Franco-Prussian War, after which he assisted E. du Sommerard in organizing the *Art de France* exhibition in London; studied art in the collections at Cluny and the Louvre, in particular cameos and precious stones in the Louvre's Galerie d'Apollon that later influenced his own cameo and cut-glass work; 1874, assumed the directorship of his family's firm. By 1884, he had produced a large body of work, including some in Islamic and medieval styles. Other designs were cast with up to four layers of glass and included air bubbles, enamels, and gold and platinum paillons, illustrating flowers, insects, vegetation, and, rarely, the human form. Through a search for wood bases for his glassware, he became interested in the grains of exotic woods and, 1884, began designing furniture. The first series of Gallé's furniture, reflecting 18th-century cabinetwork with Renaissance-type carving, was shown at 1889 *Exposition Universelle*, Paris. He showed pieces that could be inexpensively machine produced and waxed (never polished or varnished); 1884, began using opaque glass influenced by the Brandt collection of Chinese glass at Kunstgewerbemuseum, Berlin; 1889, beginning to reduce the number of layers in his acid-etched glasswork to three, called himself the 'vulgarizer of art'; produced notable unique pieces as well as limited editions known as the *grand genre* and *demi-riche*. By this time the Gallé workshop produced many pieces neither of his hand nor of his design. By 1884, his unique pieces and prototypes were produced in Nancy and his industrial glass by Burgun und Schverer, Meisenthal. 1886, he established a fully equipped cabinetmaking facility with steam sheds, workshops, sawmills, stores, offices, and showrooms; amassed a large library of reference works; grew plants, grouped by species, which he used as models for his marquetry; for his complicated decorative inlays, kept a stock of over 600 veneers; 1897, received patents for marquetry and *patinage* (texturing). His *verres sculptés* produced c. 1900 appeared to be more sculpture than vessels. 1901, he founded Alliance Provinciale des Industries d'Art (aka École de Nancy), serving as its first president. His wife and daughters briefly managed the firm from his 1904 death to 1905, when his two sons-in-law and manager Émile Lang took over, assisted by Victor Prouvé; it closed in 1931. Gallé's dissertations on the applied arts were published posthumously as *Ecrits pour l'art—floriculture, art décoratif, notices d'exposition (1884–1889)* (Paris: Librairie Renouard/H. Laurens, 1908).

Émile Gallé. Vase. c. 1900. Glass, h. approx. 9 1/2" (24.1 cm). Fund. Mfr.: Emile Gallé, France. Edgar Kaufmann, Jr. Fund. MoMA.

Exhibitions/citations In Paris: work first noticed at 1878 *Exposition Universelle*, Paris, and shown at 1884 Salon of Union Centrale des Arts Décoratifs. Appeared as a glass artist at 1884 *Exposition Universelle* (showing 300 pieces, some in Islamic and medieval styles); 1889 *Exposition Universelle*, Paris; top prizes (for glassware, furniture, and collaborative work), 1900 *Exposition Universelle*; École de Nancy's 1904 exhibition, Pavillon de Marsan, the Louvre. 1900, Légion d'Honneur.
Bibliography Émile Gallé, 'Le mobilier contemporain orné d'après la nature,' *Revue des arts décoratifs*, vol. XX, 1900: 333–41, 365–77. Louis de Fourcaud, *Émile Gallé*, Paris: Librarie d l'Art, 1903. R. and L. Grover, *Carved and Decorated European Art Glass*, Rutland, Vermont: Tuttle, 1970: 121–29. J. Bloch-Dermant, *L'art du verre en France 1860–1914*, Paris: Denöel, 1975: 90. Philippe Garner, *Émile Gallé*, London: Academy, 1976. Yvonne Brunhammer et al., *Art Nouveau Belgium, France*, Houston: Rice University, 1976. Alastair Duncan, *Art Nouveau and Art Déco Lighting*, New York: Simon & Schuster, 1978. Jessica Rutherford, *Art Nouveau, Art Deco and the Thirties: The Furniture Collections at Brighton Museum*, Brighton: The Royal Pavilion, Art Gallery and Museums, 1983: 13–14.

Gallen-Kallela, Akseli (aka Axel Gallén 1865–1931)

Finnish painter and designer.

Training Painting, Taideyhdistyksen Piirustuskoulu, Helsinki; 1881–84, Académie Julian and atelier of Fernand Cormon, both Paris.
Biography 1905, Akseli Gallen-Kallela simplified and changed his name to Axel Gallén; was a pioneer and the prime exponent of the Finnish National Romantic Movement. His work covered a wide range of crafts media. 1928, he painted the ceiling frescoes of Suomen Kansallismuseo (Finnish national museum) in Helsinki. His textiles, including *ryijy* rugs, were produced with flamelike motifs arranged asymmetrically and most woven by the Suomen Käsityön Ystävien (friends of Finnish handicraft).
Exhibitions/citations Gold medal (Iris room), 1900 *Exposition Universelle*, Paris, where he painted frescoes for the Finnish pavilion. Had his own section at 1914 Biennale di Venezia and at 1915 *Panama-Pacific Exposition*, San Francisco. Work subject of 1906–08 retrospective in Hungary, and of 1971 exhibition, Nationalmuseum, Stockholm (catalog below).
Bibliography Onni Okkonen, *A. Gallen-Kallela: piirustuksia = teckningar = drawings*, Porvoo: W. Söderström, 1947. Onni Okkonen, *Akseli Gallen-Kallelan taidetta*, Porvoo: W. Söderström, 1948. Onni Okkonen, *A. Gallen-Kallela: elämä ja taide*, Porvoo: W. Söderström, 1949. Cat., Eva Nordenson (ed.), *Finskt sekelskifte*, Stockholm: Rabén & Sjögren, 1971. Seppo Knuuttila, *Akseli Gallen-Kallelan Väinämöiset*, Helsinki: Suomalaisen Kirjallisuuden Seura, 1978. Kirsti Gallén-Kallela, *Isäni Akseli Gallen-Kallela*, Porvoo: W. Söderström, 1964.

Gallerey, Mathieu

French decorator, furniture designer, and metalworker; born and active Paris.

Biography Gallerey was active in a workshop at 2, rue de la Roquette, Paris, where he produced furniture, lighting, rugs, and wallpaper. Early on, his designs reflected the rustic, provincial French style. However, Gallerey's starkly simple dining-room suite at the 1937 *Exposition* in Paris was in the Art Déco manner. 1904–24, he was a member of the Société des Artistes Décorateurs. In some of his work, he called on beaten copper to produce a sculptural effect, developed earlier by Art Nouveau exponents; 1942, designed and furnished his own villa in Saint-Mandé.
Exhibitions/citations In Paris: work first shown and received second prize (dining-room suite, furniture competition), 1900 *Exposition Universelle*, Paris. Exhibited at 1908 Salon of Société Nationale des Beaux-Arts; 1912 Salon of Société des Artistes Décorateurs, editions of Salon d'Automne, 1937 *Exposition Internationale des Arts et Techniques dans la Vie Moderne*,.
Bibliography Émile Sedeyn, *Le mobilier*, F. Rieder, 1921. Léon Deshairs (intro.), *Modern French Decorative Art: A Collection of Examples of Modern French Decoration*, Paris: Albert Lévy, c. 1925–30. Pierre Kjellberg, *Art déco: les maîtres du mobilier, le décor des paquebots*, Paris: Amateur, 1986: 78.

Galloway and Graff
American terracotta manufacturers; located Philadelphia.

History 1868, William Galloway and John Graff set up a partnership in Philadelphia to continue the activities of a previous business begun in 1810. Located on Market Street, the firm produced utilitarian and ornamental terracotta ware including urns, pedestals, sundials, benches, bird baths, flower boxes, fountains, and architectural ornamentation. Its objects were made from clays found in Pennsylvania, Maryland, and New Jersey. 1876, it began producing vases and plaques based on antique models, possibly inspired by ancient Greek vases seen in the Danish Pavilion at 1876 *Centennial Exposition*, Philadelphia; 1889, moved its plant to Walnut Street; by 1893, was conducting business under the name William Galloway; 1911, was incorporated as Galloway Terra-Cotta Company, when Galloway's son William B. Galloway became its president; closed in c. 1941.
Exhibitions/citations Work (including vases copied from examples in the British Museum, London) shown at 1876 *Centennial Exposition*, Philadelphia. First prize, 1893 *World's Columbian Exposition*, Chicago; grand prize, 1904 *Louisiana Purchase Exposition*, St. Louis.
Bibliography Edwin AtLee Barber, *The Pottery and Porcelain of the United States...*, New York: Feingold & Lewis, 1909. Doreen Bolger Burke et al., *In Pursuit of Beauty: Americans and the Aesthetic Movement*, New York: The Metropolitan Museum of Art/Rizzoli, 1986.

galuchat
> See shagreen.

Gambardella, Claudio (1953–)
Italian architect and designer; born Naples.

Training To 1980 under Riccardo Dalisi, Facoltá di Architettura, Seconda Università degli Studi di Napoli (SUN).
Biography 1981–81, Gambardella taught under Dalisi at SUN in Naples and, from 1984, a faculty member there; also taught design and applied arts, Istituto Superiore di Design, Naples; has been active as an architect, designer, and researcher into local arts-and-crafts industries as they relate to employment and tourism, and the curator of a number of exhibitions; has written widely. Design work includes 1986 Merlino table clock, 1991 Mare Nostrum table by Paolo Mariano, 2000 ceramics by Franco Raimondi, others.
Exhibitions Work included in exhibitions in Paris, New York, and Italy, including 1983 *Oggetti Progetti/Uno*, Naples; 1986 *Tic-Tax/Expo Arte*, Bari; 1986 *Forum Design*, Naples; 1991 *Per Abitare con l'Arte*, Milan; 1992 *Alabastro–Oggetti Fatti ad Arte*, Milan; 1993 *Design, Miroir du Siècle*, Grand Palais, Paris; 1996 invitational exhibition/competition *Fatto ad Arte*, TODI; 1996 *Caserta–Passagi si Senso* and 2000 *Dafne o il Compimento del Classico*, Abitare il Tempo fair, Verona; 2000 *Le Diversità/Colori Locali*, Fortenza da Basso, Florence.
Bibliography Fumio Shimizu and Studio Matteo Thun (eds.), *The Italian Design: Descendants of Leonardo da Vinci*, Tokyo: Graphic-sha, 1987. *Interni*, no. 364, Oct. 1986. Fumio Shimizu and David Palterer, *The Italian Furniture*, Japan: Graphic-sha, 1991. *Architektur & Wohnen*, no. 3, June–July 1991. *Industrial Design–European Masters/3*, Barcelona: Atrium, 1992. Cat., *Design, miroir du siècle*, Paris: Flammarion, 1993. By Gambardella: 'Arredo Urbano a Napoli/Edicole,' *Domus*, no. 656, Dec. 1984; *Il progetto leggero–Riccardo Dalisi: 20 anni di design*, Naples: Clean, 1988; 'Le prospettive dell'architetto' (Paolo Portoghesi profile), *Interni*, no. 378, March 1988; 'Gli anni '70,' in Almerico de Angelis (ed.), *Design: storia e storie–le storie parallel*, Naples: NC, 1994.

Games, Abram (1914–1996; b. Abraham Games)
British graphic artist and industrial designer; born London.

Training Two terms, St. Martins School of Art, London; life class in drawing.
Biography 1932–36, Games was an office boy at commerical-art studio Askew-Young, London; became a freelance graphic designer with work including 1930s–50s posters for the British War Office, British post office, London Transport, Shell, British Petroleum, BOAC, Guinness, and others, and his graphics for 1951 *Festival of Britain* exposition, London. From 1942, he was an official war artist, designing printed propaganda for British Ministry of Information; was one of the last graphic artists to draw directly and traditionally on a lithographic stone rather than reproducing his work by means of the new photographic

Bertel Gardberg. Tea strainer. 1955. Silver and teak, overall 1 x 2 1/2 x 4 1/2" (2.5 x 6.4 x 11.5 cm). Mfr.: Bertel Gardberg, Finland. Given anonymously. MoMA.

technique. He is known as one of the great poster designers of the 20th century. Games also learned to mold and cast metal and thus designed the widely published and highly sculptural 1947 coffee percolator produced from 1949 by Cona Coffee Company, reworked in 1959, and still in production. Original it was built of disused airplane aluminum, plentiful at the end of World War II. Early 1960s, he redesigned the body and workings of the Gestetner duplicating machine; although, due to the decline of the use of mimeographic duplicators (invented in 1881) and the introduction of xerographics and also to Hungarian émigré Dávid Gestetner's death, it was not put into production.

Bibliography Michael Farr, *Design in British Industry: A Mid-Century Survey*, London: Cambridge, 1955: 145. Jeremy Myerson and Sylvia Katz, *Conran Design Guides: Kitchenware*, London: Conran Octopus, 1990.

Gammelgaard, Jørgen (1938–91)
Danish designer; born Bispebjerg.

Training 1957, apprentice cabinetmaker, C.B. Hansen's furniture workshop; 1959–62, Kunsthåndværkskolen; 1962–64, visiting student, department of furniture and spatial art, Kunstakademiets Arkitektskole, all Copenhagen.
Biography 1957–59, Gammelgaard was a journeyman cabinetmaker, A.J. Iversen; 1962–64, designer in the various offices of architects/designers Grete Jalk, Steen Eiler Rasmussen, and Mogens Koch; 1965–67, was assigned by UNESCO as a consultant in furniture making and design in Samoa; 1967–68, served in the air force. 1968–69 period: he was a designer in the office of architect/designer Arne Jacobsen, designed furniture for the Rødovre Public Library, was assigned by UNESCO as a furniture consultant in the Sudan and Ceylon (now Sri Lanka). 1970, he was a designer in the office of architect Jørgen Bo, designed lamps and cutlery by Design Forum, and was a designer of furniture and exhibitions in the office of an architect. 1971–73, he taught, department of furniture, Kunsthåndværkskolen, and consulted, department of furniture development, Teknologisk Institut. 1973, he set up his own design office and was a juror and examiner, Kunsthåndværkskolen; 1976–79 with Grete Jalk, cofounded Cabinetmakers' Autumn Exhibition (SE); 1976–79, designed furniture by Karl Andersson & Söner, upholstered leather furniture by Ivan Schlechter, and exhibitions of the SE. 1980, he developed a hydraulic mini-tractor by Linexa and designed furniture by Erik Jørgensen Møbelfabrik; 1982, contract and domestic furniture by Schiang Møbler; 1983, exhibitions at Marienlyst Castle in Helsingør; 1984–86, chairperson, Committee on Arts and Crafts and Industrial Design, Danish State Art Foundation; 1986, visiting professor, department of industrial design, Kunsthåndværkskolen; 1987, professor, department of furniture and spatial art, Kunstakademiet; 1989, furniture and lighting for Frederiksborg Castle in Hillerød; 1990 office furniture by MH Stålmøbler.
Exhibitions/citations Lamps, furniture, and accessories included in Danish State Art Foundation exhibition. Work subject of 1995 exhibition, Copenhagen (catalog below). As a student at Kunsthåndværkskolen, silver and bronze medals in an arts-and-crafts project and

participated in Cabinetmakers' Guild competitions; 1971 Møbelprisen (Danish furniture award); 1986 annual prize, Kunsthåndværkerrådet (Danish council of arts and crafts); 1986 annual prize, Dansk Designråd (Danish design council).
Bibliography Frederik Sieck, *Nutidig Dansk Møbeldesign – en kortfattet illustreret beskrivelse*, Copenhagen: Bondo Gravesen, 1990. Cat., Per Mollerup, *Jørgen Gammelgard*, Copenhagen: Kunstindustrimuseet, 1995.

Gammelgaard, Niels (1944–)

Danish architect and designer; born Copenhagen.

Training To 1970, architecture, Det Kongelige Danske Kunstakademi, Copenhagen.
Biography 1969 with four other architects, Gammelgaard founded Box 25 Architects, active to 1978; from 1970, taught, department of industrial design, Det Kongelige Danske Kunstakademi, Copenhagen; also taught, Det Kongelige Danske Kunstakademi, and the Arkitektskolen, Århus; 1978 with Lars Mathiesen (1950–), founded Pelikan Design. 1986–91, Gammelgaard worked on his own but, 1992, re-established Pelikan Design where, with Mathiesen, designed Decision public-seating bank, Labyrint and Wing screen-walls, and Plano table by Fritz Hansen. Other work includes 1973 Sofiegården student housing, 1976 Kvarterlygten (Neigborhood lamp) by Louis Poulsen, designs (with Mathiesen and alone) from 1975 by IKEA, 1980 child's Tribike by Rabo, café chair by Fritz Hansen, 1994 Opus chair by Bent Krogh, office furniture by Duba, Ypsilon lounge chair by Metteograssi, 1995 equipment/furniture for the Danish railway company carriages.
Citations For work by Fritz Hansen: 1983 Top Ten European design award, Cologne; 1996 Danish ID Award; Red Dot award (three times), Design Zentrum Nordrhein Westfalen, Essen; 1980 Dansk ID Prize (for Tribike, with Mathiesen), 1991 and 1996 Scan-Prize, Utmärkt Svensk Form (three times), 1993 Upholstered Furniture Design Award Europe, 1993 Danish Furniture Award, 1996 Brunel Award for Outstanding Visual Design in Public Railway Design; other prizes in Scandinavia and Japan.
Bibliography Robert A.M. Stern (ed.), *The International Design Yearbook*, New York: Abbeville, 1985/1986.

Gamperl, Ernst (1965–)

German designer and cabinetmaker; born Munich.

Training 1984, completed his academic studies; apprenticeship as a cabinetmaker and turner, qualifying as journeyman in both in 1989–90.
Biography Gamperl began his professional career as a carpenter and continues to call on his craft skills in his furniture creations; 1990, set up a cabinetmaking workshop in Trauchgau/Allgäu and joined the Bayerische Gesellschaft der Kunstgewerbe (Bavarian society of arts and crafts); 1992, established a new workshop in Bidingen/Allgäu; has a deep-seated love of nature, particularly of the Lake Garda region of Northern Italy where he resides; in his furniture, emphasizes the natural grain, texture, and color of woods, which he enhances by hand-polishing.
Exhibitions From 1991, work subject of numerous German and international exhibitions.

Gandini, Marcello (1938–)

Italian automobile designer.

Biography 1965, Gandini turned from being active as an independent designer to work at Bertone coachworks, succeeding designer Giorgetto Giugiaro within a year's time there; was probably Bertone's most influential designer and assisted in the creation of possibly the most revolutionary sports-car concepts ever. His 1966 Lamborghini Miura (named for a Spanish fighting bull) was the first of the supercars. Others have include 1974 Countach, 1971 Lancia Stratos, 1972 Fiat X1/9, the popular 1982 Citroën BX. Late 1970s, he became an individualist and focused on a number of industrial-vehicle and car designs; after 15 years, left Bertone and became a freelance stylist of cars, including 1980 Lamborghini Diablo (modified by Chrysler), 1989 Cizeta V16T ('c' and 'z' in Cizeta being the sounds of auto manufacturer Claudio Zampolli's initials), 1990–91 Bugatti EB110, 1991 Iso Grifo, and 1995 Maserati Shamal. Gandini's bodies feature difficult entry, almost no headroom, poor visibility, and deficient aerodynamics—none a deterent to supercar enthusiasts; prefers the angular, wedge shape; has designed no mass-made, in-production cars.
Exhibitions In addition to others at numerous earlier shows, the dramatic V16T (delivered 1991) shown at 1988 Salon de l'Auto, Geneva.
Bibliography Penny Sparke, *A Century of Car Design*, London: Mitchell Beazley, 2002.

Garcés, Jordi (1945–); Enric Soria (1937–)

Spanish architects and designers; born Barcelona.

Training To 1970, architecture school, Barcelona.
Biographies Garcés and Soria worked together in the Martorell-Bohigas-Mackay studio; subsequently, set up their own association, whose work has been widely published. Product designs have included 1973 Silvestrina cylinder lamp by Bd Ediciones de Diseño and 1990 Banc Sócrates bench by Escofet.
Exhibitions/citations Subject of numerous venues. 1987, 1989, and 1991 Premi FAD d'Arquitectura (best Barcelona building citation).
Bibliography '200 logements, architects: Jordi Garces and Enric Soria,' *L'architecture d'aujourd'hui*, no. 244, Apr. 1986: 40–41. 'Edificio de viviendas y jardines centrales en Mollet del Vallès, Barcelona: Jordi Garcès y Enric Sòria, arquitectos,' *Diseño*, no. 153, 1994: 70+.

Garcia Garay, Jorge (1945–)

Argentine designer and entrepreneur; born Buenos Aires; active Barcelona.

Training 1974, degree in architecture, Facultad de Arquitectura, Universidad de Buenos Aires.
Biography After schooling, Garay set up his own firm in Buenos Aires; 1979 settled in Barcelona with his wife Lili Rosenzuit and, the same year, established Garcia Garay Design, designing and producing furniture and lighting, eventualy primarily lighting; became a naturalized Spanish citizen.
Exhibitions/honors Work included in a number of exhibitions. 1979, 1986 awards, ADI/FAD (industrial-design and decorative-arts associations), Spain.
Bibliography *The International Design Yearbook*, New York: Abbeville, 1988, 1989, 1991, 1998, 2000, 2001. Emma Dent Coad, *Spanish Design and Architecture*, New York: Rizzoli, 1990. V. Lorenzo Porcelli, *International Lighting Design*, Rockport, Maine: Rockport, 1991. Guy Julier, *New Spanish Design*, London: Thames & Hudson, 1991. Mel Byars, *50 Lights...*, Hove: RotoVision, 1997. Robert Blaich, *New Notable Product Design*, Rockport, Maine: Rockport, 1995. Jeremy Myerson, *International Lighting Design*, London: Laurence King, 1996.

Gardberg, Bertel (1916–)

Finnish jeweler and metalworker.

Education 1938–41, Taideteollinen korkeakoulu, Helsinki.
Biography Gardberg first worked in Copenhagen and, subsequently, moved to Helsinki, where he maintained a studio 1949–66; designed silver and stainless-steel tableware by the Georg Jensen Sølvsmedie in Copenhagen; Les Galeries Lafayette department store in Paris; and Kilkenny Design Workshops in Dublin; although known for his metalwares, also worked in wood and stone; 1951–53, taught, Taideteollinen korkeakoulu, Helsinki; attempted to revive Ireland's decorative arts and promote craftsmanship locally through his service as artistic director, Kilkenny Design Workshop in Dublin 1966–68, and head of design and technical director of Rionor in Kilkenny 1968–71. Other cutlery and stainless-steel models were produced by Fiskars, Hackman, and Hopeatehdas, and wooden pieces and ecclesiastical and domestic silver by Noormarkun Kotiteollisuus. 1973, he set up a studio in Pohja, Finland, where he continued his activities in woodworking, metalwares, and silver jewelry, into which he incorporated, as previously developed in Ireland, precious and semi-precious stones.
Exhibitions/citations Work shown at 1955 exhibition, Gothenburg; 1956 exhibition, Copenhagen. 1961 Lunning Prize; gold medals at 1954 (10th) and 1957 (11th) and four silver medals at 1960 (12th) editions of Triennale di Milano; 1982, elected member, Academy of Finland.
Bibliography Erik Zahle (ed.), *A Treasury of Scandinavian Design*, New York: Golden Press, 1961. John Haycraft, *Finnish Jewellery and Silverware*, Helsinki: Otava, 1962. Cat., *Georg Jensen Silversmithy: 77 Artists, 75 Years*, Washington: Smithsonian, 1980. Cat., David Revere McFadden (ed.), *Scandinavian Modern Design 1880–1980*, New York: Abrams, 1982. Barbro Kulvik, 'Craftsmanship Is a Way of Life,' *Form Function Finland*, no. 1, 1983: 34–39. Cat., Kathryn B. Hiesinger and George H. Marcus III (eds.), *Design Since 1945*, Philadelphia: Philadelphia Museum of Art, 1983. Cat., *The Lunning Prize*, Stockholm: Nationalmuseum, 1986.

Gardella, Ignazio (1905–1999)

Italian architect-designer; born and active Milan.

Education To 1931, engineering, Politecnico, Milan; to 1949, architecture, Istituto Universitario di Architettura, Venice.
Biography Gardella began his career as an architect and town planner with interior decoration and rebuilding schemes including 1934 theater in Busto Arsizio; entered the competition for the tower on the Piazza del Duomo in Milan, followed by his design for 1937 Dispensario Provinciale e Laboratorio di Igiene e Profilassi, Alessandria (Italy); became active in industrial design and designed 1940 folding butterfly chair by Vigano; 1949 with Corrado Corradi Dell'Acqua, Luigi Caccia Dominioni, and set up the Azucena shop in 1947 with the intention of having a place to experiment and produced high-quality furniture and furnishings. Gardella wrote for the journal *Casabella* during Ernesto Rogers's editorship 1954–65; was professor of architectural composition, Istituto Universitario di Architettura, Venice. In the 1950s, Anna Castelli Ferrieri joined Gardella, becoming the architect and designer who was to realize his designs; worked with Gardella for 15 years on public-housing and furniture projects. Gardella was among the first to break with Italian Rationalism, reviving the neoclassical architectural tradition. His classical façade for 1945 Villa Borletti and Olivetti headquarters building, Ivrea, placed him at the center of the 1950s controversies discussed in Rogers's *Casabella*. Gardella designed the Digamma armchair by Gavina; street lighting for the Piazza San Babilia, Milan; pioneering plastic furniture with Castelli Ferrieri by Kartell; furniture by Rima, and 1960 Olivetti showroom in Düsseldorf. His buildings included 1950–51 IACP 'Mangiagalli' quarter (with Franco Albini) in Milan; 1950 – 53 transformation of Terme Regina Isabella in Lacco Ameno d'Ischia; 1954–58 apartment building in Zattere; 1955–59 Olivetti refectory building in Ivrea; 1963–66 Chiesa di Sant'Enrico in Metanopoli; 1968–71 building for the technical offices of Alfa Romeo (with Ferrieri and Jacopo Gardella) in Arese; 1968 competition project for the new theater in Vicenza; 1981–82 project for the reconstruction of Teatro Carlo Felice (with Aldo Rossi and Fabio Reinhart) in Genoa. He was a member of CIAM, INU, MSA, and IN-Arch, and, from 1956, of Associazione per il Disegno Industriale (ADI); executive committee member, 1960 (12th) Triennale di Milano, and administrative counselor of its 1964 (13th) and 1968 (14th) editions and a juror.
Exhibitions/citations 1947 House for Three People shown at RIMA exhibition. Shelving and cabinets for Spezzo shown at 1948 (7th) Triennale di Milano, receiving a gold medal. Designed Standard pavilion, 1951 (9th) Triennale di Milano, receiving a gold medal for furniture by Azucena and showed his work at chair exhibition of 1954 (10th) edition. First national 1955 Olivetti prize (architecture); 1972 MIA gold medal (with Ferrieri, oval polyester table by Kartell). Work subject of 1986 exhibition, Gund Hall Gallery, Cambridge, Mass.; 1992, Padiglione d'Arte Contemporanea, Milan; 1998–99 exhibit, Centro Culturale 'Città di Cremona,' Santa Maria della Pietà, Italy (catalog below).
Bibliography Giulio Carlo Argan (intro.), *Ignazio Gardella*, Milan: Comunità, 1959. Andrea Branzi and Michele De Lucchi, *Design Italiano degli Anni '50*, Milan: Ricerche Design Editrice, 1985. Cat., Alberto Samonà, *Ignazio Gardella e il professionismo italiano*, Rome: Officina, 1981. M. Porta (ed.), *L'Architettura di Ignazio Gardella*, Milan: Etas, 1985. Paolo Zermani, *Ignazio Gardella*, Bari: Laterza, 1991. Gianluca Frediani and Michele Capobianco, *Ignazio Gardella e Ischia*, Rome: Officina, 1991. Paolo Zermani, *Ignazio Gardella*, Rome: Laterza, 1991. Cat., Maria Cristina Loi et al., *Ignazio Gardella architetture*, Milan: Electa, 1998.

Gardère, Adrien (1972–)

French designer; born and active Paris.

Training École Nationale Supérieure des Arts Appliqués–Boulle; École Nationale Supérieure des Arts Décoratifs; both Paris.
Biography Gardère spent his youth in India; eventually established a studio in Paris; has designed for Conran, Driade, Hermès, Puiforcat, and Ligne Roset. His 1995 Inoxydable desk and étagère in plywood with stainless-steel receptacles was edited by Néotù and Melampo Notte lamp range with articulated shades produced by Artemide.

Garouste, Elizabeth (1949–); Mattia Bonetti (1953–)

French and Italian furniture designers. Garouste: born Paris; active Marcilly (Eure). Bonetti: born Lugano; active Paris.

Training Garouste: École Camondo, Paris, and in theater and costume design. Bonetti: Centro Scolastico per l'Industria Artistica, Italy.
Biography Garouste began collaborating on design with her husband/painter Gérard Garouste; designed stage sets and costumes for Fernando Arrabal; was a stylist for Marie Berani; collaborated with Andrée Putman. Bonetti was a photographer and had an interest in textiles. Garouste commissioned Bonetti to redesign the graphics and window displays for her parents' store. From early 1980s, they began working together, with first commission to decorate (with Gérard Garouste) Le Privilège restaurant in Le Palace nightclub in Paris; officially launched their collaboration with the first series of their *objets primitifs* and *objets barbares*, first shown 1981 at the interior-design firm Jansen. The sobriquet 'New Barbarians' originated with their work edited by Néotù: 1981 Chaise Barbare of iron and horsehide, 1981 Cage Haute étagère, 1981 Table à Onze Pieds, and 1983 Lampadaire Tripode. 1982, they designed sets and costumes for the play *On loge la nuit café à l'eau* at Théatre National de Chaillot in Paris; participated in 1983 revue *L'ennemie* at Centre Georges Pompidou in Paris. Subsequently, also edited by Néotù: 1984 Menhiz console, 1981 Cage Haute étagère, 1986 Bahut Rhinocéros cabinet, 1985 Napoli lamp, 1985 Prince Impérial chair, 1986 Table Bronze coffee table, 1988 Armoire Cathédrale, Semainier Arc en Ciel cabinet, Le Jour et La Nuit armchair, and others. In Paris, they designed 1987 furniture and interiors for Christian Lacroix's clothing salon, rue du Faubourg Saint-Honoré; 1987 Restaurant Géopoly, rue du Faubourg Montmartre; Hachette offices, boulevard Saint-Michel; and offices of publisher J.C. Lattes. They studied the use of glass in furniture at Centre de Recherche sur le Verre (CIRVA); were closely associated with Manufacture Nationale de Sèvres, from which their 1988 Cabinet de Sèvres was inspired; designed 1989 Trapani Collection glassware and a dinner service by Daum; created 1990 cosmetics packaging designs for Nina Ricci and bedroom and living-room décor and furnishings for Princess Gloria von Thurn und Taxis's castle in Bavaria and restaurant entry and bookstore there. Also designed restaurant furnishings by Anthologie Quartett; 1991 limited-edition case goods, chair, and table in bamboo and unfinished wood by Lou Fagotin; and 1991 crystal and ceramics by Daum.
Exhibitions/citations Work first shown (1981) at Jansen, Paris, and, subsequently, included in and subject of a large number of venues. 1981 sponsorship (for Chaise Barbare) and 1989 Carte Blanche production support (for Patchwork collection), VIA (French furniture association).
Bibliography Sophie Anargyros, *Intérieurs 80*, Paris: Regard, 1983. François Baudot, 'Une soirée manifeste néo-moderne,' *Beaux-Arts*, no. 4, 1983. Cat., *Mattia Bonetti, Elizabeth Garouste*, Bordeaux: Musée des Arts Décoratifs de la Ville de Bordeaux, 1985. Cat., Margo Rouard Snowman, *The Most Contemporary French Furniture*, London: Victoria and Albert Museum, 1988. Stephen Calloway et al., *Elizabeth et Mattia Bonetti*, Marseille: Aveline, 1990. Alex Buck and Matthias Theodor Vogt (eds.), *Garouste and Bonetti*, Frankfurt: form, 1996. Art Books International, 1997. Pierre Staudenmeyer et al., *Elizabeth Garouste & Mattia Bonetti*, Paris: Dis Voir, 1998. Elisabeth Vedrenne, *Elizabeth Garouste & Mattia Bonetti 1981–2001*, Brussels: Ante Post, 2001. Elisabeth Vedrenne, *Elizabeth Garouste & Mattia Bonetti, 1981–2001*, Paris: Lettre Volée, 2002.

Gascoin, Marcel (1907–1986)

French furniture designer and decorator.

Training Under Henri Sauvage, architecture, École Nationale Supérieure des Arts Décoratifs, Paris.
Biography From 1950, Gascoin designed furniture in wood; specialized in furniture arrangements; developed a theory of the organization of living spaces; from 1934 to World War II, was a member, Union des Artistes Modernes (UAM). Many young designers, including Pierre Guariche, Pierre Paulin, Michel Mortier, and René-Jean Caillette, worked in Gascoin's *bureau d'études*, a kind of studio supportive of internships, after World War II.
Exhibitions In Paris: work shown at 1930 (1st) exhibition of UAM, by invitation and where he met UAM leader Robert Mallet-Stevens; 1934 competition designing cabins of steel oceanliners organized by Office Technique pour l'Utilisation de l'Acier (OTUA); 1936 competition of school furniture; 1949–50 (1st) *Formes Utiles* exhibition, Pavillon de Marsan of the Louvre; 1956 (1st) Triennale d'Art Français Contemporain. 1947, in charge of presenting seven apartments, *Urbanisme et Habitation* exhibition, Grand Palais.
Bibliography Renée Moutard-Uldry, 'Marcel Gascoin,' *Art et décoration*, vol. LXVI, 1937. Marie-Anne Febvre-Desportes, 'Rationalisme practique et fantaisie démonstrative, Marcel Gascoin,' *Art et décoration*, no. 4, 1947. Yolande Amic, *Intérieurs: le mobilier français 1945–1964*, Paris: Regard, 1983. Arlette Barré-Despond, *UAM*, Paris: Regard, 1986.

Cat., *Les années UAM 1929–1958*, Paris: Musée des Arts Décoratifs, 1988. Patrick Favardin, *Les décorateurs des années 50*, Paris: Norma, 2002: 96.

Gate, Simon (1883–1945)

Swedish artist-craftsperson; born S. Fågelås, Saraborg.

Training From 1902, Kungliga Tekniska Högskolan, Stockholm.
Biography 1915, Gate and Edward Hald became the first artists appointed at the Orrefors Glasbruk. Gate was associated with the firm's inexpensive modern glass work, which remained collectors' items until his death; 1920s with Hald and glass-blower Knut Bergqvist, developed the *graal* technique. *Graal* art glass was produced by covering a thick layer of clear glass with a thin colored layer that is cut away to reveal the clear background, then heated to lend a smooth appearance and covered with another layer of clear glass before being blown into a final shape. In Gate's three decades at Orrefors, he designed a wide variety of utilitarian and decorative glass.
Exhibitions Work shown internationally including in 1917 *Ideal Homes Exhibition* (organized by the Svenska Slöjdforeningen), Liljevach's Art Gallery, Stockholm; 1925 *Exposition Internationale des Arts Décoratifs et Industriels Modernes*, Paris; 1983–84 *Svenskt Glas '83*, Stockholm (catalog below); 1996 exhibition, Bard Graduate Center for Studies in the Decorative Arts, New York (catalog below).
Bibliography Arthur Hald (ed.), *Simon Gate, Edward Hald en Skildring av människorna och konstnärliga*, Stockholm: Norstedt, 1948. Cat., *Svenskt glas '83: prisbelönt design*, Stockholm: Nationalmuseum, 1983. Jennifer Hawkins Opie, *Scandinavia: Ceramics and Glass in the Twentieth Century*, New York: Rizzoli, 1989. Hokkaidoritsu Kindai Bijutsukan, *Lyricism of Modern Design: Swedish Glass 1900–1970*, Sapporo: Asahi Shimbun, 1992. Cat., Anne-Marie Ericsson, *The Brilliance of Swedish Glass, 1918–1939: An Alliance of Art and Industry*, New Haven: Bard Graduate Center/Yale University, 1996. Kerstin Wickman (ed.), *Orrefors: A Century of Swedish Glassmaking*, Stockholm: Byggförlaget-Kultur, 1998.
> See Orrefors.

Gates, John Montieth (1905–1979)

American architect and glass designer; born Elyria, Ohio.

Training Harvard University, Cambridge, Mass.; Columbia University, New York.
Biography 1932, Gates became vice-president of design to supervise quality and aesthetics in the Steuben Division of Corning Glass Works, Corning, N.Y.; developed an imaginative marketing program to increase sales during the Great Depression of the 1930s. Under his guidance, the firm introduced glass by Samuel Ayers, Edwin Fuerst, and Sidney Waugh. Gates participated in the design of Steuben's first (1934) shop and Corning-Steuben's 1937 House of Glass building (with Geoffrey and William Platt) at 718 Fifth Avenue—both New York. Gates commissioned 27 international artists, including Paul Manship and Isamu Noguchi, to execute designs for the 1940 limited-edition engraved glass-object collection.
Exhibitions Organized stands at 1937 *Exposition Internationale des Arts et Techniques dans la Vie Moderne*, Paris; 1939–40 *New York World's Fair: The World of Tomorrow*; 1940 *Twenty-seven Artists in Crystal* (a Gates project), Steuben gallery, New York.
Bibliography Cat., Janet Kardon (ed.), *Craft in the Machine Age 1920–1945*, New York: Abrams with American Craft Museum, 1995.

Gates Potteries, The

American pottery manufacturer; located Terra Cotta, Ill.

History 1881, The Gates Potteries was founded by William Day Gates as a subsidiary of the American Terra Cotta and Ceramic Company. The Gates works produced plain, undecorated garden pottery which it continued to make throughout its history; 1895, added green-glazed Teco (from TErraCOtta) ware to its production of tiles and decorative architectural items. The brand was established to produce inexpensive art ware cast from molds. Frank Lloyd Wright, William LeBaron Jenney, Max Dunning, William B. Mundie, Howard Van Doren Shaw, and Hugh M.G. Gardner executed Teco designs, which they used in their Prairie School-interiors. Teco shapes, styles, and motifs were influenced by aquatic plants and classical motifs and reflected the architectonic forms of the Prairie School. Chief chemist Elmer Groton developed Teco's legendary matt glaze with a lustrous, waxy texture, which varies from silvery pale green to deep moss green. Rose, gray, blue, gold, yellow, and four brown, and several new green matt glazes were added in 1910. The range, sold through its own offices, showrooms, mail-order catalogs, and magazine advertisements, grew to include over 500 shapes. From 1912, the pottery's activities were cut back due to falling sales, and, 1922, art-pottery production was discontinued. 1930, the plant closed when the parent firm was sold.
Exhibitions/citations 1900, Teco was first shown and featured in a number of subsequent venues. Teco was subject of 1989 exhibition, Erie Art Museum, Erie, Pa. (catalog below). Highest awards at 1904 *Louisiana Purchase Exposition*, St. Louis, Mo., US.
Bibliography William D. Gates, 'The Revival of the Potter's Art,' *Clay-Worker*, no. 28, Oct. 1897: 275–76. Sharon S. Darling, *Chicago Ceramics and Glass: An Illustrated History from 1871 to 1933*, Chicago: Chicago Historical Society/University of Chicago, 1979. William C. Gates, Jr, *The City of Hills and Kilns: Life and Work in East Liverpool, Ohio*, East Liverpool, Ohio: East Liverpool Historical Society, 1984. Cat., *American Art Pottery*, New York: Cooper-Hewitt Museum, 1987. Cat., Sharon S. Darling, *Teco: Art Pottery of the Prairie School*, Erie, Pa.: Erie Art Museum, 1989.

Piero Gatti, Cesare Paolini, and Franco Teodoro. Sacco chair. 1968. Leather and polystyrene beads, h. 45 x dia. 33" (114.3 x 83.8 cm). Mfr.: Zanotta, Italy. Gift of the mfr. MoMA.

Gatti, Piero (1940–); Cesare Paolini (1937–1983); Franco Teodoro (1939–)

Italian graphic and industrial design collaboration. Gatti and Teodoro: born Turin. Paolini: born Genova. .

Biography 1965, Gatti, Paolini, and Teodoro set up a design studio in Turin. Their highly successfuy 1969 Sacco bean-bag seat, filled with polyurethane pellets and still in production, is an example of 1960s–70s Anti-Design rebellion against conventional furniture and furnishings. Courageously produced by Zanotta, it is the ultimate in flexible form. The manufacturer claimed that the 12 million plastic granules within the seat's envelope would adapted instantly to the sitter's body, providing firm but comfortable support. The envelope is vinyl or leather, and the seat weighs 13 lb (6 kg).
Bibliography Cat., *Modern Chairs 1918–1970*, London: Lund Humphries, 1971. Victor Papanek, *Design for the Real World*, New York, 1974: 103–04. *Moderne Klassiker: Möbel, die Geschichte machen*, Hamburg: Gruner + Jahr, 1982: 91. Casciani Stefano and Emilio Ambasz *Mobili come architetture: il disegno della produzione Zanotta*, Milan: Arcadia, 1984: 160. Cat., Kathryn B. Hiesinger and George H. Marcus III (eds.), *Design Since 1945*, Philadelphia: Philadelphia Museum of Art, 1983. Mel Byars with Arlette Barré-Despond, *100 Designs/100 Years: A Celebration of the 20th Century*, Hove: RotoVision: 150–51. Paola Antonelli (ed.), *Objects of Design: The Museum of Modern Art*, New York: The Museum of Modern Art, 2003: 259.

Gaudernack, Gustav (1865–1914)

Bohemian silversmith; active Norway.

Training 1880–81, industrial design, Vocational School for Glass and Metal Industry; 1885–87, Ceramics Vocational School, Tetschen (now Děčín, Czech Republic); 1888–91, Kunstgewerbeschule, Vienna.
Biography 1891, Gaudernack settled in Norway and designed glassware for Christiania Glasmagasin, Kristiania (now Oslo); 1892–10, was artistic director of metalwork, David-Andersen firm, Kristiania. Gaudernack arrived at a new technique, which made it possible to produce large objects in *plique-à-jour* enamel on which finely detailed naturalistic motifs could be produced; 1910, set up his workshop in Kristiania and produced silver, filigree, and enamel; from 1912, taught, Statens Håndverks-og Kunstindustriskole, Kristiania.
Exhibitions/citations Work shown at 1898 exhibition, Bergen; 1907 Salon, Paris. Silver medal, 1900 *Exposition Universelle*, Paris; grand prize (with David-Andersen), 1904 *Louisiana Purchase Exposition*, St. Louis; gold medal, 1914 *Centenary Exhibition*, Frogner, Kristiania.
Bibliography Alf Bøe, 'Gustav Gaudernack, Tegninger og utførte arbeider,' in *Kunstindustrimuseet i Oslo Årbok*, 1959–62: 41–72. Jan-Lauritz Opstad and Rolf Gaudernack, *Gustav Gaudernack: En europeer i norsk jugend*, Oslo: Kunstindustrimuseet i Oslo, 1979. Cat., David Revere McFadden (ed.), *Scandinavian Modern Design 1880–1980*, New York: Abrams, 1982. Annelies Krekel-Aalberse, *Art Nouveau and Art Déco Silver*, New York: Abrams, 1989.

Gaudí i Cornet, Antoni (1852–1926)

Spanish architect and designer; born Reus.

Training 1873–78, architecture, Escola Superior d'Arquitectura, Barcelona.
Biography 'Antonio' is the sometime spelling of his forename. At the Barcelona architecture school, Gaudí was influenced by the Gothic revival tradition; admired Eugène-Emmanuel Viollet-le-Duc's *Entretiens sur l'architecture* (Paris: Q. Morel, 1863–72). Gaudí, like other Catalan architects of the last quarter of the 19th century, benefited from the lack of an architectural tradition in Barcelona (excluding the Catalonian Gothic style). His father was a metalworker and, likewise, Gaudí's 1879 cast-iron lamp designs show an interest in metalwork. An idiosyncratic version of Art Nouveau evolved in his 1883–88 Casa Vicens and 1886–89 Palau Güell, both in Barcelona and influenced by Arabian art. His 1883–1926 crypt and transept of the cathedral of La Sagrada Familia, sculptural and unfinished, represent his most visionary work and show the influence of medieval art. His fondness for *objets trouvés* was expressed in the stucco façades, into which he incorporated broken tiles and pot shards. So consuming was his interest in the cathedral that he lived for a time on the premises. He brought to his architecture a talent for sculpture, painting, ironsmithing, ceramics, mosaics, and furniture making. His interest in new materials reflected the influence of the Art Nouveau movement. He designed site-specific furniture and furnishings and paid attention to every element of a building, down to its most minute details, like Henry van de Velde on the Bloemenwerf in Uccle and Hector Guimard on the Castel Béranger in Paris. He pursued this attention to detail in the partitions and furniture for the ground floor of 1898–1900 Casa Calvet, the bone-like asymmetrical forms of the of c. 1907 furniture and furnishings for the first floor of Casa Batlló, and the benches in the crypt of 1908 Colonia Güell church in Santa Coloma de Cervelló, near Barcelona. Gaudí's work continues to exert an influence on Barcelona's architects. The 1902–04 chair for the Calvet apartment house, reissued in limited production from 1980s, is possibly his most recognizable piece of furniture design. He was killed by a trolley car in Barcelona.
Exhibitions Drawings subject of 1977 exhibition, New York, and numerous venues worldwide.
Bibliography José F. Ráfols, *Gaudí*, Barcelona: Canosa, 1929. J. Bergós, *Gaudí: l'home i l'obra*, Barcelona: Ariel, 1954. Henry-Russell Hitchcock, *Gaudí*, New York: The Museum of Modern Art, 1957. James Johnson Sweeney and Josep Lluís Sert, *Antoni Gaudí*, New York: Praeger, 1960, 1970 (rev. ed.). George R. Collins, *A Bibliography of Antonio Gaudí and the Catalan Movement 1870–1930*, Charlottesville, Va., 1973. Josef A. Widemann, *Gaudí: Inspiration in Architektur und Handwerk*, Munich: Callwey, 1974. Cat., George R. Collins, *The Drawings of Antonio Gaudí*, New York: Drawing Center, 1977. Luis Peña et al., *Gaudí diseñador = Gaudí designer*, Barcelona: Blume, 1978. Riccardo Dalisi, *Gaudí: Furniture and Objects*, Woodbury, N.Y.: Barron's, 1980. Rainer Zerbst, *Antoni Gaudí i Cornet, Una vida dedicada a la arquitectura*, Cologne: Taschen, 1989. Gijs Van Hensbergen, *Gaudí*, London: HarperCollins, 2001. Paola Antonelli

Antoni Gaudí i Cornet. Side chair. 1905–07. Oak, 29 5/8 x 20 3/4 x 15 1/4" (75.2 x 52.7 x 38.7 cm), seat h. 17 5/8" (44 cm). Mfr.: Casa Ribas Seva, Spain. Purchase. MoMA.

(ed.), *Objects of Design: The Museum of Modern Art*, New York: The Museum of Modern Art, 2003: 125–26.

Gauguin, Paul (1848–1903)

French painter, sculptor, and graphic and decorative designer; born Paris.

Biography Gauguin is best known for his paintings of women in the South Seas; was the leader of the Pont-Aven artists' group and one of the painters who became involved in the decorative arts at the end of the 19th century; designed a large number of ceramic pieces, carved furniture, and other decorative items, and produced a small group of wooden vessels. Gauguin's career can be divided into three periods. During the first and most prolific period, 1886–87, he worked in the ceramics studio of Ernest Chaplet, rue Blomet, Paris. On cylindrical vases and cups, Gauguin's signature appeared with Chaplet's and Haviland's marks. He produced motifs in *cloisonné* with gold highlights. Other pieces were less successfully hand molded. Gauguin's second period was begun with his return to Paris from Martinique, 1887. In the rue Blomet studio, he worked with Auguste Delaherche, who had taken over the premises from Chaplet. Departing further and further from traditional ceramics in his forms, Gauguin now spent more time on technique, clay composition, and glazes. With most of his completed pieces given to his family in Copenhagen and friends, he had little success with sales. In his third period, 1889–90, he was attracted to sculpture and, except for stoneware executed in c. 1893–95, abandoned ceramics altogether. He died in Atuona on the Îsles Marquises, South Pacific Ocean. His son Jean Gauguin (1881–1961) worked for Bing & Grøndahl Porcelænsfabrik.
Bibliography Yvonne Brunhammer et al., *Art Nouveau Belgium, France*, Houston: Rice University, 1976, biblio.

Gaultier, Jean-Paul (1952–)

French fashion and furniture designer; born Arcueil; active Paris.

Biography Gaultier is best known as a fashion designer. He began his career working the the fashion houses of Pierre Cardin and, subse-

quently, of Jacques Esterel and Jean Patou; 1976, established his own, eventually highly successful fashion enterprise in Paris. In a brief effort into industrial design, he created a 1989–90 collection of domestic objects by 3 Suisses and 1992 chest of drawers made of leather luggage and chairs with over-sized industrial wheels, sponsored by VIA (French furniture association).
Exhibitions Made by JPG and Voyage au Tibet furniture shown at *Commodes comme Mode*, Galerie VIA, Paris.
Bibliography Arlette Barré-Despond (ed.), *Dictionnaire international des arts appliqués et du design*, Paris: Regard, 1996.

Gauthier, Jerôme (1970–)
French designer.

Biography Gauthier's work has included 1997 Beam shelves, 1998 Spime wood stacking chair by Soca Line, 1995 Karla Mazoo chair/table/stool suite by Soca Line, 2000 1+1 side chair and Wind lounge chair/ottoman, 2001 Slat wood armchair, Band console and table, Fit lounge chair, Happy side table by Cinna
Citations 1997 and 1999 Appel Permanent grant, VIA. (French furniture association).
Bibliography Mel Byars, *50 Tables...*, Hove: RotoVision, 1997. Mel Byars, *Design in Steel*, London: Laurence King, 2002. www.via.asso.fr

Gautier-Delaye, Pierre (1923–)
French industrial designer and decorator; active Paris.

Training 1947–51, École Nationale Supérieure des Arts Décoratifs, Paris.
Biography 1951–58, Gautier-Delaye was director of the interior-design department, Compagnie de l'Esthétique Industrielle (CEI), Paris (established by Raymond Loewy); 1958, set up his own design office at 99, rue Saint-Honoré, Paris; 1960–70, was active in interior, furniture, product, and graphic design for clients including Vergnières, Jacob Delafon (sanitary fixtures) and Formica (packaging). For Air France: ticket-office interiors and furnishings world-wide, c. 1970 entire interior of Boeing 747 airplane with textiles by Sheila Hicks, 1988 upgrade of *Concorde* interior, and other Air France commissions.
Citations 1956 René Gabriel Prize; 1970 best offices on Fifth Avenue (to Air France for Gautier-Delaye façade), City of New York commission.
Bibliography *Ensembles mobiliers*, Paris: Charles Moreau, no. 33, 1954. Arlette Barré-Despond (ed.), *Dictionnaire international des arts appliqués et du design*, Paris: Regard, 1996. Patrick Favardin, *Les décorateurs des années 50*, Paris: Norma, 2002: 204.
> See CEI (Compagnie de l'Esthétique Industrielle).

Gavina: Marco Zanuso Sr. and Richard Sapper. Lambda chair. 1959. Painted sheet metal, 30 3/4 x 15 3/8 x 17" (78.1 x 39 x 43.2 cm). Mfr.: Gavina, Italy (1964). Gift of the mfr. MoMA.

Gavina, Dino (1922–)
Italian furniture entrepreneur; born Bologna.

Biography 1960, Dino Gavina founded the firm Gavina as a subsidiary of his eponymous Dino Gavina company. Architect/designer Carlo Scarpa was appointed its titular president. The designs of Franco Albini and the earlier 1920s models of Marcel Breuer were reproduced. Breuer's 1928 B32 chair, renamed Cesca (after Breuer's daughter Francesca), became highly successful in mass production by Gavina and was followed by the reissue of the 1924 Laccio tables, 1925 Wassily chair, 1935 bentwood chaise, and 1955 Canaan desk. Its most distinguished neo-Liberty design was the 1959 Sanluca armchair by the Castiglioni brothers with its curvaceous form. Gavina produced the Tomasa folding chair, taken from a 15th-century painting by Florentine painter Paolo Uccello (1397–1475). Having met Kazuhide Takahama at 1954 (10th) Triennale di Milano, Gavina commissioned him to design furniture for the firm, starting with 1965 Marcel, Raymond, and Suzanne sofas. The firm produced the 1966 Malitte (or Muro) modular-seating configuration designed by Surrealist painter Matta. Other designers included Ignazio Gardella, Tobia Scarpa, Vico Magistretti, Renzo Masetti, and Marco Zanuso Sr./Richard Sapper. 1962, Gavina formed Flos for lighting manufacture, with board members Maria Simoncini and Cesare Cassina and was instrumental in setting up Gemini. 1968, Gavina sold the firm to Knoll International and, 1970, established Simón International to produce yet another furniture line. 1996, Simón was taken over by Ultramobile of Calcinelli di Saltara (Pesaro-Urbino), Italy, to continue the production.
Exhibitions 2000 *Dino Gavina, UltraMobile: 50 opere di Dino Gavina*, Complesso Museale di San Francesco, Trevi.
Bibliography Virgilio Vercelloni, *The Adventure of Design: Gavina*, New York: Rizzoli, 1987. Cat., Leslie Jackson, *The New Look: Design in the Fifties*, New York: Thames & Hudson, 1991. Cat., Vittorio Sgarbi et al., *Dino Gavina, UltraMobile: 50 opere di Dino Gavina*, Begagna: ESG 89, 2000.
> See Ultramobile.

Gavoille, Kristian (1956–)
French architect and furniture designer; born Brazzaville (now in Republic of the Congo); active Paris.

Training To 1982, École d'Architecture, Toulouse.
Biography 1984, Gavoille settled in Paris; 1984–86, collaborated with several architecture firms in Toulouse and Paris and worked at Services d'Architecture de la Ville de Paris (city architecture office); 1985–91, worked in Philippe Starck's studio on numerous projects and established his own design office in 1992. He designed 1986 table-service objects for Château de Belle Fontaine in Paris; from 1988, designed for Disform and Néotù; 1988 and 1989 theater sets. Other work has included 1988 Table Divine and Guéridon Divin, 1989 Athéo armchair; 1999 Kings Ford Smith sofa by Néotù; Le Trabendo bar and music hall in Parc de la Vilette, Paris; 1993 interior and Monmien heat-formed-plastic chair for Café Gavoile in Amiens; 1995 interior of store and employee restaurant of Kookaï in Paris and provinces; 1996 dressing room of La Compagnie Bleue fitness center, Paris; 1997 Dooble lounge chair by Soca Line; Lumignonne sconce by Ardi; 1997 vitrine and store design of Marithé + François Girbaud in Paris; 2000 Kloc rug/pillow by Cinna; 2001 Urbain lamp by Abel. From 1994, Gavoille taught, École Nationale Supérieure des Arts Décoratifs, and 1993, 1995, 1997, at École Camondo; both Paris. He has become the artistic director of Ardi home accessories.
Exhibitions/citations Work first shown at Disform and Néotù stands, 1988 Salone del Mobile, Milan. 1988, 1989, and 1993 Appel Permanent grants and 1991 Carte Blanche citation, VIA (French furniture association); Creator of the Year, 1992 Salon du Meuble, Paris.
Bibliography Odile Filion, *Architecture créé*, May 1988. *Design français*, Paris: Flammarion, 1988. *Intramuros*, Feb. and July 1988. Philippe Louguet, *Kristian Gavoille*, Paris: Regard, 1995. www.via.asso.fr.

GDA (Gérard, Dufraisseix et Abbot)
French porcelain manufacturer; located Limoges.

History 1797, a firm for the production of porcelain was founded by François Alluaud and, 1877–81, was directed by Charles Field Haviland. Haviland, a cousin of Charles and Théodore Haviland of Haviland & Cie., had married into the Alluaud family. This original Alluaud/Haviland firm was taken over by Gérard, Dufraisseix et Morel in 1882. 1890, Morel withdrew from the association to experiment with high-fired decoration. Thence, the firm operated under the name Gérard, Dufraisseix & Cie. until it assumed the name GDA (for Gérard, Dufraisseix et Abbot) in 1900, when Abbot, an American, became a director and managed its activities in the US. From 1901, GDA also produced ceramics for Siegfried Bing's gallery/shop L'Art Nouveau, Paris.
Bibliography Yvonne Brunhammer et al., *Art Nouveau Belgium, France*, Houston: Rice University, 1976, biblio.

GDV (Girault, Demay et Vignolet)
French ceramics firm; located Bruère.

History 1877, GDV was founded by merchants Louis Girault and Jean Vignolet and ceramicist Claude Demay.
Exhibitions/citations Work shown at 1889 and 1900 (gold medal) editions of *Exposition Universelle*, Paris.
Bibliography *Europäische Keramik, 1880–1930*, Darmstadt: Hessisches Landesmuseum, 1986: 101.

Gebert, Jacob (1965–)
German designer; born Freiburg.

Training 1990–94, interior, product, and architectural design, Schule für Gestaltung, Basel, Switzerland.
Biography 1994, Gebert established his own studio; has designed for a number of firms, including Belux, Nels Moormann (1996 Spanoto table with force-fitted legs) and Vitra (Taino side chair). 1998, taught, Schule für Gestaltung in Basel and, 1999, Staatliche Hochschule für Gestaltung in Karlsruhe.
Exhibitions Work included in 1998 exhibition organized by Institut für Auslandsbeziehungen (IFA), Stüttgart, reorganized for traveling from 2004 (catalog below).
Bibliography Mel Byars, *50 Tables: Innovations in Design and Materials*, Hove: RotoVision, 1997. Cat., *bewußt, einfach—Das Entstehen einer alternativen Produktkultur*, Stüttgart: Institut für Auslandsbeziehungen, 1998

Gecchelin, Bruno (1939–)
Italian architect-designer; born and active Milan.

Training To 1959, architecture, Politecnico, Milan.
Biography 1962, Gecchelin began his professional career in 1962. With Ettore Sottsass, he designed the Fiat Coima camper, Fiat Panda automobile, and Olivetti typewriters, calculators, and computer terminals. Individual work has included office furniture by Bazzani; lighting by Antonangeli, Arteluce/Flos, iGuzzini Illuminazione, O luce, Skipper, Stilnovo, and Tronconi; electronics by Aermec-Riello and Matsushita; accessories by Fratelli Guzzini, Metaform, and Rede; glass by Venini; furniture by Ycami; refrigerators and gas stoves for Indesit; and others. The 1988 Atelier 75 range was designed to commemorate the 75th anniversary of the founding of Fratelli Guzzini.
Citations 1982, 1983, 1987, 1989, and 1991 awards, Industrie Forum Design (iF), Hanover; 1989 and 1991 Premio Compasso d'Oro. Participated in 1981 and 1988 BIO industrial design biennials, Ljubljana.
Bibliography Tomás Maldonado, *Disegno industriale: un riesame*, Milan: Feltrinelli, 1991. Gabriele Lueg and P. Pfeiffer, *Halogen: 20. Jahre neues Licht*, Lauphein: Novus, 1991. Anty Pansera (ed.), *Dizionario del design*, Florence: Cantini, 1995. *Moderne Klassiker—Möbel, die Geschichte machen*, Munich: Schöner Wohnen, 1996. Charlotte and Peter Fiell, *70's Decorative Art*, Cologne: Taschen, 2000. Michele De Lucchi (ed.), *The International Design Yearbook*, London: Laurence King, 2001.

Geddes, Norman Bel (b. Norman Melancton Geddes 1893–1958)
American industrial and theatrical designer; born Adrian, Mich.; active New York; father of actress Barbara Bel Geddes.

Training c. 1908, Art Institute of Chicago and in Cleveland.
Biography 1913, Bel Geddes worked first as an advertising draftsperson at an agency in Detroit, where, after six months, he became an art director; 1916, wrote a play, following which he designed six theatrical productions in Los Angeles, the first being Zoe Akins's *Papa*; designed over 200 play and opera sets, including the renowned one for Max Reinhardt's *The Miracle* (1926); 1918, was stage designer for the Metropolitan Opera Company, New York; 1925, settled in Hollywood and designed film sets for Cecil B. De Mille and D.W. Griffith; produced, directed, and designed plays, including *Jeanne D'Arc* with Eva Le Gallienne in Paris and *Lysistrata* with Miriam Hopkins and Fay Bainter in Hollywood; 1927, became an 'industrial designer,' a title somewhat new then. His technologically-orientated outlook was expressed in his book *Horizons* (Boston: Little, Brown, 1932), stylishly bound in blue-and-silver printed cloth, and in his and Otto Koller's model for 1929 Super Airliner 4. He designed 1928 painted-metal bedroom suite by Simmons, 1928–30 windows (vitrines) of Franklin Simon department store, New York, 1929 stoves by SGE (Standard Gas Equipment Corporation of New York) based on a standardized-height system, scales by Toledo, 1931 radios by Philco, radio cabinets by RCA (Radio Corporation of America), 1932 interiors for J. Walter Thompson advertising agency in New York, 1934 Manhattan and Skyscraper cocktail sets by Revere Copper and Brass, 1940 red-white-blue Patriot table radio by Emerson Radio and Phonograph, 1935 Soda King syphon bottles with Worthen Paxton (1905–1977) by Walter Kidde Sales, an automobile by Graham-Paige; became an influential prophet predicting, for example, the automobile superhighway system and the popularity of air conditioning. His work in standardization for home furnishing equipment, especially in the kitchen, was pioneering. 1930s, Eero Saarinen was his pupil, and he employed Eliot Noyes, who worked on the early IBM electric typewriter design under Geddes. Geddes was an exponent of streamline styling. He was the first of the consultant designers to gain public recognition when a profile of him appeared in a 1930 issue of *Fortune* magazine. Geddes archive is housed in the University of Texas, Austin. Died in New York.
Exhibitions Designed General Motors' *Futurama* building and interior display, 1939–40 *New York World's Fair: The World of Tomorrow*, resulting in his book *Magic Motorways* (New York: Random House, 1940). Work included in numerous exhibitions and subject of 1979 *Norman Bel Geddes: An Exhibition of Theatrical and Industrial Designs*, Michener Galleries, Austin, Tex., US.
Bibliography Norman Bel Geddes with William Kelley, *Miracle in the Evening*, Garden City, N.Y.: Doubleday, 1960 (published posthumously). Cat., Jennifer David Roberts, *Norman Bel Geddes: An Exhibition of Theatrical and Industrial Designs*, Austin: University of Texas, 1979. John Heskett, *Industrial Design*, London: Thames & Hudson, 1980. Penny Sparke, *A Century of Car Design*, London: Mitchell Beazley, 2002.

Gefle Porslinsfabrik
Swedish porcelain factory.

History 1910, Gefle was established at Gävle on the same site as earlier O. Forsell Kakel-och Fajansfabrik tileworks; 1913, was reorganized, with designer Arthur Percy working there; became known for its well-designed table and decorative wares; 1936, was bought by Upsala-Ekeby group; closed in 1979.
Bibliography Jennifer Hawkins Opie, *Scandinavia: Ceramics and Glass in the Twentieth Century*, New York: Rizzoli, 1989.

Gehl, Ebbe (1942–)
Danish furniture designer.

Training 1963–66, Kunsthåndværkskolen, Copenhagen.
Biography 1959–63, Gehl worked for Rud. Rasmussen; 1966–67, collaborated with Nanna Ditzel; 1967–69, taught at Edinburgh College of Art; 1970, set up an architecture office with Søren Nissen. Furniture designs were produced by Carl Hansen & Søn, Sannemanns Møbelfabrik, A. Mikael Laursen, and Jeki.
Exhibitions Work shown at 1975 Danish furniture exhibition, Berlin; 1976 *SCAN*, Washington, D.C.
Bibliography Frederik Sieck, *Nutidig Dansk Møbeldesign – en kortfattet illustreret beskrivelse*, Copenhagen: Bondo Gravesen, 1990.

Gehry, Frank Owen (b. Frank Goldberg 1930–)
Canadian architect, designer, and artist; born Toronto; active Los Angeles.

Training 1949–51 and 1954, architecture, University of California in Los Angeles; 1956–57, Graduate School of Design, Harvard University.

Biography For a time, was professor of design at Yale and Harvard universities; Gehry was influenced by Richard Neutra, Rudolf Schindler, and the Case Study Program sponsored by journal *Arts + Architecture*, which included Charles Eames's own 1949 house, Santa Monica, Cal.; early on, produced commercial drawings for developer John Postman. His architectural drawings are rendered in a deliberately crude style. 1954, he designed Wright-like furniture for dayrooms, Fort Benning, Ga. 1953–54, he was architectural designer, Victor Gruen Associates; 1955–56, planner and designer, Robert and Company Architects, Atlanta; 1957, architectural designer and planner, Hideo Sasaki Associates, Boston; 1957–58, architectural designer, Pereira and Luckman, Los Angeles; 1958–61, designer and planner, André Remondet, Paris; 1961, planner, Pereira and Lickman, Paris; 1962, returned to the US and set up a practice with another young architect; 1967 founded his current firm, Frank O. Gehry and Associates, Los Angeles, where, from the beginning, he was assisted by Greg Walsh; mid-1970s, came to public notice with the design of his own Santa Monica home; collaborated with artists Claes Oldenburg and Richard Serra and designed stage sets for choreographer Lucinda Childs. Widely published, his furniture and architecture attempted to be sculptural in form with minimal construction and inexpensive industrial materials. 1969–73, he produced corrugated cardboard furniture. His best-known furniture designs included Easy Edges corrugated paper chairs, designed and produced from 1971 (reissued 1982 as Rough Edges in a less rigid and more plastic interpretation); 1979–82 Experimental Edges followed. From 1987, models of the paper chairs were produced by Vitra. He designed the 1987 Bubbles lounge chair. Mid-1970s, real-estate firm Rouse Company was his main client, for which he executed designs for housing, shopping malls, and its corporate headquarters, Columbia, Md. 1976, he became a proponent of Deconstructivist architecture; 1983, created his first 'fish-light,' commissioned by Formica in ColorCore plastic laminate. 1984, Formica produced his Ryba fish lamps as well as his Snake lamps. The fish has been a recurring theme since childhood and his astrological sign. Gehry was snubbed when the addition to Los Angeles County Museum of Art was commissioned from Hardy Holzman Pfeiffer Associates, and the Museum of Contemporary Art from Arata Isozaki; created a 1989–92 collection of furniture in woven wooden strips and 1999 FOG side chair and armchair (named for the designer's initials) by Knoll and designed the limited-edition fish-form hand-blown goblet produced by Swid-Powell. Architects who worked in his office included Thom Mayne and Michael Rotundi of Morphosis, and Frank Israel. His exhibition designs included 1968 exhibition of the work of Billy Al Bengston, Los Angeles County Museum of Art; 1980 *The Avant-Garde in Russia, 1910–1930*, Los Angeles County Museum of Art; and 1986 Pitti Uomo menswear collection, Florence and Turin. Buildings included 1962 studio and house of graphic designer Lou Danziger; 1972 corrugated-metal house and studio of artist Ron Davis, Malibu, Cal.; building for his own office and for artist Chuck Arnoldi, Venice, Cal.; 1976–79 studio and gallery for print publisher Gemini Graphic Editions, Los Angeles; 1978 Wagner house (unrealized), Malibu; 1978 Familian house (unrealized), Santa Monica; 1978–79, 1991, and onward, his own house alterations, Santa Monica; 1983 Norton house, Venice, Cal.; 1983 Temporary Contemporary building, Museum of Contemporary Art, Los Angeles; 1983–84 California Aerospace Museum, Exposition Park, Los Angeles; 1986 Sirmai-Peterson house, Thousand Oaks, Cal.; 1986 Information and Computer Sciences (Engineering Research Lab), University of California in Irvine, Cal.; 1987 Fish Dance Restaurant, Kobe, Japan; 1989 Vitra Design Museum and Vitra factory, Weil am Rhein, Germany; Walt Disney Concert Hall of c. 1989, Los Angeles; 1991 Chiat / Day/ Mojo building, Venice, Cal.; 1991 Vitra building, Basel; 1991 retail center, Vila Olimpica, Barcelona; 1992–94 American Center, Paris; 1992–93 Entertainment Center, Euro Disneyland, Marne-la-Vallée; 1997 Guggenheim Museum, Bilbao, Spain; 2004–07 Art Gallery of Ontario, Toronto.

Exhibitions/citations Work subject of 1986 *The Architecture of Frank Gehry* touring the US; 1991 *Projets en Europe*, Centre Georges Pompidou, Paris; 2000 *Frank O. Gehry Furniture*, Brazos Project, Houston; 2001 *Frank O. Gehry: The Art of Architecture*, Guggenheim Museum, New York (catalog below). Work shown at 1972 (Easy Edges chairs) and 1982 (Rough Edges chairs) exhibitions, Max Protetch Gallery, New York, and a 1983 Philadelphia exhibition (catalog below). Other work at 1974 *Contemporary Home Environs*, La Jolla Museum of Contemporary Art, California; a Fairfield County exhibition (catalog below); 1981 *Collaboration* with Serra; 1984–85 exhibition of Formica ColorCore fish lighting, Metro Pictures, New York; 1985 performance with Oldenburg, Venice, Cal.; 1988 *Deconstruction Architecture*, The Museum of Modern Art, New York. Numerous awards, including 1989 Pritzker Architecture Prize; fellow, American Institute of Architects (AIA); gold medal, Royal Architectural Institute of Canada.

Bibliography Cat., Lisa Phillips (intro.), *Shape and Environment: Furniture by American Architects*, New York: Whitney Museum of American Art, 1982. Cat., Kathryn B. Hiesinger and George H. Marcus III (eds.), *Design Since 1945*, Philadelphia: Philadelphia Museum of Art, 1983. Peter Arnell and Ted Bickford, *Frank Gehry: Buildings and Projects*, New York: Rizzoli, 1985. Olivier Boissière and Martin Filler, *Frank Gehry: Vitra Design Museum*, London: Thames & Hudson, 1990: 64. Frank Gehry, 'Up Everest in a Volkswagen,' *Design Quarterly*, 1992. Cat., *Frank Gehry: New Bentwood Furniture Designs*, Montréal : Montréal Museum of Decorative Arts, 1992. Coosje van Bruggen, *Frank O. Gehry: Guggenheim Museum Bilbao*, New York: Guggenheim, 1998. Cat., Jean-Louis Cohen et al., *Frank O. Gehry: The Art of Architecture*, New York: Abrams, 2001. Paola Antonelli (ed.), *Objects of Design: The Museum of Modern Art*, New York: The Museum of Modern Art, 2003: 164.

Frank O. Gehry. Easy Edges Body Contour rocker. 1971. Laminated corrugated fiberboard. Mfr.: Easy Edges, US. Gift of the mfr. MoMA.

Gelman (b. Gelman Alexander 1967-)

American multidisciplinary designer; born Moscow, USSR.

Training 1988, bachelor's degree in fine art, Moscow Art School. **Biography** 1987–93, Gelman was an independent consultant; from 1993, a partner and creative director, Access Factory studio, New York; 1996 briefly, artistic director, Swatch Design Lab, New York; 1997, founded Design Machine studio, New York. Gelman has been active in graphic, product, furniture, and interior design as well as film, new-media writing, criticism, and education. In New York, commissions have included identity elements for The Art Directors Club, New York; interior/exterior of Time Labs fitness-club building; interior/exterior of HK restaurant. Gelman designed his own line of products, including skateboards, T-shirts, buttons, pillows, rugs, stationery, home furnishings, and lighting. From 1996, has taught at institutions, including School of Visual Arts, Parsons School of Design, The Cooper Union for the Advancement of Science and Art, Yale University, and Media Lab (as a Design Fellow) of Massachusetts Institute of Technology. He wrote the book *Substraction: Aspects of Essential Design* (Hove: RotoVision, 2000).
Exhibitions/citations Work included in 2000 National Design Triennial, Cooper-Hewitt National Design Museum; 2000 *The Process Show*; both New York. Subject of 1998 *Substraction*, Space Yui; 2000 *Design by Substraction*, AXIS Gallery; both Tokyo. Nominee for 2000 DaimlerChrysler Design Award; finalist/communications design, 2000 National Design Award.
Bibliography Mel Byars, *50 Tables...*, Hove: RotoVision, 1997. Mel Byars, *50 Lights...*, Hove: RotoVision, 1997. *Gelman*, Beijing: China Youth, 2001. Yuichi Yamada, 'Design by Substraction,' *Design News*, Summer 2000. Helen Walters, 'Less Is More,' *Creative Review*, Feb. 2000. Chris Reinewald, 'Alexander Gelman,' *Items*, Mar. 2001. Hironori Okybo, 'Gelman: Design by Substraction,' *Design News*, Mar. 2001. Lanny Sommese, 'Gelman: The Miles Davis of Design,' *Graphis*, Sept.-Oct. 2003.

Gencol, Hakan (1964–)

Turkish industrial designer; born Malatya; active Manisa, Turkey.

Training 1987, bachelor's degree in industrial design, Middle East Technical University (METU), Ankara, Turkey. 1988 Domus Academy, Milan. **Biography** 1989–92, Gencol worked in a number of architecture and design studios in Milan and was a correspondent for *Arkitekt* magazine; 1992–2000, was a consultant in urban, interior, and industrial design, graphics, and architecture to his family's firm, Gencol & Gencol; 1995, part-time professor in fashion/textiles, Dokuz Eylül Üniversitesi (DEU), Izmir; 1996–98, part-time professor in industrial-design master's program, Izmir Yuksek Teknoloji Enstitusu (IYTE, institute of technology); 2000, part-time professor, Ýstanbul Bilgi Üniversitesi, Istanbul; from 2001, head of industrial design for audio/video products, Vestel Consumer Electronics, Manisa, Turkey; in Milan, has collaborated with Adalberto Dal Lago, Stefano Giovannoni, Paolo Nava, Hans von Klier, and on a number of products, such as furniture, lighting, sunglasses, graphics, and automobile seating, for significant manufacturers.
Citations 1995 Conceptual Project (Fatal Attraction magnetic button for clothing), ETMK (organization of industrial designers), Ankara.
Bibliography Cat., *Designers' Odyssey*, Ankara: ETMK, 1994: 28. *Maison française*, no. 30, Oct. 1997: 52–53; no. 73, June 2001: 32–33.

General Hardware
> See Corning.

Genêt et Michon

French lighting manufacturers; located Paris.

History 1911, Philippe Genêt (1882–) and Lucien Michon (1887-1963) founded Genêt et Michon, the lighting, furniture, and chair manufacturer. 1919, the firm began to specialize in lighting and produced fixtures for the Palais de l'Élysée in Paris and for consulates and ministries. After extensive experiments, Genêt and Michon discovered that thick pressed glass multiplies reflections and increased the intensity of illumination more than thin glass of other forms. A mixture of silica, soda, and lime was melted at 1,300° F. (700° C) and poured into a steel mold. The highly secret formula, unchanged until 1938, had no pigments added in order to retain the brightness and glow. Its pressed glass was sometimes etched and combined with lead crystal; glass beads were occasionally incorporated into fixtures in the 19th-century manner. The firm is credited with having introduced the illuminated ramps that bordered a room at 1925 Paris *Exposition*; 1920s, was a pioneer (with René Lalique and Jean Perzel) of the suspended illuminated sphere; produced ceiling *dalles*, lamps, lusters, wall brackets, epergnes, and illuminated friezes, tables, door architraves, cornices, vases, pilasters, and columns. By 1930, its complex designs, incorporating bunches of grapes, had given way to simpler forms with a more refined finish on the pressed glass. The firm designed lighting for 1935 oceanliner *Normandie*, collaborated with decorators including Jacques-Émile Ruhlmann, Paul Follot, and Michel Dufrêne on lighting and glass, and produced numerous small Art Déco furniture pieces.
Exhibitions Lighting fixtures and interiors shown at 1922–38 Salons of Société des Artistes Décorateurs, 1922–24 editions of Salon d'Automne, and others. Work shown at 1924 Grand Lighting Competition; 1923 (1st) or 1925 (2nd) *Esposizione Biennale delle Arti Decorative e Industriali Moderne*, Monza; 1934 (2nd) and 1935 (3rd) editions of Salon de Lumière; Pavillon de Lumière, 1937 *Exposition Internationale des Arts et Techniques dans la Vie Moderne*, Paris.
Bibliography Gabriel Henriot, *Luminaire moderne*, Paris: Charles Moreau, 1937: plates 20–23, [n.d.]. Alastair Duncan, *Art Nouveau and Art Déco Lighting*, New York: Simon & Schuster, 1978. Pierre Kjellberg, *Art déco: les maîtres du mobilier, le décor des paquebots*, Paris: Amateur, 1986.

James Gentes. Aerohead bicycle racing helmet. 1988. Expanded polystyrene (EPS) foam and Lycra, 7 3/4 x 13 3/4 x 7 1/4" (19.7 x 35 x 18.4 cm). Mfr.: Giro, US. Gift of the mfr. MoMA.

Genévrière, Marcel (1885–1967)
> See Dominique.

Génisset, Jean-Pierre (1911–1998)

French furniture designer; born and active Paris.

Training École des Arts Appliqués; École Nationale Supérieure des Arts Décoratifs; both Paris.
Biography 1936, Génisset joined La Crémaillère; from 1941, worked with friend André Renou; 1971, departed.
Bibliography Pierre Kjellberg, *Art déco: les maîtres du mobilier, le décor des paquebots*, Paris: Amateur, 1986. Patrick Favardin, *Les décorateurs des années 50*, Paris: Norma, 2002: 150.

Gensoli, Maurice (1892–1972)

Algerian ceramicist; born Oran.

Training Under a master glassmaker in Oran.
Biography From 1921, Gensoli was a freelance designer at Manufacture Nationale de Sèvres, where he became chief of the porcelain in 1925 and of the design studio in 1928. He remained at Sèvres to 1959, where he executed pieces that featured waves, sea shells, exotic animals, and human figures in a Cubist style; was highly knowledgeable about ceramics technology; designed the fountains on oceanliners 1927 *Liberté* and 1935 *Normandie.*
Exhibitions/citations Work shown regularly at Salons of Société des Artistes Décorateurs and editions of Salon d'Autmone; 1925 *Exposition Internationale des Arts Décoratifs et Industriels Modernes* (decorative porcelain panels), Paris. A number of prizes and diplomas; elected Chevalier in 1938 and Officier in 1952 of the Légion d'Honneur.
Bibliography *Mobilier et décoration*, no. 4, May 1954. Yvonne Brunhammer, *Le cinquantenaire de l'Exposition de 1925*, Paris: Musée des Arts Décoratifs, 1976.

Gentes, 'Jim' James (1957-)

American bicycle racer and designer.

Biography 1985, Gentes left a position as a designer at the Blackburn bicycle-accessories firm, Santa Cruz, Cal., where he was a designer, to found Giro Sports Design in Santa Cruz. His first Giro product was an aerostyle triathlon helmet. 1986, he introduced the ProLite, a lightweight, Lycra-sheathed helmet, based on wind-tunnel tests, which he had previously conducted. This model introduced Giro's subsequent considerable success; however, some initial experimental prototypes had a strange appearance and were based on information gathered from professional-bike-racing trials. Gentes has also been known to make the tools that have realized his not-alway-successful ideas, yet enough to create a highly successful enterprise. A large number of Giro helmet models, adopted by prominent athletes and popular with the public, have been introduced. 1995, Giro Sports Design was bought by Bell Sports, and Gentes continued to work on the Giro brand.
Bibliography Steve Frothingham, 'Bell Sports Adds Giro to Roster,' *Bicycle Retailer and Industry News*, vol. 5, no. 1, 1 Jan. 1996.

Géo (b. Roger Feraud 1890–1964)

French decorator and furnituremaker; born La Ciotat.

Training École Nationale Supérieure des Arts Décoratifs, Paris.
Biography Active from 1920s in Neuilly, near Paris, Géo designed furniture and suites in incised lacquer, his specialty, and also lighting and rugs in geometric motifs. From 1928, he designed swiveling chairs. His furniture was produced by various French and foreign firms, including Cromos in France. After World War II, he specialized in rigid tubular-metal furniture and tables in perforated metal and chromed or painted metal as well as chairs with plastic and interwoven cord. Commissions included oceanliners; hotels (such as areas of the George V in Paris), Ministère de la Poste in Paris, French consulates; and a residence in Tunis. His name in literature is often incorrectly spelled 'Fenand.' He died in Neuilly-sur-Seine.
Exhibitions 1933–61, work shown at Salons of Société des Artistes Décorateurs.
Bibliography Pierre Kjellberg, *Art déco: les maîtres du mobilier, le décor des paquebots*, Paris: Amateur, 1986.

Geranzani, Piero (1928-)

Italian industrial designer; born Monza.

Biography 1949, Geranzani began as a graphics designer of advertising in the studio of Serafino Campi; 1954, established his own studio, serving clients such as Lane BBB, MV motocycles and helicopters, Rotaprint, and realizing advertising campaigns, catalogs, and posters; 1956, began working for Candy as an industrial designer and became well known for 1959 Candy Fullmatic washing machine (designed with the Candy design staff) by Officine Meccaniche Eden Fumagalli in Monza. His designs for Candy of refrigerators, air conditioners, and small domestic appliances followed. From 1962 within his new studio, he began working for other clients such as Arrigoni, Velosolex, Galbani, Ramazzotti Amaro, and Grappa Fiordivite, and, from 1972, was active within yet another studio. The Geranzani agency has continued to design award-winning appliances and electronics for clients such as Candy, Rowenta, and Zerowatt.
Citations 1952 Gran Premio d'Italia; 1959 Premio Compasso d'Oro (Candy Fullmatic); 1965 Palma d'Oro della Pubblicità; others.
Bibliography Penny Sparke, *Design in Italy, 1870 to the Present*, New York: Abbeville, 1988.

Gerlach, Ernest (1890-)

American silversmith.

Biography 1914, Gerlach established The Cellini Shop at Chicago Ave. and Davis St. in Evanston, Ill., and, 1934 with Hans Gregg, established Cellini Crafts at the same locations. 1969 and 1957, respectively, the firms were purchased by Randahl.
Bibliography Sharon S. Darling with Gail Farr Casterline, *Chicago Metalsmiths*, Chicago Historical Society, 1977.

Germanaz, Christian (1940-)

French industrial and furniture designer; born Bourth; active Paris.

Training École Boulle and École Nationale Supérieure des Arts Décoratifs; both Paris.
Biography 1966, Germanaz designed a range of office furniture, including the best-known 1968 Half and Half seat, by Airborne; 1970, set up his own design office and realized many public interiors, including those for hotels, restaurants, and hospitals; as an interior architect, designed art galleries, museums, and Manufacture Nationale de Sèvres. He designed exhibition sets for the Grand Palais in Paris, others in Caen and at École Nationale des Beaux-Arts in Paris. Also designed stage sets for dancer Maurice Béjart and seating, including 1982 Comedia sofa by Roche-Bobois. He has taught interior design, École Nationale Supérieure des Arts Décoratifs, Paris.
Exhibitions/citations Work included in 1990 exhibition, Paris (catalog below). VIA's Carte Blanche production support (Comedia chair, included in exhibition of VIA [French furniture association] at Bloomingdale's department store, New York); 1996 Prix de l'Académie d'Architecture.
Bibliography Cat., *Les années VIA 1980–1990*, Paris: Musée des Arts Décoratifs, 1990. François Mathey, *Au bonheur des formes, design français 1945–1992*, Paris: Regard, 1992.

Gero

Dutch metalworking factory; located Zeist.

History 1909–13, a factory was formed from the foundation of the M.J. Gerritsen operation with production only in spoons and forks in three patterns. Its production was drastically limited during World War I, when it produced buttons, waistband hooks, emblems, and soldier uniform numbers. 1917, the Gero brand name was registered (to become the official name of the factory in 1925). 1918, an apprenticeship program was set up, when R. Lubach became head engraver. The firm began to produce pewterware. Orders from Dutch colonies spurred its success. (1921, Gerritsen left the firm and set up competing manufacturer Sola.) 1923, a number of objects were designed by C.J. van der Hoef. Early 1920s to post-1950, Gero's most important designer was Georg Nilsson, the Dane trained by Georg Jensen in Copenhagen who initially worked at Gero's branch in Denmark. The management, which was dissatisfied with van der Hoef, placed Thomas Hooft in charge of pewter design. Hooft, who had been working at the firm from 1918, was more familiar with the technical demands of production. Jan Eisenloeffel executed only one design for Gero, 1929 Model 70 cutlery. 1930, 1931, and 1933, A.D. Copier designed a set of bowls and vases. R. Hamstra designed its emblem and catalogs. 1929–33, Gero experienced financial difficulties due to the Great Depression and, 1931, began producing 18/8 stainless steel under the Zilmeta brand. 1945, the factory was severely damaged by bombing but, after the war, was rebuilt and became successful; 1947, the subsidiary Nieuw-Weerdinge near Emmen was established. Gero remains active.
Bibliography Cat., *Industry and Design in the Netherlands, 1850/1950*, Amsterdam: Stedelijk Museum, 1985.

Gerritsen en Van Kempen (Koninklijke)

Dutch silver manufacturer; located Zeist.

History Koninklijke Gerritsen en Van Kempen was founded in 1924. 1934–77, Gustav Beran, a native of Vienna and pupil of Josef Hoffmann, was the head designer at the firm, which merged with Van Kempen en Begeer in Voorschoten in 1960.
Exhibition Beran's work shown at Gerritsen en Van Kempen's stand, 1937 *Exposition Internationale des Arts et Techniques dans la Vie Moderne*, Paris.
Bibliography Annelies Krekel-Aalberse, *Art Nouveau and Art Déco Silver*, New York: Abrams, 1989.

Gerth, Ruth (d. 1952)

American designer.

Biography Calling themselves Gerth and Gerth, Ruth Gerth and William Gerth (possibly her brother) were metalworkers originally in the Arts and Crafts mode, later turning to modernism. They may have been active in New York State before settling in Chicago. The Gerths designed a number of tabletop items and home accessories, such as a watering can and a small table lamp produced from plumbing floats and others in brass or chromium-plate by Chase Brass and Copper Co. in Waterbury, Conn. Their double candlestick for Chase was a notable, simple modern statement. Other clients included Bates Manufacturing Co. and R.E. Dietz. 1936, Ruth was president, Artists' Guild, an association of freelance artists.
Bibliography R.S. McFadden, 'Designers' Ability Salvages Waste,' *Design*, vol. 35, no. 3, Sept. 1933: 20–24. Donald-Brian Johnson and Leslie A. Piña, *Chase Complete: Déco Specialties of the Chase Brass & Copper Co.*, Atglen, Pa.: Schiffer, 1999.

Christian Ghion. Butterfly Kiss armchair. c. 2002. Dacryl, h. 29 1/8 x w. 23 5/8 x d. 45 1/4" (74 x 60 x 115 cm). Mfr.: prototype Cappellini, Italy.

Geyling, Remigius (1878–1974)

Austrian stage designer, painter, and craftsperson; born Vienna.

Biography On the occasion of the 1908 (16th) anniversary of the Emperor Franz Joseph's accession to the throne of Austria, Geyling designed (with Heinrich Lefler, Berthold Löffler, and Oskar Kokoschka) the costumes for historical and folklore tableaux.
Bibliography Robert Waissenberger, *Vienna 1890–1920*, Secaucus, N.J.: Wellfleet 1984.

Ghia, Giacinto (1887–1944)
> See Karmann, Wilhelm.

Ghion, Christian (1958–)

French designer; born Montmorency.

Training Diploma, École du Louvre, Paris.
Biography 1988–97, Ghion collaborated with Patrick Nadeau; 1997 with others, created the D.G. designer-rights group. Design work with Nadeau has included 1995 Maria-Louisa pearwood table; 1996 Oh! Marie-Laure one-piece ash plywood table by G.N. Éditions; 1996 Fire Side sofa and 1998 H.A.N. side chair by Idée. Design work as an individual has included 1998 Ego vase by Cinna, 1998 Blé Sur ceramic flower vase by Evans & Wong, 1998 Ruche PVC/cotton ceiling light by Ligne Roset, 1999 Ovo glass vases by Ligne Roset, 2000 Insideout glass vase and 2002 Insideout Murano glass vase by XO, 2000 Blue Lagoon gel-capsule chaise longue, 2001 Tour à CD rotating table to hold CDs by Lemarchand, faïence dinner service by Silvera, products by mail-order firm 3 Suisses and by Evans and Wong, a new Japanese restaurant in Paris, multimedia spaces for the Ministère de la Culture of France, lamps by En Attendant les Barbares, 2002 Shadow chaise longue in Corian by Cappellinni, 2001 Sugar seating collection by Abdi. Is a professor at the various Écoles des Beaux-Arts in Reims, Saint-Étienne, and Rennes.
Exhibitions/citations Director of Design Lab (25 designers' work), 2002 Salon du Meuble, Paris. 1989, 1992, 1994, 1995, 1996, and 1997 Appel Permanent grants, VIA; 1991 co-winner (with Nadeau) Grand Prix de la Ville de Paris; 1995 study scholarship from Association Française d'Action Artistique (AFAA).
Bibliography Mel Byars, *50 Tables...*, Hove: RotoVision, 1997. Mel Byars, *50 Beds...*, Hove: RotoVision, 2000. www.via.asso.fr

Ghyczy, Peter (1940–)

Hungarian designer; born Budapest.

Training University of Aachen.
Biography After his studies, Ghyczy was commissioned by Reuter Products to design 1969–72 plastic furniture, including the 1969 28252 armchair (reissued as GN2) in plastic with fabric-inset upholstery and RO3 illuminated glass shelf (reissued as GN3) for the Form + Life Collection in Germany. He has since become known primarily for 1968 Senftenberger Ei (garden egg) flip-top indoor/outdoor fiberglass-reinforced polyurethane chair. It was reissued in 2001 as GN1, in high-impact polystyrene with a stainless-steel hinge and a turntable beneath the 'egg.' 1972, he established his own firm Ghyczy Selection in Swalmen, the Netherlands, in order to be able to control production and distribution of his design work. In the Ghyczy Novo collection are more recent works such as 2001 GN4 lightweight table in expanded polypropylene.
Bibliography www.ghyczy.nl.

Giacometti, Alberto (1901–1966); Diego Giacometti (1902–1985)

Swiss artist-designers; both active Paris, brothers.

Training Alberto Giacometti: in Geneva and Paris.
Biography 1922, Alberto Giacometti moved to Paris, where he was joined a few years later by his brother Diego. At first they shared a studio space on the rue Froidevaux; 1927, moved into the adjacent workroom at 46, rue Hippolyte-Maindron; 1927–33, designed accessories for the Desny firm in Paris; 1928, began to design and produce lighting, bronze vases, candlesticks, medallions, mantelpieces, andirons, and other accessories for the clients of Parisian decorator Jean-Michel Frank. At this time, Alberto was making little money on his fine art activities; later commented, 'I attempted to make vases, for example, as well as I could, and I realized that I was working on a vase exactly as I did on sculpture.' The specific role of each brother in the production of their wares for Frank is not clear. Alberto may have designed the pieces, and Diego oversaw their casting. Alberto designed the large stone sculpture *Figure* (1932) for the garden of vicomte and vicomtesse de Noailles's villa in Hyères. After Frank's business diminished, Diego found work designing perfume bottles and fashion accessories. From the early 1950s, he began making bronze furniture. Alberto insisted that Diego sign his work with his first name to avoid confusion but yet made sure that Diego was recognized in his own right. From Alberto's 1966 death, Diego continued to cast pieces of their early tables and floor lamps. From this time on, Diego's new furniture and furnishings reflected an interest in nature, particularly animals. An example of his later work is illustrated by the group of objects produced for Musée Picasso, Hôtel Salé, Paris. 1992, a group of vendors and manufacturers was charged with counterfeiting Diego's bronze furniture.
Exhibitions Work subject of 1985 *Diego Giacometti*, Greenberg Gallery, St. Louis, and Marisa del Re Gallery, New York; 1986 *Diego Giacometti: Möbel und Objekte aus Bronze*, Museum Bellerive, Zürich; others.
Bibliography James Lord, *Giacometti*, New York: Farrar, Straus, Giroux, 1985: 122, 210–11, 212, 214, 253, 331. Françoise Francisci et al., *Diego Giacometti: catalogue de l'œuvre*, Paris: EOLIA, 1986. Daniel Marchesseau, *Diego Giacometti*, New York: Abrams; Paris: Hermann; 1987. François Baudot, *Diego Giacometti*, Paris: Assouline, 1998. Cat., Christian Klemm et al., *Alberto Giacometti*, New York: The Museum of Modern Art; Zürich: Kunsthaus Zürich; 2001.

Giacosa, Dante (1905–1996)

Italian automobile designer and engineer; born Rome; active Turin.

Training Secondary school, Alba; 1926, engineering degree, Politecnico, Turin.
Biography Giacosa is considered by some critics to have been the father of the small Italian automobile. From 1927, he worked at Fiat in Turin where he was the chief designer, early on working on military vehicles; from 1928, worked on commercial vehicles and diesel engines. At the time, Oreste Lardone was the chief designer there. Fiat head Giovanni Agnelli ordered Lardone to design a 'people's car' to be built, like Britain's Morris 8 and Germany's Volkswagen. The Fiat attempt was a favorite project of Italian premier Benito Mussolini but a failure, and Lordone was thus dismissed. However, as a response, Giacosa created the 1936 canvas-topped Fiat 500 (affectionately nicknamed 'Topolino' ('Mickey Mouse' in Italian) with a water-cooled rear-wheel drive and a forward-placed engine, created under the supervision of Antonio Fessia. When production was resumed in 1945, the 500 sold for 720,000 lire (36 months' salary of the average Italian industrial worker)—not cheap as intended and hardly 'the people's car.' Also after World War II and then in charge of Fiat's entire design division, Giacosa developed the 1946 Cisitalia 202, 1950 Fiat 1400, 1956 forward-engine rear-wheel drive Fiat 600 and a group of rear-engined models such as 1957 Nuova 500 (a reissue of the Topolino). He also designed 1964 Autobianchi Primula, 1969 Fiat 128 that changed the front-wheel drive, the boxy model 124, and the 1971 model 127—all presaging Fiat's small and midsize models. For a number of years, Giacosa taught, Politecnico, Turin; 1970, retired from Fiat; died in Turin. Some critics claim that he made Fiat what it became at the peak of its success. Attempting to revive the original 500 model, Fiat produced the 1991 Cinquecento (500) mini-model.
Citations 1959 Premio Compasso d'Oro (for Fiat 500).
Bibliography Dante Giacosa, *Forty Years of Design at Fiat*, Milan: Automobilia,1979. Penny Sparke, *A Century of Car Design*, London: Mitchell Beazley, 2002.

Giannelli, Márcio (1977–)
> See Nó Design.

Gibbons, Austin Cedric (1893–1960)

Irish film-set designer; son of an architect; born Dublin; active US.

Training Art Students League, New York
Biography Cedric Gibbons worked for his father briefly; 1915, became a set dresser for films, assisting art director Hugo Ballin at Edison Studios, New York, and, within two years, was a full art director; soon accompanied Ballin to Hollywood, where he was hired by Samuel Goldwyn in 1918, when Ballin resigned as an art director to direct and produce. 1924, Gibbons joined the staff of newly formed Metro Goldwyn Mayer (MGM) and assumed the novel title 'supervising art director.' He went on to replace painted backdrops with three-dimensional sets and, thus, was dubbed the person who 'put the glove on the mantelpiece.' He managed a staff of talented unit art directors, not always recognized in screen credits, including Ben Carré, Merrill Pye, Richard Day, and Arnold Gillespie; 1924, signed a contract with MGM that gave him sole credit for every film the studio made in the US; was in control of the wardrobe, set-dressing, matte-painting, special effects, and photography sections of the studio. The 1925 *Exposition Internationale des Arts Décoratifs et Industriels Modernes*, Paris, profoundly influenced his approach, as seen in sets from *Greed* (1923), his first, to *Our Dancing Daughters* (1928), with its expansive Art Déco interiors. Other glamorous films popularizing Art Déco followed, including *Our Modern Maidens* (1929) and *Our Blushing Brides* (1930), creating a craze for affectations that included venetian blinds, dancing figurines, and indirect lighting in middle-class décors of the time. Gibbons has been widely credited with the c. 1928 design of the Oscar statuette for the Academy of Motion Picture Arts and Sciences (which he himself won 11 times, 1929–56, and once for 'consistent excellence' in 1950); however, the statuette was created by Los Angeles sculptor George Stanley, who, after sketches were submitted by several local artists, was commissioned by Gibbons. (The statuette is 24-karat-gold plated, manufactured today by R.S. Owens & Co. in Chicago, and 13 1/2" (33.5 cm) high and weighs 8 1/2 lbs./3.6 kg.) 1930–41, Gibbons was married to actress Delores Del Rio. His streamlined showcase office on the MGM lot was designed by Merrill Pye, one of his set-design assistants, who worked with him on *Our Blushing Brides* (1930). Hobart Erwin and Frederick Hope (under Gibbons) designed *Dinner at Eight* (1933), the set that incorporated the 'white telephone' look. Gibbons was congratulated by architects for his French Revolution sets for *Marie Antoinette* (1938), although its aesthetics were highly exaggerated. 1917–55, Gibbons had screen credits for more than 1,500 films. He died in Hollywood, Cal.
Bibliography John Hambley and Patrick Downing, *The Art of Hollywood*, London: Thames Television, 1979. Howard Mandelbaum and Eric Myers, *Screen Deco: A Celebration of High Style in Hollywood*, New York: St. Martin's, 1985. Ephraim Katz et al., *The Film Encyclopedia*, New York: Harper, 2001 (4th ed.).

Gibson, Natalie

British textile designer.

Training 1956–58, painting, Chelsea School of Art, London.
Biography 1958–61, Gibson printed textiles at Royal College of Art, London; designed for numerous firms including Connaissance, Fieldcrest, Habitat, and Heal's; became primarily active in fashion; designed fabrics by Bini & Stehli, Mantero, and Fidelis, and clothing for Cacharel, Chloë, Galeries Lafayette, and MAFIA; was senior lecturer, St. Martins School of Art, London.
Exhibitions Work in shown in numerous venues.
Bibliography Robert A.M. Stern (ed.), *The International Design Yearbook*, New York: Abbeville, 1985/1986.

Giedion, Sigfried (1888–1968)

Bohemian art historian and designer; born Prague; active Switzerland.

Training Engineering, Technische Hochschule, Vienna, 1916–22, art history, Zürich and Berlin, and under Heinrich Wölfflin at Universität München.
Biography 1923, Giedion met Walter Gropius at the Bauhaus in Weimar and, 1925, Le Corbusier in Paris; 1928–56, was general secretary, Congrès Internationaux d'Architecture Moderne (CIAM), of which he was a cofounder; published books *Bauen in Frankreich, Eisen, Eisenbeton* (Leipzig: Klinkhardt & Biermann, 1928) and *Befreites Wohne: 85 Bilder* (Zürich: O. Füssl, 1929). 1931 with Werner Max Moser and Rudolf Graber, he cofounded the Wohnbedarf department store in Zürich, specializing in home furnishings, and was head of the technical division 1934–35. His international contacts with designers such as Alvar Aalto, Le Corbusier, Marcel Breuer, László Moholy-Nagy, and Herbert Bayer proved decisive in Wohnbedarf's growth. 1932, Giedion designed bronzeware for the BAG factory, Turgi (Switzerland), a firm which he helped to reorganize, and designed its c. 1932 indi lamp series with 'Hin' Hindrich Bredendieck. He reorganized steel-furniture company EMBRU-Werke in Rüti, Switzerland, for modern-design furniture production and designed its factory. 1938, Giedion delivered a paper in the Charles Eliot Norton Lectures at Harvard University and, from early 1940s, wrote books in English, beginning with *Space, Time and Architecture: The Growth of a New Tradition* (Cambridge, Mass.: Harvard University, 1941 and subsequent eds.). This is his best-known book and highly influential, particularly in defining modern architecture and its discussion of transparency, examining the leading modern figures and movements, and the roots of the ideas of the founding fathers. Under the tutelage of Heinrich Wölfflin, Giedion developed a theory of 'anonymous' history in his writings, best revealed in his speculative book *Mechanization Takes Command: A Contribution to Anonymous History* (New York: Oxford University, 1948), which continues to be highly regarded. Other books followed, including *Walter Gropius: Work and Teamwork* (New York: Reinhold, 1954), *Architecture, You and Me...* (Cambridge, Mass.: Harvard University, 1958), *The Eternal Present...*, (2 vols., New York: Pantheon, 1962 and 1964), and *The Beginnings of Architecture...* (New York: Pantheon, 1964). He dispatched the manuscript of his last book, *Architecture and the Phenomena of Transition...* (Cambridge, Mass.: Harvard University, 1971) to the publisher on the day of his death.
Bibliography Stanislaus von Moos, 'Sigfried Giedion zum Gedenken,' in *Schweizerische Bauzeitung*, 1968, no. 26, 467–68. Paul Hofer and Ulrich Stucky, *Hommage à Giedion: Profile seiner Persönlichkeit*, Basel/Stuttgart: Birkhäuser, 1971. Friederike Mehlau-Wiebking et al., *Schweizer Typenmöbel 1925–35, Sigfried Giedion und die Wohnbedarf AG*, Zürich: gta, 1989. Sokratis Georgiadis, *Sigfried Giedion: An Intellectual Biography*, Edinburgh: Edinburgh University, 1993.

Gien, Société Nouvelle des Faïenceries de

French ceramics manufacturer; located Gien.

History 1821, the faïence factory in Gien was purchased by Thomas Hulm, an Englishman known as 'Hall'; is still located on its original site,

Sigfried Giedion and Hin Bredendiek. indi floor lamp. c. 1932. Steel tubing and sheet steel, extendable h. 61 5/8–73 7/16" (156.5–186.5 cm). Mfr.: BAG, Türgi, Switzerland, for Wohbedarf store, Zurich, Switzerland. Courtesy Quittenbaum Kunstauktionen, Munich.

the 15th-century convent of Minime on the river Loire. A landmark in its production was its 1875 Renaissance Fond Bleu faïence. The factory was commissioned by European royal families to produce dinner services; made tiles for the interior walls of the stations of the Métro in Paris; became known for its inexpensive faïence ware. Its freelance designers from the 1970s have included Isabelle de Borchgrave, Jean-Pierre Caillères, Jacqueline Deyme, Christian Duc, Eliakim, Garouste and Bonetti, Pascal Mourgue, Paco Rabanne, Martin Székely, and Jean-Michel Wilmotte.
Exhibitions/citations 1839 (bronze medal), 1844 (bronze medal), 1855 (bronze medal), 1867 (silver medal), 1878 (gold medal), 1889 (grand prize), and at 1900 *Expositions Universelles*, Paris; 1873 (bronze medal) *Third Annual International Exhibition*, London; 1873 (bronze medal) *Welt-Ausstellung*, Vienna; 1876 (gold medal), *Centennial Exposition*, Philadelphia; 1878 exhibition (bronze medal) in Amsterdam; 1879–80 (gold medal) *Sydney International Exhibition*.
Bibliography Roger Bernard and Jean-Claude Ronard, *La faïence de Gien*, Brussels: Sous le Vent, 1981. Roger Bernard and Jean-Claude Renard, *Gien Faïence*, Gien: Société Nouvelle des Faïenceries de Gien, 1985. Michèle-Cécile Gillard, *Faïence de Gien: formes et décors*, Paris: Massin, 1988. Cat., *L'Art de Vivre: Decorative Art and Design in France, 1789–1989*, New York: Vendôme, 1989.

Gignoux, Michèle (1944–)

French designer, painter, and fashion designer.

Training Charpentier workshop, Paris.
Biography Calling herself a 'Pop romantic' artist, she invented the 1967 Cube photo frame in Plexiglas by Bac Design; designed 1989 Vertige chair in fluorescent colors and Formica, shown in various galleries including that of VIA (French furniture association) in Paris; became known for her 'illuminated jacket' and 'photomontages.'
Bibliography Cat., *Michèle Gignoux: Gladys Fabre, Béatrice Fraenkel, Inès de la Fressange, Linda Henderson, Barbara Rose*, Paris: Galerie Franka Berndt Bastille/Galerie VIA/Difference, 1989. Arlette Barré-Despond (ed.), *Dictionnaire international des arts appliqués et du design*, Paris: Regard, 1996

Gigou, Louis

French locksmith and lighting designer.

Biography Gigou designed door handles, finger plates, escutcheons, and keys and also a variety of lighting forms in bronze, wrought iron, and steel with ornamental copper overlays. His distinctive lighting, produced chiefly 1919–25, includes table lamps, sconces, and floor lamps. After this time, he specialized in locksmithing.
Exhibitions Metalwork shown at various Salons of Société des Artistes Décorateurs, Paris.
Bibliography Guillaume Janneau, *Le luminaire et les moyens d'éclairage nouveaux*, Paris: Charles Moreau, 1st series: plates 26, 43, [n.d.]. Léon Deshairs (intro.), *Modern French Decorative Art: A Collection of Examples of Modern French Decoration*, Paris: Albert Lévy, c. 1925–30. Alastair Duncan, *Art Nouveau and Art Déco Lighting*, New York: Simon & Schuster, 1978.

Gilardi, Piero (1942–)

Italian artist and designer; born Turin.

Biography Gilardi is more an artist than a designer. But his three designs have become legendary: 1967 Pavé Piuma floor mat, 1968 Sassi (rocks) seating, and 1974 Massolo pseudo-archeological artifact. They were produced by Gufram in its proprietary Guflac expanded polyurethane and derived from the same material as much of his fine art. His first one-person show, 1963 *Macchine per il Futuro* (machine of the future), and his first pieces (1965) in polyurethane foam were exhibited in Paris, Brussels, Cologne, Hamburg, Amsterdam, and New York. 1968, he turned from standard art to the new artistic trends of the late 1960s (Arte Povera, Land Art, and Antiform Art)—a pursuit also of Joe Colombo and Gaetano Pesce. Gilardi took part in organizing the first two, landmark international exhibitions of the new genres, at the Stedelijk Museum in Amsterdam and the Kunsthalle in Berne. 1969, he began a continuing quest to analyze and experience a so-called Art/Life experience; tavelled to Nicaragua, the Southwest in the US, and Mexico; first half of 1980s, began investigating new technologies, realized through the 1985 *Ixiana* installation in the Parc de La Vilette in Paris, intended for the public to experience digital technology. He remains quite actively involved in the theoretical analysis of an art that calls on new media and writes the column 'Return to the Future' in *Flash Art* magazine. Today, working in his Studio B&D in Milan, he created the art for Vase no. 29 in Alessi's vase series. His more accessible art work includes 2002 *Fiore Tropicale,* a three-dimensional expanded-polyurethane piece, 11 7/8 x 11 7/8" (30 x 30 cm), in his Nature Carpets series. Recently, with musician Ricardo Colella, he developed a series of 'dancing,' illuminated electronic devices, called *Albero Danzante* (dancing trees).
Exhibitions Work included in numerous venues.
Bibliography Cat., *Piero Gilardi*, Bologna: Galleria La Nuova Loggia 1967. *ADI Annual 1976*, Milan: Associazione per il Disegno Industriale, 1976. Cat., Marco Meneguzzo, *Piero Gilardi: Tappeti natura 1966–1985*, Milan: Galleria Seno, 1985. Albrecht Bangert, *Italienisches Möbeldesign*, Munich: Bangert, 1989. Dan Cameron and Massimo Melotti, *Piero Gilardi*, New York: Artinvest, 1991. Richard Flood and Frances Morris, *Zero to Infinity: Arte Povera 1962–1972*, Minneapolis: Walker Art Center, 2001. Cat., Franco Mello, Ennio Chiggio, and Stefano Casciani, *The Rock Furniture = Il Design della Gufram negli anni del rock*, Turin: Castello di Rivoli, 2001. Paola Antonelli (ed.), *Objects of Design: The Museum of Modern Art*, New York: The Museum of Modern Art, 2003: 258.

Gilbert, Alfred Carlton (1884–1962)

American inventor; born Salem, Ore.

Training To 1909, Medical School, Yale University, New Haven, Conn.
Biography As a child, Gilbert was an aficionado of magic tricks, at which he became proficient, so much so that he was able to fund his university tuition by performing as a magician. While at Yale, he founded Mysto Manufacturing Co., which sold magic kits for children; 1909, turned from medicine to expanding his toy business; 1911 while in New York, became inspired by an electrical power-line tower that was being built of thin steel beams and, thus, invented a child's construction set based on the same principles. It included flat metal braces with evenly spaced holes to accommodate bolts, screws, gears, pulleys, and other appurtenances. However, British toymaker Meccano made a similar set. Nevertheless, 1913, Gilbert marketed his Musto Erector Structural Steel Builder, which soon became the most popular toy ever—the Erector Set. He also invented the 1936 Gilbert Chemistry Outfit for Boys (becoming simply the Gilbert Chemistry Set); was elected the first president, Toy Manufacturers Association (TMA), US. 1998, A.C. Gilbert's Discovery Village theme park opened at National Toy Hall of Fame in Gilbert's birthplace, Salem, Ore.
Bibliography Al M. Sternagle and William M. Bean, *Greenberg's Guide to Gilbert Erector Sets*, Brookfield, Wis.: Kalmbach, vol. 1, 1993; vol. 2, 1997. Steven Lubar and Kathleen M. Kendrick, *Legacies: Collecting America's History at the Smithsonian*, Washington, D.C.: Smithsonian, 2001. Bruce Watson, *The Man Who Changed the Way Boys and Toys Were Made*, New York: Viking Penguin, 2002.

Gili, Anna (1960–)

Italian designer; born Orvieto; active Milan.

Training 1980–84, Istituto Superiore per le Industrie Artistiche (ISIA), Florence.
Biography 1984, Gili began as a freelance designer. Work has included 1991 Murai table by Cassina, 1991 Tonda armchair by Cappellini, 1995 Stelle mosaic table and 1999 Noah's Ark series of hand-painted crystal goblets and mosaic pictures by Bisazza, 1996 Rigati series and 2000 Bulbi vases by Salviati, 2000 Teddy Bear drinking glass by Ritzenhoff, 2000 Manhattan and 2001 jewelry collections by Nicolis Cola, and 2002 Op Art box, table clock, and compass by Swarovski, ceramics by Tendentse, lighting and fabrics by Francis Cot, jewelry by Cleto Munari. She has contributed to design journal *Ollo*; from 1984, designed a number of installations.
Exhibitions Vestito Sonoro project shown at Padiglione d'Arte Contemporanea, Milan; Seibu, Tokyo; Kunstmuseum, Düsseldorf. Gin vase by Porcellane Richard Ginori, Cielo and Nuvola laminates by Abet Laminati, and Razio armchair by Poltrona Frau included in 1992 *Nuovo bel design: 200 nuovi oggetti per la casa*, Salone del Mobile, Milan.
Bibliography Paolo Rinaldi, 'Carla Ceccariglia e Anna Gili,' *Casa Vogue*, no. 214, 1989. *Modo*, no. 148, Mar.–Apr. 1993: 120. Fumio Shimizu, *Pioneers of Product Design*, Tokyo: Creo, 1994. Cat., *Nuovo bel design: 200 nuovi oggetti per la casa*, Milan: Electa, 1992. Cat., *New Design In Glass*, Kunstmuseum, Dusseldorf, 1996. Cat., *Design im Wandel*, Munich: Bangert, 1996. *The International Design Yearbook*, New York: Abbeville, 1996, 1997, 2000. Andrea Branzi, *Aldo Cibic Designer*, Milan, 1999. Lina Kälin, 'Lo stile di Anna Gili,' *Gioia Casa*, no.1, 2000. M. Erlhoff et al, *Anna Gili, Mental Bodies*, Milan: L'Archivolto, 2001.

Gill, Arthur Eric Rowton (1882–1940)

British sculptor, graphic artist, engraver, and typographer; born Brighton.

Training 1900–03 under Edward Johnston, Chichester Art School; Central School of Arts and Crafts, London.
Biography 1900–03, Gill was apprentice to architect W.D. Caröe; 1913, converted to Roman Catholicism; 1913–18, carved the Stations of the Cross at Westminster Cathedral, London; c. 1918, cofounded a semi-religious crafts community, the Guild of St. Joseph and St. Dominic in Ditchling, Sussex; 1920, cofounded Society of Wood Engravers; 1924, settled in Capel-y-ffin, Wales and began a collaboration with the Golden Cockerel Press; designed numerous typefaces, including 1927 Perpetua and 1928 Gill Sans by Monotype; 1928, settled in and set up a printing press in Pigotts, Buckinghamshire. His graphic-design commissions came from various publishers, including Clarendon Press, Cloverhill Press, Cranach Press, Dent, Faber & Faber, and Limited Editions Club (US). 1929–31, he produced sculpture for BBC Broadcasting House, London, and, 1936, for League of Nations building, Geneva. Gill's silver designs of c. 1930 were produced by H.G. Murphy of The Worshipful Company of Goldsmiths. 1930, Gill designed a casement clock for Edward W. Hunter of the Sun Engraving Co, and the typography and embellishments of 1937 postage stamps (with the king's image by Edmund Dulac) for King George VI's coronation.
Citations 1935 honorary associate, Royal Institute of British Architects; 1936, elected Honorary Royal Designer for Industry, UK; 1937, associate, Royal Academy; 1937, honorary associate, Royal Society of British Sculptors.
Bibliography Eric Gill, 'Paintings and Criticism,' *The Architecture Review*, Mar. 1930. Eric Gill, *Autobiography*, London: Jonathan Cape, 1940. Robert Speaight, *The Life of Eric Gill*, London: Methuen, 1966. Donald Attwater, *A Cell of Good Living: The Life, Works and Opinions of Eric Gill*, London, G. Chapman, 1969. Roy Muller, *Eric Gill: The Man Who Loved Letters*, London, Muller, 1973. Cat., *Thirties: British Art and Design Before the War*, London: Arts Council of Great Britain/Hayward Gallery, 1979. Annelies Krekel-Aalberse, *Art Nouveau and Art Déco Silver*, New York: Abrams, 1989.

Piero Gilardi. Sassi (rocks). 1968. Painted polyurethane foam, largest 17 3/4 x 27 1/2 x 21 5/8" (45.1 x 69.9 x 55 cm). Mfr.: Gufram, Italy. Gift of the mfr. MoMA.

Gilles, Willem (1923–2002)
Dutch industrial designer and educator; born Alkmaar; active the Netherlands and Canada.

Training Polytechnic, Dordrecht.
Biography Gilles practiced engineering design and, from 1949, product design and, from 1953, part-time teaching of industrial design; co-founded KIO, a Dutch association of industrial designers; worked with others to established Bureau of European Design Associations (BEDA). In the Netherlands, he designed school furniture, enameled cast-iron and sheet-metal kitchenware, sanitaryware, heating equipment, washing machines, and others. In Belgium, he designed the ID program and layout of a polyethylene and polyether plant. 1963–73 taught, Akademie voor Industriële Vormgeving, Eindhoven, where he was the director from 1970; moved to Canada and, 1973–85, directed and taught, School of Industrial Design, Carleton University, Ottawa; 1985–92, founded and taught, Centre for Industrial Design Research, Carleton University; 1992, retired. He wrote a number of articles and the book *Form Organisation* (Oxford: Butterworth-Heinemann, 1991).
Citations Honorary member, KIO, the Netherlands; 1992, appointed emeritus professor of industrial design and, 1997, granted honorary doctor of engineering degree, Carleton University.

Gillgren, Sven Arne (1913–1992)
Swedish metalworker.

Training 1933, in engraving under C.F. Hallberg; 1936, Kungliga Tekniska Högskolan, Stockholm.
Biography From 1937, Gillgren was a designer at Guldsmedsaktiebolaget in Stockholm, where he was artistic director 1942–75; from 1944, designed for goldsmithy G. Dahlgren in Malmö. Sweden's neutrality during World War II permitted artisans like Gillgren to produce luxury crafts. His designs show an interest in folk motifs. 1937–1975, he designed for Gense in Eskilstuna; created cutlery for Swedish institutions and silver for churches in Sweden and abroad; 1955–70, was the principal teacher in the department of metalworking and industrial design, Konstfackskolan (formerly Kungliga Tekniska Högskolan); 1975, set up his own studio in Stockholm.
Citations First prize, 1958 Stockholm Handicraft Society competition; first prize, 1960 *International Design Competition for Sterling Silver Flatware*, Museum of Contemporary Crafts, New York; 1963 prize of honor, Swedish Design Center; 1964 Prince Eugen Medal; 1966 Eligius Prize.
Bibliography Cat., David Revere McFadden (ed.), *Scandinavian Modern Design 1880–1980*, New York: Abrams, 1982.

Gilliam, Kenneth (1952–)
American retailer and designer; active San Francisco.

Biography Early 1990s, collaborated with retailer and designer Dan Friedlander (1951–); designed furniture in a 1960s style, produced by Design America; for a time recently, was the principal of the Design Contiuum studio branch in San Francisco until the branch there was closed.
Bibliography Arlene Hirst, 'Design Class at Last,' *Metropolitan Home*, Nov. 1990: 101.

Gilliard, Joseph W. (1914–)
American ceramicist, metalsmith, and teacher; born Taylors, S.C.

Biography Gilliard taught, Hampton Institute, Va., where he greatly influenced generations of African-American ceramics students. His own forms and glazes were innovative. He invented a wheel to accommodate the throwing of vessels up to 39" (100 cm) wide; experimented with glazes and high temperatures to produce unique effects like gold-flecking; 1940s, pursued organic forms and, subsequently, abstract ones; was also a competent metalsmith of lathe-turned metal as components of ceramic vessels.
Citations 50-Year-Pin recipient, American Ceramics Society.
Bibliography Cat., Janet Kardon (ed.), *Craft in the Machine Age 1920–1945*, New York: Abrams with American Craft Museum, 1995.

Gimson, Ernest (1864–1919)
British architect and designer; born Leicester.

Training 1881 under architect Isaac Barradale, apprenticeship, Leicester; Leicester School of Art.
Biography On William Morris's recommendation, Gimson joined the architecture office of J.D. Sedding in 1886; met brothers Ernest and Sidney Barnsley; learned chair-turning under Herefordshire craftsperson Philip Clisrett and studied plaster work; 1895, established his own workshop in the Cotswolds with the Barnsley brothers. 1901, they were joined by Peter van der Waals, a Dutch cabinetmaker then living in London. 1902, The Daneway Workshops were set up by Gimson and the Barnsley brothers at Daneway House in Gloucestershire. The partnership was dissolved in c. 1905, and Gimson continued on his own. Gimson's furniture ranged from simple, vernacular rush-seated chairs to elaborate cabinets with rich inlays and veneers. He refused to join the Design and Industries Association because he did not want his work to be produced by machinery.
Exhibitions Work shown at Arts and Crafts Exhibition Society events.
Bibliography W. R. Lethaby et al., *Ernest Gimson, His Life and Work*, Stratford-upon-Avon: Shakespeare Head, 1924. Cat., *Ernest Gimson*, Leicester: Leicester Museums and Art Gallery, 1969. Cat., *Ernest Gimson and The Cotswold Group of Craftsmen*, Leicester: Leicester Museums, 1969. *British Art and Design, 1900–1960*, London: Victoria and Albert Museum, 1983.

GINChUK
> See INKhUK.

Guinochet, Jean-Louis (1945–)
French designer.

Biography Guinochet's work has included 1986 Collection d'Artistes sideboard (homage to painter Pierre Soulages) by Passerelle, 1986 Manhattan kitchen system by Chabert Duval, 1988 Khéops table and chair by Magne, 1990 Calligraphe desk by Vinco, Table du Fumeur Diva, 1987 Diva smokers' table by Grange, 1987 Particule et Acacia armchair by Atoll, 1987 PL de Philips by Résistex, 2000 stool/chair in twigs by Lou Fagotin, 2002 Transatlantic seating by Sifas, 2003 Sienna Collection (14-piece furniture range, resisting UV damage) by Hall Designs in the US. By Ligne Roset: 2000 Planet table, Vide Poches table lamp, Franges rug ranges, 2002 Damier coffee table, 2003 O'val lamp, and others by Ligne Roset. He works primarily independently but also with Anne Guinochet (1949–).
Citations 1986 Kitchen of the Year. Designs sponsored by VIA (French furniture association): in 1980 (for Feûtre chair with Anne Guinochet), 1986 (for Manhattan kitchen), 2000 (for 1999 roto-molded stool), and 2003 (for Transatlantic seating).
Bibliography www.via.asso.fr.

Gioacchini, Nilo (1946–)
Italian industrial designer; born Osimo; active Florence.

Biography 1968–69, Gioacchini worked in industrial-design studio Nizzoli Associati in Milan; 1970 with Gianni Ferrara and Carlo Bimbi, established industrial-design studio Gruppo Internotredici in Florence,

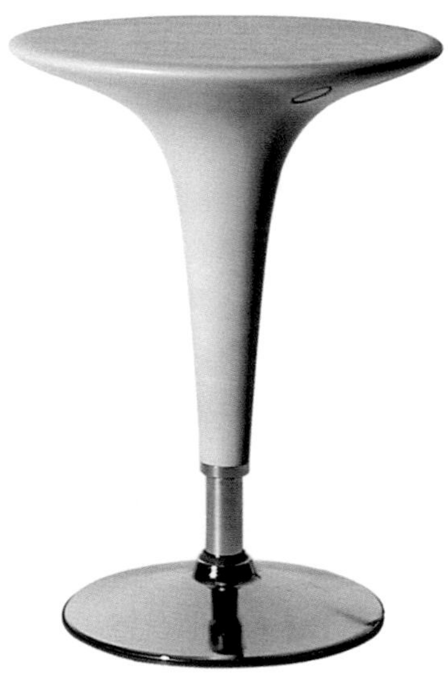

Stefano Giovannoni. Bombo adjustable table. c. 1998. Steel and polypropylene, h. 25 1/2–35 3/8 x dia. 21 5/8" (65–90 x 55 cm). Mfr.: Magis, Italy.

designing furniture, sanitary fittings, and table accessories; became a member, Associazione per il Disegno Industriale (ADI).
Exhibitions/citations Their work shown at 1967 *Universal and International Exhibition (Expo '67)*, Montréal; 1971 (9th) Mostra Selettva del Mobile, Cantù, sponsored by Rassegna (where Internotredici's 1,076 sq. ft. [100 m²] apartment was shown); 1972 *Italy: The New Domestic Landscape*, The Museum of Modern Art, New York; 1973 BIO 5 industrial-design biennial, Ljubljana; *Italia Oggi* exhibition, Gimbel's department store, Pittsburgh, Pa., US; Italian design pavilion, 1975 *Salon d'Ameublement*, Lausanne. Internotredici received its first citation, at 1968 (8th) Ottavo Concorso Internationale del Mobile, Trieste, and a first prize at its 1969 (9th) edition and the Bayer prize at its 1970 (9th) edition; first and second prizes, 1971 Concorso Nazionale (for plastic-laminated furniture sponsored by Abet-Print); first prize in 1972 competition for alabaster objects by Volterra.
Bibliography *ADI Annual 1976*, Milan: Associazione per il Disegno Industriale, 1976.

Giordano, Paolo (1954–)
Italian designer; born Naples; active Milan.

Training To 1978, architecture, Politecnico, Milan.
Biography 1978–95, Giordano worked as an artistic and a professional photographer, creating photomontages, architectural photography, and still life for magazines, including *Abitare* and *Casa Vogue*; 1996 with wife Nuala Goodman, founded I + I company in Milan for the design and production of domestic objects and textiles. In addition to their own-produced/marketed products, some of their clients have included Boffi (from 2000) and Molteni (from 2002) for the design of customized products coordinated with the firms' furniture.
Bibliography *The International Design Yearbook*, Abbeville: New York, 1996, 1997, and 2000. Jeremy Myerson and Jennifer Hudson (eds.), *International Lighting Design*, London: Laurence King, 1996. *World of Interiors*, Jan. 2001.
> See Goodman, Nuala.

Giorgetti
Italian furniture and kitchen-furnishings firm; located Meda.

History 1898, Giorgetti was founded in Meda, an area that had become known for the traditional handcrafting of ebony and for its skilled craftspeople who paint wood and furniture. Late 1980s, Giorgetti began to work exclusively with designer Massimo Scolari, who later called in others to design for the firm, including Nicola Adami, Umberto Asnago, Leon Krier, Chi-Wing-Lo, Antonello Mosca, and Laura Silvestrini. 60% of its production is exported.

Giovannetti Collezioni d'Arredamento
Italian furniture firm; located Pistoia.

History 1965, Benito Luigi Giovannetti founded the eponymous firm and began to produce innovative furniture, including Bazaar enclosed seating unit by Superstudio and 1971 Anfibio convertible couch by Alessandro Becchi. Other earlier commissioned designers included Pierluigi Bacci, Fabio De Poli, Sergio Giobbi, Paolo Piva, Roberto Tapinassi. Most recent designs include the 2000 Isa chaise longue by Antonella Scarpitta and Norberto Delfinetti, 2000 Roly-Poly lounge chair by Guido M. Rosati, 2003 Gabbiano chaise longue by Carin Silva Gil. 50% of its production is exported.
Citations 1979 Premio Compasso d'Oro (for Anfibio).

Giovannoni, Stefano (1954–)
Italian architect and interior and industrial designer; born La Spezia.

Training To 1978, Facoltá di Architettura, Università degli Studi, Florence.
Biography From 1979, Giovannoni has taught and conducted research, Facoltà di Architettura, Università degli Studi, Florence; is a master professor, Domus Academy, Milan, and Università del Progetto, Reggio Emilia. He collaborated with Guido Venturini under the name King Kong, whose symbol in the form of little men icons, or Girotondi, was applied to products by Alessi from 1985. Giovannoni specializes in the design of plastic and metal products; has become well known for his goods by Laufen, Oras, Seiko, and Siemens. Other Alessi work has included 1989–2001 Girotondo range (trays, baskets, kitchen wares, jewelry, under the King Kong name), 1999–2002 Mami range (cutlery and pots), 2002 Alessi bathroom collection (ceramics, faucets, bath tubs and fixtures, textiles) by Alessi with others. By other firms: 1997–2002 Bombo range (stools, chairs, and tables) by Magis; 1998 Volcano and 1999

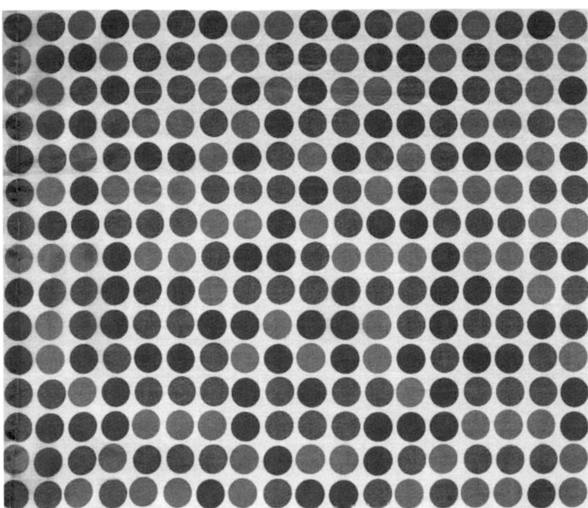
Alexander Girard. Circles sheer fabric. c. 1952. Silk gauze, 89 x 44 1/2" (226 x 113 cm). Mfr.: Herman Miller Furniture Co., US. Gift of the mfr. MoMA.

Octopussy watches by Alba-Seiko; 2002 Twoo and 2001 Flash lamp and flashlight (torch) by Flos and Alessi-Flos, respectively.
Exhibitions/citations Designed Italian pavillon, 1991 *Les Capitales Européennes du Nouveau Design*, Centre Georges Pompidou, Paris. 1994 and 1996 Design Plus awards, Ambiente fair, Frankfurt; 1999 award, Industrie Forum Design (iF), Hanover; 1996 and 1998 Premio Compasso d'Oro.
Bibliography Nally Bellati, *New Italian Design*, New York: Rizzoli, 1990. Matthias Dietz and Fumio Shimiizu, *Euro Design*, Tokyo: Graphic-sha, 1993. Claudia Neumann, *Design Lexikon Italien*, Cologne: DuMont, 1999. Eva Karcher and Manuela von Perfall, *Italienisches Design*, Munich: Heyne, 2000. Charlotte and Peter Fiell, *Designing the 21st Century*, London: Taschen, 2001. Mel Byars, *Design in Steel*, London: Laurence King, 2002.

Gips, A.F. (1861–1943)
Dutch metalworker and teacher; active Delft.

Biography c. 1900, Gips designed silver for the Koninklijke Utrechtsche Fabriek van Zilverwerk C.J. Begeer, Utrecht.
Exhibitions Gips's silverwork by Begeer, including a tea set, shown at 1900 *Exposition Universelle*, Paris.
Bibliography Annelies Krekel-Aalberse, *Art Nouveau and Art Déco Silver*, New York: Abrams, 1989.

Girard, 'Sandro' Alexander Hayden (1907–1993)
American textile, wallpaper, furniture, and exhibition designer; born New York.

Training To 1929, Royal Institute of British Architects, London; to 1931, Royal School of Architecture, Rome; 1935, New York University.
Biography Girard worked in architectural offices of others in Florence, Rome, London, Paris, and New York; 1930, opened his own office in Florence; 1932, set up an architecture and design office in New York; 1937, moved to Detroit, Mich., and established an office there; designed interiors of 1943 Ford and 1946 Lincoln automobiles; 1951–52, was a color consultant on 1948–56 General Motors Technical Center, Warren, Mich. (architect, Eero Saarinen); 1952, began designing textiles for Herman Miller Furniture Company, Zeeland, Mich., having been brought there by friend Charles Eames; 1952, became director of Herman Miller's fabric division under design director George Nelson. Work included upholstery fabrics and casement goods as well as exuberant, colorful, large-patterned prints for Herman Miller; 1953, opened an office in Santa Fe, N.M.; 1957 interior of film director Billy Wilder's home in Los Angeles; 1956 interiors of La Fonda del Sol restaurant in New York, and 1966 interior and furniture (produced by Knoll) of L'Étoile restaurant in New York; 1965 corporate-identity graphics program for Braniff Airlines. His work, particularly in the field of textile design, was influenced by his large collection of folk art. 1961, he established the Girard Foundation in Santa Fe, an international collection of toys and related objects. The Textiles & Objects shop, established with Herman Miller, proved unsuccessful. Girard's design archive is housed in the Vitra Design Museum in Weil am Rhine, Germany.

Exhibitions/citations Exhibition designs included Italian Pavilion and interior-design model rooms of Florentine Artisans Guild at 1929–30 *Exposición Internacional de Barcelona*, Spain; 1949 *An Exhibition for Modern Living* (showing an array of objects from dog leashes and sunglasses to glassware, silver, and furniture; catalog below), Detroit Institute of Arts; 1950 *Design for Modern Use: Made in the* USA, US and touring Europe, organized by The Museum of Modern Art, New York; 1968 *El Encanto de un Pueblo* exhibition at 1968 *Hemisfair '68*, San Antonio, Tex. Work subject of 2001 *The Opulent Eye of Alexander Girard*, Cooper-Hewitt National Design Museum, New York. Museum of International Folk Art (housing Girard's personal collection), located Sante Fe, N.M., US (see 1968 catalog below). 1965, elected Honorary Royal Designer for Industry.
Bibliography Cat., A.H. Girard and W.D. Laurie Jr. (eds.), *An Exhibition for Modern Living*, Detroit: Detroit Institute of Arts, 1949. 'Out-Maneuvering the Plain Plane,' *Interiors*, vol. 125, Feb. 1966: 99–105. Cat., Alexander H. Girard (photos by Charles and Ray Eames), *El Encanto de un Pueblo: The Magic of a People* (folk art and toys from the collection of the Girard Foundation), New York: Viking, 1968. Jack Lenor Larsen, 'Nelson, Eames, Girard, Propst: The Design Process at Herman Miller,' *Design Quarterly 98–99*, 1975. Ralph Caplan, *The Making of Herman Miller*, New York: Whitney, 1976. Cat., Kathryn B. Hiesinger and George H. Marcus III (eds.), *Design Since 1945*, Philadelphia: Philadelphia Museum of Art, 1983. Cherie Fehrman and Kenneth Fehrman, *Postwar Interior Design, 1945–1960*, New York: Van Nostrand Reinhold, 1987. Henry Glassie, *The Spirit of Folk Art: The Girard Collection at the Museum of International Folk Art*, New York: Abrams, Santa Fe, 1989. Leslie Piña, *Alexander Girard Designs for Herman Miller*, Atglen, Pa.: Schiffer, 1998.

Giro
> See Gentes, 'Jim' James.

Gismondi, Emma
> See Schweinberger-Gismondi, Emma.

Gismondi, Ernesto (1931–); Artemide

Italian lighting designer, entrepreneur, and teacher; born San Remo; active Milan.

Training Aeronautical engineering, Politecnico, Milan, and Scuola Superiore di Ingeneria, Rome.
Biography 1959, Gismondi founded the Artemide lighting company, which became a leader in lighting design and manufacture; invested in other firms in Milan, including Alias and several Memphis collections; is known for his ability to identify new trends. When Memphis's efforts were discontinued by Ettore Sottsass in 1988, Gismondi established Meta-Memphis to produce the designs of fine artists, rather than industrial designers, at high prices, but achieved little of the success enjoyed by Sottsass's original Memphis production. From 1984, Gismondi taught rocket tech-nology, Politecnico, Milan, and at institutions in New York, Los Angeles, and Milan. The 1972 Tizio lamp by Richard Sapper has proved to be Artemide's most successful product and the best-selling lamp ever by any other firm and a primary source of the firm's income
Artemide An enterprise that has produced lighting fixtures and plastic furniture; including 1966 Demetrio 45 table in reinforced resin, followed by the Stadio range, both by Vico Magistretti; 1969 Boalum snake-like tubular lighting by Gianfranco Frattini and Livio Castiglioni was over 6 ft. (180 cm) long. Other Artemide's designers include Gismondi himself (such as 1975 Sintesi lamp range), Richard Sapper, Vico Magistretti, Antonio Citterio, Steven Lombardi, F.A. Porche, Gregory H. Tew, Angelo Mangiarotti, Ettore Sottsass, Michele De Lucchi, Giancarlo Fassina, Jean Jacques Villaret, Carlo Forcolini, Mario Botta, Enzo Mari, Mario Bellini, Carlotta de Bevilacqua, Luciano Vistosi, Lella and Massimo Vignelli, Emilio Ambasz, CP&PR Associati, Eric Gottein, Mitchell Mauk, Sergio Mazza, De Pas/D'Urbino/Lomazzi, Örni Halloween, and Mario Morenco. Sapper's 1978 Tizio lamp, a primary source of the firm's income, became the bestselling lamp in history. Another, 2000 Yang polypropylene table lamp by Bevilacqua, was highly successful. The 'Modern Classic' series reintroduced 18 lamps that had been out of production for a number of years, including Sergio Mazza's 1959 Alfa, Castiglioni and Frattini's 1970 Boalum, Aulenti's 1975 Patroclo. The Artemide Group operates—through 23 subsidiary or controlled companies and 31 exclusive distributors—worldwide with manufacturing in Italy, France, Germany, and the US.
Bibliography Cat., Milena Lamarová, *Design a Plastické Hmoty*, Prague: Uměleckoprůmyslové Muzeum 1972: 168. Giancarlo Iliprandi and Pierluigi Molinari (eds.), *Industrial designers italiani*, Fagagna: Magnus, 1985: 110. Cat., Hans Wichmann, *Italien Design 1945 bis heute*, Munich: Die Neue Sammlung, 1988. Jeremy Myerson and Sylvia Katz, *Conran Design Guides: Lamps and Lighting*, London: Conran Octopus, 1990: 75.
> See de Bevilacqua, Carlotta.

Gispen, Willem H. (1890–1981)

Dutch metalworker and lighting and furniture designer; born Amsterdam; active Rotterdam.

Training To 1916 under Willem Kromhout, architecture, Koninklinke Academie voor Beeldende Kundsten, Technische Wetenschappen, Rotterdam.
Biography Gispen became an architect's draftsperson; worked briefly as designer in an artistic wrought-iron factory; 1911–12, traveled in England, coming into contact with Arts and Crafts ideas and works; was a member, Nederlands Vereening voor in Ambachts-en Nijverheids-kunst (Netherlands union for handicraft and industrial art), founded in 1904; 1915, opened a factory in the Netherlands; made wooden furniture before he began working with steel; 1916, established the Gispen Fabriek voor Metaalbewerking (Gispen metalwork factory) at Voorhaven 101, Rotterdam, where he designed and produced outdoor public and domestic furniture. 1916–24, Gispen designed domestic and public metalwork; his stair railings were used in the 1911–16 Sheepvaarthuis, Amsterdam. His steel-tube bending was accomplished by filling the cores with sand, heating, and bending by hand. Soon after, he used machines for bending; 1920 with Kromhout, J.J.P. Oud, M.J. Granprè Molière, and van de Vlught, founded the architects' circle de Opbouw ('Construction'), Rotterdam; 1920, joined Vakgroep voor Drukkunst, Bindkunst en Leerbewerking (VANK); 1922, received the first of several commissions from architect L.C. van der Vlught, for a stairway and balcony railings for the Scala theater, Rotterdam; 1924, turned from handicraft to mechanization; 1925 when Mart Stam returned to the Netherlands, became involved in the debate between Functionalism and formalism; 1926, put Giso lighting range on the market; 1929, set up a factory in Culemborg, encouraged by commissions for 1927 *Weissenhofsiedlung* exhibition, Stuttgart, and growth of his sales in Europe. His designs were produced by 100 employees; C.J. Hoffman was his chief assistant. The 1924–29 Van Nelle Tobacco, Coffee and Tea Factory, Rotterdam, by van de Vlught and J.A. Brinkmann (begun by Brinkmann's father) was

Ernesto Gismondi. Miconos table lamp. 1999. Polished chromium-plated metal and mouth-blown glass, h. 23 5/8 x dia. 9 7/8" (60 x 25cm). Mfr.: Artemide, Italy.

Battista Giudici and Gino Giudici. Lilo outdoor lounge chair. 1935–36. Galvanized-steel tubing, wood, and canvas, 39 x 21 5/8 x 42 7/8" (99 x 55 x 109 cm). Mfr.: Fratelli Giudici, Italy. Courtesy Quittenbaum Kunstauktionen, Munich.

furnished in 1929 with bent tubular-steel furniture and lighting by Gispen, including hanging lamps, small wall and desk lamps, writing desks and chairs for the main offices and small round tables (nos. 501 and 1053) in tubular steel with blue glass tops. By 1929, Gispen had a showroom in Amsterdam, where he sold lighting and furniture. 1932, he opened showrooms in The Hague; 212, rue La Fayette, Paris; 190 Kensington Church Street and High Holborn, London; 8 East Circus Street, Nottingham. 1930s, Gispen and Jan Schröfer designed furniture independently of each other for the De Cirkel factory. For town hall in Hilversum, architect Willem Dudok used an array of Gispen furniture, including Van Nelle chair (no. 103) in leather upholstery, chromed-framed desk (no. 602) with a black top, glass-topped occasional tables, Van Nelle chair (no. 203) with 'Gisolite'-plastic arms in the canteen, armchair no. 401 in the public waiting room, and a circular table. J.W. Buys used Gispen's chairs nos. 101 and 201 in the offices of Volharding, The Hague. Brinkmann and van der Vlught used Gispen dining chairs (no. 103) and easy chairs (no. 407) in 1933 Sonneveld house in Rotterdam. All these commissions incorporated the Giso lamps. Gispen furnished 1933 AVRO radio buildings in Hilversum; fitted oceanliner *Dagenham* (first vessel to use tubular-steel furniture), used by Ford Motor Company for transporting its employees; 1928, designed his own flat incorporating his own furniture; during World War II, was imprisoned in Scheveningen after cosigning a letter of protest against the Kulturkammer (chamber of culture), which all artists were obliged to join; when freed, moved to Gelderland and took up painting. After the war, the artistic range at the factory was reduced in favor of office furniture, and, 1949, Gispen resigned. 1940–50, he was chairperson of Bond voor Kunst in Industrie (BKI); 1950–53, taught a weekend industrial-design course, Koninklijke Academie, The Hague; designed wooden furniture and ran a ceramics factory; 1951, turned away from his manufacturing business to paint and draw for pleasure; 1953, founded the Kembo factory and designed furniture and lighting inspired by the Scandinavians and Italians. Other firms produced his work, including Emmein Staal, Polynorm, and Riemersma. Early 1960s, he stopped designing furniture; turned to designing bungalows on the Costa Brava and a house in The Hague; 1969, took etching lessons at the Haagse Academie; from 1970, regularly showed graphic art; died in Rotterdam.

Exhibitions Gispen's lighting was included in J.J.P. Oud's interiors at the 1927 *Weissenhofsiedlung*, Stuttgart. Work subject of 1980 lamp exhibition, Stedelijk Museum, Amsterdam (catalog below).

Bibliography W.H. Gispen, *Het Sirend Metaal in de Bouwkunst*, Rotterdam: R. Grusse, 1925. Barbie Campbell-Cole and Tim Benton (eds.), *Tubular Steel Furniture*, London: The Art Book Company, 1979: 28–45. Cat., *Gispen Lampen 1916–1980*, Amsterdam: Stedelijk Museum, 1980. Cat., *Industry and Design in the Netherlands 1850/1950*, Amsterdam: Stedelijk Museum, 1985: 268–71. André Koch, *Industrieel ontwerper W.H. Gispen (1890–1981): Een modern electicus (1890–1981)*, Rotterdam: De Hef, 1988.

Giudici, Battista (1903–70); Gino Giudici (1914–)

Swiss designers; born Locarno; brothers.

Biography Battista and Gino Giudici collaborated on design in their workshop Fratelli Giudici in Locarno, specializing in metalwork; developed 1935–36 Lilo outdoor lounge chair, with two positions, which they patented in 1938; 1936, constructed a metal stool and table; 1946, developed a prefabricated garage.

Bibliography Friederike Mehlau-Wiebking et al., *Schweizer Typenmöbel 1925–35, Sigfried Giedion und die Wohnbedarf AG*, Zürich: gta, 1989: 228.

Giugiaro, Giorgetto (1938–)

Italian industrial designer; born Garessio.

Training 1952–54, technical and graphic design, Accademia di Belle Arti, Turin.

Biography 1955–59, Giugiaro worked in the design center of Fiat automobile firm, Turin; 1960–65 with the sports-car entrpreneur Nuccio Bertone, was head of the styling center at Carrozzeria Bortone, Turin; 1965–67, director of projects and styling center at Ghia, Turin; 1968 with Aldo Mantovani, founded ItalDesign–Giugiaro to work on automobile styling; designed the last version of 1978 Nikon F3 and F4 cameras, imbuing them with ergonometric attributes. Primarily a distinguished car designer, his work has also included Necchi sewing machines, such as 1982 Logica by his product-design firm Giugiaro Design, formed in 1981. By mid-1980s, ItalDesign was employing about 200 designers, engineers, and computer specialists. Giugiaro has designed over 40 production models and a number of prototypal automobiles, including 1960 Alfa Romeo 2600 Sprint, 1961 Aston Martin DB4, 1965 Fiat 850 Spider, 1971 Alfa Romeo Alfasud, 1974 Volkswagen Golf, 1980 Fiat Panda three-door, five-seat hatchback, 1983 Fiat Uno, 1998 Bugatti 118 prototype, and 2001 Maserati spider. His studio styled the early-1980s Seiko Chronograph, representing the 1980s symbols of high technology. ItalDesign's commissions have also included sports equipment and street furniture for the city of Turin, 1983 Marielle pasta by Voiello, and men's clothing and accessories.

Citations 1984, honorary doctorate in design, Royal College of Art, London; 1996, honorary doctorate in design, Rusenski Universitet 'Angel Kunchev,' Rousse, Bulgaria.

Bibliography Alfonso Grassi and Anty Pansera, *Atlante del design italiano 1940/1980*, Milan: Fabbri, 1980: 94, 243, 300. G. Gardini and M. Bugli (eds.), *Design Giugiaro: la forma dell'automobile*, Milan: Automobilia, 1980. Akira Fujimoto (ed.), 'Giugiaro & ItalDesign' special ed., *Car Styling*, vol. 35 1/2, 1981. Cat., Kathryn B. Hiesinger and George H. Marcus III (eds.), *Design Since 1945*, Philadelphia: Philadelphia Museum of Art, 1983. Akira Fijimoto (ed.), *Giugiaro Design*, Tokyo: San'ei Shobo, 1985. Bruno Alfieri, *Catalogue raisonné Giugiaro*, Milan: Automobilia, 1987. Paula Gribaudo (ed.), *Giugiaro Design: The Non-Automotive Projects*, Milan: L'Archivolto, 1993. Rodolfo Bosio, *Giugiaro, l'auto e Torino*, Milan: Il sole 24 ore libri, 1994. Giuliano Molineri (ed.), *Giugiaro Italdesign: Come creare un'automobile...*, Milan: Automobilia, 1995. Bruno Alfieri, *Car Men 4: Giorgetto Giugiaro*, Milan: Automobilia, 1999. Laura Giugiaro, *Vent'anni di Giugiaro Design 1981–2001*, Milan: Electa, 2001.

Giunta, Marco (1966–)

Italian designer.

Training Architecture, Politecnico, Milan.
Biography 1992–96, Giunta was a consultant to Zerodisegno and to Quatrocchio; from 1994, has taught, Politecnico, Milan, and also institutions in Antwerp and Genova; 1995, established his own studio Disegni to specialize in the design of furniture, packaging, displays for shops.
Bibliography Michele De Lucchi (ed.), *The International Design Yearbook*, London: Laurence King, 2001.

Gizard, Eric (1960–)

French designer; born Phnom Penh, Cambodia; active Paris.

Training 1981–84, École des Arts Appliqués, Duperré.
Biography In Paris: 1984–85, Gizard worked in the office of decorator Michel Boyer and, 1986, in architecture office B.E.D; 1987, established his own firm, collaborating with Desgrippes Gobé et Associés on architectural projects for Air France, Stéphane Kelian, Go Sport, Chronopost, and Groupe André. 1998, he set up Eric Gizard Associés (E.G.A.) with Jean-Michel Picot, Dominique Daillet, and Alexandre Dugognon; has designed a number of interiors, offices, showrooms, commercial spaces, private apartments, and products, including 1998 theater of Institut Molière in Rio de Janeiro; 1997 office interiors and furnishings of reception area of the French Embassy in Zimbabwe; 1999 president's and council offices of SNCF (French national railway); 2001 boutique of Daum on the rue de la Paix, Paris, and on Madison Avenue, New York; 2003 airplane interiors and lounge of Air France; and a number of other commissions.

Gjerdrum, Reidun Sissel (1954–)

Norwegian ceramicist.

Training In ceramics, Kunstakademiet, Trondheim.
Biography 1979–81, she worked at Municipal Workshop for Arts and Crafts, Trondheim; in 1981, set up her own workshop, where for some ceramic production she called on Japanese *raku* firing, resulting in a crackle pattern in the glaze.
Bibliography Cat., David Revere McFadden (ed.), *Scandinavian Modern Design 1880–1980*, New York: Abrams, 1982.

Gjerløv-Knudsen, Ole (1930–)

Danish furniture designer.

Training To 1952, furniture department, Kunsthåndværkskolen; to 1955, furniture department, Det Kongelige Danske Kunstakademi; both Copenhagen.
Biography 1955–57 and 1960–62, Gjerløv-Knudsen worked with architect Kay Kørbing; 1957–60, with architect Vilhelm Lauritzen; from 1962, with architect Torben Lind. From 1962, he taught furniture design, Kunsthåndværkskolen, where he was the rector of the department of furniture design; from 1977, participated in Dansk Designråd and Industrelle Designere Danmark (IDD). Was known for his demountable canvas-wood 'camp' furniture; designed one-piece polyethylene chair (with Lind) by Orth Plast, 1964 cot and 1962 Moduline lounge chair (with Lind) by France & Søn (sold by Cato), and 1970s Orth Plast 4652 plastic molded chair, and 1999 Comma table (with Lind) by PP Møbler. He developed 1999 steel-frame deck- and armchair in the Danish State Workshops, Gl. Dok, Copenhagen.
Exhibitions Work shown at Museum of Contemporary Crafts, New York; 1975–77 *Dansk Miljø*, touring Europe; others.
Bibliography Frederik Sieck, *Nutidig Dansk Møbeldesign – en kortfattet illustreret beskrivelse*, Copenhagen: Bondo Gravesen, 1990.

Gläser AG
> See Wogg.

Glaser, Milton (1929–)

American graphic designer; born and active New York.

Training The Cooper Union for the Advancement of Science and Art, New York.
Biography 1954, Glaser, Ed Sorel, Reynold Ruffins, and Seymour Chwast established Push Pin Studios in New York, where Glaser was president 1954–74. 1974, Glaser set up his own independent studio in New York; redesigned periodicals, including *New York*, *Paris Match*, and *The Washington Post*, and architectural interiors based on supergraphics for the Grand Union grocery-store chain and restaurants in the World Trade Center, New York; from 1961, has designed as many as 500 posters, the best-known being the late-1960s Bob Dylan poster for Columbia Records. His 'I [heart symbol] NY' motif to promote New York State tourism was subsequently much pirated. He designed the dinnerware and graphics for the Rainbow Room in Rockefeller Center, New York, and table/kitchenware in wood for the Twergi range by Alessi. Has become one of the most influential and important figures in design, particularly graphics, today.
Exhibitions/citations In earliest venues, work subject of 1970s exhibitions at The Museum of Modern Art, New York; Musée des Arts Décoratifs, Paris; Musée Provisoire d'Art Moderne, Brussels. Other one-person venues: at Musei di Porta Romana, Milan, in 2000; AIGA National Design Center Gallery, New York, in 2000; Philadelphia Museum of Art, in 2000–01. 1972 medal, American Institute of Graphics Art (AIGA); 1979, elected Honorary Royal Designer for Industry, UK.
Bibliography *Milton Glaser: Graphic Design*, New York: Overlook, 1973. Cristina Taverna and Andrea Rauch, *I [heart symbol] NY: Milton Glaser, opere 1960–2000*, Milan: Nuages, 2000. Milton Glaser, *Art Is Work: Graphic Design, Interiors, Objects, and Illustrations*, New York: Overlook, 2000.

Glasgow School
> See Mackintosh, Charles Rennie.

Glasshouse Gallery and Workshop, The

British glassware workshop.

History 1969 Sam Herman, Peter Layton, and others established The Glasshouse Gallery and Workshop at 65 Long Acre in London. The artists there have included Annette Meech, David Taylor, Fleur Tookey, and Christopher Williams. The furnaces and ovens were on view to the public at the gallery premises.1980s–90s, it was the only gallery in central London showing and producing contemporary glassware, both functional and non-functional; played a major role in the development of British studio glass; has been recognized for fostering innovation and experimentation.

Gleadowe, Richard Morier Yorke (1888–1944)

British silver designer; active London.

Biography Gleadowe taught art at Winchester College and was Slade Professor of Fine Art at Oxford University; from late 1920s, was active as a silver designer for Edward Barnard and for H.G. Murphy and, 1930s, for Wakely and Wheeler. (At Barnard's, the chaser was B.J. Colson and engraver George Friend.) Under the influence of Gleadowe, a general growing interest in engraving developed, and his work often showed detailed pictorial engraving. He produced a number of important commemorative pieces and presentation objects for The Worshipful Company of Goldsmiths and others; 1934, gave a series of BBC radio talks on British art.
Exhibitions/citations Work shown at 1979 exhibition, London (catalog below); from 1939, was a member, Court of Assistants; 1943, appointed Commander of Royal Victorian Order (for work on Stalingrad Sword given by King George VI to citizens of Stalingrad, now Volgograd).
Bibliography R.M.Y. Gleadowe and W.G. Constable, 'British Art—BBC Talks Pamphlet (no. 730),' London: British Broadcasting Company, 1934. Cat., *Thirties: British Art and Design Before the War*, London: Arts Council of Great Britain/Hayward Gallery, 1979. Annelies Krekel-Aalberse, *Art Nouveau and Art Déco Silver*, New York: Abrams, 1989.

Glidden Pottery; Glidden McLellan Parker Jr. (1913–1980)

American commercial pottery; located Alfred, N.Y. Parker: born Phillips, Maine.

History Founded in 1940, Glidden Pottery was active until its 1959 closing; used modern production methods of slip casting and ram pressing; produced cups, bowls, plates, beakers, casseroles, and others, in 300–400 shapes that were individually glazed and decorated; became a large commercial firm, making hundreds of thousands of objects during its lifetime—6,000 pieces weekly in 1953, for example. Glidden McLellan Parker Jr., the founder, was also a designer there who hired others such as Fong Chow (at Glidden 1953–57) and Sergio Dello Strologo as designers; some designers served as expert moldmakers and decorators. 1958, the pottery closed. Parker had received a bach-elor's degree from Bates College, Lewiston, Maine, 1931–35; 1935–56, studied philosophy, film history, and German theater, the university, Vienna; and, 1937–39 under Donald Schreckengost, studied pottery, New York State College of Ceramics, Alfred. Parker died in Sante Fe, N.M.
Exhibitions 2001 retrospective (catalog below).
Bibliography Cat., Margaret Carney, *Glidden Pottery*, Alfred, N.Y.: Schein-Joseph International Museum of Ceramic Art, 2001.

Global Tools

Italian design group.

History The members of the Global Tools group came from the studios of Archizoom, Gruppo 9999, Superstudio, UFO, and Zziggurat and included Remo Buti, Riccardo Dalisi, Gianni Pettena, and Ettore Sottsass. 1973, they convened in the offices in Milan of the review *Casabella* to found the organization; proposed to set up 'a system of laboratories in Florence dedicated to prompting the study and use of natural technical materials and their relative behavioral characteristics. The object of Global Tools is to stimulate the free development of individual creativity.' In fact, it served as a forum for radical architectural and Radical-Design ideas of the 1970s–80s.
Exhibition Work included in *Radicals: Architettura e Design 1960–75*, 1996 (6th) Mostra Internazionale di Archittettura, Venice.
Bibliography Franco Raggi, 'Radical Story,' *Casabella*, no. 382, 1973: 45.

Glusberg, Gaspar (1959–)

Argentine designer; born Buenos Aires.

Training To 1984, Facultad de Arquitectura, Universidad de Buenos Aires; to 1993, management of medium-size firms, Instituto de Altos Estudios Empresariales, Universidad Austral, Argentina.
Biography In Buenos Aires, Glusberg was a designer, the design director, and a board member of Modulor 1986–98, at Sointu in 1998 and Kunstdesign in 2000. He has designed a number of products and lighting; 2002, settled in the US.
Bibliography Mel Byars, *50 Products...*, Hove: RotoVision, 1999.

Lyn Godley and Lloyd Schwan. Crinkle lamp. 1996. Vinyl and steel, h. x dia. 11" (27.9 cm). Mfr.: Godley Schwan, US. Gift of the mfr. MoMA.

Gnamuš, Marijan (1930–)

Slovenian designer; born Slovenj Gradec.

Training To 1960, Fakulteta za Arhitekturo, Univerza v Ljubljani.
Biography 1956, Gnamuš cofounded the Slovenj Gradec Art Pavilion; 1956–59, worked at Udarnik factory on sports aircraft and façade elements; 1961–63, at Construction Centre of Slovenia; 1963 cofounded *Sinteza* visual-arts magazine; 1968–1985, worked at Iskra in Ljubljana; 1985–1998, lectured, department of design, Akademija za Llikovno Umetnost (ALU, academy of fine arts), Ljubljana. Designs included 1971 Digimer 1 universal digital instrument and 1973 Pobi battery filler, both by Iskra.
Exhibitions/citations Participated in 1963–68 BIO industrial-design biennials (honorary awards at 1971, 1973, 1975, and 1977 editions), Ljubljana; 1974 Prešeren Fund Award, Slovenia; 1975 award, Industrie Forum Design (iF), Hanover.
Bibliography Stane Bernik, *Slovenska arhitektura, urbanizem, oblikovanje in fotografija 1945–1978*, Ljubljana, 1979.

Gočár, Josef (1880–1945)

Czech architect; born Semín, Pardubice.

Training 1903–05 under Jan Kotěra, Baugewerbeschule (school of industrial design), Prague.
Biography 1905–08, Gočár worked in the office of Kotěra; 1911–14, published an artistic review; became known for his furniture design; from 1929, taught, Akademie Výtvarných Umení (academy of fine arts), Prague; 1911, became a member of the Bohemian Artists' Group. His Functionalism could be seen in his 1935 filling station for Fanto in Prague. Buildings included 1910 Wenke department store in Jaroměř; 1911 House of Flack Mother of God in Prague; and 1928–32 Wenceslas Church in Prague.
Exhibitions Participated in Czech interiors at 1914 *Deutscher Werkbund-Ausstellung*, Cologne.
Bibliography Josef Gočár, P. Janák, and F. Kysela, *Tschechische Bestrebungen um ein Modernes Interieur*, Prague, 1915. *Josef Gočár*, Ghent: 'Meister der Baukunst,' 1930. Marie Benešová, *Josef Gočár*, Prague: Nakl. Ceskoslovenskych vytvarnych umělců, 1958. Zdeněk Wirth, *Joseph Gočár: Hradec Králové*, Vienna/Berlin: Aida, 1930. Vladimír Šlapeta, *Czech Functionalism*, London: Architectural Association, 1987: 124.

Godley, Lyn (1956–)

American designer and teacher; born Oberlin, Ohio; wife of Lloyd Schwan.

Training 1978, bachelor of fine arts, Ohio State University, Columbus; 1980, master of fine arts, University of Wisconsin, Madison.
Biography 1979 with Lloyd Schwan, Godley set up the firm Godley-Schwan in New York, where they initially made jewelry, tabletop accessories and other items and collaborated on the design of furniture sold through their firm. Their limited-production pieces were produced in a workshop in Brooklyn, N.Y. Also independently, Godley has been active as a designer, and a product-design consultant to Nestlé Corp., has organized a number of exhibitions, and taught 3-D design, Department of Art, Moravian College, Bethlehem, Pa., 2002–03, and product design, Parsons School of Design, New York, from 1997; has lectured widely.
Exhibitions Sculptural seating and case goods (with Schwan) first shown internationally at 1988 Salone del Mobile, Milan; from 1987, work included in a large number of exhibitions in the US and Europe, including 2003 *U.S. Design 1975–2000*, Denver Art Museum, Denver, Colo., and traveling.
Bibliography 'The New American Entrepreneurs,' *Metropolis*, May 1991: 70. Mel Byars, *50 Lights: Innovations in Design and Materials*, Hove: RotoVision, 1997. Cat., R. Craig Miller (intro.), *U.S. Design 1975–2000*, Munich: Prestel, 2002.

Godwin, Edward William (1833–86)

British architect; born Bristol; active Bristol and London.

Biography Godwin trained under and worked for William Armstrong, city surveyor, architect, and civil engineer in Bristol, and soon took over projects from Armstrong; 1854, set up his own practice in Bristol; 1857–59, lived in Ireland, working with his engineer brother but with no significant commissions. His first (1857) commission of consequence was a church in Saint Johnston, County Donegal, Ireland. Inspired by Ruskin's interpretation of the Gothic, he designed the town halls of

Northampton in 1861 and Congleton in 1864; was also highly influenced by the *International Exhibition on Industry and Art of 1862*, London, and, thus, experimented with interiors in his own residence in Bristol, where he arranged Japanese prints on plain-colored walls, Persian rugs on bare floors, and 18th-century furniture; 1862, began collecting Japanese artifacts at a time when few others were interested. 1865, he moved to London and set up his own office and, 1866, worked with a fellow admirer of Gothic and Japanese design, William Burges. 1864–71, Godwin was in partnership with Henry Crisp. 1866, he began designing wallpaper by Jeffrey & Co. and furniture by others in various styles from c. 1867, the year his work on Dromore Castle in Ireland was completed. His best-known work is the stark Anglo-Japanese art furniture made by William Wall. The Art Furniture Company also manufactured his designs for a short time, with subsequent production by others, including Collinson and Lock, Gillow, Green and King, and W.A. Smee. The term 'Anglo-Japanese' has been coined for the slender lines and geometric forms of Godwin's art furniture, often produced in ebonized wood without moldings, carving, or ornamentation. 1874–78, he collaborated with friend and painter James Whistler; designed 1876 houses in a vernacular style for the Bedford Park Estate in Chiswick (Britain's first garden suburb), but was replaced on the project later by Richard Norman Shaw. Godwin was named 'one of the most artistic spirits in England' by Oscar Wilde, who lived in the Godwin-decorated house (in 1884) at 34 Tite Street in Chelsea, London. Godwin was a prolific writer and became interested in costume and set designs toward the end of his life. His designs of the 1870s influenced subsequent applied art and interiors and anticipated modern design in Germany and France at end of the 19th century.

Exhibitions/citations His first winning competition entry was the Italian-Gothic design for Northampton town hall. Suite of furniture (with Whistler's painted panels) by William Wall shown at 1878 *Exposition Universelle*, Paris. Work subject of 2000 *E.W. Godwin: Aesthetic Movement Architect and Designer*, Bard Graduate Center, New York (1999 catalog below).

Bibliography Elizabeth Aslin, *Nineteenth Century English Furniture*, New York: Yoseloff, 1962: 63–64. Elizabeth Aslin, 'The Furniture Designs of E. W. Godwin,' *Victoria and Albert Museum Bulletin 3*, Oct. 1967: 145–54. Cat., Cleo Witt and Karin Walton, *Furniture by Godwin and Breuer*, Bristol: Bristol City Art Gallery, 1976. E.W. Godwin, *Art Furniture and Artistic Conservatories*, New York: Garland, 1978. Clive Wainright and Charlotte Gere, *Architect-Designers: Pugin to Mackintosh*, London: Fine Art Society, 1981: 32. Elizabeth Aslin, *E.W. Godwin: Furniture and Interior Decoration*, London: John Murray, 1986. Doreen Bolger Burke et al., *In Pursuit of Beauty: Americans and the Aesthetic Movement*, New York: The Metropolitan Museum of Art/Rizzoli, 1986. Cat., Susan Weber Soros (ed.), *E.W. Godwin: Aesthetic Movement Architect and Designer*, New Haven: Yale, 1999.

Goldberg, Bertrand (1913–77)

American architect and furniture designer.

Training Architecture, Harvard University, Cambridge, Mass.; Bauhaus, Dessau, Germany; Armour Institute (now Illinois Institute of Technology), Chicago.

Biography 1937, Goldberg opened an architecture office in Chicago; pursued Bauhaus principles; was also an industrial and furniture designer; built steel, also realized as plastic, and plywood furniture installed in his own architecture; developed plastic freight cars; designed Marina City in Chicago as a centrally radiating residential-commercial-recreational center.

Exhibition A plywood chair and settee made in Mexico shown at 1939–40 *New York World's Fair: The World of Tomorrow*.

Bibliography Cat., Janet Kardon (ed.), *Craft in the Machine Age 1920–1945*, New York: Abrams with American Craft Museum, 1995.

Goldfinger, Ernö (1902–1987)

Hungarian architect and designer; born Budapest; active Paris and London.

Training 1922–23, Atelier Jaussely; 1923, École des Beaux-Arts; 1924, Atelier Perret; 1926–28, École d'Urbanisme at the Sorbonne, all Paris.

Biography 1925, Goldfinger set up with others the Atelier Perret in a wing of the Palais du Bois, designed by Auguste Perret, at the Porte Maillot, near the Bois de Boulogne, Paris. 1925–29 with fellow Hungarian architect A. Szivessy, aka André Sive, Goldfinger set up a partnership; 1926, left the Atelier Perret and joined the Atelier Defrasse; in 1927, attended the *Weissenhofsiedlung*, Stuttgart, with Pierre Chareau, and designed a cover for the magazine *L'organisation ménagère*; attended 1929 conference of Congrès Internationaux d'Architecture Moderne (CIAM) conference, Frankfurt, and designed the first version of the Safari chair, later produced for photographer Lee Miller, and 1931 Entas stacking metal chair. Some of his furniture was made by Paul & Marjorie Abbatt Ltd. He devised 1932 (final version) Heliometer machine to measure an installation; designed 1933 The Outlook house conversion and new studio block for M. Lahousse, Cucq, et Le Touquet (his first complete building); 1933, sailed to Athens as secretary of the French delegation to the CIAM, a floating congress that produced the Athens Charter; 1934, settled in St. John's Wood, London, with an office at 7 Bedford Square; 1935, moved to a flat in Highpoint, Highgate, designed by Tecton architects. 1936 with Gerald Flower, Goldfinger set up an architecture partnership. Goldfinger's 1937 proposal to build on the site of four 19th-century cottages in Willow Road, Hampstead, London, provoked opposition from the local area protection society. His own 1939 house at 2 Willow Road is part of The National Trust and is today visitable. Goldfinger was supported by Flora Robson, Roland Penrose, and Julian Huxley; was a member, Modern Architecture Research Group (MARS); 1945 with Colin Pen, set up a partnership; 1946, opened an office alone at 69–70 Piccadilly and, with fellow Hungarian Pierre Vago, founded Union Internationale des Architectes (UIA). 1971, Goldfinger was elected an associate of the Royal Academy; 1972, set up an office in the still-fashionable Trellick Tower (which he designed 1968–72) at 19 Golborne Road; was one of the most important Modern architects of 1930s and, particularly, after World War II in Britain. His great grandson is now producing models of his furniture in the UK.

Work In Paris (except where noted) included his own 1925 apartment interior, 29, rue Abel-Hovelaque; 1926 apartment interior and furniture for paint manufacturer M. Coutrot; film sets (with Robert Delaunay), with 'H' chairs for *Le p'tit parigot* (1926, director, René Le Somptier); 1926 furniture for Thonet design competition; 1926 furniture for Lehmann family in Berlin; first (1926) of his apartments, for Suzanne Blum; 1926 library, Aghion House (originally designed by Auguste Perret), Alexandria, Egypt; 1927 Central European Express travel bureau, rue Godot-de-Mauroy, for M. Grossmann, with the interior in metal-faced plywood; 1927 tailor M. Lidvall's fitting-room interior; 1927 apartment of American journalist Edward Morgan Besser Titus (Helena Rubinstein's husband), rue Delambre; 1927 Helena Rubinstein's salon, Grafton Street, London, and a number of other interiors. Exhibition work included the 1928 Alpina (snakeskin goods) exhibition stand, Foire de Paris, and at British Industries Fair, London. He designed the 1928 glass showroom furniture for Helena Rubinstein; 1929 Myrbor shop-front project (realized design by André Lurcat) and furniture for its proprietrix Marie Cuttoli. Other commissions included those in England as well as the 1963 French government tourist office (with Charlotte Perriand; later altered) and SNCF tourist office, Piccadilly, London; 1963 Westminster Bank, Alexander Fleming House, Elephant and Castle; 1963 Odeon Cinema, Elephant and Castle; 1966 French government tourist office and SNCF office, 127, avenue des Champs-Élysées, Paris; 1967 housing, Edenham Street, North Kensington; 1968 wooden house Teesdale, Westville Road, Windlesham, Surrey, for Mr. and Mrs. J. Perry.

Exhibition design Designed exhibitions in London: children's section of 1935 *Dorland Hall Exhibition*, London; 1942 travel-poster exhibitions (with his wife) commissioned by Army Bureau of Current Affairs (ABCA), the Admiralty, and Air Force Education; 1943 *The Cinema* exhibition of ABCA; 1944 *The LCC Plan for London* exhibition of ABCA; 1944 *Traffic*, *Planning Your Kitchen*, *Health Centres*, and 1945 *Planning Your Neighbourhood* exhibitions of ABCA; 1945 *Wartime Production* (with Misha Black), Oxford Street, London; 1946 *A National Health Service* and *Planning Your Home* exhibitions of ABCA; entertainment complex and 30 vending kiosks at 1951 *Festival of Britain*; and 1956 *This Is Tomorrow*, Whitechapel Gallery.

Exhibitions/citations Work included in 1979–80 *Thirties* exhibition, Hayward Gallery; and subject of 1983 exhibition, Architectural Association; both London. 1971, elected an associate of the Royal Academy; 1975, elected a Royal Academician.

Bibliography Cat., James Dunnett and Gavin Stamp (eds.), *Ernö Goldfinger*, London: Architectural Association, 1983. Rebecca Milner, 'Erno Goldfinger: The Architect as Furniture Designer,' in Edwin Heathcote (ed.), *Furniture + Architecture*, New York: Wiley-Academy, 2002.

Goldman, Jonathan (1959–)

American artist, performer, and designer.

Training National Theater Institute, Eugene O'Neill Theater Center, Waterford, Conn.; 1979, Middlesex Polytechnic School for the Performing Arts; 1981–82, Pennsylvania Academy of Arts; to 1985, Center for

Edward William Godwin. Table. c. 1875. Wood and brass, 28 3/4 x 40 x 40" (73 x 101.6 x 101.6 cm). Mfr.: attributed to William Wall, UK. Gift of Paul F. Walter. MoMA.

Advanced Visual Studies, Massachusetts Institute of Technology (MIT), Cambridge, Mass.
Biography 1986, Goldman established Goldman Arts in Boston; designed 1990 300 ft (91 m) ribbon for opening of Trump Taj Mahal Casino, Atlantic City, N.J., and numerous other installations from 1985. His wife Nicole Novick Goldman was president of the firm. 1980s, Goldman called himself an environmental sculptor and designed the Sawtooth lamp, incorporating an electric fan that inflated the shape and cooled the bulb; Hairy Chair in navy blue upholstery with inflatable yellow spikes; Venus Fly Trap chair, 50" (127 cm) tall in forest green upholstery surrounded by bright blue cones. 1980, he taught electronic imagery, MIT; 1985–86, art and dance, Brown University; 1987–90, fine art, Boston Architecture Center.
Exhibitions/citations From 1985, work included in numerous group exhibitions and, from 1990, subject of large number of one-person venues. Grants: Cambridge Public Art Competition, 1983; WBZ Fund for the Arts-Visual Arts Grant, 1986; National Endowment for the Arts/Rockefeller Foundation, 1987; International Festival Associations, 1990; Industrial Fabrics Association International, 1991.

Goldschmidt, Denis (1939–)
French industrial designer.

Training Architecture, École Nationale Supérieure des Beaux-Arts, Paris.
Biography 1961–62, Goldschmidt collaborated with Harold Barnett and Georges Patrix; 1964–67 with Jean Guilleminot, set up design office Atelier G, working on exhibitions, product design, and corporate-identity programs.
Citations 1972 urban-furniture award (telephone booth by Mercelec), sponsored by CCI.
Bibliography Gilles de Bure, *Le mobilier français 1965–1979*, Paris: Regard/VIA, 1983: 74.

Goldsmiths' and Silversmiths' Company
British silversmiths; located London.

History 1898, Goldsmiths' and Silversmiths' Company was founded in London as a manufacturer and retailer; 1930s, produced the designs of Bernard Cuzner, S.J. Day, Leslie Durbin, Arthur Edward Harvey, and Harold Stabler.
Bibliography Annelies Krekel-Aalberse, *Art Nouveau and Art Déco Silver*, New York: Abrams, 1989.

Gomber, Henrike (1955–)
German ceramicist; born Dernbach.

Training 1971–74 under potter Rudi Stahl, apprenticeship; 1975–76, materials engineering, Fachhochschule, Nuremberg; 1976–80, product design, Fachhochschule, Krefeld.
Biography 1981–84, she designed earthenware, decorative ceramics, and architectural ceramics at Ceramano; from 1985, was a product designer for Scheurich Keramik in Kleinheubach am Main, where she designed 1988 casserole and soufflé dishes, and for Kahla/Thüringen Porzellan in Kahla, Germany.
Bibliography Cat., Design Center Stuttgart, *Women in Design: Careers and Life Histories Since 1900*, Stuttgart: Haus der Wirtschaft, 1989.

Gomez, Didier (1953–)
French interior and furniture designer; born Moulins.

Training Drawing, École Nationale Supérieure des Beaux-Arts; singing, Conservatoire de Musique; both Paris. Autodidactic in interior design.
Biography Gomez was a professional opera singer; 1978, turned to furniture design and marketed his work under the name First Time; 1985, opened his office in Paris and has since designed a large number of corporate headquarters, boutiques, offices, and other interiors worldwide, including private residences of movie actors and interiors of the enterprises Yves Saint Laurent, Jean-Paul Gaultier, Mauboussin, Pomellato, Cartier, and Rolex; from 1994 with Jean-Jacques Ory, has received larger commissions such as department stores, museums, and airports; was consultant art director to the Carrousel du Louvre retail/exhibition space, Paris. By Lignet Roset: designed 1995 Tichka lounge chair, 1996 Médina and Menara side tables, 1996 Nomad seating ensemble, 1997 Wicky Manila-hemp club chair, 1997 Phare floor lamps, 1997 French Line lounge chair, 1999 Fugue chaise longue. Others: 1996 Deauville metal/wood side chair by Cinna; Pasco metal/fabric side chair by Artelano; furniture by Macé.
Bibliography www.via.asso.fr.

Gomperz, Lucie Marie (1902–)
> See Rie, Lucie.

Gonzo, Elisabeth
> See EG + AV.

Good Design
American design exhibitions held 1950–55.

History The *Good Design* exhibitions/awards, first only at the Chicago Merchandise Mart, in Jan. 1950 and, 1950–55, also at The Museum of Modern Art, recognized what the museum's director René d'Harnoncourt and Mart general manager William O. Ollman called 'the best examples of modern design in home furnishings.' The events were financially supported by the Mart. The exhibition sets were designed by Charles and Ray Eames (1950), Finn Juhl (1951), Paul Rudolph (1952), Alexander Girard (1953–54), Daniel Brennan and A. James Speyer (1954). Examples were selected from items submitted by manufacturers or requested by the jury, consisting of one prominent retailer and one designer, in addition to Edgar Kaufmann Jr., the Museum of Modern Art curator who served as the permanent Good Design chair-

Gorham: Donald Colflish. Coffee service. 1969. Silver and ebonized wood, pot h. 11 5/8" (29.5 cm), sugar bowl h. 4 5/16" (11cm), creamer h. 6 5/16" (16.5cm), tray dia. 15 15/16" (40.5 cm). Mfr.: Gorham, US. Courtesy Quittenbaum Kunstauktionen, Munich.

person. Selection committee members at various times included Serge Chermayeff (1950), Philip Johnson (1951), Eero Saarinen (1951), Florence Knoll (1953), others. The event was widely advertised and supported by retail stores, and a Good Design label was attached to selected designs for sale to the public. Thrice yearly-exhibitions ocurred in parallel with design conferences in Aspen, Col., which were organized by Egbert Jacobsen, director of design at Container Corporation of America. (The Canadian National Industrial Design Committee was similar to Good Design.)
Bibliography 'Good Design,' *Interiors*, vol. 113, Aug. 1953: 88–89, 146–48. Jonathan M. Woodham, *Twentieth-Century Ornament*, New York: Rizzoli, 1990. Esbjørn Hiort, *Finn Juhl: Furniture, Architecture, Applied Art*, Copenhagen: The Danish Architectural Press, 1990. Terence Riley and Edward Eigen, 'Between the Museum and the Marketplace: Selling Good Design,' *The Museum of Modern Art at Mid-Century: At Home and Abroad* (Studies in Modern Art 4), New York: The Museum of Modern Art, 1994: 150–79.

Goodden, Robert Yorke (1909–)

British architect and designer; born Over Compton, Dorset.

Training 1926–31, Architectural Association, London.
Biography From 1932, Goodden was in private practice. His varied output included wallpapers, domestic machine-pressed glassware by Chance Bros., 1953 Coronation hangings for Westminster Abbey, gold- and silverwares, ceremonial metalwork, glassware for King's College in Cambridge, metal-foil murals for the 1961 oceanliner *Canberra*, engraved and sandblasted glass murals by Pilkington, and, with R.D. Russell, the design of the 1969–71 Western sculpture and Oriental galleries and the print room of the British Museum. 1948–74, Goodden was professor of jewelry, silversmithing, and industrial glass, Royal College of Art, London.
Exhibitions/citations Designed sports section of 1946 *Britain Can Make It* exposition and sections of 1951 *Festival of Britain* exposition including the Lion and Unicorn Pavilion (with R.D. Russell); both London. 1947, elected Honorary Royal Designer for Industry, UK.
Bibliography Fiona MacCarthy and Patrick Nuttgens, *An Eye for Industry*, London: Lund Humphries, 1986.

Goodman, Nuala (1962–)

Irish designer; born Dublin; active Milan.

Training 1980–84, National College of Art and Design, Dublin.
Biography 1984, Goodman worked at Sottsass Associati in Milan; 1984–85, was active as a freelance designer in fine art and painting and designed clothing collections by Biffi in Milan, Luisa in Florence, and Papete in Riccione, textiles by Fantoccoli in Como. 1996 with husband Paolo Giordano, established I + I company in Milan for the design of home accessories, handmade in India and Nepal and distributed worldwide. Design work has also included 1992 Eva watch by Swatch and 1994 Memory Containers painted boxes by Alessi.
Bibliography *The International Design Yearbook*, Abbeville: New York, 1995 and 1996. *World of Interiors*, Jan. 2001.
> See Giordano, Paolo.

Gorham; Jabez Gorham (1792–1869)

American silversmiths; located Providence, R.I.

History Gorham is one of the oldest silver factories in the US. Jabez Gorham, after a seven-year apprenticeship with Nehemiah Dodge of Providence, R.I., established a jewelry-making business with four other men in 1813. The firm, in its jewelry production, was known for its 'Gorham chain,' said to be of exceptional quality. The partnership was dissolved in 1818, and Gorham continued alone to 1831, when he took in Henry L. Webster, who made coin-silver spoons. 1837, jeweler William G. Price joined the firm. Jabez Gorham took his son John Gorham into the firm, which became J. Gorham and Son, and retired in 1848. John Gorham was in partnership with his cousin Gorham Thurber for a short period during the 1850s and remained the titular director for 30 years, increasing mechanization and production and converting the plant to steam power. He installed a British stamping machine for the fast manufacture of cutlery, began production of silver hollow-ware, and established a company sales program. Gorham was one of the first firms to produce silverware with the aid of machinery. In Britain in 1852, Gorham discovered the electroplating process at Elkington that, 11 years later, he introduced at Gorham's plant in Providence. 1863, the firm was named the Gorham Manufacturing Company, and, 1868, adopted the silver standard and greatly increased its production. 1878, John Gorham declared bankruptcy and was replaced by William Crins, a Providence businessman. 1894, Crins was succeeded by Edward Holbrook (1849–1910), who had joined the firm in 1870. As a wholesaler, the Gorham firm supplied jewelers and small shops, including Black, Starr and Frost in New York; Shreve in San Francisco, and Spaulding in Chicago. 1850–1915, the firm's workmen and most of its well-known designers came from Britain, including George Wilkinson of Birmingham, who arrived in 1854 at Gorham, where he was chief designer 1860–1891; Thomas J. Pairpoint, formerly with Lambert and Rawlings, who was responsible for Renaissance Revival and historicist designs and at Gorham 1868–77; and A.J. Barrett, who came to Gorham in the late 1860s. Holbrook managed a small group of highly skilled silversmiths who produced the designs of a group of artists under the leadership of William Christ-

mas Codman (1839–1921), who came to Providence in 1891 from London. c. 1900, the group's silverwork was sold under the trade name Martelé, with most of the pieces in a hand-hammer finish. 1891–1914, Codman was the chief design director at Gorham, where he produced handmade silver in the Art Nouveau style. 1897, Codman's Martelé range of hollow-ware was produced in 0.950 silver (the Britannia Standard) rather than 0.925 sterling. The Martelé range initially included only vases, beakers, and bowls and was followed by complete tea sets and dinner services. Handmade Martelé pieces in a diluted Art Nouveau style, as well as Louis XV patterns, were produced and sold through Spaulding in Paris. Gorham's Athenic range combined silver with other metals. From 1925, Danish silversmith Erik Magnussen produced designs for the firm in motifs characteristic of the Danish Modern style, although his triangular-faceted Lights and Shadows of Manhattan coffee service showed an American influence. Julius Randahl was one of Gorham's silversmiths. 20th-century production expanded into bronze casting. By the 1920s, Gorham had bought out several other East Coast silver manufacturers, including Whiting Manufacturing Company. c. 1985, the Gorham plant was moved to Smithfield, R.I.
Exhibitions The Century Vase by Thomas J. Pairpoint and George Wilkinson shown at 1876 *Centennial Exposition*, Philadelphia.
Bibliography Larry Freeman, *Early American Plated Silver*, Watkins Glen, N.Y.: Century House, 1973: 46–48. Dorothy T. Rainwater (ed.), *Sterling Silver Holloware*, Princeton, N.J.: Pyne Press, 1973: 7. Charlotte Gere, *American and European Jewelry 1830–1914*, New York: Crown, 1975. Charles H. Carpenter Jr., *Gorham Silver, 1831–1981*, New York: Dodd, Mead, 1982. Cat., Doreen Bolger Burke et al., *In Pursuit of Beauty: Americans and the Aesthetic Movement*, New York: Metropolitan Museum of Art/Rizzoli, 1987. Annelies Krekel-Aalberse, *Art Nouveau and Art Déco Silver*, New York: Abrams, 1989.

Gorska de Montaut, Adrienne (b. Adrienne Gorska 1899–1969)

Polish architect, decorator, and furniture designer; born Moscow; active Paris.

Training To 1924, frequented École Spéciale d'Architecture, Paris.
Biography 1919, Gorska settled in Paris; collaborated in a design office with architect/husband Pierre de Montaut (1892–1947), with whom she specialized in cinema design. c. 1930, Reginald Ford commissioned them to design cinemas for the Cineac group. They designed both interiors and furniture, especially models in chromium-plated metal, for offices, apartments, and cinemas. Gorska may have had a lasting collaboration with the little-known designer called Madame Lipska; even so, they designed the loft-type apartment of c. 1920s of hairdresser Antoine (b. A. Antoni Cierplikowski, 1884–1976) and 1920–30 interior of Barbara Harrison's renovated house on the rue Voirerin (now rue Maréchal-Leclerq) in Rambouillet. Gorska designed her paintersister Tamara de Lempicka's 1929 two-storey high apartment and its furniture at 7, rue Méchain, Paris (building architect, Robert Mallet-Stevens); 1920s–30s, had other clients, including Marquis Somni Picenardi in Paris. She was a member, Union des Artistes Modernes (UAM); taught Eileen Gray architectural drawing; died in Beaulieu-sur-Mer.
Bibliography Pierre Kjellberg, *Art déco: les maîtres du mobilier, le décor des paquebots*, Paris: Amateur, 1986. Arlette Barré-Despond, *UAM*, Paris: Regard, 1986. Baroness Kizette de Lempicka with Charles Phillips, *Passion by Design, The Art and Times of Tamara de Lempicka*, New York: Abbeville, 1987. Gilles Néret, *Tamara de Lempicka, 1898–1980*, Cologne: Taschen, 1992.

Gosweiler, Herbert V. (1915–1991)
> See Philco.

Gould, Ernest (1884–1954)

American metalworker; active Chicago.

Biography With Edmund Bocker, Gould established the Chicago Art Silver Shop in 1912 at 11 East Illinois Avenue in Chicago.
Bibliography Sharon S. Darling with Gail Farr Casterline, *Chicago Metalsmiths*, Chicago: Chicago Historical Society, 1977.

Goulden, Jean (1878–1947)

Alsacian painter, musician, and craftsperson; born Charpentry, Meuse; son-in-law of François-Louis Schmied.

Training École Alsacienne; and in medicine; both Paris.
Biography 1906, Goulden published his thesis on the physiology of the heart; 1908, became a consultant to hospital Laënnec in Paris; discovered Byzantine enamels, while near Mount Athos in Macedonia during World War I; returned to Paris and persuaded Jean Dunand to teach him the art of *champlevé* enameling; through Dunand, was friendly with Jean Lambert-Rucki, Paul Jouve, and François-Louis Schmied; produced works in silver, polished or gilded copper or bronze with *champlevé* enamel highlights, in the form of boxes, caskets, vases, flower stands, lamps, and candlesticks. His shapes were geometric with decorations composed like painting. His caskets were covered with overlapping and uneven block motifs, and his Cubist pendulum clocks were among his finest work. Goulden had a studio in Paris to 1928, when he moved to Reims. His objects are rare, totaling only c. 180 known items, including *coupes*, clocks, cigarette boxes, small boxes, and silver plaques for bindings by Georges Cretté and Schmied. His large book on his travels in Macedonia was bound by Schmied in crushed black morocco with silver-metal mounts and colored enameled champs.
Exhibitions From 1924, work with Dunand, Jouve, Lambert-Rucki, and Schmied shown at Galerie Georges Petit and Galerie Charpentier, both Paris. Work shown independently and annually at Salons of Société des Artistes Décorateurs. Work with Dunand subject of 1973 commemorative exhibition, Galerie du Luxembourg, Paris (catalog below).
Bibliography Cat., Jean Dunand, *Jean Goulden*, Paris: Galerie du Luxembourg, 1973. Victor Arwas, *Art Déco*, New York: Abrams, 1980. Pierre Cabanne, *Encyclopédie art déco*, Paris: Somogy, 1986: 196. Alastair Duncan and Georges de Bartha, *Art Nouveau and Art Déco Bookbinding*, New York: Abrams, 1989. Bernard Goulden, *Jean Goulden*, Paris: Regard, 1989.

Goupy, Marcel (1886–1954)

French potter and glass artist; active Paris.

Training Architecture, sculpture, and interior decoration, École Nationale Supérieure des Arts Décoratifs, Paris.
Biography Goupy was a painter, silversmith, and jeweler to 1909, when he met Georges Rouard, who had recently opened the Maison Geo. Rouard on the avenue de l'Opéra in Paris. As Rouard's artistic director to 1954, Goupy designed a large amount of glassware, much of which was enameled inside and out, and porcelain and ceramic dinnerware. Most of Goupy's porcelain was produced by Théodore Haviland in Limoges. He also designed wares in silver and, for the Le Sylve design studio of Le Bûcheron at the Au Bon Marché department store, Paris; 1918–36 in his own atelier, produced distinguished enameled and applied-gold glassware vases, bowls, and other vessels.
Exhibitions Work shown at 1923 Exhibition of Contemporary Decorative Arts and in various pavilions including Rouard's at 1925 *Exposition Internationale des Arts Décoratifs et Industriels Modernes*, Paris, where he was vice-president of the glass jury.
Bibliography Yvonne Brunhammer et al, *Art Nouveau Belgium, France*, Houston: Rice University, 1976. Victor Arwas, *Art Déco*, New York: Abrams, 1980. Cat., *Verriers français contemporains: art et industrie*, Paris: Musée des Arts Décoratifs, 1982.

Govin, Bernard (1940–)

French designer and interior architect; born Amiens; active Nice.

Training Industrial design and interior architecture, École des Arts Appliqués; Institut d'Esthéthique Industrielle; both Paris.
Biography Govin is equally an interior and furniture designer; 1963, set up his own studio; designed 1967 Asmara undulating modular seating system and 1975 Satan furniture range by Ligne Roset. Other clients have included Mobilier International (Octa chair), Saporiti Italia (Elliptique chair), Airborne, Allia Doulton (marble bathtubs), Dunlopillo (beds), Mondial Design (1972 Anémone bed). 1972 with Christian Adam, Govin designed the 'archimeuble' environment and architectural interiors for the mayor of Orléans, interior of SNIAS de l'Aérospatiale, and a hotel in Nice.
Exhibitions From 1963, work regularly shown at Salons of Société des Artistes Décorateurs; including in 1968 *Les Assises du Siège Contemporain* (Asmara modular system), Musée des Arts Décoratifs, Paris.
Bibliography Bernard Govin and Christian Adam, 'Le nouvel habitat archimeuble, ou comment constituer son cadre de vie sur mesure,' *L'architecture d'aujourd'hui*, June 1972. Bernard Govin, 'Lit et architecture,' *Hexaform*, no. 1, 1975. Cat., *Acquisitions 1982–1990 arts décoratifs*, Paris: Fonds National d'Art Contemporain, 1991. Cat., Sophie Tasma Anargyros et al., *L'école française: les créateurs de meubles du 20ème siècle*, Paris: Industries Françaises de l'Ameublement, 2000.

Graber, Karl Emil Rudolf (1902–71)

Swiss entrepreneur; born Basel.

Biography Early 1920s, Rudolf Graber settled in Munich and worked as a volunteer in a bookstore; subsequently, worked in the typewriter office of Flachschreibmaschinen Karl Endrich in Zürich; 1927–30, was a salesperson for Elliott-Fischer und Sundstrand bookkeeping and adding machines in Cologne; returned to Switzerland and, 1931 with Sigfried Giedion and Werner Max Moser, cofounded the Wohnbedarf de-partment store in Zürich; invested all his capital in the store and served as the director of the sales division. 1935, Wohnbedarf became the sole property of Graber and his mother. During an era of conservative taste, he sold antiques in the store alongside modern furniture; 1947, began to work with Hans Knoll, who had set up a furniture-design and manufacturing facility in the US.
Bibliography Friederike Mehlau-Wiebking et al., *Schweizer Typenmöbel 1925–35, Sigfried Giedion und die Wohnbedarf AG*, Zürich: gta, 1989.

Grachev, Mikhail & Semeon

Russian silversmiths and enamelers; located St. Petersburg.

Biography 1866, the Grachev brothers established their eponymous firm; 1896, were granted an Imperial warrant. The Grachev firm's aristocratic customers preferred *guilloché* enamel; provided them with *cloisonné* and *champlevé*-enamel objects; closed after the 1917 Russian Revolution.
Bibliography Annelies Krekel-Aalberse, *Art Nouveau and Art Déco Silver*, New York: Abrams, 1989.

Graffi, Carlo (1925–1985)

Italian designer and architect; active Turin.

Biography Furniture of the early 1950s by Graffi and Franco Campo has been erroneously attributed to Carlo Mollino in various literature, particularly a dining table of c. 1953 with a *millepedi* carved-maple base and a clear-glass top. They designed it when they were young and working as architects under Mollino, who eventually owned the table and a set of side chairs. The pieces are examples of the so-called Organic School of Turin and were made by the same craftspeople whom Mollino used for his own work: Appelli & Varesio in Turin and Ettore Canali in Brescia. Like Mollino, Graffi and Campo had a predilection for intricately constructed, flamboyant furniture. Late 1950s, they left Mollino's studio and worked independently of Mollino, designing a number of Italian houses and interiors. Graffi designed, possibly alone, an idiosyncratic c. 1950 *chaise-coquille* stool with a tufted cushion on a fibro-cement shell with metal legs and a 1956 freestanding room divider/bookcase by Mobili Italiani Moderni (M.I.M), Italy.
Bibliography 'Una serie di mobili,' *Domus*, July 1953: 47. Yvonne Brunhammer and Guillemette Delaporte, *Les styles des années 30 à 50*, Paris: Baschet, 1987: 127. Albrecht Bangert, *Italian Furniture Design: Ideas, Styles, Movements*, Munich: Gebundene Ausgabe 1988: 123. Auction cat., *20th–21st Century Design Art*, New York: Phillips, de Pury & Luxembourg, 21 Dec. 2001: lot 176–77.

Gramigna, Giuliana (1929–)

Italian designer, writer, and journalist; born and active Milan.

Biography 1956, Gramigna began her professional career; became a member, Associazione per il Disegno Industriale (ADI); from 1961, was an associate of architect Sergio Mazza, collaborating with him on furniture by Bacci, Cinova, Full, and Poltrona Frau; lighting by Artemide, Martinelli, and Quattrifolio; interior architecture; appliances by Krupp Italia; and fabrics by Texital. She designed ceramics by Gabbianelli, including wall tiles and 1969 Pomona ceramic dinnerware. From the 1966 founding of *Ottagono* to 1988, was editor of the journal.
Citations 1961 first prize, Cedit-Piastrella competition; diplomas, 1964 (13th) and 1968 (14th) Triennale di Milano.
Bibliography Cat., *Italy: The New Domestic Landscape*, New York: The Museum of Modern Art, 1972. *ADI Annual 1976*, Milan: Associazione per il Disegno Industriale, 1976. 'Sergio Mazza e Giuliana Gramigna,' *Interni*, no. 282, Sept. 1978: 54–57. Alfonso Grassi and Anty Pansera, *Atlante del design italiano 1940/1980*, Milan: Fabbri, 1980. Cat., Kathryn B. Hiesinger and George H. Marcus III (eds.), *Design Since 1945*, Philadelphia: Philadelphia Museum of Art, 1983. *Modo*, no. 148, Mar.-Apr. 1993: 120. Sergio Mazza and Giuliana Gramigna, *Milano: un secolo di architettura milanese dal Cordusio alla Bicocca*, Milan: Hoepli, 2001. Giuliana Gramigna and Paola Biondi, *Il design in Italia dell'arredamento domestico*, Milan: Alemanni, 2000. Giuliana Gramigna, *Repertorio dell'arredamento domestico*, Turin: Allemandi, 2002.
> See Mazza, Sergio.

Grand Feu Art Pottery

American ceramics manufactory; located California.

History Active c. 1912–16, Grand Feu Art Pottery was founded in California by Cornelius Brauckman (c. 1866–c. 1954), about whom little is known. Its output was of a high quality and aesthetically distinctive. Generically, 'grand feu' is a ceramic ware fired at 2500° F. (1400° C), maturing its body and glaze simultaneously. 'Grand feu' is both porcelain and gres, and Grand Feu Art Pottery specialized in the latter. Grand Feu produced a vitrified body, calling it 'gres-cerame,' that was neither pure nor translucent. Brauckman did not apply color but rather relied on the natural effects produced by an interaction of heat and glaze. His wares are considered to be on the highest level of any produced in the US.
Exhibitions/citations Gold medal (to Brauckman), 1915 *Panama-California Exposition*, San Diego. Grand Feu work shown at 1916 (1st) Annual Arts and Crafts Salon, Los Angeles.
Bibliography Paul Evans in Timothy J. Andersen et al., *California Design 1910*, Salt Lake City: Peregrine Smith, 1980.

Grange, Jacques (1944–)

French interior and furniture designer; active Paris.

Biography 1970s and 1980s, Grange worked for Yves Saint Laurent, designing his private houses and offices also 1990 Saint Laurent boutique for haute-couture accessories in Paris (including one-of-a-kind historicist furniture). Other work has included furniture and furnishings for firms as well as interiors for individual clients such as Pierre Bergé, Princess Caroline of Monaco, Isabelle Adjani, and the 1998 bar of the Restaurant Ducasse in Paris. 1990, Grange was commissioned by Ian Schrager to design the refurbished interiors of the Barbizon Hotel in New York; 2000 at the Galerie du Passage, Biennial, Carrousel du Louvre, Paris, among other stands, recreated the complete 1935 leather-walled smoking room designed by Jean-Michel Frank (containing furniture by Jean Royère and Emilio Terry) for the Guerlain family in Paris; 2000, designed a furniture collection by John Widdicomb in Grand Rapids, Mich., US, which typified his synthesis of 18th- and 19th-century French furniture styles with 1930s–40s masterworks; became known for his so-called French-salon-style of interior design. Some critics, by the first years of 21st century, were touting Grange as being 'the world's best living decorator.'
Exhibitions/citations Widdicomb furniture introduction, 2000 furniture fair, Highpoint, N.C., US; designed stands of Galerie Mermoz, Robert Vallois, and Galerie du Passage, 2000 Biennial, Carrousel du Louvre, Paris. One of 2001 Giants of Design, *House Beautiful* magazine.
Bibliography Esther Henwood, 'Of Love and Accessories,' *Vogue Décoration*, no. 26, June–July 1990: 61–63. Stephen Mudge, *Paris Rooms: Portfolios of 40 Interior Designers*, Gloucester, Mass.: Rockport, 1999. François Baudot and Jean Demachy, *Elle Decor: The Grand Book of French Style/Style Elle Decor*, Boston: Bullfinch, 2001; Levallois-Perret: Filipacchi, 2001.

Grange, Kenneth Henry (1929–)

British industrial designer; born and active London.

Training 1944–47, Willesden School of Arts and Crafts, London; 1947–49, in illustration.
Biography In London: 1948, Grange was a design assistant at Arcon Chartered Architects; 1949–50, architectural assistant at Bronek Katz and Vaughn; 1950–52, designer with George Bower; and 1952–58, designer at Jack Howe and Partners; 1958–71, was active in his own design consultancy; 1972 with Theo Crosby, Ala Fletcher, Colin Forbes, and Mervyn Kurlansky, cofounded the Pentagram studio, which subsequently set up branch offices in New York and San Francisco. Grange was influenced by the sculptural simplicity of German postwar design, such as that of Braun; redesigned products for Kenwood, including 1960 reworking of the Chef food mixer. 1987–88, he was president, Chartered Society of Designers. From the late 1980s an increasing number of his clients were Japanese. Shiseido (toiletry bottles), and tile manufacturer Inax (bathroom fittings). His industrial design work includes 1959 Brownie 44A camera, 1964 Brownie Vecta camera, 1970 Instamatic camera, 1975 Pocket Instamatic camera, all by Kodak; 1960 parking meter by Venner; 1960 Chef food mixer, 1966

Chefette hand mixer, 1967 rechargeable electric knife, all by Kenwood; 1963 Milward Courier electric shaver by Needle Industries; 1972 Safety razor and 1977 Royale razor by Wilkinson Sword; 1965–67 hat-and-coat systems by A.J. Binns; 1968–72 corporate symbol, sewing machines, calculators, and typewriters by Maruzen, 1971–73 125 high-speed train body by British Rail; and 1979 Parker 25 fountain pen.
Exhibitions/citations Work subject of 1983 *Kenneth Grange at the Boilerhouse: An Exhibition of British Product Design*, Victoria and Albert Museum, London (catalog below). 1959–81 awards, Design Council; 1963 Duke of Edinburgh's Prize for Elegant Design (Courier electric shaver); 1969, elected Honorary Royal Designer for Industry, UK; 1984 Commander of the British Empire (CBE); 1996, gold medal (for lifetime achievement), Chartered Society of Designers.
Bibliography Peter Grob (ed.), *Living by Design: Pentagram Design Partnership*, London: Lund Humphries, 1978: 224–83. Cat., *Kenneth Grange at the Boilerhouse: An Exhibition of British Product Design*, London: The Conran Foundation, 1983. Fiona MacCarthy and Patrick Nuttgens, *An Eye for Industry*, London: Lund Humphries, 1986. 'The Camera,' London: Design Museum, 1989. Jeremy Myerson and Sylvia Katz, *Conran Design Guides: Kitchenware*, London: Conran Octopus, 1990.

Granger, David
> See Bang Design.

Granpré Molière, M.J. (1883–1972)
Dutch architect.

Biography From 1924, Granpré Molière was professor, mechanical-engineering department, Technische Hogeschool, Delft; 1927, became a Catholic; inspired a large number of architecture students who formed the ad-hoc Delft School group; was a fierce opponent of machine production, Functionalism, and Rationalism; propagated the use of natural materials and ornament.
Bibliography Gert Staal and Hester Wolters, *Holland in Vorm: Vormgeving in Nederland 1945–1987*, 's-Gravenhage: Stichling Holland in Vorm, 1987.

Grant, Duncan (1885–1978)
British painter, muralist, and designer; born Rothiemerchus, Inverness, Scotland.

Training 1902–05, painting, Westminster School of Art, London; 1905–07, Slade School of Fine Art, London; 1906–07, Jacques-Émile Blanche's La Palette, Paris.
Biography From 1911, Grant was a member of the Camden Town group of painters; after 1912 meeting of critic Roger Fry, joined Omega Workshop in Fitzroy Square, London, the artists' community founded by Fry; 1913–19 with Fry and Vanessa Bell, was codirector of Omega Workshops, living with Bell from 1916; at the workshops, designed textiles, pottery, and furnishings, including painted furniture with Bell, Wyndham Lewis, Henri Gaudier-Brzeska, and Nina Hamnett. Grant was a central figure of the Bloomsbury Group and continued collaborating with Bell on 1920s–30s on interiors, rugs, printed furnishings, embroideries, and tableware in a painterly style. His rugs illustrated a deliberate irregularity derived from folk art. He designed the sets and costumes for Jacques Copeau's productions of 1914 *Twelfth Night* and 1917 *Pelléas et Mélisande*, both in Paris; continued to be active in theater design throughout his life; 1916, moved into Charleston house in Sussex with Bell and David Garnett, living there for most of his life. The house was decorated and redecorated by Grant, Bell, and others of the Bell family for over six decades. Grant and Bell designed 1926 décor of Clive Bell house at 50 Gordon Square and Mrs. St. John Hutchinson's house at 3 Albert Gate, Regent's Park, both London. 1927–38, Grant spent summers painting in south of France; for interiors, created ornamentation applied to almost all surfaces; 1931, became a member, London Artists' Association; 1932, designed ballet *The Enchanted Grove* produced by Old Vic-Sadler's Wells; 1932, was commissioned by Allan Walton to design printed fabrics on linen, cotton, cotton velvet, and cotton-rayon satin weave, including the legendary *Daphne and Apollo* motif. He also designed 1934 Old English Rose bone-china dinner service by E. Brain, realized three panels for 1934 oceanliner *Queen Mary* (that were rejected by Cunard Lines' chairman as being 'too modern'); late 1930s, decorated ceramics by Phyllis Keyes.
Exhibitions Work shown at 1915 Vorticist group exhibition, London; 1934, with the AIA. Ceramics shown at 1934 *Modern Art for the Table*, Harrod's department store, London, organized by Thomas Acland Fennemore. Work subject of exhibitions at Carfax Gallery, 1920; Tate Gallery, London, 1959; Scottish National Gallery of Modern Art, 1975; Bluecoat Gallery, Liverpool, 1980 (catalog below).
Bibliography Richard Shone, *Bloomsbury Portraits: Vanessa Bell, Duncan Grant and Their Circle*, London. Phaidon, 1976. Cat., *Thirties: British Art and Design Before the War*, London: Arts Council of Great Britain/Hayward Gallery, 1979. Cat., Richard Shone and Judith Collins, *Duncan Grant designer*, Liverpool: Bluecoat Gallery, 1980. Fiona MacCarthy and Patrick Nuttgens, *An Eye for Industry*, London: Lund Humphries, 1986. Stephen Calloway, *Twentieth-Century Decoration*, New York: Rizzoli, 1988: 153. Simon Watney, *The Art of Duncan Grant*, London: Murray, 1990.

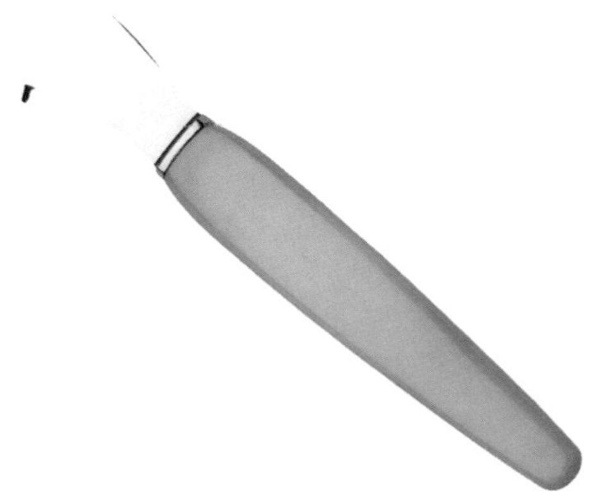

Grasoli-Werk Gebr. Grah. Orange peeler. c. 1950. Plastic handle and stainless steel blade, l. 5 1/2" (14 cm). Mfr.: Grasoli-Werk Gebr., Grah, Germany. Gift of the mfr. MoMA.

Grasoli-Werk Gebr. Grah
German utensils manufacturer; located Solingen.

History The firm was founded by the Grah brothers; for a time, was managed by family member Hans-Robert Grah (1911–1998); has produced a number of kitchen utensils known for their high standards of production, materials, and design; remains a family-managed firm.
Citations 1954, 1957 (two citations), 1958, 1959, 1960, 1964, and 1967 (two citations, utensils designed by Rido Busse) awards, Industrie Form Design (iF), Hanover.

Grasset, Eugène-Samuel (1841–1917)
Swiss architect, writer, jeweler, and designer; born Lausanne.

Training Under Eugène-Emmanuel Viollet-le-Duc, in architecture.
Biography An early admirer of Japanese art, particularly prints and paintings, he made decorative sculpture and worked as an architect in Lausanne. He settled in Paris in 1871. His first work to bring him general recognition was the illustration *Les quatre fils d'Aymon*, begun in 1881. From 1854, he designed a series of distinctive jewelry pieces for Vever; taught a course on Parisian decorative arts, École Normale d'Enseignement du Dessin, rue Vavin, Paris. His furniture commissions included a complete interior of c. 1880–85 for Louis Gillot's photographic studio on the rue Madame, Paris, the furniture for which showed influences of Renaissance architecture combined with Art Nouveau's fauna-flora motifs, stemming from the Middle Ages. Grasset designed mosaics, ceramics, and stained-glass windows and, 1905–07 with Frantz Jourdain, all the lettering for La Samaritaine department store in Paris. Windows, usually religious, were made by Félix Gaudin and included Grasset's famous Joan of Arc windows for the cathedral, Orléans. Grasset was a prolific poster artist, even with commissions from the US; published books *La plante et ses applications ornementales* (Paris: Libraire Centrale des Beaux-Arts, 1896) and *Méthode de composition ornementale* (Paris: Libraire Centrale des Beaux-Arts, 1905) for and with the help of his students and very influential in the Art Nouveau movement.

Rody Graumans. 85 Lamps Lighting Fixture. 1992. Lightbulbs, cords, and sockets, h. x dia. 39 3/8" (100 cm). Mfr.: Droog Design, the Netherlands. Patricia Phelps de Cisneros Purchase Fund. MoMA.

Exhibitions Work first shown at Salon de la Rose Croix and, subsequently, at editions of Salon de la Libre Esthétique and Salon d'Automne. Au Printemps department store window and panels shown at 1900 *Exposition Universelle*, Paris.
Bibliography Yvonne Brunhammer et al., *Art Nouveau Belgium, France*, Houston: Rice University, 1976. Charlotte Gere, *American and European Jewelry 1830–1914*, New York: Crown, 1975: 189. Victor Arwas, *Berthon & Grasset*, London: Academy, 1978. Anne Murray-Robertson, *Grasset: pionnier de l'art nouveau*, Lausanne: 24 heures, 1981. Yves Plauchaut and Françoise Blondel, *Eugène Grasset: Laussane 1841–Sceaux 1917*, Paris: Marchand, 1981. Arlette Barré-Despond and Suzanne Tise, *Jourdain*, Paris: Regard, 1988.

Gråsten, Viola (1910–)

Finnish textile designer; active Sweden.

Training Taideteollisuuskeskuskoulu, Helsinki.
Biography Influential as a colorist and textile designer, Grasten's first work on *ryijy* rugs was inspired by Finnish folk art. 1945–56, she produced geometric and figurative patterns; from 1956 to the end of 1960s, was artistic director of Mölnlycke textiles, Gothenburg: 1970s, was a freelance designer, with clients including Kasthall and Borås.
Bibliography Erik Zahle (ed.), *A Treasury of Scandinavian Design*, New York: Golden Press, 1961. *Design in Sweden*, Stockholm: The Swedish Institute, 1972: 69. Cat., Kathryn B. Hiesinger and George H. Marcus III (eds.), *Design Since 1945*, Philadelphia: Philadelphia Museum of Art, 1983.

Graumans, Rody (1968–)

Dutch designer.

Biography Graumans is best known for 1992 85 Lamps lighting fixture by Droog Design. It is essentially 85 bare incandescent light bulbs hanging from individual black standard electrical wires, gathered at the top, to form a chandelier. He has confessed, 'I am not into that "less is more" stuff. I just work in lowly situations, like with an ordinary lightbulb, things that do not have much value. I like the idea of getting power out of inferiority. You can't avoid using a lightbulb; it is always part of a lamp's construction. And you shouldn't... [try to] escape [it] by sticking a shade over it.'
Exhibitions Work included in 1996 *Contemporary Design from the Netherlands*, The Museum of Modern Art, New York; 2002–03 *Moins & Plus*, Musée d'Art Moderne, Saint-Étienne, France; numerous others.
Bibliography Ida van Zijl, *Droog Design, 1991–1996*, Utrecht: Centraal Museum, 1997. Renny Ramkers and Gijs Bakker (eds.), *Droog Design: Spirit of the Nineties*, Rotterdam: 010 Publishers, 1998. Paola Antonelli (ed.), *Objects of Design: The Museum of Modern Art*, New York: The Museum of Modern Art, 2003: 277.

Graves, Michael (1934–)

American architect; born Indianapolis, Ind.; active Princeton, N.J.

Training 1968, architecture, University of Cincinnati; to 1959, Graduate School of Design, Harvard University; 1960–62, American Academy in Rome.
Biography Late 1950s and early 1960s, Graves was an artist in a studio shared with Richard Meier on 10th Street, New York; from 1962, taught architecture as Schirmer Professor of Architecture, Princeton (N.J.) University; 1964, set up his own architecture practice in Princeton. His early work was inspired by classical art and Cubist painting; he used color on his structures to create metaphorical landscapes; early 1970s, became known as one of ad-hoc New York Five group of architects and, from early 1970s, only for his drawings until 1982, when his postmodern Public Services Building, Portland, Ore., was completed. (The other New York Five architects were Peter Eisen-man, Charles Gwathmey, John Hejduk, and Richard Meier.) At this stage, Graves was better known for his furniture and furnishings than for his architecture; 1977, his first furniture collection was produced by Sunar Hauserman, and he produced widely published furniture designs for Memphis, early 1980s, including 1981 Plaza dressing table. His 1985 stainless-steel teapot with its 'fledgling' whistle for Alessi became a popular icon of postmodern design, selling more than 500,000 pieces. The 1985 MG2 armchair and MG3 club chair were produced by Sawaya & Moroni. Graves's designs reflected the influences of mass-produced 1930s–40s goods, early 19th-century neoclassical designs, and the Wiener Werkstätte. He and ten other architect / designers designed services for Alessi's 1983 Tea and Coffee Piazza project. He designed 1988 carpet designs for the Dialog collection of Vorwerk and ceramics by Swid Powell, including 1985 Big Dripper coffee pot. His 1989 Kyoto Collection of furniture was produced by Kenneth Smith's Arkitektura firm. His furniture originally intended for the Disney corporate offices was produced by Dunbar 1990 but designed earlier. 1993, he opened his own retail shop in Princeton, N.J.; designed 1993 Mickey Mouse teapot; 1999, began a lucrative relationship with Target stores that produced an extensive range of low-price kitchen and tabletop wares that sold in very large numbers. Buildings include, in the US: 1967 Hanselmann house, Fort Wayne, Ind.; 1972 Snyderman house, Fort Wayne, Ind.; 1977–78 Fargo-Moorhead Cultural Center; 1978 New Children's

Johanna Grawunder. Medusa vase. 2001. Hand-modeled, mouth-blown glass, h. 9 3/4 x w. 13 5/8" (25 x 35 cm). Mfr.: Salviati., Italy.

Museum; 1979–82 Public Services Building, Portland, Ore.; 1982–85 Humana building, Louisville, Ky.; 1990 Newark Museum wing; 1989 Disney World Dolphin Hotel and 1990 Swan Hotel in Orlando, Fla.; 1989–90 Whitney Museum of American Art addition, New York; Museum of Art at Emory University, Atlanta, Ga.; library in San Juan Capistrano, Cal.; and Pegase di Domaine Clos winery in the Napa valley of California. Graves and others developed the resort site plan, Euro Disneyland, Marne-la-Vallée, where he designed its New York Hotel. In his own residence, he has mixed Biedermeier furniture with his own designs.
Exhibitions/citations Furniture shown at Whitney Museum of American Art exhibition and Philadelphia exhibition (catalogs below). Dining table and chairs shown at 1985 (17th) Triennale di Milano. *Progressive Architecture* award; Arnold W. Brunner Prize in architecture; National American Institute of Architects (AIA) award; 1999 gold IDSA/*Business Week* award; others.
Bibliography Kenneth Frampton and Colin Rowe, *Five Architects: Eisenman, Graves, Gwathmey, Hejduk, Meier*, New York: Wittenborn, 1972. Mario Gandelsonas and David Morton, 'On Reading Architecture: Eisenman and Graves—An Analysis,' *Progressive Architecture*, no. 53, Mar. 1972: 68–88. Allan Greenberg, 'The Lurking American Legacy,' *Architectural Forum*, no. 138, May 1973: 54–55. Cat., Lisa Phillips (intro.), *Shape and Environment: Furniture by American Architects*, New York: Whitney Museum of American Art, 1982: 36–37. Marilyn Bethany, 'The Architect as Artist,' *The New York Times Magazine*, 25 Apr. 1982: 96. Officina Alessi, *Tea and Coffee Piazza...*, Milan: Crusinallo, 1983. Cat., Kathryn B. Hiesinger and George H. Marcus III (eds.), *Design Since 1945*, Philadelphia: Philadelphia Museum of Art, 1983. Cat., Carlo Guenzi, *Le affinità elettive*, Milan: Electa, 1985.

Graven Images
> Kirkpatrick, Janice.

Grawunder, Johanna (1961–)

American designer; born San Diego, Cal.; active Milan.

Training To 1984, California Polytechnic State University, San Luis Obispo, with final-year study in Florence.
Biography From 1985, Grawunder has worked in architecture/design studio Sottsass Associati and, 1989, becoming a partner, active in architecture, design, and technological lighting concepts. Design work has included that for clients such as Acme Studio, Christofle, Egizia, Giotto, Salviati, and WMF. Architecture work, with the studio, has included Wolf House in Colorado, Olabuenaga House in Hawaii, Yuko House in Tokyo, Contemporary Furniture Museum in Ravenna, golf club and resort and residential village in China, and houses in Australia, Singapore, and Belgium. From 1985, has taught or teaches in Florence at California State University extension; Royal College of Art, London; Hochschule der Kunste, Berlin; and Domus Academy, Istituto Europeo di Design, and Futurarium, Milan.

Gray, Eileen Moray (1879–1976)

Irish architect and designer; born Enniscorthy, County Wexford; active France.

Training 1898–1902, painting and drawing, Slade School of Fine Art, London; 1900–02, lacquerwork at D. Charles furniture workshop, Dean Street, London; 1902–05, Atelier Colarossi, Paris; Académie Julian, Paris.
Biography 1907, Gray settled in Paris; from 1907, studied lacquerwork with Seizo Sugawara; c. 1910, began to work on decorative panels and screens and, subsequently, furniture, desks, bookcases, and beds as one-of-a-kind pieces for rich clients. 1914, she made her first complete object, Le Destin four-panel screen in deep-red lacquer, for the residence of couturier Jacques Doucet at 43, avenue du Bois (now avenue Foch), Paris, along with some additional notable designs. She regretted the exclusivity of her work and devoted much thought from 1914 to furniture that might be batch-produced and more widely sold. During World War I, she worked in London in a studio near Cheyne Walk, Chelsea. 1918, she returned to Paris, accompanied by Sugawara; 1919–22 during her exotic first period, designed the apartment of modiste Suzanne Talbot (Mme. Mathieu Lévy), rue de Lota, Paris, where the imaginative setting included luxurious furniture alongside avant-garde work, including her legendary lacquered screens and the widely published 'gondola' daybed. Only 11 known examples of the 1922 Talbot-apartment screens were produced up to 1971; six in black, five in white lacquer. 1922–30, Gray

Eileen Gray. Screen. 1922. Lacquered wood and metal rods, 74 1/2 x 53 1/2 x 3/4" (189.2 x 135.9 x 1.9 cm). Mfr.: Jean Désert, France. Hector Guimard Fund. MoMA.

operated a shop at 217, rue du Faubourg Saint-Honoré, Paris, under the fictitious name Jean Désert, where she sold limited-production pieces of furniture, furnishings, lighting, and carpets. c. 1923, she was commissioned to produce rugs and furniture for the villa of vicomte and vicomtesse de Noailles, Hyères, through the intervention of its architect Robert Mallet-Stevens. Even though Gray's main interest lay with lacquerwork, her rugs were successful. 1910, she met British artist Evelyn Wyld, and they became companions. And, thus, Gray's carpets were woven by female apprentices in the 1920s in Wyld's business, Atelier du Tissage on the rue Visconti. Associating with the Parisian beau monde, Gray's clients included architects Jean-Charles Moreux, Henri Pacon, and Charles Siclis, and collectors Jacques Doucet, Henri Laurens, Elsa Schiaparelli, Maharaja of Indore, and the Countess of Oxford. 1924, Gray designed furniture (produced in 1927) for 1924 oceanliner *Transatlantique*; c. 1925, designed her first pieces of furniture in metal and a 1926 functional chair based on a desk-chair model. Gray's geometric orientation began to appear as early as 1923, at the Salon of Société des Artistes Décorateurs (where it was not well received by the critics). However, the Salon installation was admired by Walter Gropius and J.J.P. Oud. And Oud arranged to have her work published for the first time internationally, in Dutch periodical *Wendingen* (no. 6, Sept.–Oct. 1924). 1925, she was encouraged by architect Jean Badovici to pursue architecture; 1927–29, outfitted her own house, E 1027, Roquebrune-Cap-Martin, with Badovici's assistance. The interiors were clean, sparse, comfortable, and multifunctional, with collapsible furniture in tubular steel, glass, plate glass, and painted wood. She became more interested in architecture and closed Galerie Jean Désert in 1930; designed Badovici's apartment 1931 at 17, rue Châteaubriand, Paris, with her furniture and rugs; 1932, turned over E 1027 to Badovici and built the house Tempe à Pailla, near Castellar, also in the Alpes Maritimes, occupying it alone; c. 1938, outfitted an apartment in Saint-Tropez. During World War II, she occupied a château restored by Henri Pacon and brothers Jan and Jöel Martel and harbored a number of artists; after the war, began to work on the reconstruction of the house Maubeuge for Jean Badovici and returned to Castellar. Little known after World War II, she received some little notice with the publication of images of E 1027, Tempe à Pailla, and certain furniture in the 1956 exhibition catalog of *25 Années de l'UAM* and in a 1959 article in journal *L'architecture d'aujourd'hui*. Her furniture suitable for mass production was not made until early 1970s, when she was in her 90s and when interest in her work revived.

Exhibitions/citations Work (Symbolist-inspired bas-relief) first shown at 1913 Salon of Société des Artistes Décorateurs and at its 1923 (Room-Boudoir for Monte Carlo), 1924, and 1933 editions; 1922 Salon d'Automne; 1930, 1932, and 1956 exhibitions of Union des Artistes Modernes (UAM); Pavillon des Temps Nouveaux, 1937 *Exposition Internationale des Arts et Techniques dans la Vie Moderne*, Paris; 1937 *Le Décor de la Vie de 1909 à 1925*, Pavillon Marsan, Musée des Arts Décoratifs, Paris; 1970 *Modern Chairs*, Whitechapel Gallery, London; some pieces shown at 1976 *1925* exhibition, Musée des Arts Décoratifs, Paris; 1976 *Cinquantenaire de l'Exposition de 1925*, Musée des Arts Décoratifs, Paris; 1979 *Paris-Moscou*, Centre Georges Pompidou, Paris. 1952, she participated in a project for an exhibition of UAM, Musée d'Art Moderne, Paris. Work subject of 1970 exhibitions, Graz and Vienna; 1972 exhibition sponsored by the Royal Institute of British Architects, Heinz Gallery, London; 1975 touring American exhibition, sponsored by Architectural League of New York; 1979 exhibition sponsored by the Scottish Arts Council; 1980 *Eileen Gray and les Arts Décoratifs*, Rosa Esman Gallery, New York; 1979–80 exhibition, The Museum of Modern Art, New York, and Victoria and Albert Museum, London; 1992 *Eileen Gray*, Design Museum, London. 1972, admitted into Royal Society of Art, London; 1972, elected Honorary Royal Designer for Industry, UK; 1973, elected honorary fellow, Institute of Architects, Ireland.

Bibliography 'L'appartement de Suzanne Talbot,' *L'illustration*, no. 7, 1933: 357. Joseph Rykwert, 'Eileen Gray: Pioneer of Design,' *Architectural Review*, 1972: 357. Eveline Schlumberger, 'Eileen Gray' (interview), *Connaissance des arts*, no. 258, 1973: 72. J. Stewart Johnson, *Eileen Gray: Designer*, New York: The Museum of Modern Art, 1979. Cat., *Les années UAM 1929–1958*, Paris: Musée des Arts Décoratifs, 1988: 186–87. Philippe Garner, *Eileen Gray: Design and Architecture, 1878–1976*, Cologne: Taschen, 1993. Stefan Hecker and Christian F. Müller, *Eileen Gray*, Barcelona: Gustavo Gili, 1993. Michel Raynaud, *De léclectisme au doute: Eileen Gray et Jean Badovici: suivi de, La beauté du geste*, Paris: Altamira, 1994. Peter Adam: *Eileen Gray: Architect/Designer, A Biography*, New York: Abrams, 2000. Caroline Constant, *Eileen Gray*, London: Phaidon, 2000. Paola Antonelli (ed.), *Objects of Design: The Museum of Modern Art*, New York: The Museum of Modern Art, 2003: 78–79.

> See Wyld, Evelyn.

Gray, Milner Connorton (1899–1997)

British industrial and graphic designer; born Blackheath, London.

Training Painting and design, Goldsmiths' College School of Art, London University.

Biography 1917–19, Gray worked in the first war camouflage unit; 1922, set up the design consultancy Bassett-Gray; 1930, became one of the eight founding members of Society of Industrial Artists (SIA; later Society of Industrial Artists and Designers), of which he was honorary secretary 1932–40 and president 1943–48 and 1968; c. 1934, designed graphics for the packaging of Golden Mushrooms, with air vents at the sides and clear film in a circular window on top. 1935–38, he was a council member, Design and Industries Association (DIA); 1932–40, was a senior partner, design consultancy Industrial Design Partnership; was influenced by the work of Henry Dreyfuss and Raymond Loewy; 1937–40, was principal, Sir John Cass School, and had numerous other teaching positions; from 1943, was a founding partner with Misha Black of Design Research Unit (DRU); played a leading role in the development of design consultancy in Britain; during World War II, worked with Black and others for the Ministry of In-formation designing propaganda exhibitions, including *Dig for Victory*. He was a prominent member, chair, or president of almost every British and international body in graphic and industrial design. Best-known as a graphic artist, he designed corporate identity programs for British Rail, Courage breweries, and Austin Reed; (with William Vaughan for events in London) developed prototype domestic wares for the 'Ideal' fitted-kitchen installation at 1946 *Britain Can Make It* exhibition and was responsible for the overall design of the exhibition, and, jointly, for signage of 1951 *Festival of Britain*, and designed 1955 Pyrex glass kitchenware (with Kenneth Lamble) for James A. Jobling and the emblem for Queen Elizabeth II's 1977 Silver Jubilee.

Exhibitions/citations Package designs shown 1979–80 *Thirties* exhibition, Hayward Gallery, London (catalog below). Master in the Art-Workers' Guild; 1937, elected Honorary Royal Designer for Industry, UK; 1963, Commander of the British Empire (CBE); diploma, 1957 (10th) Triennale di Milano; large number of other honors.

Bibliography Michael Farr, *Design in British Industry: A Mid-Century Survey*, London: Cambridge, 1955: 145. Cat., *Thirties: British Art and Design Before the War*, London: Arts Council of Great Britain/Hayward Gallery, 1979. Avril Blake, *Milner Gray*, London: The Design Council, 1986. Jeremy Myerson and Sylvia Katz, *Conran Design Guides: Kitchenware*, London: Conran Octopus, 1990.

Graydon-Stannus, Elizabeth

Irish glassmaker; active Battersea, London.

Biography Mrs. Graydon-Stannus, an antiques dealer, was an authority on English and Irish glass. 1925, she began the production of glass in her workshop Graydon Glass at 69–71 High St. in Battersea with, later, showrooms in London and the US; employed about a dozen workers; by 1926, production was in full force. The staff included A. Noel Billinghurst, the chief designer and deputy; James Manning, the chief daytime glass blower; George Hollings, the chief night-time glass blower; and someone named Everet, the cutter. Initial wares were traditional English and Irish glass and essentially fakes of other glass, and, also from 1926, decorative- and tableware, later named Gray-Stan. Most of the Gray-Stan was designed by Billinghurst. c. 1935–36, Manning left and established a small glass department at the Bromley School of Art, and the Graydon Glass factory closed. The claim, encouraged by its practice of reproducing fakes, that there was also a factory in France that made Lalique-like glass is apocryphal.

Citations She was elected a fellow, Royal Society of Arts.

Bibliography Cat., *Thirties: British Art and Design Before the War*, London: Arts Council of Great Britain/Hayward Gallery, 1979.

Grcic, Konstantin (1965–)

German designer; born and active Munich.

Training 1985–87, cabinetmaking, Parnham College, Dorset, England; 1988–90, design, Royal College of Art, London.

Biography Grcic worked in the office of Jasper Morrison, London; 1991, established his own eponymous design practice in Munich; has designed widely published furniture, housewares, lighting, jewelry, and exhibitions for international clients, including Babybloom, Cappellini, Chi Ha Pura, ClassiCon, Driade, Flos, littala/Hackman, Montina, Moormann, Porzellan-Manufaktur Nymphenburg, Proto Design, SCP, Whirlpool Europe, and Wireworks. Designed furniture for Munich Tourist Information office (with David Chipperfield) and exhibitions for Authentics, as well as products for the latter.

Exhibitions/citations Won 1999 competition for design of public square in Canary Warf, London; guest of honor with extensive exhibition of work, 2000 (17th) Intérieur design biennial, Courtrai, Belgium.

Bibliography Fumio Shimizu, *Euro Design*, Tokyo: Graphic-sha, 1993. *Intramuros*, no. 52, Jan.–Feb. 1994: 24–27. Volker Albus et al., *13 nach Memphis: Design zwischen Askese und Sinnlichkeit*, Munich: Prestel, 1995. *Architektur & Wohnen*, no. 33, Winter 1996: 78–81. *Interni*, no. 471, June 1997: 128–29. *Azure*, Nov.–Dec. 1997: 52–55. *Abitare*, no. 371, Mar. 1998: 156; no. 372, Apr. 1998: 173. *Domus*, no. 820, Nov. 1999: 42–51. Mel Byars, *50 Beds…*, Hove: RotoVision, 2000. Michael Erlhoff, *50 Jahre Italienisches und Deutsche Design*, Bonn: Kunst- and Ausstellungshalle der Bundesrepublik Deutschland, 2000. Mel Byars, *On/Off: New Electronic Products*, New York: Universe, 2001. www.konstantin-grcic.com.

Green, A. Romney (1872–1945)

British furniture maker, craftsperson, and sailor; brother of architect Curtis Green..

Biography Green was influenced by Ernest Barnsley and Godfrey Blount early on; a proponent of the Arts and Crafts movement in furniture. Eric Gill's woodcuts appeared in his book *Woodwork in Principle and Practice* (1918). His furniture showed influences of 19th-century styles. 1930s, Green and Stanley W. Davies of Windermere, while unassociated, both worked in the same style.

Bibliography Cat., *Thirties: British Art and Design Before the War*, London: Arts Council of Great Britain/Hayward Gallery, 1979.

Green, Taylor (1914–)

> See Van Keppel, Hendrik.

Konstantin Grcic. Mayday portable lamp. 1998. Diffuser polypropylène, 20⅞ x 8 7/16" (53 x 21.5 cm). 1998. Mfr.: Flos.

Greene, Charles Sumner (1868–1957); Henry Mather Greene (1870–1954)

American architects, designers, and brothers; born Brighton, Ohio; active Pasadena, Cal.

Training Both: Calvin Milton Woodward's Manual Training School, University of Washington, St. Louis, Mo., an institution strongly influenced by John Ruskin and William Morris. To 1890, Charles studied architecture, Massachusetts Institute of Technology (MIT), Cambridge, Mass.; to 1892, Henry also there.
Biography 1891–94 in Boston, Charles worked for architects H. Lawford Warren and, subsequently, Winslow and Whetherall; 1891–94, Henry worked for architects Stickney and Austin, and, subsequently, Shepley, Rutan and Coolidge, and Chamberlin and Austin. The brothers visited 1893 *World's Columbian Exposition*, Chicago, where they were greatly influenced by the Japanese section that included a structure known as Ho-o-den by Frank Lloyd Wright. Another influence may have come from Edward Morse's book *Japanese Homes and Their Surroundings* (1885). 1893, they set up an architecture office, Pasadena, Cal.. Their first furniture was influenced by Bradley's designs for the magazine *The Ladies' Home Journal* of 1901 and begun in that year. Bradley's style had in turn been influenced by British designers Hugh Baillie Scott, Charles Rennie Mackintosh, and C.F.A. Voysey. 1903, the brothers set up an office, Los Angeles; from 1905, worked in a highly refined style. By 1906, their practice was flourishing, and most of the houses for which they are known today were produced in the next few years. Their first significant patron was Adelaide Tichenor, for whom they built their first (1904) Craftsman bungalow in Long Beach, Cal. Praised by Gustav Stickley in *The Craftsman* and Charles R. Ashbee, 1909, their lyrical work lacked the heaviness of some other Arts and Crafts pieces. They proceeded to build in and around Pasadena and Los Angeles a type of building known as the California Bungalow, of which the most impressive examples were 1907 Blacker and 1908 Gamble houses, Pasadena, and 1909 Pratt and Thorsen houses farther north. These blended the Arts and Crafts emphasis on materials, Chinese and Japanese approaches, and the simplicity of local Franciscan missions of Spanish Colonial architecture. Other buildings include 1896 Edward B. Hosmer house, 1902 James A. Culbertson house, 1903 Arturo Bandini house, 1904 Edgar W. Camp house, 1904 Jennie A. Reeve house, 1906 Robinson house, 1907 Freeman Ford house. The Greenes' furniture and cabinetry incorporated intricate inlay and sensuous lines. The Greenes, like Frank Lloyd Wright, included Stickley furniture in earlier residences, but increasingly designed their own furniture and furnishings from 1904, whose constructions took an exasperatingly long time to complete. The partnership began to founder when Charles moved to Carmel, Cal., 1916. It was finally dissolved 1922, when Charles designed some furniture alone and Henry practiced architecture alone.
Exhibitions Work included in 1982 *Shape and Environment: Furniture by American Architects*, Whitney Museum of American Art, Fairfield County, Conn.; 1989 *From Architecture to Object*, Hirschl and Adler gallery, New York; 1987–88 *'The Art That Is Life': The Arts and Crafts Movement in America, 1875–1920* touring the US.
Bibliography Esther McCoy, *Five California Architects*, New York: Reinhold, 1960. Karen Current, *Greene & Greene: Architects in the Residential Style*, Fort Worth, Tex.: Amon Carter Museum of Western Art, 1974. Janann Strand, *A Greene and Greene Guide*, Pasadena: G. Dahlstrom, 1974. Randell L. Makinson, *Greene & Greene*, vol. 1, *Architecture as a Fine Art*; vol. 2, *Furniture and Related Designs*, Salt Lake City, Utah: Peregrine Smith, 1977, 1979. Cat., Lisa Phillips (intro.), *Shape and Environment: Furniture by American Architects*, New York: Whitney Museum of American Art, 1982: 38–39. Cat., Wendy Kaplan (ed.), *'The Art That Is Life': The Arts and Crafts Movement in America, 1875–1920*, Boston: Museum of Fine Arts, 1987. Edward R. Bosley, *Greene & Greene*, London: Phaidon, 2000.

Greenwood Pottery

American pottery; located Trenton, N.J.

History Trained as a dipper and kiln stoker in Staffordshire (England), William Tams settled in the US with his son James Tams (1845–1910). After working for a short time at Young's pottery in New Jersey, William opened a pottery with partner William Barnard. James joined his father's pottery, where James P. Stephens and Charles Brearly had become partners in the firm known as Brearly, Stephens and Tams, and succeeded him in 1866. The firm was incorporated in 1868 as Greenwood Pottery Company. James Tams was president, and James Stephens was secretary and treasurer. To 1875, the pottery produced industrial white-granite and cream-colored tableware for restaurants, hotels, steamships, and railroads, and ceramic hardware including doorknobs and electrical insulations. 1878, it began production of the American China range, whose success resulted in the acquisition of the older Eagle Pottery and Burroughs and Mountford Pottery. 1870s, some of its industrial ware was decorated. 1870s–80s, the firm began producing thin, translucent white porcelain. 1882, when the plant was destroyed by fire and rebuilt, decorating departments and showrooms were added. 1883, an English porcelain decorator called Jones, formerly at Royal Worcester Porcelain Company, joined Greenwood, and other artisans from Worcester followed. This hiring resulted in ware indistinguishable from English examples. Greenwood's deep blue glaze on vases imitated the Bleu du Roi of Sèvres and was usually decorated in raised gold, silver, or bronze color. Its artistic ceramic production was short lived. From 1891, Greenwood returned to industrial whiteware.
Bibliography Jennie J. Young, *The Ceramic Art: A Compendium of the History and Manufacture of Pottery and Porcelain*, New York: Harper, 1879. Edwin AtLee Barber, *The Pottery and Porcelain of the United States...*, New York: Feingold & Lewis, 1909. *The Work of the Potteries of New Jersey 1865 to 1876*, Newark: Newark Museum Association, 1914. Doreen Bolger Burke et al., *In Pursuit of Beauty: Americans and the Aesthetic Movement*, New York: The Metropolitan Museum of Art/Rizzoli, 1986.

Grégoire, Marc (1905–1996)

French inventor.

Biography 6 April 1938, the first Teflon substance was accidentally discovered by Roy Plunkett at Du Pont while experimenting with a number of gases. He realized that the resulting waxy solid was very slippery and impervious to corrosive chemicals. Plunkett abbreviated the name of the substance, known as polytetrafluoroethylene (PTFE), a solid version of fluorocarbons (or freon), to 'Teflon,' now a Du Pont proprietary name. 1948, full-scale commercial production began but was limited to industrial applications. However, because Teflon will adhere to practically nothing, cracks and crevices must be applied on a surface to have a primer cling. Today, sandblasting is used before applying the primer, into which the Teflon is embedded. 1956 in Paris, based on an idea from his wife Colette to prevent an omelette's stick-

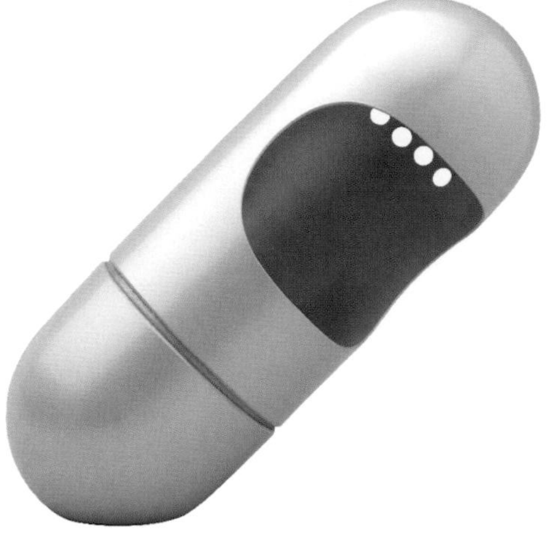

Vittorio Gregotti, Giotto Stoppino, and Lodovico Meneghetti. Equilibrium table lamp (no. 537). 1967. Laquered aluminum, h. 8 x dia. 3 3/4" (20.3 x 9.5 cm). Mfr.: Arteluce, Italy. Gift of the mfr. MoMA.

ing to a frypan and his using the adherence method, Marc Grégoire was able to affix a thin layer of Teflon onto aluminum cookware, thus creating the first nonstick frying pan. Within several years, he was manufacturing more than a million T-Fal-coated pans annually; Grégoire's patented name for Teflon was Tefal or T-Fal®. 2 May 1956, he founded the Société Tefal, later Tefal S.A., with some initial sales difficulty and resistance but with subsequent great success. Christmas 1960, United Press International journalist Thomas Hardie introduced the Tefal pans in the US through Macy's department store, New York. By 1968, Tefal had become France's largest manufacturer of non-stick cookware; 1974, introduced non-stick waffle iron and other innovative models followed; was incorporated into SEB. Gregoire died in Tourrette-sur-Loup.

Gregori, Bruno (1954–)

Italian designer; brother of architect Giorgio Gregori.

Training Accademia di Belle Arti di Brera, Milan.
Biography One of the founders of Studio Alchimia in 1976, Gregori was particularly active in its graphics program; in addition to graphic design for the journal *Domus*, has worked on various furniture-design projects. Furniture with Alessandro Mendini, another Alchimia cofounder, included 1984 Tower Furniture cabinet, 1984 Atomaria lamp, 1984 Zabro table-chair (hand-painted by Gregori), 1985 Calamobio cabinet, 1985 Cerambrice silkscreen desk, 1985 Macaone table.
Exhibitions Participated in 1979 *Form Design* exhibition, Linz.
Bibliography Robert A.M. Stern (ed.), *The International Design Yearbook*, New York: Abbeville, 1985/1986. Kazuko Sato, *Alchimia*, Berlin: Taco, 1988.

Gregori, Giorgio (1957–1995)

Italian architect and designer; born Rome; active Milan.

Training Faculty of Architecture, Politecnico, Milan.
Biography From 1984, Giorgio Gregori was the architecture coordinator for Alchimia and, from 1980, for Studio Alchimia; participated in projects including Summer Architecture, Unfinished Architecture, and Black Out.
Exhibition Work (Ala sofa by Arflex) shown at 1992 *Nuovo bel design: 200 nuovi oggetti per la casa*, Salone del Mobile, Milan.

Gregorie, 'Bob' Eugene T. (1908–2002)

American automobile designer; born New York.

Biography 1927, Gregorie worked at Elco Boat Works in New Jersey; from 1928, at Cox and Stevens yacht design studio in New York; 1929, moved to Detroit, Mich., and, for a time, under Harley Earl at General Motors, and at Brewster coachbuilders; from 1931 to his 1945 retirement, worked at Ford Motor Company as a body draftsperson at Lincoln and in 1935, when he became Ford's head of the new design department, refined the 1936 Lincoln Zephyr as the 1938 model (based on John Tjaarda's 1932 Briggs Dream Car), but Gregorie was not its sole designer. He introduced the first (1938) horizontal radiator grille on an American production car. Designs include 1933–34 and 1935–37 Fords, 1939 Mercury, 1939 Lincoln Continental, 1940s Ford and Mercury bodies, and 1949 Lincoln. On Ford Motor Company director Edsel Ford's 1943 death, Gregorie left Ford and the next year was brought back by Henry Ford II but, 1945, finally retired to St. Augustine, Fla., where he died some time later.
Bibliography Henry L. Dominguez, *Edsel Ford and E.T. Gregorie: The Remarkable Design Team and Their Classic Fords of the 1930s and 1940s*, Warrendale, Pa.: Society of Automotive Engineers, 1999. Penny Sparke, *A Century of Car Design*, London: Mitchell Beazley, 2002.

Gregorietti, Salvatore (1941–)

Italian designer; born Palermo; active Milan.

Biography 1963, Gregorietti began his professional career; was an associate of the studio Unimark International; became a member, Associazione per il Disegno Industriale (ADI). Work included lighting and metal and glass table accessories. Clients included Atkinsons, Brionvega, La Rinascente, Molteni, Motta, Pirelli, Sonzogno, and Standa. His Nalu table lamp was produced by Sirrah and Alice hanging light by Valenti.
Citations 1979 (for the journal *Ottagono,* with Giuliana Gramigna and Sergio Mazza) Premio Compasso d'Oro.
Bibliography *ADI Annual 1976*, Milan: Associazione per il Disegno Industriale, 1976.

Gregotti, Vittorio (1927–)

Italian architect and designer; born Novara (Italy).

Training 1948–1952, Politecnico, Milan.
Biography Gregotti was a partner with Ludovico Meneghetti and Giotto Stoppino in Architetti Associati in Navara 1952–64 and in Milan 1964–67; 1968–74, was in private practice in Milan; 1974, with Pierluigi Cerri and Hiromichi Matsui, established the architecture firm Gregotti Associati; 1964–78, taught at Politecnico, Milan and, from 1978, at Istituto Universitario di Architettura, Venice; was guest professor at universities in Tokyo, Buenos Aires, São Paulo, Berkeley (Cal.), and Lausanne; was an editor on several journals including associate editor of *Casabella-continuità* 1952–60, *Edilizia moderna* (responsible for monographs) 1962–64, and *Il verri* (responsible for architecture section) 1963–65; from 1980, was director of *La rassegna italiana* and a member of the editorial board of the journal *Lotus*; published a number of books including *New Directions in Italian Architecture* (1968) and *Il territorio dell' architettura* (1986). Architecture included 1956 – 57 Italian neo-Liberty block of flats for the Bossi company, Cameri, near Novara; 1962–67 town plan for Novara; 1969 project for the Quartiere Zen (with Francesco Amoroso, Salvatore Bisogni, Hiromichi Matsui, and Franco Purini), Palermo; from 1970, building projects for Università degli Studi, Palermo; 1975 competition project for new branch of Università degli Studi, Calabria (with Emilio Battisti, Hiromichi Matsui, Pierluigi Nicolin, Franco Purini, Carlo Rusconi Clerici, and Bruno Viganò), near Cozenza; 1980 project for ACTV (Venice transport company) boatyards (with Augusto Cagnardi, Pierluigi Cerri, and Hiromichi Matsui), Guidecca; 1983–84 area of via Corassari (with members of his studio), Modena.
Exhibitions/citations Work shown at Triennale di Milano from 1951; 1979 *Architettura*, Palazzo delle Stelline, Milan; 1979 *Design & design*, Palazzo delle Stelline, Milan, and Palazzo Grassi, Venice; 1982 *Maquettes d'architectes*, Centre d'Art Contemporain, Geneva, and Le Nouveau Musée, Lyons-Villeurbanne; and numerous other venues worldwide. First prize, 1964 (13th) Triennale di Milano; 1960 (with others), 1967, 1994 (two citations with others) Premio Compasso d'Oro; first prize, Housing Development Competition, Istituto Autonomo Case Popolari (ICAP), Parlero; first prize entry, 1971 Università degli Studi, Florence, competition; first prize entry, 1973 Università degli Studi, Calabria, competition. 1974–76, director of architecture and visual-arts section, Biennale di Venezia.
Bibliography Vittorio Gregotti, *New Directions in Italian Architecture*, New York: Braziller, 1968. 'Vittorio Gregotti,' *Architecture and Urbanism*, July 1977. Manfredo Tafuri, *Vittorio Gregotti, progetti e architetture*, Milan: Electa, 1982. P. Lovero, 'La generazione dello Z.E.N. Evora, Vitoria, Palermo: tre quartieri a confronto,' *Lotus International*, no. 36, 1982: 17–45. S. Brandolini and P.-A. Croset, 'Gregotti associati, G 14 Progettazione—Studio GPI. Cadorna-Pagano: un progetto per il centro di Milano,' *Casabella 48*, no. 513, 1984: 52–63. Juli Capella and Quim Larrea, *Designed by Architects in the 1980s*, New York: Rizzoli, 1988.

Grenander, Alfred (1863–1931)
Swedish industrial designer; born Sköfde.

Biography Grenander was an early member of the Deutscher Werkbund; designed many pieces of furniture along highly functional lines produced by Berliner Möbelfabrik, and stations and passenger cars for the Berlin elevated tramway.
Bibliography Penny Sparke, *Introduction to Design and Culture in the Twentieth Century*, Allen & Unwin, 1986.

Gresham, David
> See Design Logic.

Gresley, Herbert Nigel (1897–)
British engineer and designer.

Training Under Francis Webb in Crewe and John Aspinal in Horwich.
Biography 1905, he became the carriage and wagon superintendent of the Great Northern Railway, succeeding H.A. Scott as locomotive superintendent, 1911; from 1923, was chief mechanical engineer of the London and North Eastern Railway; subsequently, developed new features of carriage and wagon designs; was best known for his de-signs of Britain's largest, most powerful, and fastest steam locomotives, particularly the streamline *Mallard* engine. Gresley designed a special carriage for the fast service between London and Edinburgh, commemorating the 1936 coronation of King George VI. In two shades of blue, the *Coronation* used Rexine on surfaces and uncut moquette for upholstery and carpets. Its exterior was trimmed in chrome-plated metal.
Exhibitions Engine maquettes were shown at 1979–80 *Thirties: British Art and Design Before the War*, Hayward Gallery, London (catalog below).
Bibliography Cat., *Thirties: British Art and Design Before the War*, London: Arts Council of Great Britain/Hayward Gallery, 1979.

Gretsch, Hermann (1895–1950)
German architect, engineer, and product designer; born Augsburg; active Stuttgart.

Biography 1930s, Gretsch worked for the Porzellanfabrik Arzberg and others. His best-known design was the 1931 Form 1382 undecorated domestic white porcelain dinnerware, whose basic shape influenced the work of several designers. He worked in the modern style in Germany during the Nazi period; when the Nazis closed the Deutscher Werkbund, he became head of its replacement, the Bund Deutscher Entwerfer (association of German designers); wrote and edited numerous publications on design for mass production. Considered a 20th-century classic, Form 1382 was produced by Arzberg and was a synthesis of his design approach and theories; designed the 2050, 2200, and 1954 2000 ceramic ranges by Heinrich Löffelhardt, 1936 Form 98 by Schönwald, and 1955 Blattnetz by KPM, Berlin; died in Stuttgart.
Exhibitions/citations Gold medal (Form 1382), 1937 *Exposition Internationale des Arts et Techniques dans la Vie Moderne*, Paris; an award, 1936 (6th) Triennale di Milano.
Bibliography Penny Sparke, *Introduction to Design and Culture in the Twentieth Century*, London: Allen & Unwin, 1986. Cat., *100 Jahre Porzellanfabrik Arzberg 1887–1987*, Hohengerg: Museum der Deutschen Porzellanindustrie, 1987. Jeremy Myerson and Sylvia Katz, *Conran Design Guides: Tableware*, London: Conran Octopus, 1990.

Hermann Gretsch. Pitcher. 1948. Glazed porcelain, h. 9 1/2 x dia. 5 3/4" (24.1 x 14.6 cm). Mfr.: Porzellanfabrik Arzberg, Germany. Gift of H. E. Lauffer Co., Inc. MoMA.

Greubel, Jürgen (1938–)
German industrial designer.

Biography Greubel was employed by Braun to design its products, including 1970 MP50 (Multi-press/4154) kitchen juicer (with Dieter Rams), 1971 HL 70 desk fan (with Rheinhold Weiss), and 1971 HLD 6/61 hair dryer. Other work: 1986 furniture range by Vitsœ, including the 862 chair, and 1992 Optipen medical instrument by Hoechst.
Citations 1993 award, Industrie Forum Design (iF), Hanover.

Grewenig, Leo (1898–1991)
German ceramicist; born Heusweiler (Saarland).

Training 1924–25, Bauhaus, Weimar.
Biography His work reflected the theory of simplicity of Otto Lindig, who became head of the Bauhaus pottery department in 1923. Handles added to his vessels of c. 1924 made the pieces easier to handle and lent distinction to the design.Grewenig's later work rejected the historicist forms that had influenced his earlier Bauhaus work.
Bibliography Cat., *The Bauhaus: Masters and Students*, New York: Barry Freidman, 1988.

Griegst, Arje (1938–)
Danish silversmith and designer.

Training In Rome and Paris.
Biography 1963–65, he taught at Bezalet Academy of Arts and Design, Jerusalem; from 1965, designed silver for the Georg Jensen Sølvsmedie and ceramics for Royal Copenhagen Porcelain factory.
Bibliography Cat., *Georg Jensen Silversmithy: 77 Artists, 75 Years*, Washington: Smithsonian, 1980.

Grierson, Martin (1932–)
British furniture and interior designer.

Training To 1953, Central School of Arts and Crafts, London.
Biography 1960, Grierson became an independent designer; 1975, opened a workshop in London, where his own designs were made; lectured occasionally at Central School of Art and Design.
Citations Furniture designs received numerous international awards including in 1959 Arflex-Domus competition.
Bibliography A. Best, 'Design Review: Martin Grierson: Cabinetmaker,' *Architectural Review*, vol. CLXIII, no. 974, Apr. 1978: 229–31. Robert A.M. Stern (ed.), *The International Design Yearbook*, New York: Abbeville, 1985/1986.

Grierson, Ronald (1901–)
British textile, carpet, and wallpaper designer.

Training Hammersmith School of Art; Grosvenor School of Modern Art.
Biography 1927–28, Grierson designed posters and interiors; from early 1930s, learned weaving techniques. Jean Orage wove some of his rugs and tapestry designs; others were produced by craftspeople in India in knotted wool on cotton warps that produced a close pile. His motifs included elements of Continental modernism, with influences from Synthetic Cubism. His numerous clients for textile, carpet, and wallpaper designs included Campbell Fabrics, Old Bleach Linen, S.J. Stockwell, Tomkinsons, and Wilton Royal Carpet Factory. He and his wife produced embroideries. 1945–48, he taught at Camberwell School of Art and, until 1977, at the Hampstead Garden Suburb Institute; published the book *Woven Rugs* (1952).

Exhibitions 1930s, work shown at most of major decorative- and industrial-art exhibitions, and subject of 1936 one-person exhibition, Redfern Gallery, London. Examples of his embroidery, rugs, and linoprints included in 1979-80 exhibition *Thirties: British Art and Design Before the War*, Hayward Gallery, London (catalog below).
Bibliography Cat., *Thirties: British Art and Design Before the War*, London: Arts Council of Great Britain/Hayward Gallery, 1979. Jonathan M. Woodham, *Twentieth-Century Ornament*, New York: Rizzoli, 1990.

Griffen, Smith and Co.

American pottery; located Phoenixville, Pa.

History During the peak of its popularity in 1880s, Griffen, Smith and Co. was the most successful producer of majolica in the US; 1867, at Starr and Church Streets, Phoenixville, began as the Phoenix Pottery, Kaolin and Fire Brick Co.; produced simple industrial wares and bricks for the furnaces of the Phoenix Iron Company (owned by John Griffen), located in an adjacent plant; by 1872, when the pottery was managed by W.A.H. Schreiber and J.F. Betz and Schreiber and Co., produced yellow, white, and Rockingham (manganese brown glaze) wares and terracotta animal heads used as decoration on tavern façades. 1877, the premises were leased to Levi B. Beerbower and Henry Ramsay Griffen (son of John Griffen), who produced simple white ironstone china (aka graniteware). 1879, it was reorganized as Griffen, Smith and Hill, whose partners were Henry R. Griffen, brother George S. Griffen, David Smith, and William Hill. The Griffens had graduated in civil engineering from Rensselaer Polytechnic Institute, Troy, N.Y. Smith was an Englishman who had worked at potteries in Stoke-on-Trent and Trenton, N.J. 1880, Hill left, and the name became Griffen, Smith and Co. By 1879, the pottery was producing Etruscan-type Majolica from clays in New Jersey, Pennsylvania, and Delaware. Some designs were based on English 18th-century models. Its begonia-leaf tableware and sunflower motif, developed in England in 1870s, were extremely popular in the 1880s. Also 1880s, it produced hard- and soft-paste porcelain and jetware in a black glaze with gold decoration. By 1886, it employed 50 decorators, including Susan Argue O'Neill and Susan Kelley Coyne. David Smith left 1889. J. Stewart Love (Henry Griffen's father-in-law) assumed directorship of the firm, which became Griffen, Love and Co. Due to majolica's diminished popularity at the end of 1880s and an 1890 fire that destroyed most of the plant, its majolica production ceased, and its name became Griffen China. For a time, Thomas Scott Callowhill (formerly of Royal Worcester Porcelain and Doulton) was a decorator at Griffen. The pottery closed but, 1894–1902, continued as Chester Pottery of Pennsylvania, later as Penn China and finally as Tuxedo Pottery.
Exhibitions Work shown at 1884–85 *World's Industrial and Cotton Centennial Exposition*, New Orleans.
Bibliography Edwin AtLee Barber, *The Pottery and Porcelain of the United States...*, New York: Putnam's, 1893. Henry R. Griffen, *Clay Glazes and Enamels, with a Supplement on Crazing, Its Cause and Prevention*, Indianapolis: T.A. Randall, 1896. Charles Rebert, *American Majolica, 1850–1900*, Des Moines, Iowa: Wallace-Homestead, 1981. Doreen Bolger Burke et al., *In Pursuit of Beauty: Americans and the Aesthetic Movement*, New York: The Metropolitan Museum of Art/Rizzoli, 1987.

Grigoriev, Boris (1886–1939)

Russian painter, graphic and theater artist; born Moscow; active St. Petersburg and Paris.

Training 1903–07, Stroganov School, Moscow; 1907–12, Petersburg Academy School.
Biography 1912–14, Grigoriev lived in Paris and produced drawings for St. Petersburg magazines *Satirikon*, *Novy Satirikon*, and *Lukomor'e*; returned to St. Petersburg and worked on the interior design of The Comedians' Camp cabaret and on the graphic and pictorial series *Russia*; 1919, settled in France again but was associated with various Russian publishing houses and magazines; taught, Russian Academy, Paris; died in Cannes, France.

Gris
> See Riart, Carles.

Grittel, Émile (1870–1953)

German ceramicist, painter, and sculptor; born Strasbourg (now France).

Biography Grittel was encouraged to pursue stoneware by Georges Hoentschel and Jean Carriès; 1894, when Carriès died, Grittel made a portrait of him entitled *Carriès au chapeau*; worked both in Saint-Amand-en-Puisaye with Eugène Lion and in his own Paris studio in Clichy, where he fired stoneware by Hoentschel. His own ceramics included pieces inspired by Japanese art with apples and pears and dark monochromatic glazes and gold, and vases with naturalistic reliefs.
Bibliography Yvonne Brunhammer et al., *Art Nouveau Belgium, France*, Houston: Rice University, 1976.

Griziotti, Laura (1942–)

Italian architect and designer; born Seregno; active Milan.

Training To 1966, architecture, Politecnico, Milan.
Biography 1967, she began her professional career; became a member, Associazione per il Disegno Industriale (ADI); 1967–74, collaborated with architect and designer Cini Boeri; 1974, set up her own studio, Milan; participated in the planning of 1971 industrial design exhibition of ADI at the Design Centre, Brussels; with Boeri, designed 1970–71 Serpentone seating and 1973 Strips upholstered furniture, both by Arflex; with architect Pietro Salmoiraghi, designed 1975 seat for machine operators by Misal.
Bibliography *ADI Annual 1976*, Milan: Associazione per il Disegno Industriale, 1976.

Groag, Jacqueline (1903–86)

Czech textile designer and ceramicist; born Prague; active Paris and London.

Training In Vienna.
Biography 1937, she settled in Paris, where she designed dress prints for Jeanne Lanvin, Elsa Schiaparelli, and others; 1939, settled in London and began designing textiles for clothing and furnishings; broke away from stereotypical floral prints of the time; early 1950s, designed silkscreen motifs for ceramic dinnerware produced by Johnson, Matthey, and colorful textile motifs in typical amorphic printed patterns for David Whitehead. Her designs appeared on wallpaper, laminates, carpets, greeting cards, and even Liberty book matches. She worked for Alastair Morton's Edinburgh Weavers, Bond-Worth carpets, British Rail, De la Rue, 1951 *Festival of Britain*, and others.
Citations 1984, elected Honorary Royal Designer for Industry, UK.
Bibliography Fiona MacCarthy and Patrick Nuttgens, *An Eye for Industry*, London: Lund Humphries, 1986. Michael Farr, *Design in British Industry: A Mid-Century Survey*, London: Cambridge, 1955.

Groenekan, Gerard A. van de
> See van de Groenekan, Gerald A.

Gropius, Walter Adolph (1883–1969)

German architect; born Berlin; active Germany, Britain, and the US.

Training Architecture, Technische Hochschule, Munich, 1903–05, and Berlin, 1905–07.
Biography 1908–1910, Gropius worked in the office of Peter Behrens in Berlin, where he designed office interiors and furnishings for the Lehmann department store in Cologne; 1910, set up his own architecture practice with Adolf Meyer in Berlin-Neubabelsberg; 1911, joined the Deutscher Werkbund, an association promoting the marriage of creative designers to machine production, and, 1912–14, was editor of its *Jahrbücher* (yearbook); with Meyer, designed 1911–13 Fagus shoe-last factory, Alfeld an der Leine. The factory building, a landmark in the so-called Machine Style, projected a steel skeleton and pulled the structures supporting elements to the inside, permitting extensive glass exterior walls and, thus, becoming the first consistent realization of what was later to be called the 'curtain wall.' 1913, he designed the furniture for Karl Hertzfeld in a neoclassical style reminiscent of Behrens, a diesel locomotive by Königsberg, interiors at 1913 Ghent exhibition, furnishings and interiors for 1913 Langerfeld and Mendel houses, and 1914 steel furniture (with Adolf Meyer) for battleship *Von Hindenburg*. At 1914 *Deutscher Werkbund-Ausstellung*, Cologne, Gropius displayed a model factory, office building, and machinery hall, and railway sleeping-car interior for the Deutsche Reichsbahn, and silver by Arthur Krupp in Berndorf. 1915, Gropius married writer/composer Alma Maria Mahler-Werfel (Vienna 1879–New York 1964), former wife (1902–11) of composer Gustav Mahler. (They divorced, and she married writer Franz Werfel in 1929.) 1919, Gropius was appointed director of the Grossherzoglich-Sachsen-Weimarische Hochschule für angewandte Kunst and of the

Walter Gropius, Louis McMillen, and Katherine de Souza. TAC 1 tea service. 1968. White-glazed porcelain, teapot h. 4 3/4" (12.2 cm), creamer h. 2 5/8" (6.7 cm), sugar bowl h. 3 1/16" (7.8 cm). Mfr.: Rosenthal, Germany. Courtesy Quittenbaum Kunstauktionen, Munich.

Grossherzogliche Kunstakademie in Weimar, which had been merged into a single entity to bridge the gap between art and industry, named the Staatliches Bauhaus. Of note are his 1920 Cube armchair and 1923 hanging tubular lamp for his own Bauhaus office, reminiscent of the 1920 lighting fixture by Gerrit Rietveld. 1925, the Bauhaus moved to Dessau (where he designed its 1925–26 building and the director's and department-heads' houses) and was renamed the Bauhaus Dessau. (1928, Gropius resigned; see the Bauhaus.) Concurrent with the Bauhaus, he and Meyer reestablished their architecture practice in 1920 in Berlin. 1924, Gropius cofounded Der Ring (later known as Zwölferring or Zehnerring, depending on the number of members). His major early projects included 1921–22 house for timber merchant Sommerfeld, 1921 abstract sculpture *Monument to the March Dead*, Weimar; 1922 entry *Chicago Tribune* building competition; with assistants, c. 1924–26 house and furnishings of Karl Benscheidt Jr.; with Ernst Neufert, produced some white-painted wood furniture. 1925–34, Gropius was active in his own practice, working on the Siemensstadt housing estate; a prefabricated house at 1927 *Weissenhofsiedlung*, Stuttgart; 1925 furniture for the Feder department store, Berlin; 1929–33, conventional bodies by Adler Automobilwerk; was assisted by Marcel Breuer, Herbert Bayer, and László Moholy-Nagy on 1930 *Deutscher Werkbund-Ausstellung*, Paris; 1934, settled in Britain, where he worked in association with E. Maxwell Fry 1934–36; 1936–37, was a partner in an architecture practice with Fry; published *The New Architecture and the Bauhaus* (1935). After discussions between Gropius and Jack Pritchard 1935, Pritchard's firm Isokon began furniture production. 1936, Gropius became controller of design at Jack Pritchard's Isokon furniture company in the UK, for which Gropius designed a 1935 perforated-aluminum trash bin and 1936 plywood chair and table. Along with other refugees, he lived in Jack Pritchard's 1934 Lawn Road flats, Hampstead, London. 1937, he left London and settled permanently in the US. Breuer took over the position. 1937–52, Gropius was professor of architecture, Graduate School of Design, Harvard University; built his own 1937–38 house, Lincoln, Mass.; 1937–42, was in partnership with Marcel Breuer, also an emigré; 1946, cofounded The Architects' Collaborative (TAC), Cambridge, Mass. TAC exemplified his belief in teamwork such as, for example, with Louis McMillen and Katherine de Souza on the design of 1969 TAC 1 tea set and 1969 TAC 2 coffee set produced by Rosenthal in Germany. A version of the tea set was produced with decoration known as Bauhaus Homage II by Herbert Bayer. Rosenthal also produced 1975 Gropius rainbow-patterned dinnerware designed with Otto Piene of TAC. Architecture included (with Breuer) housing in Chelsea, London; 1937 Woods house (for Jack Donaldson), Shipbourne, Kent; processing laboratories, Denham, Buckinghamshire; 1937–39 Impington Village College, Cambridgeshire, and numerous unrealized projects. His work in the US included 1952 Pan Am Building (now Met Life), New York, and 1957 Temple of Oheb Shalom, Baltimore, Md. A proponent of standardized elements for house construction, he was against 'the idea of prefabrication... seized by manufacturing firms who came up with the stifling project of mass producing whole house types instead of component parts only' (Herbert, 1984: 318). He died in Boston. His 1922–23 armchair for the Faguswerk in Alfeld and armchair for his own Bauhaus office (and derived sofa) are being reproduced by Tecta in Lauenförde, Germany.
Exhibitions/citations Work shown at 1969 Bauhaus exhibition, Stuttgart. Subject of exhibition, Zürich; 1972 touring exhibition, sponsored by the International Exhibitions Foundation; 1974 touring exhibition, organized by the Bauhaus-Archiv; 1992 *Walter Gropius Total Theatre Design*, Busch-Reisinger Museum, Cambridge, Mass. TAC 1 tea set received 1969 International Vicenza Prize. Other citations: gold medal (interiors), 1913 *Exposition Universelle et Industrielle*, Ghent; 1954 Matarazzo International Grand Prize in Architecture, São Paulo; 1956 Royal Gold Medal, Royal Institute of British Architects; 1958 award, *Grosses Verdienstkreuz mit Stern*; 1959 gold medal, American Institute of Architects (AIA); 1961 Gold Albert Medal, Royal Society of Arts; 1963 Gurlitt Medal; 1947, elected Honorary Royal Designer for Industry, UK.
Bibliography Walter Gropius, *Idee und Aufbau des Staatlichen Bauhauses*, Munich and Weimar: Bauhausverlag, 1923. James Marston Fitch, *Walter Gropius*, New York and London: George Braziller, 1960. Marcel Franciscono, *Walter Gropius and the Creation of the Bauhaus in Weimar*, Urbana, Ill.: University of Illinois, 1971. Gilbert Herbert, *Dream of the Factory-Made House: Walter Gropius and Konrad Wachsmann*, Cambridge, Mass.: MIT, 1984. Reginald Isaacs, *Gropius: An Illustrated Biography of the Creator of the Bauhaus*, Boston: Bullfinch, 1983 and subsequent eds. Cat., Stuhlmuseum Burg Beverungen, *Der Kragstuhl*, Berlin: Alexander, 1986. Dieter Hezel (ed.), *Architekten, Walter Gropius* (bibliography), Stuttgart: IRB, 1995. Sabine Kraft, *Gropius baut privat: Seine Wohnhäuser in Dessau (1925/26) und Lincoln, Mass. (1938)*, Marburg: Jonas, 1997.

Gross, Karl (1869–1934)

German sculptor and silversmith; active Dresden and Munich.

Training Under Fritz von Miller; studied Kunstgewerbeschule, Munich.
Biography In 1898, he became professor, Kunstgewerbeschule, Dresden. Theodor Heinze and Hermann Ehrenlechner of Dresden produced his silver designs. He designed furniture and porcelain. His cutlery patterns were produced by Bruckmann & Söhne, Heilbronn. He worked for the Vereinigte Werkstätten für Kunst im Handwerk, Munich.
Bibliography Annelies Krekel-Aalberse, *Art Nouveau and Art Déco Silver*, New York: Abrams, 1989. Cat., *Metallkunst*, Berlin: Bröhan Museum, 1990: 588.

Grossman, Greta Magnusson (b. Greta Magnusson 1906–1999)

Swedish designer and architecture; active California.

Training In furniture, textiles, and metalwork; Kungliga Tekniska Högskolan, Stockholm.

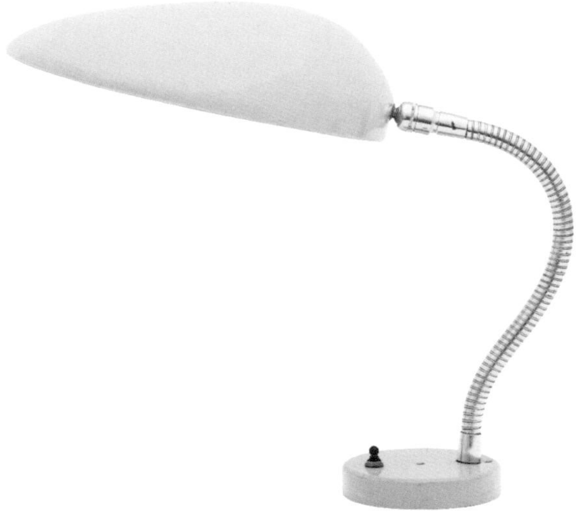

Greta Magnusson Grossman. Lighting Fixture. c. 1948. Grey enamel reflector and base, l. 27 1/2" (69.9 cm), shade l. 14" (35.6 cm). Mfr.: Ralph O. Smith Co., US. Gift of the mfr. MoMA.

Biography After her earlier studies, she worked with a cabinetmaker for a year and, subsequently, opened her own store and upholstery workshop and simultaneously attended the royal technical school; c. 1939 with her husband, visited the US and stayed on permanently in Los Angeles; 1940s–1950s, decorated houses and shops in California in a Swedish modern style popular in that US state at the time, which were widely published in John Entenza's *Arts & Architecture* magazine; by 1942, was designing for Barker Brothers and, during the next two decades, for Glenn of California, Modern Line, and Sherman Bertram, incorporating rope, natural wood, and cane seats into her furniture work; designed early 1950s range of lighting by Ralph O. Smith and c. 1952 Wilshire Group of furniture by Martin/Brattrud; 1950s, taught industrial design, University of California, and Art Center School (today Art Center College of Design), both Los Angeles; designed a number of interiors and houses, including her own.

Grot, Anton (1884–1974)

Film set designer; born in Kelbasin, Poland; active the US.

Biography Grot's earliest film designs were from 1913 at the Lubin studio, having emigrated to the US in 1909. His ink and charcoal sketches showed meticulous continuity from sequence to sequence, lighting positions, and camera angles. As Warner Brothers' supervision art director, he designed the precisely paced and organized films of Busby Berkeley. Grot's sense of space, starkness, and economy can be seen in Berkeley's *Gold Diggers of 1933* (1933), *Footlight Parade* (1933), and *Gold Diggers of 1935* (1935). Notable is Grot's gigantic setting for the 'mechanical ballet' in *Lilies of the Field* (1930), in which actress Corinne Griffith becomes the radiator mascot on a giant automobile. For the huge nightclub setting for Berkeley's 'Lullaby of Broadway' musical number in *Gold Diggers of 1935*, Grot went far beyond the Art Déco style, while evoking German Expressionism.
Bibliography Howard Mandelbaum and Eric Myers, *Screen Deco: A Celebration of High Style in Hollywood*, New York: St. Martin's, 1985.

Grotell, Maija (b. Majlis Grotell 1899–1973)

Finnish ceramicist; born Helsingfors, Finland; active Finland and the US.

Training To c. 1920–21 under Alfred William Finch, Taideteollinen korkeakoulu, Helsinki; postgraduate studies in ceramics and textiles.
Biography 1927, Grotell emigrated to the US; lived in New York and travelled to Alfred (N.Y.) University to study pottery under Charles Fergus Binns; 1928–38, was associated with Craft School of Henry Settlement, New York; 1938–66, was head of ceramics department, Cranbrook Academy of Art, Bloomfield Hills, Mich., where students included Peter Voulkos, Carlton Ball, Harvey Littleton, and Charles Lakofsky. She singlehandedly shifted pottery from an avocation to a profession. Grotell produced a large body of one-of-a-kind pottery; 1966, retired; and died in Pontiac, Mich. Maija Grotell Papers housed at Syracuse (N.Y.) University Library.
Exhibitions/citations Ceramics shown at numerous exhibitions, including 2001 venue, Bard Graduate Center, New York (catalog below). More than 25 major awards.
Bibliography Robert Judson Clark et al, *Design in America: The Cranbrook Vision 1925–1950*, New York: Abrams, 1983. R. Craig Miller, *Modern Design, 1890–1990*, New York: Abrams, 1990. Cat., Pat Kirkham (ed.), *Women Designers in the USA 1900–2000: Diversity and Difference*, New Haven: Yale University, 2001.

Groult, André (1884–1967)

French furniture, textile, and wallpaper designer; born and active Paris.

Biography 1910s and 1920s, Groult worked in the traditional 18th- and early 19th-century style associated with Louis Süe and André Mare, with furniture that evoked a feeling of comfort and security. 1912, he became interested in elegant wallpaper and toile (boldly printed, ornate fabric patterns). He published his own drawings as well as those of Marie Laurencin, d'Espagnat, Albert Laprade, Dresa (André Saglio), and Paul Iribe. His masterpiece was probably the anthropomorphic *chiffonier* in shagreen, shown at the 1925 Paris *Exposition*. 1925, he produced silver designs for Christofle. He was fond of furniture and walls in straw-yellow veneer.
Exhibitions From 1910, work shown at editions of Salon d'Automne and at Salons of Société des Artistes Décorateurs. Designed lady's bedroom in Une Ambassade Française and parts of the Fontaine and Christofle/Baccarat pavilions, including the musical instrument and garden sections of the Grand Palais, at 1925 *Exposition Internationale des Arts Décoratifs et Industriels Modernes*, Paris.
Bibliography Léon Deshairs (intro.), *Modern French Decorative Art: A Collection of Examples of Modern French Decoration*, Paris: Albert Lévy, c. 1925–30. Victor Arwas, *Art Déco*, New York: Abrams, 1980. Yvonne Brunhammer, *Art Déco Style*, London: Academy, 1983. Pierre Kjellberg, *Art déco: les maîtres du mobilier, le décor des paquebots*, Paris: Amateur, 1986. Félix Marcilhac, *André Groult (1884–1966): décorateur-ensemblier du XXème siècle*, Paris: Amateur, 1997.

Groupe 7
> See Gruppo Sette.

Gruber, Jacques (1870–1936)

Alsacian stained-glass artist, designer, and teacher; born Sundhausen, Alsace.

Training École National Supérieure des Beaux-Arts, Paris, under Gustave Moreau.
Biography Gruber was distinguished as a designer in the Art Nouveau idiom; 1894–97, worked for the Daum glassworks, designing complex figurative vases; learned the art of engraving, rendering decorations for Wagner's operas; taught and profoundly influenced painter and tapestry designer Jean Lurçat, poster designer Paul Colin, and architect André Lurçat at École des Beaux-Arts, Nancy; designed furniture for Majorelle, ceramics for the Mougin brothers, and bookbindings for René Wiener; was a founder of the École de Nancy; 1900, set up his own practice to design and manufacture furniture, acid-etched cameo glass that was incorporated into his furniture pieces, wallpaper, and stained glass, closing in 1914. The glass for the tea room and cupola of Les Galeries Lafayette department store, Paris, are by Gruber. His interest in furniture gradually diminished, although he had previously designed models with Adolphe Chanaux. 1914, he moved to a studio in the Villa d'Alésia, Paris, and concentrated on secular and religious stained glass in a full-blown geometric style retaining figuration. His commissions included the choir of the cathedral in Verdun, steel factory in Nancy, and French embassies. 1936, his son took over the business.
Exhibitions Work shown at Salons of Société des Artistes Décorateurs from 1908 and Société des Artistes Français, Salon d'Automne, and at Musée Galliéra, Paris. Stained-glass panels were in a number of pavilions and shown at 1925 *Exposition Internationale des Arts Décoratifs et Industriels Modernes*, Paris. Received numerous awards.
Bibliography Yvonne Brunhammer et al., *Art Nouveau Belgium, France*, Houston: Rice University, 1976, biblio.

Grueby, William H. (1867–1925); Grueby Pottery

American potter; active Boston.

Biography From 1882, Grueby worked at the J. and J.G. Low Art Tile Works, Chelsea, Mass., until c. 1890, when he organized a short-

lived company which produced architectural faïence in Revere, Mass.; 1892, (with Eugene R. Atwood) established Atwood and Grueby, part of the larger Fiske, Coleman and Co., where architectural ceramics and glazed bricks for interior and exterior decoration were produced; supervised the Fiske, Coleman pavilion at 1893 *World's Columbian Exposition*, Chicago, where he became familiar with the flambé technique of French artist-potters Ernest Chaplet and Auguste Delaherche; after Atwood and Grueby was dissolved in 1893, established his own firm, Grueby Faïence, Boston, and produced architectural faïence and terracotta tiles inspired by 15th-century Italian ceramics by Luca della Robbia, Moorish designs, and Chinese ceramics; 1897, discovered the matt glazes for which he became well known, and began to produce art pottery. The matt glaze was received with enthusiasm by the public and pottery manufacturers. Grueby produced some surprisingly modern forms in the Arts and Crafts idiom. His wares were admired by Gustav Stickley, in whose journal *The Craftsman* Grueby's work was praised. 1897–1902, George Prentiss Kendrick was the designer at the pottery, followed by French architect Addison B. Le Boutiller. Grueby was responsible for the glazes. From 1899, the art pottery had the Grueby Pottery mark, the Grueby Faïence mark appearing only on architectural faïence. Siegfried Bing in Paris, through his gallery/shop L'Art Nouveau, sold Grueby's works to prestigious collections including the Musée des Arts Décoratifs, Paris. Decorations were drawn by women graduates of the School of the Museum of Fine Arts, Boston, and the Cowles Art School. Motifs were based on vegetal images suggested by Grueby's green glaze and its dense texture. 1907, the busi-ness was restructured as Grueby Pottery. Grueby incorporated another pottery whose production was limited to architectural faïence. After a 1913 fire, Grueby Faïence and Tile was rebuilt and production continued until 1919, when the firm was acquired by C. Pardee Works, Perth Amboy, N.J.
Exhibitions/citations Work shown at 1895 exhibition, Architectural League of New York; 1897 exhibition of Boston Society of Arts and Crafts; 1900 *Exposition Universelle* (gold medal for enamels and glazes, silver medal for pottery design, gold medal for matt enamels), Paris; 1901 *Pan-American Exposition* (jointly with Gustav Stickley), Buffalo; 1901 exhibition, St. Petersburg; 1902 *Esposizione Internazionale d'Arte Decorativa Moderna*, Turin. Showed 40 objects (with French architect designer Addison Le Boutillier) and received grand prize, 1904 *Louisiana Purchase Exposition*, St. Louis. Work subject of 1981 exhibit, Everson Museum of Art, Syracuse, N.Y.; 1994 exhibit, Hood Museum of Art, Hanover, N.H., US. Received numerous medals during its active history.
Bibliography Yvonne Brunhammer et al., *Art Nouveau Belgium, France*, Houston: Rice University, 1976. Robert W. Blasberg, *The Ceramics of William H. Grueby: Catalog of an Exhibition at the Everson Museum of Art*, Syracuse: Everson Museum of Art, 1981. Cat., *American Art Pottery*, New York: Cooper-Hewitt Museum, 1987. Susan J. Montgomery, *The Ceramics of William H. Grueby: The Spirit of the New Idea in Artistic Handicraft*, Lambertville, N.J.: Arts & Crafts Quarterly, 1993. *Grueby Pottery: A New England Arts and Crafts Venture—The William Curry Collection*, Hanover, N.H.: Dartmouth College, 1994.

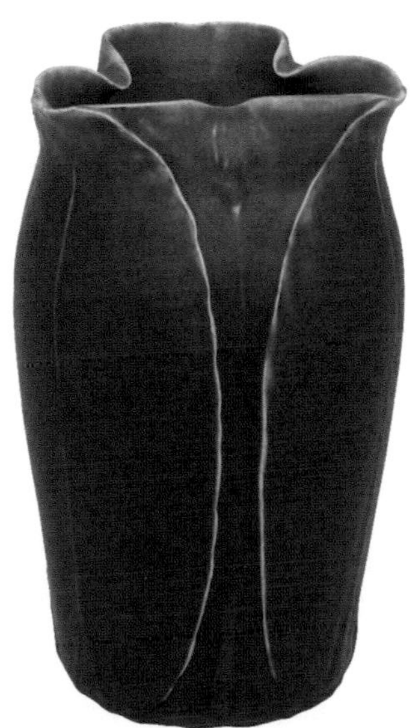

Grueby Pottery. Vase. 1898–1902. Pottery, h. 7 3/4" (19.7 cm). Mfr.: Grueby Pottery, US. Department Purchase Fund. MoMA.

Gruppo Architetti Urbanisti 'Città Nuova.' Nesso table lamp. 1964. Fiberglass-reinforced polyester resin, h. 13 x dia. 21" (33 x 53.3 cm). Mfr.: Artemide, Italy. Gift of the mfr. MoMA.

Gruppo Architetti Urbanisti 'Città Nuova'
Italian design group.

History The group is best known for 1967 Nesso table and wall lamp (with Giancarlo Mattioli) by Artemide. The fixture, reflecting the aesthetics of the 1960s and the popularity of orange at the time, was the result of a competition sponsored by *Domus* magazine. The ABS plastic was injection molded and then hot-curved in stages.
Bibliography *Progetti e architetture, 1961–1991: Gruppo Architetti Urbanisti 'Città Nuova,'* Milan: Electa, 1992.

Gruppo G14
Italian studio.

History Active from late 1960 in so-called Anti-Design initially as well as more orthodox work individually outside the group and with others, the consortium was formed by young architects Gianfranco Facchetti (1939–), Umberto Orsoni (1940–), Gianni Pareschi (1940–), Giuseppe Pensotti (1939–), and Roberto Ubaldi (1940–). Due to its unusual nature and a statement of the Anti-Design of the time, the group's 1970 Fiocco undulating lounge chair (by Busnelli) was widely published. Orsoni (with Angelo Cortesi) designed certain installations/functions at Malpensa and Linate airports, near Milan, and various structures (with Facchetti and other architects). Gianni Pareschi's furniture clients have included Estel Office Furniture Division Bambini Office, Ciatti, Scavolini, and others. He and Ubaldi designed 1997 interiors of Jerusalem's Club Hotel Eilat, the first theme hotel in and the largest in Middle East. Pensotti and Ubaldi (with Marcello Pozzi) designed 1987 urban train station, Ferrovie Nord, Milan.
Bibliography 'Milano Ferrovie Nord—SSU,' *L'Arca*, no. 7, June 1987.

Gruppo 9999
Italian architecture and design group; active Florence.

History 1967, the group was founded by Giorgio Birelli, Carlo Caldini, Fabrizio Fiumi, and Paolo Galli in Florence to practice Radical architecture and art, espousing a kind of ecological utopia. 1968, its members staged a 'design happening' on Ponte Vecchio, Florence. Another of its efforts included the interior environment for the 1969 Space Electronic discothèque, Florence. 1972, at the large dance hall in Florence that the group managed, it organized the seminar 'S-S-Space World Festival No. 1' on conceptual and behavioral architecture, attended by Italian and foreign participants. It published the book *Memories of Architecture* (1973).
Exhibitions A theoretical project shown at 1972 *Italy: The New Do-*

mestic Landscape, The Museum of Modern Art, New York. Work included in *Radicals: architettura e design 1960–75*, 1996 (6th) Mostra Internazionale di Archittettura, Venice.
Bibliography Andrea Branzi, *La casa calda: esperienze del nuovo disegno italiano*, Milan: Idea, 1982. Penny Sparke, *Introduction to Design and Culture in the Twentieth Century*, London: Allen & Unwin, 1986.

Gruppo Sette

Italian architecture association.

History 1926, Gruppo Sette (group [of] seven) was organized by the young Milanese architects Luigi Figini, Guido Frette, Sebastiano Larco, Adalberto Libera, Gino Pollini, Carlo Enrico Rava, and Giuseppe Terragni. They published a four-part manifesto in the journal *Rassegna*, launching the Italian Rationalist movement in architecture with an attempt to relate the European avant-garde movement in architecture with Italy's classical past. The fascist regime opposed the group from its first exhibition of Rationalist architecture, 1927; they were accused of being 'fashionable Europeans' by Edoardo Persico. 1928, the group Movimento Architettura Razionale (MAR) was started by the Gruppo Sette. The situation was complicated by the formation of Movimento Italiano per l'Architettura Razionale (MIAR), the publication of P.M. Bardi's *Rapporto sull architettura (per Mussolini)*, the establishment of Bardi's journals *Quadrante* and *Casa-bella* (with Giuseppe Pagano and Persico as editors of the latter), and Gruppo Sette's own exhibitions in New York and abroad. The Italian avant-garde scene around this time included elements of the Futurists' second phase and the efforts of Gio Ponti and his journal *Domus*. The fascist regime set up a rival to the MIAR.
Exhibitions Group's work first shown at 1927 (3rd) Monza *Esposizione Biennale delle Arti Decorative e Industriali Moderne* and at its 1930 (4th) event, 1927 *Werkbund-Ausstellung*, Stuttgart and elsewhere.
Bibliography Pietro Betta, 'Il "Gruppo 7" e l'architettura nuova' in *L'Architettura italiana*, year XII, no. 2. Barbie Campbell-Cole and Tim Benton (eds.), *Tubular Steel Furniture*, London: The Art Book Company, 1979: 46–47. Hanno-Walter Kruft, 'Rationalismus in der Architektur—eine Begriffsklärung,' *Architectura*, vol. 9, 1979. Vittorio Magnago Lampugnani (ed.), *Encyclopedia of 20th-Century Architecture*, New York: Abrams, 1986: 141. Penny Sparke, *Design in Italy, 1870 to the Present*, New York: Abbeville, 1988. Richard A. Etlin, *Modernism in Italian Architecture, 1890–1940*, Cambridge: MIT, 1991.

Gruppo Strum

Italian architecture and design organization.

History Based in Turin, Gruppo Strum was founded in 1966 by Pietro Derossi, Giorgio Ceretti, Carla Giammarco, Riccardo Rosso, and Maurizio Vogliazzo. It became an active participant in Italy's Radical Design movement of the late 1960s; used the technique of handing out picture stories to explain the socio-political background of the architectural culture of the time. Its members took an experimental approach, using architecture as an instrument for political propaganda. Its 1971 Pratone (big meadow) furniture piece, designed by Derossi, Ceretti, and Rosso and produced by Gufram, was made of flexible polyurethane foam painted green, and was one of the few examples from an Anti-Design group actually to be produced. 'Gruppo Strum' was derived from 'GRUPPO per una architettura STRUMentale' (group for instrumental architecture).
Exhibitions Mounted Mediatory City shown at 1972 *Italy: The New Domestic Landscape*, The Museum of Modern Art, New York. Work included in *Radicals: Architettura e Design 1960–75*, 1996 (6th) Mostra Internazionale di Archittettura, Venice.
Bibliography Andrea Branzi, *La casa calda: esperienze del nuovo disegno italiano*, Milan: Idea, 1982. Penny Sparke, *Introduction to Design and Culture in the Twentieth Century*, London: Allen & Unwin, 1986. Cat., Hans Wichmann, *Italien Design 1945 bis heute*, Munich: Die Neue Sammlung, 1988.

Gualtierotti, Gianfranco (1944–..)

Italian furniture producer; born Rome.

Training To 1964, I.T.I.S. A. Pacinotti (technical school), Pistoia.
Biography 1967, Gualtierotti became active in the mass production of furniture and eventually began working for major firms and alongside various architects and designers. 1970–74, headed the engineering office of a chemical company,. working with furniture makers. Collaborated on the design of airline seats, including those fitted in European DC-10s, European Airbuses, and the Italian president's DC-9. 1975, he was the director of a large furniture manufacturer; 1977, became a freelance designer chiefly of objects and seating systems; since 1985, worked with Alessandro Mazzoni Delle Stelle.
Citations 1985, first prize, Italian Design Competition, Rome; 1987, second prize, NeoCon, Chicago.
> See Mazzoni Delle Stelle, Alessandro.

Guariche, Pierre (1926–1995)

French furniture designer; born Paris.

Training École Nationale Supérieure des Arts Décoratifs, Paris.
Biography c. 1949–52, Guariche worked for Marcel Gascoin, where he met Michel Mortier; 1953–57, was associated with Mortier and Joseph A. Motte; they signed their designs 'A.R.P.' Guariche designed inexpensive serially-produced furniture models that were both practical and soberly elegant. 1950s, his furniture became known for its use of metal, including lacquered tubular steel, and modular elements. For his chairs, he pioneered the use of plastic foam and 'no-sag' and 'free-span' springs. The 1952–53 Tonneau was the first molded-plywood chair commercially produced in France, edited by Steiner in Paris (followed by the similar 1953 Tulipe chair). His lamps of the 1950s were produced by Disderot, France. His work also included the Catherine hemispherical pivoting chair and the Radar foam-rubber chair. 1960 Vallée blanche lounge chair was produced by Huchers Minvielle and compared to Le Corbusier's 1929 lounge chair. Other furniture was produced by Airborne and Steiner. Guariche died in Bandol.
Bibliography Pascal Renous, *Portraits de créateurs*, Paris: H. Vial, 1969. Yolande Amic, *Intérieurs: le mobilier français, 1945–1964*, Paris: Regard/VIA, 1983: 86–87. Patrick Favardin, *Les décorateurs des années 50*, Paris: Norma, 2002: 212.

Gudme-Leth, Marie (1910–)

Danish textile designer; active Copenhagen.

Training Industrial Art School for Women, Copenhagen; Det Kongelige Danske Kunstakademi, Copenhagen; Kunstgewerbeschule, Frankfurt.
Biography 1931–48, Gudme-Leth was head of the textile department, Kunsthåndværkerskolen, Copenhagen; 1935, cofounded Dansk Kattuntrykkeri, Copenhagen, where she was director until 1940; printed bold graphic patterns, some based on folk themes; 1940, set up her own silkscreen workshop for printing textiles.
Exhibitions/citations Work shown at 1954–57 *Design in Scandinavia*, touring the US; 1956–59 *Neue Form aus Dänemark*, touring Germany; 1958 *Formes Scandinaves*, Musée des Arts Décoratifs, Paris; 1982 exhibition, New York (catalog below). Gold medals, 1937 *Exposition Internationale des Arts et Techniques dans la Vie Moderne*, Paris, and 1951 (9th) Triennale di Milano.
Bibliography Cat., David Revere McFadden (ed.), *Scandinavian Modern Design 1880–1980*, New York: Abrams, 1982.

Gudmundsson, Annika (1951–)

Swedish industrial designer; active Gothenburg and Stockholm.

Training 1971–75, industrial design, University of Gothenburg.
Biography 1977, she joined the Industridesign Kunsult group, Gothenburg, where she executed designs for graphics and products, including objects rendered in metal and plastics by Guldsmeds; from 1981, was an industrial designer at Made Arkitektkontor in Stockholm.
Bibliography Cat., Kathryn B. Hiesinger and George H. Marcus III (eds.), *Design Since 1945*, Philadelphia: Philadelphia Museum of Art, 1983.

Gué
> See Champion, Georges.

Guéden, Colette (1905–1999)

French object, furniture, jewelry, and interior designer; born Cholon, Vietnam.

Biography 1931 when René Guilleré died, Guéden and Guilleré's widow Charlotte Chauchet-Guilleré became codirectors of Primavera, the decorating studio of Au Printemps department store, Paris. 1939, Guéden was sole director of Primavera; 1947, was commissioned by the wife of French president Vincent Auriol to design a child's room in the Palais de l'Élysée; 1965, organized a large exhibition for the centenary of Printemps that influenced public taste in furniture design.

Exhibitions Work shown at 1928–40 Salons, Salon des Artistes Décorateurs.
Bibliography *Ensembles mobiliers*, Paris: Charles Moreau, vol. 6, nos. 30–31, 1945. Patrick Favardin, *Les décorateurs des années 50*, Paris: Norma, 2002: 30.

Guénot, Albert-Lucien (1894–1993)

French decorator and furniture designer; born Arcueil-Cachan.

Training École Boulle, Paris.
Biography Guénot worked as a designer in the workshop of Maurice Dufrêne, where he became familiar with the Style Moderne; 1914–18, worked in sculptured wood with Laurent Malclès; from 1920, in sculpture with Paul Follot; 1922, for ironworker Edgar Brandt; and briefly for architect René Crevel. From 1923 and for the rest of his career, he was at the Pomone design studio of Bon Marché department store, Paris; became the *chef d'atelier* under director Follot; 1932 succeeded René Prou as its director, remaining there until 1955. Guénot designed the interiors of the hotels Château Frontenac (with decorative painting by Dumouchel) and George V, Paris, 1935 oceanliner *Normandie*, 1961 oceanliner *France*, and offices of Maison Militaire de l'Élysée. He died in Paris.
Exhibitions From 1920, work shown at Salons of Société des Artistes Décorateurs; from 1927, Salons d'Automne; 1925 *Exposition Internationale des Arts Décoratifs et Industriels Modernes*, Paris; 1931 *Exposition Coloniale*, Paris; 1937 *Exposition Internationale des Arts et Techniques dans la Vie Moderne*, Paris; installments of Salon des Arts Ménagers; numerous exhibitions abroad.
Bibliography *Restaurants, dancing, cafés, bars*, Paris: Charles Moreau, no. 38, *Ensembles mobiliers*, vol. 2, Paris: Charles Moreau, 1937. R. Moutard-Uldry, *Dictionnaire des artistes décorateurs*, Paris: Mobilier et décoration, 1953–57: Nov. 1953. *Ensembles mobiliers*, Paris: Charles Moreau, nos. 27–28, 1954. Pierre Kjellberg, *Art Déco: Les Maîtres du mobilier, le décor des paquebots*, Paris: Amateur, 1986: 83–84. *Meubles, 1920–1937*, Paris: Musée d'Art Moderne de la Ville de Paris, 1986.

Pierre Guariche. Tonneau side chairs. 1952–53. Painted steel tubing, painted bent plywood, and vinyl, 31 1/8 x 20 1/8 x 17 7/8" (79 x 51 x 45 cm). Mfr.: Steiner, France. Courtesy Quittenbaum Kunstauktionen, Munich.

Guens, Van
> See Rameckers, Clemens.

Guenzi, Carlo (1941–)

Italian industrial designer; born Venice; active Milan.

Training To 1966, Faculty of Architecture, Politecnico, Milan.
Biography 1965–76, Guenzi was editor of journal *Casabella*; designed a system of institutional infant furniture produced by Jolli; was a member, Associazione per il Disegno Industriale, (ADI); organized roundtable conferences in Rimini, San Marino, and Verrucchio; 1975 (8th) and 1976 (9th) Biennale del Mobile, Mariano Comese and Cantù; 1973 *Design als Postulat* and 1976 *Gestaltung von Kindertagesstatten*, Internationales Design Zentrum (IDZ), Berlin; 1974 *Contemporanea Incontri Internazionali d'Arte*, Rome; 1975 avant-garde and popular-culture exhibition, Bologna; 1976 conference on conditions in the workplace and ergonometrics, Pescara.
Bibliography *ADI Annual 1976*, Milan: Associazione per il Disegno Industriale, 1976.

Guerriero, Alessandro (1943–)

Italian architect and designer; born and active Milan.

Training Architecture, Politecnico, Milan, refusing his to-be-granted 1968 degree.
Biography 1976, Guerriero cofounded Studio Alchimia, which became a vital Italian avant-garde design group; produced the 1977 Endless Furniture concept, a mixture of design, fashion, and performance devised and directed by Alessandro Mendini with contributions by designers Andrea Branzi, Achille Castiglioni, Ugo La Pietra, Ettore Sottsass, and others, and painters Sandro Chia, Enzo Cucchi, Nicola de Maria, and Mimmo Paladino; 1983, edited *Décoration*, Paris; 1982, cofounded Domus Academy, Milan; from 1984, was artistic director at Zabro; 1988, opened the store Museo Alchimia, Milan, a retail outlet for Alchimia's products. His architecture includes 1986 civic tower, Gibellina, Sicily; 1988 Casa della Felicità (for the Alessi family); 1995 Museum of Art (with Coop Himmelblau, Michele De Lucchi, Alessandro Mendini, Philippe Starck), Groningen, Netherlands. 1987, he cofounded Domus Academy, Milan; 1992, established Museo del Nuovo Design, in turn inspiring 1992 *Nuovo Bel Design* exhibition, Triennale of Milan. Recent work has included a football stadium, Milanofiori; a building to celebrate 30 years of the Sirte canal, Libyan desert; exhibition in Turin to commemorate 100 years of Fiat; Radiosity, Milan, from 1996; Museum of Communication for Benetton; 1999, founding of Futurarium, a design, art, and architecture school in Milan.
Exhibitions Among many with Alchimia, *Città Alchimia* (a large-scale venue, in collaboration with the former East-German town, which explored the problem central to Guerriero's thought: man as a sum of individualities), Erfurt.
Bibliography Barbara Radice, *Elogio del banale*, Milan: Studio forma Alchimia, 1980. Andrea Branzi, *Architettura innamorata*, Milan: Studio Forma Alchimia, 1980. Andrea Branzi, *Moderno postmoderno millenario*, Milan: Studio Forma Alchimia, 1980. Rosa Maria Rinaldi, *Il mobile infinito*, Milan: Alchimia Editore, 1981. Fulvio Irace, *Stanze un'idea per la casa*, Milan: Alchimia, 1981. Helmut Gsoellpointner, Angela Hareiter, *Laurids Ortner, Design ist Unsichtbar*, Vienna: Löker, 1981. Guia Sambonet, *Alchimia*, Turin: Allemandi, 1986. Kazuko Sato, *Alchimia*, Berlin: Taco, 1988. Gillo Dorfles, *Il kitsch antologia del cattivo gusto*, Milan: Mazzotta, 1990. Stefano Casciani, *Design in Italia 1950–1980*, Milan: Gian Carlo Politi Editore, 1991. Giacinto di Pietrantonio, *Incontri con architettura e design*, Milan: Gian Carlo Politi, 1991.
> See Alchimia.

Guévrékian, Gabriel (1900–1970)

Turkish architect and furniture designer; born Constantinople (now Istanbul).

Training From 1921, Kunstgewerbeschule, Vienna.
Biography 1919–21, he practiced architecture with Oskar Strnad and Josef Hoffmann in Vienna, executing small houses and interiors; 1921, moved to Paris, where he worked with Henri Sauvage; 1922–26, collaborated with Robert Mallet-Stevens and designed five residences on the rue Mallet-Stevens, Auteuil, and residences of Jacques Doucet in Marley-sur-Seine and Paul Poiret in Melun-sur-Seine. 1923, through Mallet-Stevens, Guévrékian designed the 'Cubist garden' of the villa of vicomte and vicomtesse de Noailles, Hyères; 1920s, designed furniture in a stark, somewhat quirky, modern style, often incorporating plated bent-metal tubing; 1928, cofounded Congrès Internationaux d'Archi-

tecture Moderne (CIAM), and, 1930, Union des Artistes Modernes (UAM). The decorating firm D.I.M. commissioned him to execute various lighting fixtures for its interiors. For the lighting requirements of his own interiors, he consulted with lighting engineer André Salomon. A 1929 Guévrékian-Salomon lighting fixture may have been inspired by the earlier 1928 Couronne lumineuse model by Eugène Printz. 1927, he designed the renovated Paris apartment of photographer Thérèse Bonney, 1937–40, worked in the office of architects Connell, Ward and Lucas, London; 1946–48, was instructor and head of the architecture department, French Academy, Saarbrücken, Germany; designed 1948–49 *brise-soleils* type office building, Casablanca; settling in the US in 1948, taught architecture, Alabama Polytechnic Institute, Auburn, Ala.
Exhibitions Water and Light garden (next to Konstantin Melnikov's Russian pavilion) shown at 1925 *Exposition Internationale des Arts Décoratifs et Industriels Modernes*, Paris, where he was a member of the architecture jury and vice-president of the musical instruments sections. As a member of UAM, showed at its 1930 (1st) exhibition (a 1930 hotel project in Buenos Aires); 1931 exhibition (a hammock and various architecture projects), Galerie Georges Petit, Paris; 1932 UAM exhibition (a hotel project in Juan-les-Pins and metal window prototype); 1933 UAM exhibition (a service station model for the Société des Pétroles in Languedoc).
Bibliography Alastair Duncan, *Art Nouveau and Art Déco Lighting*, New York: Simon & Schuster, 1978. Arlette Barré-Despond, *UAM*, Paris: Regard, 1986. Elisabeth Vitou et al., *Gabriel Guévrékian une autre architecture moderne*, Paris: Connivences, 1987. Cat., *Les années UAM 1929–1958*, Paris: Musée des Arts Décoratifs, 1988.

Guffanti, Luigi Maria (1948–)

Italian industrial designer; born and active Milan.

Biography 1970, Guffanti began his professional career and has been active in public housing, tourism, and interior architecture; served as the editor of journals *Milanocasa* and *Sinàat Italia*. He became a member, Associazione per il Disegno Industriale (ADI). Some of Guffanti's clients have included Bora (camping trailers), Candle-Riboli (lighting), Cantieri Sciallino (motor yacht), Elnagh (mobile homes and trailers/caravans), and a number of others have followed.
Bibliography *ADI Annual 1976*, Milan: Associazione per il Disegno Industriale, 1976.

Gufram

Italian furniture manufacturer; located Balangero.

History 1952 in Turin, the Gugliermetto brothers founded Gugliermetto Fratelli Mobile, a small firm for the artisanal production of chairs. 1966, the name was changed to the acronym, Gufram, based on GUliermetto FRAtelli Mobile, when the firm began to make high-design furniture in small quantities. 1966 was also the same year as the founding of two Italian Radical Design groups, Archizoom and Superstudio. 1967, Gufram introduced 1967 Multipli (multiples) collection and produced 1967 Pavé Piuma floor mat, 1968 Sassi (rocks) seating, and 1974 Massolo fake archeological artifact by artist Piero Gilardi, already experienced in polyurethane. Tullio Regge designed 1970 Detecma donut-like chair. Others included 1971 Bocca foam sofa by Studio 65 (based on a model by Salvadore Dalí and named Marilyn by the US importer). Turin architects Giorgio Ceretti, Pietro Derossi, Riccardo Rosso designed 1971 Pratone (meadow) so-called seating. Franco Mello designed 1970 Erba table and, with Guido Drocco, 1972 Cactus coat rack. The 1970 Farfalla seat was not produced. All were formed in cold-expanded polyurethane that was self-healing or painted. Franco Mello has observed about the landmark moment, 'There were poetic and cost judgements made. But there was little or no thought given to marketing. There were the collaborations and the quick comings and goings of designers and architects who invented [the new models]. It was a small handicraft operation, an unrealistic company, in a territory absolutely disowned by others... The time was 1966. There were euphoria and disorganization. The objects were born quickly. The polyurethane "bread" was cut with skill—with blades, hack-saws, glue, scissors, varnish. It wanted you to think with your hands. And at Gufram, hands were better than machines.' From 1978, Gufram turned to the production of conservative armchairs for theatres, public arenas, and schools; 2003–04, became part of Poltrona Frau Group.
Exhibitions Examples of Multipli collection included in a large number of exhibitions. Gufram subject of 2002 exhibition, Manica Lunga, Castello di Rivoli, Turin (catalog below).
Bibliography *Provokationen Design aus Italien*, Hanover: Werkbund, 1982. Enzo Frateili, *Il disegno industriale italiano 1928–1981*, Turin: Celid, 1983. Ezio Mauzini, *La materia dell'invenzione: materiali e progetto*, Milan: Arcadia, 1986. R. Craig Miller, *Modern Design 1890–1990*, New York: The Metropolitan Museum of Art/Abrams, 1990. Cristina Morozzi and Silvio San Pietro, *Mobili italiani contemporanei*, Milan: Archivolto, 1996. Andrea Branzi, *Il design italiano 1964–1990*, Milano: Elemond, 1996. Cat., Stefano Casciani (ed.), *Design italiano nei musei del mondo 1950–1990*, Milano: Abitare Segesta, 1998. Cat., Franco Mello, Ennio Chiggio, and Stefano Casciani, *The Rock Furniture = Il Design della Gufram negli anni del rock*, Turin: Castello di Rivoli, 2002. www.gufram.com.

Willy Guhl. Schlinge outdoor chair. 1954. Abestos cement, 22 1/4 x 21 7/8 x 29 1/2" (56.5 x 55.5 x 75 cm). Mfr.: Eternit, Switzerland. Courtesy Quittenbaum Kunstauktionen, Munich.

Hans Gugelot and Reinhold Häcker (1903–1976). Carousel-S slide projector. 1963. Painted aluminum and plastic, 6 x 11 1/4 x 10 5/8" (15.2 x 28.6 x 27 cm). Mfr.: Kodak, Germany. Gift of Kodak A.G., Germany. MoMA.

Gugelot, Hans (1920–1965)

Dutch-Swiss architect and industrial designer; born Makassar (now Ujung Pandang, Indonesia); active Germany.

Training 1940–42, architecture in Lausanne; 1942–46, Eidgenössische Technische Hochschule (federal technical college), Zürich.
Biography 1946–54, Gugelot worked with Max Bill and designed his first furniture, produced by Horgen-Glarus; 1954, met Erwin Braun of the Braun appliance firm, where he was a designer until 1965; 1960–65, he was active in his own design studio, Institut Gugelot, Ulm; from 1954, was head of product-design department, Hochschule für Gestaltung, Ulm, where, he argued that a product should function efficiently without disguise or decoration and exerted a great influence on the forms adopted by postwar manufactured domestic goods. Gugelot's designs featured muted grays, black, right angles, and no ornamentation. An expression of this approach can be seen in Braun's 1956 Phonosuper record player (with Rams), nicknamed *Schneewittchensarg* (Snow White's coffin), and which illustrated the design principles for which Braun became known. Gugelot's 1962 Sixtant electric shaver by Braun set a new international standard. For others, Gugelot also designed a sewing machine by Pfaff and M125 storage unit by Bofinger furniture company; 1959–62, was a consultant to the U-bahn of Hamburg; continued to practice architecture. He died in Ulm.
Exhibitions Work shown at 1963 *Ulm Hochschule für Gestaltung 1963*, touring; 1974 *50er Jahre Bundespreis 'Die gute Industrieform'* exhibition, Rat für Formgebung (German design council), Munich. Work subject of an exhibition in Munich (catalog below).
Bibliography Alison and Peter Smithson, 'Concealment and Display: Meditations on Braun,' *Architectural Design*, July 1966: 362–63. François Burkhardt and Inez Franksen (ed.), *Dieter Rams &*, Berlin: Gerhardt, 1980–81. Cat., Hans Wichmann (ed.), *System-Design Bahnbrecher: Hans Gugelot 1920–1965*, Munich: Die Neue Sammlung, 1984.

Guhl, 'Willy' Wilhelm (1915–)

Swiss designer; born Stein am Rhein.

Training 1930–33, furniture making in Schaffhausen; 1934–38 under Wilhelm Kienzle, interior design, Kunstgewerbeschule, Zürich.
Biography 1939, Guhl established his own studio in Zürich; designed 1954 Schlinge garden chair and table by Eternit (in cement-fiber bond, reissued from 1998) and 1959 Guhl side chair in wood and cane by Dietiker. 1943, he became a member, Schweizerischer Werkbund (SWB). His 1948 abstract furniture game (reissued from 1996) was employed by him in his classes (from 1951) at Kunstgewerbeschule, Zürich, and has been claimed to have highly influenced Swiss industrial design. 1967, he traveled in the US and Canada. The Willy Guhl prize to students has been established.
Exhibition Work first shown, 1943 *Unsere Wohnung*, Zürich, and subject of 1985 exhibition, Zürich (catalog below)
Bibliography Cat., *Willy Guhl: Gestalter und Lehrer* (Schweizer Design—Pioniere 2), Zürich: Museum für Gestaltung, 1985.

Guido, Anthony (1960–)

American industrial designer; born Portsmouth, N.H.

Training To 1982, Ohio State University, Columbus.
Biography Taught design in Germany; later worked at Esslinger Design in Altensteig, Germany, on the SnowWhite project of Apple Computer in 1985; joined the staff of Esslinger's frogdesign studio in California, and, with others, participated in the design of numerous Apple products, including 1981–82 Apple IIc and 1985 IIGS, 1985 Macintosh SE, 1984–85 Jonathan project, 1986 Macintosh Portable. 1987, Guido left frogdesign and, with another ex-frogdesign staff member, developed 1989 Twister concepts (predating 1990 Powerbook) for Apple; directed the graduate-design program, University of the Arts, Philadelphia.
Bibliography Paul Kunkel, *Apple Design: The World of the Apple Industrial Design Group*, New York: Graphis, 1997.

Guiguichon, Suzanne (1901–1985)

French decorator and furniture designer; born and active Paris.

Training Under Maurice Dufrêne, school on the rue Madame, Paris.
Biography From 1929, Guiguichon was active as a designer with Maurice Dufrêne at La Maîtrise design atelier of Les Galeries Lafayette, Paris, designing, for the most part anonymously, furniture, clocks, lighting, fabrics, rugs, and accessories; 1930, set up her own studio at 54, rue de Clichy, Paris. Her furniture produced by various manufacturers in the Faubourg Saint-Antoine area, particularly Speich Frères. She worked for both private and contract clients; was commissioned to design an office for the mayor of the 6th arrondissement, Paris, and 1947, bedrooms of French President Vincent Auriol in the Château de Rambouillet and the Palais de l'Élysée in Paris. She taught École de l'Union Centrale des Arts Décoratifs, Paris.
Exhibitions/citations A bedroom (with Gabriel Englinger) shown in La Maîtrise pavilion at 1925 *Exposition Internationale des Arts Décoratifs et Industriels Modernes*, Paris, receiving a gold medal. 1930s, work regularly shown at Salons of Société des Artistes Décorateurs and editions of Salon d'Automne, and at 1935 *Exposition Universelle et Internationale de Bruxelles*; 1937 *Exposition Internationale des Arts et Techniques dans la Vie Moderne*, Paris.
Bibliography *Ensembles mobiliers*, vol. 2, Paris: Charles Moreau, 1937; vol. V, no. 5, 1945; no. 2, 1954. Pierre Kjellberg, *Art déco: les maîtres du mobilier, le décor des paquebots*, Paris: Amateur, 1986.

Guild, Lurelle Van Arsdale (1898–1985)

American industrial designer and writer; active Darien, Conn.

Training Painting, Syracuse (N.Y.) University.
Biography Guild's name is prounced to rhyme with 'child,' not with 'spilled.' He initially designed for the theater and turned to industrial design in 1920s; by 1920, was selling cover artwork to magazines *House & Garden* and *The Ladies' Home Journal*; subsequently, collaborated with wife Louise Eden Guild on illustrations for *Woman's Home Companion*, *McCall's*, *House Beautiful*, and other magazines; 1927, became an industrial designer and, subsequently, realized 1,000 product designs or more a year. His drawings, based on a knowledge of mechanical engineering, could be used without alterations by his

Lurelle Guild. Wear-Ever water kettle (no. 1403). c. 1923–33. Aluminum with plastic handle and lid knob, overall approximate h. 8 1/2 x w. 9 1/2" (21.6 x 24.1 cm). Mfr.: The Aluminum Cooking Utensil Co., US. Gift of the designer. MoMA.

clients' engineers. He produced working models in his workshop and sometimes tested his designs by displaying them in department stores. His streamlined c. 1937 Electrolux Model 30 vacuum cleaner with sleigh feet is among his best-known designs. Guild redesigned the electric washing machine, reducing the controls from five to one. His 1934 aluminum-and-glass-ball compote by Alcoa's Kensington division is an elegant example of his work. A skilled metalworker, his work by Kensington was extensive. Guild's 1932 pots and kettles by Wear-Ever were practical, innovative, and ubiquitous. His 1935 Alcoa aluminum showroom, dubbed a 'museum,' in New York, was a streamline design with a model railroad car on view and lighting fixtures, furniture, and plinths all in aluminum. He designed numerous domestic accessories and lights by Chase Brass and Copper in Waterbury, Conn.; much of the lighting was historicist in nature, reflecting Guild's unashamed readiness to accommodate popular taste and his dictum, 'Beauty alone does not sell.' His streamline designs ranged from tabletop accessories such as ashtrays to heavy kitchen equipment, the 1934 oil burner by May, and a refrigerator by Norge. Guild was a prolific writer early in his career of articles on antique furniture for women's magazines; was interested in Early American crafts; moved an entire Early American village from New Hampshire to Darien, Conn., where he lived and worked. The Guild archive is housed in the library of Syracuse (N.Y.) University.
Exhibitions Work included in 1934 *Philadelphia Art Alliance Dynamic Design* (Wear-Ever pots and pans); 1942 *Aluminized America*, Marshall Field's department store, Chicago; 2000 *Aluminum by Design*, touring the US (catalog below); 2000 *American Modern, 1925–40: Design for a New Age* and touring the the US (catalog below).
Bibliography *Fortune*, Feb. 1934: 90. Harry V. Anderson, 'Contemporary American Designers,' *Decorators Digest*, Feb. 1935: 42–43, 82, 84. David Heskett, *Industrial Design*, London: Thames & Hudson, 1980. Martin Grief, *Depression Modern: The Thirties Style in America*, New York: Universe, 1975: 60, 174–79. Ralph Caplan, *By Design*, New York: McGraw-Hill, 1982: 37. Cat., Sarah Nichols et al., *Aluminum by Design*, New York: Abrams, 2000. Cat., J. Stewart Johnson, *American Modern, 1925–1940...*, New York: Abrams, 2000.
> See Alcoa (Aluminum Company of America).

Guild of Handicraft

British crafts group; located London and, subsequently, Chipping Campden, Gloucestershire.

History 1888, Charles Robert Ashbee founded the Guild of Handicraft in London. Some of its early (1898) silversmiths included J.K. Bailey, David Cameron, William Hardiman, and W.A. White. Enamelers Fleetwood C. Varley and David Cameron used copious enamel and cabochon-cut semi-precious stones and mother-of-pearl, an approach soon copied by other English silversmiths. Ashbee translated Benvenuto Cellini's 16th-century manuals *Trattato dell'Oreficeria* and *Trattato della Scultura* for his Guild metalworks. Ashbee's own work was separate from that of the Guild's collective talent. Its artisans in London produced furniture designed by H.M. Baillie Scott for the palace of the Grand Duke Louis IV of Hesse-Darmstadt. 1902, Guild members moved to Chipping Campden. Their work was shown worldwide and became a source of inspiration to many. Unable to compete with firms that produced cheaper goods, the Guild closed in 1907. Ashbee noted, 'An artist under the conditions of Industrialism has no protection; any trades can steal his design.'
Exhibitions Work from its inception shown worldwide; subject of 1988 exhibition, Cheltenham Art Gallery & Museums (catalog below).
Bibliography C.R. Ashbee, *Modern English Silverwork*, 1909. Alec Miller, 'C. R. Ashbee and The Guild of Handicraft,' unpublished typescript in Victoria and Albert Museum MSS Collection, 1952. Alan Crawford, *C.R. Ashbee, Architect, Designer and Romantic Socialist*, New Haven: Yale, 1985. Cat., by Annette Carruthers and Frank Johnson, *The Guild of Handicraft 1888–1988*, Cheltenham: Cheltenham Art Gallery & Museums, 1988. Annelies Krekel-Aalberse, *Art Nouveau and Art Déco Silver*, New York: Abrams, 1989.

Hector Guimard. Armchair. c. 1899–1900. Walnut and leather, 32 3/8 x 30 3/4 x 21" (82.3 x 78.1 x 53.3 cm), seat h. 20 3/4" (52.7 cm). Gift of Madame Hector Guimard. MoMA.

Guillemard, Marcel (1886–1932)

French decorator and furniture designer; born and active Paris.

Training In furniture design at Krieger, furniture makers in the Faubourg Saint-Antoine area, Paris.
Biography Guillemard was active as a furniture and interior designer; from late 1920s, worked with Louis Sognot in the Primavera decorating workshop of Printemps department store in Paris, where, 1918–29, he was chief of the section of design and decoration, sometimes collaborating with architect G. Wibo, including on the tearoom at Printemps; was the force behind the Printemps's annual fairs and the new techniques of window display and merchandising. Guillemard's early work was reminiscent of 18th- and 19th-century French styles.
Exhibitions 1922 Salon of Société des Artistes Décorateurs (dining room with Charlotte Chauchet-Guilleré); work shown at editions of Salon d'Automne; Primavera pavilion (dining room) at 1925 *Exposition Internationale des Arts Décoratifs et Industriels Modernes*, Paris.
Bibliography *Restaurants, dancing, cafés, bars*, Paris: Charles Moreau, no. 16, 1929. Alastair Duncan, *Art Nouveau and Art Déco Lighting*, New York: Simon & Schuster, 1978: 185. Pierre Kjellberg, *Art Déco: les maîtres du mobilier, le décor des paquebots*, Paris: Amateur, 1986.

Guilleré, René (1878–1931)

French entrepreneur, tastemaker, and lawyer; active Paris; husband of Charlotte Chauchet-Guilleré.

Biography 1901, Guilleré was a founder, Société des Artistes Décorateurs, of which he was president in 1911, became legal advisor to Société des Sculpteurs Modeleurs; was active in the management of Au Printemps department store in Paris, in which he established the Primavera decorating workshop in 1913. His wife Charlotte Chauchet-Guilleré was the first director of Primavera.
Bibliography Pierre Kjellberg, *Art déco: les maîtres du mobilier, le décor des paquebots*, Paris: Amateur, 1986.

Guillon, Jacques S. (1922–)

Canadian furniture designer; born Paris; active Toronto; son of an Canadian architect.

Training To 1952, architecture, McGill University, Toronto; in furniture design, Montréal.
Biography 1940, Guillon came to Canada with his family; returned to Europe as a Royal Canadian Air Force pilot; 1952–54, practiced architecture with Max Roth; 1954, established his own industrial-design firm. 1958, the firm became Jacques S. Guillon & Associates in Montréal and specialized in major transportation and product-design projects, with clients such as Air France, Aluminium Company of Canada, Morgan Trust, and Canadian General Electric Company. He and his wife Pego McNaughton owned and operated Pego's, stores which sold Scandinavian furniture in Montréal (1954–62) and Québec City (1956–61) and made some furniture through Guillon's Ebena Manufacturing division. 1962, the Ebena was bought by Art Woodwork (and in turn was bought by Sunar Industries). Guillon has become best known for

1950 lightweight laminated-wood and nylon-cord side chair, designed while at McGill University and, subsequently, produced by three different manufacturers, including Modernart of Canada. He also designed mid-1960s heavy-framed furniture by Paul Arno in Montréal. Within his firm, known as the first multidisciplinary office of designers in Canada, he and others designed the early-1960s logo and carriages (body, frame, and interiors) of Montréal underground transportation system. The logo, inspired by the London Underground's symbol, is a white upside-down arrow within a circle on blue background. By 1979, the Guillon firm was known as GSM Design Produit & Transport Inc. (based on partners Guillon, Smith, and Macquart). Swiss graphic designer Laurence Marquart added visual communication to the firm's services. 1983, was called simply GSM Design. 1987, Guillon retired.
Exhibitions/citations Participated in mounting scientific exhibit in Pavilion of Man, 1967 *Universal and International Exhibition (Expo '67)*, Montréal, and many others at National Museum of Science and Technology, Ottawa. 1954 award (for fireplace grid), National Industrial Design Committee (NIDC); 2000 Gagnant du Prix Sam-Lapointe, Institut de Design, Montréal.
Bibliography Cat., *Seduced and Abandoned: Modern Furniture Designers in Canada, the First Fifty Years*, Toronto: The Art Gallery at Harbourfront, 1986. 14–15, 20. Rachel Gotlieb and Cora Golden, *Design in Canada Since 1945: Fifty Years from Teakettles to Task Chairs*, Toronto: Knopf Canada, 2001.

Guillot, Émile (aka E. Guyot; A. Guyot)
French architect and furniture designer; born Le Perreux.

Biography Guillot designed for Thonet Frères, Paris, which produced his furniture to 1957. He also had an independent practice. Some of his furniture (possibly all) was produced by Thonet-Czechoslovakia because the inventory of Thonet Frères (no longer connected to Thonet Mundus) also included bentwood furniture made by Thonet-Czechoslovakia. c. 1930, he was associated with the organization Union des Artistes Modernes (UAM) in Paris, but little else is known about him—the reason for the various French phonetic spellings of his name.
Exhibition His Thonet furniture shown at 1930 (1st) UAM exhibition; 1930 Salon (B290 cabinet and B261 armchair) of Société des Artistes Décorateurs, both Paris.
Bibliography René Chavance, 'Le meuble métallique en série,' *Mobilier et décoration*, no. 12, Dec. 1929: 221. Cat., *Les années UAM 1929–1958*, Paris: Musée des Arts Décoratifs, 1988.
> See Thonet Frères.

Guimard, Hector (1867–1942)
French architect and furniture designer; born Lyon.

Training 1882–85 under architects Eugène Train and Charles Génuys, École Nationale Supérieure des Arts Décoratifs, Paris; 1889 under Gustave Gaulin, École Nationale Supérieure des Beaux-Arts, Paris.
Biography Guimard designed the interior of the restaurant Grand Neptune (his first commission) on the quai d'Auteuil, Paris, and several houses in Paris and its environs. By the time of his 1893 villa for Charles Jassedé on the avenue de Clamart (now place Charles-de-Gaulle), Paris, Guimard had already achieved an architectural maturity expressed by buildings that completely integrated exteriors with interiors. His unorthodox aesthetic was inspired by the Henri II style and Gothic Revival through Eugène-Emmanuel Viollet-le-Duc's *Entretiens sur l'architecture*. (Paris: Q. Morel, 1863–72). Guimard's 1894–97 Castel Béranger apartment house in Paris typified his style: florid ornamentation and cast-iron stairways and balconies with asymmetrical, winding plant-like forms. 1894, Guimard discovered English Domestic Revival architecture and saw Victor Horta's recently completed Hôtel Horta in Brussels. Guimard devoted much attention to public areas as well as private apartment interiors, designing complete furnishings, ceiling ornaments, floor and wall coverings, fireplaces, and lighting fixtures. His most prolific period was 1898–1901, when he constructed 1898–1900 Maison Coilliot in Lille, 1899–1900 Castel Henriette in Sèvres, and 1901 Humbert de Romans Concert Hall in Paris. Commissioned by Compagnie Générale du Métropolitain in 1903, Guimard is best known for his rythmical cast-iron Paris Métro (subway) station entrances, a design idiom that he pursued, in the free form of his carved wooden furniture, with bronzes executed in collaboration with chiseler M. Philippon. At his summit, Guimard's style was elegant, if severe, and free of the mannerism that characterized his later works, such as 1902–05 Maison Nozal, 1910 Villa Flore, and 1911 Hôtel Mezzara. After World War I, his interest in materials and his innovative spirit appeared in his own country home in Vaucresson, where he incorporated tubular asbestos elements designed by architect Henri Sauvage. 1920, he issued his first serially produced standardized furniture; 1921, built his first standardized apartment building and worker's house. As the Art Nouveau style fell into disrepute, his earlier successes were forgotten. Was a founding member, Société Le Nouveau-Paris. 1938, he settled in New York.
Exhibitions Active in numerous venues, he designed a small pavilion and Pavillon d'Électricité at 1889 *Exposition Universelle*, Paris, and won 1899 façade competition (for Castel Béranger, 14, rue La Fontaine, Auteuil, now Paris), when he organized an exhibition of the building. Work subject of exhibitions at Galerie du Luxembourg, Paris, 1971; Musée Municipal, Saint-Dizier; Landesmuseum, Münster, 1975; The Museum of Modern Art, New York, 1980; Musée des Arts Décoratifs et des Tissus, Lyon, 1991 and 1993. Work shown at 1900 *Exposition Universelle*, Paris, and 1925 *Exposition Internationale des Arts Décoratifs et Industriels Modernes*, Paris, and Salons of Société des Artistes Français from 1890, Salons of Société Nationale des Beaux-Arts from 1894, 1971 *Guimard, Horta, Van de Velde* exhibition, Musée des Arts Décoratifs, Paris.1902, became a member, Société des Artistes Décorateurs, showing at its Salons from 1904.
Bibliography Hector Guimard, 'An Architect's Opinion of l'Art Nouveau,' *Architectural Record*, June 1902: 130–33. F. Lanier Graham, *Hector Guimard*, New York: The Museum of Modern Art, 1970. Gillian Naylor and Yvonne Brunhammer, *Hector Guimard*, New York: Rizzoli, 1978. David Dunster (ed.), *Hector Guimard*, London: Academy, 1978. Claude Frontisi, *Hector Guimard, architectures*, Paris: Les Amis d'Hector Guimard, 1985. Georges Vigne, *Hector Guimard et l'art nouveau*, Paris: Hachette/Réunion des Musées Nationaux, 1990. Cat., Philippe Thiébaut (ed.), *Guimard*, Lyon: Musée des Arts Décoratifs et des Tissus, 1991. Cat., *Guimard: colloque international* (12–13 June 1992), Paris: Musee d'Orsay. 1994. Paola Antonelli (ed.), *Objects of Design: The Museum of Modern Art*, New York: The Museum of Modern Art, 2003: 128–29.

Guixé, Martí (1964–)
Catalan designer; born and active Barcelona.

Training 1983–85, interior design, Elisava (Escola Superior de Disseny), Barcelona; 1986-87, industrial design, Politecnico, Milan.
Biography 1994–96, Guixé was a design consultant to KIDP in Seoul; 1998, designed Camper shops on Old Bond Street, London, and on El Triangle, Barcelona. He designed 1998 Flamp lamp by H2O, Barcelona, and 1999 Apron kitchen collection by Authentics; participated in Oranienbaum design project and 2001 'do create' design project by Droog Design. Other design work: Autoband toy and 2000 Kid's Spamt tool kit and H2O chair by H2O, Barcelona; layout for *La vuelta al mundo* magazine of Escuela Técnica Superior de Arquitectura in Alicante; food pack by El Sindicato Agency, Barcelona; products including 2002 Signature vase by Die Imaginäre Manufaktur (D.I.M.) (products made by the blind); bag collection by Authentics; widely published temporary Camper shop on the via Montenapoleone in Milan; Camper shop in New York; *Intramuros* magazine's 'Cabane' during the Biennale Off in Saint-Etienne, France; self-produced roll of sticky tape, to be formed into a football (soccer) shape. Other clients have included Alessi, Chupa Chups, and Vitra.
Exhibitions/citations Work subject of large number of exhibitions from 1997 *SPAMT*, H2O Gallery, Barcelona. Work in numerous group exhibitions: 1999 *Design und Zeit*, Kunst Halle, Krems, Austria; 2000 *Do for Droog Design*, Rotterdam, Milan, and Paris; 2001 *Workspheres*, The Museum of Modern Art, New York; *Droog Design in the AA*, London.; 2002–03 *Sonic Process* (MP Tree), MACBA, Barcelona and Centre Georges Pompidou, Paris; 2003 *Martí Guixé*, mu.dac (Musée de Design et d'Arts Appliqués Contemporains), Lausanne. 1985 ARQ INFAD medal for interior design; 1999 Ciutat de Barcelona design prize.
Bibliography 'Martí Guixé: A Revolutionary in the Institutions,' *Domus*, no. 799, 1997. *M.Guixé/Fish Futures*, Barcelona: H2O, 1998. 'Wer hat Angst vor Martí Guixé?,' *form*, no. 165, 1999. 'Guixé à nos pieds,' *Intramuros*, no. 83, 1999. 'Martí Guixé interroger le réel,' *Intramuros*, no. 90, 2000. Sarah Robins, 'Maveric Mandorla,' *Monument*, no. 39, 2001. 'Marté Guixé,' *Axis*, no. 91, May–June 2001: 129. Ed van Hinte (ed.), *Martí Guixé 1:1*, Rotterdam: 010, 2002. Paola Antonelli (ed.), *Objects of Design: The Museum of Modern Art*, New York: The Museum of Modern Art, 2003: 281.

Gulassa, David (1961–2001)
American designer and sculptor; born Walnut Creek, Cal.

Training Renaissance Art School, Oakland, Cal.
Biography 1990, Gulassa established his eponymous firm in Seattle,

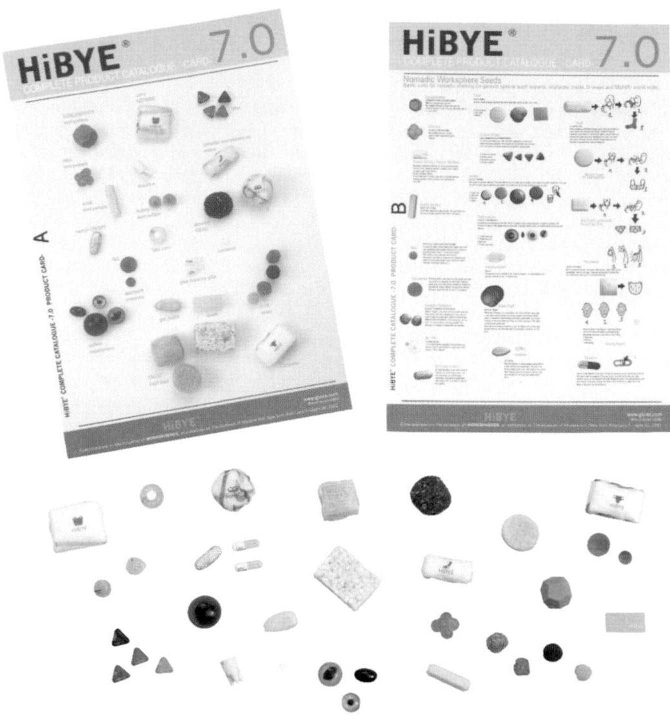

Martí Guixé. HiBye 'pills' and instruction card. 2000. Various materials, from minimum h. 1/16 x dia. 1/4" (0.2 x 0.6 cm) to maximum h. x dia. 1 3/4" (4.4 cm), catalogue card h. 12 1/4 x 8 1/4 x 3" (31.1 x 21 x 7.6 cm). Mfr.: the designer, Spain (prototypes). Workspheres Exhibition Fund. MoMA.

Wash., specializing in furniture, lighting, vases, and interior design. Commissions included metalwork for 1990 St. Ignatius Chapel (Steven Holl, architect) in Seattle and construction of 1998 Washington State's World War II Memorial in Olympia, Wash. Also became known for his wood, glass, and concrete work in full-interior commissions. Died in Seattle, where firm David Gulassa & Company continues.
Bibliography Cat., R. Craig Miller (intro.), *U.S. Design 1975–2000*, Munich: Prestel, 2002.

Gulbrandsen, Nora (1894–1978)

Norwegian designer; born Kristiania (now Oslo).

Training Statens Håndverks-og Kunstindustriskole, Kristiania.
Biography Gulbrandsen was recommended by the Landsforeningen Norsk Brukskunst (Norwegian association for applied arts) for employment at Porsgrund Porselænsfabrik in Porsgrunn, where she was artistic director 1928–45; in a program of renewal at Porsgrund, introduced modern designs and décor in a semblance of Art Déco. Her 1920s ceramics showed Chinese influences, and her spirals and circles suggested speed and movement and also incorporated cubes and cylinders. She designed ceramics for mass-produced sets as well as one-of-a-kind pieces and glass-ware, textiles, book jackets, bookbinding, and wallpaper; 1946, left Porsgrund and set up her own pottery-design studio and, from 1960s, designed silver by David-Andersen.
Exhibitions Work shown at 1927 exhibition sponsored by Norske Kunsthåndverkere (Norwegian society of arts and crafts), Bergen.
Bibliography Cat., David Revere McFadden (ed.), *Scandinavian Modern Design 1880–1980*, New York: Abrams, 1982. Fredrik Wildhagen, *Norge i Form*, Oslo: Stenersen, 1988. Jennifer Hawkins Opie, *Scandinavia: Ceramics and Glass in the Twentieth Century*, New York: Rizzoli, 1989. Cat., Anne Wichstrøm, *Rooms with a View: Women's Art in Norway 1880–1990*, Oslo: The Royal Ministry of Foreign Affairs, 1990: 24.

Guldsmedsaktiebolaget (aka GAB)

Swedish silversmiths; located Stockholm.

History 1867, Guldsmedsaktiebolaget was founded in Stockholm. By the time Jacob Ängman had joined GAB in 1907 as artistic director, the operation had become Sweden's leading modern silversmithy. Ängman led the way for modern Swedish silver design with notable examples like 1916 Three Holy Kings jewel casket. Like Nils Fougstedt's work for Hallberg, Ängman's silverware was forerunner of the quality of design that established Sweden's high reputation in 1930s. GAB's 1920s–30s designers included Just Andersen, Maja-Lisa Ohlsson, and Folke Arström. 1961, GAB merged with C.G. Hallberg.
Bibliography Annelies Krekel-Aalberse, *Art Nouveau and Art Déco Silver*, New York: Abrams, 1989.

Gullaskruf Glasbruk

Swedish glass factory.

History 1895, a factory was founded in Gullaskruf for the production of window glass; 1920, was closed but, 1925, was reorganized by engineer William Stenberg and his daughter. Stenberg designed molds for everyday glassware, the specialty of the firm that later included decorative wares designed by Hugo Gehlin and Arthur Percy. The firm began to include colored glass and experimented with various techniques such as semi-opaque glass. 1975, Gullaskruf was amalgamated with Royal Krona; subsequently, with Orrefors.
Bibliography Jennifer Hawkins Opie, *Scandinavia: Ceramics and Glass in the Twentieth Century*, New York: Rizzoli, 1989.

Gulotta, Gerald (1921–)

American tableware designer and teacher; active New York.

Biography Gulotta was an international designer, whose work was realized in the US, Europe, and the Far East for clients including Block, Ceramicas S. Bernardo, Cristais de Alcobaca-Atlantis, Dansk, Ionia, Porcelanas del Bidasoa, Sociedad de Porcelanas, and Tienshan. From late 1960s, he was a professor; organized and directed government-sponsored 1974 *Industrial Design Workshop 74* in Portugal; 1976–77, developed the first foundation curriculum in industrial design for a new school of design at the University of Guadalajara in Mexico; 1982 in China, lectured on industrial design, Central School of Arts and Crafts of Beijing University in Hunan; and College of Arts and Crafts in Jingdezhen.
Citations First prize, 1971 Premio Internacional, International Ceramic and Glass Competition, Valéncia; 1998 Good Design award, Chicago Athenaeum.

Gundlach-Pedersen, Oscar (1887–1970)
Danish designer and architect.

Training Det Kongelige Danske Kunstakademi, Copenhagen.
Biography Gundlach-Pedersen designed buildings in Denmark; from 1911, worked at the Georg Jensen Sølvesmedie, Copenhagen, where he was the assistant director from 1926–54. Designs for the firm included 1931Parallel silver cutlery and Jensen's first stainless-steel cutlery, Mitra, and 1937 Nordic silver cutlery, as well as hollow-ware.
Exhibitions/citations 1920s–30s, work shown at numerous exhibitions in Copenhagen. Received gold medal, 1925 *Exposition Internationale des Arts Décoratifs et Industriels Modernes*; diploma of honor, 1937 *Exposition Internationale des Arts et Techniques dans la Vie Moderne*; both Paris.
Bibliography Cat., *Georg Jensen Silversmithy: 77 Artists, 75 Years*, Washington: Smithsonian, 1980.

Günther, Kelp (aka 'Zamp')
> See Haus-Rucker-Co.

Gur, Tal (1962–)
Israeli industrial designer; born Kfar Yehoshua; active Kibbutz Gilgal.

Training 1992–96, industrial design, Bezalel Academy of Art and Design, Jerusalem; 2000, in traditional Japanese papermaking, in Mino City, Japan.
Biography Gur designs and has had produced a range of products, particularly lighting, that employs his-own-developed rotational-molding and other innovative techniques. The rotational process realizes similar but essentially one-of-a-kind items in colorful plastics. From 1996, has lectured, Department of Industrial Design, Bezalel Academy of Art and Design.
Exhibitions/citations From 1998, work included in large number of exhibitions. 1998 and 2001 Crate & Barrel grants for Israeli domestic products, The Israel Museum, Jerusalem; first prizes, 1998 and 1999 Contemporary Design Competition, Interior Design Society of Israel; 2000 Premio Ambiente for environmental design, Pantalleria, Italy; 2001 (1st) Design Award, Ministry of Culture, Israel.

Gurschner, Gustav (1873–1970)
German sculptor and designer; born Mühldorf, Bavaria.

Training Art school, Bozen (now Bolzano, Italy); Königliche Akademie der bildenden Künste, Vienna.
Biography Gurschner settled in Vienna; produced monumental sculpture groups and portrait busts; turned to small domestic objects, including door knockers, ashtrays, hand mirrors, inkwells, and dishes. Most of these items were sold by A. Forster in Vienna. He created the 1909 memorial to the 1905 meeting between King Edward VII of Britain and Emperor Franz Josef of Austria-Hungary at Marienbad (now Mariánské Lázně, Czech Republic), and medals for automobile races honoring Gordon Bennett and Herbert von Herkomer. In his lighting, Gurschner often incorporated the well-worn theme of naked women and sometimes sea shells. His small workshop staff produced metalwork and for a time ventured into jewelry and furniture production.
Exhibitions Work shown at 1898 (1st) Wiener Sezession exhibition and, subsequently, at various exhibitions in Vienna, and in Munich, Monte Carlo, and Paris, including 1900 *Exposition Universelle* there.
Bibliography Cat., *Jugendstil 20er Jahre*, Vienna: Künstlerhaus Galerie, plates 2–5. Hans Vollmer, *Allgemeines Lexikon der Bildenden Künstler des 20. Jahrhunderts*, vol. II, Leipzig: Seemann, 1955: 339. Alastair Duncan, *Art Nouveau and Art Déco Lighting*, New York: Simon & Schuster, 1978.

Gusrud, Svein (1944–)
Norwegian furniture designer.

Biography By Studio HÅG in Oslo, Gusrud designed the widely published 1982 Balans Activ ergonomic stool (with Hans Christian Mengshoel) and innovative 1983 prototype transportation seating; with Oddvin Rykkens and Peter Opsvik, led the development of the ergonomic stool and seating popular in the early 1980s.
Bibliography Cat., David Revere McFadden (ed.), *Scandinavian Modern Design 1880–1980*, New York: Abrams, 1982. Fredrik Wildhagen, *Norge i Form*, Oslo: Stenersen, 1988.

Gustafson, Knut L. (1885–1976)
Swedish silversmith; born Stockholm; active Chicago.

Training Apprenticeship in Stockholm.
Biography c. 1910, Gustafson settled in Chicago and became associated with the Jarvie Shop, the Lebolt firm, and the Randahl Shop; 1932, founded the Chicago Silver Company. His firm produced most of its hollow-ware by spinning; however, some patterns bear noticeable hammer marks. He later concentrated on cutlery, most of it decorated with a simple leaf pattern; during 1940s, patented the hammered cutlery patterns Oak Leaf and Nordic; 1906, sold the dies for these two patterns to Spaulding in Chicago. His Chicago metalsmithies were located at 1741 W. Division St. 1923–30, 165 N. Wabash 1930–35, and 225 S. Wabash 1935–45.
Bibliography Sharon S. Darling with Gail Farr Casterline, *Chicago Metalsmiths*, Chicago Historical Society, 1977. Annelies Krekel-Aalberse, *Art Nouveau and Art Déco Silver*, New York: Abrams, 1989.

Gustavsberg
Swedish ceramics factory.

History 1640, Gustavsberg was founded as a brickworks on Värmdö island, 15 miles (25 km) from Stockholm. It later produced practical and decorative ceramic ware; made English china, Parianware figures, color-glaze majolica, and, later in 19th century, flambé-glaze stoneware; 1869–1937, it expanded substantially; stocked imported patterns as well as work by Gunnar Gunnarsson Wennerberg and August Malmström. 1897–1908, Wennerberg was the artistic director, when imitation Wedgwood Jasperware was produced at Gustavsberg. He later designed dinnerware patterns, large vases, and urns in simple Art Nouveau motifs. Wennerberg's pupil Josef Ekberg designed for the factory 1897–1945, calling on Art Nouveau plant forms. 1917, Wilhelm Kåge became the artistic director. Gustavsberg, one of the largest factories producing domestic tablewares in Sweden, was sold to Kooperative Förbundet 1937. In succession, Stig Lingberg and Karin Björquist were artistic directors. 1987, the firm was bought by the Finnish firm Arabla and, 1988, amalgamated with Rörstrand, becoming Rörstrand-Gustavsberg. 1990, Rörstrand-Gustavsberg was bought by Hackman. 2000, Gustavsberg became a brand of the Villeroy & Boch Group.
Bibliography *150 år Gustavsberg* Stockholm: Nationalmuseum, 1975–76. Jennifer Hawkins Opie, *Scandinavia: Ceramics and Glass in the Twentieth Century*, New York: Rizzoli, 1989.

Guyot, E.; A. Guyot
> See Émile Guillot.

Guzman, Roberto (1962–)
> See Comma.

Guzzini (aka Fratelli Guzzini)
Italian manufacturer; located Recanati.

History 1912, Fratelli Guzzini began with a couple of initial products designed by Enrico Guzzini and ten products during 1922 to c. 1941 by Pierino Mariano Guzzini. From early 1950s, wares were designed by an in-house staff and some commissioned designers. Today, it manufactures a wide range of domestic wares, including those for the kitchen and lighting in metal and particularly in plastics. Bruno Gecchelin designed the 1989 range of four kitchen utensils to commemorate the 75th anniversary of the founding of the firm, located today in Recanati. At one time, the firm had branches in Yugoslavia (now Croatia) and Canada. Recent designers have included Rodolfo Bonetto, frogdesign, Bruno Gecchelin, Giugiaro Design, Franco Guzzini, Furio Minuti, Ambrogio Pozzi, Rossari-Maggioni Associati, Paolo Tilche, and others. Adolfo Guzzini, a director of the firm, became a member, Associazione per il Disegno Industriale (ADI). 30% of its production is exported. 1958, iGuzzzini Illuminazione (later named) was established (see below).
Citations 1954, 1956, 1971, 1981, 1987 (three citations), 1989 (five citations), 1991 (six citations), 1998 Premio Compasso d'Oro.
Bibliography Jeremy Myerson and Sylvia Katz, *Conran Design Guides: Kitchenware*, London: Conran Octopus, 1990: 44, 74. *ADI Annual 1976*, Milan: Associazione per il Disegno Industriale, 1976.
> See Gecchelin, Bruno; Guzzini Illuminazione.

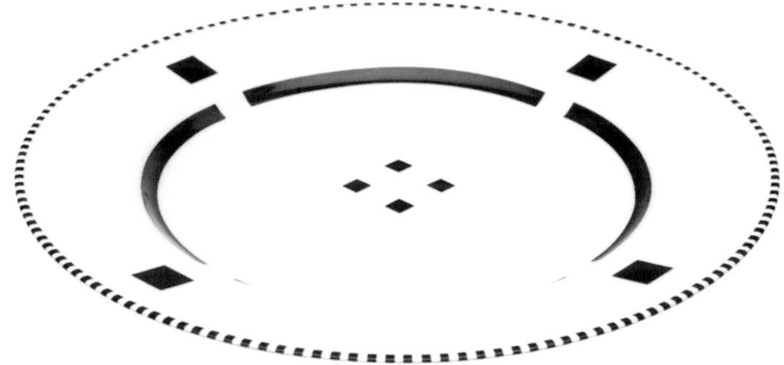

Charles Gwathmey and Robert Siegel. Tuxedo plate. 1984. Porcelain, h. 1 1/4 x dia. 12" (3.2 x 30.5 cm). Mfr.: Swid Powell, US. Marshall Cogan Purchase Fund. MoMA.

Guzzini Illuminazione (aka iGuzzini Illuminazione); Gruppo Guzzini

Italian lighting firm; located Recanati.

History 1958, Harvey Creazioni was developed by the five sons of Mariano Guzzini (of the Guzzini products family); from 1964, directed by Adolfo Guzzini (1941–). 'Harvey' refers to the invisible rabbit in the American play *Harvey* (1950) by Mary Chase and 1950 movie version (director, Henry Koster). The firm's first lamps were c. 1960 Rafalet by Karl Roters, 1969 Alicante by Emanuele Ponzio, and c. 1972 Cli-clak by the Guzzini staff. From 1967, was called Harvey Guzzini DH (Design House); from 1963, called iGuzzini Illuminazione or Gruppo Guzzini. Innovative and technologically advanced, iGuzzini has commissioned designs by Gae Aulenti, Piero Castiglioni, Perry King/Santiago Miranda, Renzo Piano, Gio Ponti, and others. Installations include those in the Louvre and the Centre Georges Pompidou, both Paris; Vatican Museum, Rome; Ferrari showrooms; North Greenwich Transport Interchange and Heathrow Airport, London; Mercedes Design Centre, Stuttgart; J. Marie Tjimbaou Cultural Centre, New Caledonia. Other fixtures have included the Nuvola street lamp by Piano Design Workshop, Cestello modular-lighting system by Aulenti and P. Castiglioni, Lingotto lighting system by Renzo Piano. 1994, Gruppo Guzzini acquired Sirrah lighting firm; is now composed of iGuzzini Illuminazione, Rede, Sirrah/Guzzini, Telma, and Teuco; 1995, opened a research/study center; exports 60% of its production.
Citations To iGuzzini Illuminazione: 1991 (five citations), 1994 (three citations), and 1998 (four citations) Premio Compasso d'Oro; 2000 Intel Design Prize; 2000–02 awards, Industrie Forum Design (iF), Hanover; 2000–02 Intel Design Prizes; 2001 Leonardo Quality Prize.
> See Guzzini.

Harvey Guzzini. Table lamp. Late 1960s. Glass, h. 11 1/4" (28.5 cm). Mfr.: Harvey Guzzini DH (Design House), Italy. Courtesy Quittenbaum Kunstauktionen, Munich.

Gwathmey, Charles (1938–)

American architect; born Charlotte, N.C.; active New York.

Training Under Louis Kahn and Robert Venturi, University of Pennsylvania, Philadelphia; and under Paul Rudolph, James Stirling, and Shadrach Woods, School of Architecture, Yale University.
Biography 1964–66, Gwathmey was professor of design, Pratt Institute, Brooklyn, N.Y.; subsequently, taught at Yale University, Princeton University, Harvard University, and University of California, Los Angeles; initially came to prominence with 1965–67 house and studio for his parents on Long Island, N.Y., which reveals the influenced of Le Corbusier; 1966 with Richard Henderson, set up an architecture partnership in New York followed by a partnership with Robert Siegel from 1968; early 1970s, became known as one of adhoc New York Five group of architects. From 1980s with Siegel, designed six dinnerware services (including the Anniversary set) by Swid Powell, furniture (including Derby desk) by Knoll, de Menil table series by International Contract Furnishings (ICF), and a tapestry by V'Soske. Large number of architectural commissions includes Gwathmey's completition of Le Corbusier's ramp of the Carpenter Center, Harvard University, and interior design. They also designed the controversial 1991–92 addition to Frank Lloyd Wright's Guggenheim Museum in New York. Architects working in the Gwathmey-Siegel office have included Rank Lupo and Daniel Rowen.
Exhibitions/citations Work included in 1969 *New York Five*; 1974 *Five Architects*, Princeton University. A number of awards to the partnership includes 1982 Architecture Firm Award, and 1981 gold medal, New York American Institute of Architects (AIA).
Bibliography Kay and Paul Breslow (eds.), *Charles Gwathmey and Robert Siegel: Wohnbauten 1966–1977*, Fribourg: Office du Livre, 1979. Stanley Aberchrombie, *Gwathmey Siegel*, New York: Whitney, 1981. Robert A.M. Stern (ed.) *The International Design Yearbook*, New York: Abbeville, 1985/1986. Annette Tapert, *Swid Powell: Objects by Architects*, New York: Rizzoli, 1990. Brad Collins (ed.), *Gwathmey Siegel: Buildings and Projects 1965–2000*, New York: Universe, 2000. Brad Collins (ed.), *Gwathmey Siegel Houses*, New York: Monacelli Press, 2000.

Poul Henningsen. PH-Zapfen (Artichoke) lamp (detail). 1958. MoMA.

Haase, Lawrence H. (1908–)
American metalworker; active Chicago.

Training 1932–33, Design School, Chicago Art Institute; Bauhaus, Berlin; 1933, Black Mountain College, N.C.
Biography Several times, Haase visited Walter Gropius in his architecture studio in Berlin. In his later work in the US, Haase was greatly influenced by that of Josef Albers and Vasilii Kandinsky; was friends with Albers and his wife Anni who were later teachers at Black Mountain College. Haase worked at General Motors, Detroit, Mich., and the product-development department of Sears, Roebuck & Co., Chicago; subsequently, set up his own manufacturing business in Chicago to produce innovative plastic products for the automotive, appliance, and packaging industries.
Bibliography Cat., *The Bauhaus: Masters and Students*, New York: Barry Friedman, 1988.

Haavardsholm, Frøydis (1896–1984)
Norwegian furniture designer.

Biography Haavardsholm was active from first quarter of 20th century. he designed early modernist furniture that was typically Norwegian in that realistic images were incorporated into the designs.
Bibliography Fredrik Wildhagen, *Norge i Form*, Oslo: Stenersen, 1988: 76.

Häberli, Alfredo (1964–)
Argentine-Swiss designer; born Buenos Aires; active Zürich.

Training To 1991, Höhere Schule für Gestaltung, Zürich.
Biography 1977, Häberli moved to Switzerland; 1988–89, worked for Siemens, New York, and Produkt Entwicklung Roericht, Ulm; from 1988, designed numerous exhibitions at Museum für Gestaltung, Zürich, some with Christophe Marchand; 1993, set up a studio with Marchand and, subsequently, worked alone or, to 1999, when the partnership was dissolved. His partnership or individual work has been realized for firms such as Alias, Authentics, Edra, Driade, Luceplan, Thonet, Zanotta. From 2000, Häberli developed products for Asplund, Bd Ediciones de Diseño, Cappellini, Danese, De Padova, Hackman, littala, Leitner, Luceplan, Magis, Offecct, Rörstrand.
Exhibitions/citations Work shown in numerous exhibitions in Europe. 1998 award (for 1997 Move It table, with Marchand, by Thonet), Industrie Forum Design (iF), Hanover.
Bibliography *Spoon: 100 Designers, 10 Curators, 10 Design Classics*, London: Phaidon, 2002. Mel Byars, *Design in Steel*, London: Laurence King, 2002. Björn Dahlstrom and Konstantin Grcic, *Alfredo Häberli: Sketching My Own Landscape*, Amsterdam: Frame, 2002.
> See Marchand, Christophe.

Hablik, Wenzel (1881–1934)
Austro-Hungarian architect, painter, designer, and interior decorator; active Itzehoe.

Training Kunstgewerbeschule, Vienna; Academy, Prague.
Biography Hablik was a contemporary of Bruno Taut, who also like Hablik was active in the Expressionist movement in architecture. But, like no other, Hablik earlier and more consequentially developed his utopian and visionary ideas. He was also a painter, commerical artist, interior designer, and craftsperson (including textiles and metalwork), probably best expressed as a *Gesamtkunstwerk* for his own house in Itzehoe, Germany, now Wenzel-Hablik-Museum (established in 1995).
Bibliography Cat., *Hablik, Designer, Utopian, Architect, Expressionist, artist, 1881–1934*, London: The Architectural Association, 1980. Anneliese Krekel-Aalberse, *Art Nouveau and Art Déco Silver*, New York: Abrams, 1989: 255. Jürgen Häusser, *Wenzel Hablik: Architekturvisionen 1903–1920*, Darmstadt: J. Häusser, 1998.

HackmanGroup
Finnish housewares and kitchen equipment manufacturer.

History The story of Hackman began in 1777, when Johan Friedrich Hackman (1755–1806) of Bremen, Germany, moved to Vyborg, in southern Finland at the time. With preceding enterprises, he eventually established six saw mills and was active in shipping 1801–05. 1806, his widow Marie Hackman (1776–1855) took over the management, and his son Johan Friedrich Hackman Jr. (1801–79) became a full partner in 1829. Even though the area of the plants became a duchy of Russia in 1809, through J.F. Hackman Jr.'s enterprising spirit the businesses nevertheless prospered, with trading, importation/exportation, and acquisitions. 1876, Hackman entered into a new business—a cutlery factory in Nurmi, near Vyborg. On J.F. Hackman Jr.'s 1879 death, his son Wilhelm Hackman (1842–1925), part owner from 1866, succeeded him as head of the firm, with Carl-August Ekström (1823–1900), Wilhelm's brother-in-law, as part owner. Numerous investments continued, and the cutlery factory was moved to Sorsakoski in 1891. The area soon developed into a center of metalworking and, during World War I, Hackman supplied barbed-wire scissors and bayonets to Russia. There were a number of losses of various Hackman plants during the

war, but, from 1924, the Sorsakoski plant's manufacture of stainless-steel knives was greatly increased, realizing success. And, a few years hence, complete cutlery sets were introduced. 1925, Wilhelm's sons Leo Hackman (d. 1948) and Henry Hackman (d. 1950) and Edvin Ektröm, Gunnar Ekström, and C.G. Wolff became the managers of the firm, which also had holdings in a pulp mill and household-chemical plants. Due to the outbreak of World War II and the Soviet Union's 1939 attack on Finland, Hackman produced war materiel for the Finnish Defense Forces. On Henry Hackman's 1950 death, his sons Herrick Hackman and Gunnar Ekström managed the firm, which remained active in forestry and the wood and heavy-metalworking sectors. From 1950, the firm produced steel pots and pans and, 1950s, steel household wares, designed by Kaj Franck, Bertel Gardberg, and Nanny Still, which became popular worldwide. From 1972, the firm has been managed by numerous non-Hackman-family men. A large number of acquisitions followed, including the late-1980s purchase of Hammarplast and Sarvis to create Hackman Form. 1988, the firm became publicly held. 1989, Hackman acquired the Høyang-Polaris pot-and-pan factory in Norway, the Nilsjohan and Skultuna factories in Sweden, and the Klöverblad factory in Denmark. 1990, the corporation bought Finland's Arabia porcelain plant (founded in 1874), Sweden's Gustavsberg porcelain plant (founded in 1825), Rörstrand (founded in 1726), Finland's Iittala glassworks (founded in 1881), and Nuutajärvi (founded in 1793, already acquired by Iittala), and, thus, Hackman Tabletop was formed. (Some brands have since been sold by Hackman to other holding groups.) From 1991, the heavy industries were sold off. 1993, Hackman bought Fürst Bestecke, a German cutlery manufacturer. 1994, Hackman Housewares and Hackman Tabletop merged into Hackman Designor. 1994, Hackman Designor bought Oy ALU Ab. 2000, Hackman Designor Oy Ab changed its name to Designor Oy Ab. 2002, iittala was chosen as the international brand of the company, retaining the original 1955 'i' logo, designed by Timo Sarpaneva when Iittala was independent. 2003, Designor acquired BodaNova–Höganäs Keramik. 2003, Designor Oy Ab's name was changed to iittala oy ab, with an initial lowercase 'i.' Hence, the HackmanGroup is now composed of two divisions: Metos and iittala. Metos manufactures dishwashing equipment and offers services and systems to professional kitchens. The other division, iittala, is composed of the Arabia, Hackman, Høyang-Polaris, iittala, and Rörstrand brands. Høyang-Polaris pots and pans have been designed by Björn Dahlström and Nanny Still. Hackefors, Kløverblad, Nilsjohan, and Polaris are used as so-called Power Brand names in the household-goods market. 2002, Pekka Lundmark (1964–), formerly a senior vice-president at Nokia and, subsequently, a partner of Startupfactory, was appointed HackmanGroup's president and CEO. 2002 net sales of its Scandinavian-designed and -made products was $352 million/346 million euros. Employees number about 3,000.
> See Arabia; Gustavsberg; Höganäs Keramik, Iittala Lasi; Nuutajärvi-Notsjö; Rörstrand Porslinsfabriker.

Hadelands Glassverk

Norwegian glassware manufacturer; located Jevnaker.

History 1762, a factory was established on property in Jevnaker owned by the Danish-Norwegian state under Christian VI; 1765, started production of colored glass bottles, pharmaceutical glass, and fishing floats; 1852, began to produce colorless glass, leading to tablewares; 1898, became part of shareholding company A/S Christiana Glasmagasin with a shop in Kristiana (now Oslo) and three factories: Hadelands (decorative and utility wares), Høvik Verk (lighting), and Drammens Glassverk (window glass). Continued production throughout World War II with designs by Sverre Pettersen, its first full-time designer and art director 1928–49. From 1937, sculptor Ståle Kylingstad (1903–) worked there. From 1936, Willy Johansson (along with his father Wilhelm Johansson) was a master glassblower, instrumental in improving the quality and quantity of its tablewares, and was a designer and became head of design, production, and artwares 1947–88. Other designers have included Herman Bongard to 1955, Arne Jon Jutrem from 1950 (art director at Hadelands from 1985), and Severin Brørby from 1956. 1955–1967, Benny Motzfeldt, worked there and later left to be head of design at Randsfjords Glassverks. A number of other distinguished designers have worked for the firm, including the present one, Lena Hansson (1962–), and current chief designer and art director Maud Gjeruldsen Bugge (1962–). 1835 to 1980s (a 150-year saga), the Berg family had been closely associated with Hadelands, where Jens W. Berg (1922–) was managing director 1951–80.

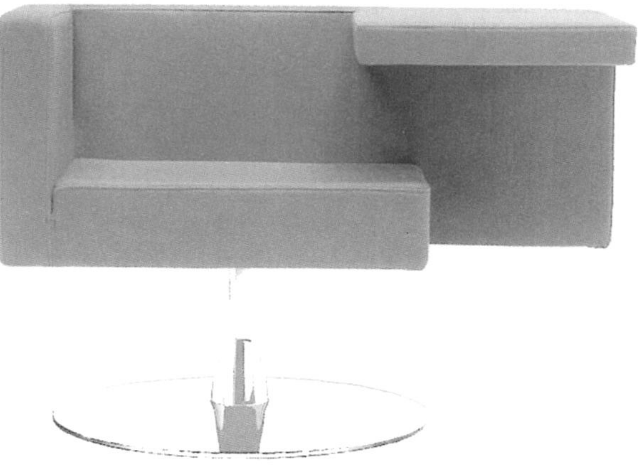

Alfredo Häberli. Solitaire seat with writing surface. c. 2002. Wood, cold foam with flame fiber, fabric, and chrome lacquer, h. 28 x w. 36 5/8 x d 24 3/8" (71 x 93 x 62 cm). Mfr.: Offecct, Sweden.

Exhibitions/citations Work (by W. Johansson) shown at 1933 (5th) Triennale di Milano and subsequently, including 1954 (10th) Triennale di Milano, where Johansson received the diploma of honor.
Bibliography Arne Jon Jutrem, *Glas og glassfórmere på Hadeland*, Årbok: Nordenfjeldske Kunstindustriemuseum, 1958. *Glas Er Vart Material*, Oslo: Hadelands, 1961. I.M. Lie, *Hadelandsglass 1950–1900*, Oslo: Huitfeldt, 1977. Jennifer Hawkins Opie, *Scandinavia: Ceramics and Glass in the Twentieth Century*, New York: Rizzoli, 1989. Leslie Jackson, *20th Century Factory Glass*, London: Octopus, 2000.

Hadid, Zaha (1950–)

Iraqi architect; born Bagdad; active London.

Training To 1971, mathematics, American University of Beirut; 1972–77, diploma prize, Architectural Association, London.
Biography In London: Hadid has taught, Architectural Association; 1977 joined Rem Koolhaas and Elia Zenghelis, Office of Metropolitan Architect; 1980, began her own practice and, to 1987, her own studio at the Architectural Association. She became well known for her award-winning 1983 The Peak competition entry in Hong Kong, a private club and residential complex. She called on radical methods of representation and credited early Russian Suprematist exercises as influences on her work. Work has included furniture such as 1987 Wavy Back sofa with Michael Wolfson by Edra and 1999 Z-Scape by Sawaya & Moroni. Architecture includes 1985 apartments, London; 1985 interiors and furniture, Bitar, London; 1986 Kurfürstendamm office building, Berlin; 1986 IBA Housing, Berlin; 1987 Tomigaya, Tokyo; 1991–93 fire station, Vitra factory, Weil am Rhien; 1998 Holloway Road Bridge, University of North London; 1998 Zentrum für zeitgenössische

Hadelands. Vase. 1980s. Colorless glass with white threads and orange strips, h. 5 1/8" (13 cm). Mfr.: Hadelands Glassverk, Norway. Courtesy Quittenbaum Kunstauktionen, Munich.

Kunst, Rome; 1998–2003 Rosenthal Center for Contemporary Arts Center (first museum by a female architect in the US), Cincinnati, Ohio; 1999 Center for Contemporary Arts, Rome; 1999 Bergisel ski-jump, Innsbruck, Austria; 2001 The Temporary Guggenheim, Tokyo; 2000 National Library, Québec; 1999–2000 Mind Zone, Millennium Dome, London; from 2001 Fährterminal, Salerno; 1999–2002 Bergisel Sprungschanze, Innsbruck; Science Center, Wolfsburg (from 2000), Vista Master Plan, Singapore (from 2001), Spittelau-Viadukt, Wien (from 1994), BMW-Zentralgebäude, Leipzig (from 2002). 1986, she was visiting professor (and Kenzo Tange chairperson 1994), Harvard University School of Design, Cambridge, Mass.; visiting professor, Columbia University, New York. Her paintings and drawings have been widely published.
Exhibitions/citations Work subject of exhibitions, including Guggenheim Museum, New York, 1978; Architectural Association, 1983; GA Gallery, Tokyo, 1985; The Museum of Modern Art, New York, 1988; Graduate School of Design; Harvard University, 1994; Waiting Room, Grand Central Station, New York, 1995, subject of 2000 exhibition (first major solo venue of her work), Institute of Contemporary Art, London; 2003 *Zaha Hadid, Architektur*, Österreichisches Museum für angewandte Kunst, Vienna.1982 gold medal (for apartment conversions, Eaton Place, London), *Architectural Digest* magazine. First place awards: 1986, competition in Kufurstendamm, Berlin; 1989, for art and media center Dusseldorf; 1994, for the Cardiff Bay Opera House. 1983 first prize, The Peak competition, Hong Kong; 2004 Pritzker Architecture Prize. Wavy Back Sofa shown at 1991 *Mobili Italiani 1961 –1991: Le Varie Età dei Linguaggi* exhibition, Salone del Mobile, Milan. As an exhibition designer, 1990 *Exhibition for Video Art*, Gronningen; 1992 *Great Utopia*, Guggenheim Museum, New York. Work included in numerous venues.
Bibliography *Planetary Architecture* (folio of work), Z. Hadid and Architectural Association, London, 1983. Y. Futagawa, (ed.), *GA Architecture: Zaha M. Hadid*, ADA Edita, Tokyo, 1986. Aaron Betsky, *Zaha Hadid: The Complete Buildings and Projects*, London: Thames & Hud-son, 1998. *Zaha Hadid LF one (Landscape Formation one) in Weil am Rhein*, Basel: Birkhäuser, 1999. Documentary video, Steve Gebhardt, *Zaha Hadid and the Museum* (Contemporary Arts Center, Cincinnati), 2003.
> See Sawaya & Moroni.

Hadley, Albert (1920–)

American interior designer; born Nashville, Tenn.; active New York.

Training Art and design, Peabody College, Nashville; c. 1946–48, Parsons School of Design, New York.
Biography Hadley first worked at Bradford's furniture store, then for decorating firm A. Herbert Rogers, both in Nashville; during World War II, served in 861st Aviation Engineer Battalion, in London; 1948, graduated from Parsons, where he taught at the school c. 1949–54. In New York: 1954–57, Hadley established his own decorating business, and, 1957–62, worked at interior design firm McMillen, where his assignments included the restoration of the Rosedown Plantation in Louisiana; 1963, formed a partnership with Mrs. Henry 'Sister' Parish 2nd. Hadley has become known for his attention to architecture and the arrangement of art and furniture. Parish-Hadley Associates gained a worldwide reputation for its interiors for privileged and wealthy clients. Hadley designed 1993 range of furniture by Baker. 1994, 'Sister' Parish died; 1999, Hadley closed Parish-Hadley and set up his own smaller business.
Bibliography Mark Hampton, *The Legendary Decorators of the Twentieth Century*, New York: Doubleday, 1992. Sister Parish, Albert Hadley, and Christopher Petkanas, *Parish Hadley: Sixty Years of American Design*, Boston: Little, Brown, 1995. Apple Parish Bartlett, Susan Bartlett Carter, Albert Hadley, *Sister: The Life of the Legendary American Interior Decorator Mrs. Henry Parish II*, New York: St. Martin's, 2000.

Haefeli, Max Ernst (1901–1976)

Swiss architect and designer; born Zürich.

Training 1919–23 under Karl Moser, architecture, Eidgenössische Technische Hochschule, Zürich.
Biography 1923–24, Haefeli worked in studio of Otto Bartning in Berlin; 1924–25, joined his father's architectural office Pfleghard und Haefeli; 1926, set up independent practice; 1926, designed renovation of Girsberger bookstore in Zürich, including design of chairs and tables; 1927, became head of Kollektivgruppe Schweizer Architekten; 1927–28, designed Rotachhäuser building in Zürich, an early example of the modern Neues Bauen style in Switzerland and a breakthrough in Zürich architecture. Late 1920s, he collaborated closely with Ernst Kadler-Vögeli and manufacturer Horgen-Glarus in Switzerland; 1928–31, was a member of the planning team for 1931 Siedlung Neubühl in Zürich; taught, Kunstgewerbeschule and Abendtechnikum Juventus, both in Zürich; 1937, became cofounder of architectural firm Haefeli, Moser und Steiger (HMS). HMS designed the Kongresshaus and 1942–51 cantonal hospital, both Zürich, of which Haefeli was responsible for the skin and interior spatial scheme. Subsequent work included the planning and building of swimming pools, cemeteries, zoos, and commercial buildings.
Exhibitions c. 1927 *Form ohne Ornament* (chair and table models for Girsberger bookstore), Zürich; as head of Kollektivgruppe Schweizer Architekten, 1927 *Weissenhofsiedlung* (furniture and accessories for several apartments by Mies van der Rohe), Stuttgart. c. 1931 *Das Neue Heim* (furniture produced by Wohnbedarf store), Zürich.
Bibliography Friederike Mehlau-Wiebking et al., *Schweizer Typenmöbel 1925–35, Sigfried Giedion und die Wohnbedarf AG*, Zürich: gta, 1989: 228.

Max E. Haefeli and Walter Custer. Volksschrank cabinet. 1933. Birch-veneer plywood and solid wood, 61 x 35 7/16 x 21 7/16" (155 x 90 x 54.5 cm). Mfr.: initially, Fischer carpentry workshop, Switzerland, and, subsequently, Jaeggi, Switzerland, for Wohbedarf store, Zurich, Switzerland. Courtesy Quittenbaum Kunstauktionen, Munich.

Haerdtl, Oswald (1899–1959)

Austrian architect and designer; born Vienna.

Training 1916-21 under Josef Hoffmann, Kunstgewerbeschule, Vienna.
Biography 1922, Haerdtl (or Härdtl) was an assistant and, from c. 1928, partner in Josef Hoffmann's architectural firm; 1935–59, taught, Kunstgewerbeschule in Vienna; has become best known as a designer rather than an architect, rendering graceful, delicate drinking sets, gift items, candlesticks, and crystal lighting by J. & L. Lobmeyr in Vienna, including 1924 Tableset no. 240 (aka The Ambassador), 1950 Tableset no. 257 (aka The Commodore), furniture, interiors, and domestic items, and, c. 1930, a number of his silver objects by Klinkosch.
Exhibitions Assisted Josef Hoffmann on Austrian pavilion at 1925 *Exposition Internationale des Arts Décoratifs et Industriels Modernes*, Paris; designed a pavilion, 1934 *Exposition de l'Habitation*, Paris. Tableset no. 257 was designed to be shown at 1951 (9th) Triennale di Milano.
Bibliography Günther Feuerstein, *Vienna—Present and Past: Arts and Crafts—Applied Art—Design*, Vienna: Jugend und Volk, 1976: 49, 50, 51, 53, 80. Cat., *Oswald Haerdtl 1899–1959*, Vienna: Hochschule für angewandte Kunst, 1978. Annelies Krekel-Aalberse, *Art Nouveau and Art Déco Silver*, New York: Abrams, 1989. Cat., Adolph Stiller, *Oswald Haerdtl Architekt und Designer 1899–1959* (Architektur Zentrum Wien), Salzburg: Pustet, 2000.

Hafner, Dorothy (1952–)

American ceramicist and designer; born Woodbridge, Conn.

Training To 1974, bachelor's degree in fine art, Skidmore College, Saratoga Springs, N.Y., and post-graduate studies there.
Biography Hafner at first produced designs by hand in Pop-Art or comic-book style with flamboyant colors; 1970–90, designed a signature ceramic range by Tiffany & Co. in New York; 1980s, was the principal designer at Rosenthal for cutlery and ceramics such as 1987 Flash tea set; was the first woman among Rosenthal Studio-Linie's designers; late 1990s and early 2000s, constructed complex free-standing glass panels and glass vases.
Exhibitions/citations Work subject of exhibitions in the US, including at Heller Gallery, New York, where her mouth-blown/fused glass was first shown in 1995. 1983 certificate of honor, Women in Design International, Ross, Cal.; 1985 Westerwald Prize for Industrial Ceramics, Westerwald, Germany; 1986 New York Foundation for the Arts Fellowship; 1988 Design Excellence, Stuttgart Design Center, Germany; 1988 (1st) International Tabletop Award, Dallas, Tex.; 1997 Fellissimo Design Award, New York Foundation for the Arts.
Bibliography Yvònne Joris (intro.), *Functional Glamour*, 's-Hertogenbosch: Museum Het Kruithuis, 1987: 56–67. Albrecht Bangert and Karl Michael Armer, *80s Style: Designs of the Decade*, New York: Abbeville, 1990: 138, 231. Cat., R. Craig Miller (intro.), *U.S. Design 1975–2000*, Munich: Prestel, 2002.

Hagenauer, Carl (1871–1928)

Austrian metalworker; active Vienna; father of Karl, Franz, and Grete Hagenauer.

Training Apprentice at goldsmiths Würbel & Czokally, Vienna.
Biography Carl Hagenauer was a journeyman goldsmith under Bernauer Samu in Preßburg (now Bratislava, Slovakia), becoming a gold chaser; 1898, set up his own workshop at Werkstätten Hagenauer, Vienna, where he produced bronzeware designed by himself and others and small metal sculptures by old masters; produced metalware designed by Josef Hoffmann, Otto Prutscher, E.J. Meckel, and others.
Exhibitions Work in numerous exhibitions, including those in Paris, London, and Berlin where he won prizes. Subject of 1971 exhibition at Österreichisches Museum für angewandte Kunst, Vienna.
Bibliography Cat., *Werkstätten Hagenauer, 1898–1971*, Vienna: Österreichisches Museum für angewandte Kunst, 1971. Cat., *Metallkunst*, Berlin: Bröhan Museum, 1990: 105–589.
> See Hagenauer, Werkstätten.

Hagenauer, Karl (1898–1956)

Austrian metalworker; born Preßburg (now Bratislava, Slovakia); active Vienna; son of Carl Hagenauer; brother of Franz and Grete Hagenauer.

Training Under Josef Hoffmann and Oskar Strnad, Kunstgewerbeschule, Vienna; and architecture.
Biography From 1919, Karl Hagenauer worked in his family's workshop, designing and producing domestic ware in silver, bronze, copper, enamel, ivory, stone, and wood that revealed the influences of Josef Hoffmann and the Wiener Werkstätte. On his father's 1928 death, Karl became director of the firm (with brother Franz Hagenauer and sister Grete Hagenauer), which was expanded to include a furniture workshop and sales stores in Vienna and Salzburg; became active in interior design; was a member of the Österreichischer Werkbund and the Österreichische Werkstätten.
Exhibition Work included in 1971 exhibition, Österreichisches Museum für angewandte Kunst, Vienna (catalog below).
Bibliography Cat., *Werkstätten Hagenauer, 1898–1971*, Vienna: Österreichisches Museum für angewandte Kunst, 1971. Cat., *Metallkunst*, Berlin: Bröhan Museum, 1990: 105–589.
> See Hagenauer, Werkstätten.

Hagenauer, Werkstätten

Austrian metalsmiths; located Vienna.

History Werkstätten Hagenauer greatly influenced the applied arts in Austria in styles ranging from the Jugendstil and the Wiener Werkstätte to modernism. 1870–1914, Viennese bronze work had become particularly and generally distinguished. In Vienna, the influence of the Ringstrasse construction and growing prosperity fostered production of metalwork that included candelabra, lamps, vases, watches, andirons, writing utensils, bookends, ashtrays, bar items, and other domestic accessories. By 1898, the Viennese metalworking industry had included more than 230 factories and workshops. 1898 was the year Carl Hagenauer established Werkstätten Hagenauer, where he used his knowledge of gold, silver, and other metals in styles akin to Jungendstil and exported his wares worldwide. 1919, his son Karl joined the firm. Karl defied the Jungendstil of Oskar Strnad's generation and sought a contemporary foreign genre. From 1920s, the Hagenauer workshop expanded from metalworking into domestic accessories and furniture that called on an array of materials, particularly following Julius Jirisek's participation in the firm; produced works by outside designers Otto Prutscher, E.J. Meckel, and Josef Hoffmann. Its metalwork in plated silver and chromium incorporated carved woods and bronzes. 1932, French designer René Coulon collaborated with Jacques Adnet on tempered-glass furniture by Hagenauer. 1956, the firm closed.
Exhibitions Work subject of 1971 exhibition, Österreichisches Museum für angewandte Kunst, Vienna.
Bibliography Cat., *Werkstätten Hagenauer, 1898–1971*, Vienna: Österreichisches Museum für angewandte Kunst, 1971. Annelies Krekel-Aalberse, *Art Nouveau and Art Déco Silver*, New York: Abrams, 1989. Cat., *Metallkunst*, Berlin: Bröhan Museum, 1990.

Oswald Haerdtl. Ambassador Service glasses. 1924. Gold-lustre crystal, tallest (champagne glass) h. 8 1/2 x dia. 4 1/16" (21.6 x 10.3 cm), shortest (wine glass) h. 7 13/16 x dia. 3 3/4" (19.8 x 9.5 cm). Mfr.: J. & L. Lobmeyr, Austria. Gift of A. J. Van Dugteren & Sons, Inc. MoMA.

Hagener Silberschmiede

German silversmiths; located Hagen.

History 1910, Hagener Silberschmiede (Hagen silver workshop) was established by Karl Ernst Osthaus. Its silverwares were designed by J.L.M. Lauweriks, director of the Handfertigkeitsseminar; F.H. Ehmcke; and E.H. Scheidler. On Lauweriks's recommendation, Frans Zwollo Sr. became its head designer. In a short-lived experiment, the silversmithy aimed to rival the Wiener Werkstätte. 1914, it closed due to the outbreak of World War I, when Zwollo returned to the Netherlands.
Bibliography Cat., *Franz Zwollo en zijn tijd*, Rotterdam: Museum Boymans-van Beuningen, 1982. Annelies Krekel-Aalberse, *Art Nouveau and Art Déco Silver*, New York: Abrams, 1989.

Hahn, Otto (1873–1953)

German silversmith; active Bielefeld and Berlin.

History c. 1910, Hahn produced hollow-ware designed by Hans Perathoner, a sculptor from the southern Tyrol. (Perathoner created the 1909 linen weavers' memorial, Bielefeld's best-known landmark.) Charles Rennie Mackintosh's 1904 christening cutlery for his godchild Friedrich Eckart Muthesius was marked 'C. Hahn, Berlin.' 1930s, Otto Hahn designed and made modern silver.
Bibliography Annelies Krekel-Aalberse, *Art Nouveau and Art Déco Silver*, New York: Abrams, 1989.

Haigh, Paul (1949–); Barbara H. Haigh (1948–)
Paul: British designer and architect; born Leeds. Barbara: American design director; born New York; husband and wife.

Training Paul: to 1972, architecture and design studies, Leeds University; 1975, post-graduate studies, Royal College of Art, London. Barbara: interior design, Pratt Institute and New York School of Interior Design, both New York.
Biography Paul worked for Knoll International in Milan; 1978, emigrated to the US to design exclusively for Knoll. Following the 1982 opening of Knoll Design Center in New York, he set up his own architectural and design studio Haigh Space in New York. 1982, his wife Barbara joined the firm. (1974–81, she had been the design manager of new products at Knoll.) 1990, Haigh Architects + Designers moved to Greenwich, Conn. Architecture includes Knoll Design Center, New York; 1990 Vitra office, Fogelsville, Pa.; 1993 Caroline's Comedy Club, New York; 1992-93 prototype retail outlet of Mikasa (ceramics), Secaucus, N.J.; 1999 retail design for Brooks Brothers (clothing) and Steuben Store (crystal), both New York. Design work has include 1984 Tux chair and table by Bieffeplast; glass collections by Baccarat and by Steuben; desk systems, seating, and office products by Herman Miller; in-store display fixtures for Rosenthal and for Bulgari, US. Paul has taught architecture at Parsons School of Design, New York, and lectured worldwide.
Exhibitions/citations 1986 *40 under 40* review of American architects by and Paul Haigh named as one of the 'Emerging Voices' by the Architectural League of New York. Drawings and projects shown in group and solo exhibitions, including SoHo Guggenheim Museum and 1990 Cooper-Hewitt National Museum of Design, both New York; 1990 Dentsu Gallery, Tokyo; Royal College of Art, London; 2003, Parsons School of Design, New York. Awards: Record Houses Award for Framingham Residence, Remsemburg, N. Y., *Architectural Record* journal; several American Institute of Architects (AIA) awards and two National Honor Awards (for 1992 Paramount Hotel and 1995 Caroline's Comedy Theater, both New York), American Institute of Architects (AIA); 1991 Lumen Award (for lighting design); 1994 merit award (for Caroline's Comedy Club, New York), United States Institute of Theater Technology; several citations, Annual Design Review editions, *I.D.* magazine; Institute of Business Designers (IBD): 1987 Gold Award (for Sinistra chair by Berndardt) and 1987 Silver Award (for Enigma chair collection by Bernhardt); International Furniture Competition awards, *Progressive Architecture* journal; 1988 East Meets West Competition, Japan; 1990 Virtu 5 Design Award (for '...thin end of the wedge' table collection, Ottoman Empire), Canada; fellow, Worldesign Foundation; jury chairperson, Interiors Awards Committee, AIA; member, Architectural League of New York.
Bibliography www.haigharchitects.com.

Haile, 'Sam' Thomas Samuel (1909–1948)
British painter and ceramicist; husband of ceramicist Marianne de Trey.

Training 1931–34, Under William Staite Murray, pottery, Royal College of Art, London.
Biography Haile designed modern stoneware and slipware reminiscent of contemporary painting; 1935, taught pottery, Leicester College of Art; 1936, taught and worked in London; 1939 with Trey, traveled to the US and taught, New York State College of Ceramics, Alfred, N.Y., and at College of Architecture, University of Michigan, Ann Arbor, Mich.
Bibliography Cat., *Thirties: British Art and Design Before the War*, London: Arts Council of Great Britain/Hayward Gallery, 1979.

Haimi
Finnish furniture manufacturer.

History 1943, Haimi was founded in Helsinki; 1965, began using plastics in furniture, with the bulk of its products in fiberglass and acrylics. Yrjö Kukkapuro's designs for Haimi included the renowned 1965 Karuselli 412 and 1969 Haimi 415 fiberglass chairs, 1966 Chair 414 k, and Design Y table and chairs, 1970 Saturnus sofa. Eventually, Haimi was succeeded by Avarte.
Exhibitions Work shown at 1966 (1st) Eurodomus, Genoa; 1968 Eurodomus II, Turin; 1966 *Vijtig jaar zitten*, Stedelijk Museum, Amsterdam.
Bibliography Cat., Milena Lamarová, *Design a Plastické Hmoty*, Prague: Uměleckoprůmyslové Muzeum, 1972: 56, 58, 188.

Karl Hagenauer. Ashtray. 1946. Oxidized brass bowl and polished brass top, overall h. 1/2 x dia. 4 1/8" (1.3 x 10.5 cm). Mfr.: Werkstätten Karl Hagenauer, Austria. Gift of Rena Rosenthal, Inc. MoMA.

Haines, William (1900–1973)
American film actor and interior designer; born Stauton, Va.; active Los Angeles.

Biography Haines won a photo contest in New York sponsored by the Goldwyn film company and moved to Hollywood. 1927, he became one of only ten Metro-Goldwyn-Mayer (MGM) actors whose name was placed above the title; lived in a house on North Stanley Avenue, Hollywood, where he dabbled in interior design, critical of the hodge-podge of historical styles popular in the 1920s. Before turning from the film business, he had already begun decorating professionally; was a partner of Mitchell Foster in an antiques shop; 1930, left MGM and established an interior design firm on the Sunset Strip called Haines Foster; incorporated English antiques and decorated the Hyams/Berg house (architect, Paul R. Williams) in Beverly Hills; decorated the Jack and Ann Warner house (architect, Roland E. Coate); collaborated with architect J.E. Dolena on the enlarged Beverly Hills house of film-director George Cukor in a so-called Regency Modern style. The Cukor house was distinguished by its oval sitting room with copper-covered cornice-lighting, copper fireplace, copper lampshades, suede walls, leather-laced curtains (a Haines trademark), and coral-colored leather-and-fabric side chairs. The Cukor design was an example of Haines's unusual materials-and-textures combinations. His taste was idiosyncratic yet rooted in traditionalism. During World War II, the Haines-Foster partnership was discontinued. After the war, Haines established the decorating firm William Haines Designs in Beverly Hills. 1946, Ted Graber (decorator of the family rooms in The White House for president Ronald Reagan) joined the firm. Late 1940s, Haines worked in a modern style akin to Richard Neutra, R.M. Schindler, and Charles Eames, illustrated by Haines's Sidney and Frances Brody house (architect, A. Quincy Jones) in Los Angeles. The Haines-Jones collaboration resulted in six more houses, including another for Hyams and Berg, Walter Annenberg's 1966 desert house 'Sunnylands' and 1969 'Winfield House,' and the American ambassador's residence in Regent's Park, London.
Bibliography Pilar Viladas, 'Decorating's Leading Man,' *House & Garden*, Aug. 1990: 100+.

Haité, George Charles (1855–1924)
British textile designer and painter; born Bexley, Kent.

Biography Haité was prolific, successful, and one of the most important pattern designers in the late Victorian period; wrote the books *Plant Studies for Artists, Designers, and Art Students* (London: Bernard Quaritch, 1886) and *How to Draw Floral and Vegetal Forms* (1870). He called on conventionalized patterns derived from nature and *japonisant* art for ceiling designs by J. Tollman & Co., wallpapers by Arthur Sanderson & Sons and Essex & Co., and fabrics by G. P. & J. Baker. He also designed small decorative objects such as 1896 interior fittings for the studio of E. Davis that included metallic electroliers decorated with leaves and flowers and four copper *repoussé* grilles representing the Four Seasons. 1911, he donated 60 examples of the textile work of his father, George Haité (1825–1871), to the Victoria and Albert Museum, London. His father, who died of small pox, asserted

toward the end of his life that designers were 'slaves to the fashion of the hour, the style of the season and the middleman' and, frequently, declared that he would not allow his son to follow him into the textile trade, which contrarily he did.
Bibliography Stuart Durant, *Ornament from the Industrial Revolution to Today,* Woodstock, N.Y.: Overlook, 1986: 42, 323.

Hajdu, Etienne (1907–1996)
Hungarian sculptor; born Turda, Romania; active Paris.

Training Under Antoine Bourdelle, in sculpture.
Biography Hajdu, a naturalized French citizen, designed 1976 Diane dinnerware which showed a dancing white abstract pattern on a deep-blue background, and, for Manufacture Nationale de Sèvres, a 1970 dinner service. His 1967–71 Colonnes à Mallarmé bronze sculpture was acquired by FRAC Bretagne in 1983, installed 1986. He died in Bagneux, France.
Exhibitions/citations Work included in numerous exhibitions. 1969 Grand Prix National des Arts.
Bibliography *Les carnets du design*, Paris: Mad-Cap Productions/ APCI, 1986: 21.

Halabala, Jindřich (1903–1978)
Moravian architect and furniture designer; born Koryčany (now in Czech Republic).

Training 1922–26 under Pavel Janák, Vysoká Škola Uměleckoprůmyslová (VŠUP, academy of arts, architecture, and design), Prague.
Biography 1930–50, Halabala was head architect at the Spojené UP Závody, Brno; 1930s, collaborated on standard (or type) furniture systems; designed two versions of 1931 elastic tubular-steel chairs; was a consultant and publisher on modern interior design.
Bibliography Jan van Geest and Otakar Máčel, *Stühle aus Stahl, Metallmöbel 1925–1940*, Cologne: König, 1980. Alena Adlerová, *České užité umění 1918–1938*, Prague: Odeon, 1983.

Halcyon Art Pottery
American ceramics manufactory; located Halcyon, near San Luis Obispo, Cal.

History 1904, a Theosophist group established a sanatorium in Halcyon, Cal., and, 1909, the Temple Home Association; 1910, opened a school and art pottery with Alexander Robertson as instructor and director of pottery. (He had been active in his own Roblin Art Pottery, San Francisco, which closed after the 1906 earthquake.) The students were responsible for much of the decoration of Halcyon's pottery. Its often unglazed forms, lending themselves to modeling and carving, were frequently overwrought. An image of the lizard was the most popular modeled decoration. Robertson's wares included incense burners, clay whistles, paperweights, vases, bowls, and pitchers. The pottery became successful and was the basis for the Industrial School of Arts and Crafts in Halcyon. 1913, the pottery closed, following a revision of the association's charter.
Bibliography Paul Evans in Timothy J. Andersen et al., *California Design 1910*, Salt Lake City: Peregrine Smith, 1980: 65.

Hall China Co.: Eva Zeisel. Hallcraft/Tomorrow's Classic sauce boat and ladle, 1949. Glazed earthenware, sauce boat 6 1/4 x 6 1/2 x 5 1/4" (15.9 x 16.5 x 13.3 cm), ladle 4 x 4 1/2 x 1 7/8" (10.2 x 11.4 x 4.7 cm). Mfr.: Hall China Co., US (1952). Gift of Della Rothermel in honor of John Patrick Rothermel. MoMA.

Hald, Dagny (1936–); Finn Hald (1929–)
Norwegian ceramicists; husband (Dagny) and wife (Finn).

Training Dagny Hald: 1951, Academie delle Belle Arti, Faenza, Italy; 1952–54, Statens Håndverks-og Kunstindustriskole, Oslo; 1955, workshops of Marianne and Lars Thiirslund, and of Kaare B. Fjeldsaa, Blommenholm.
Biography From 1956, the Halds were active in their own studio; became best known for their 1970 gnome-like ceramic figures; as clay artists, were unwilling to work for a ceramics factory. Work has also included a number of ceramic vessels, architectural elements, furniture, and illustrations (particularly for books), and, by Finn Hald, stoves by Ceramic Store Company in Oxford, UK.
Bibliography Fredrik Wildhagen, *Norge i Form*, Oslo: Stenersen, 1988: 160. Jennifer Hawkins Opie, *Scandinavia: Ceramics and Glass in the Twentieth Century*, New York: Rizzoli, 1989. *Ut i verden: Grafikk av Dagny Hald av Finn Hald*, Bjørnemyr: Frifant, 2001.

Hald, Nils Tov Edward (1883–1980)
Swedish glassware designer, ceramicist, and painter; born Stockholm.

Training 1903–04, professional studies in England and Germany; 1904–06, Technische Akademie, Dresden; 1907, painting, Artists' Studio School, Copenhagen; Artists' League School, Stockholm; 1908–12 under Henri Matisse, in Paris.
Biography 1917–27, Edward Hald worked as a freelance designer at Rörstrand porcelain factory, Lidköping; 1924–33, designer and art director at Karlskrona porcelain factory. Concurrently, from 1917, his designs were produced by the Orrefors Glasbruk, where he was artistic director 1924–33 and managing director 1933–44, and developed the *graal* technique of blowing glass with colored decoration incorporated within the walls of his vessels. 1920s, he worked in ceramics; until late 1970s, was associated with Orrefors.
Citations Grand prize, 1925 *Exposition Internationale des Arts Décoratifs et Industriels Modernes*, Paris; 1945 Prince Eugen Medal; 1939, elected Honorary Royal Designer for Industry, UK; member of Svensk Form (Swedish Society of Crafts and Design); honorary fellow of Society of Glass Technology, Sheffield.
Bibliography Cat., *Edward Hald målare Konst industripianjär*, Stockholm: Nationalmuseum, 1983. Jennifer Hawkins Opie, *Scandinavia: Ceramics and Glass in the Twentieth Century*, New York: Rizzoli, 1989. Mel Byars with Arlette Barré-Despond, *100 Designs/100 Years: A Celebration of the 20th Century*, Hove: RotoVision, 1999: 52–53. George Fischler and Barrett Gould, *Scandinavian Ceramics and Glass: 1940s to 1980s*, Atglen, Pa.: Schiffer, 2000.

Haley, Reuben (1872–1933)
American glass designer, metalsmith, sculptor; born Pittsburgh, Pa.

Biography Working as a sculptor and metalsmith, Haley was chief designer from 1911–25 at United States Glass, a conglomerate of 13 manufacturers, where he eventually became a vice-president. 1925 when the firm was sold, he refused the position of president and departed. Haley reopened his own Metal Products Company (originally active briefly c. 1910 in a space rented from Consolidated Lamp & Glass Works in West Virginia). And at Metal Products, he designed Mexican-style art glass and the Ruba Rombic range (37 items produced from 1927–32). He was one of few who first modeled his glass designs in clay, an approach which may account for the symphony of flat planes on each piece of the Ruba Rombic group, probably derived from European, particularly Czech, Cubism. The Ruba Rombic saga of production is a complicated one. Haley designed patterns by Morgantown Glass Works in West Virginia and for Indiana Glass Company in Dunkirk, Ind., and a line of art pottery by Muncie Pottery Company in Muncie, Ind.
Bibliography Cat., Janet Kardon (ed.), *Craft in the Machine Age 1920–1945*, New York: Abrams with American Craft Museum, 1995.
> See Consolidated Lamp & Glass Company.

Hall China Company, The

American ceramics factory.

History 1903, former assets of the East Liverpool Potteries Company were dispensed to Robert Hall in East Liverpool, Ohio, and he founded The Hall China Company. Bed pans and combinets were the first products. On Hall's 1904 death, his son, Robert Taggert Hall, took over the management. 1903–11, Robert Taggert Hall investigated glazes to accommodate the high heat required for bisque firing; with superintendent Robert Meakin, discovered that a leadless glaze was the solution. Financial problems grew when vandals destroyed much of the plant. Even so, with Francis I. Simmers in charge of sales, the venture succeeded. 1920, Robert Taggart Hall died and Simmers became president of the firm, which began making stoneware items for food preparation/service that were smooth, non-absorbent, and shiny, contrary to the influx of imported wares. 1919, Hall China bought Goodwin Pottery Company and teapots were introduced. 1927, a third plant was opened. From 1933, decorated cooking china, teapots, and coffeemakers were produced. Notable products included 1940 streamline pitcher by J. Palin Thorley and 1952 Tomorrow's Classic dinnerware and serving pieces by Eva Ziesel (some production of which featured applied motifs designed by others in a dubious taste). Eva Zeisel's 1942–45 Museum White, 1949 Tomorrow's Classic, and 1956 Century were produced under the Hall trademark of Hallcraft. Container sets for use in refrigerators were produced for Montgomery Ward, Hotpoint, Westinghouse, and General Electric. Hall China also produced a number of pieces for other ceramics firms. The firm's full œuvre has become very large. From 1990s, some designs from the past were reentered into production: 1936 Ball pitcher, 1937 Donut teapot, 1954 Rivera pitcher, 1969 Duck casserole, 1940 Thorley streamline pitcher, and others.
Bibliography Harvey Duke, *Superior Quality: Hall China: A Guide for Collectors*, Otisville, Mich.: Depression Glass Daze, 1977. Jeffrey B. Snyder, *Hall China*, Atglen, Pa.: Schiffer, 2001. Margaret Whitmyer and Kenn Whitmyer, *Collectors Encyclopedia of Hall China*, Paduka, Ky.: Collectors Books, 2001 (3rd ed.).
> See Thorley, Joseph Palin.

Hallbergs Guldsmeds

Swedish silversmiths; located Stockholm.

History 1900, Hallbergs Guldsmeds produced the silver work of designer Ferdinand Boberg, who worked in a naturalistic Art Nouveau style. 1920s, director C.G. Hallberg's designers included Edvin Ollers, Niels Fougstedt, Elis Bergh, Hakon Ahlberg, and, 1930s, Sylvia Stave. 1961, the firm merged with Guldsmedsaktiebolaget (GAB).
Bibliography Annelies Krekel-Aalberse, *Art Nouveau and Art Déco Silver*, New York: Abrams, 1989.

Haller, Fritz (1924–)

Swiss architect, designer, and town planner; born Solothurn.

Training Apprenticeships under various architects, in Switzerland; under Willem van Tijen and H.A. Maaskant, in Rotterdam.
Biography 1949, Haller set up an architectural practice in Solothurn; 1966–71, was guest professor, University of Southern California, Los Angeles; concurrently, collaborated on movement studies with German architect Konrad Wachsmann. From 1977, Haller taught, Technische Universität, Karlsruhe; became known for his structural-steel industrial building systems. From his work on a building for metal-construction firm USM in Karlsruhe, Haller developed the Maxi system for spanning very wide spaces, originally developed for smaller spans. Calling on his experiences with large building projects, designed 1962–70 modular-furniture system still produced today by joint-venture firm USM Haller; early 1970s, designed Midi building system for medium-distance spans in industrial construction; with Franz Füeg, was one of the best-known members of Solothurn school of architecture. Haller wrote books on town planning: *Totale Stadt, ein Modell* (Olten: Walter, 1968) and *Totale Stadt, ein globales Modell: Integral urban, a global model* (Olten: Walter, 1974). In Switzerland: structures include 1951–55 (1st phase) and 1958–62 (end phase) Wasgenring School, Basel; 1958–64 Canton School, Baden; 1960–64 buildings for USM, Münsingen; 1961–66 Höhere Technische Lehranstalt, Brugg-Windisch; and 1980–82 Railways Training Center (with Hans Zaugg and Alfons Barth), Murten, which first employed the Midi system on a large scale.
Bibliography 'Die Solothurner Schule,' *Bauen + Wohnen*, vol. 36, nos. 7–8, 1981. Thomas Herzog in Vittorio Magnago Lampugnani (ed.), *Encyclopedia of 20th-Century Architecture*, New York: Abrams, 1986.

Shoji Hamada. Plate. 1960. Glazed ceramic. h. 2 1/4 x dia. 10 1/2" (5.7 x 26.7 cm). Mfr.: Shoji Hamada, Japan. Gift of Walter Bareiss in honor of Arthur Drexler and Arthur Drexler Fund. MoMA.

Cat., Hans Wichmann, *System-Design: Fritz Haller, Bauten, Möbel, Forschung*, Munich: Die Neue Sammlung, 1989.

Halling-Koch, Annagrete (1947–)

Danish ceramicist; born Copenhagen.

Training Ceramics, Kunsthåndværkerskolen, Copenhagen.
Biography Halling-Koch worked at Bing & Grøndahl Porcelænsfabrik in Copenhagen, where she designed and decorated ceramics; she also designed textiles for others.
Exhibitions Work shown in Copenhagen and the US.
Bibliography Robert A.M. Stern (ed.), *The International Design Yearbook*, New York: Abbeville, 1985/1986.

Halseth, Eivind (1972–)

Norwegian industrial designer.

Training 1995–99, Department of Industrial Design, Arkitekthøgskolen i Oslo (AHO), Norway; 1997–98, product design, Art Center College of Design, Pasadena, Cal.; 1994, mathematics and science, Universitet i Trondheim, Norway.
Biography From 2000, Halseth has been a partner in Permafrost Designstudio; 1999, taught in Department of Industrial Design, Arkitekthøgskolen i Oslo; designed 1998 cabinet handle by Artista in Oslo, 1999 toothbrushes by Øxeth Angelfoss, 1999 illustrations for the Tell publishing house.
Exhibitions/citations Work included in 1998 *The Future Elderly*, Oslo City Hall; 1999 *Young Millennium Design*, Norsk Form, Norwegian Forum for Design and Architecture; 1999–2000 *Future communications*, Technical Museum, Oslo. 1997 winner, Ericsson Electronics Design Competition; 1999 and 2000 Talent of the Year, Norska Designrådet (Norwegian design council).
Bibliography Mel Byars, *Design in Steel*, London: Laurence King, 2002. www.permafrost.no.
> See Permafrost, for group activities.

Hamada, Shoji (1894–1978)

Japanese potter; born Tokyo.

Training 1913–16 under Kanjiro Kawai, ceramics, Technical College, Tokyo; 1916–20, ceramics reseach, Kyoto.
Biography Hamada became known for chemical experimentation, notably in ancient Korean and Chinese ceramics glazes; 1919, met Bernard Leach in his workshop in Abiko and accompanied him back to England, starting a 60-year association; 1920–23, shared a studio with Leach in St. Ives, Cornwall; 1924, returned to Japan and set up a studio in Mashiko, a traditional village of artisans north of Tokyo, where he specialized in simple plates; 1910s–20s, developed the idea of Mingei (popular art), which had been created by philosopher Soetsu Yanagi, a friend of Leach; produced simple forms, including unusual sake bottles inspired by models of Okinawa, also teapots, vases, and plates in the molded or turned grès ware of Mashiko. Hamada's work was characterized by the great liberty he took with shapes and the spontaneity of his decorations.
Exhibitions/citations Work included in 1962 *Grès d'Aujourd'hui, d'Ici et d'Ailleurs*, Château de Ratilly (France); 1962 *Maîtres Potiers Contemporains*, Musée des Arts Décoratifs, Paris. 1955, officially appointed a living national treasure in Japan.

Bibliography Bernard Leach, *Hamada: Potter*, Tokyo and New York: Kodansha, 1975; reprinted 1997. *The Quiet Eye: Pottery of Shoji Hamada and Bernard Leach*, Monterey, Cal.: Monterey Peninsula Museum of Art, 1990.

Hamanaka, Katsu (1895–1982)
Japanese designer and artist.

Training Painting and interior decoration, School of Kushiro, Hokkaido.
Biography 1924, Hamanaka settled in Paris; 1935 under Jules Leleu's direction, decorated the Trouville dining room of 1935 oceanliner *Normandie*; was a technical collaborator with many prominent designers in Paris, including Jacques Adnet, Maurice Dufrêne, Pierre-Paul Montagnac, and Jacques-Émile Ruhlmann. Hamanaka was one of the rare specialists working with true lacquer (partially sap from the tree called *Urushi-no-ki* in Japanese, or *Rhus vernicifera* or *Rhus verniciflua*, a deciduous tree of the surnac family).
Exhibitions 1926–38, work shown at Salons in Paris and exhibitions organized by the Japanese embassy in Paris.
Bibliography Cat., Aaron Lederfajn and Xavier Lenormand, *Le Louvre des Antiquaires présente: 1930 quand le meuble devient sculpture*, Paris, 1986.

Hamel, Maria Christina (1958–)
British designer; born New Delhi; active Milan.

Training To 1979, Politecnico, Milan.
Biography 1972, Hamel settled in Milan; collaborated on projects with Ugo La Pietra, Ambrogio Rossari, Alessandro Mendini, and the Alchimia group; 1984-85, was an assistant instructor under Mendini, Hochschule für angewandte Kunst, Vienna; 1990, taught, National Institute of Design, Ahmedabad, Gujarat, India. Clients have included Alessi, Lipparini, FGB, Kartell, Moretti, Salviati, Sica, Swarovski, Tissot.
Exhibitions Work shown at 1992 *Nuovo Bel Design: 200 Nuovi Oggetti per la Casa* (Devuja ceramic dinner service by Mondo, Pavone glass vase, and Ellis vase by Richard Ginori), Salone del Mobile, Milan. Solo exhibitions: 1992 *Une Zebra à Pois*, Galleria Colombari, Milan; 1993 *Mille Bolle Blu*, Galleria Crispi, Verona.
Bibliography *Modo*, no. 148, Mar.–Apr. 1993: 121. Giuliana Gramigna and Paola Biondi, *Il design in Italia dell'arredamento domestico*, Turin: Allemandi, 1999.

Hamilton, Hugh
Canadian furniture designer; active Toronto.

Training Ontario College of Art.
Biography 1969–72 with partner Philip Salmon, Hamilton was active in Salmon-Hamilton Design Consultants in Toronto. (Salmon studied at Central School of Technology, Toronto.) They became active as designers of tubular-steel and plywood furniture. Their c. 1969 stool with one-piece bent tubular-steel base was patented and produced by Bentube and marketed by Form Canada. Subsequently, Hamilton and Salmon sold the license for production to Kinetics Furniture in Toronto. Also in the original group was a low stool (not footrest) and Zee chair and bookcase. Haworth bought Kinetics and continues production of the stool. Amisco in Québec also makes the stool with lower production values.
Bibliography Cat., *Seduced and Abandoned: Modern Furniture Designers in Canada, the First Fifty Years*, Toronto: The Art Gallery at Harbourfront, 1986: 25. Rachel Gotlieb and Cora Golden, *Design in Canada Since 1945: Fifty Years from Teakettles to Task Chairs*, Toronto: Knopf Canada, 2001.

Hamilton Beach
> See Wolcott, Frank E.

Hamm, Isabel (1964–)
German ceramicist and glassware designer.

Training 1981–84, ceramics apprenticeship, Limburg, Germany; 1987, master's degree in crafts, Marburg, Germany; 1985–88, Fachschule für Keramikgestaltung, Höhr-Grenzhausen, Germany; 1996–98, master's degree, Royal College of Art, London.
Biography 1989–96, Hamm was active in her own ceramics studio in Cologne; 1987–92 was a member of X99 design group; 1990, participated in Memory Container workshop of Alessi, Italy; 1990–95, realized photo and video projects with ceramics in Cologne; 1997, first began working in glass, at Royal College of Art; from 1998, has been primarily active as freelance designer of tableware in Cologne and in the production of glassware by herself; 2000, taught in ceramics department, Polytechnic Fachhochschule Niederrhein, Krefeld, Germany; 2001, taught in product-design department, Hochschule für Bankwirtschaft, Saarbrücken, Germany; 2001, collaborated with Steffen Kaz, Milan. Clients have included Iceberg Home Collection, Mercantile, Odin, Schött, Salviati, Wächtersbach Keramik, and WMF.
Exhibitions/citations Work shown at numerous venues since 1988 *Arbeitsproben* group show, Hessischer Werkbund, Frankfurt, and 1991 *Transmöbel*, Cologne and Milan, both with X99 design group. Exhibitions include 1989 *Marlboro Design Förderpreis*, Frankfurt and Munich; 1999 *Double Games* (solo show), Galerie Andrea Leenarz, Cologne; 1999 *New Work in Glass*, Vessel, London; 2000 *Bunker* European designers, Bratislava, Slovakia. 1991, designed ceramics for Apple Computers stand, Fairform, Berlin; 1999 Viva television music award (for Comet Ana Motjér).

Hammerplast
Swedish manufacturer.

History 1947 in Sweden, brothers Carl and Hugo Hammargren began manufacturing articles in plastics, called Hammarplast. (The same year in Norway, the Panco plastics firm was founded, and, with the 1921 founding of the Sarvis plastics firm, claims are that the Finnish plastics industry began. Subsequently, Dyno Industrier—acquired by Industri Kapital in 2000—became a leading producer of household plastics in Denmark.) Late 1980s, the Sarvis and Hammarplast firms, Panco's brand name, and Dyno's consumer-products division were acquired by Hackman, to form Hackman Form. 1991, Hackman acquired Plastcenter (founded 1941 in Gislaved, Sweden), which, at the time, was the largest producer of garden products in Scandinavia. From 1998, Hammarplast has been part of the Hammarplast group (Hammarplastgruppen AB), owned by Swedish families Hermansson and Bergendahl and also by Industrifonden (a Swedish investment fund). The Hammarplast group is comprised of three entities: Hammarplast, Hammarplast Landén, and Hammarplast Medical. Hammarplast's 1950s production included 1950s Sigvard Bernadotte's Birgitta bowl; 1960s Swisch sled; 1980s microwave resistant wares, high-temperature-resistant kitchen utensils, and stackable containers; 1990s ecologically sensitive products; later, those in steel.
Bibliography Mel Byars, *Design in Steel*, London: Laurence King, 2002

Hammel, Rudolf (1862–1937)
Austrian architect, designer, and teacher; active Vienna.

Biography 1899 (also the year of Josef Hoffmann's and Koloman

Isabel Hamm. Fish vase. 2000. Mouth-blown glass, h. 17 1/8 x w. 5 1/8" (5 x 13 cm). Mfr.: the designer, Germany.

Moser's appointments), Hammel became professor, Kunstgewerbeschule, Vienna; 1898–1903, designed silverware by firms Josef Bannert, and 1902 for A. Pollak. He also designed furniture for numerous manufacturers at beginning of 20th century, also for glass, porcelain, metal, textiles, and wood, principally inspired by the British Arts and Crafts style; initiated the publication of technical magazine *Wohnräume*, for cabinet makers (25 issues from 1903–15); was active in the Österreichisches Museum für angewandte Kunst, Vienna.
Exhibitions/citations 1902, silverwares by Bannert shown at *Esposizione Internazionale d'Arte Decorativa Moderna*, Turin; interiors and furniture at 1904 *Louisiana Purchase Exposition*, St. Louis, Mo.; and a large number of others; and received many awards.
Bibliography Annelies Krekel-Aalberse, *Art Nouveau and Art Déco Silver*, New York: Abrams, 1989.

Hammer, Marius (1847–1927)
Norwegian silversmith; active Bergen.

History Hammer established his eponymous silversmithy in Bergen, one of Norway's largest; became best known for his *plique-à-jour* enameled spoons, popular with tourists and exported in large quantities; produced 'Norwegian brilliant enamel work' spoons offered in 1896 and 1898 Christmas catalogs of Liberty's in London. From 1905, one of Hammer's designers of modern silver was Emil Hoye, a Dane who was artistic director 1910–16 and whose work was influenced by Mogens Ballin and later by Georg Jensen. Hoye continued to design for Hammer, even after he set up his own workshop.
Bibliography R.W. Lightbown, *Catalogue of Scandinavian and Baltic Silver*, London: Victoria and Albert Museum, 1975: 147. Annelies Krekel-Aalberse, *Art Nouveau and Art Déco Silver*, New York: Abrams, 1989.

Hammond, Henry Fauchon (1914–1989)
British ceramicist; active Farnham, Surrey.

Training 1934–38 under William Staite Murray, pottery, Royal College of Art, London; and in mural painting.
Biography Hammond produced mainly stoneware that showed fluent brushwork; from 1939, taught, Farnham School of Art; 1946, began producing stoneware pieces with slipware finishes, calling on local clays; became head of the ceramics department, West Surrey College of Art and Design, Farnham.
Exhibitions Work shown at 1937 *Exposition Internationale des Arts et Techniques dans la Vie Moderne*, Paris; 1979–80 *Thirties* exhibition, Hayward Gallery, London (catalog below).
Bibliography Cat., *Thirties: British Art and Design Before the War*, London: Arts Council of Great Britain/Hayward Gallery, 1979.

Hanada, Yoshie (1954–)
Japanese glass designer.

Training To 1976, Department of Art, Musashino Junior College of Art, Tokyo; 1981–86, Staatliche Akademie der bildenden Künste, Stuttgart, Germany.
Exhibitions Work shown at 1985 *New Glass in Japan*, Badisches Landesmuseum, Karlsruhe, Germany; 1985 *Zweiter Coburger Glaspreis*, Kunstsammlungen der Weste, Coburg, Germany; *Glass '87 in Japan* and *Glass '90 in Japan*, Tokyo; 1991 (5th) Triennale of Japan Glass Art Crafts Association, Heller Gallery, New York.
Bibliography Cat., *Glass Japan*, New York: Heller Gallery and Japan Glass Art Crafts Association, 1991: no. 7.

Handel, Philip
American lighting manufacturer.

History 1885, Adolph Eyden and Philip Handel established a glass-decorating firm in Meriden, Conn. 1893, Handel bought out Eyden, forming Handel and Co.; 1902, established a foundry to facilitate the production of metal bases to accompany the style of the glass diffusers. 1903, the name was changed to The Handel Co. The firm specialized in glass lamp diffusers and also made vases, tobacco jars, and *tazzas*. Handel's goods were produced by a large studio of artists and craftspeople. Its lighting fixtures ranged from large ceiling- and floor-lamp models to small nightlights. The firm did not make its own glass but bought machine-rolled glass blanks. Individually cut sheets were used for floral and geometric lampshades, and the blanks were reverse-painted. Artists produced effects by enameling, etching, and filigreeing metal overlays and by applying a chipped frosted finish to the outsides. 1941, the firm closed.

Hammarplast: Karl-Axel Andersson and Morgan Ferme. Thermos. 1986. Plastic and glass, 11 1/4 x 7 1/2 x dia. 6" (28.6 x 19.1 x 15.2 cm). Mfr.: Hammerplast, Denmark. Friends of the Department Fund. MoMA.

Bibliography Alastair Duncan, *Art Nouveau and Art Déco Lighting*, New York: Simon & Schuster, 1978. Robert De Falco and John Hibel, *Handel Lamps: Painted Shades and Glassware*, Staten Island, N.Y.: H&D, 1986. Carole Goldman Hibel et al., *The Handel Lamps Book*, Pittsfield. Mass.: Fontaine, 1999. Martin M. May, *Great Art Glass Lamps: Tiffany, Duffner & Kimberly, Pairpoint, and Handel*, Atglen, Pa.: Schiffler, 2003

Handler, Laura (1947–)
American industrial designer; active Milan and New York.

Biography 1981–83, Handler worked with Sottsass Associati, Krizia, Pomellato, and others in Milan; 1983, set up her own design firm in New York and designed clocks, tabletop accessories, leather goods, housewares; also designed atomizers for Prescriptives cosmetics and worked on projects for Pomellato and Alessi; developed Safari cosmetics line for Ralph Lauren; taught, Parsons School of Design, New York. Other clients have included Macy's, Williams-Sonoma, Fissler, Magniform, The May Company, Lenox China, Montgomery Ward, WMF, Dansk, Waechtersbach, Estée Lauder, Colgate-Palmolive, Calvin Klein, Fabergé, and Revlon.
Citations Awards (for 1986 thermos and folding clock and 1991 modular votive-candle holder by Design Ideas), *I.D.* magazine.

Hannah, Bruce R. (1941–)
American industrial designer and teacher; active New York.

Training To 1963, industrial design, Pratt Institute, Brooklyn, N.Y.
Biography With Andrew Morrison, Hannah designed 1967 seating group by Knoll; has since been an active industrial designer, concerned with socially and environmentally responsible design; with Morrison, designed 1972 seating and 1974 office-furniture range by Knoll. Hannah has taught, Industrial Design Department, Pratt Institute, Brooklyn, N.Y.; 1976, established his own design firm Hannah Design. Design work includes 1989 Orchestra desk accessories (with Ayse Birsel) and 1990 Hannah Desk System by Knoll; 1986, was appointed chairperson in 1986, Graduate Industrial Design Department, and chairperson in 1988, Industrial Design Department, Pratt Institute. Subsequently the Graduate and Undergraduate Departments were merged. Hannah and George Covington wrote the book *Access by Design* (Van Nostrand Reinhold, 1996) and *Becoming a Product Designer: A Guide to Careers in Design* (John Wiley & Sons, 2003).
Exhibitions/citations Co-organized 1998-99 *Unlimited by Design*, Cooper-Hewitt National Design Museum, New York and touring. 1991, named Cooper-Hewitt Museum's first designer-in-residence; 2000 Fed-

Bruce R. Hannah and Andrew Ivar Morrison. Armchair (no. 2021). 1971. Vinyl upholstery and polyester-coated cast aluminum, 28 x 25 5/8 x 28 3/4" (71 x 65 x 72 cm). Mfr.: Knoll International, US. Courtesy Quittenbaum Kunstauktionen, Munich.

eral Design Achievement Award (for exhibitions, with others); 1992 Bronze Apple Award (for first conference on Universal Design); Design of the Decade (1990s) (for Hannah Desk System by Knoll), IDSA/ *Business Week* magazine; 1998 National Design Education Award, Industrial Designers Society of America (IDSA); and a number of other citations from IDSA.

Hans, Ineke (1966–)

Dutch designer.

Training Product design in Arnhem, Netherlands; 1995, master's degree in furniture, Royal College of Art, London.
Biography From 1995, Hans designed furniture by Habitat in the UK, and others such as Artifort in the Netherlands; from 1998, was active in the Netherlands; designed playful one-of-a-kind and multiple-production furniture/furnishings that could be mistaken for intended use by children. She taught, Gerrit Rietveld Academie, Amsterdam; was visiting teacher, Hochschule für Angewandte Kunst, Vienna, and Bauhaus-Universität, Weimar. Furniture has included 1997 Eat Your Heart Out (16 ways to make one stacking chair), 1997 Ordinary table/chairs set in recycled plastic, 1997 Undercover lounge chair, and 1998 Hole in One pierced vase.
Exhibitions Showed work at 1997 and 1998 100% Design fair, London.

Hansen, Andreas (1936–)

Danish furniture designer.

Training Apprenticeship in cabinetmaking, in Ringe, Denmark, becoming a journeyman joiner in 1957; to 1962, Kunsthåndværkerskolen, Copenhagen; 1962–63, furniture department, Det Kongelige Danske Kunstakademi, Copenhagen; subsequently, study tours in Florence, Rome, and Venice.
Biography Early 1960s while concurrently touring Italy, Hansen worked in the offices of Mogens Koch and of Vilhelm Wohlert; 1963, set up his own studio; designed furniture by Hadsten Trœindustri, Form 75, and N. Eilersen, and domestic and office lighting and accessories by others, mainly Danish firms; 1968–88, taught, Billedkunstskolerne (school of visual arts), Det Kongelige Danske Kunstakademi, and 1970–73, at Kunsthåndværkerskolen; 1974, traveled for study in Egypt.
Bibliography Frederik Sieck, *Nutidig Dansk Møbeldesign – en kortfattet illustreret beskrivelse*, Copenhagen: Bondo Gravesen, 1990.

Hansen, Bente (1943–)

Danish ceramicist; born Copenhagen.

Training 1960–64, Danmarks Designskole, Copenhagen.
Biography 1964–70, Hansen worked at Bing & Grøndahl Porcelænsfabrik and, 1978–82, at Royal Copenhagen Porcelain Factory. 1968, he established his own workshop in Copenhagen; 1992–96, was head of ceramics and glass department, Danmarks Designskole; 1991–96, was a committee member of Danmarks Nationalbank Jubilee Foundation of 1968.
Exhibitions/citations From 1967, work included in a large number of exhibitions in Europe, Iceland, and the US. 1964 silver medal, Teknisk Skoles Prisopgave, Denmark; 1982 Ole Haslunds Grant, Denmark; 1982 and 1989 Danmarks Nationalbank Jubilee Foundation; 1985 three-year working grant, Statens Kunstfond, Denmark; 1986 special prize, Saltzbrand, Koblenz, Germany; 1990 Kunsthåndværkerrådets Årspris, Denmark; 1991 Estonian State Culture Prize, Tallin; 1997 Thorvald Bindesbøll Medal.

Hansen, Frida (1855–1931)

Norwegian textile designer; born Hillevåg-by-Stavanger.

Training 1871, in painting.
Biography 1882, Hansen set up an embroidery workshop in Stavanger; became familiar with the historical textile traditions of Norway, though she did not base her work on others' designs; combined art and craft and developed a distinctive style that incorporated realistic images with abstract motifs. 1889, she completed her first tapestry and learned weaving on a standing loom at Kjerstina Hauglum in Sogn; 1890, set up her own studio; 1892, moved to Kristiania (now Oslo), where she became director of weaving workshop Det Norske Billedvaeveri (DNB). Hansen was a pioneer in reviving old weaving techniques and in the use of natural plant dyes; is known for 'transparent weaving,' in which she left open areas of the warp that contrasted with broad, richly colored expanses. She collaborated with Gerhard Munthe on tapestries and, 1890s, became the most important practitioner of Norway's weaving renaissance, though she was a maverick in her style and choice of subject matter. She wrote the book *Husflid og kunstindustri i Norge* (1899).
Exhibitions/citations Work shown at 1893 *World's Columbian Exposition*, Chicago; subject of 1973 and 1991 exhibitions, both Kunstindustrimuseet, Oslo (catalogs below). Gold medals (for work for DNB),

Fritz Hansen: Arne Jacobsen. Stacking side chair. 1951. Molded plywood, chrome-plated tubular steel, and rubber, 30 x 20 1/2 x 21" (76.2 x 52.1 x 53.3 cm). Mfr.: Fritz Hansen, Copenhagen. Gift of Richards Morgenthau Co. MoMA.

Johannes Hansen: Hans Jørgen Wegner. Round Chair. 1949. Oak and cane, 30 x 24 5/8 x 21 1/4" (76.2 x 62.5 x 54 cm), seat h. 17" (43.2 cm). Mfr.: Johannes Hansen, Denmark. Gift of Georg Jensen, Inc. MoMA.

1900 *Exposition Universelle*, Paris.
Bibliography Frida Hansen, *Europeeren i norsk vevkunst*, Oslo: Kunstindustrimuseet, 1973. Anniken Thue, *Frida Hansen: En europeer norsk tekstilkunst omkring 1900*, Stravange: Univ. Forl., 1986. Fredrik Wild hagen, *Norge i Form*, Oslo: Stenersen, 1988: 41–42. Cat., Anne Wichstrøm, *Rooms with a View: Women's Art in Norway 1880–1990*, Oslo: The Royal Ministry of Foreign Affairs, 1990: 18. Cat., Anniken Thue, *Frida Hansen og de andre...: transparente portierer 1897–1930*, Oslo: Kunstindustrimuseet, 1991.

Hansen, Fritz
Danish furniture manufacturer; located Allerød.

History 1872, Hansen founded a wood-turning business which introduced industrial processes into furniture making as well as innovative technology and extensive research. 1933, the firm was involved in a legal dispute with Lorenz-Thonet over a cantilever chair design. 1930s, it produced the furniture designs of Mart Stam, Arne Jacobsen, Fritz Schlegel, and Magnus Stephensen, and later the work of Gunnar Andersen, Jens Ammundsen, Ebbe Clemmensen, Piet Hein, Peter Hvidt, Grete Jalk, Jørgen Kastholm, Ib Kofod-Larsen, Orla Holgård-Nielsen, Verner Panton, Henrik Rolf, and Hans Wegner.
Bibliography Frederik Sieck, *Nutidig Dansk Møbeldesign – en kortfattet illustreret beskrivelse*, Copenhagen: Bondo Gravesen, 1981, 1990. Cat., David Revere McFadden (ed.), *Scandinavian Modern Design 1880–1980*, New York: Abrams, 1982. Mel Byars with Arlette Barré-Despond, *100 Designs/100 Years: A Celebration of the 20th Century*, Hove: RotoVision, 1999: 128–29. Poul Hviburg-Hansen, *Danish Furniture Design Through 125 Years: Fritz Hansen, 1872–1997*, Copenhagen: Trapholts, 1997.
> See Jacobsen, Arne.

Hansen, Hans (1884–1940); Karl Gustav Hansen (1914–)
Danish silversmiths.

Biography 1906, Hans Hansen established a silversmithy in Kolding; 1930s, produced modern silverwares. Karl Gustav Hansen designed for his father's firm, where he was the artistic director 1940–62 and the artistic consultant and designer from 1962. Also, concurrently, he was a consultant designer to Rosenthal. Karl Gustav became known for his unblemished silver surfaces and precisely planned and crafted geometric forms.

Bibliography Cat., David Revere McFadden (ed.), *Scandinavian Modern Design 1880–1980*, New York: Abrams, 1982. Annelies Krekel-Aalberse, *Art Nouveau and Art Déco Silver*, New York: Abrams, 1989.

Hansen, Johannes
Danish furniture manufacturer; located Søborg.

History Johannes Hansen established an eponymous manufacturing company, which produced many of the chairs and some tables designed by Hans Wegner, who was more than half the age of Hansen. 1940, Wegner met Hansen, who was chairperson of the Copenhagen Guild of Handicrafters and an accomplished furniture maker. 1941, Wegner showed his first furniture in the Hansen store at Bredgade 65, Copenhagen. One of the landmark Wegner/Hansen pieces is 1949 Round chair, or simply the Chair in the US (now made by P.P. Møbler, the producers of other former Wegner/Hansen examples). Wegner said the relationship with Hansen, which lasted over 25 years, was 'like a game.... We had to have something novel to display every autumn. I drew it, and Johannes Hansen made it. We were happy if we could just sell the chairs we had made for the exhibition. That was as far as our hopes went.' Wegner was not paid for the developmental work, only a royalty if the furniture sold. When the Round chair was introduced in 1949 and achieved success by appearing on the cover of *Interiors* magazine in the US, a club in Chicago placed an order for 400 examples. Hansen claimed that his workshop could not make 400 chairs and declined the request. However, the club owners persisted, and 400 chairs were delivered to them a few years hence.
Exhibitions/citations. Numerous to Wegner for Hansen work.
> See Wegner, Hans.

Hansen, Roald Steen (1942–)
Danish architect and furniture designer.

Training To 1967, Kunsthåndværkerskolen, Copenhagen; to 1972, department of furniture design, Det Kongelige Danske Kunstakademiets Arkitektskole, Copenhagen; 1974–76, Danish Academy of Science and Art, Rome.
Biography 1962, Hansen became a journeyman joiner; 1967–70, worked in the office of Arne Jacobsen; 1972–74, in the office of Knud Peter Harboe; 1980–81, in the office of Henning Larsen; designed furniture by Bjarne Bo Andersen, Søren Horns, and Brdr. Sondt.
Exhibitions/citations Work shown at 1971 Exempla, Munich; 1972 Danish art and design exhibition, Viborg. Work subject of 1975 *Børn og Møbler*, Kunstindustrimuseet, Copenhagen. Received 1971 Johannes Krøiers Legat, 1976 Danish furniture prize, 1984 Design Award, American Society of Interior Designers (ASID).
Bibliography Frederik Sieck, *Nutidig Dansk Møbeldesign – en kortfattet illustreret beskrivelse*, Copenhagen: Bondo Gravesen, 1981: 74.

Hansen, Rolf (1922–)
Norwegian ceramicist.

Training 1942, Statens Håndverks-og Kunstindustriskole, Oslo; 1943, advertising, commercial school, Oslo; 1944 under Trygve Mosebekk; 1944–46, apprenticeship at Åros Keramikkfabrik, Royken.
Biography 1947–c. 1957, Rolf Hansen worked in shape design at the Kongsberg Keramikk Arnold Wiigs Fabrikker in Halden, and, 1958, at Plus; became a freelance consultant.
Bibliography Fredrik Wildhagen, *Norge i Form*, Oslo: Stenersen, 1988: 122. Jennifer Hawkins Opie, *Scandinavia: Ceramics and Glass in the Twentieth Century*, New York: Rizzoli, 1989.

Hansen, Theophil von (1813–1891)
Danish architect; born Copenhagen; active Vienna.

Training Academy, Copenhagen.
Biography 1838–46, Hansen lived in Athens, where he became acquainted with Byzantine architecture; 1846, settled in Vienna; became one of the historicists to give the *Gründerzeit* style its particular Viennese flavor in architecture, painting, sculpture, and the applied arts and designed 1864 Déjeuner porcelain dinner service and 1866 Service (no. 103) engraved crystal range. He is best known for his 1883 neoclassical Parliament building; 1890s, was one of the designers of the Ringstrasse in Vienna. He died in Vienna.
Bibliography Günther Feuerstein, *Vienna—Present and Past: Arts and Crafts—Applied Art—Design*, Vienna: Jugend und Volk, 1976. Robert Waissenberger, *Vienna 1890–1920*, Secaucus, N.J.: Wellfleet, 1984.

Haraszty, Eszter (1910–)
Hungarian textile, interior, and clothing designer; active Budapest and New York.

Biography 1930s, Haraszty set up a screen-printing studio in Budapest; after World War II, resorted to printing on bed sheets, window shades, and other salvaged woven goods; 1947, settled in the US and became a consultant designer to Knoll; 1949–55, was director of Knoll Textiles, during the revolutionary period in commercial upholstery fabrics; designed Knoll's Transportation Cloth; at Knoll, hired Marianne Strengell and Evelyn Hill to produce handwoven designs, and Angelo Testa to design prints; encouraged designers Stig Lindberg, Sven Markelius, and Astrid Sampe to travel to the US. Her mixing of oranges and pinks was audacious even for the colorful 1950s. Designs included 1951 Knoll Stripes, 1953 Fibra, and 1956 Triad. 1958, she opened her own design studio in New York; wrote books *Needlepainting: A Garden of Stitches* (New York: Liveright, 1974), *The Embroider's Portfolio of Flowers* (New York: Liveright, 1981), and others.
Exhibitions/citations Fibra fabric and others at 1950s *Good Design* exhibitions/awards, The Museum of Modern Art, New York, and Chicago Merchandise Mart; 2000–01 *A Woman's Touch: Designing Textiles in America, 1945–1969*, Museum of Fashion Institute of Technology, New York. International Design Award (for Triad fabric), American Institute of Designers (AID).
Bibliography 'The Exhilarated World of Eszter Haraszty,' *Interiors*, vol. 114, May 1955: 92–99. Eric Larrabee and Massimo Vignelli, *Knoll Design*, New York: Abrams, 1981: 92–93. Cat., Kathryn B. Hiesinger and George H. Marcus III (eds.), *Design Since 1945*, Philadelphia: Philadelphia Museum of Art, 1984. Cherie Fehrman and Kenneth Fehrman, *Post-war Interior Design, 1945–1960*, New York: Van Nostrand Reinhold, 1987.

Harcourt, Geoffrey (1935–)
British furniture designer; born London.

Training 1957–60, High Wycombe School of Art and Royal College of Art, London.
Biography 1960–61, Harcourt worked at Latham, Tyler and Jensen in Chicago, and with Jacob Jensen in Copenhagen; 1961, opened his own studio in London, specializing in furniture design; from 1962; began designing seating by Artifort in the Netherlands, which produced more than 20 models of his furniture designs, including 1968 F510 lounge chair, serpentine 1973 Cleopatra (no. C248) sofa, 1974 F590/F510 lounge chairs. He also designed for other furniture companies, some in Japan. His chairs were popular with airport designers.
Bibliography Michael Farr, *Design in British Industry: A Mid-Century Survey*, London: Cambridge, 1955.

Hardman and Co., John
British ecclesiastical metalworkers.

History Hardman and Iliffe was originally a button maker in Birmingham. John Hardman (1811–1867) was a partner in Elkington, a large Birmingham manufacturer and electroplating firm; 1838, set up his own business, John Hardman and Co., with A.W.N. Pugin as the chief designer, to manufacture church furnishings in the Gothic style. Describing itself as 'mediaeval metalworkers,' the firm executed metalwork designed by Pugin for the Houses of Parliament in London; ecclesiastical designs; and Pugin's famous marriage jewelry. Hardman continued to produce jewelry in the same style as Pugin's marriage jewelry adapted from his own designs or those of William Burges. Some of Hardman's jewelry was marked 'AP,' to represent Pugin's own 'AWP' monogram, which appeared exclusively on Hardman/Pugin metalwork.
Exhibitions Jewelry in the Pugin manner shown at *International Exhibition of 1862*, London.
Bibliography Charlotte Gere, *American and European Jewelry 1830–1914*, New York: Crown, 1975.

Härdtl, Oswald
> See Haerdtl, Oswald.

Hardy, Patrice (1944–)
French architect and furniture designer.

Biography For ten years, Hardy worked with Pascal Mourgue in Paris; later designed furniture and boats, including the Hop trimaran (with the Institut National d'Études et de Recherches Navales).
Bibliography Agnès Lévitte and Margo Rouard, *100 quotidiens objets made in France*, Paris: APCI/Syros-Alternatives, 1987: 51. Arlette Barré-Despond (ed.), *Dictionnaire international des arts appliqués et du design*, Paris: Regard, 1996.

Eszther Haraszty. Tracy sheer fabric. 1952. Silk gauze, 55 x 43 1/2" (139.7 x 110.5 cm). Mfr.: Knoll Textiles, US. Gift of the mfr. MoMA.

Häring, Hugo (1882–1958)
German architect and designer; born Biberach.

Training Under Theodor Fischer, Technische Hochschule, Stuttgart; under Gurlitt, Schumacher, and Wallot, Technische Hochschule, Dresden.
Biography 1903–04, Häring practiced architecture in Ulm, and 1904–14 in Hamburg; 1915–21, worked as an architect in Allenburg on projects in East Prussia (now Poland); after World War I, became a member of Novembergruppe; c. 1921, set up his own architectural practice and workshop, Berlin; 1924, was active in the founding of Zehnerring (circle of ten), an avant-garde architectural association, which opposed Berlin city architect Ludwig Hoffmann. 1926, Häring became secretary of Zehnerring, when it was enlarged to become Der Ring; attended first (1928) Congrès Internationaux d'Architecture Moderne (CIAM) in La Sarraz, Switzerland; lectured on and published books and essays concerning organic building. c. 1930, Häring's ideas, localized at first, became popular. He was empathetic with the work of Hans Scharoun, Alvar Aalto, and Louis Kahn; became best known for 1922–23 Gut Garkau farm complex, near Lübeck; 1935–43, was director, private art school Kunst und Werk, Berlin, which specialized in Beaux-Arts design. The Beaux-Arts discipline was contrary to his being a pioneer in furniture design, particularly the cantilever chair.
Exhibitions Participated in 1924 *Berliner Architekturausstellung*. Work shown at 1932 *Werkbund-Ausstellung*, Vienna; a chair design shown at 1986 *Der Kragstuhl* exhibition, Stuhlmuseum Burg Beverungen (catalog below).
Bibliography Hugo Häring, 'Wege zur Form,' *Die Form*, vol. 1, 1925. Hugo Häring, 'Geometrie und Organik,' *Baukunst und Werkform*, vol. 9, 1951. Heinrich Lauterbach and Jürgen Joedicke (eds.), *Hugo Häring: Schriften, Entwürfe, Bauten*, Stuttgart, 1965. Hugo Häring, *Die Ausbildung des Geistes zur Arbeit an der Gestalt*, Berlin, 1968. Jürgen Joedicke (ed.), *Das andere Bauen-Gedanken und Zeichnungen von Hugo Häring*, Stuttgart: Krämer, 1982. Cat., *Der Kragstuhl*, Berlin: Alexander, 1986: 133. Jürgen Joedicke in Vittorio Magnago Lampugnani (ed.), *Encyclopedia of 20th-Century Architecture*, New York: Abrams, 1986: 143–44.

Haring, Keith (1958–1990)
American artist; active New York.

Biography Haring is best known for his graffiti-like paintings, initially on the black paper used to obviate discontinued billboard advertisements in the New York subway, for which he was sometimes arrested. He went on to become internationally famous and highly regarded for his more legitimate drawings, paintings, and prints. His design work

includes 1988 On Taro and On Giro tables (with artist Toshiyuki Kita) by Kreon; 1989 a nine-piece bronze furniture set (with art dealer Sam Havadtoy), including a writing table, three-panel screen, and coffee table; and early 1990s ceramic dinnerware by Villeroy & Boch. Haring set up a trust to fund research into Aids, from which he died; it promotes the use of his images on toys, T-shirts, and other items.
Exhibitions A large number worldwide.
Bibliography Cat., *Keith Haring: Peintures, sculptures et dessins*, Bordeaux: CAPC, 1985. *New York Magazine*, Feb. 25, 1991: 18. John Gruen, *Keith Haring: The Authorized Biography*, New York: Prentice-Hall, 1991. Germano Celant (ed.), *Keith Haring*, Munich: Prestel, 1992. *In Your Face*, New York: MALCA Fine Art, 1997. www.haring.com.

Harkrider, John (1899–1982)

American theater and film-set designer; born Texas.

Biography 1920s, Harkrider designed costumes for the Ziegfeld Follies in New York; settled in Hollywood and became supervising art director at Universal film studios; designed the interior of Club Raymond and redecorated Silver Sandal nightclub for the film *Swing Time* (1936), including its costumes (with Bernard Newman). Club Raymond (inspired by real establishments: the Rainbow Room in New York and Clover Club in Hollywood) had a quilted ceiling, seating for 300, a glass elevator, and a simulated view of New York at night. The Silver Sandal décor was redesigned by Harkrider into a glittering fantasy of black and silver and the setting for the Fred Astaire and Ginger Rogers 'Never Gonna Dance' sequence in *Swing Time*; the set was equipped with silver tablecloths and Saturn-ring lamps, a dance floor with a black-and-grey concentric diamond motif, and a curving staircase that rose up to huge windows revealing a starry night behind the musicians. Harkrider designed sets for other films, including *My Man Godfrey* (1936), the floating penthouse nightclub in *Top of the Town* (1937), and the so-called Jungle Moderne cabaret in *Three Smart Girls* (1937). Also designed the costumes for a number of films such as *Top of the Town* (1937), and still others uncredited, such as *Whoopee!* (1930). He died in Los Angeles.
Bibliography Howard Mandelbaum and Eric Myers, *Screen Deco: A Celebration of High Style in Hollywood*, New York: St. Martin's, 1985.

Harmon Powell, David
> See Powell, David Harmon.

Harni, Pekka (1956–)

Finnish industrial designer.

Biography Harni has been active in numerous projects in the fields of renovation and interior decoration; as an industrial designer, designed ceramics by Arabia and textiles by Marimekko. His Arabia Basic Ceramics (ABC) dinnerware in two forms and three colors by Arabia claims to have '1,001 possible combinations of use.' He taught architecture and design, Taideteollinen korkeakoulu, Helsinki, and Lapin Yliopisto (university of Lapland), Rovaniemi, Finland; has lectured and conducted workshops worldwide.
Exhibitions/Citations Participated in 2001 *Céramique-Design-Industrie* exhibition, Uzès, France. Design Plus prize, 1999 Ambiente fair, Frankfurt.

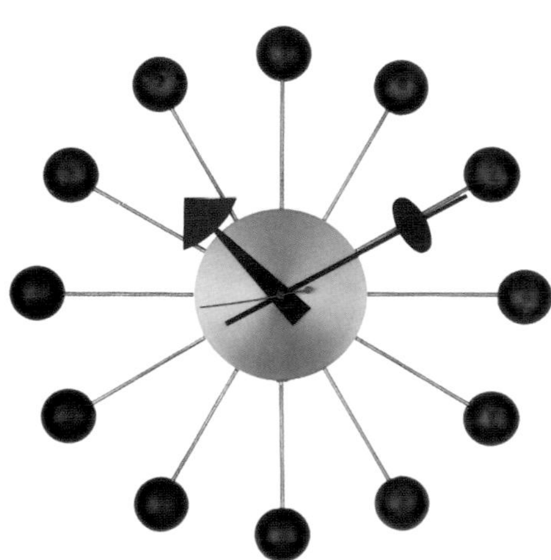

Irving Harper, George Nelson Associates. Ball clock (no. 4755). 1947. Painted wood and sheet steel or brass, dia. 13" (33 cm). Mfr.: Howard Miller Clock Co., US. Courtesy Quittenbaum Kunstauktionen, Munich.

Harper, Irving (1917–)

American designer.

Biography Harper was active in various design offices in New York, where, 1930s, he worked in studio of Gilbert Rohde on the Plexiglas, the Anthracite, and the Home Furnishings Focal stands at 1939–40 *New York World's Fair: The World of Tomorrow*. After World War II, he worked at Raymond Loewy Associates; 1947–63, at George Nelson Associates. As a staff designer at Nelson, he solely created 1956 Marshmallow sofa by and the 1940s undulating 'M' logo for Herman Miller, and Ball and other clocks (annually designing a group of eight or so models) by Howard Miller Clock Company (1954–55). His Marshmallow sofa (only 100 were made due to their intricacy, but which was reintroduced by Herman Miller and by Vitra in 1999) was designed during a single week-end, according to Harper's account. 1963 with Phillip George, Harper founded Harper+George design studio in New York, serving clients such as Braniff Airlines, Jack Lenor Larsen, and Hallmark Cards. They designed the Chrysler Pavilion at 1964 *New York World's Fair*. 1983, Harper retired, but, 2000, served as the consultant on 1950s Nelson office-designed fabrics being reissued by Maharam.
Bibliography Paul Makovsky, 'Vintage Modern,' *Metropolis*, June 2001.

Harrison, Marc (1936–)

American industrial designer.

Training Pratt Institute, Brooklyn, N.Y., and Cranbrook Academy of Art, Bloomfield Hills, Mich.
Biography From 1959, Harrison taught, Rhode Island School of Design, Providence, R.I.; in his design work, focused on ergonomic and human-factor concerns; in his design studio, specialized in industrial and medical equipment, including the patented 1972 Red Cross blood-collecting process used in the US, and subway equipment for Massachusetts Bay Transit Authority. From 1978, he was principal designer of products by Cuisinart and redesigned its food-processing range.
Bibliography Marc Harrison, 'Design for the Donor,' *Industrial Design*, vol. 20, Nov. 1973: 20–29. 'Product Portfolio,' *Industrial Design*, vol. 28, July–Aug. 1981: 20. Cat., Kathryn B. Hiesinger and George H. Marcus III (eds.), *Design Since 1945*, Philadelphia: Philadelphia Museum of Art, 1983.

Hart, George H. (1882–1973)

British silversmith and designer.

Biography Hart was a member of C.R. Ashbee's Guild of Handicraft in Chipping Campden, Gloucestershire; after the Guild's closing in 1908, worked as a silversmith and designer at Huyshe and Warmington in Chipping Campden.
Bibliography Annelies Krekel-Aalberse, *Art Nouveau and Art Déco Silver*, New York: Abrams, 1989.

Hartman, Cedric (1929–)

American lighting and furniture designer.

Biography Hartman executed designs for lighting and furniture produced in his own factory The Afternoon Company in Omaha, Neb.; designed the widely published, award-winning 1966 pharmacy or reading lamp (no. 1 or no. VW), which was subsequently much imitated. The company is extant, as Cedric Hartman CE Lighting, with an inventory of other fixtures.
Exhibitions Pharmacy lamp shown in 1983 Philadelphia exhibition.
Bibliography 'The 25 Best-Designed Products,' *Fortune*, vol. 95, May 1977: 271. Cat., Kathryn B. Hiesinger and George H. Marcus III (eds.), *Design Since 1945*, Philadelphia: Philadelphia Museum of Art, 1983.

Hartwein, Peter (1942–)

German industrial designer; born Weilheim.

Training 1960–62, in joinery; 1962–65, Werkkunstschule, Kaiserslautern, Germany.
Biography 1965–70, Hartwein worked in several architecture studios in Munich; from 1970, has been active at Braun, where he has designed a large number of its products, including 1976 Visacustic 1000 st film

Cedric Hartman. Reading lamp (no. 1 and VW). 1966. Nickel-plated brass and stainless steel, h. 36 3/4" (93.3 cm). Mfr.: The Afternoon Company, US. Gift of the mfr. MoMA.

projector, 1980 T1/A1/C1 high-fidelity system (with Dieter Rams), and 1991 D 5525 electric toothbrush; is in charge of the BraunPrize exhibitions.
Citations For Braun products: product design awards in 2000 (for Oral-B OxyJet 3D Center) and 1995 (for Oral-B Plak Control D 7525 Z), Industrie Forum Design (iF), Hanover; Red Dot awards in 1998 (for Oral-B Interclean) and 2002 (for Oral-B child's toothbrush, with Till Winkler), Design Zentrum Nordrhein Westfalen, Essen.

Hartwig, Josef (1880–1955)
German sculptor; born Munich; active Weimar and Frankfurt.

Training 1993–97, in stone cutting and subsequently in sculpture, Munich; 1904–08, art, Academy, Munich.
Biography 1897, Hartwig supervised the stone cutting of the renowned relief by August Endell of the Photoatelier Elvira in Munich; 1910–21, was a *Werkmeister* in Berlin; 1921–25, *Werkmeister* in the stone/wood-carving workshops at the Bauhaus, Weimar; designed the now-famous 1924 Schachspiel (chess set), illustrating Bauhaus machine aesthetics, and in a box with graphics by Joost Schmidt; 1925–45, taught, Städelschule, Frankfurt; from 1945, led the restoration workshop of the public sculpture collection Lubig-Haus in Frankfurt.
Bibliography Lionel Richard, *Encyclopédie du Bauhaus*, Paris: Somogy, 1985: 153. Auction cat., *Bauhaus*, London: Christie's, 1989. *Sammlung-Katalog 3*, Berlin: Bauhaus-Archiv, 1987.

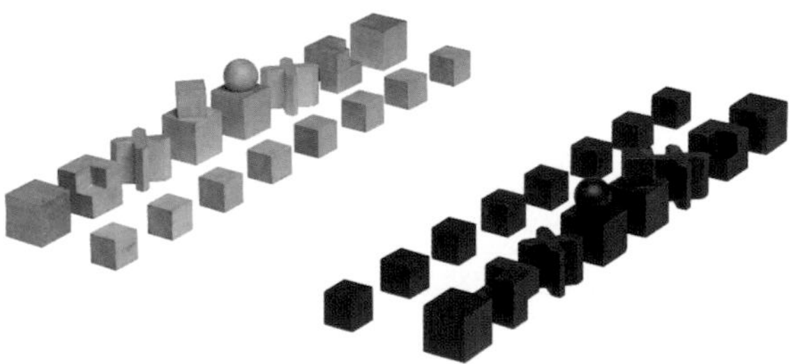

Josef Hartwig. Chess set. 1924. Pear wood, natural and stained black, largest 1 7/8 x 1 1/8 x 1 1/8" (4.8 x 2.9 x 2.9 cm), smallest 7/8 x 7/8 x 7/8" (2.2 x 2.2 x 2.2 cm). Mfr.: Bauhaus, Germany. Gift of Alfred H. Barr Jr. MoMA.

Harvey, Arthur Edward
British architect and silversmith; active Birmingham.

Biography Harvey was head of industrial-design department, Birmingham Central School; 1930s, was one of several designers, artists, and architects designing mass-produced silver and electroplate wares for Mappin and Webb in Sheffield, Goldsmiths' and Silversmiths' Company in London, Hukin & Heath and Deakin & Francis, both in Birmingham.
Bibliography Annelies Krekel-Aalberse, *Art Nouveau and Art Déco Silver*, New York: Abrams, 1989.

Harvey, Jeremy (1945–)
British designer; born Scotland.

Biography Harvey is best known for his 1978 Hello There (no. F007) cast-aluminum side chair, reentered into production by Artifort in 2001 and considered one of the first Postmodern expressions in the Dutch furniture industry. He is a designer at Axis Design Group in London.

Haseler, W.H.
British silversmiths; located Birmingham.

History 1870, William Hair Haseler founded his eponymous silversmithy in London; from 1901, was in partnership with Liberty's in London; 1899–27, produced the successful Cymric range of silver in the Arts and Crafts style sold at Liberty's. Other Liberty jewelry may have been manufactured at Haseler's premises at 34 Hatton Garden, London. 1900, Haseler moved to Hylton Street, Birmingham; 1901–04, was known as Haseler Bros. Silversmiths at 89 Hatton Gardens. Design attribution of the Cymric line is uncertain because the designs were often altered for production, and because Liberty required its designers to be anonymous until the journal *The Studio* published Cymric designs by Birmingham silversmiths Oliver Baker and Bernard Cuzner, and Maud Coggin, and enameler Cecil Aldin. Talented chaser Harry Craythorn was head of Haseler's design department. Other early designers included Jessie Jones, Thomas Hodgetts, and Charles Povey. Though dissolved in 1927, the Haseler smithy continued afterward to provide Liberty's with silver items.
Bibliography Charlotte Gere, *American and European Jewelry 1830–1914*, New York: Crown, 1975: 203. Annelies Krekel-Aalberse, *Art Nouveau and Art Déco Silver*, New York: Abrams, 1989.

Hasenauer, Karl von (1833–1894)
Austrian architect; born and active Vienna.

Biography 1870s, Hasenauer was one of the designers of the Vienna Ringstrasse, the circular boulevard lined with monumental buildings developed after a proclamation of 1857 to enlarge the city. He was one of the historicists who gave the *Gründerzeit* style its particular Viennese flavor in architecture, painting, sculpture, and the applied arts; became a professor and head, special school of architecture, Akademie der bildenden Künste, Vienna, where he was succeeded in 1894 by Otto Wagner.
Bibliography Robert Waissenberger, *Vienna 1890–1920*, Secaucus, N.J.: Wellfleet, 1984: 171, 172, 267. Renate Wagner-Rieger (ed.), *Die Wiener Ringstrasse*, vol. 8, Wiesbaden: Steiner, 1978: 216.

Hashimoto, Kazuyo (1941–)
Japanese glass designer.

Training To 1963, sculpture, Kyoto-shiritsu Bijutsu Daigaku (Kyoto City college of arts; now Kyoto-shiritsu Geijutsu Daigaku, or Kyoto City university of arts); 1994 under Robert Mickelsen and 1995 under Susan Plum, Pilchuck Glass School, Stanwood, Wash., US; 1996 under Polish flameworker Anna Skibska.
Biography 1963, Hashimoto joined Kamei Glass Company in Osaka, designing tableware; 1965, was married and stopped working. 1973–89 returned as a freelancer, designing for Daiwa Glass Company; 1982–92, made glass sculpture in optical glass, with assistance from skilled craftspeople, who did the finishing. After studies under Skibska, Hashimoto came to flameworking; however, her career has covered 28 years as a designer of utilitarian glass and as a prominent artist of laminated optical glass.

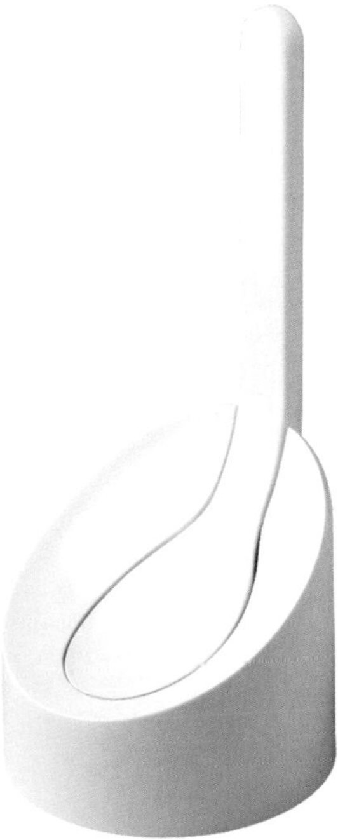

Makio Hasuike. Cucciolo toilet brush holder. 1976. ABS polymer and rubber, overall h. 13 1/4 x dia. 5 15/16" (33.7 x 15.1 cm). Mfr: Gedy, Italy. Gift of IDC Marketing Ltd. MoMA.

Exhibitions/citations Work subject of 1983 and 1984 exhibitions, Gallery Marronnier, Kyoto. Work shown at 1986 Japan Ebna Art Competition; *Glass '87 in Japan*, *Glass '90 in Japan*, and *Glass '96 in Japan* and was selected for the 1997 *Kyoto Art and Craft Exhibition*, all Tokyo; and 1991 (5th) Triennale of Japan Glass Art Crafts Association, Heller Gallery, New York. 1986 EMBA Art Contest, Japan.
Bibliography Cat., *Glass Japan*, New York: Heller Gallery and Japan Glass Art Crafts Association, 1991: no. 8.

Haskins, Michael (1944–1991)
American interior and product designer; active New York.

Training To 1973, Bowling Green (Ohio) State University.
Biography Haskins first worked with Benjamin Thompson on the design of Faneuil Hall Marketplace in Boston (first phase in 1976); was associated with design development for Thompson's Design Research stores headquarters in Boston; designed interiors of the Hay-Adams Hotel, Washington; E. Braun linen shop, Madison Avenue, New York; Bullocks Pavilion store, San Mateo, Cal.; Scarborough soap and perfume flagship store, Los Angeles; offices (with Charles Pfister) of architects Skidmore, Owings and Merrill; offices of Cannon Mills, New York; designed products by the Gear home-furnishings store chain and by Marimekko.
Bibliography 'Michael Haskins, 44, Interior Designer, Dies,' *The New York Times*, Apr. 1991.

Hassall, Thomas (1878–1940)
British ceramics designer.

Training Burslem School of Art.
Biography 1892–1940, Hassall worked for Spode, where he was artistic director 1910–40 and where his brother Joe Hassall was the chief engraver; designed decorations on ceramics by W.T. Copeland in Stoke-on-Trent, including c. 1935 Ming pattern stoneware.
Bibliography Cat., *Thirties: British Art and Design Before the War*, London: Arts Council of Great Britain/Hayward Gallery, 1979.

Hassenpflug, Gustav (1907–1977)
German architect, furniture designer, and writer; born Düsseldorf.

Training 1926–28 under Hannes Meyer and Mart Stam, furniture, industrial design, and painting, Bauhaus, Dessau.
Biography 1929–31, Hassenpflug worked with Marcel Breuer in Berlin; 1931–34, was an architect and city planner in Russia with Ernst May and Moisei Ginzburg; 1934, returned to Germany and worked for the Eisenmöbelfabrik L. und C. Arnold in Stendal/Altmark (near Berlin), as a designer of school furniture, then worked as designer for EMBRU-Werke tubular-steel furniture company in Rüti, Switzerland, where his activities included the development of garden, cinema, school, and hospital furniture. 1940–45, he worked with Egon Eiermann; subsequently, became an independent architect; 1945, received commissions to rebuild Berlin hospitals; 1946, was appointed the chairperson of urban and regional planning, Hochschule für Architektur, Weimar; 1950–56, was director, Landeskunstschule, Hamburg; 1956, became professor of building design, Technische Hochschule, Munich. He wrote the books *Bauentwurfslehre* (building design) (with Ernst Neufert, 1934–36), *Möbel aus Stahlrohr und Stahlblech* (tubular steel and sheet steel furniture) (1935), *Stahlmöbel* (steel furniture) (1960), and *Stahlmöbel für Krankenhaus und ärztliche Praxis* (steel furniture for the hospital and medical practice) (1963).
Exhibitions High-rise building shown at 1957 *Interbau* exhibition, Berlin.
Bibliography Friederike Mehlau-Wiebking et al., *Schweizer Typenmöbel 1925–35, Sigfried Giedion und die Wohnbedarf AG*, Zürich: gta, 1989: 228–29. Christian Grohn, *Gustav Hassenpflug: Architektur, Design, Lehre, 1907–1977*, Düsseldorf: Marzona, 1985.

Hassenpflug, Marie (1933–)
German metalworker.

Training Werkkunstschule, Krefeld; enameling, Werkkunstschule, Düsseldorf.
Biography 1961, Hassenpflug set up her own workshop in Düsseldorf; from 1971, designed for Georg Jensen Sølvsmedie in Copenhagen.
Bibliography Cat., *Georg Jensen Silversmithy: 77 Artists, 75 Years*, Washington: Smithsonian, 1980.

Hasuike, Makio (1938–)
Japanese industrial designer; born Tokyo; active Milan.

Training To 1962, industrial design, Tokyo National University of Fine Arts and Music.
Biography 1962, Hasuike worked for Seiko, designing more than 20 timepieces, and for the 1964 Osaka Winter Olympiad; 1963, settled in Milan, worked as a designer, and, subsequently, in the studio of Rudolfo Bonetto; became a member of the Associazione per il Disegno Industriale (ADI); 1968, set up his own design studio in Milan, where he established MH Way in 1982, a firm to manufacture and market bags and accessories; from 1982, taught, Domus Academy, Milan, and cofounded the master's-degree program in strategic design and was teacher in the Facoltà di Disegno Industriale, Politecnico, Milan. Clients have included Gaggia, Frau, Gruppo Merloni, Bialetti, Cantieri Posillipo, Gela, Molveno-Cometti, Cedit (ceramic tiles), Montedil , and Italora. Other work includes a television set by Seimart Elettronica; plastic bathroom accessories (with Olaf Von Bohr), including well-known toilet brush by Gedy; all-glass Dama console by Fiam Italia; and a dinner service by Società Ceramiche Revelli.
Exhibitions/citations Participated in 1973 (15th) Triennale di Milano. 1979 (two citations), 1981 (two citations), 1984 (two citations), 1987 (three citations individually and with Luca Meda), 1989 (three citations), 1991 (two citations individually and with Marc-René-Marie de Jonghe), 1994 (five citations), 1998 (four citations), Compasso d'Oro; numerous others.
Bibliography Giancarlo Iliprandi and Pierluigi Molinari (eds.), *Industrial designers italiani*, Fagagna: Magnus, 1985: 116. Interview with Hasuike, *The Sun*, no. 351, Oct. 1990: 110–11. 'Makio Hasuike, borse e oggetti di un designer imprenditore,' *Domus*, no. 742, Oct. 1992: 68–73. 'L'isola felice di Makio Hasuike,' *Interni*, no. 446, Dec. 1994: 186–92. Anty Pansera, *Dizionario del design italiano*, Milan: Cantini, 1995. 'Italian design, Makio Hasuike,' *Nikkei Design*, Aug. 1995: 40. Andrea Branzi, *Il design italiano 1964–1990*, Milan: Electa, 1996. 'Makio Hasuike e il vecchio lavatoio di un cortile milanese,' *Abitare*, no. 390, Dec. 1999: 156-57.

Hattori, Kintaro (1860–1934)
> See Seiko.

Haugesen, Niels Jørgen (1936–)
Danish architect and furniture designers born Vivild.

Training To 1961, furniture design, Kunsthåndværkerskolen, Copenhagen.

Biography 1956, Haugesen became a journeyman joiner; 1962–64, worked in the office of architect Sven Kaj-Larsen in Stockholm; 1964–66, with Orla Mølgård-Nielsen; 1966–71, with Arne Jacobsen. Haugesen has taught furniture design, Skolen for Brugskunst, Copenhagen; 1971, set up his own design studio; 1980–95, collaborated on furniture design with textile designer Gunvor Haugesen. Designed furniture by OD-Møbler, recently by Tranekær Furniture (from 1989 with Gunvor Haugesen), and others, including the widely published 1977 wire and sheet-metal stacking chair by Hybodon. He is best know for 1978 X-line chair by Hybodan and 1986 Haugesen folding table by Fritz Hansen. By Bent Krogh: 1992 Nimbus conference table/chairs, 1994–97 Xylofon outdoor furniture, 1998 Fleur chair, and 2000 X-Line chair.
Exhibitions/citations Work shown at 1960, 1961, and 1964 Cabinetmakers' Guild exhibition, Kunstindustrimuseet, Copenhagen; 1964 *Form i Malmö*; 1966 *Vijftig jaar zitten*, Stedelijk Museum, Amsterdam. First prize, 1963 Swedish Forestry Society competition; 1965 second prize, Danish Forestry Society competition; 1965 second prize, Nordic competition, Swedish furniture industry; 1968, 1969, and 1987 Danmarks Nationalbank Jubilee Foundation; 1982 and 1987 awards, Danish State Art Foundation; 1987 Dansk ID Prize; 1989 first prize, Danish Forestry Society competition; 1996 Danish Furniture Prize (with Gunvor Haugesen).
Bibliography Frederik Sieck, *Nutidig Dansk Møbeldesign – en kortfattet illustreret beskrivelse*, Copenhagen: Bondo Gravesen, 1981: 55.

Haupt, Karl Hermann (1904–1983)
German designer.

Training 1922–25, painting, Kunstgewerbeschule, Burg Giebichenstein; 1925, Bauhaus, Dessau; under Johannes Itten, Textilfachschule, Krefeld.
Biography There is a 1925 pencil drawing of a chair designed by Haupt that may have been produced. 1926–31, he worked in a textile factory; subsequently, was a pattern-drawer in a weaving factory; 1951 – 53, taught, Hochschule für angewandte Kunst; subsequently, became a scientific designer and photographer, Akademie der Wissenschaften, Berlin.
Bibliography Cat., *The Bauhaus: Masters and Students*, New York: Barry Friedman, 1988.

Haus-Rucker-Co
Austrian architecture and design group.

History 1967, Haus-Rucker-Co was founded in Vienna as an experimental arhictecture and design group by Laurids Ortner (Linz 1941–), Günther Zamp Kelp (Bistritz, Romania, 1941–), and Klaus Pinter (Schärding 1940–). Ortner and Kelp had studied architecture; Pinter painting. Based on utopian concepts, their initial projects spanned architectural design and *Aktionskunst* such as 1967 Balloon for Two in Vienna and 1971 Shell Around [the] Haus Lange Museum in Krefeld, and the utopian 1967 Pneumacosm mini-environment (unrealized). 1970, the group opened another studio in Düsseldorf and Manfred Ortner joined; and, 1971, a third in New York; became known as exponents of 1960s–70s Radical Design and for 'provisional' (or disposable) architecture to accommodate changes in the environment; realized a number of spectacular/provocative projects such as Eatable Architecture (a model erected in New York's Central Park, for the park's centenary, and popular with the public); designed 1975 Quart modular range of storage furniture by Elst and, 1977–83, furniture, offices, and the showroom at Renngasse 6–8, Vienna, of Bene office-furniture company (and, from 1987, Laurids Ortner as a designer for Bene). 1977, Pinter left the group. The remaining couple designed 1980 Forum Design exhibition, Linz; 1981–87, was active in Berlin; won the 1987 competition for the Messepalast large exhibition complex in Vienna. 1987, Kemp set up an architecture practice, and brothers Laurids Ortner and Manfred Ortner (Linz 1943–) set up Ortner & Ortner Baukunst in Vienna and Berlin. All have taught at a number of institutions, particularly L. Ortner, Hochschule für Künstlerische Industrielle Gestaltung.
Exhibitions/citations Participated in Documenta 5 (1972), 6 (1977), and 8 (1987), Kassel; Kunsthalle, Düsseldorf and Berlin; Triennale di Milano; events at Centre George Pompidou, Paris. Work subject of 1977 *Architecture de la Ville*, Centre Georges Pompidou; 1992 *Haus-Rucker-Co Objekt, Konzept, Bauten 1967–1992* (retrospective), Kunstehalle, Vienna (catalogs below). Included in *Radicals: architettura e design 1960–75*, 1996 (6th) Mostra Internazionale di Archittettura, Venice. 1979 Kunstpreis Berlin (for Akademie der Künste, Berlin).
Bibliography Heinrich Klotz (ed.), *Haus-Rucker-Co: 1967 bis 1983*, Brunswick/Wiesbaden: F. Vieweg, 1984. Hugh Honour et al., *Lexikon der Weltarchitektur*, Munich: Prestel; 1987: 267. Günther Feuerstein, *Vienna–Present and Past: Arts and Crafts—Applied Art—Design*, Vienna: Jugend und Volk, 1976: 62, 64, 80. Cat, *Haus-Rucker-Co: Denkräume – Stadträume 1967–1992*, Klagenfurt: Ritter, 1992. Arlette Barré-Despond (ed.), *Dictionnaire international des arts appliqués et du design*, Paris: Regard, 1996.

Paul Haustein. Coffee service. c. 1904. Pewter-silver alloy, coffee pot: 7 x 5 x 9 1/2" (17.8 x 12.7 x 24.2 cm), sugar bowl h. 3 7/8 x dia. 4" (9.9 x 10.2 cm), creamer 3 5/8 x 2 3/4 x 5 3/4" (9.2 x 7 x 14.6 cm). Mfr.: Gerhardi & Co., Germany. Phyllis B. Lambert Fund. MoMA.

Haussmann Robert (1931–); Trix Haussmann (b. Trix Högl 1933–)
Architects and industrial designers. Haussmann born Zürich. Högl born Chur. Husband and wife; active Zürich.

Training Högl: to 1963, architecture and urban planning, Eidgenössische Technische Hochschule (ETH), Zürich. Haussmann: in Zürich and, under Gerrit Rietveld, Amsterdam.
Biography Robert Haussmann designed 1955 RH 301 lounge chair with an uncanny resemblance to Ludwig Mies van der Rohe's 1929 Barcelona chair. 1967, the husband/wife team founded their office Allgemeine Entwurfsanstalt in Zürich; from 1978, participated with the Alchimia group in Milan, which produced some of their objects; designed 1984 Broken, 1985 Black Stripes, and 1987 Zürich dinnerware by Swid Powell, and a large body of other work, including buildings, interiors, restorations, products, as well as furniture by Teo Jacob, Wogg, and others. Considered Postmoderns, they operate within the doctrine of *Allgemeine Entwurfsanstalt* (furniture as an architectural statement). Architecture has included the Galleria in Hamburg. They teach at ETH; he there 1979–81 and, from 1986, Staatliche Akademie der bildenden Künste, Stuttgart.
Exhibitions Work shown at 1989 *Mobilier Suisse*, Galerie des Brèves du CCI, Centre Georges Pompidou, Paris; subject of 2002 *Trix und Robert Haussmann: Ein alphabetischer Spaziergng*, Museum für Gestaltung, Zürich.
Bibliography Kazuko Sato, *Alchimia*, Berlin: Taco, 1988. Frank R. Werner, *Robert + Trix Haussmann*, Fellbach: Axel Menges, 1998.

Haustein, Paul (1880–1944)
German enamelist, metalworker, ceramicist, and furniture and graphic designer; born Chemnitz; active Darmstadt and Stuttgart.

Training Kunstgewerbeschule, Dresden and Munich.
Biography Haustein experimented with enamelwork and produced some designs in metal by the Vereinigte Werkstätten für Kunst im Handwerk in Munich and, from 1906, simple designs with rich abstract foliate scroll ornamentation by Bruckmann & Söhne in Heilbronn; 1903, was one of the artists at the Darmstadt colony of the Grand Duke Louis IV of Hesse-Darmstadt. Haustein was interested in silver and copper, which he combined in highly original ways and in one early example applied enamel to copper. His 1903–05 silver designs, like those of Hans Christiansen, were produced by E.L. Viëtor, the court silversmith at Darmstadt. Haustein taught the applied-arts master course in Nuremberg established by Peter Behrens in 1901–02; from 1905, taught metalworking, Kunstgewerbeschule, Stuttgart, of which Bernhard Pankok was the director. Haustein's tureen shown at 1910 Brussels *Ex-*

position was one of the first examples of the Art Déco style and a reaction against Henry van de Velde's plain, functional forms.
Exhibitions/citations Work shown at exhibitions in Darmstadt; 1904 *Louisiana Purchase Exposition*, St. Louis, Miss., where he won a prize; Bruckman stand at 1910 *Exposition Universelle et Internationale*, Brussels.
Bibliography Cat., *Ein Document Deutscher Kunst*, vol. 4, Mathildenhöhe: Die Künstler der Mathildenhöhe, 1976: 85–91. Annelies Krekel-Aalberse, *Art Nouveau and Art Déco Silver*, New York: Abrams, 1989.

Haviland
French porcelain factory.

History 1843, David Haviland, an American, established the Haviland pottery works in Limoges, where his son Charles Haviland was director 1866–1921. 1873, Félix Bracquemond opened a research studio in Auteuil, near Paris, where designs were created for production by the Limoges factory in soft-paste porcelain or *faïence fine*. 1875 in Auteuil, Ernest Chaplet began producing barbotine decorations, whose designs were painted by the studio's own artists or freelance painters and sculptors. These vases did not sell well and were discontinued. 1881, Bracquemond left Auteuil. 1882, a studio was established on the rue Blomet, Vaugirard commune, Paris, directed by Chaplet to 1885. The Auteuil studio continued to 1914 under a manager named Jochum, producing decorations for porcelain made in Limoges.
Bibliography Yvonne Brunhammer, *Art Nouveau Belgium, France*, Houston: Rice University, 1976.

Havinden, Ashley Eldrid (1903–1973)
British painter and graphic and textile designer.

Training Drawing and design, Central School of Arts and Crafts, London.
Biography 1923, Havinden became a trainee in the advertising agency W.S. Crawford in London, where he became a board member and director of art and design in 1929 and was vice-chairperson of the agency from 1960. His clients included Milk Marketing Board, General Post Office, Brewers' Society, and Simpson's department store, London. From 1933, he designed rugs and textiles for the interior-decorating firm J. Duncan Miller; through Wells Coates, met Walter Gropius, Marcel Breuer, László Moholy-Nagy, and Herbert Bayer; 1935, created advertising for Morton Sundour Fabrics. 1930s, Havinden's rug and printed and woven designs were produced by Campbell Fabrics in London and by Wilton Royal Carpet Factory. His scroll motifs, birds in flight, and ribbon patterns were produced on fabrics by Alastair Morton's Edinburgh Weavers in Carlisle. He designed the book pavillion at 1937 *Exposition Internationale des Arts et Techniques dans la Vie Moderne*, Paris; 1956, was president, Society of Industrial Artists. Havinden is known both as an abstract painter and poster designer and wrote the books *Line Drawing for Reproduction* (London: Studio Publications, 1933) and *Advertising and the Artist* (London: Studio Publications, 1956).
Exhibitions Rugs and fabrics were the subject of 1937 exhibitions at Duncan Miller Gallery, paintings at London Gallery Ltd. (during 1936–50), and advertising work at Lund Humphries Gallery, all London. Fabrics were shown at 1939 *Golden Gate International Exposition*, San Francisco; paintings at 1939 *Abstract Paintings by Nine British Artists*, Lefevre Gallery, London ; fabrics, rugs, and graphics at 1979–80 *Thirties* exhibition, Hayward Gallery, London (catalog below).
Bibliography Cat., *Thirties: British Art and Design Before the War*, London: Arts Council of Great Britain/Hayward Gallery, 1979. Stuart Durant, *Ornament from the Industrial Revolution to Today*, Woodstock, N.Y.: Overlook, 1986.

Haworth: Brian Alexander (1963–). Flo Cell storage unit. 1997. Fiberglass, aluminum, steel, leather, and ABS polymer, 24 x 37 x 20" (61 x 94 x 50.8 cm). Mfr.: Haworth, US (prototype). Gift of the mfr. MoMA.

Havlíček, Josef (1899–1961)
Czech architect, sculptor, painter, furniture designer, and theoretician; born Prague.

Training 1916–24, České Vysoké Učení Technické (Czech technical university), and, 1923–26 under Josef Gočar, Akademie Výtvarných Umení (academy of fine arts); both Prague.
Biography 1925–26, Havlíček worked in Gočár's studio and, 1927–28, in Osvald Polívka's architecture studio; 1922, with Karel Honzík, set up his own studio called H&H. His first artworks and architecture were influenced by Cubism, and his architecture adhered to the 'tectonic organism.' 1920s, Havlíček became one of the leading proponents of modernism in Czechoslovakia; from 1923 until its close in 1931, was a member of the Devětsil group; designed for Polívka in the International Style, influenced by Le Corbusier. H&H produced 1929–30 Koldom community house and first phases of 1932–34 Všeobecný penzijní ústav building, Prague, one of the most important International Style structures in Europe. Died in Prague.
Bibliography Josef Havlíček, *Návrhy a stavby: 1925–60*, Prague, 1964. Cat., Devětsil: Czech *Avant-Garde Art, Architecture, and Design of the 1920s and 30s*, Oxford: Museum of Modern Art; London: Design Museum, 1990. Cat., *Prague, 1900–1938: capitale secrète des avants-gardes*, Dijon: Musée des Beaux-Arts, 1997.

Hawkes, T.G.
> See Carder, Frederick C.

Haworth
American furniture manufacturer.

History 1948 in his garage, G.W. Haworth (1912–) founded Modern Products company as a small manufacturer of custom wood products. 1954, the firm began making modular office partitions (an early panel system for the construction of 'cubicles' as they have become known); 1971, introduced Modern Office Modules (MOM) and offered the first of what is today's acoustical-panel configurations and the universal panel hinge for flexible open-office plans; 1976, introduced ERA-I, the world's first prewired modular panel, to eliminate extension cords and hard wiring and also introduced monocoque panel construction, somewhat like airplane-wing construction, for high strength without stress points; 1981, set up its new corporate headquarters, in Holland, Mich.; 1984, produced its one millionth UniGroup panel; 1986, introduced The Power Base, the industry's first eight-wire power system with three dedicated circuits, for dedicated electrical-power sources and a reduction of destructive electrical interference. 1975, the corporate name was changed to Haworth. 1988–93, the corporation expanded substantially worldwide with the purchase of firms Mueller, Myrtle, Kinetics, and Lunstead in Europe; Comforto in Germany; Ordo, and Mobilier International in France; Castelli in Italy; and Cortal and Seldex in Portugal; and developed relationships in Asia. 1992, Haworth became the first US office-furniture manufacturer to be registered for ISO-9001 standards; holds more than 150 international patents; 1993, acquired Globe Business Furniture. Worldwide sales exceeded $2 billion/2.2 billion euros in 2000, employing more than 10,000 people.
Citations Winner, 1997 Best of Competition (for TAS seating), 1998 Gold Tooling Solutions, 1999 Gold Award (for JumpStuff office system), 2000 Best Of NeoCon (for JumpStuff), all NeoCon, Chicago; 1997 Gold Excellence Award (for Office Explorations), IDSA/*Business Week* magazine; three awards, 1998 Annual Design Review, *I.D.* magazine; 1998 Award for Design Excellence, ADEX, *Design Journal*; others. To H.W. Haworth himself: 1987 honorary degree, Kendall College, Evanston, Ill.

Edith Heath. Teapot. 1947. Glazed stoneware, pot 6 3/4 x 8 1/2 x 7 1/2" (17.1 x 21.6 x 19.1 cm), lid 1 1/4 x 3 x 2 3/4" (3.2 x 7.6 x 7 cm). Mfr.: Heath Ceramics, US. Gift of the mfr. MoMA.

Hayek, Nicholas G. (1925–)
> See Swatch.

Haynes and Co., D.F.

American ceramics manufacturer.

History 1880, a pottery was established by Henry and Isaac Brougham and John Tunstall at Nicholsen and Decatur Streets in Baltimore, Maryland. 1882, David Francis Haynes (d. 1908), formerly a crockery jobber in Baltimore, bought the firm, expanding it from an operation with one kiln into one of the most successful art potteries in the US. Haynes had sold ceramics in Lowell, Mass.; 1856, traveled in England, visiting the Staffordshire potteries; worked for Abbott Rolling Iron Works in Baltimore, and, 1858, for the oil and lamp merchant Ammidon, which had begun producing crockery; 1872, became a partner in Ammidon and, 1877, became its sole owner, renaming the firm D.F. Haynes and Co; 1882, bought the Chesapeake Pottery; from 1879, was closely associated with Maryland Queensware, through which he sold the entire production of his wares; designed some ceramics and, more successfully, sold and marketed his firm's ceramics; 1877–78, hired Englishmen Lewis Taft to handle the supervision of the bodies, glazes, and kilns, and Frederick Hackney to handle artistic production, including mold making. Hackney probably developed Clifton ware (similar to majolica) and Avalon ware (ivory bodies). 1890–1910, the firm's most successful production was in Parian tea roses mounted on velvet, portrait medallions of bulls, and an historicist porcelain clock case. 1882, Chesapeake Pottery was enlarged; financially overstretched, Haynes sold it in 1887 to Edwin Bennett of Baltimore. 1890, Haynes, with partner E. Houston Bennett (Edwin Bennett's son), bought back the firm, renaming it Haynes, Bennett and Co. 1895, Bennett retired, and Frank R. Haynes became a partner. 1896, the name became D.F. Haynes and Son. 1914, the firm closed.
Exhibitions/citations Prizes, 1901 *Pan-American Exposition*, Buffalo, N.Y., and 1904 *Louisiana Purchase Exposition*, St. Louis, Mo.
Bibliography 'David F. Haynes', *Baltimore American*, 28 Aug. 1908: 14. Ulrich Thieme and Felix Becker (eds.), *Allgemeines Lexikon der bildenden Künstler*, vol. 16, Leipzig, 1923: 182. Cat., *The Potter's Craft in Maryland: An Exhibition of Nearly Two Hundred Examples of Pottery Manufactured 1793 to 1890*, 1955. Paul J. FitzPatrick, 'Chesapeake Pottery,' *Antiques Journal*, no. 33, Dec. 1978: 16–19, 48. Doreen Bolger Burke et al., *In Pursuit of Beauty: Americans and the Aesthetic Movement*, New York: The Metropolitan Museum of Art/Rizzoli, 1986.

Heal, Ambrose (1872–1959)

British furniture designer; born and active London.

Training Slade School of Fine Art, London.
Biography 1890-93, Heal served as an apprentice cabinet maker at Plucknett in Warwick; 1893, joined the family firm (established 1810); 1896, began to show his furniture designs at exhibitions, which were in the Arts and Crafts idiom and primarily in solid oak with sturdy craftsmanship and simple, stark lines; was a member of the Art-Workers' Guild; 1915, played a role in the formation of the Design and Industries Association (DIA). From early 1930s, he adopted the more fashionable modern approach to furniture, following the style of his designers J.F. Johnson and Arthur Greenwood. C.F.A. Voysey also designed for him. Heal brought modernism to the mass trade in Britain; after visiting 1923 Gothenburg Exhibition, introduced Swedish glassware to Britain and sold Swedish furniture. 1950s, the firm employed many young British designers, especially of textiles. 1983, Heal's was acquired by the Habitat Group under Terence Conran, which in-cluded Habitat.
Honors 1933, Ambrose Heal was knighted; 1939, elected Royal Designer for Industry, UK.
Bibliography Kenneth Farr, *Design in British Industry: A Mid-Century Survey*, London: Cambridge, 1955. Cat., *Thirties: British Art and Design Before the War*, London: Arts Council of Great Britain/Hayward Gallery, 1979. Cat., Leslie Jackson, *The New Look: Design in the Fifties*, New York: Thames & Hudson, 1991: 125.

Heath, Adrian (1920–1992)

British industrial designer; active Denmark; husband of Ditte Heath.

Training To 1951, Achitectural Association, London.
Biography 1951–52, Adrian Heath worked for furniture firm Jacob Kjær in Copenhagen and, later, for Ernest Race in London and Peter Hvidt and Orla Mølgård-Nielsen in Copenhagen; opened an office with his wife Ditte Heath in Hadsten, Denmark. Clients included Søren Horn, Gimson & Slater, F.D.B. Denmark, France & Søn. 1963–68, he lectured on furniture design at Edinburgh College of Art; from 1969, taught industrial-design history at Arkitekskolen in Århus. Work included furniture, exhibition design, and lighting. One of his best known furniture designs is 1968 laminated wood/canvas Chair 194 (with his wife) by France & Søn.
Exhibitions/citations Work shown at 1963–69 annual exhibitions, Copenhagen Cabinetmakers' Guild; Chair 194 at 1970 *Modern Chairs 1918–1970* exhibition, Whitechapel Gallery, London (catalog below). 1961 design award (office furniture), Timber Development Association, London; 1961 award, Danish Furniture Manufacturers' Association competition; 1963 award, *Daily Mirror* International Furniture Competition,.
Bibliography *Designers in Britain 6*, London, 1964. Cat., *Modern Chairs 1918–1970*, London: Lund Humphries, 1971. Adrian Heath, Ditte Heath, Aage Lund Jensen, *300 Years of Industrial Design: Function, Form, Technique 1700–2000*, London : Herbert, 2000.

Heath, Ditte (1923–)

Danish interior, furniture, and furnishings designer; active Denmark; wife of Adrian Heath.

Training To 1948, Bygningsskole, Det Kongelige Danske Kunstakademi, Copenhagen.
Biography Ditte Heath worked for the Architects' Cooperative Partnership, the London County Council Architects Department, and architects Ole Buhl, Peter Hvidt, and Orla Mølgård-Nielsen. She was a librarian at Arkitekskole, Århus; with her husband, Adrian Heath, she opened an office in Hadsten, Denmark. Their clients included Søren Horn, Gimson & Slater, F.D.B. Denmark, and France & Søn. Her range of objects included furniture and lighting.
Exhibitions Work shown with Adrian Heath.
Bibliography Cat., *Modern Chairs 1918–1970*, London: Lund Humphries, 1971. Frederik Sieck, *Nutidig Dansk Møbeldesign – en kortfattet illustreret beskrivelse*, Copenhagen: Bondo Gravesen, 1981, 1990.

Heath, Edith (1911–)

American painter, sculptor, and ceramicist.

Training 1934–40, painting and sculpture, Art Institute of Chicago; ceramic chemistry, University of California.
Biography 1844, Edith Heath and her husband, Brian, opened a studio/pottery in the garage of their home in California. She was helped by many assistants and produced a range of hand-thrown dinnerware that sold in a San Francisco department store. 1947, she abandoned hand-throwing for mass-production and, with her husband, established a small factory, producing the famous Coupe ovenproof range of stoneware (produced from 1948 to today). Even though most of the Coupe pieces were mass-produced, some parts were handmade to insinuate a handcrafted appearance. 1960, Heath Ceramics began producing tiles used for the sheathing of the Pasadena Art Museum in Pasadena, Cal. With her husband, Edith Heath controls all aspects of the

production and implementation of the demanding standards for production. Even though past the age of 90, she continues to be active in the plant in Sausalito, Cal., with a staff of about 20.
Exhibitions/citations Work subject of 1944 exhibition, Palace of the Legion of Honor Museum, San Francisco. Awarded 1971 gold medal (for architectural tile), American Institute of Architects (AIA).
Bibliography Edith Heath, 'Pottery and Dinnerware,' *Arts + Architecture*, vol. 66, Sept. 1949: 38–39. Don Wallance, *Shaping America's Products*, New York: Reinhold, 1956: 93–96. Cat., Kathryn B. Hiesinger and George H. Marcus III (eds.), *Design Since 1945*, Philadelphia: Philadelphia Museum of Art, 1983.

Heaton, Maurice (1900–1990)
Swiss glassware designer; born Neuchatel; active New York

Training 1920–21, engineering, Stevens Institute of Technology, Hoboken, N.J.
Biography 1914, Heaton settled with his family in New York; was introduced to glassmaking by his father, stained-glass designer Clement J. Heaton, who was also the son of a glass artist. From late 1920s, Maurice Heaton pursued innovative methods for producing glass designs; experimented with translucent white-enamel glazes on hand-cut, bubbly glass sheets; was able to produce enamel spirals by working on a potter's wheel. Through the Architectural League of New York, his work became well known and was sold through the galleries of Eugene Schoen and Rena Rosenthal in New York. For several interior schemes, Heaton was commissioned by Schoen to execute large glass murals, the most impressive of which was *The Flight of Amelia Earhart Across the Atlantic* for 1932 interior of the RKO theater in Rockefeller Center, New York. He was interested in producing affordable art glass; remained active in his studio in Rockland County, N.Y., until he died there.
Bibliography Eugene Clute, 'Craftsmanship in Decorated Glass,' *Architecture*, July 1931: 11. 'An Illuminated Glass Mural,' *Architecture*, Dec. 1932: 351. Eleanor Bitterman, 'Heaton's Wizardry with Glass,' *Craft Horizons*, June 1954: 13. 'Heaton, Maurice,' *Who's Who in American Art*, 1980. Karen Davies, *At Home in Manhattan: Modern Decorative Arts, 1925 to the Depression*, New Haven: Yale, 1983: 61.

Hébert, Julien (1917–1994)
Canadian industrial designer, teacher, and sculptor; born Rigaud, Québec; active Montréal.

Training To 1941, École des Beaux-Arts, Montréal; 1944, master's degree in philosophy, Université de Montréal; 1947–48 under Ossip Zadkine, in Paris.
Biography 1948 or 1949, Hébert returned to Montréal to teach fine art at the École des Beaux-Arts; 1951–61 with partner Yves Grouix, produced wooden/steel office desks, tables, and commodes under the name Grébert. Hébert designed a 1954 aluminum-tube garden chair with a canvas cover by Siegmund Werner in Montréal, 1955 biomorphic 'ribbon'-edge coffee table by Snyder's in Waterloo, Ontario, 1963 trapezoid school desks by Paul Dumont in Montréal. Hébert organized 1956 *Good Design in Aluminum* exhibition, National Gallery of Canada; 1956–66, taught design, École du Meuble (later known as Institute des Arts Appliqués); designed 1967 La Ronde official logo (with former pupil Marcel Girard) of 1967 *Universal and International Exhibition (Expo '67)*, Montréal, and managed the design of the Canadian and Québec pavilions at 1970 *Japan World Exposition (Expo '70)*, Osaka; 1970s, organized industrial-design department, Université de Montréal. 1981–85, he was a member of Canada Council. As a sculptor, his aluminum pieces are installed in the foyer of Place des Arts (1963), Montréal, and on the Opera Hall ceiling (1966) of National Arts Centre, Ottawa.
Citations Received award in 1951 (1st) industrial design competition in Canada, among others; 1953 grant to study industrial design, Massachusetts Institute of Technology (MIT), Cambridge, Mass., US.
Bibliography Cat., *Seduced and Abandoned: Modern Furniture Designers in Canada, the First Fifty Years*, Toronto: The Art Gallery at Harbourfront, 1986: 16. Rachel Gotlieb and Cora Golden, *Design in Canada Since 1945: Fifty Years from Teakettles to Task Chairs*, Toronto: Knopf Canada, 2001.

Hebey, Isabelle (1935–1996)
French industrial and furniture designer; active Paris.

Training Psychology and sociology, École du Louvre, Paris.
Biography 1966–90, Hebey designed all of Yves Saint Laurent's Rive Gauche boutiques worldwide. Other design work included 1971 interior (with Aérospatiale agency) of the Concorde airliner; 1979–82 interiors of the Honda Accord automobile; 1988–90 furniture and interiors of the new French Ministère de l'Economie des Finances; 1984 personal desk of Danielle Mitterrand, the wife of the French president; interior of and furniture for the South Arch of La Grande Arche de la Défense building complex (architect, Otto von Sprekelsen).
Bibliography Gilles de Bure, *Le mobilier français 1965–1979*, Paris: Regard, 1983. François Mathey, *Au bonheur des formes, design français 1945–1992*, Paris: Regard, 1992.

Hecht, Sam (1969–)
British industrial designer; born London.

Training Royal College of Art, London.
Biography After schooling, Hecht became active as an interior and industrial designer; subsequently, joined the Studio design group in Tel Aviv; after which in San Francisco, began a collaboration with the IDEO design consortium; has designed equipment by AT&T and NEC and office interiors for IDEO clients; eventually, joined the IDEO staff in Japan, designing primarily hi-tech products for clients such as Matsushita, NEC, Seiko, and others; lectures in Japan.
Citations 1998 award, exhibition category, D&AD, London.
Bibliography Jasper Morrison (ed.), *The International Design Yearbook*, London: Laurence King, 1999. Paola Antonelli (ed.), *Objects of Design: The Museum of Modern Art*, New York: The Museum of Modern Art, 2003: 183.

Heetman, Joris (1857–)
> See Liberati, Anne.

Hefetz, 'Safi' Joseph Guy (1962–)
Israeli industrial designer; born Haifa; active Tel Aviv.

Training 1990, bachelor's degree in design, Bezalel Academy of Art and Design, Jerusalem; 1995, training course in Unigraphics format, organized by Makit for qualification in the format; 1996, training course in Solid Works format, organized by Systematics.
Biography 1989–90, Hefetz worked as a designer at architecture firm Springer; 1990–94, was an independent designer; 1994–2002, deputy director and project manager, Design Department, Creo-Scitex, Tel Aviv; from 2002, partner, I2D design studio, Tel Aviv. From 1993, he has been a lecturer, Department of Industrial Design, Bezalel Academy, and, from 2002, in charge of Class A program and Teaching Committee there; from 1993, coordinator of teaching Class B, Department of Design, Hadassah. Hefetz has participated in a number of product designs, including 1992 computer-interface programs, portable computer system, Mokdanit home emergency-call system for cardiac patients, 1993 portable pan-top computer, and 1994 control/monitoring unit by Tadiran; 1992 digital printer by Indigo; 1993 taxi terminal by Hi-G-Teac; 1995 redesign of automatic flat-bed scanner and 1996 flat-bed scanner by Scitex.
Exhibitions/citations Work shown in a large number of exhibitions. 1993 Crate & Barrel award (for Mokdanit project), Department of Design, Israel Museum; 2001 award (for back panel of a digital camera), Industrie Forum Design (iF), Hanover.
Bibliography *Mokdanit Project*, Jerusalem: Israel Museum, 1993. Giora Urian, *From the Israel Museum to the Carmel Market: Israeli Design*, Ramat-Hasaron: Urian / The Architect's Encyclopedia, 2001. *iF Annual*, Hanover: Industrie Forum Design, 2001. Cats., Vanni Pasca and Ely Rozenberg, *Industrious Designers = Giovani designer israeliani*, Verona: Abitare il Tempo, 2001 and 2002.

Hegermann-Lindencrone, Effie (1860–1945)
Danish ceramicist.

Training 1880–85, Under Pietro Krohn and others, Tegneskolen for Kvinder.
Biography 1885–86, Hegermann-Lindencrone worked at Københavns Lervarefabrik in Valby; 1886–1945, was a designer at Bing & Grøndahl Porcelænsfabrik in Copenhagen, known for her pierced ceramic vessels; designed ceramics in the first quarter of the 20th century that continued the late 19th-century Scandinavian naturalistic style.
Exhibitions/citations Diploma of honor, 1925 *Exposition Internationale des Arts Décoratifs et Industriels Modernes*, Paris.
Bibliography Cat., David Revere McFadden (ed.), *Scandinavian Modern Design 1880–1980*, New York: Abrams, 1982. Jennifer Hawkins Opie, *Scandinavia: Ceramics and Glass in the Twentieth Century*, New York: Rizzoli, 1989.

Heiberg, Jean (1884–1976)

Norwegian artist and designer.

Training Painting, Munich and Paris, including under Henri Matisse.
Biography Heiberg was a follower of Henri Matisse and other Fauvists. His significant participation in industrial design came in c. 1930, when Alf Rolfson rejected the commission to add visual appeal to the pre-existing Bakelite telephone model designed by engineer Johan Christian Bjerknes for Norsk Elektrisk Bureau. The Bureau was a subsidiary of the Swedish firm Ericsson, whose directors decided that a new telephone model was required to serve the rapidly developing world telephone-service market. Rolfson turned over the assignment to Heiberg, who had just returned from Paris and had become professor at Statens Håndverks-og Kunstindustriskole in Oslo. Heiberg conjured the 1930 or 1931 Bakelite telephone, based on the discipline of a sculptor and initially developed the form as a plaster maquette. The shape may have been influenced by Cubism with elements of neoclassical architectural stylobate (the flatness in a row of columns). Made by Ericsson from 1932 as no. DBH 1001 (or no. EB 32), the Heiberg tabletop phone was also distributed in Turkey, Greece, and Italy and was also produced under license in France and the US. It soon became the standard model of the Televerket (Swedish telephone company) and was introduced by the BPO of Britain as the Tele 332, developed with Ericsson Telephones Ltd., UK.
Bibliography Jesper Engelstoft (ed.), *Lexikon över modern skandinavisk konst*, Copenhagen: Raben & Sjögren, 1958. Cat., *Art and Industry*, London: Boilerhouse Project, Victoria and Albert Museum, 1982. Fredrik Wildhagen, *Norge i Form*, Oslo: Stenersen, 1988: 108. Danielle Schirman (director), *Le téléphone en Bakélite*, television program coproduced by Arte France et al., 25 minutes, 2003.

Heikkilä, Simo (1943–)

Finnish furniture, exhibition, and interior designer; born Helsinki.

Training To 1967, Taideteollinen korkeakoulu, Helsinki.
Biography Heikkilä was an assistant and collaborating designer at Marimekko fabrics; 1970s–80s with Yrjö Kukkapuro, worked on furniture and the design of the subway stations in Helsinki; with Yrjö Wiherheimo, on accessories and furniture by Vivero in Helsinki and, independently, for a number of manufacturers, from Asko in 1968 to Bruno Mathsson in 1999. Though starkly industrial in appearance, their furniture was comfortable. 1979–83, Heikkilä researched in and experimented with interior furnishings; 1975–81, 1984–88, and from 1995, taught architecture and interior design, Teknillinen korkeakoulu, Helsinki; 1971–75, at Helsingin Teknillinen korkeakoulu; 1973–75, at Teknillinen korkeakoulu, Tamperei; visiting professor in Bergen 1985–88 and in Gothenberg 1995–96.
Exhibitions Palus Fini Articus glass-and-wood chair and table shown at 1985 (17th) Triennale di Milano.
Bibliography Cat., David Revere McFadden (ed.), *Scandinavian Modern Design 1880–1980*, New York: Abrams, 1982. Cat., Carlo Guenzi, *Le affinità elettive*, Milan: Electa, 1985. Auction cat., *Asta di modernariato 1900–1986, Auction 'Modernariato,'* Milan: Semenzato Nuova Geri, 8 Oct. 1986: lots 99–100.

Heiligenstein, Auguste (1891–1976)

French glass and ceramics designer; born Saint-Denis.

Training Apprenticeship at Legras glassworks.
Biography Heiligenstein worked at Prestat and at Baccarat as a glass painter, specializing in gold relief decoration; from 1910, was active as a commercial artist; 1919, was hired by Marcel Goupy to produce enameled glass to Goupy's specifications for Maison Geo. Rouard in Paris on pieces signed by Goupy only; showed his work at Rouard's until 1926, when he switched to Edgar Brandt's gallery and worked as ceramicist and glass designer; for Florence Blumenthal, designed glass with enameling in an image by Léon Bakst; 1931–35, designed for Pantin; c. 1933, founded Syndicat des Artisans d'Art.
Exhibitions/citations 1923, work (glassware) first shown, at Musée Galliéra, Paris; subsequently, at Salon of Société des Artistes Français, where he received awards, including 1947 medal of honor. 1960, elected Officier of the Légion d'Honneur.
Bibliography Félix Marcilhac, 'Auguste Heiligenstein,' *Encyclopédie Connaissance des Arts*, no. 295, Sept. 1976. Victor Arwas, *Art Déco*, New York: Abrams, 1980. Cat., *Verriers français contemporains: art et industrie*, Paris: Musée des Arts Décoratifs, 1982.

Hein, Piet (aka Kumbel 1905–1996)

Danish author, inventor, mathematician, artist, and metalworker; born Copenhagen.

Training Kobenhavns Universitet and Kungliga Tekniska Högskolan, Stockholm; private painting schools, Denmark and Sweden.
Biography Hein was known throughout Scandinavia as Kumbel, the author of thousands of popular poems, which he named 'grooks,' published from 1940. 1960s, Hein was a town-planning consultant on the Sergel's Square project in Stockholm, where, in an attempt to solve traffic problems, he developed the concept of the Superellipse, a shape that melds between an oval into a rectangle; developed the shape for 1968 Superellipse tables and chairs (with Bruno Matthson) by Fritz Hansen, a firm for which he also designed lighting, metalwork, china, glass, and textiles; used the Superellipse for buildings in Paris, Canada, Chicago, and Mexico City. Other work included 1967 Sine lamp (based on the flattened curve) by Uniline and 1960s Superegg sterling-silver box by Georg Jensen Sølvsmedie. 1969–76, Hein lived in England; aside from practical design, wrote on the relationship between art and science.
Exhibitions/citations Work shown at 1974 *I Ord og Rum* exhibition, Kunstindustrimuseet, Copenhagen; exhibitions in Washington, D.C., Philadelphia, and elsewhere. 1968 Alexander Graham Bell Silver Bell award, 1971 Dansk ID Prize; 1971 Die Gute Industrieform, Berlin; 1972 honorary doctoral degree, Yale University, New Haven, Conn., US; 1974 honorary doctorate degree, Odense University, Denmark; 1983 Nobel Lecture, Sweden; 1989 annual award, Dansk Designråd (Danish design council); 1985 Ingenio et Arti (official Danish distinction medal) from Danish Queen Margrethe II; 1990 Tietgen medal.
Bibliography Carl E. Christiansson, 'Bruno Mathsson: Furniture Structures Ideas,' *Design Quarterly*, no. 65, 1966: 7–9. Cat., *Georg Jensen Silversmithy: 77 Artists, 75 Years*, Washington: Smithsonian, 1980. Frederik Sieck, *Nutidig Dansk Møbeldesign – en kortfattet illustreret beskrivelse*, Copenhagen: Bondo Gravesen, 1981. Cat., Kathryn B. Hiesinger and George H. Marcus III (eds.), *Design Since 1945*, Philadelphia: Philadelphia Museum of Art, 1983.

Heine, Klaus Achim (1955–)
> See Fischer, Uwe.

Heisey and Company, A.H.

American glassware manufacturer.

History Augustus H. Heisey (Hanover, Germany, 1842–1922) moved to Merrittown, Pa., US, with his family, but returned to Germany after his mother died; worked in the printing trade to 1861, when he became a glass clerk with the King Glass Company in Pittsburgh, Pa. From 1862, Heisey served in the US Civil War; then returned to work in the glass industry, becoming first a shipping clerk and later a salesperson at Ripley & Company in Pittsburgh; 1870, married Susan N. Duncan, the daughter of George Duncan Sr. who soon became the sole owner of the Ripley Glass Company and who renamed it Geo. Duncan & Sons. Heisey, his wife, and his brother-in-law later became part owners of the Duncan Glass Company. 1895, Heisey moved to Newark, Ohio, where he established a glass factory, operational from 1896. On Heisey's 1922 death, his sons E. Wilson Heisey and T. Clarence Heisey became managers of the firm and were successful as directors to 1957, when the works closed. Its trademark 'H' in a red logenze, its animal-shaped glass, and its extensive color range became widely known. The Heisey Glass Museum, operated by the Heisey Collectors of America club, is located in the 1831 Samuel D. King house with an adjoint permanent exhibition at the Institute of Industrial Technology in Newark.

Held, Marc (1932–)

French designer; born in and active near Paris.

Training In kinesitherapy and dramatic arts; in furniture design, Germany.
Biography Held was a professor of physical education; 1960, cofounded and directed Archiform, a study center for industrial and interior design and architecture which attracted designers, architects, and former students of the École Boulle in Paris; 1965, established the magazine *Échoppe*. His L'Échoppe boutique was one of the first furniture-design shops in Paris. To 1966, he designed numerous private apartment interiors. 1966–68, was active as an interior architect with assignments, including that of Hôtel Les Dromonts in Avoriaz; designed three chairs by Knoll, including widely published 1967 Culbuto chair (produced from 1970). Other work: 1969 plastic molded fur-

niture for the houses of architect Georges Candilis, 1973 Limoges porcelain dinner service by Coquet; 1971, numerous pieces of plastic furniture (sold by L'Échoppe) produced by Créateurs et Industrielles (distributed by Prisunic), including a tea-cart, writing desk, and bed; 1974 Lip wrist-watch collection. Held became active as an independent architect for clients such as IBS; laid out the interior of 1987 oceanliner *Wind Star*. Archiform designed the grand drawing room of Palais de l'Élysée in Paris for president François Mitterrand, interior of the Lintas advertising agency in Paris, and the interior of oceanliner 1956 *Jean Mermoz* (the rebuilt *Serenade*). While very successful in 1980s, Held retired to Greece and wrote books on the architecture of the island of Skopelos.
Exhibitions Participated in 1968 (14th) Triennale di Milano. Work (molded plastic furniture) shown in architecture section, French pavilion, 1970 (3rd) Eurodomus, Palazzo dell'Arte, Milan; 1988 *Design Français: 1960–1990: Trois Décennies exhibition*, Centre Georges Pompidou, Paris. Designed 1969 *Construction et Humanisme* exhibition, Cannes.
Bibliography Cat., Milena Lamarová, *Design a Plastické Hmoty*, Prague: Umĕleckoprůmyslové Muzeum, 1972: 112. Cat., *Marc Held: 10 ans de recherches*, Nantes: Musée des Arts Décoratifs, 1973. Cat., *Design français 1960–1990: trois décennies*, Paris: APCI/Centre Georges Pompidou, 1988. 'Albert Memmi raconto Marc Held,' *Jardin des modes*, Mar. 1989. François Mathey, *Au bonheur des formes, design français 1945–1992*, Paris: Regard, 1992: 191, 251.

Helg, Franca (1920–1989)
Italian architect and designer.

Training To 1943, architecture, Politecnico, Milan.
Biography Helg was a member of Istituto Nazionale Urbanistica (INU) and of Accademia di San Luca; taught, Politecnico, Milan; 1951, joined Franco Albini's studio in Milan, eventually renamed Studio di Architettura Franco Albini e Franca Helg. She was active in the studio with Albini, from 1962 with Antonio Piva, and from 1965 with Marco Albini. With Albini and individually, she taught at Technische Hochschule in Munich; Universidad Católica, Córdoba, Argentina; and in Peru and Ecuador. With Albini, she designed 1950 wicker chair by Bonacina, 1955 club chair by Arflex, c. 1960s sound equipment by Brionvega, 1963 Milan subway stations (with Antonio Piva and Bob Noorda), 1979 restaurant at Palazzo Lascari in Turin, 1982 government museum in Varese, 1984 post office in Gorizia. But much of the furniture designed in the Albini studio may have been from Helg's hand alone.
Bibliography Alfonso Grassi and Anty Pansera, *Atlante del design italiano 1940/1980*, Milan: Fabbri, 1980. Andrea Branzi and Michelle De Lucchi, *Design italiano degli anni '50*, Milan: Editoriale Domus, 1980. Fumio Shimizu and Studio Matteo Thun (eds.), *The Italian Design: Descendants of Leonardo da Vinci*, Tokyo: Graphic-sha, 1987: 330. Cat., Hans Wichmann, *Italien Design 1945 bis heute*, Munich: Die Neue Sammlung, 1988.

Heller Designs: Massimo Vignelli. Max-2 stacking cups (shorter of two versions in the series). 1970. Melamine, 2 3/4 x 6 1/4 x 7 1/2" (7 x 15.9 x 19.1 cm). Mfr.: Heller Designs, US. Gift of the mfr. MoMA.

Helios
British textile manufacturer; located Bolton, Lancashire.

History 1937, Helios was established by Thomas Barlow of Barlow and Jones, a furnishings and dress-fabrics firm in Bolton. From mid-1930s, Marianne Straub, an important contributor to the design and manufacture of British woven textiles, designed contemporary fabrics for the power looms at Helios, including her c. 1940 Pony dobby cotton.
Bibliography Cat., *Thirties: British Art and Design Before the War*, London: Arts Council of Great Britain/Hayward Gallery, 1979.

Hellsten, Lars (1933–)
Swedish glassware designer.

Training 1957–63, Konstfackskolan, Stockholm; 1954, sculpture and ceramics, Konstindustriskolan, Gothenburg.
Biography 1964–72, Hellsten worked at the glassworks in Skruf and, from 1972, at Orrefors Glasbruk; exploited the transparency of glass, incorporated globular architectonic forms, and produced hot-worked, non-functional glass sculptures as well as utilitarian glassware; taught, Konstfackskolan.
Exhibitions The Red Square glass sculpture shown at a 1982 New York exhibition.
Bibliography Cat., David Revere McFadden (ed.), *Scandinavian Modern Design 1880–1980*, New York: Abrams, 1982. Jennifer Hawkins Opie, *Scandinavia: Ceramics and Glass in the Twentieth Century*, New York: Rizzoli, 1989.

Heller Designs
American manufacturer; located New York.

History 1971, Alan Heller (1940–) founded Heller Design in New York to make well-designed domestic products available at reasonable prices, the first of which was 1970 Max-2 stacking cups by Massimo Vignelli (produced from 1971) and 1978 Max-2 lidded pitcher, all in Melamine. Furniture production has included 1998 Bellini chair by Mario Bellini Studio, 1999 Tavollini table/stool, and 2000 Arcobellini chair by Mario and Claudio Bellini, followed by 2001 Calla chair by Willliam Sawaya, 1969 chair (reissued 2002) by Vico Magistretti. Also has produced a line of containers and tabletop objects.
Citations 2001 Premio Compasso d'Oro (Bellini chair); 1999 Design Distinction (for furniture), Annual Design Review, *I.D.* magazine; 1999 bronze award (for Bellini chair), Industrial Designers Society of America (IDSA); Best-Seating Award, International Contemporary Furniture Fair (ICFF), New York; Good Design award, Chicago Athenaeum.

Henning, Arthur (1880–1959)
German designer.

Biography Among other work, Henning designed the c. 1932 cheerful, checkered-pattern dinner service of c. 1932 by Friedrich Kaestner in Oberhohndorf in Saxony.
Bibliography Cat., *Porzellan aus Zwickau, Friedrich Kaestner: Firmen- und Stilgeschichte*, Zwickau: Städt Museum, 2000.

Henning, Gerhard (1880–1967); Gerda Henning (1891–1951)
Swedish sculptor and weaver; husband and wife; Henning: born Stockholm; Gerda: born Fåborg; active Denmark.

Training In sculpture.
Biography From 1901, sculptor Gerhard Henning, a part of a Bohemian circle of artists in Gothenberg, often focused on the female form. 1908–25 at Royal Copenhagen Porcelain Manufactory, he designed figurines with exotic costumes and combined traditional elements of the 18th and 20th centuries; also designed patterns for textiles produced by his accomplished wife Gerda, whom he had married in 1918. She died in Copenhagen; he in Hellerup. The Gerhard Henning Grant, a 3-year stipend, was established by The State Arts Council of Sweden.
Exhibitions Gerhard Henning work subject of 2003–04 exhibition, Västra Kupolhallen, Gothenberg.
Bibliography Cat., David Revere McFadden (ed.), *Scandinavian Modern Design 1880–1980*, New York: Abrams, 1982. Lisbeth Tolstrup et al. (ed.), *Tekstilkunst i Danmark 1988–98*, Valby : Borgen, 1999. *Scandinavian Journal of Design*, no. 5, 1995. Vibeke Klint, 'Memories of the Weaver Gerda Henning,' *Danish Journal of Design History*, vol. 5, 1995.

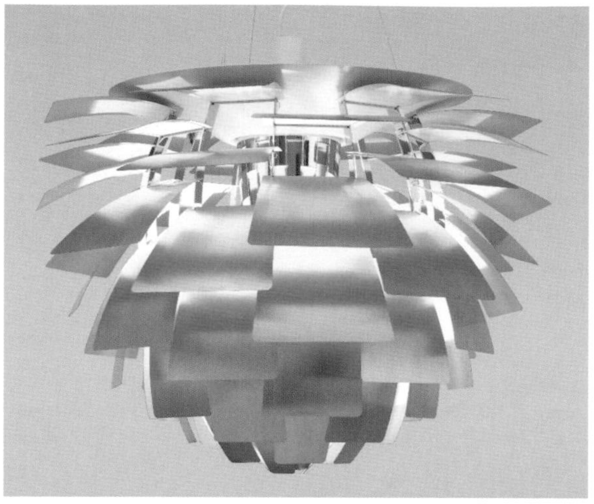

Poul Henningsen. 1958 PH-Zapfen (Artichoke) lamp. 1958. Copper and steel, h. 28 3/8 x dia. 33 1/4" (72.1 x 84.5 cm). Mfr.: Louis Poulsen & Co., Denmark (1999). Gift of the mfr. MoMA.

Henningsen, Poul (1894–1967)

Danish architect, writer, and designer; born Ordrup.

Training 1911–14, architecture, Danmarks Tekniske Højskole; 1914–17, Polyteknisk Læreanstalt, Copenhagen.
Biography From 1920, Henningsen worked as an independent architect in Copenhagen; is best known for 1924 PH multi-shade ceiling and table lamp range by Louis Poulsen in Copenhagen, still in production and installed in the 1929–30 Tugendhat house in Brno by its architect Ludwig Mies van der Rohe and, 1926, in the Forum building in Copenhagen. 1929, Henningsen's lamps began worldwide distribution. 1941, he designed backdrop lamp for Tivoli Gardens in Copenhagen and, later, a series of lighting fixtures that, like the PH, had three or more diffusing saucers, including 1957 PH5 and 1958 PH-Zapfen (Artichoke) hanging lamps. Henningsen also designed houses and theater interiors, keeping traditional forms wherever possible; 1926–28 with Kaare Klint, Henningsen edited the journal *Kritisk Revy*, which was influential in spreading the Functionalist gospel in Denmark
Exhibitions/citations PH lamps were the subject of 1994 exhibition, Kunstindustrimuseet, Copenhagen. Gold medal, 1925 *Exposition Internationale des Arts Décoratifs et Industriels Modernes*, Paris.
Bibliography Cat., Kathryn B. Hiesinger and George H. Marcus III (eds.), *Design Since 1945*, Philadelphia: Philadelphia Museum of Art, 1983. Morten Thing, *Kommunismens kultur: DKP og de intellektuelle 1918–1960*, Copenhagen: Tiderne Skifter, 1993. Tina Jørstian and Poul Erik Munk Nielsen (eds.), *Light Years Ahead: The Story of the Lamps*, Copenhagen: Louis Poulsen, 1994 (Eng. and Danish eds.). www.louis-poulsen.com.

Henriksen, Niels Georg (1855–1922)

Danish sculptor and silversmith.

Biography Henriksen was artistic director at the metalsmithy A. Michelsen, which produced his work with chased and embossed naturalistic flower, thistle, iris, and poppy motifs.
Exhibitions Silverware by A. Michelsen shown at 1900 *Exposition Universelle*, Paris.
Bibliography Annelies Krekel-Aalberse, *Art Nouveau and Art Déco Silver*, New York: Abrams, 1989.

Henrion, Frederick Henri Kay (1914–1994)

French exhibition and graphic designer; born Nuremberg; active Paris and London.

Training 1932–33, graphic design, École Paul Colin, Paris.
Biography 1936, Henrion settled in London and was also active in Paris to 1939; 1943–45, designed all the exhibitions of the British Ministry of Agriculture; 1945, was a consultant to the US Office of War Information. His poster work included those for the British General Post Office, BOAC, London Transport, and CoID. He designed the corporate identity of KLM (Royal Dutch Airlines); 1951–82, was a principal of Henrion Design Associates, which became Henrion Design International in 1971 and Henrion, Ludlow and Schmidt in 1981. He became a consultant in 1982 and was president of the Society of Industrial Artists 1961–63. His numerous books included *Design Coordination and Corporate Image* (with Alan Parkin) (1969), *Top Graphic Design* (1983), and *AGI Annals* (1989).
Exhibitions/citations Participated in 1938 *British Empire Exhibition*, Glasgow; 1939–40 *New York World's Fair: The World of Tomorrow*; the Agriculture and Natural Scene and the Country (natural history) (with Brian O'Rorke) pavilions at 1951 *Festival of Britain*, London; 1967 *Universal and International Exhibition* (*Expo '67*), Montréal. 1939 poster for the General Post Office shown at 1979–80 *Thirties* exhibition, Hayward Gallery, London. 1959, elected Honorary Royal Designer for Industry, UK.
Bibliography Cat., *Thirties: British Art and Design Before the War*, London: Arts Council of Great Britain/Hayward Gallery, 1979. Fiona MacCarthy and Patrick Nuttgens, *An Eye for Industry*, London: Lund Humphries, 1986.

Henry, Hélène (1891–1965)

French textile designer; born Champagney; active Paris.

Biography 1918, Henry set up hand looms in Paris to weave modern fabrics in her own patterns of abstract printed motifs and textures; wove for designer friends such as Jacques-Émile Ruhlmann, Pierre Chareau, Maurice Dufrêne, Francis Jourdain, René Herbst, and Robert Mallet-Stevens. Henry was one of the first fabric designers to use artificial yarns combined with wool and cotton; participated in the decoration of numerous houses, cinemas, and oceanliners; decorated the reception area of the League of Nations in Paris; 1929, cofounded Union des Artistes Modernes (UAM) and was a member of its first executive committee.
Exhibitions Work shown at many exhibitions, including 1920 edition of Salon d'Automne; in Pierre Chareau's library of Ruhlmann's Une Ambassade Française pavilion at1925 *Exposition Internationale des Arts Décoratifs et Industriels Modernes*, Paris; from 1930, UAM expositions; Sélection Formes Utiles at Salon des Arts Ménagers; 1956 (1st) Triennale d'Art Français Contemporain, Musée des Arts Décoratifs, Paris.
Bibliography Jean Fuller, 'L'œuvre d'Hélène Henry,' *Art et industrie*, Sept.–Oct. 1933. Léandre Vaillat, 'Le décor de la vie,' *Le temps*, 28 June 1933. Pierre Migennes, 'Hélène Henry et les tissus de ce temps,' *Art et décoration*, vol. 65, 1936. Yvonne Brunhammer, *Le cinquantenaire de l'Exposition de 1925*, Paris: Musée des Arts Décoratifs, 1976: 131. Victor Arwas, *Art Déco*, New York: Abrams, 1980. Arlette Barré-Despond, *UAM*, Paris: Regard, 1986. Cat., *Les années UAM 1929–1958*, Paris: Musée des Arts Décoratifs.

Henschel, Erich (1907–); Ruth Henschel-Josefek (1904–1982)

Erich Henschel: German painter and decorator; born Görlitz. Ruth Henschel-Josefek: German fabric designer; born Gleiwitz (now Gliwice, Poland). Husband and wife.

Training 1930–33, Erich Henschel studied at the Bauhaus, Berlin, where Ruth Josefek studied.
Biography The Henschels met at the Bauhaus; 1947, set up their own studio in Löwenstein-Hirrweiler.
Bibliography Lionel Richard, *Encyclopédie du Bauhaus*, Paris: Somogy, 1985: 192. Cat., Gunta Stölzl, *Weberei am Bauhaus und aus eigener Werkstatt*, Berlin: Bauhaus-Archiv, 1987: 152. Sigrid Wortmann-Weltge, *Bauhaus Textiles: Women Artists and the Weaving Workshop*, San Francisco: Chronicle, 1993.

Hentschel, William (1882–1962)

American ceramicist; active Cincinnati, Ohio.

Training Art Students League; ceramics, Columbia University; both New York.
Biography 1907–39, Hentschel was ceramics decorator at Rookwood Pottery in Cincinnati; late 1920s with Lorinda Epply, produced some of Rookwood's most individual work.
Exhibitions With Epply, ceramics by Rookwood were shown at 1926–27 *American Industrial Art, 10th Annual Exhibition of Current Manufacturers Designed and Made in the United States*, The Metropolitan Museum of Art, New York.
Bibliography Hentschel, William, *Who's Who in American Art, 1940–*

41, vol. 3, Washington, D.C., American Federation of Art, 1947. Virginia Raymond Cummins, *Rookwood Pottery Potpourri*, Silver Spring, Md.: Cliff R. Leonard and Duke Coleman, 1980. Karen Davies, *At Home in Manhattan: Modern Decorative Arts, 1925 to the Depression*, New Haven: Yale, 1983: 40.

Hepworth, Barbara (1903–1975)

British sculptor and designer; born Wakefield, Yorkshire; wife first of artist John Skeaping and second of artist Ben Nicholson.

Training 1920–21, Leeds College of Art; 1921–24, sculpture, Royal College of Art, London; 1924–25, British School in Italy; carving under Giovanni Ardini.
Biography 1926, Hepworth settled in London; 1929–39, lived in Hampstead; from 1931, worked with Ben Nicholson; 1931–35, was a member of Seven and Five Society, London; 1933, became a member of Abstraction-Création, Paris; 1933–35, was a member of Unit One. 1937, Hepworth and Nicholson were commissioned by Alastair Morton to design fabric patterns for his Edinburgh Weavers' Constructive Art range. Edinburgh Weavers produced Hepworth's Pillar fabric with highly textured yarns which were weft inlaid and cropped on the surface around the motifs. 1939–45, Hepworth owned and operated a plant nursery and market garden in St. Ives, Cornwall; designed sets and costumes for a 1951 production of *Electra* at the Old Vic Theatre and 1954 Michael Tippet's opera *The Midsummer Marriage* at the Royal Opera House, both London; from 1939 until her death there, lived in St. Ives. She became an accomplished, highly regarded, and proliftic scuptor with significant public commissions.
Exhibitions/citations 1928, work (sculpture with John Skeaping and William Norman) first shown, at Beaux Arts Gallery, London. From 1933, Hepworth showed textiles at Lefevre Gallery, London. Her work has been included in or the subject of more than 70 exhibitions, including 1930 exhibition, Arthur Tooth and Sons, London; 1932 and 1933 exhibitions (with Nicholson; including eight hand-printed textiles), Lefevre Gallery; 1950 Biennale di Venezia; 1969 retrospective exhibition at Tate Gallery, London. Work shown at 1934 Unit One exhibition, Mayor Gallery, London, and touring; 1935 *Abstraction-Création* exhibition, Paris; 1936 *Art Non-Figuratif*, Paris; *Abstract and Concrete*, Oxford; 1937 *Abstract Art*, American Institute of Architecture (AIA); 1937 *Constructive Art*, London Gallery; 1979–80 *Thirties* exhibition (Pillar fabric and sculpture pieces), Hayward Gallery, London (catalog below). 1958, was appointed Commander of the British Empire (CBE).
Bibliography J.L. Martin et al. (eds.), *Circle: International Survey of Constructive Art*, London: Faber & Faber, 1937. Alan Bowness, *Barbara Hepworth*, London, 1971. Cat., *Thirties: British Art and Design Before the War*, London: Arts Council of Great Britain/Hayward Gallery, 1979. Muriel Emanuel et al. (eds.), *Contemporary Artists*, New York: St Martin's, 1983: 402–03. M. Gale and C. Stevens, *Barbara Hepworth: Works at the Tate Gallery Collection and the Barbara Hepworth Museum St. Ives*, London: Tate Gallery, 1999.

Herbst, René (1891–1982)

Architect and designer; born and active Paris.

Biography From 1908, Herbst had architectural practices in London and Frankfurt, before settling in Paris; became a leader in the Functionalist movement, shunning ornament. His work incorporated polished and plated metal, and what is called today 'bungee cord' (a type of rubber tube wrapped in cloth threading with hooks on the ends for creating a seating surface when used in multiples). On his furniture he used leather and frequently fabric designed by Hélène Henry. 1927–37, Herbst was artistic advisor (with André Vigneau as artistic director) of the Siégel window-display/mannequin firm, Paris, where he exerted an appreciable influence. He designed 1928 Sandows chair, for which he is best known due to its much-later subsequent reproduction and whose name was derived from *sandows* (named after bodybuilder Eugen Sandows). This chair type was made in small quantities. 1929–32, Herbst published four articles on lighting in the journal *Lux*, advising readers to consult a lighting engineer, an approach compatible with the ideas of architect Robert Mallet-Stevens. Some of his lighting was sold by Cottin. André Salomon, lighting engineer at the small firm Perfécla, advised Herbst on lighting, including the double-winged ceiling fixture shown at the 1928 Salon d'Automne. Herbst's lighting fixtures were not of a consistently high quality of manufacture. All in Paris: Herbst designed 1930 Prince Aga Khan and 1928 Rosenberg, 1929 Peissi (director of Office Technique pour l'Utilisation de l'Acier, OTUA), 1931 Aghion, 1932 Schneider, c. 1948 Gessler, and 1948 Delagrave apartments. Also designed c. 1932 furniture in chromium-plated tubular steel for the Maharajah of Indore in India; numerous boutiques, stores, and houses of commerce, including interiors of shops in Paris: Jean Puiforcat (silver), Henriette Léon (handbags), Isabey (perfume packaging), Robj (ceramics), Siégel (mannequins), and Luminex (laminates). As one in the group which left the Salon of Société des Artistes Décorateurs, Herbst cofounded Union des Artistes Modernes (UAM) in 1929, and, with Hélène Henry, Francis Jourdain, Raymond Templier, and Robert Mallet-Stevens, was a member of its executive committee. 1931–61, Herbst was artistic advisor of OTUA (steel association); founded *Parade* review; with Jourdain, was in charge of UAM's 1930 (1st) exhibition; on Mallet-Stevens's 1945 death, served as the president of UAM and represented the organization at a committee organized by OTUA for the Étude d'Aménagement Métallique des Paquebots (technical office for steel production in oceanliner design); until 1961, designed all UAM exhibitions concerning the French iron-and-steel industry; 1950 – 69, was president of UAM's Formes Utiles; described himself and other UAM members as 'the puritans of art'; 1942, vice-president, Société des Artistes Décorateurs. 1946, vice president, Salon d'Automne; chief architect of French section at 1954 (10th), 1957 (11th), and 1960 (12th) editions of Triennale di Milano; architect of Pavillon de la Sidérurgie Française at 1961 *International Exposition*, Moscow.
Exhibitions/citations From 1921, work shown regularly at editions of Salon d'Automne, and from 1924 at Salons of Société des Artistes Décorateurs; furniture designs shown at all the international expositions of the time. Was a jury member of 1925 *Exposition Internationale des Arts Décoratifs et Industriels Modernes*, Paris, where he designed stands (for himself, Pleyel, Cusenier, Dumas) on pont Alexandre-III and for Siégel and couturière Lina Mouton. Work shown at exhibitions of UAM 1930–37; lighting shown at 1934 (2nd) and 1935 (3rd) editions of Salon de la Lumière; French section (with Charlotte Perriand, Le Corbusier, Pierre Jeanneret, Louis Sognot, Fernand Léger) at 1935 *Exposition Universelle et Internationale de Bruxelles*. Furniture for multiple usage and other models included in UAM pavilion at and was architect/designer of Pavillon de la Publicité at 1937 *Exposition Internationale des Arts et Techniques dans la Vie Moderne*, Paris. A chair included

René Herbst. Sandows side chair. 1928. Nickel-plated steel tube and bungee cord, 26 x 17 x 19 1/2" (66 x 43.2 x 49.5 cm). Gift of Marshall S. Cogan in honor of Barbara Jakobson. MoMA.

in 1968 *Les Assises du Siège Contemporain*, Musée des Arts Décoratifs, Paris. Work subject of 1999 *La Maison de René Herbst*, Galerie de Beyrie, New York. 1924 Blumenthal Prize; 1935, appointed Chevalier of Légion d'Honneur.
Bibliography André Boll, 'René Herbst,' *Art et décoration*, vol. 62, 1933. 'René Herbst, promoteur de séries métalliques,' *Le décor d'aujourd'hui*, no. 35, 1946. Alastair Duncan, *Art Nouveau and Art Déco Lighting*, New York: Simon & Schuster, 1978. Victor Arwas, *Art Déco*, New York: Abrams, 1980. Odile Fillion, 'René Herbst, l'homme d'acier,' *Architecture intérieure crée*, no. 194, 1983. Pierre Kjellberg, *Art déco: les maîtres du mobilier, le décor des paquebots*, Paris: Amateur, 1986. Arlette Barré-Despond, *UAM*, Paris: Regard, 1986: 414–21. Cat., *Les années UAM 1929–1958*, Paris: Musée des Arts Décoratifs, 1988. Solange Goguel, *René Herbst*, Paris: Regard, 1990. Mel Byars with Arlette Barré-Despond, *100 Designs/100 Years: A Celebration of the 20th Century*, Hove: RotoVision, 1999: 34–35. Paola Antonelli (ed.), *Objects of Design: The Museum of Modern Art*, New York: The Museum of Modern Art, 2003: 83, 250.

Herbst Lazar Bell

American industrial design firm; located Chicago.

History 1963, the firm was established to offer research, planning, industrial design, engineering, and prototyping services to a large rostrum of clients, including Compaq, Craftsman, Gillette, Kodak, Hewlitt-Packard, Motorola, and Sunbeam.
Exhibitions Work included in 2000 National Design Triennial, Cooper-Hewitt National Design Museum, New York; 2002 *U.S. Design*, touring the US (catalog below). Design of the Decade (1990s) three citations, IDSA/*Business Week* magazine; 2000 Red Dot award (Eclipse petrol pump by Marconi), Design Zentrum Nordrhein Westfalen, Essen; numerous others.
Bibliography Cat., Donald Albrecht et al., *Design Culture Now: The National Design Triennial*, New York: Princeton Architectural Press. 2000. Mel Byars, *On/Off: New Electronic Products*, New York: Universe, 2001. Cat., R. Craig Miller (intro.), *U.S. Design 1975–2000*, Munich: Prestel, 2002.

Heritage, Rachel (1958–)

British industrial designer; born London; daughter of Robert Heritage.

Training 1978–81, furniture design, Kingston Polytechnic (now Kingston University); 1982–85, furniture design, Royal College of Art, London.
Biography 1981–82, Heritage worked at the design and architectural studio Cini Boeri Associati in Milan for clients, including Fusital (door hardware), Tronconi (lighting), and Knoll (contract furniture); 1985 with brother Paul Heritage, set up Heritage Design in London, active in furniture and lighting design.
Exhibitions/citations Work shown at 1985 exhibition, ASB Gallery, London; 1986 *Style '86*, Olympia, London; 1988 *Design It Again*, Design Centre, London. 1981 Ambrose Heal Award, 1982 Antocks Lairn Bursary, 1985 Concord Lighting Award.
Bibliography Cat., Design Center Stuttgart, *Women in Design: Careers and Life Histories Since 1900*, Stuttgart: Haus der Wirtschaft, 1989: 268–71.

Erik Herløw. Covered storage containers. c. 1945–55. Anodized aluminum, silver-color h. 4 x dia. 4 3/4" (10.2 x 12.1 cm), gold color h. 2) x dia. 4 3/4" (5.1 x 12.1 cm). Mfr.: Dansk Aluminum Industri, Denmark. Purchase Fund. MoMA.

Heritage, Robert (1927–)

British furniture and product designer; born Birmingham; father of Rachel Heritage.

Training 1942–46, Birmingham College of Art; 1948–52 under R.D. Russell, Royal College of Art, London.
Biography 1951–53, Heritage was a staff designer for furniture manufacturer G.W. Evans; 1953, set up his own studio, designing furniture and lighting for British and foreign firms. His early furniture by Archie Shine showed the influence of R.D. Russell's simple, understated approach. He was consultant designer to Rotaflex and to Beaver and Tapley; 1974–85, was professor of furniture design, Royal College of Art, while maintaining an active design studio with his wife, Dorothy. Heritage's high-tech lighting, including 1973 Pan Parabolic track lamp by Concord/Rotaflex, was widely published. He designed the technically innovative 1968–69 QE2 cast-aluminum chair by Race Furniture in Sheerness, in aluminum alloy, with a special adhesive for the leg connection, as well as Race's less imaginative 1969 Apollo office side chairs, cutlery by Yote, furniture by Archie Shine Furniture, and household appliances.
Exhibitions/citations Work shown at *British Week* exhibitions in Copenhagen, Milan, Lyon, Brussels, and Gothenburg. 1969, QE2 chair first shown at the Design Centre, London. 1969 Council of Industrial Design annual award for QE2 chair, also shown at 1970 *Modern Chairs 1918–1970*, Whitechapel Gallery, London (catalog below). High-tech lighting shown at 1983–84 *Design Since 1945*, Philadelphia Museum of Art (catalog below). Has received more British Design Council awards than any other person; from 1958, eight design awards (including four for furniture), Council of Industrial Design; 1966 British Aluminium award. 1963, elected Honorary Royal Designer for Industry, UK.
Bibliography Michael Farr, *Design in British Industry: A Mid-Century Survey*, London: Cambridge, 1955: 8+. 'Race: Case Histories,' London: Race Furniture, 1969: 19–25. Cat., *Modern Chairs 1918–1970*, London: Lund Humphries, 1971. Fiona MacCarthy, *British Design since 1880*, London, 1982. Cat., Kathryn B. Hiesinger and George H. Marcus III (eds.), *Design Since 1945*, Philadelphia: Philadelphia Museum of Art, 1983. Fiona MacCarthy and Patrick Nuttgens, *An Eye for Industry*, London: Lund Humphries, 1986.

Herlitz, John E. (1942–)

American automobile designer; born New York.

Training Industrial design, Pratt Institute, Brooklyn, N.Y.
Biography 1964, Herlitz joined design staff of Chrysler Corporation in Detroit, Mich.; assignments included restyling 1967 Plymouth Barracuda and completely new design of 1970 model, the latter thought to be a landmark in 'muscle cars.' Herlitz became chief of interior design at Chrysler in 1977, director of exterior design in 1981, senior vice-president of product design in 1998, under Thomas Gale and Trevor Creed. Herlitz, just as Gale did, retired from Chrysler in 2001.
Bibliography Jim McGraw, 'Another Master Designer Departs,' *The New York Times*, 9 Feb. 2001: F1.

Herløw, Erik (1913–1991)

Danish architect and designer.

Training To 1941, architecture, Det Kongelige Danske Kustakademi, Copenhagen.
Biography 1945, Herløw set up a design studio in Copenhagen; became head of Det Kongelige Danske Kunstakademi; designed stainless-steel and sterling-silver wares by A. Michelsen, aluminum cooking wares by Dansk, and 1954 Obelisk cutlery by Universal Steel; from 1955, was artistic director, Royal Copenhagen Porcelain Manufactory; from 1959, designed jewelry by Georg Jensen Sølvsmedie.
Bibliography Arne Karlsen, *Made in Denmark*, New York: Reinhold, 1960: 13, 86–93, 114–115. *Contemporary Danish Design*, Copenhagen: The Danish Society of Arts and Crafts and Industrial Design, 1960. Cat., Kathryn B. Hiesinger and George H. Marcus III (eds.), *Design Since 1945*, Philadelphia: Philadelphia Museum of Art, 1983.

Herman, Sam (1936–)

American glass designer and teacher, born Mexico.

Training Under Leo Steppern, sculpture, University of Wisconsin at Madison; 1966 under Harvey Littleton and Dominick Labino, in glass making; 1966, Edinburgh College of Art; 1967, Royal College of Art, London.
Biography 1969–74, Herman was an influential teacher at Royal Col-

Herman Miller Furniture Company: Charles Eames and Ray Eames. Lounge chair and ottoman. 1956. Molded rosewood veneer over plywood, leather, cast aluminum, rubber-shock mounts, and stainless-steel glides, chair 33 x 33¾ x 33" (83.8 x 85.7 x 83.8 cm), ottoman 16 x 26 x 21" (40.6 x 66 x 53.3 cm). Mfr.: Herman Miller Furniture Co., US. Gift of the mfr. MoMA.

lege of Art, where he became a tutor in glass. His work was close to that of his mentors Labino and Littleton. 1969 with Graham Hughes (the chairperson of the British Crafts Centre), he cofounded The Glasshouse Gallery and Workshop on Neal Street, London, which eventually moved to nearby Long Acre. Herman founded the New Wave Glass movement in Australia, living there from 1974–80 and establishing Jam Factory glass workshop in Adelaide. 1970s in Belgium, he collaborated with Louis Leloup, the chief designer at Val Saint Lambert, on glass objects; delivered a seminal lecture at 1984 conference of Decorative Arts Society in Brighton, UK, where he restated the principles of the Studio Glass movement.
Bibliography Frederick Cooke, *Glass: Twentieth-Century Design*, New York: Dutton, 1986: 105–06.

Herman Miller Furniture Company
American furniture manufacturer; located Zeeland, Mich.

History 1923, Herman Miller Furniture Company was founded in Zeeland, Mich., to manufacture furniture in various classical styles, with D.J. DePree as its head. The firm was named for DePree's father-in-law, who was not associated directly with it. DePree reluctantly and gradually converted the firm to the modern style in the 1930s through the efforts of Gilbert Rohde, who was hired as the design director in 1932. On Rohde's 1944 death, New York architect George Nelson assumed the position, bringing in a stable of designers including Charles and Ray Eames, Isamu Noguchi, and Nelson's own New York staff. From late 1940s, Herman Miller was the mass-producer of the Eameses' classic molded-plywood chair as well as a large inventory of other models subsequently. Nelson Associate's 1959 CSS Storage System was produced to 1973. Architect Gordon Bunshaft's 1960 Union Carbide building, New York, furnished by Herman Miller, was an example of fully formed functional planning with interiors integrated with external design. This landscape-office layout demanded furniture flexible enough to provide different design solutions for every type of office use, while being mass-produced. Herman Miller responded with systems furniture based on interchangeable panels from which desk tops, shelves, and storage units were hung. The 1962 Action Office 2 system by Robert Probst revolutionized office design and became the first commercially successfully functioning furniture system. Many of Herman Miller's designs were executed in the Nelson design office in New York in collaboration with the Herman Miller staff in Zeeland. Various Herman Miller products were designed by people other than Nelson himself: Steelframe storage and seating systems by John Pile, Sling Sofa by John Svezia, and EOG office system by Ernest Farmer. The new Ethospace system was launched in 1986 and designed by Bill Stumpf, who was a vice-president of Herman Miller 1970–73. From 1990s and still located in Zeeland, Mich., the firm has reintroduced a number of its classics of the 1940s–60s. More recent production to serve primarily the office market has been designed by freelancers Yves Behár, Ayse Birsel, Eric Chan, Poul Christiansen, Asympote (Hani Rashid and Lise Anne Couture), and others.
Exhibitions/citations Work included in a large number of venues. 2003 Presidential Commendation, International Interior Design Association (IIDA); 1999, 2000, 2002 Platinum List, 1986–99 Most Admired recognition, 1992 Hall of Fame (to Max DePree, Herman Miller chairperson), *Forbes* magazine; 2002 Dow Jones Sustainability Index (DJSI); 1990 American Business Hall of Fame (to D.J. DePree); 2003 National Design Award, Cooper-Hewitt National Design Museum, New York; Design of the Decade (1990s) (for Ergon chair), IDSA/*Business Week* magazine; a number of others and, particularly, to individually to designers.
Bibliography George Nelson, *Storage*, New York: Whitney, 1954. Ralph Caplan, *The Design of Herman Miller*, New York: Whitney, 1976. George Nelson, *George Nelson on Design*, New York: Whitney, 1979. David Hanks, *Innovative Furniture in America*, New York: Horizon, 1981. Margery B. Stein, 'Teaching Steelcase to Dance,' *The New York Times Magazine Business World,* Apr. 1, 1990. George Nelson (ed.), *The Herman Miller Collection, 1952*, New York: Acanthus, 1995 (reprint). Leslie S. Piña, *Herman Miller 1939 Catalog: Gilbert Rohde Modern Furniture Design with Value Guide*, Atglen, Pa.: Schiffer, 1998. Leslie Piña, *Alexander Girard Designs for Herman Miller*, Atglen, Pa.: Schiffer, 1998. Leslie S. Piña, *Classic Herman Miller*, Atglen, Pa.: Schiffer, 1998. www.hermanmiller.com.
> See DePree, Dirk Jan; Eames, Charles; Nelson, George.

Hermant, André (1908–1978)
French architect and furniture designer.

Training École Spéciale d'Architecture, Paris.
Biography From mid-1930s, Hermant designed sheet-metal and glass furniture; 1936, became a member of the Union des Artistes Modernes (UAM); after World War II, participated in the reconstruction of the port of Le Havre under the direction of Auguste Perret; 1948–52, was vice-president of UAM and originated the idea of its 'Formes Utiles' program manifested through the 1949–50 (1st) exhibition at Pavillon de Marsan, the Musée du Louvre, Paris, which became the annual Sélection

Formes Utiles at Salon des Arts Ménagers 1950–83. Herman was the architect of 1969 Musée Marc Chagall in Nice.
Exhibitions Designed the architecture gallery in UAM pavilion and Pavilion of Rubber, 1937 *Exposition Internationale des Arts et Techniques dans la Vie Moderne*, Paris. 'Economical' prefabricated house shown at 1954 (11th) Salon de l'Habitation sponsored by Salon des Arts Ménagers and later built for Dr. Faure as the Formes Utiles house in Port-Marly.
Bibliography André Hermant, 'Questions techniques dans la construction des H.B.M.,' *L'architecture d'aujourd'hui*, no. 7, July 1935. André Hermant, *Formes Utiles*, Paris: Salon des Arts Ménagers, 1959. Arlette Barré-Despond, *UAM*, Paris, 1986: 422–25. Cat., *Les années UAM 1929–1958*, Paris: Musée des Arts Décoratifs, 1988.

Hermès

French leather-goods manufacturer and retailer; located Paris.

History 1837, Thierry Hermès founded the firm in Paris as a harness-maker. From 1880, it manufactured saddles; 1920s, expanded its operation greatly, when handbags, traveling bags, couture, men's and women's sportswear, jewelry, watches, perfume, and scarves were added to its range; after World War II, established new branches worldwide. Jean-Michel Frank designed 1929 white-leather hand-sewn desk and, 1930s, monumental double doors in leather with gilded bronze handles by Alberto Giacometti, and oak and leather camping armchair. 1930 and 1940s, Paul Dupré-Lafon designed desks and armchairs. Well-known products include 1930s À Coins Rapportés suitcase, 1930s Sac-à-Dépêches (satchel handbag, called Kelly bag after Princess Grace of Monaco, from 1956), 1938 Chaîne-d'Ancre bracelet, and 1956 Brides-de-Gala scarf. Other notable works include 1929 trunk for Bugatti 'La Royale' automobile, 1976 interior of *Corvette* twin-engine jet airplane, and 1987 Espace carbon fiber suitcase. From 1983, Rena Dumas designed Hermès branch interiors worldwide as well as 1986 Pippa portable folding writing desk, folding stool, and folding chaise longue. 1988–92, Hilton McConnico designed its exhibitions in Paris, Tokyo, and Milan and 1989 new packaging for Amazone perfume. Its designers of leather goods have included Robert Dumas (1962), Catherine de Karolyi (1986), and Jean-Louis Dumas (1989); of couture, Victor Vasarely (1960s), Catherine de Karoli (from 1966), Bernard Sanz (1978–88), and Eric Bergère (1981–88); of watches, Jean-Louis Dumas (1978) and Henri d'Origny. Tableware has included Christiane Vauzelles's 1984 Les Pivoines china dinnerware, Laurence Thioune's 1986 Toucans china dinnerware, Zoe Pauwels's 1988 Marqueterie de Pierres d'Orient et d'Occident, Philippe Mouquet's 1992 Moisson crystal and cutlery, and Rena Dumas's 1991 Complice silverplated teapot. 1926–78, Annie Beaumel decorated the Hermès shop windows. From 1961, Leila Menchart worked with Beaumel and, from 1978, decorated the windows. However, the customers are more interested in the Hermès labels, rather than the designer. From 1978, Hermès has been directed by Jean-Louis Dumas-Hermès, fifth-generation member of Hermès family, who mandates that the firm's designers remain anonymous. Hermès (now part of the Castille group) is a member of Comité Colbert.
Exhibitions/citations Silver medal, *Exposition Universelle de 1867*; gold medal, *Exposition Universelle de 1878*; grand prize, 1889 and 1900 editions of *Exposition Universelle*; all Paris. Numerous other prizes and exhibitions.

Hermes, Gertrude (1902–)

British illustrator, sculptor, and designer.

Training 1919–20, Beckenham School of Art; 1922–25, wood-engraving and sculpture, Brook Green School, London.
Biography From 1926, Hermes collaborated with her husband Blair Hughes-Stanton on wood-engraved illustrations in *The Pilgrim's Progress*; produced sculptures (including portrait busts) and decorative furnishings; was a member of the Gregynog Press. Her best-known work may be illustrations for books *The Story of My Heart* by Richard Jeffries (Harmondsworth: Penguin, 1938) and *The Compleat Angler* by Izaak Walton (Harmondsworth: Penguin, 1939). 1932, she produced the mosaic floor and carved center stone of the fountain and door furniture for the Shakespeare Memorial Theatre, Stratford-upon-Avon; 1935, became a member of the London Group; 1938, was admitted to National Register of Industrial Designers.
Exhibitions 30-foot (9-m) glass window included in British Pavilion, 1937 *Exposition Internationale des Arts et Techniques dans la Vie Moderne*, Paris; three glass panels in British Pavilion at 1939–40 *New York World's Fair: The World of Tomorrow*; engravings (with six other engravers from Britain) at 1939 Venice international exhibition; 1930 *Willows and Water Lilies* wood engraving at 1979–80 Thirties exhibition, Hayward Gallery, London (catalog below).
Bibliography Cat., *Thirties: British Art and Design Before the War*, London: Arts Council of Great Britain/Hayward Gallery, 1979.

Helena Hernmarck. Yin-Yang/Mao tapestry. 1971. Cotton, wool, nylon, linen, plastic, and sequins, 55 x 55" (139.7 x 139.7 cm). Mfr.: the designer, Sweden. Estée and Joseph Lauder Design Fund. MoMA.

Hernmarck, Helena (1941–)

Swedish textile designer; active Connecticut; wife of Niels Diffrient.

Biography Hernmarck worked as an independent textile designer, producing large tapestries for public spaces, including Sweden House in Stockholm and Federal Reserve Bank in Boston. Her images amalgamated the traditional with the modern, and old techniques with new. Mid-1960s, she moved to Montréal; subsequently, to London; then, to New York, where she set up her own studio.
Bibliography Cat., David Revere McFadden (ed.), *Scandinavian Modern Design 1880–1980*, New York: Abrams, 1982.

Heron Parigi
> See Parigi, Paolo.

Herter Brothers

American furniture manufacturer and interior design firm; located New York.

History Gustave Herter (Stuttgart, Germany, 1830–1898) worked for the architect Leins, designing interior woodwork for the royal palace in Berg, Germany; 1848, settled in New York, where he worked for Tiffany, Young and Ellis to 1851, when he became a cabinetmaker in his own workshop at 48 Mercer Street. He was associated with cabinetmaker Edward W. Hutchings, through whom he may have met Auguste Pottier. 1852–54, Herter's workshop was at 56 Beekman Street. 1853, Herter had a brief partnership with Pottier; c. 1856, moved to 547 Broadway. 1859, his half-brother Christian Herter, who had previously studied in Stuttgart and at the École des Beaux-Arts in Paris, also settled in New York; after a short time working for Tiffany, in 1865 joined Gustave's firm, which was renamed Herter Brothers. Encouraged by Gustave, Christian returned to Paris and studied there 1868–70 under Pierre-Victor Galland. Christian later commissioned murals from Galland for inclusion in the commissions of various clients, including William H. Vanderbilt. 1870, Christian returned to the US and bought out his brother's interest in the firm; 1870–83, achieved international recognition through his progressive American furniture company, whose designs were influenced by the art furniture of E.W. Godwin of England. c. 1876, the time of the *Centennial Exposition*, Philadelphia, the firm began producing finely crafted furniture in the new Anglo-Japanese style, in light and ebony woods with asymmetrical patterns. From 1876,

Christian Herter imported embroideries, wallpaper, Chinese porcelain, Persian pottery, and Japanese *objets d'art* to complement his furniture. 1870, William Baumgarten became a designer at Herter and was the director 1881–91. French émigré Alexandre Sandier worked for the firm in the 1870s and, subsequently, was in charge of the art department at the Manufacture Nationale de Sèvres. Sandier's designs for Herter were similar to Godwin's. William B. Bigelow and Francis H. Bacon were also designers there, the latter leaving in 1881 and later joining A.H. Davenport. Architect and designer Wilhelm Kimbel worked for the firm in c. 1890. Throughout 1870s, Herter Brothers produced respectable historicist models in 18th- and early 19th-century English styles. It furnished its clients with its own-designed textiles, mosaics, stained glass, plasterwork, carpets, and lighting. Its 1879 commission for the decoration of the William H. Vanderbilt house (completed 1882) at Fifth Avenue and 51st Street, New York, was its most prestigious commission and widely published. The building was designed by Herter employees John B. Snook and Charles B. Atwood. 1883–91, Herter Brothers was managed by William Baumgarten and, 1891–1906, by William Nichols. Its lavish commissions continued, including c. 1883 Oliver Ames Jr. house in Boston, 1884 W.D. Washburn house in Minneapolis, and 1889 St. Elizabeth's Roman Catholic Church in Philadelphia. 1902, Herter supplied furniture to McKim, Mead & White's redecorated rooms in The White House in Washington (the cost of the whole redecoration was $167 million). Much of the contents of the Herter's showrooms and gallery were sold in 1905, followed by the firm's formal dissolution in 1906.
Exhibitions Gustave Herter showed work at 1853–54 *Crystal Palace* exhibition (Renaissance buffet produced with Erastus Bulkley and rosewood étagère for T. Brooks, Brooklyn), New York's first 'world's fair.' Also at 1876 *Centennial Exposition*, Philadelphia; New York State building (Pompeian-theme vestibule with murals by Charles Caryl Coleman) at 1893 *World's Columbia Exposition*, Chicago. Work subject of 1980 *Christian Herter and the Aesthetic Movement in America*, Washburn Gallery, New York; 1994–95 *Herter Brothers: Furniture and Interiors for a Gilded Age*, touring the US.
Bibliography Cat. Mary Jean Smith Madigan, *Eastlake-Influenced American Furniture, 1870–1890*, Yonkers, N.Y.: Hudson River Museum, 1973. William Seale, *The Tasteful Interlude*, New York: Praeger, 1975: 74–75. Cat., David Hanks, *Christian Herter and the Aesthetic Movement in America*, New York: Washburn Gallery, 1980. Doreen Bolger Burke et al., *In Pursuit of Beauty: Americans and the Aesthetic Movement*, New York: The Metropolitan Museum of Art/Rizzoli, 1986. Cat., Katherine S. Howe et al., *Herter Brothers: Furniture and Interiors for a Gilded Age*, New York: Abrams/Museum of Fine Arts, Houston, 1994.

Hertz, Peter
Danish silversmiths; active Copenhagen.

History 1834, Peter Hertz (aka Peter Herz), the oldest silver factory in Denmark, was founded in Copenhagen; produced designs by Thorvald Bindesbøll, Just Andersen, and Johan Rohde. Mogens Ballin's and Bindesbøll's work by Hertz presaged the Cubist forms of the 1920s.
Bibliography Annelies Krekel-Aalberse, *Art Nouveau and Art Déco Silver*, New York: Abrams, 1989.

Hesse, Kurt
German designer.

Training In architecture and design in Germany.
Biography At the beginning of his career, Hesse designed domestic furnishings; 1952, began to design lighting, working for a German lighting firm; 1978, set up his own studio in Milan, with clients including PAF lighting and Brillant Leuchten.
Citations 1978 award (for a fixture by Brillant Leuchten), Industrie Forum Design (iF), Hanover.

Heyde, Marcus (1967–)
> See Trondesign.

Heymann-Marks, Margarete (1899–1988)
> See Marks, Margarete.

Heythum, Antonín (1901–1954)
Czech architect and set and furniture designer; born Brüx Most (now in Czech Republic).

Biography From 1924, Heythum was a member of the Devětsil group; wrote *Pictorial Poems*; designed stage sets in a Constructivist style; 1926, cofounded the Osvobozené Divadlo (the liberated theater), where he influenced the early stage style of the theater group; 1927–29, was the chief set designer of České Divadlo (Czech theater), Olomouc; experimented with the use of standard parts in mass-produced furniture. Heythum moved to the US before the outbreak of World War II. His teaching at the University of Syracuse, Syracuse, N.Y., and his practical knowledge went into his book *Design for Use: A Study of Relationships Between Things and Men* (with his wife Charlotta Malecká Heythum, 1944), in which he espoused a Functionalist approach to interior design. Produced a design for a 1929 collapsible couch (a proposed solution for small flats) and two 1930 variants of a cantilevered tubular-metal chair design; wrote on the design and production of such chairs (in *Stavba*, no. 8, 1932: 131–32). His economical use of space was illustrated by his 1903 layout for a one-room apartment. He was a professor, Californian Institute of Technology; 1945, professor of architecture, Columbia University, New York; after World War II, taught in Switzerland. His papers are in the Smithsonian Archives of American Arts, Washington, D.C. He died in Rottach.
Exhibitions 1930s, designed a number of exhibition pavilions including Czechoslovak pavilions at 1935 *Exposition Universelle et Internationale de Bruxelles*; 1939–40 *New York World's Fair: The World of Tomorrow*; and San Francisco (unrealized). Designed several exhibitions at Uměleckoprůmyslové Muzeum, Prague. Subject of 1941 *The Work of Antonín and Charlotta Heythum*, Avery Hall, Columbia University, New York.
Bibliography Milena Lamarová, 'Antonín Heythum a interiér,' *Umění*, XXXV, 1987: 139–144, Academia Praha. Cat., *Devětsil: Czech Avant-Garde Art, Architecture, and Design of the 1920s and 30s*, Oxford: Museum of Modern Art and London: Design Museum, 1990.

Heywood Brothers; Heywood-Wakefield
American furniture manufacturer.

History 1826, Levi Heywood founded Heywood Brothers and Co. in Gardner, Mass., which became one of the largest American producers of chairs, including Windsor style and bentwood models; 1870s, developed new methods for bending rattan and experimented with wrapped cane and reed. 1897, Heywood bought Wakefield Rattan and became Heywood Brothers and Wakefield. Henry Heywood, a nephew of Levi, took over the management of the firm, and factories were set up in several cities. Selling to an international market, Heywood-Wakefield produced wicker ware, including chairs, cradles, baby carriages, tête-à-têtes, sofas, screens, window shades, and umbrella stands up to 1930s, when it began the production of imaginative and modern furniture in light-colored woods. 1979, the firm closed, but, 1992, Leonard Riforgiato, owner of South Beach Furniture Co. in Miami, and investment banker Andrew Capitman bought the remains of the old firm; by 1993, the re-formed Heywood-Wakefield Company was reproducing examples of early models, particularly of the 1930s, that had already become highly desirable to collectors. 1994, Riforgiato acquired the rights to the Heywood-Wakefield trademark and logo and restarted production of more than 35 examples of streamlined furniture from the 1940s, in yellow birchwood as before.
Bibliography Andrea Di Noto, 'The Presence of Wicker,' *Connoisseur*, vol. 214, June 1984: 78–84. Doreen Bolger Burke et al., *In Pursuit of Beauty: Americans and the Aesthetic Movement*, New York: The Metropolitan Museum of Art/Rizzoli, 1986. www.heywoodwakefield.com.

Hibbard, 'Le Baron' Thomas
> See Darrin, 'Dutch' Howard A.

Hicks, David Nightingale (1929–1998)
British designer; born Coggeshall, Essex; active London.

Training Central School of Arts and Crafts, London.
Biography 1953, Hicks became an independent designer, designing the widely published interiors of his mother's house in South Eaton Place, London; 1956–59 with Tom Parr, was active in decorating firm Hicks and Parr; 1960–70, in David Hicks Ltd.; from 1970, in David Hicks International Marketing Ltd. with offices in Australia, Belgium, France, Germany, Pakistan, and Switzerland. 1960, Hicks began to design textiles and carpets; from 1982, womenswear; from 1977, costume jewelry, eyeglasses, shoes, and menswear through the David Hicks Association of Japanese Manufacturers. He was a member and master of the Worshipful Company of Salters, and fellow of Royal Society of Arts, London. Hicks became known for his luxurious English interiors and eclectic mixture of styles and materials, 'bringing Mod to Mayfair' or nearing kitsch, according to some detractors. However,

Hicks described his approach as 'the art of accentuating the best and covering up the worst.' He has been acknowledged for having transformed the domestic British toilet from an unpleasant room into an elegant environment. His *David Hicks on Decoration* (London: Frewin 1966) was the first of many books; designed interiors for royal and wealthy private clients, such as Prince Charles, Vidal Sassoon, and King Fahd of Saudi Arabia, and public interiors, including the original nightclub on the 1969 oceanliner *Queen Elizabeth II*, Raffles nightclub in Chelsea, ten Peter Evans Eating Houses, and numerous offices.
Bibliography S. Patterson, 'The Bigger the Challenge the Better I Like It,' *Réalités*, Mar. 1970. R.J. Vinson, 'La salle de bains de David Hicks,' *Connaisance des Arts*, Nov. 1972. Ann Lee Morgan (ed.), *Contemporary Designers*, London: Macmillan, 1984: 282. Mark Hampton, *The Legendary Decorators of the Twentieth Century*, New York: Doubleday, 1992. Ashley Hicks, *David Hicks: Designer*, London: Scriptum, 2003.

Hicks, Sheila (1934–)

American textile designer; active France.

Training 1954–58 under Josef Albers and Rico Legrun, painting, Yale University, New Haven, Conn.
Biography Early 1960s in Central and South America, Hicks began weaving and producing fabrics influenced by traditional methods and by Albers's Constructivist approach; in India, worked in a handloom factory producing commercial textiles, including her 1968 Badagara heavy double-sided cloth with a deep relief woven by the Commonwealth Trust in Kerala. Still in production in 1980s, Badagara was used as a wall hanging. 1967, Hicks set up a studio in Paris named Ateliers des Grands Augustins, while teaching and working worldwide. In Chile, Morocco, and Israel, she encouraged large-scale local production using traditional methods; in Paris, produced numerous large hangings and wallcoverings for various installations, including (with Warren Platner) the conference room at the Ford Foundation Building in New York, 1969 conference center of United Arab League in Mecca, the entrance of 1972 CB 12 tower of IBM in La Défense, near Paris, and 1980s fabrics for Air France's Boeing 747 airplane interior (interior design by Pierre Gautier-Delaye).
Bibliography Cat., Kathryn B. Hiesinger and George H. Marcus III (eds.), *Design Since 1945*, Philadelphia: Philadelphia Museum of Art, 1983. Monique Lévi-Strauss, *Sheila Hicks*, New York: Van Nostrand Reinhold, 1974. Cat., *Sheila Hicks*, New York: Modern Master Tapestries, 1974. Mildred Constantine and Jack Lenor Larsen, *Beyond Craft: The Art Fabric*, New York: Van Nostrand Reinhold, 1973: 172–93. Cat., Konstantina Hlaváckovà et al., *Sheila Hicks*, Prague: Uměleckoprůmyslové Muzeum, 1992.

Hielle-Vatter, Marga (1913–)

German fabric designer.

Training In Dresden and Vienna.
Biography From 1933, Hielle-Vatter designed fabrics woven at her own mill; became known for her complex geometric patterns with long repeats, including 1981 Alcudia fabric by her own factory Rohi Stoffe in Geretsried, Germany.
Exhibitions/citations Alcudia pattern in 1983–84 exhibition, Philadelphia (catalog below). Silver medal, 1957 (11th) Triennale di Milano.
Bibliography Jack Lenor Larsen and Jeanne Weeks, *Fabrics for Interiors*, New York: Van Nostrand Reinhold, 1975. Cat., Kathryn B. Hiesinger and George H. Marcus III (eds.), *Design Since 1945*, Philadelphia: Philadelphia Museum of Art, 1983. Cat., Hans Wichmann, *Von Morris bis Memphis, Textilien der Neuen Sammlung, Ende 19. bis Ende 20. Jahrhundert*, Basel: Birkhäuser, 1990.

Hiemstra, Chris (1942–)

Dutch industrial designer and administrator; born Voorburg.

Training Gerrit Rietveld Academie, Amsterdam, and Academie van Beeldende Kunsten, the Hague; 1965–68, industrial design, Koninlelijie Academie voor Geeldende Kunsten, the Hague.
Biography For three years, Hiemstra worked an assistant in the studio of Kho Liang Ie in Rotterdam; 1967, was active as a freelance designer; from 1968, became associated with the industrial-design studio of Harry J. Swaak; from 1971, was a designer at Lumiance (formerly Hiemstra Evolux), responsible for product development and presentation from 1976.
Citations Five Product Design Awards in 1980 and seven in 1982, Industrie Forum Design (iF), Hanover; 1983 Kho Liang Ie Prijs (with Swaak); and others.
Bibliography Robert A.M. Stern (ed.), *The International Design Yearbook*, New York: Abbeville, 1985/1986.

Higgins, David Lawrence (1936–)

British industrial designer; born and active Stratford-upon-Avon.

Biography 1959–69, Higgins was active in various large firms, including in the studio of consultants Wilkes & Ashmore in England, for three years; for two years at Philips in Eindhoven; for four years on Olivetti projects in the studio of Ettore Sottsass; and in the Information System Group of General Electric in Schenectady, N.Y. 1969, he set up David Higgins Associates, specializing in graphic and industrial design and electronic machinery for industry and domestic electrical appliances. 1970 with other industrial designers, he formed Incateam design group, with associates in Germany, the Netherlands, Switzerland, Norway, and Italy; became a member of Associazione per il Disegno Industriale (ADI).
Bibliography *ADI Annual 1976*, Milan: Associazione per il Disegno Industriale, 1976.

High-Tech

Architectural and decorating style of the 1970s and 1980s.

History Early 1970s, High-Tech was initiated by architects Richard Rogers, Norman Foster, Nicholas Grimshaw, and others. In domestic interiors, designers rejected elegant materials and furnishings and used

Sheila Hicks. The Evolving Tapestry: He/She. 1967–68. Linen and silk, 'He' 32 x 30 x 22" (81.3 x 76.2 x 55.9 cm), 'She' 34 1/2 x 19 1/2 x 14" (87.6 x 49.5 x 35.6 cm). Mfr.: the designer, US. Given in Memory of Arthur Drexler by Sheila Hicks, Jack Lenor Larsen, and Henry and Alison Kates; and Department Purchase Funds. MoMA.

industrial products and equipment, such as tables intended for restaurants and garage tool cabinets used as bedroom chests of drawers. The originator of the early brand of minimalism in interior design in the US was Joseph Paul D'Urso, who installed, as examples, flat industrial carpeting, polished-metal swinging doors, and, on several occasions, the 1927 Chaise Longue à Reglage Continu by Le Corbusier/Jeanneret/Perriand with its cover removed to expose the metal-slat supports.
Bibliography Joan Kron and Suzanne Slesin, *High-Tech: The Industrial Style and Source Book for the Home* (New York: Potter, 1978).

Hildebrand, Margret (1917–)
German fabric designer and ceramicist; born Stuttgart.

Training Staatliche Kunstgewerbeschule, Stuttgart, Kunstschule für Textilindustrie, Plauen.
Biography From 1934, Hildebrand worked at Stuttgarter Gardinenfabrik, where she was director 1956–66. She tried to amalgamate the functional approach of design with mass-production; designed ceramics, some with Elsa Fischer-Treyden by Rosenthal; became Germany's best-known fabric designer following World War II; from 1956, taught textile design, Hochschule für bildende Künste, Hamburg.
Citations Gold medal,1954 (10th) Triennale di Milano.
Bibliography Josef Alfons Thuna et al., *Margret Hildebrand*, Stuttgart: Gerd Hatje, 1952. Margret Hildebrand, 'Der tapfere Käufer,' in *Zeitgemässe Form: Industrial Design International*, Munich, 1967: 109–11. Cat., Kathryn B. Hiesinger and George H. Marcus III (eds.), *Design Since 1945*, Philadelphia: Philadelphia Museum of Art, 1983. Cat., Hans Wichmann, *Von Morris bis Memphis, Textilien der Neuen Sammlung, Ende 19. bis Ende 20. Jahrhundert*, Basel: Birkhäuser, 1990.

Hill, Evelyn (1925–2003)
American textile designer.

Training Under Josef Albers, Black Mountain College, N. C.; Institute of Design, Chicago.
Biography 1950s, Hill designed fabrics by Knoll and by Cohama, introducing bright color combinations and fabrications in wool and monofilament for commercial interiors; 1954, married George Anselevicius (who became dean emeritus, School of Architecture and Planning, University of New Mexico) and became known as Evelyn Anselevicius; was an independent weaver in San Miguel de Allende, Mexico; early 1980s, settled in Albuquerque, N.M.
Exhibitions/citations Work first achieved recognition at 1953 *Good Design* exhibition/award, The Museum of Modern Art/Chicago Merchandise Mart. Textiles for commercial interiors were shown at 1983–84 *Design Since 1945* exhibition, Philadelphia Museum of Art. 1973 award for excellence (integration of art and architecture), American Institute of Architects (AIA), Kansas City, Missouri.
Bibliography 'Evelyn Hill,' *Everyday Art Quarterly*, no. 25, 1953: 181–9. Mildred Constantine and Jack Lenor Larsen, *Beyond Craft: The Art Fabric*, New York: Van Nostrand Reinhold, 1973: 108–11. Cat., Kathryn B. Hiesinger and George H. Marcus III (eds.), *Design Since 1945*, Philadelphia: Philadelphia Museum of Art, 1983.

Hill, Oliver (1887–1968)
British architect and designer.

Training Architectural Association, London.
Biography Edwin Lutyens, a friend of Hill's father, encouraged Hill to become an apprentice to a firm of builders. 1907–10, Hill was an apprentice to the architect William Flockhart; 1910, set up his own architectural practice; from 1918, was successful as a designer of country and town houses and an interior designer; early 1930s, designed furniture by Heal's. His interior-design work included Maryland, a house in Hurtwood; North House, Westminster; and art historian Kenneth Clark's house in Hampstead. Architecture included 1931–33 Midland Hotel for the LMS Railway in Morecambe, Lancashire; 1933 *British Industrial Art in Relation to the Home* exhibition, as coordinating architect and designer, at Dorland Hall, London; 1930–32 Gayfere House, London; 1933–35 Miss Newton house in Holthanger, Wentworth, Surrey; house in Virginia Water, Surrey; 1934–35 scheme for Frinton-on-Sea, Essex; British pavilion at 1937 *Exposition Internationale des Arts et Techniques dans la Vie Moderne*, Paris; unrealized projects, including a primary school in London.
Bibliography Cat., *Thirties: British Art and Design Before the War*, London: Arts Council of Great Britain/Hayward Gallery, 1979.

Hill, Reginald Henry (1914–1975)
British silversmith; active London.

Training Central School of Arts and Crafts, London.
Biography 1930, Hill was an apprentice to a silversmith; became a prolific silver designer to Elkington in Birmingham, Wakely and Wheeler in London, and, later, C.J. Vander in London; taught silversmithing, Central School of Arts and Crafts.
Bibliography Cat., *Thirties: British Art and Design Before the War*, London: Arts Council of Great Britain/Hayward Gallery, 1979. Annelies Krekel-Aalberse, *Art Nouveau and Art Déco Silver*, New York: Abrams, 1989.

Hille
British furniture manufacturer; located London.

History 1906, Hille was established in London by Russian émigré Salamon Hille, originally a restorer of 18th-century furniture in London's Whitechapel area. After World War II, Leslie Julius, Hille's grandson, was successful in selling modern furniture. Designers included Robin Day, Roger Dean, and Fred Scott. Day's polypropylene 1963 Mark II (or Polyprop) chair was Hille's most successful product, selling more than 12 million pieces. 1982, Hille merged with Ergonom as Ergonom Hille Ltd. and, 1989, was sold to Wassall, a large conglomerate, with Ergonom becoming an office-furniture brand, along with Wassall's Evertaut and Toone brands.
Exhibitions/citations Gold medal (for Robin Day's furniture by Hille), 1951 (9th) Triennale di Milano. Work subject of 1981 exhibition, Victoria and Albert Museum, London.
Bibliography Cat., Sutherland Lyall, *Hille: 75 Years of British Furniture*, London: Elron, 1981. Penny Sparke, *Introduction to Design and Culture in the Twentieth Century*, London: Allen & Unwin, 1986. Cat., Leslie Jackson, *The New Look: Design in the Fifties*, New York: Thames & Hudson, 1991: 125.

Hiller, Dorothée (1945–)
German industrial designer; born Schorndorf, Württemberg.

Training 1966–67, in joinery; 1967–71, interior and furniture design, Staatliche Akademie der bildenden Künste, Stuttgart.
Biography 1971, Hiller joined the firm D-Team-Design in Stuttgart, where she was manager from 1972. Her work (with Rainer Bohl) included 1978 Bima Profi industrial chair range by Biedermann, 1986 FD 90 kitchenware range by Fissler, 1985 Multibox sink unit by Blanc, and 1988 Triangle chair (with Bohl and Heike Salomon) by Drabert Söhne. She established Dorothée Hiller & Partner Design, designing for clients such as PowerPull products.
Bibliography Cat., Design Center Stuttgart, *Women in Design: Careers and Life Histories Since 1900*, Stuttgart: Haus der Wirtschaft, 1989: 88–101.

Hillfon, Hertha (1921–)
Swedish ceramicist.

Training 1953–57, Konstfackskolan, Stockholm.
Biography 1959, Hillfon set up a ceramics workshop; was one of the artisans who extended the range of ceramics in the 1960s by producing non-functional ceramics as art. Her applied images often included depictions of everyday objects, such as clothing.
Exhibitions Participated in 1960 (12th) Triennale di Milano. 1957 Medal for Proficiency and Industry of the Society for Industrial Design, 1962 Lunning Prize.
Bibliography Cat., David Revere McFadden (ed.), *Scandinavian Modern Design 1880–1980*, New York: Abrams, 1982. Jennifer Hawkins Opie, *Scandinavia: Ceramics and Glass in the Twentieth Century*, New York: Rizzoli, 1989.

Hills, David (1923–)
American glassware designer.

Training Pratt Institute, Brooklyn, N.Y.
Biography 1948–52, Hills was a glassware designer at Steuben, creating more than 20 production vessels such as pitchers, candlesticks, urns, vases, and tumblers; designed some exhibition pieces for Steuben and 1949 bud vase—one of Steuben's most popular items of the 1950s and still in production.
Bibliography Cat., Kathryn B. Hiesinger and George H. Marcus III (eds.), *Design Since 1945*, Philadelphia: Philadelphia Museum of Art,

Matthew Hilton. Wait stacking chair. 1999. Polypropylene, h. 30 1/2 x w. 18 3/4 x d. 20 1/2" (77.5 x 47.5 x 51 cm). Mfr.: Authentics, antipresent, Germany.

1983. Mary Jean Smith Madigan, *Steuben Glass: An American Tradition in Crystal*, New York: Abrams, 1982.

Hils, Peter (1967–)

German designer; born Rottweil; works and lives Berlin.

Training Apprenticeship in typesetting; product and environmental design, Fachhochschule, Potsdam; Hochschule der Künste, Berlin; Nanyang Polytechnic (NYP), Singapore.
Biography Hils designed advertising and rendered illustrations for firms, including Haribo, Fischer-Technik, and Polaroid; 2000, set up his own studio and designed products such as 1999 Build-a-Brush set and Quickie bath brush by Die Imaginäre Manufaktur (DIM). Other clients have been Design-Initiative Brandenburg, Vitrashop, and Vogt + Weizenegger (the managers of DIM), Berlin.

Hilton, Matthew (1957–)

British furniture, product, and interior designer; born Hastings; active London.

Training 1975–76, Portsmouth College of Art; 1976–79, furniture and three-dimensional design, Kingston Polytechnic (now Kingston University).
Biography For five years, Hilton worked for the product-design consultancy CAPA on high-tech products; 1984, established his own studio to design furniture, lighting, and interiors, including a 1986 furniture range by Sheridan Coakley. Hilton is best known for 1987 Antelope aluminum and wood side table with its animal-like legs and 1988 Flipper aluminum and glass low table with rotating fin-shaped legs. From 1992, his design work was produced by a number of European companies including Disform, Sawaya & Moroni, XO, Montis, and Perobell. 2000, Driade produced his nine-piece collection of tables, seating, and a bed and, 2003, Bd Ediciones de Diseño his Pouf Ottoman chair/ottoman. From 2000, Hilton was head of design, Habitat.
Exhibitions His first furniture design shown (1985) at Joseph Pour La Maison, London. Furniture by Sheridan Coakley shown at 1986 and 1988 editions of Salone del Mobile, Milan; 1988 (1st) International Contemporary Furniture Fair (ICFF), New York. Work subject of 1992 exhibition, Ferens Art Gallery, Hull.
Bibliography Albrecht Bangert and Karl Michael Armer, *80s Style: Designs of the Decade*, New York: Abbeville, 1990: 60–61, 231. *Contract*, July 1990: 26. Catherine McDermott et al., *Matthew Hilton: Furniture of Our Time*, London: Lund Humphries, 2000.
> See Authentics.

Hingelberg, Frantz

Danish silversmiths.

History 1897, the Frantz Hingelberg firm was founded in Århus. Its stable of craftspeople included Svend Weihrauch, who worked as a silversmith and designer from 1928. For silver drinking vessels for hot liquids, Weihrauch added strips of wood to handles and under bases.
Exhibitions 1935 *Exposition Universelle et Internationale de Bruxelles*, silver by Weihrauch first shown outside of Denmark.
Bibliography Annelies Krekel-Aalberse, *Art Nouveau and Art Déco Silver*, New York: Abrams, 1989.

Hinkola, Vesa
> See Snowcrash.

Hiort-Lorenzen, Peter (1943–)

Swedish architect and furniture designer.

Training To 1962, carpenter's apprenticeship, Helsingør Shipbuilding Yard; 1962–65, Kunsthåndværkerskolen; 1965–68, Møbelskole, Det Kongelige Danske Kunstakademiet; all Copenhagen.
Biography 1968–70, Hiort-Lorenzen worked at Kilkenny Design Workshop in the castle yard of Kilkenny, Ireland; 1966–68, in Svenson's design firm; 1970–71, in Niels Fagerholt's design firm. 1972, established a design studio and, from 1977, was in partnership with Johannes Foersom; 1975, lecturer at Danmarks Designskole. Hiort-Lorenzen became a partner and board member in Eleven Danes; designed furniture by Høng Stolefabrik, C. Danel, Albæk Møbler, and Skive Møbelfabrik; interior design for SAS and Copenhagen Airport; products by Danfoss, Vølund A/S, and others. Work with Fersom has included 1984 Rotor sofa and 1985 Pipeline modular sofa by Erik Jørgensen, 1996 Campus by Lammhults, and 1996 dining room chair by Kvist Møbler.
Bibliography www.lammhults.se.
> For citations: See Foersom, Johannes

Hirche, Herbert (1910–2002)

German industrial designer; born Goerlitz, Silesia (then Germany, now chiefly eastern Czech Republic and southwestern Poland).

Training 1930–33, Bauhaus, Dessau and Berlin.
Biography In Berlin: 1934–38, Hirche collaborated with Ludwig Mies van der Rohe and Lilly Reich; 1940–45, with Egon Eiermann; 1945–48, with Hans Scharoun; from 1948, taught, Hochschule für angewandte Kunst, Berlin-Weißensee. After World War II, he taught, Staatliche Akademie der bildenden Künste, Stuttgart, where he became a professor of interior architecture and furniture 1952–75; worked at Braun, designing electric appliances. Other work: 1960 Wilkhahn furniture-company office building in Bad Münder and furniture by Deutsche Werkstätten and by WK-Verband. Hirche's 1953 upholstered lounge chair and 1969 Santa Lucia rattan/tubular-metal armchair are currently being produced by Richard Lampert in Stuttgart.
Exhibitions Designed a dining-room furniture system for 1957 *Interbau* exposition, Berlin. Work subject of an exhibition, Stuttgart.
Bibliography Cat., *Herbert Hirche, Architektur, Innenraum, Design, 1945–1978*, Stuttgart: Staatliche Akademie der bildenden Künste, 1978. Cat., Hans Wichmann, *Deutsche Werkstätten und WK-Verband, 1898 – 1990*, Munich: Prestel, 1992: 327. 'Mort de l'architecte Herbert Hirche,' *La liberation*, 31 Jan. 2002.

Hirschberg, John (1949–)
> See Berlinetta.

Hislop, David

British watchmaker, jeweler, silversmith, and vendor; active Glasgow.

Biography 1904–05, Hislop was a watchmaker and jeweler in Glasgow; became a dealer of silver and electroplated wares designed by Charles Rennie Mackintosh and the vendor for the christening set made by C. Hahn in Berlin designed by Mackintosh for his godchild Friedrich Eckart Muthesius, son of the German architect; sold Mackintosh-designed cutlery (probably produced by Elkington) used at the Cranston tearooms in Glasgow.
Bibliography Annelies Krekel-Aalberse, *Art Nouveau and Art Déco Silver*, New York: Abrams, 1989.

Hitier, Jacques (1917–1999)
French decorator and furniture designer.

Training École Boulle, Paris.
Biography 1930–34, Hitier worked at the Primavera decorating studio of Au Printemps department store in Paris; from 1946, taught, École Boulle in Paris and designed furniture, particularly tubular-metal models for schools; 1960, decorated and furnished the officers' dining room of 1961 oceanliner *France*.
Exhibitions From 1948, work shown at Salons of Société des Artistes Décorateurs; from 1950, at Salon des Arts Ménagers.
Bibliography Pascal Renous, *Portraits de créateurs*, Paris: H. Vial, 1969. Patrick Favardin, *Les décorateurs des années 50*, Paris: Norma, 2002: 108.

Hjelle, Lars
> See Jordan.

Hlava, Pavel (1924–)
Czech artist and glassware designer.

Training 1939–42, School of Glassmaking, Železný Brod; 1943–48, Vysoká Škola Uměleckoprůmyslové (VŠUP, academy of arts, architecture, and design), Prague.
Biography Hlava designed numerous glass tableware items and domestic cut- and engraved-glass items in a wide color range; 1952–58, was associated with Art Center for Glass Industry in Prague, and, from 1958, with Institute for Interior and Fashion Design; from 1969, designed glass tableware in the Rosenthal Studio-Linie; 1980s, was active in the design of large-scale abstract decorative glass objects.
Bibliography Cat., *Modernes Glas*, Frankfurt: Museum für Kunsthandwerk, 1976. *Czechoslovakian Glass: 1350–1980*, Corning, N.Y.: The Corning Museum of Glass, 1981: 167. Cat., Kathryn B. Hiesinger and George H. Marcus III (eds.), *Design Since 1945*, Philadelphia: Philadelphia Museum of Art, 1983.

Hobbs, Brockunier and Co.
American glassware manufacturers; located Wheeling, W.V.

History John L. Hobbs (1804–1881), a superintendent of the cutting department and salesperson at New England Glass Company, and James B. Barnes, the engineer who designed and constructed the firm's first furnace, bought Plunkett and Miller Glasshouse in Wheeling, W.V. They began to produce leaded glass for solar chimneys, jars, vials, tumblers, and scent bottles. 1849, Barnes was succeeded by his son James F. Barnes, who changed the firm's name to Hobbs, Barnes and Co. 1864, the factory successfully produced a cheap flint-glass substitute, called lime glass, an innovation that influenced the entire glass industry. In colorless opal and lime glass, the firm produced cut and engraved flint wares and pressed wares in numerous patterns. By 1879, Hobbs, Barnes and Co. had become one of the largest American glass factories; early 1880s, attained a favorable reputation through its 'fancy glass,' including crackle or frosted glass ware called Craquelle, with spangled glass added to its inventory in 1883; 1886, began producing its Peachblow brand of art glass, made from white opal glass coated with an amber-to-ruby shaded layer and resembling porcelain. Through an 1886 agreement by Brockunier, Hobbs and Co. and New England Glass Co., the production of pressed amberina glass was begun. c. 1887, the success of its art glass had waned. The firm became known as J.H. Hobbs Glass but closed in 1891 and, with 17 other glass factories in the area, was purchased by United States Glass.
Bibliography Albert Christian Revi, *American Pressed Glass and Figure Bottles*, New York: Nelson, 1964: 182–92. Cat., Eason Eige, *A Century of Glassmaking in West Virginia*, Huntington, W.V: Huntington Galleries, 1980: 4–15. Cat., T. Patrick Brennan, *The Wheeling Glasshouses*, Wheeling, W.V: Oglebay Institute / Mansion Museum [n.d.].

Hobson, Stephen (1942–)
American industrial designer, active Palo Alto, Cal.

Training Stanford University, Stanford, Cal.
Biography Hobson worked for Norse Micrographics, Coates & Welter, and Hewlett-Packard; 1980, became a principal in ID Two (later organized as IDEO), the American industrial-design studio of Design Developments in London; was a project coordinator of the team who designed the 1981–1982 Compass, one of the first portable computers.
Bibliography 'The Compass Computer: The Design Challenges Behind the Innovation,' *Innovation*, Winter 1983: 4–8. Cat., Kathryn B. Hiesinger and George H. Marcus III (eds.), *Design Since 1945*, Philadelphia: Philadelphia Museum of Art, 1983.

Hoek, Ben (1964–)
Dutch designer.

Training To 1986, architecture, Middlebaar Technische School, The Hague.
Biography 1980, Hoek designed his first furniture; 1987–95, worked for the Cepezed architectural office in Delft; 1993, established his own furniture-design and production enterprise, often working with folded sheet steel and specializing in tables initially; designed 1995 TE.10 and TE.11 tables and 2001 Nexus wall system by Spectrum.

Hoentschel, Georges (1855–1915)
French decorator, ceramicist, and collector.

Biography Hoentschel was strongly influenced by *japonisant* decoration, like that of Jean Carriès, with whom he conducted research on stoneware. In this Japanese manner, Hoenstschel decorated his pieces with gold-overflow glazes and metal mountings. After Carriès's 1894 death, he acquired a house in Montriveau, where he worked with Émile Grittel; was active as interior decorator and furnishings designer; toward the end of his life, settled in Paris, where he worked in Grittel's studio. 1898 at age 16, Armand-Albert Rateau worked for Hoentschel.
Exhibitions Work shown at Salons of the Société Nationale des Beaux-Arts. Decorated and furnished Salon du Bois, Union Centrale des Arts Décoratifs pavilion, 1900 *Exposition Universelle*, Paris.
Bibliography Yvonne Brunhammer, *Art Nouveau Belgium, France*, Houston: Institute for the Arts, Rice University, 1976.

Hoff, Paul (1945–)
Swedish ceramicist and glassware designer; born Stockholm.

Training 1963–68, postgraduate courses, Konstfackskolan, Stockholm.
Biography From 1969–74 and 1982–87, Hoff worked at Gustavsberg porcelain factory; 1972–82, was a designer at Kosta Boda glassworks; 1982, set up own design company; c. 1987 when it was founded, was artistic advisor to Studioglas Strömbergshyttan in Hovmantorp, Småland; from 1988, worked at Rörstrand-Gustavsberg;
Exhibitions Work shown in Europe, Japan, Australia, and the US.
Bibliography Jennifer Hawkins Opie, *Scandinavia: Ceramics and Glass in the Twentieth Century*, New York: Rizzoli, 1989.

Hoffmann, Jochen (1940–)
German industrial designer; active Bielefeld.

Training Hochschule für bildende Künste, Brunswick.
Biography 1970, Hoffman set up his own design studio, Büro für Produktgestaltung. Work has included 1985 Trio articulated sofa by Franz Fertig, and, recently, Rico lounge chair and Zento sofa by Cor.
Bibliography Albrecht Bangert and Karl Michael Armer, *80s Style: Designs of the Decade*, New York: Abbeville, 1990: 42–43, 231.

Hoffmann, Josef Franz Maria (1870–1956)
Moravian architect and designer; born Pirnitz (now Brtnice, Czech Republic); father of Wolfgang Hoffmann.

Training 1887–91, architecture, Höhere Staatsgewerbeschule, Brünn (now Brno, Czech Republic); 1892–95 under Karl von Hasenauer and Otto Wagner, Akademie der bildenden Künste, Vienna.
Biography 1896, Hoffmann worked in studio of Otto Wagner; 1897, became a founding member of the Wiener Sezession; was responsible for organizing an early Sezession exhibition; from 1899, taught, Kunstgewerbeschule, Vienna, as part of reforms begun by Arthur von Scala; 1900, designed a suburb in Vienna where he built four 1901–05 villas; 1903 with Koloman Moser and banker/arts patron Fritz Wärndorfer (later joined by C.O. Czeschka), established the Werkstätte Productiv-Gemeinschaft von Kunsthandwerkern in Wien. It was a group of workshops and crafts studios in Vienna inspired by C.R. Ashbee's Guild of Handicrafts and which helped to pioneer the 1920s style. Hoffmann kept in close contact with Charles Rennie Mackintosh and his Glasgow School of Art; was a follower of the modernism in Belgium and France. His œuvre was wide ranging and large, including metalwork, accessories, furniture, lighting, and textiles. Some of Hoffman's furniture designs were produced by J. & J. Kohn, particularly his c. 1905 Sitzmaschine reclining chair (no. 670). He is known for the

Gesamtkunstwerk (total work of art) of the Kabaret Fledermaus in Vienna and other commissions. For the Lobmeyr firm, he designed numerous drinking sets, flower bowls, and glasses in clear, enamel-painted cut crystal. His major work as an architect includes 1904–05 Purkersdorf sanatorium, and 1905–24 Palais Stoclet, Brussels, for which, with Gustav Klimt, he created a complex exterior architecture, interiors, furnishings, and decorations. 1912, Hoffmann founded the Österreichischer Werkbund; at 1914 *Deutscher Werkbund-Ausstellung* in Cologne, came into contact with the work of Gropius and the new forms of contemporary art and architecture. From 1922, his Kunstgewerbeschule student Oswald Haerdtl worked in Hoffmann's architectural office and c. 1928 became a partner. 1980s, Beffeplast reproduced early Hoffmann metal grid-design accessories. Other firms have reissued his furniture, and Woka of Vienna his lighting.
Exhibitions Designed rooms for the Kunstgewerbeschule and the Wiener Sezession at 1900 *Exposition Universelle*, Paris. Participated in 1902 *Esposizione Internazionale d'Arte Decorativa Moderna*, Turin; 1902 exhibition, Österreichisches Museum für Kunst und Industrie, Vienna; 1914 *Deutscher Werkbund-Ausstellung*, Cologne. A room setting was installed at 1928 *Exposition of Art in Industry at Macy's*, New York; terraced houses shown at 1932 *Internationale Werkbundsiedlung*; Austrian Pavilion at 1934 Biennale di Venezia. Work subject of 1977 exhibition, Fischer Fine Arts, London; 1981, Galerie Metropol, New York; 1983, Fort Worth Art Museum, Tex.; 1983, Museum Bellerive, Zürich; 1987–93 touring exhibition, originating at Österreichisches Museum für angewandte Kunst, Vienna; 1991 *Josef Hoffmann: Drawings and Objects from Conception to Design*, touring the US.
Bibliography Dorothee Müller, *Klassiker des modernen Möbeldesign: Otto Wagner–Adolf Loos–Josef Hoffmann–Koloman Moser*, Munich: Keyser, 1980. Eduard F. Sekler, *Josef Hoffmann: das architektonische Werk...*, Salzburg: Residenz, 1982. Peter Vergo, 'Fritz Warndorfer and Josef Hoffmann,' *Burlington Magazine*, vol. CXXV, 1983: 402–10. Cat., *Josef Hoffmann, Ornament zwischen Hoffnung und Verbrechen*, Vienna: Österreichisches Museum für angewandte Kunst/Hochschule für angewandte Kunst, 1987. Alessandra Muntoni, *Il Palazzo Stoclet di Josef Hoffmann, 1905–1911*, Rome: Multigrafica, 1989. Torsten Bröhan, *Glaskunst der Moderne: von Josef Hoffmann bis Wilhelm Wagenfeld*, Munich: Klinkhardt & Biermann, 1992. Peter Noever (ed.), *Josef Hoffmann Designs*, Munich: Prestel, 1992. Paola Antonelli (ed.), *Objects of Design: The Museum of Modern Art*, New York: The Museum of Modern Art, 2003: 35–36.

Hoffmann, Wolfgang (1900–1969)

Austrian designer; born Vienna; son of Josef Hoffmann; husband of Pola Hoffmann.

Training Under Oskar Strnad and Josef Frank, architecture, Kunstgewerbeschule, Vienna.
Biography For two years, Hoffmann worked in the office of his father Josef Hoffmann in Vienna. He married Pola Hoffmann (Stryz, Poland, 1902–), whom he had met at the Kunstgewerbeschule (a student there under Oskar Strnad). 1925, they emigrated to the US, where they became residential interior decorators and worked for Joseph Urban in the branch of the Wiener Werkstätte in New York. Leaving Urban and working briefly also for architect Ely Jacques Kahn, the Hoffmanns set up an office on Madison Avenue and, late 1920s and early 1930s, designed one-of-a-kind furniture for private clients. Wolfgang's early work included the Little Carnegie Playhouse and other theaters, stores, and apartments, mostly in Manhattan. For the second exhibition (c. 1929) of the American Designers Gallery in New York, as objects for sale, Wolfgang designed a dinning room with curtains and a lampshade by Pola. By 1932, he had become interested in pewter accessories, lighting, and furniture. Also 1932, Wolfgang assisted Joseph Urban in developing the color scheme for 1933–34 *A Century of Progress International Exhibition*, Chicago, and was commissioned to design the interior and furniture for the Lumber Industries House pavilion at the fair. Work at the fair brought Hoffmann to the attention of Howell Co., headquartered in Geneva, Ill., and later, in St. Charles, Ill., where he was the resident designer 1934–42. 1934, he redesigned the reception area of the Howell administration building; became active as a designer of furniture and furnishings, including numerous models of bent tubular-steel furniture, in the style of Marcel Breuer, for

Josef Hoffmann. Sitzmaschine chair with adjustable back (no. 670). c. 1905, Bent beechwood and sycamore panels, 43 1/2 x 28 1/4 x 32" (110.5 x 71.8 x 81.3 cm). Mfr.: J. & J. Kohn, Austria. Gift of Jo Carole and Ronald S. Lauder. MoMA.

Howell. He settled in Chicago to supervise the manufacture of his Howell work. Pola Hoffmann became known primarily as a textile designer, although she collaborated with her husband on c. 1930 metal tabletop accessories by Early American Pewter Co. in Boston. 1930s, the Hoffmanns divorced and dissolved their business partnership. 1936, Wolfgang patented several tubular-metal chair designs, including an outdoor chair, open-arm lounge chair, club chair, and chaise longue; 1935–36, designed numerous smoking stands; from c. 1942 to 1960, Hoffmann turned from design, becoming active as a professional photographer.
Exhibitions Hoffmanns' work shown at 1928 and 1929 American Designers Gallery exhibitions, New York. Hoffmanns' pewterware for Early American Pewter Co shown at 1930–31 *Decorative Metalwork and Cotton Textiles*, American Federation of Arts, New York; 1983 *At Home in Manhattan*, Yale University, New Haven, Conn. Rooms in Lumber Industries House at and the fair's general color system (with Urban) for 1933–34 *A Century of Progress International Exhibition*, Chicago.
Bibliography Harry V. Anderson, 'Contemporary American Designers,' *Decorators Digest*, May 1936: 38–41, 78. 'Pola Hoffmann' in Alice Irman Prather-Moses, *The International Dictionary of Women Workers in the Decorative Arts*, Metuchen, N.J.: Scarecrow, 1981. Marta K. Sironen, *A History of American Furniture*, East Stroudsburg, Pa: Towse, 1936: 140–41. Karen Davies, *At Home in Manhattan: Modern Decorative Arts, 1925 to the Depression*, New Haven: Yale, 1983: 77.

Hofman, Jiří (1935–)
Czech industrial designer.

Training Střední Uměleckoprůmyslové Škole (school of applied arts), Liberec.
Biography Hofman was head of a government department, which managed Plastimat Liberec, and for which he produced his first design in plastics in 1956, and 1970 disposable ice-cream cup and food containers; collaborated with I. Jakeš.
Bibliography Cat., Milena Lamarová, *Design a Plastické Hmoty*, Prague: Uměleckoprůmyslové Muzeum, 1972: 114.

Hofman, Vlastislav (1884–1964)
Czech architect, designer, and painter; born Jitschia (now Jičín, Czech Republic).

Training 1902–07 J. Fanta, J.E. Koula, and J. Schulz, České Vysoké Učení Technické (Czech technical university), Prague.
Biography Hofman worked in the building department of the Prague magistrate; was a member of the Artěl Cooperative and of Mánes Association of Plastic Artists; 1911, left Mánes and joined the Group of Plastic Artists; wrote a number of theoretical essays for magazines; 1912, left the Group of Plastic Artists and returned to Mánes; was an initiator of the Czech modern movement, with a range of activities including architecture, applied arts, painting, and, from 1919, theater set design, primarily collaborating with Karel Hilar; contributed to the development of Czech Cubism through theoretical treatises; died in Prague.
Exhibitions/citations Gold medal, 1925 *Exposition Internationale des Arts Décoratifs et Industriels Modernes*, Paris; grand prize, 1937 *Exposition Internationale des Arts et Techniques dans la Vie Moderne*, Paris; grand prize, 1940 (7th) Triennale di Milano.

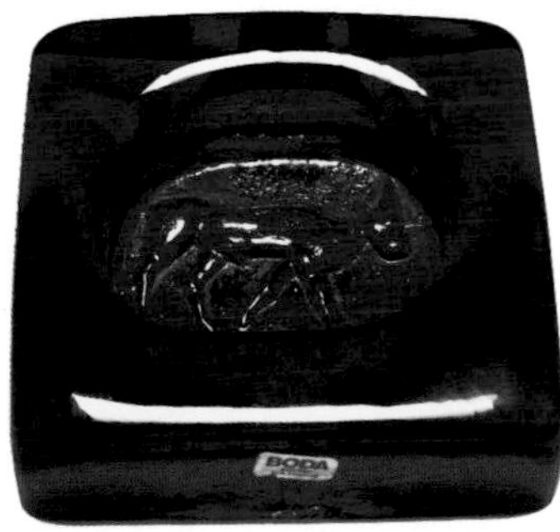

Erik Höglund. Ashtray. c. 1970. Form-poured glass, w. and d. 3 15/16" (10 cm). Mfr.: Boda Glasbruk, Sweden. Courtesy Quittenbaum Kunstauktionen, Munich.

Bibliography Alexander von Vegesack et al., *Czech Cubism: Architecture, Furniture, and Decorative Arts, 1910–1925*, New York: Princeton Architectural Press, 1992. Cat., *Prague, 1900–1938: capitale secrète des avants-gardes*, Dijon: Musée des Beaux-Arts, 1997.

Hogan, James (1883–1948)
British glass craftsperson.

Training Central School of Arts and Crafts; Camberwell School of Art; both London.
Biography Hogan was a member of the Art-Workers' Guild; became the artistic director of James Powell, makers of Whitefriars glass; designed glass for serial production, handmade pieces, stained glass for American churches, and two 100 ft (30 m) windows for Liverpool Cathedral (architect, Giles Gilbert Scott).
Citations 1936, elected Honorary Royal Designer for Industry, UK.
Bibliography Fiona MacCarthy and Patrick Nuttgens, *Eye for Design*, London: Lund Humphries, 1986.

Höganäs-Billesholms
Swedish ceramics factory; located Höganäs.

History 1797, the pottery was established; during 19th century, produced a wide range of ceramic table and decorative wares, including some in the Art Nouveau style in c. 1900; 1903, changed its name to Höganäs-Billesholms. 1915–18, Berndt Friberg worked as a thrower; 1916, Edgar Böckman became the artistic director. 1926, the factory closed.
Bibliography Jennifer Hawkins Opie, *Scandinavia: Ceramics and Glass in the Twentieth Century*, New York: Rizzoli, 1989.

Höganäs Keramik
Swedish ceramics factory; located Höganäs commune.

History 1909, Höganäs Kermik was founded in southern Sweden; became known for its high-quality stoneware; 1997 with Orrefors Kosta-Boda and other glass factories, was merged with Royal Copenhagen to form Royal Scandinavia, to be only a brand as BodaNova-Höganäs Keramik. However, in 2000, Royal Scandinavia was bought by an investment group which soon divested. And, in 2002, HackmanGroup bought BodaNova-Höganäs Keramik and, eventually, included them as separate brands within its iittala division, which was established in 2003. Some of the recent designers of its imaginative everyday dinnerware (mugs, plates, and bowls) have included Ann-Britt Haglund (1961–), Carl-Johan Skog (1970–), Eva Hanner (1961–), Marie-Louise Hellgren (1958–), Örjan Johansson (1944–), Cecilia Stööp (1965–), Maria Uggla (1962–), Lovisa Wattman (1967–), Åsa Westerhult (1964–), and Ann-Carin Wiktorsson (1968–).
Bibliography Leslie Jackson, *20th Century Factory Glass*, London: Octopus, 2000.
> See HackmanGroup; Royal Scandinavia.

Höglund, Erik (1932–1998)
Swedish glassware and metalworker.

Training Sculpture, Kungliga Tekniska Högskolan, Stockholm.
Biography 1953–73, Höglund was a glass designer at Boda; 1950s, became known for the inclusion of metallic particles and fine or uneven bubbles in vessel walls. His glass contrasted with the elegant, sophisticated wares of 1950s. From 1973, he was a visiting professor, Pitchuck Glass Center, Standwood, Wash.; from 1978–81, freelance designer at Pukeberg and at Lindshammer; 1986, was a freelance designer to Urigstads Kristallihytta and, c. 1987, to Studioglas Strömbergshyttan.
Exhibitions/citations 1957 Lunning Prize. Work shown in numerous exhibitions in Sweden and abroad.
Bibliography Cat., David Revere McFadden (ed.), *Scandinavian Modern Design 1880–1980*, New York: Abrams, 1982. Jennifer Hawkins Opie, *Scandinavia: Ceramics and Glass in the Twentieth Century*, New York: Rizzoli, 1989.

Hohulin, Samuel E. (1936–)
American industrial designer.

Biography From 1964, Hohulin was the chief industrial designer at The Eureka Company, Bloomington, Ill.; was assisted by Kenneth R. Parker Jr. (1957–) in the design of a number of Eureka vacuum cleaners, including 1982 Mighty Mite in brightly colored plastic casing and known for its small, compact size. With Gregory W. Lueb-

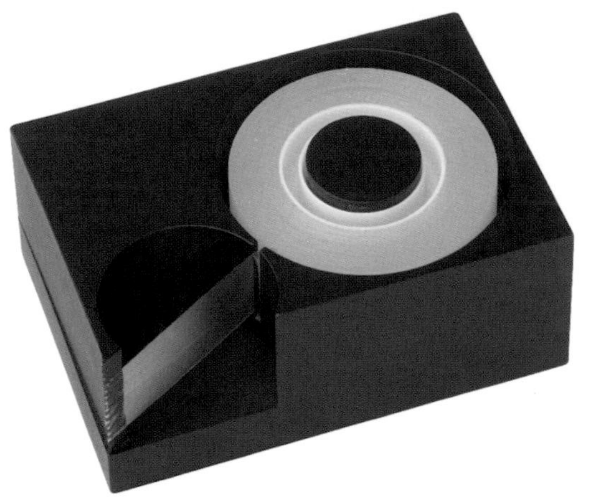

Torben Holmbäck. Tape block. 1982. Anodized aluminum, 2 3/4 x 4 1/8 x 1 3/4" (7 x 10.5 x 4.5 cm). Mfr.: Strategi/Holmback, Denmark. Gift of the mfr. MoMA.

bering, Hohulin also designed the Victory model and, with Parker and Sue Pike, the Freedom cord-free vertical model.
Exhibitions/citations Mighty Mite shown at 1983–84 *Design Since 1945*, Philadelphia Museum of Art. 1990 (Freedom vacuum cleaner), 1996 (Victory vacuum cleaner) IDSA/*Business Week* awards.
Bibliography Cat., Kathryn B. Hiesinger and George H. Marcus III (eds.), *Design Since 1945*, Philadelphia: Philadelphia Museum of Art, 1983. Wolf von Eckardt, 'Fashionable Is not Enough,' *Time*, vol. 121: Jan. 3, 1983: 76–77.

Holdaway, Bernard
British furniture designer.

Biography Holdaway is best known for 1966 Tomotom furniture range, in pressed paper, based on the tube and the spindle, in conjunction with Peter Neubart of Hull Traders in Lancashire, the producer; has taught, Kent Institute of Art and Design.
Bibliography Jonathan M. Woodham, *Twentieth-Century Ornament*, New York: Rizzoli, 1990: 246–47.

Holiday, Henry George Alexander (1839–1927)
British artist and designer.

Training From 1854, painting, Royal Academy Schools, London.
Biography Through fellow students Simeon Solomon, William De Morgan, and W. Richmond, Holiday became associated with the Pre-Raphaelites; worked as a stained-glass cartoonist and succeeded Edward Burne-Jones at James Powell, manufacturers of Whitefriars glass, where he designed some of its best work. His glass windows were known for his freer hand and better organization of images than the confined perspectives and narrow framework of Morris and Co.'s early glass designs. Holiday's work included embroideries (often with his wife Catherine, who produced a number of embroidered panels for Morris), mosaics, enamels, and murals.
Exhibitions Work first shown (1857) at Royal Academy, London.
Bibliography Isabelle Anscombe and Charlotte Gere, *Arts and Crafts in Britain and America*, New York: Rizzoli, 1978.

Holl, Steven (1947–)
American architect and designer; born Bremerton, Wash.

Training 1970, bachelor's degree in architecture, University of Washington, Seattle; 1976, Architectural Association, London.
Biography 1976, Holl set up his own firm to design architecture, furniture, textiles, and tableware. Architecture has included 1988 Hylbrid Building, Seaside, Fla.; 1991–92 D.E. Shaw & Co. office, New York; 1994 storefront of Art and Architecture, New York; 1989–92 Stretto house, Dallas, Tex.; 1993–97 Museum of Contemporary Art, Helsinki; 1998 Cranbrook Institute of Science, Bloomfield Hills, Mich. He designed tableware by Swid Powell and rugs by V'Soske; 1991–92, taught, Columbia University, New York.
Citations 1982, 1984, 1986, 1987, 1991 *Progressive Architecture* citations; 1990 Brimmer Prize; 1992 and 1993 Honor Awards, American Institute of Architects (AIA).
Bibliography Cat., R. Craig Miller (intro.), *U.S. Design: 1975–2000*, Munich: Prestel, 2002.

Holland, Nick (1946–)
British industrial designer and teacher.

Biography Holland taught, Royal College of Art, London, before he set up an industrial-design practice, designing hydraulic equipment at first; from 1973, was the general manager of Design Objectives, a small home-accessories manufacturer, where housewares design was his specialty; 1976–82, was head of design development at Staffordshire Potteries; 1982, established his own manufacturing company, Nicholas John; 1983, set up Nick Holland Design Group in Cardiff, where a wide range of products were designed, including kitchenware; designed 1988 electronic scale, with ABS housing incorporating a new weighing mechanism, by Waymaster.
Bibliography Jeremy Myerson and Sylvia Katz, *Conran Design Guides: Kitchenware*, London: Conran Octopus, 1990: 43, 75–76.

Hollein, Hans (1934–)
Austrian architect and designer; born Vienna; active Vienna and Düsseldorf.

Training To 1956, engineering and architecture, Bundesgewerbeschule, Akademie der bildenden Künste, Vienna; 1958–60 under Frank Lloyd Wright and Ludwig Mies van der Rohe, Illinois Institute of Technology (ITT), Chicago; 1960, College of Environmental Design, University of California, Berkeley.
Biography 1964, Hollein set up an office in Vienna, becoming active as architect, urban planner, and designer; early in his career, became the most prominent figure in progressive exhibition design in Austria. His 1964–65 Retti candleshop in the Kohlmarkt, Vienna, synthesized illusionist dream architecture and the machine aesthetic of the airplane. Because the street on which his Metek boutique was located was dark, he solved the problem with a striking décor. His 1974 Schullin jewelry store in Graben, Vienna, was presented as a deconstructed 'jewel.' In shop after shop, he linked the street environment to the interior and, because of this approach, has been identified as the successor of fellow Austrians Otto Wagner, Adolf Loos, Josef Hoffmann, and Oswald Haerdtl. 1965–70, he was editor of journal *Bau*, Vienna; from 1967, taught, Staatliche Kunstakademie, Düsseldorf; from 1976, was a professor, Akademie der bildenden Künste, Vienna. His architecture incorporated details in expensive materials, primarily marble, brass, and chrome. His 1984–85 Marilyn sofa by Poltronova and 1983 tea set by Alessi contributed to his popularity. He designed 1981 Schwarzenberg briar-wood table by Memphis; became known for combining traditional and industrial materials with a kitsch/Pop sensibility. 1994–96 and 2000, was curator of Austrian exhibitions at Biennale di Venezia. Clients have included Herman Miller, Knoll, Yamagiwa, Wittmann, American Optical Corporation, Cleto Munari, Swid Powell, and Baleri. Design work has included 1980 candelabrum and metalware accessories by Rossi & Arcandi, 1984 Mitzi sofa by Poltronova, 1990 Avant-Garde piano (with electric lid opener) by Bösendorfer. Other architecture and interior architecture has included 1963 Aircraft-Carrier City project; 1967–69 Richard Feigen Gallery (now Hannae Hori store), East 79th Street, New York; 1966 *Selection 66* and *Austriennale* exhibitions at the Triennale di Milano; 1970 *Tod* (death) exhibition, Städtisches Museum, Mönchengladbach; 1970–75 Siemens central office, Munich; 1970–72 Carl Friedrich von Siemens Foundation, Nymphenburg; 1971–72 Media-Linien (Media-Lines), Olympiad Village, Munich; 1972–82 Abteiberg municipal museum, Mönchengladbach; 1976–78 Österreichisches Verkehrsbüro, Vienna; 1976–78 Museum of Glass and Ceramics, Tehran, in an old Qajar mansion; 1979 public school, Vienna; 1981–82 Schullin II jewelry store, Vienna; 1981 museum of applied art, Vienna; 1987–91 Museum für Moderne Kunst, Frankfurt; 1983 IBA condominium, Berlin; 1983 Kulturforum, Berlin; 1981–83 Ludwig Beck shop, Trump Tower, New York; 1984–85 *Dream and Reality, Vienna 1870–1930* exhibition, Vienna; numerous others subsequently.
Exhibitions/citations Work shown widely, including at 1985 (17th) Triennale di Milano; and included in *Radicals: Architettura e Design 1960–75*, 1996 (6th) Mostra Internazionale di Archittettura, Venice. Subject of a number of exhibitions, including 1995 at Historisches Museum der Stadt, Vienna. Numerous prizes and honors, including 1966 Reynolds Memorial Award, 1983 Grand Austrian State Award, 1983 German Architecture Award, 1985 Pritzker Architecture Prize.

Bibliography Cat., *Hans Hollein/Walter Pichler, Architektur*, Vienna, 1963. Cat., *Dortmunder Architekturausstellung 1976*, Darmstadt: Institut für Neue Technische Form, 1976. Günther Feuerstein, *Vienna—Present and Past: Arts and Crafts—Applied Art—Design*, Vienna: Jugend und Volk, 1976. Robert A.M. Stern (ed.), *The International Design Yearbook*, New York: Abbeville, 1985/1986. Officina Alessi, *Tea and Coffee Piazza: 11 Servizi da tè e caffè...*, Milan: Crusinallo, 1983. Cat., Carlo Guenzi, *Le affinità elettive*, Milan: Electa, 1985. *Nouvelles tendances: les avant-gardes de la fin du XXe siècle*, Paris: Centre Georges Pompidou, 1986. Juli Capella and Quim Larrea, *Designed by Architects in the 1980s*, New York: Rizzoli, 1988. Cat., *Hans Hollein, opere 1960–1988*, Florence: Academia delle Arti del Disegno, 1988. Albrecht Bangert and Karl Michael Armer, *80s Style: Designs of the Decade*, New York: Abbeville, 1990. Silvio San Pietro (ed.), *Hans Hollein—Agenda 1994*, Milan: L'Archivolto, 1993.

Holmbäck, Torben (1933–)

Danish designer; active Copenhagen.

Training Rungsted State Gymnasium; 1954, trainee, Joshua B. Powers Ltd., an international publishers' representative.
Biography 1955–57, Holmbäck was head of department, Joshua B. Powers; 1958, copywriter, Eberlin advertising agency; 1959–69, director, advertising department, *Stiftstidender* provincial newspapers; 1970–78, director, advertising department, Berlingske group of periodicals; 1979–1985, his own Holmbäck Mediastrategy; 1985–98, his own Holmbäck Design; 1985–2002, Member of Danish Designers (mDD) and board member 1992–97. 1999 Torben Holmbäck, Sebastian Holmbäck, Louise Campbell, and Cecilia Enevoldsen initialed *Walk the Plank*, a traveling exhibition of Danish designers' and manufacturers' work (later to be sold via the Internet) and another *Plank* installment followed.
Exhibitions/citations Work included in 1993 *Design, Miroir du Siècle*, Grand Palais, Paris; others. Received 1986 G-prize for industrial design, Japan; 1988 Dansk ID Prize; 1989 award, Industrie Forum Design (iF), Hanover; others.

Holmboe, Thorolf (1866–1935)

Norwegian ceramicist and textile designer.

Training 1889–90, painting in Berlin and at Atelier Fernand Cormon, Paris; sculpture, Statens Håndverks-og Kunstindustriskole, Oslo.
Biography From c. 1895, Holmboe was a member of the late 19th-century Symbolist artists' group in Scandinavia; 1908–11, designed underglaze porcelain decoration at Porsgrunds Porselænsfabrik, in a more restrained manner than that practiced at Royal Copenhagen Porcelain Manufactory. He also illustrated and designed books.
Exhibitions Work shown at 1900 *Exposition Universelle*, Paris; 1909, in Venice, Rome, and Vienna; 1912 in Vienna; and 1915 *Panama-Pacific International Exposition*, San Francisco.
Bibliography Cat., David Revere McFadden (ed.), *Scandinavian Modern Design 1880–1980*, New York: Abrams, 1982. Jennifer Hawkins Opie, *Scandinavia: Ceramics and Glass in the Twentieth Century*, New York: Rizzoli, 1989.

Holmegård Glasværk

Danish glassware manufacturer; located Holmegård commune.

History A glassworks using peat fuel was planned by Count C.C.S. Danneskiold-Samsøe, the owner of the Holmegård Marsh area in South Zealand, Denmark. 1825, a glassworks was founded there by his widow Countess Henriette Danneskiold-Samsøe, who made an agreement with Christian Wendt, a Norwegian, of the Hadelands Glassverk to set up the first furnaces, making only bottles initially. From 1835, glassworkers from Bohemia and Germany produced traditional European models there. 1835, cutting was introduced; from 1837, enamelling began. 1847, a second facility was established at Kastrup on Amager island, near Copenhagen, to make bottles at first; 1867, tableware followed and, 1875–80, pressed glass was subsequent. 1873, Kastrup was sold to finance Holmegård's expansion. 1905–06 Margarethe, a commissioned design by Svend Hammershøi (1873–1948), was the first new-design ware. Margarethe, one of two of his patterns, was produced to 1959. 1907, the bottle-making facilities in Denmark were sold (but not Holmegård) to found the Kastrup Glasværk. There was a commitment to employ designers, of whom the first was Orla Juul Nielsen from 1924–29, followed by architect Jacob E. Bang, from 1927. Bang designed the Primula and Viola patterns. (Bang left the glass industry in 1942 and returned in 1957.) Under Bang, the firm produced stoneware figurines, decorative wares, and lighting. 1942, Bang was succeeded by Per Lütken, who continued the production of modern forms. Inspired during study tour of Italy at the time of the 1950s editions of the Triennale di Milano, Lutken introduced major changes in production and style. His style incorporated fluid forms in slightly colored glass, some with etching, and hot metal applied to formed shapes of others. 1965, Holmegård merged with Kastrup to form Kastrup & Homegård Glasværks, with Lütken as the chief designer in charge of a large team producing free-blown glass objects to his 1998 death. 1975, the factory in Hellerup closed; 1979, Kastrup's production ceased; 1990, the factory in Odense was closed. 1985, the firm was acquired by Royal Copenhagen, then formed with others as Royal Scandinavia. 1998, the container glassmaking operation of Holmegård was sold to PLM. However, in 2000, Royal Scandinavia was bought by an investment group but, eventually, dismantled into various reorganized entities.
Exhibitions Work shown at 1937 *Ten Years of Danish Art Glassware* and numerous of other venues hence.
Bibliography Robert A.M Stern (ed.), *The International Design Yearbook*, New York: Abbeville, 1985/1986. Jennifer Hawkins Opie, *Scandinavia: Ceramics and Glass in the Twentieth Century*, New York: Rizzoli, 1989. Leslie Jackson, *20th Century Factory Glass*, London: Octopus, 2000.
> See Royal Scandinavia.

Holmes, Frank Graham (1878–1954)
> See Lenox, Walter Scott.

Holmes, Kenneth (1878–1954)

British industrial designer.

Biography Holmes designed c. 1934 vase by Lenox in Trenton, N. J. Early 1950s with N.R.G. Poynton and students of Leicester College of Art, he designed a stainless-steel cruet set for BOAC airlines, cutlery by Mitchells and Butler, and an electroplated coffee/tea set by Gladwin. With other students, he designed a coffee/tea service in plastic and stainless steel by Andrew Brothers.
Exhibitions 1934 *Machine Art* (c. 1934 vase by Lenox), The Museum of Modern Art, New York.
Bibliography Michael Farr, *Design in British Industry: A Mid-Century Survey*, London: Cambridge, 1955: 163–64.

Holophane Corporation

Lighting manufacturer.

History 1893 working in a Paris laboratory, French scientist André Blondel and Greek engineer Spiridion Psaroudaki received a US patent for a glass globe with parallel, vertical prisms that would brightly diffuse light. 1894, they sold their US rights in the Holophane glassware company to Louis N. Bruner. ('Holophane' was derived from the Greek for 'a completely luminous appearance.') 1895, Geo. A. Macbeth Company in Pittsburgh, Pa., acquired the glass-globe rights and the Holophane trademark from Bruner, which, in 1896, were again transferred, to Otis Mygatt, a Harvard University graduate, and, thus, founded Holophane Company in London. 1898, Holophane Glass Company was incorporated in the US with offices in New York. 1890s, the firm manufactured reflectors and globes for carbon lamps, gas burners, acetylene, and oil lamps. It was highly successful in England, selling lighting manufactured by others under the Holophane name. 1911, General Electric contracted with Holophane in the US to make and exclusively sell Holophane products; c. 1912, General Electric began combining Holophane glass with a range of frosted, milk-white glassware by Fostoria. From 1916, Holophane was managed by Charles Franck. 1920, the 'pleated' glass diffusers began to be installed in large, open factory spaces for bright, overall illumination, and its Traficon model used in traffic lights and signage. 1935–36 Lobay Luminaire model, a version by Americans Vearl S. Wince and Kurt Franck, was the first to incorporate exposed metal-rod struts to hold the heavy pressed-glass reflector in place, before the struts became a standard Holophane feature. 1930s, Holophane lighted NBC's Radio City broadcasting studios in New York and the 1937 coronation of George VI in Westminster Abbey in London; 1953, again in Westminster Abbey, provided supplemental lighting for Elizabeth II's coronation. Problems over payment of estate taxes for chairperson Guy Campbell (who died in 1962), forced the sale of the firm to Holophane's British entity in 1966. By 1970s, when the high-tech style in designer interiors débuted, Holophane lighting had outgrown exclusive industrial application. 1971, the firm merged with Johns-Manville; 1989, was purchased by private investors and became a publicly held firm; is today an Acuity Brands

Friedl Holzer-Kjellberg. Dinner plate. 1954. Glazed porcelain, h. 3/4 x dia. 10 1/8" (1.9 x 25.7 cm). Mfr.: Arabia, Finland. Phyllis B. Lambert Fund. MoMA.

company. Holophane introduced early 1990s Messenger for internal lighting of signage and 1998 Mongoose armless roadway lighting. 1994, Holophane purchased Antique Street Lamps of Buda, Tex., and 1996, fluorescent lighting firm MetalOptics of Austin, Tex. Today an international company, headquarters are in Newark, Ohio.
Bibliography Mel Byars, 'To Be Continued,' *Metropolitan Home*, Nov.-Dec. 1999: 80+. www.holophane.com.

Holscher, Knud (1930–)
Danish architect and designer.

Training Architecture, Det Kongelige Danske Kunstakademi, Copenhagen.
Biography Holscher doubled as an industrial designer and architect on commissions, including the Copenhagen airport and Bahrain Museum; 1967–96, a partner in architecture firm Krohn & Hartvig Rasmussen; 1968–87, was a professor of architecture, Det Kongelige Danske Kunstakademi; 1960–64, was associated with Arne Jacobsen, serving as supervising architect on Jacobsen's 1960–64 St. Catherine's College in Oxford, UK; from 1970, was a principal of Knud Holscher Industrial Design. Work included sanitary fittings by Ifö Sanitär/Ceranova; 1973 stainless-steel hardware by d line international; from 1974, metalwork by Georg Jensen, including 1975 stainless-steel wire serving pieces; 1996 Milewide sound barriers and road equip-ment for the Danish Road Authority.
Exhibitions/citations Received numerous architectural and design awards, including three British awards (including 1966, for Modric hardware), 1970 Eckersberg Medal, six Dansk ID Prizes, 1979 Danish Wood Award, 1993 Knud V. Engelhardt's Memorial Fund grant, 1993 C.F. Hansen Medal, and won a number of architectural competitions for schools, sports pavilions, town centers, and universities in Scandinavia and abroad.
Bibliography ' "Modric" Architectural Ironmongery,' *Design*, no. 209, May 1966: 36–37. Cat., *Georg Jensen Silversmithy: 77 Artists, 75 Years*, Washington: Smithsonian, 1980. Cat., Kathryn B. Hiesinger and George H. Marcus III (eds.), *Design Since 1945*, Philadelphia: Philadelphia Museum of Art, 1983.

Göran Hongell. Aarne shot glass. 1948. Turned mold-blown glass, h. 2 15/16 x dia. 2" (7.5 x 5.1 cm). Mfr.: Iittala Lasi, Finland. Given anonymously. MoMA.

Holt, Steven Skov (1957–)
American designer; born Santa Barbara, Cal.

Biography Holt worked at Zebra Design in Cologne, Germany, and at Smart Design in New York; from 1992, was director of strategy, frogdesign, New York; from 1995, was director of industrial design programs, California College of Arts and Crafts, San Francisco; has been editor, *I.D.* magazine; subsequently, at frogdesign, San Francisco.
Bibliography Cat., R. Craig Miller (intro.), *U.S. Design 1975–2000*, Munich: Prestel, 2002.

Holt Le Son, Lucie (1899–)
American painter, sculptor, decorator, and designer; born Philadelphia, Pa.; active US and Paris; wife of Jean-Léon Le Son.

Biography Active 1920s–30s, Le Son designed interiors and, from 1927, wood-carved mannequins and screens by Siégel, the store-display manufacturer; 1928, began designing furniture that incorporated chromium-plated metal and frequently used fabrics by Hélène Henry.
Exhibitions From 1926, Holt Le Son was the first American to show at annual editions of Salon d'Automne, and from 1927 at Salons of Société des Artistes Décorateurs (SAD) and other years at Salon d'Automne (mannequins and screens at 1927 editions of both). At 1928 SAD Salon (travel-agency décor with partly lacquered fibrous-cement panels); 1929 SAD Salon (central salon of a ship produced by Art du Bois). At 1930 (1st) exhibition (hotel room and bath produced by Labor Métal), Union des Artistes Modernes (UAM); and 1931 *Exposition Coloniale* (furniture in different-color woods), Paris.
Bibliography Pierre Kjellberg, *Art déco: les maîtres du mobilier, le décor des paquebots*, Paris: Amateur, 1986.

Holzer, Rainer Michael
> See Coop Himmelb(l)au.

Holzer-Kjellberg, Friedl (1905–1993)
Austrian ceramicist; active Helsinki.

Biography 1924–70, Holzer-Kjellberg was a designer for Arabia pottery in Helsinki, where she was the artistic director from 1948; became known for her one-of-a-kind stoneware vessels and Chinese 'rice' pattern porcelain bowls, whose effect was created by cutting a pattern into very thin porcelain, with the opening covered by a translucent glaze.
Bibliography Cat., David Revere McFadden (ed.), *Scandinavian Modern Design 1880–1980*, New York: Abrams, 1982.

Homann, Alfred (1948–)
Danish architect and designer.

Training To 1976, architecture, Det Kongelige Danske Kunstakademi, Copenhagen.
Biography 1972, Homann worked at Schooley & Cornelius design studio in Ohio, US, and, 1972–79, in Wilhelm Wohlert's design studio in Denmark; 1978, set up his own design studio; 1984–87, partner of Penta Design; consultant, Danmarks Designskole; has been active in building design and the restoration of old structures; designed lighting and furniture, including Ensemble chair and NB 10 chair in bent plywood and steel tubing chair by Fritz Hansen.
Honors 1978 award, Industrie Forum Design, Hanover; 1987 Dansk ID Prize; 1988 ION Award, Netherlands; 1992 Design Innovation Award, Germany.

Hongell, Göran (1902–1973)
Finnish glasware designer.

Training Decorative art, Taideteollinen korkeakoulu, Helsinki.
Biography Hongel taught decorative painting, Taideteollinen korkeakoulu; 1932, began working at Iittala glassworks and, from 1940, at Karhula glassworks; is best known for mass-production glassware; after World War II, began designing Functionalist glass-

Saara Hopea-Untracht. Pitcher. 1951. Blown glass, h. 6 3/4 x dia. including handle 6 9/16" (17.1 x 16.6 cm). Mfr.: Nuutajärvi Glass Works, Finland. Gift of Barbro Kulvik and Antti Siltavuori. MoMA.

ware, without decoration.
Bibliography Cat., David Revere McFadden (ed.), *Scandinavian Modern Design 1880–1980*, New York: Abrams, 1982.

Honzík, Karel (1900–1966)

Czech architect, furniture designer, graphic artist, set designer, architectural theoretician, and writer; born Le Croisic.

Training 1918–25, České Vysoké Učení Technické (Czech technical university), Prague.
Biography From 1923 until its 1931 demise, Honzík was a member of Devětsil group, and, from 1926, chairperson of its architecture section ARDEV. His early designs were in the style of the Puristická Čtyřka group, close to Evžen Linhart's contemporary works, and realized in Honzík's own Purist design for 1925–26 suburban house on Za Strahovem in Prague (a project taken over from Krejcar) and 1926–28 apartment block on Starokošiřská St. in Prague. 1928 with Josef Havlíček, Honzík set up H&H studio. The International Style, to which he turned, is illustrated by his 1929–30 suburban house on Nad Cementárnou St., as well as collaborative projects with Havlíček. From 1924, Honzík was an architectural theoretician; 1926, began his polemic with Teige on the Constructivist 'elimination of art'; believed that an emphasis on art enhanced the utilitarian character of architecture; died in Prague.
Exhibitions Participated in 1923 Bauhaus exhibition, Weimar.
Bibliography Cat., *Devětsil: Czech Avant-Garde Art, Architecture, and Design of the 1920s and 30s*, Oxford Museum of Modern Art / London Design Museum, 1990. Cat., *Prague, 1900–1938: capitale secrète des avants-gardes*, Dijon: Musée des Beaux-Arts, 1997.

Hood, Raymond Mathewson (1881–1934)

American architect; born Pawtucket, R.I.

Training Brown University, Providence, R.I.; 1900–1903, bachelor's degree, Massachusetts Institute of Technology (MIT), Cambridge, Mass.; 1905–11, École des Beaux-Arts, Paris.
Biography 1907, Hood began working for architecture firm Cram, Goodhue and Ferguson in Boston but soon left for Pittsburgh to work for Henry Hornsbostel, becoming his chief designer; 1914, settled in New York and partnered with Rayne Adams, and, 1924–31, collaborated with architects Jacques-André Fouilhoux and Frederick A. Godley in the partnership Raymond, Fouilhoux and Godley; 1931, practiced architecture alone; 1932, established a partnership with Fouilhoux. 1922, with John Mead Howells, Hood won the *Chicago Tribune* Tower competition (built in 1925), being selected from 260 entries, including those of Walter Gropius, Eliel Saarinen, and Adolph Loos. Hood turned from historicism to a modern style influenced by Art Déco, using almost no external ornamentation by 1930. As one of three architectural teams, Hood and Fouilhoux participated in design of 1932–40 Rockefeller Center in New York, where the curtain-wall façade was introduced into what became known as the Inter-national Style. Hood's buildings included 1924 American Radiator building, 1929–30 *Daily News* building, and 1930 McGraw-Hill building, all New York. His work included furniture design.
Exhibitions Apartment house loggia and business executive's office installed at 1929 (11th) *The Architect and the Industrial Arts: An Exhibition of Contemporary American Design*, The Metropolitan Museum of Art, New York. Work subject of 1982 exhibition, New York.
Bibliography Arthur Rappan North, *Raymond M. Hood*, New York: Whittlesey House, 1931. Walter H. Kilham, *Raymond Hood, Architect*, New York: Architectural Book, 1973. John B. Schwartzman, *Raymond Hood: The Unheralded Architect*, Charlottesville, Va., 1962. Cat., Robert A.M. Stern, *Raymond M. Hood*, New York: Institute for Architecture and Urban Studies, 1982. Gerd Hatje in Vittorio Magnago Lampugnani (ed.), *Encyclopedia of 20th-Century Architecture*, New York: Abrams, 1986: 153–54. R. Craig Miller, *Modern Design 1890–1990*, New York: Abrams, 1990.

Hoontrakul, Martin
> See Propaganda.

Hoosemans, François (aka Franz Hoosemans)

Belgian jeweler and silversmith; active Brussels.

Biography With Égide Rombaux, Hoosemans produced works of distinction, including a range of candelabra and table lamps.
Exhibitions Silver candelabra with nude female ivory figures by Rombaux shown at 1897 exhibition, Musée Royal de l'Afrique Centrale in Tervuren, Belgium. Other work in Belgian pavilion, 1900 *Exposition Universelle*, Paris.
Bibliography Cat., *Werke Um 1900*, Berlin: Kunstgewerbe Museum, 1966: nos. 14 and 15. R. Barilli, *Art Nouveau*, London: Paul Hamlyn, 1966: 45. M. Rheims, *L'objet 1900*, Paris, 1964. Annelies Krekel-Aalberse, *Art Nouveau and Art Déco Silver*, New York: Abrams, 1989.

Hooykaas, H.

Dutch silversmiths; located Schoonhoven.

History 1875, the firm was founded; 1920s, produced the modern silver designs of Harm Ellens.
Bibliography Annelies Krekel-Aalberse, *Art Nouveau and Art Déco Silver*, New York: Abrams, 1989.

Hopea-Untracht, Saara (1925–1984)

Finnish interior, furniture, glassware, and lighting designer, metalworker, and ceramicist; born Porvoo; active Helsinki and Porvoo.

Training Interior design, Taideteollinen korkeakoulu, Helsinki.
Biography 1946–52, she was an independent interior designer; was also a furniture designer for Mobilia in 1946–48 and lighting for Taito in 1948–52; from 1951–80 off and on, constructed himmelis (traditional Finnish straw or stalk hangings). 1952–59, she worked at Nuutajärvi glassworks as associate of Kaj Franck; executed utility and decorative glassware designs, including the first (1951) Finnish nesting range in molded-blown colored glass; also under Franck, worked at Arabia; from 1960–67, was active as a freelance enamelist; later, specialized in silver jewelry and enameling and was the artistic director at her family's firm Ossian Hopea in Porvoo.
Exhibitions/citations Work included in 1953 exhibition, Helsinki; 1954 exhibition, Brussels; 1954–57 *Design in Scandinavia*, touring the US; 1955 *H 55*, Hälsingborg, Sweden; 1956–57 *Finnish Exhibition*, touring West Germany; 1961 *Finlandia* in Zürich, Amsterdam, and London. Editions of Triennale di Milano: silver medals, 1954 (10th) (glassware), 1957 (11th) (glassware), 1960 (12th) (jewelry).
Bibliography '15 Contemporary Finnish Designers,' *Design Quarterly*, no. 37, 1957: 12–13. Tuula Koli, 'Saara Hopea-Untracht—Tapio Yli-Viikäri,' *Form Function Finland*, no. 3, 1982: 12–13. Cat., Kathryn B. Hiesinger and George H. Marcus III (eds.), *Design Since 1945*, Philadelphia: Philadelphia Museum of Art, 1983. Cat., David Revere McFadden (ed.), *Scandinavian Modern Design: 1880–1980*, New York: Cooper-Hewitt Museum, 1982. Jennifer Hawkins Opie, *Scandinavia: Ceramics and Glass in the Twentieth Century*, New York: Rizzoli, 1989.

Hopf, Benjamin (1971–)
> See büro für form.

Horák, Bohuslav (1954–)
Czech sculptor and designer.

Biography 1988, Horák joined design group Atika, established in 1987 and based in Prague. Atika produced his 1988 A Rotten Luck Easy Chair in welded iron wire and leather and 1988 Flammenschrank cupboard in stained wood and metal. His designs emphasized non-industrial production methods, incorporated traditional materials, including leather and wood, and exhibited a high regard for nature.
Bibliography Albrecht Bangert and Karl Michael Armer, *80s Style: Designs of the Decade*, New York: Abbeville, 1990.

Horejc, Jaroslav (1886–1983)
Czech sculptor and designer; born Prague.

Training Specialized School of Jewelry; and, 1906–10, Vysoká Škola Uměleckoprůmyslová (VŠUP, academy of arts, architecture, and design); both Prague.
Biography From 1912, Horejc collaborated with the cooperative Artěl and designed Cubist ceramic vases; 1918–48, was a professor of metalwork, VŠUP, Prague; designed metal latticework and screens with architect Jan Kotěra and others, and important work in glass, including four famous cut and engraved pieces: 1921 Bacchus, 1922–23 Canaan, 1923 Dance, and 1924 Three Goddesses. He also designed noteworthy jewelry in an Art Déco style and 1937 cut-glass monumental relief The Earth and the Men for the Palace of Nations in Geneva. Died in Prague.
Exhibitions/citations Grand prize (for a cut-glass collection), 1925 *Exposition International des Arts Décoratifs et Industriels Modernes*, Paris.
Bibliography Alena Adlerová, *České užité umění 1918–1938*, Prague: Odeon 1983. Cat., J. Horneková, *Jarosvlav Horejc: Výběr z díla, Výstava k 85*, Prague: Uměleckoprůmyslové Muzeum, 1971. Cat., *Prague, 1900–1938: capitale secrète des avants-gardes*, Dijon: Musée des Beaux-Arts, 1997.

Horgen Möbelfabrik; Horgen-Glarus
Swiss furniture manufacturer; today located Glarus.

History 1882, Horgen Möbelfabrik was founded by Emil Baumann in Horgen, Switzerland, to make chairs and tables according to a high craft tradition; 1902, established a second plant in Glarus, Switzerland, and, thus the name Horgen-Glarus came to be; from 1926, produced modern wood furniture sold by Wohnbedarf and others and designed by Swiss architects Ernst Haefeli, Arnold Itlen, Werner M. Moser, Flora and Rudolf Steige and artist/pedagogue Max Bill; furnished the Swiss Pavilion at 1929–30 *Exposición Internacional de Barcelona*, with chairs by Swiss architect Hans Hofmann. Wilhelm Kienzle designed trapezoidal kindergarten tables for the firm. Its best-known chairs were designed by Hans Bellmann: 1951–52 Einpunkt side chair, reentered into production currently, and 1954 GA side chair in bentwood and tubular steel. The factory at one time employed 200 people—today only 22, but still calling on hand methods for production. 2000, the firm was bought by Markus and Tanja Landolt Virchaux. Its current freelance designers include Urs Esposito, Dan Hodler, Jean-Claude Mahler, and Hannes Wettstein.
Bibliography Friederike Mehlau-Wiebking et al., *Schweizer Typenmöbel 1925–35, Sigfried Giedion und die Wohnbedarf AG*, Zürich: gta, 1989.

Hornby, Frank (1863–1936)
British inventor; born Liverpool.

Training Left school aged 16.
Biography From 1879, Hornby worked in his father's grocery business; 1887, began working as a bookkeeper for a Liverpool meat-importing firm under David Elliott. With no engineering or mechanics training and in his spare time at first, Hornby made toys for his two sons from hand-cut sheet metal and interchangeable parts; by perforating 1/2" (1 cm) wide metal strips at 1/2" (1 cm) intervals and using nuts and bolts to assemble them, he soon discovered that he had invented a viable construction toy. With money borrowed from Elliott (who also became a business partner), Hornby received a 1901 patent for his Mechanics Made Easy that was a set of 15 pieces but not affordable by the average British child and family at the time. 1906, the business began making a profit. 1907, Hornby separated from Elliott and started a firm and re-named his product Meccano, which he manufactured himself in a facility in Liverpool. Early models were crude, but the sets became more sophisticated, with gears and other parts available, although for years the only change Hornby made to the system was a shift from tin to a cardboard box. 1913–14 with soaring sales, factories were set up in Paris and Berlin and, 1916, in Masonic Hall, New York. The Liverpool facility was expanded, but the majority of production was soon shifted to munitions to serve Britain's World War I effort. From 1916, Hornby published the *Meccano Magazine*. 1920, Hornby Trains (a new line of clockwork trains) were introduced, followed by electric train sets in 1920s. 1931, Hornby was elected a Member of Parliament. 1934 Dinky Toys (a quick-and-easy-to-assemble system) were introduced, followed by Dublo electric trains from 1938. 1964, the Meccano firm was bought by Lines Group, operating under the name Meccano Ltd. and, from 1970, under the name Meccano-Triang. But, 1979, the latter became bankrupt after it was bought by Airfix Group. 1980, Meccano production ceased in Britain, but subsidiaries abroad continued. 1981, Airfix was liquidated, and the names of Meccano and Dinky Toys were bought by General Mills Toy Group, US, which already owned Miro-Meccano, Paris. 1990, the Miro-Meccano firm continued Meccano production in the US and Argentina. 2000, the Meccano firm, having been restructured with new directors and headquarters in Calais, was bought by Nikko of Japan, a maker of radio-controlled toys.
Bibliography B.N. Love, *Meccano Constuctors' Guide*, Hemel Hempstead: Model and Allied, 1971. Joseph Maduca, *The Meccano Magazine 1916–1981*, London: New Cavendish, 1987. Roger Beardsley, *The Hornby Companion*, London: New Cavendish, 1992. Mike and Sue Richardson, *Dinky Toys & Modelled Miniatures 1931–1979*, London: New Cavendish, 1992. Anthony McReavy, *The Toy Story: The Life and Times of Inventor Frank Hornby*, London: Ebury, 2002.

Horgen-Glarus: Max Bill. Kreuzzargenstuhl (no. 5–050). 1951. Painted solid birch and laminated birch, 30 7/16 x 16 1/2 x 20 1/16" (77.3 x 42 x 51 cm). Mfr.: Horgen-Glarus Möbelfabrik, Switzerland. Courtesy Quittenbaum Kunstauktionen, Munich.

Horta, Victor (1861–1947)
Belgian architect and designer; born Ghent; active Brussels.

Training 1876, architecture at the academy in Ghent; to 1881, Académie des Beaux-Arts, Brussels.
Biography An enthusiastic disciple of Eugène-Emmanuel Viollet-le-Duc, the Baron Horta took on the design of a building and its entire contents, including chandeliers, furniture, door handles, and key escutcheons. He was also sympathetic with Viollet-le-Duc's view that structure

was in itself an architectural expression. Horta worked for some time in the office of the neoclassical architect Alphonse Balat. From 1892, he rejected historicism and developed his own style, in which he exposed the framework of a building, including its iron pillars, balustrades, and window frames. This exercise created an association between the framework and the interior furnishings. The iron supports as a decorative element became known as the 'Horta line.' He is best known for his own 1898–11 house, now a museum, on the rue Américaine in Brussels. Horta became the leading practitioner of the Belgian Art Nouveau idiom in architecture. His design of 1892–93 Hôtel Tassel in Brussels was outstanding for its combination of craft and industrial techniques; it was the first house in which iron was used extensively. From 1912, he was a professor, Académie des Beaux-Arts, Brussels, serving as the school's head 1927–31. His later architecture was classical and austere, with Art Nouveau waves replaced by straight lines. His other buildings in Brussels included 1893 Autrique House, 1895–96 Winssinger house, 1894 Frison house, 1895–1900 Hôtel Solvay, Château de la Hulpe, 1896–99 Maison du Peuple, for the Socialist Party (with the first iron-and-glass façade in Belgium), 1897–1900 Baron van Eetvelde house, 1900 Hôtel Aubecq, 1901 À l'Innovation department store, 1922–28 Palais des Beaux-Arts (principal example of Horta's later straight lines replacing waves). He wrote the books *Considérations sur l'art moderne* (Brussels, 1925). and *L'enseignement architectural et l'architecture moderne* (Brussels, 1926).
Exhibitions Work included in 1971 *Guimard, Horta, Van de Velde*, Paris (catalog below). Subject of 1991–92 *Victor Horta: architetto e designer (1861–1947)*, Palazzo dei Diamanti, Ferrara, Italy; 1997 *Horta: Art Noveau to Modernism*, Palais des Beaux-Arts, Brussels (catalog below).
Bibliography Robert L. Delevoy, *Victor Horta*, Brussels: Elsevier, 1958. Pierre Puttemans and Jean Delhaye, *Victor Horta*, Saint-Gilles: Administration Communale, 1964. P. Portoghesi and F. Borsi, *Victor Horta*, Rome: Del Tritone, 1969. Cat., *Guimard, Horta, Van de Velde*, Paris, 1971. A. Hoppenbrouwers et al., *Victor Horta architectonographie*, Brussels: Confédération Nationale de la Construction, 1975. A. Duncan, *Art Nouveau and Art Deco Lighting*, New York: Simon & Schuster, 1978: 50–51. Françoise Aubry and Jos Vandenbreeden, *Horta: Art Nouveau to Modernism*, Ghent: Ludion, 1996.

Horwitt, Nathan George (1889–1990)

Russian industrial designer; active New York.

Training City University of New York; New York University; Art Students League, New York.
Biography Late 1920s, Horwitt formed Design Engineers in New York, an industrial-design studio, where he experimented with the digital clock and patented ideas, trying to sell them to manufacturers. The enterprise lasted three years. After World War II, he worked at pharmaceutical firm E.R. Squibb as an advertising copywriter, later becoming director of advertising. He designed 1930 Beta chair, the 'frameless' picture frame (marketed as the Bruquette system), and 1970 (no. 4601) numberless black-face clock (by Howard Miller Clock Company). Earlier (1947), he designed the numberless watch face. He patented the numberless concept in 1958 and 1959 and purportedly said, 'There might have been 15 Swiss watch companies which I tried to gain for my design between 1956 and 1960—without any success.' After The Museum of Modern Art had included the watch (produced by Vacheron-Constantin-LeCoultre) in its permanent collection in 1960, Movado introduced it in 1961 and called it 'The Museum Watch' in its advertising. Horwitt pursued litigation with Movado, resulting in their paying him $29,000 and subsequent parlaying the basic design of a dot in a circle into a entire range of fashion goods. Movado repatented the design as no. 6709 in 1999. The Horwit archive is housed in Cooper-Hewitt National Design Museum, New York.
Exhibitions 1934 *Machine Art* (Beta chair) and 1991 *Art of the Forties* (watch), both The Museum of Modern Art, New York.
Bibliography Joan Cook, *The New York Times,* obituary, 20 June 1990: B8. Cat., Riva Castleman (ed.), *Art of the Forties*, New York: The Museum of Modern Art, 1991: 133.

Hosak-Robb, Bibs (1955–)

German industrial designer; born Neu-Ulm.

Training 1975–80, industrial design, Fachhochschule, Munich; 1981–84, Royal College of Art, London.
Biography 1980–81, Hosak-Robb worked for Bosch-Siemens Hausgeräte in Munich; from 1981, was a consultant designer to clients, including BMW, WMF, Schlagheck Schultes Design studio, Trak Sport Articles, and Tristar Sports. Her work included 1983 Edo silver cutlery

Nathan George Horwitt. Wristwatch face. 1947. White gold with enameled dial, dia. 1 5/16" (3.3 cm). Mfr: Vaceron Constantin-Le Coultre, Switzerland. Gift of the designer. MoMA.

by Robbe & Berking and 1988 KunstDisco Seoul dining/eating concept, including the Göffel (fork/spoon) utensil by Carl Mertens.
Bibliography Cat., Design Center Stuttgart, *Women in Design: Careers and Life Histories Since 1900*, Stuttgart: Haus der Wirtschaft, 1989: 116–19.

Hose, Robert H. (1915–1977)

American industrial designer.

Training To 1937, architecture, University of Minnesota, Minneapolis; Massachusetts Institute of Technology (MIT), Cambridge, Mass.
Biography 1939, Hose began work at Bell Telephone Laboratories in New Jersey in a small industrial-design department there to which Henry Dreyfuss had been a consultant from 1930. Up to 1920s, there was no distinction between the technical design and the styling in the telephone. During World War II, Hose and Dreyfuss collaborated on over 100 communications projects. 1946, Hose became an associate in industrial design office of Dreyfuss in New York, working on Model 500 desk telephone project, and was later a partner. 1953–54, was president, Society of Industrial Designers. 1961, Hose left Dreyfuss and set up his own studio.
Bibliography Arthur Pulos, *The American Design Adventure 1940–1975*, Cambridge: MIT Press: 1988: 23.

Hosken, 'Fran' Franziska (1919–)

American designer; active Boston, Mass.; wife of James Hosken.

Training Smith College, Northampton, Mass.; mid-1940s under Gyorgy Kepes, Institute of Design, Chicago.
Biography 1938, Hosken emigrated to the US from Austria; married and settled in Boston after her studies; designed home furnishings, furniture, and accessories; 1948, established Hosken, Inc., to realize her work through manufacture to sale. She was particularly productive 1947–50; is little known; nevertheless, her work, which included flexible, low-cost modern design, was published in journals such as *Everyday Art Quarterly* in 1948 and *Furniture Forum* in 1949.
Exhibitions Work partially the subject of 2001 *With an Eye on Good Design: The Work of Angelo Testa and Franziska Hosken*, Lin Weinberg Gallery, New York.

Hosoe, Isao (1942–)

Japanese designer; born Tokyo; active Milan.

Training To 1967, mechanical engineering and aerospace technology, Hihon University, Tokyo.
Biography 1965, Hosoe settled in Italy; to 1974, collaborated with

Alberto Rosselli in Milan. Working in the studio Gruppo Professionale, he designed furniture, furnishings, and lighting by Bilumen, Cesame, Elle, Flores, Kartell, Omfa, Reguitti, Rima, Saporiti Italia, and Valenti. He also designed lighting by Yamagiwa in Tokyo and office furniture and furnishings by Arflex, Facomet Italia, HC, Martini, and Sasea; was a consultant designer to ICA, Camera di Commercio di Pesaro, and Fiat; designed automobile bodies by Boneschi, Orlandi, and Fiat; 1981, established Design Research Center in Milan; working in plastics early 1980s, designed Picchio cantilever ABS table lamp by Luxo Italiana and Snake free-standing articulated wall system (with Ann Marinelli) by Sacea and, in another material, 1991 Oskar table and chair by Cassina. His award-winning design work for technical products tells much of his and his studio's history in this area. He has taught, Politecnico, Milan; became a member of Associazione per il Disegno Industriale (ADI); 1986, established Hosoe Design in Milan.
Exhibitions/citations Work included in 1972 *Italy: The New Domestic Landscape*, The Museum of Modern Art, New York, and a large number of others subsequently. Premio Compasso d'Oro: 1970 (Meteor motor coach with Alberto Rosselli by Fiat-Orlandi), 1981 (transportation seat by CML), 1987 (Snake articulated wall with Marinelli by Sacea; Modulus domestic robot with others by Sirius), 1989 (Space 330 mini-disk holder with Pozzoli by Mass Plast), 1998 (FMP 270 Pulsar with others by Sacmi Forni; Integral TH13 telephonic terminal with others by Robert Boch). Gold medal, 1973 (15th) Triennale di Milano; honorable mention, 1973 BIO 5 industrial-design biennial, Ljubljana; 1974 Premio SMAU Industrial Design, Salone della Machina e Attrezzature per l'Ufficio, Milan.
Bibliography *ADI Annual 1976*, Milan: Associazione per il Disegno Industriale, 1976. Alfonso Grassi and Anty Pansera, *Atlante del design italiano 1940/1980*, Milan: Fabbri, 1980. Robert A.M. Stern (ed.), *The International Design Yearbook*, New York: Abbeville, 1985/1986. Cat., Hans Wichmann, *Italien Design 1945 bis heute*, Munich: Die Neue Sammlung, 1988. *Modo*, no. 148, Mar.–Apr.1993: 121.

Houillon, Louis

French silversmith; active Paris.

Biography Houillon was considered the best enameler of his day; from 1867, was the chief enameler at the P. Soyer workshop; subsequently, established his own atelier; 1878–89, worked for Felize at Boucheron. Étienne Tourette and Philippe Wolfers were pupils in Houillons workshop in Paris.
Exhibitions From 1878, Houillon and Tourette exhibited jointly. Work included in Salons of Société Nationale des Beaux-Arts 1884, Société des Artistes Français 1901, and Sociéte des Artistes Décorateurs 1904, 1906, 1908.
Bibliography Cat. *Die Fouquet, 1960–1960, Schmuckkünstler in Paris*, Museum Bellerive, Zürich, 1984: 64. Annelies Krekel-Aalberse, *Art Nouveau and Art Déco Silver*, New York: Abrams, 1989.

Houtzager, Cees
> See Studio Pro.

Høvelskov, Jørgen

Danish architect and designer.

Biography Høvelskov is or was primarily an architect and little known himself. However, his best-known work is the 1963 Harpen (harp) chair by Chris-tensen & Larsen with production shifted, possibly from 1968, to P. Jeppenens Møbelfabrik (now P.J. Furniture), both Denmark. There may have been an original model from which the final Harpen chair was a refinement. Its composition is solid ash for the frame and thin streched rope, or string, for the back and seat. The construction details include a metal joint where the wood frame intersects. The chair reflects both tradition and innovation—with a Scandinavian crafts approach to manufacture and in a form like no other, even though string for seating has been employed by others. The shape is based on the bow of a Viking ship and, due to the strings, reflects a harp.

Howard Miller Clock Company

American timing-device manufacturer; son of Herman Miller.

History Howard C. Miller (1905–1995), a German émigré, learned clock making under his father in the Black Forest region of Bavaria. From 1926, he focused on making cases for mantel clocks in this workshop founded in Zeeland, Mich., US, to which he emigrated during World War I. In 1930s, the firm was reorganized and took on its present name; during World War II, produced anti-aircraft covers for Ford

Howard Miller Clock Company: Nathan George Horwitt. Wall clock (no. 4601). 1969– 70. Metal lacquered case and glass front, d. 2 3/8 x dia. 12 13/16" (6 x 32.5 cm). Mfr.: Howard Miller Clock Co., US. Gift of the mfr. MoMA.

Motor Co. in Detroit. Before the war, in addition to traditional models, the firm made distinguished table and wall clocks designed by Gilbert Rohde in 1930s and, from 1947 through the George Nelson Associates studio, by Irving Harper. Also through the Nelson studio, William Renwick's 1947 Bubble lamp range (with plastic sprayed over a wire frame) was made. The Rohde/Nelson connections with Howard Miller came through their mutual association with Herman Miller, his father who was the general manager of Colonial Manufacturing. Colonial made grandfather clocks, also in Zeeland. Throughout the years, the Howard Miller firm has imported movements from Germany. (Even though the Herman Miller Furniture Company was named for Herman Miller, the firm itself was founded and directed by Herman's son-in-law D.J. DePree. Rhode and Nelson were the sequential artistic directors of Herman Miller.) Howard Miller also produced Nathan Horwitt's 1970 (no. 4601) single-dot black-face wall clock. The firm continues today but without the design talent of the 1950s, directed by Howard's sons Jack and Philip Miller. 1983, the firm bought the Hekman Furniture Co. The Harper/Nelson clocks have achieved a popularity today, possibly due to an interest in the kitsch Pop design of the 1950s, and nine models are being reproduced by Vitra Design Museum in Weil am Rhein, Germany.
Bibliography Cat., Martin Eidelberg (ed.), *Design 1935–1965: What Modern Was*, New York: Musée des Arts Décoratifs/Abrams, 1991.
> See Harper, Irving; Nelson, George; Renwick, William, Rohde, Gilbert.

Høye, Emil (1875–1958)

Danish silversmith; active Bergen and Kristiania (known as Oslo from 1925).

Biography 1905, Høye settled in Bergen; 1910–16, was the artistic director of Marius Hammer, one of Norway's largest silversmithies, which produced large quantities of souvenir silver spoons for tourists and export. After setting up his own workshop, Høye continued to create silver designs for Hammer. His work was influenced by Mogens Ballin and later by Georg Jensen.
Bibliography Annelies Krekel-Aalberse, *Art Nouveau and Art Déco Silver*, New York: Abrams, 1989.

Hubbard, Elbert Green (1856–1915)

American furniture designer.

Biography 1894 and 1895, Hubbard met William Morris; inspired by Morris's Kelmscott Press, founded the Roycroft Press in East Aurora, near Buffalo, N.Y.; also founded the Roycrofters, an Arts and Crafts community, and organized workshops, lectured, and wrote as a highly effective champion of the Arts and Crafts philosophy. He established a group of enterprises, including for book publishing and binding, furniture production, and leather- and metalware. There were more than 400 people in the utopian Roycroft community, based on some of the principles of the British Arts and Crafts movement but with a commercial slant of its own. The Roycrofters operated a restaurant which served the many tourists, who discovered its activities through its publications (*Little Journeys* pamphlets, *The Philistine* monthly journal, and mail-

order catalogs advertising gift items and souvenirs). Hubbard cofounded the Larkin Company in Buffalo. 1915, he and his wife died aboard the oceanliner *Lusitania*. His son Elbert Hubbard Jr. became the director of the Roycrofters until the community closed in 1938.
Bibliography Freeman Champney, *Art and Glory: The Story of Elbert Hubbard*, New York: Crown, 1968. Anne Yaffe Phillips, *From Architecture to Object*, New York: Hirschl and Adler, 1989: 24. Cat., Leslie Greene Bowman, *American Arts and Crafts: Virtue in Design*, Los Angeles: Los Angeles County Museum, Boston: Bulfinch, 1990.

Huber, Patriz (1878–1902)

German architect and interior, furniture, and silver designer; born Stuttgart; active Darmstadt and Berlin.

Training Under his father Anton Huber, Kunstgewerbeschule, Mainz; under painter L. von Langenmantel, in Munich.
Biography Huber became interested in architecture, interior decoration, and design, and, 1899–1902,a member of the Darmstadt artists' colony of Grand Duke Louis IV of Hesse-Darmstadt. 1901–02, he collaborated with Theodor Fahrner, who made Huber's jewelry designs in a workshop in Pforzheim. 1902, Huber set up his own studio. Martin Mayer in Mainz was the primary producer of thousands of pieces of Huber's silver designs. Huber's simple geometrical ornamentation with angular spirals influenced Munich court silversmith Carl Weishaupt, who borrowed Huber's designs. Huber committed suicide in Berlin.
Exhibitions Installations by Huber in Glückert and Habich houses, including his furniture, umbrella handles, stoppers, and boxes, all at Darmstadt artists' colony in 1901. 1903 commemorative exhibition of his work shown in Darmstadt.
Bibliography Charlotte Gere, *American and European Jewelry 1830–1914*, New York: Crown, 1975. Annelies Krekel-Aalberse, *Art Nouveau and Art Déco Silver*, New York: Abrams, 1989. Deanna F. Cera (ed.), *Jewels of Fantasy: Costume Jewelry of the 20th Century*, New York: Abrams, 1992. Cat., *Patriz Huber, Ein glied der Darmstädter Künstlerkolonie*, Darmstadt: Museum Künstlerkolonie, 1992.

Hucker, Thomas (1955–)

American furniture designer.

Training 1973, under Daniel Jackson, and, 1974–76, under Leonoro Hllgner, both in Philadelphia, Pa.; 1976–80 under Jere Osgood, Program in Artisanry, Boston (Mass.) University; 1989, industrial design, Domus Academy, Milan.
Biography 1982, Hucker was an artist-in-residence in the architecture department, Tokyo National University of Fine Arts and Music, and set up his own design studio for one-off production of furniture and lighting. Clients included Dansk (1986–90 table-top designs and crystal stemware) and Bernini (1990 wooden furniture). Designed a 1991 furniture range by Palazzetti.
Exhibitions Work shown in 1989 *New American Furniture*, touring the US; 2004 *Academy Timbers: Furniture by Kalle Fauset and Thomas Hucker* (furniture produced from the original 1856 timbers of the Philadelphia Academy of Music), Wexler Gallery, Philadelphia, Pa.; 2004 *The Maker's Hand: American Studio Furniture, 1940–1990*, Museum of Fine Arts, Boston.
Bibliography Peter D. Slatin, *Thomas Hucker*, New York: Peter Joseph Gallery, John Kelsey and Rick Mastelli (ed.), *Furniture Studio: The Heart of the Functional Arts*, The Furniture Society, 1999.

Hukin & Heath: Christopher Dresser. Covered soup tureen and ladle. 1880. Electroplated silver with wooden handles and knob, tureen h. 6 3/8 x rim dia. 9 1/4" (16.2 x 23.5 cm), lid dia. 9" (22.9 cm), ladle l. 12 3/4" (32.4 cm). Mfr.: Hukin & Heath, UK. Gift of Mrs. John D. Rockefeller 3rd. MoMA.

Huggins, Vera (d. 1975)

British ceramics designer and decorator.

Biography In 1923, she began working as a designer in the painting studios at Doulton, Lambeth, where her work included Royal Doulton ceramc lamp bases; c. 1940–50, produced a small amount of export stoneware.
Exhibitions Huggins showed original signed ceramic pieces at 1935 exhibition, Royal Academy, London. Other work at 1937 *Exposition Internationale des Arts et Techniques dans la Vie Moderne*, Paris; international events in Johannesburg, Sydney, and New York.
Bibliography Cat., *Thirties: British Art and Design Before the War*, London: Arts Council of Great Britain/Hayward Gallery, 1979.

Hugo, François (1899–1981)

French jeweler and metalworker; father of Pierre Hugo.

Biography At an early age, Hugo met and befriended Jean Cocteau, Max Ernst, André Derain, Jean Arp, and Pablo Picasso; developed a process of hammering precious metals in a bronze mold, resulting in an accurate and light reproduction of an original; produced Picasso's first (1956) designs in silver. Other metal works of artists soon followed. Hugo produced Salvador Dalí's well-known 1957 Mollusc cutlery in silver gilt and glass.
Bibliography *Applied Arts by 20th Century Artists*, Christie's Geneva, 1991.

Huguenin, Suzanne

Swiss textile designer, active New York and Mesingen, Switzerland.

Training 1952–55, apprentice/assistant to Eszter Harastzy, who headed Knoll Textiles.
Biography 1955–63, Huguenin succeeded Harastzy as head of Knoll Textiles that produced textiles for the commercial market; developed Nylon Homespun upholstery-fabric range, woven with nylon carpet yarn (previously only available in a filament form with an undesirable glossy appearance); from 1964, was a freelance textile designer in New York and Switzerland.
Bibliography Eric Larrabee and Massimo Vignelli, *Knoll Design*, New York: Abrams, 1981: 93. Cat., Kathryn B. Hiesinger and George H. Marcus III (eds.), *Design Since 1945*, Philadelphia: Philadelphia Museum of Art, 1983.

Hukin & Heath

British crystal and silver firm.

History 1875, Hukin & Heath was founded by J.W. Hukin and J.T. Heath in Birmingham. Christopher Dresser, as a freelance designer closely associated with the firm, created silver pieces for the firm from 1878. A.E. Harvey designed for the firm in 1930s. The parts on some items such as the retaining straps on pepper grinders were sup-plied by Geugeot Frères in France.
Bibliography Annelies Krekel-Aalberse, *Art Nouveau and Art Déco Silver*, New York: Abrams, 1989. Stuart Durant, *Christopher Dresser*, London: Academy; Berlin: Ernst & Sohn, 1993.

Huldt, Johan (1942–)

Swedish designer; born Stockholm.

Training To 1968, Konstfackskolan, Stockholm.
Biography Huldt founded Innovator Design studio; 1974–76, was director, Swedish Furniture Research Institute; from 1983, was chairperson, Svenskainred Ningsarkitekters Riksforbund.
Bibliography Robert A.M. Stern (ed.), *The International Design Yearbook*, New York: Abbeville, 1985/1986.

Hummel, Richard O. (c. 1899–c. 1976)
> See Cowan, R. Guy.

Hunebelle, André (1896–1985)
French designer, producer of glassware, lighting, metalwork, accessories, and film maker; born Meudon.

Training Mathematics, École Polytechnique, Paris.
Biography 1922–39, Hunnebelle was a designer and decorator at 2, avenue Victor-Emmanuel-III, Paris; in addition to bibelots, produced small furniture pieces in glass and metal; 1937–39, was a newspaper administrator; 1941–74, was a film producer and director of c. 15 films, including *Feu sacré* (1941–42), *Leçon de conduite* (1945), *Rendez-vous à Paris* (1946), *Carrefour du crime* (1947), *Métier de fous* (1948), *Millionaire d'un jour* (1949), *Massacre en dentelles* (1951) (winner of the Prix du Meill), *Ma femme est formidable* (1951), *Mon mari est merveilleux* (1953). He was a member, Comité Directeur du Syndicat Français des Production et Exportation des Films.
Bibliography Claude Morava, *L'art moderne dans la verrerie: illustré par quelques œuvres du maître verrier André Hunebelle*, Paris: Hunebelle, 1937. Philippe Décelle, *Opalescence: le verre moule des années 1920–1930*, BrusselsFondation pour l'Architecture, 1986 (reprinted 2000). Carolus Harmann, *Glasmarken Lexikon, Signaturen, Fabrik- und Handelsmarken 1600–1945, Europe and America*, Stuttgart: Arnoldsche, 1997. Victor Arwas, *Glass: Art Nouveau to Art Déco*, London: Academy, 1987.

Hunt, Martin (1942–)
British ceramicist and glass designer.

Training 1960–63, Gloucestershire College of Art; 1963–66, Royal College of Art, London.
Biography In 1966, Hunt and ceramics designer David Queensberry established Queensberry Hunt design group. Hunt worked for Hornsea Pottery, Bing & Grøndahl Porcelænsfabrik, Wedgwood, Rosenthal, Thomas Glass, Watson's Potteries, Doulton, Ravenshead, Judge International, and Pilkington Glass; designed 1977 Concept vitrified-clay dinnerware (with Colin Rawson) by Hornsea Pottery and Tournée porcelain range by Thomas; 1976–86, was head of the department of glass, Royal College of Art; from 1998–99, was visiting professor, Ceramics and Glass, School of Applied Art, Royal College of Art; and teaches at other institutions. Continues to be active in Queensberry Hunt Design Consultancy, which remains in touch with new lifestyle trends and eating habits.
Citations Four awards, Design Council (including one jointly with James Kirkwood for ceramic lamps and three for Hornsea Pottery dinnerware sets; and for Concept dinnerware); 1981, elected Honorary Royal Designer for Industry, UK.
Bibliography Fiona MacCarthy and Patrick Nuttgens, *An Eye for Industry*, London: Lund Humphries, 1986. Jeremy Myerson and Sylvia Katz, *Conran Design Guides: Tableware*, London: Conran Octopus, 1990: 33, 75.

Hunter, Alec (1899–1958)
British textile designer and weaver; son of Edmund Hunter.

Training Drawing and design, Byam Shaw School of Art, London.
Biography Hunter's father, Edmund Hunter, was the owner of St. Edmundsbury Weaving Works in Haslemere and, subsequently, of a hand-weaving mill in Letchworth, which produced fine dress and furnishing fabrics for domestic and ecclesiastical use. Alec became a partner. 1928, the firm was bought by Morton Sundour Fabrics and became the basis for the establishment of Edinburgh Weavers in Carlisle. Alec Hunter settled in Carlisle; oversaw Edinburgh Weavers' production prior to Alastair Morton's direction; 1932–58, became production manager at both Edinburgh Weavers and Warner and Sons in Braintree, where he and Theo Moorman controlled the style and design of its production; was an advisor to freelance designers on cloth construction and yarns, and fostered experimentation with power-loom production.
Bibliography Cat., *Thirties: British Art and Design Before the War*, London: Arts Council of Great Britain/Hayward Gallery, 1979.

Hunter, Edmund (1866–1937)
British fabric designer; father of Alec Hunter.

Training Silver Studio, London.
Biography 1902, Hunter founded the St. Edmundsbury Weavers in Surrey, which produced mostly handloom-woven plain and figured silks incorporating gold and other metal threads; 1908, moved to Letchworth and began using power looms. Subsequently, production included silk scarves and dress fabrics for Liberty's and linings for Burberry's clothing.
Exhibitions 1912 venue of Arts and Crafts Exhibition Society.

Hunter, Eileen (aka Laura Hunter)
British textile designer and writer; daughter of Edward Hunter.

Biography Her father Edward Hunter was the founder and chairperson of, among others, Sun Engraving, process engravers and block printers. 1933–39, Eileen Hunter was active in her own firm, Eileen Hunter Fabrics, in Grafton Street and on Bond Street, both London, where she designed fabrics that were block printed by Warner and Sons in Braintree; had offices in Paris, New York, Canada, and the Netherlands; disliked the popular pallid, washed-out colors in the textile patterns of the 1930s; wrote numerous articles on design and textiles for publications, including *Vogue* and *Decoration*; under the *nom-de-plume* of Laura Hunter, wrote books, including *Vanished with the Rose* (London: Hutchinson, 1964), *The Profound Attachment* (London: Deutsch, 1969), *Christabel, the Russell Case* (London: Deutsch, 1973), and *Tales of Waybeyond* (London: Deutsch, 1979).
Exhibitions Hunter participated in most of the major decorative arts exhibitions of her time including 1935 *British Art in Industry*, Royal Academy, London; 1937 *Exposition Internationale des Arts et Techniques dans la Vie Moderne*, Paris; 1934 *Children's Exhibition* (modern nursery), Chesterfield House, London.
Bibliography Cat., *Thirties: British Art and Design Before the War*, London: Arts Council of Great Britain/Hayward Gallery, 1979.

Hunter, Ross
> See Kirkpatrick, Janice.

Hunzinger, George (1835–1898)
American furniture maker; born Germany; active Brooklyn, N.Y.

Training In cabinetmaking, family business, Germany.
Biography Hunzinger was born in Germany to a family of cabinet makers who had been active since 17th century; 1855, emigrated to New York (much like other German cabinet makers including the Herter borthers); was spurred on by the new technology and inventions in America. He became a prolific inventor and a leader in 'patent furniture' and received 21 patents for furniture inventions, from 1860 until his 1898 death, including extension, swivel top, and nesting tables; reclining and folding chairs, convertible beds, platform rockers, a woven seat in a fabric-covered steel wire. Unlike his contemporaries, Hunzinger was more involved with engineering than style; received an early patent for a side chair with a diagonal brace that formed the front leg; later and similarly, 1873 folding chair with a cantilevered seat. Like Michael Thonet, he had a modern interest in sales/marketing and widely distributed catalogs and, somewhat like Thomas Chippendale, offered the same piece with a choice of woods, finishes, and upholstery. His work presaged the spare, abstract designs of America's 20th-century machine aesthetic.
Bibliography Doreen Bolger Burke et al., *In Pursuit of Beauty: Americans and the Aesthetic Movement*, New York: The Metropolitan Museum of Art/Rizzoli, 1986: 479. Barry R. Harwood, *The Furniture of George Hunzinger: Invention and Innovation in Nineteenth Century America*, New York: Brooklyn Museum, 1997.

Hürlimann, Heinrich Otto (1900–1964)
Swiss textile designer; born Wald.

Training 1924–26, weaving, Bauhaus, Weimar.
Biography Hürlimann was active in Herrliberg, Switzerland, as a coworker of Johannes Itten. With colleague Gertrud Dirks-Preiswerk and former Bauhaus teacher Gunta Stölzl, Hürlimann founded the firm SPH to produce furniture, textiles, and carpets. The firm was renamed S+H Stoffe when Dirks-Preiswerk left. 1937, Hürlimann left the company; 1926–62, taught textile design, Kunstgewerbeschule, Zürich.
Bibliography Friederike Mehlau-Wiebking et al., *Schweizer Typenmöbel 1925–35, Sigfried Giedion und die Wohnbedarf AG*, Zürich: gta, 1989: 229.

Husson, Henri (1852–1914)
French designer, born Les Vosges; active Paris.

Biography Husson experimented with silver and gold incrustations that produced painterly effects. c. 1900, his work was discovered and sold by gallery owner H. Heibrand. From 1902, Husson realized great success through his designs of vases, boxes, and jewelry that incorporated plant and animal ornamentation.

Richard Hutten. Table/lamp. c. 1999. Oak, steel, and fabric, h. 43 1/4 x w. 19 5/8 x l. 19 5/8" (110 x 50 x 50 cm). Mfr.: REEEL, the Netherlands.

Bibliography Annelies Krekel-Aalberse, *Art Nouveau and Art Déco Silver*, New York: Abrams, 1989.

Husson, Thierry (1951–)

French furniture and environmental designer.

Biography 1986, Husson began collaborating with Fabienne Arietti in Paris. They designed 1986 Babylone chair and Arbélette triangular small folding table, sponsored by VIA (French furniture association) and produced by their own Édition AH!. A suite of Babylone furniture was installed in the 1987 office of Jack Lang, the French Ministère de la Culture at the time, and in the Assemblée Nationale.
Exhibitions/citations Work shown at 1987 Salon du Meuble, Paris, receiving the young creator's prize for contemporary furniture. Work received 1987, 1989, 1990, 1991 VIA production-aid support.
> See Arietti, Fabienne.

Hutten, Richard (1967–)

Dutch designer; born Zwollerkerspel.

Training To 1991, Akademie voor Industriële Vormgeving, Eindhoven.
Biography 1991, Hutten established a design studio in Rotterdam and worked on a number of furniture and design projects for products, interiors, and exhibitions; c. 1992, developed his 'No sign of design' and 'Table upon table' concepts; from 1993, was a member of Droog Design, an ad hoc Dutch 'group.' Some Hutten furniture was installed in the Philippe Starck-designed interiors of the Delano Hotel in Miami and Mondrian Hotel in Los Angeles. Clients have included H.R.H. Queen Beatrix, Centraal Museum in Utrecht, E&Y Tokyo, Englender, Donna Karan, Harvink, Hidden, Idée, Karl Lagerfeld, KPN Telecom, Maxfield, Moss, Planet, Pure Design, REEEL (outlet for Droog Design), Sawaya & Moroni, and SMAK. His work by Droog Design—such as 1991 Table-chair, 1997 Bronto child's chair, and 1994 The Cross table/benches—helped him to achieve some international prominence. Other work has included the design of Centraal Museum Bookshop, De Refter cafeteria of the Centraal Museum, and Thonik Studio; 1996–98, taught product design, Academy Beeldende Kunsten, Maastricht.
Exhibitions Work shown worldwide in numerous venues, including 1996 *Contemporary Design from the Netherlands* (1994 stool and couch prototypes), The Museum of Modern Art, New York.
Bibliography Alessandro Mendini (ed.), *The International Design Yearbook*, New York: Abbeville, 1996. 'Richard Hutten,' *Axis*, no. 78, March–April 1999: 2. www.richardhutten.com.

Hutton, John

New Zealand glassware designer; active Britain.

Biography After World War II, Hutton became one of the most accomplished engravers and etchers of contemporary glass; 1960s, was hired by Whitefriars Glass; designed a series of vases with acid-etched motifs taken from his own designs for the west window of Coventry Cathedral. Hutton was associated with Laurence Whistler, another reviver of stipple engraving, whose forms Whitefriars produced to his specifications.
Bibliography Frederick Cooke, *Glass: Twentieth-Century Design*, New York: Dutton, 1986: 75.

Hutton, John (1947–)

American furniture, fabric, and wallpaper designer; born Massachusetts

Training In New York and San Francisco.
Biography 1978, Hutton succeeded Angelo Donghia as the design director of Donghia Furniture and Textiles in New York. Hutton works in a quasi-modern style, much like Donghia, with a traditional flavor loosely likened to 1980s French designs and reminiscent of 1950s curvaceous forms; created designs for furnishings, fabrics, wallpaper, and furniture, including 1988 San Marco sofa and 1988 Luciano club chair by Donghia. c. 2000, Hutton left the Donghia firm; legal difficulties ensued as a result, and he nevertheless established his own offices in New York, the Netherlands, and France, with clients such as Bench, Flexform (2001 furniture collection), Sutherland, Holly Hunt, HBF. His body of work includes more than 200 design pieces, in addition to public and residential interiors.
Exhibition First one-person show, Galerie VIA, Paris.
Bibliography *Metropolitan Home*, Apr. 1990: 80. Arlene Hirst, 'World Class at Last,' *Metropolitan Home*, Nov. 1990: 102. Albrecht Bangert and Karl Michael Armer, *80s Style: Designs of the Decade*, New York: Abbeville, 1990.

Hutton and Sons, William

British silversmiths.

History 1800, William Hutton and Sons was founded in Sheffield; sold some of its wares through various retail vendors in London, including the Goldsmiths' and Silversmiths' Company. From 1901, Kate Harris designed Art Nouveau silver for the firm, whose inventory also included clocks, paperweights with leather, and other wares in the first decade of the 20th century, reminiscent of Liberty's wares. Was active to at least World War II.
Bibliography Annelies Krekel-Aalberse, *Art Nouveau and Art Déco Silver*, New York: Abrams, 1989.

Huxtable, L. Garth (1911–1989)

American industrial designer; husband of architecture critic Ada Louise Huxtable; active New York.

Training To 1933, Massachusetts College of Art, Boston, Mass.
Biography Mid-1930s, Huxtable was active as an industrial designer; for over 20 years to 1970, designed a number of domestic hand tools by Miller Falls Company, with Leonard C. Pratt, its vice-president for developmental engineering. (1962, Miller Falls was purchased by Ingersoll-Rand.) Huxtable's Miller Falls work included a 1969 power-tools series. He was part of a team that designed table and serving ware for Restaurant Associates' La Fond del Sol restaurant (head designer, Alexander Girard) in New York. Huxtable also designed Restaurant Associates' Newarker coffee shop and restaurant in Newark, N. J. In New York: restaurants in the Plaza Hotel, The Metropolitan Opera in Lincoln Center, and Tower Sky Lobbies restaurant (not realized) in The World Trade Center. 1958, he was commissioned by architect Philip Johnson to design glassware and silver serving pieces, designed with his wife Ada Louise Huxtable (1921–), for 1960 The Four Seasons restaurant in the Seagram Building on Park Avenue, New York. His archive is housed in American Heritage Center, University of Wyoming, Laramie, and some papers in San Francisco Airport museum.

L. Garth Huxtable and Ada Louise Huxtable (1921–). Serving dish. 1958. Silver-soldered metal, h. 1 3/4 x dia. 4 3/4" (4.5 x 12 cm). Mfr.: International Silver Company, US. Gift of The Four Seasons, Inc. MoMA.

Hvidt, Christian (1946–)

Danish industrial designer.

Training 1966, in toolmaking; to 1971, in mechanical engineering with product development, Danmarks Tekniske Højskole, Copenhagen.
Biography 1980, Hvidt established his own design firm; 1980–91, was a board member, Danish Association of Furniture Designers and Interior Architects (MMI), of which he was chairperson 1985–89. Work has included furniture and furniture systems by Fritz Hansen and Søborg Møbelfabrik, street lamps and bollards by Jakobsson, street furniture in concrete by Unicon Beton, and housewares by Bodum.
Citations 1984 award, Le Klint Foundation; 1981, 1982, and 1984 awards, Industrie Forum Design (iF), Hanover.

Hvidt, Flemming (1944–)

Danish furniture designer.

Training To 1970, Kunsthåndværskerskolen, Copenhagen.
Biography From 1973, Hvidt collaborated with Jørgen Bo, Peter Hvidt, and Orla Mølgård-Nielsen; 1974–78, was a consultant, Teknologisk Institut, Tastrup.
Exhibitions From 1966, prizes in furniture and industrial design competitions, including 1979 Danish Furniture Prize, Association of Danish Furniture Industries.
Bibliography Frederik Sieck, *Nutidig Dansk Møbeldesign – en kortfattet illustreret beskrivelse*, Copenhagen: Bondo, 1981, 1990.

Hvidt, Peter (1916–1986)

Danish architect and cabinetmaker.

Training To 1940, architecture and cabinetmaking, Kunsthåndværkerskolen, Copenhagen.
Biography 1942, Hvidt opened an office where various designers worked, including Orla Mølgård-Nielsen 1944–75, Hans Kristensen from 1970, and British designer Adrian Heath. Clients included Fritz Hansen, France & Søn, Allerød, Møbelexport, and Søborg Møbelfabrik. 1942–45, he taught, Kunsthåndværkerskolen; designed 1944 Portex chair, one of the first Danish stacking chairs—but much of his 1940s output was traditional. 1950 AX range of chairs and tables (with Mølgård-Nielsen) by Fritz Hansen marked the introduction of the laminate-glueing process (originally used in tennis-racket manufacture) in furniture making. The design encouraged a new interest in Danish furniture by others and became the first Danish chair with a seat and back (removable and packaged separately) made of double-curved laminated wood (inspired by the innovations of Charles and Ray Eames in the US). Hvidt also pioneered knock-down furniture.
Exhibitions/citations Work with Mølgård-Nielsen at 1956–57 *Neue Form aus Dänemark*, touring Germany; 1958 *Formes Scandinaves*, Musée des Arts Décoratifs, Paris. Diplomas of honor (with Mølgård-Nielsen) at 1951 (9th) and 1954 (10th) editions of Triennale di Milano. AX chair in 1951 *Good Design* exhibition/awards, The Museum of Modern Art, New York, and Chicago Merchandise Mart; 1966 *Vijftig jaar Zitten*, Stedelijk Museum, Amsterdam; 1970 *Modern Chairs 1918–1970*, White-chapel Gallery, London; 1980 *Scandinavian Modern Design 1880–1980*, Cooper-Hewitt National Design Museum, New York; 1983–84 exhibition, Philadelphia (catalogs below).
Bibliography Esbjørn Hiort, *Danish Furniture*, New York: Architectural Book, 1956. Erik Zahle (ed.), *A Treasury of Scandinavian Design*, New York: Golden Press, 196. *Mobilia*, July 1960: 21. Cat., *Modern Chairs 1918–1970*, London: Lund Humphries, 1971. Frederik Sieck, *Nutidig Dansk Møbeldesign – en kortfattet illustreret beskrivelse*, Copenhagen: Bondo Gravesen, 1981, 1990. Cat., David Revere McFadden (ed.), *Scandinavian Modern Design 1880–1980*, New York: Abrams, 1982. Cat., Kathryn B. Hiesinger and George H. Marcus III (eds.), *Design Since 1945*, Philadelphia: Philadelphia Museum of Art, 1983.

Hvorslev, Theresia (1935–)

Swedish silver designer.

Training 1956–58, Staatliche Höhere Fachschule für das Edelmetallgewerbe, Schwäbisch-Gmünd; 1960, Konstfackskolan, Stockholm.
Biography 1960–64, Hvorslev trained as a silversmith at Georg Jensen Sølvsmedie and Bernadotte & Björn, both in Copenhagen; designed silver hollow-ware, tableware, cutlery, and jewelry.
Exhibitions/citations From 1964, work in numerous exhibitions worldwide. Several international design awards, including 1967, 1971, and 1974 Diamonds International Award, DeBeers.
Bibliography *Svenskt Silver Inför Åttiotalet*, Stockholm, 1979. Cat., *Georg Jensen Silversmithy: 77 Artists, 75 Years*, Washington: Smithsonian, 1980.

Hydman-Vallien, Ulrica (1938–)

Swedish glassware designer and ceramicist; born and active Stockholm.

Training 1958–61, Konstfackskolan, Stockholm.
Biography 1963, Hydman-Vallien set up her own workshop in Åfors; from 1972 to the present, designed for Kosta Boda glassworks; is best known for her vividly colored ceramic sculpture; from 1979, worked for Rörstrand glassworks; 1981–88, taught, Pilchuck Glass Center, Standwood, Wash., US; ; has also designed printed textiles and carpets by Kinnasand; has introduced myth into her work, thus creating a classical Scandinavia spirit, and also been active as a ceramicist and fine artist, including 1995–96 lithograph series of 35 prints called *Karlekens Labyrint* (labyrinth of love).
Exhibitions Work shown in New York, Tokyo, London, Paris, Tel Aviv, and Stockholm; 1975 *Adventures in Swedish Glass*, Australia; numerous others worldwide.
Bibliography Cat., David Revere McFadden (ed.), *Scandinavian Modern Design 1880–1980*, New York: Abrams, 1982. Jennifer Hawkins Opie, *Scandinavia: Ceramics and Glass in the Twentieth* Century, New York: Rizzoli, 1989.

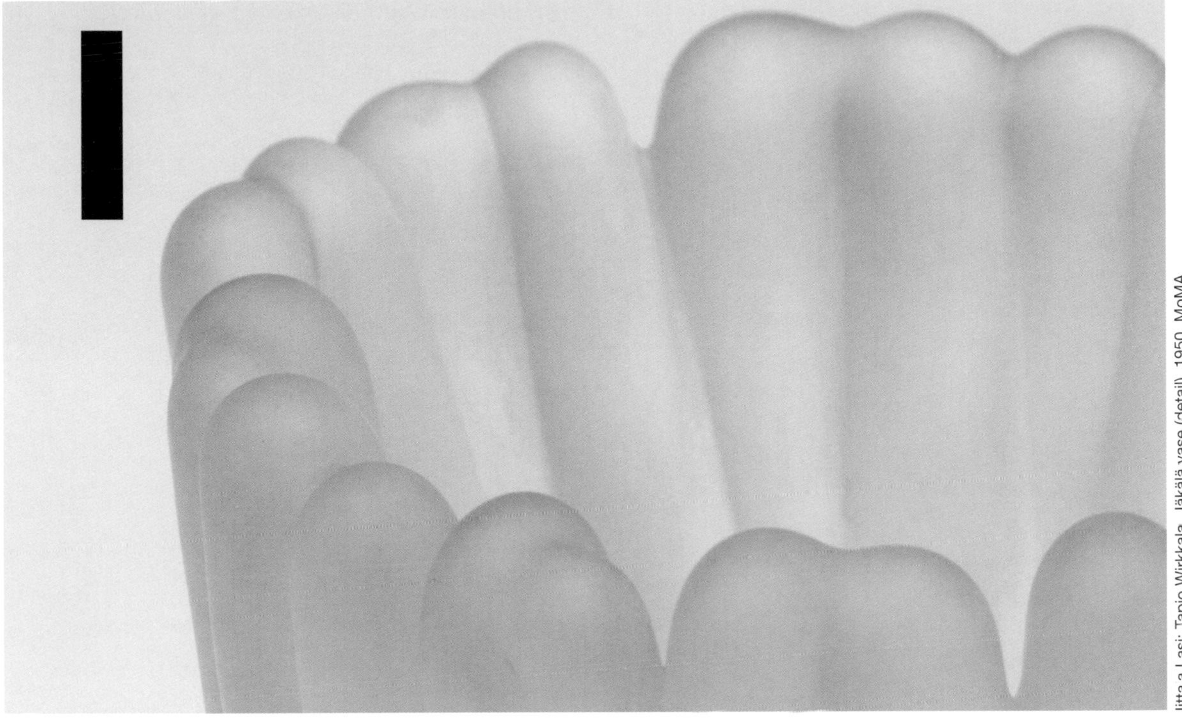

Iitta a Lasi: Tapio Wirkkala. Jäkälä vase (detail). 1950. MoMA.

Iakulov Georgii Bogdanovich (1884–1928)
> See Yakulov, Georgii Bogdanovich.

Ibens, Paul (1939–); Claire Bataille (1940–)
Belgian designers.

Training Both to 1961, interior design, Nationaal Instituut voor Bouwkunst en Stedebouw. Bataille: to 1962, Hoger Kunstonderwijs. Both Antwerp.
Biography 1968, Ibens and Bataille began working together and established Claire Bataille & Paul ibens Design (with a small 'i' in 'ibens') in Antwerp. The partners have designed a large number of domestic and office interiors and those of restaurants, stores, and showrooms and have become known for their pure, reductivist, and neutrally colored spaces. Their furniture, lighting, and glass has included 1988 78+ prefabricated construction system, 1995 chair by Elbe, 1994 H2O office furniture by Bulo, 1996 Palladio crystal-glass set by Val Saint Lambert, 1996 Table Y and stool by Obumex, 1997 Clair Obscur sofas by Durlet, 1998 Ag+ cutlery by Wiskemann, 1998 Shadow light fixture by Light, and 1998 Table 95+ by Hennie De Jong, 1998 bench and table by Apart, 2002 lazy susan and plate by When Objects Work, and furniture to customers' specifications. 1996, ibens & Bataille bvba was established for the exclusive production of Ibens-and-Bataille-designed furniture and objects. Interior-architecture work: a number of boutiques from 1973 and clean, austere domestic and public interiors, including 1974 Courthout house (architect, Lieven Langohr) in Schilde, 1995 Apartment K on the Belgian seaside, 1998 Groenhoven in Malderen, 1998 Van Hoecke offices (civil engineer, Julien Wymeersch) in St.-Niklaas, and 2000 House P in Brussels. Architecture with others from 1971: Convent of Sisters of the Holy Family (with R. Pluys), Sint Job, 't Goor; and shops from 1980 Delbeke apartments/shops, Antwerp.
Citations In a number of exhibitions/fairs from 1982 Intérieur biennial, Courtrai. Work subject of 2003 exhibition, Design Museum, Ghent. Received award, 1963 (2nd) *Daily Mirror* International Furniture Competition; 1980 Sigle d'Or, Design Centre, Brussels; 1997 Trophy for Galvanization, Progalva Benelux; 2001 Editors' Award, International Contemporary Furniture Fair (ICFF), New York; 2001 Henry Van de Velde Prize (for professional career), Vizo, Brussels.
Bibliography Cynthia Inions, *One Space Living*, New York: Watson-Guptill, 1999. Paco Asensio et al., *Minimalist Interiors*, New York: Watson-Guptill, 2000. Catherine Slessor and A.E.J. Morris, *See-Through Houses: Inspirational Homes and Features in Glass*, London: Ryland Peters & Small; 2002. Koen Van Synghel et al., *Claire Bataille, Paul ibens: projecten et objeten = projects et objects 1968–2002*, Gent: Ludion, 2003.

IBM
American computer manufacturer.

History 1914, Thomas J. Watson Sr. (Campbell, N.Y., 1874–1956) joined Computing-Tabulating-Recording Co. (CTR, incorporated in 1911) as the general manager; 1915, became president. The firm produced scales and time clocks and gradually added other products; 1924, changed its name to International Business Machines (IBM). Watson the elder was renowned for his encouragement of aggressive salesmanship. Thomas J. Watson Jr. (Dayton, Ohio, 1914–Greenwich, Conn., 1993), who recognizing the value of good design, joined the firm in 1937 and became the president in 1952 and chairperson in 1956. Watson the younger hired Eliot Noyes as the head design consultant to serve 1956–77. Noyes had earlier become associated with the firm while he was designing one of its first typewriters in the office of Norman Bel Geddes in New York. Noyes commissioned the foremost architects of the day to design IBM's buildings, including Ludwig Mies van der Rohe, Edward Larrabee Barnes, Marcel Breuer, and Eero Saarinen. Charles Eames created the company's public presentations, including a number of international exhibitions and films. Noyes also hired Paul Rand to design the graphics. Noyes designed 1959 Executive and 1961 Selectric electric typewriters and 1961 Executary dictating machine. After Noyes's 1977 death, German designer Richard Sapper became its industrial-design consultant in 1980. Its first personal computer (PC), introduced in 1981, marked a major milestone in computing and led to the growth of the PC-compatible market, with the creation of companies such as Compaq, Dell, and 3Com, and a major boost to the fortunes of Microsoft, Novell, and Borland. By 1980s, the design program was managed within IBM's corporate communications department in Stamford, Conn. Late 1980s, Edward Tufte became a consultant on interface graphics and published the book *The Visual Display of Quantitative Information* (Cheshire, Conn.: Graphics Press, 1987, 2nd ed. 2001) and six others. Richard Sapper and Sam Lucente designed the 1989 Leapfrog laptop computer. More recent products, through the IBM Japan Design Center, include 2000 NetVista X40 flat-panel PC (by Kazuhiko Yamazaki, Hisashi Shima, Bob Steinbugler, Bob Tennant, Ron A. Smith, John Karidas, Richard Sapper), WatchPad (Yamazaki, Nariaki Mieki, Shima, Shigeru Yoshida), XD-400 DVD ROM drive (Yamazaki), ThinkPad X30 and Trans-Note (Shima, Yamazaki, David Hill, Sapper, others), Butterfly monitor (Yamazaki and Kazuo Nakada). Sapper designed the 1992 ThinkPad 700 (and other permutations, with others, a version used on the International Space Station) and 2000 NetVista X40 cases. Purportedly, the ThinkPad form was inspired by the *shoukadou bentou* (black *bento*, or Japanese lunch box). Engineer John Karidis designed the ThinkPad 701C keyboard.

IBM: Richard Sapper and Sam Lucente (1958–). Leapfrog portable computer. 1989. Carbon-fiber reinforced plastic, magnesium-alloy, ABS polymer, and other materials, closed 1 1/2 x 10 5/8 x 13 3/4" (3.8 x 27 x 35 cm). Mfr.: IBM, US (1993). Gift of the mfr. MoMA.

By 2002, IBM had sold 15 million ThinkPads.
Citations 2001 Red Dot Best of the Best (ThinkPad and TransNote), 2001 (WatchPad) and 2003 (ThinkPad X30) Red Dot awards, Design Zentrum Nordrhein Westfalen, Essen; 2001 (NetVista X40) and 2002 (NetVista X41), Industrie Forum Design (iF), Hanover; 2001 and 2002 (NetVista X40 and X41) Best Product Designs of the Year, Industrial Designers Society of America (IDSA); Design of the Decade (1990s) bronze citation (ThinkPad), IDSA/*Business Week* magazine; large number of other citations.
Bibliography Buck Rodgers, *The IBM Way: Insights into the World's Most Successful Marketing Organization*, New York: Harper, 1987. Thomas J. Watson and Peter Petre, *Father Son & Co.: My Life at IBM and Beyond*, New York: Bantam, 1990. John Drexel (ed.), *The Facts on File Encyclopedia of the 20th Century*, New York: Facts on File, 1991: 458. Peter Dormer (intro.), *The Illustrated Dictionary of 20th-Century Designers: The Key Personalities in Design and the Applied Arts*, New York: Mallard, 1991.

Ibuka, Masaru (1908–1997)
> See Sony.

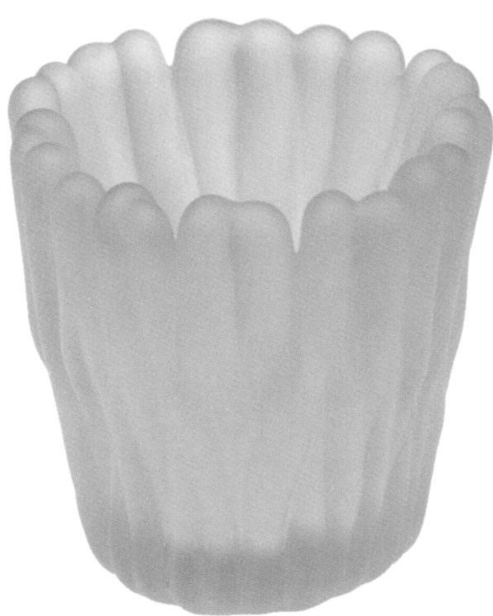

Iittala Lasi: Tapio Wirkkala. Jäkälä vase. 1950. Crystal, h. x dia. 3 1/2" (8.9 cm). Mfr.: Iittala Lasi, Finland. Gift of the Finnish Ministry of Com-merce and Industry. MoMA.

ICF (International Contract Furnishings)
American furniture company.

History 1962, Sam Friedman founded ICF in New York to sell in the US furniture by Artek (Alvar Aalto's firm in Finland). ICF also became known for introducing other modern European design to US stores or outlets, including the reproductions or new designs of Josef Hoffmann, Mario Botta, Philippe Starck, and Richard Neutra. While still importing goods today, the conglomerate also makes and finishes some examples in the US; has expanded its range to include Unika Vaev textiles, Nienkämper, and Helikon.
Bibliography www.icfgroup.com.
> See Unika Vaev.

ICSID
International professional organization; located Paris.

History 1957, International Council of Societies of Industrial Designers (ICSID) was founded in Paris; cooperates with UNESCO; brings together designers worldwide and is associated with more than 50 design societies from 40 countries; is involved with professional practice standards, the promotion of design in developing countries, design education, and design-related terminology; holds conferences biannually.

ID Two
American industrial design studio.

History 1979, ID Two was established in Palo Alto, Cal., as an American branch of Design Developments, a London industrial design firm headed by Bill Moggeridge. Clients included Conversion Technologies and Decision Data. The studio designed 1981–82 Compass computer (a high-density unit in a magnesium case produced by Grid Systems, one of the first portable computers, and a project coordinated by Stephen Hobson). Hobson was a principal in the firm, which eventually became IDEO with offices worldwide.
Exhibitions Compass computer shown at 1983–84 *Design Since 1945* exhibition, Philadelphia Museum of Art (catalog below).
Bibliography Cat., Kathryn B. Hiesinger and George H. Marcus III (eds.), *Design Since 1945*, Philadelphia: Philadelphia Museum of Art, 1983. *Central to Design, Central to Industry*, London: Central School of Art and Design, 1983: 95–96. 'The Compass Computer: The Design Challenges Behind the Innovation,' *Innovation*, Winter 1983: 4–8. Mel Byars with Arlette Barré-Despond, *100 Designs/100 Years: A Celebration of the 20th Century*, Hove: RotoVision, 1999.
> See IDEO.

Idée
Japanese furniture manufacturer; located Tokyo.

History 1984, Tentuo Kurosaki established Idée; produced furniture by Philippe Starck, Marie-Christine Dorner, Shiro Kuramata, and others; introduced the first designs of Marc Newson. Today, Idée is a shop that sells its own goods and those produced by others, and sponsors an annual design competition.

Ie, Kho Liang
> See Liang Ie, Kho.

IDEO
American industrial-design studio.

History The studio grew out of ID Two industrial-design studio in London and has became a large operation with offices worldwide. 1991, it was founded by British émigrés Bill Moggeridge and Mike Nuttall and American engineer David Kelley. Before then, Moggeridge had become known for the first laptop computer (1981–82 Compass by Grid Systems, with others), Nuttall for products by his own studio (Matrix), and Kelley for the first in-production mouse (1982, by Apple). They set out to change industry's mindsets about design by building models within real settings. The five-studio complex in Palo Alto, Cal., houses electronics laboratories and model-making facilities and a staff comprised of designers, engineers, anthropologists, and researchers. Its more than 200 clients include BMW, Nike, Pepsi, Steelcase, Canon, and GM/Hughes. In additon to California, there have been eight other IDEO studios on three continents.
Citations Two silver Design of the Decade (1990s) citations, IDSA/*Business Week* magazine; numerous others.

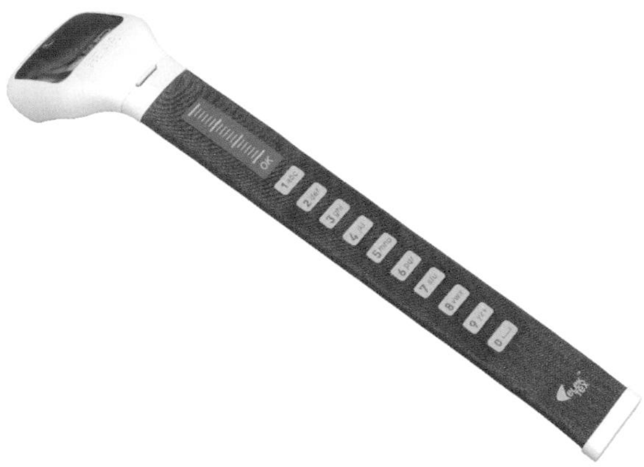

IDEO: Sam Hecht. Watchphone. 2000. Polyurethane rubber with ElekTex laminate and board, 1 1/16 x 1 13/16 x 8 7/16" (1.8 x 4.6 x 21.5 cm). Mfr.: Samsung, Korea. Gift of the mfr. MoMA.

Bibliography Jeremy Myerson, *IDEO: Masters of Design*, New York: teNeues, 2001.
> See Moggeridge, Bill.

Iittala Lasi; Karhula

Finnish glass factory.

History 1881, Iittala Lasi (also known as Iittalan Lasitehdas) was founded by Swedish glass-blower Petter Magnus Abrahamsson and initially staffed by Swedish workers who produced high-quality glassware. 1889, Karhula was founded by William Ruth, originally producing bottles and table glass, including cut and etched lead crystal. 1915, Karhula was bought by A. Ahlström, which, 1917, also bought Iittala to form Karhula-Iittala. After the merger, Iittala continued with mouth-blown tableware, and Karhula with mainly bottles and pressed glass. To 1920, Karhula continued to mouth-blow bottles, with some machinery installed; 1936, introduced automation; 1925, commissioned Eric O.W. Ehrström to design engraved glass. 1930s, Karhula-Iittala sponsored several design competitions (at its 1932 event, the first prize to Aarre Putro and second prize to Aino Aalto; at its 1936–37 event, the first prize to Alvar Aalto). Other award recipients were brought into the fold of commissioned designers. To 1940s, Iittala made traditional glass, primarily drinking glasses; 1947–54, was completely transformed into a design-oriented firm, which garnered international renown. Its mouth-blown- and pressed-glass production was assumed by Karhula. From 1954, Karhula specialized in only container glass, with glass-fiber production 1958–82. After Tapio Wirkkala received the first prize in its 1946 competition, he was appointed the chief designer at Iittala. From 1950, Timo Sarpaneva designed for the firm, including the company's 1955 'i' logo. Other designers included Jorma Vennola. Eventually, Iittala became the largest utility and art-glass producer in Finland. 1987, Nuutajärvi was merged with Iittala to become part of Iittala's Pro Arte department, or Iittala-Nuutajärvi, which also included the acquisitions of Humppila (founded in 1970) and Napapiiri (founded in 1982). 1985, A. Ahlström bought a major share of Riihimäki, and, 1988, Karhula and Riihimäki were combined to form Ahlström Riihimäki Lasi. 1990, Riihimäki was closed, and, 1995, Karhula was sold to Owens-Illinois of the US. 1990, Iittala-Nuutajärvi became part of Hackman Tabletop and, 2002, part of Hackman's newly established Designor division. 2003, Designor was renamed iittala (with an initial lowercase 'i'), as one of Hackman's two divisions; the other is Metos. Nuutajärvi is now a brand sold under the iittala name. Early designs, such as glassware by Aino and Alvar Aalto, continue to be produced. The more recent generation of designers has included Harri Koskinen, Marc Newson, Konstantin Grcic, Annaleena Hakatie (1966–), Nathalie Lahdenmäki (1974–), Kari Uusitalo (1958–).

Bibliography Jennifer Hawkins Opie, *Scandinavia: Ceramics and Glass in the Twentieth Century*, New York: Rizzoli, 1989. Leslie Jackson, *20th Century Factory Glass*, London: Octopus, 2000.

IKEA

Swedish furniture, furnishings, and housewares store chain.

History 1943 at age 17, Ingvar Kamprad (1926–) founded IKEA, which was named for the initials of his name ('IK'), followed by 'E' for the farm Elmtaryd, and 'A' for the village of Agunnaryd in Sweden, where he was born. The business was established on a gift from his father of money to be used for such purposes, as a reward for succeeding at school. Originally, Kamprad resold pens, picture frames, table linen, watches, jewelry, wallets, and nylon stockings that he had bought cheaply. 1945, IKEA published its first advertisements; 1953, opened a furniture showroom; 1955, began commissioning exclusive furniture designs and instituted the flat-packing of knock-down models; 1965, opened a large store in Stockholm; hired Marian Grabinski to design the popular 1963 MIP bookcase/cabinet system and developed relationships with Polish manufacturers. 1973, first IKEA store outside Scandinavia opened in Zürich. 1974, Skopa plastic chair, unorthodox for its time, was developed by Olle Gjerlöv-Knudsen and Torben Lind and produced by a bowl and bucket manufacturer. 1985, the first IKEA store opened in the US. 1997, Children's IKEA was introduced. More recent IKEA designers, such as Thomas Sandell, who designed 1995 PS bench and other furniture, went on to achieve fame. Kamprad became known as 'the self-assembled billionaire' and for being frugal. From 1980, the IKEA Group has been owned by the Netherlands-registered charity Stichting Ingka ('Ingka is for 'INgrar KAmprad) Foundation, which also bought Habitat in 1997 and which is under the private control of Ingvar Kamprad. From 1976, Kamprad and his family have lived in Epalinges, Switzerland.
Exhibitions/citations IKEA's Democratic Design stand at 1995 Salone del Mobile, Milan (creating a stir because the firm had not until then been considered cutting-edge). 1999 *H 99* exhibition, Sweden.

IKEA: Carl Öjerstam. Storvik lounge chair. 2002. Clear-lacquered rattan, 30 3/8 x w. 41 3/8 x l. 51 1/8" (77 x 105 x 130 cm). Mfr. IKEA, Sweden.

1987 Utmärkt Svensk Form prize (excellent Swedish design for 1985 Moment by Niels Gammelgaard); 1999 Red Dot award, Design Zentrum Nordrhein Westfalen, Essen.
Bibliography Martin C. Pedersen, 'Ikea, The Great Interior Equalizer,' *Graphis*, no. 305, Sept.–Oct. 1996: 42–48. Christopher A. Bartlett, 'Ingvar Kamprad and IKEA' in Christopher A. Barlett and Sumantra Ghoshal (ed.), *Managing Across Borders: The Transnational Solution*, Boston: Harvard Business School, 2002 (2nd ed.).

Ikuta, Susumu (1934–)

Japanese ceramicist; born Kyoto; active Chapel Hill, N.C.

Training Late 1950s, ceramics in night classes, New York; from 1973 under Kobei Katoh and his son Takuo Katoh, in traditional ceramics techniques, Japan.
Biography Ikuta worked as a fashion designer in Tokyo; 1958, moved to New York to work for the milliner Lilly Daché; 1973, returned to Japan, where he studied underglaze decoration and potting techniques at Kohbei-Gama; 1978, came back to the US; worked with underglaze blue and white designs initially, later supplemented with underglaze iron and copper oxides combined with overglaze enameling; decorated porcelain forms with Western insect and plant motifs.
Bibliography Frederick Baekeland, 'Modern Japanese Studio Ceramics,' *Orientations*, June 1988: 6–7. Mary Frakes, 'Summery Abundance,' *Elle Decor*, Nov. 1990: 60.

Ilvessalo, Kirsti (1920–)

Finnish textile designer.

Training Taideteollinen korkeakoulu, Helsinki.
Biography From 1950s, Ilvessalo was a designer for Marimekko in Helsinki; was active in rugmaking in the riya technique.
Exhibitions Work shown at 1954–57 *Design in Scandinavia*, touring the US; 1958 *Formes Scandinaves*, Musée des Arts Décoratifs, Paris; 1961 *Finlandia* in Zürich, Amsterdam, and London.
Bibliography Cat., David Revere McFadden (ed.), *Scandinavian Modern Design 1880–1980*, New York: Abrams, 1982.

Illo, Patrik (1973–)

Slovakian designer; born Považská Bystrica.

Training 1992–98, Glass Department, Vysoká Škola Výtvarných Umení (academy of fine arts), Bratislava.
Biography While in secondary school, Illo learned the craft of glass design and production at Rona Crystal factory, Slovakia's largest, in Lednické Rovne and has been the full-time master there; has investigated and pushed the possibilities of traditional hand methods. His simple, minimal, and functional wares account for c. 80% of the factory's production. Illo forms and produces the award trophies in glass for the annual International Film Festival in Bratislava.
Exibitions Work included in 1997 *Talente*, Munich; 1998 *Dialogues*, Copenhagen; *Contemporary Slovak Glass*, London in 1999, and Rome in 2000.

Imans, Pierre

Dutch sculptor and mannequin designer/manufacturer; active Paris.

Biography From before 1900, Imans was active in a mannequin factory in Paris where, by 1920s, his establishment was located at 10, rue de Crussol. He became known for his faultlessly finished imitation human skin in wax and eyes that moved on smiling faces; 1922, developed 'carnesine' or 'carnisine' (a gypsum-gel mixture) to simulate skin; developed a secret formula that was mainly plaster with gelatin; subsequently, produced models in various synthetic materials and wood for placement in store vitrines worldwide and also figures in the images of well-known actresses and politicians. But Imans, called by some 'the patron saint of mannequins,' is probably best known for his molded *papier-mâché*/wax combination figures that set a standard called on by competitors such as Siégel & Stockman, also in Paris. Imans and Siégal were inspired by abstract, Cubist sculpture.
Exhibitions/citations Anatomical *papier-mâché*-wax busts shown at 1900 *Exposition Universelle*, Paris, and other work at Salons of Société des Artistes Décorateurs and editions of Salon d'Automne; 1915 *Panama-Pacific International Exposition*, San Francisco; 1925 *Exposition Internationale des Arts Décoratifs et Industriels Modernes* (in charge of 'street art' and his own pavilion on the pont Alexandre-III), Paris. First prize, 1911 *Esposizone Internazionale dell'Industria e del Lavoro*, Turin.
Bibliography Nicole Parrot, *Mannequins*, Paris: Colona, 1981; London: Academy, 1982.

Indore, Maharaja of (Prince Yeshwant Rao Holkar Bahadur 1908–1956)

Indian patron and ruler of Indore (now Madhya Pradesh).

Training Oxford University.
Biography His full name/title was Major General Maharajahiraja Raj Rajeshwar Sawai Shree Sir Yeshwant Rao Holkar Bahadur, G.C.I.E. He succeeded on 26 Feb. 1926 as the Maharaja of Indore and, from 1930, achieved the full ruling powers of the Mahratta state in central India; was influenced by the Western avant-garde in Paris and a friend and patron of sculptor Brancusi; was introduced to European art during his studies at Oxford University and, 1929, befriended Friedrich Eckart Muthesius, the son of Hermann Muthesius, who founded the Deutscher Werkbund. From 1925, he planned a modern palace, to be known as Manik Bagh (garden of rubies). 1929–33, Muthesius collaborated with Klemens Weigel on the design of the décor, which included the private apartment of the Maharaja, banquet hall, ballroom, music room, and many guest suites. Much of the furniture and lighting was designed by Muthesius, with other furniture by Jacques-Émile Ruhlmann, Le Corbusier and his team, Louis Sognot, Charlotte Alix, and others; with carpets by Ivan Da Silva Bruhns, chandeliers by René Lalique, and silver by Jean Puiforcat. Eileen Gray furnished two Transat chairs (one of which sat beside the Maharaja's metal and mirrored bed by Sognot) and the dramatic Satellite chandelier. There was other tubular furniture by PEL (Practical Equipment Ltd.) of London. The technical equipment, marble flooring, furniture, and lamps were made to Muthesius's designs and specifications in Germany. Three ships filled with furniture, steel doors, and marble sailed from Hamburg for Indore. 1970, the perfectly preserved palace was discovered by journalist-photogapher Robert Descharnes, at which time the heirs of the Maharaja, who had carefully attended to the domicile, were unsuccessful in commissioning Gray to design more furniture for the pool area. Because the privileges of maharajas and thus the Holkar family were abolished in 1971, the family abandoned the palace and household. Manik Bagh (its contents sold in 1980 at a Sotheby's auction in Montecarlo) was in its 1930s heyday much discussed and widely published. But the building today is the headquarters of the Madhya Pradesh Customs and Central Excise Office in Indore.
Bibliography Peter Adam, *Eileen Gray, Architect/Design*, New York: Abrams, 1987: 143, 187–89. Reto Niggl, *Eckart Muthesius 1930: Der Palast des Maharadschas in Indore: Architektur und Interieur = The Maharaja's Palace in Indore: Architecture and Interior Designer*, Stuttgart: Arnoldsche, 1996.
> See Muthesius, Eckhart.

Inflate

British design group; located London.

History 1992, the idea of Inflate, as a design group and a manufactuer, was conceived by Nick Crosbie (1971–), whose assessment project at Central St. Martin's School, London, focused on PVC film and the high-frequency welding of plastic films. 1995, Crosbie founded Inflate with brothers Michael Sodeau (1969–) and Mark Sodeau (1970–). Eventually, Crosbie became the artistic director, and Mark Sodeau the production manager. (1990–93, Crosbie received a bachelor's degree in industrial design, Central St. Martin's School; 1993–95, master's degree in industrial design, Royal College of Art, London. 1989–92, Mark Sodeau received a bachelor's degree in aeronautical engineering, City University, London; Michael Sodeau studied product design at Central St. Martin's School.) 1997, with new staff members and freelance designers such as Michael Marriott, Inflate developed a new range of dip-molded PVC products to complement the original inflatable wares. 1997, Michael Sodeau left the company and was replaced by Paul Croft (1973-). The business was boosted by a contract for a range of architectural-size pneumatic structures for *Swiss Expo 2001*. 1998, a distribution service was developed for Inflate's own products as well as for other wares produced in studios in the UK, such as Eurolounge and Jam. 1999, work included reusuable packaging by Boots (the chemists) and Big M portable architecture for English Heritage. 2000, Inflate designed an accessories line by Pod International and bathroom products by Habitat; designed/produced its first rotationally molded products (2000 Snoozymodular bed and 2000 Sir Stikkle by Crosbie and Paul Crofts) as a move into large-scale furniture and lighting for the retail and contract market. Inflate's first TV commercial (with Brave Films) was produced. 2001, the group designed the Volvo stand

for new concept car in Detroit and Bubble Chair (with Ushida Findlay) for Crayola. Products have continued with, Strip Light pneumatic fixture, Memo pneumatic chair, Towel Wall Grip, and Magnet table (first in a magnetized range). Inflatables range from 1995 egg cup (Sodeau); table light, fruit bowl, UFO, wine rack, ashtray, picture frame, mirror, sugar shaker, and star light (Crosbie) to 1997 FS screen and lounge chair (Crosbie). Dip-molded products range from 1997 Mr & Mrs Prickly, Ripple light, and Chunks of Light (all Crosbie); Digital Grass (Mark Garside), and piggy bank (Steve Bretland) to 1999 Cactooth (Doimo) and 2000 Tonsil, Lozenge, and Soap Lounger (Inflate studio). Inflate sells through retail shops and the internet.
Exhibitions/citations Work included in a number of venues worldwide. 1996 (for table light) and 1999 (for exhibition stand and product) 100% Design/*Blueprint* award; 2000 Laurent Perrier Design Award; 2001 Peugeot Design Award (for Snoozy).
Bibliography Lynda Ralph Knight, 'Challenging the Norm,' *Design Week*, 28 May 1999. 'The Next Big Thing,' *Blueprint*, Feb. 1999. 'Blow Up', *i-D* (London journal), June 1999. 'The Story About Inflate's Journey So Far,' *Graphics Beef*, Jan. 1999. Alexander Payne, *Once Upon a Line: Mark Sodeau*, London: Black Dog, 2000. www.inflate.co.uk.
> See Sodeau, Michael.

Ingrand, Max (1908–1969)
French glass designer.

Training École Nationale Supérieure des Arts Décoratifs; École Nationale Supérieure des Beaux-Arts; both Paris.
Biography Ingrand became involved in glass design, active in France, Europe, and the Americas; designed the illuminated glass fountain in the Rond Point on the avenue des Champs-Élysées, Paris; decorated the residence of President Bourguiba of Tunisia at Skanes. He designed for Saint-Gobain glassworks and for Verre et Lumière. Work included the wavy, thin-walled 1957 Mouchoir (handkerchief) vase by Fontana-Arte and 1953 stained-glass windows in Église de Saint-Pierre de Montmartre, Paris. He was a counsellor, Commerce of Trade; vice-president, Société des Artistes Décorateurs; president, Association Française de l'Éclairage; was appointed Chevalier of the Légion d'Honneur.
Bibliography Patrick Favardin, *Le style 50: un moment de l'art français*, Paris: Sous Le Vent-Vilo, 1987: 74–80.

Inkehans-Arnhem
> See Hans, Inke.

INKhUK (institute of artistic culture)
Russian specialized learning institution; active 1921–24.

History 1920, INKhUK (INstitut KHUdozhestvennoy Kultury) was founded in Moscow under the auspices of IZO NKP (fine-arts department of Narkompros, the people's commissariat for enlightenment, formed 1918). Its members included artists, architects, theoreticians, and art historians who attempted to associate the production of a work of art with its interpretation. The institute was responsible for the theory and methodology of art and education. Kandinsky attempted to organize its research program according to principles he had set out before the 1917 Russian Revolution in his essay 'On the Spiritual in Art.' His approach was counter to the politicized avant-garde, and he also attempted to synthesize three-dimensional representation with other art forms. INKhUK had branches in Petrograd, Vitebsk, and other Soviet cities.
Bibliography Igor Golomstock, *Totalitarian Art in the Soviet Union, The Third Reich, Fascist Italy and the People's Republic of China*, New York: Icon, 1990: 66. S.O. Khan-Magomedov, *Vhutemas: Moscou, 1920–1930*, Paris: Regard, 1990. Cat., *The Great Utopia: The Russian and Soviet Avant-Garde, 1915–1932*, New York: Guggenheim Museum, 1992.

Innocenti, Ferdinado (1891–1966); Lambretta
Italian vehicle entrepreneur; born Brescia region. Scooter.

Biography/history After his education and being fascinated by mechanics, Innocenti joined his family's hardware store; expanded the business to include the purchase and sale of raw steel and iron; 1931, moved to Rome to set up his own company, which was to be financed by a bank that collapsed. He instead turned to selling steel pipe produced by another firm; 1926 with the help of governmental grants, set up his own steel-pipe warehouse in Rome and, 1933, began to manufacture an innovative scaffolding system. Also 1933, the firm, then known as Fratelli Innocenti, moved to the Lambrate (MI); received a number of important contracts and, subsequently, began to make a variety of automobile parts. By 1934, the firm was employing 200 people and others in nine locations in other areas of Italy; mid-1930s, based on prospects of an impending war, began manufacturing bomb casings and aircraft-hanger frames; built a 4 million sq. ft. (400 thousand m²) building that took three years to construct but, nevertheless, was completely destroyed during World War II. 1946, production once more began, and a new plant was built. 1947, Ferdinando's son Luigi joined the firm, after graduating in engineering. Like Enrico Piaggio, Ferdinando recognized the need for personal transportation. Inspired by military motorcycles he had seen in Rome, he entered into discussions with airplane/helicopter engineer Corradino D'Ascanio. They failed to agree on a concept, and D'Ascanio joined Piaggio to work on aircraft design, where he eventually designed Piaggio's 1946 Vespa. Even though some claim that engineer Pierluigi Torre designed the Innocenti scooter (with Ferdinado Innocenti and the firm's general director Guiseppe Lauro), it was probably by engineer Cesare Pallavicino in 1945–46, who had developed progressive Italian fighter airplanes by Caproni, where he worked from 1933. Nevertheless, Innocenti produced the 1947 125cc Lambretta, which was named after Lambrate, the town of the plant's location. It became very successful and a formidable competitor of the Vespa. On Ferdinando's 1966 death, his son Luigi took over direction of the firm. By 1970, scooter sales had appreciably decreased. 1971, the firm stopped manufacturing Lambrettas. 1972, the tools for manufacturing the DL-series scooter were sold to Scooters of India.
Exhibitions First Lambretta shown at 1947 Salon de l'Auto, Paris.
Bibliography Vittorio Tessera, *Innocenti Lambretta*, Vimodrone (MI): G. Nada, 1995. Franco Miroglio, *Lambretta: nascita, ascesa e caduta della grande rivale della 'Vespa,'* Rome: Alpi, 1997.
> See Piaggio.

Inoue Pleats
Japanese fabric company; located Fukui.

History 1943, Inoue Pleats began producing pleated fabrics; from 1953, with the introduction of acetate yarn, used thermoplasticity in pleating process; established Pleeets retail store in Tokyo.
Exhibitions Work included in 1999 *Structure and Surface: Contemporary Japanese Textiles*, New York and St. Louis (catalog below).
Bibliography Cat., Cara McCarty and Matilda McQuaid, *Structure and Surface: Contemporary Japanese Textiles*, New York: Abrams/The Museum of Modern Art, 1999.

Institut d'Esthétique Industrielle
> See Viénot, Jacques.

Inflate: Nick Crosbie. Glass jar. c. 1997. PVC and glass, h. 7 x dia. 4 3/8" (18 x 11 cm). Mfr.: Inflate, UK.

International Silver Company

American silversmiths; located Meriden, Conn.

History 1898, International Silver Company was founded by independent New England silversmiths; between the world wars, produced distinguished sterling and silverplate designs. Some pieces were designed by in-house artists (such as Ernest R. Beck, Edward J. Conroy, Jean G. Theobald, Alfred G. Kintz, Leslie A. Brown, and Frederick W. Stark) and also by leading commissioned industrial designers, architects, and artists (such as Eliel Saarinen, Alfons Bach, Donald Deskey, Paul Lobel, and Lurelle Guild). Guild designed 1934–35 line of silverplate tableware and Saarinen-designed 1933–35 prototype globular tea service (by Wilcox Silverplate Division); however, Saarinen also designed in-product wares. Other International Silver items combined silver with semi-precious stones or new plastics. Some designs were less original, such as the purloined Georg Jensen 1915 Konge (or Acorn) cutlery by Johan Rohde and Blossom pattern. International Silver is today the world's largest manufacturer of silverware.
Bibliography W. Scott Braznell, *American Silver Museum Newsletter*, Meriden, Conn., 1989. Annelies Krekel-Aalberse, *Art Nouveau and Art Déco Silver*, New York: Abrams, 1989.

International Style

Style associated with the architecture of the modern movement.

History 1931, the term International Style was coined by Alfred H. Barr Jr. in connection with Philip Johnson and Henry-Russell Hitchcock's 1932 *Modern Architecture—International Exhibition* (with the ccompanying book *International Style: Architecture Since 1922*) at The Museum of Modern Art, New York, of which Barr was director. Barr saw in the designs of Le Corbusier, Ludwig Mies van der Rohe, J.J.P. Oud, Walter Gropius, and others the first new approach in Western architecture since the 13th century. The name was drawn from the 15th-century international style of painting in Europe. The exhibition introduced the work of Mies van der Rohe to Americans and traveled for seven years around the US, including to such unlikely places as the Sears, Roebuck & Co. store in Chicago and Bullock's Wilshire department store in Los Angeles. Barr wrote the foreword to the catalog and persuaded publicist Edward Bernays to spread news of the event, with front-page coverage in *The New York Times*. American architects included Frank Lloyd Wright, Claus and Daub, Hood and Fouhilhoux, Howe and Lescaze, and Tucker and Howell. Other architects included Alvar Aalto, Josef Albers, Gunnar Asplund, Hans Borkowsky, Marcel Breuer, Brinkman and Van Der Vlugt, Erik Bryggman, Le Corbusier/Pierre Jeanneret, Eixenlohr/Pfennig, Otto Eisler, Joseph Emberton, Figini/Pollini, Brohuslav Fuchs, Walter Gropius, Max Haefeli, Haesler/Völker, Kellermüller/Hofmann, Kocher/Frey, L.H. de Koninck, Josef Kranz, Ludvik Kysela, Labayen/Aizpurua, J.W. Lehr, André Lurçat, Markelius/Ahren, Mendelsohn / Reichel, Theodor Merrill, Ludwig Mies van der Rohe, Richard Neutra, J.J.P. Oud, Lilly Reich, Jan Ruhtenberg, Hans Scharoun, Hans Schmidt, Karl Schneider, Stam/Moser, Steger/Egender, Eskil Sundahl, Lois Welzenbacher, Mamoru Yamada, Nicolaiev/Fissenko, and various government architecture agencies.
Exhibitions Subject of 1992 *International Style Exhibition 15 and MoMA*, Arthur Ross Architecture Gallery, Buell Hall, Columbia University, New York (catalog below).
Bibliography Henry-Russell Hitchcock, *Modern Architecture: Romanticism and Reintegration*, New York: Payson & Clark, 1929. Theo van Doesburg, 'Obnova umjetnost i architekture u Evropi,' *Hrvatska Revija*, 4, 1931, 8: 419–32. Alfred H. Barr, Jr. (foreword), *Modern Architecture: International Exhibition*, New York: Museum of Modern Art, 1932. Henry-Russell Hitchcock, 'The International Style Twenty Years After,' *Architectural Record*, 1951. *Alfred H. Barr, Jr.: A Memorial Tri-bute*, New York: Museum of Modern Art, 1981. Richard Power (ed.), 'Revising Modernist History,' *Art Journal*, Summer 1983 (special issue). Alice Goldfarb Marquis, *Alfred H. Barr, Jr., Missionary for the Modern*, Chicago: Contemporary Books, 1989. Cat., *The International Style: Exhibition 15 and The Museum of Modern Art*, New York: Rizzoli/cba, 1992.

International Tile and Trim

American ceramics manufacturer.

History 1882, John Ivory founded International Tile and Trim at 92 Third Street, Brooklyn, N.Y. The funding and machinery to start the firm came from Britain, as did many artisans, including printers and engravers. Fred H. Wilde, who later wrote a history of the firm, had worked for Haw, one of the largest tile manufacturers in Britain, before settling in the US in 1885, when he began working for International Tile and Trim. The firm's work was similar to the British tiles of the 1875–85 period, with allegorical draped female figures from classical literature. 1884, a branch of the firm was established in Britain. 1888, the firm was purchased by New York Vitrified Tile Co.
Bibliography Jill Austwick and Brian Austwick, *The Decorated Tile: An Illustrated History of English Tile-Making and Design*, London, 1980: 43–45, 59–63. Doreen Bolger Burke et al., *In Pursuit of Beauty: Americans and the Aesthetic Movement*, New York: The Metropolitan Museum of Art/Rizzoli, 1986: 442.

Introini, Vittorio (1935–)

Italian architect, town planner, industrial designer, and teacher.

Training To 1961, architecture, Politecnico, Milan.
Biography From 1963, Introini worked as consultant designer at Saporiti and later for its affiliate Proposals; designed Saporiti furnishings, including 1969 library system and its 1975 showroom in New York; taught, Politecnico, Milan.
Bibliography Enrichetta Ritter, *Design italiano: i mobili*, Milan, Rome: C. Bestetti, 1968: 175. 'Saporiti Italia on Fifth Avenue,' *Interior Design*, vol. 47, Feb. 1976: 142–43. Cat., Kathryn B. Hiesinger and George H. Marcus III (eds.), *Design Since 1945*, Philadelphia: Philadelphia Museum of Art, 1983. Cat., Hans Wichmann, *Italien Design 1945 bis heute*, Munich: Die Neue Sammlung, 1988.

Inventum

Dutch appliance manufacturer; located De Bilt/Bilthoven.

History 1908, the firm was established; 1915, was named Inventum and produced electrical teamakers and toasters and, from late 1940s, radios. Its only artist may have been A.W. Verbeek in 1928. The firm remains active today.
Bibliography Cat., *Industry and Design in the Netherlands 1850/1950*, Amsterdam: Stedelijk Museum, 1985.

Iosa Ghini, Massimo (1959–)

Italian designer and artist; born Borgo Tossignano; active Bologna and Milan.

Training In Florence; to 1989, architecture, Politecnico, Milan.
Biography Iosa Ghini began his design career as a comic-strip artist and illustrator for periodicals *Alter Linus*, *Frigidaire*, *Heavy Metal*, *Fashion News*, and *Vanity*; 1981, became a member of Zak-Ark group. He supplied comic-book-type illustrations to *Per luì* magazine and rock magazines in the US; worked on projects with Swatch, Solvay, and Centro Moda Firenze; at the time, was best known for illustrating comic books; from 1984, designed for the firm AGO; from 1982, designed discothèques, video projects, and magazines; from 1985, was a consultant to RAI television network in Italy, designing sets, art movies, and graphics. From 1986, he has designed furniture, including for Memphis's 1986 12 New Collection, the Roy wood and metal table for its 1987 collection, the widely published 1987 Bertrand sideboard in wood and metal, and the Juliette armchair in metal with plastic and straw webbing. He also designed his first furniture collection (1987) Dynamic by Moroso and 1988 Bolidio discothèque in New York. He has taught and lectured at Istituto Europeo di Design, Domus Academy, and Vitra Design Museum. His furniture and furnishings were produced in amorphic forms in neo-1950s streamlined style. The style is a manifestation of the Movimento Bolidista which Iosa Ghini conjured in 1986 in Bologna with Pierangelo Caramia and others and claimed, among a number of assertions, 'that ideology is a useless and harmful brake.' His clients have included Fiam Italia (for which he designed the all-glass Volgente étagère and Genio and Incontro tables), Bieffeplast, Bonaldo, Hoesch, Duravit, Dornbracht, Stildomus.
Exhibitions/citations Work shown at 1991 *Mobili italiani 1961–1991: le varie età dei linguaggi*, Salone del Mobile, Milan; 1989, first one-person exhibition of graphics and objects, Inspiration Gallery, Axis Centre, Tokyo. Work also included in exhibitions in Los Angeles, New York, Tokyo, Milan, Vienna, Paris, Geneva, Singapore, Cologne, and Berlin. Jury member, 1992 Intérieur biennial, Courtrai, Belgium. Won 1988 competition for Centre Georges Pompidou plaza, Paris; 1988 Roscoe award, US.
Bibliography Fumio Shimizu and Studio Matteo Thun (eds.), *The Italian Design: Descendants of Leonardo da Vinci*, Tokyo: Graphic-sha 1987: 325. *Modo*, no. 148, Mar.–Apr.1993: 121. Mel Byars, *Design in Steel*, London: Laurence King, 2002. Maurizio Corrado et al., *Massimo Iosa Ghini, 15 anni di progetti = 15 Years of Projects*, Milan: Electa, 2002.

International Silver Company. Four-piece set of cutlery. 1937. Stainless steel, knife): l. 9 x w. 3/4" (22.9 x 1.9 cm), teaspoon l. 6 x w. 1 1/4" (15.2 x 3.2 cm). Mfr: International Silver Company, US. Purchase. MoMA.

Ipnos

Italian furniture company; located San Stino di Livenza.

History Ipnos was founded to produce furniture for small living spaces. Products include Dopp range of tables on castors that can be individually regulated to various heights, and transformable beds and seating—using wood, veneer, metal, MDF, and cotton fabrics. Models have included Dopp articulated table range and Andros table in the figure of a person, and Andromaca chair-storage cabinet.
Citations 1998 Premio Catas (for Puzzle folding MDF chair by Stefano Jus), Catas research association.
Bibliography www.ipnosangelswithus.com.

Iribe, Paul (b. Paul Iribarne Garay 1883–1935)

French designer and illustrator; born Angoulême; active Paris and Hollywood, Cal.

Biography Iribe worked as a caricaturist for journals *Le rire*, *L'assiette au beurre*, *Le cri de Paris*, and others and, 1908, founded *Le témoin*. As a member of the world of high fashion, he influenced taste by illustrating a fashion portfolio for Paul Poiret; later, set up a decorating studio, where he designed furniture, fabrics, wallpaper, and *objets d'art,* after collaborating with Pierre Legrain. His furniture—at first finely carved, then simpler—was veneered with amaranth, ebony, Brazilian rosewood, and colored shagreen, with inlays in contrasting colors. Couturier Jacques Doucet, who had sold his distinguished collection of 18th-century furniture, commissioned Iribe to furnish his entire apartment at 46, avenue du Bois (today avenue Foch), Paris; Iribe hired Pierre Legrain as assistant. Iribe's modernism always tended to the baroque, inclined toward a 19th-century sense of luxury, with chairs that engulfed the sitter. 1914, Iribe settled in Hollywood, Cali., and worked as theatrical designer for film directors, including Cecil B. De Mille. The lush sets for De Mille's *The Affairs of Anatol* (1921) and *Cleopatra* (1934) were among Iribe's better-known accomplishments. With architects Umbdenstock and Hourtieg, he wrote a 1926 manifesto against modern art, and, as a traditionalist, he was opposed to Union des Artistes Modernes (UAM). 1930, he returned to France and illustrated periodicals and books including a trilogy for Nicolas wines; designed the Lanvin emblem representing Jeanne Lanvin dressed for a ball with her daughter Marie-Blanche at her knee, and costume jewelry for Coco Chanel, who became a close friend; 1935, founded journal *Le mot*.
Bibliography Victor Arwas, *Art Déco*, New York: Abrams, 1980. Raymond Bachollet et al., *Paul Iribe*, Paris: Denoël, 1982. Cat., Aaron Lederfajn and Xavier Lenormand, *Le Louvre des Antiquaires présente: 1930 quand le meuble devient sculpture*, Paris, 1986. Pierre Kjellberg, *Art déco: les maîtres du mobilier, le décor des paquebots*, Paris: Amateur, 1986.

Iris

Finnish domestic goods manufacturer.

History 1897, Iris workshops were established in Porvoo in the spirit of William Morris and John Ruskin by Louis Sparre of Sweden and Finnish painter Akseli Gallen-Kallela; produced ceramics, textiles, metalwork, lamps, and furniture and complete interiors for customers in Finland and St. Petersburg; also sold to retail shops in Paris and St. Petersburg. Alfred W. Finch, who was brought to Finland by Sparre, was director of the ceramics section. 1902, the firm closed.
Exhibitions Work shown at 1900 *Exposition Universelle*, Paris. Subject of 2000 *Soome Disain 1900*, Soome Instituut, Tallinin, Estonia.
Bibliography Jennifer Hawkins Opie, *Scandinavia Ceramics and Glass in the Twentieth Century*, New York: Rizzoli, 1989.
> See Sparre, Louis.

Ironrite Ironer Company, The

American manufacturer; located Detroit and Mount Clemens, Mich.

History 1911, Herman A. Sperlich and John H. Uhlig established the Sperlich and Uhlig Company to manufacture custom machinery and were engineers to and performed experimental work for others; 1917, began washing-machine production. Their major client was the Crystal Company, which moved from Detroit in 1920, and, thus, forced the entrepreneurial pair to find another product. Therefore, Dec. 1921 after extensive research into the potential and need for a domestic clothes ironer, they invented the first fully automatic clothes ironer, the table-type two-part steam Ironrite ironer (no. 46) that was rather large, suitable for the laundry room of a house. The J.L. Hudson department store, Detroit, was Ironrite's first retail dealer. 12 May 1927, the firm's name was changed to the Ironrite Ironer Company and some time later to Ironrite Inc. The ironers were produced in Mt. Clemens, Mich., where a plant had been established at the end of World War II. 1940s–50s, 'Ironrite' (or mangler) became an American household name. Sperlich designed the swivel-back late-1940–early-1950s Health Chair as an adjunct to the ironer itself, at which a housewife or maid sat to operate the device. Sept. 1959, Ironrite merged with Dielectric Products and Engineering Company of Raymond, Maine, a manufacturer of electronic components. 1961, ironer production stopped, and the Mt. Clemens plant was sold to a bicycle manufacturer.

Irvine, James (1958–)

British designer; born London; active Milan.

Training 1978–81, bachelor of arts degree, industrial and furniture design, Kingston Polytechnic (now Kingston University); 1981–84, master's degree in furniture design, Royal College of Art, London.
Biography 1984, Irvine settled in Milan; 1984–93, was a design consultant to Olivetti on industrial products with Michele De Lucchi, while concurrently working in De Lucchi's studio 1985–87; 1985, helped found design corsortium Solid, led by De Lucchi; 1988 in Tokyo, within a cultural-exchange program organized by Olivetti, conducted research in industrial products at Toshiba Design Center; 1988, established his own studio in Milan, with clients Alessi, Abet Laminati, Cappellini, Vitra, SCP, Design Gallery Milano, and others. 1990, he was a visiting lecturer, Domus Academy, Milan; from 1990, visiting lecturer, Istituto Europeo di Design, Milan; from 1992 with Jasper Morrison, coordinated the design of the Progetto Oggetto collection of objects by Cappellini; from 1993–97, was an associate/partner responsible for industrial design at Sottsass Associati in Milan. 1999, he designed the Üstra city bus fleet of Hanover, Germany; 131 buses have since been built by Mercedes-Benz. Recent clients have included Artemide, B&B Italia, Danese, Duravit, Swedese, WMF, Alfi, Magis, Whirlpool, Arabia, Mabeg, and Canon.
Exhibitions Included in 1986 *12 New Memphis* and 1988 *Solid*. Designed and coordinated 1993 *Citizen Office* exhibition, Vitra Design Museum, Weil am Rhein, Germany. Work subject of his first (1993) exhibition, at Konstfackskolan, Stockholm, and of 1999 exhibition at Asplund, Stockholm. Participated in Whirlpool's 1999 Microwave project, shown at 2000 Salone del Mobile, Milan.
Bibliography Mel Byars, *On/Off: New Electronic Products*, New York: Universe, 2001: 32. www.james-irvine.com.

James Irvine. X5 rug. 1999. Wool, 78 3/4 x 98 1/8" (200 x 250 cm) or 59 x 78 3/4" (150 x 200 cm). Mfr.: Asplund, Sweden.

Isbrand, Hans (1941–); Lise Isbrand (1942–)

Danish furniture designers, active Albertslund.

Training Cabinetmaking, Skolen for Brugskunst, Copenhagen.
Biography 1965, the Isbrands opened an office in Albertslund; became consultants to architects M. Hammer, H. Moldenhawer, Herman Olsen, Ole Hagen, and Arne Jacobsen; have designed a range of objects including furniture, radio and TV sets, shop display units, and 1966 PJ35 chair in laminated wicker cane and chromium, produced by P. Jeppesen Møbelfabrik (today P.P. Møbler, Allerød). And more recently: 1998 screen and 2000 table by Cabale and 2002 C one-piece flexible seat and 2003 Lav armchair by P.P. Møbler.
Exhibitions Work shown at 1966 *Formes Danoises*, Monaco; 1967 *Danish Arts and Crafts and Industrial Design*, Copenhagen; 1968 *Two Centuries of Danish Design*, Victoria and Albert Museum, London; 1970 *Modern Chairs 1918–1970* (PJ35 chair), Whitechapel Gallery, London.
Bibliography Cat., *Modern Chairs 1918–1970*, London: Lund Humphries, 1971. Frederik Sieck, *Nutidig Dansk Møbeldesign – en kortfattet illustreret beskrivelsee*, Copenhagen: Bondo Gravesen, 1981, 1990.

Ishibashi, Chuzaburo (1948–)

Japanese glass designer.

Training To 1972, Tama Art University, Tokyo; 1980, bachelor's degree, Stourbridge School of Art, Stourbridge, UK.
Biography 1972–76, Ishibashi worked as designer at Joetsu Crystal, Gumma, Japan.
Exhibitions Work was included in 1985 New Glass in Japan, Badisches Landesmuseum, Karlsruhe; 1986 *Expression en Verre*, Musée des Arts Décoratifs, Lausanne; 1987 *Glass from Stourbridge*, Birmingham Museum of Art; 1988 *Arte en Vidro*, Museu de Arte, São Paulo; 1990 *Glass '90 in Japan*, Tokyo; and 1991 (5th) Triennale of Japan Glass Art Crafts Association, Heller Gallery, New York; numerous others.
Citations Numerous, including Bayerischer Staatspreis.
Bibliography Cat., *Glass Japan*, New York: Heller Gallery and Japan Glass Art Crafts Association, 1991: no. 10.

Ishii, Koji (1946–)

Japanese glass designer.

Training To 1971, Tokyo University of Arts.
Biography 1971–77, Ishii worked for Hoya Crystal, Tokyo; 1977, set up his own glass studio.
Exhibitions Work shown at 1990 *Glass '90 in Japan*, Tokyo, and 1991 (5th) Triennale of the Japan Glass Art Crafts Association, Heller Gallery, New York. Work subject of exhibitions at Seibu department store, Tokyo, 1979; Takashimaya store, Yokohama, 1981; Tokyo Central Arts Gallery, 1982. Featured in 1988 *World of Art*, NTB–TV, numerous others, Japan; participated in 1976 Hot Glass Seminar, London.
Bibliography Cat., *Glass Japan*, New York: Heller Gallery and Japan Glass Art Crafts Association, 1991: no. 11.

Ishimoto, Fujiwo (1941–)

Japanese textile designer; born Ehime; active Finland.

Training Design and graphic art, Tokyo National University of Fine Arts and Music.
Biography 1964–70, Ishimoto worked at Ichida clothing company in Tokyo; 1970, settled in Finland and, 1970–74, was designer at Decembre; 1974, joined Marimekko, where he worked for 30 years as designer of printed fabrics. He has became known for his black-and-white palette and use of nature themes at Marimekko, where he incorporated geometric patterns similar to the Marimekko work of Maija Isola; from early 1980s, has designed some 15 patterns a year for Marimekko, over 300 of which have gone into production; from 1989. Ishimoto also designed for Arabia pottery, including Illusia dinnerware (with Heikki Orvola).
Exhibitions/citations Fabrics shown in venues in Scandinavia, Central Europe, Japan, and the US. Subject of 2001 *On the Road: Fujiwo Ishimoto*, Amos Andersonin Taidemuseo, Helsinki. Received 1983 Roscoe Prize, US; honorable mention award, Finland Design Exhibition; 1989 grant from Cultural Foundation of Arabia ceramics; 1991 industrial design award, Finnish government; 1983, 1989, and 1993 honorable mentions, Finnish Design; 1994 Kaj Franck Design Prize.
Bibliography 'Marimekko Oy,' *Domus*, no. 599, Oct. 1979: 76–77. Bella Obermaier, 'Castle of the Winds,' *Mobilia*, no. 298, 1981: 25–32. Cat., Kathryn B. Hiesinger and George H. Marcus III (eds.), *Design Since 1945*, Philadelphia: Philadelphia Museum of Art, 1983. Marja-Terttu Vuorimaa, 'Marimekko Exports Know-How,' *Form Function Finland*, no. 2, 1983: 10–11. Albrecht Bangert and Karl Michael Armer, *80s Style: Designs of the Decade*, New York: Abbeville, 1990.

Isokon
> See Pritchard, Jack (1899–1992).

Isola, Maija (1927–2001)

Finnish painter and fabric designer.

Training Taideteollinen korkeakoulu, Helsinki.
Biography 1949, Isola joined Printex, where her colorful and bold patterns on printed textiles brought the firm renown in 1950s–60s; used bed sheeting as material on which to silkscreen huge geometric designs for Printex; from 1951, used the same method for producing clothing and furnishings fabrics by Marimekko. Her early work was abstract; later, she introduced patterns influenced by Byzantine decorations and the eastern folk motifs of the Finnish/Russian region of Karelia.
Bibliography Erik Zahle (ed.), *A Treasury of Scandinavian Design*, New York: Golden Press, 1961. David Davies, 'Fabrics by Marimekko,' *Design*, no. 236, Aug. 1968: 28–31. 'Marimekko Oy,' *Domus*, no. 599, Oct. 1979: 76–77. Charles S. Talley, 'Contemporary Textile Art,' *Scandinavia*, Stockholm, 1982: 130–31. Cat., David Revere McFadden (ed.), *Scandinavian Modern Design 1880–1980*, New York: Abrams, 1982. Cat., Kathryn B. Hiesinger and George H. Marcus III (eds.), *Design Since 1945*, Philadelphia: Philadelphia Museum of Art, 1983.

Isozaki, Arata (1931–)

Japanese architect and designer; born Oita, Kyushu.

Training To 1954 under Kenzo Tange, Tokyo Kogyo Daigaku (university of Tokyo).
Biography Isozaki has become one of Japan's best known architects of the last quarter of 20th century. His work has been direct, sometimes humorous, with geometric, solid forms. 1954–63, he worked in office of architect Kenzo Tange; 1963, set up his own architectural practice, while collaborating with other architects and studios. He was a visiting professor, University of California, Los Angeles; University of Hawaii; Rhode Island School of Design; Columbia University, New York; Yale University, New Haven, Conn.; and lectured at numerous institutions, including universities in the US, Canada, and Australia. He designed dinnerware by Swid Powell, rugs included in 1988 Dialog range by Vorwerk, 1973–83 Monroe chair and table by ICF, 1981 Fuji cabinets by Memphis, bed at *Affinità Elettiva* of 1985 Triennale di Milano, 1986 jewelry by Cleto Munari. With Tange, he was chief architect for 1970 *Japan World Exposition (Expo '70)*, Osaka, and 1965–66 reconstruction plan (international competition winner, with Tange) of Skopje, Yugoslavia

(destroyed by 1963 earthquake; now the capital of Macedonia). Isozaki architecture includes 1955–58 Kagawa prefectural offices, Takamatsu; 1957–58 city hall, Imabari; 1959–60 town plan for Tokyo; 1971–74 Gumma Prefecture Museum of Fine Arts, Takasaki; 1972–74 Kitakyushu City Museum of Art; 1972–74 Fujimi country club house, Oita; 1972–75 Kitakyushu central library; 1974–75 Shukosha building, Fukoka; 1976–78 Kamioka town hall, Gifu; 1977–78 audio-visual center, Oita; 1979–82 Tsukuba civic center; 1981–86 Museum of Contemporary Art, Los Angeles; 1983 Palladium discothèque, New York; 1986 new city hall, Tokyo; 1986 Los Angeles Museum of Modern Art; 1986–90 Art Tower Mito, Ibaragi (Japan); 1992 Guggenheim Museum Soho, New York; 1997 Mirage City; 2000 Volksbank on Potsdamer Platz, Berlin-Tiergarten; 2000 Police Station, Okayama. As a theorist, he wrote the series of articles, 'The Dismantling of Architecture' published in *Bijutsu Techo* magazine (to 1973).
Exhibitions/citations Work shown at 1968 (15th) Triennale di Milano; 1976 and 1980 Biennali di Venezia; 1976–77 *ManTRANSforms*, Cooper-Hewitt National Design Museum, New York; 1977 Biennale di São Paulo; *Dal Cucchiaio alla Città*, 1983 Triennale di Milano; *Affinità Elettiva* (Floor = Furniture bed) 1985 Triennale di Milano. Work subject of 1985 exhibition, Japan House, New York; 1991, Museum of Contemporary Art, Los Angeles (catalog below). Special prize for his work on *Expo '70*; 1967 and 1975 annual prizes, Architectural Institute of Japan; 1983 award, *Interiors* magazine; 1986 gold medal, Royal Institute of British Architects; 1978, elected honorary member, Accademia Tiberina, Rome; 1983, Bund Deutscher Architekten; 1988 memorial award of Arnold B. Brunner, American Academy of Fine Arts and Literature); 1992 National Honor Award, American Institute of Architects (AIA).
Bibliography Cat., Carlo Guenzi, *Le affinità elettive*, Milan: Electa, 1985. Juli Capella and Quim Larrea, *Designed by Architects in the 1980s*, New York: Rizzoli, 1988. David B. Stewart and Hajime Yatsuka (essays), *Arata Isozaki: Architecture, 1960–1990*, Los Angeles: Museum of Contemporary Art; New York: Rizzoli, 1991. Francesco dal Co et al., *Arata Isozaki*, Milan: Electa, 1995. Philip Drew, *Arata Isozaki*, London: Phaidon, 1996. *Arata Isozaki: Four Decades of Architecture*, New York: Universe, 1998.

Issel, Alberto (1848–1926)
Italian furniture designer; born Genoa; active Turin.

Biography By the time of the exposure of his work at 1902 Turin *Esposizione*, Issel was already well-known and active in his own substantial workshop, which employed more than 70 craftspeople. He designed in the Stile Floreale with carved, lyrical floral decorative features; was also a painter of marine, pastoral, and military subjects.
Exhibitions Work shown at 1898 exhibition and 1902 *Esposizione Internazionale d'Arte Decorativa Moderna*, both Turin. Drawing room shown in 2003 *La Collezione Wolfson 1880–1945*, Palazzo della Regione, Genoa.
Bibliography Cat., Gabriel P. Weisberg, *Stile Floreale: The Cult of Nature in Italian Design*, Miami: The Wolfsonian Foundation, 1988.

Issigonis, 'Alec' Alexander Arnold Constantine (1906–1988)
British automobile designer; born Smyrna, Turkey.

Training Three years, Battersea Polytechnic.
Biography 1922, Issigonis arrived in England, having had a British father who died during the journey from Turkey; 1928–34, worked as a draftsperson in the office of Edward Gillett (the developer of a semi-automatic car transmission), London; from 1934, in the drawing office of Humber automobiles in Cambridge; from 1936 under Robert Boyle, worked at Morris automobiles in Cowley, where Issigonis developed an independent suspension and rack-and-pinion steering; from early 1940s, worked on the design of the Mosquito (later known as 1948 Morris Minor) that became the British 'people's car' of 1950s. When he first saw his Minor, he called it 'a poached egg.' Through 1970s, he also contributed to most of the Austin/Morris cars, including 1959 Mini, 1962 1100, 1964 1800, and 1969 Maxi. His highly influential 1959 BMC Mini was short but spacious, featuring a transverse transmission/engine layout and the first front-wheel drive; it was a fuel-saving answer to the Suez Canal Crisis, which greatly diminished British oil importation. 1961, John Cooper and Issigonis created the racer versions: Morris Mini-Cooper and Austin Mini-Cooper.
Citations 1967 British knighthood.
Bibliography Laurence Pomeroy, *The Mini Story*, London: Temple, London, 1964. John Tipler, *Mini Cooper: The Real Thing*, St. Paul, Minn.: Motorbooks International, 1993. Karen Pender, *The Secret Life of the Morris Minor*, Dorchester: Veloce, 1995. Penny Sparke, *A Century of Car Design*, London: Mitchell Beazley, 2002.

Italcomma
Italian furniture manufacturer and distributor; located Montelabbate (Pesaro).

History From 1980, Italcomma was the sole distributor of Thonet bentwood chairs and accessories in Italy; 1995, began expanding its own range of contemporary chairs and tables while emphasizing innovative materials and avant-garde design. Its various divisions include home furniture, contract, and health care (rest homes/hospitals).

Itten, Johannes (1888–1967)
Swiss theoretician and teacher; born Süderen-Linde.

Training 1913–16 under Adolf Hölzel, painting, Stuttgarter Akademie.
Biography 1916, Itten founded Itten-Shule (his own art school), Vienna; 1919–23, was a master at the Bauhaus, Weimar, devising the preliminary course that became a new pedagogic concept for training artists. His approach was too mystical for pragmatic Bauhaus director Walter Gropius, who dismissed him in 1923; 1926–31, managed his own Itten-Schule in Berlin; 1931–38, was director, Textilfachschule, Krefeld, and director, Kunstgewerbeschule, Zurich; from 1949, was collaborator, then from 1952, director, Museum Rietberg (for non-European art), Zurich; died in Zurich.
Exhibitions Work subject of exhibitions at Westfälisches Landesmuseum für Kunst und Kulturgeschichte, Munich, 1980; Bern 1984; Zurich and Heidelberg 1988–89; Krefeld 1992; Bauhaus-Archiv, Museum für Gestaltung, Berlin, 1994–95.
Bibliography Willy Rotzler (ed.), *Johannes Itten, Werke und Schriften*, Zurich: Orell Fussli, 1978. Cat., *Johannes Itten, Künstler und Lehrer*, Bern: Kunstmuseum, 1984. Cat., *Johannes Itten und die Höhere Fachschule für Textile Flächenkunst in Krefeld*, Krefeld: Deutsches Textilmuseum, 1992. Cat., *Das Frühe Bauhaus und Johannes Itten: Katalogbuch anlässlich des 75. Gründungsjubiläums des Staatlichen Bauhauses in Weimar*, Ostfildern-Ruit: Hatje, 1994.

Iuliis, Daniele De
> See De Iuliis, Daniele.

Ive, Jonathan (1967–)
British industrial designer; born London.

Training Industrial design, University of Newcastle.
Biography 1990, Ive cofounded Tangerine design partnership in London, where the 1992 concepts for Apple Computer's Juggernaut investigation led him to become a designer in IDg (Industrial Design Group) of Apple Computer, Cupertino, Cal., where his first design was 1992 Newton Message Pad 110 (Lindy). 1996, he became the director of IDg, when Robert Brunner left Apple; was later promoted to senior director and broke away from Brunner's conservative approach to realize the group's highly successful iMac family of computers from 1998, including Power Mac G4, flat-panel monitors, 2000 Titanium PowerBook G4, 2001 iPod MP3 player. These and other products contributed to Apple's ascendancy as a leader in computer design.
Citations 2002 Red Dot Best of the Best (iPod, with others) and 2003 Red Dot award (12" and 17" PowerBooks, with others), Design Zentrum Nordrhein Westfalen, Essen.
Bibliography Paul Kunkel, *Apple Design: The World of the Apple Industrial Design Group*, New York: Graphis, 1997.
> See Jobs, Steven P.

Ivester, Gavin
American industrial designer; born San Jose, Cal.

Training Mid-1980s, San Jose State University.
Biography From 1981, Ivester worked at Apple Computer as a parts sorter, then in the engineering department, and, 1982–86 concurrent with his university studies, in Apple's Industrial Design Group (IDg). He designed 1987 Macintosh IIcx (Apple's first in-house-designed product in SnowWhite project); codesigned 1989 Knowledge Navigator and concepts for Goldilocks; supervised the design of 1989–89 Macintosh Portable; designed 1989 Personal LaserWriter, 1990–91 PowerBook (with Robert Brunner), 1990 PowerBook Duo, and early concepts for the Newton MessagePad; 1992, left Apple and, with Lawrence Lam, founded Tonic Industrial Design in Palo Alto, Cal. Ivester specializes in footwear collections and brand building.

Jonathan Ive and Apple IDg (Industrial Design Group). iMac desktop computer. 1998. Polycarbonate and other materials, 15 x 15 x 17" (38.1 x 38.1 x 43.2 cm). Mfr: Apple Computer, US. Gift of the designers. MoMA.

Bibliography Paul Kunkel, *Apple Design: The World of the Apple Industrial Design Group*, New York: Graphis, 1997.

Iwata, Hisatoshi (1925–)

Japanese glass designer; son of glass designer Toshichi Iwata.

Training To 1950, crafts, Tokyo University of Arts.
Biography Iwata was on the board of trustees of *Nitten* (Japanese fine-arts exhibitions) in Kofukai; lifetime member and founder in 1972 of Japan Glass Art Crafts Association; for a time, called on slightly opaque white glass to create his Flowing Clouds series.
Exhibitions/citations Work shown at 1945 *Nitten*; 1978, 1981, 1984, 1987, and 1990 *Glass in Japan* exhibitions; 1991 (5th) Triennale of Japan Glass Art Crafts Association, Heller Gallery, New York. Subject of 1997–98 Contemporary Glass Art from Japan: Toshichi Iwata & Hisatoshi Iwata, *Pioneers of Contemporary Japanese Glass Art, Kemper Museum of Contemporary Art*, Kansas City, Missouri. Received 1976 prize of Minister of Education at 1976 (8th) annual *Nitten* exhibition, Tokyo; 1981 (23rd) Mainichi Art Prize; 1982 (38th) prize, Japan Art Academy, numerous others.
Bibliography Cat., *Glass Japan*, New York: Heller Gallery and Japan Glass Art Crafts Association, 1991: no. 11.

Iwata, Itoko (1922–)

Japanese glass designer.

Biography Iwata is the progenitor of a family of glass designers and specialist; was president of Iwata Glass, Tokyo; 1984, was a member of International Council of Pilchuck Glass School, Stanwood, Wash., and was a trustee of The Corning Museum of Glass, Corning, N.Y., and cofounder and secretary general, Japan Glass Art Crafts Association. With others, wrote the book *A History of Glass in Japan* (Tokyo, Kodansha, 1973).
Exhibitions Work shown at 1978, 1981, 1984, 1987, and 1990 *Glass in Japan*, Tokyo; 1991 (5th) Triennale of Japan Glass Art Crafts Association, Heller Gallery, New York, numerous others.
Bibliography Cat., *Glass Japan*, New York: Heller Gallery and Japan Glass Art Crafts Association, 1991: no. 14.

Iwata, Ruri (1951–)

Japanese glass designer.

Training To 1977, Tokyo National University of Fine Arts and Music.
Biography Iwata was director of the family firm Iwata Glass, Tokyo.
Exhibitions/citations Work shown at 1990 *Glass '90 in Japan*, Tokyo; 1991 (5th) Triennale of the Japan Glass Art Crafts Association, Heller Gallery, New York, numerous others. Participated in 1988 (3rd) Interglas Symposium, Crystalex, Nový Bor (now Czech Republic). 1989 (14th) Yoshidaisoya Architecture Art Prize.
Bibliography Cat., *Glass Japan*, New York: Heller Gallery and Japan Glass Art Crafts Association, 1991: no. 15.

IZO (department of fine arts)

Russian educational institution.

History 1918, IZO was established as the fine arts department of Narkompros (the people's commissariat for enlightenment). Its wide-ranging brief covered painting, graphics, sculpture, and architecture. IZO's head was artist David Shterenberg; most members of the artistic board were Leftists and Constructivists, including Natan Al'tman, Vladimir Baranov-Rossiné, Nikolai Punin, Vladimir Maiakovskii, and Osip Brik. Vladimir Tatlin was appointed head of the artistic section in Moscow and Al'tman of its counterpart in Petrograd. Its early activities were considered by the Party leadership to be ineffective and even sometimes harmful; Narkompros's head was Anatolii Lunacharskii. Lenin ordered the reorganization of Narkompros in 1920 and became personally involved. INKhUK (institute of artistic culture) was organized under IZO NKP to handle art and artistic education. INKhUK's first president was Vasilii Kandinsky, followed by Osip Brik. 1922, David Shterenberg was dismissed as the head of IZO NKP. To this time, IZO NKP had been the only buyer of art and the distributor of State orders, subsidies, rations, advances, and other material goods, but, with the partial return of capitalism, a new bourgeoisie arose, which was soon able to patronize the arts. Theories of Constructivism and 'production art' continued to inspire the German Bauhaus, Dutch De Stijl, British Tekton, and other institutions/movements in Europe and the US, but, within the Soviet Union, the last major avant-garde exhibition was 1923 *Artists of All Tendencies 1919–23* in Petrograd (today St. Petersburg). The avant-garde, which had been a highly enthusiastic supporter of the Bolshevik takeover, became one of its victims.
Bibliography S. Fitzpatrick, *The Commissariat of Enlightenment*, Cambridge: Cambridge University, 1970. Igor Golomstock, *Totalitarian Art in the Soviet Union, The Third Reich, Fascist Italy and the People's Republic of China*, New York: Icon, 1990: 14, 36. Cat., *The Great Utopia: The Russian and Soviet Avant-Garde, 1915–1932*, New York: Guggenheim Museum, 1992.

J

Hella Jongerius. My Soft Office power patch (cetail). 2000. MoMA.

Jack, George Washington Henry (1855–1932)

British architect; born Long Island, N.Y.; active Britain.

Training Under Horatio K. Bromhead, in architecture, Glasgow.
Biography From c. 1890, Jack was the chief furniture designer at Morris and Co., London; 1880, began working in Philip Webb's London architectural practice, which he took over in 1900; wrote *Wood-carving: Design and Workmanship* (New York: Appleton, 1903; London: John Hogg, 1903), included in John Hogg's 'The Artistic Crafts' series of technical handbooks.
Bibliography Stuart Durant, *Ornament from the Industrial Revolution to Today*, Woodstock, N.Y.: Overlook, 1986.

Jackson, Dakota (1949–)

American furniture designer; active New York.

Biography Jackson was born into a family of magicians and performers; began his career as a consultant to stage magicians and to rock musicians, who wanted illusion incorporated in their performances; early 1970s, was also a dancer with the Laura Dean and Tricia Brown troupes; c. 1970, produced his first furniture design (commissioned by Yoko Ono for John Lennon); 1991, introduced his Vikter range of furniture, including the Stacking Chair; has been a prolific designer of interiors and furniture, with showrooms in the US (including one designed by Jackson and Peter Eisenmann in Pacific Design Center, Los Angeles) and a manufacturing facility in Queens, New York. Jackson sometimes calls on the imaginative use of new materials; frequently assigns curious and occasionally unpronounceable names to his pieces, of which many early models are still in production.
Exhibitions/citations In New York: work shown in *High Styles: Twentieth Century American Design* (Saturn stool), Whitney Museum of American Art; 1991 *Explorations: The New Furniture*, American Crafts Museum; 1992 theme installation documenting creation and development of the Vik-ter chair, Cooper-Hewitt National Design Museum. Award (for ark and chapel at Temple Jeremiah, Winnetka, Ill.), American Institute of Architects (AIA).
Bibliography 'The New American Entrepreneurs,' *Metropolis*, May 1991: 69.

Jacober, Aldo (1939–)

Italian architect and designer.

Training Politecnico, Milan.
Biography 1964, Jacober set up his own office in Milan.
Exhibitions/citations Work shown at 1967 Corso Internazionale del Mobile, Cantù; 1966–69 Saloni del Milan. First prize (for Trieste folding chair, with Pierangela D'Aniello), 1966 Fiera di Trieste; first prize, 1966 *Mostra Internazionale dell' Arredamento* (MIA), Monza.

Jacobs, Carl (1925–)

Danish furniture designer.

Biography 1950–51, Jacobs worked for Kandya, London, for which he designed the 1950 Jason stacking chairs produced in a bent beech shell and with turned wooden legs for use in restaurants, offices, schools, and homes. Its plywood shell, bent without the use of steam heat, was shaped by a pneumatic jig and glued in place with a synthetic resin. Jacob made some 27 prototypes before reaching the desired shape. One large man on the shoulders of another tested the immensely strong construction. The chair was used in the South Bank Restaurant and other sites at 1951 *Festival of Britain*, London. Production ceased in c. 1970.
Bibliography Michael Farr, *Design in British Industry: A Mid-Century Survey*, London: Cambridge, 1955: 8ff. Cat., *Modern Chairs 1918–1970*, London: Lund Humphries, 1971.

Jacobs, J.A. (1885–1968)

Dutch silversmith; active Amsterdam.

Biography From or in 1917, Jacobs was a teacher in the silver department, Kunstnijverheidschool Quellinus (renamed Instituut voor de Kunstnijverheid in 1924), Amsterdam. A 1922 *bonbonnière* with ornamentation typical of Amsterdam School of Expressionist Dutch architecture serves as an example of his metalwork.
Bibliography Annelies Krekel-Aalberse, *Art Nouveau and Art Déco Silver*, New York: Abrams, 1989.

Jacobsen, Arne (1902–1971)

Danish designer; born Copenhagen.

Training To 1927, Det Tekniske Selskabs Skoler, Copenhagen; under Kay Fisker, architecture, Det Kongelige Danske Kunstakademi, Copenhagen.
Biography 1927–30, Jacobsen worked in the office of Paul Holsoe; 1930, opened his own office in Hellerup; was influenced by 1930s modern architecture, including that of Le Corbusier, Gunnar Asplund, and Ludwig Mies van der Rohe, and, thus, became Denmark's first exponent of Functionalism. His first major commission was 1930–34 Bellavista housing project in Copenhagen. 1950, Jacobsen began to design furnishings for mass production and, from 1952, his best-known work,

Aldo Jacober. Trieste folding chair. 1966. Lacquer painted wood with woven straw seat, open 28 x 21 1/4 x 18" (71 x 54 x 45.7 cm), closed (not shown) 21 1/4 x 30 3/4 x 2" (54 x 78.1 x 5.1 cm). Mfr: Alberto Bazzini, Italy. Gift of the mfr. MoMA.

by Fritz Hansen, includes 1952 Ant (no. 3100 with three legs, no. 3101 with four), 1958 Swan and Egg chairs, 1956 Series 7 group. Among his earliest production, the 1951 three-legged stacking chair in plywood and steel was developed for factory production by Fritz Hansen. Swan and Egg chairs were designed for the glass-sheathed 1958–60 SAS Hotel in Copenhagen. The 1956 no. 3107 side chair was adapted from the Ant chair, with optional casters and arms. He also designed tables by Hansen. His 1957 cutlery by A. Michelsen appeared in 1969 film *2001: A Space Odyssey*. 1967 Cylinda Line stainless-steel tableware range by Stelton proved highly popular. Much of Jacobsen's work is still in production. Clients included Allerød (furniture from 1932), Louis Poulsen (lighting), Stelton and Michelsen (silver and stainless steel), I.P. Lunds (bathroom fixtures), Grautex (textiles), Aug. Millech (textiles), and C. Olesen (textiles). 1960–64 St. Catherine's College building, Oxford, is a manifestation of his interest in controlling all elements of the physical environment, integrating architecture, interior furnishings, and utilitarian objects. Other architecture included 1937 Sterling House, Copenhagen; 1939–40 town hall (with Erik Møller), Århus; 1942 town hall (with Flemming Larsen), Søllerød; 1952 Massey-Harris exhibition and factory building, Glostrup; 1952–56 Munkegård School, Gentofte; 1955 Jespersen office building, Copenhagen; 1955 housing scheme, Søholm; 1955 town hall, Rødovre; 1956 Carl Christensen factory, Ålborg; 1961–67 Danish National Bank, Copenhagen; 1962–70 main administration building of Hamburgische Elektrizitäts-Werke, Hamburg; 1970–73 city hall building (completed by Hans Dissing and Otto Weitling), Mainz. 1956–65, he was professor emeritus, Det Kongelige Danske Kunstakademi & Arkitekskole, Copenhagen.

Exhibitions/citations House of the Future (with Flemming Lassen), circular with rooftop helipad, shown at 1929 exhibition; other work at 1954–57 *Design in Scandinavia*, touring the US; 1968 *Formes Scandinaves*, Paris; 1960–61 *Arts of Denmark*, touring the US; 1968 *Two Centuries of Danish Design*, London; 1966 *Vijftig Jaar Zitten*, Stedelijk Museum; 1968 *Les Assises du Siège Contemporain*, Musée des Arts Décoratifs, Paris. Work subject of 1959 exhibition, Royal Institute of British Architects, London; 1968 exhibition, Glasgow; 1987–88 *Arne Jacobsen: Architecte et Designer Danois 1902–1971*, Musée des Arts Décoratifs, Paris; and numerous one-person 2002 events making his 100th birthday anniversary. Silver medal, 1925 *Exposition Internationale des Arts Décoratifs et Industriels Modernes*, Paris; 1928 gold medal, Det Kongelige Danske Kunstakademi; 1936 Eckersberg Medal; 1954 Prize of Honor, Biennale of São Paulo; 1956 C.F. Hansen Medal; grand prize and silver medal, 1957 (11th) Triennale di Milano; 1960 Grand Prix Internationale, *L'architecture d'aujourd'hui* journal; 1962 medal of honor, Danish Architectural Association; 1962 Prince Eugen Medal; 1963 Fritz-Schumacher-Preis der Freien Hansestadt, Hamburg; 1963 bronze medal and honorary corresponding member, Royal Institute of British Architects; 1967 and 1969 *I.D.* magazine awards; 1967 (for Cylinda Line) and 1969 (for Vola bathroom fixtures), Industrial Design Prize, Denmark; 1969 gold medal, *Pio Manzu*, San Marino; 1969 Die Plakette, Akademie der Künste, Hamburg; 1970 Wood Prize, Denmark; 1971 gold medal, Academie d'Architecture de France.

Bibliography J. Pedersen, *Arkitekten Arne Jacobsen*, Copenhagen 1954. Cat., *Arne Jacobsen: Architecture, Applied Art*, London: Royal Institute of British Architects, 1959. Tobias Faber, *Arne Jacobsen*, New York: Praeger, 1964. Cat., *Les Assises du Siège Contemporain*, Paris: Musée des Arts Décoratifs, 1968. Poul Erik Shriver and E. Waade, *Arne Jacobsen*, Copenhagen: Danish Bicentennial Committee, 1976. Sara S. Richardson, *Arne Jacobsen: Danish Master—A Bibliography*, Monticello, Ill.: Vance Bibliographies, 1989. Poul Erik Tøjner and Kjeld Vindum, *Arne Jacobsen, Architekt & Designer*, Copenhagen: Dansk Design Centre, 1994. Erik Moller et al., *Arne Jacobsen*, New York: Rizzoli, 1995. Carsten Thau and Kjeld Vindum, *Arne Jacobsen*, Copenhagen: Arkitektens, 1998. Mel Byars with Arlette Barré-Despond, *100 Designs/ 100 Years: A Celebration of the 20th Century*, Hove: RotoVision, 1999: 128–29. Jane Sandberg (ed.), *Arne Jacobsen og den Organiske Form*, Copenhagen: Kunstforeningen, 1999. *Arne Jacobsen, Architect & Designer*, Copenhagen: Dansk Design Center, 2000. Paola Antonelli (ed.), *Objects of Design: The Museum of Modern Art*, New York: The Museum of Modern Art, 2003: 139.

Jacobsen, Jacob (1901–1996)

Norwegian industrial designer.

Training In engineering.

Biography Initially, Jacobsen worked in the textile industry in England and Switzerland; was director of Jac. Jacobsen in Oslo; adapted his 1937 Luxor L-1 lamp from George Carwadine's British Anglepoise prototype and bought the Anglepoise rights in 1937 to produce it in Norway; by 1940s, had a monopoly on the product, produced today by Luxo; was a major innovator in lighting design in early 20th century.

Bibliography Cat., Leslie Jackson, *The New Look: Design in the Fifties*,

Carl Jacobs. Jason chair. 1950. Beech, 28 1/2 x 20 x 18" (72.4 x 50.8 x 45.7 cm). Mfr: Kandya, UK. Gift of the mfr. MoMA.

Arne Jacobsen. Chair Serie 7 (no. 3107). c. 1952. Chrome-plated steel tubing and molded plywood with black lacquer, 30 1/4 x 18 x 20" (76.8 x 45.7 x 50.8 cm). Mfr: Fritz Hansen, Denmark. Gift of Mr. Jacques and Mrs. Anna B. Dutka. MoMA.

New York: Thames & Hudson, 1991. Cat., David Revere McFadden (ed.), *Scandinavian Modern Design 1880–1980*, New York: Abrams, 1982. Fredrik Wildhagen, *Norge i Form*, Oslo: Stenersen, 1988.
> See Carwardine, George.

Johansen, Oskar (1974–)
> See Permafrost.

Jakobsen, Hans Sandgren (1963–)

Danish designer; born Copenhagen.

Training To 1986, in cabinet making; 1986–90, industrial design, Danmarks Designskole, Copenhagen.
Biography While in school, Jakobsen studied Shaker craftsmanship in US; 1986–87, worked at Rud. Rasmussens Snedkerier; for three months, was a designer at Cobo Design, Nagoya, Japan; 1991–97, was an assistant to Nanna Ditzel; from 1997, worked independently. He designed the Viper screen-wall in cardboard or aluminum by Fritz Hansen. Other clients included VIA (Nevada, US), Kohseki (Kyoto, Japan), and, in Denmark, Art Andersen & Copenhagen, Kunsforeningen Gammel Strand, Stilling Furniture, Fritz Hansen, Frederica Furniture, and Codex. From 1991, he was a member of design group Spring Beginning; from 1994, a member of Snedkernes Efterrsudstilling (SE) society.
Exhibitions/citations Work shown worldwide. For several years, Jubilee scholarship, Dansk Nationalbank. For Fritz Hansen products: 1998 Designpreis, Baden Württemberg; 1998 Red Dot award, Design Zentrum Nordrhein Westfalen, Essen; 1998 award, Industrial Design Society of America (IDSA); 1998 award, Industrieform (iF) Prize, Hanover; 1999 G-Mark Good Design award, Japanese Industrial Design Promotion Organization (JIDPO).

Jalk, Grete (1920–)

Danish furniture designer.

Training All Copenhagen: 1940–42, design school; to 1946, Kunsthåndværkerskolen; under Kaare Klint, furniture, Det Kongelige Danske Kunstakademi; 1940–43, apprenticeship.
Biography 1954, Jalk set up her own design studio; 1955–60, taught furniture design; 1956–62 and 1968–74, was associated with Mobilia store; designed the widely published 1963 two-piece multiple-fold plywood chair by P. Jeppesens Møbelfabrik (today P.J. Furniture) and other models by Fritz Hansen and Poul Jeppesen.
Exhibitions/citations Work shown at 1946–60 exhibitions, Copenhagen Cabinetmakers' Guild; 1951 (9th) Triennale di Milano; from 1956, at furniture fairs in Europe; 1968 *Two Centuries of Danish Design*, Victoria and Albert Museum, London; 1968 *Les Assises du Siège Contemporain*, Musée des Arts Décoratifs, Paris. First prize, 1946, 1961, 1963 Cabinetmakers' Guild; 1953 prize, Georg Jensen; 1955 first prize, Grdr. Dahl wallpaper; 1963 (2nd) award (one-piece circular plywood chair), *Daily Mirror* International Furniture Competition; 1981 first prize, Danish State Art Foundation.
Bibliography Cat., *Les assises du siège contemporain*, Paris: Musée des Arts Décoratifs, 1968. F. Sieck, *Nutidig Dansk Møbeldesign – en kortfattet illustreret beskrivelse*, Copenhagen: Bondo Gravesen, 1981, 1990. N. Oda, *Danish Chairs*, San Francisco: Chronicle Books, 1999.

Jallot, Léon-Albert (1874–1967)

French artisan and designer; born Nantes; active Paris; father of Maurice Jallot.

Biography 1890, Jallot began to make furniture; 1898–1901, was the manager of furniture workshop of Siegfried Bing's gallery/shop L'Art Nouveau, Paris; 1901, cofounded Société des Artistes Décorateurs; 1903, established his own decorating workshop, where he designed and made furniture, fabrics, carpets, tapestries, glassware, lacquer, and screens; was skillful in use of rabbeted wood; drew plans for his own house and for that of painter André Derain on the rue Douanier-Rousseau, Paris. Jallot was the first to turn away from the excessively floral ornamentation of Art Nouveau and to advocate the pursuit of linearism. As early as 1904, when his only decoration was the grain of the wood, he championed rich materials rather than overwrought forms to suggest luxury; from 1921, in partnership with his son Maurice, he designed a wide variety of furniture and furnishings. His furniture had simple lines and flat surfaces which were lacquered, painted, or shagreen- or leather-covered. 1920s, the Jallots began to use synthetic materials and metal in their work. Léon's standard light fixtures were sold by Favre. After c. 1927, when he and Maurice began to design rooms with almost entirely indirect lighting, fixtures for their interiors

Grete Jalk. Lounge chair. 1963. Teak, 29 1/2 x 24 3/4 x 27 1/4" (74.9 x 62.9 x 69.2 cm). Mfr: Poul Jeppesen, Denmark. Gift of Jo Carole and Ronald S. Lauder. MoMA.

were designed by Jean Perzel, G. Fabre, and Eugène Capon. The Jallots produced fluted columns lit from within for 1920 Salon of Société des Artistes Décorateurs and a peripherally illuminated pelmet for 1928 Hôtel Radio (including interiors and a restaurant by Maurice), boulevard de Clichy, Paris.
Exhibitions Work shown at Salons of Société Nationale des Beaux-Arts from 1908; Société des Artistes Décorateurs from 1906; editions of Salon d'Automne from 1919; grand salon of Une Ambassade Française and L'Hôtel du Collectionneur (man's bedroom with Georges Chevalier, and Jallot produced the furniture designed by Henri Rapin and Pierre Selmersheim) at 1925 *Exposition Internationale des Arts Décoratifs et Industriels Modernes*, Paris.
Bibliography Alastair Duncan, *Art Nouveau and Art Déco Lighting*, New York: Simon & Schuster, 1978. *Restaurants, dancing, cafés, bars*, Paris: Charles Moreau, nos. 39–44, 1929. *Ensembles mobiliers*, Paris: Charles Moreau, vol. 5, nos. 6–7, 1945. Victor Arwas, *Art Déco*, New York: Abrams, 1980. Cat., Aaron Lederfajn and Xavier Lenormand, *Le Louvre des Antiquaires présente: 1930 quand le meuble devient sculpture*, Paris, 1986. Pierre Kjellberg, *Art déco: les maîtres du mobilier, le décor des paquebots*, Paris: Amateur, 1986: 94, 97.

Jallot, Maurice (1900–1971)

French furniture designer and decorator; born and active Paris; son of Léon Jallot.

Training To 1921, École Boulle, Paris.
Biography 1921, Maurice Jallot began collaborating with his father Léon, from whom he eventually took over the business, but was more of a modernist than his father. To 1950, Maurice regularly worked with the Maîtrise decorating studio of Les Galeries Lafayette department store in Paris and with Le Mobilier National; was also active as a decorator and designed a number of store and apartment interiors, including a stair railing (produced by Raymond Subes), rugs, stained glass, and geometric-motif furniture panels.
Exhibitions Work first shown under Maurice's name alone at 1927 (18th) Salon of Société des Artistes Décorateurs; Une Ambassade Française pavilion (furniture suite for the reception salon), 1925 Exposition Internationale des Arts Décoratifs et Industriels Modernes, Paris.
Bibliography Pierre Kjellberg, *Art déco: les maîtres du mobilier, le décor des paquebots*, Paris: Amateur, 1986. Cat., Sophie Tasma Anargyros et al., *L'école française: les créateurs de meubles du 20ème siècle*, Paris: Industries Françaises de l'Ameublement, 2000.

Janák, František (1951–)

Czech glass designer and teacher; born Havlíckuv Brod.

Training 1961–67, apprenticeship in glass cutting, Bohemia Glassworks in Svetlá nad Sázavou; 1967-71, Specialized School of Glassmaking, Kamenicky´ Šenov; 1975-81 under Staislav Libensky, Vysoká Škola Umělecko-průmyslová (VŠUP, academy of arts, architecture, and design), Prague.
Biography 1971–72, Janák was director, Bohemia Glassworks in Svetlá nad Sázavou; 1972–75, glass cutter at Vytvarna Remesla cooperative in Prague; 1981–85, freelance glass artist in his own studio in Dolni Mesto; 1985–88, glass designer at UBOK (institute of interior and fashion design) in Prague. 1989–93, Janák was a freelance glass artist in his own studio in Prague; 1993–95, a glass designer at LINEA-UBOK in Prague; 1995–97, a visiting professor at Toyama Institute of Glass Art, Toyama, Japan. 1997–98, he returned to Prague, again as a freelance glass designer; 1998–2000, was a professor at and the head of the department of cut glass of Specialized School of Glassmaking in Kamenicky´ Šenov; 2000–01, a visiting associate professor at Rochester (N.Y.) Institute of Technology, US; from 2001, has been once again a freelance artist in his own studio.
Exhibitions/citations Work included in a number of exhibitions from 1982 *Jugend Gestaltet*, Munich, Germany, to 2002 *Glass, Sculptures, Paintings*, Glassicenter, Kamenicky´ Šenov. 1981 Rector Prize, VŠUP, Prague; 1982 Urkunde Jugend gestaltet, Munich; 1985 (2nd) Coburger Glaspreis, Coburg, Germany; first prize, 1986 (4th) Quadrennial, Erfurt, Germany; diploma, 1988 *The World Crafts Council-Europe* exhibition, Stuttgart, Germany; Pavel Hlava prize, 1995 International Exhibition of Glass, Kanazawa, Japan.

Janák, Pavel (1882–1956)

Czech architect, designer, and teacher, born Prague.

Training Under J. Schulz, České Vysoké Učení Technické (Czech technical university), Prague; under J. Zitek, Deutsche Technische Hochschule, Prague; 1906–08 under Otto Wagner, Akademie der bildenden Künste, Vienna.
Biography 1908–09, Janák worked in Jan Kotěra's studio in Prague; 1908, became a member of Union of Architects of Mánes Association of Plastic Artists, and participated in founding of Artěl cooperative; 1911, resigned from Mánes and joined the Group of Plastic Artists, serving as the architect of its first (1912) exhibition; 1912, cofounded Prague Artistic Workshops; 1914, cofounded Association of Czech Accomplishment; from 1924, was the chairperson of the Czechoslovakian Werkbund (SČSD); 1917, returned to Mánes; 1921–25, was the editor of magazine *Výtvarná práce*; 1921–42, was a professor of architecture, Vysoká Škola Uměleckoprůmyslová (VŠUP, academy of arts, architecture, and design), Prague; 1936, became the chief architect of Prague Castle. Janák was an important urbanist; died in Prague.
Exhibitions Work subject of 1982–84 two-place exhibition: Emmauskloster, Prague, and Semper-Depot of Akademie der bildenden Künste, Vienna (c. 1984 catalog below).
Bibliography Marie Benesová, *Pavel Janák*, Prague, 1959. Cat., Olga Herbe-nová und Vladimir Slapeta, *Pavel Janák, 1882–1956: Architektur und Kunstgewerbe*, Prague: Kunstgewerbemuseum Prag [Uměleckoprůmyslové Muzeum], c. 1984. Alexander von Vegesack et al., *Czech Cubism: Architecture, Furniture, and Decorative Arts, 1910–1925*, New York; Princeton Architectural Press, 1992. Cat., *Prague, 1900–1938: capitale secrète des avants-gardes*, Dijon: Musée des Beaux-Arts, 1997.

japonisme

Style in the decorative arts.

History The opening up of trade with Japan following American Commodore Matthew Perry's 1853 expedition increased interest in Japanese art in the West, particularly in France. One early interpreter of the style was artist Félix Bracquemond, a friend of the Goncourt brothers. His 1866 table service for the comte de Rousseau was produced by Lebœuf et Millet in Creil. Enthusiasm for the style was heightened by the profusion of Japanese prints and wares at the 1867 *Exposition Universelle* in Paris. Exponents of *japonisme* adopted Japanese motifs and images and imitated its ceramics techniques. 1874, when Théodore Deck developed *émaux-en-relief* process of enamel glazing in deep, saturated colors, the process was adopted by porcelain factories, including the large facility in Bordeaux managed by Albert and Charles Vieillard. The Vieillards produced ironstone, stoneware, earthenware, and hard-and-soft-paste porcelain. 1880–1910, *japonisme* became an integral aspect of the Art Nouveau style. Siegfried Bing, the proprietor of gallery/shop L'Art Nouveau, Paris, was more sensitive than anyone else to the pulse of Art Nouveau and wrote the books *Le japon artistique: documents d'art et d'industrie* (Paris: Japon Artistique, 1888–91) and *La culture artistique en Amérique* (Paris, 1896), the latter based on his visit to 1893 *World's Columbian Exposition*, Chicago. Christopher Dresser, who visited the 1876 *Centenary Exposition*, Philadelphia, went to Japan, acquired a large number of objects for Tiffany & Co. in New York, and wrote the book *Japan: Its Architecture, Art, and Art Manufactures* (London: Longmans, Green, 1882). Japanese influences were seen in the US in the work of, among others, Louis Comfort Tiffany, who had close ties with Bing in Paris, and in Britain through the enterprise of Arthur Lasenby Liberty as early as 1862.
Bibliography Cat., Gabriel P. Weisberg, *Art Nouveau Bing*, New York: Abrams, 1986. Cat., L. d'Albis, *Japonisme à la manufacture Vieillard 1875–1890, projets de céramiques*, Paris: Galerie Fischer-Kiener, 1986. Mary L. Myers, Amédée de Caranza entry, *Recent Acquisitions: A Selection 1986–1987*, New York: The Metropolitan Museum of Art, 1987. Jacob Baal-Teshuva, *Louis Comfort Tiffany*, Cologne: Taschen, 2001.
> See Art Nouveau.

Jaray, Paul (1889–1974)

Austrian engineer and designer; born Vienna.

Biography Before and during World War I, Jaray took part in studies of German navy airships; after the war, turned to car design and patented a number of aerodynamic car bodies and principles, often conflicting with those of another Viennese inventor, Edmund Rumpler, resulting in lawsuits. Jaray was a stubborn purist who refused to deviate from his ideas; late 1920s and early 1930s, further developed his aerodynamic principles in pursuit of what he considered to be the 'perfect' form with a long-sloping back profile for auto bodies. The form was eventually employed by a number of German firms. But it proved imperfect, and Hans Ledwinka, one of Europe's most brilliant automobile engineers, developed an alternative based on Jaray's initiative. The Ledwinka

interpretation was employed in a very advanced aerodynamic truck, the Tatra Type 87, produced in Czechoslovakia and featuring an air-cooled rear engine and central-beam frame. Earlier, Jaray had been successful in developing the use of his J-Wheel (or J-Rad), particularly appropriate in the construction of bicycles and eventually in airplanes and automobiles, to minimize air resistance. 1922–23, the Hesperus factory in Stuttgart produced about 2,000 armchair wheels, very successful in the Netherlands, based on the Jaray wheel concept. Much was published at the time on the Jaray J-Wheel bicycle that offered high efficiency compared to other contemporary models. He died in St. Gallen, Switzerland.
Bibliography Wolfgang Schmarbeck, *Tatra, die Geschichte der Tatra Automobile*, Lübbecke, Germany: Uhle & Kleimann, 1976. *Auto Tatra Aerod Car*, St. Paul, Minn.: Motorbooks International. Miroslav Gomola, *Automobily Tatra—Luxusní vozy z Koprivnice 1920–1940,* Brno, Czech Republic: AGM CZ, 2000. Miroslav Gomola, Gavin Farmer, and Jan Tulis, *Automobiles Tatra—Aerodynamic Cars from Koprivnice*, Brno: AGM-Gomola, 1999. Kees Smit, *Tatra Aerodynamic Cars, 1933–1975*, Brno: AGM CZ. Miroslav Gomola, *Hadimrs̆ka: aneb Nesmrtelnedmapades̆á*, Brno: AGM CZ.
> See Ledwinka, Hans.

Jarrige, Jacques (1962–)
French architect and designer; born Paris.

Training In architecture.
Biography Jarrige, who describes himself as an artist–artisan, has designed furniture, some examples of which appear to be single pieces of curvaceous wood. His tables, sideboards, cabinets, and lamps have been compared to those of Antoni Gaudí's Catalan school.
Exhibitions French-design venue (1999 Luca table by Cat-Berro), 2000 Salon du Meuble, Paris.
Bibliography Cat., Sophie Tasma Anargyros et al., *L'école française: les créateurs de meubles du 20ème siècle*, Paris: Industries Françaises de l'Ameublement, 2000.

Jarvie, Robert Riddle (1865–1941)
American metalworker; born New York; active Chicago.

Biography Jarvie was employed by Chicago Department of Transportation at turn of 19th century; 1893–1917, registered as a silversmith in Chicago; 1900, showed his work for the first time; 1901–04, in *House Beautiful* magazine, advertised himself as 'the candlestick maker' and was indeed largely supported by the success of his candlesticks. By 1905, he had opened The Jarvie Shop. Émigrés J.P. Petterson from Norway and Knut L. Gustafson from Sweden worked for Jarvie. From c. 1912, he produced noteworthy gold and silver trophies, including 1912 Aero Club trophy, 1917 trophy for a University of Illinois dairy exposition, and annual trophies for the Union Stock Yard Company and International Live Stock Exposition. Other work: hand-beaten copper bowls, sconces, vases, trays, and bookends. He called on geometric patterns derived from Native American motifs and realized intriguing Art Nouveau and Arts and Crafts forms. 1920, he went out of business.
Exhibitions Work first shown, at 1900 *Arts and Crafts Society Exhibition*, Chicago; at a 1902 exhibition (candlesticks), Chicago Art Institute.
Bibliography Sharon S. Darling with Gail Farr Casterline, *Chicago Metalsmiths*, Chicago Historical Society, 1977. Cat., Anne Yaffe Phillips, *From Architecture to Object*, New York: Hirschl and Adler, 1989: 100. Annelies Krekel-Aalberse, *Art Nouveau and Art Déco Silver*, New York: Abrams, 1989. *Metropolitan Home*, Nov. 1990: 54.

Järvisalo, Jouko (1950–)
Finnish designer; born Varkaus; active Helsinki.

Biography Järvisalo has been active as an interior architect and freelance designer. Practicing from 1983 in an interior-design studio, has served clients such as Artek, Asko, Inno, Mobel Oy, Yosoy, Aksi, Lamilux, and Peltola; for others, designed c. 1986 Flap wood-and-metal chair by Inno-Tuote, 1997 lightweight Kova chair by Mobel Original Design, and 1996 Flight chair, sofa and tables by Avarte.
Citations Citations include 1999 Pro Finnish Design award (for Kova).
Bibliography Robert A.M. Stern (ed.), *The International Design Yearbook*, New York: Abbeville, 1985/1986.

Jasper Seating Company
Furniture manufacturer; located Jasper, Ind.

History By founding a furniture factory nine months before the Oct. 1929 American Stock Market crash, Jasper Seating was able to profit from the Old World craftsmanship of accomplished German woodworkers, who had immigrated to southern Indiana in 19th century. Its armchair no. 303, continuously produced since the firm was established, was part of its initial range of wooden institutional seating whose manufacture was and continues to be complemented by its own lumberyard milling facility and rare steam-bending operation. A version of the anonymous, archetypically American design of the no. 303 appeared as early as 1910 in both side-chair and swivel-base versions. The original no. 303 featured a flat, round-edge seat but this was changed to a more friendly sculptured saddle seat. The firm's current inventory includes a number of historicist and contemporary chairs, as well as tables.
Bibliography Mel Byars, 'To Be Continued,' *Metropolitan Home*, Nov.–Dec. 1999: 80+.

Jastrzebowski, Adalbert (1885–)
Polish designer.

Training School of Fine Art, Cracow.
Exhibitions At 1925 *Exposition Internationale des Arts Décoratifs et Industriels Modernes*, Paris; Jastrzebowski designed the dining room at the Polish pavilion (with architect Josef Czajkowski) and sgraffito walls of the pavilion courtyard, and organized Polish exhibitions in the Grand Palais. He taught at the School of Fine Art, Cracow.
Bibliography *Écoles professionnelles de la République Tchécoslovaque*, Prague: Imprimerie Industrielle, 1925. Great Britain Department of Overseas Trade (with an introductory survey), *Reports on the Present Position and Tendencies of the Industrial Arts as Indicated at the International Exhibition of Modern Decorative and Industrial Arts, Paris, 1925*, Harrow: H.M.S.O. Press, 1927. Maurice Dufrône, *Ensembles mobiliers, Exposition Internationale 1925*, Paris: Charles Moreau, 1925; Woodbridge, Suffolk: Antique Collectors' Club 1989: 160.

Jaulmes, Gustave-Louis (1873–1959)
Swiss architect and designer; born Lausanne; active Paris.

Training In architecture.
Biography Jaulmes was an architect before turning to decorative painting in 1901, to furniture design in 1910, and tapestry design in 1915. He received important commissions including for the Musée Rodin in Paris; designed tapestries and upholstery fabrics by Compagnie des Arts Français (CAF); joined CAF on its 1919 founding by Louis Süe and André Mare. While at CAF, Jaulmes executed several notable tapestries such as *Le départ des troupes américaines de Philadelphie pour la France*, and murals inspired by Berain and du Cerceau depicting garlands, gathered fabric, and draperies in a lush 18th-century style. His upholstery fabrics were usually woven by his wife. He designed furniture by decorating firm Damon; decorated (with Süe and Mare) the avenue des Champs-Élysées and designed the cenotaph commemorating World War II; painted murals for Théâtre de Chaillot and Musée des Arts Décoratifs, Paris, and the proscenium curtain of Grand-Théâtre, Lyon, along with tapestries and paintings for numerous other theaters, monuments, casinos, and hotels; 1944, elected member of Académie des Beaux-Arts, Paris.
Exhibitions Work shown at Salons of Société Nationale des Beaux-Arts from 1906, editions of Salon d'Automne from 1908 and of Salon des Artistes Indépendants from 1909. 1910, began to show furniture. At 1925 *Exposition Internationale des Arts Décoratifs et Industriels Modernes*, Paris: painted areas of L'Hôtel du Collectionneur and Une Ambassade Française pavilions, six paintings illustrating *Les mois en fête* in Salle des Fêtes of the Grand Palais, and participated in Musée d'Art Contemporain organized by Compagnie des Arts Français.
Bibliography Léon Deshairs (intro.), *Modern French Decorative Art: A Collection of Examples of Modern French Decoration*, Paris: Albert Lévy, c. 1925–30. Yvonne Brunhammer, *Le cinquantenaire de l'Exposition de 1925*, Paris: Musée des Arts Décoratifs, 1976: 132. Victor Arwas, *Art Déco*, New York: Abrams, 1980. Pierre Cabanne, *Encyclopédie art déco*, Paris: Somogy, 1986: 201–02.

Jean, Nathalie (1963–)
Canadian architect and designer; active Montreal and Milan.

Training 1986, architecture degree, Montreal.
Biography Jean worked at Peter Rose Architect in Montreal; subsequently, became a TV and theater set designer at Alliance Entertainment; worked at the studio of artist/architect Melvin Charney in Montreal; 1988, settled in Milan and, 1988–91, collaborated with Sottsass Associati and, 1991–93, with Aldo Cibic; 1993, established her own studio in Milan for interior design, primarily of fashion boutiques and exhibition design

for Pomellato, Italseta, Alberta Ferretti, Lineapiù; products by Rosenthal; various interiors for fashion magazine *Io Donna*.
Exhibitions/citations While at Melvin Charney, collaborated on the winning competition design of the gardens of Centre Canadien d'Architecture (CCA), Montreal, exhibited at 1992 Biennale di Venezia.

Jeanneney, Paul (1861–1920)
French ceramicist; born Strasbourg.

Biography Jeanneney was a collector of Far Eastern ceramics. After the 1894 death of Carriès, Jeanneney learned stoneware techniques based on Carriès's; 1902, moved from Strasbourg to Saint-Amand-en-Puisaye. His work was influenced by Chinese stoneware with flambé glazes and Japanese *trompe-l'œil* stoneware, similar to that of Carriès. Jeanneney made gourd vases, bowls, bottles, and round vases, inspired by Korean *chawans*; created the *champignon* vase decorated with bracket fungus, with a wooden lid; produced stoneware versions of a head of Balzac and heads of the Burghers of Calais, both by Auguste Rodin.
Bibliography Yvonne Brunhammer et al., *Art Nouveau Belgium, France*, Houston: Institute for the Arts, Rice University, 1976.

Jeanneret, Pierre (1896–1967)
Swiss architect, designer, and painter; born Geneva; cousin of Le Corbusier.

Training In architecture, Geneva.
Biography 1920, Jeanneret settled in Paris, where he first worked in the architectural office of the Perret brothers and, from 1922, as an architect in office of Le Corbusier. He collaborated with Le Corbusier and Charlotte Perriand on seminal furniture designs, although his specific contribution is not known; 1923, met Purist painter Amédée Ozenfant, who had a strong influence on Jeanneret's own painting; 1927 with Le Corbusier, wrote 'Five Points Towards a New Architecture' (originally published in *Almanach de l'architecture moderne*, Paris 1926). The treatise was a manifesto of their architectural aesthetic. From 1930, Jeanneret was a member of Union des Artistes Modernes (UAM). He designed and patented the Scissor chair, originally produced in France in 1947 and, 1948–66 as no. 92 by Knoll Associates in the US. Purportedly, it was the first Knoll chair to be upholstered. The chair was constructed of maple with circular brass struts and included foam-rubber cushions upholstered in a linen-and-jute fabric. He also designed other credited furniture of his own. After World War II, Jeanneret experimented with prefabrication techniques and collaborated with Jean Prouvé on prefabricated housing and with Georges Blanchon on the town planning of Puteaux, France; from 1950, worked on government buildings in Chandigarh, India, and was lauded as the principal architect over Le Corbusier (the only time). Jeanneret designed a number of other public buildings but was and remains in the shadow of Le Corbusier; died in Lausanne, and his ashes were scattered on the Sukhna Lake in Chandigarh, as he had requested.
Exhibitions Furniture (with Le Corbusier and Perriand) shown at 1929 Salon d'Automne and 1930 (1st) UAM exhibition; subsequent UAM exhibitions (with Le Corbusier's architectural projects, models, and photographs of various completed buildings). 1999 extensive exhibition of Jeanneret photography of Chandigarh project in India.
Bibliography S. Randhawa, *L'architecture d'aujourd'hui*, no. 136, Feb.–Mar. 1968: VI. Arlette Barré-Despond, *UAM*, Paris: Regard, 1986: 426–27. *Dictionnaire encyclopédique de l'architecture moderne et contemporaine*, Paris: Vilo, 1987: 182. Catherine Courtiau, 'Pierre Jeanneret,' in *Le Corbusier, une encyclopédie*, Paris: Centre Georges Pompidou/CCI, 1987. Cat., *Les années UAM 1929–1958*, Paris: Musée des Arts Décoratifs, 1988: 198–99.
> See Le Corbusier.

Jeep
> See Probst, Karl K.

Jeffers, 'Grace' Gracemarie Antoinette Jeffers (1967–)
American designer, design historian, and consultant; active New York.

Training 1990, bachelor's degree, School of the Art Institute of Chicago, Illinois; 1996, master's degree in history of the decorative arts; The Bard Graduate Center, New York.
Biography 1982–90, she was active in Grace Jeffers Designs; 1991–93, was sales representative/product developer at Maya Romanoff, New York; 1993–94, marketing director, Bendheim Architectural Glass (glass

Pierre Jeanneret. Scissor chair. 1947. Maple, brass struts, web supports, foam, and cotton fabric, 28 3/8 x 22 13/16 x 26 3/8" (72 x 58 x 67 cm). Mfr.: Knoll Associates, US. (1948–66). Courtesy Quittenbaum Kunstauktionen, Munich.

importers), Passaic, N.J.; from 1995, has been partner of Inside Design, a consultancy for design, curatorial services, marketing, and public relations, including for Wilsonart and Airstream; lectures, writes, and teaches.
Exhibitions/citations From 1994, has curated a number of exhibitions, including 1994–95 *Crosscurrents of Modernism: Early 20th-Century Masterpieces from the Virginia Museum*, Bard Graduate Center, New York. A number of citations, including 1999 Modernism Award, *Metropolitan Home* magazine.

Jeffrey & Co.
British wallpaper manufacturer.

History 1836, Jeffrey and Wise was established at St Helen's Place, London; 1838, moved to Kent and Essex Yard, Whitechapel, London; by 1840, had begun using cylinders to print some of its designs, a technology derived from calico cloth printing; produced washable wallpaper invented by Crease, a paper stainer. 1842, Robert Horne became a partner, and the name became Jeffrey, Wise and Horne, changed again in 1843 to Horne and Allen. A wallpaper shown at 1851 London *Great Exhibition*, admired for the flatness of its design, was one of the first of the firm's productions of the 1870s–80s period. By 1862, its name was Jeffrey & Co., in Whitechapel, with partners including William Allen, Alfred Brown, and Edward Hamilton. 1864, the firm merged with Holmes and Aubert, a producer of hand-printed, flocked, and leaf-metal papers at 64 Essex Street, Islington, London, where Jeffrey's headquarters then moved. Dissatisfied with his own production of papers, William Morris in 1864 commissioned Jeffrey to print his 1862 Daisy pattern, the first Morris paper made widely available to the public. The firm continued to print Morris papers to 1930, using the same pearwood blocks. Jackson Graham assigned to Jeffrey the printing of Owen Jones's complicated papers (requiring 58 separate wood blocks) for the Viceroy's Palace in Cairo. On William Allen's 1866 retirement, Metford Warner became a junior partner. 1871, after deaths of Alfred Brown and Edward Hamilton, Warner became the sole proprietor; elevated Jeffrey's production to an art, as shown in the Royal Albert Hall in 1873. He commissioned designs from leading British designers and architects of the day such as Lewis F. Day, J.D. Sedding, C.F.A. Voysey, William Burges, Walter Crane, E.W. Godwin, Christopher Dresser, and Bruce J. Talbert. Charles Locke Eastlake designed the popular 1869 Solanum pattern. 1872, Godwin's work was first printed and, 1880s, became popular in the US. From 1875, Ipswich architect Brightwen Binyon's idea of a combination of papers for dado, filling, and frieze became popular. To 1920s, Metford Warner managed the firm with his sons Albert, Marcus, and Horace. On Metford Warner's 1930 death, the firm was bought by Sanderson, which in 1940 acquired Morris's printing blocks, still in use today.

Exhibitions/citations 1851 *Great Exhibition of the Works of Industry of All Nations* (wallpapers), London; 1873 *Annual Exhibition of All Fine Arts* (first shown as fine art), Royal Albert Hall, London; 1876 *Centennial Exposition*, Philadelphia (three-part paper based on Chaucer's *Legend of Good Women*, by Walter Crane, receiving two gold medals). Gold medals 1878, 1889, and 1900 editions of *Exposition Universelle*, Paris; gold medal, 1893 *World's Columbian Exposition*, Chicago; international prizes throughout late 19th century; grand prize, 1908 *Franco-British Exhibition*, London.
Bibliography Alan Victor Sugden and John Ludlam Edmondson, *A History of English Wallpaper, 1509–1914*, London: Batsford, 1926: 209–12. E.A. Entwisle, *A Literary History of Wallpaper*, London: Batsford, 1960: 41–45. Catherine Lynn, *Wallpaper in America: From the Seventeenth Century to World War I*, New York: Norton, 1980. Doreen Bolger Burke et al., *In Pursuit of Beauty: Americans and the Aesthetic Movement*, New York: The Metropolitan Museum of Art/Rizzoli, 1986.

Jenaer Glaswerke
> See Schott und Genossen Glaswerke.

Jencks, Charles A. (1939–)
American architect, designer, and critic; born Baltimore, Md.; active London.

Training Literature and architecture, Harvard University, Cambridge, Mass.; architecture, London University.
Biography From 1968, Jencks taught, Architectural Association, London, and, from 1974, at University of California, Los Angeles. His writings on postmodern architecture have become widely known. He designed influential and widely published buildings and furniture, some of which, with symbolic ornament, was initially executed for the 'Summer Room' of a London house; pieces which had limited manufacture included 1984 Sun table with the image of a *trompe-l'œil* solar disk, and Sun chair produced by Sawaya & Moroni. Jencks was one of 11 architect designers commissioned for 1983 Tea and Coffee Piazza project by Alessi, his example calling on classical columnar shapes. Jencks's numerous books included *Meaning in Architecture* (edited with George Baird, London: Barrie & Rockliff/Cresset, 1969), *Architecture 2000: Predictions and Methods* (London: Studio Vista, 1971), *Adhocism: The Case for Improvisation* (with Nathan Silver, London: Secker & Warburg, 1972), *Modern Movements in Architecture* (London: Pelican, 1973), *The Language of Post-Modern Architecture* (London: Academy, 1978 rev. ed.), *Signs, Symbols and Architecture* (with Geoffrey Broadbent and Richard Bunt, New York: Wiley, 1980), *Skyscrapers–Skycities* (New York: Rizzoli, 1980), *Post-Modern Classicism* (London: Architectural Design, 1980), *Current Architecture* (London: Academy, 1982), *Towards a Symbolic Architecture: The Thematic House* (London: Academy, 1985), and *Post-Modernism: The New Classicism in Art and Architecture* (London: Academy, 1987).
Bibliography Officina Alessi, *Tea and Coffee Piazza*, Milan: Crusinallo, 1983. Robert A.M. Stern (ed.), *The International Design Yearbook*, New York: Abbeville, 1985/1986. *Les carnets du design*, Paris: Mad-Cap Productions/APCI, 1986: 71. Juli Capella and Quim Larrea, *Designed by Architects in the 1980s*, New York: Rizzoli, 1988.

Jensen, Arthur Georg (1866–1935); Georg Jensen Sølvsmedie
Danish metalworker and enterprise; born Faavad.

Training Apprenticeship as a goldsmith; c. 1895–1901, sculpture, Det Kongelige Danske Kunstakademi, Copenhagen.
Biography/history Jensen served his apprenticeship in Copenhagen for a time under Holm and, 1884, became a journeyman; c. 1898 with Christian Joachim, made ceramics in the workshop of painter/designer Mogens Ballin, near Copenhagen. Jensen worked in Aluminia pottery and in Bing & Grøndahl Porcelænsfabrik, Copenhagen; 1904, began designing jewelry and silverwares and, the same year with one assistant, opened his own small shop Georg Jensen Sølvsmedie, which eventually became large, successful, and highly productive. He disliked classical (or historicist) reproductions and wanted to make modern design commercially successful; his own designs were influenced by nature. Jensen's success may be partially attributed to his ability to attract and foster the talents of Johan Rohde, Gundorph Albertus, Harald Nielsen, and Sigvard Bernadotte, and others. Post-World War II designers Henning Koppel and Tias Eckhoff continued the high level of innovation at Jensen's. Almost all of the original designs continue today to be made by hand. Jensen also used stainless steel, originally a wartime substitute for silver. It gained popularity after World War I, and Jensen's postwar stainless-steel pieces were distinguished. By 1920, Jensen had opened a showroom on Fifth Avenue in New York; its success was assured when publisher William Randolph Hearst bought the entire inventory at 1915 *Panama–Pacific International Exposition*, San Francisco. (1915 Acorn pattern by Rohde and 1919 Blossom pattern by Jensen himself were plagiarized by International Silver Company in the US.) Finn Juhl executed glassware designs for the firm. On Jensen's 1935 death, the management of the firm passed to his son Jørgen Jensen, to 1962. 1972, Royal Copenhagen Porcelain Factory, which already owned A. Michelsen, bought Georg Jensen. 1975, Georg Jensen and A. Michelsen were amalgamated. 1985, Georg Jensen and A. Michelsen merged with Royal Copenhagen Porcelain Factory and Kastrup & Holmegård Glasswærks under the umbrella name of Royal Copenhagen. Continuing, Royal Copenhagen bought the Illums Bolighus furnishings store in Copenhagen in 1985; Hans Hansen Silversmiths in 1991; Orrefors Kosta Boda, BodaNova-Höganäs Keramik, and Venini in 1997, and, and eventually others, to form the overall group known as Royal Scandinavia. However, in 2000, Royal Scandinavia was bought by an investment group and eventually dismantled into various entities.
Exhibitions/citations Jensen work shown to acclaim in every major international exhibition of the applied arts in the first three decades of the 20th century, including 1900 *Exposition Universelle*, Paris (honorable mention with Petersen for ceramics); 1905 *Exposition Internationale*, The Hague; 1909 exhibition, Århus (Denmark); 1909 exhibition, Musée des Arts Décoratifs, Paris; 1910 *Exposition Universelle et Internationale*, Brussels (gold medal); 1913 edition of Salon d'Automne, Paris; 1915 *Panama-Pacific International Exposition*, San Francisco (first prize); 1925 *Exposition Internationale des Arts Décoratifs et Industriels Modernes*, Paris (grand prize); 1929–30 *Exposición Internacional de Barcelona* (grand prize). More recently, 2003 Red Dot Best of the Best (for Quack thermos flask by Maria Berntsen), Design Zentrum Nordrhein Westfalen, Essen. Work subject of 1966 exhibition, Goldsmiths' Hall, London; 1980 *Georg Jensen Silversmithy: 77 Artists, 75 Years*, Smithsonian Institution, Washington (catalog below).
Bibliography Cat., *Georg Jensen Silversmithy: 77 Artists, 75 Years*, Washington: Smithsonian, 1980. Cat., David Revere McFadden (ed.), *Scandinavian Modern Design 1880–1980*, New York: Abrams, 1982. Jørgen E.R. Møller, *Georg Jensen, the Danish Silversmith*, Copenhagen: G. Jensen & Wendel, 1985. Melissa Gabardi, *Les bijoux des années 50*, Paris: Amateur, 1987. Janet and Bill Drucker, *Georg Jensen: 20th Century Designs*, Atglen, Pa.: Schiffer, 2002.
> See Royal Scandinavia.

Jensen, Helge Vestergård (1917–)
Danish furniture designer.

Training To 1942, furniture design, Kunsthåndværkerskolen; Møbelskole, Det Kongelige Danske Kunstakademiet; both Copenhagen.
Biography 1937, Jensen served as an apprentice; 1942, worked with architect Kaare Klint; 1944–46, with architect Mølgård Nielsen; 1946–48, with architect Palle Suenson; from 1950, with architect Vilhelm Lauritzen; 1950, set up his own design practice; designed furniture by Søren Horn and the widely published 1955 Racket chair with strung nylon-cord and a 'floating' headrest.
Awards 1954–58 and 1960–63 Danish furniture prizes.
Bibliography Frederik Sieck, *Nutidig Dansk Møbeldesign – en kortfattet illustreret beskrivelse*, Copenhagen: Bondo Gravesen, 1981: 50. Noritsugu Oda, *Danish Chairs*, San Francisco: Chronicle, 1999.

Jensen, Henning (1924–)
Danish architect and furniture designer.

Training To 1948, architecture, Det Kongelige Danske Kunstakademi, Copenhagen.
Biography 1948–58, Jensen worked at the office of architect Palle Suenson; 1958–61, was the chief architect, Federation of Retail Grocers; 1951–64, taught in architecture school, Det Kongelige Danske Kunstakademi; designed furniture by Munch Møbler, Christensen og Larsen, and others.
Exhibitions/citations Work shown at 1962 and 1965 Cabinetmakers' Guild exhibitions (with Hanne and Torben Valeur); 1965 Danish Society of Arts and Crafts (with the Valeurs), Charlottenborg; 1960, 1963, 1972, and 1976 Spring Exhibition (with Torben Valeur), 1962 *Young Nordic Designers*, Röhsska Konstslöjdmuseet, Gothenburg; 1962 *Moderne Dänische Wohnkultur*, Vienna. 1988 citation (furniture system by Munch Møbler), Den Danske Designpris.

Bibliography Frederik Sieck, *Nutidig Dansk Møbeldesign – en kortfattet illustreret beskrivelse*, Copenhagen: Bondo Gravesen, 1981, 1990.

Jensen, Jacob (1926–)

Danish industrial designer.

Training To 1951, industrial design, Kunsthåndværkerskolen, Copenhagen.
Biography From 1951, Jensen worked in the office of Bernadotte & Bjørn, where he was the office manager 1954–59; 1958, set up Jacob Jensen Design in Copenhagen; 1959–61, was assistant professor of industrial design, University of Chicago; from 1960, a partner in Latham, Tyler & Jensen, New York and Chicago; 1958, moved his Danish design firm to Hejskov in Jutland; created more than 500 industrial products by Danish and foreign companies. As one of Bang & Olufsen's primary designers during 1965–91, he became best known for a large number of designs for the firm such as 1970 Beolit 600 portable radio, 1972 Beogram 4000 turntable, 1986 Beocenter 9000 sound system, and numerous others. office chairs by Labofa, 1976 Comet telephone by Kristian Kirks Telefonfabriker (today Kirk Telecom), toys by LEGO, kitchen appliances by Gaggenau, astronomical clock/watches/telephone/Jensen-One car by Max René, loudspeakers by Dantax. Other product clients: Rosti (kitchenware), Lasat Caddy (computer accessories), JO JO (electrical accessories), NEG Micon (windmills), Boform (office furniture), Berg Furniture, Labofa (furniture). Graphic-design clients: Lasat Communications, Ringkjøbing Amt, KT Electronic, Madsen, Marker Scandinavia, and Dantax. 1997, he wrote the autobiography *Anderledes, men ikke mærkeligt* (different, but not strange). From 1989, Timothy Jacob Jensen has managed the firm, with Nigel Hapwood as the art director.
Exhibitions/citations Work subject of 1978 exhibitions at The Museum of Modern Art, New York, and in Århus and Copenhagen, and included in 1990 Bang & Olufsen exhibition, Paris; continuing with others. 1978 award, Industrial Designers Society of America (IDSA); 1983 Thorvald Bindesbøll Medal, Akademirådet, Denmark; 1970, 1976, 1978 1994 Industrial Design Prize; 1967 (three citations), 1968 (two citations), 1970, 1971, 1991, 1992, 1998 awards, Industrie Forum Design (iF), Hanover; 1986, 1991, 1994 (two citations), and 1998 G-Mark Good Design, Japanese Industrial Design Promotion Organization (JIDPO); 1977 Gold SIM; 1970 Dansk ID Prize; 1990 (Bang & Olufsen corporate ID, with Acton Bjørn), Den Danske Designpris; Ridderkors (cross of the order of knighthood), Denmark; others.
Bibliography Svend Erik Moller, 'A Non-Specializing Specialist,' *Danish Journal*, vol. 76, 1973: 30–32. Jens Bernsen, *Design: The Problem Comes First*, Copenhagen: Danish Design Council, 1982: 90–95. Cat., Chantal Bizot, *Bang & Olufsen, design et technologie*, Paris: Musée des Arts Décoratifs, 1990. Cat., *Jacob Jensen Design*, Copenhagen: Det Danske Kunstindustriemuseum, 1993. Jens Bang, *Bang & Olufsen: fra vision til legende = From Vision to Legend*, Denmark: Vidsyn, 2000. Paola Antonelli (ed.), *Objects of Design: The Museum of Modern Art*, New York: The Museum of Modern Art, 2003: 239. www.jacob-jensen.com.
> See Bang & Olufsen.

Jacob Jensen. Jydsk Telefon desk model (no. 76E). 1977. Plastic, 3 5/8 x 7 1/8 x 8 7/8" (9.2 x 18.1 x 22.5 cm). Mfr.: Kristian Kirks Telefonfabriker, Denmark. Gift of the designer. MoMA.

Jensen, Jens Jacob Herring Krog (1898–1978)

Danish ceramicist; born Fynen, Jutland; active Cincinnati, Ohio.

Training Ryslinge and Askov Academy, Jutland.
Biography 1927, Jensen moved to the US and, 1928–48, worked at Rookwood Pottery in Cincinnati; decorated pottery, sometimes inspired by contemporary painters in Europe; introduced glazes that produced floating images and curdled color areas; was also a canvas painter; died in Maysville, Ky.
Exhibitions Represented the US at 1939 *Golden Gate International Exposition*, San Francisco. Rookwood stand (with wares by William Hentschel and Wilhelmine Rehm), 1931 (12th) *Exhibition of Contemporary American Industrial Art*, The Metropolitan Museum of Art, New York.
Bibliography Karen Davies, *At Home in Manhattan: Modern Decorative Arts, 1925 to the Depression*, New Haven: Yale, 1983: 56. Herbert Peck, *The Book of Rookwood Pottery*, New York: Crown, 1968. Cat., Kenneth R. Trapp, *Toward the Modern Style: Rookwood Pottery, the Later Years, 1915–1950*, New York: Jordan-Volpe Gallery, 1983.

Jensen, Jørgen (1895–1966)

Danish designer; son of Georg Jensen.

Training 1914 under Leonhard Ebert, in silversmithing in Munich.
Biography 1923–36, Jensen ran a silversmithy in Stockholm; designed silver cutlery and jewelry; after his father's 1935 death, managed Georg Jensen Sølvsmedie to 1962, and contributed mainly larger silverworks, such as bowls, jugs, and tea sets.
Bibliography Michael Farr, *Design in British Industry: A Mid-Century Survey*, London: Cambridge, 1955: 41.

Jensen, Søren Georg (1917–1982)

Danish designer; son of Georg Jensen.

Training From 1936, apprenticeship in the family silversmithy; 1945, silversmithing and sculpture, Det Kongelige Danske Kunstakademi, Copenhagen.
Biography 1962–74, Jensen was head of design department at Georg Jensen Sølvsmedie; 1974, turned to sculpture.
Exhibitions/citations Work included in 1980 *Georg Jensen Silversmithy: 77 Artists, 75 Years*, Washington (catalog below). Gold medal at 1960 (12th) Triennale di Milano; 1974 Thorvald Bindesbøll Medal, Akademirådet, Denmark.
Bibliography Graham Hughes, *Modern Silver Throughout the World*, London: Studio Vista, 1967: no. 19. Cat., *Georg Jensen Silversmithy: 77 Artists, 75 Years*, Washington: Smithsonian, 1980. Cat., Kathryn B. Hiesinger and George H. Marcus III (eds.), *Design Since 1945*, Philadelphia: Philadelphia Museum of Art, 1983.

Jeppesen Møbelfabrik, P.
> See P.J. Furniture.

Jess, Marga (1885–1953)

German silversmith; active Lüneburg.

Training Under Karl Johann Bauer, Lehr- und Versuchs ateliers für angewandte und freie Kunst (Debschitz-Schule), Munich.
Biography Active from 1912, Jess was the first fully qualified female silversmith in Germany. Compared to Emmy Roth's work in Berlin, Jess's silver designs showed a tentative modernism; her designs included raised ornamentation and spirals as well as realistic images in, for example, a 1940 brooch for the Third Reich's 'Wir fahren gegen Engelland' (we sail for England) with Norse/Norman figures to symbolize the SS's hoped-for invasion of England.
Exhibitions Work subject of 1996 *Marga Jess, 1885–1953: Goldschmiedekunst zwischen Tradition und Moderne*, Museum für das Fürstentum, Lüneburg.
Bibliography Annelies Krekel-Aalberse, *Art Nouveau and Art Déco Silver*, New York: Abrams, 1989.

Jirasek, Julius (1896–1966)

Architect and designer; active Vienna.

Training Under Oskar Strnad, Architecture, Kunstgewerbeschule, Vienna.
Biography While a prisoner-of-war in Russia, Jirasek became interested in the ethnographic art of the Urals; on his 1923 return to Vienna, re-entered the Kunstgewerbeschule; became an independent archi-

tect in Vienna, where he designed residential and shop interiors; by 1930, was working at Werkstätten Hagenauer, which produced his designs for silver jewelry, ceramics, lighting, glassware, and furniture and where he was a major contributor to the firm's success.
Exhibitions/citations Work shown at 1971 *Werkstätten Hagenauer 1898–1971 und Hochschule für angewandte Kunst, Meisterklasse für freies Gestalten in Metall* exhibition, Österreichisches Museum für angewandte Kunst, Vienna. 1951 prize for the applied arts, Vienna.
Bibliography Cat., *Werkstätten Hagenauer, 1898–1971*, Vienna: Österreichisches Museum für angewandte Kunst, 1971.

Jiricná, Eva (1938–)

Czech interior designer; born Prague; active London; daughter of an architect.

Training To 1963, České Vysoké Učení Technické (Czech technical university); Akademie Výtvarných Umení (academy of fine arts); both Prague.
Biography 1968, Jiricná settled in London and worked for a year as an architect with the Greater London Council schools division; for eight years, was an associate at Louis de Soissons Partnership, working principally on the Brighton Marina development; 1979 with David Hodges, set up an independent interior-design practice; from 1980, designed interiors for fashion retailer Joseph Ettedgui, including c. 1982 Le Caprice restaurant in London. 1981–82 in London, she designed the Kenzo shop, and Joseph Tricot on Sloane Street. 1985–87, she designed L'Express café, Pour La Maison, Joseph Tricot in Paris, and a second residence for Ettedgui. 1985, she formed Jiricna Kerr Associates and designed Joseph Bis on Draycott Avenue, Joe's Café, Joseph Pour la Ville, Legends nightclub and restaurant, The Sanctuary, Vidal Sassoon hair salon in Frankfurt, Thompson Twins apartment refurbishment and a recording studio. 1987, her design firm became Eva Jiricna Architects. She designed c. 1984 folding table and chair manufactured by TAG Design Partnership for Formica Colorcore; office furniture by Techno of the UK. Jiricná's studio collaborated with Richard Rogers + Partners on the interiors of the Lloyds building, with Czech designer Jan Kaplicky on Harrods store's Way In department, and 1988 entrance to Vitra building in Weil am Rhein, Germany. Recent commissions: bridges (including 1991 Koliste Footbridge, Brno), exhibitions (including 1996 *Africa: Art of a Continent*, Royal Academy of Art, London), leisure (including 2002 Hotel Josef, Prague), apartments (including 2002 penthouse, Belgrave Court, Canary Wharf, London), shops (shop of Royal Academy of Arts, London), buildings (2002 AMEC headquarters, London). Has become known for her dramatic staircases, particularly in glass.
Exhibitions/citations Work included in c. 1984 *New British and French Colorcore* (folding table and chair by TAG for Formica Colorcore); 1996 *Designs of the Times*, Moore College of Art, Philadelphia, Pa., US. 1980–82 *AD/Architectural Design* magazine awards (for her own residence, Joseph Ettedgui's first residence, and Kenzo Shop); and numerous others. 1993, President Havel's member of the Prague Presidential Council; 1997, Royal Academician, 1996, Fellow Royal Society of Arts; 1994 *Architects Journal*/Bovis Design Award; 1994, Commander of Order of the British Empire (OBE) for services to interior design.
Bibliography Robert A.M. Stern (ed.), *The International Design Yearbook*, New York: Abbeville, 1985/1986. Liz McQuiston, *Women in Design: A Contemporary View*, New York: Rizzoli, 1988. Eva Jiricna, *Staircases*, New York: Watson-Guptill, 2001.

Joachim, Christian (1870–1943)

Danish ceramicist.

Training 1889–92 and 1895, Det Kongelige Danske Kunstakademi, Copenhagen.
Biography 1897–1900, Joachim made ceramics with Georg Jensen in a workshop outside Copenhagen; 1901–33, worked for Royal Copenhagen Porcelain Manufactory, where his restrained neoclassical forms were sometimes decorated by Arno Malinowski; 1904, became director of the Aluminia pottery in Copenhagen; 1922–33, was the artistic director of Royal Copenhagen Porcelain and of Aluminia.
Exhibitions/citations Grand prize, 1925 *Exposition Internationale des Arts Décoratifs et Industriels Modernes*, Paris. 1939, elected Honorary Royal Designer for Industry, UK.
Bibliography Cat., David Revere McFadden (ed.), *Scandinavian Modern Design 1880–1980*, New York: Abrams, 1982: 266. Jennifer Hawkins Opie, *Scandinavia: Ceramics and Glass in the Twentieth Century*, New York: Rizzoli, 1989.

Jobling & Co., James A.

British glassware manufacturer; located Sunderland.

History 1921, James A. Jobling & Co., a division of Wear Flint Glass Works (founded in 1855), was established from a former operation and transformed into a updated, profitable enterprise by Ernest Jobling-Purser (1875–1959). 1921, he decided to purchase from Corning Glassworks the rights to manufacture the borosilicate glass Pyrex; from 1922, initially produced Pyrex in forms developed by Corning but soon had new items designed to satisfy British taste; by mid-1920s, manufactured oven-to-table kitchen/tableware which, according to its advertisements, added 'charm to your table with its glistening transparency amid your silver and glass.... Your dishes will keep hotter than they did in those unsightly obsolete metal and earthenware dishes.' 1934, Harold Stabler redesigned Jobling's 1931 Utility Streamline range. Jobling's Wearside factory produced Stabler's 1939 range of oven-to-table ware with sprayed-on colors in green, yellow, and blue, later withdrawn due to wartime shortages. Just before his 1949 retirement, Purser sold Jobling to Pilkington Brothers, which in 1950 sold 60% to holding company Thomas Tilling. 1954, the remaining 40% was bought by Corning. 1952–59, John D. Cochrane was Jobling's first full-time designer and, 1952–69, Milner Gray and Kenneth Lamble (of Design Research Unit consultancy) were commissioned. After Thomas Tilling sold its interests to Corning in 1973, Jobling became Corning Ltd. in 1975. 1994, Corning sold the Jobling factory and Pyrex rights to the Newell Company, which, as the Newell Group, bought Anchor Hocking in 1987 as well as a large number of other operations.
Exhibitions Jobling work shown at 1929 *Industrial Art for the Slender Purse*, sponsored by British Institute for Industrial Art, Victoria and Albert Museum, London.
Bibliography Frederick Cooke, *Glass: Twentieth-Century Design*, New York: Dutton, 1986: 60–62. Robert Charleston (ed.), *The Glass Circle 6*, Woodbridge: Antique Collectors' Club Woodbridge 1989. Leslie Jackson, *20th Century Factory Glass*, London: Octopus, 2000.

Jobs, Gocken (1914–)

Swedish textile designer and ceramicist.

Biography Jobs worked in her family's studio, which was active from 1940s in Leksand, province of Dalarna, where she handprinted fabrics and produced ceramics; worked alongside her sister Lisbet Jobs-Söderlung (1909–1961). The operation, which felicitously fused craftmanship and industrial production, was known for its meticulous work. Their house/workshop is preserved today in Leksand .
Exhibitions Work subject of 2003–04 *Jobs: Keramik och Textil av Lisbet och Gocken Jobs*, Leksands Konstmuseum
Bibliography Cat., David Revere McFadden (ed.), *Scandinavian Modern Design 1880–1980*, New York: Abrams, 1982. Delia Gaze and Leanda Shrimpton (eds.), *Dictionary of Women Artists*, 2 vols., Chicago/London; Fitzroy Dearborn, 1997.

Jobs, Steven P. (1955–); Apple Computer

American entrepeneur and inventor; born San Francisco.

Training Reed College, Portland, Ore.
Biography Jobs began building his first computer as a teenager; 1970, met future partner Stephen Wozniak, who was also trying to build his first computer; traveled to India. By 1975, Jobs had returned to Silicon Valley, Cal., and, with Wozniak, attended meetings of Homebrew Computer Company. When Wozniak completed the computer later called the Apple I, Jobs secured orders for 50 examples. 1 Apr. 1976, Jobs, Wozniak, and 'Mike' A.C. Markkula founded Apple Computer Company (today a publicly held corporation located in Cupertino, Cal.). Jobs and Wozniak's 1977 Apple II computer, with casing designed by Jerry Manock, not only made the company the fastest growing in US history but also contributed to the popularity of the personal computer, which would eventually transform the printing, publishing, advertising, and graphic design industries. However, the Lisa and the Apple II were unsuccessful, but the circumstances were remedied by the subsequent Manock-designed 1983 Macintosh 124K, which cost $3,195 (£2,320, rate at the time). Yet, the product needed a more sophisticated look, and, 1983, Jobs assigned full control of design to Hartmut Esslinger and his studio. Sept. 1985, Jobs was ousted from Apple, and John Scully became the chairperson. Jobs went on to establish the NeXT Computer Company, when he also purchased Pixar from George Lucas. 1995, Pixar became a public offering on Wall Street and Walt Disney Productions released the

Steven P. Jobs and Jerry Manock. Macintosh 128K home computer. 1983. ABS polymer casing, 13 3/4 x 9 3/4 x 10 3/4" (34.9 x 24.8 x 27.3 cm), excluding keyboard and mouse. Mfr.: Apple Computer, US. Gift of the mfr. MoMA.

first Pixar animated film, *Toy Story*. (Eventually, Pixar became highly successful and severed its agreement with Walt Disney in 2004.) With 80% share of the stock, Jobs became Pixar's chief executive officer and the chairperson; 1996, sold the NeXT Software firm to Apple for $433 (£287) million and, the same year, returned to Apple as an advisor to new chairperson Gilbert Amelio. 1999, when Robert Brunner resigned as head of Apple's IDg (Industrial Design Group), Jonathan Ive assumed the position. IDg had been established as a in-house entity for the design of Apple products; its staff members have included Bart Andre, Danny Coster, Daniele De Iuliis, Richard Howarth, Duncan Kerr, Matthew Rohrbach, Doug Satzger, Cal Seid, Christopher Stringer, Eugene Whang. They are the team, with Ive, that designed, for example, the iBook laptop comuter. (Other staffers, see below.)
Citations to Apple Design of the Decade (1990s) silver (1991 PowerBook by staff and Lunar Design), IDSA/*Business Week* magazine; numerous others.
Bibliography Paul Kunkel, *Apple Design: The World of the Apple Industrial Design Group*, New York: Graphis, 1997. Mel Byars with Arlette Barré-Despond, *100 Designs/100 Years...*, Hove: RotoVision, 1999. Paola Antonelli (ed.), *Objects of Design: The Museum of Modern Art*, New York: The Museum of Modern Art, 2003: 242-46.
> See staff members, accompanied by individual Apple products: Barbera, Larry; Bissell, Brad; Brunner, Robert; De Iuliis, Daniele; Dresselhaus, Bill; Esslinger, Hartmut; Guido, Anthony; Ive, Jonathan; Ivester, Gavin; Jordan, Richard; Lam, Lawrence; Manock, Jerry; Meyerhöffer, Thomas; Oyama, Terry; Parsey, Tim; Peart, Stephen; Pfeifer, Herbert; Pierce, Susanne; Riley, Raymond; Stewart, Jim.

Joel, Betty (b. Betty Stewart Lockhart 1894–1985)

British furniture, textile, and interior designer; born Hong Kong.

Biography She met David Joel while he was in the navy in the Far East; 1918, they married and, c. 1919 together, established the firm Betty Joel Ltd. on Hayling Island in Hampshire and later a showroom at 177 Sloane Street in London. None had formal design training. Her early work combined Arts and Crafts and Georgian styles. She emphasized the quality of manufacture and high-design principles; by 1920s, had developed a strong personal style of simple lines and sophisticated forms; often used so-called Empire woods (exotic ones from British colonies such as Indian laurel and Australian silky oak) and other luxury materials such as ivory. She became best known for her fancy furniture designs in satin and frills (belated versions of 1920s French models) and geometric-motif carpets, but some were in chrome, glass, and mirror, including 1935 flower table and other pieces for John Colville in Auchengray, UK. c. 1935, she opened a new workshop, which was designed by H.S. Goodhart-Rendel, in Kingston-upon-Thames, Surrey, and a new showroom at 25 Knightsbridge in London and, 1937, Goodhart-Rendel redesigned the showroom's facade. Joel's carpets, finer and denser than others of the time, were hand-knotted in Tientsin, China, on a cotton warp and clipped into grooves around the edges of the motifs. She designed radio cabinets for K.B. Kolster Brandes (produced by cabinet makers Holmes Bros. in Walthamstow). Late 1930s, she designed case-goods produced by G. Ashley and W.R. Irwin at Token Works, Portsmouth. Clients included Louis Mountbatten, Winston Churchill, H.R.H. The Queen Mother, the Duchess of York, Lord Beaverbrook, Coutts Bank, and Metro-Goldwyn-Mayer Pictures. 1930s, she was adversely criticized for her overly luxurious work that deviated from rigid modernist principles; she intended to create elegant but comfortable interiors for ordinary people. 1937, she retired, divorced, and closed her business. To 1950s, her husband continued the business and revived some of her designs.
Exhibitions Bedroom with a revolving bed installed at 1935 *British Art in Industry*, Royal Academy, London; other work at 1979–80 *Thirties* exhibition, Hayward Gallery, London (catalog below).
Bibliography Cat., *Thirties: British Art and Design Before the War*, London: Arts Council of Great Britain/Hayward Gallery, 1979. Auction cat., *British Design*, London: Phillips, 25 Sept. 2001. Cat., Raymond Foulk and Jenny Lewis, *Betty Joel: Celtic Spirit from the Orient*, London: Foulk Lewis Collection, 1996.

Johannsson, Leo (1956–)

Icelandic furniture designer; born Reykjavik.

Training To 1983, Konstfackskolan, Stockholm.
Biography 1983–92, Johannsson was active in his own studio, I 3 Interior Architects; subsequently, has been program manager of furniture design at Carl Malmsten Centrum för Träteknik och Design (composed of Carl Malmsten furniture-production facilities in Stockholm and a research group in Linköping). The Centrum is one of four faculties at Linköpings Universitet.
Exhibitions/citations Showed work and received awards in Sweden and abroad.

Johansfors Glasbruk

Swedish glass factory.

History 1889, glass painter A. Ahrends established a decorating workshop in Broakulla, Småland; 1891 with partner F.O. Israelsson, established the Johansfors Glasbruk there; to c. 1900, specialized in

painting on glass rendered elsewhere; from mid-1920s, was favorably acknowledged for its engraved glass. Factory engravers included Folke Walwing (1907–), and artists included Gunnar Håkansson. The plant began to produce utility and table glass. From 1950, Sixten Wennerstrand managed the operation, rebuilt and updated the factory, and hired Bengt Orup, who was the artistic director 1952–73. Wennerstrand departed in 1972, when Johansfors was bought by the Åforsgruppen, a consortium already amalgamated with Kosta Boda glassworks. From this time, the designers there were Bertil Vallien and Anna Ehrner. 1990, Kosta Boda was bought by Orrefors and Johansfors was then closed. 1992, Johansfors was re-established by some former employees but is today owned by Magnor Glassverk of Norway.
Bibliography Jennifer Hawkins Opie, *Scandinavia: Ceramics and Glass in the Twentieth Century*, New York: Rizzoli, 1989. Leslie Jackson, *20th Century Factory Glass*, London: Octopus, 2000.

Johanssdottir, Sigridur (1948–)

Icelandic textile designer.

History Johanssdottir has been an independent textile designer in her own studio in Reykjavik, often weaving fabrications from the designs of her husband Leifur Breidfjord.
Bibliography Cat., David Revere McFadden (ed.), *Scandinavian Modern Design 1880–1980*, New York: Abrams, 1982.

Johansson, Willy (1921–1993)

Norwegian glassware designer.

Training 1939–42, Statens Håndværks -og Kunstindustriskole, Oslo.
Biography Willy Johansson's father Wilhelm was at the Hadelands Glassverk in Jevnaker, where Willy himself joined the glassmaking workshop in 1936 as an apprentice. He worked closely with sculptor Ståle Kyllingstad, and, from 1947, was a designer and became head of design, production, and artwares to his 1988 retirement. He was best known for the white rim on his clear or smoked glasswares and the simplicity of what became known as Scandinavian modern. The Johanssons made an appreciable contribution to the expansion of the range and improvement of the quality of Hadelands's tablewares. Willy designed mass-produced as well as one-of-a-kind wares. Designs included 1949 Willy blown stemware, 1966 Snorre tumblers, 1968 Halling wine glasses, 1982 Ocean vases. His stemware still in production: 1969 Oslo, 1971 Peer Gynt, 1983 Sonja, and 1988 Lord. 1945–47, he taught in the night school of Statens Håndværks -og Kunstindustriskole.
Citations 1954 (10th) (diploma of honor), 1957 (11th) (gold medal), and 1960 (12th) (silver medal), editions of Triennale di Milano.
Bibliography Cat., Kathryn B. Hiesinger and George H. Marcus III (eds.), *Design Since 1945*, Philadelphia: Philadelphia Museum of Art, 1983. 'Revolution in Scandinavian Design: Willy Johansson,' *Crafts Horizons*, vol. 18, Mar. 1958: 32. Eileene Harrison Beer, *Scandinavian Design: Objects of a Life*, New York: Farrar, Straus & Giroux, 1975. Cat., David Revere McFadden (ed.), *Scandinavian Modern Design 1880–1980*, New York: Abrams, 1982. Jennifer Hawkins Opie, *Scandinavia: Ceramics and Glass in the Twentieth Century*, New York: Rizzoli, 1989. Leslie Jackson, *20th Century Factory Glass*, London: Octopus, 2000.

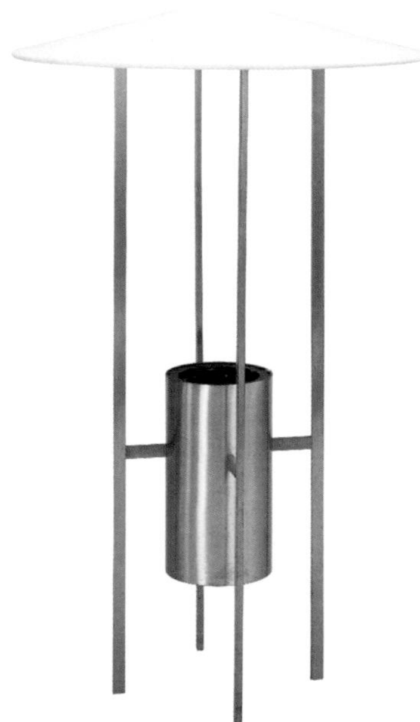

Philip Johnson and Richard Kelly (1910–1977). Floor lamp. 1950. Brass and painted metal, overall h. 42 x dia. 25" (106.7 x 63.5 cm). Mfr.: Edison Price, US (1959). Gift of Philip Johnson. MoMA.

Johansson-Pape, Lisa (1907–1989)

Finnish exhibition architect and interior, textile, and lighting designer.

Training 1927, Taideteollinen korkeakoulu, Helsinki.
Biography 1928–30, Johansson-Pape designed furniture by Kylmäkoski and, 1928–37, textiles for Suomen Käsityön Ystävien (friends of Finnish handicraft), of which she was the artistic director from 1952; 1937–49, was a furniture, textile, and interior designer at Stockmann in Helsinki; from 1949, designed Rational and practical models for the Stockmann Orno lamp company. Work also included ceramics, glass, and textiles.
Exhibitions/citations First and second prizes and diploma of honor, 1937 *Exposition Internationale des Arts et Techniques dans la Vie Moderne*, Paris; 1951 (9th) (silver medal), 1954 (10th) (gold medal), and 1960 (12th) (silver medal) editions of Triennale di Milano.
Bibliography Marja Kaipainen, 'Lisa Johansson-Pape—Lauri Anttila,' *Form Function Finland*, no. 3, 1982: 6–11. Cat., David Revere McFadden (ed.), *Scandinavian Modern Design 1880–1980*, New York: Abrams, 1982. Cat., Kathryn B. Hiesinger and George H. Marcus III (eds.), *Design Since 1945*, Philadelphia: Philadelphia Museum of Art, 1983.

Johnová, Helena (1884–1962)

Czech sculptor and ceramicist; born Soběslav.

Training Vysoká Škola Uměleckoprůmyslová (VŠUP, academy of arts, architecture, and design), Prague; 1909–11 under Michael Powolny, Kunstgewerbeschule, Vienna.
Biography In Vienna, Johnová founded a ceramics firm that closed in 1920, and created a number of figurines and vessels in small series; 1919–42, was a professor, VŠUP, Prague; for a Czechoslovakian Werkbund (SČSD) competition, she designed a ceramic tea-and-coffee set that showed modern influence; 1930s, created a number of monumental objects on floral themes.
Bibliography Antonin Novotný, *Helena Johnová*, Prague: Zikes, 1940. Alena Adlerová, *České užité umění 1918–1938*, Prague: Odeon, 1983.

Johnson, Philip Cortelyou (1906–)

American architect; born Cleveland, Ohio; active New York.

Training 1923–30, philosophy and, 1940–43 under Walter Gropius and Marcel Breuer, architecture, Harvard University, Cambridge, Mass.
Biography While at Harvard, Johnson worked in his own architectural office in Cambridge, Mass.; from 1930, was director of the Depart-ment of Architecture, The Museum of Modern Art, New York. 1932, he staged the first architecture exhibition at the museum—*Modern Architecture—International Exhibition* (coorganized with Henry-Russell Hitchcock). This venue was followed by another, the first on design at the museum—1934 *Machine Art*; 1934, he left the museum to pursue right-wing political causes; 1940–43. returned to architectural studies at Harvard University; 1947–55, was again at the museum as the director of the Architecture and Design Department and organized and wrote the book for the museum's 1947 *Mies van der Rohe* exhibition (as well as a number of other exhibitions). He arranged Mies's first trip to New York; from 1956, has been a trustee of the museum (to the present). From 1954, Johnson worked as an architect in New York, where, 1964–67, collaborated with partner Richard Foster and, from 1967, with partner John Burgee; was effective in promoting the International Style and modern and contemporary design through gifts and loans to museums, particularly The Museum of Modern Art. Johnson later rejected the International Style in architecture and, with Burgee, designed the pedimented 1979–84 AT&T building in New York (sold to Sony in

1990, to become Sony Plaza). Johnson's earlier and subsequent architecture has included his own 1949 Glass House, New Canaan, Conn.; 1949–50 Mrs. John D. Rockefeller 3rd's townhouse, 252 East 52nd Street, New York; 1952 Winton house, Wayzata, Minn.; 1953 garden of and subsequent additions to The Museum of Modern Art; 1954–56 Tifereth Israel Synagogue, Port Chester, N.Y.; 1960 Roofless Church, New Harmony, Ind.; 1954–58 Seagram Building (assisting Mies van der Rohe) and its Four Seasons Restaurant interiors (with William Pahlmann; and 1997 renovation), New York; 1956 Synagogue, Port Chester, N.Y.; 1960–61 Rehovot Nuclear Plant, Rehovoth, Israel; 1961 Amon Carter Museum, Fort Worth; 1962 Sheldon Memorial Art Gallery, University of Nebraska, Lincoln, Neb.; 1963–68 Kunsthalle, Bielefeld, Germany; 1962–64 New York State Theater, Lincoln Center, New York; 1964–66 Kline Biology Tower, Yale University, New Haven, Conn.; 1963 Sheldon Memorial Art Gallery, University of Nebraska, Lincoln; 1968–73 IDS Center (with Burgee), Minneapolis, Minn.; 1971 Boston Public Library Extension, Boston; 1975–76 Pennzoil Place (with others), Houston, Tex.; 1980 Water Garden (with Burgee), Fort Worth, Tex.; 1980 Community Church–Crystal Cathedral, Garden Grove, Cal.; 1982 United Bank of Denver Center (with Burgee; now Wells Fargo Center) , Denver, Colo.; 1983 Transco Tower (with Burgee and Morris-Aubry; now Williams Tower), Houston; 1983 Republic Bank Center (with Burgee; now NCNB), Houston; 1984 AT&T Building (now Sony Plaza), New York; 1985 International Place, Boston; 1987 Bank One Center (with Burgee), Dallas, Texas; 1989–95 Lewis house (with Frank Gehry), Cleveland; 1995 Celebration—Disney World town planning (with others), Orlando, Fla.; 1996 Fine Arts Center, Seton Hill College, Greensburg, Pa. However, from 1989, Johnson has been semiretired, devoting time mainly to his own projects but consulting to Johnson Burgee Architects and with Alan Richie, subsequently forming Philip Johnson Richie Fiore Architects. His 1908–2001 papers are housed in J. Paul Getty Museum, Los Angeles, Cal.
Cititations 1979 Pritzker Architecture Prize; numerous others.
Bibliography Henry-Russell Hitchcock and Philip Johnson, *The International Style: Architecture Since 1922*, New York: Museum of Modern Art, 1932. Philip Johnson, *Machine Art*, New York: Museum of Modern Art, 1934. Philip Johnson, *Mies van der Rohe*, New York: Museum of Modern Art, 1947. Henry-Russell Hitchcock (intro.), *Philip Johnson: Architecture 1949–1965*, New York: Holt, Rinehart & Winston, 1966. Robert A.M. Stern (ed.), *Philip Johnson, Writings*, New York: Oxford: 1979. Nory Miller, *Johnson/Burgee: Architecture*, New York: Random House, 1979. Cat., Philip Johnson and Mark Wigley, *Deconstructivist Architecture*, New York: The Museum of Modern Art, 1988. Alice Goldfarb Marquis, *Alfred H. Barr Jr.: Missionary for the Modern*, Chicago: Contemporary Books, 1989. Franz Schulze, *Philip Johnson: Life and Work*, New York: Knopf, 1994. David Whitney and Jeffrey Kipnir (eds), *Philip Johnson, The Glasshouse*, New York: Pantheon, 1993. John T. O'Connor and Hilary Lewis (eds.), *Philip Johnson: The Architect in His Own Words*, New York: Rizzoli, 1994. Terence Riley et al., *Philip Johnson and the Museum of Modern Art*, New York: The Museum of Modern Art, 1998. Stover Jenkins and David Mohney, *The Houses of Philip Johnson*, New York: Abbeville, 2001. Richard Payne et al., *The Architecture of Philip Johnson*, Boston: Bulfinch, 2002.

Johnson, Rob (1965–)

American furniture, lighting, and vehicle designer; born Spokane, Wash.

Training In welding and other industrial techniques, New York
Biography 1979, Johnson moved to New York and began makiing matt-black wrought-iron and welded furniture; early 1990s with Jerry Morrell, designed glass-topped tables. Features of his design work included mismatched legs and pseudo-flawed tops. With leather designer Toshiki, he produced steel-rod chairs with leather seat covers, incorporating foam-filled domes and pyramids. His furniture and lighting in distinctive calligraphic profiles incorporated rubber and found industrial parts. Curl chair is one of his best-known pieces.
Bibliography Stephen Perrine, 'Furniture at 50 Miles an Hour,' *Elle Decor*, Nov. 1990: 52.

Jonassen, Severin (1913–)
> See Philco.

Jonchery, Charles-Émile (1873–1937)

French designer; active Paris.

Training Under Aimé Miller and Antoine Gauthier.
Biography Jonchery's work included portrait medallions, busts, garniture clocks, candelabra, and table lamps in plaster, bronze, and marble.
Exhibitions 1883–1922, sculpture shown at Salons of Société des Artistes Français, where, 1903, he showed La Vague (the wave) lamp.
Bibliography *Revue des Arts Décoratifs*, 1901: 262. Salon catalog, Société des Artistes Français, 1903. *Allgemeines Lexikon der bildenden Künstler*, 1955. Auction catalog, Hôtel Drouot, 20 June 1975, Lot 92. Alastair Duncan, *Art Nouveau and Art Déco Lighting*, New York: Simon & Schuster, 1978.

Hella Jongerius. My Soft Office power patch. 2000. Technogel, synthetic fur, plastic, 1 x 42 x 30 1/2" (2.5 x 106.7 x 77.5 cm). Mfr.: Jongeriuslab, the Netherlands. Gift of the designer. MoMA.

Jones, A.E. (1879–1954)

British silversmith; active Birmingham.

Training Birmingham Central School of Art.
Biography Jones worked at the Birmingham Guild of Handicrafts; 1902, set up a silver department within his father's firm; like other Arts and Crafts metalsmiths, produced hammered surfaces combined with pierced or interlaced rims.
Bibliography Annelies Krekel-Aalberse, *Art Nouveau and Art Déco Silver*, New York: Abrams, 1989.

Jones, Andrew (1966–)

Canadian architect and designer; forn Brantford, Ontario; active Toronto.

Training 1991, bachelor's degree in architecture, University of Toronto; 1997, master's degree in furniture design, Royal College of Art, London.
Biography Jones teaches furniture design, graduate program in architecture, University of Toronto; from 1998, has taught, Faculty of Architecture, Landscape, and Diesign, University of Toronto; from early 2000, has been active as an interior architect and furniture designer in Toronto and London; designed the Gym chair and table series by Keilhauer.
Bibliography Rachel Gotlieb and Cora Golden, *Design in Canada Since 1945: Fifty Years from Teakettles to Task Chairs*, Toronto: Knopf Canada, 2001.

Jongerius, Hella (1963–)

Dutch designer; born De Meern.

Training 1988–93, Akademie voor Industriële Vormgeving, Eindhoven.
Biography 1993, Jongerius began her career as a designer; initially, became known for her work through the Droog Design cooperative. Work has included 1994 Soft Vase and bathroom mat, both in polyurethane by DMD (Droog Design's production associate), The Hague; 1996 Pushed Washtub (washbasin) in polyurethane; 1995 Knitted

Lamp in fiberglass; 1998 Slightly Damaged Dinner Service by Koninklijke Tichelaar Makkum; 1998 pot collection; 2000 Felt Stool, Embroidered Porcelain/Tablecloth, and Long Neck/Groove Bottle glass/porcelain/packing-tape vases. Her 1999 Kasese Sheep Chair and Kasese Foam Chair, both by Rep Air in Rijswijk, were inspired by early ethnic African examples. 2000, she founded JongeriusLab, which produces some of her designs.
Exhibitions/citations An invited participant in 1997 high-tech experimental program, Technische Universiteit, Delft, resulting in the Knitted Lamp. Work included in 1996 *Contemporary Design from the Netherlands*, and My Soft Office, a commission for 2001 *Workspheres* (catalog below), both The Museum of Modern Art, New York. With Gijs Bakker, work subject of exhibition, Pittsburgh. Work included in *Design World 2000*, Konstindustrimuseet, Helsinki; individually the subject of 2003 exhibition, Design Museum, London. 1998 Incentive Award (for Soft Washbowl), Amsterdam Art Foundation for Industrial Design; 2003 Designprijs, Rotterdam; 2004 Designer of the Year, Salon du Meuble, Paris.
Bibliography *The International Design Yearbook*, London: Laurence King, 1995, 1996, and 1997. Renny Ramkers and Gijs Bakker (eds.), *Droog Design: Spirit of the Nineties*, Rotterdam: 010, 1998. Cat., Paola Antonelli, *Workspheres*, New York: The Museum of Modern Art, 2001. Paola Antonelli (ed.), *Objects of Design: The Museum of Modern Art*, New York: The Museum of Modern Art, 2003: 178. Louise Schouwenberg, *Hella Jongerius*, London/New York: Phaidon, 2003.

Jordan

Norwegian toothbrush firm.

History 1837, Danish comb maker Wilhelm Jordan founded a factory that he moved to Kristiana (now Oslo), where he set up a workshop for comb production and, soon after, established a brush factory. 1927, the firm became the first toothbrush maker in Norway. Jordan's toothbrushes at the time were sold under the brand name Pronto, but, 1969, this changed to Jordan. By 1937, Jordan was making 225,000 toothbrushes yearly, and, by 1968, 25 million. From 1958, brushes were sold internationally and packaged in clear plastic containers. 1970, Jordan bought Swedish paintbrush firm Anza and, 1998, British toothbrush maker Wisdom. Jordan eventually became known for its innovatively designed or technologically advanced toothbrushes such as 1973 T-4 spoon-handled toothbrush (designed by Lars Hjelle); 1992 Jordan Magic, the world's first color-changing model to indicate exhausted use; and 1997 Philips-Jordan electric toothbrush.
Citations 1986 Company of the Year (also 150th anniversary of the company), Norway.
Bibliography Fredrik Wildhagen, *Norge i Form*, Oslo: Stenersen, 1988: 190. www.jordan.no.

Patrick Jouin. Fol.d chair. 2001. Polypropylene and chromium-plated tubular steel. 2001, h. 31 7/8 x w. 17 x 20" (81 x 43 x 52cm). Mfr.: XO, France.

Jordan, Richard

American industrial designer; active California.

Training Product design, Stanford University, Berkeley, Cal.
Biography From 1978, Jordan was a designer at Apple Computer in Cupertino, Cal., where he worked on the design of a number of computers, including Apple III, Twiggy, Apple IIGS, Macintosh II. After frogdesign's participation in all Apple designs was discontinued in 1986–87, Jordan managed Apple's Industrial Design Group (IDg) in 1988–89. He hired Giorgetto Giugiaro to further the design of the SnowWhite project, which was never implemented; 1990, hired Bob Brunner to manage IDg and formed a new image for Apple's in-house design work.
Bibliography Paul Kunkel, *Apple Design: The World of the Apple Industrial Design Group*, New York: Graphis, 1997.

Jørgensen, Erik-Ole (1925–2002)

Danish furniture designer.

Training 1944, in furniture upholstery; 1946–48 under Kaare Klint, Det Kongelige Danske Kunstakademi, Copenhagen; to 1948, Kunsthåndværkerskolen, Copenhagen
Biography 1941–44, Jørgensen was active as a freelance furniture designer; 1953–64, was associated with manufacturer L.F. Foght; 1958–64, with Dux and with Sverige; 1971, with Halling-Koch Designcenter. Also, 1952–72, operated his own furniture production operation and designed fabrics by Kvadrat; became known for his 1974 J146-J149 sofa series by Kvist Møbler.
Exhibitions/citations Work shown at 1954 (10th), 1957 (11th), 1960 (12th) editions of Triennale di Milano. 1977 Award of the Year, Earl's Court Fair, London.
Bibliography Frederik Sieck, *Nutidig Dansk Møbeldesign – en kortfattet illustreret beskrivelse*, Copenhagen: Bondo Gravesen: 1990.

Joubert, René (d. 1931)

French decorator and furniture designer; active Paris.

Biography Joubert worked for decorating firm Jansen and, later, for Diot et Bouché; from 1912, was active as a furniture designer; after World War I with Georges Mouveau, established decorating firm Décoration Intérieure Moderne (D.I.M.), Paris.
Exhibitions From 1921, work shown at Salons of Société des Artistes Décorateurs, Paris (from 1926, with Philippe Petit).
Bibliography *Encyclopédie des métiers d'Art*, vol. I, p. 34, Paris: Albert Morancé. Pierre Kjellberg, *Art déco: les maîtres du mobilier, le décor des paquebots*, Paris: Amateur, 1986.
> See D.I.M.

Jouin, Patrick (1967–)

French environmental and industrial designer; born Nantes.

Training To 1992, ENSCI (Les Ateliers), Paris.
Biography 1992, Jouin worked at Compagnie des Wagon-Lits; 1993–94 under Philippe Starck, in the Tim Thom studio of Thomson multimedia; 1995–99, in Starck's studio; from 1999, in his own studio. His work has included 1995 Boos speakers (with Starck) by Thomson; 1995 Television 55 (with Starck) by Saba; 1995 Aloo cordless telephone and 1995 Don O radio/cassette player by Thomson; 1998 Facto chair and table by Fermob; Fluxus trestle table, Cosmic Thing and 1999 Morphée sofa, all 1997 by Ligne Roset; 1999 Al étagère by Proto Design; 1999 Wave dinnerware (for restaurateur Alain Ducasse) by Gien; 2000 Cute Cut sofa by Moderno; 2000 interior architecture of Alain Ducase restaurant and 2001 bar, both in Plaza Athenée hotel, Paris; 2000 59 Poincaré restaurant, Paris; 2001 Fo.ld folding chair by XO; plastic surgeon's office, Nantes; 2001 Audiolab acoustical player for museum tours. 1998 with Thierry Gaugain and Jean-Marie Massaud, Jouin founded Luxlab group, which designed 1999 Sol Mutable real-grass environmental installation.

Éric Jourdan. Tolozan chaise longue. c. 2002. Steel, thermoformed polystyrene, polyethylene, and wood veneer, h. 33 1/2 x w. 30 x l. 54 1/4" (85 x 76.2 x 137.8cm). Mfr.: Ligne Roset, France.

Exhibitions/citations Work regularly shown at editions of Salon du Meuble, Paris, and other furniture fairs. 1996 and 1997 Appel Permanent grant and 1998 Carte Blanche production support, VIA (French furniture association); 1998 Prix de Presse Internationale, Salon du Meuble, Paris; 1998 (for Facto chair) and 1999 (for bed/sofa) Label du VIA.
Bibliography Sophie Tasma Anargyros, 'Patrick Jouin: Portrait du designer,' *Intramuros*, no. 87, Feb.–March 2000, 41–45. Sophie Lemoine, 'De la poésie pour le quotidien,' *Le Figaro*, 11 Feb. 2000. Pascale Cassgnau and Christophe Pillet, *Beef, Brétillot/Valette, Matali Crasset, Patrick Jouin, Jean-Marie Massaud: petits enfants de Starck?*, Paris: Dis Voir, 2000. Mel Byars, *50 Beds...*, Hove: RotoVision, 2000. Mel Byars, *Design in Steel*, London: Laurence King, 2002.

Jourdain, Francis (1876–1958)

French painter, graphic artist, and designer; born and active Paris; son of Frantz Jourdain; father of Frantz-Philippe Jourdain.

Training 1894 under Joseph Chéret, in drawing; under Eugène Carrière and Paul-Albert Besnard, Atelier Gervex.
Biography 1912, Jourdain began his career as a painter and showed his canvases with Paul Cézanne, Henri Matisse, Henri de Toulouse-Lautrec, Vasilii Kandinsky, and Maurice Denis at editions of the Salon des Indépendants. Inspired by Adolf Loos's famous 1908 pamphlet 'Ornament und Verbrechen' ('Ornament and Crime'), in 1912 Jourdain set up his own workshop, Ateliers Modernes, where he designed and made furniture for mass-production in inexpensive materials and also produced one-of-a-kind pieces. He opposed Paul Follot's voluptuous *style tapissier* and preferred balanced proportions and harmonious and simple colors. By the end of World War I, Jourdain had set up a factory separate from his showroom and retail shop Chez Francis Jourdain on the rue de Sèze, Paris. He designed furniture, fabrics, wallpaper, and ceramics, and decorated apartments, offices, airplanes, and railway cars; designed the tea room, restaurant, wooden garden chairs, and smoking car for the Compagnie Paris–Orléans railroad company. 1923–33, work also included some furniture for and the decoration of some rooms of the villa in Hyères of the vicomte and vicomtesse de Noailles (architect, Robert Mallet-Stevens, with whom Jourdain had worked on other commissions from 1922). Also with Mallet-Stevens as architect, Jourdain designed interior of 1928 Bally shoe showroom on the boulevard des Capucines, Paris, including its metal furniture, showcases, and display units. He created innovative lighting, including a distinguished four-armed ceiling fixture, for Mallet-Stevens's own 1927–28 house at 12, rue Mallet-Stevens, Auteuil; fresco of Les Grands Magasins de la Samaritaine, Paris (with the store's architect, his father Frantz Jourdain). He published *Intérieurs* (1929), which illustrated his work and that of Mallet-Stevens, Le Corbusier, Pierre Chareau, and Gerrit Rietveld; was a friend of Jean Renoir, Jules Vallès, Octave Mirbeau, and Émile Zola; was associated with Elie Faure, Fernand Léger, Léon-Paul Fargue, Léon Moussinac, and Aragon. For Jean Vigo, he designed the barge in the film *L'Atalante* (1934); published articles, books, and monographs, militantly supporting Rationalism; 1929, cofounded Union des Artistes Modernes (UAM); 1938 with Pierre Chareau, Louis Sognot, and Jacques Adnet, designed the reception area and administration offices of the Collège de France; was known for applying to walls clock faces with only numerals and hands (with the works built-in); was one of the true originals of 1920s–30s. He spent much of the time during World War II in hiding or with the Resistance; after the war, wrote monographs on Pierre Bonnard, Henri de Toulouse-Lautrec, Albert Marquet, and Félix Valloton; was also a novelist and published *Sans remords ni rancune: souvenirs épars d'un vieil homme né en 76* (Paris: Corréa, 1953) and *Né en soixante-seize* (Paris: Pavillon, 1951) and his memoir *De mon temps: propos tenus à un moins de vingt ans par un moins de cent ans* (Paris: F. Maspero, 1963). 1946, he was president, Comité d'Honneur, Mallet-Stevens Club; 1948, honorary president, UAM; from 1949, principal director, *Formes Utiles* exhibitions.
Exhibitions/citations Before 1912, paintings first shown at Salon of Société Nationale des Beaux-Arts. To 1938, work shown at editions of Salon d'Automne (founded by his father, Frantz Jourdain), beginning with a dining room and bedroom at its 1913 installment. Designed a smoking room and gymnasium in Une Ambassade Française pavilion and Compagnie Paris–Orléans railway smoking car at 1925 *Exposition Internationale des Arts Décoratifs et Industriels Modernes*, Paris. From 1930, work shown at UAM exhibitions. Designed a modest ensemble composed of interchangeable and variously arranged furniture called Essai de Désencombrement pour Jeune Travailleuse Intellectuelle et Manuelle at 1937 *Exposition Internationale des Arts et Techniques dans la Vie Moderne*, Paris, and, installed in the Salon de la Lumière pavilion there, illuminated tables designed with lighting engineer André Salomon. Work subject of 1976 *Francis Jourdain (1876–1958)* exhibition, Saint-Denis. Received grand prize, 1911 *Esposizione Internazionale dell'Industria e del Lavoro*, Turin.
Bibliography Francis Jourdain, 'Les besoins individuels et l'art décoratif,' *Art et décoration*, vol. 65, 1936. Léon Moussinac, *Francis Jourdain*, Paris: Pierre Cailler, 1955. Cat., *Francis Jourdain (1876–1958)*, Saint-Denis: Musée d'Art et d'Histoire, 1976. Arlette Barré-Despond, *UAM*, Paris: Regard, 1986: 428–33. Meredith L. Clausen, *Frantz Jourdain and the Samaritaine: Art Nouveau Theory and Criticism*, Leiden: Brill, 1987. Cat., *Les années UAM 1929–1958*, Paris: Musée des Arts Décoratifs, 1988: 200–202. Arlette Barré-Despond and Suzanne Tise, *Jourdain*, Paris: Regard, 1988. Mel Byars with Arlette Barré-Despond, *100 Designs/100 Years: A Celebration of the 20th Century*, Hove: RotoVision: 38–39. *Francis Jourdain: un parcours moderne 1876–1958*, Paris: Somogy, 2000.

Jourdain, Frantz-Calixte-Raphaël-Ferdinand-Marie (1847–1935)

French architect, writer, and critic; born Antwerp; active Paris; father of Francis Jourdain.

Training From 1867, École Nationale Supérieure des Beaux-Arts, Paris.
Biography 1903, Jourdain created the Salon d'Automne in response to the spring Salons of groups such as Société Nationale des Beaux-Arts and Société des Artistes Français, which he considered too academic. The work of architects, decorative artists, furniture designers, jewelry designers, and binders was shown, in an attempt to end the schism between the fine and applied arts. He encouraged his friend Émile Zola to write the editorial 'J'accuse' in defence of Captain Dreyfus; 1898, became a founding member of Ligue des Droits de l'Homme (human rights association); was a prolific journalist, novelist, and playwright. His major architectural work and masterpiece was 1905–07 Samaritaine department store in Paris, one of the best examples of steel, glass, and concrete architecture in Paris. Its Art Nouveau design was influenced by Victor Horta's 1901 L'Innovation store, Brussels, and Louis Henri Sullivan's 1899–1906 Carson-Pirie-Scott department store, Chicago. His other architecture included 1892 villa in Saint-Leu. Others, in Paris: 1894 Edouard Schenck house (one of first concrete houses in Paris), 9, rue Vergniaud; perfumery pavilion at 1900 *Exposition Universelle*; 1907 Magasin 2 of La Samaritaine; 1926 Pont-Neuf extension (with Henri Sauvage) of La Samaritaine; 1912 building, 16, rue du Louvre; 1914 La Samaritaine de Luxe.
Citations 1894, appointed Chevalier of the Légion d'Honneur.
Bibliography Victor Arwas, *Art Déco*, New York: Abrams, 1980. Pierre Cabanne, *Encyclopédie art déco*, Paris: Somogy, 1986: 202–04. Meredith L. Clausen, *Frantz Jourdain and the Samaritaine: Art Nouveau Theory and Criticism*, Leiden: Brill, 1987. Arlette Barré-Despond, *Jourdain*, Paris: Regard, 1988. Arlette Barré-Despond and Suzanne Tise, *Jourdain*, New York: Rizzoli, 1990.

Jourdain, Frantz-Philippe (1906–1990)

French architect; active Paris; son of Francis Jourdain.

Training École Spéciale d'Architecture, Paris.
Biography Jourdain's first important commission was the 1928 villa in Grandchamps; 1934, became a member of Union des Artistes Modernes (UAM); with André-L. Louis, designed several low-cost modern buildings, including two 1934–36 villas at Grandchamps.
Exhibitions All in Paris: 1931 UAM exhibition (milliner's atelier); competition organized by Office Technique pour l'Utilisation de l'Acier (OTUA) (with Louis, project for the design of an oceanliner cabin) at Salon d'Automne; with Louis, *3e Exposition de l'Habitation*, sponsored by journal *L'architecture d'aujourd'hui* and Groupe des Cinq; 1935 Salon de la Lumière (furniture, ensembles, and models). With Georges-Henri Pingusson, the design of the UAM pavilion at 1937 *Exposition Internationale des Arts et Techniques dans la Vie Moderne* (furniture designs), Paris.
Bibliography Jean Porcher, 'Une villa par Frantz Philippe Jourdain,' *Art et décoration*, vol. 59, Dec. 1930. Cat., *Les années UAM 1929–1958*, Paris: Musée des Arts Décoratifs, 1988: 203. Arlette Barré-Despond, *Jourdain*, Paris: Regard, 1988. Arlette Barré-Despond and Suzanne Tise, *Jourdain*, New York: Rizzoli, 1990.

Jourdan, Éric (1966–)

French environmental designer, interior architect, and teacher; born and active Paris.

Training To 1987 under François Bauchet, École des Beaux Arts, Saint-Étienne; École Nationale Supérieur des Arts Décoratifs, Paris; and with Luigi Colani.
Biography Jourdan spent four months working under Philippe Starck in the Tim Thom design studio of Thomson multimedia. He designed 1988 Ker side chair and 1998 Klin lounge chair edited by Néotù; 1996 guardrail (with François Bauchet) at the river Seine embankment, commissioned by General Council of Val-de-Marne, France; 1998 Collection Tropicale cabinet commissioned by French Ministère de la Culture; 2000 Collection Traversants by Gilles Peyroulet; 2000 Marguerite pitcher by Arcodif; signage for Chevreuse; 2000 shelf unit edited by Galerie Valentin, Paris; furniture series edited by Cottard gallery, Stockholm. He teaches, École des Beaux-Arts, Saint-Étienne, and occupied the first chair (endowed by Habitat for one year) at École Nationale Supérieure des Beaux-Arts, Paris.
Exhibitions Work included in 1987 exhibition of young designers, Galerie Néotù, Paris; 1987 *Exposition Desco* at Zeus, Milan; 1987 exhibition, Galerie VIA (French furniture association), Paris; Zeus stand, 1988 Salone del Mobile, Milan; VIA stand, 1988 Salon du Meuble, Paris; 1980 *Nos Années 80*, Fondation Cartier, Jouy en Josas; numerous others. From VIA: 2002 Appel Spécifique (for multimedia environment with Tolozan armchairs/ottoman by Ligne Roset); and 1988, 1989, 1993, 1994, and 2004 Appel Permanent grants and 1995 Carte Blanche production support.
Bibliography *Casa Vogue*, Dec. 1987. Christine Colin, *Design aujourd'hui*, Paris: Flammarion, 1988. Cat., *Desco*, Milan: Zeus, 1987. Cat., Sophie Tasma Anargyros et al., *L'école française: les créateurs de meubles du 20ème siècle*, Paris: Industries Françaises de l'Ameublement, 2000. www.via.asso.fr.

Jouve, Georges (1910–1964)

French ceramicist; active Paris.

Training Apprenticeship in architecture; to 1930, École Boulle; to 1931, Académie de la Grande Chaumière; subsequently, Académie Julian; all Paris.
Biography 1940 during World War II, Jouve was a prisoner in Lorraine and, 1941, escaped to Nyons, France, where he produced his first ceramics; 1942, opened a small workshop and created a number of pieces based on a Christian-religion theme; 1943, moved to Dieulefit, a village known for its potteries, met Etienne Martin and Wols H.P. Poché, and illustrated several books by Clara Malraux for publisher Enfant-Poète; 1944, was invited by Jacques Adnet to participate in exhibitions of Adnet's Compagnie des Arts Français (CAF); in Paris, left a place on the Île Saint-Louis in Paris to established an atelier on the rue de la Tombe-Issoire and turned from pottery to ceramics; 1954, moved to Aix-en-Provence; 1963, made relief murals for a school (architect, René Colon) in Dieppe, nine large panels for École de Sarreguemines (architect, Roland Flageul), Éléctricité de France headquarters (EDF) in Paris, and the large polyester sculpture *Espoir* for Institut de Rééducation (architect, Margarites) in Marseille. Jouve became known for his exuberant work, particularly in 1950s; after a long illness, died in Aix-en-Provence.
Exhibitions In Paris, sold work through Galerie Steph Simon; from 1944, showed work at Salons of Société des Artistes Décorateurs. Work included in a number of other venues worldwide.

Joy, Daven (1961–)

American designer; born Los Angeles.

Training 1988, bachelor of art's degree, University of California, San Diego.
Biography 1989, Joy worked on architectural projects at North American Stijl Life in San Francisco; 1991, on media projects under Michael Boyd; 1992, founded Park Furniture; currently, is active in Pacifica, Cal. Clients have included Sony, Gap, Banana Republic, Manhattan Hotel in Tokyo, Warner Brothers.
Citations 1998, Best Body of Work, International Contemporary Furniture Fair (ICFF), New York.
Bibliography Cat., R. Craig Miller (intro.), *U.S. Design 1975–2000*, Munich: Prestel, 2002.

Jozancy, Luc
> See Rhinn, Eric.

Jucker, Carl Jacob (1902–1997)

Swiss metalworker; born Zurich.

Training 1918–1922, Kunstgewerbeschule, Zurich; 1922–23 under Georg Muche, metalworking shop, Bauhaus, Weimar.
Biography Many of Jucker's lamp models were made for the interior of 1923 Haus am Horn exhibition at the Bauhaus. He claimed that he designed, or perfected for serial production, the all-glass version of Wilhelm Wagenfeld's 1924 Bauhaus (or MT 8 or Glaslampe) table lamp, but there is possibly no documentation to confirm this. Jucker may also have worked with Marcel Breuer on the development of tubular-steel furniture; 1923, returned to Switzerland and became designer at Jezler silverware factory in Schaffhausen; taught in Zurich and in Schaffhausen; was a member of design team for the yacht *Lacustre*. Bauhaus-Archiv / Museum für Gestaltung in Berlin lists 'Karl' as the spelling of his forename. Died in Schaffhausen.
Bibliography Friederike Mehlau-Wiebking et al., *Schweizer Typenmöbel 1925–35, Sigfried Giedion und die Wohnbedarf AG*, Zurich: gta, 1989: 229. Cat., *Die Metallwerkstatt am Bauhaus*, Berlin:

Bauhaus-Archiv, 1992: 216–19, 317. Magdalena Droste, *The Bauhaus Light by Carl Jacob Jucker and Wilhelm Wagenfeld*, Frankfurt: form, 1998.

Judd, Donald (1928–1994)

American sculptor and designer; born Excelsior Springs, Mo.; active New York and Marfa, Tex.

Training 1948, briefly, Art Students League, New York; from 1948, College of William and Mary, Williamsburg, Va.; from 1949, philosophy, Columbia University, New York; again, Art Students League.
Biography 1959, Judd wrote for magazine *Art News*; 1953–65, was a contributiong editor to *Arts Magazine*; early 1960s, turned from painting to sculpture; taught art at various institutions. 1960s and 1970s, Judd created Minimal Art sculpture; designed minimalist furniture, including that in aluminum by Dutch firm Janssen. Aluminum chairs, for example, were designed in 1984 and produced from 2000, but much of his so-called furniture is in wood. 1986, Judd was instrumental in establishing The Chinati Foundation/La Fundación Chinati in Marfa, Tex., an independent, non-profit, publicly funded institution that exhibits his work and that of John Chamberlain, Dan Flavin, and others.
Exhibitions/citations In New York: first (1956 and 1957) one-person shows, at Panoras Gallery; third (1963) one-person show, at Green Gallery; from 1966, numerous one-person shows at Leo Castelli Gallery; subsequently, others worldwide. Work subject of a comprehensive 1987 exhibition, touring Eindhoven, Düsseldorf, Paris, Barcelona, and Turin; 1988 touring exhibition, organized by Whitney Museum of American Art. 1966 and 1976 National Endowment for the Arts grant; 1968 Guggenheim Memorial Foundation grant; 1993 Stankowski Foundation prize, Stuttgart.
Bibliography *Donald Judd: Complete Writings, 1959–1975*, Halifax: Nova Scotia College of Art and Design Press; New York: New York University, 1975. Muriel Emanuel et al. (eds.), *Contemporary Artists*, New York: St. Martin's, 1983 2nd ed. Donald Judd, *Texte de Donald Judd*, Paris/New York: Galerie Maeght Lelong, 1987. Cat., Piet de Jong et al. (organizers), *Donald Judd Furniture: Retrospective*, Rotterdam: Museum Boymans-van Beuningen, 1993.

Juhl, Finn (1912–1989)

Danish industrial designer and decorator.

Training Under Kaare Klint, Arkitektskole, Det Kongelige Danske Kunstakademiet, Copenhagen.
Biography 1937, Juhl began a longstanding collaboration with Niels Vodder's firm, which at first made furniture by hand. Over the next decade, their work consistently won awards from the Danish Cabinetmakers' Guild. With his restrained designs in furniture, Juhl broke with the Functionalist style; 1939, designed a soft-edged sofa by Niels Vodder, which offered a new approach to Danish design while reflecting the forms of Jean Arp; received many awards for 1942 house he built for himself. Danish design's coming to international attention in the late 1940s was largely due to Juhl. He was partially influenced by primitive, especially African, sculptural forms; 1944–55, was a senior teacher, Skolen for Boligindretning (school of interior design) of the Frederiksberg Tekniske Skole. In addition to Vodder, clients included Allerød (furniture), France & Søn (furniture), Georg Jensen (glassware), Kay Bojesen (turned teak bowls), General Electric (refrigerators), Bing & Grøndahl Porcelænsfabrik (dinnerware), and Unika-Vaev (carpets). 1945 sculptural lounge chair and 1949 plain Chieftain chair are exemplars of Juhl's work. He designed 1951 extensive furniture range by Bakers Brothers Furniture in Grand Rapids, Mich., US, which introduced his work to the US. Other ranges were later produced by Bovirke in Europe. Juhl was known for his 'floating seat,' as seen in the Baker group, which rested on crossbars rather than on the chair frame. 1951, Juhl designed the Trusteeship Council Chamber, UN headquarters, New York. His first major exhibition-design commission, from Edgar Kaufmann Jr., was 1951 *Good Design* exhibitions/awards, The Museum of Modern Art, New York, and Chicago Merchandise Mart. 1952, he designed a room in Kunstindustrimuseum, Trondheim. His sculptural use of wood and elaboration of structural forms were notable. Juhl designed 1960 trophy of Kaufmann International Design Award, first won by Charles and Ray Eames 1960, and 1966 Export Oscar trophy of National Association for Danish Enterprise.
Exhibitions/citations Work shown at 1950 and 1955 *Good Design* exhibitions/awards, The Museum of Modern Art, New York, and Chicago Merchandise Mart; 1951 (9th) (diploma of honor), 1954 (10th), and 1957 (11th) (gold medal) editions of Triennale di Milano; (1945 easy chair) 1945 Copenhagen Cabinetmakers' Guild event; 1954–57 *Design in Scandinavia*, touring the US; 1956–59 *Neue Form aus Dänemark*, touring Germany; 1958 *Formes Scandinaves*, Musée des Arts Décoratifs, Paris; 1960–61 *The Arts of Denmark*, touring the US; 1966 *Vijftig Jaar Zitten*, Stedelijk Museum, Amsterdam; 1968 *Two Centuries of Danish Design*, Glasgow, London, and Manchester; 1968 *Les Assises du Siège Contemporain*, Musée des Arts Décoratifs, Paris; 1970 *Modern Chairs 1918–1970*, Whitechapel Gallery, London. Work subject of exhibitions at Charlottenborg Autumn venue in 1970; in Cantù, Italy, in 1973; at Kunstindustrimuseet, Copenhagen, in 1982. 1944 C.F. Hansen prize; 1947 Eckersberg Medal; diploma (for 1955 Villabyernes Bio cinema in Vangede), Gentofte Municipality; 1964 prize (for design), American Institute of Architects (AIA), Chicago; 1978, elected Honorary Royal Designer for Industry, UK; 1984, Knight of the Order of the Dannebrog.
Bibliography Frederik Sieck, *Nutidig Dansk Møbeldesign – en kortfattet illustreret beskrivelse*, Copenhagen: Bondo Gravesen, 1981, 1990. Cat., David Revere McFadden (ed.), *Scandinavian Modern Design 1880–1980*, New York: Abrams, 1982. Esbjørn Hiort, *Finn Juhl: Furniture, Architecture, Applied Art*, Copenhagen: The Danish Architectural Press, 1990. Noritsugu Oda, *Danish Chairs*, San Francisco: Chronicle Books, 1999.

Juhlen, Sven-Eric (1940–)
> See Ergonomi Design Gruppen.

Jujol i Gibert, Josep Maria (1879–1949)

Spanish architect; born Tarragona, Catalonia; active Barcelona.

Training Escola Superior d'Arquitectura, Barcelona, directed by Lluís Domènech i Montaner.
Biography Jujol was a member of the younger generation of Catalan *modernista* architects. An apprentice under Antoni Gaudí, he has, perhaps unfairly, been labeled as nothing more than a simple follower; may have indeed been a Gaudí collaborator, as seen in his work on Gaudí's buildings: iron railings for 1906–12 Casa Milà La Perdrera, and mosaic decorations for Park Güell and Batlló apartment building, all in Barcelona. Jujol's decorative work presaged the Surrealists and Expressionists, and his own architecture—churches, shops, a theater, and other public buildings—included the remodeling of 1914–31 Casa Bofarull, near Tarragona. Residences included 1913–16 Torre de la Creu in Sant Joan Despí (aka Casa dels Ous or 'house of eggs,' named for its curvaceous lines) and 1923–24 Casa Planells in Barcelona.
Exhibitions Work subject of 1998 exhibition, El Col•legi d'Arquitectes de Catalunya, Barcelona.

Finn Juhl. Armchair (no. 45). 1945. Teak and wool, each: 31 3/4 x 24 x 31" (80.6 x 61 x 78.7 cm). Mfr.: Niels Vodder, Denmark. Edgar Kaufmann, Jr., Fund. MoMA.

Bibliography Ignasi de Solà Morales, *Jujol*, Cologne: Taschen, 1990. Thomas S. Hines, 'Brilliant Career of the Little-Known Catalan Modernist,' *Architectural Digest*, Nov. 1993: 74–86. Dennis Dollens, *Josep Maria Jujol: Five Major Buildings 1913–1923*, New York: Sites/Lumens, 1994. Ronald Christ (intro.), *The Architecture of Jujol*, Santa Fe, New Mexico: Sites/Lumens, 1996.

Julmat, The

American metalsmithy.

History The Julmat, producing works in Arts and Crafts style, was founded in 1910 by Julius O. Randahl and Matthias William Hanck in Park Ridge, Ill. The designers followed the early style of their mentor, Clara Welles, creating hammered-surface pieces in austere forms.
Bibliography Sharon S. Darling with Gail Farr Casterline, *Chicago Metalsmiths*, Chicago Historical Society, 1977.

Jung, Dora (1906–1980)

Finnish textile designer.

Training Taideteollinen korkeakoulu, Helsinki.
Biography Jung was a designer of fabrics at Tampella linen works, Tampere; 1932, set up her own studio in Helsinki; became known for her high standards; was a prominent weaver in Finland for more than 50 years of both mass-production and unique pieces.
Exhibitions/citations Work shown independently and in group exhibitions, including Gothenburg 1955 and Copenhagen 1956. Gold medal, 1937 *Exposition Internationale des Arts et Techniques dans la Vie Moderne*, Paris; grand prizes, 1951 (9th), 1954 (10th), and 1957 (11th) editons of Triennale di Milano. 1979, elected Honorary Royal Designer for Industry, UK.
Bibliography Cat., David Revere McFadden (ed.), *Scandinavian Modern Design 1880–1980*, New York: Abrams, 1982.

Jung, Gunilla (1905–1939)

Finnish designer.

Training Taideteollinen korkeakoulu, Helsinki; 1936, Institut Supérieur des Arts Décoratifs, Brussels.
Biography Jung designed lamps, silver, textiles, and enamel; 1932, set up her own studio in Helsinki; specialized in damask weaving, both mass-produced by Tampella and individually commissioned from clients, including Suomen Pankki (national bank of Finland), Kansallisteatteri (Finnish national theater), and Finlandia Hall, Helsinki. Her silver designs were first produced by Taito and later, in 1930s, by Viri and by Kultasepat. She worked with Frans Nykänen, the director at both silversmithies at different times; designed dinner service for Finnish silversmiths Lennart Baugartner, her largest commission.
Exhibitions/citations Work included in 1983–84 *Design Since 1945* (1957 Linenplay machine-woven damask), Philadelphia Museum of Art. Gold medal, 1937 *Exposition Internationale des Arts et Techniques dans la Vie Moderne*, Paris; grand prizes, 1951 (9th), 1954 (10th), and 1957 (11th) editions of Triennale di Milano.
Bibliography Benedict Zilliacus, *Finnish Designers*, Helsinki, 1954. Erik Zahle (ed.), *A Treasury of Scandinavian Design*, New York: Golden Press, 1961. Eeva Siltvuori, 'I Never Tire of Watching a Gull's Glide,' *Form Function Finland*, no. 2, 1981: 58–63. Charles S. Talley, *Contemporary Textile Art: Scandinavia*, Stockholm: Carmina, 1982. Cat., Kathryn B. Hiesinger and George H. Marcus III (eds.), *Design Since 1945*, Philadelphia: Philadelphia Museum of Art, 1983. Annelies Krekel-Aalberse, *Art Nouveau and Art Déco Silver*, New York: Abrams, 1989.

Junkers, Hugo (1859–1935)

German engineer, inventor, and entrepreneur; born Rheydt.

Training From 1878, engineering, Universität Berlin; 1881–83 and 1884–85, engineering, Rheinisch-Westfälische Hochschule, Aachen; 1887, electrical engineering and economics in Berlin.
Biography 1883, Junkers became manager of his father's textile firm in Rheydt, but returned to Aachen in 1884 for further study and concurrently worked in Aachen. 1890, he founded Versuchsstation für Gasmotoren von Oechelhaeuser & Junkers, Dessau, for production of gas engines. 1892, he established Hugo Junkers Civilingenieur Dessau; after other entrepreneurial activity, first took on design of airplanes in 1908 and, 1913–14, built a wind tunnel in Aachen; 1915, developed the first of his all-metal airplanes, Junkers J1. 1917, with Anthony Fokker, began serial production of airplanes, the first being 1917–18 Junkers J9 for Junkers-Fokker Flugzeugwerke AG. After

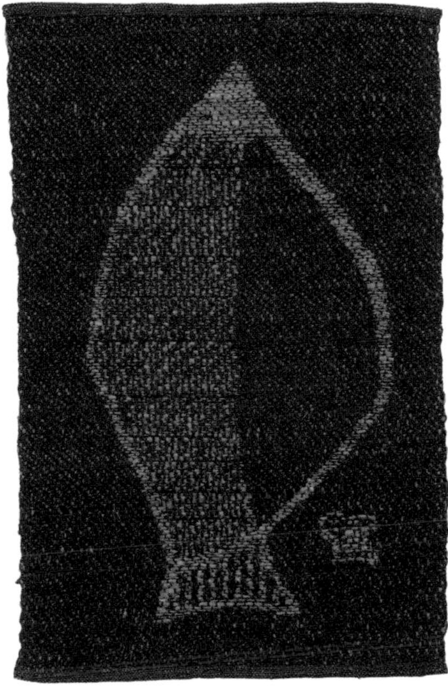

Dora Jung. Fish textile. Unknown date. Satin damask. 20 x 12 3/4" (50.8 x 32.4 cm). Mfr.: the designer, Finland. Given anonymously. MoMA.

Junkers's death, the firm became Germany's top Nazi weapons factory. c. 1919–30, Junkers designed a suitcase in Duralumin.
Exhibitions 2000 *Aluminum by Design* (suitcase), touring.
Bibliography Günter Schmitt, *Hugo Junkers und seine Flugzeuge*, Stuttgart: Motorbuch, 1986. Manfred Griehl, *Junkers Bombers*, Poole, Dorset: Arms and Armour; New York: Sterling, 1987.

Jutrem, Arne Jon (1929–)

Norwegian glassware and textile designer and metalworker.

Training 1946–50, lithography, Statens Håndværks -og Kunstindustriskole, Oslo; 1952, painting, Académie Léger, Paris, under Fernand Léger.
Biography From 1940s, Jutrem designed graphics, furniture, textiles, carpets, ceramics, metalwork, and, principally, glassware, particularly, 1950–62, for Hadelands Glassverk, Jevnaker. His liquid forms were full of movement, with undulating surfaces. Some pieces incorporated bursts of bubbles; others were more sculptural with grotesque additions. 1960s, he designed large kitchen appliances; 1962–64, was a consultant designer to Holmegård Glasværk, Copenhagen, where his work included a range of decorative and utilitarian glassware, including vases, bowls, plates, pitchers, and stemware with engraved decoration, strong colors, and matt finishes. 1963, he cofounded the new Landsforbundet Norske Brukskunst and, from 1965–66, its chairperson; from 1964–72, board member, Norsk Designcentrum; from 1965–70, chairperson and board member, Statens Håndværks -og Kunstindustrieskole; 1967, worked at Plus Glasshytte; from 1967, executed public commissions in glass, enamel, and metal.
Exhibitions/citations Work shown at 1967 *Universal and International Exhibition (Expo '67)*, Montreal. Work subject of 1979 exhibition, Oslo (catalog below). 1959 Lunning Prize; gold medal (for glassware), 1954 (10th) Triennale di Milano.
Bibliography 'Thirty-four Lunning Prize-Winners,' *Mobilia*, no. 146, Sept. 1967. Cat., *Arne Jon Jutrem*, Oslo: Kunstindustrimuseum, 1979. Cat., David Revere McFadden (ed.), *Scandinavian Modern Design 1880–1980*, New York: Abrams, 1982. Kathryn B. Hiesinger and George H. Marcus III (eds.), *Design Since 1945*, Philadelphia: Philadelphia Museum of Art, 1983. Cat., *The Lunning Prize*, Stockholm: Nationalmuseum, 1986. Fredrik Wildhagen, *Norge i Form*, Oslo: Stenersen, 1988: 127. Jennifer Hawkins Opie, *Scandinavia: Ceramics and Glass in the Twentieth Century*, New York: Rizzoli, 1989.

Južnič, Bohumíl (1895–1963)

Slovakian designer; born Požege (today in Slovenia).

Training Self-taught.

Biography Južnič was originally an army officer; from 1931, worked at Krásná Jizba (the beautiful room), which, together with the Czechoslovakian Werkbund (Svaz Československého Díla, SČSD), was instrumental in spreading Functionalist design in prewar Czechoslovakia; designed mainly metal tableware and, by end of 1930s, ceramics, glass, and wood.

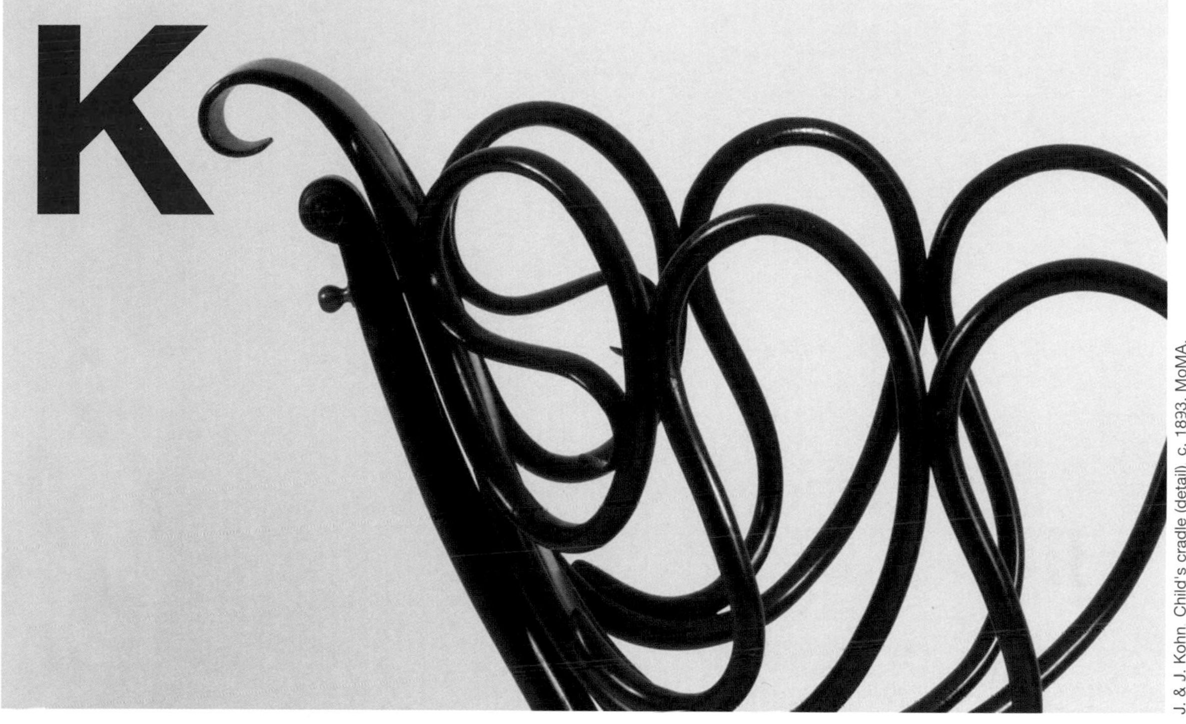

J. & J. Kohn Child's cradle (detail) c. 1833. MoMA.

K8 industridesign

Norwegian design studio; located Oslo.

History 14 April 1998, K8 industridesign (also known as Koockidoodle 8 industridesign) was established by Bjørn Bye (Oslo, 1971–), Johan Schreiner (Palo Alto, Cal., US, 1965–), and Marius Andresen (Gjøvik, 1971–). Work has included 1997 Najag (hydrofoil kayak prototype), 1998 'happygolucky' tabletop objects in concrete, 1998 Handsfree telephone (concept) by Nokia, 1998 packaging for Stabburet, 1999 decoration of Jordal Secondary School, 2000 Swing and Smart hospital-patient lifter, 2000–03 Xplory urban transporation of children by Stokke Children, from 2001 grocery-market thermometer by Instrutek, from 2002 board game by Brand Solutions, 2003 horse-training cart by Tore Haugen, others. 1998, Bye and Schreiner graduated from Department of Industrial Design, Arkitekthøgskolen, Oslo. Andresen graduated from Department of Industrial Design, Arkitekthøgskolen, Oslo, and attended ENSCI (Les Atelier), Paris. They have taught creativity and design. Other members of the studio: Mathias Hanssen (1977–), who earned a bachelor's degree in product design, Brunel University, Uxbridge, UK, and Lars-Frederik Forberg (1976–), a master of technology degree in product design, Norges Teknisk-Naturvitenskapelige Universitet (NTNU), Oslo.
Exhibitions/citations Young Talent Awards, Norska Designrådet (ND, Norwegian design council). Norsk Form awards: 1994 (for Schreiner and Lars Monrad Vaage, wheelchair design), 1996 (Andresen for welding mask), 1997 (Andresen and Schreiner, for Koil kayak), 2002 (Smart patient lifter). 1999 Product of the Month (Andresen, for Basso Flexo). Award (Andresen, with Steffen Anger, for fiberglass bicycle), World Bike competition, Paris. 2003 Young Designers of the Year, Norwegian Center for Architecture and Design; others.
Bibliography www.k8.no.

Kadlec, Zdeněk (1933–)

Czech industrial designer; born Zlín; active Uherské Hradiště.

Biography Kadlec was head of department of plastics, Vystudoval Střední Uměleckoprůmyslové Škole (secondary school of applied arts) in Uherské Hradiště; began producing designs in plastics, in collaboration with Tesla factory in Liptovsky Hrádek, on the occasion of a 1962 telephone-design competition sponsored by the Union of Plastic Artists, in which he came second. His first design, working individually, was a vacuum-molded bar unit for Frigera Beroun.
Bibliography Cat., Milena Lamarová, *Design a Plastické Hmoty*, Prague: Uměleckoprůmyslové Muzeum, 1972: 116.

Kadushin, Ronen (1964–)

Israeli designer; born Haifa.

Training To 1991, industrial design, Bezalel Academy of Art and Design, Jerusalem.
Biography Kadushin worked for various domestic- and office-furniture design firms before becoming a partner in furniture- and industrial-design firm D>W (Design to Work Ltd.), Tel Aviv; 1997–98, taught furniture design, Bezalel Academy of Art and Design, and, later, furniture design and creativity at Hadassa College, Jerusalem, and Vital School of Design, Tel Aviv.
Exhibitions/citations Work included in and subject of a number of exhibitions. Several design prizes.
Bibliography Giora Urian, *From the Israel Museum to the Carmel Market: Israeli Design*, Ramat-Hasaron: Urian–The Architect's Encyclopedia, 2001. Mel Byars, *Design in Steel*, London: Laurence King, 2002.

Kagan, Vladimir (1927–)

German furniture designer; born Worms am Rhein; active New York.

Training Architecture, Columbia University, New York.
Biography 1938, Kagan settled in the US; 1947, joined his father's woodworking shop; late 1940s, began designing furniture; designed 1947–48 Delegates' Cocktail Lounge in first United Nations headquarters, Lake Success, N.Y.; 1949 opened his first shop on East 65th Street, New York, and 1950, moved to 57th Street. His corporate clients have included General Electric, Monsanto, Prudential Insurance, Pioneer Industries, Warner Communications, American Express, Kenyon and Eckhart advertising, Walt Disney Enterprises, A&P groceries store, Kingdom of Saudi Arabia. He has worked for private clients such as Marilyn Monroe, Xavier Cougart, Lilly Pons, Gary Cooper, and Shermann Fairchild; established Vladimir Kagan Design Group; became active as an interior-design consultant to the home-furnishings and contract industries. After closing his factory and showroom, he continued to design for manufacturers such as Directional, Giorgio Collection, The Lane Company, Alpha Metallix, Preview Furniture, American Leather, Ello, and David Lynch. Other interior design clients have included the Du Pont family, Wilmington, Del.; and Black Clawson headquarters, New York. He was president of American Society of Interior Designers (ASID) and president of its New York Chapter; chairperson of Advisory Commission of School of Art and Design; member of Architectural League and American Society of Furniture Designers. He has taught at Parsons School of Design and lectured widely on modern

architecture and furniture design; is best known for his anthropomorphic designs of 1950s, especially a particular sweeping low-back sofa. 2000, Club House Italia introduced the Kagan New York Collection. From 2002, some of his 1950s designs, in the newly named Skulpture collection, were reproduced by Ralph Pucci, New York. His wife is needlework design and author Erica Wilson.
Exhibitions/citations Work shown at an edition of *Good Design* exhibition/award, The Museum of Modern Art, New York, and Chicago Merchandise Mart; 1991 *Organic Design* exhibition, Design Museum, London. Work subject of 1980 *Three Decades of Design*, Fashion Institute of Technology, New York. 2002 Lifetime Achievement Award, American Society of Furniture Designers.

Kåge, Algot Wilhelm (1889–1960)

Swedish ceramicist.

Training 1908–09, painting, Valand Art School, Gothenburg; under Carl Wilhelmsson in Stockholm; 1911–12 under Johan Rohde, Artists' Studio School, Copenhagen; Plakatschule, Munich.
Biography Kåge was initially active as a poster designer; joined the Gustavsberg ceramics factory, where, from 1917, he designed ceramics and was artistic director to 1949 (succeeded by Stig Lindberg, who had been at Gustavsberg from 1937). Kåge took the company in a new direction and encouraged use of modern designs and introduced stacking designs, simple forms, and heat-resistant dinnerware. His 1917 Liljebala (blue lily) dinnerware exemplified the attempt to raise design standards in inexpensive everyday wares. His designs included 1933 Praktika, Marina, and Pyro. His molded stoneware of 1950s, named Farsta after the island on which Gustavsberg is located, was influenced by Mexican and Chinese forms.
Exhibitions/citations Grand prize, 1925 *Exposition Internationale des Arts Décoratifs et Industriels Modernes*, Paris. Work shown at 1959 (20th) *Ceramic International Exhibition*, The Metropolitan Museum of Art, New York; 1975 *Gustavsberg 150 ar*, Nationalmuseum, Stockholm. Work subject of 1917 exhibition, Liljevalchs Art Gallery, Stockholm; 1953, Nationalmuseum, Stockholm.
Bibliography Nils Palmgren, *Wilhelm Kåge: konstnär och Hantverkare*, Stockholm: Nordisk Rotogravyr, 1953. Cat., *Wilhelm Kåge, Gustavsberg*, Stockholm: Nationalmuseum, 1953. Cat., *Gustavsberg 150 ar*, Stockholm: Nationalmuseum, 1975. Björn Hedstrand, *Servisgods från Gustavsberg av Wilhelm Kåge 1917–1945*, Motala, 1975. Cat., Kathryn B. Hiesinger and George H. Marcus III (eds.), *Design Since 1945*, Philadelphia: Philadelphia Museum of Art, 1983. Jennifer Hawkins Opie, *Scandinavia: Ceramics and Glass in the Twentieth Century*, New York: Rizzoli, 1989. George Fischler and Barrett Gould, *Scandinavian Ceramics and Glass: 1940s to 1980s*, Atglen, Pa.: Schiffer, 2000.

Kahlcke, Hartwig (1942–)
> See Seiffert, Florian.

Kähler, Herman August (1846–1917)

Danish ceramicist.

Training Under sculptor H.V. Biesen; and in ceramics factories in Berlin and Zurich.
Biography 1872, Kähler took charge of his father's pottery workshop in Næstved, where the designs of Thorvald Bindesbøll, Karl Hansen-Reistrup, and O. Eckmann were produced.
Exhibitions Work shown at 1889 *Exposition Universelle*, Paris; 1893 *World's Columbian Exposition*, Chicago; 1899 exhibition of Münchner Sezession; 1900 *Exposition Universelle*, Paris.
Bibliography Cat., David Revere McFadden (ed.), *Scandinavian Modern Design 1880–1980*, New York: Abrams, 1982.
> See Kähler Keramik.

Kähler Keramik

Danish ceramics factory.

History 1839, the factory was established by Christian Herman Kähler at Naestved, South Zealand; to 1888, specialized in production of earthenware stoves. 1872, Kähler's son Herman August Kähler took over as director and introduced redware to the line that he had shown with some success in 1880s; produced architectural ceramics, including those by sculptor K.F.C. Hansen-Reistrup; into 1920s, continued to produce lusterware designed by Herman Kähler himself and his brother Nils A. Kähler. 1913 and 1917–41, Jens Thirslund was the chief designer and, 1919, introduced painted lusters.
Exhibitions 2002 *Kähler Ceramics 1839–1969*, Kunstindustrimuseet, Copenhagen.
Bibliography Jennifer Hawkins Opie, *Scandinavia: Ceramics and Glass in the Twentieth Century*, New York: Rizzoli, 1989.

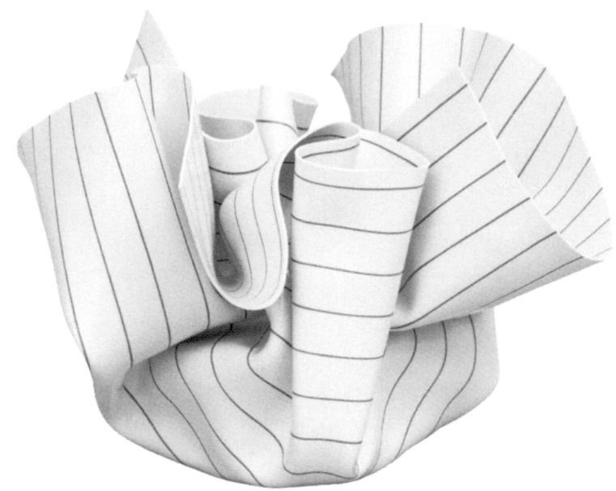

Tibor Kalman. Legal-size Paperweight. 1984 (manufactured 1994). Vinyl and lead, 3 3/8 x 3 1/2 x 4 1/2" (8.6 x 8.9 x 11.4 cm). Mfr: M & Co Labs, US (1994). Rob Beyer Purchase Fund. MoMA.

Kahn, Ely Jacques (1884–1972)

American architect and designer; born New York.

Training To 1903, architecture, Columbia University, New York; to 1911, École des Beaux-Arts, Paris.
Biography 1915, Kahn taught design at Cornell University, Ithaca, N.Y.; 1917, joined architects Buchman & Fox in New York; visited 1925 *Exposition Internationale des Arts Décoratifs et Industriels Modernes*, Paris, which resulted in his shift to modernism, even though initially having been influenced by the Beaux-Arts; 1925–31, designed 30 buildings in New York and, from 1929, interiors, furniture, and furnishings for, among others in New York, Frederick Rose apartment on Park Avenue, Mrs. Maurice Benjamin's apartment, and a number of stores. He became known for his use of vivid colors in architecture, possibly influenced by his collaboration with English émigré colorist Leon Solon. He wrote the books *Design in Art and Industry* (New York: Scribner's Sons, 1935) and *A Building Goes Up* (New York: Simon & Schuster, 1969).
Exhibitions Designed 1928 *Exposition of Modern French Decorative Art*, Lord & Taylor store, New York. Was in charge of Industrial Arts Section at 1933–34 *A Century of Progress International Exhibition*, Chicago. With Paul-Philippe Cret, directed young industrial designers' section at *Contemporary American Industrial Art, 1934* (including his textiles); *Contemporary American Industrial Art: 1940 Fifteenth Exhibition*; both The Metropolitan Museum of Art, New York.
Bibliography Arthur Tappan North, *Ely Jacques Kahn, 1884–1972*, New York: Whittlesey, 1931; New York: Acanthus, 1995 reprint. Karen Davies, *At Home in Manhattan: Modern Decorative Arts, 1925 to the Present*, New Haven: Yale, 1983. Robert A.M. Stern et al., *New York 1930*, New York : Rizzoli, 1987.

Kähönen, Hannu (1948–)

Finnish industrial designer.

Training 1967–71, graphic design and, 1971–75, industrial design, Taideteollinen korkeakoulu, Helsinki.
Biography 1981, Kähönen founded Creadesign industrial-design consultancy and has designed numerous products, ranging from Helsinki City trash bins and solar-powered machinery to graphic design and the Helsinki City low-body tram. Other work by him and his staff has included mobile phones by Benefon, such as the Spica, fireplaces by Tulikivi, locks by Abloy, skis by Karhu, sporting goods by Berner Osakeyhtiö, and product identity for Timberjack

Group. The studio's number of clients exceeds 40. From 1977, Kähönen taught, Taideteollinen korkeakoulu, Helsinki; has lectured worldwide.
Exhibitions/citations Work shown at more than 25 venues in Europe, Asia, and the US. A number of citations, awards, and scholarships, including 2000 jubilee medal of Helsinki's 450 years; 2001 Pro Finlandia medal, Finnish government.

Kaipiainen, Birger (1915–1988)
Finnish ceramicist.

Training 1933–37, Taideteollinen korkeakoulu, Helsinki.
Biography 1937–54, Kaipiainen was a designer at Arabia pottery in Helsinki, where he decorated Olga Osol's 1953 Tapetti dinnerware (produced to 1964); 1948–50, worked for Richard Ginori in Florence and Milan; 1954–58, at Rörstrand in Lidköping; 1958, returned to Arabia; used a painter's technique on ceramic forms. Kaipiainen became one of Finland's best-known ceramic artists; called on a color-saturated palette, which earned him the titles 'prince of ceramics' and 'king of decorators'; was inspired by Russian Orthodox and Italian Renaissance art. 1937–54 and 1958–88 in Arabia's art department in Finland, and 1954–58 in Rörstrand's in Sweden, he created mostly one-of-a-kind pieces. 1969 Paratiisi by Arabia was his only dinnerware design.
Exhibitions/citations Work shown at 1954–57 *Design in Scandinavia*, touring the US, 1961 *Finlandia* in Zurich, Amsterdam, and London. Work subject of exhibitions in Helsinki, Malmö, Gothenburg, Milan, and New York. 1951 (9th) (diploma of honor) and 1960 (12th) (grand prize) Triennali di Milano; 1963 Pro Finlandia; 1982 Prince Eugen Medal; 1997, honorary title of professor.
Bibliography Cat., David Revere McFadden (ed.), *Scandinavian Modern Design 1880–1980*, New York: Abrams, 1982. Jennifer Hawkins Opie, *Scandinavia: Ceramics and Glass in the Twentieth Century*, New York: Rizzoli, 1989.

Kairos, Studio
Italian design group.

History 1980, Massimo Bonetti (Turin 1949–), Giuseppe Manente, (Mestre, 1947–), and Abramo Mion (Mirano, 1951–) founded Studio Kairos for industrial design principally. They had previously worked separately. (*Kairos* in classical Greek means 'right point,' 'right place,' or 'right degree.') Work has included 1996 Pab storage units, 1997 Alanta wordrobe, and others by B&B Italia; c. 1987 Cucina Futura by Dada/Molteni; and c. 1987 Scarpone da Sci by Dolomite; all award winners. Also hardware by Colombo.
Citations 1984, 1987, 1989, 1994 Premio Compasso d'Oro (for products by B&B Italia, Dada/Molteni, and Dolomite); 1984 Möbel des Jahres (for Armadio Sisamo), *Schöner Wohnen* magazine; 1989 prize, Esposizione Internazionale Biennale dei Mobili per Ufficio (EIMU), Milan.

Kaiser, Robert (1925–)
American furniture designer; born Detroit; active Toronto.

Training After World War II, Meinzinger Art School, Detroit; design, Institute of Design, Illinois Institute of Technology, Chicago.
Biography 1950, Kaiser emigrated to Canada and became a technical illustrator for airplane manufacturers A.V. Roe Canada and De Havilland Aircraft of Canada and designed a retail stores for Cameron McIndoo and at Kinsella Design; freelanced as a furniture designer and, subsequently, joined the Primavera Design Group, Toronto, which produced his 1956 Occational chair in walnut and crossed steel rods with fabric seat and back, considered today to be a classic of Canadian design. He is known for his wide range of residential and contract furniture for manufacturers in Ontario. He taught, Ontario College of Art 1960–65 and 1970–89, and Ryerson Polytechnical Institute 1984–95.
Exhibitions/citations Suite of knock-down furniture in Suite of the Future in the Habitat pavilion, *Universal and International Exhibition (Expo '67)*, Montreal. For Occational chair: 1956 award, National Industrial Design Council, Canada; included in Canadian exhibit, 1957 (11th) Triennale di Milano.
Bibliography Cat., *Seduced and Abandoned: Modern Furniture Designers in Canada, the First Fifty Years*, Toronto: The Art Gallery at Harbourfront, 1986: 18. Rachel Gotlieb and Cora Golden, *Design in Canada Since 1945: Fifty Years from Teakettles to Task Chairs*, Toronto: Knopf Canada, 2001.

Kalawantavanich, Satit
> See Propaganda.

Kalff, Louis (1897–1976)
> See Philips.

Kalinsky, Stuart Alan (1951–)
American product designer; active New York.

Biography 1982, Kalinsky set up a toothbrush manufacturing business; designed molded Lucite-handle toothbrushes with embedded lace, gingham, chintz, leopard pattern, sequins, confetti, glitter, paisley, stripes, and other materials, including objects floating in water. He produced toilet accessories and fulfilled commissions for toothbrushes from corporate clients; patented a process for sealing materials in thick acetate sheets, which were then turned on a lathe and buffed.
Exhibitions Toothbrushes shown at 1990 *The Plastics Age*, Victoria and Albert Museum, London.
Bibliography Deborah Hofmann, 'Stylemakers,' *The New York Times*, 23 Dec. 1990: Sec. 1, p. 26.

Kalman, Tibor (1949–1999)
Hungarian graphic and product designer; born Budapest.

Training New York University, New York.
Biiography 1970–79, Kalman was design and publicity director for Barnes and Noble bookstores; 1979, set up his own design firm, M&Co, New York; 1991, became editor of Benetton's *Colors* magazine; 1995, reopened M&Co, where clients included Talking Heads, 42nd Street Redevelopment of New York, and Jonathan Demme. He became known for his unique and decidedly individualistic approach to design, evident in products made by his own firm, including a range of clocks now issued by The Museum of Modern Art, New York, and in radical *Colors* magazine. When terminally ill, he designed his own funeral ceremony, including the printed program, executed as a cheap restaurant menu. He wrote the book *Chairman Rolf Fehlbaum* (New York: Princeton Architectural Press, 1998, on Vitra furniture company director, and *(un) Fashion*, with wife Maira Kalman (New York: Abrams, 2000). The M&Co firm is now managed by his wife.
Bibliography Liz Farrelly, *Tibor Kalman: Design and Undesign*, New York: Watson-Guptill, 1998. Michael Bierut et al. (eds.), *Tibor Kalman: Perverse Optimist*, New York: Princeton Architectural Press, 1998. *T. Bor: Tiborocity Exhibition*, New York: The Little Bookroom, 2002. *Colors: Tibor Kalman, Issues 1–13*, New York: Abrams, 2002. Cat., R. Craig Miller (intro.), *U.S. Design 1975–2000*, Munich: Prestel, 2002.

Kalo Shops
> See Welles, Clara Barck.

Kamiyama, Shunichi (1947–)
Japanese glass designer.

Training To 1970, Tokyo University of Arts.
Biography 1970, Kamiyama became a designer at Hoya Crystal, Tokyo; is a board member, Japan Glass Art Crafts Association.
Exhibitions Work shown at numerous editions of 1990 *Glass in Japan*, Tokyo, from 1978; 1983 *Little Objects*, Japan Glass Art Crafts Association; 1991 (5th) Triennale of Japan Glass Art Crafts Association, Heller Gallery, New York.
Bibliography Cat., *Glass Japan*, New York: Heller Gallery and Japan Glass Art Crafts Association, 1991: no. 16.

Kan, Shiu-Kay (1949–)
British lighting designer; born Hong Kong; active London.

Training Architecture, Central London Polytechnic; 1976, Architectural Association, London.
Biography As a qualified architect, Kan worked for Foster Associates and Fiorucci, both London; 1979, established SKK Lighting in London. His first lighting model was 1979 Kite Light; the second was 1981 Griffe with a dichronic-halogen fitting. Others have included Magic Lantern and Inflatable Xmas Tree. Interested in new technologies, Kan produced low-voltage lighting and motorized models. His 1983–88 Motorized Robotic Light that moved across the ceiling on horizontal conductive cables by programmable remote control was installed as an initial fitting in the Design Museum in

London. He expanded his business to include a consultancy for contract lighting, a production subsidiary for developing new fittings, and a retail store. More recent commissions have been lighting for Mark Knopfler, Memorial Gate on Constitutional Hill for the Prince of Wales, and a large city development at Lion Plaza, all London. New products include c. 2001 Micro Paper Chase.
Citations 1983 lighting award, Philips, the Netherlands.
Bibliography Jeremy Myerson and Sylvia Katz, *Conran Design Guides: Lamps and Lighting*, London: Octopus, 1990.

Kandinsky, Vasilii Vasilievich (1866–1944)

Russian painter, printmaker, and theorist; born Moscow; active Russia, Germany, and France.

Training 1886–92, law, Moscow University (1893, taught in the law faculty there); 1900, under Franz von Stück, Akademie der bildenden Künste, Munich.
Biography 1889, Kandinsky participated in an ethnographic expedition to the Vologda Province, which kindled an interest in folk art; 1896, decided to dedicate himself to art; 1897–99, moved to Germany and studied at A. Azbé's school in Munich where, 1902–14, he lived and worked but made frequent trips to Russia, providing an important link between artistic groups in both countries. He was also a magazine correspondent, teacher, and organizer of artistic groups. He cofounded the group Phalanx in 1901, cofounded the New Artists' Association in 1909, and founded Der Blaue Reiter group in 1911, which became one of the most important links between experimental art in Germany and in Russia. Kandinsky wrote his first major theoretical text, *Über das Geistige in der Kunst* (on the spiritual in art) (Munich: R. Piper, 1912); 1914–21, lived and exhibited in Moscow. From 1918, he was one of the chief organizers of artistic life in Russia; 1918, became a member of the collegium of IZO Narkompros and developed a plan for a network of contemporary art museums; 1919–21, was professor, State Free Arts Workshops, Petrograd; 1920, became an honorary professor, Moscow University, and a member, Institute for Artistic Culture (INKhUK). 1921, he was vice-president, Russian Academy for Artistic Science; 1921, designed several motifs for porcelain at the State Porcelain Factory; Dec. 1921, went to Berlin and then on to Weimar to teach at the Bauhaus; wrote his second theoretical book, *Punkt und Linie Zu Fläche: Beitrag zur Analyse der malerischen Elemente...* (point and line to plane...) (ninth in Bauhausbücher series, Munich: Albert Langen, 1926); was invited by Ludwig Mies van der Rohe to render decorations for three ceramic walls of a music room at 1931 *Deutsche Bauausstellung*, Berlin. 1933, he moved to France and was active as a painter and writer to his death at Neuilly-sur-Seine, near Paris.
Exhibitions 1909–10, exhibited over 40 works at the Izdebsky Salon, Odessa; other work at 1912 Salon des Indépendants, Paris; 1910, with the Knave of Diamonds, Moscow; 1912–14, with Der Blaue Reiter, Munich. 1922–44, work subject of several exhibitions every year in Europe and the US.
Bibliography Jelena Hahl-Koch, *Kandinsky*, New York: Rizzoli, 1993. Vivian Endicott Barnett and Armin Zweite, *Kandinsky Watercolors and Drawings*, Munich: Prestel-Verlag, 1992. John Milner, *A Dictionary of Russian and Soviet Artists*, Woodbridge, Suffolk: Antique Collectors' Club,1993.

Kaneko, Steven T. (1962–)

Industrial designer; lives in Seattle, Washington.

Biography All in California: Kaneko was an industrial designer at Fluke Corporation and at Hewlett-Packard Company, designing electronic-measuring instruments; worked at Technology Design on the design of consumer electronics, computer peripherals, and medical diagnostic equipment; from 1991, has been design director, Windows Hardware Experience Group of Microsoft Corporation, Redmond, Wash., where he has designed, alone and with others, and patented a number of computer-related products, including mice; also commissions outside consultancies, such as frogdesign, for branding and assistance on in-house design; has supervised the design/development of mice, keyboards, cordless phones, digital speakers, and the redesign of Microsoft's logo (chosen from as many as 175 proposals) by frogdesign. Is a member, Industrial Designers Society of America (IDSA).
Citations 1998 IDSA98 Showcase (ergonomic IntelliMouse Trackball, with Carl Ledbetter, Edie Adams, and Hugh McLoone), IDSA; 1997, elected one of 40 most influential in technology design, *I.D.* magazine; numerous others.

Kantack, Walter

American lighting designer; born Meriden, Conn.

Training Pratt Institute, Brooklyn, N.Y.
Biography Kantack worked in drafting room of Edward F. Caldwell decorating firm, New York; 1915, began working at Sterling Bronze as a designer; 1917, set up his own design firm and was a specialist in custom lighting to 1932. He was vice-president, Architectural League of New York; honorary member, American Institute of Decorators (AID); member of the Hoover Delegation to 1925 *Exposition International des Arts Décoratifs et Industriels Modernes*, Paris.
Exhibitions/citations Late 1920s and early 1930s, work shown in exhibitions of industrial design, The Metropolitan Museum of Art, New York. 1934 gold medal, American Institute of Architects (AIA).
Bibliography Harry V. Anderson, 'Contemporary American Designers,' *Decorators Digest*, Aug. 1935: 45–49.

Kapka, Mark (1960–)

American designer.

Training Industrial design at San Jose State University, Cal.
Biography For nine years, Kapka worked as a staff designer at Metro furniture company in Oakland, Cal., where he designed a number of pieces of furniture, showrooms, and exhibits. From 1997, he worked independently in San Francisco for various manufacturers and has designed seating by Keilhauer, training-room furniture by Howe, and home-office furniture by OFFI & Company.

Karasz, Ilonka (1896–1981)

Hungarian designer; born Budapest; sister of Mariska Karasz.

Training Royal School of Arts and Crafts, Budapest.
Biography 1913, Karasz emigrated to the US; became active first as a graphic artist then as a designer, painter, and teacher. She designed fabrics by Lesher-Whitman, Cheney, Susequehanna Silk Mills, Belding, Standard Textile, Mallinson, Du Pont Rayon Division, and Schwarzenbach-Huber. She taught at Modern Art School, New York, and sold her work at bookshop/gallery The Sunwise Turn, which specialized in hand-dyed textiles and embroideries. She designed c. 1928–39 metalware by Paye & Baker Manufacturing; 1928–29, was a member of the executive committee of American Designers Gallery, and, 1930–c. 1933 of American Union of Decorative Artists and Craftsmen (AUDAC). Her work revealed an Eastern European crafts approach. She was also active as a designer of ceramics, silver, wallpaper, and furniture and illustrator of books and covers for *The New Yorker* magazine.
Exhibitions 1928 and 1929 American Designers Gallery exhibitions (c. 1934 Lamelle tea service by Buffalo China); 1934 *Contemporary American Industrial Art*, The Metropolitan Museum of Art; both New York.
Bibliography Harry V. Anderson, 'Contemporary American Designers,' *Decorators Digest*, Dec. 1935: 46–53. Karen Davies, *At Home in Manhattan: Modern Decorative Arts, 1925 to the Depression*, New Haven: Yale, 1983. Jonathan M. Woodham, *Twentieth-Century Ornament*, New York: Rizzoli, 1990. Cat., Pat Kirkham (ed.), *Women Designers in the USA, 1900–2000: Diversity and Difference*, New York: Bard; New Haven: Yale, 2000.

Karasz, Mariska (1898–1960)

Hungarian designer; born Budapest; sister of Ilonka Karasz.

Training Under Ethel Traphagen, The Cooper Union for the Advancement of Science and Art, New York.
Biography 1914, a year after her sister, Karasz emigrated to the US; specialized in handworked textiles; 1920s, designed women's and children's clothing; called on primary colors and geometric forms in small-scale convertible furniture, including a 1935 tubular-steel bassinet, convertible to a pram, by Saks Fifth Avenue; 1939, designed clothing patterns, published in women's magazines, embroideries and metalware.
Exhibitions 1930 and 1931 exhibition, American Union of Decorative Artists and Craftsmen (AUDAC); 1928 *International Exposition of Art in Industry* (child's rug), Macy's department store, New York, and touring ten US cities.
Bibliography Harry V. Anderson, 'Contemporary American Designers,' *Decorators Digest*, Dec. 1935: 46–53. Karen Davies, *At Home in Manhattan: Modern Decorative Arts, 1925 to the Depression*, New Haven: Yale, 1983. Jonathan M. Woodham, *Twentieth-Century*

Ornament, New York: Rizzoli, 1990. Cat., Pat Kirkham (ed.), *Women Designers in the USA, 1900–2000: Diversity and Difference*, New York: Bard; New Haven: Yale, 2000.

Karhula
> See Iittala Lasi.

Karlsen, Arne (1927–)
Danish architect and furniture designer.

Training To 1950, Arkitektskole, Det Kongelige Danske Kunstakademiet, Copenhagen.
Biography 1948–50, Karlsen worked at Faellesforeningen for Danmarks Brugsforeninger Møbeltegnestue (FDB, Danish association of consumer-cooperatives' furniture-design studio); 1950–55, worked for Mogen Koch; 1955, established his own office; 1950–56 and 1964–65, taught, Arkitektskole, Det Kongelige Danske Kunstakademi; 1955–60, editor, Dansk Kunsthåndværk; 1965, taught furniture and design, Arkitektskolen, Århus, where he was rector 1968–72 and a professor from 1981; from 1968, was a member, Akademirådet (academy of fine arts), and, 1973–75 and 1977–80, the president of the academy and its council. He wrote a number of books on the applied arts, including, *Contemporary Danish Design* (Copenhagen: Danish Society of Arts and Crafts and Industrial Design, 1960) and, as the editor, *Danish Design at the Millennium: Five Exhibitions, Five Essays* (Copenhagen: Christian Ejlers, 1997).
Bibliography Frederik Sieck, *Nutidig Dansk Møbeldesign – en kortfattet illustreret beskrivelse*, Copenhagen: Bondo Gravesen, 1981, 1990.

Karlskrona Porslinsfabrik
Swedish ceramics factory.

History 1918, the factory was established for the production of artware and tableware. Edvard Hald served as artistic director 1924–33, and was succeeded by Sven-Erik Skawonius 1933–39. 1942, the firm was amalgamated into Upsala-Ekeby and, 1968, closed.
Bibliography Jennifer Hawkins Opie, *Scandinavia: Ceramics and Glass in the Twentieth Century*, New York: Rizzoli, 1989.

Karmann, Wilhelm; Carrozzeria Ghia
German automobile coach builders; located Osnabrück. Italian coach designers; located Turin

Biography 1901, Wilhelm Karmann the elder (1864–1952) purchased Klases coach builders (established in 1874) and changed the name to his own; 1902, began building his own coaches and soon after automobile bodies; by 1914, was making bodies for Opel, Minerva, and FN, many of them convertibles. The company grew appreciably and was saved during the Great Depression of the 1930s by a relationship with Adler motor company, known for its attractive, leak-proof convertibles, and, 1931, Karmann built Model A convertibles for Ford. The Karmann plant was commandeered by British forces after World War II, when the factory turned to producing only tools, dies, and body parts until a Volkswagen agreement in 1948; began making export Beetle chassis in 1949. On his father's 1952 death, Wilhelm the younger (Osnabrück, 1914–Osnabrück, 1998), an accomplished engineer not a designer, became the director of the firm. Having earlier been approached by Volkswagen to design a sports car on a Beetle chassis, Karmann contacted the Carrozzeria Ghia in Turin (begun as Carrozzeria Ghia & Gariglio in 1915 by Giacinto Ghia [Turin, 1887–Turin, 1944] and his partner Gariglio and called simply Carrozzeria Ghia from 1926). It was suggested by then-Ghia-owner Felice Mario Boano, who knew little of Karmann or Volkswagen, that Luigi Segre (1919–1963), the commercial director of Ghia, reconnoiter a Beetle from French VW importer Charles Ladouche, which Segre stripped down at Ghia for careful study. The design, eventually to be known as the Karmann Ghia coupé, was designed by Boano and the Ghia staff in 1953 (some say also by Segre), with production from 1955, a convertible from 1956, and Type 3 from 1961–69. But all were discontinued in 1975, when the last body appeared to be little different from the first example. (From 1953, Ghia was owned by Segre but was bought in 1967 by Leonidas Trujillo, the son of Dominican dictator Rafael Trujillo.) The Karmann Ghia was somewhat successful. Karmann also hired Giorgetto Giugiaro to design a number of successful bodies, including 1967 Maserati Ghibli and 1971 De Tomaso Pantera. 1970, Ghia was purchased by Ford and incorporated into the Ford design studio while remaining in Italy, where the 2000 StreetKa concept was created to be one of the few notable examples since the Ford acquisition. Wilhelm Karmann GmbH is still active.
Biography Valerio Moretti, *Ghia*, Milan: Automobilia, 1991. Laurence Meredith, *Essential Volkswagen Karmann Ghia: The Cars and Their Story, 1955–74*, St. Paul, Minn.: Motorbooks International, 1994. Malcolm Bobbit, *Karmann-Ghia Coupe and Convertible*, Dorchester: Veloce, 2002.

Peter Karpf. NXT stacking chair. 1991. Laminated beech, 29 1/4 x 20 3/8 x 15 1/2" (74.2 x 51.7 x 39.4 cm). Mfr.: Swedese Möbler, Sweden. Gift of the mfr. MoMA.

Karnagel, Wolf (1940–)
German designer and teacher; born Leipzig.

Training Under Bodo Kapmann, Hochschule der Kunst, Brunswick.
Biography Karnagel worked as associate designer at Staatliche Porzellan-Manufaktur (KPM) in Berlin. He designed two ranges by Rosenthal Studio-Linie: 1969 Joy glass and 1980s Pandio glass; also 1986 Epoca cutlery range by Wilkens in Bremen, and 1967 Stambul mocha service by KPM. Other clients included Lufthansa airlines from c. 1973 to recently with, for Lufthansa's first-class carriage, Rosenthal Studio-Linie and, subseqently, Hutschenreuther and also Schönwald porcelain dinnerware. Possibly not all were designed by Karnagel; however, he designed more than 100 sets for the airline; has been a professor of design, Hochschule der Künste, Berlin.
Citations Numerous awards include 1999 Red Dot award (for Ballerina stemware by Theresienthaler Krystallglasmanufaktur in Zwiesel), Design Zentrum Nordrhein Westfalen, Essen.
Bibliography Frederick Cooke, *Glass: Twentieth-Century Design*, New York: Dutton, 1986. Albrecht Bangert and Karl Michael Armer, *80s Style: Designs of the Decade*, New York: Abbeville, 1990.

Karpf, Peter (1940–)
Danish furniture designer; born Copenhagen.

Training 1957, at the Fritz Hansens furniture company; 1961, Kunsthåndværkerskolen, Copenhagen.
Biography Karpf has designed furniture by Iform, including the Voixa collection; and 1968 The Wing chair by Christiansen & Larsen. From 1991, he became best known for his distinctive NXT, ECO, TRI, OTO, XUS, and VUW bentwood stacking chairs by Iform, with three-letter titles and that employ the use of technologically innovative plywood

construction and manufacturing techniques which Karpf developed.
Exhibitions/citations Work included in venues in Sweden and abroad. 1967 grant (for a plastic building material), National Endowment for the Arts; 1993 Forsnäs award (for NXT); 2000 Ecology Design Award and design award (for ECO) and 2001 (for OTO), Industrie Forum Design (iF), Hanover; 2001 Red Dot award (for NXT), Design Zentrum Nordrhein Westfalen, Essen; 2002 Bruno Mathsson Prize.
Bibliography Mel Byars, *50 Chairs...*, Hove: RotoVision, 1996.

Karppanen, Mikko (1955–)
Finnish glassware designer.

Biography From 1983, Karppanen designed glassware at Iittala, Finland, and became its youngest designer. Some of his glassware featured new watercolor-like decoration. Examples by Iittala include 1995 Ice Cube votive-candle holder and 1988 Theba vase and a number of other models: Kanto, Lumilinna, Scilla, Silmu, and Tähti. He is is a senior lecturer, Kerava Institute, Kerava.

Karra, Alexandra (1962–)
Greek industrial designer; born Katerini.

Training 1980–85, architecture, Aristotelian University of Thessaloniki; 1987–88, industrial design, Domus Academy, Milan.
Exhibitions/citations Prize for a series of objects in 'Pyramid' section of 1986 Panhellenic Competition of Furniture Design—Furnidec, Thessaloniki. Her work was included in 1986 (8th) Biennial of Young Artists of Europe and the Mediterranean, Thessaloniki; 1987 (3rd) *European Exhibition of Creation SAD '87*, Grand Palais, Paris; 1988 *Bagno Extra: A Bath of Sense and Sensuality*, Cersale '88, Bologna.
Bibliography Cat., Design Center Stuttgart, *Women in Design: Careers and Life Histories Since 1900*, Stuttgart: Haus der Wirtschaft, 1989.

Kartell
Italian domestic goods manufacturer; located Noviglio (MI).

History 1949, Kartell was founded by chemical engineer Giulio Castelli (1920–) he studied under Giulio Natta, Politecnico, Milan; was a chemical engineer and technical consultant and specialized in and was an innovator of plastics. (Later in his career, Castelli was a member of the promotion committee of Associazione per il Disegno Industriale [ADI] and its president for four years; from 1962, jury of Premio Compasso d'Oro.) Early on, he founded Kartell in 1949 to produce household articles in plastics, adding lamps in 1958 and furniture in 1967. Initially, he hired his wife Anna Castelli Ferrieri and Ignazio Gardella as consultant designers. Kartell set up the Labware division to make products for use in chemical laboratories. Others of its first generation of designers included Olaf von Bohr, Giotto Stoppino, Joe Colombo, Gae Aulenti, Anig Sarian, Piero Lissoni, Paolo RIzzatto, Alberto Meda, Marco Zanuso, Sergio Asti, Pierluigi Spadolini, Ferruccio Laviani, and Pietro Felli. Kartell's range has encompassed the celebrated 1965–67 stacking chair by Colombo and Philippe Starck's 1989 Dr. Glob chair. 1991 collapsible table series by Antonio Citterio was widely published. Designs include von Bohr's 1970 Modular bookshelves 4930–7, Stoppino's Stackable Tables 4905–7, Columbo's Table Lamps 4008, 4088, and 4029, Asti's Writing Tray 4640, Starck's 1998 La Marie clear chair, Ron Arad's FPE (Fantastic Plastic Elastic) chair, and many works by Castelli Ferrieri. A large number of successful products, which often take up to three years to develop, have followed. Since its purchase in 1988 by Claudio Luti (the son-in-law of Giulio Castelli who formerly worked with Gianni Versace), Kartell has thrived. The firm exports 75% of its produce to over 60 countries, particularly to Germany; established 16 flagship stores and 140 shops within various department stores. To mark Kartell's 50th anniversary, its museum (architect, Ferruccio Laviani) was opened 12 April 2000 in Naviglio to display more than 1,000 historical products.
Exhibitions/citations Work shown at 1972 *Italy: The New Domestic Landscape*, The Museum of Modern Art, New York. Work subject of a 2000 exhibition (a Kartell donation to the museum), Centre Georges Pompidou, Paris. Gold and silver medals at numerous editions of the Triennale di Milano; from 1954 to the present, a large number Premio Compasso d'Oro; 1965 Interplast award; 1968 Oscar Plast award; first prize, 1968 Fiera del Mobile, Trieste; 1967, 1968, and 1972 prizes, Mostra di Articoli Casalinghi e Ferramenta (Macef); silver medal, 1972 Bauzentrum, Vienna; 1973 Bundespreis Produktdesign, Rat für Formgebung (German design council), Frankfurt; 1974 Casa Amica prize. Products selected for 1968 BIO 3 and 1973 BIO 5 industrial-design biennials, Ljubljana.
Bibliography Cat., Milena Lamarová, *Design a Plastické Hmoty*, Prague: Umĕleckoprůmyslové Muzeum, 1972: 60, 62, 192. Augusto Morello and Anna Castelli Ferrieri, *Plastiche e design = Plastic and Design*, Milan: Arcadia, 1984/1988. *ADI Annual 1976*, Milan: Associazione per il Disegno Industriale, 1976. Cat., *Kartell Museo*, Milan: Fondazione Museo Kartell, 1999. Cat., *La donation Kartell: un environnement plastique 1949–2000*, Paris: Centre Georges Pompidou, 2000.

Kashiwabara, Hiroyuki (1942–)
Japanese glass designer.

Training To 1968, Nihon University, Tokyo.
Biography 1968, Kashiwabara began work at Sasaki Glass in Tokyo, where he became the chief designer.
Exhibitions Prize for Excellence, 1978 *Japan Crafts* exhibition; Functional Design Prize, 1986 (30th) *Anniversary Exhibition of Crafts Design Association*; Achievement Award, 1988 *International Exhibition of Glass Craft*, Industrial Gallery of Ishikawa Prefecture, Kanazawa. Work shown at 1982 *Modern Japanese Crafts*, touring Southeast Asia; 1987 and 1990 *Glass in Japan*, Tokyo; 1991 (5th) Triennial, Japan Glass Art Crafts Association, Heller Gallery, New York; numerous others.
Bibliography Cat., *Glass Japan*, New York: Heller Gallery and Japan Glass Art Crafts Association, 1991: no. 17.

Kastelec, Albert (1930–)
Slovene designer; born Medno.

Training To 1949, Secondary Graphic Arts School, Ljubljana.
Biography Kastelec has been a freelance industrial designer, whose work has included 1968–70 Universal electrical hand tools by Iskra and 1974 Stimulator PO 10 produced by the Institute for the Rehabilitation of the Disabled, Ljubljana.
Citations 1970 Prešeren Fund Award, Slovenia.

Kastholm, Jørgen (1931–)
Danish architect and furniture designer; born Roskilde.

Training 1954–58 under Arne Jacobsen, Skole for Boligindretning, Frederiksberg; 1959, Grafisk Højskole.
Biography 1954, Kastholm began as a journeyman; worked for furniture makers Fritz Hansen and Ole Hagen; 1960, set up a studio in Holte; 1962–70, was a partner of Preben Fabricius as well as, 1971, with Arne Jacobsen, about whom he wrote a book. 1972, Kastholm moved to Düsseldorf. Designs included furniture for Alfred Kill International and Ivan Schlechter, and cutlery, textiles, lighting, and books; from 1975 or 1976, he taught furniture design at Universität-Gesamthoch-schule, Wuppertal. He designed 1962 tractor-seat-like Sciar Chair 63 by Ivan Schlechter; 1964 FK6725 (Tulip) armchair with casters (with Preben Fabricius) by Alfred Kill in Fellbach; and 1985 Geo-Line armchair, echoing 1930s models by others, by Franz Wittmann.
Exhibitions Work shown at 1966 *Vijftig Jaar Zitten*, Stedelijk Museum, Amsterdam; 1968 *Les Assises du Siège Contemporain*, Musée des Arts Décoratifs, Paris (catalog below); Ringling Museum, US, 1969; Royal Albert Hall, London. 1962 Sciar Chair 63 shown first time, at *New Forms* exhibition, Charlottenborg Museum, Copenhagen. Received 1968 Illum Prize; 1969 Ringling Museum Award; 1969, 1972, 1974, 1976, 1985 Bundespreis Produktdesign, Rat für Formgebung (German design council); Design Center Stuttgart 1972–77; Design Center Munich; 1973 grand prize, Museo de Arte Moderne, Brazil.
Bibliography Cat., *Les assises du siège contemporain*, Paris: Musée des Arts Décoratifs, 1968. Cat., *Modern Chairs 1918–1970*, London: Lund Humphries, 1971. Hans Wichmann, *Industrial Design Unikate und Serienerzeugnisse*, Munich: Die Neue Sammlung, 1985. Robert A.M. Stern (ed.), *The International Design Yearbook*, New York: Abbeville, 1985/1986. Frederik Sieck, *Nutidig Dansk Møbeldesign – en kortfattet illustreret beskrivelse*, Copenhagen: Bondo Gravesen; 1990.

Kastrup Glasværk
Danish glass manufacturer

History 1847, Kastrup was founded; produced glass designed by Jacob Bang and others; 1965, merged with Holmegård Glasværk. 1985, the merged company in turn merged with Royal Copenhagen; 1997, was further amalgamated with Boda Nova, Höganäs Keramik, Orrefors, Kosta Boda, and Venini to form Royal Scandinavia. However, in 2000, Royal Scandinavia was bought by an investment group and eventually dismantled into various entities.
> See Holmegård; Royal Scandinavia.

Katavolos, William (1924–)

American designer; active New York and Cold Spring, N.Y.

Training To 1949, industrial design, Pratt Institute, Brooklyn, N.Y.; 1964, physics, New York University.
Biography 1949–55, Katavolos was a partner with Ross Littell and Douglas Kelley on furniture, textile, and dinnerware designs for Laverne Originals. Commissioned by Erwine and Estelle Laverne, they executed their first furniture collection, Laverne's 1949 New Furniture Group of chairs and tables in leather, chrome, glass, and marble. The 1952 'T' chair (no. 31C) was initially a wooden-dowel prototype with production in chromium-plated steel, possibly designed by Katavolos alone, as is his claim; others assert its having been designed with Littell, Kelley, and Alton Kelley (1940–). 1955–57, Katavolos worked at George Nelson Associates, New York, designing 1956–57 Omni Pole shelving system, Williamsburgh Restoration exhibit systems, and Smithsonian Museum exhibition system, and collaborating on the Experimental House. He was a freelance designer for the Agricultural Pavilion and Solar Energy Pavilion, US exhibition, 1957 Salonika Fair, Greece; designed ceiling tension-ring structure for interior dome of 1959 *American National Exhibition*, Moscow; 1959–63, taught design, Sarah Lawrence College, Bronxville, N.Y;. designed the 1965 experimental school building Education Tower; 1965 partition systems (with J. Luss) for offices of Time–Life, New York; and 1969 hospital and surgical products by Johnson & Johnson. 1973, Katavolos was chairperson of the curriculum, School of Architecture, Pratt Institute, and, from 1975, a professor there. 1979, he was invited by Technicon University, Haifa, to participate in the town planning of North Jerusaleum; 1985, became a partner of Ergo Design, Boulder, Colo.; 1990–91, was consulting designer to Marai International, New York and Tokyo. He wrote the book *Organics* (Hilversum: De Jong, 1962) and produced the film *Correlations* (1968).
Exhibitions/citations 1953 and 1955 *Good Design* exhibitions/awards (Laverne work and Katavolos's textile designs), The Museum of Modern Art, New York, and Chicago Merchandise Mart. From 1958, work shown in worldwide touring exhibition, sponsored by the US government. 'The Chemical City' shown at 1961 *Visionary Architecture* exhibition, The Museum of Modern Art, New York. 1952 award for best US furniture design (for 'T' chair), American Institute of Architects (AIA); 1975 George Becker grant (for production of Hydronic Energy House), Higgins Hall, Pratt Institute.
Bibliography 'Good Design,' *Interiors*, vol. 113, Aug. 1953: 88–89, 146–48. Roberto Aloi and Agnoldomenico Pica, *Mobili tipo*, Milan: Ulrico Hoepli, 1956: 97, 121, 187, 216. Clement Meadmore, *The Modern Chair: Classics in Production*, New York: Van Nostrand Reinhold, 1975: 98–101. Cat., Kathryn B. Hiesinger and George H. Marcus III (eds.), *Design Since 1945*, Philadelphia: Philadelphia Museum of Art, 1983.

William Katavolos, Douglas Kelley, Ross Littell, and Alton Kelley (1940–). 'T' side chair. 1952. Chrome-plated steel, enameled steel, and leather, 32 x 23 x 22 7/8" (81.3 x 58.4 x 58.1 cm). Mfr.: Laverne Originals, US. Gift of the mfr. MoMA.

Kauffer, Edward McKnight (b. Edward Kauffer 1890–1954)

American graphic artist and designer; born Montana; active London; husband of Marion Dorn.

Training In painting, US.
Biography Kauffer added 'McKnight' to his name in honor of Joseph E. McKnight, the patron of his 1913 study trip to Paris. 1914, Kauffer settled in Britain; 1915, received his first important commission, a poster design for the London Underground, from its publicity manager Frank Pick, eventually one of Kauffer's major clients for the next quarter century. 1921, Kauffer gave up painting to concentrate on commercial art and design and became best known for his lively posters. Clients included Eastman, J.C. Eno, The Gas, Light and Coke Co, General Post Office, Orient Line steamships, Empire Marketing Board, Great Western Railway, Shell Mex, and British Petroleum. He illustrated books including *Don Quixote de la Mancha* (London: Nonesuch, 1930) by Miguel de Cervantes, *Triumphal March* (London: Faber & Faber, 1931) by T.S. Eliot, and *Dream of Destiny, an Unfinished Novel,* and *Venus Rising from the Sea* (London: Cassell, 1932) by Arnold Bennett, numerous book jackets, and a cover for *The Studio* journal. He designed theater costumes and sets including those for the 1937 ballet *Checkmate* (composer, Arthur Bliss; choreographer, Ninette de Valois), by Vic-Wells Ballet (later Sadler's Wells Ballet and Royal Ballet), Théâtre des Champs-Elysées, Paris. From 1920s, Kauffer designed rugs, with modernist motifs, by Wilton Royal Carpet Factory, as did his wife Marion Dorn. They were among the first British designers to equal the standards of the carpet designs of the French *artistesdécorateurs*. 1940, they moved to New York.
Exhibitions 1929 exhibition (Wilton rugs with Dorn), Arthur Tooth decorators, London; 1979–80 *Thirties* exhibition (graphics and rugs), Hayward Gallery, London (catalog below). Work subject of 1955 memorial exhibition, Victoria and Albert Museum, London; 1989–90 exhibition, Cooper-Hewitt National Design Museum, New York. 1936, elected Honorary Royal Designer for Industry, UK.
Bibliography E. McKnight Kauffer, *The Art of the Poster: Its Origin, Evolution & Purpose*, London: C. Palmer, 1924. Michael Farr, *Design in British Industry: A Mid-Century Survey*, London: Cambridge, 1955: 192. Cat., *Thirties: British Art and Design Before the War*, London: Arts Council of Great Britain/Hayward Gallery, 1979. Mark Haworth-Booth, *E. McKnight Kauffer: A Designer and His Public*, London: Gordon Fraser, 1979.
> See Dorn, Marion.

Kauffer, Elizabeth

American designer; active New York.

Biography Kauffer was originally associated with Gilbert Rohde, the design director of Herman Miller Furniture Company; later, became the color coordinator for Herman Miller; 1960 designed a group of table lamps by Nessen Studio, Yonkers, N.Y., that featured bases in Italian marble.
Bibliography *Home Lighting and Accessories*, Apr. 1985: 22–26.

Kaufman, Yaacov (1945–)

Israeli designer; born Russia; active Tel Aviv and Milan.

Training Sculpture, Bat-Yam Institute of Art, Bat-Yam, Israel.
Biography Kaufman is head of the master's-degree design program, Bezalel Academy of Art and Design, Jerusalem; has designed for clients, including Arflex, Edizioni Galleria Colombari, I.B. Office, Lumina Italia, Luxo, Porro, Seccose, Segno, and SisustusikkunaTecno; has received a number of patents for the articulation elements of lamp arms and patents for furniture and exposition design, ergonomic seating, composite-wooden surfaces, and others.
Exhibitions/citations From 1980, work shown in venues in London, Amsterdam, Milan, Paris, Nordrhein Westfalen, and New York, and

subject of exhibitions in New York, Milan, Tel Aviv, and Haifa. 1987 Forma Finlandia prize (for portable raft); 1988 Form Design 88 prize (for Eye halogen lamp), Milan; 1989 Sandberg Prize, The Israel Museum, Jerusalem; 1989 judges' special award, Kai World Scissors and Shears Design Competition, Japan; 1991 (for Attiva ergonomic chair by Secco) and 1994 (for S 22 folding chair by Tecno) Premio Compasso d'Oro; 1997 honorable mention, Wood of Finland competition, Finland.

Kaufmann Jr., Edgar (1910–1989)

American museum curator, historian, and philanthropist; born Pittsburgh, Pa.; active New York.

Training In painting, New York, Vienna, Florence, and London; 1934–35, Frank Lloyd Wright's Taliesin Foundation, Scottsdale, Ariz.
Biography 1935, Kaufmann joined the family's Kaufmann's Department Store in Pittsburgh and became the merchandise manager for home furnishings. Frank Lloyd Wright designed 1935–37 office of Kaufmann's father, Edgar J. Kaufmann Sr. (1885–1955), in the department store, and 1936–38 Liliane S. and Edgar J. Kaufmann Sr. country home, 'Fallingwater,' Bear Run, Pa. (The office is now part of the Victoria and Albert Museum collection, London, and the home was designated a National Historic Landmark in 2000.) At The Museum of Modern Art, New York: 1940, Kaufmann became a curator in the Department of Industrial Design; served in the army and returned as the director of the department. 1947, the department was merged with the Department of Architecture, under the directorship of Philip Johnson and when Kaufmann became Research Associate and Consultant in Industrial Design, to 1955. In the position as director, he had succeeded John McAndrew after Eliot Noyes and the brief tenure of Suzanne Wasson-Tucker. Kaufmann focused the museum's permanent design collection on products and objects from Europe, particularly Italy and Scandinavia. His publications while at the museum attempted to educate the public in the high-aesthetic standards of design; from 1950, managed the first series of *Good Design* exhibitions/awards at the museum and at the Chicago Merchandise Mart. On his father's 1955 death, he inherited 'Fallingwater' and, 1963, donated the house and a large parcel of adjunct land to the Western Pennsylvania Conservancy with a $500,000 endowment. (His mother Liliane S. Kaufmann [1889–1952], an active participant in Kaufmann's Department Store and a philanthropist, had died prior to her husband.) 1979, a pavilion on the property was designed by Kaufmann's companion Paul Mayen. Kaufmann was for many years adjunct professor of architecture and art history, Columbia University, New York; published numerous essays and books on architecture and design, including *Fallingwater: A Frank Lloyd Wright Country House* (New York: Abbeville, 1986); 1978, cofounded and directed Architectural History Foundation.
Exhibitions Organized numerous exhibitions at The Museum of Modern Art, New York, and 1970 *The Rise of American Architecture 1815–1915*, The Metropolitan Museum of Art, New York; *1999 Merchant Prince and Master Builder: Edgar J. Kaufmann [Sr.] and Frank Lloyd Wright*, Carnegie Museum of Art, Pittsburg.
Bibliography Leon Harris, *Merchant Princes*, New York: Harper and Row, 1979. Edgar Kaufmann Jr., *Prize Designs for Modern Furniture from the International Competition for Low-Cost Furniture Design*, New York: The Museum of Modern Art, 1950, Edgar Kaufmann Jr., *What is Modern Design?*, New York: The Museum of Modern Art, 1950. Edgar Kaufmann Jr., *What is Modern Interior Design?*, New York: The Museum of Modern Art, 1953. Paul Goldberger, 'Edgar Kaufmann Jr., 79, Architecture Historian,' *The New York Times*, 1 Aug. 1989. Christopher Wilk, *Frank Lloyd Wright: The Kaufmann Office*, Victoria and Albert Museum, 1993. Rona Roob, 'Edgar Kaufmann, Jr., Fallingwater and The Museum of Modern Art,' *MoMA Magazine*, winter / spring 1994: 68.

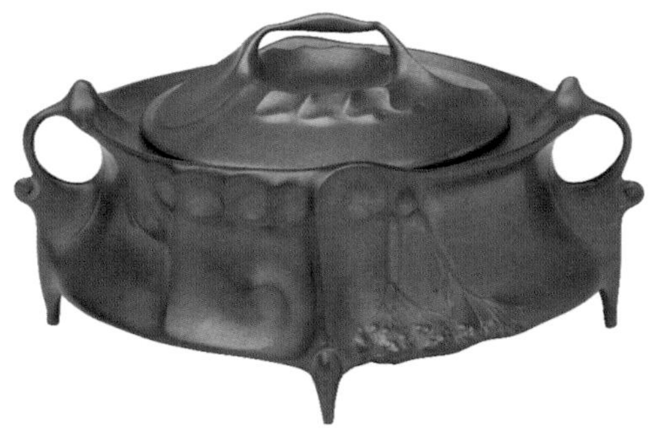

J.P. Kayser: Hermann Fauser (1874–1947). Biscuit box. 1902–04. Pewter, body 4 1/2 x 9 x 7 1/2" (11.4 x 22.8 x 19 cm), lid h. 1 9/16 x dia. 5 3/8" (3.9 x 13.7 cm). Mfr.: J.P. Kayser Sohn, Germany. Estée and Joseph Lauder Design Fund. MoMA.

Kawabe, Sachiko (1958–)

Japanese designer; born Tokyo.

Training Women's Art University, Tokyo.
Biography Kawabe set up her own design office and executed 1988 Kan Kan lacquered wood tableware range produced by Yamada-Heiando.
Bibliography Albrecht Bangert and Karl Michael Armer, *80s Style: Designs of the Decade*, New York: Abbeville, 1990: 142, 151, 232.

Kawakami, Motomi (1940–)

Japanese furniture designer; born Hyogo Prefecture.

Training To 1964, industrial design, Tokyo National University of Fine Art and Music, and graduate studies there.
Biography 1966–69, Kawakami worked in Angelo Mangiarotti studio in Milan; designed 1968 Fiorenza Chair, a form in a continuous band with slits for flexibility and drainage when used outdoors, produced by Alberto Bazzani, Milan. 1971, established his own studio for product and interior design; has been design professor, Tokyo National University of Fine Arts and Music, Aichi Prefectural University of Fine Arts and Music, and other institutions. Various work has included Crescendo chair by Arflex, Blitz folding chair by Skipper, and 1980–87 Tsurumi Tsubasa (or Wing) Bridge over the bay of Yokohama.
Exhibitions/citations Work shown in furniture fairs in Cologne, Paris, and Milan. Also at 1966 (1st) Eurodomus, Genoa; 1968 (2nd) Eurodomus, Turin; 1970 *Modern Chairs 1918–1970* exhibition, Whitechapel Gallery, London. Received 1967 MIA award, Mostra Internazionale Arredamento, Monza, 1976 award, Japan Interior Designers Association; first prize (for Blitz chair), 1977 Open International Chair Design Competition, American Institute of Architects (AIA), US; 1981, 1982, 1999 award, Industrie Forum Design (iF), Hanover; 1991 Mainichi Design Prize; 1992 Kitaro Kunii Industrial Design Award; 1995 Tanaka Prize (for Yokohama bay bridge), Japan Society of Civil Engineering; 1966 Yokohama Civic Design Award; gold prize, 1998 G-Mark Good Design Award, Japanese Industrial Design Promotion Organization.
Bibliography Cat., *Modern Chairs 1918–1970*, London: Lund Humphries, 1971. Angelo Mangiarotti, *Motomi Kawakami Design with Precision and Flexibility*, Osaka: Aram Art Press, 2001.

Kawasaki, Kazuo (1949–)

Japanese designer, born Fukui City.

Training To 1972, Kanazawa College of Art, Kanazawa, Ishikawa.
Biography To 1979, Kawasaki was the creative director of the product-design department at Toshiba electronics; 1979–80, a freelance consultant designer; from 1980, president of Ex-Design; designed 1987 X and I scissors by Takefu Knife Village in Takefu, Fukui Prefecture, and 1989 Carna folding wheelchair by SIG Workshop. He has been a lecturer, Fukui University; instructor at Kanazawa University of Arts; and technical advisor to the Fukui Prefecture.
Bibliography Albrecht Bangert and Karl Michael Armer, *80s Style: Designs of the Decade*, New York: Abbeville, 1990: 220, 232. Paola Antonelli (ed.), *Objects of Design: The Museum of Modern Art*, New York: The Museum of Modern Art, 2003: 279.

Kay, John Illingworth (1870–1950)

British designer and teacher; born Kirkcaldy, Scotland; active London.

Biography Kay was an intimate of Harry Napper of Silver Studio and textile/fabric designer Lindsay Philip Butterfield; 1892–1900, worked at the Silver Studio and rendered book covers, textiles, and wallpaper designs; from 1900–22, worked at wallpaper manufacturer Essex & Co.; concurrently, may also have designed for firms such as Baker, Morton Sundour, Grafton's, and Liberty's, revealing influences from C.F.A. Voysey and the Continental Art Nouveau style; left Essex to teach at Central School of Arts and Crafts, London.

Bibliography Stuart Durant, *Ornament from the Industrial Revolution to Today*, Woodstock, N.Y.: Overlook, 1986.

Kayser, Fredrik A. (1924–1968)
Norwegian furniture designer.

Training Statens Håndverks -og Kunstindustriskole, Oslo.
Biography Kayser designed furniture by Rastad & Relling and by Vatne Lenestolfabrikk; from 1956, was an independent designer.
Bibliography Cat., David Revere McFadden (ed.), *Scandinavian Modern Design 1880–1980*, New York: Abrams, 1982. Fredrik Wildhagen, *Norge i Form*, Oslo: Stenersen, 1988: 152–153.

Kayser, J.P.
German pewter foundry; located Krefeld-Bochum.

History 1844 in Kaiserswerth (near Düsseldorf), the Leuconide Metallwarenfabrik Factory and the trading company J.P. Kayser und Sohn were amalgamated. 1862, J.P. Kayser was established as a pewter foundry, directed by Jean Kayser. 1885, the facility in Krefeld-Bochrum was enlarged and updated. 1894, its design studio was set up in Cologne by Engelbert Kayser (1840–1911), who became known as the 'father of Kayserzinn' (a thumb-pressure method of shaping pewter objects) and who designed pewterware for the firm; also introduced copper and antimony into the formula, for brightness and durability. 1894–1912, the firm was the leading producer of pewterware. By 1900, 500 workers were active in the firm, which shortly grew to 800. J.P. Kayser produced salvers, jardinières, candlesticks, and candelabra in the Art Nouveau style, sold through Liberty in London, and others. Designers included Hugo Leven (1874–1956), Karl Geyer (1858–1912), Hermann Fauser (1874–1947), Karl Berghof (1881–1967), and Düsseldorf hunting-scene painter Johann Cristian Kroner (1838–1911). To at least 1925, Kayser was active.
Exhbitions/citations 1900 *Exposition Universelle* (gold medal), Paris; 1902 *Esposizione Internazionale d'Arte Decorativa Moderna* (gold medal), Turin; *German National Trade Exhibition*, Düsseldorf; 1904 *Louisiana Purchase Exposition*, St. Louis, Mo.
Bibliography Cat., *Jugendstil*, Darmstadt: Hessisches Landesmuseum, 1965. Cat., G. Woeckel, *Jugendstilsammlung*, Kassel: Staatliche Kunstsammlungen, 1968. Cat., *Liberty's 1875–1975*, London: Victoria and Albert Museum, 1975. Alastair Duncan, *Art Nouveau and Art Déco Lighting*, New York: Simon & Schuster, 1978. Cat., *Metallkunst*, Berlin: Bröhan Museum, 1990: 284–343.

Keilhauer, Ed (1932–)
Yugoslovian furniture manufacturer; born Putinci; active Canada.

Training Late 1940s, apprenticeship in saddle making and upholstery in Europe.
Biography 1951, Keilhauer emigrated to Canada and worked for a number of large local domestic-furniture manufacturers; 1955, established Fine Art Upholstering and, for the next 25 years, worked closely with product and interior designers on custom interiors and, early 1960s, upholstery work for commercial furniture manufacturers. 1981, he founded the firm Keilhauer to produce furniture of his own design. The firm is managed today by his five sons and has become large, exclusively devoted to seating. c. 1990, it began to produce office seating with ergonomic features and, subsequently, with more contemporary designs, such as its 2001 product range that included Net chair (in a stiff-woven polyester by Eoos), Junior adjustable office chair by Tom Deacon, MoJo table/console by Tom McHugh, and Jim table range by Andrew Jones. Its Confer chair and Eglinton seating series were designed by Scot Laughton. The firm's advertising is imaginative and sophisticated.
Citations Large number of awards, from 1988 Bronze award (for the Keilhauer stand), IIDEX/NeoCon, Canada, to two 2003 Best of Canada awards (for Canal furniture range by Scot Laughton and Felt seating by Brent Cordner).
Bibliography www.keilhauer.com.

Keler, Peter (1898–1982)
German architect, graphic designer, and painter; born Kiel.

Training 1920–25, Bauhaus, Weimar.
Biography Keler is best known for his brightly painted 1922 cradle that reduced the design to a blue circle, a yellow triangle, and a red square. His work was influenced by the theories of Bauhaus teacher

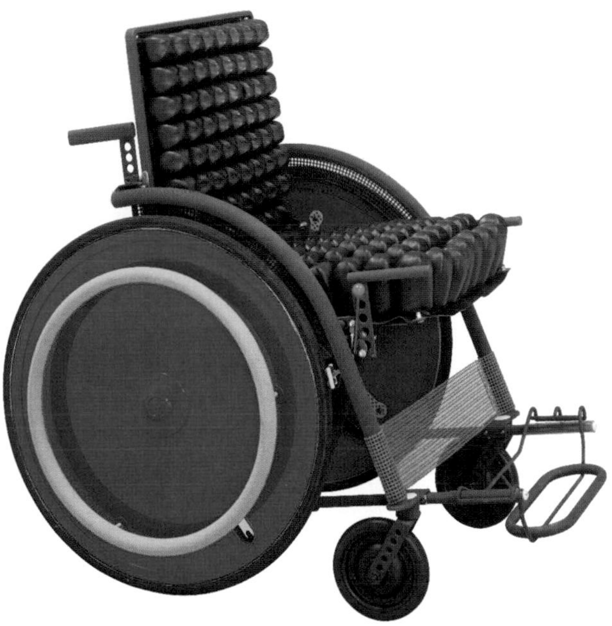

Kazuo Kawasaki. Carna folding wheel chair. 1989. Titanium, rubber, and aluminum honeycomb, 33 x 22 x 35 1/4" (83.8 x 55.9 x 89.5 cm). Mfr: SIG Workshop Co., Japan. Gift of the designer. MoMA.

Vasilii Kandinsky. He designed other furniture that was more mundane such as 1925 armchair based on the campaign chair with a swivel back. 1927–42 and 1947, he taught, Bauhaus, Weimar; had been labeled a 'degenerate artist' by the Nazis. His crib and Der Rote Kubus club chair are being reproduced by Tecta in Lauenförde.
Exhibitions/citations 1922 cradle was included 1923 exhibition, Bauhaus, Weimar. Work was the subject of 1978 exhibition, Halle.
Bibliography Lionel Richard, *Encyclopédie du Bauhaus*, Paris: Somogy, 1985: 196. Cat., *The Bauhaus: Masters and Students*, New York: Barry Friedman, 1988.

Keller, Miles (1959–)
Canadian designer; born Montreal.

Training Architecture, University of British Columbia, Vancouver; 1981, bachelor's degree, University of Calgary; to 1988, industrial design, Ontario College of Art, Toronto.
Biography 1989 with Helen Kerr, Keller cofounded Kerr Keller Design, Toronto; 1996–2001, president, Association of Chartered Industrial Designers of Ontario (ACIDO). 1997, he left Kerr Keller Design to form Carbon Design, Toronto, a studio specializing in ergonomic seating and, among others, 2000 Fluid chair by Herman Miller (realized through CAD software, and appeared in the film *A.I.* (2001; director, Steven Spielberg); a member, boards of *Financial Post* Design Effectiveness Awards committee and of Humane Village International Design Conference, both Canada
Citiations To Keller: 1988 Annual Design Review, *I.D.* magazine; 1987–96 award, Virtu/Directions in Canadian Design. Good Design awards, Chicago Athenaeum: 1996 (for 1996 Plato dishrack by Umbra), 1999 (for Oss stacking chair by Allseating), 1996 (1996 Plato dishrack by Umbra), 1999 (Oss stacking chair by Allseating), 2001 (2000–01 Fluid task chair by Allseating).
> See Kerr, Helen.

Keller Frères, Gustave
> See Gustave Keller Frères.

Kelley, Douglas (1928–)
American designer.

Training Pratt Institute, Brooklyn, N.Y.
Biography 1949–55, Kelley collaborated with Ross Littell and William Katavolos on furniture, textile, and dinnerware designs by Laverne Originals. Erwine and Estelle Laverne commissioned them to design

Laverne's 1949 New Furniture Group of chairs and tables in leather, chrome, glass, and marble. The 1952 T chair (no. 31C), credited to all three designers, was initially executed by Katavolos with wooden-dowel legs and ultimately manufactured in chromium-plated steel and leather. Kelley participated in the design of the 1965 Elna Lotus sewing machine, with CEI and Roger Riche; eventually, settled in London.
Exhibitions/citations With others at 1953 and 1955 *Good Design* exhibitions/awards, The Museum of Modern Art, New York, and Chicago Merchandise Mart. 1952 award for best US furniture (with others, for 'T' chair), American Institute of Decorators (AID).
Bibliography 'Good Design,' *Interiors*, vol. 113, Aug. 1953: 88–89, 146–48. Roberto Aloi and Agnoldomenico Pica, *Mobili tipo*, Milan: Ulrico Hoepli, 1956: 97, 121, 187, 216. Clement Meadmore, *The Modern Chair: Classics in Production*, New York: Van Nostrand Reinhold, 1975: 98–101. Cat., Kathryn B. Hiesinger and George H. Marcus III (eds.), *Design Since 1945*, Philadelphia: Philadelphia Museum of Art, 1983.

Kelp, Günther
> See Haus-Rucker-Co.

Kenmochi, Isamu (1912–1971)
Japanese designer; born Tokyo.

Training Tokyo National University of Fine Arts.
Biography 1932, Kenmochi and Kappei Toyoguchi under Bruno Taut began working on a standard prototype chair. (Taut was teaching woodworking and bamboo crafts at Industrial Laboratory in Gunma Prefecture.) 1951, Kenmochi designed the format of *Kagaku Asahi* science magazine (a format continuing in use today); 1952, with Riki Watanabe and Sori Yanagi, cofounded the Japan Industrial Designers Association; 1955, established Isamu Kenmochi Design Associates; created a variety of interior designs for Keio Plaza hotel; became known for 1960 Lounge Chair in wicker. Other work included 1955 bentwood stacking stool by Akita, 1961 T3048M bentwood and steel-legged dining chair by Tendo, and 1967 low table. Kenmochi was director, Industrial Arts Institute, Tokyo.
Citations 1958 Gold medal (for Japanese stand), *Exposition Universelle et Internationale de Bruxelles* (*Expo '58*).

Kenwood
British domestic kitchenware manufacturer; located Havant, Hampshire, UK.

History 1947, Kenwood was founded by Kenneth Wood (d. 1997) in a garage in Woking, registered it as Kenwood Manufacturing Company, and produced his first appliance, 1947 A100 turnover toaster, a retrograde side-opening model; 1948, established a factory at Hipley Street, Woking, and made his second product, A200 food mixer, the forerunner of his sophisticated 1950 Chef A700 food mixer. The A700 may have been highly influenced by the design of Braun products. He expanded his range into irons, with one of the first steam irons in Britain, 1955 Steam-o-Matic A801 (the first steam iron was introduced in the US in 1948). By 1956, the firm employed over 400 workers; 1959, bought Peerless & Ericsson Limited, the first reverse public takeover. 1960, Kenneth Grange redesigned the Chef, a design now widely regarded as the iconic shape of a food mixer. The Chefette A320 hand mixer was launched in 1960, when Kenneth Wood resigned. 1962, the plant was moved to New Lane in Havant. Matchmaker Hair Rollers were introduced in 1968, when Kenneth Wood sold the firm to Thorn Electrical Industries. Claims are that Kenwood's 1979 Processor De-Luxe A530 was the first food processor, a distinction rather held by Carl Sontheimer's 1973 Cuisinart. 1988, Kenwood introduced cordless appliances to its line; 1992, became Kenwood Appliances plc; 1993, acquired Waymaster scales and water-filtration company. Still active, the firm remains in the vanguard of good design in Britain, with over 75% of its products exported.
Exhibitions Chef A700 shown at 1950 *Ideal Home*, London.
Bibliography Jeremy Myerson and Sylvia Katz, *Conran Design Guides: Kitchenware*, London: Conran Octopus, 1990: v11. www.kenwood.net.

Isamu Kenmochi. Stool (no. S-302). 1963. Rattan and fabric-upholstered cushion, h. 14 1/4 x dia. 15 1/4" (36.2 x 38.7 cm). Mfr.: Yamakawa Rattan Co., Japan. Gift of the mfr. MoMA.

Kerr, Helen (1959–)
Canadian designer; born Montreal.

Training Environmental science, University of Waterloo; industrial design, Ontario College of Art and Design, Toronto.
Biography Kerr is the principal of Kerr and Company, founded 1988, which is active in industrial design—ranging from contract furniture and housewares to more technical mass-production objects—serving clients, including Umbra, Keilhauer, Krug, Corning, and J.P. Getty Museum. She has taught, Ontario College of Art and Design; is a member, Toronto Design Forum, and member of the board, Virtu, an organization promoting Canadian design. 1989 with Miles Keller, she cofounded Kerr Keller Design, Toronto, and Keller departed in 1997.
Exhibitions Kerr and Company work included in 2001–02 *Habitat: Canadian Design Now*, Winnipeg Art Gallery, Manitoba.

Kersting, Walter Maria (1889–1970)
German architect, engineer, and graphic designer; born Münster.

Training Technische Hochschule, Hanover.
Biography Kersting became a member of Deutscher Werkbund; from 1926, taught, Werkkunstschule, Cologne; is best known for 1933 VE 301 Volksempfänger (people's radio), which was first produced as a 1928 prototype. The design was independent of the National Socialist Government's approval for mass-produced goods, an official approval otherwise not being possible due to the stark Functionalist form of the Bakelite cabinet. Nevertheless, production began in 1933. By 1939, 12.5 million examples of the VE 301 Volksempfäger, or similar models, had been produced by Hagenuh in Kiel—an unprecedented number of examples for Europe. During World War II, German citizens could receive only those radio stations that were controlled by the Nazi Ministry for Public Enlightenment and Propaganda, thus obfuscating news from elsewhere. The '301' of model no. VE 301 refers to '30/1' or the 30th day of January, the date Hitler became German chancellor in 1933. A subtle swastika pattern was woven into the speaker grille cloth.
Bibliography Hans Wichmann, *Industrial Design Unikate und Serienerzeugnisse*, Munich: Die Neue Sammlung, 1985. Cat., *Plastics + Design*, Munich: Die Neue Sammlung, 1998. Mel Byars with Arlette Barré-Despond, *100 Designs/100 Years: A Celebration of the 20th Century*, Hove: RotoVision, 1999: 78–79. Auction cat., *Modernes Design—Kunsthandwerk nach 1945*, Munich: Quittenbaum, 1 June 2002: lot 30.

Ketoff, Sacha (1949–)
French sculptor and designer.

Training 1969–70, Accademia di Belle Arti di Brera, Milan; 1971, architecture, École Nationale Supérieure des Beaux-Arts, Paris.
Biography 1971, Ketoff collaborated with Architetti Associati and with Superstudio group in Florence; 1970s, was also a sculptor and created the artwork *Aircrash* (1977); later, designed books, film sets, and furniture, beginning with 1975 Experimental Seat. His first manufactured furniture was realized as 1980 Tabula Rassa table and Elektrika

Walter Maria Kersting. VE 301 Volksempfänger (peoples' radio). 1933. Phenolic plastic, other plastics, fabric, and metal, 15 1/2 x 10 3/4 x 6 1/16" (39 x 27.5 x 15.5 cm). Mfr.: Georg Seipt, Germany. Courtesy Quittenbaum Kunstauktionen, Munich.

chair by Écart International. He designed 1985 Géometrika watch, 1989 Sapiens lamp by PAF, and 1989 curtained screen system by Hatchi Design; 1990, taught, École Camondo, Paris; subsequently, École des Beaux-Arts, Perpignan. Ketoff is best known for 1985 WEO desk lamp (with André Livigne) by Aluminor Luminaires. ('WEO' refers to American aviators, the 'Wilbur Et Orville' Wright brothers).
Exhibitions/citations Designed the 1983 *L'Empire du Bureau* exhibition, Musée des Arts Décoratifs, Paris. Work shown in numerous exhibitions including 1989 *L'Art de Vivre*, Cooper-Hewitt National Design Museum, New York. Work subject of 1975 exhibition, Galerie Space, Paris. Won 1985 Lampes de Bureaux competition (WEO lamp) sponsored by French Ministry of Culture and Agence pour la Promotion de la Création Industrielle (APCI).
Bibliography Gilles de Bure, *Le mobilier français 1965–1979*, Paris: Regard/VIA, 1983. Robert A.M. Stern (ed.), *The International Design Yearbook*, New York: Abbeville, 1985/1986. Auction cat., *Memphis: La Collection Karl Lagerfeld*, Monaco: Sotheby's, 13 Oct. 1991. Arlette Barré-Despond (ed.), *Dictionnaire international des arts appliqués et du design*, Paris: Regard, 1996.

Khahn, Quasar (1934–)
> See Quasar.

Khouri, David (1960–)
> See Comma.

Khoury, Georges (1958–)
French designer and interior architect.

Biography Khoury designed 1987 Agathe silver-crystal oil-and-vinegar set by Puiforcat in the tradition of designs of 1920s–30s by Jean Puiforcat, and other items for the firm; was active in various industrial design projects, including marine design.
Bibliography *Les carnets du design*, Paris: Mad-Cap Productions/ APCI, 1986: 56.

Kielland, Gabriel (1871–1960)
Norwegian architect and glassware and furniture designer.

Training 1891–92, painting, Munich; 1892–94, Weimar; 1894, Paris.
Biography From 1890s, Kielland was active in Trondheim, where he was a painter, director of a private art school, and designer of posters and furniture for Nordenfjeldske Kunstindustrimuseum, which he furnished in an English interpretation of Art Nouveau. His proto-modern furniture in undecorated wood was known for its simplicity, straightforward quality, and power.
Bibliography Cat., David Revere McFadden (ed.), *Scandinavian Modern Design 1880–1980*, New York: Abrams, 1982.

Kienzle, Wilhelm (1886–1958)
Swiss furniture designer and metalworker; born Basel.

Training 1901–02, apprenticeship in carpentry at Zehnle und Bussinger, Basel, and, 1903–05, a furniture draftsperson there, while concurrently at Gewerbeschule, Basel.
Biography 1908, Kienzle worked as a metalworker, chaser, and belt-buckle maker for Riggenbach in Basel; 1909, was a designer in a furniture factory in Freiburg, Germany, and opened his own studio in Munich, where, to 1911, he realized furniture designs for crafts and for industrial production, as well as interior decoration; achieved recognition for his poster designs; later, worked in architectural office of Ino A. Campbell in Munich and, 1914, in architecture office of Peter Behrens in Neu-Babelsberg, near Berlin; 1914–16 under Valentin Witt, worked at K.B. Hofmöbelfabrik in Munich. 1918–51, he was teaching assistant and then director of interior carpentry classes, Kunstgewerbeschule, Zurich. Work included 1931 Kienzle bookshelf by EMBRU-Werke, a telephone table by Wohnbedarf store (probably produced by EMBRU-Werke), trapezoid kindergarten tables by Horgen-Glarus, shoe rack by Wohnhilfe, and household utensils by Therma.

Frederick John Kiesler. Nesting coffee tables. 1935–38. Cast aluminum, large element 9 1/2 x 34 x 25" (24.1 x 86.4 x 63.5 cm), small element 9 1/2 x 22 x 16 1/4" (24 x 55.9 x 41.3 cm). Gift of Carlo M. Grossman and Josie G. Lindau in memory of their parents Isobel and Isidore Grossman. MoMA.

Robert J. King. Coffee service. 1958. Sterling silver and teak, coffee pot 8 1/8 x 9 5/8 x 5 1/2" (20.6 x 24.5 x 14 cm), creamer 3 7/8 x 5 1/2 x 2 7/8" (9.8 x 14 x 7.3 cm), sugar bowl h. 1 7/8 x dia. 3 7/16" (4.7 x 8.7 cm), spoon 4 7/8 x 1 5/8 x 1/2" (12.4 x 4.1 x 1.3 cm), tray h. 11/16 x dia. 13 3/4" (1.8 x 34.9 cm). Mfr.: Robert J. King, US. Gift of the designer. MoMA.

Exhibitions Participated in 1926 and 1928 *Das Neue Heim* (the new home) exhibitions. Decorated Apartment for the First Five Years of Marriage at 1931 *Wohnausstellung*, Neubühl settlement, Zurich.
Bibliography Friederike Mehlau-Wiebking et al., *Schweizer Typenmöbel 1925–35, Sigfried Giedion und die Wohnbedarf AG*, Zurich: gta, 1989: 229. Lotte Schilder-Bär and Norbert Wild, *Designland Schweiz Gebrauchsgüterkultur im 20. Jahrhundert*, Zurich, Pro Helvetia, 2001.

Kiesler, Frederick John (1890–1965)

Romanian architect and industrial and furniture designer; born Cernauti, Romania (now Ukraine); active Vienna and New York.

Training 1908–09, Technische Hochschule; 1910–12, painting and printmaking, Akademie der bildenden Künste; both Vienna.
Biography After c. 1918, Kiesler worked as a stage and interior designer in Vienna and Berlin; from 1920, collaborated briefly with Adolf Loos; 1923, joined the De Stijl group in the Netherlands and developed the design of his Endless House and Theater. The concept, based on an egg shape, featured a flexible interior, inexpensive heating, and fewer than usual joints. Kiesler was closely associated with the group G, founded by Werner Graeff, Hans Richter, and Ludwig Mies van der Rohe. He created 1924 L+T (Leger und Trager) hanging system for galleries and museums; was artistic director and architect of 1924 *International Exhibition of New Theater Technique*, Konzerthaus, Vienna; was architect and director of the Austrian pavilion, designing its theater and architecture sections (including his 'Raumstadt' exhibition design), at 1925 *Exposition Internationale des Arts Décoratifs et Industriels Modernes*, Paris. 1926, settled in New York, where, 1926–28, he was in partnership with Harvey Wiley Corbett; 1930–c. 1933, member of American Union of Decorative Artists and Craftsmen (AUDAC); 1934–37, director of scenic design, Julliard School of Music; 1936–42, director of Laboratory for Design Correlation, School of Architecture, Columbia University. He directed the installation of 1947 *Exposition Internationale de Surréalisme*, Paris; 1956–62, was in partnership with Armand Bartos, New York. Although Kiesler built few buildings, his inventions influenced architects and artists. From 1936, he concentrated on interior and furniture design; 1937, designed his 'space' house and furniture that included the biomorphic 1935–38 Nesting Coffee Tables in cast aluminum and 1942 Multi-Use Rocker and Multi-Use Chair in his 1942 'Abstract Gallery' for Peggy Guggenheim's Art of This Century Gallery, New York, in which Kiesler put Surrealist canvases to spatial use. Originally intended for mass-production (though designed for fabric designer Alma Mergentine's New York apartment), the Two-Part Nesting Tables were realized by Jason McCoy gallery, New York, from 1990 and, subsequently, by another in Italy. His only realized architecture was 1929 Film Guild Cinema, New York, with an eye-shaped projection screen and 1957–65 Shrine of the Book (with former student Armand Bartos), the repository of the Dead Sea Scrolls.
Exhibitions Work included in 1982 *Shape and Environment: Furniture by American Architects* [drawings], Whitney Museum of American Art, Fairfield County, Conn.; 2000 *Aluminum by Design* (tables), touring the US. Subject of 1975 exhibition, Vienna; 1990 and 1992, Jason McCoy gallery, New York; 1988 *Friedrich Kiesler—Visionär, 1890–1965*, Museum moderner Kunst, Vienna, and touring; 1996, Centre Georges Pompidou, Paris (catalog below).
Bibliography Frederick Kiesler, *Inside the Endless House—Art, People and Architecture: A Journal*, New York: Simon & Schuster, 1964. Cat., *Frederick Kiesler: Environmental Sculpture*, New York: Guggenheim Museum, 1964 and 1966. 'Kiesler by Kiesler,' *Architectural Forum*, Sept. 1965. 'Frederick Kiesler 1923–1964,' *Zodiac*, no. 19, 1969: 18–49. Cat., *Frederick Kiesler*, Vienna: Hochschule für angewandte Kunst, 1975. Roger L. Held, 'Endless Innovations: The Theories and Scenic Design of Frederick Kiesler,' doctoral dissertation, Ohio: Bowling Green State University, 1977. Cat., Lisa Phillips (intro.), *Shape and Environment: Furniture by American Architects*, New York: Whitney Museum of American Art, 1982. Dieter Bogner (ed.), *Friedrich Kiesler*, Vienna: Löcker, 1988. Barbara Lesák, *Die Kulisse explodiert: Friedrich Kieslers Theaterexperimente und Architekturprojekte, 1923–1925*, Vienna: Löcker, 1988. 'Fitting Together 30s Design,' *The New York Times*, Dec. 20, 1990: C3. Cat., Chantal Béret, *Frederick Kiesler: artiste-architecte*, Paris: Centre Georges Pompidou, 1996. Alexander Payne and James Zemaitis, *The Coffee Table Coffee Table Book*, London: Black Dog, 2003.

Kihlman, Henrik (1961–)

Finnish silversmith; active Helsinki.

Training Political science, University of Turku; to 1987, goldsmithing, Lahti Design Institute; 1998, design degree, Polytechnic, Lahti.
Biography Kihlman has attempted to revive the almost extinct craft of silversmithing in Finland; is active in his own workshop in Helsinki. Sometimes he adopts details from non-metalic wares such as wooden objects. He has taught woodwork, metalwork, and silversmithing at several institutions and colleges; designed and made altar cross, candlesticks, and chalices at Church of St. John, Helsinki.
Exhibitions Several venues in Finland and Sweden as well as private exhibitions.

Kimber, Cecil (1888–1945); Morris; MG

British automobile designer, engineer, and entrepreneur; born London.

Biography 1915, Kimber was an assistant to the chief engineer at Sheffield-Simplex; 1916, moved to AC Cars in Thames Ditton and, 1919, to E.G. Wrigley in Birmingham; 1921, to Morris Garages. 1920s,

he imagined a sports car for the masses. As a supervising manager under automobile industrialist William Morris from 1922, he developed the first MG auto 1928, incorporating exisiting mechanics, including engines, into a purpose-built chassis. In the pre-war years, the J, P, and T models of the MG followed. Kimber died in a train accident. In 1960s, T and Midget models were introduced. MGB, MGC, and MG V8 sports cars of the mid-1950s to late 1970s marked the end of the MG production. The marque was revived with MGF model, begun 1991 by Rover designers led by Gerry McGovern, who studied at Royal College of Art, London. The F became the first completely new MG since 1962 B (1993 R V8 model was merely a facelift of the MGB). MG Rover Group now owns Rover and MG.
Exhibitions MGF introduction, 1995 Auto Salon, Geneva; MGF Supersports introduction, 1998 Auto Salon, Geneva.
Bibliography Chris Harve, *Great Marques MG*, London: Octopus, 1983. David Knowles, *MG The Untold Story*, London : Windrow & Greene 1997. Malcolm Green, *MG Sports: An Illustrated History of the World-Famous Marque*, Surrey: Bramley, 2nd ed., 1997.

Kindt-Larsen, Edvard (1901–1982); Tove Kindt-Larsen (1906–1994)

Danish architect and furniture designers; husband and wife.

Training Edvard: to 1922, Bygningsteknisk Skole, Friedersberg; to 1927, Arkitekskole, Det Kongelige Danske Kunstakademiet, Copenhagen. Tove: Arkitekskole, Det Kongelike Danske Kunstakademi.
Biography Upon completion of his architecture studies, Edvard designed an award-winning project for a grand hotel on the lakes of Copenhagen. His subsequent architecture attracted favorable attention, particularly for his own 1962 home in Klampenborg. However, he worked mainly on exhibitions and industrial design, including furniture; 1945–53, was the principal, Kunsthandværskolen, Copenhagen. From 1937, he and Tove were active in their own architecture/design office. Their work included folding lamps by Le Klint as well as, for others, furniture, silver, glassware, and jewelry, including 1952 EKL wristwatch by Georg Jensen Sølvsmedie; from 1960, worked with textiles. Furniture clients included Gustav Bertelsen.
Citations 1931 gold medal at Det Kongelige Danske Kunstakademi; 1938, 1940, 1941, and 1943 first prizes, Danish Cabinetmakers' Guild; 1949 Eckersberg Medal; second prize, A. Michelsen's 1940 jubilee competition; second prize, Holmegård's 1946 glass competition; 1946 prize, Danish Cabinetmakers' Guild; 1957 first prize, Riihimäen Lasi Nordic competition; first prize, Georg Jensen Sølvsmedie's 1965 competition for cutlery. (Most awards granted jointly to Edvard and Tove.) To Tove: 1956, 1958, 1959, 1960, and 1961 prizes, California State Fairs and expositions.
Bibliography Frederik Sieck, *Nutidig Dansk Møbeldesign – en kortfattet illustreret beskrivelse*, Copenhagen: Bondo Gravesen, 1981, 1990.

King, Jessie Marion (1875–1949)

British designer and illustrator; born Glasgow.

Training Glasgow School of Art; South Kensington School of Art, London.
Biography King was primarily a book illustrator; taught, Glasgow School of Art; became a prominent member of the ad hoc Glasgow School of artists and designers with Charles Rennie Mackintosh and his wife Margaret Macdonald. King was a participant in the Arts and Crafts movement; created designs for fabrics and wallpaper and, by Liberty's, the Cymric range of jewelry and silverwork, and other jewelry by Murrle, Bennett and Co. She was influenced by the elongated figural forms of Aubrey Beardsley; designed bookcovers, murals, and mosaics and illustrated numerous books, including Rudyard Kipling's *The Jungle Book*, William Morris's *The Defence of Guenevere and Other Poems*, John Milton's *Comus*, Oscar Wilde's *A House of Pomegranates*. Her colors, childlike at first, became more intense though delicate. The shift to a stronger palette appeared after she had seen Léon Bakst's exotic costumes and sets for Ballets Russes in Paris in 1911.
Exhibitions/citations With the Mackintoshes and MacNairs, King exhibited at 1902 *Esposizione Internazionale d'Arte Decorativa Moderna* (gold medal for her drawings and watercolors), Turin.
Bibliography Charlotte Gere, *American and European Jewelry 1830 – 1914*, New York: Crown, 1975. Diana L. Johnson, *Fantastic Illustration and Design in Britain, 1850–1930*, Providence: Rhode Island School of Design; New York: Cooper-Hewitt Museum, 1979. Toni Lesser Wolf, 'Women Jewelers of the British Arts and Crafts Movement,' *The Journal of Decorative and Propaganda Arts*, no. 14, Fall 1989: 32–33, 43.

King, Perry Alan (1938–)

British designer; born London; active Milan.

Training To 1965, Birmingham College of Art.
Biography From 1956, King designed office machinery at Olivetti; with Hans von Klier, on the corporate-design program of C. Castelli. He worked on the design of dictating machines by Süd-Atlas Werke in Munich and electronic apparatus and control systems by Praxis in Milan. He designed furniture and a catalog produced by Planula in Agliana, Italy, and, with Ettore Sottsass, 1969 Valentine typewriter; from 1972, was the design coordinator of Olivetti's corporate-identity program and designed a typeface for Olivetti. From 1975, he collaborated with Santiago Miranda in Milan on the project Limited Horizons. King–Miranda Associati executed environmental, industrial, furniture, interior, and graphic designs; posters and catalogs for Olivetti; corporate-identity programs for others; lighting by Arteluce (including 1977–78 Donald table lamp), Flos (many examples with Giancarlo Arnaldi), Cable office system and Air Mail chair by Marcatré, and power tools by Black and Decker. Their 1985 Aurora glass pendant lamp by Arteluce presaged designs by others. Other design work: 1988 Bloom bookshelf system by Tisettanta, 1987 Bergamo Murano glass bowl by VeArt, 1991 Lucerno lighting range for public areas of Expo '92 in Seville. King became a member of Associazione per il Disegno Industriale (ADI) and Society of Industrial Artists and Designers (SIAD).
Exhibitions Work shown at 1979 *Design Process Olivetti 1908–1978*, Frederick S. Wight Art Gallery, University of California, Los Angeles; subsequently as King-Miranda, numerous other venues worldwide.
Bibliography 'When Is a Dot not a Dot?,' *Design*, no. 317, May 1975: 22. *ADI Annual 1976*, Milan: Associazione per il Disegno Industriale, 1976. Cat., Kathryn B. Hiesinger and George H. Marcus III (eds.), *Design Since 1945*, Philadelphia: Philadelphia Museum of Art, 1983. Albrecht Bangert and Karl Michael Armer, *80s Style: Designs of the Decade*, New York: Abbeville, 1990. Hugh Aldersey Williams, *King and Miranda: The Poetry of the Machine*, New York: Rizzoli, 1991. > See Santiago, Miranda.

King, Robert J. (1917–)

American silversmith.

Training 1947–49, silversmithing and enameling, School for American Craftsmen, Rochester Institute of Technology, Rochester, N.Y.
Biography 1949–62, King worked at Towle silversmiths as a designer; designed its 1951 Contour pattern and other cutlery and hollowware; 1962–77, worked for International Silver and, concurrently, produced handcrafted jewelry, enamels, and silver table pieces.
Bibliography Cat., Kathryn B. Hiesinger and George H. Marcus III (eds.), *Design Since 1945*, Philadelphia: Philadelphia Museum of Art, 1983. Lee Nordness, *Objects: U.S.A.*, New York: 1970: 178.

King, Spencer (1926–)

British automobile designer.

Biography For a time, the rugged British-made Land Rover, a counterpart of the Jeep produced in America, was the crude 1948–58 Defender Series I. However, Rover's management was receptive to innovation and welcomed Spencer King's suggestion for a major redesign of the vehicle. The new 1970 Range Rover was much more comfortable and included a smooth, efficient V8 engine and four-wheel drive. Sold as the Land Rover, it soon attracted numerous customers and established a standard for SUVs (sports-utility vehicles).
Bibliography Graham Robson, *The Land-Rover: Workhorse of the World*, North Pomfret, Vt.: David & Charles, 1976. Graham Robson, *The Range Rover Land-Rover*, North Pomfret, Vt.: David & Charles, 3rd ed., 1988 James Taylor, *The Land-Rover 1948–1988: A Collector's Guide*, Croydon, England: Motor Racing Publications, 1988. Matthijs Devreede, *Land Rover*, Philadelphia: Xlibris, 1999. Martin Hodder, *Land Rover: Simply the Best*, Haynes, 1999.

Kinsbourg, Renée (1888–1958)

French decorator and furniture designer; born Rouen; active Paris.

Biography Kinsbourg designed furniture in a 'baroque' Art Déco manner, some examples produced by Les Arts de France; also designed rugs, wallpaper, and numerous interiors, including c. 1928 residence of jeweler Alfred Van Cleef.
Exhibitions From 1924, work shown at editions of Salon d'Automne;

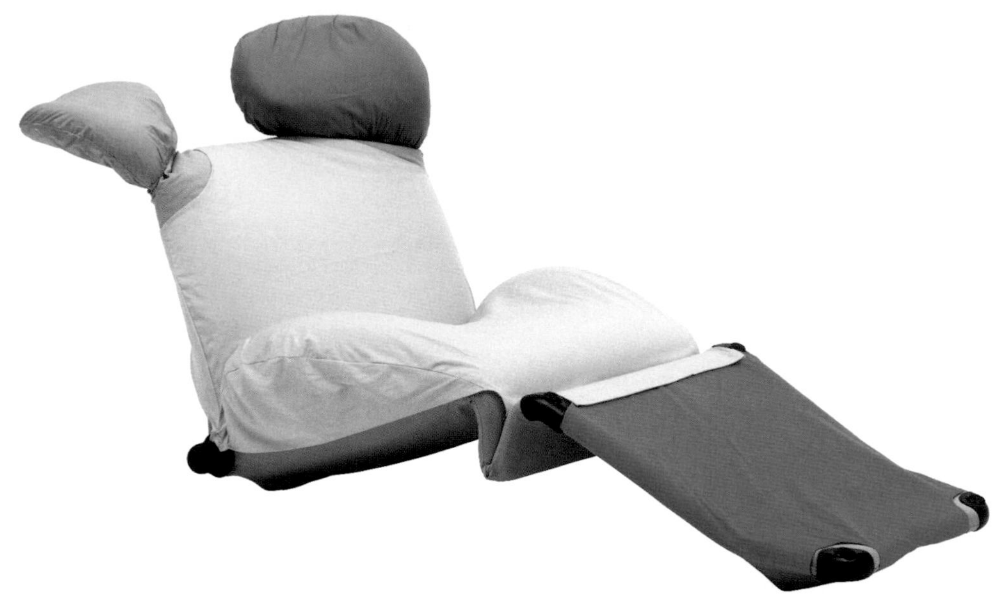

Toshiyuki Kita. Wink lounge chair (no. 111.01). 1980. Polyurethane foam, steel, and Dacron, overall upright 40 5/8 x 33 x 31 5/8" (103.2 x 83.8 x 80.3 cm), seat h. 14 3/4" (37.5 cm), reclining 24 3/8 x 33 x 75 3/4" (61.9 x 83.8 x 192.4 cm). Mfr: Cassina, Italy. Gift of Atelier International. MoMA.

from 1927, Salons of Société des Artistes Décorateurs; 1928 *Exposition Générale d'Art Appliqué*, Musée Galliéra, Paris.
Bibliography Pierre Kjellberg, *Art déco: les maîtres du mobilier, le décor des paquebots*, Paris: Amateur, 1986.

Kinsman, Rodney (1943–)

British industrial designer.

Training Central School of Arts and Crafts, London.
Biography 1966 with Jerry Olejnik and Bryan Morrison, Kinsman established OMK Design as a design group serving furniture manufacturers. 1967, OMK began limited production of its own conservatively modern designs. For others, Kinsman designed 1970 Omstack chair, 1984 Grafitti shelving system, and other furniture by Bieffeplast, including 1984 Graffiti shelving system, 1985 models in bent tubular metal in a style reminiscent of 1930s British designs. Other work: 1990 multiple-module outdoor public seating for British Rail (produced by Trax in London) with optional upholstery, arms, and alternate underframes.
Exhibitions/citations Several awards to OMK. Kinsman's work has been widely shown and published.
Bibliography Robert A.M. Stern (ed.), *The International Design Yearbook*, New York: Abbeville, 1985/1986. *Design 5*, London: Design Museum, Winter 1990.

Kiock, Valerie (1970–)
> See N2.

Kirk, Arthur Nevill (1881–1958)

British metalworker; born Lewes, Sussex; active England and US.

Training From 1916, Brighton School; to 1920, Central School of Arts and Crafts, London.
Biography 1920–27, Kirk taught metalworking and miniature painting, Central School of Arts and Crafts; 1924–27, was the director, Chalice Well Crafts School, Glastonbury; 1927, emigrated to the US on the invitation of George G. Booth to instruct at Art School of the Detroit Society of Arts and Crafts; 1929 with Charles Price and Margaret Biggar as assistants, became director of the metal workshop, Cranbrook Academy of Art, Bloomfield Hills, Mich. His work there consisted of expensive objects set with precious stones and applied enamel that showed influences of Omar Ramsden and Alexander Fisher. Some pieces were in a geometrical version of the Art Déco style. 1933, the Cranbrook workshop became a victim of the Great Depression, and Kirk moved his studio to private quarters. He became an ecclesiastical metalworker in Detroit; taught, Wayne State University, Detroit, until Parkinson's disease forced his retirement.
Bibliography Robert Judson Clark et al., *The Cranbrook Vision*, New York: Abrams/The Metropolitan Museum of Art, 1983. Annelies Krekel-Aalberse, *Art Nouveau and Art Déco Silver*, New York: Abrams, 1989. Cat., Janet Kardon (ed.), *Craft in the Machine Age 1920–1945*, New York: Abrams with American Craft Museum, 1995.

Kirkpatrick, Janice (1962–)

British designer and teacher; born Scotland.

Training 1974–80, Dumfries Academy; 1980–85, Glasgow School of Art.
Biography 1985, Kirkpatrick graduated with Ross Hunter from the Glasgow School of Art; with Hunter, cofounded Graven Images design studio in Glasgow, which executes both national and international commissions involving cooperation among staff designers, architects, musicians, and filmmakers. 1990–2000 works included Balsa bar interior in Glasgow, Barbazza bar interior in Inverness; Blue Square business center in Glasgow; Cube music and dance club in Musselburgh (near Edinburgh), Room at the Top nightclub in Bathgate, Tinderbox café in Glasgow and London, complete redesign of Glasgow-based broadsheet *The Herald*, design projects for the UK government through the British Council, including international exhibitions on diverse themes, such as football, the color red, and Islam. Kirkpatrick teaches/lectures at various British institutions; has written for *Architectural Journal*, *Design Week*, *Design Review*, *The Herald*, and other periodicals. She has been a BBC Design Awards juror, a director of The Lighthouse (Scotland's Centre for Architecture, Design and the City), a governor of the Glasgow School of Art, a trustee of the National Endowment for Science, Technology and the Arts (NESTA), UK, and a judge of 2000 Design Sense Award for sustainable design organized by London's Design Museum.
Exhibitions/citations Kirkpatrick (with others) has designed and organized exhibitions and festivals of design and architecture, including *Glasgow 1999* and design of 1999 *The Shape of Colour: Red* at Victoria and Albert Museum, London. Received 1984 Newbery Medal; citations from Royal Society of Arts, Scottish Film Council and Conran Foundation Archive Collector; elected fellow, Royal Society of Arts.
Bibliography Neil Cameron, *Graven Images*, Basel: Birkhäuser/Frame, 2002.

Kiss, Paul (1885–1962)

Hungarian metalworker; born Bélabalva (now Romania); active Paris.

Biography 1907, Kiss settled in Paris, where he worked for metalworkers Edgar Brandt and Raymond Subes; after World War I,

set up a workshop and showroom on the rue Delhomme, Paris; designed and produced (sometimes with Paul Fehér) domestic ironwork and public monuments, and restored historic monuments. Clients included kings of Egypt and Siam (now Thailand). He designed and forged the Porte du Monument aux Morts de la Guerre in Levallois-Perret. He incorporated motifs of birds and plants, some figures, and geometric forms into his wrought-iron lighting, stands, consoles, doors, grilles, and railings. Kiss's lighting fixtures, some of which resembled Michel and Jules Nics's, were old-fashioned but of a high technical quality, with the slenderest attenuations and mounts holding alabaster, engraved glass, and marble shades and panels.
Exhibitions Silver medal for the monument at Levallois-Perret shown at 1924 Salon of Société des Artistes Français. Work shown at Salons of Société des Artistes Français, Société des Artistes Décorateurs 1926 and 1927, and 1925 *Exposition Internationale des Arts Décoratifs et Industriels Modernes* (including a pair of wrought-iron doors for Savary pavilion); all Paris.
Bibliography Guillaume Janneau, *Le luminaire et les moyens d'éclairage*, 1st series, Paris: Charles Moreau, plates 30, 43, [n.d.]. George Denoinville, 'Paul Kiss ferronier d'art,' *Mobilier et décoration*, Dec. 1925: 21–27. Pierre Lahalle, 'Les ferronneries de Paul Kiss,' *Mobilier et décoration*, Jan. June 1929: 35–40. Alastair Duncan, *Art Nouveau and Art Déco Lighting*, New York: Simon & Schuster, 1978. Jessica Rutherford, *Art Nouveau, Art Déco and the Thirties: The Furniture Collections at Brighton Museum*, Brighton: The Royal Pavilion, Art Gallery and Museums, 1983: 35. Pierre Kjellberg, *Art déco: les maîtres du mobilier, le décor des paquebots*, Paris: Amateur, 1986.

Kita, Toshiyuki (1942–)

Japanese furniture and interior designer; born and active Osaka and Milan.

Training 1962–64, industrial design, Naniwa College of Art (known as Osaka University of Arts from 1966), Osaka.
Biography 1964–67, Kita worked at Osaka Aluminum Company in Japan; 1969 as an independent designer, began to work for clients in Japan and Milan; on Bernini furniture, collaborated with Silvio Coppola, Giotto Stoppino, and Bepi Fiori. He is best known for 1980 Wink articulated lounge chair by Cassina, which took four years to design. Other clients have included Tribu, Interflex, and Shar, and other work; 1983 Kick table by Cassina, 1983 Tomo lamp by Lucci, 1983 Tabola Altabasso table by Casadue; 1983 Icchio lamp by Yamagiwa, 1983 Bone-Rest chair by Johoku Mokko, 1986 Urushi dinnerware range by Koshudo, 1989 Always table, 1994 Ibuki monument in Wakayama (Japan), 2000 Wide 28 ultra-thin TV monitor and other models by Sharp. With artist Keith Haring, designed 1988 On Taro and On Giro tables by Kreon. His designs are known for combining humor, technology, and comfort. 1993, he was an honorary visiting tutor, Hochschule für angewandte Kunst, Vienna; is interested in traditional Japanese lacquer goods and paper products; designed rotating theater in the Japanese Pavilion at 1992 *Exposición Universal de Sevilla (Expo '92)*; was chairperson, 1995 G-Mark Good Design Award, Japanese Industrial Design Promotion Organization (JIDPO).
Exhibitions/citations 1981 Salone del Mobile (Wink chair), Milan; 1983–84 *Design Since 1945*, Philadelphia Museum of Art; 1987 *Nouvelles Tendences*, Centre Georges Pompidou, Paris; 1991 *Mobili Italiani 1961–1991: Le Varie Età dei Linguaggi*, Milan; 1991 exhibition, Hiroshima Modern Art Museum; chair and interior, rotating theater, Japanese Pavilion, 1992 *Exposición Universal de Sevilla (Expo '92)*; 1991 exhibition, Hiroshima Modern Art Museum. Work subject of 2001 and 2002 *L'anima del design*, Milan; 2001 Museum für Kunst und Gewerbe, Hamburg. Received 1975 Japan Interior Design Award (furniture designs); 1981 Kitaro Kuni Industrial Arts Prize; 1983 product-design award, Institute of Business Designers (IBD)/ *Contract* magazine, US; 1985 Mainichi Design Award; 1990 Delta d'Oro, ADI/FAD (industrial-design/decorative-arts associations), Spain.
Bibliography 'Arredi su dimensioni modulari,' *Ottagono*, no. 38, Sept. 1975: 110–15. Cat., Kathryn B. Hiesinger and George H. Marcus III (eds.), *Design Since 1945*, Philadelphia: Philadelphia Museum of Art, 1983. Cat., *Kagu-mobilier japonais*, Tokyo: Shibaura Institute of Technology, 1985. *Nouvelles tendances: les avant-gardes de la fin du XXe siècle*, Paris: Centre Georges Pompidou, 1986. Albrecht Bangert and Karl Michael Armer, *80s Style: Designs of the Decade*, New York: Abbeville, 1990. *Toshiyuki Kita: Movement as Concept*, Tokyo: Rikuyosha, 1990. *Toshiyuki Kita: The Soul of Design*, Osaka-shi: Amus Arts, 2001.

Kitaoka, Setsuo (1946–)

Japanese interior designer; born Kouchi Prefecture.

Training To 1974, Kuwazawa Design Research Institute.
Biography 1974, Kitaoka began working for Yamaguchi; 1977, established his own eponymous design studio in Tokyo; has designed boutiques for Yohji Yamamoto, Kenzo Takada, and Takeo Kikuchi, and Barney's New York; products by Uchino Body & Bath Co.; beauty salons, exhibitions, condomidiums and a number of private interiors in Japan.
Exhibitions/citations Work included in 1994 *Japan Design Since 1950*, Philadelphia, traveling worldwide (catalog below). Designed the chairs with shoes employed in the promotional literature of 2002 Tokyo Designer's Week. Several display-design awards.
Bibliography 'Chrome and Steel Furniture,' *Interiors*; July 1988: 142–43. lbrecht Bangert and Karl Michael Armer, *80s Style: Designs of the Decade*, New York: Abbeville, 1990: 69, 232. *Setsuo Kitaoka: Interior Designer*, Japan, 1989. Kathryn B. Hiesinger and Felice Fischer, *Japanese Design: A Survey Since 1950*, Philadelphia: Philadelphia Museum of Art, 1994

Kitchen, Shona
> See KRD.

Kittelsen, Grete Prytz (1917–)

Norwegian jewelry designer and metalworker.

Training Statens Håndværks -og Kunstindustriskole, Oslo; in France; School of the Art Institute of Chicago.
Biography c. 1945, Kittelsen designed enamel and silver jewelry for J. Tostrup, Oslo; produced vessels alone and with Gunnar S. Gundersen. Her work included enameled stainless steel and the stand for Tostrup in the Norwegian Pavilion of 1954 (10th) Triennale di Milano.
Citations 1952 (2nd) Lunning Prize. 1954 (10th) (grand prize); 1952 enamel exhibition (Kittelsen's new work), Kunstindustrimuseet, Oslo; 1957 (11th) (gold medal), and 1960 (12th) (gold medal) editions of Triennale di Milano.
Bibliography Cat., David Revere McFadden (ed.), *Scandinavian Modern Design 1880–1980*, New York: Abrams, 1982. Jan-Lauritz Opstad, *Grete Prytz Kittelsen Emaljekunst og design*, Oslo: Oslo Museum of Applied Arts, 1978.

Kittelsen, Theodor (1857–1914)

Norwegian ceramicist and book illustrator.

Training 1884–87, in painting in Munich.
Biography Early 1900s, Kittelsen was a designer of ceramics for Porsgrunds Porselænsfabrik, Porsgrunn; was known for his illustrated books of folk tales, particularly those including trolls and fairies, and for his children's books.
Bibliography Cat., David Revere McFadden (ed.), *Scandinavian Modern Design 1880–1980*, New York: Abrams, 1982.

Kjær, Jacob (1896–1957)

Danish designer and cabinetmaker.

Biography 1915, Kjær became a journeyman silversmith; 1918–20, a joiner in Copenhagen and, 1921–22, at the Kunstgewerbemuseum in Berlin; 1922–24, apprentice joiner in Paris; from 1926, was a journeyman in Copenhagen and was active as a furniture designer.
Exhibitions Work shown at 1929–30 *Exposición Internacional de Barcelona*; 1935 *Exposition Universelle et Internationale de Bruxelles*; 1937 *Exposition Internationale des Arts et Techniques dans la Vie Moderne*, Paris; 1939–40 *New York World's Fair: The World of Tomorrow*; 1951 (9th) Triennale di Milano.
Bibliography Frederik Sieck, *Nutidig Dansk Møbeldesign – en kortfattet illustreret beskrivelse*, Copenhagen: Bondo Gravesen, 1981.

Kjærholm, Poul (1929–1980)

Danish furniture designer; born Øster Vrå.

Training 1948, apprenticeship as a cabinet maker with Grønbech; to 1952, cabinetmaking and furniture design, Kunsthåndværkerskolen; from 1955, Det Kongelige Dansk Kunstakademi; both Copenhagen.
Biography 1952–56, Kjærholm taught, Møbelskole, Kunsthåndværkerskolen, and, from 1955, at Det Kongelige Dansk Kunstakademi. Though trained as a cabinetmaker, he designed furniture exclusively

for mass-production. 1955–82, much of his furniture was produced by his friend Ejvind Kold Christensen in Hellerup. He is best known for 1955 PK 20 chair, 1956 leather sofa, 1956 PK 22 easy chair in wickerwork or leather, and 1957 PK 11 armchair by Fritz Hansen; 1965 PK 13 arm chair by P.P. Møbler (1991); and 1965 PK 24 (Hammock chair); 1976 maple/wickerwork folding chairs by Christensen for Louisiana Museum for Moderne Kunst, Humlebæk, Denmark; 1977 dining room of Royal Porcelain concert hall and 1978 restaurant Kanalen.
Exhibitions/citations Work included in a large number of exhibitions worldwide. 1957 (12th) (grand prize) and 1960 (13th) (gold medal and designed the Danish industrial-design stand) at editions of Triennale di Milano, 1958 Lunning Prize, 1960 Eckersberg Medal, 1965 Engelhardt Legacy, Prix de la Critique at 1968 (3rd) Biennale des Arts Graphiques Appliqués, Brno, 1973 Dansk ID prize; from 1962–71, fellow of Akademirådet (royal academy).
Bibliography Cat., *Les assises du siège contemporain*, Paris: Musée des Arts Décoratifs, 1968. Cat., *Modern Chairs 1918–1970*, London: Lund Humphries, 1971. 'One Hundred Great Danish Designs,' *Mobilia*, nos. 230–33, Dec. 1974: nos. 12–14. Frederik Sieck, *Nutidig Dansk Møbeldesign – en kortfattet illustreret beskrivelse*, Copenhagen: Bondo Gravesen, 1981, 1990. Per Møllerup, 'Poul Kjaerholm's Furniture,' *Mobilia*, nos. 304–05, 1982: 1–24. Cat., *The Lunning Prize*, Stockholm: Nationalmuseum, 1986. Noritsugu Oda, *Danish Chairs*, San Francisco: Chronicle Books, 1999. Erik Krogh, Ole Palsby, and Christoffer Harlang, *Poul Kjærholm*, Copenhagen: Arkitektens, 1999.

Kjarval, Sveinn (1919–1981)
Icelandic furniture and interior designer.

Training Kunsthåndværkerskolen, Copenhagen.
Biography With an interest in Icelandic traditions, Kjarval designed furniture in 1950s–60s, based on Danish forms. His furniture was influential on other Icelandic designers and called on the use of natural native materials.
Bibliography Cat., David Revere McFadden (ed.), *Scandinavian Modern Design 1880–1980*, New York: Abrams, 1982.

Kleemann, Georg (1863–1932)
German jewelry, wallpaper, and ceramics designer and illustrator; born Oberwurmbach.

Training Kunstgewerbeschule, Munich.
Biography Kleeman was an apprentice in the workshop of Theodor Spieß, under whom he designed wallpaper and ceramics and illustrated books; from c. 1901, collaborated with Theodor Fahrner; from 1887, was a professor of design, Kunstgewerbeschule, Pforzheim; wrote the book *Moderner Schmuck* (1900); supplied jewelry designs to Carl Herrmann, Lauer & Wiedmann, Victor Mayer, Rodi & Wienenberger, Söllner, and Zerenner in Pforzheim.
Exhibitions A number of works were shown at 1903 *Fine Metals Exhibition*, Stuttgart.

Klein, Jacque (b. Jacques Klein 1899–1963)
French decorator and furniture designer; born Malaunay (Seine et Marne); active Paris.

Biography No to be confused with Jacques-François Klein, Jaque Klein designed wallpaper and rugs for Les Galeries Lafayette department store, Paris; 1942, established his own furniture-editing firm, J. Klein, at 31, rue de Miromesnil, Paris. Some of his furniture was produced by Delepoulle and by Gouffé.
Exhibitions Work shown at Salons d'Automne 1922–28, Salon of Société des Artistes Décorateurs (dining-room suite with Laurent Malclès) in 1922 and continued after World War II, and Salon d'Automne (bedroom by Delepoulle) in 1922.
Bibliography *Ensembles mobiliers*, Paris: Charles Moreau, vol. 5, no. 28, 1945; nos. 35–36, 1954. Pierre Kjellberg, *Art déco: les maîtres du mobilier, le décor des paquebots*, Paris: Amateur, 1986.

Kleinhempel, Gertrud (1875–1948)
German designer and teacher; born Leipzig.

Training In drawing in Dresden and Munich.
Biography Kleinhempel directed a private applied-arts school in Dresden with her brothers Fritz and Erich; at turn of century, was a designer at Dresdner Werkstätten für Handwerkunst; from 1907, taught textile design, Handwerker und Kunstgewerbeschule, Bielefeld, and

Poul Kjærholm. Triennale chair (no. P 22). 1956. Chrome-plated steel and cane, 29 x 25 x 24" (73.7 x 63.5 x 61 cm). Mfr.: Ejvind Kold Christensen, Denmark. Gift of Georg Jensen, Inc. MoMA.

was a professor there from 1921. She was one of the few female designers to receive recognition in the late 1910s–early 1920s. Her restrained interiors emphasized function and featured a crafts-oriented simplicity.
Bibliography Cat., Hans Wichmann, *Deutsche Werkstätten und WK-Verband, 1878–1990*, Munich: Prestel, 1992.

Kleiser, Lorentz (1871–1963)
American textile designer, interior decorator, and painter; born Elgin, Ill.

Training 1892 under a mural painter, apprenticeship in Oslo; studied in Munich.
Biography 1900, Kleiser returned to the US; became a designer and mural painter for a decorator in New York; 1914, began handweaving tapestries and founded Edgewater Tapestry Looms. Kleiser was internationally known for his tapestries, on which he lectured at The Metropolitan Museum of Art and at New York University.
Exhibitions 1935 exhibition of tapestries, touring the US; 1936, first exhibition of paintings, at Ehrich-Newhouse Galleries, New York.
Bibliography Cat., Janet Kardon (ed.), *Craft in the Machine Age 1920–1945*, New York: Abrams with American Craft Museum, 1995.

Klemm, Walther (1883–1957)
German woodcarver, illustrator, and teacher; born Karlsbad.

Training Großherzogliche Hochschule für bildende Kunst, Vienna; 1913, Kunstgewerbeschule, Weimar, under Henry van de Velde.
Biography Klemm joined an artists' colony in Dachau, Bavaria; taught at Hochschule für bildende Kunst, Weimar, where his students included Karl Peter Röhl, Johannes Malzahn, Robert Michel, and Ella Bergman-Michel. Toward end of 1910s, some students, including the Michels, rebelled against the school's 'antiquated' drawing methods. 1919–21, Klemm was a master at the Bauhaus, Weimar, where Röhl, Malzahn, and the Michels had become students; was known as an illustrator and also considered an outstanding woodcarver.
Bibliography Lionel Richard, *Encyclopédie du Bauhaus*, Paris: Somogy, 1985: 1957.

Klenell, Matti (1972–)
Swedish interior architect and designer; active Stockholm.

Training 1994–99, master of fine arts degree, Konstfack, Stockholm; 1997, Det Kongelige Danske Kunstakademi, Copenhagen.

Biography 1998–2000, Klenell worked at Nyréns Arkitektkontor; later, designed furniture for manufacturer Offecct. Through his participation in the Our studio, other clients have included Miljöexpo, Pyra, Agata, and Örsjö Industrier. From 2000, has been head of the design course, Anders Beckman School of Design, Stockholm.
Exhibitions/citations Work subject of 2002 unique-glass exhibition, Galleri Inger Molin, Stockholm; and included in 2001 *3D+ Stagomg Swedosj Design*, touring Belgium, Ireland, Germany, Sweden; *Generation X: Young Nordic Design*, traveling the world from 2000; 1998–2000 *Young Swedish Design*, traveling. 1997 Marianne and Sigvard Bernadotte artists scholarship, 1999 St Johannislogen scholarship, 2000 Ljustus Prize, 1997–2000 Young Swedish Design diploma, 2001 International Artists Studio Program in Stockholm (IASPIS) for contribution to international cultural-exchange project.

Klerk, Michel de
> See de Klerk, Michel.

Klinkosch, J.C.

Austrian silversmiths; located Vienna.

History 1797, J.C. Klinkosch was founded; 1902, produced the silver designs of Otto Wagner and, in 1920s, a number of pieces designed by Otto Prutscher and Oswald Haerdtl.
Exhibitions Silver by Wagner shown at Austrian stand at 1902 *Esposizione Internazionale d'Arte Decorativa Moderna*, Turin, and 1902 winter exhibition at Österreichisches Museum für Kunst und Industrie, Vienna.
Bibliography Annelies Krekel-Aalberse, *Art Nouveau and Art Déco Silver*, New York: Abrams, 1989.

Klint, Le; Tage Klint (1884–1953)

Danish lamp manufacturer.

History c. 1900, P.V. Jensen Klint, the designer of the Grundtvig Church in Copenhagen, needed an appropriate shade for a stoneware oil lamp, so he pleated paper into a lampshade. Subsequently, the technique became a preoccupation of the Klint family to 1943, when Tage Klint founded the company Le Klint. In plastic-coated paper or plastic sheets, the eventual range of lamp designs became extensive. In addition to early models by Ebsen and Kaare Klint (unrelated to Jensen Klint), designers have included Henning Seidelin, Tove and Edvard Kindt-Larsen, Andreas Hansen, Philip Ludvigsen/Thomas Krause, Hvidt og Mølgaard, Poul Christiansen, Erik Hansen, Aage Petersen, and others; more recently, brass-base models by Philip Bro Ludvigsen and ceiling fixtures by Robert Kasal. To acknowledge its 60th birthday in 2003 and 50 years since Tage Klint's death, Le Klint reissued the original 1943 adjustable table lamp by Tage Klint.

Klint, Ebsen (1915–1969)

Danish industrial designer; son of Kaare Klint.

Training Arkitektskole, Det Kongelige Danske Kunstakademiet, Copenhagen.
Biography 1938–39, Ebsen Klint was an industrial designer for Philips; 1959–62, designed school furniture with Børge Mogensen and physiotherapist Eigil Snorrason, produced in four different sizes. Klint is best known for his 1947 folded-paper lighting fixtures by Le Klint. (Le Klint was directed by Tage Klint, who was unrelated to Kaare and Ebsen Klint.)
Bibliography Arne Karlsen, *Furniture Designed by Børge Mogensen*, Copenhagen, 1968. Svend Hansen, 'Le Klint,' *Mobilia*, no. 206, 1972. Cat., Kathryn B. Hiesinger and George H. Marcus III (eds.), *Design Since 1945*, Philadelphia: Philadelphia Museum of Art, 1983.

Klint, Kaare (b. Kaare Jensen-Klint 1888–1954)

Danish architect, furniture designer, and theorist; born Frederiksberg, Vartov; active Copenhagen; son of architect/painter Peder Vilhelm Jensen-Klint (1853–1930).

Training Teknisk Skole; Møller-Jensen's art school; additionally under his father and Carl Petersen (professor of building), Det Kongelige Danske Kunstakademi; all Copenhagen.
Biography 1920, Klint set up an office in Copenhagen; 1924, founded department of furniture and, 1944, became professor at Det Kongelige Danske Kunstakademi, Copenhagen, where Finn Juhl was one of his pupils. Early on, Klint designed furniture by N.M. Rasmussen and N.C. Jensen Kjær; later, designed chiefly for Rud Rasmussen, producer of his 1933 deck chair. Rasmussen still produces his designs. Klint designed a collection of furniture and furnishings by Holger Rasmussen for the Fåborg Museum 1914–15 ; Thorvaldsens Museum, Copenhagen, 1922–25; and Det Danske Kunstindustrimuseum, Copenhagen, 1924–54. His plastic-coated folded-paper lighting range, with son Ebsen Klint, is still in production by Le Klint (a business of Tage Klint, not a relative of Kaare).
Exhibitions/citations Designed/organized exhibitions and work included in a numerous of venues worldwide as well as subject of 1956 memorial exhibition, Det Danske Kunstindustrimuseum, Copenhagen. Grand prize, 1929–30 *Exposición Internacional de Barcelona*, Spain; grand prize, 1935 *Exposition Universelle et Internationale de Bruxelles*; 1954 Eckersberg Medal; 1954 C.F. Hansen Medal; 1949, elected Honorary Royal Designer for Industry, UK.
Bibliography Cat., *Les assises du siège contemporain*, Paris: Musée des Arts Décoratifs, 1968. Cat., *Modern Chairs 1918–1970*, London: Lund Humphries, 1971. Cat., David Revere McFadden (ed.), *Scandinavian Modern Design 1880–1980*, New York: Abrams, 1982. Noritsugu Oda, *Danish Chairs*, San Francisco: Chronicle Books, 1999.

Klint, Tage (1884–1953)
> See Le Klint.

Klint, Vibeke (1927–)

Danish textile designer; born Fåborg; active Klampenborg.

Training 1949–50, under Gerda Henning, Kunsthåndværkerskolen, Copenhagen; 1951, under Jean Lurçat, at Aubusson (France); under Pierre Wemaëre, at Saint-Céré and in Brittany.
Biography 1951, Klint set up her own studio; from 1956, was an industrial fabric designer for C. Olesen/Cotil and others; is a member of the Dansk Designråd (Danish design council) and has become renowned in Denmark.
Exhibitions/citations Work shown at 1956–57 *Neue Form aus Dänemark*, touring Germany; 1958 *Formes Scandinaves*, Musée des Arts Décoratifs, Paris; 1960–61 *The Arts of Denmark*, touring the US; 1980 *Scandinavian Modern Design 1880–1980*, Cooper-Hewitt National Design Museum, New York; a number of others in Europe and the US. Silver medals, 1954 (10th) and 1975 (11th) editions of Triennale di Milano; 1958 Michelsens Jubilee medal; 1967 Cotil Prizes; 1972 Eckersbergs Medal,1987 Dansk Kunsthåndværks prize, 1992 Danmarks Nationalbank Jubilee Foundation; 1960 Lunning Prize.
Bibliography Cat., *The Lunning Prize,* Stockholm: Nationalmuseum, 1986. Annette Graae (ed.), *Tekstilkunst i Danmark 1960–87*, Valby: Borgen, 1987. Vibeke Klint, 'Memories of the Weaver Gerda Henning,' *Danish Journal of Design History*, vol. 5, 1995. Inge Alifrangis, *Det danske ægte tæppe = Danish Handmade Rugs and Carpets*, Copenhagen: Rhodos, 1996. Inge Alifrangis: *Væveren Vibeke Klint = Vibeke Klint, The Weaver*, Copenhagen: Rhodos, 1997.

Kliun, Ivan Vasil'evich (b. Ivan Vasil'evich Kliunkov 1873–1943)

Russian sculptor and interior designer.

Training 1890, Drawing School, Association for the Encouragement of the Arts, Warsaw; 1900, F. Rerberg's and I. Mashkov's private studio, Moscow
Biography From 1907, Kliun was a follower of Kasimir Malevich; 1917–21, headed the exhibitions bureau of IZO NKP; 1918–21, was a member of INKhUK (institute of artistic culture), and taught at SVOMAS (free art studios); 1925, became a member of 4 Arts group.
Exhibitions Work shown at 1922 *Erste Russische Kunstausstellung*, Berlin; 1913 exhibitions of Union of Youth; 1916–17 exhibition of Bubnovy Valet (Jack of Diamonds).
Bibliography Cat., *Kunst und Revolution: Russische und Sowjetische Kunst 1910–1932*, Vienna: Österreichisches Museum für angewandte Kunst, 1988.

Klotz, Blanche-Jeanne (1885–)

French decorator and furniture designer; born Paris.

Biography From c. 1925, Klotz was active as a designer of interior schemes; designed furniture influenced by rustic early 19th-century French forms; 1927–28, worked in a more Rationalist style, shown in 1928 dining room of M.E. Fould and 1929 décor of a Parisian banker; designed a cabin with lacquered aluminum furniture, stainless-steel lighting, and fabrics by Hélène Henry for 1935 oceanliner *Normandie*.

1930, she became a member of Union des Artistes Modernes (UAM); 1935, began a collaboration with cabinetmaker Schmit on the rue de Charonne, Paris, which produced her furniture in limited editions; 1938, became director of artists' group Mai 36 and designed the office of Pen Club on the rue Pierre-Charron, Paris, and several villas in Provence, including aluminum furniture, steel lighting, and décor for a roon in the villa (architect, Robert Mallet-Stevens) of vicomte and vicomtesse de Noailles, Hyères. By 1954, was active in an atelier at 25, rue Henri-Rochefort, Paris.
Exhibitions Work shown at 1928, 1934, and 1936 Salons of Société des Artistes Décorateurs and in the 1950s; 1925 *Exposition Internationale des Arts Décoratifs et Industriel Modernes* (studio-hall for a mountain chalet), Paris; 1930 (1st) UAM exhibition (an office); interior decoration of the Togo paviliona 1931 *Exposition Coloniale*, Paris.
Bibliography *Ensembles mobiliers*, Paris: Charles Moreau, nos. 40-41, 1954. Pierre Kjellberg, *Art déco: les maîtres du mobilier, le décor des paquebots*, Paris: Amateur, 1986: 102. Arlette Barré-Despond, *UAM*, Paris: Regard, 1986: 226, 523.

Klug, Ubald (1932-)

Swiss designer and interior architect; born St. Gallen; active Paris; husband of Brazilian-born potter Helena Klug.

Training 1949–52, apprenticeship in tapestry and interior decoration; 1952–55 under Willy Guhl, interior decoration, Kunstgewerbeschule, Zurich.
Biography After working in the offices of architects in Zurich and Helsinki, Klug moved to Paris, where he worked with sculptor François Stahly 1958–61 and attended lectures by Jean Prouvé; became the technical director of a sanitary ware and kitchen manufacturer in Bern; 1966, finally settled in Paris, where, from 1968, he worked at design agency MAFIA in Paris; 1972, established his own office for architecture and interior architecture. Commissions have included the design of exhibitions, fair stands, showrooms, shops, and restaurants in France, Germany, and Switzerland. He has designed products for the furniture, watch, textiles, glass, and ceramics industries. For some furniture/furnishings such as the Spiga coat tree by Röthlisberger, he has called on the use of plywood. Other work has included widely published 1973 Terrazza Furniture System by DeSede, 1983 Bed to Live In by Wogg, and carpets by Carpet Concept and by Melchnau.
Citations Four design prizes for his c. 1999 Shell armoire (by Röthlisberger), including Designpreis, Baden Württemberg; Swiss Design Prize; 1999 Red Dot award, Design Zentrum Nordrhein Westfalen, Essen; 1998 Top 10 award, Industrie Forum Design Hanover.

Klutcis, Gustav Gustavovich (aka Klutsis and Klucis) 1895–1944)

Latvian artist and graphic, poster, and applied arts designer; born near Riga.

Training 1913–15, studied City Art School, Riga; 1915–17, Drawing School, Association for the Encouragement of the Arts; 1918, private studio of I. Mashkov, Moscow; 1919–20, K. Korovin's and A. Pevsner's studio; 1921, Faculty of Painting, VKhUTEMAS.
Biography 1918, Klutcis participated in the art workshop in Moscow, led by Voldemar Andersen, organized by the infantry regiment in which he was serving. Klutcis painted scenes of army activities; c. 1918, enrolled in SVOMAS/VKhUTEMAS and, by 1919–20, was creating posters and pursuing his interests in typography and architecture; 1920–22, was influenced by El Lissitzky, particularly in his approach to spatial relations and color in graphics and photomontages; became a member, INKhUK (institute of artistic culture); from 1924, taught, VKhUTEMAS; 1925, produced photomontages for Vladimir Maiakovskii's poem 'V.I. Lenin' and similar work for other theater activities; 1927, codesigned *Chetryre foneticheskikh romana* (four phonetic novels) by Aleksej E. Kruchenykh; 1928, cofounded the group October, serving in its photo section to the group's 1932 disbandment; was fairly inactive from the end of 1930s.
Exhibitions Work shown at 1922 *Erste Russische Kunstausstellung*, Berlin; 1925 *Exposition Internationale des Arts Décoratifs et Industriels Modernes* (was the director and one of the interior designers of the Soviet pavilion), Paris; 1927 *Lissitzky's All-Union Polygraphical*, Moscow; 1928 Pressa (international press fair), Cologne; 1932 and 1933, was the interior and graphic designer of Soviet exhibitions in the US, France, Spain, and Brazil; 1933 and 1934 poster exhibitions, Belgium, Italy, and Britain; 1930 October group exhibition. 1938, stopped showing his work, which was nevertheless subject of 1959 and 1970 exhibitions in Riga.
Bibliography L. Oginskaia, 'Khudozhnik-agitator,' *Dekorativnoe iskusstvo*, Moscow, 1971, no. 5: 34–37. M. Ostrovskii (ed.), *Sto pamiatnykh dat. Khdozhestvennyi kalendar*, Moscow, 1974: 17–20. Cat., Stephanie Barron and Maurice Tuchman, *The Avant-Garde in Russia, 1910–1930*, Cambridge: M.I.T., 1980: 172. Cat., *Kunst und Revolution: Russische und Sowjetische Kunst 1910–1932*, Vienna: Österreichisches Museum für angewandte Kunst, 1988. S.O. Khan-Magomedov, *Vhutemas: Moscou, 1920–1930*, Paris: Regard, 1990.

Knag, Christian Christopher (1855–1942)

Norwegian cabinetmaker and furniture designer.

Biography 1878, Knag set up his own workshop and salesroom in Bergen, where he specialized in inlaid goods, with landscape motifs in the Art Nouveau style.
Exhibitions/citations Gold medal, 1900 *Exposition Universelle*, Paris; grand prize, 1904 *Louisiana Purchase Exposition*, St. Louis. Work subject of 1909 exhibition, Kunstindustrimuseet, Oslo.
Bibliography Cat., David Revere McFadden (ed.), *Scandinavian Modern Design 1880–1980*, New York: Abrams, 1982.

Knight, Laura (1877–1970)

British painter and ceramics decorator; born Long Eaton, Derbyshire; active Newlyn, Cornwall.

Training 1892, Nottingham School of Art.
Biography Knight was a juror of 1922 Carnegie International competition, Pittsburgh; designed both shapes and decorations, under Clarice Cliff's supervision, for 1933–34 Circus range of ceramics tableware by Arthur J. Wilkinson in Burslem. Further work included 1937 Geroge VI Coronation ceramics by Wedgwood and glassware by Stuart Crystal. 1939–40, she was an official war artist and, 1946, an official artist at the war-tribunal trial of the Nazis in Nuremberg; became well known for her paintings of circus life, ballet dancers, and gypsies; wrote the books 1936 *Oil Paint and Grease Paint* (autobiography) (Harmondsworth: Penguin, 1936) and *The Magic of a Line* (London: William Kimber, 1965).
Exhibitions From 1903 exhibitions (paintings), Royal Academy, London; 1934 *Modern Art for the Table* (glassware), Harrods department store, London.
Bibliography Cat., *Thirties: British Art and Design Before the War*, London: Arts Council of Great Britain/Hayward Gallery, 1979. Caroline Fox, *Dame Laura Knight*, Oxford: Phaidon, 1988

Knight, Phil
> See Bowerman, Bill.

Knoll

American and international furniture manufacturer.

History 1938, the firm (initially called HG Knoll) was established by Hans Knoll on East 72nd Street, New York. 1955, his wife Florence Knoll assumed directorship. 1959, firm was sold to Art Metal Inc, with W. Cornell Dechert as president and Florence Knoll as design consultant to both firms. By 1960s, Knoll had 20 showrooms in the US and 30 around the world. 1965, Robert Cadwallader replaced Florence Knoll as president. Graphic design and advertising had been executed by Herbert Matter, who also resigned in 1965, and one of Cadwallader's first moves was to appoint Massimo Vignelli in Matter's place. The firm imported some designs, including Ilmari Tapiovaara's 1946 Domus armchair produced by Keravan Puuteollisuus. 1971, Knoll Planning Unit was dissolved. Furniture designers added to the stable included Gae Aulenti, Cini Boeri, Joe d'Urso, Carles Riart, and Vignelli (hitherto as the design director of the firm). Other designers' work included Charles Pfister's 1975 table, Robert Venturi's 1978–84 chairs, table, and sofa, Andrew Morrison and Bruce Hannah's 1967 seating and Morrison's 1974 office furniture, Richard Meier's 1978–82 tables and chairs, Ettore Sottsass's 1983 and 1986 chairs and sofas, and Frank Gehry's 1989–92 bentwood collection and his 1999 FOG side chair and armchair. Knoll has always called on the finest materials and craftsmanship. In the firm's Mies reproduction range, stainless steel (not the original chromium plating) was used. Continuing after many changes of ownership, Knoll has attempted to maintain its status while adding less-expensive lines of systems, furniture, and furnishings. In a successful effort to enliven its textile line, fashion fabric designer Jhane Barnes was commissioned in late 1980s. Initially, Knoll did not sell through its own retail outlets; both 1969 showroom at Georg Jensen's, Madison Avenue, New York, and 1974 Blooming-

Florence Knoll. 541 sideboard. 1952. Walnut veneer, 26 3/8 x 51 1/4 x 18 7/8" (67 x 130 x 46cm). Mfr.: Knoll Associates, Greenville, Pa., US. Courtesy Quittenbaum Kunstauktionen, Munich.

dale's plan failed. 1993, Knoll began selling directly to the general public with greater success.
Exhibitions (See Knoll Bassett, 'Shu' Florence.)
Bibliography 'To the Trade and Beyond,' *Industrial Design*, Oct. 1974: 44–55. Edward Larrabee and Massimo Vignelli, *Knoll Design*, New York: Abrams, 1981. *Contemporary Designers*, London: Macmillan, 1984: 332–33. Margery B. Stein, 'Teaching Steelcase to Dance,' *The New York Times Magazine, The Business World*, Apr. 1, 1990. Steven and Linda Rouland, *1938–1960 Knoll Furniture*, Atglen, Pa.: Schiffer, 1999. www.knoll.com.
> See Knoll Bassett, Florence 'Shu'; Knoll, Hans.

Knoll Bassett, 'Shu' Florence (b. Florence Schust 1917–)

American interior, furniture, and textile designer, architect, and entrepreneur; born Saginaw, Mich.; active New York.

Training 1932–34, under Eliel and Eero Saarinen, architecture, Kingswood School, Bloomfield Hills, Mich.; intermittently 1934–39, Cranbrook Academy of Art, Bloomfield Hills; 1936–38, Architectural Association, London; 1940–41, under Ludwig Mies van der Rohe, Illinois Institute of Technology, Chicago.
Biography Knoll was highly influenced by her distinguished teachers; from 1941, worked for architects Wallace K. Harrison, New York, and for Walter Gropius and Marcel Breuer, Cambridge, Mass.; 1943, joined furniture manufacturer Hans Knoll (having met him in 1941) and formed the Knoll Planning Unit in New York out of his extant furniture business with manufacturing facilities in Greenville, Pa. 1943–65, she was the director of Knoll's Planning Unit and of furniture and textile design development, the interior planning service for the fledgling company. 1946, she married Hans Knoll, and they transformed his HG Knoll firm into Knoll Associates. Florence Knoll exerted a profound influence on modern furniture and interiors after World War II. 1945, began the reproduction of Ferrari Hardoy/Kurchan/Bonet 1938 Butterfly sling chair (no. 198); in 1947 of Mies van der Rohe's 1929 Barcelona Chair and 1930 low glass-and-steel Dessau table (originally for the Tugendhat House in Brno); and included Eero Saarinen's 1948 fiberglass-shell Womb chair (an evolution from early-1940s molded-plastic experiments conducted with Charles Eames), 1952 Diamond chair by Harry Bertoia (another Florence Knoll Cranbrook colleague). Knoll's woven fabrics designed by Anni Albers, Evelyn Hill, Eszter Haraszty, and Suzanne Huguenin were innovatory in their specificity to the office environment. Florence Knoll herself designed many of the firm's more functional pieces, including desks with modular storage, much-imitated 1950s cabinets, and 1954 lounge chairs and sofas, as what she termed 'fill-in pieces' for interiors. (1958, she married Harry Hood Bassett, Hans Knoll having died in 1955.) Her 1961 oval desk/table on a plated-metal central column is notable. Her interior designs of the time established a standard for corporate headquarters. Saarinen's 1957 standard office chairs became ubiquitous. 1960, Knoll added Mies's 1930 Bruno chair (initially reproduced for Philip Johnson's Four Seasons restaurant in the Seagram Building, New York) and, 1964, his 1927 Weissenhof chair, 1930 Tugendhat chair, and 1930 Berlin leather couch. 1968, when the company acquired Gavina, licenses were obtained to manufacture Breuer and Scarpa designs and, from 1969, as a result of the Gavina acquisition, Franco Albini's 1958 Floating Mini-Desk and Breuer's 1925 Wassily chair, 1925 Laccio table, and 1927 Cesca chair were added to the Knoll line. 1968–91, Knoll sold 250,000 copies of Cesca chair. Others designing for Knoll included George Nakashima and Isamu Noguchi. 1951, first Knoll subsidiary was set up, in Germany. All of Knoll's foreign subsidiaries were also manufacturers. Florence Knoll executed highly influential interior designs that included 1948 and 1957 Rockefeller family installation, 1958 H.J. Heinz building, 1962 Cowles Publications building, 1964 Columbia Broadcasting Company (CBS) building, and Knoll showrooms worldwide. Her interior design projects conveyed the self-assurance and sophistication for which she became known, although she regarded her own designs as relatively insignificant at the time. Her Rationalist and architecturally integrated interiors were based on the concept of an open-plan layout where junior and secretarial staff sat together in a central area and executives' offices were located along the window walls. With architects Skidmore Owings and Merrill, she further refined her ideas in 1957 Connecticut General headquarters, Hartford, Conn. 1955–65, she was president of Knoll but, 1959, sold the firm to Art Metal Inc, serving as a design consultant to both Knoll and Art Metal until her 1965 retirement. 1969, the firm became Knoll International; 1977, it was acquired by General Felt Industries and, 1990, by Westinghouse, which sold it in 1996. Other Knoll designs have include 1979 Seating Series by Niels Diffrient, 1981 Desk System by Bruce Hannah, 1989–92 Gehry Collection bentwood slat furniture and 1999 Fog chair by Frank Gehry. Maya Lin designed furniture for Knoll in solid stone, 1998 The World Is (Not) Flat furniture collection, and, to celebrate Knoll's 60th anniversary (1938) through Maya Lin, Shea + Latone, 1998 Latitude lounge chair, 1998 Stones tables/stools range, and others. The Florence Knoll Bassett Papers of 1932–2000 are housed in the Smithsonian Archives of American Art, Washington, D.C.
Exhibitions/citations 1950s, Knoll work shown at *Good Design* exhibitions/awards, The Museum of Modern Art, New York, and Chicago Merchandise Mart. Subject of 1972 *Knoll au Louvre* exhibition, Musée des Arts Décoratifs, Paris, and 1975 *A Modern Consciousness: D.J. DePree, Florence Knoll*, Renwick Gallery, Washington. 1954 (1st) International Design Award, American Institute of Decorators (AID); 1961 gold medal for industrial design, American Institute of Architects (AIA); 1992 IDSA design award (for 1991 Orchestra desk by Lin), Industrial Designers Society of America (IDSA); 2002 National Medal of Arts (for dedication to 20th-century modern design).
Bibliography Cat., *Knoll au Louvre*, Paris: Musée des Arts Décoratifs, 1972. Cat., *A Modern Consciousness:* D.J. DePree, *Florence Knoll*, Washington, D.C.: Renwick Gallery, 1975. Eric Larrabee and Massi-

Archibald Knox. Jewel box. c. 1900. Silver, mother-of-pearl, turquoise, and enamel, 4 x 11 1/2 x 6 1/2" (10.2 x 29.2 x 16.5 cm). Mfr: H. C. Craythorne/ Liberty & Company, UK. Gift of the family of Mrs. John D. Rockefeller 3rd. MoMA.

mo Vignelli, *Knoll Design*, New York: Abrams, 1981: 76–89. *Contemporary Designers*, London: Macmillan. Elaine Louie, 'The Many Lives of a Very Common Chair,' *The New York Times*, 7 Feb. 1991: C10.

Knoll, Hans (1914–1955)

German furniture manufacturer; born Stuttgart; son of furniture manufacturer Walter Knoll; active Germany, UK, and US.

Training In Switzerland and England.
Biography 1938, Knoll was sent by his father to Britain to help promote the family firm's new line of Elbo easy chairs made in Borghams and at Gordon Russell in High Wycombe and sold under the Knoll name in the showroom of Plan, the British furniture firm of Serge Chermeyeff. Knoll moved to the US to work as a designer; unsuccessful at this, set up his own workshop in Pennsylvania, later moving to another factory in Greenville, Pa., near where the Knoll factory is located today. 1938, he opened a showroom on East 72nd Street, New York; 1938, established HG Knoll Furniture Company, a one-man operation to have made and to sell simple, modern furniture. The 1941 chairs of Jens Risom, Knoll's first designer, reflected the scarcity of materials in the immediate postwar period. 1946, Knoll married Florence Schust and formed Knoll Associates, with showroom/offices on Madison Avenue, New York, with her financial support. 1947, Hans began working with Rudolf Graber of Wohnbedarf department store, Switzerland; died in an automobile wreck in Havana, Cuba. From his 1955 death to 1959, Florence Knoll managed the firm. Until she retired in 1965, she worked as a design consultant to the firm under others' ownership.
Bibliography Edward Larrabee and Massimo Vignelli, *Knoll Design*, New York: Abrams, 1981. Akio Izutsu, *The Bauhaus: A Japanese Perspective and A Profile of Hans and Florence Schust Knoll*, Tokyo, 1992.
> See Knoll Bassett, Florence 'Shu.'

Knoll (Ledersitzmöbelfabrik Wilhelm Knoll; Willy Knoll)

German furniture manufacturers; active Stuttgart.

Biographies 1898, Willy Knoll (1878–1954), the son of Wilhelm Knoll (1839–1907), was a leatherworker in his father's factory in Stuttgart. 1906, the firm became known as Ledersitzmöbelfabrik Wilhelm Knoll. 1907, Willy took over management from his father; moved the business to Forststrasse 71 in Stuttgart, where he introduced technical and aesthetic innovations. Based on the success of his models, the firm became respected worldwide and an important European manufacturer. Knoll emphasized the comfort of its chairs, particularly its first Klubfauteuil (club chair). The firm produced chairs with wood frames and tied-on upholstery. Its Derby armchair was published in *Innen-Dekoration* (in a 1908 advertising of Knoll). Shifting from historicist to modern styles, the firm sold its new range through outlets in Vienna and St. Petersburg. Knoll patented springs, new materials, and new techniques for upholstery and constructed resilient and self-supporting loose cushions. 1912, the firm Nestra was set up, with improved manufacturing technique and with leather upholstery free from the frame. A new factory in Stuttgart was set up to produce chairs. Knoll began making sofas in the same way as it made its chairs. 1925, the firm known as Walter Knoll was founded; it produced the 1928 Prodomo range and 1930s tubular-steel furniture with thick, loose cushions. (1937, the Herrenberger Sitzmöbel firm was established in Herrenberg; by 1954, had an outlet in Paris.) 1985, Wilhelm Knoll firm took over Herrenberger Sitzmöbel. The Knoll firm continues today in Herrenberger. Its recent commissioned designers have included Eoos studio, PearsonLloyd, Norman Foster, Wolfgang C. R. Mezger studio,
Citations Red Dot awards: 2001 (six citations), 2002 (two citations), and 2003 (three citations), Design Zentrum Nordrhein Westfalen, Essen; 2003 award, Industrie Forum Design (iF), Hanover; others.
Bibliography Adolf Schneck, *Das Polstermöbel*, Stuttgart: Julius Hoffmann, 1933. *Ensembles mobiliers*, Paris: Charles Moreau, no. 32, 1954. Barbie Campbell-Cole and Tim Benton (eds.), *Tubular Steel Furniture*, London: The Art Book Company, 1979: 13, 24. Arno Votteler and Herbert Eilmann, *125 Jahre Knoll: Vier Generationen Sitzmöbel-Design*, Stuttgart: Karl Krämer, 1990.

Knorr, Donald (1922–)

American architect and designer; born Chicago.

Training To 1947, architecture, University of Illinois, Champaign; postgraduate design studies, Cranbrook Academy of Art, Bloomfield Hills, Mich.
Biography 1947, Knorr joined the architecture office of Eero Saarinen in Ann Arbor, Mich., where he worked on projects such as 1948–56 General Motors Technical Center, Warren, Mich., and, with Saarinen, on the development of furniture, such as office chairs (Nos. 71 and 72) to be produced by Knoll Associates; never designed furniture of his own that surpassed the model entered in The Museum of Modern Art's 1948–50 Low-Cost Furniture Competition; 1949 with his textile-designer wife (also formerly a Cranbrook student), moved to San Francisco and joined the staff of Skidmore, Owings and Merrill architecture office; 1951, opened own practice, Don Knorr and Associates, from 1957–76 known as Knorr-Elliott Associates, both San Francisco, and became known for residential and commerical architecture; from c. 1970, was a partner in Lane-Knorr-Plunkett in Anchorage, Alaska; and,

Donald R. Knorr. Side chair. 1948–50. Sheet metal, steel rods, rubber foam, and fabric, 30 1/4 x 23 x 19" (76.8 x 58.4 x 48.3 cm). Mfr: Knoll Associates, US. Gift of the mfr. MoMA.

from 1976, concurrently in Don Knorr and Associates, San Francisco.
Citations One of two first-prize winners in seating category (1948–50 chair, subsequently produced by Knoll), 1948–50 International Competition for Low-Cost Furniture Design, The Museum of Modern Art, New York.
Bibliography Cat., Martin Eidelberg (ed.), *Design 1935–1965: What Modern Was*, New York: Musée des Arts Décoratifs/Abrams, 1991.

Knox, Archibald (1864–1933)

British metal designer; born Tromode, Isle of Man.

Training 1878–84, Douglas School of Art, Isle of Man.
Biography To 1896, Knox taught at Douglas School of Art; 1897, moved to London, first teaching at Redhill School of Art; was assisted in his metalwork by Christopher Dresser; from 1898, designed for Liberty's and the inspiration behind Liberty's Cymric and Tudric patterns that were influential in 1890s Celtic revival. He designed silver that was among the most refined of the Edwardian era; 1898, textiles by Silver Studio, which he also used as an agency for his design work. 1899, Knox became the design master, Kingston-upon-Thames Art School; from 1899 at Liberty's, designed interlace decoration, enamel work, Donegal carpets (produced c. 1902), pottery, and textiles; 1900–04, lived on Isle of Man and sent his designs to Liberty's. His work was sold at Liberty's to 1930s, although Knox stopped designing for the firm before World War I. 1906–07, he taught, Wimbledon Art School; 1912, visited the US, where he designed carpets by Bromley and lectured at Pennsylvania School of Industrial Art, both in Philadelphia; 1911–39, was active in his own Knox Guild of Craft and Design; 1913, returned to Isle of Man, where he painted and taught; 1917, designed the gravestone of Arthur Lasenby Liberty, the late proprietor of Liberty's.
Exhibitions 1964 *Centenary Exhibition of the Work of Archibald Knox, Manx Artist and Designer*, Manx Museum, Douglas.
Bibliography Charlotte Gere, *American and European Jewelry 1830–1914*, New York: Crown, 1975. A.J. Tilbrook, *The Designs of Archibald Knox for Liberty & Co.*, London, Ornament, 1976. Anthony Jones, 'Knox of Manx and Liberty's of London: In the Ministry of the Beautiful,' in T.J. Edelstein, *Imagining an Irish Past: The Celtic Revival 1840–1940*, Chicago: David and Alfred Smart Museum of Art, 1992. Stephen A. Martin (ed.), *Archibald Knox*, London: Academy, 1995.

Kobayashi, Masakazu (1944–)

Japanese textile designer.

Training University of Arts, Kyoto.
Biography 1966–75, Kobayashi worked as a textile designer at Kawashima; incorporated traditional textile techniques and aesthetics into his work; executed both production fabrics and large-scale fiber works. The repeated lines and stripes of his 1982 Space Age fabric by Sangetsu evoked *komon*, a textile-dyeing technique which calls on paper patterns with small motifs. Other works suggestive of traditional weavings included 1977 W to the Third Power and, with threads suspended in frame, 1979 Meditation.
Bibliography Mildred Constantine and Jack Lenor Larsen, *Beyond Craft: The Art Fabric*, New York: Van Nostrand Reinhold, 1973. Cat., Kathryn B. Hiesinger and George H. Marcus III (eds.), *Design Since 1945*, Philadelphia: Philadelphia Museum of Art, 1983.

Kobayashi, Mitsugi (1932–)

Japanese glass designer.

Training To 1957, Tokyo National University of Fine Arts and Music.
Biography Kobayashi was a trustee, Japan Glass Art Crafts Association; an associate member, *Nitten* (Japan fine-arts exhibitions), Tokyo; a member, Japan Modern Decorative Arts Association; and juror, 1989 *Japan Modern Decorative Arts* exhibition Tokyo.
Exhibitions/citations In Tokyo: 1980 *Japan Modern Decorative Arts* (Governor's Prize) and 1973 *Japan Modern Decorative Arts* (Prize of Modern Decorative Arts). Work shown at 1978 *Modern Decorative Arts in Japan*, National Museum of Modern Art, Tokyo; 1982 *World Glass Now '82*, Hokkaido Museum of Modern Art, Sapporo; 1985 *New Glass in Japan*, Badisches Landesmuseum, Karlsruhe; 1990 *Glass '90 in Japan*, Tokyo; 1991 (5th) Triennale of Japan Glass Art Crafts Association, Heller Gallery, New York; numerous others. Work subject of 1986 exhibition at Nogoya, Tokyo.
Bibliography Cat., *Glass Japan*, New York: Heller Gallery and Japan Glass Art Crafts Association, 1991: no. 17.

Mogens Koch. Safari folding chair. 1932. Wood, leather, and brass, 34 7/16 x 21 1/8 x 14 5/16" (87.5 x 53.7 x 36.3cm). Mfr.: Rud Rasmussens Snedkerier, Rud, Denmark. Courtesy Quittenbaum Kunstauktionen, Munich.

Kobayashi, Naomi (1945–)

Japanese fabric designer; born Tokyo.

Training 1965–69, Musashino Art University, Tokyo.
Biography Kobayashi lives in a mountainous area near Kyoto; incorporates Japanese paper, cotton, and paper thread into her fabrications; has become a significant figure in the field of textile design.
Exhibitions Work included in 1999 *Structure and Surface: Contemporary Japanese Textiles*, New York and St. Louis. From 1969, numerous other group exhibitions; participated in Biennial of Tapestry, Lausanne. From 1981, many one-person exhibitions and, recently, has chosen to exhibit with her husband/artist Masakazu Kobayashi (1944–).
Bibliography Cat., Cara McCarty and Matilda McQuaid, *Structure and Surface: Contemporary Japanese Textiles*, New York: Abrams/The Museum of Modern Art, 1999.

Koch, Mogens (1898–1992)

Danish architect and designer; active Copenhagen.

Training To 1925, Arikteksole, Det Kongelige Danske Kunstakademiet, Copenhagen.
Biography 1934, Koch set up his own studio. His best-known furniture is 1928 Byggereol (folding bookcase), 1932 Foldestol (folding or Safari chair), 1936 Øreklapstol (no. 50 wing-back chair or 'ear-flap chair'), and Lænestol (no. 51 easy chair) in mahogany and leather. The Foldestol chair was produced from 1960 and the Øreklapstol from 1964 by Rud Rasmussens Snedkerier. He also designed furniture by Ivan Schlechter, Cado, Danish CWS, and Interna; carpets; fittings; silver; and fabrics for the restoration of Danish churches. He wrote the books *Moderne dansk kunsthåndværk* (Copenhagen: Thaning & Appel, 1948) and *Geometri og bygningskunst* (Copenhagen: Christian Ejlers' Forlag, 1993); was the architect of 1950–71 Roskilde Doomchurch and designed furniture and decorations for the Danske Kirke (Danish church) in London. 1950–68, Koch was professor of building construction/art, Det Kongelige Danske Kunstakademi; 1956, was a visiting lecturer, Massachusetts Institute of Technology (MIT), Cambridge, Mass.; 1962, a lecturer, Industrial Art Institute, Tokyo.
Exhibitions/citations Work regularly shown at editions of Triennale di Milano and included in 1925 *Exposition Internationale des Arts Décoratifs et Industriels Modernes*, Paris; 1937 *Exposition Internationale*

des Arts Décoratifs et Techniques dans la Vie Moderne, Paris, and a number of other exhibitions worldwide. 1938 Eckersberg Medal; 1963 C.F. Hansen Medal; 1990 Classics Award, Dansk Design Centre; 1990 Danmarks Nationalbank Jubilee Foundation.
Bibliography Arne Karlsen and Axel Thygesen, *Om Mogens Koch Arbejder*, Copenhagen: Landsforeningen dansk kunsthaandværk, 1964. Erik Zahle, *Scandinavian Domestic Design*, London: Methuen, 1963. Axel Thygesen, *Tilegnet Mogens Koch*, Copenhagen: Nyt Nordisk/Arnold, 1968. Frederik Sieck, *Nutidig Dansk Møbeldesign – en kortfattet illustreret beskrivelse*, Copenhagen: Bondo Gravesen, 1981, 1990.

Koch & Bergfeld

German silversmithy.

History 1829, Koch & Bergfeld was founded in Bremen. Before 1910, Christoph Kay trained there. 1900–10, the firm produced designs of Hugo Leven, Albin Müller, and Henry van de Velde and 1920s–30s designs of Gustav Elsass and Bernhard Hoetger, although it attached less importance than other smithies to working with renowned independent artists. Court jeweler Theodor Müller designed a 335-piece dinner service, assigned to Koch & Bergfeld, for marriage of Grand Duke Louis IV of Hesse-Darmstadt. The head of the firm's design studio was Heinrich von der Cammer, who was succeeded in 1904 by sculptor Hugo Leven. 1909, Leven left to become director, Königlich Preussische Zeichenakademie, Hanau, and was succeeded at the smithy by Gustav Elsass. Leven was kept on as artistic advisor. Wilhelm Wagenfeld first trained as a silversmith in the Koch & Bergfeld factory, which was bought by Villeroy & Boch in 1989.
Exhibitions Müller's centerpieces for Hesse-Darmstadt and two other services, including the silver designs of Albin Müller, were shown at 1910 *Exposition Universelle et Internationale*, Brussels.
Bibliography Annelies Krekel-Aalberse, *Art Nouveau and Art Déco Silver*, New York: Abrams, 1989. Cat., *Metallkunst*, Berlin: Bröhan Museum, 1990. Bernhard Heitmann, *Handwerk und Maschinenkraft: die Silbermanufaktur Koch & Bergfeld in Bremen*, Hamburg: Museum für Kunst und Gewerbe, 1999.

Kodak
See Eastman, George.

Koenig, Giovanni Klaus (1924–1989)

Italian architect, designer, critic, and teacher; born Turin.

Biography Koenig collaborated with Roberto Segoni; designed 1970 Jumbo Tram (in production from 1975) in Milan; 1977 underground train in Rome; and 1978–79 ALe.804 and ALe.884 electric express trains of the Ferrovie dello Stato (FS)/Trenitalia. He taught, Facoltà di Architettura, Università degli Studi, Florence, where in 1960s, with Pierluigi Spadolini, he was instrumental in establishing a bachelor's-degree program in industrial design and where, later, the Centro Studi Giovanni Klaus Koenig was founded. As a critic, he was known to be cutting and sarcastic; was a prolific writer for *Domus*, *Ottogano*, and other journals and of books/essays on modern architecture and design.
Bibliography Paolo Portoghesi (ed.), *Dizionario enciclopedico di architettura e urbanistica*, vol. 3, Rome: Istituto Editoriale Romano, 1968: 301. Vittorio Gregotti, *Il disegno del prodotto industriale: Italia 1860–1980*, Milan: Electa, 1982. Cat., Hans Wichmann, *Italien Design 1945 bis heute*, Munich: Die Neue Sammlung, 1988. Claudio Messina, *Me ne vado e sbatto l'uscio: Giovanni Klaus Koenig: architetture*, Firenze: Alinea, 1994. Giovanni Klaus Koenig, *Architettura del Novecento*, Venice, 1995.

Kofod-Larsen, Ib (1921–)

Danish architect and designer.

Training Arkitekskole, Det Kongelige Danske Kunstakademiet, Copenhagen.
Biography Kofod-Larsen's furniture designs were produced in 1950s by Fritz Hansen and by Christensen og Larsen, some in small editions by the latter. The Larsen chair, probably better known than the designer himself, is characterized by a curved bentwood back with low-sloping sides and is elevated from the back end of the seat on a wooden or steel-rod frame.
Citations Annual prize, Danish Cabinetmakers' Guild; first prize, 1948

J. & J. Kohn. Child's cradle. c. 1893. Ebonized bentwood, 80 1/4 x 56 1/4 x 25 7/16" (203.8 x 142.9 x 64.6 cm). Mfr: Jacob & Josef Kohn, Austria. Gift of Barry Friedman. MoMA.

Holmegård Glasværks competition.
Bibliography Frederik Sieck, *Nutidig Dansk Møbeldesign – en kortfattet illustreret beskrivelse*, Copenhagen: Bondo Gravesen, 1990.

Kogan, Belle (1902–2000)

Russian-American designer; active the US.

Training Mechanical drawing, high school; Pratt Institute, Brooklyn, N.Y. (one semester); Art Students League, Manhattan, N.Y.; summer 1920, New York University.
Biography 1906, Kogan immigrated with her parents from Russia to the US; after high school, taught mechanical drawing in Brooklyn to make money to attend Pratt Institute, but was able to attend only for a very short time; designed jewelry settings while at the Art Students League. c. 1929, she was hired as a freelance designer of pewter and silver objects at Quaker Silver Company in Attleboro, Mass.; 1931, established her own studio in New York, becoming one of the first designers in America to experiment with plastics in jewelry, including celluloid toilet articles and clocks, Bakelite jewelry, and a chromium toaster with a plastic base. Kogan faced opposition from the male members of her profession and rejection by manufacturers because of her sex. After much difficulty in early 1930s, she had an established business by 1939 with three female staff designers. Clients included Reed & Barton, Bausch & Lomb, Boonton Molding (1950s plastic dinnerware ranges), Libbey Glass, and Dow Chemicals. 1938, she designed 100 new vase shapes produced by Red Wing Pottery and agressively marketed as 'the Belle Kogan 100.' She again designed for the firm 1949–63, including 1963 Prismatic art-pottery range. (Red Wing closed in 1967.) 1938, Kogan cofounded New York chapter of American Institute of Decorators (AID), which later became Interior Designers Association (IDA). 1970, she closed her office.
Citations 1994 Personal Recognition Award, Industrial Designers Society of America (IDSA).
Bibliography Cat., Pat Kirkham (ed.), *Women Designers in the USA, 1900–2000: Diversity and Difference*, New York: Bard, New Haven: Yale, 2000.

Kogoj, Oskar (1942–)

Slovene industrial designer; born Miren.

Training To 1966, diploma studies in industrial design, Facoltà di Design e Arti, Università degli Studi, Venice.
Biography 1969–70, Kogoj worked at Meblo furniture factory in Nova Gorica (a new town built in 1948), Slovenia; from 1971, was a freelance designer; 1972–75, lectured at Università degli Studi in Florence and in Venice; first became known for his 1968 Red Object plastic wagon; was interested in organic forms primarily in plastic and designed cutlery, kitchenware, furniture, and children's toys, including 1988–90 Valovnica series of bottles and glasses. His ergonomic approach was manifested in his Gondola range of easy chairs, for which he developed a pattern from impressions of the seated human body, and in his plastic cutlery. Designed bottles for Batic farm and vineyard, Sempas, Slovenia.
Exhibitions Cutlery shown at 1983–84 *Design Since 1945*, Philadelphia Museum of Art.
Bibliography 'Design in Action: Prototype Plastic Flatware,' *Industrial Design*, vol. 19, Oct. 1972: 60–61. Cat., Gillo Dorfles and Peter Krečič, *Zoran Kržičnik*, Nova Gorica, 1972. 'Child Care,' *Industrial Design*, vol. 24, May 1977: 49–51. Cat., Kathryn B. Hiesinger and George H. Marcus III (eds.), *Design Since 1945*, Philadelphia: Philadelphia Museum of Art, 1983.

Kohlmann, Étienne (1903–1988)

French designer and interior decorator; born and active Paris.

Training 1916, at age 13, apprenticeship as a cabinetmaker at aviation factory Nieuport; to 1922, École Boulle, Paris.
Biography Kohlmann was an accomplished cabinetmaker from an early age; 1922 for one year, worked for a cabinetmaker in Faubourg Saint-Antoine area of Paris; 1923–38 with Maurice Matet, was codirector of Studium decorating department of Les Grands Magasins du Louvre, Paris; at Studium-Louvre as it was also known, sometimes collaborated on designs with Maurice Matet and Dubard, and eventually became the artistic director. His work included a large amount of furniture as well as luxury interiors and the lounge of 1927 oceanliner *Île-de-France*, a number of Paris shop interiors for Le Mobilier National, and, often with architect Barrot, a number of private commissions. From 1928, he included metal in his furniture designs. The rugs,

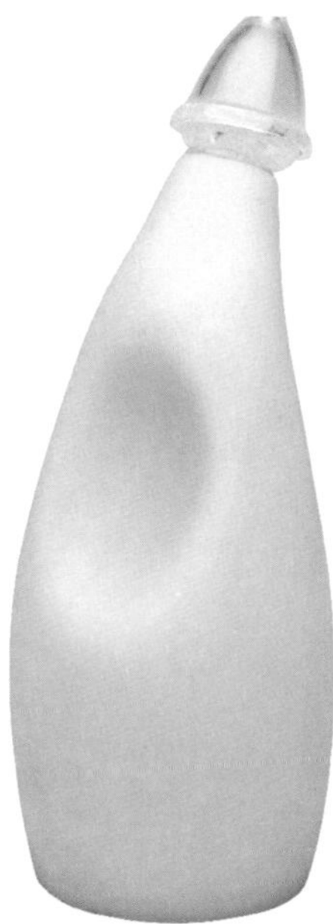

Oscar Kogoj. Aspirator. 1974. Rubber and plastic, 4 1/2 x base dia. 1 1/2" (11.5 x 3.8 cm). Mfr.: Ciciban Shoe & Children's Ware Factory, Yugoslavia (now Croatia). Gift of the manufacturer. MoMA.

upholstery fabrics, and murals for his commissioned interiors were produced by Mlle. Max Vibert. 1934, he designed offices of the laboratories of Dr. Debat in Garches and other commissions, including stores, hotels, restaurants, and numerous residences. On his less-than-successful lighting for Studium-Louvre, he received occasional technical assistance from Jean Lévy and from lighting engineer P. Juget. Kohlmann also designed lighting by Holophane. By 1954, his workshop was located at 22, quai du Louvre, Paris.
Exhibitions All in Paris: work shown at Salons of Société des Artistes Décorateurs 1924–42, editions of Salon d'Automne from 1923, and 1947 edition of Salon des Tuileries; 1925 *Exposition Internationale des Arts Décoratifs et Industriels Modernes* (participated in Studium-Louvre's pavilion and in others); 1931 *Exposition Coloniale*; 1934 (2nd) and 1935 (3rd) (fixtures by Holophane) Salon de la Lumière; 1939–40 *New York World's Fair: The World of Tomorrow*, 1937 *Exposition Internationale des Arts et Techniques dans la Vie Moderne* (lacquered metal chandelier and wall brackets by F. Gagneau, and, with Eugène Printz, general illumination of corridors and vestibules of the Pavillon de la Lumière), Paris.
Bibliography Guillaume Janneau, *Le luminaire et les moyens d'éclairage nouveaux*, 1st series, Paris: Charles Moreau, plates 32, 36, [n.d.]. *Ensembles mobiliers*, Paris: Charles Moreau, vol. 6, nos. 44–48; nos. 35–36, 1954. Alastair Duncan, *Art Nouveau and Art Déco Lighting*, New York: Simon & Schuster, 1978. Pierre Kjellberg, *Art déco: les maîtres du mobilier, le décor des paquebots*, Paris: Amateur, 1986. Cat., Sophie Tasma Anargyros et al., *L'école française: les créateurs de meubles du 20ème siècle*, Paris: Industries Françaises de l'Ameublement, 2000.

Kohn, Jacob & Josef

Moravian furniture manufacturer.

History 1869, Michael Thonet lost his monopoly for producing bentwood furniture on the expiry of his patent. 1850, the Kohn family founded a lumber-producing firm in Holleschau, Moravia (now Holešov, Czech Republic), where local craftspeople were hired. 1867, Jacob Kohn (1791–1868) went into partnership with son Josef (1814–1884) on 8 Nov. 1867, forming Jacob & Josef Kohn. 1869, the firm built its first factories in Wsetin, Moravia (now Vsetin, Czech Republic), and, 1870, began production. With its business growing rapidly, the firm established other factories in Litsch, Moravia, 1869; Krakau (Cracow, Poland), 1871; Teschen, Austrian Silesia (now where Těšin, Czech Republic, and Cieszyn, Poland, meet), 1871. And large factories in Radomsk (now Radomsko, Poland), 1885, and Holle-

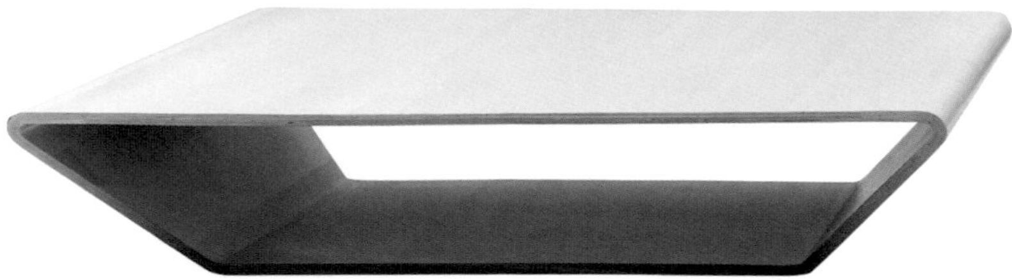

Eero Koivisto and Ola Rune. Brazilia coffee table. c. 2002. Laminated plywood, h. 11 x w. 39 3/8"–47 1/4 x l. 39 3/8"–47 1/4" (28 x 100–120 x 100–120cm). Mfr.: Swedese.

schau (now Holešov, Czech Republic), 1890. There were smaller facilities in Ratibor and Keltsch, both in Moravia. Also in Wagstadt (now Bilovec), Skotschau, and in Jablunkau (now Jablonka, Poland) in Silesia. Kohn became Thonet's major competitor, although, by 1893, there were more than 50 other bentwood-furniture firms in Western and Eastern Europe. By 1882, Kohn had important sales branches in Berlin, Hamburg, London, and Paris. Kohn copied Thonet's styles at first but, by 1900, had begun manufacturing bentwood furniture designed by accomplished people such as Gustav Siegel, a pupil of Josef Hoffmann. 1899, Siegel was appointed head of design. Kohn was to play an important role in architect-designed bentwood furniture and produced the first architect-designed bentwood chair, by Adolf Loos for the billiard room of 1899 Café Museum in Vienna. Kohn's success at 1900 *Exposition Universelle*, Paris, ushered in the production of furniture by eminent architects, including Josef Hoffmann, Koloman Moser, and Otto Wagner. Siegel and and Otto Wagner were probably responsible for early Art Nouveau models by Kohn. One of Kohn's best-known products may be the c. 1905 Sitzmaschine reclining chair (no. 670) by Hoffmann. Other designers included Marcel Kammerer, Josef Urban, and Leopold Bauer. By 1904, Kohn's 6,300 employees were producing 5,500 pieces of furniture daily in 407 different models in four facilities. 1914, the firm merged with Mundus; 1918, moved to Zurich. 1922, Thonet merged with Kohn; 1923, operated under the name Mundus-Handel und industrielle Gesellschaft (Mundus commercial and industrial firm), with 20 factories and 10,000 workers. 1932, 'Kohn' disappeared from the firm's business in Germany.
Exhibitions/citations Work shown at 1876 *Centennial Exhibition*, Philadelphia. Grand prize (for rooms by Siegel, including by Moser), 1900 *Exposition Universelle*, Paris.
Bibliography Giovanna Massobrio and Paolo Portoghesi, *La Seggiola di Vienna: storia dei mobili in legno curavto*, Turin: Martano, 1976. *Jacob und Josef Kohn: Der Katalog von 1916*, Munich: Graham Day, 1980. Graham Day, 'The Development of the Bent-Wood Furniture Industry, 1869–1914,' in Derek E. Ostergard (ed.), *Bent Wood and Metal Furniture 1850–1946*, New York: The American Federation of Arts, 1987. Paola Antonelli (ed.), *Objects of Design: The Museum of Modern Art*, New York: The Museum of Modern Art, 2003: 124.

J. Jurriaan Kok and Jacobus Lucas Verhoog (1878–). Candy jar. 1900. Eggshell porcelain with painted decoration, overall 4 1/2 x 3 1/2 x 3 1/2" (11.5 x 8.9 x 8.9 cm). Mfr: Haagsche Plateelbakkerig Rozenburg, the Netherlands. Gift of Don Page. MoMA.

Koivisto, Eero (1958–)

Swedish teacher, architecture, and interior and furniture designer; born Karlstad; active Stockholm.

Training 1989, Konstfackskolan, Stockholm; 1992, architecture and product design, Parsons School of Design, New York; 1993, architecture and interior design, Taideteollinen korkeakoulu, Helsinki; 1994, master of fine arts degree, Konstfack (formerly Konstfackskolan), Stockholm; 1995, design leadership, Taideteollinen korkeakoulu, Helsinki.
Biography Koivisto was artistic director at Konstfack; 1993, with Mårten Cleasson and Ola Rune, established Claesson Koivisto Rune Arkitektkontor; both Stockholm. The group has designed a wide range of furniture by Offecct, including the Cornflake chair and Window table. Other clients have included BodaNova, Cappellini, David Design, IForm, IKEA, Lammhults, Lindelöfs Interiör, and Trussardi. Architectural commissions: 1997 Scandinavia Online (Internet firm), 1998 Gucci store, and 1998 One Happy Cloud (Japanese restaurant); all Stockholm.
Exhibitions/citations Partnership work subject of 2002 exhibition, Arkitekturmuseet, Stockholm. Received 1991 Scandinavia–Japan Sasakawa Foundation grant; 1992 first prize (apartment design with Rune), HSB Stockholm competition; 1993 Nordplus grant (with Rune); 1997 Swedish Artists Fund.
Bibliography Terence Riley et al., *Claesson Koivisto Rune*, Barcelona: Editorial Gustavo Gili: 2001.
> See Claesson, Mårten.

Kok, J. Jurriaan (1861–1919)

Dutch ceramicist and architect; born Rotterdam.

Training Architecture, Polytechnische School, Delft.
Biography 1883–93, Kok was a practicing architect in The Hague and, 1894–1913, an alderman for the public-works department of The Hague and worked at Haagsche Plateelbakkerig Rozenburg, a delftware factory. At first at Rozenburg, he was an aesthetics adviser; from June 1894, the manager; and, from 1895, the general manager. He introduced a number of production-process improvements there including, with chemist M.N. Engelen, imaginative chemical porcelain-making methods such as plaster-mold shaping and high-temperature biscuit firing. This made the production of very thin eggshell porcelain objects possible. The slipcasting facilitated the forming of Kok's exaggerated shapes, especially handles. Through his efforts, Rozenburg became highly successful. However, due to diminished import/export tariffs, the factory was forced to close during World War I. Kok died in The Hague.
Bibliography *The Grove Dictionary of Art*, London: Macmillan, 2000 (Netherlands, the, §VII, 4: Ceramics, after 1830); www.groveart.com.

Kokke, Ruud-Jan H.M. (1956–)

Dutch interior and furniture designer; born Velp; active Oosterbeek.

Training College of Social Studies; Koninklijke Nederlandse Akademie van Wetenschappen (KNAW), Amsterdam.
Biography 1986, Kokke set up his own independent design studio; has designed Kokkechair (first designed in 1984 with thin ash lathing), Kokkechair (with beech plywood seat and back), beds by Auping, a

Ray Komai. Side chair. 1949. Chrome-plated steel and molded wood. Mfr.: JG Furniture Co., US. Gift of the mfr. MoMA.

walking stick by Becker (commissioned by the Museum Boymans-van Beuningen in Rotterdam), a child's bentwood chair by Live and Play of Doorn in the Netherlands, 1990 Wander (no. TC) bentwood stacking stools by Designum in Laag Keppel, transportable soccer court in Amsterdam (by Streetlife of Leiden), chair for a restaurant in Groningen, a natal-care center in Arnhem, Timbra side chair/armchair by Eromes Wijchen; others. Clients have included Chabotmuseum in Rotterdam (the Chabot chair), Fonds voor de Kunsten in Amsterdam, Museum voor Moderne Kunsten in Arnhem, SSHW in Wageningen, Vormgevingsinstituut in Amsterdam.
Exhibitions/citations Work shown at 1996 *Contemporary Design from the Netherlands* (TC stool), The Museum of Modern Art, New York. Received Designprijs (for soccer court), Rotterdam; first prize (for walking stick), Gelderland Design Prize; 1996 Red Dot Highest Design Quality award (for Kokkestock), Design Zentrum Nordrhein Westfalen, Essen; first prize (for Wander no. TC stool), International Contemporary Furniture Fair (ICFF), New York; Form '92 (for Wander no TC stool), Frankfurt; award (for Moment bench) Industrie Forum Design (iF), Hanover; others.

Kokko, Valto (1933–)
Finnish designer.

Biography 1963, Kokko began working at littala glassworks as a designer of lighting fixtures; later, as head of the visual department, designed packaging, exhibitions, and promotional literature and supervised photography and industrial films. From late 1970s, Kokko became active in design of domestic utilitarian glassware, including 1978 Otso drinking glasses by littala.

Kolte, Olof (1964–)
Swedish designer; born Stockholm.

Training To 1990, civil engineering, Konstfackskolan, Stockholm; 1986–87, exchange student, École Spéciale des Travaux Publics du Bâtiment et de l'Industrie (ESTP), Paris; 1995–96, guest student in architecture and design, Det Kongelige Danske Kunstakademiet, Copenhagen; 1998, master of arts degree, Royal College of Art, London.
Biography 1990–95, Kolte worked as a civil engineer in Mexico City, Mexico; Malmö, Sweden; and Riga, Latvia. Since 1991, he has been a freelance designer for David Design in Malmö, designing products including 1993 High Funk table legs, 1993 Hot Drain kettle heater, 1993 Consolidate bracket, 1994 Jigsaw plywood CD shelf, 1996 Cylinder table lamp, 1998 Spice Boy spice shelf, 2000 Bowl vacuum-formed lamp range in four versions. 1998, he established his own design practice in London; currently, active in Malmö, serving other clients, including IKEA, Pergo, Skultuna Messingsbruk, White Arkitekter, and Wireworks.
Bibliography Mel Byars, *50 Tables...*, Hove: RotoVision, 1997.

Komai, Ray (1918–)
American graphic, industrial, and interior designer.

Training Interior, industrial, and graphic design, Art Center College, Los Angeles.
Biography 1944, Komai settled in New York, where he worked in advertising; 1948 with Carter Winter, set up a graphic-design and advertising studio. Komai's 1949 molded plywood chair with a split seat and bent-metal legs was produced by J.G. Furniture, which also produced his other chairs, tables, and upholstered seating designs. From c. 1945, he designed wallpaper and textiles in figurative and abstract motifs (inspired by art of Pablo Picasso, Paul Klee, and Cubist painters) by Laverne International in New York. 1952–60, he was associate art director at Advertising Forum; 1963–76, a designer at the United States Information Agency and created the sets of cultural exhibitions in Germany, Austria, India, and Japan.
Exhibitions/citations 1950 *Good Design* exhibition/award (1949 split-seat chair), The Museum of Modern Art, New York, and Chicago Merchandise Mart; 1983–84 *Design Since 1945* (plywood chair and textiles by Laverne), Philadelphia Museum of Art.
Bibliography William J. Hennessey, *Modern Furnishings for the Home*, New York: Reinhold, vol. 1, 1952; New York: Acanthus, 1997. George Nelson (ed.), *Chairs*, New York: Whitney, 1953; New York: Acanthus, 1994. Cat., Kathryn B. Hiesinger and George H. Marcus III (eds.), *Design Since 1945*, Philadelphia: Philadelphia Museum of Art, 1983. Cherie Fehrman and Kenneth Fehrman, *Postwar Interior Design, 1945–1960*, New York: Van Nostrand Reinhold, 1987. Cat., Martin Eidelberg (ed.), *Design 1935–1965: What Modern Was*, New York: Musée des Arts Décoratifs/Abrams, 1991.

Komatsu, Makoto (1943–)
Japanese designer; born Tokyo; active Gyoda, Saitama.

Training To 1965, Crafts Design Department, Musashino Art Junior College (now College of Art and Design, Musashino Art University), Tokyo.
Biography 1965–69, Komatsu worked in the crafts-design office,

Ruud-Jan H.M. Kokke. Wander stacking stool (no. TC). 1990. Birch plywood, 16 15/16 x 14 5/8 x 12 1/8" (43 x 37.2 x 30.8 cm). Mfr.: Designum, the Netherlands. Gift of the mfr. and Kikkerland Design, Inc. MoMA.

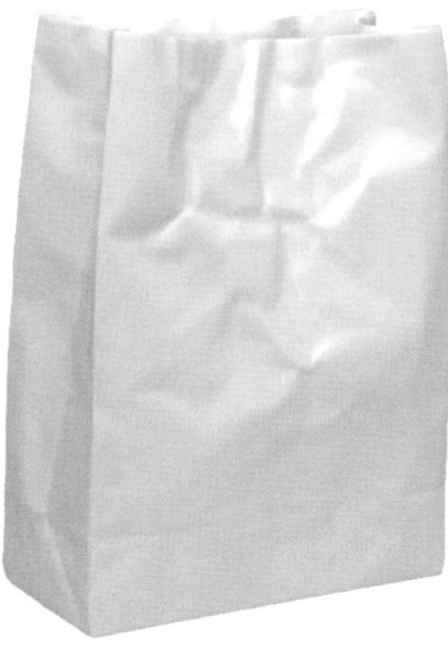

Makoto Komatsu. Crinkle Super Bag vase (no. K-2). 1975. Glazed cast porcelain, 9 7/8 x 7 1/4 x 3 7/16" (25.1 x 18.4 x 8.7 cm). Mfr.: Ceramic Japan Co., Japan. Gift of the designer and Emilio Ambasz Fund. MoMA.

Musashino Art University; 1970–73, in the design studio, Gustavsberg ceramics factory, Sweden; 1973, established his own studio in Gyoda, Saitama, Japan; 1975, participated with Fam product-design group; is best known for his 1975 Crinkle vessels in porcelain that purposefully look like crinkled paper bags and 1980 Crumple tumblers. (Tapio Wirkkala's similar 1977 'bag' porcelain vase, with a brown exterior, was produced by Rosenthal.) Other wares: 2000–02 Kuu thin series of pierced ceramics and 1986 Soyushi and 1989 Spin aluminum produced by computer-numerically-controlled machinery. He is a professor, Masashino Art University, and a lecturer: Aichi Prefectural University of Art, Kyoto City University of Art, and Ishikawa Prefectural Kutani Ware Technical Training Institute in Terai.
Exhibitions/citations From 1975 *Hands Series* one-person venue, Craft Gallery, Ginza Matsuya. Work shown in a large number of exhibtions, including at the Victoria and Albert Museum, London, and Museo Internazionale delle Ceramiche, Faenza. Numerous design awards, including 1976 bronze medal, Design Forum 75, Japan Design Committee; grand prize, 1986 (1st) International Ceramics Competition, Mino, Japan; grand prize, 1987 (30th) Ceramics Design Competition.
Bibliography Mel Byars, *50 Products: Innovations in Design and Materials*, Hove: RotoVision, 1998.

Komplot Design
> See Berlin, Boris.

Koolhaas, Rem (1944–)
Dutch architect; born Rotterdam.

Training From 1965, Architectural Association, London.
Biography After working as a copywriter in the Netherlands, Koolhaas studied architecture in London and worked with Elia Zenghelis. 1965, they became partners in the Office for Metropolitan Architecture (OMA), London, and were joined by artists Zoe Zenghelis and Madelon Vriesendorp. The group was influenced by disparate disciplines and forms, including the work of neo-Suprematist Ivan Leonidov and 1960s Continuous Monument by Aldolfo Natalini and Superstudio. Koolhaas and Elia Zenghelis entered 1975 competition for housing complex on Roosevelt Island, New York. Mid-1970s, Koolhaas collaborated with Laurinda Spear on 1979 Spear house, Miami Beach, Fla., completed by Spear's firm Arquitectonica. Koolhaas published *Delirious New York: A Retroactive Manifesto for Manhattan* (1978), which presented fantasy projects reflecting OMA's philosophy. OMA's work has included 1978 Parliament extension (with Zaha Hadid), The Hague; 1981 design submitted for 1984 *Internationale Bauausstellung*, Berlin; 1988 Netherlands Dance Theater, The Hague; 1991 Nexus World Kashii, Japan; 1992 Kunsthal, Rotterdam; 1994 Grand Palais, Lille; 1997 Educatorium, Utrech. With Bruce Mau and others, he prepared the book *S,M,L,XL*: OMA (Rotterdam: 010, 1995).
Exhibitions/citations Work included in *Radicals: Architettura e Design 1960–75*, 1996 (6th) Mostra Internazionale di Architettura, Venice. 2000 Pritzker Architecture Prize.
Bibliography 'OMA,' *Architectural Design*, vol. 47, no. 5, 1977. Cat., *OMA Projects 1978–1981*, London, 1981. Kenneth Frampton in Vittorio Magnago Lampugnani (ed.), *Encyclopedia of 20th-Century Architecture*, New York: Abrams, 1986: 190–91. 'Rem Koolhaas, Post-Nationalist Architect,' *The New York Times*, 11 Sept. 1994.

Kopka, Alfred (1894–1987)
German metalworker; born Tourcoing, France.

Training Under Josef Wilm, Kunstgewerbeschule, Berlin.
Biography 1921, Kopka became master of the metal workshop at the Bauhaus, Weimar; taught metalworking, Vereinigte Staatsschulen für freie und angewandte Kunst (formerly Kunstgewerbeschule), Berlin, and, 1923–31, in Breslau (now Wroclaw, Poland).
Exhibitions A chased service shown at 1922 *Deutsche Gewerbeschau*, Munich.
Bibliography Annelies Krekel-Aalberse, *Art Nouveau and Art Déco Silver*, New York: Abrams, 1989. Cat., *Die Metallwerkstatt am Bauhaus*, Berlin: Bauhaus-Archiv, 1992: 317.

Koppel, Henning (1918–1981)
Danish architect and designer; active Copenhagen.

Training 1936–37, sculpture, Det Kongelige Danske Kunstakademi, Copenhagen; 1938–39 under Charles Malfrey, Académie Ranson, Paris.
Biography 1940–45, Koppel was a refugee in Stockholm, when he first designed silver and gold jewelry and worked for both Svensk Tenn and Orrefors. He worked for Georg Jensen Sølvsmedie 1945–81, Bing & Grøndahl Porcelænsfabrik 1961–81, freelancer to Louis Poulsen (lighting and clocks) from 1967, freelancer to Orrefors Glasbruk from 1971. He designed 1962 Form 24 tea set by Bing & Grøndahl; was best known for his sleek sculptural designs, particularly the silver items by Jensen over a 35-year period. 1950s, his style came to fruition in expressive, languorous silver work. His innovative work varied from abstract and glamorous silver tea-and-coffee sets with limpid handles and sensuous spouts to inexpensive stainless-steel organic pieces. His 1954 silver fish dish with a cover for Jensen has been widely published and exhibited. Known primarily for his metalwork, he designed a 1960 wall clock by Louis Poulsen.
Exhibitions/citations A featured designer at 1966 *Centenary Exhibition*, Goldsmiths' Hall, London. Silver work shown at 1954–57 *Design in Scandinavia*, touring the US; 1956–59 *Neue Form aus Dänemark*, touring Germany; 1958 *Formes Scandinaves*, Musée des Arts Décoratifs, Paris; 1960–61 *The Arts of Denmark*, touring the US; 1975 *Adventures in Swedish Glass*, Australia; 1982 *Scandinavian Modern Design 1880–1980*, Cooper-Hewitt National Design Museum, New York. Work subject of 1982 commemorative exhibition of Jensen silver work, Kunstindustrimuseet, Copenhagen. Numerous awards, including 1953 Lunning Prize; gold medals at 1951 (9th), 1954 (10th), and 1957 (11th) editions of Triennale di Milano; 1963 International Design Award, American Institute of Decorators (AID).
Bibliography Viggo Sten Møller, *Henning Koppel*, Copenhagen, 1965. Graham Hughes, *Modern Silver Throughout the World*, New York: Crown, 1967: 237, plates 22–31. *Henning Koppel in D B & D*, Copenhagen: Danish Society of Arts and Crafts and Industrial Design,

Harri Koskinen. Block lamp. 1995–96. Hand-cast glass, cord, and electrical switch, 3 3/4 x 6 1/2 x 4" (9.5 x 16.5 x 10.2 cm). Mfr.: Design House Stockholm, Sweden (1999). Gift of the mfr. MoMA.

1972: 7–10. Cat., *Georg Jensen Silversmithy: 77 Artists, 75 Years*, Washington: Smithsonian, 1980. Cat., *Henning Koppel: En mindeudstilling, sølvarbejder for Georg Jensen Sølvsmedie*, Copenhagen: Kunstindustrimuseet, 1982. Cat., *The Lunning Prize*, Stockholm: Nationalmuseum, 1986: 54–57. Cat., Martin Eidelberg (ed.), *Design 1935–1965: What Modern Was*, New York: Musée des Arts Décoratifs/Abrams, 1991. Niels-Jørgen Kaiser, *Henning Koppels verden*, Copenhagen: Gyldendal, 2000.

Köpping, Karl (1848–1914)

German painter, graphic designer, and chemist.

Training Chemistry, Akademie der bildenden Künste, Munich.
Biography The first work of Köpping (or Koepping) involved reproductive engraving in Berlin. 1890, he returned to etching; became the director, Meisterateliers für Kupferstich und Radierung (master studios for engraving and etching) at Akademie der bildenden Künste, Berlin; from c. 1896, executed fragile, iridescent flower-form glass in the Art Nouveau style, including drinking glasses, much of it produced by Friedrich Zitzmann in Wiesbaden. From 1895, he first began to design glass objects in vegetal forms with high stems; 1896, became the editor of *Pan*, which was devoted to Art Nouveau and reproduced images of his own glass and etchings.
Bibliography Cat., Helmut Ricke, *Reflex der Jahrhunderte: Die Glassammlung des Kunstmuseums Düsseldorf*, Leipzig: Museum des Kunsthandwerks Grassimuseum, 1989: 213.

Kopriva, 'Erna' Ernestine (1894–1984)

Austrian ceramicist; born Vienna.

Training 1914–19 under A. Hanak, Josef Hoffmann, and Oskar Strnad, Kunstgewerbeschule, Vienna.
Biography 1919–28, Kopriva was among the women ceramicists, who gained importance in the Wiener Werkstätte; from 1928, was an assistant in textile design under Josef Hoffmann at the Kunstgewerbeschule; from 1944, taught, Werkstätte für Stoffdruck und Tapeten at the Kunstgewerbeschule, where she was a professor from 1953.
Bibliography Günther Feuerstein, *Vienna—Present and Past: Arts and Crafts—Applied Art—Design*, Vienna: Jugend und Volk, 1976. Cat., *Expressive Keramik der Wiener Werkstätte 1917–1930*, Munich: Bayerische Vereinsbank, 1992: 1130–31.

Kørbing, Kay (1915–)

Danish furniture designer.

Training To 1938, Tekniske Skole, Copenhagen; to 1942, Arkitekskole, Det Kongelige Danske Akademiet, Copenhagen.
Biography Some of Kørbing's furniture designs were produced by Gotfred H. Pedersen, including a 1955 fiberglass side chair with bent tubular-metal legs. 1955–57, he worked with Ole Gjerløv-Knudsen (1930–); designed the interiors of the ships of the Det Forenede Dampskibs-Selskab (DFDS) ships: *Tor Britannia*, *Color Viking*, *England*, *Winston Churchill*, *Sagafjord*, *Dana Regina* (some with DFDS's own industrial designer Niels Krygger).
Bibliography Frederik Sieck, *Nutidig Dansk Møbeldesign – en kortfattet illustreret beskrivelse*, Copenhagen: Bondo Gravesen, 1981. Bruce Peter, *Danish Ship Design: The Work of Kay Fisker and Kay Kørbing*, Ramsey, Isle of Man: Ferry Publications, 2004.

Korhonen, Harri (1946–)

Finnish designer; born Helsinki.

Biography Korhonen is director and chief designer of Inno-Tuote Oy of Espoo, for which he has designed furniture, lighting, and interior fittings such as coat racks and hooks, including witty 1985 couch/chair/lamp combination and more serious 2002 Select Medium chair range. For manufacturers Vivero and Avarte, he created furniture designs in minimalist forms in the style of Charles Eames's early work and that of Gerrit Rietveld.
Bibliography Robert A.M. Stern (ed.), *The International Design Yearbook*, New York: Abbeville, 1985/1986.

Korolainen, Ari Olavi (1956–)

Finnish building architect and industrial designer; born Oulu; active Lahti; husband of fashion designer Carita Korolainen.

Biography In response to his experience of being an active architect with a great deal of paper to manage, in 1986 Korlainen founded the

Karl Köpping. Liqueur glass. c. 1900. Mouth-blown glass, h. 4 5/8 x dia. 2 3/8" (11.8 x 6 cm). Mfr.: Lehrwerkstatte für Glasinstrumentmacher/Großherzogliche Sächsische Fachschule, Germany. Given anonymously. MoMA.

carrying case firm Private Case in Lahti, Finland. The firm calls on the use of 100-percent recycled cardboard in its products, the first of which was the 101 briefcase. Has also produced custom designs for clients such as IBM, Hertz, Holiday-Inn, AT&T, Coca-Cola, Agfa, Finnair, Neste, Nokia, and Sampo.
Exhibitions/citations Private Case products included in numerous exhibitions. Citations included Good Finnish Design award; honorable mention (designs by Private Case), Pro Finnish Design.

Korpershoek, Matijs (1969–)

Dutch designer; born Leeuwarden.

Training To 1996, Akademie voor Industriële Vormgeving, Eindhoven.
Biography From 1996, Korpershoek has worked with the Droog Design group; designed c. 2000 Changing Candlelight candle by Salviati.
Bibliography Ingo Maurer (ed.), *The International Design Yearbook*, London: Laurence King, 2000: 107.
Citations 1997 Industrial Project Quality Award (Dutch furniture recognition).

Korschann, Charles (b. Karl Korschann 1872–)

Moravian sculptor, decorator, and medalist; born Brünn (now Brno, Czech Republic).

Training Schools of fine art in Vienna, Berlin, and Copenhagen.
Biography 1894–1906, Korschann lived in Paris; 1906–14, in Berlin and Frankfurt; 1914–19, in Crakow. He returned to Brno and became a professor. While in Paris, he executed a series of small Art Nouveau bronzes, many cast by the foundry Lochet; became known for his portrait busts of famous people, including one (1904) of Alphonse Mucha for the Moravské Zemské Muzeum in Brno. His wares included clocks, inkwells, centerpieces, and lighting, in bronze and plaster.
Exhibitions Work included in various venues, including Salons of Société des Artistes Français 1894–1905.
Bibliography *Allgemeines Lexikon der bildenden Künstler*, 1955. Cat., G. Woeckel, *Jugendstilsammlung*, Kassel: Staatliche Kunstsammlungen, 1968. Yvonne Brunhammer et al., *Art Nouveau Belgium, France*, Houston: Institute for the Arts, Rice University, 1976. Alastair Duncan, *Art Nouveau and Art Déco Lighting*, New York: Simon & Schuster, 1978.

Korsmo, Arne (1890–1968)

Norwegian interior, furniture, and exhibition designer, and teacher.

Training Norges Tekniskne Högskole, Trondheim.
Biography 1929, Korsmo set up his own design office; 1936–56, was the director, Statens Håndverks -og Kunstindustriskole, Oslo; from

1956, a professor, Norges Tekniske Högskole; 1953, designed cutlery by J. Tostrup in Oslo and wood and bent-metal tubular furniture.
Exhibitions/citations 1954 (10th) Triennale di Milano. Designed both Norwegian sections at 1937 *Exposition Internationale des Arts et Techniques dans la Vie Moderne*, Paris, and 1954 (10th) Triennale di Milano; received a grand prize and gold medal at the latter.
Bibliography Cat., David Revere McFadden (ed.), *Scandinavian Modern Design 1880–1980*, New York: Abrams, 1982. Fredrik Wildhagen, *Norge i Form*, Oslo: Stenersen, 1988: 102.

Kortzau, Ole (1939–)
Danish designer.

Training To 1966, Arkitektskole, Det Kongelige Danske Kunstakademiet, Copenhagen.
Biography Kortzau worked for architects Palle Suenson 1966–67, Knud Holscher 1967–68, and Arup Associates in London 1970–72; from 1973, has been active in his own design studio in Copenhagen and since has been primarily active in fine-art graphics; however, from c. 1978, has designed for Royal Copenhagen Porcelain Manufactory, Georg Jensen Sølvsmedie, Holmegård Glasværk, Kvadrat textiles, Ege Axminster, and Hvalsø, and also furniture.
Bibliography Cat., *Georg Jensen Silversmithy: 77 Artists, 75 Years*, Washington: Smithsonian, 1980. Jennifer Hawkins Opie, *Scandinavia: Ceramics and Glass in the Twentieth Century*, New York: Rizzoli, 1989.

Koskinen, Harri (1970–)
Finnish designer; born Karstula.

Training Taideteollinen korkeakoulu, Helsinki.
Biography Koskinen's work has included 1996 Atlas candle-holder collection, 1999 Klubi drink glasses, 2000 Muotka two-part vase, and lanterns in the Relations range by Iittala glass; 2000 Koskinen outdoor-cooking utensils by Hackman Tools; Air air-tight food containers by Arabia. His best-known work may be 1995–96 Block lamp and subsequent 2000 Mini Block lamp (made of two separatable solid sections of clear glass) by Design House Stockholm. Other clients: Issey Miyake and Schmidinger Modul. 2000, he established his own design company Friends of Industry Ltd.
Exhibitions/citations Work included in *Generation X: Young Nordic Design*, traveling the world from 2000; *Design World 2000*, Taideteollisuusmuseo, Helsinki. 2000 Young Designer of the Year, Finland. For Block lamp: 1998 Excellent Swedish Design 1998; 1999 Design Plus award, Ambiente fair, Frankfurt; 1999 Best New Products award, *Accent on Design* exhibition, New York International Gift Fair.

Kosta Boda
Swedish glass manufacturer.

History Early 18th century, the forests of fir and birch trees used in glass-furnaces attracted glassmakers to the Swedish villages of Boda, Johansfors, and Åfors. 1742, a glass factory was established and named for county governors A. Koskull and Bogislaus Stål von Holstein; the main product was window glass made by German craftspeople. It soon became Sweden's leading producer of household glass. Boda was founded in 1864, Åfors in 1876, both by glassblowers from Kosta. From the turn of 19th century, designers included Gunnar Wennerberg, Alf Wallander, Edvin Ollers, and Elis Bergh. c. 1900, Kosta commissioned Wennerberg to design carved cameo-glass vessels. Kosta Boda produced a much-copied design for a drinking glass with a bubble incorporated into its thick base, produced in 1938 as the Pippi glass. 1950, Vicke Lindstrand (formerly of Orrefors) became the artistic director. From 1953, notable artwares were designed by Lindstrand, Erik Höglund, Ulrica Hydman-Vallien, Bertil Vallien, Ann Wärff (later Ann Worff), Goran Wärff, Signe Persson-Merlin, and Gunnel Sahlin. 1970, Boda Nova was established to produce ceramics, textiles, cork, fireproof glass, and stainless-steel goods. Prior (1946), Kosta, Boda, and Åfors merged; 1970, Kosta Boda was renamed Åforsgruppen; 1972, acquired by Johansfors; 1975, amalgamated into Upsala-Ekeby and renamed Kosta Boda; 1977, it acquired Skruf and Måleräs Glasbruk from Royal Krona; 1981, established Boda Smide forging department; 1983, was acquired by Proventus; 1990, further consolidated, with Orrefors to form Orresfors Kosta Boda. 1997, Orrefors Kosta Boda, BodaNova-Höganäs Keramik, and Venini amalgamated to form Royal Scandinavia. However, in 2000, Royal Scandinavia was bought by an investment group and eventually dismantled into various reorganized entities.
Exhibitions/citations Work shown internationally, beginning with 1900 *Exposition Universelle* (numerous individual, group and individual designer awards), Paris. With Orrefors, work subject of 1975 *Adventure in Swedish Glass: 16 Artists from Kosta-Boda and Orrefors*, sponsored by Svenska Slöjdföreningen, Australian Gallery Directors' Conference; 1986 exhibition, Kosta Boda Djurgården, Stockholm (catalog below).
Bibliography Jennifer Hawkins Opie, *Scandinavia: Ceramics and Glass in the Twentieth Century*, New York: Rizzoli, 1989. Arteus. Margareta Arteus (ed.), *Kosta 250: 1742–1992, 250 Years of Craftsmanship*, Kosta: Kosta Boda, 1992. Ralf Turander et al., *Gunnel Sahlin & Kosta Boda*, Stockholm: Tåg, 2000. Leslie Jackson, *20th Century Factory Glass*, London: Octopus, 2000.
> See Royal Scandinavia.

Kotarbinski, Mieczylas (1890–1943)
Polish painter, graphic artist, and interior designer.

Training In fine art, Warsaw and Cracow.
Exhibitions 1920s, Kotarbinski taught at School of Applied Arts, Warsaw; designed study/office (produced by Michel Herodeck of Warsaw) in a version of Cubism, using rare Polish woods, at 1925 *Exposition Internationale des Arts Décoratifs et Industriels Modernes*, Paris.
Bibliography Maurice Dufrêne, *Ensembles mobiliers*, Paris: Charles Moreau, 1925; Woodbridge, Suffolk: Antique Collectors' Club, 1989.

Kotěra, Jan (1871–1923)
Moravian architect; born Brünn (now Brno, Czech Republic).

Training Baugewerbeschule, Pilsen (now Plzeň, Czech Republic); 1894–97 under Otto Wagner, Akademie der bildenden Künste, Vienna.
Biography Kotěra's 1906–12 municipal museum at Königgrätz (now Hradec Králové, Czech Republic) was the first structure in Europe to apply the ideas of Frank Lloyd Wright. 1900–10, Kotěra exerted a major influence on modern architecture in Czechoslovakia; became a member of the Siebener Club in Vienna, an early association of Wiener Sezessionists. 1898–1910, he was a professor at Akademie Výtvarných Umení (academy of fine arts), Prague, and 1910–23, at Vysoká Škola Uměleckoprůmyslová (VŠUP, academy of arts, architecture, and design), Prague. 1898–1903, the students in his academy studio pursued glass design. His 1903 punchbowl, refined in 1910, is a milestone in modern glass design. 1898, Kotěra designed railway-carriage interiors by Wagon and Tender Company Franz Ringhoffer & Smichow (Waggon- und Lokomotiv-Fabrik Franz Ringhoffer & Smichow—now Tatra) in Prague, and, subsequently, a number of private and public interiors, including restaurants and banks. His furniture designs combined a modernist attitude with a master's conception of detail. His buildings included 1905–16 water tower, Prague; 1905–07 National House, Prossnitz (now Prostějov); 1913 Lemberger Palais, Lwów (now in Poland). He died in Prague.
Bibliography Jan Kotěra, *Práce má a mých žáků 1898–1901* (me and my pupils' work 1898–1901), Vienna, 1901: 168. Cat., *Czechoslovakia Glass 1350–1980*, New York: Dover, 1981. Vladimír Šlapeta, *Czech Functionalism*, London: Architectural Association, 1987: 8. Cat., *Prague, 1900–1938: capitale secrète des avants-gardes*, Dijon: Musée des Beaux-Arts, 1997.

Kotík, Jan (1916–2002)
Czech painter, and industrial and glassware designer; born Turnau (now Turnov); son of artist illustrator Pravoslav Kotík.

Training 1936–41 under Benda, Vysoká Škola Uměleckoprůmyslová (VŠUP, academy of arts, architecture, and design), Prague.
Biography Kotík produced free-blown forms made at the Plastic Art Center of the glassworks at Nový Bor. 1949–64, his work, sometimes engraved by Čestmír Čejnar, showed an advanced sense of the possibilities of glass He was active at Nový Bor at the same time as René Roubíček in off-hand-shaped (tubular mouth-blown) glass, engraved glass, and glass panels in dramatic three-dimensional forms; particularly in 1960s, brought the Abstract Expressionism of the current fine art to glass engraving. He has been more recognized as a highly active painter; was a member of artists' guild Group 42 and of Sdružení Éeských Umìlcù Grafiku/Hollar (SÈUG = society of Czech graphic artists/Hollar); 1974, cofounded the Systhema group. His early period is linked with the civilization programme of Group 42 and is based on the post-Cubist stylization of reality; from 1992, was a member, Akademie der Künste, Berlin; died in Berlin, where he had lived from 1969.
Exhibitions/citations Work shown at 1937 *Exposition Internationale*

des Arts et Techniques dans la Vie Moderne (bronze medal), Paris; 1958 *Exposition Universelle et Internationale de Bruxelles (Expo '58)* (diploma of honor; showed stained-glass panel *Glassmakers)*; 1957 (11th); 1960 (12th) editions of Triennale di Milano. Paintings subject of 1984 exhibition, Albright-Knox Art Gallery, Buffalo (catalog below). 1966 scholarship, Cité Internationale des Arts, Paris.
Bibliography Cat., *Czechoslovakia Glass 1350–1980*, New York: Dover, 1981: 168. Cat., *Jan Kotik: The Painterly Object*, Buffalo: Buffalo Fine Arts Academy, 1984. Frederick Cooke, *Glass: Twentieth-Century Design*, New York: Dutton, 1986: 90.

Kovar, Zdenek (1917–)

Czech teacher and industrial designer; born Vsetin; active Zlín.

Training 1939–43 under Vincenc Makovsky, Vystudovala Střední Uměleckoprůmyslovou Škola (secondary school of applied arts), Gottwaldov (today Zlín, Slovakia).
Biography While a student at the Gottwaldov secondary school, Kovar worked with avant-garde sculptor Makovsky (1900–1966) on the design of R50 lathe machines for which Kovar designed the control levers. Kovar also designed the handles of various tools, particularly for the industry of shoe manufacture, a trade in which he had originally trained. After graduation, he became an industrial designer at the Moravské Akciové Strojírny (MAS) engineering plant in Gottwaldov; from 1949, taught machine and tool design at Vystudovala Střední Uměleckoprůmyslovou Školou in Zlín, which eventually moved to Uherské Hradiště (today in the Czech Republic) and where he trained a number of first-generation (1950s) Czech industrial designers. He established a machine- and tool-design studio in Gottwaldov and, 1959, was on the faculty of the VŠUP in Prague, there to 1982, when he retired. Examples of his work are housed in the Národni Technické Muzeum in Prague.
Bibliography www.ntm.cz=ntext/ak-80-c.htm
> See Richtr, Alois.

Koz, Dafne (1964–)

Turkish designer; born Ankara; active Milan.

Training1981–85, Italian language and literature, Ankara Üniversitesi, Turkey; 1987–88, bachelor's degree and, 1989, master's degree in industrial design, Domus Academy, Milan.
Biography 1989, Koz settled in Milan, where, 1991–92, she worked with Ettore Sottsass in architecture/design studio of Sottsass Associati; 1992, established her own eponymous studio, working on interior planning commissions for private houses, 1991–92 furniture by Steel, 1993 David People and 1995 Aprido clothing stores in Turkey, 1993–94 tabletop objects by R-S-V-P, 1994 Aski tray by Ala Rossa, 1994 container by Cappellini, 1994 Tomo 40-piece office-furniture system by Alparda, 2001 Relax furniture with lighting and 2001 Diogene lamp system by FontanaArte, and 2001 Ray fruit basket by Alessi, 2002 drinking glasses and vases by Egizia, and others.
Exhibitions Work included in numerous venues in Europe, Asia, and South America.

KPM
> See Staatliche Porzellan-Manufaktur.

Kraechter, Andreas (1966–)
> See Trondesign.

Kralij, Niko (1921–)

Slovene furniture designer; born Zavrh.

Training 1946–52, Fakulteta za Arhitekturo, Univerza v Ljubljana; 1964–65, on a Ford Foundation scholarship in the US.
Biography 1952–60, Kralj worked at the Stol furniture factory, where he established the first industrial-design bureau in Yugoslavia; 1957, worked with Olaf Pir and Ilmari Tapiovaara; 1960–1992, taught, Fakulteta za Arhitekturo (faculty of architecture), Ljubljana; was an advisor to the United Nations; 1966–67, program developer, art advisor, designer, and development manager for several Israeli companies; lectured, University of Jerusalem. He has primarily designed office and school furniture, exploring folding systems for serial production, and over 60 chairs by Stol, including the well-known 1952 Rex chair (1955 folding version and subsequent versions); holds over 100 patents in furniture production; has written over 100 articles on design.
Exhibitions/citations Work included in a large number of venues. Many citations include the first award (1957) of Neue Gemeinschaft für Wohnkultur–Sozialwerk, Stuttgart; awards, 1957, 1963, 1965 Concorso Internazionale del Mobile, Cantù; medals, 1957 and 1973 editions of Triennale di Milano; several medals, 1960 and 1961 citations, *International Patent Exhibition*, Brussels; 1962 Prešeren Fund Award, Slovenia; award, 1972 International Furniture Competition, Barcelona; silver medal, 1973 Ideen-Erfindungen-Neuheiten Ausstellung (IENA, product-invention fair), Nuremberg.
Bibliography M. Murko and Niko Kralj, *Industrijsko oblikovanje*, Belgrade, 1970

Kramer, Ferdinand (1898–1985)

German architect and furniture designer; active Frankfurt.

Training 1919, Bauhaus, Weimar; 1919–22, in architecture in Munich.
Biography 1920, Kramer became a member of the Deutscher Werkbund; from 1925 under Ernst May, worked at the Hochbauamt building-construction office in Frankfurt, where, subsequently, he became the artistic director. 1925–26 Kramer-Ofen (Kramer-stove) was produced by Buderus. He managed the municipal architecture department of Frankfurt and designed *typenmöbel* (standardized furniture) by Hausrat for new housing developments. Another example, a diminished-size version of his 1927 black-lacquered bentwood side chair, produced by Thonet, was installed in the Frankfurt elementary schools as a standard model. 1938, he moved to the US and worked in the design studio of Norman Bel Geddes and office of architects Kahn & Jacobs, both New York; 1946, became a member, American Institute of Architects (AIA); designed Rainbelle furniture range produced 1948–51; 1952, returned to Germany and became the director, architecture department, Universität Frankfurt.
Exhibitions Work subject of 1991–92 exhibition, originating at Museum für Gestaltung, Zurich, traveling to Deutscher Werkbund in Frankfurt and Bauhaus in Dessau (catalog below).
Bibliography Ferdinand Kramer, 'Die Thonet Industrie,' *Die Form*, no. IV, 1929. Barbie Campbell-Cole and Tim Benton (eds.), *Tubular Steel Furniture*, London: The Art Book Company, 1979: 12. Cat., *The Bauhaus: Masters and Students*, New York: Barry Friedman, 1988. Cat., Claude Lichtenstein (ed.), *Ferdinand Kramer, der Charme des Systematischen: Architektur, Einrichtung, Design*, Zurich: Museum für Gestaltung, 1991.

Kramer, Frisco (1922–)

Dutch designer.

Biography Kramer was influential in the Netherlands as an industrial and furniture designer and member of movements and groups such as the Goed Wonen foundation of 1950s, which was involved in the restoration of materials and housing after World War II. Inspired by the work of the Eameses in the US, he designed molded-plywood and steel chairs by De Cirkel, including 1953 Revolt chair. 1950s, taught popular courses, Academie van Beeldende Kunsten, the Hague; designed industrial products such as 1958 Davoronde oil heater by Davo; 1963, cofounded Total Design group, which he left in 1967. He designed 1972 Mehes office-furniture range by Ahrend/Oda and 1986 experimental seat/bed unit by De Waal. The Mehes system (acronym of Mobility, Efficiency, Humanization, Environment, and Standardization) was an open-plan office system similar to Robert Propst's 1968 Action Office by Herman Miller.
Exhibitions 1954 Triennale di Milano (Revolt chair, a metal table, and a hanging cupboard). Work subject of 1977–78 exhibition, Stedelijk Museum, Amsterdam (catalog below).
Bibliography Cat., *Stoelen*, Delft: Technische Hochschule, 1974. Cat., Wil Bertheux et al., *Friso Kramer*, Amsterdam: Stedelijk Museum, 1978. Klaus-Jürgen Sembach, *Neue Möbel*, Stuttgart: Hatje Cantz, 1982. Gert Staal and Hester Wolters, *Holland in Vorm: Vormgeving in Nederland 1945–1987*, 's-Gravenhage: Stichling Holand in Vorm, 1987. Auction cat., *Modernes Design Kunsthandwerk nach 1945*, Munich: Quittenbaum, 1 June 2002: lots 260–63.

Krásná Jizba Družstevní Práce (aka KJ) (cooperative work's the beautiful room)

Czech design studio.

History Active 1927–48, Krásná Jizba Družstevní Práce—or KJ—was established by the publishing house Družstevní Práce to sell arts and crafts, decorative arts, graphic design, and objects for the home. Its first director was painter Emanuel Frinta. From 1929, Ladislav Sutnar was its artistic director. KJ was influential in encouraging the accep-

Frisco Kramer. Revolt chair. 1954. Painted steel and black plastic, 31 5/8 x 17 3/4 x 16 3/4" (80.4 x 45.2 x 42.5cm). Mfr.: Horgen-Glarus Möbelfabrik, Switzerland. Courtesy Quittenbaum Kunstauktionen, Munich.

tance of modern design, partly through the magazine *Panorama*, co-edited by Sutnar and publicity photographer Josef Sudek. Late 1920s, KJ began a successful collaboration with a group of young designers and artists. 1928 *Exhibition of Contemporary Culture* (similar to 1927 *Weissenhofsiedlung* exhibition, Stuttgart) in Brünn (now Brno) was an important turning-point. KJ sold designs by Sutnar, Ludvika Smrčková, Bohumil Južnič, Ladislav Žák, Antonín Kybal, Jan Vaněk, Jan Emil Koula, and others; lighting fixtures produced by the Inwald firm; tubular-steel furniture designed by Marcel Breuer, produced by Thonet-Mundus; and textiles, ceramics, and lighting from the Bauhaus. From 1936, KJ was located in central Prague in a Functionalist building at Národní Třída 36; 1948, was amalgamated with the Center for Art and Folk Crafts and lost its commitment to modern design, or new approaches to design.
Bibliography Alena Adlerová, *České užité umění 1918–1938*, Prague: Odeon, 1983.

Krasnik, Antoinette
Austrian painter and designer; active Vienna.

Training Under Koloman Moser, Kunstgewerbeschule, Vienna.
Biography While at Kunstgewerbeschule, Krasnik designed glass, porcelain, silver, and jewelry; with Jutta Sika and Robert Holubetz, was considered to be of the Schule Moser (Koloman Moser's followers/students). She designed silver by Alexander Sturm, including 1902 cigarette case with a stylized dragonfly in blue *plique-à-jour* enamel; rendered the circular stencil-applied pattern of Jutta Sika's well-known 1901–02 porcelain by Wiener Porzellanmanufaktur Josef Böck.
Exhibitions 1902–03 winter exhibition (cigarette case by Sturm), Österreichisches Museum für Kunst und Industrie, Vienna.
Bibliography Annelies Krekel-Aalberse, *Art Nouveau and Art Déco Silver*, New York: Abrams, 1989.

KRD (Kitchen Rogers Design)
British design consultancy, located London.

History 1997, Kitchen and Rogers established KRD. Shona Kitchen (1968–) has studied furniture design, department of interior design, Glasgow School of Art. Ab Rogers (1968–) completed the City & Guilds advanced cabinetmaking course, Royal College of Art, London. KRD's work has includes 1999 Responsive Space interactive installation, Kelvingrove Gallery, Glasgow; Naked'interactive living room, Collins, as part of the 1999 Glasgow City of Architecture initiative; domestic interiors; new office of RCN agency, London; 2001 Comme des Garçons shop, Paris; *Futures and Derivates Exhibitions*, Barbican Centre, London; exhibition stand of the Deutsche Börse; two exhibition stands at *Spectrum 98* (Royal College of Art furniture fair); the set of a TV cookery program; London Beach Store (sports equipment), London; 2000 Monster fiberglass three-place seat by Edra.
Bibliography www.edra.com.

Krebs, Nathalie (1895–1978)
Danish civil engineer and ceramicist; born Århus.

Training Civil engineering, Danmarks Tekniske Højskole, Copenhagen.
Biography 1929 with Gunnar Nylund, Krebs set up stoneware pottery studio Nylund og Krebs in Copenhagen. 1930, Nyland left and Krebs assumed management of the works, naming it Saxbo and collaborating with Eva Stæhr-Nielsen from 1932. Krebs went on to develop dynamic relationships with Stæhr-Nielsen and Edith Bruun Sonne, who had been under contract at Saxbo 1938–39. Krebs pursued oriental-influenced glazes, and Stæhr-Nielsen designed the shapes, both contributing to what became known as the 'Saxbo style.' 1968, Saxbo closed. Krebs died in Copenhagen.
Exhibitions/citations Work included in 1954–57 *Design in Scandinavia*, touring the US; 1956–59 *Neue Form aus Dänemark*, touring Germany; 1958 *Formes Scandinaves*, Musée des Arts Décoratifs, Paris; 1960–61 *The Arts of Denmark*, touring the US. Gold medal (to Saxbo), 1957 (11th) Triennale di Milano; others.
Bibliography Cat., David Revere McFadden (ed.), *Scandinavian Modern Design 1880–1980*, New York: Abrams, 1982.Robin Hecht, *Scandinavian Art Pottery: Denmark and Sweden*, Atglen, Pa.: Schiffer, 1999.

Krehan, Max (1875–1925)
German ceramicist; born Thuringia.

Biography Apr. 1920, Krehan met Walter Gropius; 1920–25, taught pottery at the ceramics annex of the Bauhaus in Dornburg.
Bibliography Lionel Richard, *Encyclopédie du Bauhaus*, Paris: Somogy, 1985: 157. Cat., *Keramik am Bauhaus*, Berlin: Bauhaus-Archiv, 1989: 265.

Krejcar, Jaromír (1895–1949)
Czech architect, furniture designer, graphics artist, and architectural theoretician; born Hundsheim, Austria.

Training 1917–21 under Jan Kotěra, Akademie Výtvarných Umení (academy of fine arts), Prague.
Biography From 1922 to its close in 1931, Krejcar was a member of the Devětsil group and its leading architect; was editor of compendium *Život II* and journal *Disk*; 1922, worked in office of architect Josef Gočár; 1923, set up his own office in Prague. He was the Bauhaus representative in Czechoslovakia and a friend of Karel Teige. Krejcar designed 1924 and 1926 suburban house in Prague-Zbraslav, of Devětsil chairperson Vladislav Vančura; 1927 reconstruction of Fromek's Odeon publishing house, Prague; 1927–28 reconstruction of Teige's flat with interiors at 14 Črnî St., Prague; 1926–27 building (with his wife Milena Jesenská) at 35 Spálené St., Prague; family house of German writer Brete Reiner, who lived in Prague. The Reiner house featured many modern innovations, including built-in bookcases and cupboards, a three-part couch with drawers for bedding, colored carpets, and upholstery in a simple geometrical motif; it also featured Krejcar tables, armchairs, and swiveling chairs by a furniture company in Sudoměřice. An example of Devětsil's industrial/nautical style can be seen in Krejcar's 1925 street wing of the store Olympic. After 1925, he pursued Constructivist and Bauhaus approaches; 1933–35, was active in USSR; 1946–48, was a professor of architecture, České Vysoké Školy Technické (Czech technical university), Brno; 1948, settled in London, where he lectured at Architectural Association. He died in London.
Exhibitions 1923 Bauhaus exhibition, Weimar; 1927 exhibition of OSA group, Moscow. Designed the Czech pavilion at 1937 *Exposition Internationale des Arts et Techniques dans la Vie Moderne*, Paris.
Bibliography Karel Teige, *Práce Jaromíra Krejcara, Václav Petr*, Prague, 1933. Jaromír Krejcar, *Lázeňský dům* (spa hotel), Prague: Knihovna Lazreňské Techniky, 1933. Cat., *Devětsil: Czech Avant-*

Garde Art, Architecture, and Design of the 1920s and 30s, Oxford Museum of Modern Art and London Design Museum, 1990. Cat., *Prague, 1900–1938: capitale secrète des avants-gardes*, Dijon: Musée des Beaux-Arts, 1997.

Krenchel, Herbert (Danish, 1922–)
See Ørskov & Co. A/S.

Kriege, Jan (1884–1944)

Dutch sculptor and silversmith; active Woerden.

Training Apprenticeship, workshop of C.J. Begeer, Utrecht.
Biography 1919, Kreige set up his own workshop; from 1932, taught metalwork, Instituut voor de Kunstnijverheid, Amsterdam.
Bibliography Annelies Krekel-Aalberse, *Art Nouveau and Art Déco Silver*, New York: Abrams, 1989.

Kriptonite Italia

Italian lighting and clock firm; located Peschiera Borromeo.

History 1985, Kriptonite Italia was founded to specialize in production of inexpensive but high-quality goods that combine cutting-edge design and functionality. The firm uses aluminum as its main material for the manufacture of domestic and public clocks; more recently, has made book shelves, waste bins, and other small items; credits no designers; exports 45% of its production.

Kristalunie

Dutch glass firm; located Maastricht.

History 1827, Petrus L. Regout set up a glass-cutting works in Maastricht. 1838, the firm began manufacturing its own glass, mainly tableware. c. 1850, its wares were angular and decorated with vertical faceting. Its services, that became more elaborately aesthetic after 1890, included the Model 22. 1925, Regout and his son's firm Stella merged to form Kristalunie. Commissioned designers included architect Ed. Cuypers in c. 1927, architect J. de Meijer in c. 1927, Jan Eisenloeffel in c. 1928, P. Zwart 1927–29, and G.M.E. Bellefroid (for the Stramino drinking glass set) in c. 1939. Regout's first full-time designer was graphic artist W.J. Rozendaal (who had worked at the sister company De Sphinx from 1924–28) at Kristalunie 1928–33 and part-time 1933–37. After his departure, Rozendaal also created some designs 1937–38. The firm experienced growth after World War II, and became part of the Vereenigde Glasfabrieken; from 1978, produced only packaging glass (for beverage, etc., firms).
Bibliography Cat., *Industry and Design in the Netherlands, 1850/1950*, Amsterdam: Stedelijk Museum, 1985: 190–95.

Kristiansen, Bo (1944–)

Danish ceramicist.

Training Kunsthåndværkerskolen, Copenhagen.
Biography 1968, Kristiansen set up a studio in Gudhjem; 1979, relocatied to Copenhagen; created stoneware vessels, some calling on the application of typographic (letters) images.
Exhibitions Work included in 1969, 1973, and 1980 exhibitions, Bornholms Museum, Copenhagen; 1973 exhibition, Det Danske Kunstindustrimuseum, Copenhagen; 1971 *International Ceramics*, London; 1975–77 *Dansk Miljø*, touring Eastern Europe; 1981 *Danish Ceramic Design*, University Park, Pennsylvania; 1982 *Scandinavian Modern Design 1880–1980*, Cooper-Hewitt National Design Museum, New York (catalog below). Work subject of exhibitions at Galerie Inart, Amsterdam, 1980; Galerie der Kunsthandverk, Hamburg, 1981.
Bibliography Cat., David Revere McFadden (ed.), *Scandinavian Modern Design 1880–1980*, New York: Abrams, 1982.

Kristiansen, Kai (1929–)

Danish furniture designer.

Training To 1950 under Kaare Klint, Det Kongelige Danske Kunstakademi, Copenhagen.
Biography From 1949, Kristiansen was a journeyman cabinetmaker; 1955, set up his own design workshop; 1937–69, designed furniture by Magnus Olesen in Roslev; other times, by others.
Bibliography Frederik Sieck, *Nutidig Dansk Møbeldesign – en kortfattet illustreret beskrivelse*, Copenhagen: Bondo Gravesen, 1981.

Krizman, Tomislav (1882–1955)

Croatian graphic designer, product designer, and teacher; born Orlovac.

Training 1902–05, Kunstgewerbeschule, Vienna; 1905–07, Akademie der bildende Künste, Vienna.
Biography On completion of his schooling, Krizman returned to Zagreb and became a graphics artist, graphics designer, product designer, and scenographer. 1908, he cofounded the Meduli arts association; 1911, established a private school of arts and crafts; from 1912, taught at Škola Úžitkového Vývarníctva (school of arts and crafts); 1915, cofounded The Spring Salon exhibition venue; from 1922, was professor at Skola za Umjetnost i Obrt (college of arts and crafts, now Akademija Likovnih Umjetnosti—academy of fine arts); 1925, founded the association Djelo (work of art) for promotion of traditional crafts within industrial production; from 1934, was art director, Muzej Moderne Umjetnosti (gallery of modern art), Zagreb; 1920s and 1930s, wrote a number of articles on the significance of arts and crafts in a local context and the book *On Graphic Art* (1952) and others. From 1911, he designed ceramics, porcelain, stoneware, glass, and paper objects, as well as furniture. Also designed book covers, stage sets, and posters, particularly for plays and concerts. His mid-1920s work was influenced by Josef Hoffmann and the Wiener Werkstätte, illustrated by Krizman's coffee and tea cups by Pfeiffer & Lowenstein in Czechoslovakia. Later, in 1920s, Krizman moved toward the Art Déco style. The Association 'Djelo' Krizman was established to recognize traditional folk ornament expressed on objects primarily by local Croatian manufacturers.
Exhibitions Work included in numerous exhibitions in Zagreb. Was art director of Pavilion of Kingdom of Serbs, Croats, and Slovenes at 1925 *Exposition Internationale des Arts Décoratifs et Industriels Modernes*, Paris. Work subject of 1954 and 1955 exhibitions, Arts Pavilion, Zagreb.
Bibliography Cat., Smiljka Domac-Ceraj, *Tomislav Krizman*, Zagreb: Arts Pavilion, 1995. Fedja Vukic, *A Century of Croatian Design*, Zagreb: Meandar, 1998.

Krog, Arnold (1856–1931)

Danish architect and ceramicist.

Training 1874–80, architecture, Det Kongelige Danske Kunstakademi, Copenhagen.
Biography 1878–81 while a student, Krog worked on the interior decoration and interior repairs of the Frederiksborg Palace in Hillerød; 1883, worked in the design office of architect Henrik Hagemann; from 1884, worked at Royal Copenhagen Porcelain Factory, where he was artistic director 1885–1916 and developed a style of underglaze decoration.
Exhibitions Work shown at 1888 *Scandinavian Exhibition of Industry, Agriculture and Art*, Copenhagen; 1889 and 1900 editions of *Exposition Universelles*, Paris.
Bibliography Cat., David Revere McFadden (ed.), *Scandinavian Modern Design 1880–1980*, New York: Abrams, 1982. Jennifer Hawkins Opie, *Scandinavia: Ceramics and Glass in the Twentieth Century*, New York: Rizzoli, 1989.

Krogh, Henrik (1886–1927)

Swedish textile designer, metalworker, and ceramicist.

Biography Krogh was active as a designer of ceramics and metalwork. Some of his tapestries were woven by Märta Måås-Fjetterström in her workshop in Båstad, just north of Malmö, which she began in 1919.
Bibliography Cat., David Revere McFadden (ed.), *Scandinavian Modern Design 1880–1980*, New York: Abrams, 1982.

Krohn, Lisa (1963–)

American industrial designer; born and active New York; also active Los Angeles.

Training 1984, under Rowena Reed Kostellow, bachelor of arts degree, Brown University, Providence, R.I.; 1985–86 three-dimensional form, New York,; 1998, master of fine arts degree, Cranbrook Academy of Art, Bloomfield Hills, Mich.
Biography 1985, Krohn worked at Smart Design in New York; 1985–87, editor at Industrial Designers Society of America, New York; 1987–88, designer and research consultant at Johnson & Johnson,

New York; 1988, designer and research consultant, Herman Miller Research, Ann Arbor, Mich.; 1988–89, designer in studio of Mario Bellini, Milan. 1989, Krohn became a founding partner of Abel Industrial design collaborative, New York, which made products, graphics, furniture, lighting, and interior and stage set designs for clients including NYNEX (New York telephone company, now Verizon), Estée Lauder, George Kovacs Lighting, Alessi, Steelcase Design Partnership, and Ultradata; 1988, visiting lecturer, University of Monterrey, Mexico; from 1989, a visiting critic, industrial design department, Parsons School of Design, New York. Her best-known products include 1988 wrist communicator, 1994 Tuffet stool, Cyberdesk head-attached communicator, and 1997 Phonebook answering machine; has designed lighting, furniture, and textiles for Columbia Pictures, Disney, Estée Lauder, Herman Miller, Knoll, Steuben. From 1992, she has taught, environmental-design department, Center College of Design, Los Angeles; Southern California Institute of Architecture, and California Institute of the Arts.
Exhibitions/citations 1995 *Mutant Materials in Contemporary Design*, The Museum of Modern Art, New York, and touring. Grand prize, 1987 Forma Finlandia prize; 1988 Fulbright Scholarship; 1994 grant, National Endowment for the Arts, US; 1996 Young Designer Award, Brooklyn Museum; 1997 Top 40 Innovators, *I.D.* magazine; 1997 Chrysler Design Award.
Bibliography Cat., Paola Antonelli, *Mutant Materials in Contemporary Design*, New York: The Museum of Modern Art/Abrams, 1995. Cat., R. Craig Miller (intro.), *U.S. Design 1975–2000*, Munich: Prestel, 2002.

Krohn, Pietro (1840–1905)
Danish ceramicist.

Biography 1885–97, Krohn was the artistic director, Bing & Grøndahl Porcelænsfabrik, Copenhagen; was also active as a painter, costume designer, and illustrator; became the first director, Det Danske Kunstindustrimuseum, Copenhagen.
Bibliography Cat., David Revere McFadden (ed.), *Scandinavian Modern Design 1880–1980*, New York: Abrams, 1982.

Krol, Leo (1955–)
> See Lumiance.

Kroll, Boris (1913–1991)
American textile designer; born Buffalo, N.Y.

Training Apprenticeship under a furniture designer and his brother Hammond Kroll.
Biography 1930 with wife Helen, Boris Kroll established a printed-fabric business using handscreening methods; 1938, established Cromwell Designs, which at first produced modern furnishing fabrics on a hand loom, with a bathtub for dyeing yarns; 1939, began using power looms; 1946, set up Boris Kroll Fabrics in New York; used cotton and novelty spun rayon; 1956, was invited by the government of India to advise on updating hand-loom production. The firm expanded its original specialization to fabrics woven on a jacquard loom, where complex patterns were produced for the mass market. By 1991, the firm had 16 showrooms in the US and a large manufacturing plant in Paterson, N.J.
Exhibitions/citations Work shown at 1983–84 *Design Since 1945*, Philadelphia Museum of Art (catalog below). Work subject of 1977 and 1980 exhibitions, East Hampton, N.Y. and Fashion Institute of Technology, New York (catalogs below). 13 citations at 1953 *Good Design* exhibition/award, The Museum of Modern Art, New York, and Chicago Merchandise Mart. To Kroll himself: 1971 honorary degree in textiles, Philadelphia College of Textiles and Science.
Bibliography 'A New Home for the House of Boris Kroll,' *Interiors*, vol. 111, Dec. 1951: 115–18, 180–81. Cat., *Boris Kroll: Exhibition of Jacquard Woven Tapestries Designed by Master Weaver*, East Hampton, N.Y.: Guild Hall, East Hampton, 1977. Cat., *Boris Kroll—Tapestries and Textiles*, 1980. Cat., Kathryn B. Hiesinger and George H. Marcus III (eds.), *Design Since 1945*, Philadelphia: Philadelphia Museum of Art, 1983. 'Celebrating Design Innovation,' *Designers West*, Apr. 1991: 32. Obituary, 'Boris Kroll, 77, Owner of a Fabrics Company,' obituary, *The New York Times*, 9 June 1991.

Krondahl, Hans (1929–)
Swedish textile designer.

Training 1955–60, Konstfackskolan, Stockholm.
Biography 1960, Krondahl set up a studio in Brösarp; 1959–75, was a consultant designer to Nordiska Kompaniet, where he created designs for pictorial weavings and tapestries and printed furnishing fabrics in cotton, velvet, and fiberglass. His motifs were produced in large geometric and stylized figurative patterns and bright colors. 1974–75, Krondahl taught and worked in Scandinavia and the US; 1975–77, designer for Argos in Oak Grove Village, Ill.; 1979–80, was a UNIDO (United Nations) advisor in textile design and product development in Indonesia. From 1981, he taught, Konstfackskolan, Stockholm; Kunstindustriskole, Oslo; Konstindustriskolan, Gothenburg.
Exhibitions/citations Work subject of 1982 exhibition, Museet Kulturhuset, Borås. 1965 Lunning Prize.
Bibliography Cat., *Hans Krondahl*, Borås, Sweden: Museet Kulturhuset, 1982. 'Thirty-four Lunning Prize-Winners,' *Mobilia*, no. 146, Sept. 1967. Charles S. Talley, *Contemporary Textile Art of Scandinavia*, Stockholm: Carmina, 1982: 73–76. Hans Krondahl, 'Swedish Design,' *Handwoven*, Mar.–Apr.1983: 29–33. Cat., Kathryn B. Hiesinger and George H. Marcus III (eds.), *Design Since 1945*, Philadelphia: Philadelphia Museum of Art, 1983. Cat., *The Lunning Prize*, Stockholm: Nationalmuseum, 1986: 162–65.

Kruithof, Patrick (1968–)
Dutch designer; born Naarden.

Training 1986–93, design section in industrial design engineering, Technische Universiteit, Delft; 1991–92, Elisava (Escola de Disseny Superior), Barcelona.
Biography 1994 with Eelco Rietveld, cofounded De Denktank design studio in Rotterdam; 1998, was an ecodesign consultancy to several small and large firms; 2001, founded The Moment Company, The Wish Balloon Experience, and The Real Marquis de Castagne Experience. Projects, some with production, have included 1995 Curva ruler, 1996 Penta exhibition system, 1996 Luce rubber lamp, 1998 Frozen fruitbowl, 1999 Firestarter for campfires, 2001 Queen Electric knitted lamp, and 2002 ceramics with a memory. From 1997, he has conducted research into various technologies and ecodevelopment, Fasal thermoplastic wood, Pragon thermoplastic starch, rubber-refuse applications for Vredestein Fietsbanden, and wooden-refuse application for Hunter Douglas.
Exhibitions Work included in 1996 *Re(f)use, Making the Most of What We Have*, Arango traveling exhibition; 1997 *Glamorous Green*, Material Connexion, New York; 1999 *RenewRecycleReuse*, Idée, Tokyo; 2000 *Replay*, Design Gallery Vivid, Rotterdam.

Krupp, Arthur (1856–1938)
Austrian designer; born Vienna.

Biography From 1879, Krupp was director of Berndorfer Metallwarenfabrik in Berndorf, where he realized silverwares designed by Walter Gropius, including bowls, compotes, and candlesticks.
Exhibitions Work shown at 1914 *Deutscher Werkbund-Ausstellung* (Gropius designs), Cologne.
Bibliography Annelies Krekel-Aalberse, *Art Nouveau and Art Déco Silver*, New York: Abrams, 1989 Cat., *Metallkunst*, Berlin: Bröhan-Museum, 1992: 20.

Kryptonite
> See Zane, Frank S. (1948–).

Kuckuck, Henner (1940–)
German designer and sculptor; born Berlin.

Training 1960–62, Fakultät Architektur, Technische Universität, Brunswick, Germany; 1962–68, sculpture, Hochschule für bildende Künste, Berlin (1968 master's studies under Hans Uhlman).
Biography Kuckuck was a public sculptor before 1990, when he became an industrial designer, primarily of furniture, active in New York.
Exhibitions/citations Work included in numerous group venues and subject of venues in New York. 1992 gold medal (for Spine chair) and 1994 Design Distinction Award, Annual Design Review, *I.D.* magazine; 1994 Felissimo Art and Design Award.
Bibliography Cat., R. Craig Miller (intro.), *U.S. Design 1975–2000*, Munich: Prestel, 2002.

Kundalini
Italian lighting and furniture firm; located Milan.

History Founded 1996, Kundalini S.r.l.—Corpi di Illuminazione Interiore primarily produces lighting fixtures in innovative and unusual

shapes; also makes furniture accessories; employs state-of-the-art technology/materials or manipulates traditional ones, while retaining a handicraft approach to production. Inventory has included Float Sutra daybed by Kundalinidesign.com, Soft Cube wooden stool by Room8, 1997 E.T.A.-Extra Terrestrial Angel floor lamp by Guglielmo Berchicci.
Bibliography Mel Byars, *50 Lights...*, Hove: RotoVision, 1997. Mel Byars, *50 Products...*, Hove: RotoVision, 1999.

Kudriashev, Ivan Alekseevich (1896–1970)

Russian artist and designer; born Moscow.

Training From 1913, Moscow Institute of Painting, Sculpture, and Architecture.
Biography For the first anniversary celebration in Moscow of the 1917 Russian Revolution, Kudriashev produced Agitprop designs for automobiles; 1920, participated in interior designs for Summer Red Army Theater and First Soviet Theater in Orenburg; 1920s, investigated luminosity and refractivity in painting and painted in the so-called Engineerist style associated with Kliment Redko (1897–1956).
Exhibitions Work included in 1922 *Erste Russische Kunstausstellung*, Berlin; 1925 *First State Traveling Exhibition of Paintings* from Moscow; 1925 (1st), 1926 (2nd), and 1928 (4th) exhibitions of Obshchestvo Khudozhnikov-Stankovistov (OST, exhibition society of easel artists), Moscow. 1928, stopped showing his work.
Bibliography Cat., Stephanie Barron and Maurice Tuchman, *The Avant-Garde in Russia, 1919–1930: New Perspectives*, Cambridge, Mass: MIT, 1980: 176. Cat., *The Great Utopia: The Russian and Soviet Avant-Garde, 1915–1932*, New York: Guggenheim Museum, 1992.

Kufus, Axel (1958–)

German designer and cabinetmaker; born Essen.

Training From 1977, apprenticeship in building and cabinetmaking, becoming a journeyman in 1979; 1983, master craftsman's certificate, Holzfachschule, Bad Wildungen; 1985–87, Hochschule der Künste, Berlin.
Biography 1979–82, Kufus worked with sculptor Richard Mühlemeier in Bischofsheim/Rhön and set up a wood and bronze workshop, producing his own designs; 1984–86, worked with sculptor Ulrike Holthöfer in Kassel, Düsseldorf, and Berlin, and experimented with furniture and objects; 1986–94, was co-owner of Crelle Werkstatt (woodshop) in Berlin, designing, producing, and marketing his own serially produced furniture; 1989–92 with Andreas Brandolini and Jasper Morrison, created projects for urban spaces through their firm called Utilism International; from 1990 with Sibylle Jans, has been co-owner of the Werkstudio in Berlin, designing products, interiors, exhibitions, and primarily furniture; from 1993, has been professor of product design, Bauhaus-Universität, Weimar. Work has included 1987 Mesa five-piece plywood table and, by Adus 1989 FNP System Regal 1:1 shelving system. Other clients have included Atoll, Cappellini, Magis, Nils Holger Moormann, Casawell Gruppe, and Ninkaplast.
Exhibitions/citations Work included in international venues. Received 1991 Red Dot award, Design Zentrum Nordrhein Westfalen, Essen; 2001 award, Industrie Forum Design (iF), Hanover; 2001 Good Design award, Chicago Athenaeum; 1998 Kölner Klopfer.
Bibliography Volker Albus and Christian Borngräber, *Design Bilanz*, Cologne: DuMont, 1992. Mel Byars, *50 Tables: Innovations in Design and Materials*, Hove: RotoVision, 1997. www.kufus.de.

Kukkapuro, Yrjö (1933–)

Finnish designer; born Viipuri.

Training 1954–58, Taideteollinen korkeakoulu, Helsinki
Biography 1959, Kukkapuro opened an office in Kauniainen; 1969–74, was a teacher in architecture department, Helsingin Teknillinen korkeakoulu; 1974–80, was a professor, Taideteollinen korkeakoulu, Helsinki, where he was the rector 1978–80; 1965, began calling on the use of plastics and, from 1980, was head designer of furniture firm Haimi and its successor Avarte; has designed site-specific furniture, though appropriate for general application. His best-known work is 1964 Karuselli 412/412J lounge chair in fiberglass on a pedestal base and leather upholstery by Haimi, still in production now by Avarte. Others by Avarte include 1964 Ateljee 810 lounge chair/sofa, 1966 Ventus bench, 1970–72 Remmi 817 lounge chair/sofa, 1981 sp 730 table, 1991 Sirkus desk chair, 1999 Sirkus ES desk chair.
Exhibitions/citations Work shown at 1959, 1964, and 1968 annuals of Suomen Taideteollisuusyhdistys (Finnish society of crafts and design); 1960 (12th) and 1968 (14th) editions of Triennale di Milano;

Yrjö Kukkapuro. Funktus 552 armchair. c. 1998. Tubular steel, birch plywood, and upholstery, l. 33 1/4 x w. 21 5/8 x d. 22 3/8" (85 x 55 x 57 cm). Mfr.: Avarte, Finland.

1962 50th Anniversary Gala of Ornamo (Finnish association of designers); 1963 *60 Years of Finnish Industrial Design*, Stockholm; 1964 and 1967 *Finlandia Industrial Design*, traveling Europe and US; 1966 *Vijftig Jaar Zitten*, Stedelijk Museum, Amsterdam; 1966 (1st) Eurodomus, Genoa; *Art of Living*, 1967 Salon of Société des Artistes Décorateurs, Paris; 1968 (2nd) Eurodomus, Turin; others (catalogs below); 1999 *5x5 Stoelen*, Museum voor Sierkunst en Vormgeving, Gent, 1999; 2003–06 *Scandinavian Design: Beyond the Myth*, traveling. Work subject of 1962 exhibition, Finnish Design Center; 1992 Scandinavian Design Center, Düsselforf.. Received 1966 Lunning Prize; 1970 Design Award, Finland; 1982 Artek Prize; 1983 Pro Finlandia award; 1984 award, Institute of Business Designers (IBD), US; 1995 Kaj Franck Design Prize; 2001 Best Selection, Design Zentrum Nordrhein Westfalen, Essen; 2002 member, Royal Society of Arts.
Bibliography Cat., Milena Lamarová, *Design a Plastické Hmoty*, Prague: Uměleckoprůmyslové Muzeum, 1972: 120. Cat., *Les assises du siège contemporain*, Paris: Musée des Arts Décoratifs, 1968. Robert A.M. Stern (ed.), *The International Design Yearbook*, New York: Abbeville, 1985/1986.

Kumbel
> See Hein, Piet (1905–1996).

Kunert, Heidemarie (1958–)

German industrial designer; born and active Berlin.

Training 1977–83, industrial design, Hochschule der Künste, Berlin.
Biography From 1983, Kunert has been an independent consultant designer; 1984–85, designed exhibitions, including the stand and corporate-identity program of the 'Big Tech' and Kaufhold; has coordinated workshops on corporate design; 1986 with Marina Donner, set up design office Amazonas Design in Berlin.
Exhibitions/citations Work shown at 1987–88 *Berlin Ways–Products and Design from Berlin* in Berlin, Zurich, Stockholm, and Barcelona. Received 1988 Mia Seeger Preis, Stuttgart.
Bibliography Cat., Design Center Stuttgart, *Women in Design: Careers and Life Histories Since 1900*, Stuttgart: Haus der Wirtschaft, 1989: 52–63.

Kunovská, Júlia (1949–)

Slovakian designer; born Košice; active Bratislava.

Training 1968–74, faculty of architecture, Slovenská Technická Uni-

verzita, Bratislava.
Biography Kunosova has designed interiors, exhibitions, furniture, tableware, textiles, and jewelry; 1990 with two others, opened the Gallery X for applied arts and design, Bratislava .
Exhibitions/citations Work included in 1984 *Design of the Century*, Prague, and 1999 World Competition of Arts and Crafts, Kanazawa, Japan. From 1990, work subject of several exhibitions. Received 1978, 1979, and 1980 gold medals (for furniture), International Fair of Industrial Products, Brno; 1979 first prize, Czechoslovak Competition of Upholstery Furniture; 1980 thematic and main prizes, International Triennial of Furniture, Poznan, Poland; 1986 prize (wood work) and honorable mention (textile work), International Biennial of Art and Crafts, Bratislava; 1996 award, World Crafts Council; honorable mention (for Torso bowl), 1999 World Competition of Arts & Crafts, Kanazawa, Japan.

Kupittaan Savi
Finnish ceramics factory.

History 1712, Kupittaan, Finland's oldest pottery, was founded as a brickworks in Kupittaa; 1915, began the production of domestic ceramics used primarily for experimentation involving acid-resistant ceramics and fire-resistant bricks. When designer Kerttu Suvanto-Vaajakallio was hired, the firm increased its production of table and kitchenwares and began exporting to the US and Germany; 1969, closed.
Award Silver medal for works by Laine Taitto, Linnea Lehtonen, and Marjukka Paasivirta at 1954 (10th) Triennale di Milano.
Bibliography Jennifer Hawkins Opie, *Scandinavia: Ceramics and Glass in the Twentieth Century*, New York: Rizzoli, 1989.

Kuppenheim, Louis
German enamel manufacturer; located Pforzheim.

Biography Late 19th century, Louis Kuppenheim (1814–1889) founded his eponymous firm, which became one of the leading enamelers in Germany. c. 1900, the workshop produced enameled pieces designed by Hans Christiansen of Darmstadt. Christiansen's objects included cigarette boxes and cases with enameled lids that showed a preference for colorful naturalistic motifs. Others, like women's powder compacts, liberally interpreted Alphonse Mucha images.
Bibliography Annelies Krekel-Aalberse, *Art Nouveau and Art Déco Silver*, New York: Abrams, 1989.

Kuramata, Shiro (1934–1991)
Japanese furniture and interior designer; son of a scientific-institute director, born Tokyo.

Training To 1952, woodworking, Municipal Polytechnic Secondary School, Tokyo; to 1956, Department of Living Design, Kuwazawa Institute of Design.
Biography 1954, Kuramata joined Teikokukizai furniture factory; from 1957, worked in the interior-design departments of major Japanese department stores, including San-Ai Co. promotion department, Matsuya store, Tokyo, in 1965; 1965, opened his own design office in Tokyo. His first noteworthy furniture was 1970 Revolving Cabinet. Commissions included interiors for Issey Miyake's clothing boutiques (1984 Paris, 1986 Tokyo, 1987 worldwide); Seibu store (1987 Tokyo); Lucchino Bar; and Caffe Oyx. From 1965, he designed more than 300 boutiques and restaurants. The Furniture in Irregular Form 1 and 2 wavy cabinets (by Furnishing and Decorating Department of Fujiko Manufacture and Sales in 1970 and by Cappellini from 1986) won him acclaim, while illustrating his quirky, surreal sense of humor and self-confessed love of drawers. Much of his early Japanese furniture was produced by Aoshima Shoten, Ishimaru, and Fijiko. His ultimate statement in high-tech romanticism, Blues in the Night table, has dozens of red diode tubes that glow inside transparent acrylic. His large 1972 lamps by Yamagiwa were made of milk-white plastic sheets, heated and hung over poles, creating naturally formed curves. From 1975, was a consultant for Mainichi Design Awards; 1988, bought 1927 house designed by Robert Mallet-Stevens for Joël and Jan Martell, rue Mallet-Stevens, Paris (and sold by his estate 1992); set up an office in the rue Royale, Paris; designed Copacabana woman's handbag. Working with the Memphis group and its director, Ettore Sottsass, 1981–83: 1981 Imperial three-part cabinets, 1983 Kyoto cement and glass side table, 1987 Sally side table with a broken-glass top. Other design work: 1972 lamp Fantôme, 1978 Marilyn Monroe chest of drawers by Lappelini, 1964 49 Drawers by Aoshima Shoten, 1968 Pyramid furniture and 1970 revolving cabinet by Ishimaru, 1976 glass chair for Mhoya Glass Shop, 1977 Solaris by Aoshima Shoten, 1983 Star Peace table by Ishimaru, 1985 Begin the Beguine chair homage to Josef Hoffmann, 1986 How High the Moon metal-mesh chair by Terada Tekkojo (later, by Vitra; two-person version sold at Bonham's, London, for £12,650, 1998 auction), 1986 Sing Sing armchair by XO, 1988 BK 86000 bar stool by Pastoe, 1988 Miss Blanche chair in clear acrylic resin with embedded paper roses by Ishimaru (sold at Christie's, London, for £46,000, 1997 auction), 1991 washstand by Rapsel. Kuramata took a minimalist approach to his furniture and interiors, reflecting traditional Japanese austerity, although the results combined Eastern and Western sensibilities and a self-confessed fascination with drawers. He brought a level of sophistication to Japanese design never before seen; was beloved by many peers and the press; generously embraced the efforts of fellow international designers; traveled widely. His studio is now managed by his wife.

Shiro Kuramata. Miss Blanche armchair. 1988. Paper flowers, acrylic resin, and aluminum, 36 7/8 x 24 7/8 x 20 1/4" (93.7 x 63.2 x 51.4 cm). Mfr: Ishimaru Co., Japan (1997). Gift of Agnes Gund in honor of Patricia Phelps de Cisneros. MoMA.

Exhibitions/citations Work shown in numerous exhibitions including 1978 *MA Espace/temps au Japon*, Musée des Arts Décoratifs, Paris, and various Memphis exhibitions. 1972 Mainichi Design Award, 1981 Japan Culture Design Award, 1990 Ordre des Arts et des Lettres. Work subject of 1996–99 exhibition in Tokyo, San Francisco, New York, Montreal, Paris, Vienna.
Bibliography *Memphis, the New International Style*, Milan: Electa, 1981. Cat., *The Works of Shiro Kuramata 1967–1981*, London: Aram Designs, 1981; Tokyo: Parco, 1981. Cat., *Kagu-mobilier japonais*, Tokyo: Shibaura Institute of Technology, 1985. 'Kuramata,' *City*, Sept. 1986. 'Les scènes des années 80,' *Beaux-Arts*, Apr. 1989. *Acquisitions arts décoratifs 1982–1990*, Paris: Fonds National d'Art Contemporain, 1991. Cat., Arata Isozaki et al., *Shiro Kuramata*, Tokyo: Foundation Arc-en-Ciel, 1996. Paola Antonelli (ed.), *Objects of Design: The Museum of Modern Art*, New York: The Museum of Modern Art, 2003: 166, 275, 269.

Kuramoto, Yoko (1950–)
Japanese glass designer.

Training To 1972, department of crafts and industrial design, Musashino Art University, Tokyo; 1980, Pilchuck School of Glass, Stanwood, Wash., US.
Biography From 1982, Kuramoto worked at Ito & Kuramoto Glass Studio, Yamanishi; 1986, was a designer at Martiglass.

Exhibitions Work has been included in numerous editions of *Glass in Japan*, Tokyo, from 1984; 1985 *New Glass in Japan*, Badisches Landesmuseum, Karlsruhe; 1988 *International Exhibition of Glass Craft*, Industrial Gallery of Ishikawa Prefecture, Kanazawa; 1988 *World Glass Now '88*, Hokkaido Museum of Modern Art, Sapporo; 1989 *Arte en Vidro*, São Paulo Art Museum; 1991 (5th) Triennial of Japan Glass Art Crafts Association, Heller Gallery, New York; 1999 *2000 Years of Japanese Glass*, Suntory Museum of Art, Osaka; others. Work subject of 1981 exhibition, Takashimaya Gallery, Yokohama; 1985, Isetan Fine Arts Salon, Tokyo; 1995, Gallery Nakama, Tokyo.
Bibliography Cat., *Glass Japan*, New York: Heller Gallery and Japan Glass Art Crafts Association, 1991: no. 19.

Kurchan, Juan (1913 -75)
> See Ferrari Hardoy, Jorge.

Kurita, Yasuhisa (1945-)

Japanese glass designer; active Tokyo.

Training To 1969, sculpture, Faculty of Fine Arts, Tokyo University of Education; 1974–75 under Bertil Vallien, Konstfackskolan, Stockholm.
Biography Kurita was a designer at Hoya Crystal in Tokyo; is a board member, Japan Glass Art Crafts Association.
Exhibitions Work has been included in numerous editions of *Glass in Japan*, Tokyo, from 1981; 1982 *New Glass Review 3*, The Corning Museum of Glass, Corning, N.Y.; 1983 *Little Objects*, Japan Glass Art Crafts Association; 1991 (5th) Triennale of the Japan Glass Art Crafts Association, Heller Gallery, New York; others.
Bibliography Cat., *Glass Japan*, New York: Heller Gallery and Japan Glass Art Crafts Association, 1991: no. 20.

Kurokawa, Kisho (1938-)

Japanese architect and furniture designer.

Training To 1964, architecture, Faculty of Architecture, University of Tokyo.
Biography Active as an architect from 1970, Kurokawa designed 1970 Sony Tower, Osaka; 1984 Roppongi Prince Hotel, Tokyo; 1984 Wacoal Kojimachi Building, Tokyo; 1983 Japanese Studies Center, Bangkok; 1983 Japanese-German Culture Center, Berlin; 1983 National Bunraku Theater, Osaka; and a number of others. His books include *Architecture of the Street* (1983), *A Cross Selection of Japan* (1983), and *Thesis on Architecture* (1982). He has designed distinctive furniture by Tendo and by Kosuga, and Edo range of chairs and tables by PPM Corporation in Tokyo and Fractal range in wood by Flores Design Edition in Dusseldorf.
Exhibitions Work shown in numerous exhibitions in New York, Paris, London, Dublin, Moscow, Milan, Florence, Rome, Budapest, and Sofia; and subject of others.

Masayuki Kurokawa. Fieno scuba (self-contained underwater re-breathing apparatus). 1993. Injection-molded polycarbonate-polyester blend, 6 1/4 x 13 7/8 x 20 1/8" (15.9 x 35.2 x 51.1 cm). Mfr.: Grand Bleu, Japan. Gift of the designer. MoMA.

Bibliography Robert A.M. Stern (ed.), *The International Design Yearbook*, New York: Abbeville, 1985/1986. Cat., *Kisho Kurokawa: Retrospective*, Paris: Maison de la Culture du Japan, 1998

Kurokawa, Masayuki (1937-)

Japanese furniture and lighting designer, born Nagoya.

Training 1961, architecture degree, Nagoya Institute of Technology, ; to 1967, Graduate School of Architecture, Waseda University, Tokyo.
Biography 1967, he set up Masayuki Kurokawa Architect and Associates and has realized a number of architectural commissions. His lighting designs have been diverse, some fixtures by Matsushita, including 1984 Angolo Slit T Bar wall light. Other work: 1986 flat-wave speaker produced by Seidenko, 1987 Archi Version K pencils by Sakura Color Products, 1987 Kite ceiling light by Yamagiwa, 1986 Ingott-Batta knockdown furniture, 1987 K series faucets by Toto, 1987 Rabat and Delhi wristwatches by Citizen, 1987 writing desk by Wogg, 1989 Giga and 1992 Interface door knobs by Miwa Lock, 1989 EN series bronze tableware by Takenaka Works, 1990 Bio-Lite Pro desk lamp by Yamagiwa/Hayashibara Biochemical Laboratories, 1990 Libro bookshelf by Tostem, 1991 platinum-and-gum jewelry by Urban Gold, 1993 Fieno scuba gear by Grand Bleu. He has been a professor, Graduate School of Art, Nihon University, Koriyama City, Fukushima Prefecture, Japan.
Citations 1970 International Design Competition (mass-production house); 1973 competition Interior Vertical Element of a House; 1976 annual prize, Japan Interior Designers Association; six citations (for tables and lighting), Industrie Forum Design (iF), Hanover; 1986 Mainichi Design Award; 1994 Good Design award, Chicago Athenaeum; a number of others.
Bibliography *Masayuki Kurokawa: Multifacetted Architect/ The Japan Architect 280*, Tokyo: Shinkenchiku-sha, 1980. *The Works of Masayuki Kurokawa/Space Design*, Tokyo: Kajima Institute, 1981. *5 Sensors of an Age*, Tokyo: Rikuyo-sha, 1985. *Masayuki Kurokawa: Product Design*, Tokyo: Rikuyo-sha, 1993.

Kurz, Petra (1962-)

German product designer; born Schwäbisch-Hall.

Training 1979–82 under Susanne Lüftner, Unterricht für Freie Kunst,; to 1983, design, Fachhochschule für Gestaltung, Schwäbisch-Gmünd.
Biography 1988, Kurz has been a freelance designer of textiles, color, and lighting; 1989, worked at Design Center, Stuttgart, organizing and designing 1989 (2nd) exhibition and catalog of *Design-Börse Stuttgart* and catalog of *Frauen im Design* exhibition; 1989, with two partners, set up a design office in Schwäbisch-Gmünd.
Citations Honorable-mention award, 1988 (1st) *Design-Börse Stuttgart*; Mia Seeger Preis.
Bibliography Cat., Design Center Stuttgart, *Women in Design: Careers and Life Histories Since 1990*, Stuttgart: Haus der Wirtschaft, 1989: 354–55.

Kustodiev, Boris Mikhailovich (1878–1927)

Russian painter, graphic artist, theatrical designer, and sculptor; born Astrakhan; died Leningrad.

Training 1896–1903, Academy of Fine Arts, St. Petersburg. 1904 on an Academy grant, in France and Spain.
Biography 1905, Kustodiev designed posters and illustrated satirical magazines; 1909–10, executed a number of sculptures which are represented in the Russian Museum; 1910, became a member of the revived V Mir Iskusstva (the world of art) group and later painted a well-known picture of the group's members meeting in a green dining room (now displayed in the Russian Museum, St. Petersburg); 1918, after the Revolution he was involved in Agitprop decorations; 1919, participated in the First State Free Exhibition of Artworks in Petrograd and his name appeared on the 1919 list of artists for acquisitions by the envisaged Museum of Painterly Culture. 1920, the Petrograd Soviet commissioned him to paint a large canvas of the Second Congress of the Communist International and he was also given a one-person show; 1923, designed two famous figurines for the State Porcelain Factory and other designs followed.
Exhibitions Work included in Serge Diaghilev's exhibition of Russian art, 1906 Salon d'Automne, Paris; 1907–10 Union of Artists exhibitions; 1922 *Erste Russische Kunstausstellung*, Berlin; 1923 *Exhibition of Paintings of Petrograd Artists of All Tendencies 1919–23*, Petrograd; 1925 *Exposition Internationale des Arts Décoratifs et Industriels*

Modernes, Paris. Work subject of 1928, 1947, 1952, 1968 exhibitions.
Bibliography V.E. Lebedeva, *Boris Kustodiev*, Moscow: Progress, 1981. Nina Lobanov-Rostovsky, *Revolutionary Ceramics*, London: Studio Vista, 1990. John Milner, *A Dictionary of Russian and Soviet Artists*, Woodbridge, UK: Antique Collectors' Club, 1993.

Kutzner, Ingrid (1949–)

German industrial designer; born Börssum.

Training 1965–68, apprenticeship as a draftsperson in an architectural office; 1969–76, industrial design, Hochschule der bildenden Künste, Brunswick.
Biography 1976, Kutzner worked as an industrial designer at Richardson and Smith Inc. in Columbus, Ohio, US, and, 1977, at Institut für Produktgestaltung of AEG in Frankfurt, where she established 'design linea' in 1983; 1984, was a guest professor of product design, Ohio State University, Columbus. Designs have include included 1980 Aqualux mouthspray, 1981 Rotofix universal cutter, and 1982 modular desk system, all by AEG.
Bibliography Cat., Design Center Stuttgart, *Women in Design: Careers and Life Histories Since 1900*, Stuttgart: Haus der Wirtschaft, 1989: 130–31.

Kuypers, Jan (1925–)

Dutch industrial designer; son of a furniture manufacturer; active Toronto, Canada.

Training To 1947, Academie van Beeldende Kunsten, The Hague; from 1955, Massachusetts Institute of Technology (MIT), Cambridge, Mass., US.
Biography Kuypers moved to England from Holland and, 1951, to Canada; set up a design department at Imperial Furniture Manufacturing in Stratford, Ontario, where he was the chief designer to 1960, when he became a partner of E. Orr and Associates, Toronto. 1961 with Julian Rowan and Frank Dudas, he founded a design agency (known as DKR from 1967) in Toronto, with furniture including seating for IIL International. (Subseqently, DKR became KAN Industrial Design, one of the longest-active design firms in Canada. Kuypers may have been Canada's most important furniture designer of 1950s. Examples of his work are numerous, including 1957 bent-plywood armchair by Imperial; 1983 Anthro chair (with Ed Halstab) and 1979 Muffin chair by Harter Furniture; and 1990 Solido 3-D eye goggles for use in IMAX-Dome (Omnimax) theaters.
Bibliography Cat., *Seduced and Abandoned: Modern Furniture Designers in Canada, the First Fifty Years*, Toronto: The Art Gallery at Harbourfront, 1986: 21. Rachel Gotlieb and Cora Golden, *Design in Canada Since 1945: Fifty Years from Teakettles to Task Chairs*, Toronto: Knopf Canada, 2001.
> See Dudas, Frank.

KVT (Koninklijke Vereenigde Tapijtenfabrieken)

Dutch rug factory; located Rotterdam and Moordrecht.

History 1797, Deventer Tapijtfabriek was founded in Rotterdam; 1819, became the best known of three merged factories, which formed the Koninklijke Vereenigde Tapijtenfabrieken. King Willem III was a shareholder and client and encouraged its historicist styles with gifts of expensive illustrated books to the firm's design department. Its workers wove cowhair and other simple carpets and rugs and, from c. 1820, hand-knotted Smyrna carpets. The sons of one of the company founders, G. Birnie, were the designers (including Johan Willem Birnie, the manager 1820–48). Much of the work at this time was imitation Turkish, Persian, and other Oriental carpet adaptations, and European Renaissance, French, and Empire styles. The fabrication that became known as Deventer was highly successful from 1850s. Rugs and carpets were made to measure. From turn of 19th century, both historicist and modern styles were made. The 's-Gravenhaagsche Smyrnatapijtfabriek (founded 1901 in The Hague) organized design competitions, one of which (1901) had the theme 'Modern Style'; its winner was Chris Lebeau. 1895, the factory was to be closed, but friends of artist Thomas A.C. Colenbrander, who designed for the company, took over the firm, to be Amersfoortsche Tapijtfabriek in 1896. J.G. Mouton was a new stockholder, W.P.A. Garjeanne a director, and Colenbrander the 'aesthetic advisor.' The Amersfoort company became successful and Colenbrander's carpets widely known. 1919, Amersfoort was amalgamated into Deventer Tapijtfabriek. Commissioned designers for the two companies included H.P. Berlage, Th. W. Nieuwenhuis, J.W. Gidding, C.A. Lion Cachet, W. Penaat, J.J. Gompertz, J. van den Boch, and C. van der Sluys. After the merger, more machine-made rugs were produced. After 1930, its only freelance designer was Jaap Gidding. New designs began to be realized in 1950s.
Exhibitions/citations Deventer received prizes at 1851 *Great Exhibition of the Works of Industry of All Nations*, London, and 1878 *Exposition Universelle*, Paris. Koninklijke Tapijtfabriek Werklust (one of the firms founded in 1854 in Rotterdam) showed work at 1900 *Exposition Universelle*, Paris, and 1902 *Esposizione Internazionale d'Arte Decorativa Moderna*, Turin.
Bibliography Cat., *Industry and Design in the Netherlands, 1850/1950*, Amsterdam: Stedelijk Museum, 1985.

Kybal, Antonín (1901–1971)

Czech painter, textile artist, and textile producer; born Nové Město nad Metují.

Training Vysoká Škola Uměleckoprůmyslová (VŠUP, academy of arts, architecture, and design); and philosophy, Univerzity Karlovy (Charles university); both Prague.
Biography 1928, Kybal set up his own textile studio in Prague; became a member of the Czechoslovakian Werkbund (SČSD); collaborated at Krásná Jizba (the beautiful room); 1948–71, was a professor, VŠUP, Prague; 1920s–30s, was the leading influence in the modern style of textiles for domestic use and became important in the production of handmade prints; designed a large number of hand- and machine-woven carpets; collaborated with leading Czech architects; designed furnishing fabrics for family houses, interiors of Prague Castle in 1936, and League of Nations, Geneva, in 1937. He published articles in magazines *Žijeme* in 1931, *Panorama* in 1935, *Architektura* in 1942, and others. He died in Prague.
Exhibitions/citations 1958 *Exposition Universelle et Internationale de Bruxelles (Expo '58)* (gold medal).
Bibliography Alena Adlerová, *České užité umění 1918–1938*, Prague: Odeon, 1983. Cat., *Prague, 1900–1938: capitale secrète des avants-gardes*, Dijon: Musée des Beaux-Arts, 1997.

Kysela, František (1881–1941)

Czech designer and teacher; born Kouřím.

Training 1900–04 and 1905–08 under K. Mašek, Vysoká Škola Uměleckoprůmyslová (VŠUP, academy of arts, architecture, and design); 1904–05 under H. Schwaigr, Akademie Výtvarných Umení (academy of fine arts); both Prague.
Biography From 1913, Kysela was a professor, VŠUP, Prague, and from 1921, taught applied graphics; 1908, joined Mánes Association of Plastic Artists and, 1909, was elected to its executive; was a member of the Artěl Cooperative. 1911, he left Mánes and joined the Group of Plastic Artists; worked in editorial offices of *Uměleckýměsíčník*; 1917, rejoined Mánes; was active in various disciplines, especially the applied arts; created frescoes, paintings on glass windows, textile designs for clothing and upholstery, jewelry, tapestries, postage stamps, banknotes, book illustrations, stage sets, and theater costumes, including those for Bedřich Smetana's operas at the Národní Divadlo (national theater), Prague. He died in Prague.
Exhibitions/citations Grand prize and gold medal, 1925 *Exposition Internationale des Arts Décoratifs et Industriels Modernes*, Paris.
Bibliography Alexander von Vegesack et al., *Czech Cubism: Architecture, Furniture, and Decorative Arts, 1910–1925*, New York: Princeton Architectural Press, 1992. Cat., *Prague, 1900–1938: capitale secrète des avants-gardes*, Dijon: Musée des Beaux-Arts, 1997.

State Porcelain Factory (aka Lomonosov Porcelain Factory). Nikolai Suetin. Teapot (detail). c. 1923. MoMA.

La Farge, John Frederick Lewis Joseph (1835–1910)

American artist, stained-glass designer, and decorator; born and active New York.

Biography 1856, La Farge left employment in a law firm in New York, traveled to France, and met author Théophile Gautier and poet Charles-Pierre Baudelaire through his cousin, journalist-critic Paul de Saint-Victor. In France, La Farge copied and studied old masters' art works at the Louvre and studied for a few weeks in the studio of Théodore Chassériau. 1857, he returned to the US via England, where he visited the *Manchester Art Treasures Exhibition* with its works by the Pre-Raphaelites; 1858, set up his own studio in the 10th Street Studio Building, New York; met architect Richard Morris Hunt, who encouraged La Farge to pursue painting and to study under his brother William Morris Hunt in Newport, R. I. La Farge's 1860s work bore a similarity to that of Claude Monet. c. 1865, he began to create decorative paintings, receiving a commission from architect Henry Van Brunt for the 1865 dining room of builder Charles Freeland in Boston but, due to illness, was replaced by Albion Bicknell. 1875, he began working in stained glass, influenced by Edward Burne-Jones, Ford Madox Brown, and Dante Gabriel Rossetti, all of whom he had visited in England in 1873. La Farge's stained-glass methods revolutionized the craft in America. He introduced opalescent glass, which offered tonality and eliminated traditional painting details, used first on his window in the Henry G. Marquand residence in Newport, R. I., in c. 1880. He went on to produce several thousand stained-glass windows. Commissioned by architect H.H. Richardson, from 1876 La Farge also realized notable murals and architectural details—most of which he directed personally—for Trinity Church in Boston. Other murals included those for St. Thomas's Church in 1877, Church of the Incarnation in 1885, and Church of the Ascension 1886–88, all New York. 1880–85, he directed the La Farge Decorative Art Company for interior decoration; early 1880s in New York, participated in the decoration of the Japanese Parlor of the William H. Vanderbilt residence, and dining room and watercolor room of the residence of his son, Cornelius Vanderbilt II, both completed in cooperation with artist/sculptor Augustus Saint-Gaudens. 1880s–90s, La Farge traveled to Japan and the South Pacific, where he drew watercolors that illustrated his memoirs; wrote a number of books, including *Considerations on Painting: Lectures Given in the Year 1893 at the Metropolitan Museum of New York* (New York/London: Macmillan, 1895), *Great Masters* (New York: McClure, Phillips, 1903), and *The Higher Life in Art* (New York: McClure, 1908).
Exhibitions 1862, first still-life paintings and figurative art shown, at National Academy of Design, New York. Work subject of 1936 exhibition, The Metropolitan Museum of Art, New York; 1987, Pittsburgh and Washington, D.C. (catalogs below).
Bibliography Cat., Metropolitan Museum of Art, *An Exhibition of the Work of John La Farge*, New York: Blanchard Press, 1936. H. Barbara Weinberg, *The Decorative Work of John La Farge*, New York: Garland, 1977. James L. Sturm, *Stained Glass from Medieval Times to the Present: Treasures to Be Seen in New York*, New York: Dutton, 1982: 34–46. Doreen Bolger Burke et al., *In Pursuit of Beauty: Americans and the Aesthetic Movement*, New York: The Metropolitan Museum of Art/Rizzoli, 1986: 47–48. Cat., Henry Adams et al., *The Art of John La Farge: Essays*, Washington: National Museum of American Art, 1987. James L. Yarnall, *Recreation and Idleness: The Pacific Travels of John La Farge*, New York: V. Jordan Fine Art, 1998.

La Godelinais, René (aka Renan de La Godelinais 1908–1986)

French furniture maker and decorator; born Fougères.

Biography To 1929, La Godelinais collaborated with Jacques-Émile Ruhlmann and, to 1938, with Alfred Porteneuve; designed for Michelin and locks/metal fittings by Fontaine and silver by Puiforcat. He serially produced furniture for hotels; from 1949, was a member of Union des Artistes Modernes (UAM). His furniture featured elements such as painted metal, rattan, and removable upholstery. He died in Paris.
Exhibitions Showed work in various venues, including 1937 *Exposition Inter-nationale des Arts et Techniques dans la Vie Moderne*, Paris; 1958 *Exposition Universelle et Internationale de Bruxelles* (*Expo '58*). He organized (with René Herbst, Charlotte Perriand, and André Hermant) 1949 (1st) *Formes Utiles* exhibition, Pavillon de Marsan, Louvre, Paris.
Bibliography Pierre Kjellberg, *Art déco: les maîtres du mobilier, le décor des paquebots*, Paris: Amateur, 1986/1990. Arlette Barré-Despond (ed.), *Dictionnaire international des arts appliqués et du design*, Paris: Regard, 1996

La Mache, Didier (1945–)

French designer and manufacturer.

Training Art and industrial design, École Nationale Supérieure des Arts Décoratifs, Paris, and Royal College of Art, London.
Biography La Mache produced and sold his own lighting, furniture, and accessories, including 1987 Ciel Bauhaus! table lamp; designed 1987 Bleu Électre table lamp, sponsored by VIA.
Bibliography François Mathey, *Au bonheur des formes, design français 1945–1992*, Paris: Regard, 1992: 307–08, 376.

La Nave

Spanish design consultancy; located Valéncia.

History 1984, design studios Caps i Mans and Enebecé were merged to form multidisciplinary design consultancy La Nave, which received numerous public commissions in Valéncia, including from the Valéncia regional government. Composed of 10 core members from various backgrounds, its staff has included Sandra Figuerola, Marisa Gallén Castelló, 1958, and Luís Gonzáles—fine artists; Paco Bascuñán and Lorenzo Company—graphic designers; and Carlos Bento—an architect. Gallén and Figuerola designed 1987 Fried-Eggs inflatable for pools and 1989 inflatable pool by Torrente Industrial (TOI), 1988 writing pad by Don Antonio, and 1989 linens by Castilla Textil. Daniel Nabot and Nacho Lavernia designed 1986 automobile ski racks and water fountain by Indústrias Saludes. 1991, La Nave was dissolved. Firuerola and Gallén established a design/communications agency in Valéncia, which has designed for Alessi, Atrium, Coco Fundacio Mediambiental, Green Chilli, Goldwin Athletic Wear, Gandia Blasco, La Mediterranea, and others.
Bibliography Guy Julier, *New Spanish Design*, London: Thames & Hudson, 1991.'Entrevista a Marisa Gallen y Sandra Figuerola,' *Experimenta*, no. 36, Oct. 2001.

La Pietra, Ugo (1938–)

Italian architect, designer, theoretician, and writer; born Bussi sul Tirino (PE); active Milan.

Training To 1964, architecture, Politecnico, Milan.
Biography From 1962, La Pietra has been active in investigating the relationship between objects and users, even as early as 1960 taking a multidisciplinary approach, adopting ideas from conceptual, environmental, social, narrative art, the cinema, literature, neo-eclecticism, architecture, and Radical Design. He has published and taught concerning his conclusions and theories; worked with and/or co-founded a number of associations, including Gruppo del Cenobio, Gruppo La Lepre Lunare, Global Tools, Cooperativa Maroncelli, Fabbrica di Comunicazione, Libero Laboratorio, as well as with individual architects, designers, and artists. 1964, La Pietra set up his own studio and became a design consultant to furniture, accessories, and lighting manufacturers; has worked for clients, including Arosio, Busnelli, Elam, Jabik & Colophon, Moro, Poggi, Sima, Vecchione, and Zama. From 1965, his numerous books include *Autoarchiterapia* (Milan: Jabik & Colophon, 1975), *Abitare la città* (Florence, Alinea, 1983), and *Ad arte—1985–1995: dieci anni di ambienti e oggetti per abitare con arte* (Florence, Alinea, 1995), in addition to an extensive list of articles. 1971–74, he was editor of journal *IN*; 1973–74, of *Progettare in più* and *Fascicolo*; 1976–79, of *Brera Flash* and *Fascicolo* and, 1978–86, was the design-section editor, *Domus*; c. 1984, became artistic director, Gruppo Industriale Busnelli; to 1974, was assistant lecturer, Facoltà di Architettura, Politecnico, Milan and, 1967–79, at Facoltà di Architettura, Università degli Studi 'G. d'Annunzio,' Pescara; from 1977, was instructor of industrial and environmental design, Istituto Statale d'Arte Villa Reale, Monza, and architecture professor, schools of architecture in Palermo and Turin. 1990, opened a gallery in Milan, where he showed his own work; became a member, Associazione per il Designo Industriale (ADI). Designs by Busnelli include 1984 Pretenziosa armchair, 1984 Agevole sofa, 1984 Flessuosa sofa, 1985 Autorevole armchair, 1985 At-Tese chair and table, 1985 Incrocio table and chair, and 1986 Articolata chair. Other clients: Boffi, Bottega dei Vasai, Cooperativa Ceramiche di Imola, Interflex, Luceplan, Marangoni, Marioni, Memphis, Up & Up, Zanotta, and JC Decaux (1993 public lighting) in Paris.
Exhibitions Participated in over 300 exhibitions in Italy and abroad, including at Museum of Contemporary Crafts, New York; IDZ, Berlin; Architectural Association, London; Institut de l'Environnement, Paris; Landesmuseum Joanneum, Graz; Museum am Ostwall, Dortmund; and 1968 (14th) (experimental environment) Triennale di Milano. Exhibition designs include 1980 *50 Years of Architecture*, Milan; *Cronografie*, 1982 Biennale di Venezia; audio-visual section, 1979 (16th) Triennale di Milano; *La Casa Telemática*, 1983 (61st) Fiera Campionaria Internazionale, Milan; 1972 *Italy: The New Domestic Landscape* (1971 Uno sull'altro bookcase by Poggi), The Museum of Modern Art, New York. First prize, 1975 (1st) architecture-film festival, Nancy; 1979 (for bedroom set by Arosio Giacobbe e Figli/Fratelli Viscardi) and 1987 (for furniture by Busnelli) Premio Compasso d'Oro.
Bibliography Germano Celant, 'Ugo La Pietra,' *Casabella*, nos. 304 and 316, 1966 and 1967. Cat., Eligio Cesana, *La Pietra*, Lecco: Galleria Stefanoni, 1966. Alberto Prina, 'Ugo La Pietra o la ricerca morfologica,' *Formaluce*, no. 4, 1968. Emilio Ambasz (ed.), *Italy: The New Domestic Landscape*, New York: The Museum of Modern Art, 1972: 55. Alfonso Grassi and Anty Pansera, *Atlante del design italiano 1940–1980*, Milan: Fabbri, 1980: 303. Cat., Lucius Burckhardt, *Design ist Unsichtbar*, Linz: Löcker, 1981. Andrea Branzi, *La casa calda: esperienze del nuovo disegno italiano*, Milan: Idea, 1982. Cat., *Ugo La Pietra 1960–1990, percorsi in punta di penna*, Milan: Galleria Avida Dollars, 1990. Grazia Ambrosio, 'Ugo La Pietra esploratore della realtà...,' *Arte*, no. 27, 1996.

Max Laeuger. Vase. 1923. Majolica, h. 3 1/8" (7.9 cm). Mfr.: Max Laeuger, Karlsruhe Majolikamanufaktur, Germany. Courtesy Quittenbaum Kunstauktionen, Munich.

La Spada, Alessandro (1967–)

Italian designer; born Reggio Calabria; active Milan.

Training 1987–90, diploma in interior design, Istituto Superiore di Architettura d'Interni, Milan.
Biography 1991–94, La Spada worked for Sawaya & Moroni on the development of interior design and furniture prototypes; from 1994, has taught furniture design, Istituto Superiore di Architettura d'Interni; 1994–95, designed metal furnishing accessories by Siryo Gruppo; 1995, conducted decoration research for Richard Ginori ceramics; 1995 with Francesco Tibaldi, established Falt Design in Milan for the design of interior and furnishing accessories, 1997 prototype of upholstered electrically mechanical seating for Nippon Brox, and 2001 seating by Brian Form; from 2002, has been manager of the art studio of Numerodue. Other designs include 1996 Mouse trolley and Meridiano table for Sormani Esse 81; 1996 Coc Love Pulser stool and Mito d'Europa lounge chair by Kundalini; from 2000, extensive furniture and lighting for Numerodue; 2001 beds by Porro & Porro.
Bibliography Maurizio Corrado, *Nuove tendenze e progetti nella architettura d'interni*, Milan: De Vecchi, 1988. Maria Gallo and Patrizia Ledda, *Make Love with Design*, Bologna: Costa & Nolan/Phoenix, 1999. Ingo Maurer (ed.), *The International Design Yearbook*, London: Laurence King, 2000.

La Trobe-Bateman, Richard (1938–)

British designer.

Training 1957–64, sculpture, St. Martin's School of Art, London; 1965–67, furniture, Royal College of Art, London.
Biography 1968, La Trobe-Bateman set up his first workshop in London, where he designed and produced wood furniture; 1978, set up a second workshop in Somerset; 1968–77 taught scupture, St. Martin's College of Art; from 1989, has been a lecturer in furniture design, Loughborough College of Art and Design.
Exhibitions Work shown at 1982 *Maker's Eye;* 1987 *Contemporary Applied Arts*; 1991 *Beyond the Dovetail*, Crafts Council; all London.
Bibliography *Decorative Arts Today*, London: Bonhams, 1992: no. 41a.

Labino, Dominick (1910–1987)

American ceramicist and glassware designer.

Training From 1953, glassmaking, University of Wisconsin, Madison.
Biography Mid-1960s, Labino was the most productive of the first group in Harvey Littleton's studio-glass program, University of Wisconsin; was involved in glass technology. Labino, formerly the director of research at Johns-Manville Glass Fibers Division, was a pioneer of

the Studio Glass Movement, led by Littleton. Labino developed two free-form techniques: immersion pieces made from many layers, and large off-hand forms produced by opening up asymmetrical bubbles and stretching with pincers. Sam Herman was a student of Labino's in 1966.
Bibliography Frederick Cooke, *Glass: Twentieth-Century Design*, New York: Dutton, 1986: 105.
> See Littleton, Harvey.

Lachenal, Edmond (1855–1930)
French sculptor and ceramicist; born Paris; father of Raoul Lachenal.

Biography 1870, Lachenal joined the studio of Théodore Deck and later became the director; 1880, established his own studio in Malakoff, near Paris, and, 1887, at Châtillon-sous-Bagneux. He made pottery in the Persian style influenced by Deck and decorated with stylized figures, landscapes, greenery, and flowers; 1890, perfected a finish whose glaze surface was partially dulled with hydrofluoric acid; experimented with metallic luster glazes with Keller of Guérin; showed the results of these experiments along with ceramic sculptures after works by Rodin, Fix-Masseau, Epinay, and Madrassi at Galerie Georges Petit, Paris. Lachenal became interested in enameled glass and began to work at Daum in Nancy. His vase forms at this time were inspired by plant motifs, fashionable then. He produced small figurines and animal forms. Beginning of 20th century, he left ceramics and turned his studio over to his son Raoul Lachenel and his wife.
Exhibitions From 1884, work shown annually at Galerie Georges Petit; 1900 *Exposition Universelle* (suite of stoneware furniture), Paris.
Bibliography Yvonne Brunhammer et al., *Art Nouveau Belgium, France*, Houston: Institute for the Arts, Rice University, 1976. *Europäische Keramik 1880–1930: Sammlung Silzer*, Darmstadt: Hessisches Landesmuseum, 1986. Elisabeth Cameron, *Encyclopedia of Pottery and Porcelain*, London: Faber & Faber, 1986: 192.

Lachenal, Raoul (1885–1956)
French ceramicist; son of Edmond Lachenal.

Biography Lachenal succeeded his father Edmond in his studio in Châtillon-sous-Bagneux; from 1904, exhibited incised-relief and geometric-motif stoneware or colored glazes within *cloisonné*, outlined in deep orange; used matt and gray *flambé* effects in rare colors; 1911, moved to Boulogne-sur-Seine; later on, produced porcelain and serial and one-of-a-kind pieces; was fond of ovoid shapes, simple decoration, and black-and-white contrasts.
Bibliography Yvonne Bruhammer, *Les années '25,'* Paris: Musée des Arts Décoratifs, 1966: 108. Yvonne Brunhammer, *Le cinquantenaire de l'Exposition de 1925*, Paris: Musée des Arts Décoratifs, 1976: 133. Elisabeth Cameron, *Encyclopedia of Pottery and Porcelain*, London: Faber & Faber, 1986: 192.

Lachevsky, Dominique
> See Naggar, Patrick.

Lacloche, Galerie
French exhibition space and furniture producer.

History To 1970s, Galerie Lacloche was managed by Jacques Lacloche in Paris; produced and sold widely published designs in small editions, including Roger Tallon's large 1965 chair in polished aluminum with polyester foam, his 1964 Helicold staircase (produced 1966), and Bernard Rancillac's 1967 Elephant Chair. An eclectic enterprise, the gallery also presented a number of exhibitions, including 1960 Leonardo Cremonini painting exhibition, 1962 *Les Premières Tapisseries d'OssipZadkine*, 1966 *L'Objet 2*, 1969 *Bijoux et Sculptures d'Eau* (sculptor Gyula Kosice's work); 1970, *Attractions* (Alice Hutchins's art constructions), 1977 Georges Jeanclos exhibition.
Bibliography Gilles de Bure, *Le mobilier français 1965–1979*, Paris: Regard, 1983: 51, 65.

Lacombe, Georges (1868–1916)
French carver; born Versailles.

Training Under Alfred Roll, painting; Académie Julian, Paris.
Biography 1892, Lacombe became a member of the artists' group Nabis, and 1893, showed his paintings with the group; 1893–94, took up wood carving; produced furniture and panels carved in a style relating to Gauguin's. He never sold his work, which was given to friends and neighbors.
Bibliography Yvonne Brunhammer et al., *Art Nouveau Belgium, France*, Houston: Institute for the Arts, Rice University, 1976.

Lacoste, Gerald (1909–c. 1995)
British architect, designer, and painter.

Biography 1933, Lacoste designed the decorative glass for Casani's Club and the music room in glass for 1934 Queen's Gate Place, both London; is best known for his 1934 silvery-gray-green glass fireplace with a glass-tile hearth by Pilkington and surrounding mirrored wall for Norman Hartnell's showroom on Bruton Street, London. 1938, designed Lord Mountbatten's flat; after 1945, designed schools and residences, mostly in Essex; was a captain in the British Expeditionary Force (BEF).
Bibliography Cat., *Thirties: British Art and Design Before the War*, London: Arts Council of Great Britain/Hayward Gallery, 1979.

Lacroix, Boris-Jean (1902–1984)
French designer; born Paris.

Biography Lacroix was a prolific designer of lighting, wallpaper, bookbinding, furniture, and interiors; 1924, began working for couturière Madeleine Vionnet as a designer of dresses, handbags, and costume jewelry; soon after, decorated and designed her private residence. His designs were commissioned by Jean-Michel Frank and Jean Dunand. He designed furniture and chairs in Cubist forms for himself, produced by cabinetmaker Régamey; had other clients including Damon, for whom he created a great many modern lamps in engraved mirror and frosted-glass tubes, and private clients. He suggested that his lighting had no purpose other than to be harmonious with modern interiors and predicted that lighting fixtures would become obsolete; created practically every model of domestic lighting, including table lamps, illuminated ceilings, and picture frames. Most of his polished and matt-finished nickel-plated copper lamps incorporated glass; yet some were realized only in metal. Damon used its special enamel-diffusing glass or the plain frosted variety. His articles were published in *Lux* in the late 1920s. 1945, he became a member, Union des Artistes Modernes (UAM); pursued some lighting and interior design independently. He died in Paris.
Exhibitions From 1927, shown at editions of Salon d'Automne and Salons of Société des Artistes Décorateurs.
Bibliography Guillaume Janneau, *Le luminaire et les moyens d'éclairage nouveaux*, 2nd series, Paris: Charles Moreau: plates 22–24, 3rd series: plates 27–33, [n.d.]. *The Studio*, July–Dec. 1929: 643. *Lux*, Jan. 1929: 15, Dec. 1929: 170, Dec. 1934: 150. Alastair Duncan, *Art Nouveau and Art Déco Lighting*, New York: Simon & Schuster, 1978. Cat., Aaron Lederfajn and Xavier Lenormand, *Le Louvre des Antiquaires présente: 1930 quand le meuble devient sculpture*, Paris, 1986. Pierre Kjellberg, *Art déco: les maîtres du mobilier, le décor des paquebots*, Paris: Amateur, 1986/1990. Arlette Barré-Despond, *UAM*, Paris: Regard, 1986: 523. Cat., Sophie Tasma Anargyros et al., *L'école française: les créateurs de meubles du 20ème siècle*, Paris: Industries Françaises de l'Ameublement, 2000.

Lade, Jan (1944–)
Danish interior architect and furniture designer.

Training To 1969, Skolen for Brugskunst, Copenhagen.
Biography 1970 with Svein Asbjørsen, Lade founded the studio Møre Designteam; created the 'Split' concept of seating; designed 1970 Ecco chairs by L.K. Hjelle og Hjellegjerde Møbelfabrikk in Sykkylven and 1985 ergonomic seat/bed/lounge unit designed to place the sitters' legs higher than their heart for supposed beneficial effects on circulation.
Bibliography Robert A.M. Stern (ed.), *The International Design Yearbook*, New York: Abbeville, 1985/1986. Fredrik Wildhagen, *Norge i Form*, Oslo: Stenersen, 1988: 171–72.

Laeuger, Max (1864–1952)
German architect, potter, painter, sculptor, and designer; born Lörrach.

Training 1880–84, painting and interior design, Kunstgewerbeschule, Karlsruhe; 1892–93, Académie Julian, Paris.
Biography 1885–90, Laeuger taught, Kunstgewerbeschule, Karlsruhe and worked at the potteries in Kandern during his holidays. From 1893, he began to create lead-glazed slipware, some models of which were made in the J. Armbruster workshop in Kandern; founded and directed a crafts pottery in Kandern, where plates were painted with metal

Laguiole: Philippe Starck. Folding knife, 1986. 440A stainless steel and polished aluminum, open 1/2 x 7 x 1/2" (1.2 x 17.8 x 1.2 cm). Mfr.: Forge de Laguiole, France. David Whitney Collection, Gift of David Whitney. MoMA.

oxides over white slip. Some models were crackled and bubbled, while others were faint and smoky due to reduction firing. From 1898, Laeuger was a professor, Universtät Karlsruhe; 1907, cofounded the Deutscher Werkbund; designed in a proto-Art Déco style; 1916, set up a studio in the Staatlichen Majolikamanufaktur in Karlsruhe; concurrently, taught at institutions, including Staatliche Akademie der bildenden Künste (known as the Badische Landeskunstschule), Baden, from 1920–22. 1920s, he turned from painted decoration to techniques with glazes and slips fired to create subtle effects. Work included vases, bowls, plaques, and experimentation with ceramic sculpture in animal forms (particularly elephants) and female figures. His turquoise glaze became known as Laeuger blue.
Bibliography Stuart Durant, *Ornament from the Industrial Revolution to Today*, Woodstock, N.Y.: Overlook, 1986: 249. Elisabeth Cameron, *Encyclopedia of Pottery and Porcelain*, London: Faber & Faber, 1986.

Lafaille, Maurice (1902–1988)
French painter and furniture designer; born and active Paris.

Training Cabinetmaking, École Boulle, Paris.
Biography Lafaille worked as a cabinetmaker for a manufacturer in the Faubourg Saint-Antoine area of Paris; 1928, became the director of shop L'Intérieur Moderne in Paris and designed a luxurious bedroom (with Fraysse) for Mme. Francis Carco, among other work.
Exhibitions 1925–26, work (as painter) shown at Salon d'Automne and, from 1927 (as decorator, with furniture by Atelier Français), at Salons of Société des Artistes Décorateurs.
Bibliography Pierre Kjellberg, *Art déco: les maîtres du mobilier, le décor des paquebots*, Paris: Amateur, 1986/1990.

Lagaay, Harm M. (1946–)
Dutch automobile designer; born The Hague.

Biography 1970–77, Lagaay was a member of the design team of Porsche automobile company's Research and Development Center in Weißach, near Stuttgart, Germany, headed by 'Tony' Anatole Lupine (Latvia 1930–). (Lupine had spent 17 years at General Motors before moving to GM's Opel division in Germany and then joined Porsche, where he was responsible for the realization of 1975 Porsche 924 that Lagaay designed.) 1977, Lagaay assumed Lupine's position as design director. Lagaay's other Porsche models include 1989 Panamericana, 1992 model 968, 1993 Boxter (concept version), 1994 model 993, 1996 model 928, and 1997 model 996.
Citations 1997 Good Design Award (for 1996 Boxster), Chicago Athenauem.
Bibliography Penny Sparke, *A Century of Car Design*, London: Mitchell Beazley, 2002.

Lagares, Marcelo Joulia (1958–)
> See Naço, Studio.

Laguiole, Forge de
French cutler; located Aubrac, Auvergne.

History The origin of the legendary Laguiole knife is unclear, but the year of its introduction may be 1829, a claim of today's Forge de Laguiole. Created by French peasants on the Aubrac plateau of Auvergne, this versatile tool was eventually owned by almost every French citizen. In addition to the sharply honed, curvaceous, pointed, narrow blade, it was fitted with a pick for crafting leather straps and harnesses, or a screw for removing bottle corks. From time to time, versions—plain or precious—featured wood, horn, or ivory handle plates, and a four-leaf clover, fleur-de-lys, 'Napoleonic bee,' or, especially, the 'Aubrac fly' (the insect) at the blade's hinge. 1950, artisanal production of the knife was shifted to industrial production in Thiers, the cutlery center of France. 1987, Gérard Boissins re-established production of the knife in the village of its origin, Laguiole (provincially pronounced 'Lahyuhl'). Traditional versions of the knife have been joined by restyled examples; the 1986 Philippe Starck model became the first 'designer Laguiole' and commemorated Forge de Laguiole's re-establishment. Starck is also the architect of the company's 1987 building/factory (enlarged 1990 and 1995) in Villefranche-de-Rouergue, its 1991 shop in the village of Laguiole and its 1991 gallery/shop in Paris. He also designed another model, 1992 Jojo Long Legs cheese knife. Various Laguiole knives have also been designed by Yan Pennor in 1990, architect Éric Raffy in 1994, the Hermès staff in 1995, Courrèges (two models) in 2002, and others. And a number of vintage designs have been reissued as reproductions. 1989, Pennor redesigned the Laguiole logo, developed a corporate-identity program, and smoothed and simplified the 'Aubrac fly.'
Exhibitions/citations Comité Colbert chose the 1988 Philippe Starck knife for inclusion at 1989 *L'Art de Vivre*, Cooper-Hewitt National Design Museum, New York. 1992 Jojo Long Legs cheese knife shown at 1992 *Exposición Universal de Sevilla (Expo '92)*, where it received European Community Design Prize. 1991 Grand Prix Français de l'Objet Design (for Pennor's knife), and Design Plus award (for 1993 Sommelier wine waiter's knife), 1996 Ambiente fair, Frankfurt.
Bibliography *European Community Design Prize*, Paris: Commission of the European Community, 1992. Mel Byars, 'To Be Continued,' *Metropolitan Home*, Nov.–Dec. 1999: 80+. Daniel Crozes, *Le Laguiole: une lame de légende*, Rodez: Rouergue, 1996.
> See Coutellerie à Thiers, La.

Lahalle, Pierre (1877–1956)
French architect, furniture designer, and interior decorator; born Orléans.

Training École Nationale Supérieure des Arts Décoratifs, Paris.
Biography c. 1902, Lahalle began designing furniture with Maurice Lucet (Orléans 1877–1941) and, 1907, was joined by Georges Levard. They moved from Art Nouveau to Art Déco styles based on 18th-century designs that they simplified and stylized, using fine woods with ivory and mother-of-pearl inlays. Their color combinations of wood and lacquer, polychrome, and gilding were dramatic. The three worked as partners and individually. With Levard, Lahalle designed furniture for various firms in Paris, including the Studium decorating department of Les Grands Magasins du Louvre, and occasionally worked for La Primavera decorating department of Au Printemps department store. He died in Versailles.
Exhibitions Work (often with Levard) shown at editions of Salon d'Automne and (alone 1921; with Levard from 1922) Salons of Société des Artistes Décorateurs; pavilion of the Studium at 1925 *Exposition Internationale des Arts Décoratifs et Industriels Modernes* (salon and boudoir with Levard and André Fréchet); all Paris.
Bibliography Victor Arwas, *Art Déco*, New York: Abrams, 1980. Pierre Kjellberg, *Art déco: les maîtres du mobilier, le décor des paquebots*, Paris: Amateur, 1986/1990.

Lahdenmäki, Nathalie (1974–)
Finnish and French ceramicist.

Training Master's degree in art, department of ceramics and glass, Taideteollinen korkeakoulu, Helsinki.
Biography Both a Finnish and a French citizen, she is a researcher and teacher, UIAH; works as a freelance designer for Arabia pottery (such as Fire candleholders) and Iittala glassworks (such as 1997 Natal candleholders).
Exhibitions/citations Work included in numerous group exhibitions. Honorary mention, 1998 (5th) International Ceramics Competition, Mino, Japan.

Laituri, Dave (1962–)

American industrial designer.

Training 1984, bachelor of science degree in industrial design, Ohio State University, Columbus, Ohio; 1984, postgraduate study, Staatliche Akademie der bildende Künste, Stuttgart, Germany; 2002, master's degree in business administration and design management, University of Westminster, London.
Biography 1985–88, Laituri worked as a staff designer, General Motors, Warren, Mich.; 1988–90, associate designer, Fitch, Worthington, Ohio; 1996–99, a principal, Company X, Palo Alto, Cal., where he designed an Internet home computer and Internet kitchen computer and worked for clients, including Hasbro Interactive, Interval Research, and Softbook Press; 1990–99, was partner and senior designer, Lunar Design, Palo Alto, for clients, including Apple Computer, Hewlett-Packard, and Steelcase; from 1999, worked at Polaroid Corporation, Wayland, Mass., where he has supervised the design of the i-zone digital camera and Instant Combo camera and other projects.
Citations Awards to Lunar and/or manufacturers' staffs. Good Design, Chicago Athenaeum: 1996 (for 1996 512 Ultrasound System, and C256 Ethocardiography System by Acuson) and 2001 (for 1999–2000 Ultrapulse Medical Laser by Coherent Medical); 1997 (10th) Annual Excellence in Design (for SoftGrip Pipettes by Hamilton), American Appliance Association; 1999 Gold Award, Medical Design Excellence Award (for LightSheer Diode Laser System, with Lunar Design staff), Human Factors and Ergonomics Society, US.
> See Lunar Design.

Lalanne, Claude (1927–); François-Xavier Lalanne (1927–)

French artists, designers, and architects; Claude Lalanne born Paris; François-Xavier Lalanne born Agen; wife and husband.

Training Claude Lalanne: architecture, École des Beaux-Arts; École Nationale Supérieure des Arts Décoratifs. François-Xavier Lalanne: Académie Julian. All Paris.
Biography 1956, the Lalannes began collaborating, although they mainly work separately, and, 1967, married. They have become best known for their animal-form furniture and accessories in various media. Claude Lalanne's work has included 1966 Les Couverts silver cutlery and 1987 Crocodile II copper/bronze/leather armchairs. François-Xavier Lalanne's work has included 1976 Rhino Ouvrant copper container, 1977 Hippopotame bronze/wood/silver cabinet, 1984 Gorille de Sûreté bronze/steel cabinet, 1985 Grand Âne Bate bronze container, 1987 Le Poisson Boîte bronze bookholder, and 1987 Le Taureau copper/wood/leather cabinet. They have continued with other work such as 1997 Family of Sheep in bronze and cement.
Exhibitions 1952, François-Xavier Lalanne first showed paintings. 1964, their first joint exhibition at Gallery J, Paris, followed 1966 by Galerie Alexander Iolas, Paris, and 1967 Art Institute of Chicago. Their work subject of 1975 exhibition, Centre National d'Art Contemporain, Paris (catalog below). Their work included in group exhibitions: 1977 *Artiste/Artisan?*, Musée des Arts Décoratifs, Paris; 1978 *L'Art et la Ville—Art dans la Vie*, Fondation Nationale des Arts Graphiques et Plastiques, Paris; 1979 *Weich und Plastisch*, Kunsthaus, Zürich. 1967–75, work shown at Alexander Iolas galleries, Paris, New York, Milan, Geneva, Athens, and Madrid; subsequently at Marisa Del Re Gallery, New York and Paris. More recently 1997, 1998, and 1999 JGM Gallerie Paris and Miami. Work on permanent display, Galerie Artcurial, Paris.
Bibliography Cat., *Les Lalanne*, Paris: SMI, 1975. Gilles de Bure, *Le mobilier français 1965–1979*, Paris: Regard, 1983: 53–54. Cat., John Russell, *Les Lalannes—Claude and François-Xavier Lalanne*, New York: Marisa Del Re Gallery, 1988.

René Lalique. Biches vase. 1938. Unpolished colorless pressed glass, h. 6 11/16" (17 cm). Mfr.: Lalique, France. Courtesy Quittenbaum Kunstauktionen, Munich.

Lalique, Marc (1900–1977)

French glassmaker; active Paris; son of René-Jules Lalique.

Biography On the 1945 death of his father, Marc Lalique succeeded in the management of the Lalique firm but discontinued the production of glass in favor of crystal; is best known for his 1951 eight-leaf circular table and Nina Ricci's 1948 *L'Air du Temps* perfume flacon with two doves in flight on the stopper and other flacons for Nina Ricci.
Bibliography Marc and Marie-Claude Lalique, *Lalique par Lalique*, Lausanne: Edipop, 1977.

Lalique, Marie-Claude (1935–2003)

French glassware designer; daughter of Marc Lalique.

Training École Nationale Superieure des Arts Décoratifs, Paris.
Biography 1977, she became chairperson of the Lalique family firm on the death of her father Marc Lalique, assuming responsibility of the company after having been an active designer for many years, and became its sole designer. 1992, she created her first perfume scent and its flacon, 'Lalique.' 1993, the company launched a series of annual limited-edition fragrances and, 1998, reissued some limited-edition Lalique hood ornaments, following a new men's fragrance.
Bibliography *Les carnets du design*, Paris: Mad-Cap Productions/APCI, 1986: 39.

Lalique, René-Jules (1860–1945)

French glass designer, jeweler, furniture designer, painter, and sculptor; born Ay (Marne); active Paris.

Training Apprenticeship under goldsmith Louis Aucoc, Paris; 1878–80, studies in London; École Nationale Superieure des Arts Décoratifs, Paris.
Biography Lalique's early jewelry designs, stylistically conventional and technically unsophisticated, were sold to various jewelry manufacturers and published in the trade journal *Le bijou*. 1884, he met Jules Destape, who had a successful small jewelry workshop in Paris, which Lalique bought in 1885; continued to furnish a number of Parisian jewelers with designs, including Cartier, Boucheron, and his former master Aucoc. 1887, Lalique moved to a larger space and, 1890, moved once again to a new studio at 20, rue Thérèse and avenue de l'Opéra, where he designed and made jewelry in gold decorated with precious stones, increasingly introducing original designs. 1890–92, he studied enameling and experimented with new processes, realizing a range of soft colors characteristic of Art Nouveau. 1891–94, he made much of the stage jewelry for Sarah Bernhardt and an Egyptian-style tiara in aluminum and glass for Mme. Barthet; 1894, began to incorporate figurative designs (flowers, animals, insects, female figures, landscapes) into his work; 1895–1912, assembled a series of 145 pieces for Calouste Gulbenkian. By 1896, he had become prolific in the production of spectacular jewelry, showing it at the 1900 *Exposition Universelle*, Paris. Lalique created a new style of jewelry influenced by Renaissance and Japanese art. His reputation grew when museums began buying his work. An interest in glass led him to include pieces of crystal, carved into figurative forms, in his c. 1905 jewelry. His sculpture was executed in bronze, ivory, and silver. He began experimentations in glass (having invented a new process for molding glass in 1902) with the large 1904 molded-glass panel for the entry door of his house in the cours-la-Reine in Paris, some scent bottles, and sculpture. 1906–07, Lalique's career went into its second

Thomas Lamb. Steamer lounge chair. 1977. Bent birch plywood with canvas-covered cushions, overall 38 x 24 3/4 x 60 3/4" (96.5 x 62.9 x 154.3 cm), seat h. 17" (43.2 cm). Mfr.: Du Barry Furniture, Canada. Gift of the designer. MoMA.

phase, when François Coty commissioned him to design scent bottles in pressed glass. Establishing his own workshop in 1908 in Combs-la-Ville, he used both *cire perdue* (lost-wax) and other molding methods. From c. 1910, his interest in glasswork was reflected in his late jewelry pieces in simple glass plaquettes. Anticipating the importance of glass in 20th-century architecture, 1913, he designed and furnished over 200 window panes for the Coty building on Fifth Avenue, New York. He established another workshop in Wingen-sur-Moder, Alsace, where it remains today. He abandoned jewelry in favor of pressed glass. Even though he finished pieces with hand-polishing and cutting, he called on semi-industrial techniques to blow-mold and stamp. Lalique's 1920s–30s production was prolific, designing some 350 models of vases and bowls in molded clear, colored, or opalescent glass and a range of tableware, car mascots, jewelry, lighting, and scent bottles. He rediscovered the highly stable 'demi-crystal' and created one-of-a-kind pieces by the *cire perdue* process; exploited the use of glass in indirect interior lighting; 1922, created a number of boxes in aluminum, including for cosmetics firm Roger & Gallet (and had earlier pioneered the use of aluminum in jewelry, such as the 1899 Berenice Tiara). 1930s with René Prou, he designed the luxurious Istanbul Orient Express train salon carriages, also fitted with his glass and silver. 1932, he produced a wide range of glass designs for 1935 oceanliner *Normandie*. His work was widely copied by others including Sabino, Hunebelle, and Etling in France, and glassmakers worldwide. He died in Paris, and, from 1945, the business was directed by his son Marc Lalique, who designed Nina Ricci's 1948 *L'Air du Temps* flacon—not René. The firm is a membe of the Comité Colbert.
Exhibitions/citations Work (jewelry and silver incorporating enamel and glass) was first shown at 1894 Salon of Société des Artistes Français and 1900 *Exposition Universelle*, both Paris. Subsequently, 1902 *Esposizione Internazionale d'Arte Decorativa Moderna*, Turin; 1903 at Grafton Galleries, London; 1905 at Agnew's, London. 1912, first exhibition showing his glassware; from 1911, Salons of Société des Artistes Décorateurs. Work shown at 1925 *Exposition Internationale des Arts Décoratifs et Industriels Modernes*, Paris, including at his own pavilion; 1934 (2nd) Salon de la Lumière, Paris. 1897, elected Chevalier of Légion d'Honneur. Jewelry subject of 1991 exhibition, Musée des Arts Décoratifs, Paris (catalog below).
Bibliography Yvonne Brunhammer et al., *Art Nouveau Belgium, France*, Houston: Institute for the Arts, Rice University, 1976. Marc and Marie-Claude Lalique, *Lalique par Lalique*, Lausanne: Edipop, 1977. Victor Arwas, *The Glass of René Lalique*, London: Academy, 1980. Victor Arwas, *Art Déco*, New York: Abrams, 1980. Jessica Rutherford, *Art Nouveau, Art Deco, and the Thirties: The Furniture Collections at Brighton Museum*, Brighton: The Royal Pavilion, Art Gallery and Museums, 1983: 36–37. Félix Marcilhac, *René Lalique 1860–1945, maître verrier*, Paris: Amateur, 1989. Cat., Yvonne Brunhammer et al., *René Lalique: bijoux verre*, Paris: Union Centrale des Arts Décoratifs, 1991.

Lalique Haviland, Suzanne (1899–1993)

French painter and decorator; daughter of René Lalique.

Training Under Eugène Morand.
Biography She married into the Haviland ceramics family and produced designs in porcelain for the Manufacture Nationale de Sèvres and Haviland in Limoges, and fabrics and wallpaper; sold a painted screen to Jacques Doucet.
Exhibitions Work shown at 1915 Salon d'Automne and later at editions of Salon des Tuileries, Salons of Société Nationale des Beaux-Arts, and, from 1913, Société des Artistes Décorateurs.

Lallemant, Robert (1902–1954)

French ceramicist and decorator.

Training Ceramics, École des Beaux-Arts, Dijon; and in ceramics under Raoul Lachenal.
Biography 1928, Lallemant set up his own workshop and designed/produced limited-production ceramic items as sculpture, vases, and lamp bases, and designed for Au Printemps department store, Paris; was also active as an interior decorator. 1929, he became the only ceramics member, and likewise a cofounder of Union des Artistes Modernes (UAM). 1939, he ceased his design activities to join his family's public-works enterprise.
Exhibitions 1926–28, work shown at Salons of Société des Artistes Décorateurs; ceramics and metal, wood, and glass furniture at the events of UAM from its first (1930) exhibition to 1937.
Bibliography Lucie Delarue-Mardrus, 'Les céramiques de Lallemant,' *ABC antiquités, beaux-arts, curiosités*, no. 219, Apr. 1983: 37. Cat., *Robert Lallemant ou la céramique mécanisée*, Paris: Galerie Jacques de Voo, 1984. Pierre Kjellberg, *Art déco: les maîtres du mobilier, le décor des paquebots*, Paris: Amateur, 1986/1990. Arlette Barré-Despond, *UAM*, Paris: Regard, 1986: 434–53. Cat., *Les années UAM 1929–1958*, Paris: Musée des Arts Décoratifs, 1988: 204–05.

Lam, Izabel (1948–)

American tableware designer; born Hong Kong.

Training From, 1972, Parsons School of Design, New York.
Biography 1972, Lam moved to New York for studies and remained; 1975–80, has worked in the fashion industry, including for Geoffrey Beene; 1985, designed art jewelry under her own name; 1988, initiated tableware, including 1990 Sphere cutlery and Morning Tide glassware in a delicate biomorphic style for which she has become known, with her services first used (1997) by restaurants and hotels.
Bibliography Arlene Hirst, *Metropolitan Home*, June 1990: 31.

Lam, Lawrence

American industrial designer.

Training To 1985, San Jose State University, Cal.
Biography Lam worked at a number of design studios in Silicon Valley, Cal.; was senior vice-president, Puma; worked in the IDg (Industrial Design Group) of Apple Computer, Cupertino, Cal.; managed the completion of the design of the PowerBook Duo, Juggernaut investigation, Blackbird concepts, and other Apple projects and products, including the chief design of the Epic. 1996 with former Apple designer and brand-builder Gavin Ivester, he formed Tonic Industrial Design, Palo Alto, Cal., principally creating prototypes.
Bibliography Paul Kunkel, *Apple Design: The World of the Apple Industrial Design Group*, New York: Graphis, 1997.

Lamb, Thomas (1938–1997)

Canadian furniture designer; born Orillia, Ontario.

Training To 1964, furniture design, Ryerson Institute of Technology, Toronto.
Biography From 1964, Lamb worked for Al Faux at Design Collaborative, Toronto; co-designed furniture/furnishings for University of Guelph; worked with Robin Bush on furniture for the Ontario pavilion at 1967 *Universal and International Exhibition (Expo '67)*, Montréal.

He assisted Faux on the design of the widely published drafting table produced by Norman Wade; 1968, established his own studio, serving residential- and contract-furniture manufacturers. Work included 1969 Wave beachchair (prototype, never produced) for Bunting Furniture Company, Philadelphia; 1977 Steamer chair (the first Canadian design included in the permanent collection of The Museum of Modern Art, New York, and is still in production). Production of the Steamer chair, original by Dominion Chair Company in Nova Scotia, was switched to Du Barry Furniture, then to Ambiant Systems, and finally to Lamb himself through Steamer Furniture Company in Malaysia. 1982–90, Lamb appreciably helped to transform the Nienkämper firm of Toronto from a Knoll International subcontractor into an important Canadian furniture company of original designs. Other work: 1987 Embassy table for the chancery (architect, Arthur Erickson) of the Canadian Embassy, Washington, D.C.
Citations Eedee Craft Design Award (for Wave chair), Ontario Government; 1982 Rosco Award (for Steamer chair), Resource Council of New York; 1983 Gold Award of Excellence (for Steamer chair), Institute of Business Designers (IBD), US.
Bibliography Cat., *Seduced and Abandoned: Modern Furniture Designers in Canada, the First 50 Years*, Toronto: The Art Gallery at Harbourfront, 1986: 27. Rachel Gotlieb and Cora Golden, *Design in Canada Since 1945: Fifty Years from Teakettles to Task Chairs*, Toronto: Knopf Canada, 2001.

Lamb, Thomas Babbitt (1898–1988)

American industrial designer; born New York.

Training Art Students League; New York University; both New York.
Biography From 1900, Lamb worked as a textile designer; eventually established his own textile-design office; 1920s, wrote and illustrated children's books and had his cartoons published. He wrote the monthly column 'Kiddland Movies' in *Good Housekeeping* magazine, which resulted in a line of children's products. During World War II, he developed a crutch armrest for soldiers with broken limbs; designed 1952 line of cutlery by Alcas that featured the first scientifically developed ergonomic handle, the Lamb Wedge-Lock handle.
Bibliography Carroll Ganz, *100 Years of Design: A Chronology 1895–1995*, www.idsa.org/whatis/100yr.

Lambert, Théodore

French architect, decorator, and furniture designer; born Besançon.

Biography Some of Lambert's furniture was produced by Decaux (not JC Decaux); for his décors, produced locks, lighting, *passementerie* (fringe and trim), and other accouterments and fittings.
Exhibitions From 1907, work shown at Salons of Société Nationale des Beaux-Arts and, from its 1901 founding to 1923, at Salons of Société des Artistes Décorateurs, with no listing in its directory after 1927.
Bibliography *Ensembles mobiliers*, vol. 2, Paris: Charles Moreau, 1937. Pierre Kjellberg, *Art déco: les maîtres du mobilier, le décor des paquebots*, Paris: Amateur, 1986/1990.

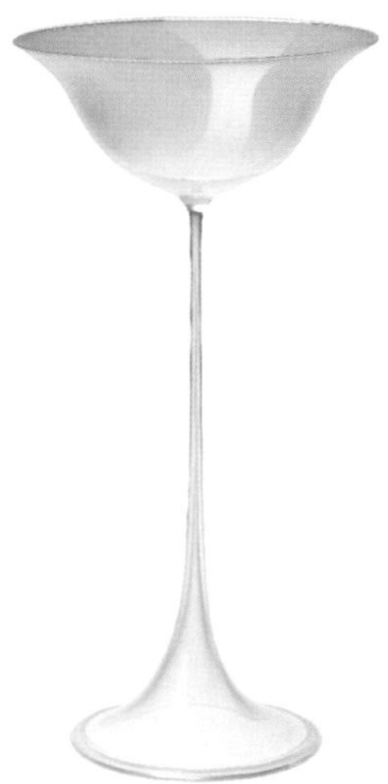

Nils Landberg. Vase. 1957. Glass, h. 13¾ x dia. 7" (34.9 x 17.8 cm). Mfr.: Orrefors, Sweden. Philip Johnson Fund. MoMA.

Lambert-Rucki, Jean (1888–1967)

Polish painter and sculptor; born Crakow.

Training School of Fine Arts, Crakow.
Biography 1911, Lambert-Rucki settled in Paris and shared a room with artist Amedeo Modigliani. His most notable achievements, influenced by Cubism, were realized with Jean Dunand, including 1920s–30s lacquered panels and decorative pieces designed by him and deftly executed by Dunand with whimsical animal motifs. 1936–37, Lambert-Rucki created jewelry designs inspired by West African art and machine aesthetics for Georges Fouquet (1862–1957) in Paris; was friendly with architects Robert Mallet-Stevens and Georges-Henri Pingusson; 1930, became a member, Union des Artistes Modernes (UAM); from 1930, devoted his efforts to religious art.
Exhibitions From 1920 all in Paris, work shown at Salon des Indépendants; 1922–24, Section d'Or group; 1924, Salon d'Automne; Galerie Léonce Rosenberg, Paris; from 1933, Salon des Tuileries; 1942, Salon of Société des Arts Décorateurs. Work included in 1925 *Exposition Internationale des Arts Décoratifs et Industriels Modernes* (smoking room of Une Ambassade Française pavilion with Dunand); 1930s exhibitions of UAM, including four 1930 sculptures; 1936 (3rd) Salon de la Lumière; UAM pavilion (monumental bas-relief), 1937 *Exposition Internationale des Arts et Techniques dans la Vie Moderne*, all Paris.
Bibliography Auction cat., *Collection Karl Lagerfeld: art-déco*, Paris: Drouot, 1975. Sylvie Raulet, *Bijoux art déco*, Paris: Regard, 1984. 'Lambert-Rucki,' in Sammlung Brohan, *Kunst der 20e und 30e Jahre*, Berlin: Karl Brohan, 1985. Arlette Barré-Despond, *UAM*, Paris: Regard, 1986: 436–37. Cat., *Les années UAM 1929–1958*, Paris: Musée des Arts Décoratifs, 1988: 206–07.

Lambretta
> See Innocenti, Ferdinado (1891–1966).

Lancel, Henri

French decorator and furniture designer; active Paris.

Training After World War I, drawing and painting, École Bernard-Palissy; École Nationale Supérieure des Arts Décoratifs; both Paris.
Biography Lancel was friendly with Jean Dunand, Jacques-Émile Ruhlmann, and Pierre Legrain of the Groupe des Cinq. 1928–30, he lived in South America and Cuba and worked in exotic woods; 1930–40, lived in Belgium; 1945, returned to France and designed furniture, most of which was produced by Mobiliers et Ameublement Français (MAF), Au Bûcheron (1958 bentwood and tubular steel chair), and for 1961 oceanliner *France* (chest of drawers and articulated mirror).
Bibliography Pascal Renous, *Portraits de créateurs*, Paris: Vial, 1969.

Landault, Roger (1919–1983)

French ceramicist and furniture designer.

Training 1933–37, École des Arts Appliqués, Paris.
Biography With all activities in Paris, Landault produced ceramics for La Crémaillère; subsequently, worked at the Studium decorating department of Les Grands Magasins du Louvre, where he was the artistic director 1945–55; had clients including individuals, hotels, and enterprises.
Citations 1955 René Gabriel Prize.
Bibliography Pascal Renous, *Portraits de créateurs*, Paris: Vial, 1969. Patrick Favardin, *Les décorateurs des années 50*, Paris: Norma, 2002:

Land Rover
> See King, Spencer.

Landberg, Nils (1907–1991)

Swedish engraver and glassware designer.

Training 1925–27, Slöjdföreningens Skola (now Högskolan för Design ock Konsthantverk), Gothenburg; and school of glass engraving, Orrefors Glasbruk.
Biography 1927–72, Landberg was a designer at Orrefors Glasbruk, where he was first an engraver and later a designer of glass, including tableware, art pieces, and architectural decorations; had a prefer-

Michael A. Landes, Norbert Berghof, and Wolfgang Rang. Kabuki dining chairs (no. F 12, for the Kabuki restaurant, Frankfurt). 1990. Steel, leather, painted wood, and fabric, 43 1/2 x 17 1/2 x 21 1/4" (110.5 x 44.5 x 54 cm). Mfr.: Draenert Studio, Germany. Courtesy Quittenbaum Kunstauktionen, Munich.

ence for freely blown thin and delicate glass. 1960s, he designed tall drinking glasses with delicate bowls and slender stems, and also studio glass.
Exhibitions Gold medal at 1954 (10th) Triennale di Milano. Work shown at 1937 *Exposition Internationale des Arts et Techniques dans la Vie Moderne*, Paris; 1939–40 *New York World's Fair: The World of Tomorrow*; 1948 and 1957 in Zürich; 1954–57 *Design in Scandinavia*, touring the US; 1958 *Formes Scandinaves*, Musée des Arts Décoratifs, Paris; 1959 in Amsterdam; 1980 *Scandinavian Modern Design 1880–1980*, Cooper-Hewitt National Design Museum, New York; 1983–84 *Design Since 1945*, Philadelphia Museum of Art (catalogs below).
Bibliography Cat., 'Nils Landberg,' *Design Quarterly*, no. 34, 1956: 16–17. Erik Zahle (ed.), *A Treasury of Scandinavian Design*, New York: Golden Press, 1961: 281: no. 22. Eileene Harrison Beer, *Scandinavian Design: Objects of a Life Style*, New York: Farrar, Straus, & Giroux, 1975. Cat., David Revere McFadden (ed.), *Scandinavian Modern Design 1880–1980*, New York: Abrams, 1982. Kathryn B. Hiesinger and George H. Marcus III (ed.), *Design Since 1945*, Philadelphia: Philadelphia Museum of Art, 1983. Jennifer Hawkins Opie, *Scandinavia: Ceramics and Glass in the Twentieth Century*, New York: Rizzoli, 1989.

Landes, Michael A. (1948–)
German architect and designer; born Frankfurt.

Training Architecture, Technische Universität, Darmstadt.
Biography 1980–86, Landes lectured in architecture, Technische Hochschule, Darmstadt; 1981, set up an architectural partnership with Norbert Berghof and Wolfgang Rang.
> See Berghof, Norbert.

Landry, Abel (1871–1923)
French architect and designer; born Limoges; active Paris.

Training École des Arts Décoratifs, Limoges; École des Beaux-Arts, Paris; and under William Morris in London.
Biography Landry became associated with Julius Meier-Graefe's shop La Maison Moderne, which made the majority of his objects, mostly in porcelain and metal. He preferred to create total interiors, including wallpaper, curtains, carved paneling, and art work for the walls; was a member of La Poignée with Victor Prouvé and Jules Brateau; used stone and ceramics for exterior ornamentation in the private homes and villas he designed in Paris, Bordeaux, and Coteaux, and apartment buildings in Lyon and Marseille. His approach was similar to that of Georges de Feure, contained no superfluous ornamentation, and was easily adaptable to mass production. After Meier-Graefe's Paris shop closed, Landry's work was sold at Déroullia et Petit, Au Printemps department store, and Maison Ballauf et Petitpoint, all Paris. He died in Paris.
Exhibitions Work shown with La Poignée from 1904, and wrought-iron chandeliers, gilt and silvered bronze ceiling lamps, table lamps, and *flambeaux* at Salons of Société des Artistes Décorateurs from 1906 and editions of Salon d'Automne 1906–13.
Bibliography *Deutsche Kunst und Dekoration*, 1902–03 issue: 179, 551, 555. Yvonne Brunhammer et al., *Art Nouveau Belgium, France*, Houston: Institute for the Arts, Rice University, 1976. Alastair Duncan, *Art Nouveau and Art Déco Lighting*, New York: Simon & Schuster, 1978: 79–80.

Lane, Danny (1955–)
American painter and furniture designer; born Urbana, Ill.; active London.

Training 1975–77 Byam Shaw School of Art; 1977–80 under Cecil Collins, painting, Central School of Arts and Crafts; both London.
Biography 1975, Lane moved to London to work with stained-glass designer Patrick Reyntiens; 1981, set up his own studio in the West End of London and, 1982, moved to Metropolitan Workshops in Hackney; 1983–85, established the cooperative Glassworks also in Hackney, where he and his workers used glass inventively to create one-of-a-kind furniture and furnishings and production models by Zeus in Italy and also Angaraib, Etruscan Chair, and Stacked Chair. By 1986, his studio was realizing large-scale architectural works. c. 1986, he collaborated with Ron Arad's One-Off workshop on commissions, including the executive offices of clothing company Bureaux, for which Lane designed dramatic glass screens. At Glassworks, he designed 1986 stacked chair and table, using layered clear glass unevenly cut; designed 2001 first-floor cocktail bar of Lucorum café, Barnsley, UK; created his shapes by hammering armor-plate glass; designed 1988 Shell and Atlas glass tables by Fiam Italia, c. 1989 work in wood, 1994 140-pillar balustrade of staircase to the mezzanine of the glass gallery of the Victoria and Albert Museum in London, 1998 tubular borosilicate glass fountains in Shanghai.
Exhibitions Work included in 2001 *Sculpture in the Close*, Jesus College, Cambridge, UK; *Design World 2000*, Konstindustrimuseet, Helsinki. Work subject of exhibitions at One-Off, London, c. 1984; Yves Gastou, Paris, 1988; Themes and Variations, London, 1988; Dilmos, Milan, 1988; Art to Use, Frankfurt, 1989; Galerie Margine, Zürich, 1990; Crucial, London, 1990; Ateliers im Museum Kunsterkolonie, Darmstadt, 1993; Mathildehohe, Darmstadt, 1993; Rohsska Museet, Gothenburg, 1994; numerous others.
Bibliography Albrecht Bangert and Karl Michael Armer, *80s Style: Designs of the Decade*, New York: Abbeville, 1990. *Acquisitions 1982–1990 arts décoratifs*, Paris: Fonds National d'Art Contemporain, 1991. Andrew Moor, *Architectural Glass Art: Form and Technique in Contemporary Glass*, London: Mitchell Beazley, 1997.

Lanel, Luc (1893–1965)
French designer.

Biography Lanel designed the Transat silver service, composed of numerous pieces, by Orfèvrerie Christofle for 1935 oceanliner *Normandie*; various wares for 1953 oceanliner *Cambodge* (now *Sella Solaris*); other silver pieces and a *dinanderie* collection by Christofle.
Exhibitions Work shown at 1920–22, 1924–25, 1928–31 annual Salons of Société des Artistes Décorateurs, Paris.
Bibliography Léon Deshairs (intro.), *Modern French Decorative Art: A Collection of Examples of Modern French Decoration*, Paris: Albert Lévy, c. 1925–30. Luc Lanel, *Centenaire de l'orfèvrerie Christofle 1839–1939*, Paris: Daragnès, 1941. *Luc Lanel: La orfebrería*, Barcelona: Vergara, 1958.

Lang, Annette (1960–)
German industrial designer; born Hamburg.

Training 1980–85, Staatliche Akademie der bildenden Künste, Stuttgart.
Biography In Milan: 1985–86, she worked at the the studio of Matteo Thun and, 1986–87, in the studio Antonio Citterio; 1987–88, was a

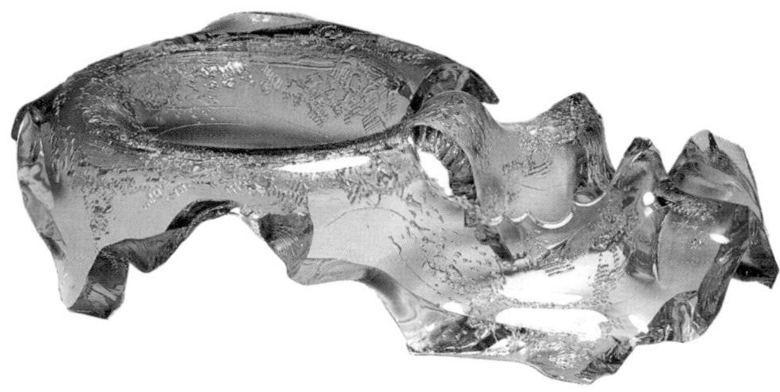

Danny Lane. Crab bowl (one of a kind). c. 2000. Kiln-formed glass, h. 7 x l. 28 1/2 x dia. 15 3/4" (18 x 72 x 40 cm). Mfr.: the designer, UK.

freelance designer at Sottsass Associati. She has been active as a designer of household articles, furniture, lighting, mobile telephones, personal computers, office furniture, and exhibition systems; designed 1988 Fantasy cutlery by ICM and 1988 Chaiseletto chaise longue in tubular steel with bicycle wheels by Valsazino; from 1988, with Richard Sapper, taught, Staatliche Akademie der bildenden Künste, Stuttgart.
Bibliography Cat., Design Center Stuttgart, *Women in Design: Careers and Life Histories Since 1900*, Stuttgart: Haus der Wirtschaft, 1989: 132–35.

Lange, Gerd (1931–)

German designer; born Wuppertal.

Training To 1956, Werkkunstschule, Offenbach am Main.
Biography 1956–61, Lange designed interiors, products, and exhibition; From 1964, in his Kapsweyer studio, specialized in furniture and lighting mainly for contract manufacturers. His furniture for German firms included Thonet in Frankenberg (1973 Flex 2000 side chair and 1985 Thonet-Cut stacking chair), Wilhelm Bofinger in Ilsfeld (1966 Farmer knock-down chair), Schlapp in Neu-Anspach, and Drabert in Minden, and lighting for Staff and Kartell. His 4035 sconce was produced by Kartell.
Exhibitions/citations From 1964, work shown annually at *Die gute Industrieform* exhibitions, Hanover, and at 1964 *Student Rooms Exhibition*, Hanover; 1965 *Die gute Industrieform*, Design Centre, London; 1966 *Vijftig Jaar Zitten*, Stedelijk Museum, Amsterdam; 1968 *Contemporary Furniture*, Munich; 1970 *Rat für Formgebung*, Darmstadt. Two first prizes (chair designs), 1969 Bundespreis 'Gute Form,' Rat für Formgebung (German design council), Frankfurt; 1974 product-design award (five citations for lamps by Staff KG), Industrie Forum Design (iF), Hanover.
Bibliography Cat., *Modern Chairs 1918–1970*, London: Lund Humphries, 1971: no. 70. 'A Chair for All Seasons from Thonet,' *Contract Interiors*, no. 136, July 1977: 20. Cat., Kathryn B. Hiesinger and George H. Marcus III (eds.), *Design Since 1945*, Philadelphia: Philadelphia Museum of Art, 1983.

Langenbeck, Karl (1861–1938)

Ceramics designer; active the US.

Biography Langenbeck joined American Encaustic Tiling, Zanesville, Ohio, where he experimented with new glazes and Parian wares; 1894 with Herman Mueller (also of American Encaustic), founded Mosaic Tile, Zanesville; departing 1908, formed Mueller Mosaic, Trenton, N.J.
Bibliography Doreen Bolger Burke et al., *In Pursuit of Beauty*, New York: The Metropolitan Museum of Art/Abrams, 1986.

Langenmayr, Albert (1951–)

German furniture designer; born Lauingen; active Berlin.

Training 1980–86, Hochschule der Künste, Berlin; 1980–86, apprentice in cabinetmaking, becoming a master in 1986.
Biography From 1982, Langenmayr has designed the interiors of houses in Berlin and the US; became known for his artful and technically sophisticated furniture designs. His 1990 Tension table incorporated suspension-bridge engineering, and his Storch I armchair and Storch II side chair were each held together by a single screw.
Exhibitions Work shown at 1984 *IBA—Idee, Prozess und Ergebnis*, Martin-Gropius-Bau, Berlin; 1986 *Transit Berlin-West: Möbel und Mode*, IDZ Berlin, Hochschule der Künste, Berlin; 1988 *Berlin: les avant-gardes du mobilier*, Galerie Néotù, Paris.
Bibliography Christian Borngräber, *Prototypen der Designwerkstätt*, Berlin: Ernst and Sohn, 1988. Cat., Angela Schönberger et al., *Berlin: les avant-gardes du mobilier*, Paris: Néotù, 1988.

Lanux, Eyre de
> See de Lanux, 'Lise' Eyre.

Lanvin, Jeanne (1867–1946)

French fashion designer; active Paris.

Biography 1885, Lanvin opened her fashion house, rue Marché Saint-Honoré, Paris; her clients included actresses, notably Yvonne Printemps. The emblem designed by Paul Iribe for the firm depicted Lanvin dressed for a ball with her daughter Marguerite (later renamed Marie-Blanche) at her feet. Armand-Albert Rateau designed Lanvin's fashion house and managed the Lanvin-Décoration department of interior design on the rue du Faubourg Saint-Honoré. Lanvin's apartment in the 1920–22 townhouse at 16, rue Barbet-de-Jouy that she had built next to that of her daughter was also designed by Rateau and partially reconstructed in 1985 in the Musée des Arts Décoratifs, Paris. 1950, Marie-Blanche Lanvin hired designer Antonio Canovas del Castillo; 1963–84, Jules-François Crahay was a stylist at Lanvin. From 1985, Maryll Lanvin was a designer. 1989, the firm was purchased by Midland Bank and, 1990, became part of Orcofi. 1990, Claude Montana became the director of haute couture.
Exhibitions Work shown at 1925 *Exposition Internationale des Arts Décoratifs et Industriels Modernes*, Paris; 1927 exhibitions, Prague and Athens; 1931 *Exposition Coloniale*, Paris; 1935 *Exposition Universelle et Internationale de Bruxelles*; 1937 *Exposition Internationale des Arts et Techniques dans la Vie Moderne*, Paris. A Lanvin fashion show was held on the 1935 oceanliner *Normandie* during its maiden voyage from Paris to New York. 1938, elected Chevalier of the Légion d'Honneur.
Bibliography Éveline Schlumberger, 'Au 16 rue Barbet-de-Jouy avec Jeanne Lanvin,' *Connaissance des arts*, no. 138, Aug. 1963: 62–71. Yvonne Brunhammer, *Le cinquantenaire de l'Exposition de 1925*, Paris: Musée des Arts Décoratifs, 1976: 134.

Lanza, Aldo (1942–)

Italian designer; born Turin; active Brescia.

Training To 1968, architecture, Politecnico, Milan.
Biography 1968, Lanza began his professional career; has had clients in Italy including Alexia and Gufram; designed plastic furniture by Valenti, bath accessories by Bilumen, and 1965 4850 stacking chair in ABS (with Georgina Castiglioni and Giorgio Gaviraghi) by Kartell; became a member, ADI (Associazione per il Disegno Industriale).
Bibliography *ADI Annual 1976*, Milan: Associazione per il Disegno Industriale, 1976.

Lanzani, Paola (1933–)

Italian architect and designer; born Nerviano; active Milan.

Biography Lanzani joined Ordine degli Architetti in Milan and Gescal public housing; 1960–65, worked in a studio in Bogotà, Colombia, where she designed residences, buildings, and furnishings; was consultant designer to Shell Colombia, Ervico, and Olivetti; taught technical design, American University, Bogotà. 1966, she returned to Italy

and worked on the renovation and architectural interiors of La Rinascente department stores in Milan and Turin, and was a consultant designer to the Richard-Ginori store, and to Lanerossi in Lecce and Mestre. 1971 with Franco Menna, she set up a studio in Milan, designing the stores of Croff Centro Casa, products, and interior architecture; 1972, became a member, Associazione per il Disegno Industriale (ADI).
Exhibitions Work shown at 1968 (14th) and 1973 (15th) editions of Triennale di Milano; various Eurodomus editions Ljubljana.
Bibliography *ADI Annual 1976*, Milan: Associazione per il Disegno Industriale, 1976.

Lap, Janja (1929–)
Slovene designer; born Ljubljana.

Training 1947–56, Faculty of Architecture, Univerza v Ljubljani; 1963–65, Royal College of Art, London.
Biography 1957–61, Lap worked in the State Architecture Office in Ljubljana; 1961–63, at Akademija Likovnih Umjetnosti (ALU, academy of fine art), Ljubljana. 1967–77, was a freelance designer, and also part-time lecturer, Sheffield University, UK. 1977–89, worked as a designer at Iskra electronic-component firm, Ljubljana; 1989–90, lectured, Mosul University, Iraq; from 1990, was been a freelance designer and part-time lecturer, Univerza v Ljubljani. Work has included 1961–63 glass designs for Rogaška, Slovenia; 1975 renovation and 1977 design of residences in Menorca, Spain, and Oxford, UK.
Bibliography Richard Sapper (ed.), *The International Design Yearbook*, London: Laurence King, 1998.

Lapidouse, Sylvie (1954–)
French furniture designer.

Biography 1987, Lapidouse established an interior-architecture and design office. In Paris, she has designed two multi-purpose rooms at the Carrousel du Louvre, the headquarters reception lobby of Nord-Est Industrie, the espresso bar of Emporio Armani, L'Homme Bleu perfume display counter for Lanvin, layout of boutique Clio Blue, layout of Guerlain beauty institute; all Paris. She laid out Serap department store, Lyon. Furniture designs include 1986 Epsilon chair by Avant Scene and 1990 wood Diver-Desk, inspired by Oliver Sacks's book *The Man Who Mistook His Wife for a Hat* (London: Duckworth, 1985).
Bibliography *Vogue décoration*, no. 26: 21. www.via.asso.fr.

Lapidus, Morris (1902–2001)
Russian architect; born Odessa.

Training To 1927, architecture, Columbia University, New York.
Biography With his parents, Lapidus emigrated as an infant to New York; began working in an architectural firm as a draftsperson, while concurrently designing retail-store interiors; became primarily known for hotels in South Florida, such as 1955 Fontainebleau (now Fontainebleau Hilton), 1955 Eden Rock (now Eden Rock Renaissance Resort & Spa), and 1956 Americana (now Sheraton Bal Harbour), many of which are intact today; also designed interiors of Rainbow shop, Brooklyn, N.Y., in c. 1939 and Bond clothing store, Brooklyn, N.Y., in 1949. His work (more than 1,200 buildings, including about 250 hotels) was panned by the critics of the time, but opinion had changed at the end of the 20th century, when kitsch became desirable, some critics by then labeling his work Postmodern. He himself even called the Fontainebleau 'the world's most pretentious hotel'; it was featured in the film *Goldfinger* (1964), based on the Ian Fleming spy novel about James Bond. Lapidus wrote the books *An architecture of Joy* (Miami: E. A. Seemann, 1979), *Architecture: A Profession and a Business* (New York: Van Nostrand Reinhold, 1967), and *Too Much Is Never Enough*, an autobiography (New York: Rizzoli, 1996). 1984, he retired but, late 1990s with Miami architect Deborah Desilets, returned to design 1997 Roots store and Aura restaurant, both Toronto; an unbuilt Miami hotel and office building; and products, including a pen, a watch, and neckties.
Exhibitions/citations 1967 *40 Years of Art and Architecture: Morris Lapidus*, Joe & Emily Lowe Art Gallery, University of Miami; 1970 exhibition, Architectural League, New York. American Originals award, 2000 (1st) National Design Awards, Cooper-Hewitt National Design Museum; 2001 honor, Society of Architectural Historians convention, Eden Roc hotel, Miami Beach.
Bibliography John W. Cook and Heinrich Klotz, *Conversations with Architects...*, New York: Praeger, 1973. *Hotel Architecture and the Work of Morris Lapidus: A Selected Bibliography*, Monticello, Ill.: Vance Bibliographies, 1985. Lamia Doumato, *Morris Lapidus: A Bibliography*, Monticello, Ill.: Vance Bibliographies, 1988. Martina Düttmann and Friederike Schneider (eds.), *Morris Lapidus: Architect of the American Dream*, Basel: Birkhäuser, 1992 (also ed. in German). 'Qui êtes-vous Morris Lapidus?,' *Architecture interieure crée*, no. 251, Nov.–Dec. 1992: 118–23. Morris Lapidus, *Too Much Is Never Enough: An Autobiography*, New York: Rizzoli, 1996. Jonathan Ringen, 'Morris Lapidus Architect,' Metropolis, Jan. 2001.

Laporte-Blairsy, Léo (1865–1923)
French sculptor and lighting designer; born Toulouse.

Training Under Alexandre Falguière.
Biography Laporte-Blairsy began as a sculptor and engraver of large monuments and busts; late 1890s, reduced the scale of his work and became known for his Art Nouveau sculptural lighting with its high aesthetics and technical innovation; was one of the first to use incandescent bulbs in a manner not possible with combustion light; designed lamps, statuettes, vases, letter openers, and epergnes in bronze, marble, and plaster. His biscuit porcelain ware was produced by Manufacture Nationale de Sèvres. He executed objects in gold, silver, and translucent enamel, mostly sold by M. Houdebine. Other lighting was produced by the foundry Susse Frères. Some of his lamps or 'luminous fantasies' told a story (La Fillette au Ballon was about a young girl who bought a balloon from Les Grands Magasins du Louvre), while others were based on historical themes, and still others were pure decoration.
Exhibitions Work shown at 1887 Salon of Société des Artistes Français, including smaller-scale works at its 1898 edition.
Bibliography *Revue des arts décoratifs*, 1901: 260. *L'art*, 1902: 40–47. *Éclairage de 1900 à nos jours*, Brussels: L'Écuyer, nos. 31, 33, and 43. *Deutsche Kunst und Dekoration,* 1903–04 issue: 105. Alastair Duncan, *Art Nouveau and Art Déco Lighting*, New York: Simon & Schuster, 1978.

Larche, François-Raoul (1860–1912)
French sculptor; born Saint-André-de-Cubzac.

Training From 1878 under François Jouffroy, Alexandre Falguière, and Eugène Delaplanche, École Nationale des Beaux-Arts, Paris.
Biography Initially Larche realized monumental sculpture but, at the end of the 19th century, turned to mass-produced castings of smaller pieces, such as lamps, goblets, ashtrays, vases, and centerpieces made by Siot-Décauville and by Susse Frères. He is best known for gilt-bronze table lamps (also cast by Siot-Décauville) in the swirling form of American dancer Loïe Fuller in her famous flowing costume and other Fuller statues, the most famous of which is the c. 1897 La Danse du Feu. (Fuller performed rather flamboyantly at the Folies-Bergère in Paris.) Larche executed the sculpture group *La Loire et ses affluents*, commissioned in 1910 for the place du Carrousel in Paris, a number of works on Christian themes, and the c. 1919 monument to the dead of World War I on the Île-sur-Tet, France.
Exhibitions/citations Work first shown at 1881 Salon of Société des Artistes Français and, from 1884, regularly at École Nationale des Beaux-Arts, where, 1886, received grand prize of Prix de Rome. Gold medal, 1900 *Exposition Universelle*, Paris,
Bibliography Cat., *Exposition des œuvres de Raoul Larche, statuaire et peintre, et de Raymond Sudre, statuaire et peintre*, Paris: 57, rue Chardon Lagache [n.d.]. *Le Modern Style*, Paris: Baschet, 1974: 172. Yvonne Brunhammer et al., *Art Nouveau Belgium, France*, Houston: Institute for the Arts, Rice University, 1976.

Larcher, Dorothy (1884–1952)
British textile designer; active Painswick, Gloucestershire.

Training Hornsey School of Art, London.
Biography From early 1920s, Larcher and Phyllis Barron collaborated on textile production and design. 1930, production was moved to Painswick, Gloucestershire, where they produced dressmaking and furnishing textiles using new and historic French blocks. 1939, their fabrics were sold through Little Gallery on Ellis Street, London. Commissions included soft furnishings for the Duke of Westminster's yacht *The Flying Cloud* and the Senior Common Room of Girton College in Cambridge. With Enid Marx, they were the foremost exponents of hand-block-printed fabrics in the first half of the 20th century in Britain. They rejected aniline dyes in favor of vegetable dyes; revived the discharge-printing method; were best known for their bold monochromatic prints on unbleached cotton and linens.

Bibliography Cat., *Thirties: British Art and Design Before the War*, London: Arts Council of Great Britain/Hayward Gallery, 1979.

Larger, Sophie (1972–)
French designer; born Nancy.

Training École Nationale Supérieure des Arts Décoratifs; ENSCI (Les Ateliers); both Paris.
Biography Born to a family of engineers, Larger has become known for her unusual seating, which is highly use-flexible and calls on new materials, an example of which is 1997 Glüp hassock (stuffed with small plastic pellets) by Ligne Roset and sponsored for production by VIA (French furniture association); also 2003 Ouff inflatable chair by Inoui. For her one-of-a-kind Fluff armchair, she called on Alucobond, an aluminum-and-plastic-sandwich sheet.
Exhibitions Work included in 2004 *Design d'Elle*, Galerie VIA (French furniture association), Paris.
Bibliography Cat., Sophie Tasma Anargyros et al., *L'école française: les créateurs de meubles du 20ème siècle*, Paris: Industries Françaises de l'Ameublement, 2000.

Larsen, Ejner (1917–)
Danish furniture designer.

Training To 1940, cabinetmaking, Møbelskole, Kunsthåndværkerskolen, Copenhagen.
Biography 1942–57, Larsen was an instructor at Det Kongelige Danske Akademi in Copenhagen; 1942–52, worked for cabinet maker Jacob Kjær and for architects Mogens Koch, Peter Koch, and Palle Suenson; 1947 with Askel Bender Madsen, set up his own design studio. Some of their furniture was produced by Willy Beck. 1952–70, Larsen was architect at Christiansborg Palace (and the department architect 1966–79); 1977, was a court and state inspector.
Exhibitions Work shown at editions of the Triennale di Milano and included in 1954–57 *Design in Scandinavia*, touring the US, 1960–61 *The Arts of Denmark*, touring the US, 1965 exhibition of Danish arts and crafts, Das Kantonale Gewerbemuseum, Berne.
Bibliography Frederik Sieck, *Nutidig Dansk Møbeldesign – en kortfattet illustreret beskrivelse*, Copenhagen: Bondo Gravesen, 1990.

Larsen, Ib Kofod-
> See Kofod-Larsen, Ib.

Larsen, Jack Lenor (1927–)
American textile designer; born Seattle.

Training 1945–50, Washington University, Seattle; 1951–52, Cranbrook Academy of Art, Bloomfield Hills, Mich.
Biography 1952, Larsen opened his own workshop in New York and received his first commission from architecture firm Skidmore, Owings, and Merrill, for draperies for 1952 Lever House, Park Avenue, New York. At this time, he began machine-weaving fabrics with the appearance of handweaving; they were subsequently much imitated. 1958, he set up Larsen Design Studio for experimentation, consultation, and fabrication for large architecture projects; designed fabrics for the decorating trade and institutional and airline use; lectured and traveled widely, studying textile design. Larsen's textile innovations included the first printed-velvet upholstery fabrics, the first (1961) stretch upholstery fabric, and the first warp-knit Saran-monofilament casement fabric (including the 1960 Interplay). He created cabin upholstery fabrics for Pan American airlines in 1969 and for Braniff airlines 1972–78; the theater curtain for Filene Center for Performing Arts, Wolf Trap, Va., in 1971; quilted banners for Sears Tower, Chicago, in 1974; 1981 upholstery fabric for Cassin in 1967, and for Vescom. He wrote numerous books with others, including *Elements of Weaving...* (with Azalea Thorpe; Garden City, N.Y.: Doubleday 1978) and *Beyond Craft: The Art Fabric* (with Mildred Constantine; New York: Van Nostrand Reinhold, 1973), as well as *Jack Lenor Larsen: A Weaver's Memoir* (see below).
Exhibitions/citations Work subject of 1967 *Andean Arts*, Otis Art Institute of Los Angeles County; 1969 exhibit, Designer/Craftsman Guild and Fort Wayne Art Institute, Indiana; 1977 exhibit, Stedelijk Museum, Amsterdam; 1981 *Jack Lenor Larsen: 30 ans de création textile = 30 Years of Creative Textiles*, Musée des Arts Décoratifs, Paris (catalog below). Gold medal, 1964 (13th) Triennale di Milano; 1983, elected Honorary Royal Designer for Industry, UK.
Bibliography Larry Salmon, 'Jack Lenor Larsen in Boston,' *Craft Horizons*, no. 23, Apr. 1971: 14–23. Mildred Constantine, 'Jack Lenor

Jack Lenor Larsen. Leather Cloth upholstery fabric. 1955. Leather, vinyl, and nylon, 109 x 38" (276.9 x 96.5 cm). Mfr.: Jack Lenor Larsen, US. Given anonymously. MoMA.

Larsen: The First 25 Years,' *American Fabrics and Fashions*, no. 113, summer 1978. Cat., *Jack Lenor Larsen: 30 Years of Creative Textiles*, Paris: Musée des Arts Décoratifs, 1981. Cat., Kathryn B. Hiesinger and George H. Marcus III (eds.), *Design Since 1945*, Philadelphia: Philadelphia Museum of Art, 1983. Robert A.M. Stern (ed.), *The International Design Yearbook*, New York: Abbeville, 1985/1986. Jack Lenor Larsen, *Jack Lenor Larsen: A Weaver's Memoir*, New York: Abrams, 1998.

Larsen, Johannes (1912–)
Danish engineer.

Training In civil engineering, Copenhagen.
Biography 1967, Larsen opened his own office in Vanlose; designed a range of objects, including furniture, milking machines, and 1967–68 Cylinder Cushion 272 floor seat by France & Søn.
Exhibitions Cylinder Cushion 181 lounger first shown, at 1968 Annual Furniture Fair at Christianhus, Horsholm, Denmark.
Bibliography Cat., *Modern Chairs 1918–1970*, London: Lund Humphries, 1971.

Larsens, Bjørn A. (1926–)
Norwegian furniture designer.

Biography Active from 1950s, Larsens worked for Trio Fabrikker from 1952 and the Postverket from 1957.
Citations 1973 Japanese design prize (for bicycle model, with Terje Meyer and Jan Sverre Christiansen).
Bibliography Fredrik Wildhagen, *Norge i Form*, Oslo: Stenersen, 1988: 153.

Larsson-Kjelin, Ann (1953–)
Swedish textile designer.

Training To 1974, Institutionen Textilhögskolan, Högskolan, Borås.
Biography From 1977, she was associated with the firm Marks Pelle Vävare; in addition to domestic textiles, contributed to a number of public works; teaches textile design, Institutionen Textilhögskolan.
Bibliography Robert A.M. Stern (ed.), *The International Design Yearbook*, New York: Abbeville, 1985/1986.

Lassus, Kristiina (1966–)
Finnish designer; born Helsinki; active Finland and Italy.

Training 1992, master's degrees, design leadership and, 1995, interior architecture and furniture, both Taideteollinen korkeakoulu, Helsinki.
Biography Lassus was a consultant and the design coordinator to Artek; a consultant, a furniture designer, and a designer of interior

Johannes Larsen. Cubo adjustable cushion. 1967–68. Fabric-covered polyurethane foam, folded h. 22 1/16 x dia. 20 7/8" (56 x 53 cm). Mfr.: France & Søn, Denmark. Gift of John Stuart, Inc. MoMA.

architecture to others in Finland and elsewhere; has designed objects and furniture by Alessi, Zanotta, Poltronova, and others. Work includes 1995 Tundra trivets and 2002 Uma incense burner by Alessi and 1997 Clea side chair and ottoman, and 1995 Puro table by Zanotta. 1993, she founded her first studio D'Imago for product design, interior architecture, and design consultancy and, 2003, a second, Kristiina Lassus Studio, in Stresa (VB), Italy. She has been the product manager of Silva Wetterhoff, then design coordinator of Artek, both Finland, and, 1998, became design manager of Alessi. Her 2000 Strawbowls, made from an agricultural by-product by the Finnish firm Strawbius Oy for Alessi, were based on Lassus's ecological and conservational concerns.
Exhibition/exhibition Work included in *Generation X: Young Nordic Design*, traveling the world from 2000. Designed Strawbius bowls originally for 1999 *Find* exhibition. 2000 Fair to Nature; 2001 Design Plus award, Ambienti fair, Frankfurt; 2001 Premio Compasso d'Oro

László, Paul (1900–1993)
Hungarian architect, decorator, and designer.

Biography 1923, László moved to Vienna and established a decorating firm; within a short time, worked on decorating commissions throughout Europe. 1927, he settled in Stuttgart; 1936, moved to Los Angeles and decorated interiors of celebrity clients, including Cary Grant, Elizabeth Taylor, Barbara Stanwyck, Robert Taylor, and Barbara Hutton. In Los Angeles, he designed stores for Bullock's Wilshire, Goldwater's, Robinson's, and Orbach's and, in Las Vegas, most of the casinos and showrooms in Howard Hughes's hotels. László's style was an exuberant one, associated with the 1950s on the West Coast. His work included textiles and lighting, some furniture by Saltman California and little-known 1940s upholstery and furniture by Herman Miller.
Bibliography Obituary, 'Paul Laszlo, 93, Dies; Architect to Celebrities,' *The New York Times*, 9 Apr. 1993: D21.

Latham, Richard S. (1920–1991)
American industrial designer.

Training 1940–41 under Ludwig Mies van der Rohe, engineering and design, Illinois Institute of Technology (IIT), Chicago.
Biography In Chicago: from 1942 under Anne Swainson, Latham worked in the Bureau of Design, Montgomery Ward; 1945–55, Latham was a product designer for Raymond Loewy; directed Loewy's Chicago office for most of this period, producing work such as casings for Hallicrafters radios and televisions. With Loewy, designed and planned the marketing for 1954 Service 2000 range of ceramic dinnerware by Rosenthal and, under his own name, designed glassware by Rosenthal Studio-Linie. 1955 in Chicago, Latham was active in the design office Latham Tyler Jensen, with designer George Jensen (Danish from the West Coast, not Georg Jensen), architect Robert Tyler, and others, with offices in Long Beach, Cal., and in Copenhagen (with Jacob Jensen from 1959–61), serving clients such as Xerox, Argus cameras, Ampex electronics, and Bang & Olufsen. From c. 1995, Latham was president, International Council of Societies of Industrial Design (ICSID).
Bibliography Richard S. Latham, 'Is This Change Necessary?,' *Industrial Design*, vol. 5, Feb. 1958: 66–70. Richard S. Latham, 'The Artifacts as a Cultural Cipher,' in Laurence B. Holland (ed.), *Who Designs America?*, Garden City, N.Y.: Anchor, 1966: 257–80. Richard S. Latham, 'Der Designer in USA: Stilist, Künstler, Produktplaner?' *form*, no. 34, 1966: 28–31. Cat., Kathryn B. Hiesinger and George H. Marcus III (eds.), *Design Since 1945*, Philadelphia: Philadelphia Museum of Art, 1983. Ralph Caplan, 'Design Heads and Tales/Richard Latham, FIDSA (1920–1991),' *Innovation* (IDSA quarterly journal), vol. 11, no. 1, 1992.

Laube, Sandra (1967–)
German designer; born Frankfurt; active Italy.

Training 1987–93, Istituto Superiore per le Industrie Artistiche (ISIA), Florence; 1993, scholarship, Minneapolis (Minn.) College of Art and Design (MCAD), and internship at 3M, St. Paul, Minn., US; from 2000, course in collaboration with Università degli Studi, Florence, and Fashion Institute of Technology, New York.
Biography 1995 with art director Biagio Cisotti, Laube established design studio Cisotti Laube in Florence. The partnership was founded on the design of furniture by B.R.F. in Colle Val d'Elsa (SI), directed by Fabio Biancucci, with work for the firm such as 1995 Blob cupboards, 2000 Giolito modular sofa, and 2001–02 Loop bookcase system. For other clients: 1995 Olivia chair by Certaldese; 1996 Nella stacking chair by Poltronova; 1997 Motion carpet by Namaste; 1998 Millefoglie chair, 1998 Cincin table, and 1999 Frisbi barstool by Plank: 2001 Nuvole vase by Vilca; others.
Bibliography *The International Design Yearbook*, London: Laurence King, 1996 and 1998. Cristina Morozzi and Silvio San Pietro, *Contemporary Italian Furniture*, Milan: L'Archivolto, 1996.
> See Cisotti, Biagio.

Laubersheimer, Wolfgang (1955–)
German designer; born Bad Kreuznach.

Training Metal sculpture, Kunsthochschule, Cologne.
Biography 1982, Laubersheimer cofounded Group Unikate and, 1985, Group Pentagon, both Cologne; 1989, founded Laubersheimer Werkstätten in Bad Kreuznach and cofounded the Initiative Design Horizonte in Frankfurt; has designed for Swatch, Phillip Morris, AEG, Daimler-Benz, Tiffany, SEAT, Les Galeries Lafayette, and Lancaster. Teaching activities: 1989, lecturer, J.W. Goethe-Universität, Frankfurt; 1990, visiting professor, University of California at Los Angeles; 1991, visiting professor, Design Institute, Hong Kong; 1991, professor, Fachhochschule, Cologne; 1995, conceived and designed first multi-media cafés with Internet terminals in Germany.
Exhibitions/citations Work shown throughout Germany and in São Paulo, New York, Milan, Basel, Nagoya, and Los Angeles.

Kristiina Lassus. Strawbowls. 2000. Straw, large h. 5 1/8 x dia. 11 7/8" (13.5 x 30 cm), small h. 7 1/2 x dia. 8 5/8" (10 x 22 cm). Mfr.: Alessi, Italy.

1989 Design Plus prize, Ambiente fair, Frankfurt.

Lauda, Giovanni (1956–)

Italian architect and designer; born Naples; active Milan.

Training In architecture.
Biography 1989–92, Lauda worked at Morozzi & Partners in Milan; designed several household objects by Sedie & Company, Uchino, Play Line, Radice, Artas; home and store furniture by Tramontano Gioielli, and Royal; commercial mountings by Nolan, Replastic, and Fissler. 1998 Passepartout seating unit (with Dante Donegani) was produced by Edra. From 1993, director, design-culture course in the master of industrial design program, Domus Academy, Milan. 1993 with Dante Donegani, set up design studio D&L. Lauda has lectured at SDA Bocconi (Scuola di Direzione Aziendale), Milan; Facoltà di Architettura, Politecnico, Milan; in Tokyo; Thai Interior Design Association (TIDA), Bangkok; Faculty of Architecture, Istanbul Teknik Üniversitesi (ITU); Universidad Pontificia Bilivariana, Medellin, Colombia. Designed the exhibition *Rodin and Michelangelo, Il Giardino di San Marco*.
Exhibitions Participator in exhibition design and catalog editor, 1996 *Il design italiano dal 1964 al 1990*, Palazzo della Triennale, Milan.
Bibliography Michele De Lucchi (ed.), *The International Design Yearbook*, London: Laurence King, 2001.
> See Donegani, Dante.

Laudani, Marta (1954–)

Italian designer; born Verona; active Rome.

Training 1979, architecture degree, Università degli Studi, Rome.
Biography 1980, Laudani established her own studio in Rome; 1981–85, participated in a number of international architecture competitions, including residential part of Lützowplatz, Berlin; maritime station, port of Piombino; Piazza dei Mulini, Positano; urban park, port, and Manifattura Tabacchi, Bologna; entrance to the town of Tivoli; urban part of Certaldo Alto, Florence; 1985, replanned Piazza of Parco dei Caduti del 19 luglio 1943, Rome, winning entry (master stages 1989–90), '48 Green Areas in Rome.' From 1987, she has designed furniture, textiles, and lighting with Marco Romanelli; 1987–95, was a contributing writer to *Domus* magazine; 1992–2000, vice-president, Associazione Jacqueline Vodoz e Bruno Danese in Milan; from 2001, has been professor of furnishings and interior architecture, Facoltà di Architettura, Università degli Studi 'La Sapienza,' Rome; has written articles, essays, and books on design.
Bibliography Mauro Baracco, 'New Directions in Contemporary Italian Architecture,' *Transition*, no. 40, 1993. Maruska Scotuzzi, 'Progettare al femminile,' *Blu & Rosso*, Oct. 1993. Stefano Casciani, 'Oggetto-Ambiente,' *Abitare*, no. 328, Apr. 1994: 176–83. Marta Laudani and Marco Romanelli, *Paradigmaticità delle arti decorative*, Milan: Associazione JV & BD, 1995. 'Le opere di Marta Laudani e Marco Romanelli,' *Costruttori Romani*, Nov.–Dec. 1996: 84. Marco Romanelli and Marta Laudani, *Design Nord-Est: Bianconi, Bonfanti, Pinton, Rinaldi, Scarpa, Valle*, Milan: Abitare Segesta, 1996. Cat., Enzo Biffi Gentili, *Il disegno ceramico: Gagnère, Laudani, Romanelli, Szekely*, Milan: Electa, 1999. *The International Design Yearbook*, London: Laurence King, 1999 and 2002.
> See Romanelli, Marco.

Laughlin Pottery

American ceramics manufacturer; located East Liverpool, Ohio.

History 1871, brothers Shakespeare and Homer Laughlin founded a small pottery in East Liverpool, Ohio. It was one of the first potteries in the US to produce whiteware. Starting with 60 employees, it produced about 6,000 pieces of dinnerware per day; by 1874, was known as The Ohio Valley Pottery. 1879, Shakespeare left the firm, which was managed by Homer 1879–81. 1889, William Edwin Wells joined the firm. 1897, Homer sold out completely to Wells, Marcus Aaron, and others. The firm moved to nearby Laughlin Station, where it had begun full production by 1903, in two new buildings and a third purchased from another company. 1906, a fourth plant was built in Newell, W. V., which began full production in 1907. 1913, a fifth plant was added and, 1923, a sixth with a continuous tunnel kiln. The new production technique proved so successful that further plants were added in 1927 and 1929. At its peak, 2,500 workers produced 360,000 pieces of dinnerware per day in 1,500,000 square feet (140,000 m²) of production space. 1929, all the East Liverpool factories were closed, and only the Newell site remained. 1930, Wells was succeeded by his son Joseph Mahan Wells. Under the Aarons' management, the production included Oven Serve (oven-to-table ware) and Kitchen Kraft. 1927, British émigré Frederick Rhead became the artistic director and designed the legendary 1935 Fiesta dinnerware (reintroduced as a lead-free product in 1986) in the brightly colored glazes, that became strongly associated with the Homer Laughlin firm. Rhead's Harlequin and Rivera soon followed. But all was not modern; many wares were historicist in nature. 1936, a colorful decal pattern was applied to the Nautilus range, creating the Harmony line. 1942, Rhead died of cancer and, 1945, was replaced by Don Schreckengost (brother of Viktor Schreckengost) as the artistic director. 1960, Joseph M. Wells became the chairperson and his son Joseph M. Wells Jr. executive vice-president. Homer Laughlin's 1,600 workers today produce over one million pieces of dinnerware per week. 1984 after a succession of artistic directors, Jonathan O. Perry assumed the position. From 1989, Marcus L. Aaron 2nd has been the president, replacing his father Marcus L. Aaron 1st, who had been at the firm for 65 years.
Exhibitions Grand prize, 1876 *Centennial Exposition*, Philadelphia; and 1939–40 *New York World's Fair: The World of Tomorrow.*
Bibliography Sharon and Bob Huxford, *The Collector's Encyclopedia of Fiesta*, Paducah, Ky.: Collector Books, 1984. Jo Cunningham, *Homer Laughlin China: 1940s & 1950s*, Atglen, Pa.: Schiffer, 2000. Jo Cunningham and Darlene Nossaman, *Homer Laughlin China: Guide to Shapes and Patterns*, Atglen, Pa.: Schiffer, 2002.
> See Rhead, Frederick.

Laughton, Scot (1962–)

Canadian industrial designer.

Training Ontario College of Art (now Ontario College of Art and Design), Toronto.
Biography Soon after finishing his studies, Laughton founded manufacturing company Portico, with two partners. The Strala lamp, designed while Laughton was at school, was one of Portico's first products. 1992, he established his own studio, where he has designed the Confer chair and Eglinton seating range by Keilhauer, Tufold table series by Nienkämper, 1998–99 Juxta storage/furniture system and 1999 Bravo coat-hook system and other products by Umbra, and furniture, including 1997 Jim stool and others, by Pure Design. He teaches, Ontario College of Art and Design.
Exhibitions/citations 1999–2000 *Virtu 12* magazine annual, Toronto; 1987 Top Ten Designs (for Strala lamp), *Time* magazine; 1999 Good Design award (for Juxta system), Chicago Athenaeum; 2003 Best of Canada (for Canal furniture range by Keilhauer), Design Exchange, Toronto.

Laurent, Micheline (1894–)

French fabric designer; born Paris; wife of architect Georges-Henri Pingusson.

Biography 1932, Laurent and Pingusson became members of UAM (Union des Artistes Modernes). She worked on her husband's design of the Hôtel Latitude; specialized in curtains, pillows, and table linen.
Exhibitions Work shown at UAM pavilion, 1937 *Exposition Internationale des Arts et Techniques dans la Vie Moderne*, Paris.
Bibliography Arlette Barré-Despond, *UAM*, Paris: Regard, 1986: 523.

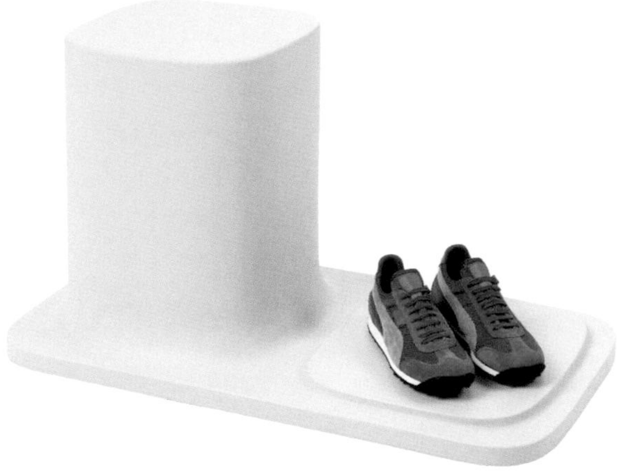

Scot Laughton. Situ flexible seat. 2002. Fiberglass and polyurethane-foam core, covered with post-painted close-cell urethane skin, h. 17 x w. 18 x l. 32 1/2" (43.2 x 45.7 x 82.5 cm). Mfr.: Lolah, Canada.

Lauriola, Vincenzo
> See Carallo, Nunzie Paola; Di Somma, Giuseppe.

Lauro, Agostino (1861–1924)

Italian designer and entrepreneur; active Turin.

Biography By 1890s, Lauro had a reputation as an entrepreneur and designer with numerous private commissions, including c. 1900 villa at Sordevolo and assignments for the decoration of public buildings in Turin; operated a furniture gallery that was patronized by distinguished clients on the via Genoa of Turin; designed furniture in the prevailing Stile Liberty (or Stile Floreale).
Exhibitions The Palazzina Lauro, designed by architect Giuseppe Velati-Bellini, was built for the 1902 *Esposizione Internazionale d'Arte Decorativa Moderna*, Turin. Exhibited in numerous international expositions.
Bibliography Cat., Gabriel P. Weisberg, *Stile Floreale: The Cult of Nature in Italian Design*, Miami: The Wolfsonian Foundation, 1988.

Lauro, Guiseppe
> See Innocenti, Ferdinado.

Lauro, Mario Rosario (1940–)

Italian industrial and graphic designer; born and active Naples.

Biography 1963–65, Lauro was active in research, analysis, and project design on the reconstruction of the northern section of Naples; was an architect in the partnership Lauro, Palomba, Pasca in Naples. From 1966, he has been involved in publishing and designed public furniture at Sudesign 75 pavilion of 1975 Festa Provinciale de l'Unità, Naples; 1975 with Palomba and Pasca, designed the publication for Centro Ricerche Artigianato e Design of the cities of Campagna and Ellisse; became a member, Associazione per il Disegno Industriale (ADI).
Citations Honorable-mention recognition (for his La Nuova Città project on restoration of Naples), Premio Internazionale Adriano Olivetti.
Bibliography *ADI Annual 1976*, Milan: Associazione per il Disegno Industriale, 1976.

Lausitzer Glaswerke
> See Vereinigte Lausitzer Glaswerke.

Lauweriks, Johannes Ludovicus Mattheus (1864–1932)

Dutch architect and designer; active Amsterdam, Düsseldorf, and Hagen, Germany.

Biography 1894–1903, Lauweriks taught, Haarlemsche School voor Kunstnijverheid, and, 1904–09, at Kunstgewerbeschule, Düsseldorf, where the director was Peter Behrens. 1909–16, he was director of Handfertigkeitsseminar in Hagen, instructing crafts teachers, and worked for banker/art patron K.E. Osthaus; 1908–09, published the journal *Ring*. (*Ring* was modeled on the journal *Wendingen*, to which Lauweriks contributed.) Under Frans Zwollo Sr. at Hagener Silberschmiede, he designed most of its silver. On Lauweriks's recommendation, Zwollo became the first metalwork teacher at Haarlemsche School voor Kunstnijverheid (1897–1907) and director of Hagener Silberschmiede, where the aim was to rival the Wiener Werkstätte. Lauweriks believed that the mathematical proportions of an object's form determined its expressivity and used spirals because they produced undulating contours. 1916, he became director, Kunstnijverheidschool Quellinus (renamed Instituut voor de Kunstnijverheid in 1924), Amsterdam; subsequently, played an important role in the formation of the Amsterdam School of architecture.
Exhibition Work subject of 1987 exhibition, Museum Boymans-van Beuningen, Rotterdam.
Bibliography Cat., *Frans Zwollo Sr 1872–1945 und seine Zeit*, Rotterdam: Museum Boymans-van Beuningen, 1982. Wim de Wit (ed.), *The Amsterdam School: Dutch Expressionist Architecture*, 1915–1930, Cambridge, Mass.: MIT, 1983. Annelies Krekel-Aalberse, *Art Nouveau and Art Déco Silver*, New York: Abrams, 1989. Guglielmo Bilancioni, *Architectura esoterica: geometria e teosofia in Johannes Ludovicus Mattheus Lauweriks*, Palermo: Sellerio, 1991.

Lavarello, Marcello (1921–)

Italian architect and interior designer; born and active Genoa.

Biography 1954, Lavarello began his professional career; designed the interiors of oceanliners 1951 *Giulio Cesare*, 1953 *Cristoforo Colombo*, 1957 *Leonardo da Vinci*, and 1962 *Michelangelo*, and exhibitions, including *Ente Fiera* in Genoa, *Industria Italiana* in Moscow, 1971 and 1976 *Euroflora* in Genoa; and four-star hotels and numerous houses in Italy and offices in Genoa, Milan, Brescia, Rome, Vienna, and Paris, and churches, chapels, gardens, and aircraft. Became a member, Associazione per il Disegno Industriale (ADI).
Bibliography *ADI Annual 1976*, Milan: Associazione per il Disegno Industriale, 1976.

Laverne, Erwine (1909–2003) and Estelle Laverne (1915–1997)

American artists, designers, and entrepreneurs; husband and wife.

Training Both: under Hans Hofmann, painting, Art Students League, New York.
Biography 1938, they established Laverne Originals with design studios on the old estate of L.C. Tiffany in Oyster Bay, N.Y. (on Long Island); by the 1950s, had relocated to 160 East 57th Street in New York and became known as Laverne International. They initially designed the furniture, fabrics, and wallcoverings themselves, including the popular Marbalia range of marbled murals by Erwine. From c. 1945, Ray Komai designed some of their printed cotton and linen fabrics. 1949–55, the Lavernes commissioned William Katavolos, Ross Littell, and Douglas Kelley to design furniture, textiles, and dinnerware, including the New Furniture Group of chairs and tables. Laverne produced Katavolos, Littell, and Kelley's 1952 'T' chair (model 31C). The 1957 Invisible group of see-through Perspex molded-plastic furniture designed by the Lavernes was produced using techniques developed by them and later licensed to others. The flower names of their pieces —Daffodil, Lily, and Jonquil—reflected their spirituality. The 1957 Lily and 1960 Buttercup chairs were the best known, with a single cushion as the only essentially 'visual' element. They also designed the 1958 Lotus chair, and 1960 Tulip fiberglass chair with an aluminum base. A 1961 group of lighthearted tall planters in colorfully painted aluminum were called Golliwog.
Exhibitions/citations 1953 and 1955 *Good Design* exhibitions/awards (Katavolos, Littell, and Kelley's work for Laverne, including textiles), The Museum of Modern Art, New York, and Chicago Merchandise Mart; 1968 *Please Be Seated* exhibition (clear Plexiglas chair), American Federation of Arts; 1983–84 *Design Since 1945* exhibition ('T' chair, fabric by Komai, and 1957 Champagne clear Plexiglas chair), Philadelphia Museum of Art. 1952 award for best US furniture ('T' chair) and 1961 award (Golliwog planters), American Institute of Decorators (AID).
Bibliography 'Good Design,' *Interiors*, vol. 113, Aug. 1953: 88–89, 146–48. Roberto Aloi and Agnoldomenico Pica, *Mobili tipo*, Milan: Hoepli, 1956. Cat., *Please Be Seated*, New York: American Federation of Arts, 1968: no. 68. Clement Meadmore, *The Modern Chair: Classics in Production*, New York: Van Nostrand Reinhold, 1979. Cat., Kathryn B. Hiesinger and George H. Marcus III (eds.), *Design Since 1945*, Philadelphia: Philadelphia Museum of Art, 1983. Charlotte Fiell and Peter Fiell, *1000 Chairs*, New York: Taschen, 2000. Elaine Mayers Salkain, 'The Invisibles.' *The New York Times*, 8 April 2004.

Laverrière, Janette (1909–)
Swiss interior architect and decorator; born Lausanne.

Training École Cantonale de Dessin et d'Art Appliqué, Lausanne; Gewerbeschule, Basel.
Biography Laverrière worked in the office of her architect father Alphonse Laverrière, and, 1932–33, in the workshop of Jacques-Émile Ruhlmann; from 1944, was quite active designing a number of public and private interiors; 1929, was a founding member of Union des Artistes Modernes (UAM). Some of her furniture was asymetical in form. She realized a significant body of work, including ceramics with Georges Jouve in 1950; 1961–72, taught, École Camondo, Paris.
Exhibitions/citations All Paris: from 1936, showed work regularly in Salons of Société des Artistes Décorateurs and Société des Arts Ménagers, active member from 1938; also 1937 *Exposition Internationale des Arts et Techniques dans la Vie Moderne* (gold medal for a furniture range, with Maurice Pré); participated in editions of Salon des Arts Ménagers. Work subject of 1987 exhibition organized by VIA (French furniture association), Paris. Was cited by Société d'Encouragement à l'Art et à l'Industrie; also by the Société Formica at 1948 Salon of Société des Artistes Décorateurs. Work subject of 1987 exhibition, Galerie VIA.
Bibliography *Mobilier et décoration*, no. 3, April 1956. Patrick Favardin, *Les décorateurs des années 50*, Paris: Norma, 2002: 124.

Laviani, Pietro Ferruccio (1960–)
Italian architect and designer, born Grumello Cremonese.

Training 1984, diploma in design and, 1986, university degree, both Politecnico, Milan.
Biography Laviani designed for Memphis's 1986 12 Nuovi Memphis collection and its 1987 collection; was a founder of and contributed designs to the work of the Solid design group. His other work includes 1986–87 furniture collection Residenza sulla Terra by Malobbia International and large amount of furniture, furnishings, and products for Abet Laminati, Adachi Group, Alfox, Delux, Biette, Città 'Conveniza, Credito Bergamasco, Elam, Kagome, Mandarina Duck, Martini Prefabbricati, Olivetti Synthesis, Origin, Pelikan, Polaroid, RB Rossana, Swatch, Signifiée, Unilever. 1986–91, Laviani was a partner, Studio De Lucchi, Milan, and Oil Milano; 1990, designed the history section of Groningen Museum, Netherlands (with Michele De Lucchi and Geert and coordinated by Alessandro Mendini); 1990, was head of industrial-design seminars, Politecnico, Milan. From 1991, he designed the corporate logos, graphics, literature, and/or exhibition stands (particularly at Salone del Mobile, Milan) for and/or furniture by a large number of clients, including Kartell, Moroso, Bros's, Imel, Emmemobili, Busnelli, Emmebi, Technogym, Molteni, Cos, Dada-Alta Cucina, Flos, and Piombo, and public interiors in Italy, France, Germany, Brazil, and China. Other work, as a prolific, versatile designer: 1996 with Achille Castiglioni, *Gio Ponti* and *Vico Magistretti* exhibitions, both Salone del Mobile, Milan, and 1999 stage set of *Ricominciare* TV program for RAI (Italian broadcasting company). 2000, Laviani designed the Museo Kartell in Navilgio (MI), Italy, to mark the manufacturer's 50th anniversary; it displays more than 1,000 historical products.
Exhibitions Work included in a number of exhibitions, including 1990 *Creativitalia*, Japan and 1991 *European Capitals of New Design* (Morandotti silverware collection), Centre Georges Pompidou, Paris. Was in charge of 1991 *Techniques Discrètes,* Musée des Arts Décoratifs, Paris (catalog below); other exhibitions.
Bibliography Cat., Manolo de Giorgi and Paola Antonelli (eds), *Techniques discrètes: le design mobilier en Italie, 1980–1990*, Rome: Istituto Nazionale per il Commercio Estero; Milan: Assarredo; Paris: Musée des Arts Décoratifs, 1991.

David Law, Massimo Vignelli, and Lella Vignelli. Handkerchief chair, 1985. Glass-fiber reinforced polyester and plastic-coated metal rods, 29 x 22 1/8 x 18 1/4" (73.7 x 56.2 x 46.4 cm). Mfr.: Knoll International, US. Gift of the manufacturer. MoMA.

Lavonen, Maija (1931–)
Finnish textile designer.

Training Institut for Industriel Design, Helsingfors.
Biography Lavonen designed mass-produced textiles by Marimekko and for Tampella and fabricated one-of-a-kind pieces using techniques, including 'riya' and double weaves. Her work has been recognized as having made a significant contribution to 20th-century Finnish applied arts.
Exhibition Work included in 1980 *Scandinavian Modern Design 1880–1980* (1977 riya rug), Cooper-Hewitt National Design Museum, New York; 1983 *Scandinavian Touch*, Taideteollisuusmuseo, Helsinki. Work subject of 1996 exhibition, Näyttely Rovaniemen Taidemuseossa, Rovaniemi, Finland (catalog below); 2002 *Sekä—Että* (with Oiva Toikka), Oulun Taidemuseo, Oulun, Finland.
Bibliography Cat., David Revere McFadden (ed.), *Scandinavian Modern Design 1880–1980*, New York: Abrams, 1982. Cat., *Maija Lavonen: teoksia vuosilta 1970–1996 = Works from the Years 1970–1996*, Helsinki: Kyriiri, 1996.

Law, David (1937–)
American designer; born Pittsburgh.

Training Art Center College of Design, Los Angeles.
Biography 1967, Law began as executive designer for the Detroit and Chicago branches of Unimark International; 1972, cofounded Design Planning Group in Chicago; 1975, became manager of packaging design at JC Penney, New York; 1978, joined Massimo and Lela Vignelli's studio in New York, where he has designed printed and architectural graphics, packaging, exhibitions, products, furniture, and interior design; collaborated with Massimo Vignelli and Lella Vignelli on 1985 Handkerchief chair by Knoll and 1985 Serenissimo table by Acerbis International, and on 1986 Bordin and Aneic cutlery by Sasaki. Other clients: Knoll, Poltrona Frau, Bernhardt, Hickory Business Furniture, Stendig, Krueger International, Steelcase, SunarHauserman, Poltrona Frau, Joseph Magnin, Puritan Fashions, Sara Lee, IBM, and Xerox. Law has become senior vice-president and a partner of Vignelli Associates and Design Director of Vignelli Designs, and has independently designed a number of other products.
Bibliography Albrecht Bangert and Karl Michael Armer, *80s Style: Designs of the Decade*, New York: Abbeville, 1990.

Lawson, Geoff (1944–1999)
British automobile designer; born Leicester.

Training Leicester College of Art; master's degree in furniture design, Royal College of Art, London.
Biography From 1969, Lawson worked at Vauxhall (General Motors' British subsidiary) as a designer and, subsequently, on cars and trucks in Europe and the US for General Motors, eventually becoming chief designer; from 1984, was chief designer at Jaguar, where he reinterpreted the style aesthetic developed by Jaguar founder William Lyons. Lawson, during his tenure and until his death, designed all Jaguar's models, including 1988–94 XJ6, 1998–2003 XJ8, and 1996-to-pre-

sent XK8. The nose of the 2000-to-present XK8 S-Type was a distinguished accomplishment. 2000, Jaguar opened the Geoff Lawson Studio for the exploration of advanced design concepts, directed by Julian Thomson.
Citations 2001 Red Dot Best of the Best award (for Jaguar S-type), Design Zentrum Nordrhein Westfalen, Essen.
Bibliography Martin Buckley, *Jaguar: Fifty Years of Speed and Style*, St. Paul, Minn.: Motorbooks International, 1999. Buckley Martin and Mann James, *Jaguar XJ-Series*, London: Windrow & Greene, 1992.

Lax, Michael (1929–1999)
American designer.

Training New York State College of Ceramics, Alfred, N.Y.; and in Finland and Rome.
Biography Lax set up his own design office in New York; executed designs for exhibitions, environments, graphic-information systems, furnishings, wallcoverings, and lighting. His clients included Copco, Corning, Dunbar, Formica, Kimberley-Clark, Lightolier, and Salton.
Exhibitions Glass bowls by Dunbar were included in 1952 *Good Design* exhibition/award, The Museum of Modern Art, New York, and Chicago Merchandise Mart, and also work in 1983–84 *Design Since 1945*, Philadelphia Museum of Art.
Bibliography Jay Doblin, *One Hundred Great Product Designs*, New York: Van Nostrand Reinhold, 1970: no. 99. Cat., Kathryn B. Hiesinger and George H. Marcus III (eds.), *Design Since 1945*, Philadelphia: Philadelphia Museum of Art, 1983.

Layton, Peter (1937–)
Czech glass designer and ceramacist; born Prague.

Training Ceramics, Bradford College of Art and Technology (today Bradford College), Bradford; ceramics, Central School of Art, London.
Biography Layton taught ceramics at various colleges in the US and UK; subsequently, 1969, cofounded the Glasshouse Gallery and Workshop, London; 1970, set up his own glass workshop in Morar, Scotland; 1976, founded Glassblowing Workshop in London; cofounded British Artists in Glass (BAG), of which he was the chairperson 1983–84; was the British delegate to 1985 (1st) International Glass Conference, Japan, and at 1985 (2nd) International Glass Symposium, Nový Bor, Czech Republic.
Exhibitions Numerous in Europe, the US, Australia, and Japan.
> See The Glasshouse Gallery and Workshop.

Lazzeroni, Roberto (1950–)
Italian designer; born Pisa.

Training 1970–75, Accademia di Belle Arti, Florence.
Biography Lazzeroni was active in the Radical Design movement and in conceptual art in Florence, where he set up his eponymous studio in 1980 and today in Cascina (PI); early 1980s, began to be active in industrial design; from 1988, has been the artistic director of the wooden-furniture Ceccotti Collezioni (a division of Aviero Ceccotti's company). At Ceccotti, Lazzeroni works with a number of the company's commissioned designers such as André Dubreuil, Yamo, Christophe Pillet, Jasper Morrison, and others. Lazzeroni is also active as a versatile designer of furniture by Acerbis, Bertocci, Casamilano,

Giulio Lazzotti. Covered peanuts bowl. 1981. Marble and slate, overall h. 2 1/4 x dia. 7 1/16" (5.7 x 17.9 cm). Mfr.: Casigliani, Italy. Gift of the mfr. MoMA.

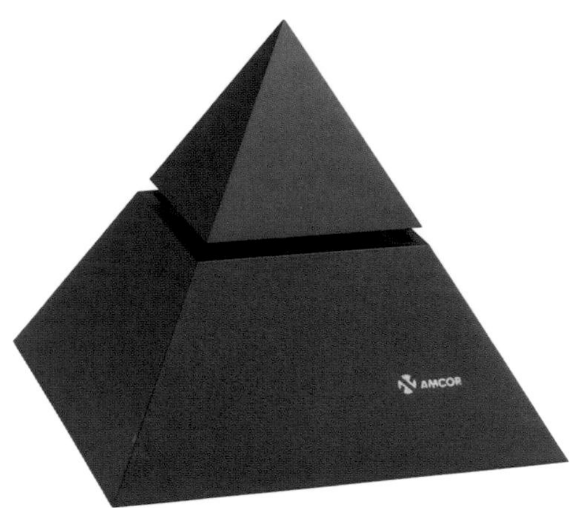

Michael Lax. Modulion 10 Ionizer. 1980. Plastic, 5 5/8 x 6 5/16 x 6 5/16" (14.3 x 16 x 16 cm). Gift of the designer. Mfr.: Amcor, Israel. MoMA.

Cidue, Confalonieri, Driade, Frighetto, Gandi, Gervasoni, Gufram, Moroso, Plank, Raspel, and Ycami, including the White Land kitchen system by Aurora and Emporio kitchen furniture by bisbis.com. Also works for Luminara, Levante, and IPE Cavalli.
Exhibitions Work included in 1991 *Techniques Discrètes*, Musée des Arts Décoratifs, Paris (catalog below); 1993 *Dall'Albergo alla Nave*, Tecnhotel, Genoa; 1993 *La Fabbrica Estetica: Il Ultima Generazione del Design Italiano*, Grand Palais, Paris; 1999 *Contruire il mobile*, Milan.
Bibliography Cat., Manolo de Giorgi and Paola Antonelli (eds), *Techniques discrètes: le design mobilier en Italie, 1980–1990*, Rome: Istituto Nazionale per il Commercio Estero; Milan: Assarredo; Paris: Musée des Arts Décoratifs, 1991.

Lazzotti, Giulio (1943–)
Italian architect and interior and product designer; born and active Pietrasanta (LU).

Training Under Salvator di Pasquale, architecture in construction theory, Università degli Studi, Florence.
Biography 1972–82, Lazzotti was the artistic director of C.A.M.P., a consortium of marble artisans from 100 firms; 1973–75, taught, Università degli Studi, Florence; 1991–93, taught marble design, Accademia di Belle Arte, Carrara; 1991–96, was the creative director of various exhibitions in Milan of Japanese sculptor Kan Yasuda and the editor of books on Yasuda; 1995–97, organized conferences on marble and urban design, University of Taiwan, and on marble and urban design at 1995–96 Internazionale Marmo & Macchine fair in Carara; to 1999, was urban-design consultant to the City Council of the historical center of Pietrasanta. Clients for architecture, interior design, and design have included Alane's Garden, Arata Paolo, Artipresent, Bernini, Casigliani, Design Within Reach, Disenia, Effepi, Gaiac, Iveco, Krieger, La Sedia, Mageia, Roche-Bobois, Sica, Smith & Hawken, Stone International, Stoneforms, The Conran Shop, Up & Up, Zona, and Xtramo.
Citations 1978 Oscar for best interior design and 1982 first prize in design, Moving fairs, Paris; Top Ten prize, 1999 Salone Internazionale della Sedia (Promodedia), Udine; 1999 Premio Torre Guinigi–Lucca (for urban design of Pietrasanta historical center).

Le Chevallier, Jacques (1896–1987)
French lighting and furniture designer; born and active Paris.

Training 1911–15, École Nationale Supérieure des Arts Décoratifs, Paris.
Biography Le Chevallier's interest in stained glass eventually resulted in the 1920–45 partnership with Louis Barillet. They established a stained-glass workshop on the rue Alain-Chartier, Paris. Work included painting, tapestries, engraving on wood, lighting, and secular and religious items. 1927–30, Le Chevallier designed a variety of geometric/angular aluminum lamps evoking the machine age and incorporating metal, exposed rivets and screws, hinges, and counterweights; also often collaborated with Raymond Koechlin; designed lighting for Pierre Chareau's office (architect, Robert Mallet-Stevens). Other designs,

similar to Boris Lacroix's, were more refined. He was commissioned by the interior-design group Décoration Intérieur Moderne (D.I.M.) to produce various components in their ensembles; 1929, cofounded Union des Artistes Modernes (UAM). 1945, he established his own workshop in Fontenay-aux-Roses, France, and produced stained glass with Barillet and designed mosaics and tapestries; 1948, founded Centre d'Art Sacré and participated in the renovation of cathedrals in Besançon, Toulouse, and Angers.

Exhibitions Work shown at Salons of Société des Artistes Décorateurs, editions of Salon d'Automne and of Salon des Indépendants, UAM exhibitions from 1930, and 1937 *Exposition Internationale des Arts et Techniques dans la Vie Moderne*, Paris (stained glass later installed in Notre Dame Cathedral, Paris). Several lamps were included in 2000-03 *Aluminum by Design* touring exhibition, organized by Carnegie Art Museum, Pittsburgh.

Bibliography René Drouin, 'Au quatrième salon de l'UAM,' *L'architecture d'aujourd'hui*, no. 5, June 1933. Jacques Le Chevallier, *Les cahiers d'art—documents*, no. 110, Geneva: Pierre Cailles, 1959. Alastair Duncan, *Art Nouveau and Art Déco Lighting*, New York: Simon & Schuster, 1978: 177. Victor Arwas, *Art Déco*, New York: Abrams, 1980. Cat., Aaron Lederfajn and Xavier Lenormand, *Le Louvre des Antiquaires présente: 1930 quand le meuble devient sculpture*, Paris, 1986. Cat., *Les années UAM 1929–1958*, Paris: Musée des Arts Décoratifs, 1988: 208–09. Cat., Sarah Nichols et al., *Aluminum by Design*, Pittsburgh: Carnegie Art Museum, 2000.

Le Corbusier (b. Charles-Edouard Jeanneret-Gris 1887–1965)

Swiss architect; born La Chaux-de-Fonds; active Paris.

Training From 1900 under Charles L'Éplattenier, metal engraving, École d'Art, La Chaux-de-Fonds.

Biography 1908, Le Corbusier worked with Josef Hoffmann at the Wiener Werkstätte, refusing a permanent job; 1908, with Tony Garnier in Lyon and Henri Sauvage in Paris. 1908–09 in Paris, he was an apprentice in the Perret brothers' architecture office, becoming familiar with reinforced-concrete methods before becoming a member (1910–11) of the staff of Peter Behrens's office in Berlin, where he became interested in mass-produced furniture and, in the office came into contact with Mies van der Rohe and Walter Gropius. 1917, he returned to Paris and met Amédée Ozenfant, with whom he developed a style of painting called Purism, and wrote the manifesto, with Ozenfant, *Après le cubisme, le purisme* (1918; translated into English in the catalog, Carol S. Eliel, *L'Esprit Nouveau: Purism in Paris, 1918–1925*, Los Angeles: Los Angeles County Museum of Art/Abrams, 2001). This publication was followed by *La peinture moderne* (Paris: Crès, 1925). He used the pseudonym Le Corbusier (his maternal grandfather's name) as an author from 1920, as an architect from 1922, and as a painter from 1928. His interest in Greek architecture and the machine was discussed in *Vers une architecture* (Paris: Crès, 1923), a collection of articles from the periodical *L'esprit nouveau: revue international d'esthétique* (Éditions de l'Esprit Nouveau, 1920–25), which he, Ozenfant, and poet Paul Dermée coedited. The articles created a sensation (under the by-line 'Corbusier-Saugnier,' the latter being Ozenfant's pseudonym). From 1922, Le Corbusier and his cousin Pierre Jeanneret worked in the architecture office at 35, rue de Sèvres, Paris. 1924–38, Jean Badovici documented their projects in the journal *L'architecture vivante*. Le Corbusier's buildings and writings were to have a revolutionary effect on the international development of modern architecture. Le Corbusier and Jeanneret's pavilion L'Esprit Nouveau at the 1925 Paris *Exposition*, and Le Corbusier's white concrete houses of the period, manifested what was later dubbed the International Style of architecture, of which Le Corbusier's 1929–31 Villa Savoye at Poissy is a prime example. The pavilion L'Esprit Nouveau created a scandal that precipitated Le Corbusier and others' 1929 departure from the Société des Artistes Décorateurs to form Union des Artistes Modernes (UAM). Even at the 1937 *Exposition Internationale des Arts et Techniques dans la Vie Moderne*, Paris, his pavilion Temps Nouveau was relegated to Porte Maillot, far from the fair grounds. 1927, he began to design tubular furniture in association with Jeanneret and Charlotte Perriand, who, as a student of architecture, joined the Le Corbusier/Jeanneret studio in 1927. She probably designed most of the furniture, although this was never openly confirmed by her. Not interested in originality, the team based the designs of their best-known metal models on mass-produced wooden furniture, as in 1928 Siège à Dossier Basculant (swivel-back chair). All the furniture of the Le Corbusier/Jeanneret/Perriand team was first produced by Thonet Frères in Paris. 1930, they designed the scheme for the office of the administrator of the review *La semaine à Paris* (architect, Robert Mallet-Stevens). Some of the team's furniture has become icons of 20th-century design, partly through their realization as reproductions from the mid-1970s, beginning with 16 or so models by Heidi Weber in Zürich. From the 1930s, Le Corbusier concentrated on architecture and planning, and his work in the 1950s made a distinct break with the formalism of his earlier International Style and turned toward freer expression. His much quoted term 'machine for living,' referring to a house one lives in, is often incorrectly interpreted as expressing a cold indifference to the provision of human shelter. He died in Cap Martin.

Architecture 1920–22 Citrohan house (shown at 1922 Salon d'Automne); 1922 Ville Contemporaine project; 1922 Ozenfant house, Paris; 1922 three-million-person city project; 1922 Villa Besnos, Vaucresson; 1923 Lipchitz house, Boulogne-sur-Seine; 1923 La Roche and Jeanneret houses, Auteuil, Paris; 1925 city-garden, Pessac, near Bordeaux; L'Esprit Nouveau pavilion, 1925 *Exposition International des Arts Décoratifs et Industriels Modernes*, Paris; 1925 Plan-Voisin project for Paris; 1926 Cook house, Boulogne-sur-Seine; Cité Frugès and Armée du Salut, Paris; 1927 competition for the Palace of the League of Nations, Geneva; 1927 Stein house, Garches; two houses at 1927 *Weissenhofsiedlung*, Stuttgart; 1929–31 Savoye house, Poissy; 1929–

Le Corbusier, Pierre Jeanneret, and Charlotte Perriand. Chaise longue (LC/4). 1928. Chrome-plated and painted steel, fabric, and leather, 26 3/8 x 23 x 62 3/8" (67 x 58.4 x 158.4 cm). Mfr.: Thonet Frères, France. Gift of Thonet Industries, Inc. MoMA.

31 Centrosoyus building, Moscow; 1930–32 Clarté apartment house, Geneva; 1930–32 Pavillon Suisse, Cité Universitaire, Paris; 1931 competition for Palace of the Soviets, Moscow; 1932–33 Cité du Refuge, Paris, 1932 Raoul La Roche house, Paris; 1932 Pierre Jeanneret house, Paris; 1936–43 Ministry of Health and Education (executed by Lúcio Costa, Oscar Niemeyer, and Affonso Eduardo Reidy), Rio de Janeiro; 1947–50 Secretariat building of United Nations (executed by Wallace K. Harrison and Max Abramovitz), New York; 1947–52 Unité d'Habitation, Marseille; housing in Nantes-Rezé (1952–57), Berlin (1956–58), Meaux (1957–59), Briey-en-Forêt (1957–60), and Firminy-Vert (1962–68); 1950–54 church of Notre-Dame-du-Haut, Ronchamp; 1950–51 general plan (with Maxwell Fry and Jane Drew) and capitol area with government buildings, Chandigarh (India); 1952–56 Jaoul house, Neuilly-sur-Seine; 1957–60 monastery of Sainte-Marie-de-la-Tourette, Eveux-sur-l'Arbresle; four buildings in India 1955–56; 1961–64 Carpenter Center for the Visual Arts, Harvard University, Cambridge, Mass.; 1965 Maison de la Culture, stadium, and Unité d'Habitation, Firminy.
Exhibitions In 1921, work (group of paintings) shown at Galerie Druet, Paris. Built pavilion L'Esprit Nouveau at *1925 Exposition Internationale des Arts Décoratifs et Industriels Modernes*, Paris. Equipement Intérieur d'une Habitation installed at 1929 Salon d'Automne. Furniture (extension table, pivoting and lounge chair by Thonet, and six chairs in the hall by architect Robert Mallet-Stevens) shown at 1930 (1st) UAM exhibition, Paris; model of Ville Radieuse and photographs of Villa Savoye at UAM 1931 exhibition; the project for the Centrosoyuz in Moscow at UAM 1932 exhibition; the town plan for Obus-d'Alger at UAM 1933 exhibition. The three architects designed Salle d'Étude pour l'Appartement d'un Jeune Homme in the fine-arts section of French pavilion at 1935 *Exposition Universelle et Internationale de Bruxelles*. Savoye house model shown at 1932 *Modern Architecture—International Exhibition*, The Museum of Modern Art, New York. As his last project associated with UAM, Le Corbusier (with Jeanneret/Perriand) designed the toilet prototype shown in UAM pavilion at 1937 *Exposition Internationale des Arts et Techniques dans la Vie Moderne*, Paris. Le Corbusier's Philips pavilion at 1958 Brussels *Exposition* featured Poème Électronique multi-media presentation with other artists. Work subject of 1987 centenary exhibition, Centre Georges Pompidou, Paris; 1992 *Le Corbusier Domestique: Furniture/Tapestries 1927–67*, Carpenter Center for the Visual Arts, Cambridge, Mass.; 2002 *Der junge Le Corbusier...*, Museum Langmatt Sidney und Jenny Brown, Baden, Switzerland, traveling as 2002–03 *Le Corbusier Before Le Corbusier...*, Bard Graduate Center, New York. (Catalogs below.)
Bibliography Willy Boesiger (ed.), *Le Corbusier: œuvre complète*, Zürich: Architecture Erlenbach, 1930 and onward. Henry-Russell Hitchcock, *Le Corbusier*, New York: The Museum of Modern Art, 1935. Stamo Papadaki (ed.), *Le Corbusier: Architect, Painter, Writer*, New York: Macmillan, 1948. Stanislav von Moos, *Le Corbusier: Elemente einer Synthese*, Frauenfeld: Huber, 1968. Charles Jencks, *Le Corbusier and the Tragic View of Architecture*, London: Allen Lane, 1973. Cat., André Bauchant, *16 Werke aus der Sammlung Le Corbusier*, Zürich: Heidi Weber, 1975. Renato De Fusco, *Le Corbusier designer i mobili del 1929*, Milan: Casabella, 1976. Renato De Fusco, *Le Corbusier, Designer: Furniture, 1929*, Woodbury, N.Y.: Barrons, 1977. Arlette Barré-Despond, *UAM*, Paris: Regard, 1986. *Le Corbusier, une encyclopédie*, Paris: Centre Georges Pompidou/CCI, 1987. Gilles Ragot and Dion Mathilde, *Le Corbusier en France, réalisations et projets*, Paris: Electa Moniteur, 1987. Cat., *Les années UAM 1929–1958*, Paris: Musée des Arts Décoratifs, 1988. Cat., Stanislaus von Moos and Arthur Rüegg (eds.), *Le Corbusier Before Le Corbusier: Applied Arts, Architecture, Painting, Photography*, 1907–1922, New Haven/London: Bard Graduate Center/Yale University, 2002. Cat., *Der junge Le Corbusier: Möbel, Reiseskizzen, Fotografie, Architektur, 1907–1923*, Baden: Museum Langmatt Sidney und Jenny Brown, 2002. Paola Antonelli (ed.), *Objects of Design: The Museum of Modern Art*, New York: The Museum of Modern Art, 2003: 80–81.
> See Perriand, Charlotte.

Le Klint
> See Klint, Le.

Le Quément, Patrick (1945–)

French automobile design director.

Biography Le Quément worked at Simca and, subsequently, was active in his design studio Style International in Paris; 1968–85, worked at Ford motor company in Detroit, Mich., and then at Volkswagen for a short time; from 1987, has directed the styling of Renault automobiles, where he encourages the firm to consider cars within a broad cultural context and foster original thinking; is a member of the management committee of Renault operations and reports only to Renault Group's chairperson/CEO Louis Schweitzer (1943–). 1988, Le Quément created the Renault's Department of Industrial Design, combining the efforts of 65 designers and 90 or so modelmakers of about 14 different nationalities; from 1997, has been in charge of design in two areas: general auto design (managed by Antony Grade), and VU/VI (*véhicules utilitaires/véhicules industriels*) and industrial design (managed by Jean-Paul Marceau). Other departments include those of future design, concept cars, and color studies. 1995, Le Quément also became responsible for quality control, a double assignment unusual in the auto industry. His Renault car designs included 1994 Argos concept car, 1996 Twingo, and 1999 Mégane Scenic.
Citations 1992 Prix National de la Création Industrielle, France; 1996, elected Chevalier of the Légion d'Honneur; 1998, appointed president of the administrative counsel, ENSCI (Les Ateliers), Paris.
Bibliography Georges Mason, *Patrick Le Quément: Renault Design*, Milan: Automobilia, 2000. Penny Sparke, *A Century of Car Design*, London: Mitchell Beazley, 2002.

Le Son, Lucie Holt
> See Holt Le Son, Lucie.

Le Teo, Catherine (1957–)
> See Blet, Théo.

Leach, Bernard Howell (1887–1979)

British ceramicist; born Hong Kong; active St. Ives and Devon.

Training From 1897, Slade School of Fine Art, London; London School of Art; engraving under Frank Brangwyn; from 1911 under Ogata Kenzan, in pottery, Japan.
Biography From 1909, Leach lived in Japan, where he taught design and engraving and studied and where, 1911, he discovered pottery and met potter Ogata Kenzan 6th, a master of a long line of Japanese potters. Leach traveled to China 1916–18 and, subsequently, Korea. 1920, after helping Kenzan build a new stoneware kiln near Tokyo, he established a pottery at St. Ives in Cornwall with associate Shoji Hamada. Leach investigated the techniques and styles of early English pottery, including the traditions of country slipware; developed slipware pieces and original ideas, both influenced by his Japanese training; introduced to Britain the Japanese concept of a potter's complete responsibility for all stages of creative activity and the unity of the results; 1920s, shared his ideas and facilities with many potters. During 1930s when he became well known and when his son David joined the pottery, Leach was freer to travel and teach and, thus from 1932, taught, Dartington Hall, Devon, and, 1934, accepted the invitation of National Craft Society to visit Japan, where he traveled for a year with Soetsu Yanagi and Shoji Hamada and worked in various potteries. 1935, Leach visited Korea again and, 1936 back in Britain, set up a pottery at Dartington Hall, a boarding school. Gathering material while at the school, he wrote *A Potter's Book* (London: Faber & Faber, 1940) with introductions by Soetsu Yanagi and Michael Cardew; and other publications followed (see below). (Cardew first met Leach and Hamada at St. Ives in 1923.) Leach was the leading exponent of studio pottery in Britain, and, through his writing and teaching, extremely influential.
Exhibitions/citations 1932, appointed Commander of the Order of the British Empire (CBE); 1966, Order of the Sacred Treasure (second class), Japan; 1973, made Companion of Honour (CH). Work included in numerous exhibitions.
Bibliography Bernard Leach, *A Potter's Outlook*, London: New Handworkers' Gallery, 1928. Bernard Leach, *Kenzan and His Tradition...*, London: Faber, 1966. Bernard Leach, *A Potter's Work*, London: Jupiter, 1977. Carol Hogben, *The Art of Bernard Leach*, London: Faber, 1978. Bernard Leach, *Beyond East and West: Memoirs, Portraits, and Essays*, London: Faber, 1978. Cat., Shoji Hamada, *The Quiet Eye: Pottery of Shoji Hamada and Bernard Leach*, Monterey, Cal.: Monterey Peninsula Museum of Art, 1990. Marion Whybrow, *The Leach Legacy: The St. Ives Pottery and Its Influence*, Oviedo, Fla.: Gentle Breeze, 1996. Edmund De Waal, *Bernard Leach*, Seattle: University of Washington, 1998.

Lebeau, 'Chris' Joris Johannes Christiaan (1878–1945)

Dutch decorator and designer; born Amsterdam.

Training 1895–99, Kunstnijverheidschool Quellinus (renamed Instituut

Auguste Ledru. Dinner-table bell. c. 1900. Cast bronze, h. 5" (12.8 cm). Mfr.: Susse Frères, France. Courtesy Quittenbaum Kunstauktionen, Munich.

voor de Kunstnijverheid in 1924), and Rijksacademie voor Beeldende Kunsten; both Amsterdam.
Biography By 1899, Lebeau was teaching art at the Burgeravondschool in Amsterdam; shortly after, began as a professional designer with wall decorations commissioned for the Netherlands pavilion at the 1900 *Exposition Universelle*, Paris, and, at the same time, began working in batik in the workshop of Agathe Wegerif-Gravenstein in Appeldoorn. Lebeau executed numerous folding screens in batik, some double-sided; 1923–26, worked at Leerdam glassworks, where he designed idiosyncratic wares but refused to design wine glasses due to being a teetotaler. c. 1930, he designed a fabric by Schellens & Marto for the Royal Palace, Tilburg.
Exhibitions Work was the subject of 1966 exhibition, Gemeentemuseum, the Hague. Won 1901 design competition on the theme 'Modern Style' of 's-Gravenhaagsche Smyrnatapijtfabriek carpet weavers, the Hague.
Bibliography Cat., *Chris Lebeau*, The Hague: Gemeentemuseum, 1966. M. Komaneck and V.F. Butera, *The Folding Image Screens by Western Artists of the Nineteenth and Twentieth Centuries*, New Haven: Yale University Art Gallery, 1984.

Lebedeva, Mariia Vasil'evna (1895–1942)
Russian painter, graphic artist, book designer, decorative artist, and ceramics designer.

Training To 1917 under Ivan Bilibin, drawing school of the Society for the Encouragement of the Arts, Petrograd.
Biography 1919–23, she created designs for application to porcelain wares that portrayed symbolic and fantastic themes, produced at the State Porcelain Factory, Petrograd; 1924–27, taught decorative arts at Vitebsk Technical School of Art and, 1924–27, at Minsk College of Fine Arts; 1934–40, worked at Lomonosov (formerly State Porcelain Factory), Leningrad (now St. Petersburg).
Bibliography Cat., *Kunst und Revolution: Russische und Sowjetische Kunst 1910–1932*, Vienna: Österreichisches Museum für angewandte Kunst, 1988. Nina Lobanov-Rostovsky, *Revolutionary Ceramics*, London: Studio Vista, 1990.

Lebovici, Yonel (1937–1998)
French designer; born Paris to Breton mother and Rumanian father.

Training 1953–55, degree in aeronautics; from 1955, art, Academie de la Grande Chaumière and also École des Arts Appliqués; from 1957, École des Arts et Métiers; all Paris.
Biography From 1959 for a short time, Lebovici worked with light metals at Sud Aviation; subsequently, was active as a test pilot, professional Be-Bop dancer in Saint-Germain-des-Prés area of Paris, and an extra-actor in films; 1962, became greatly influenced by Serge Mansau, who introduced Lebovici to glass blowing; 1969, left Mansau and set up his own workshop and prolifically designed a wide range of products, including furniture, lighting, glassware, toys, posters, advertising materials for clients Jansen, Cardin, Club Med, Lancel, others; was active as both a designer and a sculptor. Works range from, early on, 1965 magnetic puzzle and 1965 Aquarophile aquarium to, later, 1990 bar-code lamps and 1990 Lumière Tamisée (tennis racket) lamp. He invented the first low-voltage, cordless lamps (Spiders series), later used by NG first to produce the Variation range.
Exhibitions Work (Aquarophile) first shown, at 1965 Eurodesign fair, Nancy. Subsequent work included in and subject of a number of exhibitions, including 2003 venue, Paris (catalog below).
Bibliography Robert A.M. Stern (ed.), *The International Design Yearbook*, New York: Abbeville, 1985/1986. Cat., Delphine and Yorane Lebovici, *Yonel Lebovici 1937–1998*, Paris: 15 Square de Vergennes, 2003.

Lecoq, Jacqueline (1932-)
> See Philippon, Antoine.

Ledru, Auguste (1860–1902)
French metal and glass designer and sculptor.

Training In sculpture, ateliers of Augustin Dumont and of Bonnassieux (aka Jean-Marie Bienaimé).
Biography Ledru, Joseph Chéret, and Raoul Larche were among the first designers to concentrate on the female form in the Art Nouveau style. Glassmaker René Lalique married Ledru's daughter, Augustine-Alice Ledru.
Bibliography Salon catalog, Paris: Société des Artistes Français, 1901. *Éclairage de 1900 à nos jours*, Brussels: L'Écuyer, no. 29. *Allgemeines Lexikon der bildenden Künstler*, Leipzig: E.A. Seemann, 1955. Alastair Duncan, *Art Nouveau and Art Déco Lighting*, New York: Simon & Schuster, 1978. Philippe Dahhan, *Élairs 1900*, Paris: Amateurs, 2000.

Ledru, Léon (1855–1926)
French glassmaker.

Biography Ledru was manager of the design department of the Cristalleries du Val Saint Lambert in Belgium for 38 years. Though Ledru designed traditional pieces, he became known for his innovations in technique, color, and decoration, brought about by his long association with Val Saint Lambert chemist Aldolphe Lecrenier.
Exhibitions Through work the firm showed at 1897 *Exposition Internationale*, Brussels, he stimulated interest in avant-garde design. The crystal factory's vases, influenced by Henry van de Velde and shown at 1901 exhibition of La Libre Esthétique group, Brussels, were distinctly modern. Pieces shown at 1900 *Exposition Universelle*, Paris, had floral decoration in a more naturalistic style, much like the work of the École de Nancy and Émile Gallé.
Bibliography Yvonne Brunhammer et al., *Art Nouveau Belgium, France*, Houston: Institute for the Arts, Rice University, 1976. Alastair Duncan, *Art Nouveau and Art Déco Lighting*, New York: Simon & Schuster, 1978.

Ledwinka, Hans (1878–1967)
Austrian automobile engineer and designer; born Klosterneuburg.

Training Technische Fachschule für Maschinenbau, Vienna.
Biograpy 1850, Ignaz Schustala established a wagon-making enterprise in Nesseldorf, Moravia (now Koprivnica, Czech Republic), and expanded into making railroad cars. The firm became known as Nesselsdorfer Wagenbau-Fabriks-Gesellschaft. On Ledwinka's 1897 arrival at Nesselsdorfer Wagenbau Fabriks-Gesellschaft (later called Tatra-Werke), the firm bought a one-cylinder Benz to analyze/dissect and as a result decided to make automobiles itself. 1899, Ledwinka, who was the self-appointed but unofficial chief automotive engineer at the firm, redesigned a multi-functional transmission to replace the one in Nesselsdorfer's first (1897) Benz imitation. 1905–45, he was the technical director there. Having developed fast S-type models for racing, Ledwinka found himself at odds with the Nesselsdorfer management, departed, and, 1916, began working for Steyr, where he designed a series of very original heavy trucks and luxury autos. But Steyr had no facilities to produce small cars. 1921, Ledwinka returned to Nesselsdorfer, whose car was now known as the Tatra, due to its abilitity to climb the Tatra mountains in what is today the Czech Republic. Late 1920s, he developed the air-cooled rear-engine mounted on a new frame; the engine was very noisy, but the body featured new aerodynamic principles. Ledwinka became known for his broad, rather than specialized, interests in automobile design and construction and also in bodywork and chassis. He pioneered the backbone

chassis that was combined with an integrated drive train and an all-independent wing-axle suspension; designed 1933 Tatra 570 with an aerodynamic body, air-cooled rear-V8 engine, and tubular chassis, very advanced for its time. Ledwinka's most notable model may be the 1932 Tatra Type 57, and the streamling of his 1937 Type 87 is highly dramatic with long drawn-out rear and wind scoops. The 1937–38 Type 97 (by Ledwinka's son Erich, who in 1936 had succeeded Übelacker as Tatra's chief designer) was the most advance small car anywhere at the time but expensive at almost six times the price of the first Volkswagen Beetle (KdF-Wagen). Some critics assert that Ledwinka (who followed the 1928–33 Tatra aerodynamic work of Paul Jaray, and whose work was closely watched by Ferdinand Porsche) established the initial principles for the subsequent development of Porsche's Volkswagen Beetle. But, with the seizure of Czechoslovakia by Germany in 1938–39, the Tatra operation was doomed. 1945, Ledwinka moved to Munich, where he died. 2001, SDC International bought Tatra from the Czech government, by which time Tatra had become an undistinguished truck manufacturer.
Exhibitions 1897, the first Nesselsdorfer car model shown in Vienna.
Bibliography Wolfgang Schmarbeck, *Tatra, die Geschichte der Tatra Automobile*, Lübbecke, Germany: Uhle & Kleimann, 1976. Miroslav Gomola, Gavin Farmer, and Jan Tulis, *Automobiles Tatra—Aerodynamic Cars from Koprivnice*, Brno, Czech Republic: AGM CZ, 1999. Miroslav Gomola, *Automobily Tatra—Luxusní vozy z Koprivnice 1920–1940,* Brno, Czech Republic: AGM CZ, 2000.
> See Jaray, Paul.

Lee, Mother Ann (1736–1784)
> See Shaker furniture.

Lee and Sons, Arthur
British textile firm; located Birkenhead, Lancashire.

History 1888, Arthur H. Lee founded his eponymous firm as a weaver, printer, and embroiderer in Warrington, moving in 1908 to Birkenhead; produced some important Art Nouveau textiles by leading designers in 1890s and early 1900s; subsequently, specialized in reproduction woven fabrics and embroidery for furnishings and upholstery. The firm was an agent for Mariano Fortuny's printed textiles. Arthur Lee and Sons closed in 1972.
Bibliography Valerie Mendes, *The Victoria and Albert Museum's Textile Collection; British Textiles from 1900 to 1937*, London: Victoria and Albert Museum, 1992.

Leerdam Glasfabriek
Dutch glassware manufacturer; located Leerdam.

History 1875, C.A. Jeekel set up glass factory Hardglasfabriek Jeekel in Leerdam, near Rotterdam. 1878, Jeekel, J.J. Mijnssen, and O.H.L. Nieuwenhuyzen established Glasfabriek Jeekel, Mijnssen & Co. to produce crystal and half-crystal wares. 1891, the name was changed to NV Glasfabriek Leerdam. From 1915, its first consultant designer was architect Karel Petrus Cornelis de Bazel (1869–1923), who, to 1923, was primarily concerned with the design of a pressed-glass service. 1917–26, graphic artist Cornelis de Lorm (1875–1942) designed for Leerdam; one of his first designs was a drop-shaped carafe with barrel-shaped drinking glasses. 1919–26, Christian Johannes Lanooy (1881–1948) designed domestic glassware. 1923–31 intermittently, architect H.P. Berlage came to Leerdam and designed a glass breakfast and dinner service. Piet Zwart, Berlage's associate, adapted a 1924 bright yellow pressed-glass breakfast set in a hexagonal shape (originally for avid German art collector Helene Kröller-Müller). Painter and graphic artist J.J.C. Lebeau (while at Leerdam 1923–26) designed a carafe, water glasses (not wine glasses, because he was a teetotaler), a finger bowl, and a fruit plate. A new management/worker arrangement (the first in the Netherlands) was created, and the plant was reorganized by P.S. Gerbrandy. A.D. Copier's Unica series of glassware, designed c. 1925, remained in production until after World War II. (1923, Copier and Lebeau began experimenting with free-blown art glass, to be known as the Unica series, whose development continued after World War II.) 1920–30, numerous designers, including Frank Lloyd Wright, produced decorative glassware motifs; even though Wright designed 16 pieces, including glassware and a full dinner service, only a tall green cut-glass vase was produced. From 1914, Copier was the only full-time design supervisor; he worked under J. Jongert 1918–23. Copier supervised the work of de Bazel and de Lorm and, 1920, began designing himself. At the firm from 1904, P.M. Cochius was put in charge of the general artistic management of the factory. c. 1937, I. Falkenberg-Liefrinck, J.A.H.F. Nicolas, and W. Stuurman designed tableware and ornamental glass objects. 1938, Leerdam was amalgamated into Vereenigde Glasfabrieken in Schiedam to form NV Vereenigde Leerdam Glasfabriek (Leerdam united glassworks). 1940, Copier established the Leerdam Glass School, where Floris Meydam 1949–85, Sybren Valkema 1948–66, Willem Heesen 1950–70, and G.J. Thomassen from 1951 were trained. 1953, the firm became NV Koninklijke Nederlandsche Glasfabriek Leerdam (while remaining a subsidiary of NV Vereenigde Glasfabrieken). 1959, Kristalunie in Maastricht joined the group. From 1959, the production of both factories was sold jointly until 1978, when domestic glassware was in Leerdam. Automated production of drinking glasses had already begun in 1958. 1968, the Glasvormcentrum (glass form center) was established. 1950s–60s designers included Henro Marius Laupman (1912–1992), Isabel Giampietro, Martien van der Eertwegh (1939–), Simon van der Marel (1944–), Gerard Jacobus Thomassen (1926–), Yje Theo Jansen (1926–), Jacobus Franciscus Linssen (1936–), and Brigitte Altenburger (1942–). 1980s–90s designers were Mieke Pontier (1945–), Vilma Henkelman (1944–), Olaf Stevens (1954–), and Winnie Teschmacher (1958–). 1971, Copier officially retired but stayed on to 1988 and further experimented with the Unica series. Currently, Leerdam primarily produces machine-made stemware, including utility glassware for others such as IKEA. By 1984, there were 1,800 employees at Leerdam and Maastricht. 2002, Royal Leerdam was acquired by Libbey Inc.
Exhibitions/citations Unica series shown at 1925 *Exposition Internationale des Arts Décoratifs et Industriels Modernes*, Paris, where Copier received a silver medal; and subject of a number of venues.
Bibliography Cat., *Glasschool Leerdam*, Amsterdam: Stedelijk Museum, 1947. Cat., *Leerdam Unica...*, Ghent: Museum voor Sierkuns, 1979. Cat., *Industry and Design in the Netherlands, 1850/1950*, Amsterdam: Stedelijk Museum, 1985. Leslie Jackson, *20th Century Factory Glass*, London: Octopus, 2000. Annet van der Kley-Blekxtoon, *Leerdam Glas 1878–1998*, Lochem: Antiek, 1999.

Leerdam Glasfabriek: Andries Dirk Copier. Urn. c. 1946. Glass, h. 8" (20.3 cm). Mfr.: NV Vereenigde Leerdam Glasfabriek, the Netherlands. Purchase. MoMA.

Lefler, Heinrich (1863–1919)
Austrian designer; born Vienna.

Biography 1900, Lefler and his brother-in-law Joseph Urban, with whom he often collaborated, founded the Künstlerbund Hagen (better known as the Hagenbund). Unlike the Wiener Sezession, the Hagenbund did not erect a new building for its own use but had a market-hall office (known as the Zedlitzhalle). Lefler and Urban handled the 1902 adaptation of the building, whose conversion revealed Leftler and Urban's crafts background, though they incorporated Sezession ornamentation throughout.
Exhibitions A room by Lefler and Urban designed at 1897 winter exhibition, Österreichisches Museum für Kunst und Industrie. Work subject of 1975 exhibition, Eigenverl. d. Museen d. Stadt Wien (catalog below).

Bibliography Robert Waissenberger, *Der Hagenbund*, Vienna: Eigenverl. der Museen der Stadt, 1975. Günther Feuerstein, *Vienna—Present and Past: Arts and Crafts—Applied Art—Design*, Vienna: Jugend und Volk, 1976: 23, 35, 80. Robert Waissenberger, *Vienna 1890–1920*, Secaucus, N.J.: Wellfleet, 1984.

LEGO
> See Christiansen, Ole Kirk.

Legrain, Pierre-Émile (1889–1929)

French designer of furniture, furnishings, and bookbindings; born Levallois-Perret; active Paris.

Training From 1904, sculpture, painting, and theater design, École des Arts Appliqués Germain-Croix, Paris.
Biography Legrain submitted cartoons in 1908 for Paul Iribe's satirical reviews *Le témoin*, *L'assiette au beurre*, *Le mot*, and *La Baïonnette*. Iribe invited Legrain to collaborate with him on projects, including furniture and interior design, jewelry for Robert Linzeler, and dress designs for Paquin. From 1912, Legrain designed geometric bookbindings for couturier Jacques Doucet and, subsequently, was put in charge of decoration and furniture for Doucet's studio on the rue Saint-Jacques, Neuilly. Legrain quickly became one of the most creative designers of bookbinding in the world and used a number of professional binders to execute his designs, particularly René Kieffer; for a period from 1919, he worked exclusively with Kieffer on bookbindings. Doucet also commissioned Legrain to design the bindings for his recently acquired collection of books by contemporary authors, including André Gide, André Suarès, Paul Claudel, and Francis Jammes, and Legrain worked on the binding designs in Doucet's dining room, sometimes assisted by Doucet himself. The exhibition of Legrain's work at the 1919 Salon proved a tremendous success, encouraging book collectors to embrace modernism enthusiastically. His newly acquired clients numbered Louis Barthou, baron R. Gourgaud, Georges and Auguste Blaizot, and baron Robert de Rothschild in Paris, and Florence Blumenthal and Daniel Sickles in the US. 1923, Legrain was invited by decorators Briant et Robert to set up his workshop in their establishment at 7, rue d'Argenteuil. c. 1925, Doucet commissioned him to decorate his Neuilly studio, whose architect was Paul Ruau. In addition to Kieffer, Legrain used binders Salvadore David, Georges Canape, George Huser, Georges Levitsky, Henri Nouilhac, Germaine Schroeder, Stroobants, Jeanne, Collet, Desmoules, Aufschneider, Dress, Vincent, and Lordereau. His work's success at the 1925 Paris *Exposition* encouraged him to set up his own bindery in 1926 on the avenue Percier and soon after on the rue Saint-Jacques. His bindings are known for their high level of craftsmanship, originality, and use of exotic materials. Legrain understood Cubism and African art, and the furniture he designed for Doucet shows both influences. One of his best-known pieces was the Pleyel piano in plate glass and copper, with its works visible, designed for the house of Pierre Meyer on the avenue Montaigne in Paris. He designed interiors, including a number of pieces of custom furniture, for friends of Doucet, including two apartments for milliner Jeanne Tachard, a suite of rooms for Maurice Martin du Gard, a bedroom for the vicomte and vicomtesse de Noailles, houses on the rue Villejust in Paris, and at La Celle-Saint Cloud, and commissions from Suzanne Talbot and Mme. Louis Boulanger. He designed a leather camera case for Kodak, a desk set for the Palais de l'Élysée, and cigarette boxes for Lucky Strike and Camel. He was a member of Groupe des Cinq, with Pierre Chareau, Dominique, Jean Puiforcat, and Raymond Templier. 1929, Legrain cofounded Union des Artistes Modernes (UAM) and designed the logotype for the group, dying in Paris shortly before its first exhibition. In barely 12 years, he produced some 1,300 designs for book covers and revolutionized an ancient craft. 1931–32, Legrain's widow produced certain of his bindings.
Exhibitions Doucet exhibited 20 of Legrain's binding designs at 1919 Salon of Société des Artistes Français. Legrain, Robert Mallet-Stevens, Chareau, Ruhlmann, and Paul Poiret collectively designed the pavilion La Réception et l'Intérieur d'un Appartement Moderne at 1924 Salon d'Automne. Participated in 1925 *Exposition Internationale des Arts Décoratifs et Industriels Modernes*; and from 1926, in exhibitions of Groupe des Cinq; plate-glass piano shown at 1929 exhibition of Groupe des Cinq, Galerie de la Renaissance, Paris.
Bibliography Léon Rosenthal, 'Pierre Legrain, relieur,' *Art et décoration*, Mar. 1923: 65–70. Léon Deshairs, *Les arts décoratifs modernes 1918–1925*, Paris, 1925. Philippe Dally, 'Les techniques modernes de la reliure,' *Art et décoration*, Jan.–June 1927: 15–17. Joseph Breck, 'Bookbindings by Legrain,' *Bulletin of The Metropolitan Museum of Art*, no. 11, Nov. 1932: 235–36. Ernest de Crauzat, *La reliure française de 1900 à 1925*, Paris: R. Kieffer, 1932, vol. 1: 180-87, vol. 2: 15-31. Roger Devauchelle, *La reliure en France de ses origines à nos jours*, Paris: Rousseau-Girard, 1959. Victor Arwas, *Art Déco*, New York: Abrams, 1980. Alastair Duncan, *Art Déco Furniture*, London and New York: Thames & Hudson, 1984. Jacques Guignard, *Pierre Legrain et la reliure: évolution d'un style*, Paris: Léon Rosenthal. Pierre Kjellberg, *Art déco: les maîtres du mobilier, le décor des paquebots*, Paris: Amateur, 1986/1990. Arlette Barré-Despond, *UAM*, Paris: Regard, 1986. Cat., *Les années UAM 1929–1958*, Paris: Musée des Arts Décoratifs, 1988. Alastair Duncan and Georges de Bartha, *Art Nouveau and Art Déco Bookbinding*, New York: Abrams, 1989.

Legrand, Roger (1925–)

French furniture designer; active Belfort.

Biography 1960s, Legrand is best known for his 1964 Pan U elements in bentwood produced by Steph Simon; was technical director of Knoll International; cofounded Atelier de Recherche et de Création (ARC) of Le Mobilier National.
Exhibitions Participated with Pierre Faucheux and Jean-Marie Serreau in French section (grand prize and gold medal), 1964 (13th) Triennale di Milano.
Bibliography Gilles de Bure, *Le mobilier français 1965–1979*, Paris: Regard/VIA, 1983: 6–7.

Legras & Cie.

French glass factory; located Saint-Denis, near Paris.

History Verreries et Cristalleries de Saint-Denis et des Quatre-Chemins, of which Auguste J.F. Legras became manager in 1864, was renamed Legras et Cie. and became one of France's principal glassworks be-fore 1914. By 1900 (under the management of François-Théodore Legras, succeeded by Charles Legras in 1909), it produced a wide range of tableware, mainly vases and some table lamps in cameo, enameled, and intaglio-carved glass. Its wares depicted pastoral scenes and seascapes. Legras took over the Vidié glassworks in Pantin in 1897 and, by 1908, employed over 1,500 workers. Charles Legras admired Gallé and attempted to imitate his work, but the glassworks' produce was not exceptional. After World War I, the firm was reorganized as Verreries et Cristalleries de Saint-Denis et de Pantin Réunies.
Exhibitions/citations Gold medal, 1888 *Exposición Universal de Barcelona*; grand prizes, 1889 and 1900 editions of *Exposition Universelle*, Paris.
Bibliography Ray and Lee Grover, *Carved and Decorated European Art Glass*, Rutledge, Vt.: Tuttle, 1970: 130–31. Helga Hilschenz, *Das Glas des Jugendstils*, Munich: Prestel, 1973: 317–24. Yvonne Brunhammer et al., *Art Nouveau Belgium, France*, Houston: Institute for the Arts, Rice University, 1976. Alastair Duncan, *Art Nouveau and Art Déco Lighting*, New York: Simon & Schuster, 1978: 82–83.

Lehmann, Andreas (1948–)

Swiss designer.

Biography 1986 with Beat Frank, Lehmann established the Atelier Vorsprung design studio in Berne, Switzerland. They have specialized in abstract sculpture intended for seating such as the 1989 Sitzkreuz furniture/sculpture that was installed in a hotel foyer in France, at a school for actors, and shown in a touring exhibition.
Bibliography Albrecht Bangert and Karl Michael Armer, *80s Style: Designs of the Decade*, New York: Abbeville, 1990: 80, 232.

Leischner, Margaret (1907–1970)

German textile designer; born Bischofswerden; active London.

Training In Dresden and, 1927–30, Bauhaus, Dessau.
Biography 1931, she headed the Dye Workshop at the Bauhaus, where she was an assistant to Gunta Stölz; 1931, designed woven textiles at Dresdener Deutsche Werkstätten; 1932–36, was head of the weaving department at the Modeschule in Berlin; 1938–42, was head designer at Team Valley Weaving Industries in Gateshead, a British furnishing fabric manufacturer; 1944–50, was a consultant designer to R. Greg and, for a time, to Fothergill and Harvey for car upholstery and radio-speaker baffle cloth; 1948–63, headed the weaving department, Royal College of Art, London; 1959, designed Tintawn sisal carpeting by Curragh Tintawn Carpets Ltd. (division of Irish Ropes) and was a consultant to Chemstrand for its Acrilan acrylic fiber (now a Solutia trademark).

Lektro Products. Packard Lifetime Lektro-Shaver. 1935. Bakelite casing and metal, 1 3/8 x 1 13/16 x 3 7/8" (3.5 x 4.5 x 9.8 cm). Mfr.: Lektro Products, US. Gift of Paul L. Loewenwarter. MoMA.

Citations 1969, was elected Honorary Royal Designer for Industry, UK; fellow, Society of Industrial Arts.
Bibliography Fiona MacCarthy and Patrick Nuttgens, *An Eye for Industry*, London: Lund Humphries, 1986. Cat., Gunta Stölzl, *Weberei am Bauhaus und aus eigener Werkstatt*, Berlin: Bauhaus-Archiv, 1987: 158. Cat., *The Bauhaus: Masters and Students*, New York: Barry Friedman, 1988. Sigrid Wortmann Weltge, *Women's Work: Textile Art from the Bauhaus*, San Francisco: Chronicle, 1993.

Lejambre, A. and H.

American furniture manufacturer; located Philadelphia.

History Jean-Pierre-Alphonse Lejambre emigrated to the US during the second decade of the 19th century and established an upholstery shop in Philadelphia. After his 1843 death, his wife Anna managed the firm with their son Alexis, who became a partner in c. 1853. By 1853, they were producing and importing French furniture, curtains, trimmings, and cornices. Alexis died young in 1862 and Anna Lejambre became a partner in 1865 and, likewise, her cousin Henri Lejambre, who had worked with the firm since 1850s. 1867, the name became A. and H. Lejambre (for Anna and Henri). 1860s–70s, the company produced massive pieces of furniture in the French Renaissance style, then popular in Philadelphia, and some English-style pieces. From Anna's 1878 death, A. and H. Lejambre was managed by Henri, his son Eugène Lejambre, and his various nephews. However, the enterprise achieved meager success, and it thus ceased its production in c. 1907.
Bibliography Peter L.L. Strickland, 'Furniture by the Lejambre Family of Philadelphia,' *Antiques*, vol. 113, Mar. 1978: 600–13. Doreen Bolger Burke et al., *In Pursuit of Beauty: Americans and the Aesthetic Movement*, New York: The Metropolitan Museum of Art / Rizzoli, 986: 449.

Lektro Products

American manufacturer; located Milford, Conn.

History 1934, Dictography Products, Inc., was founded by Archie Moulton Andrews in New Milford, Conn. He had been an employee of the Schick electric razor company before departing to establish Dictography, whose name was eventually changed to Lektro Products, Inc. Prior to Schick, Andrews had been the head of Hupp Motor Co., makers of the Huppmobile, and for a time of Dictaphone. (Dictograph machines were used by office executives to dictate letters for secretaries to transcribe.) The first model that Lektro produced was the 1935 Packard Lifetime Lektro-Shaver, which became highly successful. Subsequently, the firm produced for a short time the Model T with three cutting heads and a vibrating motor, in a Bakelite case. Purportedly, of the 1,200,000 electric shavers in use in the US by 1936, 400,000 were by Lektro. The Packard Twin-Dual had two cutting heads. Howard McGuire was president of Lektro during the firm's most successful period. 1953, the firm closed.
Bibliography Phillip L. Krumholz, *Value Guide for Barberiana and Shaving Collectibles*, Bartonville, Ill.: Ad Lib, 1988. Phillip L. Krumholz, *A History of Shaving and Razors*, Bartonville, Ill.: Ad Lib, 1988.

Leleu, Jules-Émile (1883–1961)

French sculptor and designer; born Boulogne-sur-Mer.

Training Under Théophile Deman, Académie des Beaux-Arts, Boulogne-sur-Mer; private academy, Brussels; École Jean Goujon, Paris, under Secame; École des Arts Appliqués, Paris.
Biography From 1901, Leleu and his brother Marcel Leleu directed their father's painting business, and Jules-Émile began working as an interior designer. After World War I, he established his own interior-design studio and furniture workshop in Paris. His 1920s–30s furniture designs were produced in his cabinet making workshops in Boulogne. He followed a pattern established by Louis Süe / André Mare and Jacques-Émile Ruhlmann in designing in a classical, massive, and lavish 'baroque' Art Déco form, but akin to the Louis XVI style. 1920s, his furniture designs were more delicate, with an extensive use of exotic woods. 1930s, his lines and techniques became simpler, and he developed a modern style of his own. 1924, he set up showrooms at 65, avenue Victor-Emmanuel III (now avenue Franklin-Roosevelt), Paris. His monumental style was particularly appropriate to commissions for official and semi-official décors, including numerous French embassies and civic and royal residences. He designed the décors of and supplied furniture for more than 20 oceanliners, including the lecture room on 1927 *Île-de-France*, interiors (with rugs by Ivan Da Silva Bruhns) on 1931 *L'Atlantique*, first-class cabins on 1935 *Normandie*, and used metal for the first time on 1961 *France*; designed the dining room of the Palais de l'Élysée in Paris in 1937, where his modern-style furniture first appeared. He executed décors in the Palace of the League of Nations in Geneva and French embassies in Japan, Brazil, Turkey, Poland, and the Netherlands. He often collaborated with artists and friends, including metalworker Edgar Brandt, architect André Lurcat, and lacquerist Jean Dunand. After World War II, he continued the family business, while designing interiors, furniture, carpets, fabrics, and lighting with his son André and daughter Paule. He died in Paris.
Exhibitions From 1905, sculpture shown at Salons of Société des Artistes Français. Design work first shown (1922), Salon of Société des Artistes Français; then, 1922–27 and 1929–42 Salons of Société des Artistes Décorateurs and editions of Salon d'Automne and Salon des Tuileries. At 1925 *Exposition Internationale des Arts Décoratifs et Industriels Modernes*, Paris, he made the chairs for the Grand Salon designed by Henri Rapin and Pierre Selmersheim and the music room by Sèzille; designed and made a suite of living-room furniture for his own stand on the Esplanade des Invalides there. His 1931 Hôtel Nord-Sud in Calvi, Corsica, shown at 1932 *Modern Architecture—International Style*, The Museum of Modern Art, New York.
Bibliography *Ensembles mobiliers*, Paris: Charles Moreau, no. 20, 1954. Cat., *Decorative Arts 1925 Style*, New York: Didier Aaron, 1979. Victor Arwas, *Art Déco*, New York: Abrams, 1980. Jessica Rutherford, *Art Nouveau, Art Deco, and the Thirties: The Furniture Collections at Brighton Museum*, Brighton: The Royal Pavilion, Art Gallery and Mu-seums, 1983: 37. Pierre Kjellberg, *Art déco: les maîtres du mobilier, le décor des paquebots*, Paris: Amateur, 1986/1990. *Jules et André Leleu*, Paris: Vecteurs, 1989. Cat., Sophie Tasma Anargyros et al., *L'école française: les créateurs de meubles du 20ème siècle*, Paris: Industries Françaises de l'Ameublement, 2000.

Lemarchands, Vincent (1960–)

French designer; born Lyon.

Biography 1980–87 with Jacques Bonnot, Frédérick du Chayla, and Claire Olivès, Lemarchands was a member of the Totem group in Lyon; 1884, cofounded the Caravelle association to organize exhibitions; from 1985, taught design, École Régionale des Beaux-Arts, Saint-Étienne, France; organized 1986 Caravelles 1 international quadrennial of design in Grenoble, Lyon, and Saint-Étienne; organized 1991 Caravelles 2 in Lyon, Villeurbanne, Villefranche-sur-Saône, Saint-Étienne, and Le Puy-en-Velay; organized 1998 *Design 98*, Saint-Étienne; 1999, cofounded La Stéphanoise de Design, a collective of de-signers, artists, and architects in Saint-Étienne.
> See Totem.

Lemelson, Jerome H. (1923–1997)

American inventor; born Staten Island, N.Y.; son of a physician.

Training Three engineering degrees (1947, 1949, and 1951), New York University, New York.
Biography As a youth, Lemelson experimented with model airplanes, an interest that he developed into a career when he became a designer of defense systems for America during World War II; subsequently and for the remainder of his life, was active as an independent inventor; 1974, licensed his audio-cassette-drive mechanism to Sony, which led to the Walkman. His first patent application (1977) was for the camcorder, but it was rejected. 1981, he sold about 20 patents for data and word-processing systems to IBM; 1976–79, was a member of US Advisory Committee on patents; over a four-decade period, received an average of one patent grant per month—more than 500 in all—including for the cordless phone, fax machine, industrial robots, and crying baby dolls; 1994 with his wife Dorothy, established the Lemelson Foundation for recognizing American invention, which funds the Lemelson-MIT Awards Program at Massachusetts Institute of Technology (MIT), Cambridge, Mass.

Lemmen, Georges (1865–1916)

Belgian painter; born Schaerbeek.

Biography Lemmen was an active member of Belgium's avant-garde movement, in contact with the pioneers of Art Nouveau in Belgium and Henri de Toulouse-Lautrec in France. His work was initially in the Impressionist style. Like other members of artists' group Les Vingt, he was active in reviving interest in the decorative arts; designed rugs, tapestries, ceramics, jewelry, and mosaics, and illustrated books and posters. Some of his jewelry was designed for Philippe Wolfers, and Toulouse-Lautrec purchased a tapestry for which Lemmen designed the cartoon. Lemmen designed the typeface for Henry van de Velde's 1908 edition of Nietzsche's *Also sprach Zarathustra: ein Buch für Alle und Keinen* (Leipzig: Insel). Van de Velde considered Lemmon to be pessimistic and thought his later work akin to that of Hermann Obrist and Otto Eckmann.
Exhibitions From 1899, work shown at annual salons of Les Vingt, and later of La Libre Esthétique.
Bibliography Marcel Nyns, *Georges Lemmen*, Antwerp, De Sikkel, 1954. Yvonne Brunhammer et al., *Art Nouveau Belgium, France*, Houston: Institute for the Arts, Rice University, 1976. Stuart Durant, *Ornament from the Industrial Revolution to Today*, Woodstock, N.Y.: Overlook, 1986. Roger Cardon, *Georges Lemmen: (1865–1916): monographie générale suivie du catalogue raisonné de l'œuvre gravé*, Antwerp: Pandora, 1990. Roger Cardon, Georges Lemmen, 1865–1916, Antwerp: Crédit Communal/Snoeck–Ducaju & Zoon/Pandora, 1997.

Lemongras; Carmen K.M. Cheong (1970–); Mortiz Engelbrecht (1964–)

German design studio. Cheong: born Singapore. Engelbrecht: born Berlin.

History/biographies 1987–91, Carmen K.M. Cheong studied product design under Franke Drake, Temasek Polytechnic, Singapore; from 1991, worked as a furniture designer at chemical-laboratory furniture manufacturer Morgan & Grundy (now APMG) in Manchester, UK; 1996, received a master of art degree in industrial design, Royal College of Art, London, with numerous citations. 1983, Moritz Engelbrecht studied interior design, University of San Francisco, US. Active in Munich during 1984–92, he received a degree in economic engineering, Technische Hochschule, Munich; 1987, cofounded Pontius & Pilatus, an interior- and furniture-design studio, and, 1993, Emdrei interior-design consultancy; 1994–96, received a master of art degree in furniture design from Royal College of Art, where he met Cheong. Realizing that the UK was not the best place to work as industrial designers, they established Lemongras for the design of products, furniture, interiors, and packaging, in Munich in 1997.
Bibliography Mel Byars, *Design in Steel*, London: Laurence King, 2002.

Lenci, Fabio (1935–)

Italian designer; born and active Rome.

Training In Rome.
Biography 1966, Lenci set up a shop for contemporary furniture in Rome and began to explore the use of new plastics and manufacturing techniques in the production of his own furniture designs, including his Chain armchair with suspended upholstered tubes between plate-glass sides. 1975 with Giovanna Talocci, he established Studio Lenci Talocci; for a time, collaborated with Carlo Urbanati and Patrizia Lalle. His clients in Italy have included Bonacina, Poltrona Frau, Ellisse, G.B. Bernini, Iform, Incom, Sleeping International System Italia, and Tenco. He has designed furniture, interiors, textiles, lighting and sanitary fixtures, including the 1974 Aquarius bath/shower unit by Teuco-Guzzini (from 1975); became a member, Associazione per il Disegno Industriale (ADI).
Exhibitions 1970 polyurethane table-chair set and table by Bernini shown at 1972 *Italy: The New Domestic Landscape*, The Museum of Modern Art, New York.
Bibliography Emilio Ambasz (ed.), *Italy: The New Domestic Landscape*, New York: The Museum of Modern Art, 1972: 122. *ADI Annual 1976*, Milan: Associazione per il Disegno Industriale, 1976. Sylvia Katz, *Plastics: Designs and Materials*, London, 1978: 96. Cat., Kathryn B. Hiesinger and George H. Marcus III (eds.), *Design Since 1945*, Philadelphia: Philadelphia Museum of Art, 1983. *Modo*, no. 148, Mar.–Apr.1993: 121.

Lendecke, Otto (1886–1918)

German draftsman, graphic artist, fashion and book designer; born Lemberg (now Lvov, Ukraine).

Biography Lendecke lived in Paris for a time and worked briefly with Paul Poiret; from 1911, was associated with the Wiener Werkstätte and, 1915, settled in Vienna and designed theater sets and costumes for the Werkstätte. From 1917, he published fashion magazine *Die Damenwelt* (ladies' world) and contributed to others, including *Wiener Mode*, *Die Dame*, and 1914–15 fashion folder *Die Mode*.
Bibliography Deanna F. Cera (ed.), *Jewels of Fantasy: Costume Jewelry of the 20th Century*, New York: Abrams, 1992.

Lennon, Dennis (1918–1991)

British architect and furniture designer and maker.

Biography 1946–48, Lennon was an assistant designer in the architecture office of Maxwell Fry in London; became director of Rayon Industry Design; 1950, formed architectural-design firm Dennis Lennon and Partners and was prolific in the post-World War II years; 1950s–60s, worked on the interiors of Cumberland Hotel, Jaeger shops, 1969 oceanliner *Queen Elizabeth II*, Peter Jones department store, and Sekers. Other interior schemes included those for Commercial Union Bank, Sainsbury's, Vickers, Mercantile and General Bank, Bank of America, and Rothschilds Intercontinental. (The Lennon practice is where Terence Conran first began designing furniture in 1951, after studying at Central School of Arts and Crafts, London.)
Bibliography Ernö Goldfinger, *British Furniture Today*, London, 1951. Michael Farr, *Design in British Industry: A Mid-Century Survey*, London: Cambridge, 1955. Robert Harling (ed.), *Studio Dictionary of Design and Decoration*, New York: Viking, 1973. Sutherland Lyall, *Hille: 75 Years of British Furniture*, London: Elron, 1981.

Lenoble, Émile (1875–1940)

French ceramicist.

Training École Nationale Supérieure des Arts Décoratifs, Paris.
Biography After a seven-year apprenticeship, Lenoble turned in 1904 from earthenware to stoneware and high-temperature firing. Henry Rivière, his mentor and a connoisseur of Middle Eastern and oriental art, introduced Lenoble to Korean pottery and Sung ceramics, which became a major influence on Lenoble's work. c. 1910, he began producing gray enamelwork. In his studio in Choisy-le-Roy, near Paris, Lenoble's hand-thrown pots, cylindrical vases, bottles, and bowls were made from kaolin mixed with stoneware for a delicacy and lightness. His motifs were simple, geometric (chevrons and spirals), and floral (flowers and stylized leaves). 1920–30, his work showed a Chinese influence and was realized in a variety of colors such as turquoise, lapis-lazuli, yellows, browns, and celadon.
Bibliography Pierre Cabanne, *Encyclopédie art déco*, Paris: Somogy, 1986: 213.

Lenox, Walter Scott (1859–1920); Frank Graham Holmes (1878–1954)

American ceramicists; born and active Trenton, N.J.

Biography From 1875, Walter Scott Lenox worked as a decorator and designer for potteries in Trenton, N.J., a major pottery center; from

1881, was design director of Ott & Brewer and, subsequently, of Willets Manufacturing—both, even though eventual failures, making domestic thin, cream-colored Irish Belleek, popular with the Victorian public. 1889, Lenox established his own pottery, Lenox's Ceramic Art Company, in Trenton, N.J. The location was near good transporation and sources of clay. He gained a favorable reputation quickly. Apparently indefatigable, Lenox continued to go to the pottery daily toward the end of his life, despite being blind, paralysed, and needing to be carried. He was assisted in the business by Harry Brow. Lenox had been dogged to overcome negative attitudes toward American-made china; from 1902, began offering custom patterns by artists such as William Morley and, from 1910, transfer prints; 1906, changed the name to Lenox Incorporated. After Lenox's 1920 death, the operation was managed by Brown, Frank Graham Holmes, and William Clayton. William Bromley Sr. also assisted but soon left. 1905–54, Holmes was the chief designer. The firm's success was greatly assisted when, in 1917, President Woodrow Wilson ordered a 1,700 piece Lenox dinner set (produced in 1918) for use in The White House in Washington, D.C. The commissions continued with Franklin D. Roosevelt (1934), Harry S. Truman (1951), Ronald Reagan (1981), Bill Clinton (2000), and more than 300 US embassies and (half) 25 of state governors' mansions. Through 1930s, the firm's president was Harry Brown. Oven-proof ceramics were added to its range in 1972, handblown lead crystal in 1966, and silver cutlery in 1991. Its specialty continues to be ivory-colored porcelain.
Exhibitions/citations Work was shown at 1926–27 *American Industrial Art, Tenth Annual Exhibition of Current Manufactures Designed and Made in the United States*, The Metropolitan Museum of Art, New York. To Holmes: 1927 Craftsmanship Medal, American Institute of Architects (AIA); 1943 silver medal, American Institute of Decorators (AID); 1928, work included in 34 Lenox pieces chosen for display by Musée National de Céramique, Sévres, France.
Bibliography *Lenox China: The Story of Walter Scott Lenox*, Philadelphia: for private circulation, 1924. Karen Davies, *At Home in Manhattan: Modern Decorative Arts, 1925 to the Depression*, New Haven: Yale, 1983.

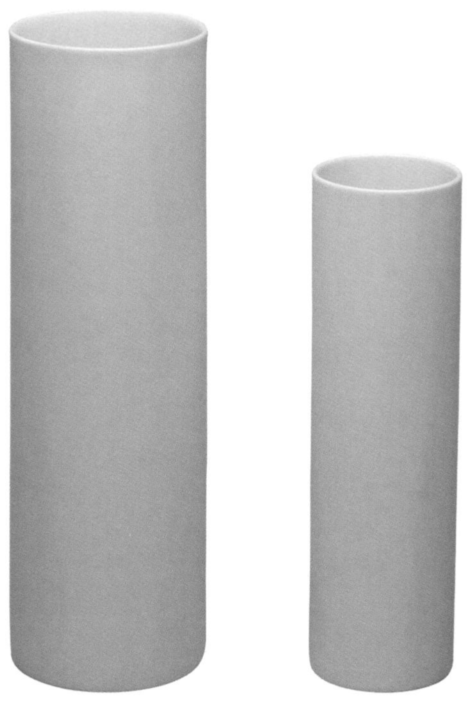

Lenox: Frank Graham Holmes. 1908. Glazed porcelain, left h. 10 1/4 x dia. 3 1/8" (26.1 x 8 cm), right h. 8 x dia. 2 3/8" (20.3 x 6 cm). Mfr.: Lenox, US (c. 1940). Gift of the mfr. MoMA.

Lenti, Paola (1958–)

Italian designer; born Alessandria; active Meda (Milan).

Biography 1999, Lenti pursued the new popularity of wool felt in home furnishings in late 1990s. 1999, she began to produce her own designs of felt rugs and seating such as the Linea undulating chaise longue (absent of a base), and Rope 04 chaise in another material, Atollo sofa and hassock, and Kubo stool and hassock. Other wares included containers and vases in glass and ceramics, rugs, and blankets. She has also called on synthetic so-called Rope for her Mat rugs and Twist seating.
Exhibitions Subject of 2003 venue, Material ConneXion, New York.

Léonard-Agathon (aka Léonard-Agathon van Weydeveldt 1841–1923)

Belgian designer; born Lille.

Training École des Beaux-Arts, Lille.
Biography Léonard-Agathon settled in Paris and became a member of Société des Artistes Français in 1887 and of Société Nationale des Beaux-Arts in 1897; was naturalized French in 1887. He changed his family name to his surname Léonard due to feeling that Weydeveldt was too difficult for a French person to pronounce; executed portrait medallions, rose-quartz and green Egyptian marble statuettes and groups, bronze, ivory, plaster, and flambé earthenware. He is primarily known for his female figurine group Jeu de l'Écharpe (game with a scarf) commissioned by Manufacture Nationale de Porcelaine in Sèvres, in white bisque and, subsequently, by Susse Frères in bronze. He died in Paris.
Exhibitions/citations Jeu de l'Écharpe figurines were first (1897) shown at Salon of the Société Nationale des Beaux-Arts in Paris, and subsequently (as the Sèvres version), in the Sèvres pavilion at 1900 *Exposition Universelle*, Paris. Work subject of 2003 exhibitions at Musée d'Art et d'Industrie André-Diligent (La Piscine in Roubaix) and at Musée Départemental de l'Oise in Beauvais. 1902, was elected Chevalier of the Légion d'Honneur.
Bibliography *Deutsche Kunst und Dekoration*, 1900–01: 177. Martin Battersby, *Art Nouveau*, London, 1969: 34. Alastair Duncan, *Art Nouveau and Art Déco Lighting*, New York: Simon & Schuster, 1978. Ingelore Böstge and Emmanuelle Héran, *Agathon Léonard, le geste Art nouveau*, Paris: Somogy, 2003.

Leonardi, Cesare (1935–)

Italian industrial designer and architect; active Modena.

Training To 1970, architecture, Università degli Studi, Firenze.
Biography 1961, Leonardi opened his own office in Modena and, 1962, Franca Stagi became a partner in the Leonardi initiative. They went on to specialize in architecture, urban planning, and industrial design and designed furniture by Bernini, Fiam Italia, and Peguri; plastic products by Elco; lighting by Lumenform; and a number of products by other firms. Their best-known design, the sculptural 1967 Dondolo rocking chair (in molded-fiberglass, polyester reinforced) by Elco in Venice, has become a classic.
Exhibitions Furniture shown at 1968–69 editions of Internationale Möbelmesse, Cologne, and Salone del Mobile, Milan (Donaldo chair first shown there in 1968); 1970 *Design for Living, Italian Style*, London; Donaldo subsequently included, at 1970 *Modern Chairs 1918–1970*, Whitechapel Gallery, London, and 1983–84 *Design Since 1945*, Philadelphia Museum of Art.
Bibliography 'Tavolini da soggiorno in vetroresina, impignabili,' *Domus*, no. 483, Feb. 1970: 43–44. Cat., *Modern Chairs 1918–1970*, London: Lund Humphries, 1971: no. 119. Cat., Kathryn B. Hiesinger and George H. Marcus III (eds.), *Design Since 1945*, Philadelphia: Philadelphia Museum of Art, 1983.

Leonidov, Ivan Ilich (1902–1959)

Russian architect; born Vlasikh, near Kalinin.

Training From 1919, art school, Tver; from 1921, fine art, VKhUTEMAS, Moscow; to 1928, Lenin Institute, Moscow.
Biography 1921, Leonidov settled in Moscow, becoming a painter and studying at the VKhUTEMAS, where, under the influence of Aleksandr Vesnin, he turned from painting to architecture. 1926, his school project for *Izvestia* newspaper's printing plant showed a fully realized expression of Constructivism. 1928, he became a lecturer at the Lenin Institute. As a Constructivist/Suprematist architect affected by Russian traditionalism, his style changed from dynamic, glass-walled structures to somewhat 'baroque' structures, illustrated by his 1933 Narkomtiazprom-competition entry. Leonidov was able to produce only one notable building, the 1932 amphitheater and stairway for the

Ordjohikedze sanatorium in Kislovodsk. After World War II, he worked exclusively as an exhibition designer.
Exhibitions/citations 1921, entered a number of architecture competitions, receiving several prizes. School project for the Lenin Institute of Moscow shown at 1927 (1st) exhibition of OSA (union of contemporary artists), Moscow.
Bibliography Selim O. Khan-Magomedov, 'Ivan Leonidov,' *Sovietskaia Architektura*, 16, 1964: 103–16. S.O. Khan-Magomedov, 'I.I. Leonidov 1902–1959,' in O.A. Shvidovsky (ed.), *Building in the USSR, 1917–1932*, New York: Praeger, 1971. Selim O. Khan-Magomedov, *Ivan Leonidov*, Moscow: Stroiizdat, 1971. S.O. Khan-Magomedov, *I. Leonidov*, Moscow, 1973. Vieri Quilici and M. Scolari (eds.), *Ivan Leonidov*, Milan, 1975. Vieri Quilici and S.O. Khan-Magomedov, *Ivan Leonidov*, New York: Institute for Architecture and Urban Studies/ Rizzoli, 1981. Andrei Gozak and Andrei Leonidov, *Ivan Leonidov: The Complete Works*, London: Academy, 1988. S.O. Khan-Magomedov, *Vhutemas: Moscou, 1920–1930*, Paris: Regard, 1990. Cat., *The Great Utopia: The Russian and Soviet Avant-Garde, 1915–1932*, New York: Guggenheim Musem, 1992.

Leonori, Luca (1951–)
Italian designer; born and active Rome.

Training To 1973, design, Università Internazionale dell'Arte (UIA), Florence; to 1976, architecture, Università degli Studi 'La Sapienza,' Rome.
Biography From 1976, Leonari worked with the Studio Passarelli and, concurrently from 1978, at Pallucco, both Rome, on architectural projects; from 1985, in the graphic and design group Grafite, with architects L. De Lorenzo, F. Piferi, and S. Stefani.
Bibliography Fumio Shimizu and Studio Matteo Thun (eds.), *The Italian Design: Descendants of Leonardo da Vinci*, Tokyo: Graphic-sha, 1987.

Lepape, Georges (1887–1971)
French painter, illustrator, and designer.

Training Under Fernand Cormon, École Nationale Supérieure des Beaux-Arts; Atelier Humbert; both Paris.
Biography At École des Beaux-Arts, Lepape met André Marty, Pierre Brissaud, and Charles Martin, all known for their illustrations in fashion magazines and books; met Georges Braque, Francis Picabia, and Marie Laurencin at Atelier Humbert. 1909, Lepape was discovered by couturier Paul Poiret and interpreted Poiret's revolutionary ideas and creations into drawings and watercolors; illustrated the portfolio *Les choses de Paul Poiret vues par Georges Lepape* (Paris: Poiret, 1911); 1912, was commissioned by Jean-Louis Vaudoyer to design the sets of *La nuit persane* at Théâtre des Arts, Paris; 1912–25, rendered illustrations for the fashion magazine *Gazette du bon ton*; 1915, designed for the ballet-pantomime *Le coup manqué* for the revue *Rip* at the Théâtre de l'Athénée and, 1916, another set for a ballet for *Rip* at Théâtre de Marigny. 1923, he designed the set for Maurice Maeterlinck's *L'oiseau bleu*; before World War I, supplied Poiret with original couture ideas as well as some fabric designs; went on to design film sets; 1924–38, taught, New York School of Fine and Applied Arts.

William Lescaze. Salt and pepper shakers. c. 1935. Aluminum and plastic, each 1 3/4 x 2 x 5/8" (4.4 x 5.1 x 1.6 cm). Mfr.: Revere Copper and Brass, US. Dorothy Cullman Purchase Fund. MoMA.

Bibliography Cat., *Decorative Arts 1925 Style*, New York: Didier Aaron, 1979. Victor Arwas, *Art Déco*, Abrams, 1980. Claude Lepape and Thierry Defert, *Georges Lepape ou l'élégance illustrée*, Paris: Herscher, 1983. Pierre Cabanne, *Encyclopédie art déco*, Paris: Somogy, 1986: 213.

Leporskaia, Anna Aleksandrovna (1900–1982)
Russian painter, interior designer, decorative artist, and porcelain designer and painter; wife of Nikolai Suetin.

Training 1918, Under A. Radakov; from 1922, Pskov School of Decorative Arts; Under K. Petrov-Vodkin, A. Savinov, and V. Sinaiskii Academy of Arts, Petrograd .
Biography 1925, she was an associate of GINKhUK in the department of Kazimir Malevich and active in interior decoration and book illustration. 1930–31, she was involved with design at the Krasny Theater and at the Muzikalnaia Komedia Theater, Leningrad (now St. Petersburg); in 1934, designed the interior of the Cultural Center of the Industrial Cooperative with husband Suetin; from 1945, designed porcelain forms; and, from 1948, was a designer at the Lomonosov Porcelain Factory, Leningrad. From 1952, she was a member, examining committee, College of Decorative Arts, Leningrad.
Exhibitions/citations Participated in 1937 *Exposition Internationale des Arts et Techniques dans la Vie Moderne*, Paris; the installation of the 1939–40 *New York World's Fair: The World of Tomorrow*; with Suetin, 1940 *National Agricultural Exhibition*; Leningrad stand at the *Great War of Defence* exhibition. Received Repin State Prize.
Bibliography Cat., *Kunst und Revolution: Russische und Sowjetische Kunst 1910–1932*, Vienna: Österreichisches Museum für angewandte Kunst, 1988. Cat., *The Great Utopia: The Russian and Soviet Avant-Garde, 1915–1932*, New York: Guggenheim Museum, 1992.

Lera, Roberto (1945–)
Italian architect and designer.

Biography His first work in plastics was the 1969 table for Fratelli Merati. He worked for Sormani; was involved with the journal *La stampa sera* in Turin; 1969, designed Linea B's first plastic production.
Bibliography Cat., Milena Lamarová, *Design a Plastické Hmoty*, Prague: Uměleckoprůmyslové Muzeum, 1972: 120.

Lescaze, William (1896–1969)
Swiss architect and designer; born Onez, near Geneva; active Paris and the US.

Training To 1914, Collège de Genève; 1915, École des Beaux-Arts, Geneva; 1919 under Karl Moser, master's degree in architecture, Eigenössische Technische Hochschule, Zürich.
Biography 1919–20, Lescaze worked on projects for the Committee for the Reconstruction of Devastated France and, for a time in Paris, in the architecture office of Henri Sauvage. 1919–21, he emigrated to the US and worked as a draftsperson for architects Hubbell and Benes in Cleveland, Ohio; 1921–23, for Walter R. McCormack, the chief of the Bureau of Design of the Cleveland Board of Education, as a draftsperson of schools and a planner and designed a 1922 warehouse. 1923, he set up his own practice in New York with a commission for the townhouse of Simeon Ford at Sutton Place and Sutton Square, New York; 1929–33, collaborated with George Howe in New York and Philadelphia. Lescaze and Howe are best known for the 1929–32 Philadelphia Savings Fund Society (PSFS) building, one of the most distinguished skyscrapers of all time and a notable early International Style structure. Lescaze designed 1931–36 buildings at Dartington Hall, Devon. Other architecture included Edgewood School (in collegiate neo-Gothic style) in Greenwich, Conn.; interiors (in a Paris modern vocabulary) at 1929 Macy's *Exposition* in New York; progressive schools (with Howe) in Philadelphia in 1929 and in New York in 1931; 1930–31 Frederick Vanderbilt House, New Hartford, Conn., one of the first International Style residences in the US; 1938 radio studios of Columbia Broadcasting System (CBS), Hollywood; 1942 Longfellow apartment building, Connecticut Ave./Rhode Island Ave., Washington D.C.; 1950 100-unit residential complex Spinney Hill, Manhasset, N.Y.; 1955 Borg-Warner building, Chicago; and 1962 Church Peace Center building, New York. After the dissolution of the partnership with Howe, Lescaze designed the Unity house in the Pocono mountains of Pennsylvania, and Williamsbridge public housing in Brooklyn, N.Y. Becoming active after World War II in the decorative arts and metalwork, he designed office spaces, including 711 Third Avenue building (demolished and

replaced by the ING building), New York. His most notable product designs and furniture were for the PSFS building and the CBS building in Hollywood, including metal cantilever chairs and upholstered seating. He designed furniture and lighting for Bertel house, 1928 de Sièyes house, his own 1933–34 house at 211 East 48th Street, New York, and 1928 Andrew Geller Shoes stores. Also designed a 1932 clock, desk set, coat rack, desks, chairs, and ceiling lighting fixture for the PSFS building; c. 1935 salt-and-pepper shakers by Revere Copper and Brass; 1936 microphone and 1945 mobile truck unit for CBS. He died in New York.

Exhibitions Work included in 1927 *Art in Industry* (paintings, furniture, fabrics, and accessories), Halle Brothers department store, Cleve-land; 1928 *Exposition of Art in Industry at Macy's* (a room setting), New York; Central Gallery of 1935 *Contemporary American Industrial Art, 1934* (living room) and 1940 *Contemporary American Industrial Art* (four-year-old's room), The Metropolitan Museum of Art, New York. Work subject of 1992 *William Lescaze*, Institute for Architecture and Urban Studies, New York (and Basel; catalog below). Lescaze's and Howe's work shown in 1931 European touring exhibition; included in 1932 *Modern Architecture—International Exhibition*, The Museum of Modern Art, New York.

Bibliography William Lescaze, *On Being an Architect*, New York: Putnam's, 1942. L. Wodehouse, 'Lescaze and Dartington Hall,' *Architectural Association Quarterly*, vol. 8, no. 2, 1976. Cat., *William Lescaze*, New York: Institute for Architecture and Urban Studies, 1992. Welling Lanmon Lorraine, *William Lescaze, Architect*, Philadelphia: The Art Alliance, 1987. Cat., Lindsay Stamm Shapiro, *William Lescaze*, Basel: Wiese, 1993.

Lethaby, William Richard (1857–1931)

British architect, draftsperson, and theorist; born Barnstaple, Devon.

Training Royal Academy Schools, London.

Biography Lethaby worked as an apprentice in the offices of Alexander Lauder at Barnstaple; from 1877 under the architect Norman Shaw in London and, 1881, became his principal assistant. Lethaby was strongly influenced by William Morris and Philip Webb and admired medieval art; cofounded Art-Workers' Guild and created some of the most original buildings of the Arts and Crafts movement. 1896, he and George Frampton were appointed joint advisors of the newly organized Central School of Arts and Crafts, London, the first school of arts and crafts with workshops in various crafts, as a prototype for the Bauhaus. At the school, he became the joint principal, with Frampton, and remained there to 1911. 1900, Lethaby became the first professor of art at Royal College of Art, London. He set out to break down the barriers between high and popular art, using the commonplace and the familiar to inspire the craftsperson and designer. 1915, he cofounded Design and Industries Association; published important theoretical books on art, craft, and design; was editor of the influential *The Artistic Crafts Series of Technical Handbooks* (London: John Hogg, 1906; and further eds.). His notable buildings include 1891 Avon Tyrell house, Hampshire; 1899 Eagle Insurance building, Birmingham; 1900–02 country church, Brockhampton, Ross-on-Wye, Herefordshire.

Bibliography W.R. Lethaby, *Architecture, Mysticism and Myth*, London: Percival, 1892. W.R. Lethaby, *Leadwork, Old and Ornamental and for the Most Part English*, London: Macmillan, 1893. W.R. Lethaby, *Architecture: An Introduction to the History...*, London: Williams & Norgate, 1912. W.R. Lethaby, *Designing Games*, Leicester, 1929. W.R. Lethaby, *Form in Civilization*, London: Oxford University, 1922. W.R. Lethaby, *Philip Webb and His Work*, London: Oxford University, 1935. Godfrey Rubens, *William Richard Lethaby: His Life and Work 1857–1931*, London: Architectural Press, 1986. Sylvia Backemeyer and Theresa Gronberg (eds.), *W.R. Lethaby, 1857–1931: Architecture, Design and Education*, London: Lund Humphries, 1984. Stuart Durant, *Ornament from the Industrial Revolution to Today*, Woodstock, N.Y.: Overlook, 1986: 220, 325. Vittorio Magnago Lampugnani (ed.), *Encyclopedia of 20th-Century Architecture*, New York: Abrams, 1986: 200–01.

Lettré, Emil (1876–1954)

German silversmith; born Hanau; active Vienna, Budapest, Paris, and Berlin.

Training Königliche Preussische Zeichenakademie, Hanau; and in Vienna.

Biography Lettré worked under Fritz von Miller in Munich and in Vienna, Budapest, and Paris; from 1905, had a silversmithy in Berlin, where British silversmith Henry Wilson practiced for some years and, 1912, H.G. Murphy worked as an apprentice. The condensed, severe form of Lettré's production with its stylized animals presaged later styles by others. His objects, mostly silver and with simple geometric designs, were produced in his workshop; were always simple, with smooth forms and fine linear chasing. 1920s, Lettré-designed cutlery was produced by Bruckmann & Söhne in Heilbronn. 1933, he was appointed director, Staatliche Zeichenakademie, Hanau.

Exhibitions Work included in a 1906 exhibition, Dresden; 1914 *Deutscher Werkbund-Ausstellung*, Cologne; 1937 *Exposition Internationale des Arts et Techniques dans la Vie Moderne*, Paris.

Bibliography Charlotte Gere, *American and European Jewelry 1830–1914*, New York: Crown, 1975. Cat., *Emil Lettré, Andreas Moritz: Zwei deutsche Silberschmiede im 20. Jahrhundert*, Cologne: Museen der Stadt and Kunstgewerbemuseum, 1976. Annelies Krekel-Aalberse, *Art Nouveau and Art Déco Silver*, New York: Abrams, 1989. Cat., *Metallkunst*, Berlin: Bröhan-Museum, 1990.

Levanti, Giovanni (1957–)

Italian designer; born Palermo.

Training To 1983, Facoltà di Architettura, Università degli Studi, Palermo; 1985, master's degree in industrial design, Domus Academy, Milan.

Biography Levanti has participated in a number of design and architecture projects; was active with the Memphis group, designing 1987 Nastassja side chair and 1987 Alfonso leather-and-metal bench by Memphis; 1985–90, worked in the studio of Andrea Branzi in Milan; 1995–97, was professor, Scuola di Specializzazione in Disegno Industriale, Facoltà di Architettura, Università di Palermo; 1997, 1999, and 2000, was the project leader of the master in industrial design program, Domus Academy; 1998–2002, taught industrial design, Istituto Superiore per le Industrie Artistiche (ISIA), Faenza; collaborated with Francesco Biondo; has designed furniture, furnishings, products, and lighting by Alessi, Campeggi, Domodinamica, Edra, Foscarini, Gloria, Marutomi, Polluccoitalia, Salviati.

Exhibitions/citations Work shown in 1986 *12 Nuovi Memphis* exhibition, Milan, and others with the Memphis group; 1987 Biennal de Barcelona; 1989 *I nuovissimi modo*, Padova; 1989 *Il gioco delle arti*, Palazzo della Triennale, Milan; 1994 *Artedesign*, Milan; 1996 *Vedere & vendere*, Pitti Casa, Florence; 1996 *Design e identità*, Louisiana Museum for Moderne Kunst, Humlebæk, Denmark; 2001 *Italia e Giappone: Design come Stile di Vita*, Yokohama; numerous others. Design Plus award, 2000 Ambiente fair, Frankfurt; 2001 Premio Compasso d'Oro.

Bibliography Fumio Shimizu and Studio Matteo Thun (eds.), *The Italian Design: Descendants of Leonardo da Vinci*, Tokyo: Graphic-sha, 1987, 326. Nally Bellati, *New Italian Design*, New York: Rizzoli, 1990. M. Borgia, 'Un progettista della nuova generazione,' *Modo*, no., 142, 1991. Fumio Shimizu, *Euro Design*, Tokyo: Graphic-sha, 1993. Loredana Mascheroni, 'Xito Giovanni Levanti,' *Domus*, no. 817, 1999. Mel Byars, *50 Beds...*, Hove: RotoVision, 2000. Eva Karcher and Manuela von Perfall, *Design*, Munich: Heyne, 2000. Viviana Trapani, 'Giovanni Levanti Designer,' *DDN*, no. 86, 2001.

Levard, Georges

> See Lahalle, Pierre.

Léveillé, André (1880–1962)

French artist and textile and jewelry designer.

Biography Léveillé produced patterns and weaves for industrial textile fabrication. 1920s, the motifs in his paintings were called on by Georges Fouquet for jewelry.

Bibliography Sylvie Raulet, *Bijoux art déco*, Paris: Regard, 1984. David McFadden (ed.), *L'Art de Vivre*, New York: Vendôme, 1989.

Leven, Hugo (1874–1956)

German sculptor, designer, and metalsmith; active Düsseldorf, Bremen, and Hanau.

Biography Leven is best known for his designs for the Kayserzinn pewter factory; 1904, succeeded Heinrich von der Cammer as head of the design studio of Koch & Bergfeld in Bremen, where Leven was succeeded by Gustav Elsass in 1909. However, Leven stayed on as artistic advisor. He designed silver for silversmiths Conrad Anton Beumers in Düsseldorf; from 1909, was director, Königlich Preussische Zeichenakademie, Hanau.

Bibliography Annelies Krekel-Aalberse, *Art Nouveau and Art Déco Silver*, New York: Abrams, 1989. Cat., *Metallkunst*, Berlin: Bröhan-Museum, 1990: 592.

Levi-Montalcini, Gino (1902–1974)

Italian architect and designer; born Milan.

Training Facoltà di Architettura, Turin.
Biography At the architecture school in Turin, Levi-Montalcini met Giuseppe Pagano, with whom he worked steadily to 1930. They realized some of the first Italian Rationalist structures, such as the 1928–30 Gualino office building on the corso Vittorio Emanuele II and 1931 project on the via Roma (with the MIAR group), both Turin. Pagano moved to Milan and became involved with the fascist party, and Levi Montalcini remained true to Rationalist architecture and was involved with Pier Maria Bardi's journal *La Casa Bella* (later *Casabella*), participated in competitions of Triennale di Milano, designed structures in Piedmont (such as villas on the Turin hill and the holiday camp in Bardonecchia). After World War II, taught, Facoltà di Ingegneria, Politecnico, and then in Palermo, Padova, and Facoltà di Architettura, Turin. Subsequent work included 1950–52 electrical station (with Passanti and Ceresa) in Chivasso. As an industrial designer, he is best known for tubular-steel and leather furniture, such as 1932 Chichibio telephone table (with Pagano), being reproduced today by Zanotta. He died in Turin.
Bibliography Penny Sparke, *Introduction to Design and Culture in the Twentieth Century*, London: Allen & Unwin, 1986.
> See Pagano, Giuseppe.

Levin, Moisei Zelikovich (1896–1946)

Russian stage designer.

Training To 1915, Vilno Art School, Lithuania.
Biography 1921, Levin produced his first stage designs and joined the Constructivists; designed the set of B. Lavrentiev's play *Razlom* (collapse) (1927) and, from 1923, for films, including *Puteshestvie v Arzrum* (a journey to Erzerum) (1936, Lenfilm studio). For a time, it was believed the Kazakh national film industry began with Levin's *Amangel'dy* (1938), even though actuallly entirely realized by Lenfilm studio. After Kazakhstan's independence, the assertion was revised to acknowledge its initiation as being marked by *Poem of Love* (1953, Kazakfilm studio), the first movie directed by Shaken Aimanov (1914–1970).
Bibliography Cat., *Kunst und Revolution: Russische und Sowjetische Kunst 1910–1932*, Vienna: Österreichisches Museum für angewandte Kunst, 1988.

Levin, Richard

British exhibition, graphic, and television designer.

Biography Levin designed stands for 1936 *Building Trades Exhibition*, 1949 *Bakelite Exhibition*, and 1951 *Festival of Britain*; all London. He collaborated on graphic designs with Lázsló Moholy-Nagy.
Exhibition Nov. 1935 and Feb. 1936 covers of the magazine *Self Appeal* (designed with Moholy-Nagy) shown at 1979–80 *Thirties* exhibition, Hayward Gallery, London (catalog below).
Bibliography Cat., *Thirties: British Art and Design Before the War*, London: Arts Council of Great Britain/Hayward Gallery, 1979.

Lévy, Alfred

Furniture designer and publisher; active Paris.

Biography From 1919, Lévy worked at Louis Majorelle's furniture manufacture firm In Nancy; after Majorelle's death, was the manager and artistic and technical director of the firm; mid-1930s, was joined there by Paul Beucher. Subsequently, Lévy was also active as an author and publisher of numerous books on French design such as *Modern French Decorative Art: A Collection of Examples of Modern French Decoration* (c. 1925–30, with the Introduction by Léon Deshairs).
Exhibitions Furniture and interior design shown at Salons in Paris including, 1929–31 and 1933–35, of Société des Artistes Décorateurs. Alfred Lévy and Majorelle designed the study in the Nancy pavilion at 1925 *Exposition Internationale des Arts Décoratifs et Industriels Modernes*, Paris.

Levy, Arik (1963–)

Israeli designer; born Tel Aviv; active Paris.

Training To 1991, industrial design, Art Center College of Design (Europe), La Tour-de-Peilz, Switzerland.
Biography 1986–88, Levy specialized in graphic design; settled in Paris, where he taught at ENSCI (Les Ateliers) 1992–94 and in workshops in various European universities; designed 1992 set for a modern-dance performance at the Grand Théâtre de Genève and, subsequently, sets for Nederlands Dans Theater, Suomen Kansallisbalotti (Finnish national ballet), Batsheva Dance Company in Israel; 1994 stage design of requiem opera *Flamma Flamma*, Belgium; with Pippo Lionni, established (L)design in Paris for the design of products, lighting, corporate-image programs, packaging, display, point of purchase, interiors of stores, exhibitions, and stage sets for international clients. Extensive list of clients includes Ligne Roset.
Exhibitions/citations From 1991, work included in a number of exhibitions. Won 1991 Seiko Epson's International Art Center Award (thus taking part in the firm's design program in Japan); 1997 Movement Français de la Qualité—Les Affiches pour la Qualité 97, Paris; 1999 Design Plus award (for Seed porcelain lamp), Ambiente fair, Frankfurt; 1999 Grand Prix International de la Critique (in the lighting section, for Cloud lamp), Salon du Meuble, Paris; 1999, 2000, and 2001 Label VIA and 2000 Carte Blanche production support, VIA (French furniture association), Paris; 2000 Best of Category (for a lamp), *L'Express* magazine; 2000 award (for a lamp), Industrie Form Design (iF), Hanover; 2001 George Nelson Award, *Interiors* magazine.
Bibliography Mel Byars, *On/Off: New Electronic Products*, New York: Universe, 2001. Cat., Vanni Pasca and Ely Rozenberg, *Industrious Designers = Giovani designer israeliani*, Verona: Abitare il Tempo, 2001 and 2002. Mel Byars, *Design in Steel*, London: Laurence King, 2002.

Hugo Leven. Biscuit jar (no. 4505). 1902. Silver-plated pewter, overall: 17 x 27 x 27" (43.2 x 68.6 x 68.6 cm). Manufacturer: J.P. Kayser, Germany. Gift of Faber Donoughe. MoMA.

Lévy, Claude (1895–1942)

French painter, architect, and designer; born Nantes.

Biography From 1918, Lévy worked for the Primavera decorating department of Au Printemps department store, Paris, under its director René Guilleré (her husband). She designed a number of chairs, faience vases, animal figures in white crackled grès ware; was active as a decorator of shops and offices, including that of the journal *La semaine à Paris* (architect, Robert Mallet-Stevens, late 1920s) and c. 1928 façade and interior of Édouard Loewy bookstore, both Paris; and interior ensembles in the US. 1930, she became a member, Union des Artistes Modernes (UAM). Not physically well, she retired to Menton in 1930, where she met painter Henri Matisse, who influenced her subsequent activities as a painter.
Exhibitions From 1921, work shown at Salons of Société des Artistes Décorateurs; from 1921, Salons d'Automne; 1930 (1st) UAM exhibition (Coin Fantasque chrome tube armchair with leather cushions, produced by Primavera).
Bibliography Pierre Kjellberg, *Art déco: les maîtres du mobilier, le dé-*

David Lewis. Beovox Cona subwoofer loudspeaker. 1988. ABS polymer, h. 10 1/2 x dia. 17" (26.6 x 43.2 cm). Mfr.: Bang & Olufsen, Denmark. Gift of the mfr. MoMA.

cor des paquebots, Paris: Amateur, 1986/1990. Arlette Barré-Despond, *UAM*, Paris: Regard, 1986: 302, 532.

Lévy, Lucien (aka Lucien Lévy-Dhurmer 1865–1953)

French ceramicist; born Algiers.

Training Painting, lithography, design, and ceramics, Paris municipal school of drawing and sculpture.
Biography 1887–95, Lévy was a ceramicist, while concurrently working at Clément Massier's factory in Golfe-Juan, France, as the artistic director. Lévy signed his name Lévy-Dhurmer from 1896; may have been responsible for the rediscovery of the metallic luster glaze technique, common in Middle Eastern ceramics from the 9th century and in Hispano-Moresque pottery of the 15th century, although the sheen on pieces by Massier and Lévy-Dhurmer has not lasted. He used primarily light-colored earthenware with gold highlights, and somber-glazed stoneware. His forms were both simple, and also elaborate in the Islamic style. His painted or modeled decorations usually depicted typical Art Nouveau images. His interest in painting was revived during an 1895 trip to Italy. After 1900, he traveled throughout Europe and North Africa, particularly the Mediterranean coast, painting landscapes and drawing figure studies. For a private 1910–14 home on the Champ de Mars in Paris, he painted murals and designed furniture and paneling for the living room, dining room, and library.
Exhibitions 1892 Salon (his copy on porcelain of Alexandre Cabanel's painting *La naissance de Vénus*), Paris; from 1882, editions of Salon des Artistes Français and, from 1897, Salons of Société Nationale des Beaux-Arts; from 1930, editions of Salon d'Automne. Was a member of Société de Pastellistes Français and of Société des Orientalistes.
Bibliography Yvonne Brunhammer et al., *Art Nouveau Belgium, France*, Houston: Institute for the Arts, Rice University, 1976.

Lewis, David (1939–)

British industrial designer; active Copenhagen.

Training Central School of Arts and Crafts, London.
Biography 1960–68, Lewis collaborated with Jacob Jensen on the design of radios and TV sets for various Danish firms; from 1962, was assistant designer at Bang & Olufsen and, 1965 (the same year from which Jensen's also designed for B&O), on the Beolab 5000 and developed the 'slide rule' device for regulating volume and tone. 1967, Lewis set up his own workshop in Copenhagen; from 1968, collaborated with Henning Moldenhawer on products for Bang & Olufsen and other industrial clients. Lewis also designed 1979 Gori boat propeller by Gori Marine, 1982 Odontoson 3 and Odontosyringe 2 dental instruments by Goof, 1989 Multimec switch by Mec. From 1980, he primarily designed for Bang & Olufsen, specializing in TV-set and electronics casings, including 1970 Beovision 600 and 1974 Beovision 3500 TVs (both with Henning Moldenhawer), 1985 Beovision MX 2000, 1989 Beolink 1000 remote-control unit, 1991 Beosystem 2500 sound system (with graphics by Sally Bearsley), 1996 BeoSound 9000 multiple-CD player. From 1993, he has been responsible for all B&O casings such as 1999 BeoLab 1 tower.
Exhibitions/citations Work included in 1990 *Bang & Olufsen: Design et Technologie*, Musée des Arts Décoratifs, Paris. 1979, 1982, 1986, 1990, and 1994 Dansk ID Prizes; 1988 Design Prize of the European Community.
Bibliography Cat., Chantal Bizot, *Bang & Olufsen: design et technologie*, Paris: Musée des Arts Décoratifs, 1990: 8–9. Jens Bang, *Bang & Olufsen: Fra vision til legende = From Vision to Legend*, Denmark: Vidsyn, 2000.

Lewis, E. Walmsley

British architect.

Biography Lewis was best known for his blue-and-green Art Déco design of the 1930 New Victoria Cinema in Westminster, London, with its dramatic auditorium ceiling influenced by Hans Poelzig's 1918–19 Großes Schauspielhaus, Berlin.
Bibliography Jonathan M. Woodham, *Twentieth-Century Ornament*, New York: Rizzoli, 1990: 66.

Lexon

French electronics and writing-instruments manufacturer.

History 1991, Lexon introduced its first collection of 28 products; 1992, purportedly created the 'aluminum' trend in product design. Products have included 1991 Missile pen and Equation calculator, 1992 Futura calculator, 1995 Zero calculator, 1996 microfiber luggage with aluminum handles, 1997 Tykho soft-plastic radio, and 1998 Jerry computer mouse. From 1995, the large product collection was divided into categories. Marc Berthier and Jean-Marie Massaud began to design for Lexon in 1994, Sebastian Bergne in 1995; others have included Eric Berthes, Elise Berthier, Matali Crasset, Pierre Garner, Frédéric Lintz, Martin Luck/Marc Barandard/Cyril Fuchs, Takhasi Tato, and Teo Williams. The Marc Berthier's Tykho radio was featured on the March 2000 cover of *Time* magazine.
Exhibitions/citations Work included in 1993 *Design, Miroir du Siècle*, Grand Palais, Paris. Numerous design awards.
Bibliography www.lexon-design.com.

L'Herbier, Marcel (1888–1979)

French film director; born and active Paris.

Training Collège Stanislas; École des Hautes Etudes Sociales; a licence in law; and at the Sorbonne; all Paris.
Biography L'Herbier published his first book, *Dans le jardin de jeux secrets* (1914); was the first director to incorporate modern architecture/furnishings in film sets. Elements of the new style appeared in

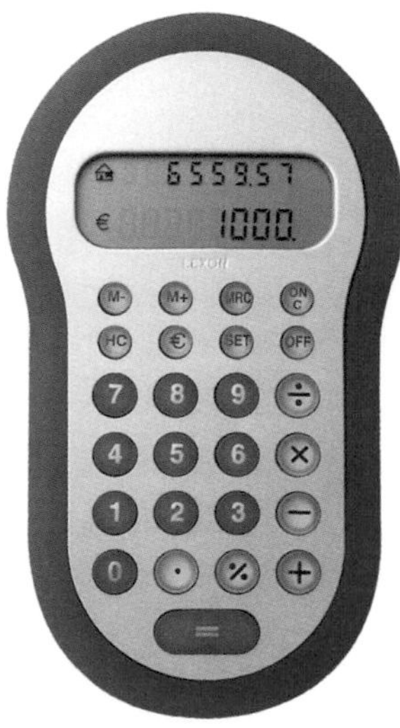

Lexon: Theo Williams. Handy calculator. c. 2001. Silicone rubber and aluminum, h. 5 x w. 2 7/8 x d. 1/2" (12.8 x 7.2 x 1.2 cm). Mfr.: Lexon, France.

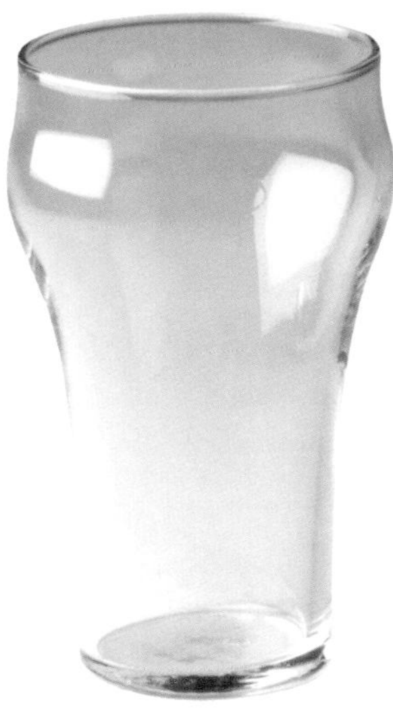

Libbey Glass Company. Soda-fountain tumbler. Pre-1956. Glass, h. 5 1/8 x dia. 3" (13 x 7.6 cm). Mfr.: Libbey Glass Company, division of Owens-Illinois Glass Company, US. Department purchase. MoMA.

his *Le carnaval des vérités* (1919), designed by Michel Dufet and Claude Autant-Lara. L'Herbier's most daring venture was *L'inhumaine* (1923), with contributions by art directors Alberto Cavalcanti and Autant-Lara, artist Fernand Léger, jewelry designer Raymond Templier, designer Pierre Chareau, and architect Robert Mallet-Stevens. Paul Poiret designed the costumes, Pierre Chareau some furniture, Jean Puiforcat, René Lalique, and Jean Luce glassware and carpets. Darius Milhaud wrote the music. The film was shocking to contemporary audiences of the time, accustomed to historicist sets. L'Herbier continued to use modern sets for his films, including *Eldorado* (1921), *Le vertige* (1926), *Feu Mathias Pascal* (1925), *L'argent* (1927), *Le parfum de la dame en noir* (1929), *Forfaiture* (1927), and *La nuit fantastique* (1942). 1943, he founded film school Institut des Hautes Études Cinématographiques (IDHEC); wrote the book *Intelligence du cinématographe*, (Paris: Corrêa, 1946).
Exhibitions Work subject of 1985 (14th) *Mostra Internazionale del Cinema Libero*, Porretta Terme, Italy (catalog below).
Bibliography Noël Burch, *Marcel L'Herbier*, Paris: Seghers, 1973 Jean-Pierre Brossard, *Marcel L'Herbier et son temps: une documentation*, La Chaux-de-Fonds: Cinédiff, 1980. Howard Mandelbaum and Eric Myers, *Screen Deco: A Celebration of High Style in Hollywood*, New York: St. Martin's, 1985. Cat., Michele Canosa, *Marcel L'Herbier: XIV Mostra internazionale del cinema libero di Porretta Terme*, Parma: Pratiche, 1985. Jonathan M. Woodham, *Twentieth-Century Ornament*, New York: Rizzoli, 1990. *Petit Robert: Dictionnaire universel des noms propres*, vol. 1, Paris, 1991.
> See de Noailles, vicomte Charles.

Liaigre, Christian (1945–)

French interior and furniture/furnishings designer; active Paris.

Training École Nationale Supérieure des Arts Décoratifs, Paris.
Biography 1970s, Liaigre was artistic director of furnishings company Nobilis; 1982, set up his own design office in Paris; designed 1990 interior of Hotel Montalembert, Paris, and, subsequently, worked on Mercer Hotel, New York, private offices of Valentino Couture, Paris, a showroom and stores of Marc Jacobs, Selfridges in London, and the residences in various places of Kenzo, Calvin Klein, Karl Lagerfeld, Carole Bouquet, and Rupert Murdoch. Other commissions: Lloyd's in London; French embassies in New Delhi, Warsaw, and Ottawa; Hotel Guanahani in the West Indies; Société Générale de Belgique in Brussels; Julien Cornic art bookshops in Paris and Tokyo; Strenesse (German fashion brand) in Tokyo; also Ralph Lauren. It has also designed products such as: 1991 sycamore travel furniture by Louis Vuitton; 1992 Remember lamp by Manufactor; and his own-designed, distributed, and marketed furniture, including rough-hewn Brancusi-esque tables as well as other more highly finished models. Critics favorably compare his furniture to Pierre Chareau's and Jean-Michel Frank's and claim he combines traditions of the French decorator with feng shui.
Citations 1989 Carte Blanche production support, VIA (French furniture association).
Bibliography Cat., *Les années VIA*, Paris: Musée des Arts Décoratifs, 1990. Cat., Sophie Tasma Anargyros et al., *L'école française: les créateurs de meubles du 20ème siècle*, Paris: Industries Françaises de l'Ameublement, 2000.

Liang Ie, Kho (1927–1975)

Indonesian industrial designer; active Rotterdam.

Training 1950–54, Instituut voor Kunstnijverheidonderwijs (IVKNO), Amsterdam.
Biography 1949, Liang Ie emigrated to the Netherlands; primarily designed for Dutch firms, such Artifort in Maastricht, which produced 1968 C 684 sofa (installed in his interior design of 1962–69 Schiphol airport, Amsterdam). He also designed for CAR in Katwijk (such as 1960 wood-planks armchair) and Royal Mosa ceramic tiles; became highly regarded in the Netherlands, acknowledged by the Kho Liang Ie applied arts prize of the Amsterdam Fonds voor de Kunst, the country's highest design prize. Kho Liang Ie & Associates remains active in Amsterdam.
Biography Ineke van Ginneke, *Kho Liang Ie, Interieurarchitect/industrieel ontwerper*, Rotterdam: 010, 1986.

Libbey Glass Company; Owens-Illinois Glass Company

American glassware manufacturers.

History 1818, Libbey Glass was founded. But, 1878 when William L. Libbey (1827–1883) leased the New England Glass Company glassworks in Cambridge, Mass., he changed the name to the unwieldy moniker 'New England Glassworks, L. L. Libbey and Sons, Proprietors.' Joseph Locke (1846–1936) patented his discovery of heat-senstive Amberina glass there in 1883. From 1883, William Libbey's son Edward Drummond Libbey (1854–1925) managed the operation, by then known as W.L. Libbey & Son. 1888, Edward closed the factory and moved it to Toledo, Ohio, with the new name Libbey Glass Company. The years 1890–1915 there were known as the 'Brilliant Period,' when it became the largest cut-glass factory in the world. 1883–1940, it produced Locke's colored, ornamental glassware, including 1885 Pomona, 1886 Peach Blow, 1886 Wild Rose, 1887 Agata, and 1889 Maize, using new processes developed by Locke. From Edward Libbey's 1925 death, the firm was controlled by J.D. Robinson and his sons. 1931, they hired A. Douglas Nash, who introduced high-quality 1933 Libbey-Nash Glassware. (Nash was formerly the manager at Tiffany Furnaces.) In the modern arena, Libbey is known for its 1939 Embassy stemware for the *New York World's Fair* by Walter Dorwin Teague and Edwin W. Fuerst. 1936, Libbey Glass became a part of Owens-Illinois Glass Company and a major producer of domestic and utility glassware. (1903, Owens Bottle Machine Company had been established to market new automatic bottle-making machineery invented by Michael J. Owens. When the firm began making bottles, the name was changed to Owens Bottle Company in 1919 and, after amalgamating with Illinois Glass company in 1929, the entity was named Owens-Illinois Glass Company.) As the Libbey Glass division, it produced the designs of Freda Diamond, including 1949 Stardust stemware, 1950 Classic tumbler, and 1957 Golden Foliage table glass. Diamond had also been hired for her advice, which included the production of low-cost wares as boxed sets. In contrast, 1940–45 ornamental lead-crystal glassware by Edwin W. Fuerst was put into production. The Scandinavian-inspired and inexpensive 1960s Accent Stemware glass range in smoke-gray was one of its most successful products. For patterns applied to its party-style drinking glasses, an epoxy-resin printing process was employed. Eventually, only machine-made tableware was produced by Libbey; its last handcrafted glassware was the 1940 Modern American series. Libbey-brand glass continues to be made (including its classic soda-fountain tumbler), though mainly for restaurants. Libbey sold its glass-making operations to form Libbey-Owens-Ford, or LOF; 1985, was acquired by Pilkington plc., now Pilkington Libbey-Owens-Ford; 2000, was dissolved as a brand into Pilkington. 1987, Kohlberg Kravis Roberts & Company acquired Owens-Illinois, and the Libbey division name became Libbey Glass Inc. Now as a separate entity, Libbey Inc. acquired Royal Leerdam (B.V. Koninklijke Nederlandsche Glasfabriek Leerdam) and Syracuse China. Under its Libbey Tableware subsidiary, imports cutlery, hollow-ware, and ceramic dinnerware.

Liberty & Co. Inkstand. c. 1903–04. Pewter and enameled copper decoration, 3 1/2 x 6 x 6" (8.9 x 15.2 x 15.2 cm). Mfr.: Liberty & Co., UK. Purchase Fund. MoMA.

Bibliography E. William Fairfield, *Fire & Sand: The History of the Libbey-Owens Sheet Glass Company*, Toledo, Ohio: Libbey-Owens-Ford, 1960. *Art in Glass: Guide to the Glass Collections*, Toledo, Ohio: Toldeo Museum of Art, 1969. Harold Newman, *An Illustrated Dictionary of Glass*, London: Thames & Hudson, 1977: 183–84. Carl U. Fauster, *Libbey Glass Since 1818: Pictorial History and Collectors Guide*, Toledo, Ohio: Len Beach, 1979.
> See Diamond, Freda; Pilkington.

Libera, Adalberto (1903–1963)

Italian architect; born Villa Lagarina, Trento; active Rome.

Training 1921, in architecture, Parma; from 1925, Regia Scuola di Architettura, Rome; to 1927, Università di Roma.
Biography 1927 in Cologne, Libera was invited to become a member of Gruppo Sette (Group of Seven), originally organized in 1926 and in which Libera replaced Ubaldo Castagnoli as a full-fledged member. With architecture critic Gaetano Minnucci, Libera organized 1928 (1st) *Esposizione dell'Architettura Razionale* in Rome, which offered an opportunity for young Rationalists to compete with academic architects. He was the secretary of Movemento Italiano per l'Architettura Razionale (MIAR), a group of architects in Rome who, unsuccessfully attempted to have the fascist regime adopt Rationalist architecture; 1937, Rationalism was officially condemned. Libera and Guido Frette, with Luigi Figini and Gino Pollini (Gruppo Sette members) and Piero Bottoni, designed the Casa Elettrica for Montedison at 1930 (4th) Biennale di Monza, the first public expression of modern architecture in Italy.
Work Including the CSAC pavilion, 1928 (2nd) *Esposizione di Architettura Razionale* in Rome; 1931–34 elementary school competition, piazza Raffaello Sanzio, Trento; 1933–34 post office building (with M. de Renzi); Italian pavilion, 1935 *Exposition Universelle et Internationale de Bruxelle*; 1942 *E 42* exposition (unrealized), Rome; 1937 exhibition, Circo Maximo, Rome; his best-known work, 1938–43 Villa Malaparte, Capri; 1949 housing block, Trento; 1951 tobacconist's interior, Milan; 1955 housing block, via Pessina, Cagliari; 1956–58 office building, via Torino, Rome; 1959 Pfizer laboratory, Latina; 1959 Rome Olympiad Village (with others).
Exhibitions Work subject of 1989 exhibitions at Museo Provinciale d'Arte, Trento, and at Palazzo della Triennale, Milan (catalog below).
Bibliography A. Alieri et al., 'Adalberto Libera,' *L'architettura—cronache e storia*, nos. 124–33, 1966. Paolo Portoghesi (ed.), *Dizionario enciclopedico di architettura e urbanistica*, Rome: Istituto Editoriale Romano, 1968. Giulio Argan, *Adalberto Libera*, Rome: Editalia, 1975. Barbie Campbell-Cole and Tim Benton (eds.), *Tubular Steel Furniture*, London: The Art Book Company, 1979: 47. Cat., *Adalberto Libera: Opera completa*, Milan: Electa, 1989. Marida Talamona et al., *Casa Malaparte*, New York: Princeton Architectural Press, 1992. Michael McDonough, *Malaparte: A House Like Me*, New York: Crown, 1999.

Liberati, Anne (1961–); Joris Heetman (1957–)

French and Dutch furniture designers; active Paris.

Training Liberati: Atelier Met de Penninghen, Paris. Heetman: Akademie voor Industriële Vormgeving, Eindhoven.
Biography For three years, they were staff members in design office Endt Fulton Partners in Paris; 1987, were freelance designers and, the same year, set up their own design office Chaperon et Méchant Loup. Furniture has include Pin Up and Le Horta cabinets by Néotù.
Exhibitions Work included in 2004 *Design d'Elle*, Galerie VIA (French furniture association), Paris; also at VIA, subject of 1990 exhibition.
Bibliography Cat., *Les années VIA 1980–1990*, Paris: Musée des Arts Décoratifs, 1990: 186.

Liberty, Arthur Lasenby (1843–1917); Liberty and Company

British entrepreneur; born Chesham. Enterprise from 1875.

Biography From 1862, Liberty worked for the Great Shawl and Cloak Emporium on Regent Street, London, whose sales had been spurred by a growing interest in Japanese goods. 1864–75, he was manager of the firm's Oriental Emporium; 1875, established his own business on the same street, two decades before Siegfried Bing set up his gallery / shop L'Art Nouveau in Paris. And Liberty's operation became successful. 1883, he acquired additional quarters on Regent Street, named Chesham House, after his birthplace. 1884, he established a costume shop, managed by E.W. Godwin, that sold progressive clothing influenced by Paris styles; 1888–89, visited Japan and later wrote a book on his trip; sold Japanese metalwork and Indian enamels, which he had mounted in Britain. The furniture-design studio was managed by Leonard F. Wyburd, who designed its rustic Athelstan range of furniture. 1880s–90s, Liberty's furniture styles ranged widely from fashionable Moresque and Arabic to historicist and modern. Liberty's furniture was popular throughout Europe, including being available for purchase in Paris, Vienna, Berlin, and Brussels. Gustave Serrurier-Bovy set up a Liberty concession in his shop in Nancy. Liberty imported the work of Continental designers, including Richard Riemerschmid, a practice the firm continued to 1950s. Liberty's customers and oriental-art enthusiasts included E.W. Godwin, William Burges, Dante Gabriel Rossetti, Edward Burne-Jones, and James Whistler. Liberty realized that crafts metalwork would become popular and began commissioning British designers and craftspeople; became involved with Christopher Dresser from 1890s, with Archibald Knox who designed the firm's 1899 Cymric and 1901 Tudric silver patterns, and with Rex and Harry Silver. Liberty later adopted Tudor-revival designs but cease their production at the end of 1920s. Most of the Cymric range was made 1900–27 by W.H. Haseler of Birmingham. Identical pieces were also produced by the firms Murrle, Bennett, and the as-yet-unidentified 'L.C. and Co' (as some wares have been stamped). Liberty's had a policy of not revealing the names of its designers, who included Oliver Baker, A.E. Jones, Arthur Gaskin, Bernard Cuzner, Harry Craythorn, C. Carter, Jessie M. King, Thomas Hodgetts, Charles Povey, Jessie Jones, and Maud Coggin. Patterns from designers were often not executed in their original forms, making attribution difficult. The influence and popularity of Liberty's work were such that in Italy one of the names by which Art Nouveau became known was Lo Stile Liberty. The store is still located on Regent Street, with branches worldwide. Some of its textile and wallpaper designs are commissioned from freelance designers.
Exhibitions/citations Work subject of 1975 *Liberty's 1875–1975* centenary exhibition, Victoria and Albert Museum, London (catalog below). 1913, Arthur Lasenby Liberty was knighted.
Bibliography Alison Adburgham, *Liberty's: A Biography of a Shop*, London: Allen & Unwin, 1975. Cat., *Liberty's 1875–1975*, London:

Ernst Lichtblau. Platter. 1950. Baked enamel on aluminum, h. 7/8 x dia. 15" (2.2 x 38.1 cm). Mfr.: Joseph Franken Decorative Accessories, US. Gift of the mfr. MoMA.

Victoria and Albert Museum, 1975. Shirley Bury, 'New Light on the Liberty Metalwork Venture,' *Bulletin of the Decorative Arts Society*, 1975. Annelies Krekel-Aalberse, *Art Nouveau and Art Déco Silver*, New York: Abrams, 1989. Stephen Calloway, *Liberty of London, Masters of Style and Decoration*, London: Thames & Hudson, 1992.

Libidarch

Italian radical architecture group.

History 1971, Libidarch was founded in Turin by Edoardo Ceretto, Maria Grazia Daprà Conti, Vittorio Gallo, Andrea Mascardi, and Walter Mazzella. Active only to 1975, the group was involved in research on 'poor' and 'banal' urban projects; produced the video *A Proposal for the Methodological Definition of 'Poor' Architecture* (1972). Some of their work was produced by Busnelli. Certain members reconvened later to participate in exhibitions, including a 1983 event in the Parc de la Villette, Paris.
Exhibitions As a group, participated in 1973 (15th) Triennale di Milano, and biennial of architecture, São Paulo.
Bibliography Andrea Branzi, *La casa calda: esperienze del nuovo disegno italiano*, Milan: Idea, 1982.

Lichtblau, Ernst (1883–1963)

Austrian architect and furniture and interior designer; born Vienna; active Vienna and the US.

Training 1902–05 under Otto Wagner, Akademie der bildenden Künste, Vienna.
Biography Lichtblau was a professor, Höheren Staatsgewerbeschule, Vienna; 1912, designed silver with enamel by Alfred Pollak; c. 1920s, set up his own workshop in Vienna; 1939, settled in the US and taught, Rhode Island School of Design, Providence, R.I.; was active through 1950s and designed 1950 vessels in baked-enamel aluminum by Joseph Franken Decorative Accessories, New York.
Bibliography Günther Feuerstein, *Vienna—Present and Past: Arts and Crafts-Applied Art—Design*, Vienna: Jugend und Volk, 1976: 49, 80. Astrod Gmeiner and Gottbried Pirhofer, *Der Österreichische Werkbund*, Saltzburg/Vienna: Residenz, 1985: 235. Annelies Krekel-Aalberse, *Art Nouveau and Art Déco Silver*, New York: Abrams, 1989.

Lichtenstein, Roy (1923–1997)

American artist and designer; born New York; active New York State.

Training 1939–40 under Reginald Marsh, Art Students League, New York; 1940–43 and 1946–49, Ohio State University, Columbus.
Biography 1949–51, Lichtenstein taught, Ohio State University; 1957–60, New York State University, Oswego; 1960–63, Douglass College, Rutgers University, New Jersey. 1963, he settled in New York. His Abstract Expressionist period preceded his Pop Art style, for which he is best known. His large images were reproduced in primary colors revealing the Ben Day dots of the comic strips that inspired his work. Mid-1960s, he converted famous works of art into comic-strip interpretations. His 1966 dinner service in heavy institutional china was produced by Jackson China and 1990s porcelain by Bernardaud. Fond of the kitsch, he showed a mastery of color and composition in his work; later in his career, was able to translate his two-dimentional images into three-dimensional sculpture, sometimes in brass; had a predilection for illustrating interiors. His furniture insinuated the 1930s Art Déco style. His rug designs were included in two 1988 Dialog ranges by Vorwerk. 1982, he rented a loft in New York and owned a studio in Southampton, N.Y. (near New York City). He died of pneumonia. The Roy Lichtenstein Foundation was established in New York.
Exhibition First one-person exhibition (1951), Carlebach Gallery, New York; also 1969 retrospective, Soloman R. Guggenheim Museum, New York, and numerous others before and after.
Bibliography *Roy Lichtenstein Sculpture*, London: Leo Castelli and The Mayor Galleries, 1977: 4. Volker Fischer, *Bodenreform: Teppichboden von Künstlern und Architekten*, Berlin: Ernst und Sohn, 1989. Cat., Milton Esterow, *Roy Lichtenstein, Interiors: Collages*, Vienna: Galerie Ulysses, 1992. Diane Waldman, *Roy Lichtenstein*, New York: Rizzoli, 1993. Lawrence Alloway, *Roy Lichtenstein*, 2 vols., New York: Abbeville, 1999.

Lidköpings Porslinsfabrik

Swedish ceramics factory.

History 1900, Nymans Porslinsmaleri was established in Lidköping to paint and decorate blank ware; 1911, was renamed Lidköpings Porslinsfabrik and began its own porcelain production; by c. 1920, commissioned freelance designer Einar Forseth; 1927, was bought by Arabia; 1932, was bought by Rörstrand, which moved its own Rörstrand production from Gothenburg to Lidköping. 1939, Lidköpings was absorbed as a brand name into Rörstrand. Through a number of subsequent mergers, Rörstrand became part of the HackmanGroup in 1990.
Bibliography Jennifer Hawkins Opie, *Scandinavia: Ceramics and Glass in the Twentieth Century*, New York: Rizzoli, 1989.

Dorothy Liebes Designer's sample of wall fabric. c. 1930–47. Jute and wool, 7 x 5 1/4" (17.8 x 13.3 cm). Mfr.: Dorothy Liebes Textiles, US. Gift of the designer. MoMA.

Liebes, Dorothy Wright (aka Mrs. Rehlman Morin 1899–1972)

American textile designer; born Santa Rosa, Cal.; active San Francisco and New York.

Training 1919, bachelor's degree, San Jose State Teachers College, Cal.; 1923, bachelor's degree in applied design, University of California, Berkeley; 1928, master's degree in art education, Columbia University, New York.
Biography She served an internship at Rodier, the French textile firm; 1930, set up her own design studio in San Francisco, where she specialized in custom-handwoven goods for architects and decorators. 1940, she received her first commission for large-scale production fabrics from Goodall Fabrics in Sanford, Maine; 1948, moved her design studio to New York and, c. 1958, abandoned her custom work in favor of industrial consultation and textile design for mass production. Her commissions included work for Du Pont in 1955, Bigelow-Sanford in 1957, and Sears, Roebuck & Co. in 1969. She became one of the first American textile designers to apply the handmade techniques of weaving to mass production, in fabrics noted for their bright-color combinations and unconventional yarns and materials such as sequins, leather strips, grass, plastics (particularly Lurex), Stock Market ticker tape, and bamboo. She died in New York.
Exhibitions Work was the subject of 1970 retrospective exhibition sponsored by Du Pont, Museum of Contemporary Crafts, New York.
Bibliography Cat., Dorothy Liebes (coordinator), *Nylon Rug Designs: An Exhibition*, Wilmington, Delaware: E.I. Du Pont de Nemours, Textile Fibers Dept., 1958. Cat., *Dorothy Liebes*, New York: Museum of Contemporary Crafts, 1970. Cat., Janet Kardon (ed.), *Craft in the Machine Age 1920–1945*, New York: Abrams with American Craft Museum, 1995.

Lie-Jørgensen, Thorbjørn (1900–1961)

Norwegian metalworker and painter.

Training Under silversmith Henrik Lundat Notodden, apprenticeship; under Henrik Lund, Statens Håndverks-og Kunstindustriskole, Oslo;

painting, Statens Kunstakademi, Oslo.
Biography His and others's efforts led to Scandinavian modern design from classical Funtionalism; 1927, worked at the firm David-Anderson in Oslo and made important contributions to the renewal of its metalware production. 1939, he left to become department head, Statens Håndverks-og Kunstindustriskole, to 1961. And while at the school, he continued to design for David-Anderson.
Citations Gold medal, 1954 (10th) Triennale di Milano, and another gold medal in a 1955 competition in Munich; won 1948 silver-tableware competition for the town hall, Oslo.
Bibliography Cat., David Revere McFadden (ed.), *Scandinavian Modern Design 1880–1980*, New York: Abrams, 1982. Fredrik Wildhagen, *Norge i Form*, Oslo: Stenersen, 1988: 88.

Liévore, Alberto (1948–); Liévore Altherr Molina

Argentine designer and architect; born Buenos Aires.

Training In architecture, Universidad de Buenos Aires.
Biography 1972, Liévore set up Hipótesis, a showroom/shop within his own studio; subsequently with Norberto Chaves, founded the Grupo Berenguer (later joined by Jorge Pensi and Oriel Pibernat), combining teaching/theoretical and practical design work; 1977 with Pensi, established a design practice in Barcelona, like other Argentine émigrés such Carlos Rolando, América Sánchez, and J. García Garay. Liévore and Pensi designed many of the 1984 exhibition stands for Selección International de Diseño de Equipamiento para el Habitat (SIDI), which acted as an international launch pad for Spanish design; also designed early-1980s Latina furniture range by Perobell. From 1984, Liévore and Pensi began to work separately, and Pensi pursed furniture and lighting. Liévore set up his own design studio, specializing in products (including furniture and lighting), consultation, and artistic direction for various firms. He designed the widely published 1988 Manolete one-arm chair and 1987 Helsinoor armchair (with Pensi) by Perobell. Was instrumental in the development of Maderón, a material made from almond shells, used in the molding of furniture such as his 1989 Rothko side chair. 1991, Pensi, Jeanette Altherr (Heidelberg 1965–), and Manel Molina (Barcelona 1963–) founded design studio Liévore Altherr Molina in Barcelona. Altherr, who had collaborated with Liévore from 1989, previously studied industrial design in Darmstadt and Barcelona. Molina had studied interior and industrial design at Eina (Escola de Disseny i Art) in Barcelona and, 1985–89, had collaborated with Miquel Milá on the design of interiors and products. The Liévore Altherr Molina group designed 890 chair by Thonet (their first together) and for firms in Spain, Germany and Italy, including Andreu World, Arper, Casamilano, Disform, Do+Ce, Ferlea, Foscarini, Halifax, Lema, Orizzonti, Perobell, Prenatal, Sellex, Tisettanta, and Verzelloni.
Exhibitions/citations Liévore: 1995 *Mutant Materials* (Rothko chair), New York, and traveling (see catalog below). Liévore Altherr Molina: 1999 National Design Prize, Spain, and Delta de Plata, ADI/FAD; National Furniture Design Competition Award, Feria Internacional del Mueble, Valéncia.
Bibliography Guy Julier, *New Spanish Design*, London: Thames & Hudson, 1991. Cat., Paola Antonelli, *Mutant Materials in Contemporary Design*, New York: The Museum of Modern Art / Abrams, 1995. Mel Byars, *50 Chairs...*, Hove: RotoVision, 1996. Mel Byars, *50 Beds...*, Hove: RotoVision, 2000.
> See Pensi, Jorge.

Lifshitz, Raviv (1968–)

Israeli designer.

Training 1992–96, Industrial Design Department, Bezalel Academy of Art and Design, Jerusalem.
Biography 1997–2000, Lifshitz worked in the design center Vital in Tel Aviv; from 1997, has worked at Eureka Technologies Group; independently, has pursued theoretical products by reprocessing anonymous designs into new ones, like the Umbrellight (an umbrella frame as a lamp), Ironic chair (ironing board as a seat), and Agency chair (a bicycle backrack as a seat), all 2000.
Exhibitions 2001 *Design 21*, Fellissimo, New York; 2001 *Re Use*, artists' gallery, Tel Aviv; 1999 *Young European Design*, traveling; and subject of 2000 *A Gesture to the Anonymous Designer*, Periscope, Tel Aviv.
Bibliography Mel Byars, *Design in Steel*, London: Laurence King, 2003.

Ligne Roset
> See Roset, Ligne.

Likarz-Strauß, Maria (b. Maria Likarz 1893–1971)

Austrian draftsperson, ceramics decorator, painter, and fashion and accessories designer; born Przemyśl (now in Poland).

Training 1908–10 under O. Friedrich, Kunstschule für Frauen und Mädchen, Vienna; 1911–15 under A. von Kenner and Josef Hoffmann, Kunstgewerbeschule, Vienna.
Biography 1912–14, she was member of Neuer Werkbund Österreichs and of Wiener Frauenkunst (Vienna women's art group); 1916–17 and 1920, taught, Kunstgewerbeschule Burg Giebichenstein, Halle, Germany, having left Vienna and returning in 1920 to work for the Wiener Werkstätte. 1912–14 and 1920–31, she designed fashion postcards and designed textiles, leather, lace, pearl work, and in other media for the Wiener Werkstätte and contributed to 1914–15 fashion folder *Die Mode*. Her jewelry incorporated pearls and enamel. 1938, she left Vienna again, this time for Italy.
Exhibitions Venues of the Wiener Frauenkunst: 1930 *Wie sieht die Frau* and 1933 *Die Schöne Wand*; included in 2003–04 exhibition of centenary of Wiener Werkstätte, Österreichisches Museum für angewandte Kunst, Vienna (catalog below).
Bibliography Deanna F. Cera (ed.), *Jewels of Fantasy: Costume Jewelry of the 20th Century*, New York: Abrams, 1992. Cat., Peter Noever (ed.), *Yearning for Beauty: For the 100th Anniversary of the Wiener Werkstätte*, Ostfildern-Ruit: Hatje Cantz/Österreichisches Museum für angewandte Kunst, 2003.

Liljedahl, Bengt (1932–)

Swedish metalworker.

Training To 1953, Konstfackskolan, Stockholm; 1958, École Nationale Supérieure des Arts Décoratifs, Paris.
Biography 1954, Liljedahl set up his own workshop in Stockholm, producing silver hollow-ware.
Bibliography *Svenskt Silver Inför Åttiotalet*, Stockholm, 1979. Cat., David Revere McFadden (ed.), *Scandinavian Modern Design 1880–1980*, New York: Abrams, 1982.

Liljefors, Anders B. (1923–1970)

Swedish ceramicist; born the US.

Training 1942–43, sculpture and painting, Grünewalds Målarskola, Stockholm; 1945–47, Det Kongelige Danske Kunstakademi, Copenhagen; and in Paris.
Biography 1947–53 and 1955–57, Liljefors worked for Gustavsberg porcelain works; c. 1947, set up his own workshop in Karlskrona; produced a number of sculpture pieces, addition to functional objects; from 1950s, was one of the potters who redefined the role of the craft potter.
Exhibitions Work subject of one-person exhibitions at the Nordiska Kompaniet in Stockholm in 1952; another in Stockholm; and in Gothenburg, 1957. Work included in numerous group exhibitions.
Bibliography Cat., David Revere McFadden (ed.), *Scandinavian Modern Design 1880–1980*, New York: Abrams, 1982. Jennifer Hawkins Opie, *Scandinavia: Ceramics and Glass in the Twentieth Century*, New York: Rizzoli, 1989.

Limbert, Charles P. (1854–1923)

American furniture designer and maker.

Biography 1880s, Limbert worked for furniture firm John A. Colby in Chicago; 1889, set up the Limbert and Klingman Chair Co. in Grand Rapids, Mich., with Phillip Klingman. The firm was closed in 1894, when C.P. Limbert and Co. was formed. 1902, Limbert established the Holland Dutch Arts and Crafts furniture company in Grand Rapids and in Holland, Mich. He marketed eclectic designs based on Mission furniture models; 1904–06, produced mostly his own imaginative work. Limbert's trademark pierced rectangles with rounded corners echoed some of C.R. Mackintosh's, C.F.A. Voysey's, and Hugh Baillie Scott's designs. Limbert's tables had flaring bases and tops with sides protruding beyond the legs of the table. Like other designers in the Grand Rapids area, he was sympathetic with the work of Josef Hoffmann in Austria and Mackintosh in Scotland. Though strongly influenced by others, Limbert synthesized the more lyrical European style with the American Arts and Crafts aesthetic. While his 1905 Square-Cut Café Chair and 1906 Oval Center Table were inspired by the chairs in Mackintosh's Willow Tea Rooms in Glasgow, Lambert's table is more graceful and dynamic.

Exhibitions Work shown at 1904 *Louisiana Purchase Exposition*, St. Louis.
Bibliography *Limbert's Holland Dutch Arts and Crafts Furniture*, New York: Turn of the Century, 1981. Anne Yaffe Phillips, *From Architecture to Object*, New York: Hirschl and Adler, 1989: 70, 78.

Limoges
French ceramics factory; located Limoges.

History 1736, the Limoges factory was established for the production of domestic ceramic ware. From 1768, kaolin (fine white clay) and petuntse (aka china stone) were quarried near Limoges and used at Sèvres. 1771, hard-paste porcelain began to be produced under the patronage of the comte d'Artois, brother of Louis XVI. André Massier was the first to produce all-French porcelain wares. 1784, the Limoges factory was taken over by Louis XVI himself and became the Manufacture Royale to produce plain white ware. After 1789 French Revolution, numerous factories were established in the area, including those of Pierre-Léon Sazerat and François Alluaud. By 1840, the area had more than 30 manufacturers; they were joined by New York merchant David Haviland, who took over the Alluaud factory. Still known for its ordinary fine tablewares, the area remains the center of porcelain production in France.
Exhibition Work subject of 1996 venue, Musée du Luxembourg, Paris, organized by Réunion des Musées Nationaux et Musée National Adrien Dubouché (catalog below).
Bibliography Sharon Wood, *Haviland-Limoges*, Watkins Glen, N.Y.: Century House, 1951. J. d'Albis and C. Romanet, *La porcelaine de Limoges*, Paris, 1980. Nathalie Valière, *Un américain à Limoges: Charles Edward Haviland (1839–1921), porcelainier*, Tulle: Lemouzi, 1992. Cat., *Chefs-d'œuvre de la porcelaine de Limoges*, Paris: Réunion des Musées Nationaux, 1996.

Lin, Maya (1959–)
American architect, sculptor, and furniture designer; born Athens, Ohio.

Training 1981, bachelor of arts degree and, 1986, master's degree in architecture, Yale University, New Haven, Conn.
Biography Lin won 1981 Vietnam Veterans Memorial design competition (completed 1982), Washington, D.C., for which she created a black-granite sculpture-wall and for which she is best known. Now admired, the construction was widely opposed at the time of its installation in favor of a more traditional monument. As an architect, she also designed 1989 Civil Rights Memorial, Southern Poverty Law Center, Montgomery, Ala.; 1991 The Women's Table, Yale University; 1993 Groundswell garden, Ohio State University; 1994 14-foot-long (4.3 m) clock at Pennsylvania Station, New York; 1995 *Wave Field* sculpture, University of Michigan, Ann Arbor; and several houses. She designed furniture in solid stone and 1998 The World Is Not Flat furniture by Knoll; to celebrate Knoll's 60th anniversary (founded 1938). As Maya Lin, Shea + Latone, she designed a non-rectilinear chaise longue à la Ludwig Mies van der Rohe, also by Knoll.
Exhibition Work subject of 2000 exhibition, The Cooper Union for the Advancement of Science and Art, New York. 1999 Industrial Design Award of Excellence (for chaise longue by Knoll), IDSA/*Business Week* magazine.
Bibliography Julie V. Iovine, *Metropolitan Home*, Apr. 1990: 108. Documentary film, Freida Lee Mock (dir.), *Maya Lin: A Strong, Clear Vision*, American Film Foundation, Sanders & Mock Productions, 1994 (granted a 1995 Oscar for best documentary film feature, from Academy of Motion Picture Arts and Sciences). Cat., R. Craig Miller (intro.), *U.S. Design 1975–2000*, Munich: Prestel, 2002.

Lincoln Logs
> See Wright, John Lloyd.

Lindau, Börge (1932–1999)
Swedish furniture and interior designer.

Training 1957–62, Slöjdföreningens Skola (now Konstindustriskolan), Gothenburg.
Biography Lindau and Bo Lindekrantz met at the Slöjdföreningens Skola in Gothenburg; from 1964, worked together after a brief interlude at an architecture firm in Hälsingborg; from 1965, were active primarily for Lammhults furniture company and designed a furniture range calling on chromium-plated bent-metal tubing and, from 1977, partnered with Peter Hiort-Lorentzen on Lammhults and other work; 1984, established Blá Station Åhus. Work included flexible display system for Form Design Center in Malmö, 1963 Opalen stackable armchair (still in production), 1968 S-70-1 chromium tubular-steel stackable stool, furniture for a day nursery in Hälsingborg, furnishings for 1969 library in Norrköping, 1970 Peking stackable hook-on armchair in chromium tubular steel, 1972 X75-2 tubular-metal folding chair, 1982 Duet 8 upholstered lounge chair in tubular steel and birch, 1985 Planka chair, 1998 and 2002 Alias office chairs.
Citations With Lindau: 963 Probok Prize; 1969 Lunning Prize; 1975 prize, Föreningen Svenska Industridesigner (SID); 1983 best contract furniture, SIR (national Swedish association of interior architects); 1984 Forsnäs Prize; best home furniture, Forsnäs Prize.
Bibliography Cat., David Revere McFadden (ed.), *Scandinavian Modern Design 1880–1980*, New York: Abrams, 1982. Cat., *The Lunning Prize*, Stockholm: Nationalmuseum, 1986: 198–201. www.lammhults.se.
> See Hiort-Lorentzen, Peter; Lindekrantz, Bo.

Lindberg, Stig (1916–1982)
Swedish ceramicist and textile designer; active Stockholm.

Training 1935–37, Kungliga Tekniska Högskolan, Stockholm; 1937–40 under Wilhelm Kåge, at Gustavsberg porcelain factory; and in Paris.
Biography Lindberg specialized in ceramics, although he also designed plastics, textiles, appliances, enamels, glassware, and graphics; from 1937, worked at Gustavsberg and was influenced by its artistic director Wilhelm Kåge (seen in Lindberg's 1949 soft-silhouette dinner service). At Gustavsberg, Lindberg suceeded Kåge as the artistic director, to 1978, and designed decorative and utilitarian ceramics and developed painted decorations for enamelware. 1945–47, he designed for Målerås glassworks and, from 1947, hand-printed textiles for Nordiska Kompaniet in Stockholm; 1957–70, was senior lecturer, Konstfackskolan. Lindberg also painted large-scale murals and public works; from 1980, was active in his studio in Italy.
Exhibitions/citations Work subject of exhibitions in Europe, Japan, and the US; shown at 1939–40 *New York World's Fair: The World of Tomorrow*; 1954–57 *Design in Scandinavia*, touring the US; 1955 *H 55*, Hälsingborg; 1958 *Formes Scandinaves*, Musée des Arts Décoratifs, Paris; 1975 *Gustavsberg 150 ar*, Nationalmuseum, Stockholm (catalog below). Gold medals, 1948 (8th) and 1957 (11th) editions of Triennale di Milano and grand prizes at the 1951 (9th) and 1954 (10th) editions; 1955 gold medal in Cannes; 1957 Gregor Paulsson trophy; 1968 Prince Eugen Medal; 1973 gold medal, Concorso Internazionale della Ceramica d'Arte, Faenza.
Bibliography 'Stig Lindberg,' *Everyday Art Quarterly*, no. 25, 1953: 14–15. Berndt Klyvare et al., 'Stig Lindberg,' *Graphis*, vol. 15, July 1959: 308–15. Berndt Klyvare and Dag Widman, *Stig Lindberg—*

Stig Lindberg. Covered container. 1957. Hand-thrown stoneware, overall h. 6 7/8 x dia. 3 1/4" (17.5 x 8.2 cm). Mfr.: AB Gustavsberg Fabriker, Sweden. Gift of the mfr. MoMA.

Swedish Artist and Designer, Stockholm: Rabén & Sjögren, 1963. Cat., *Gustavsberg 150 ar*, Stockholm: Nationalmuseum, 1975. Cat., Kathryn B. Hiesinger and George H. Marcus III (eds.), *Design Since 1945*. Philadelphia: Philadelphia Museum of Art, 1983. Jennifer Hawkins Opie, *Scandinavia: Ceramics and Glass in the Twentieth Century*, New York: Rizzoli, 1989. George Fischler and Barrett Gould, *Scandinavian Ceramics and Glass: 1940s to 1980s*, Atglen, Pa.: Schiffer, 2000.

Lindblad, Gun (1954–)

Swedish glassware designer; born Lapland.

Training 1977–81, glass and ceramics, Konstfackskolan, Stockholm.
Biography 1982–87, Lindblad was a designer at Kosta Boda glassworks; from 1987, was active in his own studio in Stockholm; from c. 1987, artist-in-residence, California College of Arts and Crafts, Los Angeles; from 1987, consultant at Strömbergshyttan.
Exhibitions Work shown in Norway, Finland, Sweden, Switzerland.
Bibliography Jennifer Hawkins Opie, *Scandinavia: Ceramics and Glass in the Twentieth Century*, New York: Rizzoli, 1989.

Lindekrantz, Bo (1932–)

Swedish furniture and interior designer.

Training 1957–61, Konstindustriskolan, Gothenberg.
Biography 1964 with Börge Lindau, Lindekrantz cofounded an architecture office and collaborated on furniture designs produced by Lammhults. They designed furniture that often incorporated chromium-plated bent metal tubing.
Bibliography Cat., David Revere McFadden (ed), *Scandinavian Modern Design 1880–1980*, New York: Abrams, 1982.
> See Lindau, Börge.

Lindfors, Stefan (1962–)

Finnish sculptor and interior and furniture designer; born Maarianhamina, Åland islands.

Training 1982–88, master's degree, department of interior architecture and furniture design, Taideteollinen korkeakoulu, Helsinki.
Biography 1988, Lindfors designed the stage set for the evening-news television program, Yleisradio (YLE, Finnish broadcasting company); 1988 Scaragoo articulated table lamp that lights up when touched (designed with and produced by Design M/Ingo Maurer of Munich; 1993 Draco armchair by Asko. 1989, Lindfors designed interiors and furniture for the restaurant of Taideteollisuusmuseoon (museum of applied arts), Helsinki; has been active in the design of graphics, architecture, scenography, and performance-like lectures, as well as jewelry, lamps, sculpture, and products by Alessi, Hackman, Marimekko, Martela, Kalevala Koru, and Asko. 1993, he was hired by Kansas City Art Institute as the tenured Distinguished Professor of Design and Chair of the Design Department; and lectures worldwide. Public installations include the outdoor clocktower by Swatch at 1996 Atlanta Summer Olympiad, US; the tower clock in Lapinlahti, Finland; installations at Gershwin Hotel and at Mercer Hotel, both New York. From 1999, he designed products by P.O. Korhonen (furniture including 1999 Abaqus chair), Iittala glass, and Arabia ceramics, and children's chairs for the Kiasma restaurant of Nykytaiteen Museo Kiasmat (museum of contemporary art; architect, Steven Holl), Helsinki.
Exhibitions/citations Sculpture subject of 1988 exhibition, Gallery Titanik, Turku, Finland. Silver medal, 1986 (17th) Triennale di Milano, and other awards; 1992 Georg Jensen prize, Copenhagen; 1992 Väinö Tanner Trailblazer Award. Work included in *Design World 2000*, Konstindustrimuseet, Helsinki; 1995 *Mutant Materials*, New York (catalog below).
Bibliography Albrecht Bangert and Karl Michael Armer, *80s Style: Designs of the Decade*, New York: Abbeville, 1990. Paola Antonelli, *Mutant Materials in Contemporary Design*, New York: The Museum of Modern Art/Abrams, 1995. *The International Design Yearbook*, New York: Abbeville, 1996.

Lindenfeld, Lore (b. Lore Kadden) (1921–)

German textile designer.

Training 1945–48 under Josef and Anni Albers, Black Mountain College, Black Mountain, N.C.
Biography 1938, Kadden emigrated to the US; during World War II, was aided by a group of Harvard University faculty wives to live in Cambridge, Mass., US. After she studied in North Carolina and married Peter Lindenfeld, she stopped weaving but returned in 1970s; made several trips to Europe and Japan, where weaving, drawing, and stitchery inspired her; in her fabrications, replaced cotton and wool fibers with nylon netting, polyester, paper, Mylar, and other non-traditional materials.
Exhibitions Work subject of 1997 exhibition, Black Mountain College (catalog below); included in 2000–01 *A Woman's Hand; Designing Textiles in America*, Fashion Institute of Technology, New York.
Bibliography Cat., Sigrid Wortmann Weltge, *Lore Kadden Lindenfeld: A Life in Textiles, 1945–1997*, Black Mountain, N.C.: Black Mountain College Museum and Arts Center, 1997.

Lindh, Richard (1929–); Francesca Lindh (1931–)

Finnish ceramicists; husband and wife.

Training 1952–53, Taideteollinen korkeakoulu, Helsinki.
Biography 1953–55, the Lindhs shared a studio in Helsinki and, from 1955, worked for the Arabia pottery in Helsinki, where Richard was head of the industrial-art department from 1960 and artistic director 1973–c. 1985.
Exhibitions/citations Work included in 1955 *H 55*, Hälsingborg, Sweden; 1961 *Finlandia* in Zürich, Amsterdam, and London; 1957 (11th) and 1960 (12th) editions of Triennale di Milano. First prize in a competition, Museum of Contemporary Crafts, New York.
Bibliography Cat., David Revere McFadden (ed.), *Scandinavian Modern Design 1880–1980*, New York: Abrams, 1982. Jennifer Hawkins Opie, *Scandinavia: Ceramics and Glass in the Twentieth Century*, New York: Rizzoli, 1990.

Lindig, Otto (1895–1966)

German ceramicist; born Prößneck.

Training 1919–25, Bauhaus, Weimar.
Biography Lindig was an enthusiastic supporter of the pottery workshop at the Bauhaus, contending that it should be included in the school's core curriculum. When it was separated into design and production workshops, Lindig supervised the production segment, combining handwork and mass-production methods. At the Bauhaus pottery department in Dornburg, his work was elegant in form and called on semi-opaque glazes that resulted in a wide variety of finishes on one-of-a-kind pieces. His work signaled a break from historicist forms toward modern mass production. His tenure at the Bauhaus pottery department in Dornburg was 1925–30. He designed ceramics in, or from, 1930 for Staatliche Majolikamanufaktur Karlsruhe.
Bibliography Cat., *The Bauhaus: Masters and Students*, New York: Barry Friedman, 1988. Cat., *Otto Lindig—der Töpfer*, Karlsruhe: Museum der Stadt Gera/Badisches Landesmuseum, 1990.

Lindiger-Löwy, Gideon (1952–); Lone Lindinger-Löwy (1956–)

Danish industrial designers; husband and wife. Gideon: born London. Lone: born Copenhagen. Both: active Copenhagen.

Training Both: design, Det Kongelige Danske Kunstakademi, Copenhagen.
Biography 1982, the Lindinger-Löwys set up their own studio, with Bang & Olufsen as their first client and, 1983, conducted research in lighting for Louis Poulsen. His design work has included 1983 Beocom 1000 and Beocom 2000 telephones, 1986 Beolab Penta tall speaker system, and 1988 Beolab 3000 and 5000 speakers by Bang & Olufsen. Also designed 1984 plastic jewelry by Buch and ceramics by Bing & Grøndahl Porcelænsfabrik, including 1987–88 Stripes and Stars dinnerware range.
Bibliography Cat., Chantal Bizot, *Bang & Olufsen: design et technologie*, Paris: Musée des Arts Décoratifs, 1990: 10. Jens Bang, *Bang & Olufsen: Fra vision til legende = From Vision to Legend*, Denmark: Vidsyn, 2000.

Lindstrand, 'Vicke' (Viktor Emmanuel, 1904–1983)

Swedish glassware designer; born Gothenburg

Training 1924–27, Slöjdföreningens Skola (now Konstindustriskolan), Gothenburg.
Biography 1928–40, Lindstrand was a glassware designer at Orrefors Glasbruk; 1935–36, at Kariskrona Porslinsfabrik; 1936–50, at Upsala-Ekeby (art director there from 1943–50). 1950–73, he was the design director at Kosta Boda glassworks, while concurrently active

Richard Lindh and Francesca Lindh. Double teapot. 1956. Glazed earthenware, large pot (top) 5 1/4 x dia. 6 1/4" (13.3 x 15.9 cm), small pot (bottom) h. 3 x dia. 4 3/8" (7.6 x 11.1 cm). Mfr.: Arabia, Finland. Phyllis B. Lambert Fund. MoMA.

in his own studio in Århus. His free-form work was often engraved.
Exhibitions Lindstrand's 22 ft. (7 m) high windows were installed in the Swedish pavilion, 1937 *Exposition Internationale des Arts et Techniques dans la Vie Moderne*, Paris, and his public glass fountain installed at 1939–40 *New York World's Fair: The World of Tomorrow*. Other work shown at editions of Triennale di Milano from 1933 (5th) edition, 1930 Stockholmsutställningen, 1955 *H 55* exhibition in Hälsingborg, and 1959 in Amsterdam.
Bibliography Cat., *Glas in Schweden 1915–1960*, Munich: Kunstmuseum Düsseldorf, 1986. Helmut Ricke and Lars Thor, *Schwedische Glasmanufakturen*, Munich: Prestel, 1987. Jennifer Hawkins Opie, *Scandinavia: Ceramics and Glass in the Twentieth* Century, New York: Rizzoli, 1989. George Fischler and Barrett Gould, *Scandinavian Ceramics and Glass: 1940s to 1980s*, Atglen, Pa.: Schiffer, 2000.

Lindvall, Jonas (1963–)
Swedish furniture designer and interior architect; born Malmö.

Training 1989–93, interior architecture, Högskolan för Design och Konsthantverk (HDK), Göteborgs Universitet; 1992, visiting student, furniture department, Royal College of Art, London; 1993, visiting student, furniture department, Det Kongelige Danske Kunstakademi, Copenhagen.
Biography Lindvall's large body of furniture design has included 1994 Sputnik chair and Belly Up chest by David Design, 1998 Metropolis adjustable armchair and Potemkin adjustable table by Kockums, 1998 Noa stacking chair and Lui armchair by Skandiform, 2001 Norton lamps by Annell Ljus och Form, 2001 Inka JL rug by Asplund. Architecture, exhibition design, and interior architecture has included 1992 new gate of Skabersjö Castle in Skabersjö, Sweden; 1993 Izakaya Koi restaurant in Malmö, Sweden; 1995 Mac Mekarna computer office in Malmö; 1995 *Design in Sports* exhibition at Röhsska Museet, Gothenburg; 1997 Flos Scandinavia showroom and office in Malmö; 1999 Annell Ljus och Form office, Sweden; 2000 Texon Automation office building in Limhamn, Sweden; 2000 Sigtuna Stads Hotell in Sigtuna, Sweden; 2001 stands of Skandiform and Interstudio at Scandinavian Furniture Fair, Stockholm; a number of houses and apartments.
Exhibitions/citations Work included in 1991 *Young Furniture Designers of Scandinavia*, Copenhagen; 1992 *Nordic Design Students*, Copenhagen; 1992 *Future Furniture*, Royal College of Art, London; 1993 *Kunsthantverkgewerb*, Munich, 1993, Galleri Doktor Glas (furniture), Stockholm; 1996 *Not So Simple*, New York; 1999 *Empty Spaces*, Europäische Patentamt (EPA), Munich; 1999 *Neues Scandinavia*, Die Neue Sammlung, Munich; 2000 *Chairexpo*, Arkitekturmuseet, Stockholm; 2001 chair exhibition of the Arkitekturmuseet at Stockholm Furniture Fair. Work subject of 2004 *Sacred Boxes*, Galerie Pascal Cottard-Olsson, Stockholm. 1991–98, Josef Frank, Estrid Ericsson, Drafoord, Erasmus, and Hordic Council scholarships; 1998–2000 Excellent Swedish Design annual citations; 2001 Furniture of the Year Award, Sweden.

Linea B
Italian domestic goods manufacturer.

History Linea B first began production in plastics with 1969 Gabbiano stool designed by Roberto Lera. The firm produced small furniture pieces and accessories. Its witty designs began to draw attention at the furniture venues of the early 1970s.
Exhibition 1972 Tovaglia fiberglass table designed by Studio Tetrach included in the 1972 *Design a Plastické Hmoty*, Uměleckoprůmyslové Muzeum, Prague (catalog below).
Bibliography Cat., Milena Lamarová, *Design a Plastické Hmoty*, Prague: Uměleckoprůmyslové Muzeum, 1972: 64, 194.

Linhart, Evžen (1898–1949)
Czech architect, interior designer, and painter; born Kouřim.

Training 1918–24, České Vysoké Učení Technické (Czech technical university), Prague.
Biography From 1924, Linhart worked at the city building department in Prague. 1922–26, his designs were distinguished by their subtle use of light and detailing and followed the style of the Puristická Čtyřka group. From 1923 to its 1931 end, he was a member of the Devětsil group. His own house, where he lived only 1927–29, showed three innovative examples of his design activity: a long and shallow sideboard with asymmetrical paneling and doors on rollers in a Constructivist style, three retractable pedestal tables, and a nickel-plated standard lamp. He was accompanied by fellow Devětsil member Jan Rosůlek on a visit to Paris and, to the 1927 *Die Wohnung* exhibition in Stuttgart. Whereas his friend Jaroslav Frágner emphasized Functionalism, Linhart expressed aesthetic ideas in the interior of his own 1927–29 house at 46 Na Viničních Horách St. in Prague-Dejvice. The deep coloring of the internal walls, the numerous built-in elements in spray-coated concrete, and the impressive ramp with white banisters attest to Le Corbusier's profound influence. The wood and metal furniture was standard models by Thonet but included a Linhart-designed sideboard, a metal lamp, and a set of simple tables. And the Le Corbusier influence is further revealed by Linhart's 1931–32 family house at 50 Na Ostrohu St. in Prague (designed with Antonin Heythum). He died in Prague.
Exhibitions Participated in 1923 Bauhaus exhibition, Weimar.
Bibliography Cat., *Devětsil: Czech Avant-Garde Art, Architecture, and Design of the 1920s and 30s*, Oxford: Oxford Museum of Modern Art/ London: Design Museum, London, 1990. Alexander von Vegesack (ed.), *Czech Cubism: Architecture, Furniture, and Decorative Arts 1910–1925*, New York: Princeton Architectural Press and Vitra, 1992. Cat., *Prague, 1900–1938: capitale secrète des avants-gardes*, Dijon: Musée des Beaux-Arts, 1997.

Linke, Norbert (1939–)
German industrial designer; born Stuttgart; active Milan.

Biography 1962 Linke began his professional career and has served clients including Bosch (domestic electrical appliances), Brunell (silverware), Concord (cutlery), S.T. Dupont, Hofman Rheem (irons), Sama (coffeemaking machines), Silma (film projectors), Vallecchi FPCT (technical publishing), Walter Frank, and Weco (optical equipment), as well as a number of others. 1970s, he designed television sets by Philco; is a member of the Verband Deutscher Industrie Designer (VDID) and Associazione per il Disegno Industriale (ADI) in Italy; has served on a number of juries in Germany.
Bibliography *ADI Annual 1976*, Milan: Associazione per il Disegno Industriale, 1976.

linoleum
Floor covering.

History 1860, linoleum was developed by Frederick Walton in Britain. Searching for an inexpensive floor covering, Walton coated flax cloth with a mixture of gum, cork dust, resin, and linseed oil. The name linoleum is an amalgamation of Latin words *linum* (flax) and *oleum* (oil). The 'floor cloth,' which preceded 'linoleum,' was made by applying an oil-based paint to canvas. Since linoleum was springier, longer-

El Lissitzky (attribution). Plate, c. 1923. Turned earthenware, h. 1 x dia. 7 5/8" (2.5 x 19.4 cm). Gift of Manfred Ludewig. MoMA.

lasting, easy to clean, and waxable, it became popular with the Victorians. 1908 in Pittsburgh, Thomas Armstrong created linoleum in a wide range of colors and patterns, including a simulation of wood, flowered chintz, and Cubist art. The pattern that simulated cobblestones was Armstrong's most popular. Linoleum has been popular for a time as a medium for art prints, either when lithographic stones were not available because of war shortages or when a special effect is desired, still today. It was also used in the printing of posters. Because its applied surface design wears off through continued use, linoleum has come to be replaced by vinyl, a synthetic polymer that accepts impregnated designs and is more durable, offering resistance to heavy abrasion and pointed shoe heels. With the nostalgia and kitsch movement of 1980s, vinyl has been produced in the linoleum motifs of the past.
Bibliography Diane di Costanzo, *Metropolitan Home*, Oct. 1990: 54. Gerhard Kaldewei (ed.), *Linoleum: History, Design, Architecture 1882–2000*, Ostfildern-Ruit: Hatje Cantz, 2000.

Linossier, Claudius (1893–1953)
French metalworker.

Biography Linoissier moved to Paris from Lyon and worked as a silversmith and goldsmith before joining Jean Dunand for three months to learn *dinanderie* (metalwork). Like Dunand, he specialized in geometric and abstract patterns. Though Linossier produced work of quality, it lacked innovation, with the repeated use of the same techniques and motifs.
Exhibitions/citations Work included in several stands at 1925 *Exposition Internationale des Arts Décoratifs et Industriels Modernes*, Paris; Salon of Société des Artistes Français; Salon d'Automne; from 1921, Salon of Société des Artistes Décorateurs. 1932, was elected to the Légion d'Honneur.
Bibliography Victor Arwas, *Art Déco*, New York: Abrams, 1980.

Lion Cachet, Carel Adolph (1864–1945)
Dutch designer.

Biography Lion Cachet was an interior architect and applied-arts designer of some note, best known for his *Nieuwe Kunst* furniture designs which expressed a refined Arabian nature, some of which were produced by Pander. He designed ceramics by De Distel, Goedewaagen, De Porceleyne Fles, and De Sphinx; rugs by KVT; bookbindings, some featuring batik work; glass by Leerdam; and 10-gulden paper money with Rembrandt's likeness. He sometimes collaborated with Th. Nieuwenhuis. 1879–89, Lion Cachet also designed ceramics by Linthorpe Pottery in Middlesborough, UK; 1910–40, worked for Schellens & Marto fabric firm on various commissions, including for use in oceanliner interiors, such as for Stoomvart Maatschappij Nederland (Netherlands steam navigation company); 1928–31, wallpaper by Rath & Doodeheefvre.
Exhibition Work subject of 1994 exhibition, Assen and Rotterdam.
Bibliography Cat., Antoinette Does-de Haan et al., *C.A. Lion Cachet, 1864–1945*, Assen: Drents Museum; Rotterdam: Museum Boymans-van Beuningen, 1994.

Lipofsky, Marvin (1938–)
American glassware and ceramics designer, and teacher.

Training Bachelor of fine arts, industrial design, University of Illinois; two master's degrees in sculpture, University of Madison, Wis., where he was one of Harvey Littleton's first advanced-degree students.
Biography Lipofsky became head of ceramics and introduced glass as an art form to the design department, University of California, Berke-ley. He was interested at first in asymmetrical, misshapen forms but, 1970s, produced work that was sometimes comic and often kitsch; travels widely and has worked collaboratively on sculptural works.
Citations Numerous international awards, and (twice) National Endowment for the Arts Fellowship, US.
Bibliography Frederick Cooke, *Glass: Twentieth-Century Design*, New York: Dutton, 1986: 105.

Lippe, Jens von der (1911–)
Norwegian ceramicist.

Training Statens Håndværks-og Kunstindustriskole, Oslo; Staatliche Keramische Fachschule, Schlesien (now Silesia, Poland); Istituto Statale d'Arte per la Ceramica, Faenza.
Biography 1933, Lippe and his wife Margrethe set up their own pottery workshop in Oslo. 1939–75, Lippe taught, Statens Handverks og Kunstindustriskole, Oslo, and head of its ceramics department from 1956.
Bibliography Cat., David Revere McFadden (ed.), *Scandinavian Modern Design 1880–1980*, New York: Abrams, 1982.

Lippincott, J. Gordon (1909–1998)
American industrial designer.

Training Engineering, Swarthmore (Pennsylvania) College; Columbia University, New York.
Biography 1943, Lippincott opened a design office in New York; was joined by Walter P. Margulies in 1944. Eventually, the firm Lippincott & Margulies became an important consultancy in package and product design. The agency served clients such as Waterman, Paramount Pictures, Republic Aircraft, Fuller Brush Co., Walgreen Drug Stores, RCA, General Electric, Macy's department store, Mead-Johnson drugs, Northwest Airlines, and Barbizon Plaza Hotel in New York. Margulies was the first person to recognized and conceptualize modern corporate-identity as a consulting business. The L&M office styled vacuum cleaners, office duplicating equipment, fountain pens, and packaging for cosmetics and perfume, as well as heavy-industrial equipment, including sea airplanes, boats, the interior of the Tucker automobile, and development of corporate logos and names. Through his large staff, he designed gasoline stations, stores, theaters, hotel interiors, and supermarkets. By 1966 or earlier, Lippincott, who was essentially a product-designer with little interest in corporate identity, left the firm. 1986, Marsh & McLennan Companies bought Lippincott & Margulies from Clive Chajet, and L&M became part of Mercer Management Consulting. 2003, L&M was reformed by Marsh & McLennan, with branding specialists culled from Mercer, as Lippinott Mercer with headquarters currently in New York.
Bibliography J. Gordon Lippincott, *Design for Business*, Chicago: Paul Theobald, 1947. Michael T. Kaufman, 'J. Gordon Lippincott...,' *New York Times*, 7 May 1998: sec. B, p. 11.

Vera Lisková. Tumbler. 1948. Crystal, h. 2 7/8 x dia. 3 5/8" (7.3 x 9.2 cm). Mfr.: J. & L. Lobmeyr, Austria. Gift of A. J. Van Dugteren & Sons, Inc. MoMA.

Lippmann, Herbert (1889–1978)

American architect and designer; active New York.

Training Architecture, Columbia University, New York.
Biography For the Lowell apartment house on East 63rd Street, New York, Lippmann and partner Henry C. Churchill commissioned metalwork from Edgar Brandt and Walter von Nessen. Lippmann designed and furnished several suburban New York houses. Inspired by the 'skyscraper' furniture of Paul Frankl, he designed in the angular French Art Moderne style (in contrat to 'baroque' Art Déco) and used veneers in a Viennese manner.
Bibliography Cervin Robinson and Rosemarie Haag Bletter, *Skyscraper Style: Art Deco*, New York: Oxford, 1975: 15–16. R.W. Sexton, *The Logic of Modern Architecture*, New York: Architectural Book Publishing, 1929: 73–75. Karen Davies, *At Home in Manhattan: Modern Decorative Arts, 1925 to the Depression*, New Haven: Yale, 1983.

Lipska, Madame

Russian dressmaker and interior designer; born Russia; active Paris.

Training Under theater-scenery and costume designer Léon Bakst.
Biography 1920s, Lipska, little known including her presumably unknown forename, established a couture shop on the avenue des Champs-Élysées, Paris; designed the apartment of the marquis Somni Picenardi in Paris, c. 1930 renovation (with Adrienne Gorska) of the Château de Rambouillet (the house of Barbara Harrison), and c. 1933 duplex apartment of perfumer Antoine.

Lisková, Vera (1924–1979)

Czech glassmaker.

Biography Lisková was effective in turning borosilicate lampworking into a fine art; was a pioneer in flameworking; from 1970s, became favorably recognized by critics and respected by collectors. She influenced a number of Eastern European lampworkers, including Anna Skibska and Barbara Idzikowska of Poland. Lisková designed a number of distinctive simple clear-glass vessels. The Vera Liskova Lecture Fund was established at the Glass Center of Salem Community College, Salem, N.J., US.

Lissitzky, El (b. Lazar Markovich Lissitzkii 1890–1941)

Russian artist and architect; born Polshchinok, near Smolensk.

Training 1909–14, architecture, Technische Hochschule, Darmstadt; 1915–16, Riga Polytechnic.
Biography On the invitation of Marc Chagall, Lissitzky taught graphics and architecture in Vitebsk 1917–19; 1919, joined Kazimir Malevich's UNOVIS group, through which he transformed Malevich's Suprematism into his own PROUN (PROyect OUtverjdenya Novogo, or project for the affirmation of the new), an effort to move painting into architecture, or, in his words, 'The Proun is the station where one changes from painting to architecture.' Founded in Titebs, PROUN was active 1919–22. Lissitzky designed the 1920 sloping steel speaker's platform for Lenin. 1921, he taught at VKhUTEMAS (the official Soviet design institute) and, 1922–25, in Germany and Switzerland. He designed the cover of the *Wendingen* monograph (Nov. 1922) on Frank Lloyd Wright. Lissitzky, who traveled often in 1920s, associated with Dada artists, Bauhaus designers (including Ludwig Mies van der Rohe), and De Stijl members (such as Theo van Doesburg). Thus, he was an important link between Russian Constructivism and the Western European avant-garde. He and Mart Stam (whom he had met in 1914) designed 1924–25 Wolkenbügel (cloud props) project, which was a cantilevered office block on large piers. In Germany, he designed the PROUN Space at 1923 *Greater Berlin Art Exhibition* in Eindhoven and the first (1926) *Exhibition Room* (international art exhibition) in Dresden. 1925, he returned to VKhUTEMAS and, from 1926, taught furniture and interior design in its metalwork and woodworking department. He cofounded Constructivism; thereafter, was primarily an exhibition and typographical designer. The exceptions to this activity are a chair for 1928 *Pressa-Austellung* in Cologne and conference table and auditorium chair that showed a clear Bauhaus influence for 1930–31 *Hygiene-Ausstellung* in Dresden. The *Pressa-Austellung* and *Hygiene-Austellung* furniture is now being reproduced by Tecta in Lauenförde. He experimented constantly with interior design, graphics, book design, typography, photography, and photograms. His 1941 *Provide More Tanks* propaganda poster was his last work.
Exhibitions Decorative paintings titled *The Leader* and *Jericho* shown at 1917 exhibition of V Mir Iskusstva (the world of art) group, Petrograd. Work included in many exhibitions in Russia and abroad, including 1922 *Erste Russische Kunstausstellung*, Berlin. Work subject of exhibitions at Galerie Gmurzynska, Cologne, in 1976; Museum of Modern Art, Oxford, in 1977; and numerous 1990 international venues to mark the centenary of his birth.
Bibliography Horst Richter, *El Lissitzky: Sieg über die Sonne—Zur Kunst des Konstruktivismus*, Cologne: Galerie Christoph Czwiklitzer, 1958. Sophie Lissitzky-Küppers, *El Lissitzky: Life, Letters, Texts*, Greenwich, Conn.: New York Graphic Society, 1968. Kenneth Frampton, 'The Work and Influence of El Lissitzky,' *Architect's Year Book*, no. 12, 1968: 253–68. El Lissitzky, *Russia: An Architecture for World Revolution*, Cambridge: MIT, 1970. Jan Tschichold, *Werke und Aufsätze von El Lissitzky (1890–1941)*, Berlin, 1971. Cat., *El Lissitzky*, Cologne: Galerie Gmurzynska, 1976. Cat., *Lissitzky*, Oxford: Museum of Modern Art, 1977. Cat., *Der Kragstuhl*, Stuhlmuseum Burg Beverungen, Berlin: Alexander, 1986: 134. Margarita Tupitsyn, *El Lissitzky: Beyond the Abstract Cabinet: Photography, Design, Collaboration*, New Haven: Yale, 1999.

Piero Lissoni. Paper chair. c. 1998. Wood, tubular steel, and fabric, h. 29 7/8 x w. 22 5/8 x d. 18 1/2" (76 x 58 x 47 cm). Mfr.: Cappellini, Italy.

Lissoni, Piero (1956–)

Italian architect and designer; born Seregno; active Milan.

Training To 1985, architecture, Politecnico, Milan.
Biography 1978-79, Lissoni began his career working at Studio 14 in Milan; 1980-81, designed the corporate-identity program, kitchen systems, shops, and exhibition stands of Casakit; 1982, conducted studies for the Linate and Malpensa airports (near Milan). Other 1980s clients included Effeti Cucine (corporate-identity program), Estel (graphics and photographic program), Linate Airport (departure lounge), Lema (L25 furniture system), Boffi Cucine (becoming art director and designer). 1986 with Nicoletta Canesi in Milan, established Studio Lissoni for industrial, interior, graphic, store, and exhibition design, which has subsequently become large, serving clients including Living (furniture, ID program, new offices, and factory), Iren Uffici (office furniture), Matteograssi (becoming art director), Star-Treviso, Porro, Takashimaya (Kobe shopping center logo and trademark), Yoshimura architecture studio (trademark and logo), Artemide, InterForm (furniture showroom), Foscarini, Lema (becoming art director), Cassina, Cappellini, Eurisko (offices), Kartell, Alessi, Flos/Antares, Units (Boffi-Cappellini partnership), Welonda (Wella group), Allegri, Liv'it. Lissoni has designed several private houses and hotels; is known for his stark minimalism, exemplified by kitchen systems by Boffi.
Exhibitions/citations Work included in *30 architetti e la qualità della casa* exhibition, Milan. Premio Compasso d'Oro: 1991 (for Esprit kitchen by Boffi) and 2001 (for WK6 kitchen by Boffi, One cabinet system by Kartell, and HT by Porro). A number of other exhibitions and awards.
Bibliography Silvio San Pietro and Paola Gallo, *Nuovi negozi in Italia*

3, Milan: L'Archivolto, 1995. Silvio San Pietro and Cristina Morozzi, *Contemporary Italian Furniture*, Milan: L'Archivolto, 1996. Charlotte and Peter Fiell, *1000 Chairs*, New York: Taschen, 1997. Patrizia Malfatti, *Piero Lissoni a Milano: naturalità assoluta in abitare*, Milan: Abitare Segesta, 1998. Claudia Neumann, *Design Lexicon Italien*, Cologne: DuMont, 1999. Ingo Maurer (ed.), *International Design Yearbook*, London: Laurence King, 2000. Sara Manuelli, 'Renaissance Man,' *Design Week*, Nov. 2000. Mel Byars, 'Simple is Never Simple: One by Piero Lissoni with Patricia Urquiola,' *Echoes*, no. 36, May 2001: 24–25. Almerico De Angelis, *Design—The Italian Way*, Milan: Modo, 2001. Nelda Rodger, 'Piero Lissoni's Studio Designs', *Azure*, Sept.–Oct. 2002.

Lithonia Lighting
> See Holophane Corporation.

Littell, Ross (1924–2000)

American designer, active New York.

Training Pratt Institute of Arts, Brooklyn, N.Y.
Biography 1949–55, Littell collaborated with fellow Pratt students William Katavolos and Douglas Kelley on furniture, textile, and dinnerware designs for Laverne Originals. Commissioned by Erwine and Estelle Laverne, they executed 1949 New Furniture Group of chairs and tables in leather, chrome, glass, and marble. The team's three-legged 1952 'T' chair (model 31C) (but possibly by Katavolos alone, who rendered a prototype with wooden dowels) was produced in chromium-plated steel. Individually, Littell designed 1987 RL 2 side chair by Atelier in Italy. Littell's 1968 Luar (no. PLR 1) double pedestal, woven-leather chair is currently made by ICF. After the partnership dissolved, mid-1950s, Littell designed textile prints for curtains by Knoll; later, traveled to Europe as a Fulbright scholar and shot c. 2,200 photographs of patterns, such as cobblestones in Paris, which resulted in textile patterns inspired by mathematical ideas; subsequently, lived in Italy and Denmark and created sculpture called *Luminars*, a number of fabrics by Kvadrat, including a tri-dimensional example still in production, and products in Ørskov's Form & Favre range. He retired in Santa Barbara, Cal., where he died.
Exhibitions 1952 AID award (T chair for best US furniture); Fulbright Scholarship. The group's work shown at 1953 and 1955 *Good Design* exhibitions/awards (including Littell's textiles), The Museum of Modern Art, New York, and Chicago Merchandise Mart; 1983–84 *Design Since 1945* exhibition of the Philadelphia Museum of Art.
Bibliography 'Good Design,' *Interiors*, vol. 113, Aug. 1953: 88–89, 146–48. Roberto Aloi and Agnoldomenico Pica, *Mobili tipo*, Milan: Hoepli, 1956. Clement Meadmore, *The Modern Chair: Classics in Production*, New York: Van Nostrand Reinhold, 1975: 98–101. Cat., Kathryn B. Hiesinger and George H. Marcus III (eds.), *Design Since* 1945, Philadelphia: Philadelphia Museum of Art, 1983. 'Ross Littell: Portrait of an International Designer', *Living Architecture*, no. 8. 'Kvadrat: New textiles by Ross Littell,' *Living Architecture*, No. 16.
> See Katavolos, William.

Little, Mary (1958–)

British furniture designer; born Northern Ireland.

Training To 1981, Ulster Polytechnic, Northern Ireland; to 1985, Royal College of Art, London.
Biography Little's design career began with a 1981 occasional table and 1985 armchair for her bachelor's and master's degrees shows. She made and painted the Davis Table designed by Floris van den Broecke for Richard Ball's book *Master Pieces* (Poole: Blandford, 1983/1984), and exhibition (see below); was a design assistant to architecture firm Faulkner Brown Hendy Watkinson Stonor, working on furniture for leisure centers. She produced furniture for shops and restaurants for interior designers Maurice Broughton Associates. A 1985 armchair combined elements of Catalan, Scandinavian, and late-punk styles into a functional piece of furniture that was widely published. As a freelance designer in Milan from 1986, she worked for Daniela Puppa, Franco Raggi, Emilio Ambasz, Nanni Strada, and Massimo Morozzi. Her diverse work has included bathroom accessories, chairs, belts, dining tables, tea sets, bags for schoolchildren, lamps, and sofas. She designed 1988 lighting by Memphis, various work by Vitra, and 2002 Luna and 2002 Ana felt/wood vessels (with Austrian designer Peter Wheeler); taught at the Glasgow School of Art, Loughborough College of Art and Design, and Wimbledon School of Art.
Exhibitions/citations Work subject of 1996 *Have a Seat: The Köln Project*, Galerie Andrea Leenarts, Cologne, Germany; 1996 *Coat of Arms Collection*, Gallery Valerie, London. Included in 1983 *Experimental Furniture*, Octagon Gallery, Belfast; 1983 *Young Blood*, Barbican, London; 1983 *Master Pieces*, Hille store showroom, London, and Oxford Museum of Modern Art; 1985 exhibition, ASB Marketing, London; 1985 *La Créativité Britannique*, Au Printemps department store, Paris; 1985 *Armchairs*, Néotù gallery, Paris; 1986 *Enjeu de l'Objet*, Caravelles, Musée des Arts Décoratifs, Lyon; 1986 *Les Assises du Siège Contemporain*, Musée des Arts Décoratifs, Paris (catalog below); numerous others have followed, including 1999 *A Grand Design*, Victoria and Albert Museum, London, and 2002 *Functional Fine Art*, Braunstein/Quay Gallery, San Francisco. Received 1993 Harald Hyam Wingate Trust and 1992 Oppenheim-John Downes Memorial Trust, UK.
Bibliography Cat., *Les assises du siège contemporain*, Paris: Musée des Arts Décoratifs, 1986. Liz McQuiston, *Women in Design: A Contemporary View*, New York: Rizzoli, 1988. *Acquisitions 1982–1990 arts décoratifs*, Paris: Fonds National d'Art Contemporain, 1991.

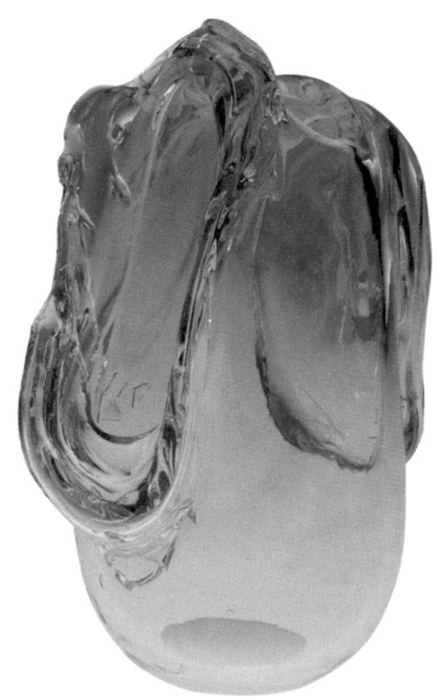

Harvey Littleton. Vase. 1963. Glass, 9 3/4 x 7 1/2 x 4 7/8" (24.8 x 19 x 12.4 cm). Mfr.: the designer, US. Greta Daniel Fund. MoMA.

Littleton, Harvey K. (1922–)

American glassware designer; born Corning, N.Y.; active the US and Britain.

Training 1939–42 and 1946–47, University of Michigan, Ann Arbor, receiving a bachelor's degree in design; 1941 and 1949–51, Cranbrook Academy of Art, Bloomfield Hills, Mich., receiving a master's degree in ceramics; 1945 under Nora Braden, Brighton School of Art, Brighton, UK.
Biography Littleton is known as the father of the Studio Glass Movement. Serving in Britain during World War II, he enrolled in Nora Braden's pottery classes near Brighton. 1945, he joined Corning Glassworks in Corning, N.Y.; from 1946, taught part-time, Toledo Museum of Art, Toledo, Ohio, and, from 1951, at University of Wisconsin, Madison. 1957, he studied Hispano-Moresque pottery and was commissioned by the Corning Glass Museum to do research on Spanish glass; traveled to Venice to study Murano glassmakers' techniques and set up an artists' group in the US based on their practices. Summer 1962, he turned from ceramics to glass when the Toledo Museum of Art invited him to conduct a glassblowing workshop, a landmark seminar in which Littleton introduced the idea that glass could be melted, mixed, blown, and worked in a studio by an artist as a sculptural medium with little reference to mass-produced glass vessels. Littleton had developed the approach with Dominick Labino, the director of research at Johns-Manville Glass Fibers Division. Littleton's graduate course in the University of Wisconsin attracted Marvin Lipofsky and Dale Chihuly, among others, as students. 1975, Littleton retired from teaching and settled in Spruce Pine, N.C. to produced his most technically challenging work: the sinuous Lyrical Movement and Implied Movement groups, the Descending forms, and the Crowns series with multiple exu-

berant arcs. 1990s, he pioneered intaglio vitreography, art prints on paper produced from glass plates created with various treatments.
Exhibitions/citations Work subject of 1984–86 exhibition, touring five US cities, from Atlanta; 1999–2000 exhibition, touring three US cities, from Charlotte, N.C. (catalogs below); others. A large number of group exhibitions and grants.
Bibliography Robert Judson Clark et al., *The Cranbrook Vision*, New York: Abrams/The Metropolitan Museum of Art, 1983. Cat., Joan Falconer Byrd (essay), *Harvey K. Littleton: A Retrospective Exhibition*, Atlanta: High Museum of Art, 1984. Cat., Mary F. Douglas, *Harvey K. Littleton: Reflections, 1946–1994*, Charlotte, N.C.: Mint Museum of Art, 1999.

Littmann, Ludwig (1942–)

German industrial designer; born Mühlheim.

Biography From 1970s, Littmann designed a number of products by Braun in Kronberg, Germany, including 1981–88 UK 400 food processor (with Hartwig Kahlcke), 1982 MPZ 4 citrus presss, 1987 MR 300 HC hand mixer, 1989 HT 57 toaster, 1990 MP 75 centrifuge, 1991 400 T coffee maker, 1992 MPZ 6 citrus press, and numerous recent models.
Citations Was one of four students who received 1972 (1st) Braun-Prize. A number of awards such as 1995 (for Braun Espresso Cappuccino Pro E300 maker) and 1996 (Multiquick control plus vario MR 550 CA) awards, Industrie Forum Design (iF); 2002 Red Dot (for Braun Multiquick hand mixer), Design Zentrum Nordrhein Westfalen, Essen.

Lloyd, Marshall Burns (1858–1927); Lloyd Loom

American furniture manufacturer; born Minneapolis, Minn.; active Menominee, Mich.

Biography and history 1883, Lloyd rented a blacksmithy in St. Thomas, South Dakota, where he established the Lloyd Scale Company to produce a combination sack-holder and scale device. 1894, he became president of the firm C.O. White; invented a method for manufacturing bedsprings and mattresses; bought C.O. White and, 1900, changed its name to Lloyd Manufacturing Co. 1906, he moved the plant to Menominee, Mich., where he was mayor of the town 1913–17. 1914, the firm began producing baby carriages in vegetal reeds as part of its range of prams and handcarts. 1917, Lloyd patented a new system for producing wicker products. He also innovatively used kraft paper twisted over steel wire that he developed as a substitute for wicker, when the importation of rattan and cane was interrupted by World War I. The phrase 'woven fiber' was coined to replace the humble term 'twisted paper.' Claiming that the fiber was hygienic and resistant to humidity, dirt, and warping, Lloyd used it to produce over 100 furniture models and, by 1940, over 10 million units had been sold. A sign in Lloyd's office, whose walls were covered in the Lloyd Loom woven fiber, read, 'I never do what anyone else can do.' 1921, Lloyd Loom became part of the firm Heywood-Wakefield. After 1920, the French rights were sold to René Duval and Pierre Mouronval, both in the wicker business. They furnished some Lloyd-type furniture to 1927 oceanliners *Île-de-France* and *Champlaine*. 1922, a German factory was set up, organized in Fulda by Lloyd with workers who had been trained in Menominee. 1920s–30s, Lloyd Loom furniture was a household name in American and also in Britain. 1924, Lloyd retired from the Menominee factory but remained as a director of Heywood-Wakefield and maintained an independent experimental workshop near Menominee with a dozen assistants.
Bibliography Lee J. Curtis, *Lloyd Loom Woven Fiber Furniture*, New York: Rizzoli, 1991.

Lluscà, Josep (1948–)

Spanish designer; born and active Barcelona.

Training From 1968, design, Eina (Escola de Desseny i Art), Barcelona; École des Arts et Métiers, Montréal.
Biography 1972, Lluscà established Lluscà & Asociados in Barcelona and pursued a wide range of design disciplines, later specializing in furniture and lighting. His clients have included Norma Europa. Associating himself with sculptors, his work incorporated elements from Antoní Gaudí and 1950s Rationalism. He worked on the development of an office-chair mechanism that resulted in 1989 Lola range by Oken. 1985–87, he was vice-president, ADI/FAD (industrial design/decorative arts associations) and a member, Design Council of the Generalitat de Catalunya (Catalonian government); taught, Eina, Barcelona; was a member of the Council of Barcelona Design Center (BCD). Work has included 1986 Andrea chair (based on 1944 three-legged chair by Charles Eames) by Andreu World, 1989 Ketupa lamp (with silversmith Joaquín Berao) and 1986 Anade 4169 lamp by Metalarte, and 1988 BCN armchair by Enea. Other clients: A^3, Alcatel, Ascue, Bluet, Carlsberg, and Antonio Puig.
Citations 1974, 1986, 1988, 1999 Delta d'Oro and Delta de Plata awards, ADI/FAD; 1990 National Design Prize, Spain; 1991 Bronze Industrial Design Excellence Award, Industrial Designers Society of America (IDSA), US; 1991 and 1992 Bronze Award, Institute of Business Designers (IBD), US; 1993 Red Dot award, Design Zentrum Nordrhein Westfalen, Essen; 1993 and 1998 awards, Industrie Forum Design (iF), Hanover; 1998 Best of NeoCon, Chicago; others.
Bibliography Marco Romanelli, 'Josep Llusca: progetti 1986-1990,' *Domus*, no. 709, Oct. 1989. Albrecht Bangert and Karl Michael Armer, *80s Style: Designs of the Decade*, New York: Abbeville, 1990: 108, 232. Guy Julier, *New Spanish Design*, London: Thames & Hudson, 1991.

Lobel, Paul (1899–1983)

Romanian metalworker; active New York.

Biography Lobel, an émigré to the US and a studio jeweler, designed and made silver jewelry and a number of vessels and other utilitarian ware in plane, geometric forms; was a consultant designer to International Silver Company and to Regal Art Glass Company. He was also commissioned by Hupmobile Company in Hartford, Conn., and Barbizon Plaza and St. Moritz hotels, New York. He died New York. His 1938–71 papers are housed in the Smithsonian Institution Archives and Manuscripts Catalog, Washington, D.C., donated by his widow Maizie Lobel.
Exhibitions Work included in 1934 *Contemporary American Industrial Design Art* (1934 tea service by International Silver/Wilcox Silverplate), The Metropolitan Museum of Art; 1946 *Modern Handmade Silver*, The Museum of Modern Art; both New York.
Bibliography R. Craig Miller, *Modern Design 1890–1990*, New York: Abrams, 1990. Cat., Janet Kardon (ed.), *Craft in the Machine Age 1920–1945*, New York: Abrams with American Craft Museum, 1995.

Lobmeyr, J. & L.

Austrian glassware manufacturer.

History 1823, Josef Lobmeyr (Grieskirchen 1792–Vienna 1855) began as a glassware retailer off the Karnterstraße in the center of Vienna; 1837–51, operated two unsuccessful glass factories in Slovenia (now Croatia): in Matienthal from 1937 and in Zwechewo. He went on to collaborate with factories in Bohemia and Bavaria, with cutting/engraving in Steinschönau (now Kamenický Šenov), and with others. From 1841, he produced about 100 different drinking glass models in clear, cut, engraved, and enamel-painted crystal and, subsequently, lighting fixtures and mirrors in bronze and crystal, as well as the first electrified chandeliers, in 1883. On Josef Lobmeyr the elder's 1855 death, his sons Josef the younger (1828–1864) and Ludwig (1829–1917) became the managers of the firm, and, soon after, the firm became known as J. & L. Lobmeyr. Ludwig Lobmeyr designed as well as served as the principal director of the firm after his brother Josef's 1864 death. Ludwig commissioned designs from Viennese designers, including architect Theophil von Hansen, and was associated with the Österreichisches Museum für angewandte Kunst (founded in 1864). Known for its fine craftsmanship and high aesthetic standards, the firm supplied the Austrian court and aristocracy with services and began producing mousselin glass designed by Ludwig Lobmeyr in 1856. At this time, Lobmeyr's products were in historicist designs, although its drinking glasses were sometimes simple and austere. 1902, Ludwig Lobmeyr's nephew Stefan Rath (1876–1960) took over management of the firm, when production consisted of Art Nouveau and later Art Moderne styles. The work of Wiener Sezession codirector Josef Hoffmann was commissioned by Rath; some of Hoffmann's are still in production, including models TS 238 and TS 240 in glass chiffon (black lacquer on mouth-blown glass with two different etched motifs). Adolf Loos's unadorned 1931 Service water pitcher and glasses (no. 248, with Oskar Strnad) were made by Lobmeyr. A number of other commissioned designers and engravers followed. 1938, Rath's son Hans Harald Rath (1904–1968) became manager of the Viennese headquarters. 1948, the Steinschönau workshop was nationalized by the Czech government, where Stefan stayed until 1951. 1968, the firm was taken over by Hans Harald Rath's sons Harald (1938–), Peter (1939–), and Hans Stefan (1943–), the latter chiefly a lighting designer. More recent designers have included Monica Flood-Grimburg, Matteo Thun, Jaromir Tisljar, and Paul Wieser. The firm remains active.

J. & L. Lobmeyr: Oswald Haerdtl. Ambassador Service wine decanter. 1925. Mouth-blown muslinglass, overall h. 15 1/2 x dia. 5 3/8" (39.4 x 13.7 cm). Mfr.: J. & L. Lobmeyr, Austria. Given anonymously. MoMA.

Bibliography Stephan Rath, *Lobmeyr*, Vienna, 1963. Cat., *150 Jahre Österreichische Glaskunst: Lobmeyr 1923–1973*, Vienna, 1973. W. Neuwirth, *Orientalisierende Gläser von J. und L. Lobmeyr*, Vienna, 1981. Leslie Jackson, *20th Century Factory Glass*, London: Octopus, 2000.
> See Rath, Stephan (1876–1960).

Locatelli, Antonio
> See Studio Pro

Lock, Josef Michael (1875–1964)

German sculptor and designer; born Jagstfeld.

Biography Lock's silver designs were produced by Bruckmann & Söhne in Heilbronn, where he was artistic director and also a teacher in Bruckmann's school.
Bibliography Annelies Krekel-Aalberse, *Art Nouveau and Art Déco Silver*, New York: Abrams, 1989: 137–38, 175, 257. Reinhard W. Sänger, *Das deutsche Silber-Besteck*, Stuttgart: Arnoldsche: 1991: 156–57.

Locke, Joseph (1846–1936)
> See Libbey Glass.

Lötz Witwe (Glassfabrik Johann Lötz Witwe)

Bohemian glassware factory; located Klostermühle.

History 1836, a glassmaking facility was established in Klášterský Mlýn, Bohemia (now Klostermühle, Germany) by Johann Baptist Eisner von Eisentein. From 1843, his son-in-law Friedrich Hafenbrädl directed the operation and in turn, 1849, sold the firm to Eisner's brother-in-law Martin Schmid. 1851, it was bought by Dr. Franz Gerstner (1816–1855) and his wife Susanna (1809–1887) and, 1852, she became the sole proprietrix. She was formerly married to Johann Lötz (1778–1848), who had operated a glassworks in Goldbrunn. On Lötz's 1848 death, or possibly initiated before his demise, the Lötz factory in Klostermühle was operated by his wife under the name Glasfabrik Johann Lötz-Witwe ('widow Johann Lötz's glassworks' in English). 1879, she passed it on to her grandson Max Ritter von Spaun (1856–1909). Under Ritter's guidance and the efforts of managing director Eduard Prochaska (1851–1922), Lötz flourished, expanded, updated the facilities, and gained international recognition by winning prizes at world's fairs. It began to produce early imitations of semi-precious stones, including jasper, aventurine, and chalcedony. It also produced Art Nouveau vessels based on Tiffany's 'favrile' (or *glaser à la Tiffany*, an iridescent-glass technique or type of carnival glass), including tableware, vases, rosewater sprinklers, lamps, and candlesticks in a vivid range of colors. It made the glass shades for Gustav Gurschner's bronze-sculpture lamps. Prochaska (at Lötz to 1914) also designed some products. Its commissioned designers included Franz Hofstätter, Robert Holubetz, Antoinette Krasnik, Koloman Moser, and Jutta Sika. Leopold Bauer created more than 60 models. From 1905, Lötz shifted from the Art Nouveau style, and Josef Hoffmann, Otto Prutscher, and Adolf Beckert designed for the firm. 1898–1920s, Lötz was contracted to produce glass for Lobmeyr. 1908, von Spaun's son, also named Max, assumed directorship of the firm, which became insolvent in 1911 and was reorganized as a new entity in 1913: Johann Lötz Witwe GmbH. Adversely affected by a 1930 major factory fire and the Great Depression, all production eventually stopped in 1948.
Exhibitions/citations First showed wares at 1878 *Exposition Universelle*, and received grand prizes at the 1889 and 1990 editions; all Paris.
Bibliography Cat., Dr. G. Woeckel, *Jugendstilsammlung*, Kassel: Staatliche Kunstsammlungen, 1968. Cat., *Loetz Austria*, Munich: Stuck-Villa, 1972. H. Hilschenz, *Das Glas des Jugendstils*, Munich, 1973: 390–91. *L'art verrier à l'aube du XXe siècle*, Lausanne: Galerie des Arts Décoratifs, 1973: 73–79. *Objekte des Jugendstils*, Bern: Benteli, 1975. Alastair Duncan, *Art Nouveau and Art Déco Lighting*, New York: Simon & Schuster, 1978: 123–24. Waltrand Neuwirth, *Loetz Austria 1905–1918*, Vienna: 1986. Leslie Jackson, *20th Century Factory Glass*, London: Octopus, 2000.

Loewy, Raymond Fernand (1893–1986)

French designer; born Paris; active Paris and New York.

Training In electrical engineering in Paris.
Biography 1909, Loewy designed, built, and sold a successful airplane model; 1919, settled in New York, where he was employed for a short time as a windowdresser at R.H. Macy & Co. department store; c. 1923–28, was a fashion illustrator—one of his main clients was magazine *Harper's Bazaar*; designed 1923 trademark for Neiman

Johann Lötz-Witwe. Vase. c. 1895. Iridescent glass, h. 5 1/2 x dia. 3 1/2" (14 x 8.9 cm). Mfr.: Glasfabrik Johann Loetz Witwe, Austria. Joseph H. Heil Bequest. MoMA.

Marcus department store in Texas and advertisements for Kayser hosiery and a 1928 fashion brochure for Bonwit Teller store in New York. His first significant industrial design was the 1929 redesigned casing of a duplicating machine by Sigmund Gestetner, using modeling clay to give a sleek shape, a technique later employed by others in the design of automobile bodies. However, his boastful touting of streamline styling, like in his 1933 pencil-sharpener prototype, was more for publicity's sake than to demonstrate a scientifically valid function. His interest in car design was illustrated by 1934 Hupmobile and, for Studebaker, 1947 Champion, 1953 European-styled Starline coupé, and 1962 Avanti. Also designed 1934 Sears Coldspot refrigerator cabinet, his first major achievement; 1934 Purma Special acrylic-plastic camera by Purma Camera Ltd. (England); 1936 Argus A for International Research, Michigan, the first mass-produced American 35mm camera; 1940 redesign of Lucky Strike cigarette package. 1936–52 with Carl Otto, he designed for British manufacturers, from a London office; 1951, established CEI (Compagnie de l'Esthétique Industrielle), Paris (managed by Pierre Gautier-Delaye 1951–58). His work included packaging, Coca Cola dispensers (1943 counter-mounted is most notable), locomotive engines and passenger-car interiors, Greyhound coaches, 1967–72 interiors for NASA's Skylab. He and/or his staff designed the interior of US President Kennedy's Boeing 707 Air Force One airplane. Other work, through various cities' Loewy studios, included postage stamps, trademarks, radios, electric shavers, china, textiles, furniture. Dinnerware by Rosenthal included 1967 Aries and 1954 Service 2000 (with Richard Latham). By 1937, Loewy's staff included 38 architects, technicians, and engineers; in 1939, 100; in 1951, over 140. Thus, much of the work credited solely to Loewy himself was designed by others with his possible supervision, including the automobile bodies. His books include *The Locomotive: Its Esthetics* (London: The Studio, 1937), *Never Leave Well Enough Alone* (New York: Simon & Schuster, 1951, subsequently translated into numerous languages), and *Industrial Design* (Woodstock, N.Y.: Overlook, 1979). He died in Monte Carlo.
Exhibitions/citations Work subject of 1976 *The Designs of Raymond Loewy*, Renwick Gallery, Washington, D.C.; 1990–91 *Raymond Loewy: Pioneer of American Industrial Design*, organized by International Design Zentrum, Berlin, and touring. 1939, was elected Honorary Royal Designer for Industry, UK.
Bibliography C.F.O. Clarke, 'Raymond Loewy Associates: Modern American Industrial Designing,' *Graphis*, vol. 2, Jan.–Feb. 1946: 94–97. David Pleydell-Bouverie and Zlec Davis, 'Popular Art Organised: The Manner and Methods of Raymond Loewy Associates,' *Architectural Review*, vol. 110, Nov. 1951: 319–26. Cat., *The Designs of Raymond Loewy*, Washington, D.C.: Renwick Gallery, 1976. Cat., Angela Schönberger et al., *Raymond Loewy: Pioneer of American Industrial Design*, Munich: Prestel, 1990. Philippe Tretiack, *Raymond Loewy and Streamlined Design*, New York: Universe, 1999. Mel Byars, 'Raymond Fernand Loewy,' in John A. Garraty et al. (eds.), *Oxford American Biography*, New York: Oxford, 1999. Mel Byars with Arlette Barré Despond, *100 Designs/100 Years: A Celebration of the 20th Century*, Hove: RotoVision, 1999: 80–81.
> See CEI (Compagnie de l'Esthétique Industrielle).

Heinreich Löffelhardt. Teapot (part of a service). 1959. Mouth-blown heat-resistant glass, h. 5 1/4" (13.3 cm).Mfr.: Jenaer Glaswerk, Schott & Gen., Germany. Gift of the mfr. MoMA.

Löffelhardt, Heinrich (1901–1979)

German ceramics and glassware designer; born Heilbronn.

Training 1920–23, in silversmithing at Bruckmann & Söhne, Heilbronn; 1924–28 under Georg Kolbe, in sculpture, Berlin.
Biography 1929–36, Löffelhardt was active as a sculptor; 1937–41, worked at the Vereinigte Lausitzer Glaswerke in Weisswasser under its artistic director Wilhelm Wagenfeld. After World War II, Wagenfeld arranged for Löffelhardt's appointment as director of design at Landesgewerbeamt (district trade and craft offices) in Stuttgart. Succeeding Hermann Gretsch, 1952–54, Löffelhardt was artistic director of Arzberg and of Schönwald porcelain factories, his work following closely Gretsch's prewar models, including 1954 Arzberg 2000, 1953 Schönwald 411, 1957 Arzberg 2025, 1958 Schönwald 511, 1961 Schönwald 498, and 1963 Arzberg 2075 dinner services. Succeeding Wilhelm Wagenfeld, 1954–77, he was design director of Jenaer Glaswerk, Schott & Genossen in Mainz and its affiliate company Vereinigte Farbglaswerke in Zwiesel. At Vereinigte Lausitzer, he was responsible for a number of utility glass ranges considered innovative in 1950s–60s. He continued as a consultant designer with Schott & Genossen, working for its utility glass and lighting divisions. He designed the 1959 range of heat-resistant borosilicate glass (similar to Wagenfeld's), in-

Raymond Loewy Associates. Communications receiver (no. S-40A). 1947. Steel casing, 8 7/8 x 18 1/2 x 9 5/8" (22.5 x 47 x 24.5 cm). Mfr.: The Hallicrafters Co., US. Gift of the mfr. MoMA.

State Porcelain Factory (aka Lomonosov Porcelain Factory). Nikolai Suetin. Teapot. c. 1923. Porcelain with overglaze painted decoration, h. 4 1/2" (14 cm) x diam. 4 1/2" (11.4 cm). Mfr.: State Porcelain Factory, USSR (now Russia). Estée and Joseph Lauder Design Fund. MoMA.

cluding a tea set, cups and saucers, plates, and bowls. While mass production caused Löffelhardt's early glassware to be discontinued, 240 million units of his Neckar white-wine glass by Vereinigte Farbglaswerke had been sold by 1978. He died in Stuttgart.
Exhibitions/citations Work subject of 1980 *In Memoriam Heinrich Löffelhardt...* in Karlsruhe. The dishes and Arzberg dinnerware included in 1983–84 *Design Since 1945* (dishes and Arzberg dinnerware), Philadelphia Museum of Art; *Glass of the Avant-Garde*, traveling from 2001. (All catalogs below.) Grand prizes (for 1959 Arzberg 2050 dinnerware and 1955 redesign of Wagenfeld's heat-resistant dishes), 1960 (12th) Triennale di Milano; prizes (for Arzberg dinnerware), 1961 and 1962 Salone Internazionale della Ceramica, Vicenza.
Bibliography Cat., *In Memoriam Heinrich Löffelhardt, 1901–1979: Design für die Glas und Porzellanindustrie*, Karlsruhe: Badisches Landesmuseum, 1980. Cat., Kathryn B. Hiesinger and George H. Marcus III (eds.), *Design Since 1945*, Philadelphia: Philadelphia Museum of Art, 1983. Cat., Torsten Brohan and Martin Eidelberg, *Glass of the Avant-Garde: From Vienna Secession to Bauhaus*, Munich: Prestel, 2001.

Löffler, Berthold (1874–1960)

Austrian painter, designer, ceramicist, illustrator, and graphics artist; born Nieder-Rosenthal (Ružodol, Czech Republic).

Training Under F. Matsch the elder and Koloman Moser, Kunstgewerbeschule, Vienna.
Biography From 1900, Löffler was a painter and graphic designer; 1909–35, was a professor, Kunstgewerbeschule, Vienna, where he taught Oscar Kokoschka; 1906 with Michael Powolny, cofounded Wiener Keramik, a high point in the decorative phase of late Art Nouveau. The workshop produced ceramics for the Wiener Werkstätte, showing folkloric influences, including some Russian. The workshop's tiles were installed in some of Josef Hoffmann's commissions (Kabaret Fledermaus, Sanatorium Purkersdorf, and Palais Stoclet). Löffler was also known for his distinctive poster designs in 1910s; was one of the initial members, Österreichischer Werkbund; died in Vienna.
Exhibitions Work subject of 1978 and 2000 venues in Vienna (catalog of the latter below).
Bibliography Günther Feuerstein, *Vienna—Present and Past: Arts and Crafts—Applied Art—Design*, Vienna: Jugend und Volk, 1976. Cat., *Berthold Löffler*, Hochschule für angewandte Kunst, Vienna, 1978. Robert Waissenberger, *Vienna 1890–1920*, Secaucus, N.J.: Wellfleet 1984. Cat., *Berthold Löffler*, Vienna: Universität für angewandte Kunst, 2000

Lohmann, Jan (1944–)

Danish metalworker.

Training 1966–68, in a workshop in Switzerland.
Biography 1968, Lohmann set up his own workshop, Copenhagen; 1976, studied on tours to Peru, Mexico, Guatemala, Ecuador, and New York.
Exhibitions/citations Work was included in 1974 exhibition, Det Danske Kunstindustrimuseum, Copenhagen; 1975–77 *Danske Miljø*, Eastern Europe; 1978 and 1980 exhibitions, Gallery for Contemporary Silver and Goldsmith's Art, Copenhagen. Received 1966 silver medal from Goldsmiths' Guild; 1972, 1976, and 1978 Goldsmiths' Guild Scandinavian Design Award.
Bibliography Cat., David Revere McFadden (ed.), *Scandinavian Modern Design 1880–1980*, New York: Abrams, 1982.

Lomazzi, Paolo (1936–)
> See De Pas, Gionatan.

Lomonosov Porcelain Factory (aka Imperial Porcelain Factory, and State Porcelain Factory)

Russian ceramics factory; located St. Petersburg.

History The Imperial Porcelain Factory, located on what is now the Obukhovskoii Oboronii Prospekt in St. Petersburg, was established in the first half of the 18th century. Its early production, exclusively for the imperial court, included dinner services, vases, figurines, presentation services, and furnishings for royal residences and yachts. From World War I, it also produced wares for the army and its hospitals. 1917, the facility was renamed the State Porcelain Factory, and, 1925, again reverted to the Lomonosov Porcelain Factory, named for scientist Mikhail Vasil'evich Lomonosov (1711–1765). After the Nov. 1917 Bolshevik Revolution, the factory's operation was briefly under the Commissariat of Agriculture and, from 1918, under Narkompros (the people's commissariat for enlightenment). At this time, Sergei Chekhonin, a consultant to the Commissariat of Agriculture, organized a group to discuss the problems of the artistic industries in the country. IZO NKP (fine-arts department of Narkompros) was involved in the factory's production, and David Shterenberg (IZO NKP's head), along with energetic reformers Petr Vaulin and Chekhonin, were the directors of the factory. There were 12 workers in the painting section and 100 factory workers. The artists in 1918 included Mikhail Adamovich, Rudolf Vilde, Grigori Zimm, Vasilii Timorev, Varvara Freze, Yelizaveta Rozendorf, Elena Danko, Mariia Ivashintsova, Elizaveta Potapova, and Aleksandra Shehekotikhina-Pototskaia. 1918, Zinaida Kobiletskaia (who had previous worked there 1912–14) rejoined the staff. 1919, Ekaterina Bolsheva, Liubov' Gaush, Alisa Golenkina, Mariia Kirilova, Mariia Lebedeva, Varvara Rukavishnikova, and others joined the staff. The established artists, who created designs for the State Porcelain Factory, included Natan Al'tman, Veniamin Belkin, Mstislav Dobujinskii, Vladimir Lebedev, Vasilii Kandinsky, and Valentin Sherbakov. The factory also applied Agitprop designs onto the porcelain blanks of the pre-revolutionary period. However, there were a few silhouettes exclusive to the post-Revolution period by Kazimir Malevich and Nikolai Suetin, some being reproduced today by the original factory.
Bibliography Nina Lobanov-Rostovsky, *Revolutionary Ceramics*, London: Studio Vista, 1990. Cat., Ian Wardropper, *News from a Radiant Future: Soviet Porcelain from the Collection of Craig H. and Kay A. Tuber*, Chicago: Art Institute of Chicago, 1992. Cat., Deborah Sampson Shinn, *Soviet Porcelains (1918–1985)*, New York: Cooper-Hewitt National Museum of Design, 1992.

Loos, Adolf (1870–1933)

Moravian architect and designer; born Brünn (now Brno, Czech Republic); active Austria.

Training Reichenberg Polytechnik and Technische Hochschule, Dresden.
Biography 1893–96, Loos traveled in America and worked as a mason and floorlayer; saw the work of the Chicago School of architects such as William Le Baron Jenny, Burnham and Root, and Louis Sullivan; 1896, settled in Vienna and began to write and work as a designer and architect, turning away from the Wiener Sezession style and abandoning all decoration and ornamentation. His first series of articles condemned the aesthetics of painter Gustav Klimt and the styles of Joseph Maria Olbrich and Josef Hoffmann; they were published in journal *Neue Freie Presse* (1897–98). He codified his thesis in the seminal essay 'Ornament und Verbrechen' (ornament and crime) (1908). Loos worked for a time with architect Otto Wagner and admired Scottish architects Charles Rennie Mackintosh and Hugh Baillie Scott; his own architecture drew on neoclassicism and Karl Friedrich Schinkel's work. Loos's 1910 Steiner house was one of the first domestic dwellings in reinforced concrete and included many innovations

such as a new use of internal space, pure straight lines, horizontal windows, and Cubist solids. 1920–22, he was in charge of municipal housing in Vienna and entered his visionary Doric-column project in the 1922 *Chicago Tribune* competition. 1923–28, he lived in Paris, where he designed the 1926–27 house and interior of Dadaist artist Tristan Tzara, with African masks, tube lighting over the doors, and 17th-century chairs. Other Loos structures included 1906 Karma house (renovation) in Clarens, near Montreux, 1907 Kärntner Bar in Vienna, 1910 commercial block on the Michaelerplatz in Vienna, 1922 Rufer house in Vienna, 1928 Möller house in Pötzleinsdorf, 1930 Kuhner house in Payerback, and 1930 Müller house in Praha-Stresovice. The latter, for I. František Müller and his wife Milada, expresses Loos's desire for completely functional surroundings, his *Raumplan* (space planning), and usage of midlevel floors. Loos felt that the house was his most beautiful, but its realization ran into trouble with bureaucratic approval due to its austerity. Loos claimed, 'The building must be dumb on the outside and reveal its wealth on the inside.' 1948, the house was seize by the new government to become a storage space for the Uměleckoprůmyslové Muzeum in Prague, later as a publishing house, and finally as headquarters of the Marxist-Leninist Institute. The Müllers and their daughter Eva were assigned to only a bedroom and the study. Dr. Müller died in 1951, and his wife lived there until her 1968 death. Through the intervention of Leslie Van Duzer (see 1994 book below), great give-and-take, and high-profile publicity through the international press, the city of Prague acquiesced in 1995, paid 30 million koruna ($1 million) for the house, and turned it over to the Muzeum Hlavního Města of Prague, which organized an impressive, thorough restoration led by architect Václav Girsa (1945–). Apart from Loos's architecture, he designed little; a 1899 bentwood chair for the Café Museum by J. & J. Kohn (now by Thonet), and the starkly simple 1931

Adolph Loos. Side chair. 1899. Steam-bent beech wood and cane, 34 x 17 7/16 x 20 7/16" (86.4 x 44.3 x 51.9 cm), seat h. 17 13/16" (45.2 cm). Mfr.: J. & J. Kohn, Austria. Estée and Joseph Lauder Design Fund. MoMA.

Service water pitcher and glasses (no. 248, with Oskar Strnad) by Lobmeyr, originally for Loos's 1907 American Bar on Kärntner Durchgang, Vienna, continue to be produced. For his own use, he chose 18th-century furniture.

Bibliography Adolf Loos, 'Ornament und Verbrechen' essay, Vienna, 1908 (in Adolf Loos, *Ornament and Crime: Selected Essays*, Riverside, Cal.: Ariadne, 1998). A. Marilaun, *Adolf Loos*, Vienna-Leipzig: WILA, 1922. Bruno Taut, J.J.P. Oud et al., *Adolf Loos, Festschrift zum 60: Geburtstag, am 10. Dezember 1930*, Vienna: Richard Lanyi, 1930. H. Kulka, *Adolf Loos, das Werk des Architekten*, Vienna: Anton Achroll, 1931. Ludwig Münz and Gustave Künstler, *Adolf Loos: Pioneer of Modern Architecture*, London: Thames & Hudson, 1966. Dorothee Müller, *Klassiker des modernen Möbeldesign: Otto Wagner—Adolf Loos—Josef Hoffmann—Koloman Moser*, Munich: Keyser, 1980. Berkhard Rukschcio and Roland Schachel, *Adolf Loos—Leben und Werk*, Salzburg/Vienna: Residenz, 1982. Adolf Loos, *Spoken into the Void: Collected Essays*, Cambridge, Mass.: MIT, 1982. Cat., Yehuda Safran and Wilfried Wang, *The Architecture of Adolf Loos*, London: Arts Council of Great Britain, 1985. Rukschcio Burkhardt, *Adolf Loos, Leben und Werk*, Salzburg and Vienna: Residenz, 1987. Gabriele Leug, *Design im 20. jahrhundert*, Cologne: Museum für angewandte Kunst, 1989: 67. Eva B. Ottillinger, *Adolf Loos: Wohnkonzepte und Möbelentwürfe*, Salzburg: Residenz, 1994. Kent Kleinman and Leslie Van Duzer, *Villa Müller: A Work of Adolf Loos*. New York: Princeton Architectural Press, 1994. Ivana Edwards, 'Adolf Loos's Multilevel Masterpiece: The Müller House,' *Metropolis*, Feb. 2001.

Looze, Hervé de
> See de Looze, Hervé.

Lorena, Eliana (1957–)

Italian designer; born Novara; active Milan.

Training 1975–78, art history, Università Statale, Milan.
Biography 1977, Lorena began her career with Fiorucci, then went on to the Centro Design department of Montefibre, both Milan. 1979–86, she worked in the studios of Andrea Branzi and of Castelli Design; 1989, with husband Aldo Petillo, established MCA&Partners.
> See Petillo, Aldo.

Lorenz, Anton (1891–1964)

Hungarian furniture designer and manufacturer; active Berlin.

Biography 1928, Anton Lorenz joined the firm Standardmöbel Lengyel shortly after its formation in Berlin by Marcel Breuer and Kálmán Lengyel. This furniture venture was not successful, and Breuer sold his rights to the firm, although his 1927–28 designs were not transferred to the firm. 1928, Lorenz began to produce his own-designed upholstered steel armchairs, including his patent no. 348590, often mistakenly attributed to Breuer. Breuer's famous B32 and B34 chairs with and without arms were produced by Standardmöbel and also by Thonet, with which Breuer had entered into an agreement in 1928 for slightly different versions. 1929, Thonet bought Standardmöbel. A 1929 lawsuit between Lorenz and Thonet was based on Thonet's assertion that rights to Breuer's cantilever chair were to be included in the Standardmöbel sale. Lorenz's newly formed firm Deutsche Stahlmöbel (DESTA) was included in the dispute. 1930, Lorenz won the suit and, 1932, secured an injunction to stop Thonet producing the L32 and L34 cantilever chairs; Thonet thereafter produced the chairs under a license agreement with Lorenz. Lorenz discontinued his own production and concentrated on selling his rights to the chairs abroad, while Thonet was in charge of their production. 1931, Lorenz lodged a complaint with the firm C. Beck und A. Schultze (CEBASCO) in Ohrdruf concerning chairs designed by Erich Dieckmann. CEBASCO signed a license agreement with Lorenz that lasted to 1934. Lorenz also claimed that the production of a chair designed by Heinz Rasch and produced by L. und C. Arnold infringed Lorenz's 1929 patent; since the chair was proved to have been produced from 1928, the claim was dropped. In a 1933 court case between Fritz Hansen and the Lorenz-Thonet team, the latter's copyright was upheld. 1934, Gispen won in a case concerning the cantilevering principle brought against Gispen by Thonet in Rotterdam. Lorenz-Thonet also lost a 1934 case against A.W. Nilsons Fabriker in Malmö. Because of the volume of production in foreign countries, it was not possible for Lorenz to keep his hold over the cantilevering principle. Though DESTA was closed in 1933, Lorenz used the firm's name to 1935. Late 1930s, he settled in the US and, after World War II, introduced his highly popular Barca Lounger. He died in the US.

Ross Lovegrove. Agaricon table lamp. 2001. Polycarbonate with silk-opaque treatment, h. 11 x dia. 15¾" (28 x 40 cm). Mfr.: Luceplan, Italy.

Exhibitions Lorenz's 1928 model upholstered steel armchairs shown at 1931 *Deutsche Bauausstellung* (German building exhibition), Berlin.
Bibliography Barbie Campbell-Cole and Tim Benton, *Tubular Steel Furniture*, London: The Art Book Company, 1979: 13, 20. Otakar Máčel, 'Avant-Garde Design and the Law: Litigation over the Cantilever Chair,' *Journal of Design History*, vol. 3, nos. 2 and 3, 1990: 125–32.

Louis, Armand
> See Atelier Oï.

LOV (Labor Omnia Vincit)
Dutch furniture manufacturer; located Oosterbeek.

History 1910, Oosterbeeksche Meubelfabriek LOV (Labor Omnia Vincit, or work conquers all) was established by G. Pelt, who wished to bring about social and political reform and to based LOV's organization on 'copartnership,' whereby the employees participated in the company management and worked in the factory under safe and healthful conditions. An enthusiastic proponent of the machine, Pelt was not sympathetic with Morris's views on the ennoblement of craftsmanship. Nevertheless, LOV products were largely handmade and, thus, quite expensive, with an extensive use of mahogony and walnut. H.F. Mertens, who was the factory manager from 1911, designed demountable bent tubular-steel furniture for Loeb's UMS furniture factory. The firm used numerous consultant designers such as J. Crouwel, J.B. van Loghem, A.H. Jansen, and C. Alons. Though never avant-garde, LOV's furniture reflected current trends. The factory executed large orders for the Rotterdam City Hall and the Troelstra resort in Beekbergen. 1935, the plant closed, and Pelt's original goal to make inexpensively constructed and reliable workers' furniture was never realized.
Bibliography Cat., *Industry and Design in the Netherlands, 1850–1950*, Amsterdam: Stedelijk Museum, 1985.

Lovegrove, Ross (1958–)
Welsh designer; born Cardiff.

Training To 1980, Manchester Polytechnic; 1983, master's degree in design, Royal College of Art, London.
Biography 1980s, Lovegrove worked at frogdesign in Altensteig, Germany; was a consultant to Knoll International in Paris and then joined Atelier Nîmes, consulting to Cacharel, Louis Vuitton, Hermès, Du Pont, and others; designed 1991 FO8 stacking one-piece fiberglass side chair by XO. Other work has included 1993 prototype zircon-Y (ceramic) razor by K.L. Laboratories; 1995 DAF, RL, and Apollo chairs and Teso table and 1997 Bluebell armchair (much like a George Nelson version) by Driade; 1997 Magic cantilevered chair by Fasem; 1999 Go aluminum-polycarbonate chair by Bernhardt; 1998 Pod lamp by Luceplan; 1999 Fluidium lamp (update of the Lava lamp) by Mathmos; 1999 and 2000 kitchenware by Hackman Tools. Other clients: Alias, Apple Computers, British Airways, Cappellini, Fratelli Guzzini, Kartell, Knoll, Herman Miller, Mazda, Moroso, Olympus cameras, Philips, Pottery Barn, Sony Research, Tag Heuer. Some of his design forms have been influenced by English sculptor Henry Moore; however, others are more Rational. He was the editor, *The International Design Yearbook* (London: Laurence King, 2002).
Exhibitions/citations Work in 1995 *Mutant Materials*, New York; 2000–03 *Aluminum by Design*, organized by Carnegie Art Museum, Pittsburgh, and touring (catalogs below). Also at Axis Center, Japan; Centre Georges Pompidou, Paris; Design Museum, London; Solomon R. Guggenheim Museum; New York. Elected fellow, Chartered Society of Designers; numerous other citations.
Bibliography Cat., Paola Antonelli, *Mutant Materials in Contemporary Design*, New York: The Museum of Modern Art/Abrams, 1995. Mel Byars with Arlette Barré-Despond, *100 Designs/100 Years: A Celebration of the 20th Century*, Hove: RotoVision, 1999. Cat., Sarah Nichols et al., *Aluminum by Design*, New York: Abrams, 2000.

Low Art Tile Works, J. and J.G.
American ceramic tile manufacturer; located Chelsea, Mass.

History John Gardner Low (1835–1907) worked at Chelsea Keramic Art Works in early 1870s and painted vases in a classical Greek style. Inspired by 1876 Philadelphia *Exposition*, he and his father John Low founded the firm J. and J.G. Low in 1877 and various family members became managers subsequently. After 1883, it was renamed J.G. and J.F. Low. The firm was the first to combine art with mass production in its decorative tiles; 1883, began to produce vessels. 1889, J.G. Low patented the 'natural process,' employed in England from 1840, of pressing leaves, fabrics, and flowers into clay tiles; he later discovered that the same patterns could be pressed into a second clay tile to realize an intaglio version. 1878, Low hired George W. Robertson, who had worked at the Chelsea Keramic Art Works. 1880s, British sculptor Arthur Osborne was one of Low's artists. Low's wares were sold through more than 30 distributors in the US. Its tiles were applied to fireplace surrounds and walls, and for various ornamental purposes, including clocks. Magee Art Castings of Chelsea, Mass., produced Low's brass- and metalwork, including umbrella stands and picture frames. Low's tiles were used on the cast-iron stove under the name Art Westminster produced by Rathbone, Sard and Co. of Albany, N.Y. Low produced elaborate ceramic soda fountains for drugstores. 1902, the firm stopped production.
Exhibitions/citations Silver medal, 1879 *Industrial Exposition*, Cincinnati; gold medal, a 1880 British competition. Work shown at 1882 exhibition, Fine Art Society, London; and subject of 1903 exhibition, Worcester Art Museum, Worcester, Mass., US.
Bibliography Everett Townsend, 'Development of the Tile Industry in the United States,' *Bulletin of the American Ceramic Society*, vol. 22, May 15, 1943: 129. Lura Woodside Watkins, 'Low's Art Tiles,' *Antiques*, vol. 45, May 1944: 250–52. Julian Barnard, *Victorian Ceramic Tiles*, Greenwich, Conn., 1972. Barbara White Morse, 'The Low Family of Chelsea, Massachusetts, and Their Pottery,' *Spinning Wheel*, vol. 33, Sept. 1977: 28–33. Doreen Bolger Burke et al., *In Pursuit of Beauty: Americans and the Aesthetic Movement*, New York: The Metropolitan Museum of Art/Rizzoli, 1986: 449–50.

Löw, Glen Oliver
> See Citterio, Antonio.

Lown, Aaron (1968–)
American designer.

Biography Lown came to prominence with the 1994 Hi Ho prototype stool in sand-cast aluminum and leather. Other work has included 2003 BYO Bag (for transporting wine to a party, in scuba suit material) by Built NY and Safe Condom Keeper (produced with Krohn Design). Built NY is a design/manufacturing firm directed by Lown, John Roscoe Swartz, and Carter Weiss.
Exhibitions Hi Ho stool included in 1995 *Mutant Materials*, New York, and traveling; 2000-03 *Aluminum by Design*, organized by Carnegie Art Museum, Pittsburgh, and touring (catalogs below).
Bibliography Cat., Paola Antonelli, *Mutant Materials in Contemporary Design*, New York: The Museum of Modern Art/Abrams, 1995. Cat., *Aluminum by Design*, Pittsburgh: Carnegie Art Museum, 2000.

Loy, Mina (b. Mina Gertrude Lowy 1882–1966)
American writer, designer, actress, and model; born London.

Biography From late 1920s, Loy worked in her shops in Paris and New York, somewhat financially supported by Peggy Guggenheim. Loy produced hundreds of lamps and lampshades with her daughter Joella; subsequently, sold the enterprise due to its interferring with

her writing and painting and also possibly due to her being not good at business. She claimed, and some sources verify, that her lamps were frequently plagiarized. One of her best known is the distinctive Calla Lilly table lamp of c. 1927. Loy was also a photographic model for Man Ray, a stage actress, and the only female member of the Futurist group. She has only recently been widely acknowledged as an accomplished poet. In an often-quoted 1921 letter from Ezra Pound to Marianne Moore, he ironically inquired, '... is there anyone in America except you, Bill [William Carlos Williams] and Mina Loy who can write anything of interest in verse?' Her first book of poems was published in 1923, followed by segments of her long autobiographical poem 'Anglo-Mongrels and the Rose' (1923–25) and others.
Bibliography Corolyn Burke, *Becoming Modern: The Life of Mina Loy*, New York: Farrar, Straus & Giroux, 1996. Maeera Shreiber and Keith Tuma (eds.), *Mina Loy: Woman and Poet*, Orono, Maine: National Poetry Foundation, 1998.

Lubs, Dietrich (1938–)

Industrial designer; born Berlin.

Biography From 1970s as a design director with Dieter Rams, Lubs has designed products by Braun, particularly timepieces, including 1979 ET 33 calculator (with Rams), 1980 ABW 21 quartz clock/barometer, 1982 ABW 30 wall clock, 1987 ST 1 calculator, 1989 AB 313 rsl travel clock, 1987 ST 1 credit-card size calculator, 1989 AW 10 wristwatch, 1990 ET 88 calculator, 1992 AW 50 wristwatch, and, more recently, 1998–2001 ThermoScan plus IRT 3520.

Lucchini, Alberto Valento (1947–)

Italian designer; born Cuneo; active Milan.

Biography 1972, Lucchini began his professional career, when he began designing for Sormani (furniture, accessories, and lighting) and Brevetto (heavy industry) Other clients: magazine *Nuovi Orizzonti* of the Italian tourist board (graphic design) from 1973, Mopoa (clocks) from 1974, Velca Legnano (furniture) from 1975, and Gabbianelli (tableware) from 1975. He is a member, Associazione per il Disegno Industriale (ADI).
Citations Designed furniture for 1972 Interieur biennial competition, Courtrai, Belgium. Honorable mention, 1973 International Pottery Design Competition.
Bibliography *ADI Annual 1976*, Milan: Associazione per il Disegno Industriale, 1976.

Lucci, Roberto (1942–)

Italian designer; born Milan.

Training 1960–61, Institute of Design, Chicago; 1962–64, Corso Superiore Disegno Industriale, Venice.
Biography Lucci and Paolo Orlandini (1941–) worked with Marco Zanuso and Richard Sapper to 1973, when they began their independent studio, serving a number of clients within their studio Lucci Orlandini Design. Extensive work has included lamps and chairs by Artemide, Martinelli Luce, and Segno; products by Antonelli and ArcLinea; television sets by Brionvega; refrigerators by Candy-Kelvinator; furniture by Magis; and office furniture by Velca. Other work: fully recyclable, low-cost, lightweight chairs with synchronized self-adjusting back supports, most notable of which are 1992 A1000 by Lamm/Shelby Williams, 1994 Soho by Knoll, and 2000 Chela chair by Versteel/Lamm. From 1974, they have taught, Istituto Europeo di Design, Milan, and at universities in Australia, Brazil, Belgium, Colombia, Italy, New Zealand, Switzerland, and the US. Codesigned-work: more than 350 products, including chairs of which more than three million units have been produced.
Exhibitions Work shown at editions of Triennale di Milano, Chicago Athenaeum, and Museum für Kunst und Gewerbe in Hamburg.
Bibliography Robert A.M. Stern (ed.), *The International Design Yearbook*, New York: Abbeville, 1985/1986. Roberto Lucci and Paolo Orlandini, *Product Design Models*. New York: Van Nostrand Rein-hold, 1990. Charlotte and Peter Fiell, *1000 Chairs*, Cologne: Taschen, 1997. *Modo*, no. 148, Mar.–Apr. 1993: 121. Mel Byars, *50 Chairs...*, Hove: RotoVision, 1996. Mel Byars, *50 Beds...*, Hove: RotoVision, 2000.

Luce, Jean (1895–1964)

French ceramicist and glassware designer; born Paris.

Biography Luce worked in his father's ceramics shop, which made table crockery; 1923, opened his own shop, although he was not able to take over its direction until 1931. From 1931, specialized in ceramics and glass for the table and concentrated on the double problem of shape and decoration; painted by hand or from stencils in linear and naturalistic motifs in a spare Art Moderne manner, highlighted with gold for the luxury pieces. His early work included clear enameled decoration, and, from c. 1924, was sandblasted. He designed porcelain and glass for 1935 oceanliner *Normandie,* adopted by the Compagnie Générale Transatlantique for their other ships; early 1930s, designed glassware by Cristalleries de Saint-Louis and, late 1950s, stainless-steel cutlery by Sola France; 1937, became a member, Union des Artistes Modernes (UAM); taught, École des Arts Appliqués, Paris; was a technical advisor to Manufacture Nationale de Sèvres. Mid-1980s, Les Verreries de la Rochere reproduced Luce's mouth-blown drinking glasses from original designs of c. 1925. 1988–91, an earlier coffee-tea set was reproduced by Lumen Center.
Exhibitions 1921, work first shown, at Musée Galliéra, Paris, and, subsequently, at editions of Salon d'Automne and, from 1914, of Société des Artistes Décorateurs. Was a juror, 1925 *Exposition Internationale des Arts Décoratifs et Industriels Modernes* and 1937 *Exposition Internationale des Arts et Techniques dans la Vie Moderne* (with work included in the UAM pavilion); both Paris. Was responsible for glassware/plate section of 1949–50 (1st) *Formes Utiles*, Pavillon de Marsan, the Louvre, and exhibited in its 1953 and 1958 editions.
Bibliography Victor Arwas, *Art Déco*, Abrams, 1980. *Les carnets du design*, Paris: Mad-Cap Productions/APCI, 1986: 40. Arlette Barré-Despond, *UAM*, Paris: Regard, 1986: 456–58, Cat., *Les années UAM 1929–1958*, Paris: Musée des Arts Décoratifs, 1988: 220–21.

Luceplan

Italian lighting firm; located Milan.

History 1978, Luceplan was founded by architects Riccardo Sarfatti, his wife Sandra Severi Sarfatti, and Paolo Rizzatto; produces lighting for the home, office, public spaces, and showrooms; takes a sophisticated approach and calls on advanced technology and materials; is environmentally aware. Some models may be years in the development in its high-tech facilities. The firm invests heavily (7%) on research and development; employs over 70 people. Its inventory has included 1984 Berenice, 1986 Constanza, and 1989 Titania by Alberto Meda and Rizzatto, and 1994 Lucilla by Rizzatto. Recent fixtures include 2001 Carrara floor lamp by Alfredo Häberli and 2001 Agaricon table lamp by Ross Lovegrove. From 1995, Luceplan has been Italy's third largest lighting manufacturer.
Citations 1981, 1987 (two citations), 1989, 1991, 1994 (two citations) Premio Compasso d'Oro; 1988 Lampe d'Argent and 1990 Lampe d'Or, Concours de la Création Artistique, Salon International du Luminaire (SIL), Paris; 1988 Forum Design Prize, Cosmit, Milan; 1992 Design Plus prize, Ambiente fair, Frankfurt; 1992 Product Award, 1991 Light-ing Fair, New York; 1994 European Community Design Prize; 1995 and 1996 awards, Industrie Forum Design (iF), Hanover; 1999 prize, SWIATLO '99, Warsaw.
Bibliography 'Materials and Design,' *Domus*, no. 756, Jan. 1994. Mel Byars, *50 Lights...*, Hove: RotoVision, 1997. 'Light Stories,' *DDN*, no. 45, Oct. 1996. 'The New Way of Doing Business,' *Lighting Design*, Oct. 2003.

Lucet, Maurice (1877–1941)
> See Lahalle, Pierre.

Lucini, Ennio (1934–)

Italian packaging, product, and graphic designer; active Milan.

Biography Lucini has designed small objects for the home in ceramics and glass by Gabbianelli, metalware by Barazzoni, hemispherical Ponte di Brera drinking glasses (from 1965 by Ponte di Brera, 1968–75 by Gabbianelli), and 1968 Tummy stainless-steel cooking pots by Barazoni. His extensive client list includes La Rinascente-Upim, Anonima Castelli, Bossi Tessuti, Central Adams, Christian Dior, De.Bi., Du Pont, Estée Lauder (Aramis and Clinique cosmetic ranges), Fanini Fain, Fiori, Fratelli Guzzini, Fratelli Rossetti, Gabbianelli (ceramics and glass), Les Galeries Lafayette store in Paris, Gavina, Henraux Marmi, Istituto Commercio Estero, Istituto Franco Tosi, Lema Lidman, Ligure Lombarda, Malferrari, Mc. IN Comifan, Midy, Mira Lanza, Pierrel, Pirelli, Poltrona Frau, Poggi, Prodotti Roche, Richard Ginori, Rootes Autos, Saifi, Schiffini, Snia Viscosa, Sorgente dei Mobili, Stella Unitex, Vefer, Itres, Paolo Barazzoni, and P.A. Bonacina. He coordinated corporate-image programs for Anonima Castelli, Barazzoni, Cafecrem, C. Broumand, Centro Duchamp, Itres, Ligure Lombarda, Fanini Fain, Falconi,

Luceplan: Paolo Rizzatto. Constanzina table lamp (no. D13pi). 1992. Silk-screen polycarbonate and aluminum, overall h. 20 1/4 x dia. 9 7/8" (51.4 x 25.1 cm). Mfr.: Luceplan, Italy. Gift of the mfr. MoMA.

Galeries Lafayette, Mc. IN Comifan, Palazzo Durini, and Ponte di Brera. He was a graphic designer for magazines *Design Italia*, *Forme*, *Pacco*, and *Stilitaria* and, 1975–80, art director of *Domus*. He became a member, Associazione per il Disegno Industriale (ADI); cofounder, Art Directors Club Milano (ADCM); 1968, taught graphic design, Scuola Umanitaria, Milan.
Exhibitions/citations Work shown at 1968 (14th) Triennale di Milano; the various Eurodomus fairs in Ljubljana in the past; 1983–84 *Design Since 1945* (Tummy range and Ponte di Brera glasses), Philadelphia (catalog below). Received 1979 Premio Compasso d'Oro (for Tummy pots by F.lli Barazzoni).
Bibliography *ADI Annual 1976*, Milan: Associazione per il Disegno Industriale, 1976. 'Designers d'oggi: Ennio Lucini,' *Interni*, Apr. 1979: 54–55. Cat., Kathryn B. Hiesinger and George H. Marcus III (eds.), *Design Since 1945*, Philadelphia: Philadelphia Museum of Art, 1983. Carla Caccia, 'Parliamo di design con... Ennio Lucini,' *Arredorama*, Jan. 1983: 9–14.

Luckhardt, Wassili (1889–1972); Hans Luckhardt (1890–1954)

German architects and designers; both born Berlin; brothers.

Training Wassili: Technische Hochschule, Berlin-Charlottenburg, and in Munich and Dresden. Hans: Technische Hochschule, Karlsruhe.
Biography The Luckhardts were signatories of the 1919 Architecture Program issued by the Arbeitsrat für Kunst and contributed letters and drawings to the 'Utopian Correspondence' of Bruno Taut. 1921–54 in Berlin, they worked in partnership, for a time from 1924, with Alfons Anker (1872–1958). Their first Expressionist structures were 1921 Museum for Hygienics in Dresden and 1922 Institutsgebäude, Berlin-Zehlendorf. Other buildings included 1926–27 Hirsch office building, Berlin; 1928–29 Telschow house, Berlin; 1929 Alexanderplatz rearrangement projects, Berlin-Mitte, Berlin pavilion at 1951 *Constructa-Ausstellung*, Hanover; 1933 Medical College, Preßurg (now Bratislava, Slovakia), and, one of their last, 1958 Institut für Pflanzenphysiologie, Berlin-Zehlendorf. From mid-1920s, they took a Rationalist approach; however, their most accomplished plans were not built due to being thwarted by World War II. Continuing to work in Berlin after the war, their unornamented designs showed a certain elegance, with well-defined silhouettes. They designed notable bent tubular-steel furniture. From 1952, Hans was a professor at Hochschule für bildende Künste, Berlin, and, from 1956, Wassili at Akademie der bildenden Künste, Berlin. Hans died in Bad Wiessee, and Wassili in Berlin.
Exhibitions Work co-subject of 1990 exhibition, Akademie der Künste, Berlin (catalog below).
Bibliography Udo Kultermann (ed.), *Wassili und Hans Luckhardt: Bauten und Entwürfe*, Tübingen: Ernst Wasmuth, 1958. Hans Luckhardt, letters in *Die Gläserne Kette: Visionare Architekturen aus dem Kreis um Bruno Taut 1919–1920*, Berlin: Akademie der Künste, 1963. Helga Kliemann, *Wassili Luckhardt*, Tübingen: Ernst Wasmuth, 1973. Vittorio Magnago Lampugnani (ed.), *Encyclopedia of 20th-Century Architecture*, New York: Abrams, 1986: 204. Cat., *Brüder Luckhardt und Alfons Anker*, Berlin: Akademie der Künste, 1990.

Ludvika, Smrčková (1903–1991)

Czech glass artist, painter, and graphic designer.

Training Under Emil Dítě, V.H. Brunner, and František Kysela, Vysoká Škola Uměleckoprůmyslová (VŠUP, academy of arts, architecture, and design); and Univerzity Karlovy (Charles University); both Prague.
Biography She began her career in glass under Brunner, following the simple shapes of Constructivism shown at the 1925 Paris *Exposition*; 1928–48, taught, Czech secondary schools in Příbor, Litomyšl, Kladno, and Prague; from 1928, was a member, Czechoslovakian Werkbund (SČSD); 1930–48, worked mainly for the firm Ruckel in Nižbor; collaborated with the agency Krásná Jizba (the beautiful room) and introduced simple, dynamic shapes (often formed by cutting the edges) into table glassware; 1930s, designed vases and bowls with geometric cut motifs and, from 1948, for the firms Inwald and Skloexport and for the Center of Glass Industry and Fine Ceramics in Prague; 1960s–70s, she experimented with engraved and painted glass; was also active in painting, graphics, book design, and book-binding design.
Awards Grand prize, 1935 *Exposition Universelle et Internationale de Bruxelles*; grand prize and gold medal, 1937 *Exposition Internationale des Arts et Techniques dans la Vie Moderne*, Paris.
Bibliography Alena Adlerová, *České užité umění 1918–1938*, Prague: Odeon, 1983. Cat., *Tschechische Kunst der 20+30 Jahre, Avantgarde und Tradition*, Darmstadt: Mathildenhöhe, 1988–89.

Lukens, Glen (1887–1967)

American ceramicist and teacher; born Cowgilll, Mo.

Training Under Myrtle French, ceramics, Art Institute of Chicago.
Biography Lukens's development of a potter's wheel by adapting a sewing machine was noticed by the US Surgeon General, who thus hired him to direct a pottery program to help rehabilitate solders wounded in World War I; by 1924, taught craft courses in California; from 1936 to mid-1960s, was a professor of ceramics, School of Architecture, University of Southern California. In his own work, he used desert stones and oxides to produce unusual, strong yellow, turquoise,

Ennio Lucini. Mangiafumo ashtray. 1968. Ceramic, h. 2 3/8 x dia. 4 3/4" (6 x 12.1 cm). Mfr.: Gabbianelli, Italy. Gift of the mfr. MoMA.

and green colors in earthenware and thick glazes.
Exhibitions/citations Work shown at 1937 *Exposition Internationale des Arts et Techniques dans la Vie Moderne* (representing West Coast of US), Paris; 1939–40 *New York World's Fair: The World of Tomorrow*. Organized first (1938) all-California *Ceramic Art Exhibition*. First prize (for Yellow Bowl), 1936 *National Ceramic Exhibition*, Syracuse, N.Y., US.
Bibliography Cat., Janet Kardon (ed.), *Craft in the Machine Age 1920–1945*, New York: Abrams with American Craft Museum, 1995.

Lumiance

Dutch lighting manufacturer.

Biography Harry Swaak founded Lumiance (formerly Hiemstra Evolux) in Haarlem and was the CEO. The firm's name is a contraction of French words LUMIère and ambiANCE. Leo Krol (1955–), who had worked at Frans de la Haye and at Philips to 1989, joined the Lumiance design studio. The product line has included 1993 Primostar Pino table lamp by Ronald Meijs (1962–), models by Bonini Spicciolato Associates, and numerous others. Lumiance became a brand within the Sylvania Lighting International group.
Exhibitions/citations 1996 *Contemporary Dutch Design from the Netherlands* (1993 Primostar Pino), The Museum of Modern Art, New York. A number of awards, including 1994 European Design Competition and a large number of citations from Industrie Forum Design (iF), Hanover. Swaak himself received 1983 Amsterdamse Kunstprijzen, Amsterdams Fonds voor de Kunst; 2001 Red Dot award (for Pixo halogen spots), Design Zentrum Nordrhein Westfalen, Essen. Swaak with Chris Hemistra: 1983 Kho Liang Ie Prijs.

Lumina
> See Cimini, Tommaso.

Lunar Design

Industrial design studio; located Palo Alto and San Francisco, Cal.

History 1985, Lunar Design was founded; currently employs a large staff of designers, engineers, and marketing people. Jeff Smith is the CEO, and John Edson, president. 1990–99, Dave Laituri was a partner and senior designer. Work has included 2001 Xootr eX3 light-weight electrical scooter (designed with Technique Applied Science and Nova Cruz) and 1999 Hewlett-Packard slim Pavilion 2755C personal computer. Other clients have included BSA, Philips, Microsoft, and Sunrise Technologies.
Exhibitions/citations 1995 *Mutant Materials* (Lush Lily set), The Museum of Modern Art, New York, and traveling (catalog below). From Lunar Design's founding: 1998–2000, over 200 awards from Good Design, Chicago Athenaeum; Annual Award Reveiw, *I.D.* magazine; Industrie Forum Design (iF), Hanover; American Institute of Graphic Design (AIGA) awards; *Print* magazine; Premio SMAU Industrial Design, Salone della Machina e Attrezzature per l'Ufficio, Milan; *form* magazine; Industrial Designers Society of America (IDSA); and others, including Design of the Decade (1990s) two silver citations, IDSA/*Business Week* magazine.
Bibliography Cat., Paola Antonelli, *Mutant Materials in Contemporary Design*, New York: The Museum of Modern Art/Abrams, 1995. www.lunar.com.

Lund, Johan (1861–1939)

Norwegian designer and silversmith; active Christiania (Kristiania from 1877, Oslo from 1925) and Drammen.

Biography Lund designed and executed silver by David-Andersen around the time of the firm's shift from *champlevé* and *cloisonné* enamel to *plique à jour*, a technique in which Lund worked at the turn of the century. 1894–98, he was director, Norsk Filigransfabrik. 1899, settled in Drammen.
Exhibitions Oil lamp by David-Andersen with a large *plique-à-jour* shade included in the Norwegian stand at 1893 *World's Columbian Exposition*, Chicago.
Bibliography Annelies Krekel-Aalberse, *Art Nouveau and Art Déco Silver*, New York: Abrams, 1989.

Lundin, Ingeborg (1921–1991)

Swedish glassware designer; active Stockholm.

Training 1941–46, Kungliga Tekniska Högskolan/Konstfackskolan, Stockholm.
Biography 1947–71, Lundin worked at the Orrefors Glasbruk. Her 1955 Äpplet (apple) vase epitomized her dynamic blown-glass work as well as the best aspects of 1950s Scandinavian modern style. Other glass works included 1954 Timglas (hourglass) and 1954 Bamby vases. Her subtle forms well exploited the plasticity and quality of crystal.
Exhibitions/citations Work subject of 1959 exhibition in Stockholm; included in 1957 (11th) and 1960 (12th) editions of Triennale di Milano, 1954–57 *Design in Scandinavia*, touring the US; 1955 *H 55*, Hälsingborg; 1958 *Formes Scandinaves*, Musée des Arts Décoratifs, Paris; 1957 exhibition, Zürich; and 1959 exhibition, Amsterdam. 1954 Lunning Prize.
Bibliography Cat., David Revere McFadden (ed.), *Scandinavian Modern Design 1880–1980*, New York: Abrams, 1982. Cat., *The Lunning Prize*, Stockholm, Nationalmuseum, 1986: 58–61. Helmut Ricke and Lars Thor, *Schwedische Glasmanufakturen*, Munich: Prestel, 1987.

Lunning Prize

Danish-American design award.

History Frederik Lunning, who previously served as the head of the shop of Georg Jensen Sølvsmedie in Copenhagen, established the branch of the Georg Jensen Sølvsmedie in 1923 in New York. Based on an idea of Kaj Dessau and marking the 70th birthday of Lunning, he established the Lunning Prize in 1951 in his own name with the intention of stimulating design excellence in the decorative arts. Over a two-decade period, its recipients included Hans J. Wegner and Tapio Wirkkala, 1951; Carl-Axel Acking and Grete Prytz-Kittelsen, 1952; Tias Eckhoff and Henning Koppel, 1953; Ingeborg Lundin and Jens H. Quistgaard, 1954; Ingrid Dessau and Kaj Franck, 1955; Nanna and Jørgen Ditzel and Timo Sarpaneva, 1956; Hermann Bongard and Erik Höglung, 1957; Paul Kjærholm and Signe Persson-Melin, 1958; Arne Jon Jutrem and Antti Nurmesniemi, 1959; Torun Bülow-Hübe and Vibeke Klint, 1960; Bertel Gardberg and Erik Pøen, 1961; Hertha Hillfon and Kristian Vedel, 1962; Karin Björquist and Börje Rajalin, 1963; Vuokko Eskolin-Nurmesniemi and Bent Gabrielsen, 1964; Eli-Marie Johnsen and Hans Krondahl, 1965; Erik Magnussen and Kristi Skintveit, 1967; Björn Weckström and Ann and Göran Wärff, 1968; Helga and Bent Exner and Börje Lindau and Bo Lindekrantz, 1969;

Wassili Luckhardt and Hans Luckhardt. Side Chair (no. ST14). 1931. Tubular steel and molded plywood, 34 5/8 x 21 3/16 x 24 3/16" (88 x 53.8 x 61.5 cm). Mfr.: Deutsche Stahlmöbe (DESTA), Germany. Museum purchase. MoMA.

Per Lütken. Dish. 1952. Light-blue glass, dia. 11 13/16" (30 cm). Mfr.: Holmegård Glasværk, Denmark. Courtesy Quittenbaum Kunstauktionen, Munich.

Kim Naver and Oiva Toikka, 1970. 1970, the prize was discontinued.
Bibliography Cat., *The Lunning Prize*, Stockholm: Nationalmuseum, 1986.

Lunt Silversmiths; A.F. Towle & Son Company

American metalware manufacturer; Greenfield, Mass.

History William Moulton 4th (1814–), of a family of Massachusetts silversmith reaching back to late 17th century, began making silver cutlery and hollow-ware for the daughters and wives of the sea captains and gentry on the Massachusetts coast. Anthony F. Towle moved from Hampton, Mass., and became an apprentice under Moulton in Newburyport. 1855 with William P. Jones, Towle established an independent smithy; subsequently, purchased Moulton's business and, 1857, formed Towle and Jones. 1890 with his son, Towle moved the smithy to Greenfield, Mass. At Towle and Jones in 1882, George C. Lunt was an apprentice engraver under Towle the elder. Later, Lunt studied design and modeling with sculptor Max Bachman in Boston, after which he returned to A.F. Towle & Son Company as a designer. 1902, Lunt founded Lunt Silversmiths and purchased the factory, dies, tools, and trademarks of A.F. Towle & Son; was the treasurer, general manager, and chief designer of the new firm. 1901, Rogers, Lunt & Bowlen Company was established, alongside Lunt Silversmiths, both of which are still in family hands. 2000, Lunt Silversmiths acquired French cutlery/hollow-ware/housewares manufacturer Dasso Group with its Couzon, Cuisinox, and Durol brands. Currently, Lunt manufactures over a thousand different items such as Embassy Scroll cutlery, chosen as the official tableware for all US embassies and consulates worldwide. For over 25 years, Nord Bowlen (1909–), who had studied industrial design at Rhode Island School of Design in Providence, was head of Lunt's design department. His work included the commercially unsuccessful 1954 Contrast sterling silver cutlery with black injection-molded nylon handles.
Bibliography 'Annual Design Review,' *Industrial Design*, Dec. 1956: no. 148. Cat., Kathryn B. Hiesinger and George H. Marcus III (eds.), *Design Since 1945*, Philadelphia: Philadelphia Museum of Art, 1983.

Lurçat, André (1894–1970)

French architect and furniture designer; born Bruyères, Vosges; brother of Jean Lurcat.

Training 1911–13, École Municipale des Beaux-Arts; 1918–23, École Nationale Supérieure des Beaux-Arts, Paris.
Biography 1928, André Lurçat cofounded Congrès Internationaux d'Architecture Moderne (CIAM) and was head of its commission on urbanism. His 1920s furniture was in geometrical forms influenced by Cubism, as was his architecture. In France, he designed pioneering structures such as 1925–26 Seurat artist studios in Paris, 1925 Gromaire house in Versailles, 1926 Bomsel house in Versailles, 1926–27 painter Guggenbuhl's house on the rue Nansouty in Paris, and 1927 sculptor Froriep de Sallis's house in Boulogne-Billancourt. Many of his unrealized domestic buildings were radical for the time and the country. 1930, he published the manifesto *Architecture*, built the Hôtel Nord-Sud in Calvi on the Mediterranean, and joined a Marxist group that focused on urbanism. He designed 1931–33 École Karl-Marx primary school in Villejuif, near Paris, with frescoes by his brother Jean Lurçat. 1932, he opened his own architecture office in Paris; 1929, became a member, Union des Artistes Modernes (UAM). He was fervent admirer of and frequent visitor to the Soviet Union, studied architecture there with others of the Villejuif group, and was the only foreign architect allowed to compete for the USSR Sciences Academy Building competition. His interest in monumentality and axiality was reflected in his buildings for the reconstruction of Maubeuge and the renovation of Saint-Denis after World War II, and in his essay *Formes, composition et lois d'harmonie* (1953–57).
Exhibitions First showed the Seurat artist studios, at an edition of Salon d'Automne. Participated in 1925 *Exposition Internationale des Arts Décoratifs et Industriels Modernes*, Paris; in 1925 opening of the Bauhaus in Dessau; in exhibition of Viennese plastic arts in France.
Bibliography André Lurçat, 'Urbanisme et architecture,' *L'architecture d'aujourd'hui*, no. 1, May–June 1945. 'André Lurçat,' *Architecture, mouvement, continuité*, no. 40, 1976: 5–38. Jean-Louis Cohen, 'L'architecture d'André Lurçat (1894–1970), autocritique d'un moderne,' doctoral thesis, Paris: École des Hautes Études en Sciences Sociales, 1985. Arlette Barré-Despond, *UAM*, Paris: Regard, 1986: 452–53. Cat., *Les années UAM 1929–1958*, Paris: Musée des Arts Décoratifs, 1988: 222–23. *Andre Lurçat architecte, l'œuvre lorraine*, (Itinéraires du Patrimoine, no. 94), Metz: Serpenoise, 2000. Martine Joly, *L'architecte André Lurçat*, Paris: Picard, 2000.

Lurçat, Jean (1892–1966)

French painter and tapestry designer; born Bruyères (Vosges); brother of André Lurcat.

Training From 1912 infrequently, École Nationale Supérieure des Beaux-Arts; Académie Colarossi; atelier of graveurist Bernard Naudin; all Paris.
Biography 1912, Jean Lurçat settled in Paris; 1913, founded a journal with three friends; 1917, designed his first two tapestries, *Filles vertes* and *Soirée dans Grenade*, made by his mother; 1919, left for Geneva. 1920, he visited Berlin, Munich, and Rome and worked with Victor Prouvé in Nancy; from 1920, lived on the rue Nollet, Paris, where he met Pierre Chareau, for whom he later produced tapestries for the Bernheim family's Château de Villefix and for Chareau's Maison de Verre, Paris. 1921, designed sets and costumes for Georges and Ludmilla Pitoëff's dance company and, subsequently, for others, including (having traveled to New York) the new American Ballet Company. 1940, he met François Tabard; after seeing the 14th-century *Apocalypse* tapestry in Angers, became devoted to textile work and revived medieval techniques and a nomenclature of colors and fringes. From 1957, he produced a large number of hangings including *Le chant du monde*. Was also active as a painter, lithographer, ceramicist, and wallpaper designer. c. 1930, he joined Union des Artistes Modernes (UAM).1959, composed the ceramic-mosaic façade of the Église de Maubeuge (architect, André Lurçat), Paris; 1965, traveled to Mexico and Greece. He died in Saint-Paul-de-Vence.
Exhibitions Rugs in the Myrbor stand at 1925 *Exposition Internationale des Arts Décoratifs et Industriels Modernes*, Paris. Work subject of 1953 exhibition, Musée Réattu, Arles; 1992 *Jean Lurçat: le combat et la victoire: Aubusson 92: centenaire*, Aubusson; 1944, 20 tapestries, Galerie Carré, Paris; participated in 1962 (1st) Biennale Internationale de la Tapisserie, Lausanne. 1959, was elected a member, Escola das Artes, Portugal, and Académie Royale, Belgium.
Bibliography *Jean Lurçat: Tapestries = Jean Lurçat: tapisseries*, Eind-

hoven: printed by Lecturis, 1971. *Sammlung Bröhan: Kunst der 20er und 30er Jahre*, vol. 3, Berlin: Karl H. Bröhan, 1985. Arlette Barré-Despond, *UAM*, Paris: Regard, 1986: 454–55. Gérard Denizeau and Simone Lurçat, *L'œuvre peint de Jean Lurçat: catalogue raisonné, 1910–1965*, Lausanne: Acatos, 1998.

Luthersson, Petur B. (1936–)

Icelandic furniture, interior, and lighting designer.

Biography Luthersson designed the interiors of private and public spaces and has been Iceland's most important furniture designer. His domestic and office furniture was produced in wood and metal. A 1969 aluminum hanging light was produced by Amundi Sigurdhsson in Reykjavik, and a wide range of other lighting, in spun aluminum.
Bibliography Cat., David Revere McFadden (ed.), *Scandinavian Modern Design 1880–1980*, New York: Abrams, 1982.

Lütken, Per (1916–1998)

Danish glassware designer; active Copenhagen.

Training 1937, painting and technical drawing, Kunsthåndværkerskolen, Copenhagen.
Biography From 1 May 1942, Lütken became the design director at Holmegård Glasværk, succeeding former design director Jacob Bang and for a time pursuing Bang's modern forms. However, Lütken became inspired by 1950s editions of the Triennale di Milano and went on to introduce major changes in Holmegård's production and style. He applied hot metal to formed glass shapes. As one of Denmark's most important glass designers, his work incorporated fluid forms in lightly colored glass, some with etching that produced a satin finish. When Kastrup Glasværk merged with Holmegård in 1965, he remained at Holmegård to manage a large staff. Lütken wrote the book *Glass Is Life* (Copenhagen: Nyt Nordisk/Arnold, 1986) about his being inspired and challenged by glass over five decades.
Exhibitions Participated in 1951 (9th) Triennale di Milano. Work was included in the 1954–57 *Design in Scandinavia*, touring the US; 1956–59 *Neue Form aus Dänemark*, touring Germany; 1958 *Formes Scandinaves*, Musée des Arts Décoratifs, Paris; 1960–61 *The Arts of Denmark*, touring the US; 1962 *Creative Craft in Denmark Today*, New York; 1980 *Scandinavian Modern Design 1880–1980*, Cooper-Hewitt National Design Museum, New York; 1983–84 *Design Since 1945*, Philadelphia Museum of Art (catalog below). Work subject of 1992 *Fifty Years Seen Through Glass: Per Lütken*, Glasmuseet, Ebeltoft, Denmark.
Bibliography *150 Years of Danish Glass*, Copenhagen: Kastrup & Holmegård Glassworks, nos. 209–37, [n.d.]. Arne Karlsen, *Made in Denmark*, New York: Reinhold, 1960: 50–55, 119. 'Per Lütken,' in *DB&D*, Copenhagen: Danish Society of Arts and Crafts and Industrial Design, 1972: 21–22. Erik Lassen and Mogens Schlüter, *Dansk Glas: 1925–1975*, Copenhagen: Nyt Nordisk/Arnold, 1975. Cat., David Revere McFadden (ed.), *Scandinavian Modern Design 1880–1980*, New York: Abrams, 1982. Jennifer Hawkins Opie, *Scandinavia: Ceramics and Glass in the Twentieth Century*, New York: Rizzoli, 1989.
> See Holmegård Glasværk.

Lutyens, Candia

British entrepreneur; granddaughter of Edwin Lutyens.

Biography 1990, Lutyens set up a firm to reproduce Edwin Lutyens's sofas, chairs, and tables. Production included his 1928 Pall Mall and 1931 Spiderback chairs, both originally designed for a London plumbing company showroom; the c. 1900 mahogany-and-upholstered so-called Napoleon chair used in his own house; and 1930 New Delhi Circleback chair for the Viceroy's house in India.
Bibliography Cat., *Lutyens: The Work of the English Architect Sir Edward Lutyens*, London: Arts Council, 1981. Suzanne Slesin, 'Lutyens's Furniture from the Originals,' *The New York Times*, 25 July 1991: C3.

Lutyens, Edwin Landseer (1869–1944)

British architect and designer; born London.

Training 1885–87, South Kensington School of Art, London.
Biography 1887, Lutyens worked under architect Ernest George in the firm George and Peto, where he met Herbert Baker, later a colleague in New Delhi. He was influenced by Richard Norman Shaw and Philip Webb. Edward Hudson publicized the work of the young Lutyens in *Country Life* magazine. His earliest designs were for garden furniture. For his first married home, in Bloomsbury, Lutyens designed most of the few furnishings within the sparse setting, and later returned repeatedly to those initial furniture themes. Historicist pieces for the house included an oak refectory table with heavy pillar supports, and a four-poster bed and dressing table. 1889, he received his first architecture assignment and set up his own practice. His approach embraced the Arts and Crafts movement, Queen Anne, English Regency, Mughal, and neoclassicism. Lutyens's 1906–12 Folly Farm in Sulhampstead, Berkshire, broke new ground in its architecture and interior design, incorporating crisp white painted woodwork and ceilings, glossy black walls, red fretwork, and lacquered furniture. Among his extensive furniture designs was a wooden garden settee with the characteristics of padded upholstery, still in production and widely produced and published. 1905, he designed 21 chairs for the boardroom of *Country Life*. By the end of World War I, his furniture had become bolder, and his ideas about decorating uncompromising. Lutyens's eccentric taste was expressed in his residence on Mansfield Street in London, which included his own-designed chairs inspired by Napoleon's *méridiennes*, with one arm lower than the other to accommodate a draped leg. He was the architect of 1919–20 Cenotaph in London; 1921–24 Queen Mary's dolls' house (a miniaturized structure); 1926 Thiepval Arch war memorial on the Somme; many English country houses and one in Normandy, France. His 1912–31 large complex of government buildings, New Delhi, including Viceroy's House, resulted in his best-known examples of massively scaled lighting, tables, and chairs. For smaller rooms in the viceroy's residence and minor offices, his hand was freer: in the nursery, there were light-hearted chandeliers with animal cut-outs, and an amorphous clock. Another clock had hands that extended as they rounded the oval dial. Furniture and lighting for the 1928–31 offices of sanitary-fittings firm Crane Bennet on Pall Mall, London, were reinterpretations of some of the New Delhi designs. Furniture for 1934–35 Reuters and Press Association building, London, reflected the designs for his own house in Bloomsbury almost 40 years earlier. 1942, he conceived the 'RA Plan for London,' based on the 1938 Bressey-Lutyens Report. From 1938, he was president of the Royal Academy.
Architecture Numerous Arts and Crafts-style country houses in England, including Deanery Garden in Sonning; the neo-baroque houses 1906 Heathcote in Ilkley and 1905–08 Nashdom in Taplow; English Free Style work at Hampstead Garden Suburb in London; and neo-Georgian houses. After World War I, he designed commercial and government buildings, including 1924–39 Britannic House, the Midland Bank head office, and townhouses, all in London. 1930s, his major commission was the Metropolitan Cathedral of Christ the King in Liverpool, in a style reminiscent of Christopher Wren that Lutyens called 'Wrenaissance.' It was to be the world's second-largest Christian church, and Lutyens was prepared for construction to take 100 years. The foundation stone was laid in 1933; most of the crypt was completed by 1939; work was abandoned in 1941; costs after World War II prohibited completion of the Lutyens design. Other commissions included 1933–36 Champion Hall, and 1937–38 Middleton Park (with Robert Lutyens), both in Oxford. His only house in France (Varengeville-sur-Mer), commissioned by banker Guilliaume Mallet in 1898, is surrounded by the 24-acre (9.7-hectare) garden Bois des Moutiers, created by him and Gertrude Jekyll.
Exhibitions/citations 18 in (13.2 m) model for 1929 Liverpool cathedral shown at 1934 exhibition, Royal Academy, London; and, with drawings and photographs of New Delhi, at 1979–80 *Thirties* exhibition, Hayward Gallery, London (catalog below). Work subject of 1978 exhibition, The Museum of Modern Art, New York, and 1981 *Lutyens: The Work of the English Architect Sir Edwin Lutyens (1869–1944)*, London. 1918, knighted; 1921 gold medal, Royal Institute of British Architects (RIBA); 1924 medal, American Institute of Architects (AIA); 1933, was made a master of Art-Workers' Guild; 1942 Order of Merit.
Bibliography Edwin Lutyens, 'What I Think of Modern Architecture,' *Country Life*, vol. 69, 1931: 775–77. A.S.G. Butler, with George Stewart and Christopher Hussey, *The Architecture of Sir Edwin Lutyens*, London: Country Life, 1950. Christopher Hussey, *The Life of Sir Edwin Lutyens*, London: Country Life, 1950. Cat., *Thirties: British Art and Design Before the War*, London: Arts Council of Great Britain/Hayward Gallery, 1979. Cat., *British Art and Design, 1900–1960*, London: Victoria and Albert Museum, 1983. Stephen Calloway, 'Lutyens as Furniture Designer,' *Christie's International Magazine*, February 1991: 6–10. Jane Brown, *Lutyens and the Edwardians: An English Architect and His Clients*, London/New York: Viking, 1996.

Elizabeth Wilhide and Candia Lutyens, *Sir Edwin Lutyens: Designing in the English Tradition*, New York: Abrams, 2000.

Luxton, John (1920–)

British glassware designer.

Training 1936–39, Stourbridge School of Art; 1946–49, Royal College of Art, London.
Biography 1949, Luxton began designing cut-glass crystal for Stuart & Sons, including tumblers glasses in robust silhouettes. The Edge picture frame and some vases are still in production: Prism vases and Edge tumbler/vase. These 1950 designs, discovered in a old Stuart portfolio, were returned to production and supervised by Luxton while in his 80s, and he recently designed a new range, though in retirement.
Bibliography Frederick Cooke, *Glass: Twentieth-Century Design*, New York: Dutton, 1986: 78.

Lycett, Edward (1833–1910)

British ceramicist; born Newcastle-under-Lyme; active New York.

Training Under Thomas Battam, apprenticeship at an early age at Copeland and Garrett, Stoke-on-Trent.
Biography 1852, Lycett worked in Battam's decorating shop in London, where he painted copies of Greek vases in the British Museum; 1861, settled in New York and opened his own decorating workshop on Greene Street, where about 40 people eventually worked. At first he painted earthenware vases produced by Williamsburg Terra Cotta, Long Island, N.Y., and painted imported Sèvres and Haviland porcelain blanks. Known for his raised goldwork and rich over- and underglazed dark blue, he was adept at rendering realistic images of fish, birds, fruit, and vegetables. 1865, he was commissioned by John Vogt to paint the monogrammed china service (on the blanks by another designer) of US president Abraham Lincoln. Late 1860s, Lycett added classrooms to his workshop, offering women's pottery-painting lessons. His firm produced painted washbasins and porcelain panels incorporated into furniture. Architect Richard Morris Hunt commissioned Lycett to decorate large enameled-iron panels for 1871–73 Van Rensselaer building, New York. Lycett left his son William in charge of the workshop while he taught china painting at St. Louis School of Design in 1877 and in Cincinnati. At this time, the studio was known as Warrin and Lycett. 1879–82, he was active in a china-painting workshop at 4 Great Jones Street with partner John Bennett. 1884–90, Lycett was artistic director of Faience Manufacturing Co., Brooklyn, N.Y., experimenting with fine-grade white porcelain and producing iridescent metallic glazes on Persian lusterware. 1890, he retired to Atlanta, Ga., to assist his son William, who had set up a china-painting workshop there in 1883.
Exhibitions Work for Copeland and Garrett shown at 1851 *Great Exhibition of the Works of Industry of All Nations*, London; other work in 1878 exhibition of Cincinnati Women's Art Museum.
Bibliography Edwin Atlee Barber, 'Recent Advances in the Pottery Industry,' *Popular Science Monthly*, no. 40, Jan. 1892: 297–98. Edwin Atlee Barber, *The Pottery and Porcelain of the United States...*, New York: Feingold & Lewis, 1893. Doreen Bolger Burke et al., *In Pursuit of Beauty: Americans and the Aesthetic Movement*, New York: The Metropolitan Museum of Art/Rizzoli, 1986.

Lynggaard, Finn (1930–)

Danish ceramicist and glassware designer.

Training 1951–55, painting and ceramics, Det Kongelige Danske Akademi in Copenhagen.
Biography 1958, Lynggaard set up his own ceramics workshop and much later became a pioneer in Danish studio glass. He attributes his turning to glass to nights spent in 1971 in the hot-glass workshop of Sheridan College, Oakville, Ontario, Canada, where he was a guest ceramics instructor. His glass work is known for its deeply colored floral motifs on clear grounds. 1985, he founded the Glasmuseet in Ebelstoft, a town where he has a studio with his wife Tchai Munch (1954–). He wrote the books *Kyohei Fujita: The Man and His Work* (Copenhagen: Bogen, 2001), *Glas—en introduktion* (Copenhagen: Borgen, 2002), and others; is a member, International Council, Pilchuk Glass School, Stanwood, Wash., US.
Exhibitions Participated in 1960 (12th) Triennale di Milano. Work included in 1960–61 *The Arts of Denmark*, touring the US; numerous others subsequently.
Bibliography Cat., David Revere McFadden (ed.), *Scandinavian Modern Design 1880–1980*, New York: Abrams, 1982. F. Lyngaard-Sködt, *Finn Lynggaard: the grand old man i europaeisk glas*, Ebeltoft: Glasmuseet, 1994.

Lyons, Susan (1954–)

American textile designer; born New York.

Training 1976, bachelor of art's degree, Williams College, Williamstown, Mass.
Biography 1976 with two other Williams College students, Lyons founded Alliance Editions for textile-printing design; 1979–84, designed for Clarence House and Boris Kroll Fabrics; from 1989, has been director of design at Design Tex, New York, and, with William McDonough, designed 1992 environmentally safe upholstery.
Citations 2000 Design Sense award (with Rohner Textile and William McDonough), Design Museum, London.
Bibliography Cat., R. Craig Miller (intro.), *U.S. Design 1975–2000*, Munich: Prestel, 2002.

Lyons, William (1901–1985)

British automobile entrepreneur and designer; born Blackpool.

Biography 1922, Lyons began his automotive career with the building of motorcycle sidecars; subsequently, produced special bodywork for a number of British mass-produced automobiles; 1922, established Jaguar Cars Ltd.; 1948, introduced what was to become a classic, the Jaguar XK120 roadster with a twin overhead camshaft six-cylinder engine; also styled the SS and all Jaguar saloons himself until and including the first XJ. From the 1959 Mark IX, the saloons were fitted with sumptuous leather-and-wood interiors. 1950s, Jaguar won seven racing competitions at Le Mans, France. Under Lyons's direction, Malcolm Sayer (formerly with Bristol Aircraft) designed the Jaguar 1951 C-, 1954 D-, and 1961 E-types; however, Sayer's post-Lyons-era 1975 XJS coupé was aesthetically unsuccessful. 1984, the year before Lyons's death, Geoff Lawson was appointed chief designer and, subsequently, created a long line of attractive, successful models. The highly refined 1989 and 1990 XJR-15, designed by Peter Stevens and built by TWR in Kevlar and carbon fiber, regained Jaguar's winning streak at Le Mans.
Citations 1956, knighted.
Bibliography Martin Buckley, *Jaguar: Fifty Years of Speed and Style*, St. Paul, Minn.: Motorbooks International, 1999.
> See Lawson, Geoff; Stevens, Peter.

Lysell, Ralph (1907–)

Swedish industrial designer; active the US, Germany, and Sweden.

Biography After working in the US and Germany, Lysell returned to Sweden; 1939–45, worked for Ericsson, where he assisted Hugo Blomberg on the initial concept of the Ericofon telephone. 1949–54, Lysell, Blomberg, and Gösta Thames developed the design and engineering for the telephone.
Bibliography Hugo Blomberg, 'The Ericofon—The New Telephone Set,' *Ericsson Review*, vol. 33, no. 4, 1956: 99–109. Cat., Kathryn B. Hiesinger and George H. Marcus III (eds.), *Design Since 1945*, Philadelphia: Philadelphia Museum of Art, 1983.
> See Ericsson, Telefonaktie-bolaget L.M.; Blomberg, Hugo.

Bruno Munari. L'Ora X clock (detail) 1945. MoMA.

Måås-Fjetterström, Märta (1873–1941)

Swedish textile designer.

Biography 1919, she set up a workshop in Båstad and became a leading textile artist and a master of composition, form, and line. As a weaver, she greatly contributed to the development of the modern rug and influenced the development of many important artists; combined a painterly approach with traditional textile techniques in abstract motifs and strong colors. Barbro Nilsson succeeded her as director of the workshop for many years, still in operation. 1948, the workshop was from Märta Måås-Fjetterström's original Strandgården to the present house (architects, Ivar and Anders Tengbom).
Bibliography Cat., David Revere McFadden (ed.), *Scandinavian Modern Design 1880–1980,* New York: Abrams, 1982.

Macchi Cassia, Antonio (1937–)

Italian industrial designer; born and active Milan.

Training Mechanical engineering, Switzerland.
Biography 1967, Macchi Cassia became a member, Associazione per il Disegno Industriale (ADI), and committee director there 1971–73; 1968–70, was active in Studio Bonfanti-Macchi Cassia-Porta; 1969–81, was an industrial-design consultant to Olivetti and to Steiner International; for Olivetti, participated in the design of a number of products, including 1981 M20 (with Ettorre Sottsass and Michele De Lucchi, its being first Italian personal computer). 1971 with R. Beretta, Macchi Cassia set up a studio in Milan. His clients included La Rinascente (graphics), Mellin d'Italia (graphics and package design), Ascensori Falconi (control devices), Arteluce (lighting), Stilnovo (lighting), Radiomarelli (television sets), Condor (television sets), Artemide (research on furniture components), Tosimobili (furniture systems), Focchi, Crouzet (measuring instruments), Burgo Scott, Totalgas, and Condor. He taught, Istituto Europeo del Design (IED), Milan; ISIA (Istituto Superiore per le Industrie Artistiche), Rome; and, from 1994, industrial design, Politecnico, Milan.
Bibliography *ADI Annual 1976–2000*, Milan: Associazione per il Disegno Industriale, 1976. Cat., Giovanni Giudici (ed.), *Design Process: Olivetti 1908–1983*, Ivrea: Olivetti, 1983. Hans Wichmann, *Italien Design 1945 bis heute*, Munich: Die Neue Sammlung, 1988.

Macdonald, Alex (1965–)

British furniture designer; born Cheltenham.

Training Furniture production, Parnham College, Dorset.
Biography 1983–85, Macdonald worked in furniture production at Howard and Constable in Hackney; from 1988, has been active independently, producing prototypes for well-known designers and architects; from 1993, set up a design/manufacturing business, producing furniture to his own simple and well-crafted designs. Work includes a bent-birch child's stacking chair by Akta in London.
Bibliography *Axis*, vol. 89, July 1999.

Macdonald, Frances (1874–1921); Margaret Macdonald (1865–1933)

British artists and designers; sisters; both born Newcastle-under-Lyme.

Training Glasgow School of Art.
Biography At the Glasgow School of Art they met their future husbands J. Herbert MacNair and Charles Rennie Mackintosh, with whom they were members of The Four. Influenced by the Arts and Crafts movement, the Pre-Raphaelites, and the revival of Celtic and Japanese art, they developed an arch but elegant personal style of design and decoration. 1894, The Four organized an exhibition of furniture, metalwork, and embroidery. Their work was published in *The Studio*. The sisters opened their own studio on Hope Street, Glasgow, in c. 1894. Their style rejected the medievalism of John Ruskin and William Morris and combined Katsushika Hokusai's mannerism with Aubrey Beardsley's elongated figures; this bizarre combination encouraged critics to label their early work (c. 1893–97) the 'Spook School' of Celtic expression. Margaret Macdonald's influence can be seen in the work of husband Mackintosh from the time of their marriage. As a graphics designer, she also designed the menus and other image work for Miss Cranston's Tea Rooms in Glasgow, for which Mackintosh designed the interiors and furniture; she also stitched embroideries. Frances Macdonald taught enameling and gold- and silversmithing, Glasgow School of Art; her few jewelry pieces, leaded glass, and plaster-and-wire wall decorations influenced the jewelry work of the *fin de siècle* as well as her pupils such as Agnes B. Harvey. By the century's end, they began to use cast aluminum in wares such as table mirrors.
Exhibitions The Four showed their work at 1895 *L'Œuvre Artistique*, Liège; 1896 *Arts and Crafts Exhibition*, London; 1900 (8th) Secession Exhibition, Vienna; 1902 *Esposizione Internazionale d'Arte Decorativa Moderna* (including Frances's jewelry and *repoussé* silver panels), Turin; and in Budapest, Dresden, Munich, and Moscow. The MacNairs showed jewelry at *1901 Education Exhibition*, St. George's Hall, Liverpool.
Bibliography Charlotte Gere, *American and European Jewelry 1830–1914*, New York: Crown, 1975. Anthea Callen, *Women Artists of the Arts and Crafts Movement 1870–1914*, New York: Pantheon, 1979.

David Brett, 'The Eroticization of Domestic Space: A Mirror by C.R. Mackintosh,' *The Journal of Decorative and Propaganda Art*, Fall 1988: 6–13. Toni Lesser Wolf, 'Women Jewelers of the British Arts and Crafts Movement,' *The Journal of Decorative and Propaganda Arts*, no. 14, Fall 1989: 40–41. David Brett, *C.R. Mackintosh: The Poetics of Workmanship*, London: Reaktion, 1992.

Mächtig, Saša Janez (1941–)

Slovene architect and designer; born Ljubljana.

Training 1960–66, Fakulteta za Arhitekturo, and 1966–68, Filozofska Fakulteta, both Univerza v Ljubljani.
Biography 1966–84, Mächtig was a freelance architect and designer; from 1984, taught, Faculty of Arts, Univerza v Ljubljani; 1975–84, developed and established the industrial-design curriculum, Univerza v Ljubljani; 1987–92, organized conferences of International Council of Societies of Industrial Designers (ICSID) in Ljubljana; 2001, was vice-president of executive board, Erasmus/Cumulus European Higher Education Network of Art and Design. Work has included 1968 Europa café pavilion (a self-supporting prefabricated steel structure covered by transparent reinforced polyester), 1967 Kiosk K67 by Imgrad, 1981 Euromodul prefabricated bus-shelter modules, 1984 recyclable trash bin by Donit, 2001 MET 3 modular bus-shelter system.
Citations 1973 Prešeren Fund Award, Slovenia.

Mack, Daniel (1947–)

American furniture designer; born Rochester, N.Y.; active New York and Warwick, N.Y.

Training Anthropology, University of Toronto; to 1975, media studies, The New School for Social Research, New York.
Biography Mack was active as a radio/television journalist and teacher; 1970s, worked for Canadian Broadcasting Corporation, was an interviewer on WRVR radio station in New York, and was a producer of documentaries for *Today* TV program on NBC in the US. 1979, he began to make twig furniture and, eventually, played a major role in the revival of 19th-century rustic furniture. Though made from natural and found forms, the rectilinearity and high backs of his chairs suggest the work of Frank Lloyd Wright and Charles Rennie Mackintosh. He wrote *Making Rustic Furniture* (New York: Sterling/Lark, 1992); taught media studies, The New School for Social Research (now New School University), and, 1986– 90, furniture making, Center for the Arts, Lake Placid, N.Y.

MacKenzie, Warren (1924–)

American potter; born Kansas City, Mo.

Training Ceramics at an art school; dissatisfied with the quality of his training, went with his wife Alix in 1949 to study under Bernard Leach, St. Ives, Cornwall, UK.
Biography MacKenzie was greatly influenced by Leach, who taught him the quality of life in addition to pottery techniques; lived for two years in the Pottery Cottage with Leach; 1952 with his wife, returned to the US and began as a lecturer, University of Minnesota. They moved into a farmhouse and built a kiln where he threw pots on a kick wheel. Until her 1962 death, Alix decorated the pots of Warren, whose use of color was skillful and confident and whose work has become highly regarded and desirable.
Bibliography Margaret Carney, *Charles Fergus Binns: The Father of American Studio Ceramics* (including catalogue raisonné), New York: Hudson Hills Press with International Museum of Ceramic Art, 1998.

Mackintosh, Charles Rennie (1868–1928)

British architect and designer; born and active Glasgow; husband of Margaret Macdonald.

Training 1884 under architect John Hutchinson, apprenticeship; 1885–89, Glasgow School of Art.
Biography 1889, Mackintosh met J. Herbert MacNair in the office of architects J. Honeyman and Keppie, a major Glasgow partnership, where they were draftspeople. 1890s, Mackintosh became a leading figure of The Four of the Glasgow School of Art with MacNair and Margaret and Frances Macdonald, designing posters and metalwork that were published in *The Studio*; 1894 with MacNair and the Macdonalds, organized an exhibition of furniture, metalwork, and embroidery. Their work—including leaded glass, furniture, book illustration, and jewelry—was influenced by the Arts and Crafts movement, Pre-Raphaelites, and the revival of Celtic and Japanese art. Working in a

Charles Rennie Mackintosh. Side chair. 1897. Oak and silk, 54 3/8 x 20 x 18" (138.1 x 50.8 x 45.7 cm), seat h. 17" (43.2 cm). Gift of the Glasgow School of Art. MoMA.

Scottish idiom and neo-Gothic style, the group became known as the Glasgow School and throughout Europe as the 'Spook School,' of Celtic expression. (Jessie Marion King, Talwyn Morris, and George Walton Mackintosh were also associated with the group.) Became a prolific designer of furniture, textiles, and graphics, and accomplished watercolorist. As the leader of Art Nouveau in Britain, he made an appreciable contribution to design and architecture; 1900, married Margaret Macdonald, the same year as invitation to 8th Wiener Sezession exhibition, where the group was highly influential. The 1894 corner tower of the *Glasgow Herald* building was Mackintosh's first executed structure. While still at Honeyman and Keppie, he won 1896 competition to design the new Glasgow School of Art building, realized in two stages, 1897–99 and 1907–09; also designed 1897–1910 Miss Catherine Cranston's Tea Rooms in Glasgow. His Glasgow School of Art building and interiors, little publicized at the time, are now considered a brilliant example of proto-modernism. Purportedly, he designed only two pieces of jewelry: a necklace with pendant in the form of a flight of birds (made by Margaret Macdonald, and more recently frequently copied) and a ring. He also designed 1897–98 Queen's Cross Church in Glasgow, 1899–1901 Windyhill at Kilmalcolm, and 1902–04 publisher Walter Blackie's Hill House in Helensburgh. 1914, he moved to London, where his design work included furniture and printed fabrics. His work was known throughout Europe but not widely accepted in Britain. He became a close friend and mentor of Josef Hoffmann. Mackintosh's reputation was enhanced by the publication (by Hermann Muthesius) of a portfolio of his competition designs for 'House for an Art Lover.' 1916–17, Mackintosh's work for W.J. Bassett-Lowke house at 78 Derngate, Northampton, included the use of plastics and other adventurous-for-the-time materials, influenced by Chinese design. In some cases, his designs for silver and electroplated cutlery that reveal

the mark of David Hislop were possibly produced by Elkington in Birmingham. However, his 1904 silver christening-set for Hermann Muthesius's son was produced by Hahn in Berlin. The extent of the Margaret Macdonald-and-Mackintosh collaboration cannot now be determined but was obviously close and extensive, revealed by their own apartment at 120 Main Street, Glasgow. 1915–early 1920s, he completed numerous textile designs; 1919, designed fabrics by W. Foxton in London; 1920, gave up architecture entirely in favor of watercolor painting, later living in Port-Vendres in the Pyrénées from 1923–27. His silver cutlery patterns were reproduced from 1984 by Sabattini Argenteria, including Black and White vase, 1904 ewer and bowl (shown in a bedroom at 1903 Dresdner Werkstätten exhbition and for Catherine Cranston and Major Cocrane at Hill House), 1903 Willow bowl, 1904 Cranston candlestick or flower holder, 1904 christening fork and spoon, 1902 cutlery (for Jessie Newberry), and 1900–03 MMM, along with a number of his furniture designs reproduced by Cassina and others.
Exhibitions/citations Several architectural students' competitions, including 1890 Alexander Thomson traveling scholarship. With the Macdonalds and MacNair as The Four, organized 1894 exhibition of their work at Glasgow School of Art; showed their work at 1895 *L'Œuvre Artistique*, Liège. Mackintosh won second prize in 1901 Grand Duke Louis IV of Hesse Darmstadt's design competition under auspices of journal *Zeitschrift für Innendekoration*; designed Scottish section at 1900 (8th) Wiener Sezession exhibition and Scottish section at 1911 *Esposizione Internazionale d'Arte Decorativa Moderna*, Turin. In addition to the latter two expositions, Mackintosh, his wife, and the MacNairs showed their work in London in 1896, in Moscow in 1903, and in Budapest, Dresden, and Munich. Mackintosh's work subject of 1968 exhibition, Glasgow; 1996–97, traveling Scotland and US (catalogs below).
Bibliography Hermann Muthesius, 'Charles Rennie Mackintosh, Glasgow: Das Haus eines Kunstfreundes,' *Meister der Innen-Kunst*, vol. 2. Darmstadt: Alexander Koch, 1901. Nikolaus Pevsner, *Ch. R. Mackintosh*, Milan: Il Balcone, 1950. Cat., Andrew McLaren Young, *Charles Rennie Mackintosh, Architecture, Design and Painting*, Glasgow: Scottish Arts Council, 1968. Filippo Alison, *Charles Rennie Mackintosh as a Designer of Chairs*, London: Warehouse Publications, 1974. Roger Billcliffe, *Architectural Sketches and Flower Drawings by Charles Rennie Mackintosh*, London: Academy, 1977. Roger Billcliffe, *Charles Rennie Mackintosh: The Complete Furniture Drawings and Interior Design*, Guildford and London: Lutterworth, 1979. Jackie Cooper (ed.), *Mackintosh Architecture: The Complete Buildings and Selected Projects*, London: Academy, 1978. Alan Crawford, *Charles Rennie Mackintosh*, London: Thames & Hudson, 1995. Cat., Wendy Kaplan, *Charles Rennie Mackintosh*, New York: Abbeville, 1996. Paola Antonelli (ed.), *Objects of Design: The Museum of Modern Art*, New York: The Museum of Modern Art, 2003: 26.

Mackmurdo, Arthur Heygate (1851–1942)
British architect, designer, and economist; born London.

Training From 1869 under Gothic Revivalist architects Chatfield Brooks and James Brooks, apprenticeships.
Biography c. 1874, Mackmurdo was encouraged by John Ruskin to become an architect; 1875, set up an office in the Strand in London and met William Morris and James Abbott McNeill Whistler; developed a singular style of striking simplicity, which brought him wide renown; was influenced by a diverse group such as Victor Horta, Gustave Serrurier-Bovy, Charles Rennie Mackintosh, and C.F.A. Voysey. (Voysey later became a friend and pupil.) 1882, Mackmurdo, Herbert P. Horne, Selwyn Image, and Bernard Creswick founded The Century Guild, a cooperative association of craftspeople and artists inspired by Morris and Ruskin. The group designed interiors and produced wallpaper, furniture, carpets, and metalwork, successfully shown at exhibitions in London, Manchester, and Liverpool. The principles of The Century Guild inspired C.R. Ashbee. Known as one of the originators of Art Nouveau, Mackmurdo was also involved in typography, textile design, and graphics; was an author of books, including *Wren's City Churches* (Orpington: G. Allen, 1883), whose cover design of flame-like curves is thought the earliest example of Art Nouveau. 1884 at The Century Guild, he founded the periodical *The Hobby Horse*, attempting to synthesize all the arts, including music and literature. The periodical was original in its design and typography and one of the most important and influential journals of the time. From 1886, he designed simple, elegant, and original furniture, strongly influencing Voysey. His architectural work included 1889 parts (with H. Horne) of Savoy Hotel in London and 1899 Mortimer Mempes house. 1904, he retired to Essex and concentrated on social and economic issues and writing for next four decades.
Exhibitions Work subject of 1967 and 1979 exhibitions (catalogs below).
Bibliography Yvonne Brunhammer et al., *Art Nouveau Belgium, France*, Houston: Institute for the Arts, Rice University, 1976. Cat., *The Eccentric A.H. Mackmurdo, 1851–1942*, Colchester: The Minories, 1979. Cat., *A.H. Mackmurdo and the Century Guild Collection*, London: William Morris Gallery, 1967.

MacNair, James Herbert (1868–1955)
British architect, designer, and illustrator.

Training Glasgow School of Art.
Biography 1889, MacNair met Charles Rennie Mackintosh, while working for architects J. Honeyman and Keppie in Glasgow. They met sisters Margaret and Frances Macdonald at Glasgow School of Art. MacNair was not happy as an architect and turned to the decorative arts. 1899, MacNair married Frances Macdonald, thus becoming Mackintosh's brother-in-law. His work was influenced by the same Celtic forms and mysticism as the Macdonalds'. Much of Frances and Herbert MacNair's work became indistinguishable after their marriage.
Exhibitions The group organized 1894 exhibition of their work at Glasgow School of Art. The Four showed their work at a number of exhibitions, including 1902 *Esposizione Internazionale d'Arte Decorativa Moderna*, Turin, where the MacNairs exhibited two tables: one with jewelry by themselves and jewelry with enamels by Lily Day, an enamelist and jeweler who taught in architecture and applied-arts department, Liverpool University.
Bibliography Charlotte Gere, *American and European Jewelry 1830–1914*, New York: Crown, 1975: 205. Toni Lesser Wolf, 'Women Jewelers of the British Arts and Crafts Movement,' *Journal of Decorative and Propaganda Arts*, no. 14, Fall 1989: 40–41.
> See Mackintosh, Charles Rennie.

Madsen, Askel Bender (1916–)
Danish furniture designer.

Training Furniture design, Kunsthåndværkerskolen, to 1940; and Det Kongelige Danske Kunstakademi; both Copenhagen.
Biography 1940–43, Madsen worked for architects Kaare Klint and Arne Jacobsen; from 1954, was active in decorating in Copenhagen; 1946–54, taught furniture design, Kunsthåndværkerskolen; 1947 with Ejner Larsen, set up a studio. Much of their furniture was produced by Willy Beck.
Exhibitions Work first shown in 1943; subsequently, in editions of Triennale di Milano, 1954–57 *Design in Scandinavia*, toured the US, 1960–61 *The Arts of Denmark*, toured the US, 1965, Gewerbemuseum, Bern.
Bibliography Frederik Sieck, *Nutidig Dansk Mobeldesign–en kortfattet illustreret beskrivelse*, Copenhagen: Bondo Gravesen, 1990.

Madsen, Eric Rørbæk (1915–)
Danish industrial designer.

Training In engineering.
Biography From 1937, Madsen worked at Bang & Olufsen, where he became the chief engineer, specializing in acoustics; 1958, began the development of the firm's first platinum stereo turntable and designed 1955 *BM 3* ribbon microphone and 1958 tangential turntable pick-up arm; 1975, left B&O and Denmark for Spain to study solar energy.
Bibliography Jens Bang, *Bang & Olufsen: Fra vision til legende = From Vision to Legend*, Denmark: Vidsyn, 2000.

MAFIA
> See Arnodin, Maïmé.

Magg, Helmut (1927–)
German designer; born Munich.

Training In crafts methods; subsequently, under Josef Hillerbrand, Akademie der bildenden Künste, Munich.
Biography 1950s, Magg designed for the Deutsche Werkstätten, where, in 1960s, was the second most productive worker there, after Josef Hillerbrand; from 1950, taught spatial-relationship courses, Munich Akademie, where he earlier studied, and from 1957, Fachschule für Korbflechterei, Lichtenfels; from 1981, professor, Akademie der bildenden Künste, Nuremberg.

Helmut Magg. Desk. 1950s. Wood veneer and plastic laminate, 33 1/16 x 39 3/8 x 23 7/16" (84 x 100 x 59.5 cm). Mfr.: WK-Möbel, Deutsche Werkstätten, Germany. Courtesy Quittenbaum Kunstauktionen, Munich.

Bibliography Hans Wichmann, *Deutsche Werkstätten und WK-Verband 1988–1990: Aufbruch zum neuen Wohnen*, Munich: Prestel, 1992. Cat., *Design—Made in Germany*, Cologne: Kunsthaus Rhenania Köln, 2000.

Maggiori, 'Bepi' Giuseppe (1951–)

Italian designer and entrepreneur; born and active Rimini.

Training To 1978, in architecture, Florence.
Biography Maggiori collaborated with Marco Zanuso Jr. on the design of furniture for several firms. 1983, Marriori, Zanuso, Luigi Greppi, and Pietro Greppi cofounded lighting firm Oceano Oltreluce. From 1982, Maggiori wrote on design for *Casa Vogue*; organized exhibitions, including 1982 *Camera Design* in Milan, 1982 *For Sale* in Vienna, 1982–83 *Möbel Perdu* in Hamburg, 1982 *Conseguenze Impreviste: Art, Fashion, Design* in Prato, 1983 *Design Balneare* in Cattolica, 1982 *Mobili Mobili* in Lerici, and 1983 *Light* in Milan. 1983, he cofounded Movimento Bolidista, based on neo-1950s streamlining concepts.
Exhibitions Participated in 1979 (16th) Triennale di Milano.
Bibliography Andrea Branzi, *La casa calda: esperienze del nuovo disegno italiano*, Milan: Idea, 1982.

Magis

Italian furniture and accessories company; located Motta di Livenza, Treviso.

History July 1976, Magis was founded by Eugenio Perazza who called on high-tech processes for the production of furniture accessories; eventually turned to high design and furniture. Its products have included Stefano Giovannoni's 1997 Bombo seating range, Richard Sapper's 2000 Aida table, Jasper Morrison's 1993 Bottle wine-bottle rack, Michael Young's 2001 MY 082 table range and 2001 MY 083 table, Enzo Mari's 2000 Ypsilon table and 2001 Togo coat rack, Marcello Ziliani's 2001 Flò extendable stepladder, Björn Dahlström's 2000 Joystick walking stick, and a large number of other products over the years. Other designers have included Harry Allen, Marc Berthier, Klaus Hackl, James Irvine, Sven Jonke, Christoph Katzler, Marc Newson, Karim Rashid, Toshiyuki Kita, Jerszy Seymour, and the Bouroullec brothers. 85% of its goods are exported.
Citations Premio Compasso d'Oro: 1981, 1984, 1987, 1991 (three citations), 1994 (four citations), 1998 (three citations), 2001 (two citations).
Bibliography www.magisdesign.com.

Magistretti, 'Vico' Ludovico (1920–)

Italian architect, furniture and interior designer, and urban planner; born and active Milan.

Training 1945, architecture degree, Champ Universitaire Italien, Lausanne, Switzerland.
Biography 1945, Magistretti joined his father's architecture office. Like many postwar designers, he pursued design as well as architecture during Italy's reconstruction period, although initially architecture, town planning, and the interior layouts of buildings. Early work includes 1955 civic center for Campana in Argentina; 1956 Torre del Parco office building; and 1970 Hispano Olivetti training center in Barcelona. His 1946 bookcase had expanding tubes pressed to floor and ceiling. He designed numerous bookcases such as 1950 ladder-like shelving that leans against a wall. c. 1960, he began designing consumer products independently and his relationship with Cassina began; 1959 Chrimate (for Crimate country club) with a rush seat on a brightly orange-stained wooden frame by Cassina is part traditional, part modern, reminiscent of 19th-century Italian country chairs (in production today by De Padova). The whimsical Pan chair and table by Cassina was less accessible. He was one of the first Italian designers to work in plastics, eventually realizing, as examples, 1966 Stadio table; 1969 Selene chair (now by Heller), 1963–66 Demetrio table and stacking chair, all by Artemide. From 1960s, his clients included Asko, Azucena, B&B Italia, Conran, Knoll, La Rinascente, Montina Fratelli, Oca, Poggi, and Stendig. As a consultant designer, he worked with only one assistant and architect in his office. Work was widely published. By Artemide: 1966 Chimera light, 1967 Eclisse table lamp, and 1970 Gaudi and Vicario chairs by Artemide. By Cassina: 1973 Maralunga chair, 1983 Veranda 3 sofa, 1977 Nuvola Rossa folding bookcase, 1981 Sinbad chair (derived from a horse blanket), 1981 Kalaari 440 lamp, 1985 Edison table, 1986 Cardigan modular seating. By O luce: 1977 Atollo lamp, 1980 Kuta lamp, 1980 Nara lamp, 1984 Idomeneo lamp. Also: 1980 cutlery by Rossi & Arcandi, 1986 Planet lamp by Venini, 1986 Vidun table and 1989 Silver aluminum desk chair by De Padova, 1990 Campiglia kitchen system by Schiffini, Samarcanda folding easy chair by Campeggi. All part of a large body of other work. From early 1960s, 80% of Magistretti's product designs are still in production. He was honorary visiting professor, Royal College of Art in London; 1961, guest professor, Istituto Universitario di Architettura, Venice; from 1967, Accademia di San Luca, Rome; 1975, Collegi d'Arquitectes de Catalunya (COAC), Barcelona; 1986, School of Architecture, Tokyo; taught, Domus Academy, Milan; other institutions, in Brazil, England, and Germany. He was committee member, Edilizia Comune di Milano; competition board member, 1951 (9th) and 1954 (10th) editions of Triennae di Milano; member, technical jury, 1960 (11th) Triennale; became a member, ADI (Associazione per il Disegno Industriale). Recently, continuing prolifically, has collaborated with Patricia Urquiola (including mid-1960s Flower armchair and Loom sofas) and Birgit Lohmann on seating and, independently, designed a large number of recent furniture by De Padova, 1992 Palomar lamp by FontanaArte; 1996 Maui and Maui-Kea and 1999 Moorea chairs by Kartell; 1997 Vico, VicoDuo, VicoSolo, and VicoLounge by Fritz Hansen.
Exhibitions/citations From 1948, has participated in almost all the editions of Triennale di Milano, receiving first-prize awards at 1948 (8th) and 1954 (10th) editions and gold medal at 1951 (9th) edition.

Magis: Jasper Morrison. Bottle storage module. 1993. Injection-molded polypropylene and anodized aluminum, 10 1/4 x 9 x 14 3/16" (26 x 22.9 x 36 cm). Mfr.: Magis, Italy. Gift of the mfr. MoMA.

Premio Compasso d'Oro (and on juries): 1957 silver medal from Comune di Milano; 1950 Vis prize; 1954, 1955, 1967 (four citations), 1970 (three citations), 1979 (three citations), 1981 (two citations), 1984, 1994 (three citations), 1998 (with Diver Viss). Others: 1986 gold medal, Society of Industrial Artists and Designers, London. 1983, elected honorary member, Royal College of Art, London, and of Royal Incorporation of Architects, Scotland. Work included in a large number of exhibitions and subject of 1996 exhibition, Salone di Mobile, Milan. Chairs by Fritz Hansen received some of the most prestigious design prizes, including 1998 award, Industrie Forum Design (iF), Hanover.
Bibliography Cat., *Milano 70/70: un secolo d'arte, Dal 1946 al 1970*, vol. 3, 1972: 304–05. Cat., *Design Process Olivetti: 1908–1978*, Los Angeles: Frederick S. Wight Art Gallery, 1979. Alfonso Grassi and Anty Pansera, *Atlante del design italiano 1940/1980*, Milan: Fabbri, 1980: 283. Cat., Kathryn B. Hiesinger and George H. Marcus III (eds.), *Design Since 1945*, Philadelphia: Philadelphia Museum of Art, 1983. Juli Capella and Quim Larrea, *Designed by Architects in the 1980s*, New York: Rizzoli, 1988. Vanni Pasca, *Vico Magistretti Designer*, London: Thames & Hudson, 1991. Fulvio Irace and Vanni Pasca, *Vico Magistretti: Architetto e design*, Milan: Electa, 1999.

Magnussen, Erik (1884–1961)

Danish metalworker; born openhagen; active Copenhagen, Chicago, and Los Angeles.

Training In modeling and silversmithing; 1907–09, Kunstgewerbeschule, Berlin.
Biography To some extent, Magnussen taught himself to make jewelry; 1902, worked as a chaser for Viggo Hansen in Denmark and as a metalsmith to Otto Rohloff in Berlin; 1909, set up his own workshop in Copenhagen, influenced, as so many others were in Denmark, by Thorwald Bindesbøll and Georg Jensen; 1925, settled in the US on the invitation of Gorham Manufacturing, which wanted a European artist to produce modern forms, and where he was the art director to 1929. Magnussen's designs were produced with the soft curves, hammered surfaces, and restrained ornament characteristic of the Danish style. 1929, he began working for August Dingeldein & Son, which had factories in Germany and a retail store in New York; 1932 in Chicago, opened his own workshop; 1933–38, worked in Los Angeles. When American Union of Decorative Artists and Craftsmen (AUDAC) established a chapter in Chicago in 1932, Magnussen was its vice-president. 1938–39, he designed for the International Silver Company in Meriden, Conn. 1920s–30s, his output was primarily for useful objects, including tea and coffee sets, tazzas, bowls, and similar. His best-known, though untypical, work was 1927 Lights and Shadows of Manhattan silver coffee service by Gorham, with a trapezoid tray and salad set; the silver facets of its Cubist forms were burnished, gilded, and oxidized. 1939, he returned to Copenhagen and to a more conservative approach.
Exhibitions/citations Work was included in 1901, 1904, and 1907 exhibitions, Kunstindustrimuseum, Copenhagen; 1930, Art Center, New York; 1931 Architectural League of New York; 1922 Salon d'Automne, Paris; 1926, 1927, and 1937, The Metropolitan Museum of Art, New York; 1931 and 1937, Brooklyn Museum of Art, Brooklyn, N.Y.
Bibliography Charles H. Carpenter Jr., *Gorham Silver: 1831–1981*, New York: Dodd, Mead, 1982. Annelies Krekel-Aalberse, *Art Nouveau and Art Déco Silver*, New York: Abrams, 1989. Cat., Janet Kardon (ed.), *Craft in the Machine Age 1920–1945*, New York: Abrams with American Craft Museum, 1995.

'Vico' Ludovico Magistretti. Atollo table lamp (no. 233). 1977. Aluminum and polyurethane plastic, h. 26 x shade dia. 19 1/4 x base dia. 8" (66 x 48.9 x 20.3 cm). Mfr.: O luce, Milan. Gift of the mfr. MoMA.

Magnussen, Erik (1940–)

Danish designer; born Copenhagen.

Training To 1960, ceramics, Kunsthåndværkerskolen, Copenhagen.
Biography Magnussen set up his own workshop, where he designed stoneware, glassware, cutlery, tableware, lighting, and furniture for various clients; from 1962, worked at Bing & Grøndahl Porcelænsfabrik; from 1975, for Stelton; from c. 1976–77, with Kevi furniture; from 1978, as a hollow-ware designer at Georg Jensen Sølvsmedie in Copenhagen. 1972, he replaced Arne Jacobsen who was the principal free-lance designer at Stelton to 1971, and the Magnussen-Stelton marriage proved highly successful with the introduction of new designs and plastic wares, including 1977 range of water pitchers, teapots, and containers. He sought to reduce his designs to essentials, to make pieces interchangeable and stackable, and to lend them temperature-retaining forms. His 1968 steel-and-fabric Z-stolen (Z chair) was produced by Torben Ørskov. Other clients: Licht und Form (porcelain lamps), Fritz Hansen (furniture), and Paustian. He taught, Det Kongelige Danske Kunstakademi, Copenhagen; has a studio in Klampenborg, Denmark.
Citations 1967 Lunning Prize; 1972, 1978, 1987, and 1990 Dansk ID Prizes; 1977 Danish Furniture Award; 1983 Designer of the Year, Dansk Designråd (Danish design council); 1996 Thorvald Bindelsbøll Medal; 1997 Red Dot award, Design Zentrum Nordrhein Westfalen, Essen; gold medal, G-Mark Good Design award, Japanese Industrial Design Promotion Organization (JIDPO); 2001 elected Royal Designer for Industry, UK; others.
Bibliography Cat., *Georg Jensen Silversmithy: 77 Artists, 75 Years*, Washington: Smithsonian, 1980. Cat., Kathryn B. Hiesinger and George H. Marcus III (eds.), *Design Since 1945*, Philadelphia: Philadelphia Museum of Art, 1983. Cat., David Revere McFadden (ed.), *Scandinavian Modern Design 1880–1980*, New York: Abrams, 1982. Cat., *The Lunning Prize*, Stockholm: Nationalmuseum, 1986. Jennifer Hawkins Opie, *Scandinavia: Ceramics and Glass in the Twentieth Century*, New York: Rizzoli, 1989.

Magnusson Grossman, Greta (1906–1999)
> See Grossman Magnusson, Greta.

Magnusson, Gunnar (1933–)

Icelandic furniture and interior designer.

Biography One of the foremost Icelandic designers, Magnusson furnished public spaces and taught; designed furniture known for its exposed construction and overt simplicity.
Bibliography Cat., David Revere McFadden (ed.), *Scandinavian Modern Design 1880–1980*, New York: Abrams, 1982.

Magris, Roberto (1935–2003)

Italian industrial designer; born and active Florence.

Training Università degli Studi, Florence.
Biography 1955–67, Magris worked as an industrial and graphic designer and illustrator. 1967, Magris, his brother Alessandro Magris, Adolfo Natalini, Cristiano Toraldo di Francia, and Piero Frassinelli set up Superstudio Design Architettura Ricerca in Florence. Magris designed heavy construction equipment, train cars, exhibition and interior-design schemes, ceramics, glassware, and optical equipment. With gruppo 9999, he proposed the Scuola Separata per l'Architettura

Concettuale Espansa (S-Space); 1973–75, was active in Global Tools, an experimental creative collective. Magris also produced a series of films on architecture. He became a member, ADI (Associazione per il Disegno Industriale).
Exhibitions Work included in 1972 *Italy: The New Domestic Landscape*, The Museum of Modern Art, New York; 1973 (15th) Triennale di Milano; 1973–75 exhibition (with Superstudio), touring the US and Europe.
Bibliography *ADI Annual 1976*, Milan: Associazione per il Disegno Industriale, 1976.

Maharaja of Indore (1908–1956)
> See Indore, Maharaja of.

Mahdavi Hudson, India (b. India Mahdavi c. 1963)

Irano-Egyptian interior and furniture designer; born in Iran to Iranian father and Egyptian mother; active Paris.

Training École Freinet, near Nice, France; seven years at École Nationale Supérieure des Beaux-Arts, Paris. In New York: graphic design, School of Visual Arts; furniture design, Parsons School of Design; industrial design, The Cooper Union for the Advancement of Science and Art.
Biography Mahdavi returned to Paris from her studies in New York and, for seven years, was art director of Christian Liaigre's studio before establishing her own studio, IMH Interiors, Paris, in 1999. From c. 2000: she designed the Townhouse Hotel (commissioned by Jonathan Morr), Miami; Joseph store, London; Eric Bergère clothing boutique, Paris; Empire Hotel (commissioned by Ian Schraeger), New York. From 2002: she designed Givenchy flagship store, Paris; private club, Bombay; and lodge, Siwa Oasis, Egypt. Best-known product is the Célibataire, a floor tray almost 3 m (118 in.) long. Her simple furniture includes Venus desk, Kiss Me table lamps, and Good Hope chair by Joseph. 2001, furniture/furnishings were first sold in the US, at Arcila-Duque gallery, Miami.
Exhibitions/citations Work included in 2004 *Design d'Elle,* Galerie VIA (French furniture association), Paris. Designer of the Year, 2004 Maison & Objet, Villepinte, France.

Maher, George Washington (1864–1926)

American furniture designe; born Mill Creek, W. V.

Training 1887, apprenticeship in architecture office of Joseph Lyman Silsbee, alongside Frank Lloyd Wright and George Grant Elmslie.
Biography 1887, Maher left the Silsbee office and opened his own architecture practice. His early work was ornate and monumental. From 1905, he began to work in a less elaborate style, influenced by C.F.A. Voysey. A notable example of this later style is his 1912 Rockledge house for E.L. King in Homer, Minn., where the principal architectural device was a segmented arch with short flanges set on canted buttresses. His chairs included such architectonic features as the arch, guttae, tapered stiles, and wide bases. Certain architectural devices appeared throughout his houses; his lamps, for example, featured segmented arches, guttae, and stained-glass motifs that were linked with the exterior landscape, thus *Gesamtkunstwerk* (whole work of art). Maher, a Prairie-school architect, collaborated with Claude & Stark architects in Madison, Wis.; showed an awareness of Peter Behrens and other Europeans. Mahler commited suicide.
Bibliography Brian A. Spencer (ed.), *The Prairie School Tradition/The Prairie Archives of the Milwaukee Art Center*, New York: Whitney, 1979. Anne Yaffe Phillips, *From Architecture to Object*, New York: Hirschl and Adler, 1989: 78.

Maiakovskaia, Liudmila Vladimirovna (1884–1963)

Russian textile designer.

Training 1904–10, textile printing, Stroganov School of Applied Art, Moscow.
Biography 1909, she worked in the silk mill of Muss and was head of the painting workshop at the Manufacture of Prokhorovo, under Oskar Griun; 1921–30, taught at VKhUTEMAS and VKhUTEIN; from 1931, lectured, Institute of Textiles, Moscow.
Exhibitions Participated in 1925 *Exposition Internationale des Arts Décoratifs et Industriels Modernes*, Paris.
Bibliography Cat., *Kunst und Revolution: Russische und Sowjetische Kunst 1910–1932*, Vienna: Österreichisches Museum für angewandte Kunst, 1988. Cat., *The Great Utopia: The Russian and Soviet Avant-Garde, 1915–1932*, New York: Guggenheim Museum, 1992.

Hansjerg Maier-Aichen. LIP wastepaper baskets. 1993. Injection-molded polypropylene, large 13 1/4 x 12 x 6" (33.7 x 30.5 x 15.2 cm), small 9 1/2 x 9 1/8 x 5 1/4" (24.1 x 23.2 x 13.3 cm). Mfr.: Authentics, division of artipresent, Germany. Gift of the mfr. MoMA.

Maier-Aichen, Hansjerg (1940–)

German design director.

Training Interior architecture in Wuppertal; painting, Staatliche Hochschule der bildenden Künste, Munich; 1972, master of fine arts degree, Art Institute of Chicago.
Biography Maier-Aichen taught in Chicago, Münster, and Karlsruhe; 1972–74, lived in Italy on the Villa-Romana and Villa-Massimo (Rome prizes) grants; 1974, began working at the family firm, artipresent GmbH, and, to 1980, was an artist showing work in Europe and the US; 1980, established the Authentics trademark at artipresent for the design and marketing of household goods, particularly for the kitchen and bath in simple forms primarily in colorful, translucent polypropylene; later added glass goods to the line; instituted lawsuits, attempting to stem the tide of plagiarizing competition, especially from Asia. The Authentics firm eventually closed. 1976–85, Maier-Aichen was a consultant in design and marketing to the European Community Commission; from 1997, has been a member of the board, Rat für Formgebung (German design council), Frankfurt; from 1999, taught, Central Saint Martins College of Art and Design, London; from 2002, taught product design, Staatliche Hochschule für Gestaltung, Karlsruhe; remains a designer and strategic-design consultant for various European and American firms.
> See Authentics.

Mairet, Ethel M. (b. Ethel Partridge 1872–1952)

British weaver; born Barnstaple, Devon.

Biography 1903–06, she lived in Ceylon (now Sri Lanka), and, 1906–10, in Chipping Campden, Gloucestershire, UK, where she had close contact with C.R. Ashbee and his Guild of Handicraft. 1911–12, she began weaving in Saunton; 1918, moved to Ditchling, Sussex, where she set up her workshop Gospels. (Eric Gill also worked in Ditchling at the time.) Gospels became a meeting place for weavers, including Marianne Straub, Margery Kendon, Valentine Kilbride, and, from 1917, Elizabeth Peacock. Mairet sought a fresh approach to hand-weaving and to its relationship to power looms; was particularly knowledgeable about vegetable dyes; is the acknowledged leader of the hand-weaving revival in England; had a keen color sense. Gospels produced a wide range of hand-woven goods known for their excellent hang, drape, and harmonious colors. A prolific writer, Mairet wrote an Afterword to *The Dipavamsa and Mahavamsa and their Historical Development in Ceylon* (1908) translated by E.M. Coomaraswamy and her books included *The Future of Dyeing, or, the Conflict Between Science and Art in the Making of Colour* (1915), *A Book on Vegetable Dyes* (Hammersmith, Douglas Pepler, 1916), *An Essay on Crafts and Obedience* (Ditchling: Douglas Pepler 1918) with husband Philip A. Mairet, *Vegetable Dyes...* (Ditchling: St. Dominic's Press, 1931), *Hand-Weaving Today, Traditions and Changes* (London: Faber, 1939), *Hand-Weaving and Education* (London: Faber, 1942), and *Hand-Weaving Notes for Teachers* (London: Faber, 1949).
Exhibitions/citations Weavings included in 1979–80 *Thirties*, Hay-

ward Gallery, London (catalog below). 1938, elected Honorary Royal Designer for Industry, UK.
Bibliography Cat., *Thirties: British Art and Design Before the War*, London: Arts Council of Great Britain Hayward Gallery, 1979. Fiona MacCarthy and Patrick Nuttgens, *An Eye for Industry*, London: Lund Humphries, 1986.

Maîtrise, La

French decorating studio; located Paris.

History 1922, La Maîtrise was established as the decorating and design studio of Les Galeries Lafayette department store, Paris; from its beginning to 1952, was directed by Maurice Dufrêne. Commissions included the decoration of apartments and townhouses as well as furniture and furnishings. Dufrêne's regular collaborators were Suzanne Guiguichon, Gabriel Englinger, Eric Bagge, Fernand Nathan, Geneviève Pons, Jacques Adnet, René Drouet, and others. Édouard Bénédictus designed tapestries.
Exhibitions Work subject of an exhibition at 1922 Salon d'Automne. La Maîtrise's seven-room pavilion at 1925 *Exposition Internationale des Arts Décoratifs et Industriels Modernes*, Paris.
Bibliography Guillaume Janneau, 'La Maîtrise,' *La renaissance de l'art français et des industries de luxe*, no. 8, May 1925: 221–29. Michael B. Miller, *The Bon Marché: Bourgeois Culture and the Department Store, 1869–1920*, Princeton: Princeton University, 1981. Pierre Kjellberg, *Art déco: les maîtres du mobilier, le décor des paquebots*, Paris: Amateur, 1986/1990. Patrick Favardin, *Les décorateurs des années 50*, Paris: Norma, 2002: 306.

Májek, Miloš (1926–1978)

Czech designer; born Sázava nad Sázavou.

Training School of glassmaking, Železný Brod.
Biography 1950s, Májek was active as a designer of consumer products, including glass frames, mail boxes, irons, vacuum cleaners, and pumps. He introduced aerodynamic and organic forms into the design of everyday goods; had clients such as Chirana (dentist lighting and pharmaceutical interiors in late 1960s).
Bibliography Milena Lamarová, *Průmyslový design*, Prague: Odeon, 1984.

Majorelle, Louis (1859–1926)

French designer and cabinetmaker; born Toul.

Training From 1877, in painting in Nancy, and, subsequently under Jean Millet, École des Beaux-Arts, Paris.
Biography 1878, Majorelle took over his family cabinet-making and ceramics enterprise in Nancy; late 1880s, began designing modern furniture; was the most dynamic practitioner of School of Nancy, working of course in Art Nouveau style; supported by active merchandizing, produced great quantities of highly decorated commercial furniture and more elaborate pieces using exprensive materials such as mahogany, burr walnut, and ormolu. The firm's catalog included a wide range of furniture models in both historicist and Art Nouveau styles. He is known primarily for his unconventional furniture; designed pianos, desks, armchairs, and, when his workshop included metalworking, wrought-iron banisters, ormolu, iron mounts, and lighting; produced the metalwork for Daum, which in turn produced glassware for Majorelle's lighting. Majorelle designed lamp bases with cloth shades similar to Louis Comfort Tiffany's; 1901, became vice-president, École de Nancy; after World War I, moved into the Art Déco idiom with more severe forms and restricted ornamentation. His residence in Nancy was designed by Henri Sauvage. The firm continued after Majorelle's death under the management of Alfred Lévy, its artistic and technical director, who, mid-1930s, was joined in Atelier Majorelle by Paul Beucher. The firm had showrooms in Nancy, Paris, and Lyon.
Exhibitions Work shown at Salon des Artistes Décorateurs from 1904 and 1903 exhibition of École de Nancy, Paris. With Alfred Lévy, designed the study in Nancy pavilion, 1925 *Exposition Internationale des Arts Décoratifs et Industriels Modernes*, Paris.
Bibliography P. Juyot, *Louis Majorelle: artiste décorateur maître ébéniste*, Nancy, 1927. Yvanhoé Rambosson, 'Majorelle,' *Mobilier et décoration*, July 1933: 284–93. Hugh Honour, *Cabinet Makers and Furniture Designers*, London: Weidenfeld and Nicolson, 1969. Pierre Kjellberg, *Art déco: les maîtres du mobilier, le décor des paquebots*, Paris: Amateur, 1986/1990. Roselyne Bouvier, *Majorelle: une aventure moderne*, Metz: Bibliothèque des Arts; Serpenoise, 1991. Alastair Duncan, *Louis Majorelle: Master of Art Nouveau Design*, New York: Abrams, 1991.

Makepeace, John (1939–)

British furniture designer.

Training Denstone College, Staffordshire, and under Keith Cooper.
Biography 1961, Makepeace began designing furniture; 1964, set up a workshop in Farnborough Barn, Banbury, moving in 1976 to Parnham House in Dorset, where he established the Parnham Trust and School for Craftsmen in Wood, in 1977. 1989, he started training students in product design and development and to use wood thinning, a waste product.
Exhibitions Work shown at 1973 *Craftsman's Art*, London; 1982 *The Maker's Eye*, London; 1990 *New Art Forms Exposition*, Chicago; 1991 *Beyond the Dovetail*, London. Work subject of exhibitions, New Art Centre, London, 1971, and Fine Art Society, London, 1977.
Bibliography Robert A.M. Stern (ed.), *The International Design Yearbook*, New York: Abbeville, 1985/1986. *Decorative Arts Today*, London: Bonhams, 1992: no. 45a. *John Makepiece Furniture*, Beaminster: John Makepeace Furniture/Parnham House, 1991. Jeremy Myerson, *Makepeace: A Spirit of Adventure in Craft & Design*, London: Octopus, 1995.

Mäkiniemi, 'Elissa' Elsa Kaisa Mäkiniemi (1922–1994)
> See Aalto, Hugo Alvar Henrik.

Malcourant, Véronique (1954–)

French furniture designer; born Vichy.

Biography All in Paris: 1975–77, Malcourant was an illustrator at Maxime Fillon; 1978 with François Germond, established a furniture workshop and was an apprentice in marquetry and lacquerwork; 1979–86 with Jean-Michel Cornu, set up a furniture-design studio; 1998 with Cornu, established Bistro Design, and participated with Design Fax; 1986–99, was an independent designer; 1999, cofounded the Université du Symbole for teaching, symposia, and corporate-identity programs; 2000, established the firm Renaissance. She has designed furniture, lighting, exhibition stands, and others for long list of clients: Avant-Scène, Akaba, Amat, Bidasoa, BST (Groupe Bisset

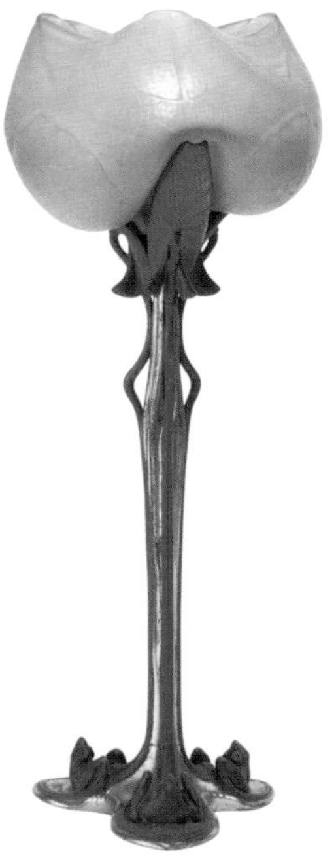

Louis Majorelle. Table lamp. c. 1900. Gilded and patinated bronze and acid-etched glass, 27 1/4 x 11 1/2 x 11 1/2" (69.2 x 29.2 x 29.2 cm). Mfr.: Louis Majorelle and Daum Frères, France. Joseph H. Heil Bequest (by exchange). MoMA.

Industries), Chantal Thomass, Christofle, DIM, exhibition of French designers at *Expo 2000* in Hanover, Fluocaril, Hôtel de la Monnaie, Kanebo, La Cornue, L'Oréal, Armani, Paloma Picasso, Helena Rubinstein, Musée de la Poste, Paris-Tokio, Qualipige, Roquefort Société, Saint-Gobain, Shell, Toshiba, and Van Cleef & Arpels. Has taught at Strate Collège, Issy-les-Moulineaux, France, and, 1991–95, École Supérieure de Design Industriel, Paris.
Citations 1988 and 1989 Point de Mire, Centre Georges Pompidou, Paris; 1989 Delta d'Oro, ADI/FAD (industrial-design/decorative arts associations), Spain; 1989 laureate, Club de la Presse, Moving fair, Paris; 1989 Grand Prix, Strategie du Design; Washington Trademark Design Award, 1990 Salon International des Arts Ménages, Paris; 1991, 1993, 1997, 1989 Janus de l'Industrie, Institut Français du Design; 1993 Supon Design Group's First Competition of International Self-Promotion.

Maldonado, Tomás (1922–)

Argentine teacher; born Buenos Aires.

Biography 1955–67 on the invitation of design theoretician and artist/designer Max Bill, Maldonado taught, Hochschule für Gestaltung (HfG), Ulm, where he was chancellor from 1964–66. 1965, he was Lethaby Lecturer, Royal College of Art, London; 1976–84, professor of letters and philosophy, Università di Bologna and, subsequently, professor of environmental design, Politecnico, Milan; 1979–83, managing editor, journal *Casabella*; has written extensively on architecture, including books *Max Bill* (Buenos Aires: Nueva Visión, 1955), *La speranza progettuale* (Turin: Einaudi, 1970, 2nd. ed. 1992), and *Avanguardia e razionalità* (Turin: Einaudi, 1974) and on the information revolution in *La speranza progettuale* (Turin: Einaudi, 1970), *Reale e virtuale* (Milan: Feltrinelli, 1992) and *Critica della ragione informatica* (Milan: Feltrinelli, 1997). He wrote about pedagogy, with Gui Bonsiepe, in the article 'Science and Design,' *Ulm* (vols. 10–11, May 1964: 16–18).
Citations 1966, was appointed a fellow of Council of Humanities, Princeton University
Bibliography Andrea Branzi, *La casa calda: esperienze del nuovo disegno italiano*, Milan: Idea, 1982. Cat., *Hochschule für Gestaltung Ulm... Die Moral Der Gegenstände*, Berlin: Bauhausarchiv, 1987: 273.

Malevich, Kazimir Severinovich (1878–1935)

Russian artist artist and designer; born near Kiev.

Training 1895–96, Kiev Drawing School; 1903, Institute of Painting, Sculpture, and Architecture, Moscow.
Biography 1910–12, Malevich was influenced by neo-Primitivism, subsequently by Cubism and Futurism; 1913, participated in the Futurist conference in Uusikirkko, Finland (now in Russia); designed the décor for Aleksei Kruchenykh's 1923 Futurist opera *Pobeda nad solntsem* (victory over the sun); illustrated Futurist booklets, including *Troe* (three), *Porosiata* (piglets), and *Vozropshchem* (*let's g-r-r-rumble*). 1914, Malevich met Futurist artist Filippo Tommaso Marinetti on his arrival in Russia. 1915, Malevich formalized his own Suprematism, a version of abstract art, in which geometrical forms play on white backgrounds; explained it as 'the supremacy of pure emotion,' expounding upon it in the theoretical essay 'Ot kubizma i futurizma k suprematizmu: Novyi zhivopisnyi realizm' (from Cubism and Futurism to Suprematism: the new painterly realism*)*. From 1918, he was involved in IZO NKP (fine-art department of Narkompros); published the tract 'O novykh sistemakh v iskusstve' (on new systems in art) in Vitebsk, where he took over the directorship of the art school from Marc Chagall after the Revolution. Malevich founded POSNOVIS/UNOVIS (followers of new art/affirmers of new art), around which talented students gathered, including Il'ia Chashnik, El Lissitzky, and Nikolai Suetin. 1920, Malevich designed the cover of the first *Tsikl lektsii* (cycles of lectures) by art critic Nikolai Punin; moved to Petrograd with some of his students and, 1922, set up a branch of INKhUK (institute of artistic culture). His ceramics were produced by the Lomonosov factory, where he, Suetin, and Chasnik worked briefly in 1922–23. 1920s, he produced architectural models and designed textiles; traveled to Warsaw and Berlin for his 1927 one-person exhibitions authorized by the Soviet government. He anticipated the fate of the Soviet avant-garde and, thus, entrusted his archives to his German friends, together with the approximately 70 works shown in the 1927 exhibition; they wound up in the Netherlands and since, particularly from the beginning of the 21st century, have been in litigation concerning their ownership. The note accompanying the exhibition, known as Malevich's Testament, begins, 'In case I die or am innocently imprisoned....' 1927, Malevich visited the Bauhaus, and the same year his theories were published as *Die Gegenstandslose Welt* (the groundless world) (Munich: Albert Langan, 1927, later published in English as *Suprematism—The Non-Objective World* (1927). From 1930, when his painting style became more figurative, his property was confiscated by the governmental regime, and he was held for a time as a German spy. 1990, Rossi & Arcandi in Italy reissued an edition of 50 examples of his square silver tray and, recently, his Lomonosov ceramics have been reissued by the original factory.
Exhibitions Participation in Mikhail Larionov's c. 1912 *Jack of Diamonds* exhibition. 1911–17: contributed to numerous avant-garde exhibitions, including *Donkey's Tail*, *0–10* (first public showing of Suprematist works), and *The Store*. Also, 1919 *Tenth State Exhibition: Non-Objective Creation and Suprematism*, and numerous other 1920s exhibitions in Russia and abroad. Work subject of 1927 exhibitions, Warsaw and Berlin; 1990–91 exhibition, touring the US, organized by National Gallery of Art, Washington; 1980 *Œuvres de Casimir Severinovitch Malévitch (1878–1935): avec en Appendice les Œuvres de Nicolaï Mikhaïlovitch Souiétine (1897–1954)*, Centre Georges Pompidou, Musée National d'Art Moderne, Paris; 2000, Palazzo Forti, Verona.
Bibliography Joop Joesten (tr. by Howard Dearstyne), *Kasimir Malevich, The Non-Objective World*, Chicago: Theobald, 1959. Troels Andersen, *Malevich*, Amsterdam: Stedelijk Museum, 1970. Cat., Stephanie Barron and Maurice Tuchman, *The Avant-Garde in Russia, 1910–1930*, Cambridge: MIT, 1980: 194. Larissa A. Zhadova, *Malevich: Suprematism and Revolution in Russian Art, 1910–1930*, London: Thames & Hudson, 1982. Cat., John Bowlt, *Kazimir Malevich 1878–1935*, Washington: Smithsonian, 1990. Cat., Krystyna Gmurzynska-Bscher et al. (eds.), *Malewitsch, Suetin, Tschaschnik*, Cologne: Galerie Gmurzynska, 1992. John Milner, *Kazimir Malevich and the Art of Geometry*, New Haven: Yale, 1996. Bruno Duborgel, *Malevitch: la question de l'icône*, Saint-Étienne: Université de Saint-Etienne, 1997. Di Giorgio Cortenova and Evgenija Petrova, *Kasimir Malevich e le sacre icone russe: avanguardia e tradizioni*, Milan: Electa; Verona: Palazzo Forti, 2000.

Malinowski, Arno (1899–1976)

Danish sculptor and metalworker.

Training 1919–22, Det Kongelige Danske Kunstakademi, Copenhagen; 1914–19, apprenticeship under Danish Royal Court engraver S. Lindahl.
Biography From 1921–35, Malinowski executed figurines for Royal Copenhagen Porcelain Manufactory and decorated others, forms, including those of designer Christian Joachim; from 1934–39, taught, Kunsthåndværkerskolen, Copenhagen; 1936–65, designed jewelry by Georg Jensen Sølvsmedie, Copenhagen, including the medal by Jensen for 70th birthday of King Christian X, worn by thousands of Danes during World War II and, thus, a patriotic symbol.
Exhibitions/citations Silver medal, 1925 *Exposition Internationale des Arts Décoratifs et Industriels Modernes*, Paris; 1933 Eckersberg Medal.
Bibliography Cat., *Georg Jensen Silversmithy: 77 Artists, 75 Years*, Washington: Smithsonian, 1980. Cat., David Revere McFadden (ed.), *Scandinavian Modern Design 1880–1980*, New York: Abrams, 1982. Jennifer Hawkins Opie, *Scandinavia: Ceramics and Glass in the Twentieth Century*, New York: Rizzoli, 1989.

Malinowski, Ruth (1928–)

Austrian textile designer; active Denmark and Sweden.

Training Kunsthåndværkerskolen, Copenhagen.
Biography She settled in Copenhagen with her parents; during World War II, lived in Sweden; 1945, returned to Copenhagen and, 1948, set up her first workshop and worked for various studios and supplied fabrics or designs to Den Permanente, Unikavaev, and Cotil; had a highly active career. Her designs were simple, flat geometric, and painterly.
Exhibitions Work subject a number of one-person exhibitions from Nationalmuseum, Stockholm, in 1968.
Bibliography Annette Graae (ed.), *Tekstilkunst i Danmark 1960–87*, Valby: Borgens Forlag, 1987.

Mallet-Stevens, Robert (1886–1945)

French architect and designer; born and active Paris.

Training 1905–10, École Spéciale d'Architecture, Paris.
Biography Mallet-Stevens garnered some initial attention, at 1913 edition of Salon d'Automne, where he installed a hall and music room, notable for their vibrant color, purity, and clarity. He called on geometric shapes in his furniture in painted metal and nickel-plated tubular steel; was the first architect to introduce new concepts of simplification and Functionalism to the rich tastes of France; was influenced by

Josef Hoffmann's crusade against the excesses of Art Nouveau. Mallet-Stevens wrote about his views in a series of articles in 1911–12 issues of reviews *Le home*, *Tekné*, *Lux*, and *L'art ménager*. 1922, he published *Une cité moderne*, portfolio of architecture drawings with a preface by Frantz Jourdain; from 1923 with Ludwig Mies van der Rohe and Theo van Doesburg, was associated with journal *L'architecture moderne*; from 1924, taught, École Spéciale d'Architecture, Paris. His structures—Influenced by Cubism, Charles Rennie Mackintosh, and as mentioned Hoffmann—were severely geometrical with intricate planes, rectangular solids, and white stucco surfaces—rigorously rejecting superfluous ornamentation. Mallet-Stevens's notable designs include 1925 Alfa Romeo showroom at 36, rue Marbeuf, Paris. Film maker Marcel L'Herbier hired Mallet-Stevens, art directors Alberto Cavalcanti and Claude Autant-Lara, artist Fernand Léger, and furniture designer Pierre Chareau to participate in the film *L'inhumaine* (1923–24); its ultra-modern design was shocking to audiences accustomed to neo-classical settings. Mallet-Stevens designed subsequent sets for films *Le secret de Rosette Lambert* (1920), *Jettatura* (1921), *La singulière aventure de Neil Hogan, jockey* (1921), *Le vertige* (1926), and 13 others. His maquettes and film sets offered a platform for architectural experimentation. He designed the 1924–33 villa (and some of its furnishings) of the vicomte and vicomtesse de Noailles in Hyères, with contributions by associates Francis Jourdain, Djo-Bourgeois, Pierre Chareau, Blanche Klotz, and others as collaborators. With Paul Ruau, he designed the 1924 villa (unrealized) of Jacques Doucet at Marly; took over the Château Yvelines (which had been discontinued due to Paul Poiret's bankruptcy) in Mézy-sur-Seine; 1926 Collinet townhouse, Boulogne; and 1928 casino in Saint-Jean-de-Luz. Other works in Paris: late-1920s Café du Brésil, avenue de Wagram; 1928–29 offices of periodical *Semaine à Paris* (with stained-glass windows by Louis Barillet and furnishings by others), 1930 apartment house (in which Tamara de Lempicka had a studio), 7, rue Méchain; 1935 firehouse-barracks, rue Mesnil; and various stores and shops. In Istanbul, a distillery. The 1927 group of stucco-clad white houses along the rue Mallet-Stevens in Auteuil (now Paris), was his most complete complex, where there was a house for himself (no. 12) and the studio for the Martel twins (no. 10), with whom he often worked. He frequently used tubular steel in his furniture designs, painted bright colors as well as white and light green. A tubular-steel side chair with a curved metal back and vertical flat stays, later reproduced by Écart International, has become an icon of 20th-century design. From the 1980s, other furniture models have been reproduced. Only for 1931–32 Villa Cavroix at Croix did he create all the furniture designs alone. His early lighting designs were produced by Baguès, Fabre, and Martin. Mallet-Steven's subsequent lighting was produced by Perfécla, the firm of André Salomon with whom Mallet-Stevens created the wall and ceiling lamps for the shop of Paul Poiret and the entrance hall to 1930 (1st) exhibition of Union des Artistes Modernes (UAM), Paris. For his own residence in Auteuil, various lighting was designed by Chareau and Jourdain. 1946, UAM members established the Club Mallet-Stevens, an information center for art and modern architecture.
Exhibitions Extensive design and architectural work shown at 1912, 1913, and 1914 editions of Salons d'Automne, Paris. Organized 1924 exhibition, which combined the work of the De Stijl designers, Chareau, and Jourdain. Designed the tourism pavilion for the garden of Une Habitation Moderne at 1925 *Exposition Internationale des Arts Décoratifs et Industriels Modernes*, Paris. As a 1929 founding member, UAM, and its first president, showed work at all its exhibitions from 1930. At the apex of his career, executed five pavilions, including Pavillons de l'Hygiène, de l'Electricité, du Solidarité Nationale, and du Tabac, and Café du Brésil pavilion, 1937 *Exposition Internationale des Arts et Techniques dans la Vie Moderne*, Paris. Showed a series of illuminated balloons (hung axially above the river Seine), 1935 (3rd) Salon de la Lumière, Paris.
Bibliography Maurice Raynal et al., *Dix ans de réalisations: Rob. Mallet-Stevens en architecture et en décoration*, Paris: Charles Massin, 1930. Léon Moussinac, *Mallet-Stevens*, Paris: G. Crès, 1931. 'Architecture Moderne,' *L'architecture d'aujourd'hui*, no. 8, 1932. Alastair Duncan, *Art Nouveau and Art Déco Lighting*, New York: Simon & Schuster, 1978: 178. Cat., *Rob Mallet-Stevens architecte*, Brussels: Archives d'Architecture Moderne, 1980. Jean Claude Delorme and Philippe Chair, *L'école de Paris: 10 architectes et leur immeubles, 1905–1937*, Paris, 1981: 61–70. Arlette Barré-Despond, *UAM*, Paris: Regard, 1986: 458–65. Jean-François Pinchon (ed.), *Rob. Mallet-Stevens, architecture, mobilier, décoration*, Paris: Philippe Sers, 1986; Cambridge: MIT, 1990 English ed. Cat., *Les années UAM 1929– 1958*, Paris: Musée des Arts Décoratifs, 1988: 224–25. François Carassan et al., *Villa de Noailles*, Paris: Plume/Flammarion, 2001.

Malmsten, Carl (b. Charley Per Henrik Malmsten 1888–1972)

Swedish furniture and textile designer and maker.

Training Pahlmanns Handelsinstitut and Kungliga Tekniska Högskolan, Stockholm; 1910, economics in Lund; 1910–12 under cabinetmaker Per Jönsson, in Stockholm; 1912–15, handicrafts and architecture under Carl Bersten in Stockholm.
Biography Malmsten was a freelance furniture and interior designer in Stockholm; 1916–19, was active in his own workshops in Tunnelgatan; 1919–22, in Arbertargatan; 1940–50, in Krukmakargatan; and, 1950–72, in Renstiernagatan. He called on Gustavian forms in his chairs, wooden sofas, and small tables, installed in his austere rooms, which anticipated the Swedish modern style. He included elements of late 18th-century painting; experimented with paint finishes; to 1923, worked at Stockholm Town Hall; designed 1924–25 Stockholm Concert Hall; 1928, founded Olof School, Stockholm, where he was the director to 1941; 1945, founded Nyckelvik School (for handicrafts and folk art), Stockholm, and, subsequently, Capellagården School (for creative work), Vickelby. His enterprise Carl Malmsten Möbelfabricks AB continues in Åfors.
Exhibitions/citations Work shown at 1917 Blanche Konstsalon (art fair), Stockholm; 1923 and 1956 exhibitions, Gothenburg; Swedish pavilion at 1925 *Exposition Internationale des Arts Décoratifs et Industriels Modernes*, Paris; 1939–40 *New York World's Fair: The World of Tomorrow*. Work subject of 1944 retrospective, Nationalmuseum, Stockholm. First and second prizes (furniture design), 1916 event, Stockholm Town Hall; 1926 Litteris et Artibus Medal; 1945 Prince Eugen Medal.
Bibliography Cat., David Revere McFadden (ed.), *Scandinavian Modern Design 1880–1980*, New York: Abrams, 1982. Stephen Calloway, *Twentieth Century Decoration*, New York: Rizzoli, 1988.

Malmström, August (1829–1901)

Swedish ceramicist.

Training 1849–56, painting, Kungliga Konsthögskolan, Stockholm; 1857–58, in Paris; 1859–60, in Italy.
Biography From 1867, Malmström taught, Kungliga Konsthögskolan and, subsequently, became the director; 1868–74, was a designer at Gustavsberg porcelain works, where he and Daniel J. Carlsson revived traditional Viking designs. Carlsson painted the decoration on Malmström's forms.
Bibliography Cat., David Revere McFadden (ed.), *Scandinavian Modern Design 1880–1980*, New York: Abrams, 1982.

Maloof, Sam (1916–)

American furniture designer and maker; born Chino, Cal.; active California.

Training Self-taught.
Biography 1934, Maloof began to work as a graphics artist at Padova Hills Theater, Claremont, Cal.; worked for industrial designer Harold Graham, also in Claremont, designing interior displays for Bullock's department store, Los Angeles; 1947, worked with artist Millard Sheets (1907–1989); 1948, established his own furniture workshop and, about the same year, received his first furniture commission, a suite for the home of industrial designer Henry Dreyfuss; from c. 1945–50, furniture commissions from interior designers Kneedler-Fouchere; 1953, settled in Alta Loma, Cal., where he built a workshop in 1954 and is still active today; 1959, worked as designer, woodworker, and technician for Dave Chapman Inc, Chicago, Ill., as a consultant on a US State Department project in Lebanon and El Salvador. For at least 50 years, he worked in a freehand style, using a bandsaw and incorporating dado-rabbetted joinery; became known as the 'king of the rocker' because he made a large number of rocking chairs.
Exhibitions Work first shown, 1948 Los Angeles County (California) Fair. Subject of 1976 *Please Be Seated*, Museum of Fine Arts, Boston; 2001–02 *The Furniture of Sam Maloof*, Renwick Gallery, Smithsonian American Art Museum, Washington, D.C. Included in 2001 *Contemporary Art Furniture: Sam Maloof, John Cederquist, Wendy Maruyama*, Arizona State University Art Museum, Tempe. Named craftsman/trustee, American Crafts Council, 1973–76; a fellow there, 1975; a trustee there, 1979.
Bibliography William Kayden (producer), *On the Go*, film, production: NBC Television, 1959. Maynard Orme (producer), *Sam Maloof, Woodworker*, film, production: Oregon Public Broadcasting, 1973. Julie Hall, *Tradition and Change: The New American Craftsman*, New York:

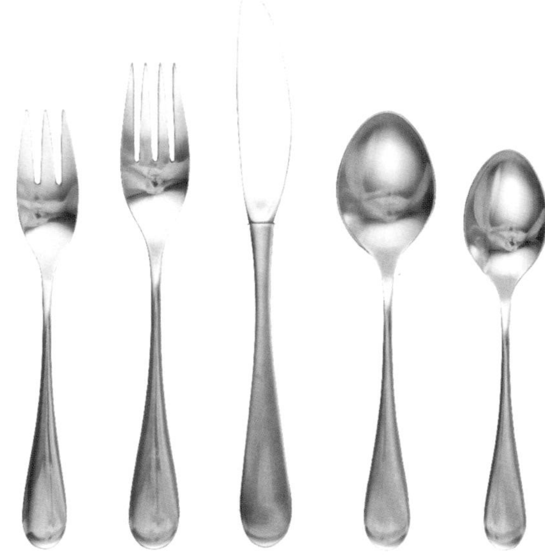

Ellen B. Manderfield. Oneida/Heirloom Omni Stainless cutlery. 1975. Satin finish stainless steel, knife 8 5/8 x 13/16 x 5/16" (21.9 x 2.1 x 0.8 cm), teaspoon 6 1/8 x 1 1/4 x 1/8" (15.5 x 3.2 x 0.3 cm). Mfr.: Oneida, US (c. 1979). Gift of the mfr. MoMA.

Dutton, 1977. Barbaralee Diamondstein (presenter), *Handmade in America*, film, production: ABC Television, 1982. Film, Bob Smith (producer), *Sam Maloof: The Rocking Chair*, production: Smith Broadcasting Group, 1983. Jonathan Pollock (photographer), *Sam Maloof, Woodworker*, Tokyo: Kodansha, 1983; reprinted 1989. Jeremy Adamson, *The Furniture of Sam Maloof,* New York: Norton, 2001.

Maly, Peter (1936–)

Czech designer; born Trautenau, Bohemia (now Trutov, Czech Republic); active Hamburg.

Training To 1960, interior design, Fachhochschule, Detmold.
Biography 1960–70, Maly led the interior-design team at *Schöner Wohnen* magazine; 1970, set up his own studio in Hamburg for interior and product design with a small staff and became one of the leading furniture designers in Europe; has also designed exhibitions, photo sets, and showrooms/stores. Clients have included Cor (award-winning 1984 Zyklus chair) and Ligne Roset (working for it from 1982, designing numerous pieces of furniture, such as 1983 Maly bed). Other work: award-winning 737 chair by Thonet, 1998 Vivace piano by Carl Sauter, and furniture by Behr. He has taught woodworking, Fachhochschule, Detmoth.
Citations 1983 and 1985 awards, Design Center Stuttgart; 1984 Best Furniture of the Year (for Zyklus chair), *Schöner Wohnen* magazine; prize winner, 1985 Made in Germany competition; 1986 Bundespreis 'Die Gute Form,' West Germany; 1986 Du Pont International Awards; 1989 Hommage de l'industrie aux Créateurs, Paris; two 1995 Red Dot awards, Design Zentrum Nordrhein Westfalen, Essen; 1996 award, Industrie Forum Design (iF), Hanover; 1997 Designpreis Schweiz; 2001 Good Design award, Chicago Athenaeum; and others.
Exhibitions Work subject of 2001–03 *Peter Maly: Arbeiten 1967–2001*, Museum für Kunst und Gewerbe, Hamburg
Bibliography Alex Buck and Matthias Vogt, *Peter Maly*, Frankfurt: form, 2000.

MAM
> See Mobilier Artistique Moderne.

Mamontov, Savva (1841–1918); Elizabeth Mamontov (1847–1909)

Russian patrons of the arts. Savva: Railroad magnate. Elizabeth: Amateur singer and patrons of the arts.

Biographies 1870, the Mamontovs bought the estate of Abramtsevo near Moscow and there formed an artists' colony where the Vasnetsov brothers, Vasilii Polenov, Elena Polenova, Konstantin Korovin, Valentin Serov, Mikhail Vrubel, and many others visited, painted, and participated in the amateur theatricals staged there every summer. The colony involved the prominent Russian painters of the day with scenic and costume designs for the theater, an innovation which was to influence those of Konstantin Stanislavii (Mamontov's cousin-in-law), Serge Diaghilev's Les Ballets Russes, the Moscow Art Theater. 1885, Savva launched his Opera Privé in Moscow and brought Russian opera to the attention of his countrymen. Elizabeth, who was devoutly religious, had a small church built at Abramtsevo, which sparked a general interest in the revival of Russian medieval art and architecture.

Manderfield, Ellen B. (1916–1999)

American industrial designer.

Training Bachelor of fine arts degree, Mundelein College, Loyola University; to 1939, commercial art school elsewhere.
Biography 1939–45, she worked as a packaging and graphics designer; subsequently, supervised a staff of seven and designed TVs, portable radios, record players at Colonial Radio Corporation (later named Sylvania); 1947–51 under Anne Swainson, designed sewing machines, accordions, bathroom fixtures, lawn mowers, and other appliances at Montgomery Ward, Chicago; 1952–56, designed electronic equipment and TVs at General Electric, Syracuse, N.Y.; 1953, founded the Syracuse chapter of Industrial Designers Institute (IDI); 1956, rejected an offer to work at the Donald Deskey studio in New York and instead worked at the Oneida silversmithy until her 1986 retirement. Oneida's 1975 Omni stainless-steel cutlery represents the simplicity of her work, which nevertheless ranged from historicist to modern aesthetics, Scandinavian modern to Early American.
Citations 1957, first woman accepted for membership, American Society of Industrial Designers (ASID); 1992, first woman granted Personal Recognition Award, Industrial Design Society of Americ (IDSA).
Bibliography Cat., Pat Kirkham (ed.), *Women Designers in the USA, 1900–2000: Diversity and Difference*, New York: Bard, New Haven: Yale, 2000.

Mandrot, Hélène de (1867–1948)
> See de Mandrot, Hélène.

Mandsfelt Eriksen, Steen (1958–)

Danish industrial designer.

Training To 1993, industrial design, Det Kongelige Danske Kunstakademi, Copenhagen.
Biography 1994–96, Mandsfelt Eriksen worked as an industrial designer on Danish Private Railway's IC2 train, in research/development department of ABB Scandia (later named ADtranz); 1998–99, worked on the development of ergonomically oriented office and school furniture at SIS International; 1994, established his own design firm. Work has included 1994–99 radio equipment by Danitas Radio, 1995 supermarket cash register by TAB Hugin, 1995–97 work lighting by Protec Production, 1996–2000 mini-compressors and lighting by Backuum, 1996–99 vacuum cleaner by Nilfisk-Advance, 1996–98 concept de-

Angelo Mangiarotti. Table (no. T-98). c. 1998. Glass and wood, h. 28 3/8 x dia. 51 1/8" (72 x 130 cm). Mfr.: Novikos International, Italy.

velopment for LEGO Futura (play objects for children ages 4–6, by LEGO), and 1996–2000 power-drill/screwdriver combination.
Citations 1996 Danish ID Vision Prize; 1998 and 1999 Dansk ID Prizes.

Manente, Giuseppe (1947–)
> See Kairos, Studio.

Mangiarotti, Angelo (1921–)
Italian designer; born and active Milan.

Training To 1948, architecture, Politecnico, Milan; 1953–54, Institute of Design, Illinois Institute of Technology (IIT), Chicago.
Biography Mangiarotti was guest professor, Institute of Design, IIT, Chicago, where Ludwig Mies van der Rohe was the director; had a design office in Ohio; 1955, returned to Italy and 1955–60 set up Mangiarotti e Morassutti studio with Bruno Morassutti; from 1960, worked alone as architect, designer, and town planner, emphasizing industrial-production solutions. His buildings have been in the International Style, with construction elements resembling those of Pier Luigi Nervi. Mangiarotti realized prefabricated structures, primarily in reinforced concrete. He became a member, ADI (Associazione per il Disegno Industriale). Design work has included 1958 Model 44 portable sewing machine by Salmoiraghi and 1961–63 Secticon CI clock by Portescap, an example of how, during this period, Italians were combining sculpture with a Rational approach to function. 1963 chair by Cassina exemplified his concern for strong plastic silhouettes in everyday objects. He designed collapsible furniture, glassware, and metalware, including 1947 door handle (first handle by him and his first for Olivari); glass vase and marble ashtray by Knoll;1969 IN chair (self-skinned in one-piece molded multi-density polyurethane) by Zanotta; faïence tableware by Danese; 1986 La Badoera table by Poltronova; 1967 Lesbos (including 1979 Egina, 1983 vases and 1984 tea-and-coffee service by Cleto Munari, 1986 Pericle, and c. 2000 Helios) by Artemide, 1988 First Glass vase by Colle. Other glassware by Vetreria Vistosi (1967–68, 1982) and Seguso Vetri d'Arte (c. 1990). By Skipper: 1981 Asolo table, 1982 Estrual bookcase, marble accessories, marble table range, 1984 Terra Blanca table, 1985 Ganci lamp, and 1988 More table. 1970, he was a visiting instructor, University of Hawaii; 1982–84, taught, Facoltà di Architettura of universities in Palermo and Florence. Buildings include 1957 Mater Misericordiae church, Baranzate, near Milan; 1963 exhibition pavilion for Fiera del Mare, Genoa; 1964 workshop hall of Società Elmag, Lissone, near Monza; 1968 administration and factory building, Cinisello Balsamo, near Milan. 1989, he founded Mangiarotti & Associates (with 12 Japanese architects, including Motomi Kawakami) in Tokyo for architecture and design; from 1996, began designing for Baleri Italia.
Exhibitions/citations Work included in editions various of the Triennale di Milano and a large number of venues worldwide, and subject of 1985 exhibition, Kunstindustrimuseet, Oslo; *Mangiarotti: Architettura, Design e Scultura* (marking 80th birthday of Mangiarotti in 2001), Triennale di Milano. Received Premio Compasso d'Oro: 1957, 1959, 1967 (two citations), 1989, 1994 (for his body of work). 1998, was granted an honorary engineering doctorate degree, Technische Universität, Munich, Germany.
Bibliography *Angelo Mangiarotti 1955–1964*, Tokyo: Seido-sha, 1964. 'Angelo Mangiarotti,' *Architecture and Urbanism*, Sept. 1974. Giulia Veronesi, *Mangiarotti (1962–1963): profili*, Florence, 1969. Enrico D. Bona, *Angelo Mangiarotti: il processo del costruire*, Milan: Electa, 1980. *Architectural Digest*, Mar. 1964. Gillo Dorfles, *Il disegno industriale e la sua estetica*, Bologna: Cappelli, 1963. Andrea Branzi and Michele De Lucchi (eds.), *Il design italiano degli anni '50*, Milan: Ricerche De-sign, 1985. Cat., Tore Brantenberg et al, *Sammenhenger Angelo Mangiarotti*, Oslo: Kunstindustrimuseet, 1985. Juli Capella and Quim Larrea, *Designed by Architects in the 1980s*, New York: Rizzoli, 1988. Vittorio Gagone and Monica Luchi, *Disegnare il cristallo: Angelo Man-giarotti*, Milan: Idea, 1991. Guido Nardi, *Angelo Mangiarotti*, Rimini: Maggioli, 1997. Enrico D. Bona, *Mangiarotti*, Genova: Sagep, 1998. Luciano Caramel, *Il DNA della scultura—Angelo Mangiarotti*, Carrara: Internazionale Marmi e Macchine Carrara, 1999. Beppe Finessi, *Su Mangiarotti*, Milan: Abitare Segesta, 2002.

Pio Manzù. Chronotime clocks. 1968. ABS polymer casing and metal parts, each h. x dia. 2 3/4" (6.7 cm). Mfr.: Italora, Italy. Purchase and gift of Signora Pio Manzu. MoMA.

Mangiarotti, Raffaella (1965–)
Italian designer; born Genoa; active Milan.

Training 1984, classical studies, Pavia; 1985–91, Facoltà di Architettura (industrial-design thesis) and, 1991–94, doctoral degree in industrial design, Politecnico, Milan.
Biography 1992, Mangiarotti worked as architect in the offices of Marco Zanuso Sr. and, 1993 of Francesco Trabucco, both Milan. 1994–99, she was a partner in the Trabucco design office; 1999 with Matteo Bazzicalupo, established Deepdesign studio in Milan, which has executed a number of commissions. 1996–2001, she was an assistant professor of industrial design and, from 2002, professor, Politecnico.
> See Bazzicalupo, Leopoldo Matteo.

Manock, Jerry (1941–)
American industrial designer; born Los Angeles.

Training 1968, master's degree in product design, Stanford University, Berkeley, Cal.
Biography Manock worked at Hewlett-Packard and at Telesensory; 1976, became a freelance designer; 1977, met Steven Jobs of Apple Computer and designed the casing for 1977 Apple II home computer and 1983 Macintosh 124K; was appointed Apple's first industrial-design manager, responsible for hiring many of the firm's early industrial and product designers; with Terry Oyama and Jobs, designed 1978–79 Apple III; managed the 1982–83 SnowWhite Project, which introduced Helmut Esslinger and his frogdesign studio as an in-house design operation within Apple's own offices. Thus, 1983, Esslinger's group displaced Manock and others. 1984, Manock left Apple and moved to Vermont where he lives today.
Bibliography Paul Kunkel, *Apple Design: The World of the Apple Industrial Design Group*, New York: Graphis, 1997.
> See Jobs, Steven.

Mantelet, Jean (1900–1991)
> See Moulinex.

Manzù, Pio (b. Pio Manzoni 1939–1969)
Italian automobile and industrial designer; son of sculptor Giacomo Manzoni (1908–1991) with the assumed name Manzù.

Training Hochschule für Gestaltung, Ulm.
Biography 1960s–70s, Manzù worked under Dante Giacosa on the design of automobiles, taxis, and tractors by Fiat, including 1968 Fiat City Taxi, 1971 Fiat 127, 1972 Fiat 850, and others. He also designed lighting and appliances; packaging for Olivetti; wrote for magazines *form*, *Industrial Design*, *Style Auto,* and *Interiors*. Other work: 1966 Cronotime table clock by Italora; a pencil holder in ABS by Kartell; and Parentesi lamp, completed 1970 by Achille Castiglioni, produced by Flos from 1971. Much of his design work was realized posthumously due to his having died at age 30 in the car crash of his Fiat 500 while driving to Turin to visit his father.
Exhibitions/citations Work included in 1983–84 *Design Since 1945* (Parentesi lamp), Philadelphia Museum of Art; 1972 *Italy: The New Domestic Landscape* (Cronotime clock), The Museum of Modern Art, New York. 1979 Compasso d'Oro (for Parentesi lamp).
Bibliography Alfonso Grassi and Anty Pansera, *Atlante del design italiano 1940/1980*, Milan: Fabbri, 1980: 91, 177, 244, 305. Cat., Kathryn B. Hiesinger and George H. Marcus III (eds.), *Design Since 1945*, Philadelphia: Philadelphia Museum of Art, 1983.

Mappin and Webb. Platter. 1904. Silver, dia. 13" (33 cm). Mfr.: Mappin and Webb, UK. Courtesy Quittenbaum Kunstauktionen, Munich.

Mappin and Webb

British silversmiths; located Sheffield.

History 1863, Mappin and Webb was founded; 1930s, produced modern silver designed by A.E. Harvey, Keith Murray, and James Warwick. However, modern silver remained a sideline while the firm continued to produce Art Nouveau and Arts and Crafts style silverware. To 1935, A. Hatfield was its chief designer. The Paris shop was the locale for the burgled jewelry store in Jules Dassin's film *Du rififi chez les hommes* (1955). The firm exists today primarily as a retail jeweler.
Bibliography Annelies Krekel-Aalberse, *Art Nouveau and Art Déco Silver*, New York: Abrams, 1989.

Marangoni, Alberto (1943–)

Italian designer; active Milan.

Training To 1964, Accademia di Belle Arti di Brera, Milan.
Biography 1964, Marangoni began his professional career, working on graphic and industrial design in studio MID in Milan; from 1967, was a member, Associazione per il Disegno Industriale (ADI), participating in its 1973 guidance committee; 1971–73, taught graphic design, Società Umanitaria, Milan; designed museum exhibitions for IBM Italia and others. Client list has included Anic, Borsa Valori, Ciba Geigy, Falk, Fratelli Fabbri Editori, Ferrania, Honeywell, Ideal Standard, Liquigas, Mondadori, 3M Italia, Pierrel, Profina, Rizzoli, Università di Pavia, and Citroën Italia.
Exhibitions Participated in 1968 (14th) Triennale di Milano; 1968 BIO 3 industrial-design biennial, Ljubljana; 1968 *Maggio Musicale Fiorentino*, Florence; 1967 International Graphics Biennial, Warsaw.
Bibliography *ADI Annual 1976*, Milan: Associazione per il Disegno Industriale, 1976.

Marblehead Pottery

American pottery; located Marblehead, Mass.

History 1904, Herbert J. Hall established Marblehead Pottery as one of several 'handcraft shops' providing occupational therapy for 'nervously worn out patients.' The shops produced handweaving, woodcarving, and metalwork, with pottery's being the most successful. Hall hired Arthur Eugene Baggs (1886–1947), a student at School of Clay-Working and Ceramics, Alfred (N.Y.) University; by 1908, the pottery was producing almost 200 pieces a week, including vases, decorated tiles, and jardinières. Staff members were Arthur Irwin Hennessey, Maude Milner, and Hannah Tutt; the kiln person was E.J. Lewis and the thrower John Swallow. A combination of brick clay from Massachusetts and stoneware clay from New Jersey was used. The pottery moved from workrooms at the Devereux mansion of Dr. Hall to 111 Front Street, Marblehead. 1916, Baggs took over ownership of the pottery; from 1920s, was there only in the summer; 1925–28, was a glaze chemist at Cowan Art Pottery Studio, near Cleveland, Ohio; 1928–47, professor, Ohio State University. 1936, Marblehead Pottery closed.
Bibliography 'The Pottery at Marblehead: The Exquisite Work Produced on the Massachusetts Coast,' *Arts and Decoration*, no. 1, Sept. 1911: 448–49. *Marblehead Pottery*, Marblehead: Marblehead Potteries, 1919. Elizabeth Russell, 'The Pottery of Marblehead,' *House Beautiful*, no. 59, Mar. 1926: 362, 364, 366. Arthur E. Baggs, 'The Story of a Potter,' *Handicrafter*, no. 1, April–May 1929: 8–10. *American Art Pottery*, New York: Cooper-Hewitt Museum, 1987: 124.

Marchand, Christophe (1965–)

Swiss designer; born Fribourg.

Training To 1991, industrial design, Hochschule für Gestaltung, Zürich.
Biography Marchand has taught at a number of institutions; from 1998, collaborated on the design of exhibitions with Alfredo Häberli at the Museum für Gestaltung, Zürich; 1993–99, worked with Häberli or independently on industrial-design projects for firms such as Authentics, Alias, Danese, Driade, Edra, Luceplan, Thonet, and Zanotta. Recent Marchand work has included a 2002 range of chairs (Carré in an integral, self-healing foam, Wave, and Jelly) by Ycami.
Citations 1991, IKEA-Beneficence grant; 1997 Appel Permanent grant and 1998 Carte Blanche production support, VIA (French furniture association), France; 1997 Design Preis Schweiz (for Sec by Alias, with Häberli).
> See Häberli, Alfredo.

Marcks, Gerhard (1889–1981)

German sculptor and potter; born Berlin.

Training Under Georg Kolbe and Richard Scheibe, in sculpture; and in Paris.
Biography Marcks was a member, November-Gruppe, Berlin; from 1918 with Walter Gropius and others, a member, Arbeitsrat für Kunst; taught, Kunstgewerbeschule, Berlin; 1919, was appointed by Gropius as *Formmeister* of the production workshop in the ceramics annex of the Bauhaus in Dornburg. Much of Marcks's design during the Dornburg period was ornate and archaic, later became innovative. His 1924 Sintrax coffee maker by Jenaer Glaswerke of Schott & Gen. illustrates an understanding of materials and mass-production. 1925 after leaving the Bauhaus, he taught, Kunstgewerbeschule Burg Gübichen-

Gerhard Marcks. Sintrax coffeemaker. c. 1924. Heat resistant glass, wood, rubber, and metal, overall height 11 3/4 x widest dia. 5 1/2" (29.8 cm x 14 cm). Mfr.: Jenaer Glaswerk, Schott & Genossen, Germany. Philip Johnson Fund. MoMA.

stein, Halle; due to Nazi pressure, the school's activities, like those of the Bauhaus, were suspended. After World War II, he taught, Landeskunstschule, Hamburg. 1971, the Gerhard Marcks-Stiftung was established in Bremen. He died in Burgbrohl/Eifel.
Exhibitions Created sculpture for main entrance of Walter Gropius's Installation at 1914 *Deutscher Werkbund-Ausstellung*, Cologne. Work subject of 1953 exhibition, Walker Art Gallery, Minneapolis; 1969, University of California, Los Angeles, Art Galleries, and Portland (Oregon) Art Museum; 1989, Galerie Vömel, Düsseldorf; others.
Bibliography Adolf Rieth, *Gerhard Marcks*, Recklinghausen: Bongers, 1959. Cat., *Gerhard Marcks*, Los Angeles: University of California, 1969. Günter Busch, *Das plastische Werk: Gerhard Marcks*, Frankfurt am Main: Propyläen, 1977. Martina Rudloff (ed.), *Gerhard Marcks zum 90. Geburtstag: das Werk des vergangenen Jahrzehnts, 1968–1978*, Bremen: Gerhard Marcks-Stiftung, 1979. Cat., Marlina Rudloff (ed.), *Gerhard Marcks, 1889–1981: Retrospektive*, Munich: Hirmer, 1989.

Marcot, Alain

French interior architect.

Training École des Arts Décoratifs, Nice; École Nationale Supérieure des Arts Décoratifs, Paris.
Biography Marcot was an instructor and vice-president, École Nationale Supérieure des Arts Décoratifs, Paris; from 1977, a freelancer and an associate at Cabinet Concepteurs Associés; designed 1999 interiors of Hôtel Pont Royal, Paris, incorporating lighting by Isolux; established his own interior-architecture agency in Paris; is president Fédération Nationale des Syndicats Architects d'Intérieur (FNSAI).
Citations 1966 Formica prize; 1969 Prix Révélations CREAC of Union Nationale d'Industries Français d'Ameublement (UNIFA).
Bibliography Robert A.M. Stern (ed.), *The International Design Yearbook*, New York: Abbeville, 1985/1986.

Marcoussis, Louis (b. Ludwig Casimir Ladislas Markus 1878–1941)

Polish painter and textile designer; born Warsaw; active Paris.

Training From 1910 under Jan Grzegorz Stanisławski, painting, academy of fine arts, Warsaw; from 1903, under Jules Lefèbvre, Académie Julian, Paris.
Biography 1903, Markus settled in Paris and worked under Jules Lefèbvre at the Académie Julian. 1907, he abandoned painting but, 1910, once again assumed the activity, turning to Cubism. He associated with Guillaume Apollinaire (who suggested his pseudonym Marcoussis, used by Markus from 1917), Georges Braque, and Pablo Picasso; made his living by selling caricatures to satirical periodicals, including *La vie parisienne* and *Le journal*; c. 1914, devised the *papier collé* technique; from 1919–28, realized a number of paintings on glass. In the decorative arts in 1920s, he became known for his geometric-motif rugs, some of which for courturier Jacques Doucet. With the advancing German army in 1940, Marcoussis moved to Cusset, near Vichy, where he died within the year.
Exhibitions Work first shown, at 1905 edition of Salon d'Automne; 1906 edition of Salon des Indépendants; subsequently, frequently at both; 1912 Section d'Orork (painting); a large number follow, including one-person venues. Work subject of 1979 exhibition, Centre Georges Pompidou, Paris.

Mare, André (1887–1932)

French painter, decorator, and furniture designer; born Argentan (Orne); active Paris.

Training Painting, Académie Julian, Paris.
Biography 1903–04, Mare shared a studio with Fernand Léger; from c. 1911, worked closely with Roger de la Fresnaye. The decorative arts began showing up in the work he submitted to annual Salons in Paris, although he then considered himself primarily a painter. 1910 with architect Louis Süe, he began designing furniture in L'Atelier Français on the rue de Courcelles, Paris; produced radical Cubist furniture designs for Raymond Duchamp-Villon's Maison Cubiste at 1912 edition of Salon d'Automne; some time before 1914, began bookbinding, with a penchant for vellum and parchment and a vivid palette akin to Ballets Russes sets and costumes and German avant-garde painting, although his motifs were influenced by Louis-Philippe decoration. His bindings included covers for *Le temple de Gnide*, *Les Fioretti*, *La nuit vénitienne*, *Les jardins*, and *Des voyages et des parfums*. During World War I, his wife Charlotte oversaw the production of his furniture, rug, and fabric designs while he served in the armed forces. 1919 with Süe and Gustave Jaulmes, he decorated the cenotaph beneath the Arc de Triomphe for the Fêtes de la Victoire. By 1918, Mare and Süe had begun their association under the name Belle France on the avenue Friedland, Paris, and, 1919, set up as interior designers in their firm Compagnie des Arts Français (CAF) at 116, rue du Faubourg Saint-Honoré. They designed the costumes and sets for 1921 production of Maurice Ravel's *L'heure espagnole* at the Opéra, Paris. At CAF, they drew on the talents of friends such as Maurice Marinot and André Marty to take on any aspect of interior design. Others included Marie Laurencin, André Derain, and Raoul Dufy. Süe and Mare's furniture was distinguished by deep curves, carved garlands, contrasting woods, and gilded-bronze panels, inspired by the Louis-Philippe style; they also designed lighting and *objets d'art*. A portfolio of their work and projects with text by Paul Valéry was published as *Architecture* (1921). With Léandre Vaillat, Süe published *Rythme de l'architecture* (1923); Jean Badovici issued *Intérieurs de Süe et Mare* (1924). Mare managed the interior-decoration activities of the firm and the 1910–12 execution of several furniture ensembles. 1920s, Süe and Mare designed silver by Orfèvrerie Christofle and by Tétard Frères, interiors for several oceanliners, and 1925 shop of d'Orsay perfumes in Paris, including its flacons. Other clients included Helena Rubinstein and Jean Patou. 1927–28, they constructed and furnished the villa of the actress Jane Renouard at Saint-Cloud. 1928, Jacques Adnet took over as director of design at CAF. Süe returned to architecture but continued to decorate. Mare returned to painting.
Exhibitions Work first shown at 1903–04 Salons, Paris. Mare showed decorations and furnishings of Maison Cubiste at 1912 Salon d'Automne. With Süe, designed two pavilions (one for CAF, the other for Musée des Arts Contemporains) at 1925 *Exposition Internationale des Arts Décoratifs et Industriels Modernes*, Paris, where their work was included in pavilions of Christofle and Baccarat. Subject of 1971 exhibition, Ancienne Douane Strasbourg; 1986–87 with Süe, Institut Français d'Architecture, Paris (catalogs below).
Bibliography Ami Chantre, 'Les reliures d'André Mare,' *L'art décoratif*, July–Dec. 1913: 251–58. *André Mare et la Compagnie des arts français (Süe et Mare)*, Strasbourg: ISTRA, 1971. Raymond Foulk, *The Extraordinary Work of Süe and Mare*, London: The Foulk Lewis Collection, 1979. Margaret Mary Malone, 'André Mare and the 1912 Maison Cubiste,' master's-degree thesis, University of Texas at Austin, 1980. Cat., *Un demi-siècle de reliures d'art contemporain en France et dans le monde*, Paris: Bibliothèque Forney, 1984. Cat, Susan Day, *Louis Süe, 1875–1968: Architecte des années folles, associé d'André Mare*, Liège: P. Mardaga, 1986. Alastair Duncan and Georges de Bartha, *Art Nouveau and Art Déco Bookbinding*, New York: Abrams, 1989. Florence Camard, *Süe et Mare et La Compagnie des Arts Français*, Paris: Amateur, 1993.

Margold, Emanuel Josef (1889–1962)

Austrian architect, interior designer, ceramicist, and silversmith; born Vienna; active Vienna, Darmstadt, and Berlin.

Training Under Josef Hoffmann, Kunstgewerbeschule, Vienna.
Biography Margold became an assistant of Hoffmann at the Wiener Werkstätte; 1911, went to the artists' colony in Darmstadt of Grand Duke Louis IV of Hesse-Darmstadt where he and Theodor Wende were the last artists to settle there. At Darmstadt, he was a prolific designer of furniture, glass, and porcelain; 1913, was commissioned by Bruckmann & Söhne of Heilbronn to design silver, which showed fine beading, fluting, and heart-shaped leaves; treated floral decoration with an approach similar to Hoffmann's. He designed umbrella handles by K. Jordan in Darmstadt and packaging for bakery Bahlsen Keksfabrik, Hanover; 1929, settled in Berlin; was listed in 1949 Union des Artistes Modernes (UAM) manifesto as a foreign contributor.
Exhibitions/citations Grand prize (for a display presentation there), 1910 *Exposition Universelle et Internationale*, Brussels.
Bibliography Günther Feuerstein, *Vienna—Present and Past: Arts and Crafts—Applied Art-Design*, Vienna: Jugend und Volk, 1976. Cat., *Ein Dokument Deutscher Kunst*, vol. 4, Darmstadt: Die Kunstler der Mathildenhöhe, 1976: 132–43. Stuart Durant, *Ornament from the Industrial Revolution to Today*, Woodstock, N.Y.: Overlook, 1986. Annelies Krekel-Aalberse, *Art Nouveau and Art Déco Silver*, New York: Abrams, 1989.

Mari, Enzo (1932–)

Italian designer; born Novara; active Milan.

Training 1952–56, Accademia di Belle Arti di Brera, Milan.
Biography 1956, Mari first became interested in design, especially of

Enzo Mari. Java container. 1969–70. Melamine, overall h. 3 3/4 x dia. 5 5/8" (9.5 x 14.3 cm). Mfr.: Bruno Danese, Italy. Gift of the mfr. MoMA.

books and children's games; 1957, began working for Danese, for which some of his designs and ideas were for games and puzzles such as the 1957 wooden puzzle for children. From 1959, he designed experimental objects in plastics, continuing with 1962 cylindrical umbrella stand in PVC and 1968–69 reversible Tortiglione vase series in ABS plastic by Danese. From 1963, he was a member of the Nuove Tendenze movement; 1963–66, taught design methodology and graphics, Scuola Umanitaria, Milan; 1970, taught, Centro Sperimentale di Cinematografia, Rome; 1972, at Istituto di Storia dell'Arte, Università di Parma; at Accademia di Belle Arti, Carrara; Facoltà di Architettura, Politecnico, Milan. From 1965, he collaborated with his brother Elio Mari. Enzo Mari published his design and research theories in *Funzione della ricerca estetica* (1970) and other lighter titles; designed a 1972 bookcase (with Elio Mari) by Fabina; 1974 grid-pattern Quaderna table and 1979 Delfina chair by Driade; 1979 Elementare wall tiles by Gabbianelli; 1985 Tonietta chair by Driade (reentered into production c. 2001 by Robots). Other clients: Anonima Castelli, Artemide, Editore Boringhieri, Gabbianelli, Gavina-Knoll, ICF, De Padova, La Rinascente-Upim, Olivetti, Simón International, and Le Creuset. 1976–79, he was president, Associazione per il Disegno Industriale (ADI). His 1996 Service Berlin porcelain dinnerware (and subsequent additions) by Königliche Porzellan-Manufaktur (KPM) of Berlin was widely published.
Exhibitions/citations Work subject of 1984 exhibition, Palazzo Reale, Milan. Refused to execute an environment for *1972 Italy: The New Domestic Landscape*, The Museum of Modern Art, New York, and supplied an Anti-Design statement instead. Work included in 1970 Danese-products exhibition, Musée des Arts Décoratifs, Paris (catalog below); 1972 *Design a Plastické Hmoty*, Uměleckoprůmyslové Muzeum, Prague; 1983–84 *Design Since 1945*, Philadelphia Museum of Art; 1991 *Mobili Italiani 1961–1991: Le Varie Età dei Linguaggi*, Milan; numerous others. Premio Compasso d'Oro: 1960, 1967, 1979, 1987, 1989, 1991, 1994, 1998, 2001.
Bibliography Max Bill and Bruno Munari, *Enzo Mari*, Milan: Muggiani, 1959. Cat., *Contenir, regarder, jouer* (1970 exhibition), Milan: A. Lucini, 1969. Enzo Mari, *Funzione della ricerca estetica*, Milan: Comunità: 1970. Cat., Emilio Ambasz, *Italy: The New Domestic Landscape*, New York: The Museum of Modern Art, 1972. Renato Pedio, *Enzo Mari designer*, Bari: Dedalo Libri, 1980. Arturo Carlo Quintaballe, *Enzo Mari*, Parma: Università di Parma, Centro Studi e Archivio della Communicazione, 1983. 'Colloqui Di Modo: Artigianato non esiste,' *Modo*, no. 56, Jan.-Feb. 1983: 22–25. Leonetti, Francesco et al., *Enzo Mari: modelli del reale = models of the real*, Milan: Mazzotta, 1988. Antonio d'Avossa and Francesca Picchi, *Enzo Mari: il lavoro al centro*, Milan: Electa, 1999.

Mariani, Massimo (1951–)

Italian designer; born Pistoia; active Florence and Montecatini Terme.

Biography 1980 with Alberto Casciani, Mariani established Stilema Studio to design and produce furnishings for public and private clients.
Exhibitions Work shown at *Wohnen von Sinnen*, Kunstmuseum, Düsseldorf.
Bibliography Cat., Emilio Ambasz, *Italy: The New Domestic Landscape*, 1972. Fumio Shimizu and Studio Matteo Thun (eds.), *The Italian Design: Descendants of Leonardo da Vinci*, Tokyo: Graphic-sha, 1987.

Marimekko

Finnish fabric manufacturer, marketer, and retail-store chain.

History Armi Ratia (1912–1979) worked in her own weaving workshop in Vyborg until 1939, selling the rya rugs that she designed. 1949, her husband Viljo Ratia bought the firm Printex, which at the time produced oilcloth. She joined Printex and reorganized the factory to accommodate silkscreen printing by hand on thin cotton sheeting. A number of designers began producing motifs, including Maija Isola and Vuokko Eskolin-Nurmesniemi. The first dresses made in Printex's new cotton fabric were presented under the name Marimekko ('Mary's dress' in eastern Finnish dialect); and entered in the Trade Register on 25 May 1951. At a later date the entire operation took this name. 1960s, the motifs became larger and bolder, particularly in motifs by Isola, and flower and bird silhouettes were introduced. The firm also produced furniture such as 1961 Kameleontti sofa by Torsten Laakso. 1960s–70s, Marimekko products included cotton, jersey, and wool fabrications along with paper, laminated plastics, and table coverings. Through franchises worldwide today, the store also sells simple clothing for women and children along with some household accessories and furniture, including pieces by Alvar Aalto. 1985, the children of Armi Ratia (Ristomatti, his sister, and brother) sold the firm to Amer-Group. Subsequently, Marimekko was bought by the HackmanGroup.
Exhibitions Work subject of 2003 venue, Bard Center, New York (catalog below).
Bibliography *The Marimekko Story*, Helsinki: Marimekko Printex, 1964. David Davies, 'Fabrics by Marimekko,' *Design*, no. 236, Aug. 1968: 28–31. 'The Finn-Tastics,' *Sphere*, Mar. 1975. Ristomatti Ratia, 'The Legacy of Armi Ratia,' *Form Function Finland*, nos. 1–2, 1980: 10–11. Cat., Kathryn B. Hiesinger and George H. Marcus III (eds.), *Design Since 1945*, Philadelphia: Philadelphia Museum of Art, 1983. Pekko Suhonen, *Phenomenon Marimekko*, Helsinki: Marimekko Oy, 1986. Marianne Aav (ed.), *Marimekko: Fabrics, Fashion, Architecture*, New Haven: Yale, 2003.
> See Ratia, Armi; Ratia, Ristomatti.

Marinot, Maurice (1882–1960)

French painter and glassmaker; born Troyes.

Training From 1889, painting and sculpture, École des Beaux-Arts, Paris.
Biography From c. 1900, Marinot was a member of artists' group Les Fauves. 1911, his interest in glass was sparked when he visited the glasshouse of brothers Eugène and Gabriel Viard at Bar-sur-Seine, where, at first, he designed decorations applied in enamel by an artisan, and later by himself. He created bold motifs in stark colors; from 1913, learned to make glass; by 1921, had abandoned enamel decoration in favor of thick-walled, internally decorated pieces. At first he incised them deeply; later, worked at the furnace and developed special glasses produced at lower temperatures, which enabled him to construct massive and complex forms with very thick gathers laid one upon the other. His work became widely known through exhibitions and articles in journals; priced beyond the means of most people, it was sought after by museums. After World War II, Marinot returned to painting.
Exhibitions/citations Paintings shown with Les Fauves at 1905 edition of Salon d'Automne, and glassware in 1912; continuously to 1913, in International Exhibition of Modern Art (or so-called Armory Show, first modern art shown in the US), 69th Regiment Armory building, New York. Work was on continuous display at Galerie Adrien Hebrand, rue Royale, Paris; subject of 1965 exhibition, Musée de des Beaux-Arts, Lyon; 1990 (painting and glass), Musée de l'Orangerie (catalogs below). First prize in the glass section, 1937 *Exposition Internationale des Arts et Techniques dans la Vie Moderne*, Paris.
Bibliography Guillaume Janneau, *Le verre et l'art de Marinot*, Paris: Charles Moreau, 1925. *Art déco*, Brussels: Société Générale de Banque, 1925. Cat., *Marinot*, Lyons: Musée de Lyon, 1965. Cat., *Le cinquantenaire de l'Exposition 1925*, Paris: Musée des Arts Décoratifs, 1976. Cat., *Verriers français contemporains*, Paris: Musée des Arts Décoratifs, 1982. Cat., *Maurice Marinot, peintre et verrier*, Paris: Musée de l'Orangerie/Réunion des Musées Nationaux, 1990.

Mariscal, Javier (1950–)

Spanish designer; born Valéncia; active Barcelona.

Training To 1967, philosophy, Universitat de València; to 1971, graphic design, Elisava (Escola Superior de Disseny), Barcelona.
Biography Mariscal's 1970s poster designs included one (1979) for

city of Barcelona as a pictogram of the words *bar cel ona* ('bar sky wave' in Spanish). In addition to his furniture by Memphis, Mariscal designed 'neo-déco' graphics, a 1950s pop-art canine-featured comic strip character called 'Garriris' (for which he became somewhat well-known), quasi-ethnic carpets, 'neo-baroque' ersatz bronze sculpture, pop-comic zig-zag lamps, bold primary-colored Klee/Morris-like textile patterns, grinning cats, Kandinsky-like ceramics, and objects in an intentionally kitsch taste. Beginning as a cartoonist, he drew a 1974 series called 'Comix Underground' for *El Rollo Enmascarado*; 1978, began decorating houses in Barcelona and Valéncia and created his first textile range by Marieta. His first piece of furniture was the asymmetrical brightly colored 1981 Dúplex bar stool (designed for Bar Dúplex in Valéncia), by Bd Ediciones de Diseño. He came to the attention of Ettore Sottsass through the Bar Dúplex (with Fernando Salas) in Valéncia and 1981 *Muebles Amorales* (amoral furniture) exhibition (with Cortes) at Sala Vinçon, Barcelona, and thus participated in the initial 1981 Memphis exhibition, Milan (organized by Sottsass) for which Mariscal designed 1981 Hilton backwardly slanting tea cart, 1981 Colén table, and 1981 Luminaires Impossibles. Other work: 1984 fabrics by Tráfico de Modas; 1985 ceramic range by Vinçon; 1986 ceramic range by Axis; Torero and Tio Pepe chairs for 1987 Centre Georges Pompidou exhibition, Paris, that parodied Spanish culture; 1986 MOR Sillón sofa and 1986 Trampolín chair (with Cortés) by Akaba; 1986–87 fabric collection by Seibu; 1990 *The Cobi Troup* animated TV series; 1990 logotype for Onda Cero Radio and three TV spots in 3D; Cobi mascot for 1992 Barcelona Summer Olympiad; mascot for 1992 *Exposición Universal de Sevilla (Expo '92)*; 1995 Twipsy mascot for 2000 *World's Exposition*, Hanover; 1995 and 1996 furniture collections by Moroso; 2002 graphics and interiors of Gran Hotel Domine in Bilbao; 2002 corporate identity of Gran Vía L'Hospitalet in Barcelona. Subsequent furniture clients: Akaba, Adex, Nani Marquina, Pamesa, Alessi, Swatch, Vorwerk, Rosenthal, Sangetsu, and Santa & Cole.
Exhibitions Work subject of 1977 *Gran Hotel*, Galería Mec Mec, Barcelona; *Mariscal* (1982 fabric collection), Espace Actuel, Paris; 1988 *Cien Añes en Barcelona*, Barcelona; 1989 exhibition, London. Work included in 1981 *Muebles Amorales* (prototypes of furniture by Vinçon), Sala Vinçon, Barcelona; 1983–84 *Design Since 1945* (printed textiles for Marieta and furniture), Philadelphia Museum of Art; 1986 *Nouvelles Tendances: Les Avant-Gardes de la Fin du XXe Siècle*, Centre Georges Pompidou, Paris; 1987 Documenta 8, Kassel; 1986 *Barcelona*, Espace MCC, Saint-Étienne, France; *Design World 2000*, Konstindustrimuseet, Helsinki.
Bibliography *Graphic Design*, no. 76, Dec. 1979: 52. Barbara Radice (ed.), *Memphis: The New International Style*, Milan: Electa, 1981. 'Mariscal,' *De diseño*, no. 10, 1987. Guy Julier, *New Spanish Design*, London: Thames & Hudson, 1991. Emma Dent Coad, *Javier Mariscal: Designing The New Spain*, New York: Rizzoli, 1991. Guy Julier, *Mariscal*, Cologne: Taschen, 1992. Llàtzer Moix, *Biografía,* Barcelona: Anagrama, 1991. Cat., *100 años con Mariscal*, Valéncia: Generalitat de Valénciana, 1988. 'Estudio Mariscal,' *ON Diseño,* 1999 (special ed.).

Markelius, Sven (1889–1972)

Swedish architect, town planner, textile designer; born Stockholm.

Training Kungliga Tekniska Högskolan; Kungliga Konsthögskolan; both Stockholm.
Biography Markelius began his career in the office of Ragnar Östberg and participated in the Functionalist movement of the mid-1920s, influenced by Le Corbusier; 1928, cofounded Congrès Internationaux d'Architecture Moderne (CIAM); designed apartments, offices, and the 1932–34 concert hall in Hälsingborg; 1938–44, was a building administration member of Stockholm; 1944–54, was head of town-planning department and responsible for 1953–59 satellite-town Vällingby, which presaged subsequent approaches to town planning. He assisted with 1930 Stockholm Exhibition; was an author of *Acceptera* (with Gunnar Asplund and others), the manifesto of Swedish Functionalism (Stockholm: Bokförlagsaktiebolaget Tiden, 1931); designed the Swedish pavilion (that first won him recognition) at 1939–40 *New York World's Fair: The World of Tomorrow*; participated in the planning of United Nations building, New York. His other buildings included 1935 Collective House in Stockholm. He taught in Stockholm and at Yale University; 1950s, designed simple wooden furniture and, with Astrid Sampe, printed fabrics by Nordiska. Some of his textiles were marketed by Knoll Textiles. He died in Stockholm.
Bibliography Sven Markelius in C.E. Kidder Smith, *Sweden Builds...*, London: Architectural Press, 1950. 'Architecture in a Social Context: The Work of Sven Markelius,' *Architectural Record*, Apr. 1964: 153–64. Stefano Ray, *Il contributo svedese all'architettura contemporanea e lopera di Sven Markelius*, Rome: Officina, 1969. Stefano Ray, *Sven Markelius, 1889–1972*, Rome: Officina, 1989. Eva Rudberg, Sven Markelius, Stockholm: Arkitektur Förlag,1989.

Markham, Herman C. (d. 1922)

American ceramicist.

Biography Markham, a traveling salesperson living in Ann Arbor, Mich., was a rose enthusiast. He became dissatisfied with containers for displaying flowers and began throwing pots, at first with clays from his own yard; 1905 with his son Kenneth Markham, began producing pottery wares commercially. Using molds made after prototypes, these wares had the appearance of excavated relics, in forms based on classical models. 1913, they settled in National City, Cal., and set up a pottery calling on the convenience of the clays in the area. Their two types of wares were Reseau with fine texturing and delicate veins and Arabesque with a coarser rough texture. 1921, the operation closed.
Bibliography Paul Evans in Timothy J. Andersen et al., *California Design 1910*, Salt Lake City: Peregrine Smith, 1980: 76.

Marks, Margarete (aka Margarete Heymann-Marks Löbenstein 1899–1990)

German ceramicist; born Cologne; active Germany and London.

Training Kunstgewerbeschule, Cologne; Kunstakademie, Düsseldorf; 1920–21, Bauhaus, Weimar.
Biography She rendered free-form abstract pottery, greatly influenced by Vasilii Kandinsky; by 1921, had left the Bauhaus to work in a pottery at Frechen and teach at the Kunstgewerbeschule, Cologne, where she had earlier studied; 1922, worked at the Steingutfabriken Velten-Vordamm; 1923, married Gustav Löbenstein (who died in a 1927 car accident), and they founded the Haël-Werkstätten für Künstlerische Keramik in Marwitz, which was a member of the Deutscher Werkbund. 1932, the pottery closed due to worsening attitude against Jews and bad German economy and, 1935, was forcibly purchased by the Nazis. However, the pottery had been successful at one time, employing 120 people at its height and producing geometric dinnerware with colored glazes. 1935 assisted by department-store mogul Ambrose Heal, she moved to Britain; 1936 for only six months, had her own studio in the Minton factory in Stoke-on-Trent, producing her own designs under the backstamp 'Greta Pottery at Minton'; and, until 1939, was active in own workshop Greta Pottery using unglazed ware from Goss and from Wedgwood; 1938, married extra-mural tutor Harold Marks. After World War II, she worked in own studio-pottery workshop but never achieved significant success or respectability due to conservative attitudes in Stoke-on-Trent. She died in London.
Bibliography Cat., *The Bauhaus: Masters and Students*, New York: Barry Friedman, 1988. Cat., *Keramik und Bauhaus*, Berlin: Bauhaus-Archiv, 1989: 264.

Marquina i Audouard, Rafael (1921–)

Spanish architect, designer, and sculptor; born Madrid; active Barcelona.

Training 1943–49, Escola Tècnica Superior d'Arquitectura (EISAB), Barcelona.
Biography 1953, Marquina opened his own studio in Barcelona, where his first designs were a 1953 motorcyle and a tricycle by Carrocerias Terrasa Coast; 1960 with Miguel Milá and others, cofounded ADI/FAD (Associacion Diseño Industrial/Fomento Artes Decorativas) industrial-design/decorative-arts associations; 1966–68, was a professor, Elisava (Escola Superior de Disseny), Barcelona; 1968–71, was director of *especialidad diseño*, Escola Massana, Barcelona; has designed more than 50 products.
Citations 1961 and 1986 ADI Medal (both for invention of 1960 non-drip olive-oil/vinegar cruet, re-introduced by Mobles 114), ADI/FAD; first Gold Delta Award, ADI/FAD, at 1961 meeting of International Council of Societies of Industrial Design (ICSID), Venice.
Bibliography R. Marquina and S. Pey, *El libro del hogar: La casa y su decoración*, Barcelona: Danae, 1974.

Marquina, Nani (1952–)

Spanish designer; born and active Barcelona; daughter of Rafael Marquina.

Training 1970–75, Escola Massana, Barcelona.
Biography From 1975, Marquina worked at the Selles-Marquina Estudio Arquitectura, her father's firm; 1978, established her own

business, Self Decor, a combination shop/interior-design enterprise; 1980, set up her own decoration studio, specializing in fabric and carpets; designed her first collection (1981–83), by Faitesa; 1986, created her own eponymous label, introducing Cuadrícula and Ibiza carpet collections; has commissioned designers Antoni Arola, Eduard Samsó, América Sánchez, Javier Mariscal, and others for textiles by her firm, as well as her best-known carpet, 1997 Cuadros. She designed a special carpet for the 35th birthday (1994) of the Barbie doll; 1992, was vice-president, ADI/FAD (Associacion Diseño Industrial/ Fomento Artes Decorativas).
Exhibitions/citations Work included in exhibitions of Catalán design, Osaka in 1989 and New York in 1990. Also, 1995 *Primavera del Disseny*, Barcelona; 1995–2002 Casa Décor fairs; 1999 *Women Made*, Catalunya and Baleares Islands; 2002 *Pasión, Diseño Español*, Sala de Exposiciones Santo Domingo, Salamanca, traveling to Berlin and Vienna. 1988 selection, Selección Internacional de Diseño de Equipamiento para el Hábitat (SIDI) for furnishings for the home, Spain.
Bibliography Cat., *Pasión, diseño español*, Salamanca: DDI and SEACEX, 2002.

Marriott, Michael (1963–)
British designer; born London.

Training 1985, higher diploma in furniture, London College of Furniture; 1993, master of arts degree in furniture, Royal College of Art, London.
Biography After 1985, Marriott worked for a lighting-design consultancy; subsequently, held various positions in the fields of carpentry and graphic design; after 1993, established his own studio and became active as a designer of furniture, products, and exhibitions. Clients have included Mathmos, Trico, SCP, Inflate, 20/21, Oreka Kids, Die Imaginäre Manufaktur (D.I.M.), SMAK (City Museum of Contemporary Art, Ghent, Belgium). Marriott has taught and lectured at many institutions in Britain and abroad and was a tutor, master's program in product design, Royal College of Art.
Exhibitions/citations Work included in 1996 *Not So Simple*, Cologne; 1996 *Design of the Times: One Hundred Years of the Royal College of Art*, London; 1996 *Objects of Our Time*, Crafts Council, London; *Highlights: Design from Great Britain*, Cologne; 1998 *Upside Down/ Inside Out*, Copenhagen; 1999–2001 *Lost and Found*, touring Europe; 1999 *Identity Crisis*, Glasgow; 2000 *Bring Me Sunshine*, Tokyo; 2001 *Home Sweet Home*, Stockholm; *Global Tools*, Vienna. Received 1994 Crafts Council Award; 1999 Jerwood Applied Arts Prize for Furniture; both UK.
Bibliography David Redhead, *Products of Our Time*, Basel: Birkhäuser, 2000. Catherine McDermott, *20th Century Design*, Woodstock, New York: Overlook, 1997. Cat., Clare Catterall and Christopher Frayling, eds., *Design of the Times: One Hundred Years of the Royal College of Art*, Richard Dencs, 1996.

Maria Martinez and Popovi Da (1931–). Jar. 1960. Stone-polished blackware, h. 9 1/2 x dia. 10" (24.1 x 25.4 cm). Mfr.: the designers, US. Gift of the Louis Comfort Tiffany Foundation, and Celeste G. Bartos, Mr. and Mrs. Gifford Phillips, and the Cornelius N. Bliss Memorial Fund. MoMA.

Marshall, Bryan
> See Bang Design.

Martens, 'Dino' Corrado (1894–1970)
Italian glass designer; born Venice.

Training Accademia di Belle Arti, Venice.
Biography 1925 in Murano, Martens produced glass designs for Studio Ars et Labor Industrie Riunite (SALIR), a firm specializing in engraved and painted mirrors on blanks made by others; 1932–35, designed glass, including glass mosaics, by Salviati & C.; 1944–63, at the end of his career, worked for Successori Andrea Rioda and for Vetri Decorativi Ragioniere Aureliano Toso. At the latter, his ideas were produced in a great variety of distinctive forms and techniques, especially his best-known work today: vividly colorful, irregularly shaped vases of the 1950s. He died in Venice.
Exhibitions 1932 (glass mosaics by Salviati) and 1934 (vases) Biennale di Venezia; 1933 Triennale di Milano (reticello glass objects).
Bibliography Rosa Barovier Mentasti, *Venetian Glass 1890–1990*, Venice: Arsenale, 1992. Marc Heiremans, *Muraner Glas-Designer. Werkverzeichnis = Dino Martens: Muranese Glass Designer 1922–1963*, Stuttgart: Arnoldsche, 1999.

Martin, Charles (1848–1934)
French graphic artist and designer.

Training Écoles des Beaux-Arts, Montpellier; under Fernand Cormon, École Nationale des Beaux-Arts, Paris; Académie Julian.
Biography Martin was prolific as a graphic artist, including of book illustrations; also designed stage sets and costumes for plays, revues, and ballets, and furniture, furnishings, fabrics, and wallpaper for several decorators, including Groult, for whom he painted panels and screens.
Exhibitions Work shown at editions of Salon d'Automne and Salon des Humoristes.
Bibliography Léon Deshairs (intro.), *Modern French Decorative Art: A Collection of Examples of Modern French Decoration*, Paris: Albert Lévy, c. 1925–30. Victor Arwas, *Art Déco*, New York: Abrams, 1980.

Martin, Henri Étienne (1913–1995)
> See Étienne-Martin, Henri.

Martine, Atelier
French interior design studio; located Paris.

History 1911, fashion designer Paul Poiret set up the design studio Martine primarily to sell the designs of the working-class students of his École Martine. Classes for young women were at first run by Madame Sérusier, wife of Symbolist artist Paul Sérusier. Instruction was later altered to a more experimental approach through, among other activities, visits to zoos, botanical gardens, and the countryside. They designed fabrics, wallpapers, murals, and Cubist wooden furniture (made by Pierre Fauconnet) in bright colors or with busy-patterned veneers, recognizable for their colorful, flat, and often floral motifs; produced rugs, fabrics, wallpapers, and interior design schemes. Their wares were much in demand. Poiret opened an interior-decoration business through which he sold a range of wares and offered decoration consultancy to hotels, restaurants, offices, and private clients. 1924, a branch was opened in London; goods were exported widely, including to the US. 1910, Poiret met Josef Hoffmann in Vienna and was particularly attracted to the Wiener Werkstätte's folk-derived textiles in floral patterns. Raoul Dufy collaborated with the Martines and Poiret before 1912, when he joined textile firm Bianchini et Férier in Lyon, although Dufy continued to be associated with Poiret. The group designed the Chantilly deluxe suite on 1927 oceanliner *Île-de-France*. At first set up at 83, rue du Faubourg Saint-Honoré, Paris, the shop was moved to the avenue Victor-Emmanuel-III and Rond-Point des Champs-Élysées in 1924, where it remained to its 1934 closing.
Exhibitions Martine students first showed their work as sketches and patterns in two rooms at 1912 edition of Salon d'Automne; designed Poiret's three houseboats (*Amours*, *Délices*, and *Orgues*), docked near 1925 *Exposition Internationale des Arts Décoratifs et Industriels Modernes*, Paris.
Bibliography Palmer White, *Poiret*, New York: Potter, 1973. Victor Arwas, *Art Déco*, New York: Abrams, 1980. Pierre Kjellberg, *Art déco: les maîtres du mobilier, le décor des paquebots*, Paris: Amateur, 1986/ 1990. Yvonne Deslandres, *Paul Poiret, 1879–1944*, Paris: Regard, 1986, New York: Rizzoli, 1987. Jonathan M. Woodham, *Twentieth-Century Ornament*, New York: Rizzoli, 1990. Paul Poiret, *My First Fifty Years*

(biography), London: V. Gollancz, 1931 (English ed.). Alice Mackrell, *Paul Poiret*, London: Batsford, 1990.

Martinelli, Elio (1922–)

Italian lighting designer; born Lucca.

Training Painting and architecture, Accademia di Belle Arti, Florence.
Biography 1942 with others, Martinelli set up a lighting firm; 1956, established Martinelli Luce in Lucca, designing and producing plastics and metal lamps. The firm's production included plastics from the beginning, with only acrylics at first. It followed with metacrylate, melamine, ABS, and Delrin. Its designs were based on the square, the sphere, and derived forms. In addition to Martinelli himself, commissioned designers included Gae Aulenti, Sergio Asti, Giovanni Bassi, Sergio Martinelli, and Studio DA. Production was in small series.
Exhibitions Work included in 1966 (1st) Eurodomus, Genoa; 1967 (2nd) Eurodomus, Turin; 1968 (14th) Triennale di Milano; *Domus Design*, Switzerland and the Netherlands; 1972 *Design a Plastické Hmoty*, Umĕleckoprůmyslové Muzeum, Prague; and numerous since.
Bibliography *Moderne Klassiker: Möbel, die Geschichte machen*, Hamburg: Gruner + Jahr, 1982: 61. Giuliana Gramigna, *1950/1980 Repertorio*, Milan: Arnoldo Mondadori, 1985. Cat., Hans Wichmann, *Italien Design 1945 bis heute*, Munich: Die Neue Sammlung, 1988.

Martínez Lapeña, José Antonio (1941–)

Spanish architect and landscape and product designer; born Tarragona.

Training 1962, in building and, to 1968, architecture, Escola Tècnica Superior d'Arquitectura de Barcelona (ETSAB).
Biography 1968, Martínez and Eliás Torres Tur set up an architecture practice. From 1984, Martínez was a professor of design, Escola Técnica Superior d'Arquitectura del Vallès (ETSAV), Sant Cuget del Vallès; from 1980, a professor of design, Escola Tècnica Superior d'Arquitectura de Barcelona (ETSAB). He and Torres designed 1986 Lampelunas street light by Cemusa, 1986 Barcelona and 1986 Hollywood rug by BVD, and 1987 bus shelter (with José Luís Canosa) by Cemusa. From 1982, their architecture/landscape included a gallery, a park, and a hospital in Barcelona and a school in Olot.
Citations 1986 Delta d'Oro, ADI/FAD (industrial-design/decorative-arts associations); 1986, 1988, and 1992 Premi FAD d'Arquitectura Award (best Barcelona building); 2001 Premi FAD d'Espais Exteriors Award (best outdoor space); all Spain.
Bibliography Juli Capella and Quim Larrea, *Designed by Architects in the 1980s*, New York: Rizzoli, 1988.
> See Torres Tur, Eliás.

Martinez, 'Marie' María (b. María Montoya 1887–1980); Julian Martinez (1879–1943); Popovi Da (1923–1971); Tony Da (1940–)

Native American potters. Maria: born San Ildefonso Pueblo, N.M. Julian: born New Mexico. Wife, husband, son, and grandson, respectively.

Biographies María Martinez, who learned pottery from her sister Tia Nocolasa, made traditional US-Southwest-native polychrome pots at first, painted with red clays and *guaco*, a black pigment from wild spinach. From 1912, she was internationally known as 'the potter of San Ildefonso' for her polished black pots; was fêted by four US presidents. Her husband Julian, whose Indian name was Pocano, created many highly influential paintings on paper at first. Then, 1918, he discovered how to produced a matte effect on certain areas of the shiny black surfaces of pots. (Black earthenware in the area dates back to the late 19th century.) The couple also trained others in San Ildefonso in this technique, eventually resulting in a cottage industry of highly desirable wares. (The pots were not wheel turned.) 1930–43, Maria and Julian cosigned their pieces. From Julian's 1943 death to 1954, she worked with their son Adam and his wife Santana. From 1956, her second son Popovi Da collaborated with Maria on all aspects of pottery preparation and their pieces were cosigned. Popovi began putting dates on the work from c. 1959. Not wishing to detract from his mother's effort, Popovi rarely made pottery on his own. Purportedly, the first piece signed by him alone is dated 1962. (His wife was Anita Da.) Even though Popovi began with the legendary blackware, he was one of the first Pueblo potters to break from it. Tony Da (1940–), the son of Popovi, experimented with painting and jewelry making early on and, 1964 when he returned to San Ildefonso from service in the US Navy, apprenticed himself to his grandmother María. The careers of the three men in the family ended prematurely—Julian and Popovi from death and Tony from a motorcycle accident (c. 1980), which prevented his return to pottery.
Exhibitions/citations Only hours after their wedding, María and Julian left for the 1904 *Louisiana Purchase Exposition*, Saint Louis, where she performed native dances and demonstrated pottery making. María also conducted pottery demonstrations at 1915 *Panama-Pacific International Exposition*, San Francisco; 1933–34 *A Century of Progress Exposition* (granted a bronze medal from Ford Foundation), Chicago, and 1939–40 *Golden Gate International Exposition*, San Francisco. To María: numerous awards and honorary doctoral degrees internationally.
Bibliography Alice Marriott, María: *The Potter of San Ildefonso* (Norman: University of Oklahoma, 1948. Susan Peterson, *The Living Tradition of María Martínez*, New York: Kodansha, 1989. Ron McCoy, 'Tony Da,' in Lee M. Cohen (ed.), *Art of Clay: Timeless Pottery of the Southwest*, Santa Fe: Clear Light Publishers, 1993. Richard L. Spivey, *The Legacy of María Poveka Martinez*, Santa Fe: Museum of New Mexico, 2003.

Martinuzzi, Napoleone (1892–1977)

Italian sculptor and glass designer; born Murano; possibly a glass-blower's son.

Training Free Art School and Accademia di Belle Arti, both Venice; under sculptor Angelo Zanelli, Libera Accademia di Belle Arti, Rome.
Biography 1911, Martinuzzi returned to Venice to work as a freelance glass designer, but prior had been highly active and successful as a sculptor; 1917, was the favorite artist of writer/dramatist Gabriele D'Annunzio, for whom he designed glass and sculpture, culminating in a commission to design D'Annunzio's mausoleum; from 1921–31, was director, Museo Vetrario di Murano, and, concurrently, designed glass for Successori Andrea Rioda. (1922, Martinuzzi cofounded the artists' group Circolo Artistico Veneziano and, 1924, Confederazione delle Arti Plastiche.) From 1925, was the artistic director and a partner, Vetri Soffiati Muranesi Venini & C. Martinuzzi left Venini and, 1932, joined with Francesco Zecchin and founded Zecchin-Martinuzzi Vetri Artistici e Mosaici where, to 1936, he was artistic director. 1936, he turned exclusively to sculpture but returned to glass. And, 1947–53, he was artistic director of Alberto Seguso's Arte Vetro. Over time, his work ranged from chandeliers to sculpture to small animals and vases. 1953–58, he designed for Vetreria Cenedese and its successor Vetreria Gino Cenedese; 1955, for Centro Studio Pittori nell'Arte del Vetro di Murano (Fucina degli Angeli); 1960–75, for Pauly & C. His designs for Pauly were fabricated by Vetreria Alberto Barbini.
Exhibitions/citations Work shown at 1908 (1st) exhibition of Secessionist group Cà Pesaro. Glass sculpture subject of exhibition at 1952 Bienale di Venezia. Glass designs shown at 1934 Bienale di Venezia; 1951 and 1957 (salon of honor) editions of Trienale di Milano.
Bibliography Marina Barovier et al., *Napoleone Martinuzzi: Vetraio del Novecento*, Venice: Il Cardo, 1992.

Martorell Codina, Josep Maria (1925–)

Spanish architect and industrial designer; born Barcelona.

Training To 1963. architecture and town planning, Escola Tècnica Superior d'Arquitectura de Barcelona (ETSAB).
Exhibitions/citations Work (with David Mackay and Oriol Bohigas) included in 1986 *Contemporary Spanish Architecture: An Eclectic Panorama*, Architectural League of New York. They received 1959, 1962, 1966, 1978–79 and 1991 Premi FAD d'Arquitectura Award (latter for best Barcelona building); 1966 and 1976 Delta de Plata award, ADI/FAD (industrial designers association for promotion of decorative arts); first prize, 1984 Internationale Bauaussetellung, Berlin; two first prizes, Prototype Schools Competition, Ministry of Education, Madrid. 1984 Premi FAD de Restauració (best restoration work). 1990 Premi FAD d'Interiorisme (for best interiors), Spain.
Bibliography Antón Capitel and Ignacio Solà-Morales, *Contemporary Spanish Architecture*, New York: Rizzoli, 1986: 64–67.

Marucco, Pierangelo (1953–)

Italian textile and ceramics designer; born and active Milan.

Training To 1970, Liceo Artistico di Brera; subsequently, architecture, Politecnico; both Milan.
Biography 1970, Marucco set up Designers 6R5 studio, producing designs for textiles and ceramics; 1975 with Maurizio Alberti, Giuseppi Bossi, Francesco Roggero, and Bruno Rossio, set up the studio Original Designers 6R5, Milan, designing textiles for Italian clients, inclu-

ding Lanerossi, Sasatex, Taif, and Bassetti, and Spanish firms, including Griso and Jover. They designed tapestry murals by Printeco, Le Roi, Grifine Marechal, and French wallpaper firms. Marucco became a member, Associazione per il Disegno Industriale (ADI).
Bibliography *ADI Annual 1976*, Milan: Associazione per il Disegno Industriale, 1976.

Marx, Enid Crystal Dorothy (1902–1998)

British textile and graphic designer, printmaker, and illustrator; born London.

Training Central School of Arts and Crafts; painting and wood engraving, Royal College of Art; both London.
Biography 1925–27, Marx worked with Barron and Larcher fabric manufacturer; subsequently, set up her own textile-printing workshop. Her work brought her to the attention of Gordon Russell, who helped her career. A versatile and prolific designer of decorative items until her death, she executed patterned papers for books and wrapping, book jackets for Chatto & Windus and for Penguin, illustrations, trademarks, printed and woven fabrics, wallpapers, posters for London Transport, calendars for Shell, ceramics, plastics, and postage stamps. She also designed a 1937 range of modern moquette-type fabrics for London Transport. Her serviceable and richly textured textile designs were produced in muted abstract patterns of chevrons, stripes, stars, and circles. She wrote British folk-art books *When Victoria Began to Reign* (with Margaret Lambert, London: Faber & Faber, 1937; subsequent eds.) and important *English Popular Art* (with Margaret Lambert, London: Batsford, 1951; 2nd ed. 1981) and eight children's books. Marx collected folk art, now Marx & Lambert Collection of Folk Art, Compton Verney, Warwickshire; designed fabrics by Edinburgh Weavers, some printed by herself.
Exhibitions/citations Participated in 1946 *Britain Can Make It* and 1951 *Festival of Britain* (textile by Morton Sundour); shown in Utility furniture venue (catalog below); all London. Work subject of an exhibition, Camden Arts Centre, London; 1983–84 *Design Since 1945*, Philadelphia Museum of Art. 1944, elected Honorary Royal Designer for Industry, UK.
Bibliography Cat., *Enid Marx*, London, Camden Arts Centre, 1969. Cat., *CC41: Utility Furniture and Fashion, 1941–1951*: Inner London Education Authority, 1974: 30–31. Jacqueline Herald, 'A Portrait of Enid Marx,' *Crafts*, no. 40, Sept. 1979: 17–21. Fiona MacCarthy and Patrick Nuttgens, *An Eye for Industry*, London: Lund Humphries, 1986. Cynthia Weaver, 'Enid Marx: Designing Textiles for the Utility Furniture Design Advisory Panel,' in *Utility Reassessed*, Manchester University, 1999. Cynthia Weaver, 'Enid Marx at the Central School in the 1920s,' in S. Backemeyer (ed.), *Making Their Mark: Art, Craft and Design*, London: Herbert Press, A. & C. Black, 2000.

Marx, Samuel A. (1885–1964)

American interior and furniture designer and architect; active Chicago.

Biography Marx's first commission was the 1909 competition-winning design of Delgado Museum of Art, New Orleans. He designed interiors and architecture, including those of 1937 The Arts Club, 1938 Pump Room of Ambassador East Hotel, 1939 Tavern Club, and Mary and Leigh Block 1941, all Chicago; May Company department store 1940, Los Angeles; Morton D. May (and house) 1942, Ladue, Mo.; Edward G. Robinson house 1944 and Mervyn LeRoy house 1944, Beverly Hills, Cal.; 1952 Alexander Hamilton Memorial, Chicago; 1957 Pierre Marques Hotel, Acapulco; others. Designed simple made-to-order furniture, some by Quigley & Company, Chicago; often chose fabrics by Dorothy Liebes and carpets by Stanislav V'Soske.
Exhibitions His interior of Pullman train car shown at 1933–34 *A Century of Progress International Exhibition*, Chicago; 1965 exhibition of Samuel and Florene May Marx's fine-art collection, The Museum of Modern Art, New York.
Bibliography 'Meet Samuel Marx,' *House Beautiful*, Nov. 1945, no. 87, p. 120. 'Furniture that Starts as Architecture,' *House Beautiful*, Oct. 1948, no. 90, p. 297. David Lowe, *Chicago Interiors*, Chicago: Chicago Contemporary Books, 1979. Cat., Liz O'Brien and Bob Hiemstra, *Samuel Marx: Furniture and Decoration*, New York: Forty One/Liz O'Brien, 1996.

Mascheroni, John (1932–)

American furniture and industrial designer; active New York.

Training Pratt Institute, Brooklyn, N.Y.
Biography Paul Mascheroni emigrated to the US and, 1924, established a furniture company in New York. His son John joined the firm and, 1960, became the head, exploring modern design. Work ihas ncluded Sereno lamp (with Tony Palladino) and Tubo table, both by Steelcase; has designed furniture for other manufacturers such as for Swaim and for Jeffco. John's son Mark is now a member of the firm.
Exhibitions Work shown at 1969 *Plastic as Plastic* (one-piece heat-bent clear-plastic chaise longue), Museum of Contemporary Crafts, New York; 1969 Annual Design Review, Museum of Science and Industry, Chicago; 1970 *Modern Chairs 1918–1970* (Chair 424 by Steelcase) Whitechapel Gallery, London; 1970 *Product Environment*, Saint Louis and traveling. (Catalogs below).
Bibliography Cat., Terrence Cashen and David Suttle, *Product Environment*, Saint Louis: City Art Museum, 1970. Cat., *Modern Chairs 1918–1970*, London: Lund Humphries, 1971. Arlene Hirst, 'World Class at Last,' *American Home*, Nov. 1990: 102.

Jean-Marie Massaud. Lola chair. 2000. Injection-molded plastic and aluminum, h. 31 1/2 x w. 24 x d. 20 1/2" (80 x 61 x 52 cm). Mfr.: Liv'it, Italy.

Maske, Cathrine (1966–)

Norwegian glass designer; born Trondheim.

Training 1989–93, Department of Ceramics, Statens kunstakademi, Oslo; 1993–96, Department of Ceramics and Glass Design, Taideteollinen korkeakoulu, Helsinki; 1996–97, Department of Photography, Kunsthøgskolen, Bergen.
Biography Maske has become known for her dramatic applications of photography with glass itself, particularly in thick-wall vases, achieving a magnifying effect.
Exhibitions/citations Work featured in a number of exhibitions, including 1996 *Finnish Post-War Glass*, Sunderland Museum and Art Gallery, UK; 1999 *Steninge World Exhibition of Art Glass*, Steninge Slott Kulturcenter, Märsta, Sweden; 1998 *Aktuelles Design aus dem Norden*, Museum für Kunst und Gewerbe, Hamburg, and Die Neue Sammlung, Munich; *Generation X: Young Nordic Design*, traveling the world from 2000. 1997 prize for young designers, Norsk Form; 1998 Young Design award, Norska Designrådet (ND, Norwegian design council); 1998 Scheiblers Legat, prize for young artists.

Massaloux, Laurent (1968–)
> See Radi Designers.

Massana, Josep Maria (1947–)

Spanish designer and entrepreneur; born and active Barcelona.

Training To 1969, Escola Massana, Barcelona.
Biography 1968–72 with Josep Maria Tremoleda (Barcelona, 1946–), Massana was active in their studio Equip de Disseny in Bar-

celona; 1971 with Mariano Ferrer Thomàs, Carles Riart, and Bigas Luna, cofounded design team Gris in Barcelona. Much of Massana's activities have been with Tremoleda, also a graduate (1969) of Escola Massana. 1973 also with Tremoleda and Mariano Ferrer Thomàs, established and managed '114,' a furniture shop and interior-design studio and, 1981, Mobles 114, an enterprise, that markets/commissions residential and commercial furniture, lighting, and accessories. Work with Tremoleda includes 1975 Gira lamp, 1975 Tria shelving sys-tem, 1994 Síria bathroom accessories, and 1999 Kiosk table, all by Mobles 114, and 1994 Ateneu armchair by Perobell; also designs with others. > See Mobles 114.

Massarelli, Leonardo (1979–)
> See Nó Design.

Massari, Noti
> See Toso, Aureliano.

Massaud, Jean-Marie (1966–)
French designer; born Toulouse.

Training To 1990, ENSCI (Les Ateliers), Paris.
Biography Massaud worked in several design agencies in Asia and France, including Philippe Starck's in Paris; 1994, established his own studio in Paris and has been active in interior design, scenography, industrial design, and other activities. European and Japanese clients have included Authentics, Baccarat, Back, Cacharel, Cappellini, Comet, Domeau & Pères, E&Y, Golden Whale, Habitat, ICM, Lancôme, Lanvin, Lexon, Liv'it, Ligne Roset, Magis, Mazzega, Mizuno, Offecct, Paloma Picasso, Tronconi, Technal. 1998–2000, he was furniture-design chairperson, École Nationale Supérieure des Arts Décoratifs, Paris; and visiting teacher, ENSCI, Paris; École Nationale Supérieure des Arts Décoratifs, Reims, and École Cantonale d'Art, Lausanne. With Thierry Gaugain and Patrick Jouin, he cofounder the Luxlab group in 1998, which designed 1999 Sol Mutable (mutable soil) real-grass installation; 2000 with Danile Pouzet, became active in architecture.
Exhibitions/citations Work included in a number of exhibitions, and subject of 1999 venue, Musée des Arts Décoratifs, Paris. 1994 (two citations) and 1999 Premio Compasso d'Oro; Chair of the Year, 1995 Salone Internazionale della Sedia (Promodedia), Udine; 1996 National Product Design Award, Australia; 1996 award, Industrie Forum Design (iF), Hanover; 1996 Grand Prix de la Presse et de la Critique and 1999 Nombre d'Or, Salon du Meuble, Paris.
Bibliography Mel Byars, *50 Beds...*, Hove: RotoVision, 2000. Pascale Cassgnau and Christophe Pillet, *Beef, Brétillot/Valette, Matali Crasset, Patrick Jouin, Jean-Marie Massaud: petits enfants de Starck?*, Paris: Dis Voir, 2000. Mel Byars, *On/Off: New Electronic Products*, New York: Universe, 2001. Vannick Grannec (preface), *Jean-Marie Massaud*, Paris: Pyramyd, 2003.

Massier, Clément (1844–1917)
French ceramicist; born Vallauris.

Training In his father's pottery.
Biography 1864, Massier set up his own workshop; from 1883, produced *faïence-vernissée* ceramics in Golfe-Juan, near Cannes, where numerous potters, including Jacques Sicard, were trained. 1886, Massier produced his first luster glaze. 1885–95, young painter Lucien Lévy-Dhurmer managed Massier's enterprise. Manus Alexandre and Jean-Baptiste Barol often collaborated with Massier, whose influence led to the establishment of new workshops for lusterware. Many manufacturers and artists referenced his work as a model for lusterware production. The Massier factory continues as a family business.
Exhibitions Work (with Optat Milet of Manufacture Nationale de Sèvres) shown at 1878 and 1889 editions of *Exposition Universelle*, Paris.
Bibliography *Europäische Keramik 1880–1930, Sammlung Silzer*, Darmstadt: Hessisches Landesmuseum, 1986: 128.

Massoni, Luigi (1930–)
Italian industrial designer; born Milan; active Cermenate.

Biography 1954, Massoni began his professional career; 1959, founded Mobilia, an association of furniture industrialists and one of the first centers for the promotion of Italian design; 1965–75, collaborated with the firm Guzzini and designed a number of products (Jolly bed tray currently in production) and developed Guzzini's corporate-image program; from 1972, was president and responsible for architecture and industrial-design department of A&D; from 1956–63, editor, *Marmo tecnica architettura*; from 1962, has been editor and designer, journal *Forme*; from 1963–66, editor, *Popular Photography*; from 1973, artistic director, Centro Forms; became a member, Associazione per il Disegno Industriale (ADI). As a a designer, Italian clients have included Alessi from 1953 (with a bar set, his first industrial design), Boffi (kitchen systems) from 1959, Poltrona Frau (furniture) from 1967, Fratelli Guzzini (plastic tableware and accessories) from 1964, Nazareno Gabrielli (leatherwork) from 1969, Gallotti & Radice (crystal) from 1969, and Palini (school furniture) from 1974. He wrote the book *Gifts from Italy: Design and Colour* (with Raffaello Baldini, Milan: Alfieri & Lacroix, 1971).
Exhibitions Work shown at 1985 Triennale di Milano (Nodi and Cerniere containers).
Bibliography *ADI Annual 1976*, Milan: Associazione per il Disegno Industriale, 1976. Cat., Carlo Guenzi, *Le affinità elettive*, Milan: Electa, 1985. Auction cat., *Asta di modernariato 1900–1986*, Auction *'Modernariato,'* Milan: Semenzato Nuova Geri, 8 Oct. 1986: lot 102. *Modo*, no. 148, Mar.–Apr. 1993: 122.

Massoul, Félix (1872–1942)
French ceramicist; born Saint-Germain.

Training École Nationale Supérieure des Arts Décoratifs, Paris.
Biography Massoul was active in enameling with metallic flecks on faïence; frequently worked with his archeologist wife Madeleine and studied blue Egyptian faïence; used ornate decoration in two blues and developed new glazes and *pâte-sableuse* stoneware; realized forms and designs in simple geometric patterns in blue, green, and burnished gold; with his wife, wrote and lectured on historic ceramics.
Exhibitions 1895, work (with his wife) first shown; Salons of Société des Artistes Français from 1903; salons of Société des Artistes Décorateurs from 1904; other exhibitions in France and abroad.
Bibliography Yvonne Brunhammer, *The Art Deco Style*, London: Academy, 1983: 143. *Europäische Keramik 1880–1930, Sammlung Silzer*, Darmstadt: Hessisches Landesmuseum, 1986: 137. Edgar Pelichet, *La céramique art déco*, Lausanne: Grand-Pont, 1988.

Masuda, Hisanori (1949–)
Japanese designer; born Shizuoka Prefecture.

Training Under Mosuke Yoshitake, Musashino University of Art, Tokyo.
Biography For five years, Masuda stayed on at the university as a studio assistant to Yoshitake. Masuda originally lived and worked in Tokyo and, 1977, settled in Yamagata City, where he established his own studio Chushin-Kobo in 1997. Though accomplished in the use of new materials, Masuda also calls on the Yamagata Prefecture's traditional of the distinguished production of metalware (beginning in the Heian period; A.D. 794–1185), particularly of *tetsubin* (hand-made cast-iron teapots) and trivets. His other work: 1999 Oquom Tableware Collection in sand-cast recycled aluminum and gold leaf by Kikuchi Hojudo (the manufacturer founded in 1604) and Chushin-Kobo. Masuda lec-

Luigi Massoni. Stacking tumblers. 1967. Acrylic, each h. 2 15/16" (7.5 cm) x dia. 2 9/16" (6.5 cm). Mfr.: Fratelli Guzzini, Italy. Gift of Bonniers, Inc. MoMA.

tures, training center of Yamagata Metal Casting Association (of which he is vice-president); also Tohoku University of Art and Design, Yamagata City. He is director, Japan Craft Design Association.
Exhibitions/citations Catalogs below; large number of other exhibitions, and awards.
Bibliography Cat., Paola Antonelli, *Mutant Materials in Contemporary Design*, New York: The Museum of Modern Art/Abrams, 1995. Cat., *Aluminum by Design*, Pittsburgh: Carnegie Art Museum, 2000.

Matégot, Mathieu (1910–2001)

Hungarian decorator and furniture designer; born Tapio-Sully.

Training Magyar Képzõmûvészeti Egyetem (Hungarian academy of fine art); Jasnick Academy; both Budapest.
Biography Matégot began as a set designer for the Nemzeti Színház (national theater), Budapest; traveled to Italy and the US; 1931, settled in Paris, working as a window dresser, particularly for Les Galeries Lafayette department store; 1933, designed some furniture in cane on metal; while still a painter, began working in tapestry and worked with renowned tapestry gallerist/producer Marie Cuttoli; during World War II, joined the French Resistance and became a prisoner and worker in a mechanical factory, where he was inspired by Bugatti-car perforated steel; after the war, was naturalized as a French citizen; was befriended by Jean Lurçat, who encouraged him to become further involved in tapestry, some eventually woven by Manufacture d'Aubusson. Matégot patented a perforated sheet, foldable and workable lilke cloth, realized first in his three-legged 1950 Nagasaki chair with a perforated metal seat, and also employed real and imitation leather. 1950s, became known for 1955 Kobe chaise longue in metal tubing and plastic upholstery, and Copacabana chair with a curved structure, and Papillon chair, which features a pair of wings, tables, and lighting. He used metal as a basic component for his furniture and stressed function rather than decoration; 1955, discontinued the production and design of furniture and objects, became more involved with interior design; from 1960s, turned exclusively to tapestry making; 1990, established Mathieu Matégot Foundation for Contemporary Tapestry Inc. in Bethesda, Md., US. Three Matégot tapestries (woven with Australian wool, produced by Aubusson) hang in the foyer of National Library of Australia, Canberra.
Exhibitions 1955 Salon des Arts Ménagers (Kioto and Panama chairs introduced). Work subject of 2002 venue, Villa Noailles, Hyères.
Bibliography Cat., Germain Bazin et al., *Les tapisseries de Mathieu Matégot*, Paris: Galerie La Demeure, 1962. Cat., *Mathieu Matégot*, Paris: Galerie La Demeure, 1971. *Ensembles mobiliers*, Paris: Charles Moreau, nos. 13–14, 1954. Yolande Amic, *Intérieurs: le mobilier français 1945–1965*, Paris: Regard, 1983: 54. Cat., Leslie Jackson, *The New Look: Design in the Fifties*, New York: Thames & Hudson, 1991: 124. Patrick Favardin, *Les décorateurs des années 50*, Paris: Norma, 2002: 36. Philippe Jousse and Caroline Montineu, *Mathieu Matégot (1910–2001)*, Paris: Jousse, 2003.

Matégot, Xavier (1956–)

French architect and furniture designer; born Paris.

Training École Comondo; to 1989, École d'Architecture Paris–Villemin.
Biography Matégot collaborates with other architects in the design of office and domestic interiors, in Paris; has also been independently active in industrial design, specializing in hospital and medical equipment and furniture/products/exhibition stands for Solitol, Art Bloc, Sopha Medical, SBC Sopha Bioconcept, Technal. From 1984, he has been as an architect and designer. In his furniture, he blends 1930s Constructivism with 1950s eccentricity. A large body of work has included 1986 M3 one-of-a-kind but widely published chair with floating arms and seat (sponsored by VIA [French Furniture Association]); 1986 M2 bookcase, 1987 M6 sideboard, 1988 M9 sofa, and 1989 steel-aluminum-granite bench, all by Christian Farjon, as well as the interior of the firm's headquarters; 1991 Gamma medical imaging device by Sopha Médical; exhibition stand of Institut Français de Restauration des Œuvres d'Art, 1990 Salon International des Musées, Paris.
Exhibition/citations A number of exhibitions, from 1987. Received 1984 and 1987 Appel Permanent grants, VIA; 1987 Bourse Agora award. Participated in interior-architecture competitions, including Counsel General's office at Belfort; COGEDIM competition, Counsel General's office at Hauts-de-Seine; competition of Assistance Publique Hôpitaux at Paris (hospital furniture), Cultural Center in Boulogne-Billancourt (SM7 chair).

Bruno Mathsson. Eva lounge chair (no. T101). 1934. Bent laminated beech wood and hemp webbing, 31 1/2 x 19 1/4 x 28 3/8" (80 x 48.9 x 72.1 cm), seat h. 15 7/8" (40.3 cm). Mfr.: Karl Mathsson, Varnamo, Sweden (1941). Purchase. MoMA.

Bibliography Christine Colin, *Design d'aujourd'hui*, Paris: Flammarion, 1988. Suzanne Tise, 'Innovators at the Museum,' *Vogue Décoration*, no. 26, June–July 1990: 48. Cat., *Les années VIA 1980–1990*, Paris: Musée des Arts Décoratifs, 1990: 130–31. Cat., Sophie Tasma Anargyros et al., *L'école française: les créateurs de meubles du 20ème siècle*, Paris: Industries Françaises de l'Ameublement, 2000.

Matet, Maurice (1903–1989)

French decorator and furniture designer; born Colombes.

Training École Nationale Supérieure des Arts Décoratifs, Paris.
Biography From 1923, Matet worked as a designer and decorator at the Studium decorating department of Les Grands Magasins du Louvre, where he sometimes collaborated with Étienne Kohlmann and Dubard. c. 1930, he was a professor, École des Arts Appliqués, Paris; after World War II, continued to design furniture, particularly in metal and glass, and radically modern silver tableware; died in Rueil-Malmaison.
Exhibitions 1923 edition of Salon d'Automne (bedroom and office with Kohlmann). Editions of Salon of Société des Artistes Décorateurs: 1926 (dining room), 1928 (tubular-metal furniture with rubber and leather fittings by Matet, Kohlmann, Djo-Bourgeois, René Herbst, and Charlotte Perriand), 1929 (Matet's more traditional Art Déco furniture by Saddier). 1925 *Exposition Internationale des Arts Décoratifs et Industriels Modernes* (dining room of Studium Louvre pavilion). All Paris.
Bibliography Léon Deshairs (intro.), *Modern French Decorative Art: A Collection of Examples of Modern French Decoration*, Paris: Albert Lévy, c. 1925–30. Pierre Kjellberg, *Art déco: les maîtres du mobilier, le décor des paquebots*, Paris: Amateur, 1986/1990. Maurice Dufrêne, *Ensembles mobiliers, Exposition Internationale 1925*, Paris: Charles Moreau, 1925; Woodbridge, Suffolk: Antique Collectors' Club,1989.

Mathews, Arthur Frank (1860–1945); Lucia Mathews (b. Lucia Kleinhans 1870–1955)

American artists, muralists, and furniture designers; active San Francisco; husband and wife.

Training Mathews: under Boulanger and Lefèbvre, painting, Académie Julian, Paris. Kleinhans: under Arthur Mathews, Mark Hopkins Institute.
Biography 1880s while studying in Paris, Frank Mathews was influenced by the new ideas current there and by oriental art, especially Japanese woodcuts; 1890–1906, was dean, Mark Hopkins Institute, San Francisco, responsible for a faculty trained in the Beaux-Arts tradition of Paris; established a regional (California) figurative tradition in the arts. Lucia Kleinhans met Mathews while a student at Mark Hop-

kins Institute, where she was his best student; became his sometime collaborator on decorative projects. He approached his work from an architect's or muralist's perspective, while she had a more painterly style and drew watercolors and pastels of flowers, landscapes, and children. Together they produced unique handmade pieces in a Beaux-Arts, rather than an Arts and Crafts, style. By 1910, the Mathewses were at the peak of their success as leaders of San Francisco's arts community and were identified with what came to be called the California Decorative Style of 1890s–1920s. Through their business, The Furniture Shop in San Francisco, they prolifically executed frames, paintings, furniture, fixtures, and accessories. 1906–20, the shop prospered during the rebuilding of San Francisco, after the 1906 earthquake/fire. Production consisted of domestic and public pieces, including large suites of furniture, and fixtures and custom murals. Lucia was fastidious in her application of decoration to smaller pieces and picture frames. Arthur's monthly magazine *Philopolis* debated ethical and aesthetic aspects of art, town planning, and the reconstruction of San Francisco, the city to which the Mathewses were so commited that they shunned opportunities to expand their business nationally. Having fallen into obscurity, they were rediscovered in 1970s.
Bibliography Harvey L. Jones in Timothy J. Andersen et al., *California Design 1910*, Salt Lake City: Peregrine Smith, 1980: 88–93.

Mathiesen, Lars (1950–)

Danish architect and designer; born Greenland.

Training To 1957, school of architecture, Det Kongelige Danske Kunstakademi, Copenhagen.
Biography 1973–78, Mathiesen was employed by Box 25 Architects, where he worked with Neils Gammelgaard (1944–); 1978–86 with Gammelgaard, was active in Pelikan Design; 1987–91 with Poul Christiansen and Boris Berlin, was a partner in Komplot; but, 1992 with Gammelgaard again, re-established Pelikan Design. Mathiesen taught, Det Kongelige Danske Kunstakademi, Copenhagen. Best known work (with Gammelgaard) has included 1980 child's Tribike by Rabo, café chair and Wing screen wall for Fritz Hansen A/S, 1994 Opus chair for Bent Krogh, office furniture by Duba, Ypsilon easy chair for Metteograssi, interior of train carriages of Banestyrelsen (Danish national railway agency); cabinet/stand of S6-series speakers and new Mi speakers by Audiovector.
Citations Pelikan Design: five times, Dansk ID Prize; 1984 Scan-Prize; 1991 New Scandinavian Furniture Award; 1993 Upholstered Furniture Design Award Europe; 1993 Danish Furniture Award; 1996 Red Dot award, Design Zentrum Nordrhein Westfalen, Essen; 1996 Brunel Design Award.
> See Gammelgaard, Niels.

Mathsson, Bruno (1907–1988)

Swedish designer and architect; active Värnamo.

Training Under his father, in cabinetmaking and designing in Värnamo.
Biography Mathsson opened a studio in Värnamo and specialized in natural wood, principally beech; followed his research into the physiology of seating and designed furniture with organic, flowing lines. Many of his designs were produced in the family furniture factory Karl Mathsson in Värnamo, with his later designs produced by Dux Möbel. His 1934 chair and compact 1946 extension table are still in production. He has become best known for 1934 Eva and 1942 Miranda chairs, produced by Karl Mathsson; Eva was produced from 1935 and redesigned with arms in 1942. Most of his chairs were given women's names, like the leather-cushioned Karin chairs, but he also designed the upholstered Jetson chair—both in tubular steel. Early 1960s, Mathsson collaborated with Piet Hein on adapting Hein's 'super-ellipse' ideas for furniture production and on developing a versatile self-clamping leg model. As an architect and interior designer who was influenced by a 1940s visit to the US, he pioneered glass-wall construction in Sweden; was one of the leading figures in the modern movement in that country. The Bruno Mathsson Award was established in his honor.
Exhibitions/citations Work shown at 1937 *Exposition Internationale des Arts et Techniques dans la Vie Moderne*, Paris; 1939–40 *Golden Gate International Exposition,* San Francisco; 1939–40 *New York World's Fair: The World of Tomorrow*; and a large number of other venues. Subject of 1993 exhibition, Nationalmuseum, Stockholm. 1955 Gregor Paulsson trophy; 1978, was elected Honorary Royal Designer for Industry, UK.
Bibliography Cat., *Möbler Bruno Mathsson, mattor Ingrid Dessau, tygtryck Borås Wäfveri*, Stockholm: Nationalmuseum, 1958. Cat., Karl-Gustaf Gester, *Bruno Mathsson, en klassiker bland modernister*, Stockholm: Stockholm Universitet, 1986. Ingrid Böhn-Jullander, *Bruno Mathsson, Möbelkonstnären, Glashusarkitekten, Människan*, Stockholm: Signum, 1992. Carl Christiansson, *Bruno Mathsson, Dikten om Människan som Sitter*, Stockholm: Raster, 1993. Mel Byars with Arlette Barré-Despond, *100 Designs/100 Years: A Celebration of the 20th Century*, Hove: RotoVision, 1999: 96–97.

Matras, Laurent (1961–)
> See Delo Lindo.

Matsunaga, Naoki (1936–)

Japanese designer; born Tokyo; active Milan.

Training To 1961, Tokyo Kogyo Daigaku (university of Tokyo).
Biography With Rudolfo Bonetto, Matsunaga has designed tables, seating, case goods, and other domestic products for Italian clients including BCM, Candy, Cimbali, Fratelli Guzzini, Olivetti, Simail, Sair Falconi, Voxon, and Romi in Brazil; became a member, Associazione per il Disegno Industriale (ADI).
Citations First prizes, 1960 Mainichi Industrial Design competition; 1965 (1st) Japan Display Design competition; 1966 (1st) Monstra dell'Arredamento (MIA), Monza.
Bibliography *ADI Annual 1976*, Milan: Associazione per il Disegno Industriale, 1976.

Matsushita Electric Industrial Co.
> See Panasonic.

Matta (b. Roberto Sebastián Matta Echaurren 1911–2002)

Chilean Surrealist painter and designer; born Santiago.

Training College of the Sacred Heart, Santiago; 1931, architecture degree; Catholic University, Santiago; 1935–37, in office of Le Corbusier, Paris.
Biography Matta was primarily known as a painter; 1936, went to Paris and, 1937, joined the Surrealists there; 1938, settled in New York, where he produced his strongest work; 1948, returned to Europe; mid-1960s, executed designs produced by Gavina (and its successor Simón) in Italy, including 1966 Malitte (or Muro) component-seating unit (produced 1966–68), and by Knoll International's acquisition of Gavina (produced 1968–74). The system's puzzle-like, stretch-fabric-on-polyester-foam units can be stacked as a vertical square when not demounted for seating. Designs by Matta for Gavina and subsequent Simón International (the later, Dino Gavina's firm founded in 1970) are

Matta (Roberto Sebastian Matta Echaurren). Malitte component seating system. 1966. Polyurethane foam and stretch-wool upholstery, overall 63 x 63 x 25" (160 x 160 x 63.5 cm). Mfr.: Gavina, Italy (c. 1969–70). Gift of Knoll International. MoMA.

the 1972 Magritta 'apple/hat' seat and Sacco Alato ready-made 'fakes.' Ultramobile continues some of Simón's production today.
Bibliography William Rubin, *Matta*, New York: The Museum of Modern Art, 1957. Eric Larrabee and Massimo Vignelli, *Knoll Design*, New York: Abrams, 1981. Cat., Kathryn B. Hiesinger and George H. Marcus III (eds.), *Design Since 1945*, Philadelphia: Philadelphia Museum of Art, 1983. Cat., Vittorio Sgarbi et al., *Dino Gavina, UltraMobile: 50 opere di Dino Gavina*, Begagna: ESG 89, 2000. Paola Antonelli (ed.), *Objects of Design: The Museum of Modern Art*, New York: The Museum of Modern Art, 2003: 255.

Mattu, Diego (1946–)

Italian designer; born and active Rome.

Training To 1970, Corso Superiore di Disegno Industriale e Communicazioni Visive, Rome.
Biography 1970, Mattu was a research assistant, Istituto di Psicologia of Consiglio Nazionale delle Richerche (CNR), Rome; 1971, was a designer for International Company Furniture (ICF)/De Padova, worked in the design studio of Enzo Mari in Milan, and was a graphic artist in Salaroli Piludu studio, Rome. From 1972, he was a designer and graphic artist in the Commissionaria Italiana Fabricche e Arredamento (CIFA) group, Rome, working for clients such as ItalBed and Uno Pi; 1968–72, developed an exhibition system for a department store, designed machinery, rendered maps and graphics for Istituto Assistenza a Sviluppo Mezzogiorno (IASM), and designed graphics for Italsonics; was a consultant designer to Mautren-Mec in Aprilia and a designer and graphic artist for Drobeta in Pomezia, Tortora in Prato, and for Betti and for Pallucco in Rome. He has written for journals, including *Rassegna Artistica*, *Casabella*, *Esso Rivista*, *MD*, and *Albergo Moderno*; designed furniture and case goods, often in plastics; 1968–74, created the signage of the Premio Compasso d'Oro events; became a member, Associazione per il Disegno Industriale (ADI); from 1997, has taught design and visual communication, Istituto Europeo, Rome; from 2000, has designed train-carriage furniture for Trenitalia and ship furniture for Flotta Laura and for Rodriguez.
Bibliography *ADI Annual 1976*, Milan: Associazione per il Disegno Industriale, 1976. Cat., Kathryn B. Hiesinger and George H. Marcus III (eds.), *Design Since 1945*, Philadelphia: Philadelphia Museum of Art, 1983.

Maugham, Syrie (b. Gwendoline Maude Syrie Barnardo 1879–1955)

British interior and furniture designer; born and active London; daughter of Dr. Thomas John Barnardo, founder of the Barnardo Homes for Boys and Girls; wife of Henry Wellcome and W. Somerset Maugham.

Biography After a scandal-filled youth, 'Queenie,' as her father called her, developed an interest in interior design and opened her first shop (1922) at 85 Baker Street in London. She began her decorating career on her own house, the Villa Eliza, in 1926 at 213 King's Road in Chelsea, London, in which she painted almost everything white—a successful publicity ploy. Also 1926, she opened a shop in New York, had a studio on Michigan Avenue in Chicago in the 1920s, and even designed a house for British male-impersonator Vesta Tilley. Marion Dorn, Oliver Messel, and Christian Bérard designed rugs, furnishings, and murals for Syrie's clients. She sold furniture wiped with a white paint solution, creating a so-called pickled finish; became notorious for applying this treatment to fine 18th-century pieces; adopted the calla lilly as her trademark. She was parodied in Beverley Nichols's *For Adults Only* (London: J. Cape, 1932) as the Countess of Westbourne and in Evelyn Waugh's *A Handful of Dust* (London: Chapman & Hall, 1934) as Mrs. Beaver. Success encouraged her to move in c. 1924 to headquarters in Grosvenor Square in London. Her 'white look' influenced Hollywood film sets and, 1960s–70s, was emulated by American interior designer Michael Taylor with his 'California look.' By 1933, she had abandoned her all-white period for a blue one, followed by a red one, then for a Victorian one, followed by what Cecil Beaton described as being in 'the vivid colors of lobster salad.' 1930s, her rival was decorator Sybil Colefax. Her clients included Noel Coward, Tallulah Bankhead, Clare Booth Luce, Ava and Paul Mellon, Mary Pickford, and the Duke and Duchess of Windsor. She became bankrupt but, early 1950s, executed a few commissions in the US. Syrie's first (1900) marriage was to Henry Wellcome (divorcing in 1916) and second (1917) marriage to author W. Somerset Maugham (Paris 1874–Nice 1965), to 1929. She was aware of Maugham's homosexuality and his relationship with American man Gerald Haxton (a Red Cross ambulance driver whom Maugham had met during World War I in France). However, Syrie had both a miscarriage and a child, Liza, by Maugham. 1927, Maugham left England amid scandal, divorced Syrie in Nice in 1929, and settled with Haxton (who was deported from England in 1919) in the villa Mauresque on the Cap Ferat, France. The wealthy Somerset Maugham spent the rest of his life there (except in Hollywood during World War II), entertaining the rich and literati until his death.
Bibliography Richard B. Fisher, *Syrie Maugham*, London/Dallas: Duckworth, 1978. Cat., *Thirties: British Art and Design Before the War*, London: Arts Council of Great Britain Hayward Gallery, 1979. Jessica Rutherford, *Art Nouveau, Art Deco and the Thirties: The Furniture Collections at Brighton Museum*, Brighton: The Royal Pavilion, Art Gallery and Museums, 1983: 54. Mitchell Owens, 'White Magic,' *Elle Decor*, Sept.1990: 92–96.

Maugirard, Jean-Claude (1939–)

French industrial and furniture designer; active Paris.

Training 1955–60, École Boulle, Paris.
Biography 1965, Maugirard invented the Mobile Cable System (MCS) for hanging paintings and objects in exhibitions; with François Barré, designed 1967 *Sigma 3* exhibition, Bordeaux, and 1968 Fosse de Conversation with modular furniture elements in foam; 1971, worked with injection-molded plastic and designed 1971 CH 131 elements and Kangourou boxes by Formag; was artistic director, Rattan Design Group; invented a range of 'new rustic' furniture by Bruynzeel-France; taught furniture design, École Nationale Supérieure des Arts Décoratifs, Paris; from 1978–94, was director of VIA (French furniture association), Paris, after which was its artistic director.
Bibliography Gilles de Bure, *Le mobilier français 1965–1979*, Paris; Regard/VIA, 1983: 44, 61–62, 74, 100, 108–09. Arlette Barré-Despond (ed.), *Dictionnaire international des arts appliqués et du design*, Paris: Regard, 1996.

Maurandy, Daniel (1922–)

French industrial designer.

Training In law and architecture.
Biography 1960, Maurandy founded Agence Parisienne d'Esthétique Industrielle (APES); 1970s, carried out an urban design program for the town of Vitry-sur-Seine, designing public furniture, signage, and transportation; often collaborated with Gérard Guerre on certain projects, including the corporate-identity programs of Fédération Nationale d'Achat des Cadres/FNAC (hi-fi and domestic appliances), Merlin Gérin (electronics), and Nobel Bozel (chemistry). 1975, APES was amalgamated into Technès to become Technès-Maurandy.
Bibliography Cat., *Design français 1960–1990: trois décennies*, Paris: Centre Georges Pompidou/APCI, 1988. François Mathey, *Au bonheur des formes, design français 1945–1992*, Paris: Regard, 1992. Arlette Barré-Despond (ed.), *Dictionnaire international des arts appliqués et du design*, Paris: Regard, 1996.

Maurer-Becker, Dorothée

German designer; wife of Ingo Maurer.

Biography Maurer-Becker is best known for her 1969 *Uten.Silo 1* (or *Wall-All II*) rack/storage in various permutations in ABS plastics by Ingo Maurer Design M, Munich (reissued by Vitra in 2000), and *Wall-All III* rack/storage by Format Sales, US. The unit is based on experiments in 1960s working in wood.
Bibliography Cat., *Plastics + Design, Munich: Die Neue Sammlung,* 1997.

Maurer, Ingo (1932–)

German graphic and lighting designer; born Reichenau, Lake Constance.

Training In typography, Lake Constance; 1954–58, in graphic design, Germany and Switzerland.
Biography 1960, Maurer worked in the US for Kayser Aluminum and for IBM as a designer, returning to Europe in 1963, where he was active as a graphic designer; 1965, received his first commission to design a lamp; 1966, set up his own one-person lighting-design workshop Design M, designed his first fixture (1966 Bulb table lamp) and became known for his witty and innovatory ideas. His 1979 Thomas Alva Edison fixture recognized the 100th anniversary of Edison's light bulb invention. Early 1980s, his intriguing Willydilly fluorescent hanging light fixture in cotton fabric and 1983 Ilios rocking lamp (his first halogen fixture) were widely published; 1980 Bulb Bulb fixture was a Pop Art statement in the form of a giant light bulb. Maurer's Baka Ru and in-

tricate 1984 Ya Ya Ho low-voltage ceiling system used a novel high-wire cable suspension system. The latter, whose metal arms could be moved along uninsulated cables, was also one of Maurer's innovatory miniature low-voltage lights. Other designs included 1982 Bibibbibi, 1986 Fukusu, 1994 Porca Miseria broken-ceramic-dinner-plates chandelier, and numerous others subsequently. From 1999, Maurer, his staff, and the commissioned designers have been experimenting with LED technology. Lindfors Stefan's 1988 Scaragoo table lamp and fixtures by others have been produced by Design M. Ingo Maurer edited *The International Design Yearbook* (2000); has declared, 'I have always been fascinated by the light bulb because it is the perfect meeting of industry and poetry. The bulb is my inspiration.'
Exhibitions/citations Work included in a large number venues. Subject of exhibitions, including 1986 *Ingo Maurer Lumière aha SoSo*, Institut Français d'Architecture, Paris; 1989 *Ingo Maurer: Lumière Hasard Réflexion*, Fondation Cartier pour l'Art Contemporain, Jouy-en-Josas, France; 1998 *Projects 66* (with the Campana brothers), The Museum of Modern Art, New York; 1992 *Ingo Maurer, Arbeiten mit Licht*, Museum Villa Stuck, Munich; 1993 *Licht Licht*, Stedelijk Museum, Amsterdam; 2001 *Pasión por la Luz* (retrospective of 1965–2000 work), Santa Mònica Art Center, Barcelona. Appointed 1997 Designer of the Year, *Architektur & Wohnen* magazine; other awards.
Bibliography 'Ingo Maurer, poète lumière,' *Intramuros*, Sept. 1985. Cat., *Luminères*, Paris: CCI/Centre Georges Pompidou, 1985. Herbert Bauer (ed.), *Ingo Maurer: Making Light*, Munich: Nazraeli, 1996. Cat., Helmut Bauer, *Ingo Maurer: Making Light*, Tucson, Ariz.: Nazraeli, 1997. Claudia M. Clemente, *Ingo Maurer: Percorsi di luce*, Turin: Testo & Immagine, 2000. Cat., *Ingo Maurer, Pasión por la luz = Passion for Light*, Barcelona: Artar, 2001. Michael Webb et al., *Ingo Maurer*, San Francisco: Chronicle, 2003. Paola Antonelli (ed.), *Objects of Design: The Museum of Modern Art*, New York: The Museum of Modern Art, 2003: 257, 272–73.

Mayne, Thom (1944–)
American architect and design; born Waterbury, Conn.

Training 1968, bachelor's degree in architecture, University of Southern California, Los Angeles; 1978, master's degree in architecture, Harvard University, Cambridge.
Biography 1972, Mayne founded Morphosis in Santa Monica, Cal., for the design of lighting and furniture, including 1988 Nee side chair, and architecture such as 1986 Kate Mantilini restaurant, Beverly Hills; 1987–92 Crawford house, Montecinto; 1992–96 Blades house, Santa Barbara; all California; and 1995–97 Sun Tower, Seoul, Korea. He taught, University of California; Harvard, Yale, Columbia, and Miami universities; others; cofounder, Southern California Institute of Architecture (SCI-Arc).
Bibliography Cat., R. Craig Miller (intro.), *U.S. Design 1975–2000*, Munich: Prestel, 2002.

Ingo Maurer. Bulb table lamp. 1966. Chromium-plated metal and glass, h. 11¾" (30 cm) x dia. 7⅞" (20 cm). Mfr.: Ingo Maurer, Germany (1998). Gift of the designer. MoMA.

Mayodon, Jean (1893–1967)
French ceramicist.

Biography Mayodon began as a painter; 1912, produced his first ceramic pieces, strongly influenced by Persian pottery; became known for a rich color palette. His pottery was made heat resistant by the addition of powdered clay, and decoration was painted with a brush or was highlighted with gold in low relief. He fired some pieces five or six times, creating colors with a metallic sheen; during World War II, was the director, Manufacture Nationale de Sèvres.
Exhibitions After World War I, work shown at Musée Galliéra, Paris.
Bibliography Cat., *Decorative Arts 1925 Style*, New York: Didier Aaron, 1979.

Mayrhofer, Adolf von (1864–1929)
German silversmith and enameler; active Munich.

Training Apprenticeship in workshop of F. Harrach, Munich.
Biography For 12 years, Mayrhofer was an assistant to E. Wollenweber, a silversmith to the Bavarian court; 1903, set up his own silversmithy and produced hand-raised beakers and slightly curved, somewhat foreshortened boxes with undecorated areas and carved ivory and ebony finials and handles; produced *cloisonné* pieces, and on others incorporated spiral ornamentation and, 1920s, silver designed by Else Wenz-Viëtor and Hermann Haas. 1921–24, Franz Rickert and Dietrich Bruckmann, son of Peter Bruckmann, apprenticed in Mayrhofer's workshop. Mayrhofer's silver was sold in Carel Begeer's shops.
Exhibitions/citations Work included in Munich silversmiths' collective display, 1910 *Exposition Universelle et Internationale*, Brussels, receiving a gold metal; and shown at 1914 *Deutscher Werkbund-Ausstellung*, Cologne.
Bibliography Annelies Krekel-Aalberse, *Art Nouveau and Art Déco Silver*, New York: Abrams, 1989. Reinhard W. Sänger, *Das deutsche Silberbesteck 1805–1918*, Stuttgart: Arnoldsche, 1991: 158–63.

Mays, 'J.' John (1954–)
American automobile designer; born Oklahoma.

Training To 1980, Art Center College of Design, Pasadena, Cal.
Biography From 1980, Mays worked for Audi motor company in Germany and contributed to the design of the Avus concept car; 1989, returned to the US as chief designer at Volkswagen in California, in charge (with Freeman Thomas) of the 1994 Concept 1 car, later to be introduced as the new Beetle. (Thomas had been brought to Volkswagen in 1991 and was to inspire the 1999 Audi TT by Peter Schreyer.) 1993, Mays returned to Audi as design director; 1994, left Audi and worked for brand-identity company SHR Perceptual Management in Scottsdale, Ariz., primarily on strategic planning and branding conceptualization. 1997, Jack Telnack asked Mays to assumed his position as the director of the design department at Ford in Detroit, Mich. Previously, Mays's car designs have primarily been those of concept models: 1997 Mercury MC4, 1999 Mercury Cougar, and 2000 Ford 24.7. Currently, Mays is the vice-president of design at Ford, in charge of Ford, Mazda, Mercury, Lincoln, Volvo, Jaguar, Land Rover, and Aston Martin. He tells the designers under him not to follow trends.
Exhibitions 2002 *Retrofuturism: The Car Design of J. Mays*, Museum of Contemporary Art, Los Angeles, first US museum to honor a single car designer.
Bibliography Penny Sparke, *A Century of Car Design*, London: Mitchell Beazley, 2002.

Mazairac, Pierre (1943–)
Dutch designer.

Training Hogeschool voor de Kunsten, Utrecht.
Biography Mazairac worked for Dutch furniture firm UMS-Pastoe; 1979 with Karel Boonzaauer, set up a design studio, whose clients have included Metaform (EBM glass-top table) and Pastoe (1985 Vision Monolith cabinet, reinterpreted in 2003).
Bibliography Robert A.M. Stern (ed.), *The International Design Year-*

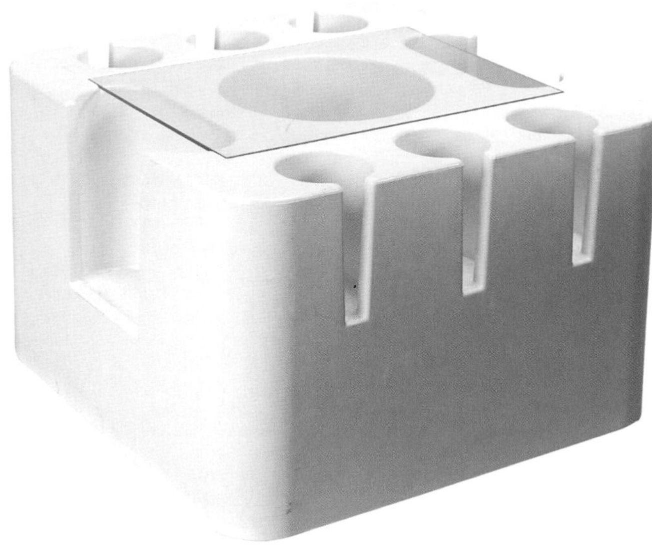

Sergio Mazza. Bacco table/bar. 1967. ABS plastic and plate glass, 15 7/8 x 24 1/8 x 24 3/16" (40.3 x 61 x 61.5 cm). Mfr.: Artemide, Italy. Courtesy Quittenbaum Kunstauktionen, Munich.

book, New York: Abbeville, 1985/1986.

Mazza, Sergio (1931–)

Italian interior architect and designer; born and active Milan.

Training To 1954, Institute of Architecture, Lausanne, Switzerland.
Biography 1955, Mazza began his professional career; 1956, opened his own office in Milan, collaborating with Giuliana Gramigna on domestic furnishings and industrial design. Clients have included Artemide (lighting and furniture), Saporiti Italia (furniture), Cinova, Poltrona Frau (furniture), Cedit (ceramics), Formica, Full, Krupp (domestic electrical appliances), and Lema. His Torlonia hanging lamp was produced by Quattrifolio. He has become known for his work in plastics, but his best-known pieces are 1968 Toga fiberglass chair and 1967 Bacco low, fitted mobile bar, both by Artemide. From 1961, continued collaborating with Gramigna on product design through their Studio SMC (Studio Mazza e Collaboratori) Architettura; 1966, founded the journal *Ottagono*, directing it to 1988; became a member, ADI (Associazione per il Disegno Industriale). He wrote the book *Milano: un secolo di architettura milanese dal Cordusio alla Bicocca* (with Gramigna, Milan: Hoepli, 2001.
Exhibitions/citations From 1954, participated in editions of Triennale di Milano. Work included in 1970 *Modern Chairs 1918–1970*, Whitechapel Gallery, London; 1972 *Italy: The New Domestic Landscape*, The Museum of Modern Art, New York; 1983–84 *Design Since 1945*, Philadelphia Museum of Art. Premio Compasso d'Oro: 1960 (for Static clock by Lorenz; Delta Grande lamp by Artemide), 1960 (for Delta Grande lamp by Artemide) and 1979 (for the journal *Ottagono* with Gramigna and Salvatore Gregorietti; Poker chair with Gramigna by Cinova).
Bibliography 'Sergio Mazza e Giuliana Gramigna,' *Interni*, no. 282, Sept. 1978: 54–57. Alfonso Grassi and Anty Pansera, *Atlante del design italiano 1940/1980*, Milan: Fabbri, 1980: 162, 168, 290. *ADI Annual 1976*, Milan: Associazione per il Disegno Industriale, 1976. *Modo*, no. 148, Mar.–Apr.1993: 122.
>See Gramigna, Giuliana.

Mazzer, Mario (1955–)

Italian designer; born San Vendemiano (Treviso).

Training 1977–79, architecture degree and certificate in industrial design, both Politecnico, Milan.
Biography 1979, Mazzer worked with Achille Castiglioni and, 1979, with Marco Zanuso Sr., both Milan; 1980, opened his own studio in Conegliano Veneto, active as an architect and industrial designer; from 1984, has been artistic director of Magis and designed for the firm; from 2000, artistic director of firms, including Bergamin, Jesse, Martex, Mimo, and View. Work has included 1993 Quinta furniture, 1994 Basic tables, and 1995 Central furniture by Acerbis; 1997 Origami desk and 1997 Plate tables by Alivar; 1989 Psiche lamp by Arcana; 1992 Parete furniture by Bonacina; 1995 Ritratto and Bernini dining tables and 1996 Girondo transformable table by Bros's; 1992 seating by Busnelli; 2002 Satori luminescent table by Cappellini; 1999/2001 Oblò kitchen system by Cappellini/Units; 1995 Merry-Hall accessories by Cidue; 1999 jewelry by Kikai Lamin; 2002 seating by Mimo. Other clients: Martex, Meson's, Mobel Italia, Morphos, Permasteelisa, Rossi di Albizzate, Uvet, Varaschin, View, Ycami, Zanette, Zanotta.
Exhibitions/citations 1987 *Italian Design*, Budapest; 1988 and 1989 (special mentions) and 1991 (winner) *Young & Design*, Milan; 1990 *30 Architects*, Milan; 1992, 1994, 1998 BIO industrial-design biennials, Ljubjana; 1993 and 1996 Abitare il Tempo fair, Verona.
Bibliography Cristina Morozzi and Silvio San Pietro, *Contemporary Italian Furniture*, Milan: L'Archivolto, 1996. Giuliana Gramigna and Paola Biondi, *Il design in Italia dell'arredamento domestico*, Turin: Allemandi, 1999. Mario Vigiak (ed.), *Thinking About Things: Mario Mazzer Designer*, Pordenone: Biblioteca Immagine, 2001.

Mazzoni delle Stelle, Alessandro (1941–)

Italian industrial designer; born and active Florence.

Training Industrial design, Istituto Superiore per le Industrie Artistiche (ISIA), Florence.
Biography 1969, Mazzoni began his professional career, founding the studio Associazione Reazionaria Design Italiani Totalement Integrati (A.R.D.I.T.I.) and started to develop an interest in furniture design, and where with others, he began research into a new utilitarian philosophy and investigation of objects with original formal traits. 1975 with the staff of Bayer engineering departments, he participated in a research project to develop system design; 1977 after closure of A.R.D.I.T.I, began working with other designers and technicians. From 1985, he collaborated with Gianfranco Gualtierotti; 1985–95, worked with Gualtierotti on various ideas; from 1988, has designed furniture by Zanotta, beginning with Europa sofa.
Exhibitions/citations Work shown at 1972 (4th) Eurodomus in Turin, 1973 (15th) Triennale di Milano, and numerous other national and international exhibitions, including 1982 *Italian Re-evolution* (Magia sofa with Pierluigi Bacci by Giovanetti), traveling the US. Received 1973 Design of the Month Award (for Memoria armchair), *Bolaffi Casa* magazine.
Bibliography *ADI Annual 1976*, Milan: Associazione per il Disegno Industriale, 1976. *Modo*, no. 148, Mar.–Apr.1993: 122.
> See Gualtierotti, Gianfranco.

Mazzucchelli, Franco (1939–)

Italian industrial designer; born and active Milan.

Biography 1968, Mazzucchelli began his professional career; became best known for his inflatable plastic objects, sometimes as giant public monuments; became a member, ADI (Associazione per il Disegno Industriale). Clients have included Arflex, Anny di Gennaro, Forme &

Superfici, Garavaglia, Habitat in Italy and Tokyo, Quirra, and Sir.
Bibliography *ADI Annual 1976*, Milan: Associazione per il Disegno Industriale, 1976.

McArthur, Warren (1885–1961)

American industrial designer and manufacturer; active Los Angeles and New York.

Training To 1908, mechanical engineering, Cornell University, Ithaca, N.Y.
Biography 1911–13, McArthur filed for ten patents for lighting designs, including one still in production, but slightly changed, by Dietz Lantern, Chicago; 1913, moved to Arizona with his two brothers and became a partner in Arizona Biltmore Hotel for which he designed some furniture. Intrigued by making furniture with standardized elements, he created his first metal furniture in c. 1924 and, from late 1920s, worked in aluminum—but at first he used gas pipes and automobile washers. Even though he patented the early use of aluminum in furniture in 1930, his lightweight furnishings, of which there were more than 600 models, did not become popular until late 1980s. 1924, McArthur designed the Wonder Bus, a tourist-promotional vehicle; 1930, established his own furniture manufacturing company in Los Angeles, where clients included movie stars and movie studios; 1933 with the California firm having become bankrupted, moved his factory to Rome, N.Y., with offices in Manhattan; 1937, again moved the factory, to Bantam, Conn. 1938, he accepted the prototype-furniture commission for Frank Lloyd Wright's Johnson Wax Building, for which he submited a prototype desk, a secretary's chair, and a low half-round table, based on Wright's drawings for metal furniture designs, but Steelcase furniture company was awarded the contract. McArthur's version of Wright's chair was rendered in aluminum. During World War II, McArthur produced aluminum and magnesium seating for aircraft bombers. Some of his furniture models, although modern in their use of aluminum, were ironically historicist in form and constructed of interchangeable standardized tubular metal parts fastened with interior screws concealed under aluminum bands. Two of his best-known pieces are 1932 Ambassador armchair/ottoman and 1933 Biltmore upholstered chair with tubular arms. 1947, McArthur founded Mayfair Industries in Yonkers, near New York. Even though interest in aluminum furniture faded after World War II, he continued some production to the 1960s. Some versions are now being reproduced by ClassiCon.
Bibliography *Four Miles South of Kitty Hawk*, New York and Bantam, Conn.: Warren McArthur Corporation, 1942. Obituary, 'Warren McArthur,' *The New York Times*, 18 Dec. 1961: 35. Sale cat., *Frank Lloyd Wright*, Chicago: Kelmscott Gallery, 1981. Jonathan Lipman, *Frank Lloyd Wright and the Johnson Wax Building*, New York: Rizzoli: 1986: 87–88, 185. Suzanne Slesin, 'It's Back to the Futuristic Machine Age,' *The New York Times*, 17 Dec. 1992: C3.

Paul McCobb. Sideboard. c. 1954. Beechwood and fiberboard, 57 11/16 x 36 x 12 1/4 or 18 3/16" (146.5 x 91.5 x 30.8 or 46.2 cm). Mfr.: Winchendon Furniture Co., US. Courtesy Quittenbaum Kunstauktionen, Munich.

McBride, Ross (1962–)

American designer; born Pittsburgh, Pa..; active Tokyo.

Training 1985, bachelor's degree in graphic design, California Institute of Arts, Valéncia, Cal.; research student in graphic design, Nippon University, Japan; Nippon Bunri University, Oita.
Biography After studios in California, McBride moved to Japan 1985; subsequently, worked in the studio of Takenobu Igarashi; 1991, established Normal graphic-design agency in Tokyo; 1997–98, turned from designing graphics to furniture, interiors, and products; 2000, established Normal as a manufacturing and marketing entity of his designs and has self-produced his 2002 Silicon Switch (sculptural electrical switches by Man Ray), Ripple (multipurpose interior fixture/stand for E&Y, Tokyo), Dolly salt/pepper shakers, Grid wall clock, and Grid bowl.
Exhibitions Regularly at E&Y store, Tokyo; 100% Design, London; 2001 Designers Block, Tokyo; others.

McClelland, Nancy Vincent (1876–1959)

American designer; born Poughkeepsie, N.Y.

Training To 1897, Vassar College, Poughkeepsie.
Biography From 1897–1901, she worked for the newspaper *Philadelphia Press*; from 1901–07, worked in the advertising department, Wanamaker's store, Philadelphia; from 1907–13, was sent by Wanamaker's to Paris, where she studied, edited her own bulletin on fashion trends, collected documentary wallpapers, and traveled widely; 1913, was transferred to Wanamaker's, New York, at which she founded the Au Quatrième decorating studio, said to be the first antiques-and-decorating department established in a department store; 1922, set up her own interior-design business at 15 East 57th Street, New York, showing antique French furniture in paneled rooms and becoming known for her historic-wallpaper reproductions, printed in France. She wrote numerous books on design and decoration, including *Historic Wall-papers* (Philadelphia/London: Lippincott, 1924), said to be the first complete history on the subject. She had a great interest in the restoration of historic museums and buildings in the US; participated in the restoration of Roger Morris-Jumel Mansion, New York; George Washington house, Mount Vernon, Va.; General Robert E. Lee headquarters, Fredericksburg, Va.; Henry Wadsworth Longfellow house, Portland, Maine; House of History, Kinderhoek, N.Y.
Citations 1930, elected Chevalier of the Légion d'Honneur; fellow, Royal Society for the Encouragement of Arts, Manufactures and Commerce, UK; for three years, national president, American Institute of Decorators (AID), becoming a fellowship member in 1948; 1946 (1st) Justin P. Allman Award (for contributing to renewal of wallpaper's popularity), Wallcoverings Wholesalers Association (now Wallcoverings Association).
Bibliography 'Nancy McClelland First to Win Justin Allman Wallpaper Award,' *The New York Times*, 11 Oct. 1946. 'Miss M'Clelland, Antiquary, Here,' *The New York Times*, 2 Oct. 1959. John Esten, Rose Bennett Gilbert, *Manhattan Style*, Boston: Little, Brown, 1990: 4.

McCobb, Paul (1917–1969)

American furniture designer.

Biography 1945, McCobb set up his own studio, working as a painter, interior decorator, and display designer; 1950 with distributor B.G. Mosberg, introduced Planner Group, his first low-cost furniture collection. His higher-priced furniture ranges—Directional, Predictor Linear, and Perimeter—were produced by Winchendon Furniture in Massachusetts and marketed and distributed by McCobb himself. His 1950s designs were also produced by H. Sacks in Brookline, Mass.,

and Calvin Furniture in Grand Rapids, Mich. Similar in concept to Charles and Ray Eames's and Eero Saarinen's designs, McCobb's interchangeable chests, cabinets, and bookcases had bench bases which also served as separate tables. His desk tops had bevelled edges to create a thinner look. He popularized modular furniture; created 'living walls' with moveable room dividers and storage systems; conjured an entirely new American style of décor and believed in giving the customer good value. His renown in 1950s was considerable, though his name was little known from 1960s.
Exhibitions Work included in 1950s *Good Design* exhibitions/awards, The Museum of Modern Art, New York, and Chicago Merchandise Mart. 1957, Bloomingdale's department store, New York, showed 348 furniture pieces in 15 room settings.
Bibliography 'McCobb's Predictor Solves Many Problems Simultaneously,' *Interiors*, vol. 111, Oct. 1951: 126–29. 'An Interior View: Paul McCobb,' *Art Digest*, vol. 26, 15 Sept. 1952: 19. George Nelson (ed.), *Storage*, New York: Whitney, 1954. Roberto Aloi and Agnoldomenico Pica, *Mobili tipo*, Milan: Ulrico Hoepli, 1956: 109. *Current Biography*, New York: H.W. Wilson, 1958. Jay Doblin, *One Hundred Great Product Designs*, New York: Van Nostrand Reinhold, 1970: no. 60.

McConnico, Hilton (1943–)

American furniture designer; born Memphis, Tenn.; active Paris.

Biography 1965, McConnico moved to Paris; became an assistant to Ted Lapidus, designing a collection of couture dresses; worked for Yves Saint Laurent, designing the firm's first ready-to-wear menswear collection, and Jacques Heim. McConnico also designed furs for Neiman Marcus in Texas; created his first film set for friend and director Bob Swaim and, from 1974, worked on 22 film-set designs and more than 30 television-commercial sets in France. Film sets included those for Jean-Jacques Beineix's films *Diva* (1981) and *La lune dans le caniveau* (1983). Other film sets were designed for François Truffaut and Claude Chabrol. From 1985, he has been active in the decorative arts; designed *pâte-de-verre* glassware by Daum, initially incorporating a cactus motif; from late 1980s, designed rugs by Toulemonde Bochart, porcelain and a silk foulard by Hermès for 1989 French Revolution bicentennial, and, under McConnico's own label, rugs and fabrics for Les Galeries Lafayette department store, Paris. 1989, he designed Musée du Cheval de Courses at Longchamps racecourse, Paris; Musée du Costume in Château-Chinon; late-1990s stage sets for Hermès; 1989 limited-edition cactus-motif rug by Art Surface, and, with partner Gilles Le Gall, refurbishment of Chaussée-d'Antin métro station, Paris; 1993 Lance table lamp by Drimmer; 1992 Paradox bowl (resin/cement material developed by McConnico and part of a suite) by Lavin; 1994 Toupary restaurant/bar in La Samaritaine department store, Paris; 2000 Voyageur bed by Tréca; 1997 H armchair by Titien/Tennessee.
Exhibitions/citations Work subject of 1990 exhibition, Memphis, Tenn. (catalog below). César (French film award for sets of *La Lune dans le caniveau)*.
Bibliography Peter S. Green, 'McConnico Unlimited,' *House & Garden*, July 1989. Suzanne Slesin, 'A Designer's Whimsical Essays in "Tex-Baroque,"' *The New York Times*, 15 June 1989: C12. Cat., Suzanne Slesin (intro.), *Hilton McConnico*, Marseille: Aveline; Memphis: Memphis Brooks Museum of Art, 1990. David Souffan, *Hilton McConnico*, Paris: Regard, 1998. www.via.asso.fr

McCoy, Michael (1945–)

Industrial designer and teacher.

Training Bachelor of arts degree, Michigan State University, East Lansing, Mich.; master of arts degree, Wayne State University, Detroit, Mich..
Biography For 24 years, McCoy was co-chairperson, department of design, Cranbrook Academy of Art, Bloomfield Hills, Mich.; 1994–95, was Distinguished Visiting Professor, Royal College of Art, London; from 1995, has been senior lecturer, Institute of Design, Illinois Institute of Technology (IIT), Chicago; is also active as a designer and a partner in McCoy&McCoy (with his wife Katherine McCoy) and in Fahnstrom /McCoy (with Dale Fahnstrom) design consultants; is a proponent of using design to humanize technology and has designed products by Philips and NEC and office furniture by Knoll, Brayton, and Steelcase.
Citations 1994 Chrysler Award for Innovation in Design (with Katherine McCoy), and a number of other major citations.
Bibliography Mary Beth Jordan, *Metropolitan Home*, Apr. 1990: 107. Hugh Aldersey-Williams et al., *Cranbrook Design: The New Discourse*, New York: Rizzoli, 1990.

McCurry, Margaret (1942–)

American architect; born Lake Forest, Ill.; wife of architect Stanley Tigerman.

Training 1964, bachelor of arts degree, Vassar College, Poughkeepsie, N.Y.; 1986–87, Loeb Fellow, Harvard University, Cambridge, Mass.
Biography First, McCurry was a packaging designer; 1964–77, worked on interiors at architects Skidmore, Owings and Merrill, Chicago, for the 1968 Container Corporation headquarters, 1968–77 National Life and Accident headquarters, 1972–74 St. Joseph Valley Bank, 1974–76 Baxter Laboratories headquarters, and 1975–77 Holiday Inn Mart Plaza. 1977, she set up her own studio in Chicago and designed the interior of Van Straatan Art Gallery, Chicago; 1982, joined Stanley Tigerman and Robert Gugman in Chicago to form Tigerman, Fugman and McCurry, which, in 1988, became Tigerman McCurry Architects, where she continues. She designed ceramics (with Tigerman), including the Heaven range and Teaside coffee and tea set and metalware by Swid Powell from the 1980s, a tea set for Alessi's 1983 Tea and Coffee Piazza project, a showroom for American Standard in New York, and the Heritage faucet range by American Standard; (with Tigerman) an outspoken voice on contemporary architecture, she designed 1990 Chicago Bar Association building; 'Wit's End' house in Sawyer, Mich.; 1984 showroom of Herman Miller, Chicago. 1987–89, was vice-president, American Institute of Architects (AIA) Chicago Chapter; became first woman to chair the National AIA Committee on Design; taught design practice, Art Institute of Chicago and University of Illinois, Chicago; board member, Textile Society. Wrote the book *Constructing Twenty-Five Short Stories*, New York: Monacelli, 2000), the title of which refers to tales of her 25 built and unbuilt projects, and *Dorothy in Dreamland* (with Stanley Tigerman, New York: Rizzoli, 1991).
Citations Award, Chicago Chapter of American Institute of Architects; appointed to 1990 Hall of Fame, *Interior Design* magazine; 1998 gold award (best furniture system), IIDA IFMA (interior-design organization), NeoCon, Chicago;
Bibliography Robert A.M. Stern (ed.), *The International Design Yearbook*, New York: Abbeville, 1985/1986. Beverly Russell, *Women of Design*, New York: Rizzoli, 1992: 174–75, 214–17. Cat., R. Craig Miller (intro.), *U.S. Design 1975–2000*, Munich: Prestel, 2002.
> See Tigerman, Stanley.

McDonald Jr., Eugene F. (1886–1958)

American consumer electronics entrepreneur; born Syracuse, N.Y.

Biography As a child, McDonald was fascinated with electronic devices; 1912, organized a finance organization for the installment-payment purchase of an automobile, a first in the industry. 1918, two young radio amateurs Karl Hassel and R.H.G. Matthews established Chicago Radio Laboratory. 1921, McDonald joined them. Based on the call letters of the amateurs' radio station, 9-ZN, they and McDonald conjured the tradename Z-Nith. 1923, McDonald founded Zenith Radio Corp., based on the tradename Z-Nith, with himself as president. 1923, he established one of the first professional broadcast stations, WJAZ; founded and became the first president of National Association of Broadcasters (NAB); was instrumental in forming the the US government's Radio Commission (later Federal Commications Commission/FCC); contributed to radio's being used as a medium for national advertising; pioneered shortwave radio for long-distance transmission/reception (outfitting Donald B. MacMillan's 1923 arctic expedition with transmitters/receivers); expanded radio into ship-to-shore, radar, and VHF and UHF television communications; was instrumental in developing some firsts: automatic push-button radio tuner, wireless TV remote controls, and subscription TV service; commissioned Robert Davol Budlong to design Zenith radio casings. McDonald served at Zenith for 45 years.
> See Budlong, Robert Davol.

McGinn, Michael
> See Sebastian, James A.

McGovern, Gerry
> See Kimber, Cecil.

McGrath, Raymond (1903–1977)

Australian architect and designer; active London.

Training 1920–21, Sydney University; 1921–25, School of Architecture, Sydney University; 1926, Brixton School of Building and Westminster School of Art, London; 1927–30, Cambridge University.

Biography 1926, McGrath settled in Britain; 1920s–30s, was a leading exponent of modernism. His first independent commission was 1929 remodeling of Mansfield Forbes residence 'Finella,' a Regency house outfitted in colored glass and copper with pink and green walls and a widely published commission that helped to promote McGrath as a leading designer and architect and resulted in his being appointed 'decoration consultant' of 1930–32 interiors of BBC Broadcasting House in London, where he headed a design team that included Serge Chermayeff and Wells Coates. He was responsible for 1935 Manchester studios of BBC; 1930, set up a practice in London; c. 1932, became more active in industrial and interior design; used glass extensively, with natural colored materials and indoor plants; 1940, settled in Ireland, where he was architect to Office of Public Works and principal architect there 1948–68. His work included 1932 lighting and Synchronome wall clock by Abbey Electric Clock Works for BBC studios; numerous exhibition stands and showrooms, including for GEC and Imperial Airways; radio cabinets by Ekco; unit furniture by Easiwork, interiors of *Atlanta* airplane of Imperial Airways; oil-dispensing equipment by Vacuum Oil; 1932 Fischers Long Bar and Restaurant, New Bond Street, London; 1932–33 Embassy Club, London; electrical section of 1933 *Ideal Home* exhibition, London; c. 1935 Kingstone store, Leicester; 1935–37 houses in Chertsey, including 1936–37 house at St. Ann's Hill with its circular two-storey spaces; 1936–39 houses in Gaulby; 1934 *Six Ages of Architecture* door panels (Greek, Roman, Chinese, Gothic, Florentine, and modern) at Royal Institute of British Architects, London; 1935 plate-glass-and-metal sales trophy for Austin Reed; with Elizabeth Craig, 1937 heat-resistant glassware (Phoenix ware) by British Heat Resisting Glass, Birmingham. He wrote the books *Twentieth Century Homes* (London: Faber & Faber, 1934) and *Glass in Architecture and Decoration* (with A.C. Frost, London: Architectural Press, 1937).
Exhibitions Work included in 1979–80 *Thirties*, Hayward Gallery, London.
Bibliography Philippe Garner, *The Encyclopedia of Decorative Arts, 1890–1940*, Secaucus, N.J.: Chartwell, 1978. Cat., *Thirties: British Art and Design Before the War*, London: Arts Council of Great Britain Hayward Gallery, 1979.

McGugan, Steve (1960–)

Canadian industrial designer; born Vancouver; active Copenhagen.

Training 1979-1981, product design, Art Center College of Design, Pasadena, Cal.
Biography 1982–84, McGugan was a staff designer at Bang & Olufsen in Struer, Denmark; 1985–87, worked in studio of David Lewis in Copenhagen; 1988, established his own studio and designed electronic and medical products, including 1985 Form 2 earphones by Bang & Olufsen, 1988 taxi-cab meter by F. Frogne, and 1989 NovoLet 1,5 insulin pen and Pharma-Plast. Other clients: Radiometer, Ericsson, Brüel & Kjær, Royal Copenhagen Porcelain Factory, Georg Jensen; is a member, Foreningen Danske Designere (association of Danish designers). He resides in Klampenborg, Denmark.
Exhibitions/citations Work shown frequently worldwide. Numerous awards include 1990, 1991, 1998 Dansk ID prize; 1993 and 1999 G prize, Japan; first prize, 1993 Forma Finlandia; 1994 Czech Republic design award; 1994 silver medal, Dansk Designråd (Danish design council); product-design award, Industrie Forum Design (iF), Hanover.
Bibliography Cat., Chantal Bizot, *Bang & Olufsen: design et technologie*, Paris: Musée des Arts Décoratifs, 1990: 11. Jens Bang, *Bang & Olufsen: Fra vision til legende = From Vision to Legend*, Denmark: Vidsyn, 2000.

McHugh, Tom (1941–)

American architect, and interior and furniture designer; born Leominster, Mass.; active Philadelphia, Pa., US.

Training 1965, bachelor of architecture, University of Notre Dame, Notre Dame, Ind.; Paolo Soleri Workshop, Arcosanti, Ariz.; Royal College of Art, London; San Francisco Art Institute; The New School for Social Research, New York.
Biography McHugh was one of the first designers to implement 'hoteling' offices (spaces for executives to work while in hotels) in America; has worked for various architectural firms in the US and UK, from 1965–66 at August Perez & Associates, New Orleans, to including Maxwell Frey & Jane Drew, London; Skidmore, Owings and Merrill, San Francisco and London; and, from 2001, at Flad & Associates, Madison, Wis., where he is a senior associate and senior interior designer. 1998, he was national chairperson of Interiors PIA (a wing of American Institute of Architects/AIA). His diverse portfolio has extended from historic preservation and a large number of architectural projects to office/shop/showroom interiors. Furniture design includes: Tisbury lounge chairs and MoJo table/console by Keilhauer and others by Brayton and CCN International; has taught or been a visiting professor at more than ten institutions in the US.
Exhibitions/citations Work included in venues in the US and Canada, including at the Cooper-Hewitt National Design Museum, New York, and National Building Museum, Washington, D.C. 1990 (for McHugh chair range), 1992 silver award (for Tisbury chair range) and 1993 bronze award (for Primavista reception desk) of Institute of Business Designers (IBD); silver award (for 2000–01 MoJo table/console) at 2001 IIDEX/Neocon, Canada; 1992 (for Tisbury chair range) and 2001 (for MoJo) Good Design awards of Chicago Athenaeum; 1995 Best Product Designs of the Year of IDSA/*Business Week* magazine; others.
Bibliography 'Appropriate Officing: Hoteling Office Design Proves to Be an Efficient Asset,' *IS*, Sept.–Oct. 1995. 'No Reservations About Hoteling,' *Building*, Oct. 1999.

McIntosh, Lawrie G. (1924–)

Canadian designer; born Clinton, Ontario; active Toronto.

Training 1946, bachelor's degree of applied science in mechanical engineering, University of Toronto; 1951, master of science degree in product design, Illinois Institute of Technology, Chicago.
Biography 1946, McIntosh worked for T.S. Simms & Co. in Saint John; 1951, established his own studio, McIntosh Design Associates, becoming active in industrial and furniture design; 1954, was president, Association of Canadian Industrial Designers (ACID); a consulting editor of journal *Product Design Engineer*; 1983–89, taught, Ontario College of Art.
Citations Gold medal (for automatic steam-and-dry iron by Steam Electric Products), 1954 (10th) Triennale di Milano. His 1976 Theratron 780 Cobalt Therapy unit by AECL was featured on a Canadian postage stamp. Granted 1981 Outstanding Achievement award, National Design Council/Design Canada/ACID.
Bibliography Cat., *Seduced and Abandoned: Modern Furniture Designers in Canada, the First Fifty Years*, Toronto: The Art Gallery at Harbourfront, 1986: 14. Rachel Gotlieb and Cora Golden, *Design in Canada Since 1945: Fifty Years from Teakettles to Task Chairs*, Toronto: Knopf Canada, 2001.

McKinney, Nanny (1926–)
> See Still McKinney, Nanny.

McLaughlin, Mary Louise (1847–1939)

American pottery and porcelain decorator; active Cincinnati, Ohio.

Training In art in Cincinnati; under Benn Pitman, School of Design, University of Cincinnati.
Biography She was a pioneer of china-painting in the US and profoundly influenced her contemporaries and subsequent ceramicists. She became initially exposed to painting through Benn Pitman and German instructor Maria Eggers in Cincinnati and was influenced by underglazed slip-decorated Haviland faïence made in Limoges. In fact, she began to copy the Limoges technique. She wrote the books *China Painting: A Practical Manual for the Use of Amateurs in the Decoration of Hard Porcelain* (Cincinnati: R. Clarke, 1877) and *Pottery Decoration under the Glaze* (Cincinnati: R. Clarke, 1885). 1877, she successfully duplicated Limoges faïence at P.L. Coultry's pottery in Cincinnati; 1879 with Laura Fry, Agnes Pitman, and Elizabeth Nourse, cofounded Cincinnati Pottery Club (which disbanded in 1890), of which McLaughlin was president and whose members fired their pieces at the Frederick Dallas Pottery and later at Maria Longworth Nichols's Rookwood Pottery to 1883. 1894, McLaughlin began experimenting at the Brockman Pottery by painting decoration on the interiors of molds with slip before casting, which she called 'American faience' (patented by her in 1894). However, she was dissatisfied with its results and soon abandoned it. 1890, she founded Associated Artists of Cincinnati, a group of metalworkers and ceramics decorators, and was its president. Her 40-inch (1 m) Ali Baba vase was the largest made in the US at the time; three examples were produced. She worked in copper for a time but returned to ceramics in 1895, producing carved ware known as Losanti that she made until 1904, the year she gave up pottery to write on history and politics. She was assisted by Margaret Hickey, who cast the porcelain and tended the kiln. 1914, McLaughlin became involved once more with metalwork, jewelry making, needlework, etching, painting, and sculpture; was active up

to her death at age 92.
Exhibitions/citations Work shown at 1876 *Centennial Exposition* (showing a carved desk, under the direction of Henry Lindley Fry and William Henry Fry), Philadelphia; in Cincinnati and New York (showing Limoges-type faïence of c. 1877); 1899 exhibition (showing 20 pieces of her Losanti ware), Cincinnati Art Museum. Received an honorable mention citation at 1878 *Exposition Universelle*, Paris; bronze medal, 1901 *Pan-American Exposition* (showing 27 pieces), Buffalo, N.Y.; silver medal (for metalwork) at 1900 *Exposition Universelle*, Paris.
Bibliography Edwin AtLee Barber, *The Pottery and Porcelain of the United States*, New York: Feingold & Lewis, 1893. Cat., *The Ladies, God Bless 'Em: The Women's Art Movement in Cincinnati in the Nineteenth Century*, Cincinnati: Cincinnati Art Museum, 1976. Joan Siegfried, 'American Women in Art Pottery,' *Nineteenth Century*, vol. 9, Spring 1984: 12–18. Doreen Bolger Burke et al., *In Pursuit of Beauty: Americans and the Aesthetic Movement*, New York: The Metropolitan Museum of Art/Rizzoli, 1986.

McLeish, Minnie (1876–1957)
British textile designer.

Biography McLeish was a freelance textile designer of bold, colorful patterns for printed furnishing fabrics; worked for several firms, notably Foxton textiles (where she was associated with Charles Rennie Mackintosh and Constance Irving) in London, and the Metz store in Amsterdam; 1920s–30s, was a prolific designer of patterns for fabrics by Morton Sundour.
Exhibitions Work included in British section, 1927 *Europäisches Kunstgewerbe*, Grassi Museum, Leipzig; in textile exhibitions in Paris and Vienna.
Bibliography Giovanni and Rosalia Ranelli, *Il tessuto moderno*, Florence, 1976: 181, 217. *Journal of the Decorative Arts Society 1890–1940*, no. 4, 1979: 26ff. Stuart Durant, *Ornament from the Industrial Revolution to Today*, Woodstock, N.Y.: Overlook, 1986: 252, 255. Cat., Hans Wichmann, *Von Morris bis Memphis: Textilien der Neuen Sammlung, Ende 19. bis Ende 20. Jahrhundert*, Basel: Birkhäuser, 1990: 445. Valerie Mendes, *The Victoria & Albert Museum's Textile Collection, British Textiles from 1900 to 1937*, London: Victoria and Albert Museum, 1992.

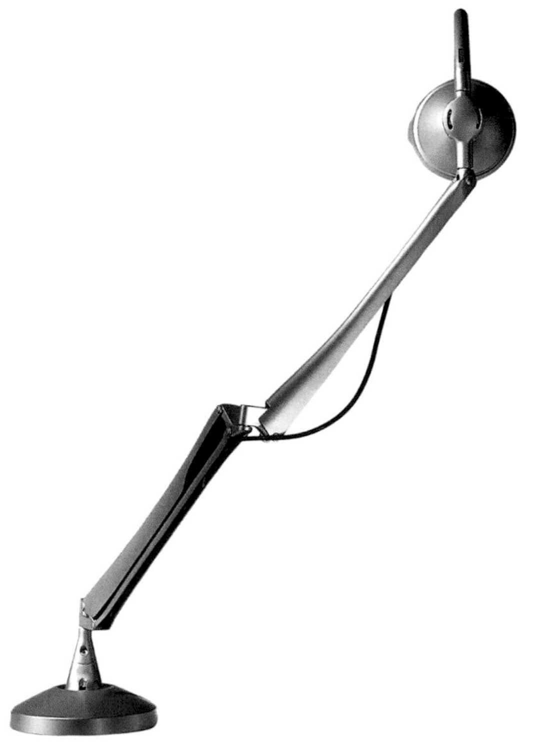

Alberto Meda and Paolo Rizzatto. Fortebraccio table lamp. c. 1998. Steel, Zamak, and thermoplastics, l. of arm 9 3/8–7 3/4" (35–45 cm). Mfr.: Luceplan, Italy.

McMillen, Eleanor (1890–1990)
> See Brown, Eleanor McMillen.

McVickers, Julia (1906–1990)
American textile designer; born Memphis, Tenn.

Training Under Marli Ehrman, Institute of Design, Chicago.
Biography 1945–80 with Else Regensteiner, she cofounded Reg/Wick Handwoven Originals in Hyde Park, Ill.; designed custom handwoven fabrics for designers and architects and for industry; cofounded, Midwest Designer Craftsmen.
Exhibition Reg/Wick handwoven fabrics subject of 1961 exhibition, Art Institute of Chicago.
Bibliography Sigrid Wortmann Weltge, *Women's Work: Textile Art from the Bauhaus*, London: Thames & Hudson, 1993.

Means, Bridget (1965–)
Australian designer and entrepreneur.

Training To 1988, degree in communication design, Parsons School of Design, New York.
Biography After schooling, Means settled in New York and became a designer of image-identity programs, packaging, and products; 1996 with Giovanni Pellone, founded Benza in Brooklyn, N.Y., for the design and production of tabletop objects and accessories; 2003, departed Benza.
Exhibitions/citations Work included in venues worldwide. Several design awards.
> See Pellone, Giovanni.

Meccano
> See Hornby, Frank.

Meda, Alberto (1945–)
Italian engineer and designer; born Lenno Tremezzina (CO); active Milan.

Training 1969, master's degree in mechanical engineering, Politecnico, Milan.
Biography From 1970–75, Meda was assistant director of production at Magneti Marelli; 1973, became technical manager, responsible for control of furniture and plastics-laboratory equipment, Kartell in Binasco, where initiated research into the use of polyurethane; 1979, began his independent professional career as engineer, designer, and consultant for product engineering and consultant to Alfa Romeo auto, Ansaldo Sistemi Industriali, Alias, Alessi, Arabia, Cinelli, Colombo Design, Brevetti Gaggia, JC Decaux, Ideal Standard, Italtel Telematica, Luceplan, Legrand, Mandarina Duck, Omron, Philips, Vitra, and others; from 1983, taught industrial technology, Domus Academy, Milan; 1984, joined Luceplan as a partner; 1986, began to design furniture, including 1987 LightLight chair and Dry table by Alias in Milan. 1989 Softlight by Alias was formed in an epoxy-resin matrix sandwiched in a beehive of Nomex and unidirectional carbon fiber. Meda and Paolo Rizzatto designed 1989 Titania aluminum-polycarbonate hanging light, 1984 Berenice lamp, 1987 Lola lamp, 1989 Titana hanging fixture by Luceplan, and 2000 Partner bookcase system by Kartell. Other Meda-alone work includes 1994 Longframe aluminum and web-fiber lounge chair and Highframe armchair version by Alias, furniture by Vitra, and c. 2000 Water ceramic jug (with filter and funnel), tray, and drinking-glass set by Arabia.
Exhibitions/citations Work included in 1992 (18th) Triennale di Milano; 1993 *Mestieri d'autore*, Siena; 1993 *Design, Miroir du Siècle*, Grand Palais, Paris; 1997 *Mutant Materials in Contemporary Design*, The Museum of Modern Art, New York, and traveling; 2001 *Italia e Giappone design come stile di vita*, Yokohama and Kobe. Work subject of 1990 exhibition, Design Gallery, Matzuia Ginza, Tokyo. 1996 exhibition (with Rizzatto), Binnen Galerie, Amsterdam; 1996 *Lighting Affinities* exhibition (with Rizzatto), Milan; 1999 Salon du Meuble (as Creator of the Year), Paris. 1992 Design Plus, Ambiente fair, Frankfurt; 1994 European Design Prize; 1995 awards, Industrie Forum Design (iF), Hanover; 1997 Best of Category (with Vitra), Annual Design Review, *I.D.* magazine; 2000 Bundespries Produktdesign, Germany. Premio Compasso d'Oro: 1987 (two citations), 1989, 1991, 1994 (three citations), 1998 (three citations).
Bibliography Cat., Manolo de Giorgi and Paola Antonelli (eds), *Techniques discrètes: le design mobilier en Italie 1980-1990*, Rome: ICI/Assarredo, 1991. *Modo*, no. 148, Mar.–Apr.1993: 122. Mel Byars, *50 Chairs...*, Hove: RotoVision, 1996. Mel Byars, *50 Lights...*, Hove: RotoVision, 1997. Mel Byars, *50 Tables...*, Hove: RotoVision, 1997.

Paola Antonelli (ed.), *Objects of Design: The Museum of Modern Art*, New York: The Museum of Modern Art, 2003: 163.

Medjeber, Chérif
> See Chérif (1962–).

Medley, Robert (1905–1994)

British painter and theater designer.

Training 1921, Byam Shaw School and Royal Academy School; 1923–26, Slade School of Fine Art, London.
Biography From 1930, Medley was a member of London Group and of London Artists' Association; from 1933, designed for the Group Theatre, founded by Rupert Doone, including costumes and sets for plays *Dance of Death* (1933) by W.H. Auden, *Sweeney Agonistes* (1935–36) by T.S. Eliot, *The Dog Beneath the Skin* (1935–36) by Auden and Christopher Isherwood, and *The Ascent of F6* (1937) by Auden and Isherwood, at the Mercury Theatre, London; wrote the article 'Hitler's Art in Munich' in journal *Axis 8* (1937).
Exhibitions Work subject of 1930 exhibition, Cooling Galleries, London. Included in 1936 *International Surrealist Exhibition* and 1979–80 *Thirties*, Hayward Gallery, London (catalog below); others.
Bibliography Cat., *Thirties: British Art and Design Before the War*, London: Arts Council of Great Britain Hayward Gallery, 1979.

Mednis, Juris (1937–)

Latvian inventor; active U.S.

Biography In New York State, Mednis was a banker at the Shore National Bank, at the Howell State Bank, and at The Bank of New York. He founded manufacturing firm Universal Symetrics in Howell, N.J., to produce and market his own-design products, such as the 1983 colorful modular container system to save space and create efficient packaging.
Citations 1990 Inventor of the Year, New Jersey Inventors Hall of Fame; 1988 (1st) The Du Pont Award for Innovation in Packaging.

Meier, Otto (1901–1982)

Swiss architect and furniture designer; born and active Basel.

Training Apprenticeship in masonry and carpentry in Basel.
Biography 1926 with Ernst Mumenthaler (1901–1978), Meier established an architecture office and contracting firm in Basel. They developed the modular furniture system 3M-Möbel, constructed by Meier himself. Their award-winning 1927 cabinets shown at *Das Neue Heim II* exhibition were also developed in lightweight plywood. 1944, they and architect August Künzel designed the housing development Drei Linden in Basel. 1972, Mumenthaler and Meier's office closed.
Exhibitions/citations First prize (to Meier and Mumenthaler), competition held at 1928 *Das Neue Heim II* exhibition, Kunstgewerbemuseum, Zürich.
Bibliography Friederike Mehlau-Wiebking et al., *Schweizer Typenmöbel 1925–35, Sigfried Giedion und die Wohnbedarf AG*, Zürich: gta, 1989: 229. Ueli Kräuchi, *Ernst Mumenthaler und Otto Meier*, Basel: Architekturmuseum, 1995.

Meier, Richard Alan (1934–)

American architect; born Newark, N. J.

Training To 1957, architecture, Cornell University, Ithaca, N.Y.
Biography 1958–59, he worked for architects Davis, Brody and Wisniewski; 1959–60, for Skidmore, Owings and Merrill; 1960–63, for Marcel Breuer and Associates; all New York. Late 1950s and early 1960s, he was an artist in a studio he shared with Michael Graves on 10th Street, New York; 1963, set up his own practice. 1964–73, Meier was professor of architecture, The Cooper Union for the Advancement of Science and Art, New York; 1975–77, at Yale University, New Haven, Connecticut; in 1977, at Harvard University, Cambridge, Mass. Early 1970s, he became known as one of ad-hoc New York Five group of architects, with Peter Eisenman, Michael Graves, Charles Gwathmey, and John Hejduk. Meier's architecture reflected the influence of Le Corbusier's 1920s Cubist forms, and for three decades Meier sought the modernist ideal, exemplified initially by the design of his parents' house in Old Westbury, N.Y. His first furniture was produced 1978, by Knoll, including 1978–82 chairs, stool, telephone stand, and chaise, of which these and others were often derivative of earlier 20th-century designers' works, including the tea set (reflective of Malevich's work) for 1983 Tea and Coffee Piazza project and 1984–96 metal-

Richard Meier. Dish. 1984. Silverplated brass, h. 1 5/16" (3.3 cm) x dia. 7 7/16" (18.9 cm). Mfr.: Lunt Silversmith, US. Marshall Cogan Purchase Fund. MoMA.

work and ceramics (quoting Josef Hoffmann's grid designs), all by Alessi. He also designed early-1980s ceramics (Joseph, Peachtree, and Anna), glassware (Spiral, Lattice, and Professor), stemware, and cutlery by Swid Powell; 1991 fabric collection by Design Tex; 1992 glass bowl and vase by Steuben; 1996 grand piano by Ibach & Sohn; c. 2000 Space dinnerware by Arabia; lighting fixtures by Baldinger, door and window hardware by Valli & Valli, clocks and watches by Markuse; others. His work may be defined as neo-modern rather than Postmodern. The film *Concert of Wills* (producer: Maysles Films, 1998) documented the travails of the building of Meiers's Getty Museum, as well.
Architecture Body of work includes his own 1965 house in Essex Fells, N.J., and a large number of other commissions, including 1980–84 Museum für Kunsthandwerk (1979 competition winner), Frankfurt; 1983 High Museum, Atlanta, Ga.; 1984–97 Getty Museum, Los Angeles; 1990–98 Camden Medical Center, Singapore.
Exhibitions/citations Work included in 1969 *New York Five* and 1966 *40 Under 40*, both New York; 1974 *Five Architects*, Princeton University; 1982 *Shape and Environment: Furniture by American Architects*, Whitney Museum of American Art, Fairfield County, Conn. Work subject of 2003 *The Undiscovered Richard Meier: The Architect as Designer and Artist*, Frankfurt. 1972 Arnold W. Brunner Memorial Prize; 1983 award, Institute of Business Designers (IBD); 1983 Roscoe Award; Reynolds Memorial Award; 1984 Pritzker Architecture Prize; 1989 gold medal, Royal Institute of British Architects; 1992 Commander of Arts and Letters, France; 1997 gold medal, American Institute of Architects (AIA).
Bibliography Kenneth Frampton and Colin Rowe, *Five Architects: Eisenman, Graves, Gwathmey, Hejduk, Meier*, New York: Wittenborn, 1972. Richard Meier, *Richard Meier, Architect: Buildings and Projects, 1966–76*, New York: Oxford, 1976. Cat., Lisa Phillips (intro.), *Shape and Environment: Furniture by American Architects*, New York: Whitney Museum of American Art, 1982: 42–43. *Richard Meier: Buildings and Projects 1965–1981*, Zürich, 1982. *Richard Meier, Architect*, New York: Rizzoli, 1984 (vol. 1) and 1991 (vol. 2). Michael Blackwood (dir.), *Richard Meier*, film, producer: Michael Blackwood Productions, 1985. Juli Capella and Quim Larrea, *Designed by Architects in the 1980s*, New York: Rizzoli, 1988. CD-ROM, *Richard Meier, Architect*, Lugano: Victory Interactive Media, 1995. www.richardmeier.com

Meier-Graefe, Julius (1867–1935)

Romanian writer, art critic, and entrepreneur; active Germany and France.

Biography 1893, Meier-Graefe met William Morris, Edward Burne-Jones, and Aubrey Beardsley; was a specialist in 19th-century French painting and a champion of Expressionism with Siegfried Bing (the proprietor of gallery/shop L'Art Nouveau, Paris). 1895, Meier-Graefe traveled in Belgium, Britain, Holland, Denmark, Germany, and Austria; embraced the role of industry and the ending of the romantic notion of the artist's isolation from industrial culture; 1897, founded journal *Dekorative Kunst*, from which he resigned as the editor in 1899 to open the shop La Maison Moderne on the rue des Petits-Champs, Paris, commissioning Henry van de Velde to design its exterior and interior. He publicized the shop as an association of artists, who were coming together for commercial purposes, and for the creation of designs appropriate for production in quantity, an idea drawn from the Münchner Vereinigten Werkstätten für Kunst im Handwerk and in contrast

to contemporary French practice. 1895, he showed Louis Comfort Tiffany's stained-glass windows, enamels, glass mosaics, and lighting at the shop; became increasingly alienated from Bing's enterprise L'Art Nouveau. 1903, Meier-Graefe was forced to close the shop and liquidate at half price, including van de Velde-designed furniture and fittings of the shop. He lost his investment and inheritance and returned to Germany, where Hermann Muthesius designed his house in 1921. But once again, Meier-Graefe left Germany for France in 1934.
Bibliography Julius Meier-Graefe, 'Einiges aus "La Maison Moderne,"' *Dekorative Kunst*, no. 5, Oct. 1899–Mar. 1900: 209–12. *Documents sur l'art industriel au vingtième siècle...*, Paris: *La Maison Moderne* magazine, 1901. Maurice Dufrêne, 'Notre enquête sur le mobilier moderne,' *Art et décoration*, no. 39, 1921: 129–43. Kenworth Moffett, *Meier-Graefe as Art Critic* (Studien zur Kunst des neunzehnten Jahrhunderts, no. 18), Munich: Prestel, 1973. Gabriel Weisberg, 'Consumerism and Modernity at Meier-Graefe's La Maison Moderne, 1899–1903,' *Design and Sign*, no. 1, 1990: 21–34. Nancy J. Troy, *Modernism and the Decorative Arts in France: Art Nouveau to Le Corbusier*, New Haven: Yale, 1991. Hugo von Hofmannsthal, *Briefwechsel mit Julius Meier-Graefe: 1905–1929* (correspondence), Freiburg im Breisgau: Rombach, 1998. Julius Meier-Graefe, *Kunst ist nicht für Kunstgeschichte da: Briefe und Dokumente* (correspondence), Göttingen: Wallstein, 2001.

Meijs, Ronald (1962–)
> See Lumiance.

Meinzer, Manfred (1943–)

German industrial designer; active Cologne and Berlin.

Training Industrial design, Art Center College, Los Angeles.
Biography Meinzer worked for Ford in Cologne and Telefunken in Berlin; 1965, became an independent designer in Hemer, Germany; has designed for Revox, where he substituted transistors for vacuum tubes and incorporated modular components into Revox's Functionalist sound equipment housing. His first important design was the 1967 Revox A77 stereo tape recorder, followed by a number of others such as 1988 B291 record player with a tangential tone-arm. For Leica: 1992 Geovid binoculars, 1996 R8 35mm SLR camera. He has designed electronics by Willi Studer and products by others.
Exhibitions/citations Work included in 1983–84 *Design Since 1945*, Philadelphia Museum of Art. Europe's Compact Camera of the Year 1998–99 (for Leica Minilux Zoom), European Imaging and Sound Association (EISA).
Bibliography Cat., Kathryn B. Hiesinger and George H. Marcus III (eds.), *Design Since 1945*, Philadelphia: Philadelphia Museum of Art, 1983.

David Mellor. Minimal cutlery. c. 2002. Stainless steel. Mfr.: David Mellor Design, UK.

Mello, Franco (1945–)

Italian designer; born Genoa; active Turin, Spineto Scrivia, and Alexandria.

Biography Mello has designed books, catalogues and posters for artists Paladino, Pistoletto, Cucchi, Chia, Penone, Paolini, De Maria, Schifano, Anselmo, Feininger, Parmiggiani, Gastini, and others; has been the curator of visual communication for the exibitions at Galleria Civica d'Arte Moderna e Contemporanea (GAM) in Turin, concerning Yves Klein, Alberto Burri, Pinot Gallizio and the Laboratorio Sperimentale of Alba, The Camel Award, and Conceptual Art/Arte Povera/Land Art. He codeveloped a TV serial for children for Rai 1 and Rai 3, with Bruno Munari, Nico Orengo, and Emanuele Luzzati; designed 1972 Cactus coat rack (with Guido Drocco) in expanded polyurethane by Gufram and 1972 Trampolino transformable table by Colli.
Exhibitions Work included in 1970 *Le Design et l'Enfant*, Céntre de Crèation Industrielle (CCI), Centre Georges Pompidou, Paris; 1972 *Italy: The New Domestic Landscape* exhibition, The Museum of Modern Art, New York; 1972–73 *Mobilier urbain*, Index Internationaux, Paris; 1973 (15th) Triennale in Milan (showing giant polyurethane letters as a game); 1973 (1st) Exposition Internationale de Jeux d'Exterieur, Place au Jeu, Lusanne; 1981 *50 Years of Italian Design*, Cologne; 1991 *CreativItalia*, Tokyo; *Avventura Internazionale*, Castello di Rivoli; 2002 exhibition of Gufram, Manica Lunga, Castello di Rivoli, Turin (catalog below); 2003 *The Theater of Italian Creativity*, New York.
Bibliography Cat., Franco Mello, Ennio Chiggio and Stefano Casciani, *The Rock Furniture = Il design della Gufram negli anni del rock*, Turin: Castello di Rivoli, 2001.
> See Gufram.

Mellor, David (1930–)

British metalworker, manufacturer, and retailer; born Sheffield.

Training 1946–48, Sheffield College of Art; 1950–54, Royal College of Art, London; 1953–54, British School in Rome.
Biography Mellor's early design work included the 1951 silver coffee set, and 1954 Pride cutlery by Walker and Hall, Sheffield. 1954, he set up his own metalsmithy and industrial-design workshop in Sheffield, the center of the metal tableware industry in Britain; designed 1963 Embassy cutlery and teapot for use in British embassies, 1965 Thrift stainless-steel set for government canteens, prisons, and hospitals, and a 1957 bus shelter in galvanized steel and vitreous enamel for the Ministry of Transport. From 1969, he has manufactured cookware, hardware, textiles, and woodenware, and eventually established a retail outlet to sell domestic kitchen supplies and tableware by himself and others in Sloane Square, London; in 1980, Manchester; and, in 1981, on James Street, Covent Garden, London. Early 1970s, he began manufacturing his own cutlery using innovative methods in Broom Hall, an historic building in Sheffield that he restored and converted into purpose-designed workshops, where all the design and development of his cutlery is pursued. He has executed commission from ITT, Abacus Municipal, Glacier Metal, H.R.H. Post Office, British Rail, James Neill Tools, and British Department of the Environment. Mellor has received silver commissions from The Worshipful Company of Goldsmiths, London; The Cutlers' Company, Sheffield; Essex University; Southwell Minster; Darwin College, Cambridge. 1981–83, he was chairperson, Design Council's Committee of Enquiry on British Consumer Goods Design Standards; from 1982, a member, National Advisory Body, Art and Design Working Group; from 1982, chairperson, Crafts Council. Often called 'the cutlery king,' he continues to be a prolific designer for his own firm.
Exhibitions/citations Work shown at Stedelijk Museum, Amsterdam, 1968; National Museum, Cardiff, 1972. 1950 National Design Competition (for silver coffee set, while a student at Sheffield College of Art), Design and Research Centre for Gold, Silver and Jewellery; 1953 silver medal from the Royal College of Art; 1957 award (for his Pride cutlery), Design Council; 1957, 1959, 1962, 1965, 1974, 1977 and other Design Council awards; 1975 Architectural Heritage Year Award for conversion of Broom Hall; 1981 Duke of Edinburgh's Royal Society of Arts Presidential Award for Design Management. 1962, elected Honorary Royal Designer for Industry, UK; 1964, fellow, Society of Industrial Artists and Designers; 1979, honorary fellow, Sheffield Polytechnic; 1981, liveryman, Worshipful Company of Goldsmiths; 1981, freeman, Cutlers' Company; 1981, Order of the British Empire (OBE); 1984, trustee, Victoria and Albert Museum, London; 2000, honorary doctorate degree, Royal College of Art; Commander of the British Empire (CBE), 2001.
Bibliography Michael Farr, *Design in British Industry: A Mid-Century*

Survey, London: Cambridge, 1955: 175. Graham Hughes, *Modern Silver Throughout the World*, London: Studio Vista, 1967. *Design*, no. 342, June 1977: 47. Fiona MacCarthy, *British Design Since 1880*, London, 1982. Cat., Kathryn B. Hiesinger and George H. Marcus III (eds.), *Design Since 1945*, Philadelphia: Philadelphia Museum of Art, 1983. Fiona MacCarthy and Patrick Nuttgens, *An Eye for Industry*, London: Lund Humphries, 1986.

Melocchi, Mario
> See OPI, Studio.

Melotti, Fausto (1901–1986)
Italian sculptor and ceramicist; born Rovereto.

Training Scuole Reali Elisabettine, Rovereto; to 1918, Università di Pisa; 1924, diploma in electronic engineering, Politecnico, Milan; frequently under Adolfo Wildt, Accademia di Brera, Milan.
Biography Melotti is best known for his sculpture; was influenced by the antihistoricism of Carlo Belli and the didactics of Fortunato Depero. In turn, his ceramic work exemplifies the malleable, painterly approach he took to sculpture. He attempted to develop new shapes in all his work; was particularlly active 1950–70 and a friend of Lucio Fontana; died in Milan.
Exhibitions Work first (1935) shown, at Galleria il Milione, Milan. 2003 *Fausto Melotti: l'opera in ceramica*, Mart Rovereto, Italy; 2003 *Fausto Melotti: grafica e scultura*, Milan.
Bibliography Domenico Bacile, *Musica visiva di Fausto Melotti*, Milan: Virgilio, 1975. Carlo Priovano, *Melotti: ottantotto disegni*, Milan: Electa, 1981.

Fausto Melotti. Cup and saucer. c. 1947. Glazed majolica, cup h. 2" (5.1 cm) x dia. 4" (10.2 cm), saucer h. 3/4" (1.9 cm) x dia. 4 5/8" (11.8 cm). Mfr.: the designer, Italy. Gift of Edgar Kaufmann, Jr. MoMA.

Memory Hotel Studio
Italian design group; located Florence.

History 1983, Fabrizio Galli and Anna Perico, who studied architecture in Florence, established Memory Hotel Studio, specializing in design and production of furniture and small products. At some point in time, they were joined by G. Barone. 1986, they and a large group of other architects and designers founded the Movimento Bolidista, whose members pursued a retro-1950s/streamline aesthetic and whose manifesto claimed, among other assertions, 'that ideology is a useless and harmful brake.'
Exhibitions From 1981, their work was included in national and international exhibitions; in 1983 *Memoria e mito balneare II: design balneare* (as Memory Hotel Studio) Centro Culturale Polivalente, Comune di Cattolica (RN), Italy (catalog below).
Bibliography Fumino Shimizu and Studio Matteo Thun (eds.), *The Italian Design: Descendants of Leonardo da Vinci*, Tokyo: Graphic-sha, 1987: 326. Cat., Stefano Casciani (ed.), *Design balneare*, Maggioli, 1986.
> See Bolidista, Movimento.

Memphis
Design cooperative and firm.

History Memphis was the group led by Ettore Sottsass, which designed furniture, fabric, glass, and ceramics, first exposed in the showroom of Arc 74, during 1981 Salone del Mobile in Milan. (Purportedly the name was derived from Bob Dylan's song 'Stuck Inside of Mobile with the Memphis Blues Again' ©1976). The Milan début caused an international sensation; was organized in opposition to the ideas of earlier Studio Alchimia, the proto-Memphis group that examined the metaphysical rather than the technological aspects of design; became commercially successful by selling items in limited quantity. Its designs incorporated a heterogeneous mixture of styles from brash 1950s tastes to ancient art. Originally stimulated by Italian bourgeois taste, Sottsass saw the designs as 'quoting from suburbia.' Its designers included Marco Zanini, Sottsass, Daniel Weil, Shiro Kuramata, George Sowden, Michele De Lucchi, Aldo Cibic, Nathalie du Pasquier, Andrea Branzi, and Javier Mariscal. Its art director was Barbara Radice. Memphis came to be seen as a highly desirable expression of contemporary culture and was a landmark in late 20th-century design. The widely published apartment in Monte Carlo of clothing designer Karl Lagerfeld, furnished exclusively in Memphis products, somewhat helped to popularize the look. The high prices of Memphis items possibly encouraged its elitist cult image. 1988, the group was disbanded on Sottsass's behest, and Ernesto Gismondi acquired the brand.
Exhibitions Work subject of 1982 exhibition, Boilerhouse, Victoria and Albert Museum; 1986 *12 Nuovi Memphis*, Milan; 1989–90, Groninger Museum, Groninger; 1991 (ceramics, silver, glass), Musées de Marseille; 2001–02, Design Museum, London.
Bibliography *Memphis, the New International Style*, Milan: Electa, 1981. Cat., *Memphis Milano in London*, The Boilerhouse Project, London: Victoria and Albert Museum, 1982. Barbara Radice, *Memphis: ricerche, esperienze, risultati, fallimenti e successi del nuovo design*, Milan: 1984 (English ed.: New York: Rizzoli, 1984). Paolo Martegani et al., *Memphis una questione di stile*, Rome, 1987. Poul ter Hofstede (ed.), *Memphis, 1981–1988*, Groningen: Groninger Museum, 1989. Brigitte Fitoussi, *Memphis*, London: Thames & Hudson, 1998. Auction cat., *Memphis: la Collection Karl Kagerfeld*, Monaco: Sotheby's, 13 Oct. 1991. Danielle Maternati-Baldouy et al., *Memphis: céramique, argent, verre*, 1981–1987, Paris: Aveline; Marseille: Musées de Marseille, 1991.

Mendini, Alessandro (1931–)
Italian designer; born and active Milan.

Training 1959, architecture, Politecnico, Milan.
Biography 1956, Mendini began his professional career; to 1970, was a partner in industrial design studio Nizzoli Associati, Milan, 1973 with others, founded Radical Design group Global Tools, creating objects, architecture, and urban-planning solutions; 1970–76, was managing editor, journal *Casabella*; 1977–81, founder and managing editor, *Mode*; 1980–85, managing editor, *Domus*; directed journal *Ollo*. Active as a design theorist from 1978, Mendini has organized exhibitions, primarily with Studio Alchimia, where he propagated the concept of Banal Design; was an advocate of Nuovo Design or Neomodernismo (a renewal of Italian design), and the author of seminars; doggedly championed banal, inconsequential, and kitsch furniture and furnishings that questioned traditional attitudes toward value and function and hoped to encourage individual thinking. 1960s–80s, he was involved in the Anti-Design movement in Italy. His best-known work was the redesign in 1978 of a sideboard with decoration inspired by Kandinsky of the 1940s, and his 1978 Poltrona di Proust (Proust's armchair) painted in a Divisionist technique for Alchimia's 1979 'Bau.Haus uno' collection. (The 1980 'Bau.Haus due' collection followed. The Proust chair was reissued by Cappellini from 1993.) His 1978–79 Kandissi sofa also by by Alchimia controversially turned fine art into kitsch. He participated in the Bracciodiferro project (a 1981 experimental furniture workshop for Cassina), when he collaborated with others and executed designs for metalware by Alessi, including a set in their 1983 Tea and Coffee Piazza project, for which he was design and communications director. Responsible in part for Alessi's success, he also designed pots and pans by the firm. Clients have included Zanotta, Fiat, Zabro, Driade, MIM, Poltronova, Elam, and Abet Laminati. From 1983, Mendini has been a lecturer in design, Hochschule für angewandte Kunst, Vienna; was a member of the scientific committee of Domus Academy, of CDM (Consulenti Design Milano), and of ADI (Associazione per il Disegno Industriale); established the Genetic Laboratory for Visual Surprises to question established values of taste and function; wrote the books *Paesaggio casalingo: die produktion Alessi...* (1979), *Architettura addio* (1981), and *Il progetto infelice* (1983). Second half of 1980s, his œuvre included painting. His large body of work has included 1970s–80s covers for *Modo*, *Casabella*, and *Domus*, 1974 Lassù (up there) burning chair (performance art), 1978 Redesigned Chairs from the Modern Movement (one-of-a-kind

Alessandro Mendini. Vaso Viso vase. 2002. Ceramic, h. 43 3/8" (110 cm). Mfr.: Alessi, Italy.

furniture), 1981 Modulando 1-4 cabinet by Alchimia, 1981 Cipriani liquor cabinet by Memphis, 1981 Redesigned Breuer Chair, 1982 Arredo Vestitivo (furniture dress) (performance art with Alchimia) for Fiorucci in Milan, 1982 Galla Placidia plastic-laminate design by Abet Laminati, 1984 Tower Furniture cabinet (with Bruno Gregori), 1984 Cristina and Riflesso rugs by Bd Ediciones de Diseño, 1985 San Leonardo Collection seating by Matteograssi, 1985 Karina bench by Baleri Italia, 1985 ceramic panel by Tendentse, 1985 Poko steel shelf by Baleri Italia, 1985 Laverda motorcycle redesign, 1985–86 Casa della Felicità showcase residence (with Francesco Mendini and Studio Alchimia) of Alberto Alessi. Other clients included FBS-Franz Schneider Brakel (door handle), Daichi (silver case, jewelry, and sculptures with Sinya Okayama), Acme (jewelry), Elam Uno (furniture), 1986 Mirabili (modular furniture with M. Christina Hamel), Up & Up (tables and bookshelves, Segno (floor lamp), 1988 first cover for journal *Ollo*, Venini (blown-glass vase), Türler (watch and jewelry with M. Christina Hamel), Zabro (a large amount of furniture and lighting, some with Bruno Gregori). Late 1980s, Mendini returned to architecture, in Atelier Mendini in Milan with his brother Francesco; one of first commission was 1989 Paradise Tower in Hiroshima (with Yumio Kabayashi). Mendini was editor of *The International Design Yearbook* (New York: Abbeville, 1996).
Exhibitions/citations 1970s, organized exhibitions, mainly with Studio Alchimia. Anti-Design work included in *The Banal Object*, 1980 Biennale di Venezia; *Robots Sentimentale* (with Alchimia), 1982 Mediazione Inter-Mediterranea (MIM); 1985 Triennale di Milano; 1987 (8th) Documenta, Kassel; numerous other venues. Work was subject of 1989–90 *Alessi/Mendini: Dix Ans de Collaboration*, Centre Georges Pompidou, Paris. Premio Compasso d'Oro: 1979 (for design of journal Modo), 1981 (for Modulando seat by Studio Alchimia; research on the interior for Centro Domus), 1987 (for San Leonardo chair by Matteograssi), and 1994 (for Alessofono contralto saxophone by Alessi).
Bibliography Rosa Maria Rinaldi, *Mobile Infinito*, Milan: Alchimia, 1981. Fulvio Irace, *Stanze: un'idea per la casa*, Milan: Alchimia, 1981. Cat., *Nouvelles tendances: les avant-gardes de la fin du XXe siècle*, Paris: Centre Georges Pompidou. 1986. Kazuko Sato, *Alchimia*, Berlin: Taco, 1988. Juli Capella and Quim Larrea, *Designed by Architects in the 1980s*, New York: Rizzoli, 1988. Stefano Casciani et al., *Alessandro Mendini*, Milan: Giancarlo Politi, 1989. Rafaella Poletti (ed.), *Atelier Mendini: un'utopia visiva*, Milan: Fabbri Editore, 1994. Cat., Marijke Martin et al., *Alessandro & Francesco Mendini, Philippe Starck, Michele De Lucchi, Coop Himmelblau in Groningen*, Groningen: Groninger Museum, 1996. Peter Weiss, *Alessandro Mendini: Design and Architecture*, Milan: Electa Architetture, 2001.

Menghi, Roberto (1920–)

Italian industrial designer; born and active Milan.

Training To 1944, architecture, Politecnico, Milan.
Biography 1950, Menghi began his professional career; collaborated with Marco Zanuso Sr. and, 1953, with Anna Castelli and Ignazio Gardella; 1953–54, assisted Franco Albini at Istituto Universitario di Architettura, Venice; from 1955 specialized in plastics and designed furniture, industrial containers, electronic equipment, glassware, and housing. Clients included Arflex, Bormioli, Gulf, Fontana, IPI, Moneta, Merioni, Pirelli, Siemens, Velca, and Venini; became a member, Associazione per il Disegno Industriale (ADI). He designed 1964 house of Giovanni Pirelli in Varese, 1966 camping shelter by ICS, 1972 Abitere tent by Moretti, washing machine by Sub Matic, plastic kitchenware and other products by Kartell, and 1963 modular kitchen by Ariston.
Citations 1956 (two citations), 1957, 1959, 1967 Premio Compasso d'Oro.
Bibliography *ADI Annual 1976*, Milan: Associazione per il Disegno Industriale, 1976. Cat., Manolo de Giorgi (ed.), *45-63. Un museo del disegno industriale in Italia*, Milan: Abitare Segesta Cataloghi, 1995.

Mengshoel, Hans Christian (1946–)

Norwegian furniture designer.

Biography In Norway, A.C. Mandal, a Danish medical doctor in the mid-1960s, discovered that 25% of desk-job workers suffered from back problems. The 1979 Balans furniture series by Håg in Oslo was developed to assuage the situation, with chairs to accommodate the occupant with an angle between the spine and the thigh at 90°, rather than the normal 120° sitting posture in traditional office chairs. The concept was developed by Hans Christian Mengshoel and implemented by designers Peter Opsvik, Svein Gusrud, Oddvin Rykkens, and others. The Balans principle was patented, and litigation ultimately ensued, but the patent was withdrawn in 1992.
Bibliography Cat., David Revere McFadden (ed.), *Scandinavian Modern Design 1880–1980*, New York: Abrams, 1982.

Menna, Franco (1943–)

Italian industrial and retail designer; born Cheti; active Milan.

Training In geometry, interior architecture, and scenic design in Rome.
Biography 1963–74 in Rome, Menna was a consultant designer in interior-design department of La Rinascente department store, and for the shop Croff Centro Casa. 1971 with architect Paola Lanzani, set up a studio to pursue commissions in industrial design and interior architecture. From 1974, he worked on the magazine *Amica*; 1972, became a member, Associazione per il Disegno Industriale (ADI), and, 1972, of Ordine dei Gironalisti Elenco Pubblicisti.
Exhibitions Participated in various Eurodomus editions; 1973 (15th) Triennale di Milano.
Bibliography *ADI Annual 1976*, Milan: Associazione per il Disegno Industriale, 1976.

Mentula, Perttu (1936–)

Finnish architect and interior, exhibition, product, graphic, and furniture designer.

Training 1958–60, Taideteollinen korkeakoulu, Helsinki.
Biography 1958–60, Mentula was an interior and product designer in the Helsinki studios of Antti Nurmesniemi and Timo Sarpaneva, and of Toivo Korhonen and Reino Lamminsoila; 1960–77, was active in his own design studio; 1964–77, a designer for the Wärtsilä Shipyards in Helsinki; from 1977, director, Studio Perttu Mentula; 1970 and 1978–80, a board member, Ornamo (Finnish association of designers); from 1974, member, Fine Arts Commission of the Helsinki Festival; 1978–80, chairperson, Sisustusarkkitehdit (SIO, Finnish interior-architects association); 1978, member, Representational Arts Commission; 1978, member, Idea Group; 1981–83, vice-president, International Federation of Interior Designers; from 1981, member, executive committee and organizing committee, Design 81 Congress; 1981, coordinator, D'81 Creative Group; from 1982, design manager, Keriland Project, Kerimäki. Designs include 1971–74 Ringside hanging chairs, Rs 656 R by Avitom, and 1961 sauna stool.

Roberto Menghi. Container for liquids. 1958. Polyethylene plastic, 15 x 11 x 5" (38.1 x 27.9 x 12.7 cm). Mfr.: Pirelli, Italy. Gift of the mfr. MoMA.

Exhibitions/citations Work included in a number of Finnish exhibitions. First and second prizes, 1963 Export Furniture Competition, Helsinki; silver medal, 1964 (13th) Triennale di Milano; 1972 (two citations) Lighting Competition Awards, Tokyo; 1973 first prize, Scandinavian Environment and Furniture Competition, Copenhagen; 1981 first prize, Community Development Competition, Kerimäki; 1983, elected honorary member, AIPI (Italian interior architects association); numerous others.
Bibliography Ulf Hård af Segerstad, *Modern Finnish Design*, New York: Praeger, 1969. Donald J. Willcox, *New Design in Wood*, New York: Van Nostrand Reinhold, 1970. Ann Lee Morgan (ed.), *Contemporary Designers*, London: Macmillan, 1984: 405–07. Sara Pendergast, *Contemporary Designers*, Detroit: St. James, 1997 (3rd ed.).

Menuez, Ross (1965–)
American designer; born New York.

Training Sculpture, Hunter College, New York.
Biography When a teenager, Menuez began exploring design, worked on a small aircraft, and aspired to work for NASA; moved to Costa Rica and returned to New York and studied at Hunter College; became interested in metalwork after building a 48" (122 cm) steel railing; worked as a metal fabricator and, subsequently, became a designer; from 1992, created furniture, lighting, and accessories, calling on stainless steel combined with nylon, Bakelite, fiberglass, silicone, and polypropylene. His interior architecture includes David Barton Gym, Halston shop, Polo shop, Coup restaurant, all New York; was a staff designer at Habitat, London, and traveled for Habitat, including to Vietnam
Exhibitions/citations Work included in 2000 *The American Design Challenge*, Totem gallery, New York; 2002 *U.S. Design 1975–2000*, Denver (Colorado) Art Museum and traveling. Was Editor's Choice for Best New Designer, 1996 International Contemporary Furniture Fair (ICFF), New York.
Bibliography Mel Byars, *50 Products...*, Hove: RotoVision, 1999. Cat., R. Craig Miller (intro.), *U.S. Design 1975–2000*, Munich: Prestel, 2002.

Menzies, William Cameron (1896–1957)
American film set designer; born New Haven, Conn.; active Hollywood, Cal.

Training Yale University; University of Edinburgh; Art Students League, New York.
Biography 1920–22, Menzies worked in special effects and design for Famous Players-Lasky in London and New York and, 1923, settled in Hollywood; became the most respected and highest paid Hollywood designer of 1920s; designed the sets for film *Serenade* (1921); was an art director for Pickford-Fairbanks, Alexander Korda, David O. Selznick, Sam Wood, and major studios. As a writer (with Norman Z. McLeod) of the film *Alice in Wonderland* (1933), he invented the 'story board' technique. Drawing on his earlier career of designing children's books, Menzies combined 'baroque' Art Déco with 1920s illustrations for juveniles for film *The Thief of Bagdad* (1924); received the first (1928) Academy Award for art direction for both *The Tempest* (1928) and *The Dove* (1928); designed the spectacular production design of *For Things to Come* (1936), filmed in Britain; created the vast mythical ship *L'Amérique* for landmark Art Déco film *Reaching for the Moon* (1931) and the speakeasy in *I Loved You Wednesday* (1933); was the production designer of *Gone With the Wind* (1939); from 1943, directed and produced films.
Citations Oscars (from American Academy of Motion Picture Arts and Sciences) for the art direction of *The Dove* (1927), *The Tempest* (1927) and *Gone with the Wind* (1939).
Bibliography Howard Mandelbaum and Eric Myers, *Screen Deco: A Celebration of High Style in Hollywood*, New York: St. Martin's, 1985.

Mercatali, Davide (1948–)
Italian designer; born and active Milan.

Training To 1973, architecture, Politecnico, Milan.
Biography Mercatali worked independently as a graphic and product designer and illustrator for advertising agencies, publishers, and his own clients, including Società Donchi Formart in Milan; 1978 with Paolo Pedrizzetti, set up an industrial-design studio where he initially designed for materials and tiles. Subsequently, he has designed promotional accessories, point-of-sale displays in retail stores, fabrics, and dinnerware. Also the Nomade seating systems with buckles and straps (with architect M. Dall'Asta), 1978 I Balocchi collection of colored faucets and bathroom fixtures (with Paolo Pedrizetti) and Calibro by Fantini, 1980s Selz cutlery in stainless steel with nylon handles by Case Casa-Industrie Casalinghi Mari. 1982 with Pedrizetti, he cofounded Associated Studio, which designs domestic goods, electrical appliances, interior decoration, lighting, accessories, and building components and tools; became a member, Associazione per il Disegno Industriale (ADI); 1984, cofounded the group Zeus for design, fashion, and fine art, which gave rise to a boutique (producing its own fabrics and clothing), an art gallery (for one-person exhibitions of its members), and a large collection of furniture. from 1989, Mercatali has coordinated Metals, a group of jewelry designers making objects and articles in metal.
Citations 1979 (I Balocchi bathroom fittings with Pedrizetti by Fantini), 1981 (Calibro bathroom fittings by Fantini), 1987 (Giotto can opener with Pedrizetti by Icam) Premio Compasso d'Oro.
Bibliography *ADI Annual 1976*, Milan: Associazione per il Disegno Industriale, 1976. Giancarlo Iliprandi and Pierluigi Molinari (eds.), *Industrial designers italiani*, Fagagna: Magnus, 1985: 143. Robert A.M. Stern (ed.), *The International Design Yearbook*, New York: Abbeville, 1985/1986. Fumio Shimizu and Studio Matteo Thun (eds.), *The Italian Design: Descendants of Leonardo da Vinci*, Tokyo: Graphic-sha, 1987: 326. Cat., Hans Wichmann, *Italien Design 1945 bis heute*, Munich: Die Neue Sammlung, 1988. *Modo*, no. 148, Mar.–Apr.1993: 122.

Davide Mercatali and Paolo Pedrizzetti. Calibro single-control mixer tap. 1978. Lacquered brass with epoxy-resin finish, 5 7/8 x 2 1/4 x 6 7/8" (15 x 5.7 x 17.5 cm). Mfr.: Fratelli Fantini, Italy. Gift of the mfr. MoMA.

Mercier Frères

French decorators and furniture makers; located Paris.

History The brothers Mercier produced their furniture in a workshop in the Faubourg Saint-Antoine area of Paris; 1925, opened Palais du Marbre decorating shop at 77, avenue des Champs-Elysées, whose artistic director was Eric Bagge from 1925–29.
Bibliography *Ensembles mobiliers*, vol. 2, Paris: Charles Moreau, 1937. Pierre Kjellberg, *Art déco: les maîtres du mobilier, le décor des paquebots*, Paris: Amateur, 1986/1990.

Merckx, Arnold (1941–)

Dutch designer.

Training To 1962, interior architecture, Academie voor Beeldende Kunsten en Technische Wetenschappen, Rotterdam; apprenticeships under Kho Liang Ie, Pierre Paulin, and others.
Biography Merckx is a member of a furniture-making family in Fristho where he worked for a time; 1978, established his own design studio, working primarily for furniture manufacturers, such as Arco and Montis. Design work includes 1998 Chap chair and sofa by Pastoe; and 2000 Spider table, Flow High dining chair, and Flow Low easy chair by Spectrum.
Citations A number of prizes.

Mère, Clément (1861–1940)

French painter, tabletier, designer, and furniture maker; born Bayonne, active Paris.

Training Under Jean-Léon Gérôme, painting, École des Beaux-Arts, Paris.
Biography Mère designed bookbindings, embroideries, and objects in the Art Nouveau manner; c. 1900, joined Julius Meier-Graefe's stable of designers/craftspeople at the shop La Maison Moderne, Paris, where he met Franz Waldraff, with whom he designed and made intricate ivory panels and wood and ivory boxes, and supplied dress fabrics, buttons, and other dressmaker's materials. On his own, Mère specialized in designing and creating costly cabinets, cases, desks, and decorative work in exotic woods and materials that were influenced by his training as a painter and a craftsperson of overlays. His shapes were classically geometric rather than Cubist.
Exhibitions Work shown at editions of Salon d'Automne, Salons of Société des Artistes Décorateurs from 1910, and of Société Nationale des Beaux-Arts.
Bibliography Victor Arwas, *Art Déco*, New York: Abrams, 1980: 303.

Mergier, Paul (1891–1986)

French aeronautical engineer, painter, metalworker, enameler, furniture maker, and decorator; born Orthez.

Training From 1920, in engineering and enameling.
Biography Mergier incorporating new methods and applications in his work, particularly pastes rather than powders to make both small and very large enamel plaques. He also painted and drew still lifes. His metalwork included figurative scenes; his furniture was covered in leather and inlaid with mother-of-pearl, ivory, and other precious materials. He wrote a book on the association between the arts and the sciences, and another on enameling techniques. He died in Paris.
Exhibitions Work was at editions of Salon d'Automne, Salon of Société des Artistes Décorateurs (from 1927), Salon of Société des Artistes Français, Salon des Tuileries, Salon des Indépendants, *Exposition Internationale des Arts et Techniques dans la Vie Moderne*; all Paris. And 1939–40 *New York World's Fair: The World of Tomorrow*.
Bibliography Pierre Kjellberg, *Art déco: les maîtres du mobilier, le décor des paquebots*, Paris: Amateur, 1986/1990.

Meriden Britannia

American silverplate factory; located West Meriden, Conn.

History A group of Britannia-ware producers consolidated their efforts and, 1852, formed Meriden Britannia. (Britannia metal itself is a silver-white alloy largely of tin, antimony, and copper, similar to pewter.) The group of seven directors included Isaac Chauncey Lewis (the firm's first president), Horace Cornwall Wilcox, and Samuel Simpson (the founder of Simpson, Hall, Miller and Co. in Wallingford, Conn.). First using Britannia metal and then nickel silver for its bases, the firm began the production of silver-plated objects, including teapots, candlesticks, epergnes, punch bowls, cutlery, and vessels; had sales offices in Chicago, San Francisco, New York, and London; was the largest silver-plate ware manufacturer in the world by 1870; 1881, opened a second factory in Hamilton, Ontario, Canada, and later a third. Its success was supported by the refinement of the electroplating process by Elkington in Britain and the 1859 discovery of silver in the Comstock Lode in Nevada. 1895, the firm purchased Wilcox and Evertson, silversmiths in New York, resulting in its 1897 fine-silver cutlery range; 1898, was amalgamated with others to form the International Silver Company.
Exhibitions Work shown at international exhibitions in the US. During 1876–93, its most effective presentation was at 1876 *Centennial Exposition* (showing Theodore Bauer's silverplated centerpiece, based on his sculpture *The Buffalo Hunt*), Philadelphia.
Bibliography Dorothy T. Rainwater and H. Ivan Rainwater, *American Silverplate*, Nashville, Tenn., and Hanover, Pa., 1968: 13–27, 39–132, 138–40. Doreen Bolger Burke et al., *In Pursuit of Beauty: Americans and the Aesthetic Movement*, New York: The Metropolitan Museum of Art/Rizzoli, 1986: 453.

Meritalia

Italian furniture and lighting company; located Mariano Comense (CO).

History Founded in 1987, the firm produces a wide range of furniture including seating, tables, and lighting in wood, metal, marble, and glass in four factories; has commissioned designers including Afra and Tobia Scarpa, Vittorio Prato, Dante Benini, Marc Newson, and Pipa Bradbury.

Merkx, Evelyne (1947–)

Dutch interior architect and designer.

Training 1979 at age 32, enrolled at Gerrit Rietveld Academie, Amsterdam.
Biography Upon graduation, Merkx set up her own interior-architecture studio; moved to a former shampoo factory, where she lives and works; with business and social partner Patrice Girod, manages the Merkx & Girod agency, with 20 staff members. Commissions have included interiors of homes, boutiques, redesign of De Bijendorf department store chain, Herna superstores, ABN Amro bank's head office in Amsterdam, first-class restaurant in Amsterdam Central Station, shopping/bar/catering section at Schiphol airport D-pier, and renovation of Concertgebouw (concert building). Her 1999 Spine table (with one side absent of legs) is being produced by Bulo in Antwerp. Purportedly, Merkx is one of Holland's top five interior architects.

Mertens, H.F.
> See LOV.

Messel, Oliver (1905–1978)

British theater, film, and interior designer; active London and Barbados.

Training Slade School of Fine Art, London.
Biography While at the Slade, Messel met Rex Whistler, with whom he took up making *papier-mâché* masks, which interested Sergei Diaghilev, who commissioned Messel to produce masks for the Ballets Russes's 1925 production of *Zéphyre et Flore*. Messel designed sets and costumes for Noel Coward's play *This Year of Grace* (1928) and film the *The Scarlet Pimpernel* (director, Harold Young, 1934), and costumes for a production of Mozart's *The Magic Flute*. Messel's work was historicist, with columns, entablatures, drapery swags, and baroque ornamentation. 1952, he designed the commemorative silk scarf and exterior decorations of the Dorchester hotel in London to celebrate the Coronation of Queen Elizabeth II. 1953 at the Dorchester, he completed the Oliver Messel Suite; 1953, the Penthouse Suite; and, 1956, the Pavilion Room. His rugs for the hotel were woven in Bangkok. 1991, the hotel's décor—inspired by Messel's designs for 1946 production of *The Sleeping Beauty* by Sadler's Wells Ballet (now Royal Ballet)—was restored under the direction of John Claridge, who had worked on the original project. Through his social connections, he was hired to design lavish parties and weddings such as the 1955 marriage of Princess Ira von Fürstenberg to Prince Alfonso von Hohenlohe-Lagenburg; 1966, Messel retired to Barbados, where he planned to paint and relax but instead began a second career designing gardens and houses, including the 'Prospero' estate. Princess Margaret lived in a Messel house in Barbados. He used non-traditional, improvisational procedures in his houses, incorporating humble materials and simple building techniques; was fond of lush garden

effects and influential in establishing much of today's architectural tone on the islands; 1959, designed the houses on 1,200-acre (500-hectare) parcel on Mustique for Lord Glenconner but died before completion of Glenconner's 'Great House,' which he jokingly dubbed an 'Indo-Asiatic ragbag.'
Bibliography John Claridge, 'Restoration Drama,' *House and Garden*, Apr. 1991: 50, 51. John Mayfield, 'Sounds and Sweet Airs,' *Elle Decor*, June/July 1991: 40, 42. Charles Castle, *Oliver Messel*, London: Thames & Hudson, 1986.

Mestral, Georges de (1907–1990)
> See de Mestral, Georges.

metal furniture
> See tubular-steel furniture.

Metalarte
Spanish lighting firm; located Barcelona.

History 1932, the Riera family founded Metalarte, specializing in metalwork and lighting made to order; from 1948, began the production of decorative, domestic lighting; purportedly, has become a pioneer in the design of lighting in Spain. Currently commissions freelance designers such as André Ricard, Josep Lluscà, Joaquín Beraoi, Enric Franch, Toni Arola, Alberto Liévori, and the Devesa brothers. The firm issues new designs annually and a catalog biannually; exports 70% of its production to Europe, South America, and the US. Franch's 1975 Calder halogen swivel table lamp represented an exception to a return to conservative production. 1980s, Metalarte again produced high-design contemporary lighting, with its 1988 Maja standard lighting and other models by Devesa, and 1989 Ketupa lamp by Lluscà and Berao.
Bibliography Guy Julier, *New Spanish Design*, London: Thames & Hudson, 1991.

Meta-Memphis
Italian furniture firm.

History 1988, Meta-Memphis, or Metamemphis, was set up when Ettore Sottsass, the original founder of Memphis (active 1981–88), decided to close the enterprise/studio. He asserted that an innovative idea has a life of five to seven years. Ernesto Gismondi, president of Artemide lighting manufacturer, purchased the Memphis brand name. 1989 in Venice, Gismondi unveiled what he called Meta-Memphis with an initial collection of 20 pieces by ten artists (in contrast to Sottsass's industrial designers), including Sandro Chia, Joseph Kossuth, Lawrence Weiner, and Michelangelo Pistoletto. Other collections followed. Sottsass disapproved of 'art furniture' and, thus, Meta-Memphis. The firm's line was priced as if it were fine art and not limited-production furniture. Some of the former designs in the original Memphis collection continued to be produced.
Bibliography Arlene Hirst, *Metropolitan Home*, Aug. 1989: 22.

Metelák, Alois (1897–1980)
Czech architect and glass designer; born Martěnice.

Training Under Jožef Plečník, decorative architecture, Vysokou Školu Uměleckoprůmyslovou (academy of arts, architecture, and design), Prague.
Biography 1924–48, Metelák was director, Středni Uměleckoprůmyslová Škola Sklářská (school of glass making), Železný Brod; 1948–52, director, Střední Uměleckoprůmyslová Školy (SUPŠ, school of jewelry) Turnov; from 1920, was a member, Czechoslovakian Werkbund (SČSD); specialized in cut, engraved, and etched glass. In 1930s particularly, his architectural training showed in the rich plasticity of his glass vases and bowls. 1920s–30s, some of his table glass acknowledged Czech modernism.
Bibliography Alena Adlerová, *Alois Metelák: Sklo z let 1924–1963*, Prague, 1963. D. Šindelář, *Současné umělecké sklo v Československu*, Prague, 1970. Alena Adlerová, *České užité uměni 1918–1938*, Prague: Odeon, 1983.

Metsovaara, Marjatta (1928–)
Finnish textile artist and designer; active Helsinki.

Training 1949, Taideteollinen korkeakoulu, Helsinki.
Biography 1954, Metsovaara set up a workshop in Helsinki; executed rich handcrafted effects calling on both traditional and synthetic materials; designed woven and printed furnishing fabrics for mass production by Uniwool and by Tampella and dress fabric by Finn-Flare, the fashion house she established with Maj Kuhlefelt in 1963; in her studio, made wool and mohair lap robes and stoles, rya rugs, and carpets.
Citations Medals at 1957 (11th) and 1960 (12th) editions of Triennale di Milano.
Bibliography Erik Zahle (ed.), *A Treasury of Scandinavian Design*, New York: Golden Press, 1961. Eileene Harrison Beer, *Scandinavian Design: Objects of a Life Style*, New York: Farrar, Straus & Giroux, 1975. Cat., Kathryn B. Hiesinger and George H. Marcus III (eds.), *Design Since 1945*, Philadelphia: Philadelphia Museum of Art, 1983.

Metthey, André (1871–1921)
French ceramicist; born Laignes.

Training In decorations and sculpture, apprenticeship.
Biography Metthey became a potter after his design/art training; 1901–06, made *flambé* stoneware in Japanese and Korean styles; after pursuing often fruitless research, was then interested in faïence in the French tradition, opening a studio in Asnières. Metthey's works were decorated by artists Odilon Redon, Georges Rouault, Henri Matisse, Pierre Bonnard, Jean Édouard Vuillard, Valtat, André Derain, Maurice de Vlaminck, and Othon Friesz. Metthey abandoned faïence for glazed earthenware; 1912, returned to stoneware; experimented with *pâte-de-verre* toward the end of his career.
Bibliography Yvonne Brunhammer et al., *Art Nouveau Belgium, France*, Houston: Institute for the Arts, Rice University, 1976.

Metz
Dutch drapery and furniture store; located Amsterdam.

History 1740, Samuel Moses Metz established a fabric store in Amsterdam which began selling products made by others; from end of 1910s to 1960s, made limited-production items, most by craftspeople, for sale in its own stores. The firm was distinguished by its design policy and association with a large number of freelance designers. Joseph de Leeuw (1876–1944), responsible for its enlightened approach to design, was owner and director from c. 1900. Products were imported from Britain (Liberty goods), France, and Austra. Dutch goods included those by Leerdam (glassware), De Distel (ceramics), and De Ploeg (fabrics). 1918–24, Paul Bromberg designed furniture and advised Metz clients on interior furnishings; was succeeded by interior architect Willen Penaat. Moderately functional furniture was designed by H.P. Berlage and K.P.C. de Bazel. However, De Leeuw had little regard for most Dutch designers and commissioned the firm's Metzco clothing and upholstery fabrics from foreigners such as Sonia Delaunay, who made bright geometric patterned fabrications. c. 1930, a style departure followed de Leeuw's meetings with architect Gerrit Rietveld (who designed for Metz until 1950s) and painter B. van der Leck. At this time and even so, numerous other Dutch designers worked for the firm, including J.J.P. Oud, Mart Stam, and I. Falkenberg-Liefrinck, and, in France, Jean Burkhalter and Édouard-Joseph Bourgeois. Graphic artists included A.M. Cassandre in 1930 and Jean Carlu in 1933. Metz made its own wood furniture, but tubular-steel models were contracted out. E. Berkovich, the supervisor of Metz's furniture workshop from 1922–46, designed 1930s furniture and lamps for Metz. Though he provided almost unbridled freedom to his consultant designers, de Leeuw did not pay them well. Today Metz & Co. is own by Liberty's of London.
Bibliography Barbie Campbell-Cole and Tim Benton (eds.), *Tubular Steel Furniture*, London: The Art Book Company, 1979: 31. Cat., *Industry and Design in the Netherlands, 1850/1950*, Amsterdam: Stedelijk Museum, 1985. Petra Timmer, *Metz & Co. De creatieve jaren*, Rotterdam: 010, 1995.

Meubles et Fonctions International (MFI)
> See Perrigault, Pierre.

Meydam, Floris (1919–)
Dutch glassware designer.

Biography Meydam produced both freely formed one-of-a-kind pieces and tableware ranges at Vereenigde Leerdam Glasfabriek, in the Netherlands, that were spare and unadorned; 1935, became an assistant to its artistic director Andries Copier; from 1943, was a trainee in the Leerdam glass school and, from 1944, taught there; returned to the factory, where he was the chief designer from 1949–89. He contributed to Leerdam's Unica range. His solid and geometrical crystal objects

Floris Meydam. Nesting Tumblers. c. 1949–53. Tapered clear crystal tumblers, tallest h. 3 3/8" (8.6 cm) x dia. 3 1/2" (8.9 cm), shortest h. 2" (5.1 cm) x dia. 2" (5.1 cm). Mfr.: N.V. Koninklijke Nederlandsche Glasfabriek Leerdam, the Netherlands. Gift of A. J. Van Dugteren & Sons, Inc. MoMA.

were realized as cylinders, spheres, and teardrops, often incorporating air bubbles, cuts, and ground sections that caught the light and played with colors. He was primarily known for his glass but also designed ceramics by Zenith, Flora, and Fris. Indeed, from 1952–66, he designed ceramics for Kunstaardewerkfabriek Regina in Gouda, including the 1958 Prince Orange tea service.
Exhibitions Work included in 1953 *Good Design* exhibition/award, The Museum of Modern Art, New York, and Chicago Merchandise Mart; 1977 Leerdam exhibition, Düsseldorf/Rotterdam.
Bibliography Cat., *Leerdam unica: 50 jaar modern nederlands glas*, Düsseldorf: Kunstmuseum, 1977. Geoffrey Beard, *International Modern Glass*, London, 1976: plates 91, 93, 253 Frederick Cooke, *Glass: Twentieth-Century Design*, New York: Dutton: 1986.

Meyer, Grethe (1918–)

Danish architect, ceramicist, and furniture and glassware designer; born Svendborg.

Training To 1947, architecture, Det Kongelige Danske Kunstakademi, Copenhagen.
Biography 1944–55, she was on the editorial staff of the anthology *Byggebogen* (the building book); 1955–60, was active in housing research at Danish Building Research Institute, collaborating with Poul Kjærgaard and Bent Salicath on research in housing and consumer products; worked frequently with Børge Mogensen and was influential in his research in the standardization of sizes of consumer products; with Mogensen, designed 1957 Boligens Byggeskabe (cabinets for the home) and Øresund cabinet-storage systems; 1959, with Ibi Trier Mørch, glassware by Kastrup and Holmegård. 1960, she set up her own drawing office; from 1960, designed tableware by Royal Copenhagen Porcelain Manufactory, including 1965 Blå Kant (blue rim) faïence dinner service and 1991 cutlery. With Mørch, she designed 1958 Stub (stump) and Stamme drinking glasses by Kastrup Glasværk, 1972 Weisstopf dinnerware, 1976 Feuerpott oven-to-table kitchenware range, and 1989 Ocean vases by Royal Copenhagen; 1991 Copenhagen steel cutlery (also 1996 Copenhagen Line cutlery) by Georg Jensen Sølvsmedie. She was a member, Akademisk Arkitektforening (AA, academic association of architects) and, from 1977, of Dansk Designråd (Danish design council).
Exhibitions/citations Work shown at editions of Triennale di Milano; 1960–61 *The Arts of Denmark*, touring the US; 1980 *Scandinavian Modern Design 1880–1980*, Cooper-Hewitt National Design Museum, New York; 1983–84 *Design Since 1945*, Philadelphia Museum of Art. Received 1965 Bojesen's Memorial Grant; 1965 (for Blå Kant), 1976, 1997 Dansk ID Prize; 1965 silver medal, Concorso Internazionale della Ceramica d'Arte, Faenza; 1972, elected Honorary Royal Designer for Industry, UK; 1973 Nordic Artist-Craftsmen and Design Prize; 1980 lifetime grant, Danish State Art Foundation; 1983 Thorvald Bindesbøll Medal, Akademirådet, Denmark.
Bibliography Arne Karlsen, *Made in Denmark*, New York: Rheinhold, 1960: 118–19. Arne Karlsen, *Møbler tegnet af Børge Mogensen: Udvalgt og beskrevet, Tegninger af forfatteren*, Copenhagen: Arkitektens Forlag, 1968. Eileene Harrison Beer, *Scandinavian Design: Objects of a Life Style*, New York: Farrar, Straus & Giroux, 1975. Jens Bersen, *Design: The Problem Comes First*, Copenhagen: Danish Design Council, 1982: 64–67. Cat., Design Center Stuttgart, *Women in Design: Careers and Life Histories Since 1900*, Stuttgart: Haus der Wirtschaft, 1989: 230–31. Jennifer Hawkins Opie, *Scandinavia: Ceramics and Glass in the Twentieth Century*, New York: Rizzoli, 1989.

Meyer, Hannes (1889–1954)

Swiss teacher and designer; born Basel; husband of textile designer Léna Bergner.

Training 1905–09, masonry and architectural drafting, Gewerbeschule, Basel; subsequently, Kunstgewerbeschule, Landwirtschaftsakademie and Technische Hochschule, Berlin; 1912–13, in England.
Biography Meyer was active in the land reform movement and designed 1919–24 Freidorf estate in Muttenz, near Basel; 1916–19, participated in housing projects in Munich, Essen, and Lausanne; from 1916 in Munich, assisted Georg Metundorf in the design of workers' housing, and thereafter for Krupp; 1919, set up his own architecture practice in Basel and, 1926, became a partner of Hans Wittwer; 1926, attended the Bauhaus, where, from 1927, taught in its architectural department, and where, 1928, succeeded Gropius as director. 1928–29, Meyer published the eight issues of the journal *Bauhaus*. Shunned architecture founded on aesthetic formalism, a position that created friction with Bauhaus teachers, including László Moholy-Nagy. Also, due to his rigorously left-wing approach to architecture and design, his tenure was short at the Bauhaus, where, 1930, Ludwig Mies van der Rohe assumed the directorship when Meyer decamped to the USSR (today Russia) with a group of his students. Active in USSR to 1936, he became a professor, College of Architecture, Moscow; 1930, designed an inventive chair with an adjustable seat. From 1936, he worked on town planning projects in Geneva; 1939–49, lived in Mexico and, 1949, in Lugano. His most important works are the 1926–27 Palace of Nations non-winning competition entry (with Hans Wittwer; and one of 377 submissions) in Geneva, 1928–30 Allgemeiner Deutscher Gewerkschaftsbund (united German workers' union) building in Bernau, near Berlin, and 1932 housing plan for Sozgorod Gorki, Russia.
Bibliography Claude Schnaidt, *Hannes Meyer, Bauten, Projekte und Schriften = Buildings, Projects, and Writings*, Teufen: Arthur Niggli, 1965; London: Alec Tiranti, 1965. Cat., *Der Kragstuhl*, Stuhlmuseum Burg Beverungen, Berlin: Alexander, 1986: 134. Werner Kleinerüschkamp, *Hannes Meyer, 1889–1954: Architekt, Urbanist, Lehrer*, Berlin: Ernst, 1989. Klaus-Jürgen Winkler (ed.), *Der Architekt Hannes Meyer: Anschauungen und Werk*, Berlin: Ernst, 1989. Cat., *The Bauhaus: Masters and Students*, New York: Barry Friedman, 1988. K. Michael Hays, *Modernism and the Posthumanist Subject: The Architecture of Hannes Meyer and Ludwig Hilberseimer*, Cambridge: MIT, 1992.

Meyer, Helena (1906–1981)
> See Bergner, Léna.

Meyer, Terje (1942–)

Norwegian furniture designer.

Biography Early on, Meyer became known for his widely published 1968 paper furniture by Strongpack and 1970 multi-media room. He also designed 1968 Uni-Line furniture range (with Mona Kinn) by Dokka Møbler and 1976 low-cost house in plastic (with Jan Sverre Christiansen). Currently, Meyer directs Meyer Design, a small but successful consultancy in Oslo, through which he designed the new high-speed express train from Oslo's central station to Gardermoen Airport for ADtranz/NSB and the Signatur trains for NSB. Also designs for Silence International (formerly SINTEF Telecom and Informatics).
Citations 1973 Japanese design prize for a bicycle model, designed with Bjørn A. Larsen and Christiansen.

Bibliography Fredrik Wildhagen, *Norge i Form*, *Oslo*: Stenersen, 1988.

Meyerhoffer, Thomas

Swedish industrial designer; born Stockholm.

Training To 1991, Art Center College of Design, Montreux.
Biography Meyerhoffer collaborated on the interior of 1996 Porsche Boxter automobile; designed computer monitors by NEC; was a consultant at IDEO Product Development in Palo Alto, Cal.; from 1995, worked at Apple Computer in Cupertino, Cal., where he designed 1997 eMate 300 laptop, which broke from Apple's conservative approach and was targeted to the youth market. 1998, formed own studio, Meyerhoffer, with clients including, Cappellini, Ericsson, and others.
Bibliography Paul Kunkel, *Apple Design: The World of the Apple Industrial Design Group*, New York: Graphis, 1997.

Michel, Eugène (1848–1904)

French glassmaker; born Lunéville, Meurthe-et-Moselle.

Biography 1867, Michel worked as an engraver and decorator for Eugène Rousseau and, subsequently, for Rousseau's successor Eugène Léveillé; c. 1900, became an independent glassmaker in Paris; like Rousseau, worked primarily with crackled glass in several different colored layers, deeply engraved, creating a dramatic effect. His work was strongly influenced by 18th- and 19th-century Chinese glassware. Lelièvre, with whom Michel collaborated for a time, made metal mountings for Michel's cut and engraved crystal bottles.
Bibliography Yvonne Brunhammer et al., *Art Nouveau Belgium, France*, Houston: Institute for the Arts, Rice University, 1976.

Michelotti, Giovanni (1921–1981)

Italian automobile designer; born and active Turin.

Biography From 1937, Michelotti worked in the workshop of Stabilimenti Farina (founded in 1906 by Giovanni Farina) in Turin, where he had become the chief design by 1939. After World War II, he left Farina and worked on his own in his home from 1949. In 1950s when coach makers were turning to design studios, Michelotti became one of those working independently. However, he has become somewhat unknown, possibly due to the absence of a direct connection with a particular firm. Even so, he designed innovative and flamboyant car bodies, many of the early examples being made by Alfredo Vignale. But Michelotti is best known for 1959 Triumph Herald and 1962 Triumph Spitfire (various editions). Also designed 1951 Ferrari 212 Export, 1961 Triumph TR4; 1959 BMW 700, 1961 BMW 1800, Renault Berlinette Alpine models of 1955 (A106) and 1958–63 (A108), and 1968 DAF 55.

Michelsen, A.

Danish silversmiths; located Copenhagen.

History 1841, Anton Michelsen (Copenhagen, 1809–1977) founded his eponymous firm, the only Danish establishment to show silver at 1900 Paris *Exposition*. 19th century and most of the 20th, it became Denmark's foremost gold- and silversmith, carrying out commissions for the royal household and the government. Early years of 20th century, Carl Michelsen (1853–1921) was the proprietor and commissioned designs from Thorvald Bindesbøll (from 1887–88), Mogens Ballin, and others. 1906, Fr. Hegel began working for the firm; his work was influenced by Bindesbøll and Holger Kyster of Kolding. Late 19th and early 20th century, Niels Georg Henriksen (1855-1922) was the artistic director and one of the first in Denmark to work in the Art Nouveau style; his work showed chased and embossed naturalistic thistles, irises, and poppies. Harald Slott-Møller, another influenced by Bindesbøll, created designs of abstract, playful ornament. 1910–80s, Michelsen issued annual Christmas spoons; 1920s, produced the designs of Kay Fisker and, 1930s, those of Palle Svenson and Kay Gottlob; and Inger Hanmann. Its 1930s stainless-steel ware was highly successful, particularly Arne Jacobsen's 1957 cutlery that appeared in the film *2001: A Space Odyssey* (director, Stanley Kubrick, 1969). 1977, Georg Jensen and Michelsen were amalgamated and, 1985, merged with Royal Copenhagen Porcelain Factory and Holmegård Glassworks under the umbrella name Royal Copenhagen Ltd. However, in 2000, Royal Scandinavia was bought by an investment group and eventually dismantled into various reorganized entities.
Exhibitions Silver shown (with Henriksen and Slott-Møller) at 1900 *Exposition Universelle*, Paris.
Bibliography Annelies Krekel-Aalberse, *Art Nouveau and Art Déco Silver*, New York: Abrams, 1989. Jacob Thage, *Danske smykker = Danish Jewelry*, Copenhagen: Komma & Clausen, 1990.
> See Royal Scandinavia.

Michon, Lucien (1887–1963)
> See Genêt et Michon.

Midavaine, Louis (1888–1978)

French accessories and furniture designer; born Roubaix.

Training École des Beaux-Arts, Roubaix.
Biography Before World War I, Midavaine worked for his family's painting and decoration enterprise in the village of Grièvement. He was injured and taken prisoner in Germany, where he discovered the techniques of lacquer through the brother of his nurse. After the war, he moved to Issy-les-Moulineaux, where he decorated objects in lacquer sold to benefit the Red Cross. The duchesse de La Rochefoucauld, the director of the Red Cross, set up Midavaine in a studio in Paris in 1917. He designed numerous modern lacquered pieces, prin-cipally in the form of animals; participated in the decoration of oceanliners, including 1935 *Normandie* and 1939 *Pasteur;* 1950, decorated the residence in the Côte d'Azur of Bao-Daï, the emperor of Annam (a part of Vietnam), and, after World War II, private residences and state interiors, including dining room of the French president of the Senate.
Exhibitions Work shown at all Salons of Société Nationale des Beaux-Arts.
Bibliography *Meubles 1920–1937*, Paris: Musée d'Art Moderne de la Ville de Paris, 1986.

Middelboe, Rolf (1917–)

Danish graphic and textile designer.

Biography 1941, Middelboe set up his own workshop, where he printed textiles and executed graphic designs; furnished printed and woven fabric designs to Danish firms, including Spindegården and to Unika-Vaev; used various techniques in his regular, screen-printed geometric motifs and increased the variety of effects through the use of positive and negative alternations.
Bibliography Arne Karlsen, *Made in Denmark*, New York: Rheinhold, 1960. Erik Zahle (ed.), *A Treasury of Scandinavian Design*, New York: Golden Press, 1961. Cat., Kathryn B. Hiesinger and George H. Marcus III (eds.), *Design Since 1945*, Philadelphia: Philadelphia Museum of Art, 1983.

A. Michelsen: Arne Jacobsen. Cutlery. 1957. Stainless steel, knife l. 7 3/4 x w. 5/8" (19.7 x 1.6 cm), teaspoon l. 6 1/8 x w. 3/4" (15.6 x 1.9 cm). Mfr.: A. Michelsen, Denmark. Gift of the mfr. MoMA.

Ludwig Mies van der Rohe. Barcelona chair. 1929. Stainless-steel bars and leather upholstery, 31 x 29 3/8 x 30" (78.7 x 74.6 x 76.2 cm), seat h. 17 3/8" (44.2 cm). Mfr.: Knoll International, US. (1953). Gift of the mfr. MoMA.

Mies van der Rohe, Ludwig (b. Ludwig Mies 1886–1969)

German architect and designer; born Aachen.

Training 1899–1901, Domschule (cathedral school) and Gewerbeschule (vocational school), Aachen; 1906–07, Staatliche Kunstschule des Kunstgewerbemuseums, Berlin.

Biography 1905, Mies moved to Berlin and worked for the Berlin borough of Rixdorf to furnish the council chamber; late 1905 (or early 1906) to 1907 in Berlin, was apprenticed to architect and furniture designer Bruno Paul, under whom he received his principal training, and studied wooden furniture design; 1908–10, worked in office of Peter Behrens in Berlin-Neubabelsberg (Le Corbusier, Walter Gropius, Hans Meyer, Jean Krämer, and Peter Grossman also worked in Behrens's office about this time on Allgemeine Elektritätsgesellschaft/AEG projects) and, 1911, supervised the construction of Behrens's 1910–11 German Embassy in St. Petersburg. Mies's 1910 competition entry for the Bismark monument project (an early but seminal work) in Bingerbrück-Bingen married the classicism of Karl Friedrich Schinkel with modernism. In fact, Mies's earliest work was inspired by Schinkel, and, thus, as an amalgamator, Mies was to become a creator of the International Style. 1911, he traveled to the Hague, planned an unrealized house for Anton Kröller and Helene Kröller-Müller, and became acquainted with Hendrik Berlage; 1913, returned to Berlin and opened his own architecture office; 1914–15, served in the military. 1921, he changed his name from simply Mies to the more distinguished-appearing Mies van der Rohe by adding his mother's maiden name Rohe (the addition first appeared in print in 1922). His 1921 glass-sheathed Friedrichstraße office building 1 project and 1922 glass skyscraper project, both for Berlin, are milestones, presaging a codified realization of the International Style to come. As a member of the Novembergruppe, he was the director of architecture exhibitions from 1922–25. 1923, he joined the Bund deutscher Architekten (BdA) and, 1924, joined the younger vanguardists of the BdA to cofound architects' organization Der Ring (later known as Zwölferring or Zehnerring, depending on the number of members), and its chairperson from 1923–25. And very shortly (1924), he joined the Deutscher Werkbund, of which he was vice-president from 1926–32; 1923–24, was joint editor of journal *G* (for *Gestaltung*, named by El Lissitsky). It was at this time (1922–23) that Mies designed a major work, the concret office building project; from 1925, was the director of the Deutscher Werkbund's exhibition/colony *Die Wohnung* in Stuttgart, heading the *Weissenhofsiedlung* building project there, which opened in 1927. Mid-1920s, Mies began work on 1927 MR cantilever curved-legged tubular-steel chair, introducing a realized example (with and without arms) at the *Weissenhofsiedlung* (where Mart Stam's and Marcel Breuer's cantilever chairs also appeared). The Mies chairs were fitted with belting fabric (Eisengarn or 'iron yarn') or with special wickerwork by Lilly Reich and also included in Reich's installation at 1927 *Mode der Dame* exhibition in Berlin. The originator of the cantilever design was Mart Stam; as Sergius Ruegenberg, an assistant of Mies, recalled, 'Mies came back from Stuttgart in Nov. 1926 and told us about Mart Stam's idea for a chair.... Mies drew the chair... and he said, "Ugly, those fittings are really ugly [referring to the pipe joints]. If only he'd [Stam would have] rounded them off—there, that looks better," and Mies drew a curve. A simple curve from his hand on the Stam sketch had made a new chair out of it!,' Ruegenberg concludes. 1927, Mies was assigned a patent for the cantilever tubular-steel chair that was first produced by locksmith Berliner Metallgewerbe Joseph Müller in Neubabelsberg from 1927–29 (the firm was renamed Bamberg Metallwerkstätten in 1931 and the chair as MR 10). Subsequent production: by Thonet from 1930–36 as MR 533 and by Knoll from 1970. He designed furniture for all his early houses, including the Werner house; for 1928–30 Tugendhat house, designed everything with assistance from Lilly Reich. From 1948, Mies's furniture designs were licensed to Knoll, whose deft marketing turned his 1920s–30s furniture pieces into status symbols. As companion pieces, Mies designed a tubular stool with a leather sling and a low table with a round glass top. His chair for 1929 Barcelona *Exposición*, known now as the Barcelona chair, is still in production, as is much of his furniture by various firms. Expensive to produce, the Barcelona was first made by Joseph Müller in 1929; by Thonet from Nov. 1931; by Knoll from 1948; today, by others, also continuing by Knoll. The commission of the 1929–30 Fritz and Grete Tugendhat house in Brno resulted in a cantilevered variant of the Barcelona chair concept with arms, and several other pieces, including a rosewood desk on tubular-steel legs and a low vitrine that served as a room divider. 1927, Mies met Lilly Reich, who eventually had a hand in the design of some of the furniture, usually credited solely to Mies, including the 1930 Berlin leather couch, shown at 1931 *Deutsche Bauausstellung*, Berlin, and, from 1964, reproduced by Knoll and today by Knoll and others. (Purportedly, Reich designed the cushions of the Barcelona chair and of others.) Mies and Reich designed the Velvet and Silk Café stand at 1927 *Weissenhofsiedlung*, Stuttgart. 1928–29, he was director of German contribution to Barcelona exhibition, where he designed the German Industry exhibitions and German Electricity pavilion; 1931–38, was a member, Preußische Akademie der Künste. 1930–32, Mies was the final director of Bauhaus in Dessau, until the Nazis, already in control of the Dessau city council, closed the school and forced the relocation to Berlin-Steglitz. The school operated there for six more months but, due to Gestapo insistance that Ludwig Hilberseimer and Vasilii Kandinsky be dismissed and other pressures, it finally closed. With Lilly Reich, Mies codirected

the Deutscher Werkbund's exhibition 1931 *Die Wohnung* in Berlin; designed one exhibit at the 1934 *Deutsches Volk—Deutsche Arbeit* exhibition and designed the German National Pavilion project (unrealized) for 1935 *Exposition Universelle et Internationale de Bruxelles*. 1936, Mies arrived in New York, traveled to various places, including Chicago, and met Frank Lloyd Wright in Taliesin in Wisconsin. Mies returned to New York and worked on the Resnor house (unrealized) for Jackson Hole, Wyo. 1938, he made one last trip to Chicago, then returned to Germany to settle his affairs for emigration to American and, thus, to Chicago in 1938. 1938–58, he served as head of architecture at the Armour Institute of Technology (which merged with Lewis College in 1940 to form Illinois Institute of Technology/IIT) and, initially, had the school hire Bauhaus colleagues Hilberseimer (who emigrated from Berlin), Walter Peterhans (who had already emigrated), and John Barney Rodgers. 1939, Lilly Reich joined him in Chicago for a short time. After his association with Reich was severed, neither of them produced any more furniture. Mies's own residence in a 1930s-style apartment house (200 East Pearson Street, where he lived until his death) was sparsely furnished with his own pieces, Japanese *tatami* mats, and drawings by former Bauhaus associate Kandinsky and others. He died in Chicago. 1986, the Deutsche Bundespost Berlin issued a postage stamp (with his portrati and a drawing of the Neue Nationalgalerie) to commemorate Mies's 100th birthday. Mies's much quoted 'Less is more' was first penned by Robert Browning in his poem 'Andrea del Sorto' (*Men and Women*, 2 vols., London: Chapman & Hall, 1855).
Architecture Including 1907 Riehl Haus, Neubabelsberg; 1911 Perls Haus, Zehlendorf; 1912 Kröller-Müller Haus project, Wassenaar, the Netherlands; 1912–13 Werner Haus, Berlin-Zehlendorf; 1913 house on the Heerstrasse, Berlin; 1921 Friedrichstrasse office building 1 project; 1914/1915–17 Urbig Haus, Berlin-Neubabelsberg; 1922 Eichstaedt Haus, Berlin-Wannsee; 1922–23 reinforced-concrete office building project; 1923 concrete country house project; 1923–24 brick country house project; 1924–26 Mosler Haus, Berlin-Neubabelsberg; 1925–27 Wolf Haus (destroyed), Guben; 1926 Monument to the November Revolution (Karl Liebknecht–Rosa Luxemburg memorial) (destroyed), cemetery, Berlin-Friedrichsfelde; 1926–27 municipal-housing development, Afrikanische Straße, Berlin; 1928 Lange Haus, Krefeld; 1928 Esters Haus, Krefeld; 1928 bank building project, Stuttgart; 1928–30 Tugendhat Haus, Brno; 1932 Gericke Haus, Berlin-Wannsee; 1932–33 Lemcke Haus, Berlin-Hohenschönhausen; Reichsbank project, Berlin; 1934 country house projects; 1934–35 Hubbe Haus, Magdeburg; 1937–41 Resnor house, Jackson Hole, Wyo.; 1939 preliminary campus plan of Armour Institute of Technology, which became Illinois Institute of Technology, for which he designed 1940–41 master plan and numerous buildings there to 1958; 1946–51 Farnsworth house, Plano, Ill.; 1953–56 no. 1300 and nos. 900–910 Lake Shore Drive apartments, Chicago; 1954–58 Seagram building (with Philip Johnson), New York; 1962–68 Neue Nationalgalerie, Berlin; 1963–69 Dominion Centre, Toronto; 1966–69 IBM regional office building, Chicago.
Furniture All completed by 1930 (with the exception of 1960s tuxedo-type sofa for Knoll) with the original catalog numbers of Bamberg Metallwerkstätten given here: chair (MR1), S chair (MR10), with arms (MR20), with upholstery cushions (MR30), and with upholstery cushions and arms; Bruno chair (MR50); Tugendhat chair (MR60) and with arms (MR70); Barcelona stool with flat leather sling (MR80); Barcelona chair (MR90), including a one-off edition in aluminum for Alcoa's headquarters, Pittsburgh, 1953; tubular lounge chairs with cushions (MR100, MR110); side chair (MR120); round side tables with notched-glass top (MR130, MR140); glass tables (MR150, MR500, MR510); coffee tables (MR520, MR530); and beds (MR600, MR610, MR620).
Exhibitions Was in charge of 1927 *Weissenhofsiedlung* exhibition, Stuttgart. With Lilly Reich, designed stands in Berlin at 1927 *Mode der Dame*, 1931 *Deutsche Bauausstellung*, and 1934 *Deutsches Volk—Deutsche Arbeit* exhibition. He designed German National Pavilion and Sede stand, 1929–30 *Exposición Internacional de Barcelona*, where his designs included two chairs (later known as Barcelona chairs), situated at right angles to an onyx wall, for King Alfonso XIII and Queen Victoria Eugénie of Spain to use as modern thrones; however, they did not. Work subject of 1936, 1948, and 1960 one-person exhibitions; 1977 *Furniture and Furniture Drawings from the Design Collection and Mies van der Rohe Archive*, and 2001 *Mies in Berlin*, all The Museum of Modern Art, New York. 2001 *Mies in America*, Whitney Museum of American Art, New York; 2001–02 *Mies van der Rohe: Möbel und Bauten in Stuttgart, Barcelona, Brno*, Vitra Design Museum, Berlin.
Bibliography Philip Johnson, *Ludwig Mies van der Rohe*, New York: The Museum of Modern Art, 1947, 1953 2nd ed., 1978 3rd ed. Ludwig Hilberseimer, *Mies van der Rohe*, Chicago: Paul Theobold, 1956. Arthur Drexler, *Ludwig Mies van der Rohe*, New York: Braziller, 1960. Ludwig Glaeser, *Mies van der Rohe: Drawings in the Collection of the Museum of Modern Art*, New York: The Museum of Modern Art,1969. Ludwig Glaeser, *Furniture and Drawings from the Design Collection and Mies van der Rohe Archive*, New York:The Museum of Modern Art, 1977. Wolf Tegethoff, *Mies van der Rohe: The Villas and Country Houses*, New York: The Museum of Modern Art, 1895. Cat., *Der Kragstuhl*, Stuhlmuseum Burg Beverungen, Berlin: Alexander, 1986: 135. Elaine S. Hochman, *Architects of Fortune*, New York: Wiedenfeld & Nicholson, 1989. Franz Schulze, *Mies van der Rohe: Critical Essays*, New York: The Museum of Modern Art, 1989. 'Documents,' *Journal of Design History*, vol. 3, nos. 2 and 3, 1990: 172–74. Otakar Máčel, 'Avant-garde Design and the Law-Litigation over the Cantilever Chair,' *Journal of Design History*, vol. 3, nos. 2 and 3, 1990: 125. Alexander von Vegesack et al., *Mies van der Rohe: Stuttgart, Barcelona and Brno: Furniture and Architecture*, Geneva: Skira-Berenice, 1999. Daniela Hammer-Tugendhat and Wolf Tegethoff (eds.), *Ludwig Mies van der Rohe: The Tugendhat House*, New York: Springer, 2000. Barry Bergdoll and Terence Riley (eds), *Mies in Berlin*, New York: The Museum of Modern Art, 2001. Josep Quetglas, *Fear of Glass: Mies van der Rohe's Pavilion in Barcelona*, Basel: Burkhäuser, 2001. Paola Antonelli (ed.), *Objects of Design: The Museum of Modern Art*, New York: The Museum of Modern Art, 2003: 88–90, 92.

Migeon, Christian (1955–); Marie-Thérèse Migeon (1955–)

French designers. Christian: born Laos. Marie-Thérèse: born Compiègne, France.

Training Marie-Thérèse: in jewelrymaking. Christian: École Boulle, Paris.
Biographies Christian began his career designing jewelry for Christian Lacroix and Yves Saint-Laurent; 1990s, turned to designing home accessories and furniture and called on the aesthetics of his Franco-Khmer heritage. He had earlier (1978) formed a partnership with Marie-Thérèse for fashion/jewelry activities. Their furniture has been produced in exotic wood, resin, enamel, and bronze. 1997, Christian became the exclusive designer of doorknobs by Poignée.
Bibliography Cat., Sophie Tasma Anargyros et al., *L'école française: les créateurs de meubles du 20ème siècle*, Paris: Industries Françaises de l'Ameublement, 2000.

Miklós, Gustave (1888–1967)

Hungarian sculptor, painter, and designer; born Budapest; active Paris.

Training Magyar Iparművészeti Egyetem (MIE, university of applied arts), Budapest; École Spéciale d'Architecture and other institutions, Paris.
Biography As an Hungarian in the French army during World War I, Miklós discovered the art of Greece and Byzantium; in Paris after the war, met Jacques Doucet, for whom he designed silverware, enamels, tapestries, and carpets for Doucet's residence on the avenue du Bois (today avenue Foch); c. 1923, turned to decorative sculpture, again executing commissions for Doucet and also for others in a Cubist style and relating to West African art; befriended François-Louis Schmied; designed furniture and supplied painted panels and carvings to Jean Dunand and others. Other work: stained glass, jewelry, and illustrations in books. 1930, he became a member, Unions des Artistes Modernes (UAM), Paris; 1940, left Paris and taught in Oyonnax.
Exhibitions Work shown at editions of Salon d'Automne; 1938 and 1942 Salons of Société des Artistes Décorateurs; 1922, Léonce Rosenberg's L'Effort Moderne gallery, Paris; 1928, La Renaissance gallery; all Paris. From 1930, work included in UAM exhibitions. Subject of 1983 exhibition, Centre Culturel Aragon, Oyonnax (catalog below).
Bibliography Cat., *Gustave Miklos, exposition rétrospective*, Oyonnax: Centre Culturel Aragon, 1983. Pierre Cabanne, *Encyclopédie art déco*, Paris: Somogy, 1986: 223. Arlette Barré-Despond, *UAM*, Paris: Regard, 1986: 470–71. Cat., *Les années UAM 1929–1958*, Paris: Musée des Arts Décoratifs, 1988: 230.

Milá, Miguel (1931–)

Spanish industrial designer; born and active Barcelona.

Training Escola Tècnica Superior d'Arquitectura de Barcelona (ETSAB), Barcelona.
Biography Milá came to industrial design via interior design; left architecture school to work in the office of architect/brother Alfonso Milá

(1924–) and Frederico Correa. One of his first designs, 1956 TMC/TM lamp by himself and others, was eventually produced by Polinax in 1961 and by Santa & Cole later, marketed from 1983 by Bd Ediciones de Diseño as the TMC/TMC lamp, with continuing modifications. Also designed 1967 BM street lamp (with Pep Bonet) by Diseño Ahorro Energético for Polinax and 1977 Ximenea fireplace unit by Diseño Ahorro Energetico. He worked on a new (1986) Metro station (with Rafael Montero), Barcelona.
Exhibitions/citations Work subject of 2003 exhibition, ARQ-INFAD, FAD (architecture/interior design association), Barcelona. Six awards, ADI/FAD (industrial designers decorative arts associations) (including 1962 for TMC lamp and 1965 for ice tongs); 1987 (1st) National Design Prize, Spain.
Bibliography Guy Julier, *New Spanish Design*, London: Thames & Hudson, 1991.

Milner, Alison (1958–)

British designer; born Sevenoaks, Kent.

Training To 1985, furniture design, Middlesex Polytechnic; to 1987, Royal College of Art, London.
Biography In freelance practice, she designed a 1986 chair, with textile designer Caroline McKintey, that was widely published and a collection of bedroom furniture for mass production by Indian craftspeople for India Works in London.
Citations 1986 Prince of Wales award; second prize (1987 Mirror Lamp), 1987 British Design in Japan competition, Design Council, UK.
Bibliography Liz McQuiston, *Women in Design: A Contemporary View*, New York: Rizzoli, 1988.

Minagawa, Masa (1917–)

Japanese industrial designer; born Tokyo.

Training To 1940 under Takao Miyashita, Industrial Arts High School, Tokyo.
Biography Minagawa was a designer for Tokyo Electric Company; from 1954, established Masa Minagawa Design in Tokyo and has specialized in the design of lighting and electrical appliances; 1957–63, lecturer, Chiba University, Chiba; 1963–83, dean, industrial-design department, Tokyo National University of Fine Arts and Music; 1963, cofounded, Japan Industrial Designers' Association.
Citations 1978 Blue Ribbon Medal from the Japanese government.
Bibliography 'Office Visit,' *Industrial Design*, Aug. 1983. Ann Lee Morgan (ed.), *Contemporary Designers*, London: Macmillan, 1984: 415–16.

Minale, Marcello (1938–)

Italian designer; born Tripoli.

Training Technical school, Naples.
Biography Minale was a designer at Taucher advertising agency, Finland; art director at Mackkinointi Uiherjuuri, Finland; to 1964, design director of Young and Rubicam advertising agency in London. 1964 with Brian Tattersfield, set up design firm Minale Tattersfield; 1982, became president, Designers and Art Directors Association, London; has designed graphics, furniture, interiors, and packaging for a range of clients, including Suchard, Boots, and Gilbey's. Others: Cubic Metre Furniture, Zanotta, and Aqualisa Showers. He wrote the book *How to Keep Running a Successful Design Company* (see below), the story of Minale Tattersfield.
Exhibitions/citations Work shown at 1979 exhibition, Design Centre, London; 1983 exhibition, Museo d'Arte Contemporanea, Milan. Received 1977 gold medal, New York Art Directors Club.
Bibliography Ann Lee Morgan (ed.), *Contemporary Designers*, London: Macmillan, 1984: 417–18. Cat., Hans Wichmann, *Italien Design 1945 bis heute*, Munich: Die Neue Sammlung, 1988. Marcello Minale, Minale Tattersfield, *How to Keep Running a Successful Design Company*, London: International Thomson Business Press, 1999.

Minoletti, Giulio (1910–1981)

Italian industrial designer; born Milan.

Training To 1931, Scuola Superiore di Architettura, Politecnico, Milan.
Biography 1947, Minoletti cofounded Istituto Nazionale di Urbanistica (INU, national institute of city planning), Milan; 1954, cofounded Premio Compasso d'Oro, under the Associazione per il Disegno Industriale (ADI). For a time, he collaborated with Franco Albini, Giancarlo Palanti, Piero Bottoni, Ignazio Gardella, Eugenio Gentili, and Mario Tevarotto (architects), and with G. Chiodi and F. Clerici (engineers) in Bologna. 1953–55, Minoletti was chairperson, Movimento di Studi per l'Architettura (MSA), Milan. Designs included 1949 ETR 300 Settebello high-speed electric train by Breda Ferroviaria, Better Living bathroom fixtures, and 1957 kitchen sinks. Minoletti's archives are housed in the Archivio del Moderno, Accademia di Architettura della Svizzera Italiana, Mendrisio, Switzerland.
Citations Gold medal, 1933 Triennale di Milano; grand prize for architecture, 1957 (11th) Triennale.
Bibliography Gio Ponti (preface), *Architetti italiani: Giulio Minoletti*, Milan: Edizioni Milano Moderna, 1959. Alfonso Grassi and Anty Pansera, *Atlante del design italiano 1940/1980*, Milan: Fabbri 1980. Cat., Hans Wichmann, *Italien Design 1945 bis heute*, Munich: Die Neue Sammlung, 1988. Cat., Manolo de Giorgi and Paola Antonelli (eds.), *Collezione per un modello di museo del design*, Milan: Fabbri, 1990. Cat., Manolo de Giorgi (ed.), *45–63: un museo del disegno industriale in Italia*, Milan: Abitare Segesta Cataloghi, 1995.

Minox cameras
> See Zapp, Walter.

Minton

British ceramics firm; located Stoke-on-Trent.

History 1793, Thomas Minton (1765–1836) bought a pottery in Stoke-on-Trent and, 1796, began the production of inexpensive blue transfer-printed earthenware. 1836, his son Herbert Minton (1793–1858) became director, expanded the range of wares, and hired artists. 1840s–50s, Henry Cole designed the shapes of tablewares with printed decorations by A.W.N. Pugin; both were friends of Herbert. (The firm was known by more than a dozen names over the years, all with 'Menton' in the title. From Herbert's 1858 death, no Minton family member was connected with the firm.) 1849, Léon Arnoux became the artistic director and introduced majolica with bright glazes, naturalistic forms, and amusing shapes popular until the 1880s. From early 1840s to end of the century, the firm produced large numbers of decorative tiles, starting with encaustic examples for flooring. The firm also made printed tiles with designs by designers such as J. Moyr Smith and Christopher Dresser. Its tiles were also used to decorate furniture. 1858, Herbert Minton's nephew Colin Minton Campbell (1827–1885) became the director, and Minton's domestic wares were intended for a mass market. 1871, Minton established the Art Pottery Studio in South Kensington, London, where earthenware decoration was taught. The Studio pursued china painting during the time of the Aesthetic Movement and was directed by William S. Coleman, who was employed by Minton from 1869. The Studio closed when its building burned down in 1875. From early 1860s, Minton's wares were influenced by Eastern and Middle-Eastern designs, motifs, and materials. When large numbers of French artists came to Britain in 1870s, Minton began the production of pieces in *pâte-sur-pâte* (relief porcelain decoration) with classical decoration. At the century's turn, its wares began to show the influence of Art Nouveau and a German interpretation of the Sezession. 1968, Minton was amalgamated into the Royal Tableware Group.
Exhibitions 1851 *Great Exhibition of the Works of Industry of All Nations* (majolica ware), London.
Bibliography Geoffrey A. Godden, *Minton Pottery and Porcelain of the First Period, 1793–1850*, New York: Praeger, 1968. Cat., Elizabeth Aslin and Paul Atterbury, *Minton, 1798–1910*, London: Victoria and Albert Museum, 1976. Paul Atterbury (ed.), *The History of Porcelain*, New York: Morrow, 1982: 155–77. Doreen Bolger Burke et al., *In Pursuit of Beauty: Americans and the Aesthetic Movement*, New York: The Metropolitan Museum of Art/Rizzoli, 1986. Paul Atterbury and Maureen Batkin, *The Dictionary of Minton*, Woodbridge, Suffolk: Antique Collectors Club, 1990.

Mion, Abramo (1951–)
> See Kairos, Studio.

Mir Iskusstva, V (the world of art)

Russian arts society and magazine; located St. Petersburg.

History 1889, V Mir Iskusstva was founded by a group of young men who became artists, critics, and aesthetes, including Serge Diaghilev (later, founder of Les Ballet Russe) and painter/writer/decorator Alexandre Benois. The artist Valentin Serov was also associated with its activities. To 1898, the group published a journal by the same name (*Mir Iskusstva*); like its sponsoring organization, the journal's goal was

to arouse interest in Russian archeology and architecture and to document contemporary developments in the applied arts elsewhere in Europe. The combination of the old with the new was peculiar to Russia but reflected the nationalist mood in Europe with its interest in traditional crafts. Léon Bakst was a contributor to the journal, which has come to represent an entire movement parallel with Art Nouveau in Western Europe. Many of the articles printed in *Mir Iskusstva* have been reprinted in Western journals. Artists in the group were chiefly concerned with the sets and costumes for ballets commissioned by Diaghilev, who first brought them to Paris in 1909. V Mir Iskusstva, the group, reflected the westward-looking artistic culture of St. Petersburg and its Artists' Association, whose chief rival was the more nationalistic and conservative League of Russian Artists in Moscow. Later, other notable participants included Ivan Bilibin, Mstislav Dobuzhinskii, Aleksandr Golovin, Igor Grabar, Boris Grigoriev, Nikolai Konstantin Somov, Konstantin Korovin, Boris Kustodiev, Pavel Kuznetsov, Yevgenii Lanceray, Nikolai Milioti, Georgii Narbut, Anna Ostroumova-Lebedeva, Kuzma Petrov-Vodkin, and Nikolai Roerich.
Bibliography Camilla Gray, *The Great Experiment: Russian Art 1863–1922*, London: Thames & Hudson, 1962 (rev. ed. 1986). Gabriella di Milia, *Mir Iskusstva—il mondo dell'arte: artisti russi dal 1898 al 1924*, Naples: Società Napoletana, 1982. Nina Lobanov-Rostovsky, *Revolutionary Ceramics*, London: Studio Vista, 1990.

Miralles, Enric (1955–2000)

Spanish architect and designer; born Barcelona.

Training To 1974, Escola Tècnica Superior d'Arquitectura de Barcelona (ETSAB).
Biography 1973–85, Miralles collaborated with Albert Viaplana and Carme Piñón; 1993, set up a practice with his wife Benedetta Tagliabue; became highly regarded and the *enfant terrible* of Spanish architecture. From 1985, he taught, ETSAB, where was the chairperson of architecture from 1996 and, concurrently from 1992, Kenzo Tange chair professor, Graduate School of Design, Harvard University, Cambridge, Mass., US. In addition to architecture, he was active as an interior designer and facilities planner and designed products such as 1979/1995 Hypóstila I/Hypóstila II shelving systems (with Luís Clotet and Óscar Tusquets Blanca) by Bd Ediciones de Diseño, and others, garnering citations. Of his many buildings, a number were in construction on his premature death at age 45.
Exhibitions/citations Work included a number of exhibitions as well as 1997 Triennale di Milano. Subject of a large number of exhibitions. Received 1980–81 Fullbright Scholar at Columbia University, New York; 1983 and 1991 Premi FAD d'Arquitectura (best Barcelona building); 1986 and 2000 Premi FAD d'Interiorisme (best interiors); 1991 IT ALSTAD for Europe; 1992 Barcelona City Hall Prize; 1993 Madrid City Prize; 1995 (1st) National Architecture Prize, Spain; 1996 Leone d'Oro prize, Biennale di Venezia.
Bibliography Mary Troy and Maggie Troy, *Enric Miralles*, Architectural Monograph no. 40, London: Academy, 1994. Benedetta Tagliabue, *Enric Miralles: opere e progetti*, Milan: Electa, 1996. Marco de Michelis and Maddalena Scimeni, *Miralles Tagliabue: architettura e progetti*, Milan: Skira, 2002.

Miralles, Pedro (1955–)

Spanish architect and designer; born Valéncia; active Madrid and Valéncia.

Training To 1980, Escuela Técnica Superior de Arquitectura, Madrid; to 1987 on a scholarship from Istituto de la Mediana y Pequeña Industria Valénciana (IMPIVA) for study at Domus Academy, Milan.
Biography Miralles worked in the office of fashion designer Jesús del Pozo and in theatrical archives. His industrial designs, with references to cinema, literature, and popular music, were produced by Luís Adelantado, Bd Ediciones de Diseño, Arflex, José Martinez Medina, and Artespaña. Work by NMF has included 1985 Acuatica chair, 1985 Dry Martini stool, 1986 Armchair 115, Voyeur folding screen, Egyptian lamp, and Calzada rug. Others: 1988 Andrews Sisters three-part interlocking tables in bubinga wood by Punt Mobles, and 1987 *Egipcia* floor lamp by Santa & Cole. His public waste bins, installed at 1992 *Exposición Universal de Sevilla (Expo '92)*, made of concrete and sheet iron with a built-in ashtray in a dodecahedron shape, were inspired by the Torre del Oro (the 13th-century 12-sided tower overlooking the Guadalquivir river, Seville).
Bibliography Juli Capella and Quim Larrea, *Designed by Architects in the 1980s*, New York: Rizzoli, 1988. Emma Dent Coat, 'Seville Expo '92,' *Metropolis*, Oct. 1991: 51. Guy Julier, *New Spanish Design*, London: Thames & Hudson, 1991.

Miranda, Santiago (1947–)

Spanish designer; born Seville; active Milan.

Training Escuela de Artes Aplicadas y Oficios Artisticos, Seville.
Biography Moving to Milan, Italy, Miranda collaborated with Perry King from 1971; 1976, founded King-Miranda Associati, a studio that executed environmental and industrial design, furniture, interior designs, and graphics. King and Miranda have designed lights by Flos, Louis Poulsen, Sirrah, Luxo, Belux and Marlin Lighting. Also designed office furniture for Marcatré and Ahrend, showrooms for Marcatré and Inter-Décor, chairs for Vecta, Tisettanta, and Cassina IXC Ltd., lighting range for the public areas of 1992 *Exposición Universal de Sevilla (Expo '92)* and interiors and contents of the Spanish Pavilion for the *Expo 2000*, Hanover. Miranda is a member, Scientific Committee, Instituto Europeo di Design, Madrid.
Exhibitions 1990 *Lonely Tools*, Barcelona, Tokyo, Amsterdam; 1992 *Drawings by King and Miranda*, London; 1996 *King and Miranda Designers*, Madrid; 1999–2002 *The Fifth Quarter*, Seville, Madrid, Copenhagen and Milan. 1989 National Design Prize and 1995 Premi Andalucia de Diseño, Spain.
Bibliography 'When Is a Dot not a Dot?,' *Design*, no. 317, May 1975: 22. Cat. Giovanni Giudicci (ed.), *Design Process Olivetti 1908–1978*, Ivrea: Olivetti, 1979. James Woudhuysen, 'Priests at Technology's Altar,' *Design*, no. 410, Feb. 1983: 40–42. Robert A.M. Stern (ed.), *The International Design Yearbook*, New York: Abbeville, 1985/1986. Hugh Aldersey-Williams, *King and Miranda: The Poetry of the Machine*, New York: Rizzoli, 1991.
> See King, Perry Alan.

Mirenzi, Franco (1942–)

Italian industrial designer; born Trieste; active Milan.

Biography 1964, Mirenzi began his professional career; worked in the office of Unimark International in Milan; has designed furniture, accessories, lighting, ceramics, hi-fi equipment, domestic electrical appliances, and exhibitions, on occasion with Bob Noorda. His clients in Italy have included Agip, Boston, Brionvega, Cedit, Citterio, Dreher, Fabbri, General Electric, Honeywell, Molteni, Norex, Sirrah, and Unifor. His Zeta lamp by Valenti was widely published. Mirenzi became a member, Associazione per il Disegno Industriale (ADI).
Citations First prize (for Modulo 3 furniture system with Noorda by Casalucci), 1971 Premio SMAU Industrial Design, Salone della Machina e Attrezzature per l'Uffizio, Milan; 1979 (corporate image with others of Agip Petroli), 1998 (Linea DPXX product line with Unimark by Nuovo Pignone) Premio Compasso d'Oro.
Bibliography *ADI Annual 1976*, Milan: Associazione per il Disegno Industriale, 1976. Giancarlo Iliprandi and Pierluigi Molinari (eds.), *Industrial Designers Italiani*, Fagagna: Tipographie Graphis, 1984. Cat., Hans Wichmann, *Italien Design 1945 bis heute*, Munich: Die Neue Sammlung, 1988.

Mission Inn

American hostelry; located Riverside, Cal.

History 1870s, Frank Miller established the Mission Inn for early tourists to California. In a Spanish-colonial style, it was constructed and altered over many years, notably c. 1902–03. The construction of elements—including of balcony railings, lighting fixtures, and door hardware—was performed on site in its catacombs. Before being applied, its iron was laid out in the sun and sprinkled with water for weathering/rusting. The furniture was supplied by Gustav Stickley, the Limberts, and other East Coast firms; when construction got underway, craftspeople working in situ included resident potters such as Cornelius Brauckman and Fred H. Robertson, who produced souvenirs. Influenced by Spanish-Mission styles, the Inn's Arts and Crafts furniture had exaggerated lines.
Bibliography Timothy J. Anderson et al., *California Design 1910*, Salt Lake City: Peregrine Smith, 1980 (reprint of 1974 ed.).

Missoni, 'Tai' Ottavio (1921–); Rosita Missoni (b. Rosita Jelmini 1931–)

Italian fabric and fashion designers; husband and wife; Missoni born Zara, Croatia; Jelmini born Italy.

Biography 1953 Missoni and Jelmini set up a small workshop and factory to knit ready-to-wear clothing in Gallarate, near Milan. Sub-

sequently, they have added menswear, fragrances, linens, and home furnishings, particularly rugs, to its inventory. 1980s, management of the firm included their two sons and a daughter. Refining their goods, they perfected certain machine-knitted fabrications such as 1961 patchwork knitwear and 1962 flame-stitch wear. Mid-1950s, the Missonis were associated with Biki of Milan and Emmanuelle Khanh of Paris and, late 1960s, established their own label.
Bibliography Gloria Bianchino et al. (eds.) *Italian Fashion*, vol. 1, Milan: Electa, 1987: 294. Cat., Hans Wichmann, *Italien Design 1945 bis heute*, Munich: Die Neue Sammlung, 1988.

Mitchell, 'Bill' William L. (1912–1988)
American automobile designer.

Training In mechanical engineering; night classes in fine art, Art Students League, New York.
Biography Late 1920s, Mitchell worked at an advertising agency in New York; on his own, sketched various automobiles like Bugattis and MGs, and others; from 1935, worked under Harley Earl at General Motors (GM) in Detroit, Mich.; from 1938, was chief designer in GM's Cadillac division; 1959, succeeded Harley Earl as the head of design at GM and became the vice-president of design. He loathed GM's conservative corporate culture and its committee system of design approval. Mitchell designed the first (1954) fiberglass-bodied Chevrolet Corvette (incorporating Francis L. Scott's simple retractable-hardtop design, from 1958), which went beyond the Europeanized body design; worked with Zora Arkus-Duntov to completely redesigned the chassis and body of the Corvette as the Sting Ray split-window coupé in 1962 (of which some consider Larry Shinoda the codesigner, while others claim Charles M. Jordan/Mitchell-staff authorship). A number of permutations of the Sting Ray soft-top model succeeded to 1975. Mitchell also designed the controversial rear-engined 1959 Chevrolet Corvair, 1963 Buick Riviera, 1967 Chevrolet Camaro, and 1967 Pontiac Firebird; 1950s–60s, was able to lend a strong brand identity to GM through these marques. Mitchell's archive of drawings and paintings is housed in Henry Ford Museum, Dearborn, Mich. He wrote *Corvette—A Piece of the Action: Impressions of the Marque and Mystique, 1953–1985* (with Allan Girdler, St. Paul, Minn.: Motorbooks International, 1985). 1977, Mitchell retired from GM.
Bibliography James Flammang, *Corvette Chronicle*, Lincolnwood, Ill.: Publications International, 1993. Penny Sparke, *A Century of Car Design*, London: Mitchell Beazley, 2002.

Miturich, Petr Vasilievich (1887–1956)
Russian artist and industrial and graphic designer; born St. Petersburg.

Training 1906–09 Kiev Art Institute; 1909–15 under Nikolai Samokish, Academy of Arts, St. Petersburg.
Biography From 1914, Miturich developed an interest in aviation, resulting in his late-1920s designs for dirigibles; 1918, became a member, Left Association of Petrograd Artists; 1918–22, worked on 'spatial graphics' and 'spatial paintings'; 1920–22, designed numerous covers for the sheet music of Artur Lurie, including *Roial v detskoi* (the piano in the nursery) and the cover of *Zangezi* by Viktor Khlebnikov. Miturich became a professor, graphics and architecture departments, VKhUTEMAS (higher artistic and technical studios); 1925–29, was a member, Four Arts group; 1928, designed children's books, including *Miau* (meow) by Alexandr Vvedenskii; from 1930, turned to painting chiefly landscapes and portraits.
Exhibitions From 1915, contributed to numerous exhibitions, including 1915 *Exhibition of Painting*, Moscow; *Contemporary Russian Painting*, Petrograd; 1915–18 exhibitions of V Mir Iskusstva (the world of art) group, Petrograd; 1924 *Esposizione Internazionale*, Venice.
Bibliography Natalia Rozanova, *Petr Vasilievich Miturich*, Moscow, 1973. Stephanie Barron and Maurice Tuchman, *The Avant-Garde in Russia, 1910–1930*, Cambridge: MIT, 1980. S.O. Khan-Magomedov, *Vhutemas: Moscou, 1920–1930*, Paris: Regard, 1990.

Miyamoto, Eiji (1948–)
Japanese textile designer; born Tokyo.

Training To 1970, Hosei University, Tokyo.
Biography 1975, Miyamoto joined his father's textile company, also worked independently and began experimenting with and designing fabrics, later supplying goods to Issey Miyake and other Japanese fashion designers. Distinguished 1987 one-of-a-kind fabrications were produced by Miyashin.
Exhibitions/citations Subject of a number of one-person venues. Work included in 1994 *Japanese Design: A Survey Since 1950*, Philadelphia Museum of Art; 1999 *Structure and Surface: Contemporary Japanese Textiles*, The Museum of Modern Art, New York and St. Louis (catalog below). 1990 Mainichi Fashion Award; Amiko Kujiraoka Prize; 1995 Companion Membership, Textile Institute of UK.
Bibliography Albrecht Bangert and Karl Michael Armer, *80s Style: Designs of the Decade*, New York: Abbeville, 1990. Cat., Cara McCarty and Matilda McQuaid, *Structure and Surface: Contemporary Japanese Textiles*, New York: Abrams/The Museum of Modern Art, 1999.

Mizutani, Soichi (1955–)
Japanese interior designer; born Fukui Prefecture.

Training To 1973, Chuo University, Tokyo; to 1975, Kyoto College of Art.
Biography From 1979, Mizutani worked at Plastic Studio & Associates; 1987, established Soichi Mizutani Design Office; 1992, was a part-time lecturer, Kuwasawa Design School and, from 1995, lecturer, interactive-design department, ICS College of Arts; all Tokyo. Interior-

Børge Mogensen. Sofa (no. 2192). 1963. Wood and leather, 42 1/2 x 60 1/4 x 34 5/8" (108 x 153 x 88 cm). Mfr.: Fredericia Stolefabrik, Denmark. Courtesy Quittenbaum Kunstauktionen, Munich.

design commissions have included 1991 Eyes showroom, Aizuwakamatsu; 1991 Yuki bar, Yagumo; 1991 Renaud Pellegrino space, Paris; 1992 Setsugekka restaurant/bar, Tokyo; 1993 stadium in Hiroo/Tokyo; 2000 development of Coup de Chance shops nationwide.
Exhibitions/citations Work subject of *Void>0*, Minamiaoyama House, Tokyo. Numerous citations include 1992 Grand Prize, Shotenkenchiku Design Competition and Best Prize; 1993 NSG Design Fair.
Bibliography *Domus* No. 747, 1993.

MM Design
Italian design group.

History 1991, the group (whose name 'MM' is the roman numeral '2000') established an office in Bressanone/Brixen in the Southern Italian Alps; is composed of seven industrial designers; has designed furniture and a wide variety of products, including sports equipment, for international clients, including De Longhi, Illy, Siemens, Samsonite, Vorwerk, Hoppe, Burton, and Mattel. Some products for other clients: 1994 Dolphin gardening tools by Golden Star, 1999 Attac snap-hook for mountain climbing by Salewa, 1999 Bombino refrigerator by Smeg, and 2000 skiing boots by Kneissl & Friends.
Citations 1999 award (Impact crampon and Attac snap-hook), Industrie Forum Design (iF), Hanover; G-Mark Good Design Award (Attac snap-hook), Japanese Industrial Design Promotion Organization (JIDPO).
Bibliography Mel Byars, *50 Sports Wares...*, Hove: RotoVision, 1999. Anna Maria Scevola and Silvio Sanpietro, *Prodotto industriale italiano contemporaneo*, Milan: L'Archivolto, 1999.

Mobilier Artistique Moderne (MAM)
French interior decorating firm; located Paris.

History 1913, Michel Dufet established Mobilier Artistique Moderne (MAM) at 3, avenue de l'Opéra, Paris, to produce modern furniture, wallpaper, fabrics, and lighting, sometimes with Louis Bureau.
Bibliography Léon Deshairs (intro.), *Modern French Decorative Art: A Collection of Examples of Modern French Decoration*, Paris: Albert Lévy, c. 1925–30. *Ensembles mobiliers*, vol. 2, Paris: Charles Moreau, 1937. Pierre Kjellberg, *Art déco: les maîtres du mobilier, le décor des paquebots*, Paris: Amateur, 1986/1990.

Mobilier National, Le
French governmental institution.

History 1633, Le Mobilier National was founded by Jean-Baptiste Colbert (1619–1683), Louis XIV's *contrôleur général* (somewhat like a finance minister). Le Mobilier National was the only state furniture depository until 1965, when French minister of culture André Malraux (Paris 1901–Verrières-le-Buisson 1976) commissioned Jean Coural (1925–2001) to create L'Atelier de Recherche et de Création with the intention of promoting contemporary French furniture and funding prototypes to encourage ultimate production. Its collection represents a complete history of French furniture from which ministers, public administrators, and embassy officials may choose pieces to furnish their offices, salons, and waiting rooms.
Bibliography 'Jean Coural, 1925–2001,' *Revue de l'art*, no 134, April 2001: 95.

Mobles 114
Spanish furniture manufacturer and design studio.

History 1973, Josep Maria Massana and Josep Maria Tremoleda established the furniture shop and design studio Mobles 114. Massana, Tremoleda, and Mariano Ferrer designed the 1977 Gira lamp as an alternative to the Flexo lamp by an unknown designer, an evolving model popular in Spain from 1940s. Classic models still in production include 1934 Torres Clavé armchair by Torres Clavé, 1956 Copenhagen ashtray by André Ricard, and 1961 Marquina non-drip oil/vinegar cruet by Rafael Marquina. Other designers of its furniture, lighting, fittings, and accessories have been Enzo Mari, Lluís Pau, Jorge Pensí, Lluís Porqueras, Carles Riart, Álvaro Siza Vieira, and Óscar Tusquets Blanca.
Citations Lage number of award, ADI/FAD (industrial-designers/decorative-arts associations) selections, including 1992 Delta d'Oro and 1986 medal (for his work over the last 25 years), ADI; 2001 National Design Prize, Spain.
> See Massana, Josep Maria.

Modernismo (aka Modernista; Catalan school)
> See Art Nouveau.

Modular
Italian furniture manufacturer; located Osteria Grande.

History 1973, Modular was founded; 1990, turned to the production of cutting-edge designs with the establishment of a young management headed by Paolo Castelli. Furniture has included the innovative 1995 Dreamspace office-furniture system, Olympiona lamp, and Maya Desnuda chaise longue all designed by Denis Santachiara. 1996, Modular bought Santachiara's Domodinamica, a firm that was producing his avant-garde furniture and accessories. Modular's inventory has also included Telos curtains; Domodinamica domestic furniture and accessories, and contract furniture; Massimo Iosa Ghini's Open stool; and Matali Crasset's 1997 Capriccio di Ugo chair.
Bibliography www.domodinamica.com.

Möckl, Ernst (1931–)
German designer; active Stuttgart.

Training 1954–59 under Max Bill, product design, Hochschule für Gestaltung (HfG), Ulm.
Biography Before attending the HfG, Möckl worked as a technical draughtsperson and technical designer in metallurgy; 1960, established his own product-design office in Stuttgart. Work includes 1958 SBM 680 knock-down armchair (with K.H. Bergmiller while at HfG) by Wilde + Spieth; 1971 one-piece plastic side chair/armchair by Horn; a number of cameras and equipment by Rollei-Werke Franke & Heidecke.
Exhibitions/citations 1971 plastic chair included in 1998 *'68–Design und Alltagskultur zwischen Konsum und Konflikt*, Kunstmuseum, Düsseldorf, and Galerie im Karmeliterkloster, Frankfurt. 1962 one-person exhibition, Design-Center Stuttgart. Received Bundespreis Produktdesign, Rat für Formgebung (German design council), Frankfurt; 1969 (five citations for cameras and equipment by Rollei) Industrie Forum Design (iF), Hanover.
Bibliography 'Der Produktgestalter Ernst Moeckl,' *form*, no. 20, 1965. Wolfgang Schepers. Cat., *'68–Design und Alltagskultur zwischen Konsum und Konflikt*, Cologne: DuMont, 1998.

Moerel, Marre (1966–)
Dutch designer; born Breda.

Training In fashion and sculpture; 1989–91, master of arts degree in furniture design, Royal College of Art, London; 1987–89, bachelor of arts degree in sculpture, Exeter School of Arts and Design, UK; 1985–87, fashion design, Akademie van Beeldende Kunsten, Rotterdam; 1984–85 Kunstakademie St. Joost, Breda.
Biography 1993, Moerel settled in New York, working as a freelance designer and artist; taught furniture design, Parsons School of Design there; has become active primarily as an interior, product, and furniture designer. Clients have included Cappellini, Covo, Fiorocci, Offecct, Ozone, Wilsonart.
Citations 1999 Best Body of Work (for Wilsonart laminates), International Contemporary Furniture Fair (ICFF), New York, and 1999 Best of ICFF, *Design Journal*; 2000 Annual Design Review (for Millennium furniture collection), *I.D.* magazine; 2001 Best New Collection (glass by Covo), Designers Block, Tokyo.

Mögelin, Else (1887–1982)
German textile designer; born Berlin.

Training To 1919, Kunstgewerbeschule, Berlin-Charlottenburg; 1919–21 under Gerhard Marcks, Bauhaus Pottery workshop, Dornburg; 1921–23, Bauhaus Weaving Workshop and Metal Workshop, Weimar.
Biography 1923–27, was active in her own textile workshop; 1927–45, directed textile instruction, Kunstgewerbeschule, Stettin, Germany (now Szczecin, Poland). 1933, the Nazis confiscated her art supplies and presumably she was inactive until after World War II. 1945–52, instructor and director of weaving, Hochschule für bildende Künste, Hamburg; 1952, retired from teaching but continued weaving.
Bibliography Sigrid Wortmann Weltge. *Women's Work: Textile Art from the Bauhaus*, London: Thames & Hudson, 1993.

Mogensen, Børge (1914–1972)
Danish furniture designer.

Training 1936–38, Kunsthåndværkerskolen, Copenhagen; 1938–42 under Kaare Klint, Møbelskole, Det Kongelige Danske Kunstakademiet, Copenhagen.

Bill Moggridge, Stephen Hobson (1942–), and Glenn Edens (1952–). Compass portable computer. 1981. Die-cast magnesium casing and injection-molded plastic, closed 2 1/16 x 11 1/2 x 15" (5.2 x 29.2 x 38.1 cm). Mfr.: Grid Systems Corp., US. Gift of the mfr. MoMA.

Biography 1938–42, Mogensen worked for various architects, including Mogens Koch and Kaare Klint; 1942–50, was chairperson, furniture-design department, FDB (association of Danish cooperative wholesale societies), for which he designed simple utilitarian pieces; 1945–47, was an assistant to Kaare Klint at Det Kongelige Danske Kunstakademi; 1945–46, worked with Hans Wegner; 1950, opened his own office in Copenhagen; 1962 with Klint, designed school furniture. Mogensen designed furniture by Karl Andersson, Søborg Møbelfabrik, Fredericia Stolefabrik, Hüskvarna, P. Lauritsen, and Erhard Rasmussen. From 1953, he was artistic consultant to C. Olesen, for which he designed wooden furniture combined with leather and fabric (fabric designed with Lis Ahlmann); designs included traditional types of Chinese-derived furniture and American-derived Windsor chairs and Shaker models. His furniture was practical and popular, some still in production. He is best known for 1945 Spokeback sofa and armchair (Knole-like dropping sides) by Fritz Hansen and 1964 Asserbo Chair 504 by Karl Andersson, but there are also conservative models such as 1969 club chair no. 2721-5 by Fredericia Stolefabrik. After extensive research into the ideal proportions and standardized measurements for objects of daily life, he designed the Øresund system with Grethe Meyer.
Exhibitions/citations 1938–62, work was regularly included in Copenhagen Cabinetmakers' Guild annual exhibitions and those of the Danish Society of Arts and Crafts and Industrial Design. Also included in 1968 *Two Centuries of Danish Design*, Victoria and Albert Museum, London; *Design Since 1945*, Philadelphia Museum of Art. Received 1945 Bissen Legacy, 1950 Eckersberg Medal, silver medal at 1953 Dansk Købestævne (Danish trade fair), 1958 award of honor from Copenhagen Cabinetmakers' Guild, 1971 Danish furniture prize. 1972, elected Honorary Royal Designer for Industry, UK.
Bibliography Bent Salicath and Arne Karlsen (eds.), *Modern Danish Textiles*, Copenhagen: Danish Society of Arts and Crafts and Industrial Design, 1959. Arne Karlsen, *Made in Denmark*, New York: Rheinhold, 1960. Erik Zahle, *Scandinavian Domestic Design*, London: Methuen, 1963. Arne Karlsen, *Møbler tegnet af Børge Mogensen: Udvalgt og beskrevet, Tegninger af forfatteren*, Copenhagen: Arkitektens Forlag, 1968. Frederik Sieck, *Nutidig Dansk Møbeldesign – en kortfattet illustreret beskrivelse*, Copenhagen: Bondo Gravesen, 1990.

Moggridge, Bill (1943–)
British industrial designer; active London (England).

Training 1965, Central School of Arts and Crafts, London.
Biography 1969, Moggridge set up his own industrial design studio in London, executing models for scientific and consumer products for American Sterilizer, Pitney Bowes, and Hoover. 1977, he moved to California and established Industrial Design Models studio in London as an entity under which he set up ID Two in Palo Alto, Cal., and Design Models in London. ID Two designed the first portable computer, 1981 Compass, by Grid Systems. 1987, Design 3 Produktdesign was established in Hanover as the German branch of Moggridge Associates of London; 1990, became an independent company, when others joined IDEO; 1999, was moved to Hamburg. 1991, IDEO, which grew out of ID Two, is now a large industrial-design firm.
Exhibitions Compass computer shown at 1983–84 *Design Since 1945*, Philadelphia Museum of Art.
Bibliography Cat., Kathryn B. Hiesinger and George H. Marcus III (eds.), *Design Since 1945*, Philadelphia: Philadelphia Museum of Art, 1983. *Central to Design, Central to Industry*, London: Central School of Art and Design, 1983. 'The Compass Computer: The Design Challenges Behind the Innovation,' *Innovation*, Winter 1983: 4–8. Mel Byars with Arlette Barré-Despond, *100 Designs/100 Years: A Celebration of the 20th Century*, Hove: RotoVision, 1999. Michele De Lucchi (ed.), *The International Design Yearbook*, London: Laurence King, 2001.
> See IDEO.

Møhl-Hansen, Kristian (1876–1962)
Danish designer and artist.

Training Painting, Det Kongelige Danske Kunstakademi, Copenhagen; and Zahrtmann School.
Biography Møhl-Hansen worked for the Georg Jensen Sølvsmedie in Copenhagen, where his 1916 silver and amber cup was produced until 1930.
Exhibitions/citations 1920 Eckersberg Medal; gold medal (for embroidered textiles), 1925 *Exposition Internationale des Arts Décoratifs et Industriels Modernes*, Paris.
Bibliography Cat., *Georg Jensen Silversmithy: 77 Artists, 75 Years*, Washington: Smithsonian, 1980.

Möhler, Fritz (1896–)
German silversmith; active Schwäbisch-Gmünd.

Training Steel engraving in his father's workshop; metalworking, technical school, Schwäbisch Gmünd; Kunstgewerbeschule, Munich.
Biography 1923, Möhler set up his own workshop in Schwäbisch-Gmünd, where he executed numerous commissions for ecclesiastical silverwork and secular pieces; was a skilled enameler and produced pieces incorporating *cloisonné* and *champlevé* enamel decoration. Before World War II in Germany, he was considered one of the most important silversmiths and contributed to the resurgence of interest in the goldsmith's craft.
Bibliography Annelies Krekel-Aalberse, *Art Nouveau and Art Déco Silver*, New York: Abrams, 1989.

Moholy-Nagy, László (1895–1946)
Hungarian painter, photographer, film maker, graphic designer, typographer, stage designer, writer, and teacher; born Bácsborsód.

Training In the law, Budapest; in drawing and painting, elsewhere.
Biography Moholy-Nagy started to draw during World War I; became interested in Kazimir Malevich's and El Lissitzky's work; 1919, moved to Vienna and, 1920, to Berlin. His art work, which reflected an interest in both Dada and Constructivism, was reproduced in the avant-garde Hungarian magazine *Ma* and shown at Herwarth Walden's Der Sturm gallery. He was friendly with the Constructivists and participated in the 1922 Dadaist-Constructivist Congress in Weimar organized by Theo van Doesburg. On the invitation of Walter Gropius, director of the Bauhaus, Moholy-Nagy was at the Bauhaus in Weimar and Dessau from 1923–28, where he practiced book design, film making, photography, and typography. And, at the Bauhaus in Weimar, he succeeded Johannes Itten as the director of the *Vorkurs* (preliminary course) and succeeded Paul Klee as the director of the metal workshop. Christian Dell, Wilhelm Wagenfeld, and Marianne Brandt were among Moholy-Nagy's pupils. He and Gropius edited the *Bauhausbücher* publication series. While at the Bauhaus, he developed the photogram; 1928, left the Bauhaus for Berlin where, 1928–33, was a stage designer, painter, photographer, and film maker and active at Erwin Piscator's Piscator Theater. 1934, Moholy-Nagy moved to Amsterdam and worked in London from 1935–37, where his graphic design work stimulated the poster scene. He worked with Richard Levin on some graphic designs, including covers of magazine *Shelf Appeal* in mid-1930s and also contributed to illustrated weekly magazines *Lilliput* and *Picture Post*. Along with other refugees, he resided in Jack Pritchard's Lawn Road flats (built in 1934) in Hampstead, London. His work in Britain included films, layout and poster designs for International Textiles, touring exhibitions and publicity materials for

Imperial Airways, posters for London Transport, publicity and display work for Simpson's department store, special visual effects for Alexander Korda's 1936 film *Things to Come* (but not in the final cut), publicity materials for Pritchard's Isokon furniture firm, exhibition displays, and cover designs and photographs. At Gropius's recommendation, he left London in 1937 and became director of the short-lived New Bauhaus in Chicago. 1939, he set up the independent School of Design, Chicago (renamed Institute of Design in 1944), which became a department under Serge Chermayeff at Armour Institute of Technology (now Illinois Institute of Technology/ITT) on Moholy-Nagy's death. Moholy-Nagy's books were influential and included *The New Vision: From Material to Architecture* (New York: Brewer, Warren & Putnam, 1932) and *Vision in Motion* (Chicago: P. Theobald, 1947). He died in Chicago.
Exhibitions Early 1920s, his Dada- and Constructivist-influenced paintings shown at Herwarth Walden's Der Sturm gallery, Berlin. Widely published modular illuminated structure shown at Werkbund stand at 1930 Salon des Artistes Décorateurs, Paris. Work subject of numerous exhibitions (many with catalogs), including London Gallery, 1936; The Royal Photographic Society, London, 1937; Art Institute of Chicago, 1947 exhibition, touring the US; Städtische Kunsthalle Mannheim, 1982–83; Bronx Museum of the Arts, New York, 1983; Museum Haus Lange, Krefeld, 1987; Tokyo Metropolitan Museum of Photography, 1990; Kunsthalle Fridericianum, Kassel, 1991; Musée des Beaux-Arts, Marseille, 1991; Magyar Fotográfiai Múzeum, Budapest, 1995; Kunsthalle, Bielefeld, 1995; Centre Georges Pompidou, Paris; Museum Folkwang, Essen, 1995–96; others. Work included in 1979–80 exhibition, Hayward Gallery, London (catalog below). Subject of 1995 Internationales László Moholy-Nagy Symposium, Bielefeld, Germany.
Bibliography Sibyl Moholy-Nagy, *Moholy-Nagy: Experiment in Totality*, Cambridge, Mass.: MIT, 1950. Hannah Weitemeier, *Licht-Visionen: Ein Experiment von Moholy-Nagy*, Berlin: Bauhaus-Archiv, 1972. Cat., *Thirties: British Art and Design Before the War*, London: Arts Council of Great Britain Hayward Gallery, 1979. Karisztina Passuth, *Laszlo Moholy-Nagy*, London: Thames & Hudson, 1985. Cat., Jutta Hülsewig-Johnen, Gottfried Jäger, and Christiane Heuwinkel (eds.), *László Moholy-Nagy, Idee und Wirkung: Anklänge an sein Work in der zeitgenössischen Kunst: Gruppe Animato...*, Bielefeld: Kerber, 1995.

Moïse, Bernard (1966–)
French designer; born Avignon.

Training 1985, applied arts in secondary school (baccalauréat F12), Marseille; 1987, BTS Architecture technician's certificate, Marseille; to 1992, ENSCI (Les Ateliers), Paris, receiving 1992 Abourse Agora citation for a distinguished project.
Biography 1992, Moïse founded Attitude Design agency for developing links between creation and economic, political, social and cultural spheres. 1994–95 with others in Paris, Moïse was active in agency Chopô-Moïse-Fritsch Associés for the design of interiors, visual communication, and products; from 1999, Moïse Associés, Paris. His own work has includes 2001 Loon electronically adjustable chaise longue by VIA (French furniture association) with Thomson multimédia, Hommage à l'Allumette candle lamp, Noot metal/mirror coat hanger, Draad floor/desk lamp by Cinna; Foll'Bille wall-mounted paper holder by Ardi; La pelle (a shovel) toilet-paper holder by Créa-Créa; furniture range by Cap-line; armchair by Soca. 1998, he designed numerous interiors, including Dalloyau boutiques, a commission from a department store in Warsaw, Spoon restaurant, and a number of private apartments. He was professor of design, École Boulle, 1997–2000; project head, ENSCI, 2002–03; both Paris.
Citations 2001 Appol Permanent grant (Loon chair), VIA; and a large number of other grants.
Bibliography Mel Byars, *50 Products: Innovations in Design and Materials*, Hove: RotoVision, 1999. www.via.asso.fr.

Moje, Klaus (1936–)
German glass designer; born Hamburg.

Training 1952–55, in his family's workshop in Hamburg; 1957–59, master's certificate, glass schools, Rheinbach and Hadamar.
Biography 1959–61, Moje worked in industry and crafts; 1961, set up a studio with Isgard Moje-Wohlgemuth; 1961–65, executed commissions for the design of stained-glass windows for churches, public buildings, and restoration projects; 1971–73, was a representative of the Arbeitsgemeinschaft des Deutschen Kunsthandwerks at World Crafts Council and became a member of its board of directors; 1976, cofounded Galerie der Kunsthandwerker (formerly Workshop Galerie), Hamburg; from 1979, was a guest lecturer, Pilchuck Glass School, Stanwood, Wash., US; Kunsthåndværkerskolen, Copenhagen; Middlesex Polytechnic (now Middlesex University), London; California College of Art and Crafts (now California College of the Arts), San Francisco; Gerrit Rietveld Academie, Amsterdam. 1982, he set up and became head of the glass workshop, Canberra School of Art (now School of Art, The Australian National University), Australia, to 1992. Critics regard Moje as Australia's most distinguished glass artist.
Exhibitions/citations From 1969, work shown in and subject of a large number of exhibitions worldwide. Received Dr. Maedebach Memorial Prize, 1985 Zweiter Coburger Glaspreis für Moderne Glasgestaltung in Europa; 2001 Australia Council Emeritus Fellowship Award, Australia Council.
Bibliography Klaus Moje, 'Material and Medium Glass,' *Kunst und Handwerk*, Oct. 1976: 364. Klaus Moje, 'Studio Glass USA,' *New Glass*, Jan. 1980: 18–25.

Moldenhawer, Henning (1914–1983)
Danish industrial designer.

Biography Moldenhawer was active in architecture and design; as an architect, created the small city Stampedammen, Denmark, where inhabitants live in a life style-enhanced social community; is best know for his product designs, particularly the transistorized stereo 1964 Beomaster 900 K radio, with a new cabinet-front, by Bang & Olufsen that set the standard for the firm's subsequent high-aesthetic pursuits. Also for the firm: 1965 Beovision 400 TV, 1966 Beovision 700 TV, 1967 Beo-vision 3000 SJ TV, 1967 Beomaster 1400 receiver, from 1968. And with David Lewis: 1970 Beovision 600 and 1974 Beovision 3500 TVs.
Exhibitions/citations Work included in 1978 Bang & Olufsen special display, The Museum of Modern Art, New York. Numerous design awards, including 1964 Industrie Forum Design (iF) (for Beomaster 900 radio), Hanover.
Bibliography Jens Bang, *Bang & Olufsen: Fra vision til legende = From Vision to Legend*, Denmark: Vidsyn, 2000.

Henning Moldenhawer. Beomaster 900 radio. 1964. Metal and plastic, 5 3/8 x 29 1/8 x 8 1/4" (13.6 x 74.3 x 21 cm). Mfr.: Bang & Olufsen, Denmark. Courtesy Quittenbaum Kunstauktionen, Munich.

Molesworth, Thomas Canada (1890–1977)

American furniture designer; born Kansas.

Training 1908–09, Art Institute of Chicago.
Biography 1931, Molesworth moved from Billings, Mont., to Cody, Wyo., where he and his wife LaVerne (b. LaVerne Johnston) established and managed Shoshone Furniture Co. (active 1931–61 and named after the Native American tribe). LaVerne designed and made drapes, curtains, and bedspreads and kept the financial records. (Cody is the town founded in 1901 by Col. William F. Cody [aka 'Buffalo Bill'].) Molesworth settled there with the intention of selling furniture and accessories in the Wild West style to tourists but did not invent the Western look in the US. Inspired by the Arts and Crafts movement and calling on the myth of the American cowboy that 'Wild Bill' established, Molesworth rather perfected the style. His first commission (1931) was probably for Carl Dunrud's Double Dee Dude Ranch in Wyoming. The 1940 furniture commission for the TE Ranch, originally the property of William Cody, featured an easy chair with Chimayo-weave cushions and moose-antler 'wings.' 1930s–1950s, his furniture flourished in US hotel lobbies, dude ranches, and private houses for a wealthy clientele, including a Wyoming ranch for Moses Annenberg (which is said to have launched Molesworth's design career), the ranch of the Rockefeller family, and a den for President Dwight D. Eisenhower in Gettysburg, Pa. Although his designs were meant to suggest primitivism, they had modern lines; after all, he had studied at the Art Institute of Chicago. Molesworth used honey-colored woods, fir and pine burls, and pastel leather upholstery trimmed in brass tacks, to reflect the romantic, yet synthetic, image of the American West purveyed by 1930s Hollywood movies. His most complete, if kitsch, architectural ensemble showed bucking broncos in linoleum, a wrought-iron and steel ashtray in a burro design with removable receptacles in its saddlebags, chairs with pierced bow-legged cowboy forms, and rope trim. Interested in the work of artist friends, he had an extensive art collection. A successful 1995 Christie's auction of the c. 1935 Molesworth contents of The Old Lodge, Glenwood Springs, Colo., helped dissiminate his reputation. His granddaughter Leslie Molesworth and her husband Tim Callahan are today reproducing some Molesworth furnishings in Rio Vista, Cal.
Exhibitions Work subject of *Interior West: The Craft and Style of Thomas Molesworth*, Buffalo Bill Historical Center, Cody, Wyo., 1989, and Gene Autry Western Heritage Museum, Los Angeles, 1990.
Bibliography Patricia Leigh Brown, 'How the West Was Done,' *The New York Times*, 5 Apr. 1990: C1ff. Elizabeth Clair Flood, *Cowboy High Style: Thomas Molesworth to the New West*, Layton, Utah: Gibbs Smith, 1992.

Mølgård-Nielsen, Orla (1907–)

Danish architect, cabinetmaker, and furniture designer.

Training Cabinetmaking and furniture design, Kunsthåndværkerskolen, Copenhagen; Under Kaare Klint Det Kongelige Danske Kunstakademie, Copenhagen.
Biography Mølgård-Nielsen introduced laminates and plywood to the Danish furniture industry; 1936–45, taught, Kunsthåndværkerskolen; 1944 with architect-cabinetmaker Peter Hvidt, opened their own office and, after World War II, they created a sectional furniture group of seating that was easy to ship and assemble. Their furniture clients included Fritz Hansen, France & Søn, and Søborg Møbelfabrik. The knock-down furniture principle was introduced by their 1950 AX range of chairs and table by Fritz Hansen, from 1960. Their AX Chair 6003 marked the introduction of the lamella-gluing principle in their furniture making and fostered international interest in Danish furniture.
Exhibitions/citations Mølgård-Nielsen and Hvidt's work included in 1950s *Good Design* exhibitions/awards, The Museum of Modern Art, New York, and Chicago Merchandise Mart; 1954–57 *Design in Scandinavia*, touring the US, 1956–59 *Neue Form aus Dänemark*, touring Germany, 1958 *Formes Scandinaves*, Musée des Arts Décoratifs, Paris, 1960–61 *The Arts of Denmark*, touring the US; 1966 *Vijftig Jaar Zitten*, Stedelijk Museum, Amsterdam; 1971 *Modern Chairs 1918–1970*, Whitechapel Gallery, London; 1983 *Design Since 1945*, Philadelphia Museum of Art. Diplomas of honor at 1951 (9th) and 1954 (10th) editions of Triennale di Milano.
Bibliography Esbjørn Hiort, *Contemporary Danish Furniture*, Copenhagen: Arkitektens Forlag, 1959. Gunnar Bratvold, *Mobilia*, July 1960: 21. Erik Zahle (ed.), *A Treasury of Scandinavian Design*, New York: Golden Press, 1961. Cat., David Revere McFadden (ed.) *Scandinavian Modern Design 1880–1980*, New York: Abrams, 1982. Frederik Sieck, *Nutidig Dansk Møbeldesign – en kortfattet illustreret beskrivelse*, Copenhagen: Bondo Gravesen, 1990. Noritsugu Oda, *Danish Chairs*, San Francisco: Chronicle Books, 1999.
> See Hvidt, Peter.

Molina, Manel (1963-)
See Liévore, Alberto.

Molinari, Pierluigi (1938–)

Italian industrial designer; born and active Milan.

Training Liceo Artistico di Brera; Accademia di Belle Arti di Brera; both Milan.
Biography 1961, Molinari began his professional career, working for clients including Ampaglas (plastics), Pozzi (seating), Aspaco (public furniture), Asnaghi (furniture), Faralia (industrial chemicals), Filab (lighting), Interzoom (furniture), Italora (clocks), Lisiline (sanitary fittings), Lineas (furniture), Merlett (plastics), Schiume (bathroom accessories), Salpol (upholstery fabrics), and Triplex (domestic electrical appliances). 1971, he became a member, Associazione per il Disegno Industriale (ADI), of which he was president from 1988–91; with Carlo Antonio Cerbaro, designed 1975 ADI exhibition, Lausanne, and 1979 *Design & Design* at Palazzo delle Stelline, Milan, and at Palazzo Grassi, Venice.
Exhibitions/citations Participated in numerous national and international exhibitions and won the 1973 gold metal at the Mostra Internazionale dell'Arredamento (MIA), Monza.
Bibliography *ADI Annual 1976*, Milan: Associazione per il Disegno Industriale, 1976. Alfonso Grassi and Anty Pansera, *Atlante del design italiano 1940/1980*, Milan: Fabbri 1980. Cat., Hans Wichmann, *Italien Design 1945 bis heute*, Munich: Die Neue Sammlung, 1988. *Modo*, no. 148, Mar.–Apr. 1993: 123.

Møller, Inger Eleonora (1886–1979)

Danish silversmith; born Otterup; active Copenhagen; wife of Just Andersen.

Training Under Georg Jensen.
Biography 1909–21, Møller worked for the Georg Jensen Sølvsmedie in Copenhagen; 1922, set up her own workshop. Her work was rendered in simple motifs soldered onto smooth surfaces, exemplified by the austere 1937 silver vegetable dish that might be mistaken for a cooking pot. She died in Bagsværd.
Exhibitions Work shown abroad first time, 1925 *Exposition Internationale des Arts Décoratifs et Industriels Modernes*, Paris. Subsequently, 1937 *Exposition Internationale des Arts et Techniques dans la Vie Moderne*, Paris; 1939–40 *New York World's Fair: The World of Tomorrow*; 1951 (9th) and 1957 (11th) editions of Triennale di Milano; 1954–57 *Design in Scandinavia*, touring the US; 1960–61 *The Arts of Denmark*, touring the US.
Bibliography Annelies Krekel-Aalberse, *Art Nouveau and Art Déco Silver*, New York: Abrams, 1989. Lise Funder, *Dansk sølv: 20. århudrede*, Copenhagen: Nyt Nordisk/Arnold, 1999.

Møller, Niels O. (1920–)

Danish cabinetmaker and furniture designer.

Training 1939, apprenticeship under a cabinetmaker; subsequently, Konstruktørskolen, Århus.
Biography Reminiscent of Gio Ponti's 1956 Superleggera chair, Møller's 1964 Chair 79 with a strip-leather seat was produced by J.L. Møller Møbelfabrik in Højberg, where he was director from 1944.
Exhibitions/citations Chair 79 first shown at 1964 *Scandinavian Furniture Fair*, Copenhagen. Received Danish bronze medal for craftsmanship.
Bibliography Cat., *Modern Chairs 1918–1970*, London: Lund Humphries, 1971. Noritsugu Oda, *Danish Chairs*, San Francisco: Chronicle, 1999.

Møller-Jensen, Jens (1938–)

Danish architect and designer.

Training 1955, toolmaking; 1964, Det Kongelige Danske Kunstakademi, Copenhagen; from 1965, in design in Italy, the US, and England.
Biography 1967, Møller-Hensen opened his own design firm and became a design consultant to DSB (Danish state railway) from 1972–90, and to Novo from 1989–99 (including 1991 design of its blood-

coagulation meter); from 1980, has been a member, Dansk Designråd (Danish design council); 1980–83, 1985–89, and 1992–95, juror of the Dansk ID Prize; from 1998, member of the board, Det Kongelige Akademi for de Skønne Kunster/Akademiraadet (the academy council). Designs include 1963 Albertslund lamp by Louis Poulsen.
Citations 1978 Knud V. Engelhardt's Memorial Grant; 1984, 1990, and 1991 Dansk ID Prizes.

Mollica, Silvana (1947–)

Italian archiect and designer; born Bergamo.

Training 1963–68, Liceo Scientifico Leonardo da Vinci; 1969–73, Faculty of Architecture, Politecnico; both Milan.
Biography All activities in Milan: 1976–77, Mollica was a consultant to Sertec; 1988–97, collaborated with Studio G14 Progettazione-Sezione Design; 1998 with Renata Fusi and Paola Mollica, established Fusi Mollica Zanotto Architetti Associati.
> See Fusi, Renata; Zanotto, Paolo.

Mollino, Carlo (1905–1973)

Italian architect and designer; born Turin.

Training Engineering; 1929, art history, Ghent art school; to 1931, Royal School of Architecture, University of Turin.
Biography Mollino began his career as an architect in his father's office in Turin; subsequently, worked independently but stayed in his father's office. His 1944 residence of Ada and Cesare Minola in Turin illustrated his Surrealist-streamlined style. His work contrasted with the more Rationalist designs emerging from Milan at this time. He was influenced by the organic forms reproduced in late-1940s issues of journal *Domus*, such as Henry Moore's sculptures, and his fantastic designs for furniture reflected these shapes. Most of his important furniture was made by the Apelli & Varesio joinery in Turin. He was also influenced by the works of Antoni Gaudí, Charles Rennie Mackintosh, Charles and Ray Eames, Le Corbusier, and Alvar Aalto. He executed a series of glass tables with one-piece bent-plywood bases, and chairs in organic forms. His wide-ranging œuvre included aeronautics, art, photography, set design, town planning, teaching, automobile bodies, clothing, furniture, interior decoration, and architecture. Much of his furniture and furnishings were site-specific and one-of-a-kind, like that for 1947-55 Casa Del Sole in Cervinia, serially produced by Apelli & Varesio and by Ettore Canali in Brescia. Late 1940s–early 1950s, Mollino designed in glass and bentwood (furniture), plastic rods (lamps), and industrial materials (shelving). He designed 1950–60 flats in Turin, 1950 house in San Remo, Teatro Regio in Turin, furnishings for a bachelor's apartment in Turin, furnishings by MUS, the radio pavilion of the Azienda Generale Italiana Petroli (AGIP) exhibition stand, and exhibitions for art, sports, and cars. 1950–60, he produced prototypes, few of which were manufactured; patented articulated lamps with Birri, cupboard-and-panel systems, and cold-bent plywood (used in his furniture); designed three-legged stools, fold-up and transforming furniture, and the 1954 Osca 1100 automobile series (never produced); was a member, Associazione per il Designo Industriale (ADI). A sense of decadent kitsch pervaded his work. Mollino was excessively preoccupied with women and himself. 1960, he bought a house on the Po river in Turin, named by him the 'Warrior's House of Rest,' but he never stayed there; was interested in the occult and particularly fascinated by the c. 1390–1352 B.C. tomb of Egyptian royal architect Kha.
Exhibitions/citations Work shown at 1954 (10th) and 1957 (11th) Triennali di Milano. Won the Reed & Barton cutlery competition. Work subject of 1989–90 *Carlo Mollino 1905–1973*, Centre Georges Pompidou, Paris.
Bibliography *Casa F.G. Minola*, Turin, 1944. 'Across the Seas Collaboration for the New Singer Collection,' *Interiors*, vol. 111, Dec. 1951: 120–29, 150. L.L. Ponti and E. Ritter (eds.) *Mobili e interni—selezione della rivista Domus,* Milan: Editoriale Domus, 1952. 'Nuovi Mobili di Mollino,' *Domus*, vol. 270, 1952: 50–53. Andrea Branzi and Michele De Lucchi, *Design italiano degli anni '50*, Milan: Ricerche Design, 1985. Giovani Brino, *Carlo Mollino: architettura come autobiografia architettura, mobili, ambientazioni, 1928–1973*, Milan: Idea, 1985, London: Thames & Hudson, 1987 (English ed.). François Burkhardt et al., *Carlo Mollino: l'étrange univers de l'architecture*, Paris: Centre Georges Pompidou, 1989. *Carlo Mollino: Chairs and Furnishings*, Milan: Institut Mathidenhöhe, 1994. Elena Tamagno, *Carlo Mollino: esuberanze soft*, Torino: Testo & Immagine, 1996.

MOLPOSNOVIS
> See UNOVIS.

Molteni

Itallan furniture company; located Giussano (MI).

History Early 1930s, Molteni was founded; has always operated contrary to current fashion; became Il Gruppo Molteni. Its production ranges fully, from the acquisition of raw materials through to finished products. 1969, the firm established Unifor for office-furniture production; 1980, bought Dada, the kitchen-furniture firm; retained Molteni &

Carlo Mollino and Alberto Bodogna. Armchair and ottoman (for Lutrario Dance Hall, via Stradella 3, Turin). 1959. Painted steel frame, brass, laminated wood, and Resinflex vinyl upholstery, armchair 29 1/2 x 21 1/4 x 22 7/16" (75.5 x 54 x 57.5 cm), ottoman 17 x 16 1/2 x 10 13/16" (43.5 x 42 x 27.5 cm). Mfr.: SC International, Italy. Courtesy Quittenbaum Kunstauktionen, Munich.

C as the firm name for home furnishing. Dada produces a range of kitchen systems with high aesthetic standards, including Futura wall unit, designed by Studio Kairos, with upwardly folding doors. Other Dada commissioned designers have included Pier Luigi Cerri, Michele De Lucchi, Ferruccio Laviani, Luca Meda, Paola Navone, Paolo Piva, and Hannes Wettstein. Molteni's commissioned designers have included Luca Meda, Aldo Rossi, Richard Sapper, Alvaro Siza, Pagani & Perversi, Rodolfo Dordoni, Hannes Wettstein, Afra and Tobia Scarpa, Cini Boeri, and Ferruccio Laviani. Unifor primarily produces office furniture noted for its clean lines, like the Less table series with very thin tops by Jean Nouvel and designs by Franco Mirenzi, Philippe Boisselier, Pierluigi Cerri, Franco Mirenzi, Aldo Rossi, and Richard Sapper.
Bibliography 'Milan à l'heure du design,' *Maison et Jardin*, Apr. 1992: 123. www.molteni.it.

Moltzer, Kim

Austrian artist and furniture designer; active Paris.

Biography Moltzer has often collaborated with Jean-Paul Barray (1930–) on the design of furniture, lighting, and decorative objects. Their best-known furniture is 1969 Penta folding lounge chair with a suspended fabric seat and nickel-plated steel-wire frame, by Wilhelm Bofinger.
Exhibitions 1970s, work shown in numerous venues.
Bibliography Gilles de Bure, *Le mobilier français 1965–1979*, Paris: Regard/VIA, 1983: 37. Arlette Barré-Despond (ed.), *Dictionnaire international des arts appliqués et du design*, Paris: Regard, 1996: 60–61.
> See Barray, Jean-Paul.

Moneo, José Rafael (1937–)

Spanish architect; born Tudela (Navarra).

Training 1961, architecture degree, Escuela Técnica Superior de Arquitectura, Madrid.
Biography 1958–61, Moneo worked in the office of architect Francisco Javier Sáenz de Oíza (Cáseda 1918–Madrid 2000) in Madrid and, 1961–62, office of architect Jørn Utzon in Hellebaek, Denmark; 1970–80, was chairperson of and taught, Escuela Técnica Superior de Arquitectura de Barcelona (ETSAB); from 1980, was a professor, Escuela Técnica Superior de Arquitectura de Madrid (ETSAM), within the Universidad Politécnica; 1965, set up his own practice in Madrid. Moneo has been an active architecture critic; uses brick to humanize his architecture and soften its extreme simplicity; 1976, was invited to teach at Institute for Architecture and Urban Studies, New York, and became associated with Irwin S. Chanin School of Architecture at The Cooper Union for the Advancement of Science and Art, New York. He was also Ospite Professor, Institute of Architecture in Lausanne and Princeton University; 1985–90, chairperson, Graduate School of Design, Harvard University, Cambridge, Mass., becoming Sert Professor there in 1991; and lectured worldwide. He cofounded and became an editorial board member of journal *Arquitecturas Bis* and wrote numerous articles. His architecture includes 1963–67 Diestre factory, Saragossa; 1967 addition to Plaza de Toros, Pamplona; 1969–71 Urumea mansion, San Sebastian; 1973–81 town hall, Logroño; 1973–76 Bankinter (with Ramón Bescós), Madrid; 1980–84 Museo de Arte Romana, Mérida, Mexico. Furniture has included El viaje paralelo del libro y de la vida desk chair and 2000 Panticosa side chair by Punt Mobles (designed for Moneo's rehabilitation of 1998 Arenberg Library of Katholieke Universiteit Leuven, Belgium, and for the restaurant of Panticosa Restaurant, Panticosa, Huesca, Spain.)
Exhibitions/citations Work subject of exhibitions at Akademie der bildenden Künst, Vienna, 1993; Architeckturmuseum, Basel, 1993; Arkitekturmuseet, Stockholm, 1993; Suomen Rakennustaiteen Museo (museum of Finnish architecture), Helsinki, 1994. Received 1974–75 Premi FAD d'Interiorisme Award (best interiors); 1992 gold medal for achievement in fine art, Spanish Government; 1993 honorary doctorate degree, Katholieke Universiteit Leuven; 1993 Arnold W. Brunner Memorial Prize in Architecture, The American Academy and Institute of Arts and Letters; 1993, Prince of Viana Prize, Government of the Province of Navarra; Schock Prize in the Visual Arts, Schock Foundation and Royal Academy of Fine Art, Stockholm; 1994 laurea ad honorem, Istituto Universitario di Architettura, Venice; 1994 Pritzker Architecture Prize.
Bibliography 'José Rafael Moneo,' *Nueva Forma*, Jan. 1975. Cat., Carlo Guenzi, *Le affinità elettive*, Milan: Electa, 1985. Auction cat., *Asta di Modernariato 1900–1986, Auction 'Modernariato,'* Milan: Semenzato Nuova Geri, 8 Oct. 1986: lot 114. Juli Capella and Quim Larrea, *Designed by Architects in the 1980s*, New York: Rizzoli, 1988.

Monk, John Lawrence (1936–)

American industrial designer; born Los Angeles; active Varese, Italy.

Biography 1960, Monk began his professional career; worked in Ettore Sottsass studio in Milan on the design of products by Lesa (domestic electrical appliances and sound equipment), Duben Haskell Jacobson (industrial machinery), Oerre (vacuum cleaners and appliances), Artsana (small medical apparati), Cafèbar (beverage dispenser with David Lawrence Higgins) in Stratford (England), Forma & Funzione (lighting), and Caravans International in Varedo. Monk designed 1969 Olivetti G 120 calculator (with Ettore Sottsass and David Higgins) by Olivetti and a medical portable aerosol device by Artsana; worked in industrial-design studio Incateam with offices in Norway, Germany, Britain, Switzerland, the Netherlands, and Italy; became a member, Associazione per il Disegno Industriale (ADI).
Citations 1970 Premio Compasso d'Oro (for G 120 calculator with others by Olivetti).
Bibliography *ADI Annual 1976*, Milan: Associazione per il Disegno Industriale, 1976.

Monpoix, André (1925–1976)

French furniture designer; active Paris.

Training From 1945, École Nationale Supérieure des Arts Décoratifs, Paris.
Biography Monpoix learned decoration from Maxime Old, René Gabriel, and Jacques Dumond, with whom he worked for four years; often collaborated with Alain Richard, designing furniture by Meubles TV.
Exhibitions From 1953, work shown at editions of Salon des Arts Ménagers and Salons of Société des Artistes Décorateurs.
Bibliography Pascal Renou, *Portraits de créateurs*, Paris: H. Vial, 1969. Gilles de Bure, *Le mobilier français 1965–1969*, Paris: Regard/VIA, 1983: 75. Patrick Favardin, *Les décorateurs des années 50*, Paris: Norma, 2002: 222.

Montagnac, Pierre-Paul (1883–1961)

French painter, architect, decorator, and furniture designer.

Training Under Eugène Carrière, and Académie de la Grande Chaumière, both Paris.
Biography From 1918, Montagnac worked for a time in the workshop of André Mare and, subsequently, pursued a career as architect and decorator, constructing housing, designing interiors, and rendering furniture. He worked equally in the fine and applied arts and designed well-constructed furniture in solid classical forms. He was dis-

Pierre-Paul Montagnac. Sideboard. c. 1930. Tropical wood and marble, 42 1/8 x 43 3/8 x 21 3/4" (107 x 110 x 56 cm). Mfr.: attrib. to Robert Sangouard, France. Courtesy Quittenbaum Kunstauktionen, Munich.

satisfied with the furniture manufacturers in the Faubourg Saint-Antoine area of Paris and had Robert Sangouard in Saint-Ouen produce his work. From 1922, Montagnac collaborated with Maurice Dufrêne at La Maîtrise decorating studio of Les Galeries Lafayette department store, Paris, contributing furniture designs there; was active as a designer of a large number of tapestries (by Manufacture Nationale des Gobelins), lighting, and ceramics. Other work: furniture in limited editions by Fontaine and for several other firms, numerous offices, stores, apartments, and suites on oceanliners 1931 *L'Atlantique*, 1935 *Normandie*, and 1939 *Pasteur*. 1930–38, he was president, Société des Artistes Décorateurs; 1940–45, studied serial furniture production, shown at 1950s editions of Salon of Société des Artistes Décorateurs and Salon d'Automne; 1947, became president, Salon d'Automne.
Exhibitions/citations 1912, work first shown in Salons in Paris. And 1920 Salon d'Automne (paintings), where he received a traveling scholarship; applied art at Salons of Société des Artistes Décorateurs from 1921, Salon des Architectes Modernes, and in Barcelona and Leipzig. Designed reception room of Esplanade des Invalides and supplied furniture for Grand Salon by Rapin and Selmersheim for Une Ambassade Française, 1925 *Exposition Internationale des Arts Décoratifs et Industriels Modernes*. Participated in and organized pavilion of Société des Artistes Décorateurs, *Exposition Internationale des Arts et Techniques dans la Vie Moderne*. All Paris.
Bibliography *Ensembles mobiliers*, vol. 2, Paris: Charles Moreau, 1937. Pierre Kjellberg, *Art déco: les maîtres du mobilier, le décor des paquebots*, Paris: Amateur, 1986/1990.

Montagni, Berizzi, Butte, Architetti
Italian architecture practice.

History 1950s, Dario Montagni, Sergio Berizzi (1930–), and Cesare Butte established their practice, Architetti Montagni, Berizzi, Butte, in Milan; invented a concept for the Phonola company—1956 TV set (no. 17/18) with a picture tube, separate from the tabletop cabinet, that can be rotated independently of the table- or floor-version cabinet. The voluptuous shape of the picture-tube casing in metal contrasts with the ridigidly geometrical cabinet box of veneered wood. In that the picture tube is separate, this Italian model is similar to the Philco Predicta TV (introduced in 1958, produced in the US) and to the Teleavia 1956 model designed by Philippe Carbonneaux (produced in France). A progressive firm, Phonola also made the 1939–40 (no. 547) five-valve desktop radio receiver in Bakelite by Livio and Pier Giacomo Castiglioni.
Bibliography Andrea Branzi and Michael De Lucchi (eds.), *Il design italiano degli anni '50*, Milan: Ricerche Design Editrice, 1985: 271. Penny Sparke, *Design in Italy, 1870 to the Present*, New York: Abbeville, 1988: 143, 145.

Monteiro, Elder António Ferreira (1972–)
Portuguese designer; born Beira, Mozambique.

Training Graphic design, António Arroio high school, Lisbon; equipment design, fine art college, Lisbon University.
Biography 1989–91, Monteiro was junior art director at Leo Burnett advertising agency; 1996, was an intern at Proto Design, and a staff member there from 2001. He has designed a stand at *Expo '98* in Lisbon. 1999: Atlantis crystal manufacturer, interior design and child's car by Sonae Corporation, and ice cream stand by Wall's in Warner Brothers spaces. 2000: brushes by D.I.M. (Die Imaginäre Manufaktur), Berlin. 2002: glass projects by MGlass.
Exhibitions/citations 1999 *Primavera del diseño—experimentáveis*, ICEP, Barcelona; 1999 *Sweet Revolution*, Salão Internacional do Móvel, Milão; *Experimenta design 99*, Convento do Beato; 2000 Experimental Design stand, Salone del Mobile, Milan; 2000 *Diseño Portugués: un compromiso con la Industria*, ICEP, Madrid; 2000 Ambiente fair, Frankfurt; 2000 Intérieur, Courtrai, Belgium; 2001 *Sinne+5*, Stilwerk, Berlin. Young Designer's Awards sponsored by Investimentos, Comércio e Turismo de Portugal (ICEP) 1996 Young Talents Award, Munich.

Montgomery, Paul (1959–)
American industrial designer.

Training 1981, bachelor's degree, College of Design, North Carolina State University; University of Georgia in Cortona (Italy); 1987, masters degree, Cranbrook Academy of Art, Bloomfield Hills, Mich.
Biography Prior to Cranbrook, Montgomery worked for Texas Instruments in Austin, Texas, and PA Technology in Princeton, N.J.; after Cranbrook, was design director of frogdesign in California. 1990 with Herbert Pfeifer (Germany 1949–), he established multi-disciplinary studio Montgomery Pfeifer in San Francisco, with clients including Alcatel, Apple, Digital Persona, Intel, Lifescan, and Microsoft; has designed computer systems, TV sets, medical and office products, and luggage, including 1993 MouseMan Cordless mouse by Logitech.
Exhibitions/citations MouseMan Cordless shown in 1995 *Mutant Materials*, New York (catalog below). Received 1987 award for a digital still camera, Industrial Designers Society of America (IDSA) frogdesign's 'frogjunior' award; Designer's Choice, *I.D.* magazine.
Bibliography Albrecht Bangert and Karl Michael Armer, *80s Style: Designs of the Decade*, New York: Abbeville, 1990: 200, 233. Cat., Paola Antonelli, *Mutant Materials in Contemporary Design*, New York: The Museum of Modern Art/Abrams, 1995.

Architetti Montagni, Berizzi, Butte (Dario Montagni, Sergio Berizzi (1930–), and Cesare Butte). TV set (no. 1718). 1956. Metal and wood. 22 x 19 x 19" (55.9 x 48.2 x 48.2 cm). Mfr.: Phonola, Italy. Given anonymously. MoMA.

Monti G.P.A., Studio
Italian architecture and design studio; located Milan.

History 1948, Studio Monti G.P.A. in Milan was established by siblings Gianemilio Monti (Milan 1920–), Pietro Monti (Corenno Plinio 1922–Milan 1990), and Anna Bertarini Monti (Milan 1923–), who had studied at the Politecnico in Milan. The Montis were members of Istituto Nazionale Urbanistica (INU); 1956, cofounders of Associazione per il Disegno Industriale (ADI); and, 1954–60, members of Movimento Studi Architettura (MSA). Gianemilio and Pietro Monti were active in the Commissione Edilizia (building commission) of the Comune of Milan, and, 1970–72, Pietro was president, Ordine degli Architetti (architects' association) of Lombardy. Their design work encompassed the 1955 bed and hallstand by ICF, 1959–65 plastic lamps for Kartell (including 1959 4334/5 sconce), 1963 furniture by Stildomus (including Orsola chest), 1972–76 lamps by Fontana, 1970–71 Boma door handles by Olivari. They also designed buildings and restaurants in Italy.
Bibliography *ADI Annual 1976*, Milan: Associazione per il Disegno Industriale, 1976. Alfonso Grassi and Anty Pansera, *Atlante del design italiano 1940/1980*, Milan: Fabbri, 1980. Giancarolo Iliprandi and Pierluigi Molinari (eds.), *Industrial designers italiani*, Fagagna: Magnus, 1985: 147. Christina Morozzi, 1956–1988 *Trent'anni e più di design*, Milan: Idea, 1988. Cat., Hans Wichmann, *Italien Design 1945 bis heute*, Munich: Die Neue Sammlung, 1988.

Montina
Italian furniture company; located San Giovanni al Natisone (UD).

History Founded in 1919, Montina was founded by three brothers: Giovanni Battista (business director), Pierceleste (sales director), and Erminio (production director), at first for the production of clothes stands and racks and toys hangers. 1920, seating was introduced. 1938, a foldable deck chair began a series of patented products. 1960, Montina began commissioning consulting designers, such as Studio TiPi, and others followed such as Tito Agnoli in 1963 and Gio Ponti in 1969, and, subsequently, Carlo De Carli, Ilmari Tapiovaara, Eero Arnio, Vico Magistretti, Ettore Sottsass, Enzo Mari, Enzo Berti, Jasper Morrison, Enrico Franzolini. Konstanin Grcic 2000 seat/stand was widely published. Older models continue to be produced, for example, Ponti's 969 side chair.

Moooi
Dutch manufacturer; located Amsterdam.

History The firm was formerly called Wanders Wonders, the manufacturing entity of designer Marcel Wanders; 2001, became known as Moooi, pronounced 'moy,' rhyming with 'toy'; also edits the work of other designers such as Bianca Nooyens, Desirée de Jong, and Jorrit Kortenhorst.
> See Wanders, Marcel.

Moorcroft
British ceramics firm; located Burslem, Staffordshire.

History Designer William Moorcroft (1872–1945) founded the pottery works c. 1925 in Burslem. All ware was hand-thrown and -turned. Moorcroft prided himself on the correctness of the shapes he produced and on a high level of craftsmanship. However, the firm's potters were not expected to innovate. Its original designs of 1920s continued to be produced into 1950s.
Bibliography Michael Farr, *Design in British Industry: A Mid-Century Survey*, London: Cambridge, 1955. Paul Atterbury, *Moorcroft*, London: Dennis & Edwards, 1990, 1993 rev. ed.

Moore, Edward Chandler (1827–1891)
American silversmith; active New York.

Biography Moore was an accomplished designer known for his fine craftsmanship; 1852, encouraged Tiffany & Co. to become the first American smithy to adopt the English sterling standard (92.5% silver). 1868, Tiffany bought Moore's workshop, and he became the director of its silver department. Late 1860s or early 1870s, there were no silver training schools in New York, so he set up a program for silversmiths in the Tiffany workshops, then located on Prince Street in New York. He was enthusiastic about the Japanese style, having seen pieces at 1867 *Exposition Universelle* in Paris. By 1871, the firm was producing Japanese-influenced cutlery patterns and, from 1873, hollow-ware. Under Moore, Tiffany produced jewelry in the Japanese style for New York's socialites. In many of Moore's pieces, he combined Western and Eastern themes and motifs.
Exhibitions/citations 1889, elected Chevalier of Légion d'Honneur, France.
Bibliography 'The Edward C. Moore Collection,' *Bulletin of The Metropolitan Museum of Art*, vol. 2, June 1902: 105–06. Henry H. Hawley, 'Tiffany's Silver in the Japanese Taste,' *Bulletin of the Cleveland Museum of Art*, Oct. 1976: 236–45. Bruce Kamerling, 'Edward C. Moore: The Genius Behind Tiffany Silver,' parts 1 and 2, *Silver*, vol. 10, Sept.–Oct. 1977: 16–20. Charles H. Carpenter Jr., 'Tiffany Silver in the Japanese Style,' *Connoisseur*, vol. 200, Jan. 1979: 42–47. Doreen Bolger Burke et al., *In Pursuit of Beauty: Americans and the Aesthetic Movement*, New York: The Metropolitan Museum of Art/Rizzoli, 1986.

Moore, Gene (1910–1998)
American designer; born Birmingham, Ala.

Training Painting, Chicago Academy of Fine Arts.
Biography 1935, Moore settled in New York; after odd jobs, was a display assistant then the display director, I. Miller shoe store; 1938, joined Bergdorf Goodman women's clothing store and the adjunct Delman's shoe department; 1945, became display director, Bonwit Teller clothing store; 1955–94, was Tiffany & Co.'s display director and created distinctive, high-profile designs in the five small vitrines along Fifth Avenue and 57th Street. His simple treatments at Tiffany were provocative vignettes, incorporating expensive jewelry in ways not before seen. Moore, who designed more than 5,000 windows in his 50-year career, also incorporated in the Tiffany windows the work of artists such as Robert Rauschenberg and Jasper Johns and was inclined to juxtapose, for example, pasta noodles against large-carat diamonds. The day after he died, the company darkened the windows he had made famous. Moore's archive is housed in the Cooper-Hewitt National Design Museum, New York.
Bibliography Gene Moore and Jay Hyams, *My Time at Tiffany's*, New York: St. Martin's, 1990.

Moore, Riette Sturge (1907–)
> See Sturge Moore, Riette H.

Moorman, Theo (1907–1990)
British weaver and designer.

Training 1925–28, Central School of Arts and Crafts, London.
Biography 1928–35, she was a freelance weaver and designer; 1935–39, worked at fabric firm Warner in Braintree, where she designed and wove fabrications by hand or power looms. She was responsible for hand-woven examples intended eventually for machine production; experimented with unusual and new yarns to produce fabrics in modern motifs and patterns, including brocades, weft inlays, and yarns such as natural fibers, trail rays, metallic strips, and cellophane. 1944–53, she was assistant regional director, Arts Council of Great Britain; from 1953, was active as a freelance weaver, known for wall hangings and ecclesiastical fabrics; 1968–78, lectured and taught in the US.
Exhibitions 1979–80 *Thirties* (hand-woven fabrications), Hayward Gallery, London (catalog below).
Bibliography Cat., *Thirties: British Art and Design Before the War*, London: Arts Council of Great Britain Hayward Gallery, 1979.

Moormann Möbel-Produktions und Handelsgesellschaft
German furniture firm; located Aschau im Chiemgau.

History 1984, the firm, known simply as Nils Holger Moormann, was founded by him in Frasdorf to design, produce, and distribute innovative and functional furniture and furniture systems. No matter the relatively unknown status of many of its commissioned designers, the work, most of it highly simple, has been distinguished. The Moormann inventory has included 1985 Lamello chair by Christian Anderegg, 1989 Buttone stools by Markus Heeb and Felix Schranz, 1990 Pap wastepaper basket by Marcus Botsch, 1993 Happy New Ears CD-holding board by Galerie Blau, 1999 Clicmore shelf system by Burkhardt Leitner Constructiv, 2000 Dr. I transparent office container by Peter Bonfig, 2000 Plötzlich table-base trestles by Christophe Marchand, 2002 Billy Clever shelf by Matthias Furch and Kai Ertel, 2002 Kant desk by Patrick Frey and Markus Boge, and 2002 book-like shelf lamp by Büro für Gestaltungsfragen (BFGF). Jakob Gebert's 1996 Spanoto demountable force-fitted table in wood was widely published; likewise, 1999 Tischbocktisch (table) by Jakob Timpe, featuring a self-locking thin wooden base.
Citations Bundespreis Produktdesign, Rat für Formgebung (German design council), Frankfurt; Top Ten, Industrie Forum Design (iF), Frankfurt; Red Dot award, Design Zentrum Nordrhein Westfalen, Essen; Good Design award, Chicago Athenaeum; 2000 Fokus Arbeitswelten, Design Center Stuttgart; and a large number of other awards.
Bibliography Mel Byars, *50 Tables...*, Hove: RotoVision, 1997. www.moormann.de.

Moos, Peder (1906–1991)
Danish furniture designer.

Training 1925, apprenticeship under a cabinetmaker; 1935–38, Det Kongelige Danske Akademiets Møbelskole, Copenhagen, under Kaare Klint.
Biography 1925–30, Moos worked as a cabinetmaker in Switzerland and France; 1935–54, was active in his own workshop in Copenhagen, and, from 1954, in Bredebro. 1941–43, he taught, Teknologisk Institut, Taastrup; 1950–53, Copenhagen Commune school; 1964–65, Tønder Seminarium (teachers' college).
Exhibitions Work was included in 1948 *Deense Kunsthandwerk*, Gemeente Musem, The Hague; 1940–63 exhibitions of Danish Handcraft Guild; 1948 *Danish Arts and Crafts*, Gemeente Museum; 1960–61 *The Arts of Denmark*, touring the US.
Bibliography Frederik Sieck, *Nutidig Dansk Mobeldesign – en kortfattet illustreret beskrivelse*, Copenhagen: Bondo Gravesen, 1990.

Morandini, Marcello (1940–)
Italian designer; born Mantua; active Varese.

Training Fine art, Accademia di Belle Arti di Brera, Milan.

Carlo Moretti. Oval tumbler. Pre-1980. Glass with a gold trim, h. 5" (12.7 cm) x dia. 2 7/8" (7.3 cm). Mfr.: Carlo Moretti, Italy. Greta Daniel Fund. MoMA.

Biography 1960, Morandini began as a professional designer in Milan; 1963, opened his own studio; 1979, moved to Sydney, Australia, and, subsequently, worked in Singapore. For several years, he designed ceramics by Rosenthal, additionally the façade of its offices in Selb. With references to 1920s decoration and De Stijl forms, his 1980s Corner unit furniture was produced by Rosenthal. For others, his body of design has included cutlery, furniture, lighting, carpets, wallpaper, doors, and folding screens.
Exhibitions 1965, first showed his three-dimensional structures, in Genoa. Work subject of 2000 exhibition, Museo d'Arte Moderna e Contemporanea Castello di Masnago, Varese (catalog below); 2003 *Marcello Morandini: Design*, mu.dac (Musée de Design et d'Arts Appliqués Contemporains), Lausanne.
Bibliography Giancarlo Iliprandi and Pierluigi Molinari (eds.), *Industrial designers italiani*, Fagagna: Magnus, 1985: 148. Cat., Hans Wichmann, *Italien Design 1945 bis heute*, Munich: Die Neue Sammlung, 1988. Albrecht Bangert and Karl Michael Armer, *80s Style: Designs of the Decade*, New York: Abbeville, 1990: 142, 188–89, 233. Cat., Emanuela Belloni (ed.), *Marcello Morandini: Art – Design 1964–2000*, Milan: Charta, 2000.

Morassutti, Bruno (1920–)

Italian industrial designer; born Padova; active Milan.

Training To 1947, in architecture in Venice.
Biography 1949–50, Morassutti worked in the Taliesin West studio of Frank Lloyd Wright, Scottsdale, Ariz.; 1955–60, collaborated with Angelo Mangiarotti as Mangiarotti e Morassutti; 1968 set up a partnership in Milan, with Mario Memoli, Giovanna Gussoni, and M. Gabriella Benevento; became a member, Associazione per il Disegno Industriale (ADI). Architecture includes 1959–60 multiple dwelling in Milan.
Exhibitions His career began with participation in 1947 (8th) Triennale di Milano. Work included in 1972 *Milano 70/70*, Museo Poldi Pezzoli, Milan.
Bibliography Cat., *Milano 70/70*, Milan, 1972. *ADI Annual 1976*, Milan: Associazione per il Disegno Industriale, 1976. Cat., Hans Wichmann, *Italien Design 1945 bis heute*, Munich: Die Neue Sammlung, 1988.

Mørch, Ibi Trier (1910–)

Danish architect and industrial designer.

Training Architecture, Det Kongelige Danske Kunstakademi, Copenhagen.
Biography Specialized in silver and glassware and collaborated with Erik Herløw from 1951–60. Mørch and Grethe Meyer designed 1958 drinking glasses (Stub stacking and Stamme models) by Kastrup Glasværk.
Bibliography 'One Hundred Great Danish Designs,' *Mobilia*, nos. 230–33, Dec. 1974: no. 47. Cat., *Danskt 50 Tal: Scandinavian Design*, Stockholm: Nationalmuseum, 1982: 36, no. 126. Cat., Kathryn B. Hiesinger and George H. Marcus III (eds.), *Design Since 1945*, Philadelphia: Philadelphia Museum of Art, 1984.

Morel, Jean-Paul
> See Chaix, Philippe.

Moretti, Carlo (1934–); Giovanni Moretti (1940–)

Italian glassmakers; active Murano.

Biographies/history End of 19th century, Vincenzo Moretti established a glass and bead factory near Venice. 1958, his grandsons Carlo and Giovanni Moretti established the Carlo Moretti company in Murano to produce engraved glassware, colored liqueur glasses, and opaline goblets. 1973, the enterprise began the production of more technically sophisticated objects, most of them in Murano glass, produced by master glass blowers. Moretti has designed hexagonal glasses with gold borders and widely published octagonal glasses; 1990, began to design special glasses for collecting. Other designers of often-frosted mouth-blown ware have included Alessandro Lenarda, Teff Sarasin, and Helge De Leo, all in 1960s; Maria Christina Hamel and Patrizia Scarzella, in 1980s; and Gian Paolo Canova.
Bibliography *Les carnets du design*, Paris: Mad-Cap Productions/ APCI, 1986: 54. Robert A.M. Stern (ed.), *The International Design Yearbook*, New York: Abbeville, 1985/1986.

Moreux, Jean-Charles (1889–1956)

French architect, painter, and designer.

Training Architecture, École Nationale Supérieure des Beaux-Arts; concurrently, history of art, École du Louvre; both Paris.
Biography 1924, Moreux began his career with a commission from the vicomte Charles de Noailles; became a highly cultivated architect, painter, and furniture designer; designed a number of townhouses, vacation houses, and studios (including those of Luc-Albert Moreau and Jos Hessel). Some of his furniture was lacquered, some in pre-

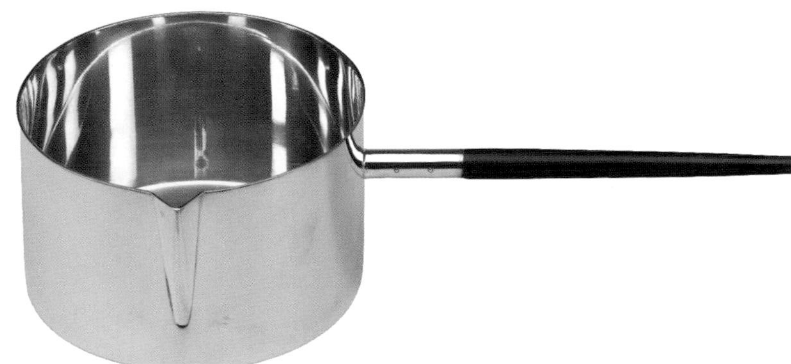

Ibi Trier Mørch. Serving pot. 1955. Sterling silver and ebony, 2 3/4 x 10 7/8 x 4 7/8" (7 x 27.6 x 12.4 cm). Mfr.: A. Michelsen, Denmark. Purchase Fund. MoMA.

cious woods, some in metal; though sometimes massive, it was elegant. His architecture and interiors included the apartment of Robert de Rothschild, 1928 music pavilion of harpsicordist Wanda Landowska, c. 1926 house of A.D. Mouradian in Saint-Cloud, 1943–44 apartment of Raphaël Lopez on the avenue Pierre-1er-de-Serbie, Paris, and Château Maulny in Sarthe. Through an acquaintaince with Bolette Natanson, he became involved with accomplished writers and musicians of the day. And, when Natanson died, Moreux rejected Functionalism, Constructivism, and Robotism completely in favor of a more romantic, theatrical style. He designed a table in ebony, crocodile, galuchat, crystal, and ivory (possibly made by Pierre Legrain) for couturier Jacques Doucet; 1931, joined Union des Artistes Modernes (UAM); collaborated for a time with architect André Lurçat; participated in the 1938 design of the apartment by Louis Süe of Helena Rubenstein in Paris; was Architecte des Palais Nationaux, including the Louvre; published *Carnet de voyage* (1954) with his architectural sketches; designed 1952 garden and 1955 library of ambassador Henry Spitzmuller in the Château de Henry in Yonne; and the gardens of Shepherd's Hotel in Cairo.
Exhibitions Participated in 1925 *Exposition Internationale des Arts Décoratifs et Industriels Modernes*, Paris; designed Martinique pavilion at 1931 UAM exhibition; 1939 and 1942 Salon of Société des Artistes Décorateurs.
Bibliography Albert Laprade, 'L'œuvre de J-Ch Moreux,' *L'architecture*, 1939. Pierre Kjellberg, *Art déco: les maîtres du mobilier, le décor des paquebots*, Paris: Amateur, 1986/1990. Arlette Barré-Despond, *UAM*, Paris: Regard, 1986: 22–21, 256, 311. Patrick Mauriès, 'Jean-Charles Moreux: néoclassicisme inspiré,' *Vogue décoration*, no. 39, Aug.–Sept. 1992: 77–81. Susan Day, *Jean-Charles Moreux, architecte-décorateur-paysagiste*, Paris: Norma, 1999. Cat., Sophie Tasma Anargyros et al., *L'école française: les créateurs de meubles du 20ème siècle*, Paris: Industries Françaises de l'Ameublement, 2000.

Morgan, David (1951–)
British industrial designer.

Training Physics, London University, and industrial design, Royal College of Art, London.
Biography He joined the design department of Thorn Lighting; 1981, established David Morgan Associates in London, through which he has specialized in lighting products, including 1986 Burlington glare-free desk lamp by Panasonic; also designs consumer products, electronics, and scientific equipment. Lighting clients include Belfer Lighting, Daiko Electric, Kreon, Louis Poulsen, Lightolier, Matsushita Electric Works, Philips Lighting, Schreder, and Thorn Lighting.
Exhibitions Burlington lamp won the 1987 British Design in Japan competition.
Bibliography Jeremy Myerson and Sylvia Katz, *Conran Design Guides: Lamps and Lighting*, London: Conran Octopus, 1990: 77.

Morgan, Simon (1959–1999)
British designer; born London.

Training To 1981, School of Three-Dimensional Design, Kingston Polytechnic (now Kingston University); 1985, Royal College of Art, London.
Biography In Milan: from 1981, Morgan collaborated with Michele De Lucchi; also from 1981, was a consultant in the Olivetti Design Studio (directed by Ettore Sottsass and George Sowden); from 1984, collaborated with Sowden; 1985, was a member of the Solid design group. In France: 1996, Morgan settled in Rocher, near Largentière, and set up his own studio, with some contacts in Milan; taught design in Marseilles; committed suicide.
> See Solid.

Morgan, William Frend De (1839–1917)
> See De Morgan, William Frend.

Morita, Akio (1921–1999)
> See Sony.

Moroso
Italian furniture company; located Cavalicco.

History 1952, Moroso was founded; specializes in upholstered furniture with attention toward handcrafting; was the first Italian firm to be certified by the international conformation of the ISO 9001 standard for quality and of the ISO 14001 for environmental management; produces furniture for homes, offices, cruise ships, hotels, restaurants, and airports; has showrooms in Milan and Amsterdam. Its commissioned designers include Antonio Citterio, Michele De Lucchi, Enrico Franzolini, Toshiyuki Kita, Rodolfo Dordoni, Massimo Iosa Ghini, Óscar Tusquets Blanca, Roberto Lazzeroni, Javier Mariscal, Ross Lovegrove. One of Achille Castiglioni's last designs is 2000 40/80 suspended-seat chair (with Ferruccio Laviani). Seating has included Patricia Urquiola's 1998 Step One, Step Two, and Step divans (her first for the firm) 2000 Lowland and Lowseat, and widely published 2002 Fjord seats. Ron Arad designed 2000 Victoria and Albert sofa and armchair and subsequent 2001 Little Albert armchair and 2001 Victoria table in rotation-molded polypropylene.
Bibliography http://www.moroso.it.

Morozzi, Massimo (1941–)
Italian architect and designer; born Florence; active Milan.

Training To 1966, in architecture, Florence.
Biography 1966 with Andrea Branzi, Gilberto Corretti, and Paolo Deganello, Morozzi cofounded and was active with Archizoom Associati to 1972, which produced industrial and architectural designs and town planning. He collaborated with Cassina on the production of Archizoom's 1973 AEO chair (credited to Deganello). 1972–77, coordinated the efforts of Montedison's Centro Design Montefibre for the promotion of furnishing and textile products. He has conducted research into color and interior decoration and introduced a new 'soft' approach to furniture design. 1976 with Branzi, Gianni Cutolo, Alessandro Mendini, Clino Trini Castelli, and Ettore Sottsass, he cofounded the consultancy Consulenti Design Milano (CDM), which handled large-scale projects including the corporate image and landscaping of Rome's Leonardo da Vinci airport, Louis Vuitton product lines, an information system for the Italian post office, a center for creative colorimetrics for the Colorterminal, the color system for Piaggo, and some of the activities of the Montefibre Design Center. 1982, Morozzi set up his own design practice, specializing in household products and industrial design for clients including Fiam Italia, Edra, Mazzei, Giorgetti, Ideal Standard, Cassina, Alessi, and Driade; worked in Japan (Nissan's concept car) and Australia; designed multi-colored, seven part 1983 Tangram table by Cassina; has lectured and held seminars in Europe and Asia; became art director of Edra and Mazzei and responsible for their graphic design; as design director (including a number of his own pieces of furniture) of Edra, has led the firm into international prominence.
Exhibitions/citations Work included in exhibitions at The Museum of Modern Art, New York, and Musée des Arts Décoratifs, Paris. 1979 (Fibermatching 25 with others for Centro Design Montefibre) and 1981 (Kanguro furniture by Metalcastelli) Premio Compasso d'Oro.

William Morris. Honeysuckle printed fabric. 1876. Cotton, 36 x 37" (91.5 x 94 cm). Mfr.: J.H. Thorp & Co., US (c. 1942). Gift of Edgar Kaufmann Jr. MoMA.

Massimo Morozzi. Cubista sofa. c. 1998. Polyurethane foam, configuration shown h. 28 3/8 x w 70 7/8 x d. 42 1/2" (72 x 180 x 108 cm). Mfr.: Edra, Italy.

Bibliography Andrea Branzi, *La casa calda: esperienze del nuovo disegno italiano*, Milan: Idea, 1982. Fumio Shimizu and Studio Matteo Thun (eds.), *The Italian Design: Descendants of Leonardo da Vinci*, Tokyo: Graphic-sha, 1987: 338. Albrecht Bangert and Karl Michael Armer, *80s Style: Designs of the Decade*, New York: Abbeville, 1990. *Modo*, no. 148, Mar.–Apr.1993: 123. Cristina Morozzi (texts) and Silvio San Pietro (ed.), *Massimo Morozzi*, Milan: L'Archivolto, 1993.

Morris, May (1862–1938)

British designer, needleworker, jeweler, and teacher; daughter of William Morris.

Biography Morris produced designs for fabrics, embroideries, and wallpaper for Morris and Co. Her work resembled that of her father. She also designed and made many pieces of jewelry, including string necklaces in various color combinations and textures. At age 12, she created the jewelry that her mother Jane wore in portraits by Dante Gabriel Rossetti, and the jewelry she herself wore in the Rossetti triple-portrait *Rosa Triplex* (1874). Her jewelry designs were based on floral and leaf forms and included cabochon semi-precious stones as well as glass such as unusual beads of Venetian glass. From 1886, she managed the embroidery shop at Merton Abbey, the site of her father's design company, and taught at Central School of Arts and Crafts in London. 1907, she was a founding member, Women's Guild of Arts and, subsequently, the chairperson; 1910, lectured in the US on embroidery, costume and pattern design, and jewelry; sold her jewelry at Fordham Gallery in Maddox Street and at Arts and Crafts Exhibition Society; wrote books *Decorative Needle Work* (London: J. Hughes, 1893) and *William Morris, Artist, Writer, Socialist* (Oxford: B. Blackwell, 1936); was the editor of her father's collected papers (London/New York: Longmans, Green, 1910–15).

Bibliography Charlotte Gere, *American and European Jewelry 1830–1914*, New York: Crown, 1975. Stuart Durant, *Ornament from the Industrial Revolution to Today*, Woodstock, N.Y.: Overlook, 1986: 219, 326. Toni Lesser Wolf, 'Women Jewelers of the British Arts and Crafts Movement,' *The Journal of Decorative and Propaganda Arts*, no. 14, Fall 1989: 32. Jan Marsh, *Jane and May Morris: A Biographical Story, 1839–1938*, London/New York: Pandora Press, 1986.

Morris, William (1834–1896)

British writer, poet, and designer; born Walthamstow, Essex; father of May Morris.

Training 1853–55, theology, Oxford University.

Biography While at Oxford, Morris met Edward Burne-Jones. They both read John Ruskin and Thomas Carlyle and planned careers in art and architecture. Morris joined the office of Gothic Revivalist architect George Edmund Street in Oxford, where he met and befriended Philip Webb, Street's senior assistant. Morris followed Street's move to London, where he shared a house with Burne-Jones from 1856. Morris began to design large, heavy furniture pieces, painting their surfaces with medieval figures and inscriptions; 1857, began to paint, guided by Dante Gabriel Rossetti. Morris and Rossetti worked together on 1857 frescoes of Oxford Union debating hall, to which Morris contributed scenes from 15th-century *Morte d'Arthur*. 1859, he married Jane Burden, later the model for Rossetti's idealized Pre-Raphaelite woman; wrote his first volume of poetry, *The Defence of Guinevere, and Other Poems* (London: Bell & Daldy, 1858). Webb designed Morris's 1859 Red House in Bexley Heath, a domestic architectural landmark. And Webb, Burne-Jones, and Morris collaborated on most of its furniture; Ford Madox Brown suggested they form a group to produce decorative works, and, 1861, Morris, Marshall, Faulkner and Co. was established with Burne-Jones, Webb, Rossetti, and Ford Madox Brown. Early commissions were mostly for stained-glass windows designed by Marshall, Burne-Jones, Webb, Brown, Rossetti, and Morris. Its tiles and pottery were painted by Faulkner's sisters Lucy and Kate, many to designs by William De Morgan. Morris learned embroidery and trained his wife, sister-in-law Elizabeth Burden, and Georgiana Burne-Jones, who ran the firm's embroidery workshop. 1862, Morris began designing wallpaper; *Daisy*, *Fruit*, and *Trellis* were printed in 1864, with wider production from 1870s, by which time they were also available in Boston. By mid-1860s, the firm had received major commissions, including 1867 refreshment room of South Kensington Museum (now Victoria and Albert Museum) and two rooms in St. James's Palace, both London. Late 1860s–early 1870s, Morris's renown as a poet grew, and, 1869, his translations of Icelandic sagas were published. By mid-1870s, the firm was in financial trouble. Morris paid off his partners and, 1875, launched Morris and Co.; 1877, began lecturing and weaving in Hammersmith; founded the Society for the Protection of Ancient Buildings; 1881, set up looms in Merton Abbey, near his friend De Morgan, an Arts and Crafts tilemaker; 1883, joined Democratic Federation, Britain's first Socialist political organization, and lectured on social and economic issues; 1890, set up Kelmscott Press where, 1891–98, beautiful handmade books were produced, one of the first being Ruskin's *The Nature of Gothic...* (Hammersmith: Kelmscott, 1892). It published 53 titles on handmade paper in limited editions, almost all designed by Morris himself in a style evoking medieval manuscripts and early printed books. Morris's socialism directly influenced Walter Crane and C.R. Ashbee. His championing of handicrafts and the decorative arts inspired guilds and groups throughout Britain, America, Germany, and Belgium. He passionately opposed industrialism, which he held responsible for material and spiritual ugliness, and his belief that beautiful and well-made objects ought to be available to the masses. His dogma contained a contra-

diction only partially resolved when his successors embraced mass production.
Exhibitions Two stall of Morris, Marshall and Faulkner at *International Exhibition of 1862*, London. Morris work in 1934 centenary exhibition, Victoria and Albert Museum, London (catalog below).
Bibliography May Morris (ed.), *The Collected Works of William Morris*, 24 vols, London: Longmans, Green, 1910–15; New York, Russell & Russell, 1966 (facsimile ed.). *Catalogue of an Exhibition in the Celebration of the Centenary of William Morris*, London: Victoria and Albert Museum, 1934. Philip Henderson, *William Morris: His Life, Work and Friends*, London: Penguin, 1967. Paul Thompson, *The Works of William Morris*, London: Quartet, 1977. David Latham and Sheila Latham, *An Annotated Critical Bibliography of William Morris*, London: Harvester Wheatsheaf; New York: St. Martins, 1991. Charles Havery and Jon Press, *William Morris: Design and Enterprise in Victorian Britain*, Manchester: Manchester University, 1991. Charles Havery and Jon Press, *Art, Enterprise, and Ethics: The Life and Works of William Morris*, London/Portland, Ore.: Frank Cass, 1996. Lucia van der Post, *William Morris and Morris & Co.*, London:Victoria and Albert Museum, 2003.

Morrison, Andrew Ivar (1939–)

American designer; born Washington state.

Training To 1963, Pratt Institute, Brooklyn, N.Y.
Biography Morrison taught at Pratt Institute, where he had met Bruce Hannah when they were students. 1967, they designed furniture, such as 1967 cast-aluminum and upholstered range and 1974 office-furniture range by Knoll, and 1960s furniture by Stendig, including a 1968 magazine rack.
Exhibitions/citations With Hannah, work was included in 1970 *Ventures in Design*, and, alone, at a venue at Design Zentrum, Stuttgart. Numerous citations.
Bibliography Cat., Hans Wichmann, *Industrial Design, Unikate und Serienerzeugnisse: Die Neue Sammlung. Ein neuer Museumstyp des 20. Jahrhunderts*, Munich: Prestel, 1985.

Morrison, Jasper (1959–)

British designer; born and active London.

Training 1979–82, bachelor of arts degree, Kingston Polytechnic (now Kingston University); 1982–85, master of design degree, Royal College of Art, London; 1984, on a scholarship, Hochschule der Künste, Berlin.
Biography 1986, Morrison established his own studio in London and designed ideosyncratic, satiric, understated furniture. He used his 1986 South Kensington flat as a launch pad to publicize his work; was a founding member, Narrative Architecture Today (NATO) group of architects, in London. His large body of work has included 1981 Handlebar table, 1983 Flower-Pot table, 1985 Wingnut chair, A Rug of Many Blossoms, and Rise table, 1986 dining chair and Thinking Man's Chair, 1987 One-Legged Table, chaise longue, and day bed, and 1988 Chair 3, all by Cappellini; 1984 Office System and Ribbed table, and 1987 Hat Stand by Aram Designs; 1982 stools and 1984 side table and Wingnut chair, 1986 console table, and 1988 sofa by SCP; 1988 3 Green Bottles that Could also Be Clear, plywood chair and three carpets, 1989 low plywood table and Panton Project by Vitra; 1988 plywood desk by Galerie Néotù; benches for 1989 Art Frankfurt fair; 1988 Door Handles I and II and 1989 range of aluminum handles by FSB. From 1992: with James Irvine, Morrison coordinated the Progetto Oggetto home-and-office-object collection by young designers produced by Cappellini; with Andreas Brandolini and Axel Kufus, organized Utilism International for the improvement of public spaces, provoking highly negative criticism by Hanoverian architects who claimed that a large amount of money was being spent with no recognizable results. Morrison was appointed consultant to the Üstra (Hanover transportation office), designing the 1995 bus stop and 1997 TW2000 tram for the city, in connection with the *Expo 2000*, Hanover. He has been active in Vienna, Graz, and Berlin urban planning; designed a chair for Couvent de la Tourette (Le Corbusier, architect), near Lyon, and 2001 furnishings for public spaces of the new Tate Modern museum, London; collaborated with potters in Vallauris, France. He edited *The International Design Yearbook* (1999).
Exhibitions/citations From 1968, work included in large number of exhibitions worldwide. Industrie Forum Design (iF) and Ecology Award (both for Hanover tram), Germany; Creator of the Year, 2000 Salon du Meuble, Paris; Creator of the Year, 2001 Maison & Objet, Villepinte, France. Created 2001 digital version of *World Without Words* at the

Jasper Morrison. Lima chair. 1995. Anodized aluminum and polypropylene plastic, 26 3/8 x 23 5/8 x 31 1/2" (67 x 60 x 80 cm). Mfr.: Cappellini, Italy. Gift of the mfr. MoMA.

Design Museum, London.
Bibliography *Contract*, July 1990: 26. Peter Dormer, *Jasper Morrison: Designs, Projects and Drawings, 1981–1989*, London: Architecture Design and Technology, 1990. Charles Arthur Boyer and Federica Zanco, *Jasper Morrison*, Paris: Dis Voir, 1999. *Jasper Morrison: A World Without Words*, Ennetbaden: Lars Müller, 1999. Jasper Morrison, *Everything but the Walls*, Ennetbaden: Lars Müller, 2001.

Morsing, Ann
> See Box Design.

Mortier, Michel (1925–)

French furniture designer.

Training 1940–44, École des Arts Appliqués, Duperré.
Biography 1945–46 with his former teacher Étienne-Henri Martin, Mortier worked in the interior-design department of Bon Marché department store, Brussels; 1949–53, was head of design at Marcel Gascoin's studio; subsequently, with Pierre Guariche and Joseph-André Motte, founded the group Atelier de Recherches Plastics (ARP); worked on sections of 1967 *Universal and International Exhibition (Expo '67)*, Montréal; 1967, set up his own agency to serve domestic and foreign clients, particularly in Canada; taught, Institut des Arts Appliqués, Montréal; returned to Paris and worked for Meubles et Fonctions International (MFI) on office and other furniture, and for Renz of Germany. He taught at École des Arts Appliqués, École Nationale Supérieure des Arts Décoratifs, and École Camondo, all Paris. His 1970s work included 1970 modular furniture by Renz, four 1973 restaurants at Aéroport Charles-de-Gaulle, and 1976 MP2 furniture by Meubles et Fonctions.
Exhibitions 1963 René Gabriel Prize. Work included in venues from editions of Salon des Arts Ménagers, Paris, to Triennali di Milano (numerous prizes).
Bibliography Yolande Amic, *Intérieurs: le mobilier français 1945–1964*, Paris: Regard/VIA, 1983. Patrick Favardin, *Les décorateurs des années 50*, Paris: Norma, 2002: 230.

Morton, Alistair J.F. (1910–1963)

British textile manufacturer and painter.

Training Edinburgh University, and Oxford University.
Biography 1931, Morton joined his family firm Morton Sundour Fabrics and supervised its first screen-printed fabrics. From 1932, he was the artistic director and the principal designer of Edinburgh Weavers in Carlisle (established in 1928 as Morton Sundour's creative design unit). He had been a follower of the modern movement from 1930s and commissioned designs from notable painters and designers. 1937, he conceived the Constructivist Fabrics range with designs

by Barbara Hepworth and Ben Nicholson. His 1937–38 Brackenfell house in Brampton was designed by J. Leslie Martin and Sadie Speight. Morton, a painter and textile designer himself, designed dress prints for Horrockses and Edinburgh Fabrics, including 1946 Unit Prints series. He studied hand spinning and weaving under Ethel Mairet in her Ditchling workshop; 1962, became the chief executive director of Morton Sundour; was a frequent lecturer, a member of Council of Industrial Design, and an assessor for the four central art schools in Scotland.
Bibliography *The Mortons: Three Generations of Textile Creations*, London: Victoria and Albert Museum, 1973. Cat., *Thirties: British Art and Design Before the War*, London: Arts Council of Great Britain Hayward Gallery, 1979. Fiona MacCarthy and Patrick Nuttgens, *An Eye for Industry*, London: Lund Humphries, 1986.

Morton, Alexander (1844–1923)
British textile manufacturer through his firm Alexander Morton & Co.; located Darvel and Carlisle.

Biography At first, Alexander Morton sold muslin made by local weavers in their homes. He began producing madras and, 1881, established a factory to weave chenilles, woollens, and three-ply carpeting; from 1890s, produced the double cloths for which the firm became known. 1896, he visited Ireland and adversely reacted to the poverty and unemployment there and, thus, opened a number of factories in Donegal that made what became highly fashionable hand-knotted carpets. Late 19th–early 20th centuries, the firm commissioned designs from leading Arts and Crafts people, including Frank Brangwyn, Lindsay Philip Butterfield, Lewis F. Day, Henry Napper, Baillie Scott, Silver Studio, and C.F.A. Voysey; supplied most high-end British shops such as Liberty's and Wylie & Lochhead. From 1900, the factory was located in Carlisle with madras and lace production remaining at Darvel. 1914, almost all of Alexander Morton & Co.'s production, except for carpets and lace, was taken over by Morton Sundour under James Morton's direction. From 1912, it had its own hand-block printing unit. Printed fabrics were transferred to Morton Sundour, and roller-printing began in 1921 and screen printing in 1931.
Bibliography Valerie Mendes, *The Victoria & Albert Museum's Textile Collection, British Textiles from 1900 to 1937* London: Victoria and Albert Museum, 1992.
> See Morton Sundour Fabrics (below).

Morton Sundour Fabrics
British textile firm.

History 1914, the firm was founded, with James Morton (1867–1943) as governing director; took over almost all of Alexander Morton & Co.'s textile production, except for lace and carpets; produced Sundour non-fading fabrics; from 1914, also produced synthetic vat dyestuffs and well-designed goods at reasonable cost.
Bibliography Valerie Mendes, *The Victoria & Albert Museum's Textile Collection British Textiles from 1900 to 1937*, London: Victoria and Albert Museum, 1992.

Moser, Koloman (1868–1918)
Austrian painter, designer, metalworker, and graphic artist; born Vienna.

Training 1889–92, painting, Akademie der bildenden Künste, Vienna; 1892–95, graphic design, Kunstgewerbeschule, Vienna.
Biography From 1892, Moser designed for fashion magazine *Wiener Mode* and, 1895, with publisher Martin Gerlach and other Viennese artists, produced the *Allegories* set of folio volumes. At this time, he met Gustav Klimt. 1895, Moser and a group of progressive artists (including Josef Hoffmann and Joseph Maria Olbrich) formed the Siebener Club (an early association of what-was-to-become Sezession exponents). 1897, the Sezession was formally introduced in Vienna as an autonomous group of artists; it followed the example of the Münchner Sezession (founded 1982) and the Berliner Sezession (founded 1893). (1905, Moser, with the Klimt group, left the Sezession.) Moser organized and designed Sezession exhibitions; 1898, was involved with the launch of Sezession journal *Ver Sacrum*, and contributed numerous illustrations to its first issue. His decorative style in graphics at this time showed naturalistic ornamentation on a square grid. From 1901, he developed his characteristic checker pattern, based on Assyrian and Egyptian art and derived from abstract floral patterns rather than black-and-white-square geometry. In his transitional period, naturalistic and abstract motifs of the Sezession style lingered alongside geometrical patterns. 1899, he became professor of painting, Kunstgewerbeschule of Österreichisches Museum für Kunst und Industrie, Vienna, and, 1900, its director, coming in contact with Josef Hoffmann. Teaching students to work in a Sezession style, he designed graphics, glass, leather, book covers, metalwork, stained-glass windows, stage sets, ceramics, and toys; as a graphic artist, designed banknotes, postage stamps, posters, and typography. 1903, Moser, Hoffmann, and financial backer Fritz Wärndorfer founded the Wiener Werkstätte, which was the Austrian equivalent of the Deutscher Werkbund. Moser was editor of Werkstätte magazine *Hohe Warte*. He also designed silver hollow-ware for Wiener Werkstätte and furniture, primarily made by commercial firms, including Caspar Hrazdil and Portois und Fix. His boxes were produced by Georg Adam Scheid and jewelry by Rozet und Fischmeister of Vienna. His work illustrates the spread of the Mackintosh style in Germany in c. 1910. He left the Werkstätte in 1907. Yet his Werkstätte designs continued to be produced for some years, even though he executed no silver designs after 1907. Moser's theater-design work began with sets (using drapes in place of convential décor) for Felix Salten's youth theater (Jung-Wiener Theater zum lieben Augustin, founded in 1901, and purportedly the first Viennese cabaret). 1907, Moser returned to painting but continued with theater design. Today, Woka of Vienna is reproducing a number of Moser's lamps.
Exhibitions 1900 (8th) Wiener Sezession exhibition (his glass for the Sezession). Work as an artist first shown at a 1911 exhibition, Miethke Gallery, Vienna. Work by Moser, Klimt, and others in a 1920 exhibition organized by Hoffmann and others. Moser's work subject of 1920 and 1971 retrospectives, Vienna, organized by art publisher Wolfrum; 1979, Hochschule für angewandte Kunst, Vienna; 1981, Galerie Metropole, New York; 1989, Musée d'Orsay, Paris (catalog below).
Bibliography Peter Vergo, *Art in Vienna 1898–1918*, London: Phaidon, 1975. Werner Fenz, Kolo Moser: *Internat. Jugendstil und Wiener Secession*, Salzburg: Residenz, 1976. Cat., *Koloman Moser*, Vienna: Hochschule für angewandte Kunst, 1979. Dorothee Müller, *Klassiker des modernen Möbeldesign: Otto Wagner—Adolf Loos—Josef Hoffmann—Koloman Moser*, Munich: Keyser, 1980. Daniele Baroni and Antonio D'Auria, Daniele, *Kolo Moser, grafico e designer*, Milan: Mazzotta, 1984. Werner Fenz, *Kolomon Moser: Graphik, Kunstgewerbe, Malerei*, Salzburg: Residenz, 1984. Cat., Marc Bascou, *Koloman Moser: un createur d'avant-garde à Vienne*, Paris: Musée d'Orsay, 1989. Christian Brandstätter (ed.), *Koloman Moser: Leben und Werk 1868–1918*, Vienna: C. Brandstätter, 2002.

Moser, Werner Max (1896–1970)
German architect, furniture designer, and writer; born Karlsruhe; son of Karl Moser.

Training 1916–21 under his father, Eidgenössische Technische Hochschule, Zürich.
Biography 1921–23, Moser worked in the office of M.H. Grandpré-Molière in the Netherlands and, 1923–26, in various architecture offices in the US, including that of Frank Lloyd Wright. 1927, Moser became a member of the Swiss group, which designed furniture for several

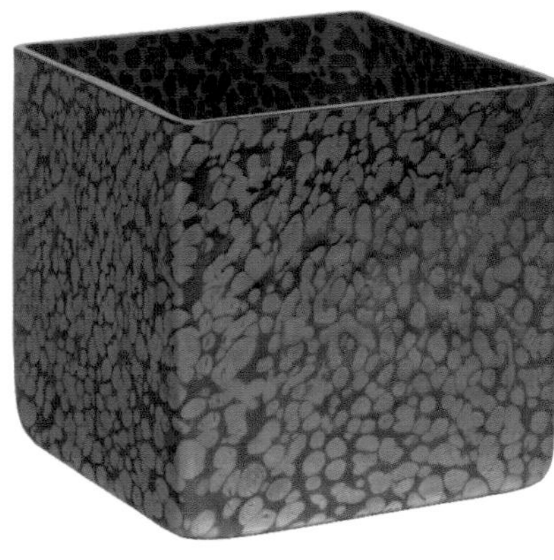

Koloman Moser. Vase. 1902. Glass, 6 x 6 x 6" (15.2 x 15.2 x 15.2 cm). Mfr.: Glasfabrik Johann Loetz Witwe, Austria. Estée and Joseph Lauder Design Fund. MoMA.

spaces in Mies van der Rohe's apartments at the *Weissenhofsiedlung* exhibition in Stuttgart. With Mart Stam and Ferdinand Kramer, Moser designed 1929–30 Budget Home in Frankfurt. 1928, he cofounded Congrès International d'Architecture Moderne (CIAM) and was the Swiss delegate to its 1931 congress. 1931 with Sigfried Giedion and Rudolf Graber, Moser co founded the Wohnbedarf furnishings store in Zürich, and, 1932, he applied for patents for furniture models known as *Wohnbedarf-Typen* (proprietary standardized furniture). With future partners Max Ernst Haefeli and Rudolf Steiger, and others, Moser designed the building and interiors of 1931–33 Neubühl settlement near Zürich; became a specialist in school and church architecture; wrote the book and organized 1933 exhibition *Das Kind und sein Schulhaus* (the child and his schoolhouse), which influenced the design of subsequent school buildings. 1938–41, he designed a church in Zürich-Altstetten, finding a sensitive solution to modern building in an historical context; 1937, formed architecture partnership Haefeli Moser Steiger; 1955, was a guest professor, Harvard University, Cambridge, Mass., US; 1958, was chairperson, Eidgenössische Technische Hochschule, Zürich, where he taught to 1963.
Exhibitions/citations Furnished the Working Apartment for a Journalist Couple included in the opening exhibition at the Neubühl. Competition project for the Kongresshaus in Zürich. The apartment design was a successful entry at 1939 *Schweizer Landesausstellung* (Swiss national exposition), Zürich. Granted 1958 honorary doctorate, Universität Stuttgart.
Bibliography Friederike Mehlau-Wiebking et al., *Schweizer Typenmöbel 1925–35, Sigfried Giedion und die Wohnbedarf AG*, Zürich: gta, 1989: 229–30.

Mott, Joseph H.

British ceramicist.

Biography Mott was a highly accomplished ceramicist and pioneer. 1880, he began working at Doulton in Lambeth, South London, where he was artistic director from 1897–1935; was an authority on ceramic glazes, colors, and bodies and worked on laboratory porcelains from c. 1914–19. Subsequently, 1920s to 1935, he worked on the development of glazes—including *flambé*, matt, semi-matt, luster, and crystalline—and designed shapes. 1935–50, Mott was retained as a counsellor in ceramics.
Bibliography Cat., *Thirties: British Art and Design Before the War*, London: Arts Council of Great Britain Hayward Gallery, 1979: 154, 297.

Motte, Joseph-André (1926–)

French furniture designer and painter.

Training In painting and sculpture; to 1948, École des Arts Appliqués, Paris.
Biography Motte worked for Au Bon Marché department store, Paris, with Albert Guenot; 1948 with Pierre Guariche and Michel Mortier, set up the design office Atelier de Recherches Plastiques (ARP), becoming an independent designer in 1951. 1954 and 1958–61, he worked on interior design for Administration de Grands Travaux and designed the chapel, transit hall, and bar at Orly airport. He also participated in the renovation of the grand gallery of the Louvre museum, Paris; was commissioned by Le Mobilier National to design office furniture for use in prefecture buildings; furnished the offices of a number of firms; designed furniture for serial production. His best-known designs include 1950 Tripode chair in steel, beechwood, and rattan by Rousier; late-1950s chairs by Steiner; and stainless-steel chairs by Moebius, which inspired several 1963 prototypes in stainless steel by Ugine Gueugnon. He designed a number of wooden tables with bentwood bases; received commissions from RATP (Paris public-transit system) and collaborated on the design of sea and river ports (Le Havre in 1962, Strasbourg and Dunkerque in 1965, Marseille in 1968–69) and airports (Roissy-Charles de Gaulle in 1969 and 1976 and Lyon Satolas in 1974). At Le Havre, he designed the maritime train station and central administration headquarters. In pedagogy, Motte was in charge of a workshop at École Nationale Supérieure des Arts Déco-ratifs, Paris.
Citations 1970 Premio Compasso d'Oro (for Graphis chair with Borsani and Gerli by Tecno).
Bibliography Yolande Amic, *Intérieurs: le mobilier français 1945–1964*, Regard/VIA, 1983: 92. Cat., Sophie Tasma Anargyros et al., *L'école française: les créateurs de meubles du 20ème siècle*, Paris: Industries Françaises de l'Ameublement, 2000. Patrick Favardin, *Les décorateurs des années 50*, Paris: Norma, 2002: 240. Arlette Barré-Despond (ed.), *Dictionnaire international des arts appliqués et du design*, Paris: Regard, 1996

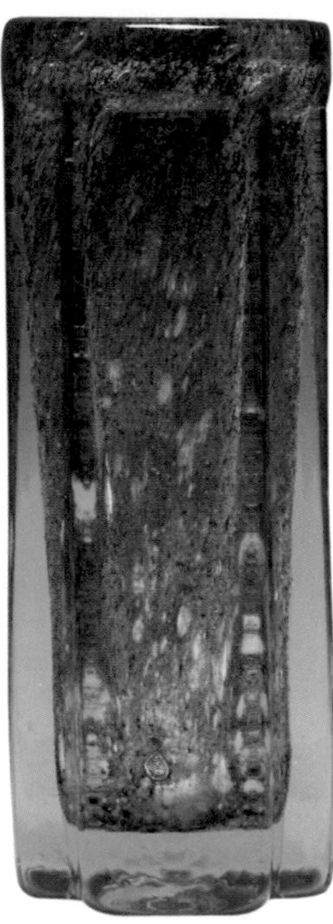

Benny Motzfeldt. Vase. c. 1970. Glass, h. 6 9/16" (16.6 cm). Mfr.: Randsfjord Glassverk, Norway. Courtesy Quittenbaum Kunstauktionen, Munich.

Motzfeldt, Benny (1909–1995)

Norwegian glassware designer; born North-Trøndelag; active Fredrikstad.

Training Graphic design, Statens Håndverks -og Kunstindustriskole, Oslo.
Biography She rendered decorations for sandblasting and engraving on crystal and glass windows. She became more interested in glass production and began working directly with glass blowers; together they experimented by adding metal dust, wire netting, and different colors. From 1955, she worked at Christiana Glasmagasin; from 1955–67, was a member of the design team at Hadelands Glassverk and, 1967–70, head of design at Randsfjords Glassverk. From 1970, she was director of Plus Centre in Fredrikstad, a small glass studio for serial production.
Exhibitions/citations Work shown at 1971 exhibition, Det Danske Kunstindustrimuseum, Copenhagen; 1979–81 Smithsonian Institution exhibition, touring the US. Work subject of 1977 exhibition, Germany. 1969 Jacob-prize.
Bibliography Cat., David Revere McFadden (ed.), *Scandinavian Modern Design 1880–1980*, New York: Abrams, 1982: 268–69, no. 288. Cat., Anne Wichstrøm, *Rooms with a View: Women's Art in Norway 1880–1990*, Oslo: The Royal Ministry of Foreign Affairs, 1990: 34. Jennifer Hawkins Opie, *Scandinavia: Ceramics and Glass in the Twentieth Century*, New York: Rizzoli, 1989.

Mougin, Joseph (1876–1961); Pierre Mougin (1880–1955)

French ceramicists; brothers; born Nancy.

Training Joseph Mougin: École des Beaux-Arts, Nancy; and under sculptor Pierron; 1896–98, under Louis-Ernest Barrias, sculpture, École National Supérieure des Beaux-Arts, Paris.
Biographies Joseph Mougin decided to become a ceramicist after seeing an 1894 exhibition of Jean Carriès's pottery; 1898 after studies at the Beaux-Arts school, was joined in Paris by his brother Pierre, and they set up a studio and kiln in Montrouge with the help of sculptor/friend Lemarquier. After two years, Lemarquier left, because the kiln was poorly constructed and would not fire properly. The Mouguin brothers worked briefly at the Manufacture Nationale de Sèvres. They

returned to Paris and set up a new kiln in Vaugirard which also had problems, but, nevertheless, they produced some innovative ceramics. Encouraged by fellow Nancy artist Victor Prouvé, they showed their work at various Paris salons, gaining favorable notices and sales to museums, collectors, and the French government. 1906, the brothers moved their operation to Nancy and became members of Émile Gallé's artists' group École de Nancy and collaborated with Prouvé, Alfred Finot, Ernest Wittmann, and Ernest Bussière on pieces in an Art Nouveau style. After World War I, the brothers made volume-production art pottery at Faïencerie de Lunéville. 1936–60, Joseph continued to produce new forms and glazes with his daughter Odile and son François. He died in Nancy, and Pierre in Gerbéviller.
Exhibitions/citations Work with Prouvé, Finot, and Bussière shown in Paris and, up to 1914, included in exhibitions of the École de Nancy. Grand prize for ceramics, 1925 *Exposition Internationale des Arts Décoratifs et Industriels Modernes*, Paris.
Bibliography Yvonne Brunhammer et al., *Art Nouveau Belgium, France*, Houston: Institute for the Arts, Rice University, 1976.

Mouille, Serge (1922–1988)
French lighting designer; born and active Paris.

Training To 1941, silversmithing, École des Arts Appliqués, Paris.
Biography 1937, Mouille worked in studio of silversmith/sculptor Gilbert Lacroix; 1945, set up a studio while teaching at École des Arts Appliqués, Paris; 1953, was commissioned by Jacques Adnet, director of Compagnie des Arts Français (CAF) to design what became Mouille's first lighting fixtures; from 1955, was a member, Société des Artistes Décorateurs and Société Nationale des Beaux-Arts; 1950s, became known for his spindly black lighting fixtures (even better known today) such as 1953 Œil, 1954 Flammes, and 1958 Saturn. A very thin floor-lamp model of c. 1950 with two diffusers was re-entered into production in 2001. From 1950s, his lamps were solidly architectonic. He designed lighting for Université d'Antony, schools in Strasbourg and Marseille, and Cathédrale de Bizerte; 1961, established Société de Création de Modèles (SCM) to encourage young lighting designers. Highly productive during 1950–64, he afterward turned to teaching, sculpting, and drawing.
Exhibitions/citations From 1956, work shown at the Steph Simon gallery, Paris. Colonnes lamps shown at 1962 Salon des Arts Ménagers et Batimat; lighting and jewelry at *Formes Françaises*, Stockholm; sculpture and metalwork for the silversmith Saglier at the Grand Palais, Paris. Diploma of honor, 1958 *Exposition Universelle et Internationale de Bruxelles* (*Expo '58*); 1963 gold medal, Société d'Encouragement à l'Art et à l'Industrie; medal of the City of Paris from directors of Métiers d'Art; 1955 Charles Plumet prize. Work subject of 1983 exhibition, Galerie 1950, Paris.
Bibliography Cat., *Serge Mouille, luminaires, 1953–1963*, Paris: Galerie 1950, 1983. Anthony Delorenzo, *Two Master Metalworkers*, New York: Delorenzo, 1983. Thierry de Beaumont, 'Serge Mouille,' *L'atelier*, no. 115, Feb. 1987. Jean-François Archieri, 'Serge Mouille: des lignes de lumière,' *Techniques et architecture*, no. 383, Apr.–May 1989. Cat., *Serge Mouille, luminaires*, Paris: Le Regard d'Alan, 1992. Mel Byars with Arlette Barré-Despond, *100 Designs/100 Years: A Celebration of the 20th Century*, Hove: RotoVision: 118–19. Cat., Sophie Tasma Anargyros et al., *L'école française: les créateurs de meubles du 20ème siècle*, Paris: Industries Françaises de l'Ameublement, 2000.

Moulinex
French home-appliances manufacturer.

History 1937, Jean Mantelet (1900–1991) established a spinning mill for hemp and Alençon textiles in Ozé, then in Germany; 1931, returned from Germany with a potato-mashing device that he had found to be interesting but ultimately ineffective. He improved on it, resulting in the 1932 *press-purée* (or *moulin à légumes*) for turning vegetables into a puree and, the same year, established a firm based on this first invention. 1956, he went on to invent the first electric coffee mill. 1957, the firm was renamed Moulinex (based on French word *moulin*, or 'mill'), which, from 1958 located in Argentan, made hair dryers and coffee mills. Subsequently, factories were established in a number of other towns. 1969, the firm became a publicly held. Early on Mantelet declared, 'In my job, it is necessary to aim at the customers. Mine, they are the women.' However and ironically, he became out of step with the customers and their product needs, and, 1974, the first signs of a crisis appeared toward the company's ultimate degradation. Even so, 1977, the firm opened a factory in the US and, 1978, in Mexico but, subsequently, dismissed 1,500 employees worldwide who were not replaced; 1980, was employing about 11,000 workers in 12 factories; 1984, bought English kettle-and-pan maker Swan; 1986, decreased employment to 8,500 workers; 1989, opened factories in England and Italy; on Mantelet's 1991 death, appointed Roland Darneau the director (replaced by Jules Coulon in 1994, by Pierre Blayau in 1996, and finally by Patrick Puy in 2000) and repurchased German firm Krups; 1996, began to close some factories; 2000, was amalgamated with Brandt; 2001, announced bankruptcy and was taken over by SEB.
Bibliography Cat., Eva Afuhs et al., *3 Installationen, Wiener Secession: Moulinex* (aka *Drei Installationen: Moulinex*), Vienna: Wiener Secession, 1992. Quim Monzo, *Olivetti, Moulinex, Chaffoteaux et Maury*, Barcelona: Quaderns Crema, 1993. www.france-ouest.com/moulinex

Moulthrop, Edward (1916–)
American architect and woodworker; born Rochester, N.Y.

Training 1939, architecture degree, Case-Western Reserve University, Cleveland, Ohio; 1941, master's degree in architecture, Princeton University, N.J.; self-taught woodworker.
Biography 1944, Moulthrop settled in Atlanta, Ga., taught architecture, Georgia Institute of Technology; 1953, opened an architecture practice and, 1972, resigned from an architecture firm; from early 1960s, was active working wooden bowls on a lathe. He typically pares a 1,600 lb. (726 kg) log down into an 80-lb. (36 kg) bowl. He has said, 'Only one tree in a thousand is interesting enough for me.'
Exhibitions/citations Work included in 1978 *The Art of the Turned Bowl*, Renwick Gallery, Washington, D.C.; many others. First award, 1962 Atlanta Arts Festival; numerous citations subsequently. 1987, elected Fellow of American Craft Council.

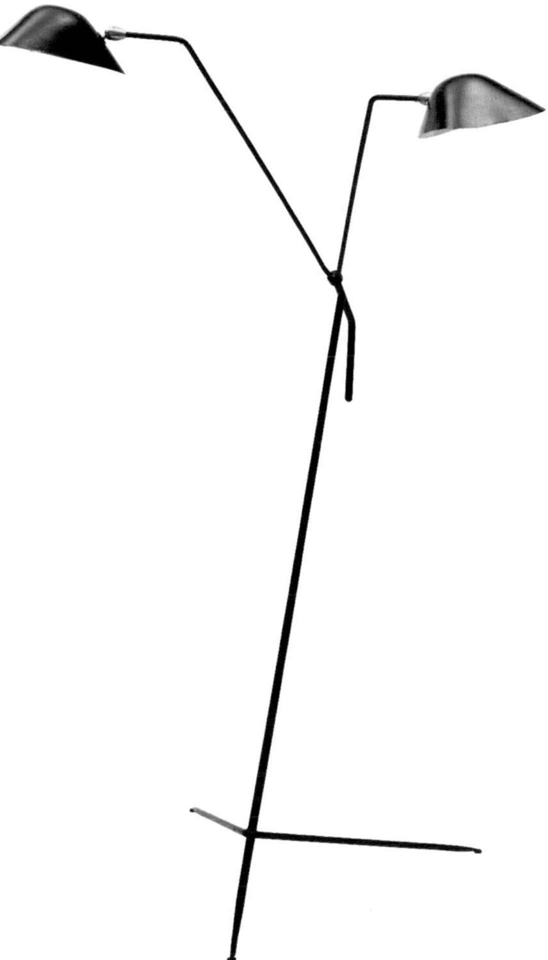

Serge Mouille. Floor lamp. 1953. Painted brass and steel, 64 3/16 x 37 x 37 3/16" (163 x 94 x 96 cm). Mfr: L'Atelier de Serge Mouille, France. Patricia Phelps de Cisneros Purchase Fund. MoMA.

Edward Moulthrop. Bowl. 1984. Rare ash-leaf maple, h. 8 1/8" (20.6 cm) x dia. 12 15/16" (32.9 cm). Mfr.: the designer, US. National Endowment for the Arts Purchase Fund and Cook and Shanosky Associates, Inc. MoMA.

Bibliography Catherine Fox, 'Edward Moulthrop,' *The Atlanta Journal*, 6 May 1984.

Mount Washington Glass

American glassware manufacturer; located South Boston and New Bedford, Mass.

History The founder of Boston and Sandwich Glass and businessman, Deming Jarves (1790–1869) set up a factory in South Boston, Mass. His son George Jarves was the comanager there, with John D. Labree at first and with Henry Comerais subsequently. Jarves and Comerais, known as the Mount Washington Glass Works, was active to 1861, when its bookkeeper William L. Libbey and clerk Timothy Howe became directors of the firm. Libbey became the sole director when Howe died. During this time, the firm produced kerosene lamps and blown, pressed, and cut glassware. 1869, Libbey moved the factory from South Boston to premises of the failed New Bedford Glass in New Bedford, Mass., installing new equipment; 1870s–80s, W.L. Libbey and Co. began to experiment with art glass. 1871, the Smith brothers were in charge of the decoration department. 1872, Libbey left and became an agent for New England Glass. His brother Henry Libbey managed the firm, which closed in 1873. Re-opened in 1874 under the management of English émigré Frederick Stacey Shirley and was named Mount Washington Glass. From 1884, it produced rose-amber glassware that was Shirley's imitation of the Amberina ware invented in 1883 by Joseph Locke at New England Glass. 1885, its Burmese glass was patented and made in more than 250 forms. 1886, Thomas Webb was given a license to produce Queens Burmese. (Queens Burmese ware, an opaque and single layered glass, was one of the most popular types of glass and commercially successful.) From 1889, the firm produced luxurious gilded and enameled opal wares, as well as brilliant-cut and engraved crystal and acid-etched cameo glass; 1880, Pairpoint Manufacturing Co. opened an adjacent factory, and Mount Washington Glass began to use silver-plated mounts. Mount Washington Glass, during Shirley's tenure 1874–94, produced a wide range of very high-quality glassware. By 1890, the factory was dubbed 'headquarters of art glassware in America.' 1894, the enterprise was brought by Pairpoint. 1895, Shirley and his partner John P. Gregory reopened Boston and Sandwich Glass, which failed the next year.

Exhibitions Awards, 1876 Centennial Exposition (cut-glass chandeliers and opal glass), Philadelphia; 1986–87 *In Pursuit of Beauty*, The Metropolitan Museum of Art, New York (catalog below).

Bibliography George S. McKearin and Helen McKearin, *American Glass*, New York: Crown, 1941. Kenneth M. Wilson, *New England Glass and Glassmaking*, New York: Crowell, 1972. Leonard E. Padgett, *Pairpoint Glass*, Des Moines, Iowa: Wallace-Homestead, 1979. Doreen Bolger Burke et al., *In Pursuit of Beauty: Americans and the Aesthetic Movement*, New York: The Metropolitan Museum of Art/Rizzoli, 1986: 457–58.

> See Pairpoint.

Mourgue, Olivier (1939–)

French designer; born Paris; active Brittany; brother of Pascal Mourgue.

Training 1946–54, interior design, École Boulle, Paris; 1954–58, interior architecture; 1958–60, École Nationale Supérieure des Arts Décoratifs, Paris.

Biography 1960, Olivier Mourgue opened an office in Paris and was a consultant to Airborne, Prisunic, Le Mobilier National, Disderot, Air France, and Renault; designed furniture, textiles, environments, and toys. His furniture covered with stretched Latex fabric on steel and foam, including 1965 Djinn chaise longue and other seating produced by Airborne, was noticeable in his interiors for the film *2001: A Space Odyssey* (director, Stanley Kubrick, 1968). Other Airborne furniture models included Tric-Trac and Whist. His 1969 carpet-covered low seating was widely published. He designed 1969 furniture and seating range for Prisunic five-and-dime store and the interiors of the *Boeing 747* for Air France. He designed a futuristic environment at 1972 *Visiona 3* (sponsored by Bayer at the Möbelmesse in Cologne), with adjunct installations by Verner Panton and Joe Colombo. He developed a wheeled design studio in 1970, an open-plan domestic environment, a soft-surface bathroom suite for himself in 1970, and studies commissioned by Renault on automobile interior volume and color in 1977. Concerned with space and mobility, Mourgue's supple, undulating forms typified French design to the world in 1960s. 1976, Mourgue moved to Brittany, where he has taught, École des Beaux-Arts, Brest.

Exhibitions/citations Djinn chaise longue first shown at 1965 Salon du Meuble, Paris. Chairs were installed in reception area of French pavilion, 1967 *Universal and International Exhibition (Expo '67)*, Montreal; 1968 Bouloum lounge chair in the French pavilion, 1970 *Universal and International Japanese Exposition (Expo '70)*, Osaka. Work subject of a 1976 exhibition, Musée des Arts Décoratifs, Nantes (catalog below). Award (for his Mobile Studio), 1968 (2nd) Eurodomus, Turin; 1968 award (for Djinn chaise longue), American Institute of

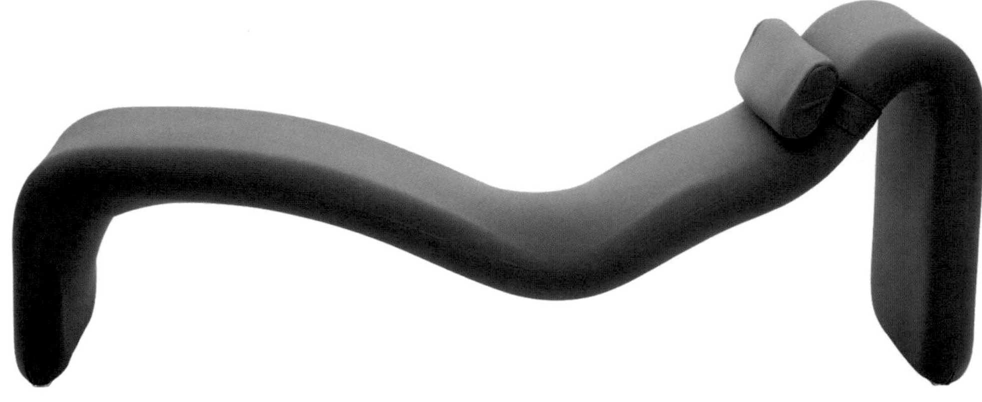

Olivier Mourgue. Djinn chaise longue. 1964–65. Tubular steel frame, foam padding, and nylon-jersey upholstery, h. 25 1/2 x l. 66" (64.8 x 167.6 cm). Mfr.: Airborne, France. Gift of George Tanier, Inc. MoMA.

Gabriele Mucchi. Genni lounge chaise longue and ottoman. 1935. Chromium-plated steel tubing, springs, foam rubber, and leather, chair 30 x 22 13/16 x 46 1/2" (76 x 58 x 118 cm), ottoman 14 x 21 1/4 x 17 1/2" (35.5 x 54 x 44.5 cm). Mfr.: Zanotta, Italy (1980s). Courtesy Quittenbaum Kunstauktionen, Munich.

Decorators (AID), Chicago; 1969 gold medal, Société d'Encouragement à l'Art et à l'Industrie; 1981 Carte Blanche production support, VIA (French furniture association); 1991 Grand Prix National de la Création Industrielle.

Bibliography Cat., *Les assises du siège contemporain*, Paris: Musée des Arts Décoratifs, 1968. Cat., *Modern Chairs 1918–1970*, London: Lund Humphries, 1971. Cat., *Design français*, Paris: CCI, 1971: no. 138. 'Visiona 3,' *Industrial Design*, vol. 19, May 1972: 42–45. J. Roger Guilfoyle, 'An Atelier for Living,' *Industrial Design*, vol. 20, Oct. 1973: 28–32. Cat., *Olivier Mourgue*, Nantes: Musée des Arts décoratifs, 1976. Cat., Kathryn B. Hiesinger and George H. Marcus III (eds.), *Design Since 1945*, Philadelphia: Philadelphia Museum of Art, 1983. Cat., *Mobilier National: 20 ans de création*, Paris: CNACGP/CCI/CNAP, 1984. *Acquisitions arts décoratifs 1982–1990*, Paris: Fonds National d'Art Contemporain, 1991. François Mathey, *Au bonheur des formes, design français 1945–1992*, Paris: Regard, 1992: 257, 264, 338.

Mourgue, Pascal (1943–)

French designer and artist; born Neuilly; active Paris; brother of Olivier Mourgue.

Training 1957 at age 14 1/2, École Boulle; subsequently, École Nationale Supérieure des Arts Décoratifs, both Paris.

Biography 1960, Mourgue began as an interior designer; from 1968, designed furniture for Vinco, Le Mobilier National, and Knoll; from 1982, created furniture, furnishing, textile, and product designs for a number of others, including 1985 Lune l'Argent chair and stool (possibly his best-known work), 1988 Ikmisou and 2000 Jour de Fête chair by Fermob; mopeds by Motobécane, and Yob trimaran (Patrice Hardy) by Kental International. His first (1994) furniture collection was produced by Cinna (a Ligne Roset division), followed by 1995 Mourgue bed, 1997 In Fine upholstered furniture, 2000 Smala modular sofa and armchair, 2000 Easy Light adjustable lamps, Ligne Câlin lounge and side chairs. By Artelano: 1971 Rio chair (for large room in Carrousel du Louvre, Paris), 1986 glass and metal three-legged café table, 1987 Atlantique furniture collection, 1993 Ligne Lolita armchair, 1995 Ligne Tempo stacking chair and 2000 Imagine convertible sofa. Other design work: carpets by Toulemonde Bochart; a sofa by Guermonprez. His furniture designs by Fermob and Ligne Roset have been extensive; the Ligne Roset examples included the Câlin chair, Dolce Vita sofa range, Pascal Mourgue tables, Roller trolleys, and 2000 Smala collection. 1988, he established the Galerie Différences near the Musée Picasso in Paris to show his fine art. Other work has included glass sculpture sponsored by Centre International de Recherche sur le Verre et les Arts Plastiques (CIRVA), Marseille. He works in a studio with longtime friend and collaborator Patrice Hardy in Montreuil.

Exhibitions/citations Glass work subject of 1989 exhibition, Galerie Scremini, Paris. 1983 first prize (Arc lounge-armchair) at the exhibition of VIA at Bloomingdale's department store, New York; 1983 Appel Permanent grant and 1984 Carte Blanche production support (Arte chaise longue), VIA (French furniture association; Creator of the Year, 1984 Salon du Meuble, Paris; grand prize, 1986 Critique du Meuble Contemporain; 1992 Grand Prix de la Création de la Ville de Paris; 1996 Grand Prix National de la Création Industrielle, Ministère de la Culture, France; winner, competition for contemporary art (Lune l'Argent chair), Fondation Cartier; 2001 (for Smala collection) and 2004 (for Lover divan seating range), Industrie Forum Design (iF), Hanover. Work included in a number of exhibitions, Paris, London, and New York.

Bibliography Cat. Margo Rouard Snowman, *The Most Contemporary French Furniture*, London: Victoria and Albert Museum, 1988. Cat. *Les années VIA*, Paris; Musée des Arts Décoratifs, 1990. Albrecht Bangert and Karl Michael Armer, *80s Style: Designs of the Decade*, New York: Abbeville, 1990. François Mathey, *Au bonheur des formes, design français 1945–1992*, Paris: Regard, 1992. Yvonne Brunhammer and Marie-Laure Perrin, *Le mobilier français 1960–1998*, Paris: Massin, 1998. Cat., Sophie Tasma Anargyros et al., *L'école française: les créateurs de meubles du 20ème siècle*, Paris: Industries Françaises de l'Ameublement, 2000.

Mouveau, Georges

> See D.I.M.

Mucchi, Gabriele (1899–2002)

Italian writer, painter, designer, architect, and engineer; born Turin; active Milan.

Training In Turin, Rome, Catania, Correggio, and Bologna; studied civil engineering.

Biography 1927–34, Mucchi was a painter in Milan, Berlin, and Paris; was identified with the avant-garde movements—from the Corrente group, which he cofounded to the Rationalist movement, in whose idiom he executed some metal furniture designs, including the 1934–36 Genni armchair/ottoman and Ambo table in bent metal tubing and wicker produced by Crespi in Emilio Pino (reissued by Zanotta from 1982). 1934, he settled in a house in Milan that became the meeting point for anti-fascists and artists of the Corrente group. Concurrently he played a creative and functional role in the Rationalist architecture of Milan and its proponents, including Pagano, Rogers, Albini, Belgiojoso, Gardella, and Zanuso. He worked with Bottoni, Lingeri, and Terragni on competitions and commissions. He designed a 1934 house on the via Marcora, one of Milan's earliest examples of Rationalist architecture. Mucchi was a member of Congrès Internationaux d'Architecture Moderne (CIAM) and of Movimento Studi Architettura (MSA); worked with Bottoni and others on the OT8 experimental district,

where he built a prefabricated house erected in 1947; the same year, drew up Milan's master plan and previously proposed the AR Plan, with Albini, Bottoni, Belgiojoso, Peressutti, Putelli, and Rogers. Other structures: 1945 farmer's house (with Bottoni and Pucci) in Valera Fratta and 1953 kindergarten in Muscoline. 1955, Mucchi turned exclusively to painting; 1956–61 in East Germany (Deutsche Demokratische Republik), taught at Berlin-Brandenburgische Akademie der Wissenschaften and at Universität Greifswald. 1960, he became active again as an architect for a time, with the Braendli house in Carona.
Exhibitions/citations Participated in numerous exhibitions including 1926 *Italian 20th Century*, Milan. At the Triennale di Milano either as architect or painter: 1933 (5th, showed a fresco and the exhibit of his Winding Sheet Chapel), 1936 (6th), 1940 (7th), and 1947 (8th). Others: 1931–33 private exhibition, Galerie Bonaparte, Paris; 1949 Magneti Marelli and House of Culture, Milan; 1955 exhibitions in Prague, Berlin, and Dresden. Subject of exhibition at Deutschen Akademie der Künste, Berlin, 1955; comprehensive exhibition in 1983, traveling to Staatliche Museen zu Berlin, Pushkin Museum in Moscow, Society of Current Art in Bremen; 1987 in Magdeburg (DDR); 2000 *Gabriele Mucchi—Zeiträume*, Kleinen Humboldt-Galerie, Berlin. Granted 1984 honorary doctorate, Humboldt-Universität, Leipzig.
Bibliography Fumio Shimizu and Studio Matteo Thun (eds.), *The Italian Design: Descendants of Leonardo da Vinci*, Tokyo: Graphic-sha, 1987: 331. Cat., Hans Wichmann, *Italien Design 1945 bis heute*, Munich: Die Neue Sammlung, 1988. Gabriele Mucchi, Norberto Bobbio (preface), *Le cccasioni perdute* (autobiography), Milan: L'Archivolto, 1994. Charlotte and Peter Fiell, *1000 Chairs*, Cologne: Taschen, 1997: 210. Cat., Raffaelle De Grada, *Gabriele Mucchi: cento anni—mostra antologica*, Cinisello Balsamo: Silvana, 1999.

Mucha, Alfons Maria (aka Alphonse Mucha 1860–1939)

Moravian decorator, painter, and graphic artist; born Ivančice, southern Moravia (now Czech Republic).

Biography Mucha first designed stage sets in Vienna; moved to Munich in 1885 and Paris in 1887; produced wall decorations for the country estate Schloß Emmahof of the count Khuen-Belasi, near Grußbach (now Hrušovany, Czech Republic); became involved in book and journal illustration and produced his first lithographs with Lemercier in Paris; combined his artistry with lithographer Champenois's business expertise; experimented with screen designs c. 1885–88, when he made a three-panel painted screen for the count Khuen-Belasi; is best-known for his poster designs for Sarah Bernhardt, of which the first example was printed in 1894. Georges Fouquet produced the jewelry Mucha designed for Bernhardt, and Mucha designed the interior of Fouquet's shop at 6, rue Royale, Paris. Mucha's furnishings, room settings, and objects attempted to relate Art Nouveau one dimensional art to the three-dimensional interior design; 1904, collaborated on jewelry designs with Louis Comfort Tiffany; 1903–22, made four successful visits to the US, where industrialist Charles Richard Crane, a Slavophile resident of Chicago, sponsored Mucha's 20-painting series *Slav Epic*. Returning in 1922 to Czechoslovakia, his design work included postage stamps and banknotes. Designs, including jewelry, were published in the 1902 pattern book *Documents Décoratifs* (new ed.: David M.H. Kern (ed.), *The art Nouveau Style Book of Alphonse Mucha: All 72 Plates from 'Documents Décoratifs' in Original Color*, New York: Dover, 1980.).
Exhibitions Work was the subject of 1980 exhibition, Grand Palais, Paris.
Bibliography Jiří Mucha, *Alphonse Mucha: His Life and Art*, London: Heinemann, 1966. Charlotte Gere, *American and European Jewelry 1830–1914*, New York: Crown, 1975. Alastair Duncan, *Art Nouveau and Art Déco Lighting*, New York: Simon & Schuster, 1978: 124. M. Komaneck and V.F. Butera, *The Folding Image Screens by Western Artists of the Nineteenth and Twentieth Century*, New Haven: Yale University Art Gallery, 1984: 165–68. Jiří Mucha, *Alfons Mucha: Ein Kunstlerleben, Aus dem Tschechischen von Gustav Just*, Berlin: Volk & Welt, 1986. Victor Arwas et al., *Alphonse Mucha: The Spirit of Art Nouveau*, Alexandra, Va.: Art Services International, 1998.

Muche, Georg (1895–1987)

German painter, graphic designer, and teacher; born Querfurt, Saxony; son of naive painter, who became known as Felix Ramholz.

Training 1913, painting, Ažbé-Kunstschule (art school of Slovene artist Anton Ažbé), Munich.
Biography From 1914 in Berlin, Muche came in contact with Der Sturm, a group of modernists, and the Galerie Der Sturm founded by Herwarth Walden (b. Georg Lewin); 1917–20 (while interruped by World War I service), taught painting, Kunstschule of the Der Sturm group; 1921–27 at the Bauhaus, was the *Formmeister* in the weaving department there; 1924, took a study trip to the US; 1926 with his architecture student Richard Paulick, designed a prefabricated house that employed steel plates and was active in other areas; 1927–30, taught, Ittenschule, Berlin; from 1931, professor of painting with colleague Oscar Schlemmer, Staatliche Akademie, Breslau, from which Muche was dismissed in 1933; c. 1934 to 1938, taught, Kunst und Werk school, Berlin, headed by Hugo Häring; 1939–1958, directed and taught the masterclass of textile art, Staatliche Ingenieurschule für Textilwesen, Krefeld; 1960, settled in Lindau (Bodensee, Lake Constance), where he became a painter and graphic artist and died.
Exhibitions 1916, first exhibition (with Max Ernst), Galerie Der Sturm, Berlin; continuing, to 1919. Designed *Haus am Horn* at 1923 Bauhaus exhibition, Weimar. One of his paintings was included in *Entartete Kunst* (degenerate art) exhibition organized by the Nazis, in Munich from 1937 and traveling to 13 cities in Germany and Austria.
Bibliography Horst Richter, *Georg Muche*, Recklinghausen: A. Bongers, 1960. Ute Ackermann and Ludwig Steinfeld, *Georg Muche: Sturm, Bauhaus, Spätwerk*, Tübingen: Wasmuth, 1995.

Muehling, Ted (1953–)

American designer.

Exhibitions To 1975, industrial design, Pratt Institute, Brooklyn, N.Y.
Biography 1976, Muehling set up his own design studio; has designed limited-production jewelry, for which he is primarily known, and home accessories. The managing director of Porzellan-Manufaktur Nymphenburg of Munich, Baron Egbert von Maltzahn, was looking to have the factory make new designer wares and happened upon Muehling and, 2000, commissioned him to design a porcelain vessel range, including a spoon collection. Muehling also contributed 3-dimensional pop-up art to *Visionaire 6: The Sea* periodical (summer 1992). From 1999, has been artistic director, Salviati glassworks.
Citations 1977 Coty award; 2000 Crysler Design Award.
Bibliography *Metropolitan Home*, Sept.1990: 89–92.

Mueller, Herman Carl (b. Hermann Carl Müller 1854–1941)

German ceramicist and tile maker; active the US.

Training In sculpture, Munich and Nuremberg.
Biography Müller settled in Cincinnati, Ohio, and anglicized his name; from c. 1887, worked at American Encaustic Tiling Company in Zanesville, Ohio, where he painted images on tiles, including classically draped figures in pastoral settings; 1894 with Karl Langenbeck, founded Mosaic Tile Company in Zanesville; departed 1908 and formed Mueller Mosaic Tile Company in Trenton, New Jersey, for the production of architectural ceramics. Zanesville and Trenton were major centers of ceramics production in the US.
Exhibitions Work subject of 1979 exhibit, N.J. State Museum (catalog below).
Bibliography H.C. Mueller, 'The Artistic Value of Fire Flashes...,' *The Clay-Worker*, Feb. 1909: 229–30. Cat., Lisa Factor Taft, *Herman Carl Mueller: Architectural Ceramics and the Arts and Crafts Movement*, Trenton: New Jersey State Museum, 1979. Cat., Doreen Bolger Burke et al., *In Pursuit of Beauty*, New York: The Metropolitan Museum of Art/Abrams, 1986. 'A Discussion of Herman Carl Mueller,' *Flash Point*, vol. 5, no. 1, Jan.-Mar. 1992.

Mühlhaus, Heike (1954–)

German designer; born Wiesbaden-Sonnenberg.

Training 1977–81 under Margot Münster, design and ceramics, Fachhochschule, Wiesbaden.
Biography 1981 with Renate von Brevern, Mühlhaus cofounded design studio Cocktail in Berlin. Their work has included a 1988 mirror and 1986 Sisters vases, marketed by Herbert Jakob Weinand in limited editions. She was a founding member, Das Europäische project; from 1992, has managed and continues to design through Cocktail; also produces limited-edition examples of other designers, work; has become known for her spherical ceramics with African-inspired patterns. Clients for mass production have included Mira-X, Blaupunkt, Belux, Alessi, and B-S.
Exhibitions Work included in or subject of 1990 *Luci del Nord*, Museo Nuova Era, Bari, Italy; 1990 *Afrikanische Straße*, Design Galerie, Berlin;

1991 *Cocktail Retrospektive*, Kunstmuseum Kloster Unser Lieben Frauen, Magdeburg; 1991 (4th) Zeitgenössisches deutsches Kunsthandwerk triennal, Museum für Kunsthandwerk in Frankfurt, Kestner-Museum in Hanover, and Grassimuseum in Leipzig; 1991 *Interferenzen—Kunst aus Westberlin 1960–1990*, Riga and St. Petersburg; 1991 *Piazzetta Palladio*, Kestner-Museum; 1991 *Cocktail Berlin*, Rokoko, Stuttgart; 1992 *Busstops*, Stiftung Niedersachsen, Hanover; *Das Europäische Haus*, 1992 *Documenta 9*, Kassel; 1993 *Wege*, Kulturhistorischen Museum, Magdeburg; *Kölner Design-Tage '93*, Industrie- und Handelskammer, Cologne.
Bibliography Cat., Design Center Stuttgart, *Women in Design: Careers and Life Histories Since 1900*, Stuttgart: Haus der Wirtschaft, 1989: 94–95. Georg C. Bertsch, Euro-Design-Guide, Munich: Wilhelm Heyne, 1991.

Müller, Albin (1871–1941)
German architect and designer; born Dittersbach; active Magdeburg and Darmstadt.

Training Kunstgewerbeschules, Mainz; Akademie der bildenden Künste, Dresden.
Biography 1900–06, Müller taught, Kunstgewerbeschule, Magdeburg; from 1906, worked at Darmstadt artists' colony of Grand Duke Louis IV of Hesse-Darmstadt, where he produced designs influenced by Peter Behrens and Josef Maria Olbrich; on Olbrich's 1908 death, became the leading architect at Darmstadt, although the fame of the colony had by then declined; designed special exhibition products for Darmstadt manufacturers, including clocks and chairs. His silver designs were produced by Koch & Bergfeld of Bremen, Johann L. Brandner, and J. Götz in Regensburg. Pewterware was produced by Eduard Hueck in Lüdenscheid, cutlery by M.H. Wilkens in Bremen, and other items by Stolbergsches Hüttenamt in Wernigerode; while a professor at Darmstadt's Technical School, designed buildings for the colony. Published in journal *Alte und neue Stadtbaukunst* (1920), his architecture was then showing the influence of Expressionism.
Exhibitions Two centerpieces were shown at 1910 *Exposition Universelle et Internationale*, Brussels.
Bibliography Annelies Krekel-Aalberse, *Art Nouveau and Art Déco Silver*, New York: Abrams, 1989. Cat., *Künstlerkolonie Darmstadt*, Darmstadt, 1990: 155.

Muller, Émile (d. 1889)
French engineer and ceramicist.

History 1854, Muller founded tileworks Grande Tuilerie d'Ivry in Port d'Ivry (Seine), where he perfected a high-fired glaze and a body resistant to abrupt temperature changes. His interest centered on tiles for monumental decoration rather than the small, regular tiles then common, so that architects could execute their own designs. The Muller factory's numerous products included revetment tiles, decorative terracotta, stoneware, and glazed bricks. The firm became Émile Müller et Cie when his son Louis Muller assumed directorship in 1889 and introduced *flambé*-glazed, high-fired stoneware copies of sculpture by Donatello, Verrocchio, Antoine Barye, Alexandre Charpentier, Eugène Grasset, and James Vibert. 1893, the factory made the glazed ceramic panels and roof tiles designed by Hector Guimard for 1895 Hôtel Jassedé, Paris. 1886, opened a new factory, and, on his 1889 death, his son Louis took over the firm under the name Émile Muller Cie.
Exhibitions/citations Grand prize and three medals, *Exposition Internationale de Bruxelles, 1897*. Participated somewhat regularly in *Exposition Universelle* editions in Paris, including receiving a grand prize at 1889 edition and executed a frieze for the monumental gateway by Anatole Guillot, named *Frise du Travail*, at 1900 edition.
Bibliography Yvonne Brunhammer et al., *Art Nouveau Belgium, France*, Houston: Institute for the Arts, Rice University, 1976.

Müller, Gerd Alfred (1932–1991)
German industrial designer; born Frankfurt-am-Main.

Training To 1952, apprenticeship as a joiner; subsequently, interior design, Werkkunstschule, Wiesbaden.
Biography From 1955, Müller worked at Braun in the Functionalist approach that the firm was then espousing; executed designs for some of Braun's best known products, including electric razors (from the 1955 300 and various models), 1957 KM 3 multi-purpose kitchen machine, and 1957 Multipress MP 32. 1960, he set up his own design studio in Eschborn, where continued to design for Braun such as 1963 MX 32 three-speed mixer and 1962 Standard razor models. He died in Eschborn.
Exhibitions 1983–84 *Design Since 1945* (kitchen machine by Braun), Philadelphia Museum of Art (catalog below).
Bibliography Cat., Kathryn B. Hiesinger and George H. Marcus III (eds.), *Design Since 1945*, Philadelphia: Philadelphia Museum of Art, 1983. *75 Jahre Deutscher Werkbund*, Frankfurt, 1983.

Müller, Hermann
> See Mueller, Herman.

Müller, Karl (1888–1972)
German silversmith; active Halle.

Training Akadamie der Künste, Berlin.
Biography 1923–58, Müller taught metalwork, Kunstgewerbeschule Burg Giebichenstein, Halle, which was more geared to commercial production than the Bauhaus. Eva Mascher-Elsässer and Hildegard Risch were students of Müller's. 1925 when the Bauhaus moved to Dessau, Wolfgang Tümpel moved to the workshop in Halle under Müller. Müller designed sculptures, domestic objects, lighting, cutlery, and other items.
Exhibitions/citations Gold medal, 1937 *Exposition Internationale des Arts et Techniques dans la Vie Moderne*, Paris
Bibliography Cat., *Karl Müller 1888–1972, 100 Arbeiten*, Halle: Staat liche Galerie Moritzburg, 1988. Annelies Krekel-Aalberse, *Art Nouveau and Art Déco Silver*, New York: Abrams, 1989. Katja Schneider, *Burg Giebichenstein*, Weinheim: VCA, Acta Humaniora 1992: 253–71, 468–70.

Muller, Keith N. (1938–)
Canadian designer.

Training To 1963, industrial design, Ontario College of Art, Toronto.
Biography From 1960s, Muller was active as a furniture, product, hospital equipment, and office-systems designer; was a space planner; with Michael Stewart (1940–), designed the popular late-1960s Image sofa and chair and 1968 MS-SC molded-plywood stacking chair (inspired by Alvar Aalto's seating and the winner of the interior-design contract for Conestoga College in Kitchener) by Ambiant Systems in Toronto. Ambiant was established by Muller and Stewart, and produced a line of other bentwood furniture, including Al Faux's mid-1960s swing-back chair for the Ryerson Institute of Technology. Muller is a founding board member, DX (Design Exchange), Toronto.

Albin Müller. Mantel clock. 1906. Cast iron, brass, alabaster, and marble, 12 3/16 x 7 9/16 x 3 7/8" (31 x 19.3 x 10 cm). Mfr.: Stolbergsches Hüttenamt, Germany. Courtesy Quittenbaum Kunstauktienen, Munich.

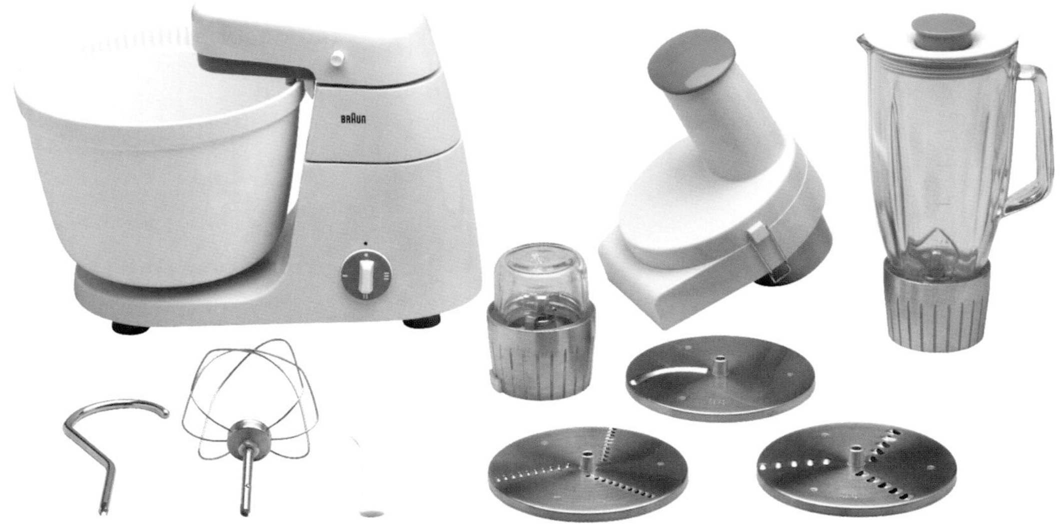

Gerd Alfred Müller and Robert Oberheim. Kitchen machine (no. KM 32). 1957. Plastic and steel, two-part machine 10 1/2 x 14 1/2 x 7 1/2" (26.7 x 36.8 x 19 cm), bowl h. 6 5/8" (16.8 cm) x dia. 9 1/2" (24.1 cm), dough hook l. 6 11/16" (17 cm), whisk l. 6 5/8" (16.8 cm). Mfr: Braun AG, Germany (1964). Gift of the mfr. MoMA.

Bibliography Cat., *Seduced and Abandoned: Modern Furniture Designers in Canada, the First Fifty Years*, Toronto: The Art Gallery at Harbourfront, 1986: 22. Rachel Gotlieb and Cora Golden, *Design in Canada Since 1945: Fifty Years from Teakettles to Task Chairs*, Toronto: Knopf Canada, 2001.

Muller Frères
French glass manufacturer; located Lunéville.

History The brothers Désiré and Eugène Muller worked in the Gallé workshop in Nancy. Three other Muller brothers—Henri, Victor, and Pierre—were later apprentices there. 1895, the family set up their own workshop on the rue Sainte-Anne in Lunéville; the glass was blown at the Hinzelin Gabeleterie in nearby Croismare under the Mullers' direction. The most common product was cameo glass, which featured up to seven layers and was acid-etched or wheel-cut. The Mullers produced tableware including pitchers, vases, and bowls, table lamps, chandeliers, and night lights in Art Nouveau and Art Déco styles. Production ceased during World War I, from 1914, but the Mullers' arrangement with Hinzelin was re-established in 1919, and production resumed. Before the firm's 1936 closing, its employees numbered 300.
Bibliography Berniece and Henry Blount, *French Cameo Glass*, Des Moines, Iowa, 1968: 134. *L'art verrier à l'aube du XXe siècle*, Lausanne: Galerie des Arts Décoratifs, 1973: 58–59. Janine Bloch-Dermant, *L'art du verre en France 1860–1914*, Lausanne: Denöel, 1974: 163. Alastair Duncan, *Art Nouveau and Art Déco Lighting*, New York: Simon & Schuster, 1978: 84–85.

Peter Müller-Munk. Cafex percolator. c. 1947. Aluminum, borosilicate glass, phenolic plastic, and stainless steel, overall h. 8 1/8" (20.6 cm) x dia. 5" (12.7 cm). Mfr: The Hartford Products Corp., US. Gift of the designer. MoMA.

Müller-Hellwig, Alen (b. Alen Hellwig, 1902–1993)
German textile designer; born Lauenburg.

Training 1920–23, Kungstgewerbeschule, Hamburg; 1923–24, Kunstgewerbeschule, Munich.
Biography From 1926–91, she was active in her own studio, Werkstatt für Handweberei in Lübeck, and, from 1934, located in the Burgtorhaus; 1937, married violin maker G. Müller. The Alen-Müller-Hellwig-Förderpreis (northern Germany handicrafts prize) has been established.
Exhibitions/citations Work shown in exhibitions, from the 1927 Leipzig fair, in Europe, South America, and the US. Received 1931 honorary prize from city of Berlin; gold medal, 1937 *Exhibition Internationale des Arts et Techniques dans la Vie Moderne*, Paris; awards, 1940 (7th) and 1951 (9th) editions of Triennale di Milano; 1954 art award from town of Schleswig-Holstein; award from Kunstgewerbeverein, Hamburg; honors from town of Lübeck.
Bibliography Sigrid Wortmann Weltge, *Women's Work: Textile Art from the Bauhaus*, London: Thames & Hudson, 1993.

Müller-Munk, Peter (1904–1967)
German designer; born Berlin; active Berlin, New York, Pittsburgh.

Training Universität Berlin; under Waldemar Rämisch, Kunstgewerbeschule, Berlin (1924, renamed Vereinigte Staatsschulen für freie und angewandte Kunst in Berlin-Charlottenburg).
Biography 1925, Müller-Munk settled in New York and worked for Tiffany & Co.; 1927, set up his own workshop in New York and, subsequently, Chicago; 1934–44, was associate professor, Carnegie Institute (now Carnegie-Mellon University), Pittsburgh, and turned to industrial design; 1935 with Donald Dohner and Robert Lepper at Carnegie Institute, established the first degree-granting industrial-design department/program in an institution of higher learning in the US. His metalwork was angular with accentuated vertical and horizontal lines, revealing his German training. He was interested in reviving ancient silver production techniques but is best known for his sleek, simple, and inexpensive-at-the-time 1935 *Normandie* chromium-plated pitcher, based on the silhouette of 1935 French oceanliner *Normandie*, mass produced by Revere Copper & Brass in Rome, N.Y. 1945, he established Peter Mueller-Munk Associates in Pittsburgh for product design and serviced a number of clients, including Bell & Howell, U.S. Steel, Waring Mixer Corporation, and Westinghouse, variously on home appliances, cameras, and commercial machinery. He

was a member, American Society of Industrial Designers (ASID), and president from 1954–55; member, International Council of Industrial Designers (ICID), and president 1957–59.
Exhibitions Work first shown and subject of a 1928 exhibition, Chase Bank Building, New York. Work included in a large number of subsequent exhibitions.
Bibliography Augusta Owen Patterson, 'The Decorative Arts,' *Town and Country*, 15 Apr. 1928: 71. Helen Appleton Read, 'The Modern Theme Finds a Distinctive Medium in American Silver,' *Vogue*, 1 July 1928: 98. Peter Müller-Munk, 'Machine-Hand,' *The Studio*, Oct. 1929: 709ff. 'Müller-Munk, Peter,' *Who's Who in America*, Chicago: Marquis, 1947. Annelies Krekel-Aalberse, *Art Nouveau and Art Déco Silver*, New York: Abrams, 1989. Cat., Janet Kardon (ed.), *Craft in the Machine Age 1920–1945*, New York: Abrams/American Craft Museum, 1995.

Mumenthaler, Ernst (1901–1978)
> See Meier, Otto.

Munari, Bruno (1907–1998)

Italian artist and designer; born and active Milan.

Biography Late 1920s–30s, Munari began his career as a sculptor and painter, showing in Futurist exhibitions in Milan; 1933, produced his first suspended kinetic objects called Useless Machines, exhibiting them in 1933 and 1945; created his first (1935) abstract-geometric picture; 1945, designed Hour X kinetic complex, later made by Danese in Milan; 1948 with Soldati, Dorfles, and Monnet, cofounded Movimento Arte Concreta (MAC); 1950, painted positive and negative pictures as experimentations in color interaction. 1950s, his earliest industrial designs appeared, including 1954 toy monkey by Pigomma. The 1957 Melamine cubic ashtray, his first effort into plastics, was the beginning of a long association with Danese. He designed a late 1950s–early-1960s series of collapsible lamps and wooden puzzles by Danese, including 1963 Calza lamp with metal hoops and white stretched fabric. Munari divided his time between the fine and applied arts, pondering aesthetics-vs.-function relationship. His 1971 space-frame environment, 1972 hanging shelves, and 1972 Abitacola bed/work/play/living structure in chromed steel rods by Robots, as well as designs by Zanotta, reflected a high-tech approach. 1967, he taught a research/experimentation course on design/communication, Harvard University, Cambridge, Mass., US; from 1970, was a professor, Politecnico, Milan; published numerous books, edited by Laterza, Einaudi, and Zanichelli; 1980 with educator Beba Restelli investigated infant creativity, establishing the Metodo Bruno Munari® and a laboratory.
Exhibitions/citations 1953, color experiments were presented in Milan, New York, Stockholm, Paris, and others cities and at Shuzo Takiguchi, Tokyo. 1962, he organized the first exhibition of 'program art,' where the works of his own and that of Group T and Group N traveled to American museums and universities. Work included in a large number of exhibitions, and subject of venues at editiions of Biennale di Venezia; Künstlerhaus, Graz, in 1970; Israel Museum, Jerusalem, in 1988; 1999 Salone del Mobile, Milan (catalog below); 1999–2000 *Omaggio a Bruno Munari*, Fondazione Bandera per l'Arte, Busto Arsizio (VA). Premio Compasso d'Oro: 1954 (three citations), 1955, 1956 (two citations), 1960 (three citations), 1979 (individually and with others), 1981, 1989, 1994 (individually and with Marco Ferreri).
Bibliography Munari, Bruno, *What I'd Like to Be*, London: Harvill, 1953. Max Bill and Bruno Munari, *Enzo Mari*, Milan: Muggiani Editore, 1959. Bruno Munari, *The Birthday Present*, New York: Collins, 1959 / 1980. *Bruno Munari's Zoo*, Cleveland: World, 1963. Bruno Munari, *Good Design*, Mantova: Corraini, 1963; Milan: All'Insegna del Pesce d'Oro, 1997. Bruno Munari, *The Discovery of the Square*, Milan: Scheiwiller, 1960; New York: Wittenborn, 1964. *Filastrocche in cielo e in terra: disegni di Bruno Munari*, Turin: Einaudi, 1968 (3rd ed.). Bruno Munari, *Art as a Craft*, Bari: Laterza, 1966. Bruno Munari, *Illegible Book N.Y. 1*, New York: The Museum of Modern Art, 1967. Enrichetta Ritter, *Design italiano: mobili*, Milan and Rome: Bestetti, 1968. Bruno Munari, *Design and Visual Communications*., Bari: Laterza, 1968. Cat., *Ricerche, visive design, visuelle,* Graz: Künstlerhaus, 1970. Bruno Munari, *Design as Art*, Harmondsworth: Penguin, 1971. Bruno Munari, *Obvious Code*, Turin: Einaudi, 1971. Bruno Munari, *Artist and Designer*, Bari: Laterza, 1971. Aldo Tanchis, *Bruno Munari: From Futurism to Post-Industrial Design*, Cambridge, Mass.: MIT, 1986; London: Lund Humphries, 1987. Marco Meneguzzo and Tiziana Quirico, *Bruno Munari*, Milan: Electa, 1986. Marco Meneguzzo, *Bruno Munari*, Rome: Laterza, 1993. *Bruno Munari*, Lubin: Biuro Wystaw Artystycznych, 1998. Cat., *Bruno Munari*, Milan: Salone del Mobile, 1999. *Air Made Visible: A Visual Reader on Bruno Munari*, Baden: Lars Müller, 1999. Paola Antonelli (ed.), *Objects of Design: The Museum of Modern Art*, New York: The Museum of Modern Art, 2003: 203, 251.

Bruno Munari. L'Ora X clock. 1945. Plastic, aluminum, and spring mechanism, d. 2 1/2" (6.4 cm) x dia. 7 7/8" (20 cm). Mfr.: Bruno Danese, Italy (1963). Greta Daniel Design Fund. MoMA.

Muller Frères. Hanging lamp. 1920s. Blackened wrought iron and unpolished clear glass with white- and colored-powder inclusions, 33 1/16 x dia. 22 7/16" (84 x 57 cm). Mfr.: Müller Frères, France. Courtesy Quittenbaum Kunstauktionen, Munich.

Munari, Cleto (1930–)

Italian entrepreneur; born Gorizia; active Vicenza.

Training Technical schools, Padua and Vicenza.
Biography From 1960–70, Munari was managing director of a machin-

ery firm; 1972, met architect Carlo Scarpa and began a close association with him when Scarpa moved to Vicenza, and, thus, greatly influenced Munari concerning the world of design and contemporary architecture; 1973, had the now-renowned Maestro gold cutlery designed by Scarpa for his own use and, 1974, began the production of Scarpa's metalware; 1977, set up an eponymous firm to produce tabletop and domestic accessories in silver, gold, semi-precious stones, and glass; 1985, established a laboratory for the design of jewelry by established designers. As part of the trend at the time to commission architects as designers, some of his first wares were designed by Sami Wirkkala in addition to Scarpa; and, subsequently, more than 100 others have included Gae Aulenti, Mario Bellini, Robert A.M. Stern, Achille Castiglioni, Vittorio Gregotti, Hans Hollein, Vico Magistretti, and Robert Venturi.
Exhibitions Work subject of 1990 *Il tesoro dell'architettura*, Palazzo Medici Riccardi, Florence; 2002 *La figura delle cose*, Museo Nazionale di Castel Sant'Angelo, Rome (catalogs below); *Micromacro* blown-glass by Alesandro Mendini at 2003 Abitare il Tempo, Verona.
Bibliography Cat., Alessandro Vezzosi, *Il tesoro dell'architettura: gioielli, argenti, vetri, orologi, 1980/1990, Cleto Munari*, Florence: EDIFIR, 1990. Enzo Buffi Bentili, *Cleto Munari, Dandy Design*, Naples: Electa, 1997. Cat., Achille Bonito Oliva, *La figura delle cose: Cleto Munari in Castel Sant'Angelo*, Naples: Electa.

Munch-Petersen, Ursula Birgitte (1937–)
Danish ceramic artist.

Training 1956–60, Det Kongelike Danske Kunstakademi, Copenhagen; 1960–61, Hjorths Terracotta Factory, Rønne; 1961–68, Bing & Grøndahl Porcelænsfabrik; 1968, visiting student, Escuela de Diseño y Artesanias, Mexico (1968); 1970–72, Skolen for Rum- og Murkunst (school for interior decoration and wall decorations), Det Kongelige Danske Kunstakademi, Copenhagen.
Biography 1978, she established her own workshop; from 1987, Royal Copenhagen Porcelain Factory; was best known for 1963 student housing complex Otto Mønsteds Kollegium, 1978 Children's Museum (Louisiana Museum for Moderne Kunst, Humlebæk, Denmark), 1992 Ursula faïence tableware by Royal Copenhagen, 1991 bridge decoration in enamel at Hvidovre Station (1992), 1999 24 large flowerpots at Botanical Garden, Copenhagen.
Citations DesignPlus award, 1992 Frankfurt Fair; 1986 Annual Award, Council for Arts and Crafts (1986); 1991 Bojesen's Memorial Grant; 1994 Thorvald Bindesbøll Medal, Akademirådet, Denmark.
Bibliography Cat., Mirjam Gelfer-Jørgensen and Teresa Nielsen, *Ursula Munch-Petersen*, Vejen: Vejen Art Museum, 1997. Jørgen Schou-Christensen, *Syv keramikere*, Copenhagen: Det Danske Kunstindustrimuseum, 1977.

Münchner Sezession (Munich Secession)
German artists' exhibition group; located Munich.

Biography Rejecting the existing exhibition association Münchner Künstlergenossenschaft, over 100 local artist dissidents met in the Kunstgewerbehaus in 1892 and named the new association Verein bildender Künstler Münchens (Munich society of visual artists). In its first four months, the group grew tenfold and became popularly known by the public and the press as the Münchner Sezession, a title it eventually officially adopted. Mounting its own show in 1893, this new group was the first art secession in German-speaking countries. Berlin followed with its own group in 1893 and thus Vienna, the more well-known Sezession, in 1897. Munich was at this time the capital of the visual arts in central Europe. The Münchner Sezession was a progressive force in German art for nearly a decade.
Bibliography Maria Makela, *The Munich Secession: Art and Artists in Turn-of-the-Century Munich*, Princeton: Princeton University, 1990.

Münchner Vereinigte Werkstätten für Kunst im Handwerk
German applied arts group.

History The success of the presentation of the works of Bruno Paul, Bernhard Pankok, Hermann Obrist, and others, in the small decorative-arts section of 1897 *Glaspalast* exhibition in Munich led to the formation of the Vereinigte Werkstätten für Kunst im Handwerk (united workshops for art in handwork). The group, directed by painter Franz August Otto Krüger, had its own workshop and a showroom and was the first of its kind in Germany. In addition to Paul, Pankok, and Obrist, designers included Peter Behrens and Richard Riemerschmid. Short-lived, the group achieved little success and soon disbanded, leaving Munich.
Exhibitions Some work of the members of the Vereinigte Werkstätten was first shown, at 1897 *Glaspalast*, Munich. Pankok, Paul, and Riemerschmid exhibited at 1900 *Exposition Universelle*, Paris; Paul at 1904 *Louisiana Purchase Exposition*, St. Louis; Troost, Schröder, and Paul at 1910 *Exposition Universelle et Internationale de Bruxelles*.
Bibliography Katherine Bloom Hiesinger (ed. and intro.), *Art Nouveau in Munich: Masters of the Jugendstil from the Stadtmuseum, Munich, and Other Public and Private Collections*, Philadelphia: Philadelphia Museum of Art and Prestel, 1988.

Murphy Radio: Type A 100 radio. c. 1946. Phenolic plastic and Plexiglas, 7 1/2 x 9 1/16 x 4" (19 x 23 x 10 cm). Mfr.: Murphy Radio, UK. Courtesy Quittenbaum Kunstauktionen, Munich.

Munthe, Gerhard (1855–1929)
Norwegian textile, furniture, and interior designer; son of Alf Munthe; active Munich.

Training Under J.F. Eckersberg, Knud Bergslien, and Julius Middletun, in painting, Oslo; 1874, in Düsseldorf; also in Munich.
Biography 1877–82, Munthe lived in Munich; called on Norwegian folk art and poetry to illustrate books and design tapestries for firms, including Det Norske Billedvæveri (DNB) and the illustrations in the 1899 deluxe edition of *Egils saga* (attribute to Sturluson Snorri, but actually by Icelandic skaldic poet Egill Skallagrimsson, a Snorri heir). As a pictorial artist, Munthe brought about the break with historicism in Norway. His 1892 dinner service was produced by Porsgrunds Porselænsfabrik; it was based on a nature-oriented, rather than an historical theme. He also designed 1895 furniture for the Holmenkollen Turisthotell, with dragons in the pierced backs of wooden armchairs.
Exhibitions/citations Gold medal, 1900 *Exposition Universelle*, Paris. Work subject of 1965 exhibition, Kunstindustrimuseet, Oslo (catalog below).
Bibliography Hilmar Bakken, *Gerhard Munthes dekorative kunst*, Oslo: Gyldenda Norsk Forlag, 1946. Hilmar Bakken, *Gerhard Munthe: en biografisk studie* (with English summary), Oslo: Gyldenda Norsk, 1952. Cat., *Gerhard Munthe om inspirasjonen til 'c'est ainsi*,' Oslo: Årbok, 1965: 94–97. Cat., David Revere McFadden (ed.), *Scandinavian Modern Design 1880–1980*, New York: Abrams, 1982. Frederik Wildhagen, *Norge i Form*, Oslo: Stenersen, 1988: 37.

Munthe-Kaas, Herman (1890–1977)
Norwegian architect and furniture designer.

Biography 1922, Munthe-Kaas set up an architecture office with Gudolf Blakstad (Gjerpen 1893–Oslo 1985). Munthe-Kaas designed in a modern style; created a Functionalist interpretation of the wing-back chair, published in journal *Form og Farve* (1924). He was an early exponent of tubular-steel furniture in Norway and designed 1929 cantilever, bent-metal, nickel-plated furniture by Christiania Jernsengfabrikk in Oslo.
Bibliography Cat., David Revere McFadden (ed.), *Scandinavian Modern Design 1880–1980*, New York: Abrams, 1982. Fredrik Wildhagen, *Norge i Form*, Oslo: Stenersen, 1988: 82.

Muona, Toini (1904–1987)
Finnish ceramicist.

Training 1927–33, Taideteollinen korkeakoulu, Helsinki; under Alfred William Finch, in ceramics.
Biography 1931–70, Muona worked at Arabia pottery factory in Helsinki; from 1963–64, at Nuutajärvi.
Exhibitions Citations at 1929–30 *Exposición Internacional de Barcelona*; 1933 (5th), 1951 (9th), 1954 (10th), and 1957 (11th) Triennali di Milano; gold medal, 1935 *Exposition Universelle et Internationale de Bruxelles*; gold medal (ceramics) and silver medal (glass), 1937 *Exposition Internationale des Arts et Techniques dans la Vie Moderne*, Paris; 1957 Pro Finlandia prize. Work subject of 1955 exhibition, Cannes, and included in 1954–57 *Design in Scandinavia*, touring the US; 1955 *H 55*, Hälsingborg; 1956–57 *Finnish Exhibition*, touring West Germany; 1958 *Formes Scandinaves*, Musée des Arts Décoratifs, Paris; 1961 *Finlandia,* in Zürich, Amsterdam, and London.
Bibliography Cat., David Revere McFadden (ed.), *Scandinavian Modern Design 1880–1980*, New York: Abrams, 1982. Jennifer Hawkins Opie, *Scandinavia: Ceramics and Glass in the Twentieth Century*, New York: Rizzoli, 1989.

Murai, Reiko
> See Tanabe, Reiko.

Murakami, Tatsuo (1950–)
Japanese glass designer; born Kanazawa.

Training 1970, industrial-design degree, Toukyou Dezaina Gakuin.
Biography 1970, Murakami began working in the design department of Shibata Hario Glass, Tokyo, makers of heat-resistant glass, and, subsequently, he became director of marketing there; is a member, Japan Crafts Design Association.
Exhibitions/citations Work was included in 1984, 1987, 1990, 1993, and 1996 *Glass in Japan*, Tokyo; 1988 *International Exhibition of Glass Craft*, Industrial Gallery of Ishikawa Prefecture, Kanazawa; 1991 (5th) Triennial of Japan Glass Art Crafts Association, Heller Gallery, New York. 1975 Ministry of International Trade and Industry Design Award.
Bibliography Cat., *Glass Japan*, New York: Heller Gallery and Japan Glass Art Crafts Association, 1991: no. 26.

Murdoch, Peter (1940–)
British furniture, interior, graphic, and industrial designer.

Training Royal College of Art, London.
Biography 1969, Murdoch opened his own studio in London; designed widely published 1963 Spotty child's chair in polyethylene-coated laminated kraft paper, printed in a large polka-dot motif (produced 1964–65 by International Paper). It was the first piece of commercial furniture made of paper; was sold flat with score lines for customer assembly. He also designed a 1967 group (including Papp chair) of his children's furniture in brightly colored plastic-coated cardboard was produced by Perspective Designs and widely distributed in Britain and abroad. The cardboard furniture earned Murdoch a reputation as a Pop designer. He was a consultant to Hille and to Price. With Lance Wyman, he designed graphics for 1968 Mexico City Olympiad, and graphics and corporate identity programs for other clients.
Exhibitions/citations Spotty child's chair shown at 1965 *Industrial Design Exhibition*, USSR; 1970 *Modern Chairs 1918–1970*, Whitechapel Gallery, London (catalog below); 1983–84 *Design Since 1945*, Philadelphia Museum of Art (catalog below). Received 1966 gold award, National Fiber Box Manufacturers, US; 1968 annual award (for 1967 children's furniture), Council of Industrial Design, UK.
Bibliography 'Children's Table, Chair and Stool: Perspective Designs Those Things,' *Design*, no. 233, May 1968: 33. Cat., *Modern Chairs 1918–1970*, London: Lund Humphries, 1971: no. 69. Cat., Kathryn B. Hiesinger and George H. Marcus III (eds.), *Design Since 1945*, Philadelphia: Philadelphia Museum of Art, 1983. Cat., Linda Brown and Deyan Sudjic, *The Modern Chair*, London, 1989. Charlotte and Peter Fiell, *1000 Chairs*, Cologne: Taschen, 2000.

Murphy, Henry George (1884–1939)
British jeweler and silversmith; active London.

Training Under Henry Wilson, Central School of Arts and Crafts, London; 1898, apprenticeship under Henry Wilson, the architect turned sculptor, metalworker, and jeweler, later working with him on ecclesiastical commissions.
Biography From 1909, Murphy taught, Royal College of Art, and then Central School of Arts and Crafts, both London; 1912–13, worked in the Berlin workshop of Emil Lettré; 1913, set up his own workshop in London; became head, jewelry and silversmithing department, Central School of Arts and Crafts, where he was the principal form 1937. His workshop at 'The Sign of the Falcon' was located in Weymouth Street in London. During the years after World War I, he moved away from the Arts and Crafts style toward the more fashionable Art Déco style; produced his own work as well as the designs of Eric Gill and R.M.Y. Gleadowe. Some of Murphy's designs reflected 1920s German and Austrian influences.
Citations 1929, freeman, Goldsmiths' Company; 1938, member, Court of Assistants; 1936, elected Honorary Royal Designer for Industry, UK.
Bibliography H.G. Murphy, 'British Silver Today,' *The Studio*, Jan. 1936: 36–42. Charlotte Gere, *American and European Jewelry 1830–1914*, New York: Crown, 1975. Cat., *Thirties: British Art and Design Before the War*, London: Arts Council of Great Britain Hayward Gallery, 1979. Annelies Krekel-Aalberse, *Art Nouveau and Art Déco Silver*, New York: Abrams, 1989.

Murphy Radio
British domestic electronics manufacturer; located Welwyn Garden City, Hertfordshire.

History c. 1929, Murphy Radio was founded by Frank Murphy and E.J. Power. The operation began with less than ten employees and grew to over 200. The enterprise specialized in military communication. However, Murphy contracted Gordon Russell to design radio cabinets. Russell in turn passed on the commission to his brother R.D. Russell, who created an influential series of veneered plywood cabinets and, 1935–36, was a staff designer at Murphy Radio and, from 1936, a consultant there. His innovative series of housings included 1932 AS and the inexpensive 1937 AD32 model. (Murphy left the firm in 1937.) As a consultant designer, R.D. Russell continued to design Murphy's radio cases after World War II, rendering bare modern veneer essays. His 1936 square floor model and 1948 A146C tapering cabinet, with its porthole-like central sound hole in large all-wood face, have been widely published. Early 1950s, he continued his work with Murphy on TV cabinets. The heyday of Murphy was over by the early 1960s.
Exhibitions Work included in 1999 *Modern Britain 1929–1939*, Design Museum, London (catalog below).
Bibliography Michael Farr, *Design in British Industry: A Mid-Century Survey*, London: Cambridge, 1955. *The Radio*, London: Design Museum, 1989. Cat., James Peto and Donna Loveday, *Modern Britain 1929–1939*, London: Alan Powers, 1999.

Murray, Keith Day Pearce (1892–1981)
New Zealand architect and designer; born Auckland; active Britain.

Training From 1918, Architectural Association, London.
Biography Murray first worked for the James Powell Whitefriars Glassworks. From 1932, he was active part-time as a ceramics and glass designer at Stevens and Williams's Brierley Hill Glassworks in Staffordshire, then, from 1933, at Wedgwood. He designed many successful shapes and decorations for both firms, some historicist, but most in a Functionalist style in simple geometric forms. His work had been influenced by the glassware he saw at 1925 *Exposition Internationale des Arts Décoratifs et Industriels Modernes*, Paris, and Swedish glassware at 1931 *Swedish Exhibition*, London. 1934, Mappin and Webb hired Murray for silver designs, including a covered silver-and-ivory cup and modern silver-plated cocktail shaker. 1936, he set up an architecture practice with C.S. White; designed the Wedgwood factory in Barlaston, Staffordshire, which opened in 1940. The celebrated matt glazes (classics of 1930s modernism in Britain) on his pottery by Wedgwood, particularly 1933–35 Matt Green and Straw glazes, were not Murray's but a development of Norman Wilson. 1946, Murray returned briefly to Wedgwood and designed sprigged ware, not commercially sold, and the Commonwealth service. He eventually returned full time to architecture, practicing in the firm of Murray, Ward and Partners in London.
Exhibitions/citations Work included in 1933 *British Industrial Art in Relation to the Home*, Dorland Hall, London; gold medal, 1933 (5th) Triennale di Milano; 1935 *British Art in Industry*, Royal Academy, London; 1935 *English Pottery Old and New*, Victoria and Albert Museum, London; *Design at Work* (Commonwealth service), Royal Society of Arts and Council of Industrial Design; 1979–80 *Thirties*, Hayward Gallery, London (catalog below). Work subject of a 1935 one-person ex-

hibition, Medici Galleries, London; cosubject of 2004 *English Glass Between the Wars: Cut Glass from 1930–1939 by Keith Murray & Clyne Farquharson*, Hamilton Art Gallery, Victoria, Australia. 1936, elected one of the first ten Honorary Designers for Industry, UK.
Bibliography Cat., *Thirties: British Art and Design Before the War*, London: Arts Council of Great Britain Hayward Gallery, 1979.
> See Wilson, Norman.

Murray, William Staite (1881–1962)
British ceramicist.

Training Camberwell School of Art, London.
Biography Initially interested in painting, Staite Murray took up pottery only in 1918 at age 37, working first in London, later moving to Bray in Berkshire. 1925–39, was an instructor, Royal College of Art, London and, from 1926, was head of the pottery department there; however, even though an influential teacher, offered no formal technical instruction to his students. He was at odds with Bernard Leach because Staite Murray considered pottery to be a fine art rather than a craft and discouraged collaboration with industry. Unlike many of his notable contemporaries, the main influence on his work came from Chinese rather than Japanese ceramics. He usually gave titles to his pieces, which, like the work of fine artists with whom he exhibited, were expensive. In addition to his pedagogy, he worked in his studio in Bray.
Exhibitions Regularly showed work (often with painters) at William Patterson Gallery and at Lefevre Gallery, both London. In 1950s, his pottery of the late 1930s shown at Leicester Gallery, London.
Bibliography Cat., *Thirties: British Art and Design Before the War*, London: Arts Council of Great Britain/Hayward Gallery, 1979.

Muthesius, Friedrich Eckart (1904–1989)
German designer and architect; born Berlin; son of Hermann Muthesius.

Training Vereinigte Staatsschule für angewandte und freie Kunst, Berlin-Charlottenburg; London Polytechnic.
Biography Charles Rennie Mackintosh designed the 1904 christening cutlery set for Friedrich Muthesius (Mackintosh's godchild). Muthesius worked for architects James & Yerbury and for Raymond Unwin and for his father Hermann Muthesius. With Klemens Weigel, Muthesius supervised the 1930–33 decoration and furnishing of the palace Manik Bagh (garden of rubies) in India of the Maharaja of Indore, whom Muthesius had met in 1928 at Oxford. He coordinated the contributions of Jacques-Émile Ruhlmann, Eileen Gray, Le Corbusier, René Herbst, Louis Sognot, Charlotte Alix, and others, although much of the furniture and lighting was designed by Muthesius himself. The writer Henri-Pierre Roché assembled the collection. 1936–39, Muthesius was consulting architect to Board of Planning and Restoration of Indore in the state of Madhya Pradesh, India, but returned at World War II's onset to Berlin, where he worked as an architect.
Exhibitions 1997 retrospective (marking 50th anniversary of Indian independence, organized by Werkbundarchiv/Martin-Gropius-Bau Berlin).
Bibliography Peter Adams, *Eileen Gray, Architect/Designer*, New York: Abrams, 1987: 187–88. Annelies Krekel-Aalberse, *Art Nouveau and Art Déco Silver*, New York: Abrams, 1989. Reto Niggl, *Eckart Muthesius, 1930: Der Palast des Maharadschas in Indore: Architektur und Interieur = The Maharaja's Palace in Indore: Architecture and Interior*, Stuttgart: Arnoldsche, 1996.
> See Indore, Maharaja of.

Muthesius, Hermann (1861–1927)
German architect, designer, and theorist; born Gross-Neuhausen; father of Friedrich Muthesius.

Training Technische Hochschule, Berlin-Charlottenburg.
Biography Muthesius worked in the offices of Wallot, and of Ende & Böckmann in Tokyo; 1896–1903, was the attaché of architecture at the Germany Embassy in London and reported on the British Arts and Crafts movement; 1898, wrote on C.R. Ashbee's Guild and School of Handicrafts in journals *Dekorative Kunst* and *Der Kunstgewerbliche Dilettantismus* and, thus, drawing attention to the London Home Arts and Industries Association, which held annual exhibitions at Royal Albert Hall. He also published two books on contemporary British architecture, followed by another on British church architecture. The three-volume *Das englische Haus* (1904–11), on the work of C.F.A. Voysey and others, contributed to a renaissance in domestic architecture on the continent. Muthesius wrote the British section in *Die Krisis im Kunstgewerbe*, edited by R. Graul, which played a key role in introducing British Arts and Crafts doctrines to German industry and paved the way for the modern movement. From 1904, he was important in the reform of German schools of design and actively promoted design in German industry; visited 1904 *Louisiana Purchase Exhibition*, St. Louis, US; 1907 as superintendent of Preußischer Handelskammer für Kunstgewerbeschule (Prussian board of trade for schools of arts and crafts), became a founding member with Peter Behrens and others of the Deutscher Werkbund, through which Muthesius was a strong advocate of standardization. He was a friend of Charles Rennie Mackintosh and chose Mackintosh as the godfather of his son Friedrich.
Exhibitions Subject of exhibitions at Architectural Association, London, in 1979 (1979 catalog below); Akademie der Künste, Berlin, in 1977.
Bibliography Julius Posener, 'Hermann Muthesius,' *Architects' Year Book*, no. 10, 1962: 45–61. Cat., Julius Posener and Sonia Günther (eds.), *Hermann Muthesius 1861–1927*, Berlin: Akademie der Künste, 1977. Cat., Dennis Sharp (ed.), *Hermann Muthesius 1861–1927*, London: Architectural Association, 1979. Hans-Joachim Hubrich, *Hermann Muthesius, Die Schriften*, Berlin: Gebrüder Mann, 1980. *Muthesius*, Milan: Electra, 1981. Fedor Roth, *Hermann Muthesius und die Idee deer harmonischen Kultur, Kultur als Einheit...*, Berlin: Mann, 2001.

MUZhYZ
> See VKhUTEMAS.

Myhr, Frode (1974–)
> See Norway Says.

Myrbach, Felician von (1853–1940)
Polish painter, designer, and graphic artist; born Zaleszczyki (now Ukraine).

Biography 1899, Myrbach became head of the Kunstgewerbeschule, Vienna, where, under him, Josef Hoffman was in charge of architecture and Koloman Moser of painting. 1903, Myrbach became a founding member of the Wiener Werkstätte.
Bibliography Robert Waissenberger, *Vienna 1890–1920*, Secaucus, N.J.: Wellfleet 1984: 125, 268.

Myrbor
French collaborative and gallery; located Paris.

History 1920s, the Myrbor workshop and gallery was established by Marie Cuttoli in Paris. 1929, André Lurçat designed its store at 17, rue Vignon. 1932, Alexander Calder first exhibited his mobiles, in the Myrbor gallery. 1929, Ernö Goldfinger designed its Marrakesh carpet factory (unrealized). Primarily a gallery for paintings and *objets d'art*, Myrbor operated a small workshop for weaving rugs and was frequently commissioned to execute the decoration of interiors. Pablo Picasso, Jean Lurçat, Joan Miró, Marcel Dufy, and Fernand Léger designed rugs made in limited editions. 1920s–30s, the popularity of these weavings led to a revival not only of the French rug but also of tapestry.
Bibliography James Dunnett and Gavin Stamp (eds.), *Ernö Goldfinger*, London: Architectural Association, 1983: 18.
> See Cuttoli, Marie.

Myrdam, Leif Heiberg (1938–)
Norwegian ceramicist.

Training Statens Håndverks -og Kunstindustriskole, Oslo; apprenticeship under Erik Pløen.
Biography 1967, Myrdam set up his own workshop.
Bibliography Fredrik Wildhagen, *Norge i Form*, Oslo: Stenersen, 1988: 164.

N

Marc Newson. Biomega bicycle (detail). 1999.

N2

Design collective; located Basel.

History Publicly débuting in 1997, N2 was a collective of Swiss designers, composed of Jörg Boner (1968–), Christian Deuber (1965–), Paolo Fasulo (1965–), Valerie Kiock (1970–), Kuno Nüssli (1970–), and This Reber. (The name N2 was derived from the N2 highway between Basel and Lucerne.) The group was involved in the design, production, and marketing of furniture/products and design of interiors. As a kind of consortium, the members acted as a support system and a working forum. Members were active individually and separately. David Braun, another member of the group, departed in 1998, and Reber departed in 1999. The N2 group eventually completely dismantled. Valerie Kiock became active in Munich in her own graphics studio; Fasulo eventually also worked in German; Nüssli established his own production company in Switzerland. Boner and Deuber work together and independently—Deuber, for example, on a project for Dornbracht Interiors, and both for Hidden/sdb. Deuber, who trained as an electrical engineer, also set up the studio Pharus Lighting Design, with clients such as Driade and Pallucco Italia.
Exhibitions First showed work, at 1997 Wohnmesse, Messe Basel. Subject of *Win-Win Situtation* (with Bibi Gutjahr—Sven-Anwar Bibi and Mark Gutjahr), 2001 Internationale Möbelmesse, Cologne.
Biobliography Mel Byars, *50 Beds: Innovations in Design and Materials*, Hove: RotoVision, 2000. Michele De Lucchi (ed.), *The International Design Yearbook*, London: Laurence King, 2001.

Nabis

French artists' group; active Paris.

History Late 1880s, a group of artists who studied at the Académie Julian in Paris congregated in the nearby Café Brady. They were Paul Sérusier (1864–1927), Édouard Vuillard (1868–1940), Maurice Denis (1870–1943), H.-G. Ibels (1867–1936), Paul Ranson (1864–1909), and Pierre Bonnard (1867–1947). 1888, led by Sérusier and Paul Gauguin (1848–1903), the artists formed the Nabis group, a name, coined by poet Henri Cazalis (1840–1909), based on the Hebrew word for 'prophets' and an ironic allusion to their attitude toward Gauguin's work, associated with a kind of religious enlightenment. Bonnard became known as the 'Nabi japonard'; his early work incorporated flat silhouettes and arabesques that were greatly influenced by Japanese prints, Symbolist painters, and the canvases of Gauguin. Before he turned to sculpture, Aristide Maillol (1861–1944) showed his work with the Nabis, whose members included musician Claude-Achille Debussy (1862–1918) for a time. The group emphasized color and form, revolutionizing traditional aesthetics in painting, printmaking, posters, book illustration, theater design, and the design of textiles, furniture, graphics, and stained glass. The group was opposed to the naturalism of Impressionism but rather was attracted to linear distortion influential among the Symbolists in literature, poetry, the theater, and journalism, as published in *Revue blanche*.
Exhibitions 1889, the Nabis mounted their last official exhibition (an homage to Odilon Redon), at Galerie Durand; 1892 Nabis exhibition, gallery of art dealer Louis-Léon Le Barc de Boutteville; both Paris.
Bibliography Fritz Hermann, *Die Revue blanche und die Nabis*, Munich: Mikrokopie, 1959. Charles Chassé, *Nabis et leur temps = The Nabis and Their Period*, New York: Praeger, 1969. Cat., Patricia Eckert Boyer (ed.), *The Nabis and the Parisian Avant-Garde*, New Brunswick, N.J.: Rutgers University/Jane Voorhees Zimmerli Art Museum, 1988. Cat., *Au temps des Nabis*, Paris: Huguette Berès, 1990. Claire Frèsches-Thory and Antoine Terrasse, *The Nabis: Bonnard, Vuillard, and Their Circle*, New York: Abrams, 1991. Albert Kostenevich, *Bonnar i khudozhniki gruppy Nabi: Kolektsii Muzeev Rossii*, St. Petersburg: Aurora; Burnemut: Parkstoun, 1996.

Naço, Studio

French group of architects and designers.

History 1985, architects Marcelo Joulia Lagares (Cordoba, Argentina, 1958–) and Alain Renk (Paris, 1962–) founded Studio Naço in Paris, becoming active in interior architecture, industrial design, and communication. They met while studying architecture at Unité Pédogogique (UP6) architecture school, Paris (and obtaining a DPLG diploma in architecture in 1990), Paris. (*Naço* means 'intuition' in the Guarani language of the Tupi-Guaranian people of South America.) The group has designed schemes for stores, including Bathroom Graffiti, Kookaï, and Michel Bachoz, and for offices and exhibitions. Their 1988 Belfort armchair in cast aluminum for the General Council's office of Belfort was sponsored by VIA (French furniture association) and produced by Le Mobilier National. The group has also designed lighting fixtures for Luminance, Electrorama, and Lucien Gau (including 1992 Ondine table lamp); electrical appliances by Dewoo; tea service and lighting by Hisense; 1999 architecture of Cité Numérique (of 3 Suisses) at Villeneuve-d'Ascq; Cinéma Pathé (Joulia with Beatrice Bérian and Denise Conrady). Also designed furniture in 2000 for offices of BDDQ & Fils, identity for the Who's Next fair, boutique of Club Med, 1999 redesign of a Suzanne Ermann shop; all Paris.
Exhibitions/citations 1988 prize (General Council's office at Belfort) and first prize (its furniture), *Objet 2000* exhibition. Work subject of 1987 and 2000 exhibitions, Galerie VIA, Paris; participated in 1997

(6th) Bienal de la Habana, Cuba, and 2000 (7th) Biennale di Architettura, Venice.

Nadeau, Patrick (1955–)

French designer; born La Rochelle.

Training 1985, diploma, École d'Architecture Paris-Villemin; post-graduate studies, Etude et Création de Mobilier (ECM), École d'Architecture de Paris-Val-de-Marne.
Biography 1989–97, Nadeau worked with Christian Ghion, designing numerous pieces of furniture, interiors, exhibitions, and sets; designed furniture by Néotù, Idée, Hatchi Design, and Sitting Collectivité, from 1993–97; lighting by Lucien Gau, Delmas Drimmer, and Tébong, from 1990–98; tabletop products by Opaque Diffusion, Futuroscope de Poitiers, Trajectoire, and Techniland, from 1990–98. Activities before 1997 were with Ghion. Nadeau has taught, École Supérieure d'Art et de Design, Reims, from 1996, and École Supérieure d'Administration et de Management, Paris, from 1998.
Exhibitions/citations From 1987, participated in a number of exhibitions. 1991 Grand Prix de la Ville de Paris (with Christian Ghion); 1994–97 annual Appel Permanent production support, VIA (French furniture association); 1995 study scholarship, Association Française d'Action Artistique (AFAA).
Bibliography Mel Byars, *50 Beds...*, Hove: RotoVision, 2000. Cat., Sophie Tasma Anargyros et al., *L'école française: les créateurs de meubles du 20ème siècle*, Paris: Industries Françaises de l'Ameublement, 2000.

Naggar, Patrick (1946–)

French architect and designer; born Cairo, Egypt.

Training To 1972, École Nationale Supérieure des Beaux-Arts, Paris; 1977–82 under Michel Serres, in philosophy.
Biography From 1972, Naggar and Domique Lachevsky have designed architecture, interiors, packaging, displays for Cacharel and Paloma Picasso perfumes, furniture by Arc International and Écart International, and other furniture: 1989 Fauteuil Elytre and 1989 Miroir 1 and Miroir 2 by Néotù. 1985, Naggar moved to the US, working as an interior designer.
Exhibitions/citations Their furniture in 1985 exhibition, Jensen showroom, Paris. 1987 *House & Garden* prize.
Bibliography Cat., Sophie Tasma Anargyros et al., *L'école française: les créateurs de meubles du 20ème siècle*, Paris: Industries Françaises de l'Ameublement, 2000.

Nakamura, Shiro (1950–)

Japanese automobile designer.

Training 1974, bachelor of art degree in industrial design, Musashino Art University, Tokyo; bachelor of science degree in transportation design, Art Center College of Design, Pasadena, Cal., US.
Biography From 1974, Nakamura worked at Isuzu Motors as the chief designer of sport-utility vehicles, vice-president of product planning, and general manager of Isuzu's design center in Kanagawa, Japan; 1985, worked at the Advanced Design Studio of General Motors in Detroit, Mich., US; 1986, returned to Isuzu, in charge of the Gemini model; from 1989, was design manager/chief designer at Isuzu in Brussels, Belgium, and Brimingham, UK; 1999, joined Nissan Motor Co., from 2001 senior vice-president and design director and coordinator of Nissan Design America (NDA) and Nissan Design Europe (NDE). He established Nissan Design Europe in London, operational from 2003; has been able to transform Nissan from dowdy to fashionable with, for example, 2002 Nissan 350ZX (a resurrection of the Z series).
Bibliography Marzia Gandini, *Shiro Nakamura: Nissan Design* (Car Men 15), Milan: Automobilia, 2003.

Nakashima, George (1905–1990)

American woodworker and designer; born Spokane, Wash.

Training To 1929, architecture, University of Washington, Seattle; 1929, École Americaine des Beaux-Arts, Fontainebleau; to 1930, architecture, Massachusetts Institute of Technology (MIT), Cambridge, Mass.
Biography 1934, Nakashima worked in the office of American architect Antonin Raymond in India and, 1937, in the office in Tokyo, where he studied Japanese carpentry techniques. 1941, he set up his first workshop, in Seattle; 1942, was interned in Idaho, when he studied with an old Japanese carpenter until Antonin Raymond arranged his release. Raymond had a farm and office in New Hope, Pa., where Nakashima moved in 1943 and started a small furniture business. He regarded his work as fine art and seldom sold to manufacturers or stores/shops. Most of his work was custom-made and site-specific. Nakashima worked with untrimmed slabs of wood, particularly black walnut and redwood, leaving rough edges and knot holes in the final piece; did most of the shaping and finishing by hand. His designs showed the influences of the Windsor chair, Shaker craftsmanship, Japanese woodworking, and contemporary forms. He made furniture and furnishings for Nelson A. Rockefeller's home in Tarrytown, N.Y., and designed interiors for International Paper Co. and Columbia University, both New York. From a piece of English walnut weighing 1,500 lbs (700 kg), he executed the 1968 heart-shaped Altar for Peace at the Cathedral of St. John the Divine, New York. At the time of his death, he was working to replace the 111-piece collection of furniture and furnishings in a Princeton, N.J., home destroyed by fire 1989. His daughter Mira Yarnall-Nakashima became vice-president of George Nakashima Woodworker.
Exhibitions/citations 1951, work shown at *Design for Use, USA*, The Museum of Modern Art, New York; 1972, Renwick Gallery, Washington; 1983–84 *Design Since 1945*, Philadelphia Museum of Art. Work subject of 1989 exhibition, American Craft Museum, New York. 1952 gold medal for craftsmanship, American Institute of Architects (AIA); 1979, elected fellow, American Craft Council; 1981 Hazlett Award, Crafts: Governor's Award for the Arts, Pennsylvania Council on the Arts.
Biobliography *George Nakashima, Woodworker*, New Hope, Pa.: Conoid Studio, 1966. Derek E. Ostergard, *George Nakashima: Full Circle*, New York: Weidenfeld & Nicholson, 1989. Wolfgang Saxon, *The New York Times* [obituary], 17 June 1990: L30. George Nakashima, *The Soul of a Tree: A Woodworker's Reflections*, Tokyo, 1981. *The Torch*, no. 91, June 1991: 8. Cat., Steven Beyer and Matilda McQuaid, *George Nakashima and the Modernist Moment*, Doylestown, Pa.: James A. Michener Art Musem, 2002

Nambé

American furniture and tabletop-object manufacturer; located Santa Fe, N.M.

History 1951, the Nambé foundry began production of tabletop objects that called on a new metal alloy (developed in the aerospace industry) with the appearance of sterling silver and durability of steel, but with no silver, lead, or pewter content. Late 1990s, Nambé produced its first designs by Karim Rashid; 1999, introduced a range of full-lead-crystal objects and, 2001, first of range of decorative lamps, by Rashid and Brian Lintner. Other designers have included Fred Bould, Neil Cohen, Aaron Johnson, Lisa Smith/Linda Celentano, Frederic Spector, and Eva Zeisel.
Exhibitions/citations Worked included in 1999–2000 *Designing the Future: Three Directions for the New Millennium*, Phildelphia Museum of Art. From 1994, a number of awards.
Bibliography *The International Design Yearbook*, New York: Abbeville, 1995 and 1997. Mel Byars (ed.), *Product Design 2*, New York: Graphis, 1997. www.nambe.com.

Nancy, École de
> See École de Nancy.

Narbut, Georgii Ivanovich (1886–1920)

Ukrainian graphic designer and illustrator.

Training To 1906, history and philology, University of St. Petersburg, and, concurrently, art lessons from painter and graphic artist Ivan Bilibin; 1907–08 under Dobuzhinsky, Elizaveta Zvantseva School, St. Petersburg; 1909–10, Simon Hollósy Schule, Munich.
Biography 1909–10, Narbut exhibited with the First Izdebsky International Salon in Odessa; 1910–17, lived and worked in St. Petersburg; 1918, returned to the Ukraine and taught, Academy of Arts, Kiev. After Narbut's death, Sergei Chekhonin, who admired his work, suggested that the State Porcelain Factory use his silhouette designs to decorate a series of objects produced by the factory specifically for trade fairs abroad.
Exhibitions 1910–17, participated in exhibitions of Union of Russian Artists, New Society, and V Mir Iskusstva (the world of art) groups, St. Petersburg.
Bibliography P. Beletsky, *G.I. Narbut*, Leningrad: Iskusstvo, 1985. Nina Lobanov-Rostovsky, *Revolutionary Ceramics*, London: Studio Vista, 1990. John Milner, *A Dictionary of Russian and Soviet Artists*, Woodbridge, Suffolk: Antique Collectors' Club, 1993.

Nardi, Claudio (1951–)

Italian architect and designer; born Prato (FI); active Florence.

Biography 1971–78, Nardi was active in interior design, first with Design Center; subsequently, International Design. 1977–79, he remained active as an interior designer and, with the cooperative Cooplan, worked on the town planning of Roccastrada. 1980 when Cooplan was dissolved, Nardi became an independent designer with work including part of *GlasHominis* exhibition sponsored by the Florence town council, *Scenic Parks* exhibition, renovation of apartments, offices and showrooms such as Luisa Via Roma, Luisa il Corso, Studio Piccinini, Ausonia offices, and Touche showroom, Rome; designed jewelry, lighting, furniture, and ceramics. He designed posters and publicity and the new shop (with Carlo Scarpa) of International Design. Other interior architecture: 1999 BP Studio, Florence; 1999 residence, Shelter Island, N.Y., US; 2000 multiplex cinema, Campi Bisenzio (FI); 2000 Hotel Leonardo Da Vinci, Florence; 2000 residence, Kuwait City; 2001 Abu Dhabi Building and Royal Palace, Abu Dhabi; others.
Bibliography Fumio Shimizu and Studio Matteo Thun (eds.), *The Italian Design: Descendants of Leonardo da Vinci*, Tokyo: Graphic-sha, 1987.

Narkompros (the people's commissariat for enlightenment)

Soviet government institution.

History 1917, Narkompros was established in Moscow under Anatolii Lunacharskii the commissar of education, who recruited artists he knew for placement in IZO (the fine-art department). Futurist artist David Shterenberg was overall president and deputy head of the Moscow IZO, with Vladimir Tatlin. Nathan Al'tman headed the Petrograd section. The department was in charge of all visual-arts activities from exhibitions to art education, including the establishment of SVOMAS (the Moscow free state art studios) in Petrograd and Moscow. IZO's board initially consisted of Shterenberg (president), Nikolai Punin (deputy head, Petrograd), Petr Vaulin, Alexei Karev, Aleksandr Matveev, Al'tman, Sergei Chekhonin, and Yatmonov. The Petrograd IZO was moderate and artistically eclectic. Vaulin, Chekhonin, and Shterenberg were also in charge of the Lomonosov Porcelain Factory. The artists who held executive positions within the system were granted the power to 'construct everything anew.'
Bibliography Nina Lobanov-Rostovsky, *Revolutionary Ceramics*, London: Studio Vista, 1990. Igor Golomstock, *Totalitarian Art in the Soviet Union, The Third Reich, Fascist Italy, and the People's Republic of China*, New York: Icon, 1990: 14–15. Cat., *The Great Utopia: The Russian and Soviet Avant-Garde, 1915–1932*, New York: Guggenheim Museum, 1992.

Nash, A. Douglas (1885–1940)

American glass artist; son of British glassmaker Arthur J. Nash.

Biography Nash worked with his father at Louis Comfort Tiffany's factory in Corona, N.Y. On Tiffany's 1919 retired, Nash purchased the assets of Tiffany's factory on Long Island, N.Y., active until 1920 as A. Douglas Associates when Louis C. Tiffany Furnaces was established. 1928 when Tiffany once again discontinued financial support, Nash and his father founded A. Douglas Corporation, continuing to produce Tiffany-style art glass and also lustered (with bubbles) and tinted glass. 1931 when the operation closed, Nash was hired to revive luxury glass at Libbey Glass Company, where he was a designer and technician; however, his wares there could not be priced for the mass market. 1935, he left Libbey; subsequently, worked for Pittsburgh Plate Glass Company and for other firms.
Bibliography Cat., Janet Kardon (ed.), *Craft in the Machine Age 1920–1945*, New York: Abrams with American Craft Museum, 1995.

Nash, Paul (1889–1946)

British painter and designer; born London.

Training 1906–08, Chelsea Polytechnic, London; from 1908, London County Council Art School; 1910–11, Slade School of Fine Art, London.
Biography 1914, Nash worked at the Omega workshops; became a member, London Group, and, 1919, of New English Art Club; 1917–19, was an official war artist; 1924–25 and 1938–40, assistant instructor, Royal College of Art, London; 1927, became a member, London Artists' Association. 1928, Curwen Press produced his patterned paper and, same year, London Passenger Transport Board used his moquette fabric for seating in rail carriages. Under the pseudonym Robert Derriman, he was an art critic for periodicals *New Witness*, 1919; *Weekend Review*, 1930–33; and *The Listener*, 1931–35. 1925–29, his first textiles were hand-printed by Mrs. Eric Kennington at her workshop Footprints. He designed dress fabrics by Tom Heron's firm Cresta Silks Ltd.; executed watercolor illustrations with collotype bases, colored by stenciling (the last to be reproduced with this technique) and printed (30 illustrations) in an edition of Thomas Browne's *Urne Buriall and the Gardens of Cyrus* (London: Cassell, 1932). Nash was a juror on the Carnegie International Competition, Pittsburgh. His 1932 bathroom design for male impersonator Tilly Losch incorporated black-glazed earthenware and silvered 'stippled cathedral' glass in a dazzling manner. 1933, he founded artists' group Unit One, whose purpose was primarily promotional; 1933–36, designed decorations for ceramic tableware by E. Brain (where T.A. Fennemore was the artistic director) and 1934 crystal by Stuart in Stourbridge; wrote *Shell County Guide to Dorset* (London: Architectural Press, 1936), *Shell County Guide to Buckinghamshire* (London: Batsford, 1937) and *Outline: An Autobiography, and Other Writings* (London: Faber & Faber, 1949). Contributed to journal *Axis 1*; 1940–45, was again an official war artist for War Artists Committee (chairperson, Kenneth Clark). Nash was one of the eight cofounders of Society of Industrial Artists and its first practicing designer to be president, from 1932–34.
Exhibitions Work subject of 1912 one-person exhibition, Carfax Gallery, London. 1914, exhibited at Friday Club; 1917, war drawings shown at Goupil Gallery and Leicester Gallery; both London. Ceramics included in 1934 *Modern Art for the Table*, Harrods store, London. Work included in 1934 exhibition of Unit One members, Mayor Gallery, London, and touring; 1936 *International Surrealist Exhibition*, London; 1937 exhibitions, Redfern Gallery and London Gallery; 1937 Surrealist Section, American Institute of Architects (AIA); 1939–40 *New York World's Fair: The World of Tomorrow*.
Bibliography Cat., *Paul Nash as Designer*, London: Victoria and Albert Museum, 1975. Cat., *Thirties: British Art and Design Before the War*, London: Arts Council of Great Britain, Hayward Gallery, 1979. Muriel Emanuel et al. (eds.), *Contemporary Artists*, New York: St. Martin's, 1983: 664. Valerie Mendes, *The Victoria & Albert Museum's Textiles from 1900 to 1937*, London: Victoria and Albert Museum, 1992.

Nason e Moretti: Umberto Nason. Bowl. 1954. Glass, h. 8¾" (22.3 cm) x dia. 4⅝" (11.7 cm). Mfr.: Cristalleria Nason e Moretti, Italy. Gift of Philip Johnson. MoMA.

Nason e Moretti

Italian glassware manufacturer; located Venice.

History c. 1923, a glass factory was founded in Venice by Ugo Nason and his sons Antonio, Giuseppe, Vincenzo, and Umberto. Those working at the foundry have included Umberto Nason from 1949–64, Ugo Nason from 1964, Paolo Nason in 1970, Marco Nason from 1980, Giorgio Nason from 1982, and Piero Nason from 1992. Its directors at one time, Umberto Nason (1889–1964) and Carlo Moretti, executed glassware of their own designs and when the firm became known as Cristalleria Nason e Moretti. 1955, Nason developed a technique whereby white glass appears on interiors and bright colors on exteriors of bowls and drinking glasses.
Exhibitions/citations Work included in 1979 *Design & design* exhibition, Milan and Venice (catalog below). To Umberto Nason: 1955 (bicolored glass vessels) and 1957 (two citations: green glass and cylindrical series) Premio Compasso d'Oro.
Bibliography Cat., *Design & Design*, Milan: Palazzo delle Stelline, 1979: 42. Cat., Kathryn B. Hiesenger and George H. Marcus III (eds.), *Design Since 1945*, Philadelphia: Philadelphia Museum of Art, 1983.

Rosita Adamoli and Robert Emmett Bright, *Inventiamo la tavola*, Milan: Fabbri, 1986.

Natalini, Adolfo (1941–)

Italian architect, designer, writer and teacher; born Pistoia; active Florence.

Training To 1966, architecture, Università di Firenze.
Biography 1966–78 with Cristiano Toraldo di Francia and others, Natalini cofounded and was active in the Superstudio group in Florence, which took a more conceptual route to design than its sister group Archizoom. Natalini specialized in town planning and, early 1960s with Superstudio members, initiated Radical Architecture. 1979, he participated in a number of projects for historical cities including Frankfurt, Jerusalem, Mannheim, Karlsruhe, Strasbourg, Parma, and Florence. From 1973, he has taught architecture, Università degli Studi di Firenze; designed 1987 Volumina secretary (with Guglielmo Renzi) by Sawaya & Moroni. Other design clients have included Poltronova, Arflex, Driade, and Mirabili. He has been the artistic director of numerous firms; wrote books *Figure di Pietra* (Milan: Electa, 1984) and *Il teatro della compagnia* (Anfione Zeto, 1989). 1991, he established Natalini Architetti with Fabrizio Natalini (no relation). Other publications include *Appunti Costruttivi: la palestra di Gorle* (Milan: Il Ferrone, 1992), *Il Museo dell'Opificio a Firenze* (Livorno: Sillabe, 1995), *Temporanea occupazione* (Florence: Alinea, 2000), and *Un edificio senese* (Sant'-Oreste: Gli Ori, 2002).
Exhibitions/citations 1986 Tercas Architettura, 1987 Architettura di Pietra, 1988 Marble Architectural Awards (MAA), 1989, Disegnare il Granito, all first prizes; 1991 winner of architectural competition for Waagstraat, Groningen, and, 1992, for a multistory parking, Verona; 1992 Premio Europeo d'Architettura, Barcelona; others. Is honorary member, Bund Deutscher Architecter (BDA), Accademia delle Arti e del Disegno, Florence, and Accademia di San Luca.
Bibliography Cat., Carlo Guenzi (ed.), *Le affinità elettive*, Milan: Electa, 1985. Pierluigi Nicolin and Vittorio Savi, *Adolfo Natalini: architetture raccontate*, Milan: Electa, 1989. Vittorio Savi (ed.), *Natalini architetti, nuove architetture raccontate*, Milan: Electa, 1996. Fabio Arrigoni (ed.), *Adolfo Natalini: disegni 1966–2001*, Milan: Federico Motta, 2002. Vittorio Fagone, *Adolfo Natalini Architettore*, Lucca: Fondazione Radianti, 2002.
> See Superstudio.

Nathan, Fernand (1875–1950)

French painter, decorator, and furniture designer; born Marseille.

Biography A painter before becoming active as an interior architect, Nathan was also a cabinetmaker and designer of lighting, printed fabrics, and furniture. His furniture reflected influences of Chippendale, Louis XVI, Directoire, Restauration, and Louis Philippe styles, some of it produced by Beyne. From 1922, he designed simple lacquered models for La Maîtrise decorating studio of Les Galeries Lafayette department store, Paris. Some of his fabric designs were produced by Cornille.
Exhibitions Work (a dining room) was first shown (1914), at Salon of Société des Artistes Décorateurs, Paris.
Bibliography *Ensembles mobiliers*, vol. 2, Paris: Charles Moreau, 1937. Pierre Kjellberg, *Art déco: les maîtres du mobilier, le décor des paquebots*, Paris: Amateur, 1986 / 1990.

National
> See Panasonic.

Natzler, Gertrud (b. Gertrud Amon 1908–1971); Otto Natzler (1908–)

Austrian ceramicists; born Vienna; wife and husband.

Training Gertrud: 1926, Handelsakademie, Vienna. Otto: Lehranstalt für Textilindustrie, Vienna. Both: 1934, under Franz Iskra, Vienna.
Biography To 1933, Gertrud Amon and Otto Natzler worked as textile designers; 1934, set up their first studio and developed a purist style in ceramics, distinct from the ornate work of those of the Wiener Werkstätte. Gertrud threw the forms; Otto handled the glazes. 1938, they emigrated to the US; 1939, settled in Los Angeles; 1939–42, taught ceramics; became known for their technical expertise, especially in their art pottery and glaze technology; 1939–71, perfected their glazes. 1976, Otto began to produce slab work.
Exhibitions Numerous awards, including a silver medal, 1937 *Exposition Internationale des Arts et Techniques dans la Vie Moderne*, Paris; first prize, Ceramic National, Syracuse, N.Y. Work shown at 1959 (20th) *Ceramic International Exhibition*, The Metropolitan Museum of Art, New York. Otto's slab constructions were shown at a 1977 exhibition, Craft and Folk Art Museum, Los Angeles, and other work elsewhere and often (catalogs below). Natzlers' work subject of 1993 exhibition, American Craft Museum, New York.
Bibliography Cat., *Gertrud and Otto Natzler Ceramics*, Los Angeles Museum of Art, 1968. Cat., *The Ceramic Work of Gertrud and Otto Natzler*, Los Angeles County Museum of Art, 1966. Cat., *Gertrud and Otto Natzler: Ceramics*, Springfield: George Walter Vincent Smith Art Museum, 1970. Cat., *Ceramic Work of Gertrud and Otto Natzler*, San Francisco: M.H. De Young Memorial Museum, 1971. Cat., *Form and Fire: Natzler Ceramics 1939–72*, Washington: Smithsonian Institution, 1973. Cat., *Natzler (1971–1977)*, Flagstaff: Northern Arizona University, 1977.

Naumov, Aleksandr Il'ich (1899–1928)

Russian theater, poster, and interior designer.

Training 1909–17, Stroganov School of Applied Art, Moscow; 1918–21, VKhUTEMAS, Moscow.
Biography From 1918, Naumov participated in several exhibitions, was a member, Obmokhu (society of young artists) and later joined the October group; designed sets for theaters in Moscow and film posters; organized exhibitions. 1928, settled in Cologne.
Bibliography Cat., *Kunst und Revolution: Russische und Sowjetische Kunst 1910–1932*, Vienna: Österreichisches Museum für angewandte Kunst, 1988.

Nautilus-Technologia Creativa Associati

Italian design group; located Milan.

History 1985, the cooperative was established by a group of young designers in charge of various areas: Vincenzo Di Dato (industrial design), Ivano Boscardini (visual design), Giacomo Schieppati (electronic hardware engineering), and Morerio Manzini (electronic software engineering). (Di Dato and Boscardini had collaborated from 1982; and they and others work together and independently.) The group specializes in industrial and visual design, electronic engineering, and the application of new technologies, with clients including Alacta, Ectasis, and Axil.
Award 1987 Premio Compasso d'Oro (for AFS 101 mountain boot, designed by P. Zanotto and Di Dato, made by Asolo).
Bibliography Fumio Shimizu and Studio Matteo Thun (eds.), *The Italian Design: Descendants of Leonardo da Vinci*, Tokyo: Graphic-sha, 1987, 327. *Modo*, no. 148, Mar.–Apr. 1993: 123.

Nava, Riccardo (1942–)

Italian industrial designer; born and active Milan.

History 1968 with Giorgio Romani, Duccio Soffientini, and Alessandro Ubertazzi, Nava set up the interior-design center DA; was associated with magazine *Interni* and the firm Faema; served on 1968 committee of Premio Compasso d'Oro; designed technical instruments and clocks and, from 1970, was a consultant on the ergonomic aspects of precision instruments. From 1975, he designed a range of sailboat equipment (including block and tackle) by Nemo in Sarsina and the Comar shipyard in Forlì. Clients in Italy have included Italora (domestic clocks and electronics), Superband (large thermoformed production), and Svaba. He became a member, ADI (Associazione per il Disegno Industriale).
Bibliography *ADI Annual 1976*, Milan: Associazione per il Disegno Industriale, 1976.
>See Ubertazzi, Alessandro.

Navarre, Henri (1885–1970)

French sculptor, architect, silversmith, and glassmaker; born Paris.

Training Apprenticeship in architecture, goldsmithing, and silversmithing; wood carving, École Bernard-Palissy, La Rochelle; stained glass and mosaics, Conservatoire des Arts et Métiers, Paris.
Biography Navarre executed a number of monumental sculptures and architectural carvings. His glass work was influenced by Maurice Marinot, and in 1924, Navarre began to make simply shaped thick walled glass vessels with internal decoration. His work in glass was produced in collaboration with André Thuret. He executed a gilded reredos for the chapel of the 1927 oceanliner *Île-de-France*.
Exhibitions Created the frieze on the Monumental Gate at 1925 *Ex-*

Gertrud Natzler and Otto Natzler. Vase Natzler (no. 2821). 1942. Glazed ceramic, h. 5 1/2" (14 cm) x dia. 6 1/2" (16.5 cm). Mfr: Gertrud Natzler and Otto Natzler, US. Gift of Edgar Kaufmann Jr. MoMA.

position Internationale des Arts Décoratifs et Industriels Modernes, Paris. Designed Grille of Honor of Colonial Museum at 1931 *Exposition Coloniale*, Paris. Work shown in Brussels, Cairo, Stockholm, Oslo, Athens, and New York, and at Salons of Société Nationale des Beaux-Arts, Société des Artistes Décorateurs from 1938, and editions of Salons d'Automne.
Bibliography Cat., *Verriers français contemporains: art et industrie*, Paris: Musée des Arts Décoratifs, 1982.

Naver, Kim (1940–)
Danish weaver and designer.

Training 1966 under Lis Ahlmann and Vibeke Klint, apprenticeship in weaving.
Biography 1966, Naver set up her own workshop and designed industrial and ecclesiastical textiles and wove tapestries and carpets. From 1971, she designed jewelry by Georg Jensen Damaskvæerveriet in Kolding. Her commissions included five 1978–79 tapestries for the reception hall of the Danmarks National Bank, Copenhagen, and, 1978, designs produced by C. Olesen-Cotil, Paustian, C. Danel, and Finnlayson. 1978, she became a member of the steering committee, Skolen for Brugskunst, Copenhagen; 1982, chairperson, Kunsthåndværkerrådet (decorative arts council), Denmark.
Award 1970 Lunning Prize.
Bibliography Cat., *Georg Jensen Silversmithy: 77 Artists, 75 Years*, Washington: Smithsonian, 1980. Cat., *The Lunning Prize*, Stockholm: Nationalmuseum, 1986.

Navone, Paola (1950–)
Italian designer; active Milan.

Training 1968–73, degree in architecture, Politecnico, Turin; 1970–73, architecture courses, Università degli Studi, Florence.
Biography Navone has collaborated with design magazines in Italy; 1974–78, worked at Centrokappa, Milan; directed research at Domus Study Center, Milan; 1975–79, was art director of Centrokappa, of a textile exhibition for Naj Oleari, and of 1950s-design and plastic-chair exhibition; 1977, was a consultant to journal *Modo*; 1979, was a design consultant to Abet Laminati and on laminate surfaces shown at 1979 (16th) Triennale di Milano; 1981, conducted research for Abet Laminati, Alessi, Driade, Fiat, and Zanotta; has been a consultant to a number of firms worldwide. She has designed furniture, furnishings, table-top objects, and textiles, including 1981 armchair range by Knoll, 1982 objects and 1984 Mizhar trays by Alessi, 1995 tabletop objects and bed linen by dHouse (Driade), 1997–2002 furniture collections by and corporate image for Gervasoni; 1997 and 1999–2002 collections by and corporate image for Orizzonti; 1998 furniture range by and shop and showrooms of Piazza Sempione; 1999 vase collections by Arcade; 2000 lamp collection by Antonangeli; 2000–2002 furniture collections by Casamilano; 2002 Eiffel kitchen by Dada; 2002 furniture by Molteni and by Natuzzi; 2002 Ping-Pong collection by Roche-Bobois; 2002 Morgana chandelier by Swarovski. Navone has lectured at architecture universities in Reggio Calabria and Florence and C.P.F Institute in Modena, and, with Giulio Cappellini, conceived and created Mondo furniture/objects division of Cappellini; designed 1999 Interni restaurant, Athens, and 2000 open-air restaurant, Mikonos;
Exhibitions/citations Designed exhibitions: *A Banal Object* (with Alessandro Mendini, Daniela Puppa, and Franco Raggi) at 1980 Biennale di Venezia; 1983 *Eat with Your Eyes* (with Kazuko Sato), Centrodomus, Milan; *Soft Touch*, 1997 Ambiente fair, Frankfurt; *Italia in Cina*, 1997 Federtessile, Beijing; exhibitions at 1999 and 2000 Pitti Immagine Casa, Florence; a number of others. Design award, 1983 (1st) Osaka Design Festival; Designer of the Year, 1999 Maison & Objet, Villepinte, France; Designer of the Year, *Architectur & Wohnen* magazine, 2000 Möble Messe, Cologne;
Biobliography Andrea Branzi, *La casa calda: esperienze del nuovo disegno italiano*, Milan: Idea, 1982.

Neagle, Richard (1922–)
American industrial designer.

Training Pratt Institute, Brooklyn, N.Y.
Biography 1949, Neagle joined a design partnership; 1954, opened his own office in Westport, Conn.; was the design director of Admiral Italiana and of Pye Electronics in Italy, and design consultant to Armstrong Cork and to Monsanto in the US. Work included furniture, radio and TV sets, refrigerators, washing machines, telephones, plastic housewares, and partition systems. His 1968 Nike chair by Sormani was among the first to be made in a vacuum-formed plastic.
Exhibitions Nike chair first shown, at 1968 Salone del Mobile, Milan; included in 1970 *Modern Chairs, 1918–1970*, London (catalog below).
Bibliography Cat., *Modern Chairs, 1918–1970*, London: Lund Humphries, 1971.

Nechansky, Arnold (1888–1938)
Austrian architect and silversmith; active Vienna and Berlin.

Training 1909–13 under Josef Hoffmann, Kunstgewerbeschule, Vienna.
Biography From 1912, Nechansky designed for the Wiener Werkstätte; 1913, silver by A. Pollak in Vienna; 1919–33, was an instructor, Kunstgewerbeschule, Berlin; 1921–33, taught metalworking, Meisterschule für Kunsthandwerk, Berlin.
Bibliography Annelies Krekel-Aalberse, *Art Nouveau and Art Déco Silver*, New York: Abrams, 1989.

Neeland, Torsten (1963–)
German designer; born Hamburg; active London, UK.

Training 1984–90, industrial design, Hochschule fur bildende Kunste, Hamburg.
Biography Neeland has designed interiors, fair stands, shops, jewelry, carriage seating for the German intercity train (GMP), and products for clients, including Donna Karan Home, Authentics, Rosenthal porcelain, Rosenthal furniture, Dornbracht, Montina, Babylon, Best Friends-Modern Jewelry, and WMF.
Citations Design Plus prizes, 1994 and 1999 Ambiente fair, Frankfurt; 1995 Karl Schneider Preis, Senate of Hamburg; 2002 Red Dot award, Design Zentrum Nordrhein Westfalen, Essen.

Neerman, Philip (1930–)
Belgian architect and designer; born Elizabethville, Zaire; active Courtrai.

Training Académie Royale des Beaux-Arts; École Nationale Supérieure des Arts Visuels, La Cambre; both Brussels.
Biography From 1972, Neerman has taught applied ergonomics in Antwerp and lectured at the universities in Lille, Compiègne, and Pretoria; for 16 years, was director of the Foundation Intérieur which organizes the Intérieur biennials of contemporary design in Courtrai; has been active as an engineer, architect, urban planner, and industrial and graphic designer. 1967, Neerman founded Industriel-Design Planning Office (IDPO), with a branch in France from 1988 and known for its studies in transportation, including the subway (underground) in Brussels (1971–75) and in Lyon and Marseille (1973–75), consultation on the Eurotunnel (1990–92), conception/development of the tramway in Strasborg (1989–94), and others.

George Nelson Associates (Ernest Farmer, attribution). Music cabinet with a radio (a unit in the EOG system, Executive Office Group). 1950. Birchwood veneer, 29 1/2 x 55 7/8 x 18 1/2" (75 x 142 x 47 cm). Mfr.: Herman Miller Furniture Company, US. Courtesy Quittenbaum Kunstauktionen, Munich.

Nelson, George (1908–1986)

American industrial designer; born Hartford, Conn.; active New York.

Training 1928–31, architecture, Yale; 1931, Catholic University of America, Washington; 1932–34, American Academy, Rome.
Biography 1936–37, Nelson wrote about International Style architects in a series of articles in journal *Pencil Points*; promoted modernism and was instrumental, through writing, in introducing Mies van der Rohe to America; 1935–43, was associate editor of journal *The Architectural Forum*, where he was consultant editor from 1944–49. 1936–41, was in partnership with William Hamby in New York where was active in architecture and interior design. Nelson pioneered the pedestrian mall in his 1942 Grass on Main Street concept; 1942–45, taught, Columbia University, New York; 1947, opened his own architecture and design office in New York; from 1953, was a partner in New York with Gordon Chadwick on architecture and industrial design projects. Although an architect by training and profession, Nelson designed few buildings; his interests lay with furniture, industrial, exhibition, and urban design, writing, and speaking. Succeeding Gilbert Rohde, Nelson was the designer director of Herman Miller Furniture Company in Zeeland, Mich., from 1946–65. His Storagewall concept received wide public notice through its preview in a 1945 issue of *LIFE* magazine and led to much work for Herman Miller, probably all of which was rendered by Nelson's staff members. Such as: John Pile's 1954 Steelframe group, seating systems, and others; Ernest Farmer's many furniture designs, including the 1971 EOG (Executive Office Group) and possibly 1956 thin-edge case goods; 1947 Platform (slat) bench models and accompanying 1946 modular system of cabinets; Irving Harper's 1954–55 Marshmallow sofa; George Mulhauser's 1956 Coconut chair; 1956 fiberglass Daf armchair; 1959 Catenary furniture group; John Svezia's 1963 Sling sofa; 1964 Action Office 1 (based on a Robert Probst concept); and Don Ervin's and George Tscherny's graphics. Herman Miller interiors included 1948 Chicago showroom; 1953 and 1956 New York showrooms; 1964 Washington showroom; and 1962 and 1966 factory building in Zeeland, Mich. (For other clients: William Renwick's 1947 Bubble lamp range and Harper's 1950s clocks by Howard Miller Clock Co.; kitchen systems by GE; 1968 Editor 2 typewriter by Olivetti; plastic dinnerware by Prolon.) Ettore Sottsass and Michael Graves worked in New York studio for a time. Nelson became responsible for discovering the distinguished rostrum of designers at Herman Miller, including Charles Eames from 1946 and Alexander Girard from 1952; was best known during his lifetime for his writing and lectures; repudiated, with others of the European circle, the commercialism of Raymond Loewy and other purveyors of styling. From late 1950s, Nelson became interested in exhibition design and concentrated on urban-design problems; with Charles Eames, designed 1959 *American National Exhibition*, Moscow; 1967 US Industrial Design pavilion, USSR; Chrysler and Irish pavilions at 1964 *New York World's Fair: The World of Tomorrow*; 1976 *USA '76: The First Two Hundred Years* traveling exhibition. Nelson wrote *Tomorrow's House* (New York: Simon & Schuster, 1945); 'Modern Furniture: An Attempt to Explore Its Nature, Its Sources, and Its Probable Future' (in *Interiors*, no. 108, July 1949: 76–117); *Problems of Design* (New York: Whitney, 1957); *On Design* (New York: Whitney, 1979). He died in New York. The Nelson archive is housed in the Vitra Design Museum, Weil am Rhine.
Exhibitions/citations Work included in 1966 *Vijftig Jaar Zitten*, Stedelijk Museum, Amsterdam; 1968 *Les Assises du Siège Contemporain*, Musée des Arts Décoratifs, Paris (catalog below); 1982 *Space and Environment: Furniture by Architects*, Whitney Museum of American Art, Fairfield, Conn.; others since. To Nelson: 1964 Industrial Arts Medal, American Institute of Architects (AIA); 1965 Alcoa Industrial Design Award; 1973, elected Honorary Royal Designer for Industry, UK.
Bibliography Cat., *Les assises du siège contemporain*, Paris: Musée des Arts Décoratifs, 1968. Olga Gueft, 'George Nelson,' in 'Nelson/Eames/Girard/Probst: The Design Process at Herman Miller,' *Design Quarterly*, nos. 98–99, 1975. Stanley Abercrombie, *George Nelson: The Design of Modern Design*, Cambridge: MIT, 1995. Michael Webb et al., *George Nelson*, San Francisco: Chronicle, 2003. Paola Antonelli (ed.), *Objects of Design: The Museum of Modern Art*, New York: The Museum of Modern Art, 2003: 194.

Nemecek, Jan (1963–)
> See Olgoj chorchoj.

Nemo
> See Domingo, Alain.

Nemo; Nemo Italianaluce

Italian lighting firm; located Rovellasca (CO).

History 1993, Nemo was founded by Carlo and Francesco Forcolini in partnership with Cassina to produce residential and office lighting; 1995, was wholly purchased by Cassina Group. 1998, Nemo bought the firm Italianluce, and, subsequently, Nemo has become a division of the Fimalac Group (with Fimalac, Cassina, and Alias). Commissioned architects and designers have included Mario Barbaglia, Marco Colombo, Carlo Forcolini, Jehs & Laub, Piero Lissoni, Vico Magistretti, and Stefano Marcato. One of its best-known fixtures is the 1984–85 Dove desk lamp (originally under the Studio PAF brand) by Barbaglia and Colombo. 65% of its produce is exported.

Néotù

French furniture and furnishings gallery; located Paris.

History 1984, Néotù was founded by Pierre Staudenmeyer and Gérard Dalmon on the rue du Renard, Paris; represented the limited-production designs of Martin Székely, Bořek Šípek, Pucci de Rossi, Sylvain Dubuisson, Elisabeth Garouste/Mattia Bonetti, and a number of others; was instrumental in establishing new French design of the 1980s, and assisted with production. 1990, a branch was established in New York and, 1992, Néotù began representing VIA (French furniture association) there. 2001, Néotù closed. Subsequently, Staudenmeyer established a new shop, Movements Modernes, on the rue Jean-Jacques-Rousseau, Paris.
> See Dalmon, Gérard.

Neter-Kähler, Greten (1906–1986)

German textile designer; born Schleswig.

Training 1924–25, apprenticeship in a handweaving studio, Munich; 1926–27, Kunstgewerbeschule, Flensburg; 1929–32, weaving workshop, Bauhaus, Dessau.
Biography 1928, she worked in a fashion house in Hamburg; 1932 settled in the Netherlands and collaborated with Kitty van der Mijll-Dekker Dekker and Hermann Fischer in a handweaving studio; 1929–34, was the wife of Herman Fischer and, from 1934, of Bob Neter; specialized in silk and linen fabrics and liturgical textiles. 1935–37, she was director of the weaving studio of De Kerkuil, Amsterdam; 1945–82, directed the textile department, Rijksschool voor Kunstnijverheid, Amsterdam, and worked as a freelance weaver and designer.
Bibliography Sigrid Wortmann Weltge, *Women's Work: Textile Art from the Bauhaus*, London: Thames & Hudson, 1993.

Neue Sachlichkeit

German artists' movement and theory.

Biography *Neue Sachlichkeit* (new objectivity) was coined by G.F. Hartlaub for his 1925 *Die Neue Sachlichkeit* neofigurative painting exhibition, Kunsthalle, Mannheim, which featured coolly and impersonally representational pictures by Max Beckmann, Otto Dix, and the ex-Dadaists George Grosz and Rudolf Schlichter, and a group of Magic Realist works. c. 1923–33, the movement emphasized a new, supposedly impersonal, manner in architecture, design, fine art, graphics, and photography. *Neue Sachlichkeit* rejected Impressionism and, in particular, Expressionism; valued Functionalism and social engagement; was acceptable to German communists, who favored proletarian art. The term came to be applied to the architecture of the Rationalist school, particularly in Germany.

Neureuther, Christian
> See Wächtersbacher Steingutfabrik.

Neutra, Richard Josef (1892–1970)

Austrian architect and designer; born Vienna; active Los Angeles.

Training To 1917, Technische Hochschule, Vienna.
Biography Neutra was initially influenced by the Viennese modernists, including Otto Wagner and Adolf Loos; 1911, discovered the work of Wright through the portfolio *Ausgeführte Bauten und Entwürfe von Frank Lloyd Wright* (Berlin: Wasmuth, 1910). After World War I, Neutra worked in Switzerland; 1919 with Karl Moser, conducted seminars, Eidgenössische Technische Hochschule, Zürich; 1919–20, worked with landscape architect Gustav Amann in Zürich; 1921, met Erich Mendelsohn while employed in the Municipal Building Office in Luckenwalde, Germany, and began working in Mendelsohn's office in Berlin; 1923, settled in the US and worked in various architecture offices there; 1924, met Louis Sullivan and Frank Lloyd Wright, both in Chicago, and worked alternately at architects Holabird and Roche in Chicago and for Wright in Spring Green, Wis. 1924 when Erich Mendelsohn visited Wright in Wisconsin, Neutra acted as translator. 1925–30, he lived in the house of and worked on architecture with fellow Austrian Rudolph Schindler in Los Angeles; 1930–39, practiced alone in Los Angeles; from 1949, began collaborating with Robert Alexander on numerous large commissions; 1965–70, was in partnership with his son Dion Neutra; designed mostly houses in the International Style furnished with simple, if ideosyncratic, site-specific furniture arranged in large open spaces, including chromium-plated tubular-steel furniture; frequently followed Wright's approach, by including built-in furniture units to create open areas. His simple, elegant structures reveal the influences of Wagner and Loos. Neutra dissolved the separation between interior and exterior spaces with expansive glazing that met at corners, absent of mullions. His best-known houses are the 1929 Lovell and 1942 Nesbitt, both Los Angeles. Other structures: 1927 competition entry (with Schindler) for League of Nations; 1932 Van der Leeuw (VDL) Research House, Los Angeles; 1935 Josef von Sternberg house, San Fernando Valley, Los Angeles; 1937 Strathmore Apartments, Los Angeles; 1927 Landfair Apartments, Los Angeles; 1938 Schiff house, Los Angeles; 1942–44 Channel Heights Housing, San Pedro, Cal.; 1946 Kaufmann house, Palm Springs, Cal.; and 1947–48 Tremaine house, Santa Barbara, Cal. His site-specific furniture (reproduced in limited editions from 1990 by Prospettive in Italy) includes 1929 Cantilever chair in tubular steel for Lovell house, a low-backed bentwood version for 1942 Branch house, and a high-backed bentwood version for 1947 Tremaine house; 1940 Camel table with wooden legs for Sidney Kahn house and 1951 revised version with metal legs for the Logar house; early-1930s asymmetrical Alpha sofa; 1942 Boomering chair with and without arms for the Nesbitt house. A prolific writer, he was a foreign member, Union des Artistes Modernes (UAM). He wrote *Wie baut Amerika?* (Stuttgart: J. Hoffmann, 1927) and *Life and Shape* (New York: Appleton-Century-Crofts, 1962).
Exhibitions Work subject of 1982 exhibition, The Museum of Modern Art, New York, and included in 1982 *Space and Environment: Furniture Design by Architects*, Whitney Museum of American Art, Fairfield County, Conn. (catalogs below).
Bibliography Willy Boesiger (ed.), *Richard Neutra: Buildings and Projects*, Zürich: Gersberger, 1951, 1959, 1966. Esther McCoy, *Richard Neutra...*, Ravensburg: Otto Maier, 1960. Esther McCoy, *Vienna to Los Angeles: Two Journeys* (Schindler/Neutra and Schindler/Sullivan letters), Santa Monica: Arts + Architecture, 1979. Thomas S. Hines, *Richard Neutra and the Search for Modern Architecture*, New York: Oxford, 1982. Cat., Arthur Drexler and Thomas S. Hines, *The Architecture of Richard Neutra: From International Style to California Modern*, New York: The Museum of Modern Art, 1982. Cat., Lisa Phillips (intro.), *Shape and Environment: Furniture by American Architects*, New York: Whitney Museum of American Art, 1982: 48–49. Manfred Sack and Dion Neutra, *Richard Neutra...*, Zürich: Verlag für Architektur, 1992. Manfred Sack, *Richard Neutra*, Zürich: Artemis, 1994. Barbara Lamprecht, *Neutra: Complete Works*, Cologne: Taschen, 2000.

Nevalainen, Markus (1970–)
> See Snowcrash.

Newcomb Pottery

American pottery; located New Orleans.

History c. 1884, Ellsworth Woodward (1861–1939) formed the Tulane Decorative Arts League, a group of about 30 women who had an interest in handicrafts. 1886, H. Sophie Newcomb Memorial College for women was founded at Tulane University. 1887, Woodward became head of its art program and was joined by his brother William Woodward and Gertrude Roberts (later Gertrude Smith). c. 1887–90, William Woodward and a small number of his evening-class students operated New Orleans Art Pottery, joined briefly by George E. Ohr, already an established potter in Biloxi, Miss. 1894, Ellsworth Woodward set up a pottery on the college grounds. Mary Given Sheerer, an accomplished china painter from Cincinnati, Ohio, became his assistant, began teaching china painting and pottery design, and, to 1931, remained there. Clays and glazes were tested during Newcomb College Pottery's first year. Early on, most of clays came from Bayou Bogufalaya; others were mixed at Newcomb, from elsewhere in the South. A two-year training program was established. 1896–1927, Joseph Fortune Meyer held the potter's job. As at Rookwood, Newcomb women designed and produced the decorations while men potted, fired, and glazed. The pottery was intended to provide continuing education to the graduates of the art school. Undergraduate decorators were used at first; later, about ten graduate women were hired. During the pottery's history, about 90 'art craftsmen' or decorators maintained a high quality.
Exhibitions/citations 1896, first public exhibition and sale of Newcomb Pottery wares. Bronze medal, 1900 *Exposition Universelle*, Paris.
Bibliography Kenneth E. Smith, 'The Origin, Development, and Present Status of Newcomb Pottery,' *American Ceramic Society Bulletin*, no. 17, June 1938: 257–60. Robert W. Blasberg, 'Newcomb Pottery,' *Antiques*, no. 94, July 1968: 73–77. Suzanne Ormond and Mary E. Irvine, *Louisiana's Art Nouveau: The Crafts of the Newcomb Style*, Gretna, La.: Pelican, 1976. Jessie Poesch, *Newcomb Pottery: An Enterprise for Southern Women, 1895–1940*, Exton, Pa.: Schiffer, 1984. *American Art Pottery*, New York: Cooper-Hewitt Museum, 1987.

Newson, Marc (1962–)

Australian industrial designer; born Sydney.

Training Jewelry design, College of Art, Sydney.
Biography Early on, Newson designed furniture by Tentuo Kurosaki of Idée in Tokyo; worked with Ron Arad in London; became known for the 1985 Lockheed Lounge steel chaise, installed in the lobby of the 1990 Paramount Hotel, New York; designed black 1990 Pod clock, circular from the front and elliptical from the side, inspired by turn-of-the-century Cartier models. 1991, settled in Paris, where he designed the Helice lamp by Flos, Gello table by 3 Suisses, Orgone glass by Cappellini, and Bluton chair by Moroso, 1993 TV Chair/TV

Marc Newson. Biomega bicycle. 1999. Super-formed aluminum frame, h. 26 3/8 x w. 6 7/8 x l. 32 5/8" (67 x 17 x 83 cm). Mfr.: Biomega, Denmark.

Table by Moroso. Interior design includes Coast and Mash & Air, London; Sÿn Studio, Tokyo; WYLT boutique chain of Walter van Beirendonck. 1997, he moved to London and designed furniture by Vitra and B&B Italia, interior of a private jet, Megapode and Isopode watches by Ikepod, a lamp by Flos, and products by Magis and by Alessi. 2002, resettled in Paris; has become prolific.
Exhibitions/citations Designer of the year, 1992 Salone del Mobile, Milan; Creator of the Year, 1993 Salon du Meuble, Paris. 1995 Bucky sculpture (inspired by R. Buckminster Fuller), shown at Galerie d'Art Contemporain, Fondation Cartier, Paris. Work subject of 2001–02 *Marc Newson—Design Works*, Powerhouse Museum, Sydney.
Bibliography Alice Rathsthorn, *Marc Newson*, London: Booth-Clibborn, 2000. Conway Lloyd Morgan, *Marc Newson*, New York: Universe, 2003. www.marc-newson.com.

Nicholls, David Shaw (1959–)

British architect and designer; born Bellshill, Scotland; active New York and Milan.

Training To 1984, Edinburgh College of Art, and Domus Academy, Milan.
Biography 1980–82, Nicholls established Asflexi to design and produce metal furniture; 1984–85, worked in the design office Sottsass Associati, Milan, on projects including Snaporaz Restaurant in Los Angeles; Academy Bridge in Venice; and Esprit showrooms in Europe. From 1985, he was active in his own studio and designed Bar Montmartre in Milan, and several fashion showrooms and residences in Italy; 1987, settled in New York and pursued architecture and interior design. Sergio Palazzetti commissioned from him the 1991 DSN sofa and chair for Palazzetti's Maverick Collection. Others: Arno chair, Aria and Arianne tables, and Aston credenza by Beast; scent bottle and display systems for Elizabeth Arden; Gardens, Pompeii, Piazza, and Chivalry rugs by DSN; and Mari, Bride 'n' Groom, and 1993 Seven Palaces dinnerware, 1994 range of rugs; tabletop accessories by Swid Powell. Nicholls established a firm in New York for his-own-design carpets (produced in Nepal and India) and floor textiles.
Exhibitions Work shown at *British Designer Craftsmen*, 1980 Edinburgh International Festival; 1981 *Charles Rennie Mackintosh and International Furniture*, Fine Arts Society, London; 1985 (3rd) Biennale di Architettura, Venice; from 1990 (1st) International Contemporary Furniture Fair (ICFF), New York.
Bibliography 'The New American Entrepreneurs,' *Metropolis*, May 1991: 66–67.

Nichols, Maria Longworth (1849–1932)
> See Rookwood Pottery.

Nicholson, Ben (1894–1982)

British painter, sculptor, and textile designer; husband of Barbara Hepworth.

Training 1910–11, Slade School of Fine Art, London.
Biography 1924–36, Nicholson was a member, artists' group Seven and Five Society; 1924, painted his first abstract canvas; 1932, became a member, Association Abstract-Création, Paris; 1933, of artists' group Unit One. 1937, he was coeditor, art journal *Circle*. With his second wife, Barbara Hepworth, he designed fabrics for 1937 Constructivist Fabrics range by Edinburgh Weavers, under artistic director Alastair Morton. 1943–58, lived in St. Ives, Cornwall; 1948, designed limited-edition screen-printed silk squares by Zika Ascher; painted the mural at Regatta Restaurant of 1951 *Festival of Britain*, London; 1958–72, lived near Ascona, Switzerland, working on a concrete relief for 1964 Documenta III in Kassel.
Exhibitions/citations Work subject of one-person exhibitions: Adelphi Gallery, 1922, and Lefevre Gallery, 1932, 1933, 1935, 1937, and 1939; both London; 1969 retrospective, Tate Gallery, London; 1978–79 retrospective, Albright-Knox Art Gallery, Buffalo, N.Y. Work included in almost 100 exhibitions, including British section, 1939–40 *New York World's Fair: The World of Tomorrow*. First prize, 1952 Carnegie International Competition, Pittsburgh; 1968 Order of Merit, UK.
Bibliography Herbert Read, *Ben Nicholson: Paintings, Reliefs, Drawings*, London: Lund Humphries, 1948. Herbert Read, *Ben Nicholson: Paintings*, London: Methuen, 1962. Cat., Steven A. Nash, *Ben Nicholson: 50 Years of His Art*, Buffalo, N.Y.: Albright-Knox Art Gallery, 1978. Cat., *Thirties: British Art and Design Before the War*, London: Arts Council of Great Britain/Hayward Gallery, 1979. Muriel Emanuel et al. (eds.), *Contemporary Artists*, New York: St Martin's, 1983: 675–76. Valerie Mendes, *The Victoria & Albert Museum's Textile Collection, British Textiles from 1900 to 1937*, London: Victoria and Albert Museum, 1992.

Nicholson, Roger (1922–1986)

British painter, muralist, and designer.

Biography Nicholson taught graphic design, St. Martin's School of Art; 1958–84, was professor of textile design, Royal College of Art; both London. He was a consultant designer to several major manufacturers; late 1950s and 1960s, designed wallpaper patterns in the Palladio Collections by Sanderson.
Bibliography Stuart Durant, *Ornament from the Industrial Revolution to Today*, Woodstock, N.Y.: Overlook, 1986: 283, 296, 327.

Nics Frères; Michel and Jules Nics

Hungarian metalworkers and furniture makers; brothers; active Paris.

Biography From c. 1907, Michel and Jules Nics were active at 98, avenue Félix-Faure, Paris, and became known for their fine ironwork, equal to the highest standards of 18th- and 19th-century French work; made consoles, balustrades, dumb waiters, iron gates, balcony railings, and various lighting fixtures. Their chandeliers, *torchères*, and sconces were constructed in wrought iron with opalescent-glass shades or panels. Their invariably applied *martelé* finish imbued their work with some distinction, though they were not innovators. 1925, they were commissioned to render wrought-iron furnishings for a hairdressing salon by Jacques-Émile Ruhlmann.
Exhibitions Participated in 1914 Salon of Société des Artistes Fran-

çais; from 1910, Salons of Société des Artistes Décorateurs.
Bibliography Guillaume Janneau, *Le luminaire et les moyens d'éclairage nouveaux*, 2nd series: plate 31, 3rd series: plates 34–36, [n.d.]. Jean Lort, 'La ferronnerie moderne des frères Nics,' *Mobilier et décoration d'interieur*, Apr.–May 1923: 27–31. Alastair Duncan, *Art Nouveau and Art Déco Lighting*, New York: Simon & Schuster, 1978: 179. Pierre Kjellberg, *Art déco: les maîtres du mobilier, le décor des paquebots*, Paris: Amateur, 1986/1990.

Niedecken, George Mann (1878–1945)

American furniture designer and maker and interior designer; born and active Wisconsin.

Training 1890, Wisconsin Art Institute; 1897–98, Louis Millet's decorative-design class at School of the Art Institute of Chicago; 1899–1900, in Paris.
Biography Niedecken described himself as an interior architect, functioning successfully as the intermediary between client and architect. In some of his earliest (1896–97) drawings and watercolors, he recorded the landscape around his native state of Wisconsin; toured Europe, returned home, and began showing his work with the Society of Milwaukee Artists. c. 1904–20, he created Prairie-style murals for a number of domestic interiors, many of which were designed by Frank Lloyd Wright; was familiar with and influenced by British Arts and Crafts, French Art Nouveau, Wiener Sezession, Jugendstil, and, of course, the work of Wright. His business associate F.H. Bresler was a furniture maker, print dealer, and art importer, who specialized in American Arts and Crafts materials, Chinese ceramics, and Japanese prints. Bresler helped Niedecken realize his first interior-design commissions and invested in the firm of Niedecken-Waldbridge, which supervised the 1907–10 production of Wright furniture made by F.H. Bresler Co. in Milwaukee. With Wright, Niedecken designed 1904 Bresler Gallery showroom and, alone, some interiors and furniture for Wright's structures.
Exhibitions Work subject of 1981 and 1995–96 exhibitions, Milwaukee Art Museum (catalogs below).
Bibliography George M. Niedecken, 'Relationship of Decorator, Architect and Clients,' *The Western Architect*, May 1913: 42–44. David A. Hanks, *The Decorative Designs of Frank Lloyd Wright*, New York: Dutton, 1979: 215–17, passim. Cat., *The Domestic Interior (1897–1927): George M. Niedecken, Interior Architect*, Milwaukee: Milwaukee Art Museum, 1981. Cat., Cheryl Robertson and Terrence Marvel, *Frank Lloyd Wright and George Mann Niedecken: Prairie School Collaborators*, Milwaukee and Lexington, Mass.: Milwaukee Art Museum/ Museum of Our National Heritage, 1999.

Nielsen, Erik (1857–1947)

Danish ceramicist.

Training 1885–86, Det Kongelige Danske Kunstakademi, Copenhagen.
Biography Nielsen was an apprentice woodcarver; c.1886–87, worked at Royal Copenhagen Porcelain Manufactory and collaborated with Arnold Krog on one-of-a-kind ceramics; was influenced by naturalism and Japanese designs; from 1887–1947, was a medalmaker and signing artist at Royal Copenhagen and produced models for Kähler Keramik.
Bibliography Cat., David Revere McFadden (ed.), *Scandinavian Modern Design 1880–1980*, New York: Abrams, 1982. Jennifer Hawkins Opie, *Scandinavia: Ceramics and Glass in the Twentieth Century*, New York: Rizzoli, 1989.

Nielsen, Harald (1892–1977)

Danish silver designer; active Copenhagen; brother-in-law of Georg Jensen, married to his sister Johanne.

Biography From 1909, Nielsen was an apprentice at Georg Jensen Sølvsmedie. Jensen's comment on Nielsen's 1927 Pyramid cutlery pattern was purportedly, 'It's neat but it won't sell'; however, Nielsen's geometric design become one of the firm's top-three best-selling patterns. Nielsen worked as a designer of tableware and jewelry at Jensen; was one of Georg Jensen's closest colleagues and his brother-in-law; from Jensen 1935 death, was the firm's artistic director for almost 30 years. A prolific designer, his work covered the entire field of silver from jewelry and some famous designs in tableware to bowls, coffee/tea sets, jugs, and dishes, distinguished by smooth, undecorated forms with straight edges and sharp angles. Nielsen's work included 1947 Old Danish cutlery.
Bibliography *Georg Jensen Sølv: Nogle nye arbejder tegnet af Harald Nielsen*, Copenhagen: Jensen & Wendel, 1933. Christian Ditlev Reventlow, 'The Artists of Georg Jensen Silver,' in *Fifty Years of Danish Silver in the Georg Jensen Tradition*, New York: Georg Jensen, [n.d. c. 1954]. *Harald Nielsen: et tilbageblik på en kunstners arbejde ved 60-årsdagen*, Copenhagen: Georg Jensen, 1952. Graham Hughes, *Modern Silver Throughout the World 1880–1967*, London: Studio Vista, 1957: 94. Cat., *Georg Jensen Silversmithy: 77 Artists, 75 Years*, Washington: Smithsonian, 1980.

Harald Nielsen (covered container) and Georg Jensen. Spice set. c. 1935. Sterling silver with blue enamel inside covered container), covered container h. 2 1/16" (5.3 cm), spoon l. 2 1/16" (5.2 cm), open dish dia. 1 5/16" (3.4 cm), spoon l. 1 5/8" (4.2cm). Mfr.: Georg Jensen, Denmark. Courtesy Quittenbaum Kunstauktionen, Munich.

Nielsen, Jens (1937–1992)

Danish architect and designer.

Training To 1965, School of Architecture, Det Kongelige Danske Kunstakademi, Copenhagen.
Biography 1959–71, Nielsen wrote for several Danish newspapers and trade periodicals; 1964–71, was secretary, Selskabet for Industriel Formgivning; 1971, head of design, DSB (Danish state railways), and, 1979–84, chief architect there and, again, head of design; 1974–75, visiting professor, Koninklijke Academie voor Schone Kunsten, Antwerp; 1967, cofounded IDD (association of industrial designers Denmark); 1977, cofounded Dansk Designråd (Danish design council); created graphics and industrial designs for Danish and foreign firms, including design program of DSB and development of its new trains, ferries, and building system.
Citations Honorary fellow, American Institue of Architecture (AIA); 1982 Knud V. Engelhardt's Memorial Grant; 1984 Bruno Matthson Award; 1986 Annual Award, Dansk Designråd; 1991 Dansk ID Prize; international design award, Japan Design Foundation.
Bibliography E. Ellegaard Frederiksen et al. (eds.), *Jens Nielsen*, Copenhagen: Dansk Design Centre, 1996.

Nienkämper

Canadian furniture manufacturer.

History 1960, Klaus Nienkämper (Duisburg, Germany, 1940–) emigrated to Canada; 1968, founded and still manages his eponymous firm in Toronto, which has grown into a company known for its hand craftsmanship. It produces office and lounge seating, conference tables, casegoods, shelving, and tables in wood, metal, and leather. Products include Vox videoconferencing system by Mark Müller (the head of the firm's design department); 2000 Wavelength seating and tables by Karim Rashid. Other commissioned designers have included Tom Deacon and Scot Laughton. The firm has become a leader in contemporary furniture design in Canada.
Citations Best of NeoCon, Best of Show, Gold Award, and Best Booth—NeoCon, Chicago, from 1998; 1997 *Virtu II* award, and 1998 Annual Design Review (both for Target Shelving by Müller), *I.D.* magazine; 1997 IIDA Apex Award (for casegoods by Müller); 1998 Best of Canada (for Vox tables and Target Shelving); 2000 Good Design award (for Seating Collection 2000 by Rashid), Chicago Athenaeum; 2001 Best of Canada Design Award (for Wavelength seating by Rashid), *Canadian Interiors* magazine; numerous others.
Bibliography www.nienkamper.com.

Nies-Friedlaender, Cordula Kianga (1958–)

German industrial designer; born Kassel.

Training 1978–79, apprenticeship at Daimler-Benz; 1979–84, product design, Staatliche Akademie der bildenden Künste, Stuttgart; 1985–87, Royal College of Art, London.
Biography 1984–85, she was an independent designer with clients including FAG in Frankfurt and Schmidt Motor Sport in Nuremberg. 1986, she worked at the industrial design studio Moggridge Associates and, from 1987, as a designer in the architecture office Foster Associates, both in London. Her work has included office furniture by Tecno, sale systems for Esprit London, interior decoration, and planning and detail studies in architecture.
Bibliography Cat., Design Center Stuttgart, *Women in Design: Careers and Life Histories Since 1900*, Stuttgart: Haus der Wirtschaft, 1989: 138–41.

Nieuwenhuis, Theodoor Willem (aka Theodorus Wilhelmus 1866–1951)

Dutch artist and interior and product designer.

Biography Nieuwenhuis designed advertising posters (1918) for Philips and other graphics, including lithography of plant life (1905); 1928–31, wallpaper for Rath & Dodeheefver; is best known for furniture, clocks, lamps, and textiles; also ceramics, particularly by De Distel.
Bibliography Jan Ritzema Bos, *Nederlandsche planten: 50 Oorspronkeluke Litho's in Kleuren van Th. Nieuwenhuis and L. Klaver*, Amsterdam: S.L. van Looy, 1905. *Dijsselhof, Lion Cachet en Nieuwenhuis: Drie ontwerpers*, Amsterdam: Prententenkabinet (Stadhouderskade 42), 1972.

Nike
> See Bowerman Jr., 'Bill' William Jay.

Niklová, Libuše (1934–1981)

Czech industrial designer; born Zlín.

Training Plastics design, College of Decorative Arts, Gottwaldov (now Zlín, Czech Republic).
Biography Niklová designed for Fatra Napajedla. Rubber toys by Gumotex Břeclav were her first venture in plastics. 1961, she began calling on PVC and polyethylene for inflatable toys, seating, boats, and other items, including 1968 children's toys by Fatra. She died in Zlín.
Exhibitions/citations Work shown in numerous exhibitions in Czechoslovakia and abroad, including 1967 *Design in Czechoslovakia*, London. Outstanding Product of the Year (toy designs), Czechoslovak CoID.
Bibliography Cat., Milena Lamarová, *Design a Plastické Hmoty*, Prague: Uměleckoprůmyslové Muzeum, 1972: 136.

Nilsson, Barbro (b. Barbro Lundberg 1899–1983)

Swedish textile designer; born Lundberg.

Training 1913–17 under Johanna Brunsson and Alma Jakobsson, weaving, Brunsson Vavskola; 1917–20, Kungliga Tekniska Högskolan, Stockholm; 1920–24, Högre Konstindustrielle Skolan, Stockholm.
Biography 1919–41, she was an instructor, Brunssons Vävskola; 1924–25, director and chief instructor (with Maria Nordenfelt), Craft and Design Seminarium (now Högskolan för Design och Konsthantverk), Göteborgs Universitet; 1924–25, instructor, Aftonskolan, Stockholm; visiting instructor, Kungliga Tekniska Högskolan, Stockholm, and Kunsthandværkerskolen, Copenhagen. 1927, she set up her own workshop in Stockholm; 1942–71, was artistic director, AB Märta Måås-Fjetterström in Båstad, a position she assumed after Måås-Fjetterström's death.
Exhibitions/citations Work included in 1954–57 *Design in Scandinavia*, touring the US, 1955 *H 55*, Hälsingborg; 1958 *Formes Scandinaves*, Musée des Arts Décoratifs, Paris. 1948 Litteris et Artibus Medal; 1954 Prince Eugen Medal.
Bibliography Cat., David Revere McFadden (ed.), *Scandinavian Modern Design 1880–1980*, New York: Abrams, 1982.

Nilsson, Wiwen (aka Edvin Wiwen-Nilsson 1897–1974)

Swedish silver designer; born Lund.

Training In the workshop of his father Anders Nilsson; Königliche Preussische Zeichenakademie, Hanau, Germany; Paris studio of Georg Jensen while at Académie de la Grande Chaumière and Académie Colarossi.
Biography From 1923, Nilsson worked in his father's workshop in Lund, where he became the manager in 1928. 1920s–30s, he worked in a geometrical style, which incorporated cylinders, hemispheres, and sharp angles into large vessels. Under Nilsson's and Erik Fleming's leadership, Swedish silver acquired a character uniquely its own.
Exhibitions/citations Work shown at 1939–40 *New York World's Fair: The World of Tomorrow*; 1955 *H 55*, Hälsingborg, 1954–57 *Design in Scandinavia*, touring the US; 1958 *Formes Scandinaves*, Musée des Arts Décoratifs, Paris. Gold medal, 1925 *Exposition Internationale des Arts Décoratifs et Industriels Modernes*, Paris; 1955 Gregor Paulsson trophy; 1956 gold medal, Swedish Goldsmiths' and Jewellers' Guild; 1958 Prince Eugen Medal.
Bibliography Cat., David Revere McFadden (ed.), *Scandinavian Modern Design 1880–1980*, New York: Abrams, 1982. Sylvie Raulet, *Bijoux art déco*, Paris: Regard, 1984. Annelies Krekel-Aalberse, *Art Nouveau and Art Déco* Silver, New York: Abrams, 1989.

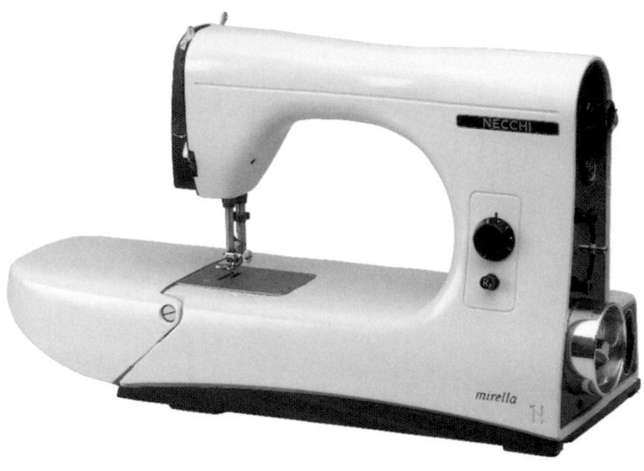

Marcello Nizzoli. Mirella sewing machine. 1956. Enameled aluminum, 11 x 19 1/2 x 7" (27.9 x 49.5 x 17.8 cm). Mf.: Necchi, Italy. Gift of the mfr. MoMA.

Ninaber van Eyben, Bruno (1950–)

Dutch designer; born Boxtel; active Delft.

Training Jewelry design, Jan van Eyck Akademie, Maastricht.
Biography Ninaber van Eyben's one-of-a-kind or limited-edition design commissions for special occasions include products ranging from an artificial kidney to a typewriter; also designed the new coinage (1980, produced from 1982, prior to the euro) of the Netherlands and 1998 obverse of the Dutch euro coinage (selected in a closed competition). 1985, he cofounded the 'nlplk' design consultancy (Ninaber/Peters/Krouwel Industrial Design). Other work has included a 1973 bracelet watch, renowned 1976 black rubber-cord necklace watch, 1977 fluorescent lighting system, 1994 lipped ruler (with the 'nlplk' group) by Randstad Uitzendbureau—all still in production. 1997, he established his own eponymous design studio, operating with a small staff.
Exhibitions/citations 1996 *Contemporary Design from the Netherlands* (lipped ruler), The Museum of Modern Art, New York. Second (1979) recipient of Kho Liang Ie applied-arts prize of Amsterdam Fonds voor de Kunst; numerous others.
Bibliography Jan Teunen (ed.), *Bruno Ninaber van Eyben*, Rotterdam: 010, 2002.

9999
> See Gruppo 9999.

Nissen, Søren (1944–)

Danish architect and furniture designer.

Training To 1965, apprenticeship, furniture manufacturer Rud. Rasmussen; to 1968, Kunsthåndværkerskolen, Copenhagen.
Biography From 1970, Nissen worked with Ebbe Gehl. Their furniture designs were produced by Ry Møbler.
Exhibitions Work included in 1975 *Danske Fyrretræsmøbler*, Berlin; 1976 *SCAN*, Washington, D.C.
Bibliography Frederik Sieck, *Nutidig Dansk Møbeldesign – en kortfa*

tet illustreret beskrivelse, Copenhagen: Bondo Gravesen, 1990.

Nixon, Harry
> See Noke, Charles John.

Nizzoli, Marcello (1887–1969)
Italian industrial designer; born Boretto.

Training 1910, architecture, materials, and graphics, Scuola di Belle Arti, Parma.
Biography Initially a painter, Nizzoli was later involved with the design of fabrics, exhibitions, and graphics, including 1926 posters for Campari; 1934–36 with Edoardo Persico, became a partner in a studio where they designed two 1934 Parker Pen shops in Milan, Hall of Gold Medals at 1934 *Aeronautical Exhibition,* a tubular-steel advertising structure in the Galleria Vittorio Emanuelle II in Milan, and the primary exhibit (Victory salon) at 1936 (6th) Triennale di Milano. 1931, industrialist Adriano Olivetti set up an advertising department in Olivetti's corporate headquarters, where Nizzoli began in 1936, to become a product designer of machines that have become classics. Work for Olivetti: 1948 Lexikon 80, 1950 Lettera 22, 1959 Diaspron 82 typewriters, and 1956 Divisumma 24 and Summa 40 adding machines. From 1950, he was also an architect to Olivetti. From 1948, he collaborated with G.M. Oliveri; designed 1955 automatic Supernova and 1956 Mirella sewing machines by Necchi (the latter a variation of the Lydia Mk2). In all of Nizzoli's work, the machinery is housed in organically curved casings, with attention paid to the outline and the applied graphics.
Exhibitions/citations Work shown in numerous exhibitions, and subject of 1968 exhibition in Milan. Gold medal (for Supernova), 1968 (14th) Triennale di Milano. Premio Compasso d'Oro: 1954 (for BU sewing machine by Necchi and Lettera 22 portable typewriter by Olivetti), 1957 (for Mirella sewing machine by Necchi), and 1960 (for Replic duplicating machine by Spada). 1961, elected Honorary Royal Designer for Industry, UK; 1962, honorary doctorate in architecture, Politecnico, Milan.
Bibliography L. Sinisgalli, *Biografia e bibliografia di Nizzoli: la botte e il violino*, no. 1, 1964. Germano Celant, *Marcello Nizzoli*, Milan: Comunità, 1968. Cat., Germano Celant and Gillo Dorfles, *Marcello Nizzoli*, Milan: Comunità, 1968. Cat., Benedetto Gravagnuolo (ed.), *Gli studi Nizzoli, architettura e design, 1948–1983*, Milan: Electa, 1983. Cat., Giovanni Giudici (ed.), *Design Process: Olivetti 1908–1983*, Ivrea: Olivetti, 1983: 381–82. Arturo Carlo Quintavalle (intro.), *Marcello Nizzoli*, Milan: Electa, 1990. Sibylle Kicherer, *Olivetti, a Study of the Corporate Management of Design*, New York: Rizzoli, 1990. Mangone Fabio and Godoli Ezio, *Marcello Nizzoli, design d'architettura*, Milan: Electa, 1992. Paola Antonelli (ed.), *Objects of Design: The Museum of Modern Art*, New York: The Museum of Modern Art, 2003: 224–25.
> See Oliveri, G. Mario.

Nó Design
Brazilian design studio; active São Paulo.

History The studio was founded by Flavio Di Sarno (1978–), Leonardo Massarelli (1979–), Márcio Giannelli (1977–), Pablo Casas (1979–); has designed a number of home furnishings and accessories; imaginatively and innovatively calls on recycled materials for the production of wares, including Runned Over bowls from reprocessed vehicle tires and Moth chair from shopping bags.

Noailles, de
> See de Noailles, vicomte Charles.

Nocq, Henri Eugène (1868–1944)
French sculptor and medalist; born Paris.

Training Under sculptor Henri Chapu.
Biography An occasional illustrator and graphic designer, Nocq was best known for his metalwork, including lamps, mirrors, jewelry, domestic accessories, and, especially, medals/medallions. As a critic and historian, he wrote numerous journal articles and, a major work on silver marks, the seminal book *L'orfèvrerie civile française du XVIe au début XIXe siècle* (with P. Alfassa and J. Guerin, Paris: Albert Lévy, 1927, two vols.), which accompanied the 1927 exhibition at the Pavillon de Marsan, Musée du Louvre, Paris.
Exhibitions/citations From 1887, work shown at editions of Salon des Artistes Français, at which he received an honorable-mention citation at 1889 edition and showed jewelry with sculptor Krieger at 1898 edition; 1897–1912, Salons of Société Nationale des Beaux-Arts; silver medal, 1900 *Exposition Universelle*, Paris. Was elected Chevalier of the Légion d'Honeur.
Bibliography Yvonne Brunhammer et al., *Art Nouveau in Belgium, France*, Houston: Institute for the Arts, Rice University, 1976.

Nogard Derain, Charlotte (b. Charlotte Nogard 1949–)
French designer and graphic and fine artist; wife of Gilles Derain.

Training École Nationale Supérieure des Arts Décoratifs, Paris; École de la Cambre, Brussels; École Rembrandt, Amsterdam; and École du Louvre, Paris.
Biography She has designed fabrics for Teskid in Italy, graphic design and packaging for Herboristerie du Palais Royal, and film posters for Paramount-Gaumont. Her murals and decorations appeared in the Ragtime bar in Cannes. She designed 1989 rugs for Géométrie Variable, including designs for children; 1987 package designs for toiletries by Prince Abdul Aziz Bin Khalifa Al Thani; continues as an artist with numerous exhibitions.

Noguchi, Isamu (1904–1988)
American sculptor and designer; born Los Angeles; active New York.

Training 1917, in cabinetmaking, Japan; 1921–22, Columbia University, New York.
Biography 1918, Noguchi returned to the US from Japan and, c. 1922, assisted the director of the Leonardo da Vinci Art School, New York. 1920s–30s, he created portrait busts; 1927–29, was Constantin Brancusi's assistant in Paris, where he met Alberto Giacometti. From 1932, Noguchi lived mainly in New York, where he was a sculptor. First used aluminum in the sculpture *Miss Expanding Universe* (1932); designed 1937 helmet-like Bakelite Radio Nurse by Zenith Radio of Chicago; 1940 glass motifs for Steuben Glassworks; a 1939 free-form glass-topped coffee table for the house of A. Congers Goodyear, the president of The Museum of Modern Art, New York. There were other variations of the table, including the version (IN50) mass-produced from 1944 by Herman Miller, discontinued 1973, and returned to production, 1984, by Herman Miller and, earlier, by other firms. Other Herman Miller furniture: 1944 IN20 (Fin) dining table, IN52 (Fin) coffee table, and IN22 (Fin) stool; 1946 IN70 sofa and matching IN71 ottoman (in limited editions to 1948). Noguchi designed ceramics produced in Japan; married expressive biomorphic forms with oriental elegance in his furniture designs. His sculpture gardens, including example at Bienecke Rare Book Library, Yale University, New Haven, Conn., fused design, sculpture, and architecture. The range of 1944 and 1951–66 Chochin-type (paper lantern in Gifu style) lighting fixtures made of mulberry paper and spirally woven bamboo, by Ozeki in Gifu, Japan, and called Akari (light), are still in production today. For mass production, he designed a playful 1954 rocking stool-table and

Isamu Noguchi. Radio Nurse speaker. 1937. Bakelite resin, h. 8 1/4" (21 cm) x dia. 6 1/2" (16.5 cm). Mfr: Zenith Radio Corporation, US. Gift of the designer. MoMA.

1955 group of wire-and-Formica tables by Knoll, and biomorphic tables, sofa, and ottoman for Herman Miller. The IN70 free-form upholstered sofa and ottoman have been reproduced by others from 1980s and, by Vitra, a number of Noguchi designs, particularly from 2003. 1985, he established a garden museum in Long Island City, N.Y., to exhibit his work; died in New York.
Exhibitions Designs and sculpture included in and subject of numerous exhibitions.
Bibliography Isamu Noguchi, 'Japanese Akari Lamps,' *Craft Horizons*, vol. 14, Sept. 1954: 16–18. Isamu Noguchi, 'Akari,' *Arts + Architecture*, vol. 72, May 1955: 14, 31. *Isamu Noguchi*, New York: Whitney Museum of Art, 1968. *Noguchi's Imaginary Landscapes*, Minneapolis: Walker Art Center, 1978. Videorecording, Bruce W. Bassett, *Isamu Noguchi*, director/producer, Bruce W. Bassett for Whitgate Productions, 1980. *Isamu Noguchi:Space of Akari and Stone*, San Francisco: Chronicle, 1986. Charlotte and Peter Fiell, *Modern Furniture Classics Since 1945*, London: Thames & Hudson, 1991. Bruce Altshuler, *Isamu Noguchi*, New York: Abbeville, 1994. Videorecording, *Isamu Noguchi: Stones and Paper*, producer: Princeton, N.J.: Films for the Humanities & Sciences, 1997. Paola Antonelli (ed.), *Objects of Design: The Museum of Modern Art*, New York: The Museum of Modern Art, 2003: 131.

Noirot, Emmanuelle (1961–)
> See Torck, Emmanuelle.

Noke, Charles John (1858–1941)
British ceramicist.

Training Worcester Royal Porcelain under Charles Binns.
Biography 1889, Noke became a modeler at Doulton in Burslem, Staffordshire; 1893–98, modeled vases (including Columbis and Diana) and figures (including Holbein and Rembrandt wares). Late 1890s to early 1900s, he began experimenting with the reproduction of Sung, Ming, and early Ch'ing dynasty blood-red *rouge flambé* and *sang-de-boeuf* glazes with Cuthbert Bailey and John Slater. c. 1906, Noke and William Edmund Grace introduced 'series' wares. 1914–36, he was artistic director at Doulton; c. 1914, introduced Titania ware and, c. 1915, Sung ware; with Harry Nixon and his son Cecil Jack Noke, developed *flambé* glaze designs and introduced Chang ware, named after southern Sung potter Chang the Elder. 1936, Noke retired and was succeeded by his son. To 1940, all his glazes were in production, and, by 1965, Sung and *rouge flambé* glazes were re-entered into production.
Bibliography Cat., *Thirties: British Art and Design Before the War*, London: Arts Council of Great Britain Hayward Gallery, 1979.

Nolan, Harry E.
American furniture designer and inventor; active Des Moines, Iowa.

Biography 1922, Nolan patented an eccentric 'lawn chair' based on the cantilever principle. Later, it was the basis of the 1931 legal action in Berlin, in which Anton Lorenz sued Thonet over rights to Lorenz's and other tubular-steel furniture. Nolan's design used solid steel rods rather than the tubular steel used by Lorenz, Ludwig Mies van der Rohe, Marcel Breuer, and Mart Stam.
Bibliography Barbie Campbell-Cole and Tim Benton (eds.), *Tubular Steel Furniture*, London: The Art Book Company, 1979: 14. 'Documents,' *Journal of Design History*, vol. 3, nos. 2 and 3, 1990:171–72.

Noll, Alexandre (1880–1970)
French sculptor and furniture designer.

Biography 1920, Noll began working in wood; 1925, showed his work at the La Crémaillère shop in Paris; explored the plastic nature of wood in furniture, furnishings, and vessels that hovered between fine art and utility. Like his sculpture, each piece was one-of-a-kind and clearly handmade. In addition to furniture, he produced numerous household objects.
Bibliography Patrick Favardin, *Le Style 50: un moment de l'art français*, Paris: Sous Le Vent—Vilo, 1987: 66–73. François Mathey, *Au bonheur des formes, design français 1945–1992*, Paris: Regard, 1992: 208–09. Olivier, Jean-Elie and Pierre Passebon, *Alexandre Noll*, Paris: Regard, 1999. Cat., Sophie Tasma Anargyros et al., *L'école française: les créateurs de meubles du 20ème siècle*, Paris: Industries Françaises de l'Ameublement, 2000.

Nord, Beban
> See Box Design.

Nordström, Patrick (1870–1929)
Swedish ceramicist; active Denmark.

Training 1889–90, Svenska Slöjdföreningens Skola, Gothenburg; 1894–95, Tekniska Yrkesskolan, Lund.
Biography 1902–07, Nordström was active in his own workshop on the Bakkegårdsalle, Copenhagen; 1907–10, in Vanlose, Denmark; 1911–23, worked at Royal Copenhagen Porcelain Factory and, subsequently, in his own workshop in Islev in Denmark from 1923–29. A pioneer in Danish stoneware, he became known for his unusual glazes.
Exhibitions Work shown at 1900 *Exposition Universelle*, Paris; 1914 *Baltic Exhibition*, Malmö; 1982–83 *Scandinavian Modern Design 1880–1980*, Cooper-Hewitt National Design Museum, New York. Work subject of 1956 exhibition, Det Danske Kunstindustrimuseum, Copenhagen.
Bibliography Cat., David Revere McFadden (ed.), *Scandinavian Modern Design 1880–1980*, New York: Abrams, 1982. Jennifer Hawkins Opie, *Scandinavia: Ceramics and Glass in the Twentieth Century*, New York: Rizzoli, 1989.

Norguet, Patrick (1969–)
French designer.

Training To 1993, mechanical engineering, Institut Universitaire de Technologie (IUT), Le Mans; to 1996, École Supérieure de Design Industriel (ESDI), Paris.
Biography 1997–98, Norguet worked at Louis Vuitton, responsible for visual identity; 1998, established his own studio in Paris, active as a product, interior, and set designer. Work has included the widely published 2000 Rainbow methacrylate-striped chair, 2001 Rive Droite sofa and armchair (with Emilio Pucci fabric), and 2001 Empty table by Cappellini; 2001 Apollo 71 sofa, Apollo pedestal chair, What's Up chaise/sofa, Ny02 armchair by Artifort; 2002 Go vase and others in Limoges porcelain by Artoria; Ancolie vases for Musée des Arts Décoratifs, Paris. Other clients have included Givenchy, Dior, Marithé et François Girbaud, Renault, Van Cleef & Arpels, Moroso, and Liv'it.

Noriyuki, Otsuka (1960–)
Japanese interior designer; born Fukui Prefecture.

Training 1981, Tokyo Designer Gakuin College.
Biography Noriyuki worked at Plastic Studio & Associates in Tokyo; 1983–84, traveled in Europe; 1989, established her own eponymous design office. Work includes 1989 Maha bar/restaurant in Tokyo, Ondine shoe store in Sapporo, 1994 furniture by Pleats Box.
Exhibitions Work subject of 1994 *Otsuka Noriyuki—Beyond Scenery*, Omotesando, Tokyo.

Norton, Ian
> See Dudas, Frank.

Norway Says
Norwegian design collaborative.

History 2000, Norway Says was founded by some graduates of schools in Bergen and Oslo in an effort, according to its manifesto, to improve Norway's design reputation, which lagged behind other Nordic countries. The studio is composed of five designers/interior architects: Torbjørn Anderssen (Elverum, 1976–), Tore Borgersen (Trønsberg, 1966–), Andreas Engesvik (Svolvær, 1970–), Frode Myhr (Tromsø, 1974–), and Espen Voll (Trondheim, 1965–). Norway Says commissions have included 2001 KPI 1,000-CD cabinet (a wedding present to Prince Haakon and Princess Mette Marit, commissioned by the Norwegian Prime Minister), 2001 Pancras chair/stool/table by Iform, 2002 April seating by Vestre, and 2002 Dock chair by Globe Furniture; also products by Saporiti Italia, Habitat, and Pure Design, and, in Norway, Vestre, Hovden Møbel, Skisma Industrier, and Slettvoll. Designers in the group work in tandem with one or another or independently, some through their own practices.
Exhibitions/citations Work included 2001 exhibition, Rom gallery for architecture, Oslo; 2001 Innotown Design Festival, Ålesund Art Center, Ålesund; 2001, Kunstindustrimuseum, Bergen; 2002 *Milan in a Van: The Best of the Milan Furniture Fair*, Victoria and Albert Museum, London. Received 2003 International Design Award (for Anderssen's Papermaster magazine rack by Swedese), Norska Designrådet (Norwegian design council).
Bibliography *The New York Times*, 20 Apr. and 19 Oct. 2000. *Design Week*, no. 8, 2000. *Wallpaper**, Aug. 2000 and Apr. 2002. *Frame*,

Patrick Norguet. Rive Droite armchair. 2001. Plywood, polyurethane, steel, and fabric design by Pucci, h. 26 7/8 x w. 38 1/4 x d. 29 5/8" (69 x 98 x 76 cm). Mfr.: Cappellini, Italy.

July–Aug. 2001. *Abitare*, Sept. 2001. *Domus*, nos. 840 and 841, Oct. and Sept. 2001. *Atrium*, Nov. 2001. Charlotte Fiell, *Scandinavian Design*, London: Taschen, 2002.

Nouvel, Jean (1945–)

French architect and designer; born Fumel.

Training 1966–71, DPLG architecture (governmental diploma), France.
Biography 1970, Nouvel set up his first office with architect / scenographer François Seigueur; 1985, established his own architecture practice and, 1988 with others, Nouvel, Cattani & Associés; 1994, established Ateliers Jean Nouvel (AJN), Paris, the current and largest of his architecture practices with 40 active projects at any one time in 13 countries, and, subsequently, Jean Nouvel Design (JND) for industrial design; 1976, founded 'Mars 1976' movement; 1980, became a founding member and artistic director, Biennale de l'Architecture, Paris. He has been active in numerous projects for the theater, working with scenographer Jacques Le Marquet on the Théâtre de Jean-Maire Serreau, the Cartoucherie de Vincennes, part of the Théâtre de Belfort, and the Opéra in Lyon. As an architect, is best known for the 1981 – 87 Institut du Monde Arabe (with sun-sensitive lenses on the south window wall, as well as interiors and reception-room furnishings), Paris. Other architecture: part of 1977 renovation, Gaieté Lyrique, Paris; 1978 renovation and extension of clinic Centre Médico-Chirurgical (with Gilbert Lézènes), Bezons; 1979 Collège Anne Frank (with Lézènes), Antony; 1981–83 municipal theater renovation (with Lézènes and Dominique Lyon), Belfort; 1989 Tour sans Fin building, La Défense (with Emmanuel Cattani), France; 1991–94 Cartier headquarters, Paris; 1992 factory of Cartier, Villeret, Switzerland. His furniture in general is simplified to its barest form, and late-1980s examples were reminiscent of Louis Cuny's 1920s work. He designed 1996 Quasi Normal and Normal office furniture; Carte Blanche range by Bulo; 1987 BAO articulated aluminum chest (prototype), IAC table, unnamed folding table, and extending bookshelves (all Carte Blanche production support from VIA—unrelated to the furniture by Bulo), a collection by Knoll; 1989 cold-molded polyurethane divan in his Profils range by Ligne Roset. 1988, designed the installation of *Les Années 50* exhibition, Centre Georges Pompidou, Paris. 1991, was elected vice-president, Institut Français d'Architecure; served as the editor, *International Yearbook of Design* (1995).
Exhibitions/citations Furniture shown at 1988 French-furniture exhibition, Victoria and Albert Museum, London (catalog below). Work included in 1998–99 *Premises* exhibition of French art, architecture, and design, Guggenheim Museum Soho, New York, and subject of 1995 exhibition, Architektur Zentrum, Vienna; 2002, Centre Georges Pompidou, Paris; others. 1983 silver medal, Facultad de Arquitectura, and honorary doctorate, Universidad de Buenos Aires; 1987 architecture grand prize (for Institut du Monde Arabe) and 1993 (for Opéra, Lyon), Équerre d'Argent; 1987 special mention, Aga Khan Prize; Creator of the Year, 1987 Salon du Meuble, Paris; 1990 *Architectural Record* prize (for 1987–89 Saint James hotel-restaurant, Bouliac); 1987 Carte Blanche production support from VIA, to produce a range of aluminum furniture; best French building; 1983, Chevalier of the Ordre des Arts et Lettres; 1983 silver medal, Academie d'Architecture; 2001 Praemium Imperiale award, Japan; 2001 gold medal, Royal Institute of British Architects (RIBA).
Bibliography Patrice Goulet, *Jean Nouvel*, Paris: Electa Moniteur, 1987. Cat., Garth Hall and Margo Rouard Snowman, *Avant Premiere: Contemporary French Furniture*, London: Éprouvé, 1988. Cat., *Les années VIA, 1980–1990*, Paris: Musée des Arts Décoratifs, 1990. Olivier Boissière, *Jean Nouvel*, Zürich: Artemis, 1992. Olivier Boissière, *Jean Nouvel*, Paris: Terrail, 1996. Aurora Cuito and Cristina Montes (eds.), *Jean Nouvel*, Kempen: teNeues, 2002.

Novembre, Fabio (1966–)

Italian architect and designer; born Lecce.

Training 1992, degree in architecture, Politecnico, Milan.
Biography Novembre has designed furniture, including 2001 Org table with a clear-glass top and 171 red legs of rope, only six of which are for structural support; also by Cappellini: 2001 Net carpet and 2002 And sofa; 1988 Honlywood chair by B&B Italia; 1991 Mediterranea chaise longue by Pierantonio Bonacina. From 2000, he has been the artistic director of Bisazza mosaics firm.
Bibliography Beppe Finessi and Fabio Novembre, *Domus*, no. 809, Nov. 1998: 96–103. Leo Gullbring, *Fabio November*, Basel: Birkhäuser, 2001.

Novotný, Otakar (1880–1959)

Czech architect and designer; born Benešov.

Training To 1903 under Jan Kotěra, Vysoká Škola Uměleckoprůmyslová (VŠUP; academy of arts, architecture, and design), Prague.
Biography After 1903, Novotný worked in Kotěra's studio; 1902, became a member, Mánes Association of Plastic Artists, and served as its chairperson from 1913–15 and 1920–32; 1929–54, was professor, VŠUP, Prague; was commissioner of exhibitions in Paris, Rome, and Vienna. He was influenced by Henrik Berlage's brick architecture in the Netherlands; became an important exponent of Cubism in architecture and design. Commissions included the exhibition halls for the Association of Czech Accomplishment at 1914 *Deutscher Werkbund-Ausstellung*, Cologne; 1946 Charles Eames exhibition; 1927–30 Mánes Association building, Prague.
Exhibitions/citations Grand prize, 1925 *Exposition Internationale des Arts Décoratifs et Industriels Modernes*, Paris.
Bibliography Alexander von Vegesack et al., *Czech Cubism: Architecture, Furniture, and Decorative Arts, 1910–1925*, New York: Princeton Architectural Press, 1992.

Noyes, Eliot Fette (1910–1977)

American architect and industrial designer; born Boston; active New Canaan, Conn.

Training 1928–32, architecture, Harvard University, Cambridge, Mass.; 1932–35 and 1937–38 under Walter Gropius and Marcel Breuer, Harvard Graduate School of Design.
Biography Noyes became an advocate of the modern European

Eliot Noyes. Selectric electric typewriter. 1961. Painted metal and plastic, 7 1/16 x 17 11/16 x 15 3/4" (18 x 45 x 40 cm). Mfr.: IBM, US. Courtesy Quittenbaum Kunstauktionen, Munich.

design ethic after reading Le Corbusier's book *Vers une architecture* (Paris: Crès, 1923) and Gropius's published teachings. 1938, Noyes worked in the office of architects Coolidge, Shepley, Bulfinch and Abbot in Boston and, 1939–40, in the office of Gropius and Breuer in Cambridge. On Gropius's recommendation, he served as first director of industrial design (1940–42 and 1945–46), The Museum of Modern Art, New York, where he was curator of 1940 *Organic Design in Home Furnishings* competition/exhibition among others. 1946–47, he worked in the office of industrial designer Norman Bel Geddes, where he designed the IBM Model A electric typewriter. When the Bel Geddes design firm closed, Noyes was retained by IBM to set up a corporate program of design along the lines of Olivetti; from 1947, was concurrently in private practice in New Canaan, Conn. 1956–77, was corporate design director of IBM, where he rejected annual model changes and concessions to marketing; took the same approach for other clients, including Westinghouse from 1960–76, Mobil from 1964–77, Pan Am from 1969–72, and as president of MIT from 1972–77. Noyes appointed graphic designers sympathetic with his approach (much like Gropius), such as Paul Rand to IBM, Ivan Chermayeff to Mobil, and Breuer and other prominent architects to design IBM buildings worldwide. Noyes was instrumental in shaping the image of the major companies for which he worked. His product designs for IBM included 1959 Executive, 1961 Selectric electric typewriters (conceived on paper from 1950), 1960 Executary dictating machine (hardly distinguishable from a Braun product), 1961 Golfball No. 72 electric typewriter, and 1440 Data Processing System. He designed many of IBM's mainframe computers as well as corporate office buildings and interiors for IBM and others. His 1964 Mobil filling station was adopted as a standard model for the company's stations worldwide. His 'balloon' house at Hobe Sound, Fla., was constructed by spraying wet concrete onto a large inflated balloon to create a hemisphere. Other houses incorporated open plans with spaces delineated by furniture or fireplaces and featured natural materials, including stone and wood, as in some houses by Breuer. 1947–54, he wrote a column on design for *Consumer Reports* magazine; 1965–70, was president, International Design Conferences, Aspen, Colo. In his office, Noyes displayed a child's version of Harley Earl's automobile fascia to illustrate to his staff and clients 'false principles' and vulgarity in design. He died in New Caanan, Conn.
Exhibitions/citations 1954 design award for distinguished American modernism (Noyes's own house, New Canaan), *Progressive Architecture* journal.
Bibliography Eliot Noyes, *Organic Design and Home Furnishing*, New York: Museum of Modern Art, 1941. Walter McQuade, 'An Industrial Designer with a Conspicuous Conscience,' *Fortune*, Aug. 1963: 135–38, 183–88, 190. 'The Work of Eliot Noyes and Associates,' *Industrial Design*, June 1966. 'Eliot F. Noyes (1910–1977), obituary, *Industrial Design*, June 1966. Jay Doblin, *One Hundred Great Product Designs*, New York: Van Nostrand Reinhold, 1970: no. 93. Cat., Kathryn B. Hiesinger and George H. Marcus III (eds.), *Design Since 1945*, Philadelphia: Philadelphia Museum of Art, 1983. Vittorio Magnago Lampugnani (ed.), *Encyclopedia of 20th-Century Architecture*, New York: Abrams, 1986: 252.

NSF (Nederlandsche Seintoestellen Fabriek)
> See Philips.

Nummi, Yki (1925–1984)
Finnish lighting and interior designer and colorist; born China to son of a missionary.

Training 1945–47, in mathematics and physics, Helsinki and Turku; 1946–50, painting, Taideteollinen korkeakoulu, Helsinki.
Biography 1950–58, Nummi was a designer in the design department of Orno Metalfactories, creating lamps for hospitals, sanatoria, churches, and other contracts. 1950–75, he designed lighting for Stockmann, Helsinki. His fixtures incorporated innovative materials, including colored and white acrylics, opaline glass, aluminum, and brass. 1951–65, he designed series of white and transparent acrylic lamps, including 1956 Modern Art, named due to its acceptance into The Museum of Modern Art collection; was a board member of the Orno company and of Ornamo (Finnish association of designers); from 1958, head of color-design department of paint manufacturer Schildt & Hallberg; early 1960s, designed a color plan for Helsingin Tuomiokirkko (Helsinki cathedral). As a result of 1960 Lentävä Lautanen (sky flyer) hanging lamp (today made by Adelta, Germany), he is acknowledged as being one of the first Finns to use plastics / acrylics for lighting. He collaborated with Lisa Johansson-Pape as

Yki Nummi. Table lamp. 1955. Acrylic, overall h. 15 5/8" (39.7 cm) x dia. 11 1/4" (28.6 cm). Mfr: Stockmann-Orno, Finland. Phyllis B. Lambert Fund. MoMA.

color specialist at Stockman/Orno, Kerava. Later became an independent designer of lighting, furniture, and furnishings; wrote on color, lighting, and design principles.
Exhibitions/citations Designed 100W/24 main spotlights for *Exposition Universelle et Internationale de Bruxelles*. Work shown in 1954–57 *Design in Scandinavia*, touring the US; 1955 *H 55*, Hälsingborg; 1958 *Formes Scandinaves*, Musée des Arts Décoratifs, Paris, 1956–57 *Finnish Exhibition*, touring West Germany; 1961 *Finlandia* in Zürich, Amsterdam, and London. Lighting honored at 1954 (10th), 1957 (11th), and 1960 (12th) Triennale di Milano; received 1971 Pro Finlandia prize.
Bibliography Erik Zahle (ed.), *A Treasury of Scandinavian Design*, New York: Golden Press, 1961. Cat., David Revere McFadden (ed.), *Scandinavian Modern Design 1880–1980*, New York: Abrams, 1982.

Nurmesniemi, Antti Aarre (1927–2003)
Finnish interior and industrial designer; born Hämeenlinna; active Helsinki; husband of Vuokko Eskolin.

Training To 1950, interior design, Taideteollinen Oppilaitos, Helsinki.
Biography 1949–50, Nurmesniemi was a furniture designer in the design office of Stockmann department store, Helsinki; 1951–56, was furniture and interior designer in office of architect Viljo Revell, Helsinki and, 1954–55, was active in the office of architect Giovanni Romano, Milan; designed interiors for hotels, restaurants, and banks. 1956, he returned to Finland and set up his own design studio; created popular designs for furniture (sometimes with his wife Vuokko Eskolin) by various firms and his own firm; lighting; glassware; wallpaper; textiles; transportation (with Börje Rajalin); and metalwork, including 1958 Finel coffee pot (a standard in Finnish homes) in two sizes by Wärtsilä-Arabia; numerous interior designs, including public and corporate offices, restaurants, hotels, banks; a widely published 1952 sauna stool, for the Palace Hotel, Helsinki (produced in mass by G. Soderstrom); 1974 railway carriages for President of Finland and Council of State. Clients included Artek (furniture and lighting) from 1957–60, Merivaara (furniture) from 1963–66, Vecta Möbel (furniture) in 1978, Fujitsu (telephone) in 1984, Cassina (furniture) in 1985, Piiroinen from 1990, and others. He was active in restoration projects, lectured worldwide, designed a large number of exhibitions. His work combined the bareness of modernism with the traditions of Finnish design. He was president, Ornamo (Finnish association of designers); from 1982, was a member, European Council of Science, Art and Culture.
Exhibitions/citations Work included in numerous venues and subject of 1992 exhibition (catalog below) and 2003 exhibition, Helsinki. Received 1959 Lunning Prize; grand prizes at 1957 (11th) and 1964 (13th) (for sauna stool) editions of Triennale di Milano and a grand prize at its 1960 (12th) edition; first prize, 1955 competition of Suo-

men Taideteollisuusyhdistys (Finnish society of crafts and design) for 80th-anniversary exhibition; 1975 Finnish State Design Award; 1981 medal, Society of Industrial Artists and Designers (now The Chartered Society of Designers), UK; 1986, elected Honorary Royal Designer for Industry, UK; 1991 Japan Design Foundation Award.
Bibliography Erik Zahle (ed.), *A Treasury of Scandinavian Design*, New York: Golden Press, 1961. 'Thirty-four Lunning Prize-Winners,' *Mobilia*, no. 146, Sept. 1967. Cat., *Modern Chairs 1918–70*, London: Lund Humphries, 1971: no. 35. Marja Kaipainen, 'Some Call Them Purists,' *Form Function Finland*, no. 2, 1981: 12–16. Cat., David R. McFadden (ed.), *Scandinavian Modern Design 1880–1980*, New York: Abrams, 1982. Cat., *The Lunning Prize*, Stockholm: Nationalmuseum 1986. Cat., Marja-Liisa Bell et al., *Antti Nurmesniemi: ajatuksia ja suunnitelmia = To Reflect and to Design*, Helsinki: Kaupungin Taidemuseo, 1992.

Nurmesniemi, Vuokko (b. Vuokko Eskolin 1930–)

Finnish textile designer; wife of Antti Nurmesniemi.

Training 1948–52, ceramics, Taideteollinen korkeakoulu, Helsinki.
Biography 1952–53, she designed ceramics and glassware for Wärtsilä-Arabia; 1953, turned to textile design and began working for Marimekko; 1953–60, was Marimekko's chief designer, responsible for fabrics and clothing. Her color range for Marimekko was warmer than that of its earlier range of vivid geometric prints. She created large graphic images often called panels because they were frequently hung flat. Concurrently at Marimekko, she designed for Borås in Sweden and Pausa in Germany; 1964, set up her own design firm Vuokko in Helsinki, producing clothing, fashion accessories, and fabrics. Some of her husband Antti Nurmesniemi's furniture designs were executed in collaboration with the Vuokko firm.
Citations 1957 (11th) (gold medal) and 1964 (13th) (grand prize with Antti Nurmesniemi) editions of Triennale di Milano; 1964 Lunning Prize; 1968 Pro Finlandia prize.
Bibliography 'Thirty-four Lunning Prize-Winners,' *Mobilia*, no. 146, Sept. 1967. Marja Kaipainen, 'Some Call Them Purists,' *Form Function Finland*, no. 2, 1981: 13–16. Charles S. Talley, *Contemporary Textile Art: Scandinavia*, Stockholm: Carmina, 1982: 136–38. Cat., David Revere McFadden (ed.), *Scandinavian Modern Design 1880–1980*, New York: Abrams, 1982. Cat., Kathryn B. Hiesinger and George H. Marcus III (eds.), *Design Since 1945*, Philadelphia: Philadelphia Museum of Art, 1983. Cat., *The Lunning Prize*, Stockholm: Nationalmuseum, 1986.

Nüssli, Kuno (1970–)
> See N2.

Antti Nurmesniemi. Sauna sool. 1952. Laminated birch and teak, 16 3/4 x 16 7/8 x 16 3/4" (42.5 x 42.8 x 42.5 cm). Mfr: G. Soderstrom, Finland. Gift of Palace Hotel, Helsinki. MoMA.

Nuutajärvi-Notsjö

Finnish glass factory.

History Until 1987, Nuutajärvi was Finland's oldest glass factory. Its history began in 1793, when the Notsjö glass factory was established at Nuutajärvi by Swedes to produce mainly window panes and bottles; from 1851, began to make pressed-glass objects; 1853, was bought by Adolf Törngren, who improved production methods and used higher-quality raw materials; 1861–78, manufactured ceramics; 1865, set up its own glass shop at Stockmann, which evolved into the largest and best-known department store in Helsinki. 1946–48, Gunnel Nyman was hired as the designer, who created a close working relationship between designer and glassworker and set high standards for glass design. 1950, the facility was closed for a short time due to a fire and, subsequently, bought by Wärtsilä. 1950–76, Kay Franck was the artistic director of Nuutajärvi and, with Saara Hopea, of Arabia, both Wärtsilä companies. Bottle production was discontinued, and art glass and household glass were emphasized. 1963, Oiva Toikka became the artistic director. Designers included Kerttu Nurminen, Heikki Orvola, and Markku Salo. 1987, Nuutajärvi was amalgamated with Iittala and, subsequently, became a part of Iittala's Pro Arte department.
Exhibitions Catalogs below.
Bibliography Cat., *Nuutajärvi: kartano ja lasipruuki: Näyttely, Suomen kansallismuseo = Notsjö: herrgård och glasbruk: utställning, Finlands Nationalmuseum*, Helsinki: Suomen Kansallismuseo, 1983. Jennifer Hawkins Opie, *Scandinavia: Ceramics and Glass in the Twentieth Century*, New York: Rizzoli, 1989. Tuula Poutasuo, *Nuutäjarvi: 200 vuotta suomalaista lasia = Nuutäjarvi: 200 Years of Finnish Glass*, Helsinki: Hackman, 1993. Cat., *Oiva Toikka: Glass from Nuutajarvi*, Helsinki: Amos Anderson Konstmuseum, 1995.

Nykänen, Frans Evald (1893–1951)

Finnish silversmith; born St. Petersburg; active Helsinki.

Training In his father's workshop in Sortavala, Sweden (now Finland).
Biography Nykänen founded Viri, which produced silver items in small series, and worked for others; from 1918, was director of Taito silversmiths, where one of the consultant designers was Gunilla Jung. At the time, Nykänen was considered the best chaser in Finland.
Bibliography Annelies Krekel-Aalberse, *Art Nouveau and Art Déco Silver*, New York: Abrams, 1989.

Nylund, Gunnar (1904–1997)

Danish ceramicist; born Paris, France.

Training In architecture in Finland and Denmark.
Biography Nyland turned to ceramics due to an economic recession, which thwarted a practice in architecture; began his ceramics career at Bing & Grondahl Porcelænsfabrik, Denmark; 1929 with Nathalie Krebs, set up Nylund og Krebs, a stoneware-pottery studio in Copenhagen, which became Saxbo in 1930, when Krebs took over its management. (Saxbo was active to 1968.) From 1931, Nylund worked at Rörstrand, where he was the artistic director to 1937, remaining to 1956. The 1932 Candia pattern is one of his best known by Rörstrand. During his prolific tenure, he created a range of wares from dinner services to ornamental, even monumental, objects. From 1956, he worked freelance, continuing to manifest the influence of Chinese pottery, but remained associated with Rörstrand for most of his life.
Bibliography Cat., David Revere McFadden (ed.), *Scandinavian Modern Design 1880–1980*, New York: Abrams, 1982. George Fischler and Barrett Gould, *Scandinavian Ceramics and Glass: 1940s to 1980s*, Atglen, Pa.: Schiffer, 2000.

Nyman, Gunnel Gustafsson (1909–1948)

Finnish glassware, furniture, and textile designer.

Training 1928–32 under Arttu Brummer, Taideteollinen korkeakoulu, Helsinki.
Biography Nyman worked for all the renowned Finnish glass manufacturers of the 20th century: Riihimäki from 1932–47, Karhula from 1935–37, Nuutajärvi-Notsjö from 1946–48, and Iittala from 1946–47—and was active in both production and studio glass. Her style was characterized by a strong sense of form, the plastic quality of molten glass, and a subtle articulation of surface and mass. 1935–37, she also designed furniture (by Taito), textiles, and lighting fixtures.
Exhibitions/citations 1933 (third prize) and 1936 (second and third prizes), Riihimäki glass competition; 1936 (second and third prizes),

Karhula glass competition; gold medal (for glass) and silver medal (for furniture), 1937 *Exposition Internationale des Arts et Techniques dans la Vie Moderne*, Paris; gold medal (glass), 1951 (9th) Triennale di Milano.
Bibliography Cat., David Revere McFadden (ed.), *Scandinavian Modern Design 1880–1980*, New York: Abrams, 1982. Frederick Cooke, *Glass: Twentieth-Century Design*, New York: Dutton, 1986: 52, 83. Jennifer Hawkins Opie, *Scandinavia: Ceramics and Glass in the Twentieth Century*, New York: Rizzoli, 1989.

Nymølle Fajansfabrik

Danish ceramics factory.

History c. 1937, Schou Ravnholm established the Fuurstrøm pottery factory in Kongens Lyngby to manufacture inexpensive earthenware. (Schou Ravnholm was a retail firm that sold imported ceramics and inexpensive goods.) After World War II, Fuurstrøm commissioned Jacob Bang to supervise more artistic wares made in the factory, renamed Nymølle Fajansfabrik. 1946, Bang invited Bjørn Wiinblad to design at the firm. 1946–56, most of the line was designed for copper-plate engraving of transfer prints by Wiinblad. 1974, the firm went into bankruptcy; 1976, was purchased by Wiinblad.
Bibliography Jennifer Hawkins Opie, *Scandinavia: Ceramics and Glass in the Twentieth Century*, New York: Rizzoli, 1989.

Torben Ørskov & Co.: Herbert Krenchel. Krenit bowl (detail). 1953. MoMA.

O
> See Fevre, Francis.

O luce
Italian lighting firm; lcoated San Giuliano Milanese (Milan).

History 1945, Giuseppe Ostuni established the firm that has become the oldest Italian lighting-design company still active. Designers have included the Castiglioni brothers, Franco Buzzi, Tito Agnoli, Forti, Bruno Gecchelin, Mario Antonio Arnaboldi, Gianemilio Monti, and Marcello Minale. It was with designs like Joe and Gianni Colombo's 1962 Acrilica table lamp (no. 281) that O luce's output became more revolutionary. Other models have included 1963 no. 175 in white perspex with a swivel shade by Marco Zanuso; and 1965 Spider, 1968 Coupé, and 1971 Colombo (first indoor halogen lamp) by Joe Colombo. Early 1970s, the Verderi family bought O luce, and Vico Magistretti became the artistic director and chief designer. From early 1990s, Hannes Wettstein and Riccardo Dalisi designed for the firm. 1995, Marco Romanelli became the artistic director with designs by Sebastian Bergne, Hans Peter Weidmann, Marta Laudani, and Romanelli himself. The 1997 Estella lamp models were the Campana brothers' first product to be serially produced. 2000, Toni Cordero began collaboration with the firm.
Exhibitions/citations 1972 *Italy: The New Domestic Landscape* (Spider), The Museum of Modern Art, New York; 1999–2000 *The State of Things* (Laterna), Berlin, Brunswick, and Cologne. Premio Compasso d'Oro: 1964 (gold medal for Colombo model) and 1968 (recognition for Spring) Triennale di Milano. 1955 (nos. 363 and S154), 1956 (no. 4161 and Polivinile), 1967 (Spider by Colombo), 1979 (Atollo by Magistretti), 1981 (Nara 420 by Magistretti), 1984 (Slalom), 1989 (Personal by Gecchelin), 1991 (Sister 365 by Dalisi), and 2001 (Lanerna and Nuvola). Other citations: 1968 International Design Award (Coupé and Spring), American Institute of Decorators (AID), Chicago; 1999 Prix d'Excellence (Lid), *Marie Claire Maison* magazine.

Oberheim, Robert (1938–)
German industrial designer; born Gedern.

Training Werkkunstschule, Wiesbaden.
Biography From 1972, Oberheim was the second director of the design studio of Braun, the domestic electrical appliance manufacturer, where, among others, he designed 1957 Multipurpose food processor (no. KM 32, with Gerd Alfred Müller), 1965 S 8 T camera, 1970 D 300 slide projector, 1971 FP 30 movie projector, 1972 Intercontinental razor (with Florian Seiffer), 1982 PSK 1200 hair dryer, 1992 GCS portable (handbag) hair curler, and a large number of other products.

Obrist, Hermann (1862–1927)
Swiss sculptor and designer; born Kilchberg, Switzerland; active Germany.

Training In medicine and natural sciences; from 1888, in ceramics; subsequently in sculpture, Académie Julian, Paris.
Biography 1886, Obrist turned to art, prompted by a vision of a radiant city; 1892, settled in Florence, concentrating on marble techniques; 1894, established a studio for embroidery in Munich. Obrist, Peter Behrens, Bruno Paul, Bernhard Pankok, and Richard Riemerschmid followed the lead of Koloman Moser and Josef Hoffmann's Wiener Werkstätte and founded the Münchner Vereinigte Werkstätten für Kunst im Handwerk (Munich united workshops for art in handwork) in 1897. It aimed to sell everyday objects designed by modern designers. Obrist was one of the leading designers of the Jugendstil and designed furniture and textiles. 1901 with Wilhelm von Debschitz, Obrist cofounded the Lehr- und Versuchsateliers für angewandte und freie Kunst, known as the Debschitz-Schule, whose rostrum of graduates became distinguished.
Exhibitions Work included in 1988 exhibition, Philadelphia (catalog below).
Bibliography Frederick Cooke, *Glass: Twentieth-Century Design*, New York: Dutton, 1986: 36–38. Stuart Durant, *Ornament from the Industrial Revolution to Today*, Woodstock, N.Y.: Overlook, 1986: 47, 327. Cat., Kathryn Bloom Hiesinger (ed.), *Die Meister des Münchner Jugenstils*, Munich: Stadtmuseum, 1988: 79–87.

Obrtel, Vít (1901–1988)
Czech architect, book, set, and furniture designer, poet, and theoretician; born Olomouc.

Training 1918–25, České Vysoké Učení Technické (Czech technical university), Prague.
Biography From 1923 until its close in 1931, Obrtel was a member of the Devětsil group; worked in the Prague city construction department and at the postal-and-telegraph ministry; 1925, moved to Paris. His early architecture work bridged Cubism and the style of the Puristická Čtyřka group, while strongly influenced by neoclassicism. Mid-1920s, he began working in the International Style and, by the end of 1920s, became interested in Hugo Häring's organic architecture. Obrtel designed 1927–28 family house at 561 Nábřeží Dukelských Hrdinů in Rožnov pod Radhoštěm and 1927–28 house with a bakery at 65 Husova St. in Jičín. By 1926, Obrtel was known as a book illustrator and for his Constructivist covers; converted his typographic designs into three dimensions in a 1927 stage set for the Osvobozené Divadlo (liberated theater). His essays on architecture were published in maga-

Robert Oberheim. Nizo 80 movie camera. 1968. Aluminum and plastic, 4 3/4 x 10 3/8 x 2" (12.1 x 26.3 x 5.1 cm). Mfr: Braun, Germany. Gift of Braun North America. MoMA.

zines *Tam-tam*, *ReD*, *Fronta*, *Plán*, and *Kvart*. From 1926, he opposed architect Karel Teige's scientific-Constructivist theories; died in Prague.
Exhibitions Work included in 1923 Bauhaus exhibition, Weimar; 1990 touring exhibition of Devětsil (catalog below).
Bibliography Cat., *Devětsil: Czech Avant-Garde Art, Architecture, and Design of the 1920s and 30s*, Oxford Museum of Modern Art, Oxford and London Design Museum, 1990. Cat., *Prague, 1900–1938: capitale secrète des avants-gardes*, Dijon: Musée des Beaux-Arts, 1997.

Oceano Oltreluce

Italian lighting manufacturer; located Casate Novo (Lecco).

History 1983, Oceano Oltreluce was founded by Marco Zanuso Jr., Luigi and Pietro Greppi, and Bepi Maggiori, who have also contributed designs to the products; produced Denis Santachiara's 1985 Sparta lamp stanchions and numerous other lighting models by less well-known designers, such as Josè Manuel and Carvalho Araùjo, Mario Belloni, Silvia Cortese, Mauro Galfrè, Kazuyo Komoda, Pino Montalti, Enrico Crespi, Titi Cusatelli, and Francesco Ruffini and Margherita Quinto. Its inventory has also included aluminum fixtures by the in-house design staff through its Alluminia division.
Bibliography Fumio Shimizu and Studio Matteo Thun (eds.), *The Italian Design: Descendants of Leonardo da Vinci*, Tokyo: Graphic-sha, 1987.

Oddo, Adriano M. (1948–)

Italian designer; born Cairo, Egypt; active Milan.

Training To 1973, in architecture.
Biography Oddo's clients included Sormani (furniture, furnishings, and lighting), Mopoa (clocks), 1974; Velca (furniture), 1975; Gabbianelli (tableware), 1975. 1972, he patented a mechanical knuckle joint; produced signage for 1972 Interieur design biennial, Courtrai; 1973, designed magazine *Nuovi Orizzonti* for the Italian tourist bureau; taught, Facoltà di Architettura, Politecnico, Milan, and at Liceo Artistico Statale, Novara; became a member, Associazione per il Disegno Industriale (ADI).
Citations Honorable mention, 1973 Concorso Internazionale della Ceramica d'Arte, Faenza.
Bibliography *ADI Annual 1976*, Milan: Associazione per il Disegno Industriale, 1976.

Odom, William Macdougal (1884–1942)

American teacher; born Georgia; active New York and Paris.

Training To 1908 under William Merritt Chase, New York School of Fine and Applied Art; under Leopold Stokowski, in music; design and architecture, École des Beaux-Arts, Paris.
Biography Later dubbed 'Mr. Taste,' Odom had by 1920 persuaded Frank Parsons, under whom he taught at New York School of Fine and Applied Art, to open a branch of the school in Paris. Odom lived on the place des Vosges in Paris in a 17th-century townhouse furnished in period French furniture and fitted with typical *boiserie* walls. He subsequently returned to New York; 1915–16 with Parsons, led study trips abroad. Through Odom's social connections, the students were able to visit public and private buildings of importance in France and, 1921, a branch of the school was established in Paris. c. 1922, Odom became head of the school's department of interior architecture and decoration, where he emphasized architecture and exerted a lasting influence on interior design. 1930–42, he was president of the school, and he renamed it Parsons School of Design in 1941. He never decorated professionally and could not tolerate working with clients. In the décors for himself, almost everything was arranged symmetrically and often fitted out in pairs of furniture pieces and objects. At his behest, he was buried in London, and part of his furnishings went to Musée des Arts Décoratifs, Paris.
Bibliography 'The Influence of William Odom on American Taste,' *House & Garden*, July 1946. John Esten and Rose Bennett Gilbert, *Manhattan Style*, Boston: Little, Brown, 1990: vii, 6–7.

Oerke, Thilo (1940–)

German industrial designer; born Celle.

Training 1964–68 under Mattias Janssen, Technische Universität, Berlin, and, under Arno Votteler, Hochschule für bildende Künste, Brunswick.
Biography Oerke worked in the office of Arno Votteler, designing electronic equipment by Blaupunkt; 1968–70, designed for Siemens and for Blaupunkt. Other clients have included Perpetuum Ebner, Dual, Intel, Europhon, Thomson-Brandt-Dual, Rosita Tonmöbel. One of his best-know designs is c. 1971 Vision 2000 spherical radio/cassette unit on a pedestal by Rosita Tonmöbel.
Citations 1969 Bundespreis 'Gute Form,' Rat für Formgebung (German design council), Frankfurt.
Bibliography Cat., *Made in Germany*, Cologne, 2001: 199, no. 108. Auction cat., *Modernes Design Kunsthandwerk nach 1945*, Munich: Quittenbaum, 4 Dec. 2001, lot 36.

Oerley, Robert (1876–1945)

Austrian architect, painter, and designer; born and active Vienna.

Biography Oerley was a founding member of the Hagenbund and, 1907–39, a member of the Wiener Sezession; designed furniture and was an architect; created motifs printed on silk by Backhausen.
Bibliography Günther Feuerstein, *Vienna—Present and Past: Arts and Crafts—Applied Art—Design*, Vienna: Jugend und Volk, 1976: 42, 81. Astrid Gmeiner and Gottfried Pirhofer, *Der Österreichische Werkbund*, Salzburg/Vienna: Residenz, 1985: 239.

Oestreicher Birman, Lisbeth (b. Lisbeth Oestreicher 1902–1989)

German textile designer; born Carlsbad (now Karlovy Vary, Czech Republic).

Training 1926–30, Bauhaus weaving workshop, Dessau.
Biography She produced prototypes for firms Polytex and Pausa and designed dress patterns for publishing firms Ullstein and Bayer while at the Bauhaus; in 1930, settled in the Netherlands and set up her own studio, working as a freelance designer to 1942; 1942–45, was interned in the Nazi's Durchgangslager (transit camp) in Westerbork, the Netherlands. 1945, she married Otto Birman and became a freelance designer.
Bibliography Wolfgang Wangler, *Bauhaus-Webereu am beispiel der Lisbeth Oestreicher = Bauhaus-Weaving of Lisbeth Oestreicher*, Cologne: Zeitschrift 'Symbol,' 1985. Sigrid Wortmann Weltge, *Women's Work: Textile Art from the Bauhaus*, London: Thames & Hudson, 1993.

Offredi, Giovanni (1927–)

Italian product designer and interior architect; born and active Milan.

Training Technical and artistic studies.
Biography 1963–65, Offredi began his professional career; after a brief period working as an architect, began to design furniture and products for clients in Italy such as Crassevig (bentwood furnishings, including the Johan clothes rack), MC di Marco Contini, Bando Line, Crassevig, ITT, GiPi of G. Pizzitutti, GM Arredamenti, Tosi Mobili, Bazzani, Ultravox (sound equipment), Sirrah, Abaco & Mobiam, Face Alcatel, Saporiti Italia, and Sintesi (kitchens). His cabinet and kitchens by Snaidero began with the Contralto range and continued with

Kalya, Pragma, and Krios. 1973–90, he was an active member of Associazione per il Disegno Industriale (ADI).
Exhibitions/citations Participated in 1985 Bayer Visiona, Frankfurt. 1957 Plasti Riv, 1965–70 Mia Print, 1968 prize at Fiera di Trieste, 1981 (Swing Rete lounge chair by Saporiti Italia) and 1984 (Silos container/sideboard by Saporiti Italia) Premio Compasso d'Oro; First Prize (1985, Futura telephone by Alcatel-Face) Premio SMAU Industrial Design, Salone della Machina e Attrezzature per l'Ufficio, Milan; prizes at the Biennale di Mariano and the Fiera di Monza; others.
Bibliography *ADI Annual 1976*, Milan: Associazione per il Disegno Industriale, 1976. Sergio Saporiti and Giorgio Saporiti, *Il nostro lavoro con Offredi*, Marnate, 1978. Giancarlo Iliprandi and Pierluigi Molinari (eds.), 'Italian Industrial Designers' in *Omnibook No. 2*, Udine: Magnus, 1985. Fumio Shimizu and Studio Matteo Thun (eds.), *The Italian Design: Descendants of Leonardo da Vinci*, Tokyo: Graphic-sha, 1987: 334. Sonia P. Grianti, 'Incontro con Giovanni Offredi,' *Case e Giardino*, Oct. 1989. *Modo*, no.148, Mar.–Apr. 1993: 123.

Ofner, Hans (1880–1939)
Austrian designer; born St. Pölten.

Training Under Josef Hoffmann, Kunstgewerbeschule, Vienna.
Biography Ofner designed 1911 interiors of two villas (manufacturer Schießl's and lace producer Fred Gidderudge's) and 1913 interior of the extension, Hotel Pittner, all St. Pölten; also designed furniture, including by J.J. Müller of Linz, and tabletop objects in metal, featuring the square perforations for which the Wiener Werkstätte became known; was an accomplished illustrator of interiors; died in Salzburg.
Exhibitions While at the Kunsgewerbeschule, showed handcrafted objects, partially made by himself, at City Hall in St. Pölten. Exhibited at Galerie Zimmermann, Munich; 1908, Kunstsalon Zimmermann, Munich; 1909 Kunstschau, Vienna.
Bibliography Cat., *Wierner Werkstätte—Die ewige Moderne: Ihre Künstler und deren Schüler*, Vienna: Ble Etage–Wolfgang Bauer, 2003–04.

Ogawa, Isao (1944–)
Japanese designer; born Tokyo; active Milan.

Biography 1965, Ogawa began his professional career; 1971–74, worked in the Studio Ammannati e Vitelli and designed furniture, furnishings, and lighting; became a member, ADI (Associazione per il Disegno Industriale).
Exhibitions/citations Work shown at 1966 (with Makoto Shimazaki, and Akiraka Takaghi) and 1968 G-Mark Good Design awards, Japanese Industrial Design Promotion Organization (JIDPO); 1973 (15th) Triennale di Milano (with other Japanese designers).

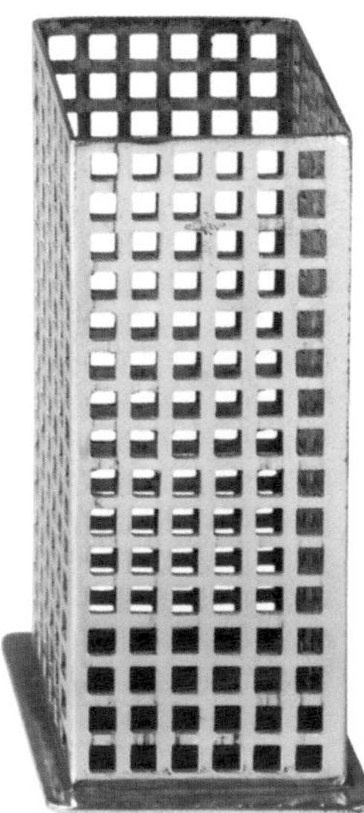

Hans Ofner. Vase. c. 1905. Perforated metal, 3 3/4 x 1 7/8 x 1 7/8" (9.5 x 4.7 x 4.7 cm). Mfr: Argentor, Austria. Given anonymously. MoMA.

George Ohr. Bowl. c. 1900. Glazed ceramic, h. 4" (10.2 cm) x dia. 8" (20.3 cm). Mfr.: the designer, US. John D. Rockefeller 3rd Purchase Fund. MoMA.

Bibliography *ADI Annual 1976*, Milan: Associazione per il Disegno Industriale, 1976.

Ohr, George Edgar (1857–1918)
American potter; active Biloxi, Miss.

Training 1879–81, Under family friend Joseph Fortune Meyer apprenticeship as a potter.
Biography c. 1882, Ohr set up a pottery in Biloxi, Miss., where he produced earthenware characterized by boldly colored, bent, and twisted designs combining whimsy and art, and resembling the later modern works of others. During his activity, he was rarely recognized outside Mississippi and dubbed 'the mad potter of Biloxi'; worked alone, though sometimes his son Leo Ohr helped him prepare the clay; threw on a handmade wheel with clays from the Tchouticabouffe and Pascagoula rivers. His forms are unlike those of any other American work but show a similarity to Christopher Dresser's ceramics from 1879 by Linthorpe in Middlesbrough, UK. c. 1909, Ohr stopped potting but hoped to sell his œuvre to a national collection. He stored over 6,000 pieces in the attic of the Ohr Boys Auto Repair Shop in Biloxi which remained there until the early 1970s, when they were sold and dispersed.
Exhibitions/citations Work shown at 1884 *World's Industrial and Cotton Centennial Exhibition* (over 600 uniquely shaped pieces), New Orleans; 1904 *Louisiana Purchase Exposition* (received a prize for originality), St. Louis; 1900 *Arts and Crafts Exhibition*, Buffalo, N.Y.; and subject of 1983 *George E. Ohr: An Artworld Homage*, Garth Clark Gallery, New York; included in images of Jasper Johns paintings shown at 1983 exhibition, Leo Castelli Gallery, New York.
Bibliography Robert W. Blasberg, *George E. Ohr and His Biloxi Art Pottery*, Port Jervis, N.Y.: Carpenter, 1973. Garth Clark, *The Biloxi Art Pottery of George Ohr*, Jackson: Mississippi Department of Archives and History/Mississippi State Historical Museum, 1978. Robert W. Blasberg, *The Unknown Ohr: A Sequel to the 1973 Monograph*, Milford, Pa.: Peaceable, 1986. Garth Clark et al., *The Mad Potter of Biloxi: The Art & Life of George E. Ohr*, New York: Abbeville, 1989. Eugene Hecht, *After the Fire: George Ohr: An American Genius*, Lambertville, N.J.: Arts and Crafts Quarterly, 1994.

Öhrström, Karl Edvin (1906–1994)
Swedish glass designer; born Burlöv.

Training In Stockholm: 1928, Kungliga Tekniska Högskolan; and, from 1928 under Carl Milles and Nils Sjörgren, Kungliga Konsthögskolan. In Paris: Académie Colarossi; under Charles Despiau, Maison Watteau; and, under Fernand Léger, Académie Moderne.
Biography Early on, Öhrström created a number of concrete, bronze, and granite public sculptures; from 1961, primarily worked in glass and metal. He was first hired by Orrefors Glasbruk to oversee and introduce new glass at 1937 Paris *Exposition* and, 1936–58, designed glassware by Orrefors, where he worked in the new bubble-filled Ariel glass technique, capturing images not before possible, like the Dalí-esque/Surrealist figures in The Gondolier vase. He made study trips throughout Europe, Asia, Mexico, and the US.
Exhibitions/citations 1937 *Exposition Internationale des Arts et Techniques dans la Vie Moderne* (for glass by Öhrström), Paris; 1996

Karl Edvin Öhrström. Vase. 1940. Bubble-filled Ariel glass technique, h. 6 11/16" (17 cm). Mfr.: Orrefors Glasbruk, Sweden. Courtesy Quittenbaum Kunstauk-tionen, Munich.

Swedish glass exhibition, Bard Graduate Center, New York (catalog below); numerous others. Grand prize, 1954 (10th) Triennale di Milano.
Bibliography Cat., Nina Stritzler-Levine et al., *Brilliance of Swedish Glass, 1918–1939: An Alliance of Art and Industry*, New Haven: Yale, 1996.

Okano, Yuh (1965–)

Japanese textile designer.

Training Rhode Island School of Design, Providence, R.I., US.
Biography She is an active textile designer as well as an instructor of textile fiber technique, Otsuka Textile Design Institute.
Exhibitions/citations Work subject of solo and in group exhibitions, including 1999 *Structure and Surface: Contemporary Japanese Textiles*, New York and St. Louis (catalog below).
Bibliography Cat., Cara McCarty and Matilda McQuaid, *Structure and Surface: Contemporary Japanese Textiles*, New York: Abrams/The Museum of Modern Art, 1999.

Okayama, Sinya (1941–)

Japanese designer; born Osaka.

Biography Late 1970s, Okayama became active as a designer; 1985, met Alessandro Mendin as a result of *Contemporary Landscape—From the Horizon of Post-Modern Design* exhibition, National Museum of Modern Art, Kyoto, in which was included the 1981 *Unfinished Furniture* collection by Alchimia (Mendini's group). Okayama's restructuring of the Alchimia section caught Mendini's approving attention. As a result, Okayama has been collaborating with Mendini since then on furniture, lighting, sculpture, carpets, and jewelry. Examples of this collaboration have been the 1985 Alchimia cabinet by Alessandro Mendini with art direction by Okayama and magnetic painting by Cleila Ravone and 1994 Mr. Lady and 1994 Opening table by Okayama and Mendini. From 1981, Okayama has on occasion been designing under his own name, including 1984 Crocodile bench (with ten electrically illuminated tufting buttons) and 1989 Kotobuki plinth (based on a Japanese caligraphy character), Macho armchair, and Ayame lamp. 1992 100% Make Up vase (shape by Mendini, motif by Okayama) was produced in a limited edition by Alessi/Tendentse.
Bibliography Kazuko Sato, *Alchimia*, Berlin: Taco, 1988. *Alessandro Mendini*, Milan: Giancarlo Politi, 1989. Frans Haks, *Alessandro Mendini Sketchbook*, Groningin: Groninger Museum, 1988

Olbrich, Joseph Maria (1867–1908)

Austrian artist, architect and designer; born Troppau (now Opava, Czech Republic); active Vienna and Darmstadt.

Training From 1882 under Camillo Sitte and others, Staatsgewerbeschule, Vienna; 1890 under Karl von Hasenauer, Akademie der bildenden Künste, Vienna.
Biography From 1894, Olbrich worked for Otto Wagner and became friends with Josef Hoffmann; 1897 with Hoffmann, Koloman Moser, and Gustav Klimt, cofounded the Wiener Sezession and codesigned (with Klimt) its 1897–98 Exhibition Hall on the Karlsplatz in Vienna. 1899, Olbrich became a participant in the Darmstadt artists' colony of the Grand Duke Louis IV of Hesse-Darmstadt, where he was responsible for a portion of the Art Nouveau architecture and decoration at the Mathildenhöhe complex and the Grand Duke's house at the 1901 exhibition, and in a number of houses for colleagues. In some ways anticipating Expressionism, his buildings at Darmstadt exerted an influence on later architecture. 1907, Olbrich cofounded the Deutscher Werkbund. His silver designs were not successful, with only a handful surviving (candelabra, tea-table pieces, tea caddies, sugar bowls, and biscuit barrels), all evidently by Bruckmann & Söhne in Heilbronn. He designed a number of pieces of jewelry (often set with mother-of-pearl and opaque stones) by D. und M. Loewenthal and by Theodor Fahrner; created some electroplated cutlery patterns and numerous lighting fixtures, including pewter, brass, and silver items, electric ceiling models, and gas sconces. His designs were clean and functional, reflecting Charles Rennie Mackinstosh and Viennese school members' fondness for cubes and rectangles. His death from leukemia occured only ten years after his first major commission, the Sezession Exhibition Hall.
Exhibitions/citations 1893 Prix de Rome while in his third year at Akademie der bildenden Künste, Vienna. Designed one of two domestic houses built for 1901 *A Document of German Art* exhibition, Darmstadt. Work included in an exhibition and the subject of 1967 and 1990 exhibitions, Darmstadt (catalogs below), traveling to Vienna and Berlin.
Bibliography *Ideen von Olbrich*, Vienna: Gerlach & Schenk, 1904; Stuttgart: Arnoldsche, 1992 (reprint). *J.M. Olbrich, Architektur*, 30 portfolios, Berlin: Wasmuth, 1901–14. *Joseph Olbrich's Zeichnungen für Baukunst u. Kunstgewerbe*, Berlin: Holten, 1912. Joseph August Lex, *Joseph M. Olbrich*, Berlin: Wasmuth, 1919. Hans-Günther Sperlich, *Versuch über Joseph Maria Olbrich*, Darmstadt: Justus von Liebig,

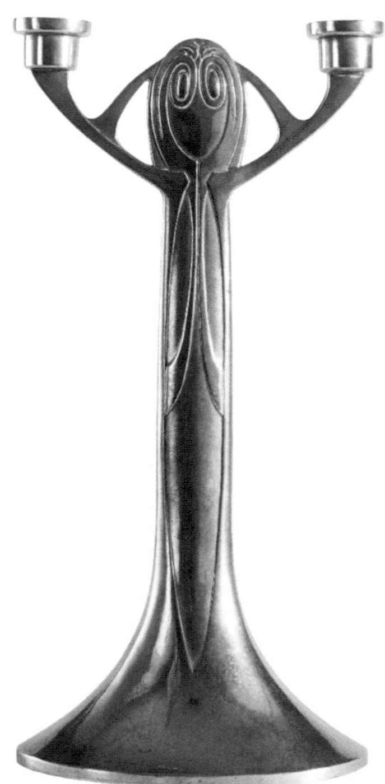

Joseph Maria Olbrich. Candelabrum. c. 1901. Pewter, h. 14 1/4" (36.2 cm) x dia. 6 13/16" (17.3 cm). Mfr: Edelzinn E. Hueck, Austria. Philip Johnson Fund. MoMA.

1965. Cat., *Joseph M. Olbrich, 1867–1908, Das Werk des Architekten*, Darmstadt: Hessisches Landesmuseum, 1967. Karl Heinz Schreyl, *Joseph Maria Olbrich: Die Zeichnungen in der Kunstbibliothek Berlin*, Berlin: Mann, 1972. Ian Latham, *Joseph Maria Olbrich*, London: Academy, 1980. Annelies Krekel-Aalberse, *Art Nouveau and Art Déco Silver*, New York: Abrams, 1989. Cat., *Museum Künstlerkolonie Darmstadt*, Darmstadt: the museum, 1990: 183–215. Ezio Godoli (intro.) *Idee: Architetture e Interni Viennesi/Joseph Maria Olbrich*, Florence: Cantini, 1991.

Old-Bleach Linen Company

British textile manufacturer; located Randalstown, Northern Ireland.

History 1864, the firm was founded by C. J. Webb; operated a weaving mill and printing shed, producing screen printing equal in quality to its woven goods; produced embroidery, dress and furnishing linens, damask table linens; from 1908, published quarterly periodical *The Embroideress* (with James Pearsall & Co., manufacturers of knitting wools and embroidery yarns). The firm furnished table linens to royalty and oceanliners of the Cunard Line. 1930s, it commissioned designers Marion Dorn, Norman Webb, J.L. Lindsay, Ronald Grierson, and Mansouroff. 1955, the enterprise closed. Archival business documents are housed in Public Record Office of Northern Ireland.
Bibliography Cat., *Thirties: British Art and Design Before the War*, London: Arts Council of Great Britain/Hayward Gallery Gallery, 1979. Valerie Mendes, *The Victoria & Albert Museum's Textile Collection, British Textiles from 1900 to 1937*, London: Victoria and Albert Museum, 1992.

Old, Maxime (1910–1991)

French decorator and furniture designer; born Maisons-Alfort.

Training École Boulle, Paris; to 1928–34, apprenticeship in Jacques-Émile Ruhlmann's workshop.
Biography In Ruhlmann's workshop, Old learned the precise production methods of the master; participated in the furnishing of oceanliners, including 1931 *Atlantique*, 1928 *Liberté*, 1951 *Ville de Marseille*, and 1952 *Flandre*. After World War II, he was commissioned by the French government to produce furniture ensembles for the Ministère de l'Economie des Finances et de l'Industrie and by the legation in Helsinki. He designed all the furnishings (mahogany and woven-cane furniture) for Hôtel Marhaba, Casablanca, characteristic of his 1950s work. He was active in a workshop at 37, rue de Chanzy, Paris. His designs and furniture were known for refinement and elegance and he was active well into the 1980s, having changed his style to simpler forms and, from 1960, beginning to incorporate metal.
Exhibitions Work shown at 1937 *Exposition Internationale des Arts et Techniques dans la Vie Moderne*; Salons of Société des Artistes Décorateurs regularly from 1935 (vice-president in 1949) and editions of Salon des Arts Ménagers; 1947–48 Salon de l'Imagerie; all Paris; and 1997 exhibition, Galerie Nationale de la Tapisserie, Beauvais.
Bibliography *Ensembles mobiliers*, Paris: Charles Moreau, vol. 6, no. 25, 1945; no.19, 1954. Yolande Amic, *Intérieurs: le mobilier français, 1945–1964*, Paris: Regard/VIA, 1983: 42–43. Yves Badetz, *Maxime Old: architecte-décorateur*, Paris: Norma, 2000.

Olgoj chorchoj

Czech design partnership; located Prague.

History Czech designers Michal Fronek (1966–) and Jan Nemecek (1963–) were fellow students, under Borěk Šípek, at Vysoká Škola Uměleckoprů-myslová (VŠUP, academy of arts, architecture, and design), Prague; 1990, formed Olgoj chorchoj design group; have specialized in furniture and interior design and call on a range of traditional Czech craft materials from cold-cast glass for tabletops (an original Czech technique) to plywood and laser-cut aircraft alloys for bracelets. They designed the headquarters of Sony Music and of Young & Rubicam advertising agency, both Prague. The name of their Milan exhibition, *Twinwall*, also refered to a concept involved in the production of vases, candleholders, and other tabletop objects made by melding together two sheets of Pyrex glass.
Exhibitions Initially, achieved wide recognition at Salone del Mobile, Milan; work included in 2001 *Art & Interior*, Muzeum Moderniho a Soucasneho Umeni (trade fair palace/museum of modern and contemporary art) of Národní Galerie (national gallery), Prague.
Bibliography Richard Sapper (ed.), *The International Design Yearbook*, London: Laurence King, 1998.

Olgoj chorchoj. OCH_Sony dish. 1999. Glass; 2 3/4 x 7 7/8 x l. 15 3/4" (7 x 20 x 40 cm). Mfr.: Lhotsky, Czech Republic.

Oliveri, G. Mario (1921–); Nizzoli Associati

Italian industrial designer; born Palermo; active Milan; and studio.

Training To 1952, architecture, Politecnico, Milan.
Biography 1947, Oliveri began working with Marcello Nizzoli, specializing in industrial design and architectural projects for Olivetti, including 1948 Lexikon 80 typewriter, 1950 Unifamigliari housing for Olivetti employees in Ivrea, 1955–58 Ente Nazionale Idrocarburi (ENI) headquarters buildings in San Donato Milanese, 1961–63 Azienda Nazionale Idrogenazione Combustibili (ANIC) in Gela, Sicily. 1958–60, Oliveri and Nizzoli designed a gasoline pump for Agip and a telephone for Satnat. 1955–97, Oliveri designed covers for journal *L'Architettura*. On Nizzoli's mid-1960s retirement, Oliveri continued his activity with various associates and partners in the firm that assumed various names (1965–71, Nizzoli Associati with Paolo Viola, Alessandro Mendini, and Antonio Susini; 1973 – 82, Studio Nizzoli with Susini and Viola; and 1982–92, Group Nizzoli with Viola). The firm's Italian clients included Stilnovo (lighting and accessories), Zucchetti (Z 80 faucet range), Ceccato (service-station equipment), Fidenza (glass lighting fixtures), Lombardini (spark plugs), Solari (heating appliances), and Fiamm (horns and batteries for automobiles). From 1972 under the Nizzoli Sistemi partnership, Oliveri designed agricultural machinery, trailers, and mobile homes (caravans) (with G. Giuliani, R. Ingegnere) by Laverda; toilet fittings (with Giuliani, Ingegnere, Picciani, and Matessi) by Ideal Standard; lighting and kitchenware in glass (with Giuliani and Picciani) for Fidenza. Oliveri has been a member, Associazione per il Disegno Industriale (ADI). From mid-1980s, the Nizzoli studio has reduced its activities, concentrating on research and competition participation. 1995, Group Nizzoli Architettura, with Oliveri, Domenico Cavallo, Nicola and Michele Premoli, and Gabriele Tosi, was established. Affiliation with other Italian and foreign groups has realized projects, including 1997 feasibility study of Mount Mottarone as a tourist resort, 1998–2001 office-building restorations in Milan, 2000 improvement plan for Origani quarter in Milan, several stores worldwide, interior design, and appliances.
Exhibitions/citations Work subject of 1983 exhibition, Palazzo Dugagni, Milan; exhibition of post-1948 work, 2001 Triennale di Milano and New York University, New York (catalog below).
Bibliography Germano Celant, *Nizzoli*, Milan: Comunità, 1967. *ADI Annual 1976*, Milan: Associazione per il Disegno Industriale, 1976. 'Gli studi Nizzoli,' *D'ARS*, no. 102, 1983: 194 – 95. 'A colloquio con G. Mario Oliveri,' *D'ARS*, no. 103, 1984: 122–31. 'The Commercial Architecture,' *Shoten Kenchiku*, vol. 31, 1986: 239 – 244. Giorgio Muratore et al. (eds), *Guida all'architettura moderna: Italia gli ultimo trent'anni*, Bologna: Zanichelli, 1988. Luigi Spinelli (ed.), *G. Mario Oliveri e gli studi Nizzoli: Architecture and Design Since 1948*, Milan: Editoriale Domus, 2001.

Olivès, Claire (1958–)

French designer; born El-Biar, Algeria.

Biography 1980–86, Olivès was a member of the Totem group; 1987 – 93, worked as a freelance designer; 1995–2000, graphic designer, WAG interactive-communicationations consultancy (later named W-I), Paris.
Exhibitions 1993 one-person exhibit, Galerie Cour Intérieur, Paris; 1999 ephemeral group installation in a park on the theme of invisibility, Bratislava, Slovakia.
> See Totem.

Olivetti, Camillo (1868–1943); Olivetti

Italian office machinery and furniture firm; located Ivrea.

History 1908, the Olivetti office machinery company was founded by Camillo Olivetti, who designed the firm's, and Italy's, first typewriter, 1908–10 M1. He manufactured it on a moving assembly line similar to the one introduced by Henry Ford in 1913. Late 1920s, he visited the US to observe new manufacturing techniques and to study new products; in fact, the M1 may have been based on an Underwood typewriter model. Early on, the Olivetti factory occupied fortress-like brick factory buildings. Olivetti commissioned Luigi Figini and Gino Pollini to design a complex including factory, workers' housing, and hospital. The housing was completed in 1939 and the factory in 1940. Its nursery school was replaced in 1940–41 with a new building also by Figini and Pollini. From 1938, Olivetti's son Adriano (1901–1960) was president of the firm and initiated the policy of commissioning consultant designers. Marcello Nizzoli, hired in 1938 to work in the advertising office, designed its 1940s–50s graphics and went on to create some of Olivetti's renowned products, including 1948 Lexikon 80 and 1950 Lettera 22 typewriters, and 1956 Divisumma 24 calculator. 1950s, art director Giovanni Pintori designed displays for store windows as well as graphics, while Leo Lionni designed Olivetti's magazine advertising. Prior to Lionni, Olivetti's artists included Xanti Schawinsky and Costantino Nivola. Hired in 1957, Ettore Sottsass created designs for computers, typewriters, and systems furniture, including his 1968 Valentine portable typewriter (with Perry King) and 1968 Lettera 36 typewriter. His Synthesis 45 system of furniture answered the need in the 1970s for new shapes, materials, and ergonomic considerations in office design. Sottsass's system was distinguished by bright colors and bold, witty plastic details characteristic of the 1970s, when there was a more relaxed attitude toward work. Sottsass was in charge of the design of systems and furniture, collaborating with Albert Leclerc, Bruno Gecchelin, George Sowden, and Masanori Umeda. Mario Bellini was in charge of consumer products (consultant there from 1965), collaborating with Antonio Macchi Cassia, Michele De Lucci, Gianni Pasquini, and Sandro Pasqui. The Premio Compasso d'Oro citations (below) for disguished design also document Olivetti's product-design history. Olivetti, which became essentially only a holding company, taken over by cable/tire giant Pirelli in 2001 and, as a producer of high-design products, is now defunct. 1986, L'Archivio Storico Olivetti was established, on the initiative of Paul Mancinelli (former general secretary of Olivetti), in Ivrea on the occasion of the company's 90th anniversary, and directed by Giovanni Maggia from 1987–94; was organized as L'Associazione per l'Archivio Storico Olivetti in 1998 with its factories, offices, shops, housing, and agricultural and social facilities as part of a museum system, which was opened in 2001 by the Ivrea Town Council.
Exhibitions M1 typewriter introduced at 1911 *Esposizione Internazionale dell'Industria e del Lavoro*, Turin. Products were shown at numerous international fairs, included in important exhibitions, and were subject of 1952 and 1979 exhibitions, New York and Los Angeles (catalogs below). A number of honors, including Premio SMAU Industrial Design, Salone della Machina e Attrezzature per l'Ufficio, Milan; two 2000 awards (for Jet-Lab 600 and ArtJet 10), Industrie Forum Design (iF), Hanover. Premio Compasso d'Oro awards: 1954 (for Lettera 22 typewriter), 1959 (for Elea calculator by Sottsass), 1962 (for Spazio office furniture by BBPR, 1964 (for CMC 77004 magnetic-character machine by Bellini), 1967 (for Auctor Multiplex MUT/40A by Benetto), 1967 (for company publication by Pintori), 1970 (nine citations), 1979 (for Inspector Midi 130 W measuring machine by Bonetto and Naoki Matsunaga; advertising literature; body of work), 1979 (three citations), 1981 (four citations), 1984 (four citations), 1987 (for ETV 250 computer by Bellini; Delphos office furniture by Sottsass and De Lucchi), 1989 (for Miram 200 telephone by Sowden and Morgan; ET 55 Personal typewriter by Belllini), 1991 (for OFX 420 fax machine by Sowden and Simon; four other citations), 1994 (body of work; three other citations), 1994 (three citations), 2001 (for ArtJet 10 ink-jet printer).
Bibliography 'Olivetti: Design in Industry,' *The Museum of Modern Art Bulletin*, New York: The Museum of Modern Art, 1952. Mario Labò, *L'aspetto estetico dell'opera sociale di Adriano Olivetti*, Milan: La Rinascente, 1957. Cat., Hans Fischli and Willy Rotzler (eds.), *Stile Olivetti; Geschichte und Formen einer italienischen, Industrie*, Zürich, Kunstgewerbemuseum, 1961. Bruno Caizzi, *Camillo e Adriano Olivetti*, Turin: Unione tipografico–editrice torinese, 1962. Cat., *Design Process Olivetti 1908–1978*, Los Angeles: Frederick S. Wight Art Gallery, 1979. Giuseppe Berta, *Le idee al potere: Adriano Olivetti tra la fabbrica e la comunità*, Milan: Comunità, 1980. Cat., Giovani Giudicci (ed.), *Design Process: Olivetti 1908-1978*, Ivrea: Olivetti, 1979. Valerio Ochetto, *Adriano Olivetti*, Milan: Mondadori, 1985. Sibylle Kicherer, *Olivetti: A Study of the Corporate Management of Design*, New York: Rizzoli, 1990. Mel Byars with Arlette Barré-Despond, *100 Designs/100 Years: A Celebration of the 20th Century*, Hove: RotoVision, 1999: 32–33. Giorgio Soavi, *Adriano Olivetti: una sorpresa italiana*, Milan: Rizzoli, 2001. www.olivetti.com.

Ollers, Edvin (1888–1959)

Swedish glassware designer, metalworker, and ceramicist.

Biography 1917, Ollers worked for the Kosta Glasbruk and, 1918–20, for the Rejmyre Glasbruk in Rejmyra; 1931–32, returned to Kosta; designed glassware for mass production in inexpensive soda glass with natural bubbles and blisters; also designed in pewter, silver, and ceramics.
Exhibitions Work included in 1982 exhibition, New York (catalog below).
Bibliography Cat., David Revere McFadden (ed.), *Scandinavian Modern Design 1880–1980*, New York: Abrams, 1982.

Ollestad, Andreas (1857–1936)

Norwegian ceramicist.

Biography From 1886, Ollestad worked at Egersunds Fayancefabrik in Egersund, where, from 1905, was production manager and introduced the Art Nouveau style; designed ceramic pieces that integrated decoration and modeled relief.
Exhibitions Work included in 1982 exhibition, New York (catalog below).
Bibliography Cat., David Revere McFadden (ed.), *Scandinavian Mo-*

Olivetti: Mario Bellini. Divisumma 18 electronic printing calculator. 1972. Cast-injected ABS polymer body, flexible synthetic rubber skin, and melamine, 1 7/8 x 9 3/4 x 4 3/4" (4.8 x 24.8 x 12.1 cm). Mfr.: Ing. C. Olivetti & C., Italy. Gift of Kenneth Walker. MoMA.

dern Design 1880–1980, New York: Abrams, 1982.

Olofs, Max (1889–1969)
German sculptor and silversmith; active Munich.

Training Under Fritz von Miller, Kunstgewerbeschule; Bayerischen Akademie der Wissenschaften; both Munich.
Biography 1919, Olofs set up a workshop in Munich with Johann Scheidacker and René Sammann; the latter two left c. 1922.
Exhibitions Work included in 1990 exhibition, Munich (catalog below).
Bibliography Annelies Krekel-Aalberse, *Art Nouveau and Art Déco Silver*, New York: Abrams, 1989. Cat., *Münchner Schmuck 1900–1940*, Munich: Bayerisches Nationalmuseum, 1990: 90–92.

Olsen, Hans (1919–)
Danish furniture designer.

Training 1941, apprenticeship as a cabinetmaker; to 1943, Kunsthåndværkerskolen, Copenhagen.
Biography 1953, Olsen became an independent designer of furniture by Bondo Gravesen, Frem Røjle, and Schou Andersen Møbelfabrik.
Citations 1965 International Design Award.
Bibliography Frederik Sieck, *Nutidig Dansk Møbeldesign – en kortfattet illustreret beskrivelse*, Copenhagen: Bondo Gravesen, 1990.

Olsen, Harald (1851–1910)
Norwegian architect and furniture and glassware designer, metalworker, and enamelist.

Biography 1880s, Olson practiced architecture in Kristiania (now Oslo); was a designer at Hadelands Glasverk in Jevnaker and designed silver and enamelwork by J. Tostrup and David-Andersen, both in Oslo. His curvaceous furniture designs showed French and Belgian influences, and some of his furniture was produced by Christiania Handværks -og Industriforening and De Samvirkende Fagforeninger.
Exhibitions Work included in 1982 exhibition, New York (catalog below).
Bibliography Cat., David Revere McFadden (ed.), *Scandinavian Modern Design 1880–1980*, New York: Abrams, 1982.

Omega Workshops
British cooperative producing furniture, furnishings, ceramics, and textiles.

History 1913, the Omega Workshops were set up by painter, art critic, and lecturer Roger Fry to create employment for his young avant-garde artist friends. He aimed to unite art and design and recruited artists rather than craftspeople; used the Wiener Werkstätte and Paul Poiret's Atelier Martine as models. A range of domestic furnishings and goods, including pottery, was designed in an attempt to escape the prevailing historicism in Britain at the time. The group designed the 1914 interior of Cadena Café at 49 Westbourne Grove, London, including waitresses' uniforms, murals, rugs, and lighting. Some of the Workshops' pottery was put into limited commercial production; it presaged the angular shapes of the British modern movement of a decade later. Omega's linens were printed in France. With studios in Fitzroy Square in London, Omega's designers included Fry, Vanessa Bell, and Duncan Grant. Wyndham Lewis worked there briefly, but, 1914, left to establish The Rebel Art Centre, feeling that the work of the Omega painters was outmoded and finding few buyers for the Workshops' wares. The group's activities attracted the participation of leading artists of the day, including David Bomberg, Paul Nash, and graphic designer McKnight Kauffer. The Workshops' painted furniture was decorated in designs contrived to fit the geometry of a piece rather than arbitrarily applied. The main motifs were nudes and flowers, except for Lewis's abstract patterns. The most successful work was by Fry himself, particularly pottery and the Cubist-inspired textile range Amenophis. 1920, Workshop activities ceased.
Exhibitions Work subject of and included in 1946 and 1983 exhibitions, London (catalogs below).
Bibliography Cat., *Omega Workshops: Furniture, Textiles and Pottery 1913–1918*, London: Victoria and and Albert Museum, 1946. Richard Shone, *Bloomsbury Portraits: Vanessa Bell, Duncan Grant and Their Circle*, London: Phaidon, 1976. Francis Spalding, *Roger Fry*, London: Elek/Granada, 1980. Isabelle Anscombe, *Omega and After: Bloomsbury and the Decorative Arts*, New York: Thames & Hudson, 1981. Judith Collins, *The Omega Workshops*, Chicago: University of Chicago, 1984. Cat., *The Omega Workshops: Alliance and Enmity in English Art 1911–1920*, London: Anthony d'Offay Gallery, 1984. Alan and Veronica Palmer, *Who's Who in Bloomsbury*, Brighton: Harvester, 1987.

OMK Design
British design group; located London.

Biography 1966, OMK Design was established by Jerry Olejnik, Bryan Morrison, and Rodney Kinsman, all trained at Central School of Arts and Crafts, London. The group produced its own furniture, including its well-known 1969 T5 chair and 1970 Omstack chair, the latter design credited to Kinsman.
Exhibitions/citations OMK Design's work shown at 1966 exhibition, Redfern Gallery, London; 1970 *Ideal Home*, London; 1970 *Expo '70*, Osaka; 1970 *International Airport Exhibition*, Amsterdam; 1969 *Décor International* (T5 chair), London; 1971 exhibition (T5 chair), London (catalog below). Received 1969 Observer Design Award.
Bibliography Cat., *Modern Chairs 1918–1970*, London: Lund Humphries, 1971. www.omkdesign.co.uk.

One Foot Taller
British design studio/consultancy; located Glasgow.

History 1995, Katty Barac (Cape Town, South Africa, 1972–) established a studio in Scotland for the design and production of furniture, and Will White (Hertford, UK, 1972–) joined in 2000. The pair have also offered consultancy to restaurants, retailers, and other projects. Work (all Glasgow producers and places) has included 1995 Java Internet Café; 1998 telephone table; 1998 *Chasm* for Harrold, Glasgow; 1999 China lamp (with Fireworks); 1999 *Ravine* and 1999 *Canyon* chairs for Harrold; 2000 SOBA bar and restaurant; The Arches Theatre (2000–03 redevelopment of old Arches Theatre, Glasgow, with Timo-rous Beasties); 2001 domestic products by Plastic Mouldings. Also designed 2002 Pop storage by Habitat and 2003 recycled boxes (with k two products). Barac and White have said, 'We are often thought of as "recyclers." Although it is exciting when useful materials can be found this way, recycling is not our sole interest.'
Exhibitions/citations Work included in 2000 *Lost and Found: Critical Voices in New British Design*, Warsaw and Bordeaux; 2001 *Home Alone*, Glasgow Art Fair. 1996 Start Up of the Year Award for Innovation, The Glasgow Development Agency. For Chasm chair: Blueprint Editor's Award, 1998 100% Design show, London; 1999 Peugeot Design Award; 1999 Millennium Product Status citation.
Bibliography www.onefoottaller.com.

Onken, Oscar (1858–1948)
American entrepreneur; active Ohio.

Biography Onken was a prominent businessperson and philanthropist. Based on his being impressed with the Gustav Stickley and the Austrian stands at1904 *Louisiana Purchase Exposition*, St. Louis, Onken founded The Shop of the Crafts in Cincinnati in 1904; hired Hungarian designer Paul Horti, who had designed the fair's Austrian stand. There was a distinctly European flavor to The Shop's furniture, with inlays, applied carvings, and painted motifs.
Bibliography Cat., Anne Yaffe Phillips, *From Architecture to Object*, New York: Hirschl and Adler, 1989: 80. Cat., Wendy Kaplan (ed.), *'The Art That Is Life': The Arts and Crafts Movement in America, 1875–1930*, Boston: Museum of Fine Arts, 1987: 248.

Opbouw, de; de 8 en Opbouw
Dutch architecture group.

History 1920, Wilhelm Gispen, Willem Kromhout, J.J.P. Oud, M.J. Granpré Molière, and L.G. van de Vlught founded the architecture association 'de Opbouw' (construction), which was particularly active in Rotterdam 'to promote more exclusively modern ideas,' according to Gispen, 'about architecture and to keep the movement free from commercial influence.' Early 1920s, Oud was chairperson, a position assumed by Mart Stam in 1925. For three decades, the group represented the Functionalism of Congrès Internationaux d'Architecture Moderne (CIAM). Other members included Piet Zwart, G. Kiljan, A. Bodon, P. Schuitema, and J. Niegeman. 1932, it merged with 'de 8' to become 'de 8 en Opbouw.'
Bibliography Barbie Campbell-Cole and Tim Benton (eds.), *Tubular Steel Furniture*, London: The Art Book Company, 1979: 29. Gert Staal and Hester Wolters, *Holland in Vorm*, 's-Gravenhage: Stichting Holland in Vorm, 1987.

OPI, Studio
Italian design cooperative.

Biography 1955, Franco Bettonica (1927–) and Mario Melocchi established Studio OPI and designed smoking, desk, and bar accessories in stainless steel and plastics by Melocchi's own-associated firm Cini e Nils in Milan. Well known are their 1972 Cuboluce lamp in an ABS box, plastic accessories, and a number of other lighting fixtures.
History Studio OPI's work included in 1972 and 1983 exhibitions, New York and Philadelphia (catalogs below).
Bibliography Cat., Emilio Ambasz (ed.), *Italy: The New Domestic Landscape*, New York: Museum of Modern Art, 1972. Cat., Kathryn B. Hiesinger and George H. Marcus III (eds.), *Design Since 1945*, Philadelphia: Philadelphia Museum of Art, 1983. Cat., Hans Wichmann (ed.), *Design Italien 1945 bis heute*, Munich: Die Neue Sammlung, 1988.

Oppenheim, Meret (1913–1985)
German artist; born Berlin.

Training 1918–30, studied at various German and Swiss schools; 1929–30 and 1938–40, Kunstgewerbeschule, Basel; 1932–33, Académie de la Grande Chaumière, Paris.
Biography From 1932, Oppenheim was an independent artist in Paris, associated with Surrealists Alberto Giacometti, Sophie Taeuber, and Hans Arp, encounters which possibly ignited her imagination; at 23, garnered initial and lasting recognition for the fur-wrapped cup/saucer/spoon (*Breakfast in Fur*, 1936) that eventually served as one of the defining images of Surrealism. From 1948, lived in Bern; became a heroine of the women's rights movement, asserting, 'Nobody gives you freedom; you have to take it.' Her work included photography, sculpture, furniture, and performances. She created 1939 Table aux Pieds d'Oiseau (realized in small quantities as 1972 Traccia table by Simón in Italy; from 1993, reissued by Ultramobile).
Exhibitions 1936 International Surrealist Exhibition (first exposure of *Breakfast with Fur*), New Burlington Galleries, London. From 1936 at Galerie Schultess, Basel, work subsequently subject of more than 30 exhibitions, including at Institute of Contemporary Arts, London, 1989 (see other catalogs below), and 1996 *Meret Oppenheim: Beyond the Fur Lined Teacup*, Solomon R. Guggenheim Museum, New York.
Bibliography Alfred H. Barr, *Fantastic Art, Dada and Surrealism*, New York: The Museum of Modern Art, 1936. Cat., Hans Christoph von Tavel, *Meret Oppenheim*, Solothurn, 1974. Cat., Patrick Walberg, Meret Oppenheim et ses jeux d'été, Paris, 1974. Cat., Jürgen Glaesemer, *Meret Oppenheim: Arbeiten von 1930–1978*, Hamburg: Kestner-Gresellschaft, 1978. Muriel Emanuel et al (eds.) *Contemporary Artists*, New York: St Martin's, 1983: 701–02.

Opron, Robert (1932–)
French automobile designer.

Biography On Flaminio Bertoni's 1964 death, Opron became head of design at the Citroën motor works. He may have assumed the position with difficulty, considering the cutting-edge image that Bertoni had earlier created. Opron's bodies by Citroën included 1970–75 SM, 1970–81 GS (first as the Projet G), and 1974–89 CX (the last of Opron-supervised Citroën bodies), all considered by some to be 'true' Citroëns in the Bertoni manner. From 1977, Opron worked at Renault where he designed/supervised 1981 R9, 1982 R11, 1989 R19, 1990 R19 Chamade, and the unique 1978 Fuego (derived from the R18); some critics have noted Citroën SM charactistics in the Fuego. Concerning Renault's image, the 1972 Renault logo (still in use but with the stripes removed in 1990) was designed by Hungarian artist Victor Vasarely (1908–1997) and called the 'rhombe,' becoming the first logo to be solely applied on the firm's autos without the name 'Renault.' It had been preceded by seven logos, from 1900.
Exhibitions 1970 Salon de l'Auto (SM model), Geneva; 1974 Auto Salon (CX model), Paris; 1978 Salon de l'Auto (Fuego), Geneva.

Opsvik, Peter (1939–)
Norwegian furniture designer.

Training 1960s under Ulrich Burandt, in ergonomics; design schools in Bergen and Oslo; 1970s, in Britain, and 'Folkwangschule für Gestaltung' (Umbenennung der Handwerker- und Kunstgewerbeschule), Essen.
Biography 1965–70, Opsvik was a designer at Tandberg Radio Factory; subsequently, collaborated with Hans Christian Mengshoel on development of ergonomic seating; from 1972, was a freelance designer, whose work included 1972 Tripp Trapp stool-chair by Stokke Fabrikker in Skodje; became best known for the widely published 1981 Balans Variable ergonomic stool also by Stokke Fabrikker; with Oddvin Rykkens and Svein Gusrud, further developed innovations in ergonomic stool seating, popularized in early 1980s. Opsvik also designed early-2000s Capisco and Credo office-chair ranges by HÅG.
Exhibition/citations Work shown at 1982 exhibition, New York (catalog below). 1997 European Design Prize (child's Tripp Trapp chair).
Bibliography Cat., David Revere McFadden (ed.), *Scandinavian Modern Design 1880–1980*, New York: Abrams, 1982. Fredrik Wildhagen, *Norge i Form*, Oslo: Sternersen, 1988: 187.
> See Mengshoel, Hans Christian.

Studio OPI (Franco Bettonica and Mario Melocchi). Cylindrical Collection condiment containers. 1972. Polycarbonate and stainless steel, tallest 5 1/2" (14cm) x dia. 2 1/8" (5.4 cm). Mfr.: Cini & Nils, Italy. Gift of the mfr. MoMA.

Optic
> See Timmermans, Hugo.

Origlia, Giorgio (1943–)
Italian industrial designer; born Turin; active Milan.

Training To 1968, architecture, Politecnico, Milan.
Biography 1973, Origlia began his professional career as a designer in the studio of Mario Bellini, working on lighting by Artemide and the Pianeta Ufficio institutional furniture system by Marcatré.
Exhibitions Bellini's Kar-a-sutra prototype, on which Origlia participated, was included in 1972 *Italy: The New Domestic Landscape*, The Museum of Modern Art, New York.
Bibliography Giorgio Origlia, *Eating as Design*, Milan: Electa, 1981.

Oriol, Maite (1953–)
Spanish architect and designer; born Barcelona.

Training Escuela de Arquitectura Técnica de Navarra, Pamploná; in interior design, Barcelona.
Biography 1983, Oriol settled in Italy, where she works at Beneti Design Associati; has designed products, including 1982 Surco ashtray and 1982 Escuardra waste bin (both with Juancho de Mendoza) by Bd Ediciones de Diseño in Barcelona.

Orivit-Metallwarenfabrik
German silversmiths; located Cologne-Braunsfeld.

History Orivit was founded by Ferdinand Hubert Schmitz; 1896–1908, produced nearly 2,800 models. 'Orivit' was an alloy with a low silver content. For a short time, the firm made silver hollow-ware on the new Huberpresse machine, which stamped out pieces with simple ornamentation under hydraulic pressure. 1905, Orivit taken over by Württembergische Metallwaren Fabrik (WMF); 1928, stopped production.
Exhibitions Silver service shown at 1904 *Louisiana Purchase Exposition*, St. Louis; 1990, in Berlin (see catalog below).
Bibliography Annelies Krekel-Aalberse, *Art Nouveau and Art Déco Silver*, New York: Abrams, 1989. Cat., *Metallkunst*, Berlin: Bröhan-Museum, 1990: 382–87.

Orivit-Metallwarenfabrik. Tea pot, 1904. Pressed and pierced pewter, h. 5 7/8" (15 cm). Mfr.: Orivit-Metallwarenfabrik, Germany. Courtesy Quittenbaum Kunstauktionen, Munich.

Orlandini, Paolo (1941–)

Italian designer; born Grosseto.

Training 1960–65, School of Architecture, Politecnico, Milan.
Biography Orlandini worked with Marco Zanuso and Richard Sapper to 1973, when he worked with Roberto Lucci or independently for a number of clients under the Lucci Orlandini Design umbrella in Milan.
> See Lucci, Roberto.

O'Rorke, Brian (1901–1974)

New Zealand architect and interior designer; active Britain.

Training Architecture, Cambridge University and Architectural Association, London.
Biography O'Rorke's style was uncompromisingly modern. The 1932 music room he designed for Mrs. Robert Solomon in London included a swirl-motif rug by Marion Dorn. O'Rorke established a small studio that specialized in interior design, particularly for ships, aircraft, and trains; designed interiors for oceanliners 1935 *Orion* (commissioned by Colin Anderson), 1946 *Vickers Viking,* 1948 *Orcades* (which broke from traditional modes), and interiors of other ships of the Orient Line; was the architect for 1947 Orient Steam Navigation building in Sydney; designed a number of houses, including a semi-detached house complex and 1933–36 Ashcombe Tower for Major Ralph Rayner; designed The Natural Scene and the Country (natural history) pavilions (with F.H.K. Henrion), 1951 *Festival of Britain*, London.
Bibliography Cat., *Thirties; British Art and Design Before the War*, London: Arts Council of Great Britain/Hayward Gallery Gallery, 1979.

Orrefors Glasbruk

Swedish glassware manufacturer; located Orrefors.

History 1726, an ironworking factory was established on the property of Halleberg (the Orrefors estate) in Socken, Småland; 1898, began the production of ink bottles. 1913, Johan Ekman purchased the estate and placed forester Albert Ahlin in charge. Ekman produced art glass with little success at first, until he hired Simon Gate in 1916 and Edward Hald in 1917 as designers; they were members of the Slöjdföreningen (Swedish crafts society). The two artists had done no glass designing before. Gate and Hald collaborated with the glass blowers and with former cutter Gustav Abels on reviving engraved glass. With master glass blower Knut Bergqvist, they developed the *graal* technique in 1916. 1933, Gate became the artistic director of Orrefors. Orrefors also produced a full range of tableware. Designers Edvin Öhrström and Vicke Lindstrand and blower Gustav Bergqvist developed the bubble-filled Ariel glass technique. 1889, the Sandvik glassworks was leased, which was purchased by Orrefors in 1918; the facility specialized in plain, inexpensive table and household soda glass and expanded the Orrefors range. Orrrefors today operates a school for glass blowers and engravers, from among whom it draws its workforce. Other designers have included Nils Landberg, Gunnar Cyrén, Eva Englund, and Lars Hellsten. Sometime after Gullaskruf was amalgamated with Royal Krona in 1975, it was then incorporated into Orrefors. Orrefors bought Strömbergshyttan in 1974; the SEA and the Alghuit glassworks in 1984; was consolidated with Kosta Boda in 1990, forming Orrefors Kosta Boda. 1997, Venini, Orrefors Kosta Boda, BodaNova–Höganäs Keramik, and others became a group of brands to form Royal Scandinavia. However, in 2000, Royal Scandinavia was bought by an investment group and eventually dismantled into various reorganized entities.
Exhibitions/citations Three grand prizes and three gold medals, 1925 *Exposition Internationale des Arts Décoratifs et Industriels Modernes*, Paris. Included in 1937 *Exposition Internationale des Arts et Techniques dans la Vie Moderne* (glass by Öhrström), Paris. Work subject of 1970 exhibition, Röhsska Museet, Gothenberg (catalog below).
Bibliography *Orrefors*, Stockholm: Bröderna, 1951. Cat., Agnes Hellners and Thomas Baagøe, *Orreforsglas*, Gothenberg: Röhsska konstslöjdmuseet, 1970. *Orreforsglas*, Gothenberg: Röhsska Konstslöjdmuseet, 1975–76. Jennifer Hawkins Opie, *Scandinavia: Ceramics and Glass in the Twentieth Century*, New York: Rizzoli, 1989. Ann Marie Herlitz-Gezelius, *Orrefors: A Swedish Glassplant*, Stockholm: Atlantis, 1984. *Gunnar Cyrén: Glas, Silver, stål och plast, det bästa under 30 år: utställning i samarbete med Orrefors Glasbruk*, Orrefors: Orrefors Glasbruk, 1990. Kerstin Wickman (ed.), *Orrefors: A Century of Swedish Glassmaking*, Stockholm: Byggförlaget-Kultur, 1998. *Kärlek till glas: Agnes Hellners samling av Orreforsglas*, Sweden: Stiftelsen Kungstenen/Rastor, 1998.
> See Royal Scandinavia.

Ørskov & Co.

Danish manufacturer; located Espergærde.

History 1953, Ørskov was founded by Torben Ørskov (Copenhagen, 1928–) to produce tabletop wares, fabrics, toys, and dinnerware. Designers today include Karin Carlander, Jørgen Møller, Henrik Jeppesen, Hans Bølling, Jacek Szmidt, and, from the onset, a large number of others such as Bo Bonfils, Torun Bülow-Hübe, Arne Jacobsen, Finn Juhl, Henning Koppel, Ross Littell, Erik Magnussen, Henrik Steen Møller, Ole Palsby, and Rud Thygesen. Its 1953 Krenit acid-proof enamel-on-steel bowl range by Herbert Krenchel (Danish, 1922–) may be better known now as a desirable 'collectible' than when introduced. 1950s–80s, products made by various firms were sold through Ørskov's Form & Farve shops, owned by Torben Ørskov and Knud Aage Nielsen (who left the firm in the 1970s); currently, distributes its own production worldwide as Ørskov & Co., which is managed by the founder's son Jeppe Ørskov (Copenhagen, 1963–), while his father continues to a degree to work with the early designers.
Bibliography www.orskov.com.

Orsoni, Umberto (1940–)
> See Gruppo G14.

Ortner, Laurids (1941–)
> See Haus-Rucker-Co.

Orvola, Heikki (1943–)

Finnish designer.

Biography Orvola has designed glass by Iittala, ceramics by Arabia and Rörstrand, textiles by Marimekko, and cast-iron and enameled products. Late 1990s work by Arabia: Illusia ceramic dinnerware (with Fujiwo Ishimoto). Work by Iittala: 1972 Aurora drinking glasses/decanter, 1988 Kivi votive-candle holder, 1996 Evergreen vivid-green vases, 2001 Annual Cube art object.
Citations 1984 Pro Finlandia prize; 1994 grant (for 15 years) from the State of Finland; 1997 Design Plus prize (24h ceramic dinnerware by Arabia), Ambiente fair, Frankfurt; 1998 Kaj Franck Prize; others.

Osgerby, Jay (1969–)
> See Barber Osgerby Associates.

Osko, Blasius (1975–)
> See Deichmann, Oliver.

Østergaard, Steen (1935–)

Danish furniture designer.

Training To 1960, Kunsthåndværkerskolen, Copenhagen.
Biography 1962–65, Østergaard worked with architect Finn Juhl and, 1965, set up his own design studio. Østergaard's first plastic object—1970 Chair 290 in polyamid by France & Søn in Denmark—is purportedly the first chair to be extruded as a single unit. Its fiberglass reinforced-polyester molded shell was upholstered on the inside and

Orrefors: Gunnar Cyrén. Bowl. 1967. Glass, h. 2" (5.1 cm) x dia. 14 1/2" (36.8 cm). Mfr.: Orrefors, Sweden. Gift of Bonniers, Inc., New York. MoMA.

supported by an underframe of chromium-plated metal. His stacking chair and other plastic models were produced by Cado.
Exhibitions/citations Work shown in exhibitions at Kunstindustrimuseet, Stockholm, in 1962 and 1964; Erikholm, in 1965; London, in 1970; Milan, in 1971; Boutique Danoise, Paris, in 1972; Prague, in 1972. First prize, 1963 Corso Internazionale del Mobile, Cantù; 1966 Johannes Krøiers prize; 1966, recognition in San Cataldo.
Bibliography Cat., Milena Lamarová, *Design a Plastické Hmoty*, Prague: Uměleckoprůmyslové Muzeum, 1972: 138. Frederik Sieck, *Nutidig Dansk Møbeldesign – en kortfattet illustreret beskrivelse*, Copenhagen: Bondo Gravesen, 1990.

Østern, Bjørn Sigurd (1935–)

Norwegian metalworker.

Training 1955–56, Kunsthåndverkskole, Bergen; 1956–61, Statens Håndverks -og Kunstindustriskole, Oslo.
Biography From 1961, Østern was a designer at David-Andersen.
Exhibitions Work shown at 1982 exhibition, New York (catalog below).
Bibliography Cat., David Revere McFadden (ed.), *Scandinavian Modern Design 1880–1980*, New York: Abrams, 1982.

Otsuka, Noriyuki (1960–)

Japanese interior designer; born Fukui Prefecture.

Training To 1981, Tokyo Designer Gakuin College
Biography Otsuka worked at Plastic Studio & Associates; 1983–84, traveled in Europe; 1989, established Otsuka Noriyuki Design Office. His commissions have included design of 1989 Maha restaurant/bar, Tokyo; 1992 Ondine shoe shop, Sapporo; 1994 Pleats Box furniture.
Exhibitions/citations Work subject of 1994 *Otsuka Noriyuki—Beyond Scenery*, Omotesando, Tokyo. Citations included 13th and 14th Shop and Interior Design Contest Awards, NGK; 1992 award, Inter/Intra Space Design Selection, AGC; 1993 Encouragement Award, Commercial Space Design; 1993 Award, Nashop Lighting Competition.

Otte-Koch, Benita (1892–1976)

German fabric designer; born Stuttgart.

Training 1911–13, in drawing in Düsseldorf, receiving a teacher's certificate; 1920–25, Bauhaus, Weimar.
Biography 1925–33, she was the artistic director of handweaving, Kunstgewerbeschule Burg Giebichenstein, Halle; 1929, married interior designer and photographer Heinrich Koch; 1933–34, was freelance designer in Prague; 1934–57, director of Bodelschwinghsche Anstalten, Bethel (near Bielefeld).
Bibliography Lionel Richard, *Encyclopédie du Bauhaus*, Paris: Somogy, 1985: 204. Katja Schneider, *Burg Giebichenstein*, Weinheim: Acta Humaniora/VCH, 1992: 314–23, 462–63. Sigrid Wortmann Weltge, *Women's Work: Textile Art from the Bauhaus*, London: Thames & Hudson, 1993.

Otto, Karl (1904–1975)

German designer; born Berlin.

Training To 1929 under Hans Poelzig, architecture, Technische Hochschule, Berlin; apprentice in the studios of Poelzig and Ludwig Mies van der Rohe.
Biography 1931–34, Otto first worked as a freelance designer, in Berlin, Mannheim, and Osnabrück; participated in World War II reconstruction in Gifhorn and Osnabrück; from 1950, was director, Werkkunstschule, Hanover, and taught industrial-design classes, the first of their type in Germany; 1955–69, was director, Staatliche Hochschule für bildende Künste, Berlin. He specialized in the architecture of schools and published books that were considered standards in the field of school architecture at the time; 1954, was a founder and planning member of Rat für Formgebung (German design council) and of the Deutscher Werkbund; designed 1954 Arno plywood-and-tubular-metal side chair by L. & C. Stendal, reissued by the firm from 1998; died in Berlin.

Oud, Jacobus Johannes Pieter (1890–1963)

Dutch architect, town planner, and designer; born Purmerend.

Training In Amsterdam: 1903–06 under P.J.H. Cuijpers, Kunstnijverheidschool Quellinus (after 1924 renamed Instituut voor de Kunstnijverheid), Amsterdam; 1908–10, Rijksnormaalschool voor Teekenonderwijzers, Amsterdam. In Delft: 1910–11, Technische Hogeschool (technical college), Delft.
Biography 1907–08, Oud apprenticed in the architecture offices P.J.H. Cuijpers and Jan Stuyt, both Amsterdam; 1911, under Theodor Fischer, Munich; and, 1913, under Willem Dudok, Leiden. 1915–16, he met Theo van Doesburg and Gerrit Rietveld and became an active member of the De Stijl group (formed in 1917) and, also came into contact with the Elementarists. Oud was surprisingly successful in translating De Stijl's difficult theories into practice; admired Dutch architect H.P. Berlage and was an exponent of the Dutch approach to Neue Sachlickheit; opened his own architecture offices in Purmerend and Leiden; 1918–33, was the city architect of Rotterdam, responsible for the radical 1920 Tussendijken and Spangen housing estates and rose to prominence with his designs for Rotterdam districts of Kiefhoek and Oud-Mathenesse. He designed and furnished a group of five terraced houses (with W.H. Gispen's lamps) at 1927 *Weissenhofsiedlung* in Stuttgart. Gispen produced Oud's 1930 counterbalanced piano lamp. His work also included 1917 terraced housing (project) on the promenade in Scheveningen, 1919 factory in Purmerend, 1922–24 housing layouts in Oud-Mathenesse, 1924–25 Café de Unie in Rotterdam, 1925 housing layouts in the Hook of Holland, 1928–29 Kiefhoek development in Rotterdam, 1938–42 Shell building in The Hague, 1952–60 Cio-Children's Convalescent Home near Arnhem. His architecture and unusual furniture shared De Stijl's emphasis on cubic volumes. He attended the opening of 1923 Bauhaus exhibition in Weimar; was instrumental in widening Eileen Gray's reputation after he saw her work at 1923 Salon of Société des Artistes Décorateurs; 1927, designed tubular-steel chairs and tables for his modifications to Villa Allegonda in Katwijk. Some furniture was produced by a local motorcycle manufacturer, and chairs were painted light blue with springed seats; other furniture was produced by Metz. From c. 1935, he took a Functionalist approach, for which he was severely criticized; 1933–54, was an independent architect in Rotterdam and, from 1954, in Wassenaar, where he died.
Exhibitions/citations Work included in 1932 *Modern Architecture—International Exhibition*, The Museum of Modern Art, New York, and subject of exhibitions in Munich in 1965 and Rotterdam in 2001 (catalogs below). Honorary doctorate, Technische Hogeschool, Delft.
Bibliography *J.J.P. Oud, Holländische Architektur* (Bauhausbuch 10),

Munich: Albert Langen, 1929. Henry-Russell Hitchcock, *J.J.P. Oud*, Paris: Cahier d'Art, 1931. Giulia Veronesi, *J.J. Pieter Oud*, Milan: Il Balcone, 1953. J.J.P. Oud, *Mein Weg in 'De Stijl,'* Rotterdam: Nijgh & Van Ditmar, 1961. Cat., Wend Fischer, *J.J.P. Oud: Bauten 1906–63*, Munich: Die Neue Sammlung, 1965. Barbie Campbell-Cole and Tim Benton (eds.), *Tubular Steel Furniture*, London: The Art Book Company, 1979: 38. Ed Taverne et al., *J.J.P. Oud, Poetic Functionalist, 1890–1963: The Complete Works*, Rotterdam: Netherlands Architecture Institute (NAi), 2001.

Oval
> See Timmermans, Hugo.

Ovchinnikov

Russian silversmiths; located Moscow.

History 1853, Ovchinnikov firm was founded by Pavel Akimovich in Moscow, the most important in Russia alongside Fabergé. The firm championed traditional Russian silversmithing and, 1883, was granted an Imperial warrant. Typically, pieces were covered with *cloisonné* enamel in overall patterns of multi-colored arabesques on silver-gilt grounds. Its *champlevé* wares frequently incorporated simpler, brightly colored geometric motifs based on folk-art themes. Pavel Akimovich's sons Mikhail, Aleksandr, Pavel, and Nikolai became directors of the firm, which closed after the 1917 Russian Revolution.
Exhibitions/citations Awards (enamel wares), 1893 *World's Columbian Exhibition*, Chicago, and 1900 *Exposition Universelle*, Paris.
Bibliography Annelies Krekel-Aalberse, *Art Nouveau and Art Déco Silver*, New York: Abrams, 1989.

Overbeck Pottery

American ceramics studio; located Cambridge City, Ind.

History 1911, the Overbeck Pottery was set up in the home of the Overbeck sisters in Cambridge, Ind. They were: Margaret (1863–1911), Mary Frances (1878–1955), Elizabeth (1875–1936), and Hannah (1870–1931). (Evidently, sisters Harriet [1872–1951] and Ida [1861–1946] and the only brother, Charles Borger Overbeck [1881–1913], were not directly involved in the pottery.) Margaret taught art at DePauw University, Greencastle, Ind., worked one summer at a pottery in Zanesville, Ohio (a major ceramics center in the US), and, thus, was the driving force behind setting up the pottery studio. Even though she and her sisters achieved her ambition, she died a year after its inception. The three active surviving sisters, who had studied art, design, and ceramics, were active in the pottery. Mary Frances (a student of Arthur W. Dow at Columbia University, New York) was in charge of glazing and designed some wares. Hannah (a student at Cincinnati Art Academy and Indiana State University) was essentially the designer and decorator. Elizabeth (a student under Margaret initially and under Charles F. Binns at Alfred [N.Y.] University) wheel-threw the shapes and developed the glazes, whose formulas were never revealed but thought to be now in the possession of their nephew. The sisters contributed designs to and wrote criticism for Adelaide Alsop Robineau's journal *Keramic Studio*; believed, 'Borrowed art is bad art,' at a time when European and Japanese designs/formulae were being copied. 1955, the pottery closed. The Museum of Overbeck Art Pottery has been established in the Cambridge City Public Library.
Citations Regularly, awards in venues in Paris, Chicago, New York, Syracuse, Baltimore, St. Louis, Detroit, citites in Indiana, and on a regular basis and at 1915 *Panama-Pacific International Exposition*, San Francisco.
Bibliography *Artists in Indiana Then and Now: The Overbeck Potters of Cambridge City, 1911–1955*, Muncie, Ind.: Ball State University, 1975. Kathleen R. Postle, *The Chronicle of the Overbeck Pottery*, Indianapolis: Indiana Historical Society, 1978. *American Art Pottery*, New York: Cooper-Hewitt Museum, 1987: 122.

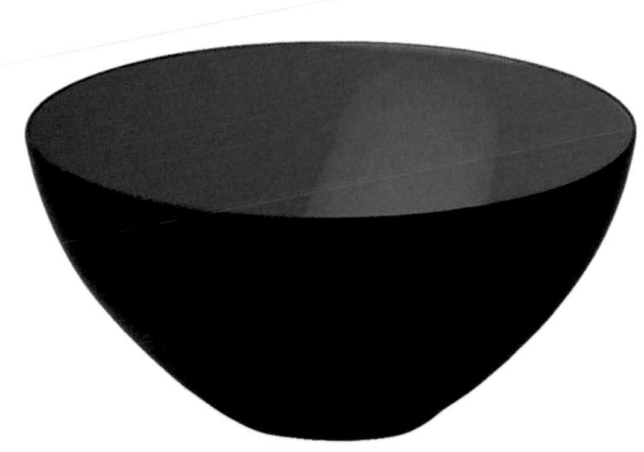

Torben Ørskov & Co.: Herbert Krenchel. Krenit bowl. 1953. Acid-proof enameled steel, h. 5 3/4" (14.6 cm) x dia. 10" (25.4 cm). Mfr.: Torben Ørskov & Co., Denmark. Given anonymously. MoMA.

Owen, Joshua K. (1970–)

American industrial designer; born Philadelphia; son of an archaelogist father.

Training 1988–89, Overseas Student Program, Tel Aviv University; 1993, bachelor of fine arts degree in visual studies, Cornell University, Ithaca, N.Y.; 1997, master of fine arts degree in furniture design, Rhode Island School of Design, Providence.
Biography 1994–95, Owen was guest artist-in-residence, Risley Residential College for the Arts, Cornell University; 1996–97, taught at Rhode Island School of Design; 1998–99, at College of Art and Design; from 1999, at Philadelphia University. 1997, He founded his own design firm, owenLOGIKdesign, for industrial and graphic design, Philadelphia; has been a frequent guest speaker, critic, and juror. His clients have included Andrew Krouk, Anthropologie, Combanimals, Cornell University, Culture & Commerce, Daroff Design, Droog Design, Feast.com, IBM, Material ConneXion, Nike, Olive Design, Umbra, and Wilsonart.
Citations 1993 Michael Rapuano Memorial Award for Distinction in Design, and others.
Exhibitions Work included in a number of exhibitions from 1997 *Nine Artists*, Herbert K. Johnson Museum of Art, Cornell University, to 2002 *U.S. Design: 1975–2000*, Denver Art Museum, Denver, Colo. (catalog below). Subject of 1994 *Furniture by Joshua K. Owen*, Clive Tjaden Gallery, Cornell University.
Bibliography Cat., R. Craig Miller (intro.), *U.S. Design 1975–2000*, Munich: Prestel, 2002.

Owens-Illinois Glass Company
> See Libbey Glass Company.

Oxo International

American housewares manufacturer; located Elmyra, N.Y.

History 1949–60, Sam Farber (1922–) worked at his father Louis Farber's firm, Sheffield Silver Co.; 1960, founded Copco, a kitchenware manufacturer. (Also, Sam Farber's uncle Simon Farber had founded Farberware in 1900, a cookware and knife specialist.) Copco began producing items useful for people with disabilities, such as its bowl-shaped chopping block with a rocker knife and the large loops and knob handles on pots and lids. However, it was not until Sam Faber's 1988 retirement that he became personally aware of the necessity of serving the disabled or infirm, partitally due to his wife Betsey's arthritis. At the time, most manufacturers focused on easy, inexpensive production, rather than facility of use. Thus, Farber came out of retirement in 1989 and established Oxo International for the production of kitchenware for older, disabled users. The palindrome 'Oxo' was chosen for its hortizontally, vertically, and upside-down readibility. Farber was assisted by son John Farber, who took a leave-of-absence as vice-president at Prudential Bache financial firm. Industrial designers Patricia Moore and the Smart Design staff of New York were hired for small royalties and produced appropriate work in 1990. Garden tools were introduced in 1994, and barbecue tools were subsequent. By 1999, the product line had increased to 350 items, including the Swivel Peeler. The Peeler, one of the first 15 items and in the Good Grips range, was the most successful. Its finned handle is double-injection-molded black Santoprene. Other manufacturers have since emulated items in the Good Grips range. More recently, the cheaper Good Grip Basics range was added to counter competition. With little spent on advertising, Oxo has nevertheless remained highly successful. 1992, Farber sold Oxo to General Housewares, and 1995, he retired again and chose Alex Lee (1961–) as the director of product development, later president. 1998, Corning Consumer Products subsidiary (including Oxo) of General Housewares was sold to Borden, which formed its own subsidiary, World Kitchen, with the

Oxo International: Smart Design. Good Grips paring knife. 1989. Stainless steel and Santoprene rubber, 7 3/4 x 1 3/8 x 1" (19.7 x 3.5 x 2.5 cm). Mfr.: Oxo International, US. Gift of the designers. MoMA.

acquisition. 1999, World Kitchen in turn bought the EKCO Group and, subsequently that year, General Housewares, which, as stated, owned Oxo, as well as Chicago Cutlery and other brands.
Exhibitions/citations Included in 1995 *Mutant Materials*, New York and traveling (catalog below). A large number of awards since Oxo's formation, including from Arthritis Foundation, US; Design Zentrum Nordrhein Westfalen, Essen; Good Housekeeping Institute award, *Metropolitan Home* magazine; including 1992 Best Product Designs of the Year, IDSA/*Business Week* magazine.
Bibliography 'Get a Grip,' *Business Week*, 29 Nov. 1999: 90. 'Grab Hold of the Future,' Innovation, fall 1992: 20. 'What Works for One Works for All,' *Business Week*, 20 Apr. 1992: 112. Cat., Paola Antonelli, *Mutant Materials in Contemporary Design*, New York: The Museum of Modern Art/Abrams, 1995.

Oyama, Terry (1941–)

American industrial designer.

Training Art Center College of Design, Pasadena, Cal.
Biography Oyama has worked at Singer, GVO, and Litronic; from 1980, was a designer in the Apple II project of Apple Computer, Cupertino, Cal.; with Apple's directors Stephen Jobs and Jerry Manock, designed 1981–83 Macintosh. Oyama said subsequently, 'Even though Steve [Jobs] didn't draw any of the lines, his ideas and inspiration made the design what it is. To be honest, we didn't know what it meant for a computer to be "friendly" until Steve told us' (Kunkel, 1997). Following freelance designer Helmut Esslinger's 1983 arrival at Apple, Oyama left in 1984 and joined Radius Systems and, subsequently, designed its successful Pivot monitor.
Bibliography Paul Kunkel, *Apple Design: The World of the Apple Industrial Design Group*, New York: Graphis, 1997.

Ozenfant, Amédée (1886–1966)

French painter and theoretician; born Saint-Quentin.

Training 1904–05, drawing, École Municipale de Dessin, Saint-Quentin; in 1905, architecture in the studio of Guichard et Lesage, Paris; in 1905 under André Dunoyer de Segonzac, Roger de La Fresnaye, and Charles Cottet, painting, Académie 'La Palette à Montparnasse,' Paris.
Biography 1905, Ozenfant settled in Paris; 1915 with Pablo Picasso, Max Jacob, and Guillaume Apollinaire, cofounded the review *L'élan* in Paris and was its editor from 1915–17. He used the pseudonym De Rayet in some writings; 1917–25, worked closely with Le Corbusier (then known as Charles-Edouard Jeanneret Gris) to develop ideas on painting and jointly to publish Purist manifesto *Après le cubisme* (1918). 1920–25 with Le Corbusier and poet Paul Dermée, Ozenfant coedited the periodical *L'esprit nouveau: revue internationale d'esthétique* (Éditions de l'Esprit Nouveau, 1920–25), the source from which Le Corbusier culled his book *Vers une architecture* (Paris: Crès, 1923). 1924 with Fernand Léger, Ozenfant opened a school of painting; worked again with Le Corbusier on the Pavilion de l'Esprit Nouveau at 1925 *Exposition Internationale des Arts Décoratifs et Industriels Modernes*, Paris; 1935–38, was a lecturer in art history, French Institute, London; wrote the book *Art* (1928), which became a classic; 1939 settled in New York, where he opened Ozenfant School of Fine Art and, 1942–54, had a weekly informal radio program as an artistic commentator for 'Voice of America'; 1943, became a naturalized US citizen; however, returned to France in 1965, re-assuming French citizenship.
Exhibitions/citations Work subject of *Ozenfant & Jeanneret (peintures puristes)*, Paris (catalog below) and 1985 exhibition, Musée Antoine Lécuyer, Saint-Quentin. Received 1962 medal of honor, Lund University, Lund, Sweden; 1949, elected Chevalier of the Légion d'Honneur and, 1962, Ordre des Arts et des Lettres.
Bibliography Amédée Ozenfant and Le Corbusier, *Après le cubisme*, Paris: Galerie Thomas, 1918. Cat. Maurice Raynal, *Ozenfant & Jeanneret (peintures puristes)*, Paris: Galerie E. Druet, 1921. Karl Nierendorf, *Amédée Ozenfant*, Berlin: Karl Nierendorf, 1931. Cat., John Golding, *Ozenfant*, New York: M. Knoedler, 1973. Suzan L. Ball, *Ozenfant and Purism: The Evolution of a Style 1915–1930*, Ann Arbor: UMI, 1981. Muriel Emanuel et al. (eds.), *Contemporary Artists*, New York: St. Martin's, 1983: 664. Cat., Françoise Ducros (ed.), *Amédée Ozenfant*, Saint-Quentin: Musée Antoine Lécuyer, 1985. William W. Braham, *Modern Color/Modern Architecture: Amédée Ozenfant and the Genealogy of Color in Modern Architecture*, Aldershot, UK, and Burlington, Vt.: Ashgate, 2002. Françoise Ducros, *Ozenfant*, Paris: Cercle d'Art, 2002.

Ferdinand Porsche and Volkswagenwerk. Volkswagen Type 1 sedan (detail). 1938. MoMA.

P.J. Furniture; P. Jeppesen Møbelfabrik

Danish furniture manufacturer; located Store-Heddinge.

History P.J. Furniture, formerly P. Jeppesen Møbelfabrik, carefully handcrafts furniture designed by accomplished architects, including models by Ole Wanscher such as PJ-149 Colonial chair, PJ-112 chair, Rungstedlund line, and a number of others, some continuing in production today. Jørgen Høvelskov's 1963 Harpen (harp) chair was originally made by Christensen & Jensen and, c. 1968, placed into production by P. Jeppesen Møbelfabrik. P.J. Furniture's more recent consultant/designers are Greta Jalk, Hans Olsen, Wilhelm Wohlert, Gorm Lindum, Jørgen Posborg, Troels Grum-Schwensen, and Morten Gøttler. The firm is still family owned.
Bibliography www.pj-furniture.com.

PP Møbler

Danish furniture manufacturer; located Allerød.

History 1953, the workshop was established by Ejnar Pedersen (Vejen, 1923–) to manufacture and sell furniture designed by accomplished Danish architects such as Ole Gerløv-Knudsen, Jørgen Høj, Poul Kjærholm, Marianne Wegner Sørensen, and Hans Jørgen Wegner. The firm calls on the closely monitored artisanal skills of its workers; employs 20 people; makes furniture such as Wegner's The Flag Halyard (PP 225), Valet chair (PP 250), Peacock (PP 550) chair, and about 20 other historical models by Wegner. 1999, management passed from Ejnar Pedersen to Søren Holst Pedersen (Allerød, 1951–).
Citations Prins Henriks Medal of Honor (to PP Møbler's Australian/New Zealand dealer Peter Bromhead); 1999 and 2000 Kundeprisen; 2000 and 2001 The Customers Award; 2001 The Bo Bedre Classical Award (for Flag Halyard chair).
Bibliography www.ppdk.com.

Pabst, Daniel (1826–1910)

German furniture designer and cabinetmaker; born Langenstein; active Philadelphia.

Training Technical high school, Darmstadt.
Biography 1849, Pabst became one of the hundreds of German craftspeople and furniture workers who settled in Philadelphia in the mid-19th century; was a journeyman furniture maker for a short time and, 1854, opened his own workshop at 222 South Fourth Street in Philadelphia. 1860–70, his financial partner was Francis Krauss, a confectioner. From 1870, his workshop was located at 269 South Fifth Street. He designed highly carved 1860s furniture in a Renaissance-Revival style for clients including Bullitt, Disston, Furness, Ingersoll, Newbold, McKean, Parry, Wistar, and Wyeth. He made a c. 1868 furniture suite for historian Henry Charles Lea; from 1860, produced carved centennial spoons for University of Pennsylvania each year; 1870s, turned to the neo-Gothic style in work that appears to be influenced by British designers Bruce J. Talbert and Christopher Dresser. Frank Furness may have designed cabinets made by Pabst, and Pabst himself may have collaborated with Henry Pratt McKean and his son Thomas on the woodwork and furniture for the US president Theodore Roosevelt's house on Long Island, N.Y. 1894, Pabst's son joined the workshop, which closed in 1896.
Exhibitions/citations Award (for a walnut side board), 1876 *Centennial Exposition*, Philadelphia. Desk shown at 1904 *Louisiana Purchase Exposition*, St. Louis. 1910; 1973 furniture in exhibition, Philadelphia (catalog below), was honored by University of Pennsylvania.
Bibliography Cat., James F. O'Gorman, *The Architecture of Frank Furness*, Philadelphia: Philadelphia Museum of Art, 1973: figs. 14–1, 15–1. David A. Hanks and Page Talbott, 'Daniel Pabst, Philadelphia Cabinetmaker,' *Philadelphia Museum of Art Bulletin*, vol. 73, Apr. 1977: 4–14. David Hanks, 'Daniel Pabst, Philadelphia Cabinetmaker,' *Art and Antiques*, vol. 3, Jan.–Feb. 1980: 94–101. Doreen Bolger Burke et al., *In Pursuit of Beauty: Americans and the Aesthetic Movement*, New York: The Metropolitan Museum of Art/Rizzoli, 1987.

Packard
> See Lektro Products, Inc.

Padrnos, Jan (1967–)

Czech designer; born Kutná Hora.

Training 1982–85, secondary schools of machinery in Pilsen and Třebič; 1985–90, faculty of machinery, České Vysoké Učení Technické (Czech technical university), Prague.
Biography After schooling, Padrnos traveled around the world; rejected a career as a mechanical engineer and, initially, answered an employment advertisement for a furniture salesperson, a position he accepted and thus began his interest in the field; from 1995, has been a freelance designer of a variety of furniture—from casegoods to tables, in wood, metal, glass, and Corian. His designs are made by his own firm Black Box in Třebič, which he founded and registered on his birthday in 2000.
Exhibitions/citations Work shown in Milan and New York. Work first (2001) subject of an exhibition, at Gallery 6, Prague; 2001 at Moravian Gallery, Brno. 2000 award (for Ulita bookcase) at Tendence (art, design, and interiors fairs), Prague.

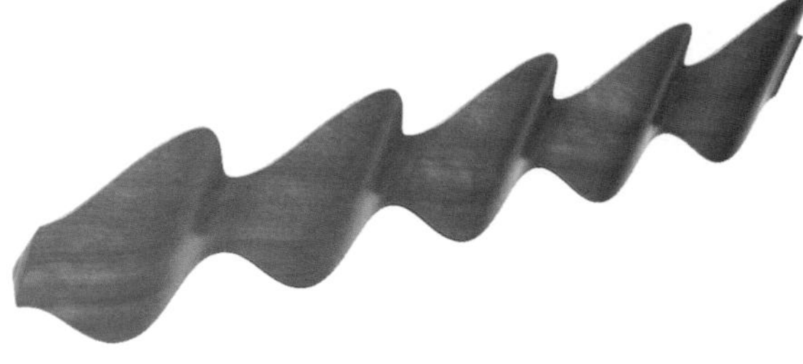

Montse Padrós i Marqués and Carlos Riart. Ona coatrack. 1992. Beechwood and metal, 38 3/16 x 7 1/2 x 2 5/16" (97 x 19.1 x 5.9 cm). Mfr.: Mobles 114, Spain (1996). Gift of the mfr. MoMA.

Padrós i Marqués, Montse (1952–)

Spanish designer; born Barcelona.

Training To 1978, Elisava (Escola de Disseny Superior), Barcelona.
Biography In Barcelona: 1974–78, Padrós worked in design studio Martorell, Bohigas & Mackay; 1979–81, in the design studio of architect Joaquim Prats; 1983–86, at the Town Council of Badalona; 1987–90, in the studio Associates Design; from 1991, in his own studio. His interior-design work has included medical center Digest in Badalona, Work in Barcelona: clothing store In Situ, Casa Pedreño, offices of Fanjoya, music bar El Badiu, pharmacy Giró, and pharmacy Torrens. In Queixans, Girona: music bar El Badiu. Products have included Parellada lamp by Santa & Cole and Ona clothes rack by Mobles 114. From 1989, member of the board, ADP (Associació de Dissenyadors Professionals).
Citations 1992 Delta d'Oro, ADI/FAD (industrial-design/decorative-arts associations), Spain; 1992 selection, Selección Internacional de Diseño de Equipamiento para el Hábitat (SIDI), Barcelona; 1994 Grand Prix de la Presse et de la Critique, 1994 Salon du Meuble, Paris; 1995 Premio de Diseño, Professional Designers Association (ADP).

Pagano, Giuseppe (b. Giuseppe Pogatschnig, aka Giuseppe Pagano-Pogatschnig 1896–1945)

Italian architect; born Parenzo (now Poreč, Croatia).

Training To 1924, architecture, Politecnico, Milan.
Biography Pogatschnig changed his name to the more-Italian Pagano, when he enlisted in the Italian army in 1915. With Gino Levi-Montalcini, he designed 1928–30 Gualino office building in Turin and several exhibition buildings at 1928 *Esposizione di Torino*, considered the earliest Rationalist structures in Italy. The 1928 *Esposizione* provided a platform for experimentation by young architects, including Alberto Sartoris, Lavinia Perona, Levi-Montalcini and Pagano, who formed the Gruppo dei Sei in 1928, led by Edoardo Persico. Pagano and Levi-Montalcinis were invited to design the Italian pavilion at 1930 *Exposition Internationale de la Grande Industrie, Science et Application Art Wallon*, Liège. From 1931, Pagano was one of the advisors of *Architettura* (the revision of journal *Architettura e arti decorative*); 1930–43 with Persico, worked on the editorial staff of Pier Maria Bardi's journal *La casa bella*, later *Casabella*, of which Pagano was the editor from 1933. He was the second leading exponent of Italian Rationalism along with Giuseppe Terragni and played a significant role as its theoretician through his writings. Pagano's Rationalist buildings were condemned by some contemporary critics as architecture reduced to engineering. With Piero Bottoni and Mario Pucci, he proposed a permanent 'experimental neighborhood' to be undertaken by the Triennale di Milano in 1934–36. Terragni, the BBPR architect team, and Pagano separately entered the 1936 competition for the Palazzo del Littorio on the via dell'Impero in Rome. His article 'Discorso sull'architettura italiana di oggi' (Discussion of Italian architecture today) was read to architecture groups in Copenhagen, Stockholm, and Helsinki and published in *La tecnica fascista* (1939). In it, Pagano endorsed 'the triumph of modern life promoted by fascism' and praised the 1932 *Mostra della Rivoluzione Fascista* (exhibition of the fascist revolution). He designed 1932 Institute of Physics (part of the university precinct in Rome, planned by Massimo Piacentini) and 1938–41 Universitá Bocconi (with Predaval) in Milan for which he designed bentwood seating Maggioni; for others, also designed bent tubular-steel furniture. Pagano was a fascist from 1920 but left the Fascist Party in 1942 and participated in the Resistance, and died in Mauthausen concentration camp.
Exhibitions Architecture jury member, 1942 *Esposizione Universale di Roma*. Designed the steel high-rise (with others), 1933 (5th) Triennale di Milano, and director of its 1936 (6th) edition. Participated in 1937 *Exposition Internationale des Arts et Techniques dans la Vie Moderne*, Paris.
Bibliography Gino Levi-Montalcini, 'Giuseppe Pagano,' *Agorà*, Nov. 1945. Sam Polistina, 'Giuseppe Pagano,' *Avant!*, 29 Sept. 1945. Giancarlo Palanti, *Giuseppe Pagano Pagatschnig: architetture e scritti*, Milan: Domus, 1947. Carlo Melograni, *Giuseppe Pagano*, Milan: Il Balcone, 1955. Barbie Campbell-Cole and Tim Benton (eds.), *Tubular Steel Furniture*, London: The Art Book Company, 1979: 47. Antonino Saggio, *L'opera di Giuseppe Pagano tra politica e architettura*, Bari: Dedalo, 1984. Alberto Bassi and Laura Castagno, *Giuseppe Pagano*, Rome: Laterza, 1994. Anty Pansera et al., *Flessibili splendori: i mobili in tubolare metallico/il caso Columbus*, Milan: Electa, 1998.

Pagnon, Patrick (1953–); Claude Pelhaître (1954–)

French furniture designers; active Paris.

Training École Nationale Supérieure des Arts Décoratifs (ENSAD); École Boulle, Paris.
Biography 1981, Pagnon and Pelhaître set up an office, specializing in interior and furniture design. Their furniture is frequently conceived as modular and adaptable systems, some by Artelano, Bauman, Habitat, Le Mobilier National, and, for example, 1993 mobile shelving/cabinets, Crescendo variable-height table, Ipso Facto glass/steel table by Cinna. 1979, they established the furniture section of ENSAD.
Exhibitions/citations Work included in 1990 exhibition, Paris (catalog below). 1984 Carte Blanche production support (for Straty range of furniture by Ligne Roset, in the Domus collection), VIA, Paris. 1985 (for Straty) and 1989 SM d'Or, Salon du Meuble, Paris; 1989 Prix de l'Industrie; 1989 Janus de l'Industrie.
Bibliography Cat., *Les années VIA 1980–1990*, Paris: Musée des Arts Décoratifs, 1990: 140. Cat., Sophie Tasma Anargyros et al., *L'école française: les créateurs de meubles du 20ème siècle*, Paris: Industries Françaises de l'Ameublement, 2000. Arlette Barré-Despond (ed.), *Dictionnaire international des arts appliqués et du design*, Paris: Regard, 1996.

Pahlmann, William (1900–1987)

American interior designer; born Illinois; active New York.

Training From 1927, interior design, Parsons School of Design, New York; 1930, Parsons School of Design, Paris.
Biography Pahlmann worked as a traveling salesperson and actor before studying design; from 1933, was active as an interior designer and became known for his colorful, eclectic 1930s model rooms for Lord & Taylor department store, New York, where he worked from 1936–42; 1946, opened his own design firm, New York; wrote newspaper column 'A Matter of Taste'; was a member, American Institute of Decorators (AID); designed numerous houses in Texas and interiors of 1959 restaurant Four Seasons (architect, Philip Johnson) in Seagram Building (architects, Mies van der Rohe and Johnson), and restaurant Forum of the Twelve Caesars, both New York; had numerous clients including playwright/actor Abe Burrows, Tiffany director Walter Hoving Sr., and Broadway producer Billy Rose; wrote *The Pahlmann Book of Interior Design* (New York: Crowell, 1955). Decorators in his office included Anne Winkler, Dorothy Tremble, A.J. Conner, Daren Pierce, Jack Hartrick, and George Thiele. Pahlmann designed the interiors of Memorial Student Center at Texas A&M University in College Station. His archive, received mid-1980s, is housed in the University's Technical Reference Center, and the University offers the annual William Pahlmann Endowed Scholarship.
Bibliography John Esten and Rose Bennett Gilbert, *Manhattan Style*, Boston: Little, Brown, 1990: 10. Mark Hampton, *The Legendary Decorators of the Twentieth Century*, New York: Doubleday, 1992.

Pairpoint

American glass manufacturer; located New Bedford, Mass.

Biography 1837, Pairpoint Crystal was founded as the Mount Washington Glass Co., which, 1894, merged with Pairpoint Silver Co. to become Pairpoint Manufacturing. Thomas J. Pairpoint (1847–1902), who formerly worked at Gorham Manufacturing Co., was the first superintendent of Pairpoint Manufacturing. The firm is best known for its

electric lamps with puffy, ribbed, or flat glass shades with scenic- or flower-motif reverse-painting and cast-metal bases made in the original New Bedford, Mass., factory, from 1907–29. When orders were slow, the artisans painted watercolors of the lamps for the sales catalogues. Still active today, the factory produces vases, tabletop objects, plates, bells, and other items mouth-blown by artisans, many from Europe, at the Pairpoint Glass Works, Sagamore, Mass.
Bibliography Leonard E. Padgett, *Pairpoint Glass*, Des Moines, Iowa: Wallace-Homestead, 1979. Doreen Bolger Burke et al., *In Pursuit of Beauty: Americans and the Aesthetic Movement*, New York: The Metropolitan Museum of Art/Rizzoli, 1986: 457. Edward and Sheila Malakoff, *Pairpoint Lamps*, Atglen, Pa.: Schiffer, 1991. Louis O. St. Aubin Jr., *Pairpoint Lamp Catalog: Shade Shapes Ambero Through Panel*, Atglen, Pa.: Schiffer, 2001

Pajeau, Charles H. (1875–1952); Tinkertoy
American stone mason and inventor.

Biography Charles H. Pajeau, formerly a granite worker who made tombstones, was inspired to develop what eventually became known as the Tinkertoy while observing children playing with pencils, sticks, and empty thread spools. In his garage in 1913, he developed a more sophisticated, but still simple, system as a substitution—a collection of identical flattened wooden spools, with eight peripheral holes and one through the center, into which could be inserted 1/4" (0.5 cm)-dia. wooden dowels. Thus, the pieces made it easy for a young child to build three-dimensional architectonic structures, and possibly more interesting to a young mind than the 'gifts' and blocks by German educator Frederich Fröbel (1782–1852), founder of the kindergarten. Soon after, according to legend, Pajeau and Robert Pettit, a stockbroker, met while commuting to work by train, from suburban Evanston, Ill., to Chicago. They complained to each other about their dissatisfaction with their jobs. Pajeau told Pettit about his toy and, thus, in 1913, they formed a partnership as the Toy Tinkers Company in Evanston to market the product, which they called the Thousand Wonder Toy (later renamed Tinkertoy). It was introduced at the 1914 American Toy Fair but received no interest. However, different stories tell of its eventual success. One is that they tried again in Chicago at Christmastime by hiring midgets dressed in elf clothing, who played with the constructions in a department-store display window. Another story is that they persuaded a druggist in Evanston to place a Tinkertoy-built windmill in the window of his pharmacy with a electric fan to turn the blades. One or another or both of these ploys was effective, and, within the first year, Pajeau and Pettit had sold a million sets, and, thence, the toy became a classic. The Pajeau-Pettit partnership lasted for almost 30 years. Eventually, the rights were sold to the Child Guidance educational-toy company, which in turn sold it to Hasbro in 1985, which markets it today as a Playskool product. The elements that were sold in a cylindrical paper container with a screw-on metal lid were little changed until Playskool (a subsidiary of Hasbro) marked Tinkertoy's 80th birthday of 1993 with a 1992 all-plastic redesign in brighter colors and fittings that facilitate the building of larger structures.
Bibliography Craig Strange, *Collector's Guide to Tinker Toys*, Paducah, Ky.: Collector Books, 1996.

Pairpoint Glass Works. Table lamp. c. 1910. Cast bronze and back-painted pressed glass, h. 26" (66 cm). Mfr.: Pairpoint Glass Works, US. Courtesy Quittenbaum Kunstauktionen, Munich.

Pakhalé, Satyendra (1967–)
Indian designer; born Washim.

Training 1985–89, bachelor's degree in engineering, Visvesvaraya Regional College of Engineering, Nagpur, India; 1989–91, master's degree in design, Industrial Design Centre, Indian Institute of Technology, Bombay; 1992–94, advanced product design, Art Center College of Design (Europe), La Tour de Peilz, Switzerland.
Biography 1991–92, Pakhalé worked as an industrial designer at Bajaj Auto Ltd., Puna, India; 1992–93, junior product designer, frogdesign, Altenstig, Germany; 1995–98, was a senior product designer at Philips, Eindhoven. 1998, he established his own studio in Amsterdam; 2001, was head of the ceramics department, Hogeschool, 's-Hertogenbosch; 2001–02, head of Man & Activity department and 2002, head of Man & Living department, both at Akademie voor Industriële Vormgeving, Eindhoven. Wide range of products, furniture, and automobiles has included fiber and ceramic chairs, a hanger, vessels, wicker lamp, and others for clients, including Alessi, Cappellini, Cor Unum, Habitat, Magis, Mexx International, Totem shop, and Zeritalia.
Exhibitions/citations From 2000, work included in a number of exhibitions, and subject of 2002 *Satyendra Pakhalé: From Projects to Products*, Stedelijk Museum, Amsterdam. Numerous awards and grants, including 1993 bronze prize, LG Electronics Design Competition; 1994, 1998, 1999 Distinction Awards, *I.D.* magazine.
Bibliography *New and Notable Product Design 2*, Gloucester, Mass.: Rockport, 1995. Michele De Lucchi (ed.), *The International Design Yearbook*, London: Laurence King, 2001. Renny Ramakers, *Less + More: Droog Design in Context*, Rotterdam: 010, 2002. Daniel Rozensztroch, *Cintres – Hangers*, Paris: Le Passage, 2002.

Palais du Marbre
French decorating workshop.

History 1925, Palais du Marbre was established as the modern furniture and decorating store of the firm Mercier Frères at 77, avenue des Champs-Élysées, Paris. 1929, Eric Bagge became its artistic director.
Exhibitions Participated in 1925 *Exposition Internationale des Arts Décoratifs et Industriels Modernes*, Paris.
Bibliography Pierre Kjellberg, *Art déco: les maîtres du mobilier, le décor des paquebots*, Paris: Amateur, 1986/1990.

Paley, Albert (1944–)
American metalworker; born Philadelphia.

Training To 1969, Tyler School of Art, Temple University, Philadelphia.
Biography From 1968, Paley has taught crafts at various institutions; trained as a blacksmith and became known for architectural metalwork made with traditional wrought-iron techniques and also modern hydraulic presses; has designed metal furniture, gates, railings, and staircases; has been active in his own workshop with other artisans in Rochester, N.Y. Art Nouveau and simple Romanesque architectural forms can be seen in his work. He also has designed/made jewelry in precious metals. Most recent commissions: 2003 Sentinel at Rochester Institute of Technology; 2002 Constellation sculptural relief on the façade of Wellington Place, Toronto, Canada; 2000 portal gates of Naples Museum of Art, Naples, Fla. He teaches as the Charlotte Fredericks Mowris Professor in Contemporary Crafts, School for American Crafts in College of Imaging Arts and Sciences at Rochester Institute of Technology.
Exhibitions/citations Numerous citations, including 1982 Award of Excellence (for 1980 gates of New York State Senate Chambers), American Institute of Architects (AIA). Work subject of exhibitions, including at Memorial Art Gallery. University of Rochester, in 1985; Peter Joseph Gallery, New York, in 1992; University of the Arts, Philadelphia,

in 1991; Renwick Gallery, Washington, in 1991; Roanoke (Virginia) Museum of Fine Arts/
Bibliography Edward Lucie-Smith, *Art of Albert Paley: Iron, Bronze, Steel*, New York: Abrams, 1996. Videorecording, *Albert Paley: Man of Steel*, writer/director Tony Machi, producer: Princeton, N.J.: Films for the Humanities & Sciences, 2001.

Pallavicino, Cesare
> See Innocenti, Ferdinado.

Pallucco, Paolo (1950–); Pallucco Italia

Italian architect, furniture designer, and manufacturer; born Rome. Enterprise located Castagnole di Paese (TV).

Training In architecture in Rome.
Biography 1980, Pallucco established the eponymous firm Pallucco, which produced new designs of his own and of others (including the Simón firm), and reissued modern classics; 1984, established Pallucco Design, through which his own designs were managed separately. His work includes 1984 Fra Dolcino shelving and other furniture pieces (with Mareille Rivier), including 1987 Tankette table with moveable tank-like metal treads. Other items by the firm included 1984 Lizie armchair designed by Régis Protière and the 1907 floor-lamp (reproduction) by Mariano Fortuny. 1990, the enterprise became Pallucco Italia and, subsequently, the inventory has appreciably expanded to include furniture, lighting, and accessories by Pascal Bauer, Denis Santachiara, Enrico Franzollini, Pallucco himself, and others. Its 2003 Bellatobrand collection was designed by Luciano Bertoncini and others.
Bibliography Albrecht Bangert and Karl Michael Armer, *80s Style: Designs of the Decade*, New York: Abbeville, 1990: 82, 234. Fumio Shimizu and Studio Matteo Thun (eds.), *The Italian Design: Descendants of Leonardo da Vinci*, Tokyo: Graphic-sha, 1987: 327. www.pallucco.com.

Palmqvist, Sven Ernst Robert (1906–1984)

Swedish glassware designer.

Training From 1927–30, glass-engraving school, Orrefors Glasbruk; 1932–34, Kungliga Tekniska Högskolan, Stockholm; 1934–36, sculpture, Kungliga Konsthögskolan, Stockholm; and in Germany, Czechoslovakia, Italy, the US, including France, under Paul Cornet and Aristide Maillol at Académie Ranson, Paris.
Biography 1930–72, Palmqvist was a designer at Orrefors Glasbruk, where his work signaled a return to the graceful lines of pre-Functionalist glasswares; 1954, invented a new technique for forming glass bowls by spinning molten glass in a centrifugal mold to eliminate hand finishing; 1950–81, created a series of delicately blown crystal forms (in the boldly colored Ravenna technique that featured simple non-figurative inlaid patterns) at Orrefors, where he was later (1972–84) a freelance designer.
Exhibitions/citations Light and Dark wall, constructed from blocks of Ravenna glass and gray-and-white crystal, shown at *Union Internationale des Telecommunications*, Geneva, and reinstalled at 1967 *Universal and International Exhibition (Expo '67)*, Montreal. Work included in 1937 *Exposition Internationale des Arts et Techniques dans la Vie Moderne*, Paris; 1939–40 *New York World's Fair: The World of Tomorrow*; 1958 *Formes Scandinaves*, Musée des Arts Décoratifs, Paris; 1958 touring exhibitions of Orrefors glass; 1982 and 1983 exhibitions, New York and Philadelphia (catalogs below.) Gold medal and grand prize (for spun-glass objects), 1957 (11th) Triennale di Milano; grand prize, 1976 Biennale di Venezia; 1977 Prince Eugen Medal.
Bibliography 'Sven Palmqvist,' *Design Quarterly*, no. 34, 1956: 21–23. Erik Zahle (ed.), *A Treasury of Scandinavian Design*, New York: Golden Press, 1961: 287, nos. 217, 219, 23. Cat., David Revere McFadden (ed.), *Scandinavian Modern Design 1880–1980*, New York: Abrams, 1982. Cat., Helmut Ricke and Ulrich Gronert, *Glas in Schweden, 1915–1960*, Munich: Prestel/Dusseldorf: Kunstmuseum, 1986. Jennifer Hawkins Opie, *Scandinavia: Ceramics and Glass in the Twentieth Century*, New York: Rizzoli, 1989. George Fischler and Barrett Gould, *Scandinavian Ceramics and Glass: 1940s to 1980s*, Atglen, Pa.: Schiffer, 2000.

Sven Palmqvist. Bowl. 1960. Glass, h. 7 5/8" (19.4 cm) x dia. 14 1/4" (36.2 cm). Mfr: Orrefors Glasbruk, Sweden. Philip Johnson Fund. MoMA.

Palomba, Roberto (1963–); Ludovica Palomba Serafini (1961–)

Italian architects and designers; husband and wife; active Verona. Roberto: born Cagliari. Ludovica: born Rome.

Training Both: in architecture, 'La Sapienza' of Università degli Studi Rome, Roberto to 1991, Ludovica to 1993.
Biography They individually designed sets (for The Spoleto Ballet and RAI television network), renovation of historical gardens (of city hall of Rome), and architecture (residences, hotels, and shops). From 1994, they have collaborated as Palomba-Serafini particularly on bathroom sanitary equipment and also on furniture and lighting by Boffi, Cappellini, De Vecchi, Dornbracht, Foscarini, Lemi, Liv'it, Prandini, Moab 80, Salviati, Tronconi, and others. They are or have been the artistic directors of and designers to Bosa, Crassevig, Ceramica Flaminia, and Kos.
Exhibitions/citations Curators and exhibitors, 1993 Abitare il Tempo fair, Verona. Work included in 1997 *Under 35*, ADI (Associazione per il Disegno Industriale), Milan; 1998 *Face Galleria del Design Italiano* (organized by *Abitare* magazine), New York; 2000 *Aperto Vetro*, Venice. Second prize (for Anna chair by Crassevig), 1999 Young & Design, Milan; prize, 2001 Design Plus (for Acquagrande sanitary fittings by Ceramica Flaminia), Ambiente fair, Frankfurt; selection (for Link and Twin Column by Ceramica Flaminia) of 2001 Premio Compasso d'Oro.
Bibliography *Abitare*, no. 386, July–Aug. 1999. Jasper Morrison (ed.), *The International Design Yearbook*, New York: Abbeville, 1999. *Design Report*, no. 11, Nov. 2000.

Palsby, Ole (1935–)

Danish designer.

Training As a stockbroker; self-taught as a designer.
Biography From 1958, Palsby worked with a graphic designer and pioneered the marketing of certain Danish- and foreign-furniture models, particularly modular kitchens and building construction; 1960, became a designer in his own right; 1964, opened an art gallery; 1975, became an independent designer; 1986, set up a design studio in London; has worked for more than 25 years on the development of design of kitchenware and is best known for 1997 Eva Trio pots and pans, 1985 Alfi spherical vacuum bottle and, by WMF, metalware, including Combination cutlery and a popular wire fruitbasket; has pursued simple and functional forms while considering economics and the appropriateness of materials.
Citations 1994 Annual Award, Dansk Design Centre; design prize, Stuttgart Centre; Japanese Design Prize; 2000 award, Industrie Forum Design (iF), Hanover.
Bibliography Michele De Lucchi (ed.), *The International Design Yearbook*, London: Laurence King, 2001.

Palterer, David (1949–)

Israeli architect and designer; born Haifa; active Florence.

Training To 1979, Facoltà di Architettura, Università degli Studi, Florence.
Biography 1979–89, Palterer was an assistant professor under Adolfo Natalini at the university in Florence; taught design courses elsewhere, including at Syracuse (N.Y.) University, 1985; Werkbund, Stuttgart, 1985, and Stätliche Akademie der bildenden Künste, 1992–93, Stuttgart, to the Commune of Tychy, Poland, 1995; faculty of engineering in Perugia, 1995. 1983 with Bořek Šípek, he established design/production firm Alterego, Amsterdam; from 1995, was director of ceramics and porcelain design, Centro di Formazione Professionale, San Colombano (FI). He has designed furniture, furnishings, lighting, and

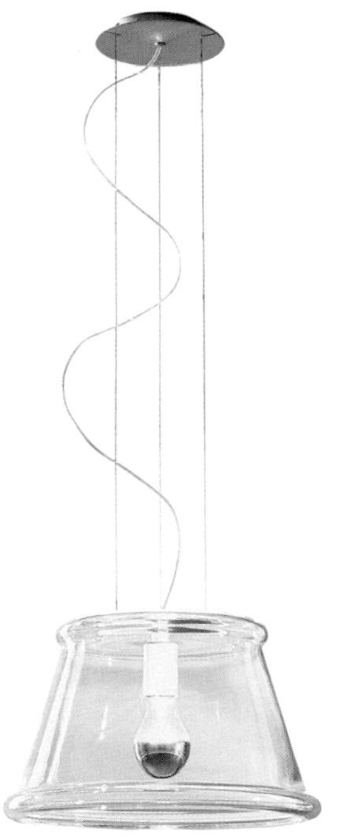

Roberto Pamio. Ivette hanging lamp. c. 1998. Metal and glass, h. max. 90 1/2" (230 cm) x dia. 15" (38 cm). Mfr.: Fabbian Illuminazione, Italy.

various products by Acerbis, Alterego, Artelano, Artemide, Arzberg, La Battaglia di Leplanto, Blome, Cleto Munari, Draenert, Daum, Driade, Ritzenhoff, Sardinia Crystal, Swid Powell, Up & Up, Vilca, Yamagiwa, and Zanotta. His buildings include San Casciano theater, Florence airport, and parks in Pesaro, Italy, and Tel Aviv, Israel; restoration/enlargement of Teatro San Casciano (with Zangheri); Florence airport terminal; modification of Philip Morris offices; Mito restaurant (in Isozaki's cultural center in Jerusalem); San Casciano agricultural-tourist center; Tenuta Castel S. Pietro; and a project for the historical center of Haifa, Israel. He wrote the book *The Italian Furniture* (with Fumio Shimizu, Japan: Graphic-sha, 1991); has organized a number of exhibitions, including 1990 *Cleto Munari*, Medicean Museum, Florence; 1994, 1995, 1996 *San Valentino Orom*, Camera di Commercio, Terni. He was three times curator of Toscana section; 1995 *Pistoia—Ospite d'Onore*, Foire Comtoise (Franche-Comté fair), Besançon.

Panasonic Company. Toot-a-Loop radio (no. R-72). c. 1972. ABS polymer, h. 2 3/4" (7 cm), dia. 6" (15.2 cm). Mfr: Panasonic Company, US. Gift of Anne Dixon. MoMA.

Citations Won competitions in Italy and abroad, including 1979 *L'interno dopo la forma dell'utilem*, Triennale di Milano; re-evaluation (with Natalini) of the old-city plan of Parma; London jewelry-store project, *Architectural Review* international competition, London. Received 1996 Red Dot award (Arzberg *Flying Object* project), Design Zentrum Nordrhein Westfalen, Essen. Glass work subject of 1996 *David Palterer Vetri: Design Collection—Sardinia Crystal*, D&D, Milan.
Bibliography 'New Wave Designers in Firenze,' *Japan Interior Design*, no. 293, 1982. Anna Gazzi, 'I "mostri" di David Palterer,' *Area*, no. 40, 1988. Adolfo Natalini, *David Palterer in Riflessioni—non solo in vetro*, Milan: Galleria Paola e Rossella Colombari, 1991. Giuseppe Alleruzzo, 'David Palterer,' *La casa nuova 4/5*, Rome: LCN, 1993. Marco Romanelli, 'Raccontare David Palterer,' in *Driadebook*, Milan: Skira, 1995. Gilles de Bure, 'David Palterer: les objets ont une âme,' *Beaux Arts* no. 133, 1995. Silvio San Pietro and Norberto Medardi (eds.), *David Palterer*, Milan: L'Archivolto, 1996.

Pamio, Roberto (1937–)

Italian architect and designer; born Mestre (VE); active Scorzè (VE).

Training To 1968, architecture, Istituto Universitario di Architettura, Venice.
Biography 1961, Pamio began his career as an architect and furniture and industrial designer; with Renato Tosso, collaborated on furniture and lighting. Large rostrum of clients has included Artemide (lighting), Gabbianelli (ceramics), Zanussi (electrical appliances), Peguri (furniture), Stilwood (furniture), Arc Linea (kitchen furniture), Cidue, FAI (bulldozers), Leucos (lighting), Arflex (office furniture), and others. Has designed a large number of international buildings, from 1977 Dolomiti hotel, Misurina, to 1993 reconstruction/addition to Arc Linea's headquarters/plant, Caldogno, and many retail shops.
Citations 1985, 1989, 1990, 1993 awards, Institute of Business Designers (IBD); 1985, 1987, 1989, 1991 Roscoe Awards; 1967 (for bed by Peguri), 1987 (for Rondo table by Cidue), 1991 (for LG 102 Legend Collection furniture by Matteograssi) Premio Compasso d'Oro; 1988 iF (Industrie Forum Design); 1989 award, Salon International de Design Intérieur de Montréal (SIDIM) ; first prize, 1999 Celebration of the 2nd Millennium Contest, Italy.
Bibliography *Moderne Klassiker: Möbel, die Geschichte machen*, Hamburg: Gruner + Jahr, 1982: 139. Giancarlo Iliprandi and Pierluigi Molinari (eds.), *Industrial designers italiani*, Fagagna: Magnus, 1985: 162. Hans Wichmann, *Italien Design 1945 bis heute*, Munich: Die Neue Sammlung, 1988. *Modo*, no. 148, Mar.–Apr. 1993: 124.

Panasonic; National; Technics; Matsushita

Japanese electronics-equipment manufacturer.

History 1918, Konosuke Matsushita (Wakayama 1894–Osaka 1989 founded Matsushita Electric Co. in Osaka, Japan, which has since grown from 3 employees to almost 300,000. Today, Panasonic, National, and Technics are essentially brands. 1918, Matsushita himself invented a two-socket light bulb. And a number of products/inventions followed, including 1923 battery-powered bicycle lamp, 1927 electric iron, 1931 automatic electric iron (first example), 1936 ocillating electric fan (first example) and 1936 incandescent bulb (first example), 1946 all-wave radio, 1950 straight fluorescent tube (first example), 1952 17" black-and-white TV set, 1952 electric blender, 1952 portable radio, 1958 tape recorder (first for home use), 1959 miniaturized transitor radio, 1960 17" color TV set, 1970 direct-dive turntable (Technics), 1973 fax machine (Japan's first), 1979 VHS home tape recorder. 1927, 'National,' the group's original brand name, was first used on a box-shaped battery-powered lamp; subsequently, on home appliances in Japan, also in Asia, the Middle East, and Africa. However and no doubt due to confusion, the 'National' brand name was discontinued in 2003, replaced by 'Panasonic.' 1955, 'Panasonic' first appeared on speakers for export; and, currently, on audio/video equipment, information/communications equipment, and factory automation equipment in Japan, and all products in the Americas, Europe, and Oceania. On others in Asia, the Middle East, and Africa. 1965, 'Technics' was first used for high-grade audio speakers in Japan and, currently, on audio products and musical instruments worldwide. For Panasonic products, the firm has commissioned a number of designers, including Leopoldo Matteo Bazzicalupo and Denis Santachiara, but, primarily, its equipment is anonymously designed by the in-house staff. Today, the mother firm, Matsushita Electric Industrial Co., is a very large enterprise, global in scope, and produces a wide range of domestic and industrial electronics.
Citations Two 2003 Best of Innovations awards and eleven honorary

awards, Consumer Electronics Association, Las Vegas, Nev.
Bibliography www.panasonic.co.jp/global/top.html.

Panco
> See Hammarplast.

Pander

Dutch furniture manufacturer; located Gouda (1863–65), the Hague (1865–85), Amsterdam (1885–1915), Rotterdam (1915–85).

History 1882, Hendrik Pander expanded his housewares store and carpet business to include curtains, linoleum, blankets, and furniture. 1887, he set up a furniture factory with models designed in Louis XVI and 'Old Dutch' styles. His machine-made furniture was sold to stores and interior furnishings on special orders. 1914–34, Hendrik Wouda worked at the firm as an interior architect and became the head of the department Modern Interior Art. 1914–16, F. Spanjaard was a designer there; 1917–23, Cor Alons worked under Wouda. Interior architect Paul Bromberg, having previously worked for Metz, was a member of the Pander staff from 1924–34. Through the efforts of Wouda and Bromberg, Pander clients were offered a choice of modern models; Wouda's work was austere and cubical, while Bromberg's was more sculptural. 1917, a large factory complex was built in the Hague; it produced furniture for domestic and foreign sales. 1927, Pander acquired the Maatschappij tot Vervaardiging van Vliegtuigen (Maastricht airplane-production company). From 1930, furniture was produced both by traditional joinery techniques and by mass-production methods. 1933–41, tapestry artist and interior architect S.F. Semeij worked in the Modern Interior Art Department; 1934, Wouda and Bromberg departed. Subsequent consultant designers included architect L.C. van der Vlugt, J. H. van den Broek, J. Wils, F.A. Eschauzier, J. van Erven Dorens, and decorative artist C.A. Lion Cachet. French designer E.B. Dubourcq worked for Pander from 1938–c. 1941, during which time contemporary designs were dropped. 1985, Pander went into liquidation.
Bibliography Cat., *Industry and Design in the Netherlands,1850/1950*, Amsterdam: Stedelijk Museum, 1985: 260–63.

Pankok, Bernhard (1872–1943)

German designer and graphic artist; born Münster.

Training Apprenticeship in restoration and decoration in Münster; to 1892, in painting in Düsseldorf and Berlin.
Biography 1892–1902, Pankok worked in Munich, contributed to the journal *Jugend*, and designed rather heavy-handed Art Nouveau-style furniture. Following the lead of Koloman Moser and Josef Hoffmann's Wiener Werkstätte, in 1898 Pankok, Hermann Obrist, Bruno Paul, Peter Behrens, and Richard Riemerschmid founded the Münchner Vereinigte Werkstätten für Kunst im Handwerk (Munich united workshops for art in handwork). The enterprise aimed to provide everyday objects designed by accomplished modern artists. 1902, Pankok settled in Stuttgart, where was director, Staatliche Kunstgewerbeschule, from 1913–37. He designed 1900 Lange house, interior of steamship *Friedrichshafen*, and a 1911 aluminum-tube chair for a Zeppelin.
Exhibitions Work subject of 1973 and 1988 exhibitions, Stuttgart (catalogs below); and 1970 *Pankok—Riemerschmid—Paul: Interieurs Münchner Architekten um 1900*, Museum Villa Stuck, Munich.
Bibliography Sonja Günther, *Interieurs um 1900: Bernhard Pankok, Bruno Paul, und Richard Riemerschmid...*, Munich: Wilhelm Fink, 1971. Cat., *Bernard Pankok 1972–1943...*, Stuttgart: Württembergische Landesmuseum, 1973. Cat., *Bernhard Pankok: Malerei, Grafik, Design im Prisma des Jugendstils*, Munich: Westfälisches Landesmuseum, 1986.

Pantin, Cristallerie de

French crystal factory; located Pantin.

History 1851, E.S. Monot founded the Cristallerie de la Villette, specializing in cut clear-glass production. 1855, it was renamed Cristallerie de Pantin, when it was moved to the town of the same name in the northeastern suburb of Paris. Adding color techniques in the 1860s, Pantin was known for its opalescent and iridescent glass. The operation became known as Monot et Stumpf and as Monot Père et Fils. And, when Monot retired c. 1886, was reorganized as Stumpf, Touvier, et Viollet. From 1888, it produced glass in an Art Nouveau style, including iridescent, enameled, and frosted glass as well as imitations of semi-precious stones under its artistic director Touvier. 1900, its director Stumpf was succeeded by Camille Turré de Varreux, under whom it expanded its production to include cased glass with finely detailed, etched, and wheel-cut decorations, and table services by Dutch architect Hendrik Berlage (1900) and Camille Tutré de Varreux (1910). 1900, the operation became Cristallerie de Pantin once again; then, 1919, merged with Legras to become Verrerie et Cristallerie de St Denis et Pantin Réunies, in Saint-Denis, to its c. 1939 closing.
Exhibitions Imitations of rock crystal and Venetian glass at 1878 Exposition Universelle, Paris.
Bibliography Yvonne Brunhammer et al., *Art Nouveau in Belgium, France*, Houston: Institute for the Arts, Rice University, 1976.

Verner Panton. Stacking side chair. 1959–60. Polyurethane plastic, 32 1/8 x 19 1/4 x 22 5/8" (81.6 x 48.9 x 57.5 cm). Mfr: Vitra-Fehlbaum, Germany (1968). Gift of Herman Miller, Switzerland. MoMA.

Panton, Verner (1926–1998)

Danish architect and designer; born Gantofte, Funen Island; active primarily Copenhagen, and Binningen, Switzerland.

Training 1944–47, Tekniske Skole, Odense; 1947–51, architecture, Det Kongelige Danske Kunstakademi, Copenhagen.
Biography Panton was introduced to product design through his relationship with lighting designer Poul Henningsen, first at the Kunstakademi in Copenhagen. (1950, Panton married Henningsen's stepdaughter, Tove Kemp, but they soon separated.) 1950–52, Panton worked in the studio of Arne Jacobsen on 1951–52 Ant chair, and also on experimental furniture, later claiming that he 'learned more from him than anyone else.' 1955, Panton set up his own studio in Binningen, Switzerland. 1955, Fritz Hansen made Panton's first mass-produced furniture—the Tivoli and Bachelor chairs. 1957, he designed customer-assembled, limited-edition weekend home (Cardboard House) and 1960 Plastic House, both garnering appreciable attention, as did the 1958 Komigen restaurant (for his inn-keeper parents) and the installation for which he also created the Cone Chair, by Plus-Linje); 1960, designed an inflatable chair and other pieces for the Astoria Hotel in Norway; 1962, briefly resided in Cannes and, 1963, settled in Basel (with wife-to-be Marianne Person-Oertenheim), where he began a relationship with the Herman Miller/Vitra furniture company; 1969, completed his Living Towers in Paris and the interiors of the headquarters of magazine *Der Spiegel* in Hamburg (the latter including his Flower Pot hanging lamps, but with Bertoia's wire side chairs); contributed futuristic installations (Fantasy Landscape Room) at 1968 and 1970 *Visiona 1* and *2* (sponsored by Bayer at the Möbelmesse in Cologne). At 1972 *Visiona 3*, Panton contributed another 'landscape,' this time with adjunct installations by Joe Colombo and Olivier

Mourgue. To 1973, Panton designed the interiors of Grüner + Jahr publishers in Hamburg and a number of other dynamic public spaces, distinctive for his explosive use of color and pattern. Through Panton's relationship with Vitra, he was able to realize a one-piece, cantilever plastic chair. However, this design Stacking chair (or Panton chair as it became known) was first produced in c. 1960 by Dansk Acryl Teknik as prototypes in a polyurethane foam. With appreciable technical assistance from the Vitra staff from 1965, the mass production of Panton chair began in 1968 and, thus, became purportedly the world's first functional one-piece plastic chair. (His 1965 S chair by Thonet was similar in shape to the plastic Panton and was the first single-piece cantilevered chair in plywood.) His prolific œuvre also included: seating by Plus-Linje (Peacock, Heart Cone, and Wire Cone chairs, all 1960); 1964 Flying chair and 1969 Living Tower by Herman Miller/Vitra; floor coverings and furnishing textiles (including by Mira-X in Suhr, Switzerland, from 1969); lighting by Louis Poulsen (including 1960 Moon and 1968 Flower Pot hanging lamps and 1970 Panthella floor/table lamps); 1973 1-2-3 furniture system by Fritz Hansen. He was isolated by living in Switzerland and somewhat unknown until interest in his work was spurred by examples of his furniture and lighting that began to appear in the press in the mid-1990s, particularly in the UK. Additional interest was spurred by IKEA's 1994 production of the Vilbert chair; Habitat followed in late 1990s into 2001 or so with a number of earlier-design reproductions The Panton chair, still in production by Vitra, continues to be popular. He died in Copenhagen.
Exhibitions/citations Flying chairs and Shell lamps created much attention at 1964 Internationale Möbelmesse, Cologne. Other work included in a number of international exhibitions. He designed his own exhibition (before he died), 1998 *Verner Panton: liset og farven* (light and color), Trapholdtmuseum, Kolding, Denmark (catalog below). Also subject of 2000 touring exhibition, organized by Vitra Design Museum, Weil am Rhine (catalog below). 1963 and 1968 International Design Awards, American Institute of Decorators (AID), US; 1967 Rosenthal Studio Prize, Germany; 1967 Poul Henningsen prize; an award, 1968 (2nd) Eurodomus, Turin, Italy; a medal, 1968 Österreichisches Bauzentrum (Austrian furniture venue); 1969 diploma of honor, 1972 Bundespreis Produktdesign, Rat für Formgebung (German design council), Frankfurt; 1973 Knight of Mark Twain Award, Kirkwood, Mo., US.
Bibliography 'Experimentator in Design,' *form*, May 1969: 2–7. Cat., *Qu'est-ce que le design?*, Paris: CCI, 1969. Cat., *Modern Chairs 1918–1970*, London: Lund Humphries, 1971. Frederik Sieck, *Nutidig Dansk Møbeldesign – en kortfattet illustreret beskrivelse*, Copenhagen: Bondo Gravesen, 1990. *Verner Panton*, Copenhagen: Bording Grafik, 1987. Charlotte and Peter Fiell, *1000 Chairs*, Cologne: Taschen, 1997. Cat., Verner Panton, *Verner Panton: Liset og Farven*, Kolding: Trapholdtmuseum, 1998. Cat., Alexander von Vegesack and Mathias Remmie, *Verner Panton: Das Gesamtwerk*, Weil Am Rhein: Vitra Design Museum, 2000 (2002 English ed.) (book and CD-ROM). Jens Bernsen, *Verner Panton: Space, Time, Matter*, Copenhagen: Danish Design Centre, 2003.Paola Antonelli (ed.), *Objects of Design: The Museum of Modern Art*, New York: The Museum of Modern Art, 2003: 158.

Paolozzi, Eduardo Luigi (1924–)

British sculptor, printmaker, and designer; born Leith (Scotland).

Training 1943, Edinburgh College of Art; 1944, Slade School of Fine Art, London.
Biography 1947–50, Paolozzi worked in Paris; 1950, returned to London and, 1950s, introduced the imagery of American mass consumerism into British art; was a member, Independent Group, Institute of Contemporary Arts, London. At its early-1950s meetings, the group considered themes including automobile styling, popular culture, advertising, and science fiction. Paolozzi has been a leading artist and has taught: 1949–55, textile department, London Central School of Arts and Crafts; 1955–58, sculpture, St. Martin's School of Art, London; 1960–62, visiting professor, School of Fine Arts, Hamburg; from 1968, ceramics, Royal College of Art, London; from 1978, ceramics, Fachhochschule, Cologne; from 1981, sculpture, Akademie der bildenden Künste, Munich. He designed ceramics by Rosenthal; 1970 Variations on a Geometric Theme ceramic tableware by Wedgwood (issued in a limited edition of 200 sets); 1984 mosaic decoration of Tottenham Court Road station of London Underground.
Exhibitions/citations Work shown at 1956 *This Is Tomorrow*, Whitechapel Gallery, London; in various other venues, including one-person European exhibitions. Large number of citations include honorary-doctorate degrees from numerous institutions; 1968, Commander of the British Empire (CBE); 1981, honorary member, Architectural Association, London.
Bibliography Winfried Konnertz, *Eduardo Paolozzi*, Cologne: DuMont, 1984. Cat., Richard Cork (ed.), *Eduardo Paolozzi Underground*, London: Royal Academy/Weidenfeld & Nicolson, 1986. Fiona Pearson, *Paolozzi*, Edinburgh: National Galleries of Scotland, 1999. Robin Spencer (ed.), *Eduardo Paolozzi: Writings and Interviews*, Oxford/New York: Oxford University, 2000.

Pap, Gyula (1899–1983)

Hungarian painter, draughtsperson, lithographer, and metalworker; born Orosháza; active Dessau, Germany.

Training To 1925 under Johannes Itten, Bauhaus, Weimar.
Biography Pap is one the best known of the Bauhaus metalsmiths; while there, designed a tea-diffuser device and 1922 brass menorah (at the Jewish Museum, New York). Pap's 1923 very simple floor lamp a with chromed steel pole, horizontal glass disk, and exposed bulb has been reproduced from c. 1989 by Tecnolumen, Germany. 1934, Pap returned to Hungary and, from 1945, was a curator, János Szántó Kovács Museum, Orosháza. As an artist, Pap was influenced by Viennese and German Expressionism; had Cubist and Surrealist periods, followed by Monumentalism; late 1970s, pursued abstract, non-figurative art. Many figurative artworks include images of Pap's native town of Orosáza and the Great Hungarian Plane. He died in Budapest.
Exhibitions 1923 floor lamp included in *Haus am Horn* of 1923 exhibition, Bauhaus, Weimar. Work subject of *Gyula Pap 2000—Bonn, Berlin, Budapest*, Stadt Museum, Bonn.
Bibliography *Neue Arbeiten der Bauhauswerkstätten* (Bauhausbücher 7), Munich: Albert Langen, 1925. Haulisch Lenke, *Pap Gyula*, Budapest: Corvina, 1974. Annelies Krekel-Aalberse, *Art Nouveau and Art Déco Silver*, New York: Abrams, 1989: 149, 258.

Papanek, Victor J. (1925–1999)

Austrian writer, teacher, and product designer; born Vienna; active in the US.

Training 1942–50, The Cooper Union for the Advancement of Science and Art, New York; 1949 under Frank Lloyd Wright, Taliesin and Taliesin West; 1954–55, Massachusets Institute of Technology (MIT), Cambridge, Mass.; 1956, Institute of General Semantics, Chicago.
Biography 1939, Papanek emigrated to the US; 1950–57, pursued an interest in anthropology, living and working for a time with the Navajos, Inuits, and Balinese; from 1964, was an independent product-development designer and became a design consultant to Volvo, Dartington Industries, Planet Products, World Health Organization, Midwest Applied Science, and others; 1954–59, taught, Ontario College of Art, University of Toronto; 1959, was a visiting professor, Rhode Island School of Design, Providence; 1959–62, associate professor, State University of New York, Buffalo; dean, School of Design, California Institute of the Arts, Valencia, Cal.; 1976–81, head of design departments at several institutions including Kansas City Art Institute, Missouri; from 1981, consultant professor of architecture and design, University of Kansas, Lawrence, Kansas; founding member of industrial design organizations, including Industrial Designers Society of America (IDSA). Though an active product designer, he is now better-known for his theorizing and numerous books, including the highly influential *Design for the Real World: Human Ecology and Social Change* (intro. by R. Buckminster Fuller, New York: Pantheon, 1972). Papanek championed a consciousness concerning design-centered human, ecological, and ethical issues and pragmatically espoused, 'The only important thing about design is how it relates to people.'
Exhibitions/citations Work included in various exhibitions; and subject of 1974 venue, Gallery Grada, Zagreb. Numerous citations, including 1988 Distinguished Designer, National Endowment for the Arts, US; 1989 IKEA Foundation International Award.
Bibliography Ann Lee Morgan (ed.), *Contemporary Designers*, London: Macmillan, 1984.

Pareschi, Gianni (1940–)
> See Gruppo G14.

Parigi, Heron; Paolo Parigi (1936–)

Italian furniture manufacturer; located Borgo San Lorenzo (FI). Paolo Parigi: industrial designer; born Borgo San Lorenzo.

History 1880, the firm was founded by Giovanni Parigi to make hand-crafted furniture, using a minimum number of parts and pieces; pro-

Vittorio Parigi and Nani Prina. Orix desk. 1970. Injection-molded plastic, chromium-plated steel, and plate glass, 32 11/16 x 40 3/4 x 25" (83 x 103.5 x 63.5 cm). Mfr.: Molteni, Italy. Courtesy Quittenbaum Kunstauktionen, Munich.

duced a number of historicist forms early on; became known for its 1965 Heron drawing table by Paolo Parigi, when the name of the firm thus became Heron Parigi. Other drawing tables followed: 1970 Delta and 1975 A90. Other products have included 1975 Polo office chair and 1985 Flap folding chair. Designed by Paolo Parigi: 1989 Canasta chair series with wide-tape backs, no. 999 aluminum armchair, Centina system of desks and shelving. Paolo Parigi (who began his design career in 1958 as a graphic design and in 1962 as an industrial designer) is a partner of this family firm; has also been active in his own studio Parigi Design. His recent work includes Lunar Trix all-aluminum combination table. He is a member, Associazione per il Disegno Industriale (ADI).
Citations To Paolo Parigi: 1973, 1975, 1982 Premio SMAU Industrial Design, Salone della Machina e Attrezzature per l'Ufficio (to P. Parigi), Milan; 1979, 1981, 1987, and 1999 Premio Compasso d'Oro; 1986 and 1987 Industrie Forum Design (iF), Hanover; 1987 Goed Industrieel, Antwerp; 1998 Innovations Award, NeoCon, Chicago; 1999 G-Mark Good Design Award, Japanese Industrial Design Promotion Organization (JIDPO); and a large rostrum of others.
Bibliography *ADI Annual 1976*, Milan: Associazione per il Disegno Industriale, 1976. Giancarlo Iliprandi and Pierluigi Molinari (eds.), 'Italian Industrial Designers' in *Omnibook No. 2*, Udine: Magnus, 1985: 164. Hans Wichmann, *Italien Design 1945 bis heute*, Munich: Die Neue Sammlung, 1988.

Parigi, Vittorio (1937–)

Italian industrial designer; born Borgo San Lorenzo, Florence; active Milan.

Training To 1964, in architecture.
Biography 1960, Parigi began his professional career; designed a range of plastic bedroom furniture by Molteni, including 1970 Orix desk (with Nani Prina) in ABS and tubular steel, and a storage system by Citterio; has worked for clients in Italy such as Sormani, Sordelli, Lem Blu-Red, and Zevi, and sailboats and mobile homes (caravans) by others. Parigi has collaborated with architects Mezzedini in Ethiopia and Bazzoni in Milan; is a member, ADI (Associazione per il Disegno Industriale).
Bibliography *ADI Annual 1976*, Milan: Associazione per il Disegno Industriale, 1976.

Parish, 'Sister' (aka Mrs. Henry Parish 2nd; b. Dorothy B. Gilbert 1910–1994)

American interior decorator; active New York.

Biography Parish was called 'Sister' by her older brother Frankie, a name that lasted; grew up on 712 Fifth Avenue, New York, the building now housing Henri Bendel store; 1930, married banker Henry Parish 2nd. While on their honeymoon in Paris, she decided to become a decorator. The Parishes' house on Gracie Square, Manhattan, New York was decorated by Eleanor Brown of McMillen. When the Parishes took a small house in New Jersey, 'Sister' Parish designed the interiors herself and, at the beginning of her professional design career, was asked to design the time-worn interiors of the Essex Hunt Club, Peapack, N.J., and, 1933, established 'Mrs. Henry Parish II Inc.' Other early work included the homes of friends in Far Hills, N.J. She opened a shop on Madison Avenue in Manhattan. Her decorating style was layered with themes from the past. Parish came to prominence in the early 1960s through her work with others on the redecoration of The White House in Washington, D.C. (directed by Mrs. John Kennedy). 1963, Parish formed Parish-Hadley Associates with Albert Hadley, who brought a more contemporary approach to the firm's activities. She perfected the 'English manor-house look.' Though also known for her décors of great richness, in her own house in Dark Harbor, Maine, patchwork quilts and rag rugs were combined with painted floors and stiff organdy curtains, creating a synthetic nostalgia. Parish-Hadley designed a 1994 range of furniture by Baker. Albert Hadley went on to work independently after Mrs. Parish's death.
Bibliography Mark Hampton, *House & Garden*, May 1990: 145–49, 214. Mark Hampton, The *Legendary Decorators of the Twentieth Century*, New York: Doubleday, 1992. Sister Parish, Albert Hadley, and Christopher Petkanas, *Parish Hadley: Sixty Years of American Design*, Boston: Little, Brown, 1995. Apple Parish Barlett and Susan Bartlett Crater (oral history of her daughter and granddaughter), *Sister: The Life of Legendary American Interior Decorator Mrs. Henry Parish II*, New York: St. Martin's, 2000.
> See Hadley, Albert.

Parisi, Ico (1916–1996)

Italian artist, architect, and designer; born Palermo; active Como.

Training 1931–35, in building construction in Como; 1949–52, under Alberto Sartoris, architecture, Institute Atheneum, Lausanne.
Biography 1935–36, Parisi worked in the office of architect Giuseppe Terragni in Como, for whom he photographed (1937) the renowned Casa del Fascio there. Also in Como: 1937–38, Parisi was an independent film maker; 1939, a freelance stage designer and, subsequently, was a freelance designer and visual artist. He collaborated with his wife Luisa Parisi and, 1948–95, they were active in their studio La Ruota for art and design activities; 1950s, designed some furniture, ceramics, and glass in a modern style; had clients in Italy, including Spartaco Brugnoli, Fratelli Rizzi, Terraneo, and Zanolli e Sebellin; 1956, became a member Associazione per il Disegno Industriale (ADI), and, 1952, of Art Club di Milano; 1935–40 with others, was active as founding member of Gruppo Como of architects and, 1936 with others, of the Alto Quota group of architects, Como. He was a prolific designer of furniture, particularly in late 1960s to 1980s. His personal archive is in the Pinacoteca Civica, Como, the town where he died.
Exhibitions/citations Work included in numerous exhibitions. From 1945 (1st), participated in the *Mostra dell'Arredamento*, Como; showed pioneering furniture at 1948 Salon des Artistes Décorateurs, Paris; 1948 *Mostra del Giornalismo*, Milano; 1949 historical *Mostra dell'arredamento of Fede Cheti*, Milan; 1950 fair in Bergamo; 1951 (9th) and 1954 (10th) Triennali di Milano; 1974 *IN-Arch*, Rome; 1976 Biennale di Venezia. Work subject of 1979 and 1981 exhibitions, Rome and Ferrara (catalogs below). 1937 film prize, City of Como; diploma of honor, 1954 (10th) Triennale di Milano; 1955 (for two chairs by Cassina) Premio Compasso d'Oro; gold and silver medals, 1957 Colori e Forme fair, Como; 1959 Lurago d'Erba Gold Medal; 1971 Knight of Mark Twain Award, Kirkwood, Mo., US; 1974 Premio Marco Aurelio, Rome.
Bibliography 'Recente lavori di Ico e Luisa Parisi,' *Casa Vogue*, Jan.–Feb. 1973. *ADI Annual 1976*, Milan: Associazione per il Disegno Industriale, 1976. Ico Parisi, *Operazione arcevia: comunità esistenziale*, Como: Cesare Nani, 1976. Cat., Massimo Piani et al., 'Ico Parisi, monografia,' in *Terra & terra tre*, Cerro: Cerro Lavavanese, 1986. *Ico Parisi & architetture*, Modena: Galleria Civica,1990. Cat., Luigi Cavadini and Flaminio Gualdoni, *Ico Parisi, architetture, design, utopie*, Lugano: Fidia, 1991.

Parker Jr., Glidden McLellan
> See Glidden Pottery.

Parker Jr., Kenneth R. (1957–)
> See Hohulin, Samuel E.

Parkin, Laurice (1971–)
> See Five Twenty One Design.

Parsey, Tim (1960–)

British industrial designer; born near London.

Training To 1981, Central School of Art and Design, London.
Biography Parsey worked in the ID Two design studio in San Francisco; 1991 with Daniele De Iuliis, transferred to Apple Design (one of ID Two's clients) in Cupertino, Cal. and designed Apple products, including 1991 StyleWriter (SpeedRacer), 1992 Lego, and 1991–93 Newton, MessagePad 100 (Junior), 1992 Color StyleWriter Pro (Fantasia). Parsey proposed the separation of Apple products into separate business and consumer categories, resulting in products such as TVs and telephones. He left Apple and became vice-president of product design and development at the US branch of ACCO office in Chicago; from c. 2000, was vice-president of consumer design at Personal Communications Sector of Motorola and developed the 2001 V.60 mobile phone. (1984, Motorola had pioneered the world's first mobile phone.) From Sept. 2003, Parsey has been vice-president of product design at Mattel toys.
Bibliography Paul Kunkel, *Apple Design: The World of the Apple Industrial Design Group*, New York: Graphis, 1997. Paola Antonelli (ed.), *Objects of Design: The Museum of Modern Art*, New York: The Museum of Modern Art, 2003: 243.

Parsons, Frank Alvah (1866–1930)

American teacher; born Chesterfield, Mass.; active New York.

Training Wesleyan Academy, Mass.; subsequently in art, England, France, Italy, and Austria; 1905, bachelor's degree in art education, Columbia University, New York.
Biography From 1901, Parsons taught fine art, Horace Mann School of Teachers College, Columbia University. 1904, William Merritt Chase began to offer interior-decoration courses at the New York School of Fine Art, which Chase founded in 1896. From 1904 at the school, Parsons taught design theory, costume design, and interior decoration and was the sole school director from 1908 to his death; established programs in photography in 1915 and architecture in 1919. Students were taught drafting, color, elevation drawing, period design, and constructive and decorative architecture. 1912–20, Parsons wrote a number of books on fashion, advertising, and interior design, such as *Interior Decoration: Its Principles and Practice* (Garden City, N.Y.: Doubleday, Page & Co., 1915). He established courses focusing on materials (rugs, fabrics, and wallpapers) and cost accounting. 1911, Parsons himself established an annual lecture series at The Metropolitan Museum of Art, which was active to his death. 1915–16, he and former student William Odom conducted study tours abroad to study historical styles 'in their natural environment.' Odom persuaded Parsons to open a branch in Paris in 1921, thus becoming the first American art-and-design school to found a campus abroad. Odom, who became head of the school, renamed it Parsons School of Design in 1941, and it became a division of New School for Social Research (now New School University) in 1970. A master's-degree program in the decorative arts was established in cooperation with Cooper-Hewitt Museum. Today, the school offers a wide range of certified and advanced degree programs and courses, including in fashion, interior, furniture, and industrial design, film studies, fine art, others.
Bibliography Marjorie F. Jones, *A History of the Parsons School of Design, 1896–1966*, doctoral thesis, New York: New York University, 1968, 1969. John Esten and Rose Bennett Gilbert, *Manhattan Style*, Boston: Little, Brown, 1990: 5–6.
> See Odom, William; Truex, Van Day.

Parthenay, Jean (1919–)

French industrial designer; active Paris.

Training École Nationale Supérieure des Arts Décoratifs, Paris.
Biography 1948–78, Parthenay worked at Agence Technès with Roger Talon, Daniel Maurandy, and Roger Riche, and supervised the studio's industrial-design work for Poclain, SEB, Calor, Thomson, and other clients; from 1971, taught, École des Arts Appliqués, Paris; 1980 with others, founded studio Objectif Design, where the Alpha X (one of the first alphanumeric telephones) was designed.
Exhibitions/citations Work included in 1988 exhibition, Paris (catalog below). 1965, 1966, 1968, and 1976 industrial design awards for hydraulic shovels by Poclain.
Bibliography Cat., *Design français 1960–1990: trois décennies,* Paris: Centre Georges Pompidou/APCI, 1988. François Mathey, *Au bonheur des formes, design français 1945–1992*, Paris: Regard, 1992: 322–25. Arlette Barré-Despond (ed.), *Dictionnaire international des arts appliqués et du design*, Paris: Regard, 1996

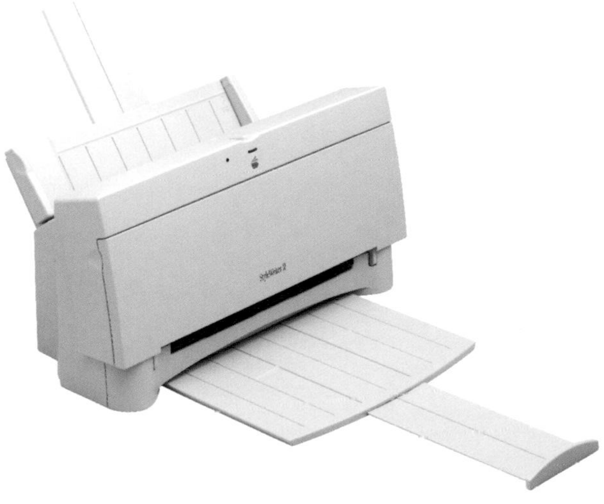

Tim Parsey. Stylewriter II printer. 1992. ABS polymer and other materials, 7 1/4 x 13 5/8 x 8" (18.4 x 34.6 x 20.3 cm). Mfr: Apple Computer, US. Gift of the mfr. MoMA.

Parzinger, Tommi (1903–1972)

German silversmith and industrial designer; son of a sculptor; born Munich.

Training Kunstgewerbeschule, Munich; and in Vienna and Berlin.
Biography Parzinger received favorable attention for his porcelain produced by KPM and wallpaper, fabric, interiors, books, and posters by or for others. He won a 1932 poster-competition prize, the recompense of which was a trip to the US on the steamship *Bremen*. In order to collect the prize, he was told that he must join the Nazi Party. Instead, he received a visa from the US Embassy and emigrated in 1935, to New York. One of his first commissions was designing silver, brass, and crystal pieces and furniture for Rena Rosenthal's shop on Madison Avenue. 1939, he established Parzinger Inc. on East 57th Street (renamed Parzinger Originals in 1946) for special-order and limited-edition furniture and accessories. 1939–42, his work was published internationally in periodicals *LIFE, Arts and Decoration*, *The Connoisseur*, and *The Studio*; after World War II, continued to be active primarily in furniture and accessories production. His clients included Charak Modern, Willow & Reed, Hofstatter, and Salterini. Other clients: Lightolier (lighting), F. Schumacher (fabrics), and Dorlyn (brasswork). 1949, Donald Cameron became an associate in his business.
Exhibitions Silverwork included in 1937 exhibition, Brooklyn Museum of Art; 1937 exhibition and 1940 *Contemporary American Industrial Art*, The Metropolitan Museum of Art, both New York; decorative-arts section, 1939–40 *Golden Gate International Exposition*, San Francisco.
Bibliography Cat., Janet Kardon (ed.), *Craft in the Machine Age 1920–1945*, New York: Abrams/American Craft Museum, 1995. Jeff Book, 'Heir of Refinement,' *Departures*, July–Aug. 1999.

Pasanella, Marco (1962–)

American furniture designer; born and active New York.

Training To 1984, Yale University, New Haven, Conn.
Biography 1985–86, Pasanella was an associate, Pasanella + Klein Architects, and, subsequently, Pasanella, Klein, Stolzman, Berg Architects; 1990, established The Pasanella Company (renamed The Polenta Group in 1999) for the design and manufacture of furniture

Sandro Pasqui and Gianni Passini. Cobra telephone. 1983. ABS polymer, 2 3/8 x 9 x 2 5/8" (6 x 22.9 x 6.7 cm). Mfr.: Italtel Telematica, Italy. Gift of the mfr. MoMA.

and furnishings; from 1987, has been a freelance writer and photographer for magazines *Elle*, *Harper's Bazaar*, *International Design*, and *Casa Vogue* (Spain); 1987–90, was a contributing editor of magazine *Taxi*; wrote the book *Living in Style Without Losing Your Mind* (New York: Simon & Schuster, 2000) and writes the monthly column 'Room for Improvement' for *The New York Times*; teaches in Interior Design Department, Parsons School of Design, New York. One of his best known works is the 1991 sideways rocking chair. Other work has ranged from housewares and furniture as well as the interior of Sunset Beach Hotel & Restaurant, Shelter Island, N.Y.; graphics; CD-ROM and video projects; and set designs for Clinique.
Citations 1987 and 1988 Design Excellence award, *I.D.* magazine, and 1991 competition '2001: How Will We Live?,' sponsored by Sony, *Metropolis* magazine, and Parsons School of Design; Design 100, *Metropolitan Home* magazine.

Pasca di Magliano, Emmanuele (1941–)

Italian industrial designer; born Homs, Tripolitania (Libya); active Naples.

Biography 1963–65, Pasca di Magliano was active in research, analysis, and project design on the reconstruction of the northern section of Naples through partnership Studio Lauro, Palomba, Pasca in Naples; 1975 with Palomba and Lauro, designed the publication *I legni* for Centro Ricerche Artigianato e Design of the cities of Campagna and Ellisse; became a member, Associazione per il Disegno Industriale (ADI).
Citations Partnership received an honorable mention (for the project on the theme 'La Nuova Città' concerning the restoration of the northern section of Naples), Internazionale A. Olivetti competition.
Bibliography *ADI Annual 1976*, Milan: Associazione per il Disegno Industriale, 1976.

Pascal, Marc (1959–)

Australian designer.

Training Bachelor's degree in industrial design, Melbourne Institute of Technology; bachelor of fine arts degree in painting and printmaking, Victorian College of the Arts, Southbank, Victoria.
Biography As a producer and designer in his own practice in Melbourne, Pascal established M2 Products, and made the Worvo jnr. lamp range. For the series, he employs translucent (or transparent) polypropylene and polyester that he die cuts and dyes, then clips to cast-polyester elliptical rings and weaves by hand—a process used by dressmakers. Other products have included 2001 Frond and Uleabè lamps, and Vaase vase in porcelain and stoneware with six openings. 1993–2001, he was an adjunct lecturer, departments of industrial design and applied design, Melbourne Institute of Technology.
Exhibitions/citations Regular exhibitions. Several grants and awards.

Pascaud, Jean (1903–1996)

French decorator and furniture designer; born Rouen.

Training To 1924, engineering, École Centrale des Arts et Manufactures, Paris.
Biography After 1925 *Exposition Internationale des Arts Décoratifs et Industriels Modernes*, Paris, Pascaud turned to the applied arts—in particular, furniture. c.1935, his furniture began to incorporate silvered glass. Commissions came from French ministries and embassies, Le Mobilier National, the Château de Rambouillet, various private and other public organizations, and oceanliners, such as 1935 *Normandie*, 1939 *Pasteur*, and 1953 *Laos*. Some of his eclectic furniture was rather dramatic; for example, a large 1948 black cabinet was supported by imposing individual kneeling white caryatids; while other models were far more simple.
Exhibitions/citations From early 1930s, work shown in Salons and expositions in France and abroad; 1997 *Trente/Quarante*, Barry Friedman Ltd., New York; 2000 French furniture exhibition, Salon du Meuble, Paris (catalog below). Grand prize, 1937 *Exposition Internationale des Arts et Techniques dans la Vie Moderne*, Paris.
Bibliography *Ensembles mobiliers*, vol. 2, Paris: Charles Moreau, 1937. *Ensembles mobiliers*, vol. 5, no.13, Paris: Charles Moreau, 1945. Pierre Kjellberg, *Art déco: les maîtres du mobilier, le décor des paquebots*, Paris: Amateur, 1986, 1990. Cat., Sophie Tasma Anargyros et al., *L'école française: les créateurs de meubles du 20ème siècle*, Paris: Industries Françaises de l'Ameublement, 2000.

Pasini, Gianni (1941–)

Italian designer; born Venice; active Milan.

Biography 1965, Pasini began his professional career serving clients, including Olivetti, Fabbrica Italiana, Magneti Marelli, and Crinospital; became a member, Associazione per il Disegno Industriale (ADI). In the Olivetti information bureau, he designed a text-editing system, minicomputer, copier, and other electronic machinery; from 1974 with Sandro Pasqui, was active in their design studio Pasqui e Pasini.
Citations 1982 and 1984 (with Pasqui) Premio SMAU Industrial Design, Salone della Machina e Attrezzature per l'Ufficio, Milan.
Bibliography *ADI Annual 1976*, Milan: Associazione per il Disegno Industriale, 1976. Giancarlo Iliprandi and Pierluigi Molinari (eds.), 'Italian Industrial Designers,' in *Omnibook No. 2*, Udine: Magnus, 1985: 166. Hans Wichmann, *Italien Design 1945 bis heute*, Munich: Die Neue Sammlung, 1988.

Pasqui, Sandro (1937–)

Italian industrial designer; born Castello; active Milan.

Biography 1963, Pasqui began his professional career, working for Olivetti until 1967; from 1968, was active in his own studio for clients including Magneti Marelli, Crinospital, and Olivetti; participated in congresses sponsored by Associazione per il Disegno Industriale (ADI), of which he was a member; 1974 with Gianni Pasini, set up design studio Pasqui e Pasini. By Olivetti, designs have included Auditronic 770 and Logos 270 office machines (with Mario Bellini and Derk Jan de Vries) and 1978 Lettera 10 portable typewriter (with others).
Exhibitions/citations Participated in the *Milano 70-70* exhibition. 1970 (Logos 270 with Bellini) and other Premio Compasso d'Oro citations to Pasqui e Pasini: 1987 (Cobra telephone and Omega 1000 telephone terminal by Italtel Telematica), 1991 (industrial sewing machine by Rimoldi); 1994 (Linea UT telephone equipment by Italtel Telematica).
Bibliography *ADI Annual 1976*, Milan: Associazione per il Disegno Industriale, 1976. Giancarlo Iliprandi and Pierluigi Molinari (eds.), 'Italian Industrial Designers,' in *Omnibook No. 2*, Udine: Magnus, 1985: 166. Hans Wichmann, *Italien Design 1945 bis heute*, Munich: Die Neue Sammlung, 1988.

Pastoe
> See UMS (Utrechtsche Machinale Stoelen Meubelfabriek).

Pastore, Gino (1950–)

Italian designer.

Biography Pastore established the design school Istituto Superiore per le Industrie Artistiche (ISIA), Rome; from 1972, has been active in interior and industrial design and has collaborated with Ykiko Tanaka.
Citations A citation, *1984 Una Sedia Italiana per gli USA*, Salone Internazionale della Sedia (Promodedia), Udine.
Bibliography Giancarlo Iliprandi and Pierluigi Molinari (eds.), 'Italian Industrial Designers' in *Omnibook No. 2*, Udine: Magnus, 1985: 168. Hans Wichmann, *Italien Design 1945 bis heute*, Munich: Die Neue Sammlung, 1988.

Patout, Pierre (1879–1965)
French architect and designer.

Training To 1903, École Nationale Supérieure des Beaux-Arts, Paris.
Biography Patout was one of the creators of the *style paquebot*, the luxurious style of oceanliner interiors of 1920s–30s. Thus, his work included interiors and furnishings for areas of oceanliners 1926 *Île-de-France* (including the first-class dining room with ceiling dalles of light by René Lalique), 1931 *L'Atlantique* (with Jacques-Émile Ruhlmann), and 1935 *Normandie*. c. 1928, he designed the Robert Bély department store, boulevard Haussmann, Paris. His dramatic taste was illustrated by his own 1929 residence at 3–5, boulevard Victor, Paris, where Auguste Perret's influence was obvious. As architect of 1932 annex of Les Galeries Lafayette department store, Paris, he installed the same opulence as in his oceanliner interiors, including the simple, if heavy, façade on the rue de la Chaussée-d'Antin side of the store, punctuated by grand columns sheathed in back-lit glass. He designed several townhouses, 1934 'Paquebot' building at 2, boulevard Victor, 1930 building on square Henri-Paté, 1928 apartments at 5, rue du Docteur-Blanche, Maison Lombard, and 1929 Hôtel Mercédès; all Paris.
Exhibitions Work shown at Salons of Société des Artistes Décorateurs from 1926; 1925 *Exposition Internationale des Arts Décoratifs et Industriels Modernes* (architect of grand gateway Porte de la Concorde, with René Binet; pavilion of Manufacture Nationale de Sèvres; and Hôtel du Collectionneur). Designed pavilion of Société des Artistes Décorateurs at 1937 *Exposition Internationale des Arts et Techniques dans la Vie Moderne*, Paris; French pavilion (with Robert Expert) at 1939–40 *New York World's Fair: The World of Tomorrow*.
Bibliography *Restaurants, dancing, cafés, bars*, Paris: Charles Moreau, nos. 8–9, 1929. Pierre Cabanne, *Encyclopédie art déco*, Paris: Somogy, 1986: 224. Nancy J. Troy, *Modernism and the Decorative Arts in France: Art Nouveau to Le Corbusier*, New Haven: Yale, 1991.

Patrix, Georges (1920–1992)
French industrial designer; active Paris.

Training Universities in Caen and Cologne, and École Nationale Supérieure des Beaux-Arts, Paris.
Biography 1947, Patrix began his career as a consulting engineer; 1950, set up his own office, specializing in industrial design and architecture; from 1960s, designed more than 2,200 factories throughout Europe and products (for Air France, including 1966 metal tray for in-flight meals, still in use), packaging (for Nescafé and Pernod), and machine tools; with Michel Ragon, Iona Friedman, Nicolas Schoffer, and Walter Jonas, cofounded, Groupe International d'Architecture Prospectif; wrote the book *L'Esthétique Industrielle* (1961).
Exhibitions Work included in 1988 exhibition, Paris (catalog below).
Bibliography Cat., *Design français 1960–1990: trois décennies,* Paris: Centre Georges Pompidou/APCI, 1988. François Mathey, *Au bonheur des formes, design français 1945–1992*, Paris: Regard, 1992: 83, 117.

Patti, Thomas (1943–)
American glass designer; born Pittsfield, Mass.

Training 1962, Boston (Mass.) Museum School; 1967, bachelor's degree and, 1969, master's degree, both in industrial design, Pratt Institute, Brooklyn, N.Y.; 1969, New School for Social Research, New York.
Biography Patti is a highly regarded glass artist who manipulates form into unique configurations; late 1960s and early 1970s, combined two distinctly different glass media—flat and blown. For example, he fused a blown-bubble form onto a flat glass sheet. Possibly his work can be linked to two disciplines of painting—minimalism and color-field painting.
Exhibitions Work subject of exhibitions at The George Walter Vincent Smith Art Museum, Springfield, Mass., in 1980, and Galerie Internationale du Verre, Biot, France, in 1993. Numerous group venues.
Bibliography Catalogs for above exhibitions. Cat., Lloyd E. Herman, *American Glass: Masters of the Art*, Washington, D.C.: Smithsonian Institution Traveling Exhibition Service, Seattle: University of Washington, 1998.

Pau i Corominas, Lluís (1950–)
Spanish designer; born Castellfollit de la Roca, Catalunya.

Training Interior, graphic, and industrial design, Eina (Escola de Desseny i Art), Barcelona.
Biography 1973, Pau established Interiors Disseny Pau (IDP) for interior design, with architects and urban planners Martorell-Bohigas-Mackay. He has designed a large number of exhibitions, public interiors, and sets, as well as furniture, products, signage systems, and a public telephone booth for Retevisión.
Exhibitions/citations Work included in or subject of 1971 *TINT-1* exhibition, Banyoles; 1976 Biennale di Venezia; 1985 *Carteles Españoles de Utilidad Pública*, Centre d'Art Santa Mònica, Barcelona; 1990 (1st) and 1992 (2nd) Mostra Internacional de Disseny, Barcelona; *MBM: Josep Martorell, Oriol Bohigas, David Mackay, Albert Puigdomènech, Lluís Pau* traveling exhibition, Madrid 1993, Barcelona 1993, Rotterdam 1994, San Marino 1997, Genova 1998. Received Delta d'Oro, ADI/FAD (Associacion Diseño Industrial/Fomento Artes Decorativas), Spain; 1981 Monuments signage-system prize; 1990 Premi FAD d'Interiorisme (for best interiors); 1994 Bronze Laus Prize; 1994 Gold Laus Prize and Premi FAD d'Espais Efímers (for ephemeral interiors); 1996 Excellence Laus prize; 1999 Premi Interiorisme Prize of 1st Bienal d'Arquitectura de les Comarques Centrals (BACC)'; 1999 Santiago Marco Medal; 2002 Amic d'Eina (Escola de Desseny i Art), Barcelona.

Pauchard, Xavier (1880–1948)
French industrialist and technician; born Saint-Léger-sous-Beuvray.

Biography 1909, Pauchard set up and managed a boiler-making workshop; 1933, added a sheetmetal division called Tolix, which was employing c. 100 workers by 1948. Even though he may have been known as a simple plumber, he was nevertheless one of the pioneers of galvanization in France; designed a since-ubiquitous range of furniture in galvanized and pressed sheet metal, including chairs and tables. His 1934 Model A outdoor side chair—that has become better known than its designer and has been considered an anonymous design by many—was modified by his son Jean Pauchard in 1956 as the A56 chair. Xavier Pauchard also designed spades for children, some public furniture, and housewares. The firm continues to be active in Autun (where Pauchard died), producing the Model A56 chair and coordinating tables, a stool, and armchair version, some painted.
Bibliography Cat., Sophie Tasma Anargyros et al., *L'école française: les créateurs de meubles du 20ème siècle*, Paris: Industries Françaises de l'Ameublement, 2000. www.tolix.fr.

Paul, Bruno (1874–1968)
German architect, cabinetmaker, designer, and teacher: born Seifhennersdorf.

Training From 1886, Kunstgewerbeschule, Dresden; from 1894 under Paul Höcker and Wilhelm von Diez, painting, Akademie für Kunst, Munich.
Biography 1892, Paul settled in Munich. He followed the lead of Koloman Moser and Josef Hoffmann's Wiener Werkstätte and, with Peter

Thomas Patti. Vase. 1976. Blown laminated plate glass, h. 5 3/4 x w. 5 3/4" (14.6 x 14.6 cm). Mfr.: the designer, US. Gift of Douglas Heller and Joshua Rosenblatt. MoMA.

Bruno Paul. Bookcase desk. 1905. Oak, brass, and leather writing surface, 30 1/2 x 69 x 3 1/8" (78 x 175 x 79 cm). Mfr.: Münchner Vereinigte Werkstätten für Kunst im Handwerk, Germany. Courtesy Quittenbaum Kunstauktionen, Munich.

Behrens, Hermann Obrist, Bernhard Pankok, Richard Riemerschmid and, others, cofounded the Münchner Vereinigte Werkstätten für Kunst im Handwerk (Munich united workshops for art in handwork) in 1898. The aim of the enterprise was to sell everyday objects designed by modern designers/architects. Mies van der Rohe, who moved to Berlin, was an apprentice to Paul in late 1905 (or early 1906) to 1907. Paul designed simple, practical 1908 Typenmöbel (standardized furniture) for the Vereinigte Werkstätten. His furniture embodied the most elegant style achievable through machine production. (Karl Schmidt's factory Dresdner Werkstätten für Handwerkskunst produced some of Paul's furniture designs.) Concurrently, Paul contributed illustrations to journal *Jugend* and Munich magazine *Simplicissimus*. 1907, he cofounded the Deutscher Werkbund; taught, Kunstgewerbeschule, Berlin (1924, renamed the Vereinigte Staatsschulen für freie und angewandte Kunst, Berlin-Charlottenburg), where he was the director from 1924–33 and which had an appreciable influence on the development of industrial design in Germany. Paul taught Walter von Nessen, Waldemar Raemisch, Alfred Kopka, and Kem Weber the importance of careful workmanship in the tradition of the Werkbund and Wiener Sezession aesthetics. He designed the interiors of 1909 oceanliner *Kronprinzessin Cecilie*. Some of his domestic interiors had the lyrical qualities of 1820s-30s watercolors. He realized furniture in both neo-Biedermeier and modern styles and architecture from an amalgam of Italian Renaissance, Jugendstil, Art Déco, and the International Style. His architecture included the Hainerberg house (before 1909), near Königstein am Taunus; Pützsche Sanatorium (before 1909), near Bonn; 1914–21 Museum Dahlem (with others), Berlin-Zehlendorf; 1914 *Deutsche Werkbund-Ausstellung* buildings, Cologne; 1925 Das Plattenhaus, Hellerau; 1928-30 Kathreiner-Hochhaus, Kleistpark, Berlin-Schöneberg; 1928-29 Traub house, Prague-Střešovice. He died in Berlin.
Exhibitions Work shown at 1900 *Exposition Universelle*, Paris; 1928 *Exposition of Art in Industry at Macy's* (a room setting), Macy's department store, New York; 1904 *Louisiana Purchase Exposition*, St. Louis; 1910 *Exposition Universelle et Internationale*, Brussels; and subject of 1992 exhibition, Munich (catalog below).
Bibliography Joseph Popp, *Bruno Paul*, Munich: Bruckmann, 1916. S. Friedrich Ahlers-Hestermann, *Bruno Paul: oder die Wucht des Komischen*, Berlin: Mann, 1960. Sonja Günther, *Interieurs um 1900: Bernhard Pankok, Bruno Paul, und Richard Riemerschmid als Mitarbeiter der Vereinigten Werkstätten für Kunst im Handwerk*, Munich: Wilhelm Fink, 1971. Lothar Lang (ed.), *Bruno Paul* (Klassiker der Karikatur, no. 1), Munich: Rogner & Bernhard, 1974. Stephen Calloway, *Twentieth-Century Decoration*, New York: Rizzoli, 1988: 114, 118, 121. Cat., Alfred Ziffer (ed.), *Bruno Paul, Deutsche Raumkunst und Architektur zwischen Jugendstil und Moderne*, Munich: Klinkhardt & Biermann, 1992. Sonja Günther, *Bruno Paul 1874–1968*, Berlin: Mann, 1992.

Paul, Francis

French lighting designer.

Biography From early 1930s until the beginning of World War II, Paul's lighting designs were advanced in their forms and conception. His models, designed for mass production, included chromed chandeliers, standard lighting in various metals including copper, and vases for direct, indirect, and semi-direct illumination. His early work was sold by Décor et Lumière; later models (including a stainless-steel ceiling light for 1935 oceanliner *Normandie*) were sold by René Pottier.
Exhibitions Lighting included in Salons of Société des Artistes Décorateurs; 1934 (2nd) and 1935 (3rd) editions of Salon de la Lumière; Pavillion de la Lumière at 1937 *Exposition Internationale des Arts et Techniques dans la Vie Moderne*; all Paris.
Bibliography Guillaume Janneau, *Le luminaire et les moyens d'éclairage nouveaux*, 2nd series, Paris: Charles Moreau, 1925: plate 13. Gabriel Henriot, *Luminaire moderne*, Paris: Charles Moreau, 1937: plates 31, 32. Alastair Duncan, *Art Nouveau and Art Déco Lighting*, New York: Simon & Schuster, 1978: 156, 179–80.

Paul, Marina (1960–)

Italian designer; born and active Milan.

Training 1989, bachelor's degree in architecture, Politecnico, Milan.
Biography After the Politecnico, Paul extended her personal studies of Muslim architecture, traveling to Fez, Morocco, in 1989, and Tozeur, Tunisia, in 1990. 1991 with Scansetti and Giorgio Gurioli, she cofounded Sýn, a design and research studio, to pursue the use and production of new materials and techniques. (Gurioli departed in 1995.)
Exhibitions Participated in the organization of exhibitions, including 1991 *Il Nuovo Bagno*, Bologna; 1991 *MIB–il Salotto Occidentale*, Forlì; 1993 *The Creative Bathroom* (with Alberto Prina and Francesco Scansetti), Frankfurt and London; 1992 *Design Future Philosophy* (with Scansetti and Giancarlo Iliprandi), Singapore.
> See Scansetti, Francesco.

Paul Revere Pottery

American ceramics firm; located Boston.

History The Saturday Evening Girls Club in Boston was a cultural and social organization for young women, mainly from poor Jewish- and Italian-immigrant families. Edith Brown and Edith Guerrier started a pottery as an addition to the club's activities with the goal of providing the girls with an income. Mrs. James J. Storrow provided the money to set up a small kiln in 1906 and continued to financially support the pottery. Glazing and firing were handled by a hired ceramicist from the Merrimac Pottery, Newburyport, Mass. By 1908, production had begun in the basement area of a settlement house in Brookline, Mass., and subsequently moved to a larger space in the Library Club House, 18 Hull Street, Boston, with a small staff. The historical nature of the neighborhood suggested the name in c. 1912 of Paul Revere Pottery (Revere's having been a Colonist patriot), although it was also known as the Bowl Shop. Simple floral and figural motifs were incised or outlined in black onto plain and decorated vases, electric lamps, dinner services, bowls, candlesticks, and tea sets. The pottery became known for its breakfast sets for children, often with custom monograms. Its wares were almost all hand thrown by the young women who had trained for one year. 1915, Mrs. Storrow funded a new building at 80 Nottingham Road, Brighton, Mass. The facilities housed four

kilns and a staff of 20, although it was never profitable. 1932 when Edith Brown died, the pottery began to have financial difficulties, but, with Mrs. Storrow's support, it survived to 1942.
Bibliography Mira B. Edson, 'Paul Revere Pottery of Boston Town,' *Arts and Decoration*, no. 2, Oct. 1911: 494–95. 'The Paul Revere Pottery: An American Craft Industry,' *House Beautiful*, no. 51, Jan. 1922: 50, 70. *American Art Pottery*, New York: Cooper-Hewitt Museum, 1987.

Paulin, Pierre (1927–)

French designer; born and active Paris.

Training From 1946 under Maxime Old, École Camondo, Paris.
Biography Paulin designed 1953 Chair 157, an early effort and his first plastic chair, in polyester, ABS, and elastomers by Artifort of Maastricht. c. 1955, he became one of the first to work in elasticized fabrics, initially for furniture by Thonet, including 1956 Paulin chair in steel and wood, and Formica desk. 1958–59, worked in the Netherlands, Belgium, Germany, the US, and Japan. Mid-1960s, set up his own design studio in Paris, designing automobile interiors for Simca, telephones by Ericsson, and packaging for Christian Dior, and designed a succession of sculptural furniture composed of a tubular-steel structure covered in foam and upholstered in the previously explored elasticized fabric, by Artifort. These models departed dramatically from his 1950s upholstered seating on black tubular-metal legs by Thonet. At the ADSA design-consultancy agency, he collaborated with Roger Tallon on 1980 Dangari plastic outdoor chair. Artifort, a client from 1958, produced iconic chairs such as 1959 chair no. 560 and stool no. 561 (reproduced as the Mushroom model by Habitat from c. 2000–01), 1959 Orange Slice, 1965 Butterfly no. 675, 1966 Ribbon no. 582, 1965 Langue (tongue) no. 577, 1973 two-part no. 598, and others. Some have either been in production since their introduction or reissued. 1967–78, Paulin participated in refurbishing and public seating of the Musée du Louvre; 1968, executed commissions from Le Mobilier National, resulting in 1971 'endless' sofa by Alpha. Other work for Le Mobilier National: the 1970 furniture and decoration of President Georges Pompidou's private quarters (including Elysée chair by Alpha), Palais de l'Élysée, Paris, and, 1983–84, of President François Mitterrand's office in the Palais; and special symbolic seating for the French pavilion at 1970 *Japan World Exposition (Expo '70)*, Osaka. Appliances have include 1986 Jet Line 10 iron in ABS and metal by Calor. Paul has became inactive and lives on a farm.
Exhibitions/citations Work included in Jaarbeurs fairs from 1962 (Chair 582 shown in 1965 edition), Utrecht; Salon du Meuble, Paris, from 1963; exhibitions in Paris 1988, London 1971, and Philadelphia 1983 (catalogs below). Subject of exhibitions at Musée des Arts Décoratifs, Paris, in 1983; at Galerie Alain Gutharc, Paris, in 2000.

Pierre Paulin. Chair (no. 300). 1965–66. Fiberglass-reinforced polyester and stretch-fabric-covered latex foam, 23 x 32 x 28" (58.4 x 81.3 x 71.1 cm). Mfr: Artifort, the Netherlands. Gift of the mfr. and Turner-T Ltd. MoMA.

Gold medals: 1958 *Exposition Universelle et Internationale de Bruxelles (Expo '58)*; 1968 (14th) Triennale di Milano; 1970 *Japan World Exposition (Expo '70)*, Osaka. Other citations, including 1969 award (for Chair 582), American Society of Interior Design (ASID).
Bibliography Cat., *Les assises du siège contemporain*, Paris: Musée des Arts Décoratifs, 1968. Cat., *Modern Chairs 1918–1970*, London: Lund Humphries, 1971. *Design Français*, Paris: CCI, 1971. Cat., Kathryn B. Hiesinger and George H. Marcus III (eds.), *Design Since 1945*, Philadelphia: Philadelphia Museum of Art, 1983. Cat., *Acquisitions 1982–1990 arts décoratifs*, Paris: Fonds National d'Art Contemporain, 1991. François Mathey, *Au bonheur des formes, design français 1945–1992*, Paris: Regard, 1992. Anne Chapoutot, *Pierre Paulin: un univers de formes*, Paris: Du May, 1992. Elisabeth Vedrenne and Anne-Marie Fevre, *Pierre Paulin*, Paris: Dis Voir, 2001.

Paulsson, Gregor (1889–1977)

Swedish architect and theorist.

Biography 1920–23, Paulsson was director of Svenska Slöjdforeningen (Swedish design council). He published the book *Vackrare vardagsvara* (more beautiful things for everyday use) (1919), which became highly influential in Sweden and contributed appreciably to the 1930 *Stockholmsutställiningen* (Stockholm exposition), of which he was the codirector (with Gunnar Asplund). Swedish design is still steeped in the spirit of Paulsson. The Gregor Paulsson award-statuette has been established by the Svenska Slöjdforeningen.
Exhibitions Work included in 1968 exhibition, Paris (catalog below).
Bibliography Cat., *Les assises du siège contemporain*, Paris: Musée des Arts Décoratifs, 1968. Penny Sparke, *Introduction to Design and Culture in the Twentieth Century*, London: Allen & Unwin, 1986.

Pawson, John (1949–)

British architect and designer; active London.

Training Eton; and Architectural Association, London.
Biography From the design of the 1981 van Royen apartment in London, which marked the founding of his practice and has been followed by a number of private and public buildings and other spaces by Pawson, he became known for his stark, super-refined structures and interiors. He rejects applied ornamentation and goes beyond the utopian and social agenda of bare traditional modernism. Other work has included 1998 residences of Karl Lagerfeld, worldwide Calvin Klein stores, and a large number of other commissions, including art galleries. For his interiors, he includes his own-design starkly simple furniture and furnishings, mostly one-of-a-kind and site specific. His product design has included 2000 bathroom system by Obumex, 2000 Demeyere cookware, 2002 furniture collection by Driade, and tabletop accessories by When Objects Work.
Bibliography Bruce Chatwin et al., *John Pawson*, Barcelona: Gustavo Gili, 1992 and 1998 editions. John Pawson, *Minimalism*, London: Phaidon, 1998. Deyan Sudjic, *John Pawson Works*, London: Phaidon, 2000. John Pawson and Annie Bell, *Eating and Living*, London: Ebury, 2001.

Peach, Harry Hardy (1874–1936)

British industrialist; born Toronto, Canada.

Training To 1886, Wyggeston and Queen Elizabeth I College, Leicester.
Biography 1902, Peach set up as a bookseller in Leicester; from 1918, was a member of the Fabian Society, from which his interest in politics eventually turned to a concern for design; 1906 searching for a cane chair for his father-in-law, began a lengthy discussion with teacher/designer Benjamin Fletcher on cane furniture production; 1907 with Fletcher's students at his art school in Leicester who supplied the designs, set up Dryad Handicrafts. Peach followed the success of the Dryad Handicrafts with the 1912 establishment of Dryad Metal Works with with designer/metalworker William Pick; however, it was unsuccessful. Concerning Dryad Handicrafts' efforts, the 1911 Bachelor's Joy armchair was probably designed by Albert Crampton. Fletcher designed the 1907 Alcover high-back armchair and c. 1910 Abundance chair and settee. The firm was later named Dryad Furniture Company and furnished cane chairs for the 1919 Vickers Vimy Passenger Aeroplane; furniture for 1934 oceanliner *Queen Mary*; cane/tubular-steel furniture designed by Oliver Bernard for Cumberland Palace Hotel at Marble Arch, London. Some furniture was exported to Japan, South America, and, from 1908, to the US. 1915, Peach cofounded the Design and Industries Association, London.
Exhibitions/citations Gold medals (to Dryad), 1910 *Japan-British Ex-*

hibition, London, and 1911 *Festival of Empire* (aka *Festival of Empire Imperial Exhibition and Pageant of London*), Crystal Palace. Silver medal, 1910 *Exposition Universelle et Internationale de Bruxelles*. Work shown at 1908 *Franco-British Exhibition*, 1910 *London Arts and Crafts Exhibition*, 1911 *House or Home*, London; 1911 *Esposizione Internazionale dell'Industria e del Lavoro*, Turin; 1914 *British Arts and Crafts Exhibition*, Paris.
Bibliography Pat Kirkham, *Harry Peach: Dryad and the DIA*, London: The Design Council, 1986.

Peacock, Elizabeth (1880–1969)
British textile designer and teacher.

Biography 1917 with Ethel Mairet, Peacock began to weave; 1922, set up her own workshop; 1931, cofounded Guild of Weavers, Spinners and Dyers; was known for producing the eight banners of 1934–38 commissioned by Leonard and Dorothy Elmhirst for the Great Hall in Dartington; was a spinner, dyer, and weaver and, 1940–57, an influential teacher.
Exhibitions Work subject of 1970 *Memorial Exhibition*, West Surrey College of Art and Design, Farnham; 1978 exhibition, Crafts Study Centre, Bath; 1979-80 *Thirties*, Hayward Gallery, London (catalog below).
Bibliography *Elizabeth Peacock*, Bath: Crafts Study Centre, 1978. Cat., *Thirties: British Art and Design Before the War*, London: Arts Council of Great Britain/Hayward Gallery Gallery, 1979.

Pearson, Ronald Hayes (1924–1996)
American metalsmith; born New York.

Training University of Wisconsin; from 1947, School for American Craftsmen (now School for American Crafts), Alfred (N.Y.) University.
Biography From 1952, Pearson lived in Rochester, N.Y., where he and three other craftspeople set up Shop One, the first artist-owned crafts gallery in the US; was best known as a jewelry designer but also active as a sculptor, industrial designer, teacher, and crafts-community activist; taught and was a board member, Haystack Mountain School of Crafts, Deer Island, Maine, where he settled in 1971 and died. Ronald Hayes Pearson Design Studio & Gallery is still extant, on Deer Island. The Ronald Hayes Pearson Scholarship Fund for metals students has been established at Haystack.
Citations 1987, honorary doctoral degree, Portland (Maine) School of Art (now Maine College of Art); 1996 gold medal, American Craft Council; nominated by Governor Angus King of Maine for the National Treasure Award, University of North Carolina.

PearsonLloyd
British design consultancy; located London.

History All activities in London: Luke Pearson studied industrial design, Central Saint Martins School of Art, and, 1993, received a master's degree in furniture design, Royal College of Art. Prior to PearsonLloyd, Pearson worked at Ross Lovegrove's Studio X and with Daniel Weil at Pentagram. Tom Lloyd studied furniture design in Nottingham and, 1993, received a master's degree in industrial design, Royal College of Art. 1997, they set up the PearsonLloyd partnership and serve clients such as Poltronova, Hitch Mylius, Westminster City Council, Tse Cashmere, CArtemide, DZLicht, Boxfresh, Cashmere by Design, Carhartt Europe, The Princes Foundation, Walter Knoll, Knoll International, and others. Commissions have included 2003 passenger seating (with Acro Engineering and automobile designers DesignQ) for 'Upper Class' area of Virgin Air airplanes. Both partners are visiting professors, École Cantonale d'Art de Lausanne, Switzerland.
Citations A number of awards, including 2001 Premio Compasso d'Oro; 2000, 2001, and 2002 FX Design Awards Best Funiture; 2002 and 2003 Red Dot awards, Design Zentrum Nordrhein Westfalen, Essen; others.

Peart, Stephen (1958–)
British industrial designer; born near Durham.

Training Bachelor of arts degree, Sheffield City Polytechnic; 1981, master of arts degree, Royal College of Art, London.
Biography From 1982, Peart worked at Esslinger Design in Alternsteig, Germany, and made an appreciable contribution to the studio's concepts for the 1982–83 SnowWhite project of Apple Computer. He settled in California and worked at Helmut Esslinger's frogdesign studio; shaped almost every printer, keyboard, mouse, and monitor

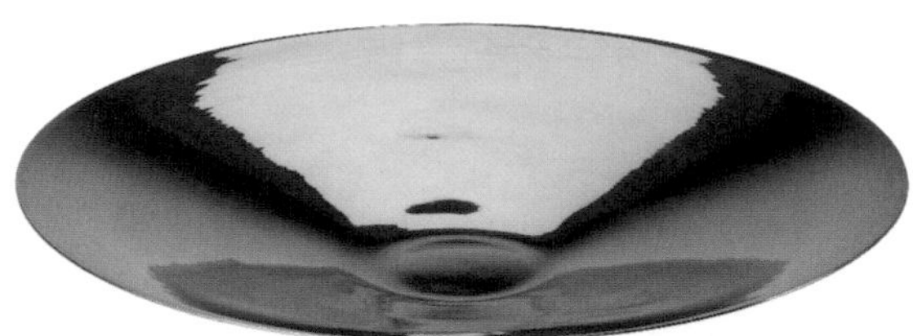

Ronald Hayes Pearson. Bowl. c. 1950-51. Spun bronze, h. 1 9/16" (4 cm) x dia. 11 7/8" (30.2 cm). Mfr.: the designer, US. Gift of Bonniers, Inc. MoMA.

developed by Apple from 1983–87 and designed 1984 LaserWriter I and 1984 LaserWriter II, 1985 ADB mouse, and 1985 ImageWriter LQ. 1988, Peart left frogdesign and founded Vent Design Associates in Campbell, Cal., while continuing to design for Apple for which he developed the Goldilocks concepts and the design of 1992 Apple adjustable keyboard. Vent Design work has included sports equipment, a PC (vertical computer/printer/jukebox) for GE's Concept House of the Future, Pittsfield, Mass. Other clients have been Compaq, Knoll International, Nike, Herman Miller, and Plantronics.
Exhibition/citations Work included in 1995 *Mutant Materials* (catalog below); 2000 National Design Triennial, Cooper-Hewitt National Design Museum; both New York. 1994 Distinction Award and 1996 Best of Category, Annual Design Review, *I.D.* magazine; 1996 Good Design award, Chicago Athenaeum; 1997 bronze award (for 'hat' computer monitor by Virtual Vision), Industrial Design Society of America.
Bibliography Paul Kunkel, *Apple Design: The World of the Apple Industrial Design Group*, New York: Graphis, 1997. Cat., Paola Antonelli, *Mutant Materials in Contemporary Design*, New York: The Museum of Modern Art/Abrams, 1995. Mel Byars, *50 Sports Wares...*, Hove: RotoVision, 2000. Cat., R. Craig Miller (intro.), *U.S. Design 1975–2000*, Munich: Prestel, 2002.

Peche, Dagobert (1887–1923)
Austrian architect, painter, metalworker, glass and ceramics artist, and jewelry designer; born St. Michael, near Salzburg; active Vienna and Zurich.

Training 1906–11, in engineering; subsequently, architecture, Akademie der bildenden Künste, Vienna.
Biography 1912, Peche began designing ceramics and rugs for industry. Particularly for ceramics, he developed a highly distinctive idiom, amalgamating decorative elements from the baroque and rococo. 1915, he joined the Wiener Werkstätte, where he was the codirector from 1917–23; the association fostered the architectonics of his lamps of c. 1920, that were more classically ornamented than his later, more abstract, work. 1917–19, he designed and directed the Wiener Werkstätte's shop in Zurich. Peche and Josef Hoffmann were the most important designers at the Werkstätte at this time. Peche's metalwork included dense ornamentation and rich decoration. He introduced completely new, playful forms, often in basic materials such as *tôle* (sheet metal) and cardboard; even so, inexpensive raw materials had been necessitated by the conditions created by World War I. After the war, he produced utilitarian silver objects as well as purely decorative silver ornaments, an example of which is the 1920 50th birthday gift presented to Hoffmann by the Wiener Werkstätte; its articulated 'fruits' represent sculpture, painting, and architecture. After a long illness, he died in Mödling at age 36.
Exhibitions Work subject of exhibitions at Hochschule für Angewandte Kunst, Vienna, in 1923; in Salzburg, in 1987; at Österreichisches Museum für angewandte Kunst, Vienna, in 1923 and 1998 (catalogs below).
Bibliography Max Eisler, *Dagobert Peche*, Vienna/Leipzig, Gerlach & Wiedling, 1925 (reprint 1992). Cat., Hans Ankwicz-Kleehoven, *Dagobert Peche*, Vienna: Österreichisches Museum für angewandte Kunst, 1923. Cat., Nikolaus Schaffer, *Dagobert Peche, 1887–1923 in seinen Zeichnungen*, Salzburg: Salzburger Museum Carolino Augusteum, 1987. Cat., Peter Noever, *Die Überwindung der Utilität: Dagobert Peche und die Wiener Werkstätte*, Ostfildern: Hatje, 1998.

Pécs Pottery
> See Zsolnay Porcelánmanufaktúra.

Pedrizzetti, Paolo (1947–)

Italian architect and designer.

Training 1969–73, architecture, Politecnico, Milan.
Biography Pedrizetti was active in publishing and boating and, 1973–78, in building design and building-site management; from 1979 with Davide Mercatali, designed products through their studio in Milan; 1982, opened his own independent design studio and, the same year with Mercatali, formed an associated studio to design furniture, furnishings, lighting, and electronics; 1988–94, was editor-in-chief of magazines *Blu & rosso* and *Bagno & bagni*; 1988 with wife Raffaella Mattia, founded Paolo Pedrizzetti & Associati; 1993, was a promoter of the cultural organization ABC Incontri sul Progetto; from 1995, was associated with the magazine *Il Bagno oggi e domani*. 1997, his architect/son Davide Pedrizetti joined the studio. Clients over the years have included Domus, Eleusi, Edilkamin, Noto (Zeus collection), Icom, Metaform, Gedy, Regia, Vismaravetro, Valli & Valli, Macrom, Tubes, Koziol, Valex, Nito, Snips, Malmoli.
Exhibitions/citations 1981, 1987, 1991 Premio Compasso d'Oro; 1984 and 1996 awards, BIO industrial-design biennials, Lublijana; 1987, 1989, 1990 Tecnhotel award, Associazione per il Disegno Industriale (ADI); 2002 Progetto e Qualità award, ADI.
Bibliography Alfonso Grassi and Anty Pansera, *Atlante del Design Italiano*, Milan: Fabbri, 1980. Giancarlo Iliprandi and Pierluigi Molinari (eds.), *Industrial Designers Italiani*, Fagagna: Magnus, 1985: 166. *The International Design Yearbook*, New York: Abbeville, 1986, 1987, 1988, 1989. Hans Wichmann, *Italien Design 1945 bis heute*, Munich: Die Neue Sammlung, 1988. Alfonso Grassi and Anty Pansera, *L'Italia del design*, Turin: Marietti, 1986. *Modo*, no. 148, Mar.–Apr. 1993: 124. *Creativitalia: The Joy of Italian Design*, Milan: Electa, 1990. Stefano Cascinai, *L'architettura presa per mano*, Milan: Idea, 1992. Anty Pansera, *Dizionario del design italiano*, Milan: Cantini, 1995. Mel Byars, *On/Off: New Electronic Products*, New York: Universe, 2001.
> See Mercatali, Davide.

Peduzzi-Riva, Eleanore
> See Riva, Eleanore Peduzzi.

Peduzzi, Richard (1943–)

French painter, interior architect, and scenic and furniture designer; active Paris.

Training Under Charles Auffret, in drawing and sculpture.
Biography 1967, Peduzzi met theater director Patrice Chéreau and, from 1969–89, designed all his productions at the Théâtre des Amandiers in Nanterre; 1979, was commissioned by Michel Laclotte, chief curator of the Musée du Louvre, Paris, to work on the interior architecture, museography, and new presentation of art works; 1988, was commissioned by Jean Coural, ex-director of Le Mobilier National, to design a furniture collection; as an interior architect, restored the library and museum of Opéra Garnier, Paris, and designed 1990 Opéra chair by Plan Venise, for its library, and more than 20 sets, including those of Shakespeare, Marivaux, Wedekind, Koltes, and Heiner Müller plays, and of Rossini, Wagner, Alban Berg, and Mozart operas; with Chéreau and Daniel Barenboim, worked on Mozart's *Don Giovanni* at 1994 Salzburg Festival; from 1991, was the principal, École Nationale Supérieure des Arts Décoratifs, Paris; from 2002, the director, Académie de France in Rome (succeeding Bruno Racine, who held the post from 1997 and who was in turn appointed president, Centre Georges Pompidou, Paris).
Bibliography François Mathey, *Au bonheur des formes, design français 1945–1992*, Paris: Regard, 1992: 236. 'Nominations,' *Le Figaro*, 25 Aug. 2002: 16.

Pel; Practical Equipment Ltd.

British furniture manufacturer; located Oldbury, Birmingham.

History 1914–19 during World War I, the tubular-steel industry in Britain was stimulated by a demand for materials. 1919, a number of the manufacturers joined to form Tube Investments, including the two major firms Accles and Pollock, and Tubes Ltd. 1927, Tube Investments formed Tube Products to exploit the new arc-welding process. It supplied most of the manufacturers of tubular-steel furniture in England during 1930s. 1927–30, Tube Investments absorbed ten small steel tube companies. 1929, Accles and Pollock established a department at its Paddock Works in Oldbury, where tubular-steel furniture frames were produced on a small scale to their own designs; the upholstery was undertaken by other firms. Its 1930 SP1 spring pattern chair (with a chromed frame, and with a cane or seagrass back and seat woven by inmates of the Birmingham Institute for the Blind) was one of its first, and best, designs; this model was one of the four Accles and Pollock products to be included in Pel's range of 1932 to come. Practical Equipment Ltd. was set up in 1931 with P.G. Carew as the managing director (who was also a director of Tube Investments, and son-in-law of Arthur Chamberlain), George Hackett as technical manager, and theater designer Oliver Bernard as the consultant designer. Carew and Hackett had seen Bernard's 1930 Strand Palace Hotel in London, where he used two steel chairs (probably by Thonet); they became enthusiastic about the designer and the potential of steel tubes for domestic use. Carew, a member of the Design and Industries Association, was aware of design issues, although his lack of commercial experience showed in Pel's amateurish launch. A showroom was opened in 1932 at 15 Henrietta Street in London, where an array of tubular-steel furniture was displayed. Starting with 18 employees, the firm occupied a corner of Accles and Pollock's Paddock factory. To avoid confusion with Practical Furniture Ltd., the firm was renamed simply 'Pel' in 1932. In 1930s, Pel produced bent-metal tubing for bedding, tables, seating, and case goods that were painted or nickel plated. Its first catalog was published to coincide with 1932 *Ideal Home* exhibition in London. Riding the wave of the popularity of chromed tubular steel, the firm produced versions of 1920s German models and also models designed by Bernard and by Serge Chermayeff. Its products were fashionable but inexpensive. Pel's 1932 steel nesting chairs designed by Chermayeff for the BBC's 1928–32 Broadcasting House in Langham Place, London, were made with canvas seats by Pel for Plan; 100 chairs could be stowed in a 20 square-foot (1.86 m^2) space. He also designed other Plan-by-Pel models for the Broadcasting House commission. By 1936, there were RP6 chairs in 11 broadcasting enterprises all over the world. The firm

Stephen Peart and Bradford Bissell. Animal wet suit. 1988. Molded neoprene and nylon jersey. Mfr: O'Neill, US. Gift of the designers. MoMA.

Joseph designed Pel's 1933–36 HT21 steel, rubber, and wood table, and 1936 SB9B steel and rexine chairs for the Prudential Assurance offices. Bernard left Pel in 1933, and he was not replaced with a full-time design consultant. Pel's customers included designers McKnight Kauffer, Marion Dorn, Arundel Clarke, Duncan Miller, and Betty Joel. Its bathroom stools were used by the hotel Claridges, its steel furniture in tartan upholstery by the Metropole in Brighton, and other models by the Berkeley and the hotel Savoy in London. Its range was retailed by Heal's, Harrods, and, in Camden Town, by Bowman's. 1934, Pel won its largest order, to furnish bungalows, administrative buildings, and sports clubs for Iraq Petroleum. Also 1934, Pel acquired rights to the RP6 stacking chair from its designer Bruno Pollock; it had been producing the RP6 since 1932 and had been sued by Pollock's agent in Britain. Pel was able to collect royalties until 1951 from other manufacturers, such as Cox and Kingfisher. Pel produced furniture to the specifications of Wells Coates for his 1935 Embassy Court in Brighton and for Erich Mendelsohn and Chermayeff for their 1935 De La Warr Pavilion in Bexhill-on-Sea. Later, Pel made up furniture for Coates's own flat in Yeoman's Row in Knightsbridge, London. The design and manufacture of Accles and Pollock's earlier furniture range had been supervised by Hackett, who left Pel in 1936 to work in another section of Tube Investments. The success of Pel was probably due to the efforts of Oliver Bernard and his enlightened management. (Pel competitors such as Cox, Steelchrome, and Biddulph Industries never hired professional designers, and their wares were designed by the directors.) Pel's competitors had to buy raw tubing from a sister firm of Pel's. 1938, Pel's production was restricted to stretchers in green tubing and wire mesh; during World War II, Pel furnished naval vessels. After the war, Pel was installed in its own premises, though production was hampered by cumbersome post-war procedures for purchasing steel. A Pel 1993 chromed tubular-steel bed was reissued by Alivar in Italy.
Exhibitions Pel steel furniture first shown, at 1932 *Ideal Home*, London, and, subsequently, 1933 *British Industrial Art in Relation to the Home* (Pel furniture in Chermeyeff's Weekend House interior installment), Dorland Hall, London. Pel furniture subject of 1977 exhibition, Architectural Association; incuded in 1979–80 *Thirties*, Hayward Gallery; both London (catalogs below).
Bibliography Cat., Dennis Sharp et al., *Pel and Tubular Steel Furniture of the Thirties*, London: Architectural Association, 1977. Cat., *Thirties: British Art and Design Before the War*, London: Arts Council of Great Britain/Hayward Gallery Gallery, 1979. Barbara Tilson, 'Plan Furniture 1932–1938: The German Connection,' *Journal of Design History*, vol. 3, nos. 2, 3, 1990: 145–55.

Pelcl, Jiří (1950–)

Czech designer and architect, born Postrelmov (today Czech Republic).

Training 1972–78, architecture, Vysoká Škola Uměleckoprůmyslová (VŠUP, academy of arts, architecture, and design), Prague; 1983–84, furniture design, Royal College of Art, London.
Biography Pelcl became active in the design of interiors and some architecture, eventually primarily furniture and a pedagogue; 1987, co-founded the avant-garde artistic group Atika, which was aligned with the Radical Design of Italy; 1989, became a member of Nové Skupiny (new group); has written widely and lectured at a number of institutions, including Gerrit Rietveld Academie in Amsterdam, University of California in Berkeley, Yale University in New Haven (Conn.), Royal College of Art, ENSCI (Les Ateliers) in Paris, and Southern California Institute of Architecture in Los Angeles; 1990, estalbished his own studio Atelier Pelcl, Prague; 1992–94, artistic director, design gallery Genius Loci, Prague; from 1997–2002, was head Department of Architecture and Design, VŠUP, Prague, and head of the school from 2002. Some critics claim his work to be more playful than that of his Czech contemporaries. He has designed interiors, porcelain, glass furniture, and other products for numerous firms and architecture and building renovations, including of Gustav Mahler birthplace, Kaliste (near Humpolec), in c. 1999. Commissions have also included 1990 Vaclav Havel's study, Prague Castle; 1994 St. Laurence Church, Prague; Czech embassies in Rome (1995) and in Pretoria (1997).
Exhibitions/citations Work subject of more than 20 one-person venues, to 2002, in London, Prague, Brno, Villach, Spittal, Bratislava, Žilna, and Norimberk; and included in numerous exhibitions worldwide, including *Czech Design '99*, Totem design store, New York; 2001 *Art and Interior*, Národní Galerie (national gallery), Prague. 2001 *Designum* magazine award (*Lindberg* office furniture by Nábytek Exner).
Bibliography *Architektura ČSR*, no. 1, 1988 and nos. 5–6, 1990. *Casa Vogue*, no. 204, 1989. *Architecture Intérieure Crée*, No. 232, 1989. *Intramuros*, nos. 10–11, 1989. *Maison et Jardin*, no. 360, 1990. *Modo*, no. 121, 1990. *Interni*, no. 412, 1991, and no. 482, 1998. *International Crafts*, London: Thames & Hudson, 1991 and 1992. *Metropolis*, Jan. 1992. *Architektur & Wohnen*, Apr. 1994. *Česká architektura 1994–95*, Prague: Obec Architektů, 1995. *Nuevo Estilo*, no. 9, 1998. *The International Design Yearbook*, London: Laurence King, 1996, 1998, 2001.

Jiří Pelcl. Novito coffee cup. c. 1997. Porcelain, h. 3" (7.5 cm) x dia. 2 3/4" (7 cm). Mfr.: Novito, Czech Republic.

Pelhaître, Claude
> See Pagnon, Patrick.

Pellegrini, Silvano D. (1939–)

Italian designer; born Foggia; active Milan.

Biography Pelligrini has been active in Milan on various projects in reinforced concrete and worked for a time in Paris; 1969, established a studio and has served clients in Italy, including MTZ Settore (design), DID Industrial Design, Maxform Collezioni (furnishings), and CAAI. His metal furniture models (such as Tuscania, Nubecula, and Denebola chairs) were produced by Maxform and furnishings by Venia, and Cama boat by LM Kado in Paris. Pellegrini is a member, Associazione per il Disegno Industriale (ADI).
Exhibitions 1966–67, participated in exhibitions in Milan, Turin, Foggia, Rome, and Brescia.
Bibliography *ADI Annual 1976*, Milan: Associazione per il Disegno Industriale, 1976.

Pellone, Giovanni (1964–); Benza

Italian designer and entrepreneur. American design/production firm.

Training Interior design, Parsons School of Design; industrial design, Pratt Institute; both New York.
Biography 1985, Pellone settled in New York and became a freelance product, package, and graphic designer and established a design consultancy with graphic designer Bridget Means (Australia, 1965–). 1996 with Means, he cofounded Benza in Brooklyn, N.Y., for the design and production of tabletop objects, accessories, and lighting by themselves and others. Products have included 2001 Paperclip clock by Harvey Bernstein, 1994 Jojo aluminum candlestick and bud vase by Anthony Di Bitonto, 1996 Zago trash bin and 1999 Pin Up felt clock by Pellone and Means, 1996 Urchin resin container by Roberto Zanon and Satomi Yoshida-Katz, 1998 Cloud Nine bonded-marble bathroom accessories by Laurene Leon Boym, 1998 Boing dish by Pellone, 2000 Soft felt picture frame by Andrew Schloss, 2001 Fuzzy desk clock by Mayuko Saul and Pellone, and 2003 Time Out clock by Karim Rashid. Other designers: Harry Allen, Jeffrey Bernett, and Daniel Streng. 2003, Means departed Benza with Pellone remaining as the principal.

Penaat, Willem (1875–1957)

Dutch interior and furniture designer; born Deventer.

Training From 1894, Rijksnormaalschool voor Teekenonderwijs, and Rijksacademie voor Beeldende Kunsten; both Amsterdam.

Jorge Pensi. Hola stacking chair. c. 1998. Metal tubing and polyurethane, h. 32 1/2 x. w. 22 3/8 x d. 22 1/2" (52 x 57 x 54 cm). Mfr.: Kusch+Co. Sitzmöbel-werke, Germany.

Biography 1900, Penaat became artistic director of the furniture workshop associated with earthenware factory Amstelhoek, Amsterdam, where he designed simple furniture, sold through the showroom of Binnenhuis, Amsterdam. 1902, he departed the furniture factory and dissolved the contract with Binnenhuis. 1903 with Jan Eisenlöffel and others, Penaat established the workshop De Woning (the home), Amsterdam; 1923 to c. 1950, was active as an interior designer for Metz & Co. store, Amsterdam and the Hague; worked on the cathedral in Utrecht and meeting room and coffee area of Amsterdam's city hall. His early furniture was in a provincial style with chair seats often in rush, illustrated by an undistinguished 1905 painted wood side chair in the Gemeetemuseum, the Hague. However, his work into the 20th century evolved into a modern, Rational style. Penaat designed all the elements—from furniture to brass door knobs—of the 'Restauratie 1923' of 1923–25 in Sneek. He died in Amsterdam.
Exhibitions Early work included in 1994 *Kunst rond 1900*, Gemeentemuseum, The Hague.
Bibliography Tuci de Loor-Alons et al. (eds.) *Willem Penaat, Meubelontwerper en organisator* (1875–1957), Rotterdam: 010, 1988.

Penati, Marco (1951–)

Italian engineering consultant and designer; born and active Muggiò (MI).

Training 1968, diploma in techniques of furniture production.
Biography 1970s, Penati worked at Sormani furniture firm and, subsequently, was the technical director of furniture firm Zanotta. He has widely lectured on the research and engineering of furnishing products, at Politecnico, Milan; Istituto Superiore per le Industrie Artistiche (ISIA), Florence; Istituto Professionale di Stato (IPSIA), Lissone; and Institute of Art & Design of Malta College of Arts Science and Technology (MCAST); from 1988, worked as research and engineering consultant to companies in the furnishing sector; from 1994 as a designer, has been a partner of studio Sigla in Milan, with Marina Bani and Patrizia Scarzella.
> See Scarzella, Patrizia.

Pengelly, Simon (1967–)

British designer.

Training Furniture making and design, Rycotewood College; to 1988, Kingston Polytechnic (now Kingston University).
Biography Pengelly began making furniture at an early age, winning an international competition at age 15 for cabinet making; from 1988, worked at Conran Design and Habitat design studios, London; has designed furniture by Isokon Plus.
Citations 2002 Best Overall Contributor, 100% Design fair, London.

Pensi, Jorge (1946–)

Argentine architect and designer; born Buenos Aires; active Barcelona.

Training In architecture, Buenos Aires.
Biography Pensi was initially active in Buenos Aires; 1975, moved to Spain and gained Spanish citizenship; 1977, settled in Barcelona; 1976, joined Grupo Berenger, founded in 1972 by Alberto Liévore and Norberto Chaves. 1981, Pensi established his own design studio, specializing in furniture, lighting, and graphics; from 1987, mainly collaborated with Diego Slemenson and, from 1995, with Constanze Schütz, and also with Pensi's wife Carmen Casares on graphic design and, from 1996, with Eduardo Campoamor on architecture and interiors. Clients have included Akaba, Amat, Arruti, B. Lux, Coin-ma, Disform, Do+Ce, IBM, Kron, Mecrimar, Niessen, *ON Diseño* magazine, Perobell, Punt Mobles, RS, Santa & Cole, SEAT Design Club, Soko Ibérica, Uraldi, Zurich Cia. Seguros. Pensi designed 1984 exhibition stands (with Liévore) for ADP and, for Perobell, much of the furniture in the early-1980s Latina range (including 1987 Helsinoor armchair) and its corporate identity. Other work has included 1988 Toledo aluminum chair and table by Amat marketed by Knoll, and 1989 Orfila chair marketed by Thonet. From 1989, his international client list has also included Akaba, Andreu World, Cassina, Ciatti, Crassevig, Driade, Kusch+Co, Inno Interior, Alvar Aalto Museum, Olympia, and others, in Argentina, France, Portugal, Singapore, and Korea. Recently, Pensi has lectured, taught, and conducted seminars in various countries.
Citations 1989 prize from Gremio Provincial de Comerciantes de Muebles; 1997 National Design Prize (for body of work), Ministerio de Industria y Energía, Spain; two 1997 Red Dot awards (Capa and Hola! side/armchairs by Kusch), Design Zentrum Nordrhein Westfalen, Essen.
Bibliography Guy Julier, *New Spanish Design*, London: Thames & Hudson, 1991. Nelly Schnaith, *Jorge Pensi*, Barcelona: Gustavo Gili, 1994. Oriol and Carles Pilbernat, *Intuitions Jorge Pensi: The Reference Book of International Industrial Design*, Barcelona: Loft, 2001.

Pensotti, Giuseppe (1939–)
> See Gruppo G14.

Pentagram

International industrial and graphic design and architecture firm.

History 1972, Pentagram was established in London, growing out of the 1950s graphic-design consultancy of the firm Forbes, Fletcher and Gill. However, Pentagram was founded by a group of five design-

Pentagram, Robert Brunner, John Tang (1959–), Peter Cazalet (1969–), Benjamin Chia, and Bob Olodort (1946–). Stowaway portable keyboard. 1999. Injection-molded ABS polymer and stamped and formed aluminum, closed w. 5 1/8 x d. 3 5/8" (13 x 9.2 cm), open w. 13 7/8 x d. 5 1/8" (35.2 x 13 cm). Mfr.: Think Outside, US. Gift of the design firm. MoMA.

ers (Theo Crosby, Kenneth Grange, Colin Forbes, Mervyn Kerlandky, and Alan Fletcher, hence the name *penta* for 'five'). Grange is the industrial designer known for his work for Kenwood. Each partner has a specialty in architecture or interior, exhibition, or graphic design. Eventually branches were also established in New York, San Francisco, and Austin, Tex. Subsequent members included Marvyn Kurlansky, John McConnell, Paul Scher, Daniel Weil, and others. For one and half years, graphic designer Bruce Mau worked there. Currently, its work, primarily in graphics, has included the redesign of periodicals *The Guardian*, *@issue*, *Architecture*, *Metro-polis*, and others. The Pentagram Prize student award has been established. Today, the studio has over 50 staff members in London alone, with seven partners.
Citations A number of awards for graphic design; also 1997 bronze award (for Infinia computer by Toshiba America) and 1999 silver (for Silicon Graphics Work Station, with manufacture's staff) IDSA/*Business Week* awards.
Bibliography Peter Gorb, *Living by Design*, London: Lund Humphries, 1978 Penny Sparke, *Introduction to Design and Culture in the Twentieth Century*, London: Allen & Unwin, 1986. David Gibbs (ed.), *Pentagram: The Compendium*, London: Phaidon, 1998.
> See Grange, Kenneth Henry.

PER, Studio
Spanish architecture and design partnership; active Barcelona.

History 1964, the umbrella partnership was formed in Barcelona to include two separate (architecture and design) workshops. In architecture section were Óscar Tusquets Blanca and Lluís Clotet Ballús, and in the other Christian Cirici and Pep Bonet. All had been students of Frederic Correa. They have been meticulous in their detailing of furniture, interiors, and buildings, resolutely opposed to orthodox architectural norms, and expressed their views in critical published texts and through their architecture. Tusquets and Clotet designed 1968 Penina house in Cardedeu, 1972 Belvedere 'Georgina' weekend house in Llofriu, and 1974 Vittoria house in Pantelleria, Italy. Cirici and Bonet's work, more conservative, has included 1973 Profitos furniture factory in Polinyà, 1974 Tokyo housing block in Barcelona, and Bonet's own 1976 house in Vilamajor. The group was effective in gaining some in-ternational recognition for themselves and for contemporary Spanish design in general. The furniture of all members of the team has been widely published. (See individual entries.)
Bibliography 'Studio PER,' *Architecture and Urbanism*, no. 4, 1977. David Mackay in Vittorio Magnago Lampugnani (ed.), *Encyclopedia of 20th-Century Architecture*, New York: Abrams, 1986: 323.

Percy, Carl Arthur Carlsson (1886–1976)
Swedish ceramicist and glassware and textile designer.

Training 1905–08, Konstnärsföbundets Skola, Stockholm; 1908 under Henri Matisse, art in Paris.
Biography 1922–29, Percy was a designer at Gefle porcelain works in Gävle; from 1943–51, at Karlskrona porcelain works; from 1936, designed printed fabrics for Elsa Gullberg; from 1951–70 worked at Gullaskruf glassworks.
Exhibitions/citations Work subject of 1957 and 1980 exhibitions, Stockholm, (catalog below), and in Gävle, 1971. Work shown at 1925 *Exposition Internationale des Arts Décoratifs et Industriels Modernes* (diploma of honor), Paris; 1929–30 *Exposición Internacional de Barcelona*; 1930 *Stockholmsutställningen* (Stockholm exhibition); 1937 *Exposition Internationale des Arts et Techniques dans la Vie Moderne*, Paris; 1939–40 *New York World's Fair: The World of Tomorrow*; 1955 *H 55* exhibition, Hälsingborg; 1982 exhibition, New York (catalog below). Received 1957 Prince Eugen Medal.
Bibliography Cat. Anne-Marie Ericsson, *Arthur Percy: konstnär och formgivare*, Uddevalla: Tryckt hos Bohuslänigens, 1980. Cat., David Revere McFadden (ed.), *Scandinavian Modern Design 1880–1980*, New York: Abrams, 1982. Jennifer Hawkins Opie, *Scandinavia: Ceramics and Glass in the Twentieth Century*, New York: Rizzoli, 1989.

Peregalli, Maurizio (1951–)
Italian designer; born Varese; active Milan.

Training Autodidact, Milan.
Biography From 1980, Peregalli designed showrooms and shops of Giorgio Armani; 1984 with five other designers, established Zeus in Milan, a selling gallery for furniture, ceramics, glass, and textiles; was a partner of Noto, an interior-design and manufacturing company established in 1984, which produced his 1982 Poltrona armchair (with Sergio Calatroni) and 1986 Poltrocino Cromo armchair (part of the Zeus collection). He has been the artistic director and director of the design collections and exhibitions of Zeus and in charge of the promotion of its international designers.
Bibliography Albrecht Bangert and Karl Michael Armer, *80s Style: Designs of the Decade*, New York: Abbeville, 1990. *Modo*, no. 148, Mar.–Apr. 1993: 124.
>See Zeus.

Peressutti, Enrico (1908–1976)
Italian architect and designer; born Pinzana al Tagliamento, Udine.

Biography 1951–52, Peressutti taught at Architectural Association, London; 1952, at Massachusetts Institute of Technology (MIT), Cambridge, Mass.; 1953–59, at Princeton University; 1957 and 1962, at Yale University.
> See BBPR.

Peretti, Elsa (1940–)
Italian jewelry designer; born Florence; active New York, Rome, and Sant Martí Vell (Spain).

Biography 1968, Peretti settled in New York and eventually became a fashion model and jewelry designer. Her first jewelry was a small teardrop and miniature silver bud vase, both pendants on a chain as necklaces. The vase holding a flower was first shown at 1968 show of the clothing of Giorgio di Sant'Angelo (Italian, 1933–1989). Early 1970s as a model and designer of jewelry, she worked closely with Halston (Ray Halston Frowick, American, 1932–1990). 1974, she began designing jewelry exclusively for Tiffany. Though her designs have been produced in materials ranging from diamonds and gold to bamboo and lacquer, she may be best known for the use of sterling silver, the metal she called on from the late 1960s. Her work incorporates motifs based on heart shapes, bones, scorpions, beans, snakes, and other forms. Halston also commissioned Peretti for package designs for his Revlon cosmetics line, including a heart-shaped compact and lipstick cases. In addition to traditional silver and gold jewelry by Tiffany, her work has included teapots, candlesticks, cutlery, and leather goods. From c. 1982, she began rebuilding the village Sant Martí Vell, near Barcelona, home of craftspeople with whom she works on her products and where she established Fundación Elsa Peretti.
Exhibitions Work subject of 1990 exhibition, Museum of the Fashion Institute of Technology, New York.
Bibliography 'Show of Peretti Designs Celebrates Tiffany Era,' *The New York Times*, 26 Apr. 1990. Anne-Marie Schiro, 'Classic Hearts and Imperishable Beans,' *The New York Times*, 23 June 1992: B8.

Perkal, Nestor (1951–)
Argentine interior architect and designer; born Buenos Aires; active Paris.

Training 1977, architecture diploma, Facultad de Arquitectura, Universidad de Buenos Aires, Buenos Aires.
Biography Perkal settled in Paris and, 1982, opened a gallery of new design, where the work of the Memphis group was first shown in France; 1985, moved the gallery from near to Centre George Pompidou to the Marais area, where it was active to 1994. 1987–94, was artistic director, metalware firm Algorithme and commissioned a number of designers to contribute to La Collection. Perkal has curated a large number of exhibitions from 1987.1993–96, he taught, École des Arts Décoratifs, Limoges; 1995–96, École Camondo, Paris; Étude et Création de Mobilier (ECM), the Paris–Conflans achitecture school; visiting professor on the framework of 1998 Biennial Internationale du Design, Saint-Étienne. 1991, he founded and directed the Centre de Recherches sur les Arts du Feu and de la Terre (CRAFT), Limoges. He designed 1987 Oz lamp by Drimmer; 1992 house in Jouy-en-Josas, France; 1992 Grand Hôtel silver-plated tabletop objects by Algorithme; 1993 house in Rueil Malmaison, France; 1993 Buis Limoges-porcelain lamp by Artcodif; 1993 Les Rivières furniture/furnishing emsemble by Lou Fagotin; 1996 house in Limoges; 1997 café of Maison Européenne de la Photographie, Paris; Morticia vase (made for 1998 *La Vie en Rose* exhibition, Fondation Cartier, Paris); 1999 Le Chemin des Philosophes fabric by Sommer; 2000 Imroz bed by Isoroy; 2000 Serre et Espace TV (shown at Galerie Chez Valentin, Paris); 2000 Buis lamp by Artcodif of Musée des Arts Décoratifs; 2001 FUSEI collection (shown at Galerie Gilles Peyroulet, Paris); 2002 Aucellus lamps by Veronese; 2003 Jardins à Vivre school furniture, through Chambre des Métiers, Limousin; 2003 Viva Mexico collection by Drimmer.

Charlotte Perriand, Le Corbusier, and Pierre Jeanneret. Revolving armchair (No. LC/7). 1929. Chrome-plated steel and leather, 29 3/4 x 22 x 21 1/4" (75.6 x 55.9 x 54 cm), seat h. 21 5/8" (54.9 cm). Mfr: Thonet Frères, France. Gift of Thonet Industries, Inc. MoMA.

Exhibitions/citations Work included in more than 30 exhibitions and subject of five exhibitions from 1993–2002. Villa Kujoyama scholarship, residence at Kyoto; 1994 Appel Permanent grant, VIA (French furniture association); national grand-prize trophy (for 1998 Combien de Temps vase by Salviati), Ministère de la Culture, France; elected Chevalier of the Ordre des Arts et des Lettres.
Bibliography Christine Colin, *Design d'aujourd'hui*, Paris: Flammarion, 1988. Arlette Barré-Despond (ed.), *Dictionnaire international des arts appliqués et du design*, Paris: Regard, 1996. Mel Byars, *50 Beds...*, Hove: RotoVision, 2000. *Intramuros*, no. 95 June-July, 2001. www.via.asso.fr.

Permafrost Designstudio

Norwegian design studio; located Oslo.

History Jan. 2000, Permafrost was founded in Oslo by a group of four industrial designers and architects. They have been active in a range of activities from development and branding to products, transportation, interior design, and architecture. Products have included 1998 shoplifting-proof cabinet handle, 1998–99 Alfa BC hiking boot by Alfa Skofabrikk, 1998 Sony MDR V1000 professional disk-jockey headphones; 1999–2000 Stolen Jewelry (jewelry, packaging, advertising), 1999–2000 Tanberg Silverline WAP mobile telephone; 2000 FoldABowl folding snack bowl; 2001 Dual Shock Controller (for Playstation 2) by Sony; c. 2000 trophy for Norsk Rikskringkasting (NRK, Norwegian broadcasting company). The studio members are frequently lecturers at their alma mater, which is the Department of Industrial Design of the Arkitekthøgskolen i Oslo (AHO).
Principal partners biographies Tore Vinje Brustand (Baerum, 1976–), Eivind Halseth (Trondheim, 1972–), Oskar Johansen (Oslo, 1974–), and Andreas Murray (Oslo, 1975–), all graduates of Department of Industrial Design, Arkitekthøgskolen i Oslo (AHO). (In addition: Halseth, three semesters, Art Center College of Design, Pasadena, Cal., US; Johansen, one semester, ENSCI [Les Ateliers], Paris; Murray, one semester, Eesti Kunstiakadeemia, Tallinn, Estonia).
Individual citations 1997 1st prize, future communication (to Halseth), Ericsson Mobile Communications; 1st prize, student workstations, Arkitekthøgskolen, Oslo; 1st prize, 1998 Plastens Tur & Retur (to Murray, for recycled-plastic six-pack drink carton); 1st prize, 1998 Velo Borealis (to Brustand, for child's bicycle); 1977 (to Johansen, for scooter for wheelchair users), 1999 (to Halseth, for three-wheel scooter), and 2000 Talent of the Year (to Halseth and Brustand, cabinet handle), Norska Designrådet (ND, Norwegian design council).
Group exhibitions Permafrost work included in *Generation X: Young Nordic Design*, traveling the world from 2000; 2001 Designers Block, London.
Bibliography www.permafrost.no.
> See Halseth, Eivind.

Perriand, Charlotte (1903–1999)

French designer; born and active Paris.

Training 1920–25, École de l'Union Centrale des Arts Décoratifs, Paris.
Biography 1927–37, Perriand worked with Le Corbusier and his cousin Pierre Jeanneret in Paris and was responsible for the furniture designs for their 'machines for living.' She deserves credit for possibly all the design of the furniture rendered in the Le Corbusier office during this time, with the possible exception of case goods; however, during her lifetime, refused to acknowledge her full participation due to, according to her, the lack of documentation, but the unrevealed reasons may have be otherwise. The protypes of the renowned 1929 range were paid for by her mother. The Le Corbusier-atelier furniture includes 1928 LC/1 sling chair (also by Cassina from 1965), 1928 LC/4 chaise longue (also by Cassina from 1965), 1929 LC/7 revolving armchair (also by Cassina from 1978), and, on her own while in Japan, 1955 Tokyo chair and other furniture for *Synthèse des Arts* exhibition, Tokyo. 1929, she cofounded UAM (Union des Artistes Modernes); 1930, met Fernand Léger, beginning a long-standing friendship; 1940 with Jean Prouvé, Pierre Jeanneret, and Georges Blanchon, set up an office on the rue La Cases, Paris, to design temporary prefabricated housing in aluminum, including huts, dormitories, dining halls, art rooms, and factory extensions. 1940, she was invited by the Japanese Ministry of Commerce and Trade to become an advisor on industrial arts production (like Bruno Taut in 1933); mounted two exhibitions on French design there; wrote the book *Contact with Japan* (with architect Junzo Sakakura, 1942); 1943–46, lived in Indochina; 1946, returned to France; 1946–49, designed furnishings for holiday resorts in Méribel-les-Allues (Savoie); 1950, created kitchen prototypes for Unité d'Habitation building (architect, Le Corbusier), Marseille; 1953 furnishings for Maison de l'Étudiant (including low tables 118"/300 cm long), rue Saint-Jacques, Paris, and for Hôtel de France, Conakry, and 1953 bookcases (with Prouvé) for Maison de la Tunisie, Cité Universitaire, Paris. 1955–74, Galerie Steph Simon edited some of Perriand and Jean Prouvé's furniture. She also designed furnishings for Air France office (with P. Bradok), London, in 1957, and in Tokyo (with Sakakura and Pen Suzuki) in 1959; 1959 furnishings for the student and common rooms, Maison du Brésil at Cité Universitaire (architects, Le Corbusier and Lucio Costa). 1959–70, she participated in the refurbishment of various conference rooms, United Nations, Geneva; 1960, designed furnishings for chalets in Méribel-les-Allues; 1962 furnishings (with Maria Elisa Costa) for an apartment in Rio de Janeiro; 1964–82, interiors and furnishings for hotels in Les Arcs (Savoie); was president of the jury, 1983–84 International Competition for New Office Furniture, Paris, sponsored by Ministère de la Culture, France; 1980s, was a consultant to Cassina, manufacturer of reproductions of the Le Corbusier/Jeanneret/Perriand furniture. She designed 1941 *Tradition, Selection, Creation* exhibition, Japan; wrote her autobiography *Une vie de création* (Paris: Jacob, 1998 French ed.; New York: Monacelli, 2001 English ed.).
Exhibitions Work included in a large number of exhibitions and Salons, from 1925 *International Arts and Crafts Exhibition*, Paris, and subject of venues at Musée des Art Décoratifs, Paris, in 1949 and 1985; Takashimaya department store (showing Synthèse des Arts/ Tokyo chair), Tokyo, in 1955; Musée National d'Art Moderne (furniture), in 1965; Musée National Fernand Léger, Paris; Musée des Arts Décoratifs, Paris, 1985.
Bibliography Charlotte Perriand, 'Wood or Metal?,' *The Studio*, vol. 97, 1929. Charlotte Perriand, 'L'habitation familiale: son développement économique et social,' *L'architecture d'aujourd'hui*, no. 1, 1935. Cat., *Charlotte Perriand: un art de vivre*, Paris: Flammarion, 1985. Cat., *Der Kragstuhl* (Stuhlmuseum Burg Beverungen), Berlin: Alexander, 1986. Arlette Barré-Despond, *UAM*, Paris: Regard, 1986. Cat., *Les années UAM 1929–1958*, Paris: Musée des Arts Décoratifs, 1988. Cat., Design Center Stuttgart, *Women in Design: Careers and Life Histories Since 1900*, Stuttgart: Haus der Wirtschaft, 1989: 248–55. Cat., *Charlotte Perriand, Fernand Léger, une connivence: Musée National Fernand Léger, Biot*, Paris: Réunion des Musées Nationaux, 1999. Mary McLeod (ed.), *Charlotte Perriand: An Art of Living*, New York: Abrams, 2003. Paola Antonelli (ed.), *Objects of Design: The Museum of Modern Art*, New York: The Museum of Modern Art, 2003: 81.

Sigurd Persson. Covered casserole. 1957. Enameled cast iron. Mfr.: Kockums Emaljerverk, Sweden. Gift of the mfr. MoMA.

Perrigault, Pierre (1931–)

French furniture manufacturer; active Paris.

Training 1947–51, École Boulle, Paris; 1951–52, in management in Britain.
Biography c. 1953, Perrigault managed the first Knoll Associates furniture showroom in Lyon, where he subsequently established Galerie Lambert and exhibited the work of young French designers, including Pierre Paulin and Etienne Fermigier; 1959, established the shop Meubles et Fonctions International (MFI) on the boulevard Raspail, Paris, and edited and exhibited the work of French and foreign designers, including Michel Mortier, Jean-Paul Barray, Daniel Pigeon, Arne Jacobsen, Verner Panton, Poul Kjaerholm, and Hans Guguelot; 1980 with Jean-Louis Berthet, was copresident of Salon of the Société des Artistes Décorateurs (SAD) and organized *1930–1980 Cinquante ans de créateurs SAD* exhibition, which documented SAD's 50-year history, Grand Palais, Paris.
Bibliography François Mathey, *Au bonheur des formes, design français 1945–1992*, Paris: Regard, 1992: 381–82. Diane Saunier, *Pierre Perrigault, l'architecte du mobilier, 1950–2000*, Paris: Meubles et Fonctions, 2000.

Perry, Mary Chase (aka Mary Chase Stratton 1867–1961)

American ceramicist.

Training 1887–89, clay modeling and sculpture, Art Academy of Cincinnati, Ohio; under painter Franz A. Bischoff, in Detroit.
Biography After teaching china painting in Asheville, N.C., she returned to Detroit in 1893 and opened a small workshop; initially applied overglaze porcelain decorations on vessels fired in kilns used for the production of false teeth. With kiln owner Horace James Caulkins, inventor of the 1892 gas-fired Revelation China Kiln for art potteries, Perry promoted its use and demonstrated its features throughout the US. By 1898, she was experimenting on her own and became known for her essays on watercolor design and china painting; after 1900, wrote for Adelaide Alsop Robineau's journal *Keramic Studio*; 1903, withdrew from membership in National League of Mineral Painters and, with Caulkins, founded Revelation Pottery, which soon became known as Pewabic Pottery, named after the upper-Michigan-state region of Perry's birth. Her early Art Nouveau wares were influenced by Louis Comfort Tiffany, William Grueby, Auguste Delaherche, and early Chinese pottery and were produced in simple forms with iridescent glazes. 1906, she developed a new pottery workshop designed by the firm of William Buck Stratton, whom she married in 1918. Pewabic's work was encouraged by Charles Lang Freer, the Detroit art connoisseur. 1908, architect Ralph Adams Cram used Pewabic tiles for the interior pavement of St. Paul's Cathedral in Detroit. The pottery received numerous other architectural commissions and concentrated on tiles for flooring, mosaics, and other architectural features. Perry perfected crystalline and volcanic glazes and, 1909, introduced her renowned Persian (or Egyptian) blue glaze; from 1924 to late 1940s, taught classes at the pottery. When her health began to fail, Ella J. Peters took over the direction of the enterprise, which operated to 1965, when it was incorporated into Michigan State University. 1968, the pottery was reopened and is today a pottery studio and museum in Detroit.
Exhibitions 23 pieces were shown at 1904 *Louisiana Purchase Exposition*, St. Louis.
Bibliography Marjorie Hegarty, 'Pewabic Pottery,' *Detroit Institute of Arts Bulletin 26*, no. 3, 1947: 69–70. Thomas Brunk, 'Pewabic Pottery,' in *Arts and Crafts in Detroit, 1906–1976: The Movement, The Society, The School*, Detroit: Detroit Institute of Arts, 1976. Lillian Myers Pear, *The Pewabic Pottery: A History of its Products and its People* (bicentennial ed.), Des Moines: Wallace-Homestead, 1976. Fred Bleicher et al., *Pewabic Pottery: An Official History*, Ann Arbor: Ars Ceramica, 1977. Cat., *American Art Pottery*, New York: Cooper-Hewitt Museum, 1987: 112–13.

Persico, Edoardo (1900–1936)

Italian architect; born Naples.

Biography A 1928 exhibition held in Turin provided a platform for experimentation by young architects, including Alberto Sartoris, Lavinia Perona, Giuseppe Pagano, and Gino Levi-Montalcini (architect of the 1929 Gualino office building with Pagano). They formed the Gruppo dei Sei, led by Persico. After 1928, Persico became involved in architecture when he arrived in Milan, where he first worked at Pier Maria Bardi's art gallery and, subsequently, Galleria del Milione; became an editorial staff member of journal *La Casa Bella* (later *Casabella*). For the latter, he designed austere covers and, from early 1930s, transformed it into an influential publication. He also wrote important articles in Gio Ponti's journal *Domus* and a number of other periodicals and books. Persico became known for his opposition to Italian Ratio-nalist architecture. Early 1930s with Marcello Nizzoli, set up a design partnership. Persico's work included two 1934 Parker Pen Shop (with Nizzoli) in Largo Santa Margherita, Milan; 1934 tubular-steel advertising structure in the Galleria Vittorio Emanuele II (with Nizzoli), Milan; 1935 Honor Court (with Nizzoli and Giancarlo Palanti); 1935 Parker Pen Shop (with Nizzoli), Corso Vittorio Emanuele II, Milan; *Sala della Vittoria* (victory salon) exhibition at 1936 (6th) Triennale di Milano.
Exhibitions/citations Work subject of 1985 exhibition, Facoltà di Architettura with l'Istituto Italiano per gli Studi Filosofici, Naples (1987 catalog below). Gold medal (with Nizzoli), 1934, *Italian Aeronautical Exhibition*, photographic venue, *Sala delle Medaglie d'Oro,* Palazzo dell'Arte, Milan.
Bibliography Giulia Veronesi, *Difficoltà politiche dell'architettura in Italia, 1920–1940*, Milan: Politecnica Tamburini, 1953. Giula Veronesi (ed.), *Tutte le opere: 1923–1935*, Milan: Comunità, 1964. Barbie Campbell-Cole and Tim Benton (eds.), *Tubular Steel Furniture*, London: The Art Book Company, 1979: 46. Cat., Cesare De Seta, *Edoardo Persico*, Naples: Electa, 1987. Penny Sparke, *Design in Italy, 1870 to the Present*, New York: Abbeville, 1988. Richard A. Etlin, *Modernism in Italian Architecture, 1890–1940*, Cambridge: MIT, 1991.

Persson, Sigurd (1914–2003)

Swedish metalworker and glassware designer; born Hälsingborg.

Training Under his father Fritiof Persson in Hälsingborg, in silversmithing; 1937–39, Akademie für angewandte Kunst, Munich; 1942, Kungliga Tekniska Högskolan, Stockholm.
Biography 1941, Persson established his own silver workshop and designed/produced jewelry and cutlery, including 1953 cutlery for Kooperative Förbundet (cooperative society of Sweden); designed in-flight dinnerware for various airlines and was a designer at Kosta Boda glassworks; wrote the book *Modern Swedish Smycken* (1950).
Exhibitions/citations Work subject of the exhibition, Malmö Museum. Work included in significant exhibitions in Sweden 1950; 1954–57 *Design in Scandinavia*, touring the US; in Sydney in 1954; in Pforzheim in 1955; 1955 *H 55*, Hälsingborg; in Havana in 1956; in New York in 1982 (catalog below). Medals at the 1951 (9th), 1954 (10th), 1957 (11th) and 1960 (12th) editions of Triennale di Milano, 1959 competition for cutlery sponsored by Scandinavian Airlines, 1970 Prince Eugen Medal, 1967 Swedish Prize for Artists, and Gregor Paulsson Trophy.
Bibliography Sigurd Persson, *Modern Swedish Smycken*, Stockholm, 1950. Cat., *Sigurd Persson Design*, Malmö: Malmö Museum, 1961. Erik Zahle (ed.), *A Treasury of Scandinavian Design*, New York: Golden Press, 1961. Cat., *Sigurd Persson*, Stock-holm: Galerie Burén, 1972. *Sigurd Persson Silver*, 1979 (*Sigurd Persson Smycken*, Stockholm: Seelig, 1980). Cat., David Revere McFadden (ed.), *Scandinavian Modern Design 1880–1980*, New York: Abrams, 1982. *Sigurd Persson: skulptur, plastiken, sculpture*, Stockholm: Arne Tryckare, 1983. *Sigurd Persson glas*, Stockholm: Königsbach-Stein, 1986. *Sigurd Persson: 10 nya kannor + 10 tidigare kannor*, Stockholm: Brödema Ljungberg Tryckeri, 1999.

Persson-Melin, Inga (1936-)

Training Kungliga Tekniska Högskotan, Stockholm
Biography From 1959, she was a designer of dinnerware and decorative objects at Rörstrand ceramics factory in Lidköping; 1971, established her own workshop but, subsequently, returned to Rörstrand, where she designed 1972 Pop porcelain dinnerware that illustrated new forms and colors more reflective of earthenware and other work.
Exhibitions/citations Work included in 1996–97 group show, Röhsska Museet, Gothenberg. 1958 Lunning Prize; 1969 gold medal, Concorso Internazionale della Ceramica d'Arte, Faenza.
Bibliography Lennart Lindkvist (ed.),*Design in Sweden*, Stockholm, 1972:39. Cat., Kathryn B. Hiesinger and George H. Marcus III (eds.), *Design Since 1945*, Philadelphia: Philadelphia Museum of Art, 1983.Jennifer Hawkins Opie, *Scandinavia: Ceramics and Glass in the Twentieth Century*, New York: Rizzoli, 1989. Cat., *Torun Vivianna Bülow-Hübe, Ingrid Dessau, Signe Persson-Melin: klassiker i svensk formgivning*, Gothenberg: Röhsska Museet, 1996.

Persson-Melin, Signe (1925–)

Swedish glassware designer and ceramicist.

Training 1945–46 and 1948–50 under Robert Nilsson, ceramics and sculpture, Konstfackskolan, Stockholm; 1947–48 under Nathalie Krebs, ceramics, Det Kongelige Danske Kunstakademi, Copenhagen; from c. 1949–50, apprenticeship at Andersson & Johansson, Höganäs.
Biography From 1951–66, she worked in her own studio in Malmö; from 1967–77, was a designer at Kosta Boda glassworks; 1970, became one of the first designers at Boda Nova; from 1980–87, worked at Rörstrand in Lidköping; 1985, became the first professor of design in Sweden, at Konstfackskolan, Stockholm; has designed ceramics by Höganäs and by Design House Stockholm.
Exhibitions/citations Work subject of exhibitions, Stockholm in 1953; Gothenburg, in 1954; Malmö in 1954. Included in 1996–97 group show, Röhsska Museet, Gothenberg (catalog below). Work shown at editions of Triennale di Milano; 1954–57 *Design in Scandinavia*, touring the US; 1975 *Adventures in Swedish Glass*, Australia; in New York in 1982; Stockholm in 1986 (catalogs below). 1958 Lunning Prize; Excellent Swedish Design (for Design House Stockholm ceramics).
Bibliography Cat., David Revere McFadden (ed.), *Scandinavian Modern Design 1880–1980*, New York: Abrams, 1982. Cat., *The Lunning Prize*, Stockholm: Nationalmuseum, 1986: 98–103. Jennifer Hawkins Opie, *Scandinavia: Ceramics and Glass in the Twentieth Century*, New York: Rizzoli, 1989. Cat., *Torun Vivianna Bülow-Hübe, Ingrid Dessau, Signe Persson-Melin: klassiker i svensk formgivning*, Gothenberg: Röhsska Museet, 1996.

Perusat, Pierre (1908–)

French ironworker; born Bordeaux.

Training Under his father, in locksmithing.
Biography Perusat worked for wrought-iron artisans Édouard and Marcel Schenck and Adalbert Szabó in Paris; early 1930s to 1962, was active in his own workshop in Bordeaux and influenced by wrought-iron designer Edgar Brandt; designed/produced firedogs, tables, consoles, radiator covers, staircases, banisters, and grilles for clients in Bordeaux.
Bibliography Pierre Kjellberg, *Art déco: les maîtres du mobilier, le décor des paquebots*, Paris: Amateur, 1986/1990.

Perzel, Jean (1892–1986)

Austrian designer; born Bruck; active Munich and Paris.

Biography At a young age, Perzel painted on glass and became a stained-glass artist in Munich; from 1919, worked in several workshops in Paris, including Jacques Gruber's; realized that the current forms of electrical lighting were merely electrified interpretations of the oil lamp or the candlestick. He first produced lamps with shades in the technique of Romanesque church windows; 1923, set up his own workshop Jean Perzel Luminaires at 3, rue de la Cité Universitaire, Paris, where his lighting incorporated metal supports and reflectors with clear, opaque, American, and tinted glass, sometimes with rough edges; became one of the first to study the lighting of grand interior spaces such as those found in oceanliners of the time, the Palace of the League of Nations in Geneva, the cathedral in Luxembourg, and the train station in Mulhouse. He designed lighting for the Henry Ford house in Detroit, US, the Savoy hotel in London, and residences in Bangkok, and the palace of the Maharaja of Indore in India. His aim

Jean Perzel. Table lamp. 1930s. Glass, brass, and paint, h. 29¾" (75.5 cm). Mfr.: the designer, France. Courtesy Quittenbaum Kunstauktionen, Munich.

in domestic lighting was to create surfaces that diffused both evenly and efficiently. Thus, he developed a frosted (or sandblasted) inner glass surface that was enamel-painted to modify its opacity. He also used beige- and pink-tinted enamels and nickel-plated or lacquered mountings. Though his lamp range was limited, he concentrated his mass production on a few models, including table lamps, chandeliers, ceiling lights, columns, ceiling dalles, and illuminated tables. Decorators Maurice Jallot and Lucien Rollin, the Tétard brothers, architect Michel Roux-Spitz, and others commissioned Perzel to design lighting for their décors. 1933, Perzel passed his knowledge on to his nephew François, who became director of the workshop in 1951. François in turn passed on the business to his son Olivier in 1981, and the firm continues today.
Exhibitions/citations Work was included in editions of Salon d'Automne from 1924, Salons of Société des Artistes Décorateurs from 1926–39, and the Société Nationale des Beaux-Arts, including a number of international exhibitions. 1926 Salon des Artistes Décorateurs (famous Drops of Water in Roux-Spitz's Central Rotunda). Lighting was included in 1930s Salons de la Lumière; 1925 *Exposition Internationale des Arts Décoratifs et Industriels Modernes*; both Paris. Received numerous citations, including being elected to the Légion d'Honneur in 1937.
Bibliography *Lux*, Dec. 1928: 174, Sept. 1929: 119, June–Aug. 1930: 108, Sept. 1931: 101, Dec. 1934: 150. Alastair Duncan, *Art Nouveau and Art Déco Lighting*, New York: Simon & Schuster, 1978. Pierre Cabanne, *Encyclopédie art déco*, Paris: Somogy, 1986.

Pesce, Gaetano (1939–)

Italian architect, designer, and sculptor; born La Spezia; active Padova, Venice, Paris, and New York.

Training 1958, Istituto Universitario di Architettura, Venice; 1959–65, Instituto Superiore del Disegno Industriale, Venice.
Biography Pesce opened an office in Padova, where, 1959, he became a founding member, Gruppo N; experimented in programmed art and collaborated with the Zero group in Germany, Groupe de Recherche d'Art Visuel in Paris (at this time known as Motus), Paris, and Gruppo T in Milan. 1961, he was active at Hochschule für Gestaltung, Ulm; 1962, began to design and, 1964, to explore plastics and, 1968, to design furniture. 1964, he began to exhibit his works, followed by *Primo Manifesto per un'Architettura Elastica* (first manifesto for an elastic architecture) at the 1965 Society in Architecture conference in Jyvaskyla, Finland. He rejected the smooth contours of early 1960s Italian design in favor of the charac-

Trude Petri-Rabin. Urbino dinnerware (part of a service). 1930–32. Glazed porcelain sugar bowl and cover h. 4" (10.2 cm) x dia. 3" (7.6 cm), coffee cup h. 1 3/4" (4.4 cm) x dia. 4" (10.2 cm), saucer dia. 6 1/8" (15.6 cm), teapot and cover h. 7" (17.8 cm) x dia. 4" (10.2 cm), creamer h. 3" (7.6 cm) x dia. 2 3/4" (7 cm). Mfr.: Staatliche Porzellan-Manufaktur (KPM), Germany. Gift of Frasers. MoMA.

teristics of Pop Art and the kinetic and conceptual-design movements. His first work in plastics was the innovative 1969 UP series by B&B Italia (including doughnut-shaped UP 1 armchair and UP 7 giant foot, and UP 5 and 6 reissued in 2000); was a participant in the Anti-Design movement with Ugo La Pietra and active in avant-garde design groups, including Gruppo Strum and UFO. His work in fine art, audio-visual presentations, architecture, and design was realized through kinetic objects, multiples, and serigraphs. He explored what he saw as an alienation between people and objects in consumer culture; used distortion and exaggeration to draw attention to this; among other manifestations, created nihilistic pieces of 'decaying' design. His design work has included 1971–72 Reconstruction of an Underground City and a Habitat for Two People in an Age of Great Contaminations, 1972–73 Golgotha Suite, 1975 Sit Down armchairs (that used polyester innovatively), 1980 Sansone tables and Dalila Uno, Due, and Tre armchairs, all by Cassina; 1983 Suite of Nine Pratt Chairs; 1986–89 thermo-formed bottle for Vittel water; 1986–88 Unequal Suite of tables; and 1986 Airport, Square, and Bastone lamps. His 1986 Feltri chair by Cassina in thick, cheap, recyclable felt and a quilted fabric brought him close to his goal of creating individualistic and expressive forms of architecture/furniture. His approach remained unorthodox for 1980 Tramonto a New York (Manhattan Sunrise) seating by Cassina, in which an upholstered 'sun' rose over foam cushions in a weave suggesting buildings. Other work includes 1985–86 interior of photographer/collector Marc-André Hubin on the avenue Foch, Paris; 1990 Organic Building, Osaka, Japan; 1992 543 Broadway side chairs by Bernini; 1995 Spaghetti (in the Fish collection) and 1998–99 Baby Crosby (in the Open Sky collection) by Pesce Ltd. and in resin; 1997 chandelier, Musée des Beaux-Arts, Lille; 1999 *Warhol, a Factory* exhibition, Guggenheim Museum, Bilbao; 1998 house in Salvador de Bahia, Brazil; 1999 limited-editon works by De Padova; 2002 resin furniture by Zerodisegno; 2003 Smorfia chair; a number of others. He has taught architecture, Istituto Universitario di Architettura, Venice, and Pratt Institute, Brooklyn, N.Y.; 1987, was a visiting professor, Faculdade de Arquitetura e Urbanismo, Universidade de São Paulo (FAU-USP), Brazil; from late 1970s, École d'Architecture, Strasbourg, influencing a new generation of designers. He established two New York firms to produce/market his products: Fish Design and Open Sky.
Exhibitions Late 1950s, art shown in galleries in various Italian cities. Design work shown extensively worldwide, including 1972 *The New Domestic Landscape*, The Museum of Modern Art, New York (catalog below). Subject of exhibitions in Italy and other countries; Yale University, New Haven, Conn., the US; 1965, Hochschule für Gestaltung, Ulm; 1965 exhibition, Finnish Design Center, Helsinki; in Paris in 1975 (catalog below); Musée des Arts Décoratifs, Montreal, in 1984; Musée d'Art Moderne, Strasbourg, in 1986; Peter Joseph Gallery, New York, in 1991; Centre Georges Pompidou, Paris, in 1996 (catalog below).
Bibliography Cat., *Modern Chairs 1918–1970*, London: Lund Humphries, 1971. Cat., Emilio Ambasz (ed.), *Italy: The New Domestic Landscape*, New York: The Museum of Modern Art, 1972. Cat., Gaetano Pesce, *Le futur est peut-être passé*, Paris: Musée des Arts Décoratifs, 1975. France Vanlaethem, *Gaetano Pesce: Architecture, Design, Art*, Milan: Rizzoli, 1989. Cat., *Gaetano Pesce*, Tel Aviv: Tel Aviv Museum of Art; New York: Peter Joseph Gallery, 1991. Cat., *Gaetano Pesce: le temps des questions*, Paris: Pompidou, 1996. Mel Byars, *50 Products: Innovations in Design and Materials*, Hove: RotoVision, 1999. Mel Byars with Arlette Barré-Despond, *100 Designs/100 Years: A Celebration of the 20th Century*, Hove: RotoVision, 1999: 162–63.

Peteranderl, Angelika (1958–)

German industrial designer; born Munich.

Training 1979–83, industrial design, Fachhochschule, Munich, and at BMW and Siemens.
Biography 1983–84, she was an independent designer of medical and engineering apparatus and instruments; from 1985, worked as a designer in the communication and information systems group of Siemens in Munich, for which she designed 1985 Mobida 4 portable personal computer, 1985–86 MX 500 and 1987 MX 300 multi-user computers, and 1987 7.500 department computer.
Citations 1978 and 1989 Industrie Forum Design (iF), Hanover.
Bibliography Cat., Design Center Stuttgart, *Women in Design: Careers and Life Histories Since 1900*, Stuttgart: Haus der Wirtschaft, 1989: 142–45.

Petersen, Arne (1922–)

Danish metalworker.

Biography Petersen learned techniques of silver and goldsmithing at the firm C.C. Herman in Copenhagen; 1948, joined the Georg Jensen Sølvsmedie, working in its hollow-ware department from 1976. His best-know design is Jensen's 1975 bottle opener in stainless steel soldered with brass.
Exhibitions Work included in exhibitions in Washington 1980 and touring, and in Philadelphia 1983 (catalogs below).
Bibliography Cat., *Georg Jensen Silversmithy: 77 Artists, 75 Years*, Washington: Smithsonian, 1980. Cat., Kathryn B. Hiesinger and George H. Marcus III (eds.), *Design Since 1945*, Philadelphia: Philadelphia Museum of Art, 1983.

Petillo, Aldo (1939–)

Italian designer; born Rome.

Training 1958–60, engineering and 1960–63, achitecture, Università degli Studi 'La Sapienza,' Rome; 1980, master's degree in strategic design, London.
Biography From 1973, Petillo lived in the UK and West and Southern Africa, particularly Mozambique; 1980 with his wife Lorena Eliana, established MCA & Partners studio in Milan, for strategic design (products, exhibitions, events, and public spaces) and product development, supervising all engineering phases; 1987, created the brand 'Metals,' for which he was the artistic director from 1987–90. Design work has included 1986 MTM 600cc motorcycle by Eduro, 1991 and 2002 furniture by Malofancon (and artistic director), 1992 new coatings on architectural glass by Pittsburgh Plate Glass (PPG) and for Eckart-Werke; 1993 colors and graphics for the Vespa 50cc motorbike by Piaggio,

1994 colors and materials for office furniture by Marcatre, 1995 computer keyboard by Korg, 1996–2001 color forecast plan for Mandarina Duck, 1997 color plan and graphics for Daelim, 1998 new plastic for Montell, 1999 new-car forecast for Lancia, 2000 trends and color forecast for Fila, 2001 handbag by Moncler, 2002 new-car concept for Fiat, 2002 corporate image of Seibu Bank.
Citations 1998 (with Andrea Dichara) award (for IS40 interactive music workstation by Korg Italy), Industrie Forum Design (iF), Hanover.
Bibliography *Domus*, no. 794, June 1997. *Design Report*, no. 10. *Ottagono*, no. 112, Sept.–Nov. 1994. *Gap Casa*, no. 88. *Interni*, no. 431. Cat., Andrea Branzi (ed.), *Italia-Giappone: design come stile di vita/10 paesaggi italiani*, Kobe: Nihon Keizai Shimbun, 2001.

Petit, Philippe (1900–1945)

French painter, decorator, and furniture designer; active Paris.

Training École Bernard-Palissy, Paris.
Biography Petit worked first at the Primavera design studio of Au Printemps department store in Paris with Louis Sognot and Marcel Guillemard. 1924–31, he worked at Décoration Intérieure Moderne (D.I.M.), replacing D.I.M. partner Georges Mouveau and collaborating with the remaining partner René Joubert. Joubert et Petit executed numerous commissions for interior schemes and furniture models and designed furniture, both together and individually, produced in the firm's own workshop.
Exhibitions On the pont Alexandre-III (D.I.M.'s stand) and Une Ambassade Française pavilion (dining room with Joubert), 1925 *Exposition Internationale des Arts Décoratifs et Industriels Modernes*. Work shown at editions of Salon d'Automne; Salons of Société des Artistes Décorateurs (with Joubert) from 1926; 1937 *Exposition Internationale des Arts et Techniques dans la Vie Moderne* (furniture with Joubert by Degorre). All Paris.
Bibliography Cat., *Decorative Arts 1925 Style*, New York: Didier Aaron, 1979. Victor Arwas, *Art Déco*, New York: Abrams, 1980. Pierre Kjellberg, *Art déco: les maîtres du mobilier, le décor des paquebots*, Paris: Amateur, 1986/1990.
> See D.I.M.

Petit, Pierre-Étienne (1900–1969)

French painter, architect, decorator, and furniture designer.

Training 1914–18, cabinetmaking, École Boulle, Paris.
Biography Petit worked initially at Siègel, a mannequin and store-design firm; 1924–27, was a decorator and designer of furniture, lighting, and grillework; 1928, set up his own workshop and, from 1930, collaborated with prominent painters, sculptors, glassware designers, and ceramicists; from 1935, was active as an architect of townhouses, vacation houses, and stores, including site-specific furniture, décor, and rugs in geometric motifs.
Exhibitions 1928 Salon d'Automne (dining room based on Cubist forms); Salon of Société des Artistes Décorateurs from 1927.
Bibliography *Ensembles mobiliers*, vol. 2, Paris: Charles Moreau, 1937. Pierre Kjellberg, *Art déco: les maîtres du mobilier, le décor des paquebots*, Paris: Amateur, 1986/1990.

Petri-Rabin, Trude (b. Trude Petri 1906–1989)

German ceramicist; born Hamburg; active Germany and the US.

Training From 1927, porcelain, Vereinigte Staatsschulen für freie und angewandte Kunst, Berlin, and Staatliche Porzellan-Manufaktur, Berlin.
Biography Like Marguerite Friedländer-Wildenhain, Petri produced entirely unornamented objects; called on a high glaze on porcelain to create pieces suggesting industrial production; with Friedländer-Wildenhain, produced 1930 porcelain designs for Staatliche Porzellan-Manufaktur, Berlin, where she was employed 1925–33. Her 1930–32 Urbino dinner service (figurative works by Ludwig Gies) by Staatliche Porzellan-Manufaktur (KPM) showed Bauhaus and Deutscher Werkbund influences; the service included a plate with a base to replace the traditional flat-rimmed plate. 1931, Petri added concentric gilded rings to Marguerite Friedländer's 1930 Halle dinner service by KPM; to 1938, designed vases, ashtrays, and chandeliers by KPM; also designed 1938 Arkadisches Service with unglazed medallions decorated by sculptor Sigmund Schütz and in a pattern suggested by Deutscher Werkbund member Günther von Pechmann, director of KPM from 1929 and dismissed for political reasons in 1938. Other designs by KPM included 1931 Neu-Berlin and 1947–48 Urbino Oval porcelain dinner services and, by Arzberg, 1985 City service. 1950, she moved to Chicago but continued to work for KPM, producing bar bottles in white and celadon porcelain; 1950 vases, ashtrays, and Igel (hedgehog) salt and pepper; 1953 vases and Urbino salad service; and 1966 porcelain chess set. Her best known design is the eponymous petri dish for bacterial-culture formations, which has become standard and anonymous in professional science laboratories.
Exhibitions/citations Work included in 1988 exhibition, New York (catalog below). Gold medal (for 1930 Urbino covered bowl in the Urbino service), 1937 *Exposition Internationale des Arts et Techniques dans la Vie Moderne*, Paris; an award (for white and celadon bar bottles), 1954 (10th) Triennale di Milano.
Bibliography Erich Köllmann, *Berliner Porzellan: Ein Brevier*, Brunswick: Klinghardt & Biermann, 1958, 1963. Barbara Mundt, *40 Jahr Porzellan: Siegmund Schütz zum 80, Geburtstag*, Berlin: Arenhövel, 1986. Margarete Jarchow, *Berliner Porzellan im 20. Jahrhundert*, Berlin: Reimer, 1988. Cat., *The Bauhaus: Masters and Students*, New York: Barry Friedman, 1988. Cat., Design Center Stuttgart, *Women in Design: Careers and Life Histories Since 1900*, Stuttgart: Haus der Wirtschaft, 1989.

Pettersen, Sverre (1884–1959)

Norwegian glassware and industrial designer.

Training At what is now called Statens Håndverks -og Kunstindustriskole, Kristiania (now Oslo).
Biography 1928, Pettersen became chief designer, Glasmagasinet; late 1920s, designed pressed glass by Høvik Glass; from 1926, worked at Hadelands Glasverk, where he was the artistic director from 1928–49; from c. 1930, was director, Statens Håndverks -og Kunstindustriskole and was active in the design of ceramics, textiles, and books; from 1947, was head of the design office, Christiana Glasmagazin.
Exhibitions Work shown in 1982 exhibition, New York (catalog below).
Bibliography Cat., David Revere McFadden (ed.), *Scandinavian Modern Design 1880–1980*, New York: Abrams, 1982. Fredrik Wildhagen, *Norge i Form*, Oslo: Stenersen, 1988: 86. Jennifer Hawkins Opie, *Scandinavia: Ceramics and Glass in the Twentieth Century*, New York: Rizzoli, 1989: 167.

Petterson, John Pontus (1884–1949)

Norwegian metalworker; active New York and Chicago.

Training Silversmithing, Statens Håndverks -og Kunstindustriskole, Kristiania (now Oslo).
Biography 1905–11, Petterson worked for Tiffany in New York; 1911, settled in Chicago, where he worked for Robert Jarvie for some years; c. 1912, founded The Petterson Studio, a home workshop at 5618 S. Homan Ave., Chicago, producing only hand-raised silver, as in the Kalo and Jarvie Shops.
Bibliography Sharon S. Darling with Gail Farr Casterline, *Chicago Metalsmiths*, Chicago Historical Society, 1977. Annelies Krekel-Aalberse, *Art Nouveau and Art Déco Silver*, New York: Abrams, 1989.

Pettersson, Lars (1969–)

Swedish designer; born and active Stockholm.

Training 1994–99, master's degree, Konstfack, Stockholm; 1997, Taideteollinen korkeakoulu, Helsinki; 1998, architecture, Kungl Tekniska Högskolan (KTH), Stockholm.
Biography 1998, Pettersson established his own furniture- and interior-design office and, 1998–2000: designed the interiors of Nyréns architecture office in Stockholm and of the Kungl Tekniska Högskolan (on the campus in Haninge); thermometer by Ericsson; Bo 01 in Malmö; restoration of Naturhistoriska Riksmuseet in Stockholm. Other subsequent work: 2001 Felengaki appartment on Östermalm, Stockholm; 2001 exhibition design of LAR, Arkitekturmuseet, Stockholm; 2000 catwalk and exhibition design, Anders Beckman School of Design, Stockholm, and Centre Culturel Suédois, Paris; 2000 office-table (with Morgan Rudberg) for public-relations office Prime, Stockholm; 1997–2001 furniture by Proventus Design, Snowcrash, Artek, David Design, Nola Industrier, Söderbergs Möbler, and Horreds Möbler.
Exhibitions/citations Work included in various venues and fairs. From 1995, a number of awards and scholarships.

Pétursdóttir, Katrín (1967–)

Icelandic designer.

Training 1989-95, Ecole Supérieure de Design Industriel (ESDI), Paris.
Biography 1995, Pétursdóttir worked on cosmetics advertising at

Estée Lauder, Paris; from 1996, on products by Alessi, in the studio of Philippe Starck, Paris; 1997, on products by Italian manufacturers, in the studio of Ross Lovegrove, London. 1998–99, Pétursdóttir developed a welded-PVC range of clothing by 66oN and other products; 1998, moved with British designer Michael Young (having met him the year prior) to Iceland to set up their MY Studio Ltd. and also established jewelry company S.M.A.K. there. 1999, she established Young&Beautiful, a department within MY Studio, and developed tumblers for milk by Ritzenhoff, calendars, soap, and posters; 1999, began drawing illustrations for magazine *Casa Brutus* and for Escalator Records, both in Japan; designed 2000 stage set of a television program for Sjadu (produced by Pluton Productions) and 2000 graphics image and campaign for Astro nightclub, Reykjavik.
> See Young, Michael.

Pevsner, Nikolaus Bernhard (1902–1983)

German art historian and critic; active Britain.

Biography Pevsner began his career at Universität Göttingen; 1935, settled in Britain and lectured at Oxford, Cambridge, and London Universities. 1929, Gordon Russell opened a shop in Wigmore Street, London, where Pevsner was the manager and, until 1939, a buyer. His affection for the ideals of the European modern movement colored his writings and ideas, but he nevertheless became an influential writer on modern architecture and design; 1960s, was among the first to realize that an expressive, non-Rational, non-autocratic approach to architecture was emerging, which consciously rejected the tenets of modernism. He has become best known for his books *Pioneers of the Modern Movement from William Morris to Walter Gropius* (London: Faber & Faber, 1936), reprinted as the partially revised and rewritten *Pioneers of Modern Design: From William Morris to Walter Gropius* (Harmondsworth: Penguin, 1960), and the portable guides known as *The Buildings of England* (Harmondsworth: Penguin, 1951–74). Concerning the latter, Pevsner wrote 32 of the guides himself and ten with others, and four were written by others—46 in total. Other works: *An Enquiry into Industrial Art in England* (Cambridge: Cambridge University, 1937), *The Sources of Modern Architecture and Design* (London: Thames & Hudson, 1968), and *Studies in Art, Architecture and Design* (London: Thames & Hudson, 1968).
Bibliography Michela Rosso, *La storia utile: patrimonio e modernità nel lavoro di John Summerson e Nikolaus Pevsner: Londra 1928–1955*, Torin: Comunità, 2001.

Pewabic Pottery
> See Perry, Mary Chase.

Peyricot, Olivier (1969–)

French designer.

Training 1989–94, Ecole Supérieure de Design Industriel (ESDI), Paris.
Biography 1991, Peyricot began as a professional designer; 1996, founded IDs design studio, Paris; is creative director, IDSland studio (founded in 2000 with Sylvie Chanchus), for products in a Paris office and graphics in Toulouse and currently with Cédric Scandella and Ned Baldessin. Work includes 1995 bookcase/seat, divan, two tables, small table, roller unit by Néotù; 1996 Panorama hanging plastic screen and 1996 Perso wall-mounted toothbrush holder by Axis; 1999 double-sided glass vase by Ad Hoc; CD holder by Ycami; temporary boutique (with Scandella) of Mandarina Duck, London; and 2002 Body Props by Edra. By Glassex: 1997 Fusion sofa by Arsenal, 1999 Bilding vertical sofa, Saturne circular seat (in shape of a swimming pool), Scream sofa with floors, and Nétanone chair. Peyricot taught at ESDI, Paris, 1993–95; École Nationale Superieure des Arts Décoratifs (ENSAD), Limoges, 1998–99; ENSCI (Les Ateliers), Paris, 1999–2000; École Camondo, Paris, 2000–01; École Superieure d'Art et de Design (ESAD), Reims, from 2001.
Citations 2003 Carte Blanche production support (for Doison Mobile /Coison Souple), VIA (French furniture association).
Bibliography Mel Byars, *50 Products...*, Hove: RotoVision, 1998. Anne Bonny, *Les années 90*, Paris: Regard, 2000. www.via.asso.fr

Pezdirc, Vladimir (1950–)

Slovene designer; born Ljubljana.

Training 1969–74, Istituto Statale d'Arte, Venice.
Biography 1974–78, Pezdirc worked as a designer at the LTH Škofja Loka, refrigerator manufacturer; 1978, established his own studio,

Roberto Pezzetta and Zanussi Industrial Design Center. Zoe washing machine. 1996. Various materials, h. 33 1/2 x w. 23 5/8 x d. 21 5/8" (85 x 60 x 55 cm). Mfr.: Electrolux Zanussi, Italy.

Kvadrat Design (not associated with the Danish fabric house). Work has included 1977 solar cooker, 1977 bactericide lamp, 1977–79 backpack and tent by Prevent, and 1982 automated crutch for the disabled by Soša.

Pezzetta, Roberto (1946–)

Italian industrial designer; born Treviso.

Biography 1969–74, Pezetta worked in the industrial-design department of Zoppas Elettrodomestici; except for a short stint at Nordica from 1974, has worked at the household appliance firm Zanussi, becoming head of the industrial-design department in 1982; designed 1987 Wizard Collection refrigerator. Though inventive, widely published, and favorably received by the design world, the refrigerator was not favored by customers. However, his and the Zanussi design staff's recent, successful, and technologically advanced inventory has included 1996 Zoe and 1999–2000 IZ washing machines and, 1994–98 Oz refrigerator. The more advanced designs have been labeled a new 'species' of domestic appliance, breaking from, for example, a refrigerator as a clinical white box. 1993, he became director of design of Electrolux European Management Design. (Swedish manufacturer Electrolux bought Zanussi in 1984.) Pezzetta's products for others have included a wall clock by Wikidue, the Giubileo lamp by Slamp, and the Etty scale by Guzzini.
Citations Most with the Zanussi design staff. Premio Compasso d'Oro: 1987 (Wizard Collection refrigerators), 1989 (three citations), 1991 (Matura 9140 washing machine with Zanussi design staff), 1998 (Soft Tech stove with Zanussi design staff). Chicago Athenaeum: 1999 (two citations), 2000 (IZ washing machine), and 2002 Good Design award (Oz refrigerator). Gold medals at industrial design events in the Netherlands and at BIO industrial-design biennials, Ljubljana.
Bibliography *Issue 2*, London: Design Museum, 1989. Albrecht Bangert and Karl Michael Armer, *80s Style: Designs of the Decade*, New York: Abbeville, 1990. Mel Byars, *On/Off: New Electronic Products*, New York: Universe, 2001.

Pezzini, Gabriele (1963–)

Italian industrial designer; born Charleroi.

Training 1977–82, photography, State Art Institute, Ascoli Piceno; 1984–90, industrial design, Istituto Superiore per le Industrie Artistiche (ISIA), Florence.

Biography 1988–90, Pezzini worked as a freelance designer for Bitre in Pistoia; 1991–93, senior product designer at Allibert in Grenoble; 1993, opened his own design studio, while remaining a consultant to Allibert to 1993 and to other clients; 1996–97, design manager/consultant, Allibert/Evolutif; 1999, moved his studio to Milan. Other clients have included, from 2000, Guzzini and, from 2001, Area Plus, do create, and aedo-to.com Website (in charge of column 'New Materials'). 2001, he founded and managed virtuallydesign.com; has participated in research projects for several organizations; 1990–93, cofounded Made gallery in Florence; 1994–96, created the brand Nobody Productions. 1988–90, he was professor of jewelry design, Scuola Arti Orafe, Florence. Visiting professor: 1993–94, ISIA, Florence; 1997, Industrial-Design Department, Facoltà di Architettura, Università degli Studi, Genoa; 2000, Bratislava University; 2000, industrial-design department, Politecnico, Milan; 2001, Rhode Island School of Design, Providence, R.I., US. 2001–02, he was a tutor in design history, industrial-design department, Facoltà di Architettura: Università degli Studi, Genoa, and Università degli Studi di Camerino, Ascoli Piceno. Work has included 1992 Eye bathroom basket by Allibert; 1994 Eolo coat hanger by Zeritalia; 1995 Europa chair, 1996 World contract seating, 1997 Brazil garden furniture by Allibert/Evolutif; 1998 Spider ski sunglasses by Decathlon; 1999 Arm-fon professional hair dryer by Wella Italia; 2000 Frame table by Edizioni Eusebi; 2001 Space Low table by Sica; 2001 Compact bathroom accessory and Drawer bathroom stool, 2001 Handle tray, and 2002 Building moving ladder by Virtuallydesign.com; 2001 Water Pot bathroom taps by Krover; 2002 Lite chair by Ifuoricasa; 2002 Match Radio portable radio by Area Plus.
Exhibitions Work shown at 1998 Biennale Internationale du Design, Saint Étienne, France; 2000 *Nuove Trame*, Pitti Casa, Florence.
Bibliography Mel Byars, *On/Off: New Electronic Products*, New York: Universe, 2001. Mel Byars, *Design in Steel*, London: Laurence King, 2002.

Pfeifer, Herbert (1946–)

German industrial designer; born near Altensteig.

Training Design, Fachhochschule für Gestaltung, Schwäebisch-Gmünd.
Biography 1976, Pfeifer began working at Esslinger Design (known as frogdesign from 1983) in Altensteig, Germany, serving clients such as AEG, Hansgrohe, Louis Vuitton, and Wega; 1984, transferred to Esslinger's frogdesign branch in California, becoming the vice-president of design and the general manager to 1990. The studio's clients were 3M, Alessi, General Electric, Kimberly Clark, Logitech, and Sun Microsytems. He was particularly active in developing products by Apple Computer. Pfeifer left frogdesign and, 1990 cofounded with Paul Montgomery (also formerly of frogdesign) the Montgomery Pfeifer design studio, San Francisco, provide corporate-identity, industrial-design, and interactive-design services.
Bibliography Paul Kunkel, *Apple Design: The World of the Apple Industrial Design Group*, New York: Graphis, 1997.
> See Montgomery, Paul.

Pfister, Charles (1939–1990)

American interior and furniture designer and architect; active San Francisco.

Training Architecture and design, University of California at Berkeley.
Biography 1965–81, Pfister was a designer of corporate interiors in the San Francisco branch of architects Skidmore, Owings and Merrill, where he became active in mass-production design and was an associate partner and the director of the interior-design department. He was known for interiors of elegant simplicity. 1981 with James Leal and Pamela Babey, he established Charles Pfister Associates in San Francisco, where the extensive list of clients included Deutsche Bank in Frankfurt and Citicorp in the US. He created the interiors of 21 Club restaurant, New York; Square One restaurant, San Francisco; Grand Hotel, Washington; Shell central headquarters, The Hague; United Overseas Bank, Singapore; and a hotel in a 13th-century monastery in Milan. He designed rugs for V'Soske, seating for Metropolitan and Bernhardt, and lighting for Boyd and Casella. His office furniture and accessories for Knoll included the 1975 range of clear glass ashtrays and bowls produced by Vistosi in Murano. His 40-piece 1990 Premier Collection of residential furniture produced by Baker was said by him to owe its design to a variety of sources, including the work of Terence Robsjohn-Gibbings (to whom the range was dedicated), 19th-century Russia, 18th-century Sweden, and 'steamship moderne.' He also designed case goods, seating, and tables by Baker Executive Office. 1988, the firm was renamed The Pfister Partnership, with offices in San Francisco and London. He died from Aids.
Bibliography Carolyn Englefield (ed.), *House & Garden*, July 1990: 124–31, 136. Lois Wagner Green, *Elle Decor*, Sept.1990: 172. 'Celebrating Design Innovation,' *Designers West*, Apr. 1991: 30.

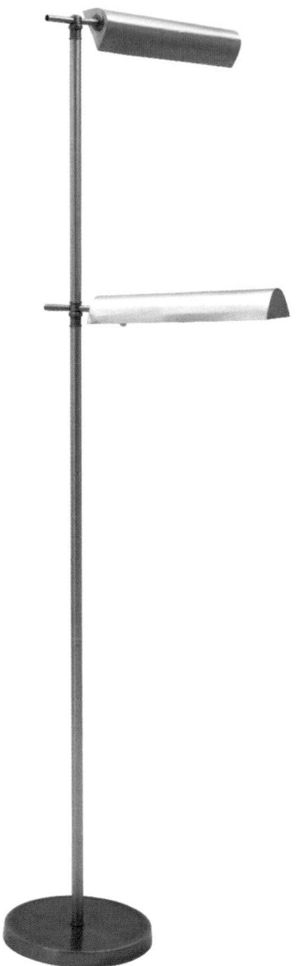

Peter Pfisterer. Floor lamp. c. 1935. Metal, h. 67" (170.2 cm). Mfr.: Mutual Sunset Lamp Mfg. Co., US (1941). Purchase Fund. MoMA.

Pfisterer, Peter (1907–)

Swiss designer.

Training Architecture, Vienna.
Biography After architecture studies, Pfristerer worked in Switzerland and France; 1933, immigrated to the US; 1933–40, worked with modern architect Richard Neutra; was greatly influenced by Neutra's stark angularity, exemplified by Pfisterer's geometry; has become especially known for a certain table lamp of c. 1935, though little is known of its history.

Pfohl, Karl (1826–1894)

Bohemian glass engraver; active Bohemia, Germany, and France.

Biography After activities in Haida (now Nový Bor, Czech Republic), he worked in Wiesbaden, Nassau (before its 1866 annexation by Prussia), and, ultimately, in his brother's workshop in Steinschönau (now Kamenický Šenov, Czech Republic). The workshop became known for engraved red and blue cased-glass vessels. Pfohl was also active in Paris for two periods—1858–64 and 1866–72; engraved hunting scenes and large compositions featuring historical and mythological themes after images by Flemish Old Master painters, such as Peter Paul Rubens, and also of Guido Reni and Bartolomé Esteban Murillo. A number of North Bohemian engravers subsequently continued Pfohl's style.

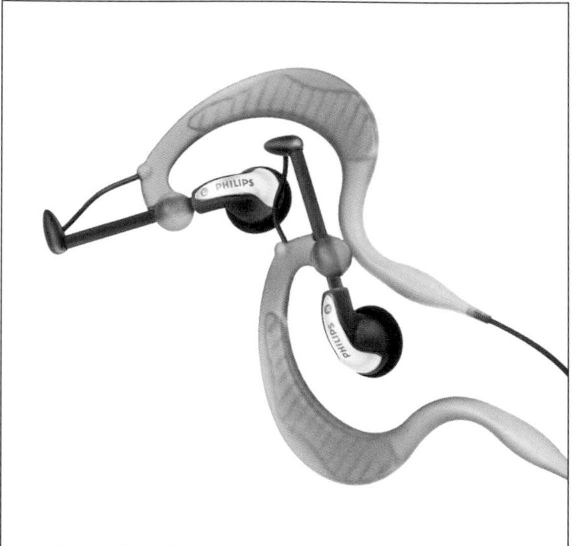

Philips in-house design. Outdoor sports earphones (no. HS 700). c. 2000. Plastics, h. 4 x w. 2 x l. 1/2" (4 x 5 x 1.5 cm). Mfr.: Philips Electronics, the Netherlands.

Bibliography John Fleming and Hugh Honor, *Dictionary of the Decorative Arts*, London: Penguin, 1989: 629.

Philco

American electronics firm; located Philadelphia.

History 1892, Philco was founded in Philadelphia; 1929, called on assembly-line techniques and produced the first truly low-priced radios; became a leading manufacturer of audio products, adding domestic stoves, refrigerators, air conditioners, and other appliances to its line; 1950s, produced a series of TV set housings in historicist cabinets but with technologically advanced features and large screens. An exception, the Predicta range of floor and table models had screens that swivelled on blonde-wood bases; the screen of the portable version could be moved about a room, while the chassis remained stationary. The Predicta was introduced to the American public on Sept. 1958 Miss America TV show/contest, sponsored by Philco. 1954–60, Herbert V. Gosweiler (1915–1991) was the manager of the product-design group and a promoter of a futuristic TV design with the appearance of being part of the wall. Severin Jonassen (1913–) designed 1958 Holiday 21-inch tabletop version. Catherine Winkler (1906–1989), a German emigrant to the US, designed 1959 'gas pump' (or 'barber-pole' or 'cyclops') version (no. 4654). And the name of Richard Whipple (1916–1964) appears on the patent for both. (Winkler may have also designed the Old Spice men's-cologne sailing-ship logo.) The Predicta has been chosen as the trademark TV of the MZTV (Museum of Television), Toronto.
Exhibitions Work included in 1983–84 exhibition, Philadelphia (catalog below).
Bibliography '15 Years of Industrial Design,' *Industrial Design*, vol. 16, Apr. 1969: 50. Cat., Kathryn B. Hiesinger and George H. Marcus III (eds.), *Design Since 1945*, Philadelphia: Philadelphia Museum of Art, 1983. *Old Timer's Bulletin* (Antique Wireless Association), May 1994. *Echoes Report*, Summer 1996.
> See Montagni, Berizzi, Butte, Architetti.

Philippon, Antoine (1930–1995); Jacqueline Lecoq (1932–)

French designers.

Training Philippon: École Boulle, Paris. Lecoq: École Nationale Superieure des Arts Décoratifs, Paris.
Biography Philippon worked for a time with Marcel Gascoin, who had a profound effect on his work. And Lecoq spent several months there. 1954, they set up their own studio and designed furniture for offices and stores in France, Germany, and Austria. Their austere furniture in cubical volumes included a 1958 hanging cabinet by Bofinger, a similar 1962 white lacquered credenza by Behr, and furniture by Airborne. An example of their rigorously simple forms is the 1958 60 chair. Their exhibition stands included those for Behr.
Bibliography Yolande Amic, *Intérieurs: le mobilier français, 1945–1964*, Paris: Regard/VIA, 1983: 106–09. Patrick Favardin, *Les décorateurs des années 50*, Paris: Norma, 2002: 264.

Philips (aka Royal Philips Electronics)

Dutch electrical appliance manufacturer; located Eindhoven.

History 1891, Gerard and Anton Philips founded the Philips firm in Eindhoven, where an initial staff of ten produced light bulbs. 1919, its first subsidiary was established in Brussels. Radio valves were manufactured from 1918 and, by 1924, other radio components were added to its range, marking the beginning of the collaboration between NSF (Nederlandsche Seintoestellen Fabriek) and Philips; the former designed and made the rectifiers for Philips light bulbs. Philips-NSF's earliest designer was probably H.A. van Anrooy in the early 1920s. From 1925, Louis Kalff (1897–1976) was the artistic director of advertising. The 1925 Queen's Set radio cabinet that NSF presented to Princess Juliana was designed by architect W.M. Dudok. 1930, Willem Penaat was commissioned as a designer, while he working for Metz. Philips poster artists included Th. W. Nieuwenhuis for light bulbs, 1918, and A.M. Cassandre for radios, 1930s. The firm's first appliance was a tea warmer; 1927, its first radio sets appeared. Philips did not itself manufacture all of its products; at first, NSF designed and made the radio cabinets with Philips components. 1947, NSF was amalgated into Philips. Other workshops also made furniture cabinets for Philips. 1926, Bakelite was first supplied by Ebena and was later replaced by Philips's own 'Philite.' Its notable radio designs have included 1931 932-A in Bakelite-impregnated paper printed in a wood pattern, 1932 730-A in wood with push buttons, 1937 461A (Overture) in all-black Bakelite, and 1938 752-A in wood and Bakelite. From 1938, Louis Kalff was the artistic director (best-known his design of a table lamp of c. 1955). The directors of Philips's Concern Industrial Design Centre (CIDC) have been Norwegian Knut Yran, its founder, from 1966–69, American Robert Blaich from 1980, Italian Stefano Marzano from 1991. Today, Philips Design operates within the Philips Electronics entity; is located in the Eindoven headquarters with branches in Europe, US, and Asia; comprises 500 professionals of more than 30 nationalities working in disciplines from design to the human sciences. 1998, Philips Design became an independent unit within Philips Group.
Exhibitions/citations Work subject of 1999 *La casa prossima futura = The Home of the Near Future*, Salone del Mobile, Milan, and Saks Fifth Avnue, New York (catalog below). Large number of awards, including 1995 Designprijs (to Jan Erik Baars, Caroline Brouwer, and Jan Paul van der Voet/Philips Corporate Design), Rotterdam; 1996 Kho Liang le Prize (for Philips Alessi household products), Netherlands; 2000 and 2001 awards, Industrie Forum Design (iF), Hanover; 2001 Red Dot award, Design Zentrum Nordrhein Westfalen, Essen; 2000 and 2001 (20 citations) Erkenningen Goed Industrieel Ontwerp (good industrial-design award), Association Designlink, Netherlands; 2001 Annual Design Review, *I.D.* magazine; 1999 2003 Red Dot award, Design Zentrum Nordrhein Westfalen, Essen.
Bibliography Barbie Campbell-Cole and Tim Benton (eds.), *Tubular Steel Furniture*, London: The Art Book Company, 1979: 30. John Heskett, *Philips: A Study of the Corporate Management of Design*, London: Trefoil, 1989. Stefano Marzano (preface), *Visions of the Future*, Eindhoven: Philips/Blaricum: V+K, 1996 and subsequent eds. Josephine Green (intro.), *La casa prossima futura*, Eindoven: Philips, 1999. Cat., www.design.philips.com.
> See NSF (Nederlandsche Seintoestellen Fabriek).

Piaggio; Vespa

Italian entrepreneurs; Rinaldo and Enrico: born Genoa.

Biography/history The first of the Piaggio family's enterprises was a woodworking shop in Sestri, which evolved into a workshop of artisanal cabinetmakers. 1884, Rinaldo Piaggio (1864–1938), at age 20, transformed the operation into the larger, more sophisticated endeavor Società Rinaldo Piaggio. When Rinaldo died and because there were no living female heirs, the firm's divisions were passed onto his sons Armando (1901–1978)—in Finale e Sestria—and Enrico (1905–1965)—in Pisa in 1917. Enrico moved the firm to Pontedera, near Genoa, in 1924 and where the only Piaggio operation is active today. During World War II, the factory built ships and soon after served the railway and aircraft industires, including constructing the streamline 1936 MC2 train (housed today in the Museo Piaggio in Pontedera). Also during World

War II, the firm expanded greatlly and, in addition to its formerly established activities, was building steamboats and oceanliners. 1945 at the end of the war, the firm was forced by the Allies to cease certain production, particularly of aircraft, and to pursue non-military activities. Thus, 1946, Piaggio began to manufacture scooters to serve a dire need for personal transportation in European urban areas; was assisted by investment funds from the US; hired well-known airplane/helicopter engineer Corradino D'Ascanio (Popoli, 1891–Pisa, 1981) to design its first scooter, the 1946 Paparino. (To 1914, D'Ascanio had studied mechanical engineering, Politecnico, Turin; after World War II and briefly, worked at the Innocenti plant but left to join Piaggio, at first on aircraft design.) The Piaggio scooter was based on a wrecked German example, used by paratroopers, that had been found in Italy. It became the prototype. However, the Paparino was not successful until a few design changes were made, when it was thus realized as the very popular Vespa (wasp). Its name purportedly came from Enrico's exclamation, 'Sembra una vespa!' (It looks like a wasp!). However, demand for scooters slowed at the end of 1950s. But the marriage of Enrico's daughter Antonella to Fiat heir Umberto Agnelli helped mutually to support both enterprises, especially Piaggo. Piaggo was able to outlast competitor Innocenti's Lambretta scooter due to Piaggio's foreign-manufacture agreements, particularly in Third World low-labor-cost countries such as India and Indonesia. 1961, Cushman Motors of the US sold imported Vespas under license, initially called the Cushman-Vespa, but it received resistance from dealers due to its foreign origin. Sears, Roebuck & Co. sold Vespas for a time through its stores and catalogs. When Innocenti stopped production of the Lambretta in 1971, Piaggio became more successful. Former licensees, such as Bajaj in India and PGO in Taiwan, continue today to produce classic Vespa copies; Piaggio litigation has been ineffective to stop their production. From late 1980s, Piaggio has manufactured scooters much like all others to fend off the threat by Far East production, while retaining the Vespa as more or less the same as the original model. By Vespa's 50th birthday, 15 million units had been sold worldwide—from the first 98cc Paparino in 1946 to more than 90 different models to date.
Exhibitions 1999 *Vespa: A Twentieth Century Design Icon*, The European Academy for the Arts & Accademia Italiana, London.
Bibliography Roberto Leardi, *Vespa: un miracolo italiano*, Rome: Alpi, 1996. Eric Brockway et al., *Vespa: An Illustrated History*, Newbury Park, Ca.: Haynes, 1998. Roberto Leardi, *Vespa: storia di una leggenda*, Rome: Polo, 1999. *Vespa: Style in Motion*, San Francisco: Chronicle, 2003.
> See Innocenti, Ferdinado (1891–1966).

Picasso, Pablo Ruiz (1881–1973)

Spanish painter, sculptor, graphic artist, ceramicist, and designer; born Málaga; active France.

Training In Pontevedra, La Coruña, and Barcelona.
Biography In Barcelona, Picasso published the review *El renacimiento*. 1900–04, lived in both Paris and Barcelona during the time of his Blue Period, when he painted images of the poor; 1904, settled in Paris, associating with avant-garde artists and writers, including Guillaume Apollinaire. He met influential connoisseurs, including Sergei Shchukin and Leo and Gertrude Stein. During his c. 1905–08 Rose Period, he depicted acrobats, dancers, and harlequins and, at this time, produced his first sculpture; 1906, met Henri Matisse. His 1906–09 Negro Period, when he attempted to analyze and simplify form, was influenced by Paul Cézanne's work and West African sculpture. He painted *Les desmoiselles d'Avignon* (1906–07), a landmark in 20th-century painting, the signal of Cubism's arrival, a violent revolt against Impressionism, and a painting understood by few others than Henri Matisse and André Derain. Until 1937, it was not shown to the public. From 1907 to World War I's beginning, Picasso developed Cubism with Georges Braque and Juan Gris; 1917 with Jean Cocteau, designed costumes and sets for ballet *Parade à Rome* and some subsequent productions of Sergei Diaghilev's Les Ballets Russes in Paris; 1920s, worked in a style of Monumental Classicism; from c. 1925, produced works embodying anguish and emotional tension, leading to the painting of *Guernica* (1937), originally produced for the Spanish Pavilion at 1937 *Exposition Internationale des Arts et Techniques dans la Vie Moderne*, Paris. How-ever, his sculpture was foreshadowed by the drama of his paintings. Picasso was one of the first to make sculpture from found objects, including his widely published *Tête d'un Taureau, Métamorphose* (1943), made from a bicycle handlebar and saddle. As a draftsperson, etcher, lithographer, linocutter, and book illustrator, his graphics were of a quality and importance equal to his painting. 1946,

Pablo Picasso. Têtes pitcher. c. 1956. Cream faïence, h. 5 1/8" (13 cm). Mfr.: Madoura, France. Courtesy Quittenbaum Kunstauktionen, Munich.

he moved to south of France, where he visited a pottery exhibition in Vallauris and expressed an interest in the Madoura stall. Suzanne and Georges Ramié invited him to use the kilns there. 1947, his pottery designs began to be produced, many still in production and essentially images on standard shapes. His 1956 silver plates were the result of his association with François Hugo and Douglas Cooper. Picasso is unquestionably the best-known and most versatile and prolific artist of the 20th century; was a key figure in developments in the visual arts during most of the first half of 20th century, though the brilliance of his pre-World War II output greatly eclipsed his subsequent work.
Bibliography G.E. Goodman, 'Twenty-Five Years of Decor,' *The Dancing Times* (London), Oct. 1935: 45-48. Suzanne and Georges Ramié, *Céramiques de Picasso*, Paris: Skira, 1948. Cat., *Picasso et le théâtre*, Toulouse: Musée des Augustins, 1965. Douglas Cooper, *Picasso, théâtre*, Paris: Cercle d'Art, 1967. *Picasso in the Collection of the Museum of Modern Art, including Remainder-Interest and Promised Gifts [by] William Rubin*, Greenwich, Conn.: The Museum of Modern Art, 1972. François and Pierre Hugo, *Picasso 19 plats en argent*, London: Lever Galleries, 1977. Ray Anne Kibbey, *Picasso: A Comprehensive Bibliography*, London: Garland, 1977. Alain Ramié, *Picasso: catalogue de l'œuvre céramique édité, 1947–1971*, Vallauris: Madoura, 1988. Videotape, *Treize journées dans la vie de Pablo Picasso* (in three parts), directors: Pierre-André Boutang, Pierre Daix, and Pierre Philippe, producer: La Sept/Arte, France, 1999.

Picasso, Paloma (1949–)

French fashion, cosmetics, and furnishings designer; daughter of Pablo Picasso and Françoise Gilot; wife first of businessman Rafael Lopez-Cambil and second of osteopath Eric Thevenet.

Biography *Paloma* means 'dove' in Spanish and was derived from her father's symbol designed for the conference of the World Committee of Peace Partisans, Paris, sponsored by the PDF (Parti Communiste Français) in spring 1949, at the time of Paloma's birth. Early 1980s, she began her design career and created signature fashion accessories, including handbags and jewelry by Tiffany. 1984, her cosmetics line by L'Oréal was launched. Early 1990s, she established a shop on the rue de la Paix, Paris; from 1987, has designed a range of glassware, ceramics, and cutlery by Villeroy & Boch. She also designed La Maison fabric range by Motif Designs and eyeware by Optyl.
Bibliography *Metropolitan Home*, Sept.1990: 42. Cat., Wilhelm Siemens (ed.), *Designwelt Paloma Picasso: zehn Jahre Paloma Picasso, Villeroy & Boch: ein Gemeinschaftsprojekt, Villeroy & Boch = The Design World of Paloma Picasso: Ten Years Paloma Picasso, Villeroy & Boch*, Hohenberg an der Eger: Mettlach / Deutsches Porzellanmuseum, 1997.

Piccaluga, Aldo (1936–); Francesco Piccaluga (1938–)

Italian architects and industrial designers; brothers; both born Genoa.

Training To late 1950s, architecture, Università degli Studi, Rome.
Biography 1960s, the Piccaluga brothers established a studio in Beirut,

where their father was an Italian diplomat; 1968 (enccouraged by *Expo '67* in Toronto), moved to Canada and set up a small practice in Toronto; have designed furniture and lighting for their projects, including interiors for fashion and advertising offices and restaurants. Their only mass-produced furniture is 1970 System Sigma range of spun steel tables and stools (installed in malls) by Synthesis of Toronto. Other work: 1977 Aztec wall lamp by Systemalux in Toronto and Montreal.
Bibliography Cat., *Seduced and Abandoned: Modern Furniture Designers in Canada, the First Fifty Years*, Toronto: The Art Gallery at Harbourfront, 1986: 24. Rachel Gotlieb and Cora Golden, *Design in Canada Since 1945: Fifty Years from Teakettles to Task Chairs*, Toronto: Knopf Canada, 2001.

Picciani, Enrico (1945–)
Italian industrial designer: born Chieti; active Milan.

Training 1963–67, Istituto Superiore per le Industrie Artistiche (ISIA), Florence.
Biography 1969, Picciani settled in Milan where he began working in the studio of Marcello Nizzoli; 1973 with Arduino Dottori and Roberto Ingegnere, cofounded studio ERA (Enrico Roberto Arduino), Milan, where he designed products, graphics, and packaging. Clients have included Lombardini (agricultural machinery), Ceccato (car-wash stations), Laverda Feraboli (agricultural machinery), Solar (heating devices), Fidenza Vetraria (glassware), Fiamm (automobile batteries and tires), Zucchetti (faucets), Ideal Standard (sanitary fittings), Evoluzione, Laverda (mobile homes, or caravans), Pozzi-Ginori, and Pirelli. He became a member, Associazione per il Disegno Industriale (ADI).
Bibliography *ADI Annual 1976*, Milan: Associazione per il Disegno Industriale, 1976. *Modo*, no. 148, Mar.–Apr. 1993: 124.

Pick, Frank (1878–1941)
British theorist and administrator; born Spalding, Lincolnshire; active London.

Biography Pick was a founding member, Design and Industries Association; 1908, became publicity officer of the London Underground and, 1912–38, was head of the office of commercial management of the expanding Underground; became the mastermind behind the 1920s–30s redesign of the Underground, for which he employed graphic designer Charles H. Holden, architect Edward Johnston, poster designer McKnight Kauffer, and Charles Paine to design the image of the newly unified public subway system. In addition to Kaufer, Pick also commissioned a number of other prominent artists of the day to design posters which have become legendary. To 1939, he managed the Ministry of Information. The renowned 1931 Underground line-diagram map of the system, designed by Henry C. Beck, has become an internationally acknowledged solution of simplification, emulated by other urban-transportation systems worldwide.
Bibliography Frederique Huygen, *British Design: Image and Identity*, London: Thames & Hudson, 1989. Jonathan Riddell and William T. Stearn, *By Underground to Kew: London Transport Posters 1908 to the Present*, London: Studio Vista, 1994. Ken Garland, *Mr Beck's Underground Map,* Harrow Weald: Capital Transport, 1994. Oliver Green, *Underground Art: London Transport Posters, 1908 to the Present*, London: Laurence King, 2001.

Pierce, Susanne (1967–)
American industrial designer; born Philadelphia.

Biography Pierce began her professional career as a freelance designer at Apple Computer, Cupertino, Cal.; collaborated on the design of 1990 PowerBook 100 and 1991–92 Newton Message Pad 100 (Junior); designed the ADB Mouse II (or Topolino); developed concepts for 1992 MacLike Things and 1993 award-winning Baby Badger; 1996, left Apple and returned to her freelance practice in San Francisco.
Bibliography Paul Kunkel, *Apple Design: The World of the Apple Industrial Design Group*, New York: Graphis, 1997.

Piferi, Filippo (1950–)
Italian designer; born Rome.

Training In architecture.
Biography Piferi was active in furniture and graphic design; from 1979, worked as a designer with Pallucco in Rome; 1985 with L. De Lorenzo, L. Leonori, and S. Stefani, founded the studio Grafite in Rome.
Bibliography Fumio Shimizu and Studio Matteo Thun (eds.), *The Descendants of Leonardo: The Italian Design*, Tokyo: Graphic-sha, 1987.

Christophe Pillet. Easy Mechanics Sky hanging lamp. 1999. Painted metal and chromium-plated metal, h. 10 3/4" (27.5 cm) x dia. 27 5/8" (55 cm). Mfr.: Tronconi, Italy.

Pigeon, Daniel (1934–1996)
French interior and furniture designer; born and active Paris.

Training École Nationale Supérieure des Arts Décoratifs, Paris.
Biography 1979, Pigeon was a founding member, VIA (French Furniture association); designed furniture produced by Prisunic, Habitat, and Seibu and some children's furniture that opens like a fan; for a few years, collaborated with Marc Berthier; with Jean-Claude Maugirard, codirected the furniture workshop, École Nationale Supérieure des Arts Décoratifs, Paris. Some of his furniture has been edited by and exhibited at Meubles et Fonctions International (MFI).
Exhibitions/citations Work included in 1990 exhibition, Paris (catalog below). Won 1981 VIA/IPEA competition for kit furniture (Sake produced by Bruyzneel and by Ciolino); 1983 prize (rattan chair designed for VIA exhibition), Bloomingdale's, New York. Received 1985 Carte Blanche production support, VIA.
Bibliography Cat., *Les années VIA 1980–1990*, Paris: Musée des Arts Décoratifs, 1990. François Mathey, *Au bonheur des formes, design français 1945–1992*, Paris: Regard, 1992: 117, 194, 246. Cat., Sophie Tasma Anargyros et al., *L'école française: les créateurs de meubles du 20ème siècle*, Paris: Industries Françaises de l'Ameublement, 2000.

Piippo, Marjaleena (1963–)
Finnish ceramicist.

Training To 1987, Taideteollinen korkeakoulu, Helsinki.
Biography With her husband Markku Piippo, she has designed ceramics using the synthetic feature of 'casting defects.' They became known for their experimental spirit in a wide range of ceramic objects called 'the Piippos' for their firm Pii-Pot. Marjaleena Piippo also designed textiles, design, interiors, and graphics.
Exhibitions/citations Work included in several exhibitions, Finland and elsewhere, including 1998 exhibition of Finnish design, Mino, Japan. First prize (for Muksa cup), 1999 Forma Tuote exhibition.

Pilchuck Glass School
American institution.

History 1971, Pilchuck Glass School was founded in Stanwood, Wash., by glass designer Dale Chihuly, supported by patrons Anne Gould

Hauberg and John H. Hauberg. He established a retreat to offer artists an opportunity to work with and learn about glass in a bucolic setting, overlooking the Puget Sound. Eventually numerous people were attracted to the institution, which has become the world's largest and most comprehensive educational center for artists working in glass, and an international model for visual-arts education. There are two hot-glass shops, a studio building with a kiln shop, a coldworking studio, a flat shop for torch work, a wood- and metal-shop, a glass-plate printmaking studio, a gallery, and a library. Some of the most accomplished glass makers have studied there.
Bibliography Tina Oldknow, *Pilchuck: A Glass School*, Seattle: Pilchuck Glass School/University of Washington, 1996.

Pilkington's Royal Lancastrian Pottery and Tile Company

British ceramics factory.

History 1882, the Pilkington family, who owned glassworks and coal-mines, and William Burton, previously a chemist at Wedgwood, founded a ceramics factory near Manchester. Burton's brother Joseph was the director. The firm produced tiles, and, from 1897, vases were produced until 1903 by the Lancashire factory or acquired from other sources and glazed on the premises. The Burton brothers perfected a luster-decorating process and a new hard transparent glaze, beginning large-scale production in 1903. The firm's consultant artists included C.F.A. Voysey, Lewis Foreman Day, and Walter Crane. 1937, the factory discontinued its domestic wares, while continuing to produce tiles. 1948–57, it once again produced ornamental ware.
Exhibitions Wares were shown at 1900 *Exposition Universelle*, Paris.
Bibliography A.J. Crass, *Pilkington's Royal Lancastrian Pottery and Tiles*, London: Richard Dennis, 1980.

Pilkington

British glass manufacturer.

History 1826, the firm was founded as St. Helens Crown Glass Company, the Greenall & Pilkington in 1829. It began with the technical knowledge and ability of John William Bell and funding from three local families (Bromilows, Greenalls, and Pilkingtons). William Pilkington was one of the original shareholders who was subsequently joined by his elder brother Richard. 1945, the firm bought Chance Brothers. From mid-1930s when ICI first developed the process, Pilkington has been supplying glass to the acrylic-casting industry. Essential to its business was, and continues to be, float glass, invented in 1952 by Alastair Pilkington. In facilities worldwide, it manufactures clear, tinted, and coated glass for buildings; clear and tinted glass for vehicles; very thin float glass for the electronics industry; glass and plastic-composite glazing for airplanes and trains; and a wide range of other fenestration products, including Activ, introduced in 2001, the world's first self-cleaning glass. The firm (named Pilkington Glass in 1849) remained privately held to 1970, when it went public on the London Stock Exchange. From 1982, began buying large stakes in Libbey-Owens-Ford, the US's largest manufacturer of building and automotive glass. 1985, Libbey, a manufacturer of domestic and restaurant glassware, sold its glass operations to form Pilkington Libbey-Owens-Ford, or Pilkington LOF, and, 2000, dissolved into simply Pilkington. Libbey Inc. exists as a separate entity.
Bibliography T.C. Barker, *Pilkington Brothers and the Glass Industry*, London: Allen & Unwin, 1960. T.C. Barker, *The Glassmakers, Pilkington: The Rise of an International Company 1826–1975*, London: Weidenfeld & Nicolson, 1977.
> See Libbey Glass Works; Pollitzer, Sigmund.

Pillet, Christophe (1959–)

French designer; active Paris.

Training 1985, diploma, École Nationale Supérieure des Arts Décoratifs, Nice; 1986, master's degree, Domus Academy, Milan.
Biography 1986–88, Pillet collaborated with Martine Bedin, Milan; 1988–93, worked in the studio of Philippe Starck, Paris; from 1993, has been an independent freelance artist and designer; each year from 1996, has designed the contemporary-design area of the Salon du Meuble, Paris. Work has included furniture and product design, interior design, architecture, and set design for clients such as Bally, Cappellini, JC Decaux, Trussardi, Daum, Écart International, Edra, E&Y, Lancôme, L'Oréal, Magis, Mazzega, Moët et Chandon, Moroso, Schopenhauer, Shiseido et Whirlpool. He also designed Catherine (Catherine Malandrino's boutique), New York, and the Universe Voyager Bag by Pantone. Other work includes 1995 Y chair and 1997 Sunset Lounge chair by Cappellini, 1997 saddle seats and Duplex adjustable floor lamp by Écart, 1998 Terrace chair by Cambrai Chrome, 1999 Twins glass group by Daum, 1999 Gallery table by Gilles Peyroulet, 1999 Video Lounge furniture group by Domeau & Pérès, 2001 Elysée modular seating by Edra.
Exhibitions/citations Work included in a number of international exhibitions. Creator of the year, 1994 Salon du Meuble, Paris; 1994 Carte Blanche production support, VIA (French furniture association); Excellence Prize in Lighting, 1995 Salon International du Luminaire, Paris.
Bibliography Pascale Cassgnau and Christophe Pillet, *Beef, Brétillot/Valette, Matali Crasset, Patrick Jouin, Jean-Marie Massaud: petits enfants de Starck?*, Paris: Dis Voir, 2000. Mel Byars, *On/Off: New Electronic Products*, New York: Universe, 2001. www.via.asso.fr

Pillivuyt; Alpico

French porcelain factory.

History To make ceramic cooking wares for professional chefs, the Pillivuyt family established a factory in the porcelain area of France, near Limoges, in 1818. The founding was five years after the word 'soufflé' was coined for the multiple-serving version of the individual 18th-century-vintage *ramequin* (ramekin). For this and other recipes, Pillivuyt's oven-safe cast-porcelain bakeware became known for its extreme hardness, like fine china but resistant to crazing, cracking, and discoloration. This was accomplished against the workers' resistance to the overuse of the molds. 1826, Albert Pillivuyt, a son of the factory owner, set up his own ceramics enterprise to furnish table- and kitchenware to French hotels and restaurants. Workers today at Alpico (an acronym of <u>Al</u>bert <u>Pi</u>llivuyt <u>CO</u>mpagnie) continue to use some of the same 180-year-old molds that Albert commandeered from the family firm. Current production maintains the traditional firing of fine clays at 2,600° F. (1,425° C) to produce microwave-safe bakeware that can travel from the refrigerator/freezer to the oven to the dinner table to the dishwasher. Should there be chips on today's Alpico non-porous, lead- and cadmium-free glaze, the dense porcelain beneath will resist bacterial growth. Generations ago, Yves Deshoulières bought Alpico, the largest manufacturer of high-quality porcelain in France. (Late 1980s, still separately active Pillivuyt commissioned Jean-Pierre Caillères to design dishes for use in microwave ovens.)
Bibliography Mel Byars, 'To Be Continued,' *Metropolitan Home*, Nov.–Dec. 1999: 80+.

Pincombe, E. Helen (1908–)

British ceramicist; born India.

Training Pottery, Camberwell School of Art and Central School of Arts and Crafts, both London.
Biography 1925, she became a teacher of pottery, Royal College of Art, London; after World War II, set up her own pottery workshop in Oxshott, Surrey.
Bibliography Cat., *Thirties: British Art and Design Before the War*, London: Arts Council of Great Britain/Hayward Gallery, 1979.

Pininfarina, Battista (b. Battista 'Pinin' Farina 1893–1966); Giovanni Farina (1884–1957)

Italian automobile coach builder. All born and active Turin.

Biography Giovanni Farina was an apprentice to a coachbuilder; 1906, set up his own workshop to repair cars and horse-drawn vehicles, which was kown as Stabilimenti Farina from 1917. Eventually, it became famous for the design and coachbuilding of early models by Fiat, Lancia, Cisitalia, and Ferrari, one of its first was 1929 Fiat 525 D'Orsay cabriolet. Alfredo Vignale, while at Farina, designed 1946 Cisitalia 202 MM (Mille Miglia), the competition version of the 202 GT model and the successor of the 202 D coupé in aluminum. Farina also built early Ferrari models, including Ferrari 166 Inter Coupé and one of Farina's last, the hand-built Lancia Aurelia B50 coupé in a light alloy. 1951, the enterprise closed. Three of Giovanni's brothers worked for the firm, including Battista 'Pinin' Farina (whose nickname 'Pinin,' or 'the youngest in the family' in Italian, was derived from his being the tenth of 11 siblings). Battista had been working there since age 11. 1930, Battista established his own firm, Carrozzeria Pinin Farina in Turin, an operation with 90 or so employees, financially supported by a rich aunt and Vincenzo Lancia, also a partner. Originally, the operation produced one-of-a-kind prototypes and small editions of 5 to 10 special models for direct sale. Battista became known for having excellent business and

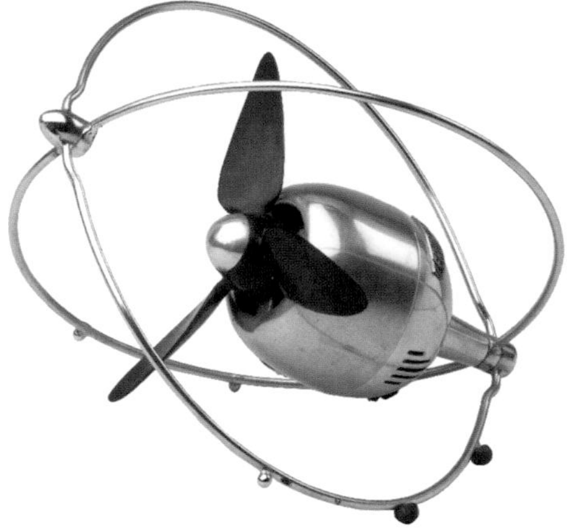

Ezio Pirali. Electric fan (no. V.E. 505). 1953. Aluminum, chromed steel, and rubber. Mfr.: Fabbriche Elettrotecniche Riunite, Italy. Gift of Philip Johnson. MoMA.

aesthetic senses; predicted that the design of auto bodies would eventually become a major selling element to attract buyers. By 1939, there were 500 employees producing 800 units annually. After World War II, Farina established a small factory for sports-car bodies, where he encouraged his designers to be innovative. 1958, the company was relocated to a new site in Grugliasco, near Turin. 1961, the family name was changed to Pininfarina, and the company name was also changed. On Batistta's 1966 death, the management and control of the enterprise was passed to his son, Sergio Pininfarina, and son-in-law, Renzo Carli. The firm has become the most highly regarded and most aesthetically accomplished car-design firm and coachbuilder worldwide. The bodies that the Pininfarina studio has designed for Ferrari since 1952 have become almost inseparable from the mark.
Bibliography Press Howell (ed.), *Pininfarina: Sixty Years*, Vimodrone (MI): Giorgio Nada, 1995. Antoine Prunet, *Pininfarina: Seventy Years*, New York: Rizzoli, 2000.
> See Michelotti, Giovanni; Pininfarina, Sergio.

Pininfarina, Paolo (1958–)

Italian automobile and product designer; born Turin; youngest of three sons of Sergio Pininfarina.

Training To 1982, mechanical engineering, Politecnico, Turin.
Biography Paolo Pininfarina interned at Honda in Tokyo; 1984, joined the board of Pininfarina Studies and Research; from 1987, managed General Motors's 'GM 200' program, which realized a number of prototypes, and he worked on the Cadillac Allante; subsequently left GM and set up Pininfarina Extra studio for industrial design, interiors, and architecture. The first products included writing instruments, sunglasses, watches, clothing, sporting goods, and kitchens.
Citations 1996 Good Design award (for Ola kitchen by Snaidero), Chicago Athenaeum; 1998 Product Innovation award (for Sanidero kit-chen), *Kitchen and Bath* magazine.

Pininfarina, Sergio (1926–)

Italian coach builder; born Turin; son of Battista Pininfarina.

Biography From 1951, Sergio Pininfarina worked in his family's Pininfarina auto-body design firm; on his father's 1966 death, became head of the firm with his brother-in-law Renzo Carli; developed the firm's coach-building activities into an advanced, low-unit production system; was probably more effective than his father at establishing the world renown of the firm; was not a designer himself but rather an effective manager, with high aesthetic standards, of the firm's design staff. Under his direction, the early, retrograde bodies of Jaguar were appreciably improved by Pininfarina. By 1989, the Pininfarina Group employed 1,700 people and produced c. 30,000 cars. The firm has become the most highly respected car-design firm and coachbuilder worldwide. Its designs have included 1932 DiLambda, 1935 Alfa Romeo 6C 2300, 1937 Lancia Aprilia, 1939 Lancia Astura, 1955 Peugeot 403 Berlina, 1956 Alfa Romeo Giulietta Spider 1300, 1956 250 GT, 1966 Alfa Romeo Duetto Spider, 1968 Daytona, 1984 Testarossa, and a number of others subsequently.
Bibliography Riccardo P. Felicioli, *Car Men 3: Sergio Pininfarina, Pininfarina Studi & Richerchi*, Milan: Automobilia, 1998.
> See Fioravanti, Leonardo.

Pinková, Andrea (1975–)

Slovakian designer; born and active Banská Bystrica.

Training School of Applied Arts, Kremnica; Academy of Fine Arts and Design, Bratislava; 6-month grant for study, École des Beaux-Arts, Saint-Étienne, France.
Biography Pinková designs toys, games, and domestic accessories.
Exhibitions Participation in a number of exhibitions, including 1996 BIO industrial-design biennial, Ljubljana; 1998, 2000, 2001, 2002 Fórum Designu, Nitra, Slovakia; 1999 Biennale Internationale du Design, Saint-Étienne, France.

Pinnavaia, Paola (1966–)

Italian industrial designer; born Milan; active Rome.

Training 1986–90, product-design department, Istituto Superiore per le Industrie Artistiche (ISIA), Rome; 1992, courses, Domus Academy, Milan.
Biography From 1990, Pinnavaia worked as industrial designer at Texas Instruments in Nice, Tokyo, and Dallas, focusing on marketing, communications, project engineering, and experimentation in new methods linked to team work. 1992, she was assigned by Texas Instruments to research/design department, Center of Industrial Design, Italy, where she contributed to the strategy of consumer products by predicting the trends and future demands of European consumers. 1994, she opened her own studio Ondesign in Rome to serve national and international manufacturers of consumer electronics. Work has included 1992 TI-30 calculator range by Texas Instruments, 1996 One Touch Easy GSM mobile phone by Alcatel, 2000 Hit Organ electronic keyboard for children by Bontempi, 2001 Oceano telephones by Industrie Dial Face, 2001 Archivia drawing/printing stand by Fellowes-Leonardi, 2001 cosmetics packaging by Lumson, stainless-steel radiator by Cordivari, and *Dal Merletto alla Motocicletta* exhibition at 2002 (10th) Biennale Donna, Ferrara.
Citations Red Dot award (for 1997 One Touch Easy Dual Band GSM mobile phone by Alcatel), Design Zentrum Nordrhein Westfalen, Essen; Good Design award (for 1999 Ospro PDA by Oregon Scientific), Chicago Athenaeum; Design Distinction award (for 2000 Foglia bath radiator by Cordivari), *I.D.* magazine.

Pinter, Klaus (1940–)
> See Haus-Rucker-Co.

Piper, John (1903–1992)

British painter and designer; born Epsom, Surrey.

Training 1928–29, Royal College of Art, London.
Biography From 1927, Piper was art critic for journal *The Nation*. 1933, he became a member of the London Group and, 1934–35, of the artists' group Seven and Five Society. 1935–37, he collaborated with his second wife Myfanwy Evans on art journal *Axis*. He wrote for the Architectural Press and on the Shell Guides, with John Betjeman; 1940–41, was an official war artist, painting bomb-devastated buildings and landscapes in Britain. He designed stage sets for *Trial of a Judge* (1938) by Stephen Spender and stage sets and costumes for operas by Benjamin Britten, including *Rape of Lucretia* (1946), *Albert Herring* (1947), and *Billy Budd* (1951). He designed 1959 stained glass for Coventry Cathedral; 1965 stained glass for Metropolitan Cathedral, Liverpool; 1965 memorial window for Benjamin Britten in Aldeburgh Parish Church, Suffolk; and a large 1965–66 tapestry for Chichester Cathedral, Sussex.
Exhibitions Work shown in 1948 exhibition, Curt Valentine Gallery, New York; 1942 *English Romantic Artists*, London; 1979–80 *Thirties*, Hayward Gallery, London (catalog below). Work subject of exhibitions at Museum of Modern Art, Oxford, 1979; Tate Gallery, London, 1983.
Bibliography Cat., *Thirties: British Art and Design Before the War*, London: Arts Council of Great Britain/Hayward Gallery, 1979.

Pirali, Ezio (1921–)

Italian engineer and industrial designer.

Biography Pirali was managing director of Fabbriche Elettrotecniche Riunite (now Zerowatt), the Italian manufacturer of domestic electrical appliances; developed the firm's products and contributed to their

styling; has become best known for minimalist 1953 V.E. 505 tabletop electric fan and 1954 model, the latter minus the protective housing grid and with a chromed tubular-steel stand, by Fabbriche Elettrotecniche Riunite.
Exhibitions/citations 1954 (for V.E. 505 electric fan) Premio Compasso d'Oro. Work included in 1979 and 1983–84 exhibitions, Milan and Philadelphia (catalogs below).
Bibliography Cat., *Design & design*, Milan: Palazzo delle Stelline, 1979: 29. Cat., Kathryn B. Hiesinger and George H. Marcus III (eds.), *Design Since 1945*, Philadelphia: Philadelphia Museum of Art, 1983. Hans Wichmann, *Italien Design 1945 bis heute*, Munich: Die Neue Sammlung, 1988.

Piretti, Giancarlo (1940–)
Italian designer; born Bologna.

Training To 1960, art education, Istituto Statale d'Arte, Bologna.
Biography 1963–70, Piretti taught interior design, Istituto Statale d'Arte, Bologna; from 1960–72, worked as a designer of office and domestic furniture at Anonima Castelli in Bologna, which produced Piretti's first plastic work: 1967 Plia folding chair. He developed numerous innovative furniture designs, primarily seating that was prefabricated, modular, and suitable for the assembly-line production techniques at Anonima Castelli, such as 1969 Plana folding armchair, 1971 Platone folding desk chair and table, and Pluvium umbrella stand. He collaborated with Emilio Ambasz on award-winning designs, including two ranges of ergonomic seating, and Dorsal and 1974–75 Vertebra by Anonima Castelli. They also designed 1984 Logotec and 1985 Oseris low-voltage spotlight ranges by Erco Lighting, and 1988 Piretti Collection of 50 chairs by Krueger of the US. From 1984, Piretti worked for Castilia.
Citations 1971 (for Plia chair) and 1979 (Vetebra chair) Premio SMAU Industrial Design, Salone della Machina e Attrezzature per l'Ufficio, Milan; prize (for Plia chair) at 1971 BIO 4 industrial-design biennial, Ljubljana; 1973 Bundespreis Produktdesign, Rat für Formgebung, (German design council), Frankfurt; 1977 gold medal (for Vertebra chair, with Ambasz) and 1980 Industrial Design Award (for Logotec lighting), Institute of Business Designers (IBD). Premio Compasso d'Oro: 1981 (for Vertebra with Ambasz), 1987 (for Delungo table and Dilemma clothes-hanger scale by Castilia), 1989 (for Dorikos office-desk system by B&B Italia), 1991 (for Piretti Collection chairs by C.O.M.s. Coop.), 1998 (for Piego extension table and Tat-Amo sofa-bed by Pro-Cord).
Bibliography Albrecht Bangert and Karl Michael Armer, *80s Style: Designs of the Decade*, New York: Abbeville, 1990. Cat., Kathryn B. Hiesinger and George H. Marcus III (eds.), *Design Since 1945*, Philadelphia: Philadelphia Museum of Art, 1983. 'Vertebra Seating System,' *Domus*, no. 572, June 1977: 38–39. *Moderne Klassiker: Möbel, die Geschichte machen*, Hamburg: Gruner + Jahr, 1982: 13–14. Fumio Shimizu and Studio Matteo Thun (eds.), *The Italian Design: Descendants of Leonardo da Vinci*, Tokyo: Graphic-sha, 1987: 338.

Pistoletto, Michelangelo (1933–)
Italian sculptor, painter, and designer.

Biography Pistoletto was a cofounder of the Italian *arte povera* movement in Berlin; is best known for his Superreal mirror paintings and produced sculptures and installations that have been widely published. 1989, he designed furniture by Meta-Memphis, including 1989 Tutti Designers wall lamp in neon with its accompanying silkscreened aluminum briefcase to hold the transformer.
Bibliography Albrecht Bangert and Karl Michael Armer, *80s Style: Designs of the Decade*, New York: Abbeville, 1990.

Pitman, Agnes (1850–1946)
American wood carver and ceramics decorator; born Sheffield; daughter of Benn Pitman and Jane Bragg Pitman; active Cincinnati, Ohio.

Training Under William Henry Fry, in wood carving; 1874 under Maria Eggers, in china painting; to 1877, design, University of Cincinnati School of Design.
Biography 1853 with her family, she settled in Cincinnati; 1870s with her mother, carved the furniture, doors, and woodwork that her father designed; 1873, assisted her father in his wood carving classes at School of Design, University of Cincinnati; 1870s, taught wood carving at Mercantile Library Building and at Woodward High School; was a member, Women's Art Museum Association; 1879, became a founding member of Cincinnati Pottery Club and continued to be active in wood, ceramics, and wall decoration.

Giancarlo Piretti. Planta clothes stand. 1972. ABS polymer, 66 7/8 x 14 15/16" (170 x 38 cm). Mfr.: Anonima Castelli, Italy. Courtesy Quittenbaum Kunstauktionen, Munich.

Exhibitions Work shown at 1872 (3rd) *Annual Cincinnati Industrial Exhibition* (furniture produced with her mother and designed by her father); Cincinnati Room (chest of drawers with carved floral motif), Women's Pavilion at 1876 *Centennial Exposition*, Philadelphia; in 1870s industrial exhibitions in Cincinnati; 1878 Cincinnati loan exhibition, Women's Art Museum Association; Cincinnati Room (painted wall decorations in the interior) in Women's Pavilion at 1893 *World's Columbian Exposition*, Chicago.
Bibliography Cat., *The Ladies, God Bless 'Em: The Women's Art Movement in Cincinnati in the Nineteenth Century*, Cincinnati: Cincinnati Art Museum, 1976: 68. Anthea Callen, *Women Artists of the Arts and Crafts Movement, 1870–1914*, New York: Pantheon, 1979: 164, 165, 169–70, 225. Doreen Bolger Burke et al., *In Pursuit of Beauty: Americans and the Aesthetic Movement*, New York: The Metropolitan Museum of Art/Rizzoli, 1987: 461–62.

Pitman, Benn (1822–1910)
British teacher and wood carver; born Trowbridge, Wiltshire; father of Agnes Pitman; active Cincinnati, Ohio.

Training Early 1830s, apprenticeship as an architect in Bath.
Biography His brother Isaac Pitman had a school in Bath and also invented a system of phonetic shorthand (phonography). Benn Pitman taught the system throughout Britain for a decade until Isaac suggested that he promote the method in US. 1852, they moved to Philadelphia and, 1853, settled in Cincinnati. Pitman set up the Phonography Institute and wrote, designed, and illustrated numerous textbooks on the shorthand method; 1856, invented relief engraving for printing. Through Henry Lindley Fry and his son William Henry Fry, who also settled in Cincinnati and whom he probably had met in Bath, Pitman developed an interest in wood carving; 1873, set up the wood carving department, School of Design, University of Cincinnati, where he taught many women from wealthy Cincinnati families to 1893; encouraged his students (who included Laura Fry, M. Louise McLaughlin, Adelaide Nourse, and his daughter Agnes) to use clay modeling as a preliminary to carving; 1874, established china-painting classes at the

school; 1877 with the Frys, and their students, began the decoration of the organ of Cincinnati Music Hall; was a follower of John Ruskin and saw in nature an endless source of ornamental motifs and decoration as an integral part of useful objects. Pitman's own highly ornamented house in Cincinnati is extant today. 1889, he became a lecturer in decorative design, Art Academy of Cincinnati; 1880s, wrote widely on wood carving and decoration, including books *American Art—Its Future Dependent on Improved Social Conditions...* [15 lectures on decorative art, delivered during 1890–91 term, to the students of Cincinnati Art Academy] (Cincinnati, 1891) and *A Plea for American Decorative Art* [published for 1895 Cotton States and International Exposition, Atlanta] (1895). 1893, William Fry took Pitman's post at Art Academy of Cincinnati, and Pitman resumed his work in phonography, writing several books on the subject, such as *A Plea for Alphabetic Reform* (1905).
Exhibitions Work shown at 1872 (3rd) *Annual Cincinnati Industrial Exhibition* (wood carvings by him, his wife, and daughter); 1883 *Cincinnati Industrial Exhibition* (a bed, highly carved by wife Adelaide Nourse with painted panels by her sister Elizabeth Nourse).
Bibliography Kenneth R. Trapp, ' "To Beautify the Useful": Benn Pitman and the Women's Woodcarving Movement in Cincinnati in the Late Nineteenth Century,' in Kenneth R. Ames (ed.), *Victorian Furniture: Essays from a Victorian Society Autumn Symposium*, Philadelphia, 1872: 173–92. Cat., Kenneth R. Trapp (ed.), *Celebrate Cincinnati Art*, Cincinnati: Cincinnati Art Museum, 1982: 48–55, 67–70. Doreen Bolger Burke et al., *In Pursuit of Beauty: Americans and the Aesthetic Movement*, New York: The Metropolitan Museum of Art/Rizzoli, 1987.

Piva, Antonio (1936–)

Italian architect and designer: born Padova; active Milan.

Training To 1962, Istituto Universitario di Architettura, Venice.
Biography From 1962, Piva taught, Facoltà di Architettura, Politecnico, Milan; 1962, began his professional career, working in the architecture partnership Franco Albini, Franca Helg, Antonio Piva, Marco Albini in Milan, and collaborated on 1962 Metropolitana Milanese (Milan subway), 1984 post office in Gorizia, and 1985 restoration of Castello di Masnago in Varese. 1968–72, he taught design, Corso Superiore di Disegno Industriale, Venice; became a member, Associazione per il Disegno Industriale (ADI); 1975, advised on the founding of a museum in Venezuela for UNESCO; 1983, taught, Universidad Federal de Bahia, Salvador, Brazil; from 1985, wrote the column 'Museografia' in *Il Sole 24ore* newspaper and has promoted and directed seminars, lectures, and postgraduate courses on museology and museography at Facoltà di Architetturae, Politecnico, Milan; judged architectural competitions; was active in the organization of architecture and design at Contemporary Art Hall, Milan, and New York International Design Center, Long Island City; designed silver, glass, and a tea set by San Lorenzo, and lighting by Sirrah.
Bibliography *ADI Annual 1976*, Milan: Associazione per il Disegno Industriale, 1976. Andrea Branzi and Michele de Lucchi, *Design Italiano degli Anni '50*, Milan: Ricerche Design Editrice, 1985. *Moderne Klassiker: Möbel, die Geschichte machen*, Hamburg: Gruner + Jahr, 1982: 58. Giancarlo Iliprandi and Pierluigi Molinari (eds.), *Industrial Design Italiani*, Fagagna: Magnus, 1985: 19. Fumio Shimizu and Studio Matteo Thun (eds.), *The Italian Design: Descendants of Leonardo da Vinci*, Tokyo: Graphic-sha, 1987: 330.

Piva, Paolo (1950–)

Italian designer; born Adria; active Venice.

Training To 1973, in architecture in Venice.
Biography 1970, Piva began his professional career; has designed kitchen systems, seating, and case goods for clients, including Dada, Giovannetti, Poliform, B&B Italia, De Sede, Fama, Burelli Cucine, Mobel Italia, Saima, and Lumenform in Italy, and, in Austria, Wittmann, Thonet, and Team 7. His Easy System seating was produced by Open of S. Lucia di Piave. He became a member, Associazione per il Disegno Industriale (ADI); with Manfredo Tafuri, organized and designed the 1980 *Vienna Rossa* exhibition in Rome; 1980, designed embassies in Kuwait and Qatar and, 1981, the interiors of a chain of dress shops.
Bibliography *ADI Annual 1976*, Milan: Associazione per il Disegno Industriale, 1976. *Modo*, no. 148, Mar.–Apr. 1993: 124.

Pizzinato, Michele (1968–)

Italian architect and designer; born Milan.

Training 1987–93, Politecnico, Milan; 1993–94 Escuela Técnica Superior de Arquitectura, Madrid.
Biography 1993–95, Pizzinato worked in an architect studio in Madrid; 1995, in the studio of Giovanni Drugman in Milan, with whom he has been a partner from 1999; designed 1997 Talvez movable bookcase by Squadramobile and other furniture with Drugman.
> See Drugman, Giovanni.

Plan

British furniture dealer.

History Established in 1932, Plan became one of the more notable retailers of modern furniture in Great Britain in 1920s and 1930s. Tubular steel, plywood, and upholstery fabrics in geometrics and stripes were used in the construction of its furniture based on German models. F.H. Miles was Plan's first director; its founder was architect and designer Serge Chermayeff, who had discontinued his relationship with Waring and Gillow in 1931. Even before Plan was set up, its furniture, identical to Pel's, appeared in 1931–32 BBC studios designed by Chermayeff and was published in *Architectural Review*. All of Plan's furniture was produced by other firms. Its wooden models were manufactured by Henry Stone of Banbury, tubular steel furniture by Pel of Oldbury, hand-knotted rugs by Morton Sundour, upholstery fabrics by Donald Brothers, and lighting by Best and Lloyd of Smethwick. Plan was located in the Chermayeff offices in the Pantheon building on Oxford Street, London. Early Plan models may have been assembled by Pel from parts supplied by Walter Knoll of Stuttgart and upholstered with material imitating Walter Knoll's in Germany. 1936, Plan was sold to German refugee Walter Trier and British designer F.J. Porter. 1938, Walter Knoll sent his son Hans to Britain to promote their new line of Elbo easy chairs made in Borghams and by a firm in High Wycombe, and sold under the Walter Knoll name in the same showroom with Plan models. The Knoll-Plan venture failed, and Plan closed in 1938.
Exhibitions Plan furniture was first shown, at 1933 *British Industrial Art in Relationship to the Home* exhibition, Dorland Hall, London, where the 'Weekend House' of Chermayeff was installed.
Bibliography Barbara Tilson, 'Plan Furniture 1932–38: The German Connection,' *Journal of Design History*, vol. 3, nos. 2 and 3, 1990: 145–55.

Plan Créatif

French design firm.

History 1985, Plan Créatif was established by Claude Braunstein and Clément Rousseau in Paris with associates Gérard Lecœur and David McKay and other offices in Geneva and London. Work has included-electric irons, 1986 Porphyre mixer tap by Porcher, the 1991 pilot's station of Airbus A330 airplane, Casino store concept, signage of 1992 Winter Olympiad in Albertville (France), 1996 Amarys telephone by France Telecom, 1996 Bouygues Telecom logo, 1998 euro/franc converter for Crédit Agricole bank, 1999 L'Arbre Urbain signage pole for RATP (Paris urban-transportation system), and a large number of other products. Employs a staff of about 40.
Honor 1986 Janus award, Ministère de l'Industrie.
Bibliography François Mathey, *Au bonheur des formes, design français 1945–1992*, Paris: Regard, 1992: 346, 362–64. Mel Byars, *50 Products...*, Hove: RotoVision, 1998.
> See Braunstein, Claude.

Plastimat Jablonec nad Nisou (aka Plastimat)

Czech manufacturer specializing in plastics; located Liberec.

History 1946, a number of small prewar enterprises were expropriated and amalgamated into Plastimat Jablonec nad Nisou. It produced small domestic products and toys, followed by household accessories. Plastimat called on a range of plastics processes and materials and produced industrial moldings and semi-manufactured goods. 1957, it established a design studio, where, by 1972, its head was Jiří Hofman. Design consultants included architect Josef Saal and instructor Gustav Hlávka at Vysoká Škola Uměleckoprůmyslová (VŠUP, academy of arts, architecture, and design), Prague. Plastimat's products have been the 1965 tableware for Czechoslovakia Airlines by I. Jakeš and a 1972 polystyrene decorative screen by Josef Saal. Hofman's work for Plastimat included the 1966 coffee box, 1968 beer jug and beaker, and 1970 disposable ice-cream cup and food containers. The factory and its designers consulted a small group of retailers to monitor the marketplace, an effort which nevertheless largely failed to satisfy consumer demand.
Exhibitions Work included in 1972 exhibition, Prague (catalog below).
Bibliography Cat., Milena Lamarová, *Design a Plastické Hmoty*,

Warren Platner. Table and stools (nos. 3715 and 1719). 1966. Clear plate glass, nickle-plated steel rods, and fabric upholstery, table h. 28 x 41 3/8" (71 x 105 cm), stool 20 1/2 x 17" (52 x 43 cm). Mfr.: Knoll Associates, US. Courtesy Quittenbaum Kunstauktionen, Munich.

Prague: Uměleckoprůmyslové Muzeum, 1972: 68, 69, 200.

Platner, Warren (1919–)

American architect and designer; born Baltimore.

Training Architecture, Cornell University, Ithaca, N.Y.
Biography Platner worked in the offices of Raymond Loewy, Eero Saarinen, I.M. Pei, and Kevin Roche and John Dinkeloo; 1953–57, designed 1966 range of vertical steel-wire tables and chairs by Knoll; devised the method and tooling for production himself—more than 1,400 welds required to produce the lounge chair in the line. The wires created a deliberate moiré effect. 1967, he set up his own design studio in North Haven, Conn., where he designed office furniture for Knoll and Lehigh and worked on commissions including architecture, interiors, lighting, and furnishings; designed the Georg Jensen Design Center and the Windows on the World restaurant in World Trade Center, both New York; Water Tower Place, Chicago.
Exhibitions Work included in 1983–84 exhibition, Philadelphia (catalog below).
Bibliography Warren Platner, 'Designing in Steel,' *Industrial Design*, vol. 16, June 1969: 62–66. 'Prototypes and Principles,' *Industrial Design*, vol. 17, Sept. 1970: 54–59. Barbaralee Diamonstein, Ward Bennett, et al., *Interior Design: The New Freedom*, New York: Rizzoli, 1982: 238–43. Cat., Kathryn B. Hiesinger and George H. Marcus III (eds.), *Design Since 1945*, Philadelphia: Philadelphia Museum of Art, 1983.

Plečník, Jožef (aka Josip or Josef Plešník 1872–1957)

Slovene architect and designer; born Laibach (now Ljubljana); active Vienna, Laibach, and Prague.

Training Kunstgewerbeschule, Graz; 1895–97 under Otto Wagner, Akademie der bildenden Künste, Vienna.
Biography Plečník worked for Otto Wagner in the office of the city railway project in Vienna, where staff designed more than 30 railway stations as well as bridges and viaducts. Plečník's most notable work was the 1903–05 shop and apartment block near the Domkirche St. Stephan (cathedral) in Vienna for manufacturer J.E. Zacherl. Plečník called on iron construction and granite slabs held in place by vertical sections, both the latest techniques of the time. Also innovative were the undulating walls that terminated below the roof line in carved atlantes. (The sculpture of Archangel Michael by Ferdinand Andri was added in 1909.) Plečník's second major Viennese work was the Kirche des Heiligen Geistes (church of the Holy Ghost) on the Schmelz, where he again also employed new techniques, here in concrete construction. Plečník was recommended by Wagner to succeed him at the Akademie der bildenden Künste, Vienna, in 1911 but was rejected in favor of Leopold Bauer, another of Wagner's pupils. 1911–21, Plečník taught at Vysoká Škola Uměleckoprůmyslová (VŠUP, academy of arts, architecture, and design), Prague; practiced architecture in 1920s–30s in Prague and Ljubljana; with the restorative architecture, executed notable and unusual decorative art for Prague Castle; from 1921 to his death, was head of architecture department, Tehnicna Fakulteta, Univerza v Ljubljani.
Exhibitions/citations Gold medal for exhibition design, 1904 *Louisiana Purchase Exposition*, St. Louis. Work subject of 1989 *Jozef Plečník Architecte* touring exhibition, originating at Centre Georges Pompidou, Paris; 1996 *Josip Plecnik: Architecture for the New Democracy*, Prague Castle; numerous others.
Bibliography Cat., François Burkhardt et al. (eds.), *Jože Plečník, architecte: 1872–1957*, Paris: CCI/Centre Pompidou, 1986. Marjan Music, *Jožef Plečník*, Ljubljana: Partizanska knj., 1986. Peter Krecic, *Plecnik: The Complete Works*, London: Academy; Berlin: Ernst & Sohn, 1993. Cat., *Josip Plečník: Architekt Prazského hradu*, Prague: Správa Pražského hradu, 1996.

Plesl, Rony (1965–)

Czech glass and product designer; born Jablonec nad Nisou.

Training 1980–84, Special High Art School, Železný Brod, Czechoslovakia; 1984–90 under V.K. Novák and Jiří Harcuba, scupture studio, Vysoká Škola Uměleckoprůmyslová (VŠUP, academy of arts, architecture, and design), Prague; 1990, La Ailla Arson, Nice, France
Biography Plesl worked at Barovier & Toso in Italy from 2001, at Bonacina in Italy, Schott Zwiesel in Germany; and at others. 1991–99, he taught in the Studio of Glass Blowing, Czech Republic; 2002 with Petr Siefert, established a full-service design agency to offer services from design and manufacturer to advertising and photography but is best known as a glass designer.
Exhibitions/citations Numerous one-person exhibitions, primarily in Europe, from 1993; and group venues, from 1990. Selected for Quality Design for 1999, Design Centrum České Republiký; First prize for best design, 2000 SIBO glass/ceramics fair, Czech Republic.

Pleydell-Bouverie, Katherine (1895–1985)

British ceramicist.

Training 1921–23, pottery, Central School of Arts and Crafts, London; 1924 under Bernard Leach, St. Ives, Cornwall.
Biography Aided by Japanese engineer, chemist, and potter Tsuronosuke Matsubayashi , she set up a pottery workshop in 1925 in Coleshill, Wiltshire, where, 1928–36, she worked with Norah Braden. They experimented with wood and vegetable ash glazes. 1946–1980s, she was active in pottery workshop she set up in Kilmington Manor, Wiltshire.
Bibliography Cat., *Thirties: British Art and Design Before the War*, London: Arts Council of Great Britain/Hayward Gallery, 1979. *Katherine Pleydell-Bouverie*, Bath: Crafts Study Centre, 1980.

Pløen, Erik (1925–)

Norwegian ceramicist.

Training In ceramics at Schneider & Knutzen workshop, near Oslo.
Biography 1946, Pløen set up his own pottery workshop in Ljan and

produced hand-thrown vessels; 1957, broke with established pottery traditions and explored self-expression, abandoning unity. 1963–64, he was a visiting professor, University of Chicago.
Exhibitions/citations Work was included in numerous exhibitions. 1961 Lunning Prize.
Bibliography Cat., David Revere McFadden (ed.), *Scandinavian Modern Design 1880–1980*, New York: Abrams, 1982. Cat, *The Lunning Prize*, Stockholm: Nationalmuseum, 1986: 126–29. Frederik Wildhagen, *Norge i Form*, Oslo: Sternersen, 1988: 159.

Plumet, Charles (1861–1928)

French architect and designer; born Cirey-sur-Vezouze (Meurthe-et-Moselle); active Paris.

Biography Having practiced in the Art Nouveau style before World War I, Plumet was one of those who sought the modern style through a synthesis of the arts; was a member of artists' group L'Art dans Tout and, 1903 with Frantz Jourdain, became a founding member of the Salon d'Automne; designed furniture with Tony Selmersheim, shown in various 1920s Salons, and built elegant townhouses in the 16th arrondissement, including on avenue Victor-Hugo, nos. 39 and 50 (now Musée Dapper), both in Paris. Designer of masonry buildings and furniture, he was chief architect of the 1925 *Exposition Internationale des Arts Décoratifs et Industriels Modernes*, Paris, where he erected four massive towers in no identifiable style that flanked the four corners of the Esplanade des Invalides; the structures housed restaurants. Also designed 1921 atelier of sculptor Joseph Bernard at 24, avenue Robert-Schuman, Boulogne-Billancourt. He died in Paris. The Charles Plumet prize has been established.
Bibliography Jean Badovici, *Maisons de rapport de Charles Plumet*, Paris: Morance, 1923. Pierre Cabanne, *Encyclopédie art déco*, Paris: Somogy, 1986: 226. Pierre Kjellberg, *Art déco: les maîtres du mobilier, le décor des paquebots*, Paris: Amateur, 1986/1990. Arlette Barré-Despond and Suzanne Tise, *Jourdain*, Paris: Regard, 1988.

Plus Glasshytte

Norwegian ceramics and glass factory; located Fredrikstad.

History 1958, the cooperative workshop Plus was founded by Per Tannum. The original intension was to supply designers and models to industry but became a place of craftspeople's workshops. From 1970, Plus Glasshytte was managed by Benny Motzfeldt.
Bibliography Jennifer Hawkins Opie, *Scandinavia: Ceramics and Glass in the Twentieth Century*, New York: Rizzoli, 1989.

Plus-linje
> See Unika-Vaev.

Plypetch, Chaiyut (1964–)
> See Propaganda.

Poelzig, Hans (1869–1936)

German architect and designer; born Berlin.

Training 1888–95 under Karl Schäffer, Technische Hochschule, Berlin.
Biography 1899–1916, Poelzig worked in his own office in Breslau (now Wroclaw, Poland); 1900–16, taught, Kunst und Kunstgewerbeschule (after 1911, called Akademie für Kunst und Kunstgewerbe), Breslau, where he was the director from from 1903; 1916–20, was municipal architect of Dresden and taught at Technische Hochschule there; from 1920, was head of a studio at Preussiche Akademie der Künste, Berlin; 1923, became professor, Technische Hochschule, Berlin-Charlottenburg, where pupils included architects-to-be Konrad Wachsmann, Rudolf Schwartz, Julius Posener, and Egon Eiermann. Poelzig turned to monumental buildings with work including the *tour-de-force* of Expressionism realized in his reconstruction of Max Reinhardt's Schumann Circus as the 1918–19 Großes Schauspielhaus, Berlin. The influence of the structure can be seen in E. Walmsley Lewis's New Victoria Cinema interior in London. Poelzig set up an architectural practice in Berlin and designed a 1911 office building in Breslau; 1911 water tower, Posen (now Poznan, Poland); 1911–12 chemical factory, Luban (now Poland); 1913 Centenary Exhibition (with Max Berg), Breslau; 1920–22 Salzburg Festival Theater; 1928–31 IG Farben administration complex, Frankfurt am Main; and Festival Hall project, Salzburg. He died in Berlin.
Exhibitions 1931, 1986, 1997 venues (catalogs below).
Bibliography Cat., *Poelzig und seine Schule*, Berlin: Wasmuth, 1931. Theodor Heuss, *Hans Poelzig, Lebensbild eines deutschen Baumeisters*, Tübingen: Rainer Wunderlich, 1939/1955. Julius Posener (ed.), *Hans Poelzig: Gesammelte Schriften und Werke*, Berlin: Mann, 1970. Cat., *Das dramatische Raum: Hans Poelzig, Malerei, Theater, Film*, Krefeld: Museum Haus Lange/Museum Haus Esters, 1986. Julius Posener, *Hans Poelzig: Reflections on his Life and Work*, New York: Architectural History Foundation; Cambridge, Mass.: MIT, 1992. Marco Biraghi, *Hans Poelzig: architectura, ars magna, 1869–1936*, Venice: Arsenale, 1992. Cat., *Hans Poelzig: Bauten für den Film*, Frankfurt am Main: Deutsches Filmmuseum, 1997.

Poggi, Carlo

Italian furniture manufacturer; located Pavia.

History 1890, the eponymous firm was founded by Carlo Poggi. A significant moment in the history of the enterpirse came in 1949 when Carlo's sons Ezio and Roberto met Franco Albini. He had designed the Rifugio Pirovano house (with Gino Colombini) in Cervinia, a landmark in regional modernism. Poggi's cabinet makers had built the furnishings for the interiors. It was then that the Poggi brothers hired Albini as their firm's exclusive designer, from 1950–68. His Poggi work included 1950 Luisa chair, 1950 LC525 armchair in cane, 1951 Cicognino table, 1956 PS16 rocking chair, and others. Subsequent commissioned designers have included Mario Bellini, Achile Castiglioni, Ugo La Pietra, Ennio Lucini, and Vico Magistretti.
Exhibitions 1972 *Italy: The New Domestic Landscape* (La Pietra's 1971 Uno sull'altro bookcase), The Museum of Modern Art, New York; numerous other venues worldwide.
Bibliography Cat., Leslie Jackson, *The New Look: Design in the Fifties*, New York: Thames & Hudson, 1991: 126.

Pohl, Josef (1894–1975)

Czech lighting designer.

Training 1929–33, Bauhaus, Dessau and Berlin.
Biography Pohl designed the 1929 precursor of the adjustable architect's lamp, a model produced by Gerd Balzer. (A similar lamp was produced by Körting und Mathieson as part of its Kamden range, and George Carwardine designed the Anglepoise in 1932.) Pohl and others at the Bauhaus also executed a prototype adjustable wall lamp, illustrated in *Staaliches Bauhaus, Weimar 1919–1923*, by K.J. Jucker. 1932, Balzer and Pohl organized Bauhaus students' work, which resulted in a conference and furniture-design competition.
Exhibitions Work included in 1988 and 1992 exhibitions, New York and Berlin (catalogs below).
Bibliography Cat., *The Bauhaus: Masters and Students*, New York: Barry Friedman, 1988. Cat., *Die Metallwerkstattam Bauhaus*, Berlin: Bauhaus-Archiv, 1992: 319.

Pöhlmann, Josef (1882–1963)

German silversmith; active Munich and Nuremberg.

Biography 1908, Pöhlmann set up his own workshop; taught in the metal workshop, Gewerbliche Fortbildungsschule, Nuremberg; 1919–45, taught silversmithing, Kunstgewerbeschule, Nuremberg, where one of his pupils was Ludwig Riffelmacher; designed early-1920s silver that was frequently simple and incorporated enameled columbines and larkspur reminiscent of the work of 16th-century silversmith Wenzel Jamnitzer of Nuremberg.
Bibliography Annelies Krekel-Aalberse, *Art Nouveau and Art Déco Silver*, New York: Abrams, 1989.

Poillerat, Gilbert (1902–1988)

French designer.

Training To 1921, chasing, École Boulle, Paris.
Biography 1921–27, Poillerat worked for metalworker Edgar Brandt on the rue Marat, Auteuil (now rue de Passy, Paris), as a designer and creator of wrought-iron furniture and furnishings; from 1927, was in charge of the new wrought-iron section of Baudet, Donon et Roussel, the carpentry and metal-construction workshop; designed and produced grillework, tables, chairs, consoles, screens, lighting, and firedogs, many to commissions from André Arbus, Jean Pascaud, Serge Roche, Lucien Rollin, and others. Working in a variety of media from jewelry to clothing, Poillerat's metalwork was rendered with characteristic winding calligraphic forms. He designed the 1934 ornamental door with folk scenes for a scholarly group in Maisons-Alfort, inexpensive jewelry for couturier Jacques Heim, a bronze door for 1935 oceanliner *Normandie*, and worked on the Bibliothèque Nationale, Palais de

Chaillot, Musée du Louvre, and Eiffel Tower. 1946, he became a professor, École Nationale des Arts Décoratifs, and set up his own workshop; eventually abandoned furniture and furnishings in favor of monumental wrought-iron work. His numerous commissions included public and governmental buildings such as the Palais de l'Élysée and designed the 1957 façade ironwork of the new synagogue in Strasbourg; often worked with Jacques Adnet.
Exhibitions Work shown for the first time, at Salon d'Automne (a grille); subsequently, at Salons of Société des Artistes Décorateurs from 1929.
Bibliography *Ferronnier d'aujourd'hui*, Paris: Charles Moreau, 1962. Pierre Kjellberg, *Art déco: les maîtres du mobilier, le décor des paquebots*, Paris: Amateur, 1986/1990. François Baudot, *Gilbert Poillerat, maître ferronnier*, Paris: Hazan, 1993.

Point, Armand (1861–1932)
French artist; born Algiers.

Biography Point was a leader in the movement to purify modern art by returning to an earlier tradition; strongly influenced by John Ruskin and the Pre-Raphaelites, attempted to emulate 15th- and 16th-century styles, like those of Leonardo da Vinci and Sandro Botticelli; founded Hauteclaire, a community of artists and craftspeople at Marlotte, where he oversaw the production of bronzes, embroideries, ceramics, enamels, and other decorative pieces.
Exhibitions Work shown with the Salon de la Rose Croix group from its 1892 beginning; Point designed its 1895 and 1896 exhibition posters.
Bibliography Yvonne Brunhammer et al., *Art Nouveau Belgium, France*, Houston: Institute for the Arts, Rice University, 1976.

Poiret, Paul (1879–1944)
French couturier and entrepreneur; active Paris.

Biography Poiret's meeting couturier Jacques Doucet was a decisive point in his career, when he thus began handling all of Doucet's graphic production and fashion designs. His costumes for famous personalities also brought him fame, including a mauve-and-black coat for Réjane for the stage production *Zana* and costume for Sarah Bernhardt in *L'aiglon*. The Doucet association ended after a dispute. Poiret became a pattern maker at Worth's couture house; 1904, opened his own establishment at 5, rue Auber, Paris, where he achieved success with a new natural style which freed women from their corsets. Several years later, he eliminated tight skirts. From 1909, Poiret's couture showroom was located in a townhouse he restored at the intersection of rue du Faubourg Saint-Honoré and avenue Victor-Emmanuel-II (now avenue Franklin-D.-Roosevelt) in which he gave dazzling parties attended by the *beau monde* of the day, including André Derain, André Dunoyer de Segonzac, Raoul Dufy, Jean-Louis Forain, Kees van Dongen, and dancers Isadora Duncan, Carlotta Zambelli, and Régina Badet. Poiret entertained principally at the Pavillon du Butard in the Bois de Fausses-Reposes; organized parties for the aristocracy; and designed theater sets. Poiret befriended avant-garde painters, particularly André Derain and Maurice de Vlaminck. Paul Iribe illustrated Poiret's portfolio *Les robes de Paul Poiret racontées par Paul Iribe* [ten pochoir images in a 250-copy edition] (Paris: Poiret, 1908) and Georges Lepape the *Les choses de Paul Poiret vues par Georges Lepape* [pochoir images in a 1,000-copy edition] (Paris: Maquet for Poiret, 1911). The 'new female,' as revealed in Iribe's and Lapape's drawings, was born. They wore Poiret clothes influenced by the Orient and the fashions of the Directoire: high waist lines, *décolletés*, flowing and shimmering fabrics, turbans, large embroidered coats, strong contrasting colors. Poiret's style rapidly became popular, though, after World War I, it was increasingly out of touch with the androgynous *garçonne* (boy-like) style popular in 1920s. 1911, Poiret founded the École Martine, a school for young women who were taught to paint freely from nature; wanted to break with the fussy, timid styles of the time; employed gifted working-class girls to create fresh and naïve motifs. The results of the Martine enterprise were realized as textiles, wallpapers, and carpets and characterized by a colorful, loose graphic style drawn by the students and sold through the Maison Martine. By 1919, the Martine school began producing bold and often painted furniture. On one project, a pair of shagreen and inlaid-ivory small chests, Poiret appears to have collaborated with Adolphe Chanaux c.1921. 1925, Poiret sold part of his collection of paintings to save his business, and his fortunes declined inexorably thereafter.
Exhibitions Work shown at Salons of Société des Artistes Décorateurs from 1924; on the pont Alexandre-III at 1925 'Exposition Internationale des Arts Décoratifs et Industriels Modernes,' Paris, where he equipped three barges, named *Amours*, *Délices*, and *Orgues*, decorated with Dufy-designed fabric in tufted ceilings and wall hangings. Work subject of 1974 exhibition, Musée Jacquemart-André (catalog below); 1986 with Nicole Groult, Musée de la Mode et du Costume, Musée Galliéra, Paris.
Bibliography Paul Poiret, *En habillant l'epoque*, Paris: Bernard Grasset, 1930; *My First Fifty Years*, London: Gollancz, 1931. Palmer White, *Poiret*, New York: Potter, 1973. Julien Cain (preface), *Poiret le magnifique*, Paris: Musée Jacquemart-André, 1974. *Poiret*, London: Academy, 1979. Yvonne Deslandres with Dorothée Lalanne, *Poiret: Paul Poiret 1897–1944*, Paris: Regard, 1986; New York: Rizzoli, 1987. Alice Mackrell, *Paul Poiret*, London: Batsford, 1990.
> See Martine, Atelier.

Polato, Piero (1936–)
Italian product and set designer and writer; born Vicenza; active Milan.

Training 1955–59, master of art degree, Istituto Statale d'Arte 'P. Selvatico,' Padova.
Biography 1960, Polato settled in Milan where he has designed more than 400 TV stage sets for RAI (Italian television network), Tedesca (Italian-Swiss television network), and TSI (Swiss television network); more than 125 educational TV programs for TSI from 1976–82 and RAI DSE 1991–92; more than 100 products, ranging from telephones, tabletop objects, lighting, to utilitarian objects for home and office, and exhibitions. Other clients have included Avancart, Agip, Canon Europa, Emme, Ferrari automobiles, Fiat Lancia automobiles, Italiana Luce, La Rinascente store, Octanorm Italia, Robots, SAIET Telefoni, Telecom Italia, UNESCO, Zucchi Telerie. Taught metallurgy, Istituto Superiore per le Industrie Artistiche (ISIA), Urbino.
Citations Awards at 1977 and 1984 'BIO' industrial-design biennial Ljubjana; 1981, 1987, 1988, 1991 Premio Compasso d'Oro; Form prize, 1997 Tendance fair, Frankfurt; 1981, 1983, 1991 Premio SMAU Industrial Design, Salone della Machina e Attrezzature per l'Ufficio, Milan; 1997 Complimenti prize, 1997 Schwizer Fachmesse Ornari, Bern.
Bibliography *ADI Annual 1976*, Milan: Associazione per il Disegno Industriale, 1976. Piero Polato, *Lavori in legno*, Milan: Mondadori, 1978. Piero Polato, *Educazione visiva*, Milan: Mondadori, 1981. *Dinamica della conoscenza e comunicazione interdisciplinare*, Rome: Istituto dell'Enciclopedia Treccani, 1985: 101–21. *Design italiano: Compasso d'Oro ADI*, Cantù: Galleria del Design e della'Arredamento, 1988: 44–49. Cat., Piero Polato, *Il modello nel design: la bottega di Giovanni Sacchi*, Milan: Hoepli, 1991.

Polglase, Van Nest (1898–1968)
American film set designer; born Brooklyn, N.Y.

Biography From 1919 as a designer at RKO motion-picture studio, Hollywood, Polglase became known for his 'Big White Set,' as seen in 1930s musical motion pictures with Fred Astaire and Ginger Rogers. From 1920s, he designed sets that could then be designed in white because arc lamps (that necessitated pink and green colors for stage-set illumination) had been replaced by incandescent bulbs. And the change from orthochromatic to more sensitive panchromatic film stock made a crisp, glossy effect possible. With his assistants, Polglase decorated Ginger Rogers's house in Hollywood. On *Top Hat* (1935), as the supervising art director, he had five unit art directors under him, including Carroll Clark, and 110 people to handle such particulars as carpets and furniture. His recreation of Venice for *Top Hat* soared two storeys, occupied two adjoining sound stages, and included winding canals, three bridges, a piazza, dance floors, balconies, and terraced cafés. His first film was probably *A Kiss in the Dark* (1925) and his last *Slightly Scarlet* (1956).
Bibliography Howard Mandelbaum and Eric Myers, *Screen Deco: A Celebration of High Style in Hollywood*, New York: St. Martin's, 1985. Ephraim Katz, *The Film Encyclopedia*, New York: Harper & Row, 1990.

Poli, Flavio (1900–1984)
Italian glassware designer; born Chioggia; active Venice.

Training In ceramics.
Biography 1929 at age 29, Poli entered the field of glass design, when he began a two-year association with Industrie Vetri Artistici Murano (I.V.A.M.); 1934, became the artistic director of Artistica Vetreria e Soffieria Barovier Seguso e Ferro and, 1937, acquired the shares owned by Luigi Olimpo Ferro, when Ferro left the firm and, 1963, Poli also left to join Società Veneziana di Conterie e Cristallerie. He also created 1952 designs by Studio Ars et Labor Industrie Riunite (S.A.L.I.R.), primarily a mirror/object engraving firm; late 1950s, executed heavy vases,

Flavio Poli. Vase. 1954. Glass, h. 13 1/2" (34.3 cm). Mfr.: Artistica Vetreria e Soffieria Barovier Seguso e Ferro, Italy (1957). Phyllis B. Lambert Fund. MoMA.

bowls, and drinking glasses in bold contrasting colors exemplary of innovatory Murano glass of the time.
Exhibitions/citations Work shown at 1932, 1948, 1950, 1952, and 1962 editions of Biennale di Venezia; 1958 *Exposition Universelle et Internationale de Bruxelles* (*Expo '58*); 1959 and 1983–84 exhibitions, Corning, N.Y. and Philadelphia.. (catalogs below). Prizes at editions of the Triennale di Milano; 1954 (two citations), 1955, 1959 Premio Compasso d'Oro.
Bibliography Cat., *Glass 1959*, Corning, N.Y.: The Corning Museum of Glass, 1959. Hans Vollmer, *Allgemeines Lexikon der bildenden Künstler des 20. Jahrhunderts*, vol. 6, Leipzig, 1962. Gio Ponti, 'Alta Fedeltà: Vetro di Flavio Poli,' *Domus*, no. 410, 1964: 50–52. Cat., Kathryn B. Hiesinger and George H. Marcus III (eds.), *Design Since 1945*, Philadelphia: Philadelphia Museum of Art, 1983. Marc Heiremans, *20th-Century Murano Glass*, Stuttgart: Arnoldsche, 1996.

Poli, Franco (1950–)

Italian designer; born Padova.

Training 1969–74, Istitutio Universitario di Architettura; 1970–71, Università Internazionale dell'Arte; both Venice.
Biography 1969–70, Poli worked as a freelancer in the architecture office of Paolo Maretto in Padova; 1974, began his individual professional career and was the artistic director of Lenzi in Quarrata (PT); 1975, opened the studio Metrocubo in Padova and was the artistic director of Gommatex of Prato (PO); 1977, opened the store Babele in Verona; 1979 – 82, was the artistic director of Bernini in Carate Brianza (MI) and, 1982–84, of B.F.B. kitchen firm in Fossombrone (PU); 1986, established a studio in Venice; 1987, was visiting professor, Università Internazionale dell'Arte, Florence; 1990–95, professor of design, Accademia di Belle Arti, Venice; 1991–96, visiting professor, Politecnico, Milan; 1994, founded Associazione del Design Veneto (A.D. Veneto), Padova; 1997, teacher and tutor, Consiglio Nazionale delle Richerche (C.N.R.) in Mesagne; 1998, set up a studio in Verona; 1999, founded Camera Italiana del Design (C.I.D.) in Milan; 1999–2001, artistic director of Pizzitutti (division of Matteograssi); 2001, artistic director of Omnidec Or in Molteno (LC). He has designed a large number of products including fabrics, furniture, tabletop objects, and lighting for clients, including Artieri del Legno, Bellato, Bernini, Busnelli, Cangrande, Cidue, Delta, Diamantini e Domeniconi, First, Frau Aviation, Giorgetti, Giovannetti, I.P.E., Oggi Italia, Piú Luce, Plana, Poltrona Frau, Stilnovo, Xilo, others. Poli has written a number of journal articles.
Exhibitions Work subject of 1998 'Franco Poli, il designer che esalta i pregi del legno,' Salone Internazionale della Sedia (Promoedia), Udine.
Bibliography Giuliana Gramigna, *1950–1980 repertorio, immagini e contributi per una storia dell'arredo italiano*, Milan: Mondadori, 1985. 'Intervista al designer Franco Poli,' *Report*, no. 13, Nov.–Dec. 1989: 37. 'Diseño in Milan,' *ON Diseño*, no. 155, 1994: 104. L. Lazzaroni, *35 anni del design al Salone del Mobile*, Milan: Cosmit, 1996. Cristina Morozzi and Silvio San Pietro, *Contemporary Italian Furniture*, Milan: L'Archivolto, 1996. A. Pozzi, 'Franco Poli, il designer che esalta i pregi del legno,' *Promosedia*, June 1998: 44–49. Giuliana Gramigna and Paola Biondi, *Il design in Italia dell'arredamento domestico*, Turin: Allemandi, 1999.
> See Seguso Vetri d'Arte.

Policar, Jean-Michel (1970–); Elsa Francès (1966–)

French industrial designers. Policar: born Versailles; active Paris. Francès: born and active Paris.

Training Policar: École Nationale Supérieure des Arts Appliqués et des Métiers d'Art. Francès: ENSCI (Les Ateliers); both Paris.
Biography From 1993 under Philippe Starck, they worked in the design studio Tim Thom of Thomson multi-média on products by Thomson, Sheba, and Telefunken. After Starck's 1995 departure from Thomson, they designed Thomson's Collection Line of product ideas; from 1999, were design managers of the Thomson Life and Thomson Scenium ranges. From 2001 at Tim Thom, Policar directed color and materials research, and Francès the design strategy. 1999, they were sponsored by Alcatel and ENSCI (Les Ateliers) to organize a research group to focus on stylistic futurology and the portable telephone (presented at 2000 CeBIT fair, Hanover). Their innovative lighting by Ligne Roset has included Dé Lumineux illuminated table (produced from 1999), 2000 On Air, 2002 La Conic, and 2002 So Watt lamps. 2002 Eh Bain bathroom project, sponsored by Création de la Délégation aux Arts Plastiques (DAP).
Exhibitions/citations Work included in 2004 *Design d'Elle*, Galerie VIA (French furniture association), Paris. 1998, 2000, 2002 Appel Permanent grants, VIA; 1998 Grand Prix de la Presse et de la Critique (for Dé Lumineux illuminated table, subsequently by Ligne Roset), 1994 Salon du Meuble, Paris.
Bibliography Mel Byars, *On/Off: New Electronic Products*, New York: Universe, 2001.

Polinsky, Glenn (1963–)

American designer; active San Francisco.

Training Industrial design, University of Washington, St. Louis, Mo.
Biography Polinsky worked at Friedman Design, San Francisco, designing products for public and domestic furniture manufacturers. His Balerafon Chair was produced by Brueton Industries. After Friedman, he founded and directed In Form, a manufacturer of contemporary home products, whose clients included the Solomon R. Guggenheim Museum, The Museum of Modern Art, Starbucks, and Crate & Barrel; 2000, became the design director of Modo, Beaverton, Ore., manufacturer of mobile hospital furniture that facilitates the use of high-tech equipment.
Citations 1988 *I.D.* magazine Annual Award (paper cutter); 1988 IDSA award (for a paper cutter), Industrial Designers Society of America (IDSA); 1988 Workspace Competition (for a computer desk), LIMN store, San Francisco.

Pollack, Mark (1954–)

American textile design; born Baltimore, Md.

Training 1976, bachelor of fine arts degree, Rhode Island School of Design, Providence.
Biography 1988 with Rich Sullivan and Susan Doty Sullivan, Pollack established Pollack & Associates, New York, and, 1988, introduced its first textile collection; 1995, first residential collection. 1998, the firm's name was simplified to Pollack.
Bibliography Cat., R. Craig Miller (intro.), *U.S. Design 1975–2000*, Munich: Prestel, 2002.

Pollak, Alfred (d. 1909)

Austrian silversmith; active Vienna.

History 1878, the firm of Alfred Pollak was founded; produced designs by Arnold Nechansky, Ernst Lichtblau, Hans Bolek, and Rudolf Hammel,

and students of the Kunstgewerbeschule, Vienna.
Exhibitions Work shown at 1902 *Esposizione Internazionale d'Arte Decorativa Moderna* (silverwork of Hammel and students of the Kunstgewerbeschule made by Alfred Pollak), Turin.
Bibliography Annelies Krekel-Aalberse, *Art Nouveau and Art Déco Silver*, New York: Abrams, 1989. Waltrand Neuwirth, *Wiener Gold und Silberschmiede und ihre Punzen 1867–1922*, Vienna: Neuwirth, 1977: 112–16.

Pollini, Gino (1903–1991)

Italian architect and designer; born Rovereto.

Training From 1927, Politecnico, Milan.
Biography Pollini often collaborated with Luigi Figini. 1926 with Figini and others, Pollini cofounded the Gruppo Sette, the architectural fraternity that launched Italian Rationalist architecture with the publication of its 1926–27 four-part manifesto. 1928, Pollini joined the Fascist Party. 1930, Pollini and Piero Bottoni replaced Carlo Enrico Rava and Alberto Sartoris as delegates to the Congrès Internationaux d'Architecture Moderne (CIAM), and they participated to 1946. Pollini and Figini with Adalberto Libera and Guido Fretti (all Gruppo Sette members) and Piero Bottoni designed the Casa Elettrica for Montedison at 1930 (4th) *International Exposition of Decorative Arts*, Monza, where an all-electric kitchen was featured, based on German and American models. Pollini had earlier designed the 'Appartamento Elettrico' at the 1929 *Esposizione dell'Alto Adige*, Bolzano. 1932 with Bottoni, Pollini organized the international exhibition *Lotizzamento Razionale*, Milan. Through 1930s, Pollini worked in the Italian Rationalist style; with Figini, designed 1934–35 Olivetti building in Ivrea, built 1939–41; with Figini and Xanti Schawinsky, designed 1935 Studio 42 typewriter by Olivetti.
Exhibitions 'Villa-Studio per un artista' (with Figini) installed at 1933 (5th) Triennale di Milano; 1934 competition project (with Gian Luigi Banfi, Lodovico Belgiojoso, Arturo Danusso, Luigi Figini, Enrico Peressutti, and Ernesto Rogers) at Palazzo del Littorio, Rome; 1938 Malparte house (with Mario De Renzi and Figini) on the piazza delle Forze Armate, Capri, shown at 1942 *Esposizione Universale di Roma*; 1983 in Milan (catalog below). Work subject of 1996 exhibition, Museo di Arte Moderna e Contemporanea di Trento e Rovereto (catalog below).
Bibliography Eugenio Gentili Tedeschi, *Figini e Pollini*, Milan: Il Balcone, 1959. Cesare Blasi, *Figini e Pollini*, Milan: Monumità, 1963. Luigi Figini and Gino Pollini, 'Origini dell'architettura italiana alla cultura internazionale,' *L'architettura d'aujourd'hui*, vol. 22, no. 41. Cat., *Design Process: Olivetti 1908–1983*, Milan: Olivetti, 1983: 377. Richard A. Etlin, *Modernism in Italian Architecture, 1890–1940*, Cambridge: MIT, 1991: 227, 233, 390, 494, 523–24, 554, 641n32. Vittorio Savi, *Figini e Pollini: Architetture, 1927–1989*, Milan: Electa, 1990. Cat. Vittorio Gregotti (curator), *Luigi Figini, Gino Pollini: opera completa*, Milan: Electa, 1996.

Pollitzer, Sigmund (1918–1980)

British painter, decorative glass designer, and writer; born London.

Training In London, Switzerland, and Hanover.
Biography Pollitzer worked on the commissions of architect and designer Oliver Bernard, including 1930 Cumberland Hotel and 1932 Marble Arch Corner House, both in London. Pollitzer and Kenneth Cheeseman were protégés of Bernard. 1933–38, Pollitzer was chief designer at Pilkington Glass, for which he created showrooms in Glasgow, Leeds, Nottingham, St. Helens, and Piccadilly in London, and the firm's stand at 1937 *Glass Train*, a publicity project fitted with a range of decorative glass and shown at railway stations throughout Britain. His decorative glass features were included in some interiors by Cheeseman, including those for British Vitrolite in 1934 and the 1934 Kirk Sandall Hotel (architect, T.H. Johnson), near Doncaster. Other commissions included accoutrements for 1936 oceanliner *Queen Mary*; 1937 McVitties Guest Restaurant; 1938 oceanliner *Mauretania*; 1938 Gaumont theater, Haymarket, London; and at 1937 *Exposition Internationale des Arts et Techniques dans la Vie Moderne*, Paris; 1938 *British Empire Exhibition*, Glasgow; 1939–40 *New York World's Fair: The World of Tomorrow*.
Exhibitions 1933 *British Industrial Art in Relation to the Home* (bedroom designed by Oliver Hill), Dorland Hall; 1935 *British Art in Industry*, Royal Academy; 1979–80 *Thirties* exhibition, Hayward Gallery (glassware designs) (catalog below); all London.
Bibliography Cat., *Thirties: British Art and Design Before the War*, London: Arts Council of Great Britain/Hayward Gallery, 1979.

Pollock, Bruno

Austrian furniture designer.

Biography Pollock designed a stacking chair (patented 12 June 1930) in tubular steel produced from c. 1932 as model RP7. Its stacking principle facilitated mass production and revolutionized auditorium seating. British furniture manufacturer Cox was involved in a 1934 legal action with competitor Pel over Pel's 1931 RP6 stacking chair, the rights to which Pel had purchased from Pollock.
Exhibitions Work included in 1977 exhibition, London (catalog below).
Bibliography *The Cabinet Maker*, July 1931. Cat., Dennis Sharp et al., *Pel and Tubular Steel Furniture of the Thirties*, London: Architectural Association, 1977. Barbie Campbell-Cole and Tim Benton (eds.), *Tubular Steel Furniture*, London: The Art Book Company, 1979: 20, 56.

Pollock, Charles (1930–)

American industrial designer.

Training Bachelor of art degree in industrial design, Pratt Institute, Brooklyn, N.Y.
Biography Pollock worked in the industrial-design office of George Nelson, New York, where he designed 1958 fiberglass armchair with tapering tubular metal legs by Herman Miller; 1958, set up his own design office where he designed 1960 no. 657 sling chair with leather seat and steel-frame support and 1965 12E-1 fiberglass-shell/upholstered office side- and armchair, both by Knoll; subsequently, designed chairs by Thonet and 1981 Penelope thermoplastically engineered steel-mesh chair, originally by Castelli, now by Haworth. He is not the brother, also named Charles Pollock, of American artist Jackson Pollock.
Citations 1991 Excellence by Design Award in Industrial Design, Pratt Institute.
Bibliography *Dal cucchiaio alla città nell'itinerario di 100 designers*, Milan, 1983. John Pile, *Dictionary of 20th-century Design*, New York: Facts-On-File, 1990: 206–07. Hans Wichmann, *Die Realisation eines neuen Museumtyps*, 1980–90, Munich: Die Neue Sammlung, 1990.

Poloni, Arnaldo (1931–)

Italian industrial designer; born Bergamo; active Milan.

Biography Poloni has designed television sets, sound systems, and electronic equipment for clients including Compania Generale Elettricità (CGE), SNT, Siemens, Minerva, Körting, and Grundig Italiana. He was a member, ADI (Associazione per il Disegno Industriale).
Bibliography *ADI Annual 1976*, Milan: Associazione per il Disegno Industriale, 1976.

Poltrona Frau
> See Frau, Renzo.

Pomone

French decorating studio.

History 1922, the Pomone design and decorating studio was established at Au Bon Marché department store, Paris. The store itself was founded by Aristide Boucicaut (Bellême 1810–Paris 1877) in a small building on the rue du Bac in 1848 and in an enormous new building in 1869 (completed 1887), begun by architect Alexandre Laplanche, succeeded by Louis-Charles Boileau. From 1923, Paul Follot was artistic director of Pomone and, to 1928, the director. 1928, René Prou succeeded Follot and, 1932, became director. 1932–55, Albert Guénot was a designer there, sometimes collaborating with Prou.
Exhibitions 2002 *Le Bon Marché, 150 ans au cœur du 7e arrondissement*, Marie du 7e Arrondissement, Paris.
Bibliography *Les Grands Magasins du Bon Marché*, Paris, 1914. Michael B. Miller, *The Bon Marché: Bourgeois Culture and the Department Store, 1869–1920*, Princeton: Princeton University, 1981.

Pompe, Antoine (1873–1980)

Belgian architect, teacher, and designer; son of a jeweler; active Brussels.

Training Precious metalwork, Académie Royale des Beaux-Arts, Brussels; 1890–91, drawing courses, Kunstgewer-blicheschule, Munich.
Biography Pompe began as a goldsmith; 1893–96, worked with master ironmongers; 1897–98, with builders/founders. From 1899, he was a draftsperon in the office of architect Adrien Delpy in Brussels; subsequently and to 1903, was active in the decorative-arts and cabinet shop of Georges Hobé; 1904, became a partner of architect Adhémar

Lenner, and they won the 1908 restricted competition of the Palace Hotel, Brussels, for which Pompe designed the furniture. 1910–20, he was a partner of Fernand Bodson, and they designed 1914 Maison du Peuple (unexecuted) in Liège and 1919 Batavia complex (with Raphaël Verwilghen) in Roeselare. Pompe was a contemporary of Henry van de Velde and belongs to the second generation of Belgian moderns. His architecture includes his first house, 1910 Institut Orthopédique Van Neck (now Institut de Rythmique Jaques-Dalcroze de Belgique, a dance school, from 1983), rue Henri Wafelaerts, Brussels. Classified as an historic landmark in 1981, it was a decisive step in Belgian architecture with its pre-Cubist expressive geometry. In addition to architecture, he designed silver cutlery and hollow-ware in c. 1903 in the style of van de Velde. Pompe is the only turn-of-the-century Belgian architect whose silver designs have survived, although they may never have been produced. He died in Brussel at age 106.
Exhibitions Work subject of 1973–74 exhibition, Musée d'Ixelles.
Bibliography *Antoine Pompe: ou, l'architecture du sentiment...*, Ixelles: Musée d'Ixelles, 1973. Annelies Krekel-Aalberse, *Art Nouveau and Art Déco Silver*, New York: Abrams, 1989.

Pond, Edward (1929–)
British designer; born London.

Training Textiles and lithography, South East Essex Technical College; Royal College of Art, London.
Biography From 1950s, Pond designed textiles and wallpapers for manufacturers in Britain and abroad; 1960s, embraced Pop Art and Op Art motifs and some historicist patterns; 1969, founded the shop Paperchase; 1976, established Edward Pond Associates, where a range of design disciplines are being pursued.
Bibliography Jonathan M. Woodham, *Twentieth-Century Ornament*, New York: Rizzoli, 1990: 324.

Pons, Geneviève (1924–)
French decorator and furniture designer; active Paris.

Training 1941–44, École Nationale Supérieure des Arts Décoratifs; 1944–46, Centre d'Art et Technique, Musée Nissim Camondo; both Paris.
Biography 1946–48, Pons worked in the Primavera design studio of Au Printemps department store, Paris, managed by Colette Guéden; made a trip to the US and then worked for a year in a department store in Ottawa, Canada; back in Paris, was the manager from 1952–72 of La Maîtrise design studio of Les Galeries Lafayette department store. Pons's interiors and furniture were simple and rational; however, sometimes called on woven fibers for seating and handwoven fabrics.
Exhibitions/citations Showed work at Société des Artistes Décorateurs, a member from 1947; and at editions of Salon des Arts Ménagers from 1952. Received 1948 Prix Plumet, Société d'Encouragement à l'Art et à l'Industrie.
Bibliography *Ensembles mobiliers*, Paris: Charles Moreau, nos. 3–4, 1954. *Mobilier et décoration*, No. 9, Dec. 1955. Patrick Favardin, *Les décorateurs des années 50*, Paris: Norma, 2002: 306.

Pontabry, Robert
French designer.

Biography Pontabry designed the kiosks at 1925 *Exposition Internationale des Arts Décoratifs et Industriels Modernes*, Paris, and a woman's desk for 1927 competition organized by the Union Centrale des Arts Décoratifs.
Bibliography Pierre Kjellberg, *Art déco: les maîtres du mobilier, le décor des paquebots*, Paris: Amateur, 1986/1990.

Ponti, 'Gio' Giovanni (1891–1979)
Italian architect and designer; born and active Milan.

Training 1918–21, architecture, Politecnico, Milan.
Biography 1921, Ponti worked in an architectural office in Milan with Mino Fiocchi and Emilio Lancia. 1923–30, he designed Wiener Werkstätte-inspired ceramics produced by Richard Ginori, where he worked from 1923–28. He was director of the Biennale di Monza (later named Triennale di Milano) from 1925–79, where he was the head of the executive board from 1924–39; 1956, became a founding member, Associazione per il Disegno Industriale (ADI); from 1927, worked with glassmaker Paolo Venini; 1923–36 with Lancia, worked in a studio in Milan; 1928, founded the journal *Domus* and, 1938–41 and 1948–79, was its first editor; 1933–45 with Antonio Fornaroli and Eugenio Soncini, worked in a studio in Milan. Piero Fornasetti became a student of Ponti

Gio Ponti. Superleggera side chair (no. 646). 1951. Wood and wicker, 32 3/4 x 16 5/8 x 18 1/4" (83.2 x 42.2 x 46.4 cm). Mfr.: Cassina, Italy. Gift of the mfr. MoMA.

and, subsequently, a protégé and an assistant, collaborating with Ponti on a number of projects in their distinctive 17th-century-image-applying technique, designed by Ponti and decorated by Fornasetti. From 1930s, Ponti designed printed fabrics, cutlery, ceramics and ceramic tiles, automobile bodies, lighting, sewing machines, enamels by Paolo di Poli, mosaics by Gabbianelli, 1951 cutlery by Krupp of Essen, 1953 sanitary equipment by Ideal Standard (including a toilet that has become a classic), and stage sets at La Scala in Milan. His work was modern in essence but drew on traditional motifs and imagery, illustrating the eclecticism of the early years of fascism. Before abandoning his neoclassical approach, he served on the executive committee of 1933 (5th) Triennale di Milano; 1936–61, taught, Politecnico, Milan; became Italy's best known postwar architect. For his first (1936) Montecatini building in Milan, designed everything, including door knobs and sanitary fittings. 1945, he founded the journal *Stile*, of which he was the director to 1947. His widely published 1948–49 espresso machine by La Pavoni owed a great deal to American streamline design of this period. 1952–76, Ponti was in partnership with Alberto Rosselli and Antonio Fornaroli and, after Rosselli's 1976 death, with Fornaroli. His best-known building is 1956 Pirelli office tower (with Rosselli, Fornaroli, and engineer Pier Luigi Nervi), damaged by an airplane in 2002 but rehabilitated. Ponti was influential on a number of younger designers and employees, including Lino Sabatini and Richard Sapper, who worked in his office 1958–59. Ponti's best-known furniture design is 1951 Superleggera side chair (no. 646), by Cassina from 1957, a play on vernacular Italian forms and still in production. His clients for furniture included Arflex, Cassina, Singer, and the Nordiska Kompaniet. He wrote nine books and a large number of journal articles and edited eight books alone and with others.
Exhibitions/citations Work shown at 1923 (1st) *Esposizione Biennale delle Arti Decorative e Industriali Moderne*, Monza; 1928 *Exposition of Art in Industry at Macy's* (room setting), Macy's department store, New York; 1951 (9th) Triennale di Milano (cutlery by Krupp); 1956 Biennale di Venezia (glass by Venini); 1971 and 1983–84 exhibitions (Superleggera chair), London and Philadelphia (catalogs below). Was general supervisor of 1961 *Italia 61*, Turin; 1966 (1st) Eurodomus, Genoa; 1968 (2nd) Eurodomus, Turin. Work was subject of 1965 *The Expression of Gio Ponti*, University of California, Los Angeles; 1987 in Faenza (catalog below); 2001, Queens Museum, New York; 2002, Design Museum, London. Numerous awards, including 1956 National Grand Prize; 1954 and 1957 Premio Compasso d'Oro; honorary degree, Royal College of Art, London.
Bibliography 'Espressione di Gio Ponti,' *Aria d'Italia,* vol. 8, Milan:

Daria Guarnati, 1954. Nathan H. Shapira, 'The Expression of Gio Ponti,' *Design Quarterly*, nos. 69–70, 1967. Cat., *Modern Chairs 1918–1970*, London: Lund Humphries, 1971. Cat., G.C. Bojani (ed.), *L'opera di Gio Ponti alla manifattura di doccia*, Faenza: MIC, 1977. G.C. Bojani et al. (eds), *Gio Ponti: ceramica e architettura*, Faenza: MIC, 1987. Lisa Licitra Ponti, *Gio Ponti: The Complete Work* 1923–1978, Cambridge: MIT, 1990. Gloria Arditi and Cesare Serratto, *Gio Ponti: venti cristalli di architettura*, Venice: Il Cardo, 1994. Ugo La Pietra et al., *Gio Ponti*, Milan: Rizzoli/Coliseum, 1995. Cat., Fulvio Irace (ed.), *Gio Ponti*, Milan: Cosmit, 1997. Cat, *Gio Ponti: le maioliche*, Milan: Biblioteca di via Senato, 2000. Lucia Miodini, *Gio Ponti: gli anni trenta*, Milan : Electa, 2001. Massimo Martignoni, *Gio Ponti, gli anni di stile 1941–1947*, Milan: Abitare, 2002. Arcila M. Torres, *Gio Ponti*, Milan: Gribaudo, 2002.

Ponzio, C. Emanuele (1923–)

Italian designer.

Biography From 1965 with Cesare Casati, Ponzio was active in Studio DA (Designer Associati); designed interiors of hotels, banks, and government buildings; served clients including Phoebus, Nai Ponteure, and Autovox. Ponzio and Casati's 1968 Pillola 'medicine capsule' lamps have become widely known as a prime example of 1960s Anti-Design.
Bibliography Giancarlo Iliprandi and Pierluigi Molinari (eds.), 'Italian Industrial Designers,' in *Omnibook No.2*, Udine: Magnus, 1985: 81. Hans Wichmann, *Italien Design 1945 bis heute*, Munich: Die Neue Sammlung, 1988.
> See Casati, Cesare; Sormani; Studio DA; Anti-Design.

Poor, Henry Varnum (1888–1970)

American ceramicist; born Chapman, Kan.; active New York.

Training Economics and art, Stanford University, Stanford, Cali.; 1910, Slade School of Art, London; 1911, Académie Julian, Paris.
Biography 1912, Poor returned to the US from France and taught art at Stanford University and at California School of Design (now Mark Hopkins Institute of Art), San Francisco; c. 1918, settled in New York and turned to ceramics as a means of income and, 1920s, completely abandoned painting. In his ceramic work, he used the Persian technique of painting and etching on damp slip before applying the glaze; built his studio Crowhouse in Rockland County, N.Y.; subsequently, sold his utilitarian pieces through art galleries in Manhattan. He had no interest in the warping of plates but rather sought spontaneity in decoration and form; from mid-1930s, worked infrequently in ceramics; 1946, became first president, Skowhegan School of Painting and Sculpture, Maine; early 1950s, was artist-in-residence, American Academy in Rome, and painting instructor, Columbia University, New York; wrote about aesthetics in ceramics in *A Book of Pottery: From Mud to Immortality* (Englewood Cliffs, N.J.: Prentice-Hall, 1958).
Exhibitions 1923, first showed ceramics, Montross Gallery, New York; work subject of 1983 exhibition, Pennsylvania State University (catalog below). Gold medal, Architectural League of New York.
Bibliography Alfred Dupont Chandler, *Henry Varnum Poor, Business Editor, Analyst, and Reformer*, Cambridge: Harvard, 1956. Karen Davies, *At Home in Manhattan: Modern Decorative Arts, 1925 to the Depression*, New Haven: Yale, 1983: 55. Cat., Harold E. Dickson et al., *Henry Varnum Poor, 1887–1970: A Retrospective Exhibition*, University Park: Museum of Art, Pennsylvania State Univeristy, 1983. R. Craig Miller, *Modern Design 1890–1990*, New York: Abrams, 1990.

Popova, Liubov' Sergeevna (1889–1924)

Russian artist and designer; born Ivanovskoye, Moscow Province.

Training 1907–08, art, Stanislav Zhukovskii's and Konstantin Yuon's private studios, Moscow; private studio of Impressionist painter Stanislav Zhukovshii; 1912–13, Académie 'La Palette à Montparnasse,' Paris.
Biography Popova was originally a Constructivist, who abandoned the 'dead ends of representation' to become an 'artist constructor'; became successful in combining Cubism (discovered while in France), Russian icons, and Italian Renaissance art. 1910, Popova traveled to Italy and became acquainted with Giotto's and Pintoriccio's works; 1910–11, traveled to St. Petersburg, Rostov, Yaroslavl, Suzdal, Pereslavl, and Kiev and discovered the work of Mikhail Vrubel and icon painting; 1912 with Viktr Bart, Vladimir Tatlin, and Kirill Zdanevich, set up The Tower studio, and worked in Tatlin's studio; 1912–13, worked and studied in Paris, visiting the studios within Académie 'La Palette à Montparnasse' under Henri Le Fauconnier and Jean Metzinger, where she met Vera Pestel and Nadezhda Udal'tsova. 1913, Popova returned to Russia, working again with Tatlin, Udal'tsova, and Alekandr Vesnin; 1915, developed her own version of non-figurative painting, 'pictorial architectonics'; 1916, joined Kasimir Malevich's Supremus group (or Suprematists); 1919–21, executed painterly constructions; 1918, taught at SVOMAS / VKhUTEMAS; 1920, became a member of INKhUK; rejected studio painting and experimented with designs for books, ceramics, textiles, and dresses; 1922, created sets and costumes for Meyerhold's production of Fernand Crommelynck's farce *The Magnanimous Cuckold* (1922) and *Zemia Dybom* (earth in turmoil) (1923); designed dresses and textiles for the First State Cotton-Printing Factory (Tsindel textile works), near Moscow, 1923–24. In her fecund career, she journeyed from Russian avant-garde and Cezannism to Cubism, Futurism, and Suprematism, through to Constructivism, easel painting, and industrial design. She died in Moscow of scarlet fever contracted from her son.
Exhibitions 1914–16 participating in all Russian avant-garde exhibitions, work shown at 1914 and 1916 exhibitions of Bubnovy Valet (Jack of Diamonds), Moscow; *Tramway V*; *0–10*; and *The Store*. Contributed to 1918 (5th) *From Impressionism to Non-Objective Art* state exhibition; 1919 (10th) *Non-Objective Creation and Suprematism* state exhibition; 1921 *55 = 25* exhibition and 1922 *Erste Russische Kunstausstellung*, Berlin; 1980 and 1992 exhibitions, Los Angeles and New York (catalogs below); 2000–01 *Amazons of the Avant-Garde*, Guggenheim Museum, New York (catalog below). Work subject of posthumous 1924 exhibition, and 1980 venue at State Tretyakov Gallery (catalog below), both Moscow.
Bibliography Cat., *L.W. Popova: 1889–1924, Exhibition of Works from the Centennial Exhibition*, Moscow: State Treyakov Gallery, 1980. Dmitrii Vladimirovich Sarabianov and Natalia L. Adaskina, *Lioubov Popova*, New York: Abrams, 1990. Magdalena Dabrowski, *Liubov Popova*, New York: The Museum of Modern Art, 1991. Cat., *The Great Utopia: The Russian and Soviet Avant-Garde, 1915–1932*, New York: Guggenheim Museum, 1992. S.O. Khan-Magomedov, *Vhutemas: Moscou, 1920 1930*, Paris: Regard, 1990: 420–23. Dmitri V. Sarabianov and Natalia L. Adaskina, *Popova*, Paris: Seuil, 1989; New York: Abrams, 1990. Dmi-trii Sarabianov and Vladimirovich Sarabianov, *Liubov Popova: Zhivopis*, Moscow: Galart, 1994. Cat., John E. Bowlt and Matthew Drutt (eds.), *Amazons of the Avant-Garde: Alexandra Exter, Natalia Goncharova, Liubov Popova, Olga Rozanova, Varvara Stepanova, and Nadezhda Udaltsova*, New York: Abrams, 2000.

Porsche, Ferdinand (1875–1951); Dr. Ing. h. c. F. Porsche; Volkswagen

Automobile engineer and firms.

Biography 1900, Porsche, born in Bohemia (now Czech Republic), built his first automobile, a front-wheel car with an electric nave-mounted engine, for carriage builder Jacob Lohner, Vienna; 1906, became chief designer at Austro-Daimler, where he was the managing director from 1916; from 1923, wass technical director, Daimler, Germany (which amalgamated with Benz in 1926 to form Daimler-Benz). At Daimler-Benz Porsche conceived the formidable SS and SSK; from 1928, worked for the Steyr firm. With the intention of becoming an independent consulting engineer, he dismissed the airplane engine designer and the gear-box specialist at Steyr and hired his former collaborators at Austro-Daimler and 20-year-old son 'Ferry.' 1931, Porsche established the consultancy Dr. Ing. h.c. F. Porsche GmbH, Konstructionbüro für Motoren-Fahrzeug-Luftfahrzeug und Wasserfahrzeugbau. One of Porsche's first commissions on his own was a large luxury car for Wanderer, which he fitted with wing-integrated headlights and a long plunging back end. Concurrently, he also undertook independent studies concerning a small, cheap automobile, called the Type 12 (which Daimler had earlier rejected), with a body by Erwin Komenda that resembled a large Wanderer. Porsche received an order from motorcycle manufacture Zündapp for a new prototype of a small car with a rear engine, central-beam chassis, four-wheel independent suspension, and alligator closing luggage compartment and spare wheel—built in 1932 but abandoned. Porsche saved the 85,000-mark payment for the Zündapp prototype. Jan. 1933, the project was further pursued by Porsche as the Type 32, which had been ordered by NSU motorcycle manufacturer, with an air-cooled 4-cylinder engine. A small *Volkswagen* (people's car)—based on Hitler's full-workforce and grand economic ambitions—was to be offered as a worker enticement, a project about which Hitler was passionate. May 1934, Porsche and Hitler met in Berlin, and Hitler, then chancellor of the Reich, presented his ideas about the Volkswagen. It was to accommodate two adults and three children, have an air-cooled engine, achieve 62 miles/hour (100km/hour), feature 6.3 quarts (6 liters) of gasoline per 62 miles (100km), and cost the consumer nor more than 1,000 marks. Based on the Zündapp and NSU experiences, 1930s aerodynamic body-shape principles, and the early work of Edmund Rumpler, Paul Jaray, and Hans Ledwinka, Porsche was suc-

Ferdinand Porsche and Volkswagenwerk. Volkswagen Type 1 sedan. 1938. Steel, 708 x 126 x 160" (149.9 x 153.7 x 406.4 cm). Mfr: Volkswagen, Germany. Acquired with assistance from Volkswagen of America, Inc. MoMA.

cessful in creating the milestone for a large sum of money. It was realized as the 1938 Volkswagen. Porsche was assisted by two auto manufacturers, but he failed to meet the ten-month deadline. After great travail, an appropriate, very simple motor had been developed; the body and chassis finalized, and a factory near Hanover was built to make the KdF-Wagen (*Kraft durch Freude Wagen*—car of strength through joy), opened on 26 May 1938. Hitler was delighted. However, over half the plant was destroyed by Allied bombs in 1944. Porsche was arrested in 1945, sent to Dijon, and released through a 500,000-franc bail in 1947. The same year of his release, Porsche founded his own automobile-manufacturing firm (planned during his French incarceration) and built his first sports car, a 1948 hand-made aluminum-bodied prototype called the Type 356 and in production with a steel body after 1949. The 356 A, as it is now known, was followed by a large number of models and innovations (including possibly the most successful, the 911) and a respectable racing history. 1949, Porsche was hired as a VW consultant and paid a generous royalty on every car built. More recent models have included 911 Carrera Coupé designed by Harm Lagaay, 911 GT2 by Lagaay and Anthony Hatter; 911 GT3 by Lagaay, Wolfgang Möbius, and Matthias Kulla; 911 Turbo by Lagaay and Pinky Lai; 959 PSK 4-wheel drive; and SUV (small utility vehicle).
Exhibitions/citations Porsche's System Löhner-Porsche shown at 1900 *Exposition Universelle*, Paris. Received 1905 Poetting Prize as Austria's outstanding automotive designer. Red Dot awards, Design Zentrum Nordrhein Westfalen, Essen, to the in-house designers: 1998 (911 Carrera Coupé) and three 2002 (for 911 GT2, 911 GT3, 911 Turbo).
Bibliography W. Robert Nitske, *The Amazing Porsche and Volkswagen Story*, New York: Comet, 1958. William Boddy, *Volkswagen Beetle: Type 1, The Traditional Beetle*, London: Osprey, 1982. Terry Shuler et al., *The Origin and Evolution of the VW Beetle*, Princeton, N.J.: Princeton Publishing, 1985. Paul Frere, *Porsche 911 Story*, Sparkford, UK: Haynes, 1997. Michael Thiriar, *Porsche Speedster: The Evolution of Porsche's Light-Weight Sports Car 1947 to 1994—356 and 911*, St. Paul, Minn.: Motorbooks International, 1998. Laurence Meredith et al., *Original VW Beetle*, Bideford, UK: Bay View Books, 1999. Dan Ouellette, *Bug Book*, Santa Monica, Cal.: Angel City, 2000. Paola Antonelli (ed.), *Objects of Design: The Museum of Modern Art*, New York: The Museum of Modern Art, 2003: 208–09.

Porsche, 'Butzi' Ferdinand Alexander (1935–)

German designer; active Germany and Austria; son of automobile designer/engineer Ferdinand 'Ferry' Porsche (1910–98); grandson of Porsche automobile founder Ferdinand Porsche (1875–1951).

Training Hochschule für Gestaltung, Ulm.
Biography Porsche worked for engineering company Bosch before joining the family automobile firm Porsche GmbH in its design-engineering department; became the company's chief designer and created two car bodies, including the celebrated 1963 911 and Targa; 1972, set up his own design studio in Zell-am-See, Austria, where he has designed various products, including watches, pipes, sunglasses, and leather goods. In 1980s as part of the trend toward luxury, he designed expensive, popular wares, also furniture, lighting, and electrical products for other firms such as Poltrona Frau, Artemide, Inter Profil, Ycami. Work has included 1985 lighting range by Luci that included the Platone ceiling, Parete PL wall, Lettura PL floor, and Soffitto pendant lamps; PAF Jazz lamp by PAF; and a large body of subsequent work. All of his designs have manifested his stark Ulm-School training.
Exhibitions/citations 1991 *Mobili italiani 1961–1991: le Varie Età dei linguaggi* (1984 Antropovarius leather seating by Poltrona Frau), Salone del Mobile, Milan; numerous other exhibitions worldwide. Large number of honors, including 2003 Red Dot award (for Data Bank by LaCie), Design Zentrum Nordrhein Westfalen, Essen.
Bibliography Albrecht Bangert and Karl Michael Armer, *80s Style: Designs of the Decade*, New York: Abbeville, 1990. Werner Dagefür, *Auf dem Weg zum Oldtimer: Design and Technik europäischer Klassiker aus den Jahren 1945–1970*, Hamburg: Gruner + Jahr, 1991. *Mobili italiani 1961–1991: le varie età dei linguaggi*, Milan: Cosmit, 1992. Uta Brandes, *Ferdinand Alexander Porsche, Designer: Damit das Denken am Leben bleibt*, Göttingen: Steidl, 1992.

Porsgrunds Porselænsfabrik (aka Porsgrunn Porselensfabrikk)

Norwegian ceramics factory; located Porsgrunn.

Biography 1885, Porsgrunds Porselænsfabrik, the first porcelain factory in Noway, was founded by Johan Jeremiassen (Kviteseid, 1843–1889), who hired Carl Maria Bauer as its technical manager. Its early production was in traditional underglaze painted and transfer-printed motifs, including those of Royal Copenhagen and Meissen. c. 1900, the Nordic style was introduced in patterns by Gerhard Munthe, Henrik Bull, Thorolf Holmboe, and others. On Jeremiassen's 1889 death, the firm was managed by his brother-in-law Gunnar Knudsen, a member of the Stortinget (national assembly) of Norway and, subsequently, the prime minister of Norway from 1908–11. Successful modern forms and patterns began to be produced with the hiring of designers Hans Flygenring in 1920 and Nora Gulbrandsen, an exponent of Art Déco style, who was the artistic director from 1928–45. Tias Eckhoff became the artistic director in 1952. Other designers have included Anne Marie Edegaard, Konrad Galaaen, and Eystein Sandnes. By 1980s, Porsgrunds was Norway's largest porcelain factory, with Stein Devik as its manager. The historical Porsgrunds collection is housed in Den Gamle Tollbod (the old custom house), Porsgrunn City Museum.
Citations Awards have included five citations, 1972 Industrie Forum

Design (iF), Hanover; a number of others.
Bibliography Alf Bøe, *Porsgrunds Porselænsfabrik: bedrift of produksjon gjennom åtti år*, Oslo: Tanum, 1967. Fredrik Wildhagen, *Norge i Form*, Oslo: Stenersen, 1988. Jennifer Hawkins Opie, *Scandinavia: Ceramics and Glass of the Twentieth Century*, New York: Rizzoli, 1989.

Porteneuve, Alfred (1896–1949)

French furniture designer; nephew of Jacques-Émile Ruhlmann.

Training To 1928, architecture, École Nationale Supérieure des Beaux-Arts, Paris.
Biography Porteneuve worked with the cabinetmaker/designer Jacques-Émile Ruhlmann in Paris. On Ruhlmann's 1933 death, Porteneuve opened his own workshop at 47, rue de Lisbonne, Paris, designing furniture that abandoned Ruhlmann's use of exotic woods in favor of fruit woods, laminates, and metal. He decorated and furnished numerous apartments, governmental and commercial offices, and interiors of 1939 oceanliner *Pasteur*; sometimes collaborated with Jean Dunand.
Exhibitions With Ruhlmann, participated in the design of L'Hôtel du Collectionneur pavilion at 1925 *Exposition Internationale des Arts Décoratifs et Industriels Modernes*, Paris.
Bibliography *Ensembles mobiliers*, vol. 2, Paris: Charles Moreau, 1937. Florence Camard, *Ruhlmann*, Paris: Regard, 1983. Pierre Kjellberg, *Art déco: les maîtres du mobilier, le décor des paquebots*, Paris: Amateur, 1986/1990.

Porter, Bruce (1865–1953)

American designer, painter, poet, and critic; born and active San Francisco.

Biography Porter designed gardens, painted murals, and created numerous church windows in San Francisco, San Mateo, Stockton, and Pacific Grove, including windows for Christ Episcopal Church in Coronado and for Children's Home in San Diego; all California. He and Gelett Burgess edited the journal *The Lark*, writing some of its essays and poetry, designing cover design, and rendering illustrations. Porter wrote the preface to the book *Art in California* (1909); was a member of Les Jeunes, a group of San Francisco bohemians; secretary, San Francisco Guild of Arts and Crafts; best known for his monument to Robert Louis Stevenson at Portsmouth Square, San Francisco.

Porthault, Madeleine (1905–1979); Daniel Porthault (1901–1974)

French producers and vendors of household linens; active Paris.

Biographies Madeleine began working for couturière Maggy Rouff in Paris. Rouff, the daughter of the directors of the house of Drecoll, sent

Ferdinand Porsche and Christian Schwamkrug. FinePix 6800 digital camera. 2001. Aluminum and magnesium, h. 3 7/8 x w. 3 1/8 x d. 1 3/8" (9.8 x 8 x 3.6 cm). Mfr.: Fuji Photo Film Co., Japan.

Paolo Portoghesi. Cutlery. 1982–84. Sterling silver, longest (dinner knife) l. 9 1/8 x w. 15/16" (23.2 x 2.4 cm) to shortest (teaspoon) l. 4 1/4 x d. 1" (10.8 x 2.5 cm). Mfr: Cleto Munari, Italy. Gift of the mfr. MoMA.

Madeleine to the US, where she designed, sold, and took measurements for clothing orders sewn in Paris; returned to Paris and married Daniel Porthault, the owner of a lingerie firm that supplied Rouff. 1920, Daniel created the D. Porthault enterprise to produce household linens and, 1925, was joined by Madeleine. 1933, a factory was established in Rieux-en-Cambrésis to weave linens for embroidery and printing. 1950, its first factory was purchased for printing linens. Prints on linen fabric are reproduced by hand with wooden blocks. The first clients included wealthy people, such as the Ford and Mellon families in the US. 1955, Madeleine designed the carnation print for the Duchess of Windsor. 1956, the firm was commissioned to make linens with a goldfish motif for Aristotle Onassis's yacht *Christina*. Other clients have included the Rothschilds, the Shah of Iran, the Kennedys, and French presidents. Its first shop was located on the rue de la Grange Batelière, Paris. 1960, Porthault opened its first boutique on East 57th Street, New York, and, 1966, a boutique on the avenue Montaigne, Paris; some have been moved to other locations and others added since. Eventually the firm was managed by the Porthaults' son Marc and his wife Françoise. Porthault's delicate screen-printed and hand-embroidered linens are considered to be some of the finest worldwide. Marc Porthault designed the 1965 four-leaf-clover motif and matching Limoges porcelain for Louise de Vilmorin, 1985 print of ducks, rabbits, and brass horns, and 1986 tulip print. 1991, the firm reissued the satin sheets with images of Grecian maidens in antique lace, originally created for Barbara Hutton. Its design studio is in Levallois-Perret. The firm, still family owned, is a member of the Comité Colbert.
Bibliography Christopher Petkanas, 'Customs of the Country,' *House & Garden*, May 1991: 146–53, 192.

Portoghesi, Paolo (1931–)

Italian architect, designer, and teacher; born Rome.

Training To 1957, Università degli Studi, Rome.
Biography 1958, Portoghesi set up his own architectural office in Rome; 1962–66, was professor of architecture at the university in Rome, where he was president from 1968–76; 1967–77, taught, Politecnico, Milan, where he was the dean from 1980, taught, Università degli Studi 'La Sapienza,' Rome; from 1979, directed the architecture section of the Biennale di Venezia, of which was president from 1983; 1969–83, was the editor of journal *Controspazio*; from 1977, of *Taca* (the journal of the Istituto di Storia dell'Architettura); and, from 1983, of *Eupalino*. He designed 1982–84 silver cutlery by Cleto Munari, 1985 Rabirio desk by Ceccotti, 1986 Sesguialtera lamp by Societa del Travertino Romano, Liuto seat by Poltronova, and 1986 Aldebarhan table by Officina Romana del Disegno. His books have included *After Modern Architecture* (New York: Rizzoli, 1982) and *Postmodern: The Architecture of the Industrial Society* (New York: Rizzoli, 1983). His hexagonal tea set was one of 11 in Alessi's 1983 Tea and Coffee Piazza project. Has been a member of Accademia degli Arti e del Disegno in Florence from 1977, of Accademia Lingustica in Genoa from 1977, and of Accademia Nazionale di San Luca from 1984. A leading postmodern architect and

town planner, his architecture includes 1959 Baldi 1 house and Papanice house, both Rome; 1968–78 Istituto Tecnico Industriale Statale dell'Aquila, L'Aquilla; 1973 International Airport Terminal, Khartoum; 1974 Royal Palace, Amman; 1977 Mosque of Rome and Center for Islamic Culture; 1977 Thermal Center, Musignano, Canino; 1978–83 headquarters of the Accademia di Belle Arti, L'Aquilla; 1978 Mosque, Rome; 1981–87 housing for Enel workers, L'Aquila; 1984 Popolare del Molise, Campobasso; 1987–89 Sala di Soggiorno (Tettucio plant), Montecatini Terme.
Exhibitions/citations Work included in numerous exhibitions and galleries in the US and Europe, such as *Affinità Elettive* (Città del Sogno alcove bed) at 1985 Triennale di Milano. Subject of several Italian exhibitions. 1974 honorary degree, University of Lausanne. Won competition for the town of Salerno.
Bibliography Carole Cable, *Paolo Portoghesi: A Selected Bibliography of Books and Articles by and about Him*, Monticello, Ill.: Vance Bibliographies, 1983. Giancarlo Priori, *L'architettura ritrovata: Opere recenti di Paolo Portoghesi*, Rome: Kappa, 1985. Cat., Claudio D'Amato, *Paolo Portoghesi: opere*, Modena: Panini, 1985. Juli Capella and Quim Larrea, *Designed by Architects in the 1980s*, New York: Rizzoli, 1988. Cat., Mario Pisani, *La Piazza come 'luogo degli sguardi': Paolo Portoghesi*, Rome: Gangemi, 1990. Mario Pisani, *Paolo Portoghesi*, Milan: Electa, 1992. Cat., Cristina Di Stefano and Donatella Scatena, *Paolo Portoghesi: designer*, Rome: Diagonale, 1998. Giovanna Massobrio et al., *Paolo Portoghesi, architetto*, Milan: Skira, 2001.

Portzamparc, Elizabeth de (1954–)

Brazilian designer; born Rio de Janeiro; active Paris.

Training To 1980 under Paul-Henri Chombart de Lauwe, urban sociology, École des Hautes Études en Science Sociale, Paris.
Biography At age 18, she settled in France and, subsequently, became a French citizen; 1977–80, was director, Atelier d'Urbanisme, Antony; married architect Christian de Portzamparc; 1975–76, was active in research; established EDP studio and, from 1975, designed exhibitions, interiors, furniture, lighting, including 1987 furniture of Café Beaubourg, Paris, including the interior with her husband. Recent products: 1998 public furniture for Bordeaux tramway, desks by Strafor, sanitary fittings by Duravit, and lamps by Véronèse; 1996 objects by Baccarat (produced in 1998). Also designed interiors of Les Grandes Marches restaurant and 2001 Pathé Munt cinema, both Paris; Grande Bibliothèque, Montreal; French Embassy, Berlin; and a number of others. 1987, she founded Éditions du Tracé Intérieur for her furniture production; 1998, established Galerie Mostra, Paris.
Exhibitions/citations Work shown at Galerie Mostra; Galerie Citroën, Amsterdam. Subject of 1999 exhibition, Parque Das Ruinas, Rio de Janeiro. Medal of merit for design and interior architecture, Fondation Candido Mendes, Rio de Janeiro.
Bibliography *Christian de Portzamparc*, New York: Princeton Architecture Press, 1995.

POSNOVIS
> See UNOVIS.

Post-it® note
> See Fry, Arthur.

postmodern

Architecture/design term.

History 'Postmodern' was first used in the context of literary criticism by Jean Baudrillard and Jacques Derrida, among others. The idea was first applied to 1960s architecture by British art historian Nikolaus Pevsner, who realized that an expressive, non-Rational, non-autocratic type of architecture was emerging that rejected many of modernism's tenets. 1970s, American architecture historian and critic Charles Jencks extended Pevsner's ideas, defining postmodern as a range of architecture that, moving beyond modernism's constraints, included works by American architects Michael Graves and Robert Venturi and by Luxembourgian architect Leon Krier (who practiced in London from 1974). postmodernism made references to mass culture and embodied pluralism, eclecticism, historicism, humor, the linguistic (or semiotic) meanings of constructed forms, and emotionally satisfying solutions in design. 'postmodern' has also become a term used to describe those products of 1970s–80s which rejected the Functional Bauhausian/Ulm-design-school approach, using criteria for design which undermined, or possibly mocked, modernism. The work of Ettore Sottsass and his Memphis studio group—with its celebration of dubious taste, brash colors, ironic wit, dislocation, playful historical references, and eclecticism—characterized postmodern design after 1981. Postmodern architects in Japan, the US, and Spain contributed to the movement, as well as a number of prominent manufacturers such as Alessi in Italy and Knoll in the US. The movement ebbed somewhat in 1990s, when its frivolity began to seem out of step with the mood of economic pessimism and environmental concerns. Modernism looked likely to have more staying power than its supposed successor, because postmodernism seemed stalled at the point of a negative definition: what it was not. Known by the new soubriquet, 'po-mo' had fallen into disfavor, especially in the UK, by the beginning of the 21st century.
Bibliography Jean Baudrillard, *L'échange symbolique et la mort*, Paris: Gallimard, 1976. Paolo Portoghesi, *After Modern Architecture*, New York: Rizzoli, 1982. Charles Jencks, *The Language of Post-Modern Architecture*, London: Academy, 1984. Mark Poster (ed.), *Jean Baudrillard: Selected Writings*, Stanford: Stanford University, 1988. Jean Baudrillard, 'The End of Production,' *Polygraph*, nos. 2–3, 1988: 5–29. Michael Collins, *Post-Modern Design*, London: Academy, 1991.

Carl Hugo Pott Jr. Cutlery (no. 2722). c. 1957. Nickel-plated 18/8 stainless steel, longest (dinner fork) 8" (20.3 cm), shortest (butter knife) 6 1/8" (15.5 cm). Mfr.: C. Hugo Pott, Germany. Given anonymously. MoMA.

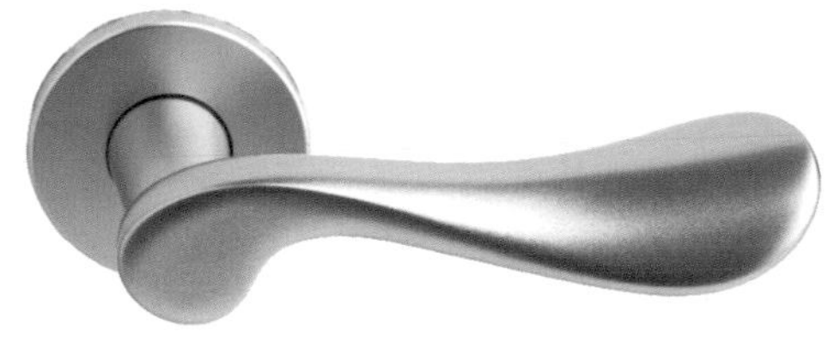

Johannes Potente. Door handle (no. 1020). 1953. Aluminum, 1 3/8 x 5 1/4 x 2 15/16" (3.5 x 13.3 x 7.5 cm). Mfr.: Franz Schneider Brakel (FSB), Germany (1998). Gift of the mfr. MoMA.

Potente, Johannes (1908–1987)

German engraver, toolmaker and instructor.

Biography For a number of years from 1953, Potente was a designer at the FSB door-handle firm, a family business founded in 1881 in Franz Schneider Brakel (FSB), Germany. His renowned handles have been recognized as following the four laws of grip, as later codified by designer/pedagogue Otl Aicher: 1. thumb stop, 2. index finger indentation, 3. roundness, and 4. grip volume. Potente's presence at FSB was powerful, and his dicta indisputable. So renowned is his work that a small book volume has been devoted to a single example (see below).
Bibliography Andrea Scholtz, *Die Türklinken 1020 von Johannes Potente: The Door Handle 1020 by Johannes Potente*, Frankfurt: form, 1998. Otl Aicher et al., *Johannes Potente, Brakel: Design der 50er Jahre*, Cologne: Walter König, 1999.
> See Braun, Jürgen.

Pott Jr., Carl Hugo (1906–1985); C. Hugo Pott GmbH

German metalworker.

Training In damascening and galvanizing, Städtische Fachschule für Metallgestaltung, Solingen; Forschungsinstitut für Edelmetalle und Metallchemie (FEM), Schwäbisch-Gmünd.
Biography 1920s–30s, Carl Hugo Pott Jr. became interested in the tenets of the Deutscher Werkbund, the Bauhaus, and various advanced-design movements in Germany; 1932, joined the metalwares firm founded (1904) by his father Carl Hugo Pott and eventually completely changed the design of the firm's products into simple unadorned forms, abandoning the heavily ornamented work of the time. After World War II, Carl the younger's designs and those of others commissioned by him were widely published, repeatedly winning awards. The firm also became known for the high quality of its production. Others whom Pott commissioned to design for the firm included Josef Hoffmann, Hermann Gretsch, Wilhelm Wagenfeld, Hans Schwippert, Elisabeth Treskow, and Don Wallance, who, from 1990, have been followed by Friedrich Becker, Ljubisa Misic, Ralph Krämer, and Tobias Huys. 1985–2001, firm was managed by Hannspeter Pott and, from 2001, by Stefanie Georg and Horst Löhnert. Ralph Krämer (Saarbruck 1955–) has been one of its more distinguished and prolific designers, who established his Büro für Gestaltung in Saarbruck in 1983.
Exhibitions/citations Diploma of honor (Carl the younger's 1935 no. 2716 cutlery), 1937 *Exposition Internationale des Arts et Techniques dans la Vie Moderne*, Paris (where his work was first shown); silver medal, 1940 (7th) Triennale di Milano; numerous awards at events in Milan, Düsseldorf, Brussels, and Ljubljana. 1998 Red Dot Best of the Best (for a cheese fork and knife by Krämer), Design Zentrum Nordrhein Westfalen, Essen.
Bibliography Heinz Georg Pfaender, 'Der Designer Carl Hugo Pott,' *Architektur und Wohnform*, vol. 74, 1966: 371–74. Graham Hughes, *Modern Silver Throughout the World*, New York: Crown, 1967: pl. 63–67. Cat., Kathryn B. Hiesinger and George H. Marcus III (eds.), *Design Since 1945*, Philadelphia: Philadelphia Museum of Art, 1983. Mel Byars, *Design in Steel*, London: Laurence King, 2002.

Poulsen, Louis

Danish lighting manufacturer; located Copenhagen.

Biography 1874, a wine importing business known as Kjøbenhavns Direkte Vin-Import-Kompagni (Copenhagen direct wine importation company) was founded by Ludvig R. Poulsen. But it closed in 1878. 1892, he opened a second business for selling tools and electrical supplies and, 1896, employed his nephew Louis Poulsen. On Ludvig's 1906 death, Louis assumed the management of the firm and, 1908, moved it to Nyhavn 11, Copenhagen, where it remains today as the headquarters. 1911, Sophus Kaastrup-Olsen (d. 1938) became a partner and the name was changed to Louis Poulsen & Co. 1917, Kaastrup-Olsen became the sole owner but retained the name, and the enterprise rapidly grew. Poul Henningsen's widely published PH three-saucer ceiling lamp for the firm was first installed in the Forum building, Copenhagen, in 1926, with production having been encouraged by its winning a gold metal at 1925 Paris *Exposition*. Another early installment included 1929–39 Tugendhat house in Brno (architect, Ludwig Mies van der Rohe). Lamps based on Henningsen's PH series as well as other early designs are still in production, including 1958 PH5 and 1958 PH-Zapfen (Artichoke) hanging lamps. From 1950, Poulsen began using plastics in its production, including acrylics for shades, diffusers, and other fittings. Late 1960–early 1970s, Arne Jacobsen designed for Poulsen; Verner Panton executed numerous designs (including 1960 Moon model) for the firm and Miranda/King a bollard; others have also contributed to the inventory.
Exhibitions/citations Henningsen won a 1924 competition for the design of lamps in the Danish pavilion, 1925 *Exposition Internationale des Arts Decoratifs et Industriels Modernes*, Paris, and a gold medal from the Exposition committee; numerous other exhibitions and citations for his lighting designs by Poulsen.
Bibliography Cat., Milena Lamarová, *Design a Plastické Hmoty*, Prague: Uměleckoprůmyslové Muzeum, 1972: 202. Tina Jørstian and Poul Erik Munk Nielsen (eds.), *Light Years Ahead: The Story of the Lamps*, Copenhagen: Louis Poulsen, 1994 (Eng. and Danish eds.). www.louis-poulsen.com.

Poulsen, Tage (1940–)

Danish furniture designer.

Training To 1964, Kunsthåndværkerskolen, Copenhagen; 1959, apprenticeship in cabinet making.
Biography Poulsen became a designer for Gramrode Møbelfabrik, Hirtshals Savværk, Eigil Rasmussen, and Goth; 1965, set up his own design studio.
Citations 1974 Danish furniture prize; 1975 Johannes Krøiers award.
Bibliography Frederik Sieck, *Nutidig Dansk Møbeldesign – en kortfattet illustreret beskrivelse*, Copenhagen: Bondo Gravesen, 1990.

Povey, Albert John Stephen (1951–)

British furniture and interior designer; born London.

Training 1976–79, furniture design, Royal College of Art, London, under Robert Heritage.
Biography 1981, Povey became a freelance designer; 1981–83, designed the British American Tobacco exhibition and worked for various clients; 1983, opened a design studio in King's Cross, London, where he designed 1985 Diametric range of furniture, including the

Louis Poulsen: Verner Panton. Moon hanging lamp. 1960. Painted metal, h. 15" (38 cm). Mfr.: Louis Poulsen, Denmark. Courtesy Quittenbaum Kunstauktionen, Munich.

Curved-Rail Bed, Y Trestle Table, and Eclipse Sofa, all in steel, and furniture for Phoenix Café in Kensington. A specialist in metal furniture, his work included 1986 Macstack Table for Macfarlanes Solicitors, Akrosystem modular shelving, Utility Chair, and Tulip Lighting. 1988, he opened the Diametric retail shop in Covent Garden, London; designed furniture and lighting for Tilby and Leeves advertising agency and Stacking Steel File Tray for the BBC (British Broadcasting Corporation). Other clients included Lincoln Hannah, Sloane Helicopters, TV Register Group, Quandrance Communications, and Relocation Project Management. 1990, Povey opened a factory in Cannock, Staffordshire, then in Uttoxeter; became known for his clever interpretations in steel of classic British styles, including Queen Anne and those of Charles Rennie Mackintosh.
Bibliography Mel Byars, *50 Chairs...*, Hove: RotoVision, 1996.

Powell, Alfred Hoare (1865–1960); Louise Powell (b. Louise Lescure 1882–1956)
British potters; husband and wife.

Training Alfred Powell: Slade School of Fine Art, London.
Biography To 1892, Alfred Powell worked for architect J.D. Sedding. The Powells were active in the Arts and Crafts movement; were friends of Ernest Barnsley from their time in London. A screen with panels by Louise Powell for 1916 *Arts and Crafts Exhibition* in London was further installed in their house. They became well-known as pottery decorators, particularly Alfred for Wedgwood from 1903–30 as well as many pieces by Rodmarton. 1930s, the Powells visited the plant regularly and bought blanks that they fired there.
Exhibitions Regularly showed their work at editions of Arts and Crafts Exhibition Society, London.
Bibliography *British Art and Design, 1900–1960*, London: Victoria and Albert Museum, 1983.

Powell, David Harmon (1933–)
British designer.

Biography 1954–60, Powell worked on the development of melamine tableware at British Industrial Plastics; 1960–68, was the chief designer of Ekco Plastics in Southend. He beame a specialist in the use of plastics and executed innovatory designs for Ekco's industrial and domestic products, including 1968 Nova injection-molded-plastic stacking tableware, Ekcoware kitchen storage containers, and 1970 semi-disposable cutlery. 1968, Powell set up his own studio and became the first tutor in molded plastics, Royal College of Art, London.
Citations 1970 award, Council of Industrial Design.
Bibliography John Heyes, 'Getting It Right the First Time,' *Design*, no. 271, Jan. 1967: 47–53. 'Disposable Plastics Cutlery,' *Design*, no. 258, June 1970: 45. Cat., Kathryn B. Hiesinger and George H. Marcus III (eds.), *Design Since 1945*, Philadelphia: Philadelphia Museum of Art, 1983.

Powell, Edmund Barnaby (1891–1939)
British glassware designer; son of James Crofts Powell.

Training 1909–14, Architectural Association, London.
Biography 1918, Powell joined the family firm of James Powell & Sons of the Whitefriars Glassworks in Wealdstone, Middlesex, where he subsequently became the director and designer of decorative and domestic glassware. He specialized in decorative glassware on a large scale, based on the malleable qualities of blown glass. With a few British contemporaries, Powell and his Whitefriars colleague William Wilson brought favorable worldwide recognition to British glasswork.
Bibliography Cat., *Thirties: British Art and Design Before the War*, London: Arts Council of Great Britain/Hayward Gallery, 1979.

Powell, James; Harry J. Powell (1855–1922)
British glassware manufacturer/entrepreneurs.

History 1834, London wine merchant James Powell bought the Whitefriars Glassworks. c. 1880–c1908, James and Harry J. Powell produced their own glass designs and those of commissioned designers, executing Venetian styles in green soda glass. The firm based its patterns on 16th- to 19th-century Italian and Dutch paintings and also reissued Philip Webb's and Thomas Jackson's glass designs. James Powell's grandson Harry Powell (1855–1922) made important contributions to the firm's designs of late 19th and early 20th centuries, at a time when the company was making respectable high-quality glass. Harry Powell initially called on 17th-century Venetian forms and later, particularly for export after 1900, turned to Art Nouveau. He studied ancient glass and the aging effects of oxidisation and, late 1910s, retired. 1919, the firm was named James Powell & Sons (Whitefriars) Ltd., with the parentheses. 1928 following the factory's move to Wealdstone, William Wilson joined the firm, which produced modern forms in 1930s. 1963, the enterprise was named Whitefriars Ltd. and is today known for its industrially produced art glass.
Exhibitions Work shown at 1900 *Exposition Universelle*, Paris; 1903 Arts and Crafts exhibition, London.
Bibliography Frederick Cooke, *Glass: Twentieth-Century Design*, New York: Dutton, 1986. Leslie Jackson, *Whitefriars Glass: The Art of James Powell & Sons*, London: Richard Dennis, 1996.

Powolny, Michael (1871–1954)
Austrian sculptor, ceramicist, and teacher; born Judenburg.

Biography 1905 under the aegis of the Wiener Werkstätte, Powolny and Berthold Löffler founded the Wiener Keramik, which represented a high point in the decorative phase of late Jugendstil, or Art Nouveau. The workshop produced ceramics showing folkloric influences from as far afield as Russia. c. 1910, Powolny designed glassware for J. & L. Lobmeyr, produced by Loetz, some with handles from the glass mass and others with no handles. While some of his glass was rendered in vivid colors, opaline glass with stripes was his signature design (reflective of Koloman Moser's 1903 'Zebra decor'). He died in Vienna.
Exhibitions Work included in 1986–87 Loetz glass exhibition, Österreichisches Museum für Angewandte Kunst, Vienna, and Oberösterreichisches Landesmuseum, Linz (catalog below).
Bibliography Günther Feuerstein, *Vienna—Present and Past: Arts and Crafts—Applied Art—Design*, Vienna: Jugend und Volk, 1976. Robert Waissenberger, *Vienna 1890–1920*, Secaucus, N.J.: Wellfleet 1984. Cat., Waltraud Neuwirth, *Loetz Austria, 1900: Glas*, Vienna: Neuwirth, 1986. Elisabeth Frottier, *Michael Powolny: Keramik und Glas aus Wien 1900 bis 1950: Monografie und Werkverzeichnis*, Vienna: Böhlau, 1990.

Pozzi, Ambrogio (1931–1997)
Italian industrial designer; born Varese; active Gallarate (MI).

Biography From 1951, Pozzi worked in the family firm Ceramica Franco Pozzi in Gallarate and redesigned its traditional products in an award-winning Functional style. His renowned 1970 Compact stacking coffee service was designed for machine production in three sizes. He set up his own design practice with clients including Riedel, Rossi, Guzzini, Harveiluce, Pierre Cardin, Rosenthal, Norex, La Rinascente department store. Other work has included 1968 Duo dinnerware and 1987 limited-edition cup and saucer included in Collector's Cup range by Rosenthal; 1970–71 first-class inflight ceramic dinnerware (with Joe Colombo) by Richard Ginori; and ceramics and glass by Ritzenhoff, from 1995. He became a member, ADI (Associazione per il Disegno Industriale).
Exhibitions Participated in all editions of 1954–73 Triennale di Milano. Work included in 1980 and 1983 exhibitions, Faenza and Philadelphia

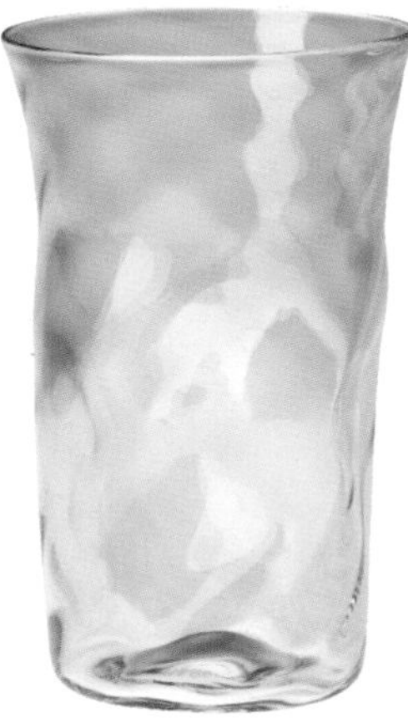

Harry J. Powell. Tumbler. c. 1900. Glass, h. 4 3/8" (11.1 cm) x dia. 2 3/4" (7 cm). Mfr.: Whitefriars Glassworks, UK. Mrs. Armand P. Bartos Purchase Fund. MoMA.

(catalogs below). 1958–64, 1966, and 1970 first prizes for industrial design, Vicenza; 1968 and 1973 gold medals (the latter for the porcelain service with Colombo for Alitalia) and 1970, Concorso Internazionale della Ceramica d'Arte, Faenza; 1967–74 Bundespreis Produktdesign, Rat für Formgebung (German design council), Frankfurt, and a member of its juries, 1969–70; 1971–74 industrial design competition, Valencia; numerous awards, Industrie Forum Design (iF), Hanover. To the family firm, two 1970 Premio Compasso d'Oro (for Compact coffee service and for TR 113 tableware).
Bibliography *Premio Compasso d'Oro*, 1971: 122–25. *ADI Annual 1976*, Milan: Associazione per il Disegno Industriale, 1976. Cat., *Arte e design*, Faenza: Palazzo delle Esposizioni, 1980. Cat., Kathryn B. Hiesinger and George H. Marcus III (eds.), *Design Since 1945*, Philadelphia: Philadelphia Museum of Art, 1983.

Pozzi, Giancarlo (1924–)
Italian industrial designer; born Turin; active Milan.

Biography 1950, Pozzi began his professional career; 1963–67, collaborated with architect Alberto Rosselli; 1970–74, with Achille Castiglioni; and within Studio Ponti/Fornaroli/Rosselli. His clients included Feal, Fiat, Moviter, Lancia, Omsa, Cassina, Montecatini, Vis-Securit, Malugani, and Arflex. He became a member, Associazione per il Disegno Industriale (ADI); mid-1960s with Franco Santi Gualtieri under Rosselli's directorship, was the editor of journal *Domus*; was a cofounder of the Premio Compasso d'Oro.
Bibliography *ADI Annual 1976*, Milan: Associazione per il Disegno Industriale, 1976.

Practical Equipment Ltd.
> See Pel.

Pratt, Davis J. (1917–1987)
American designer.

Biography After World War II, Pratt designed furniture, including a 1948 self-made inflated-tube lounge chair; also a 1951 dining chair with rattan over steel, designed with Harold Cohen for their firm Designs in Production.
Exhibitions Good Design exhibition/award (dining chair), The Museum of Modern Art, New York.

Pré, Maurice (1907–1988)
French decorator and furniture designer; born and active Paris.

Training From 1924, École Boulle, Paris.
Biography Pré worked for eight years in the studio of Jacques-Émile Ruhlmann; went to Switzerland to work for architect Alphonse Laverrière in Lausanne; 1934, returned to Paris and was active as a decorator for Patout, Démaret, and Alfred Portcneuve; from 1935, was an independent designer; 1946, suceeded René Gabriel at École des Arts Appliqués, Paris, and, 1947, became professor of composition, École Nationale des Beaux-Arts, Nancy; 1955, taught, École Boulle; was known for combining different materials (metal, wood, Formica) in furniture. Quite versatile, he designed rugs, lighting, mass-produced tabletop items, decorations on faience, and porcelain by Manufacture Nationale de Sèvres.
Exhibitions Participated with Jacques-Émile Ruhlmann at 1925 *Exposition Internationale des Arts Décoratifs et Industriels Modernes*; independently at 1937 *Exposition Internationale des Arts et Techniques dans la Vie Moderne.* Work shown regularly at Salons of Société des Artistes Décorateurs and editions of Salon d'Automne, Salon de l'Imagerie, and Salon des Arts Ménagers.
Bibliography *Mobilier et décoration*, No. 1, Feb. 1955. Pascal Renous, *Portraits de créateurs*, Paris: H. Vial, 1969. Patrick Favardin, *Les décorateurs des années 50*, Paris: Norma, 2002: 142.

Pree, D.J. De
> See DePree, Dirk Jan.

Preiss, Johann Philipp Ferdinand (aka Fritz Preiss 1882–1943)
German designer; born Ernbach.

Training In ivory-carving under Philipp Willmann.
Biography Preiss began a successful collaboration with Otto Poertzel (1876–1963); worked in Berlin during the years that Demêtre Chiparus was active in Paris. Though Preiss and Chiparus both created chryselephantine statuettes of bronze and ivory, their styles and appeal are very different. Working in a smaller scale, Preiss is known for the fine quality of his ivory carving and for the cold-painted clothing of his figures. His images of athletic children and youths represent contemporary German ideals of athletic prowess and perfection, including *The Archer, Posing*, and *Thoughts*. The association with Poertzel resulted in many of their figures being similar in form. 1906, Preiss and his partner Walter Kassler opened a foundry in Berlin (active until Preiss's death). 1929, they bought the rival workshop Rosenthal und Maeder. Preiss's bronzes were enormously popular in Germany and abroad, sold by galleries such as Phillips & MacConnal in London and Bournemouth.
Bibliography Auction cat., *Christie's New York*, 26 May 1983: Lots 448, 449, 450.

Davis J. Pratt. Chair. 1948. Fabric-covered inflated-tube seat and metal rods. Mfr.: the designer, US. Gift of the designer. MoMA.

Preiswerk, Gertrud (aka Gertrud Dirks-Preiswerk 1902–)
Swiss textile designer; born Basel.

Training 1926–30, Bauhaus, Dessau; 1929, summer courses, Johanna Brunson's weaving school, Stockholm; in silk-power loom operation, Vereinigte Seidenwebereien, Krefeld.
Biography She settled in Hildesheim; 1931–33, was active in SPH-Stoffe of Zurich, the furniture and fabrics firm she founded with Gunta Stölzl and Heinrich Otto Hürlimann. To 1933, SPH-Stoffe designed for the Wohnbedarf housewares store, Zurich.
Bibliography Cat., Gunta Stölzl, *Weberei am Bauhaus und ams eigener Werkstatt*, Berlin: Bauhaus-Archiv, 1987: 148. Cat., *The Bauhaus: Masters and Students*, New York: Barry Friedman, 1988. Friederike Mehlau-Wiebking et al., *Schweizer Typenmöbel 1925–35, Sigfried Giedion und die Wohnbedarf AG*, Zurich: gta, 1989: 226. Sigrid Wortmann Weltge, *Women's Work: Textile Art from The Bauhaus*, London: Thames & Hudson, 1993.

Premsela, Benno (1920–)
Dutch textile and exhibition designer.

Training Under A. Bodon, interior design, Nieuwe Kunstschool, Amsterdam.
Biography 1949–51, Premsela worked in the furniture department of Bijenkorf, the largest department store in Amsterdam at the time, where he was the head of display and interior design from 1956–63; 1951–53, worked in Italy and designed and printed textiles; 1956 with interior designer Jan Vonk, set up a studio in Amsterdam, and, 1987, they established the BRS Premsela Vonk design consultancy. 1963–69, Premsela was an exhibition designer for the Centrum voor Industriële Vormgeving in Amsterdam; from 1967, was responsible for the prod-

Benno Premsela. Mirror (no. DS-84). 1964–71. Laminated wood and glass mirror, dia. 19 11/16" (50 cm). Mfr.: Spectrum, the Netherlands. Courtesy Quittenbaum Kunstauktionen, Munich.

uct development and design of carpets/rugs at Van Besouw in Goirle; from 1972, designed wallcoverings by Vescom; from 1975, upholstery fabrics by Gerns & Gahler. His two vases in the Unica series marked the 40th anniversary (1993) of Cor Unum Ceramics & Art in 's-Hertogenbosch.
Exhibitions/citations Work subject of an exhibition, Amsterdam, and included in 1983–84 exhibition, Philadelphia (catalogs below). 1985 Sikkens Prize (for career work).
Bibliography Cat., *Benno Premsela onder anderen*, Amsterdam: Stedelijk Museum, 1981. Cat., Kathryn B. Hiesinger and George H. Marcus III (eds.), *Design Since 1945*, Philadelphia: Philadelphia Museum of Art, 1983.

Preobrazhenzkaia, Daria Nikolaevna (1908–1972)

Russian textile designer.

Training 1924–29, in the textile factory of VKhUTEMAS/VKhUTEIN.
Biography 1929–31, she was a textile designer at the textile mill in Ivanovo-Voznesensk and, subsequently, at the Trikhgornaya Manufacture in Moscow.
Exhibitions Participated in several Soviet exhibitions abroad.
Bibliography Cat., *Kunst und Revolution: Russische und Sowjetische Kunst 1910–1932*, Vienna: Österreichisches Museum für angewandte Kunst, 1988.

Prestini, James L. (1908–1993)

Italian woodworker; born Waterford, Connecticut.

Training Apprenticeship first as a machinist; 1938, furniture-design apprenticeship under Carl Malmsten, Stockholm; to 1930, mechanical engineering, Yale University, New Haven, Conn., US; 1938, University of Stockholm; 1939, Institute of Design, Illinois Institute of Technology, Chicago; 1943–53, Armour Research Foundation, Chicago; 1953–56, in sculpture in Italy.
Biography Prestini was the son of first-generation Italian émigrés. Working as a golf caddy, he met Thomas J. Watson Sr., the IBM chairperson, who enabled him to attend Yale University. From the early 1930s, Prestini became an accomplished woodworker and was admired by Functionalist designers for his thin, symmetrical woodwork, realized by spinning. These turned wood vessels—with a handcrafted appearance and for which he has become best known—were produced through semi-mechanical means. He taught mathematics, design, and engineering in various institutions, including from 1939–46 and 1952–53 at Institute of Design at Illinois Institute of Technology, Chicago. In mid-1950s while in Italy, he worked for Knoll International on furniture design but returned to the US and, from 1956 on the suggestion of Prof. Jesse Reichek and invitation of Dean William W. Wurster, taught at University of California, Berkeley, and was active as a sculptor. 1962, he was a design-education consultant to the West German government; 1962–63, in India; and, 1964, in the US. 1975, he retired; died in Berkeley. The Prestini archive is housed in the Archives of American Art, Smithsonian Institution, Washington, D.C.
Exhibitions/citations Work included in 1983–84 exhibition, Philadelphia (catalog below); 1948 *International Competition for Low-Cost Furniture Design* (one-piece plastic molded chair), The Museum of Modern Art, New York. Work subject of numerous exhibitions, including 1969 venue, San Francisco Museum of Art (catalog below). First prizes, *Contemporary Crafts* at 1952 Los Angeles County Fair; diploma of honor (wood and plywood designs), 1954 (10th) Triennale di Milano; 1972 R.S. Reynolds Memorial Sculpture Award, American Institute of Architects (AIA); diploma of collaboration, 1973 (15th) Triennale di Milano; 1975 Berkeley Award, University of California; 1962–63 Ford Foundation Fellow; 1972–73 Guggenheim Fellow.
Bibliography Edgar Kaufmann, Jr., *Prize Designs for Modern Furniture*, New York: The Museum of Modern Art, 1950: Edgar Kaufmann Jr. (essay), *Prestini's Art in Wood*, Lake Forest, Ill.: Pocahontas, 1950. Cat., *James Prestini: Sculpture from Structural Steel Elements*, San Francisco: San Francisco Museum of Art, 1969. John Kelsey, 'The Turned Bowl,' *Fine Woodworking*, Jan.–Feb. 1982. *James Prestini, 1938–1988*, Berkeley, Cal.: Creators Equity Foundation, 1990. 'James L. Prestini, 85, Sculptor and Teacher' (obituary), *The New York Times*, 31 July, 1993: 50.

Preti, Ermenegildo (1918–)

Italian aircraft engineer and automobile designer.

Biography Early on, Renzo Rivolta was the director of Isothermos, an Italian manufacturer of refrigerators, which turned to producing scooters in 1940s. Rivolta intended to produce autos but was thwarted by the circumstances of World War II; met aircraft engineer Ermenigildo Preti, who had already received a 1950 patent for an egg-shaped minicar with a single door in front. Preti had been inspired by the airplanes used in the war that featured front-opening doors for large cargo entry; used a watermelon-shaped wood model to demonstrate his idea to Rivolta. 1951, a prototype was developed with two wheels in the front and one in the rear. However, when this proved unstable, the final 1953 four-wheel, two-seat production model (to be called Isetta Iso) was developed with wheels 19" (48.3 cm) apart and a rear engine; the dimensions were 89 x 53" (225 x 134 cm) and weight 726 lb. (330 kgs). The Isocarro, a truck version, was also built. The car had a chain transmission; the truck a shaftdrive with wider-spaced wheels. Licenses were sold to manufacturers in Belgium, Brazil, England, France, and Spain. The BMW license for German and UK production proved the most lucrative. 1955–62, BMW made about 150,000 units with the motor of its R/27 motorcycle. Other licensees made about 50,000 units but very few by Rivolta's firm from 1953–55. Production continued through 1964. On Renzo Rivolta's 1966 death and at the time of the oil crisis, his son Piero took control of the enterprise and unwisely decided that the firm was to enter Formula One racing with Frank Williams. 1975, Iso closed.
Exhibitions 1953 Salone Internazionale del'Automobile, Turin; 1957 Salon de l'Automobile, Paris.
Bibliography Rainer W. Schlegelmilch et al., *BMW*, Cologne: Könemann, 1999. R.M. Clarke, *Isetta BMW/ISO/Velam 1953–61*, Surrey: Brooklands, 1984. Winston Goodfellow, *Isorivolta: The Men, the Machines*, Vimodrone: Giorgio Nada, 2001.

James Prestini. Bowl (no. 24). c. 1928–39. Hand-turned Mexican mahogany, h. 5 1/4" (13.4 cm) x dia. 12 3/16" (31 cm). Mfr.: the designer, US (c. 1939). Edgar Kaufmann, Jr., Fund. MoMA.

Price, Charles Douglas (1906–)

American silversmith; active Bloomfield Hills, Mich.

Biography 1927, when Arthur Nevill Kirk became director of the metal workshop, Cranbrook Academy of Art, Bloomfield Hills, Charles Price and Margaret Biggar became his assistants. 1935–37, Price taught silversmithing and metalworking at Cranbrook, where he also produced the designs of school's director Eliel Saarinen.
Bibliography Annelies Krekel-Aalberse, *Art Nouveau and Art Déco Silver*, New York: Abrams, 1989.

Price, Ursula Morley (1936–)

British ceramicist.

Training To 1957, design and painting, Camberwell School of Art, London; To 1959, painting and drawing, Slade diploma, University College, London.
Biography From mid-1970s, Price has been producing ceramic vessels with paper-thin walls. She called on punching and pulling to produce the desired results and shunned supports during firing. Subsequently, she turned to bottle forms; recently, has pursued bottle forms with *trompe l'œil* painted surfaces; has become known for her 'Japanese flanges,' 'ruffles,' and 'whizzes.'
Exhibitions Numerous group venues.

Ursula Morley Price. Vase. 1981. Glazed porcelain, 9 1/8 x 7 3/4 x 2 5/8" (23.2 x 19.7 x 6.7 cm). Mfr.: the designer, UK. Mrs. John D. Rockefeller 3rd Purchase Fund. MoMA.

Primavera

French decorating studio; located Paris.

History 1913, René Guilleré, a founder of the Sociéte des Artistes Décorateurs, established the Primavera decorating studio of Printemps department store on the boulevard Haussmann, Paris. 1920s–30s, the efforts of the studio were pace-setting in the decorative arts. On the 1931 death of Guilleré, his widow Charlotte Chauchet-Guilleré and Colette Guéden became codirectors. 1939, Guéden took over as head of Primavera. Philippe Petit first worked at Primavera alongside Louis Sognot and Marcel Guillemard. René Buthaud organized its Longwyn Pottery enterprise in Meurthe-et-Moselle and at Sainte-Radegonde.
Exhibitions Primavera pavilion (architect, Henri Sauvage) at 1925 Exposition Internationale des Arts Décoratifs et Industriels Modernes, Paris. Chauchet-Guilleré, Jean Burkhalter, Guillemard, Henri Moser, Pierre Lahalle, Sognot, Claude Lévy, Mlle. Tavernier, M.-M. R. Coquery, and Mme. Souguez participated in the pavilion.
Bibliography Pierre MacOrlan, *Le Printemps*, Paris: Gallimard, 1930. Pierre Kjellberg, *Art déco: les maîtres du mobilier, le décor des paquebots*, Paris: Amateur, 1986/1990. Patrick Favardin, *Les décorateurs des années 50*, Paris: Norma, 2002: 310.

Prina, Alberto (1941–)

Italian industrial designer; born and active Milan.

Training Liceo Artistico di Brera, Milan.
Biography 1960–62, Prina worked on a project for machine tools; 1964–66, with plastic laminates for kitchen systems; 1966–68, was the art director of the magazine *Votre Beauté*. 1968, he set up a studio for graphic and industrial design and publicity with clients, including Mobilificio Garavaglia (furniture and kitchen systems), Gruppo Emme (furniture and shelving systems), Metalpilter (silverplate tableware), Vetreria Pavese (glassware for the bath); MaxForm (accessories and furnishings), Ranco Controls (electronic equipment), Harvey Guzzini (lighting), Forme e Superfici, Lamter (lighting), Lamperti (lighting), Nenzi, DID (furniture and accessories), First (upholstered furniture), Volani, Fratelli Guzzini (metal tabletop accessories), Interspazio (furnishings), and Teuco (bathroom fixtures). 1968, he founded the magazine *Formaluce*, where he was director to 1971; 1972–74, taught publication design, Istituto Europeo di Design, Milan; designed numerous exhibitions; became a member, Associazione per il Disegno Industriale (ADI).
Bibliography *ADI Annual 1976*, Milan: Associazione per il Disegno Industriale, 1976.

Prina, Nani (1938–)

Italian architect and industrial and graphic designer; born and active Milan.

Training Politecnico, Milan.
Biography 1968, Prina began his professional career in industrial design. Prina's writing and publishing activities have been extensive. He was active in research in plastics, and his first design was a 1968 one-piece bed by Molteni in Giussano (MI). Other Italian clients have included Aba Design, Bazzani, Cassina, Cazzaniga, FEG, Roller, and Sormani. He became a member, Associazione per il Disegno Industriale (ADI).
Exhibitions Work shown 1972 exhibition, Prague (catalog below).
Bibliography *ADI Annual 1976*, Milan: Associazione per il Disegno Industriale, 1976. Cat., Milena Lamarová, *Design a Plastické Hmoty*, Prague: Uměleckoprůmyslové Muzeum, 1972: 146.

Printz, Eugène (1889–1948)

French decorator and furniture designer; born Paris.

Biography Printz worked in the workshop of his father on the rue du Faubourg Saint-Antoine, Paris, where he formed a staff of experimental practitioners; called on traditional materials in his modern furniture, including forged iron, plated metals, and leather; showed a preference for exotic woods, including sycamore, wild cherry, Rio rosewood, palissandre, and palm kekwood; set up his own workshop at 12, rue Saint-Bernard, Paris, where he designed and produced cabinets and rugs and also art (drawings and and paintings). 1930, Printz created the interior scheme of the boudoir of the princesse de la Tour d'Auvergne in the Château de Grosbois, private office of Jeanne Lanvin, reception salon of Field Marshal Louis Lyautey, and arrangement of the Musée de la France d'Outre-Mer on the occasion of 1931 *Exposition Coloniale*, Paris. He became interested in lighting and, 1930s, wrote on the subject for the journal *Lux*; felt that lighting should be considered at the very beginning of an interior-design project. His *couronne lumineuse* (crown of light), shown at a 1928 Salon, was widely imitated, including by architect Gabriel Guévrékian and lighting engineer André Salomon in 1929. He opened his own gallery at 81, rue de Miromesnil, Paris; designed offices, banks, press bureaux, and interior schemes in Britain, Belgium, the US, and Mexico. He also designed sets for *Domino* and *Jean de la Lune* at Théâtre de l'Athénée, Paris, commissioned by Louis Jouvet. On the eve of World War II with Dominique, Maurice Jallot, Jules Leleu, and René Prou, Printz formed the group Décor de France. After the war, he designed furniture produced in limited editions.
Exhibitions 1925, work first shown; then regularly in annual editions of Salon d'Automne and Salons of Société des Artistes Décorateurs from 1926. Made his international debut at 1925 *Exposition Internationale des Arts Décoratifs et Industriels Modernes*, Paris. 1928 Salon d'Automne (widely published chandelier in gray metal). Designed one of the salons (the other by Jacques-Émile Ruhlmann) at 1931 *Exposition Coloniale*, Musée des Colonies, Paris. With Étienne Kohlmann, at Pavillon de la Lumière, 1937 *Exposition Internationale des Arts et Techniques dans la Vie Moderne*, Paris, where he also designed the general lighting of corridors and vestibules, showed a *table jardinière* that could be lighted, and worked on Société des Artistes Décorateurs pavilion there.
Bibliography *Lux*, June 1928: 89, Jan. 1929: 14, Feb. 1929: 34, Feb. 1930: 10, Sept. 1931: 101–03. Gabriel Henriot, *Luminaire moderne*, Paris: Charles Moreau, 1937: plate 1. Alastair Duncan, *Art Nouveau and Art Déco Lighting*, New York: Simon & Schuster, 1978: 181. Guy Bujon and Jean-Jacques Dutko, *Eugène Printz*, Paris: Regard, 1986.

Jack Pritchard; Isokon: Marcel Breuer. Long Chair chaise longue. 1935–36. Molded and cutout plywood and upholstery, 32 1/2 x 55 1/2 x 23 5/8" (82.5 x 141 x 60 cm). Mfr.: The Isokon Furniture Company, UK. Gift of Judith Price. MoMA.

Prisunic

French store chain; located Paris.

History Christmas 1931, the first Prisunic 'five-and-dime' store was opened beside the main building of Au Printemps department store on the rue Caumartin, Paris, under the banner: *prix unique* (one price), which sounds like *prisunic* when pronounced. Three-, five-, and ten-franc items were sold (equivalent to sales in a five-and-dime store). 1954, Jacques Gueden hired Denise Fayolle to work for Prisunic. 1954–59, she developed a new corporate identity. 1955, a chain of 200 store outlets was established. 1959, the first contemporary furniture, clothing, tableware, and household goods were produced. 1968, Prisunic published its first catalog that, with subsequent editions, included high-style but practical, inexpensive furniture and furnishings by Gae Aulenti, Marc Berthier, Terence Conran, Marc Held, Andrée Putman, Danielle Quarante, and other established designers. 1992, Prisunic was merged into the Pinault-Printemps consortium and, 1997, into Les Galeries Lafayette/Monoprix group with 322 Prisunic stores by 2002.
Bibliography Gilles de Bure, *Le mobilier français 1965–1979*, Paris: Regard, 1983: 78, 82–83.
> See Arnodin, Maïmé.

Pritchard, Jack (1899–1992); The Isokon Furniture Company

British entrepreneur and manufacturer.

Training To 1922, engineering and economics, Cambridge University.
Biography 1922, Pritchard began working for Michelin tires in France and, 1925, for Venesta Plywood in Britain. After seeing Le Corbusier's 'L'Esprit nouveau' pavilion at the 1925 *Exposition Internationale des Arts Décoratifs et Industriels Modernes*, Paris, he invited the architect to design a stand for Venesta; also worked with Lászió Moholy-Nagy and hired Wells Coates to design a stand for Venesta at 1931 *British Empire Trade Exhibition*, Manchester. 1931 with his wife Molly and Coates, he was to apply 'modern functional design to houses, flats, furniture and fittings' by founding The Isokon Furniture Company and, 1935 after discussions with Walter Gropius, began producing furniture. 1936, Pritchard appointed Gropius as the controller of design, a position assumed by Marcel Breuer in 1937 after Gropius's immigration to the US. Isokon primarily produced furniture in plywood. One of its best-known designs was 1935–36 Long Chair chaise longue Others were 1936 Short Chair, 1936 Armchair and Sofa, and 1936 Nest of Tables, all by Marcel Breuer, and 1936 Penguin Donkey bookcase by Egon Riss (restyled by Ernest Race 1963; restyled again by Azumi 2003). The Donkey was conjured to hold paperback books published by Penguin Books. However, because the free-formed seats of the Long Chair, the firm's first design, had to be imported from Estonia, production was slow and sparse. 1939 when World War II began, production came to a halt. There were pre- and post-war productions and reproductions of the chair. 1934, Coates designed the Lawn Road Flats, Hampstead, one of the first International Style concrete buildings, on land purchased in 1929 by Pritchard and where Pritchard's family and refugees Breuer, Moholy-Nagy, and Gropius lived for a time. Though Pritchard designed furniture pieces himself, his major contribution was the introduction of the International Style of architecture to Britain. 1982, Windmill Furniture bought the rights to the Isokon name and earlier designs and recently included new pieces in the Isokon Plus range, including Wing Unit cabinet by Michael Sodeau, Loop coffee table by Barber Osgerby, and others by James Harris, Simon Pengelly, Hein Stolle. Isokon Plus was established as a retail outlet, London.
Exhibitions Subject of 1980 *Isokon*, Newcastle upon Tyne (catalog below).
Bibliography Cat., Cheryl Buckley, *Isokon*, Newcastle: University of Newcastle upon Tyne, 1980. Jack Pritchard, *View from a Long Chair: The Memoirs of Jack Pritchard*, London: Routledge & Kegan Paul, 1984. Peter Dormer (intro.), *The Illustrated Dictionary of 20th-Century Designers: The Key Personalities in Design and the Applied Arts*, New York: Mallard, 1991: 120. Anthony Hoyte, 'Isokon Unrealized: An Examination of the Projects Undertaken by Walter Gropius for the Isokon Company 1934–1937,' master's degree thesis in the History of Design course, London: Royal College of Art/Victoria and Albert Museum, 1991. www.isokonplus.com.

Prix, Wolf Dieter (1942–)

Austrian architect and designer; born and active Vienna.

Training Technical University, Vienna, Austria; Southern California Institute of Architecture; Architectural Association, London.
Biography 1968, Prix and Helmut Swiczinsky, Deconstructivist architects, established the architecture studio Coop Himmelb(l)au in Vienna. Prix designed furniture produced by Vitra Edition, including the 1989 Vodöl armchair, a play on the Viennese pronunciation of the French *fauteuil* (chair). The chair is an askew interpretation of Le Corbusier's 1928 Grand Confort club chair with its tublar bent-metal frame partially askew and resting on an incongruous steel I-beam. Prix and Swiczinsky designed a 1974 mobile kitchen produced by Ewe-Küchen

and work for others. 1984, Prix was an adjunct professor, Architectural Association; 1990, visiting professor, Harvard University; 1995–97, Architectural Counselor to Federal Ministry of Science, Research and the Arts, Austria; from 1998, faculty member, Columbia University, New York; currently, architectural chair, Universität für angewandte Kunst, Vienna. Architectural work includes a number of signifiant international structures.
Exhibitions/citations As partner of Coop Himmelb(l)au, work included in 1988 *Deconstructive Architecture*, The Museum of Modern Art, New York. Work subject of 1992 exhibition, Paris. Member, European Academy of Science and Arts.
> See Coop Himmelb(l)au.

Probst, Karl K. (1883–1963); Jeep; Willys-Overland Motors

American automobile engineer; born W. V. Automobile model and firm.

Training To 1903 under Kettering, Ohio State University, Columbus.
Biography/history End of 19th century, Probst built his first automobile. Others followed, including 1917 Milburn Electric, far lighter than competing models. Probst, who became known for his transience, worked for a number of minor auto firms, such as Chalmers, Lozier, Peerless, and Reo; 1940, became a temporary chief engineer at American Bantam Car Co. in Butler, Pa. The claim that Probst designed the Bantam Reconnaissance Car or BRC (later nicknamed the Jeep, the legendary 500-lb./227kg utility vehicle) may not be true. However, he had the ability quickly to produce working drawings. And speed was essential to satisfy, and thus capture, the US Quartermaster Corps' very-short-notice contract application sent out to Bantam and 134 other manufacturers on 11 July 1940. Calling on Bantam's small-car expertice, the first Jeep for wartime use, according to some sources of revisionist history, was primarily designed and completely constructed by Bantam mechanics/engineers Harold Crist, Chet Hemphling, and Ralph Turner with administrative assistance from Bantam's president Frank Fenn and his staff. The original Bantam Jeep was completed 21 Sept. 1940 and delivered 23 Sept. 1940 to the US Army's Camp Holabird in Maryland. Willys-Overland of Toledo, Ohio, which did not win the contract due to lateness, had no participation in the Jeep's invention, though asserted otherwise over the years. Also, Army personnel probably did not participate in the conception and design of the vehicle. Even so, Willys became the largest World War II producer (and Ford, the second largest) of the vehicle which it called the Quad, and, after the war, trademarked by Willys as 'Jeep.' (Purportedly, 'Jeep' was derived from the acronym 'GP' for a General Purpose vehicle.) Concerning Willys's history, John North Willys bought Standard Wheel Company in 1908; changed the name variously over the years, finally to Willys-Overland in 1939. 1940, the firm incorporated its American-saloon engine and based the body on Bantam's original. The firm had produced about 360,000 Jeeps by 1945, when it then began making the CJ (Civilian Jeep) line, with the CJ2A as the first model. 1953, Willys was bought by Kaiser, which changed the name to Willys Motor Company. 1963, the Willys name disappeared, when the corporation was renamed Kaiser-Jeep, which in turn merged with American Motors in 1970. 1975, Willys-Overland was reorganized as a wholesale/retail parts business. 1987, Chrysler bought American Motors and, thus, acquired the 'Jeep' name and the line. 1998, Chrysler merged with the Daimler-Benz Coporation to form the DaimlerChrysler Coporation.
Bibliography Herbert R. Rifkind, *The Jeep; Its Development and Procurement under the Quartermaster Corps, 1940–1942*, Washington, D.C.: Historical Section, General Service Branch, General Administrative Services, Office of Quartermaster General, 1943. Ray Cowdery and/or Rudolf Steiner, *All American Wonder Military Jeep*, vols. 1 and 2, Minneapolis, Minn.: Victory, 1990. Graham Scott, *Essential Military Jeep: Willys, Ford and Bantam Models 1941–45*, St. Paul, Minn.: Motorbooks International, 1996. Patrick R. Foster, *The Story of Jeep*, Iola, Wisc.: Krause, 1998. Chris Horton, *Encyclopedia of the Car*, Hertfordshire: Regency House, 1998.

Procházka, Antonín (1882–1945)

Czech artist and designer; born Važany, near Vyškova.

Training 1903–04, Vysoká Škola Uměleckoprůmyslová (VŠUP, academy of arts, architecture, and design); 1904–06 under V. Bukovac and H. Schwaigr, Akademie Výtvarných Umení (academy of fine arts); both Prague.
Biography 1910, Procházka was accepted (after a previous rejection) into the Mánes Association of Plastic Artists; became a teacher of drawing in Ostrava; was one of the first to respond to Cubism through Cubo-Expressionist paintings and others bordering on analytical Cubism; c. 1915, approached Orphism in his painting; designed Cubist architecture and furniture of some note. He died in Brno.
Exhibitions Participated in 1907 (1st) and 1908 (2nd) exhibitions of the Group of Eight, Prague; 1912 exhibition of Sonderbund, Cologne.
Bibliography Alexander von Vegesack et al., *Czech Cubism: Architecture, Furniture, and Decorative Arts, 1910–1925*, New York: Princeton Architectural Press, 1992. Cat., *Prague, 1900–1938: capitale secrète des avants-gardes*, Dijon: Musée des Beaux-Arts, 1997.

Procopé, Ulla (b. Ulrika Procopé 1921–1968)

Finnish ceramicist.

Training To 1948, Taideteollinen korkeakoulu, Helsinki.

Probst, Karl K.; Jeep; Willys-Overland Motors: Truck: Utility 1/4 Ton 4X4, M38A1 (Jeep). 1952. Steel body, 73 3/4 x 60 7/8 x 338 5/8" (187.3 x 154.3 x 335.3 cm). Mfr.: Willys-Overland Motors, US (1953). Gift of DaimlerChyrsler Corporation Fund. MoMA.

Biography 1948–67, Procopé designed domestic ceramics produced by Arabia, where she worked as a model planner under Kaj Franck. Work included 1957 Liekki flameproof stacking dinnerware range with lids for dishes and 1960 Ruska stoneware range in a textured warm-brown color.
Exhibitions/citations Work included in 1956–57 *Finnish Exhibition*, touring West Germany; 1958 Formes Scandinaves, Musée des Arts Décoratifs, Paris; 1961 *Finlandia*, Zurich, Amsterdam, and London; 1982 and 1983–84 exhibitions, New York and Philadelphia (catalogs below). Diploma of honor, 1957 (11thl) Triennale di Milano; gold medals, ceramic exhibitions, Sacramento, Cal., in 1962 and 1963; San Francisco in 1963; Utrecht in 1963.
Bibliography Erik Zahle (ed.), *A Treasury of Scandinavian Design*, New York: Golden Press, 1961. Benedict Zilliacus, 'Discreet and Important,' *Ceramics and Glass*, no. 1, 1969: 2–3. Leena Maunula, 'A Hundred Years of Arabia Dishes,' *Ceramics and Glass*, Nov. 1973: 20. Cat., David Revere McFadden (ed.), *Scandinavian Modern Design 1880–1980*, New York: Abrams, 1982. Cat., Kathryn B. Hiesinger and George H. Marcus III (eds.), *Design Since 1945*, Philadelphia: Philadelphia Museum of Art, 1983. Jennifer Hawkins Opie, *Scandinavia: Ceramics and Glass in The Twentieth Century*, New York: Rizzoli, 1989.

Proctor-Silex Co.
> See Wolcott, Frank E.

Proetz, Victor Hugo (1897–1966)

American architect and designer; born St. Louis, Mo.

Training To 1923, School of Architecture, Armour Institute (now Illinois Institute of Technology/IIT), Chicago.
Biography 1932, Proetz designed a collection of furniture, furnishings, and lighting for the John Lohmann House in Old Lyme, Conn.; 1937, decorated Lord and Lady Mountbatten's penthouse in London; 1943, became director of interior decorating department of the Lord & Taylor department store in New York. Proetz was a close friend and associate of Charles Nagel (1899–1992), an architect and the director of St. Louis Art Museum. The Victor Proetz Collection, covering 1920–71, of correspondence, photographs, design plans is housed in St. Louis Art Museum. Another collection, his c. 1930 to 1965 papers, is housed in the Archives of American Art, Smithsonian Institution, Washington, D.C.
Citations Award (for work on the Park Plaza Hotel, St. Louis).

Prokop, Miroslav (1896–1954)

Czech designer of lighting fixtures.

Training Electrotechnology, České Vysoké Učení Technické (Czech technical university), Prague.
Biography From 1929, Prokop was a member, Czechoslovakian Werkbund (SČSD); concentrated on the technical problems of lighting; 1927–43, designed a number of lighting fixtures for serial production; collaborated with leading Czech modern architects and, 1930s, collaborated with Zdeněk Pešánek on lighting sculptures. Prokop designed lighting for outdoor and neon advertising.
Bibliography Alena Adlerová, *České užité umění 1918–1938*, Prague: Odeon, 1983.

Propaganda

Thai designer/manufacturer collaborative; located Bangkok, Thailand.

History 1994, a group of young designers formed the ad hoc group Propaganda in Bangkok; 1996, opened their first shop. Self-proclaimingly 'taking a humorous approach to the way we live with life,' the group has transformed everyday objects into humorous implements, such as the Tooth (a large plastic tooth for holding tooth brushes), Pick-a-Tooth (tooth-pick holder), Tooth Lamp (lighting fixture), and Sweet Tooth (candy holder). Products have been designed for the bathroom, leisure living, and dining. Its staff designers include Nakool Tachaputthapong (1967–), Martin Hoontrakul (1975–), Chaiyut Plypetch (1964–), and Kunlanath Sornsriwichai (1972–). Satit Kalawantavanich is the creative director of the firm now known as Propagandist Co. Ltd.
Exhibitions/citations Work shown at 2000 (2nd) Biennale Internationale du Design, Saint-Étienne, France; 2001 *Propaganda Breaking New Ground*, The Emporium, Bangkok. 1996 and 1998 B.A.D. awards; 1999 International Merit Award; Certifications of Form, 2000 and 2002 Tendence fair, Frankfurt; 2000 (for Saltepper salt/pepper shaker) and 2001 (for Dish Up) Good Design award, Chicago Athenaeum; 2001 Red Dot award (for Ap-Peel fruit bowl/knife), Design Zentrum Nordrhein Westfalen, Essen; others.

Propst, Robert (1921–2000)

American designer; born Marino, Colorado.

Training To 1943, University of Denver, Colo.; to 1950, University of Colorado, Boulder.
Biography 1946–48, Probst was head, department of art, Tarleton College, Dublin, Tex.; late 1940s, also active as a graphic designer and sculptor; 1953, established his firm Propst Co. in Denver, where he designed architectural sculpture, ecclesiastical interiors, and playground equipment, and speculative product development, and was active with aircraft and institutional equipment companies. 1960, his firm, incorporated into Herman Miller Furniture Company, formed the research-and-development segment of its activities in Ann Arbor, Mich. From 1960, he was president and research director of Herman Miller Research Corp., and was given carte blanche by Herman Miller head D.J. DePree for product development. For Herman Miller, Propst developed the concept for 1964 Action Office 1 system (realized by the designers of George Nelson Associates) and subsequent 1968 Action Office 2 with modified components, which catapulted the firm from a modest producer of seating and tables to the world's second largest office furniture manufacturer. Propst's other design work for Herman Miller included 1964 Perch chair, 1967 Pediatrics bed, 1969 Co/Struc hospital-furniture system (introduced in 1971). Also a 1970 vertical timber harvester. He was granted over 120 patents and was active to his death.
Exhibitions/Citations Venues at the Walker Art Center in Minneapolis, Minn.; Smith-sonian Institution, Washington, D.C.; and the Henry Ford Museum. 1964 Best Collection of the Year award, *Home Furnishings Daily* trade newspaper; 1970 (21st) Annual International Design Award, American Institute of Decorators (AID); 1972 Distinguished Service Citation, Institute of Business Designers (IBD); 1976 Design Review, *Industrial Design* magazine.
Bibliography 'Nelson, Eames, Girard, Propst: The Design Process at Herman Miller,' *Design Quarterly* 98–99, 1975. Yvonne Abraham, 'The Man Behind the Cubicle,' *Metropolis*, Nov. 1998.

Protière, Régis (1948–)

French architect and designer; active Paris.

Training École Nationale Supérieure des Arts Décoratifs, Paris.
Biography Protière has designed public spaces, commercial architecture, exhibitions, objects, and furniture, including 1984–85 library and cafeteria of Musée d'Art Moderne de la Ville de Paris and Lizie chair by Pallucco; 1987, set up his own design office and, in 1990, a shop.
Exhibitions/citations Work included in 1990 exhibition, Paris (catalog below). 1980 Appel Permanent grant (cardboard/steel-wire Trois Jeunes Tambours), VIA (French furniture association); 1988 Prix de la Critique for contemporary furniture (Frère Jacques armchair).
Bibliography Cat., *Les années VIA 1980–1990*, Paris: Musée des Arts Décoratifs, 1990: 148–49.

Prou, René-Lucien (1889–1948)

French decorator and furniture designer; born Nantes; active Paris.

Training To 1908, painting, École Bernard-Palissy, Paris.
Biography 1908, Prou designed his first work as the shop foreperson of furnishings/interior-design house Gouffé in the Faubourg Saint-Antoine, Paris, where he became the chief designer. 1912, he was called the first decorator of the *goût moderne* (modern taste). Prou designed the council room of Comptoir d'Escompte, Paris, and apartment of the French ambassador, Paraguay. From 1929, his work became simpler, eschewing ornamentation. c. 1930 in his workshop at 80, rue de Rome, Paris, he began designing wrought-iron furniture produced by Edgar Brandt, Raymond Subes, and other metalworkers. 1929, he designed the interiors and furnishings of about 500 train carriages of the Compagnie Internationale des Wagons-Lits and, 1930s with René Lalique, of salon train carriages of the Istanbul Orient Express. He also designed the interiors of other train carriages, including those of the 1922 Paris-Deauville train line (aka *Train Bleu*). He received numerous other important commissions, including a piano by Pleyel, some furniture by Henri Lévy, dining rooms of 1924 oceanliner *De Grasse* and other oceanliner interiors, including 1921 *Paris*, 1926 *Île-de-France*, 1931 *L'Atlantique*, 1935 *Normandie*, and complete interiors for a dozen other oceanliners, including *Champlain*, *La Fayette*, *Cuba*, and *Florida*. Other work: dining room of Waldorf-Astoria hotel, New York; board room of the Palace of the League of Nations, Geneva; Mitsubishi department store, Tokyo; and the oceanliner pier in Le Havre.

From 1937, he was associated with his brother Jean-René Prou and worked in his own offices and boutique at 50, rue du Faubourg Saint-Honoré, Paris; From 1928, worked for the Pomone decorating department of Bon Marché department store, Paris, where he was a sometime collaborator of Albert-Lucien Guénot; 1932, succeeded Paul Follot as the director of Pomone, which produced his limited-production dining-room and bedroom furniture and was known as the *moderne aimable et souriant* (likable and smiling face of modernism); remained active as a painter and taught at various schools, including briefly École Nationale Superieure des Arts Décoratifs, where Louis Sognot succeeded Prou on his death in Paris.
Exhibitions Work shown at Salons of Sociéte des Artistes Décorateurs from 1923; with Eric Bagge, designed the Chambre de Mademoiselle of Une Ambassade Française pavilion at 1925 *Exposition Internationale des Arts Décoratifs et Industriels Modernes*, Paris.
Bibliography *Ensembles mobiliers*, Paris: Charles Moreau, vol. 6, nos. 1–7, 27, 1945. Léon Deshairs (intro.), *Modern French Decorative Art: A Collection of Examples of Modern French Decoration*, Paris: Albert Lévy, c. 1925–30. Pierre Kjellberg, *Art déco: les Maîtres du mobilier, le décor des paquebots*, Paris: Amateur, 1986/1990. Cat., Sophie Tasma Anargyros et al., *L'école française: les créateurs de meubles du 20ème siècle*, Paris: Industries Françaises de l'Ameublement, 2000.

PROUN
> See Lissitzky, El.

Prouvé, Jean (1901–1984)

French metalworker, engineer, builder, and furniture designer; born Paris; son of Victor Prouvé.

Training 1916–19 under Émile Robert, art metalworking, Nancy; 1919–21 under Hungarian blacksmith Adalbert-Georges Szabó, Paris.
Biography Prouvé's early furnishings commissions brought him into contact with avant-garde designers and architects in France, including Le Corbusier, Pierre Jeanneret, Robert Mallet-Stevens, and Paul Herbé. Known for his use of metal in his furniture design, he rejected traditional techniques in favor of the electrical welding of sheet metal; 1923, opened his own studio in Nancy and received various building commissions; 1923, designed his first furniture; 1930, established Les Ateliers de Jean Prouvé, and, after World War II, relocated to Maxéville, near Nancy. His workshop also made furniture designed by Jacques-Émile Ruhlmann and Charlotte Perriand; particularly distinctive was the 1952 furniture he designed with Perriand, such as Bibliothèque Mexique (bookcase) for Cité Universitaire, Paris. c. 1930, he developed the *mur rideau* (curtain wall), a replaceable, movable wall system, the first of its kind, and based on industrial light metal stanchions and was intended to serve the mass culture. The *mur rideau* system was installed in architects Eugène Beaudouin and Marcel Lods's 1938 Club House on the Buc airfield and their 1935 Maison du Peuple in Clichy, and, 1958, in a secondary school in Bagnols-sur-Cèze. Prouvé intended to serve a mass culture through his lightweight prefabricated components that were easy to transport and erect. His other structures included 1949 prefabricated houses, Meudon-Bellevue; 1957 temporary school (engineer, S. Ketoff), Villejuif; 1953 apartment block (with Lionel Mirabaud), Paris; 1956 units with prefabricated concrete cores for the Abbé Pierre; 1957 spa building (with Maurice Novarina), Evian; 1958 school (with Daniel Badani and Marcel Roux-Dorlut), Bagnols-sur-Cèze; 1959 houses, Meudon-Bellevue; 1958 'Sahara'-type prefabricated houses; 1963 and 1967–69 Free University (with Candilis, Josic and Woods, and Man-fred Schiedhelm), Berlin-Dahlem; 1967 Congrès Grenoble, 1967 office tower (with Jean de Mailly and Jacques Depussé), La Défense, Paris; and 1968 Total service stations. 1932, he designed furniture for Université de Nancy; 1929, was a cofounder of Union des Artistes Modernes (UAM), exhibiting at its subsequent venues; frequently worked with collaborators. All his furniture, with the exception of reproductions from the 1980s, was sold exclusively by Steph Simon in Paris. Active in workshops in Maxéville in 1944–54, he opened his own consulting firm in Paris. From 1980s, reproductions of his 86-3 chair were made by Bermude and B-80 chair by Tecta, 2001, Vitra acquired the rights to produce Prouvé furniture. He died in Nancy.
Exhibitions From 1930, work included in a number of exhibitions, including those of UAM (Union des Artistes Modernes) and 1937 *Exposition Internationale des Arts et Techniques dans la Vie Moderne* (Prouvé grand staircase in the UAM pavilion), both Paris; and subject of 1964 exhibition, Paris; 1983 exhibition, Institut Français d'Architecture, Paris; 1989 *Jean Prouvé Meubles 1924–1953*, Musée des Arts Décoratifs, Bordeaux; 1990–91 *Jean Prouvé Constructeur*, Paris and Nancy; 1993, Centre Georges Pompidou, Paris; 1977, and numerous 2001 venues to acknowledge his birth year.
Bibliography *Le métal, présenté par Jean Prouvé*, Paris: Charles Moreau, 1929. Cat., *Jean Prouvé*, Paris: Musée des Arts Décoratifs, 1964. Benedikt Huber and Jean-Claude Steinegger (eds.), *Jean Prouvé: une architecture par l'industrie = Architektur aus der Fabrik = Industrial Architecture*, Zurich: Artemis, 1971. Cat., Pierre Baertschi and Mauro Riva, *Rétrospective de l'œuvre de Jean Prouvé = Rückblick auf das Werk von Jean Prouvé*, Geneva: Centre de Documentation et d'Architecture, 1977. Dominique Clayssen, *Jean Prouvé: l'idée constructive*, Paris: Dunod, 1983. Cat., *Jean Prouvé*, Paris: Centre Georges Pompidou, 1993. Cat., Nathalie Prat, *Jean Prouvé*, Paris: Galerie Jousse Seguin, Galerie Enrico Navarra, 1998. Cat., *Jean Prouvé, 1904–1984: constructeur*, Paris: Réunion des Musées Nationaux, 2001. Armelle Lavalou (ed.), *Jean Prouvé par lui-même*, Paris: Linteau, 2001.

Jean Prouvé. Folding chair. 1930. Steel and linen, 40 3/8 x 17 5/8 x 18 3/4" (102.6 x 44.8 x 47.6 cm). Mfr.: L'Atelier de Jean Prouvé, France. Gift of Jo Carole and Ronald S. Lauder. MoMA.

Prouvé, Victor (1858–1943)

French painter, sculptor and decorator; born Nancy; father of Jean Prouvé.

Biography Victor Prouvé worked with Louis Majorelle and Émile Gallé, designing glassware, ceramics, and decorations in wood marquetry; on Gallé's 1904 death, assumed the leadership of the École de Nancy; made jewelry and decorative bronze pieces and produced patterns for lace and embroidery; in tooled and polychromed leather, created cushions, portières, plaques, caskets, and bindings, and embellished them with the fauna and flora of Alsace-Lorraine. His best-known binding was *Salammbô* (1893) by Gustave Flaubert; others included *L'art symboliste* and *La chanson des gueux*. Prouvé and René Wiener, another of the founders of the École de Nancy, created innovatory pictorial and figurative bindings.
Exhibitions From 1892, work included in annual exhibitions of Champs de Mars group, Paris; 1894 Cercle pour l'Art of La Libre Esthétique group, Brussels; 1919 Salon of Société des Artistes Décorateurs. Work subject of 2001 exhibition, Paris (catalog below).
Bibliography Madeleine Prouvé, *Victor Prouvé, 1858–1943*, Paris: Berger-Levrault, 1958. Yvonne Brunhammer et al., *Art Nouveau Belgium, France*, Houston: Institute for the Arts, Rice University, 1976. Cat., *Le cuir au musée*, Nancy: Musée de l'École de Nancy, 1985. Alastair Duncan and Georges de Bartha, *Art Nouveau and Art Déco Bookbinding*, New York: Abrams, 1989. Sophie Marcellin and Denis

Ozanne, *Victor Prouvé, 1858–1943: portraits*, Paris: S. Marcellin & D. Ozanne, 2001.

Proventus

Swedish investment group; located Stockholm.

History Proventus has invested in a range of companies, large and small. They include Aritmos, a wholly owned subsidiary, which develops and manufactures sports and leisure goods; Monark Stiga, producers of bicycles and fitness and gardening equipment; United Tiles, which makes ceramic tiles and clinkers for flooring and walls; Kinnasand, weavers of curtain and upholstery fabrics; and Artek furniture. Extensions of the firm are Proventus Inc. in the US and Proventus-Clali in Israel. 2001, Pio Barone Lumaga was appointed CEO of Art & Technology by Proventus (originally an amalgamation of Artek and Artek's Art & Technology division) and of Snowcrash (acquired in 1998). 2002, the later was discontinued and certain products were assumed by David Design in Malmö.

Prutscher, Otto (1880–1949)

Austrian architect, furniture designer, jeweler, and designer; born and active Vienna.

Training From 1897 under Josef Hoffmann, Kunstgewerbeschule, Vienna.
Biography Soon after the 1903 founding of Wiener Werkstätte, Prutscher became a textile, metalware, book, and glassware designer there in a style greatly influenced by Hoffmann; designed glassware by E. Bakalovits; from 1910, taught, Kunstgewerbeschule, Vienna
Exhibitions Work shown at 1900 *Exposition Universelle*, Paris; 1902 *Esposizione Internazionale d'Arte Decorativa Moderna*, Turin. Subject of 1997 exhibition, Vienna (catalog below).
Bibliography Max Eisler, *Otto Prutscher*, Leipzig: Friedrich Ernst Hübsch, 1925. Günther Feuerstein, *Vienna—Present and Past: Arts and Crafts—Applied Art—Design*, Vienna: Jugend und Volk, 1976: 35, 81. Torsten Bröhan (ed.), *Glaskunst der Moderne*, Munich: Klinkhardt und Biermann, 1992: 60, 154–61, 163, 460. Cat., Matthias Boeckl, Gabriele Koller, Erika Patka, *Otto Prutscher: 1880–1949*, Vienna: Hochschule für angewandte Kunst, 1997.

Prydkunstnerlager

Norwegian decorative-arts group.

History 1929, the Prydkunstnerlager was organized by a group of decorative artists, who had broken away from the Brukskunst association and wanted to substitute vernacular Norwegian traditionalism and folklore, a recurring theme in Norwegian design throughout the 20th century, for international neoclassicism.
Bibliography Fredrik Wildhagen, *Norge i Form*, Oslo: Sternersen, 1988.

Otto Prutscher. Compote dish. c. 1907. Flashed and cut glass, h. 8" (20.3 cm) x dia. 5 7/8" (15 cm). Mfr.: E. Bakalowits & Söhne, Austria. Estée and Joseph Lauder Design Fund. MoMA.

Prytz, Thorolf (1858–1938); Jacob Prytz (1886–1962)

Norwegian designers and metalworkers; born and active Kristiania (known as Oslo from 1925); father and son.

Training Statens Håndverks -og Kunstindustriskole, Kristiania (now Oslo); in Paris.
Biography From 1885,Thorolf Prytz was associated with his family's firm J. Tostrup in Kristiania, of which he was the director from 1890–1912. His silver designs were inspired by local fauna and flora. 1912, Jacob Prytz succeeded his father as the director of the firm and, from this time, proceeded to shape the development of design in Norway. Jacob's Functionalist ideas about form appreciably influenced Norwegian designers in 1920s–30s. Gustav Gaudernack was the head of and taught silversmithing at Statens Håndverks -og Kunstindustriskole. On Gaudernack's 1914 death, Jacob Prytz assumed his position at the school, where he was the rector from 1945. 1918, he cofounded the Applied Arts Association, of which he was the chairperson from 1920–39. 1946–48, Prytz was also the chairperson, National Applied Art Federation.
Exhibitions Work included in 1938 Salon, Paris; 1982, in New York (catalog below).
Bibliography Cat., David Revere McFadden (ed.), *Scandinavian Modern Design 1880–1980*, New York: Abrams, 1982. Fredrik Wildhagen, *Norge i Form*, Oslo: Stenersen, 1988: 67–68. Annelies Krekel-Aalberse, *Art Nouveau and Art Déco Silver*, New York: Abrams, 1989.

Pryzrembel, Hans (1900–1945)

German metalworker; born Halle.

Training From 1924, Bauhaus, Weimar and Dessau, under László Moholy-Nagy; in 1928, completed his apprenticeship as a silversmith.
Biography From 1919, Pryzrembel worked as a silversmith in Leipzig and often produced work for practical uses. Though a modernist, he called on hammered silver and brass and incorporated semi-precious materials, including ebony. He also designed table and ceiling lamps.
Exhibitions Work included in 1992 exhibition, Berlin (catalog below).
Bibliography Annelies Krekel-Aalberse, *Art Nouveau and Art Déco Silver*, New York: Abrams, 1989: 258. Cat., *Die Metallwerkstatt am Bauhaus*, Berlin: Bauhaus-Archiv, 1992: 240–50, 319.

Puiforcat, Jean-Émile (1897–1945)

French silversmith; born Paris.

Training Under his father Louis-Victor Puiforcat, in silversmithing; under Louis-Aimé Lejeune, in sculpture.
Biography 1921, Puiforcat set up his own workshop in Paris and rejected traditional decoration in favor of simple geometrical forms; combined his silverware with lapis lazuli, ivory, jade, rock crystal, and other semi-precious materials. c. 1926 with Pierre Chareau, Pierre Legrain, Dominique, and Raymond Templier, Puiforcat became a founding member of the Groupe des Cinq; 1930, a founding member, Union des Artistes Modernes (UAM). Interior designers André Domin and Marcel Genevrière of the firm Dominique designed and furnished Puiforcat's residence in Biarritz. A prolific designer, Puiforcat's commissions included dining silver for Maharaja of Indore, 1935 oceanliner *Normandie*, a wide range of silver objects and cutlery, and religious and sports sculptures. He was influenced by the work of mathematician Matila Ghyka on the Golden Section. The Puiforcat enterprise is still active, not by the Puiforcat family, and continues production of early wares and has introduced newer items, including 2003 Virgule cutlery.
Exhibitions Work shown at the editions of Salon d'Automne from 1921 and Salons of Société des Artistes Décorateurs from c. 1921. In Paris: at 1925 *Exposition Internationale des Arts Décoratifs et Industriels Modernes*; in his own stand at 1937 *Exposition Internationale des Arts et Techniques dans la Vie Moderne*; 1926 and 1927 with Groupe des Cinq, at Galerie Barbazanges; 1929, independently at Galerie Renaissance.
Bibliography René Herbst, *Jean Puiforcat, orfèvre sculpteur*, Paris: Flammarion, 1951. Françoise de Bonneville, *Jean Puiforcat*, Paris: Regard, 1986. Arlette Barré-Despond, *UAM*, Paris: Regard, 1986: 496–99. Cat., *Les années UAM 1929–1958*, Paris: Musée des Arts Décoratifs, 1988.

Pukebergs Glasbruk
Swedish glass factory.

History 1871, a glass factory was established in Pukeberg, Småland; 1894, was bought by lamp manufacturer Arvid Böhlmark and began producing lamps; 1930s under works manager Carl Hermelin, began to produce decorative glassware; c. 1959, introduced household and decorative glassware by accomplished designers, including Ann and Göran Wärff in 1959 and Eva Englund from 1964; 1984, was acquired by Gashbron and continues to be active.
Bibliography Jennifer Hawkins Opie, *Scandinavia: Ceramics and Glass in the Twentieth Century*, New York: Rizzoli, 1989.

Pulos, Arthur J. (1917–1997)
American industrial designer; born Vandergrift, Pa.

Training 1935–39 under Alexander Kostellow, Peter Müller-Munk, and F. Clayter, Carnegie Institute of Technology, Pittsburgh; 1939–41 under Victoria Avakian, Fred Cuthbert, and Robert Motherwell, University of Oregon, Eugene.
Biography 1958, Pulos established Pulos Design Associates, Syracuse, N.Y.; 1946–55, was associate professor of design, University of Illinois, Urbana;1955–82, chairperson, Department of Design, Syracuse (N.Y.) University, and, from 1982, professor emeritus there; 1940s–50s, was a silversmith; eventually, wrote books on industrial design, including *The American Design Adventure, 1940–1975* (1988), and *American Design Ethic* (1983). While an active writer and teacher, Pulos designed a number of products such as instruments by Welch Allyn, power tools by Rockwell, and dictation machines by Dictaphone.
Citations 1939, 1940, 1942 design awards, Associated Artists of Pittsburgh; 1947 and 1950, Wichita Art Association; 1953, Detroit Institute of Arts; 1953, Brooklyn Museum of Art; 1954, Art Institute of Chicago; 1982 Chancellor's Citation for Achievement, Syracuse (N.Y.) University; 1952–53 fellow, Ford Foundation.
Bibliography Ann Lee Morgan (ed.), *Contemporary Designers*, London: Macmillan, 1984: 499–500.

Punt Mobles
Spanish furniture manufacturer; active Valencia.

History 1980, Punt Mobles's founders Vicent Martínez and Lola Castelló produced their own furniture designs in a workshop in Valencia, making furniture kits. In time, the firm began to produce more sophisticated models at higher prices, such as Martínez's Halley table, Pedro Miralles's 1988 Andrews Sisters three interlocking tables. 1992 Lola Castelló and Vicent Martínez's Papallona folding table, Terence Woodgate's 1996 Alfil upholstered seating, Vicent Martínez's 1996 Ritmica coat rack, Jorge Pensi's 1997 Temps wooden stacking chair, as well as storage systems and shelving. Commissioned designers have also included Pepe Cortés and Pedro Miralles.
Citations 1983, 1984, 1991 honorable mention, Feria de Valencia; 1985 and 1989 prizes, Instituto de la Mediana y Pequeña Industria Valenciana (IMPIVA), Valéncia; 1986, 1990, 1991, 1993 selections, ADI/FAD (industrial-design and decorative-arts associations), 1995 Delta de Plata prize, ADI/FAD; 1987 and 1989 prizes, Selección Internacional de Diseño de Equipamiento para el Hábitat (SIDI), Barcelona; 1993 Premios Príncipe Felipe Madrid; 1992 and 1994 European Community Desingn Prize; nomination, 1994 BIO industrial-design biennial, Lubijana.
Bibliography Guy Julier, *New Spanish Design*, London: Thames & Hudson, 1991.

Puotila, Ritva (1935–)
Finnish textile designer.

Training To 1958, stage set design, Taideteollinen korkeakoulu, Helsinki.
Biography Puotila was freelance textile designer for firms in Finland and abroad; from 1959, worked for Suomen Käsityön Ystävien (friends of Finnish handicraft) and Finnrya; 1961–85, for linen factory Tampella; from 1961, for American Dansk International Designs. Work included furnishings-fabric and fashion-textile collections; devised color, fabric designs, and coordinated ensembles by Denbo of Sweden and by others; glass by Hadelands Glassverk of Norway. She was design consultant to a United Nations development cooperation program in Thailand; mid-1980s, discovered industrial paper yarn when working for Tampella, the Finnish linen factory that used paper yarn in its production of insulating cables; 1987 with son Mikko Puotila, founded the company Woodnotes to make textiles from spun paper yarn. Eventually, the firm began producing a wide range of paper-yarn products including carpets, upholstery, and partition fabrics, window blinds, place-mats, bags, and cases, in addition to a collection of handwoven fabrics and unique art pieces. As the firm's artistic director, Ritva designs all its products, and Mikko manages the business affairs. Generally, her design motifs—made from basic Finnish raw wood fiber—are simple geometric patterns in natural colors. The durable, non-allergenic products are sold in more than 40 countries and have been installed in the European Union Council headquarters, Brussels, and Mântyniemi (Finnish president's residence), Helsinki.
Exhibitions/citations Work subject of 2002 exhibit of textile art and paper, Institut Finlandais, Paris. Numerous citations, including a gold medal (a rug) at 1960 (12th) Triennale di Milano; 1996 Finland Prize (to Ritva Puotila), Finnish Ministry of Education; 1996 award (to Woodnotes for spun-paper-yarn collection), Ornamo (Finnish association of designers); 2000 Kaj Franck Design Prize; 2001 Textile Artist of the Year, Tekstiilitaiteilijat (TEXO, Finnish association of textile artists).

Punt Mobles: Jorge Pensi. Temps side chair. 1997. Cherry or beech, h. 30 7/8 x w. 16 3/8 x d. 19 1/2" (79 x 42 x 50 cm). Mfr.: Punt Mobles, Spain.

Puppa, Daniela (1947–)
Italian architect and designer; born Fiume; active Milan and Paris.

Training To 1970, Politecnico, Milan.
Biography 1970–76, she was a writer for and editor of *Casabella*; 1977–83, chief editor, design journal *Modo*; and consultant to fashion magazine *Donna*; executed interiors for Driade, Gianfranco Ferrè, Montres, and GFF Duty Free, FontanaArte, Granciclismo sports machines, and Morassutti/Metropolis. Her prolific body of work includes fabrics by Alchimia, Limonta, and Stucchi, and furniture and furnishings by Driade, Vistosi, Kartell, Flos, Carrara, Matta, FontanaArte, Sisal Collections, Tendentse, Irmel, and Ligne Roset. Other work: 1984 Newport table/bench by Cappellini; tableware (including a 1984 cup in porcelain and saucer in Melamine) for Tachikichi department store, Japan; theater sets for the group Magazzini Criminali, including its *Nervous Breakdown* (1981); since its founding, teacher in the graduate-degree program, Domus Academy, and a teacher, Politecnico, both Milan. She has been the artistic director of Nazareno Gabrielli; designed textiles by Alchima; the head of design of Limonta fabrics; 1985–91, responsible for ID program of Croff home-decoration stores of Gruppo La Rinascente; designed fashion accessories by Arte e Lavoro; 1989–92, was art director of and designed leather goods and sportswear by Nazareno Gabrielli; 1999–2001, fashion accessories for Gianfranco Ferré; from 1993, leather accessories for Christian Dior; 1997–98, new products by

Habitat. She has collaborated with Franco Raggi on exhibitions, fair stands, stores, and showrooms.
Exhibitions Co-organized exhibitions, including *L'Oggetto Banale* at 1980 Biennale di Venezia and 1979 (16th) (*Sezione Design*), and 1983 (17th) (*La Casa delle Triennale*) editions of Triennale di Milano. Work was included in 1982 *Provokationen Design aus Italien*, 1982 Hanover exhibition; *La Neomerce* for Montedison at 1985 (17th) Triennale di Milano; *Donne Designers Italiane* at 1985 ADI-Takashimaia exhibition, Tokyo; 1988 *Design e Futuro delle Metropoli*, Triennale of Milan; 1992 and after, Abitare il Tempo, Verona; 2001 (10th) Biennale Donna, Ferrara.
Bibliography Andrea Branzi, *La casa calda: esperienze del nuovo disegno italiano*, Milan: Idea, 1982. Fumio Shimizu and Studio Matteo Thun (eds.), *The Italian Design: Descendants of Leonardo da Vinci*, Tokyo: Graphic-sha, 1987: 328. Liz McQuiston, *Women in Design: A contemporary View*, New York: Rizzoli, 1988. *Modo*, no. 148, Mar.–Apr. 1993: 125.

Purcell, William F.H. (1911–)

South African industrial designer.

Training Engineering, Cambridge University; from 1937, architecture, Massachusetts Institute of Technology (MIT), Cambridge, Mass.
Biography During World War II, Purcell served in the department of munitions and supply of the Canadian government; 1946, joined the industrial-design office of Henry Dreyfuss in New York, and, in 1949, became a partner.
Bibliography Arthur Pulos, *The American Design Adventure*, Cambridge, Mass.: MIT, 1988: 24.

Purcell, William Gray (1880–1965)

American architect and furniture designer; born Wilmette, Ill.; active Minneapolis and Philadelphia.

Training Cornell University, Ithaca, N.Y.
Biography Purcell was a member of the most successful architecture partnerships practicing in the Prairie School style: 1907–09 in Minnesota with George Feick Jr., was active in architectural practice Purcell and Feick; 1910–13, as Purcell, Feick and Elmslie; 1913–22, as Purcell and Elmslie. Purcell had met George Elmslie in the office of Louis Sullivan in Chicago during his brief employment there. The practice's various commissions included banks, many in small towns throughout the upper Midwest of the US. Like Sullivan and Wright, the team avoided obvious Beaux-Arts forms and neoclassical detailing to create a simple, indigenous American style. Their building facades with steel frames, brick faces, and pier-and-lintel articulation incorporated terracotta ornamentation, arched entryways, high clerestory windows, stained-glass windows, and site-specific furniture and furnishings. The firm took on numerous local commissions, including private residences and municipal buildings. Its most successful integration of building and interiors was the 1911–12 Merchants Bank, Winona, Minn.; exterior and interior ornamentation was conceived as a whole (or *Gesamtkunstwerk*), including brickwork, terracotta, lighting, stained glass, and furniture; the chair designs were related to 1890s chairs by Wright and similar examples by Koloman Moser of Austria. Unlike Wright, Purcell designed for comfort but, like Wright, was fond of a modular, geometric type of club chair with narrow vertical splats on three sides, installing some in the Winona bank and other interiors. Also installed in his own residence on Lake Place in Minneapolis, which he occupied from 1913–17 and which was much later turned over to Minneapolis Institute of Arts and restored in 1990 by MacDonald and Mack, architects, and Alec Wilson.
Bibliography David Gebhard (new intro.), *The Work of Purcell and Elmslie, Architects* (Jan. 1913, Jan. 1915, July 1915 issues of *Western Architect* journal), Park Forest, Ill.: Prairie School Press, 1965. Anne Yaffe Phillips, *From Architecture to Object*, New York: Hirschl and Adler, 1989: 72.

Pure Design

Canadian manufacturer; located Alberta.

History 1994, Pure Design was founded by three industrial designers, Daniel Hlus (Edmunton, Alberta, 1965–), Geoffrey Lilge (London, Ontario, 1967–), and Randy McCoy (Edmonton, Alberta, 1968–), to produce furniture, lighting, and accessories by young or experienced international designers, who have included Chris Baisa, Constantin and Laurene Boym, Stephen Burks, Butter (Lindsey Adelman and David Weeks), Douglas Coupland, Richard Hutten, Sojiro Inoue, Scot Laughton, Proctor-Rihl, Karim Rashid, Andrew Tye, Peter Stathis, and Mark Naden. June 2003, Lilge departed the firm.
Bibliography www.puredesignonline.com.

Putman, Andrée (b. Andrée Aynard 1925–)

French interior designer, furniture designer, and entrepreneur; born Paris.

Biography She married Dutch businessman Jacques Putman; worked for magazines *L'œil du décorateur* and *Femina*; 1960s, was hired as a stylist by Denise Fayolle for Prisunic, the French five-and-dime chain, where she became a pioneer in inexpensive, well-designed furniture

Andrée Putman. La Lune side table/desk. 1990. Plastic and bronze, 31 7/8 x 47 1/4 x 15 3/4" (81 x 120 x 40 cm). Mfr.: Écart International, France. Courtesy Quittenbaum Kunstauktionen, Munich.

and housewares and commissioned artists Matta (aka Roberto Sebastian Matta Echaurren), Bram van Velde, Pierre Alechinsky, and Jean Messagier to design lithographs, tableware, fabric patterns, and housewares for Prisunic. An early interior-design effort, Putman decorated the c. 1963 house of Michel Guy, who was later the French minister of culture. 1968, Putman accompanied Fayolle to the partnership formed by Maïmé Arnodin and Fayolle called MAFIA, for which Putman designed interiors, textiles, and furniture. 1971, she collaborated with Didier Grumbach on clothing and home furnishings in the shop Créateurs et Industriels and promoted young fashion designers; 1978, established the furniture firm Écart International and the design firm Écart with Jean-François Bodin. Écart reproduced the designs of Eileen Gray, Robert Mallet-Stevens, Pierre Chareau, and others of the past as well as those of contemporary designers. Putman's own early furniture was made by De Sede, lighting by Baldinger, and fabrics by Stendig. Écart's first commercial interior-design assignment was the YSL Rive Gauche boutiques in the US. This was followed by 1983 layout of the office of French minister of culture Jack Lang; numerous boutiques, including those for Karl Lagerfeld, Thierry Mugler 1980–83, Yves Saint Laurent, Balenciaga, Azzedine Alaïa, all 1985, Ebel 1987, and Hémisphères; 1987 décor of Musée des Beaux-Arts, Rouen, and Centre d'Art Plastique Contemporain, Bordeaux; Saint James Club, Paris; and Hotel im Wasserturm, Cologne. She designed the Basel Trade Fair, restored Le Corbusier's Villa Turque (Ebel's public relations bureau) in La Chaux-de-Fonds (Switzerland), and designed 1990 *Les Années VIA 1980–1990* exhibition at Musée des Arts Décoratifs, Paris. Putman became best-known for her black-and-white palette in interior design, exemplified by 1985 Morgan Hotel in New York for builders Ian Schrager and Steve Rubell, for whom she also designed the interior of 1985 Palladium night club in New York. c. 1989, she began to incorporate color into her work, illustrated by dinnerware by Sasaki and rugs by Toulemonde Bochart; continued to executed numerous interior commissions, including 1995 revision of Morgan Hotel (a more colorful refurbishment of original 1985 concept); 1993 Concorde airplane interior; 1998 Galerie Lagerfeld, Paris; 1998 Lô Sushi, Paris; and furniture by Domeau & Peres, 3 Suisses, and Monoprix. A large number of commissions have followed.
Exhibitions Work subject of 1988 exhibition, Paris (catalog below).
Bibliography Cat., *Design français, 1960–1990: trois décennies*, Paris: Centre Georges Pompidou/APCI, 1988. Jane Delynn, 'Rebel with a Cause,' *Elle Decor*, Aug. 1990: 52–64. Cat., François-Olivier Rousseau, *Andrée Putman*, Paris: Regard, 1989; New York: Rizzoli, 1990. François Mathey, *Au bonheur des formes, design français 1945–1992*, Paris: Regard 1992. Sophie Tasma-Anagyros, *Andrée Putman*, London: Laurence King, 1993 and 1997 editions.
> See Écart S.A.

Pye, Merrill (1901–1975)

American theater designer, architect, and furniture designer.

Biography Pye specialized in designing film sets for musicals in Hollywood; was overshadowed by supervising art director Cedric Gibbons, under whom Pye worked at MGM movie studio; designed *Freaks* (1932), *David Copperfield* (1935), and *North by Northwest* (1959); became known for his sets for lavish musical numbers in *Dancing Lady* (1933), *Reckless* (1934), *Broadway Melody of 1936* (1935), *The Great Ziegfeld* (1936), and *Born to Dance* (1935). In *Dancing Lady*, Fred Astaire, Joan Crawford, and 41 dancers performed in front of a 20 ft. (6m) backdrop of clear cellophane curtains. Pye also designed Gibbons's luxurious streamlined personal office on the MGM lot.
Bibliography Howard Mandelbaum and Eric Myers, *Screen Deco: A Celebration of High Style in Hollywood*, New York: St. Martin's, 1985.

Q

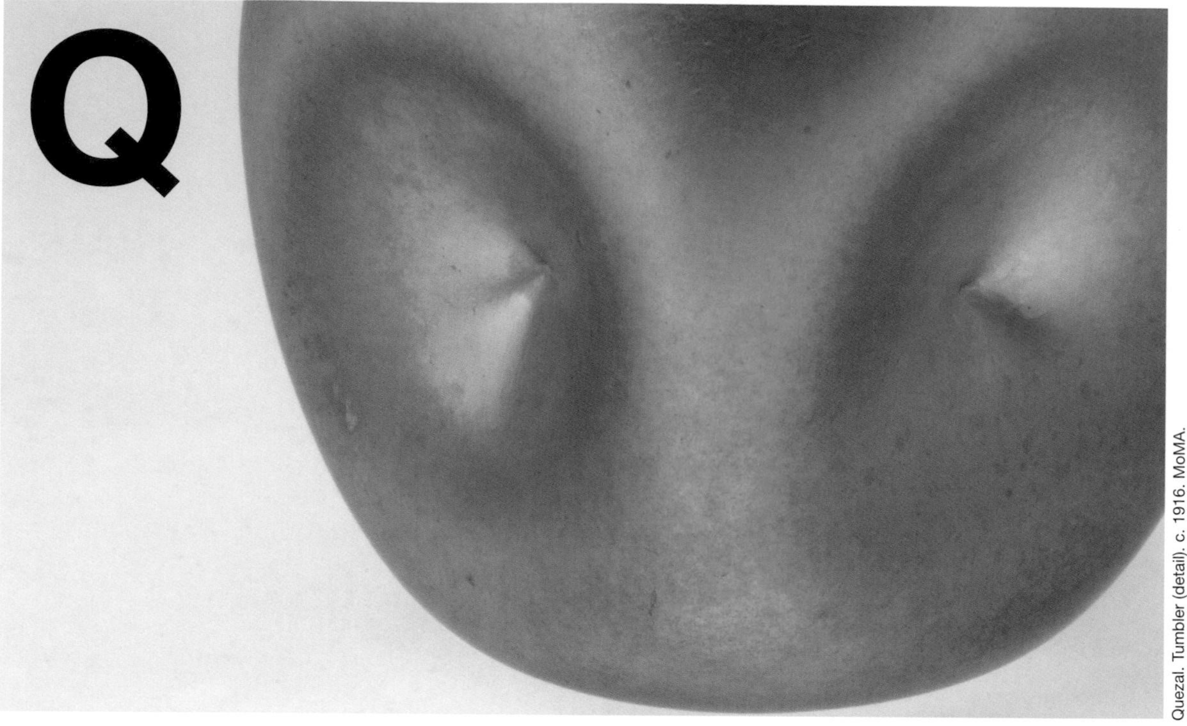

Quezal. Tumbler (detail). c. 1916. MoMA.

Quarante, Danielle (1938–)

French furniture designer; active Paris.

Training 1959–62, École Nationale Supérieure des Arts Décoratifs, and André Arbus's workshop, both Paris.
Biography She began her career in graphics and designed exhibitions; from 1966, worked on product design (children's furniture, hi-fi systems such as 1963 Bloc Source Quarante turntable/amplifier/tuner by Era, 1969 Albatros chair by Airborne, 1969 Ondine one-piece tempered-glass table); was active in research at Saint-Gobain glassworks and Usinor steel firm (today known as Arcelor); from 1974, has been a researcher and teacher, Université de Technologie de Compiègne (UTC); 1985–87, was a member of the International Council of Societies of Industrial Design (ICSID); wrote the book *Éléments de design industriel* (Paris: Economica, 2001, 3rd ed.).
Exhibitions Albatros chair by Airborne and glass table by Saint-Gobain shown at 1969 Salon, Société des Artistes Décorateurs, Paris; work included in 1988 exhibition, Paris (catalog below). Won 1970 competition sponsored by Prisunic/Shell and managed by Centre de Création Industrielle (CCI).
Bibliography Cat., *Design français 1960–1990: trois décennies,* Paris: Centre Georges Pompidou/APCI, 1988. François Mathey, *Au bonheur des formes, design français 1945–1992*, Paris: Regard, 1992: 252.

Quarti, Eugenio (1867–1931)

Italian furniture designer; born near Bergamo; active Milan.

Biography 1881 at the age of 14, Quarti began working in a furniture factory near Paris; 1888, returned to Italy and settled in Milan. After working in Carlo Bugatti's workshop for a few weeks, he set up his own work quarters. After success at 1900 *Exposition Universelle*, Paris, he moved to a larger workshop and increased his staff of three; furnished 1901–03 Palazzo Castiglioni (architect, Guiseppe Sommaruga) in Milan, and 1908 Casinò and 1925 Grand Hotel in San Pellegrino. Often collaborated with Sinnaryga and ironworker Alessandro Mazzucotelli. Quarti was a notable exponent of Art Stile Floreale (or Italian Art Nouveau), inspired by French and Austrian design; incorporated wood, silver, mother-of-pearl marquetry, carving, and cast-bronze ornamentation into his work. 1906, he considered mass-producing furniture for public buildings, including hotels.
Exhibitions/citations Work shown at 1902 *Esposizione Internazionale d'Arte Decorativa Moderna*, Turin; 1988 exhibition, Miami (catalogs below). Work subject of 1980 exhibition, Milan. Grand prize (with Bugatti), 1900 *Exposition Universelle*, Paris; prize at a 1906 exhibition, Milan.
Bibliography Cat., Eleonora Bairati et al., *L'Italia liberty: arredamento e arti decorativi*, Milan: Görlich, 1973. Cat., *Eugenio Quarti*, Milan, 1980. Cat., Gabriel P. Weisberg, *Stile Floreale: The Cult of Nature in Italian Design*, Miami: The Wolfsonian Foundation, 1988. John Fleming and Hugh Honour, *The Penguin Dictionary of Decorative Arts*, London: Viking, 1989.

Quasar (aka Quasar Khahn; b. Nguyen Manhkhan'n 1934–)

Vietnamese engineer and furniture and fashion designer; born Hanoi; former husband of Emmanuelle Khahn.

Training 1955–58, engineering, École Nationale des Ponts et Chaussées, Paris.
Biography 1958–60, Quasar worked on the viaduct in Estrées, Nord Pas de Calais, France, and, 1960–63, the Manicouagan dam in Québec, Canada; designed/produced a 1964 small urban automobile in clear acrylic plastic and 1967 Quasar Unipower car; 1969, set up design/manufacturing office Quasar-France to produce foam-rubber seating. He responded to late-1960s counter-culture—exemplified by his own bohemian lifestyle with then-wife couturière Emmanuelle Khahn and two children—by creating the 1966 inflatable-furniture in the Collection XXO, which included Relax sofa; Appolo, Satellite, and Venus armchairs; Suspensions table elements; Chesterfield sofa; transparent lamp; and 1968 inflatable house; also commissioned Philippe Starck (c. 20 years old at the time) to design some inflatables. Quasar designed 1970 menswear range by Biderman and the Hydrair KX1 boat; 1990s, returned to Vietnam and designed a bamboo bicycle, exported to Europe.
Bibliography Henry de Morant, *Histoire des arts décoratifs*, Paris: Hachette 1970: 458, 460, 478. Cat., Milena Lamarová, *Design a Plastické Hmoty*, Prague: Uměleckoprůmyslové Muzeum, 1972.

Queensberry, David, Marquess of (1929–)

British glassware designer.

Training Chelsea School of Art, London; ceramics, Central School of Arts and Crafts, London; design and technology, North Staffordshire College of Technology (now North Staffordshire Polytechnic); industrial ceramic design, Royal College of Art, London.
Biography Lord Queensberry worked in an industrial pottery in Stoke-on-Trent; was professor of ceramics/glass, Royal College of Art, London; consultant designer, Webb Corbett, for which he designed early-1960s glassware, including the starkly geometric and repetitively patterned 1963 Queensberry-Harlequin range of cut glass (tumblers,

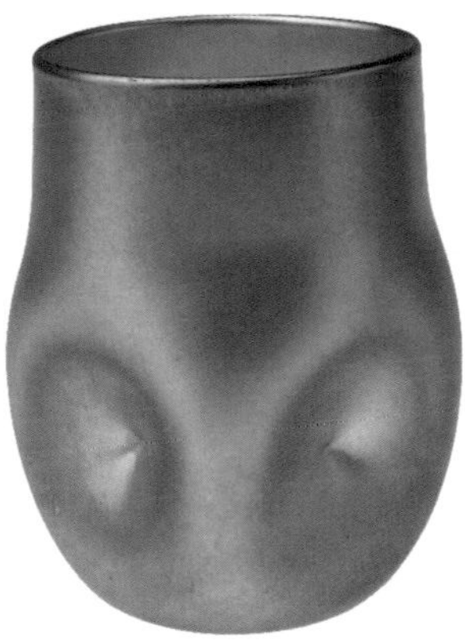

Quezal. Tumbler. c. 1916. Glass, h. 3" (7.6 cm), dia. 1 3/4" (4.5 cm). Mfr.: Quezal Art Glass and Decorating Co., US. Given anonymously. MoMA.

centerpieces, vases, and bowls). 1964 with Martin Hunt, an associate at Royal College of Art, he formed Queensberry-Hunt Design Group, working for clients, including dinnerware by Habitat, Bing & Grøndahl (1973 Delfi), and Harnsea (1976 Concept), T.G. Green (1984 Oxford), and Marks & Spencer (1988 Provence). From 1965, he was a free-lance designer for Rosenthal; on other projects, collaborated with Eduardo Paolozzi.
Exhibitions 1964 Duke of Edinburgh's Prize for Elegant Design (for Queensberry-Harlequin glass range).
Bibliography Frederick Cooke, *Glass: Twentieth-Century Design*, New York: Dutton, 1986: 78–79. Arlette Barré-Despond (ed.), *Dictionnaire international des arts appliqués et du design*, Paris: Regard, 1996: 493.

Quentin, Bernard (1923–)

French sculptor, ceramicist, and furniture designer; born Picardie, Flamicourt; active Paris.

Training École Nationale des Beaux-Arts; École Nationale Supérieure des Arts Décoratifs; both Paris.
Biography Early 1960s, Quentin was active in research at Olivetti in Italy on computer oscilloscopes and lived in the US for two years; 1965, returned to France; from 1967–76, designed inflatable objects, including PVC seating; 1977, cofounded 'Art +' artists' group; is best know as an artist/sculptor.
Exhibitions First one-person exhibition (1945), Maison de l'Université, Galerie des Etudiants d'Art, Paris; and a number of others subsequently. 1966 *Structures Moléculaires* in PVC shown at Musée des Art Décoratifs, Paris, and also there an inflatable chair included in 1967 *Les Assises du Sièges Contemporain* exhibition. 1967 exhibit of his inflatable environment, movie studio of Gunther Sachs, Neuilly, Paris, and at Blow-Up Club, Milan. Inflatables shown in French Pavilion at 1970 *Universal and International Japanese Exposition (Expo '70)*, Osaka.
Bibliography Arlette Barré-Despond (ed.), *Dictionnaire international des arts appliqués et du design*, Paris: Regard, 1996: 493.

Jens H. Quistgaard. Fjord cutlery. 1953. Teak and steel. Longest (dinner knife) 8 3/8" (21.3 cm), shortest (teaspoon) 6 1/4" (15.8 cm). Mfr.: Dansk International Designs, Denmark. Given anonymously. MoMA.

Quezal

American glassware factory.

Biography 1902, Martin Bach, Nicholas Bach, Thomas Johnson (Louis Comfort Tiffany's former glass mixer and foreman), Adolph Demuth, and Lena Scholtz cofounded Quezal Art Glass and Decorating Co. in Queens, N.Y. (Quezal is a colorful South American bird.) The group produced many pieces of luster and Favrile-type glassware and a wide range of glass tableware that included bud-vases, compotes, wine glasses, sherbets, bowls, and an obvious copy of Tiffany's Jack in the Pulpit vase. Lampshades, its speciality, were non-leaded, mouth-blown models up to 6" (15 cm) in various trumpet, lily, and bowl motifs to surround a single electric light bulb. The firm lacked innovation and produced no new designs or techniques of its own; 1905–18, experienced difficult financial times; 1921, was sold to Dr. John Ferguson, who later sold it to Edward Conlan. 1924, Quesal closed.
Bibliography Alastair Duncan, *Art Nouveau and Art Déco Lighting*, New York: Simon & Schuster, 1978: 46.

Quinet, Jacques (1918–1992)

French interior architect, furniture designer, and cabinetmaker; born Normandy.

Training In architecture.
Biography From 1947, Quinet set up his own practice and worked as an interior architect and decorator; was inspired by a range of styles from the Louis XVI style to Purism and worked in a manner similar to Ardré Arbus; became known as a perfectionist master cabinetmaker; designed the architectural interior and decoration of 1953 oceanliner *La Bourdonnais* and, eventually, passenger liner firm Messageries Maritimes became his primary client; collaborated with artists Maxime Adam, Maurice Buché, and André Wogenscky; used sycamore, mahogany, oak, and cherry in his furniture; was associated with metalsmiths Gilbert Poillerat and Raymond Subes in his 1945–65 work.
Bibliography Yolande Amic, *Intérieurs: le mobilier français, 1945– 1964*, Paris: Regard/VIA, 1983: 44–45.

Quist, Wim (1930–)

Dutch architect and designer.

Training To 1960, Academie van Bouwkunst, Amsterdam.
Biography 1960, Quist opened an architecture practice; 1968–75, was a professor of architecture/town planning, Technische Hogeschool, Eindhoven; 1975–80, was a government-appointed architect; from 1987, professor emeritus of architectonic design, Universiteit van Amsterdam (UvA); designed his first furniture, when he was a student and renewed the interest while working on 1970–77 Kröller-Müller Museum extension in Otterlo; subsequently, designed more interiors and furniture, primarily in situ with his architecture commissions of houses, offices, factories, and public buildings. 1982–84, he created his best-known furniture, for the Queen's office rooms of the Palais Noordeinde, the Hague; usually designs geometrical furniture with straight lines and no ornamentation, exemplified by 1970 BQ.01 Bank bench by Spectrum.

Quistgaard, Jens H. (1919–)

Danish wood- and metalworker and glassware designer; active Copenhagen.

Training c. 1935–44, in sculpture, drafting, silversmithing, ceramics, and carpentry; apprenticeship at Georg Jensen Sølvsmedie.
Biography After World War II, Quistgaard set up his own design studio in Copenhagen; 1954 with Ted Nierenberg of the US, founded Dansk International Designs, where he remained active to 1984. As the principal designer of Dansk (though there were a number of other commissioned designers), Quistgaard created sculptural wooden table-

ware, silverware, cookware, ceramics, cutlery, and glassware.
Citations 1954 Lunning Prize; gold and silver medals (for enameled cast-iron cooking pots by De Forenede Jerstøberier, and for cutlery at 1954 (10th) Triennale di Milano.
Bibliography Arne Karlsen, *Made in Denmark*, New York, 1960: 116–17. 'Thirty-four Lunning Prize-Winners,' *Mobilia*, no. 146, Sept. 1967. Cat., Kathryn B. Hiesinger and George H. Marcus III (eds.), *Design Since 1945*, Philadelphia: Philadelphia Museum of Art, 1983. Cat., *The Lunning Prize*, Stockholm: Nationalmuseum, 1986.

R

Gerrit Rietveld Tood Blauuwe Stoel (red blue chair) (detail). 1918. MoMA.

Raacke, Peter (1928–)

German metalworker and designer; born Hanau.

Training 1941–45, gold- and silversmithing, Zeichenakademie, and Staatliche Meisterschule für das Edelmetallhandwerk, both Hanau; 1946–47 enamelwork, Staatliche Höhere Fachschule Edelmetall-Industrie, Schwäbisch-Gmünd.
Biography Raacke is best known for his dinnerware, kitchen tools, and cookware by Hessische Metallwerke, including widely published cutlery in stainless steel: 1950 mono-t (with teak), 1959 mono-a (or sterling silver), 1959 mono 10+1, 1960 mono-e, 1966 mono-Ring (with a plastic coating), 1982 mono-Oval. He also executed designs for cardboard furniture: 1967 Papp range of modular seating, tables, stacking easy chairs, and storage units by Faltmöbel Ellen Raacke. His 1966 plastic suitcase by Hanning Kunststoffe is considered a classic. Other work: c. 1957 VOKO-Zeitgewinnsystem office furniture by VOKO (Franz Vogt & Co.). 1961–63, he was active in his own studio in Kassel and Milan; 1966–72, in Hanau/Frankfurt; 1972–80, in Hamburg; 1990–99, in Berlin. He taught at a number of institutions, including Hochschule für Gestaltung, Ulm (1962–67).
Exhibitions/citations Work included in 1971 and 1983–84 exhibitions, Nuremberg and Philadelphia (catalogs below). Subject of 2003 *Gestalten für den Gebrauch: 50 Jahre Peter Raacke Design*, Deutsches Technikmuseum, Berlin. Received 1973 Bundespreis Produktdesign (mono-a cutlery), Rat für Formgebung (German design council), Frankfurt, and others.
Bibliography 'Technologia del Provisorio, Papp, Mobili di Carta,' *Casabella*, no. 323, Feb. 1968: 55–56. 'Paper for Parents and Children,' *Design*, no. 232, Apr. 1968: 65. Cat., *Gold und Silber, Schmuck und Gerät*, Nuremberg: Gewerbemuseum, 1971. Cat., Kathryn B. Hiesinger and George H. Marcus III (eds.), *Design Since 1945*, Philadelphia: Philadelphia Museum of Art, 1983.

Rabanne, Paco (aka Francisco Rabaneva-Cuervo 1934–)

Spanish clothing and furnishings designer; born San Sebastián.

Training 1952–64, École Nationale Supérieure des Arts Décoratifs, Paris.
Biography 1960–64, Rabanne designed handbags, shoes, eye glasses, and other accessories for Dior, Givenchy, and Balenciaga; 1967, set up his own fashion house in Paris and designed clothing in plastics, paper, leather, strips of knitted fur, and metals. He named his first couture collection of plastic and aluminum dresses 'The Unwearables.' He created 1966 dresses in plastic disks and coats of neon-colored plastic diamonds sewn onto white crepe, and 1967 clothing was chain mail. From 1964, he designed costumes for films, including *Two for the Road* (1967), in which Audrey Hepburn wore his plastic dresses; *Barbarella* (1968), featuring Jane Fonda in revealing futuristic clothing; and *The Last Adventure* (1968). 1967, he became a founding member of the modern aesthetics association Groupe Verseau in Paris; developed the Calandre perfume (bottle designed by Ateliers Dinand). His firm markets furniture, and Rabanne created the 1980 Dorique faïence dinnerware in a square, askew silhouette by Faïencerie Gien.
Citations A number of prizes for fashion and perfume.
Bibliography *Contemporary Designers*, London: Macmillan, 1984. Sophie Manrique, 'Paco Rabanne de la haute couture au prêt à meubler,' *Maison française*, May 1983.

Rabinovich, Isaac Moiseievich (1894–1961)

Russian painter and designer of film and stage décors.

Training 1906–12, Kiev Art School; 1912–15, in the studio of Oleksandr Murashko.
Biography 1911, Rabinovich created the first of his many stage designs.
Exhibitions From 1914, participated in several street decorations and exhibitions; work shown at 1925 *Exposition Internationale des Arts Décoratifs et Industriels Modernes*, Paris.
Bibliography Cat., *Paris-Moscou*, Paris: Centre Georges Pompidou, 1979.

Race, Ernest (1913–1964)

British furniture and industrial designer; born Newcastle.

Training 1932–35, interior design, Bartlett School of Architecture of London University; 1937–39, weaving in India.
Biography 1935, Race was a model maker and, c. 1936, turned to lighting design, as a draftsperson under A.B. Read at the lighting manufacturer Troughton and Young. 1937, he founded Race Fabrics, selling textiles of his own design, handwoven in India (where he had visited with his aunt for four months in 1937). 1945, Race (as the designer) and J.W. Noel Jordan (as the director) founded Ernest Race Ltd., in Sheerness, which, at the time, had to use aircraft scrap metal for its raw material. 1945–54, Race was director of the firm. He used an innovative approach to materials, producing a succession of highly publicized chairs that called on bent steel rods. His 1945 BA3 chair (manufactured 1949–69 and from 1989 by Race Furniture) of stove-enameled sand-cast aluminum and other furniture in salvaged aluminum were innovations based on the scarcity of raw materials after

Peter Raacke. mono-Ring cutlery. 1966. Stainless steel and plastic-coated metal, longest (knife) 8 7/8" (22.5 cm), shortest (teaspoon) 6" (15.2 cm). Mfr.: Hessische Metallwerke, Germany. Gift of Bonniers, Inc. MoMA.

World War II. Race's firm in Sheerness produced more than 250,000 BA chairs using 850 tons of aluminum. His 1951 Antelope and Springbok chairs popularized the contemporary thin silhouette; a reproduction of the former began in 1990. Other designs included 1959 Flamingo easy chair and 1963 Sheppey settee chair. 1963, he restyled the Penguin Donkey bookcase (first designed by Egon Riss in 1936) and the Bottleship, both by Isokon. After 1954, he worked as a freelance designer. Commissions included contract design work for P&O Orient Lines, Royal Netherland Lines, and the University of Liverpool Medical School.
Exhibitions/citations BA chair and other furniture shown for first time at 1946 *Britain Can Make It*, Victoria and Albert Museum, London; 1947 metal-frame wing chair and storage units included in 1948 *International Competition for Low Cost Furniture Design*, The Museum of Modern Art, New York; Antelope and Springbok chairs and other work installed in the grounds of 1951 *Festival of Britain*, London; 1971 and 1983–84 exhibitions, London and Philadelphia (catalogs below), and numerous others. Work shown at 1951 (9th), 1954 (10th), 1957 (11th), and 1960 (12th) Triennali di Milano, where he received gold and silver medals. Other citations included three Council of Industrial Design awards for furniture; 1953, was elected Honorary Royal Designer for Industry, UK.
Bibliography 'Design Review: Trends in Factory Made Furniture by Ernest Race,' *Architectural Review*, vol. 103, May 1948: 218–20. Gillian Naylor, 'Ernest Race,' *Design*, no. 184, Apr. 1964: 54–55. 'Race: Case Histories,' London: Race Furniture Limited (submitted to the Royal Society of Arts), 1969: 3–13. Cat., *Modern Chairs 1918–1970*, London: Lund Humphries, 1971, nos. 26, 50. Hazel Conway, *Ernest Race*, London: The Design Council, 1982. Cat., Kathryn B. Hiesinger and George H. Marcus III (eds.), *Design Since 1945*, Philadelphia: Philadelphia Museum of Art, 1983. Fiona MacCarthy and Patrick Nuttgens, *Eye for Industry*, London: Lund Humphries, 1986.

Radi, Giulio (1895–1952)

Italian glassblower and designer; born Murano.

Training As a glassblower, father's workshop, Murano.
Biography 1918, Radi worked at Andrea Rioda & C. until it closed, 1921, when he cofounded Successori Andrea Rioda and was the artistic director. 1932 with Antonio Luigi Ferro, Egidio Ferro, Emilio Nason, and Galliano Ferro, he cofounded Arte Vetraria Muranese (A.VE.M.) and, from 1939 to his death in Murano, was the artistic director and, as such, designed products and conducted extensive color experiments in glass with metal oxides.
Exhibitions 1940, 1948, 1950, 1952 editions of Biennale di Venezia.

Radi Designers

French design studio; located Paris.

History 1992, Radi Designers was founded by Claudio Colucci (1965–), Laurent Massaloux (1968–), Olivier Sidet (1965–), and Robert Sadler (1966–); 1994, joined by Florence Doléac (1968–), the wife of Sadler. 2000, Colucci resigned. The group collaborates on product and exhibition design and interior architecture; amalgamates typologies, historical references, codes, usage, techniques, and forms. Members are also active independently. Work has included 1999 rug for Tarkett Sommer, 2000 public drinking fountains for SAGEP–Mayor of Paris, 2000 plastic dinnerware for Air France's economy-class section, 2000 public-bar drinking glass for Schweppes, 2000 Viquel office accessories by Kreo, 2000 public-bar Richard bottle dispenser, 2001 toiletry flacon for Issey Miyake's Le Feu d'Issey scent, and other limited-edition inventions. Doléac designed the 2002 Mise à Nu floor-level chair/rug in felt, sponsored by Fonds Municipal d'Art Contemporain (FMAC), City of Paris.
Exhibitions/citations Solo exhibitions at Galerie Emmanuel Perrotin, 1988, Paris; 1999 *Fabulation*, Foundation Cartier pour l'Art Contemporain, Paris, and 2000, Park Hyatt, Tokyo, and Art Center, Seoul); 2000 *Radi-Room*, Institut Français d'Architecture; 2001 *In Organic*, Sandra Gering Gallery, New York; 2002 *Les 10 ans de Radi*, Aux 9 Billards, Paris; 2003 *En forme la form*, Le Quartier, Le Centre d'Art Contemporain, Quimper, France, others. Various group venues since 1994. 2001 Carte Blanche, VIA (French furniture association); Creator of the Year, 2000 Salon du Meuble, Paris; public drinking fountain, Hôtel de Ville, Paris, 2000; light switch, 2000 (7th) International Design Competition, Japan; writing device, Du Pont; garden furniture, 1994 Objet 2000/Le Jardin, Paris.
Bibliography Lionel Blaisse and François Gaillard, *Temps Denses*, Besançon: Imprimeur, 1998. Mel Byars, *50 Products...*, Hove: RotoVision, 1998. *Radi Designers 'Realité Fabriquée,'* Arles: Actes Sud, 1999. Philippe Starck, 'New Generation of Designers,' *Architektur &*

Ernest Race. BA side chair. 1945. Enameled cast aluminum frame, padded plywood seat and back, and cotton upholstery. Mfr.: Race Furniture, UK. Gift of Waldron Associates. MoMA.

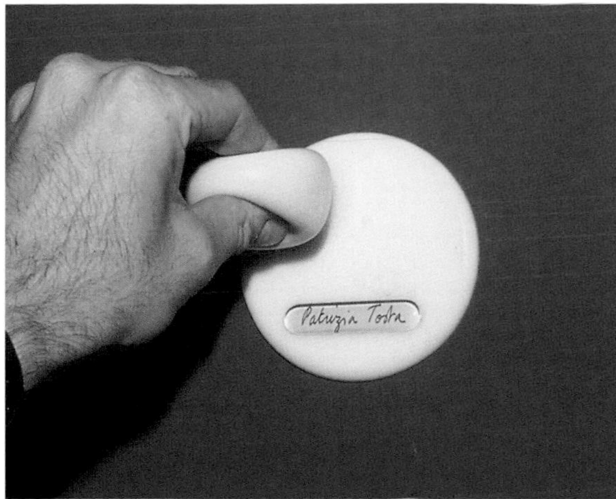

Radi Designers. Patrizia door bell. c. 1998. Silicone and polystyrene, d. 2 5/8 x dia. 3 3/4" (6.7 x 9.5 cm). Mfr.: the designers, France.

Wohnen, Hamburg, 1999. *Radi Designers à Vallauris*, Nice: Gardette, 2001. Charlotte and Peter Fiell, *Designing the 21st Century*, London: Taschen, 2001. Nathalie Chapuis, *Créateur, création en France*, Paris: Autrement, 2002. Gilles de Bure (preface), *Radi Designers*, Paris: Pyramyd, 2002. www.radidesigners.com.

Radice, Barbara (1943–)

Italian art and design director and writer; born Como.

Training Modern literature, Università Cattolica del Sacro Cuore, Milan.
Biography 1974–76, she was associate editor of art magazine *Data*, Milan; 1977, began as a freelance journalist, writing for *Modo*, *Domus*, *Casa Vogue*, *Japan SD*, *Wet*, and *Art & Auction*; 1981–88, was consulting art director in charge of exhibition and cultural activities to the Memphis group; wrote books, many about Ettore Sottsass with whom she had a personal relationship, including *Elogio del Banale* (Milan: Studio Forma Alchimia, 1980); *Memphis: ricerche, esperienze, risultati...*, Milan: Electa, 1984), *Gioielli di architetti* (Milan: Electa, 1987), B. Radice, *Ettore Sottsass* (Milan: Electa, 1993).
Bibliography Andrea Branzi, *La casa calda: esperienze del nuovo disegno italiano*, Milan: Idea, 1982. Liz McQuiston, *Women in Design: A Contemporary View*, New York: Rizzoli, 1988.

Raemisch, Waldemar (1888–1955)

German metalworker and teacher; active Berlin.

Training Early 1920s under Josef Wilm and Bruno Paul, Kunstgewerbeschule, Berlin.
Biography Raemisch taught, Vereinigte Staatsschulen für freie und angewandte Kunst (formerly called the Kunstgewerbeschule, to 1924), Berlin-Charlottenburg. Peter Müller-Munk and Frederic Buehner were his students. Raemisch designed metalware, lighting, and medals, such as 2nd-Class Olympic Breast Cross awarded to German participants in 1936 Berlin Olympiad. He also designed the 50-pfenning coin of 1923–24 and one-mark Adler coin of 1924–23 struck by the Weimar Republic. Raemisch emigrated to the US and, from 1939, taught sculpture, Rhode Island School of Design, Providence.
Exhibitions Work shown at 1922 *Deutsche Gewerbeschau* (a chased service), Munich.
Bibliography Annelies Krekel-Aalberse, *Art Nouveau and Art Déco Silver*, New York: Abrams, 1989. Hans Wichmann, *Deutsche Werkstätten und WK-Verband 1818–1990*, Munich: Prestel, 1992: 340.

Raffy, Eric (1951–)

French designer and architect.

Biography As an architect, Raffy has designed many restaurants, hotels, offices, and other establishments worldwide. As a designer, 1984 Thèbes wood stool by Raro Bordeaux, 1986 Atlantic steel furniture by Grange, 1986 Triplan bookcase by Farjon, 1986 Shangai armchair and Kangourou table and 1989 rattan furniture by Soca Line, Scarabat bookcase by Sacarabat, 1990 public furniture in granite by Art Mob, 1993 Demoiselle chair/table by Fermob, 1994 knife by Laguiole. Early 1990s, worked for couturier Paco Rabanne; taught, École d'Architecture, Bordeaux; became active in architecture and design for clients in Japan, Malaysia, Brazil, and the US.
Citations 1989 Appel Permanent grant (Thèbes stool) and 1993 Carte Blanche production support, VIA (French Furniture Association); 1987 gold medal (steel furniture by Grange), Prix de la Critique for contemporary furniture, Salon du Meuble, Paris.
Bibliography Cat., *Les années VIA 1980–1990*, Paris: Musée des Arts Décoratifs, 1990. www.ericraffy.com, www.via.asso.fr.

Raggi, Franco (1945–)

Italian architect and designer; born Milan.

Training 1963–69, architecture, Politecnico, Milan.
Biography From 1970, Raggi has been active as a designer; 1971–76, was editor of journal *Casabella* and, 1977–80, on the staff of journal *Modo*, where he was the director to 1983; 1973 with Aldo Rossi, organized the international-architecture section of the Triennale di Milan; 1973, organized the first critical exhibition of Radical Italian Design at International Design Zentrum (IDZ), Berlin, and 1975–76, the architectural exhibition *Europa/America*, Biennale di Venezia; 1979–80, was responsible for the Radical Design section at Triennale di Milano, realizing the exhibitions *Censimento del Design* and *La Casa Decorta* there; from 1985, taught architecture, Università degli Studi, Pescara. Work has included architectural structures, environments, interiors, exhibitions, publications, stage designs, and products for firms, including Artemide, Barovier & Toso, Candle, Cappellini, FontanaArte, Kartell, Luceplan, Poltronova, Roset Francia, Schopenhauer, and Tendentse. 1996–98, he was the coordinator, department of architecture, Istituto Europeo di Design, Milan, where he taught 1989–2000; and subsequently, Istituto Superiore per le Industrie Artistiche (ISIA), Florence; has been vice-director of lighting-design journal *Flare*.
Exhibitions Was an organizer and cultural coordinator of 1973 (15th), 1979 (16th), and 1983 (17th) editions of Triennale di Milano and 1975, 1976, 1977, and 1980 editions of Biennale di Venezia. Participated in 1978 *Assenza Presenza*, Bologna; 1979 *Cinquant'Anni di Architettura Italiana*, Milan; 1982 *Provokationen*, Düsseldorf; 1983 *Dal Cucchiaio alla Città*, Milan; 1983 *Una Generazione Postmoderna*, Genoa; 1985 *La Neomerce*, Milan and Paris; 1983 *Le Case della Triennale* and 1989 *Il Futuro delle Metropoli* at editions of Triennale di Milano.
Bibliography Fumio Shimizu and Studio Matteo Thun (eds.), *The Italian Design: Descendants of Leonardo da Vinci*, Tokyo: Graphic-sha, 1987. Patrizia Catalono, 'Un designer pensoso,' *Gap Casa*, no. 96, Apr. 1993. Anna Terzi, 'Come non abita il designer,' *Interni*, no. 343, Sept. 1994. Mel Byars, *50 Lights...*, Hove: RotoVision, 1997. Daniele Premoli, 'Franco Raggi: architetto e designer,' *OFX*, no. 1, Jan.–Feb. 1999.

Ragot, Christian (1933–)

French designer and architect.

Training École Boulle; École Nationale Supérieure des Arts Décoratifs; Conservatoire National des Arts et Métiers; all Paris.
Biography 1970, Ragot set up his own design office. He has designed 1967–68 Reptilampe by Autowest (distributed by Roche-Bois), 1969 Elisa line of seating (with Michel Cadestin [1942–]) by Ligne Roset, 1969 Alcove 2000 adjustable sofa in foam tubes, 1971 OS chair (edition of 15) by Réro, 1974 Canne armchair by Randsom-Choumatcher, 1985 Triamelli pasta by Panzani, a bottle for Vittel, an orbital station entry in the Archepolis competition, Spatial Monument for 1989 centenary of the Eiffel Tower. He taught, École Nationale des Beaux-Arts, Nancy, and École d'Architecture, Strasbourg; with Jean Prouvé, Andrea Branzi, and Gaetano Pesce, participated in a number of events.
Exhibitions Reptilampe shown at 1969 Salon des Artistes Décorateurs and 1970 Salon des Arts Ménagers, both Paris. Work subject of 2001 retrospective, *Pont à Mousson*; 2001 exhibition of his photographic work.
Bibliography *Domus*, no. 490, Sept. 1970: 37. *Domus*, no. 515, Oct. 1972: 40. Gilles de Bures, *Intérieurs: le mobilier français 1965–1979*, Paris: Éditions du Regard, 1983.

Raichle, Karl (1889–1965)

German metalworker; born Dettingen.

Training 1928, Bauhaus, Dessau.
Biography With Christian Dell, Marianne Brandt, and Hans Pryzembel, Raichle worked in the Bauhaus metal workshop; often produced his work in hammered pewter with ebony fittings, in the form of teapots, casseroles, and other utilitarian objects; after the Bauhaus, founded the Werkgemeinschaft Urach and, 1933, the Meersburger Zinnschmiede;

Karl Raichle: Pitcher. c. 1930. Hammered pewter, h. 9 1/2" (24 cm). Mfr.: Karl Raichle, Germany. Courtesy Quittenbaum Kunstauktionen, Munich.

belonged to a group of Utopian artists in Urach.
Bibliography Cat., *The Bauhaus: Masters and Students*, New York: Barry Friedman, 1988. Cat., *Metalkunst*, Berlin: Bröhan-Museum, 1990: 402–12.

Raimondi, Giuseppe (1941–1997)

Italian town planner, architect, and industrial designer; born Fiume; active Turin.

Training To 1967, architecture, Politecnico, Milan.
Biography 1966, Raimondi began his professional career; from 1970, collaborated with architects Sisto Giriodi, Guido Martinero, and Alberto Vaccarone in the studio A.BA.CO; designed the Mozza foam chair by Gufram and Cristal System by Cristal Art, and other work by Tarzia; became a member, Associazione per il Disegno Industriale (ADI); has written for journals including *Casabella*, *Casa Vogue*, and *Abitare*; designed a project for Museo del Pneumatico in Turin; published the book *Abitare Italia* (Milan: Fabbri, 1992). Work has included architectural structures, environments, interiors, exhibitions, publications, stage designs, and products such as 1991 upholstered seating (with Daniela Puppa) by Ligne Roset.
Citations Premio Compasso d'Oro: 1981 (for Busta Sacchetto lamp by Evoluzione; Scrittura fabric range by Tessitura Piovano), 1987 (for Delfina lounge chair by Bontempi), 1989 (for Miriade low-voltage lighting by Valenti). 1988 gold medal (for Miriade lighting system by Valenti), Toronto.
Bibliography *ADI Annual 1976*, Milan: Associazione per il Disegno Industriale, 1976. *Moderne Klassiker: Möbel, die Geschichte machen*, Hamburg: Gruner + Jahr, 1982: 75. Hans Wichmann, *Italien Design 1945 bis heute*, Munich: Die Neue Sammlung, 1988. *Modo*, no. 148, Mar.-Apr. 1993: 125.

Rajalin, Börje (1933–)

Finnish designer.

Training To 1955, department of metal design, Taideteollinen korkeakoulu, Helsinki.
Biography Rajalin worked at Bertel Gardberg's silversmithy; 1952–56, was a designer at Tillander, and, 1956, a jeweler at Kalevala Koru; 1956, set up his own studio, working as an interior, exhibition, and industrial designer. His design work included technical equipment, plastic fittings, cutlery, stainless-steel tableware, and cookware, and 1972 train carriages (with Antti Nurmesniemi) for the Helsinki subway. 1969–71, Rajalin taught, Taideteollinen Oppilaitos, and was director, Taideteollinen Ammattikoulu, both Helsinki.
Citations Gold medal (large silver screen), 1960 (12th) Triennale di Milano; 1961 AID International Design Award; 1963 Lunning Prize.
Bibliography Erik Zahle (ed.), *A Treasury of Scandinavian Design*, New York: Golden Press, 1961. Graham Hughes, *Modern Silver Throughout the World*, New York: Crown, 1967. Cat., Kathryn B. Hiesinger and George H. Marcus III (eds.), *Design Since 1945*, Philadelphia: Philadelphia Museum of Art, 1983. Cat., *The Lunning Prize*, Stockholm: Nationalmuseum, 1986.

Rakhn
> See GAkhN.

Ram

Dutch ceramics firm; located Arnhem.

History 1921, Plateelbakkerij Ram was established to produce fine ceramic bodies. Thomas A.C. Colenbrander, at Ram from 1921–25, was the designer for whom, at age 80, the company was established. Ram's wares, considered art rather than craft, were sold at exhibition auctions. 1924–35, art dealer and artist N. Henri van Lerven and, 1923–27, F. Mansveld experimented with oxide paints there; sculptor and designer H.J. Jansen van Galen created many designs. Ram's production included Colenbrander's ceramics and very hard-bodied glazes for utility ware. Colenbrander's designs were supervised by Mansveld from 1925–27. Van Lerven, a highly productive designer, created most of the products thereafter, and, on his utility ware, he incorporated single-stroke stripes and, for ornamental ware, a broad brush in a watercolor effect produced by oxide paint. After 1931, he used decalcomanias, *zilva* décor, and silver-and-gold intarsia-like flowers on blue and dark black. 1935, Plateelbakkerij Ram closed.
Bibliography Cat., *Industry and Design in the Netherlands, 1850/1950*, Amsterdam: Stedelijk Museum, 1985.

Ramaer, W.G.J.

Dutch fabric manufacturer; located Helmond.

Biography 1849 with his mother as partner, W.G.J. Ramaer began as a manufacturer of cotton, linen, and woolen goods. Interior designer Thomas W. Nieuwenhuis, of the workshop of Van Wisselingh and who designed for the firm 1909–24, encouraged the firm to make more sophisticated furnishings goods. This effort proved successful. By 1914, Ramaer had added 15 furnishing fabric patterns to its inventory and sold them worldwide. In the Netherlands, its fabrics were used by Willem Penaat, H.J.M. Walenkamp, furniture studio De Ploeg, and others. c. 1924, production of these fabrics was discontinued. 1925–61, the firm was known as Ramaer's Textielfabriek and, 1953, was taken over by Van Vlissingen; now produces machines and apparatuses and supplies services in galvanizing.
Bibliography Cat., *Industry and Design in the Netherlands, 1850/1950*, Amsterdam: Stedelijk Museum, 1985.

Ramakers, Renny
> See Droog Design.

Rambusch, Frode Christian Vlademar (1858–1924)

Danish artisan and interior and lighting designer; born Sønde Omme; active New York.

Training 1871, apprenticeship under painter Anderson in Odense; 1875–81, Det Kongelige Danske Kunstakademi, Copenhagen, and under painter Markussen; Kunstgewerbeschule, Berlin and Munich.
Biography Rambusch became a journeyman in Dresden, Berlin, Paris, Zürich, and Munich; 1889, moved to New York and worked for Arnold and Locke, a Brooklyn decorating and painting firm, where he became a foreperson and was affectionately known as the 'stencil kid'; 1893 and 1896, made two unsuccessful attempts at establishing his own workshops; 1899, established Rambusch Glass and Decorating at 175 Broadway, Manhattan, where production of lighting fixtures began in 1908. His early fixtures were made by outside artisans under the firm's supervision, with wiring completed at S.J. O'Brien; 1919, began designing for churches, including candlesticks, chalices, monstrances, crucifixes, tabernacles, and screens. Management was taken over by Rambusch's sons, Harold, William, and Viggo. 1924, Harold became president. 1947, the firm relocated to 40 West 13th Street, Manhattan. The firm's patented lighting fixtures included Lite-Paks, Shovelites, Pan-a-Lux, Annulites, and Classic Lanterns.
Exhibitions Frode Rambusch participated in 1883–94 annual exhibitions, Architectural League of New York.
Bibliography Catha Grace Rambush, 'Rambusch Decorating Company: Ninety Years of Art Metal,' *The Journal of Decorative and Propaganda Arts*, summer 1988: 6–43.

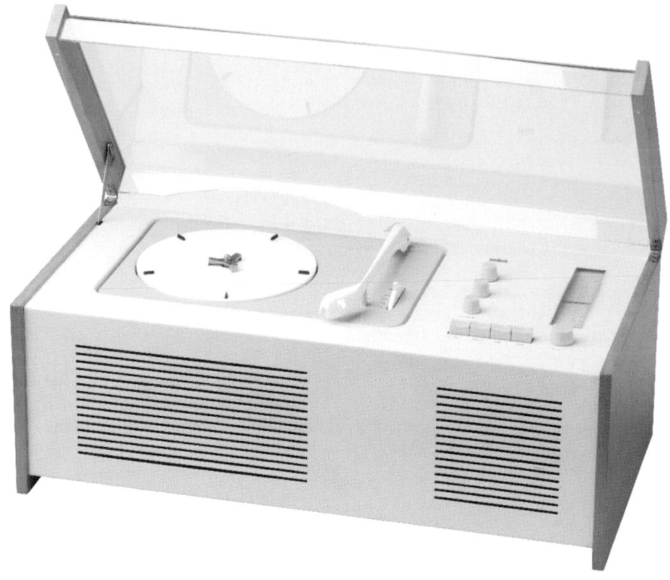

Dieter Rams and Hans Gugelot. Phonosuper radio-phonograph (no. SK 4/10). 1956. Painted metal, wood, and plastic, 9 1/2 x 23 x 11 1/2" (24.1 x 58.4 x 29.2 cm). Mfr.: Braun, Germany. Gift of the mfr. MoMA.

Rameckers, Clemens H.B. (1949–)

Dutch designer; active Paris.

Biography Early 1990s, Rameckers collaborated with Van Geuns. Both previously fashion designers, they produced together handmade furniture, ceramics, blankets, bedlinens, fabrics, and rugs designed in their Paris studio, Ravage (an acronym from RAmeckers VAn GEuns).
Exhibitions Work was the subject of a 1990 exhibition, Galerie Néotù, New York.

Ramond, Marcel

French architect and designer; born and active Paris.

Biography From 1968, Ramond was active in research in habitation, working conditions, and means of travel; 1978, established Design Management agency in Paris and served clients, including Atal, Ords, Gerbet-Grebot, Rossignol, Rodet, and Grosfillex; designed 705 folding chair in resin by Tissot, Axil seating range by Lafa Mobilier, seating by Grosfillex at the Stade de France in Saint-Denis, and 1980 Programme 9000 office furniture by Strafor. 1986, Artisanat Design Management was established as a department within the design office to assist in the development of Third World artisanal enterprises.
Citations Won 1983 competition (for Programme 9000) sponsored by Ministère de la Culture, France, and Agence pour la Promotion de la Création Industrielle (APCI); Janus award for original concept (for Isosystem desk by Haworth).

Ramos, Charles (1924–)

French furniture designer and decorator; born Bône, Algeria.

Training 1941, École des Beaux-Arts, Algiers.
Biography After World War II, Ramos lived for two years in New York; 1950, opened his own design office in Paris and worked for hotels, department stores, and several private clients; designed furniture typical of 1950s–'60s, often in wood with conical legs.
Exhibitions Work first shown, 1952 Société des Artistes Décorateurs; later, Société des Arts Ménagers, and Salon du Meuble; all Paris.
Bibliography Pascal Renous, *Portraits de créateurs*, Paris: H. Vial, 1969. Arlette Barré-Despond (ed.), *Dictionnaire international des arts appliqués et du design*, Paris: Regard, 1996.

Rams, Dieter (1932–)

German designer; born Wiesbaden; active Frankfurt.

Training 1947–48 and 1951–53, architecture and design, Werkkunstschule, Wiesbaden.
Biography Rams was associated with Otto Apel, a Frankfurt architect, and collaborated with American architecture firm Skidmore, Owings and Merrill, which was involved with the early-1950s design of US consulate buildings in West Germany. He has become legendary for his designs of a large number of austere Functional forms by Braun, where he became a designer in 1956, abandoning architecture, and, the chief designer from 1961. His work typified the spare, formal, geometric style associated with postwar German design. He has commented, 'I want to make things that recede into the background.' The 1956 Phonosuper radio-phonograph (no. SK 4/10), designed with Hans Gugelot and a testament to understatement, was known in Germany as the *Schneewittchensarg* (Snow White's coffin). His 1957 Atelier 1 unit separated the loudspeaker from the chassis, for the first time. His series of portable radios included 1956 Transistor and 1958 T3 pocket model which, combined with a small record player, became a portable radio-phonograph combination. He designed his first furniture (1957) for a firm in Eschborn that was to become Vitsoe. Vitsoe produced his 1962 RZ 62 chair and other pieces in the series; the chair was chosen by Florence Knoll for use in her residence in Florida. Vitsoe also produced Rams's 1979 Dafne folding chair and Braun his 1977 ET44 pocket calculator (with Dietrich Lubs), now regarded as a design classic. 1981, he became a professor, Hochschule für bildende Künste, Hamburg; from 1987, president, Rat für Formgebung (German design council), Frankfurt.
Exhibitions/citations His fame was enhanced when, by 1959, The Museum of Modern Art, New York, had placed his designs on exhibition. Subsequently, his work has been included in numerous other venues (catalogs below). Subject of 1989 retrospective, Museum of Art, Fort Lauderdale, Fla. Grand prizes (with other Braun designers) at 1957 (11th) and 1960 (12th) editions of Triennale di Milano; award, 1964 BIO industrial-design biennial, Ljubljana; 1966 award, American Institute of Architects (AIA); 1966 Rosenthal Studio Prize; gold medal, 1969 *International Furniture Exhibition*, Vienna; 1968, was elected Honorary Royal Designer for Industry, UK, numerous others.
Bibliography Cat., *Modern Chairs 1918–1970*, London: Lund Humphries, 1971. Dieter Rams, 'And That's How Simple It Is to Be a Good Designer,' *Designer*, Sept. 1978: 12–13. Dieter Rams, 'Die Rolle des Designers im Industrieunternehmen,' in *Design ist unsichtbar*, Vienna, 1981: 507–16. François Burkhardt and Inez Franksen, *Dieter Rams &*, Berlin: Gerhardt, 1981. Cat., Kathryn B. Hiesinger and George H. Marcus III (eds.), *Design Since 1945*, Philadelphia: Philadelphia Museum of Art, 1983. Uta Brandes, *Dieter Rams, Designer: Die leise Ordnung der Dinge*, Güttingen: Steidl, 1990. Cat., Nils Jockel, *Mehr oder Weniger, Braun—Design im Vergleich*, Hamburg: Museum für Kunst und Gewerbe, 1990. Dieter Rams, *Weniger, aber besser = Less but Better*, Hamburg: Jo Klatt Design + Design, 1995. Hans Wichmann, *Mut zum Aufbruch: Erwin Braun, 1921–1992*, Munich: Prestel, 1998. Paola Antonelli (ed.), *Objects of Design: The Museum of Modern Art*, New York: The Museum of Modern Art, 2003: 230–31.

Ramsden, Omar (1873–1939)
British silver designer; born Sheffield.

Training To 1898, Sheffield School of Art.
Biography Ramsden met Alwyn Carr at the Sheffield School of Art. Ramsden sought assistance from Carr, when he won the open contest to design the ceremonial mace for the city of Sheffield. They went to London and set up a workshop in Stamford Bridge Studios, where they completed the mace in 1899. In the early years of the St. Dunstan Ramsden–Carr workshop, the assistants were Walter Andrews, Leonard Burt, and A.E. Ulyett. Even though Ramsden is recognized as an important silversmith, most of the objects credited to him before World War I (c. 1914) were, rather, produced by Carr. Only a few of the workshop's objects were made by hand, though all had a handmade appearance. Labor-saving molding techniques were used. Church plate became a specialty. Some of the objects had Tudor-rose decoration and chased texts. In ornamentation and object type, the workshop's pieces were in 15th- and 16th-century styles, although some of the early work was in the Art Nouveau idiom. Carr and Ramsden produced objects that had wide appeal; became important practitioners in the Arts and Crafts movement; to 1914, worked together. Carr joined the army in 1914 and set up his own workshop in 1919. 1920s–30s, Ramsden, who supervised production, had many craftsmen, including various designers, chasers, and enamelers in a large workshop that specialized in embossing and finial, stem, and boss modeling. The wares during this time were produced in a picturesque neo-Tudor style.
Exhibitions Work subject of 1973 exhibition, Birmingham, and included in others, London (catalogs below).
Bibliography Cat., Peter Cannon-Brooks, *Omar Ramsden 1873–1973*, Birmingham: City Museum and Art Gallery, 1973. Charlotte Gere, *American and European Jewelry 1830–1914*, New York: Crown, 1975. Cat., *Thirties: British Art and Design Before the War*, London: Arts Council of Great Britain/Hayward Gallery Gallery, 1979. *British Art and Design, 1900–1960*, London: Victoria and Albert Museum, 1983. Annelies Krekel-Aalberse, *Art Nouveau and Art Déco Silver*, New York: Abrams, 1989.

Ramstein, Willi (1939–)
Italian industrial designer; born San Gallo; active Milan.

Training 1958–62, Hochschule für Gestaltung, Ulm.
Biography 1963, Ramstein was an assistant in industrial buildings at Hochschule für Gestaltung, Ulm; 1963–65, worked on aluminum structures in Zürich; 1967–72, participated in a housing project for the Rinascente/Upim group in Milan; 1973, was a consultant on aluminum panels to Alcan in Montréal and, 1963–73, worked on the design of shopping centers; was involved with the design of public swimming pools, including a 1975 example in Arcore; became a member, Associazione per il Disegno Industriale (ADI). His clients included Brionvega (audio/video equipment), Ceramica Laufen, Kartell (furniture), Ideal Standard (sanitary fixtures), Presbitero (building accessories), Sleeping International System, and Vebo-Arredo (stainless-steel furniture).
Exhibitions Participated in 1975 *Visiona 6* exhibition, Cologne, sponsored by Bayer AG.
Bibliography *ADI Annual 1976*, Milan: Associazione per il Disegno Industriale, 1976.

Rancillac, Bernard (1931–)
French designer and artist; born Paris.

Biography Rancillac designed the 1966 Éléphant chair in a sweeping polyester form on a welded-steel base that was produced in small numbers by Galerie Lacloche, Paris. 1985, 100 examples in a range of five colors were reissued by Michael Roudillon, Paris. Rancillac was primarily a sculptor and painter in a style near to narrative figuration.
Exhibitions 1968 *Les Assises du Siège Contemporain* (Éléphant chair), Musée des Arts Décoratifs, Paris.
Bibliography Gilles de Bure, *Le mobilier français 1965–1979*, Paris: Regard/VIA, 1983: 51. Auction cat., *Modernes Design Kunsthandwerk nach 1945*, Munich: Quittenbaum, 4 Dec. 2001, lot 133. Cat., Sophie Tasma Anargyros et al., *L'école française: les créateurs de meubles du 20ème siècle*, Paris: Industries Françaises de l'Ameublement, 2000.

Randahl, Julius Olaf (1880–1972)
Swedish silversmith; active New York and Chicago.

Biography 1901, Randahl settled in New York, where he worked for Tiffany & Co. and Gorham Manufacturing; subsequently, moved to Chicago, where he worked in the Kalo Shop from 1907 and opened his own Randahl Shop in Park Ridge, Ill., in 1911. Leading department stores, including Marshall Field & Co., sold its hollow-ware. Production was mechanized but finished by hand. Randahl was influenced by the wares of Chicago's Kalo Shop and of Copenhagen's Georg Jensen Sølvesmedie. 1957, his firm purchased the Cellini Shop and, 1969, Cellini Craft; 1965, was itself purchased by Reed & Barton.
Exhibitions/citations Silverwares shown at 1937 *Exposition Internationale des Arts et Techniques dans la Vie Moderne*, Paris, receiving a silver medal (fruit stand and candlestick).
Bibliography Annelies Krekel-Aalberse, *Art Nouveau and Art Déco Silver*, New York: Abrams, 1989.

Rang, Wolfgang (1949–)
German architect, designer, and author; born Essen.

Training Architecture, Technische Universität, Darmstadt; University of California, Los Angeles.
Biography 1981, Rang set up an architectural practice with Michael A. Landes and Norbert Berghof; 1979–85, lectured, Technische Hochschule, Darmstadt; was the architect of 2001 Observation Tower in Dietzenbach, Hesse.
> See Berghof, Norbert.

Ranson, Paul (1862–1909)
French painter and decorator; born Limoges.

Training 1880, Académie Julian, Paris.
Biography At the Académie Julian, Ranson befriended Paul Sérusier, Jean-Édouard Vuillard, Maurice Denis, Ker-Xavier Roussel, and Pierre Bonnard. 1889, they formed artists' group the Nabis with a commitment to decorative arts and met weekly in Ranson's studio. 1892 with Vuillard, Sérusier, and Bonnard, Ranson designed stage sets for the Théâtre d'Art in Paris. He also designed sets for Aurélien Lugné-Poë's new Théâtre de l'Oeuvre and drew cartoons for tapestries with women and arabesques in the Art Nouveau style, including *Le tigre* tapestry woven by Manufacture Nationale des Gobelins. 1908 with his wife, Ranson organized the Académie Ranson in Paris, where Denis, Maillol, Sérusier, Vallotton, and Bonnard taught.
Bibliography Yvonne Brunhammer et al., *Art Nouveau Belgium, France*, Houston: Institute for the Arts, Rice University 1976.

Ranzo, Patrizia (1953–)
Italian architect and designer; born and active Naples.

Training To 1981, Facoltà di Architettura, Università degli Studi di Napoli 'Federico II.'
Biography 1975, Ranzo began her work in design; from 1980, collaborated with architect Sergio Cappelli, including on 1986 Agave table by Stildomus and a large number of other products. She was a contributing writer to *Architettura e tecnologia appropriata* by V. Gangemi (1985); coauthor of *Il governo del progetto* (with Gangemi, 1986); sole author of *The Mediterranean Sensitivity as a Cultural Perspective* (1986); and, with others, *La metropoli come natura artificiale: architetture della complessità in Giappone* (1992); edited *L'era del ma*, on minimalist architecture (1996).
Exhibitions/citations Participated in a number of venues, from 1981 *La Città come Teatro* (with A. Branzi, A. Rossi, L. Thermes, F. Purini, B. Gravagnuolo, and Sergio Cappelli), Napoli Centro Zen. Received 1987 (for Agave table) Premio Compasso d'Oro; 1981 (for interiors) and 1983 (for design and architecture) awards, Women in Design international competition, California.
Bibliography Andrea Branzi, *La casa calda: esperienze del nuovo disegno italiano*, Milan: Idea, 1982. Liz McQuiston, *Women in Design: A Contemporary View*, New York: Rizzoli, 1988.
> See Cappelli, Sergio.

Rapin, Henri (1873–1939)
French artist and decorator.

Training Under Jean-Léon Gérôme and J. Blanc, École Nationale Supérieure des Beaux-Arts, Paris.
Biography Rapin worked as a painter, illustrator, furniture designer, and decorator; from 1903, designed generally simple furniture, which began to be more elaborate from c. 1910, and called on exotic materials and carved wood panels by Eve Le Bourgeois and Charles Hairon. This effort was a response to the challenge from designers of the Münchner Vereinigte Werkstätten für Kunst in Handwerk exhibiting at

the 1910 Paris Salon. c. 1924, he became a principal, Manufacture Nationale de Sèvres, and artistic director, École du Comité des Dames of the Union Centrale des Arts Décoratifs, Paris. Work included some furniture produced by Evrard and numerous interiors of theaters, music halls, and shops in Paris.
Exhibitions From 1900, work was first shown, at Salons of Société des Artistes Français; 1910 Salon d'Automne. At 1925 *Exposition Internationale des Arts Décoratifs et Industriels Modernes*, Paris: designed the stand and dining room of L'Art à l'École, the grand salon of Une Ambassade Française pavilion (with Pierre Selmersheim), Manufacture Nationale de Sèvres pavilion, and also other sections.
Bibliography Maurice Dufrêne, *Ensembles mobiliers, Exposition Internationale 1925*, Paris: Charles Moreau, 1925; Woodbridge, Suffolk: Antique Collectors' Club, 1989. Pierre Kjellberg, *Art déco: les maîtres du mobilier, le décor des paquebots*, Paris: Amateur, 1986/1990.

Rasch, Tapetenfabrik Gebrüder

German wallpaper manufacturer; located Bramsche.

History 1897, Hannoversche Tapetenfabrik Gebrüder Rasch & Co. was founded by Guido Wiecking, Hugo Rasch, and Emil Rasch in Hanover. After a 1905 fire that destroyed the plant, a new plant was built in Bramsche, its location today. As early as 1900, the firm offered a wide selection of wallpapers in historicist, marble, and Art Nouveau patterns; 1910, Rasch became one of the largest paper printers in Germany; 1926, printed its first artist-designed collection, 'Neuartige Eigenheim Tapeten' by Jeku of the studio of artists Paul Jessen and Alfred Kutzer in Cologne; end of 1920s, began to respond to the style of quieter patterns. 1930, Emil Rasch patented and promoted the Bauhaustapeten collection designed by students and teachers at the Bauhaus in Dessau (the rights to which he purchased in 1933 from Ludwig Mies van der Rohe). 1940s, designers included Maria May and Tea Ernst. 1950 Rasch-Künstler-Tapeten series included patterns by Fritz August Breuhaus, Hans Schwippert, Josef Hoffmann, Margaret Hildebrand, and, again, May and Ernst. 1950s, more than 50 artists, architects, and designers were commissioned. 1960s saw work by Salvador Dalí, Bernard Schultze, Jean de Botton, and Raimond Peynet. 1970s included Pop/Op Art images by Wolf Bauer and Klaus Dombrowski. 1980s took a flowery, Japanese turn. 1992 Zeitwände range included work by Nathalie du Pasquier, Alessandro Mendini, Bořek Šípek, Ettore Sottsass, George Sowden, Matteo Thun, and architecture team Berghof-Landes-Rang. Šípek's three-dimensional *Zed* pattern was issued with attached blown-glass crystal hemispheres. Recent additions to the Rasch group of companies have been Rasch Textil (textiles) and Rasch Druckerei und Verlag (printers and publishers).
Exhibitions/citations 'Zeitwände' collection received awards from Deutschen Designerclub and Art Directors Club Deutschland and was shown at several museums in Europe and the US.
Bibliography www.rasch.de.

Heinz Rasch and Bodo Rasch. Side chair. 1940s. Plywood and tubular steel, 34 x 17 1/8 x 19 3/8" (86.3 x 43.5 x 49.2 cm). Gift of Arthur and Elaine Cohen. MoMA.

Rasch, Heinz (1902–1996); Bodo Rasch (1903–1995)

German architects and designers; brothers. Heinz: born Berlin-Charlottenburg. Bodo: born Wuppertal-Elberfeld.

Training Heinz: 1916, Kunstgewerbeschule, Bromberg; 1920–23, Technischen Hochschulen, Hanover and Stuttgart. Bodo: 1922–27, agriculture, Stuttgart-Hohenheim.
Biography 1922, the brothers founded a factory in Stuttgart for household furnishings; became pioneers in the use of thin (1/8"/3 mm) bent plywood. Their work included advertising; posters; 1924 folding chair and bent tubular-steel chair models by L. & C. Arnold; Radio Rundfunkstuhl (broadcasting chair) linking seating in the orchestral hall of the Süddeutscher Rundfunk; 1927 Sitzgeiststuhl (chair of a sitting ghost); a stand for the Schonert & Lebrun quilt firm at the 1927 *Werbeschau* (publicity exhibition), Stuttgart; stall of the Württemberg newspapers at 1927 and 1929 *Pressa Ausstellung*, Cologne. 1925, Heinz Rasch worked on the editorial staff of *Baugilde*, the journal of the German architects' organization in Berlin, and met Mies van der Rohe and Mart Stam; edited the book *Der Stuhl* (the chair); was a pioneer in cantilever chair design; 1937–44, collaborated with Oskar Schlemmer and Franz Krause in Wuppertal; 1980s, worked toward establishing the Stuhlmuseum (chair museum) in Burg Beverungen. Architecture projects included a 1927 filling station, 1927 suspension house, and 1929 low-cost housing. Realized architecture included an office building for Dr. Herberts. At 1927 *Weissenhofsiedlung* exhibition, Stuttgart: he designed apartments (with 1924–27 chairs, 1927 desk, and adjustable ceiling light) in a building by Mies, and flats (with bed, wardrobe, night-table, and writing desk) in a building by Stam. Heinz died in Wuppertal; Bodo in Oberaichen.
Bibliography 'Heinz Rasch: Bau und Baustoffe des Neuen Hauses,' *Baukunst und Bauhandwerk*, no. 9, Sept. 1927. Heinz and Bodo Rasch, *Der Stuhl*, Stuttgart: Wedekind, 1928 and Weil am Rhein: Vitra Design Museum, 1992. Heinz and Bodo Rasch, *Wie bauen*, Stuttgart: Wedekind, 1928. Heinz and Bodo Rasch, *Zu—offen*, Stuttgart: Wedekind, 1930. Barbie Campbell-Cole and Tim Benton, *Tubular Steel Furniture*, London: The Art Book Company, 1979: 11. *Brüder Rasch: Material—Konstruktion—Form 1926–1930*, Düsseldorf: Marzona, 1981. Cat., *Der Kragstuhl*, Stuhlmuseum Burg Beverungen, Berlin: Alexander, 1986: 137. Heinz and Bodo Rasch, *Gefesselter Blick*, Baden: Lars Müller, 2001.

Rashid, Hani (1958–)
> See Asymptote.

Rashid, Karim (1960–)

Canadian designer; born Cairo; active New York.

Training 1982, bachelor of art degree in industrial design, Carleton University, Ottawa, Canada; under Ettore Sottsass and others, graduate design studies, Naples.
Biography Rashid was reared in England and Canada; subsequently, for one year, worked in the studio of Rodolfo Bonetto, Milan; returned to Canada and, for seven years, worked at KAN Industrial Designers, Toronto; at KAN 1985–90, cofounded and designed the Babel Fashion Collection; 1993, opened his own practice in New York to work with clients on products, commerical interiors, cosmetics packaging, and fashion accessories for various international firms. For ten years, he was an associate professor in industrial design, University of the Arts in Philadelphia, Pratt Institute, Rhode Island School of Design, The Ontario College of Art; has lectured internationally. Prolific work

Karim Rashid. Garbo waste bin. 1998. Injection-molded polypropylene, h. 17 x w. 13 1/2 x l. 13" (43 x 34 x 33 cm). Mfr.: Umbra, Canada.

has included 1987 mailboxes for Canada Post Corporation, 1994 *Digital Nature* exhibition for Tokyo Gas, 1991 Arp chair by Area, 1991 cordless telephones by SunMoonStar, 1997 Arp stool and 1998 Pura Café stacking chair by Pure Design, 1998 Cool tumbler for milk by Ritzenhoff, 1999 mouse pads by Totem design store, 1999 packaging for male and female Freedom scents by Estée Lauder, 1999 Morphscape laminated sheeting by Wilsonart. By Issey Miyake: 1997 handbag collection and 1997–99 packaging for male and female L'Eau d'Issey scents. By Nambé: 1998 lead-crystal vases and cast-aluminum vessels and tabletop ware. By Umbra: 1996 injection-molded polypropylene Garbo waste bin, 1998 Garbonzo waste bin, 1999 Oh polypropylene chair, 1999 Jambo tray, and 1999 Bibowl/Tribowl. Rashid was the editor, *The International Design Yearbook* (2003).
Exhibitions/citations Work subject of 1997 'Ecstasy of the Unnatural,' Idée shop, Tokyo. Sixteen *Virtu* awards, Canada, 1985–2000; 1989 '30 under 30' recognition, *Interiors* magazine; from 1991, a large number of selections, Annual Design Review, *I.D.* magazine, and likewise, from 1995, Good Design award, Chicago Athenaeum; SIT 94 seating award, London; 1998 Designer of the Year, Brooklyn Museum of Art; 1999 Daimler-Chrysler Award, US; 1999 George Nelson Award, *Interiors* magazine; 1999 silver award (Oh chair), IDEA/*Business Week*; 1999 Collab Award, Philadelphia Museum of Art; 1999 Design Effectiveness Gold Award, Design Business Association (DBA), London. Rashid designed the 'Ideal House,' 2003 *Internationale Möbelmesse*, Cologne; numerous others.
Bibliography Paola Antonelli et al., *Karim Rashid, I Want to Change the World*, New York: Universe, 2001. Mel Byars, *On/Off: New Electronic Products*, New York: Universe, 2001. Mel Byars, *Design in Steel*, London: Laurence King, 2002. Cat., R. Craig Miller (intro.), *U.S. Design 1975–2000*, Munich: Prestel, 2002. Mel Byars, 'Demain est un autre jour,' *Beaux Arts*, *Design* 2003 no. 5, June 2003: 108–11.

Rasmussen, Jørgen (1931–); Rasmussen, Ib (1931–)

Danish furniture and industrial designer; twin brothers.

Training Both: to 1955, architecture, Det Kongelige Danske Kunstakademi, Copenhagen.
Biography Jørgen Rasmussen designed office furniture and industrial fittings by Kevi in Glastrup; 1957, set up an architecture office with his twin brother, Ib Rasmussen. Jørgen's work included Kevi office-chair range by Kevi A/S from 1969 and by Fritz Hansen from 1973, still in production by the latter. The chair introduced the two-wheel enclosed caster, an innovation now standard. Other work included a 1970 office chair by Knoll.
Exhibitions/citations Jørgen's work shown at 1972 *Knoll au Louvre*, Musée des Arts Décoratifs, Paris; 1982 exhibition, New York (catalog below). The ScanCaster (two-wheel caster) was recognized with the 1998 ID Klassikerprisen, Dansk Design Center.
Bibliography Frederik Sieck, *Nutidig Dansk Møbeldesign – en kortfattet illustreret beskrivelse*, Copenhagen: Bondo Gravesen, 1990. Cat., David Revere McFadden (ed.), *Scandinavian Modern Design 1880–1980*, New York: Abrams, 1982.

Rasmussen, Leif Erik (1942–)

Danish architect and furniture designer; born Copenhagen.

Training 1962, apprenticehsip in furniture construction at cabinetmakers A.J. Iversen; 1968, furniture design, Kunsthåndværkerskolen; both Copenhagen.
Biography From 1968, Leif Rasmussen was active in architecture firm Krohn & Hartvig Rasmussen on the Odense Universitet-Center; 1972 on the Handelsbankens (bank of commerce; architect, Ole Hagen); 1975, set up his own architecture office; from 1978, was in a partnership with Henrik Rolff (with whom he worked at Krohn & Hartvig, Rasmussen, and Ole Hagen. Some Rasmussen furniture designs were produced by Hyllinge Trœindustri, and with Fritz Hansen by Bent Krogh.
Bibliography Frederik Sieck, *Nutidig Dansk Møbeldesign – en kortfattet illustreret beskrivelse*, Copenhagen: Bondo Gravesen, 1990.

Rasulo, Prospero (1953–)

Italian designer; born Stigliano di Matera.

Training Accademia di Belle Arti, Milan.
Biography Rasulo settled in Milan; 1980, opened a studio for painting, sculpture, and stage design; collaboration with Studio Alchimia, where he was accepted by Alessandro Mendini to conduct research on Mendini's Redesign and Oggetto banale concepts. With Studio Occhiomagico, he designed stage sets for videos, photos, and exhibitions. 1987 with Gianni Veneziano, he founded Oxido gallery of design, art, and architecture. Subsequently, Oxido Zoo was the trademark of a collection of furniture and art objects. Rasulo first designed furniture, art objects, carpets for his personal use, then for limited production, and since for numerous firms such as B.R.F., Foccarini, Gervasoni, Masterfly, Metals, Poltronova, and Sisal, and jewelry by Argentovivo. His body of work for Zanotta includes 2001 Tempo reversible metal table and a number of soft seats/sofas.
Exhibitions Fine art shown at Yves Gastou gallery, Paris; Colombari Galleria, Milan; and others.

Rateau, Armand Albert (1882–1938)

French furniture designer; active Paris.

Training Drawing and wood carving, École Boulle, Paris.
Biography Rateau worked as a freelance designer for several interior decorators, including for decorator and ceramicist Georges Hoentschel in 1898; 1905–14, was manager of Maison Alavoine decorating workshop; 1919, established his own workshop in Levallois and employed cabinetmakers, carpenters, sculptors, ironworkers, painters, gilders, and other craftspeople. He worked in wood at first, later lacquered and patinated metal; designed furniture, chairs, lighting, vases, ashtrays, and other domestic objects influenced by antiques from Pompeii, the Orient, and North Africa; collaborated with sculptor Paul Plumet on bronze work. Rateau was commissioned by fashion designer Jeanne Lanvin to decorate her apartment at 16, rue Barbet-de-Jouy, Paris (partially reconstructed in 1985 in the Musée des Arts Décoratifs, Paris), for which he designed some remarkable 1920–22 furniture in *vert-de-gris* bronze, strewn with daisies, butterflies, doves, and pheasants—all rendered in what he considered to be a Pompeiian style. 1921–22, he was manager of Lanvin-Sport. The c. 1925–34 Lanvin spherical La Boule perfume flacon (still produced, originally by the Manufacture Nationale de Sèvres) by Rateau was imprinted with Paul Iribe's gold image of Lanvin and her daughter. Rateau also designed Lanvin's fashion house and managed the Lanvin-Décoration department of interior design on the rue du Faubourg Saint-Honoré. Other clients included the baron and baronne Eugène de Rothschild at the Château de la Cröe, Antibes, and American art collectors George and Florence Blumenthal, who arranged for Rateau's 1919 visit to the US. He eventually turned from ornate to a more sober style and produced 1929–30 furniture for Dr. Thaleimer and Mlle. Stern; renovated the Théâtre Daunou, Paris; and, 1926, a bathroom with gold lacquered walls, Persian-style decorations, bronze furniture, and fur-covered chairs for the duchesse d'Albe in Madrid. His fondness for the overwrought and sumptuous was frequently offset by his good taste.

Exhibitions Rarely showed work at exhibitions and salons and was not associated with any group. But participated in Pavillon de l'Elégance at 1925 *Exposition Internationale des Arts Décoratifs et Industriels Modernes*, Paris.
Bibliography Éveline Schlumberger, 'Au 16 rue Barbet-de-Jouy avec Jeanne Lanvin,' *Connaissance des arts*, no. 138, Aug. 1963: 62–71. Pierre Kjellberg, *Art déco: les maîtres du mobilier, le décor des paquebots*, Paris: Amateur, 1986/1990. Alastair Duncan, *A.A. Rateau*, New York: Delorenzo Gallery, 1990. Franck Olivier-Vial and François Rateau, *Armand Albert Rateau: un baroque chez les modernes*, Paris: Éditions de l'Amateur, 1992.

Rath & Doodeheefver

Dutch wallpaper firm; located Amsterdam, Schiebroek, and Duivendrecht.

History 1860, Rath & Doodeheefver was established in Amsterdam as a family business, originally upholsterers which sold curtain and furniture fabrics and wallpaper; by 1890, had become a wallpaper wholesaler and importer; 1921, set up a factory in Schiebroek, exporting the bulk of its production. Its first collection (1924) was designed by J.W. Gidding, A. Klijn, Van Kuyck, F. Oerder, and A.J.J. de Winter. However, 1924–31 saw the peak of collaboration with freelance artists. The firm's many other designers included H.P. Berlage, who produced small-patterned motifs in consultation with the residents of his houses where the papers were applied; G.B. Broekema, 1931 and 1939; and Thomas W. Nieuwenhuis, C.A. Lion Cachet, and T. Posthuma, 1928–31. For a number of years, many designs were called on, but only for color changes and sometimes relief patterns.
Exhibitions Work was co-theme of 1927 exhibition of curtains by cotton printers Van Vissingen and wallpaper by Rath & Doodeheefver, Stedelijk Museum, Amsterdam.
Bibliography Cat., *Industry and Design in the Netherlands, 1850/1950*, Amsterdam: Stedelijk Museum, 1985: 117–21.

Rath, Hans Harald (1904–1968)

Austrian glassware designer; born Vienna.

Training In art history in Munich.
Biography 1924, Rath entered the family firm Lobmeyr in Vienna, where he became the chief designer, 1938; helped to revive the glass industry in Austria after World War II and won commissions for chandeliers in public buildings, theaters, and opera houses. Pieces designed by his son Peter Rath were installed in the Metropolitan Opera

Hans H. Rath. Alpha pitcher. 1952. Mouth-blown crystal, h. 8 1/8" (20.6 cm) x widest dia. 4 1/2" (11.5 cm). Mfr.: J. & L. Lobmeyr, Austria (1980). Gift of the mfr. MoMA.

Stephan Rath. Condiment bowl. c. 1948. Crystal, h.1 1/4" x dia. 2 5/8" (3.2 cm x 5.9 cm). Mfr.: J. & L. Lobmeyr, Austria. Gift of A. J. Van Dugteren & Sons, Inc. MoMA.

House, New York, in 1966, and John F. Kennedy Center for the Performing Arts, Washington, D.C., in 1970. Other work included the 1952 Alpha and 1967 Montréal table crystal services by Lobmeyr.
Exhibitions Work shown in 1973 and 1983–84 exhibitions, Vienna and Philadelphia (catalogs below).
Bibliography Stefan Rath, *Lobmeyr: Vom Adel des Handwerks*, Vienna: Herold, 1962. Cat., *Lobmeyr achtzehnhundertdreiundzwanzig bis neunzehnhundertdreiundsiebzig (1823–1973): 150 Jahre Österreichische Glaskunst*, Vienna: Österreichisches Museum für Angewandte Kunst, 1973. Günther Feuerstein, *Vienna—Present and Past: Arts and Crafts—Applied Art—Design*, Vienna: Jugend und Volk, 1976: 68, 81. Abby Rand, 'The Lights of Lobmeyr,' *Town and Country*, Dec. 1981: 266–67, 331–34. Cat., Kathryn B. Hiesinger and George H. Marcus III (eds.), *Design Since 1945*, Philadelphia: Philadelphia Museum of Art, 1983.

Rath, Stephan (1876–1960)

Austrian glass designer; active Vienna.

Biography Viennese glass designer Josef Lobmeyr (1792–1855) and sons Josef (1828–1864) and Ludwig (1829–1917) were the sequential directors of the Royal Glassmaking Factory. On the 1902 retirement of Ludwig Lobmeyr, his nephew Stephan Rath replaced him; 1910, became the vice-manager; 1917, possibly established his own eponymous firm.
> See Lobmeyr, J. & L.

Rathbone, R. Llewellyn (1864–1939)

British designer and metalworker.

Biography Rathbone was a cousin of Harold Rathbone, the head of Della Robbia pottery, and was related to W.A.S. Benson; produced metal fittings and utensils for projects of A.H. Mackmurdo, Heywood Sumner, and C.F.A. Voysey; was active in a workshop in Liverpool and taught metalworking at the university there from c. 1898 to 1903; became head, Art School, Sir John Cass Technical Institute, London; taught, Central School of Arts and Crafts, London; designed metalwork simpler than in his Liverpool days and produced some jewelry; wrote the books *Simple Jewellery...* (London: Constable, 1910) and *Unit Jewellery...* (London: Constable; New York: Dutton, 1921). Examples of his work were published in *Art Journal*.
Bibliography Isabelle Anscombe and Charlotte Gere, *Arts and Crafts in Britain and America*, New York: Rizzoli, 1978: 118.

Ratia, Armi (1912–1979)

Finnish textile designer; mother of Ristomatti Ratia.

Training 1935, textile design, Taideteollisuuskeskuskoulu, Helsinki.
Biography Ratia set up a weaving shop in Vyborg, where she designed and produced rya (or *ryijy*) rugs to 1939; 1949, began working at her husband Viljo Ratia's company, Printex, a producer of oilcloth, which she adapted to the production of silkscreen printing by hand on cotton sheeting. She was encouraged by Maija Isola, Vuokko Eskolin, and other designers to reproduce their patterns on fabric and, doing so, made dresses in the fabrics, first shown in 1951 under the name Marimekko ('Mary's dress' in eastern Finnish dialect). This later became

the name of the entire organization. The prints were small at first and larger, even giant, later. Primarily in the work of Isola, the designs developed into more intricate abstract patterns with bird and flower motifs being added to the line. Marimekko's 1960s–70s products included jersey, wool, and cotton fabrics, paper products, laminated plastics, and table coverings, successful in northern Europe and in the US. The Architects Collection was introduced in 1982. By 2001, the firm was employing c. 325 people and selling in c. 1,500 stores worldwide, in addition to 25 of its own stores in Finland.
Bibliography David Davies, 'Fabrics by Marimekko,' *Design*, no. 236, Aug. 1968: 28–31. 'The Finn-Tatics,' *Sphere*, Mar. 1975. Risto-matti Ratia, 'The Legacy of Armi Ratia,' *Form Function Finland*, nos. 1–2, 1980: 10–11. Cat., David Revere McFadden (ed.), *Scandinavian Modern Design 1880–1980*, New York: Abrams, 1982. Cat., Kathryn B. Hiesinger and George H. Marcus III (eds.), *Design Since 1945*, Philadelphia: Philadelphia Museum of Art, 1983.
> See Marimekko.

Ratia, 'Risto' Ristomatti (1941–)

Finnish designer; born and active Helsinki; son of Armi Ristomatti, the founder of Marimekko.

Training To 1960, Kauppakorkeakoulu, Helsinki; 1966, bachelor's degree in interior architecture, Leicester Polytechnic, UK.
Biography 1967–83, Ratia worked at Marimekko where he created the highly successful 1971 301 canvas bag (still in production); has designed for other firms worldwide, including 1969–73 domestic line of plastics under the trademark Decembre and began the Plastics and Plastics movement. 1973 with Porin Puuvilla, designed Marimekko's first line of bed sheets; soon became the firm's creative director and vice-president and eventually managed its design and licensing activities. After the 1985 sale of Marimekko to Amer-Group Ltd. by him, his sister, and brother, he established Ergonomia Design (later E&D Design); 1991, founded a branch of Studio Ratia in the US to design exclusive products for the Crate & Barrel chain. His work has included glassware, jewelry, bags, and other products in a variety of materials, including wood, plastic, linen, and silver. Some furniture, such as 1998 Palasarjasta storage units, was made by Asko. His glass vases, candle lanterns, and other designs have been made by Muurla Finland and his jewellery collection by Kultakeskus.
Citations 1973 Scandinavian Furniture Award (for Palasarjasta modular interior system).
Bibliography *The Marimekko Story*, Helsinki: Marimekko Printex, 1964. Pekko Suhonen, *Phenomenon Marimekko*, Helsinki: Marimekko, 1986. Mel Byars, *Design in Steel*, London: Laurence King, 2003.

Rationalism (Razionale)

Italian architecture and design movement.

History Rationalism was an interpretation of European Functionalism in Italy realized by the Movimento Italiano per l'Architettura Razionale (MIAR); was launched in France at the turn of the century and, 1926, in Italy with the publication of the four-part manifesto of Gruppo Sette (group of seven), formed in Milan by Gino Figini, Guido Frette, Sebastiano Larco, Adalberto Libera, Gino Pollini, Carlo Enrico Rava, and Giuseppe Terragni. They condemned Futurism for its violent ideas and rigid rejection of the past and fostered a new architecture based on logic and a distinct strand within the European modern movement. Constructivists were closer to Functionalists; Rationalists were more romantic, attempting to bring novelty to every project. Rationalists' and the traditionalists' positions appeared to be identical, although the two argued fruitlessly about technical and formal questions. A proclamation was made at 1928 (1st) *Esposizione Italiana di Architettura Razionale* in Rome, stating, 'We Italians, who devote our entire energy to this movement, feel that this is our architecture because constructive power is our Roman heritage. And Roman architecture was profoundly Rational, purposeful, and efficient.' Prolonged and bitter arguments followed, into the 1931 (2nd) *Esposizione Italiana di Architettura Razionale*, sponsored by MIAR. The earliest examples of Rational architecture in Italy were the 1927 drawings and models by the Gruppo Sette in Monza and Stuttgart; a 1928 apartment house in Como by Giuseppe Terragni and his 1929 Gualino office block in Turin; the exhibition buildings by Giuseppe Pagano and Gino Levi-Montalcini at 1928 *Esposizione di Torino*. A group of architects published the comprehensive, nine-point 'Un programma d'architettura' (1933) in the first issue (May 1933, pp. 5-6) of the review *Quadrante*, signed by Piero Bottoni, Mario Cereghini, Luigi Figini, Guido Frette, Enrico Griffini, Pietro Lingeri, Gino Pollini, Gian Luigi Banfi, Ludovico Belgiojoso, Enrico Peressutti, and Ernesto N. Rogers. It affirmed, 'Classicism and Mediterraneanism—to be understood as an attitude of mind and not as a mere adoption of forms or as folklore—is in contrast to Nordism, baroquism, or the romantic arbitrariness of some modern European architecture.' The movement was also significantly represented by Terragni's 1932–36 Casa del Fascio (Casa del Popolo) in Como, Sant'Elia's kindergarten in Como, and 1933–36 Terragni's and Lingeri's Casa Rustici at 36, Corso Sempione, Milan. The Casa del Fascio revealed an essentially intellectual quality and represented the perfection of an architectural idea, and Terragni's furniture was an expression of a whole in-situ environment (*Gesamtkunstwerk*). The second major personality of Italian Rationalism was Giuseppe Pagano, who played a significant part as the theoretician of Rationalism through his writings in *Casabella* from 1930–43. Pagano designed 1932 Institute of Physics (part of the university precinct in Rome designed by Massimo Piacentini) and 1938–41 Università Bocconi (with Giangiacomo Predaval) in Milan. 1933 was an important year in the movement's history because of the competitions for the railway station in Florence and the Palazzo del Littorio at the 1932 *Mostra della Rivoluzione Fascista* on the Via dell'Impero in Rome. Figini and Pollini continued the Rationalist tradition after Pagano's and Terragni's 1943 deaths. Figini and Pollini became known at the 1933 (5th) Triennale di Milano for their design of an artist's studio and built the Olivetti industrial park in Ivrea, from 1957. At World War II's end, the enormous problem of reconstruction created an urgent need for standardization and prefabrication. The Rationalists were completely unprepared for the situation, and the building community was confronted with unsuitable structures for industry and a shortage of skilled labor. Reconstruction proceeded by conventional means, without a clearly defined program. Respectable Italian architecture and design was not on its feet again until the late 1950s.
Bibliography Alberto Galardi, *New Italian Architecture*, New York: Praeger, 1967: 12–18. Paolo Porteghesi (ed.), *Dizionario enciclopedico di architettura e urbanistica*, Rome: Istituto Editoriale Romano, 1969. Vittorio Magnago Lampugnani, *Encyclopedia of 20th-Century Architecture*, New York: Abrams, 1986. Richard A. Etlin, *Modernism in Italian Architecture 1890–1940*, Cambridge: MIT, 1991.

Ravage
> See Rameckers, Clemens H.B.

Ravilious, Eric William (1903–1942)

British wood engraver, watercolorist, and ceramics decorator; born London.

Training 1919–22, Eastbourne School of Art; 1922–25 under Paul Nash and others, Royal College of Art, London.
Biography 1929–39, Ravilious taught, Royal College of Art. His primary activity was the execution of wood engravings for book illustrations. His work appeared in books including The *Elm Angel* (1930) by Walter de la Mare, *Twelfth Night* (1932) by William Shakespeare, *The Kynoch Press Notebook and Diary* (1933), and *The Natural History of Selborne* (1937) by Gilbert White. Influenced by the work of Paul Nash, Ravilious designed printers' ornaments for the Curwen, Golden Cockerel, and Nonesuch presses, decorations for the BBC and London Transport Board publications, advertisements for Austin Reed, and book jackets for publisher Duckworth. Ravilious, Edward Bawden, and Cyril Mahoney collaborated on 1928–29 refreshment-room murals at Morley College, London. He received his first (1935) commission from Wedgwood, over-painted enamel-colored ceramics with transfer-printed bucolic vignettes on standard ceramic blanks; designed 1935 glassware by Stuart Crystal in Stourbridge and a 1936 suite of Regency-revival furniture by Dunbar Hay (Cecilia Dunbar's Kilburn shop in London); late 1930s, became increasingly occupied with watercolor drawing; painted the wall decoration of British pavilion at 1937 *Exposition Internationale des Arts et Techniques dans la Vie Moderne*, Paris; 1938, began to pursue color lithography, inaugurated by his illustrations for *High Street* (1938); 1940, was appointed an official World War II artist. He died in air-sea mission which failed to return during the war.
Exhibitions Work included in 1979 *Thirties* and subject of centenary-birth exhibition, 2003–04 *Eric Ravilious: Imagined Realities*, Imperial War Museum, London (catalogs below).
Bibliography *Eric Ravilious 1903–1942*, Colchester: The Minories, 1972. Cat., *Thirties: British Art and Design Before the War*, London: Arts Council of Great Britain/Hayward Gallery, 1979. Helen Binyon, *Eric Ravilious: Memoir of an Artist*, New York: F.C. Beil, 1983. Maureen Batkin and Robert Dalrymple (eds.), *Ravilious & Wedgwood: The Complete Wedgwood Designs of Eric Ravilious*, London: Dalrymple,

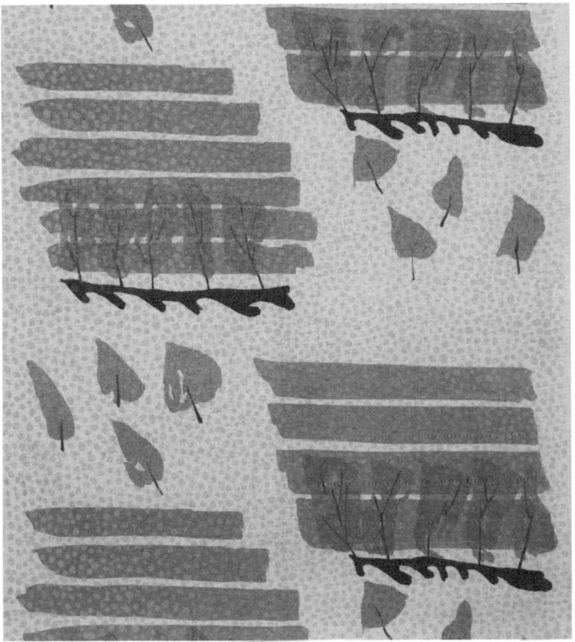

Antonin Raymond. Strips, Trunks, Trees, Dots fabric. Pre-1941. Printed cotton 88 x 50" (223.5 x 127 cm). Mfr. pre-1941. Gift of the designer, US. MoMA.

1986. Eric William Ravilious, with John Lewis, Enid Marx, and Robert Harling (contributors), *For Shop Use Only: Eric Ravilious*, Wiltshire: Garton & Co., 1993. Loyd Grossman (foreword), Frances Spalding (intro.), *Ravilious in Public*, London: Black Dog, 2002. Cat., Alan Powers, *Eric Ravilious: Imagined Realities*, London: Wilson, Philip, 2003.

Raymond, Antonin (1888–1976)

Bohemian architect and textile designer; born Kladno, Bohemia (now Czech Republic).

Training 1910, degree in architecture and engineering, České Vysoké Učení Technické (Czech technical University), Prague.
Biography Soon after university studies, Raymond moved to New York and worked in the office of architect Cass Gilbert; by 1916, was working for Frank Lloyd Wright; 1917, designed Jacques Copeau's Théâtre du Vieux Colombier in New York; during World War I, was active in army intelligence in Europe; 1920, accompanied Wright to Japan to work on 1915–22 Imperial Hotel, Tokyo, where practiced architecture from 1921–38. He was effective in introducing modern Western architecture to Japan and designed a number of buildings in the International Style in 1920s and early 1930s, which became less austere from the mid-1930s. 1939, he returned to the US and established an architecture, engineering, and design studio, New Hope, Pa. He died in Longhorne, Pa.
Citations First place in printed-fabrics category, 1940 *Organic Design in Home Furnishings* competition/exhibition, The Museum of Modern Art, New York.
Bibliography *Raymond Antonin: An Autobiography*, Rutland, Vt.: Tuttle, 1973. 'Raymond Antonin, *JA/Japan Architect*, no. 33, spring 1999.
> See Nakashima, George

Razgour, Alon (1965–)

Israeli designer; born Israel; active Timrat.

Training 1983, ceramics engineering, Women's International Zionist Organization (WIZO), Tel Aviv; 1988–92, bachelor's degree, Industrial Design Department, Bezalel Academy of Arts and Design, Jerusalem; 1993–94, business, Haifa University.
Biography 1990–92, Razgour was an industrial designer in Yaacov Kaufman's design studio in Italy; 1994, established own studio for product design and development. Clients have included Applied Spectral Imaging (ASI) (microscope camera), CW Software (Internet high-capacity server system), E.R. Lan (wireless computer communicator), Henkel (haircare-products packaging), Modclick (modular constructions and buildings), P-Cube (Internet server and definer), Ramot (jewelry-shop display units), Menan Medical (medical equipment), Saudon (invalid supporter), Strauss (food packaging), and Tadiran (air conditioner). He received 1994–95 US patent for a household product; has written for journals and newspapers.
Exhibitions Work included in 1999 exhibition of Israeli products, Egypt; 2000 international Israeli plastics exhibition, Exhibition Center, Tel Aviv; 1999 international exhibition of Israeli technologies; *Industrious De-signers = Giovani Designer Israeliani* exhibition at 2000 Abitare il Tempo, Verona, and traveling (catalog below); others. Work subject of 2000 *Multifunction Objects*, Askola design gallery, Tel Aviv, and 1999 *Open Table*, Israel Art Center, Tel Aviv.
Bibliography Cats., Vanni Pasca and Ely Rozenberg, *Industrious De-signers = Giovani Designer Israeliani*, Verona: Abitare il Tempo, 2001 and 2002. Mel Byars, *Design in Steel*, London: Laurence King, 2002.

Read, Alfred Burgess (1898–1973)

British industrial and lighting designer.

Training 1919–23, metalworking, Royal College of Art, London.
Biography 1923, Read worked at Clement Dane Advertising Studio, London; 1924–35, at French lighting firm Baguès; subsequently, visited Walter Gropius at the Bauhaus in Germany; 1925, became consultant designer to and director of Troughton and Young, where he designed pioneering lighting after World War II, including fluorescent industrial models. He worked with architects of the 1920s–30s modern movement and was instrumental in altering the character of interior lighting; gave the talk 'Design in Daily Life' on BBC radio before the opening of 1933 *British Industrial Art in Relation to the Home* exhibition at Dorland Hall, London. His lighting commissions included those for 1932 Cyril Carter house (archiect, Edward Maufe) in Yaffle Hill, Dorset. Read was a member, Society of Industrial Artists; 1950s, designed for ceramics manufacturer Carter in Poole; 1957, returned to Troughton and Young.
Citations 1940, elected Honorary Royal Designer for Industry, UK.
Bibliography Michael Farr, *Design in British Industry: A Mid-Century Survey*, London: Cambridge, 1955: 247. Cat., *Thirties: British Art and Design Before the War*, London: Arts Council of Great Britain/Hayward Gallery, 1979. Fiona MacCarthy and Patrick Nuttgens, *Eye for Industry*, London: Lund Humphries, 1986.

Read, Herbert Edward (1893–1968)

British poet, art critic, writer, and historian; born Leeds.

Biography His early poetry collections—*Songs of Chaos* (1915) and *Night Warriors* (1919)—showed influences of Imagism, the literary movement associated with Ezra Pound. Subsequent work included 1933 *The End of the War*. From 1930s, Read, a friend of T.S. Eliot, became influential in British literary and critical circles. Critical works included *The True Voice in Feeling* (1953) and *Essays in Literary Criticism* (1969). A prolific writer and lecturer, Read helped promote modernism in Britain in 1930s. His book *Art and Industry* (1934), supporting the ideas of Walter Gropius and the Bauhaus, was influential. He wrote numerous other books on art and aesthetics, including *Art and Industry: The Principles of Industrial Design* (London: Faber & Faber, 1934), *Art and Society* (London: Heinemann, 1937) and *Education Through Art* (London: Faber & Faber, 1943); was supportive of new artistic movements.
Exhibitions/citations Subject of 1993 exhibition, Leeds (catalog below). Was knighted.
Bibliography T. Duddensieg and H. Rogge, *Industrie-Kultur, Peter Behrens und die AEG, 1907–1914*, Berlin: Mann, 1979. James King, *The Last Modern: Herbert Read*, London: Weidenfeld and Nicolson, 1990. Cat., Benedict Read (ed.), *Herbert Read: A British Vision of World Art*, Leeds : Leeds City Art Galleries/Henry Moore Foundation/ Lund Humphries, 1993.

Reber, This
> See N2.

Reboldi, Arturo (1958–)

Italian designer.

Training To 1980, Accademia di Belle Arti di Brera, Milan.
Biography From 1983, Reboldi was associated with Studio Alchimia, eventually becoming an associate member.
Bibliography Fumio Shimizu and Studio Matteo Thun (eds.), *The Italian Design: Descendants of Leonardo da Vinci*, Tokyo: Graphic-sha, 1987.

Reboli, Giorgio (1942–)

Italian industrial designer; born and active Milan.

Biography 1957, Reboldi began his professional career; has designed mobile homes (caravans) by Elnagh, motor homes by Bora, lighting by Candle, and motor boats by Cantieri Sciallino; has been a consultant on building prefabrication systems. His buildings include those for civil and tourist functions. He is also active in interior architecture; editor of magazines *Milanocasa* and *Sinaat Italia*; and a member, Associazione per il Disegno Industriale (ADI).
Bibliography *ADI Annual 1976*, Milan: Associazione per il Disegno Industriale, 1976.

Reed & Barton

American silversmiths; located Taunton, Mass.

History 1824, jeweler Isaac Babbitt developed a new metal alloy he called Britannia metal, in his shop in Taunton; with friends, produced a high-quality, lustrous pewter; hired talented craftspeople, including Henry G. Reed and Charles E. Barton, who, when the firm experienced financial difficulties, took over and eventually began manufacturing under the Reed & Barton name. c. 1880, the firm became one of the first manufacturers to introduce silverplating and, eventually, a pioneer in the technology. Its respected wares were first applied with a heavy silverplate. Encouraged by the 1870s discovery of the Comstock Lode in Nevada, cutlery and hollow-ware times were produced in sterling silver from 1889. Through the 20th century, the firm has been successful. 1990s, Reed & Barton established a division to make hardwood chests for jewelry, cigars, pens, and cutlery; 1994, made the gold, silver, and bronze victory medals of the 1996 Atlanta Summer Olympiad. The firm is now one of the oldest privately held companies of any kind in the US. Acquisitions have included Theodore B. Starr (founded c. 1885) in 1924 and Daminick and Haff in 1928, both of New York; Cellini Shop/Cellini Craft of Chicago in 1965; Miller Rogaška Crystal, Rogaška, Slovenia, in 1996. Produced Robert Venturi's 1988–89 post-modern plated silver serving pieces. At one time, Carlo Mollino won a Reed & Barton cutlery competition.
Bibliography Annelies Krekel-Aalberse, *Art Nouveau and Art Déco Silver*, New York: Abrams, 1989. Charles L. Venable, *Silver in America, 1840–1940: A Century of Splendor*, New York: Abrams, 1995. Renee Garrelick, *Sterling Seasons: The Reed & Barton Story*, Taunton, Mass.: Reed & Barton, 1998.

Reeves, Ruth (1892–1966)

American textile designer; born Redlands, Cal.; active New York.

Training 1910–11, Pratt Institute, Brooklyn, N.Y.; 1911–13, California School of Design, San Francisco; 1913, Art Students League, New York; 1922–28 under Fernand Léger, Académie Moderne, Paris.
Biography Reeves became known for her handblocked textile, wallpaper, and rug designs that showed strong Cubist influence. From 1930, she was design consultant to W. and J. Slone furniture store in New York, which produced her 1930 Manhattan wallpaper and 1930 Figures with Still Life fabric. 1931, she turned from realistic images in favor of abstract forms and pure textile patterns; was a member of Designer's Gallery from 1929 and American Union of Decorative Artists and Craftsmen (AUDA) 1930–33; hand-painted wall coverings for 1932–33 Radio City Music Hall, including History of the Theater fabric covering the rear wall and balcony fascia. 1935–36, she was the first national coordinator, Index of American Design, Federal Arts Project; 1955–56, was the advisor in handicrafts (documentor of crafts traditions), Re-gistrar General of India.
Exhibitions/citations Work shown at 1930 *Decorative Metalwork and Cotton Textiles, 3rd International Exhibition of Contemporary Industrial Art*, The Metropolitan Museum of Art, New York. Paintings, drawings, and textile designs subject of 1932 exhibition, Art Center, New York. 1935, fabrics shown in Mezzanine Gallery, RCA building (now GE building), New York. Work included in 2000–01 American women designers, Bard Graduate Center, New York (catalog below). Received 1934, Guggenheim Foundation traveling fellowship to Guatemala; 1940, Guggenheim Fellowship; 1956, Fulbright Fellowship for study in India.
Bibliography Harry V. Anderson, 'Contemporary American Designers,' *Decorators' Digest*, Mar. 1935: 42–45, 59, 68, 74, 80, 82, 90. Karen Davies, *At Home in Manhattan: Modern Decorative Arts, 1925 to the Depression*, New Haven: Yale, 1983: 54. Jonathan M. Woodham, *Twentieth-Century Ornament*, New York: Rizzoli, 1990: 61, 64, 178. Cat., Pat Kirkham (ed.), *Women Designers in the USA, 1900–2000: Diversity and Difference*, New Haven: Yale, 2000.

Regondi, 'Lele' Gabriele (1949–1995)

Italian designer and entrepreneur; born Bovisio Masciago; active Bovisio Masciago and Milan.

Training To 1964, Liceo Artistico Beato Angelico, Milan; 1978, degree in architecture, Politecnico, Milan.
Biography Regondi taught design at the Liceo Artistico Beato Angelico, and, to 1992, Istituto Statale d'Arte in Monza; 1975, began working as a freelance designer and, from 1978, on furniture and furnishings, some still in production; also designed residences and exhibitions.
Citations 1979 Premio Compasso d'Oro (for Talete table by Pierluigi Ghianda).
Bibliography Fumio Shimizu and Studio Matteo Thun (eds.), *The Italian Design: Descendants of Leonardo da Vinci*, Tokyo: Graphic-sha, 1987.

Regout
> See De Sphinx; Kristalunie.

Reich, Lilly (1885–1947)

German interior architect and furniture and exhibition designer; born Berlin.

Biography One of Reich's earliest designs was a rustic metal milk pitcher of c. 1908. From 1908, she worked at the Wiener Werkstätte under Josef Hoffmann; 1911, returned to Berlin, where she was associated with Anna and Hermann Muthesius and collaborated with Else Oppler-Legband; 1912, became a member, Deutscher Werkbund, and, 1920, became the first female member of its board of directors; 1920, joined the Freie Gruppe für Farbkunst des DWB (Deutscher Werkbund); to 1924, worked for the Atelier für Innenraumgestaltung, Dekorationskunst und Mode (studio for interior design, decoration, and fashion) in Berlin; 1924–26, worked at Atelier für Ausstellungsgestaltung und Mode (studio for exhibition design and fashion) in Frankfurt. Her professional relationship with Mies van der Rohe began with the *Weissenhofsiedlung* exhibition, Stuttgart, for which they selected the exhibitors and designed stands. Its glass section had floors in black-and-white linoleum and walls of etched, clear and gray opaque glass, with chairs covered in white chamois and black cowhide and a bench table in rosewood. At the 1927 *Mode der Dame* exhibition, Berlin, she showed her expertise with textiles, and, with Mies, designed its silk exhibit. (Mies showed his tubular-steel furniture.) She was in charge of all the industrial exhibits and designed the stands in the German section of 1929–30 *Exposición Internacional de Barcelona*; the graphics and furniture were by Mies. When Mies became head of the Bauhaus in Dessau in 1930, she was already a respected interior designer. From 1932, she taught in the construction and weaving workshops at the Bauhaus and, subsequently, was head of its weaving and interior-design workshops. Mies took sole credit for their 1930 chaise-couch, a piece possibly by Reich alone. 1930, a copy was purchased by Philip Johnson for his house in New York, other acquisitions including Reich's 1930 wood and steel bookcases and 1930 writing table. When the chaise-couch was originally shown at the 1931 *Deutsche Bauausstellung* (German building exhibition), Berlin, the tension of the rubber stretched over the frame caused the piece to collapse and, apocryphally, hurt someone. Called the Berlin leather couch, it was put into production by Knoll in 1964; also produced by others since. Though Mies and Reich officially shared directorship of the *Deutsche Bauausstellung*, she created most of the work and showed her own model house along with Mies's. 1932, she moved with the Bauhaus to Berlin-Steglitz, which was soon closed. Other work included interiors and some of the furniture of Dr. Facius's 1936 apartment in Berlin-Dahlem, 1938 furniture for the children's room of the Wolf residence in Guben, 1939 furniture for the Crous residence in Berlin-Südende, and 1939 interior of Dr. Schäppi's apartment in Berlin. 1939, she traveled to Chicago to join Mies, who had settled there 1938, but, at his request, returned to Berlin to handle a long-running lawsuit against the steel firm Mauser over her and Mies's bent tubular-steel furniture designs. During the war, she designed the 1938–40 renovation of the P.A. Büren residence in Berlin-Wannsee and 1942 furniture and interior for Jürgen Reich's quarters in her house. 1943, her studio in Genthiner Strasse was destroyed by bombs. She took up temporary residence near Zittau; was drafted into the Organisation Todt, a forced-labour civil-engineering body; from 1945, worked

at the Atelier für Architektur, Design, Textilien und Mode (studio for architecture, design, textiles, and fashion) in Berlin; 1945–46, taught interior design and elementary building construction, Hochschule für bildende Künste, Berlin. She died in Berlin.
Exhibitions Work included in 1932 *Modern Architecture—International Exhibition* (interiors), The Museum of Modern Art, New York; Deutsche Textilindustrie stand, 1937 *Exposition Internationale des Arts et Techniques dans la Vie Moderne*, Paris. Exhibition work subject of 1996 exhibition, The Museum of Modern Art, New York (catalog below).
Bibliography Lilly Reich, 'Modefragen,' *Die Form—Monatsschrift für gestaltende Arbeit*, 1922. James Gowan, 'Reflections on the Mies Centennial,' *Architectural Design* 56, Mar. 1956: 6. *Mies van der Rohe: European Works*, London: Academy, 1986: 48–54. Cat., *The Bauhaus: Masters and Students*, New York: Barry Friedman, 1988. Sonja Günther, *Lilly Reich 1885–1947, Innenarchitektin, Designerin, Ausstellungsgestalterin*, Stuttgart: Deutsche Verlags-Anstalt, 1988. Otakar Máčel, 'Avant-Garde Design and the Law: Litigation over the Cantilever Chair,' *Journal of Design History*, vol. 3, nos. 2 and 3, 1990: 125–43. Cat., Matilda McQuaid, with an essay by Madgalena Droste, *Lilly Reich: Designer and Architect*, New York: The Museum of Modern Art, 1996. Paola Antonelli (ed.), *Objects of Design: The Museum of Modern Art*, New York: The Museum of Modern Art, 2003: 93.

Reichardt, 'Grete' Margarete (1907–1984)

German textile designer; born Erfurt.

Training 1926–31, fabric design, Bauhaus, Dessau.
Biography 1934, she founded her own handweaving firm; 1952–77, was a member, Verband bildender Künstler Deutschlands.
Exhibitions/citations Work included in 1987 and 1988 exhibitions, Berlin and New York (catalogs below). Gold medal, 1939 (7th) Triennale di Milano.
Bibliography Lionel Richard, *Encyclopédie du Bauhaus*, Paris: Somogy, 1985: 206. Cat., Gunta Stölzl, *Weberei am Bauhaus und ams eigener Werkstatt*, Berlin: Bauhaus-Archiv, 1987: 163–64. Cat., *The Bauhaus: Masters and Students*, New York: Barry Friedman, 1988.

Reijmyre Glasbruk

Swedish glass factory.

History 1810, a factory was established in Reijmyra, Östergötland, to produce glassware; by 1900, had become one of Sweden's leading manufacturers of pressed and engraved decorative-glass tablewares; from 1900, produced glass in the Art Nouveau style by A.E. Boman and Alf Wallander, who both joined the Reijmyra staff in 1908; installed new machinery in 1930 for pressed-glass manufacture; 1937, hired Monica Bratt as the artistic director, who designed colored glassware; after World War II, hired designers including Tom Möller; 1977, was purchased by Upsala-Ekeby.
Bibliography Jennifer Hawkins Opie, *Scandinavia: Ceramics and Glass in the Twentieth Century*, New York: Rizzoli, 1989.

Reimann, Albert (1874–1971)

German metalworker and teacher; born Gnesen; active Berlin and London.

Biography 1902, stimulated by the British Arts and Crafts movement, Reimann and his wife Klara founded the Schülerwerkstätten für Kleinplastik (school for small sculpture) in Berlin. A talented craftsperson, Reimann produced prototypes for bronze, copper, silver, gold, and pottery pieces. 1912, the school expanded into 23 departments, each with its own specialist teacher. Each student took perspective drawing, shadow construction, anatomy, art and costume history, color theory, and tailoring. By 1914, the original roll of 14 students had grown to 500. From 1912, the Schule Reimann was connected with the Höhere Fachschule für Dekorationskunst, an institution established by the Deutscher Werkbund to educate store-window decorators in cooperation with the Deutscher Verband für das kaufmännische Unterrichtswesen (German association for commercial education), and the Verband Berliner Spezialgeschäfte (Berlin association of specialty shops). From 1913, the Schule Reimann was associated with the Kunstgewerbeschule, the only institution of its kind recognized by the state government. Courses included ivory carving, painting, clothing design, architecture, spatial arts, and set, packaging, and poster design. Reimann, the sole teacher at first, was joined by Karl Heubler in 1905. Heubler headed the metalworking studio, and his students were encouraged to work independently in their own personal style. Instruction was supervised by a committee that included Hermann Muthesius, Peter Behrens, and Theo Schmuz-Baudiss. By 1927, there were 30 teachers, including Max Hertwig, who taught typography and graphic design, and painters Moriz Melzer and Georg Tappert. Later, the staff included Hans Baluschek and Paul Scheurich. Julius Klinger was head of the poster-design department. 1916, the first issue of the school magazine *Mitteilungen der Schule Reimann* was published; 1920–34, called *Farbe und Form*. The school offered professional training equal to the Kunstgewerbeschule in Vienna and, 1920s, had up to 1,000 students, many from abroad. After 1922, numerous accomplished artists from the Bauhaus were able to continue at the Schule Reimann. From 1933, Reimann himself produced tabletop accessory designs for Chase Copper and Brass Co., Waterbury, Conn., US, including silver or brass candlesticks and vessels in the Jugendstil. On the invitation of Rodney Chase, he may have visited the US during the 1930–31 exhibition of the American Federation of Arts. 1935, when the Nazis introduced the antisemitic Nuremberg Laws, Reimann, a Jew, was forced to sell the school to architect Hugo Häring; settled in London and, 1935, set up a new Schule Reimann there. 1936, the Berlin school was renamed the Werk und Zeit Privatschule für Gestaltung but was destroyed by bombs in 1943, as was Reimann's school in London.
Exhibitions Students' work shown in numerous exhibitions, including at 1906 *Grosse Berliner Kunstausstellung*, Kunstgewerbeschule, Berlin; 1906, in zoological gardens; 1908, in own building; 1909, in Kunstgewerbe Museum; at 1914 *Deutsche Werkbund-Ausstellung*, where the students decorated a row of shops. The last major contemporary exhibition of their work was in 1920 in Schönenberg.
Bibliography *Magazine of Art*, vol. 26, 1902: 65–77. Albert Reimann, *Die Reimann Schule in Berlin*, Berlin: B. Hessling, 1966. H. Duve, 'Meisterleistungen aus der Reimann-Schule,' *Die Schaulade*, no. 6, 1930: 351, 364, 372, 373. Cat., *Kunst der 20er und 30er Jahre*, Berlin: Sammlung Bröhan, 1985: 463–66. Tilmann Buddensieg (ed.), *Berlin 1900–1933, Architecture and Design*, New York: Cooper-Hewitt Museum/Mann, 1987: 110, 112. Annelies Krekel-Aalberse, *Art Nouveau and Art Déco Silver*, Abrams, 1989. Cat., *Metallkunst*, Berlin: Bröhan-Museum, 1990: 415–18. Judy Rudoe, *Decorative Arts 1850–1950: A Catalogue of the British Museum Collection*, London: British Museum, 1994.

Lilly Reich. LR small chair (no. LR 120). 1931. Leather, hardwood, and nickel-plated tubular steel, 35 1/16 x 18 1/8 x 21 5/8" (89 x 46 x 55 cm). Mfr.: The Knoll Group, US (1996). Gift of the mfr. MoMA.

Reinecke, Jean Otis (1909–1987)

American industrial designer; born Kansas.

Biography 1926, at age 17, Reinecke opened his own sign-painting shop; began his professional career as a commerical artist in St. Louis; 1934 or 1935 with salesperson James F. Barnes, founded Barnes & Reinecke, Chicago, with first assignments being designs of dioramas and architectural models for 1933–34 *A Century of Progress International Exhibition*, Chicago and, subsequently, offered product-styling services to industrial firms. By 1948, the staff had grown to 375. Reinecke designed 1947 Toastmaster by McGraw Edison (but not the first pop-up model), 1939 bullet-shaped drink mixer by Hamilton Beach, 1940 metal and 1941 plastic Scotch tape dispensers by 3M. 1948, he sold the firm to Barnes and established J.O. Reinecke & Associates in Chicago, and, 1958, also in Pasadena, Cal.; until sometime after 1975, kept the California office open; became president, Society of Industrial Designers (SID, later named IDSA), 1952. Early on, Reinecke enthusiastically advocated the use and development of plastics, considered it unreasonable to consider them fake, and wrote profusely on the subject. Barnes & Reinecke is still active today, in Arlington Heights, Ill.
Bibliography Mel Byars with Arlette Barré-Despond, *100 Designs/ 100 Years: A Celebration of the 20th Century*, Hove: RotoVision: 92–93. www.briwebsite.com.

Reiss, Henriette (1889–)

British textile designer; born Liverpool; wife of Winold Reiss.

Training Textile design in England, Munich, and Switzerland.
Biography 1914, with husband Winold Reiss, she emigrated to the US; by 1920s, was living in an artists' colony in New York State that included Marion Dorn, Ruth Reeves, and Martha Ryther; late 1920s, was a teacher.
Exhibitions Modern-design exhibitions (handhooked rugs made to designs by her husband), New England Guild, Portland, Me.; 1930, The Newark Museum, N.J.
Bibliography Cat., Janet Kardon (ed.), *Craft in the Machine Age 1920–1945*, New York: Abrams/American Craft Museum, 1995.

Reiss, Winold (1886–1953)

German artist and designer; born Karlsruhe; husband of Henriette Reiss.

Biography 1914, Reiss emigrated to the US; became known for illustrations in *Survey Graphic*, and Alain LeRoy Locke's *The New Negro: An Interpretation* (New York: A. + C. Boni, 1925), an anthology which helped launch the Harlem Renaissance. Early 1920s, in New York, Reiss decorated Medieval Grill and Congo Room in the Alamac Hotel, New York; 1920, pioneered an American interior-design motif for the Crillon restaurant and again, 1927, at a new address in New York. 1928, he became a member, American Designers Gallery, and, 1930, a member, American Union of Decorative Artists and Craftsmen (AUDAC); designed the exotic 31 ft (9.5 m) high ballroom of the 1930 addition to St. George Hotel (addition architect, Emery Roth), Brooklyn, N.Y.; 1930–31 Café Bonaparte, Beaux-Arts Apartments, New York; from 1935, a series of Longchamps restaurants, including interior design and decoration (with Albert Charles Schweizer) of its 1938 restaurant (architect, Ely Jacques Kahn) in the Empire State Building; was an accomplished mosaicist, illustrated by the panorama at 1931 Cincinnati Railroad Station (architects, Fellheimer and Wagner). Reiss had an interest in Native American motifs, possibly influenced by an association with Léon Bakst.
Exhibitions 1916–20, blockprint fabrics and rugs shown in *Albert Blum Exhibitions of Hand-Decorated Fabrics*, Art Alliance of America, New York. Work included in 1928 exhibition, American Designers Gallery; 1930 and 1931 exhibitions, AUDAC.
Bibliography Robert A.M. Stern et al., *New York 1930*, New York: Rizzoli, 1987. Mel Byars (intro.), 'What Makes American Design American?,' in R.L. Leonard and C.A. Glassgold (eds.), *Modern American Design, by the American Union of Decorative Artists and Craftsmen*, New York: Acanthus, 1992 reprint. Cat., Janet Kardon (ed.), *Craft in the Machine Age 1920–1945*, New York: Abrams/American Craft Museum, 1995.

Reitze, Achim (1966–)
> See Trondesign.

Relling, Ingmar (1920–)

Norwegian furniture and interior designer; born Sykkylven.

Training Statens Håndverks -og Kunstindustriskole, Oslo.
Biography Relling is best known for his 1965 Siesta lounge chair/ ottoman in seven-layered bentwood (noted by Victor Papanek as exemplifying exceptional ecological characteristics) and other designs by Vestlandske Møbelfabrikk in Èrsta; some work with Knut Relling, for example, the Optima Art lounge chair by Modi Scandinavia, and Rest Lux chaise longue.
Bibliography Cat., David Revere McFadden (ed.), *Scandinavian Modern Design 1880–1980*, New York: Abrams, 1982. Fredrik Wildhagen, *Norge i Form*, Oslo: Sternersen, 1988: 168.

Remy, Tejo (1960–)

Dutch designer; active Utrecht.

Training Three-dimensional design, Hogeschool voor de Kunsten, Utrecht.
Biography For his final examination at the Utrecht school, Remy created various furnishings, including the now-legendary 1991 You Can't Lay Down Your Memory chest of drawers, marketed by Droog Design. For the idea, he purportedly that he called on Daniel Defoe's *The Life and Strange Surprising Adventures of Robinson Crusoe...* (London: W. Taylor, 1719) as a metaphor. Remy was a member of the ad-hoc group Droog Design and, soon after its initial impact, departed to seek autonomy and to escape the rigid parameters of market-dictated production. Other work through Droog Design has included 1991 Milk-bottle lamp (produced from 1993) and 1991 Rag chair.
Exhibitions/citations 1996 *Contemporary Design from the Netherlands*, The Museum of Modern Art, New York; numerous others with the Droog Design group. Work subject of 2002 *S.I.G.S.I.S. (Should I Go or Should I Stay)* installment, De Appel Foundation, Amsterdam. Granted 1995 Edward Marshall Trust Award, Surrey, UK.
Bibliography Mel Byars with Arlette Barré-Despond, *100 Designs/ 100 Years: A Celebration of the 20th Century*, Hove: RotoVision, 1999: 194–95. Paola Antonelli (ed.), *Objects of Design: The Museum of Modern Art*, New York: The Museum of Modern Art, 2003: 276.
> See Droog Design.

Renaudot, Lucie (d. 1939)

French decorator and furniture designer; born Valenciennes.

Biography 1918, Renaudot became active as a decorator in Paris. Her first commissions were the tearooms Tipperary and Ça Ira. Some of Renaudot's furniture was produced by Maurice Rinck. All of P.A. Dumas's furniture production was designed by her. Various of her models were produced in limited editions, if not one-of-a-kind. She designed for 1935 oceanliner *Normandie* and executed a number of assignments in Paris and the provinces, particularly Alsace.
Exhibitions Work was first shown, at 1919 edition of Salon d'Automne, and rooms in a country house and for a young girl were installed at its 1920 edition. Participated in 1925 *Exposition Internationale des Arts Décoratifs et Industriels Modernes*; 1927 competition (a woman's office), Union Centrale des Arts Décoratifs; Salons of Société des Artistes Décorateurs; 1937 *Exposition Internationale des Arts et Techniques dans la Vie Moderne* (collaboration on a child's room in Une Ambassade Française pavilion); all Paris. Work subject of an exhibition organized by Société des Artistes Décorateurs.
Bibliography *Ensembles mobiliers*, vol. II, Paris: Charles Moreau, 1937. Léon Deshairs (intro.), *Modern French Decorative Art: A Collection of Examples of Modern French Decoration*, Paris: Albert Lévy, c. 1925–30. Pierre Kjellberg, *Art déco: les maîtres du mobilier, le décor des paquebots*, Paris: Amateur, 1986/1990.

Renk, Alain
> See Naço, Studio

Renou, André (1912–1980)

French sculptor and furniture designer.

Training 1923 under Louis Sognot, École Boulle, Paris.
Biography 1930, Renou joined La Crémaillère shop/consortium, Paris, and, 1941, became the president and director general. From 1933, Jean-Pierre Génisset joined the firm, and he and Renou collaborated to 1965 on the design/production of a number of tabletop objects and lighting, becoming among the first to produce modern knick-knacks. 1941, Renou became a member, Union des Artistes

Tejo Remy. You Can't Lay Down Your Memory chest of drawers. 1991. Metal, paper, plastic, burlap, contact paper, and paint, 55 1/2 x 53 x 20" (141 x 134.6 x 50.8 cm). Mfr.: the designer, the Netherlands. Frederieke Taylor Purchase Fund. MoMA.

Modernes (UAM); 1954–57, was chairperson, Société des Artistes Décorateurs.
Exhibitions/citations With Génisset, work shown at Salons of Société Décorateurs; and 1937 *Exposition Internationale des Arts et Techniques dans la Vie Moderne*, Paris. Gold medal, 1958 *Exposition Universelle et Internationale de Bruxelles* (*Expo '58*).
Bibliography Patrick Favardin, *Les décorateurs des années 50*, Paris: Norma, 2002: 150.

Renwick, William Crosby (1914–1992)
American industrial designer.

Training To 1940, architecture, Princeton University.
Biography 1946–51, Renwick was a product designer at Raymond Loewy Associates; 1951–57, vice-president, product design at George Nelson Associates, where he designed 1947 Bubble Lamp range for Howard Miller Clock Company, produced 1950–79 and today by others; 1957–63, was president, Renwick Thomson and Gove, industrial designers; 1963–66, design director, Dow Corning; 1966–82, design director, Brunswick sports equipment. 1962–63, he was the president, American Society of Industrial Designers (ASID).
Bibliography Ray Spilman, 'Design Heads & Tales/William Crosby Renwick,' *Innovation* (IDSA quarterly journal), vol. 12, no. 1, 1993.

Reumert, Jane (1942–)
Danish ceramicist.

Training Kunsthåndværkerskolen, Copenhagen.
Biography 1964 with Beate Andersen and Gunhild Åberg, Reumert founded the workshop Strandstræde Keramik in Copenhagen. Her ceramics are mold-cast and individually glazed. Reumert also designed for Dansk Designs, Kosta Boda glassworks, and L. Hjorts Terracotta Factory in Roenne, island of Bornholm.
Exhibitions/citations Work included in 1971 *Kunst und Kunsthandwerk aus Dänemark*, Wiesbaden; 1974 *Exempla*, Munich; 1975 exhibition, Hälsingborg Stadsmuseum; 1981 *Danish Ceramic Design*, Pennsylvania State University; 1982 exhibition, New York (catalog below); International Exhibition of Applied Art, Bratislava, in 1984; and a large number of subsequent venues. Subject of exhibitions, including at Den Permanente, Copenhagen, in 1970; Röhsska Konst-slöjdmuseet, Gothenburg, in 1977; and others to date such as retrospective, Grimmerhus Keramikmuseum, in 1995; Gallerie Bjørnen, Stockholm, in 1996; Galleri Nørby, Copenhagen, in 1997. More than two dozen awards/grants, including 1970, 1972, 1977, 1985, 1988, 1992 Danmarks Nationalbank Jubilee Foundation.
Bibliography Cat., David Revere McFadden (ed.), *Scandinavian Modern Design 1880–1980*, New York: Abrams, 1982.

Revelli di Beaumont, Mario (1905–1985)
Italian automobile designer.

Biography Count Revelli di Beaumont is not generally well known; however, he is thought to be a significant car-design pioneer and purportedly became the first independent, or freelance, auto-body designer. Before World War II, he worked for General Motors, Pininfarina, and Fiat; designed the sporty, exuberant 1933 Lancia Astura open tourer (built by Castagna) with separate front and rear seating and 1936 Cinemobile Fiat 618, equipped with a Victoria floodlight by Cinemeccanica of Milan; assisted on the 1936 Fiat Topolino; 1949, conceived the idea of the MPV (multi-purpose vehicle), claiming to presage 1957 Fiat Multipla; engineered the simple, interesting rear-engined 1961 Simca 1000 (though some sources claim the engineering to be by Dante Giacosa).

Revere Copper and Brass
American metalware manufacturer; located Clinton, Ill., and Rome, N.Y.

History 1881, John Revere, silversmith Paul Revere's grandson, became president of Revere Copper Company. 1928, six companies (Rome Brass & Copper Company, Michigan Copper & Brass Company, Baltimore Copper Mills, Dallas Brass & Copper Co., Taunton-New Bedford Copper Company, and Higgins Brass & Manufacturing Company) were merged and incorporated as the General Brass Corporation; four days later, changed name to Republic Brass Corporation. 1929, the name was changed again to Revere Copper and Brass Incorporated and a special high-design division was established at its facility in Rome, N.Y. One of its finest designs was Peter Müller-Munk's 1935 chromium-plated Normandie pitcher (not used on the 1935 French oceanliner but named for it). From 1930s, Revere produced other distinctively designed metalware. By 1933, W. Archibald Welden was a consultant designer to Revere, where he designed goods in close association with its technicians; became head of design and was instrumental in Revere's commissioning the more

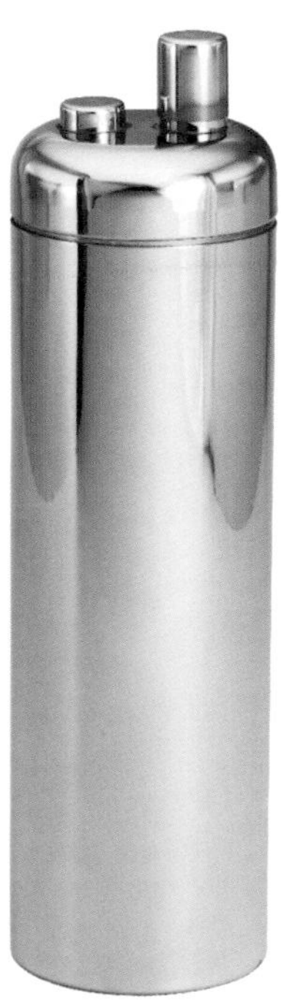

Revere: W. Archibald Welden. Zephyr cocktail shaker. c. 1938. Chrome-plated metal, h. 11" x dia. 3" (27.9 x 7.6 cm). Mfr.: Revere Copper and Brass, US. Gift of the mfr.. MoMA.

accomplished designers of the day such as Norman Bel Geddes, William Lescaze, Leslie Beaton, Elsie Wilkins, Fred Farr, Ted Mehrer, and Frederick Priess. Bel Geddes's 1934 Skyscraper and Manhattan cocktail serving sets have become icons, and Farr's 1935 Scroll bookholder is a classic of geometric simplicity. Welden's range of cocktail shakers is highlighted by c. 1938 Zephyr model. 1933, Revere acquired an interest in Warren McArthur aluminum-furniture firm, which was amalgamated into Revere's Rome Manufacturing Division. Welden's 1938 Revere Ware range of copper-bottomed cookware in stainless steel featured the now-iconic 'pistol' handle. The design resulted from an extensive study of the use, cleaning, heating, tooling, manufacturing, and consumer preferences. 1954, Welden also designed Revere's range of cookware with heat-resistant metal instead of plastic handles for the institutional market, and a number of other products. 1988, Corning purchased Revere, which became the Revere Crown division, and Revere/Crown Corning in 1990. Revere's 1993 Excel range featured the first stainless-steel pans to feature two pouring spouts, a non-stick coating, and new phenolics. 1998, Borden bought Revere Ware together with the Corning Consumer Products Division (Corelle, Corning Ware, Visions, and Pyrex brands), and Independence and Revolution non-stick aluminum cookwares were introduced. Corning Consumer Products was within Borden's subsidiary, World Kitchen. 1999, World Kitchen in turn bought the EKCO Group and, subsequently that year, bought General Housewares, an acquisition that included the Oxo, Chicago Cutlery, and other brands.
Bibliography Isaac F. Marcosson, *Copper Heritage: The Story of Revere Copper and Brass Incorporated*, New York: Dodd, Mead, 1955. Don Wallance, *Shaping America's Products*, New York: Reinhold, 1956. Cat., Kathryn B. Hiesinger and George H. Marcus III (eds.), *Design Since 1945*, Philadelphia: Philadelphia Museum of Art, 1983. Jim Linz, *Art Deco Chrome*, Atglen, Pa.: Schiffer, 1999.
> See Corning Glass Works.

Revere Pottery
> See Paul Revere Pottery.

Reynolds, Richard S. (1908–1955); Reynolds Metals

American inventor and firm.

Biography/history Reynolds worked for his uncle, tobacco entrepreneur R.J. Reynolds, during summers to 1919, when he founded his own business, U.S. Foil Co., Louisville, Ky., to make tin/lead wrappers for cigarette and candy packets. When prices for aluminum fell in 1920s, he switched from tin to brighter-appearing aluminum. 1924, he bought the firm that made Eskimo Pies, a pastry-based chocolate/marshmallow cookie (biscuit); 1926 for the first time, began using aluminum foil as a packaging material; 1927, invented Reynolds Cut-Rite Wax Paper; moved the firm's headquarters to New York; developed first high-speed, gravure-printed foil; 1928, bought Robertshaw Thermo-stat, Fulton Sylphon, and a part of Beechnut Foil companies and formed Reynolds Metals; 1938, moved the headquarters to Richmond, Va.; 1941, opened the first aluminum plant, near Sheffield, Ala. 1947, the firm invented its most-famous product, Reynolds Wrap Aluminum Foil; 1945, developed aluminum architectural siding; and opened mining operations worldwide. 1948, Richard S. Reynolds resigned as head of the firm, turning over the operations to his sons. 1982, the firm introduced Reynolds Plastic Wrap; 2000, merged with Alcoa to become the largest aluminum company in the U.S. 2002, Alcoa introduced Reynolds Wrap Release, non-stick aluminum foil.
Bibliography Richard Samuel Reynolds, *Opportunity in Crisis: The Reynolds Metals Story*, New York: Newcomen Society in North America, 1956.

Reymond, Patrick (1962–)
> See Atelier Oï.

Rezek, Ron (1947–)

American industrial designer and entrepreneur; active Los Angeles.

Training Master of fine arts degree, University of California, Los Angeles (UCLA).
Biography Rezek, whose mentor was Buckminster Fuller, was also inspired by Antonio Gaudí's work and Frank Gehry's innovative approach to raw materials. Initially, he taught in the art and architecture departments, UCLA, and at Art Center College of Design and Southern California Institute of Architecture worked for Deborah Sussman and for Gehry. 1978, Rezek set up Ron Rezek Lighting and designed playful, pragmatic lighting fixtures whose sales and distribution were handled by Artemide from 1986. Rezek's inexpensive Zink lamp was crudely plated in zinc to produce a deliberately imperfect finish. By 1989, his extensive lighting range included table lamps, sconces, pendant lamps, torchères, and 1988 Stratos ceiling fan. 1999, he founded The Modern Fan Company to break from historicist treatments and was first to offer a ceiling fan with a fluorescent light. He has consulted to Herman Miller Furniture Company, Monarch Mirror, Del Rey Lighting, Fredrick Raymond Lighting, Halsey Lighting, and Lavi Industries.
Bibliography Donna Sapolin, *Metropolitan Home*, Aug. 1989: 32E. www.modernfan.com.

Rhead, Frederick Hurten (1880–1942)

British ceramicist; born Hanley, Staffordshire; active Stoke-on-Trent, Ohio, Missouri, and California.

Biography Rhead was artistic director of the Wardle Art Pottery in Hanley, Stoke-on-Trent, UK; 1902, settled in Ohio in the US and worked for various artware ceramics factories there, including Vance/Avon with William P. Jervis. From 1903, his wares were appearing in the journal *Keramic Studio*. 1904, he became a designer at Weller Pottery, then artistic director at Roseville Pottery from 1904–08, both in Zanesville, Ohio. 1909, he worked at Jervis Pottery on Long Island, N.Y.; 1910, became an instructor in pottery at University City Pottery near St. Louis, Mo., where he was associated with Taxile Doat and Adelaide Robineau; 1911, settled in California and was hired to become the ceramicist and instructor by Philip King Brown, the organizer of the pottery at Arequipa Sanatorium in Marin County. 1913, Rhead left Arequipa and set up the Rhead Pottery in Santa Barbara, Cal. and produced landscape abstractions on pottery with the technique of fluid incised lines that reflected the California topography. (He had earlier called on the technique for Roseville's Della Robbia range.) In Santa Barbara, he created practical items, including cream-and-sugar sets and five-piece garniture sets. 1917, the firm closed. 1916–17, he published four issues of the magazine *Potter*; was the most prominent and most productive potter in California at this time; became known for his squeeze-bag technique for outlining slip and glaze infills; experimented with over 11,000 formulas for Chinese mirror-black glaze. 1917, he closed his pottery, calling his work 'a monstrosity'; 1917–27, was the research director of American Encaustic Tiling of Zanesville, Ohio; 1920, organized the art section of the American Ceramic Society and served as its chairman from 1920–25. He was artistic director from 1927 at Homer Laughlin China Company, where he was responsible for the design of his legendary Fiesta Ware in 1935 and for which he introduced the concept of mixing and matching solid color pieces within a single service. He designed a number of other patterns by Laughlin, not all modern in nature; on his 1942 death from cancer, was replaced by Don Schreckengost as the artistic director. He had been the chairperson, United States Pottery Association.
Exhibitions/citations *Fiesta Ware* introduced, 1936 *Pottery and Glass Fair*, Philadelphia; shown, Philadelphia; subject of 1986 exhibition, Erie, Pa. (catalog below). Gold medal, 1915 *Panama-Pacific International Exposition*, San Francisco; 1934 Charles F. Binns Medal, American Ceramic Society.
Bibliography Paul Evans, in Timothy J. Andersen et al., *California Design 1910*, Salt Lake City: Peregrine Smith, 1980. Cat., Sharon Dale, *Frederick Hurten Rhead: An English Potter in America*, Erie, Pa.: Erie Art Museum, 1986. Garth Clark, *American Ceramics: 1876 to the Present*, New York: Abbeville, 1987: 293+. Betty Purviance Ward and Nancy Schiffer, *Weller, Roseville and Zanesville Art Pottery and Tile*, Atglen, Pa.: Schiffer, 2000.

Rhinn, Eric (1960–)

French industrial designer.

Training École d'Architecture, Strasbourg; industrial design, École Nationale Supérieure des Arts Décoratifs, Paris.
Biography Rhinn was the designer at Usus-Solus; 1988 with Luc Jozancy, founded industrial-design and graphics studio Avant-Première, Paris, with offices in Hong Kong and New York, which specialized in educational toys, clocks, and plastic accessories; designed 1988 aluminum chair produced by Mullca and sponsored by VIA (French furniture association).
Exhibitions/citations Avant-Première work included in 1990 exhibition, Paris (catalog below). 1986 (1st) (lamp and armchair) and 1989 (aluminum side chair and armchair) Appel Permanent grants, VIA.

Bibliography *Les carnets du design*, Paris: Mad-Cap Productions/APCI, 1986: 86. Cat., *Les années VIA*, Paris: Musée des Arts Décoratifs, 1990.

Riart, Carles (1944–)

Spanish interior, exhibition, and furniture designer; born and active Barcelona.

Training 1967, industrial design, Eina (Escola de Desseny i Art), Barcelona.
Biography Early on, Riart was active in the oppressive environment of Generalissimo Francisco Franco's dictatorship in Spain and considered himself to have been a 'failure,' according to the conventional academic criteria of the time. Riart was, as one of his teachers observed, 'a soul in torment.' However, on a chance 1969 meeting with former classmate Bigas Luna (now a film director), Riart and Luna established the interior-design shop Gris in Barcelona, where they initially pursued window dressing and decoration and, eventually, designed, exhibited, and sold radical modern objects. Ending the partnership with Luna, Riart began to make his own furniture, starting with a knock-down wardrobe that he attempted (unsuccessfully) to sell from a stall outside the football stadium in Barcelona. He went on to design and produce 1976 Colilla lighting system (a row of neon inside a translucent tube), that he sold by mail (reissued by Santa & Cole in 1979 as well as other models by the firm). 1970s–80s, Riart designed chairs, tables, cabinets, lighting, and mirrors for clients including Disform, Écart, Knoll, Snark, and Tecno. Other work: mid-1980s Snooker public bar (with Santiago Roqueta, Oleguer Armengol, and Victor Mesalles) and 1985 Si-Si-Si public bar (with Gabriel Ordeig), both in Barcelona; 1973 Desnuda side chair (by Tecno by 1979); limited-edition furniture by Muebles Casas from 1980s; and furnishings by Mobles 114. His work reflected historical and 1950s models in an individual postmodern approach. His 1982 rocking chair (in commemoration of the 50th anniversary of Mies van der Rohe's pavilion at 1929–30 Barcelona *Exposición*) by Knoll has become well known. Riart has taught at Eina, Barcelona.
Exhibitions/citations 1985 *8 Spanish Designers*, Barcelona and Madrid; *Ilberdiseño 90*, San Perc de Ribas; 1990 *Mondo Materiales*, New York and Los Angeles; 1992 *Casa Barcelona*, Cultural Olympiad, Drassanes Reials, Barcelona and Madrid; 1992 Sala de Los Amigos del Centro de Arte, Museo Nacional Centro de Arte Reina Sofía, Madrid; 1994 *Catalan Furniture*, Palau Robert, Barcelona. Received 1970, 1974, 1986, 1992 Delta d'Oro, ADI/FAD (industrial-design and decorative arts associations), Spain; 1979 Premio de la Opinión, Barcelona; 1983 silver medal, Institute of Business Designers (IBD), US; 1983 Roscoe Award, US; 1986 Premi FAD d'Interiorisme Award (best interiors); two Delta de Plata and five selections, ADI, Spain; 1993 Nuevo Estilo award, Madrid; 1994 Top Ten European design award, Cologne; Grand Prix de la Presse et de la Critique, 1994 Salon du Meuble, Paris.
Bibliography 'A Barcelona Workshop,' *Domus*, no. 546, May 1975: 28. *Hogares Modernos*, no. 96, 1974: 66–67; no. 118, 1977: 18–21. 'Knoll Presents: Three Diverse Furniture Groups,' *Interior Design*, vol. 53, Dec. 1982: 134–35. Juli Capella and Quim Larrea, *25 años de diseño industrial: Los premios Delta*, Barcelona: Gili, 1986. Klaus-Jürgen Sembach et al., *Furniture Design*, Cologne: Taschen, 1988. Guy Julier, *New Spanish Design*, London: Thames & Hudson, 1991. *Moble català*, Barcelona: Departament de Cultura, Generalitat de Catalunya/Electa, 1994.

Ricard, Paul (1909–); Ricard; Pernod-Ricard

French entrepreneur; born Sainte-Marthe. And brand.

History 1932, Paul Ricard (Sainte-Marthe, 1909–) developed the formula of the Pastis de Marseille, an anise-flavored aperitif; 1939, established his eponymous firm to market the product worldwide, both in direct sales and to bars, restaurants, other hospitality establishments. The success of the firm has been attested to by the 530 million gallons (two billion liters) of Ricard sold in past 65 years. Paul Ricard has become known as a humanitarian and visionary and, with friends Pablo Picasso and Salvador Dalí, established Espace Paul Ricard in Paris, a gallery for the promotion of young artists. Fond of the sea and nature, he created research organization Institut Océanographic Paul Ricard in 1966, with navigators Alain Colas and Eric Tabarly, and several other organizations and sponsorships. 1966, the firm acquired Bisquit in Charente, adding cognac to the product line. 1972–80, Ricard was the mayor of Signes (Var); 1974, formed the group Pernod-Ricard. Since his 1975 retirement, his son Patrick Ricard has been president and Alain Chamla the director. Compared to similar enterprises, Ricard has shown an impressively high commitment to design. Serigraphed motifs for Créations & Saveurs bottles were designed by Sonia Rykiel, Tsé & Tsé Associées, Matali Crasset, Titouan Lamazou, and others, and Ricard Premium bottle by Garouste et Bonetti. For its bar/restaurant ware in the distinctive yellow-orange Ricard color, the Kréo agency commissioned Garouste et Bonetti (1996 ashtray, clock, and clear-glass carafe), Olivier Gagnère (1997 clear-glass drinking glasses), Radi Designers (1999 portion dispenser), Marc Newson (2000 pitcher), Ronan & Erwan Bouroullec (jug and ice bucket), and Pierre Charpin (cutting board). The items have been of such fine quality that, for example, the Newson pitcher has been sold at retail, not by Ricard, as a high-design collectible.
Exhibitions/citations 2001 *DeSignDeZinc* (Ricard's designer barware), Espace Ricard, Paris. Paul Ricard was elected Commandeur of the Légion d'Honneur, Officier of the Ordre National du Mérite, Chevalier of the Mérite Agricole, Chevalier of the Ordre National du Mérite Maritime, Chevalier of the Mérite Social, Chevalier of the Mérite Touristique, Dag Hammarskjoeld Peace Prize.

Ricard, André (1929–)

Spanish designer and writer; born Barcelona.

Biography Ricard discovered design in 1951, when living in London at the time of the *Festival of Britain*, and was also influenced by Raymond Loewy's book *Never Leave Well Enough Alone* (New York: Simon & Schuster, 1951) and met him 1956 in New York. He began designing packaging for his family's pharmaceutical firm. 1957, became Spain's pioneering industrial designer; attended 1959 (1st) Congress of International Council of Societies of Industrial Designers (ICSID); 1960 with Antoni de Moragas and others, cofounded ADI/FAD (industrial-design and decorative-arts association), Barcelona. 1963–67 and 1976–79, he was vice-president ICSID; designed products for clients, including 1976 Mini-Moka by Gaggia, 1972 Tatú table light by Metalarte, and perfume bottles (Puig's 1968 Agua Brava and 1981 Quorum, and Paco Rabanne's 1985 La Nuit). Other work:1965 Copenhagen plastic ashtray and 1992 Barcelona Summer Olympiad torch. The books he has written include *Diseño ¿por qué?* (what is design for?) (1982), *Diseño y calidad de vida* (design and quality of life) (1985), *Hablando de diseño* (speaking of design) (1987), and *La aventura creativa* (the creative adventure) (2001). Currently, he is the patron of Eina (Escola de Disseny i Art) Art Foundation and of Barcelona Centre de Disseny (BCD).
Exhibitions/citations Work subject of 2000 exhibition in Santander (catalog below). 1987 (1st) National Design Prize, Spain; 1993 Sant Jordi Cross, Catalunya; 1998 Chevalier des Arts et Lettres, France; 2000 Gold Artistic Medal, Barcelona.
Bibliography Emma Dent Coad, *Spanish Design and Architecture*, London: Studio Vista, 1990. Guy Julier, *New Spanish Design*, London: Thames & Hudson, 1991. Robert Hughes, *Barcelona*, New York: Knopf, 1992. Cat., *André Ricard: diseño industrial*, Santander: Fundación Marcelino Botín, 2000.

Richard, Alain (1926–)

French designer; husband of Jacqueline Iribe.

Training To 1949 under René Gabriel, École Nationale Supérieure des Arts Décoratifs, Paris.
Biography 1950s, Richard lived in the Netherlands with Henri Salomson (a former collaborator of Le Corbusier); 1952, established a research firm to study furniture and had clients such as Orly airport, Crédit Agricole, Banque de France, and RATP (design of the Métro station at Auber); was a color consultant to architects and others and active as a designer in various fields such as lighting, furniture, and interior architecture; collaborated with designer André Monpoix (on a telephone booth in ABS on a metal stanchion, produced from 1967 for the Maison de la Culture of Grenoble); 1950s, designed furniture produced by Vecchione and by Meubles TV.
Bibliography Yolande Amic, *Intérieurs: le mobilier français, 1945–1964*, Paris: Regard/VIA, 1983: 100. Patrick Favardin, *Les décorateurs des années 50*, Paris: Norma, 2002: 272. Arlette Barré-Despond (ed.), *Dictionnaire international des arts appliqués et du design*, Paris: Regard, 1996.

Richardson, Henry Hobson (1838–1886)

American architect; born St. James Parish, La.; active Paris, New York, and Brookline, Mass.

Training 1856–59, Harvard University, Cambridge, Mass.; 1859, École des Beaux-Arts, Paris.

Biography 1858–65 in Paris, Richardson worked for architects Théodore Labrouste, the brother of Henri Labrouste, and Jacques-Ignace Hittorff; 1865, settled in New York and, 1866–67, collaborated with Emlyn Littel; 1867–78, was a partner of Charles D. Gambrill and, subsequently, began a practice of his own in New York. His clients primarily were from New England, the result of friendships established at Harvard. 1874, he moved to Brookline, Mass., retaining an office in New York. From his first commission (1866 Church of the Unity in Springfield, Mass.), he began designing site-specific furniture, much of it with an affinity to William Morris's. Mid-1870s, Richardson's style incorporated Romanesque and Byzantine forms, yet was characteristic of New England regionalism. He was a member, American Society of Arts and Crafts (one of the earliest Arts and Crafts groups in the US), Boston; from 1876, created masonry buildings that were free of historicism and highly sensitive to mass and surface textures. Major architecture included 1871 Winn Memorial Public Library (with his furniture reflecting E.W. Godwin's), Woburn, Mass.; 1876 Trinity Church (primarily in brick to reflect the adjacent Back Bay-area houses), Boston; 1881 Austin Hall, Harvard University; 1882 New York State Capitol, Albany, N.Y. He was proudest of 1883–88 Allegheny County Courthouse and Jail, Pittsburgh, and 1885–87 Marshall Field Wholesale Store, Chicago. His most lyrical structure is possibly 1885 John J. Glessner House at 1800 Prairie Avenue, Chicago, completed by Charles Allerton Coolidge of Shepley, Rutan, and Coolidge. (Coolidge had previously worked in Richardson's office.) Much of the furniture that Isaac Scott designed for Richardson's 1875 Glessner residence was moved to the 1885 Glessner residence.
Exhibitions Work subject of exhibitions, New York, Boston, and Cambridge, Mass., including 1980 *Buffalo Projects: H.H. Richardson*, Burchfield Center, Western New York Forum for American Art, Buffalo, N.Y.; 1988 exhibition, Minnesota and Iowa. Work included in 1982 exhibition, Fairfield County, Conn., (catalogs below).
Bibliography Henry-Russell Hitchcock, *The Architecture of H.H. Richardson and His Times*, New York: The Museum of Modern Art, 1936. Cat., Richard H. Randall, Jr., *The Furniture of H.H. Richardson*, Boston: Museum of Fine Arts, 1962. Cat., Lisa Phillips (intro.), *Shape and Environment: Furniture Designed by American Architects*, New York: Whitney Museum of American Art, 1982: 50–51. Cat., Paul Clifford Larson with Susan M. Brown (eds.), *The Spirit of H.H. Richardson on the Midland Prairies...*, Minneapolis: University of Minnesota Art Museum; Ames: Iowa State University, 1988. Doreen Bolger Burke et al., *In Pursuit of Beauty: Americans and the Aesthetic Movement*, New York: The Metropolitan Museum of Art/Rizzoli, 1986. Margaret Henderson Floyd, *Henry Hobson Richardson: A Genius for Architecture*, New York: Monacelli, 1998.

Richtr, Alois (1927–1995)

Czech mechanic and industrial designer.

Training In electrical mechanics, Bata plant, Zlín; in drafting; 1949–1954 under Zdenek Kovar, Vystudoval Střední Uměleckoprůmyslové Škole (secondary school of applied arts) in Zlín and when it moved to Uherské Hradiště.
Biography 1955, Richtr was an industrial designer at the Kovostav Ústí nad Orlicí plant, where he and others created several measuring instruments and new shapes of spinning looms. From 1959, Richtr was head of the artistic section of Elitex Liberec Research Centre in Brno. He designed the housing of the Arachne machine, and the housing of patented hydraulic/pneumatic jet looms (with inventor Vladimir Svaty), and industrial sewing machines by Minerva. Examples of his work are in the Národní Technické Muzeum, Prague.
Bibliography www.ntm.cz/ntext/ak-81-c.htm.

Rickert, Franz (1904–1991)

German silversmith and enameler; active Munich.

Training 1921–24, apprenticeship in Adolf von Mayrhofer's workshop; 1924–27, Staatsschule für angewandte Kunst; both Munich.
Biography From 1926, Rickert worked as a silversmith and, eventually, became one of the most important silversmiths/designers in Munich and an outstanding enameler; 1935–72, taught, Staatsschule (later Akademie) für angewandte Kunst, Munich; 1950s–60s, designed numerous religious objects.
Exhibitions Work variously shown at venues, including 1937 *Exposition Internationale des Arts et Techniques dans la Vie Moderne*, Paris; 1993 exhibition, Munich (catalog below).
Bibliography Annelies Krekel-Aalberse, *Art Nouveau and Art Déco Silver*, New York: Abrams, 1989. Cat., Florain Hufnagel (ed.), *Goldschmiede Silberschmiede, Drei Generationen von der Weimarer Zeit bis heute: In memoriam Franz Rickert*, Munich: Die Neue Sammlung, 1993.

Rideout, John G. (1898–1951)
> See van Doren, Harold L.

Rie, Lucie (b. Lucie Marie Gomperz 1902–1995)

Austrian ceramicist; born Vienna; active Austria and Britain.

Training 1922–26 under Michael Powolny, fine art, Kunstgewerbeschule, Vienna.
Biography She first became active in pottery with Michael Powolny; 1926–38, was a successful potter in her own studio in Vienna and active in the Neuer Werkbund Österreichs movement; 1938, settled in Britain and, 1939, in Albion Mews, London; 1945, re-opened her pottery and button-making workshop after wartime closure and handmade one-of-a-kind buttons to order; developed an extensive range of her own ceramic glazes in order to match customers' fabrics. From 1946, German potter Hans Coper joined Rie in the Albion Mews workshop. She became known for her sophisticated domestic ceramics, including late-1950s coffee services, and for her subtle green, yellow, and pastel-pink glazes, often employing cross-hatched sgraffito decoration and a rough white tin glaze applied to pots which were fired only once. To 1971, she taught, Camberwell School of Art, London.
Exhibitions/citations As a student, pots shown at 1923 exhibition, Palais Stoclet, Brussels. Work included in 1925 *Exposition Internationale des Arts Décoratifs et Industriels Modernes*, Paris; 1930 (4th) *Esposizione Triennale delle Arti Decorative e Industriali Moderne*, Monza; 1951 (9th) and 1954 (10th) editions of Triennale di Milano; 1959 (20th) *Ceramic International Exhibition*, The Metropolitan Museum of Art, New York; 1986 *Nine Potters*, Fischer Fine Art, London. 1949, exhibited for the first time, at Berkeley Gallery, London, and, 1950 and 1956, showed work with Coper. They showed together at Röhsska Konstslojdmuseet, Gothenburg, 1955; Boymans Van Beuningen Museum, Rotterdam, 1967; Gemeentemuseum, Arnhem; Museum für Künste und Gewerbe, Hamburg, 1971; Fischer Fine Art, London, 1984. Alone, work at Arts Council Gallery, London, 1967; Sainsbury Centre for Visual Arts, Norwich, 1981; Victoria and Albert Museum, London. Work subject of 1967 *Lucie Rie: A Retrospective Exhibition of Earthenware, Stoneware and Porcelain, 1926–1967* touring exhibition, organized by Arts Council, London; co-subject of 1997 *Lucie Rie and Hans Coper: Potters in Parallel*, Barbican Art Gallery, London; and others. Gold medal, 1935 *Exposition Universelle et Internationale de Bruxelles*; silver medal, Austrian pavilion, 1937 *Exposition Internationale des Arts et Techniques dans la Vie Moderne*, Paris. 1981, was made a Commander of the British Empire (CBE).
Bibliography Tony Birks, *Lucie Rie*, Dorset: Alphabooks, 1987. R. Craig Miller, *Modern Design 1880–1990*, New York: Abrams, 1990. Cat., *Collection Fina Gomez: 30 ans de céramique contemporaine*, Paris: Musée des Arts Décoratifs, 1991: 116. Tony Birks, *Lucie Rie*, Somerset: Marston House, 1995. Cat., Conrad Bodman, Margot Coatts and Nicky Shearman (eds.), *Lucie Rie and Hans Coper: Potters in Parallel*, London: Herbert/Barbican Art Gallery, 1997.

Riedel Glas; Tiroler Glashütte

Austrian glassware manufacturers.

Training 1947–50, chemistry, Innsbruck.
Biography The venerable Riedel glass dynasty began in the 17th century when Johann Christoph Riedel (1678–1744) became a sucessful glass merchant and traveled widely, opening the Bohemian-glass market to worldwide exportation. Second-generation Johann Carl Riedel (1701–1781) was a gilder and glasscutter in his own facility. 1756, third-generation glassmaster Johann Leopold Riedel (1726–1800) built a glass factory in Antoniwald in northern Bohemia and virtually founded the village there. Fourth-generation Anton Leopold Riedel (1761–1821) abruptly turned from the production of window panes to only luxury goods. By 1890, Josef Riedel the elder (1816–94), known as 'the glass king of Bohemia,' was employing over a thousand workers. Josef Riedel the younger (1862–1924) discovered that selen will dye glass a ruby-red color and other substances a variety of other hues. At his death, the plant was employing c. 3,200 people. Eighth-generation Walter Riedel (1895–1974) managed the Tiroler Glashütte from the second quarter of the 20th century. However, the Nazis confiscated the the firm, the property, and the family home. Claus Josef Riedel (Polaun, today Horni Polubny, Czech Republic, 1925–), having escaped capture by the US Army forces at

Lucie Rie. Bowl. 1953. Glazed porcelain, h. 3 3/4" x dia. 5 1/2" (9.5 x 14 cm). Mfr.: the designer, UK. Purchase Fund. MoMA.

the end of World War II, happened upon Daniel Swarovski, of the crystal family, who knew of the Riedel family, took him in, and paid for his study of chemistry at Universität Innsbruck 1947–50. 1956 with his father Walter who had returned from the USSR the year before, Claus Josef bought an abandoned glass factory in Kufstein and renamed it Claus Josef Riedel Tiroler Glashütte. The purchase was made with the assistance of the Swarovski family. With a foundation of first working for Richard Ginori at Cristalleria Nazionale in Naples, where he became technical director, Claus Josef applied previously learned techniques to the Holdfast range at the Tiroler Glashütte and collaborated with Michael Boehm to create the Calyx range. The Calyx featured faint mold lines as an intentional design feature. Even though he did not consider himself a designer, Riedel's 1958 Exquisit and Monaco models have been widely praised. 1969, a second factory was opened at Schneegattern, notable at the time for its upgraded production techniques. 1972, a crystal grinding shop was established in Matrei. Claus Josef also independently designed for Rosenthal. Riedel was the first to declare that the shape/size of a drinking glass will appreciably affect the taste of wine. By 1996, the firm was producing 3 1/2 million machine-made and 800,000 mouth-blown pieces, 79% exported.
Exhibitions/citations Work included in *Glass 1959* and 1979 *New Glass: A Worldwide Survey* exhibitions, both Corning Museum of Glass, Corning, N.Y.; 1983–84 exhibition, Philadelphia (catalog below). Awards: 1958 *Exposition Universelle et Internationale de Bruxelles* (*Expo '58*) (grand prize for Bruxelles service); 1959 (for Special Sizes range) and 1962 (for Burg and Bridge ranges) Österreichischer Staatspreis, Vienna; 1960 (12th) Triennale di Milano (medals for Tevevisionglas, Exquisit, and Monaco ranges); Deutscher Staatspreis (for candleholders), 1961 Handwerksmesse, Munich. 1958, received Claus Josef's first award; 1957 (11th) Triennale di Milano; and, subsequently, silver medal (for drinking glasses), 1960 (12th) edition; 1982 Bundespreis Produktdesign (for Genova range), Rat für Formgebung (German design council), Frankfurt.
Bibliography 'Moderne Klassiker, pt. 13: Geschirr, Besteck, Glas,' *Schöner Wohnen*, Feb. 1982: 183. Frederick Cooke, *Glass: Twentieth-Century Design*, New York: Dutton, 1986: 96. Cat., Kathryn B. Hiesinger and George H. Marcus III (eds.), *Design Since 1945*, Philadelphia: Philadelphia Museum of Art, 1983.

Riegel, Ernst (1871–1939)

German metalsmith; born Münnerstadt; active Munich, Darmstadt, and Cologne.

Training 1887–90 under silver chaser Otto Pabst, apprenticeship in Kempten, Allgäu; from 1890 under goldsmith Fritz von Miller, in Munich.
Biography 1900–06, Riegel worked as a silversmith in his own workshop in Munich, where he taught at the municipal craft school for goldsmithing; 1907, joined the Darmstadt artists' colony of the Grand Duke Louis IV of Hesse-Darmstadt, where he was one of 23 artists, of whom only Riegel and Theodor Wende were goldsmiths. Riegel produced various mounts for the grand duke's collection of nephrite and agate bowls; was interested in historic silversmithing techniques and ornamentation; designed numerous prize/awards cups that were covered with embossed and chased foliate scrolls and flowers, and other more modern objects with soldered spiral motifs and semiprecious stones; from 1912, was a professor, Städtische Werkschule, Cologne; from 1920, was the head of the goldsmithing workshop, Institute for Religious Art, Cologne.
Bibliography Cat., *Ein Dokument Deutscher Kunst*, vol. 4, Darmstadt: Die Künstler der Mathildenhöhe, 1977: 202–10. Annelies Krekel-Aalberse, *Art Nouveau and Art Déco Silver*, New York: Abrams, 1989.

Riemerschmid, Richard (1868–1957)

German architect and designer; born Munich.

Training 1888–90, painting, Akademie des bildungen Künste, Munich.
Biography Like a number of other painters at the end of the 19th century, Riemerschmid turned to the applied arts; 1896, designed his own house in Pasing, Bavaria; was an early follower of the Arts and Crafts movement in Germany. 1897, Riemerschmid, Hermann Obrist, Bruno Paul, Bernhard Pankok, and Peter Behrens followed the lead

Claus Joseph Riedel. Exquisit stemware (pieces from a service). 1958. Glass, tallest (brandy glass) 9 3/4" (24.8 cm), shortest (liqueur glass, not shown) 6 3/4 x dia. 2 3/16" (17.2 x 5.6 cm). Mfr.: Tiroler Glashütte, Claus Joseph Riedel, Austria. Philip Johnson Fund. MoMA.

of the Wiener Werkstätte and founded the Münchner Vereinigte Werkstätten für Kunst im Handwerk (Munich united workshops for art in handwork) to sell everyday objects by modern artists. c. 1899, Riemerschmid and his brother-in-law Karl Schmidt began to investigate inexpensive furniture design and production. Riemerschmid designed an 1898–99 armchair for his music room at 1899 art exhibition in Dresden and at 1900 Paris *Exposition* (a chair manufactured by Dunbar Furniture Manufacturing Corp., Ind., from 1950 through an agreement with the designer). 1904, he began to design furniture specifically for serial machine production; 1910s, developed a range of standardized furniture for batch production and designed the 1901 interior decorations for the Munich theater; 1903–05, taught at the art school in Nuremberg. 1907, Riemerschmid, Behrens, Mies van der Rohe, Walter Gropius, and others founded the Deutscher Werkbund. 1907–13, Riemerschmid was the architect of several artists' studios in Hellerau; 1913–24, served as the director, Kunstgewerbeschule, Munich, and, 1926–31, of Werkschulen, Cologne. His cutlery designs were produced by Bruckmann & Söhne in Heilbronn and Carl Weishaupt in Munich. He was a classicist in architecture, but his design œuvre ranged eclectically from Arts and Crafts furniture and Art Nouveau ceramics to machine-made objects showing simple proto-Bauhaus geometry. He is recognized as one of the most important German designers of the 20th century.
Exhibitions 1899 German art exhibition (music room), Dresden. 1905, furniture with Karl Schmidt was shown. 1900 *Exposition Universelle* (in A Room for an Art Collector), Paris; 1910 *Exposition Universelle et Internationale*, Brussels. Work subject of 1982 exhibition, Technische Universität München, Münchner Stadtmuseum, Munich, and Germanisches Nationalmuseum, Nuremburg (catalog below).
Bibliography Herwin Schaefer, *Nineteenth-Century Modern: The Functional Tradition in Victorian Design*, New York: Praeger, 1970: 188–89. Sonja Günther, *Interieurs um 1900: Bernhard Pankok, Bruno Paul und Richard Riemerschmid als Mitarbeiter der Vereinigten Werkstätten für Kunst im Handwerk*, Munich: W. Fink, 1971. Cat., Wilfried Nerdinger (ed.), *Richard Riemerschmid: Von Jugendstil zum Werkbund*, Munich: Stadtmuseum, 1982. Michaela Rammert-Götz, *Richard Riemerschmid, Möbel und Innenräume von 1895–1900*, Munich: Tuduv, 1987. Cat., Kathryn Bloom Hiesinger, *Art Nouveau in Munich*, Munich: Prestel, 1988: 107–47. Annelies Krekel-Aalberse, *Art Nouveau and Art Déco Silver*, New York: Abrams, 1989.

Richard Riemerschmid. Armchair. 1898–99. Oak and leather, 32 13/16 x 20 7/8 x 20 7/8" (83.3 x 53 x 53 cm). Mfr.: Münchner Vereinigte Werkstätten für Kunst im Handwerk, Germany. Joseph H. Heil Fund. MoMA.

Riera, Mireia (1943–)

Spanish designer; born Barcelona.

Training Industrial and interior design, Eina (Escola de Desseny i Art), Barcelona.
Biography Riera cofounded the Bd Ediciones de Diseño firm in Barcelona; has been a contributing designer of a number of its furniture and furnishings items, including c. 1974 Luminoso mirror, 1974/1988 Sevilla wicker-and-metal-rod armchair (with Pep Bonet and Cristian Cirici), 1985 Galante floor mirror, and 1995 Little Nemo bed.
Citations 1975 Delta d'Oro (Luminoso mirror), ADI/FAD (industrial-design and decorative-arts associations), Spain.

Rietveld, Gerrit Thomas (1888–1964)

Dutch architect and furnituremaker and designer; born Utrecht.

Training 1899–1906, apprenticeship in his father's cabinetmaking workshop in Utrecht; 1906–11, trained as an architectural draftsman.
Biography Rietveld was greatly influenced by Frank Lloyd Wright's portfolio *Ausgeführte Bauten und Entwürfe von Frank Lloyd Wright* (1910). 1911, Rietveld opened his own furniture-making business in Utrecht; from 1919, was associated with the De Stijl group (founded in 1917 and led by Theo van Doesburg) through his friendship with Robert van 't Hoff and van Doesburg, whom he had met in 1918. 1919, Rietveld established himself as an architect. c. 1928, he broke from De Stijl and turned to Nieuwe Zakelijkheid (or Nieuwe Bouwen, or an approach to Functionalism, whose concerns focused mainly on the organization of society rather than on architectonics, ideas active generally 1920–60). Also 1928, Rietveld was a cofounder of Congrès Internationaux d'Architecture Moderne (CIAM). The De Stijl association inspired him to pursue the design of furniture and lighting (chairs, sideboards, tables, a wheel barrow, and hanging and desk lamps). While his chairs, as examples, may appear to have ignored concerns about physical comfort, his work rather strove for well-being and the comfort of spirit. His architectural career began with 1924 Schröder house in Utrecht that he designed with Truus Schröder-Schräder, also a De Stijl member with whom he collaborated from 1921 until his death. Rietveld kept an office in the house and lived there full-time from 1958, when his wife died. Projects with Schröder and Schräder included the 1934 terrace of houses in the Erasmuslaan and 1936 Vreeburg Cinema, both in Utrecht. Subsequently, the 1930–40s was not a particularly productive period for Rietveld, even though he taught at several institutions in the Netherlands 1942–48. 1950–60s, he designed the Netherlands pavilion at 1954 Biennale di Venezia, 1954 sculpture pavilion in Sonsbeek Park in Arnheim, and 1963–72 Rijkmuseum Vincent van Gogh (with J. van Dillen and J. van Tricht) in Amsterdam. Possibly due to Cassina's reproduction from the 1980s, his best-known work is now the 1918 chair, inspired by his De Stijl association and exploring Piet Mondrian's color use. It became the Tood Blauuwe Stoel (red blue chair), when color was added in 1923. The chair has 13 wooden lentels, two arm rests, and flat back and seat. The interrelated lintels touch but do not intersect. Like the Futurists, Rietveld preferred houses with scaffolding around them. In the Tood Blauuwe Stoel, the 'scaffolding' holds the seat and back in place. And the back and seat, to be seen as an extendable spatial continuum, break with the strict orthogonal nature of the chair. One of his late-1920s chairs was literally made from scaffolding poles clamped together. Rietveld worked with cardboard from which he made models to develop his ideas, rather than sketching them on paper. Though his medium was chiefly wood, he also produced furniture in pierced metal and a 1927 diagonal bent tubular-steel chair. Along with the 1918 chair, his 1923 Berlin chair and end table and 1934 Zig-Zag chair have also become icons of 20th-century design. (Early 1920s, Marcel Breuer at the Bauhaus became inspired by Rietveld's furniture, which can be considered abstract sculptural objects with a practical function.) Gerard van de Groenekan, as an assistant to Rietveld, made the built-in Schröder house furniture. 1924, Rietveld turned over his furniture-making business to van de Groenekan, who was 20 year old. He handmade Rietveld furniture and lighting up to 1971, when he sold the furniture-production license to Cassina.
Exhibitions/citations Bent tubular-steel and wood easy chairs and tables included in a 1930 Paris exhibition. Work subject of 1983 exhibit (furniture), Centraal Museum, Utrecht; 1989 Rietveld-birth cente-

nary exhibition, touring Chicago, New York, and Dayton, Ohio; 1990–91 exhibition (Schröder house), touring the UK; 1993 retrospective, Centre Georges Pompidou, Paris. 1963, was elected honorary member, Bond van Nederlandse Architecten; 1964, granted an honorary degree, Technische Hochschule, Delft.
Bibliography Adolf Schenck, *Der Stuhl*, Stuttgart: Julius Hoffmann, 1928: 56. Theodore M. Brown, *The Works of Gerrit Rietveld, Architect*, Utrecht: A.W. Bruna, 1958. Daniele Baroni and Frits Bless, *The Furniture of Gerrit Thomas Rietveld*, Woodbury, N.Y.: Barron's, 1978 (translation of *I mobili di Gerrit Rietveld*, 1977). Barbie Campbell-Cole and Tim Benton (eds.), *Tubular Steel Furniture*, London: The Art Book Company, 1979: 30–31. Cat., *Rietveld als Meubelmaker, Wonen met Experimenten 1900–1924*, Utrecht: Centraal Museum, 1983. Marijke Küper and Ida van Lijl, *Gerrit Th. Rietveld: The Complete Works 1888–1964*, Utrecht: Centraal Museum, 1992. Peter Vöge, *The Complete Rietveld Furniture*, Rotterdam: 010, 1993. Tobi Tobias, 'Discussion of Architect Gerrit Thomas Rietveld's Zigzag Chair,' *Dance Ink*, spring 1994, vol. 5, no. 1: 26–27. Bertus Mulder and Ida van Zijl, *Rietveld Schröder House*, New York: Princeton Architectural Press, 1999. Paola Antonelli (ed.), *Objects of Design: The Museum of Modern Art*, New York: The Museum of Modern Art, 2003: 44–45.
> See Schröder-Schräder, Truus; van de Groenekan, Gerard A.

Rietveld, Wim (1924–1985)
Dutch designer; son of Gerrit Rietveld; active the Hague.

Training Apprenticeship in a furniture factory in Utrecht; from 1950, Koninklijke Academie voor Beeldende Kunsten, The Hague.
Biography Initially, Wim Rietveld was a product designer and later head of the drawing office in a factory for industrial weighting equipment; studied in The Hague and, subsequently, was invited by W.H. Gispen to work in Gispen's firm, where he designed furniture, including 1950s models such as 1950 no. 216 (later no. 1247) and no. 216 side and armchair in bent plywood and steel rods on rubber shocks (similar to Charles and Ray Eames models). Also 1954 Oase no. 1407 lounge chair and ottoman with upholstery, Bakelite arm rests, and steel rods, (with A.R. Cordemeyer in the Meubelen voor een Eenvoudig Interieur (Furniture for a simple interior) group. Due to a lack of materials and machinery after World War II, he was force to create solid and inexpensive designs, calling on simple, traditional materials; From 1960, concentrated on transportation design; taught, Koninklijke Academie, the Hague; and Technische Hochschule, Delft, where he was an associate professor of industrial design from 1973.
Citations Gold medal (for Meubelen voor een Eenvoudig Interieur), 1954 (10th) Triennale di Milano.
Bibliography Peter Vöge, *Bab Westerveld Stoelen, Nederlandse Ontwerpen 1945–1985*, Amsterdam; 1986.

Wim Rietveld. Oase no. 1407 chair. 1954. Steel sheet and steel rods, 30 5/16 x 21 5/8 x 18 1/2" (77 x 55 x 47 cm). Mfr.: Gispen, the Netherlands. Courtesy Quittenbaum Kunstauktionen, Munich.

Gerrit Rietveld. Tood Blauuwe Stoel (red blue chair). 1918/1923. Painted wood, 34 1/8 x 26 x 33" (86.7 x 66 x 83.8 cm), seat h. 13" (33 cm). Gift of Philip Johnson. MoMA.

Riffelmacher, Ludwig (1896–)
German metalworker.

Training Metalwork, Gewerbliche Fortbildungsschule, Nuremberg, under Josef Pöhlmann; Kunstgewerbeschule, Nuremberg.
Biography 1923, Riffelmacher worked with Otto Stüber in Hamburg and, 1924, with Karl August Weiss in Pforzheim; 1924–46, was director, workshop of H.J. Wilm in Berlin, where, under Riffelmacher's supervision, massive hand-raised pieces were produced with finely engraved ornament.
Bibliography Annelies Krekel-Aalberse, *Art Nouveau and Art Déco Silver*, New York: Abrams, 1989.

Rigot, Gérard (1929–)
French artist; active Gers region.

Biography Rigot, who worked in a *naïf* style, carved one-of-a-kind fragile painted furniture in animal and plant shapes, reminiscent of the paintings of Henri Rousseau and evoking, in his own words, 'the imaginary world of childhood.' 1990, he designed a children's playground in Britain.
Exhibitions Work shown at Musée des Arts Décoratifs, Paris, 1980.
Bibliography Martine Colombet, 'Gérard Rigot and His Bestiary,' *Vogue Décoration*, no. 26, June–July 1990: 134–37.

Riihimäen Lasi
Finnish glass factory.

History 1810, the factory was established for the production of domestic glassware; 1919, began making window glass; purchased various smaller factories, including one in Riihimäen, where the Suomen Lasimuseo (Finnish glass museum) is located today; 1928, sponsored a glass design competition won by Henry Ericsson; mid-1930s, was refitted and upgraded; 1933 and 1936, sponsored other competitions entered by Alvar Aalto, Gunnel Nyman, Arttu Brummer, and others; by late 1930s, had expanded into medical and technical glass; 1941, merged with the Kauklahti and Ryttylä glassworks; after

World War II, hired new designers, including Helena Tynell and Nanny Still; 1976, became fully automated and discontinued blown-glass production; subsequently, supplied over half of the bottles and jars in Finland used for food, drink, and technochemical products; 1985, was purchased by Ahlström and 1995, sold to Owens-Illinois.
Bibliography Jennifer Hawkins Opie, *Scandinavia: Ceramics and Glass in the Twentieth Century*, New York: Rizzoli, 1989.

Riley, Raymond (1958–)
American industrial designer.

Training To 1982, University of the Arts, Philadelphia.
Biography 1986, Riley settled in California; from 1988, worked in the IDg (Industrial Design Group) of Apple Computer, Cupertino, Cal., and designed 1989 Macintosh LC; 1990, managed the design of the Apple Jaguar project in the studio of Giorgetto Giugiaro in Turin, Italy. Riley also designed 1991–92 Jaguar-inspired products (Fridge and Telecaster) and, subsequently, was active in Newton MessagePad projects. He codesigned 1993–94 Pippin project by Bandai and, 1995, departed Apple and became director of research, design, and development of the Equipment Division of Nike, Beaverton, Ore.; has been a member, Industrial Designers Society of America (IDSA).
Citations 1993 award (for Macintosh Centris 610 computer), Industrie Forum Design (iF), Hanover.
Bibliography Paul Kunkel, *Apple Design: The World of the Apple Industrial Design Group*, New York: Graphis, 1997.

Rima
> See Rinaldi, Gastone (below).

Rinaldi, Gastone (1920–)
Italian furniture designer; born and active Padua.

Training Instituto Superiore Tecnico, Padua.
Biography 1948, Rinaldi began as a designer in his father's metal-furniture and products firm, Rima, in Padua; it was one of the first furniture firms established immediately after World War II. At Rima, Rinaldi first designed furniture for schools, hospitals, and offices and for a number of years with Gio Ponti. 1952, Rinaldi created the chairs with Marco Zanuso for Zanuso's Piccolo Teatro, Milan; designed 1958 Saturno sofa, 1959 CN71 armchair, 1976 Roller chair, and 1980 Zeta armchairs for public arenas, cinemas, and theaters. 1974, he founded the firm Thema in Limena, which produced his Aurora chair in metal netting and 1979 Daphne folding chair; became a member, Associazione per il Disegno Industriale (ADI).
Exhibitions/citations DU10 and DU11 chairs (with Gio Ponti) and DU9 (the first Italian chair with a rubber seat and woven- plastic-covered-metal) shown at 1951 (9th) Triennale di Milano; silver medal (DU41 chair), 1957 (11th) Triennale di Milano. Work shown at 1952 (30th) Arte ed Estetica Industriale fair, Milan; 1976 *Design Italiano negli Anni '50*, Centrokappa, Noviglio; 1979, 1983–84, and 1988 exhibtions, Milan, Philadephia, and Munich (catalog below); 1995 *Design Italiano '45–'63*, Triennale di Milano. Subject of 1993–94 exhibition, Veneto and Milan. Premio Compasso d'Oro: 1954 (DU30 rubber-and-metal chair by Rima; plastic-web garden chair by Rima), 1955 (DU67 folding chair by Rima), 1979 (Rigi bicycle frame by Rima; Aurora chair by Thema), 1981 (Dafne chair by Thema). Citations at editions of the Triennale di Milano.
Bibliography Ernst Erik Pfannschmidt, *Metallmöbel*, Stuttgart, 1962. Vittorio Gregotti, *Il design del prodotto industriale Italia 1860-1980*, Milan: Electa, 1980. Alfonso Grassi and Anty Pansera, *Atlante del design italiano 1940-1980*, Milan, Fabbri, 1980. Cat., Hans Wichmann, *Italien Design 1945 bis heute*, Munich: Die Neue Sammlung, 1988. Anty Pansera, *Il design del mobile italiano dal 1946 ad oggi*, Rome/Bari: Laterza, 1990. Anty Pansera, *Dizionario del design italiano*, Milan: Cantini, 1995. Mel Byars, *50 Chairs...*, Hove: RotoVision, 1996. Marco Romanelli, *Design nordest: Carlo Scarpa, Gastone Rinaldi, Fulvio Bianconi, Renata Bonfanti, Gino Valle*, Milan: Abitare Segesta, 1997. *Brevetti del design italiano 1945–1965*, Milan: Electa, 2000

Rindin, Vadim Feodorovich (1920–1974)
Russian stage and film designer.

Training 1920–22, VKhUTEMAS (higher artistic and technical studies), Voronezh; 1923–24 under V. Khrakovskii, VKhUTEMAS, Moscow.
Biography 1920–22, Rindin worked in the workshop of the stage set and publicity design at the municipal theater in Voronezh; 1924, became a member of Makovets, of Omkh, and of Akhr; 1935–53, was a leading set designer at State Academic Vakhtaganov Theater; and, 1953–74, designer at the Bolshoi Theater in Moscow; 1965–74, head of the department of stage design at College of Art in Moscow. Rindin was an award-winning artist of the Soviet Russian Socialist Federation and a member of Folk Artists of the Soviet Union, and of Soviet Academy of Art.
Exhibitions/citations Work included in a 1988 exhibition, Vienna (catalog below). Received State Prize of the Soviet Union.
Bibliography Cat., *Kunst und Revolution: Russische und Sowjetische Kunst 1910–1932*, Vienna: Österreichisches Museum für angewandte Kunst, 1988.

Rintaniemi, Päivi (1956–)
Finnish ceramicist.

Training To 1987, Taideteollinen korkeakoulu, Helsinki.
Biography Her work has included the design of utility ceramics, such as cups, vases, and candlesticks. From 1987 for almost a decade, she taught, Institute of Handicraft and Design, Jurva; 1994, established her own ceramics firm, Studio Amfora in Seinäjoki, where her husband Markku Rintaniemi assists. Her work is, in part, sold through Conran's shops worldwide and, notably, through the shops of others in Japan.
Exhibitions/citations Invited to participate in 1998 ceramics exhibition, Mino, Japan. Numerous others in Finland and abroad, including 1989 and 1991 Suomi Muotoilee (Finnish design); 1991 Concorso Internazionale della Ceramica d'Arte, Faenza; 1995 Pro Arte, Jyväskylä, Finland. Work chosen for 1994 Designer/Maker Award, Taidekäsityöläiset (TAIKO, association of Finnish Designers/Makers).

Risch, Hildegard (1903–)
German metalsmith; born Halle; active Halle and Cologne.

Training 1923, Kunsthandwerkerschule Burg Giebichenstein, Halle, under Karl Müller.
Biography 1927, Risch set up a workshop in Halle with her former fellow student Eva Mascher-Elsässer. 1928, she worked with architect and designer Fritz August Breuhaus de Groot in Düsseldorf; 1929–35 in addition to being associated with Mascher-Elsässer, worked with others; from 1935, continued the activities of the workshop alone, exclusively in jewelry.
Exhibitions Work subject of 1983 exhibition, Cologne (catalog below).

Jens Risom. Low lounge chair (no. 650). 1941. Maple and leather, 36 x 11 x 20" (91.4 x 27.9 x 50.8 cm). Mfr.: Knoll Associates, US (1946). Gift of the designer. MoMA.

Bibliography Annelies Krekel-Aalberse, *Art Nouveau and Art Déco Silver*, New York: Abrams, 1989. Cat., *Hildegard Risch: Eine Goldschmiedin der Moderne*, Cologne: Galerie Mattar, 1983.

Risom, Jens (1916–)

Danish furniture designer; born Copenhagen; active in the US.

Training To 1928, Krebs Skole; to 1932, St. Anne Vester School; to 1934, Niels Brock's Business School, University of Copenhagen; 1935–38, furniture and interior design, Kunståndvaerkerskolen; all Copenhagen.
Biography 1937–39, Risom was active as a furniture and interior designer in the office of architect Ernst Kuhn, Copenhagen; 1939, settled in the US; 1939–41, was the design director at Dan Cooper, New York, where he designed furniture, textiles, and interiors; from 1941, designed the interiors of the 1940 model home by architect Edward Durrell Stone sponsored by *Colliers* magazine in Rockefeller Center, New York. 1941, he met Hans Knoll and designed the first chairs by the HG Knoll firm including 1941-design side and lounge chairs and stool in natural wood with interwoven cloth straps or leather upholstery webbing (introduced 1942, patented 1945), together with a dozen other pieces. They became virtually the only modern furniture available in the US during World War II. These designs by Knoll reflected the scarcity of raw materials. 1941–43, Risom was a freelance designer of furniture, textiles, interiors, and industrial products for other clients, including Georg Jensen; during World War II, served in the US Army; 1946–70, was active in his own eponymous firm in New York, where he was the sole designer. Unlike other designers at Knoll and Herman Miller after World War II, Risom rejected metal and plywood-molded furniture in favor of solid wood, a Scandinavian predilection. From 1990s, versions of his 1940s cloth-strap and wood chairs were reissued by Knoll. 1970, he sold his company to Dictaphone Corp., acting as the CEO. 1971, after six months, Dictaphone Corp. sold the firm, and Risom resigned and established Design Control in New Canaan, Conn. 1970–76, he was a trustee, Rhode Island School of Design, Providence.
Bibliography *Mobilia*, special edition, Sept. 1960: 1–18. 'Jens Risom Design Inc.,' *Mobilia*, special edition, Oct. 1962. Nina Bremer on Risom, in *Contemporary Designers*, London: Macmillan, 1981: 512–13. Edward Larrabee and Massimo Vignelli, *Knoll Design*, New York: Abrams, 1981. Cherie Fehrman and Kenneth Fehrman, *Postwar Interior Design: 1945–1960*, New York: Van Nostrand Reinhold, 1987: 37, 38. Cat., Martin Eidelberg (ed.), *Design 1935–1965: What Modern Was*, New York: Musée des Arts Décoratifs/Abrams, 1991.
> See Knoll, Hans.

Rittweger, Otto (1904–1965)

German designer and metalworker; born Munich.

Training 1923–28, Bauhaus, Weimar and Dessau.
Biography 1930–31, Rittweger was artistic director of the lighting firm Goldschmidt & Schwabe, Berlin.
Exhibitions Work included 1988 and 1992 exhibitions, New York and Berlin (catalogs below).
Bibliography Cat., *The Bauhaus: Masters and Students*, New York: Barry Friedman, 1988. Annelies Krekel-Aalberse, *Art Nouveau and Art Déco Silver*, New York: Abrams, 1989. Cat., *Die Metallwerkstatt am Bauhaus*, Berlin: Bauhaus-Archiv, 1992: 252–57, 319.

Riva, Eleonore Peduzzi (1939–)

Italian architect and industrial designer.

Biography 1960, Riva first began to work in plastics, her first design being the 1969 Spyros ashtray in Melamine and subsequent lighting, such as the Vacuna, by Artemide; also created designs for lighting by FontanaArte, glass by Vistosi, and for floor coverings and textiles.
Exhibitions Work included in 1972 exhibition, Prague (catalog below).
Bibliography Cat., Milena Lamarová, *Design a Plastické Hmoty*, Prague: Uměleckoprůmyslové Muzeum, 1972: 150. Mario Giovene et al., *Italian Look*, Milan: Federazione Italiana delle Industrie del Legno del Sughero e dell'Arredamento, 1972.

Riva, Umberto (1928–)

Italian architect and designer; born and active Milan.

Training To 1959, diploma in architecture, Istituto Universitario di Architettura, Venice (IUAV).
Biography Riva was a painter before graduating from the IUAV; after

Eleanore Peduzzi Riva. Dish (no. S621). 1971. Glass, h. 3 7/8 x dia. 20 5/8" (9.8 x 52.4 cm). Mfr.: Vistosi, Italy. Gift of the mfr. MoMA.

the IUAV, established an architecture practice in Milan. 1982–93, he taught, Facoltà di Architettura, Università degli Studi, Palermo; 1987–98 periodically, IUAV; 1988, Istituto Europeo di Design, Milan; 1990, the seminary in Chavenna; 1993, Facoltà di Architettura, Politecnico, Milan; 1994, was the director of planning laboratory, École d'Architecture de Nancy, France; 2002, at Università degli Studi 'La Sapienza,' Rome. Main architecture: 1960 vacation house (with Fredi Drugman), Stintino; 1966 housing cooperative, Via Paravia, Milan; 1969 vacation house, Taino; 1997 school, Faedis; 1990–95 Miggiano house, Otranto; and town planning. Product-design work: 1980 Metafora, 1989 Franceschina, 1990 Gi-Gi, 1992 Filù lamps and 1987 Adanna table by FontanaArte; 1985 Veronese, 1985 Tesa, 1987 Attesa, 1989 Sospes lamps by Barovier & Toso; 1986 chair by Poltronova; 1988 U.R. 303 and 1994 U.R. 305 office-furniture systems by I.B. Office; 1989 Side table by Acierno; 1989 Marmo table by Bigelli Marmi; 1991 carpet by Driade; 1992 chair by Bellato; 1994 Victor desk and 1996 Ale sofa and table by Schopenauer/ FontanaArte; 1997 table by Montina.
Exhibitions Responsible for decorative and industrial arts section (with others), 1964 (13th) Triennale di Milano. Participated in a number of biennials throughout Europe. Work subject of 1997 *Umberto Riva: Muovendo dalla Pittura*, Associazione J. Vodoz e B. Danese, Milan (catalog below).
Bibliography *Belice: laboratori di Progettazione*, Milan: 16th Triennale di Milano, 1982. Paolo Deganello, 'Movimenti domestici,' *Lotus International*, no. 44, New York: Rizzoli, 1985: 109–27. Guido Canella and Maria Bottero, *Umberto Riva, album di disegni (1966–1987)*, Milan: Quaderni Lotus, 1989. Maria Bottero, 'Negozio a Padova,' *Domus*, no. 742, Oct. 1992: 50–55. *Umberto Riva*, Barcelona: Gili, 1993. Nicola Flora et al, *Umberto Riva, architetto & designer*, Naples: Clean, 1994. *Pioneers of Product Design*, Tokyo: Creo, 1994. *Umberto Riva: muovendo dalla pittura*, Milan: Associazione Jacqueline Vodoz e Bruno Danese, 1997. Mel Byars, *50 Lights...*, Hove: RotoVision, 1997. *Umberto Riva: Design Album*, Milan: Electa, 1998. Aldo Aymonino, 'Umberto Riva, azioni interstiziali,' *Lotus International*, no. 102, New York: Rizzoli, 1999: 70–71.

Rivier, Mireille (1959–)

French architect and designer; born Lyon.

Training Architecture, École Polytechnique Fédérale, Lausanne.
Biography Rivier moved to Rome, where she collaborated with Paolo Pallucco at Pallucco Design and designed the witty and culturally critical 1987 Tankette table (with Pallucco), a miniature tank complete with a movable, rotating steel tread.
Bibliography Albrecht Bangert and Karl Michael Armer, *80s Style: Designs of the Decade*, New York: Abbeville, 1990.

Rivière, Théodore Louis-Auguste (1857–1912)

French sculptor; born Toulouse.

Biography From 1890, Rivière lived in Tunis for three years and taught drawing at a seminary in Carthage. He returned with some of his figurines inspired by Gustave Flaubert's historical fantasy novel *Salammbô* (1862) and attained some measure of fame; 1894, became a member, Société des Artistes Français. 1895, his *Salammbô Chez Mathô* sculpture was bought by the French government. He was known both for large sculptures and public commissions as well as for miniature groups and figurines, some as lamps, in bronze, onyx, and ivory, such as *Le voeu*, *Charles VI et Odette*, *Phryné*, and in particular *Loïe Fuller*.

Paolo Rizzatto. Clac folding chair. c. 1998. Die-cast aluminum, tubular steel, and thermoplastic, open h. 29 1/8 x w. 19 5/8 x d. 20 1/2" (74 x 50 x 52 cm). Mfr.: Alias, Italy.

Exhibitions/citations Work was first shown at 1875 Paris salon. Received a gold medal, 1900 *Exposition Universelle*, Paris.
Bibliography Yvonne Brunhammer et al., *Art Nouveau Belgium, France*, Houston: Institute for the Arts, Rice University, 1976.

Rix, Felice (1893–1967); 'Kitty' Katharina Rix (1901–)

Austrian textile and fashion designers; sisters; born Vienna.

Training Felice Rix: under Oskar Strnad, A. von Stark, R. Rothansl, and Josef Hoffmann: Kunstgewerbeschule, Vienna.
Biography They became members of the Wiener Werkstätte, through which they designed textiles and ceramics and contributed to 1914–15 fashion folder *Die Mode* and 1916 folder *Das Leben einer Dame*. 1935, Felice Rix settled in Japan; 1949–63, was a professor, Kyoto College of Art, and member, Wiener Frauenkunst (women's art association) and Neuer Werkbund Österreichs.
Bibliography Günther Feuerstein, *Vienna—Present and Past: Arts and Crafts—Applied Art—Design*, Vienna: Jugend und Volk, 1976: 35, 81. Werner J. Schweiger, *Wiener Werkstätte: Kunst und Handwerk 1902–1932*, Vienna: Brandstaetter, 1982: 267. Deanna F. Cera (ed.), *Jewels of Fantasy: Costume Jewelry of the 20th Century*, New York: Abrams, 1992. Cat., *Expressive Keramik der Wiener Werkstätte 1917–1930*, Munich: Bayerische Vereinsbank, 1992: 132–33.

Rizzatto, Paolo (1941–)

Italian designer; born and active Milan.

Training 1965, diploma in architecture, Politecnico, Milan.
Biography While at the Politecnico, Rizzatto worked as a freelancer in architecture and design; 1969–77, designed lighting by Arteluce. 1978, Rizzatto, Riccardo Sarfatti and Sandra Severi, founded Luceplan, Milan and were joined by Alberto Meda in 1984. (Rizzatto, Sarfatti, and Severi had studied together at Politecnico, Milan.) Rizzatto's architecture has included the 1972 daycare center, Segrate, Milan; 1973 vacation house, Formentera, Baleari; 1974 residential addition, Feltre, Belluno; 1976 partial house, Bazzano, Bologna; 1985 double-family housing, Montesiro, Milan; 1986 home for the elderly, Galliate, Novara; 1997 factory and headquarters of Luceplan, Milan. He has been a guest lecturer in various institutions in the US, Italy, and Russia. 1985–87, he designed furniture by Busnelli, Molteni, Kartell, Cassina, Kartell, Alias, and Thonet and worked on architecture projects with Antonio Monestiroli; some with Alberto Meda by Luceplan, designed 1980 D7 table lamp (with S. Colbertaldo), 1984 Berenice table lamp, F3/3 Kit, 1986 Constanza table and floor lamps, 1987 Lola halogen fixture, and 1989 Titania hanging and floor lamps.
Exhibitions/citations Work included in numerous exhibitions worldwide. All Luceplan lamps with Meda, except 1981 citation, with Premio Compasso d'Oro awards: 1981 (D7 with Sergio Colbertaldo), 1987 (D12), 1989 (Lola), 1991 (Titania D17), 1994 (Metropoli and Bap systems), 1995 (Metropoli), 2001 (Fortebranccio and Star Led). Others, partially: 1988 and 1992 Forum Design, Cosmit, Milan; 1992 Design Plus (Titania D17), Ambiente fair, Frankfurt; 1994 Red Dot award, Design Zentrum Nordrhein Westfalen, Essen; 1994 European Community Design Prize, Amsterdam; 1996 award, Industrie Forum Design (iF), Hanover; 1999 and 2001 SWIALTO, Warsaw; 1999 Good Design award, Chicago Anthenaeum.
Bibliography Daniele Baroni, *L'oggetto lampada forme e funzione...*, Milan: Electa, 1981. *XII Compasso d'oro—ADI*, Milan: Electa, 1981. Giovanna Albera e Nicolas Monti, *Italian Modern*, New York: Rizzoli, 1989. Cat., *Techniques discrètes: le design mobilier en Italie, 1980–1990*, Rome: Istituto Nazionale per il Commercio Estero; Milan: Assarredo; Paris: Musée des Arts Décoratifs, 1991. Gabriele Lueg and Peter Pfeiffer, *Halogen*, Cologne: Novus, 1991. Fumiu Shimizu, *Pioneers of Product Design*, Tokyo: Creo, 1994. Stefano Casciani, *The Art Factory*, Milan: Abitare Segesta, 1996. Charlotte and Peter Fiell, *1000 Chairs*, Cologne: Taschen, 1997. Mel Byars with Arlette Barré Despond, *100 Designs/100 Years: A Celebration of the 20th Century*, Hove: RotoVision, 1999. Giuliana Gramigna and Paola Biondi, *Il design in Italia*, Turin: Allemandi, 1999. Mel Byars, *The Best Tables, Chairs, and Lights*, Hove: RotoVision, 2000. *Italia e Giappone, design come stile di vita*, Tokyo: Nihon Keizai Shinburn, 2001. Silvana Annichiarico, *Non sono una signora*, Milan: Triennale di Milano, 2001.

Robeck, Sylvia (1959–)

German designer; born Berlin.

Training 1971–81, graphic design; 1982–88, industrial design, Hochschule der Künste, Berlin.
Biography 1986, Robeck became an independent consultant designer of household appliances in Produkt Entwicklung Roericht, Ulm; has worked with Jörg Hundertpfund; 1988–89, taught, Hochschule der Künste, Berlin; from 1989, worked for Addison Design Consultants, London.
Exhibitions From 1985, work included in various exhibitions.
Bibliography Cat., Design Center Stuttgart, *Women in Design: Careers and Life Histories Since 1900*, Stuttgart: Haus der Wirtschaft, 1989: 156–59.

Robert, Émile (1860–1924)

French metalworker.

Training Apprenticeship in the family ironworks.
Biography Robert was one of the last to use the forge at his family's ironworks; is credited with having revived wrought iron for domestic and architectural metalware, including banisters, consoles, vase mounts, grilles, lighting fixtures, chandeliers, and architectural ironwork. His forms were primarily vegetal, somewhat intricate before 1900 but less ornate afterward. For petroleum lighting fixtures made from materials other than iron, he used Bigot's earthenware for the reservoirs and Laumonnerie for the glass shades.
Exhibitions From 1912, work shown at Salons of Société des Artistes Français.

Robertson, Alexander W. (1840–1925)

British ceramicist; active Chelsea, Mass.; San Francisco; and Alberhill, Cal.; father of Fred H. Robertson.

Biography 1853, Robertson settled in the US; 1866, established the Chelsea Keramic Art Works in Chelsea, Massachusetts; 1884, settled in California and experimented with local clays. After several unsuccessful attempts to set up an art pottery in San Francisco, he and Linna Irelan (1846–1938) founded the Roblin Art Pottery in 1898. Robertson potted and fired, and Irelan often decorated. Her specialty was modeling, with the liberal application of little mushrooms and lizards. Robertson's work was more severe and classical, often ornamented only with finely rendered feet or handles. He used only Californian raw materials. When the pottery was destroyed in the

1906 San Francisco earthquake, it was relocated in Los Angeles in 1906. The operation there continued to 1910, when it was again relocated, to Halcyon, Cal., a utopian Theosophist colony. 1912, Robertson was hired by James H. Hill, the president of Alberhill Coal and Clay, to experiment with local clays. 1914, Robertson's last year at Alberhill, he displayed the beginnings of his art range of pottery during a lawsuit between Alberhill and the State of California over a portion of the land that held clay deposits important to the pottery. As the only potter at Alberhill, his work remained its sole output. He was briefly a resident potter at Mission Inn, which was Frank Miller's guest house for early tourists to California and where Miller brought in potters and furniture makers.
Exhibitions Work shown at 1915–16 *Panama-California International Exposition*, San Diego.
Bibliography Paul Evans, in Timothy J. Andersen et al., *California Design 1910*, Salt Lake City: Peregrine Smith, 1980: 76–77, 125.

Robertson, Fred H. (1869–1952)

American ceramicist; born Massachusetts; active San Francisco and Los Angeles; son of Alexander W. Robertson.

Biography c. 1900, Fred Robertson joined his father at the Roblin Art Pottery in San Francisco. 1906 when Roblin relocated to Los Angeles, he joined the Los Angeles Pressed Brick Company. 1914, he developed successful luster and crystalline glazes, while producing other decorative techniques. But his output was limited; however, some of his pieces with thick, flowing-lava glazes were of a higher quality than those of his uncle Hugh C. Robertson of the Dedham Pottery in Massachusetts. Though Vase-Krafts was one of the first to introduce all-ceramic lamps with pottery bases, stems, and shades, Robertson was making similar models by 1914 with glass insets furnished by the Judson Studios. Early 1920s, he worked at the Claycraft Potteries, producers of architectural tiles, and where he was joined by his son George B. Robertson at Claycraft in c. 1925. 1934, Fred Robertson established the Robertson Pottery, active until his death.
Exhibitions/citations Gold medals at 1915 Panama-Pacific International Exposition, San Francisco, and at 1915–16 Panama-California Exposition, San Diego.
Bibliography Paul Evans, in Timothy J. Andersen et al., *California Design 1910*, Salt Lake City: Peregrine Smith, 1980: 77.

Robineau, Adelaide (b. Adelaide Alsop 1865–1929)

American ceramicist; born Middletown, Conn.

Training 1899 under William Merritt Chase, painting in New York.
Biography She became a well-known decorator and member of the National League of Mineral Painters; taught briefly at Saint Mary's in Minnesota; drew watercolors and painted miniatures on ivory. 1899, with her husband Samuel Robineau and George H. Clark, she bought the magazine *China Decorator* and began publishing the journal *Keramik Studio* from 1900. 1901, the Robineaus moved to the house Four Winds that they built in Syracuse, N.Y. She became influenced by Royal Copenhagen china at first and then by the sculptural work of the Bing & Grøndahl Porcelænsfabrik in Denmark and was interested in china painting and studio pottery. 1901, she produced her first pot in the studio of Charles Volkmar; was also influenced by French ceramicist Taxile Doat and published the seminal essay 'Grand Feu Ceramics' (1903); 1903, turned from china painting to making fine porcelain; 1910–11 under Doat, taught, University City Pottery, near St. Louis, Missouri, where she produced the legendary Scarab vase, said to have taken 1,000 hours to execute. 1920–28, she taught, Syracuse (N.Y.) University.
Exhibitions Watercolors shown at annual exhibitions of the National Academy, New York, and experimental slip-cast porcelains at the 1903 Arts and Crafts exhibition, Craftsman Building, Syracuse. Work with others was declared 'the finest porcelain in the world' at 1911 *Esposizione Internazionale dell'Industria e del Lavoro*, Turin, where the American Women's League from University City received a grand prize and Robineau (who showed her Scarab vase) was granted the Diploma della Benemerenza. Other work shown at 1904 *Louisiana Purchase Exposition*, St. Louis; crystalline glazes at Art Institute of Chicago, 1904; and 1911 Salon of Société des Artistes Décorateurs, Paris; Musée des Arts Décoratifs, Paris. Received a medal and prizes from Art Institute of Chicago and societies of Arts and Crafts in Boston and Detroit. Grand prize, 1915 *Panama-Pacific International Exposition*, San Francisco; honorary doctorate, Syracuse (N.Y.) University. Work subject of 1929 memorial exhibition, The Metropolitan Museum of Art, New York (catalog below).
Bibliography *High Fire Porcelains: Adelaide Alsop Robineau, Potter, Syracuse*, New York/San Francisco: Panama-Pacific International Exposition, 1915. Samuel Robineau, 'Adelaide Alsop Robineau,' *Design*, no. 30, Apr. 1929. Cat., Joseph Breck, *A Memorial Exhibition of Porcelain Stoneware by Adelaide Alsop Robineau, 1865–1929*, New York: The Metropolitan Museum of Art, 1929. Elaine Levine, 'Pioneers of Contemporary American Ceramics: Charles Binns, Adelaide Robineau,' *Ceramic Monthly*, no. 23, Nov. 1975: 22–27. Peg Weiss, *Adelaide Alsop Robineau: Glory in Porcelain*, Syracuse, N.Y.: Syracuse University/Everson Museum of Art, 1981. Garth Clark, *American Ceramics: 1876 to the Present*, New York: Abbeville, 1987: 293 et passim. *American Art Pottery*, New York: Cooper-Hewitt Museum, 1987.

Robj; Jean Born (d. 1922); Lucien Willemetz

French shop and manufacturer.

History 1908, Jean Born set up an enterprise in Paris to sell electrical igniters, that he patented in 1910. Eventually, he changed the name to the anagram of his name, Robj, used as a trademark. In association with Lucien Willemetz in 1920, he garnered a group of sculptors, designers, and *techniciens du feu* (ceramics firers), who designed and produced a number of light-hearted bibelots and utilitarian objects such as inkwells, ashtrays, lamps, small bottles, and tumblers. He subcontracted manufacture to Boulogne-sur-Mer, Limoges, Sèvres, and Villeroy & Boch. On Born's 1922 death in an automobile accident, Willemetz organized a competition to find a replacement partner. The designers were able to have a showcase for the exposure of their work. The wares were sold in a shop on the rue de Paradis. Much of the inventory, considered to be in questionable taste at the time, included porcelain Buddhas, native Americans, Japanese geishas, Dutch boys, and Mexican sombreros. 1927–31, Willemetz sponsored annual competitions in order to find new designers. Today, Villeroy & Boch is reproducing some Robj pieces.
Bibliography Alastair Duncan, *Art Nouveau and Art Déco Lighting*, New York: Simon & Schuster, 1978: 182. Vanna Brega, *Le Ceramiche Robj 1921–1931*, Milan: Leonardo Periodici, 1995.

Roblin Art Pottery
> See Robertson, Alexander W.

Robots

Italian furniture manufacturer; located Binasco.

History 1962, Robots was established in Binasco, headed by Antonio Rebolini. 1970, a department was set up within the firm to concentrate on the development of designs in metal. It was directed by Roberto Rebolini from 1995. Its 1971 collection of domestic furnishings was designed by architects Gian Casè and Enrico Panzeri. Bruno Munari (who designed for Robots from 1970) designed 1971 Abitacolo (bed/work/play/living structure), 1972 Biplano trolley, 1973 bookcase, 1974 Vademecum carrying structure, and 1975 Divanetta. Other work: architects Nani Prina and Enrico Panzeri's 1973 table and stool; Guido de Marco and Roberto Rebolini's 1974 domestic furnishings; Piero Polato's 1975 Portarobe; Rolando Strati's 1976 6 2 X multiple.
Exhibitions/citations Work included in 1972 *Italy: The New Domestic Landscape* (Abitacolo), The Museum of Modern Art, New York. 1979 (Abitacolo; Munari bookcase; Portarobe clothes-hanger unit by Piero Polato), 1981 (Biplano), 1987 (Pieghevole chair by de Marco and Rebolini), 1989 (Zen cassette holder by Bruna Rapisarda), 1991 (Scarpiera by Polato) Premio Compasso d'Oro. To Robots: gold medal, 1973 BIO 5 industrial-design biennial, Ljubljana.
Bibliography *ADI Annual 1976*, Milan: Associazione per il Disegno Industriale, 1976. Aldo Tanchis, *Bruno Munari...: From Futurism to Post-Industrial Design*, London: Lund Humphries, 1986/1987. *Air Made Visible: A Visual Reader on Bruno Munari*, Baden: Lars Müller, 1999.

Robsjohn-Gibbings, Terence Harold (1905–1976)

British interior and furniture designer; born London; active London and New York.

Training Architecture, University of Liverpool and London University.
Biography Robsjohn-Gibbings was briefly active as a naval architect, designing passenger ship interiors, and worked as the art director for a film company; 1936, worked for Charles of London, an antiques dealer (directed by the brother of art dealer Joseph Duveen), for clients such as Elizabeth Arden and Neiman Marcus department store. 1929, Charles Duveen sent Robsjohn-Gibbings to New York,

Terence Harold Robsjohn-Gibbings. Table lamp (no. 170). 1950. Metal and linen, h. 21 1/2" x dia. 17" (54.7 cm x 43.2 cm). Mfr.: Widdicomb Furniture Co., US. Gift of the manufacturer. MoMA.

where he sold British antiques for the firm. 1933, he returned to London and designed sets for a film company. He disliked the contemporary affinity for an 'indigestible mixture of Queen Anne, Georgian, and Spanish styles,' in his words, and, 1936, opened his own office in New York with a showroom at 515 Madison Avenue, and began to incorporate touches from his earlier studies of ancient Greek furniture; culling ideas from his own portfolio of hundreds of drawings, decorated his showroom with Greek models, mosaic-floor reproductions, and honed-down furnishings. Clients included Doris Duke, Mrs. Otto (Addie) Kahn, Thelma Chrysler Foy, and Walter Annenberg. He copied the 1939 amorphic glass and wood coffee table by Isamu Noguchi, designed originally for A. Conger Goodyear, president of The Museum of Modern Art; was devoted to historicist design and considered modern art a fraud, a view expressed in his book *Mona Lisa's Moustache: A Dissection of Modern Art* (New York: Knopf, 1947); also wrote *Good-bye, Mr. Chippendale* (New York: Knopf, 1944), a spoof on 20th-century interior decoration in the US, and *Homes of the Brave* (New York: Knopf, 1954). One of his most important projects was 1934–38 Casa Encantada, the house of Mrs. J.O. Weber in Bel Air, Cal. (purchased by Conrad Hilton in 1952 and David Murdoch in the early 1980s). 1942, he designed a shocking living room with pale-blue walls, fuchsia cushions, violet chairs, and a dark-gray sofa; likewise, his 1944 red-painted bamboo chairs were upholstered in a tropical-leaf printed fabric. However, his design ideas were widely emulated. From 1946, he designed mass-market range of furniture (more than 200 pieces) by Widdicomb Furniture Co. of Grand Rapids, Mich., the firm for which he worked to 1956. 1960, he met Greek cabinetmakers Susan and Eleftherios Saridis and created a line of classical Greek furniture, still in production by Saridis. The Klismos chairs and furniture, in the Saridis line, with striped linen cushions, were included in Robsjohn-Gibbings's interiors for the early-1960s apartment of Nicholas and Dolly Goulandris in Athens, where, 1964, he settled and became the designer to the Goulandrises and Aristotle Onassis; was effective in promoting modern furniture and interiors, although he rejected Bauhaus austerity and models. Influenced by Robsjohn-Gibbings's work, Charles Pfister's 1990 furniture collection by Baker was dedicated to Robsjohn-Gibbings, who died in Athens. From 1996, 11 Widdicomb pieces were reproduced by Michael Formica through Dennis Miller Associates in New York; the revived Widdicomb Company subsequently reissued 18 Gibbings pieces, through its Bexley-Heath division.
Citations 1950 Waters Award; 1962 Elsie De Wolfe Award (with Edward J. Wormley).
Bibliography T.H. Robsjohn-Gibbings and Carlton W. Pullin, *Furniture of Classical Greece*, New York: Knopf, 1963. Edmund White, 'America's Classical Modernist,' *House & Garden*, June 1991: 100–04, 156. Reed Benhamou's entry, *Contemporary Designers*, London: Macmillan, 1981: 516–17. Jeff Book, *Departures*, Mar.–Apr. 2000.

Roche, Pierre (1855–1922)

French sculptor, metalworker, and engraver; active Paris.

Biography Roche worked in ceramics and lead casting and executed several pieces inspired by the dancer Loïe Fuller and her swirling costumes. His works based on Fuller included sketches, statuettes, and a statue for the façade of Henry Sauvage's Théâtre de la Loïe Fuller at 1900 *Exposition Universelle*, Paris. Roche's architectural sculpture included an image of St. John for the basilica of Montmartre in Paris and comedy and tragedy medallions for the theater in Tulle.
Exhibitions Work shown at Musée Galliéra; Salons of Société des Artistes Décorateurs, regularly 1904–20; Salons of Société Nationale des Beaux-Arts; all Paris.
Bibliography Yvonne Brunhammer et al., *Art Nouveau Belgium, France*, Houston: Rice University, 1976.

Rochga, Rudolf (1875–1957)

German sculptor and silver designer; born Teterow; active Munich.

Biography 1903, Rochga designed silver hollow-ware by Bruckmann & Söhne in Heilbronn; was one of the first designers at the Münchner Vereinigten Werkstätten für Kunst im Handwerk, active in wall decoration and textiles; 1903–38, taught, Lehr und Versuchswerk, Stuttgart.
Exhibitions Work included in 1990 exhibition, Berlin (catalog below).
Bibliography Annelies Krekel-Aalberse, *Art Nouveau and Art Déco Silver*, New York: Abrams, 1989. Cat., *Metallkunst*, Berlin: Bröhan-Museum, 1990: 596.

Rodchenko, Aleksandr (1891–1956)

Russian painter, designer, and graphic, theater, and cinema artist; born St. Petersburg; husband of Varvara Stepanova.

Training 1911–14 under Nikolai Feshin and Georgii Medvedev, School of Fine Art, Kazan; 1914–16, Stroganof Institute of Industrial and Fine Arts (transferred into the Free State Artistic Workshops in 1918 and in 1920 into VKhUTEMAS/VKhUTEIN), Moscow.
Biography 1915, Rodchenko, Vladimir Tatlin, Kazimir Malevich, and other avant-garde Russian artists were the principal organizers of Constructivism in Moscow. Rodchenko was a practitioner of Malevich's Suprematism and, 1917, produced the series *Movement of Colored Plains with One Projected on the Other*; 1918, adopted Linearism; from 1918, worked at IZO NKP (fine-art department of Narkompros). With Olga Rozanova, he codirected the art-industrial subsection of IZO; was head of the purchasing committee for the Museum of Painterly Culture; from 1918, worked for the theater and, 1927–30, the cinema; 1918–26, taught, Proletcult (Proletarian Culture Organization in Moscow, an independent workers' cultural and educational organization); 1918–21, worked on 'spatial constructions'; 1919–20 was a member of Zhivskulptarkh (paint/sculpt/arch) with Vladimir Krinskii, Alexandr Shevchenko, and Liubov' Popova; 1920, became a member of INKhUK; 1920–30s, professor, VKhUTEMAS/VKhUTEIN; 1923–28, worked with *Lef* (left front) and *Novyi lef* (new left front), in which some of his photographs and articles appeared; 1927, worked on Lev Kuleshov's *Zhurnalistka* (journalist), one of several films on which he participated. c. 1920–29, Rodchenko specialized in topographic design and photography; became famous as one of the founders of artistic photography. Sympathetic to Tatlin's 'artist-engineer' approach, he began more practical pursuits, including 1920s design of furniture and clothing, working with his designer wife Varvara Stepanova and others. (He is known to have designed a teapot that may never have been produced.) Rodchenko was one of the organizers of the Russian pavilion at 1925 Paris *Exposition*, where his Workers' Club had all its strictly functional furniture painted black, red, and gray—all plain and utilitarian. 1930, he joined the October group; 1930–35, returned to studio painting; early 1940s, produced a series of Abstract Expressionist canvases. He died in Moscow.
Exhibitions Ten works were included in Tatlin's 1910 *The Store*, including six rendered with a compass and ruler. Other work was included in 1921 (3rd) *Obmokhu* and 1921 *5x5 = 25*, Moscow. Interior design and furnishings for a Workers' Club was shown in one of the galleries on the Esplanade des Invalides, 1925 *Exposition Internationale des Arts Décoratifs et Industriels Modernes*, Paris. Work subject of 1983 *Alexander Rodchenko*, organized by Benteler Galleries, touring the US; 1992 *Alexander Rodchenko: Photographs*, Gantry Arts Centre, Southampton, UK; in New York (catalog below) first (1998) comprehensive retrospective in the US, The Museum of Modern Art, New York; and a large number of international photographic venues.

Bibliography Selim O. Khan-Magomedov, *Rodchenko: The Complete Work*, Cambridge: MIT, 1987. S.O. Khan-Magomedov, *Vhutemas: Moscou, 1920–1930*, Paris: Regard, 1990: 428–34. Peter Noever (ed.), *Aleksandr M. Rodchenko, Varvara F. Stepanova: The Future Is Our Only Goal*, Munich: Prestel, 1991. Cat., *The Great Utopia: The Russian and Soviet Avant-Garde, 1915–1932*, New York: Guggenheim Museum, 1992. Pierre Gallissaires (ed.), *Alles ist Experiment: Der Künstler-Ingenieur/Alexander Rodtschenko*, Hamburg: Nautilus, 1993. Magdalena Dabrowski et al., *Aleksandr Rodchenko*, New York: The Museum of Modern Art, 1998.

Roerich, Nikolai (1874–1947)

Russian painter, theater artist, philosopher, writer, mystic, and ethnographer; born St. Petersburg.

Training 1893–97, St. Petersburg Academy of Arts; concurrently, law, St. Petersburg University.
Biography Roerich studied prehistoric societies; painted historical and Symbolist canvases, including landscapes and religious and mythological subjects; from 1901, was secretary, OPKh (society for the encouragement of the arts) and, 1906–18, director of its school in St. Petersburg; 1908–14, designed for Sergei Diaghilev's Ballets Russes; 1913, wrote the plot and created set and costumes for Igor Stravinsky's *Le sacre du printemps*; 1920–22, worked on exhibitions and art education projects in the US; 1923, settled in India; from 1938 to his death, was in charge of a research station in the Himalayas; during World War II, initiated the Roerich Pact for the protection of international cultural monuments; died in Kulu Valley, Punjab, India.
Exhibitions Work shown with V Mir Iskusstva (the world of art) group (of which he was the chairperson) from 1910; Union of Russian Artists from 1903; with numerous other groups; also one-person exhibitions in Russia and abroad.

Roericht, 'Nick' Hans (1932–)

German designer.

Training 1955–59, product design, Hochschule für Gestaltung, Ulm.
Biography 1959, Roericht's senior Ulm-school-diploma project for stacking dinnerware was widely published and, from 1961 as TC 100, produced by Thomas / Rosenthal. He has specialized in systems and environmental design; 1964, Hochschule für Gestaltung, and, 1967–68, industrial design, Ohio State University, Columbus, Ohio. 1967, he began designing for Lufthansa, including interiors, furnishings, graphics, and liveries; 1968, set up his own studio (Produkt Entwicklung Roericht) in Ulm; designed stadium seating and desk systems for official offices of the 1972 Olympiad in Munich. Within the studio, he and his staff have specialized in visual communication and research and developed products for clients, including Bosch-Siemens, Nixdorf, Toto / Tokyo, and Wilkahn (such as, for the latter, 1992 Picto chair range by Burkhard Schmitz and distinctive Sitz articulating stools). From 1973, taught industrial design to the new generation of those who have become accomplished, Hochschule der Künste, Berlin.
Citations 1976 (three awards for products by Röder Söhn) and 1986 (three awards for products by NCR Computers) Industrie Forum Design (iF), Hanover.
Bibliography Gillo Dorfles, *Il disegno industriale e la sua estetica*, Bologna, 1963: no. 97. Cat., Kathryn B. Hiesinger and George H. Marcus III (eds.), *Design Since 1945*, Philadelphia: Philadelphia Museum of Art, 1983.

Rogers, Ernesto Nathan (1909–1969)

Italian architect and teacher; born Gardone, Brescia.

Training Politecnico, Milan.
Biography 1932 with others, Rogers founded the architecture office BBPR; became well known as an architect and journal editor; 1933–36, was co-editor of *Quadrante*; 1946–47, was editor of *Domus*, in which he introduced the ideas of architectural Rationalism, and, 1952–64, of *Casabella-continuità*, which became one of Europe's most influential architecture journals. From 1962, he taught, Politecnico, Milan, and, 1964, became a professor there.
Bibliography Ernesto N. Rogers, *Esperienze dell'architettura*, Turin: Einaudi, 1958. Ernesto N. Rogers, *Editoriali di architettura*, Turin: Einaudi, 1968. C. de Seta (ed.), *Elementi del fenomeno architettonico*, Naples: Guida Editori, 1981. Cat., *Design Process: Olivetti 1903–1983*, Milan: Olivetti, 1983: 374.
> See BBPR.

Rogers, Ab
> See KRD (Kitchen Rogers Design).

Rogers, Mary (1929–)

British ceramicist; born Belper, Derbyshire.

Training 1945–47, part-time, Watford School of Design; 1947–49, calligraphy, St. Martin's School of Art, London; 1960–64, ceramics, Loughborough School of Art.
Biography For several years, Rogers first worked as a calligrapher and graphic designer; 1960–64, taught ceramics part-time, Loughborough School of Art; 1987–91, worked in her own studio in Loughborough, active there for most of her career; eventually, was active in her own studio near Falmouth, Cornwall; early on, produced large coiled stoneware pots inspired by nature; from early 1970s, threw small porcelain bowls in the natural shapes of flowers, twigs, leaves, and the like; subsequently, specialized in both delicate, small porcelain objects and larger stoneware pieces, again reflecting nature. 1990s, she retired from making ceramics.
Bibliography *Ceramics Review*, no. 59, Sept.-Oct. 1979.

Roggero, Francesco (1953–)

Italian designer; born and active Milan.

Training To 1970, Liceo Artistico di Brera; from 1970, architecture, Politecnico; both Milan.
Biography 1970, Roggero established the studio Designers 6R5 in Milan with a group that designed textiles and ceramics. 1975, Roggero, Maurizio Alberti, Giuseppe Bossi, Pierangelo Marucco, and Bruno Rossio established Original Designers 6R5 in Milan. Textile clients have included Bassetti, Griso-Jover, Lanerossi, Sasatex, and Taif; also tapestries by Griffine Marechal, Le Roi, Printeco, and Sirpi; and wallpaper for various French firms. Roggero became a member, Associazione per il Disegno Industriale (ADI).
Bibliography *ADI Annual 1976*, Milan: Associazione per il Disegno Industriale, 1976.

Rohde, Gilbert (1894–1944)

Prussian industrial designer; born New York.

Training Pre-1923, Art Students League, and Grand Central Galleries, both New York.
Biography 1923–27, Rohde was a freelance illustrator for department stores Abraham & Straus, W. & J. Sloane, and Macy & Co., all New York; 1927, traveled to Paris and Germany, where he was in-spired by the modern movement and studied French furniture; c. 1928, began to design furniture incorporating Bakelite and chrome; 1927–28, decorated the fashion stores of Avedon in Connecticut. 1928–29, his interior design and furnishings for the penthouse apartment of Norman Lee at 10 Sheridan Square, Greenwich Village, were widely published. 1930–31, he designed two lines of furniture for Heywood-Wakefield in Gardner, Mass., including a renowned bentwood chair that was later reworked for Herman Miller and Kroehler. By 1939, 250,000 copies of the chair had been sold. c. 1937, he designed showrooms for Heywood-Wakefield in Chicago, for Kroehler, and several for Herman Miller; and 1942 Executive Office Group (EOG) by Herman Miller. Other furniture clients included Brown-Saltzman, Lloyd, and Valley Upholstery. From 1932, Rohde designed prolifically for Herman Miller, as its design director to 1944, as well as 1932 tub chair by Thonet and much furniture in metal by Troy Sunshade, including a 1933 Z-silhouette chair/stool; lighting and consumer appliances, including a large number of electric clocks; lectured throughout the US; was a member, American Union of Decorative Artists and Craftsmen (AUDAC), and a prolific writer and lecturer on design; design committee member, 1939–40 *New York World's Fair: The World of Tomorrow*; 1939–43, head of industrial design, School of Architecture, New York University; died in New York.
Exhibitions Work was included in many early exhibitions, including 1932 *Design for the Machine*, Philadelphia Museum; 1933–34 *A Century of Progress International Exhibition*, Chicago, where his bedroom furniture for the Design for Living house was installed. Also in New York at 1934 *Machine Art*, The Museum of Modern Art; 1934 *Art and Industry Show* of National Alliance of Art and Industry, RCA Building; *Contemporary American Industrial Art: 1940*, The Metropolitan Museum of Art; 1939–40 *New York World's Fair: The World of Tomorrow*; 1935 *Contemporary American Industrial Art, 1934* (music room), The Metropolitan Museum of Art; others.
Bibliography Sales cat., *20th Century Modern Furniture Designed by*

Gilbert Rohde. Side chair. c. 1938. Stainless steel and Plexiglas, 31 1/2 x 17 1/2 x 21" (80 x 44.4 x 53.3 cm). Gift of the Gansevoort Gallery, Jeffrey P. Klein Purchase Fund, and John C. Waddell Purchase Fund. MoMA.

Gilbert Rohde, Zeeland, Mich.: Herman Miller, 1934. Derek Ostergard and David A. Hanks, 'Gilbert Rohde and the Evolution of Modern Design, 1927–1941,' *Arts Magazine*, Oct. 1981: 98–107. Cat., David A. Hanks and Derek Ostergard, *Gilbert Rohde*, New York: Washburn Gallery, 1981. Phyllis Ross, 'Modular Meets Industry: Gilbert Rohde's Designs for Unit Furniture,' master's-degree thesis, New York: Cooper-Hewitt Museum/Parsons School of Design, 1993. Leslie S. Piña, *Herman Miller 1939 Catalog: Gilbert Rohde Modern Furniture Design with Value Guide*, Atglen, Pa.: Schiffer, 1998. Leslie S. Piña, *Herman Miller: Interior Views*, Atglen, Pa.: Schiffer, 1998. Leslie S. Piña, *Herman Miller 1940 Catalog and Supplement: Gilbert Rohde Modern Furniture Design*, Atglen, Pa.: Schiffer, 1999. Cat., J. Stewart Johnson, *American Modern, 1925–1940...*, New York: Abrams, 2000.
> See Herman Miller Furniture Company; DePree, Dirk Jan.

Rohde, Johan (1856–1935)

Danish architect, sculptor, metalworker, and textile and furniture designer.

Training In medicine; 1881–82, painting and graphics, Det Kongelige Danske Kunstakademi, Copenhagen.
Biography 1882, Rohde founded the Kunstnernes Studieskole, where he taught anatomy, and, 1908–12, was the head; designed silver for his own use, made by Georg Jensen Sølvsmedie in 1905; created his first (1906) quantity-produced silver objects by Jensen, where he worked from 1913 and eventually became one of the firm's most prolific designers. Many Jensen examples are still in production today. A Jensen best-seller, 1915 Konge (acorn), was later plagiarized by International Silver Company. Rohde's 1920 streamline pitcher was so advanced that Jensen waited five years before putting it into production. Rohde also designed textiles and furniture by others and silverware by A. Dragsted.
Exhibitions/citations Work subject of exhibitions, including at Det Danske Kunstindustrimuseum, Copenhagen, 1908, and in Stockholm, 1917. Work included in exhibitions in Berlin, 1891; 1893 *World's Columbian Exposition*, Chicago; in Århus, 1909; in Brooklyn, N.Y., 1927; in Helsinki, 1928 and 1931. Received bronze medal, 1900 *Exposition Universelle*, Paris; grand prize, 1925 *Exposition Internationale des Arts Décoratifs et Industriels Modernes*, Paris.
Bibliography Sigurd Schultz, *Johan Rohde, solv.*, Copenhagen: Fischer, 1951. Cat., *Georg Jensen Silversmithy: 77 Artists, 75 Years*, Washington: Smithsonian, 1980. Cat., David Revere McFadden (ed.), *Scandinavian Modern Design 1880–1980*, New York: Abrams, 1982. Annelies Krekel-Aalberse, *Art Nouveau and Art Déco Silver*, New York: Abrams, 1989.

Rohlfs, Charles (1853–1936)

American furniture designer and craftsman; active Buffalo, N.Y.

Biography Rohlfs became involved with furnituremaking when he produced furniture mostly for himself and friends, in his attic studio in Buffalo. His list of clients expanded to include Marshall Field department store in Chicago and individuals in Buffalo, Philadelphia, Paris, London, and Bremen. By 1898, he had expanded into commercial quarters in Buffalo and was making entire rooms of furniture for wealthy clients in other parts of the US. His simple constructions and respect for materials associated him with the Arts and Crafts movement. To distinguish his furniture from that of the Stickleys and the simple Mission style, he incorporated ornate surfaces and carving, used exaggerated proportions, and incorporated elements of medieval, Moorish, Art Nouveau, and early Norwegian styles, with a distinctly Gothic, if not peculiar, appearance.
Exhibitions Work shown at 1901 *Pan-American Exposition*, Buffalo; 1902 *Esposizione Internazionale d'Arte Decorativa Moderna*, Turin; 1904 *Louisiana Purchase Exposition*, St. Louis; 1987–88 American Arts and Crafts touring exhibition, organized by Museum of Fine Arts, Boston (catalog below).
Bibliography Cat., Wendy Kaplan, (ed.), *'The Art That Is Life': The Arts and Crafts Movement in America, 1875–1920*, Boston: Museum of Fine Arts, 1987. Michael L. James., *Drama in Design: The Life and Craft of Charles Rohlfs*, Buffalo, N.Y.: Burchfield Art Center/Buffalo State College Foundation, 1994.

Rolff, Henrik (1944–)

Danish architect and furniture designer; born Copenhagen.

Training To 1964 under Jørgen Wolff, furniture construction Jørgen Wolff, Hellerup; to 1968, furniture design, Kunsthåndværkerskolen, Copenhagen.
Biography 1968, Rolff worked at architects Krohn & Hartvig Rasmussen on the Hvidovre Hospital, and, from 1972 on the branches of the Handelsbankens (bank of commerce; architect, Ole Hagen); 1976, was employed by Magasin du Nord on a self-service/special furniture and equipment project; 1978 with Leif Erik Rasmussen (with whom Rolff worked at Krohn & Hartvig Rasmussen and Ole Hagen), set up an architecture/design office and has designed furniture by Fritz Hansen and by Bent Krogh.
Bibliography Frederik Sieck, *Nutidig Dansk Møbeldesign – en kortfattet illustreret beskrivelse*, Copenhagen: Bondo Gravesen, 1990.

Roller, Alfred (1864–1935)

Moravian set designer; born Brünn (now Brno, Czech Republic).

Training Architecture and painting, Akademie der bildenden Künste, Vienna.
Biography 1897, Roller was a cofounder and, 1902, president of the Wiener Sezession; from 1899, was professor and, from 1909, director, Kunstgewerbeschule, Vienna. 1903, composer Gustave Mahler (1860–1911) brought Roller to the Wiener Staatsoper (state opera house in Vienna), where Roller was responsible for the costumes and sets to 1909. Mahler was sympathetic with his concept of scenic design as a *Gesamtkunstwerk* (total work of art), in which lighting, color, and space were married to the music, words, and acting, as a cohesive piece. After 1909, Roller designed for a number of other theaters, including the Burgtheater; after a hiatus, returned to opera productions in 1918, working with director Franz Schalk (1863–1931) and composer Richard Strauss (1864–1949). Roller designed the sets and costumes for all the débuts of Strauss's operas in Vienna and also worked with producer/director Max Reinhardt (1873–1943); from its 1929 founding, taught, Max-Reinhardt-Seminar drama school (now part of Universität für Musik und Darstellende Kunst), Vienna. Early on, as an active member of the Wiener Sezession and Ver Sacrum

group, he created a number of now-legendary posters and journal covers that featured bold, condensed lettering. Roller died in Vienna.
Bibliography *Die Fläche: entwürfe für decorative Malerei, Placate, Buch und Druckausstellung...* (12 parts, 16 plates each, issued periodically), Vienna: Anton Schroll, 1901–02. Max Mell, *Alfred Roller*, Vienna: Wiener Literarische Anstalt, 1922. Evanthia Greisenegger, *Alfred Roller und seine Zeit*, Vienna: Böhlau, 1991. Manfred Wagner, *Alfred Roller in seiner Zeit*, Salzburg: Residenz, 1996.

Rollin, Lucien (1906–1993)
French designer.

Training From 1919 (at age 13), École Boulle, Paris.
Biography Following the École Boulle, Rollin worked in the studio of Jacques-Émile Ruhlmann; returned to the École Boulle, while he worked in the office of architect Michel Roux-Spitz; 1928, set up his own studio, taking on an eclectic range of influences, from the work of Ruhlmann and Frank Lloyd Wright to classical Greek and Louis XVI styles; was a prolific designer of Art Moderne furniture, active primarily from 1933–46. 2001, Allan Switzer, the vice-president and design director of William Switzer & Associates in Vancouver, Canada, issued a 2001 collection of Rollin-designed furniture, in exotic woods, never previously produced.
Exhibitions Participated in Ruhlmann's Hôtel du Collectionneur pavilion 1925 *Exposition Internationale des Arts Décoratifs et Industriels Modernes*, Paris. Work included in: Salons of Société des Artistes Décorateurs from 1928; French pavilion (a bedroom) at 1939–40 *New York World's Fair: The World of Tomorrow*; 1997 *Trente/Quarante: Furniture, Carpets, Lighting of the 1930s and 1940s*, Barry Friedman Gallery, New York; 2002 award (to Switzer for Rollin furniture collection), NeoCon, Chicago.
Bibliography Yvonne Brunhammer and Suzanne Tice, *French Decorative Art: The Société des Artistes Décorateurs*, Paris: Flammarion, 1990. Cat., Sophie Tasma Anargyros et al., *L'école française: les créateurs de meubles du 20ème siècle*, Paris: Industries Françaises de l'Ameublement, 2000.

Romanelli, Marco (1958–)
Italian designer and journalist, born Trieste.

Training 1983, architecture degree, Università degli Studi, Genoa; 1984, master's degree in design, Domus Academy, Milan.
Biography Activities in Milan: 1984–85, Romanelli worked in the architecture/design studio of Mario Bellini; 1986–94, was the design editor, *Domus* magazine; 1987, set up his own design studio and designed furniture, in part with Marta Laudani; from 1995, has been the design editor, *Abitare* magazine; 1992–2000, was the president, Jacqueline Associazione/J. Vodoz e B. Danese; 1994–96, the artistic director, Arlantide collection; from 1995, the artistic director, O luce; from 1996, the artistic director, Montina; from the first (1988 Trame table by Arflex to 2002 Mediterraneo tea/coffee service by Driade), most with Laudani, has designed a large amount of furniture, textiles, and lighting for other clients, including Bosa, Driade, Etno Logic Zeus, Ex-Novo, Ferlea, FontanaArte, La Palma, Montina, Seccose, Tessilart Scipioni, Up & Up, View, and Virtually Design.
Bibliography Mauro Baracco, 'New Directions in Contemporary Italian Architecture,' *Transition*, no. 40, 1993. Pino Scaglione, *Architettura contemporanea: un confronto tra generazioni*, Avenzzano: Ed'A, 1993. 'Dall' architettura degli interni al design. Le opere di Marta Laudani e Marco Romanelli,' *Costruttori Romani*, Nov.–Dec. 1996: 84. Claudia Neumann, *Design Directory Italy*, London: Pavilion, 1999. Cat., Enzo Biffi Gentili, *Il disegno ceramico: Gagnère, Laudani, Romanelli, Szekely*, Milan: Electa, 1999.
> See Laudani, Marta.

Romani, Giorgio (1946–1980)
Italian industrial designer; born and active Milan.

Training To 1968, architecture, Politecnico, Milan.
Biography 1968, Romani began his industrial design activities, in association with Riccardo Nava, Duccio Soffientini, and Alessandro Ubertazzi in the studio DA in Milan and, from 1970, collaborated with DA on traditional clocks and electronic equipment by Italora and was a consultant on clock-design application and the ergonomics of precision instruments. 1975, Romani and others of DA designed sailboat fittings by Nemo and Comar. Other clients included Sordelli, Superband, and Svaba. He became a member, Associazione per il Disegno Industriale (ADI).
Bibliography *ADI Annual 1976*, Milan: Associazione per il Disegno Industriale, 1976.
> See Ubertazzi, Alessandro.

Romanoff, Maya (1941–)
American textile designer.

Training University of California at Berkeley.
Biography With his wife Rebecca, Romanoff experimented with resist-dyeing, first employing the results in clothing and in furnishings later, and developed the process for mass production. 1970s, he introduced 'textile environments,' for which one-of-a-kind commissioned pieces, coordinated wall and floor coverings, and upholstery textiles were produced. The first was 1971 Garden Room, for the American magazine *House & Garden*; the installation included a resist-dyed canvas floor covering, a concept he further developed and introduced to the trade in 1976. He developed methods for the resist-dyeing of suede and leather. Claims are that he was the first to use quilting in domestic furnishings (however, Gaetano Pesce used quilting in 1975 Sit Down armchair by Cassina).
Citations 1976 Resources Council award (resist-dyed canvas floor covering).
Bibliography *Maya Romanoff: Fabric Impressionist*, New York: The Arsenal, 1979. Cat., Kathryn B. Hiesinger and George H. Marcus III (eds.), *Design Since 1945*, Philadelphia: Philadelphia Museum of Art, 1983: 228, VII-52.

Rombaux, Égide (1865–1942)
Belgian sculptor and medallist; active Brussels.

Training Under Charles van der Stappen and Joseph Lambeaux, in sculpture.
Biography Rombaux worked mainly in ivory, producing portrait busts, statues, and candelabra. Through his collaboration with silversmith Franz Hoosemans, Rombaux's table lamps and candelabra are distinctive. He is best known for the decoration of the Grand Palais, with chief architect Joseph Van Neck (1880–1959) at 1935 *Exposition Universelle et Internationale de Bruxelles*. The Prix Égide Rombaux was established by the Académie Royale, Belgium.
Exhibitions *Venusberg* ivory group was shown at 1897 chryselephantine exhibition at Musée Royal de l'Afrique Centrale, Tervueren. Work subject of 2003 *Studio Égide Rombaux: Bequest Valentine Bender*, Musées royaux des Beaux-Arts de Belgique, Brussels.
Bibliography Alastair Duncan, *Art Nouveau and Art Déco Lighting*, New York: Simon & Schuster, 1978: 51.

Ronchi, Domenico (1933–)
Italian architect and designer; born and active Milan.

Training To 1963, architecture, Politecnico, Milan.
Biography 1963, Ronchi became associated with the group CP & PR, active in design, architecture, and town planning; from 1964, worked at Albo; 1963–69, was an assistant professor of elementary construction; from 1964, worked on interior-design magazines published by Mondadori; designed furniture, shelving systems, ceramics, and lighting; became a member, Associazione per il Disegno Industriale (ADI). Clients included Carrara & Matta, FontanaArte, G. Pozzi, Ideal Standard, Salvarani, and Trigano Italiana.
Bibliography *ADI Annual 1976*, Milan: Associazione per il Disegno Industriale, 1976.

Rookwood Pottery
American ceramics manufacturer; located Cincinnati, Ohio.

History 1874, Maria Longworth Nichols (1849–1932) attended the first china painting classes at University of Cincinnati School of Design, along with Maria Eggers. 1879, there was competition between Nichols and M. Louise McLaughlin when the latter established the Cincinnati Pottery Club; both had worked for Frederick Dallas at his commercial pottery in Cincinnati and experimented with china painting. 1880, Nichols established Rookwood Pottery, an event marking the end of the Cincinnati women's art movement and the beginning of art pottery in the US. 1880, she hired Joseph Bailey Jr. as the superintendent and, 1881, Joseph Bailey Sr. as the artistic director. 1881–83, with instructors Clara Chipman Newton and Laura Fry, she operated the Rookwood School for Pottery Decoration. China painters working at Rookwood included Fry, Newton, and Lorinda Epply, 1904–48; William Henschel,

Rosenthal: Tapio Wirkkala. Composition cutlery. 1963. Stainless steel, longest (cake server) 8 1/2" (21.6 cm), shortest (dessert spoon) 5 1/4" (13.3 cm). Mfr.: Rosenthal, Germany. Given anonymously. MoMA.

1907–39; Albert R. Valentien, from 1881; Matthew A. Daly, from 1884; William P. McDonald, from 1884; Kataro Shirayamadani, from 1887; and William Watts Taylor, from 1883 as the manager. The enterprise became a viable financial operation; 1891, was turned over to Taylor. Rookwood's painters also included Sara Sax, in 1910s–1920s; Elizabeth F. McDermott and Edward T. Hurley, in 1900s–1940s; and Charles J. McLaughlin, in 1910s. To 1930s, Rookwood produced artistic ceramics and mass-production pieces in high-glaze and matt finishes; 1960, moved to Starkville, Miss., where a few pieces were produced to 1966. 1982, Arthur J. Townley of Michigan Center, Mich., purchased the remains of the company; 1984, began producing a limited range of ceramic novelties such as paperweights, advertising signs, and bookends with the original master molds.
Exhibitions/citations Rookwood's full range shown at 1893 *World's Columbian Exposition*, Chicago. Work subject of 1980 *Ode to Nature: Flowers and Landscapes of the Rookwood Pottery*, and 1983 *Toward the Modern Style: Rookwood Pottery, the Later Years, 1915–1950*, both Jordan-Volpe Gallery, New York (catalog below). Pieces by Valentien and Shirayamadani received a gold medal, 1889 *Exposition Universelle*, Paris. Honors to Rookwood: 1900 *Exposition Universelle*, Paris (grand prize); 1901 *Pan-American Exposition*, Buffalo (gold medal); 1902 *Esposizione Internazionale d'Arte Decorativa Moderna*, Turin (diploma of honor); 1904 *Louisiana Purchase Exposition*, St. Louis (grand prize); 1907 *Jamestown Tercentennial Exhibition*, Hampton Roads, Va. (gold medal); 1909 *Alaska-Yukon Pacific Exposition*, Seattle (grand prize). William Watts Taylor was elected Chevalier of the Légion d'Honneur.
Bibliography Herbert Peck, *The Book of Rookwood Pottery*, New York: Crown, 1968. Paul Evans, *Art Pottery of the United States: An Encyclopedia of Producers and Their Marks*, New York: Scribner, 1974: 255–60. Virginia Raymond Cummins, *Rookwood Pottery Potpourri*, Silver Spring, Md.: Cliff R. Leonard and Duke Coleman, 1980. Cat., Kenneth R. Trapp, *Toward the Modern Style: Rookwood Pottery, the Later Years, 1915–1950*, New York: Jordan-Volpe Gallery, 1983. *American Art Pottery*, New York: Cooper-Hewitt Museum, 1987. Nancy Elizabeth Owen, *Rookwood and the Industry of Art: Women, Culture, and Commerce, 1880–1913*, Athens: Ohio University, 2001.

Roqueta i Matías, 'Santi' Santiago (1944–)
Spanish designer; born Barcelona.

Training To 1991, doctoral degree, Departament d'Expressió Gràfica Arquitectònica, Escola Tècnica Superior d'Arquitectura de Barcelona (ETSAB); Catedràtic d'Universitat, Barcelona.
Biography Roqueta is a professor, school of architecture of ETSAB, and teacher, Elisava (Escola Superior de Disseny), Eina (Escola de Desseny i Art), and Llotja Escola Superior d'Arts Plàstiqes i Disseny; all Barcelona; and holds a number of other pedagogical positions. He has designed for Contacto, Mobles 114, Modulo, Santa & Cole, and Tecmo; is the director (with Jordi Miralbell) of the collections Snark and Clásicos del Diseño (by his firm, of works by Gerrit Rietveld, Giacomo Balla, Josef Hoffmann, Salvador Dalí, others), which were incorporated into Santa & Cole from 1987–88. Roqueta is also an accomplished watercolor artist. Extensive Barcelona architecture includes 1970 Ponsà, 1975 Massana, and 1985 Els Balcons restaurants; 1984 Teatre Malic; 1985 Snooker Club Barcelona; 1986 Galeria Ciento; 1998–99 BTV (Barcelona Televisió); and a number of reconstructions.
Citations 1985 FAD d'Interiorisme (Snooker Club interior); 1985 Delta de Plata (Vallvidrera armchair), ADI/FAD (industrial designa dn decorative arts association), Spain; 1992 prize, Universitat Politecnica de Catalunya, Barcelona; others.

Rorimer, Louis (1872–1939)
American designer; born Cleveland, Ohio.

Training Manual Training School, Cleveland; Kunstgewerbeschule, Munich; École des Arts Décoratifs, and Académie Julien, both Paris.
Biography Rorimer was variously active as an artist, teacher, and president of the Rorimer Brooks Studios; became well known and created a number of interior-design schemes, including in residences throughout the US and for the Statler hotel chain; was a member of the US government commission to visit 1925 *Exposition Internationale des Arts Décoratifs et Industriels Modernes*, Paris (at which the US was not represented); became a member, American Union of Decorative Artists and Craftsmen (AUDAC), New York.
Bibliography Obituary, *The New York Times*, 1 Dec. 1939: 23. Karen Davies, *At Home in Manhattan: Modern Decorative Arts, 1925 to the Depression*, New Haven: Yale, 1983: 26.

Rörstrand Porslinsfabriker
Swedish ceramics factory.

History 1726, a factory was established at Rörstrand, Stockholm, by order of King Fredrik I, to become the earliest ceramics-production facility under government-supported management. The operation began the production of faïence in cobalt blue; from 1758, made enamel-painted and gilded ceramics; 1783, bought the rival Marieberg factory and, reacting to English competition, began producing cream-colored earthenware; 1873, established the Arabia division. 1895, Alf Wallander became the artistic director and created his Art Nouveau designs. From 1917, Edward Hald worked for the firm, designing earthenware. 1926, the firm moved to Gothenburg; 1931, appointed Gunnar Nylund the artistic director; 1932, expanded to Lidköping, moving there entirely in 1936. Its tradition of hiring innovative designers continued with Signe Persson-Melin and Rolf Sinnemark and Finnish designers Oiva Toikka and Heikki Orvola. 1983, Rörstrand was purchased by Wärtsilä/Arabia, becoming Rörstrand-Gustavsberg. Today Rörstrand is a brand of Hackman's iittala division (which includes BodaNova, Arabia, Hackman, and iittala, no longer independent firms; and other brands).
Exhibitions Subject of 1999 exhibition, New York (catalog below).
Bibliography Cat., *Three Centuries of Swedish Pottery: Rörstrand 1726–1959, and Marieberg 1758–1788* (Victoria and Albert Museum),

Stockholm: Nordisk Rotogravyr, 1959. Ann Marie Herlitz-Gezelius, *Rörstrand*, Lund: Signum, 1989. Bengt Nyström, *Rörstrand Porcelain: Art Nouveau Masterpieces: The Robert Schreiber Collection*, New York: Abbeville, 1996. Cat., David Revere McFadden, *Rörstrand: Swedish Art Nouveau Porcelain from the Robert Schreiber Collection*, New York: American Craft Museum, 1999. www.designor.com.
> See Arabia.

Rosanjin, Kitaōji (1883–1959)

Japanese ceramicist; born Kamigano.

Training Primarily self-taught.
Biography Early on, Rosanjin earned his incomes as a calligrapher, seal carver, and antiques dealer; became one of the most important 20th-century potters in Japan and was also known as an accomplished cook; 1921, founded the Bishoko Club, a private restaurant, and 1925, Hoshigoaka Restaurant, Tokyo; was married five times and known as a curmudgeon; became a potter in order to make ceramics for his restaurant, due to the destruction of his antique pottery collection by the 1923 earthquake in Tokyo. He was also a scholar of ancient Japanese ceramics, publishing a 1930s treatise on the subject; lived in a traditional building complex with six kilns in Kita Kamakura, where Isamu Noguchi produced some ceramic sculpture in 1952.
Exhibitions/citations Numerous significant one-person venues, including a 1954 exhibition, The Museum of Modern Art, New York. Rejected the Living National Treasure recognition.
Bibliography Sidney B. Cardozo and Masaaki Hirano, *The Art of Rosanjin*, Tokyo/New York: Kodansha, 1987. Hirano Masaaki, *Rosanjin tōsetsu/Kitaōji Rosanjin*, Tokyo: Chuo Koronsha, 1992.

Rose, Hajo (b. Hans-Joachim Rose 1910–1989) Katja Rose (b. Käthe Schmidt 1905–)

German textile designer, photographer, and teacher; born Mannheim; husband of Katja Rose.

Training Hajo: 1930–33, Bauhaus, Dessau and Berlin. Katja: drawing and applied art, Hamburg; 1931–33, Bauhaus, Berlin; textile school, Berlin
Biography Hajo Rose, who had become known for his photography at the Bauhaus, settled in the Netherlands and, 1934–41, taught fabric design with his wife Katja, 'Nieuwe Kunstschool,' Amsterdam; 1949–52, Hochschule für Bildende Künste, Dresden; 1952–59, Fachschule für angewandte Kunst, Leipzig, where he died. After World War II, Katja had settled in Munich.
Bibliography Cat., *Katja Rose, Weberei am Bauhaus 1931–33, Bildwebereien 1964–1983*, Berlin: Bauhaus-Archiv, 1983. Lionel Richard, *Encyclopédie du Bauhaus*, Paris: Somogy, 1985: 207. Hans Wichmann, *Von Morris bis Memphis, Textilien der Neuen Sammlung, Ende 19. bis Ende 20. Jahrhundert*, Basel/Boston/Berlin: Birkhäuser, 1990: 14, 207, 449.

Kitaōji Rosanjin. Vase. 1953. Bizen ware, h. 9" (22.8 cm) x dia. 4 1/2" (11.4 cm) Mfr.: the designer, Japan. Gift of the Japan Society, Inc.. MoMA.

Rosen, Anton (1858–1928)

Danish architect and designer.

Biography Rosen designed the Palace Hotel in Copenhagen; was the principal architect of 1909 Landsudstillingen (Danish national exhibition) in Århus. About this time, he worked for Georg Jensen Sølvsmedie in Copenhagen, creating noteworthy silver objects that incorporated amber, coral, malachite, and other semi-precious stones.
Bibliography Cat., *Georg Jensen Silversmithy: 77 Artists, 75 Years*, Washington: Smithsonian, 1980.

Rosenbaum-Ducommun, Wladimir (1894–1984)

Lithuanian lawyer and art dealer; active Zürich and Ascona.

Training In law in Zürich.
Biography As a lawyer, Rosenbaum-Ducommun was active on behalf of immigrants; served as the lawyer for the construction of the Neubühl settlement in Zürich; 1931–34, was president of board of directors and stockholder of the Wohnbedarf furniture store; as a middleman for various industries, was a board member of bronzeware and lamp manufacturer BAG in Türgi; lost his law license and became an antiques and art dealer in Ascona.
Bibliography Friederike Mehlau-Wiebking et al., *Schweizer Typenmöbel 1925–35, Sigfried Giedion und die Wohnbedarf AG*, Zürich: gta, 1989: 230.

Rosenthal

German ceramics manufacturer; located Selb.

History 1870s, Philipp Rosenthal (1855–1937) settled in the US, where he worked for a porcelain factory; late 1870s, returned to Germany to manage the family business and, 1879, set up Porzellanfabrik Ph. Rosenthal & Co. AG in Erkersreuth, near Selb, and, 1897, moved to Selb; 1903, acquired Porzellanfabrik Thomas & Ens and, 1921, Erwerb der Krister Porzellan-Manufaktur AG (founded in 1831) of Waldenburg, and, 1937, Porzellanfabrik Waldersdorf (founded in 1907). 1950, the Rosenthal firm established a glass department in the factory in Bad Soden Taunus. 1959, began selling wares through in-store departments, an American technique that assured control over its image and customer relations. 1958, Rosenthal Design-Studios, under the direction of architect Renate von Brause, was set up and 1960, the Studio-Linie range and stores were introduced. Studio-Linie designs have been chosen by a panel of judges (design personalities and lay people) including Raymond Loewy (with Richard Latham), Walter Gropius (with Louis A. McMillen and others), and Wilhelm Wagenfeld, as well as a new generation, such as Bjørn Wiinblad, Timo Sarpaneva, Tapio Wirkkala, Lino Sabattini, Michael Boehm, Ettore Sottsass, Platt & Young, and numerous others. New lines have included ceramics under licenses from Versace (from 1992, including metal cutlery), Bulgari (from 1998), and Fornasetti. Its design center is also in Selb. From 1965, the firm has been known as Rosenthal AG; 1967, acquired Möbelfabrik Espelkamp. 1998, the conglomerate Waterford Wedgwood plc. acquired a major share of Rosenthal, which was increased to 90% in 2001.
Exhibitions/citations 1982 *Rosenthal: Hundert Jahre Porzellan*, Kestner-Museum, Hanover (catalog below). Numerous citations, including grand prizes at 1910 *Exposition Universelle et Internationale*, Brussels, and 1937 *Exposition Internationale des Arts et Techniques dans la Vie Moderne*, Paris; 1969 International Vicenza Prize (for Gropius-McMillan's TAC 1 tea set).
Bibliography *Philipp Rosenthal: Sein Leben und sein Porzellan*, Leipzig: Klinkhardt & Biermann, 1929. Hermann Schreiber et al., *Die Rosenthal Story: Menschen, Kultur, Wirtschaft*, Düsseldorf: Econ, 1980. Cat., Helga Hilschenz (ed.), *Rosenthal: Hundert Jahre Porzellan*, Hanover: Kestner-Museum, 1982.
> See Thomas.

Rosenthal, Rena

American entrepreneur.

Biography Some credit Mrs. Rosenthal with having established the first contemporary design shop in the US, located on Madison Avenue, New York, established early or mid-1930s. A number of designers contributed exclusive work to the establishment, including Tommi Parzinger's furniture and accessories. Early on in his career, Russel

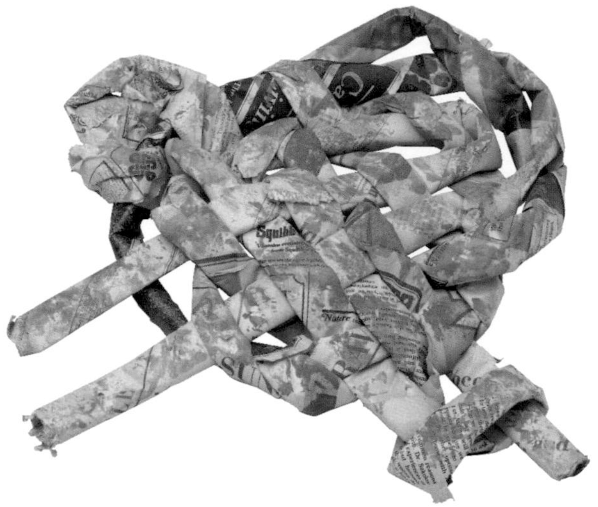

Ed Rossbach. Paper work. 1974. Newspaper and paint, h. 2 x w. 15 1/2" (5.1 x 39.4 cm). Mfr.: the designer, US. Gift of the artist. MoMA.

Wright designed masks and cast animal figures for Rosenthal. In fact, Wright's metalware and spun-aluminum serving and bar pieces were first sold at Rosenthal's, where there was an inventory of objects from a number of sources, including Fulper's 1920s–30s hand-thrown faïence vessels and 1930s Hagenauer's bronzeware.
Bibliography *The Studio Year-Book of Decorative Art: A Guide to the Artistic Decoration and Furnishing of the House*, no. 33, London: C.G. Holme, 1938. Cat., Janet Kardon (ed.), *Craft in the Machine Age 1920–1945*, New York: Abrams with American Craft Museum, 1995.

Roset, Ligne
French furniture manufacturer; Montagnieu, then Briord.

History 1860, the firm was founded by M.-Antoine Roset in Montagnieu to make bentwood walking sticks and umbrellas; by mid-1950, was producing contemporary furniture, which it continues today; is now managed by brothers Pierre and Michel Roset, fourth generation owners of the family firm. Its goods today are produced in Briord, a small Rhône-valley village, and distributed to more than 900 retail stores worldwide, its own and others. The firm calls on accomplished freelance people, both young and experienced, for the design of its products which include not only furniture, furniture systems, and storage but also lighting, accessories, and textiles (fabrics and carpets). Its stable of mostly French designers includes François Azambourg, Jeffrey Burnett, the Bouroullec brothers, Jean-Charles de Castelbajac, Delo Lindo, Thibault Desombre, Jean-Marc Gady, Christian Ghion, Jean-Louis Guinochet, Didier Gomez, Sophie Larger, Arik Levy, Peter Maly, Jean-Marie Massaud, Pascal Mourgue, and others. For a time, Michel Ducaroy was the design director.

Roseville Pottery
American pottery; located Zanesville, Ohio.

Biography 1892, Roseville was founded; became one of the largest and most successful Arts and Crafts potteries of its time. 1904–08, Frederick H. Rhead was its artistic director, who introduced sgraffito there and maintained a stylized English approach. The pottery also produced art ceramics as a sideline; 1954, was closed.
Bibliography Sharon Huxford and Bob Huxford, *The Collector's Encyclopedia of Roseville Pottery*, Paducah, Ky.: Collector Books, 1976. Cat., Leslie Greene Bowman, *American Arts & Crafts: Virtue in Design*, Boston: Bulfinch, 1990: 176.

Rosin, Mary (b. Maria Grazia Rosen 1958–)
Italian designer; born Cortina D'Ampezzo (Belluno).

Training 1978–82, diploma in painting, Academia di Belle Arti; 1981–83, history of Venetian art and architecture, Istituto Universitario di Architettura; both Venice.
Biography 1979–92, Rosin was a canvas painter. 1992, first became involved with glass as part of a project organized by the Fondazione Bevilacqua La Masa and the Vetreria de Majo glassworks in Murano. Having become enthusiastic about the medium, she turned from painting to glass while retaining the irony of Pop art which she had been pursuing in fine art. Her first major series was Detergens (made by Vittorio Ferro), a tribute to ordinary cleaning products. At Vetreria de Majo, her chandeliers included 1993 Laguna Planet, Organicosmico, and Organioptical; and 2000 Venussiano Cristal (made by Pino Signoretto), Laguna Planet Cristal, and Cosmospora. Other work: 2000 Folpi Octopus drinking glass, featuring 'pills' (made by Gianluca Pagnin), and 2000 Pears in Pills jewelry.
Exhibitions Work shown 1992–2002 at venues in Aosta, Vietri, Venice, Düsseldorf, Paris, Sapporo, and subject of 2000–01 exhibits in Cortina D'Ampezzo, Murano, and Venice (catalog below).
Bibliography 'A New Beginning,' *New Glass*, no. 2, 1993. 'Rosin and Her Magic Glass,' *Vogue gioiello*, no. 37, 1995. 'Artisans altamente di talento,' *La mia casa*, Feb. 1996. 'Medicine Alternative,' *L'Arca*, no. 152, 2000. Cat., *Strano ma vetro*, Venice: Museo Correr, 2000. 'Lustres de Murano,' *Residence Décoration*, no. 41, 2001. 'The Invasion of Carniverous Plants,' *Arte*, Jan. 2001.

Rosinski, Iréna (1956–)
Polish furniture designer; active France.

Training Academy of Applied Arts, Gdańsk; École des Beaux-Arts, Toulouse.
Biography 1980, Rosinski established a design office in Toulouse, working for furniture companies in the area; designed exhibition stands for the council of the Midi-Pyrénées region, furniture for the airport in Blagnac, and for the chamber of commerce and a hospital in Toulouse. Her furniture includes 1980–82 Praho colorful wood cabinet and 1999 Collection City collection, both by Carsalade. She teaches at the Ecole d'Architecture et de Paysage de Bordeaux, Talence; was perhaps the first French person to design furniture with high aesthetic standards distributed to superstores. Carsalade, established in 1924 by Bertrand Carsalade, first showed its furniture at the Salon du Meuble in 1986. Carsalade, which produces domestic and hotel furniture and point of purchase units, distributes to Parisian department stores, Habitat, Conforama, and others. Rosinski has also designed for Ortalide, which manufacturers for Cinna, MDF, and others.
Citations 1981 VIA/UNIFA competition (for a chair in lacquered wood and steel tubing); 1982 VIA/Conforama competition; 1983 Carte Blanche production support (for wood-and-glass dining-room furniture), VIA (French furniture association).
Bibliography Cat., *Les années VIA 1980–1990*, Paris: Musée des Arts Décoratifs, 1990: 152–53.

Rossari, Ambrogio (1943–)
Italian industrial designer; born Salò; active Milan.

Training To 1966, Corso Superiore di Disegno Industriale, Venice; master's degree in product design, Illinois Institute of Technology (IIT), Chicago.
Biography 1971, Rossari became active as a designer of domestic furnishings and lighting; is known for his bathroom fittings by Cesame and products by Guzzini and by Cesana; became a member, Associazione per il Disegno Industriale (ADI). Other clients have included Appiani, Armo, Ceim, Pirelli, Rubinetterie Giustina, Valdadige, Veca.
Citations 1987 Design Plus (for Spiegelau glasses) and Design Innovation Award, Frankfurt Fair; 1989 Essen Award (for Floria bathtub by Albatros System). Premio Compasso d'Oro: 1987 (for sink in System collection by Cesame), and 989 (for table set by Guzzini) 1991 napkin rings and dishes by Guzzini, Tempra single-lever mixing faucet by Frattini, and for Logic shower stall by 2S Cesana).
Bibliography *ADI Annual 1976*, Milan: Associazione per il Disegno Industriale, 1976. *Modo*, no. 148, Mar.–Apr. 1993: 125.

Rossbach, Ed (1914–2002)
American weaver; born Chicago.

Training 1940, bachelor's degree in painting and design, University of Washington, Seattle; 1941, master's degree in art education, Columbia University, New York; 1947, master of fine arts degree in ceramics and weaving, Cranbrook Academy of Art, Bloomfield Hills, Mich.
Biography 1940s, Rossbach began as a ceramicist and traditional weaver and, 1950s, became a basket maker; 1950s, moved to the University of California, Berkeley, where he was influentially exposed to avant-garde craftspeople; wove objects and constructions that called on non-traditional materials, such as plastics and newspaper

and forsook the use of a loom; produced playful pieces, some with Pop-culture images, and experimented with great ease; became a pioneer in fiber art.
Exhibitions Large number of group venues, primarily in the US, and one-person exhibitions, including at Textile Museum, Washington, D.C., 1990 (catalog below).
Bibliography Ed Rossbach as author of: *Baskets as Textile Art*, New York: Van Nostrand Rheinhold, 1973; and *The Nature of Basketry*, West Chester, Pa.: Schiffer, 1986. Cat., Ann Pollard Rowe and Rebecca A.T. Stevens (eds.), *Ed Rossbach: 40 Years of Exploration and Innovation in Fiber Art*, Washington, D.C.: Textile Museum, 1990.

Rosselli, Alberto (1921–1976)

Italian architect and industrial designer; born Palermo; active Milan.

Training 1938–39, in engineering; 1945–47, architecture, Politecnico, Milan.
Biography 1950, Rosselli, Gio Ponti, and Antonio Fornaroli established the architecture/design firm Studio PFR, which built notable structures, including 1956 Pirelli Tower in Milan. 1949, Rosselli edited the design section in Ponti's *Domus* journal until 1954, when Rosselli founded the journal *Stile industria* (not Ponti's *Stile*). Rosselli directed the journal to its last issue in 1963. Active also independently—1955, he opened his own office in Milan, designing vehicles by Fiat-Orlandi; furniture by Arflex, Bonacina, Kartell, and Saporiti Italia; lighting by FontanaArte; glassware by Salviati; ceramics by Cesame; also, electric clocks, domestic appliances, bathroom fixtures, and metalwork. 1956, he was a cofounder of Associazione per il Disegno Industriale (ADI) and its first president. 1957, he developed an interest in plastics, in which his first design was a bathroom unit by Montecatini. 1963, he began teaching industrial design, Politecnico, Milan. From 1967, Rosselli also collaborated with engineer and designer Isao Hosoe. 1968 one-piece fiberglass Jumbo chair is one of his best-known designs, produced 1970–78 by Saporiti; it has the appearance of a shoe and is related to his 1974 Moby Dick chaise longue. Rosselli's architectural work included the building of the *Corriere della Sera* newspaper. 1961–63, he was vice-president, International Council of Societies of Industrial Design (ICSID); from 1963, an assistant professor of industrial design, Politecnico, Milan; 1963–76, teacher, industrial design, Politecnico, Milan; a member of the committee of 1968 (14th) Triennale di Milano.
Exhibitions/citations 1967 Salone del Mobile (Jumbo chair), Milan. Work included in 1971, 1972, and 1983–84 exhibitions, London, Prague, and Philadelphia (catalogs below). Gold medals at 1954 (10th), 1957 (11th), and 1960 (12th) editions of Triennale de Milano. Premio Compasso d'Oro: 1967 (for armchair by Arflex), 1970 (for Meteor motor coach with Isao Hosoe by Fiat-Orlandi), 1987 (for body of work).
Bibliography Cat., *Modern Chairs 1918–1970*, London: Lund Humphries, 1971. Paolo Fossati, *Il design in Italia*, Turin: Einaudi, 1972: 128–38. Cat., Milena Lamarová, *Design a Plastické Hmoty*, Prague: Uměleckoprůmyslové Muzeum, 1972: 152. Giovanni Klaus Koenig et al., *Stile Industria: Alberto Rosselli*, Parma: Franco Maria Ricci, 1981. Cat., Kathryn B. Hiesinger and George H. Marcus III (eds.), *Design Since 1945*, Philadelphia: Philadelphia Museum of Art, 1983.

Rossetti, Dante Gabriel (1828–1882)

British painter and poet; born London; husband of Elizabeth Siddal.

Training In drawing under John Sell Cotman; 1848, in art under Holman Hunt.
Biography 1848, Rossetti, Holman Hunt, and John Everett Millais founded the Pre-Raphaelite Brotherhood. 1850, Rossetti and William Morris painted frescos for the Oxford Union debating hall. 1851, Morris, G.F. Watts, Edward Burne-Jones, and John Ruskin began supporting the Pre-Raphaelites and later became members. 1860s, Rossetti, like his friend James Abbot McNeill Whistler, began to collect Chinese porcelain and Japanese woodcuts. He was profoundly affected by the 1862 death of his wife Elizabeth Siddal and thus became more and more eccentric and, 1877, ceased painting; published *Poems* (London: F.S. Elllis, 1870) and his last work *Ballads and Sonnets* (London: Ellis and White, 1881). Encouraged early on by Hunt and Morris, he became involved in the applied arts and designed furniture and stained glass; was influential on the Continent and in the US, primarily through his graphic design; was involved in the formation of Morris, Marshall, and Faulkner, the Arts and Crafts decorating firm, founded by William Morris and others, and contributed designs to it.
Exhibitions/citations Work included in 1976 *Art Nouveau Belgium, France*, Rice University, Houston, Tex., and subject of 1982 'I Rossetti tra Italia e Inghilterra' conference, Città del Vasto, Rome; 1990 Dante Gabriel Rossetti exhibition, UK90 Festival, Tokyo.
Bibliography William Michael Rossetti (notes), *Dante Gabriel Rossetti as Designer and Writer*, London: Cassell, 1889; New York: AMS, 1970. Alicia Craig Faxon, *Dante Gabriel Rossetti*, New York: Abbeville, 1989. Maria Teresa Benedetti, *Dante Gabriel Rossetti*, Milan: Charta, 1998.

Rossi, Aldo (1931–1997)

Italian architect; son and grandson of bicycle manufacturers; born and active Milan.

Training Scuola dei Padri Somaschi, Lake Como; Collegio Alessandro Votas, Lecco; 1949–59, architecture, Politecnico, Milan.
Biography 1956, Aldo Rossi began his career in the studio of Ignazio Gardella in Milan; later worked with Marco Zanuso Sr.; 1955–64, worked at journal *Casabella-continuità*, where he was the editor 1961–64; 1963, was an assistant to Ludovico Quaroni in Arezzo; 1963–65, an assistant to Carlo Aymonino at Istituto Universitario di Architettura, Venice; 1969–72, taught, Politecnico, Milan; 1972–74, a guest professor, Eidgenössische Technische Hochschule, Zürich; 1974, returned to Politecnico, Milan; from 1975, chairperson of architectural composition, Istituto Universitario di Architettura, Venice; 1977, a visiting professor, The Cooper Union School of Architecture, New York, and, from 1980, Yale University, New Haven, Conn. He wrote the book *L'architettura della città* (Padua: Marsilio, 1966; Milan: Clup, 1987, new ed.). From 1971, he collaborated with Gianni Braghieri; from 1983, was the director of the architecture section, Biennale di Venezia. His few realized buildings included Teatro del Mondo (a floating wood and steel theater whose form provided the inspiration for his 1983 tea set for Alessi) at 1979–80 Biennale di Venezia. He was one of the 11 architects and designers to create a service for Alessi's 1983 Tea and Coffee Piazza project; Rossi's was housed in a glass building-like vitrine with a small flag on top and a clock in the frieze. Other coffee pots for Alessi, 90002/6 and 90002/3, again reflected the silhouettes of architecture rather than utensils. Also by Alessi, his 1985 Pressofilter incorporated the 1955 Chambord mechanism for pressing coffee grounds and was followed by 1986 Cafetière. The most memorable and refined of Rossi's designs for Alessi may be 1986 Il Conico kettle (artistic director Alberto Alessi's favorite Alessi product). From 1980s, Rossi designed furniture by Unifor; 1983 Cabina dell'Elba wardrobe cabinets, c. 1987 Milano side chair, and 1986 Theatre seating and bed (with Luca Meda) by Molteni; 1986 Il Rilievo marble table by Up & Up; marble furniture by Logoni; 1991 fabric collection by DesignTex; 1994 Il Faro ceramic-glass tea-coffee set by Rosenthal Studio-Linie. He attempted to re-create an Italian castle for 1987–89 Il Palazzo hotel, Fukuoka, Japan. His controversial, much-discussed architectural designs included 1969–73 residential building in the Monte Amiata complex, Gallaratese 2, Milan; 1971–84 competition project for the new San Cataldo Cemetery (with Gianni Braghieri), Modena; 1972–76 elementary school (with Braghieri and Arduino Cantafora), Fagnano Olona; 1977 competition project for student housing, Chieti; 1981–82 project for reconstruction of Teatro Carlo Felice (with Ignazio Gardella and Fabio Reinhart), Genoa; 1984 project for an office building (with Gianni Braghieri and others), Buenos Aires. 1986–91, he contributed to Parc de la Villette, Paris; designed 1989 Centre d'Art Contemporain à Vassivières, Limousin, France; 1995 Celebration (the Walt Disney World town), Orlando; numerous others. Rossi was director of the international architecture division, 1973 (15th) Triennale di Milano. Other books include *A Scientific Autobiography = Autobiografia scientifica* (Cambridge: MIT, 1981; Milan: Pratiche, 1999) and *Scritti scelti sull'architettura e la città 1956–1972*, Milan: Clup, 1975). He died in Milan.
Exhibitions/citations Work subject of 1979 *Aldo Rossi in America 1976 to 1979*, Institute for Architecture and Urban Studies, New York, and a 1983 exhibition, Modena. Furniture by Molteni and Up & Up shown at 1991 *Mobili Italiani 1961–1991: le Varie Età dei Linguaggi*, Milan. His first citation (with Braghieri, C. Stead, and J. Johnson) was at 1984 Internationalen Bauausstellung, Berlin, and won the competition of 1988 Deutsches Historisches Museum, Berlin-Mitte; 1989 Premio Compasso d'Oro (for the book *La conica, la cupola, e altre caffettiere*; La Cupola coffee pot; and Momento clock; all by Alessi); 1990 Pritzker Architecture Prize.
Bibliography Francesco Moschini (ed.), *Aldo Rossi: Projects and Drawings, 1962–1979*, New York: Rizzoli, 1979. Cat., *Aldo Rossi in America 1976 to 1979*, New York: Institute for Architecture and Urban Studies, 1979. Gianni Braghieri, *Aldo Rossi*, Bologna and Barcelona: Gustavo Gili, 1982. Cat., V. Savi and M. Lupano (eds.), *Aldo Rossi: opere recenti*, Modena: Panini, 1983. Gianni Braghieri, *Aldo Rossi*,

Rotterdam: 010. Juli Capella and Quim Larrea, *Designed by Architects in the 1980s*, New York: Rizzoli, 1988. Marco Brandolisio et al., *Aldo Rossi: disegni (1990–1997)*, Milan: Motta, 1999. Paolo Vitolo, *Care architetture: scritti su Aldo Rossi*, Turin: U. Allemandi, 2002.

Rossi, Pucci De
> See De Rossi, Pucci.

Rossio, Bruno (1953–)

Italian designer; born and active Milan.

Training From 1970, architecture, Politecnico, Milan.
Biography 1973, Rossio began his association with Designers 6R5 in Milan, a group that has designed textiles and ceramics; 1975, with Maurizio Alberti, Giuseppe Bossi, Pierangelo Marucco, and Francesco Roggero, established Original Designers 6R5 in Milan. Textile clients included Bassetti, Griso-Jover, Lanerossi, Sasatex, and Taif, as well as, for tapestries, Griffine Marechal, Le Roi, Printeco, and Sirpi. The group also designed wallpaper by various French firms. Rossio became a member, Associazione per il Disegno Industriale (ADI).
Bibliography *ADI Annual 1976*, Milan: Associazione per il Disegno Industriale, 1976.

Rossmann, Zdeněk (1905–1984)

Czech book designer, architect, set designer, and architectural theoretician; born Mährisch Ostrau (now Moravská Ostrava, Czech Republic).

Training 1923–28, České Vysoké Učení Technické (Czech technical university), Brno; 1928–29, Bauhaus, Dessau.
Biography From 1923 to its 1931 close, Rossmann was a member of the Devětsil group and, 1923–27, of the Brno Devětsil group; designed publications including *Pásmo* (1924–27) and the *Fronta* compendium (1927); criticized Le Corbusier's emotional Functionalism for its anti-social excess of form. Rossmann's work was based on the Bauhaus principles of Herbert Bayer and Jan Tschichold. His realized architectural work is small. Rossmann's 1929–32 stage sets for the Národní Divadlo (national theater), Bruno, were significant examples of Czech Constructivism.
Exhibitions Designed the pavilion for newspaper *Právo lidu* at 1920s *Výstava Soudobé Kultury*, Bruno.
Bibliography Cat., *Devětsil: Czech Avant-Garde Art, Architecture, and Design of the 1920s and 30s*, Oxford: Oxford Museum of Modern Art/ London Design Museum, 1990.

Roth, Alfred (1903–1998)

Swiss architect and furniture designer; born Wangen an der Aare; active Zürich.

Training 1922–26 under Gustav Gull and Karl Moser, architecture, Eidgenössische Technische Hochschule, Zürich.
Biography 1926, Roth worked in architect Karl Moser's office and, 1927 with Moser's help, worked in the office of Le Corbusier in Paris and on Corbu's houses built at 1927 *Weissenhofsiedlung* exhibition, Stuttgart, and League of Nations Building, Geneva; 1928–30, lived in Gothenborg, Sweden, where he established an architecture office with Ingrid Wallberg (the sister-in-law of Le Corbusier's brother). 1931, Roth returned to Zürich and worked in the construction office of the Neubühl Werkbund settlement. His early-1930s furniture was sold at the Wohnbedarf store in Zürich. From 1932, he was involved with the activities of the Congrès Internationaux d'Architecture Moderne (CIAM) and, 1950–56, was head of its Swiss group. 1932, he set up his own architectural office in Zürich; 1932–39, collaborated with cousin Emil Roth (1893–1980). 1935–36, the Roths and Marcel Breuer designed houses in the Doldertal in Zürich for Sigfried Giedion. Alfred Roth became editor of architecture journal *Weiterbauen*; 1932 and 1943–55, was an editorial-staff member of journal *Werk* and, 1945–52, of *Schweizerischer Baukatalog*; 1946, began publishing his *Civitas* pamphlets; wrote books, including *Die Neue Architektur* (Zürich: Girsberger, 1940; Zürich/Munich, 1975), *Das Neue Schulhaus = Das Neue Schulhaus = La Nouvelle Ecole* (Zürich: Girsberger, 1950), which earned him a reputation for being an authority on schools and commissions for them at home and abroad, and *Begegnung mit Pionieren: Le Corbusier, Piet Mondrian, Adolf Loos, Joseph Hoffmann, Auguste Perret, Henry Van de Velde* (Basel: Birkhäuser, 1973); was a foreign member, UAM (Union des Artistes Modernes), France; 1949–53, lectured at the universities of Washington, St. Louis, and Harvard; 1957, became a professor, Eidgenössische Technische Hochschule, Zürich. His own house has been privately owned since his 1998 death.
Exhibitions/citations Entered a chair design in the c. 1933 competition of Alliance Aluminum CIE France. Work subject of *Alfred Roth, Architekt*, Lehrer, Publizist, École Polytechnique Fédérale, Zürich.
Bibliography Stanislaus von Moos (intro.), *Alfred Roth, Architect of Continuity = Alfred Roth, Architekt der Kontinuität*, Zürich: Waser, 1985. Friederike Mehlau-Wiebking et al., *Schweizer Typenmöbel 1925–35, Sigfried Giedion und die Wohnbedarf AG*, Zürich: gta, 1989: 230. Canio Zarrilli, *Alfred Roth: la testimonianza di un protagonista, il movimento moderno tra le due guerre*, Florence: Alinea, 1993. Serge Lemoine (preface), Arnauld Pierre (notes), *Correspondance: Piet Mondrian, Alfred Roth*, Paris: Gallimard, 1994.

Roth, Emmy (1910–)

German silversmith; active Berlin and Voorschoten (Netherlands).

Training Under Conrad Anton Beumers in Düsseldorf.
Biography 1916, Emmy Roth established her own workshop in Berlin-Charlottenburg. Her early work showed baroque influence, but later work was plain and simple, exemplified by a fruit dish published in *The Studio* (1929). She was a member, Deutscher Werkbund; produced functional objects, hammering metal into versatile forms, including lids that also served as fruit bowls and an extendable candelabra, examples of her imaginative, well-proportioned work. Metalworker Carl J.A. Begeer met her at 1927 *Europäisches Kunstgewerbe* exhibition, Leipzig, and, on his invitation, she worked in the Netherlands 1938–39 and created austere modern table silver for industrial production by Zilverfabriek Voorschoten. 1940, she settled in the US.
Exhibitions Work shown at exhibitions, Germany and abroad, including 1927 *Europäisches Kunstgewerbe*, Leipzig.
Bibliography Annelies Krekel-Aalberse, *Art Nouveau and Art Déco Silver*, New York: Abrams, 1989. Cat., *Industry and Design in the Netherlands, 1850/1950*, Amsterdam: Stedelijk Museum, 1985: 211.

Röthlisberger Schreinerei

Swiss furniture manufacturer.

History 1928, the Röthlisberger joinery, or carpentry workshop, was established in Gümligen, near Bern; from 1958 under licence, manufactured furniture by Knoll Associates' designers. 1975 when the Knoll contract was not renewed, the firm experienced a 50% decrease in sales. To counter the impact, the Röthlisberger Kollektion, its own brand, was established in 1977 with furniture designs commissioned then and to come from Ubald Klug (Shell cabinet), Hans Eichenberger (Piedestal chest), Ueli and Susi Berger (stacked boxes as a chest of drawers), and Robert and Trix Haussmann (Mahagoni rolling shutter cabinet). Others have been Carmen and Urs Greutmann, Alfredo W. Häberli, Teo Jakob, Gerd Lange, Christophe Marchand, Koni Ochsner, and Ueli Wyser. From 1984, Peter Röthlisberger has managed the firm, known as Röthlisberger Schreinerei AG from 1985. 2002, a new building was added to the premises.

Rothschild, Jean-Maurice (1902–)

French decorator and furniture designer.

Training 1917–19, École Boulle, Paris.
Biography 1921, Rothschild began working for Jacques-Émile Ruhlmann in Paris as a designer and artisan, and participated in the design of Ruhlmann's Hôtel du Collectionneur pavilion at 1925 *Exposition Internationale des Arts Décoratifs et Industriels Modernes*, Paris. 1932, Rothschild established his own workshop at 14 bis, rue Marbeuf, Paris, and designed furniture, exemplifying classical forms and Ruhlmann's influence, produced by Muro and by Ducreuzet; end of 1920s, rejected classical forms in favor of the Rationalist approach espoused by the Union des Artistes Modernes (UAM); worked with architects, particularly Robert Expert, with whom he designed a number of chairs for 1935 oceanliner *Normandie*, including its smoking room, grill, and first-class cabins; 1937, designed the restaurant in the Eiffel Tower; 1945, began working as an interior architect; designed furniture commissioned by Le Mobilier National for the Administration de la Monnaie, for the president of the Assemblée Nationale, and for the office of president Vincent Auriol in the Palais de l'Élysée.
Exhibitions Work shown at Salons of Société des Artistes Décorateurs from 1933.
Bibliography *Ensembles mobiliers*, vol. II, Paris: Charles Moreau, 1937. *Ensembles mobiliers*, Paris: Charles Moreau, nos. 9–11, 1954. Yolande Amic, *Intérieure: le mobilier français 1945–1964*, Paris: Regard, 1983: 30–33. Pierre Kjellberg, *Art déco: les maîtres du mobilier, le décor des*

paquebots, Paris: Amateur, 1986/1990.

Rouard, Georges
French glassware and ceramics merchant; active Paris.

History Rouard produced earthenware and porcelain dinner services decorated with flowers, butterflies, and animals. He opened Maison Rouard at 34, avenue de l'Opéra, Paris, and soon after (1909) met painter, silversmith, and jewelry designer Marcel Goupy; 1913, established the group Artisans Français Contemporains. 1919, August Heiligenstein (1891–1976) produced enameled glass for Rouard to the specifications of Goupy. 1923, Heiligenstein left Rouard but showed his work there to 1926, when he went over to the gallery of Edgar Brandt. 1929–54, Goupy was Rouard's artistic director and designed glassware for the firm, much of it enameled inside and out, as well as porcelain and ceramic dinnerware. Most of the Goupy china patterns were executed by Théodore Haviland in Limoges. Rouard's was the principal vendor of François Décorchement's *pâte-de-verre* work.

Roubíček, René (1922–)
Czech glassware designer; born Prague; active Kamenický Šenov and Prague; husband of Miluse Roubíčkova.

Training 1940–44 under Jaroslav Holeček, monumental painting and sculpture, and, 1949–50 under J. Kaplicky, Vysoká Škola Umělecko-průmyslová (VŠUP, academy of arts, architecture, and design), Prague.
Biography 1945–52, Roubíček taught, specialized school of glass-making in Kamenický Šenov as a professor and designer in department of glass cutting. He also cooperated artistically with the studio of Artistic Glass in Nový Bor. His 1950s–60s work showed a sophisticated appreciation for the material. He later designed monumental glass objects; 1952–58, worked with the Art Center for the Industry of Glass and Fine Ceramics, Prague; 1953–55, was a designer in the studios of the Plastics Art Center of the national glassworks in Nový Bor, where he produced free-blown forms, active there at the same time as Jan Kotík. 1955–65, he was the chief artistic director at technical/artistic center of the national enterprise Borske Glass in Nový Bor; 1966–68, worked at Akademie Výtvarných Umení (academy of fine arts), Prague; from 1969, was a freelance artist; worked occasionally with Crystalex (successor to Borske Glass) in Nový Bor, UUR glassworks in Škrdlovice, Glasi Hergiswil in Switzerland, and AJETO glassworks in Lindava (near Nový Bor).
Citations Grand prize, 1958 *Exposition Universelle et Internationale de Bruxelles* (*Expo '58*).
Bibliography Cat., *Art in Glass/Glass in Art: Cigler, Liskova, Roubicek*, Washington, D.C.: Fendrick Gallery, 1981. Frederick Cooke, *Glass: Twentieth-Century Design*, New York: Dutton, 1986: 90.

Roubíčkova, Miluse (b. Miluse Kytkova 1922–)
Czech glass designer; born and active Prague; wife of René Roubíček.

Training 1941–44 under J. Holeček; 1945–49 under J. Kaplicky, glass and mon-umental painting, Vysoká Škola Uměleckoprůmyslová (VŠUP, academy of arts, architecture, and design), Prague.
Biography From 1948, she worked part-time for the Lobmeyr firm in Kamenicky Senov, the studio of Artistic Glass in Nový Bor, the Artistic Center of the Glass Industry and Fine Ceramics in Prague, Borske Glass (and its successor Crystalex) in Nový Bor, UUR glassworks in Škrdlovice, and Herdiswiler Glasi in Hergiswil (Switzerland)

Rougemont, Guy de (1935–)
French painter, ceramicist, and designer; active Paris.

Training 1954–58 under Marcel Gromaire, École Nationale Supérieure des Arts Décoratifs, Paris.
Biography From 1968, de Rougemont was active in the design of porcelain for Limoges, and also designed furniture and, by Bd Ediciones de Diseño, 1989 Rougemont rug. However, he is primarily an artist, and a number of his works are installed publicly, such as at Musée d'Art Moderne de la Ville de Paris, Hôpital Saint-Louis, and station of the RER (commuter train) station in Marne-la-Vallée, France.
Exhibitions/citations Participated in 1965 Biennale de Paris; 1966 Salon de Mai. From 1962, a large number of one-person venues. From 1965, work included in and subject of numerous exhibitions; is on permanent display at Galerie Artcurial, Paris. Member, Académie des Beaux-Arts; 1997, member, painting section, Institut de France.
Bibliography Cat., *Rougemont, espaces publics et arts décoratifs 1965–1990*, Paris: Musée des Arts Décoratifs, 1990.

Rousseau, Clément (1872–1950)
French sculptor and designer; born Saint-Maurice-la-Fougereuse, Deux-Sèvres; active Neuilly.

Training Under Léon Morice.
Biography From 1912, Rousseau created some highly idiosyncratic furniture for wealthy clients in Neuilly, and other objects; incorporated rich materials, including inlays of various exotic woods, shagreen, leather, ivory, and mother-of-pearl; designed in a particularly personal interpretation of 18th- and early-19th-century French styles; contributed to the revival and popularization of the use of shagreen; c. 1925, participated in furnishing Jacques Doucet's studio in Neuilly.
Exhibitions/citations From 1921, work shown at Salons of Société des Artistes Français, winning prizes; 1921 Salon of Société des Artiste Décorateurs; 1925 exhibition (lighting, furniture, clocks, and accesories), Galerie Charpentier; all Paris.
Bibliography Pierre Kjellberg, *Art déco: les maîtres du mobilier, le décor des paquebots*, Paris: Amateur, 1986/1990.

Rousseau, Clément (1948–)
French industrial designer; active Paris.

Training 1971–76, École Camondo, Paris.
Biography 1971–76, Rousseau worked at Raymond Loewy's Compagnie de l'Esthétique Industrielle, Paris; 1981–85, at PA Consulting International; 1985, with Claude Braunstein, set up the design office Plan Créatif/Crabtree Hall.
> See Plan Créatif.

Rousseau, François-Eugène (1827–1891)
French ceramicist and glass designer; born and active Paris.

Biography Rousseau inherited an establishment that specialized in the production of porcelain and faïence at 41, rue Coquillère, Paris. His 1866 Service Rousseau earthenware table service was based on Félix Bracquemond's drawings in the style of Hokusai. Rousseau worked for a time with Louis Salon. His own designs showed a distinct Japanese influence but were only executed years later, after he had turned to glass production. His flower and landscape motifs were applied by his decorators (including Eugène Michel and Alphonse-Georges Reyen) onto clear or palely colored glass. Other glassware was produced by the Appert brothers in Clichy. He greatly influenced the modern revival of glassmaking by realizing new effects through old techniques: cased glass, a Venetian and 18th-century Chinese technique of engraving on an opaque outer layer to expose a translucent inner layer; and crackled glass (for which he became famous), a 16th-century Venetian technique of immersing glass in cold water between firings. From 1885, he was associated with Ernest Léveillé.
Exhibitions Work shown at 1884 exhibition (crackled-glass objects), Union Centrale des Arts Décoratifs; 1878 *Exposition Universelle* (cased-glass objects and semi-precious stone imitations); both Paris.
Bibliography Yvonne Brunhammer et al., *Art Nouveau Belgium, France*, Houston: Rice University, 1976.

Roux-Spitz, Michel (b. Michel Roux 1888–1957)
French architect and designer; born Lyon.

Training Under Tony Garnier.
Biography Active from 1925, Roux-Spitz designed buildings in the International Style (though he rejected standardization), including 1924–29 École Dentaire, Lyon; 1929 Théâtre de la Croix-Rousse (first public building in Lyon in reinforced concrete and thin slabs); 1932 Centre des Chèques Postaux, Paris; 1933 annex to the Bibliothèque Nationale, Versailles. He managed the 1945 reconstruction of Nantes; and the construction of the Hôtel de Ville in Saint-Nazaire. He also designed furniture and interiors, including two apartments in a 1925 house on the rue Guynemer, Paris, that he built for himself. He died in Dinard.
Exhibitions Two schemes for the galleries of Cour des Méiers at 1925 *Exposition Internationale des Arts Décoratifs et Industriels Modernes*; 1926 Salon (Central Rotunda with Jean Perzel's famous Drops of Water lighting), 1928 Salon (bathroom with lighting by Perzel, silverware by Jean Puiforcat, glassware by Saint-Gobain, ironwork by Raymond Subes), 1929 Salon (dining room produced by the Société des Glaces in Boussois) of Société des Artistes Décorateurs; all Paris.
Bibliography Pierre Kjellberg, *Art déco: les maîtres du mobilier, le décor des paquebots*, Paris: Amateur, 1986/1990. *Le Petit Robert 2*, Paris: Robert, 1991: 1566.

David Rowland. 40/4 stacking chair. 1964. Chromium-plated steel, vinyl-coated steel sheet, and plastic glides, 30 x 20 x 21" (76.2 x 50.8 x 53.3 cm). Mfr.: The General Fireproofing Co., US. Gift of the mfr. MoMA.

Rowan, Doug (1925–)
Canadian industrial designer; born Edmonton.

Training Science, University of Alberta; plastics engineering, Plastics Industries Technical Institute, Los Angeles.
Biography Rowan returned to Canada from Los Angeles to design toys, housewares, fertilizers, and explosives; worked both independently and with Frank Dudas and Jan Kuypers within the design studio DKR in Toronto. The group's furniture designs included seating for IIL International. Within DKR, Rowan designed hockey helmets by Canada Cycle and Motor Company (CCM) and the first (1962) two-color plastic vacuum bottle, by Canadian Thermos Products.
Bibliography Cat., *Seduced and Abandoned: Modern Furniture Designers in Canada, the First Fifty Years*, Toronto: The Art Gallery at Harbourfront, 1986: 21. Rachel Gotlieb and Cora Golden, *Design in Canada Since 1945: Fifty Years from Teakettles to Task Chairs*, Toronto: Knopf Canada, 2001.
> See Dudas, Frank.

Rowland, David (1924–)
American industrial designer; born Los Angeles.

Training 1940 under László Moholy-Nagy, Mills College, Oakland, Cal.; 1950–51, Cranbrook Academy of Art, Bloomfield Hills, Mich.
Biography 1952–53, Rowland was a design assistant to Norman Bel Geddes in New York; 1954, established his own design office in New York; experimented with steel and plastic finishes for seating; 1956–64, developed a stacking-chair concept that resulted in the 1964 40/4 (or 40-in-4) side chair with chromium-plated steel legs and vinyl-coated seats and backs stamped from sheet metal by General Fireproofing in Youngstown, Ohio. A stack of '40' chairs reaches only '4' ft (122 cm) high, thus the name 40/4. His 1979 Sof-Tech chair by Thonet was built of tubular steel with vinyl-coated springs.
Exhibitions/citations Work shown at 1957 (11th) (gold medal for 40/4 chair) and 1964 (12th) Triennale di Milano; 1968 and 1983–84 exhibitions, Paris and Philadelphia (catalog below).
Bibliography 'United States Steel,' *Industrial Design*, vol. 12, Nov. 1965: 7–9. Cat., *Les assises du siège contemporain*, Paris: Musée des Arts Décoratifs, 1968. Olga Gueft, 'Thonet Sof-Tech Stacker,' *Interiors*, vol. 139, Aug. 1979: 66–67, 84. 'David Rowland Designs the Sof-Tech Chair for Thonet,' *Interior Design*, vol. 50, Aug. 1979: 167. Cat., Kathryn B. Hiesinger and George H. Marcus III (eds.), *Design Since 1945*, Philadelphia: Philadelphia Museum of Art, 1983.

Rowlands, Martyn (1920–)
British industrial designer; born Wales.

Training Industrial design, Central School of Arts and Crafts, London.
Biography Rowlands worked for Bakelite and, subsequently, established the design department of Ekco Plastics; 1959, set up his own practice; 1972, was vice-president of Society of Industrial Artists.
Citations Six awards (all for plastic products), Council of Industrial Design Awards, US.
Bibliography Cat., Milena Lamarová, *Design a Plastické Hmoty*, Prague: Uměleckoprůmyslové Muzeum, 1972: 154.

Rowley Gallery
British design studio; located London.

History 1898, A.J. Rowley founded the Rowley Gallery in London; designed furniture and simple, inexpensive interiors and specialized in picture framing. After World War I, Rowley hired artists, including Robert Anning Bell, Frank Brangwyn, H. Butler, and William A. Chase, to design the marquetry and stained panels made on the premises. 1920s–30s, the firm was known for its continuation of marquetry panels as well as screens, mirrors, and silver-leaf furniture and interiors, and, later, art materials. 1933, Brangwyn redesigned the exterior of the studio's quarters at 140–42 Kensington Church Street, London; three carved wood panels of craftsmen were set over Portland stone.
Bibliography Jessica Rutherford, *Art Nouveau, Art Deco and the Thirties: The Furniture Collections at Brighton Museum*, Brighton: The Royal Pavilion, Art Gallery and Museums, 1983: 55.

Royal Copenhagen Porcelain Manufactory (Den Kongelige Porcelænsfabrik)
Danish porcelain factory.

Biography 1755, the first pottery works in Copenhagen was established under the patronage of King Frederick V. Managed by Louis Fournier, a French émigré, the factory produced soft-paste and Sèvres-type porcelain. 1766 when the king died and Fournier returned to France, the factory closed. A new factory, that was opened in 1775 at the behest of the dowager queen Juliane Marie under manager Frantz Henrich Mueller, became the forerunner of the present Royal Copenhagen Porcelain Manufactory. 1790, a legendary porcelain dinner service began at the behest of the queen's son as a gift to Catherine the Great of Russia. The painted images—the lifework of Johann Christoph Bayer (Nuremberg, 1738–Copenhagen, 1812)—were derived from Flora Danica, an ongoing collection of tinted copperplate prints that depicted practically every wild plant in Denmark. (1776–1802, Bayer worked at Royal Copenhagen; 1804, Flora Danica's production temporarily stopped.) Since Catherine died before the 1,802-piece set was completed, it stayed in Denmark, sent to the royal pantry. Production consumed 12 years, averaging less than three pieces a week; however, the uninterrupted production did not begin until 1863. The examples available today are identical to Catherine's, with the Latin names of the floral images—systematized by a Swedish botanist Carolus Linneaus (1707–78)—continuing to be written on the underside of each piece. 1807, the factory was bombarded by British naval vessels under Lord Nelson. Subsequent production was artistically inferior until the factory was taken over by Philip Schou, who moved it from Köbmagergade to Smallegarde and appointed Arnold Krog, who revitalized the firm, as the artistic director. Under Krog, the firm's wares showed French and Japanese influences, and its celebrated underglaze decoration in soft grays, pinks, and blues was introduced. In the 20th century, new forms and patterns were developed, and workshops for stoneware and special glazes set up. From 1910, the production of commemorative 'Christmas spoons and forks' began. 1920s–40s, figurines were designed by sculptors Gerhard Henning, Knud Kyhn, Arno Malinowski, Jais Nielsen, and Christian Thomsen, and decorative and table wares by Axel Salto and Nils Thorsson. The largest collection of Royal Copenhagen porcelain is housed in the Kunstindustrimuseet, Copenhagen. 1923, Royal Copenhagen and Kastrup & Holmegård Glasværks opened joint foreign retail outlets. 1969, the factory began jewelry production with A. Michelsen, jewelers to the Danish court. 1985, Georg Jensen Sølvesmedie, A. Michelsen metalsmiths, and Kastrup & Holmegård Glasværks merged with the Royal Copenhagen Porcelain Factory under the umbrella name Royal

Copenhagen Ltd. 1987, Royal Copenhagen Ltd. merged with Bing & Grøndahl. 1997, Orrefors Kosta Boda, BodaNova-Höganäs Keramik, and Venini merged to become Royal Scandinavia, which has since been divested into separate entities.
Bibliography Arthur Hayden, *Royal Copenhagen Porcelain: Its History and Development from the 18th Century to the Present Day*, London: T. Fisher Unwin, 1911. Xenius Rostock, *The Royal Copenhagen Manufactory and the Faience Manufactory Aluminia: Past and Present*, Copenhagen: Berlinske Bogtrykkeri, 1939. Cat., *200 Years of Royal Copenhagen Porcelain: A Retrospective Exhibition*, Washington, D.C.: Smithsonian Institution, 1974. Bredo L. Grandjean et al., *The Royal Copenhagen Porcelain Manufactory 1775–1975*, Copenhagen: Royal Copenhagen, 1975. Jennifer Hawkins Opie, *Scandinavia: Ceramics and Glass in the Twentieth Century*, New York: Rizzoli, 1989. Mel Byars, 'To Be Continued,' *Metropolitan Home*, Nov.-Dec. 1999: 80+. Leslie Jackson, *20th Century Factory Glass*, London: Octopus, 2000.
> See Royal Scandinavia (below).

Royal Scandinavia

Danish glass-and-ceramics amalgamation.

History The formation of Royal Scandinavia is essentially a story of mergers and acquisitions, which ultimately came unraveled. By 1946, Kosta had already merged with Boda and Åfors. 1965, Kastrup and Holmegård glass manufacturers merged. 1985, Georg Jensen Sølvesmedie and A. Michelsen metalsmiths merged with Royal Copenhagen Porcelain Factory and Holmegård Glassworks and Royal Copenhagen Ltd. was formed. Also, Royal Copenhagen Ltd. bought the Illums Bolighus Ltd. furnishings store of Copenhagen in 1985 and Hans Hansen Silversmiths in 1991. When Orrefors Kosta Boda, BodaNova Höganäs Keramik, and Venini were acquired in 1997, when the name of the overall group became Royal Scandinavia Ltd., whose largest shareholder was Carlsberg Breweries. Leonhard Schrøder (1938–98), the former president of Holmegård, effected the mergers in association with Carlsberg. 1998, he died after a trip to the Far East. However, no one had been appointed or trained as a replacement. Thus, in 2000, Royal Scandinavia was bought by a group of companies—Axcel (51%) and RC Investments (21%), with Carlsberg's shares reduced from 65% to 28%. In 2001, Axcel sold Venini, Kosta Boda, and Orrefors. Also, Designor (owners of the Iittala, Arabia, Hackman, and Rörstrand brands) bought BodaNova. And divestitures and reorganizations continued.

Royal Worcester Porcelain

British ceramics manufacturer; located Worcester.

History Worcester has been long noted for its pottery industry. At least by 1751, porcelain was being produced in a factory there. 1862, W.H. Kerr left the factory, which at the time was called Kerr and Binns, and Richard William Binns (1819–1900) reorganized it as Royal Worcester Porcelain Company (an amalgamation of factories that had been operating in the area). An ivory-colored porcelain body, which accepted enamel decoration well, was introduced. Binns had a large collection of Far Eastern porcelain, and, thus influenced, Worcester's 1860s–80s Japanesque wares had enamel, gold, and other raised metallic pastework, widely copied in the US. Some designs were produced with Persian- and Indian-style decorations. 1897, Binns left the firm. Worcester, essentially a conservative operation, experimented in 1880s–90s with piercing and new glazes. Its 20th-century production focused on historicist models, and many of its 19th-century designs have remained in production.
Exhibitions *International Exhibition of 1862* (highly decorated dessert service by Kerr and Binns for Queen Victoria), London.
Bibliography R.W. Binns, *A Century of Potting in the City of Worcester, Being the History of the Royal Porcelain Works, from 1751 to 1851, to Which Is Added a Short Account of the Celtic, Roman, and Mediæval Pottery of Worcestershire*, London: B. Quaritch, 1865. R.W. Binns, *Worcester China: A Record of the Work of Forty-five Years, 1852 – 1897*, London: B. Quaritch, 1897. Henry Sandon, *Royal Worcester Porcelain from 1862 to the Present Day*, London: Barrie & Jenkins, 1973. Antoinette Fay-Hallé and Barbara Mundt, *Porcelain of the Nineteenth Century*, New York: Rizzoli, 1983. Doreen Bolger Burke et al., *In Pursuit of Beauty: Americans and the Aesthetic Movement*, New York: The Metropolitan Museum of Art / Rizzoli, 1987: 486.

Royère, Jean (1902–1981)

French decoration and furniture designer; born Paris.

Training The classics, Cambridge University.
Biography For a time, Royère worked in a bank and elsewhere in Le Havre; 1931, began his career as a decorator and worked for a furniture manufacturer in the Faubourg Saint-Antoine area of Paris. His first important commission was the 1933 design of a brasserie in the Hôtel Carlton, avenue des Champs-Élysées, Paris. 1934–42, he worked for Pierre Gouffé, managing his furniture; 1942, set up his own design office at 5, rue d'Argenson, Paris, and, 1947, at 184, rue de Faubourg Saint-Honoré; became known as the grand master of decoration in Paris, designing offices for Proche-Orient Line in US and Europe, interiors of 1962 oceanliner *France*, and the residences of King Farouk of Egypt, King Hussein of Jordan, and the Shah of Iran. In an eclectic and distinctively French style, he designed palaces, apartments, hotels, furniture, furnishings, and lighting. 1959, Royère, metalworker Gilbert Poillerat, and sculptor André Bloc designed the Beharestan (senate) in Teheran. 1970, Royère retired; sold his furniture through a 1980 auction at the Hôtel Drouout, Paris; moved to the US, and died in Pennsylvania.
Exhibitions Work shown for the first time at 1934 Salon d'Automne, then subsequently at its editions. Also Salons of Société des Artistes Décorateurs from 1935, and 1937 *Exposition Internationale des Arts et Techniques dans la Vie Moderne*, Paris. Work subject of 1999–2000 *Jean Royère: décorateur à Paris*, Musée des Arts Décoratifs, Paris (catalog below).
Bibliography Pierre Kjellberg, *Art déco: les maîtres du mobilier, le décor des paquebots*, Paris: Amateur, 1990. Cat., Marie-Claude Beaud et al., *Jean Royère, Décorateur à Paris*, Paris: Norma, 1999. *Jean Royère*, Paris: Galerie Jacques Lacoste, 2000. Cat., Catherine de Beyrie et al. (eds.), *Jean Royère*, New York and Beirut: Galerie De Beyrie/Jacques Ouaiss, 2000.

Rozanova, Ol'ga Vladimirovna (1886–1918)

Russian artist, illustrator, and theoretician; born Melenki, near Vladimir.

Training 1904–10, art studios of K. Bol'shakov and K. Yuon, and Stroganov School of Applied Art, Moscow; 1912–13, Yelizaveta Zvantseva's art school, St. Petersburg.
Biography 1911, Rozanova settled in St. Petersburg and made contact with the Union of Youth group and with Vladimir Markov (aka Waldemars Matvejs) and Mikhail Matiushin; from 1912, illustrated Futurist booklets, including her husband Aleksei Kruchenykh's *Te li le* (1914), *Zaumnaia gniga* (transrational book) (1915), *Balos* (1917), and the important albums *Voina* (war) (1916) and *Vselenskaia voina* (the universal war). 1916, she adopted Kazimir Malevich's Suprematism, participating with Malevich, Mikhail Matiushin, Liubov' Popova, composer Nikolai Roslavets, and others on the first issues of the unrealized journal *Supremus*; 1918, became a member of IZO NKP (fine-art department of Narkompros) and of Proletcult (proletarian culture organization in Moscow, an independent workers' cultural and educational association). Rozanova and Aleksandr Rodchenko directed the art-industry section of IZO, and she assisted in the formation of the State Free Art Schools (SVOMAS) in provincial towns.
Exhibitions Work included in 1913 exhibition of Bubnovy Valet (Jack of Diamonds); 1915 *Tramway V*; 1915–16 *0–10*; other exhibitions of Union of Youth; 1922 *Erste Russische Kunstausstellung*, Berlin; 2000–01 *Amazons of the Avant-Garde*, New York (catalog below). Work subject of 1919 exhibition, Moscow; 1992, Helsinki.
Bibliography Stephanie Barron and Maurice Tuchman, *The Avant-Garde in Russia, 1910–1930*, Cambridge, Mass.: MIT, 1980: 240. S.O. Khan-Magomedov, *Vhutemas: Moscou, 1920–1930*, Paris: Regard, 1990. Cat., *Olga Rozanova, 1886–1918*, Helsinki: Helsingin Kaupungin Taidemuseo, 1992. Cat., John E. Bowlt and Matthew Drutt (eds.), *Amazons of the Avant-Garde: Alexandra Exter, Natalia Goncharova, Liubov Popova, Olga Rozanova, Varvara Stepanova, and Nadezhda Udaltsova*, Abrams: Guggenheim Museum, 1999. Nina Gurianova, *Exploring Color: Olga Rozanova and the Early Russian Avant-Garde, 1910–1918*, Amsterdam: G&B Arts International, 2000.

Rozenberg, Ely (1969–)

Russian industrial designer; born Dushanbe.

Training Bezalel Academy of Art and Design, Jerusalem.
Biography 1977, Rozenberg emigrated to Israel; 1997 with Alessandro Bianchini and M. Garelick, established design studio Oz in Rome, Italy; from 1997, has been a correspondent for *Biniyan ve Diur*, the Israeli interiors and design magazine. His design work, some of his own production, frequently exploits new materials and technologies or employs them in an unusual manner, such as the incorporation of zippers in nomadic furniture and tabletop objects. Work has included 1999 Long Wave and 1999 Short Wave lamps by Pallucco Italia.

Ely Rozenberg. Tamnum bowl. 2000. Harmonius steel and zippers, h. 2 3/4 x dia. 23" (7 x 58.5 cm). Mfr.: Oz, Italy.

Exhibitions/citations First showed (lighting and seating), at Salone del Mobile, Milan; and a number of Israeli and foreign venues. Work included in 1999 *Young European Design*, traveling. Subject of 1999 exhibition, Cristiani art gallery, Turin. Organized (with Vanni Pasca) and work included in 2001 (1st) edition of *Industrious Designers* exhibition (catalog below), originating at Abitare il Tempo, Verona, and traveling, and 2002 (2nd) edition. Received 1996 first prize, competition of Radad cutlery firm; 1996 Best Domestic Israeli Product, Israel Museum, Jerusalem; 1998 Sharet Grant, American Israel Foundation; 2004 Premio Targetti Light Art, Italy.
Bibliography Cat., Vanni Pasca and Ely Rozenberg, *Industrious Designers*, Verona: Abitare il Tempo, 2001. Giora Urian, *From the Israel Museum to the Carmel Market: Israeli Design*, Ramat-Hasaron: Urian – The Architect's Encyclopedia, 2001. Michele De Lucchi (ed.), *The International Design Yearbook*, London: Laurence King, 2001. Mel Byars, *Design in Steel*, London: Laurence King, 2002.

R-S-V-P
Italian domestic-accessories firm; located Montecchio.

History 1991, R-S-V-P was founded to create small objects made from glass sheets; has used artisanal methods of production, including waterjet cutting, bending, sandblasting, and gluing, to make vases, fruit bowls, centerpieces, and other items; has commissioned designers such as Carlo Bartoli, Massimo Iosa-Ghini, Dafne Koz, Gio Pomodoro, and Ettore Sottsass to explore glass-making techniques and shapes.
Bibliography www.rsvp-oggetti-di-autore.it.

Rubik, Ernö (1937–)
Hungarian inventor.

Training Architecture, Magyar Iparmrůvészeti Egyetem (MIE, university of applied arts), Budapest.
Biography Rubik was a lecturer in the department of interior design of the university of his former study and explored three-dimensional forms, construction, and 'hidden' possibilities; in his classes, used a number of models in paper, wood, or plastic and encouraged his students to create similar constructions. And thus it was through these activities and interests that he invented his renowned Rubik's Cube puzzle in 1974. After 1978 and his demonstrating it to students and friends, the puzzle garnered local public interest, even though or maybe because it is very difficult to align the colors, which is the goal. After numerous disappointments in beginning its mass production, Rubik finally persuaded Steward Sims, vice-president of marketing, Ideal Toys, to come to Budapest, where the device could be seen almost everywhere in public. It was, thus, adopted by Ideal Toys as a product. Rubik's Cube remains popular today. Rubik continues to pursue the invention of new games and puzzles.

Rubin, Daniel and Patrick
> See Canal.

Rückert, M.J.
German silversmiths; located Mainz.

History 1901, M.J. Rückert firm was founded in Mainz and produced small silver pieces and cutlery, some designed by Patriz Huber and Hans Christiansen. Rückert made the two cutlery patterns in the Wie-ner Sezession style that Peter Behrens designed while at Darmstadt.
Bibliography Annelies Krekel-Aalberse, *Art Nouveau and Art Déco Silver*, New York: Abrams, 1989. Cat., *Metallkunst*, Berlin: Bröhan-Museum, 1990: 426–27.

Ruggeri, Cinzia (1943–)
Italian designer; born and active Milan.

Training In applied arts, Milan; apprenticeship at Carven in Paris.
Biography After studies in Paris, Ruggeri returned to Italy and became a stylist in her father's clothing firm, developing the Bloom line in 1970s, under the trademark Cinzia Ruggeri; designed costumes for the theater, women's sportswear by Kim, and a range of domestic linens by Castellini; 1980–87, was the art director of Centro Tutela Lino (CTL). From 1991, she has been dedicated to art installations and product design. Clients include Driade, Glass, Poltrona Frau, and Rapsel.
Exhibitions Participated in the 1981 Biennale di Venezia; 1982 *Italian Revolution* exhibition, California; 1983 (17th) and 1985 Triennale di Milano; 1988 *Fashion and Surrealism*, Victoria and Albert Museum, London; 1991-92 *Muneri Ruggeri Sottsass*, Milan and Rome; 1993–94 and 1995 Abitare il Tempo fair, Verona; 1998 *Antoillogica*, personal retrospective, Spazio Krizia, Milan; 2000 *Paesaggio Italiano*, Espace Electra, Paris; *Made in Italy* (curated by Gae Aulenti), Milan Triennale, 2001; Biennale Donna, Ferrara, 2002.
Bibliography Andrea Branzi, *La casa calda: esperienze del nuovo disegno italiano*, Milan: Idea, 1982.

Ruggiero, Andrea (1969–)
Italian industrial designer; born Italy.

Training 1995, bachelor of fine arts degree in product design, Parsons School of Design, New York; Domus Academy, Milan.
Biography Ruggiero was reared in Italy, China, and Austria; 1987, settled in US; collaborated with a number of design and architecture studios in New York, including Able Design, Arnell Group, Boym Design Studio, and Vignelli Associates; subsequently, worked for digital-solutions firm Razorfish, where he was responsible for developing next-generation digital-communication devices and defining new product-user scenarios; is a generalist and has been active in furniture design, packaging, corporate/brand identity, as well as interiors; was a visiting lecturer, Universidad Diego Portales, Santiago, Chile; from 1995, taught, Parsons School of Design.
Exhibitions A number of venues including, with Mike Solis, two-person 1999 *Fun[k]tion: New Basics for the Domestic Environment* exhibition, Totem design store, New York.

Ruhlmann, Jacques-Émile (1879–1933)
French designer and decorator; born and active Paris.

Biography The order of his forenames is probably Émile-Jacques, as his business stationery indicates. 1907, Ruhlmann took over the family housepainting business in Paris; was patronized by architect Charles Plumet and encouraged by couturier Jacques Doucet, Frantz Jourdain, and Tony Selmersheim and thus showed his work for the first time in 1911 (see below). He moved the business from the rue Marché Saint-Honoré to 10, rue de Maleville (the paint, wallpaper, and mirror work-

Ernö Rubik. Rubik's Cube puzzle. 1974. Plastic, 2 1/4 x 2 1/4 x 2 1/4" (5.7 x 5.7 x 5.7 cm). Mfr.: Ideal Toy Corporation, Hong Kong (1980). Gift of the mfr. MoMA.

shops) and to 27, rue de Lisbonne (the interior-design and furnishings agency). The first occasion on which he showed his work alone was a dining room with various 'classical' pieces in a circular gallery at 1913 Salon d'Automne, which established him as the primary exponent of luxury furniture. Ruhlmann's work was influenced by the Louis Philippe period and was of the highest quality, elegance, and technical and formal refinement. David David-Weill, a financier and art collector, commissioned a functional desk and cabinet to complement his collection of French 18th-century art. 1919 with painting contractor Pierre Laurent, Ruhlmann founded the Établissements Ruhlmann et Laurent to produce his work. Costly and warm woods were incorporated into simple, elegant forms. Over a year could elapse from receipt of an order to delivery. At his Hôtel du Collectionneur pavilion at 1925 Paris *Exposition*, he showed pieces that blended classical luxury with Parisian modernism, exemplifying the baroque aspects of Art Déco style. By 1928, his work showed a more sumptuous and massive approach. Ruhlmann made a contribution to the avant-garde in the form of standardized macassar-ebony modules, shown at 1929 Salon of Société des Artistes Décorateurs and intended for 'a viceroy of India,' in fact the Maharaja of Indore. He decorated the tea room of 1926 oceanliner *Île-de-France*, the meeting room of the Chambre de Commerce in Paris 1930, he designed interiors for the Palais de l'Élysée, the offices of various government ministers and administrators, the town hall of the 5th arrondissement in Paris and of the suburb Puteaux, and numerous private residences. Jean Renouardt commissioned the widely published 1930 Soleil bed in rosewood veneer. Toward the end of his short career, he began to use chrome plating and silver in his furniture; the combination of metal with luxurious woods can be found in his furniture for the palace of the Maharaja of Indore. Ruhlmann died in Paris.
Exhibitions Ruhlmann wallpaper was included in Tony Selmersheim's stand at 1911 Salon of Société des Artistes Décorateurs, and other work in its 1919–26, 1928–30, and 1932–34 editions. First showed his work alone, at the 1913 Salon d'Automne, and again in 1926. Ruhlmann built the Hôtel du Collectionneur pavilion (with contributions by Pierre Patout and a group of artists and decorators, including Jean Puiforcat, Edgar Brandt, Émile Decœur, Jean Dunand, Pierre Legrain, and Georges Bastard) at 1925 *Exposition Internationale des Arts Décoratifs et Industriels Modernes*, Paris. Ruhlmann exhibited in Madrid and Milan in 1927 and designed one of the salons at 1931 *Exposition Coloniale*, Paris. His last major display was at 1932 Salon of Société des Artistes Décorateurs. Work subject of retrospectives at Musée des Arts Décoratifs, Paris, in 1934, and Musée des Arts Décoratifs de la Ville de Bordeaux, France, in 2001 (catalogs below).
Bibliography Cat., *E.-J. Ruhlmann: exposition retrospective*, Paris : Musée des Arts Décoratifs, 1934. Penelope Hunter, *Notable Acquisitions, 1965–75*, New York: The Metropolitan Museum of Art, 1975: 229. Florence Camard, *Ruhlmann*, Paris: Regard, 1983. Pierre Cabanne, *Encyclopédie art déco*, Paris: Somogy, 1986: 233–35. Pierre Kjellberg, *Art déco: les maîtres du mobilier, le décor des paquebots*, Paris: Amateur, 1986/1990. Cat., Bruno Foucart et al., *Ruhlmann: un génie de l'art déco*, Paris: Somogy, 2001. Florence Camard et al., *Ruhlmann: un génie de l'art déco*, Paris: *Beaux Arts* magazine, 2001.

Rune, Ola (1963–)

Swedish teacher, architect, and interior and furniture designer; born Lycksele; active Stockholm.

Training 1987, Cutters Academy, Stockholm; 1990, art and design, Southwark College, London; 1992, interior and furniture design, Det Kongelige Danske Kunstakademi, Copenhagen; 1994, master of fine arts degree, Konstfack, Stockholm.
Biography Rune was the headteacher, Anders Beckman School of Design; 1993 with Mårten Cleasson and Eero Koivisto, established Claesson Koivisto Rune Arkitektkontor; both Stockholm.
Exhibitions/citations Partnership work subject of 2002 exhibition, Arkitekturmuseet, Stockholm. 1991 Scandinavia–Japan Sasakawa Foundation citation; 1992 first prize, apartment design (with Koivisto), HSB competition; 1993 Nordplus grant (with Koivisto); 1994 first prize, international furniture competition Design for Europe, Intérieur 94 biennial, Courtrai.
Bibliography Terence Riley et al., *Claesson Koivisto Rune*, Barcelona: Editorial Gustavo Gili: 2001.
> See Claesson, Mårten (for honors and work with the partnership).

Ruskin, John (1819–1900)

British social critic and writer.

Training 1837–42, Oxford University.
Biography Ruskin's influential books *The Seven Lamps of Architecture* (London: Smith, Elder, 1849) and *The Stones of Venice* (London: Smith, Elder, 1851–53) illustrate his interest in architecture and the Gothic style in particular. His writings were the mainspring of inspiration for the Arts and Crafts movement. Ruskin persuaded William Morris and Arts and Crafts followers to eschew industrial production for aesthetic and social reasons and abhorred machine-made devices and products such as railway trains, cut glass, iron, and materials that lacked handmade 'truth'; disparaged the 'fatal newness' of, for example, veneered rosewood furniture; equated the beauty of medieval craftsmanship and architecture with the joy and artisanal dignity he believed were associated with their creation; exerted an influence which reached far into 20th-century design; though an ardent historicist, foreshadowed some of the fundamental tenets of modernism, particularly by arguing that the forms of things must be faithful to the nature and materials of their construction.
Bibliography E.T. Cook and A. Wedderburn (eds.), *The Complete Works of John Ruskin*, London: George Allen, 1903–12. Gillian Naylor, *The Arts and Crafts Movement*, London: Trefoil, 1971. J.L. Bradley, *A Ruskin Chronology*, Houndmills, Basingstoke: Macmillan Press; New York: St. Martin's, 1997.

Ruskin Pottery

British ceramics manufacturer; located Smethwick.

History 1898, Edward Richard Taylor (the principal of Birmingham School of Art) founded the Ruskin Pottery in Smethwick, near Birmingham, for his son William Howson Taylor (1876–1935) to run. Influenced by the Arts and Crafts movement, the pottery was named after (but otherwise not associated with) John Ruskin and soon became highly regarded. Taylor's style was based on hand-thrown and hand-turned models with unusual glazes. Its three main areas of production were (1) mottled soufflé glazes in single colors, (2) luster finishes, and (3) high-temperature *flambé* glazes, experimented with from late 1840s by Grongiart, Salvetat, and others at Sèvres and developed there by Auguste Delaherche, Pierre-Adrien Dalpayrat, Ernest Chaplet, and Théodore Deck. Taylor was the only ceramicist in Britain to match and sometimes exceed the French technique. Mastering the process by 1919, his wares retained their high quality for almost a quarter of a century, and every piece, due to the variety of glazes, was unique. His glazes in rich tones of green, blue, purple, and red were produced in changing veined, clouded, and mottled patterns. 1935, the pottery closed on Taylor's death.
Exhibitions/citations Grand prize, 1904 *Louisiana Purchase Exposition*, St. Louis, Missouri; high citations at international exhibitions in Milan, Brussels, and elsewhere. Wares subject of 1975 exhibition, London (catalog below); 1976 exhibition, Birmingham City Museum; 1998 exhibition, Royal Cornwall Museum (catalog below).
Bibliography Cat., *Ruskin Pottery*, London: Victoria and Albert Museum, 1975. Sales cat., *Ruskin Pottery*, London: Haslam and Whiteway, 1981. Sales cat., *British Decorative Arts from 1880 to the Present Day*, Christie's London, 20 Feb. 1991, lots 212–30. Paul Atterbury, *Ruskin Pottery: The Pottery of Edward Richard Taylor and William Howson Taylor, 1898–1935, London*: Baxendale, 1993. Cat., *Ruskin Pottery: Centenary Exhibition*, Truro: Royal Institute of Cornwall, 1998.

Russell, Gordon (1892–1980)

British furniture maker and designer; born Cricklewood, London; brother of R.D. Russell.

Biography 1908, Russell worked in his father's small antiques restoration workshop, where he practiced a number of crafts and was in charge of repairs; 1910, began to design furniture; after World War I, made furniture in the manner of Ernest Gimson. By 1926, his firm Gordon Russell Ltd. was using machinery in an attempt to reconcile the best of the Arts and Crafts tradition with the efficiency of mechanized production, absorbing the theories and ideas of modernism. He was a member of the Art-Workers' Guild and an early supporter of the Design and Industries Association; 1929, set up a shop at 24 Wigmore Street, London, with Nikolaus Pevsner as manager and, 1935–39, as a buyer; visited the 1930 Gunner Asplund-organized exhibition (*Stockholmsutställningen*), Stockholm, which proved a revelation to Russell. 1935, he moved to a large showroom designed by Geoffrey Jellicoe and located a few doors away from the previous quarters; c. 1930 with his brother R.D. Russell and the firm's other designers W.H. Russell (no relation) and Eden Minns, began designing furniture in a plain modern style without ornamentation. From 1931, the firm produced radio cabinets designed by R.D. Russell for

Murphy Radio in Welwyn Garden City; these were starkly modern and influenced by a combination of the International Style and the Arts and Crafts movement. 1938 with Crofton Gane (of the Gane's store in Bristol) and Geoffrey Dunn (of the Dunn's of Bromley store), Russell initiated the Good Furnishing Group for mass-production furniture, which was discontinued with the outbreak of World War II. From 1939, Russell was influential on British domestic furniture through his involvement with the Utility Scheme; 1940, resigned as managing director of own firm, succeeded by R.H. Bee. 1943–47, he was chairperson, Board of Trade Design Panel, responsible for the production of Utility furniture; 1947–59, was director, Council of Industrial Design; 1948–49, was professor of furniture design, Royal College of Art, London, and active in the organization of 1951 *Festival of Britain*, London. The firm Gordon Russell is now a brand of the Steelcase Group.
Exhibitions/citations Work first shown in 1922, in Cheltenham; subsequently, at 1924 *British Empire Exhibition*, Wembley, and 1925 *Exposition Internationale des Arts Décoratifs et Industriels Modernes*, Paris, winning medals. Work of the Russell firm shown at 1935 exhibition, Royal Academy, London; 1937 *Exposition Internationale des Arts et Techniques dans la Vie Moderne*, Paris; 1951 *Festival of Britain*, London. Work subject of 1992 centenary exhibition in firm's own showrooms, London. 1940, elected Honorary Royal Designer for Industry, UK; fellow, Society of Arts; 1955, knighted.
Bibliography Gordon Russell, *Designer's Trade, Autobiography of Gordon Russell*, London: Allen & Unwin, 1968. Cat., *Thirties: British Art and Design Before the War*, London: Arts Council of Great Britain / Hayward Gallery, 1979. Ken Baynes and Kate Baynes, *Gordon Russell*, London: The Design Council, 1980. Fiona MacCarthy and Patrick Nuttgens, *Eye for Industry*, London: Royal Society of Arts, 1986. Jeremy Myerson, *Gordon Russell, Designer of Furniture*, London: The Design Council, 1992.

Russell, 'R.D.' Richard Dick Drew (1903–1981)

British architect and furniture and industrial designer; brother of Gordon Russell.

Training Architectural Association, London.
Biography 1929, R.D. Russell joined his brother's firm Gordon Russell Ltd., where he designed dining-room and bedroom furniture, sideboards, chests, and, most notably, radio cabinets for Murphy Radio of Welwyn Garden City, Hertfordshire. 1934–36, he was staff designer at Murphy and, 1936, a consultant there; created an influential series of veneered plywood radio cabinets, including 1932 AS model. Continuing in his own practice after World War II, he was also an influential teacher at Royal College of Art, London, where he was a professor of furniture from 1949–64. He continued to design Murphy's radio cases after the war. His 1933 A4 and 1935 A26 table models and 1948 A188C tapering concave-frame cabinet with its central speaker have recently been widely published, discussed, and admired. Early 1950s, he also worked with Murphy on TV cabinets. 1960s with R.Y. Gooden, he designed the remodeled gallery for Greek sculpture at the British Museum and, 1969–71, the Western sculpture and oriental art galleries and the print room there.
Exhibitions/citations 1944, elected Honorary Royal Designer for Industry, UK. Work subject (with Marian Pepler) of 1983–84 exhibition, Geffrye Museum, London (catalog below).
Bibliography Michael Farr, *Design in British Industry: A Mid-Century Survey*, London: Cambridge, 1955. Cat., Rosamund Allwood and Kedrun Laurie, *R.D. Russell, Marian Pepler*, London: Inner London Ed-ucation Authority, 1983. Anne Channon, 'R.D. Russell: Designer for Industry 1930–1935,' master of arts degree thesis, London: Royal Col-lege of Art / Victoria and Albert Museum, 1985. Fiona MacCarthy and Patrick Nuttgens, *Eye for Industry*, London: Royal Society of Arts, 1986. 'The Radio,' London: Design Museum, 1989. Jeremy Myerson, *Gordon Russell, Designer of Furniture*, London: The Design Council, 1992.

Ruyant, Frédéric (1961–)

French environmental designer, architect, interior architect, and teacher; born Paris.

Biography Ruyant's work has included 1999 Milky ceramic vase, 1999 Boomy swaying lamp, 1999 Mobilier en Ligne–Ligne de Mobilier unit, 2001 first-aid kit for French Red Cross, 2001 Art du Jardin environment, coat rack by Camif, Running Sofa with micro-beads by Gilles Peyroulet, Issey Miyake showroom in Paris, Gemini lamp series and 2001 Rollerglass portable bent-glass tables by Cinna, and a number of inventive, intriguing prototypes, exploring new materials and techniques.
Citations 1989, 1997, 1998, 2000 Appel Permanent grants and 2003 Carte Blanche production support, VIA (French furniture association); 1999 Creation Grant (for Mobilier en Ligne–Ligne...), Ministère de la Culture, France; 1999 Prix Lumière d'Argent.
Bibliography Mel Byars, *50 Beds...*, Hove: RotoVision, 2000.

rya

Finnish weaving process.

History Rya (or *ryijy*) is a traditional type of fabrication practiced by women in Finland. Rough yarns are handwoven into thick tapestries intended for use as carpets, marriage-bed covers, and wall hangings. 1929, Eva Brummer set up a studio in Helsinki to revive rya, and numerous others followed. (However, Eero Saarinen had been dyeing rya rugs in the 1910s.) The technique involves cutting the pile unevenly in order to create a thick relief effect, particularly popular in the 1950s and closely identified with the Scandinavian modern style of the decade.
Bibliography Cat., Kathryn B. Hiesinger and George H. Marcus III (eds.), *Design Since 1945*, Philadelphia: Philadelphia Museum of Art, 1983. Anja Louhio, *Modern Finnish Rugs*, Helsinki, 1975: 42–45.

Ryan, Mike (1961–)

American designer

Training Architecture, California Polytechnic State University, San Luis Obispo.
Biography 1984, Ryan settled in Italy to complete his final year of study at the Florence extension of the California Polytechnic; subsequently, was active in the design of interiors, products, and architecture; began working with Sottsass Associates, Milan, where he became a partner in 1989; independently, has designed objects and furniture for various Italian and foreign clients; has lectured and organized workshops on architecture and design at Istituto Europeo di Design and Domus Academy (both Milan), California Polytechnic, and Syracuse (N.Y.) University's Florence extension.
Exhibitions Work included in group architecture and design shows.

Ryggen, Hannah (1894–1970)

Swedish textile designer and teacher; born Malmö; active Norway.

Biography 1924, she settled on a small farm in Trøndelag, Norway, and began weaving in her own studio; sheared, carded, spun, and dyed the fibers herself, and wove without cartoons or sketches. The often-political subject matter of her textiles ranged from the Spanish Civil War to the plight of unmarried mothers. Her tapestries were akin to Expressionist and late-Cubist paintings.
Exhibitions Work shown at 1964 Biennale di Venezia.
Bibliography Cat., David Revere McFadden (ed.), *Scandinavian Modern Design 1880–1980*, New York: Abrams, 1982. Cat., Anne Wichstrøm, *Rooms with a View: Women's Art in Norway 1880–1990*, Oslo: The Royal Ministry of Foreign Affairs, 1990: 26.

Rykkens, Oddvin (1937–)

Norwegian furniture designer.

Biography Rykkens designed the widely published Balans Skulptor ergonomic stool; with Peter Opsvik and Svein Gusrud, was an innovator of the ergonomic seating popular in the early 1980s.
Bibliography Fredrik Wildhagen, *Norge i Form*, Oslo: Sternersen, 1988: 201.
> See Mengshoel, Hans Christian.

Ettore Sottsass and Perry King. Valentine portable typewriter (detail). 1969. MoMA.

S.A.L.I.R.
> See Studio Ars Labor Industrie Riunite (S.A.L.I.R.).

Saalburg, Guillaume (1957–)

French glassworker and engraver; active Paris.

Training In a glass engraver's workshop.
Biography Saalburg has worked as an architect and designer for business and domestic clients; collaborated with Gilles Derain, Richard Moyer, Andrée Putman, Philippe Starck, and Jean-Michel Wilmotte; participated in the design of the hall of TV broadcasting company Canal Plus. Clients have included Baleri Italia (from 1985). 1987, he established his own firm Opaque Diffusion for the production of tabletop objects and glass furniture; 1999, collaborated with La Machinerie (Pascale Simonnet and Mathias Hima, principals) on furniture and glassware for the Arthur & Fox boutiques; has been active in a number of juries, workshops, and seminars.
Exhibitions Work shown at Institut Français d'Architecture in 1987; 1990 exhibition of VIA (French furniture association), Paris (catalog below); double glass wall filled with transparent marbles (with Ronald-Cécil Sportes) at 1983 Salon of Société des Artistes Décorateurs; all Paris. In 1989 *Le verre grandeur nature* exhibition, Parc Floral, Vincennes; 2001 *Le Verre, des Créateurs aux Industriels Français (1995–2000)*, Espace Landowski, Boulogne-Billancourt.
Bibliography Cat., *Les années VIA 1980–1990*, Paris: Musée des Arts Décoratifs, 1990: 154–55.

Saarinen, Eero (1910–1961)

Finnish architect; born Kirkkonummi; active the US; son of Eliel and Loja Saarinen.

Training 1930, sculpture, Académie de la Grande Chaumière, Paris; 1934, bachelor of fine arts degree, Yale University, New Haven, Conn.
Training 1923 with his father, Eero Saarinen settled in New York; intending to become a sculptor; with his family, moved to Bloomfield Hills, Mich.; designed 1929 furniture in a joint project with his father and mother for the Kingswood School for girls; after 1934, worked on furniture design with Norman Bel Geddes, New York; 1936, returned to his father's Cranbrook Academy, Bloomfield Hills, where he taught briefly; 1937–41, practiced architecture with his father in Ann Arbor, Mich.; 1941–47, was a partner with his father and J. Robert Swan-son in Ann Arbor. With lifetime friend Charles Eames, Saarinen designed the innovative seating furniture in the Mary Seaton Room, 1940 Kleinhans Music Hall, Buffalo, N.Y., of which Saarinen and his father were the architects. 1940s, Saarinen also worked with Eames in Venice, Cal., on various projects, including 1942 sculptural plywood leg splint for the US Navy. For Hans and Florence Knoll's furniture company and beginning an association with them in 1946, Eero designed 1946 Grasshopper upholstered lounge chair/ottoman, 1948 fiberglass-shell Womb chair, and a range of office furniture. The Womb chair became a popular icon of mid-century design; Saarinen recollected that he designed it as a modern version of the traditional overstuffed club-chair model; it was a descendant of the 1940 prize-winning chair entry (with Charles Eames) at New York's Museum of Modern Art competition. Saarinen gained prominence when he won the 1948 competition for the design of the Jefferson Westward Expansion Memorial (later called Centennial Gateway Arch), St. Louis, Mo., which drew directly on an unrealized project by Italian architect Adalberto Libera (with Di Berardino) for the entrance to 1942 *Esposizione Universale di Roma*. As the architect, Saarinen created office chairs by Knoll for 1948–56 General Motors Technical Center on an artificial lake in Warren, Mich. 1950, Saarinen established an architecture/design office in Ann Arbor. His 1955–57 pedestal furniture range by Knoll, including 1955–56 Tulip armchair with a fiberglass seat and cast-aluminum pedestal, pursued his 'one piece, one material' furniture-design ideal, attempting to rid a room of a 'forest' of furniture legs. He also strove for sculptural forms in furniture, rejecting 1920s rectilinearity. His architectural accomplishments, amalgamating architecture, design, and engineering, were dramatic. Cesar Pelli, Kevin Roche, and John Dinkeloo began their careers in the architecture office of Saarinen. He died in Ann Arbor, Mich.
Architecture 1939 Smithsonian Art Gallery, Washington; 1948–56 General Motors Technical Center (with Eliel Saarinen and architecture firm Smith, Hinchman and Gryllis), Warren, Mich.; 1953–55 Kresge Auditorium and Chapel, Massachusetts Institute of Technology (MIT), Cambridge, Mass.; 1956 US Embassy, London; 1956–58 David S. Ingalls Ice Hockey Rink, Yale University, New Haven, Conn.; 1962 Trans World Airlines Terminal, Idlewild (now John F. Kennedy) Airport, New York; 1958–63 Dulles International Airport, Va.; 1956–63 John Deere administration center, Moline, Ill.; 1964 National Expansion Memorial (Centennial Gateway Arch), St. Louis, Mo.
Exhibitions/citations Work (with that of his father and mother) subject of 1932 exhibition, Detroit Institute of Arts. Tulip chair and other work have been included in a large number of exhibitions. Two first prizes (with Eames), 1940 *Organic Design in Home Furnishings* competition/exhibition, The Museum of Modern Art, New York; 1962 gold medal, American Institute of Architects (AIA), posthumously; 1966 Honors Award, AIA.
Bibliography Eero Saarinen, 'Function, Structure and Beauty,' *Archi-*

Eero Saarinen. Tulip armchair (no. 150). 1955–56. Fiberglass-reinforced polyester and cast aluminum, 31 1/2 x 25 1/4 x 23 1/2" (80 x 64.1 x 59.7 cm). Mfr.: Knoll International, US. Gift of the mfr. MoMA.

tectural Association Journal, July–Aug. 1957. Allan Temko, *Eero Saarinen*, New York: Braziller, 1962. Aline Saarinen (ed.), *Eero Saarinen on his Work 1947–64*, New Haven: Yale University, 1962. Cat., *Cranbrook: The Saarinen Years*, Detroit: Detroit Institute of Arts. Rupert Spade, *Eero Saarinen*, New York: Simon & Schuster, 1971. Cat., *Knoll au Louvre*, Paris: Musée des Arts Décoratifs, 1972. Robert A. Kuhner, *Eero Saarinen: His Life and Work*, Monticello, Ill., 1975. Cat., Lisa Phillips (intro.), *Shape and Environment: Furniture Designed by American Architects*, New York: Whitney Museum of American Art, 1982: 52–53. Robert Judson Cark et al., *Design in America: The Cranbrook Vision 1925–1950*, New York: Abrams/The Metropolitan Museum of Art, 1983. Paola Antonelli (ed.), *Objects of Design: The Museum of Modern Art*, New York: The Museum of Modern Art, 2003: 199.

Saarinen, Gottlieb Eliel (1873–1950)

Finnish architect and designer; born Rantasalmi; active Helsinki, Kirkkonummi, and Bloomfield Hills, Mich.; husband of Loja Saarinen; father of Eero Saarinen.

Training Painting, Helsingin yliopisto (Helsinki university); 1893–97, architecture, Helsingin ammattikorkeakoulu (Helsinki polytechnic).
Training To 1898, Saarinen and former fellow-student Herman Gesellius were draftspeople periodically in architect Gustaf Nyström's office. 1896, Saarinen formed a productive partnership with Gesellius and another fellow student, Armas Lindgren, in Helsinki; and, 1903–05, in the 1901–03 'Hvitträsk' house on Lake Vitträsk, Kirkkonummi, also serving as the joint studio/home of the Geselliuses, Lindgrens, and Saarinens and their employees. After 1916, 'Hvitträsk' was the Saarinen residence alone. It became a mecca for artists. Saarinen's 1916 furniture in 'Hvitträsk' and 'Suur-Merijoki' showed the influences of Mackintosh and Hugh Baillie Scott. His furniture for 1905 Malchow house was lighter and simpler; 1908 Hannes and 1910 White chairs are today made by Adelta in Dinslaken, Germany. Saarinen's wife Loja built his architectural models. He was a leader of the National Romantic movement in Finland; 1910s, began designing rya rugs; from 1912, was a member, Deutscher Werkbund; after winning second prize for 1922 Chicago Tribune Tower competition, moved with his family to the US in 1923 and returned to 'Hvitträsk' almost yearly, sometimes with Florence Schust (aka Florence Knoll); taught architecture, University of Michigan; 1924, was invited by wealthy publisher George Gough Booth to develop Cranbrook Educational Community, Bloomfield, Mich., a preparatory school for boys; 1925, designed buildings for Cranbrook Foundation (established 1927); from 1932, was the president, Cranbrook Academy of Art. He designed furniture, glass, silver, brass, and other furnishings for his own house, including 1929 chairs reproduced today by Adelta. 1929–31, his wife 'Loja' Saarinen (b. Louise Gesellius 1879–1968; sister of Herman Gesellius) designed and made rugs and textiles at the Cranbrook, including curtains and carpets for the Kingswood School for girls designed by Eliel, and made a rug designed by Frank Lloyd Wright for Edgar Kaufmann Sr.'s office, Pittsburgh. Eliel Saarinen's sketches for furniture were no more than line drawings, lacking instructions for materials and veneers; construction decisions were made by cabinetmaker and Swedish immigrant Tor Berglund, who became an instructor at Cranbrook. Saarinen's furniture collection by John Widdicomb was serially produced in bleached wood and with steel features. First half 1930s, his silver designs were produced by Arthur Nevill Kirk and Charles Price in Cranbrook's metal workshop and by International Silver, Meriden, Conn. His widely published 1934 silver-plate (also copper) urn and tray set were produced by Wilcox Silver Plate (of International Silver). Influential as a teacher, he assembled effective instructors at Cranbrook, who included Eames, Harry Bertoia, son Eero, and Swedish sculptor Carl Milles. Florence Knoll and Jack Lenor Larsen were among Eliel Saarinen's students. His books include Eliel Saarinen, *The Cranbrook Development* (Bloomfield Hills, Mich.: Cranbrook, 1931), *The City: Its Growth, Its Decay, Its Future* (New York: Reinhold, 1943) and *Search for Form: A Fundamental Approach to Art* (New York: Reinhold, 1948).
Work In Finland, Saarinen designed 1896–1923 the cupboard and swivel and stationary armchairs for the Pohjola building; 1901–03 a full range of fabrics and textiles, including upholstery fabrics and carpets, for 'Suur-Merijoki' house; numerous furnishing for the 1901–03 'Hvitträsk' house (statuary in bronze by wife Loja and paintings in dining room by Väinö Blomstedt); tables, case goods, seating, and a piano for the 1901–04 Hvittorp house; lighting, tables, seating, case goods, and shelving for the 1905–07 Remer house; desks, seating, and tables for the Helsinki Railway Station, 1904–19; 1910s–20s, tables, case goods, seating, and rya rugs, and a large amount of other furniture and furnishings. The majority of Saarinen's furniture designs were site-specific. He created numerous other pieces, resulting from his association with Suomen Käsityön Ystävien (friends of Finnish handicraft), Suomen Taideteollisuusyhdistys (Finnish society of crafts and design), and Finnish General Handicraft Society. Private furniture and furnishings commissions came from relatives, friends, and colleagues. Textiles were integral to his interiors, such as curtains and rya rugs and textiles for Suomen Käsityön Ystävien. Other work: metalware, including candlesticks, tea and coffee services, and compote dishes; from 1909, banknotes; from 1917, postage stamps and other graphic designs such as soap labels, Christmas cards, book illustrations, title pages, company signage/trademarks, emblems, book plates, posters, cartoons; more than 50 recorded paintings and portraits, landscapes, still-lifes, other works of art.
Architecture Large number of works through the Gesellius, Lindgren and Saarinen partnership from 1898–1900 Finnish pavilion at 1900 *Exposition Universelle*, Paris, to 1902–12 Suomen Kansallismuseo (Finnish national museums), with decorations by Armas Lindgren and Emil Wikström and, in 1928, Akseli Gallen-Kallela fresco. Metalwork on partnership's buildings was designed and executed by Eric O.W. Ehrström, including for Pohjola, and Hvitträsk, Hvittorp, Remer houses, Suomen Kansallismuseo, and Pohjoismaiden Osakepankki bank

Lino Sabattini. Boule teapot. 1950. Silver-electroplated brass alloy and silver alloy, 4 7/8 x 6 x 9" (12.4 x 15.2 x 22.9 cm), dia. 6" (15.2 cm). Mfr.: Sabattini Argenteria, Italy (1957). Gift of the designer. MoMA.

Marius-Ernest Sabino. Vase. c. 1925. Partially polished and partially blue-patinated black glass mouth-blown into a form, h. 6 11/16" (17 cm). Mfr.: Sabino, France. Courtesy Quittenbaum Kunstauktionen, Munich.

(with its distinctive brass doors). Saarinen alone designed 1904–19 railway station, Helsinki; 1904–13 railway station, Karelia (now Viipuri); 1906 The Hague Peace Palace competition (Saarinen's entry called 'L'homme'); 1908 Parliament House competition (won first prize; structure unrealized), Helsinki; and 1911–12 Town Hall, Lahti. From 1925, he designed buildings of the Cranbrook Foundation, Mich., and, with son Eero, 1938 Kleinhans Music Hall, Buffalo, N.Y.; Tanglewood Opera Shed, Stockbridge, Mass.; 1941–42 Tabernacle Church of Christ, Columbus, Ind. He died in Bloomfield Hills, Mich.
Exhibitions/citations Second prize, competition for a house for German publisher Wilhelm Girardt, Honnef-am-Rhein, Essen. 1910s, furniture shown at Salon d'Automne, Paris, and 1914 *Deutscher Werkbund-Ausstellung*, Cologne. Saarinen designed a dining room installed at 1929 *The Architect and Industrial Art: An Exhibition of Contemporary American Design*, The Metropolitan Museum of Art, New York. Design work of the Saarinen family shown at a 1932 exhibition, Detroit Institute of Arts. Installed Room for a Lady (with his wife), Central Gallery, 1935 (13th) *Contemporary American Industrial Art,* 1935 exhibition, The Metropolitan Museum of Art, where his 1934 silver-plate urn and-tray set was included. Silverware shown at 1937 *Exposition Internationale des Arts et Techniques dans la Vie Moderne*, Paris. Work included in 1983 *Design in America: The Cranbrook Vision 1925–1950,* touring the US (catalog below).
Bibliography Albert Christ-Janer, *Eliel Saarinen: Finnish-American Architect and Educator*, Chicago: University of Chicago, 1948. Marika Hausen, 'Gesellius-Lindgren-Saarinen,' *Arkkitehti*, 9 Nov. 1967. Cat. Robert Judson Clark et al., *Design in America: The Cranbrook Vision 1925–1950*, New York: Abrams/The Metropolitan Museum of Art, 1983. Marika Hausen et al., *Eliel Saarinen: Projects 1896–1923*, Cambridge: MIT, 1990. Gregory Wittkopp (ed.), *Saarinen House and Garden: A Total Work of Art*, New York: Abrams; Bloomfield Hills: Cranbrook, 1995.

Saarinen, 'Loja' (b. Louise Gesellius 1879–1968).
> See Saarinen, Gottlieb Eliel.

Saarinen, Eva Lisa 'Pipsan'
> See Swanson, Pipsan.

Sabattini, Lino (1925–)
Italian metalsmith and designer; born Correggio; active Bregnano and Milan.

Biography Sabattini worked as a silversmith from a very young age; learned metalworking techniques and became interested in shapes derived from the behavior of natural materials. His early work is exemplified by a 1950 teapot by W. Wolff in Germany. Moving to Milan in 1955, he met Gio Ponti, who encouraged him, and thus his work was included in a 1956 exhibition organized by Ponti, when Sabattini first came to international attention. 1955–63, he was active in Milan and, as the director of design, Christofle Orfèvrerie, Paris; created free-flowing, simple, and sculptural forms such as 1960 Como tea service by Christofle and other metalware. He also designed ceramics, glassware, and metalwork by Rosenthal, Nava, and Zani & Zani. 1964, Sabattini established his own factory Sabattini Argenteria, in Bregnano, near Como; executed the renowned 1976 Saucière Estro sauce bowl, 1986 Insect Legs silver and black titanium tableware and cutlery, and 1987 Connato silver-plated brass-alloy vase. He became a member, Associazione per il Disegno Industriale (ADI).
Exhibitions/citations Work first shown in a 1956 exhibition organized by Ponti. Regularly participated in Triennale di Milano, including 1954 (10th) and 1957 (15th) editions; 1968 *Hemisfair*, San Antonio, Texas; 1970 international exhibition, Ghent; 1983–84 *Design Since 1945*, Philadelphia Museum of Art; 1969–75 installments and 1971 gold medal, *Mostra Internazionale dell'Arredamento*, Monza; *Exempla '73*, Monaco; 1973 BIO 5 industrial-design biennial, Ljubljana; *Forme Nuove in Italia*, Tehran; numerous subsequent others. Received gold medal, 1962 *Fiera Internazionale*, Monaco; citation at exhibition of 100 years of avant-garde silver, Musée du Louvre, Paris; gold medal, World Craft Council, Munich; 1979 (for Eskimo no. B255 ice bucket) Premio Compasso d'Oro.
Bibliography Enrico Marelli, *Lino Sabattini: Intimations and Craftsmanship*, Mariano Comense: Metron, 1980. Enrico Marelli, *Lino Sabattini: 23 figure (dal '78 all '81)*, Mariano Comense: Metron, 1982. Filippo Alison and Renato de Fusco, *L'artidesign: il caso Sabattini*, Naples: Electa, 1991.

Sabino, Marius-Ernest (1878–1961)
Italian designer; born Sicily; active Paris.

Training Under his wood sculptor father; École Nationale des Arts Decoratifs and École Nationale des Beaux-Arts; both Paris.
Biography Sabino moved to France with his family at an early age; eventually became interested in the effects of electrical lighting on glass; From 1919, Sabino designed traditional lighting in wood or bronze and then soon turned to glass, produced by himself to 1930, when he hired production manager Grivois, whose stated goal was to make lighting transcend banality. Earlier (1925), Sabino developed an opalescent glass with a blue hue and used pressed and molded patterned glass in bas-relief. Ranging from very small to monumental, his lighting models included menu holders, statues, large vases, panels, ceiling tiles, pilasters, columns, stelae, bibelots, doors, and fountains. Also designed lighting for hotels, restaurants, and special lighting for 1927 oceanliner Île-de-France and others for 1935 oceanliner *Normandie*; 1935 lamps and chandeliers for the Shah of Persia. By 1939, Sabino's work had become more diverse than René Lalique's and Jean Perzel's, although of a lesser quality. Evidently, after World War II he designed nothing new. 1979, the enterprise was sold to a firm in Houston, Tex., named Sabino Crystal Company, with manufacturing continuing in France of a wide range of opalescent figurines, boudoir boxes, vases, lighting, and other items.
Exhibitions Work first shown at 1925 Salon d'Automne (subsequently, responsible for all the general illuminations in the halls, passageways, and antechambers of its annual editions); 1925 *Exposition Internationale des Arts Décoratifs et Industriels Modernes*; Salons of Société des Artistes Decorateurs from 1926; illuminated column at 1937 *Exposition Internationale des Arts et Techniques dans la Vie Moderne*; all Paris.
Bibliography *Lux*, June 1928: 88, Nov. 1928: 155, Nov. 1929: 161, Jan. 1930: 3, Sept. 1931: 101–04. *The Studio Yearbook*, 1930: 171. G. Henriot, *Luminaire moderne*, 1937: plate 12. Alastair Duncan, *Art Nouveau and Art Déco Lighting*, New York: Simon & Schuster, 1978.

Sacchi, Giovanni (aka Il Sacchi 1913–)
Italian artisanal model maker; born Sesto San Giovanni (Milan).

Training 1925–34, apprenticeship in the pattern workshop of foundry Marelli and study in mechanical drawing at night school.
Biography Sacchi worked at factory in Sesto San Giovanni for one week and, immediately bored, became an apprentice at age 12 in a small workshop to make wooden maquettes for the mechanical parts of iron molds. Subsequently, he served ten years in the army and, as part of the Resistance during World War II, was incarcerated in prison. 1948, after the war, Sacchi established a workshop on the Via Sirtori, Milan, and met industrial designer Marcello Nizzoli, for whom he bagan to make pre-production wooden maquettes, the first being of Nizzoli's 1948 Lexikon 80 typewriter, produced by Olivetti; later confessed that Nizzoli 'taught me to believe in this work'; became what biographer Piero Polato has called 'the designer's other half.' During his lifetime, he made more than 20,000 maquettes of work—from cars and clocks

to cigarette lighters and buildings—designed by about 300 designers/architets of products by 500 manufacturers, including Ermenigildo Preti's 1951–53 Iso mini-automobile. Other designers/architects included Marco Zanuso Sr., Franco Albini, Mario Bellini, Cini Boeri, Achille and Pier Giacomo Castiglioni, Anna Castelli Ferrieri, Joe Colombo, Michele De Lucchi, De Pas/D'Urbino/Lomazzi, Fortunato Depero, Enzo Mari, Bruno Munari, Giovanni Offredi, Piero Polato, Gio Ponti, Alberto Rosselli, Aldo Rossi, Richard Sapper, Roberto Sambonet, Ettore Sottsass, and Francesco Trabucco. Sacchi's models were for manufacturers such as Alcatel, Artsana, BMW, Brionvega, Campari, Chicco, Flos, Italiana Luce, Italtel, IBM, Henkel, Kartell, Molteni, Siemens, Ultravox, and Vortice. 1998 at age 85, Il Sacchi, as he became affectionately known, closed his workshop, still on the Via Sirtori, and his historic collection of more than 350 wooden maquettes was purchased by the Lombardy Council for the Collection of Italian Design at the Triennale di Milano.
Exhibitions/citations Work subject of numerous venues in Asia, Eastern and Western Europe, Russia, and South America, including possibly the most significant, 2000 exhibition, Triennale di Milano (declaring, 'I dedicate this exhibition to "my" one hundred and more designers and architects.'). 1998 career award (for 'the chisel that became a pencil'), Premio Compasso d'Oro.
Bibliography Anty Pansera, 'Between the Drawing and the Product,' *Abitare*, no. 176, July 1979. Cat., Piero Polato, *Il modello nel design, la bottega di Giovanni Sacchi*, Milan: Hoepli, 1991. Giovanni Sacchi, 'The Designer's Other Half,' *Ottagano*, no. 102, Mar. 1992: 56–64.

Sacco, Bruno (1933–)

Italian automobile designer; born Udine; active Germany.

Biography From 1959, Sacco was the design manager of Mercedes-Benz and, subsequently, became the longest-ever design manager of any auto firm—to 1999. He inspired horizontal headlights; was able to keep the Mercedes-Benz grille in place for over 30 years, no matter the body style, and thus the marque's image; became known for designing wide bodies, high rear decks, hefty shoulders, and solid 'C' pillars—which typified all Mercedes-Benz models.
Bibliography Ricardo P. Felicioli, *Bruno Sacco: Mercedes-Benz Bereich Design*, Milan: Automobilia, 1998.

Sadler, Marc (1946–)

French industrial designer; born Innsbruck, Austria; active Milan.

Training To 1968, École Nationale Supérieure des Arts Décoratifs, Paris.
Biography From 1968, Sadler was an associate at Design Center 1 and, from 1970, at France Design, both Paris; 1969, founded Déco Design in the south of France, an organization specializing in product development that incorporated materials/components from Italy and northern Europe; 1976, established his own studio, Milan, and has designed products including 1993 Alu-Kit kitchen by Boffi, 1993 Bap1 motorcycle back protector by Dainese, 1994 Drop 1 and 2 sconces by Flos-Arteluce, 1995 Apotheos shower stall, and 1998 Airstream hospital bed, both by Faram, and 2001 Tite and Mite lamps by Foscarini. Has become known for his exploitation of advanced materials and technologies; opened a workshop in Asolo (near Venice) for CAD (computer-aided design) and CAM (computer-aided manufacturing) modelmaking and technical work; established affiliations with studios in New York and Venice; has lectured at numerous institutions, including Politecnico and Domus Academy in Milan, Strate Collège and ENSCI (Les Ateliers) in Paris, École Supérieure de Plasturgie in Oyonnax, École Nationale Supérieure d'Art in Nancy, others.
Citations 1994 (two citations), 1999, and 2001 (two citations) Premio Compasso d'Oro; 1996 award, Industrie Forum Design (iF); Creator of the Year, 1997 Salon du Meuble, Paris; 1998 Brook Stevens Design Prize.
Bibliography Cat., Paola Antonelli, *Mutant Materials in Contemporary Design*, New York: The Museum of Modern Art/Abrams, 1995. Mel Byars, *50 Products...*, Hove: RotoVision, 1998.

Sadler, Robert (1966–)
> See Radi Designers.

Sagaidachnii, Evgenii Yakovlevich (1886–1961)

Russian painter, graphic artist, and stage and decorative designer.

Biography A colleague of Mikhail Larionov, Vladimir Tatlin, M. Boychuk, and M. Le-Dantu, Sagaidachny was the art director of the 1911 performance of *Tsar Maximilian* organized by Union of Youth; later in life, lived in Lvov, active primarily in the decorative arts.
Exhibitions Participated in 1910 exhibition of Union of Youth and 1912 *Donkey's Tail* exhibition.
Bibliography Cat., *Kunst und Revolution: Russische und Sowjetische Kunst 1910–1932*, Vienna: Österreichisches Museum für angewandte Kunst, 1988.

Masatoshi Sakaegi. Mug (part of the Common series). c. 1998. Melamine, h. 3 1/2" x dia. 3 1/8" (9 x 8 cm). Mfr.: Kokusai Kako Co., Japan.

Saglio, André (1869–1929)
> See Drésa, Jacques.

Saint-Gobain

French glass and crystal manufacturer; located Chapelle-Saint-Mesmin.

History In the 17th century, France was a major producer of flat glass for mirrors and windows. 1665, the factory in Saint-Gobain became the Manufacture Royale des Glaces de France; 1909, began producing laminated (or safety glass), discovered by a chemist employee (and patented 1905). The factory has a tradition for producing not only high-yield industrial glass (as well as a wide range of other products in other materials) but also inexpensive domestic products such as vases and tableware, including 1948 Duralex pressed-glass for drinking goblets, still in production. One of its more unusual and widely published products was the 1937 illuminated glass radiator by René Coulon, who was instrumental in establishing the Institut de Recherche de la Sidérurgie et Laboratoire de Recherche de Saint-Gobain (Saint-Gobain institute of iron-steel research and its research laboratory). Acquistions have included TSL Group (now Saint-Gobain Quartz) in 1988, CertainTeed in 1967, Norton in 1990, Ball Foster Glass in 1995, Poliet in 1996, and a number of other glass, plastics, and ceramics firms. By 2003, the Groupe Saint-Gobain employed more than 175,500 people in offices and factories in more than 46 countries.
Exhibitions Saint-Gobain pavilion (Coulon radiator and other products), 1937 *Exposition Internationale des Arts et Techniques dans la Vie Moderne*, Paris.
Bibliography Cat., *Les années UAM 1929–1958*, Paris: Musée des Arts Décoratifs, 1988: 166–67. *Les carnets du design*, Paris: Mad-Cap Productions/APCI, 1986: 44. Maurice Hamon, *Du soleil à la terre: une histoire de Saint-Gobain*, Paris: J.-C. Lattès, 1988. Jean-Pierre Daviet, *Une multinationale à la française: histoire de Saint-Gobain, 1665–1989*, Paris: Fayard, 1989. Maurice Hamon and Dominique Perrin, *Au cœur du XVIIIe siècle industriel: condition ouvrière et tradition villageoise à Saint-Gobain*, Paris: P.A.U., 1993.

Saint-Louis, Cristalleries de

French glass manufacturer.

History 1586, a glassworks was established in the area of Münzthal (valley of the monks) in the village of Saint-Louis-les-Bitche, province of Lorraine. The Thirty Years War (1618–48) devastated the area and thus the factory. And not until 1767 did King Louis XV decree that the glassworks be re-established as the new royal glassworks. 1781, the operation became the first in France to manufacture lead crystal (or *crystallerie)*, the monopoly for which had been held, from its 1627 invention, in Newcastle. From 1819, the enterprise was known as Compagnie des Cristalleries de Saint-Louis; 1844, began production of opaline glass; 1892, developed a technique for pressing glass into a colorless and opaque crystal; c. 1900 began the production of Art Nouveau style glassware under the name Argental. During the Art Déco period, a number of consultant designers worked for the firm, including Maurice Dufrêne, Marcel Goupy, Jean Luce, and, from 1930, Jean Sala. Gérard Ingold (1922–) was the director of Saint-Louis for over 30 years and responsible for the rebirth in 1950s of paperweight manufacture (for which the firm had earlier become well known). 1969, the Castille group (holding company of Hermès and Pochet) took over the company. 1980s, a few outside designers began to be commissioned. The firm is active today with a stable of commissioned designers, including Olivier Gagnère, Matali Crasset, and others; however, the chairperson of Castille, Jean-Louis Dumas-Hermès, encourages their anonymity.
Bibliography Cat., *Verriers français contemporains: art et industrie*, Paris: Musée des Arts Décoratifs, 1982. Gérard Ingold, *Saint-Louis: de l'art en verre à l'art du cristal de 1586 à nos jours*, Paris: Denoël, 1986. Marie Girault, *Saint-Louis: quatre siècles de cristallerie au pays de Bitche*, Tournai, Belgium: La Renaissance du Livre, 1998.

Sakaegi, Masatoshi (1944–)

Japanese designer; born Chiba.

Biography 1983, Sakaegi founded his own eponymous design studio; specializes in ceramic and melamine tableware and frequently monumental ceramic sculpture. His distinctive tableware has been produced by Kokusai Kako in Japan, and others.
Citations A number of awards, including 1995 (4th) International Ceramics Competition, Mino, Japan; one-of-ten renowned designers, 1997 (50th) prize, Concorso Internazionale della Ceramica d'Arte, Faenza; silver award for ceramics for use, 2001 (1st) CEBIKO international ceramic biennial, Kyonggi Province, Korea.
Bibliography Jasper Morrison (ed.), *The International Design Yearbook*, London: Laurence King, 1999.

Sasaki Glass Co.

Japanese glass manufacturer.

History 1902, Sakaki Sujito Shoten (or Sakaki Sujito's Glass Shop) was first established in Tokyo as a wholesaler and then to produce oil lamps; 1912, added tableware to its inventory and extended production into electric lamps; 1929, developed adhesive pigments for glass and began the firing of hand-painted items (precursor to the glass printing process); from 1931, mass produced colored cut glass equal to European quality. Under the supervision of the Japanese ministry of commerce and industry during World War II, optical glass for the military was produced. After World War II having been completely destroyed, the firm was reorganized with new objectives that were to call on contemporary design. 1950, Sasaki invented and patented a machine for pressed glass and became the first in Japan to screen-print glass; 1957, was the first Asian firm to install H-28 automated machinery, thus producing 100,000 tumblers daily. This utility glass, inexpensive compared to imported ware, proved highly successful in Japan's food services section, continuing today. Also, metalware, particularly stainless steel, became an important product. 1982, Sasaki began the production of crystal. 2002, the mother firm in Japan was merged with the Housewares Division of Toyo Glass Co. (founded as Shimada Manufacturing Co. in Osaka in 1888) to form Toyo-Sasaki Glass Co. Most products are designed by staff personnel, including design director Kiroyuki Kashiwabara, who began with the firm in 1968. So¯ri Yanagi designed for Sasaki in 1967. Also before the merger, European and American designers included Martine Bedin, Constantin Boym, Ward Bennett (late-1980s Sengai crystal range and 1985 Double Helix steel cutlery), David Law (1986 Bordin and Aneic steel cutlery), Andrée Putman, Judy Smilow, Massimo Vignelli.
Bibliography Arlette Barré-Despond (ed.), *Dictionnaire international des arts appliqués et du design*, Paris: Regard, 1996.

Sakier, George (1897–1988)

American industrial designer; born Brooklyn, N.Y.

Training From late 1910s, commercial illustration, Pratt Institute, Brooklyn, New York; engineering Columbia University Graduate School, New York; in painting in Paris.
Biography 1913 at age 19, Sakier wrote the textbook *Machine Design and Descriptive Geometry*; was introduced to art through painting camouflage patterns during World War I; after 1918 while in Paris at the war's end, began working as an engineer, designing automatic machinery and teaching machine design and engineering mathematics; 1925, became assistant art director of French *Vogue* and campaigned for the restoration of the Mayan collection stored in the Trocadéro in Paris, a collection subsequently put on view. Late 1920s, he returned to New York, became the art director of magazines *Modes and Manners* and *Harper's Bazaar*; from 1927, was the design director, bureau of design development, American Radiator and Standard Sanitary Corporation, where he designed bathtubs and wash basins, and, concurrently, was an independent designer. Work for the firm incuded a 1932 bathroom sink and the first prefabricated bathrooms, available as complete or separate units (233 examples first installed in a Washington, D.C., apartment building in 1933–34). He provided designs for other firms, notably from 1929 for almost 50 years, as the chief design consultant at Fostoria Glass in Moundsville, W.V., creating a distinctive and extensive collection of domestic glassware. Through Sakier's efforts at Fostoria, American open-stock glassware for the first time became more popular in the US than European glass-ware. He believed in providing the public with what it wanted rather than what it needed and raised no objection when one of his designs was copied and sold in inexpensive store chains or five-and-dimes. He also designed the logo of Old Schenley whiskey; By mid-1930s, his freelance-design activities were providing him with a $15,000 to $25,000 annual income.
Exhibitions/citations Galerie Julien Lévy (paintings), Paris, c. 1918. Design work including in 1934 *Machine Art*, The Museum of Modern Art, New York; 1934 *The Industrial Arts Exposition*, National Alliance of Art and Industry Inc., Rockefeller Center, New York; 1939–40 *Golden Gate International Exposition*, San Francisco; designed Science and Education Building at 1939–40 *New York World's Fair: The World of Tomorrow*. Design work subject of 1949 exhibition, Philadelphia Art Alliance and Worcester (Mass.) Museum of Art; painting in 1999 exhibition, New York (catalog below). Three *Studio Yearbook* awards.
Bibliography Harry V. Anderson, 'Contemporary American Designers,' *Decorators Digest*, July 1933: 38–41. *Fortune*, Feb. 1934: 97–98. P. McGrain (ed.), *Fostoria, the Popular Years*, Frederick, Md.: McGrain Publications, 1982. Cat., Janet Kardon (ed.), *Craft in the Machine Age 1920–1945*, New York: Abrams with American Craft Museum, 1995. Leslie Piña, *Fostoria: Designer George Sakier*, Atglen, Pa.: Schiffer, 1996. Cat., *George Sakier, Paintings and Collages*, New York: Walter Wickiser Gallery, 1999. Cat., J. Stewart Johnson, *American Modern, 1925–1940...*, New York: Abrams, 2000.

Sala, Bienvenu (1869–1939)

Spanish glassmaker and designer; born Arenys-de-Mar, Catalonia; active Paris; father of Jean Sala.

Biography c. 1905, Sala settled in Paris; established a glass workshop in the Montparnasse quarter; made vases decorated in animal and vegetal motifs; became known for his use of a particular Spanish green-tinted thick glass.
Exhibitions Work shown at Paris Salons, including editions of Société des Artistes Decorateurs from 1921; various galleries, including Galerie Drouet.
Bibliography Cat., *Verriers français contemporains: art et industrie*, Paris: Musée des Arts Décoratifs, 1982.

Sala, Jean (1895–1976)

Spanish glassmaker and designer; born Arenys-de-Mar, Catalonia; active Paris; son of Bienvenu Sala.

Training École des Beaux-Arts, Paris.
Biography c. 1905, Sala arrived in Paris with his glassmaker father; active in his father's workshop, designed vessels and chandeliers for the Cristalleries de Saint-Louis in clear crystal; c. 1953, turned from glassmaking to selling antiques.
Exhibitions Work shown regularly in Salons in Paris; in various galleries; at 1937 *Exposition Internationale des Arts et Techniques dans la Vie Moderne*, Paris.

Bibliography Cat., *Verriers français contemporains: art et industrie*, Paris: Musée des Arts Décoratifs, 1982.

Sala, Pierre (1948–1989)

French furniture and stage designer; active Paris.

Biography 1969, Sala became active as a theater producer; 1972, opened the Marie Stuart Theater, Paris; managed the theater La Potinière, Paris; 1973, established his own firm Furnitur to produce his designs such as 1983 Clairefontaine (selling 5,000 pieces), 1985 Café range, and Piranha, Heure du loup, and Mare aux canards lacquered chairs; 1985, opened a shop near the Musée d'Orsay, Paris, where he sold furniture, objects, and clothing.
Exhibitions/citations 1984, Sala's Mikado range shown at Galerie VIA (French furniture association), Paris. Won 1983 VIA/Bloomindale's competition (for Piscine's Memory Table in ceramics and *pâte-de-verre*); 1985 competition sponsored by Cartier for its headquarters on the place Vendôme, Paris.
Bibliography Cat., *Les années VIA 1980–1990*, Paris: Musée des Arts Décoratifs, 1990: 56–57.

Salli, Timo (1963–)

Finnish designer; born Porvoo; active Helsinki.

Training 1992, bachelor's degree in furniture design, Muotoiluinstituutti (Lahti design institute), Lahti; 1996, master's degree in craft and design, Taideteollinen korkeakoulu, Helsinki.
Biography 1993, Salli established his own office, Muotoilutoimisto Salli, Helsinki, for industrial design, interior architecture, and self-production of some of his own designs; concurrently from the 1996 founding of Snowcrash, was a member of the group comprised of eight other designers, who had met while students in the 1980s. The group came to the attention of an enthusiastic press with a 1997 exhibition concurrent with the Salone del Mobile, Milan (see below). Salli has designed furniture, lamps, and installations, both individually and with Snowcrash; 1997, Café 4 (four interiors of café Kaapelitehdas), Helsinki; taught, Muotoiluinstituutti, and Taideteollinen korkeakoulu. Seeking to exploit new materials, designed the 1999 TimoTimo lamp and some seating that calls on transparent and metallized polyester. Other work: 2001 Yrjö Virherheimo stove by Yesbox/Vivero and Firebox that look much like fish aquariums. Some of his chairs feature unusual folding principles. His Lontoo sconce intriguingly plays with light.
Exhibitions/citations Work included in a large number of venues, including 1997 Snowcrash exhibition (furniture), Galleria Facsimile, Milan; 1997 *Young Forum* (installation), Design Forum, Helsinki, and Nagoya Design Center, Japan; 1999 *Italy–Europa* (young European designers exhibit) (lamps), *Abitare il Tempo*, Verona; 1999 Snowcrash exhibition (lamps), Old Fashion Studio, Milan; 1999 *Scandinavian Design* (easy chair), Museum für angewandte Kunst, Cologne; 2000 *Objects & Concepts* (lamps), Taideteollisuusmuseon (museum of applied arts), Helsinki. 1997 Young Finland Prize, Helsinki; 1998 Young Design Prize, Hamburg; Three-Year (1999–2001) State Grant, Helsinki; 2002 finalist, Tubism Furniture Design Competition, Tubeurop France (a subsidiary of Usinor Tubes).
Bibliography Mel Byars, *Design in Steel,* London: Laurence King, 2002.

Salmenhaara, Kyllikki (1915–1981)

Finnish ceramicist and glass designer.

Training To 1943, Taideteollinen korkeakoulu, Helsinki.
Biography 1943–46, she worked at the Kauklahti glassworks; 1946–47, at Sakari Vapaavuori Ceramic Studio, Helsinki; 1946–47, at Saxbo; 1947–63, at Arabia pottery, Helsinki; 1961–63, taught in Taiwan; 1963–73, taught, ceramics department, Taideteollinen korkeakoulu, Helsinki, where she was the head of ceramics instruction 1973–81 and became known primarily for her reformation of the teaching of ceramics in Finland. Active up to her death.
Exhibitions/citations Work included in 1951 (9th) Triennale di Milano; 1954–57 *Design in Scandinavia*, touring the US; 1955 *H 55* exhibition, Hälsingborg; 1956–57 *Finnish Exhibition*, touring West Germany; 1961 *Finlandia,* in Zürich, Amsterdam, and London; 1980 *Scandinavian Modern Design 1880–1980* exhibition, Cooper-Hewitt National Design Museum, New York (catalog below). Work subject of 1986 exhibition, Taideteollisuusmuseon (museum of applied arts), Helsinki (catalog below). Silver medal, 1951 (9th), diploma of honor, 1954 (10th); grand prize, 1957 (11th), gold medal, 1960 (12th) Triennali di Milano; 1960 Pro Finlandia prize.
Bibliography Cat., David Revere McFadden (ed.), *Scandinavian Modern Design 1880–1980*, New York: Abrams, 1982. Cat., *Kyllikki Salmenhaara, 1915–81*, Helsinki: Taideteollisuusmuseon, 1986. Jennifer Hawkins Opie, *Scandinavia: Ceramics and Glass in the Twentieth Century*, New York: Rizzoli, 1989.

Salmoiraghi, Pietro (1941–)

Italian designer; born and active Milan.

Training To 1966, architecture, Politecnico, Milan.
Biography 1965, Salmoiraghi began his professional career; 1967, became a member, Associazione per il Disegno Industriale (ADI), and, 1973, was its president. His clients in Italy have included Cedit, Cristallerie Imperatore, Kartell, and Misal. 1965–70, he taught architecture, Politecnico, Milan; 1969, worked on a project for Ises (institute for the study of educational architecture) and, 1971, a project for Gescal (institute for the management of worker housing); 1972–73, taught courses on ergonomics, Museo Nazionale della Scienza e della Tecnologia, Milan; 1973, became a member, Società Italiana di Ergonomia; was editor of magazine *Design Italia* and a member of the restructuring committee of the Triennale di Milano. Salmoiraghi, Andries van Onck, Antonio Barrese, Cees Houtzager, and Antonio Locatelli founded Studio Pro, which specialized in industrial and visual design, architecture, and town planning. Some of its cultural and public projects have been offered *pro bono*.
Bibliography Cat., Milena Lamarová, *Design a Plastické Hmoty*, Prague: Umĕleckoprůmyslové Muzeum, 1972: 148. *ADI Annual 1976*, Milan: Associazione per il Disegno Industriale, 1976.

Salmon, Philip
> See Hamilton, Hugh.

Salo, Markku (1954–)

Finnish glassware designer; born Nokia.

Training 1972–74, Kankaanpää taidekoulu; 1974–79, Taideteollinen korkeakoulu, Helsinki.
Biography 1978, Salo was a freelance designer for lighting firm SLO Group and industrial-design studio Destern; 1979–80, worked for the studio Ergonomia Design; 1981–83, was the head of the design department of Salora electronic products; 1983–91, worked full-time at littala Lasi, where designed utilitarian glass and tableware, unique glass pieces, exhibitions, and graphics. From 1982, Salo has taught, Kankaanpää taidekoulu. He has become known for his skill, technical knowledge, and bold experimentation, exemplified by 1985 Marius goblets/decanter and, more recently, 1997 Janus stem goblets, 1998 Aava vase range, inspired by shell forms, 1998 Gabriel candle holder, and, in porcelain, 2000 Kayak fruit dish, all by littala. Other: 1998 protective collar for seedlings by Tassu-taimisuoja Co.
Exhibitions/citations From 1973, work in numerous group and one-person exhibitions worldwide. Received 1976 Extra Prize of Scan Design, 1981 first prize in Philips Luminaire Design Competition, 1988 Finnish State Award for Industrial Arts, 1990 Georg Jensen Award; 1992–2002, various scholarships; 1999 Pro Finlandia prize.
Bibliography Jennifer Hawkins Opie, *Scandinavia: Ceramics and Glass in the Twentieth Century*, New York: Rizzoli, 1989. Cat., *Markku Salo: Lasia/Glass*, Helsinki: Suomen Lasimuseo, 1991.

Salocchi, Claudio (1934–)

Italian architect, industrial designer, and teacher; born and active Milan.

Training To 1965, architecture, Politecnico, Milan.
Biography 1965, Salocchi established his own design office. His first design in plastics was 1966 Palla chair in soft polyurethane; also designed the plastic 1971 Apoggio seat based on ergonomic principles, by Sormani, and Sormani showrooms in Milan, Bologna, Turin, and Rome; was associated for a time with the group Ricerche non Finalizzate (RNF); became active as an interior architect and organizer of exhibitions and international design events; 1967, became a member, Associazione per il Disegno Industriale (ADI), and vice-president. His principal work includes 1966 Lia chair in aluminum, 1967 Ellisse range in aluminum, and 1973 Napoleone table range by Sormani; 1967 Fluo florescent light by Lumenform; S 102 kitchen system by Alberti; 1974 Free System seating, beds, and modular components and 1975 Bankor Office range of office furniture, all by Skipper. Other design clients have been Besana, Besozzi, and Rossi di Albizzate. He has taught architecture, Politecnico, Milan, and furniture and interior design, Istituto Professionale di Stato, Lissone.
Exhibitions/citations Work included in numerous exhibitions, includ-

Claudio Salocchi. Palla lounge chair and ottoman. 1969. Fabric and foam, chair 26 3/8 x 34 5/8 x 31 1/2" (67 x 88 x 80 cm), ottoman 13 x 33 1/2 x 22 7/16" (33 x 85 x 57 cm). Mfr.: Sormani, Italy. Courtesy Quittenbaum Kunstauktionen, Munich.

ing 1963 *Furniture Exhibition*, London; 1966 *European Living Art Today*, Kyoto and Tokyo; 1966 Biennale di Arredamento di Mariano Comense; 1966 (1st) Eurodomus, Genoa; 1968 (2nd) Eurodomus, Turin; 1970 (3rd) Eurodomus, Milan; 1967 *Présences d'Italie*, Paris; 1968 (14th) Triennale di Milano; 1968 *Domus Design*, Zürich; 1970 *Modern Chairs 1918–1970*, Whitechapel Gallery, London; 1972 *Design a Plastické Hmoty* exhibition, Uměleckoprůmyslové Muzeum, Prague; in exhibitions in Paris in 1967, Zürich in 1969, New York in 1970, London in 1971. Lia chair first shown, at 1966 (5th) Biennale dello Standard. Numerous subsequent exhibitions. Received Premio Compasso d'Oro: 1979 (Metrosistema furniture, S 102 kitchen, and S/I T tables by Alberti) and 1987 (Piccolo mini-kitchen by Alberti).
Bibliography Cat., *Modern Chairs 1918–1970*, London: Lund Humphries, 1971. Cat., Milena Lamarová, *Design a Plastické Hmoty*, Prague: Uměleckoprůmyslové Muzeum, 1972: 56. *ADI Annual 1976*, Milan: Associazione per il Disegno Industriale, 1976. Alfonso Grassi and Anty Pansera, *Atlante del design italiano 1940/1980,* Milan: Fabbri, 1980: 310. *Modo*, no. 148, Mar.–Apr. 1993: 125.

Salomon, André (1891–1970)
French lighting engineer; active Paris.

Training École Supérieure d'Électricité.
Biography Salomon was an engineer at Thomson electronics firm before setting up the small electrical firm Perfécla (Perfectionnement de l'Éclat). He regularly acted as a consultant to architects and designers such as Pierre Chareau, André Lurcat, and René Herbst. For architect Mallet-Stevens, he produced the innovative 1929 lighting fixture designed by Francis Jourdain in the form of a suspended concave metal ring projecting rays onto the ceiling and reflecting a soft indirect light elsewhere, a fixture possibly influenced by a 1928 prototype designed by Eugène Printz, called the Couronne Lumineuse. For Herbst, Salomon specified the precise curvature of the two wings of a 'flying' 1928 ceiling fixture. 1929, Salomon became a founding member, Union des Artistes Modernes (UAM). Mallet-Stevens also designed a wall and ceiling lightings by Salomon for Paul Poiret's shop in Paris, for the Casino in Saint-Jean-de-Luz, for the entrance hall to the 1930 exhibition of the UAM and, for others, the Bally shoe store and the Café du Brésil, both Paris. With Paul Nelson, Salomon designed the lighting for the American hospital in Neuilly and invented a 1943 system of moveable lighting for a hospital in Saint-Lô. Salomon produced lighting for 1935 oceanliner *Normandie*; after World War II, was in charge of the lighting of harbors and worked with students of Auguste Perret on the reconstruction of Le Havre and on the lighting of highways and roads. With his friend and architect Georges-Henri Pingusson, he worked on lighting for areas, including the basement theater, of the college in Boulogne-Billancourt.
Exhibitions Work included in 1928 Salon d'Automne (Herbst's double-winged ceiling fixture); 1937 *Exposition Internationale des Arts et Techniques dans la Vie Moderne* (Francis Jourdain's illuminated tables and contributions to Mallet-Stevens's Pavillon de la Lumière, ten other pavilions, and Raoul Dufy's giant work La Fée Électricité); all Paris.
Bibliography Alastair Duncan, *Art Nouveau and Art Déco Lighting*, New York: Simon & Schuster, 1978. Arlette Barré-Despond, *UAM*, Paris: Regard, 1986.

Salon des Arts Ménagers
French exhibition group for the promotion of domestic appliances.

History 1923, the first Salon des Arts Ménagers (domestic appliances fair) was initiated by Jules-Louis Breton (1872–1940)—the French undersecretary of state 1914–18; the former minister of the French agency of hygiene, assistance, and welfare; and creator and first diirector of Office National des Recherches Scientifiques et Industrielles et des Inventions (ORNI) which financed the event. The Salon, or fair, was developed 'to reward inventors for the best domestic machines [of the time].' Continuing today, citations are awarded for the best, the most economical, and, more recently, the best-designed appliances. The first edition, whose poster was designed by M. Toussaint, featured 200 exhibitors and attracted 100,000 visitors. 1940–47,annual editions were interrupted by World War II.
Bibliography Jacques Rouaud, *60 ans d'Arts Ménagers, tome 1: 1923-1939 le confort*, Paris: Syros Alternatives, 1989. 'Mechanical Dreams: Democracy and Technological Discourse in Twentieth-Century France,' in L. Winner (ed.), *Democracy in a Technological Society*, Dordrecht: Kluwer, 1992: 51–80. 'Semiotic Narratives and French Home Appliances,' *Techniques & Culture*, no. 19, Dec.1992: 23–46. 'Machine Liberation: Inventing Housewives and Home Appliances in Interwar France,' *French Historical Studies*, Apr., 1993. Jacques Rouaud, *60 ans d'Art Ménagers, tome 2: 1948–1983 la consommation*, Paris: Syros Alternatives, 1993. 'La France, la femme et la machine à laver,' in Robert Belot and R. Belot (eds.), *La technologie au risque de l'histoire*, Paris: Berg, 2000.

Salto, Axel (1889–1961)
Danish ceramicist.

Training Painting, Det Kongelige Danske Kunstakademi, Copenhagen.
Biography 1917, Salto cofounded the journal *Klingen*; 1923–25, worked at Bing & Grøndahl Porcelænsfabrik, Copenhagen; from c. 1925–c. 1933 with Nathalie Krebs, at Saxbo; from 1933, at Royal Copenhagen porcelain manufactory; 1934, designed patterns for bookbinding papers and, 1944, printed fabric by L.F. Foght; headed the project to restore 1846 Jørgen Sonne frieze on Thorvaldsens Museum, Copenhagen.
Citations Grand prize, 1951 (9th) Triennale di Milano.
Bibliography Axel Salto, *Salto's Keramick*, Copenhagen: Berlingska Bogtr., 1930. Cat., David Revere McFadden (ed.), *Scandinavian Mo-*

dern Design 1880–1980, New York: Abrams, 1982. Jennifer Hawkins Opie, *Scandinavia: Ceramics and Glass in the Twentieth Century*, New York: Rizzoli, 1989.

Salto, Kasper (1967–)

Danish furniture designer.

Training Under Jørgen Wolff, in cabinetmaking; 1989–94, design, Danmarks Designskole; 1993, one semester, Art Center, Switzerland.
Biography 1996–1997, Salto was a lecturer, Det Kongelige Danske Kunstakademi, Copenhagen, and was also appointed a member of the The Cabinetmakers' Autumn Exhibition (SE); from 1997, was an exhibition architect for the SE at the Det Danske Kunstindustrimuseum, Copenhagen; designed 1997 Runner bentwood and tubular-steel chair and 1999 Blade eccentric stacking chaise longue by Botium.
Citations 1999 Dansk ID Prize; 1999 G-Mark Good Design award, Japanese Industrial Design Promotion Organization (JIDPO); 1999 Danmarks Nationalbank Jubilee Foundation.

Salvati, Alberto (1935–)

Italian architect and designer; born Milan.

Training To 1960, in architecture in Milan.
Biography From 1960, Salvati collaborated with Ambrogio Tresoldi; 1961–64, was an assistant, Facoltà di Ingegneria, Politecnico, Milan; became active in architecture and interior and industrial design; collaborated with numerous others, most notably in his 1956–94 partnership with Ambrogio Tresoldi in architecture and interior design; worked for Centro Convenienza for the auto-highway Milan-Bergamo and on houses, motels, hotels, and shops; designed furniture and furnishings for clients, including Cassina, Delchi, Busnelli, Saporiti, and RB Rossana. He wrote, with Tresoldi, *Architettura e design* (Milan: Electa, 1980) and *Lo spazio delle interazioni* (Milan: Electa, 1985).
Citations Premio Compasso d'Oro, with Tresoldi: 1984 (for Miamina chair by Saporiti Italia) and 1987 (for Strasburgo armchair and sofa by Busnelli).
Bibliography Giancarlo Iliprandi and Pierluigi Molinari (eds.), 'Italian Industrial Designers,' in *Omnibook No. 2*, Udine: Magnus, 1985: 202. *Modo*, no. 148, Mar.–Apr. 1993: 125. Federico Bucci, *Learning to Live: Home, Architecture and Space Qualities in Salvati and Tresoldi Partnership's Research (1956–1994)*, Milan: Lybra Immagine, 1994.

Salviati, Antonio (1816–1890)

Italian glassmaker; active Vicenza.

Training In law.
Biography Salviati was first a lawyer in Vicenza; 1859, with Enrico Podio and Lorenzo Radi, cofounded Salviati dott. Antonio fu Bartolomeo, initially producing glass tiles for repairing the old mosaics of Venice and creating new ones. The remarkable 19th- and 20th-century revival of Murano glassmaking is credited to the initiative and entrepreneurship of Antonio Salviati and his associates. Aided by an investment from two Englishmen and after several name changes, Salviati acquired a hollow-ware glass factory in Murano and added hollow-ware objects to the line. Due to disagreements with the English investors, Salviati resigned in 1877, took several master glassblowers with him, and established two new operations of his own: Salviati dott. Antonio (glass hollow-ware) and Salviati & C. (mosaic glass). On his death, his sons Giulio Silvio Salviati (1898–) and Silvio Salviati and his daughter Amalia Salviati Ivancich assumed the firm's management. The successor firm, Salviati & C. S.p.A., is today owned by French investors and markets glassware made by others.

Samarawickrema, Tilak

Sri Lankan architect and designer; active Colombo.

Biography Samarawickrema designed a wool-carpet collection by Möbelstoffeweberei Lagethal of Switzerland; furnishings by Cappellini; and the book by Manikkuwadumestri Chandrasoma, *Siddhartha Gotama of the Sakya Clan: A Letter to a Grandson* (1998). He curated 1998 *The Courage of Images* (creative work of Italians and Indians traveling to India, Singapore, Japan, Bangkok, and Sri Lanka), organized by the Italian Foreign Ministry.
Exhibitions/citations Participated in 2003–04 (12th) Bienal de São Paulo. Work subject of an early-1990s exhibit, Textile Museum, Krefeld, Germany; 2001 exhibition of tapestries, Greystones-Villa, Diyatalawa, Sri Lanka. The Chandrasoma book was cited by 1998 Sahitya Award for the best-produced book of the year.

Sambinelli, Flavio (1949–)

Italian engineer and designer; born Brescia (Italy).

Training To 1969, in engineering.
Biography 1977, Sambinelli began collaborating with Carlo Giannini. He has since designed 1989 Rialto kettle and 2001 Comici pepper grinder/shaker in pear wood by Giannini, kitchens by Abiente Cucina, espresso pot by Arabica.
Citations 1984 Design Plus award (Cabiria espresso machine), Ambiente fair, Frankfurt.

Sambonet; Sambonet, Roberto (1924–1995)

Italian metalware manufacturer; located Vercelli. Roberto Sambonet: illustrator, painter, and industrial and graphic designer; born Vercelli; active Milan.

History/biography 1856, a factory for manufacturing silverwares was established in the Piedmont by the Sambonet family. Later, its designers included Vittorio Bergomi, Gio Ponti, Gigi Caccia Dominioni, and Achille and Pier Giacomo Castiglioni, and, from 1950s, Pieraldo Mortara, Edoardo Brunetti, Piero Fornara, Augusto Salviato, Osvaldo Ferraris, and Ferruccio Vercelloni. Max Huber, Heinz Waibl, Bob Noorda, and Bruno Monguzzi contributed to its corporate image. Concerning Roberto Sambonet: 1942–45, he studied architecture, Politecnico, Milan; for a time, was a professional painter; 1948–53, worked at Museo de Arte de São Paulo (MASP), and collaborated with P.M. Bardi; 1953, was apprenticed to Alvar Aalto in Helsinki; returned to Italy and was a graphic designer at La Rinascente department store and from 1957, the art director of journal *Zodiac*; 1954, joined the family firm Sambonet in Vercelli, when it first began producing stainless-steel wares. His designs were streamlined and largely free of decoration such as the 1954 fish poacher that illustrates the full potential of stainless steel as a luxury item. Based on geometrical structures, his work included cutlery and a series of nesting containers. Other highly sophisticated but functional work: 1965 Center Line stainless-steel cookware by Sambonet, 1974 ceramics by Bing & Grøndahl Porcelænsfabrik, 1977 glassware range by Baccarat (see catalog below), 1979 glassware by Seguso, 1979 glassware by Richard Ginori, silverware by Rossi & Arcandi. 1980, he taught design in Rio de Janeiro, São Paulo, and Carrara, Italy; was a member, Associazione per il Disegno Industriale (ADI).
Exhibitions/citations The firm: work shown at 1964 (13th) Triennale di Milano (a Gio Ponti design); received 1972 *Domus Inox* and Macef prizes, Mostra di Articoli Casalinghi e Ferramenta, Milan. Roberto Sambonet: 1949 exhibition (paintings and designs), Museo de Arte de São Paulo (catalog below); 1960, Galleria del Disegno, Milan; 1962,

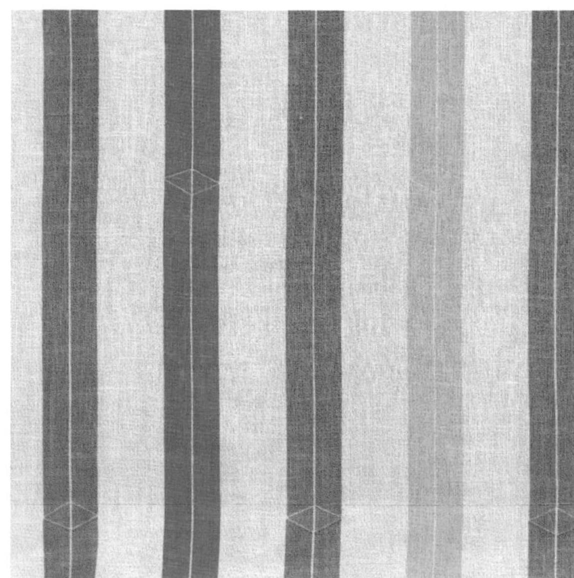

Astrid Sampe. Lazy Lines drapery fabric. 1954. Linen, 48 x 41½" (121.9 x 105.4 cm). Gift of the mfr. MoMA.

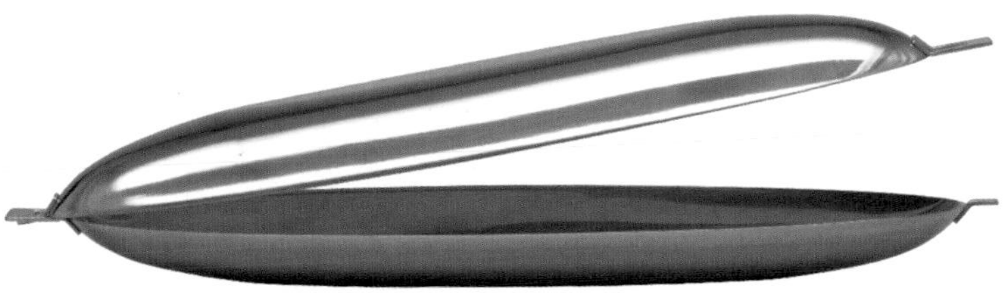

Roberto Sambonet. Fish poacher. 1954. Stainless steel, 2 3/4 x 20 1/2 x 6" (7 x 52.1 x 15.2 cm). Mfr.: Sambonet, Italy. Gift of the mfr. MoMA.

Palazzo dei Centori, Vercelli; 1963, Galleria Profili, Milan; 1966, in Pater; 1969, Il Milione; 1974 retrospective of design, graphics, and painting, Museo de Arte de São Paulo, and 1980 exhibition, Palazzo Bagatti-Valsecchi. Premio Compasso d'Oro: 1955, 1956 (three citations), 1970 (individually and Sambonet firm's entire range), 1979 (several individually and with others), and 1994. Triennale di Milano: gold medals, 1957 (11th) and 1973 (15th) and grand prize, 1960 (12th).
Bibliography Cat., P.M. Bardi (intro.), *Massa Guassú: figuras e paisagens pintadas no Brasil por Roberto Sambonet*, São Paulo: Museo de Arte de São Paulo, 1949. Paolo Fossati, *Il design in Italia 1945-1972*, Turin: Einaudi, 1972: 135–40, 239–42, plates 404–49. Alfonso Grassi, *ADI Annual 1976*, Milan: Associazione per il Disegno Industriale, 1976. Sales cat., *Baccarat: nouvelles formes d'art design par Roberto Sambonet = Baccarat: nuove forme di art design di Roberto Sambonet*, Paris: Baccarat, 1977. Alfonso Grassi and Anty Pansera, *Atlante del design italiano 1940/1980*, Milan: Fabbri, 1980: 287. Cat., *Roberto Sambonet: Design grafica pittura '74–'79*, Milan: Palazzo Bagatti Valsecchi, 1980.

Sampe, Astrid (1909–2002)

Swedish textile designer.

Training Kungliga Tekniska Högskolan, Stockholm; Royal College of Art, London.
Biography 1936, Sampe joined and, 1937–72, was head of the textile-and-design workshop of Nordiska Kompaniet, Stockholm, where she was influential as a colorist and pattern designer; with Sven Markelius, worked on the Swedish pavilion at 1939–40 *New York World's Fair: The World of Tomorrow*; 1946, introduced the use of grasscloth in Sweden; 1950s at the Wohlbeck and Kasthall rug factories, was instrumental in reviving industrially woven carpets; 1955, created a number of domestic linens in geometric and folk motifs; 1972, established her own studio in Stockholm, where she designed interiors and textiles and worked for clients, including Donald of Dundee, Knoll, Svängsta Klädesfabrik, and Almedahl-Dalsjöfors; 1975, designed the textiles and the procenium curtain of City Theater of Borås; wrote the book *Textiles Illustrated* (with Vera Diurson, 1948).
Exhibitions/citations Work included in 1937 *Exposition Internationale des Arts et Techniques dans la Vie Moderne*, Paris; 1980 *Scandinavian Modern Design 1880–1980*, Cooper-Hewitt National Design Museum, New York; 1983–84 *Design Since 1945*, Philadelphia Museum of Art (catalogs below). 1949, elected Honorary Royal Designer for Industry, UK; 1954 (10th) gold medal and 1960 (12th) silver medal, Triennale di Milano; 1956 Gregor Paulsson Trophy.
Bibliography Erik Zahle (ed.), *A Treasury of Scandinavian Design*, New York: Golden Press, 1961. Lennart Lindkvist (ed.), *Design in Sweden*, Stockholm: Svenska Institutet, 1972: 66–67. Cat., *Astrid Sampe, Swedish Textiles = Astrid Sampe, svensk industritextil*, Stockholm: Nationalmuseum, 1984. Cat., David Revere McFadden (ed.), *Scandinavian Modern Design 1880–1980*, New York: Abrams, 1982. Cat., Kathryn B. Hiesinger and George H. Marcus III (eds.), *Design Since 1945*, Philadelphia: Philadelphia Museum of Art, 1983.

Samuel, Henri (1905–1996)

French decorator.

Biography Active in Paris, Samuel practiced a high, particularly French, style of historicist decoration, or *décor de l'ancien régime*, for rich clients including the Rothschilds, Wrightmans, and Gotfreunds; furnished his own domicile with contemporary art and furniture but only a few French antiques; with Arthur Rosenblatt and Robert Kupiec, restored the Linsky Galleries at The Metropolitan Museum of Art, New York. Samuel decorated the mansion of Jose Gómez-Mena (Museo Nacional de Artes Decorativas, from 1964), Havana, Cuba. Samuel's restoration workshop in Paris was for a time headed by American craftsperson David Linker, who returned to the US in 1981. 1994, Samuel became in charge of the tapestry workshop of Lucien Delaplace (managed by son Daniel Delaplace from 1978).
Bibliography 'Linsky Galleries,' *Interior Design*, July 1985: 212–22. Mitchell Owens, 'Samuel at Ninety,' *Nest*, no. 6. Jean Bond Rafferty, 'Gentleman Decorator,' *Town & Country*, 1 Nov. 1995.

Samuelson, Alexander (b. Alexander Samuelsson 1862–1934)

Swedish glassworker and entrepreneur; born Surte.

Training In the glass industry, Sweden.
Biography 1883, Samuelson and his brother Otto (b. 1865) sailed first to the UK and then on the Wilson Line ship *Orlando* to the US, arriving in New York. Alexander decided to travel on to Chicago and changed the double 's' in his name to a single one. After a short time in Chicago, he worked at the glass plant in Steator, Ill., and, from 1895, at Everett Glass Company, Newark, Ohio, where he became a foreperson. Through his prior experience in the Swedish glass industry (known for its high quality), he was thus able to make a number of improvements to American glass. After Everett, he worked for another glass enterprise and, from 1904, for Root Glass Company in Terre Haute, Ind., whose owner was Chapman Jay Root (1864–1945). Root Glass and about 30 other glass firms were invited to design a bottle for Coca-Cola (the drink invented by John S. Pemberton in 1886), which was then being sold in the kind of standard bottle found at soda fountains. The Coca-Cola company wanted something highly recognizable, even uniquely shaped, to be found easily even in the dark. Purportedly, the rounded grooves of a coca leaf inspired the design which won the competition for Root and, thus, Samuelson. However, because the first prototype was too shapely for inexpensive manufacture, it was made somewhat thinner, but still the 'hobble skirt' shape. The bottle was patented on 16 Nov. 1915 in Alexander Samuelson's name and renewed in 1937—the first patent issued to a glass bottle solely for its unique shape. So popular did the shape become that it was early on called the 'Mae West,' a reference to the movie star's thick-waisted figure. Root received a five-cents-per-gross royalty under license, until Coca-Cola bought the rights in 1937 and trademarked it in 1960 as a 'contour bottle.' (Patents expire, but trademarks do not.) Chapman Root became rich; Samuelson received no bonus and no monetary reward.

Sandell, Thomas (1959–)

Swedish architect and designer; born Jakobstad; active Sweden.

Training To 1985, degree in architecture, Bungliga Tekniska Högskolan, Stockholm.
Biography From 1985, Sandell worked at Jan Henrikssons Arkitektkontor; 1990, opened his own office, Thomas Sandell Arkitektkontor. 1995, Sandell, Ulf Sandberg, and Joakim Uebel set up Sandellsandberg, an interdisciplinary design office, which was employing about 60 people by 2002. Sandell's early work for IKEA offered him international exposure, and, 2002, he returned as a freelance designer. Subsequently, he designed the interior of Arktekturmuseet and of Moderna Museet and several advertising agencies in Stockholm; Gåshaga Brygga project for the town hall, Lidingö; new headquarters of Ericsson, St. James Square, London; image for EU 2001 (Swedish chairmanship of the European Union). His furniture-design clients have included Artek, Asplund, B&B Italia, Cappellini, cbi, Gärsnäs, Kållermo, Mobilette, R.O.O.M., Rydéns, Tibro Kök, Tronconi. Sandell is a member, Svenska Inrednings Arkitekters Riksförbund (SIR, Swedish interior architects association) and spokesperson for Svenska Arkitekters Riksförbund (SAR, Swedish architects association). 2000, Sandellsandberg bought

Mark Sanders. No-Spill chopping board. 1988. Polypropylene plastic, 2 5/8 x 8 3/4 x 15 1/4" (6.7 x 22.2 x 38.7 cm). Mfr.: Rubycliff, UK (1990). Gift of the designer. MoMA.

the 1960 Bruno Mathsson summer house in Frösakull, Sweden, to restore and use for themselvs. 2001, Sandellsandberg was bought by internet consultancy Resco.
Exhibitions/citations Work initially shown, in IKEA stand (PS furniture), 1995 Salone del Mobile; numerous venues since. Received a number of awards.
Bibliography Claes Britton, 'Servicing Maximalism,' *Monument*, no. 41, Apr.–May 2001. Leo Gullbring, 'Buzz: IT Business Will Buy Other Architecture Firms Too,' *Frame*, no. 15, July–Aug. 2000.

Sander-Noske, Sophie (1884–1958)

Austrian designer; born Vienna.

Training Apprenticeship in Vienna.
Biography She worked at the Wiener Werkstätte and as a specialist in filigree in Paris and Amsterdam; 1911, managed a domestic-wares workshop in Cortina d'Ampezzo; 1911 and 1912, taught enameling and was head of the jewelry and metalworking departments, Haarlemse School voor Kunstnijverheid, Haarlem; established a workshop at Heuberggasse 13, Vienna. Late 1920s, designed her earliest children's furniture (published in the pages of her mother's magazine); c. 1923–25, worked at the Wiener Werkstätte, where she created freer and more lighthearted forms than those of her earlier years and designed complete interior schemes and individual furniture pieces. Also designed textiles, wallpaper, and decorative paper.
Exhibitions Work included in 1909–10, 1910–11, 1911–12, 1912–13, and 1913–14 Austrian arts and crafts exhibitions, Österreichisches Museum für Kunst und Industrie, Vienna.
Bibliography Waltrand Neuwirth, *Lexikon Wiener Gold- und Silberschmiede und ihre Punzen 1867–1922*, Vienna: Selbstverl. W. Neuwirth, 1976–77: 170–74. Stephen Calloway, *Twentieth-Century Decoration*, New York: Rizzoli, 1988: 151. Annelies Krekel-Aalberse, *Art Nouveau and Art Déco Silver*, New York: Abrams, 1989. Deanna F. Cera (ed.), *Jewels of Fantasy: Costume Jewelry of the 20th Century*, New York: Abrams, 1992.

Sanders, Mark (1958–)

British industrial designer; lives in Windsor, Berkshire.

Training 1977–80, bachelor's degree in mechanical engineering, Imperial College, University of London; 1983–85, master's degree in industrial-design engineering, Imperial College joint with Royal College of Art; both London.
Biography Sanders's body of work has included 1988 No-Spill chopping board in polypropylene and c. 2001 Strida 2 lightweight, inexpensive, rust-proof, aluminum bicycle, that purportedly folds in less than ten seconds and originally developed as an academic project; has been a design engineer and instructor; 1985, established MAS Design Products, Windsor.
Exhibitions/citations Work included in 1995 *Mutant Materials* (catalog below) and *British Design 2000*, Arango Design Foundation, traveling. Received 1988 Best New Product (for Strida bicycle), Cyclex design award; 1991 Archimedes Award for Product Design (No-Spill chopping board); others.
Bibliography 'Hit Us with Your Stick,' *Sunday Times Magazine* (London), 3 May 1987. 'Bicicletta pieghevole strida,' *Domus*, Apr. 1989. Cat., Paola Antonelli, *Mutant Materials in Contemporary Design*, New York: The Museum of Modern Art/Abrams, 1995.

Sanderson & Sons, Arthur

British textile and wallpaper firm.

Biography 1860, Arthur Sanderson (d. 1882) founded his eponymous firm, which was incorporated in 1900; began printing its own wallpaper designs from 1879 by hand-blocking (later by machines); established a furnishing fabrics printworks in Uxbridge in 1921 and wove there from 1934. The firm became known for its production from 1930 of William Morris's textiles and wallpapers, although Morris had no contact with the Sanderson firm during his lifetime. 1940 when Morris and Co. was closed, Sanderson bought from the receiver the original wallpaper blocks, log books, and pattern books; Morris wallpapers by Sanderson continue to be faithfully block-printed by hand as well as by machine. Some Morris wallpaper designs have been adapted as textiles. Patterns include 1864 Fruit (aka Pomegranate); 1864 Trellis (inspired by the view through a window of Morris's Red House; birds and flowers added by Philip Webb; was the first wallpaper designed by Morris, in 1862); 1868–70 Indian (inspired by an Indian tapestry); 1875 Marigold (a version of Larkspur, originally a wallpaper and a chintz); 1877 Chrysanthemum (used by Morris at Greenfield, near Manchester). After World War II, Sanderson began printing some fabric and wallpaper designs by machine. Today the firm also makes bed linens.
Bibliography Aymer Vallance, *The Art of William Morris: A Record*, London: G. Bell, 1897. C. Woods, *Sanderson's 1860–1985*, London: Arthur Sanderson & Sons, 1985. Valerie Mendes, *The Victoria & Albert Museum Textile Collection, British Textiles from 1900 to 1937*, London: Victoria and Albert Museum, 1992.

Sandin, Raymond C. (d. c. 1986)

Swedish industrial designer; active in the US.

Training Armory Institute (now Illinois Institute of Technology), Chicago.
Biography At age 20, Sandin settled in the US; 1935, joined the Hotpoint division of General Electric, as the only designer there; by 1935, was managing 13 designers in his department at Hotpoint, where he worked until his death. (Arthur BecVar managed the larger staff of the General Electric design department.) During World War II, he developed a service to allow Hotpoint customers to plan their kitchens, published as 'Kitchen of the Future' in a 1944 issue of magazine *Better Homes & Gardens*.
Bibliography Carroll Gantz, *100 Years of Design* (at www.idsa.org).

Sandnes, Eystein (1924–)

Norwegian glassware designer and ceramicist.

Training 1945–49, Statens Håndverks -og Kunstindustriskole, Oslo.
Biography 1951–55, Sandnes was the artistic director of Magnor glassworks and, from 1955, a freelance designer of its tableware and art glass; c. 1951, was freelance designer for S & S Helle; 1955–57, worked at Stavangerflint; from 1957, was the artistic director of Porsgrund.
Exhibitions/citations Work included in numerous venues in Norway and abroad. Received silver medal, 1960 (12th) Triennale di Milano; 1965 and 1970 prizes, Norsk Designcentrum.
Bibliography Cat., David Revere McFadden (ed.), *Scandinavian Modern Design 1880–1980*, New York: Abrams, 1982. Jennifer Hawkins Opie, *Scandinavia: Ceramics and Glass in the Twentieth Century*, New York: Rizzoli, 1989.

Sandoz, Édouard-Marcel (1881–1971)

French sculptor, metalworker, and ceramics designer.

Training Under Antonin Mercié and Jean-Antonin Injalbert, École des Beaux-Arts, Paris.
Bibliography Sandoz specialized in small animal sculptures and designed a series of polychrome porcelain items such as boxes, bottles, decanters, and tea and coffee sets in animal and other shapes made by Haviland at Limoges. The Bugnion family donated a number of his

Denis Santachiara. Giubbe Rosse sofa. c. 2002. Plastic and fabric, h. 27 1/2 x w. 75 1/2 x d. 37" (70 x 192 x 94 cm). Mfr.: Styling, Italy.

works to the Fondation de l'Hermitage, Lausanne.
Exhibitions Work shown at Salons of Société Nationale des Beaux-Arts and Société des Artistes Décorateurs; other venues in Brussels and Barcelona. Subject of a number of venues (see catalogs below).
Bibliography Maurice Genevoix, *Le bestiaire d'Édouard Marcel Sandoz*, Lausanne: La Bibliothèque des Arts, 1972. Cat., Félicien Marceau et al., *Découvrir Sandoz: statuaire du regard*, Lausanne: Grand-Pont; Paris: Bibliothèque des Arts, 1991. *Édouard-Marcel Sandoz, 1881–1971: images d'atelier*, Paris: Fondation Taylor, 1991. Félix Marcilhac, *Édouard Marcel Sandoz, sculpteur, figuriste et animalier, 1881–1971: catalogue raisonné de l'œuvre sculpté*, Paris: Amateur, 1993. Cat., *Édouard Marcel Sandoz: 1881–1971: sculpteur, figuriste et animalier*, Lausanne: Fondation de l'Hermitage, 1995. Cat., *La symphonie des animaux, exposition Édouard Marcel Sandoz*, Tokyo: Tokyo Metropolitan Foundation for History and Culture (Metropolitan Teien Art Museum), 1995.

Sans, Pete (1947–)

Spanish designer; born Barcelona; son of an abstract painter and architect.

Training To 1969, Hochschule für Gestaltung, Ulm, Germany, leaving before achieving a degree.
Biography While in secondary school, Sans worked in the studio of Catalan architect Pepe Pratmarsó; 1967–69, was a fashion designer of jerseys; after the school in Ulm, was active 1969–70 as a painter; 1971–79, was active as a graphic designer in his own studio; 1975–79, director, Nikon Gallery and Nikon school, Barcelona, and publisher of Barcelona's first, but short-lived, underground photography magazine *Papel Especial*, at the time when dictator Franco's grip was beginning to weaken. 1994, he established Petesans Sistemes Integrals, producing office furniture, the first of which was the Aula System, and his first commercially produced lighting fixture, 1979/2001 Lamparaprima (only barely a cylinder bulb and wire), first by Snark, then Taller Uno, then Santa & Cole, then by Taller Uno again; also 1989 Cálida table/floor lamps by Taller Uno, and all furniture (by Arafura Tribu in 1990) for the Institut Français, Barcelona. Other work: by Bd Ediciones de Diseño: 1985 Phidea coffee table, 1987 Coqueta wicker/steel lounge chair, and 1990 Arácnida wood table, 1993 Kadira wooden armchair, 1995 Phantasma shelf/hanger, 1997 Plomada lamp, and 1999 Eria hanging lamp. Sans has also designed for Andreu World, Garcia Garay, Metalarte, Mobles 114, Pallucco Italia, Vapor, Diseño Abato Energético.
Citations Best illumination product, 1983 Moving fair, Paris; 1985 best of Spanish design, Europalia, Brussels; 1986 (6th) Arango International Award Competition, Miami; 1988 Delta d'Oro (for Coqueta chair by Bd Ediciones de Diseño), 1995 Delta d'Oro, and 1997 selections of ADI/FAD (industrial-design/decorative-arts assocition), Barcelona; 1990 selection (for Coqueta chair, one of five for aesthetic/technical innovation), Baden-Wurtemberg; 100 Best-Design Products of 1988–90, Interieur 90 biennial, Courtral; 1992 Nuevo Estilo prize; 1993 (13th) Design Italia Prize (for Pilastra chair by Pelluco Italia).
Bibliography Mel Byars, *50 Lights...*, Hove: RotoVision, 1997.

Santa & Cole

Spanish furniture manufacturer.

History October 1985, Santa & Cole was established by brothers-in-law Gabriel Ordeig (a painter, interior designer, and former rock-band promoter) and Javier Nieto (a former economist and publisher), and by Nina Masó in a factory space that had been a part of 1929–30 *Exposición Internacional de Barcelona*. Initially as assembly space and, subsequently, a showroom, the hangar-like building was moved to the hills above Barcelona and renovated by Ordeig. At first Ordeig was the designer; Nieto managed the company, and Masó was the interiors specialist. As part of a series of eight decorated lamps, Ordeig and Masó designed 1985 La Bella Durmiente (sleeping beauty) floor lamp. Santa & Cole incorporated Snark and Clásicos del Diseño as collections within the operation (formerly owned and now directed by Santiago Roqueta with Jordi Miralbell). By 1989, Santa & Cole had more showrooms in Spain and became a distributor of Bulthaup kitchen systems. From 1989, it reissued 1969 Zeleste lamp by Angel Jové and Santiago Roqueta, Carles Riart's 1976 Colilla lamp, and Pete Sans's 1979 Lamparaprima lamp. A group of well-known international designers, including its founders, design for the firm today: Antoni Arola, Ferran Freixa, José María García de Paredes, Miguel Milá, Jordi Miralbell, Antoni de Moragas, Montse Padrós, Jorge Pensi, Mariona Raventós, de Rivera Moreno-Torres and Philippe Starck, and others.
Citations Various categories of 1986, 1990, 1992, 1995, 1997, 1998, and other-year awards, ADI/FAD (industrial-design/decorative-arts associations); 1999 National Design Prize, Spain.
Bibliography Guy Julier, *New Spanish Design*, London: Thames & Hudson, 1991.
> See Roqueta i Matías, 'Santi' Santiago.

Santachiara, Denis (1950–)

Italian designer; born Campagnola; active Milan.

Training Autodactic.
Biography 1966, Santachiara began in the design of sports cars at Centro Stile Fiat; late 1960s at the time of the Arte Povera movement, created analytical and conceptual art, while working in design; 1966, established a office for automobile design. His 1974 project for a communications system (video entertainment and information board) was designed for Milan's city center. Also 1974, he duplicated Galileo's telescope as a color-effect amusement. From 1975, he worked on

Richard Sapper. Tizio table lamp. 1971. ABS polymer, aluminum, and other materials, 46 3/4 x 42 1/2 (118.7 x 108 cm) x base dia. 4 1/4" (10.8 cm). Mfr.: Artemide, Italy. Gift of the mfr. MoMA.

'soft technology,' between art and design; from 1989, collaborated with Cesare Castelli on multi-functional novelty-furniture production, eschewing traditional values. 1990, Santichiara and Castelli founded Domodinamica, a firm for the production of interactive, experimental design. Santichiara's work addresses the social and philosophical implications of design and incorporates so-called smart materials. He has lectured, Università degli Studi, Florence; Domus Academy, Milan; Politecnico, Milan; Istituto Superiore per le Industrie Artistiche (ISIA), Rome; Gerrit Rietveld Academie, Rotterdam; ENSCI (Les Ateliers), Paris; Royal College, London. His work includes 1979 stereo earphones by BWA; 1981 Maestrale red-flag lamp; March 1982 cover design, *Uomo Vogue*; 1982 Ali lamp by FontanaArte; 1983 On-off lamp (with Raggi and Meda) by LucePlan; 1983 toothbrush by GOG, US; 1984 Work Station (with Meda and Raggi) by Italtel Telematica; 1984 Mobile infinito accessories by Alchimia; 1985 Sparta lamp stanchions by Oceano Oltreluce; 1986 plastic bicycle by Stylresine; 1986 fast-food restaurant Aquylone, Reggio Emilia; 1988 Trans armchair by Campeggi; an array of objects produced by firms worldwide and by his own, including such unorthodox items as a singing doormat. His 1987 Notturno Italiano bedside lamp in the shape of a large flattened silver lightbulb (by Yamagiwa in 1987, Domodinamica in 1990, reorganized as Modular S.r.l. for production/distribution) projects a continuous row of sheep jumping over a fence under a star-filled sky. More recent are 1995 Tato, Tatino, Tatone ottomans (with Enrico Baleri) and 1995 Mama e Granmama chair by Baleri Italia, 1997 Swing armchair without feet by Modular, 1997 Pisoló, Pistonini, and Pisola inflatable beds by Campeggi, 2000 Mister Kevin tables made of 'blown' steel refrigeration sheet and ceramic-column neon light (tributes to Nikola Tesla). Other clients: Artemide, Baleri Italia, De Padova, DNA, Erreti, Foscarini, La Murrina, Magis, Mandarina Duck, Marutomy, Panasonic, Rosenthal, Serralunga, Styling Swatch, Vitra, Zerodisegno. Santachiara has also been active in architecture and town planning.
Exhibitions/citations Curated and designed 1988 *Segni dell'Habitat* touring exhibition of Italian design and technology, sponsored by Istituto Commercio Estero (ICE); 1996–97 *New Persona* installation, Biennale di Firenze. Own work (*La Casa Telematica* project) shown for the first time, at 1973 (15th) Triennale di Milano; and, subsequently, in numerous venues worldwide. Work subject of *La Casa Onirica*, 1983 (17th) Triennale di Milano, and Grand Palais, Paris; 1987 exhibition, Vitra Design Museum, Weil am Rhein; 1990 *Santachiara: L'Estetica dell'Uso*, Civico Museo, Reggio Emilia (catalog below). 1999 Good Design award, Chicago Athenaeum; 2000 first prize, *Design World*.
Bibliography Fumio Shimizu and Studio Matteo Thun (eds.), *The Italian Design: Descendants of Leonardo da Vinci*, Tokyo: Graphic-sha, 1987. Cat., François Dagognet and Ezio Manzini, *Santachiara: l'estetica dell'uso*, Reggio Emilia: Civico Museo, 1990. Cat., Manolo de Giorgi and Paola Antonelli (eds) *Techniques discrètes: le design mobilier en Italie, 1980–1990*, Rome: Istituto Nazionale per il Commercio Estero; Milan: Assarredo; Paris: Musée des Arts Décoratifs, 1991. Stefano Casciani and Giacunto Di Pietrantonio, *Design in Italia 1950–1990*, Milan: Politi, 1991. Anty Pansera, *Storia del disegno industriale italiano*, Bari: Laterza, 1993. Cristiana Morozzi, 'Denis Santachiara,' *Intramuros*, no. 72, Sept. 1997, 32–37. Claudia Neumann, *Design Directory Italy*, London: Pavilion, 1999. Giuliana Gramigna and Paola Biondi, *Il design in Italia dell'arredamento domestico*, Turin: Allemandi, 1999. Mel Byars, *50 Beds...*, Hove: RotoVision, 2000. Cat., *Stanze e segreti*, Milan: Skira, 2000. Virginio Briatore, *Denis Santachiara*, Milan: Abitare Segesta, 2002.

Santi, Carlo (1925–)
Italian designer; born and active Milan.

Training To 1949, architecture, Politecnico, Milan.
Biography 1949, Santi began his professional career; taught urban planning, Politecnico, Milan; from 1958, member of the research center, Triennale di Milano; designed lighting and electronic equipment, 1973 plastic/steel desk lamp by Kartell, Box and Aster faucets by Stella, and products by other firms; became a member, Associazione per il Disegno Industriale (ADI).
Citations 1960 International Prize for Urban Planning, Fondazione Rocca; and 1973 Bayer Prize for Architecture.
Bibliography *ADI Annual 1976*, Milan: Associazione per il Disegno Industriale, 1976.

Santos-Dumont, Alberto (1873–1932)
Brazilian aviator; born State of Minas Gerais.

Biography Santos-Dumont was a recluse and devotee of Jules Verne. 1891, his father, a rich coffee-plantation owner, fell ill, sold his holdings, and moved to Paris with his wife and youngest son, Alberto. Alberto eventually became an aviator; 1898, made his first balloon flight; 1898–1905, built and flew 11 dirigibles; became a celebrity and won several prizes. During his flights, he could not use a pocket watch while navigating. To remedy the problem, his friend Louis-Joseph Cartier (1875–1942), the French jeweler, created a timepiece in 1904 to wear on the wrist, thus inventing the first commercially produced wristwatch. (However, English women in the 16th century wore wristwatches.) In France, Santos-Dumont pursued human flight by means other than by balloon, even though most at the time thought it impossible. Oct. 1906, the diminutive Brazilian flew his 14 Bis airplane 60 meters, 2 to 3 meters aloft. Yet, the feat was not properly witnessed, and the Wright brothers received credit two years later (1908); yet, there is some dispute as to Santos-Dumont's claim. 1910, Santos fell ill with multiple sclerosis and, 1916, returned to Brazil. He was mentally unstable, some say due to the use of airplanes in warfare, and committed suicide in Guarujá.
Bibliography Peter Wykeham, *Santos-Dumont: A Study in Obsession*, London: Putnam, 1962. Alberto Santos Dumont, Peter Wykeham (intro.), *My Airships: The Story of My Life*, New York: Dover, 1973. Mel Byars with Arlette Barré-Despond, *100 Designs/100 Years: A Celebration of the 20th Century*, Hove: RotoVision: 20–21. Henrique Lins de Barros, *Santos Dumont: O homem voa!*, Rio de Janeiro: Petrobras/Contraponto, 2000.

Saporiti Italia
Italian furniture manufacturer; located Besnate.

Biography 1945, Saporiti Industria Arredamenti was founded; introduced one of its first noteworthy designs, 1950s Mayor, Fujiama, and Etere chairs; 1967, began manufacturing in plastics. Alberto Rosselli designed its 1967 Jumbo and 1969 Moby Dick fiberglass chairs and 1970s Confidential sofa. 1980s, Saporiti Italia Gidatex, as it is known today, began incorporating Missoni fabrics; 2000, established the laboratory Contemporane A to attract international design talent; continues to make tables, seating, and bookshelves in both plastics and wood with upholstery. Designers have included Massimiliano Fuksas, Vittorio Introini, Giovanni Offredi, Giorgio Raimondi, and Antonello

Mosca. Saporiti Emages was established for computer transference of digital images of materials and finishes.
Bibliography Cat., Milena Lamarová, *Design a Plastické Hmoty*, Prague: Uměleckoprůmyslové Muzeum, 1972: 74, 204. www.saporitiitalia.it.

Sapper, Richard (1932–)

German designer; born Munich; active Munich, Stuttgart, and Milan.

Training 1952–56, philosophy, graphic design, and mechanical engineering, Technische Universität Munich.
Biography 1956–57, Sapper was a designer at Daimler Benz in Stuttgart. Settling in Italy, he worked in the studio of Gio Ponti/Alberto Rosselli in Milan 1958–59; became a member of the design department of La Rinascente department store, Milan; subsequently, joined Marco Zanuso Sr., with whom he collaborated to 1977. Specializing in high-tech products, he became best known for designing casings for consumer electronics and lighting. Sapper and Zanuso designed some of the most recognizable objects of 1960s–70s, including early-1970s scales and a kitchen timer by Terraillon. Commissioned by Brionvega from 1962, they designed 1962 Doney and 1964 Algol 11 TV sets, 1964 TS502 1° folding radio (reissued as 1977 TS505), 1969 ST201 1° 12 black box TV set (some updated and reissued from 1994); also 1965 Grillo folding telephone by Siemens. 1970–76, Sapper was a consultant to Fiat and Pirelli on experimental vehicles and automobile equipment; 1970, established his own studio in Germany and designed the skeletal low-voltage 1972 Tizio lamp, which became a cult design object, and Tantalo clock produced by Artemide. 1972 with Gae Aulenti, Sapper established a studio for the development of new systems for urban transportation, the collaboration resulting in an exhibition at 1979 (18th) Triennale di Milano. His 1979 Cafetière coffee maker and whistling 1983 Bollitore kettles, both by Alessi, combined postmodernism and high-tech styling. He created other tablewares and 1988 Uri watch by Alessi and furniture by Castelli, Molteni, and Knoll. From 1980, he has been an industrial-design consultant to IBM for all products; designed a collection of domestic furniture by Unifor; though he worked largely in his native Germany, became strongly associated with the postwar Italian design ethic; became a member, Associazione per il Disegno Industriale (ADI). In his 1970s–80s work, Sapper successfully married German precise thinking with Italian sensitivity; 1990s, began to design more high-tech products, particular the 1989 Leapfrog portable computer (with Sam Lucente) by IBM; however, has continued with clients like Alessi and domestic products by progressive firms such as Magis.
Exhibitions/citations Coorganized an exhibition of advanced technology at 1968 (14th) Triennale di Milano. Sapper, Pio Manzù, and William Lansing Plub organized *Mostra di Tecnologia* at 1968 (14th) Triennale di Milano, and other editions. Participated in 1972 *Italy: The New Domestic Landscape*, The Museum of Modern Art, New York. Premio Compasso d'Oro: 1960, 1962 (with Zanuso), 1964 (with Zanuso), 1967 (with Zanuso), 1970 (five citations, with Zanuso), 1979 (four citations), 1984, 1987 (three citations), 1991, 1994, 1998 (two citations individually; one with Francis Ferrarin). Gold medals and/or grand prizes 1964, 1966, and 1973 BIO industrial-design biennials, Ljubljana. 1969 Premio SMAU Industrial Design, Salone della Machina e Attrezzature per l'Ufficio, Milan; 1970 Bundespreis Produktdesign, Rat für Formgebung (German design council), Frankfurt.
Bibliography Paolo Fossati, *Il design in Italia, 1945–1972*, Turin: Einaudi, 1972. Alfonso Grassi and Anty Pansera, *Atlante del design italiano 1940/1980*, Milan: Fabbri, 1980. Jane Lott, 'Interview: Fifties Fantasist Turned Design Houdini,' *Design*, no. 381, Sept. 1980: 37. Giuliana Gramigna and Paola Biondi, *Il design in Italia dell'arredamento domestico*, Turin: Allemandi, 1999. Michael Webb et al., *Richard Sapper*, San Francisco: Chronicle, 2002. Paola Antonelli (ed.), *Objects of Design: The Museum of Modern Art*, New York: The Museum of Modern Art, 2003: 215, 236–37.

Saracino, Titti (1944–)

Italian designer; born and active Milan.

Training To 1968, architecture, Politecnico, Milan.
Biography 1971, she taught, Istituto Europeo di Design; designed a 1973 collection by Boom Line, 1973 porcelain range by Mangani, 1973 kitchenware and cutlery by Valco, 1974 wooden toys by Furga, 1974 baby's high chair by Isab, 1974 jewelry by Gioielleria Spallanzani, 1975 furniture collection by Gervasoni, 1976 restoration and interior design of 18th-century villa on Island of Elba, 1976 restoration and interior design of a 17th-century house in Milan, 1976 tiles by Santagostino. 1969–74, she was director of urban buildings of the Sovraintendenza Regionale Scolastica and, from 1974, director of monuments in Lombardy; became a member, Associazione per il Disegno Industriale (ADI).
Exhibitions Work shown at 1966 jewelry exhibition *Circolo della Stampa*. Designed the stand for Flexform, 1970 (3rd) *Eurodomus* exhibition, Milan, and four stands at 1972 (4th) *Eurodomus*, Turin.
Bibliography *ADI Annual 1976*, Milan: Associazione per il Disegno Industriale, 1976.

Sarfatti, Gino (1912–1984)

Italian lighting designer; born Venice.

Training Aeronaval engineering, Università degli Studi, Genoa.
Biography From 1939, Scarfatti was active in lighting design/production and established the firm Arteluce; during World War II, lived in Switzerland; was a highly innovative leader in the field of lighting in Italy in the immediate post-World War II period; initially produced brass and lacquered-metal lamps in a Rationalist style; subsequently, became more daring, incorporating exposed neon, plastics, and moveable parts, exemplified by 1966 no. 600P model. 1950s, dominated in his specialty through his own designs and those of others, including Franco Albini, Vittoriano Vigano, Ico Parisi, Gianfranco Frattini, and Marco Zanuso Sr. Early models by Sarfatti included 1954 no. 1063, 1955 no. 1055, and 1956 no. 1073 floor lamps and 1956 no. 566 table lamp. 1971, produced the first halogen table lamp. His own work was frequently installed in offices, including the Olivetti building in Barcelona, hotels, including the Hilton Hotel in Rome, schools, and ships, including the 1965 oceanliner *Michelangelo* and the identical 1965 *Raffaello*. Most notable lamp may be one of his earliest, the 1950 floor model with a tubular steel shaft and three variously colored metal diffusers on articulated stems and leather-covered shaft and stems. The legendary Arteluce shop was located on the corso Matteotti, Milan (designed with Zanuso in 1951) and on the Via della Spiga (designed in 1961 with Vigano, a close friend). 1974, Arteluce became a division/brand of Flos. Sarfatti died in Gravellona Toce.
Citations 1954 (several citations), 1955 (three citations), 1956 (two citations), 1957 (two citations), 1960 Premio Compasso d'Oro, Milan; prizes at various editions of Triennale di Milano.
Bibliography 'Cause for Applause: Lightolier's Italian Lamps and Wormley Decor,' *Interiors*, vol. 110, Nov. 1950: 130–32. Andrea Branzi and Michele de Lucchi (eds.), *Il design italiano degli anni '50*, Milan: Ricerche Design Editrice, 1985. Daniele Baroni, *L'oggetto lampada forme e funzione...*, Milan: Electa, 1981. *Moderne Klassiker: Möbel, die Geschichte machen*, Hamburg: Gruner + Jahr, 1982: 52. Cat., Kathryn B. Hiesinger and George H. Marcus III (eds.), *Design Since*

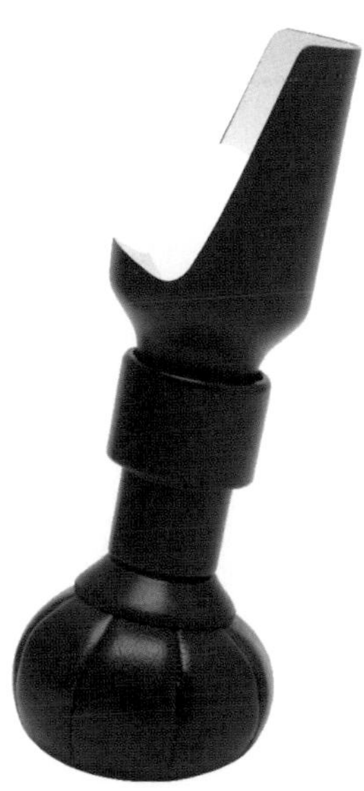

Gino Sarfatti. Lamp (no. 600P). 1966. Painted metal, synthetic leather, and lead, 8 x 3 x 3" (20.3 x 7.6 x 7.6 cm). Mfr.: Arteluce, Italy. Gift of Bonniers, Inc. MoMA.

1945, Philadelphia: Philadelphia Museum of Art, 1983.

Sargiani, Franco (1940–)

Italian graphic and industrial designer; born Modena; active Milan.

Training In architecture in Milan.
Biography Sargiani was frequently associated with the studio of architect Bruno Morassutti; from 1963, worked in design studios in Britain, Denmark, Switzerland, and Finland on industrial buildings and interior architecture; 1969 under Nino Di Salvatore, taught a course in industrial design and visualization, Scuola di Design, Novara (the school transferred to Milan in 1970 as Scuola Politecnica di Design); from 1970, designed metal tableware and graphics by Alessi, including Programma 8 range; 1969–70 packaging by Sivam and 1974–75 wallpaper and packaging by Sipea. He became a member, Associazione per il Disegno Industriale (ADI).
Bibliography *ADI Annual 1976*, Milan: Associazione per il Disegno Industriale, 1976.

Sarpaneva, Timo (1926–)

Finnish designer.

Training 1941–48, drafting, Taideteollisuuskeskuskoulu, Helsinki.
Biography 1950, Sarpaneva became head of the exhibition section and an artist at Iittala Lasi where he developed a process in the 1960s of blowing glass sculpture into wooden molds that, by burning, gave the pieces a textured surface. 1955, he designed his first utilitarian domestic-glass collection; for this series, he also designed the symbol of a lowercase 'i' in a red circle, which subsequently became the trademark of the Iittala Lasi works. From mid-1950s, he taught textile composition and printing, Taideteollinen korkeakoulu, Helsinki. 1955–56, he was the artistic director, Pori Puuvilla Cotton Mill; 1959–63, designed cast-iron cookware and wrapping papers by W. Rosenlew; 1960–62, designed rya rugs by Villayhtymä; 1962, established his own studio; 1963, designed candles by Juhava and, 1964, metalware by Primo; 1964–72, worked at Kinnassand textile mill, Sweden; 1968, designed plastics by Ensto, and glass by Corning, US, and others including Venini. An innovator of techniques and forms, he worked in the factories of his clients in order to gain mastery of the production processes and to learn from the technicians who produced his work. He designed 1968 Ambiente fabric range, printed on both sides of the weave in a process he invented; 1970 textiles by Tampella; metalware by Opa; from 1970, was a freelance designer for Rosenthal. He designed 1955 *H 55* exhibition, Hälsingborg; Finnish section of 1957 (11th) Triennale di Milano; 1961 *Finlandia*, in Zürich, Amsterdam, and London; Finnish section of 1967 *Universal and International Exhibition (Expo '67)*, Montreal; 1985 Finnish Industrial Arts Award.
Exhibitions/citations Work subject of exhibitions in Dortmund, Helsinki, and New York (catalogs below). 1951 (9th) (silver medal), 1954 (10th) (grand prize), 1957 (11th) (two grand prizes), 1960 (12th) (silver and gold medals) Triennali di Milano; two first-place awards at 1956 *American Young Scandinavian Exhibition*, US; 1956 Lunning Prizel; 1958 Pro Finlandia prize; 1985 State Award for Industrial Arts; Eurostar Prize. 1963, elected Honorary Royal Designer for Industry, UK.; 1967, granted honorary doctorate degree, Royal College of Art, London; 1976, Academia de Diseño, Mexico City.
Bibliography 'Timo Sarpaneva,' *Interiors*, vol. 128, Jan. 1969: 128–31. 'Two Faced Textiles,' *Industrial Design*, vol. 16, Mar. 1969. Cat., *Lasiaika: Glas Zeit/Timo Sarpaneva*, Dortmund: Cramers Kunstanstalt, 1985. Jennifer Hawkins Opie, *Scandinavia: Ceramics and Glass in the Twentieth Century*, New York: Rizzoli, 1989. Cat., *Timo Sarpaneva*, Helsinki: Kaupungin Taidemuseo, 1993. Cat., *Timo Sarpaneva, a retrospective* (American Craft Museum, New York), Helsinki : Helsinki City Art Museum, 1994. George Fischler and Barrett Gould, *Scandinavian Ceramics and Glass: 1940s to 1980s*, Atglen, Pa.: Schiffer, 2000.

Sartori, Franz T. (1927–)

Italian industrial designer; born Milan.

Training Architecture, Trinity Hall College, US.
Biography Sartori designed furniture for adults and children, glassware, and a range of industrial products for clients, including Arnolfo di Cambio, Vittorio Bonacina, Cristalart, Cea's Carlo Citterio, Colmob Design, Dalmine, Flexform, Imperial Chemical Industries, Luci, Carlo Parolini, Potocco, Prestige, Ritz Italora, Toiano, Stilux, Saffa, and Zanotta. He designed Tirangoli foam seating by Delta; was a professor of industrial design, Imperial College of Science, Technology and Medicine, London; taught, Istituto Statale d'Arte Stagio Stagi, Pietrasanta, Italy; was president, Design Collegio Lombardo Periti Esperti e Consulenti; president of Accademia Toscana dell'Arte e del Lavoro; president of Associazione Arredatori Progettisti,; a member of the Tribunale di Milano.
Exhibitions/citations First prize for sculpture, 1968 Concorso Nazionale Dalmine; 1970 gold medal for civic merit, Comune di Milano; first prize, 1973 *Internazionale La Modonnina*; silver medal, 1974 (17th) *Concorso giornalistico Gargagnana*; 1975 gold medal from President of the Republic of Italy. Represented Italy at 1970 *Japan World Exposition (Expo '70)*, Osaka.

Timo Sarpaneva. Carafe. 1956. Glass, h. 7 5/8 x dia. 3 5/8" (19.4 x 9.2 cm). Mfr.: Iittala Lasi, Finland. Phyllis B. Lambert Fund. MoMA.

Sarvia
> See Hammarplast.

Sason, Sixten (1912–1967)

Swedish industrial designer.

Training In silversmithing.
Biography Unlike most car designers of his time, Sixten Sason was an industrial designer and had a broad range of interests; while working on aircraft X-ray and instructional drawings for Saab, was hired by Saab engineer Gunnar Ljungstrom to improve an unattractive 1946 auto-body protype. This assignment resulted in Sason's 1950–56 Type 92 (numbers up to 91 had been assigned to aircraft). Sason went on to design 1966–74 Saab 92 Sonett II/4V/III, his first body for Saab with a fiberglass shell, an advanced use of the material at the time, and 1965 Catherina fully functional prototype. His two best auto designs are arguably the unique, aerodynamic 1956–60 Saab 93 that revealed the company's early efforts in aviation and 1960–80 Saab 96 V4 with 65 b.h.p. that garnered press favor for its individuality. As a consultant designer, Sason also created Electrolux domestic appliances, like the 1956 273 vacuum cleaner by Electrolux and many other Electrolux domestic appliances; also worked on the 'look' of the legendary square-format Hasselblad camera, which had already been conjured by Victor Hasselblad and his chief mechanic Ake Tranefors.
Bibliography *Saab, 1947-70: Models 92, 93, 95, 96, 99, Sonett I, II and III*, St. Paul, Minn.: Motor Books International. *Saab, 1956-1985*, St. Paul, Minn.: Motorbooks International, 1985. Penny Sparke, *Introduction to Design and Culture in the Twentieth Century*, London: Allen & Unwin, 1986. Eric Dymock, *Saab*, Newbury Park, Ca.: Haynes, 1997.

Sato, Kozo (1951–)

Japanese product designer; born Tokyo.

Training To 1976, Politecnico, Milan.
Bibliography 1976–80, Sato worked in the studio of Rodolfo Bonetto,

Sawaya & Moroni: Zaha Hadid. Glacier sofa. 2000. Fire-varnished wood, l. 197 x w. 49 1/4 x 19 3/4" (500 x 125 x 50 cm). Mfr.: Sawaya & Moroni, Italy.

Milan; 1983, established Kozo Design Studio, Tokyo, designing furniture and glass- and metalware; 1987–94, was a selections committee member, G-mark design products competition, Japan; 1989, Nagoya organizing committee member, International Council of Societies of Industrial Design (ICSID); 1991–92, part-time lecturer, Tama Art University. The 1993 Kozo Project table clock exemplifies the simplicity of his work, while the 1993 Kri ceiling-extending lamps by Lucitalia are technologically sophisticated.
Exhibitions/citations Work included in 1989 *Mondo Materiale*, New York, and several others. Special Prize (Group), Mainichi Design Award; 1988, 1991, and 1993 G-Mark Good Design award (for Small and Medium Enterprises), Japanese Industrial Design Promotion Organization (JIDPO).
Bibliography Mel Byars, *50 Light...*, Hove: RotoVision, 1997.

Saunders, Brenda (1949–)

British industrial designer; born Newbury, Berkshire; active London.

Training 1970–73, furniture design, Kingston Polytechnic (now Kingston University); 1973–76, Royal College of Art, London.
Biography 1976–77, she was a furniture designer in the architecture and design studio Cini Boeri Associati in Milan; 1978 with Peter Bosson, established a design studio in London, designing furniture for clients, including Olivetti, International Wool Secretariat, and American Express. 1980–86, she taught furniture and interior design, Kingston Polytechnic; from 1985, furniture and product design, Royal College of Art; 1985–86, textile and furniture design, Birmingham Polytechnic; 1985–87, at London College of Furniture; 1986–87, furniture, Manchester Polytechnic; and others. Her work has included kitchens and bathrooms, computer-related products, housewares, 1985 Parasol chair by Pel in a Cooke Mills fabric, 1986 A-Frame Bed by Sleepeezee, 1988 leather briefcase by Whitehouse and Cox. The partnership became Colebrook Bosson Saunders, designed Hana lighting stem, Harry flexible screen, Stuff-It clothes rack, and 2001 Albert mobile workstation.
Citations 1974 Burton Group Design Award; 1975 Radford Design Award; 1976 British Council Award, 1984 David Mitchell Award. To Colebrook Bosson Saunders: 2003 Produce Approval Award (for flat-screen computer monitor), British Contract Furnishing Association (BCFA).
Bibliography Cat., Design Center Stuttgart, *Women in Design: Careers and Life Histories Since 1900*, Stuttgart: Haus der Wirtschaft, 1989: 272–75.

Sauvage, Henri (1873–1932)

French architect and designer.

Training École Nationale Supérieure des Beaux-Arts, Paris.
Biography 1898–1912, Sauvage was associated with architect Charles Sarazin; 1903 with Sarazin, founded the Société Anonyme de Logements Hygiéniques à Bon Marché and built a 1912 house on the rue Vavin and a house on the rue des Amiraux, both Paris; 1900–03, became one of the first French modern architects; was a practitioner of the Art Nouveau style and known for the pavilion of Loïe Fuller at 1900 *Exposition Universelle*, Paris, and 1898 residence of Louis Majorelle in Nancy; 1919, established his own office; 1926, was associated with architect Frantz Jourdain on La Samaritaine department store extension; from 1928, taught, École Nationale Supérieure des Arts Décoratifs and, from 1931, École Nationale Supérieure des Beaux-Arts, both Paris; designed complete ensembles for Café de Paris and 1931 Decré department store in Nantes.
Exhibitions Work subject of 1976–77 exhibition, École Nationale Supérieure d'Architecture et des Arts Visuels, Brussels (catalog below).
Bibliography *L'art décoratif*, June 1902: 108. *Allgemeines Lexikon der bildenden Künstler*. 1955. Cat., *Henri Sauvage, 1873–1932*, Brussels: Les Archives, 1976. Alastair Duncan, *Art Nouveau and Art Déco Lighting*, New York: Simon & Schuster, 1978: 86. François Loyer and Hélène Guéné, *Henri Sauvage: les immeubles à gradins = Set-Back Buildings*, Liège: Mardaga, 1987. Arlette Barré-Despond and Suzanne Tise, *Jourdain*, Paris: Regard, 1988: 60–68, 144, 195. Jean-Baptiste Minnaert (ed.), *The Architectural Drawings of Henri Sauvage: The Works of an Architect-Decorator in the Collections of the Institut Français d'Architecture and the Archives de Paris*, New York: Garland, 1994.

Savnik, Davorin (1929–)

Slovene designer; born Kranj.

Training Fakulteta za Arhitekturo, Univerza v Ljubljana; and, 1969, master of arts degree, Vysoká Škola Uměleckoprůmyslová (VŠUP, school of applied arts); both Prague.
Biography 1958–73, Savnik worked at Iskra, Ljubljana and, from 1973, has been a freelance designer. Work has included 1979 Eta 80 telephone (much plagiarized, and some replicas even receiving awards) by Iskra; 1993 Megatron chair by Vitalis, Novo Mesto; and lighting, tools, watches, and electronics.
Citations 1972 and 1982 prizes, Design Center Stuttgart; 1984 award, Ministry of International Trade and Industry (MITI), Japan; gold medal, 1979 BIO 8 industrial-design biennial, Ljubljana; 1978, 1980, and 1983 awards, Industrie Forum Design (iF), Hanover.
Bibliography I. Mlašenoviš, *11 istaknutih primenjenih umetnika Jugoslavije*, Belgrade. Stane Bernik, *Slovenska arhitektura, urbanizem, oblikovanje in fotografija 1945–1978*, Ljubljana, 1979. 'The "Plagiarius" Award,' *I.D.*, Nov.–Dec. 1985.

Sawaya, William (1948–); Sawaya & Moroni

Lebanese designer and entrepreneur; born Beirut.

Training 1969–73, Institute National des Beaux-Arts, Beirut.
Biography Sawaya designed residences in Lebanon initially and then in France, Italy, Japan, Greece, and the US; 1978, settled in Italy and

established Sawaya & Moroni Architecture and Design with Paolo Moroni; 1984, founded Sawaya & Moroni Contemporary Furniture with Moroni where Sawaya directs artistic and project activities. Sawaya has become a naturalized Italian citizen. He individually and with Moroni has designed the firm's furniture, furnishings, and glass, metal, and other accessories and also commissioned designers, including Ron Arad, Uwe Fischer, Zaha Hadid, Matthew Hilton, Richard Hutten, Adolfo Natalini, Bořek Šípek, Oswald Ungers, Michael Young. For others, Sawaya has designed 2000 BArtolomeo e VAlentina child's chair for Museo Bagatti Valsecchi, 2001 Calla chair by Heller, 2001–02 football (soccer) trophies and cups for Federazione Italiana Giuoco Calcio (FIFA), and 2002 crystal items by Baccarat.
Exhibitions From 1991, work subject of venues in Basel, Hamburg, Munich, Paris, Osaka, Riom (France), and Tokyo; from 1985, included in a large number of group shows worldwide.
Bibliography Nally Bellati, *New Italian Design*, New York: Rizzoli, 1990. Ettore Mocchetti, *Le più belle case del mondo sul mare*, Milan: Mondadori, 1993. Nina Bornsen-Holtmann, *Italian Design*, Cologne: Taschen, 1993. Laura Lazzaroni, *35 anni di design al Salone del Mobile*, Milan: Cosmit/Mazzotta, 1996. Mel Byars, *50 Tables...*, Hove: RotoVision, 1997. Keith and Fiona Baker, *20th Century Furniture*, London: Carlton, 1999. Claudia Neumann, *Design Directory Italy*, London: Pavilion, 1999. Paola Biondi, *Il design dell'arredamento in Italia*, Turin: Allemandi, 2000.

Saxbo

Danish ceramics factory.

Biography 1929, Nathalie Krebs and Gunnar Nylund set up stoneware pottery studio Nylund og Krebs in Copenhagen, which became Saxbo in 1930, when Krebs took over its management. Nathalie Krebs worked in collaboration with Eva Stæhr-Nielsen, who joined the workshop in 1932. Saxbo became the most important small, independent pottery in Denmark. Krebs developed the glazes, and Stæhr-Nielsen designed the shapes. Several generations of potters active at Saxbo helped to develop the 'classic Saxbo style.' Designers there included Edith Bruun Sonne 1938–39 and Kyllikki Salmenhaara 1946–47. Tias Eckoff was an apprentice under Krebs 1947–48. And Bode Willumsen and Axel Salto (from c. 1923 to c. 1933) had a studio there. 1968, the enterprise closed.
Bibliography Jennifer Hawkins Opie, *Scandinavia: Ceramics and Glass in the Twentieth Century*, New York: Rizzoli, 1989.

Scacchetti, Luca (1952–)

Italian architect and designer; active Milan.

Training 1975, degree, Facoltà di Architettura, Politecnico, Milan.
Biography 1976–86, Scacchetti taught architectural planning, Politecnico, Milan; 1990–95, was the director, department of architecure, Istituto Europeo di Design, Milan; currently teaches elements of architecture and urban planning, Accademia di Belle Arti di Brera, Milan, and holds seminars on and teaches industrial design at Politecnico, Milan, He is active in his own architecture, design, and urban-planning office for clients worldwide. Extensive design work has included exhibitions, domestic and public furniture, furnishings, lighting, door handles, floor tiles, glassware, and bathroom fittings for clients such as Accademia, Anna Nora, Barovier e Toso, Ceramica Bardelli, Ceramica Vogue, Colombo Design, Flos, FontanaArte, Oak Design, Nito, Oma, Poltrona Frau, Roncoroni, Rossin, Sellaro, Tecno, TRE-Più, Up & Up, and Vali & Vali. From 1999, he has curated and designed cultural exhibitions at Abitare il Tempo fair, Verona.
Exhibitions/citations Work subject of 1981 *Mobili degli Efetti Meravigliosi, delle Prospettive e delle Finte Ombre e Altro*, Rome; 1982 *Vivere Architettando, Luca Scacchetti–Case*, Milan; 1986 *Luca Scacchetti, Viaggio Intorno alla mia Stanza*, Rome; 1986 *Luca Scacchetti's Approach to Modern Design–The Modernity of Traditions*, Tokyo; 1986 *El Salto del Caballo–Muebles y Objetos mas alla del Diseño*, Madrid and Frankfurt; 1990 *Luca Scacchetti, Achitetture*, Amsterdam and Madrid; 1991 *Tre Studie di Architettura*, Turin; 1991 *Luca Scacchetti, Architetture in Forme Varie*, Milan; 1993 *Sites of Earth: Sites of Mind. Travels and Projects in the Sketchbook of Luca Scacchetti*, Chicago Athenaeum. 2001 Material Excellence MC Award, Material ConneXion, New York, and 2002 Costruire Award First Prize, Milan, both for Ondapan HPL (High Pressure Laminate) panel by Gruppo Frati.
Bibliography F. Maschini, *Luca Scacchetti: forme oggetti architettura 1975/1985*, Rome: Kappa, 1986. Paolo Portoghesi, *I nuovi architetti italiani*, Bari: Laterza, 1985. S. Sanpietro and M. Vercelloni, *Nuovi negozi a Milano*, Milan: L'Archivolto, 1988. Nally Bellati, *New Italian Design*, New York: Rizzoli, 1990. Fumio Shimizu and David Palterer, *The Italian Furniture*, Tokyo: Graphic-sha, 1991. Emilio Ambasz et al., *Luca Scacchetti, Architetture,* Milan: Idea, 1991. Mel Byars, *50 Tables...*, Hove: RotoVision, 1997. Thomas Muirhead, *Milan: A Guide to Recent Architecture*, London: Ellipsis, 1998.

Scali, François (1951–)

French designer.

Training To 1974, in economics; 1979, DPLG architecture (governmental diploma), France.
Biography Scali has collaborated with Alain Domingo in Nemo, a design partnership established in 1982. They became best known for furniture designs for the Cité des Sciences et de l'Industrie, Parc de la Villette, Paris. Product design: carpets by Géométrie Variable and by Élisée Éditions, graphic design for MBK and for Motobécane, pasta by Panzani, furniture for the offices of the Caisse Nationale des Monuments Historiques et des Sites (now Centre des Monuments Nationaux) in Paris, packaging for Lesieur, furniture and furnishings by Tébong, 1985 computer screen, 1984 print lamp by Formica, and 1983 Faizzz, 1984 Mediabolo, 1983 Marini, and 1983 Moreno chairs by Nemo Édition, and the Genitron 2000 countdown clock at the Centre Georges Pompidou, Paris.
Bibliography Juli Capella and Quim Larrea, *Designed by Architects in the 1980s*, New York: Rizzoli, 1988. Didier Laroque (intro.), *Nemo: Alain Domingo, François Scali*, Barcelona: Gili, 1992.
> See Domingo, Alain.

Scansetti, Francesco (1955–)

Italian designer; born Milan.

Training To 1976, Liceo Artistico di Brera, Milan.
Biography 1975–84 with Angelo Cortesi, was active in the studio Gruppo Progettazione Integrale (G.P.I.) and designed the interiors of the Milan metropolitan airports in Linate and Malpensa; 1984 with Cortesi, designed for Kartell; 1991–92, was active within Associazione per il Disegno Industriale (ADI); taught design, Instituto Europeo di Design, Milan. 1991 with Marina Paul and Giorgio Gurioli, Scansetti cofounded the design studio Sýn (a reference to *oggetti sinbiotici*, or symbiotic objects) to investigate the use of new materials and techniques. (Gurioli left in 1995.) First products included 1991 Tra flexible-harmonic-steel book ends (with Gurioli) by Sýn, 1993 Noce nutcracker (with Gurioli), 1993 clothes hanger by Acerbis; 1995 Di humidifier, c. 1995 In photo frame, and 1995 Soft object holder and 2000 Shiatsu massage pad by Outlook-Zelco Europe. Subsequent products: 1995 Queen and 1997 UFO by Rede Guzzini; 1997 Relax polyurethane headrest; 1998 Bart, 1999 Body seating by Seven/Arflex; 1999 Gong eyeglass case by Yalos; 2001 Love seat by INSA; crystal products by Swarovski.
Exhibitions/citations Work included in 1988 *Light on Icons* (with Alberto Prina), Los Angeles and Atlanta; 1988 *Italia 2000* (with Cortesi), Moscow; 1989 Tecnhotel fair, Genoa; 1990 *Italia Presenta* (with Cortesi), Buenos Aires; 1992 *Naturalmente* (with Cortesi), 1992 (18th) Triennale di Milano; 1995 *Mutant Materials in Contemporary Design*, The Museum of Modern Art, New York. 1996 prizes, Young & Design, Milan; 1994 and 1996 prizes, BIO industrial-design biennials, Ljubljana; 1997 Design Plus prize, Ambiente fair, Frankfurt.
Bibliography Cat., Paola Antonelli, *Mutant Materials in Contemporary Design*, New York: The Museum of Modern Art/Abrams, 1995. Mel Byars, *50 Products...*, Hove: RotoVision, 1998.
> See Paul, Marina.

Scarpa, Carlo (1906–1978)

Italian architect and designer; born Venice; father of Tobia Scarpa.

Training To 1926, Accademia di Belle Arte, Venice.
Biography 1927, Scarpa established his own architecture practice in Venice. His work was influenced by the Gothic-Byzantine style of Vene-tian architecture, the work of Frank Lloyd Wright, and the De Stijl group. He also admired the Art Nouveau style, including the work of Josef Maria Olbrich; 1920s–30s, designed exhibitions and elegant interiors; created numerous furniture pieces by Gavina and others; designed the Olivetti showroom in Venice; became known for his 1932–47 distinctive and original glassware by Venini and by Studio Ars Labor Industrie Riunite (S.A.L.I.R.), and interior-design schemes. For Venini, he mixed colorless and opaque glasses, introducing colorful threads and ribbons; cut and ground glass in new ways; frosted it; made it appear ancient and corroded. For example,

his 1936 Carroso vase was composed of mouth-blown iridescent dark green and lavender glasses. The 1953–54 renovation of the Galleria Nazionale della Sicilia on the Palazzo Abbatellis, Palermo, brought him international recognition. Other commissions included a number of museum renovations, such as the Accademia in Venice, 1952; Museo Correr, Venice, 1953–60; six rooms in the Uffizi (with Ignazio Gardella and Giovanni Michelucci), Florence, 1956; the annex to the neoclassical Gipsotecca Canoviana, Possegno, near Treviso, 1956–57; 1955–61 Casa Verritti, Udine; 1961–63 Fondazione Querini Stampalia, Venice; 1964 interior design of, and restaurant in, Museo di Castelvecchio, Verona; 1970–72 Cimitero a San Vito, Treviso; 1970 –78 Brion Cemetery (posthumous), San Vito d'Altivole; 1973–81 Banca Popolare, Verona; 1975 Terrorist Outrage Monument, Brescia; 1975–78 Ottolenghi house, Bardolino; 1975–78 housing blocks, Vincenza. He taught architecture at Istituto Universitario di Architettura, Venice.1972–78, he was director, Istituto Universitario di Architettura, Venice.

Exhibitions/citations Designed the exhibitions of Paul Klee at 1948 Biennale di Venezia; of Frank Lloyd Wright at 1960 (12th) Triennale di Milano; of Erich Mendelsohn at 1960 Biennale di Venezia; 1968, of Piet Mondrian at Galleria d'Arte Moderna, Rome. Designed the Venezuelan pavilion at 1954–56 Biennale di Venezia; Italian pavilion at 1967 *Universal and International Exhibition (Expo 67)*, Montréal; information stand at 1968 Biennale di Venezia; frescoes at 1969 Florence Exhibition, London. Work was subject of 1974 exhibitions, Vicenza and London; Centre de Recherche d'Urbanisme, Paris, 1975; Accademia nazionale di San Luca, Rome, 1979; Sala Boggian at Castelvecchio, Verona, 1982; Canadian Centre for Architecture, Montréal, 1999. 1955 honorary doctorate, Accademia di Belle Arti, Venice; 1967 (Carlotta and Sedia 121 by Cassina), 1979 (Dodge table by Simón), and 1991 (posthumously, Serie 1934 by Bernini) Premio Compasso d'Oro; 1969, elected Honorary Royal Designer for Industry, UK; 1978 posthumously awarded honorary doctorate, Istituto Universitario di Architettura, Venice.

Bibliography Manlio Brusatin, 'Carlo Scarpa Architetto Veneziano,' *Contraspazio*, nos. 3–4, 1972: 2–85. Cat., T. Yokoyama and H. Toyota, 'Carlo Scarpa,' *Space Design* special issue, no. 6, June 1977. N. Miller, 'The Legendary Castle,' 'His Own Monument,' and 'A Posthumous Work'; N. Miller and G. Renalli, 'Critique'; all in *Progressive Architecture*, no. 5, 1981. Licisco Magagnato et al., *Carlo Scarpa a Castelvecchio*, Milan: Comunità, 1982. Ada Francesca Marcianò, *Carlo Scarpa*, Bologna: Zanichelli, 1984. M.A. Crippa, *Scarpa: Il pensiero, il disegno, i progetti*, Milan: Jaca Books, 1984. Francesco Dal Co and Giuseppe Mazzariol, *Carlo Scarpa: opera completa*, Milan: Electa, 1984. Maria Antonietta Crippa, *Carlo Scarpa: il pensiero, il disegno, i progetti*, Milan: Jaca, 1984. Anna Venini Diaz de Santiliana, *Venini catalogue raisonné 1921–1986*, Milan: Skira, 2000. Marino Barovier, *Carlo Scarpa: Glass of an Architect*, Milan: Skira, 1998. Cat., Nicholas Olsberg, *Carlo Scarpa, Architect: Intervening with History*, Montréal: Canadian Centre for Architecture; New York: Monacelli, 1999.

Scarpa, Tobia (1935–); Afra Scarpa (b. Afra Bianchin 1937–)

Tobia Scarpa: Italian architect and designer; born Venice; son of Carlo Scarpa. Afra Scarpa: Italian architect and designer; born Montebelluna. Active Trevignanó. Husband and wife.

Training Both: 1969, degree in architecture, Istituto Universitario di Architettura, Venice.

Biography 1957–61, Tobia Scarpa worked for Venini in Murano, where he first collaborated with his wife 1958–60. 1960, they established their own design studio in Montebelluna, where they occasionally have been active as architects; from time to time, worked with his father Carlo Scarpa (1962 Nuovola lamp by Flos and 1962–63 renovation of Italian pavilion, Biennale di Venezia), and with Gio Ponti at Cassina, designing furniture such as 1968 Ciprea armchair with a fabric slipcover over a frameless foam structure. Tobia designed furniture by Gavina from 1960 and by Knoll, but became primarily active with his wife, designing furniture, glass, cutlery, and exhibition displays; from 1962, designed the corporate-image program for Benetton shops in Europe and the US. Tobia Scarpa was a lecturer in industrial design, Academia di Belle Arte, Venice. One of his best-known designs is 1965 925 Chair in Russian leather on plywood by Cassina. For Flos lamps along with Pier Castiglioni, Tobia was commissioned by one of the founders, Dino Gavina, to design some of the first models for the firm. The Scarpas' lighting designs for Flos include 1968 Biagio in white marble (a sculptural expression of the highest level of 1960s Italian

Tobia Scarpa. Bowl. c. 1960. Blown glass, h. 2 7/8 x dia. 6 1/8" (7.3 x 15.5 cm). Mfr.: Venini & Co., Italy. Greta Daniel Design Fund. MoMA.

design), 1973 Papillion (one of the first fixtures to use new halogen technology), 1978 Ballo, 1982 Celestia, 1982 Perpetua, 1990 Vol au Vent hanging light (similar to a 1920s model by René Herbst). They were also known for their use of rare hardwoods. Their 1970s cutlery and 1992 anodized, brightly colored aluminum dishes were produced by San Lorenzo. 1980s, they began designing for firms in Spain; worked on the restoration of the plazas in Veneto and in Emilia. Other work: 1960 Bastiano divan and 1960 Vanessa metal bed by Gavina, 1964 Torcello system (table, chair, bed) by Stildomus, 1970 Sonana armchair by Cassina, 1979 Piediferro metal and marble table, 1984 Poligonon table series by B&B Italia, 1985 Salomone desk by Maxalto, 1986 Marly bookshelf and 1991 Moka table and chair by Molteni, and 1986 Ronda armchair and 1993 America armchair and sofa by Casas. Other clients: Cadel, Dimensione Fuoco, Galvani, Goppion, IB Office, Meritalia, Morseletto, Noalex, Poggi, San Lorenzo, Segno Cittá, Skipper, Unifor, VeArt/Auras, Veneta Asfalti. Their architecture, restorations, and interior-design commissions, primarily in Italy, have been extensive, from 1973 Benetton store in Selva del Montello (Treviso) to 2000 restoration of the Palazzo del Mercato Vecchio, Verona.

Exhibitions/citations 925 armchair first shown, at 1966 Salone del Mobile, Milan; 1970 *Modern Chairs 1918–1970*, Whitechapel Gallery, London; included in 1972 *New Domestic Landscape* (1968 Ciprea and 1970 Soriana armchairs by Ponti and T. Scarpa), The Museum of Modern Art, New York. Work subject of 1985 *Afra e Tobia Scarpa, Architetti e Designers*, Padiglione d'Arte Contemporanea, Milan. Premio Compasso d'Oro: 1970 (for Soriana armchair [both] and Ciprea armchair [A. Scarpa] by Cassina), 1979 (for Tamburo lamp [T. Scarpa] by Flos), 1989 (for tea set [both] by San Lorenzo).

Bibliography Cat., *Modern Chairs 1918–1970*, London: Lund Humphries, 1971. Cat., Kathryn B. Hiesinger and George H. Marcus III (eds.), *Design Since 1945*, Philadelphia: Philadelphia Museum of Art, 1983. Cat., Antonio Piva, *Afra e Tobia Scarpa, architetti e designers*, Milan: Mondadori, 1985. Cat., Daniel Boudinet, *Parere sull'architettura di Afra e Tobia Scarpa*, Milan: Mondadori, 1985. Juli Capella and Quim Larrea, *Designed by Architects in the 1980s*, New York: Rizzoli, 1988. Roberto Masiero, *Afra e Tobia Scarpa: Architetture*, Milan: Electa, 1996. Giuliana Gramigna and Paola Biondi, *Il design in Italia dell'arredamento domestico*, Turin: Allemandi, 1999.

Schaeffer, Rudolph (1886–1988)

American colorist; born Clare, Mich.

Training Thomas Normal Training School, Detroit, Mich.; 1909, Under Ernest Batchelder, design in Minneapolis, Minn.

Biography Schaeffer, a practitioner of yoga and meditation, taught lower-grade pupils in Michigan and Ohio before, at ceramicist Ernest Batchelder's instigation, moving to Pasadena, Cal., where he became an instructor at Troop Polytechnic School, succeeding Douglas Donaldson. 1914, Schaeffer was appointed by US Commissioner of Education to make a study of the role of color in the curriculum of vocational schools in Munich based on Germany's being a pioneer in new synthetic dyes. Schaeffer soon introduced new colors (turquoise, chartreuse, magenta, and other prismatic colors) into stage, interior, and crafts design classes in California and also introduced color into warp-dyed weaving goods that had traditionally been white. Dorothy Liebes publicly recognized Schaeffer for his pioneering color ideas, which changed industrial textile design in the US. Observing the value of color in the environment, he organized courses in flower arrange-

ment, which led to his self-published *Flower Arrangement* (San Francisco, 1935). 1926, he established the Rhythmo-Chromatic Design School, San Francisco, where students were taught color, textile, and environmental design. The Rudolf Schaeffer School of Design, San Francisco, is active today.
Bibliography Ann B. Angelo, 'Rudolph Schaeffer: A Memoir,' master's-degree thesis, San Francisco: John F. Kennedy University, 1980. Bonnie Mattison in Timothy J. Andersen et al., *California Design 1910*, Salt Lake City: Peregrine Smith, 1980: 87. *The Rudolph Schaeffer School of Design: Art in San Francisco Since 1915*, Berkeley, Cal.: Regional Oral History Office, The Bancroft Library, 1982

Scharff, Allan (1945–)
Danish metalworker.

Training 1963–67, apprenticeship, Georg Jensen Sølvsmedie; 1972–75, The Danish College of Jewelry and Silversmithing; both Copenhagen.
Biography 1974, Scharff established his own silversmithy and has designed glass; from 1978, was artistic consultant and a designer to Hans Hansen Sølvsmedie, Kolding; from 1978, deputy teacher, Guldsmedehøjskolen; from 1991, a designer at Holmegård Glasværk; from 1996, visiting teacher, Royal College of Art, London. Designed 1994 Infinite armband/ring, 1994 Flying Time wristwatch, 1995 gold necklace, and 1996 letter opener and orange peeler by Georg Jensen; 1995 coasters and 1995 Duet vase by Royal Copenhagen; others.
Exhibitions/citations Work in a number of venures. One-person exhibitions at Voliére–Museum of Decorative Arts, Copenhagen, in 1980; Art Galleri Boye, Århus, in 1982; Herning Museum of Fine Arts, in 1978 and 1989; Royal Copenhagen Amagertorv, in 1995; Galleria d'Arte L'Agostiniana, Rome, in 1996; Det Danske Kunstindustrimuseum, Copenhagen, in 1980. Received 1967 prize, National Board of Goldsmith Trade, Denmark; 1975 bronze and 1976 silver medals, City of Copenhagen Craftsmen Prize; 1982 and 1986 awards, Guldsmedefagets Fællesråds competition; 1985 award, Scandinavian Diamond Today competition; 1987 award, International Aurifex; 1993 award, World Crafts Councils Europe; 1995 Bayerischer Staatspreis.
Bibliography Cat., David Revere McFadden (ed.), *Scandinavian Modern Design 1880–1980*, New York: Abrams, 1982.

Schawinsky, 'Xanti' Alexander (1904–1979)
Swiss designer; born Basel.

Training In painting and architecture in Zürich, Cologne, and Berlin; 1924–29, Bauhaus, Weimar.
Biography 1926–27, Schawinsky was a theater designer in Zwickau; 1929–31, worked as a graphic designer for the city of Magdeburg; 1933, moved to Italy and became an illustrator and graphic designer in Milan, notably for Olivetti and Motta; 1936, at the invitation of Josef Albers, settled in the US and taught at Black Mountain College, North Carolina, and several universities; collaborated with Luigi Figini and Gino Pollini on 1935 Studio 42 portable typewriter for Olivetti, and with Walter Gropius and Marcel Breuer on 1939–40 *New York World's Fair: The World of Tomorrow*; 1950, began to paint and established a studio near Lake Maggiore, Italy, working in both New York and Italy. He died in Lucarno.
Bibliography Lionel Richard, *Encyclopédie du Bauhaus*, Paris: Somogy, 1985: 208. Cat., *Xanti Schawinsky*, Berlin: Bauhaus-Archiv, 1986.

Scheid, Georg Anton
Austrian silversmiths and jeweler; located Vienna.

History The firm was originally known as gold and silver jewelry manufacturer Markowitsch & Scheid. 1862, the firm was named G.A. Scheid and executed gold and silver dross, separation, and plating; from 1876, was located at 17 Hofmühlgasse, Vienna, and, 1882–1903, at 85 Gumpendorferstrasse, Vienna; produced silverwares and jewelry and became well known for its high-quality enamel work; before 1900, produced silverwares that were simple in form, unlike the busily embossed decoration and Sezession motifs in the work of contemporary Austrian silversmiths. Before the Wiener Werkstätte was established in 1903, Scheid produced the silver designs of Koloman Moser.
Exhibitions Work included in 1889 *Jubilee Exhibition*; 1896–97 *Winter Exhibition*; 1850 to 1914 Austrian arts and crafts exhibitions, Österreichisches Museum für Kunst und Industrie, Vienna; 1900 *Exposition Universelle*, Paris.
Bibliography Waltrand Neuwirth, *Lexikon Wiener Gold- und Silberschmiede und ihre Punzen 1867–1922*, Vienna: Neuwirth, 1977: 178–80. Annelies Krekel-Aalberse, *Art Nouveau and Art Déco Silver*, New York: Abrams, 1989. Deanna F. Cera (ed.), *Jewels of Fantasy: Costume Jewelry of the 20th Century*, New York: Abrams, 1992.

'Xanti' Alexander Schawinsky, Luigi Figini, and Gino Pollini. Studio 42 portable typewriter. 1935. Metal frame and fiber case, 4 5/16 x 10 7/16 x 13 3/8" (11.3 x 26.5 x 34 cm). Mfr.: Ing. C. Olivetti & C., Italy. Courtesy Quittenbaum Kunstauktionen, Munich.

Schellens & Marto
Dutch fabric manufacturer; located Eindhoven.

History Active 1887–1981, Schellens & Marto was directed by J.J. Marto 1887–96, and by members of the Schellens family 1887–1981; began production as a manufacturer of mock velvet, the process introduced by Huguenot refugees from France in the 17th and 18th centuries; started with two mechanical test looms but required partial hand production up to 1930; was using printing blocks to end of 1920s. By 1930s, double-weave looms, rather than the earlier rod looms, were used to produce two fabrics simultaneously. From 1930s, patterns were woven into the fabric in one or more colors and with one or more fabrics on a jacquard loom. Many designs were produced by the firm's staff, while others were purchased from design agencies, including Schnitzler und Vogel and Rudolf in Krefeld. Other design consultants were C.A. Lion Cachet for various 1910–40 commissions and for oceanliner interiors, including for the Stoomvart Maatschappij Nederland (Netherlands steam naviation company); C. van der Sluys 1917–19; Chris Lebeau, a designer of a c. 1930 fabric for the Royal Palace in Tilburg; Christiaan de Moor for the Dutch pavilion at 1937 *Exposition Internationale des Arts et Techniques dans la Vie Moderne*, Paris. Schellens & Marto's fabrics were primarily sold to bus and railway companies and to wholesalers who in turn sold to numerous furniture manufacturers.
Bibliography Cat., *Industry and Design in the Netherlands, 1850/1950*, Amsterdam: Stedelijk Museum, 1985: 104–05.

Schenck, Édouard (1874–1959); Marcel Schenck (1898–1946)
French metalworkers; active Toulouse; father and son.

Biography Édouard Schenck was the brother of Marcel Schenck (Toulouse 1898–1946), an architect who built 1894 Schenck house and a workshop on the rue Vergniaud, Paris. Édouard was active from the turn of the century and c. 1900 was the best-known metalworker, with Edgar Brandt and Paul Brindeau de Jarny, showing at the Salons in Paris. Schenck produced a wide range of domestic metalware based on insect and vegetal themes, including jardinières, andirons, screens, lamps, and architectural fittings. His lamps sometimes incorporated cabochons of flambé earthenware and colored glass panels. 1920s, he was joined by his son Marcel. They became

known for designing lightweight metal bases that supported historicist and aesthetically retrograde fixtures that incorporated wrought iron and/or repoussé, silvered, gilded, and patinated copper.
Exhibitions Work shown at editions of Salon d'Automne; Société des Artistes Décorateurs from 1924; 1925 *Exposition Internationale des Arts Décoratifs et Industriels Modernes*; all Paris.
Bibliography Guillaume Janneau, *Le luminaire et les moyens d'éclairage nouveaux*, Paris: Charles Moreau: 1st series, plates 37, 38; 2nd series: plates 45–46; 3rd series: plates 13–15 [n.d.]. Alastair Duncan, *Art Nouveau and Art Déco Lighting*, New York: Simon & Schuster, 1978: 86. Pierre Kjellberg, *Art déco: les maîtres du mobilier, le décor des paquebots*, Paris: Amateur, 1986 / 1990. Arlette Barré-Despond and Suzanne Tise, *Jourdain*, Paris: Regard, 1988: 44–47.

Schettini, M. Letizia (1961–)
Italian designer; born and active Florence.

Training To 1982, Istituto d'Arte, Florence.
Biography Schettini established the studio Salotto Dinamico; has been active in the design of ceramics, alabaster works, furnishings.
Exhibitions/citations Work shown in numerous exhibitions. Competition awards include 1982 *Furniture and Its Space,* and 1985 *Mainichi International ID Competition*.
Bibliography Fumio Shimizu and Studio Matteo Thun (eds.), *The Italian Design: Descendants of Leonardo da Vinci*, Tokyo: Graphic-sha, 1987.

Scheuer, Winfried (1952–)
German designer; born Calw.

Training 1976, trainee, styling department, Mercedes-Benz; to 1977, industrial design, Staatliche Akademie der bildenden Künste, Stuttgart; 1981, master's degree, Royal College of Art, London.
Biography 1983–86, Scheuer was a staff member at ID Two in San Francisco; from 1986, has been a freelance industrial designer to clients, including Authentics, Klein & More, Teunen & Teunen, and Aero; 1992–99, taught, Royal College of Art, and was a visiting lecturer, Hochschule der Kunst, Berlin, and Glasgow School of Art and Design; from 1999, professor of industrial design, Staatliche Akademie der bildenden Künste, Stuttgart; 1986–99, was an author/journalist to the journal *form* and correspondent to others.
Exhibitions 1988 Documenta Kassel; 1996 *Design of the Times: One Hundred Years of the Royal College of Art*, London; 1999–2000 *Bewusst Einfach* touring exhibition, sponsored by Institut für Auslandsbeziehungen, Stuttgart.

Schindler, Rudolph Michael (1887–1953)
Austrian architect; born Vienna; active Vienna and Los Angeles.

Training 1906–11, Technische Hochschule, Vienna; 1909–13 under Otto Wagner, Akademie der bildenden Künste, Vienna.
Biography At the academy in Vienna, Schindler was greatly influenced by Wagner's Rationalism; soon after (1914) settled in the US, where he worked for architecture firm Ottenheimer, Stern and Reichert and 1916–20, for Frank Lloyd Wright, both Chicago; 1920–21, was sent by Wright to oversee the construction of Wright's Aline Barnsdall houses in Los Angeles, where he was in private practice from 1921; 1925–26, collaborated informally with Richard Neutra, whom he had met in Vienna as a student; designed/built the 1921 furniture for his own house on North Kings Road, Hollywood, and 1925–26 Lovell Beach House, Newport Beach, Cal., and other furniture. 1930s, he designed 'unit' ('type' or standardized) furniture. The reinforced-concrete and wood architecture of his Beach House, with its spatial treatment, vertical and horizontal play, and structural articulation, showed the influences of De Stijl and, in its furniture, of Frank Lloyd Wright. Schindler realized the production of 330 of his buildings and projects over four-decade period. He died in Los Angeles.
Exhibitions Work subject of 1967 *Architecture of R.M. Schindler, 1887–1953*, Art Galleries of the University of California; 1984 exhibition, Sala de Exposiciones del MOPU, Madrid; 1985 exhibition, Museum Villa Stuck, Munich; 2001 *The Architecture of R.M. Schindler*, National Building Museum, Washington, D.C. Furniture subject of exhibitions at University of California, Santa Barbara, 1977, and University of California, Berkley, 1996. Work included in 1982 *Space and Environment: Furniture of American Architects*, Whitney Museum of American Art, Fairfield County, Conn., US.
Bibliography Esther McCoy, *Five California Architects*, New York: Reinhold, 1960. Cat., David Gebhard, *Architecture of R.M. Schindler, 1887–1953*, Santa Barbara, Cal.: University of California, 1967. David Gebhard, *Schindler*, New York: Viking, 1972. Esther McCoy, *Vienna to Los Angeles: Two Journeys*, Santa Monica, Cal.: Arts + Architecture, 1979. Cat., Lisa Phillips (intro.), *Space and Environment: Furniture Designed by American Architects*, New York: Whitney Museum of American Art, 1982: 54–55. Marla C. Berns (ed.), *The Furniture of R.M. Schindler*, Santa Barbara: University Art Museum, University of California; Seattle: University of Washington, 1997. James Steele, Peter Gössel (ed.), *Rudolf Michael Schindler*, Cologne/New York: Taschen, 1999.

Norbert Schlagheck. Agfa Family super 8 mm movie camera. 1980. Plastic, 6 1/4 x 6 1/2 x 2 1/2" (15.9 x 16.5 x 6.4 cm). Mfr.: Agfa-Gevaert, Germany. Friends of the Department Fund. MoMA.

Schlagheck, Norbert (1925–)
German industrial designer.

Training Folkwangschule, Essen.
Biography Schlagheck was the director of the household-appliances studio at Siemens; cofounded the design academy Kölner Werkschuler, Cologne; 1967 with Herbert H. Schultes, established Schlagheck Schultes Design, Munich; 1972, cofounded the ID program at Fachhochschule, Munich, where, from 1972, he has been a professor. 1991, he established Schlagheck Design, a large studio and essentially a family business with offices in Munich and New York. Schlagheck Design clients include Adidas, AGFA, Bayer, BMW, Braun, Coca-Cola, Krupp, Melita, Osram, Philips, Siemens.
Bibliography www.schlagheckdesignllc.com
> see Schultes, Herbert H.

Schlegel, Fritz (1896–1965)
Danish architect and furniture designer.

Training 1916–23, Det Kongelige Kunstakademi, Copenhagen.
Biography 1916–34, Schlegel worked with architect Edvard Thomsen; 1934, established his own architecture office; designed furniture by Fritz Hansen.
Exhibitions/citations Work shown in Stockholm in 1918; Charlottenborg in 1919, 1924, 1927, 1930, 1932, 1933, 1939; and subject of retrospective, Charlottenborg in 1941; The Hague in 1948; Paris in 1949; London and Edinburgh in 1950. Received 1924, 1927 gold medals, Danish Academy; 1926 Zacharia Jocobsen award; 1941 Eckersberg Medal.
Bibliography Frederik Sieck, *Nutidig Dansk Møbeldesign – en kortfattet illustreret beskrivelse*, Copenhagen: Bondo Gravesen, 1990.

Schlesser, Thomas (1959–)
American furniture and interior designer.

Biography Influenced by Isamu Noguchi, Schlesser designed early-1990s furniture in retro-1950s silhouettes, produced by Niedermaier, where he has been director of design. On interior architecture,

he has worked with Rebecca van de Sande of Leeser Architecture, and with Demian Repucci; has been an associate principal at Kohn Pedersen Fox Associates; all New York.
Citations 2002 Outstanding Restaurant Design (since 1999), James Beard Foundation Restaurant/Graphics Award (for Glass, with van de Sande, in New York; and for Blackbird with Repucci, Chicago).

Schloss, Andrew (1962–)

Canadian designer; born Vancouver; active New York.

Training 1987, master's degree in biomechanics, University of Oregon, Eugene, Ore., US; 1992, master's degree in industrial design, Pratt Institute, New York.
Biography 1992, Schloss established his own studio, ABS Design, New York; has designed furniture, lighting, toys, graphics, consumer products, and over 300 retail shops; teaches industrial design, Pratt Institute; lectures on retail design and identity.

Schlumbohm, Peter (1896–1962)

German chemist and inventor; born Kiel; active New York.

Training 1926, doctoral degree in physical chemistry, Universität Berlin.
Biography His early work was in refrigeration, an activity that took him to the US in 1931, and, after several other trips, he settled there in 1936 to benefit from its inventor-friendly patent laws; founded Chemex and became best known for 1941 Chemex hourglass-shaped paper-filter-type coffeemaker (still in production today), originally made in Pyrex by Corning Glass in an Erlenmeyer-flask shape with a two-part, leather-thong-held wooden grip, and requiring wartime governmental approval for the use of Pyrex. Schlumbohm designed and manufactured other domestic products, including 1949 quick water boiler, 1951 air-filtering fan, and a frying pan that required no washing; executed other functionally oriented products, many of which he engineered, manufactured, and enthusiastically promoted, and sought simple and non-mechanical methods. He held over 3,000 patents for utilitarian glassware such as goblets, cork-insullated bottle/jug coolers, and other types of water kettles. Today the Chemex Corp. is a division of International Housewares Corporation, Pittsfield, Mass. 1998, industrial designer Mark Harrison (1936–1998) collected Schlumbohm's papers, photographs, and artifacts, which were subsequently acquired by the Hagley Museum and Library, Wilmington, Del.
Exhibitions Chemex coffee maker included in 1942 *Useful Products in Wartime*, The Museum of Modern Art, New York; 1989 *Design, USA*, touring; 2000 *Chemex Exhibition*, Hagley Museum and Library; 2002–03 *Vital Forms: American Art and Design in the Atomic Age, 1940–1960*, San Diego (Cal.) Museum of Art.
Bibliography 'Two Inventors,' *Industrial Design*, vol. 7, Nov. 1960: 72–75. Ralph Caplan, 'Chemex and Creation,' *Industrial Design*, vol. 9, Dec. 1962: 121–22. Victor Papanek, *Design for the Real World*, New York: Pantheon, 1972: 105–06; London: Thames & Hudson, 1985. Cat., Kathryn B. Hiesinger and George H. Marcus III (eds.), *Design Since 1945*, Philadelphia: Philadelphia Museum of Art, 1983. Mel Byars with Arlette Barré-Despond, *100 Designs/100 Years: A Celebration of the 20th Century*, Hove: RotoVision, 1999: 94–95. Hagley Museum and Library newsletter, vol. 29, no. 4, winter 2000: 2. Paola Antonelli (ed.), *Objects of Design: The Museum of Modern Art*, New York: The Museum of Modern Art, 2003: 222–23.

Peter Schlumbohm. Chemex coffee maker. 1941. Pyrex glass, wood, and leather, h. 9 1/2 x dia. 6 1/8" (24.2 x 15.5 cm). Mfr.: Chemex, US. Gift of Lewis & Conger. MoMA.

Schmid, Carlo (1894–1988)
> See Caran d'Ache.

Schmidt, Anita (1934–)

German furniture designer; born Bretten.

Training 1953–56, philosophy, Sorbonne, Paris; at the firm C. Straub in Knittlingen and in joineries and weaving mills, including Rohi, Geretsried, and Taunusdruck.
Biography 1965 with others, she established Waldmann-Gölz-Schmidt with an exclusive arrangement with C. Straub in Germany and set up offices in Asco, Finland, and Durlet, Belgium; from 1973, was an independent designer with clients, including WK-ZE Möbel, Kill, Kaufeld, Cor, Rausch, Thörmer, Walter Knoll, Rolf Benz, Draenert, Designo, Maison, Intercane, Durlet, and Artanova. She designed furnishings for prefabrications by Hebel and fabrics and carpet. Her 1984 Cushion sofa was produced by Pro Seda.
Bibliography Cat., Design Center Stuttgart, *Women in Design: Careers and Life Histories Since 1900*, Stuttgart: Haus der Wirtschaft, 1989: 164–65.

Schmidt, Joost (1893–1948)

German woodcarver, sculptor, typographer, and teacher; born Wunstorf/Hanover; husband of Helene Schmidt-Nonné.

Training 1910–14, in Weimar; from 1919, sculpture and typography, Bauhaus, Weimar.
Biography Schmidt participated in 1920–21 Sommerfeld house (architects, Walter Gropius and Adolf Meyer) in Berlin-Dahlem, with its distinctive interiors, one of the most important early Bauhaus projects. Schmidt's design of the highly geometric carved-teak door for the Sommerfeld vestibule presaged the office walls of Edgar Kaufmann Sr. office in Pittsburgh by Frank Lloyd Wright. He taught, Bauhaus, Dessau, where he was an instructor in typography to 1932; 1928–32, was active in graphic design for advertising; after World War II, was a professor in Berlin. He died in Nuremberg.
Bibliography Heinz Loew and Helene Nonne-Schmidt, *Joost Schmidt, Lehre und Arbeit am Bauhaus 1919–1932,* Düsseldorf: Marzona, 1984. Lionel Richard, *Encyclopédie du Bauhaus*, Paris: Somogy, 1985: 166. Jonathan M. Woodham, *Twentieth-Century Ornament*, New York: Rizzoli, 1990: 114.

Schmidt, Karl (1873–1948)
> See Deutsche Werkstätten für Handwerkskunst.

Schmidt, Werner (1953–)

Swiss designer.

Biography Schmidt designed the inexpensive 1987 Alu-Falttisch aluminum demountable table which (with little, or no, credit to Schmidt) has become popular for camping use (packing down to 27 x 6" (70 x 15 cm).
Exhibition 2000–03 *Aluminum by Design* touring exhibition, organized by Carnegie Art Museum, Pittsburgh.

Schmidt-Nonné, Helene (b. Helene Nonné 1891–1976)

German textile designer, teacher and journalist; born Magdeburg; wife of Joost Schmidt.

Training In Magdeburg and Berlin; 1924–30, Bauhaus weaving workshop, Weimar and Dessau.
Biography She became a professor of drawing; 1919–24, was a secondary-school teacher; after visiting Bauhaus Week, Weimar, in

Ferdinand Hubert Schmitz. Two-arm candelabrum. c. 1900. Cast bronze with traces of gilding, h. 12 3/4 x w. 10 3/8" (32.4 x 26.4 cm). Mfr.: Orivit-Metallwarenfabrik, Germany. Phyllis B. Lambert Fund. MoMA.

Aug. 1923, decided to study there and worked in the textile workshop; 1925, married Joost Schmidt; 1933, moved to Berlin, where she was denounced by the Nazis, worked secretly, and had her studio destroyed by bombs; 1943–48 was active with her husband toward the revival of the Bauhaus ideal; 1948, became a journalist; 1953–54 on Max Bill's invitation, taught color theory, Hochschule für Gestaltung, Ulm; 1961, settled in Darmstadt; wrote a book on her husband *Joost Schmidt, Lehre und Arbeit am Bauhaus 1919 – 1932* (with Heinz Löw, Düsseldorf: Marzona, 1984).
Bibliography Heinz Loew and Helene Nonné-Schmidt, *Joost Schmidt*, Dusseldorf: Marzona, 1984. Lionel Richard, *Encyclopédie du Bauhaus*, Paris: Somogy, 1985: 208. Cat., Gunta Stölzl, *Weberei am Bauhaus und ams eigener Werkstatt*, Berlin: Bauhaus-Archiv, 1987: 165. Sigrid Wortmann Weltge, *Women's Work: Textile Art from the Bauhaus*, London: Thames & Hudson, 1993.

Schmitt, Eric (1955–)
French furniture designer; active Villiers-sous-Grez.

Training In contemporary music.
Biography Schmitt created a 1986 musical sculpture for Fondation Charles Jourdan, 1989 chair and small table by XO, for Hôtel Montalembert: 1991 ornamental objects for interior designer Christian Liaigre, 1993 *pâte-de-verre* and crystal collection and 1999 Limoge porcelain objects by Daum, 1997 two grilles for the public garden of the City of Paris, 1998 furniture for the French Embassy in Beirut, 1999 five bronze furniture pieces for Christian Liaigre.
Exhibitions First one-person venue: 13 furniture and lighting prototypes subject of 1987 exhibition, Galerie VIA, Paris; other work in VIA-sponsored exhibition (with En Attendant les Barbares, which produced his lighting fixtures Nostradamus and Louve and wrought-iron furniture range) at Habiter 87 salon. Included in 1988 *Les Cent Chaise* and 1997 *Design Français 1986–1996*, Centre Culturel, Boulogne-Billancourt; 1991 *Les Capitale Européennes*, Centre Georges Pompidou, Paris. One-person exhibitions: 1991, 1992, 1993, 1996, Néotù, Paris, and 1996, Galerie Klaus Peter Göbel, Stuttgart.
Bibliography Cat., *Les années VIA 1980–1990*, Paris: Musée des Arts Décoratifs, 1990.

Schmitt, Paul (1923–)
French design entrepreneur; born Bône (Algeria); active Paris.

Training In law and literature.
Biography 1948–88, Schmitt was the president of Le Creuset, manufacturers of enameled cast-iron cookware; commissioned Raymond Loewy to design 1958 pots, the first and only kitchen items by Loewy, and Enzo Mari to design 1973 La Mamma stew pot. 1978, Schmitt established an industrial division of Le Creuset in South Carolina, US; 1988, set up design centers in ten French provinces; was appointed design consultant to the EEC; 1988 and 1990, was a French jury member of European Design Prize.

Schmitz, Ferdinand Hubert (1863–1939)
German metalworker; active Cologne-Braunsfeld.

Biography 1894, Schmitz founded the Rheinische Broncegießerei, known as Orivit from 1900. From 1896, the factory produced objects in the proprietary pewter-like alloy Orivit and made dishes and mounts in the metal for pottery bowls as well as candelabra and silvered bronze-mounted table lamps; produced silver with the Huberpresse, a new technique of mass manufacturing stamped hollow-ware and cutlery with simple ornamentation by a hydraulic press. Its designs were of a high standard. 1905, Württembergische Metallwarenfabrik (WMF) took over the firm.
Bibliography *Deutsche Kunst und Dekoration* journal, 1900–01: 17. Cat., *Jugendstil*, Darmstadt: Hessisches Landesmuseum, 1965: 247. Cat., *Europa 1900*, Ostend Musée des Arts, Brussels: Connaissance, 1967. *Objekte des Jugendstils*, Bern: Benteli, 1975. Alastair Duncan, *Art Nouveau and Art Déco Lighting*, New York: Simon & Schuster, 1978: 126. Cat., *Metallkunst*, Berlin: Bröhan-Museum, 1990: 382–87.

Schmoll von Eisenwerth, Fritz (1883–1963)
Austrian sculptor and silversmith; born Vienna; active Munich.

Training In Karlsruhe; and Lehr- und Versuchs-Ateliers für angewandte und freie Kunst (aka Debschitz-Schule), Munich.
Biography 1909–10, he worked with architect Paul Bonatz in Stuttgart; taught, Debschitz-Schule, where he was the director from 1914–20. His silver designs produced by M.T. Wetzlar in Munich were simple and suitable for serial production. Also for serial production was his elaborate silver service by Bruckmann & Söhne in Heilbronn. He also carved plaster plates and corrected the steel dies at the factory. Other design work included furniture and ceramics. From 1919, he pursued sculpture.
Bibliography Annelies Krekel-Aalberse, *Art Nouveau and Art Déco Silver*, New York: Abrams, 1989. Cat., *Münchner Schmuck 1900–1940*, Munich: Bayerisches Nationalmuseum, 1990: 37–38.

Schmuz-Baudiss, Theodor Hermann (1859–1942)
German ceramicist; active Munich.

Training 1879–82, Kunstgewerbeschule, Munich; 1882–90, Akademie der bildenden Künste, Munich.
Biography Schmuz-Baudiss designed in the rustic manner of local Dießen pottery; from 1897, decorated ceramics in a freer manner; supplied brown-glazed stoneware to Jakob Scharvogel, with whom he conducted experiments; 1898, became a member of Vereinigte Werkstätten für Kunst im Handwerk, Munich, and pursued an extended study of porcelain production at Swaine in Hüttensteinach, Thuringia; from 1902, worked for Königliche Porzellan-Manufaktur (KPM), Berlin, where he was the director of manufactory from 1908–26 and established an underglaze department. He came to be regarded as the best ornamental designer of ceramics in Germany of the time.
Exhibition Vases shown at 1897 *Glaspalast* exhibition, Munich; Pensée dinner service by Swaine at 1900 *Exposition Universelle*, Paris.
Bibliography Cat., Kathryn Bloom Hiesinger, *Die Meister des Münchner Jugendstils*, Munich: Stadtmuseum, 1988: 154–55.

Schneck, Adolf G. (1883–1971)
German architect and designer; born Esslingen.

Training 1907–17 under Bernhard Pankok, Kunstgewerbeschule, Stuttgart; under Paul Bonatz, architecture, Königliche Technische Hochschule, Stuttgart.
Biography 1919–21, Schneck worked as an independent architect and furniture designer; designed a range of relatively inexpensive mass-

produced furniture made by various firms, including Deutsche Werkstätten, and, from 1920s, by Thonet; 1923–25 and 1933–49, taught, Kunstgewerbeschule, Stuttgart; supported the 1957 founding in Istanbul of the Uygulamalý Endüstri Sanatlarý Yüksek Okulu'ndan (UESYO, school of applied and industrial arts), today part of the Devlet Güzel Sanatlar Akademisi (DGSA, state academy of fine arts). He wrote numerous articles and a number of books. Schneck died in Stuttgart.
Exhibitions Work shown at 1924 *Die Form*, Deutscher Werkbund. Contributed to 1925 *Esposizione Biennale delle Arti Decorative et Industriale Moderne*, Monza. Designed two houses at 1927 *Weissenhofsiedlung* exhibition, Stuttgart; former and new models of bentwood chairs by Thonet in 1928 *Der Stuhl* exhibition, which he curated at the Deutscher Werkbund, Stuttgart.
Bibliography By Schneck: *Das Möbel als Gebrauchsgegenstand*, Stuttgart: Julius Hoffmann, 1929; Cat., *Der Stuhl...*, Stuttgart: Julius Hoffmann, 1928; *Das Polstermöbel...*, Stuttgart: Julius Hoffmann, 1933; *Neue Möbel vom Jugendstil bis heute*, Munich: Bruckmann, 1962. Barbie Campbell-Cole and Tim Benton (eds.), *Tubular Steel Furniture*, London: The Art Book Company, 1979: 12. *Adolf G. Schneck, 1883–1971, Leben, Lehre, Möbel, Architektur*, Stuttgart: Staatliche Akademie der bildenden Künste, 1983.

Schneider, Andreas (1867–1931)

Norwegian painter, ceramicist and furniture and textile designer.

Training 1894, ceramics in Copenhagen.
Biography 1895, Schneider set up his own workshop for ceramics; became a leading figure in the development of studio pottery in Norway; 1910, was a designer for Egersund ceramics factory; designed textiles and furniture by others.
Bibliography Cat., David Revere McFadden (ed.), *Scandinavian Modern Design 1880–1980*, New York: Abrams, 1982.

Schneider, Cristallerie

French glassware factory; located Epinay-sur-Seine, later Lorris.

History 1913, brothers Charles (1881–1953) and Ernest (1877–1933) Schneider founded the Cristallerie Schneider in the Château de la Verrerie (built 1785), the residence of the Schneider family. Charles, born in Château-Thierry, studied at the École des Beaux-Arts in Nancy under Émile Gallé and, concurrently, worked at the Gallé factory in Nancy; 1902–08, designed for Daum. At Cristallerie Schneider, Ernest was the administrator, while Charles oversaw production of art glass and was the artistic director to 1944. Charles's work was floral with bursts of color and both refined and coarse. The richness of his colors established his high reputation. The factory made mostly art glass until production declined in 1925 and was eventually discontinued. For a time, Robert Schneider (1948–), the son of founder Charles, became the director. 1962, the firm moved to Lorris, near Orléans; 1981, was closed.
Exhibitions/citations Ensemble of glassware and three 1,075-square foot (100m²) stained-glass windows for the towers surrounding the Esplanade des Invalides at 1925 *Exposition Internationale des Arts Décoratifs et Industriels Modernes*, Paris. 1926, Charles was elected Chevalier of the Légion d'Honneur.
Bibliography Yvonne Brunhammer et al., *Art Nouveau Belgium, France*, Houston: Rice University, 1976. Alastair Duncan, *Art Nouveau and Art Déco Lighting*, New York: Simon & Schuster, 1978. Cat., *Verriers français contemporains: art et industrie*, Paris: Musée des Arts Décoratifs, 1982. Pierre Cabanne, *Encyclopédie art déco*, Paris: Somogy, 1986. Victor Arwas, *Glass: Art Nouveau to Art Deco*, London: Academy, 1987.

Schoen, Eugene (1880–1957)

American architect and designer; born and active New York.

Training To 1902, architecture, Columbia University, New York.
Biography 1902 on a six-month stipend, Schoen traveled in Europe and met Josef Hoffman and Otto Wagner in Vienna and studied their work; 1905, established his own architecture practice in New York and received acclaim for his 1910 Plaza Music Hall, Manhattan (decorated by his friend Alfons Mucha). After visiting 1925 *Exposition Internationale des Arts Décoratifs et Industriels Modernes*, Paris, he began offering interior-design services from an office at 115 East 60th Street, Manhattan, where he was able to display his settings, while others were forced to show their work in department stores. He remained there until the 1929 arrival of the Great Depression forced removal to 43 West 39th Street. His furniture showed the European influences of French and German modernism, sometimes unashamedly copying Jacques-Émile Ruhlmann's features, like saber-shaped legs. Schoen also called on neoclassical forms with exotic wood veneers in an odd amalgamation of various contemporary European styles. In his own gallery, he sold his own and imported textiles and furniture and Maurice Heaton's glassware; for several interior schemes, commissioned Heaton to execute large glass murals. Heaton's *The Flight of Amelia Earhart Across the Atlantic* (large glass panels) and a photo-mural by Edward Steichen in the men's lounge were part of Schoen's interiors (with all the furnishings) of RKO theater (or Center Theater, opening in 1933) in Rockefeller Center, New York. Schoen was also an interior designer of the Center; became a consultant in the design of the New York State pavilion at 1933–34 *A Century of Progress International Exhibition*, Chicago; designed the interiors of numerous apartments, banks, theaters, department stores in Manhattan and elsewhere, including Dunhill's store interior at Rockefeller Center, an earlier store for Dunhill's, and nightclub of 1930 oceanliner *Leviathan*. Some of his furniture, such as the Chinese-influenced pieces for lawyer Henry Root Stern's apartment, Manhattan, was made by Schmieg, Hungate & Kotzian of New York (possibly the city's most prestigious cabinet makers). From 1929, his son Lee was a member of the practice. Isamu Noguchi's first (1929) one-person exhibition was at Schoen's gallery, and, at other times, the work of Maurice Heaton and Ilonka Karaz. From 1930 or 1931, Schoen was professor of interior architecture, New York University. From mid-1940s, he abandoned furniture design; died in New York.
Exhibitions/citations Work included in 1928 *Exposition of Art in Industry at Macy's* (room setting), Macy's department store, New York; 1929 (11th) *The Architect and the Industrial Arts: An Exhibition of Contemporary American Design* (child's nursery and bedroom), The Metropolitan Museum of Art, New York, and in the Central Gallery (a Schoen dining room) of the same museum's 1935 *Contemporary American Industrial Art, 1934*. He designed an exhibition at New York State Building pavilion, 1933–34 *A Century of Progress International Exhibition*, Chicago. Gold medal for crafts (a building entrance), Architectural League of New York.
Bibliography Marya Mannes, 'Gallery Notes,' *Creative Art*, Feb. 1928: 8. Nellie C. Sanford, 'An Architect-Designer of Modern Furniture,' *Good Furniture*, no. 30, Mar. 1928: 116–18. Eugene Schoen, 'The Design of Modern Interiors,' *Creative Art 2*, no. 5, May 1928: 60-63. Eugene Schoen, 'House & Garden's Modern House,' *House & Garden*, Feb. 1929: 94. Obituary, 'Eugene Schoen, Archiect, Is Dead at 77', *The New York Times*, 17 Aug. 1957: 15. Harry V. Anderson, 'Contemporary American Designers,' *Decorators' Digest*, June 1935: 41–45. Karen Davies, *At Home in Manhattan: Modern Decorative Arts, 1925 to the Depression*, New Haven: Yale, 1983: 25. Robert A.M. Stern et al., *New York 1930*, New York: Rizzoli, 1987. R. Craig Miller, *Modern Design 1890–1990*, New York: Abrams, 1990.

Schofield, Jean (1940–)

British interior and furniture designer.

Training Royal College of Art, London.
Biography 1966 with John Wright and Jill Walker, she opened a design office in London and created domestic and office furniture, lighting, and accessories; designed 1964 knock-down Chair C1 (with Wright) produced by Anderson Manson Decorations of London.
Exhibitions Chair C1 shown at 1966 *Vijftig Jaar Zitten*, Stedelijk Museum, Amsterdam; 1970 *Modern Chairs 1918–1970*, Whitechapel Gallery, London (catalog below).
Bibliography M. Gilliat, *English Style*, London: S. Bodley Head, 1967. Cat., *Modern Chairs 1918–1970*, London: Lund Humphries, 1971.

Schott & Genossen Glaswerke (aka Jenaer Glaswerk Schott & Genossen)

German glassware manufacturer; located Mainz after 1952.

History 1884, Otto Schott (1852–1935), Ernst Abbe, Carl Zeiss, and Roderich Zeiss founded the Glastechnische Laboratorium Schott & Genossen in Jena. 1884, Otto Schott developed optical glass with completely new optical properties and based glass production on scientific principles for the first time; 1887–93, invented chemically resistant borosilicate glass to withstand high temperatures. 1919, Otto Schott transfered his shareholdings to Carl-Zeiss-Stiftung and, from 1920, firm was known as Jenaer Glaswerk Schott & Genossen From 1930, the firm became known as much for its innovations and quality as for its high design, due to Wilhelm Wagenfeld, formerly of the Bauhaus. 1930–34, Wagenfeld created some of its best-known wares, much still in production today, mass-produced in heat-resistant glass,

including 1932 tea infuser, cups, and saucers; 1934 coffee percolator; and 1935 kitchenware. Early 1930s, Wagenfeld also designed a range of heat-resistant ovenware. Heinz Löffelhardt, a student of Wagenfeld's at the Vereinigte Lausitzer Glaswerke in Zwiesel in 1930s, became Schott's chief designer; was responsible for a number of suites of glasses for domestic and utility use, considered innovative in 1950s–60s. Löffelhardt was a consultant designer in utility glass and lighting divisions, when the firm moved to Mainz in 1952 and was named Schott Glas; designed its widely published 1959 range of heat-resistant borosilicate glass, including a tea set, cups and saucers, plates, and bowls. 1948 due to Soviet occupation, the enterprise was expropriated and nationalized; 1952, was moved and rebuilt in Mainz as the Schott Group. Through a number of agreements, 'VEB Jenaer Glaswerk Schott & Gen.,' Eastern Europe's leading special glass manufacturer, was incorporated into VEB Carl Zeiss Jena in 1977, and the companies in Jena and Mainz became VEB Jenaer Glaswerk (in Jena) and Schott Glaswerke (in Mainz). 1995, Schott Glaswerke became the sole owner of Jenaer Glaswerk GmbH, and, 1998, Jenaer Glaswerk GmbH was renamed Scott Jenaer Glas GmbH. However, today Schott Jenaer Glas is only a brand accompanying almost 50 others, including those for opthalmics, coatings, microlithography, photovoltaics, lighting components, fiber optics, and others. 2000, the Schott Glasmuseum was founded in Jena.
Bibliography Herbert Kühnert (ed.), *Der Briefwechsel zwischen Otto Schott und Ernst Abbe über das optische Glas 1879–1881*, Jena: Fischer, 1946. Herbert Kühnert (ed.), *Briefe und Dokumente zur Geschichte des VEB Optik Jenaer Glaswerk Schott & Genossen*, Jena: Fischer, 1953–57. Torsten Bröhan, *Glaskunst der Moderne: von Josef Hoffmann bis Wilhelm Wagenfeld*, Munich: Klinkhardt & Biermann, 1992. Walter Scheiffele et al., *Wilhelm Wagenfeld und die moderne Glasindustrie: Eine Geschichte der deutschen Glasgestaltung von Bruno Mauder, Richard Süssmuth, Heinrich Fuchs und Wilhelm Wagenfeld bis Heinrich Löffelhardt*, Stuttgart: Hatje Cantz, 1994.
> See Wagenfeld, Wilhelm.

Schreckengost, Viktor (1906–)
American ceramicist, industrial design, teacher; born Segring, Ohio.

Training 1924–29, Cleveland Institute of Art; 1929–30, ceramics and sculpture under Michael Powolny, Kunstgewerbeschule, Vienna.
Biography Schreckengost's 1930s work featured images of popular culture, including of cocktail glasses, dancers, skyscrapers, and words such as 'follies,' 'café,' and 'jazz.' 1930, he began working for Cowan Pottery Studio in Rocky River, Ohio, where he created 1931 Jazz Bowl punch set, with a jazz-theme motif, commissioned by US president's wife Eleanor Roosevelt and, subsequently, commercially produced in a small edition; 1931 when Cowan closed, continued his ceramic sculpture, while also designing mass-production ceramic tableware for firms, including American Limoges Ceramics. 1933, he was a co-organizer of American Limoges Ceramics Co. in Sebring, Ohio; also in Ohio, designed for Segring Pottery, Leigh Potters, Homer Laughlin, and Salem China. Became active as a renowned teacher, still as a nonagenarian at Cleveland School of Art, and a versatile industrial designer of a number of products including 1932–72 bicycles by Murray Company (including 1938 Champion child's pedal car) and for Sears, Roebuck & Co., including its 1965 Spaceliner bicycle. Others are 1941 Pursuit Plane child's pedal airplane, 1955 Mammoths and Mastodons bas-relief at Cleveland Zoo, and patented Salem Free Form Primitive three-leg teacup, and other models. His 1941 Beverly Hills metal lawn chair by Murray has become a standard on porches or in gardens in the US.
Exhibitions Ceramics shown at 1947 (11th) touring *Ceramic National Exhibition*, organized by Syracuse Museum of Fine Art, Syracuse, N.Y.; The Metropolitan Museum Art, New York; 1939–40 *New York World's Fair: The World of Tomorrow* (Sears bicycle). Work subject of 1976 *Victor Schreckengost: Retrospective Exhibition* and 2000–01 *Victor Schreckengost and 20th-Century Design*, both Cleveland Museum of Art (catalog below).
Bibliography Cat., Laurence Schmeckebier, *Viktor Schreckengost: Retrospective Exhibition*, Cleveland: Cleveland Institute of Art, 1976. Karen Davies, *At Home in Manhattan: Modern Decorative Arts, 1925 to the Depression*, New Haven: Yale, 1983: 81. R. Craig Miller, *Modern Design, 1890–1990*, New York: Abrams, 1990. Henry Adams, *Viktor Schreckengost and 20th-Century Design*, Cleveland: Cleveland Museum of Art, 2000. Paul Makovsky, 'Pedal to the Medal,' *Metropolis*, Jan. 2001. Video, Success by Design: Victor Schreckengost, produced by CMA, with WVIZ/PBS (TV station, Cleveland, Ohio, US), 2000.

Schreiber, Gaby (1912–)
Austrian designer; active London.

Training In art and stage and interior design in Florence, Berlin, and Paris.
Biography She was an interior designer when she arrived in London in 1930s; designed a range of modern 1940s domestic tableware by Runcolite Plastics, including a late-1940s plastic meat tray, which was widely published; 1957–63, was interior-design consultant to William Clark in Northern Ireland and a number of others, including National Westminster Bank, Westminster Foreign Bank, Gulf Oil Eastern Hemisphere, Lythe Hill Hotel in Surrey, GHP Group, Anglo-Continental Investment and Finance, Continental Bankers Agents, Myers, Peter Robinson, David Morgan, West Cumberland Hospital, Newcastle Regional Hospital Board, and Fine Fare Supermarket chain. 1965–68, she was general consultant and designer to Cunard for 1969 ocean-liner *Queen Elizabeth II* and others, and to Zarach, the Marquess of Londonderry, Crown Agents, Allen and Hanbury, and BOAC airline (today British Air); was a design consultant on plastics to Marks and Spencer and yachts for Sir Gerard d'Erlanger, Whitney Straight, and others; designed interiors for department stores, office blocks, hospitals, factories, cinemas, cabin cruisers, restaurants, and conference halls as well as domestic interiors and conversions.
Exhibitions Designed exhibition pavilions in Europe and the US. Sat on numerous national and international design juries and committees.
Bibliography Michael Farr, *Design in British Industry: A Mid-Century Survey*, London: Cambridge, 1955: 128ff. Penny Sparke, *Introduction to Design and Culture in the Twentieth Century*, Allen & Unwin, 1986. Liz McQuiston, *Women in Design: A Contemporary View*, New York: Rizzoli, 1988: 110. Ulrike Walton-Jordan, *Creativity in Exile: Gaby Schreiber and Bauhaus Principles in Britain*, Research Paper No. 5, Brighton: Centre for German-Jewish Studies, 2001.

Schreyer, Peter (1953–)
German automobile designer; born Bad Reichenhall.

Training 1975–79, industrial design, Fachhochschule, Munich; 1979–80, Royal College of Art, London
Biography 1991–92, Schreyer worked with 'J.' Mays at Volkswagen in California; 1992–93, was at Audi and then Volkswagen in Germany; 1994, became design director of Audi, where he established a strong brand identity for the marque; married a futuristic look with the retrograde aerodynamics of the Auto Union's 1930s sports cars. (Audi is an amalgamation of the four manufacturers of the former Auto Union corporation.) Schreyer's highly successful 1999 Audi TT was inspired by a doodle sketched by Freeman Thomas, who had been hired by 'J.' Mays in 1991 at Volkswagen, while Schreyer was there. Other Schreyer body designs, which appreciably helped to diminish Audi's staid image, include 1996 A3, 1999 A4 (new model), 2000 A2, and 2001 Rosemeyer. 2002, Schreyer became the design director of Volkswagen.
Citations 1994 IBCM British Steel Award; 1994, 1998, 2000, 2001 Industrie Forum Design (iF), Hanover; 1995, 1996, 1997, 1999 prizes, Design Zentrum Nordrhein; 1997 and 2000 Good Design Award, Chicago Athenaeum; 1998 and 1999 Autocar Award, US; 1994, 1996, 1997, 1998 Bundespreis Produktdesign (for furthering the German auto industry); 2003 Rat für Formgebung (German design council), Frankfurt.
Bibliography Penny Sparke, A *Century of Car Design*, London: Mitchell Beazley, 2002. Gunter Henn, *Audi Forum Ingolstadt: Tradition und Vision*, Munich: Prestel.

Schriefers, Werner (1926–)
German teacher and painter; born Viersen.

Training As a singer; subsequently, under Georg Muche, Staatliche Ingenieurschule für Textilwesen, Krefeld.
Bibliography Schriefers was a member of '1945' artists' group in Krefeld, of Deutscher Werkbund NRW (German work federation in Nordrhein-Westfalen), of Westdeutscher Künstlerbund (West German artist federation), and of 'Z' group in Wuppertal; 1990–91, chairperson, Deutscher Werkbund NRW. He became an ardent collector of post-World War I home appliances and wares, and office equipment, such as hair dryers, heat lamps, adding machines, food mixers; was influential director, Werkkunstschule, Cologne; felt that art and technology should be combined and applied to everyday life; donated his personal collection of historic products to Bergischer Universität,

Wuppertal, and Kunsthochschule, Berlin-Weißensee.
Exhibitions Subject of 1999 exhibition, Stadtmuseum, Siegburg; 2000–01 exhibition, Kunst-Museum, Ahlen; both Germany.
Bibliography Gerda Breuer and Kerstin Plüm (eds.), *Stiftung Design-Sammlung Schriefers*, Cologne: Wienand, 1997.

Schreiner, Johan (1965–)
> See K8 Industriedesign.

Schröder-Schräder, Truus (b. Truus Schräder 1889–1985)
Dutch architect; born Deventer.

Training In pharmacy.
Biography She met architect Gerrit Rietveld when he delivered some classical-design furniture copies to her home in Amsterdam, where Bruno Taut, Kurt Schwitters, and others were frequent guests. The Rietveld encounter began a life-long association with him, though she has been given little credit for their mutual architectural and design accomplishments. The canonical 1924 Schröder house in Utrecht along with its innovative furnishings was the first of a number of collaborations. Dutch painter Theo Van Doesburg declared the house to be an embodiment of the De Stijl ideal of 'the end of art.' Schröder and Rietveld's other joint projects ranged from a 1925 glass radio cabinet and 1927 project for standardized housing to the 1936 Vreeburg cinema, 1936 moveable summer houses, and the apartment block opposite the Schröder house. She lived in the Utrecht house for 60 years.
Bibliography 'Max van Rooij, Rietveld Schröder Huis De Vorm,' *Maandblad voor Vormgeving*, June–July 1975. Corrie Nagtegaal, Tr. *Schröder-Schräder, Gewoonster van het Rietveld Schröderhuis*, Utrecht: Impress bv, 1987. Paul Overy et al., *The Rietveld Schröder House*, Wiesbaden: Vieweg, 1988. *Rietveld Furniture and the Schröder House*, London: South Bank Centre, 1990. Marijke Küper and Ida van Lijl, *Gerrit Th. Rietveld: The Complete Works 1888–1964*, Utrecht: Centraal Museum, 1992. Bertus Mulder and Ida van Zijl, *Rietveld Schröder House*, New York: Princeton Architectural Press, 1999.

Schultes, Herbert H. (1938–)
German industrial designer.

Biography 1967 with Norbert Schlagheck, Schultes cofounded Schlagheck Schultes Design, Munich; from 1985, was design director of household appliances, Siemens; 1991, departed Schlagheck Design and, 2001, cofounded Schultes & Ritz design studio.
Citations 2003 Red Dot Best of the Best (System 25 kitchen by Bulthaup, with Klaus Delbeck), Design Zentrum Nordrhein Westfalen, Essen.
> See Schlagheck, Norbert.

Schudel, Paul (1951–)
> See Designum.

Schultz, Richard (1926–)
American sculptor and furniture designer.

Training Iowa State University; Illinois Institute of Technology (IIT), Chicago; Columbia University, New York.
Biography From 1951, Schultz worked at Knoll as a member of its design development group, at first working with Harry Bertoia on the wire Diamond seating range. At the request of Florence Knoll of Knoll International who wanted an outdoor-use range, Schultz designed 1960 Petal tables, 1961 steel-wire lounge chairs, and 1966 Leisure Collection outdoor seating and tables in a mesh fabric. Further pursuing outdoor furniture, he executed the design of a 1981 range. After Knoll discontinued its production of all Schultz furniture in 1988, it was reissued for a time by B&B Italia. Subsequently, with his son Peter Schultz, he established Richard Schultz Design in Palm, Pa., in 1992, with the manufacturing done by local craftspeople. Inventory includes early models, such as the Petal tables, as well as new models, such as 1996 Topiary and Confetti ranges of pierced-metal outdoor armchairs and table.
Citations 1967 International Design Award (Leisure Collection chair), American Institute of Decorators (AID).
Bibliography Cat., *Modern Chairs 1918–1970*, London: Lund Humphries, 1971: no. 84. Cat., *Les assises du siège contemporain*, Paris: Musée des Arts Décoratifs, 1968. Cat., Kathryn B. Hiesinger and George H. Marcus III (eds.), *Design Since 1945*, Philadelphia: Philadelphia Museum of Art. Eric Larrabee and Massimo Vignelli, *Knoll Design*, New York: Abrams, 1981: 158–59, 292–93.

Herbert H. Schultes and Norbert Schlagheck. Slide viewer (no. 135 B). 1976. Plastic casing, 1 1/8 x 2 3/8 x 4 9/16" (2.9 x 6 x 11.6 cm). Mfr.: Agfa-Gevaert, Germany (c. 1976–81). Gift of the mfr. MoMA.

Schumacher, F.
American fabric manufacturer; located New York.

History Frédéric Schumacher, born in Paris, was associated with Vanoutryve in Paris; acted as agent for the Brown, De Turk firm; early 1880s, traveled to the US to sell European fabrics to distributors; from 1883, was associated with fabric firm Passavant in New York; 1889, founded his own fabric firm, buying out Passavant's stock and opening an office at 935 Broadway, Manhattan; 1893, became a partner of Paul Gadebusch in a business at 222 Fourth Avenue (now Park Avenue), Manhattan. 1899, Schumacher's nephew Pierre Pozier came from France to succeed Schumacher as a stylist and purchasing agent and, 1943, became president. Distributing through interior designers, architects and retail stores, Schumacher's best-known designs have included fabrics for the Blue Room of The White House in Washington, during the presidencies of Theodore Roosevelt, Woodrow Wilson, and Calvin Coolidge; historic restoration prints for Newport and Williamsburg villages. Fabrics have been designed by Dorothy Draper, Paul McCobb, James Amster, William Pahlman, Raymond Loewy, and Frank Lloyd Wright. As early as 1909, Wright ordered Schumacher fabrics for his Robie and Coonley houses. Recently, the firm either created or purchased Gramercy, Greeff, Rosecore, Waverly, and Village brands, including Patterson, Flynn & Martin.
Bibliography David A. Hanks, *The Decorative Designs of Frank Lloyd Wright*, New York: Dutton, 1979: 217–19.

Schumacher-Percy, Ulla (1918–)
Swedish textile designer.

Training 1936–37 under Otte Sköld, in painting; 1938, Kungliga Tekniska Högskolan, Stockholm.
Biography From 1947, she was artistic director of Stockholm Domestic Crafts Association; 1949, established her own workshop, where she produced embroideries and rugs.
Exhibitions Work subject of 1957 and 1960 exhibitions, Stockholm; included in 1958 *Formes Scandinaves* exhibition, Musée des Arts Décoratifs, Paris.
Bibliography Cat., David Revere McFadden (ed.), *Scandinavian Modern Design 1880–1980*, New York: Abrams, 1982.

Schuster, Franz (1892–1976)
Austrian furniture manufacturer.

Training Kunstgewerbeschule, Vienna, under Heinrich Tessenow.
Biography From 1910s, Schuster was active in Vienna. As part of a municipal program for the construction of workers' homes after World War I, he designed a small row in the Viennese suburb Laaer Berg; at this time, also produced a modular stacking-furniture group; 1927, settled in Frankfurt; worked with Ernst May to create a furniture range in a Rationalist style suitable to the small scale of May's housing; was the artistic supervisor, Deutsche Hausratgesellschaften (household furnishings group); introduced an installment-payment plan for poor home owners, and created a range of modular furniture in wood. From

c. 1928, collaborated with the furniture firm Walter Knoll in Stuttgart; by 1930–31, had greatly expanded his range of 'unit' ('type' or standardized) furniture for state-supported or owner-occupied homes to include case goods, tables, chairs, and shelving, sold by various furniture companies and, subsequently, by Erwin Behr in Wendlingen, Stuttgart. His unit furniture may have been the basis of Serge Chermayeff's Plan range of unit furniture in England. Schuster's furniture, manifesting the more utopian aspects of 1920s–30s design philosophy, was lauded as heralding 'a new way of life' in early-1930s pamphlets and journals.
Bibliography Karl Mang, *Geschichte des Modernen Möbels*, Stuttgart: Gerd Hatje, 1978. Franz Schuster, *Ein Möbelbuch 2: Erweitete Auflage*, Stuttgart: Julius Hoffmann, 1932. 'Five Units = One Home,' *Decoration*, Jan. 1934: 7–9.

Schütt, Georg (1928–)

Danish metalworker.

Training In goldsmithing at the firm A. Michelsen, Copenhagen; in Stockholm.
Biography From 1951, Schütt worked in the design department, Georg Jensen Sølvsmedie, Copenhagen; became the public relations officer for Foreningen Dansk Møbelindustri (association of Danish furniture manufacturers). His fanlike 1958 strainer by Jensen in stainless steel is distinguished for its simplicity.
Bibliography Cat., *Georg Jensen Silversmithy: 77 Artists, 75 Years*, Washington: Smithsonian, 1980.

Schütte-Lihotzky, 'Grete' Margarete (1897–2000)

Austrian architect; born Vienna.

Training 1915–19, architecture, Königliche Akademie der bildenden Künste (from which she was the first woman to receive an architecture diploma), Vienna.
Biography Schütte designed worker housing; became known for 1927 Frankfurter Küche (Frankfurt kitchen), a standardized kitchen, still highly regarded, of which 10,000 units were incorporated into apartments in Frankfurt, Germany, some still extant. The kitchen assignment was a result of her late-1920s collaboration on the city plan of Frankfurt with Ernst May, Frankfurt's architect. She was socially conscious, antifascist, and, during World War II, was incarcerated for her involvement in resistance to the Nazis but was eventually freed. From 1938, she designed school buildings and taught, Valtion Kuvataideakatemia (state academy of fine art), Istanbul, Turkey.
Citations 1980 Architecture Award, City of Vienna; 1988 Austrian Medal for Science and Art (refused by her at the time due to its bequeathal by Austrian president Kurt Waldheim, accused of supressing his Nazi past; however, years later, was accepted by her).
Exhibition Frankfurter Küche installed at 2000–01 exhibition, Centre Georges Pompidou, Paris (catalog below).
Bibliography Walter Müller-Wulckow, *Die deutsche Wohnung der Gegenwart, Bauten der Arbeit und des Verkehrs...*, Königstein im Taunus/Leipzig: Langewiesche, 1930. *Neues Bauen, Neues Gestalten: Das Neue Frankfurt, die Neue Stadt: Eine Zeitschrift Zwischen, 1926 und 1933*, Dresden: Verlag der Kunst, 1984: 180+. Cat., Design Center Stuttgart, *Women in Design: Careers and Life Histories Since 1900*, Stuttgart: Haus der Wirtschaft, 1989: 149–73. Cat., *Les bon génies de la vie domestique*, Paris: Centre Georges Pompidou, 2000.

Schwan, Lloyd (1955–2001)

American furniture designer; born Evanston, Ill.; husband of Lyn Godley.

Training 1975–1979, School of the Art of Institute of Chicago, Minneapolis College of Art and Design, and San Francisco Art Institute.
Biography 1984–97 with Lyn Godley (Oberlin, Ohio, 1956–), Schwan was active in Godley-Schwan in New York, designing furniture, lighting, tableware, and interiors. They produced limited-production pieces in a workshop in Brooklyn, N.Y, including a distinctive, colorful wooden chest of drawers in an amorphous silhouette and, subsequently in Pennsylvania, 1996 Crinkle lamp. 1997, Schwan worked for Exit Art NYC, not-for-profit organization, as a committee member; 1997–98, the design director, Totem Design, New York; 1997–2001 in his own Lloyd Schwan/Design studio, a furniture, product, and interior-design agency for clients, including Cappellini, Box Mobles, Magis, and Asplund. He comitted suicide in Kutztown, Pa.
Exhibitions/citations A number of group and one-person exhibitions, from 1983 at the Hokin Kauffman Gallery, Chicago, to his 1998 New Furiture Collection, Totem, New York. Schwan and Godley first showed their group work (seating and case goods) at 1988 Salone del Mobile, Milan.

Schwanzer, Karl (1918–1975)

Austrian architect and furniture designer; born Vienna.

Biography From 1959, was a professor, Technischen Hochschule, Vienna; from 1963, was active in his own studio in Munich; designed mass-produced furniture and also created the panorama of the Alps in the Austrian pavilion at 1967 *Universal and International Exhibition* (*Expo '67*), Montréal, and Austrian pavilion at 1958 *Exposition Universelle et Internationale de Bruxelles* (*Expo '58*). He committed suicide in Vienna. His best-known architecture is 1970–72 Hochhaus (headquarters) of BMW, Munich.

Richard Schultz. Petal coffee table. 1960. Redwood, aluminum, and cast iron, h. 14 7/8" x dia. 42" (37.8 x 106.7 cm). Mfr.: Richard Schultz Design, US (2000). Gift of the mfr. MoMA.

Citations Numerous awards, including 1975 Großer Österreichischer Staatspreis (posthomously granted).
Bibliography Günther Feuerstein, *Vienna—Present and Past: Arts and Crafts—Applied Art—Design*, Vienna: Jugend und Volk, 1976. P. M. Bode and G. Peichl, *Architektur aus Österreich seit 1960*, Saltzburg/Vienna: Residenz, 1980.

Schwartz, Frederic (1951–)

American architect and designer; born New York.

Training 1973, bachelor's degree in architecture; 1978, master's degree in architecture, Harvard University, Cambridge, Mass.
Biography From 1978, Schwartz worked at Venturi and Rauch architects, Philadelphia, where he was the director from 1980. 1984 with others, he cofounded Anderson/Schwartz Architects; 1996, established Schwartz Architects; both New York. Interior architecture has included the Princeton Club, Joe's restaurant, Bumble & Bumble hair salon, and numerous apartments and lofts; all New York. Schwartz designed tableware by Swid Powell, bed linen by Cannon Fieldcrest, tableware, stained glass, mosaics, and other products.
Bibliography Cat., R. Craig Miller (intro.), *U.S. Design 1975–2000*, Munich: Prestel, 2002.

Schweinberger-Gismondi, Emma (1934–)

Italian designer; born Cologna Veneta.

Biography Active from 1960s, she has designed furniture and interiors; was a designer for Artemide in Milan, which produced a number of her memorable items in ABS such as 1966 Giano Vano bedside table, Elisa and 1966 Dedalo dome-shaped umbrella stand (and coordinating Dedalotto vase and Dedalino pencil holder). Lesser known is Ara detachable dining table in reinforced ABS Marbon Cycolac resin.
Exhibitions Work included in *Pop Goes the Plastic: The Visual and Cultural Aesthetic of a New Technology, 1960–1975*, traveling US from 1998.
Bibliography Hans Wichmann, *Industrial Design, Unikate, Serienerzeugnisse: Die Neue Sammlung, Ein neuer Museumtyp des 20. Jahrhunderts*, Munich. 1985: 515. Cat., Hans Wichmann, *Italien Design 1945 bis heute*, Munich: Die Neue Sammlung, 1988.

Schwippert, Hans (1899–1973)

German designer.

Biography Before World War II, Schwippert collaborated with Ludwig Mies van der Rohe in Germany; designed the apartment building, among other structures, at Bartningallee 16, Berlin; 1949, participated in the draft of the plenary of the Deutscher Bundestag in Bonn; from 1949, was chairperson, Deutscher Werkbund, Düsseldorf; frequently commissioned Albert Renger-Patzsch to photograph his buildings; was known to have designed simple wooden furniture.
Bibliography Carl Burchard, *Gutes und Böses in der Wohnung in Bild und Gegenbild...*, Leipzig: Beyer, 1933. 'Geschrieben Ende 1944,' *Baukunst und Werkform*, vol. 1, 1947: 17. *Mensch und Technik: Erzengnis, Form, Gebranch...*, Darmstadt: Neue Darmstadler Verlagsanstalt, 1952. Cat., *Realität und Vision Phänomen Weltausstellung 1851– 2000*, Hagen: Ardenku, 2000. Auction cat., *Modernes Design Kunsthandwerk nach 1945*, Munich: Quittenbaum, 1 June 2002: 17.

Scott Brown, Denise (b. Denise Lakofski; 1931–)

British architect; born Nkana, Zambia, of Latvian parents; active Philadelphia, US; wife of Robert Venturi.

Training 1948–52, architecture, University of the Witwatersrand, Johannesburg, South Africa; 1960, M.C.P., and, 1965, master's degree in architecture, University of Pennsylvania, Philadelphia.
Biography 1958, she settled in the US; 1960, began teaching architecture; 1967, joined Venturi and Rauch, Philadelphia, as architect and planner, where she became a partner in 1969. 1980, the practice became known as Venturi, Rauch and Scott Brown and, 1989, as Venturi, Scott Brown and Associates. The firm is known for its postmodern architectural style. She accomplished most of her architecture projects in collaboration with Venturi, as well as their publications, including *Learning from Las Vegas* (Cambridge, Mass.: MIT, 1972). She herself wrote *Urban Concepts* (London: Academy; New York: St. Martin's, 1990). 1960–65, she taught at the University of Pennsylvania; 1965–68, at the University of California; 1967–70, at Yale University. Her activities and recognition included hundreds of lectures, conferences, juries, selection panels, and awards in Europe, the US, and Africa. No doubt she was appreciably involved in Venturi industrial-design/product work.
Citations Numerous honorary degrees. 1987 Commendatore order of merit, Republic of Italy; 1992 National Medal of Arts, US Presidential Award; 1997 Topaz Medallion for excellence in architectural education, American Collegiate Schools of Architecture-American Institute of Architects (ACSA-AIA); 2001 Chevalier of the Ordre des Arts et Lettres, France.
Bibliography Liz McQuiston, *Women in Design: A Contemporary View*, New York: Rizzoli, 1988: 24. Cat., R. Craig Miller (intro.), *U.S. Design 1975–2000*, Munich: Prestel, 2002.
> See Venturi, Robert.

Scott, Giles Gilbert (1880–1960)

British architect.

Training Apprenticeship under architect Temple Lushington Moore.
Biography 1903, Scott established his own architectural practice; won the competition for the Liverpool Anglican Cathedral, begun in 1903 but unfinished by the time he died; 1920–21, was president, Architectural Association, London, and, 1933–35, president, Royal Institute of British Architects (RIBA); designed the renowned 1936 Model K6 red public-telephone booth that became known as the Jubilee Kiosk. British Telecom's 1988 decision to replace the booths with a new design met public protests, and a small number were reprieved. Scott also designed numerous churches and chapels in the Gothic-Revival style, including New Court at Clare College, Cambridge. His work also included 1922–60 school houses at Ampleforth College, Yorkshire; 1928–29 St. Francis Terriers Church, High Wycombe; 1930–32 Battersea power station, London (with engineer S.L. Pearce, architect J.H. Halliday); 1930–32 St. Albans Church, Golders Green, London; 1930–34 University Library, Cambridge University; 1932 St. Andrews Church, Luton; 1933–51 Guinness factory, Park Royal; 1934–45 Waterloo Bridge (with engineers Rendel, Palmer and Tritton); 1935–46 annex of the Bodleian Library, Oxford University; 1935-51 Electricity House, Bristol.
Citations 1924, was knighted.
Bibliography Adolf K. Placzek (ed.), *Macmillan Encyclopedia of Architects*, vol. 4, New York: Free Press, 1982. Cat., *Thirties: British Art and Design Before the War*, London: Arts Council of Great Britain/ Hayward Gallery Gallery, 1979. *Issue 2*, London: Design Museum, 1989.

Scott, Isaac Elwood (1845–1920)

American furniture designer, wood carver, and ceramicist; born Philadelphia.

Biography 1873, Scott moved to Chicago; became known for his fine wood carving; modeled architectural ornaments for Chicago Terra Cotta pottery; 1875, became a partner of architect Frederick W. Copeland in 'Scott and Copeland, Designers, Carvers, and Art Wood Workers.' 1875, Mr. and Mrs. John J. Glessner commissioned him to design/make furniture and furnishings for their home at 261 West Washington Boulevard, Chicago. 1879, vases for the house were made by Scott at Chelsea Keramic Art Works in Massachusetts. Scott with Asa Lyon, an architect and furniture designer, designed the 1878 coach house of the Glessner residence. Early 1880s, Scott began designing textiles and embroidery patterns; 1882–84, taught woodcarving, Chicago Society of Decorative Art; designed 1883 Glessner summer villa at The Rocks, near Littleton, New Hampshire; 1882–84, was in partnership with Henry S. Jaffray, creating interiors and designing the new headquarters of Warder, Bushnell & Glessner at Jefferson and Adams Streets, Chicago. They designed another residence and a six-storey Chicago office building. 1884, Scott moved to New York; by 1887, had designed interiors at 1129 Broadway; 1888, moved to Boston and became active in wood carving again and taught crafts at the Eliot School. When H.H. Richardson designed 1885 Glessner residence at 1800 Prairie Avenue in Chicago, Scott's earlier (1870s) furniture for the Glessners was moved into the new structure.
Exhibitions Work was included in 1875 *Inter-State Industrial Exposition* (a display of household furnishings), Chicago; 1987 *In Pursuit of Beauty*, The Metropolitan Museum of Art, New York.
Bibliography David A. Hanks, *Isaac E. Scott: Reform Furniture in Chicago: John Jacob Glessner House*, Chicago: Chicago School of Architecture Foundation, 1974. David A. Hanks, 'Isaac E. Scott, Craftsman and Designer,' *Antiques*, vol. 105, June 1974: 1307–13. Sharon Darling, *Chicago Furniture: Art, Craft, and Industry, 1933–1983*, New York: Norton, 1984.

Emma Schweinberger-Gismondi. Dedalo umbrella stand. 1966. ABS polymer, h. 13 3/8" x dia. 15 3/8" (34 x 39 cm). Mfr.: Artemide, Italy. Gift of the mfr. MoMA.

SČSD
> See Svaz Československéno Díla.

SEB, Groupe (Société d'Emboutissage de Bourgogne)
French home-appliance manufacturer.

History 1857, Antoine Lescure founded a firm at Selongey. 1944, it was re-established as Société d'Emboutissage de Bourgogne by Lescure's grandsons Jean, Frédéric, and Henri Lescure; 1953, invented a safe pressure cooker using a special clamp device that would release steam pressure automatically, if necessary, and eventually an electric fryer. (By 1999, had sold 50 million pressure cookers.) 1968, acquired Tefal and, 1972, Calor iron, hair-dryer, and portable-heater manufacturer, and, subsequently, various others; 1974, established Groupe SEB; 1974, became a public-held company; 1995, arranged a joint-venture operation with the leading clothes-iron manufacturer in China; acquired and currently produces Tefal/T-Fal and Rowenta as worldwide brands and Arno (from 1997), Volmo (from 1998), Samurai, and SEB as regional brands; 2001–02, took over the assets of bankrupted Moulinex/Krups; has become known for high-quality, well-designed household appliances, created by a distinguished design staff.
Bibliography www.groupeseb.com
> See Moulinex.

Sebastian, James A. (1942–)
American graphic designer; born Providence, R.I.

Training Bachelor's degree, marketing, Bryant College; bachelor of fine arts degree, Rhode Island School of Design, Providence.
Biography Sebastian was active in marketing, advertising, photography, and industrial and graphic design before cofounding Timeframes with Michael McGinn; designed the now-well-known 1978 Timeframe black adjustable calendar, which encouraged the founding of the studio. Other products since have included Timeframe 2, eBag, Orbital Mapping, Digital Process Tint Guide, Pause seat, Wave binder system, and Glide Top storage box. Sebastian is a board member, American Institute of Graphic Arts (AIGA); was elected to Alliance Graphique Internationale.

Sebton, Anya (1966–)
Swedish designer.

Training 1986–87, Nyckelviksskolan (art and design school), Lidingö; 1988, in art; 1993–96, Anders Beckman School of Design; Stockholm.
Biography 1987, Sebton was a photo assistant at CA publicity-photography agency; 1988–89, photo assistant/manager at Studio Tomas Gidén; 1997 with Eva Lilja-Löwenhielm, was in charge of interior-design projects for Amek advertising agency, Stockholm. Sebton and Lilja-Löwenhielm were chosen as two of 12 Swedish designers and manufacturers commissioned by the Stockholm Hotel Birger to design a guest room. Sebton's clients have also included Lammhult for furniture design, such as 1999 Multiplicity chair/ottoman.
Exhibitions Furniture (with Lilja-Löwenhielm) for an exhibition house, 1998 Nybodahöjden; new products by Zero, by Lustrum, and by Pukeberg for 1998 *Jubilee Exhibition*; design of Lammhult exhibition stand at 2000 Swedish Furniture Fair; all Stockholm. Work shown at Scandinavia International Week, 2000 International Contemporary Furniture Fair (ICFF), New York; 2000 *100% Design* fair, London.
Bibliography Paul Makovsky, 'Anya's Easy Chair,' *Metropolis*, Feb. 2001: 38. www.lammhults.se.

Secession
> See Münchner Sezession; Wiener Sezession.

Sedding, George Elton (1882–1915)
British metalworker and jeweler; son of John Dando Sedding.

Training Apprenticeship under Henry Wilson, who was formerly the chief assistant to Sedding's father, in London and Kent.
Biography 1907, Sedding returned to London from Kent and opened a small workshop at 11 Noel Street, near Oxford Circus, specializing in simple decorative objects, silver objects, and copper jewelry set with semi-precious stones in a style similar to Wilson's. As success increased, his production became more ambitious and elaborate, mainly for ecclesiastical commissions.
Bibliography Charlotte Gere, *American and European Jewelry 1830–1914*, New York: Crown, 1975.

Sedding, John Dando (1838–1891)
British architect and embroidery, metalwork, and wallpaper designer; born Eaton; father of George Elton Sedding.

Training 1858–63, apprenticeship under architect G.E. Street, becoming knowledgeable in Gothic ornamentation and architecture.
Biography 1863–65, Sedding pursued decorative design; 1865, became a partner of architect/brother Edmund Sedding in Penzance, Cornwall; 1868–74, was active in Bristol; 1874, established an office in London and, 1876, met John Ruskin. Sedding became interested in the use of natural forms in ornamentation; 1880, was appointed architect of the diocese of Bath and Wells; designed 1885 Holy Trinity Church on Sloane Street, London, and 1886 Church of the Holy Redeemer, Clerkenwell, London, in a classical style. Sedding was known to have designed embroidery, metalware, and wallpaper. His books include *Art and Handicraft* (London: K. Paul, Trench, Trübner, 1893). His chief assistant Henry Wilson assumed the affairs of the architecture office when Sedding died, and completed his unfinished commissions, including details of the elaborate French Gothic and English Perpendicular 1890 Holy Trinity Church.
Bibliography Isabelle Anscombe and Charlotte Gere, *Arts and Crafts in Britain and America*, New York: Rizzoli, 1978: 140. Adolf K. Placzek (ed.), *Macmillan Encyclopedia of Architects*, vol. 4, New York: Free Press, 1982.

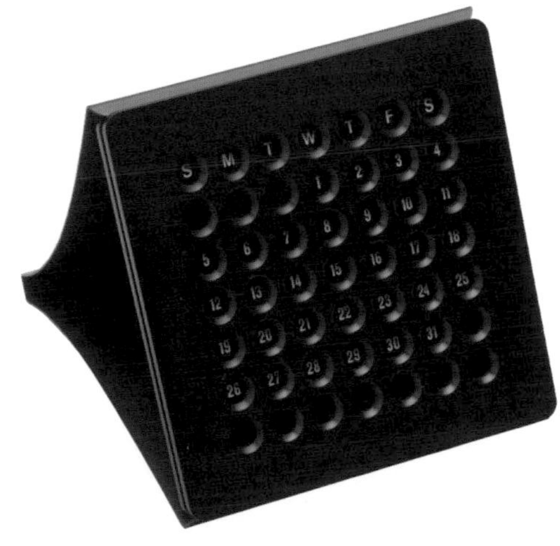

James A. Sebastian. Timeframe calendar (no. 3.5). 1978. Polystyrene, 3 1/2 x 3/8 x 3 1/2" (8.9 x 1 x 8.9 cm). Mfr.: Design Frame, US. Gift of the designer. MoMA.

Seddon, John Pollard (1827–1906)

British architect; born London.

Training 1848–51 under architect T.L. Donaldson.
Biography 1852–62, Seddon was a partner with John Pritchard in Wales and, 1884–1904, with John Coates Carter; from 1857, concurrently was active in own office. With a largely ecclesiastical clientele, by mid-1870s, he was designing country churches in Herefordshire, rebuilding a church there and altering another in Norfolk; applied medievalism to 19th-century values in a sober manner; became best known for 1864 Castle House Hotel (now University College of Wales) in Aberystwyth, Dyfed, for which his apprentice C.F.A. Voysey may have designed some decorative panels in cement at the entrance to its south wing. Seddon lost the 1884 competition for the Law Courts to George Edmund Street; designed the King René's Honeymoon cabinet for William Morris's firm, with painted panels by Ford Madox Brown, Edward Burne-Jones, and Dante Gabriel Rossetti. Some of his furniture showed Pre-Raphaelite and A.W.N. Pugin influences. Seddon incorporated bold decorative hinges; favored plain panels that featured the grain of the wood as a decorative feature; and executed designs for ecclesiastical embroideries and for numerous encaustic floor tiles by leading manufacturers. His books include *Progress in Art and Architecture, with Precedents for Ornament* (London: D. Bogue, 1852).
Exhibitions Work shown at 1874 Royal Academy venue (orphanage and chapel interiors), London; exhibit of newly-formed Morris, Faulkner and Marshall firm (a roll-top desk) at *International Exhibition of 1862*, London.
Bibliography *Journal of the Royal Institute of British Architects* (obituary), 13, 1906: 194, 221. Stuart Durant, *The Decorative Designs of C.F.A. Voysey*, London: Lutterworth, 1990: 13–14. J. Roger Webster, *Old College, Aberystwyth: The Evolution of a High Victorian Building*, Cardiff: University of Wales, 1995.

Segis

Italian furniture company; located Poggibonsi.

History 1983, Segis was founded and, subsequently, has become known for well-designed, economically priced furniture, especially chairs and tables; is managed by Franco Dominici. The firm's art director Carlo Bartoli coordinates commissioned designers such as Anna Castelli Ferrieri, Castiglia Associati, Makio Hasuike, Isao Hosoe/Etien Veeman, Roberto Romanello, Paolo Romoli. Bartoli also designs for Segis through the studio Bartoli Design. Furniture has included Please stackable polyproplylene chair by Hosoe/Veeman, Alphabet seating range by Roberto Romanello, and K table system by Bartoli Design. 80% of its production is exported.

Segre, Luigi
> See Karmann, Wilhelm.

Seguso, Archimede (1909–1999)

Italian glass designer; active Murano; son of Antonio Seguso.

Training Under his father Antonio Seguso (1984–1965) and Napoleone Barovier at Vetreria Artistica Barovier e C.
Biography There have been a number of Segusos associated with the glass industry in Murano. From 1933, Archimede Seguso was a glassblower at Vetreria Artistica Barovier e C. 1931, Barovier, Luigi Olimpo Ferro, Archimede Seguso, and his father left the firm due to the economic circumstances of the Great Depression. 1931, Archimede, his father, and his brother Ernesto (1908–86) established a small glass workshop and were joined by Barovier and Ferro in 1932. 1933, Archimede, his father, brothers Ernesto and Alberto, Barovier, and Ferro founded Artistica Vetreria e Soffieria Barovier Seguso e Ferro with Ferro and Napoleone Barovier. To 1942 when Archimede left the firm, he was a master glassblower there; from 1945 first alone and then with others, operated glass workshop Seguso Archimede; 1947, changed the name to Vetreria Archimede Seguso; up to his death in Murano, had become Murano's most celebrated living glass artisan.
Exhibition Work subject of 1991 exhibition, Palazzo Ducale, Venice (catalog below).
Bibliography Cat., *Venezianisches Glas 19. bis 20. Jahrhundert aus dem Glasmuseum Murano/Venedig*, Berlin: Kunstgewerbemuseum Schloss Köpenick, 1981: 51. Cat., Umberto Franzoi, *I vetri di Archimede Seguso*, Venezia: Arsenale, 1991. Rosa Barovier Mentasti, *I vetri di Archimede Seguso dal 1950 al 1959*, Turin: Allemandi, 2002 (trilingual).

Seguso Vetri d'Arte. Vase. c. 1937–49. Glass, h. 6 x dia. 6" (15.2 x 15.2 cm). Mfr.: Seguso Vetri d'Arte, Italy. Edgar Kaufmann, Jr. Fund. MoMA.

Seguso Vetri d'Arte

Italian glass manufacturers; located Murano.

History Through a series of starts, liquidations, and restarts, the glass enterprise Artistica Vetreria e Soffieria Barovier Seguso e Ferro began in 1933, founded by Napoleone Barovier, Luigi Olimpo Ferro, and Antonio Seguso, with Seguso's sons Ernesto, Alberto, and Archimede (later joined by their younger brother Angelo). 1937, Luigi Ferro sold his shares to the firm's artistic director Flavio Poli. Ferri departed; and the firm became known as Seguso Vetri d'Arte, but was liquidated in 1973. (While there, Poli incorporated rich colors and bubble patterns into his early work; used strong, simple silhouettes; introduced a style later known as *vetro astrale*, inspired by outer-space travel and science fiction.) 1973, Maurizio Albarelli acquired some assets of the firm to establish Sculpture Artistiche Muranesi (S.A.M.), which became bankrupted in 1976. That year it was reopened by Maurizio Albarelli as Seguso Vetri d'Arte. 1992, the name was sold to Gino Cenedese & Figlio, and Albarelli retained the factory that he sold to Formia in 1994. The workshop's rostrum of artistic directors had included Vittorio Zecchin 1933–34, Flavio Poli 1934–63, Mario Pinzoni 1963–68, and Vittorio Rigattieri 1968–73. Commissioned designers: Sergio Asti, Fulvio Bianconi, Angelo Mangiarotti, Mila Schön, Peter Shire, Ettore Sottsass, others.
Bibliography Cat., *Venini & Murano Renaissance: Italian Art Glass of the 1940s and 50s*, New York: Fifty/50, 1984.

Seibel, Ben (1918–1985)

American ceramics designer.

Biography Seibel was primarily active during 1950–70s; designed for several American potteries. Work included the successful Contempora dinnerware by Steubenville; 1952 Raymor Modern Stoneware for Raymor by Roseville; 1956 Impromptu, 1958 Informal, 1959 Inheritance, and 1964 Intaglio sets by Iroquois; 1971 ovenproof stoneware range by Haeger; and a number of designs by Mikasa. He also designed metalware and ceramics for others, such as Jenfred-Ware brass bookends and dinnerware by Forum International and by Kasuga, both Japan, possibly with motifs by others. Purportedly, Roseville, experiencing financial difficulties, hired Seibel in 1952 to design a dinnerware line that would help the firm. While the effort was not financially favorable, the venture brought Seibel to prominence. His early ceramics that are the most favored now feature very smooth finishes, in earth tones, devoid of decoration.
Bibliography Sharon and Bob Huxford, *The Collectors Encyclopedia of Roseville Pottery*, Padukah, Ky.: Collectors Books, 1980 (1995, 2nd series). Mark Bassett, *Introducing Roseville Pottery*, Atglen, Pa.: Schiffer, 2001. Cat., Brooke Kamin Rapaport and Kevin Stayton (eds.), *Vital*

Forms: American Art and Design in the Atomic Age, 1940–1960, New York: Abrams, 2001.

Seidelin, Henning (1904–1987)

Danish sculptor and designer.

Biography Seidelin was a sculptor who also designed utilitarian objects in silver, steel, porcelain, and faïence; executed 1930s silver designs by Georg Jensen Sølvsmedie, Copenhagen, such as 24-piece Savoy cutlery and a 1950 teapot. He also designed a stove by L. Lange & Co. and L 203-1 hanging lamp by Le Klint.
Exhibitions/citations Work shown at 1951 (9th) and 1954 (10th) editions of Triennale di Milano. 1951 Eckersberg Medal.
Bibliography Cat., *Georg Jensen Silversmithy: 77 Artists, 75 Years*, Washington: Smithsonian, 1980.

Seiffert, Florian (1943–); Hartwig Kahlcke (1942–)

German industrial designers.

Training Seiffert: design, Folkwangschule für Gestaltung, Essen.
Biographies 1968–72, Seiffert worked for Braun in Kronberg, Germany, designing 1970 Cassett razor, 1971 Ladyshaver razor, 1972 KF 20 coffee maker, and 1972 Cassett Standard razor in a polycarbonate. 1972–78, he was active in his own studio in Milan; from 1978, worked in Munich. While at Braun, he was a member of the design department with, among others, Hartwig Kahlcke. Also at Braun, Kahlcke designed a number of its products, including 1979 KSM 2 coffee grinder, 1980 HT 6 toaster, 1983 PV 66N iron, 1984 KF 43 coffee maker, and, with Ludwig Littmann, 1981–88 UK 400 food processor. 1988, Kahlcke joined Seiffert to form Seiffert + Kahlcke Design partnership in Wiesbaden, Germany, working for clients such as Braun, A. Eugster, Franke, Krups, Loewe, Matsushita, Moser, Rosink, Schulte-Ufer, Thomas, and Wella.

Seiko; K. Hattori & Co.

Japanese timing-device manufacturer.

History From 1873, Kintaro Hattori (1860–1934) worked as an apprentice in a foreign-goods wholesale store in Tokyo; from 1875, began working at the Kameda clock shop in Nihonbashi, near the Tokyo train station and, from 1877, the Sakata clock shop in Shimoya ward, Tokyo; 1881, established K. Hattori & Co., a retail timepiece store; within a short time, became the largest clock merchant in Tokyo; 1892, established the Seikosha supply factory for the production of wall clocks; 1895, began making watch fobs and, from 1899, alarm clocks. 1900, he traveled to America and Europe and, subsequently, returned and upgraded his manufacturing equipment. From 1902, he made table and musical clocks and, from 1913, the first Japanese wristwatches. 1917, K. Hattori & Co. became publicly held and began to make the ten-jewel Morris-type, or Seiko, watch and thus 'Seiko' became the company's trademark and appeared on its clock/watch faces from 1924. 1930, watch production was transferred to Daini Seikosha Co. (predecessor of today's Seiko). 1942, Daiwa Kogyo was established (predecessor of today's Seiko Epson). 1955, the firm introduced the quartz clock for broadcasting-station use; 1959, transistorized table clocks; 1963, portable quartz chronometers; 1969, 34SQ Seiko Astron, the world's first quart wristwatch. 1970, Seiko Time Corporation was established in the US, and, 1971, Seiko Time (UK). 1973, the 06LC was introduced as the world's first LCD quartz watch with six-digit digital display; 1975, the world's first multi-function digital watch; and 1976, the world's first quartz alarm clock. 1983, K. Hattori & Co. was renamed Hattori Seiko Co. 1983, introduced the world's first watch with sound-recording functions; 1984, the world's first watch with computer functions; 1988, quartz watch with sweep second hand; 1988, quartz watch wound by wearer's movements (no batteries required); 1988, the world's first intelligent analogue quartz watch with alarm, chronometer, and timer controlled by an IC computer on a chip. 1990, most subsidiaries began using the Seiko name, and Hattori Seiko was renamed Seiko Corporation. 1990, the firm introduced the world's first computerized diver's watch, incorporating a dive table; 1990, Receptor MessageWatch, incorporating a miniaturized FM subcarrier; 1991, Seiko Perpetual Calendar with the world's-first 'millennium-plus calendar.' From 1996, optical products and jewelry were included in the inventory.
Bibliography www.seiko.co.jp.

Pierre Selmersheim. Candlelabrum. c. 1900. Polished pewter, h. 7 5/8" (19.3 cm). Mfr.: the designer, France. Courtesy Quittenbaum Kunstauktienen, Munich.

Seiko Epson

Japanese electronic manufacturer.

History 1942, K. Hattori & Co. established the Daiwa Kogyo company. 1959, Daiwa Kogyo merged with the Suwa Plant of Daini Seikosha (now Seiko Instruments Inc.) to form Suwa Seikosha Co., which in turn established Shinshu Seiki Co. in 1961. Its Crystal Chronometer 951 (a compact tabletop quartz clock) and a printer timer were well met at the 1964 Tokyo Olympiad. 1968, the company introduced the world's first mini-printer and, 1969, Seiko Quartz 355Q, the world's-first CD-equipped digital quartz watch. 1975, the company established its first overseas sales subsidiary, Epson America and likewise the Epson brand; 1980, introduced MP-80 printer for computers, highly successful in the US; 1982, HC-20, world's first handheld computer; 1983, world's first portable color LCD TV. 1985, Suwa Seikosha Co. and Epson Corporation merged to form Seiko Epson Corporation, as it is today. 1987, introduced PC-286 personal computer; 1988, world's first self-winding quartz watch; 1989, PC-286 Note Executive, world's first laptop personal computer; 1990, Seiko Receptor, world's first watch with a pager function; 1990, mass production of world's first rare-earth (praseodymium) bonded magnet. 1992, the corporation completely eliminated the use of chlorofluorocarbons, 1993 of 1,1,1-trichloroethane (a methyl chloroform); and 1999 of chlorine-based organic solvents. 1993, Seiko Epson introduced Monsieur, world's smallest microrobot; 1994, MJ-700V2C inkjet color printer; 1994, small, lightweight ELP-3000 multi-media projector; 1996, PM-700C inkjet color printer; 1998, Intercolor LP-8000C, Seiko Epson's first laser color printor; 1998, Stylus Color 800, the first color printer used on NASA's space shuttle *Discovery*; 2000, MC-9000, a large-format inkjet color printer; 2001, PM-950C inkjet color printer, with the world's highest image resolution (2,880 dpi); 2002, Crystal Fine display in fourth-generation, high-image-quality (RGB), high-definition (200 dpi) mobile units; 2002, panel for use in projectors (100-millionth high-temperature polysilicon TFT liquid crystal); 2003, PX-V700 printer for high-clarity PX ink-technology on regular paper; 2003, Monsieur II-P microrobot prototype, featuring an ultra-slim, ultrasonic motor, and low-energy Bluetooth technology.
Citations 1992 Stratospheric Ozone Protection Award, Environmental Protection Agency, the US; 2002 Corporate Innovation Recognition Award, Institute of Electrical and Electronics Engineers (IEEE).

Selmersheim, Pierre (1869–1941)

French architect and decorator; born Paris; brother of Tony Selmersheim.

Biography With his brother Tony, Selmersheim designed lighting and collaborated on the décors of a number of buildings. Pierre decorated a 1902 apartment that, like his office interior at the 1902 Paris Salon, avoided 'superfluous ornamental forms and acrobatic accom-

plishments'; was interested in the design of household goods. By 1910, he was designing for Socard and for Gallé; 1904, became a cofounder of Société des Artistes Décorateurs. Numerous commissions included automobile designs and 1919 interior design and furnishings of a houseboat.
Exhibitions Selmersheim brothers showed furnishings at group exhibition of L'Art dans Tout; Salons of Société Nationale des Beaux-Arts, Salons of Société des Artistes Décorateurs from 1906; editions of Salon d'Automne; all Paris.
Bibliography Yvonne Brunhammer et al., *Art Nouveau Belgium, France*, Houston: Rice University, 1976. Alastair Duncan, *Art Nouveau and Art Déco Lighting*, New York: Simon & Schuster, 1978.

Selmersheim, Tony (1871–1971)
French architect and decorator; born Saint-Germain-en-Laye; brother of Pierre Selmersheim.

Biography Tony Selmersheim was initially in partnership with architect Charles Plumet. With his brother Pierre, he collaborated on furniture, furnishings, lighting, interiors of various buildings, and decoration and furniture for a first-class cabin of 1935 oceanliner *Normandie*. c. 1905, Tony designed an important range of furniture for the French Embassy, Vienna; the organ gallery of Basilique du Sacre-Cœur, Paris, and a number of offices; to 1935, worked with L. Monteil and, subsequently, with his son André Selmersheim in their studio on the boulevard Saint-Marcel, Paris, on a number of furniture designs in limited editions; was interested in mechanical objects and invented a number of tools and some machinery used in his atelier.
Exhibitions/citations Furniture ensembles from 1897, including at 1900 *Exposition Universelle*, Paris, and Salons of Société des Artistes Décorateurs from 1910. First prize in 1912 competition for the office of the president of the municipal council. All Paris.
Bibliography Alastair Duncan, *Art Nouveau and Art Déco Lighting*, New York: Simon & Schuster, 1978. Pierre Kjellberg, *Art déco: les maîtres du mobilier, le décor des paquebots*, Paris: Amateur, 1986/1990.

Semenzato, Remo (1934–)
Italian industrial designer; born Mira; active Milan.

Biography 1960–63 and 1967–69, Semenzato collaborated with architect/designer Angelo Mangiarotti and, 1965–67, with architect/designer Mario Bellini. Semenzato designed sound equipment and televisions sets, including TP252 CGE, TE355 CGE, and TX347 CGE models by Sogetel, and a number of other products; became a member, Associazione per il Disegno Industriale (ADI).
Bibliography *ADI Annual 1976*, Milan: Associazione per il Disegno Industriale, 1976.

Sempé, Inga (1968–)
French designer; born and active Paris.

Training To 1993, ENSCI (Les Ateliers), Paris; 2001, one-year fellowship, French Academy in Rome (Villa Medici).
Biography 1989, Sempé worked in the design studios of George Sowden, for Marc Newson in Paris for six months in 1994 after ENSCI, and for Andrée Putman in Paris 1997–99. 2000, she became an independent designer and has designed objects, lighting, and furniture by Cappellini (2002 monumental paper pleated lamp, with Kyoko Nakagawa), Baccarat (2003 candlestick), and Edra (2003 Brosse vertical containers, featuring industrial brushes).
Exhibitions/citations. Work included in 2004 *Design d'Elle*, Galerie VIA (French furniture association), Paris. Subject of 2003 exhibition, Musée des Arts Décoratifs, Paris. Prototype grants from VIA: 2000 articulating lamp, 2000 clock (produced with Centre de Transfert des Microtechniques), 2003 metal/rubber side chair, and others. Prix de la Critique (lighting category), 2000 Salon du Meuble, Paris; 2003 Grand Prix de la Création, Ville de Paris.
Bibliography *Axis*, vol.105, Sep. 2003.

Semprini, 'Rocky' Roberto (1959–)
Italian designer; born Rimini; active Milan.

Training 1987, architecture, Universitá di Firenze.
Biography Semprini associated himself with the Movimento Bolidista formed in 1986 in Bologna which is typified by a retro-1950s/streamline aesthetic and claims, among a number of assertions, 'that ideology is a useless and harmful brake.' Semprini has designed furniture for firms including Camaeri Arte, Esse 81, Ferrart Fly-Line, Moroso, Play-Line, Tonelli, Trivellini. Furniture includes 1993 Tatlin canapé (with Marco Cananzi) by Edra, 1994 Manta coffee table by Fiam, c. 2003 O chair by Arredaesse. He has written on design and architecture for magazines *Modo*, *Casa amica*, *Vogue*, and *L'atelier*; has lectured in seminars on the history of design and planning at Institut d'Art Visuel (IAV), Orléans; Istituto Superiore per le Industrie Artistiche (ISIA), Florence; ISIA, Faenza; Politecnico, Milan; Università del Progetto, Reggio Emilia; Istituto Europeo di Design, Milan. From c. 2001, lectures on design, Accademia di Belle Arti di Brera, Milan.
Citations 1993 Top Ten Prize (for Tatlin canapé), Düsseldorf, organized by Du Pont International; 1995 Young Design prize (Manta glass coffee table by Fiam).

Seng, Judith (1974–)
German designer; born Karlruhe.

Training 1995–2001 under Inge Sommer and 'Nick' Hans Roericht, industrial design, Hochschule der Künste, Berlin.
Biography 1998, Seng worked in the studio Industria, San Francisco; 1999 in Vogt + Weizenegger, Berlin, where she participated in the Die Imaginaire Manufaktur (DIM) project for products made by the blind/handicapped; worked in the Zeitgleich office, Berlin and, 2000, in the studio of Ronan and Erwan Bouroullec, Paris; 2001 under Achim Heine and Volker Albus, an assistant teacher, Hochschule der Künste, Berlin.
Exhibitions Work included in 1998–2001 Interieur biennials (exhibits of DIM), Courtrai; Galerie Néotù, Paris; Galeria Massimo di Carlo, Milan; 2001 *Barbe gesucht!* group exhibit, Designtransfergalerie, Berlin; 2001 Flügge group show, Berlin; *Talents*, 2001 Ambiente fair, Frankfurt.

Serré, Georges (1889–1956)
French ceramicist.

Training To 1902, apprenticeship at Manufacture Nationale de Sèvres; subsequently, traveled to Saigon to study *grès* Kmer ceramics.
Biography 1920, Serré established his own studio near the porcelain factory in Sèvres; with his friends Dejean, Gimond, Niclausse, and others, created sculpture. From 1922, Serré was encouraged by Émile Lenoble and Émile Decœur to turn to heavy stoneware and *chamotté* clay. He engraved his pieces in geometrical and simple motifs, sometimes highlighted by oxides and glazes.
Exhibitions Work shown at Salons of Société Décorateurs, frequently from 1923; 1925 *Exposition Internationale des Arts Décoratifs et Industriels Modernes*; Geo. Rouard store, Paris.
Bibliography Edgar Pelichet, *La céramique art déco*, Lausanne: Grand-Pont, 1988.

Serrurier-Bovy, Gustave (1858–1910)
Belgian architect and designer: born Liège.

Training Architecture, Académie des Beaux-Arts, Liège.
Biography Serrurier-Bovy was a follower of French architect Eugène-Emmanuel Viollet-le-Duc (1814–79). During an 1884 visit to Britain, he was introduced to the work of William Morris and the philosophy of John Ruskin, studied the Arts and Crafts movement, and thus was influenced by the movement, particularly C.F.A. Voysey's and A.H. Mackmurdo's work. Serrurier-Bovy abandoned his architectural practice to specialize in design and furniture making; 1884, opened a shop in Liège to sell Japanese, Persian, and Indian artifacts in a concession acquired from Liberty of London; 1886, opened a branch in Brussels. In Brussels on the rue de l'Université, he executed period and modern American and British interiors and sold Oriental objects and textiles; 1899, established a large furniture factory in Liège with a shop in Paris called L'Art dans l'Habitation; became a leading Belgian designer with a style of his own, which revealed inspiration from Japanese forms; typically incorporated the arched truss in his furniture.
Exhibitions 1896, organized *L'Oeuvre Artistique* in Liège, an international exposition of decorative arts to which the Glasgow School contributed a large number of exhibits. An interior for a study shown at the first (1894) installment of Salon de la Libre Esthétique and a worker's house at its 1895 edition; work at 1896 Arts and Crafts exhibition, London; 1896–1903, in the editions of Salon du Champ de Mars of Société Nationale des Beaux-Arts, Paris. Organized and designed the hall that housed the imports sections of the Tervueren colonial section at 1897 *Exposition Internationale*, Brussels; with architect René Dulong for the Pavillon Bleu, participated in 1900 *Exposition Universelle*, Paris;

participated in 1904 *Louisiana Purchase Exhibition*, St. Louis; showed a simple and innovative worker's home in the 1905, and created display stands for the 1904, 1905, and 1906 editions of Salon de l'Automobile, Paris; installed his own pavilion at 1910 *Exposition Internationale*, Brussels.
Bibliography Jacques-Grégoire Watelet, *Gustave Serrurier-Bovy, architecte et décorateur, 1858–1910*, Brussels: Palais des Académies, 1975; London: Lund Humphries, 1987. Jacques-Grégoire Watelet, *Gustave Serrurier-Bovy: à l'aube de l'esthetique industrielle*, Paris: Beaunord/Centre Wallonie-Bruxelles, 1989. Jacques-Grégoire Watelet, *L'œuvre d'une vie: Gustave Serrurier-Bovy architecte et décorateur liégeois, 1858–1910*, Alleur-Liège: Perron, 2001.

Sette, Gruppo
> See Gruppo Sette.

Sèvres, Manufacture Nationale de
French ceramics manufactory.

Biography The earliest ceramic wares in Vincennes were produced 1740–56. 1756, the Vincennes royal porcelain factory moved to Sèvres, closer to the royal court at Versailles; by 1758, employed more than 250 people; 1759, was taken over by King Louis XV's administrators. Its first duties under royal control were to provide crockery and china dinnerware for the royal household. 1876–97, Charles Lauth and Georges Vogt developed new and diverse porcelain applications that first appeared in 1880 and were shown at the 1884 Union Centrale des Arts Décoratifs exhibition. The new medium allowed for the use of almost every color nuance with certain motifs directly glazed with gold highlights. The factory was renowned for its range of blue colors, including *céleste*, *poudré*, *frotté*, *soufflé*, as well as lapis lazuli, yellow, and turquoise. Its original aim of imitating Meissen porcelain was transcended by issuing gem-like effects and *rocaille* flowers set on metal stems. At the end of 19th century, the Manufacture Nationale de Sèvres, as it became known, underwent structural changes, including divisions into artistic and technical departments. Alexandre Sandier, the director of the artistic department, had available to him four types of materials: soft-paste porcelain, stoneware, hard-paste porcelain, and Sèvres *pâte nouvelle* (one with a lower firing temperature than hard-paste porcelain); and perfected crystalline glazes (known before 1900 but always considered an unfortunate accident.) 1903–04, the factory commissioned new forms from Hector Guimard to be fully covered in crystalline glazes. Sandier made unglazed porcelain fashionable with models by Agathon Léonard inspired by Loïe Fuller at the 1900 Paris *Exposition*. Sèvres made the spherical perfume flacon of Lanvin's Argège perfume, by Armand Rateau, imprinted with Paul Iribe's gold image of Jeanne Lanvin and her daughter who are dressed for a ball. After a long hiatus, from 1960s the Sèvres management turned to contemporary designers. 1980s, Sèvres extended its practice to include private retailers and opened a showroom in Paris. The manufactory, having become known primarily for its staid historicist patterns, established an experimental workshop in 1983 for research in design to include French and foreign artists. Wares have included 1968 plate by Serge Poliakoff, 1983 *trompe-l'œil* box by Christian Renonciat, 1984 eccentric lamp by Adrian Saxe, 1987 figurines by Viola Fry, 1989 Elina frieze pattern by Bérnard Guillot, 1990 pieces by Bořek Šípek, and a cabinet in wood and Sèvres porcelain by Garouste et Bonetti. The firm is a member of the Comité Colbert.
Exhibitions Work shown at 1884 exhibition (new 1880 porcelain applications), of Union Centrale des Arts Décoratifs, Palais de l'Industrie; 1900 *Exposition Universelle* (Alexandre Sandier's new floral forms and glazes); 1925 *Exposition Internationale des Arts Décoratifs et Industriels Modernes* (modern pieces under Lechevalier-Chevignard's direction in Paris, including the introduction of a new high-temperature glass applicable to the production of glass lamp shades). Work subject of exhibitions of 19th-century porcelain in 1975 and an exhibition of 20th-century work in 1987, Musée National de Céramique, Sèvres; Desportes's drawings in 1982 exhibition and the work from 1740–93 in 1997 exhibition, Musée du Louvre, Paris; the work from 1800–47 in 1997 exhibition, Bard Graduate Center, New York (catalogs below).
Bibliography Cat., *Porcelaines de Sèvres au XIXe siècle* (Musée du Louvre), Paris: Musées Nationaux, 1975. Cat., *L'atelier de Desportes: dessins et esquisses conservés par la Manufacture nationale de Sèvres: LXXVIIe* (Musée du Louvre), Paris: Réunion des Musées Nationaux, 1982. Cat., Antoinette Fay-Hallé and Valérie Guillaume (eds.), *Porcelaines de Sèvres au XXe siècle*, Paris: Réunion des Musées Nationaux, 1987. Jean-Paul Midant, *Sèvres: la manufacture au XXème siècle*, Paris: Michel Aveline, 1992. Nicole Blondel and Tamara Préaud, *La Manufacture nationale de Sèvres: parcours du blanc à l'or*, Charenton: Flohic, 1996. Cat., Pierre Ennès with Brigitte Ducrot, *Un défi au goût: 50 ans de création à la Manufacture royale de Sèvres (1740–1793)* (Musée du Louvre), Paris: Réunion des Musées Nationaux, 1997. Cat., Derek E. Ostergard (ed.), *The Sèvres Porcelain Manufactory: Alexandre Brongniart and the Triumph of Art and Industry, 1800–1847*, New Haven, Conn.: Bard Graduate Center/Yale, 1997.

Seymour, Jerszy (1968–)
German product and furniture designer; born Berlin-Spandau; active Milan.

Training 1989, bachelor of science degree, engineering design, South Bank University; 1994, master's degree in industrial design, Royal College of Art, London.
Biography 1969 when he was one year old, Seymour was moved with his family to Canada; from 1970, lived in London; 1994, moved to Milan and for a time worked for Stefano Giovannoni; 1997, moved to New York and worked for Smart Design; 1998, moved to Paris; 1999, returned to, and established a studio in, Milan. Work combines humor not of the mainstream, and the innovative use of materials has included 1998 Captain Lovetray tray and 1999 Pipe Dreams watering can by Magis, and 1999 Playstation chaise/stool/table, 2001 Ken Kuts Murano-glass collection by Covo. Has also designed for Idée.
Exhibitions 2000 (1st) *Sputnik* exhibition (Captain Freewheelin' Franklin remote-controled tray); experimental project Bonnie & Clyde sofa/bed (full-size polyurethane-foam replica of 1985 Ford Escort coupé automobile), during 2001 Salone del Mobile, Milan. Work subject of 2002 *Playing*, Design Museum, London.

Seymour, Richard (1953–)
British designer.

Training Central School of Arts and Crafts; Royal College of Art; both London.
Biography Seymour has been the creative director for an advertising agency and freelance graphic designer on various advertising and product-development accounts; 1983 with Dick Powell, established the consultancy Seymour-Powell in London and designed for Norton (1987 police/military Commander and subsequent P55 Sport motorcycles) and for Tefal (successful line of household products, the first being 1987 Freeline cordless electric jug-kettle). A large consultancy today, other clients include Yamaha, Adidas, Adler, Aqualisa, Bajaj Electricals, BMW, Cadbury's, Calor, Casio, Clairol, Connolly, Daewoo, Dell, Dunlop, Jaguar, Le Creuset, Nokia, Norton, Philips, Tefal, Toyota, Tumi, Volvo, Waterman, Yamaha.
Bibliography Jeremy Myerson and Sylvia Katz, *Conran Design Guides: Tableware*, London: Conran Octopus, 1990: 78.

Sezession
> See Münchner Sezession; Wiener Sezession.

shagreen
Fish skin used as a veneer to cover furniture and accessories.

History Also known as *galuchat* and sharkskin, shagreen is the skin on the belly of the dogfish or shark; as a generic term, is used to describe untanned animal hides made with pebble-textured surfaces; was first made in the 17th century by Turkish and Persian herdsmen. *Galuchat* is named after Parisian craftsmen, a father and his sons named Galuchat, who made cases on the quai de l'Horloge and quai des Morjondus, Paris. Active in the 18th century, they softened and colored the skins of dogfish and sharks to cover the cases or sheaths of watches, scissors, razors, etc. British artisan John Paul Cooper specialized in unusual materials, especially shagreen, which he began using in 1903—some time before other Arts and Crafts practitioners began calling on the material and before it became popular in c. 1910, when it was used, after a long hiatus, by Clément Mère on toiletry boxes, sewing cases, and other small objects shown by him in the Paris Salons. By 1920s, Jacques-Émile Ruhlmann, Clément Rousseau, André Groult, Dominique, and other French designers used shagreen extensively, with exotic woods, on furniture. Jean-Michel Frank used it to cover whole furniture pieces. For application on furniture, the skin is soaked in a chlorine solution to bleach it, then scrubbed with a wire brush and a pumice stone to remove imperfections; is usually stained green by a copper-acetate solution but can be made pink, blue, or gray; is most effective on small objects, like those pro-

duced by Tiffany, Asprey, and Dunhill in 1920s–30s. Synthetic shagreen is available, though it is more expensive and less desirable than the real material.
Bibliography Jean Perfettini, *Le galuchat, un matériau mystérieux, une technique oubliée*, Dourdan: Vial, 1988. Alastair Duncan, 'Skin-Deep Beauty,' *Elle Decor*, May 1990: 40. De Caunes Lison Perf, *Galuchat*, Paris: Amateur, 1994.

Shaker furniture

Furniture produced by Shaker religious communities in US.

History Originating in England, 1747, the United Society of Believers in Christ's Second Appearance was a Christian sect whose ceremonies of worship included communal dancing, earning them the nicknames 'holy rollers,' 'Shaking Quakers,' or simply 'Shakers.' To escape religious persecution, a group led by Mother Ann Lee (1736–1784) settled in the US, establishing their first community in New Lebanon, N.Y., in 1787. Groups of celibate 'brothers' and 'sisters' spread to Maine, New Hampshire, Massachusetts, Rhode Island, Connecticut, New York State, Ohio, Indiana, and Kentucky. New members brought their own belongings from their motherland, including furniture. The earliest documented Shaker furniture made in the US is an 1806 case of drawers, although furniture-making almost certainly took place earlier. A pine case of drawers, inscribed 'Made by A.B. 1817,' may have been made by Anthony Brewster (1794–1838). Many of the furniture makers in the communities had been trained in cabinetmaking in England and were influenced by contemporary styles. The so-called Shaker style, developed from English country and farmhouse models, is known for its simplicity and lack of ornamentation, with built-into-wall cabinets, long trestle tables, wide-overhanging tabletops, and rocking chairs with thin vertical, curved rocker strips. Side chairs, when not in use, were hung on pegs attached to wall railings high above the floor, facilitating floor cleaning. 1887, Shaker cabinetmaker Orren N. Haskins asked, 'Why patronize the out side [sic] work or gugaws in our manufacture, when they will say we have enough of them abroad? We want a good plain substantial Shaker article, yea, one that bears credit to our profession & tells who and what we are, true and honest before the world, without hypocrisy or any false covering.' Crafts apprentices were trained by masters. The Shakers were tireless improvers of their material culture, with the motto 'hands to work and hearts to God'; their numerous inventions included the circular metal saw, automatic clothes-washing machine, and apple corer. Industrialization in the outside world, however, meant that the Shakers, who from an early date had made furniture commercially, could no longer produce goods that were competitively priced with machine-made products. The men were enticed into well-paid jobs outside the communities. With a lack of new members, communities began to close from late 19th to early 20th centuries. When the Mount Lebanon North Family community, the last of the groups, was closed in 1947, Sister Jennie Wells observed, 'Most of our visitors these days are antique collectors, and all they're interested in is buying up what little fine old handmade Shaker furniture we have left. Why, those people would grab the chairs right out from under us if we'd let them. Our furniture is very fashionable all of a sudden, you know... We're always being told how beautiful our things are. I don't say they aren't but that isn't what they were meant to be... All our furniture was ever meant to be was strong, light, and, above all, practical.'
Bibliography Edward Deming Andrews and Faith Andrews, *Religion in Wood: A Book of Shaker Furniture*, Bloomington: Indiana University, 1966. John Kassay, *Book of Shaker Furniture*, Amherst: University of Massachusetts, 1987. Jerry V. Grant and Douglas R. Allen, *Shaker Furniture Makers*, Hanover and London: University Press of New England, 1989. Timothy D. Rieman and Jean M. Burks, *The Complete Book of Shaker Furniture*, New York: Abrams, 1993. Edward Deming Andrews and Faith Andrews, *Masterpieces of Shaker Furniture*, New York: Dover, 1999. Timothy D. Rieman and Jean M. Burks, *Encyclopedia of Shaker Furniture*, Altgen, Pa.: Schiffer, 2003.

Sharp

Japanese electronics manufacturer.

History Tokuji Hayakawa (1894–1980) was a live-in apprentice to a metalworker of women's hair ornaments and precision metal products; 1912 while still an apprentice, invented a holeless Western-style belt buckle (inspired by a movie character who wore an untidy belt), which he named the Tokubijo (after his forename) and which became very popular. The same year (1912), he set up his own, small metalworking shop in Tokyo with only two employees; 1913, moved to Honjo to make patterned umbrella ferrules and the belt buckle; invented an adjustable flow faucet and received his second patent that year; 1914, moved again to a shop with a one-horse-power motor at a time when essentially all Japanese production was realized by hand; 1915, invented the Hayakawa mechanical pencil, patented in 1920 in Japan and patented in 1926 overseas, and established Hayakawa Brothers Shokai to specialize in the pencil's production. The name of the device was changed to the Ever-Ready Sharp Pencil and, subsequently, the Ever-Sharp Pencil. He established one of Japan's first assembly-line-production facilities and, by 1923, was employing 200 people. His wife and children died in, and the factory was destroyed by, the 1923 Great Kanto Earthquake. 1924, the plant was re-established in Osaka, and, 1925, developed Japan's first radio set. Innovative electronics that followed included 1931 Dyne Type 31 (with a newly developed horn speaker) and 1932 Dyne Fuji Type 33 (with a magnetic speaker). 1936, the company was renamed Hayakawa Metal Works; 1941, was requisitioned by the Japanese Army; 1942, was returned to its original name, Hayakawa Electric Industry. After World War II, the firm faced bleak financial prospects; however, was able to recover with the introduction of 1949 PR-2 portable radio and, particularly, 1951 Super Radio Set. 1953, first commerical mass production of TV sets began with TV3–14T model, ahead of others in Japan but priced at 36 times the average monthly salary of a Japanese worker with a secondary-school education. 1955, Hayakawa Electric Industry began making home appliances; 1956, established Sharp Electric as a wholesale entity; introduced its first color TV set, 1960 CV-2101, and the world's first transitor radio, 1961 BX-361 with solar cells; 1961, established the Central Research Laboratories; introduced the first Japanese microwave oven, R-10, produced from 1962, when Sharp Electronics Corporation established its first overseas sales subsidiary, in New York. 1960s, a number of advanced electronics were developed, including the world's first all-transitor electronic calculator, in 1964, and the world's first microwave oven with a turntable, 1966 R-600. 1970, the name was changed from Hayakawa Electric Industry to Sharp Corporation. Introduced 1972 SF-201 (the first wet-toner photocopier), 1972 Bill Pet (the first in-store sales terminal in Japan), 1973 EL-805 (the world's-first electronic calculator with an LED), 1975 EL-8009 compact electronic calculator, 1977 EL-8130 (the world's first card-size sensor-touch electronic calculator, 3/16" /5mm thick), 1977 1 3/16"/30mm-thick TV; 1977, Japan's first word processor, an electronic translator, and a voice-activated calculator; 1978 world's first two-channel TV picture tube; 1981 MZ-80B personal computer; 1982, world's first PC TV. 1977, the company became the first to successfully mass produce thin-film EL panels; 1985, introduced 3-D CAD (computer-aided design)/CAM (computer-aided manufacturing) systems; 1986 RE-102 toaster/microwave oven and SJ-30R7 cooking refrigerator; 1987 LED TV set and 3C-E1 Crystaltron 3-in. color TV; 1988, world's first 14-in. color TFT LCD (1 1/16"/27mm thick); 1990 UX-1 (the world's thinnest home fax machine); 1992 VL-HL1 LCD ViewCam (with numerous world's-first features) and, by 1990, had produced one million of them, and 50 million microwave ovens; 1990 Handkerchief television designed by Emilio Ambasz; 1994, the world's largest TFT LCD color TV (21 in.) and, 1995, again the world's largest (28 in.); 1999 VN-EZ1 Internet ViewCam; 1999 RE-M210 (the world's-first Internet-compatible microwave oven); 2001, TVs designed by Toshiyuki Kita; 2001, PC-MT1-H1/H1S (the world's thinnest and lightest PC notebook). Designers in-house include Nobuhiro Fujii (1968–), who studied at University of Tsukuba, who joined Sharp in 1993, for home-appliance design.
Citations 1993 Nikkei Product and Service Excellence Award; 1993–96 grand prizes, Best New Products Awards, *Nikkan Kogyo Shimbun* newspaper; 1993 and 1994 One of Best Companies and Products in Japan, *Weekly Diamond* magazine; 1994 Company of the Year, Toyo Keizai Awards; 1994 Trend Product Award and 1996 Best Product Award, *Dime* magazine; 1994 Gold Award, *Mono* magazine.
Bibliography Michele De Lucchi (ed.), *The International Design Yearbook*, London: Laurence King, 2001. Mel Byars, *On/Off: New Electronic Products*, New York: Universe, 2001: 76–79, 88. www.sharp-world.com/corporate/info.

Shapland & Petter

British cabinetmaker; located Barnstaple, Devon.

History Cabinetmaker Henry Shapland (b. 1823) founded the company; 1848, traveled to the US and was inspired by a wave-molding-machine invention and made meagre notes about it because he was only allowed to see it if he immediately left the US; as a result, estab-

lished a cabinet-making business at Raleigh wool mill, Pilton, 1854. Henry Petter, an accountant, became Shapland's partner. 1864, they bought the Raleigh factory which made to-order woodwork for shops, hotels, and banks, and mantels, stairs, and panels; fitted out Guildhall in London and Tapeley Park in north Devon, among others; supplied furniture to the Liberty and Waring & Gillow stores; employed workers after they served a seven-year apprenticeship and attended classes at Barnstaple School of Art; during World War I, made wooden airplane propellers for the Royal Flying Corps; after the war, turned from expensive hand-carved furniture to veneered work in an Art Déco style and furnished Pullman train carriages and oceanliners, but still hand-carved furniture for churches; 1924, merged with Barnstaple Cabinet Company, forming a large firm of up to 350 employees at various times.
Bibliography Information from Alison Mills, Museum of Barnstaple/North Devon, for *British Design*, London: Phillips, 25 Sept. 2001: lot 11.

Shchekotikhina-Pototskaia, Aleksandra Vasil'evna (1892–1967)

Russian designer of ceramics and book illustrator; wife of Ivan Bilibin, an artist and book illustrator.

Training Under Nikolai Roerich and Ivan Bilibin, Society for the Encouragement of the Arts, St. Petersburg.
Biography Shchekotikhina-Pototskaia designed costumes for the theater and participated in two Sergei Diaghilev productions of Les Ballets Russes. She was influenced by Russian icon art and disregarded perpective in her 1918–23 porcelain pieces for the State Porcelain Factory, St. Petersburg; 1923 with her husband and son Mstislav, settled in Alexandria. After visiting 1925 *Exposition Internationale des Arts Décoratifs et Industriels Modernes*, Paris, she lived there to 1936 and decorated porcelain made at Manufacture Nationale de Sèvres and factories in Limoges; 1936, returned to the Soviet Union; 1936–53, was active as a porcelain painter again at the State Porcelain Factory, Leningrad.
Bibliography Nina Lobanov-Rostovsky, *Revolutionary Ceramics*, London: Studio Vista, 1990. Ian Wardropper et al., *News from a Radiant Future: Soviet Porcelain*, Chicago: Art Institute of Chicago, 1992.

Shelley Potteries

British ceramics manufacturer; located Longton, Staffordshire.

History One story is that Wileman & Co. was a business at the Foley Pottery in Fenton, with Henry Wileman as its proprietor. Another is that Randle Shelley (1706–81) established a pottery in 1748. Information confirmed is that Joseph B. Shelley, who may have been related to Randle Shelley, became a partner of Henry Wileman in 1867. On Wileman's 1870 retirement, Shelley became the sole proprietor. An earthenware facility, adjunct to the factory, was closed, and only china was made, with wares featuring white or gold-line borders, produced to 1880s. 1881, Joseph's son Percy Shelley, who was university educated, joined the firm and introduced more elaboratore wares. Percy visted 1893 *World's Columbian Exposition*, Chicago, and re-cognized the value the American market would offer, and began the production of china dinnerware. And he thus commissioned artists to paint landscapes and animals on dinner plates for US export. 1896, Percy succeeded his father as the proprietor. At another facility, ornamental earthenware and underglaze-painted ware (called Intarsio) began to be made, with designs by artistic director Frederick Rhead. Other designers followed, such as Walter Slater (trained under Léon Arnoux at Minton, and at Doultons). His 1901–37 work contributed to Shelley's burgeoning favorable reputation. 1913 and soon after, Shelley's three sons joined the firm. c. 1925, Folley China became Shelley China, due to 'Foley China' not being able to be registered as a tradename. 1929, the firm Shelley Potteries Ltd. became a private limited company. and adopted the title of Shelley Potteries, Ltd. 1928, Eric Slater succeeded his father Walter as the artistic director; he had been at Foley since 1919. Eric's circle-pattern 1932 Regent shape and 1935 Vogue ceramics dinner set, with colorful geometric trim on triangular and square shapes were representative of Shelley's work at the time. (These and other more severe geometric Art Déco images and shapes are the ones for which Shelley is best known today.) On Percy's 1937 death, two of his living sons became the directors. At the end of World War II when restrictions on production were lifted, new products were quickly developed, with much of them exported. From 1948, the decorators were primarily women, having been hired directly from schools, and sophisticated machinery for efficient production was installed. 1966, Shelley Potteries ceased production, and the factory became a part of the Doulton Group, which began production of Royal Albert China. 1971, Allied English Potteries was merged with the Doulton Group, and Shelley became a Doulton brand.
Bibliography Cat., *Thirties: British Art and Design Before the War*, London: Arts Council of Great Britain/Hayward Gallery Gallery, 1979. Chris Watkins et al., *Shelley Potteries: The History and Production of a Staffordshire Family of Potters*, London: Barrie & Jenkins, 1980. Robert Prescott-Walker, *Collecting Shelley Pottery*, London: Francis Joseph, 1999.
> See Slater, Eric.

Shérif
> See Chérif.

Sheringham, George (1884–1937)

British interior and textile designer and decorative painter.

Training Painting, Slade School of Fine Art, London; and in Paris.
Biography Originally a painter, Sheringham was designing fans and silk panels by 1911; became best known as a theater designer, particularly for his work at the Lyric Theatre, Hammersmith, London, where he designed sets and costumes; produced numerous watercolor designs for fans; designed carpets and textiles by John Crossley and by Seftons, as well as posters, advertising, and book illustrations for others; was a successful architectural decorator and became known for the 1931 ballroom of Claridges hotel, London.
Bibliography G.E. Goodman, 'Notes on Decor: George Sheringham and the English School,' *The Dancing Times*, Nov. 1931: 169–71; ibid., 'Notes on Decor: The Camargo Season,' July 1932 (part 1): 365–367 and Aug. 1932 (part 2): 449+. Fiona MacCarthy and Patrick Nuttgens, *An Eye for Industry*, London: Lund Humphries with Royal Society for Arts, 1986. Valerie Mendes, *The Victoria & Albert Museum's Textile Collection: British Textiles from 1900 to 1937*, London: Victoria and Albert Museum, 1992.

Shindo, Hiroyuki (1941–)

Japanese textile designer; born Tokyo.

Training Kyoto City University of Arts.
Biography Shindo is a major designer of textiles, known for his refined approach and technical expertise; from 1997, has been the head of the textile department, Kyoto College of Art and Design; has extensively explored the range of possibilities of natural indigo dye. His work is realized through controlled dye baths that produce grades of the color blue, exemplified by his 1995 Indigo Thread Balls.
Exhibitions Work included in numerous exhibitions in France, India, and Israel; museum collections; and 1999 exhibition, New York and St. Louis (catalog below).
Bibliography Cat., Cara McCarty and Matilda McQuaid, *Structure and Surface: Contemporary Japanese Textiles*, New York: Abrams/The Museum of Modern Art, 1999.

Shiner, Cyril James (1908–)

British craftsperson and teacher; active Birmingham.

Training Under Bernard Cuzner, in Birmingham; Royal College of Art, London.
Biography Shiner was a liveryman of The Worshipful Company of Goldsmiths, where he rendered a number of formal works, including maces, medals of honor, and church plate; produced utilitarian ware, including boxes and small objects; became a freelance designer; 1930s, taught in Birmingham and designed hollow-ware by Wakely and Wheeler, London.
Bibliography Cat., *Thirties: British Art and Design Before the War*, London: Arts Council of Great Britain/Hayward Gallery, 1979. Annelies Krekel-Aalberse, *Art Nouveau and Art Déco Silver*, New York: Abrams, 1989.

Shire, Peter (1947–)

American designer; born Los Angeles; active Echo Park, California; born of an artist father.

Training To 1970, Chouinard Art Institute, Los Angeles.
Biography Prior to 1980s, Shire's work was one-of-a-kind, including glassware at Mauro Albarelli's Vistosi firm, suggesting Murano glass as lively shapes verging on sculpture. He became known for his unusual and widely varied ceramic teapots. 1981, Ettore Sottsass invited Shire to participate in the first collection of Memphis, for which

Shire designed eccentric, geometrical furniture in Pop art colors and kinetic shapes. His designs for Memphis include 1981 Brazil table, 1982 Peninsula table, 1982 Anchorage silver and lacquer teapot, 1983 Hollywood side table, 1985 Cahuenga floor lamp, 1985 Laurel table lamp, 1986 Big Sur sofa, and 1987 Peter sideboard. His multicolored 1982 Bel Air upholstered armchair was widely published as being representative of the Memphis approach. Independent of the Memphis activities, he designed a 1989 63-piece collection of furniture and furnishings made in Italy. Seguso Vetri d'Arte (Italy) produced his 1991 glass designs; Rossi & Arcandi (Italy) his work in silver; and Acme Studio (Maui, Hawaii, US) his Smudgestick pen (more an example of sculpture on a pedestal than a writing instrument) and jewelry.
Exhibitions Numerous venues, including his first one-person show in 1975, and international exhibitions from 1989.
Bibliography Julie V. Iovine, *Metropolitan Home*, Aug. 1989: 33. Auction cat., *Memphis: la collection Karl Lagerfeld*, Monaco: Sotheby's, 13 Oct. 1991. Hunter Drohojowska, *Tempest in a Teapot: The Ceramic Art of Peter Shire*, New York: Rizzoli, 1991.

Shirk, Helen (1942–)
American metalworker, born Buffalo, N.Y.

Training 1963, bachelor's degree, Skidmore College, Saratoga Springs, N.Y.; master's degrees: 1963–64 Kunsthåndværkerskolen, Copenhagen, and 1969, Indiana University, Bloomington.
Biography Shirk has become known for her metal bowls and vessels; has been a professor of art, San Diego State University, Cal.; resides in Philadelphia. Work has appeared in a number of books and journals.
Exhibitions/citations Work included in a large number of exhibitions, and subject of others, in the US and Europe. Received 1963 Fulbright Grant for study in Denmark; 1978 and 1988 Craftsman's Fellowships, National Endowment for the Arts, US; 1999, elected a fellow, American Craft Council.
Bibliography Albrecht Bangert and Karl Michael Armer, *80s Style: Designs of the Decade*, New York: Abbeville, 1990: 235. *Dictionnaire international du bijou*, Paris: Regard, 1998. Arata Isozaki (ed.), *The International Design Yearbook*, New York: Abbeville, 1998

Shukhaev, Vassilii (1887–1973)
Russian teacher, painter, and graphic, theater, and cinema artist; born Moscow.

Training 1897–1905 under Konstantin Korovin, Stroganov School of Applied Art, Moscow; 1906–12, Highest Arts School of Painting, Sculpture and Architecture, St. Petersburg.
Biography Initially, Shukhaev lived and worked in Moscow and St. Petersburg; from 1922, in Paris; 1935, returned to the USSR and was arrested and was interned in Magadan labour camp from 1937–47. From 1947, he lived in Tbilisi, Georgia, where he taught art. He was a protagonist of 20th-century Russian neoclassicism and a highly accomplished draftsperson; designed stage sets for theaters and caberets; painted portraits of literary, theatrical, and artistic celebrities of his time; died in Tbilisi.
Exhibitions From 1909.

Siard, Marcello (1939–)
Italian designer; born Trieste; active Padua.

Biography Siard designed plastic furniture by Kartell (1966 no. 4950 modular wall shelf in ABS) and by Longato Arredamenti (plastic seat and 1970 Game no. 1030 mobile bar/table in ABS), as well as the Ring table range, department store shelving, and plastic seating by others; 1962, became a member, Associazione per il Disegno Industriale (ADI); teaches, Scuola Italiana Design, Padua.
Exhibitions/citations 1972 *Italy: The New Domestic Landscape* (showing modular shelf by Kartell), The Museum of Modern Art, New York. Entered public furniture in 1962 (1st) International Furniture Design Competition. First prize, 1962 Domus Inox national competition; first prize, 1964 national furniture competition, Trieste fair.
Bibliography *ADI Annual 1976*, Milan: Associazione per il Disegno Industriale, 1976.

Sicard, Jacques (1865–1923)
French ceramicist; active Golfe-Juan, Amiens, and Zanesville, Ohio.

Biography Sicard was associated with potter Clément Massier in Golfe-Juan, near Cannes, where he learned the *reflets-métalliques* process; 1901, was hired by Weller Pottery in the US, encouraged by the popularity of Tiffany's Favrile glass and European iridescent pottery; with French assistant Henri Gellie, secretly experimented with metallic lusters that were later marketed as thrown and molded Sicardo Ware by Weller and sold at Tiffany's in 1903. 1907 when he and Gellie returned to France, iridescent pottery production was discontinued. To 1914, Sicard worked in his own pottery in Amiens.
Exhibitions Sicardo Ware included in the Weller stand, 1902 *Louisiana Purchase Exposition*, St. Louis; 1972 *The Arts and Crafts Movement in America, 1876–1916*, Princeton University Art Museum.
Bibliography Cat., Robert Judson Clark (ed.), *The Arts and Crafts Movement in America, 1876–1916*, Princeton: Princeton University, 1976. Diane Chalmers Johnson, *American Art Nouveau*, New York: Abrams, 1979: 123, no. 165. *American Art Pottery*, New York: Cooper-Hewitt National Design Museum, 1987: 106.

Sidet, Olivier (1965–)
> See Radi Designers.

Siedhoff-Buscher, Alma (1899–1944)
German designer.

Training Bauhaus.
Biography Buscher is best known for the 1923 child's toy blocks she designed while at the Bauhaus Weimar. Today it is produced by Naef Spiele in Zöfingen, Switzerland. Testament to the Bauhaus's acceptace of women in all fields, Marianne Brandt was active in its metal workshop, and Alma Buscher likewise in its cabinetmaking workshop. Buscher, the only woman in the carpentry section while the Bauhaus was in Weimar, called on cabinetmaking techniques to experiment and innovate. She also later conducted research into the play of children, which contributed to her designs for their toys and furniture. The Buscher children's furniture was some of the first Bauhaus products to be embraced by the public.
Bibliography Gillian Naylor, *The Bauhaus Reassessed: Sources and Design Theory*, New York: Dutton, 1985.

Siegel, Gustav (1880–1970)
Austrian furniture and graphic designer.

Training In cabinetmaking; from 1897, Kunstgewerbeschule; both Vienna.
Biography 1899, Siegel was appointed by Felix Kohn, the president of J. & J. Kohn, as head of its design department. Siegel and Otto Wagner were responsible for Kohn's production of early Art Nouveau furniture models, as well as subsequent modern forms. Siegel created some of Kohn's graphic design, including advertisements that were published in 1904–08 Wiener Sezession exhibition catalogs. Certain well-known Kohn pieces attributed to others such as Josef Hoffmann may rather have been designed by Siegel, particularly the 728/F tub chair and 728 shell chair installed in Hoffmann's Kabaret Fledermaus, and 728/C settee. Siegel's 415/F chair, 415/2 settee, and 1015 plant stand incorporated the same wooden-ball elements as those on Kabaret Fledermaus furniture.
Exhibition Work by Kohn shown at 1900 *Exposition Universelle*, Paris.
Bibliography Graham Day, 'The Development of the Bent-Wood Furniture Industry, 1869–1914,' in Derek E. Ostergard (ed.), *Bent Wood and Metal Furniture 1850–1946*, New York: The American Federation of Arts, 1987.

Siegel, Robert (1939–)
American architect; active New York.

Biography 1968, Siegel joined the architecture partnership of Charles Gwathmey and Richard Henderson. 1970 with Gwathmey, Siegel restructured his own practice into its present form: Gwathmey, Siegel and Associates, New York. Their furniture designs (desks and credenza) were produced by Knoll and tapestry by V'Soske. From mid-1980s, the team designed ceramics and glass (Anniversary, Chicago, and Tuxedo dinnerware, Courtney vase and candlestick, and dinnerware for American Airlines) by Swid Powell. Architectural commissions included 1992 addition/renovation of Solomon R. Guggenheim Museum, New York, and extensive residences, apartment buildings, and a number of college/university structures and campus planning worldwide. Interior design: The Capital Group, Los Angeles, 1993; Public Plaza and Atrium, Citicorp Tower, New York, 1997; EMI offices, New York, 1992; McCann-Erickson Worldwide, New York, 1989; and a large number of others.

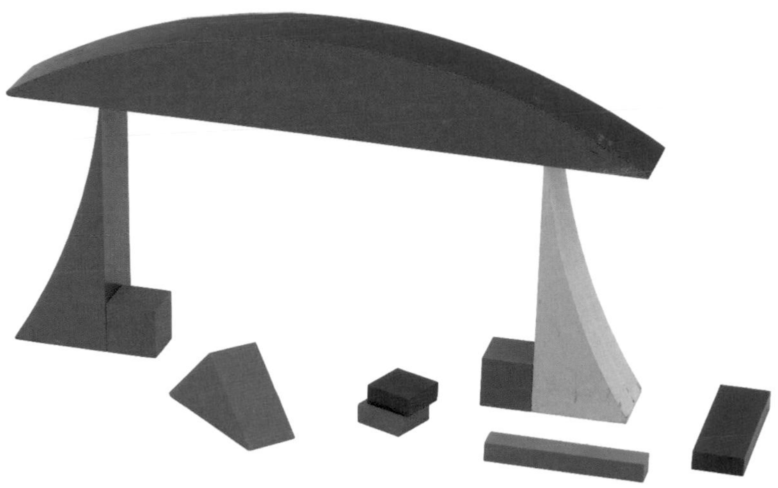

Alma Siedhoff-Buscher. Building blocks. 1923. Painted wood, configuration shown. Mfr.: Kurt Naef, Switzerland. Gift of the mfr. MoMA.

Citations By 1990, the partnership had received over 50 design awards, including 1981 gold medal (New York chapter) and 1982 National Architecture Firm Award, American Institute of Architects (AIA).
Bibliography Stanley Abercrombie: *Gwathmey Siegel*, New York: Whitney, 1981. Christine Pittel, 'The Hand of Geometry,' *Elle Decor*, Mar. 1991: 44–55. Brad Collins (ed.), *Gwathmey Siegel: Buildings and Projects 1965–2000*, New York: Universe, 2000. Paul Goldberger et al., *Gwathmey Siegel Houses*, New York: Monacelli, 2000.
> See Gwathmey, Charles.

Siégel, Victor-Napoléon (1870–1958)

Canadian businessman; active Paris.

Biography 1867, the Stockman mannequin firm was established in Paris. Siégel, who became known as the 'mannequin king,' much later joined Fred Stockman to form the firm Siégel & Stockman. Mid-1920s, René Herbst, the artistic advisor to Siégel, had an appreciable influence on the firm's work. André Vigneau—a musician, sculptor, and photographer—was the artistic director. 1927, Lucie Holt Le Son, an American working in Paris, produced mannequin bodies and panels for the firm. Other designers included Desmeures. The firm's innovations included *Cerolaque* (a wax-and-lacquer material) and a felt composition used for the construction of mannequins. Some 1920s–30s models included the likenesses of men, women, and children in realistic as well as stylized interpretations, and abstract sculptural forms and purely functional display racks. From 1927, mannequins in glass and wood were produced. By this date, Siégel operated 67 factories with branch offices in New York, Amsterdam, Copenhagen, Sydney, Stockholm, and Madrid, and a very large workshop in Saint-Ouen, France. 1927, *Vogue* magazine and its stylists, including Peter Woodruff, designed mannequins for Siégel. The firm is active today.
Exhibitions/citations Work shown at annual Salons of Société des Artistes Décorateurs and installments of Salon d'Automne, both Paris First prize for Siégel pavilion designed by Herbst (with contributions by Vigneau, Georges Polez, Léon Leyritz, Fernand Labathe, Camille Liausu, Francis Thomas, Bross, Jean Gougeon, and Herbst himself) at 1925 *Exposition Internationale des Arts Décoratifs et Industriels Modernes*, Paris.
Bibliography Alastair Duncan, *Art Nouveau and Art Déco Lighting*, New York: Simon & Schuster, 1978: 172. Nicole Parrot, *Mannequins*, Paris: Colona, 1981; London: Academy, 1982.
www.siegel-stockman.com.
> See Imans, Pierre.

Sieger, Dieter (1938–)

German industrial designer; born Münster; active Sassenberg.

Training To 1964, architecture, Werkkunstschule, Dortmund.
Biography 1965, Sieger opened his own architecture office, Münster; 1965–76, designed terraced and single-family houses in Greece, Spain, France, the US, and Saudi Arabia; 1976–82, designed sailing and motorboat interiors; from 1980, active in industrial and exhibition design; 1988, moved to Schloß Harkotten; 1991, established Sieger Design Consulting; is a member, architects' chamber in Nordrhein-Westphalen; 1997–2000 was president, Deutsche Designer Club (DDC). Today, the firm is a large multi-disciplinary essentially family agency with clients, including Alape, Arzberg, Deutsche Bahn (German railway), Dornbracht, Duravit, Hoesch, Ritzenhoff, Sony, Stiebel Eltron, and WMF; is managed by partners Dieter Sieger, Christian Sieger (1965–), and Michael Sieger (1968–). Design work has included architecture, sanitary fittings, own-brand watches, graphics/trademarks, interiors, heaters, glassware, cutlery, ceramics, packaging, and public seating.
Exhibitions/citations Work subject of 1994–95 *Dieter Sieger, Architekt, Schiffsbauer, Designer*, Stadtmuseum, Münster. Received 2002 Red Dot Best of the Best (e-Mote electronic faucets by Dornbracht), Design Zentrum Nordrhein-Westfalen, Essen.
Bibliography Christian W. Thomsen, *Dieter Sieger: Architekt–Schiffsbauer–Designer*, Tübingen: Wasmuth, 1994. Christian W. Thomsen, *Sieger Design: Strategien des Erfolgs = Strategies of Success*, Tübingen: Wasmuth, 2002.

Siemens

German electromechanical manufacturer.

History 1847, engineer/inventor Werner von Siemens (Lenthe 1816–Berlin 1892), mechanic Johann Georg Halske (Hamburg 1814–Berlin 1890), and Werner's cousin Johann Georg Siemens founded 'Telegraphen Bau-Anstalt Siemens & Halske' (or 'Telegraphen-Bauanstall von Siemens & Halske–Siemens & Halske' telegraph building company) in Berlin. Within decades, it quickly became an important force in the electrical industry, growing from a small electromechanical workshop to an early pioneer in telegraphy and public transports and today's huge electrotechnical entity with operations worldwide. Its initial success was spurred by commissions from Russia, with first contacts being made two years after Siemens's founding, for telegraph equipment and installations, including 1912 dynamo plant in St. Petersburg. However, with the 1917 Russian Revolution, Siemens's Russian operations were nationalized. Even so, Siemens workers designed 1926–32 Moscow subway (underground system) and other Russian installations, up to today. 1919, the firm established Osram incandescent-bulb company; 1935, constructed the TV set of Telefunken (owning 50% of the firm); 1939, built the production version of the electronic microscope; 1944–52, constructed the electron accelerator; the world's first cardiac pacemaker (implanted in a patient in 1958); 1959, the world's first mass-produced transistorized universal computers; 1980, developed the world's first telephone exchange with digital electronic switching. Entered the domestic electrical applicance arena with the 1957 founding of Siemens-Electrogeräte and the 1967 founding of Bosch-Siemens. Distinguished product-design consultants have included Franco Albini, Achille Castiglioni, Eric Chan, Franco Clivio, Stefano Giovannoni, Roberto Menghi, MM Design Studio, Arnaldo Poloni, Giovanni Sacchi, Schlagheck Design, Richard

Siemens & Halske. Household payphone with lockable coin-money drawer. 1920s. Bakelite, steel, and sheet steel, 7 1/16 x 6 x 9 1/2" (18 x 15.3 x 24.5 cm). Mfr.: Siemens & Halske, Germany. Courtesy Quittenbaum Kunstauktionen, Munich.

Sapper, and Marco Zanuso Sr., as well as a number of others who have worked or are working as in-house designers or design directors.
Bibliography Georg Siemens, *History of the House of Siemens: 1847–1914/The Era of Free Enterprise, vol.1; 1914–1945/The Era of World Wars*, Freiburg/Munich: Alber, 1957. J.D. Scott, *Siemens Brothers 1858–1958: An Essay in the History of Industry*, London: Weidenfeld & Nicholson, 1958. Wilfried Feldenkirchen (ed.), *150 Jahre Siemens: Das Unternehmen von 1847 bis 1997*, Munich: Siemens AG, 1997.

Sierakowski, Piotr (1957–)

Polish furniture and lighting designer; born Warsaw.

Training Industrial design, École Nationale Supérieure des Arts Visuels de La Cambre (national school for visual arts), Brussels.
Biography Sierakowski is best known for lighting; designed the Copernicus sconce, 1986 Nautilus floor light, numerous other lighting fixtures, and, with Martine Bedin, a collection of tabletop accessories by Koch + Lowy. 1992, Sierakowski, Bedin, and Mathilde Brétillot opened small production firm Manufacture Familiale, near Bordeaux; designed wooden lamps by Baldinger in the ADA collection, including 1996 Surf model.
Bibliography Albrecht Bangert and Karl Michael Armer, *80s Style: Designs of the Decade*, New York: Abbeville, 1990: 105, 236.

Siesbye, Alev Ebüzziya (1938–)

Turkish ceramicist and glass- and metalware designer; born Istanbul; active Copenhagen and Paris.

Training 1956–58, sculpture, Valtion Kuvataideakatemia (state academy of fine art); Füreya'a Ceramic Workshop; both Istanbul.
Biography 1958–60, Siesbye was a production worker at Dümler & Breiden in Höhr-Grenzhausen; 1960–62, at Eczacebasi Ceramic Factory in Istanbul; 1963–68, at Royal Copenhagen porcelain manufactory. 1969, she established her own studio in Copenhagen; from 1988 in Paris, worked freelance for clients, including Rosenthal from 1975; became known for her ceramics's pure shapes and rigorously rendered matt-enamel surfaces in blues and violets; combined Danish forms with the luminous colors of Iznik ceramics and Middle Eastern textiles.
Exhibitions Work first shown at 1982 *Koloristerne*, Copenhagen; 1987, FIAC governmental collection, Grand Palais, Paris; 1989 *L'Europe des Céramistes*, Auxerre, France; 1989 *Scandinavian Ceramics and Glass*, Victoria and Albert Museum, London; and extensively internationally, including 1997 *Dansk Keramik 1850–1997*, Sophienhölm, Denmark.
Bibliography Jennifer Hawkins Opie, *Scandinavia: Ceramics and Glass in the Twentieth Century*, New York: Rizzoli, 1989. Cat., *Collection Fina Gomez: 30 ans de céramique contemporaine*, Paris: Musée des Arts Décoratifs, 1991: 120.

Sigheaki, Asahara (1948–)

Japanese product designer; born Tokyo.

Training 1967, in Turin, Italy.
Biography From 1972, Sigheaki worked as a freelance industrial designer in Tokyo; 1976, settled in Italy and worked at Studio Abaco; from 1979, was active as a freelance industrial designer in Tokyo and Italy. Clients have included Lucitalia for which he designed 1993 Kri hanging lamp.
Exhibitions Work included in 1981 *Dal Design all'Habitat*, Bari, Italy; 1982 *Diseni Esecutivi e Designers*, Pesaro; 1983 exhibition of design, Brooklyn Museum of Art, N.Y.; 1992 *Design Zentrum München*, Deutsches Museum, Munich. 1984, 1991–95 awards, Industrie Forum Design (iF), Hanover; 1989 G-Mark Good Design award (for Small Industries), Japanese Industrial Design Promotion Organization (JIDPO).
Bibliography Mel Byars, *50 Lights...*, Hove: RotoVision, 1997: 20–21.

Sigla
> See Bani, Marina.

Siimes, Aune (1909–1964)

Finnish ceramicist.

Training To 1932, Taideteollinen korkeakoulu, Helsinki.
Biography From 1932 to her death, Siimes worked at Arabia pottery, Helsinki, on stoneware and porcelain; became known for pieces that were delicate and egg-shell thin.
Exhibitions/citations Silver medal, 1937 *Exposition Internationale des Arts et Techniques dans la Vie Moderne*, Paris; 1951 (9th) (gold medal) and 1954 (10th) (silver medal) editions of Triennale di Milano. Work shown at 1954–57 *Design in Scandinavia*, touring the US; 1955 *H 55*, Hälsingborg; 1956–57 *Finnish Exhibition*, touring West Germany; 1961 *Finlandia* in Zürich, Amsterdam, and London.
Bibliography Oili Mäki, *Taide ja työ/Finnish Designers of Today: Savi, lanka, lasi suomalaisen taiteilijan kädessä*, Helsinki: Söderström, 1954. Jennifer Hawkins Opie, *Scandinavia: Ceramics and Glass in the Twentieth Century*, New York: Rizzoli, 1989.

Sika, Jutta (1877–1964)

Austrian ceramicist and glassware designer; born Linz.

Training Under Koloman Moser, Kunstgewerbeschule, Vienna.
Biography With Robert Holubetz and Antoinette Krasnik, Sika is considered to be of the 'Schule Moser' or in the manner of Koloman Moser, which is typified by her 1901–02 porcelain service by Wiener Porzellan-Manufaktur, Josef Böck (with highly abstract flower decoration, with

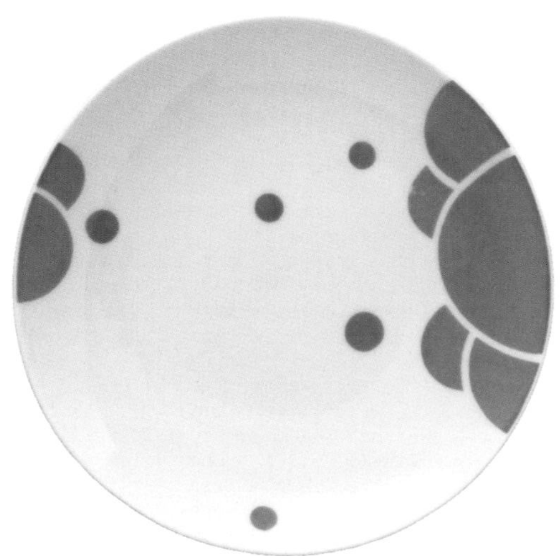

Jutta Sika. Plate. 1901–02. Porcelain and enamel, stenciled decoration, 1 1/8 x 7 1/2" (2.9 x 19.1 cm). Mfr.: Wiener Porzellan-Manufaktur, Josef Böck, Austria. Gift of Jo Carole and Ronald S. Lauder. MoMA.

'Rex' Reginald C. Silver. Flower bowl. 1903. Pewter, h. 5 7/8 x dia. 10" (15 x 25.4 cm). Mfr.: Silver Studio, UK. Phyllis B. Lambert Fund. MoMA.

Antoinette Krasnik, also a former Moser pupil). Sitka and Krasnik designed glassware by E. Bakalowits & Söhne of Vienna (which closed in c. 1914) and, c. 1910 under Moser, by Loetz. Sika also painted canvases. She died in Vienna.
Bibliography Günther Feuerstien, *Vienna—Present and Past: Arts and Crafts—Applied Art—Design*, Vienna: Jugend und Volk, 1976: 35, 81. Cat., *Women in Design*, Stuttgart: Design Center, 1989: 42–43.

Silex Co.
> See Wolcott, Frank E.

Silva Dias, Pedro (1963–)
Portuguese designer.

Training 1987, degree in product design, Faculty of Fine Art, University of Lisbon.
Biography Silva Dias taught, Universidade Técnica de Lisboa; Universidade do Porto; and, from 1996, Universidade de Lisboa. He designed a new public telephone for Portugal Telecom, signage program for Aeroporto de Lisboa, and the widely published 2002 Alcatifa (carpet) chair by Altamira in Lisbon.
Exhibitions From 1987, work shown in Portugal and abroad.

Silver, Arthur (1853–1896)
British designer and silversmith; born Reading; active London; father of Reginald and Harry Silver.

Training 1869–72 Reading School of Art; 1872 under H.W. Batley, apprenticeship in London.
Biography 1880, Silver established his own studio in London; designed and produced wallpaper, textiles, carpets, and linoleum; was commissioned by Liberty to provide wallpaper, chintz, and cretonne designs. Into 1960s, the studio's other cleints included G.P. & J. Baker, Arthur Sanderson, and John Line.
Bibliography > See Silver Studio.

Silver, Dr. Spence (1941–)
> See Fry, Arthur.

Silver Studio; 'Rex' Reginald C. Silver (1879–1965); Harry Silver (1882–1972)
British designers and silversmiths; active London; sons of Arthur Silver.

History/biographies 1880, the Silver Studio was founded by Arthur Silver (1853–1896), the father of Rex and Harry Silver. 1896, Harry Napper took over the management of the firm; 1898, left to establish his own business. From 1898, J.R. Houghton managed the studio. Napper and Houghton had sold Silver's wares to American and European firms, including Bergerot, Du Pont, Dumas, Field's, Florquin, Gros Roman, Leborgne, Macy & Co., Marshall, Parison, Vanoutryve, and Zuber. From 1901, Rex Silver managed the firm; became an important designer of textiles, silver, and pewter for Liberty. To 1916, the brothers were partners. 1899 with Bernard Cuzner and Jessie M. King, Rex Silver was one of the first London designers to become a member of Liberty's design stable for its Cymric range, which he produced to 1910. Harry Silver designed various other silverwares for Liberty. Archibald Knox joined Rex Silver, whose bowls, candlesticks, and silver clocks were very similar to Knox's work. 1920s, the American market became important. Herbert Crofts worked at the studio whose designers then included Frank Price and Lewis Jones. An outside designer was H.C. Bareham, who worked for Silver's to its 1963 closing. 1930s designers included John Aldridge, Edward Bawden, John Churton, Lucienne Day, Clifford and Rosemary Ellis, John Line, Roger Nicholson, and Lawrence Scarfe. 1880–1940, no other collection was more representative of current middle-of-the-road taste than Silver's.
Exhibition 1980–81 *The Silver Studio Collection: A London Design Studio, 1880–1963*, Museum of London, London (catalog below).
Bibliography John Brandon-Jones et al., *The Silver Studio Collection: A London Design Studio, 1880–1963*, London: Lund Humphries/ Middlesex Polytechnic, 1980. Mark Turner and Lesley Hoskins, *Silver Studio of Design: A Design and Source Book for Home Decoration*, Exeter, Devon: Webb & Bower; London: Joseph, 1988. *A Popular Art: British Wallpapers, 1930–1960*, London: Middlesex Polytechnic, 1989.

Simberg-Ehrström, Uhra-Beata (1914–1979)
Finnish textile designer.

Training Taideteollinen korkeakoulu, Helsinki.
Biography From 1935, she designed rugs for Suomen Käsityön Ystävien (friends of Finnish handicraft); from 1938, was an industrial designer at Inhemsk U11 (Native Woollens); from 1958, at Finlayson-Forssa; 1950–58, was an artist consultant to Norna Domestic Crafts.
Exhibitions/citations Work included in 1956–57 *Design in Scandinavia*, touring the US; 1955 *H 55*, Hälsingborg; 1961 *Finlandia* in Zürich, Amsterdam, and London. Diploma, 1937 *Exposition Internationale des Arts et Techniques dans la Vie Moderne*, Paris; diploma of honor, 1954 (10th); grand prize, 1957 (11th), gold medal, 1960 (12th) editions of Triennale di Milano.
Bibliography Cat., David Revere McFadden (ed.), *Scandinavian Modern Design 1880–1980*, New York: Abrams, 1982.

Simeon, Margaret (1910–)
British textile designer.

Training Chelsea School of Art and Royal College of Art, both London.
Biography Simeon was a teacher of textile printing, Royal College of Art, and freelance designer of dress, and furnishings textiles, including for Allan Walton Textiles, Campbell Fabrics, Edinburgh Weavers, and Fortnum & Mason.
Bibliography Margaret Simeon, *The History of Lace*, London: Stainer & Bell, 1979. Cat., *Thirties: British Art and Design Before the War*, London: Arts Council of Great Britain/Hayward Gallery, 1979.

Simón International
> See Gavina, Dino; Ultramobile.

Simon, Scot (1954–)
American painter and designer; active San Francisco and New York.

Training 1974, painting, Carnegie-Mellon University, Pittsburgh; 1976, San Francisco Art Institute.
Biography To 1977, Simon painted in San Francisco and New York; subsequently, began designing jewelry and belts in New York at Accessocraft and independently; executed embossed wallpaper designs and some fabrics. From 1980, work has included tableware and table linen by Mikasa and for himself. He began creating textile designs and wallcoverings, which he has since pursued exclusively.
Exhibition Work included in 1983–84 exhibition, Philadelphia Museum of Art (catalog below).
Bibliography Kathryn B. Hiesinger and George H. Marcus III (eds.), *Design Since 1945*, Philadelphia: Philadelphia Museum of Art, 1983. 'Scot Simon,' *American Fabrics and Fashions*, no. 128, 1983: 11–17.

Simon, Steph (1902–)
Gallery owner; active Paris.

Biography 1956, opened Galerie Steph Simon on the boulevard Saint-Germain, Paris; had made and sold the furniture and objects of Jean Luce, Serge Mouille, Isamu Noguchi, Jean Royère, and others, some, such as Charlotte Perriand's, almost exclusively. From 1948, Simon was the sole agent of all Jean Prouvé's furniture. Of the numerous exhibitions at the gallery, Simon mounted a 1956 venue of Serge Mouille lamps. 1974, the operation and gallery were closed.
Bibliography Patrick Favardin, *Les décorateurs des années 50*, Paris: Norma, 2002: 318–19.

Clive Marles Sinclair and Ian Sinclair. Executive pocket calculator. 1972. ABS polymer casing, 1/4 x 2 1/2 x 5 1/2" (0.6 x 6.4 x 14 cm). Mfr.: Sinclair Radionics, UK. Gift of the mfr. MoMA.

Simonet, Albert; Charles Simonet (d. 1929)

French glass- and metalworkers; brothers.

Biography Albert Simonet was a theoretician and designer, and Henri Dieupart produced his designs in molded glass. Evenness in their work was achieved with a flow of air directed into the mold immediately after pouring in molten glass. Occasionally using muted gray and violet tints, Dieupart more often left the glass uncolored. After his partnership with Dieupart, Simonet included more glass as a part of his lighting fixtures. At first, mostly floral motifs were called on, including aloe, bracken, convolvulus, honesty, hortensia, hydrangea, lily of the valley, and thistle. 1930s, geometric forms appeared, including rhomboids, squares, and lozenges. By 1933, metal had been almost entirely replaced with glass.
Exhibitions/citations Albert Simonet showed his work in 1924 (1st) *Exposition de l'Art Moderne*, Pavillon Marsan, Musée du Louvre; in the Simonet Frères stand in the Grand Palais, 1925 *Exposition Internationale des Arts Décoratifs et Industriels Modernes* and 1934 (2nd) *Salon de la Lumière*. To the Simonets: five of ten first prizes and numerous honorable-mention citations for Rooms in Homes of Families of Different Incomes, 1924 *Grand Concours de Lumière*, organized by Syndicat de l'Électricité. All Paris.
Bibliography Guillaume Janneau, *Le luminaire et les moyens d'éclairage nouveaux*, Paris: Charles Moreau, 1st series: plates 16, 39. Alastair Duncan, *Art Nouveau and Art Déco Lighting*, New York: Simon & Schuster, 1978.

Simonit, Alfredo (1937–)

Italian designer; born Romans d'Isonzo; active S. Giovanni al Natisone.

Biography 1963, Simonit began his professional career; from 1966, designed furniture for Mobel Italia, where, 1967–72, was the artistic director; 1971, began collaborating with Giorgio Del Piero, with whom he established in 1974 the design studio 'A' in San Giovanni al Natisone; became a member, Associazione per il Disegno Industriale (ADI), and highly active in the organization, even founding in 1993 a personal, ad-hoc ADI, known as Friuli Venezia Giulia (FVG).
Exhibitions/citations Showed work in Mobel Italia stand (with Del Piero), 1972 (4th) *Eurodomus*, Turin. Participated in 1963 (5th) Concorso Internazionale del Mobile, Cantù; 1965 (2nd) Concorso Nazionale del Mobile Fiera, Rome, winning a prize; 1965 Concorso Nazionale del Mobile at the fair in Trieste, winning a prize with others.
Bibliography *ADI Annual 1976*, Milan: Associazione per il Disegno Industriale, 1976.

Simonson, Lee (1888–1967)

American architect, artist, and designer; active New York.

Biography Simonson planned the 1927 *Exposition of Art in Trade at Macy's* at R.H. Macy & Co. department store, New York; 1930–32, was the president, American Union of Designers, Artists and Craftsmen (AUDAC); from 1932 to 1950s, was highly active in the decorative arts and designed sets, costumes, and lighting for as many as 25 Broadway plays, musicals, and operas. Some of his costumes for the theater are housed in The Costume Institute, The Metropolitan Museum of Art, New York. He wrote or edited a number of books on costumedesign; was one of the first group of American designers to implement the ideas of pioneers Adolphe Appia (1862–1928), Swiss stage-lighting designer, and Edward Gordon Craig (1872–1966), scenic designer. He was also highly active in the decorative arts.
Exhibition Designed The Designer's Office and Studio (with Raymond Loewy), installed at 1935 *Contemporary American Industrial Art, 1934*, The Metropolitan Museum of Art, New York.
Bibliography Lee Simonson, *Part of a Lifetime: Drawings and Designs, 1919-1940*, New York: Duell, Sloan & Pearce, 1943. R. Craig Miller, *Modern Design 1890–1990*, New York: Abrams, 1990.

Simpson, Ronald, D. (1890–1960)

British textile designer and woodworker.

Biography Simpson was a woodworker in Kendal in Cumbria, and also a textile designer at Alexander Morton from 1908, creating numerous designs for the firm, in addition to advertisements for its nonfading Sundour fabrics.
Bibliography Valerie Mendes, *The Victoria & Albert Museum's Textile Collection: British Textiles from 1900 to 1937*, London: Victoria and Albert Museum, 1992.

Sinclair, Clive Marles (1940–)

British electronics engineer and entrepreneur; born Richmond, Surrey.

Training King's College, Cambridge.
Biography 'Marles' is the maiden name of Sinclair's mother. As a teenager, he became interested in electronics and fascinated by miniaturization; 1961–79, operated Sinclair Radionics Ltd., Cambridge, and, 1962, advertised his Sinclair Micro-Microamplifier kit, 'the smallest in the world,' at 26 shillings/6 pence, and, from 1963, sold the assembled radio on which the kit was based, all by mail order. 1972, he introduced the first pocket calculator, the Executive, invented/designed with his brother Iain Sinclair (1943–); 1976, the world's first digital wristwatch; 1962 Sovereign and 1977 Microvision, the world's first first pocket-size calculator and TV. Through his firm Sinclair Research, he introduced 1980 ZX 80, a small, inexpensive personal computer (at less than £100), which sold in greater numbers than any other home computer at that time. By 1981, the firm was grossing £4.65 million; by 1982, £30 million, or seven times more. 1982, he introduced ZX Spectrum computer that could be used for game playing. However, Sinclair Motor's 1984 C5 electric car—with a motor of the type used in Italian washing machines and more like a three-wheel scooter—was a commercial flop. And at £399, requiring no license or road tax, it was based on a £7-million investment, supported by a plethora of promotional materials from C5 mugs to C5 hats. 1981–85, he operated Sinclair Browne Ltd., with Patrick Browne, concurrent with Sinclair Research. 1986, Sinclair founded Cambridge Computer and concentrated on research; was the chairperson, British Mensa, 1980–97; a visiting fellow, Robinson College, 1982–85; a professor, Department of Electronic Engineering, Imperial College of Science and Technology, London, from 1984.
Exhibitions/citations Executive calculator and Microvision television set included in 1983–84 *Design Since 1945* exhibition, Philadelphia Museum of Art (catalog below). Four awards, Design Council, UK (for Executive calculator in 1972, Sovereign calculator in 1977, Microvision television set in 1978, and ZX 81 personal computer in 1982).
Bibliography 'Clive Sinclair's New Leaf,' *Design*, no. 389, May 1981: 26–27. Myron Magnet, 'Clive Sinclair's Little Computer that Could,' *Fortune*, vol. 105, 8 Mar. 1982: 78–84. Rodney Dale, *The Sinclair Story*, London: Duckworth, 1985. Cat., Kathryn B. Hiesinger and George H. Marcus III (eds.), *Design Since 1945*, Philadelphia: Philadelphia Museum of Art, 1983.

Sindall, Matt (1958–)

British designer; active Paris.

Training Bachelor's degree, Kingston Polytechnic (now Kingston University).
Biography 1981–82, Sindall was an assistant designer of costumes and set of *Orestia* at National Theatre, London; 1982–83, interior designer for a British Rail advanced passenger train at Wrightson & Raymond, London; 1983–85 at BBC Television, was an assistant designer for various films, and TV programs such as 'Arny Johnson,'

Doctor Who Origins, *Tenko*, *Playschool*, *Crackerjack*, *Top of the Pops*, others; 1985–90, was the chief designer, Met Studio, Lon-don; 1988, cofounded organization O2, design for the environment; 1990–95, was the chief designer in the office of Jean-Michel Wilmotte, Paris; from 1995, has been a freelance designer with clients, including Banque de Luxembourg (publicity panel), Carré Noir (packaging), Eclatec (public lighting), Guinot (U.V.-transmission console), La Fuma (camping furniture), Pandora (ceramic object), Peninsula (lighting consultant), Pont à Mousson/St. Gobain (product), Renault (automobile exhibition), SCNF French train system (seating), Sunlight (lighting products), 3 Suisses (furniture collection). From 1995, has been a professor of design, École Supérieure d'Art et de Design, Reims, France. Other work: 1995 Bull leather-metal chair, 1998 Whole fiberglass table, 1998 Outshirts ceramic vase, 1998 public optical-fiber lighting models and road-inset marker with diodes by Eclatec, 1999 Chakra floor covering by Sommer/Galerie Néotù, 2000 Chaise chromatique with optical film layers, 2000 Iseeme table and bench in polycarbonate and metal film, Lightbook lamp, Red Bed/Black Bed in cut foam. Other clients have included Aéroports de Paris, Academy, Béziers Hospital, Cathay Pacific, City of Nîmes, Guerlain, Musée du Palais Saint-Pierre in Lyon, Plan Venise, Saint-Gobain, SCIC, Victoria and Albert Museum, and Wagons Lits.
Exhibitions/citations Work included in 1998 *Jus'tin petite chaise*, Paris, Rennes, and Reims; 1998 *La vie en rose*, Fondation Cartier, Paris; 1998 (1st) and 2000 (2nd) Biennale Internationale du Design, Saint-Étienne; 1999 *Sommer Time*, Galerie Néotù, Paris; 1999 *Détournement et Récupération* (for Light Cup), Paris; 2000 *État de chaise*, Cannes. Work subject of 2002 *Cité radieuse de Le Corbusier*, Briey, France. 2001 Appel Permanent grant, VIA (French furniture association).
Bibliography Mel Byars, *50 Beds: Innovations in Design and Materials*, Hove: RotoVision, 2000. www.via.asso.fr.

Sinel, 'Jo' Joseph Claude (1889–1975)

New Zealand commercial artist and designer; born Auckland; active the US.

Training From c. 1900 for five years, apprenticeship in printing at Wilson & Horton.
Biography 1911 in Auckland as a graphic designer, Sinel designed an Art Nouveau style calendar for Wilson & Horton; freelanced to lithographer Kingsley Smith; worked for Dawson Photoengravers, Abel Dykes Ltd., and Clark & Matherson. 1913, he moved to Sydney, Australia, and took odd jobs; 1915, arrived in Liverpool, UK; c. 1916, worked for Hudson, Scott & Sons in Carlisle, then Carleton Studios and C.F. Higham Ltd., both London; 1917, returned to Sydney for a few months and, 1918, emigrated to US and, 1918–19, arrived in San Francisco and, the following year, worked at advertising agencies H.K. McCann Co. and Foster & Kleiser; 1922, taught pen-and-brush lettering for one summer term, California School of Arts and Crafts; worked for Home & Livingston; with Maynard Dixon, Harold von Schmidt, Judson Starr, and David Henrickson, established an office in San Francisco and, 1923 with von Schmidt, a design office in New York; became a member of Artists Guild and Society of Illustrators and one of 14 founders of American Society of Industrial Design. He wrote *A Book of American Trade-Marks & Devices* (New York: Knopf, 1924). Clients included Dictograph, Folmer Graflex, and Ruxton automobiles. c. 1945, he returned to San Francisco and, from late 1940s, taught at California School of Arts & Crafts and at San Francisco School of Art; was active in industrial-design societies and the Aspen International Design Conferences; 1962, closed his design office in San Francisco and sold his extensive collection of American Indian artifacts and rare books; bequeathed his work archive to California College of Arts & Crafts, where he had become professor emeritus. Apocryphally, he was the first (1919) to use the term 'industrial design' in describing industrial objects pictured in a magazine advertisement. Sinel has become best known for 1928 one-cent public scale in an Art Déco 'skyscraper' form.
Exhibitions 1928 scale included in traveling exhibition of modern American design, from 2000 (catalog below).
Bibliography *Fortune*, Feb. 1934: 88. Erin K. Maline, 'Dr. Leslie & The Composing Room, 1934–1942: An Important Time in the Development of American Graphic Design,' thesis, Rochester: Rochester Institute of Technology, 1994. Cat., J. Stewart Johnson, *American Modern, 1925–1940...*, New York: Abrams, 2000.

Singer, Franz (1896–1954)

Austrian architect and furniture designer; born Vienna.

Training 1914–15 under F.A. Harta, in painting in Vienna; 1917 under Johannes Itten, Itten-Schule, Vienna; 1919–23 under Johannes Itten, Bauhaus, Weimar.
Biography 1920–24, Singer designed for the theater in Berlin and Dresden with fellow Bauhaus student Friedl Dicker; 1923–25 with Dicker, was active in the Werkstätten bildender Kunst in Berlin; 1925, moved to Vienna, where he pursued interior architecture; 1925–26,

Franz Singer. Folding sofa. Early 1930s. Chromium-plated steel tubing (fabric possibly by Friedl Dicker or Anni Wotiz), 26 x 54 3/4 x 27 3/4" (66 x 139 x 70.5 cm). Mfr.: Metz & Co., the Netherlands. Courtesy Quittenbaum Kunstauktionen, Munich.

Bořek Šípek. Red Ball vase. c. 1999. Bohemian crystal, h. 12 1/2" x dia. 17 1/8 (32 x 44 cm). Mfr.: Steltman Galleries, the Netherlands (one of a kind).

again became a partner of Dicker, at Wasserburggasse 2, Vienna, known as the Singer-Dicker workshop 1926–31; 1927, worked primarily on furniture designs in bent-steel tubing produced by firms in Austria, England, and the Netherlands and was active in the serial production of furniture; 1930–31, made his first trip to London and designed nursery and stackable furniture models there; 1930–31, moved his studio, and the Dicker-Singer collaboration was dissolved. He remained active in furniture design to 1934, when he settled in London and began working with Wells Coates on a system of modular kitchens, baths, and storage spaces for converted older apartments. After this time, Singer was active as an architect, specializing in shops such as John Lewis department store, London; was in a partnership with Hans Biel and, subsequently, with Hedy Schwarz-Abraham; 1935, wrote on housing for the London County Council; 1936, designed children's and nursery furniture; 1938, closed his studio in Vienna; 1938–54 in England, designed more nursery furniture, blackboards for a toy company, the studio of Michael Watkins, a house for W. Foges, a house at 39 Cadogan Gardens, the pavilion of Hotel Scarborough, the restaurant at Tyrell & Green, and houses of V. Kraus, Mr. and Mrs. Friedmann, V.F. Evans-Tipping, and Mr. and Mrs. Steanbrige. (Friedl Dicker, who had remained in Austria, died at the Auschwitz-Birkenau extermination camp in 1944.)
Exhibitions 1916–17, participated in Kunstschau exhibition at the Wiener Sezession and in *Österreichische Ausstellung* in Vienna; 1929 *Ausstellung Moderner Inneneinrichtungen*, Österreichisches Museum für Kunst und Industrie, Vienna. His and Dicker's work subject of 1988–89 exhibition, Hochschule für angewandte Kunst, Vienna. Dicker's in several others (see catalogs below).
Bibliography Cat., *Franz Singer/Friedl Dicker: 2X Bauhaus in Wien*, Vienna: Hochschule für angewandte Kunst, 1988. Cat., Georg Heuberger and Ursula Thürich, *Vom Bauhaus nach Terezín: Friedl Dicker-Brandeis und die Kinderzeichnungen aus dem Ghetto-Lager Theresienstadt, Frankfurt am Main: Ausstellung des Jüdischen Museums der Stadt*, 1991. Cat., Elena Makarova, *Friedl Dicker-Brandeis: ein Leben für Kunst und Lehre: Wien, Weimar, Prag, Hronov, Theresienstadt, Auschwitz*, Vienna and Munich: C. Brandstätter, 2000. Cat., Elena Makarova, *Friedl Dicker-Brandeis, Vienne 1898–Auschwitz 1944* (Musée d'Art et d'Histoire du Judaïsme), Paris: Somogy, 2000.

Singer-Schinnerl, Susi (1895–1965)
Austrian ceramicist; born Vienna.

Biography Singer-Schinnerl was a member of the ceramic workshop of the Wiener Werkstätte; 1937, settled in the US.
Bibliography Günther Feuerstein, *Vienna—Present and Past: Arts and Crafts—Applied Art—Design*, Vienna: Jugend und Volk, 1976: 35, 81. Cat., *Expressive Keramik der Wiener Werkstätte 1917–1930*, Munich: Bayerische Vereinsbank, 1992: 134–35.

Sinnemark, Rolf (1941–)
Swedish designer; born Stockholm.

Training 1956–63, Konstfackskolan, Stockholm, and, 1956–59, in the silver department there; from c. 1963, in the US, Mexico, and Europe.
Biography 1967–86, Sinnemark was a designer at Kosta Boda glassworks and, from 1967, at GAB Gense in Rörstrand.
Exhibitions Work shown in Colorado, Australia, Sweden, and Denmark.
Bibliography Jennifer Hawkins Opie, *Scandinavia: Ceramics and Glass in the Twentieth Century*, New York: Rizzoli, 1989.

Šípek, Bořek (1949–)
Czech designer; born Prague; active Amsterdam.

Training 1964–68, Vysoká Škola Uměleckoprůmyslová (VŠUP, school of applied arts), Prague; 1969, architecture, Hochschule für bildende Künste, Hamburg; in aesthetics and philosophy in Stuttgart; to 1979, architecture, Technische Hogeschool, Delft.
Biography 1977–79, Šípek worked as a scientific assistant at the Institute of Industrial Design, Universität Hannover; 1979–83, taught design theory at Universität Duisburg-Essen; 1983, realized his first major architectural comission (his sister's house in Hamburg); 1983, settled in Amsterdam, where he set up an office and explored Oriental and Occidental arts and crafts. c. 1989, he began designing tableware, accessories, and furniture in the Eidos, Malastrana, and Follies collections of Driade, Italy; became known for his domestic furnishings that merged the functional with the non-functional. His voluptuous objects in glass and metal, which systematically revisit traditional crafts techniques and materials, have included 1984 Ernst und Geduld chair and 1988 Table Satomi San by Galerie Néotù, Paris; and 1990 china by Manufacture Nationale de Sèvres, France. His widely published 1987 Sni chaise longue was produced by Driade; 1987 range of Murano mouth-blown glass by Sawaya & Moroni; other examples by the glassworks in Nový Bor, Czech Republic. Šípek continues to design glass in much the same manner as 30 years ago, such as 1998 Koten vase by Ajeto. He has designed for others, including Alessi, Alterego, Anthologie Quartett, Cleto Munari, Leitner, Moletti, Süssmuth, Swarovski, and Vitra. Was appointed Prague Castle Architect (a post previously held by Joze Plecnik) by Czech president Vaclav Havel, working 1992–96 on Plecnik's 1920s concepts and redesigning state rooms and creating new exhibition rooms. More recently, Šípek has been active as an architect for commissions such as offices of the mayor in the Beurs–World Trade Center, Rotterdam, 1987; Shoebaloo stores, Amsterdam, 1991, and Rotterdam, 1995; Léon Gulikers offices and showrooms, Gulpen, 1993; Het Kruithuis Museum extension, Den Bosch, 1994; Komatsu clothing stores, Tokyo 1996; Luxor Theater, Rotterdam, 1996. He was the editor of *The International Design Yearbook* (London: Thames & Hudson, 1993). 1997, returned to Prague.
Exhibitions/citations Work subject of *Bořek Šípek—The Nearness of Far*, Vitra Design Museum, Weil am Rhein, 1992, and Uměleckoprůmyslové Muzeum, Prague, 1993. Honorable mention for The Glasshouse, 1983 German Architecture Competition, Hamburg; 1988 Kho Liang le applied-arts prize of Amsterdam Fonds voor de Kunst; 1991 Croix of Chevalier of the Ordre des Arts et des Lettres, France; 1993 Prins Bernard Fonds Prize (architecture and applied arts).
Bibliography Albrecht Bangert and Karl Michael Armer, *80s Style:*

Designs of the Decade, New York: Abbeville, 1990. Cat., Milena Lamarová and Mel Byars, *Bořek Šípek, Blízkost dálky—architektura a design = The Nearness of Far Architecture and Design*, Amsterdam: Steltman, 1993. Pepin van Roojen and Dagmar Sedlická, *Bořek Šípek, Architect and Designer*, Amsterdam: Pepin Press. Philippe Louguet et al., *Bořek Šípek*, Paris: Dis Voir, 1998.

Sirnes, Johan (1883–1966)

Norwegian designer; active Oslo.

Biography 1914–27, Sirnes was a designer for David-Andersen in Kristiania (now Oslo), where he created expensive, highly ornamental one-of-a-kind pieces that incorporated precious stones; from 1912, taught, Statens Håndverks -og Kunstindustriskole, Kristiania.
Bibliography Fredrik Wildhagen, *Norge i Form*, Oslo: Sternersen, 1988: 88. Annelies Krekel-Aalberse, *Art Nouveau and Art Déco Silver*, New York: Abrams, 1989.

Sirrah

Italian lighting manufacturer.

History The founding of Sirrahir in Imola began with a collection of domestic lighting and interchangeable components designed by the architecture partnership of Franco Albini, Franca Helg, and Antonio Piva, introduced at 1968 (14th) Triennale di Milan. A notable early lamp for Sirrah is their 1969 Series AM/AS chrome table model. Other designers have included Vittorio Balli, Giorgina Castiglioni, Pirro Cuniberti, Salvatore Gregorietti, Glauco Gresleri, Giancarlo Mattioli, Franco Mirenzi, and Paolo Tilche. 1976, the Kaori, Kazuki, and Saori lamps designed by Kazuhide Takahama were among a new generation of lamps that featured a white fabric (heat-resistant, pliable, and washable) stretched over wire frames, and the Saori was dedicated to Lucio Fontana. Later production included 1980s Soffio by Emilio Ambasz and 1985 Sigla and 1990 Sini by René Kimma. 1994, the firm was acquired by Guzzini Illuminazione, and King-Miranda Associati were the artistic directors. Sirrah is now merely a collection.
Bibliography *ADI Annual 1976*, Milan: Associazione per il Disegno Industriale, 1976.

SITE (Sculpture in the Environment)

American architecture firm; located New York.

History 1969, SITE was established by James Wines. 1973, Alison Sky, Michelle Stone, and Emilio Sousa became partners in the firm; took architectural Deconstructivism to neo-Dada extremes with idiosyncratic, curious structures that stretched the imagination. SITE became best known for its buildings for the Best chain of stores in US, including the first in Richmond, Va. (1971–72 Peeling Project) and, subsequently, 1974–75 Indeterminate Facade, Houston, Texas; 1976–78 Tilt Showroom, Towson, Md.; and Best's business office. Commissions have also included public spaces, landscapes, interiors, graphics, and industrial products.
Bibliography *SITE Projects and Theories*, Bari: Mario Adda, 1978. Bruno Zevi and Pierre Restany, *SITE, Architecture as Art*, London: Academy, 1980. Cat., Carlo Guenzi, *Le affinità elettive*, Milan: Electa, 1985. Silvio San Pietro (ed.), *Site—Agenda 1995*, Milan: L'Archivolto, 1994.
> See Sky, Alison; Wines, James.

Sitterle, Harold (1921–); Trudi Sitterle (1921–)

American ceramic designers; husband and wife.

Biography Harold Sitterle was a graphic designer at the magazine *McCall's*; subsequently, joined his wife's workshop in Croton Falls, N.Y., near New York. 1949 to early 1970s, the Sitterles designed and produced a line of porcelain table accessories such as candleholders, sugar bowls, serving utensils, creamers, pitchers, pepper mills, and salt dishes. Widely published, their 1949 hourglass-shaped pepper mill became a popular item in their newly created porcelain business, Sitterle Ceramics Company.
Exhibitions Pepper mill shown at 1950 *Good Design* exhibition / award, The Museum of Modern Art, New York, and Chicago Merchandise Mart.
Bibliography 'Manufacturing in Microcosm: Sitterle Ceramics,' *Industrial Design*, vol. 2, Apr. 1955: 78–81. Don Wallance, *Shaping America's Products*, New York: Reinhold, 1956: 159–61. 'Trudi and Harold Sitterle,' *Design Quarterly*, no. 39, 1957: 24–27. Cat., Kathryn B. Hiesinger and George H. Marcus III (eds.), *Design Since 1945*, Philadelphia: Philadelphia Museum of Art, 1984.

Siune, Svend (1935–)

Danish metalworker and designer.

Training To 1961, Kunsthåndvaerkerskolen, Copenhagen.
Biography 1961–76, Siune was a freelance advertising artist and, subsequently, a designer of furniture and metal and plastic cutlery; became best known for 1965 Blue Shark stainless-steel cutlery by Georg Jensen Sølvsmedie, Copenhagen.
Citations Won 1966 Jensen cutlery contest (for Blue Shark cutlery).
Bibliography Cat., *Georg Jensen Silversmithy: 77 Artists, 75 Years*, Washington: Smithsonian, 1980, no. 137. Cat., Kathryn B. Hiesinger and George H. Marcus III (eds.), *Design Since 1945*, Philadelphia: Philadelphia Museum of Art, 1983.

Svend Siune. Blue Shark cutlery. 1965. Stainless steel, longest (two-piece salad servers) l. 8 1/16" (20.5 cm) to shortest (knife) l. 7 7/16" (18.9 cm). Mfr.: George Jensen Sølvsmedie, Denmark. Courtesy Quittenbaum Kunstauktionen, Munich.

Sivonen, Kari
> See Snowcrash.

Siza y Vieira, Álvaro Joaquim de Meio (1933–)
Portuguese architect and designer; born Matosinhos, near Porto.

Training 1949–55, architecture, Escola Superior de Belas Arte, Porto.
Biography 1955–58, Siza was active in an architecture practice in Porto; collaborated with architect Fernando Tavora; 1959, established his own office in Porto; designed furniture for the Faculdade de Arquitectura, Universidade do Porto, where he taught from 1966 and was a professor from 1976; also, a visiting professor, École Polytechnique Fédérale, Lausanne; University of Pennsylvania; and others. His large body of architecture has included 1986–92 Setubal Training Center, 1985 Carlos Ramos Pavilion (Faculdade de Arquitectura building), Porto; Portugese Pavilion at *Expo 2000*, Hanover; as part of a large body of architectural work. He designed 1972 Flamingo halogen table lamp by Bd Ediciones de Diseño (possibly Siza's only product for the firm); and over 30 examples of furniture, furnishings, and dinnerware by Ohm Design in 2003.
Exhibitions/citations Work subject of exhibitions including those at Museum of Contemporary Art, Milan, 1979; Alvar Aalto Museum, Finland, 1982, traveling worldwide, 1996; Fundación Canal, Madrid, 2003; *Alvaro Siza, architecte: Projets, 1961–1999*, Centre de Design, UQÀM (Université du Québec à Montréal), 2003. Won 1985 invitational competition, renovation of Campo di Marte, Venice. Received 1998 Mies van der Rohe Foundation / European Economic Community award; 1988 Prince of Wales Award, Harvard University; 1992 Pritzker Architecture Prize; a number of others.
Bibliography Juli Capella and Quim Larrea, *Designed by Architects in the 1980s*, New York: Rizzoli, 1988. Brigitte Fleck, *Alvaro Siza*, London: Routledge, 1995. Philip Jodidio, *The Work of Alvaro Siza*, New York: Taschen, 1999. Kenneth Frampton (intro.), *Alvaro Siza: Complete Works*, New York/London: Phaidon, 2000. Peter Testa, *Alvaro Siza*, Basel: Birkhäuser, 2001. 'Siza Vieira: Exclusivo para o Mundo,' *Ideias & Negóios*, Dec. 2002, 22–29.

Skeaping, John Rattenbury (1901–1980)
British sculptor and ceramics designer; husband of Barbara Hepworth.

Training Royal Academy School, London.
Biography 1926–27, Skeaping designed 14 earthenware animal figurines for Wedgwood, of which at least 12 were produced in 1933–39. Norman Wilson's 'straw' glaze was used on Skeaping's figures by Doulton. He wrote the books *Animal Drawing* (London: The Studio, 1936), *How to Draw Horses* (London: The Studio, 1941), *The Bay Tree of Mexico* (London: Turnstile, 1952), *Les sources de l'art: les animaux dans l'art* (Paris: Pierre Amiot, 1968), and *Drawn from Life: An Autobiography* (London: Collins, 1977); 1948–49, worked on terracotta sculpture assisted by potters in Zapotec, Mexico; 1953–59, taught sculpture, Royal College of Art, London.
Exhibitions His sculpture was shown in Mexico City and Oxana (Mexico) and at Royal Academy, Leicester Galleries, and Ackermann Galleries, and 1979–80 *Thirties* exhibition, Hayward Gallery (catalog below); all London.
Bibliography Cat., *Thirties: British Art and Design Before the War*, London: Arts Council of Great Britain/Hayward Gallery, 1979.

Skellern, Victor (1908–1966)
British ceramicist and designer.

Training To 1933, Royal College of Art, London.
Biography Skellern was a painter, stained-glass designer, and ceramicist; 1934–66, succeeded John Goodwin as the artistic director of Wedgwood, where he designed commemorative wares, including characters and images from Gilbert and Sullivan operas, *The Canterbury Tales*, Bayeux tapestry, and Shakespeare's plays. His 1933 Portland stained-glass window showed various scenes from the potteries at Staffordshire. Some of his decorations were applied to ceramic shapes designed by Norman Wilson at Wedgwood, including the 1935 globe-shaped dinner service. He made images on Keith Murray shapes to commemorate the 1940 move of Wedgwood to Barlaston.
Exhibitions Work included in 1935 *British Art in Industry* exhibition, Royal Academy, London; 1935 *Exposition Universelle et Internationale de Bruxelles*; 1937 *Exposition Internationale des Arts et Techniques dans la Vie Moderne*, Paris; 1979–80 *Thirties* exhibition, Hayward Gallery, London (catalog below).
Bibliography Cat., *Thirties: British Art and Design Before the War*, London: Arts Council of Great Britain/Hayward Gallery, 1979.

Barbora Skorpilová. Reek vase. c. 1997. Glass and Duralumin, 19 5/8" x dia. 9 3/8" (50 x 24 cm). Mfr.: Interier Maly, Germany.

Skogster-Lehtinen, Greta (1900–1994)
Finnish textile designer.

Biography 1921–75, she worked in her own studio and wove carpets, tapestries, and fabrics, some intended for furniture upholstery, including 1930s fabrications for architect/designer Lisa Johansson-Pape. Due to shortages created by World War II, Skogster-Lehtinen used various unusual materials, including birch bark, in her weavings.
Bibliography Cat., David Revere McFadden (ed.), *Scandinavian Modern Design 1880–1980*, New York: Abrams, 1982.

Skorpilová, Barbora (1972–)
Czech architect and interior and product designer; born Prague.

Biography Through her studio Mimolimit, Skorpilová's interior design includes Zahrada v Opere (garden in the opera) restaurant, Café Emporio, Café Nubo, 2002 Square (formerly Malostranska Kavarna) café, restaurant and cocktail bar, 2003 Boheme fashion store, all Prague. She has designed a number of jewelry, porcelain, and glass items, some in combinations of glass with Corian or aluminum; introduced 2003 line of acrylic bracelets; also writes as a journalist.
Exhibitions Work included in 1999 *Czech Design 1980–1999*, Prague; 1999 *Neomodern: Structure & Substance in Jewelry from Czech and USA*, Julie: Artisans' Gallery, New York; *Czech Design '99*, Totem Design, New York; 2003 *Contemporary Czech Glass*, Flow Gallery, Prague.
Bibliography 'Barbora Skorpilova,' *Axis*, vol. 78, Mar. 1999.

Skrufs Glasbruk
Swedish glass factory.

History 1897, a glass-making operation was established at Skruv, Småland, as a factory community, and began production of simple household glasswares; 1908, went bankrupt due to unsuccessful experimentations with new kiln types; 1909, was reorganized as Skrufs Nya Glasbruk; 1920s–30s, specialized in utility glassware for restaurants; 1948, changed its name back to Skrufs Glasbruk; 1953–78, employed Bengt Edenfalk (1924–) as its first full-time staff designer and also the artistic director, and focused production on decorative ware. (Edenfalk had studied at Konstfackskolan, Stockholm, 1947–52.) 1966, Lars Hellsten was hired, and production expanded into cast, molded, and spun glass. 1973, the company collaborated with Gullaskruf and with Björkshult; 1974–77, merged several times, resulting in the creation of Krona-Bruken, which was bought by Kosta Boda in 1977 but closed in 1980; was reopened in 1981 as a coop-

erative producing mouth-blown glass designed by Ingegerd Råman and Anette Krahner.
Bibliography Jennifer Hawkins Opie, *Scandinavia: Ceramics and Glass in the Twentieth Century*, New York: Rizzoli, 1989.

Sky, Alison (1946–)
American designer; born New York.

Biography 1969, Sky was a cofounder and principal of SITE Environmental Design to 1991, where she designed 1982–84 Willi Ware showrooms and displays. Other SITE projects of Sky's included 1984 Paz Building, Brooklyn, N.Y.; 1984 Best Products building, Milwaukee, Wis.; 1984 Brickwork Design Center, New York; 1985 Museum of the Borough of Brooklyn, N.Y.; 1985 Ansel Adams Museum and Cen-ter of Photography, Carmel, Cal.; 1986 Pershing Square Cultural Park, Los Angeles; Highway 86 at Transportation Pavilion and Plaza, *Expo '86*, Vancouver; 1986 Theater for The New City, New York. She established ON SITE books, including *Unbuilt America: Forgotten Architecture in the United States from Thomas Jefferson to the Space Age* (with Michelle Stone, New York: McGraw-Hill, 1976). Her design of 'disappearing' furniture and furnishings in a white-on-white motif for 1985 Laurie Mallet house renovation in the expansion of an 1820s residence in Greenwich Village in Manhattan was widely published. 1990s work included *Milagros Imigrando/Migrating Miracles* for US General Services Administration (GSA), Tex.; *River Sculpture* for Grove Hotel, Boise, Idaho; two thematic works for University of Connecticut, Avery Point; and 1999 *Threshold* classroom entry doors of Public Schools 83 and 360, Bronx, N.Y.
Citations Elected fellow, American Academy, Rome.
Bibliography Liz McQuiston, *Women in Design: A Contemporary View*, New York: Rizzoli, 1988: 114. Vittorio Magnago Lampugnani (ed.), *Encyclopedia of 20th-Century Architecture*, 1986: 362.
> See SITE.

Slamp (Samuel Parker)
Italian accessories and lighting range; located Pomezia.

History 1989, the Samuel Parker firm was founded. Slamp is the brand name of its economically priced range of lighting and furnishings made with new materials. Products have included the White Bamboo 'lighting tube' by Giulio Di Mauro, Slamp Fahne wall and table light by Alessandro Mendini, and C21 CD holder and Fiorenza handwoven wickerwood lamp by Francesco Paretti. The 1994–95 Wings table light by Samuel Parker's communications manager Riccardo Raco was widely published; it has employed the inexpensive material Opal-flex, frequently used by the firm for lighting , which gave the appearance of opaline glass. 50% of Slamp's production is exported.
Bibliography Mel Byars, *50 Lights...*, Hove: RotoVision, 1997.

Slang, Gerd (1925–1992)
Norwegian glassware designer.

Training Statens Håndverks -og Kunstindustriskole, Oslo.
Biography 1948–52 and 1963–72, Slang was a designer at the Hadelands Glasverk; 1952–63, worked as an independent designer; late 1960s, designed thin-wall vessels with two-side etching, including of flowers, butterflies, and textures.
Exhibition Work included in 1970 *Craftsmen from Norway* exhibition.
Bibliography Cat., David Revere McFadden (ed.), *Scandinavian Modern Design 1880–1980*, New York: Abrams, 1982. Jennifer Hawkins Opie, *Scandinavia: Ceramics and Glass in the Twentieth Century*, New York: Rizzoli, 1989. Leslie Jackson, *20th Century Factory Glass*, London: Octopus, 2000.

Slany, Erich Hans (1926–)
Czech industrial designer.

Training 1941–44, engineering in Eger, Hungary; 1948, in Esslingen, Germany.
Biography 1948–55, Slany worked for Ritter Aluminum in Esslingen, where he was a specialist in metals, plastics, and product development; 1956, established his own design studio in Esslingen; to 1959, worked in ceramics and glass under Heinrich Löffelhardt; from 1957, created numerous products, including medical equipment and electronic components for rocket construction, power tools, and plastics, including 1958 hand letterer by Rotex in France, 1958 electric drill by Boch in Germany, domestic appliances by Leifheit, and, from 1957, by Progress; 1959, cofounded German designers' association (VDID); 1969 and 1971, a juror, Bundespreis, Rat für Formgebung (German design council), Frankfurt; established Slany Design Team, Esslingen.
Exhibitions/citations Work included in 1977 *Prämiierte Produkte*, Rat für Formgebung, Darmstadt; domestic appliance for Leifheit included in 1983–84 *Design Since 1945* exhibition, Philadelphia Museum of Art (catalogs below). Work subject of 1965 *E.H. Slany: Auswahl Designarbeiten 1953 bis 1965* exhibition, Haus Industrieform, Essen. 1973 Deutscher Ornapreis (plastic tableware); 1975 Bosch prize (for Panther and Dübelblitz power tools); 1991 Red Dot Best of the Best (to Slany Design Team), Design Zentrum Nordrhein-Westfalen, Essen.
Bibliography Cat., *E.H. Slany: Auswahl Designarbeiten 1953 bis 1965*, Essen: Haus Industrieform, 1965. 'Der Designer E. H. Slany: 10 Fragen,' *form*, no. 33, Mar. 1966: 35–39. Cat., *Prämiierte Produkte*, Darmstadt: Rat für Formgebung, 1977: 14, 17. Cat., Kathryn B. Hiesinger and George H. Marcus III (eds.), *Design Since 1945*, Philadelphia: Philadelphia Museum of Art, 1983.

Slater, Eric (1902–)
British ceramicist.

Training Model-making and design, Stoke-on-Trent School of Art; design, Burslem School of Art; life art classes, Hanley School of Art; 1919–26 under Gordon M. Forsyth.
Biography 1877–1914, Slater's great-uncle John Slater was the artistic director at the Doulton ceramics factory. His father Walter Slater was the artistic director at ceramics manufacturer Foley China in Longton, Staffordshire, renamed Shelley Potteries in 1925. 1919, Eric Slater joined Foley China and, 1928, succeeded his father as the artistic director of Shelley Potteries; was responsible at Shelley for shapes, glazes, and patterns of table and decorative wares; designed the circle-patterned 1932 Regent shape and 1935 Vogue dinner set with its colorful geometric trim on triangular and square silhouettes, typical examples of Shelley's Art Déco production. Slater was the secretary, Staffordshire Artists and Designers Society.
> See Shelley Potteries for bibliography.

Slavik (b. Slavik Vassilieff 1920–)
Estonian designer; born Tallin.

Training École Nationale Supérieure des Arts Décoratifs, Paris.
Biography 1930, Slavik moved to France; later produced the tapestries Paris ma Fête and Noble Pantomime; became active as a decorator, principally of drugstores 1963 Saint-Germain-des-Près and 1965 Étoile and 1963 Renault pub; decorated private residences and designed furniture, such as bar stools with tempered-glass seats and backs.
Bibliography Arlette Barré-Despond (ed.), *Dictionnaire international des arts appliqués et du design*, Paris: Regard, 1996.

Slott-Møller, Harald (1864–1937)
Danish painter, ceramicist, and metalworker; active Copenhagen.

Training In painting.
Biography Slott-Møller's silver designs, produced by A. Michelsen in Copenhagen, was work that showed ornamentation borrowed from Thorvald Bindesbøll. Kaj Bojesen, an apprentice at Georg Jensen Sølvsmedie, produced designs of his own as well as those of Slott-Møller. For another enterprise, Slott-Møller designed ceramics for Aluminia in Copenhagen.
Exhibition Michelsen silver by Slott-Møller shown at 1900 *Exposition Universelle*, Paris.
Bibliography Cat., David Revere McFadden (ed.), *Scandinavian Modern Design 1880–1980*, New York: Abrams, 1982. Annelies Krekel-Aalberse, *Art Nouveau and Art Déco Silver*, New York: Abrams, 1989.

Slutzky, Naum J. (1894–1965)
Russian designer; born Kiev (now Ukraine); active London.

Training In Vienna; Bauhaus, Weimar; apprenticeship in Vienna.
Biography To 1924, Slutzky designed—alone and with others—lighting, metalware, and jewelry in the metal workshop at the Bauhaus, Dessau; served an apprenticeship in a goldsmithy in Vienna and became a goldsmith at the Wiener Werkstätte; 1933, settled in London and was active as a jewelry designer; 1935–40, was a lecturer in jewelry design at Central School of Arts and Crafts and, 1946–50, in product design at the school of industrial design of the Royal College of Art, both London; 1957–64, was head of the department of industrial design, College of Arts and Crafts, Birmingham.

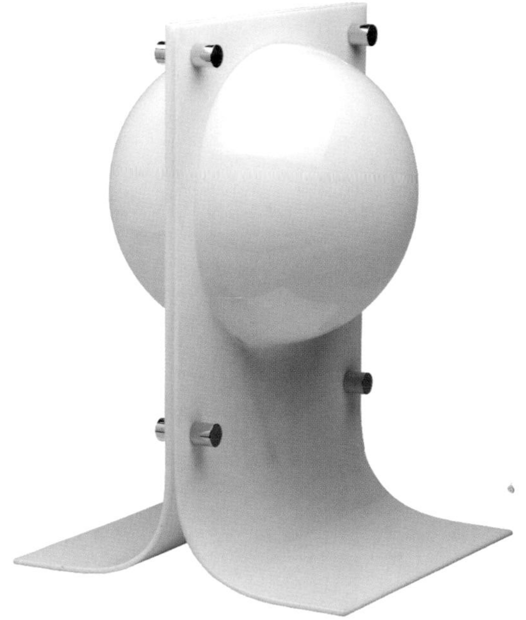

Neal Small. Area lamp (no. 1112). 1966, Acrylic and chrome-plated metal hardware, 16 7/8 x 12 x 12 1/4" (42.8 x 30.5 x 31.1 cm). Mfr.: Neal Small Designs, US. Gift of the designer. MoMA.

Bibliography Sylvie Raulet, *Bijoux art déco*, Paris: Regard, 1984. Monika Rudolph, *Naum Slutzky, Meister am Bauhaus: Goldschmied und Designer*, Stuttgart: Arnoldsche, 1990. Deanna F. Cera (ed.), *Jewels of Fantasy: Costume Jewelry of the 20th Century*, New York: Abrams, 1992.

Small, Neal (1937–)

American sculptor and designer; active New York and Pine Bush, N.Y.

Biography From c. 1965, Small worked in his own studio in New York and, subsequently to 1973, in Pine Bush, N.Y.; designed furniture, lighting, and glassware, using plastic sheets in bent, folded, and molded forms, sometimes combining them with chromed steel. His designs were produced by his own firm Neal Small Designs and by others, including Nessen lighting. 1978, he became president, Squire and Small, where he specialized in conceptual sculpture and product design for clients such as Brueton, Kovacs, and Sigma.
Exhibition Lamp for Nessen shown at 1983–84 exhibition, Philadelphia (catalog below).
Bibliography Lisa Hammel, 'He's a One-Man Furniture Craft Guild,' *The New York Times*, 7 Nov. 1967. Jocelyn de Noblet, *Design*, Paris: Stock-Chêne, 1974: 340–41. Cat., Kathryn B. Hiesinger and George H. Marcus III (eds.), *Design Since 1945*, Philadelphia: Philadelphia Museum of Art, 1983.

Smart Design

American industrial-design consultancy; located New York.

History 1981, the studio was founded as David Stowell Associ-ates and designed a 1982 line of fashion eyewear, with high-tech glass lenses, that proved to be unsuccessful no matter the high design standards. 1985, the studio became Smart Design with partners David Stowell, Tom Dair, Tamara Thomsen, and Tucker Viemeister, some of whom have since departed. The studio specializes in industrial and consumer products, packaging, corporate identity, and product graphics, including eyewear for Corning Optics and melamine tableware for Copco. The client rostrum includes Copco, Corning Ware, Black & Decker, Hewlett-Packard, Issey Miyake, Johnson & Johnson, Kellogg's, Kepner-Tregoe, Knoll Extra, LG Electronics, Timex, others. Smart Design kitchen utensils by Oxo International have been highly successful, resulting in an extensive, ongoing range. More recent staff members have included Jerszy Seymour in 1996 and David Farrage from 1996 for a time as a senior industrial designer.
Citation 1997 silver (Silicon Graphics Work Station, with manufacturer's design staff).
Bibliography Nicholas Backlund, 'Smart Moves,' *I.D.*, Sept.–Oct. 1990: 29–33. Cat., R. Craig Miller (intro.), *U.S. Design 1975–2000*, Munich: Prestel, 2002.
> See Oxo International.
Smeets, Job (1969–)
> See Timmermans, Hugo (1967–).

Smetana, Pavel (1900–1986)

Bohemian architect, furniture designer, and architecture theorist; born Zákupy.

Training 1918–23, Vysoká Škola Uměleckoprůmyslová (VŠUP, school of applied arts); 1925–26 under Pavel Janák and Josef Gočár, Akademie Výtvarných Umení (academy of fine arts); both Prague.
Biography Smetana was a member of the Devětsil group, from 1926 to its 1931 closing. He worked for major design firms in Prague. His 1920s architecture presaged the aerodynamic forms of 1930s–50s Functionalism and is exemplified by his 1926 villa shown at the third Devětsil exhibition and in his competition entry of a Catholic church in Prague Vršovice. The only structure from his Devětsil period is the 1926–29 school (with Karel Seifert) at 10 Česká St., Bratislava. 1929, Smetana designed the cupboards, armchairs, and bookcases (with Devětsil associate Karel Stráník) for the converted house of Jan and Jaroslav Novák at 215 Poštovní St., Prague.
Bibliography Cat., *Devětsil: Czech Avant-Garde Art, Architecture, and Design of the 1920s and 30s*, Oxford: Oxford Museum of Modern Art and London Design Museum, 1990.

Smeuninx, Lotte (1964–)

Belgian industrial designer; born Heusden.

Training 1982–87, in industrial design in Ghent.
Biography From 1987, Smeuninx has collaborated with Studio Alchimia in Milan and, in Belgium, the firm Struktuplas, architecture and interior designers De Gregorio & Simoni, and Jotul Martin. She participated in the Sottsass Seminar at the Domus Academy in Milan; has designed furniture, public seating, ceramics, and glassware, including 1988 Anja and Vera tea set and tea glasses by Randwyck in Maastricht.
Bibliography Cat., Design Center Stuttgart, *Women in Design: Careers and Life Histories Since 1900*, Stuttgart: Haus der Wirtschaft, 1989: 222–23.

Smilow, Judy (1958–)

American furnishings designer; born White Plains, N.Y.

Training 1976–78, Antioch College, Ohio; 1980–83, communications design, Parsons School of Design, New York; 1982–83, art therapy, The New School for Social Research, New York.
Biography 1978–80, Smilow was a technical illustrator at United Engineers in Connecticut and an art therapist at the Hawthorne Cedar Knolls Residential Treatment Center in Hawthorne, N.Y.; 1983–85, a designer in the graphics department, The Museum of Modern Art, New York. 1985, she established her own studio in Manhattan, where she has been active in the design of jewelry, dinnerware, gifts, stationery, and tabletop items. Concurrently for a time (1989–92), she collaborated with David Tisdale in a venture called Fresh Design. 1996–2000, Smilow was product developer for The Museum of Modern Art and began to specialize in tabletop objects and other products for clients, including Dansk, Formica, The Limited stores, Marimekko, Paine Webber, Sasaki, and Steuben. More than 20 of her glass tabletop designs were licensed to the Riverside Design Group and, from 2001, included metalware.
Exhibitions Work shown at 1990 *Art That Works*, Mint Museum, Charlotte, N.C.; 1987 *Pride of Place Setting*, Parsons School of Design, New York.

Smith, Alfred E. (1836–1926)
Harry A. Smith (c. 1840–1916)

British glass decorators; born Birmingham; active Birmingham and New Bedford, Mass.; brothers.

Biography William L. Smith, the father of Alfred and Harry Smith, started his career as a glassmaker at Biddle, Lloyd and Summerfield in Birmingham; before 1851, worked in his own glass-decorating workshop; was recruited by Deming Jarves to become head of the decorating department, Boston and Sandwich Glass. By 1860, the

Smart Design. Good Grips jar opener. 1989. Stainless steel and Santoprene rubber, 8 3/4 x 5 x 1" (22.2 x 12.7 x 2.6 cm). Mfr.: Oxo International, US. Gift of the designers. MoMA.

Smith brothers had joined their father in his workshop in Birmingham and, subsequently, followed him to work for Boston and Sandwich Glass. William Smith established the Boston China Decorating Works. The brothers managed Mount Washington Glass in New Bedford, Mass., and, 1874, set up their own enterprise on the premises. Exclusively practicing in glass decoration, they developed a technique for fusing color to the surface of white opaline-glass blanks that they bought from English and American manufacturers. A cylindrical vase made by various firms in Sandwich and New Bedford, including Smith Brothers (as their firm was known), was called the 'Smith Vase.' In a style associated with the Aesthetic Movement, Smith Brothers produced wares (gilded in red gold and cut, etched, and engraved) and lampshades, vases, tiles, salts, and plaques. By 1877, the firm was located on Prospect Street, New Bedford; by mid-1880s, at 28–30 William Street, New Bedford; by c. 1890, had offices and showrooms in New York. 1899, the firm closed, and Alfred Smith opened his own workshop in New Bedford but, subsequently, returned to the Mount Washington Glass factory. Harry Smith worked for a time in Meriden, Conn.
Exhibition Smith Brothers wares shown at 1876 *Centennial Exposition*, Philadelphia.
Bibliography Albert Christian Revi, *Nineteenth Century Glass: Its Genesis and Development*, Camden, N.J.: Nelson, 1967: 71, 73, 81–86. Kenneth M. Wilson, *New England Glass and Glassmaking*, New York: Crowell, 1972: 344–348. Doreen Bolger Burke et al., *In Pursuit of Beauty: Americans and the Aesthetic Movement*, New York: The Metropolitan Museum of Art/Rizzoli, 1986.

Smith, John Moyr (1839–1912)
British decorative artist; active London.

Training In architecture in the office of William Salon in Glasgow.
Biography 1860s, John Moyr Smith began working in the design studio of Christopher Dresser; was greatly influenced by the Pre-Raphaelite group; 1870s, created some designs and lithographs of furniture by Collinson and Lock; wrote the book *Ornamental Interiors Ancient & Modern* (London: Crosby Lockwood, 1887), in which he claimed that many of Dresser's designs were his own. The books he illustrated included works by William Shakespeare, Robert Burns, Plutarch, and fairy tales; his illustrations were also published in his *Ancient Greek Female Costume...* (London: S. Low, Marston, Searle, & Rivington, 1882), a version of *Costume of the Ancients* (London: William Miller, 1809) by Thomas Hope; also wrote *Legendary Studies and other Sketches for Decorative Figure Panels* (1889). From c. 1875 on a freelance basis, he drew the images for tiles by W.B. Simpson and for over 20 series of tiles by Minton. Some of the Minton tiles appeared in his *Album of Decorative Figures* (London: S. Low, Marston, Searle, & Rivington, 1882).
Exhibition Smith's Minton tiles shown at 1878 *Exposition Universelle*, Paris.
Bibliography Julian Barnard, *Victorian Ceramic Tiles*, London: Studio Vista, 1972. Jill Austwick and Brian Austwick, *The Decorated Tile: An Illustrated History of English Tilemaking and Design*, London: Pitman House, 1980. Doreen Bolger Burke et al., *In Pursuit of Beauty: Americans and the Aesthetic Movement*, New York: The Metropolitan Museum of Art/Rizzoli, 1987. Annamarie Stapleton, *John Moyr Smith 1839–1912: A Victorian Designer*, London: Richard Dennis, 2002.

Smith, Paul (1946–)
British designer; born Nottingham.

Training Evening classes, Trent Polytechnic (now The Nottingham Trent University), Nottingham.
Biography 1970, Paul Smith opened his first, quite unpretentious clothing store, Paul Smith Vêtement Pour Homme, in Nottingham; began designing clothes for the shop, assisted by wife-to-be Pauline (married in 2001); 1994, moved the shop to bigger quarters; 1976, worked as a consultant to the International Wool Secretariat; subsequently, showed his collection in Paris; 1979, opened his first shop in London and sold Filofax organizers, among others; 1982, second shop in London; by 2002, had 200 shops and 500 outlets; 1987, opened his first shop in New York and 1991, in Tokyo and Paris; 1994, designed womenswear and watches by Citizen; 2000, introduced Paul Smith Fragrances. Smith's signature ceramics, tabletop objects, and the limited-edition Mini car incorporate his ubiquitous striped pattern. He also designed a 2001 collection of furniture, including Wellington sofa and Mondo armchair (M3301) and cabinet (M2052) by Mondo Cappellini.
Exhibition/citations Work subject of 1995 exhibition, Design Museum, London. 1995 Queen's Award for Export; 2001, was knighted in Queen's Birthday Honours List.
Bibliography *Esquire*, Feb. 1993. William Gibson and Paul Smith, *You Can Find Inspiration in Everything (and, if You Can't, Look Again)*, London: Violette, 2001.

Smithson, Alison Margaret (1928–1993); Peter Smithson (1923–2003)
British architects and designers; husband and wife from 1949. Peter: born Stockton-on-Tees. Alison: born Sheffield.

Training Both: 1944–49, architecture, University of Durham, Newcastle-upon-Tyne.
Biography Active in London from 1949, Alison Smithson designed for the 1949 schools sections of the London County Council. The Smithsons were in practice together from 1950, leading a younger

Paul Smith. Mondo armchair (no. M3301). 2001. Wood, polyurethane foam, macroter lacquer, and fabric, h. 28 3/8 x w. 28 3/4 x d. 27 1/8" (72 x 73 x 69 cm). Mfr.: Mondo Cappellini, Italy.

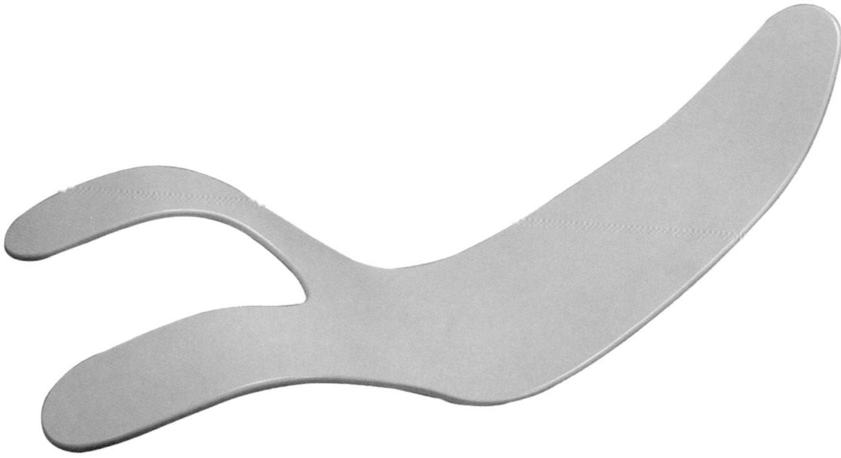

Snowcrash: Teppo Asikainen and Ilkka Terho. Chip rocking lounger. 1996. Form-pressed birch plywood and polyurethane foam; 14 5/8 x 23 5/8 x l. 55 1/8" (37 x 60 x 140 cm). Mfr.: Snowcrash, Finland.

architectural generation toward the Brutalist style and they went on to espouse that architecture, coming from context rather than content, should be exact and appropriate with a certain quiet quality to satisfy inhabitants' wishes and desires. Architecture work: 1950–54 Hunstanton Secondary Modern School, Norfolk; private houses; 1960–64 *The Economist* building on St. James's Street, London; 1963–67 Robin Hood Gardens, Tower Hamlets; 1967–69 Garden Building, St. Hilda's College, Oxford; the East India Docks residential project; the Golden Lane municipal building project, London; and University of Bath buildings in 1980s. Their best-known projects are 1951 Coventry Cathedral; 1957 Sheffield University; 1958 Infant School, Wokingham; 1959 Churchill College, Cambridge; 1964 British Embassy, Brasilia; 1973 Lucas Industries headquarters; and 1984 Maryhill Housing, Glasgow. They designed graphics from 1952, furniture from 1953, and artifacts and clothes. Their chair designs included 1955 Pogo dining-room chair in tubular steel and Plexiglas for *Ideal Homes* exhibit and the 1956 plastic Egg chair for *The House of the Future* exhibit, both part of the 1955–56 *Daily Mail Ideal Home Exhibition*, London. Their urban studies included the 1957–58 Hauptstadt, Berlin; 1962 Mehringplatz, Berlin; 1968–70 Old City in Kuwait, 1979 Damascus Gate, Jerusalem; 1980 Lutzowstrasse, Berlin; and 1982 Parc de la Villette, Paris. Peter became a highly influential teacher at Architectural Association, London. Alison Smithson's publications include *Team 10 Primer* (editor) (1968), *Euston Arch...* (1968), *Team 10 at Royaumont* (1975), *Tram Rats* (1976), *Team 10 out of CIAM* (1982), *AS in DS: An Eye on the Road* (1983), *Upper Lawn, Solar Pavilion, Folly* (1986), and, from 1951, numerous essays. Peter Smithson's include *Flying Furniture: unsere Architektur Rollt, Schwimmt, Fliegt = Our Architecture Rolls, Swims, Flies* (Axel Bruchhäuser, ed., Cologne: König, 1999). The Smithsons as co-authors: *Ordinariness and Light* (London: Faber, 1970), *Without Rhetoric: An Architectural Aesthetic*, 1955–1972 (London: Latimer New Dimensions, 1973), *The 1930's* (Berlin: Alexander, 1985), *The Charged Void—Architecture* (New York: Monacelli, 2001)
Exhibitions Smithsons' work (with Eduardo Paolozzi, Richard Hamilton, Lawrence Alloway, and others) shown at 1956 *This Is Tomorrow*, London; *Modern Chairs 1917–1970* exhibition, London;1968 (14th) Triennale di Milano and 1976 Biennale di Venezia. Work subject of 1994 *Climate Register: Four Works by Alison and Peter Smithson*, Architectural Association, London; 2003–04 *The Smithsons: From the House of Tomorrow to a House for Today*, Design Museum, London.
Bibliography Cat., *Modern Chairs 1918–1970*, London: Lund Humphries, 1971. Cat., *Der Kragstuhl, Stuhlmuseum Burg Beverungen*, Berlin: Alexander, 1986: 138. David Dunster, *Alison + Peter Smithson*, London: Academy, 1982. Liz McQuiston, *Women in Design: A Contemporary View*, New York: Rizzoli, 1988: 118. Alison and Peter Smithson, *Changing the Art of Inhabitation*, London: Artemis, 1994. Helena Webster, *Modernism Without Rhetoric: Essays on the Work of Alison and Peter Smithson*, London: Academy, 1997. Marco Vidotto, *Alison + Peter Smithson*, Barcelona: G. Gili, 1997. Obituary, Peter Salter, Peter Smithson, *The Architectural Review*, June, 2003.

Smout-Baeyens, Marie-Christine (1936–)

Belgian industrial designer; born Ghent.

Training 1955–59, industrial design, École Nationale Supérieure des Arts Visuels de La Cambre, Brussels.
Biography 1959 with husband Frank Smout, Baeyens established Obei Design; became a member of the Unie der Designers in België (UDB); 1965–75, was professor of industrial design, La Cambre, and, 1971–80, director of exhibitions, Brussels Design Center; designed furniture, lighting, appliances, equipment, machines, vehicles, glassware, ceramics, cutlery, exhibitions, and electronic equipment, initially including 1980 kitchen units for the elderly by Resocub, 1987 Génération 90 central-heating boiler by Saint Roch, and 1988 clocks by De Jaeger of Brussels.
Exhibitions Work first shown, at 1967 UBD design center, Brussels, and subsequently at its 1972, 1975, 1976, and 1980 editions. Work also included in 1975 *Selection Interdesign Bruges*, International Council of Societies of Industrial Designers (ICSID), Brussels; 1983 *Signe d'Or* in Belgium; 1986 *Belgian Designs*, Ostend; numerous others.
Bibliography Cat., Design Center Stuttgart, *Women in Design: Careers and Life Histories Since 1900*, Stuttgart: Haus der Wirtschaft, 1989: 224–27.

Smrčková, Ludvika (1903–1991)

Czech glass artist, painter, and graphic designer; born Kladno-Kročehlavy.

Training Under Emil Dítě, V.H. Brunner, and František Kysela, Vysoká Škola Uměleckoprůmyslová (VŠUP, school of applied arts); and Univerzity Karlovy (Charles University); both Prague.
Biography Smrčková began working in glass while studying under Brunner; designed a collection of bookbindings, a discipline in which she retained a lifelong interest; 1928–48, taught at secondary schools in Příbor, Litomyšl, Kladno, and Prague; from 1928, was a member, Czechoslovakian Werkbund (SČSD); 1930–48, worked primarily for Rückel in Nižbor; after 1948, was a designer at Inwald, at Skloexport, and at the Center of Glass Industry and Fine Ceramics in Prague. She collaborated with design agency Krásná Jizba (the beautiful room), introducing simple, dramatic shapes into glass tableware, often incorporating cut edges; also designed one-of-a-kind crystal pieces. Her 1930s vases and bowls in monumental architectural forms were largely geometric with high-quality cut ornamentation. 1960s–70s, she experimented with engraved and painted glass. Smrčková died in Prague.
Exhibitions/citations Work shown at 1925 *Exposition Internationale des Arts Décoratifs et Industriels Modernes*, Paris. Grand prize, 1935 *Exposition Universelle et Internationale de Bruxelles*; grand prize and gold medal, 1937 *Exposition Internationale des Arts et Techniques dans la Vie Moderne*, Paris.
Bibliography Alena Adlerová, *České užité umění 1918–1938*, Prague: Odeon, 1983. Cat., *Tschechische Kunst der 20+30 Jahre, Avantgarde*

und Tradition, Darmstadt: Mathildenhöhe, 1988–89. Cat., *Prague, 1900–1938: capitale secrète des avants-gardes*, Dijon: Musée des Beaux-Arts, 1997.

Snelling, Douglas (1916–1985)

Australian architect and designer; active Sydney.

Biography Mid-1940s for six months, Snelling was a junior partner of Douglas Honnold Architects in Los Angeles; returned to Sydney; designed popular 1947 Saran chairs in parachute webbing and Australian maple, by Functional Products in Sydney. They were greatly in the style of the 1941 webbed chairs of Jens Risom by Knoll in the US, as was a plywood chest with canted drawers in the Snelling range originally designed by Florence Knoll. The 'Snelling' line designs by Functional Products continued to 1955.
Bibliography Cat., *Featherston Chairs*, Victoria, Australia: National Gallery of Victoria, 1988.

Snowcrash; Valvomo Ltd. Architecture Studio

Finland design group; located Helsinki.

History The history of Valvomo Ltd. Architecture Studio (founded in 1993) has been somewhat misunderstood, because Snowcrash (founded in 1996) has been wrongly presumed to be a studio rather than the product range of Valvomo. And Mindworks, an audiovisual/branding studio, was founded in 1995, with clients which have included Nokia, Sonera, and Wärtsilä. The Valvomo consortium was established by Timo Salli (1963–), Ilkka Suppanen (1968–), Ilkka Terho, and Teppo Asikainen (1968–). Subsequently, designer-partners Vesa Hinkola (1970–), Markus Nevalainen (1970–), Kari Sivonen, Rane Vaskivuori, and Timo Vierros joined the group. All had known each other while students at Taideteollinen korkeakoulu, Helsinki, in late 1980s. The group had shown its work 1995–96 in Los Angeles, Copenhagen, and Helsinki, and its innovative, idiosyncratic furniture and lighting was shown at 1997 Salone del Mobile in Milan, where it garnered wide press coverage and enthusiastic interest. The first range of their work included 1996 Globlow (floor), Globlow 03 (wall), and Globlow 04 (ceiling) lamps (by Hinkola and Nevalainen) that inflate from the heat of the electrified bulbs, 1996 Chip legless chaise longue and 1997 Netsurfer computer seat/desk (both by Asikainen and Terho), 1997 Airbag frameless floor-seat (by Pasi Kolhonen, Suppanen), 1999 Desk Top computer table (by Asikainen and Terho). Subsequent work has included 2001 Loco portable work pad (by Suppanen). But many group members began to work independently, such as Timo Salli, and Jan Tromp (1969–), who joined the group after its inception. In addition to design work, the architecture under the Valvomo aegis included 1996 Nylon night club, Helsinki; 1996–97 Proidea Filmstudios, Helsinki; 1996 Stockholm comics library; 1997 Enso Fine Papers photo gallery, Finland; 1997 Marimekko clothing and textile fair stands; 1998 Soup restaurant, Helsinki; 1998 Stora Enso fair stand, Birmingham; 1999 Kaisaniemen Dynamo advertisement company, Helsinki; 1999 Artek shop, showroom, and fair stand, Helsinki; 1998–99 Cable Factory museums, Helsinki; 1999 Ogilvy & Mather advertising agency, Helsinki; 1999–2000 Razorfish media company, Helsinki; 2000 Pravda Restaurant, Helsinki; 2000 Nosturi music center/concert hall, Helsinki. 1998, the Snowcrash brand was bought by Proventus (which had already taken over Artek, including Artek's Art & Technology division, and Swedish textile firm Kinnasand). 2000, the Snowcrash showroom was moved from Helsinki to Stockholm. It became a part of the Art & Technology group of Artek. Distribution was realized worldwide. 2001, Proventus's governors appointed Pio Barone as the CEO of Snowcrash and Art & Technology. 2001, Snowcrash introduced its first office-furniture range; from 2002, began commissioning designers, other than its orginal founders, such as Israeli-in-Paris designer Arik Levy (2001 Get Set desk), Swedish designer Monica Förster, and Swedish textile designer Ulrika Mårtensson. After a reorganization, Snowcrash continues.
Exhibitions Work shown at 2001 *Designers Block* and *100% Design*, London; 2001 *B001*, first European housing exhibition, Malmö; 2001 *Workspheres*, The Museum of Modern Art, New York; 2001 Stockholm Furniture Fair; 2001 Internationale Möbelmesse, Cologne. And subject of 1997 *Future Commodities*, Salone del Mobile, Milan.
Bibliography www.snowcrash.se.; www.valvomo.com.

Giorgio Soavi. Paper weight. 1964. Steel, sphere dia. 1 3/8" (3.5 cm), cylinder h. 2 3/4" (7 cm) x dia. 3" (7.6 cm). Mfr.: Ing. C. Olivetti & C., Italy. Gift of the mfr. MoMA.

Soavi, Giorgio (1923–)

Italian designer, journalist, art critic, publisher, poet, and novelist; born Broni.

Biography Soavi has been a prolific designer of a range of desk accessories and small objects by Olivetti. During the second period of Olivetti's aesthetic success (from 1970s), he commissioned contemporary artists to illustrate the firm's desk diaries and gift books; wrote the biography *Adriano Olivetti: Una sorpresa italiana* (Milan: Rizzoli, 2001) and treatises on Fernando Botero, Jean-Michel Folon, Alberto Giacometti, and others; organized a number of fine-art exhibitions, including 2003 *Giuliano Vangi: Sei sculture a Milano*, Galleria Poleschi Arte, Milan.

Société des Artistes Décorateurs (SAD)

French decorative arts organization and sponsor of annual exhibitions.

History One of several artists' and designers' groups in Paris highly active in the first quarter of the 20th century, the Société des Artistes Décorateurs (SAD) was founded in 1901 with the intention of fostering high standards of production and design in the decorative arts, particularly through its annual Salons. René Guilleré (1878–1931), a cofounder, had been a legal advisor to the Société des Sculpteurs Modeleurs. SAD showed the work of decorative artists and industrial designers, mounting its first (1904) Salon at the Petit-Palais in Paris, where the work of Carrier-Belleuse, Roche Grosse, Grasset, Pierre Selmersheim, Lachenal, and Thesmar was shown. Afterward, its exhibitions were installed to 1923 in the Pavillon de Marsan (Musée des Arts Décoratifs) in the Musée du Louvre and, subsequently, in the Grand-Palais. 1912, the French Chamber of Deputies voted to organize a major international exhibition that would re-establish French prestige in the decorative arts. Originally planned for 1915 and rescheduled for 1922, the exhibition was finally fixed as the ambitious and highly influential 1925 *Exposition Internationale des Arts Décoratifs et Industriels Modernes*, Paris. The inclusion of industrial design (symptomatic of the weak position of the artists) gave manufacturers and merchants the upper hand. The exhibition was intended to emulate the 1902 *Esposizione Internazionale d'Arte Decorativa Moderna* in Turin. The Paris event might more accurately have been called the 1925 Salon edition of the Société des Artistes Décorateurs, as all its other annual presentations of members' work were called. By the time the 1925 *Exposition* occurred, its French members had become divided into two camps: supporters of the traditionally bent, baroque, style and those who supported the unornamented modern style. Decorator/designer/producer Jacques-Émile Ruhlmann was a practitioner of the former; architect Le Corbusier of the latter. The traditionalists tended to be the interior designers or *décorateurs*, whereas the modernists specialized in architecture and furniture design. SAD had its own pavilion, called Une Ambassade Française, an imaginary French embassy. The exhibition's title was the origin of the term 'Art Déco,' coined in the 1960s and replacing the more informative 'Art Moderne' and other terms. The seminal exhibition included pavilions from countries and of manufacturers from around the world (excluding Germany and the US, which eschewed participation). Pride of place was given to traditional design; Le Corbusier's pavilion, called L'Esprit Nouveau, was assigned to the outskirts of the fairgrounds.

Michael Sodeau. Corallo coat rack. 2001. Cane, h. 74 1/8" x dia. 29 1/4" (190 x 75 cm). Mfr.: Gervasoni, Italy.

Enthusiasm for the sumptuous traditional approach had faded but was still in place when Le Corbusier, Robert Mallet-Stevens, René Herbst, Eileen Gray, André Lurcat, Francis Jourdain, and others boycotted the 1929 SAD Salon and formed the progressive Union des Artistes Modernes (UAM), whose exhibitions displayed distinctly utilitarian forms of design and International Style architecture. The luxurious 1935 oceanliner *Normandie* was effectively the last gesture of the traditionalists, who nevertheless banded together and created opulent and widely publicized interiors and furnishings in the oceanliner's monumental spaces. The energy of the traditionalist movement and of SAD itself was thwarted due to World War II. The organization was revived after the war but was never again as strong as its former self. Even so, the Salons continue today.
Bibliography Pierre Cabanne, *Encyclopédie art déco*, Paris: Somogy, 1986. Pierre Kjellberg, *Art déco: les maîtres du mobilier, le décor des paquebots*, Paris: Amateur, 1986/1990. Yvonne Brunhammer and Suzanne Tise, *Les artistes décorateurs, 1900–1942*, Paris: Flammarion, 1990. Nancy J. Troy, *Modernism and the Decorative Arts in France: Art Nouveau to Le Corbusier*, New Haven: Yale, 1991.

Society of Industrial Arts
> See Chartered Society of Designers (CSD).

Sodeau, Mark (1970–)
> See Inflate.

Sodeau, Michael (1969–)
British designer; born and active London.

Training Product design, Central Saint Martin's College of Art and Design, London.
Biography 1995 with three others, Sodeau founded Inflate group in London for the design and production of furniture, lighting, and accessories. 1997 with Lisa Giuliani, Sandeau established an independent studio and has designed lamps, rugs, tables, shelving, ceramics, and, eventually an interior (first such Sodeau effort), for clients, including Abet Laminati, Asplund, Bute, Christopher Farr, E&Y, Isokon Plus, L'ivit, Gervasoni, SCP, Tronconi, and Wedgwood.
Bibliography Michael Sodeau, *Once upon a Line*, London: Black Dog, 2000. Ross Lovegrove, *The International Design Yearbook*, London: Laurence King, 2002.
> See Inflate.

Soénius, Ruth Jeanne (1959–)
German industrial designer; born Cologne.

Training 1978–80, photo-editing and journalism, Kölnische Rundschau, Cologne; 1980–81, wood- and metalworking and plastics processing in Cologne and Aachen; from 1981 under Klaus Lehmann and Richard Sapper, industrial design, Staatliche Akademie der bildenden Künste, Stuttgart.
Biography 1985–86, Soénius was a spokesperson for the Verband Deutscher Industrie-Designer (VDID), a regional group of professional designers in Baden-Württemberg; 1988, was an independent designer at Fabian Industrie Design in Mannheim; 1988–90, lived in the US; subsequently, has worked in the corporate industrial-design department of Siemens, where her assignment is to ensure that all Siemens products are aesthetically distinctive.
Exhibitions Work shown at 1986 *Enfaltungen* exhibition, Stuttgart, and 1987 *Muster und Modelle* exhibition, Rastatt.
Bibliography Cat., Design Center Stuttgart, *Women in Design: Careers and Life Histories Since 1900*, Stuttgart: Haus der Wirtschaft, 1989: 172–73.

Soffientini, Duccio (1946–)
Italian industrial designer; born and active Milan.

Training To 1968, architecture, Politecnico, Milan.
Biography 1968, Soffientini, Riccardo Nava, Giorgio Romani, and Alessandro Ubertazzi established the Centro DA in Milan. From 1970, he collaborated with DA on traditional clocks and electronic equipment by Italora, consulting on clock design and the ergonomics of precision instruments. 1975, the DA group designed sailboat fittings by Nemo and by Comar and, subsequently, a number of other products for clients such as Sordelli, Superband, and Svaba. Soffientini became a member, Associazione per il Disegno Industriale (ADI).
Exhibitions/citations DA designed an exhibition of the Premio Compasso d'Oro for ADI. With DA, participated in international competitions.
Bibliography *ADI Annual 1976*, Milan: Associazione per il Disegno Industriale, 1976.
> See Nava, Riccardo; Ubertazzi, Alessandro.

Soffiotti, Philippe (1972–)
French designer; born Nice.

Training BT (journeyman's certificate) in cabinetmaking; BTS (Brevet de Technicien Supérieur = advanced technician's diploma) in industrial aesthetics; École Nationale Supérieure des Arts Décoratifs, Paris.
Biography Soffiotti has designed graphics, interiors, and furniture, particularly in typically French expressionist forms; designed 1996 Lilybelle chair (school-diploma project) by Néotù, 1997 Petibaunum screen by Soca Line, others by Société Baumann and Le Mobilier National, and furniture (including 1999 Louis Pippo ambassador's desk by Degroote et Mussy) for the chancellery of the 2002 French Embassy in Singapore. He has been working in the design studio of Mario Bellini, Milan.
Citation Louis Pippo desk sponsored in 2000 by VIA (French furniture association).
Bibliography Cat., Sophie Tasma Anargyros et al., *L'école française: les créateurs de meubles du 20ème siècle*, Paris: Industries Françaises de l'Ameublement, 2000. www.via.asso.fr.

Sognot, Louis (1892–1970)
French designer and architect; active Paris.

Training École Bernard-Palissy, Paris.
Biography Sognot first worked for furniture manufacturers in the Faubourg Saint-Antoine district of Paris; 1920–30, managed the Primavera decorating studio of Au Printemps department store, Paris, with Charlotte Chauchet-Guilleré, after the death of the studio's founder René Guilleré. From 1928, collaborated closely with Charlotte Alix. Much of his and Alix's work cannot be individually attributed, although Sognot also designed alone. This was the time when Sognot began to design furniture in metal and glass. His designs also included models in precious and exotic woods, and lighting. Some of his furniture was produced by Bernel. Sognot and Alix designed a 1930 office in the building of the *La semaine à Paris* newspaper (architect, Robert Mallet-Stevens), the Polo de Bagatelle bar, the first-class doctor's office on 1935 ocean-

liner *Normandie*, the 1930 bedroom with furniture and furnishings of the Maharajah of Indore in India, the interior of poster designer Jean Carlu's atelier, furniture for the syndicate office of the City of Paris, the ticket office of an airline, metal furniture for a naval officer, a room in rattan for a young dancer, and the luxurious décors of Henry Bernstein's theaters. After World War II, Sognot collaborated with Jacques Dumond on prototype bentwood furniture intended for mass production. Their lighting showed strict adherence to the Functionalist style. Their workshop/office was the Bureau International des Arts Français, located at 15, rue de l'Abbé-Grégoire, Paris. By 1954 and working alone, Sognot's studio was located at 47, avenue Jean-Jaurès, Paris, and some of his furniture was produced by Chevallier. From 1929 in Paris, Sognot was professor of decoration, École Boulle; for a number of years, was an instructor, École Duperré; from 1938, taught, École des Arts appliqués à l'Industrie, and École Nationale Supérieure des Arts Décoratifs, becoming artist director there after the death of René Prou in 1947. Sognot was a founding member (1929), Union des Artistes Décorateurs (UAM), and a founding member (1951) of Jacques Vienot's Institut d'Esthétique Industrielle.
Exhibitions/citations Work shown at Salon d'Automne from 1923 and Salon of Société des Artistes Décorateurs from 1924, both Paris. Influenced by Cubism, designed the boudoir (with Madeleine Souguez) and bedroom in the pavilion of Primavera at 1925 *Exposition Internationale des Arts Décoratifs et Industriels Modernes*, Paris. With Alix, exhibited regularly at installments of Salon d'Automne in the 1920s and 1930s. One of Sognot's first important commissions (1929 library and reception layouts of Laboratoires Roussel in Paris) shown at 1930 (1st) UAM exhibition; interior design / furniture for the Maharaja of In-dore shown at 1930 edition of Salon d'Automne; new models of rattan furniture at 1952 Salon of Société des Artistes Décorateurs (re-ceiving a first prize) and at 1954 *Formes Utiles*, sponsored by Salon des Arts Ménagers, Paris.
Bibliography Maurice Dufrêne, *Ensembles mobiliers, Exposition Internationale 1925*, Paris: Charles Moreau, 1925; Woodbridge, Suffolk: Antique Collectors' Club, 1989: 84. Raymond Cogniat, 'Louis Sognot et Charlotte Alix, *Art et décoration*, vol. LIX, July–Dec. 1930. Louis Sognot, 'L'art décoratif contemporain,' *Cadre de la vie contemporaine*, no. 3, Aug. 1935. Alastair Duncan, *Art Nouveau and Art Déco Lighting*, New York: Simon & Schuster, 1978: 185–86. Pierre Kjellberg, *Art déco: les maîtres du mobilier, le décor des paquebots*, Paris: Amateur, 1986/1990. Arlette Barré-Despond, *UAM*, Paris: Regard, 1986. Cat., *Les années UAM 1929–1958*, Paris: Musée des Arts Décoratifs, 1988. Patrick Favardin, *Les décorateurs des années 50*, Paris: Norma, 2002: 156.

Sokolov-Skalya, Pavel (1899–1961)
Russian painter and graphic and cinema artist; born Strelnya.

Training 1909–14 under V.V. Konovalov in Saratov; 1914 or 1915–18, V.N. Meshkov's school of painting, drawing and sculpture, Moscow.
Biography 1921–24, Sokolov-Skalya was the head of artists' group Being; 1922, began teaching; from 1924, a member, AKhRR; wrote articles for newspapers and magazines; 1929, visited France and painted some landscapes; 1934–36, was the artistic director, Mosfilm movie studio; 1941–46, was the head, TASS Windows signage firm, Moscow; 1949, became a member of the Soviet academy; died in Moscow. His c. 1939 *The Train Is Moving from the Socialist Station*, with its busy typography, is today a popular, inexpensively reproduced Russian propagandist poster.
Exhibitions/citations First (1921) exhibited his work. *Defense of Tsaritsyn* panel was installed in Soviet pavilion at 1939–40 *New York World's Fair: The World of Tomorrow*. 1942, and 1949 Stalin State Prizes (for *Undergrounders of the City of Krasnodonsk* painting), Russia.

Solá, Nona Umbert (1961–)
> See Umbert Solá, Nona.

Solère; Société Contraste
French manufacturer.

History 1925, Société Solère was founded by Fernand Solère in Paris. He developed and patented a diverse range of products such as a cigarette-rolling machine, the first electric coffee grinder, and the first electric cooker. His 1950s lighting fixture—Solère's best-known invention—features a special diffusion filter, or Solersol, which purportedly produces almost no shadows, is ideally suited for use in offices of architects and engineers, but, initially, was intended to provide precise illumination in factories during machine operations. Known as the Solère Luminaire, still in production, it includes a telescopic arm extender and flexible joints that facilitate almost unrestricted articulation. Both floor, table, and wall models are today made of steel and aluminum by Société Contraste in Crécy-la-Chapelle.
Bibliography www.solere.com.

Solid
Italian design group.

History Active for only three years (1986–88) in Milan, Solid was a group of young international designers, directed by Michele De Lucchi and sponsored by entrepreneur Fulvio Brembilla; was composed of Nicholas Bewick (British 1957–), Mathilde Bretillot (French 1959–), James Irvine (British 1958–), Christian Hartmann (German 1955–), Geert Koster (Dutch 1961–), Ferruccio Laviani (Italian 1960–), Angelo Micheli (Italian 1959–), and Simon Morgan (British 1959–98). Solid's first work (1986) was produced by R.B. Rossana, a kitchen manufacturer. Due to the close association with De Lucchi, the work showed strong Memphis influences. The group attempted to create a new 'school of design' but with little direct success and was particularly interested in reviving an enthusiasm for simple Euclidian geometry. About the manifesto: 'The explosion of design of the early 1980s is now over, as is the fantasy world of colors... and also the superficial world of excessive figurativism,' according to De Lucchi. Work included a watch and bottle holder by Koster; oil/vinegar set, claret jug, colander, dishes, and bread holder by Micheli; a cook's knife and coffee pot by Bretillot; a builder's level, hammer/screwdriver/pliers and child's bank by Morgan; wine glasses and a table centrepiece by Bewick; cutlery by Laviani; and others.
Exhibitions Work introduced at a presentation in Bergamo.
Bibliography Michele De Lucchi (ed.), *Solid: una nuova collezione di oggetti per la casa*, Milan: Electa, 1987.

Solis, Mike (1969–)
American designer; born Dallas, Tex.

Training 1991, bachelor's degree, Parsons School of Design, New York.
Biography 1991, Solis established design studio Worx in Brooklyn, N.Y.; subsequently, worked at Dinoson Inc. In New York, and designed widely published furniture and lighting, including a 1995 range of furniture and home accessories; has designed retail stores in New York and Dallas such as Kirna Zabete, R 20th Century Design, Stussy, Umlaut, and Starcat; settled in Dallas. Furniture clients have included Totem and also Dune in New York.
Exhibitions/citations Showed work at K&T Lionhart Gallery, Boston; Rotunda Gallery, Brooklyn; 1996 (Editor's Award for Best New Designer) and 1998 International Contemporary Furniture Fair (ICFF), New York; a number of venues including, with Andrea Ruggiero, two-person 1999 show *Fun[k]tion: New Basics for the Domestic Environment*, Totem design store, New York. Exhibits at Salone del Mobile, Milan, with G7, a group of Americans.
Bibliography Cat., R. Craig Miller (intro.), *U.S. Design 1975–2000*, Munich: Prestel, 2002.

Solon, Albert L. (1887–1949)
British ceramicist; active Arequipa, Cal.

Biography 1913–16, Solon was the second artistic director (following Frederick H. Rhead) of Arequipa Art Pottery in Arequipa, where he introduced numerous new glazes, including some Persian faïence examples; left Arequipa and taught at the institution known today as California State University at San Jose; established Solon and Schemmel in San Jose, where he designed/made decorative wall and floor tiles; later, was a partner of Paul G. Larkin in the renamed firm Solon and Larkin.
Citation Gold medal (while at Arequipa), 1915 *Panama-Pacific International Exposition*, San Francisco.
Bibliography Paul Evans in Timothy J. Andersen et al., *California Design 1910*, Salt Lake City: Peregrine Smith, 1980.

Solon, Léon-Victor (1872–1957)
French designer and ceramicist; born Stoke-on-Trent; son of Louis-Marc-Emmanuel Solon.

Biography Léon Solon may have designed only a single produced fabric: c. 1893 Allegorical Figures by Wardle & Co. in printed tussah silk. In his primary discipline: 1900–09, he was a ceramicist and artistic director at Minton in Stoke-on-Trent, succeeding his father. At Minton, he designed Art Nouveau pottery and developed new glazes and ceramic techniques. Subsequently, settled in the US and created the polychromed sculptural friezes of Philadelphia Museum of Art (collaborating with Ely Jacques Kahn and architects Buchman & Kahn of New York); was responsible for much of the glazed tilework outside and inside Two Park Avenue (at 33rd Street), New York, and a number of other facades; wrote *Architectural Polychrome Decoration: An Analysis of Fundamental Principles of Polychromed Terra Cotta* (New York: Architectural Record, 1924), first as six articles in *Architectural Record* magazine, to which he contributed other essays.

Solon, Louis-Marc-Emmanuel (1835–1913)

French ceramicist; born Montauban (Tarn-et-Garonne); father of Léon-Victor Solon.

Training Under Lecoq de Boisbaudrant, Paris.
Biography Louis Solon worked at the Manufacture Nationale de Sèvres and experimented with the *pâte-sur-pâte* process; moved to Minton ceramics works in Stoke-on-Trent, just prior to the siege of Paris in the 1870–71 Franco-Prussian War; with his assistants at Minton, realized the now highly regarded Queen Victoria's Jubilee Vase; amassed a large personal collection of salt-glaze pottery and owned more than 3,500 books/publications on ceramics history; c. 1873, married Maria Arnoux, the daughter of Minton artistic director Leon Arnoux, and had eight sons and one daughter. He wrote the books *A Brief Account of Pâte sur Pâte* (Stoke-upon-Trent, 1908), *The Art of the Old English Pottery* (London/Derby: Bemrose & Sons, 1883), and a number of others. Solon retired in 1904 and died in Stoke-on-Trent.
Exhibition Sèvres vase, by Louis Solon and assistants, shown at 1867 *Exposition Universelle*, Paris.

Solvsten, Harbo (1915–1980)

Danish furniture designer.

Training To 1937, cabinetmaking, Tekniske Skole, Århus; to 1942, cabinetmaking, Skolen for Boligindretning (school of interior design), Frederiksberg.
Biography From 1935, Solvsten was a furniture upholsterer; 1945, established a firm for furniture manufacturing; from 1972, taught, Arkitektskolen, Århus, and, from 1976, at Skolen for Boligindretning.
Bibliography Frederik Sieck, *Nutidig Dansk Møbeldesign – en kortfattet illustreret beskrivelse*, Copenhagen: Bondo Gravesen, 1990.

Sommer, Inge (1955–)

German designer; born Paderborn; active Berlin.

Training 1979–85, industrial design, Hochschule der Künste, Berlin.
Biography 1975–78, Sommer was a goldsmith; 1984–91 with John Hirschberg, Susanne Neubohn, and Christof Walther, was active in the Berlinetta design office in Berlin on furniture, furnishings, lighting, interior, and exhibition design; from 1991, has been a lecturer in design and ecology, Foundation Bauhaus, Dessau; from 1993, has taught industrial design, Hochschule der Künste, Berlin; from 1998, has consulted on product design and visual communication.
Exhibitions Work shown in numerous exhibitions, including 1987 *Berlinetta—Möbel 84–86*, Cologne.
Bibliography Cat., Design Center Stuttgart, *Women in Design: Careers and Life Histories Since 1900*, Stuttgart: Haus der Wirtschaft, 1989: 78–81.
> See Berlinetta.

Sonne, Edith Bruun (b. Edith Rose Sonne 1910–1993)

Danish glass and ceramics designer; born Copenhagen.

Training 1930–31, Emil Rannow's art school; to 1934, Kunsthåndværkerskolen, Copenhagen.
Biography 1934–37, Sonne worked in her own studio in Hjortespring; 1938, married Gunnar Viggo Hansen Bruun (1914–79; 1938–39, was under contract to the Saxbo glass factory and was highly knowledgeable in traditional-ceramics production; from 1951, managed a group of designers at Saxbo; 1946–61, collaborated with Nathalie Krebs and Eva Stæhr-Nielsen; 1961–88, was an artist-in-residence at Bing & Grøndahl Porcelænsfabrik. She died in Frederiksberg.
Exhibition Work included in numerous venues from 1967, 1972, 1976 to 1978 Concorso Internazionale della Ceramica d'Arte, Faenza, and 1982 *Danish Ceramic Design*, Pennsylvania State University.

Sony Corporation. TV set (TV8-301). 1959. Plastic, metal, and glass, 8 1/2 x 8 1/4 x 10" (21.6 x 21 x 25.4 cm). Mfr.: Sony Corporation, Japan. Gift of Jo Carole and Ronald S. Lauder. MoMA.

Bibliography Erik Lassen, *En kobenhavnsk porcelænsfabriks historie: Bing & Grøndahl 1853–1978*, Copenhagen: Nyt Nordisk, 1978. Auction cat., *Modernes Design Kunsthandwerk nach 1945*, Munich: Quittenbaum, 4 Dec. 2001, lot 186.

Sontheimer, Carl G. (1914–1998)

American engineer, entrepreneur, and chef; born New York.

Training Engineering degree, Massachusetts Institute of Technology (MIT), Cambridge, Mass.
Biography Sontheimer spent his boyhood in France; during studies at MIT, developed an interest in microwave radiation; invented a number of technical devices, including a microwave-generated directional finder used by NASA on a moon mission; by end of 1960s, had established and then sold a successful electronics / engineering company; 1971, based on a fondness for cooking, established a business to import high-quality cooking utensils and, thus, visited a trade show about cooking in France. There, he saw a professional food-preparation machine, known as the Robot-Coup, first developed by chef Pierre Verdun in 1963. By 1971, the Verdun device had been developed into the more compact, home-use Magimix. Sontheimer purchased prototypes of the machine, acquired the US rights for production, lengthened the feeding tube, improved the cutting blade and disks, added mandatory American safety features, and named it the 'Food Processor.' He introduced his version in 1973 and improved it further in 1974. Through the help of food journalists, the Cuisinart machine, as it became known, was eventually a success, even though the pubic was at first resistant. 1988, he sold the business to an investment group, which in turn sold it to Conair Corporation in 1989. The annual Carl G. Sontheimer Prize for Excellence in Innovation and Creativity in Design was established by the Mechanical Engineering Department of MIT; first recipient was Akil Madhani in 1998. (Madhani patented the EndoWrist instrument which mimics the movement of human hands, wrists, and fingers, particular a surgeon's.)
Bibliography Mel Byars with Arlette Barré-Despond, *100 Designs/ 100 Years: A Celebration of the 20th Century*, Hove: RotoVision, 1999: 158-59. www.cuisinart.com.

Sony

Japanese electronics products firm.

History 7 May 1946, the company was founded under the name Tokyo Tsushin Kogyo Kabushikakaika (TTK, or Tokyo telecommunications/engineering corporation) by Akio Morita (1921–99) and Masaru Ibuka (1908–97). The company produced the first Japanese audiotape recorder (1950 G type), which gained the firm an access to schools and institutions throughout Japan, and, under license from Western Electric, the first successful Japanese transistor radio (1956 TR-55). 1958, TTK's corporate name was changed to Sony with the intention of sounding more Western. The firm introduced the world's-first transistorized TV set (1959 TV8-301), world's first transistorized video recorder (1961), a 5" micro TV set (1962 TV5-303), world's first domestic video recorder (1964), world's first integrated-circuit radio (1966), the Trinitron color TV tube (1968), U-matic color video cassette (1969), domestic Betamax video cassette recorder (1975), world's first Walkman personal stereo cassette player (1979), and digital audio compact disc (1980). Its success has been attributable to intelligent marketing, customer empathy, and product innovation, which continue today. Its Playstation and Playstation 2 for gaming also proved highly successful. However, the Betamax videotape system (launched 1975) was a failure (but continued to be sold in Japan). 1989, Sony took over Columbia movie studio, paying $4.7 billion (£2.9 billion/¥663billion, 1989 equivalences). 2001 with Ericsson, Sony Ericsson Mobile Communications was formed to offer joint services and advanced-technology mobile phones, including picture messaging. In-house-designs have included 1999 Vaio Z600 laptop (by Teiyu Goto) and Vaio Note X9 laptop (Shinichi Ogasawara). From 2000, Sony Entertainment has produced the Aibo robotic dog, designed by artist Hajime Sorayama. Other recent staff-designed products: NW-E3 Network Walkman (by Daisuke Ishii and Takayuki Kobayashi), CD Walkman D-E01 (by Mitsuhiro Nakamura), DVD Player DVP-F11 (by Tetsuro Miyazaka), Pascal surround-sound speakers (by Kirio Masui), DCR-IP7 network handycam (by Atsushi Kawase), CMD-J5 dual-band mobile phone (by Ken Yan,) DCR IP220 handycam (by Kaoru Sumita), PEG-NR70V Clie organizer (by Tetsu Kataoka).
Exhibitions/citations Products subject of 1982 *Sony Design*, The Boilerhouse, Victoria and Albert Museum, London. Gold medal (TV8-301), 1960 (13th) Triennale di Milano; Design of the Decade (1990s) (DSC-F1 digital still camera), IDSA/*Business Week* magazine. Red Dot awards: 2000 (Walkman D-E01, DVD Player DVP-F11, Pascal speakers, two Vaio laptops), 2001 (CMD-J5 dual-band mobile phone and NW-E3 Network Walkman), 2002 (DCR-IP7 handycam), 2003 (DCR-IP220 handycam). 2003 Red Dot Best of the Best (PEG-NR70V Clie), Design Zentrum Nordrhein Westfalen, Essen; and numerous others.
Bibliography Wolfgang Schmittel, *Design Concept Realisation*, Zurich, 1975, 169–96. Nick Lyons, *The Sony Vision*, New York: Crown, 1976. Cat., *Sony Design*, London: Victoria and Albert Museum, 1982. Akio Morita, *From a 500-Dollar Company to a Global Corporation: The Growth of Sony*, Pittsburgh: Carnegie-Mellon University, 1985. Akio Morita with Edwin M. Reingold, *Made In Japan: Akio Morita and the Sony Corporation*, New York: Dutton/Plume, 1986; New York: New American Library, 1997 reissue ed. with a variant title. Paul du Gay et al., *Doing Cultural Studies: The Story of the Sony Walkman*, London/Thousand Oaks, Cal.: Sage/The Open University, 1997. Paul Kunkel, *Digital Dreams: The Work of the Sony Design Center*, New York: Universe, 1999. John Nathan, *Sony: The Private Life*, Boston: Houghton Mifflin, 1999. Mel Byars with Arlette Barré-Despond, *100 Designs/100 Years: A Celebration of the 20th Century*, Hove: RotoVision, 1999: 170.
> See Sorayama, Hajime.

Hajime Sorayama and Sony Corporation staff. Aibo Entertainment Robot (ERS-110). 1999. Various materials, 10 1/2 x 6 x 16 1/4" (26.7 x 15.2 x 41.3 cm). Mfr.: Sony Corporation, Japan. Gift of the mfr. MoMA.

Sopha (RSCG)

French industrial design consultancy; located Paris.

History Sopha was established in Paris as part of the Sopha Group, an architecture, interior design, corporate identity, visual communications, and engineering organization. 1991, Eurocom Advertising merged with French communications group RSCG form Euro RSCG Worldwide. 1994, Euro RSCG Design, a part of Euro RSCG Worldwide, was founded through the amalgamation of Sopha and ADSA + partners. Sopha had been a subsidiary of RSCG since 1985. And ADSA + partners (established in 1985) and Roger Tallon, after various amalgamations, had been a subsidiary of Eurocom Advertising since 1987. The clients have included Société Génerale, Air France, Peugeot, RATP, Habitat, McDonald's, and design work such as Eurostar train, TGV (high-speed train), and the funicular of Montmartre in Paris. 1996, Euro RSCG Worldwide, which incorporates over 230 agencies in 75 countries, became a unit of Havas Advertising, headquartered in New York from 1997 and a vast number of mergers, acquisitions, and name changes have ensued.
Bibliography Agnès Lévitte and Margo Rouard, *100 objets quotidiens made in France*, Paris: APCI/Syros-Alternatives, 1987: 82. Arlette Barré-Despond (ed.), *Dictionnaire international des arts appliqués et du design*, Paris: Regard, 1996: 196.

Sorayama, Hajime (1947–)

Japanese illustrator; born Ehime Prefecture.

Training From 1965, Shikoku Gakuin University, Zentsuji, Kagawa Prefecture; 1967, after the publication of his *Pink Journal*, entered Chuo Art School, graduating 1968.
Biography From 1968, Sorayama worked as advertising-mockup illustrator at an advertising agency; from 1972, was active as an independent freelance illustrator; 1978, drew his first robot. 'Sexy robot' is a term which was coined to describe his images of female cyborgic forms, first created by him in 1979 and, subsequently, published as the book *Sexy Robot* (Tokyo: Genko-Sha, 1983). From 1995, his erotic art was published in *Penthouse* magazine as well a number of other periodicals and books. He has become known for a hyper-illustrated style of pin-up and heteroerotic art, some critics dubbing him the 'new Vargas,' referring to renowned pin-up artist Alberto Vargas (Peru, 1896–1982). Sorayama was the concept artist for the film *Spawn* (1997); designed a mechanical warrior for the film *Space Trucker* (1995) and, by Sony, the 1999 Aibo ERS-110 (and subsequent 1999 Aibo ERS-111, 2000 Aibo ERS-210A, 2001 Aibo ERS-220A, and 2003 Aibo-7). More recent Aibo models feature mechanics that are more futuristic and cyber-type (blinking lights, etc.) with 'learning' and 'reacting' capabilities. 'Aibo' is an acronym of Artificial Intelligent roBOT.
Exhibitions/citations A number of one-person exhibitions worldwide. 2000 Grand prize (Aibo dog), G-Mark Good Design award, Japanese Industrial Design Promotion Organization (JIDPO); 2000 Red Dot award (Aibo ERS-111), Design Zentrum Nordrhein-Westfalen, Essen.
Bibliography Paola Antonelli (ed.), *Objects of Design: The Museum of Modern Art*, New York: The Museum of Modern Art, 2003: 235.

Sørensen, Johnny (1944–)

Danish furniture designer.

Training To 1966, cabinetmaking, Kunsthåndværkerskolen, Copenhagen; 1963, apprenticeship at Helingør Skibsværft (shipyard).
Biography 1966, Sørensen and Rud Thygesen cofounded a design studio. They have collaborated on a major group of seating designs, using laminated and pressure-bent woods, sometimes in cantilever models, by Christensen og Larsen and others. With Thygesen, work

Ettore Sottsass and Perry A. King. Valentine portable typewriter. 1969. ABS polymer and other materials, 4 5/8 x 13 1/2 x 13 7/8" (11.7 x 34.3 x 35.2 cm). Mfr.: Ing. C. Olivetti & C., Italy. Gift of Olivetti Underwood. MoMA.

has included 1969–96 furniture by Fredericia and by Botium; 1980 8000 Series chairs and 1988 Swinger undulating sofa by Magnus Olesen; 1984 EB Bureau by Erik Boisen; 1994 public furniture for the Copenhagen airport. They became best known for their 1975 salt-and-pepper rasps by Rosendahl. From 1994, they have worked independently, and Sørensen continued with clients Magnus Olesen, Erik Boisen, and others.
Exhibitions/citations With Thygesen, work shown in exhibitions, including at Den Permanente, Copenhagen, 1972; Det Danske Kunstindustrimuseum, Copenhagen, 1976; in Chicago, 1977; in New York, 1982 (catalog below). Also with Thygesen, first prize, 1966 anniversary exhibition, Cabinetmakers' Guild; first prize, 1968 furniture competition, Cabinetmakers' Guild; 1969 and 1975 Danmarks Nationalbank Jubilee Foundation; 1971 honorary award, Danish Furniture Manufacturers Association; 1978 Danish Furniture Award; 1978 medal for furniture design, Institute of Business Designers (IBD), US; 1989 G-Mark Good Design award, Japanese Industrial Design Promotion Organization (JIDPO); 1992 Bruno Mathsson Award; 1994 MMI Prize; 1996 award, Industrie Forum Design (iF), Hanover; 1996 European Design Prize, European Union.
Bibliography Cat., David Revere McFadden (ed.), *Scandinavian Modern Design 1880–1980*, New York: Abrams, 1982. Frederik Sieck, *Nutidig Dansk Møbeldesign – en kortfattet illustreret beskrivelse*, Copenhagen: Bondo Gravesen, 1990. Mike Rømer, *Rud Thygesen & Johnny Sørensen: 9006 dage med design = Rud Thygesen & Johnny Sørensen: 9006 days of design*, Copenhagen: Nyt nordisk forlag A. Busck, 1991.

Soria, Enric (1937–)
> See Garcés, Jordi.

Sormani
Italian furniture manufacturer; located Arosio.

History 1961, the firm was founded by the Sormani family with a sophisticated factory operation that produced furniture and furnishings in plastics, metal, wood, and upholstery. Its first designs included Richard Neagle's 1970 Mini-Madio wardrobe in ABS plastic, Claudio Salocchi's 1966 Lia cantilevered side chair and 1970 Apoggio seat, Roberto Lera's 1970 Goga bookshelves, Studio DA's 1970 Tomorrow wine rack, Joe Colombo's 1969 Roto-Living kitchen-storage unit and 1970 Multi-Chair (two stuffed units held by a leather strap), 1970 DA 35 storage table, and Enrico Panzeri's enameled-metal table lamp. Other commissioned designers: Carlo De Carli, Davide Pizzigoni, Marco Penati. Purportedly, Neagle's 1968 Nike chair by Sormani was among the first to be made in a vacuum-formed plastic (some critics claiming it to be the very first).
Exhibitions/citations Seven examples included in 1972 *Design a Plas-tické Hmotý* exhibition, Uměleckoprůmyslové Muzeum, Prague; numerous others. 1971 Mercurio d'Oro.
Bibliography Cat., Milena Lamarová, *Design a Plastické Hmoty*, Prague: Uměleckoprůmyslové Muzeum, 1972: 76, 78, 206. Sylvia Katz, *Plastics: Common Objects, Classic Designs*, New York: Abrams, 1984.

Sornay, André (1902–2000)
French decorator and furniture maker; born Lyon.

Training École des Beaux-Arts, Lyon.
Biography Abandoning the historicist and ancient styles produced in his family's workshop, Sornay designed furniture from 1919 in simple, innovative, Cubist forms inspired by the work of friends Francis Jourdain, Pierre Chareau, and other avant-garde decorators. 1925, he opened a factory in Villeurbanne and, thence, decorated numerous apartments in Paris and Lyon, offices, houses, and libraries. 'Le style Sornay' became recognizable for the use of exposed brass nails.
Exhibitions White-sycamore ensemble at 1923 Salon d'Automne, Paris.
Bibliography Pierre Kjellberg, *Art déco: les maîtres du mobilier, le décor des paquebots*, Paris: Amateur, 1986/1990.

Sornsriwichai, Kunlanath (1972–)
> See Propaganda.

Sottsass Associati
Italian design firm; located Milan.

History 1980, Sottsass Associati studio was founded as a design/architecture studio by Ettore Sottsass, Aldo Cibic, Marco Marabelli, Matteo Thun, and Marco Zanini. Subseqently, group members have changed. Associates have included architects Johanna Grawunder and Mike Ryan, graphic designer Mario Milizia, designer James Irvine, and numerous others, while members tend to have their own indenpendent activities and young designers have used the consortium as a learning laboratory or for internships. After intially specializing in industrial design and interior planning, the studio broadened to include architecture, graphic design, and coporate-identity programs, calling on additional designers from different countries and other disciplines; currently, carries out projects of almost every kind and scope; from 1980, counts its clients in the hundreds such as electronics, oil, publishers, furniture/furnishings, lighting, and financial firms. The studio has organised shows and publications for museums worldwide; recent projects include new ERG Petroli service stations; images for Alessi and Ansaldo; furniture collections by Cassina, Knoll, Zanotta; industrial-design projects for Apple Computer, NTT, Olivetti, Philips, Zumtobel. The group has participated in numerous architecture competitions, including the reconversion of Lingotto, Turin; 'The Peak,' Hong Kong; Ponte dell'Accademia (academy bridge), Venice; MK3 Building, Düsseldorf; Twin Dome City, Fukuoka; Flower Dome stadium interior, Osaka.

Citations Premio Compasso d'Oro: 1984 (Progetto Tronics agenda and calculator with N. Linke and Progetto Columbia agenda by Nava) and 1989 (Halo Click System lighting by Philips).
Bibliography Ettore Sottsass et al, *Sottasss Associati*, New York: Rizzoli, 1988. Milco Carboni (ed.), *The Work of Ettore Sottsass and Asssociates*, New York: Universe, 1999.
> See Sottsass Jr., Ettore (below).

Sottsass Jr., Ettore (1917–)

Austrian designer; born Innsbruck; active Milan.

Training 1934–39, architecture, Politecnico, Turin.
Biography Ettore Sottsass's father Ettore Sot Sass studied at Akademie der bildenden Künste, Vienna, under Otto Wagner and, 1928, moved to Turin with his family, where he became a protagonist in the architectural debate in 1930s between Marcello Piacentini and Giuseppe Pagano over the railway-station project in Florence. 1947, Sottsass the younger began his career, also as an architect, setting up The Studio in Milan; 1956–57, worked in George Nelson's office in New York and, from 1957 or 1958, in design studio of, and was a consultant to, Olivetti. At Olivetti, he designed computers, adding machines, typewriters, systems furniture, and the first (1959) Italian electronic calculator. He became a father figure to the 1960s Anti-Design movement. Early designs include 1959 Elea 9003 computer series, 1963 Praxis and 1964 Tekne 3 typewriters, and 1969 Valentine red plastic portable typewriter (with Perry A. King) by Olivetti. From 1966, his furniture by Poltronova was influenced by Pop art and by a visit to the US, and possibly a stay in Asia. He designed 1969 subcontinental Indian inspired ceramics, radical, but rather plain, 1970 Grey furniture range, inspired by American minimalist sculpture, produced by Poltronova; 1972 Indian-inspired ceramics range (including Shiva pink ceramic 'penis' vase) by Bd Ediciones de Diseño; and 1982 Icarus office-furniture range (with Michele De Lucchi) by Olivetti. His links with Anti-Design became stronger after 1979, when he began to associate with members of Studio Alchimia. 1980, Sottsass, Aldo Cibic, Marco Zanini, and Matteo Thun established Sottsass Associati; 1980 with these and other associates, established the Memphis furniture/furnishings group whose first (1981), surprisingly successful collection was shown during the 1981 Salone del Mobile in Milan. Designs of the following period include 1988 telephone design by Enorme. And by Memphis: 1981 Casablanca and Beverly cabinets, 1981 Carlton and Survetta bookcases, Mandarin table, and 1982 Malabar console as well as fabrics, ceramics, glass, and lighting by Memphis. He closed Memphis in 1988, having decided it was an idea whose time had passed, and continued to include humor and sometimes folly in his designs for clients such as Artemide (lighting), Cleto Munari (accessories), Fusital (hardware fittings), Swid Powell (metalware and ceramics), Zanotta (furniture), and a large number of others, including luxury items (unusual for Sottsass) by Manufacture Nationale de Sèvres in 1993, Baccarat in 2001, Cartier in 2002. 1986, Sottsass, Christopher Radl and Ambrogio Borsani established publicity agency Italiana di Communicazione. Sottsass has worked for more than 100 clients worldwide, as well as architecture through Sottssas Associati, such as 1987–89 Daniel Wolf house, Ridgeway, Colo., through to 1996–98 Van Impe house, St. Lievens Houtem, Belgium.
Exhibitions/citations Work included in 1972 *Italy: The New Domestic Landscape* (an environment), The Museum of Modern Art, New York; 1979 *Design Process Olivetti 1908–78*, Frederick S. Wight Art Gallery, University of California, Los Angeles; during 1981 Salone del Mobile (Memphis-line introduction), Milan; and a large number of venues worldwide. Work subject of 1969 *Miljö för en ny planet: Ettore Sottsass jr.*, Nationalmuseum, Stockholm; 1976, International Design Zentrum, Berlin, and Biennale di Venezia; 1976–77 *Ettore Sottsass, Jr: de l'Objet Fini à la Fin de l'Objet* exhibition, Centre Georges Pompidou/CCI, Paris; 1985–95, Turin and Paris; 1987 and 1991 exhibitions, Blum Helman Gallery, New York; 1991, Trento and Rovereto; 1994, Centre Georges Pompidou; 1999 *Sottsass: l'Arte del Progetto*, Centro per l'arte contemporanea Luigi Pecci, Prato; 1999 touring exhibition, originating at Salone del Mobile, Milan (catalog below); 2003 *Ettore Sottsass: Vingt Ans de Design pour Olivetti*, Centre Georges Pompidou, Paris. 1956, 1959, 1970 (five citations individual and with others), 1987 (with De Lucchi), 1989 (two citations), 1994 (two citations) Premio Compasso d'Oro; honorable mention, 1973 BIO 5 industrial-design biennial, Ljubljana; honorary degree, Royal College of Art, London; 1992, Officer of Ordre des Arts et Lettres, France; 1993 honorary degree, Rhode Island School of Design, US; 1994 Köpfe prize, Industrie Forum Design (iF), Hanover; 1996, Lifetime Achievement award, Brooklyn Museum; 1997, Oribe award, Japan.
Bibliography Penny Sparke, *Ettore Sottsass Jr*, London: The Design Council, 1982. *Sottsass Associati*, New York: Rizzoli, 1988. *Ettore Sottsass, Jr: de l'objet fini à la fin de l'objet*, Paris: Centre de Création Industrielle, 1977. Marco Zanini, 'A Well Travelled Man,' in *Design ist unsichtbar*, Vienna, 1981: 464–74. Barbara Radice, *Memphis*, New York: Rizzoli, 1984. Paolo Martegani, Andrea Mazzoli, and Riccardo Montenegro, *Memphis una Questione di Stile*, Rome: Istituto Mides, 1984. Gilles de Bure, *Ettore Sottsass Jr*, Paris: Rivages, 1987. Barbara Radice, *Ettore Sottsass: A Critical Biography*, New York: Rizzoli, 1993. Bruno Bischofberger, *Ettore Sottsass: Ceramics*, London: Thames & Hudson, 1995. Milco Carboni (ed.), *The Work of Ettore Sottsass and Asssociates*, New York: Universe, 1999. Cat., *Ettore Sottsass*, Milan: Salone del Mobile, 1999. *Ettore Sottsass: Esercizi = Exercises,* Milan: Alberico Cetti Serbelloni, 2001. Milco Carboni and Barbara Radice, *Ettore Sottsass: Scritti 1946–2002*, Milan: Neri Pozza Editore, 2002. Paola Antonelli (ed.), *Objects of Design: The Museum of Modern Art*, New York: The Museum of Modern Art, 2003: 226.

Soudbinine, Séraphin (1870–1944)

Russian artist and sculptor; active Paris.

Training In sculpture.
Biography Soudbinine emigrated to Paris; collaborated with sculptor Auguste Rodin for ten or so years from c. 1896; traveled to the US with Polish painter Saveli Abramovich Sorine (or Sorin or Ssorin, c. 1887–), was impressed by the Pierpont Morgan collection of Asian ceramics at The Metropolitan Museum of Art (which ironically today owns an impressive Guggenheim screen by Soudbinine, see below); returned to Paris and set up a kiln and pursued ceramics production, mainly for sculpture; for some vessels, he called on *grès* porcelain which he engraved; signed pieces following his spouse's death: *en souvenir de ma femme* (in memory of my wife), evidently devoted to her. For Jean Dunand in Paris, Soudbinine designed/made doors and screens, for which Soudbinine created the overall images and carved the low-relief wood, with lacquerwork applied by Dunand. 1925–26 examples are the Fortissimo and Pianissimo screens for the music room of Mr. and Mrs. Solomon R. Guggenheim's house, Port Washington, N.Y., US. Soudbinine was also known to have created bronze sculpture, some struck by founder Alexis Rudier, Paris; also collaborated with Paul Jeanneney, who helped lesser-known sculptors, such as Soudbinine, sell their work.
Exhbitions Guggenheim screen in 1998 *Jean Dunand: Master of Art Deco*, The Metropolitan Museum of Art, New York.
Bibliography M. Komaneck and V.F. Butera, *The Folding Image: Screens by Western Artists of the Nineteenth and Twentieth* Centuries, New Haven: Yale University Art Gallery, 1984: 241–42. Félix Marcilhac, *Jean Dunand: His Life and Work*, London: Thames & Hudson, 1991.

Sougez, Madeleine (1891–1945)

French designer.

Biography 1920s–30s, Sougez designed for Au Primavera decorating department of Printemps department store, Paris, including interiors, *grés* ceramics by Sainte-Radegonde, and other wares.
Exhibitions Work included in Primavera pavilion (a kitchen), 1925 *Exposition Internationale des Arts Décoratifs et Industriels Modernes*; 1924, 1926 and 1927 Salons of Société des Artistes Décorateurs; all Paris.
Bibliography Alastair Duncan, *Art Nouveau and Art Déco Lighting*, New York: Simon & Schuster, 1978: 185.

Şouriau, Paul-Jean (1852–1926); Étienne Souriau (1892–1979)

French philosophers and theoreticians.

Training Paul: to 1873, École normale supérieure, and, 1881, doctoral degree with the thesis, 'Théorie de l'invention.'
Biography In his book *La beauté rationnelle* (Paris: F. Alcan, 1904), Paul Souriau was one of the first to propose that aesthetics and usefulness should be married, that an object can have rational beauty, and that its form should be an expression of its function—all propositions presaging industrialized aesthetics and Functionalism. He asserted, 'There is no reason for art and utilitarian objects to be separated, because the destiny of people is now being determined by the machine.' Paul Souriau also wrote the books *L'esthétique du mouvement* (Paris: F. Alcan, 1889), *La suggestion dans l'art* (Paris: F. Alcan,

1893), *L'esthétique de la lumière* (Paris: Hachette, 1913), *L'imagination de l'artiste* (Paris: Hachette, 1901), *La faïence de Langeais, ou, le destin des Boissimon, gentilshommes angevins* (Paris: Éditions France-Empire, 1987; 1996 2nd ed.), and others. His son Étienne Souriau was the director of the journal *Revue d'esthétique*, which had a strong influence on the development of modern theories of aesthetics and design. Some of Étienne's writings are included in *La correspondance des arts, éléments d'esthétique comparée* (Paris, Flammarion: 1947); also *Clefs pour l'esthétique* (Paris: Seghers, 1970) and *Le sens artistique des animaux* (Paris: Hachette, 1965).

Sowden, George James (1942–)

British designer; born Leeds; active Milan; husband of Nathalie du Pasquier.

Training 1960–64, 1966–68, architecture, Gloucestershire College of Arts and Design (part of University of Gloucestershire from 2001).
Biography 1970, Sowden settled in Milan and worked in the Olivetti design studio, headed by Ettore Sottsass, where he developed design ideas concerning information technology and designed computers and calculators; 1981, became a member of Sottsass's Memphis group and designed furniture/furnishings for its collections to its 1988 closing; concurrently worked independently and with his wife Nathalie du Pasquier; designed tableware by Bodum, including 1986 stainless-steel fruit bowl, whose pattern was produced by a sophisticated 12-stage stamping process. He has served clients such as Italtel (telephone equipment), Lorenz (time pieces with du Pasquier), and Shiznoka (electronics). 1981 Memphis designs include D'Antibes cabinet, Pierre table, Oberoi chair, Chelsea bed, and Acapulco, Excelsior, and American clocks, and, subsequently, 1982, 1983, 1985, 1986, and 1987 ceramics, fabrics, lighting, and furniture collections. 1981, he established SowdenDesign (formerly Milan Pacific) in Milan and, 1999, opened a branch in San Francisco. The studio has a large number of partners and a staff of 15 engineers, designers, graphic artists, and others and offers branding and production services and product design including Internet kiosks, pay and touch-screen Web phones, Olivetti computers and peripherals, home appliances by Ace, Alessi, Asus, Bodum, Guzzini, Olivetti, Steelcase, Swatch, Telecom Italia, and others.
Bibliography Cat., *Design Process: Olivetti 1981–1983*, Milan: Olivetti, 1983: 386. Auction cat., *Memphis: La Collection Karl Lagerfeld*, Monaco: Sotheby's, 1991. Jeremy Myerson and Sylvia Katz, *Conran Design Guides: Tableware*, London: Conran Octopus, 1990: 34, 46, 78. *Modo*, no. 148, Mar.–Apr. 1993: 126. www.georgesowden.com

Spada, Ercole (1938–)

Italian automobile designer; born Busto Arsizio.

Biography 1960, Spada began as an entry-level auto-body designer at the Carrozzeria Zagato. His first assignment there was a special body for the Aston Martin, realized as 1960 DB4 GT Zagato, an amalgamation of Spada's own approach and Zagato's already established aerodynamic forms. 1960–69, he was in charge of all design at Zagato, whose car bodies included 1960 Osca GT, 1963 Alfa Romeo Giulietta SZ, 1965 Lamborghini 3500 GTZ, 1966 Alfa Romeo Giulia TZ2, and 1972 Lancia Fulvia Sport—all have subsequently become revered collectors' items. 1977–83, Spada designed bodies for BMW series 5 and 7. From 1983, he worked with I.D.E.A. design consultancy, headed by Franco Mantegazza, on Lancia, Alfa Romeo, and Fiat bodies.
Exhibition 1960 Auto Show (DB4 GT Zagato), London.
Bibliography Penny Sparke, *A Century of Car Design*, London: Mitchell Beazley, 2002.

Spade, Batistin (1891–1969)

French decorator and furniture designer; born Marseille.

Biography 1919, Spade made a modest beginning in his own cabinetmaking and tapestry-design workshop; designed sumptuous, refined furniture and numerous interiors, including the offices of oceanline firms, banks, and insurance companies in France and abroad; 1941 and 1943, was commissioned by Le Mobilier National to design the offices of governmental officials and ambassadors; worked on 30 oceanliners, including 1927 *Île-de-France*, 1930 *Liberté* (launched first as Germany's *Europa*), 1935 *Normandie*, and 1951 *Flandre*.
Bibliography *Ensembles mobiliers*, Paris: Charles Moreau, vol. 5, no. 15, 1945. Yolande Amic, *Le mobilier français 1945–1964*, Paris: Regard/VIA, 1983: 22. Pierre Kjellberg, *Art déco: les maîtres du mobilier, le décor des paquebots*, Paris: Amateur, 1986/1990.

Spadolini, Pierluigi (1922–2000)

Italian industrial designer; born and active Florence.

Biography 1947–48, Spadolini designed systems furniture; was a co-founder of Istituto Superiore per l'Industria Artistica, Florence. He was the architect of Palazzo degli Afari, Florence; Palazzo di Giustizia, Siena; and a university and schools in Messina, Pisa, Rome, and Grosseto. His product designs ranged widely from furniture to motor yachts. He became a member, Associazione per il Disegno Industriale (ADI). His plastic furniture was produced by Kartell. Other clients included 1 P, Arflex, Autovox, Gandi, Gretz, ICS, Lesa, Magneti Marelli, and OTB.
Bibliography *ADI Annual 1976*, Milan: Associazione per il Disegno Industriale, 1976. Alfonso Grassi and Anty Pansera, *Atlante del design italiano 1940/1980*, Milan: Fabbri, 1980: 291. Giuseppe Chigiotti, *Pierluigi Spadolini, il design*, 1998.

Špalek, Josef (1902–1942)

Bohemian architect and furniture designer; born Plzeň.

Training Under Josef Gočár, Akademie výtvarných umení (academy of fine arts); and České Vysoké Učení Technické (Czech technical university); both Prague.
Biography 1928–34, Špalek worked in the studio of Jaromír Krejcar in Prague. 1920s, his most notable project is the 1928–29 monumental villa at 21 Karolíny Světlé St., Plzeň. Chosen over Karel Stráník, whose furniture was thought to be too snobbish, for this old house, in Louny of Marie Bieblová and Konstantin Biebl, Špalek designed a compact combination of bookcase, spacious couch, sideboard, and several cupboards, and included a large round table and various occasional tables from standard models by Thonet; also designed wooden furniture, including a glass-fronted extension to the sideboard in the Louny house, whose walls were painted white, and whose overall style was clearly Bauhaus influenced. He died near Moscow, a victim of Stalinist repression.
Bibliography Cat., *Devětsil: Czech Avant-Garde Art, Architecture, and Design of the 1920s and 30s*, Oxford: Museum of Modern Art; London: Design Museum, 1990.

Spalt, Johannes (1920–)
> See Arbeitsgruppe 4.

Sparre, Louis (Count Sparre 1863–1964)

Swedish furniture designer and ceramicist; active Finland.

Training 1886–90, painting, Académie Julian, Paris.
Biography 1891–1911, Count Sparre worked in Finland and, 1897, founded the Iris factory in Porvoo; subsequently worked in Stockholm; designed and illustrated books, and, with Akseli Gallen-Kallela, Eliel Saarinen, Herman Gesellius, and Armas Lindgren, was considered a pioneer in the revival of design in Finland. His bold furniture designs were rendered in emphatic geometric silhouettes.
Citation First prize, 1894 furniture competition, Suomen Käsityön Ystävien (friends of Finnish handicraft).
Bibliography Marja Supinen, *Priskurant öfver 'Aktiebolaget Iris' keramiska tillvärkningar = Hintaluettelo 'Aktiebolaget Iris' en savitaideteoksista = Tarif des fabrications de poteries de l''Aktiebolaget Iris' = Preiskurant über keramische Fabrikate der 'Aktiebolaget Iris,'* Porvoo: Porvoo Museum, 1979. Cat., David Revere McFadden (ed.), *Scandinavian Modern Design 1880–1980*, New York: Abrams, 1982.
> See Iris.

Spear, Francis (1902–)

British glass designer and maker; born London.

Training To 1926, Central School of Arts and Crafts, and Royal College of Art; both London.
Biography Spear was an assistant to Martin Travers; to 1938, taught lithography, Central School of Arts and Crafts and Royal College of Art, both London; was a radical exponent of stained glass and was commissioned to design church windows, including those at Aldeburgh in 1930, Astley Bridge in 1930, and Snaith in 1934, and the cathedral in Cape Town, South Africa, in 1957, considered by him to be his best work; also designed 1938 *St. John the Baptist* window in acid-treated flashed glass (executed by John Barker); was an occasional council member, Arts and Crafts Exhibition Society.

Bibliography Cat., *Thirties: British Art and Design Before the War*, London: Arts Council of Great Britain/Hayward Gallery Gallery, 1979.

Spear, Laurinda (1951–)

American architect and designer; born Rochester, Minn.; active Miami, Fla.

Training To 1972, Brown University, Providence, Rhode Island; to 1975, architecture, Columbia University, New York.
Biography Spear became known for the designs of Atlantis and Palace buildings in Miami; also designed banks, houses, shopping centers, condominiums, courthouses, and office towers; 1977 and 1979, was a part-time faculty member, School of Engineering and Environmental Design, University of Miami; 1977 with husband Bernardo Fort-Brescia and three associates no longer with the firm, cofounded architecture firm Arquitectonica in Miami. The first of their controversial buildings is the 1979 house (with Rem Koolhaas) for Spear's parents. 1985 with her husband, Spear established Arquitectonica Products; lived in 1990 Pink House of their own design. Initially gained recognition for 1980–82 Atlantis building with a hole, Miami. Other work has ranged from 1982–88 Banco de Credito Headquarters and 1988–94 US Embassy, both Lima, Peru, to 1997–2000 Miami City Ballet Studios and Headquarters (1997–2000), Miami Beach; 1997–2001 Aventura Government Center, Aventura, Fla.; and 1994–2002 57-story Westin Hotel, New York. Product-design work: 1984 Madonna table by Memphis, 1988 Cosmos rug by V'Soske, 1983–88 ceramics and silver serving pieces by Swid Powell, 1993–94 mirrored, rattan and sectional furniture by Flores Design Editions, 1997–99 watches and clocks by Building Timepieces by Projects,1999 door handle by Valli & Valli, 2000 the Quote pen by Acme, 2001 Whirlybird ceiling fan by Modern Fan Company. Work that has reflected her architecture: Arquitectonica neckties and scarves from 1984; 1986 Laurinda Spear Collection of laminates by Formica, 1998 Laurinda Spear Collection of fabrics by HBF Textiles, 1999 ten patterns of architectural glass by Skyline Glass Company, 2000 Linework collection of vinyl wall coverings by Wolf Gordon. Spear was a cofounder, American Institute of Architects National Committee on Design.
Exhibitions/citations Work included in numerous exhibitions from 1979, Cooper-Hewitt National Design Museum, New York. Subject of 1984–85 *Architectonics: Yesterday, Today and Tomorrow*, touring the US (catalog below). Received 1975 Progressive Architecture award (with Rem Koolhaas); 1975 design award, New York Society of Architects; 1978 Prix de Rome in Architecture; 1982 award and 1998 silver medal, American Institute of Architects (AIA), South Florida Chapter, 1983 award for Atlantis building; selection, 1986 *Architec-tural Record Houses* (for Casa Los Andes); 1992, elected fellow, AIA; 2001, elected National Academician, National Academy of Design.
Bibliography Patricia Leigh Brown, 'Having a Wonderful Time in Miami,' *The New York Times*, 25 Oct. 1990: C1, 6. Cat., Jan van der Marck (ed.), *Arquitectonica: Yesterday, Today, Tomorrow—An Exhibition of Drawings, Models, Plans and Photographs, 1977–1984*, Miami: Center for the Fine Arts, 1984. Beth Dunlop, *Arquitectonica*, Washington, D.C.: American Institute of Architects, 1991.

Spectre, Jay (1930–1992)

American interior and furniture designer; born Louisville, Ky.

Biography 1951, Spectre began his interior-design career in Louisville; 1968, established an eponymous studio in New York and designed interiors for rich clients, private jet aircraft, yachts, and offices, which showed Art Déco, Asian, and African influences with high-tech and hand-carved elements; 1985 with Geoffrey Bradfield, formed Spectre & Bradfield, and established licensing firm JSPS to sell production rights to furniture, china, rugs, and other articles designed by the Spectre firm. Product design: 1987 Neo-Deco line of furniture by Century Furniture Industry, rug designs by Louis de Poortère, outdoor furniture by Jordan Brown, Filipino-wicker furniture by Century, lighting by Sunset. Prepared by Spectre and Geoffrey Bradfield, his work was represented in the book *Point of View: Design by Jay Spectre* (Boston/London: Little, Brown/Bullfinch, 1991).
Citations Elected to 1986 Hall of Fame, *Interior Design* magazine; 1987 Award for Excellence, *Bride's* magazine.
Bibliography *Metropolitan Home*, Apr. 1990: 72. Obituary, 'Jay Spectre, 63: Interior Designer of Luxurious Homes' *The New York Times*, 17 Nov. 1992.

Basil Urwin Spence. Armchair. 1949. Laminated wood and leather, 33 1/2 x 21 1/4 x 20 3/8" (85.1 x 54 x 51.8 cm). Mfr.: H. Morris & Co., Scotland. Gift of the mfr. MoMA.

Spectrum, 't

Dutch furniture manufacturer; located 's-Hertogenbosch.

History 1941, 't Spectrum was set up as a division of Weverij de Ploeg and, after World War II, became independent; 1954, appointed Martin Visser as the head of design, for its range of Functionalist furniture, which does not reveal its crafts-built production. Visser's apparently timeless 1957 BR 02.7 sofa bed and 1960s furniture are still in production. The 1970 BQ 01 sofa by Wim Quist for the Kröller-Müller Museum in Otterlo has also remained in production from 1988. Ben Hoek designed 1995 TE10 and TE11 tables and 2001 Nexus wall system Arold Merckx designed 2000 Spider table, Flow High dining chair, and Flow Low easy chair. Another designer, of 2002 Base sofa. is Michiel van der Kley (1962–).
Citations A number of prizes include, for Nexus wall system: 1996 Best Dutch Furniture; 1997 Aluminum Award, Nederlandse Designprijs.
> See De Ploeg; Hoek, Ben; Visser, Martin; De Ploeg.

Spence, Basil Urwin (1907–1976)

British architect and exhibition and interior designer; born Bombay.

Training Architecture, Edinburgh and London.
Biography Spence was a draftsperson for Edwin Lutyens during the design of the Viceroy's House in Delhi; worked for architect Rowan Anderson; 1931, formed a brief partnership with William Kininmonth in Edinburgh and, subsequently, moved to London, where he established a practice; before World War II, built large country houses. His designs after the war included housing developments, churches, theaters, schools, civic centers, and educational institutions, including University of Sussex. He was best known for the 1954–62 rebuilding of Coventry Cathedral, having won the 1950 competition. Spence designed Scandinavian-inspired furniture for Scottish Furniture Manufacturers' Association and for Furniture Development Council. His monumental approach is illustrated by 1970 Household Cavalry Bar-

racks in Knightsbridge, London, and 1971 British Embassy in Rome.
Exhibitions Was consultant architect (chief designer, James Gardner) to 1946 *Britain Can Make It*, Victoria and Albert Museum, London. Designed Sea and Ships pavilion, 1951 *Festival of Britain* exposition, London; British Pavilion, 1967 *Universal and International Exposition (Expo '67)*, Montréal; and others.
Bibliography Michael Farr, *Design in British Industry: A Mid-Century Survey*, London: Cambridge, 1955: 216. Vittorio Magnago Lampugnani (ed.), *Encyclopedia of 20th-Century Architecture*, New York: Abrams, 1986: 315–16. Charles McKean, *Scottish Thirties: An Architectural Introduction*, Edinburgh: Scottish Academic Press, 1987. Brian Edwards, *Basil Spence, 1907–1976*, Edinburgh: Rutland, 1995.

Spencer, Edward (1872–1938)
British metalworker, silversmith, and jeweler; active London.

Biography Spencer was an entry-level designer at Artificers' Guild; 1903 when Montague Fordham took over the Guild, became the chief designer there and created silver objects with applied shagreen, mother-of-pearl, wood, coconut, and ivory. The craft aspect of his work was emphasized by visible hammer marks. Part of the Guild's success was due to Spencer's contributions, which kept up with the times. 1905, he founded the short-lived Guild of St. Michael.
Exhibitions Work regularly shown at Arts and Crafts Society and at Artificers' Guild, both London.
Bibliography Charlotte Gere, *American and European Jewelry 1830–1914*, New York: Crown, 1975: 221. Annelies Krekel-Aalberse, *Art Nouveau and Art Déco Silver*, New York: Abrams, 1989.

Sperlich, Herman A.
> See Ironrite Ironer Company, The.

Spojené Umĕleckoprůmyslové Závody (aka UP)
Czech furniture factories.

History 1921, UP (united applied-arts factory) was founded by Jan Vaněk by amalgamating a number of furniture factories in Moravia; in addition to furniture, produced metal lighting and textiles. The consortium employed 600 workers and aimed at the production of standardized (or 'type') furniture designed by Jan Grunt, Josef Gočár, Jan Vaněk, and Evžen Wiesner; 1928–35, produced 'E' range of demountable furniture and 1935–37 'H' 'sector'-type furniture range; was a member of Czechoslovakian Werkbund (SČSD) and participated in all of its exhibitions. 1947, the consortium was nationalized.
Bibliography Alena Adlerová, *České užité umění 1918–1938*, Prague, 1983.

Spook, Per (1939–)
Norwegian designer; born Oslo; active Paris.

Training In fine art; subsequently, 1957, École de la Chambre Syndicale de la Couture Parisienne, Paris.
Biography Spook worked with some of the best-known fashion designers for ten years until 1979, when he began creating his own collections; 1980, established a fashion house; designed his first (1986) ceramic dinner service (a series of four bowls with white inside and brown outside) by Les Porcelaines Lafarge; early 1990s, opened a shop in Paris.
Citations 1978 Aiguille d'Or de la Haute Couture; 1979 Dé d'Or.
Bibliography *Les carnets du design*, Paris: Mad-Cap Productions/APCI, 1986: 33.

Sportes, Ronald-Cecil (1943–)
French architect and designer; born Orléanville, Algeria; active Paris.

Training École des Arts Appliqués et des Métiers d'Arts, Paris.
Biography Sportes worked with Arne Jacobsen in Copenhagen and returned to Paris, where he worked with French and foreign architects to 1968; studied inflatable structures, including a multi-directional model by Kleber-Colombes tire company; worked at architecture firm Elsa and, subsequently, became creative and research director at Marange; 1975, established his own practice in Paris; designed interiors of Lancôme offices in New York and its headquarters in Paris, and of 1986 Concorde airplane. Other commissions: Arletty cinema, Ministère de la Justice, Cosmair office in New York, Volvo's North African headquarters in Casablanca, Museum of Science and Technology at Parc de la Villette in Paris, cultural center and museum of French wines in Osaka, Cherfien des Phosphates office in Morocco, and interior and furniture of the TGV (high-speed train) terminal in Montparnasse train station, Paris. He worked for Consulting and Engineering Cooperative for Light Industry, Beijing, on the design and production of hardwood furniture; received a commission from Chinese Ministry for Industry; designed 1983–84 interior and furniture for a room in French president Mitterrand's suite in the Palais de l'Élysée. Other product design: a 22-piece collection by JG Furniture; US; lighting by Pentalux, Italy; and furniture projects with production supported by VIA (French furniture association). Subsequent work has included the Moroccan Pavilion at *Expo 2000*, Hanover. 2001, Sportes entered into a partnership with Owens & Legge, New South Wales, Australia.
Exhibitions Work included in 1968 international exhibition on inflatable structures, Paris; 1968 (14th) Triennale di Milano; 1969 exhibition, touring the US; 1988 exhibition of contemporary French furniture, Victoria and Albert Museum, London (catalog below). Work subject of 1987 retrospective, International Design Center of New York, Long Island City, N.Y.
Bibliography Sophie Anargyros, *Le mobilier français*, Paris: Regard/VIA, 1980: 82–83. Cat., Garth Hall and Margo Rouard Snowman, *Avant Premiere: Contemporary French Furniture*, London: Eprouvé, 1988. Cat., *Les années VIA, 1980–1990*, Paris: Musée des Arts Décoratifs, 1990. Un nouveau look pour la restauration rapide,' *Architecture intérieure créé*, no. 262, Nov.-Dec. 1994: 58–61.

Spratling, William (1900–1967)
American architect and silversmith; born Sonyea, N.Y. Active New Orleans, La.; and Taxco, Mexico.

Biography 1920s, Spratling was instrumental in the emergence of modern Mexican silver; taught, Tulane University, New Orleans; 1925, settled in Taxco, where he revived the silversmithing art; used artisans in the Taxco area to produce his patterns and shapes, as a result of which Taxco became known as the silver capital of the Americas; also designed the silver-production tools and molds; in his utilitarian silver and jewelry, incorporated mother-of-pearl, hardwoods, feathers, baroque pearls, tortoiseshell, coral, amber, turquoise, jadeite, rock crystal, obsidian, and malachite. His wares, obviously handcrafted, were produced in his workshop known as Las Delicias. Products were sold at stores including Lord & Taylor, Macy's, Tiffany, and Neiman Marcus in the US and orders were placed by US President Lyndon Johnson and actors Cantinflas, Orson Welles, and Dolores del Rio. At one time, half the silverware sold in Mexico City was from Spratling's workshop. His designs sometimes incorporated ancient Meso-American motifs. A c. 1950 sugar spoon in the shape of a duck's bill (a form frequently called on) has been widely published. He wrote the book *Little Mexico* (New York: J. Cape & H. Smith, 1932). He also designed furniture by Taxco. Known today as 'William Spratling's Heirs Company,' the ranch/workshop was bought by his friend Alberto Ulrich from the former employees. 1992, the Spratling Silver retail store was opened in San Antonio, Tex., selling some of Spratling's original designs.
Exhibitions Work subject of 1987 exhibition, Taxco.
Bibliography Lucía García-Noriega y Nieto, 'Mexico Silver: William Spratling and the Taxco Style,' *The Journal of Propaganda and Decorative Arts*, Fall 1988: 42–53. Joan T. Mark, *The Silver Gringo: William Spratling and Taxco*, Albuquerque: University of New Mexico, 2000. Sandraline Cederwall and Hal Riney, *Spratling Silver*, San Francisco: Chronicle, 2000. Taylor D. Littleton, *The Color of Silver: William Spratling, His Life and Art*, Baton Rouge: Louisiana State University, 2000.

Staatliche Porzellan-Manufaktur (aka Königliche Porzellan-Manufaktur, or KPM)
German porcelain factory.

History 1763, the Königliche Porzellan-Manufaktur (KPM; royal porcelain factory) was authorized to be established by Frederick II (der Großer) of Prussia, who designated the factory's trademark: the royal blue scepter. The finest Biedermeier porcelain was made in the factory in Vienna, its wares often called 'Royal Vienna,' and in Berlin; however, the latter produced more formal work. 1919, the factory was renamed the Staatliche Porzellan-Manufaktur but continued to use the 'KPM' abbreviation, and today is back to Königliche Porzellan-Manufaktur in Berlin. 1925–28 in the modern era, it was directed by Nicola Moufang and, 1929–38, by Graf Günther von Pechmann. Both supported the modern-design ideals espoused by the Deutscher Werkbund and the Bauhaus. Using designs from the Kunstgewerbeschule in Halle, the factory made porcelain designed by Marguerite Friedlander and Hubert Griemert, and the renowned 1930–32 Urbino and 1931 Neu-Berlin dinner services by Trude Petri-

Rabin (the latter with figurative work by Ludwig Gies). However, when the Third Reich came to power, KPM was accused of employing the so-called non-Aryan Friedlander, and her name was eliminated from the 1938 catalog that marked KPM's 175th anniversary. Petri-Rabin's 1938 Arkadia dinner service (with unglazed medallions decorated by sculptor Sigmund Schütz) was suggested by Deutscher Werkbund member Günther von Pechmann, director of the Staatliche Porzellan-Manufaktur from 1929, and, in turn, von Pechmann was dismissed in 1938 for political reasons. After the war, Petri-Rabin also designed KPM's 1947–48 Urbino Oval service. Wolf Karnagel, who was an associated designer at KPM, designed its 1967 Stambul mocha service. Still active today and continuing its production of historicist styles, some more original patterns, like Urania, Berlin, and Kurland, are made for restaurant use. KPM will also create new shapes for large orders from individuals; produced Enzo Mari's 1996 Service Berlin porcelain dinnerware (and subsequent additions).
Bibliography Rudolf Forberger et al., *250 Jahre Staatliche Porzellan-Manufaktur Meissen*, Meissen: VEB Staatliche Porzellan Manufaktur, 1960. www.kpm-berlin.de.

Stabler, Harold (1872–1945)

British ceramicist, enameler, jeweler, and silversmith; born Levens, Westmorland; husband of Phoebe Stabler.

Training Under a woodcarver, apprenticeship, Kendal Art School, Cumbria; to 1902, metalworking, Keswick School of Industrial Art.
Biography 1898 while studying at the Keswick School of Industrial Art, Stabler was appointed the director of its metalwork section; 1903, left the school and began working for R.L. Rathbone in the metalworking department of the Liverpool School of Art. (Rathbone designed jewelry as a sideline.) Stabler arrived in London in early 1900s and taught, Royal College of Art, to 1907; 1907–37, was an instructor at, and later the head of, the art department, Sir John Cass Technical Institute; 1915, became a founding member, Design and Industries Association. After World War I, he turned from the Arts and Crafts idiom to that of British Art Déco. 1912–26, again taught, Royal College of Art, London; 1912 with wife Phoebe, established an enterprise in Hammersmith, where they had their own kiln, became very successful, and enjoyed working together; occasionally spent time drawing at the zoo or studying historical work at museums. They also designed architectural ceramics, including a series of World War I memorials, the largest of which (in Durban) features ceramic figures by Phoebe. 1921 with Charles Carter and John Adams, Sabler became a partner of the Carter Pottery in Poole (then called Carter, Stabler and Adams). Stabler was an accomplished ceramicist and created figurines, tiles, dinnerware, as well as ultitarian glassware in Pyrex and silverware; eventually, setting up his own workshop, designing silver and for Wakeley and Wheeler. This work was successful for mass production and introduced die-struck decoration in simple, angular motifs. Despite his crafts orientation, he was an en-thusiastic proponent of improvement in the design of everyday, machine-made domestic goods, which alienated him from some of his fellow craftspeople. His best-known silver design is a 1935 tea set by Adie Bros. 1930s, Stabler designed stainless-steel ware by Firth Vickers of Sheffield and stainless-steel hollow-ware by J. and J. Wiggin. He and his wife also modeled decorative figures and garden statues.
Exhibitions/citations Work included in exhibitions of Arts and Crafts Society, the New Gallery, and Albert Hall, all London; and in Germany, Austria, and Buenos Aires. 1936, elected Honorary Royal Designer for Industry, UK.
Bibliography Charlotte Gere, *American and European Jewelry 1830–1914*, New York: Crown, 1975. Cat., *Thirties: British Art and Design Before the War*, London: Arts Council of Great Britain/Hayward Gallery, 1979. Fiona MacCarthy and Patrick Nuttgens, *An Eye for Industry*, London: Lund Humphries/Royal Society for Arts, 1986. Annelies Krekel-Aalberse, *Art Nouveau and Art Déco Silver*, New York: Abrams, 1989. Leslie Hayward, 'Harold and Phoebe Stabler,' in *Poole Pottery Collectors' Club*, 1996: 8–9. Paul Atterbury, *Poole Pottery: Poole in the 1950's*, Somerset: Richard Dennis, 1997. Leslie Hayward and Paul Atterbury (eds), Poole Pottery, *Carter and Company and Their Successors, 1873–1998*, Somerset: Richard Dennis, 1998.

Stabler, Phoebe (b. Phoebe McCleish d. 1955)

British ceramicist, enameler, and silversmith; active London; wife of Harold Stabler.

Biography Stabler worked with husband Harold Stabler and on her own. From c. 1906, they sold ceramics designs to Doulton and to Harold's own Carter, Stabler and Adams pottery. 1906, she married Harold. They made opaque *cloisonné* enamel pendants under the guidance of Japanese craftsperson Kato; some of the pendants were not actually wearable. Other designs called on European geometric motifs in a way that exemplified British Art Déco styling. She produced garden ornaments and models primarily of women and children with colourful but simple glazes. These stoneware figures were formed in press molds, a method garnered from Chinese Tang figures, first discovered by Westerners in early 20th century, and from Greek Tanagra figure production. According to her, she and Harold encountered numerous firing problems, until the large molds were taken over by Poole Pottery (Carter, Stabler and Adams) and later sold to Doulton, Ashstead, and Worcester for larger-scale production.
Bibliography Toni Lesser Wolf, 'Women Jewelers of the British Arts and Crafts Movement,' *The Journal of Decorative and Propaganda Arts*, no. 14, Fall 1989: 34. Moira Vincentelli, *Women and Ceramics: Gendered Vessels*, Manchester: Manchester University, 2000: 239-41. > See Stabler, Harold (above).

Stæhr-Nielsen, Eva (1911-1976); Olaf Stæhr-Nielsen (1896-1969)

Danish ceramicists and metalworkers; wife and husband.

Training Eva: 1930–33, Kunsthåndværkerskolen, Copenhagen.
Biography 1932–68, Eva worked with Nathalie Krebs at the Saxbo ceramics factory and, 1968–76, at Royal Copenhagen Porcelain manufactory, both Copenhagen; from 1973, was active in her own workshop Designhuset in Lidköping; 1950s, designed silver cutlery by Georg Jensen Sølvsmedie, including 1958 Mocha spoons. Her husband Olaf Stæhr-Nielsen designed ceramics, silver, and furniture, including jewelry by Georg Jensen.
Exhibitions/citations Work included in 1954–57 *Design in Scandinavia*, touring the US; 1956–57 *Neue Form aus Dänemark*, touring Germany; 1957 exhibition, Malmö Museum; 1959 *Formes Scandinaves*, Musée des Arts Décoratifs, Paris; 1959 *Dansk Form og Miljø* exhibition, Stockholm; 1968 *Two Centuries of Danish Design*, London; at Kunstmuseum, Åborg, in 1975; in Washington, D.C., in 1980 and touring; 1982 exhibition, New York (catalogs below). To Eva: gold medals, 1937 *Exposition Internationale des Arts et Techniques dans la Vie Moderne*, Paris; and 1954 (10th) and 1957 (11th) editions of the Triennale di Milano.
Bibliography Cat., *Georg Jensen Silversmithy: 77 Artists, 75 Years*, Washington: Smithsonian, 1980. Cat., David Revere McFadden (ed.), *Scandinavian Modern Design 1880–1980*, New York: Abrams, 1982. Jennifer Hawkins Opie, *Scandinavia: Ceramics and Glass in the Twentieth Century*, New York: Rizzoli, 1989.

Stagi, Franca (1937–)

Italian industrial designer and architect; active Modena.

Training To 1962, Politecnico, Milan.
Biography 1962, Stagi became a partner in Cesare Leonardi's architecture firm in Modena. Their best-known work is 1967 Dondolo rocking chair (in molded fiberglass, polyester reinforced) by Elco in Venice, which has become a classic of Italian design. They specialized in architecture, town planning, and industrial design, including furniture by Bernini, Biarm, and Peguri and lighting by Lumenform.
Exhibitions Work included in 1970 *Design for Living, Italian Style* (Stagi's furniture), London; 1970 *Modern Chairs 1918–1970* (Dondolo rocking chair), Whitechapel Gallery, London; 1983–84 *Design Since 1945*, Philadelphia Museum of Art (catalogs below).
Bibliography Cat., *Modern Chairs 1918–1970*, London: Lund Humphries, 1971. *Casa Arredamento Giardino*, no. 19. Cat., Kathryn B. Hiesinger and George H. Marcus III (eds.), *Design Since 1945*, Philadelphia: Philadelphia Museum of Art, 1983.

Stålhane, Carl-Harry (1920–1990)

Swedish ceramicist.

Training Under Isaac Grünewald, in painting, Stockholm; Under sculptor Ossip ZadkineAcadémie, Colarossi, Paris; in Spain, Greece, Turkey, the US, Egypt, and Mexico.
Biography 1939–73, Stålhane worked at the Rörstrand ceramics factory in Lidköping and prolifically designed objects in porcelain and stoneware, ranging from non-ornamental work to more lively forms reflective of a 1950s exuberance; 1973, established his own workshop in Lidköping; 1963–71, taught ceramics, Konstindustriskolan, Gothenburg; decorated the main lounge of 1957 ocean-liner *Gripsholm* (of the Svenska Amerika Linien) with artwork called *School*

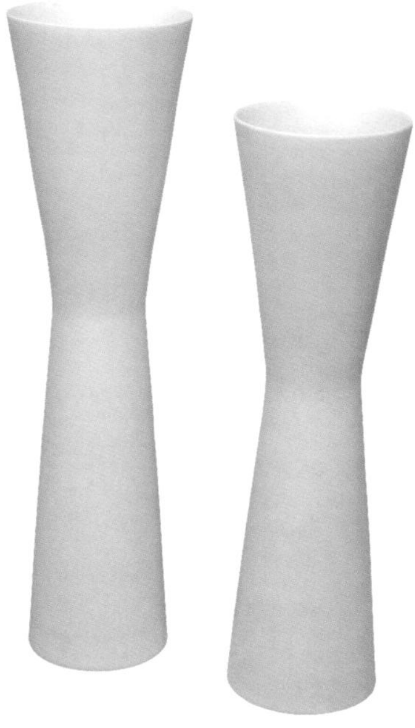

Carl-Harry Stålhane. Vases. 1950. Glazed stoneware, left h. 13 3/4" x dia. 3 11/16" (34.9 cm x 9.4 cm), right h. 12 1/8" x dia. 3 3/8" (30.8 cm x 8.6 cm). Mfr.: Rörstrands Porslinsfabriker, Sweden (1952). Gift of the mfr. MoMA.

of Fish, and lined the swimming pool with brilliantly colored mosaics by Rörstrand.
Exhibitions/citations Work subject of 1951, 1957, and 1960 exhibitions in Stockholm; 1960, in New York; and others. Gold medal at 1951 (9th) and diploma of honor at 1954 (10th) editions of Triennale di Milano; 1960 International Design Award, American Institute of Decorators (AID).
Bibliography Cat., David Revere McFadden (ed.), *Scandinavian Modern Design 1880–1980*, New York: Abrams, 1982. Jennifer Hawkins Opie, *Scandinavia: Ceramics and Glass in the Twentieth Century*, New York: Rizzoli, 1989.

Stallinga, Henk (1962–)

Dutch designer.

Biography Stallinga manufacturer and markets his own-design products through his eponymous firm, established in 1993, and designs for others; is also an active architect and interior designer, including 1997 interior of De Kring art club and a 1994 space in Stedelijk Museum, both Amsterdam, and 1997 and 2001 space in The Museum of Modern Art, New York; approaches the design of a wide range of products—from lighting and furniture to accessories and trophies—in an unusual, even surprising, manner, often with humor.
Exhibitions 1996 *Contemporary Design from the Netherlands* (1993 vase and 1993 Watt lamp), The Museum of Modern Art, New York; numerous others.
Bibliography Murray Moss and Erik Viskil, *Stallinga: This is Our Logo*, Amsterdam: BIS, Corte Madera, Cal.: Gingko, 2001. Cat., *Hallo Holland*, Amsterdam: BIS, 2002. Mel Byars, *Design in Steel,* London: Laurence King, 2002.

Stam, 'Mart' Martinus Adrianus (1899–1986)

Dutch designer; born Purmerend; active the Netherlands, Germany, and Russia; husband of architect Lotte Besse.

Training Rijksnormaalschool voor Tekenonderwijs, Amsterdam; under M. J. Granpré Molière in Verhagen, Netherlands; and under Kok in Rotterdam.
Biography Stam's career documents the interchange among the Bauhaus, Dutch Rationalism, and Constructivism. He began in the architecture offices Johan Melchior van der Mey and of M.J. Granpré Molière before leaving for Berlin in 1922. Stam became the chairperson of de Opbouw ('construction' in Dutch), the architecture group founded in 1920, whose members included W.H. Gispen, Willem Kromhout, J.J.P. Oud, Granpré Molière, and L.C. van der Vlught. While in Switzerland and Germany, he met German Constructivists, El Lissitzkii, Theo van Doesburg, and Ludwig Mies van der Rohe; entered the 1923 competition for Königsberg, in which he used reinforced concrete and glass for the design of an office-building project; worked with Lissitzky on 1924–25 Wolkenbügel (cloud props) project, based on Constructivist principles that he also later applied to the 1925 redevelopment project for the Rokin and the dam in Amsterdam. 1923, he left Berlin left for Switzerland and, 1924, worked with Hans Schmidt and he, Schmidt, and Emil Roth created the illustrated magazine *A.B.C.* and with Stam Cornavin worked on the station in Geneva, typifying the idea that architecture should serve the user. Living for a time in Paris, he returned to Holland (Rotterdam) in 1926 and worked in the office of Dutch architects J.A. Brinkman and van der Vlught on the mammoth 1926–30 Van Nelle tobacco factory, Rotterdam, for which he designed the interiors and furniture. The complex was an ambitious, pioneering work of modern industrial architecture. Stam has become best known for his design of the first (1924), or one of the first, cantilevered tubular-steel chair, initially constructed from ten pieces of gas-pipe tubing and ten elbow joints, but not industrially produced until 1926 by L. & C. Arnold, by which time Marcel Breuer and Le Corbusier had also arrived at the cantilever solution. Stam's houses nos. 28-30 (with furniture by L. & C. Arnold) at 1927 *Weissenhofsiedlung* exhibition, Stuttgart, were among the most interesting examples of domestic interior design and architecture there. 1928–29, Stam was a guest lecturer for elementary construction and town planning, Bauhaus, Dessau, where association with those working in town planning there contributed to his inspiration for the 1929–1932 Hellerhof garden-city complex in Frankfort (Main), as the town was then known. 1929–35, he traveled widely and worked in several countries, including in housing and town planning for Magnitogorsk (as part of the Gruppe May from 1930–34) with German architect Ernst May in the Soviet Union from 1930. He designed a 1932 house and furnishings (including bent tubular-steel dining and easy chairs) with Walter Schwagenscheidt (1886–1968) in Moscow; a 1932 stackable chair. 1935–48, he lived in Amsterdam, where he was the director of several institutions: Instituut voor het Onderwijzen van Industriële Kunst, Amsterdam, from 1939; became director, Akademie der bildenden Künste, Dresden, from 1948; Kunsthochschule, Berlin-Weißensee, from 1950. Stam's wife 'Lotte' Charlotte Beese (Selesia 1903–88), who studied textile design and architecture under Hannes Meyer at the Bauhaus, Dessau, from 1926–29; lived in the Soviet Union in 1930 for a few weeks (while Stam was there as part of the Gruppe May); returned to Russia and reencountered Stam; from 1935 live in Amsterdam with Stam, whom she married in 1934, divorced in 1943; studied architecture in Amsterdam from 1943–45 and, 1946, was appointed the town planner of Rotterdam, active to 1968. Stam closed his studio in 1966 and settled in Switzerland and built two houses for himself; died in Goldbach.
Exhibitions Work shown at 1927 *Die Wohnung* (houses nos. 28-30 with steel tables, desks, and shelving produced by F. Ulmer of Möhringen, Netherlands), Weissenhofsiedlung, Stuttgart.
Bibliography Giovanni Fanelli, *Architettura Moderna in Olanda, 1900–1940*, Florence: Marchi e Bertolli, 1968: 359–60. J.B. Bakema with G.H. van der Leeuw, Mart Stam, and Le Corbusier, *L.C. van der Vlught*, Amsterdam: Meulenhoff, 1968. Barbie Campbell-Cole and Tim Benton (eds.), *Tubular Steel Furniture*, London: The Art Book Company, 1979: 29. Otakar Máčel, 'Avant-garde Design and the Law: Litigation over the Cantilever Chair,' *Journal of Design History*, vol. 3, nos. 2 and 3, 1990: 125–43. Werner Oechslin (ed.), *Mart Stam: Eine Reise in die Schweiz, 1923–1925*, Zurich: Eidgenössische Technische Hochschule/Institut für Geschichte und Theorie der Architektur, 1991. Werner Möller, *Mart Stam, 1899–1986: Architekt, Visionär, Gestalter...*, Tübingen: Ernst Wasmuth, 1997. Herman van Bergeijk and Otakar Máčel (eds.), *'We vragen de kunstenaars kind te zijn van zijn eigen tijd': Teksten van Mart Stam*, Nijmegen: SUN, 1999.

Standardmöbel Lengyel (Standard-Möbel)

German furniture manufacturer.

History 1926 or 1927, Standardmöbel was established to produce bent tubular-steel furniture by Kálmán Lengyel and Marcel Breuer at Teltowerstrasse 47–48, Berlin. However, the venture proved unsuccessful, and, 1928, Breuer sold the rights to his tubular-steel furniture to Hungarian businessman Anton Lorenz, who took over the production of Breuer's furniture from Standardmöbel Lengyel. But Breuer's 1927–28 designs were not transferred to the firm. Because his famous

B32 and B34 cantilevered chairs with cane with and without wooden arms had been stored as prototypes on Standardmöbel's premises until 1929, both Thonet (with which Breuer had entered into a 1928 agreement) and Standardmöbel produced the chairs in slightly different versions simultaneously. 1929, Thonet bought Standardmöbel but not its factory. In the meantime, Lorenz had become director of Standardmöbel, and, 1929, signed an agreement with Mart Stam to produce his version of the cantilevered chair. Since Thonet asserted that the cantilevered-chair design was Breuer's, rights to which had been transferred to Thonet through the Standardmöbel sale, Thonet filed a court suit against Lorenz, whose firm Deutsche Stahlmöbel (DESTA) was injuncted into the suit. However, Lorenz won in 1930 and again on appeal in 1932; thus, Thonet was forced to to stop production of the B32 and B34 cantilevered chairs. However today, Thonet has reissued Lorenz's 1932 S146 cantilevered armchair
Bibliography Barbie Campbell-Cole and Tim Benton, *Tubular Steel Furniture*, London: The Art Book Company, 1979: 13, 20. Otakar Máčel, 'Avant-Garde Design and the Law: Litigation over the Cantilever Chair,' *Journal of Design History*, vol. 3, nos. 2 and 3, 1990: 129.

Starck, Philippe (1949-)

French product, furniture, and interior designer; born Paris.

Training 1968, École Camondo, Paris.
Biography Starck designed his first limited-edition furniture, the 1972 Joe Miller folding chair; even so, there were prototypes of others from 1967. 1969, he became artistic director of Pierre Cardin. 1970s, his career as an independent designer was largely undistinguished, although, 1976–78, he was the interior architect of La Main Bleue and Les Bains-Douches nightclubs, Paris. 1983–84 with four other designers, Starck designed and laid out a room in the quarters of French President François Mitterand in the Palais de l'Élysée (however, Mitterand's private domicile was on avenue Frédéric-Le-Play). 1984, the owner of Café Costes discovered Starck through a 1981 curved-back chair with spikey metal legs shown at Galerie VIA, Paris (which had in turn been sponsored by VIA, a French furniture association). Starck was thus hired to design Café Costes (closed 1994), and the Paris restaurant and its designer became famous soon thereafter. By 1990, 400,000 copies of what became known as the Café Costes chair had been produced by Driade. 1985, Starck became artistic director of newly formed firm XO; created a 1984 furniture collection by mail-order firm 3 Suisses. His La Cigale discothèque was realized in 1988 in Paris. In addition to Driade, he designed furniture by Baleri, Disform, Idée, and Rateri from c. 1988, accessories and dinnerware by Alessi from 1986, crystal vases by Daum in 1987, a clock by Spirale, cutlery by Sasaki, a boat interior by Beneteau, plastic bottle by Vittel in 1991, lamps by Flos, including Ará and the phallic Luci Fair, both 1988. 1987, he designed Restaurants Castel in Paris, Dijon, and Nice; Hôtel Costes in Paris; Bathmann drugstore in Zurich; and restaurants, offices, and residences in Tokyo. Starck conjured catchy titles for his furniture, such as chairs named 1982 Miss Dorn, 1983 Doctor Sonderbar (after a dirigible pilot), 1985 Mickville, 1985 Tippy Jackson, 1988 Dr. Glob. For Driade, the names of items in his Ubik line were taken from Philip K. Dicks's science-fiction novel *Ubik* (Boston: Gregg Press, 1969/1979). Starck was the editor of 1987 and 1997 editions of *The International Design Yearbook* (as the only two-time editor). He designed the 1988 exhibition of French design at Centre Georges Pompidou, later more modestly remounted in London. His design and decoration of Ian Schrager's and Steve Rubell's 1988 Hotel Royalton and 1990 Paramount Hotel, both New York, were widely published; his 1991 Royalton chair (initiated in the Hotel Royalton) was produced by Driade. After Rubell's death, the Schrager relationship led to other hotel assignments, such as the 1995 redesign of Miami's Delano Hotel. His first domestic architecture was the 1989 narrow-lot residence of Bruno Le Moult in Issy-les-Molineaux. Buildings (with various architects) have included 1989 Nani Nani café in Tokyo, 1990 Asahi brasserie in Tokyo, and 1990 Teatriz Restaurant in Madrid. With his talent for self-promotion and a supportive press and first wife (who died in 1992), Starck has become the standard-bearer for the French design community; 1990–97, headed the Tim Thom advanced-design studio of Thomson multi-média. His 1992 Fluocaril toothbrush/stand by Sanofi-Synthélabo in France was labeled, perhaps jokingly, 'the ultimate designer toothbrush.' His work through the 1990s into the 21st century has proceeded quickly and vigorously, including 2000 interpretation of 1944 Navy chair (his first American-made furniture) by Emeco and a large number of furniture designs by Kartell and other longtime clients, such as Driade. He settled in a studio outside of Paris, moved to New York and back again to Paris and now possibly in several locations; has become the best known and most prolific contemporary designer of his time, adding to his portfolio vehicles, computers, doorknobs, spectacle frames, and on and on.
Exhibitions/citations The first citation may have been 1982 Carte Blanche production support (for Miss Dorn chair), VIA. By 1987, work had been included more than three dozen exhibitions in Marseille, Rome, Munich, Düsseldorf, Kyoto, Tokyo, Chicago, Los Angeles, New York, and, of course, Paris. He designed the 1988 exhibition of French design, Centre Georges Pompidou, Paris. First (2003) one-person exhibition, Centre Georges Pompidou, Paris. Two 1995 Red Dot awards (Axor Starck faucet by Hansgrohe and Philippe Starck series bathroom by Duravit) and two 2001 Red Dot Best of the Best (Gaoua luggage and Yap backpack by Samsonite Europe), Design Zentrum Nordrhein-Westfalen, Essen; numerous others.
Bibliography Cat., *Les années VIA*, Paris: Musée des Arts Décoratifs, 1990. Olivier Boissière, *Philippe Starck*, Cologne: Taschen, 1991. François Mathey, *Au bonheur des formes, le design français 1945–1992*, Paris: Regard, 1992. Conway Lloyd Morgan, *Philippe Starck*, New York: Universe, 1998. Judith and Arthur Carmel, *Philippe Starck*, London: Carlton, 1999. Ed Cooper et al., *Starck*, Cologne: Taschen, 2000. Pascale Cassgnau and Christophe Pillet, *Beef, Brétillot/Valette, Matali Crasset, Patrick Jouin, Jean-Marie Massaud: petits enfants de Starck?*, Paris: Dis Voir, 2000. Pierre Doze, *Starck by Starck*, Cologne: Taschen, 2003. Paola Antonelli (ed.), *Objects of Design: The Museum of Modern Art*, New York: The Museum of Modern Art, 2003: 140, 146, 170–71. Full œuvre at www.philippe-starck.com.

Philippe Starck. Miss Donna table mirror. 1987. Polished aluminum and glass, 15 3/4 x 9 1/2 x 9 1/2" (40 x 24.2 x 24.2 cm). Mfr.: O.W.O., France (c. 1987–95). David Whitney Collection, Gift of David Whitney. MoMA.

Starr, Theodore B.
> See Reed & Barton.

State Porcelain Factory
> See Lomonosov Porcelain Factory.

Stathis, Peter (1960-)

American designer.

Training 1983, bachelor's degree in industrial design, Pratt Institute, Brooklyn, N.Y.; 1989, master of fine arts degree, Cranbrook Academy of Art, Bloomfield Hills, Mich.
Biography 1986–87, Stathis was senior designer at the Richard Penney Group, New York; 1989, worked at the Applied Research division of NYNEX telephone company, White Plains, N.Y.; 1989–92, was a senior

designer, Smart Design, New York; from 1992, was a principal, Virtual Studio, San Francisco. 1995–2001, he was a designer-in-residence at and head of 3-D Design Department, Cranbrook Academy of Art. Product-design work has included furniture, lighting, and housewares for clients, including Apple Computer, Black and Decker, Johnson & Johnson, Kovacs Lighting, Knoll, The Museum of Modern Art, Nambé, Oxo, Pure Design, Swatch.
Citations 2000 Best of Shown, International Contemporary Furniture Fair (ICFF), New York; IDEA/*Business Week* award; Annual Design Review, *I.D.* magazine .
Bibliography Cat., R. Craig Miller (intro.), *U.S. Design 1975–2000*, Munich: Prestel, 2002.

Stavangerflint
Norwegian ceramics factory.

History 1894, Stavangerflint was established in Stavanger; soon set up a design department that was concerned with both serial production and decorative wares; hired freelance designer Kari Nyquist, who worked for the firm from c. 1955; appointed Kaare Fjeldsaa chief designer in 1957, who became the artistic director and who at Stavangerflint remained until after the 1968 merger with Figgjo Fajanse. 1979, the firm closed.
Bibliography Jennifer Hawkins Opie, *Scandinavia: Ceramics and Glass in the Twentieth Century*, New York: Rizzoli, 1989.

steel furniture
> See tubular-steel furniture.

Steelcase
American furniture manufacturer; located Grand Rapids, Michigan.

History 1912, the firm was founded in Grand Rapids by engineer Peter M. Wege Sr. (1879–1947) and 11 associates, who initially named the firm Metal Office Furniture. Originally, it produced fireproof office safes, gradually expanding to steel desks and filing cabinets. The firm's claim to design distinction, then and now, was its 1937 commission to produce the metal office furniture designed by Frank Lloyd Wright for the Johnson Wax administration building, Racine, Wisc. Both Steelcase, whose proposal was accepted, and Warren MacArthur submitted prototypes. (MacArthur's interpretation was in aluminum). Called Steelcase from 1954, the company was perceived as a producer of durable products made in large quantities, and, at the time, it largely ignored the design community; as chairperson Robert Pew admitted, 'I hate to tell you how it was done in the 1950s. We'd take an arm from one chair, a base from another, a back from another.' Despite its lack of design sophistication, Steelcase dominated the office-furniture market due to its client base (AT&T, IBM, and others) and tightly coordinated distribution system. However, subsequently, Steelcase sought design respectability through the Steelcase Design Partnership, headed by William Crawford and a consortium of design-oriented companies associated with the industry's elite and intended to reach designers rather than end-users. Creative director of and senior advisor to the Partnership was George Beylerian, who in 1960s was an importer of high-design European domestic goods. Steelcase's status was enhanced by the Partnership's acquisition of Airborne, Atelier International (lighting and licensed Wright, Le Corbusier, and Rietveld furniture made by Cassina in Italy), Brayton (executive and lounge seating), DesignTex Fabrics (office textiles), Metropolitan Furniture (lounge seating and conference room tables), Strafor (office furniture), Vecta Contract (executive furnishings, including the Beylerian Collection), Waiko, Werndl, and, from c. 1992, its largest start-up company, Details, producing, it claimed, 'tools for a better day at work.' By 1993, Steelcase had become the largest furniture manufacturer worldwide. However, some of the brands are being discontinued or closed.
Bibliography David A. Hanks, *The Decorative Designs of Frank Lloyd Wright*, New York: Dutton, 1979: 220–21. Lois Servaas, *Steelcase, The First 75 Years*, Grand Rapids: Steelcase, 1987. Margery B. Stein, 'Teaching Steelcase to Dance,' *The New York Times Magazine*, *The Business World* section, 1 Apr. 1990.

Steelchrome
British furniture manufacturer; located London.

History 1932, Phillip Braham established the firm on Portland Street, London; had earlier trained in the coach-building trade, where he acquired a knowledge of upholstery and metalworking; was the firm's administrator, controler, and designer. Bending and welding in its own factories, Steelchrome purchased its steel tubing from Tube Products, the sister firm of Steelchrome's competitor Pel. Steelchrome specialized in bent-tubular steel for furniture, serving hairdressing/beauty salons and hospitals. Its DC111 chair was a commercial success. 1964, Braham sold the firm, which is still active in Ascot serving the food-service industry.
Bibliography Cat., Dennis Sharp et al., *Pel and Tubular Steel Furniture in the Thirties*, London: Architectural Association, 1977.

Stefani, Stefano (1953–)
Italian architect and designer; born Rome.

Training To 1977, in architecture.
Biography From 1978, Stefani collaborated with architect Laura de Lorenzo and Luca Lenori on industrial and interior design and visual communication; 1985 with architects de Lorenzo, Luca Leonori, and Filippo Piferi, founded Grifite.
Bibliography Fumio Shimizu and Studio Matteo Thun (eds.), *The Italian Design: Descendants of Leonardo da Vinci*, Tokyo: Graphic-sha, 1987.

Stefanoni, Franco (1926–)
Italian designer; born and active Lecco.

Biography 1952, Stefanoni began his professional career and designed, among other products, Stalagmite lamp by Stilnovo, lighting by Candle, seating by Base Interiors, a metal furniture range by Farina, and 1972 Martina door handle by Olivari; became a member, Associazione per il Disegno Industriale (ADI).
Exhibitions Participated in numerous competitions and exhibitions including 1985 *Uhr und Mode, Deutsche Uhrenindustrie*, Pforzheim; 1986 *Itinerari Manzoniani*, Milan.
Bibliography *ADI Annual 1976*, Milan: Associazione per il Disegno Industriale, 1976.

Stefanoni, Guido (1957–)
Italian designer; born Lecco.

Training To 1982, architecture, Politecnico, Milan.
Biography 1980, Stefanoni worked with Marco Zanuso Sr. in the design studio in MIlan; 1981–82, was assistant art director at Young & Rubicam advertising agency, Milan; 1982 with Leopoldo Freyrie, set up their own design studio; recently with F & P Architetti, restyled the Frette linen stores in Milan and Turin; was the architect of 2002 CEMB (measuring systems) building and 2003 ICMA (paper products) building, both Mandello del Lario.
Exhibitions Numerous competitions and exhibitions, including 1985 *Uhr und Mode, Deutsche Uhrenindustrie*, Pforzheim; 1986 *Itinerari Manzoniani*, Milan.
Bibliography Cat., Hans Wichmann, *Italien Design 1945 bis heute*, Munich: Die Neue Sammlung, 1988.

Steichen, Edward (b. Edouard Jean Steichen 1879–1973)
Luxembourgian photographer, painter, and designer.

Training In fine art.
Biography Steichen began his career in fine art; 1881, moved to the US; 1894 with George Niedecken and others, organized the Art Students League in Milwaukee, Wisc.; 1889, took his first photographs; 1902, became a founding member of the Photo-Secession in New York; 1911, began as a fashion photographer. He had been in-fluenced initially by Impressionist art and took to photographing nature, which gave way to portraiture; 1914–18, was the commander of the photographic division of the US Expeditionary Forces; 1923–28, was the director of photography at magazines *Vogue* and *Vanity Fair*, making numerous portraits of the *beau monde*. His abstract photographs of matchsticks (*Matches* and *Match Boxes*), sugar cubes, and other small items, which appeared in *Vogue* in 1920s, were converted into printed fabrics by Stehli Silk in 1927. 1920s, he designed glassware by Steuben, graphics, book jackets, and two 1928 pianos by Hardman and Peck as part of its Modernique range. 1945–46, Steichen served in the US Marine Corps as a war photographer. 1947 after World War II, he was head of the photography department of The Museum of Modern Art, New York, to 1962. Steichen's stylish work mirrored trends in 20th-century photography.
Exhibitions Organized 1954 *The Family of Man* (including some of Steichen's and others images), The Museum of Modern Art, in addi-

tion to others at the museum. Work subject of 2000 *Steichen's Legacy: Photographs, 1895–1973*, Whitney Museum of American Art; both New York (catalog below).
Bibliography Paul Frank, *New Dimensions*, New York: Payson and Clarke, 1928. Pierre Migennes, 'Ombres Portés et Décor de Tissus,' *Art et Décoration*, vol. 51, Jan.–June 1927: 140–42. Stuart Durant, *Ornament from the Industrial Revolution to Today*, Woodstock, N.Y.: Overlook, 1986: 256, 329. Cat., Joanna Steichen, *Steichen's Legacy: Photographs, 1895–1973*, New York: Knopf, 2000.

Steiger, Carl (1857–1946)

Swiss engineer, painter, and furniture designer; father of architect Rudolf Steiger.

Training Engineering, Technische Hochschule, Munich.
Biography Carl Steiger became a painter and was interested in aviation, building airplane prototypes; was an aviation pioneer and wrote the theoretical book *Technologie des Menschenfluges* (technology of human flight); experimented with furniture design, resulting in an early-1930s chair.
Bibliography Friederike Mehlau-Wiebking et al., *Schweizer Typenmöbel 1925–35, Sigfried Giedion und die Wohnbedarf AG*, Zurich: gta, 1989: 230.

Steiger, Rudolf (1900–1982)

Swiss architect; active Basel and Zurich; son of Carl Steiger; husband of Flora Steiger-Crawford.

Training 1919–23 under Karl Moser, architecture, Eidgenössische Technische Hochschule, Zurich.
Biography 1923–24, Rudolf Steiger worked for the firms Dumont in Brussels and Arthur Korn in Berlin; 1924 with wife Flora Steiger-Crawford, opened their own architecture practice in Basel and, 1925, moved to Zurich. 1927, he became a member of the Swiss collective, which furnished Mies van der Rohe's apartments at 1927 *Weissenhofsiedlung* exhibition, Stuttgart; 1928, cofounded Congrès Internationaux d'Architecture Moderne (CIAM); specialized in town and regional planning and, 1928–31, served on the planning team of the Neubühl Werkbund settlement in Zurich. With his wife, Steiger designed some of the furniture included in the basic inventory of the Wohnbedarf furniture store from its 1931 founding in Zurich and for which he was also the bookkeeper. 1929–37, he was a partner of Carl Hubacher, with whom he designed a 1930–32 restaurant in Zett-Haus, furnished with his stacking chairs. 1937 with Werner Max Moser and Max Ernst Haefeli, he cofounded the cooperative-office HMS for the construction of the Kongresshaus in Zurich. The Architektengruppe Kantonsspital of Zurich (the architecture office including HMS personnel, Steiger and Hermann Fietz) directed the construction of 1939–51 cantonal hospital, Zurich. From 1957, Steiger specialized in hospital architecture; 1973, cofounded Schweizerische Vereinigung für Landesplanung (Swiss union for national planning); from 1964, was the president of a professional group for regional planning in and around Zurich and a member of the board of directors, Bund Schweizer Planer (association of Swiss planners).
Citation Honorary doctorate (for achievements in hospital architecture), medical faculty, Universität Zurich.
Bibliography Friederike Mehlau-Wiebking et al., *Schweizer Typenmöbel 1925–35, Sigfried Giedion und die Wohnbedarf AG*, Zurich: gta, 1989: 231. Gilbert Frey, *Schweizer Möbeldesign 1927–1989*, Bern: Benteli, 1986.

Stelton: Arne Jacobsen. Cylinda ice bucket. 1964-67. Stainless steel, overall h. 5 3/4" x dia. 7 5/8" (14.6 x 19.4 cm). Mfr.: Stelton, Denmark (1968). Gift of Bonniers, Inc. MoMA.

Steiger-Crawford, Flora (b. Flora Crawford 1899–1991)

Swiss architect and furniture designer; born Bombay; active Basel and Zurich; wife of Rudolf Steiger.

Training To 1923 under Karl Moser, architecture, Eidgenössische Technische Hochschule (ETH), Zurich.
Biography 1923–24, she worked in the architecture office of Pfleghard und Haefeli in Zurich; 1924 with her husband Rudolf Steiger, opened an architecture office in Basel, which moved to Zurich in 1925. She drew up architectural plans and designed some furniture. With her sister, weaver Lilly Humm-Crawford, they designed the 1931 weaving studio at the Neubühl Werkbund settlement in Zurich, where they furnished a small apartment for family of six and a low-cost one-family house. Her furniture was sold by the Wohnbedarf store in Switzerland. From 1931, she worked as a sculptor in her own studio, creating portrait busts, nudes, and some draped figures in bronze, plaster, and artificial stone; 1932, became active as a landscape painter.
Bibliography Friederike Mehlau-Wiebking et al., *Schweizer Typenmöbel 1925–35, Sigfried Giedion und die Wohnbedarf AG*, Zurich: gta, 1989: 230–31.

Steiner and Co., F.

British textile firm.

History Early 19th century, Frederick Steiner emigrated to Britain; took over a fabric-printing factory (founded in 1722) in Church (near Accrington), Lancashire, making calico and dyeing textiles. The firm used known designers, who created important Art Nouveau fabrics. 1889 when others joined the Calico Printers' Association, Steiner remained independent. 1955, the firm was voluntarily liquidated.
Bibliography Valerie Mendes, *The Victoria & Albert Museum's Textile Collection, British Textiles from 1900 to 1937*, London: Victoria and Albert Museum, 1992.

Stella, Guido Balsamo
> See Balsamo Stella, Guido (1882–1941); S.A.L.I.R.

Steltman, Johannes (1891–1961)

Dutch jeweler and silversmith; active The Hague.

Training Königliche Preussische Zeichenakademie, Hanau.
Biography 1917, Steltman established the jewelry shop Joaillerie Artistique in The Hague. When silversmith Robert Mack became one of the jewelers at the shop a few years later, Steltman began producing hollow-ware in the fluid silhouettes of the Art Nouveau style. (Johannes Rohde's streamline silver pitcher of c. 1925 was of an entirely different genre from Steltman's shown at 1925 Paris *Exposition*.) Steltman became more subdued in his later work, which was smooth and severely modern. Sometimes the work of his atelier included services in the Danish style influenced by Georg Jensen.
Exhibitions/citations Gold medal (for a tea service, reminiscent of the organic work of 17th-century Dutch silversmiths and inspired by Malcolm Campbell's racing car that broke the 1923 world's speed record), 1925 *Exposition Internationale des Arts Décoratifs et Industriels Modernes*, Paris.
Bibliography Annelies Krekel-Aalberse, *Art Nouveau and Art Déco Silver*, New York: Abrams, 1989.

Stelton

Danish metalware and plastics manufacturer.

History 1960, Stelton was established to make and sell stainless-steel hollow-ware primarily for the Danish market; from 1964, commissioned freelance designer Arne Jacobsen to design its tablewares

and serving pieces, which contributed to the firm's production numbers and international sales. Stelton introduced Jacobsen's successful 1964–67 Cylinda line of stainless-steel hollow-ware; posthumously issued his Multi-Set range of serving pieces, developed from his drawings. 1975, owner/manager Peter Holmblad hired freelance designer Erik Magnussen (the replacement for Jacobsen who died in 1971) to design Stelton's stainless-steel and plastic products.
Bibliography Jennifer Hawkins Opie, *Scandinavia: Ceramics and Glass in the Twentieth Century*, New York: Rizzoli, 1989.

Stenberg, Georgii Avgustovich (1900–1933); Vladimir Avgustovich Stenberg (1899–1982)

Russian graphic, theater set, and interior designers; born Moscow; brothers.

Training 1912–17 under V.E. Yegorov and P.V. Kuznetsov, Stroganov School of Applied Art, Moscow; 1917, railroad and bridge construction in military-engineering courses, Moscow; 1917–20, SVOMAS, in the 'Studio Without a Supervisor' with fellow students Nikolai Denisovskii, Vasilii Komardenkov, Konstantin Medunetskii, Nikolai Prusakov, and Sergei Y. Svetlov.
Biography 1917, the Stenberg brothers began working together and for the theater; contributed to 1918 May Day agitprop decorations in Moscow; worked on designs of the Napoleon cinema and the Railroad Workers' Club; created agitprop decorations for the 1919 anniversary of the Bolshevik Revolution. 1919–23, they were members of the group Obmokhu (society of young artists); 1920–23, were members of INKhUK (institute of artistic culture), where they organized an exhibition of constructions; 1923–25, were closely associated with the journal *Lef* (left front); 1921 with Alexei Gan, Aleksandr Rodchenko, Varvara Stepanova, and others, were opposed to the group 'veshch' at INKhUK and rejected pure art in favor of industrial Constructivism. From 1923, they designed/illustrated posters for films, for which they are today renowned; 1922–31, created set designs and costumes for Aleksandr Tairov's Chamber Theater productions, including Aleksandr Ostrovskii's *Groza* (thunderstorm), George Bernard Shaw's *Saint Joan*, and Bertolt Brecht's *Threepenny Opera*, and, thereafter, for other theatrical productions in Russia and abroad; 1930–33, taught, All-Union Architectural and Construction Institute, Moscow. After Georgii's death, Vladimir continued to work as a stage designer; and died in Moscow.
Exhibitions/citations The Constructivist declaration was made public at Stenberg's 1922 exhibition, Poets' Café, Moscow. Work was included in 1922 *Erste Russische Kunstausstellung*, Berlin. With Aleksandra Exter, Ignatii Nivinskii, Vera Mukhina, and others, they worked on the design and decoration of 1923 *First Agricultural and Handicraft-Industrial Exhibition*. With Medunetskii, they showed their work as Constructivists at 1924 *First Discussional Exhibition of Associations of Active Revolutionary Art*, Moscow; 1927 exhibition of Soviet art, Tokyo. Work subject of 1975 exhibition (covering 1919–21), touring Paris, London, and Ontario; 1997 *Stenberg Brothers – Constructing a Revolution in Soviet Design*, The Museum of Modern Art, New York. Received a gold medal, 1925 *Exposition Internationale des Arts Décoratifs et Industriels Modernes*, Paris.
Bibliography Andrei B. Nakov, *2 Stenberg 2: The Laboratory Period (1919–1921) of Russian Constructivism*, Paris: Galerie Jean Chauvelin; London: Idea-Books, 1975. Stephanie Barron and Maurice Tuchman, *The Avant-Garde in Russia, 1910–1930*, Cambridge: MIT, 1980: 244. Cat., *The Great Utopia: The Russian and Soviet Avant-Garde, 1915–1932*, New York: Guggenheim Museum, 1992. Cat., Christopher Mount and Peter Kenez, *Stenberg Brothers: Constructing a Revolution in Soviet Design*, New York: The Museum of Modern Art/Abrams, 1997.

Stendal, L. & C.; L. & C. Arnold

German furniture manufacturer; located Württemberg, Kempen, and Schorndorf.

History 1871, metal merchant Louis Arnold and son Carl founded a garden-furniture factory in Schorndorf, later named Eisen Möbelfabrik Schorndorf; 1889, established a second factory in Stendal/Altmark (near Berlin) under the name L. & C. Arnold and, the same year, took over an old hammer factory in Ernsbach/Württemberg, which began making wooden screws; 1901, built another Arnold factory in Kempen/Niederrhein; made a well-known folding garden chair (no. 2) and sold 500,000 pieces annually. Arnold produced Heinz Rasch's 1924 bent-tubular-steel chair with swinging diagonals; by 1926, was Europe's leading tubular-steel furniture manufacturer; 1930, centralized the pro-

Magnus Stephensen. Covered serving dish. 1957. Stainless steel, dish h. 2 3/4" x dia. 7 1/4" (7 x 18.4 cm), lid dia. 7 3/16" (18.2 cm). Mfr.: Georg Jensen Sølvsmedie, Copenhagen. Phyllis B. Lambert Fund. MoMA.

duction of indoor seating and electroplating chromium in Stendal; 1936, equipped the *Hindenburg* (LZ 129) dirigible with aluminum seating. 1945–46, the Stendal factory was reorganized as VEB STIMA and chairs, tables, beds were made in East Germany. 1988–99, began trading under the name L. & C. Stendal for the first time in 100 years and reissued 1950s models. 1991, Stendal factories were integrated into a parent firm in Kempen and Schorndorf; reissued vintage models as the 1994 Arnold-Bauhaus-Collection and 1996 Arnold-Revival-Collection. Designers of Stendal's current production are not recognized.
Exhibitions/citations 1927 *Das Haus* (first chair without rear legs, by Mart Stam; steel-tubing bookcase), Manufacturers' Association stand, *Weissenhofsiedlung* exhibition, Stuttgart; 1928 *Der Stuhl* exhibition, Stuttgart, showing tubular-steel furniture by Marcel Breuer, Rasch, Stam, Mies van der Rohe, Geritt Rietveld, Le Corbusier/Jeanneret/Perriand; 1994 Orgatec (Arnold-Bauhaus-Collection shown), Cologne; 1999 Internationale Möbelmesse (Arnold-Revival-Collection shown), Cologne. Grand prize (hospital furniture), 1911 *Hygiene-Ausstellung*, Dresden; 1932 first prize (to Breuer for five seating prototypes), international aluminum competition, sponsored by International Bureau for Applications of Aluminum, Paris.
Bibliography Barbie Campbell-Cole and Tim Benton (eds.), *Tubular Steel Furniture*, London: The Art Book Company, 1979: 13, 19. Sonja Günther (intro.), *Thonet Tubular Steel Furniture Card Catalogue*, Weil am Rhein: Vitra Design Publications, 1989.

Stepanova, Varvara Fedorovna (aka pseudonyms V. Agrarykh or Varst 1894–1958)

Russian graphic, theater-set, and costume designer; born Kovno; wife of Aleksandr Rodchenko.

Training From 1910–13, School of Fine Art, Kazan; 1913–14 in Moscow, Stroganov School, also in the studios of Il'ia Mashkov and of Konstantin Yuon; from 1918, IZO NKP (fine-art department of Narkompros), Moscow.
Biography 1920, Stepanova became a member of INKhUK (institute of artistic culture); 1922, designed sets and costumes for Vsevolod Ermilievitch Meyerhold's production of Tarelkin's *Death*. Many of her designs drew on the imagery of technology. She and others argued that artists should work for the benefit of all of society pursuing direct utilitarian and social applications of their efforts aligned with mass production through advanced technology. 1923 with Liubov' Popova, Rodchenko, and others, she worked as a designer at First State Cotton-Printing Factory (Emil Tsindel textile works), near Moscow; 1923–28, was closely associated with the journals *Lef* (left front) and *Novyi lef* (new left front); 1924–25, was a professor, textile department, VKhUTEMAS (higher artistic and technical studies). From mid-1920s, she produced designs for typography, posters, and stage sets; 1930s, worked on the magazine *USSR in Construction*; died in Moscow.
Exhibitions Work included in 1914 Moscow Salon and was shown in exhibitions in the Soviet Union and abroad, including 1918 *Fifth State Exhibition*; 1919 *Tenth State Exhibition*; 1925 *Exposition Internationale des Arts Décoratifs et Industriels Modernes*, Paris; 1927 *Russian Xylography of the Past Ten Years*, Leningrad (now St. Petersburg). Her work was included in the 1921 *5x5 = 25* exhibition and 1922 *Berlin Erste Russische Kunstausstellung*; 2000–01 *Amazons of the Avant-Garde*, Guggenheim Museum, New York. One-person exhibitions include 1991, Vienna.
Bibliography A.N. Lavrentev with John E. Bowlt (intro.), *Varvara Step-*

anova, une vie constructiviste, Paris: P. Sers, 1988; *Varvara Stepanova: The Complete Work*, Cambridge, Mass.: MIT, 1988. S.O. Khan-Magomedov, *Vhutemas: Moscou, 1920–1930*, Paris: Regard, 1990: 435–38. Peter Noever (ed.), Aleksandr N. Lavrent'yev, and Angela Völker, *Aleksandr M. Rodchenko, Varvara F. Stepanova: The Future Is Our Only Goal*, Munich: Prestel, 1991. Cat., *The Great Utopia: The Russian and Soviet Avant-Garde, 1915–1932*, New York: Guggenheim Museum, 1992.

Stephensen, Magnus (1903–1984)

Danish architect, metalworker, ceramicist, and furniture designer.

Training To 1924, Teknisk Skole, Copenhagen; to 1931, architecture, Det Kongelige Danske Kunstakademi, Copenhagen; 1931, École Française d'Athènes, Athens.
Biography In a long career, Stephensen designed apartment buildings, terrace houses, schools, and waterworks, rejecting decoration and emphasizing the outlines of his structures. His ceramic tableware showed a Chinese influence. 1938–52, he designed for Kay Bojesen, 1950 silver hollow-ware and stainless-steel patterns Tanaquil and Frigate by Georg Jensen Sølvsmedie, furniture by Fritz Hansen, and ceramics by Royal Copenhagen Porcelain Manufactory and by Aluminia. His oven-to-table ceramics began the trend in Denmark toward multi-use and interchangeable dinnerware pieces.
Exhibitions/citations Work included in 1948 exhibition of the Kunsthåndværkerskolen as the subject of the school, Copenhagen; 1954–57 *Design in Scandinavia*, touring the US; 1956–59 *Neue Form aus Dänemark* touring Germany; 1958 *Formes Scandinaves*, Musée des Arts Décoratifs, Paris; 1960–61 *The Arts of Denmark*, touring US. Received 1948 Eckersberg Medal; 1971 medal of Industrielle Designere Danmark; 1951 (9th) (three gold medals), 1954 (10th) (two grand prizes), 1957 (11th) (three gold medals) and 1960 (12th) (silver medal) editions of Triennale di Milano.
Bibliography Cat., *Georg Jensen Silversmithy: 77 Artists, 75 Years*, Washington: Smithsonian, 1980, no. 140. Cat., Kathryn B. Hiesinger and George H. Marcus III (eds.), *Design Since 1945*, Philadelphia: Philadelphia Museum of Art, 1983. Arne Karlsen, *Made in Denmark*, New York: Rheinhold, 1960. Erik Zahle (ed.), *A Treasury of Scandinavian Design*, New York: Golden Press, 1961. Cat., David Revere McFadden (ed.), *Scandinavian Modern Design 1880–1980*, New York: Abrams, 1982.

Stern, Robert A.M. (1939–)

American architect and designer; born Brooklyn, N.Y.

Training To 1960, fine arts, Columbia University, New York; to 1965, architecture, Yale University, New Haven, Conn.
Biography Stern worked briefly as a designer in architect Richard Meier's office; was a planner for the City of New York to 1969, when he opened an architecture office with associate John S. Hagmann; 1977, established his own architecture practice in New York, from 1977, was a professor, Columbia University; amalgamated historical American and classical forms into a postmodern vocabulary, manifested in his furniture by Sunar-Hauserman, bedlinens by various mills, domestic tableware by Alessi, 1984 ceramics and metalware by Swid Powell, 1985 Dinner at Eight rug by Bd Ediciones de Diseño, 1986 jewelry by Acme Jewelry, a 1990 furniture collection in a retro-neo-classical style by Hickory Business Furniture, lighting by Baldinger, and products by Sasaki, Valli & Valli, and others. Stern, Michael Graves, Frank Gehry, Tigerman-McCurry, and Venturi-Scott-Brown developed the resort site plan at Euro Disney near Paris. Stern designed the 1989 hotel at Walt Disney World in Orlando, Florida, that echoed Victorian beach resorts, and other Disney buildings there including 1989 Newport Bay Hotel, inspired by his favored Shingle style, and the Cheyenne Hotel. 1965, he wrote on his theoretical views in the journal *Perspecta*, in which he rejected the International Style and espoused a return to history with an eclectic romantic style; achieved some recognition with a highly personal view of architecture in his 1986 television series *Pride of Place*, produced in the US with an adjunct book. Architects who worked in his office, currently with more than 140 people there, have included Thomas P. Catalano of Boston, Thomas A. Kligerman of Ike & Kligerman of New York, and Peter Pennoyer of New York. The two dozen books Stern wrote or edited include *New Directions in American Architecture* (New York: Braziller, 1969/1977), *George Howe: Toward a Modern American Architecture* (New Haven: Yale University Press, 1975), *New York 1900* (with others, New York: Rizzoli, 1983), and *New York 1930* (with others, New York: Rizzoli, 1987). 1998, was appointed dean and J. M. Hoppin Professor of Architecture, School of Architecture, Yale University.
Exhibitions/citations Represented the US at 1976 and 1980 editions of Biennale di Venezia. Work subject of 1982 exhibition, Newberger Museum, Purchase, N.Y., and included in exhibitions at The Museum of Modern Art, The Drawing Center, Cooper-Hewitt National Design Museum, Whitney Museum of American Art, all New York, and at Art Institute of Chicago and Walker Art Center, Minneapolis, Minn. Received 1980 and 1985 National Honor Awards, 1982 Distinguished Architecture Award, 1984 Medal of Honor of the New York Chapter, and 2001 President's Award, all from American Institute of Architects (AIA); 1999 Achievement Award, Academy of the Arts of Guild Hall, Rice University.
Bibliography Robert A.M. Stern, *Perspecta, the Yale Architectural Journal*, nos. 9–10, 1965. Robert A.M. Stern, *New Directions in American Architecture*, New York: Braziller, 1969. 'The Work of Robert A.M. Stern and John S. Hagmann,' *Architecture and Urbanism*, Oct. 1975. Peter Arnell and Ted Bickford (eds.), *Robert A.M. Stern, 1965–1980: Toward a Modern Architecture after Modernism*, New York: Rizzoli, 1981. Juli Capella and Quim Larrea, *Designed by Architects in the 1980s*, New York: Rizzoli, 1988. *Robert A. M. Stern: Buildings*, New York: Monacelli, 1996. Peter Morris (ed.), *Robert A.M. Stern: Buildings and Projects, 1993–1998*, New York: Monacelli, 1998.

Steuben Glass Works

American glassware manufacturer; located Corning, N.Y.

History 1903, Steuben Glass Works was incorporated in Corning, N.Y.; was originally established to make glass blanks and crystalware for T.G. Hawkes glass-cutting firm. When British glass designer Frederick Carder became its artistic director, the firm's range was extended to include domestic glassware, including vases, millefiori paperweights, candlesticks, goblets, and lampshades. Steuben's modern moment began in 1933, when Arthur Amory Houghton Jr., a member of the family which controlled Corning Glass Works, directed Steuben into modernism and away from Steuben's Art Nouveau approach. He sought to produce American crystal equal to Europe's best and wished to fuse 'art with technology.' 1932, he hired Walter Dorwin Teague Sr., who suggested a move toward minimalism and the rejection of colored glass in favor of Corning's new brilliant and clear 10M (the first to admit light's full spectrum) brilliance and clarity. 1932–34, Teague designed a number of items by Steuben. After World War II, Steuben continued to be the major manufacturer of fine glassware. By 1950s, it became known as a manufacturer of high-quality and high-design crystal glassware and ornamental art glass/sculpture. However, its

Steuben Glass Works. Table lamp. c. 1910–20. Brass and Aurene iridescent glass, h. 13" (33 cm). Mfr.: Steuben Glass Works, US. Courtesy Quittenbaum Kunstauktionen, Munich.

high lead content tends to make the objects, particularly utilitarian ware, brittle and easy to chip. 1950s, George Thompson was a skilled designer at Steuben of domestic glassware in the type of heavy, free-form crystal for which the firm came to be known. Steuben issued one-of-a-kind commemorative pieces presented to heads of state and their representatives. Its one-of-a-kind 1947 Merry-Go-Round Bowl by Sidney Waugh was presented by US President Harry Truman to Britain's Princess Elizabeth as a wedding present. 1954, Steuben began commissioning British designers—including Graham Sutherland, John Piper, Mathew Smith, and engraver Laurence Whistler—as part of its *British Artists in Glass* touring exhibition. Its *New Glass* annual exhibitions have been organized since 1959. The Corning Institute is one of the world's most important contributors to glassmaking and its study. Steuben became a part of Owens-Corning, but the flagship operation Steuben is not profitable. 1993, Steuben began producing more inexpensive glassware, with designs by Massimo Vignelli and others. 1998, Lino Tagliapietra of Murano, Italy, contributed work. Recently, Corning has retained Steuben but been divested of other glass operations and its consumer products division.
Exhibition 2003 *Glass and Glamour: Steuben's Modern Moment, 1930-1960*, Museum of the City of New York (catalog below).
Bibliography *The Collection of Designs in Glass by Twenty-Seven Contemporary Artists*, York: Steuben, 1940. Alastair Duncan, *Art Nouveau and Art Déco Lighting*, New York: Simon & Schuster, 1978: 46–47. Mary Jean Madigan, *Steuben Glass: An American Tradition in Crystal*, New York: Abrams, 1982 (rev. ed. 2002). Frederick Cooke, *Glass: Twentieth-Century Design*, New York: Dutton, 1986: 103. Victor Arwas, *Glass: Art Nouveau to Art Deco*, London: Academy, 1987. Cat., Donald Albrecht, *Glass and Glamour*, New York: Abrams, 2003.
> See Carder, Frederick Gates, John Monteith.

Stevens and Williams
British glassware manufacturer.

History 1880s, cameo glass was being made at three major factories in Britain: Thomas Webb, Stevens and Williams, and Richardson. 1931, the proprietor of Stevens and Williams, Hubert Williams-Thomas, sought a designer, who worked in the modern style. On Ambrose Heal's and Gordon Russell's advice, Keith Murray was retained. 1932, Stevens and Williams held an exhibition of Murray's prototypes. Murray's designs were for table glass and vases. The firm's 1946 Royalty range, originally presented to Princess Elizabeth, was designed by Tom Jones and went into production in 1950s. 1951 when the John Walsh firm closed, its designer, 'Clyne' Farquharson, was hired as Stevens and Williams's chief designer to replace Murray. Farquharson left in 1956, when Jones assumed his position as chief designer.
Exhibition First (1932) exhibition of Murray's work (prototypes) at Stevens and Williams.
Bibliography Frederick Cooke, *Glass: Twentieth-Century Design*, New York: Dutton, 1986. Roger Dodsworth, *William 'Clyne' Farquharson (1906–1972): A Short Biography*, Kingswinford: Broadfield House Glass Museum, 1986.

Stevens, Brooks (1911–1995)
American industrial designer; born and active Milwaukee, Wisc.

Training 1929–33, Cornell University, Utica, N.Y.
Biography Stevens worked briefly in a package-design studio before setting up his own studio in 1934 to redesign machinery, in Milwaukee, Wisc. 1936, he designed the world's first electric clothes drier, transforming it from the manufacturer's concept of a simple heated box into an apparatus (as the 1949 automatic clothes dryer by Hamilton Manufacturing) that had a glass window in the facade door. He also designed the world's first wide-mouth peanut butter glass jar (that allowed access to the bottom), the world's first snowmobile, world's first outboard motor, world's first mass-marketed Jeep, 1941 Petipoint iron (with Edward P. Schreyer), 1948 designs for Harley-Davidson motorcycle (with the twin engine still used today), 1958 Oscar Mayer Wienermobile (promotional vehicular gimmick in the shape of a frankfurter) in fiberglass, 1954 Lawn-Boy power lawn mower, 1956 Evinrude Lark Runabout boat, 1957 Rocket Trike tricycle by Junior Toy, automobile bodies by Volks-wagen and Alfa Romeo, 1940 Packard, 1980 AMC Cherokee automobile. Late 1940s, he worked with Formica to create Luxwood, the wood-grain laminate used on much of the furniture of the time. Stevens was the first to use color in kitchen appliances, being responsible for the ubiquitous 1950s–60s avocado-green color. Until his death, he taught, Milwaukee Institute of

Gustav Stickley. Armchair. c. 1907. Oak and leather, 29 x 26 x 27 5/8" (73.6 x 66 x 70.2 cm). Mfr.: Gustav Stickley, US. Gift of John C. Waddell. MoMA.

Art and Design, and directed the Brooks Stevens Automotive Museum. 1991, the Brooks Stevens Design Center was built at Milwaukee Institute of Art and Design. The Brooks Stevens Design studio continues today. The Brook Stevens Automobile Collection & Museum, Mequon, Wisc., closed in 1999 but was re-formed as Camelot Classic Car Repair & Storage, Milwaukee. Stevens designed for Excalibur (the first replicar-auto maker), and his son took over Excalibur's production, as SS Automobiles Inc, an enterprise active from 1964–88.
Citations Include 1966 Master Design Award (for Milwaukee Automatic Machining Center by Kearney Trecker Corp.).
Bibliography Isabel Wilkerson, 'The Man Who Put Steam in Your Iron,' *The New York Times*, 11 July 1991: C1, C6. Susan Grant Lewin (ed.), *Formica and Design: From the Counter Top to High Art*, New York: Rizzoli, 1991: 91–97.

Stevens, Irene (d. 1957)
British designer.

Biography On the 1946 death of Herbert Webb, Stevens worked at Webb & Corbett (known as Webb Corbett from 1953) in Stourbridge, where designed 1949 cut/blown glassware (produced 1953). The range included a pitcher, drinking glasses, and a fruit bowl. Her 1950s designs were influenced by Clyne Farquharson of Stevens and Williams; however, the triumvirate of Stevens, Farquharson, and Keith Murray broke from traditional British prismatic cut glass by creating more contemporary designs in which decoration was beholden to form. 1957, she left Webb Corbett to teach in the glass department of Stourbridge College. She is also said to have taught, Royal College of Art, London, and at Foley College.
Bibliography Kenneth Farr, *Design in British Industry: A Mid-Century Survey*, London: Cambridge, 1955. Frederick Cooke, *Glass: Twentieth-Century Design*, New York: Dutton, 1986.

Stevens, Peter (1945–)
British automobile designer.

Biography Stevens was a freelance designer from early in his career with almost no staff positions; late 1980s and early 1990s, styled some of the best-known racing-car bodies, including the soft-edged 1988 Stevens revision of the Lotus Elan as the M100, the stylish 1989–90 Jaguar SJR-15, and the sleek 1989 McLaren F1 with its forwardly shifted driver compartment. However, some critics claim him to be less successful with bodies for Hyundai and Proton. Due to its dynamic style, Stevens's Lotus 910 appeared in the films *Pretty Woman* (1990), *If Looks Could Kill* (1991), and *Basic Instinct* (1992). He was the chief designer at Prodrive in 1999 and at Rover in 2000, but these cannot be accurately called full-time posts; 2000, became the product-design director at Rover Group, Longbridge, Birmingham, while concurrently designing for others through his independent consultancy and serving as a visiting professor of vehicular design, Royal College of Art, London.

Stewart, Jim (1946–)

American industrial designer; born Alemeda, Cal.

Training To 1970, San Jose State University.
Biography Stewart worked for Hewlett-Packard after university; 1980, joined Apple Computer, Cupertino, Cal., to design peripheral products; with Jerry Manock, comanaged 1982–83 SnowWhite project; 1984 when Manock left Apple, assumed Manock's duties on the Macintosh computer project; subsequently, left Apple to rejoin Hewlett-Packard but returned to Apple in 1987 as the director to reorganize the IDg (Industrial Design Group); developed post-SnowWhite projects—the Goldilocks, the Three Bears, and the 1989 Macintosh Portable—eventually none successful; 1990, was assigned as manager of the printer and imaging projects in the IDg; 1994, left Apple and, subsequently, became a designer at Microsoft Corporation.
Bibliography Paul Kunkel, *Apple Design: The World of the Apple Industrial Design Group*, New York: Graphis, 1997.

Stewart, Michael (1940–)

Canadian furniture designer.

Training Art, Ontario College of Art.
Biography Stewart designed a number of popular furniture pieces, including 7000 Series public outdoor furniture; partnered with Keith Muller.
Bibliography Cat., *Seduced and Abandoned: Modern Furniture Designers in Canada, the First Fifty Years*, Toronto: The Art Gallery at Harbourfront, 1986: 23. Rachel Gotlieb and Cora Golden, *Design in Canada Since 1945: Fifty Years from Teakettles to Task Chairs*, Toronto: Knopf Canada, 2001.
> See Muller, Keith.

Stewart, Robert (1924–1995)

British designer; active Glasgow.

Training 1940s, Glasgow School of Art.
Biography 1950s–70s, Stewart was active as a designer and educator and, some claim, an inspiring, influential teacher to students going on to successful careers; from 1949, was the head of printed textiles, Glasgow School of Art, where he was the deputy director from 1982; was one of the important textile designers in Britain in 1950s with clients, including Liberty's (its chief textile designer of the period), Donald Brothers, and Edinburgh Tapestry Company; 1957, established his own company for the production of printed ceramic kitchen-ware; created graphics for Liberty's, Motif, Austin Reed, and Schweppes.
Exhibitions Work subject of 2003–04 *Robert Stewart, An Influential designer of the 20th Century*, Constance Howard Resource and Research Centre in Textiles, Goldsmiths College, University of London (catalog below).
Bibliography Liz Arthur, *Robert Stewart Design, 1946–95*, London: A. & C. Black, 2003.

Stickley, Albert; Charles Stickley; John George; Stickley (1871–1921); Leopold Stickley (1869–1957)

American furniture designers; brothers of Gustav Stickley.

Biography The Stickley brothers designed and made furniture. 1880s, Charles, Albert, and Gustav Stickley established Stickley Brothers in Binghamton, N.Y.; initially sold popular furniture by others and then designs of their own in a style that became known as Craftsman or Mission. 1891, Albert and John George established Stickley Brothers Furniture in Grand Rapids, Mich. Leopold and John George left the firm and established their own Onondaga Shop in Fayetteville, N.Y. Gustav now came into competition with his brothers. Even so, Leopold and John George were good at business and excellent furniture makers, and their firm grew rapidly; 1904, was incorporated as L. and J.G. Stickley, which is active today with the production of historic and new pieces.
Exhibition Work of L. and J.G. Stickley subject of 1995 exhibition, Parsippany, N.J. (catalog below).
Bibliography David M. Cathers (new intro.), *Stickley Craftsman Furniture Catalogs: Unabridged Reprints of Two Mission Furniture Catalogs, 'Craftsman Furniture Made by Gustav Stickley' and 'The Work of L. & J. G. Stickley,'* New York: Dover, 1979. Cat., Donald A. Davidoff et al., *Innovation and Derivation: The Contribution of L.& J.G. Stickley to the Arts and Crafts Movement*, Parsippany, N.J.: Craftsman Farms Foundation, 1995. David M. Cathers, *Furniture of the American Arts and Crafts Movement: Furniture Made by Gustav Stickley, L. & J.G. Stickley, and the Roycroft Shop*, Philmont, N.Y.: Turn of the Century, 1996.

Stickley, Gustav (b. Gustave Stickley 1858–1942)

American craftsperson, furniture designer, manufacturer, and entrepreneur; born Osceola, Wisc.; brother of Albert, Charles, John George, and Leopold Stickley.

Training Under his father, in stonemasonry.
Biography His émigré parents anglicized their German name from Stoeckel or Stöckel to Stickley. Becoming orphans after their father left them, he and his brothers (Charles, Albert, Leopold, and John George) worked in their uncle's chair factory in Pennsylvania. Subsequently like his brothers, Gustav became active in furniture making. Over the years, separate companies were established by the brothers for the production of so-called Craftsman or Mission furniture. 1880s, Charles, Albert, and Gustav Stickley established the first firm, Stickley Brothers, in Binghamton, N.Y.; however, Gustav became a competitor. 1890, his Craftsman-type oak electric chair for state corporal punishment was installed at the New York State prison in Auburn. Through his magazine *The Craftsman* and his early-20th-century furniture production, he became the greatest single influence on the American Arts and Crafts movement. Begun in 1901, the magazine expounded Stickley's philosophy, documenting his own home in Syracuse, N.Y, in 1902, and his Craftsman Farms project in Morris Plains, N.J., from 1908. Architect/designer Harvey Ellis designed the houses, furniture, and wall decorations for Stickley's United Crafts Workshop in Eastwood, N.Y. The Craftsman Farms project was an Utopian farm and school community, designed in 1907 and first introduced in 1908, probably realized in 1909, in the form of plans and elevations for the Log House and the cottages. 1910–12, the farm and school were discussed in five successive issues of *The Craftsman*. 1910, Stickley moved his family into the new Log House with furniture from his earlier Syracuse interior; sold franchises from Los Angeles to Boston; 1913, bought a large building in New York, where he established showrooms, offices, and a restaurant. Craftsman Farms was short-lived, and the move to New York proved overly ambitious, with the 1915 bankruptcy of his furniture empire and 1916 discontinuance of *The Craftsman*. The full plan for the farm was never realized. 1917, the 650-acre estate with all its furnishings sold at public auction and, 1989, became publicly owned. The furniture was dispersed. The advent of modernism and the change in public taste brought Stickley's venture to an end. Thus, even though his commitment to solid construction, 'truth in materials,' and high-quality handcrafting aligned him with the Arts and Crafts movement, his emphasis on simplicity and purity of form anticipated European Functionalism.
Exhibitions Work shown at 1904 *Louisiana Purchase Exposition*, St. Louis. Often exhibited his furniture at international exhibitions, often with the ceramics of William Greuby's designers, George P. Kendrick, and later Addison LeBoutillier. Work subject of 1992 exhibition, Parsippany, N.J. (catalog below).
Bibliography David M. Cathers (new intro.), *Stickley Craftsman Furniture Catalogs: Unabridged Reprints of Two Mission Furniture Catalogs, 'Craftsman Furniture Made by Gustav Stickley' and 'The Work of L. & J. G. Stickley,'* New York: Dover, 1979. Mary Ann Smith, *Gustav Stickley, the Craftsman*, Syracuse, N.Y.: Syracuse University, 1983. Stephen Gray and Robert Edwards (eds.), *Collected Works of Gustav Stickley*, New York: Turn of the Century, 1981/1989. Cat., A. Patricia Bartinique, *Gustav Stickley, His Craft: A Daily Vision and a Dream*, Parsippany, N.J.: Craftsman Farms Foundation, 1992. Cat., Donald A. Davidoff et al., *Innovation and Derivation: The Contribution of L.& J.G. Stickley to the Arts and Crafts Movement*, Parsippany, N.J.: Craftsman Farms Foundation, 1995. David M. Cathers, *Furniture of the American Arts and Crafts Movement: Furniture Made by Gustav Stickley, L. & J.G. Stickley, and the Roycroft Shop*, Philmont, N.Y.: Turn of the Century, 1996.

Stijl, De
> See De Stijl.

Stile Liberty
> See Art Nouveau.

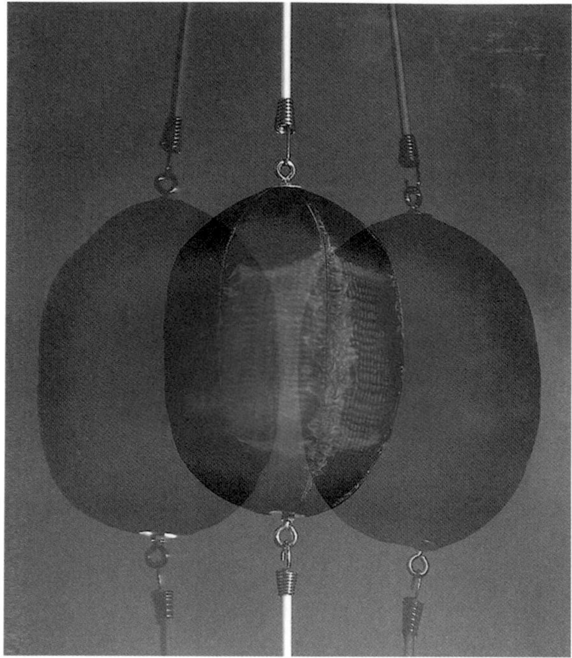

Stiletto Design/Nexus Design. Light Up Pillow. 2001. Light Club pendant light, red LEDs, 6v battery, bungee cord, 10 5/8 x 7 7/8" (27 x 20 cm). Mfr.: Stiletto Design VERTReiB, Germany.

Stiletto (b. Frank Schreiner 1959–)

German designer, born Rüsselsheim; active Berlin.

Training 1980–81, Maschinenbau,Technischen Universität, Berlin; 1982–86, visual communication, Hochschule der Künste, Berlin; 1987–88, sculpture, Kunstakademie, Düsseldorf.
Biography 1979–80, Stiletto was a metal- and locksmith in the German federal armed forces; 1981, became a video and super-8 artist; 1982, designed furniture objects; 1983, was active in holography; designed cutlery sets. His renowned 1983–84 furniture, including 1983 Consumer's Rest and the subsequent variations and 1990 Short Rest chairs, were derived from the iconic wire-grid grocery-store cart. 1991, Stiletto/Schriner established the Design Hospital (a design-and-research entity against so-called good design and the 1990s 'lifestyle' phenomenon) which designed 1991 Filzhocker felt stool and 1999 Mehr Nacht lamp. 1998 Zeitvertreib pseudo-watch jewelry was designed by 'Stiletto DESIGN VERTReiB: Heinz Landes' in Pforzheim.
Exhibitions Work included in a number of exhibitions from 1984 *Der elektronische Raum*, Berlin, to 1988 *Berlin: les avant-gardes du mobilier*, at Centre Georges Pompidou, Galerie VIA (French furniture association), and Galerie Néotù (all simultaneously, in Paris).
Bibliography Christian Borngraeber, *Prototypen: Avantgarde Design uit/aus Berlin*, Rotterdam: 010, 1986. Cat., *Berlin: les avant-gardes du mobilier*, Berlin: Design Zentrum, 1988.

Still McKinney, Nanny (b. Nanny Still 1926–)

Finnish designer; active Finland and Belgium.

Training To 1949, Taideteollinen korkeakoulu, Helsinki.
Biography 1949–76, she was a designer at Riihimäen Lasi, Finland, where she created her first glassware; 1959, moved to Brussels and designed 1962 ceramics by Cerabel Porcelain de Baudour in Belgium, and also 1965–76 ceramics by Porzellan-Fabrik Heinrich Winterling in Bavaria and 1966 and 1968 glassware by Val Saint Lambert in Belgium. The latter was mouth-blown and molded decorative and utility glassware, often in unusual shapes with textured surfaces. Subsequently executing handcrafted and industrial products, she designed wooden objects, jewelry, ceramics, lighting by Raak, and cutlery and 1987 cookware by Hackman; and, from 1977, glassware and ceramics by Rosenthal Studio-Linie; from 1986, plastics by Sarvis.
Exhibitions/citations Work subject of 1963 exhibition in Bruges (catalog below). Received diploma of honor (wooden objects), 1954 (10th) Triennale di Milano; 1972 Pro Finlandia prize.
Bibliography Erik Zahle (ed.), *A Treasury of Scandinavian Design*, New York: Golden Press, 1961. Cat., *Nanny Still Design*, Bruges: Huidevettershuis, 1963. Geoffrey W. Beard, *International Modern Glass*, London: Barrie & Jenkins, 1976, plates 97, 119, 137. Cat., Kathryn B. Hiesinger and George H. Marcus III (eds.), *Design Since 1945*, Philadelphia: Philadelphia Museum of Art, 1983. Jennifer Hawkins Opie, *Scandinavia: Ceramics and Glass in the Twentieth Century*, New York: Rizzoli, 1989.

Stockar, Rudolf (1886–1957)

Czech architect and designer; born Dolnoplazy.

Training 1904–09, architecture, České Vysoké Učení Technické (Czech technical university), Prague.
Biography Stockar worked as a freelance architect and designed furniture, interiors, and utilitarian objects; 1915–30, was the director, Artěl Cooperative; the commissioner of 1923 (1st) *Esposizione Biennale delle Arti Decorative e Industriali Moderne*, Monza. His work was somewhat influenced by Cubism and increasingly in the Art Déco style; architecture includes 1927–34 Sanatorium Sliac in Bad Sliac (now in Slovakia).
Bibliography Alexander von Vegesack et al., *Czech Cubism: Architecture, Furniture, and Decorative Arts, 1910–1925*, New York: Princeton Architectural Press, 1992.

Stockholm, Marianne (1946–)

Danish industrial designer; born Copenhagen.

Training 1967–74, Arkitektskolen, Århus.
Biography 1974–75, she worked in the office of architect Hans Knud-sen, Århus; 1975–96, taught, Arkitektskolen, Århus; 1975–83, was a freelance architect and design consultant for the handicapped, exhibitions, and houses. From 1980, she has conducted research for various institutions, particularly on ergonomics. 1983–93, she was a partner in design consultancy Stockholm / Zorea Design; from 1993, in her own studio for industrial design and has been quite active in education. Her work has included furniture, tableware, 1986 Kirk Plus wall telephone by Alcatel Kirk, 1986 Kirk Delta desktop telephone by Alcatel Kirk, 1988 Skyline graphic computer by Stantex, and a 1988 control unit for concrete pipe machines by Pedershaab Maskinfabrik. Has continued quite actively with the design of a GSM phone by Hagenug, refrigerators by Gram, mother computer by Stantext Graphic, wheelchair by Vela Electrical, Danyard cruiseliners and ferries, and numerous others. 1996–97, was the head, Designskolen, Kolding; from 1999, has been a professor in industrial design, Aalborg Universitet.
Citations 1988 and 1994 Industrie Forum Design (iF), Hanover.
Bibliography Cat., Design Center Stuttgart, *Women in Design: Careers and Life Histories Since 1900*, Stuttgart: Haus der Wirtschaft, 1989: 234–37.

Stockholm Design Laboratory
> Eriksson, Thomas.

Stockman, Fred

Belgian artist, mannequin designer, and entrepreneur; active France.

Training Tailoring in Paris under Lavigne.
Biography 1867, Stockman founded Stockman Brothers, Busts and

Nanny Still McKinney. Ashtray. 1956. Glass, h. 1 3/4" x dia. 6 1/4" (4.4 x 15.9 cm). Mfr.: Riihimäen Lasi, Finland. Phyllis B. Lambert Fund. MoMA.

Mannequins and became one of the first to show the complete female torso, rather than partial figures, in shop windows. 1922, Jérôme Le Maréchal, the director of Les Galeries Lafayette department store in Paris, asked Stockman's artisans to work from fashion drawings rather than live models. The firm is still active today, having early on amalgamated with Siegel, to become Siegel & Stockman in Paris.
Exhibitions/citations From 1878, showed his work at exhibitions in Tunis, London, Moscow, Chicago, Amsterdam, Antwerp, Brussels, and Hanoi. A medal, 1849 *Trade and Industry Exposition* (for patented 'trunk-mannequin'). Stockman was a juror and exhibitor at 1900 *Exposition Universelle*, Paris.
Bibliography Nicole Parrot, *Mannequins*, Paris: Colona, 1981; London: Academy, 1982.
> See Siégel, Victor-Napoléon.

Stockton Art Pottery

American ceramics firm; located Stockton, Cal.

History 1881, the firm was founded and, 1895, introduced Rekston art pottery, similar in treatment to Rookwood's Standard ware and Stubenville's Lonhuda ware. Rekston was an adaptation of Haviland's Cincinnati faience. From 1897, ten women worked at Stockton as artists, producing about 100 pieces of art pottery daily. Stockton ware without underglaze resembles Bennington's mid-19th-century flint-enamel glazed work. Plastic yellow California clay from the Valley Springs region was used. 1900, the factory closed.
Bibliography Paul Evans in Timothy J. Andersen et al., *California Design 1910*, Salt Lake City: Peregrine Smith, 1980: 64.

Stojan, Fabio (1953–)

Italian industrial designer and town planner; born and active Milan.

Training Scuola Politecnica di Design, Milan.

'Gunta' Adelgunde Stölzl. Tapestry. 1924. Wool, silk, mercerized cotton, and metal thread. 69 1/2 x 45" (176.5 x 114.3 cm). Mfr.: the designer, Switzerland. Phyllis B. Lambert Fund. MoMA.

Biography From 1974, Stojan collaborated with Anna Castelli, Giorgio Brambilia, and Lorenzo Tosi in a studio in Milan; became a member, Associazione per il Disegno Industriale (ADI); specialized in aspects of safety and ergonomics in town planning, working with the accident-prevention department of Montedison in Milan.
Bibliography *ADI Annual 1976*, Milan: Associazione per il Disegno Industriale, 1976.

Stolle, Hein (1923–)

Dutch architect and designer; active Amsterdam.

Training Interior design, Koninklijke Academie van Beeldende Kunsten, The Hague.
Biography Stolle's family members were furniture designers and producers. 1946 with Wim Den Boon and Kleykamp, he founded Groep studio, whose work included a waiting room at Shiphol Airport, Amsterdam; town planning of Rotterdam and the harbor; and shopping centers, housing, factories, offices, and, one of the last commissions, the botanical gardens of Floriade world horticultural exhibition. Stolle has designed furniture, some inspired by Le Corbusier and Gerrit Rietveld (once a personal friend of Stolle), as well as 1946 one piece bentwood coffee table (by Isokon Plus from 2001 as the T46). Concerning the coffee table, Stolle confesses, 'I have always wanted to have it produced; however, could never find a manufacturer with the necessary foresight, knowledge, and ability, one with bentwood technology. Therefore, the original prototype was produced in steel.'

Stoltenberg-Lerche, Hans (1867–1920)

Glassware designer; born Düsseldorf; son of a Norwegian painter.

Biography Stoltenberg-Lerche began his career in a ceramics studio in Germany; subsequently, settled in Florence, then Naples, and, 1890, in Paris, where he sculpted and painted; 1903, moved to Rome and became a glass designer; 1911–20, created glass designs by Antica Vetreria Fratelli Toso, thereby introducing French glassmaking techniques in Venice and becoming a highly important and original contributor to the development of modern Murano glass.
Exhibitions 1912, 1914, and 1920 editions of Biennale di Venezia; 1923, Monza.

Stölzl, 'Gunta' Adelgunde (1897–1983)

German textile designer; born Munich. From 1929, 'Gunta' Sharon-Stölzl; from 1942, 'Gunta' Stadler-Stölzl.

Training 1914–16, decorative arts, painting on glass, and ceramics, Kunstgewerbeschule, Munich; Staatliche Ingenieurschule für Textilwesen, Krefeld; from 1919, Bauhaus, Weimar.
Biography As the first weaver at the Bauhaus, she wove fabric for the seats of chairs by Marcel Breuer and by others and contributed textiles to Walter Gropius's 1921–22 Sommerfeld house. 1922–23, she passed the journeyman's examination at the Bauhaus with a large Smyrna carpet; 1924 encouraged by Johannes Itten, established a studio in Switzerland; 1925–26, taught, Bauhaus, Dessau, where she was one of the two women master instructors. 1927–31, she was in charge of the Bauhaus weaving department, succeeding Georg Muche. Under her leadership, Bauhaus textiles were sold through firms in Berlin, Dresden, and Stuttgart. 1931 with former Bauhaus students, she established Gertrud Dirks-Preiswerk, and, subsequently with Dirks Heinrich Otto Hürlimann, cofounded SPH, a handweaving studio and workshop for textile design in Zurich. At this time, she began working with the Wohnbedarf furniture store in Zurich. Unfortunately, a commission by Wohnbedarf led to financial problems: a large number of textiles were lost, forcing her to dissolve the SPH business. Later and again with Hürlimann, she established S+H Stoffe weaving workshop, where she continued to work even after Hürlimann had departed in 1937 to set up his own firm. She died in Zurich.
Exhibitions Work subject of exhibitions, Zurich, Bremen, and Berlin in 1987 and Dessau in 1997 (catalogs below).
Bibliography Cat., *Gunta Stölzl, Weberei am Bauhaus und aus eigener Werkstatt*, Berlin: Bauhaus-Archiv, 1987. Cat., *The Bauhaus: Masters and Students*, New York: Barry Friedman, 1988. Friederike Mehlau-Wiebking et al. *Schweizer Typenmöbel 1925–35, Sigfried Giedion und die Wohnbedarf AG*, Zurich: gta, 1989: 231. Sigrid Wortmann Weltge, *Women's Work: Textile Art from the Bauhaus*, London: Thames & Hudson, 1993. Cat., Ingrid Radewaldt et al., *Gunta Stölzl: Meisterin am Bauhaus Dessau: Textilien, Textilentwürfe und freie Arbeiten 1915–1983*, Ostfildern-Ruit: Hatje, 1997.

Stone, Arthur J. (1847–1938)

British designer and silversmith; born Sheffield; active in the US.

Training 1861–68, apprenticeship under a silversmith in Sheffield; National School of Design, New York.
Biography 1884, Stone settled in the US, where he first worked at the William B. Durgin firm, Concord, N.H.; 1887, moved to Gardner, Mass., where he worked for Frank W. Smith Silver as a designer and the head of the hollow-ware department; 1895, became a partner in J.P. Howard, New York; 1886, returned to Gardner and established his own workshop; 1901, opened a shop and joined the Society of Arts and Crafts in Boston (founded 1898), in which he was active to 1937. Stone produced historicist, traditional presentation silver from 1904, ecclesiastical silver from 1905, and domestic tableware, sometimes collaborating with Hollis French and often modifying and reinterpreting 17th- and 18th-century American and English forms. His cutlery handles were often chased with flowers or initials. The firm produced toys and other items for children, miniatures, boxes, vases, porringers, tankards, tea sets, and cutlery. Stone was one of the last independent designer-silversmiths in New England to train apprentices.
Exhibitions/citations Work included in Arts and Crafts venues in Chicago, Detroit, Cincinnati, and Philadelphia. Received 1903 and 1906 Master Craftsman and 1913 Medallist awards, Society of Arts and Crafts, Boston; silver medal (for four-piece entry at the stand of the Boston group), 1904 *Louisiana Purchase Exposition*, St. Louis.
Bibliography Elenita C. Chickering, 'Arthur J. Stone, silversmith,' *Antiques*, Jan.1986: 274–83.

Stone, Edward Durell (1902–1978)

American architect and designer; born Fayetteville, Arkansas

Training A few semesters, Arkansas State University; night class, Architecture Club, Boston, Mass.; on an architecture scholarship, Harvard University; Massachusetts Institute of Technology (MIT), Cambridge, Mass., on a two-year scholarship for European travel, but left before receiving a degree.
Biography Stone moved to Boston and, for one year, worked on one of Harvard University's buildings in the architecture office of Henry Shepley; traveled in Europe and became influenced by modernism, the Bauhaus's International Style, and Le Corbusier's machine aesthetic; returned to the US and worked for several architects; 1936, began practicing architecture on his own, including the first American interpretations of the International Style, among which was 1935 Richard Mandel house, Bronxville, N.Y., and 1938 A. Conger Goodyear vacation house, Old Westbury, N.Y. 1930s with few architecture commissions, he designed advertising graphics, lighting fixtures, the interiors of the Waldorf-Astoria Hotel and 1932 Radio City Music Hall (with Donald Deskey), both New York. However, the 1938–39 original building (by Stone with Philip S. Goodwin) of The Museum of Modern Art, New York, established his reputation as an architect of note. Other work: 1954 Hotel Phoenicia, Beirut; US Embassy, New Delhi; US Pavilion, 1958 *Exposition Universelle et Internationale de Bruxelles* (*Expo '58*); 1950s chaise, table, magazine rack, and side chair (wood and woven cane) by Fulbright Industries, Arkansas; mid-1950s 'veil-block' facade system of male dormitories (now co-educational), University of South Carolina, and his own house, New York. The 1973 Amoco building (today Ano Center), Chicago, by his firm was the tallest building at the time (today's 11th tallest). His two biographies were *The Evolution of an Architect* (New York: Horizon, 1962) and *Recent & Future Architecture* (New York: Horizon, 1967). His correspondence with Walter Gropius, Marcel Breuer, Donald Deskey, Eero Saarinen, Frank Lloyd Wright, and others is housed in the library of University of Arkansas, where he taught for a number of years.
Citation Gold medal (for 1946 El Panama Hotel), Architectural League of New York.

Stoppino, Giotto (b. Luigi Stoppino 1926–)

Italian architect and industrial designer; born Vigevano, Pavia.

Training 1945–50, architecture, Milan; 1955–57, Istituto Universitario di Architettura, Venice.
Biography 1953–63, Stoppino was a partner in the Stoppino Gregotti Meneghetti design firm in Novara and, 1964–68, in Milan; from 1968, was an independent designer in Milan; 1963, was a visiting lecturer at the university in Pavia, and, 1972, Scuola Cantonale Superiore in Lugano. Also taught, Istituto Universitario di Architettura and Facoltà di Architettura in Milan and Palermo. 1954, he became a member of Movimento Studi per l'Architettura in Milan and, 1960, of Associazione per il Disegno Industriale (ADI), of which, 1966–68 and 1971–73, was director and, 1982–84, president, and ADI delegate to the (5th) ICSID (International Council of Societies of Industrial Design) congress in Montréal. 1983, he was president of the development committee, ICSID International Congress, Milan. 1967, he began designing in plastics; his first work was 1968 4905/6-7/5 group of three stacking tables. Subsequent work included 1969 537 table lamps (with V. Gregotti and L. Meneghetti) by Arteluce, 1970 KD 32 (Tic-Tac) lamp and 1972 4676 magazine rack by Kartell, 1970 Alessia fiberglass chair by Driade, 1976 Drop 1 by Tronconi, 1984 champagne and ice bucket by Cleto Munari. For Acerbis International with Ludovico Acerbis, with whom he developed a special collaborative relationship, he designed 1981 Madison shelving system, 1983 Solemio mirror, 1983 Menhir table system in marble, 1985 Playbox system, 1986 Soffio di Vento shelving system. Other clients: Arnolfo di Cambio, Astheria, Bacci, Bellato, Bernini, Brambilla, Candle, Elco, Heller, Interior, Joint, La Rinascente, Moroni Mobili, Nicolini, Olivari, Raak, Rexite, Tronconi, and Zanotta.
Exhibitions/citations Work included in exhibitions ranging from a 1983 venue, Galleria Arte Borgogna, Milan, to 1972 *Italy: The New Domestic Landscape*, The Museum of Modern Art, New York; and a large number of others, including six editions of Triennale di Milano. Received first prize (1968 stacking tables by Kartell) at 1968 (8th) Mobile Accessorio da Vendere nei Grandi Magazzini competition in Trieste; other prizes included grand prize, 1964 (13th) Triennale di Milano; 1970 (individually and with others), 1979 (two citations individually and with L. Acerbis), 1981 (two citations), 1987 (individually and with L. Acerbis), 1991 Premio Compasso d'Oro; gold medal, 1981 BIO 9 industrial-design biennial, Ljubljana; 1981 Product Design Award, Institute of Business Designers (IBD), US.
Bibliography Cat., Milena Lamarová, *Design a Plastické Hmoty*, Prague: Uměleckoprůmyslové Muzeum, 1972: 158. *ADI Annual 1976*, Milan:

Giotto Stoppino. Nesting tables (no. 4905-6-7/5). 1966. ABS polymer, left: 16 x 18 1/2" dia. (40.6 x 47 cm), middle: 13 x 18" dia. (33 x 45.7 cm), right:. 14 1/2 x 18" dia. (36.8 x 45.7 cm). Mfr.: Kartell, Italy. Gift of the manufacturer. MoMA.

Edward Durell Stone. Bowl. 1951–52. Enameled steel, h. 4 1/2" x dia. 10 1/8" (11.4 x 25.7 cm). Mfr.: N.S. Gustin Co., US. Gift of the mfr. MoMA.

Associazione per il Disegno Industriale, 1976. Daniele Baroni, *Giotto Stoppino: dall'architettura al design*, Milan: Electa, 1983. Juli Capella and Quim Larrea, *Designed by Architects in the 1980s*, New York: Rizzoli, 1988.

Stowell, Davin (1953–)

American industrial designer; born Corning, N.Y.

Training To 1976, industrial design, Syracuse (N.Y.) University.
Biography Stowell first worked for Corning Glass Works consumer products division, Corning, N.Y.; 1978, established his first firm, Davin Stowell Associates, a consultancy to Corning Glass Works, designing consumer products and exhibitions. Employees included Tucker Viemeister and Tom Dair. 1985, the company became known as Smart Design, in New York. Stowell specialized in consumer product design, product planning, marketing communications, and graphic identity for clients including Oxo, Copco, Corning, International Playtex, Kepner-Tregoe, and 3M. He holds dozens of utility and design patents for consumer products; is a member, Industrial Designers Society of America.
Citations Numerous IDEA/*Business Week* awards; five citations, Annual Design Reviews, *I.D.* magazine.

Stráník, Karel (1899–1978)

Bohemian architect and furniture designer; born Prague; active Prague and Paris.

Training 1918–23, České Vysoké Učení Technické (Czech technical university), Prague.
Biography From 1925 until its 1931 close, Stráník was a member of the Devětsil group; assisted Le Corbusier on the L'Esprit Nouveau pavilion at 1925 *Exposition Internationale des Arts Décoratifs et Industriels Modernes*, Paris, and on plans for 1926 Cook house, Boulogne, while he was working 1925–26 in Le Corbusier's office in Paris. Returning to Prague, his 1925 competition entry for a museum adjacent to the Liberation Movement monument in Prague incorporated a classical layout with Functionalist volumes and details. He designed the 1926–29 conversion of an older ground-floor building at 215 Poštovní St. in Černošice for Jaroslav and Jan Novák, stockbrokers and collectors of Czech modern art. For the conversion, Stráník incorporated, like Le Corbusier, alternating white and colored spray-coated walls and tubular metal banisters in a setting with standard Thonet furniture. With his Devětsil friend Pavel Smetana, Stráník designed simple cupboards, armchairs, and bookcases for the Jaroslav and Jan Novák commission.
Bibliography Cat., *Devětsil: Czech Avant-Garde Art, Architecture, and Design of the 1920s and 30s*, Oxford Museum of Modern Art and London Design Museum, 1990.

Straub, Marianne (1909–1994)

Swiss weaver and designer; born Amriswil; active Britain.

Training 1928–31, Kunstgewerbeschule, Zürich; 1932–33, machine production, Bradford Technical College, West Yorkshire, UK.
Biography An experimenter, Straub used vegetable dyes in her 1920–30s textiles; worked in a Swiss cotton mill and under weaver Ethel Mairet in Britain; 1934–37, revitalized the flagging production of the Rural Industries Bureau for the Welsh Woollen Mills, including upholstery fabrics used by Gordon Russell; began weaving in her own home, while concurrently working in industrial methods in a small cotton mill. 1937–50, she was a designer at Helios, a division of Barlow & Jones, and, late 1940s, its managing director and where she worked on a dobby loom and made important advances in the production of contemporary fabrics on power looms, setting a precedent for hand weaves for mass production. 1950–70, she designed contemporary fabrics by Warner, the successor to Helios, including 1951 Festival Pattern Group, a program established by Council of Industrial Design for materials for 1951 *Festival of Britain* exposition, London. Her 1951 Surrey curtain fabric for the program (originally installed in the Regatta Restaurant at the Festival) was printed under license by 26 manufacturers. Straub was also a consultant designer to Tamesa Fabrics and Heal Fabrics; taught widely, including at Central School of Art and Design and Royal College of Art, both London. She wrote the book *Hand Weaving and Cloth Design* (1977). Her Tamesa range was used on oceanliners 1934 *Queen Mary* and 1969 *Queen Elizabeth II*. Through to 1980s, she remained active. The Marianne Straub Travel Bursary, a philanthropic fund, was founded in her honor.
Bibliography Marianne Straub, *Hand Weaving and Cloth Design*, New York: Viking, 1977. Cat., *Thirties: British Art and Design Before the War*, London: Arts Council of Great Britain/Hayward Gallery, 1979. *A Choice of Design: 1950–1980*, London: Warner and Sons, 1981: 64–65, nos. 244, 248. Mary Schoeser, *Marianne Straub*, London: The Design Council, 1984. Cat., Mary Schoeser, *Marianne Straub: A Retrospective Exhibition*, London (attri.): Warner & Sons, 1984. Mary Schoeser, *Marianne Straub,* Bridgehampton, N.Y.: State Mutual Book & Periodical Service, 1987.

Strauß, Paula (1894–1943)

German silversmith; born Stuttgart.

Training Under Paul Haustein, Kunstgewerbeschule, Stuttgart.
Biography 1920s–30s, Strauß was active in metalworking; from 1926, designed silver by Bruckmann & Söhne in Hellbronn and distinguished handwrought vessels by Halbmond und Krone (which also produced vessels in sterling silver and glass designed by others). Strauß died in Auschwitz concentration camp.
Bibliography Annelies Krekel-Aalberse, *Art Nouveau and Art Déco Silver*, New York: Abrams, 1989. Cat., *Metallkunst*, Berlin: Bröhan-Museum, 1990: 577.

streamline

A form of styling popular in the 1930s.

History With prices in the US fixed by the 1932 National Recovery Act, the need for product differentiation in the fiercely competitive Depression-affected marketplace meant that an unprecedented focus was being placed on the way a product looked. The advertising industry was developing new techniques, and consumers often saw pictures of goods before they were exposed in stores. The fledgling freelance designers leapt at the opportunity to sell their services; they came from backgrounds in commercial art, graphic design, advertising, and stage design, and promised commercial benefits for 'styling.' Designers included Norman Bel Geddes, Raymond Loewy, Henry Dreyfuss, and Walter Dorwin Teague Sr., considered the 'Big Four.' They all wrote books advocating their services. By the mid-1940s, streamline household products were commonplace. Edgar Kaufmann Jr., director of the Department of Design, The Museum of Modern Art, New York, considered streamline an anathema and saw it as a 'widespread and superficial kind of design... used to style nearly any object from automobiles to toasters. Its theme is the magic of speed expressed in teardrop shapes, fairings and a curious ornament of parallel lines—sometimes called speed whiskers. The continued misuse of these devices has spoiled them for most designers...'
Exhibitions Subject of 1984 venue, Queens, N.Y., US (catalog below).
Bibliography Edgar Kaufmann, *What is Modern Design?*, New York: The Museum of Modern Art, 1950. Tom Wolfe, *The Kandy-Kolored Tangerine Flake Streamline Baby*, New York: Farrar, Straus & Giroux, 1965. Robert C. Reed, *The Streamline Era*, San Marino, Cal.: Golden West, 1975. Cat., *Streamline Design: How the Future Was*, Flushing, N.Y.: Queens Museum, 1984. *Styling*, London: Design Museum, 1989.

Streng, Daniel (1968–)

American designer.

Training To 1995, design program, Milwaukee Institute of Art and Design, Milwaukee, Wisc.
Biography 1994, Streng established his own eponymous studio in Mil-

waukee, and, 1997 with six international designers, cofounded the Mobas consortium; has been active as an industrial and interior designer.
Exhibition Work included in 2001 *Tag Team* exhibit of ten designers, sponsored by *Surface* magazine.

Strengell, Marianne (1909–1998)
Finnish textile designer; born, Helsinki.

Training 1929, Taideteollinen korkeakoulu, Helsinki.
Biography 1930–36, Strengell designed rugs and furnishing fabrics in Helsinki and, 1934–36, by Bo Aktieselskab of Copenhagen; 1934–36, cofounded the firm Hemflit-Kotiahkeruus, specializing in fabrics, furniture, and interior design. 1937 at the invitation of schoolmaster Eliel Saarinen, she settled in Bloomfield Hills, Mich., US, where she was an instructor at Cranbrook Academy of Art and, 1942–61, head of its weaving and textile-design department. Strengell used hand and power looms at the school, where she developed prototypes for machine-woven fabrics. These fabrications emphasized textures created with new synthetic materials, also combined with natural fibers. Her 1940s hand-woven fabrics were commercially popular in the US. From 1947, she designed drapery and upholstery fabrics by Knoll and tweed and jacquard-filament automobile upholstery fabrics by Catham. Eero Saarinen used her textured materials in his 1948–56 General Motors Technical Center, Warren, Mich. Her fabrics in fiberglass (a 1935 Corning invention as 'Fiberglas') were installed in the Owens-Corning Fiberglas building, New York. She was a consultant to the governmental weaving programs of agencies in Jamaica in 1966, the Appalachia area of the US, and St. Croix in the Virgin Islands 1969–71; designed ecclesiastical and residential interiors with her second husband, Olav Hammarstrom.
Bibliography Don Wallance, *Shaping America's Products*, New York: Reinhold, 1956: 183. Eric Larrabee and Massimo Vignelli, *Knoll Design*, New York: Abrams, 1981: 91, 272. Cat., Kathryn B. Hiesinger and George H. Marcus III (eds.), *Design Since 1945*, Philadelphia: Philadelphia Museum of Art, 1983.

Strnad, Oskar (1879–1935)
Austrian architect and furniture and interior designer; born Vienna.

Biography From 1909, Strnad was a highly influential teacher at Kunstgewerbeschule in Vienna. The Wiener Möbel (Viennese furniture) was a new style, developed in 1920s, that featured solid craftsmanship without historicism. Along with Josef Frank, Strnad was the main representative of this style of interior design. Strnad was also known for theater set designs and, 1924, became the chief designer of Deutsches Volkstheater, which produced the work of avant-garde Expressionist playwrights and for which he designed sets for Ernst Křenek's *Jonny spielt auf* (1927), František Langer's *Peripherie* (1930), and others. Strnad and Adolf Loos designed 1931 Service water pitcher and drinking glasses (no. 248, by Lobmeyr), originally for Loos's 1907 American Bar at Kärntner Durchgang, Vienna.
Exhibitions His Österreichischer Edelraum (Austrian nobleman's room) was installed at 1922 *Gewerbeschau*, Munich. Work also included in the Austrian pavilion, 1925 *Exposition Internationale des Arts Décoratifs et Industriels Modernes*, Paris.
Bibliography Otto Niedermoser, *Oskar Strnad 1879–1935*, Vienna: Bergland, 1965. Günther Feuerstein, *Vienna—Present and Past: Arts and Crafts—Applied Art—Design*, Vienna: Jugend und Volk, 1976.

Strömbergshyttan
Swedish glass factory.

History 1876, the Lindfors Glasbruk was established in Hovmantorp, Småland, specializing in tableware and bottles; 1933, was leased by Edward Strömberg (1872–1946), formerly manager of Kosta, Orrefors, and Eda glass factories. He completely reorganized Lindfors, renamed it Strömbergshyttan, and began production of decorative glassware designed by his wife Gerda Strömberg (1879–1960) 1933–46 and blown by Knut Bergqvist, also formerly of Orrefors. 1930s, English designer H.J. Dunne Cooke also designed tableware and vessels. c. 1943, Strömberg bought the facility and, 1945, sold it to his son Erik (d. 1960), a chemist and technician, who had developed the subtle colors the plant's wares had assumed. 1952–75, Gunnar Nyland was the primary designer, while also serving as art director for Rörstrand ceramics to 1958. The bulk of Strömbergshyttan's production was pale-blue, high-quality, frequently engraved crystal, but some was overlaid with color and others in the Ariel bubble-infused technique. Gerda Ström-berg's forms had been highly controled, whereas Nyland's were

Marianne Strengell. Upholstery sample. 1936–75. Cotton, acetate rag, and chenille, 26 1/2 x 24 1/2" (67.3 x 62.2 cm). Mfr.: the designer, US. Given anonymously. MoMA.

fluid and biomorphic. On the 1960 death of Erik, his widow Asta Strömberg managed the firm and, 1960s–70s, was the most consequential designer, active from 1930s to 1974. The plant was updated in 1962, but a 1973 fire destroyed the factory, which was rebuilt. 1976, Strömbergshyttan was bought by Orrefors; and, 1979, closed. 1987, master glassblowers Mikael Axenbrant, Håkan Gunnarsson and Leif Persson purchased the premises in Strömbergshyttan and founded Studioglas Strömbergshyttan.
Bibliography Jennifer Hawkins Opie, *Scandinavia: Ceramics and Glass in the Twentieth Century*, New York: Rizzoli, 1989. Leslie Jackson, *20th Century Factory Glass*, London: Octopus, 2000.

Stromeyer, Gisela (1961–)
German designer; born Konstanz.

Training Technische Universität, Munich; 1989, bachelor's degree in architecture, Pratt Institute, Brooklyn, N.Y.; 1981, architect Frei Otto's studio, Stuttgart.
Biography From 1985, Stromeyer worked at FTL/Happold, a multidisciplinary engineering-design consultancy and, 1989, opened her own eponymous studio; both in New York. She has been active in interior and lighting design for residences, offices, showrooms, restaurants, and theaters with clients, including Click model agency, Disney, Elizabeth Arden, Emanuel Ungaro, MTV, Ralph Lauren, and Sony.
Bibliography Cat., R. Craig Miller (intro.), *U.S. Design 1975–2000*, Munich: Prestel, 2002.

Strum, Gruppo
> See Gruppo Strum.

Stuart & Sons
British glassware manufacturer.

History From c. 1799, glass was being made in the Red House Cone in Stourbridge when Richard Bradley bought the premises. Over the next century, numerous owners occupied the site, including Frederick Stuart (1816–1900). 1827 at age 11, he became an apprentice in the Red House and, 1881 as a master craftsperson by then, took over the lease from Phillip Pargeter and, 1885 renewed the lease. A year after his 1900 death, the Stuart family organized a limited company; 1916, bought the White House Glassworks opposite the Red House Cone; 1920, bought the the Red House from Edward Webb. 1924, 'Stuart' became a registered trademark of the company. 1927, 'Stuart Crystal' was first used. 1936, the Red House closed, with production transferred to Vine Street. The designers included F.H. Stuart and E.N. Khouri. From 1949, John Luxton designed various pieces of glassware for the firm, including goblets in a robust silhouette. 1980, Strathearn

Glass (founded in 1965) in Crieff was bought by Stuart & Sons to become Stuart Strathearn. (Herbert Dreier [1942–] was a master craftsperson at Strathearn from 1965 and with Stuart & Sons to 2001.) Strathearn designs, both glassware and paperweights, were discontinued, and Stuart & Sons placed an emphasis on lead-crystal blanks that were cut by others in Stourbridge. Two new furnaces were installed at the time. 1985–87, Iestyn Davies worked for Stuart Crystal, after leaving Stourbridge College of Art (1982–85), as the firm's colored-glass artist; designed 1986 Ebony & Gold and Dark Crystal ranges and others, produced for a short time. (1987, he established Osiris Glass at Broadfield House Glass Museum, Kingswinford; 1993, a glass studio in Stourbridge.) 1997, Stuart Crystal ceased production. 1997, the operation in Wales closed. 2001, Stuart & Sons, which had been family-owned from its founding, was bought by Waterford Wedgwood.
Exhibitions Work by Graham Sutherland, Paul Nash, Eric Ravilious, Dod Proctor, and Laura Knight shown at 1935 *British Art in Industry* exhibition of the Royal Society of Arts, London (as the only glassmakers commissioned by the British government to produce pieces for the exhibition).
Bibliography Frederick Cooke, *Glass: Twentieth-Century Design*, New York: Dutton, 1986: 70, 78. Mervyn Gulliver, *Victorian Decorative Glass: British Designs, 1850–1914*, Atglen, Pa.: 2002.
> See Luxton, John.

Stuck, Franz von (1863–1928)

German painter, sculptor, architect, and designer, born Tettenweis Lower Bavaria.

Training 1878–81, Kunstgewerbeschule; 1881–85, Königliche Akademie der Künste, both Munich.
Biography Stuck first became known as an illustrator for *Fliegende Blätter*, a Munich satirical magazine; was primarily a painter and illustrator but turned to sculpture in 1890s and became one of the important artists of the Munich Jugendstil style; 1892, cofounded the Münchner Sezession; from 1895, was a professor, Königliche Akademie der Künste, Munich; 1897–98 (with Jakob Heilmann and Max Littmann), designed his Villa Stuck with architecture, interior design, furniture, painting and sculpture as a *Gesamtkunstwerk* (total work of art).
Exhibition/citation Gold medal (Grecian-style furniture for his own house), 1900 *Exposition Universelle*, Paris.
Bibliography Heinrich Voss, *Franz von Stuck 1863–1928: Werkkatalog d. Gemälde...*, Munich: Prestel, 1973. *Franz von Stuck: Persönlickkeit und Werk*, Munich: Museum Villa Stuck, 1977. Kathryn Bloom Hiesinger, *Die Meister des Münchner Jugendstil*, Munich: Stadtmuseum, 1988: 160–61. Auction cat., Christie's, 9 Dec. 1989.

Oskar Strnad. Cigarette box (no. US 5084). 1916. Clear mouth-blown glass, overall h. 3 3/4" x dia. 2 5/8" (9.5 x 6.7 cm). Mfr.: J. & L. Lobmeyr, Austria. Gift of the mfr. MoMA.

Studio Alchimia (aka Studio Alchymia)
> See Alchimia, Studio..

Studio Ars Labor Industrie Riunite (S.A.L.I.R.)

Italian glass manufacturer; located Murano.

History 1923, Studio Ars Labor Industrie Riunite (S.A.L.I.R.) was founded by Decio Toso, son of Luigi Toso (the cofounder of Ferro Toso & C.) with Giuseppe D'Alpaos, Guglielmo Barbini, and Gino Francesconi, all formerly employed by Cristalleria Franchetti. It specialized in engraved/painted mirrors and other objects on blanks from others, at first bought from Ferro Toso. 1925, designer Dino Martens began his career there and became its first designer. From 1927, Guido Balsamo Stella was the artistic director. Also from 1927, Franz Pelzel, from Bohemia, worked there until his 1968 retirement. On the designs of Balsamo Stella, Pelzel wheel-engraved Art Déco patterns, classical figures, and life scenes. 1930s models were designed by Pelzel as well as by Vittorio Zecchin, Gio Ponti, Pietro Fornasetti, and Atte Gasparetto. Later, Pelzel and his assistants diamond-pointed or wheel-engraved modern motifs. 1940s–50s, Carlo Scarpa designed there, followed by others such as Ugo Blasi, Riccardo Licata, Serena Dal Maschio, Pietro Pelzel, Gio Ponti, Romualdo Scarpa, Ettore Sottsass, Agostino Venturini, Vinicio Vianello, Tono Zancanaro—through to Marco Zanini in 1990 and others subsequently. From 1976, the enterprise has been managed by Mario D'Alpaos and Luigi Toso, heirs of the original founders.
Exhibition 1932 Biennale di Venezia (Franz Pelzel's *inciso* vase).

Studio DA (Studio Designer Associati)

Italian consultant design group.

History Mid-1960s, architects/designers Cesare M. Casati and C. Emanuele Ponzio established design partnership Studio DA; 1965, began experimenting with plastics, developing 1965 Alda lounge chair by Comfort, the legendary 1968 Pillola lamp by Pontour, and furnishings by Sormani, including 1970 Tomorrow wine rack. Casati and Ponzio were on the editorial board of journal *Domus* and designed its headquarters in Rozzano.
Exhibitions From 1966, group work shown at major international expositions, including editions of Eurodomus and Triennali di Milano.
Bibliography Cat., Milena Lamarová, *Design a Plastické Hmoty*, Prague: Uměleckoprůmyslové Muzeum, 1972: 110.
> See Casati, Cesare; Ponzio, C. Emanuele; Sormani.

Studio Kairos
> See Kairos, Studio.

Studio Naço
> See Naço, Studio.

Studio OPI
> See OPI, Studio.

Studio PER
> See PER, Studio.

Studio 65

Italian design consortium; active Turin and Jeddah, Saudi Arabia.

History 1965, F. Audrito, A. Sampaniotis, and F. Tartaglia first established the studio in reaction to the new approach to design thinking that was fomenting in schools of the time and being provoked by the sociopolitical conflicts of 1960s. They worked on specific interventional subjects. Subsequently, the trio was joined by G. Amaudo, A. Garizio, R. Gibello, G. Paci, P. Perotti, A. Pozzo, A.M. Racchetta, A. Sampaniotou, M. Schiappa, J. Skoulas, and A. Vanara. The eventual full team created the Multipli Studio 65 collection. Its best-known design is 1970 Bocca (or Marilyn) sofa (based on the original 1934 Mae West Lips version by Salvador Dalí for Charles James; Studio 65's Marilyn by Gufram; now produced by Edra). Other designs: 1972 Capitello slanting polyurethane 'ionic capital' seat and 1973 Baby-lonia puzzle sculpture (foam covered with synthetic velvet; for random seats when unfolded). 1980s, the group became interested in international architectonic design and designed a number of architectural structures, both realized and not.
Exhibitions/citations Work included in numerous exhibitions. Received first prizes and special rewards.
Bibliography Ennio Chiggio (ed.), *Studio 65*, Milan: Electa, 1986.

Maurizio Vitta, *Studio 65: Franco Audrito*: L'Arcaedizioni, 2001. Maurizio Vitta (intro.) and Franco Audrito (text), *Lo Studio 65: architettura e design*, Milan: Arca, 1995.

Studiodada Associati

Italian design cooperative; located Milan.

History 1977, Studiodada was established by Ada Alberti, Marco Piva, Paolo Francesco Piva, Dario Ferrari, and Maurizio Maggi. They had formed the group after graduating from the Politecnico, Milan, and became active in architecture, video production, and interior, product, and graphic design.
Exhibitions Participated in numerous venues.
Bibliography Fumio Shimizu and Studio Matteo Thun (eds.), *The Italian Design: Descendants of Leonardo da Vinci*, Tokyo: Graphic-sha, 1987.

Studium (aka Studium-Louvre)

French decorating and design workshop; located Paris.

History 1923, the Studium (or the Studium-Louvre) decorating workshop was established by Société des Grands Magasins et des Hôtels du Louvre, Paris (the store itself having been originally founded in 1855 as Les Galeries du Louvre, a fashion shop on the rue de Rivoli, adjacent to Le Grand Hôtel du Louvre, and, in 1879, changed to Les Grands Magasins du Louvre, one of the largest and best-known department stores of the time). To 1938, the Studium's director was Étienne Kohlmann, who collaborated regularly with consultant designers, including architect Djo-Bourgeois, André Fréchet, Pierre Lahalle, Georges Levard, and Maurice Matet.
Exhibition The pavilion of the Studium was built at 1925 *Exposition Internationale des Arts Décoratifs et Industriels Modernes*, Paris.
Bibliography 'Studium Louvre,' *Mobilier et décoration*, Sept. 1925: 173–77. Pierre Kjellberg, *Art déco: les maîtres du mobilier, le décor des paquebots*, Paris: Amateur, 1986/1990.

Stumpf, Axel (1957–)

German designer; born Seigertshausen; active Berlin.

Training 1975–78, in universal milling technology; 1981–84, Hochschule der Künste, Berlin.
Biography Stumpf was an exponent of 1980s German avant-garde design and a designer in the Berlin Design Workshop. His 1986 Kumpel I and Kumpel II (miner) tables were built from three pickaxes and plate glass. Other work has included a 1985 strainer and the 1984 Die Rache der Kellnerin hanging lighting.
Exhibitions Participated in 1984–85 *Kaufhaus des Ostens*, Berlin, Munich, and Hamburg; 1986 *Wohnen von Sinnen*, Kunstmuseum, Düsseldorf; 1986 *Erkundungen*, Stuttgart; 1988 *Berlin: les avant-gardes du mobilier*, Centre Georges Pompidou, Galerie VIA (French Furniture Association), and Galerie Néotù (all Paris).
Bibliography Christian Borngraeber, *Prototypen: Avantgarde Design uit/aus Berlin*, Rotterdam: 010, 1986. Cat., *Berlin: les avant-gardes du mobilier*, Berlin: Design Zentrum, 1988. Albrecht Bangert and Karl Michael Armer, *80s Style: Designs of the Decade*, New York: Abbeville, 1990.

Stumpf, William (1936–)

American industrial designer; active Minneapolis, Minn.

Training To 1968, bachelor's degree in industrial design, University of Illinois, Urbana-Champlain; master's degree in environmental design, University of Wisconsin.
Biography Stumpf designed and produced the first version (1966) of the Ergon chair. 1970–73, he was vice-president in charge of research, Herman Miller, Zeeland, Mich., and became best known for his office-systems furniture; 1973, established his own consultancy in Winona, Minn.; 1977 with Donald Chadwick, set up a design partnership. For Herman Miller, Stumpf designed chairs: 1975 Ergon, 1988 Ergon 2, 2000 Ergon 3,1979–84 Equa, and 1995 Equa 2 flexing plastic (with Chadwick), as well as 1984 Ethospace open-plan office system. Strumpf and Chadwick's best-known design is the popular 1992 Aeron chair, developed through extensive, extended research and made of advanced materials. His firm became William Stumpf + Associates, then Stumpf & Weber, Minneapolis. To espouse his theories, he wrote the book *The Ice Palace That Melted Away: Restoring Civility and Other Lost Virtues to Everyday Life* (New York: Pantheon, 1998).
Exhibitions/citations Work included in numerous exhibitions, including in New York in 1995 (catalog below). 1979, cited the Designer of the 1970s by *Industrial Design* magazine; 1976 award (for Ergon chair), American Society of Interior Designers (ASID); 1984 gold award (for Equa chair) and 1985 gold award, Institute of Business Designers (IBD); 1990 Best of the Decade (Equa chair), *Time* magazine.
Bibliography Ralph Caplan, *The Design of Herman Miller*, New York: Whitney, 1976. Cat., Paola Antonelli, *Mutant Materials in Contemporary Design*, New York: The Museum of Modern Art/Abrams, 1995. Mel Byars, *50 Chairs: Innovations in Design and Materials*, Hove: RotoVision, 1996. Paola Antonelli (ed.), *Objects of Design: The Museum of Modern Art*, New York: The Museum of Modern Art, 2003: 170.

Sturge Moore, Riette H. (1907–)

British textile designer; born London; daughter of poet/artist/designer Thomas Sturge Moore.

Training Under M. La Halle, interior decoration, London; and in Paris.
Biography Sturge Moore worked for interior designer E. Curtis Moffat, furniture designer Arundell Clarke, and the furnisher Heal's, all London. From mid-1930s, she printed textiles and designed others, including those by W. Foxton in London; designed sets/costumes of 1947 production of *Dr. Faustus* and 1959 production of *Coriolanus* at Shakespeare Memorial Theatre; 1947–64, taught stage design, Bath Academy of Art, Corsham.
Exhibitions Work subject of 1938 exhibition in Heal's store, London, and included in most of the important 1930s exhibitions in London and, much later, in 1979–80 *Thirties* (1935 Ribbons jacquard cotton fabric), Hayward Gallery, London (catalog below).
Bibliography Cat., *Thirties: British Art and Design Before the War*, London: Arts Council of Great Britain, Hayward Gallery, 1979.

Sture, Alf (1915–2000)

Norwegian furniture and interior designer.

Training Statens Håndverks -og Kunstindustriskole, Oslo; from 1940, apprenticeship in cabinetmaking at Hiorth & Èstlynsen in Oslo.
Biography To 1950, Sture was a designer at Hiorth & Èstlynsen; 1950, and while continuing to design for them, established his own design studio and designed furniture and interiors for over 60 years. He was a pioneer of the disciplines in the post-World War II period. His dramatic cabinetry, while modern, called on national Norwegian values. His 1941 1036 and 1947 Kongestolen armchairs by Tonning are still in production by Tonning as is his 1959 line of ceramics by Lannem Keramikk. Tonning also produces his 1995 Amtmann armchair.
Bibliography Cat., David Revere McFadden (ed.) *Scandinavian Modern Design 1880–1980*, New York: Abrams, 1982. Fredrik Wildhagen, *Norge i Form*, Oslo: Sternersen, 1988: 120.

Sturm, Alexander

Austrian silversmiths; located Vienna.

History 1882, the firm was founded; c. 1902, produced the silver designs of Josef Hoffmann and, when the silver workshop of the Wiener Werkstätte closed c. 1930, again produced Hoffmann's work. Other distinguished wares include the 1902 cigarette case by Antoinette Krasnik with a stylized *plique-à-jour* enamel dragonfly.
Exhibition Work included 1902–03 winter exhibition (Krasnik's cigarette case), Österreichisches Museum für Kunst und Industrie, Vienna.
Bibliography Waltrand Neuwirth, *Wiener Gold und Silberschmiede und ihre Punzen 1867–1922*, vol. 2, Vienna, 1977: 238–39. Annelies Krekel-Aalberse, *Art Nouveau and Art Déco Silver*, New York: Abrams, 1989.

Stuttgart Design Center

German organization for the promotion of design in industry.

History As an organ of Baden-Württemberg's Office for the Promotion of Trade and Industry, the Design Center Stuttgart is the oldest established institution of its kind and the only government-operated design center in Germany. The center originated with the collection of the Royal Center for Trade and Crafts, as the Office for the Promotion of Trade and Industry was known in the 19th century. 1850, Ferdinand von Steinbeis, the first president of the Royal Center, set up a collection, which eventually included textiles, clocks, jewelry, appliances, toys, and commercial graphic design, organized 'to provide craftsmen in the Kingdom of Württemberg with the opportunity to observe and copy exemplary pieces of work and, at the same time, to make trades both in the Kingdom of Baden-Württemberg and elsewhere aware of

the competent craft products in this land.' 1896, the collection was housed in the new Museum of Trade and Industry, known today as the Haus der Wirtschaft. Though the collection was undamaged during World War II, the museum never reopened. Postwar exhibitions on contemporary themes such as 1949 *Living* and 1953 *The Beauty of Technology* were organized, placing a greater emphasis on the subject of design. With the need for a new institution, the Landes Baden-Württemberg established the LGA-Zentrum Form in 1962, renamed the Design Center Stuttgart in 1969.
Bibliography Cat., *Design Selection 92*, Stuttgart: Design Center Stuttgart, 1992.

Stüttgen, Gerhard (1878–1952)
German metalworker; active Cologne.

Biography Stüttgen taught, Kunstgewerbeschule, Cologne, where he instructed his students in bending steel tubing; for a time, was involved in developing a steel-frame chair with no back legs (or cantilevered). His 1923 cantilever design was revealed at the 1938 hearings of the famous court case between Mauser and Mies van der Rohe because Stüttgen had sold the rights to the frame design to Mauser in 1937.
Exhibition With little significance at the time, his tube frame was shown at 1923–24 one-person exhibition Kunstgewerbeschule, Cologne.
Bibliography Otakar Máčel, 'Avant garde Design and the Law: Litigation over the Cantilever Chair,' *Journal of Design History*, vol. 3, nos. 2 and 3, 1990.

Subes, Raymond (1893–1970)
French metalsmith; born and active Paris.

Training École Boulle, and École Nationale Supérieure des Arts Décoratifs; both Paris; and under wrought-iron designer Émile Robert.
Biography From 1916, Stubes worked in a small workshop established by Émile Robert in Enghien-les-Bains; 1919, began working for Robert's metal contracting firm Borderel et Robert at 131, rue Damrémont, Paris, where he became chief of the design department and, subsequently, director of the wrought-iron workshop. Independently, Subes collaborated with a number of architects and quickly became a leading designer and maker of metalwork; 1920s, was prolific in wrought-iron production, including the pulpit of the cathedral in Rouen. Work in Paris: the grilles of the choir entry at the Église de Saint-Germain-des-Prés, the telescoping lighting fixtures on the pont du Carrousel, the monument to General Leclerc (with sculptor R. Martin) at porte d'Orléans, and the tomb of Marshal Lyautey (with architect Laprade) at the esplanade des Invalides. 1930s, he designed/made furniture for designer Alfred Porteneuve (Jacques-Émile Ruhlmann's nephew), using chromium-plated tubular metal. He also created a large amount of ironwork for oceanliners: 1926 *Île-de-France*, 1931 *L'Atlantique*, 1935 *Normandie*, and 1939 *Pasteur.* Also in Paris: a 1931 grille for the Musée des Colonies; ironwork for the Banque de France and the National City Bank, both on the avenue des Champs-Élysées; Institut Pasteur; Caisse des Dépôts et Consignations; Musée de la France d'Outre-Mer; and Église du Saint-Esprit (doors). While his product was mainly in wrought iron (patinated, chromed, or gilded), he also worked in polished steel, bronze, and *repoussé* copper. In his lighting, he incorporated alabaster, levantine marble, frosted glass, and embroidered silk shades (produced for him by Mme. Luhuché-Méry in early 1920s). After World War II, Subes was director of the Borderel et Robert smithy and concurrently active as an independent metalworker. He died in Paris.
Exhibitions/citations First showed his work in 1919. Designed and produced a lacquered metal bookcase and console with Ruhlmann for the Hôtel du Collectionneur at 1925 *Exposition Internationale des Arts Décoratifs et Industriels Modernes*, Paris. At 1937 *Exposition Internationale des Arts et Techniques dans la Vie Moderne*, Paris, he produced the fountains for the radio pavilion and a madonna/child for the papal pavilion, and numerous screens, consoles, and grilles for other sections. 1958, was elected to Académie des Beaux-Arts.
Bibliography Henri Clouzot (intro.), *Raymond Subes, maître ferronnier: dernières œuvres*, Paris: Massin, 1931. Maximilien Gauthier, *Raymond Subes*, Paris: Gémeaux, 1949. Alastair Duncan, *Art Nouveau and Art Déco Lighting*, New York: Simon & Schuster, 1978: 187–88. Victor Arwas, *Art Déco*, New York: Abrams, 1980. Pierre Cabanne, *Encyclopédie art déco*, Paris: Somogy, 1986: 235. Pierre Kjellberg, *Art déco: les maîtres du mobilier, le décor des paquebots*, Paris: Amateur, 1986/1990.

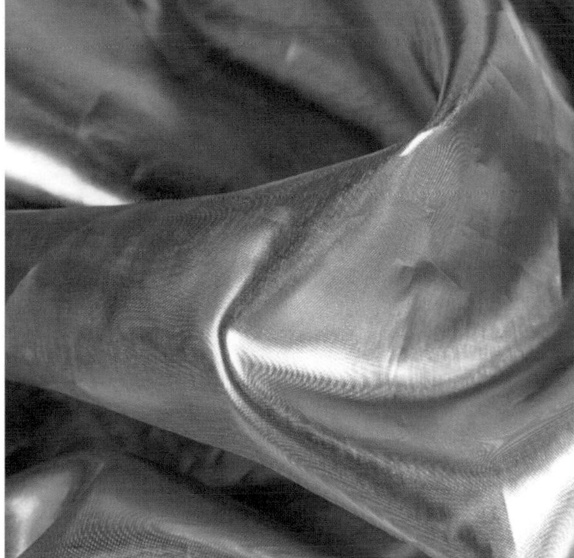

Reiko Sudo. Fabric (no. 9–134). 1990. Polyester with stainless steel finish. 245 x 44 1/4" (622.3 x 112.4 cm). Mfr.: Nuno Corporation, Japan. Gift of the manufacturer. MoMA.

Suchodolski, Sophie (1961–)
French designer.

Training To 1985, École Camondo, Paris.
Biography 1985–87, Suchodolski began her career working in commercial films and videos; from 1989, began designing objects and working with Alessi. First professional work a 1989 salt-and-pepper shaker and a bowl by Techniland. Recent work: 1996 Metropolis table lamp (one of two lighting ranges) by Habitat; 1998 Twin fruit plate, 1999 CD Building (CD rack), and 1999 Galactic hanging lamp by Cinna; 1999 Pil ashtray/rack and 1999 Iris vase by Ligne Roset. She may be best known for her 1999 Five and Lys ceramic vases by Cinna.

Sudeikin, Sergei (1882–1946)
Russian painter and theatre artist; born Smolensk.

Training Sporadically, 1897–1909 under Konstantin Korovin, Moscow College; 1909–10, St. Petersburg Academy of Fine Art.
Biography Sudeikin worked for theaters in Moscow and St. Petersburg and for Diaghilev's Les Ballets Russes; executed the designs of Bakst, Roerich, and his own; later worked for theaters in Paris, where he lived 1920–22, and New York, where he settled in 1923. He combined the refined aspects of 18th-century painting with unrefined folk primitivism, which married irony to sentimentality; died in Nyack, N.Y.
Exhibitions Work included in 1904 Crimson Rose exhibition, 1907 Blue Rose exhibition, 1908–09 Salons of the Golden Fleece; with Union of Russian Artists from 1911 and V Mir Iskusstva (the world of art) group; Diaghilev's Russian installment at 1906 Salon d'Automne, Paris.

Sudo, Reiko (1953–)
Japanese textile designer; born Ibaraki Prefecture.

Training In Japanese painting, kimono design, and traditional tapestry weaving; and textile design and art, Musashino Art University, Tokyo.
Biography 1978, Sudo established a textile design workshop; 1984, cofounded the Nuno Corporation, Tokyo, a producer of innovative fabrics, and, 1991, became its design director and has produced over 1,400 original textiles, 35 of which have been purchased for the permanent collections of 12 museums in America and other countries. Sudo is assisted by Keiji Otani. She teaches, Musashino Art University.
Exhibitions/citations Work included in venues worldwide and 1999 exhibition, New York and St. Louis (catalog below), also *Plastic Times—Plastic + Design*, Tel Aviv Museum. Two-time recipient of Roscoe Award, Cooper-Hewitt Natonal Design Museum, New York.
Bibliography Albrecht Bangert and Karl Michael Armer, *80s Style: Designs of the Decade*, New York: Abbeville, 1990. Cat., Cara McCarty and Matilda McQuaid, *Structure and Surface: Contemporary Japanese Textiles*, New York: Abrams/The Museum of Modern Art, 1999.

Süe, Louis (1875–1968)

French architect, painter, and decorator; born Bordeaux; active Paris.

Training Painting, École Nationale Supérieure des Beaux-Arts, Paris.
Biography 1895, Süe settled in Paris, where he became an architect but continued to paint, showing his canvases at the Salon des Indépendants and Salon d'Automne. 1905–07 collaborating with Paul Huillard, he designed his first houses on the rue Cassini, near the observatory in Paris. He designed furniture at this time that was marked by a German influence; became a friend of Pierre Louÿs, André Gide, and Claude Debussy. 1910 with painter André Mare, he began designing furniture in a workshop called Atelier Français on the rue de Courcelles, Paris. 1919, Süe and Mare set themselves up as interior designers in the firm Compagnie des Arts Français at 116, rue du Faubourg Saint-Honoré, Paris. Collaborators there included Marie Laurencin, André Derain, Maurice Marinot, Aristide Maillol, Charles-Georges Dufresne, Gustave-Louis Jaulmes, Paul Vera, Richard Desvallières, and Raoul Dufy. Süe and Mare's approach was inspired by the style of the Louis Philippe period and incorporated massive, theatrical forms and much gilding. They also designed mirrors, lighting, and *objets d'art*. A portfolio of their work and projects, with text by Paul Valéry, was published under the title *Architecture* (1921). With Léandre Vaillat, Süe wrote *Rythme de l'Architecture* (1923), and Jean Badovici issued *Intérieurs de Süe et Mare* (1924). Süe designed silver by Orfèvrerie Christofle, and his group designed interiors of several oceanliners, including the lounge of 1926 oceanliner *Île-de-France*, and 1925 d'Orsay perfume shop, Paris, and its flacon. 1927–28, they constructed and furnished the Art Déco villa of actress Jane Renouard in Saint-Cloud and designed couturier Jean Patou's apartment on the rue de la Faisanderie, Paris, and his country house in Ustaritz. 1928, Jacques Adnet took over as the director of design at Compagnie des Arts Français, and Süe returned to architecture, though continuing to decorate, including the c. 1929 town house of Bernard Bouvet de Monvel on the passage de la Visitation and 1938 apartment of Helena Rubinstein, both Paris. And Mare returned to painting. 1939, Süe moved to Istanbul, where he taught from 1944 at Valtion Kuvataideakatemia (state academy of fine art). 1950, collector Georges Grammont commissioned Süe to transform the Chapelle de Notre-Dame de l'Annon-ciade in Saint-Tropez.
Exhibitions Süe first exhibited (a massive desk-bookcase with Huillard) at 1911 Salon d'Automne and, at a subsequent edition, chairs with Jacques Palyart. With Mare, designed the pavilions of Compagnie des Arts Français (CAF) and Musée des Arts Contemporains at 1925 *Exposition Internationale des Arts Décoratifs et Industriels Modernes*, Paris. Showed without Mare at 1937 *Exposition Internationale des Arts et Techniques dans la Vie Moderne*, Paris. Their work subject of 1971 *André Mare et la Compagnie des Arts Français (Süe et Mare)*, Ancienne Douane, Strasbourg; 1986 Institut Français d'Architecture, Paris.
Bibliography Raymond Foulk, *The Extraordinary Work of Süe and Mare*, London: The Foulk Lewis Collection, 1979. Victor Arwas, *Art Déco*, New York: Abrams, 1980. Pierre Cabanne, *Encyclopédie art déco*, Paris: Somogy, 1986: 235–39. Susan Day, *Louis Süe, architectures*, Liège: Mardaga, 1986. Cat, Susan Day, *Louis Süe, 1875–1968: Architecte des années folles, associé d'André Mare*, Liège: P. Mardaga, 1986. Florence Camard, *Süe et Mare et La Compagnie des Arts Français*, Paris: Les Éditions de l'Amateur, 1993.

Louis Süe. Pitcher. 1931. Silverplate, h. 7 1/16" (18 cm). Mfr.: Orfèvrerie Christofle, France. Courtesy Quittenbaum Kunstauktionen, Munich.

Nikolai Suetin. Teacup and saucer. 1923. Porcelain with overglaze painted decoration, teacup h. 2 1/8" x dia. 3 5/8" (5.4 x 9.2 cm), saucer h. 1" x dia. 5 3/8" (2.5 x 13.6 cm). Mfr.: State Porcelain Factory, USSR (now Russia). Gift of Andrew Raeburn. MoMA.

Suetin, Nikolai Mikhailovich (1897–1954)

Russian artist, ceramicist, and designer; born Metlevsk Station, Kaluga; husband of Anna Leporskaia.

Training 1918–22, Vitebsk Art School.
Biography 1919. Suetin became a member of Kazimir Malevich's POSNOVIS/UNOVIS (Followers of the New Art/Affirmers of the New Art), and, along with Il'ia Chashnik, was one of Malevich's closest collaborators. 1922, Suetin, Malevich, Chashnik, Vera Ermolaeva, Lev Yudin, and others settled in Petrograd and collaborated with Malevich on Suprematist architectural constructions known as *arkhitektony* and *planity* and became affiliated with the INKhUK (Institute of Artistic Culture) there. From 1923, Suetin worked at the Lomonosov State Porcelain Factory in Petrograd, where he decorated an appreciable amount of porcelain, including tea sets, with painted Suprematist motifs; 1932–54, was head of the artistic section, where Eva Zeisel was one of his student workers. By 1930, his approach was a sort of stylized folk realism.
Exhibitions He designed the interior (with Anna Leporskaia) of 1928 *The Construction of the NKVD House*, Leningrad. Work included in 1930 *First All-City Exhibition of Visual Arts*, Academy of Arts, Leningrad; 1932 jubilee *Artists of the RSFSR During the Last 15 Years*, Academy of Arts, Leningrad; several 1930s exhibitions abroad, including 1937 *Exposition Internationale des Arts et Techniques dans la Vie Moderne*, Paris, where he assisted in the design of the Soviet pavilion. Suetin's and Malevich's work subject of 1980 exhibition, Centre Georges Pompidou, Paris. 1992 exhibition (with Malevich and Chashnik), Galerie Gmurzynska, Cologne (catalog below); also with Malerich, 1980 *Œuvres de Casimir Severinovitch Malévitch (1878–1935): avec en Appendice les Œuvres de Nicolaï Mikhaïlovitch Souiétine (1897–1954)*, Centre Georges Pompidou, Musée National d'Art Moderne, Paris; 2000, Palazzo Forti, Verona.
Bibliography L. Zhadova, 'O farfore N.M. Suetina,' in K. Rozhdestvenskii (ed.), *Sovetskow dekorativnoe iskusstvo 73/74*, Moscow, 1975: 211. L. Zhadova, 'Blokadnaia grafika N.M. Suetina,' in M. Nemirovskais (ed.), *Sovetskaia grafika 74*: Moscow, 1976: 185–90. Cat., Jean-Hubert Martin, *Malévitch: œuvres de Casimir Severinovitch Malévitch (1878–1935) avec en appendice les œuvres de Nicolaï Mikhaïlovitch Souiétine (1897–1954)*, Paris: Centre Georges Pompidou/Musée National d'Art Moderne, 1980. Cat., *The Great Utopia: The Russian and Soviet Avant-Garde, 1915–1932*, New York: Guggenheim Museum, 1992. Cat., Krystyna Gmurzynska-Bscher et al. (eds.), *Malewitsch, Suetin, Tschaschnik*, Cologne: Galerie Gmurzynska, 1992. Cat., Vasilii Rakitin, *Nikolai Mikhailovich Suetin*, Moscow: RA, 1998.

Minoru Sugahara. Tumbler. 1984. Glass, h. 5" x dia. 2 5/8" (12.7 x 6.7 cm). Mfr.: Sugahara Glass Corporation, Japan. Friends of the Department Fund. MoMA.

Sugahara, Minoru (1940–)

Japanese glassware designer; born Tokyo.

Training Wasada University, Tokyo.
Biography 1963, Sugahara joined the design staff of his family's firm, Sugahara Glass, and, 1973, became head of the design team there. Design work has included 1988 Indigo and Clear Frost square-format glass dinnerware.
Citation 1989 Japanese design award (BK & WH glassware designs).
Bibliography Albrecht Bangert and Karl Michael Armer, *80s Style: Designs of the Decade*, New York: Abbeville, 1990.

Sugasawa, Toshio (1940–)

Japanese glass designer.

Training To 1965, crafts, Tokyo National University of Fine Arts and Music.
Biography 1965, Sugasawa began working for Hoya Crystal in Tokyo, subsequently becoming chief of planning and design in the department of crystal glass there.
Exhibitions/citations Solo exhibition at 1979 *Another World*, Matsuya Gallery, Ginza, Tokyo. Work included in a large number of exhibitions, from the 1983 *Modern Japan Craft*, Fukui Prefectural Museum, Japan. Received Asahi Shimbun Prize at *World Glass Now '82*, Hokkaido Museum of Art, Sapporo.
Bibliography Cat., *Glass Japan*, New York: Heller Gallery and Japan Glass Art Crafts Association, 1991: no. 35.

Sugawara, Seizo

Japanese artisan in lacquer; active Paris.

Biography 1900, Sugawara arrived in Paris with the Japanese delegation to the *Exposition Universelle* and decided to stay there. In his own studio, he produced lacquer works that showed a synthesis of traditional Japanese techniques and geometric motifs, while experimenting with unprecedentedly opulent materials. He imported his raw materials from Japan. 1907, his work attracted the attention of Eileen Gray, who had previously worked in lacquer in Britain. She showed his wooden sculptures in her shop Jean Désert in Paris: he produced some of her lacquered works in his workshop on the rue Guénégaud. 1912, he also taught Jean Dunand the ancient and traditional procedures, advising him to replace Chinese urushi which Dunand has been using with fine Japanese urushi (sap from the tree called *Urushi-no-ki* in Japanese, or *Rhus vernicifera* or *Rhus verniciflua*, a deciduous tree of the sumac family). In turn, Dunand showed Sugawara various metalwork techniques. Late 1920s, Sugawara assisted Evelyn Wyld and Eyre de Lanux (both associates of Gray) on lacquered furniture.
Bibliography Peter Adam, *Eileen Gray, Architect/Designer*, New York: Abrams, 1987: 157, 182. Félix Marcilhac, *Jean Dunand: His Life and Work*, New York: Abrams, 1991: 28ff, 170.

Sullivan, Louis Henri (1856–1924)

American architect; born Boston; active Philadelphia and Chicago.

Training 1872–73 under William Robert Ware, architecture, Massachusetts Institute of Technology (MIT), Cambridge, Mass.; 1874–75 under Auguste-Émile Vaudremer, École des Beaux-Arts, Paris.
Biography 1873, Sullivan moved to Philadelphia, where he worked briefly in the office of Frank Furness and George W. Hewitt. The stock market crash of 1873 sent Sullivan to Chicago, where he worked for skyscraper pioneer William Le Baron Jenney. 1875 returning from his Paris studies to the US, he held a number of jobs. From 1879, he was the chief draftsperson in the Chicago office of Dankmar Adler and, 1883, became a full partner in the firm, where he was a mentor to the three eventually-to-be Prairie School architects in the office: Frank Lloyd Wright, George Grant Elmslie, and George Washington Mahler. Undistinguished at first, Adler and Sullivan's work was influenced by Richard Morris Hunt of New York, Furness of Philadelphia, the English High Victorian Gothic style, and popular French neoclassicism. Their first major commission was 1887–89 Auditorium building in Chicago. Sullivan's 1890s interiors illustrate the sureness of his mature ornamental style, and the Auditorium, restored in 1960s, is dramatic in its application of an ornamentation that envelops every surface. The 1890 Getty Tomb in Chicago was the first essay in Sullivan's monumental geometric exterior forms and ornamentation, and 1890 Wainwright Building in St. Louis, Mo., illustrates a full blossoming of the expression. His last major building was 1898–1902 Schlesinger and Mayer building (now Carson, Pirie and Scott department store), Chicago. 1895, the Adler partnership was discontinued. Sullivan became the pioneer of the modern office block and father of Prairie School architecture. He wrote seminal essays (c. 1918), serialized in *Interstate Architect*, nos. 51, 52–3, 16 Feb. 1901; 8 Feb. 1902 (first published in book form as *Kindergarten Chats on Architecture, Education and Democracy*, Lawrence, Kan. (attrib.): Scarab Fraternity Press, 1934). A *Kindergarten* essay included his famous dictum ('Form ever follows function. This is the law,' and *Autobiography of an Idea*

Louis Henri Sullivan. Door hardware. 1895. Cast bronze. door plate h. 14 x w. 4 1/4" (35.5 x 10.8 cm), knob l. 8" x dia. 2 1/2" (20.3 x 6.3 cm), key l. 2 1/4 x w. 1 1/2" (l5.7 x 3.8 cm). Mfr.: The Yale & Towne Mfg. Co., US. Gift of John Bedenkapp. MoMA.

(New York: Press of AIA, 1924) further extended his philosophy and ideas. Though Sullivan did not design moveable furniture, he had considerable influence on the decorative arts in the US through his writings, and in the development of an individual style of ornament that used finely drawn plant forms and ideas from 19th-century sources anticipating Art Nouveau; and through his influence on his assistants Wright and Elmslie. Though uniquely his own, his ornamentation was akin to that of Christopher Dresser, A.W.N. Pugin, and James Kellaway Colling. He was not commercially successful in his later years, although he built a group of small distinguished banks in the Midwest, which were some his best architectural works. The 1913 Land and Loan Office (later the Adams building), 1914 Merchant's National Bank in Grinnel, Iowa, and 1917 – 18 People's Savings and Loan Association Bank in Sidney, Ohio, are outstanding among the six banks designed 1913–19. The Adams building has leaded-glass windows in ochre and cream with counterpoints of turquoise, azure, burgundy, green, and yellow against an opalescent sky-blue ground, with upper and lower horizontal geometric borders of blue-green banded by rectangles of green and ochre centering rectangles of randomly placed bright colors. The building's large urns were made of glazed terracotta, a material used throughout the building. For the elaborate organic ornamentation on the urns, Sullivan called on some of his motifs from earlier commissions. Other work: 1885–87 Marshall Field Wholesale Store, Chicago; 1887 Selz, Schwab factory, Chicago; 1889 Walker Warehouse, Chicago; 1892 Schiller building, Chicago; 1894 Stock Exchange, Chicago; 1895 Guaranty building, Buffalo, N.Y.; 1898 Bayer building, New York; 1898–99 Gage building, Chicago; 1907–08 National Farmers' Bank, Owatonna, Minn. Sullivan was destitute at the end of his life, helped finaicially to some extent by Wright, and died in Chicago.
Exhibitions Work subject of 1986 *Louis Sullivan: The Function of Ornament*, Chicago Historical Society and St. Louis Art Museum.
Bibliography Louis H. Sullivan, *Kindergarten Chats and Other Writings*, New York: Wittenborn, Schultz, 1947. Hugh Morrison, *Louis Sullivan, Prophet of Modern Architecture*, New York: The Museum of Modern Art, 1935. George G. Elmslie, 'Sullivan Ornamentation,' *Monthly Bulletin, Illinois Society of Architects*, June–July 1935; reprinted in *Journal of the American Institute of Architects*, vol. 6, Oct. 1946: 155–58. Edgar Kaufmann Jr. (ed.), *Louis Sullivan and the Architecture of Free Enterprise*, Chicago: Art Institute of Chicago, 1956. Narcisco G. Menocal, *Architecture as Nature: The Transcendentalist Idea of Louis* Sullivan, Madison, Wis., 1981. Robert Twombly, *Louis Sullivan: His Life and Work*, New York: Viking, 1986. David Van Zanten, *Louis Sullivan: The Function of Ornament*, New York: Norton, 1986. Sarah C. Mollman (ed.), *Louis Sullivan in the Art Institute of Chicago: The Ilustrated Catalogue of Collections*, New York: Garland, 1989. Robert Twombly and Narciso G. Menocal, *Louis Sullivan: The Poetry of Architecture*, New York: Norton, 2000.

Summers, Gerald (1899–1967)

British furniture designer; born Alexandria, Egypt.

Biography 1930s, Summers (not the painter Gerald Summers 1886–1969) was the only Briton whose furniture designs rivaled those of the Continent as a contribution to the development of modern design. Comparable to Marcel Breuer and Alvar Aalto, Summers's chair designs in bent plywood represent milestones in the evolution of the modern aesthetics/production of seating, although little of his furniture was made. 1929, he founded Makers of Simple Furniture Ltd., London. The first phase of his designs from 1933 had few parallels with other British designers. With a distaste for self-promotion, he was thus overshadowed by Gordon Russell and Ambrose Heal, whose larger, well-established firms ensured their recognition. Summer was also devoid of a knowledge of, or was disinterested in, pursuing sophisticated marketing. Only a handful of his designs had been published widely by early 1990s, except in auction catalogs. The austere forms of his early painted-plywood furniture rejected his industrial apprenticeship. His furniture was characterized by an emphasis on function and absence of ornament and explored new, efficient materials and construction techniques. He showed a preference for plain, flat, and curved forms in plywood. Summers was one of the first modernists to adopt Alvar Aalto's bent plywood and organic forms for seating design. Reaching his stride by mid-1930s, Summers produced two of his best-known designs: the 1934 one-piece plywood lounge chair and the curved 1934 high-back chair. The former is a formal, technical advance over Alvar Aalto's less integrated chair designs. 1935–37, Summers's Functionalist aesthetic was applied to a wide range of pieces, including tables, beds, desks, chairs, trolleys, case goods, vases, coal bins, a gramophone casing, and children's furniture. 1938–40, Summers designed/made purpose-shaped pieces; could not compete with less expensive, imported Aalto furniture sold through British retailers such as Bowman Brothers and Aalto's Finmar. 1939, he closed the firm due to the outbreak of World War II and thus British-governmental restrictions

Gerald Summers. Lounge chair. 1934. Steam-bent birch plywood with pigmented lacquer., 29 5/8 x 23 1/2 x 35" (75.2 x 59.7 x 88.9 cm). Mfr.: Makers of Simple Furniture, UK. Barbara Jakobson Purchase Fund and Peter Norton Purchase Fund and Gift of Robert and Joyce Menschel. MoMA.

on plywood production; subsequently, opened a factory for making ball bearings.
Bibliography Martha Hart Deese, 'Gerald Summers and Makers of Simple Furniture,' master's degree thesis, New York: Cooper-Hewitt/ Parsons School of Design, c. 1990. Martha Hart Deese, 'Gerald Summers and Makers of Simple Furniture,' *Journal of Design History*, vol. 5, no. 3, 1992: 183-205.

Sunbeam
American manufacturer

History 1893, Chicago Flexible Shaft Co. was founded by John K. Stewart and Thomas J. Clark; 1895, moved from Chicago to Dundee, Ill., and made hand-crankable shaft-driven animal-fur clippers; 1900 in Chicago, opened a factory for heat-treating clipper blades; established Stewart Industrial Division to make other metal products. Another offshoot of the Chicago Flexible Shaft Co. was the 1904 production of carriage heaters. Motorized vehicles were becoming popular, but this product did not last long. Due to the seasonal nature of the animal-clipping business, Chicago Flexible continued to diversify, next by introducing an electric clothes iron in 1910. More electrical appliances followed, and, 1921, the brand name Sunbeam was used in national advertising to emphasize the reliability of these electrically powered products. 1917, a main factory was built at 5600 Roosevelt Road, Chicago. 1936, Sunbeam introduced its Shavemaster electric shaver. 1946, the name of the company was changed to Sunbeam. 1960, the controlling interest in the firm was acquired by the John Oster firm. Even though the Roosevelt Road plant has been closed for several years, the Sunbeam brand name is still being used by subsidiary plants worldwide but not on new electric shavers. Late 1970s, Sunbeam-Oster stopped making electric shavers.

Superstudio
Italian architecture and design cooperative.

History 1966, Superstudio was established in Florence by Adolfo Natalini, Christiano Toraldo di Francia, Robert Magris, Gian Piero Frassinelli, Alessandro Magris and, 1970–1972, Alessandro Poli. The group rebelled against the post-World War II orthodoxies of architecture and design, as did its sister Italian group, Archizoom, formed the same year. Aligned with student unrest and expressing metaphors with a Marxist flavor, Superstudio and Archizoom were part of the Anti-Design (or Counter-Design or Radical Design) movement of late 1960s and early 1970s. Superstudio took a conceptual approach to Anti-Design and became prominent through its late-1960s projects that straddled architecture and fine art, in a manner similar to the work of Hans Hollein in Germany. Superstudio wanted to replace product design with 'evasion design.' A manifestation of Superstudio's production was its grid-design 1971 Quaderna laminate table range by Zanotta (currently in production). The group's 1969 Il Monumento Continuo project proposed an endless framework to cover the entire surface of the earth, a mocking critique of contemporary planning. 1971–73, the group produced a series of films on the philosophical and anthropological aspects of rebuilding. Its 1972 proposal to submerge the city of Florence, with only the dome of the cathedral exposed as a tourist attraction, was a subversive contribution to the 'Save the Historic Centers' campaign of the time. Superstudio's 1973 *Fragments from a Personal Museum* exhibition proposed a Radical architecture through the use of Surrealist graphics. 1973–75, the group joined Global Tools and, from 1973, was active in research and teaching at Università degli Studi, Florence, and other institutions. 1978, its critique of architecture in a capitalist society was abandoned. Reverberations of the group's work appeared later in the projects of member Adolfo Natalini, including his 1979 unrealized project for the design of a building on the Römerberg in Frankfurt. 1982, Superstudio ended; 2001, was re-formed as Archivio Superstudio, to organize exhibitions.

Ilkka Suppanen. Hiware (or Roll Light) hanging lamp. c. 1998. Aluminum, Mylar film and carbon fiber. h. 31 1/2 x w. 55 1/8" (80 x 140 cm) x l. variable. Prototype.

Superstudio. Gherpe lamp. 1967. Plastic and metal, 13 3/4 x 20 x 7 1/2" (35 x 50.8 x 19.1 cm). Mfr.: Poltronova, Italy. Gift of Rob Beyer. MoMA.

Exhibitions Work included in 1972 *Italy: The New Domestic Landscape*, The Museum of Modern Art, New York; 1973 (15th) and 1979 (16th) editions of Triennale di Milano; 1978 and 1980 editions of Biennale di Venezia; other consequential exhibitions from 1968, including *Radicals. Architettura e Design 1960–75*, 1996 (6th) Mostra Internazionale di Archittettura, Venice. Work subject of 1973–74 *Superstudio: Fragmente aus einem persönlichen Museum*, touring Europe (catalog below); 1973–75 *Sottsass and Superstudio: Mindscapes*, touring the US; 1982 *Superstudio 1966–1982: Storia, figure, architettura*, Milan (catalog below); 2003 *Superstudio*, Design Museum, London.
Bibliography Cat., Emilio Ambasz (ed.), *Italy: The New Domestic Landscape, Achievements and Problems of Italian Design*, New York: The Museum of Modern Art, 1972. Cat., *Superstudio: Fragmente aus einem Personlichen Museum = Fragments from a Personal Museum*, Gratz: Neue Galerie aus Landesmuseum, 1973. Mildred S. Friedman, 'Sottsass and Superstudio: Minscapes' in *Design Quarterly*, no. 89 (special issue), Minneapolis: Walker Art Center, 1973. Cat., *Superstudio*, Florence: Centro Di, 1978. Cat., Izzica Gaon (ed.), *Metaphors and Allegories—Superstudio*, Jerusalem: Israel Museum, 1982. Cat., G. Pettene (ed.), *Superstudio 1966–1982: Storia, figure, architettura*, Florence: Electa, 1982. Superstudio and Moriyama Editors Studio (eds), *Superstudio and Radicals*, Tokyo: Japan Interior Design, 1982. Heinrich Klotz, 'Adolfo Natalini und Superstudio,' in *Revision der Moderne: Postmoderne Architektur 1960–1986*, Tokyo: National Museum of Modern Art, 1986. Cat., Peter Lang and William Menking (eds.), *Superstudio: Life Without Objects*, Milan: Skira, 2003.

Suppanen, Ilkka (1968–)
Finnish designer.

Training Tecknillinen korkeakoulu and Taideteollinen korkeakoulu, both Helsinki; Gerrit Rietvelt Academie, Amsterdam.
Biography For short periods, Suppanen lived in Massachusetts, US, and Amsterdam, the Netherlands; 1995, established his own studio in Helsinki, serving clients such as Artek, Cappelini, Ferrero, Castelli, Kinnasand, Proventus, and Saab, and concepts for Nokia and Haworth; 1995–2001, taught, Taideteollinen korkeakoulu; 1996, became a co-founder of Snowcrash cooperative/brand and under Snowcrash designed 1997 Airbag inflatable frameless floor-seat (with Pasi Kolhonen) and 2001 Loco-bag portable work pad for a portable computer. Working on his own, his best-known design may be 1998 Flying Carpet felt sofa by Cappellini. Suppanen's architecture has included Armi exhibition center (competition entry), Helsinki; Villa Ilo and Villa Ilo 2 built for a client on the archipelago of Finland.
Exhibitions/citations Work included in *Generation X: Young Nordic*

Design traveling the world from 2000; *Design World 2000*, Konstindustrimuseet, Helsinki (catalog below). Received 2000 Young Designer of the Year award, Finland; 1998 Dedalus prize (one of four European designers under 40), selected by Ettore Sottsass.
Bibliography *Modern Finnish Design*, New Haven: Yale University, 1998. *The International Design Yearbook*, London: Laurence King, 1998 and 1999. Yvonne G.J.M Joris, *Sense of Wonder, Chi Ha Paura...?*, Museum Het Kruithuis, 2002.*Design World 2000*, Helsinki: Konstindustrimuseet, 2000. Charlotte and Peter Fiell, *Designing for the 21th Century*, Cologne: Taschen, 2001. *Spoon 100*, London: Phaidon, 2002.
> See Snowcrash.

Suprematism
Russian abstract art style.

History Suprematism was the term coined by Russian artist Kazimir Malevich for a purely abstract art image and meant, according to him, 'the supremacy of pure sensation in the fine arts.' He first used it in reference to his paintings *Black Square on White* (1913) and *White on White* (1918); with Nikolai Suetin and a number of other followers, furthered the concept in architecture-related compositions and, in the forms of and decorations by himself and others on, ceramics at Lomonosov Porcelain Factory, St. Petersburg. There are parallels with the work and ideas of the contemporary De Stijl group in the Netherlands. 1916, Malevich founded and led the artists' group Supremus, which planned a journal of the same name, and likewise he name numerous art works *Supremus*. His theories were published as *Die Gegenstandslose Welt* (the groundless world) Munich: Albert Langen, 1927 (later published in English as *The Non-Objective World*).
Bibliography Cat., *Kunst und Revolution: Russische und Sowjetische Kunst 1910–1932*, Vienna: Österreichisches Museum für angewandte Kunst, 1988. Jaroslav Andel et al., *Art into Life: Russian Constructivism 1914–1932*, New York: Rizzoli, 1990. Cat., *The Great Utopia: The Russian and Soviet Avant-Garde, 1915–1932*, New York: Guggenheim Museum, 1992.
> See Malevich, Kazimir.

Susani, Marco (1956–)
Italian designer and architect; born and active Milan.

Training 1982, diploma in architecture, Politecnico, Milan; 1983, master's degree in industrial design, Domus Academy.
Biography In Milan: 1979–81, Susani was a graphic designer, GBA advertising agency; 1981–83, an architect, Ing. Franco Sironi architecture and engineering firm; 1984–89, a senior designer, Olivetti Design Studio (under manager Ettore Sottsass); 1986–92, the coordinator and creative director of product-design department, Sottsass Associati architecture/design studio, where he was an associate partner 1990–93; 1993–2000, the director, Domus Academy Research Center, and the director, Interaction Design Course, Domus Academy; from 2000, the director, Advanced Concepts Group, and the director, Global Design Planning, both Motorola Consumer Experience Design. Product designs have ranged from 1995 MouseMan cordless mouse by Logitech and 1992 wristwatch by Seiko to 1996–2000 vases by Egizia and 1999 decorative objects for the home by Metallia. Other clients: Bticino, JC Decaux, Logitech, Mediaset, Mitsubishi Motors, Nissan, NTT, Philips, Pirelli, Seimens/Rolm, Seiko, Telecom Italia, 3M, Veridata/CTX. Susani has organized conferences and seminars at ENSCI (Les Ateliers), Paris; Politecnico, Milan; Royal Melbourne Institute of Technology (RMIT), Melbourne; Hochschule der Kunst, Berlin; Domus Academy, Milan.
Exhibitions/citations Work shown at editions of the Triennale di Milano, 1985–92; Centre Georges Pompidou, Paris, 1986-91; Axis Gallery, Tokyo, 1993; Grand Palais, Paris, 1993. Received 1997 Top Award for Interface Design, iF (Industrie Form Design), Hanover; 1997 nomination, Moebius European Prize; 1998 grand prize, Mitsubishi International Design; 1998 nomination, Europrix; 1999 award, Pirelli Tire Design; 2001 Best of Category, Annual Design Review, *I.D.* magazine.
Bibliography Marco Susani et al., *Seamless Media*, Tokyo: NTT, 1990. Marco Susani et al., *Interface Design*, Milan: Domus Academy, 1993. Mel Byars, *50 Products...*, Hove: RotoVision, 1998.

Marco Susani and Mario Trimarchi. Flat travel trays. 1996. Polypropylene, h. 3 1/8 x w. 9 7/8 x l. 13" (8 x 25 x 33 cm). Mfr.: Serafino Zani, Italy.

Süßmuth, Richard (1900–1974)
German glassware designer; born Ruhland.

Training 1922–24, Akademie für Kunsthandwerk, Dresden.
Biography 1924, Süßmuth founded the Süßmuth Glas- und Kunstwerkstätten factory in Penzig and, after World War II, re-established it in Immenhausen, where he designed/made art glass, stained glass, and glass tableware, bridging art and utility and craft and industrial methods of production. Eventually, the firm became known as Süßmuth Glashütte and continues today. 1987, the Glasmuseum Immenhausen was established in the former Süßmuth generator plant by the Gesellschaft der Freunde der Glaskunst Richard Süßmuth (association of the friends of Richard Süßmuth Art Glass).
Exhibitions Work shown at 1950s *Good Design* exhibitions/awards, The Museum of Modern Art, New York, and Chicago Merchandise Mart; 1959 and 1983–84 exhibitions, Corning, N.Y., and Philadelphia (catalogs below).
Bibliography Cat., *Glass 1959*, Corning, N.Y.: The Corning Museum of Glass, 1959: no. 147. Cat., Kathryn B. Hiesinger and George H. Marcus III (eds.), *Design Since 1945*, Philadelphia: Philadelphia Museum of Art, 1983. Walter Scheiffele, *Wilhelm Wagenfeld und die Moderne Glasindustrie: Eine geschichte der deutschen glasgestaltung von Bruno Mauder, Richard Süssmuth, Heinrich Fuchs und Wilhelm Wagenfeld bis Heinrich Loeffelhardt*, Stuttgart: G. Hatje, 1994

Sutherland, Graham Vivian (1903–1980)
British artist, graphic artist, and designer; born London.

Training 1921–26, engraving and etching, Goldsmiths' College School of Art, London.
Biography To 1930, Sutherland worked as an artist, producing etchings in a Romantic style reminiscent of Samuel Palmer; 1926–35, taught engraving, Chelsea College of Art; 1933–34, designed decorations for ceramic tableware by E. Brain, under artistic director T.A. Fennemore, and by Arthur J. Wilkinson, under artistic director Clarice Cliff, and glassware designs by Stuart & Sons. Early 1930s, he experimented with oils and, 1934–35, returned to painting; 1941–44, was an official war artist, achieving maturity in his work; 1940s, designed fabrics by Helios; 1950s, textiles by Cresta Silks, wallpaper by Cole, crystal by Steuben, glassware by Stuart, stage costumes, and interiors. After World War II, became known for his paintings of landscapes, religious subjects, and portraiture, including *The Crucifixion* (1946) for the St. Matthew's Church in Northampton and *Somerset Maugham* (1949). He incorporated slight caricature into his work: Lady Churchill did not like Sutherland's *Winston Churchill* (1954) and destroyed it. His most popular work was 1962 Christ in Glory tapestry in Coventry Cathedral.
Exhibitions 1923–29, etchings shown at Royal Academy, London; 1934 *Modern Art for the Table* (china and glassware), Harrods department store, London; 1935 *British Art in Industry* (glassware by Stuart & Sons), Royal Society of Arts, London; art at 1936 *International Surrealist Exhibition*, London. First (1938) one-person exhibition, Rosenberg and Helft gallery, followed by 1940 exhibition, Leicester Galleries,

Richard Süßmuth. Champagne and wine glasses. 1956. Crystal, champagne glass h. 7 3/4" x dia. 2 1/4" (19.7 x 5.7 cm), wine glasses h. 5 5/8" x dia. 2 3/4" (14.3 x 7 cm). Mfr.: Richard Süßmuth Glashütte, Germany. Gift of the manufacturer. MoMA.

both London; 1992 *Graham Sutherland: Portraits*, Villa Mirabello, Varese, Italy. Fabric patterns for Helios shown at 1946 *Britain Can Make It*, Victoria and Albert Museum, London. São Paulo prize, 1952 Biennale di Venezia; glassware, china, graphic design, and artwork were included in 1979–80 *Thirties* exhibition, Hayward Gallery, London (catalog below). 1960 British Order of Merit (BOM).

Bibliography Michael Farr, *Design in British Industry: A Mid-Century Survey*, London: Cambridge, 1955. Cat., *Thirties: British Art and Design Before the War*, London: Arts Council of Great Britain/Hayward Gallery, 1979. Frederick Cooke, *Glass: Twentieth-Century Design*, New York: Dutton, 1986: 70, 78, 103. Chivers et al., *The Oxford Dictionary of Art*, Oxford: Oxford University, 1988: 483.

Sutnar, Ladislav (1897–1969)

Bohemian painter and advertising, display, and industrial designer; born Pilsen (now Plzeň, Czech Republic).

Training 1915–23, Vysoká Škola Uměleckoprůmyslová (VŠUP, school of applied arts), Univerzity Karlovy (Charles University), and České Vysoké Učení Technické (Czech technical university); all Prague.

Biography 1923–36, Sutnar was professor of design, State School of Graphic Arts, Prague; from 1926, designed the exhibitions of Czechoslovakian Werkbund (SČSD) in Czechoslovakia and abroad; from 1929, was artistic director of design agency Krásná Jizba (the beautiful room); became a board member of magazine *Panorama*, promoting good design and the modern aesthetic. His most important design work includes 1928–32 china table set, and cutlery, 1930 porcelain dinnerware, 1930–32 glass drinking set, and 1931 heat-resistant cups, tea sets, and containers by Schöne Stube of Prague. As the exhibition architect of the Czechoslovak government, he was chief designer of the Czechoslovak Hall at Internationale Buchkunst-Ausstellung, Leipzig, and of the Czech pavilion at 1939–40 *New York World's Fair: The World of Tomorrow*. A pioneering designer, he worked as a painter and for the stage, becoming one of the most notable exhibition designers of 1930s. 1939, he settled in US; from 1942, worked as a freelance designer and consulting art director to several firms; 1941–60, was director, Sweet's Catalog Service; 1951, established his own design firm; was elected a fellow, Institut International des Arts et Lettres; wrote numerous articles and books, including *Design for Point of Sale* (New York: Pellegrini & Cudahy, 1952), *Package Design: The Force of Visual Selling* (New York: Arts, 1953), and *Visual Design in Action: Principles, Purposes* (New York: Hastings House, 1961). Sutnar archive is in the Cooper-Hewitt-National Design Museum, New York.

Exhibitions/citations Subject of 2003 *Ladislav Sutnar: Prague–New York, Design in Action*, Uměleckoprůmyslové Muzeum, Prague. Received gold medal, 1929–30 *Exposición Internacional de Barcelona*; grand prize, 1936 (6th) Triennale di Milano; 14 grand prizes and gold medals, 1937 *Exposition Internationale des Arts et Techniques dans la Vie Moderne*, Paris.

Bibliography R. Roger Remington in *Contemporary Designers*, London: Macmillan, 1981: 572. Alena Adlerová, *České užité umění 1918–1938*, Prague: Odeon, 1983. Vladimír Šlapeta (essay), *Czech Functionalism*, London: Architectural Association, 1987. Sylva Petrová and J.-L. Olivié, *Verre de Bohême 1400–1989*, Paris: Flammarion, 1989.

Svarth, Dan (1942–)

Danish furniture designer and architect.

Training To 1967, Kunsthåndværkerskolen, Copenhagen; to 1969, furniture design, Det Kongelige Danske Kunstakademi; 1962, apprenticeship in cabinetmaking.

Biography 1969, Svarth worked with Herman Olsen; 1971, established his own design studio; from 1973, taught furniture design, Skolen for Brugskunst (formerly Det Tekniske Selskabs Skoler) and, from 1974, furniture and interior architecture, Det Kongelige Danske Kunstakademi. Some of his furniture was produced by Jørgen V. Hansen, Fredericia Stolefabrik, and, more recently (2000–01), by Hvalsøe Køkkener. He is a member, The Cabinetmaker's Autumn Exhibition (SE); wrote the book *Egyptisk møbelkunst fra faraotiden = Egyptian Furniture-Making in the Age of the Pharaohs* (Århus: Århus University, 1998).

Citations 1966 Johannes Krøiers award, 1966 L.F. Foghts award (of the Kunsthåndværkerskolen), 1970 and 1973 Danish State art award.

Bibliography Frederik Sieck, *Nutidig Dansk Møbeldesign – en kortfattet illustreret beskrivelse*, Copenhagen: Bondo Gravesen, 1990.

Svaz Československého Díla (SČSD) (Czechoslovakian Werkbund)

Czechoslovak artistic-industrial association; located Prague.

History 1914, Jan Kotěra founded the Czech Werkbund, which was revived in 1920 as the Czechoslovakian Workbund (SČSD). It proposed a program to support fine and folk art, enrich industrial production, improve arts and crafts education, and organize exhibitions, lectures, and consultation. It turned to modernism in 1931 and became more concerned with introducing so-called good design into industrial production and 'collaboration between engineers and artists.' Its chairpeople were Josef Gočár, followed by Pavel Janák, and Otakar Starý. There were about 500 members in 1930. 1921–23 in Prague, it organized two exhibitions that focused debate on the choice between arts and crafts production and industrial manufacture. It broke away from national decorativism in favor of modernism with its participation in 1925 Paris *Exposition* (see below) and 1928 *Contemporary Culture* in Brno. The Werkbund organized 1930–31 exhibition of Czech architecture and art, touring Geneva, Budapest, Strasbourg, and Stockholm. Also organized 1928–32 Dejvice housing project in Prague with 33 family houses as examples of modern housing. Grants were provided to artists to work in factories and workshops. The Werkbund sponsored design competitions; published catalogs, books, and periodicals, including the magazines *Výtvarná práce* (creative work) in 1921–22 and *Žijeme* (we live) 1931–33; in 1936, completed the construction of its own administrative and exhibition center, the House of Art Industry (architect, Oldřich Starý, in a purely modern style), 36 Národní St., Prague. 1948, SČSD was incorporated into the Center of Folk Art Production and discontinued its separate activities.

Exhibition Participated in 1925 *Exposition Internationale des Arts Décoratifs et Industriels Modernes,* Paris.

Sveinsdottir, Juliana (1889–1966)

Icelandic artist and textile designer.

Training 1912–17, Det Kongelige Danske Kunstakademi, Copenhagen.

Biography With her interior fabrics first appearing in 1921, she was an accomplished designer of non-figurative textiles, some of which were used in the chambers of the Højesteret (supreme court of Denmark). In her painting, she narrowed her subject matter, and her landscapes bordered on the abstract.

Exhibitions/citations Work included in editions of Triennale di Milano, including a gold medal at 1951 (9th) installment; 1954–57 *Design in Scandinavia*, traveling the US; 1958 *Formes Scandinaves*, Musée des Arts Décoratifs, Paris. Also received 1947 Eckersberg Medal.

Bibliography Cat., David Revere McFadden (ed.), *Scandinavian Modern Design 1880–1980*, New York: Abrams, 1982.

Svensson, Inez (1932–)
Swedish textile designer.

Biography 1950s, Svensson worked with Göta Trägårdh at Stobo, a Stockholm spinning mill, designing fabrics for industrial production; 1957–69, was the artistic director of Borås Wäfveri, collaborating with Gunilla Axén and Birgitta Hahn. In turn, they and seven others established studio '10-gruppen' (aka Ten Swedish Designers) in 1970 in Stockholm, with cushions as the first (1972) and, afterward, prolific collection. (1987, the ten members became five, with three remaining today.) Birgitta Hahn, Ingela Håkansson and Tom Hedqvist Svensen worked on design projects for UNESCO, including in Afghanistan; 1990–96, Svensson was the rector, Konstfack (design school); is considered a pioneer in the textile industry.
Exhibition Work with '10-gruppen' included in 2001 *Ten Swedish Designers, Thirty Years On*, Nationalmuseum, Stockholm.
Bibliography Cat., David Revere McFadden (ed.), *Scandinavian Modern Design 1880–1980*, New York: Abrams, 1982.

SVOMAS
> See VKhUTEMAS.

Swaak, Harry
> See Lumiance.

Swainson, Anne (d. 1955)
Swedish industrial designer; active the US.

Training Fine and applied arts, Columbia University, New York.
Biography Early 1920s, Swainson taught textile design, University of California, Berkeley (students included Dorothy Liebes); late 1920s, was director of design for Chase Brass and Copper, Waterbury, Conn.; 1931, director of the newly established Bureau of Design, Montgomery Ward, Chicago. By 1935, she was managing over 30 staff members (18 product designers and 14 packaging designers). She was a strict taskmistress to the staff, who redesigned a variety of products ranging from vehicle tires and arc welders to radios and toasters. Almost none was designed by Swainson alone; however, a 1938 streamline radio cabinet (patent no. 114,565, serial no. 76,577). may have been her design. She revolutionized the mail-order catalog business by turning from hand-drawn illustrations to photography; 1937, visited her native Sweden, no doubt encountering the vanguard of Scandinavian modernism, and visited the *Exposition internationale des Arts et Techniques dans la Vie Moderne*, Paris. 1930s–40s, the Montgomery Ward staff included Dave Chapman (who left in c. 1942 to open his own studio), Ray Larsen (in charge of packaging, who left to manage the graphics department of the Raymond Loewy studio), Fred Preiss (who had come from the Barnes & Reinecke studio), Herb Zeller (who left to direct design at Motorola), Jim Teague (who later formed Painter, Teague & Petertil, and, subsequently, was head of design at Warwick Radio). From late 1940s, the role of Swainson and the Bureau of Design began to shrink, and many designers left. By mid-1950s, only Swainson remained and she worked at Montgomery Ward until her 1955 death.
Bibliography Sheldon and Martha Candler Cheney, *Art and the Machine: An Account of Industrial Design in 20th-Century America*, New York: Whittlesey House, 1936; New York: Acanthus, 1992 reprint. Cat., Pat Kirkham (ed.), *Women Designers in the USA, 1900–2000: Diversity and Difference*, New York: Bard; New Haven: Yale, 2000. Some data here courtesy Christian K. Narkiewicz-Laine.

Swanson, 'Pipsan' (b. Eva Lisa Saarinen 1905–1979); Robert Swanson (1900–1981)
'Pipsan': Finnish designer; daughter of Eliel and Loja Saarinen.
Robert: American architect and designer; from Menominee, Michigan.

Training 'Pipsan': Design, Taideteollinen korkeakoulu, Helsinki.
Biography 1923, with her parents, 'Pipsan" settled in Michigan from Finland. First important projects were interiors for commissions by her father Eliel Saarinen. She taught the first formal class on contemporary furniture design at Cranbrook Academy, Bloomfield Hills, Mich., of which her father was the headmaster; 1926, eloped to marry architect J. Robert F. Swanson and established a contemporary interior-design department in his firm. (1922, Robert had received a bachelor's degree, University of Michigan, Ann Arbor.) 'Pipsan' for a number of years had designed custom furniture for clients; 1939 with Robert, introduced the Flexible Home Arrangement (F.H.A.) line of functional and flexible furniture. After World War II, they coordinated products to complement their furniture, working with 16 manufacturers. Work included products by U.S. Glass Company (they were commissioned in 1948 to design all its major goods), lighting by Mutual Sunset Lamp Company, and metalware by Cray, also printed fabrics. Mid-1940s, the Swansons founded Swanson Associates.
Citation 1957 Louise Bolender Woman of the Year Award (from tne home-furnishings industry).
Bibliography Cat., Robert Judson Clark et al., *Design in America: The Cranbrook Vision, 1925–1950*, New York: Abrams, Detroit Institute of Arts, and The Metropolitan Museum of Art, 1983. Cat., Pat Kirkham (ed.), *Women Designers in the USA, 1900–2000: Diversity and Difference*, New York: Bard; New Haven: Yale, 2000.

Swarovski
Austrian producers of cut crystal stones.

History Daniel Swarovski 1st, son of a skilled stone craftsman, founded Swarovski in Bohemia to protect an invention, an 1892 machine for cutting crystal as semi-precious stones might be cut, that revolutionized the jewelry industry. 1895, the firm was moved from the Georgenthal in Bohemia to Wattens in the Tyrol, where Swarovski was able to call on water power and soon became a major supplier of glass stones to costume jewelers in Europe and the US. The world' first rear reflectors for vehicles were introduced in 1925. Today, the firm is the leading source and creator of cut crystal and one of Austria's largest privately owned companies, still managed by descendants of the founder. It also has become a major supplier of iron-on rhinestones and patented the brand name Swarogem for green-agate and marcasite natural stones. 1976, the Swarovski Silver Crystal line of giftware and collectibles was launched. 1989 and 1992, the design of an expensive group of crystal objects and vessels was commissioned from Joël Desgrippes, Alessandro Mendini, Bořek Šípek, Andrée Putman, Ettore Sottsass, Matteo Thun, and others. The firm developed the Cubic Zirconia simulated-diamond in 1977 and a new technology for cutting precious stones in 1995. The firm introduced a watch collection and crystal 'tattoos' for skin application in 1999. Francesco Binfaré incorporated Swarovski crystal into his extravagant 2000 Flap sofa by Edra.
Bibliography Penny Sparke (ed.), *The Cutting Edge: 200 Years of Crystal: The Language Renewed...*, Wattens: Swarovski (1992, Vivienne Becker, *Swarovski: The Magic of Crystal*, New York: Abrams, 1995. www.swarovski.com

Swatch Group
Swiss holding company, primarily a watch-manufacturing consortium; located Biel.

History 1983, the Swatch Group was founded through the amalgamation of two large watchmaking entities (which produced prestigious brands such as Omega and Tissot): the Société Suisse pour l'Industrie Horlogère (SSIH), founded in 1931, and Allgemeine Scweizerrische Uhrenindustrie (ASUAG), founded in 1930. Both corporations had attempted to challenge two world financial crises that faced the timepiece industry in the West. The first was the Great Depression, from 1929, and the second was the 1970s popularity and influx into the West of inexpensive but technologically advanced timepieces and electronic products, especially from Japan. As a result of the latter, ASUAG and SSIH faced bankruptcy or the sale of their brands to non-Swiss parties. Nicholas G. Hayek (1925–) was hired to conduct an analysis of the problem, which became known as the 1983 Hayek Study. 1983 supported by bank executives, he brought the consortium, a merger of ASUAG and SSH into a single entity, called Société Suisse de Microélectronique et d'Horlogerie (aka SMH Swiss Corporation) and launched a new product—the now-legendary 1983 Swatch wristwatch. Purportedly, the Swatch technicians were inspired by LEGO blocks' injection molding and die-casting, and disposable plastic lighters' ultrasonic welding. The low-cost, high-tech, artistically appeal-ing, and cleverly promoted analog moldel with a slimness developed by young engineer Jacques Müller and his team (including Ernst Thonke and Elmar Mock) was made possible by what Hayek calls his own 'dreaming spirit.' By 1984, Max Imgrüth's vivid colors and patterns—applied to the simple plastic timepiece, and subsequently joined by the motifs of well-known artists—were to alter the fashion-watch market forever. 1988, the corporation became, and still is, the largest watch maker worldwide, representing about 25% of the world watch market. (From 1998, the firm has been known as the Swatch Group.) Its brands also include Balmain, Blancpain, Calvin Klein, Certina, Endura, FlikFlak, Hamilton, Lanco, Longines, Mido, Omega, Rado, Tissot, and others.

The consortium is active in officially timing, most of the Olympiads and other sports events, and in telecommunications and automobiles. The ambitious Hayek, who stepped down as the head in 2001, had in the 1980s considered the production and sales of an ultra-compact city car. Unsuccessful in ersuading Volkswagen into a partnership, he turned to Daimler Benz (today DaimlerChrysler), which agreed to produce and sell what became the MCC Smart car and which broke with old traditions. From late 1990, the Group began making high-tech components for computers, telecommunicators, medical applications, and electronic products and also produced low-power chips at EM Marin, quartz crystal at Micro-Crystal, and batteries at Renata. It expanded its watch line into Swatch Access (wireless accessing), Swatch Talk (a telephone in a watch), Swatch Telecom (micromechanics and microelectronics), and various other marketing ploys.
Bibliography Roland Carrera, *Swatchissimo, 1981–1991: l'extraordinaire aventure = Swatch: The Extraordinary Adventure*, Geneva: Antiquorum, 1992. Larry Ehrhard (ed.), *Almost Everything You Need to Know About Dealing and Collecting Swatch Watches*, Tavares, Fla.: Heart of America, 1996, 6th ed. Frank Edwards, *Swatch: A Guide for Connoisseurs and Collectors*, Toronto: Firefly, 1998. Mel Byars with Arlette Barré-Despond, *100 Designs/100 Years: A Celebration of the 20th Century*, Hove: RotoVision: 178–79. Paola Antonelli (ed.), *Objects of Design: The Museum of Modern Art*, New York: The Museum of Modern Art, 2003: 241.

Swedese Möbler
> See Ekström, Yngve.

Swiczinsky, Helmut (1944–)
Polish architect and designer; born Poznan; active Vienna.

Training Technical University, Vienna; Architectural Association, London.
Biography 1968 with Wolf D. Prix, Swiczinsky established the architecture firm Coop Himmelb(l)au in Vienna. (In German, *Himmelblau* means 'sky-blue' and *Himmelbau* means 'a building of skies.') 1973, Swiczinsky was a visiting professor, Architectural Association; with Prix, designed the 1974 mobile kitchen by Ewe-Küchen and the Deconstructivist 1989 Vodöl armchair by Vitra, a version of Le Corbusier's 1928 Grand Confort armchair that they dissected. (The name 'Vodöl' is based on the Austrian mispronunciation of the French word *fauteuil*.) Swiczinsky and Prix are quite active in architecture.
Exhibitions Their work was included in the 1988 *Deconstructivist Architecture* exhibition organized by Philip Johnson at The Museum of Modern Art, New York.
> See Coop Himmelb(l)au.

Swid Powell
American metalware and ceramics manufacturer.

History Swid Powell was originally established by Addie Powell and Nan Swid, wives of Knoll International executives; presented its first tableware collection in 1984. The marketing strategy was to attract many of the best-known names in architecture worldwide to design tabletop items and dinnerware. In the beginning, it commissioned Richard Meier, Robert Stern, Charles Gwathmey, Arata Isozaki, Laurinda Spear, and Stanley Tigerman with Margaret McCurry. Later the work of Hans Hollein, Javier Bellosito, Trix and Robert Haussmann, Paolo Portoghesi, and Steven Holl was added to the inventory. The firm has produced porcelain dinner services, crystal, linens, and some silver pieces, including Robert Mapplethorpe's photographic images of flowers applied to porcelain plates. Swid Powell's wares came to be known irreverently as the 'architects' plates.'
Bibliography Annette Tapert, *Swid Powell: Objects by Architects*, New York: Rizzoli, 1990.

Swiss Army Knife
> See Elsener, Karl.

Sylve, Le
French design and decoration department; located Paris.

History Le Sylve was established by the Le Bûcheron store shortly before 1925 *Exposition Internationale des Arts Décoratifs et Industriels Modernes*, Paris, although the shop had commissioned some Art Nouveau furniture at the turn of the century. Its director M. Boutillier supervised its modern-interior stand at the *Exposition*. When the staff of the atelier designed the second-class dining room of 1926 oceanliner *Île-de-France*, Boutillier was encouraged to establish the studio under the direction of Michel Dufet and art critic Léandre Vaillat. The furniture was designed by Guérin, Sénéchal, and Dufet; glass by Jean Sala and Chappellin; ceramics by Georges Serré and Marcel Goupy; silver from Georg Jensen; metalwork from Jean Dunand; paintings by Maurice Utrillo, Maurice de Vlaminck, Van Dongen, Albert Marquet, Edouard Goerg, and others; sculpture by Antoine Bourdelle, Chana Orloff, Pierre Traverse, Drivier, Guénot, Yvonne Serruys, and Albert Marque. The studio had its own separate entry on the rue de Rivoli, Paris, made by Binquet using a motif from Cassandre's poster for Le Bûcheron (of 1923, which won a grand prize at 1925 Paris *Exposition*). To 1939, Dufet was the director.
Bibliography Victor Arwas, *Art Déco*, New York: Abrams, 1980. Pierre Kjellberg, *Art déco: les maîtres du mobilier, le décor des paquebots*, Paris: Amateur, 1986/1990.

Swatch. Watch (no. GB001). 1983. Plastic and metal, 1/4 x 1 3/8 x 9 1/8" (0.6 x 3.5 x 23.2 cm). Mfr.: SMH Swiss Corporation (Société Suisse de Microélectronique et d'Horlogerie), Switzerland. Gift of the manufacturer. MoMA.

Syväluoma, Sari (1966–)
Finnish textile designer; born Vihanti.

Training 1985–87, School of Handicrafts, Nivala, Finland; 1987–90, Jurvan Käsi-Ja Taideteollisuusoppilaitos Jkto, Jurva, Finland; 1994–95, Kunsthøgskolen, Bergen, Norway; 1990–96, master of arts degree, Taideteollinen korkeakoulu, Helsinki.
Biography 1987, Syväluoma was the manager, Arts and Crafts Center, Oulainen, Finland; 1990, an assistant to textile artists Kristiina Nyrhinen and Heli Tuori-Luutonen; 1993, the junior designer of printed fabrics, Finlayson, Tampere, Finland; 1995–99, a designer of domestics, office, and public-space textiles, Sellgrens Veveri, Tingvoll, Norway; 1999, established her own studio in Oslo for clients, including Sellgrens Veveri (upholstery and curtain collections for domestic use and for public buildings), Hovden Møbel (development of textile collection for furniture collection), Norsk Form (exhibition architect), Landheim Veveri (2000–01 curtain collection), Røros Tweed (blankets/throws); is a mem-

Martin Székely. Perrier drinking glass. 1996. Glass, h. 7 1/8 x dia. 3 3/8" (15 x 8.5 cm). Mfr.: Cristal d'Arques, France.

ber of NTKD (Norwegian association of textile designers, board member from 1999), Tekstiilitaiteilijat (TEXO, Finnish association of textile artists), and Norske Kunsthåndverkere (NK, Norwegian association of arts and crafts).
Exhibitions/citations From 1997, work included in a number of exhibitions, including *Young Nordic Design*, traveling the world from 2000, and subject of 1991 *Women's Own*, Arsenaali gallery, Seinäjoki, Finland; 1993 *Dublin-Exhibition*, Taideteollinen korkeakoulu, Helsinki; 1994 *Two Spaces*, Oulainen art gallery, Oulainen, Finland; 1995 *All Men Are Heroes into Dreams*, Suomen Yhdyspankki (union bank of Finland), Helsinki; 1996 *Cycle*, Galleri Falsen, Oslo; 2001 *Blanke eller Pjuskete?*, Norsk Form, Oslo. Grants: 1992 and 1993, City of Oulainen; 1993 Erasmus IC, Finland; 1994 Nordplus, Helsinki; 1994 and 1995, UIAH, Helsinki; 2000 Oslo Culture Scholarship.
Bibliography www.sari-syvaluoma.com.

Szabó, Adalbert-Georges

Hungarian metalsmith; active Paris.

Biography 1907, Szabó became a member, Société des Artistes Décorateurs. His work before World War I was historicist and, from 1918, closer to Art Déco. He designed/hewed iron into table lamps, sconces, chandeliers, balustrades, doors, firescreens, and the chased and gilded bronze door of the dining room on 1935 oceanliner *Normandie*; was opposed to industrial techniques, particularly arc welding, and pursued traditional blacksmithing.
Exhibitions As early as 1906 and late as 1938, showed metalwork at Salons of Société des Artistes Français; 1907–40, at 25 Salons of Société des Artistes Décorateurs.
Bibliography Alastair Duncan, *Art Nouveau and Art Déco Lighting*, New York: Simon & Schuster, 1978: 187–88. Pierre Kjellberg, *Art déco: les maîtres du mobilier, le décor des paquebots*, Paris: Amateur, 1986/1990.

Székely, Martin (1956–)

French furniture designer; born and active Paris.

Training École Estienne, and École Boulle, both Paris; metalworking under a Chinese artisan.
Biography Székely began as a copper-plate engraver; 1977–78, designed furniture, including the Ar stool. His first success was a 25-piece collection of furniture for the Sauvagnat company (shown at 1979 Salon du Meuble, Paris). He designed 1980 Coin furniture collection in wood and aluminum by Skina and widely published, stark, and simple furniture models in black carbon-steel by Galerie Néotù, Paris, including 1980 Cornette chair and 1982–83 Pi chaise longue. 1984, Székely studied in Italy and met Ettore Sottsass, Paolo Deganello, and Michele De Lucchi; designed 1986 Carbone chair by Tribu; case goods in MDF and upholstered seating, including 1987 Haut Ouvert, 1987 Presse Papiers, and 1987 Stoleru armchair and sofa. Néotù edited his Chaise Toro (later mass produced), 1989 Liberata table, 1989 Armoire Leone, 1989 Lysistrata chaise longue, and 1989 Marie France fireside chair. 1987, he restored Musée de Picardie, Amiens, and the entrance hall of the George Sand villa in Nohant; 1988 office of the president of Conseil Général of Belfort; and 1988–89 shop and 1990 park of Musée de Villeneuve d'Asq. His Pi bookshelves were produced by Mega Éditions of France. 1989, he began to move away from the black metal forms for which he had earlier gained recognition. His small-series designs represented a successful collaboration between designer and producer, in this case him and Pierre Staudemeyer of Galerie Néotù, Paris. More recent work includes a champagne bucket for Dom Perignon, furniture edited by Kréo, 1993 public bench by JC Decaux, 1994 Corolle high-electricity pylon by Transel/Élétricité de France (EDF), 1994 Collection Satragno furniture range by Satragno, 1996 bar glass for Perrier, 1999 Couronne porcelain vase by Bernardaud, 1999 Eau de St. Louis flacon by St. Louis, Séville aluminum candlestick by Ardi, Nord crystal drinking glass by Val Saint-Lambert for Centre Georges Pompidou, and a wide range of other products, including ceramic public-bar-service items by Ricard in the trademark orange color.
Exhibitions/citations Work first (1982) shown at the Galerie VIA (French furniture association), Paris; subsequently, in a large number of gallery and museum venues, including in the US, Germany, France, and Israel, and many at Néotù in Paris, which represented some of his more notable early work before Néotù's 2001 closing; 1998 *Premises* (one of four French designers), Guggenheim Museum, New York. 1983 Carte Blanche production support from VIA (French furniture association); 1984 Agora award; Creator of the Year, 1987 Salon du Meuble, Paris; 1988, first prize, French art critics and VIA.
Bibliography Sophie Anargyros, *Le mobilier français*, Paris: Regard/VIA, 1980: 52–54. Cat., Garth Hall and Margo Rouard Snowman, *Avant Premiere: Contemporary French Furniture*, London: Eprouvé, 1988. Cat., *Les années VIA, 1980–1990*, Paris: Musée des Arts Décoratifs, 1990. François Mathey, *Au bonheur des formes, design français 1845–1992*, Paris: Regard, 1992: 156, 230. *Martin Székely: meublier, designer: 1983-1995*, Paris: Association Française d'Action Artistique, 1995. *Martin Szekely*, Paris: Hasan, 1998. Mel Byars, *50 Sports Wares...*, Hove: RotoVision, 1999. Cat., Enzo Biffi Gentili, *Il disegno ceramico: Gagnère, Laudani, Romanelli, Székely*, Milan: Electa, 1999.

T

Louis Comfort Tiffany. Table lamp (detail). c. 1900. MoMA.

10-Gruppen
> See Axén, Gunila.

Tachaputthapong, Nakool
> See Propaganda.

Tackett, LaGardo (1911–)
American ceramicist; active Los Angeles.

Training Sculpture and art history, Claremont College, Cal.
Biography c. 1946–54, Tackett maintained a pottery studio; taught, California School of Design, Los Angeles, where he and students from 1949 developed bisque-fired objects such as outdoor planters and smaller vessels that would be desirable to modern architects. This led to the 1950 establishment of Architectural Pottery by Rita and Max Lawrence in Manhattan Beach, Cal. Subsequently, glazed and unglazed hemispherical, cylindrical, egg- and hourglass-shaped planters for indoor/outdoor use were produced. The designers were Marilyn Kay Austin, David Cressey, Douglas Deeds, John Follis, Rex Goode, Malcolm Leland, LaGardo Tackett, and others. (The firm Vessel of San Diego, California, is now reissuing some Architectural Pottery models.) Tackett also designed 1957 range of ceramic dinnerware by Schmid International, produced in Japan; from 1963, was the manager of the objects division of Herman Miller Furniture Co.
Exhibition/citation 1951 *Good Design* exhibition/award (Architectural Pottery ware), The Museum of Modern Art, New York.
Bibliography La Gardo Tackett, 'A New Casual Structure for Ceramic Design,' *Art and Architecture*, vol. 72, Apr. 1955: 14+. M.S.S., 'New Solutions to Planting Problems,' *Interiors*, vol. 115, Feb. 1956: 114-15. Norbert Nelson, 'The Marketplace,' *Industrial Design*, vol. 10, Mar. 1963: 74–76. Cat., Kathryn B. Hiesinger and George H. Marcus III (eds.), *Design Since 1945*, Philadelphia: Philadelphia Museum of Art, 1983.

Taeuber-Arp, Sophie (b. Sophie Taeuber 1889–1943)
Swiss artist and designer; born Davos; wife of Jean Arp.

Training 1908–10, Kunstgewerbeschule, St. Gallen; subsequently, Debschitz-Schule (Lehr- und Versuchs-Atelier für angewandte und freie Kunst), Munich; 1912, Kunstgewerbeschule, Hamburg.
Biography 1891, Taeuber became a Swiss national; created collages, embroideries, sculpture, paintings, stage designs, and puppets. Her work was mostly abstract. 1915, she became a member of the SWB (Schweizerischer Werkbund) and met future husband Arp; 1916–29, taught textile design, Kunstgewerbeschule, Zürich, and, from 1916, had an independent artistic career which led her and Arp, married 1922, to contacts and collaboration with the Zürich Dada group; also jointly with Arp, created paintings and compositions in a kind of Constructivist style. 1926, she was commissioned to design the interior of Café Aubette, Strasbourg; however, eventually shared the commission with Arp and Theo van Doesburg. 1929–40, she and Arp lived in Meudon, France, where she designed and built her own studio house; 1939, joined Cercle et Carré and, 1931 or 1932, Abstract-Création group. In Meudon, she established and edited the trilingual (French, German, and English) abstract-art periodical *Plastique* (five issues 1937–39. 1941–43, she and Arp lived in a community of artists in Grasse, including Sonia Delaunay and Alberto Magnelli; died in Zürich.
Exhibition Work subject of 1964 exhibition, Paris (catalog below).
Bibliography Cat., *Sophie Taeuber-Arp*, Paris: Affaires Culturelles, Ministère d'État, 1964. Margit Weinberg-Staber, *Sophie Taeuber-Arp*, Lausanne: Éditions Rencontre, 1970. Carlyn Lanchner, *Sophie Taeuber-Arp*, New York: The Museum of Modern Art, 1981. Gregor Laschen, *Sophie Taeuber-Arp*, Rolandseck: Stiftung Hans Arp und Sophie Taeuber-Arp, Bahnhof Rolandseck, 1989.

Tagliapietra, Lino (1934–)
Italian glassworker and teacher; born Murano.s

Training 1945 under Archimede Seguso, Murano, where Tagliapietra became a master in 1955.
Biography From 1956, Tagliapietra taught glassmaking with Archimede Seguso and Nane Ferro; 1966–68, designed glass for Venini in Murano; to 1968, for Murrina; from 1968, taught glassmaking, Haystack School and Pilchuck School, Stanwood, Wash., US. He worked as master glassblower and designer at studios, including those of Galliano Ferro, Venini, La Murrina, and Effetre International; 1960s, began developing his design skills by implementing his own concepts as well as those of others; 1970s, was profoundly influenced by his participation in the symposia at La Scuola Internazionale del Vetro, Murano, where the most accomplished Muranese masters and international artists congregated; 1980s, was collaborating more and more with other artists and producing their work; became greatly influenced by working with Dutch glass designer A.D. Copier, who altered Tagliapietra's concept of glass objects as being works of art to those of utility. For the past five decades, Tagliapietra has generously shared his experience, understanding, and knowledge of traditional Venetian glassblowing, becoming largely responsible for a renaissance in glassblowing that has infiltrated studio glass and raised international standards. Mid-1980s, turned from being a traditional Venetian glassblower to a studio artist; 1990s, exclusively designed and made his own work.

Kazuhide Takahama. Saghi settee. 1972. Chrome-plated steel frame, foam, and synthetic-wool upholstery, 25 1/2 x 29 x 23 3/8" (64.8 x 73.7 x 59.4 cm), seat h. 21" (53.3 cm). Mfr.: Simón International, Italy. Gift of Architectural Supplements, Inc. MoMA.

Exhibitions Work shown worldwide including at 1988 *Uit het licht van de lagune: textiel van Norelene, glas van Tagliapietra*, Museum Boymans-van Beuningen, Rotterdam; 2000 *A.D. Copier and Lino Tagliapietra: Inspiration in Glass*, Museum Het Palais, The Hague.
Bibliography Giovanni Sarpellon (ed.), *Lino Tagliapietra: Vetri = Glass = Verres = Glas*, Venice: Arsenale, 1994. Charlotte Sahl-Madsen (ed.), *Lino Tagliapietra*, Ebeltoft, Denmark: Glasmuseum, 1996. Marino Barovier, *Tagliapietra: A Venetian Glass Maestro*, Venice: Vitrum, 1998. Titus M. Eliens (ed.), *A.D. Copier and Lino Tagliapietra: Inspiration in Glass*, Gent: Snoeck-Ducaju & Zoon; The Hague: Gemeentemuseum Den Haag, 2000.

Taira-Sakuhin, Toshiko (1921–)

Japanese textile designer; born Okinawa.

Training Under her mother Rana Taira, in traditional *basho-fu* technique; under Kichimusuke Tonomura, general weaving, in Kurashiki, Okayama Prefecture.
Biography 1948, she opened her own *basho-fu* workshop. *Basho-fu* and Taira are considered important national cultural assets. *Basho-fu*, a textile made from the fibers of the basho plant that was once popular throughout the Ryukyu and Amami Islands before World War II, is now only made in Kijoka. The weaving process is intricate.
Exhibitions/citations Work included in exhibitions in Japan, Hawaii, and Washington, D.C.; 1999 exhibition, New York and St. Louis (catalog below). 1972 appointed an Intangible National Treasure.
Bibliography Cat., Cara McCarty and Matilda McQuaid, *Structure and Surface: Contemporary Japanese Textiles*, New York: Abrams/ The Museum of Modern Art, 1999.

Takahama, Kazuhide (1930–)

Japanese architect and designer; born Muasaki.

Training To 1953, Tokyo Kogyo Daigaku (Tokyo institute of technology).
Biography From 1953, Takahama worked in the studio of architect Kazuo Fujoka in Tokyo; was a professor, School of Architecture, Kumamoto University; came to Milan for the 1957 (11th) Triennale to supervise the Japanese pavilion he had designed for installation there; met furniture impresario Dino Gavina and designed for his Gavina and subsequent Simón International firms for an extended period, resulting in about 17 pieces in 1960s–70s, such as 1963 Suzanne, 1968 Ultrarazionale collection (including minimalist Gaja steel-rod side chair, Jano stacking chair, and Kazuki flat-plane high-back armchair), 1972 Saghi settee and others. c. 1970, he settled near Bologna, Italy, where he designed 1976 Kaori, Kazuki, and Saori new generation of lamps with a stretched fabric over a wire frame, by Sirrah. Also 1981 Kaibi chair and Olinto table by B&B Italia; 1981 Len and Kumo, 1982 Totem, 1983 Tiki, 1985 Naeko and Nefer lamps by Sirrah. Today's production of some of Takahama's designs, originally by Simón, is by Ultramobile in Calcinelli di Saltara.
Citations 1979 Premio Compasso d'Oro (for 1976 Kazuki and Kaori lamps by Sirrah).
Bibliography Julí Capella and Quim Larrea, *Designed by Architects in the 1980s*, New York: Rizzoli, 1988.

Takahashi, Hideko (1950–)

Japanese textile designer; born Tokyo.

Training Under Junichi Arai, Otsuka Textile Design Institute, Tokyo.
Biography After Otsuka, she worked under Arai; from 1988, has been a part-time lecturer at Otsuka; has experimented with the use of stainless-steel yarns.
Exhibitions/citations Work included in 1999 venue, New York and St. Louis (catalog below). Subject of a number of exhibitions. Award, 1987 (1st) International Textile Competition, Kyoto.
Bibliography Cat., Cara McCarty and Matilda McQuaid, *Structure and Surface: Contemporary Japanese Textiles*, New York: Abrams/ The Museum of Modern Art, 1999.

Takematsu, Yukiharu (1963–)

Japanese architect and interior and product designer; born Nagasaki.

Training To 1986, architecture, Tama University of Art, Tokyo.
Biography From 1986, Takematsu worked at Unite Design and Planning; 1988, at Creative Intelligence Associates (CIA); 1990, at Branson Coates Architecture, London; 1991, founded Environment Protection Architectural Institute (EPA), Tokyo, and from this time has actively designed a large number of houses, restaurants, and showrooms; some furniture; and has been involved in urban planning, exhibition design, and public-art projects.
Citation 1995 Residential Architecture Award (for Ryu-Un-Inn), Tokyo Society of Architects and Building Engineers.

Talbert, Bruce James (1838–1881)

British architect and designer; born Dundee.

Training Under cabinet-carver Millar, apprenticeship; subsequently, under architect Charles Edwards.
Biography 1856, Talbert settled in Glasgow and worked in the architecture office of W.N. Tait and Campbell Douglas; early 1860s, began to design furniture and execute decorative work in a simple neo-Gothic style; from c. 1862, worked for Doveston, Bird & Hull in Manchester; shortly after, began designing silver and wrought-iron work by Francis Skidmore's firm Art Manufacturers, Coventry; 1866, settled in London and began designing furniture by Holland & Sons; wrote *Gothic Forms Applied to Furniture, Metal Work and Decoration for Domestic Purposes* (Birmingham: S. Birbeck and the author, 1867), which influenced cabinetmaking in England and the US, and *Examples of Ancient and Modern Furniture, Metal Work, Tapestries, Decorations...* (London: B.T. Batsford, 1876). Preferring 12th- and 13th-century Gothic styles, he designed furniture based on framed construction with low-relief carving, inlay, and piercing, attempting to integrate it with its architectural milieu. His ecclesiastical metalwork was produced by Cox, wallpaper by Jeffrey & Co., carpets by Brinton, ironwork by Coalbrookdale, and textiles by Cowlishaw & Nichol, Barbone & Miller, and Warner. By 1860s, Talbert had become one of the most influential industrial designers of the British Aesthetic Movement; 1876, was working in a more Jacobean style.
Exhibitions/citations 1870–76, showed architectural drawings regularly, Royal Academy of Arts, London; 1867 *Exposition Universelle* (furniture by Holland & Sons), Paris; 1873 *Weltausstellung Wien* (Pet sideboard by Gillows), Vienna; 1878 *Exposition Universelle* (Juno cabinet by Jackson and Graham), Paris. Received 1860 gold medal (architectural design) and 1862 gold medal (for drawing), Edinburgh Architectural Association.
Bibliography Elizabeth Aslin, *The Aesthetic Movement: Prelude to Art Nouveau*, New York: Praeger, 1969. Doreen Bolger Burke et al., *In Pursuit of Beauty: Americans and the Aesthetic Movement*, New York: The Metropolitan Museum of Art/Rizzoli, 1986.

Tallon, Roger (1929–)

French industrial designer.

Training In engineering, various universities, Paris.
Biography 1951, Tallon was in charge of graphic communication, Caterpillar-France, and a consultant, Du Pont European subsidiaries; 1953–72, worked at Technès, Paris (office for technical/aesthetic studies, founded in 1951 by Jacques Viénot), where he became the director in 1960. He was a cofounder of International Council of Societies of Industrial Designers (ICSID, first conference in 1957 in Paris); 1973, established Design Programmes agency; from 1984, an associate of ADSA + partners (with Pierre Paulin and others) and, from 1994, of Euro RSCG Design agency (founded through the amalgamation of Sopha and ADSA + partners). His range of objects included furniture, industrial machinery, and lighting. He designed 1957 and 1961 cameras produced by SEM, a 1957–58 coffee grinder by Peugeot, 1960 typewriter by Japy, 1964 television set by Thomson Téléavia, and 1970 drinking glasses by Daum. At this time, since French industry was slow to use the services of professional designers, most of his commissions were foreign; 1957–64, a consultant-designer to General Motors' Frigidaire refrigerators; experimented with new techniques and materials that resulted in one of his best-known pieces, the 1965 High-Back chair in aluminum and spiky polyether-foam upholstery edited by Galerie Jacques Lacloche of Paris, 1965 folding-wood TS Chair by Archigram, 1973 watches by Lip, 1977 lighting by Ercom, 1976 staircase in the Galerie Sentou, Paris. From 1970, he consulted to SNCF, designing the carriage for the 1988 high-speed TGV train by Alsthom Atlantique and Corail locomotives; taught, École Nationale Supérieure des Arts Décoratifs, Paris. More recent work has included 1996 Duplex high-speed train by SNCF (French railway), Météor subway cars of Paris Métro/RATP, 1996 marine construction system for yachts by Alligator, 1999 Chrono-Pyramidion 3rd-millennium trophy by Christofle, and 1999 Aphrosolite crystal drinking glasses by Arnolfo Cambio.
Exhibitions/citations Work shown at 1966 *L'Objet* and 1968 *Les Assises du Siège Contemporain*, both Musée des Arts Décoratifs, Paris; 1981 *Paris 1937–57*, 1988 *Les Années 50*, Centre Georges Pompidou, Paris; 1989 *L'Art de Vivre*, Cooper-Hewitt National Design Museum, New York; numerous other venues. Work subject of 1993 exhibition, Centre Georges Pompidou, Paris. Received silver medal (for a typewriter by Japy), 1960 (12th) Triennale di Milano; 1985 French national grand prize for industrial design; 1973, elected Honorary Royal Designer for Industry, UK.
Bibliography 'Da Parigi: design e idee di Roger Tallon,' *Domus*, no. 452, July 1967: 40–45. Cat., *Qu'est-ce que ce le design?*, Paris: CCI, 1969. Xavier Gilles, 'Le design selon Tallon,' *Œil*, no. 244, Nov. 1975: 57–59. Catherine Millet, 'Un designer à Paris,' in *Paris 1937–1957*, Paris: Centre Georges Pompidou, 1981. *Roger Tallon, itineraires d'un designer industriel*, Paris: Centre Georges Pompidou, 1993. Gilles de Bure and Chloé Braunstein, *Roger Tallon*, Paris: Dis Voir, 1999. Pierre Doze, 'L'échelle Tallon,' *Intramuros*, no. 97, Oct-Nov. 2001: 50–55. Catherine Millet, *Roger Tallon à Vallauris*, Nice: Grégoire Gardette, 2001.

Reiko Tanabe. Stool. 1961. Molded plywood with teak veneer, 14 1/4 x 17 x 17" (36.2 x 43.2 x 43.2 cm). Mfr.: Tendo Mokko, Japan. Gift of the mfr. MoMA.

Tamborini, Carlo (1958–)

Italian designer; born Milan.

Training 1990–93, Istituto Europeo di Design, Milan.
Biography Tamborini first worked as a freelance designer of packaging and display cabinets; collaborated with various architecture studios; from 1997, has worked in Lissoni Associatti, Milan. Designs include 1998 Velina table lamp by Codice 31; 1999 Spillo floor lamp, 2000 Spazio 1 and Spazio 2 floor lamps, 2001 Bank floor lamp, 2000 Stilo stainless-steel container, 2001 Little Wing aluminum table, and 2002 Bridge chair by Pallucco Italia; 2000 Duplex, 2001 Sag, and 2001 Slice lamps by FontanaArte/Candle; 2002 Haga armchair (with Fabio Azzolina) by Cover.
Exhibitions Participated in exhibitions of Codice 31 group.
Bibliography *The International Design Yearbook*, London: Laurence King, 2000 and 2001.

Tanabe, Reiko (b. Reiko Murai 1934–)

Japanese designer; born Tokyo.

Training To 1957, Joshibi University of Art and Design, Tokyo.
Biography From 1957, she worked at Kenji Fujimori's company; designed 1961 Murai stool (so called for her maiden name) by Tendo Mokko; 1967, established the studio Tanabe Reiko Design for architecture and the interior design of offices, hospitals, and houses.
Citations Prize in 1961 (1st) Tendo Mokko wood-furniture-design competition (for Murai stool, resulting in its production).

Tanzi, 'Pepe' Giuseppe (1945–)

Italian designer; born and active Monza; active Milan.

Training 1969, architecture, Politecnico, Milan.
Biography Tanzi has designed domestic products, publications, residences, offices, showrooms, and exhibitions/fair stands, including T.O.M. (Twinboard Over Marine) ultra-light carbon-fiber sailboat by Mako Shark. Other clients: Album (all lighting and furniture from 1987), Bernini, Biesse (all products 1971–91 and others from 1991), Boffi (1985 Grand Chef kitchen), Compagnia del Mobile/FEG, Driade (1978–80 Gabbialibera kitchen), Graepel (P.U.B., Prime Utility Box), R.O.K. (Roaming outdoor kitchen), Slurp, R.O.M. (Roll-On module stainless-steel objects), I.F.T., Matteograssi (seating), Pizzitutti (wooden products), Poliform/Varenna (1999 Planet kitchen), Pozzi & Berga, Proserpio (furniture for children from 1986), Zanotta (1989 Phi bookshelf).

Bibliography Gabriele Lueg and Peter Pfeifer, *Halogen. 20 Jahres Neues Licht*, Laupheim: Novus, 1991. Flavio Conti, *Gigi e Pepe Tanzi*, Milan: Rima, 1992. Mel Byars, *50 Products...*, Hove: RotoVision, 1998.

Tapiovaara, Ilmari (1914–1999)
Finnish interior and furniture designer.

Training To 1937, industrial and interior design, Taideteollisuuskeskuskoulu, Helsinki.
Biography 1935–36, Tapiovaara worked for Alvar Aalto in the Artek office in London; 1937, for Le Corbusier in Paris; 1952–53, for Ludwig Mies van der Rohe in Chicago. 1940s–50s, he pioneered knock-down furniture design; was a Functionalist, who approached construction so that it can be readily revealed; 1938–41, was the artistic director, Askon Tehtaat company; 1941–51, the founder and artistic and managing director, Keravan Puuteollisuus cabinetwork factory in Kerava; 1944–45, board member, Ornamo (Finnish association of designers); 1950 with his wife Annikki Tapiovaara, established a design office; 1950–52, department head, Taideteollinen korkeakoulu, Helsinki; 1952–53, assistant professor, Illinois Institute of Design (IID), Chicago. As an expert consultant: 1959–60, International Labor Organization (ILO) in Paraguay; 1964, World Council of Churches (WCC) in Geneva and Moscow; United Nations Industrial Development Organization (UNIDO) in Mauritius 1974 and 1975, Egypt 1974, Yugoslavia 1976 and 1977. 1965–69, was a visiting lecturer in interior design, Teknillinen korkeakoulu (TKK), Helsinki; 1968–71, member, Valtion Taideteollisuustoimikunnan Jäsen (state committee of industrial art). He became a versatile designer of furniture, carpets, lighting, glassware, stainless-steel cutlery, toys, and interiors. Products: Lukki I stacking chair by Lukkiseppo in Rekola (designated the 'universal chair'; for 1952 Olivetti showroom in Helsinki); 1946 Domus side and armchair by Keravan Puuteollisuus (imported by Knoll to the US); 1955 Fanett, 1958 Aslak, 1958 Mademoiselle, and 1962 Charlotte chairs by Asko; 1959 Wilhelmiina chair by Wilh. Schauman; Polar cutlery by Hackman; 1972–74 radio and stereo equipment by Centrum; 1972–74 color-planning program for paint manufacturer Winter; wall paintings and tapestries. His 1970s stabile constructions were installed in Udine, Italy; Quatre Bornes, Mauritius; and Rauma-Repola, Finland. Interior-design work included 1947 Domus Academica, Helsinki; 1951 Teekkarikylä (technology students' campus), Otaniemi, Espoo; 1957 Lauttasaaren Kirkko (Lauttasaari church), Helsinki; 1961 Hotel Marski, Helsinki; 1967 concert hall (main furnishings) in Leningrad (now St. Petersburg); Finnish pavilion, *Expo '67*, Montréal; 1960s interiors of Finnair airplanes; 1971 Intercontinental Hotel restaurant and ballroom, Helsinki.
Exhibitions/citations Work included in 1968 *Les Assises du Siège Contemporain*, Musée des Arts Décoratifs, Paris; 1970 *Modern Chairs 1918–1970*, Whitechapel Gallery, London (catalogs below). Work subject of exhibitions in Helsinki, 1949; Chicago, 1952; Stockholm, 1961; Buenos Aires, 1964. 1948 *International Competition for Low Cost Furniture Design* (knock-down fabric or leather chair) and 1950 *Good Design* exhibitions/awards, both The Museum of Modern Art, New York; 1953–57 (three first prizes), Corso Internazionale del Mobile, Cantù; 1951 (9th), 1954 (10th), 1957 (11th), 1960 (12th), 1964 (13th) editions of Triennale di Milano (six gold medals); 1963 prize, American Institute of Decorators (AID); 1963 Corso Internazionale del Mobile (first prize), Mariano Comense. 1959 Pro Finlandia prize; 1969, elected Honorary Royal Designer for Industry, UK; 1971 Valtion Taideteollisuuspalkinto (Finnish state award); 1986 prize, Suomen Kulttuurirahaston Palkinto (Finnish culture foundation); 1986, elected honoray member Sisustusarkkitehdit (SIO, Finnish association of interior architects); 1990 furniture prize, SIO.
Bibliography Benedict Zilliacus, *Finnish Designer*, Helsinki: 1954. Cat., *Les assises du siège contemporain*, Paris: Musée des Arts Décoratifs, 1968. Cat., *Modern Chairs 1918–1970*, London: Lund Humphries, 1971. Ilmari Tapiovaara: 'The Idea Was more Important than the Product,' *Form Function Finland*, 1983: 17–19. Jarno Peltonen, *Ilmari Tapiovaara: sisustusarkkitehti = Inredningsarkitekt = Interior Architect*, Helsinki: Taideteollisuusmuseo, 1984. Pilar Cós (ed.), Pekka Korvenmaa (text), *Ilmari Tapiovaara*, Barcelona: Santa & Cole, 1997.

Tarazi, Ezri (1962–)
Israeli designer and teacher; born Jerusalem.

Training 1986–90, Department of Industrial Design, Bezalel Academy of Art and Design, Jerusalem.
Biography From 1986 as a major in the Israeli Defense Forces reserves, Tarazi has been a coordinator of instructors' education for leadership in the Maritime Academy, Israeli Navy; 1986–89, a coordinator of social programs for handicapped youth, ALIN Hospital, Jerusalem; 1990–96, was project manager of industrial-design projects, DEA R&D, Jerusalem; 1993–98, freelance industrial designer; 1993–95, Tarazi was a member of the academic board and, from 1996, the director, Department of Industrial Design, Bezalel Academy; 1998–2000, partner at IDEO Israel (an affiliate of IDEO California); from 2000, founded and is CEO of Design Cells Israel. Wide range and large quantity of work has included 1990 computerized scanning system for Chinese-language word processor by Telemond, 1991 satellite navigation instrument and map by Azimuth, 1993 user interface of an optical archiving system by Imaging, 1994 home/office furniture elements by Haargaz, 1995 cooling clothing for Dead Sea Company workers by Bezalel Mop; 1996 office equipment, headquarters interiors, furniture, and work stations by Bezek, 1997 medical instruments and interface by Oridion Ergonomic Research, 1998 automobile satellite navigation instrument by Tadiran Systems, 2000 video-conferencing device (at IDEO) by Vicon, 2000–01 insulin patch (at IDEO) by Transdermics, 2000–01 Bluetooth-technology digital pen (at IDEO) by Go-Light, 2002 classroom design with PAMD syndrome, 2002 watch by MR Planet, 2002 ID programs for Maps and for Sonarics digital radio, 2002 Gemini-platform machine by Sagitta; others. From 1992, has written on design for a number of publications, including regularly for *Ha'aretz* newspaper.
Exhibitions/citations From 1996, work included in numerous exhibitions, including 2001 and 2002 *Industrious Design: Young Israeli Designers*, Abitare il Tempo fair, Verona. Subject of 2001 *Melting into the Unseen*, Periscope gallery, Tel Aviv; 2002 *Atoms of Colour*, Tel Aviv; 2002 *Re-Flex*, Bunker 325 gallery, Copenhagen; 2002 *Skinlamps*, Orian gallery, Ramat Hasharon, Israel. Received 1990 Sapir prize (industrial design); 1999–2000 entry, *Capturing Time: The New York Times Capsule Competition*, American Museum of Natural History, New York; 2002 Ministry of Culture and Science prize for Industrial Design, Israel.
Bibliography G. Urian, *From the Israel Museum to the Carmel Market: Israeli Design*, Ramat-Hasharon: *Urian: The Architect's Encyclopedia*, 2001. Cat., V. Pasca and E. Rozenberg, *Industrious Designers, Giovani designer israeliani*, Verona: Abitare il Tempo, 2001, 2002. Mel Byars, *Design in Steel*, London: Laurence King, 2002.

Tatlin, Vladimir Evgrafovich (1885–1953)
Russian artist; born Kharkov.

Training 1902–04, Moscow Institute for Painting, Sculpture and Architecture; 1904–09, Penza Art School; 1909–10 under Konstantin Korovin, Valentin Serov, and others, again Moscow Institute for Painting, Sculpture and Architecture.
Biography From 1908, Tatlin was associated with painters Mikhail Larionov and Natal'ia Goncharova; from 1911, became associated with Kazimir Malevich; designed costumes for folk operas *The Emperor Maximilian and his Disobedient Son, Adolf* (1911) produced in Moscow and the unrealized *A Life for the Czar* (1913); c. 1912, became preoccupied with structural composition and Russian icons and folk art. 1913, he traveled to Paris and met Pablo Picasso, a source of inspiration for his Painterly Reliefs; from 1914, worked on his Counter Reliefs and became close to Aleksei Grishchenko, Aleksei Morgunov, Liubov' Popova, Nadezhda Udal'tsova, and Aleksandr Vesnin. Tatlin collaborated to a minor degree with Aleksandr Rodchenko and Georgii Yakulov on the Dada-Constructivist furnishings for 1917 Café Pittoresque, Moscow, under Yakulov's guidance. From 1918, Tatlin was the head, Moscow IZO NKP (fine-art department of Narkompros); 1919–20, the director, painting department, SVOMAS/VKhUTEMAS, Moscow; worked in Petrograd on his most famous work, 1918 264" (675 cm) maquette of the *Monument to the Third International* (a spiral iron frame that supports a glass cube, cylinder, and cone, each rotating separately), shown in Moscow and Petrograd. Tatlin wished the *Monument* to unite pure art with utility, intended it to be 1,310 ft. (400 m.) high and placed over the River Neva in Petrograd. 1919 or 1921, he settled in Petrograd; as a pioneer of the Constructivist school in Russia, established a studio to pursue work focusing on 'volume, material and construction'; 1921, became the head, department of sculpture, reorganized Academy of Arts, Petrograd; designed directed, and starred in the 1923 stage production of Velimir Khlebnikov's Futurist poem/spectacle/play *Zangezi: A Supersaga in Twenty Planes* (one of the author's famous zaum works, Moscow: Tipo-lit., 1922) at INKhUK, Petrograd. 1923–24, Tatlin attempted to reform design, especially for clothing and ovens; from this time, was interested in practical design and attempted to apply engineering techniques to the construction of sculpture; 1925–27, taught courses in the 'culture of materials,' the theater and cinema section, NKP, Kiev; 1927, began

teaching woodwork, metalwork, and ceramics, VKhUTEIN, Moscow. 1927 with N.N. Rogzhin, Tatlin designed a cantilevered bentwood chair with a molded seat and supporting back legs, and also created milk-jug containers in a hand-sculpted form. Both appear to have been influenced by a similar Bauhaus language. After working on his 1929–32 Letatlin human-powered glider, he returned to painting, adopting a figurative style; after 1933 and through 1940s, worked primarily as a theater designer; died in Moscow.
Exhibitions Work included in Izdebskii's 1911 (2nd) Salon in Odessa; 1911 Union of Youth exhibition; 1911 *Contemporary Painting*, Moscow; Larionov's *Donkey's Tail* exhibition; 1912 Union of Youth exhibition; 1912 *Contemporary Painting*, Moscow; 1913 exhibition of Bubnovy Valet (Jack of Diamonds), Moscow and St. Petersburg, then to Berlin and Paris; one-person 1914 Moscow exhibition; 1915 *Tramway V* (seven Painterly Reliefs as above, influenced by Picasso's reliefs); 1915 *Exhibition of Painting*; 1915–16 *0–10*; 1922 *Erste Russische Kunstausstellung*, Berlin. He organized his own 1916 *The Store* exhibition, which included the three-dimensional works of Lev Bruni and Sofia Dymshits-Tol'staia. Tatlin's *Monument* was shown at 1920 (8th) Congress of the Soviets; canvases entirely in pink in 1922 *Union of New Trends in Art*, Museum of Artistic Culture, Petrograd; 1981 *Configuration 1910–1940 and Seven Tatlin Reconstructions*, Annely Juda Fine Art, London; 1993 *Vladimir Tatlin, Retrospektive*, Städtische Kunsthalle, Düsseldorf.
Bibliography Levana Mizrahi, *Vladimir Tatline: Chronologie, Expositions, Bibliographie*, Nanterre: Université Paris X, 1970. John Milner, *Vladimir Tatlin and the Russian Avant-Garde*, New Haven: Yale, 1983. Cat., *Der Kragstuhl*, Stuhlmuseum Burg Beverungen, Berlin: Alexander, 1986: 139. Larissa Alekseevna Zhadova (ed.), *Tatlin*, New York: Rizzoli, 1988. S.O. Khan-Magomedov, *Vhutemas: Moscou, 1920–1930*, Paris: Regard, 1990. Cat., *The Great Utopia: The Russian and Soviet Avant-Garde, 1915–1932*, New York: Guggenheim Museum, 1992. Michèle Ray-Gavras, *Tatlin e la cultura del Vchutemas: 1885–1953, 1920–1930*, Rome: Officina, 1992. Jürgen Harten (ed.), *Vladimir Tatlin: Leben, Werk, Wirkung: Ein Internationales Symposium = Tatlin*, Cologne: DuMont, 1993. Nikolai Nikolaevich Punin, *O Tatline/N. Punin*, Moscow: Literaturno-khudozh, 1994.

Tatra automobile
> See Ledwinka, Hans.

Tattersfield, Brian (1934–)
> See Minale, Marcello.

Távora, Manuel (1973–)

Portuguese designer; active London.

Training 1992–98, product design, Faculdade de Arquitectura da Universidade Técnica, Lisbon; 1998–97, postgraduate, industrial design, Glasgow School of Art/Centro Português de Design (GSA/CPD) program.
Biography Távora has worked for: 1998–99, Pedro Silva Dias Associados (product design and street furniture), Lisbon; 1999, Michael Marriott (exhibition and product design), London; 1999–2000, Maisdesign (graphics, product and industrial design), Lisbon; 2000–01, Eames Office (exhibition design and graphics), Los Angeles; 2001, Filipe Alarcão Design Studio (Porto 2001 street lamp), Lisbon; 2002, Ron Arad Associates (garden chair by Serralunga and barware by Alessi), London. Independently: fashion illustrations; brushes by Die Imaginäre Manufaktur (DIM), public seating, home-office system, and Funil lighting by Resoflex, and others; for Rede Ferroviária Nacional (REFER, Portugese railway company).
Exhibitions/citation Work included in 1998 (1st) Biennale Internationale du Design, Saint-Étienne, France; *Melting Point*, CPD/ExperimentaDesign '99, Lisbon; 2000 Portuguese Design stand, Salone del Mobile, Milan. Received special prize, Smart Scotland trophy design competition, Glasgow School of Art (GSA)/Scottish office, Glasgow.

Tayar, Ali (1959–)

Turkish architect and designer; born Istanbul; active New York.

Training Architecture, Massachusetts Institute of Technology (MIT), Cambridge, Mass.; Universität Stuttgart.
Biography 1992, Tayar established the Parallel Design Partnership, New York, and began designing products and interiors. Work includes 1994 NEA table (recycled molded MDF, cast aluminum, and glass), 2001 Rasamny indoor/outdoor folding chair, 1998–99 Plaza screen (with Atilla Rona), and Ellen's Brackets system (originally for a client named Ellen) by ICF. The screen was originally commissioned for Plaza hotel (architect, Morris Lapidus), Washington, D.C. He designed Gainsevoort Gallery, Waterloo Brasserie, and Pop restaurant (all New York); numerous other interiors. Lectured and taught, Illinois Institute of Technology, Chicago; MIT; City University of New York; University of Pennsylvania, Philadelphia; Columbia University, New York.
Exhibitions/citations 1995 *Mutant Materials* (Ellen's Brackets system) and 2001 *Workspheres* (Plaza screen), both The Museum of Modern Art, New York, and touring; 2000 *Aluminum by Design*, touring the US (catalogs below). Received 1994–98 awards, Annual Design Review, *I.D.* magazine; 1999 Editor's Award, International Contemporary Furniture Fair (ICFF), New York; 2000 *Good Design* award, Chicago Athenaeum; 2001 Best of *Interior Design* magazine.
Bibliography Cat., Paola Antonelli, *Mutant Materials in Contemporary Design*, New York: The Museum of Modern Art/Abrams, 1995. Cat., Sarah Nichols et al., *Aluminum by Design*, Pittsburgh: Carnegie Art Museum, 2000. Cat., Paola Antonelli, *Workspheres*, New York: The Museum of Modern Art, 2001. Wang Hanbai, *Design Focus: Ali Tayar*, Beijing: China Youth, 2001. Cat., R. Craig Miller (intro.), *U.S. Design 1975–2000*, Munich: Prestel, 2002.

Taylor, Gerard (1955–)

British designer; active London.

Training Glasgow School of Design; 1981, master's degree, Royal College of Art, London.
Biography From early 1980s, Taylor worked for five years in the studio of Ettore Sottsass in Milan on projects, including Esprit shops and the Memphis group's second (1982) collection, including Piccadilly lamp, and subsequent collections; 1985, became associated with Daniel Weil in London. From 1990s, work has included office systems by Skandinavisk; seating by Giroflex; retail-store concepts for Habitat, Germany, and Selfridges, UK; jewelry by Acme Studio; Wave chair and 1999 Pause club chair by Bernhardt; private residences in England and France. Other clients: Driade, Yamagiwa, Knoll, Alessi.
Bibliography Cat., *Londres, images et objets du nouveau design*, Paris: CCI/Centre Georges Pompidou, 1990. *Acquisitions 1982–1990 arts décoratifs*, Paris: Fond National d'Art Contemporain, 1991.

Taylor, Michael (1927–1986)

American interior and furniture designer; born Modesto, Cal; active San Francisco.

Training Rudolf Schaeffer School of Interior Design, San Francisco.
Biography From 1952, Taylor was a partner of Frances Milhailoff Elkins in San Francisco; 1956, established his own practice with initial clients, including Maryon Lewis and her father, Ralph Davies. Taylor frequently used logs and wicker in his furniture designs and natural stone in his sophisticated beige-on-beige interiors. His early work was influenced by Elkins and Syrie Maugham, a champion of spaces all in white. Many Taylor clients were people in show business, society, and fashion, including Gorham and Diana Knowles, Maryon Davies Lewis, Nan Kempner, Douglas S. Cramer, Steve Martin, Donald Bren, Martha Hyer, and Hal Wallis. Some California projects were the Norton Simon and Jennifer Jones house in Malibu, the John and Frances Bowes house (architect, Bernard Maybeck), architect John Lautner's house in Malibu, and Jimmy Wilson's house in Arizona. Typical designs featured ball-shaped pillows (derived from ancient China). He is credited with rediscovering the lamps and furniture of Diego Giacometti. His own work was frequently copied. Taylor had established a retail shop on Sutter Street, San Francisco and, 1985 with Paul Weaver, Michael Taylor Designs Inc. but, deeply in debt, died shortly after from Aids. Paul Weaver, after ten years at the McGuire Company, where he had become the vice-president of marketing, has continued the Taylor enterprise, marketing Taylor-manner furniture and furnishings.
Bibliography Mary Chesterfield, 'California Classics,' *Elle Decor*, winter 1990: 30, 32. Dorothea Walker, 'Taylor-Made,' *House and Garden*, vol. 163, no. 2, Feb. 1991. Mark Hampton, *The Legendary Decorators of the Twentieth Century*, New York: Doubleday, 1992.

Taylor, William Howson (1876–1935)
> See Ruskin Pottery.

Teague, Walter Dorwin Jr. (1910–)

American industrial designer; born Garden City, N.Y.; son of Walter Dorwin Teague Sr.

Training 1928–31, Massachusetts Institute of Technology (MIT), Cambridge, Mass.

Biography 1935–42, Teague the younger was head of product design at his father's design firm in New York; preferred, due to the familial connection, to be called W. Dorwin Teague; designed the widely published c. 1939 desk lamp by Polaroid with its overhanging Bakelite hood on a spun-aluminum stem (sometimes wrongly credited to Dorwin Associates employee Frank Del Guidice), and 1931 Marmon 16 and 1932 Marmon 12 automobile bodies. 1942–52, he was the head, research engineering department, Bendix Aviation, Teterboro, N.J.; 1952–67, a partner, Walter Dorwin Teague Associates, New York; from 1967, president, Dorwin Teague, Nyack, N.Y. His clients included A.B. Dick, Boeing, Bristol Myers, Caterpillar Tractor, Corning Glass Works, Dresser Industries, Du Pont, Ford, Montgomery Ward, National Cash Register, Pearson Boat, Remington Arms, Ritter Dental, Sears Roebuck, Steinway, Tappan, U.S. Atomic Energy Commission, and Volkswagen of America. Over 90 patents were assigned to him. He wrote many articles and an autobiography (see below); designed several hundred products including sports equipment, chairs, tables, settees, folding beds, boats, ski bindings, vacuum cleaners, bicycles, cash registers, glassware, radios, telephones, cameras, packaging, aircraft accessories, automobiles, buildings in Austria, Yugoslavia, and the U.S., and featured in exhibitions in seven countries.
Citations 1960 (10th) Annual Industrial Design Award; 1969 American Iron and Steel Award, best consumer product; 1969 IDSA Design Review Award; 1980 Pioneer Award for Advancement of Space Exploration Through Rocket Pioneering, the American Institute of Aeronautics and Astronautics; 1980, honorary member (for Marmon 16 automobile), Classic Car Club of America; 1952, associate fellow, American Institute of Aeronautics and Astronautics.
Bibliography W. Dorwin Teague, *Industrial Designer: The Artist as Engineer*, Lancaster, Pa.: Armstrong World Industries, 1998.

Teague, Walter Dorwin Sr. (1883–1960)

American industrial designer; born Decatur, Ind.; son of a Methodist circuit-riding minister; father of Walter Dorwin Teague Jr.

Training Art Students League, New York.
Biography 1903, Teague the elder settled in New York; was a sign painter and mail-order-catalog illustrator; from 1908, worked in the art department, Calkins and Holden advertising agency; 1910s, studied 19th-century French culture, resulting in an affection for neoclassical forms; 1911, opened his own studio, specializing in book design and advertisements, including illustrations for Community Plate and Phoenix Hosiery campaigns; may have shared offices with typographers Bruce Rogers (1870–1957) and Frederic Goudy (1865–1947); became one of the founders of Pynson Printers; mid-1920s, expanded his range, designing piano cases for Steinway and packaging for consumer goods. His first major client was Eastman Kodak. Mid-1930s, he became one of the small coterie of highly paid American industrial designers. His studio's design work included 1930s car bodies by Marmon, 1932–34 crystal by Steuben (including a bowl series incorporating an adaptation of the classical *cyma recta* motif), radios by Sparton Corp. (1934 Bluebird 506, 1935 Bluebird 504, 1935 Nocturne 1186 console, 1937 'Sled' 558), 1936 Baby Brownie and 1936 Bantam Special cameras by Kodak, 1937 Ford showroom in New York, Texaco service stations, New Haven Railroad Pullman coaches, and 1952 Scripto pen. 1932, was commissioned by Corning Glass Works president Amory Houghton to help improve the firm's Depression-hit sales; on large kitchen appliances, eliminated the clumsy apron at the foot and dropped the machinery into the legs; wrote the book *Design This Day: The Technique of Order in the Machine Age* (New York: Harcourt, Brace, 1940/1949); was profoundly influenced by Le Corbusier, argued that geometry rules all design, and analyzed the Parthenon as a paradigm of good design; designed Boeing 707 (1958) and 727 (1964) airplane interiors with Frank Del Guidice (d. 1993) (Teague's 1972 successor in the Teague studio to end of 1970s). Like Raymond Loewy and other important industrial designers, Teague was not personally involved with every project undertaken by his office but, as one of the 'Big Four' (with Loewy, Bel Geddes, Henry Dreyfuss), was an intellectual, reading Shakespeare on the train to work and writing novels. Teague died in Flemington, N.J. Still active today, Walter Dorwin Teague Associates is a large corporation with headquarters in Redmond, Wash.
Exhibitions The office work of Teague Sr. included in 1934 *Pacific International Exposition*, San Diego, and designed 1932 *Design for the Machine* exhibition, Philadelphia Museum of Art. Teague was head of the design committee, 1939–40 *New York World's Fair: The World of Tomorrow*, and designed many exhibitions, including those of Ford, Du Pont (with Robert J. Harper and A.M. Erikson), and National Cash

Walter Dorwin Teague Sr. Vase. 1932. Glass, h. 10 1/8" x dia. 11" ((25.7 x 28 cm). Mfr.: Corning Glass Works, Steuben Division, US. (c. 1932–34). Gift of the manufacturer. MoMA.

Register, which was an enormous replica of a cash register that showed the Fair's attendance figures. For the State Dining Room, Federal Building there, designed 1939 Modern American Line: Embassy stemware (with Edwin W. Fuerst) by Libbey Glass Co. Work included in 2000–02 *American Modern, 1925–1940: Design for a New Age*, touring the US, organized by American Federation of the Arts. 1951, elected Honorary Royal Designer for Industry, UK.
Bibliography Mary Siff, 'A Realist in Industrial Design,' *Arts and Decoration*, Oct. 1934: 46–47. Jeffrey L. Meikle, *Twentieth Century Limited: Industrial Design in America, 1925–1939*, Philadelphia: Temple University, 1979: 43–46. Charles Dalton Olson, 'Sign of the Star: Walter Dorwin Teague and the Texas Company, 1934–1937,' degree thesis, Ithaca, N.Y.: Cornell University, 1987. Clarence P. Hornung (ed.), *The Advertising Designs of Walter Dorwin Teague*, New York: Art Direction, 1991. Roland Marchand, 'Walter Dorwin Teague and the Professionalization of Corporate Industrial Exhibits, 1933–1940,' and Ellen Mazur Thomson, 'The Designers Go to the Fair, I: Walter Dorwin Teague and the Professionalization of Corporate Industrial Exhibits, 1933-1940,' in Dennis P. Doordan (ed.), *Design History: An Anthology*, Cambridge: MIT, 1995.

Tébong
> See Domingo, Alain.

Technics
> See Panasonic.

Tecno

Italian furniture manufacturer.

History 1954, with brother Fulgenzio Borsani, designer Osvaldo Borsani established the furniture company Tecno, which evolved from Atelier Varedo, their father's workshop in Varedo, and from the subsequently established small firm Arredamento Borsani. Among other models, Tecno produced Osvaldo Borsani's successful 1953 P40 recliner with 40 positions, 1953 D70 chair, 1962 P32 club chair with a wire base, and, more recently, Foster and Associates' 1986 Nomos table range and office system, and Mario and Claudio Bellini's 1993 Extra Dry (by Marcatré), and Crinion Associates' Compas office systems. Other recent commissioned designers: Richard Rogers, Emilio Ambasz, Gae Aulenti, Ricardo Bofill, Jean-Michel Wilmotte, Luca Scacchetti, Eugenio Gerli, and Renzo Piano. 1996, Tecno acquired the trademark and licence to produce and sell some Marcatré products.
Citations 1996 Goed Industrieel Ontwerp (for Extra Dry), Stichting Goed Industrieel Ontwerp, Amsterdam.
Bibliography Cat., *Modern Chairs 1918–1970*, London: Lund Humphries, 1971. Charlotte and Peter Fiell, *Modern Furniture Classics Since 1945*, London: Thames & Hudson, 1991. Mel Byars with Arlette Barré-Despond, *100 Designs/100 Years: A Celebration of the 20th Century*, Hove: RotoVision, 1999. www.tecnospa.com.
> See Borsani, Osvaldo.

Teco
> See Gates Potteries, The.

Tecta

Furniture manufacture; located Lauenförde.

History 1956, Hans Könecke founded Tecta, taken over by Axel and Werner Bruchhäuser in 1972 and, subsequently, began producing reproductions of original Bauhaus designs and the work of Jean Prouvé, Maximilian Seitz, Alison and Peter Smithson, and Stefan Wewerka; 1982, Tecta founded the Stuhlmuseum Burg Beverunge. Licensed furniture reproductions (through the Bauhaus and also Cassina i Maestri) include the work of Ludwig Mies van der Rohe, El Lissitsky, Gerrit Rietveld, Marcel Breuer, Erich Brendel, as well as Peter Keler's legendary 1922 cradle and George Carwardine's 1931–32 Anglepoise desk lamp, and models by Stefan Wewerka and the Smithsons. Breuer's 1926 B 40 side chair features the original-type industrial lathe-belt fabric (Eisengarn or 'iron yarn'). From 1990 to his death in 2003, Peter Smithson designed the Tecta-Landscape buidling complex and 2003 Kragstuhlmuseum/Tecta-Archiv.
Bibliography http://cgi.tecta.de.

Tedioli, Giorgio (1947–)

Italian industrial designer; born Casalbuttano; active Anzano del Parco.

Training Liceo Artistico di Brera, Milan.
Biography 1968, Tedioli began his professional career at domestic-appliance manufacturer Candy, for which he designed a 1970 air-conditioner (with Joe Columbo). From 1971, Tedioli's clients have included Giogenzana Style, Prima, Fonderie Toni, and Fondomini. He became a member, Associazione per il Disegno Industriale (ADI).
Bibliography *ADI Annual 1976*, Milan: Associazione per il Disegno Industriale, 1976.

Tefal
> See Grégoire, Marc.

Teige, Karel (1900–1951)

Czech art critic, paintor, typographic artist, and collaglst; born Prague.

Training Art history, Univerzity Karlovy (Charles university), Prague.
Biography Teige was a leading figure in Czech art and architecture between the World Wars. He wrote on art and was the editor of several avant-garde magazines, including *Disk*, *Stavba*, and *ReD*; 1923, fused art and poetry and produced the new medium of Pictorial Poems; was influenced by Soviet Constructivism and espoused 'proletarian' art; 1929, delivered a presentation at the Bauhaus, Dessau, on new forms in Czech art and was invited by Bauhaus director Hannes Meyer to organize conferences on the theme 'sociology and architecture,' a summary of which appeared in 1929 in *ReD*. Teige later specialized in typography, photomontage, and stage design, and his photomontage book covers, posters and typography were noteworthy. 1935–41, he turned to Surrealism and created complex collages based on the metamorphosis of the female body.
Exhibitions In first (early 1920s) Devětsil exhibitions (pictures and paintings in a Cubist style). Photomontage book covers, typography, and posters included in numerous avant-garde European exhibitions. Subject of 1994 *Karel Teige, 1900–1951*, Galerie Hlavního Mesta, Prague; from 2000, *Dreams and Disillusion: Karel Teige and the Czech Avant-Garde*, touring the US (first Teige appearance in the US), organized by Wolfsonian Foundation/FIU, Miami; 2000 *Karel Teige: Avant-Garde Typography and Surrealist Collage*, Czech Centre, London.
Bibliography Růžena Hamanová, *Karel Teige, 1900–1951*, Prague: Literární archív Památníku národního písemnictví, 1968. Karel Teige, *Osvobozování zivotz a poezie: studie ze čyřicátychlet*, Prague: Aurora, 1993. Eric Dluhosch and Rostislav Švácha, *Karel Teige, 1900–1951: L'Enfant Terrible of the Czech Modernist Avant-Garde*, Cambridge: MIT, 1999.

Teinitzerová-Hoppeová, Marie (1879–1960)

Czech textile artist and producer; born Čížkov u Pelhřimova.

Training Painting in Vienna and Brno; 1905–06, Vysoká Škola Uměleckoprůmyslová (VŠUP, school of arts and architecture), Prague; 1906, Weaving School, Berlin.
Biography Teinitzerová was a cofounder of the Artěl Cooperative; 1910, established own textile studio in Jindřichův Hradec; 1911–60, created a number of monumental tapestries, primarily designed by painters and was most fruitful collaborating with František Kysela; designed upholstery materials and designed/produced handmade textiles for domestic furnishings as well as for women's clothing; collaborated with Czech Cubist architects; prepared most of the natural fibers she used and devised new weaving techniques.
Exhibitions/citations Grand prize (for The Crafts tapestry), 1925 *Exposition Internationale des Arts Décoratifs et Industriels Modernes*, Paris. *The Czech Linen* (designed by Karl Putz, made by Teinitzerová) shown at 1939–40 *New York World's Fair: The World of Tomorrow*.
Bibliography Alena Adlerová, *České užité umění 1918–1938*, Odeon: 1983. Dagmar Blümlová, *Sto tváří z jihočeské kulturní historie*, Pelhřimov: Nová tiskárna, 2000.

Teixidó Sabater, Gabriel (1947–)

Spanish designer; born Barcelona.

Training 1964–69, Llotja Escola Superior d'Arts Plàstiqes i Disseny, Barcelona.
Biography Teixidó specializes in the design of furniture and lighting for a large number of clients; 1996, collaborated with Eina (Escola de Desseny i Art), Barcelona; 1998, member of the board, ADI/FAD (industrial-design and decorative-arts associations), Spain.
Citations 1986 Premio APECMO (career award); 1987 Nuevo Estilo Prize (Calando sofa by Tagano); 1987 prize (Columba lamp), Selección Internacional de Diseño de Equipamiento para el Hábitat (SIDI), Barcelona; 1988 Consell de Cambres de Catalunya Prize (Lavoro 2 office); 1995 Top Ten European design award (Tabu armchair), Cologne; 1992 and 1997 Delta award and 1997 selections of ADI/FAD (industrial-design and decorative-arts associations).
Bibliography Cat., *JAL Design 1989–1990: The Emerging Design*, Barcelona: Plural, 1990.

Tell, Åke (1926–2003)

Swedish architect and designer.

Biography Tell worked as the manager, public-spaces department, office of Sven Kai-Larsen; 1975, cofounded his own studio Darelius & Tell interior design; designed furniture, including a 1994 armchair, 1995 stool/settle, and 1996 conference table in the Fuga range by Offecct; 1997 Katell club chair and 1999 Katell armchair by Karl Andersson & Sön; and by others. He was a member of the association of Inredningsarkitekt (SIR) and Föreningen Svenska Industridesigner (SID, Swedish interior architect association).
Citation 1996 Utmärkt Svensk Form (outstanding Swedish design for Fuga chair).

Telnack, Jack (1937–)

American automobile designer; born Detroit, Mich.

Training To 1958, Art Center College of Design, Pasadena, Cal.
Biography Telnack's father worked in the Ford Motor Company plant. From 1958, Telnack was a designer at Ford, where he worked on the 1961 Ford Galaxy and created a number of important body-design milestones, including contributing to the first (1964) Ford Mustang; was eventually promoted to vice-president of design at Ford; became effective in creating a new, cutting-edge image for the firm; active in Europe, also contributed to the aerodynamics of the popular 1982 Ford Sierra, 1986 Ford Taurus, and Taurus's brother, Mercury 1986 Sable. J. Mays assumed his position at Ford and in 1998, after almost 40 years at Ford, Telnack retired to Florida.

J. and J.S. Templeton

British textile manufacturer; located Glasgow.

History 1839, J. and J.S. Templeton was founded to make chenille, Axminster, and Brussels carpets; commissioned designs by Walter Crane, Lewis F. Day, C.F.A. Voysey, Bruce Talbert, and the Silver Exhibition Society; 1860s–86, produced a series of portières (intricate hangings woven in a Jacquard pattern), many of which may have been designed by Talbert.
Bibliography Cat., The Fine Art Society in Association with Francesca Galloway, *Arts & Crafts Textiles in Britain*, London: Fine Art Gallery, [n.d.]: no. 14.

Tenisheva, Kniaginia Mariia Klavdievna (b. Maria Pyatkovskaia 1867–1929)

Russian patroness of the arts and founder of art schools and workshops; born Smolensk; died Paris.

Biography 1892, her second marriage to Prince Vyacheslav Tenishev gave her great wealth, allowing her to engage in cultural enterprises.

1894, the Kniaginia (princess) established the Tenisheva School, attendance offered free in her St. Petersburg mansion for art students preparing to enter the Imperial Academy of Fine Arts. 1895–98, the school was directed by Il'ia Repin and was attended by, among others, Ivan Bilibin, Sergei Chekhonin, and Zinaida Serebriakova. Tenisheva established a similar school in Talashkino, near Smolensk. 1904, both closed. 1897, she presented part of her collection of drawings and watercolors to the recently opened Russian Museum, St. Petersburg; 1898, contributed half the cost of publishing the journal *Mir Iskusstva* (the world of art) to the museum. But her most important contribution was to the revival and propagation of traditional Russian design, particularly peasant arts and crafts. 1893, her husband bought the Talashkino estate near Smolensk, where she organized what was to become an important center for studying and reviving the traditions of Russian applied arts. Artists of different persuasions were active there, experimenting with new ways to develop the arts and contributing to church buildings, religious art, wood carving, and neo-Russian interior design elsewhere in Russia. Tenisheva reorganized an existing peasant school and created workshops for carpentry and woodwork, for ceramics, and for embroidery. She also opened a shop, The Spring, in Moscow to sell the items produced in the workshops. The originality of the Talashkino products was closely bound to the deliberately archaic and stylized work of Sergei Malyutin (1859–1937), who directed the wood-carving workshop from 1900–03. The unique creative atmosphere that existed at Talashkino attracted many artists. And it was there, for instance, that Nikolai Roerich and Igor Stravinsky created the controversial ballet score *Le sacre du printemps* (1913). Tenisheva was one of the financial backers of Sergei Diaghilev's Ballets Russes; yet made her most enduring contribution when she built and endowed a museum of rare, antique Russian artifacts—today, the Smolensk Artistic Gallery on Tenisheva Street, one of the best regional museums in Russia. 1917, she moved to Paris.
Bibliography Nicolas Roerich, *Talachkino: l'art décoratif des ateliers Tenichef*, St. Petersburg: Sodrougestvo, 1906. Maria K. Tenisheva, *Vpechatleniia moei zhizni*, Leningrad: Iskusstvo, 1931/1991). John E. Bowlt, 'Two Russian Maecenases: Savva Mamontov and Princess Tenisheva,' *Apollo*, Dec. 1973. Mikhail Dunaev, *Smolensk: A Guide*, Moscow: Progress, 1982. L. Zhuravleva, *Kniaginia Mariia Teni-sheva*, Smolensk: Poligramma, 1994.

Terragni, Giuseppe (1904–1943)

Italian architect; born Meda.

Training 1917–21, technical school, Como; 1921–26, Politecnico, Milan.
Biography 1927–39, Giuseppe Terragni and his brother Attilio worked cooperatively in their architecture office in Como. Giuseppe's first notable architecture was a 1927 gasworks. He was a cofounder of Gruppo Sette; 1928 with Gio Ponti, joined the Italian Rationalist movement. As an exponent of Rationalism, his work exemplified Italian design's move into the mainstream of the European modern movement. Known for his uncompromising consistency, Terragni successfully combined academic neoclassicism, orthodox Rationalism, the basics of the Novecento Italiano, and the *pittura metafisica* of Giorgio de Chirico. Terragni's 1927–29 five-storey apartment block Novocomum in Como, with its simplicity and bold volumes, showed clear influences of Constructivism and caused controversy. 1920s–30s, Como was the center of experimental architecture in Italy where, due to postwar reproductions, Terragni became known for the 1930 cantilever furniture designs in tubular steel and leather installed in his Fascist headquarters Casa del Popolo (originally Casa del Fascio) in Como. His architecture also included 1936–37 Casa Bianca (influenced by Ludwig Mies van der Rohe), Seveso; structures in Milan from c. 1933; Danteum (with Pietro Lingeri) from 1936, Rome; worked on the Antonio Sant'Elia kindergarten, Como; 1938–39 Casa del Fascio (with A. Carminati), Lissone; 1939–40 Giuliani Frigerio apartment building (his last work of consequence), Como. He participated in 1933 Congrès Internationaux d'Architecture Moderne (CIAM) and in discussions leading to the Athens Charter. Terragni died in Como. Posthumously, his work was influential on the so-called New York Five group of architects, particularly Peter Eisenman.
Exhibitions Work included in 1927 (3rd) Biennale di Monza (1927 gasworks), 1927 *Werkbund-Ausstellung* (with Gruppo Sette), Stuttgart; projects at 1927 (3rd) *Esposizione Biennale delle Arti Decorative e Industriali Moderne*, Monza; 1933 (5th) Triennale di Milano (Artist's House on a Lake, with others). Work subject of 1982 *Giuseppe Terragni, 1904–1943*, touring exhibition organized by the municipality of Como with the Kunststichting of Rotterdam; 1991 *Giuseppe Terragni: Two Projects*, School of Architecture, Yale University, New Haven, Connecticut, US; 1996 Triennale di Milano.
Bibliography P. Koulermos (ed.), 'The Work of Terragni, Lingeri and Italian Rationalism,' *Architectural Design*, Mar. 1963, special issue. 'Omaggio a Terragni,' *Arte e architettura*, July 1968, no. 153, special issue. Enrico Mantero (ed.), *Giuseppe Terragni e la città del razionalismo italiano*, Bari: Dedalo, 1969. Bruno Zevi (ed.), *Giuseppe Terragni*, Bologna: Zanichelli, 1980; London: Triangle Architectural Publications, 1989. Raffaella Crespi, *Giuseppe Terragni, Designer*, Milan: Angeli, 1987. Peter Eisenman, *Giuseppe Terragni: Transfomations, Decompositions, Critiques*, New York: Rizzoli, 1991. Thomas L. Schumacher, *Surface & Symbol: Giuseppe Terragni and the Achitecture of Italian Rationalism*, New York: Princeton Architectural Press; London: ADT; Berlin: Ernst & Sohn, 1991. Antonino Saggio, *Giuseppe Terragni: Vita e Opere*, Rome/Bari: Laterza, 1995. Mirko Galli and Claudia Mühlhoff, *Virtual Terragni: CAAD in Historical and Critical Research*, Basel and Boston: Birkhäuser, 2000.

Terry, Emilio (1890–1969)

Cuban furniture designer and architect; active Paris.

Biography 1920s and 1930s, Terry became particularly known for his collaboration with Jean-Michel Frank and others in Frank's stable, including Christian Bérard and Diego and Alberto Giacometti; from 1920s, wrote and lectured on architecture from an anti-Functionalist position which fascinated the Surrealists, one of which, Salvador Dalí, painted his portrait. For the luxurious décor of his wealthy friends/clients, Terry could rarely design the furniture, most was therefore for himself. 1934, he bought the Château de Rochecotte from his brother-in-law Stanislas de Castellane and installed a number of his-own-design furniture/furnishings. (The château was owned by Terry to his death in 1969, then by Henri-Jean de Castellane to 1978, when it was purchased by the firm Marcel Joly.) From 1940s, Terry continued to be active, designing some case goods; was invited by Charles de Bestegui (who collaborated with Terry from 1939–69) and by the vicomte Charles de Noailles to work on their houses after they became disenchanted with modern architecture. Terry's designs led to a fresh, modern interpretation of traditional forms; even so he was irreverently referred to as *père du style Louis XVII* (father of the Louis XVII style).
Exhibitions Drawings and models shown at 1939 *Fantastic Arts, Dada and Surrealism*, The Museum of Modern Art, New York. Work subject of 1996 exhibition, Musée des Arts Décoratifs, Paris (catalogs below).
Bibliography Cat., Marcel Raval (intro.), *Émile Terry*, Musée Nationale d'Art Modern, 1948. *Recueil de projets d'architecture tirés des cartons de Monsieur Emilio Terry auxquels on a joint un choix de dessins d'ornements*, Paris, 1969. Cat., Jean-Louis Gaillemin (intro.), *Sièges d'Emilio Terry: projets*, Musée des Arts Décoratifs, Paris: Réunion des Musées Nationaux/Seuil, 1996. Pierre Arizzoli-Clémentel, *Tapis d'Emilio Terry: projets*, Paris: Réunion des Musées Nationaux, 1996. Emilio Terry clippings file MGZR, New York Public Library.

Teruel i Samsó, Josep J. (1952–)

Spanish designer; born Barcelona.

Training Graphic design, Llotja Escola Superior d'Arts Plàstiqes i Disseny; 1972–75, industrial design, Elisava (Escola Superior de Disseny), Barcelona; 1976–81 and 1997–2002, architecture, and 1998–2002, degree in landscape architecture, Escola Técnica Superior d'Arquitectura de Barcelona (ETSAB); all Barcelona.
Biography In Barcelona: 1974–75, Teruel worked in the studio of Àlaro Martínez-Costa, San Just Desvern; 1975–76, in the studio Arquitectura-Urbanismo-Ingeriería (AURI); 1976–89, studio of designer Josep Lluscà; 1984, became an independent designer of furniture and lighting. Work has ranged from 1985 Octubre table by Blauet to 2002 Laude office furniture by Levesta. Other clients: Blau Comercial, Carlos Jané, Enea-Eredu, Gems, Montseny, Otaola Luyando, Sellex, and Viro. 1992, Teruel founded Estudio de Diseño with Bernat Casso; teaches, Elisava and Universitat de Barcelona.
Citations 1986 selection, ADI/FAD (industrial-design/decorative-arts associations); 1986, 1987, 1988, 1990 selections, Selección Internacional de Diseño de Equipamiento para el Hábitat (SIDI), Barcelona;1990 selection, Iberdiseño-90.

Tessenow, Heinrich (1876–1950)

German architect and furniture designer; born Rostock.

Training Apprenticeship as a carpenter; subsequently, Königlich-Sächsischen Baugewerkenschule, Leipzig; 1896–1901, Fachoberschule, Munich.

Biography After his academic studies, Tessenow held several teaching positions with pupils, including Albert Speer; rejected the idea that architecture is art; from 1910, pursued the concept of craft-based, functional architecture; was disturbed by the chaos of World War I and thus pursued the building of 'organic' small towns as a solution for social cohesion; combined arts-and-crafts influences with a monumental Greek style; was able to bring the British Garden City concept to international attention and may have somewhat influenced, for example, Le Corbusier with his marriage of crafts to monumental architecture. Tassenow's furniture in simple and thin forms is reminiscent of the new classicism in his architecture. He died in Berlin. 1962, the Heinrich Tessenow Gold Medal for architecture was established.
Bibliography Muriel Emmanuel, *Contemporary Architects*, New York: St. Martin's, 1980. Dennis Sharp, *The Illustrated Encyclopedia of Architects and Architecture*, New York: Quatro, 1991.

Testa, Angelo (1921–1984)

American fabric designer and weaver; born Springfield, Mass.

Training 1938–45, New York School of Fine and Applied Arts; briefly, University of Chicago; to 1945 under Gyorgy Kepes and weaver Merli Ehrmann, as the first graduate of New Bauhaus, Chicago.
Biography 1940 after studies in New York, Testa relocated to Chicago; 1947, founded Angelo Testa and Company and followed his work through manufacture to sale; designed furniture and fabrics for Knoll and for Risom and, in addition, was a painter and sculptor. Other clients: Cohn-Hall-Marx, Forster, and Greeff. One of his best-known fabrications was 1943 Little Man figural fabric, hailed by critics as a new direction in textile design. He introduced abstract motifs into commercial textile design in the US; created patterns, including Diagonals, Space Dashes, Forms Within Forms, Line in Act, and Experiment in Space, some of which were also produced as wallpapers. Even though he executed patterns for plastic laminates, vinyls, and fiberglass panels, his work was often abstract and screen-printed on natural fibers in bold color schemes but with little ornamentation. Work also included furniture, lamps, and graphics, and murals. He died in Springfield, Mass.
Exhibitions/citations Work included in four (1950–55) *Good Design* exhibitions/awards, The Museum of Modern Art, New York; and others. Work subject of 1983 exhibition, College of Architecture, Chicago; 2001 *With an Eye on Good Design: The Work of Angelo Testa and Franziska Hosken,* Lyn Weinberg Gallery, New York.
Bibliography 'Textiles,' *Arts + Architecture*, vol. 62, Oct. 1945: 42–43. 'Angelo Testa,' *Arts + Architecture*, vol. 63, July 1946: 42–43. 'Angelo Testa,' *Everyday Art Quarterly*, no. 25, 1953: 16–17. Cat., Kathryn B. Hiesinger and George H. Marcus III (eds.), *Design Since 1945*, Philadelphia: Philadelphia Museum of Art, 1983. Cat., Angelo Testa, *Angelo Testa: 40 Years as a Designer, Painter, Weaver*, Chicago: College of Architecture, Art and Urban Planning Gallery, 1983. Cat., Janet Kardon (ed.), *Craft in the Machine Age 1920–1945*, New York: Abrams/American Craft Museum, 1995.

Tétard Frères

French silversmiths; located Paris.

History 1880, Edmond Tétard (1860–1901) took over Orfèvrerie Hugo (founded in 1851), Paris and developed it into an important silversmithy, located on the rue Béranger, Paris. On Edmond's 1901 death, management was assumed by his sons Henri, Jacques, and Georges, and the firm was thus called Tétard Frères. It produced silverwares in both historicist and Art Nouveau styles and, from and including 1920s, the more distinctive Art Déco designs. From 1919, Valérie Bizouard and Louis Tardy worked for the house, as well as the talented grandson of Edmond, Jean Tétard (1907–80). Bizouard (whose specific work was marked with a 'V' and Tardy's with an 'L') was the manager to 1936, when Tardy took over and served to 1959. Wares included tea services and platters as well as sets of cutlery available in finely crafted cases of exotic wood, such as macassar. The firm still remains somewhat active.
Exhibitions/citations Gold and two silver medals, 1889 *Exposition Universelle*; 1925 *Exposition Internationale des Arts Décoratifs et Industriels Modernes* (including Bizouard's austere ten-sided vase); 1930 *Décor de la Table* (Jean Tétard objects), Musée Galliéra; all Paris.
Bibliography Annelies Krekel-Aalberse, *Art Nouveau and Art Déco Silver*, New York: Abrams, 1989.

Thames, Has Gösta (1916–)
> See Ericsson, Telefonaktiebolaget L.M.

Theill, Christian (1954–)

German designer; born Remscheid; active Florence.

Training Industrial design, Istituto Superiore delle Industrie Artistice (ISIA), Florence.
Biography 1975, Theill settled in Italy; 1981, established his own industrial and interior-design studio with various clients, including Poltronova (furniture), Eleusi (lighting), Nova (Zeus collection), Domus, and Intermezzo; worked with several other consultant designers such as Antonio Citterio 1983. 1981–83, he taught at Università Internazionale dell'Arte, Florence; 1986–87, at Scuola Lorenzo de Medici, Florence; 1988–89, at Scuola Internazionale di Disegno, Bologna. Designed 1986 Antenna table lamp by Targetti Sankey. With Paolo Targetti, established Theill-Targetti studio in 1988. They designed furniture, furnishings, objects, lighting, graphics, and packaging; Theill designed 1993 Parascintille picture frame by Bd Ediciones de Diseño.
Citation 1981 young industrial designer award, Associazione per il Disegno Industriale (ADI).
Bibliography Fumio Shimizu and Studio Matteo Thun (eds.), *The Italian Design: Descendants of Leonardo da Vinci*, Tokyo: Graphic-sha, 1987: 329. Albrecht Bangert and Karl Michael Armer, *80s Style: Designs of the Decade*, New York: Abbeville, 1990. *Modo*, no. 148, Mar.-Apr. 1993: 126.

Theselius, Mats (1956–)

Swedish furniture designer and interior architect; born Stockholm; active Tomelilla.

Training 1979–84, Konstfackskolan, Stockholm.
Biography 1995, professor, Högskolan för Design och Konsthantverk (HDK), Göteborgs Universitet; is an active designer of furniture.
Exhibitions/citations One-person exhibitions including those at Galleri Cupido, Stockholm, 1988; Architecture gallery, Gothenburg, 1989; Ekelund/Tandan gallery, Stockholm, 1991; Gallery Rotor, Gothenburg, 1992; *Millionprogram*, housing company Poseidon gallery, 1993, and Center for Modern Art, Moscow, 1994; *Live* project, Linne Street, Gothenburg, 1994; Kraschnyj Ugol, Färgfabriken art space, Stockholm, 1996. Work included in a number of international group shows from 1983. 1984 IKEA scholarship; 1986 and 1988 Swedish state art fondation; 1989 Swedish Form society travel scholarship, 1991 and 1995 design awards, Swedish Form society; 1991 Du Pont Comfort Prize, Cologne; 1991 *Dagens Nyheter* (daily news) design prize.
Bibliography Mats Theselius, 'The Puddles Eye,' *Hype*, nos. 3–4, 1989. Mats Theselius, 'Hundrov och raketbränsle,' *Dagens Nyheter*, 11 Dec. 1989. Andreas Gedin, *Mats Theselius, Möbler/Furniture*, Värnamo, Sweden: Källemo AB, 1990. Cat., John Petter Nilsson, *Mats Theselius: en noma på språng*, Stockholm: Ekelund/Tandan, 1991. *European Masters/3*, Barcelona: Atrium, 1992. Jan Åman and Marina Timofejewa, *Komrade Mats*, Moscow: Russian Ministry of Culture/ Swedish Embassy, Moscow, 1994. Gerrit Krol, 'Low Budget—Der Diskrete Charme des Alltäglichen,' *Interni*, Dec. 1995. Marco Romanelli, 'Identita,' *Abitare*, Mar. 1996. www.theselius.com

Thesmar, André-Fernand (1845–1912)

French enamelist and ceramicist; active Neuilly.

Training Apprenticeship, the foundry of Ferdinand Barbedienne.
Biography *Cloisonné* enamel was popular in Paris in 1870s, when Thesmar learned the technique at the Barbedienne metal workshop. Thesmar settled in Neuilly, where he rediscovered *plique-à-jour* enamel in 1888 and became the first to apply it to small objects; collaborated with Hirné on mounts and Barbedienne on other work; experimented with various enameling processes; is known to have designed and/or made faience pottery.
Exhibition 1874 exhibition (with Barbedienne), Union Centrale des Beaux-Arts Appliqués à l'Industrie, Paris.
Bibliography Annelies Krekel-Aalberse, *Art Nouveau and Art Déco Silver*, New York: Abrams, 1989.
> See Barbedienne, Ferdinand.

Thiers
> See Coutellerie à Thiers, La.

Thomas

German ceramics firm.

History 1903, Fritz Thomas founded Porzellanfabrik Thomas & Ens in Marktredwitz, which became part of Rosenthal in 1908. 1960, pro-

duction was moved to Thomas am Kulm in Speichersdorf, upper Franconia. Thomas-brand porcelain is still in production. Commissioned designers have included Wolfgang von Wersin, Tapio Wirkkala, Hans Theo Baumann; however, its best-known product may be 1961 TC100 stacking tableware (1959 design) by 'Nick' Hans Roericht.
Bibliography Mel Byars and Arlette Barré-Despond, *100 Designs/100 Years: A Celebration of the 20th Century*, Hove: RotoVision, 1999.
> See Rosenthal; Roericht, 'Nick' Hans.

Thomas, Rodney (1902–)

British painter, architect, and interior and exhibition designer.

Training Painting and sculpture, Byam Shaw Art School and Slade School of Art, both London; under Leon Underwood; c. 1922–24, architecture, Bartlett School of Architecture, London University.
Training c. 1924, Thomas worked in the office of architect Giles Gilbert Scott in London and, subsequently, with his uncle Brummell Thomas; then entered the architects' department of Southern Railway, codesigning station buildings and working alongside E. Maxwell Fry and Guy Morgan in the railway offices; 1930, designed the studio interior of artist Eileen Agar in Bramham Gardens in London, 1930s, designed the interior for painter/designer Ashley Havinden, and the office interior of William Crawford in London. c. 1935–39, Thomas was the architect and designer of showrooms and exhibition stands of water-heater firm Ascot. After World War II with Edric Neal, Raglan Squire, and Jim Gear, Thomas formed the firm Arcon to design prefabricated, factory-produced houses.
Exhbitions Designed the Transport Pavilion, 1951 *Festival of Britain*, London.
Bibliography Cat., *Thirties: British Art and Design Before the War*, London: Arts Council of Great Britain/Hayward Gallery, 1979.

Thome, Elmar (1964–)

Spanish designer; born Mayen.

Biography 1978, Thome began creating sculpture, first in wood and, from 1982, in stone and metal; from 1985, he lived in both Munich and Barcelona, finally settling in the latter; designed 1990 minimalist Toma table lamp and 1997 Serie E.T. bathroom fittings by Bd Ediciones de Diseño; continues to work primarily as a sculptor of mixed-media architectonic forms, represented by Galeria Metropolitana de Barcelona.

Thompson, Benjamin C. (1918–2002)

American architect and entrepreneur.

Training 1941, bachelor's degree in fine arts, architecture, Yale University, New Haven, Connecticut.
Biography 1946, Thompson and others, including Walter Gropius, founded The Architects' Collaborative (TAC), Cambridge, Mass. 1964–68, Thompson succeeded Gropius as the chairperson of the Graduate School of Design, Harvard University. 1966, he left TAC and established Benjamin Thompson & Associates; recreated Faneuil Hall Marketplace (Quincy Place, initial phase, 1976), Boston, which inspired other festival marketplaces elsewhere in the US, including his own 1980 Harborplace in Baltimore, 1985 South Street Seaport in New York, Union Station in Washington, D.C., and others. 1953, he founded Design Research (or D/R) store, Cambridge, Mass., followed by those in New York (1964), San Francisco (1965), and the Cambridge headquarters (1969). D/R, a pioneering venture, introduced a generation of Americans to well-designed home furnishings. His wife Jane McC. Thompson was a partner in many ventures, including Harvest restaurant in Cambridge. He retired in 1993.
Citations 1987 architecture firm award and 1992 gold medal, American Institute of Architects (AIA).
Bibliography www.bta-architects.com.

Thompson, 'Jim' James Harrison Wilson Thompson (1906–1967)

American architect and entrepreneur; born Greenville, Del; active Bangkok.

Training 1924–28, Princeton University, as a family tradition; architecture, University of Pennsylvania.
Biography To 1950, Thompson practiced architecture in New York; during World War II, was assigned to the clandestine organizations, Office of Strategic Services (OSS) and Central Intelligence Agency (CIA) in Italy, France, and Asia and was rigorously trained in jungle survival. After World War II, he settled in Thailand; 1948, established Jim Thompson Thai Silk Company in Bangkok. Having abandoned architecture, he was responsible for developing the technologically advanced silk industry in Thailand, where he replaced traditional vegetable dyes with high-quality, colorfast dyes from Switzerland; made it possible for weavers to use faster, foot-operated looms and thus introduced the bright, iridescent color palette for which Thai silk is known today. 1950s–60s, sales soared, and, by 1967, Thompson had established a cottage industry of 20,000 weavers with export sales exceeding $6 million. 1967, on holiday with friends in Malaysia's Cameron Highlands, Thompson disappeared. His firm continues under different management today, and his Bangkok house is a tourist site. 1976, the James H.W. Thompson Foundation was sanctioned by Princess Maha Chakri Sirindhorn of Thailand.
Bibliography William Warren, *The Legendary American: The Remarkable Career and Strange Disappearance of Jim Thompson*, Boston, 1970. Cat., Kathryn B. Hiesinger and George H. Marcus III (eds.), *Design Since 1945*, Philadelphia: Philadelphia Museum of Art, 1983. www.jimthompsonhouse.com.

Thomsen, Tamara (1953–)

American painter and industrial designer; born Sioux Falls, S. Dak.

Training To 1976, fine art, Syracuse (N.Y.) University; to 1980, Virginia Commonwealth University, Richmond, Va.
Biography Thomsen taught painting, Virginia Commonwealth University; 1981, became a founding partner with David Stowell, Tom Dair, and Tucker Viemeister of the industrial-design practice that became Smart Design in 1985; was vice-president of graphic design and managed design programs there on accounts including AIA, Citibank, Family Care International, Kepner-Tregoe, Polder, Prodigy Services, Sam Flax, and University of Southern California.
Exhibitions Paintings in group and one-person shows in New York, Syracuse, and Richmond.

Thomas: 'Nick' Hans Roericht. Stacking tableware (no. TC 100). 1959. Glazed porcelain, soup cup (far left) h. 2 1/16" x dia. 4" (10.2 x 5.2 cm), soup-cup saucer h. 1" x dia. 6" (2.5 x 15.3 cm), soup-cup lid h. 3/4" x dia. 4" (1.9 x 10.2 cm), soup bowl (center) h. 2 1/8" x dia. 6 5/8" (5.4 x 16.8 cm), teacup (center right) h. 2 1/4" x dia. 3 1/8" (5.7 x 7.9 cm) and saucer h. 7/8" x dia. 5 1/8" (2.2 x 13 cm), teacup (far right) h. 2 1/4" x dia. 3 1/8" (5.7 x 7.9 cm). Mfr.: Thomas, division of Rosenthal, Germany (1961). Greta Daniel Design Fund. MoMA.

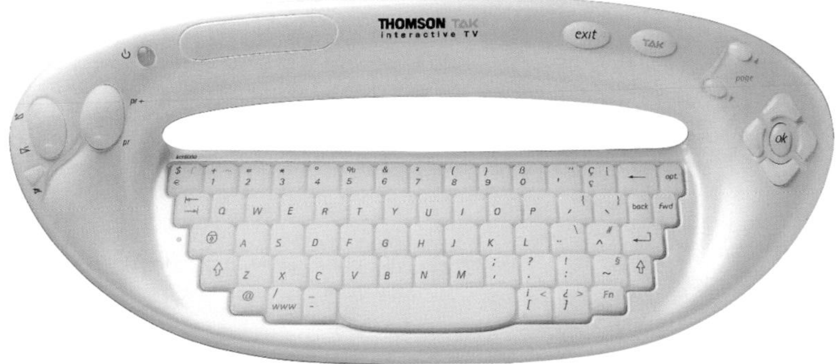

Thomson: Tim Thom studio. Tak interactive-TV keyboard. 2000. ABS plastic, h. 2 3/4 x w. 12 3/8 x l. 5" (7 x 31.5 x 12.5 cm). Mfr.: Thomson Multimédia, France.

Thomson, Elihu (1853–1937); Thomson Multimédia

British electronics entrepreneur; born Manchester. Manufacturer.

Biography/history From 1871, Thomson taught chemistry, Central High School, Philadelphia, US; 1879 with high-school science professor Edwin Houston, founded what became one of the leading electrical companies of 19th century and which was known as Thomson-Houston by 1889. The ensuing events in the history of Thomson were convoluted. 1892, the company merged with Edison General Electric Companies to form General Electric; 1893, established Compagnie Française Thomson-Houston (CFTH) in Paris, which installed the first-in-France elevated streetcar (tram) system, in Le Havre; 1920, diversified into home appliances, including heating and kitchen equipment. 1921, CFTH and Compagnie Générale d'Electricité (CGE) founded Compagnie des Lampes, and CFTH began selling radio transmitters and receivers. From 1925, Auguste Detœuf worked at the Thomson Company in Paris. 1926, CFTH's telephone department CTTH was sold to ITT National Broadcasting Company, US, and became the 'broadcast service of RCA.' 1928, Detœuf founded huge conglomerate Alsthom (Alsacienne de Construction Mécanique) and directed it for ten years. 1929, CFTH acquired Etablissements Ducretet as a foothold into radio and television, and RCA purchased Victor Talking Machine Company, acquiring its 'His Master's Voice' trademark (the 1899 painting by Francis Barraud of his brother's dog, 'Nipper,' which is listening to the horn of an early phonograph). 1930, CFTH founded Compagnie Générale de Radiologie (CGR); 1931, merged with Alsthom; 1936, bought Etablissements Kraemer, expanding into professional radio-broadcast equipment. 1937, CSF (Compagnie Générale de Télégraphie Sans Fil) introduced its first television prototype. 1938, Detœuf became chairperson of Thomson, but departed in 1940 to head Comité d'Organisation de la Construction Electrique. 1938, CFTH acquired Compagnie Générale de Radiologie (CGR). 1950, Charles Beurtheret of Thomson-Houston in France invented the Vapotron, an innovative anode cooled by water vapor. By end of 1950s, CFTH television sets accounted for about 12% of the French market. 1960, Thomson was organized into large divisions such as General Electric; 1967, merged with CSF and helped to construct the telecommunications system of the Heos satellite. 1968, the merged Thomson-Brandt took over CSF, forming Thomson-CSF, and a professional electronics company was established. 1969, Thomson-CSF was organized under the unwieldy name of Compagnie Française Thomson-Houston-Hotchkiss-Brandt. 1971, Thomson and RCA created a new company called Videocolor to produce TV picture tubes in Europe. 1976, Thomson-CSF took control of Téléphones Ericsson and LMT (Le Matériel Téléphonique); 1977, of German radio-and-TV-maker Nordmende; 1978, of Telefunken and Dual; 1981, merged with Thomson-Brandt; 1982, was nationalized in France. 1983, Thomson-CSF Téléphone and CGE merged to make a professional and consumer electronics and components business; 1985, signed a cooperative agreement with Thorn of the UK and JVC of Japan. After RCA was acquired by GE in 1986, Thomson bought RCA and GE consumer electronics from GE to become Thomson Consumer Electronics (TCE) in 1988. By 1989, RCA had sold 50 million color TV sets. Thomson introduced 1990 high-end Proscan brand; had 'Chipper', a young dog, created to join 'Nipper' in advertising; 1992, sold its electronic-household-appliances division to Italian group Elf which became Brandt. RCA introduced 1993 CinemaScreen (first widescreen TV in the US) and 1994 home-use Digital Satellite System. 1995, Thomson Consumer Electronics became Thomson multimédia (publicly held in France and the US from 1999); was integrated with Thomson Broadcast Systems (TBS); introduced 1998 Wysius (thinnest TV screen available then), 1999 Lyra (first portable digital player), 2000 Tak interactive TV. 2001, Thomson bought Technicolor; combined its multimedia plasma TV display screen with NEC's efforts. In industrial design: 1990, Thomson multimédia hired Philippe Starck as the artistic director of Tim Thom (its inhouse high-design studio) to revamp its product range– extended to include Rock 'n' Roll CD player, Lux Lux television, Babel video, Perso mobile phone and other models—with other staff designers under Starck, including Matali Crasset, Elsa Francès, Patrick Jouin, Christophe Pillet, Jean-Michel Policar.
Citations Design of the Decade (1990s) bronze (1994 Digital Satellite Receiving System), IDSA/*Business Week* magazine; numerous others.
Bibliography Elihu Thomson, *Wireless Transmission of Energy*, Washington, D.C.: Smithsonian, 1914. David O. Woodbury, *Beloved Scientist: Elihu Thomson, a Guiding Spirit of the Electrical Age*, New York: Whittlesey House, 1944. Harold J. Abrahams and Marion B. Savin (eds.), *Selections from the Scientific Correspondence of Elihu Thomson*, Cambridge, Mass.: MIT, 1971. Mel Byars, *On/Off: New Electronic Products*, New York: Universe, 2001. www.thomson-multimedia.com.

Thonet, Michael (1796–1871); Gebrüder Thonet; Thonet-Mundus

German entrepreneur; born Boppard am Rhein.

Biography/history Thonet (pronounced to rhyme with 'bonnet' in English) was born a short distance up the River Rhine from the workshop of renowned cabinetmaker David Roentgen (1743–1807). 1819, he founded his eponymous enterprise, Thonet, in Boppard am Rhein; 1842, was invited to Vienna by Prince Metternich, the chancellor of Austria, who had seen Thonet's furniture on a trip to Germany; established factories in Vienna and elsewhere and sold his furniture to members of the Austrian imperial court and to nobility, although he was interested in a wide market with mass production as his goal; 1853, handed over the business to his five sons, when the firm was thus registered as Gebrüder Thonet. 1856, the first furniture factory was founded in Koritschan (Koryčany, Moravia), near a supply of beechwood used for its innovative bentwood furniture. Subsequently, five other factories were established in Eastern Europe and, 1889, one in Frankenberg/Eder as the first production plant in Germany and where it remains today. Thonet was the most innovative of the 19th-century German furnituremakers and designers; invented the bentwood process for making chairs that resulted in low costs, durability, lightness, and flexibility, and eliminated the need for hand-carved joints and, notably, ornamentation. Earlier on, Thonet experimented with bending wood, initially gluing together veneers to make sections of furniture; later invented a new process with solid lengths of beechwood that were steamed or boiled in water and glue, which allowed for long pieces to be bent into chair frames, in some cases into fantastic forms. 1841, patents were granted in France, Britain, and Belgium for the bentwood process, and bentwood chairs were exhibited publicly in Koblenz. 1888, the firm invented the folding theater seat. By 1900,

Michael Thonet. Side chair. c. 1840–42. Laminated wood strips covered with rosewood, 36 1/4 x 16 7/8 x 16" (92.1 x 42.9 x 40.6 cm), seat h. 20 1/2" (52.1 cm). Mfr.: Gebrüder Thonet, Austria. Given anonymously. MoMA.

the company had established 52 factories in Europe. Some 50 million copies of its legendary 1859–60 'consumer chair' (no. 14) had been made by 1930; it is found in cafés worldwide and still in production. Le Corbusier admired Thonet's c. 1904 chair (no. B 9), made from six pieces of bentwood, with caning for the seat, and used it frequently in his interiors. 1920s–30s, Thonet produced some of the most distinctive examples of modern chromium-plated tubular-steel furniture (through the acquisition of other German firms), including that by Anton Lorenz, A. Bamberg, J. Hagemann, Ludwig Mies van der Rohe, and Marcel Breuer (with the artistic copyright of Mart Stam). The 1926 S 43 cantilever chair (and S 43F variant) by Mart Stam has been in continuous production. Today, the firm commissions contemporary designers such as Foster and Partners, Erik Magnussen, Ulrich Böhme, Wulf Schneider, Eddie Harlis, and others, for seating in various materials, including plastics. And Thonet is also reissuing some of its modern models. The firm continues to be managed by the Thonet family. The Thonet Museum is located in Frankenberg/Eder, Germany.
Exhibitions Subject of 1967 *Form from Process: The Thonet Chair...*, Carpenter Center for the Visual Arts, Cambridge, Mass., US; 1986–87 *L'Industrie Thonet*, Musée d'Orsay, Paris; 1989–90 *Sitz-Gelegenheiten: Bugholz- und Stahlrohrmöbel von Thonet*, Germanischen Nationalmuseums, Nürnberg; 1994–95 *Thonet: Pionier des Industriedesigns, 1830–1900*, Vitra Design Museum, Weil am Rhein, Germany.
Bibliography Christopher Wilk, *Thonet: 150 Years of Furniture*, Woodbury, N.Y.: Barron's, 1980. Christopher Wilk (intro.), *Thonet Bentwood & Other Furniture* [1904, 1905–06, and 1907 catalogs], New York: Dover Publications, 1980. Derek E. Ostergard, *Bent Wood and Metal Furniture, 1850–1946*, New York: The American Federation of Arts, 1987. Alexander von Vegesack, *Das Thonet Buch*, Munich: Bangert, 1987. Sonia Günther (intro.), *Thonet Tubular Steel Furniture Card Catalogue*, Weil am Rhein: Vitra Design Publications, 1989. Albrecht Bangert and Peter Ellenberg, *Thonet-Möbel: Bugholz-Klassiker 1830–1930...*, Munich: Heyne, 1993. Alexander von Vege-sack, *Thonet: Classic Furniture in Bentwood*, New York: Rizzoli, 1997. Andrea Gleininger, *The Chair No.14 by Michael Thonet*, Frankfurt: form, 1998. www.thonet.at.
> See Lorenz, Anton; Thonet Industries.

Thonet Frères; Bruno Weill (d. 1962); Hans Weill

Bruno Weill: Austrian architect.

Training In architecture.
Biography The association between Thonet Frères and Thonet-Mundus AG (incorporating Gebrüder Thonet) of Germany is an intricate one. 1929, Thonet Frères was established in France as an entity (in whole or in part) of international organization Thonet-Mundus AG with headquarters in Germany. Thonet Frères (or 'Thonet Brothers') was not French for Gebrüder Thonet (as in the former Gebrüder Thonet firm), but rather referred to brothers Bruno Weill and Hans Weill, who owned Thonet Fréres. The showroom, offices, and a warehouse were located in the north of Paris; the enterprise was very successful and produced the furniture of some accomplished French designers, such as Le Corbusier, Charlotte Perriand, André Lurçat, and Charles Siclis. It produced Charlotte Perriand's tubular-leg table, first shown at the Équipement Intérieur d'une Habitation installation at the 1928 Salon of Société des Artistes Décorateurs, Paris; the model was also produced by Mulke-Melder of Frystat, Czechoslovakia, under a Thonet license. Bruno Weill, an Austrian who had studied architecture, was the director of Thonet Frères and used the pseudonym Béwé (for the initials 'B.W.' of his name) as a furniture designer. Weill's own tubular-steel and wood designs (with a 'B' inventory designation) included 1928–29 B 282 table, 1928–29 B 250 office cabinet, and c. 1930 B 287 desk, and others up to 1932 or 1933. To 1957, Émile Guillot (also mistakenly known as E. Guyot and A. Guyot, due to the 'y' sound of the double 'l' in French) designed for the firm (as well as for Thonet-Czechoslovakia). When Bruno Weill died in 1962, Hans Weill sold Thonet Frères to André Leclerc. When Thonet Industries was set up in the US, Thonet Frères agreed with Thonet Industries that it would discontinue its right to Thonet copyrights in Germany and within the European Union. (However, there are some claims that Leclerc bought Thonet Fréres at the end of World War II or c. 1946; possibly he only purchased shares.) The enterprise was passed on to Leclerc's heirs and reorganized as an operation with little or no affinity to the

Gebrüder Thonet. Vienna café chair (no. 14). 1859–60. Steam-bent solid beechwood with veneer seat, 33 3/8 x 17 x 20 1/8" (84.8 x 43.2 x 51.1 cm), seat h. 18 1/4" (46.4 cm). Mfr.: Gebrüder Thonet, Austria. Purchase Fund. MoMA.

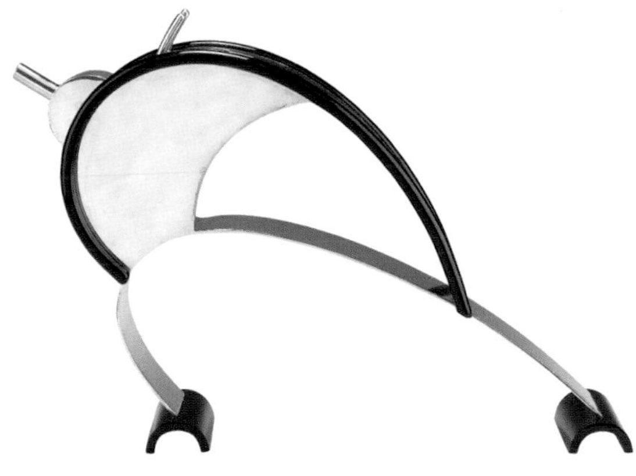

Matteo Thun. Swinging Marylin tea pot. 1985. Copper, silver metal, and black plastic, h. 18 5/8" (22.5 cm). Mfr.: Alessi, Italy, for Anthologie Quartett, Germany. Courtesy Quittenbaum Kunstauktionen, Munich.

firm's original design program. 2001, Thonet Frères was liquidated.
Bibliography Jan van Geest and Otakar Máčel, *Stühle aus Stahl, Metallmöbel 1925–1940*, Cologne: König, 1980. Cat., *Pioneers of Modern Furniture*, London: Fischer Fine Art, 1991: nos. 10–11. *Inform* (Thonet house journal), Oct. 2001: 4.

Thonet Industries

American furniture manufacturer; originally located New York.

History 1922, Gebrüder Thonet of Germany with facilities in Eastern and Western Europe was absorbed into the international enterprise Thonet-Mundus AG, headed at the time by Leopold Pilzer (1871–1950). 1938, Pilzer emigrated to the US and purchased three manufacturers—American Chair Company, North Carolina Furniture Company, and Home Furniture Company—to operate under the name Thonet Industries, Inc., with headquarters in New York. It produced the Bentply® Collection of bentwood furniture, highly influenced by the work of Charles and Ray Eames and intended for the school/health-care market. Yet its conservative production was not endowed with the high modern-design values which the mother firm had established in Germany and which had called on talented architects/designers. (Even so, Thonet Industries had the right to reproduce some historical Gebrüder Thonet and Thonet-Mundus models.) From 1973, the firm's president was James Riddering. Thonet Industries moved to York, Penn., and shifted from inhouse designers to freelancers; 1975, established a new design program, managed by Joan M. Burgasser, and commissioned Don Petit, Warren Snodgrass, David Rowland, and other independent designers. 1962, the firm became a subsidiary of Simmons mattress company (founded in 1953). 1979, Simmons was bought by Gulf & Western, which in turn (1987) sold the assets of Thonet Industries (including the rights to 200 or so historical designs) to Shelby Williams Industries. 1999, Shelby Williams along with Thonet (having dropped 'Industries') was bought by Falcon Products (founded 1959), also now owner of Howe (founded late 1920s), Johnson Tables (founded 1929), and a number of others. Today's Thonet-label inventory includes the designs of Josef Hoffmann, Ludwig Mies van der Rohe and some Gebrüder Thonet bentwood classics, as well as new seating by Beck & Beck, John Caldwell, Just Bernhard Meijer, inhouse designers, and others.

Thorley, Joseph Palin (1892–1987)

British ceramicist and archaeologist; active in the UK and US.

Biography 1924, Thorley with J.L. Kelso and W.F. Fullbright, dug together on an archaelogical expedition, inside and around Bab edh-Dhra, Jordan. Thorley wrote scholarly articles on ancient ceramics, including about the Tell Beit Mirsim excavation. He may have been the same J. Palin Thorley (as his name is distinctive) who established Thornley China Ltd., in Longton, Stoke-on-Trent, UK, in 1940, for the production of ceramics, including English Abbey-pattern dinnerware. He also designed for Wedgwood before emigrating to Ohio, US, where he designed for The Hall China Company, including ceramic containers for refrigerator use, particularly an iconic 1940 Art Déco-style pitcher (reissued in 1990s by Hall) for Westinghouse refrigerators, and possibly other 1940s–50s refrigerator ware by Hall for Hotpoint, General Electric, Montgomery Ward, and Sears, Roebuck & Co. He also designed Hall's Montecello service. From at least 1946, he lived in Williamsburg, Va.; 1951 with his wife Edith, establishing a pottery to make/sell ceramics (including official 'Williamsburg Restoration' reproductions which were stamp-signed) in what is now the Whitehall Restaurant; the Thorleys worked there until they gave up the business in 1975. Among other wares, Thorley designed the 1932 Marvel-pattern dinnerware (historicist with a rose motif), produced by Taylor Smith. 1988, The Joseph Palin Thorley Scolarship for Art and Architecture was established at College of William and Mary, Williamsburg, Va. There is some evidence that he established the Thorley Refractory Company in South Gate, Cal.
Bibliography W.F. Albright, J.L Kelso, and J. Palin Thorley, 'Early-Bronze Pottery from Bab edh-Dhra in Moab,' *Bulletin of the American Schools of Oriental Research*, no. 95. Oct. 1944: 11–13. Margaret Whitmyer and Ken Whitmyer, *Collector's Encyclopedia of Hall China*, Paduka, Ky.: Collectors Books, 2001 (3rd ed.).

Thorsteinsson, Sirgurdur (1965–)
> See Design Group Italia.

Thorup, Torsten (1944–)

Danish architect and industrial designer.

Training 1965–69 under Henning Larsen, architecture and planning, Det Kongelige Danske Kunstakademi, Copenhagen; 1969–73, psychology, Københavns Universitet.
Biography Thorup was a senior architect in the office of Henning Larsen; 1968 with Claus Bonderup, established an architecture office in Copenhagen; became a member of Danske Arkitekters Landsforbund (DAL) and of Danske Designeres medlemmer (mDD); from 1969, has designed lighting, furniture, ski equipment, and several buildings. After ending his association with Larsen, design and architecture commissions included 1981 Café Brix in Ålborg, 1981 signage for Jan Flex in Copenhagen, 1982 leather and cotton clothing by Clemme of Ålborg, and, more recently The Watch, Double Pomme wristwatch, other watches, and neckties by Georg Jensen; Pharos lamp by Focus Belysning; seating by Cubus; lamps by Fogh og Mørup. He has been associated with Jørgen Waring Studio/Architecture and Design.
Exhibitions/citations Work shown at 1979 lighting and furniture exhibition, Louisiana Museum for Moderne Kunst, Humlebæk, Denmark; 1980 *Industriforeningen*, Copenhagen; 1981 and 1982 exhibitions, Gothenburg; 1981 *Lumière*, Paris; 1982 exhibition of industrial design sponsored by Federation of Danish Architects, Ålborg. 1974 Bundespreis Produktdesign (for Semi lamp by Fogh og Mørup), Rat für Formgebung (German design council), Frankfurt; 1976 Formes Utiles prize (for Calot lamp by Focus Belysning), France; 1982 Swedish Design Prize gold medal (for Pendel no. 1 lamp by Focus Belysning).
Bibliography www.t-thorup-architects.dk.

Thun, Matteo (Count Matteo Thun-Hohenstein 1952–)

Italian ceramicist and designer; born Bolzano; active Milan.

Training To 1975, Facoltà di Architettura, Università degli Studi, Florence; sculpture, Oskar Kokoschka's Internationale Sommerakademie für bildende Kunst, Salzburg; University of California, Los Angeles.
Biography Thun was a cofounder of the Memphis group, led by Ettore Sottsass from 1980, and initially best known for his work there. He has been a prolific designer of ceramics, including the Teje and Tuja vases, Nefretiti tea set, Api ashtray, and Palma bud vase in the initial (1981) Memphis collection; and the Manitoga tray, Ontario, Erie, Superior, and Michigan bud vases, and Kariba fruit bowl, Garda amphora, and Lodoga, Titicaca, Onega, and Chad vases for the 2nd (1982) Memphis collection. 1983–95, he taught product design and ceramics, Kunstgewerbeschule, Vienna, where his students produced projects for his 'In the Spirit of the USA' assignment; dinnerware sets by the students (including Margit Denz, Renate Hattinger, Michaela Lange, Klara Obereder, and Maria Wiala) were produced by Villeroy & Boch in limited editions. Thun worked with Ettore Sottsass in Sottsass Associati; 1984, established his own architecture, communications, and design studio, now comprised of about 30 architects, engineers, and designers, and claiming a long list of prestigious clients. Thun wrote *The Baroque Bauhaus* manifesto (1985), which encourages designers of today to call on the work of designers of the past. Other work has included 1986 Via Col Vento vase by Lobmeyr; 1985 Settimana metal chest by Bieffeplast; 1988 rug by Vorwerk; 1983 ceramic

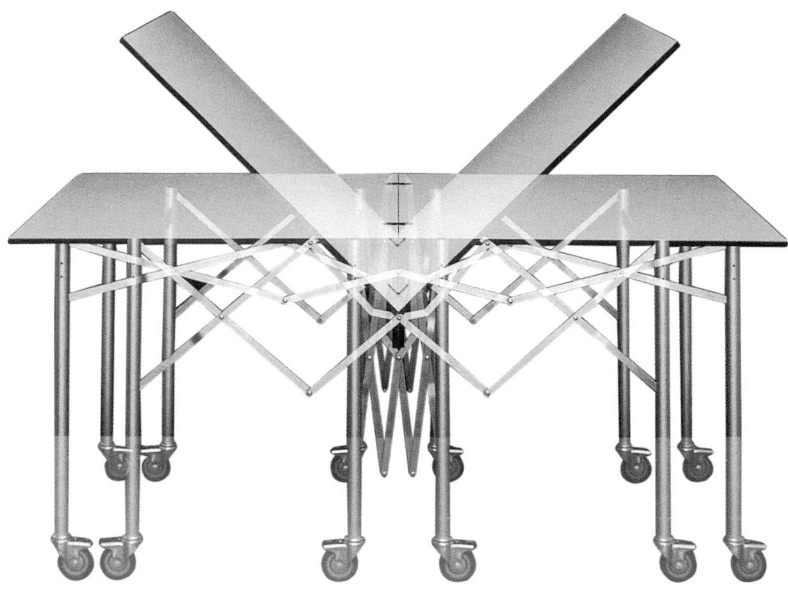

Benjamin Thut. Alu 1 folding table. c. 2000. Synthetic resin and refined steel, w. 31 1/2 x l. 63" (80 x 160 cm). Mfr.: Sele 2, Switzerland.

hanging light fixtures (including Santa Monica, Santa Ana, Santa Fe, and 1980s architectonic Stillight table lamps by Bieffeplast); 1987 Fantasia porcelain by Arzberg; 1991 Villeroy & Boch distribution center, Merzig, Germany; 1994 Bauer Kaba building, Zürich; 1997 Griffner house for mass production; from 1997, Riello fair stands and P.O.S. (point of sale) system; 1998–99 Vimar art direction; 1999 Coca-Cola warehouse/headquarters, Brüttisellen, Switzerland; 1999 Missoni shop, New York; 2000 Missoni shop, Milan; 2000 Tower One, Berlin; 2001 Side hotel, Hamburg; 2002 Cult hotel, Berlin; corporate ID programs for Dunkin' Donuts and Albert; packaging for Campari, Illy, and Vimar; a range of domestic products for Alessi, Belux, Campari, Cleto Munari, Gital, Harting, Illy, Lavazza, Leucos, Martin Stoll, Nachtmann, Swatch, Thonet, Tiffany, Unlimited Office, WMF, and Zumtobel.
Exhibitions Participated in numerous exhibitions, including with Memphis from 1981 in Milan, and at Triennali di Milano.
Bibliography Andrea Branzi, *La casa calda: esperienze del nuovo disegno italiano*, Milan: Idea, 1982. Fumio Shimizu and Studio Matteo Thun (eds.), *The Italian Design: Descendants of Leonardo da Vinci*, Tokyo: Graphic-sha, 1987. Volker Fischer, *Bodenreform: Teppichboden von Künstlern und Architekten*, Berlin: Ernst & Sohn, 1989. Alex Buck and Mattias Vogt (eds.), *Matteo Thun–Designer*, Berlin: Ernst & Sohn, 1993. Reiner Zettl and Nina Heydorn (eds.), *Industrial Happenings* (documents Thun teaching at the Kunstgewerbeschule, Vienna), Vienna: Christian Brandstätter, 1998. www.matteothun.com.

Thuret, André (1898–1965)

French glassware designer and glass engineer; active Paris.

Biography Thuret was an engineer in the glassworks of Bagneux and, subsequently, of Bezons; from 1926, was a research worker and teacher at Chimie Appliquée aux Industries de la Céramique and the glassworks of Conservatoire National des Arts et Métiers et Expert, both Paris; 1924 with friend Henri Navarre, created his first glass; suspended colored pigments by pinching the glass by fusion. His most creative period was 1940–50. To 1958, he worked in a glass factory, where he was aided by glassblowers; became an active member of the committe of Société des Artistes Décorateurs and of Union des Artistes Modernes (UAM) (sponsored by Jean Fouquet), and organizing committe of Salon d'Automne.
Exhibitions/citation Showed work in most of the Salons of his time, including Salon d'Automne in 1928 and 1932, and glass venues. Participated in 1956–57 (1st) Triennale d'Art Français Contemporain, Pavillon de Marsan, Musée du Louvre, Paris. Was appointed Chevalier of Légion d'Honneur.
Bibliography René Chavance, 'André Thuret, artiste et technicien du verre,' *Mobilier et décoration*, no. 1, Feb. 1955. Sylvie Raulet, *Bijoux art déco*, Paris: Regard, 1984. Arlette Barré-Despond, *UAM*, Paris: Regard, 1986. Cat., *Les années UAM 1929–1958*, Paris: Musée des Arts Décoratifs, 1988.

Thut, Benjamin
> See Thut, Kurt.

Thut, Kurt (1937–); Thut Möbel

Swiss furniture designer, interior architect, and architect; born Möriken. Manufacturer.

Training 1947–50, in carpentry; 1952–55 under Willy Guhl, Hans Bellmann and Hans Fischli, Kunstgewerbeschule, Zürich.
Biography/history Kurt Thut was influenced by the instructors and designers at the school he attended in Zürich and the work of Ludwig Mies van der Rohe and Charles and Ray Eames; worked in architecture studios and taught interior architecture; from 1958, created a range of furniture based on principles of the Schweizerischer Werkbund (SWB) for his family's firm, Thut Möbel AG in Möriken; 1961, set up his own studio. From 1976 when the firm's founder Walter Thut died, Kurt Thut became its manager; he possibly saved it from economic failure by, among other approaches, putting in place the use of new technologies and materials for a more efficient, creative operation. The firm today works with 12 consultant designers, directed by Kurt Thut, his son/industrial designer Benjamin Thut, and his son/aeronautical mechanic Daniel Thut. One of the firm's imaginative products is 1995 Scherenbett (no. 990, a folding bed that accommodates varying mattress widths) by Benjamin Thut.
Bibliography Mel Byars, *50 Beds...*, Hove: RotoVision, 2000.

Thygesen, Rud (1932–)

Danish furniture designer.

Training To 1966, Møbelskole, Kunsthåndværkerskolen, Copenhagen.
Biography 1966 with Johnny Sørenson, Thygesen founded a design studio in Copenhagen for the design of furniture, furnishings, and textiles; 1970–74, taught, Kunsthåndværkerskolen; with Sørensen, designed furniture by Erik Boisens and others. From 1993, they worked independently of each other.
> See Sørenson, Johnny.

Tick, Susanne (1959–)

American designer; born Bloomington, Il.

Training Bachelor of fine arts degree, University of Iowa, Iowa City.
Biography 1996 with Terry Mowers, Tick founded carpet firm Tuva

Looms; was the design director of fabric manufacturers Boris Kroll and Unika Vaev and of furniture firm Brikel Associates; subsequently, creative director of Knoll Textiles and a consultant to Interface's Prince Street and Bentley brands. All activities in New York.
Citations 1999 Design Distinction Award, Annual Design Review, *I.D.* magazine; gold award, Best of 2000 NeoCon, Chicago; 2000 *Good Design* award, Chicago Athenaeum.
Bibliography Cat., R. Craig Miller (intro.), *U.S. Design 1975–2000*, Munich: Prestel, 2002.

Tiedemann, Helene (1960–)

Swedish designer; born Malmö.

Training 1882–84, fashion, Kingsway College (now Westminster Kingsway College); 1985–88, industrial-design engineering, Central School of Art and Design (now Central Saint Martin's College of Art and Design); both London.
Biography Early 1980s, Tiedemann began as a fashion designer; from 1988 with a degree in industrial-design engineering, worked as a furniture, lighting, and home-accessories designer for London firms: Davies shop (1989 30-piece furniture and accessories ranges) and Liberty's (1990 24-piece furniture range). 1980–95, lived and worked in London and, from 1995, in Stockholm. Other work: 1992–96, 100+ furniture and products by Habitat; 1992–99 furniture by Asplund; 1993 tables and chair by E&Y Tokyo; 1994 shelving system by Conran Shop; 1994–98 products by David design; 1995 upholstered furniture by Fogia; 1996 rug by IKEA; 1999 gift packing (with Matz Borgström) for Interflora; 2000–01 furniture (with Brogström) by Skandiform; 2002 furniture by Design House Stockholm; 2002 furniture by Sagaform. She was a consultant on interior, brand, and retail-strategy programs to Fitch & Co. in 1988; David Davies Association 1988–90; Rupert Gardner Design 1996–98; Jaxvall design 1997–98; Koncept from 1998. Other clients: Harrods and Valentino. 1995–2000 in the UK, Tiedemann taught and held workshops, Royal College of Art, Kingston University, Central Saint Martin's College of Art and Design, and Anders Beckman School of Art and Design.

Tiffany, Charles Louis (1812–1902); Tiffany & Co.

American entrepreneur; born Connecticut; active New York; father of Louis Comfort Tiffany.

Biography/history 1837, Tiffany and John B. Young opened a fancy-goods and stationery store at 259 Broadway, New York. Enlarged in 1841, the store's stock was augmented with cutlery, clocks, jewelry from Paris, glass from Bohemia, and porcelain from France and Dresden. 1841, J.L. Ellis became a partner, and the firm moved to 271 Broadway, known as Tiffany, Young and Ellis. Tiffany and Young traveled to Europe and bought large, important jewelry collections, for future sale by the firm. Better quality jewelry from England, mosaic jewelry from Florence and Rome, and high-quality stock from Paris replaced the originally stocked cheap goods from Hanau and Paris. 1848, the firm began manufacturing its own jewelry; 1853, became known as Tiffany & Co. when Charles Tiffany took over the management. Gideon F.T. Reed, a Boston jeweler, became Tiffany's partner to direct the Paris branch, known as Tiffany & Reed (established by 1850 on the rue de Richelieu). From 1848, the firm made large purchases of diamonds in Paris; 1850, bought Marie Antoinette's reputed diamonds, purchased $100,000 worth of jewelry at the Eszterházy sale, and spent $500,000 at the French crown-jewels sale. 1854, the firm moved to 550 Broadway and, 1870, to 15th Street on Union Square. One of its first designers was Gustave Herter, although most of its silverwares were bought from independent New York artisans. 1851, John Chandler Moore (1802–1874), a previous maker of silver for Tiffany, was hired to produce silver hollow-ware. Though the firm sold silverplate from 1868, it became known for its sterling silver. Most of its silver cannot be assigned to a specific designer, although goods in the *japonisant* style can be credited to Moore, who saw to it that Tiffany became the first (1852) firm to adopt the English sterling standard (92.5% pure silver). 1868, Edward C. Moore (1827–1891), son of John Chandler Moore, became an officer and the silver-department director; worked at Tiffany for 40 years. A London branch was opened the same year (1868). Tiffany was at the forefront of exploiting the European and American enthusiasm for *japonisme* (producing goods from as early as 1871), probably thanks to Moore, a knowledgeable collector of Japanese art. 1876, Tiffany hired Christopher Dresser to bring back *objets d'art* from Japan; 1878, the collection of almost 2,000 pieces was sold. For other wares, its artisans practiced damascening and inlaying techniques for small *bibelots*; Japanese artisans executed some of its production. By 1873, the firm was producing hollow-ware; it became well known for the 1875 William Cullen Bryant Vase designed by James Horton Whitehouse with medallions by Augustus Saint-Gaudens. 1877, another distinguished vase was commissioned as a gift for Cincinnati philanthropist Reuben R. Springer. Louis Comfort Tiffany joined the firm of his father, who died in 1902; Louis Comfort became the artistic director. Much later, Van Day Truex, hired by Tiffany chairperson Walter Hoving in 1955, was a prolific designer for the firm to 1979; several of his designs are still in production. 1955–94, Gene Moore was the designer of Tiffany's distinctive street-window displays. The 30-year partnership with Jean Schlumberger (1907–1987) began in 1956, when Hoving opened a boutique of the French designer's jewelry and accessories, exclusive to Tiffany. From 1978, John Loring replaced Truex as the design director. More recent designers of jewelry, dinnerware, metalware, tabletop accessories, and other products have included Angela Cummings, Elsa Peretti, and Paloma Picasso.
Exhibitions/citations Wares shown at 1867 *Exposition Universelle* (silver medal), Paris; 1876 *Centennial Exposition* (award of merit), Philadelphia; 1878 *Exposition Universelle* (gold medals), Paris; 1889 *Exposition Universelle* (precious stones of North America), Paris; 1893 *World's Columbian Exposition*, Chicago; 1900 *Exposition Universelle*, Paris; 1901 *Pan-American Exposition*, Buffalo, N.Y.; 1987 *The Silver of Tiffany & Co., 1850–1987*, Museum of Fine Arts, Boston. Charles Louis Tiffany in 1878 and Edward Chandler Moore in 1889 were elected Chevaliers of Légion d'Honneur, France.
Bibliography George Frederic Heydt, *Charles L. Tiffany and the House of Tiffany & Co.*, New York: Tiffany, 1893. 'The Edward C. Moore Collection,' *Bulletin of The Metropolitan Museum of Art*, vol. 2, June 1902: 105–06. Henry H. Hawley, 'Tiffany's Silver in the Japanese Taste,' *Bulletin of the Cleveland Museum of Art*, vol. 63, Oct. 1976: 236–45. Charles H. Carpenter Jr. and Mary Grace Carpenter, *Tiffany Silver*, New York: Dodd, Mead, 1978. Norman Potter and Douglas Jackson, *Tiffany Glassware*, New York: Crown, 1988. Janet Zapata, *The Jewelry and Enamels of Louis Comfort Tiffany*, London: Thames & Hudson, 1993. W. Edmund Hood et al., *Tiffany Silver Flatware 1845–1905: When Dining Was an Art*, Woodbridge, Suffolk: Collectors' Club, 1999.
> See Moore, Gene; Tiffany, Louis Comfort; Truex, Van Day.

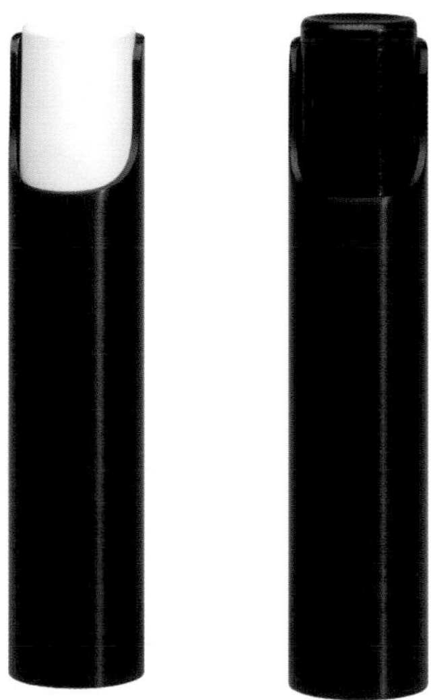

Rud Thygesen and Johnny Sørenson. Salt and pepper rasps. 1975. Metal and plastic, each h. 6" x dia. 1 1/4" (15.3 x 3.2 cm). Mfr.: PP Line, Denmark. Purchase of the Greta Daniel Fund. MoMA.

Tiffany, Louis Comfort (1848–1933)

American glassmaker, jeweler, painter, designer, and interior decorator; born New York; son of Charles L. Tiffany.

Training In painting: under George Innes, New Jersey; 1866–68, Samuel Colman, New York; to 1869, under Léon Bailly, Paris.
Biography From 1870, traveled through Spain, North Africa, and

Louis Comfort Tiffany. Table lamp. c. 1900. Bronze and glass, h. 18" x dia. 15" (45.7 x 38.1 cm). Mfr.: Tiffany Studios, US. Phyllis B. Lambert Fund. MoMA.

Egypt with Hudson River School painter Samuel Colman. Tiffany's later glasswork was influenced by the Hispano-moresque and Roman glass seen on the trip. He became influenced by the French decorative arts he saw at the 1878 *Exposition Universelle* in Paris, and by Edward C. Moore (chief designer and silver-department director at his father's firm), who encouraged him to pursue Orientalism, particularly *japonisme*. 1877 after the 1876 *Centennial Exposition* in Philadelphia, Tiffany founded the Society of American Artists with Innes, Colman, and John La Farge, which led to the 1878 formation of Louis C. Tiffany & Associated Artists. The new company received many commissions, including the 1882–83 red and blue rooms in The White House in Washington, D.C. 1870s, Tiffany began producing distinctive designs in stained glass; first (1876) designed stained glass, for the Thills Glass House in Brooklyn, N.Y.; 1880, made art glass for the Heidt Glass House in Brooklyn with a Venetian glassblower and experimented with color, luster, and opacity; was granted his first (1881) patent for luster-glass and, 1886, a patent for the process of spraying metallic chloride onto hot glass, producing a product that became known as carnival glass. 1885, he founded Tiffany Glass; 1895, was asked by Siegfried Bing to make ten stained-glass windows for Bing's gallery/shop L'Art Nouveau in Paris; they were variously designed by Pierre Bonnard, Édouard Vuillard, Paul Sérusier, and Henri de Toulouse-Lautrec. As early as 1870s, Bing was providing Tiffany with oriental objects; the collaboration placed Tiffany in touch with European artists, spurring him on to greater creativity. Encouraged by his success at 1893 *World's Columbian Exposition*, Chicago, Tiffany established a furnace in Corona, Long Island, N.Y., for the production of blown-glass pieces, inspired by Émile Gallé's work in Nancy, France; 1894, registered the trademark Favrile (from 'hand wrought' in Old Saxon). Favrile, also developed separately by John La Farge, is a kind of glass whose main characteristic is an iridescence with a metallic sheen, and it was produced by Tiffany from 1883 to 1930, when he destroyed all formulas for its making. 1895, he achieved immediate success after showing his Favrile glass at the opening of Bing's Paris shop, and, in the Salon of that year, Tiffany's glassware was bought by European museums and thence widely imitated. 1890, Tiffany established Tiffany Studios in New York to make bronze and lamps; 1900, began producing metalwork and jewelry. On his father's 1902 death, he became artistic director of Tiffany & Co. but preferred not to work at the family firm; 1902–04, spent over $2 million building his artists' colony at Laurelton Hall in Oyster Bay, Long Island. Even though he is best known for his stained glass and art glass, Tiffany also designed and produced mosaics, jewelry, furniture, textiles, and metalwork. His c. 1900 Wisteria lamp epitomizes his skill in combining colored glass and metal to create a delicate but rich illusion. 1932, Tiffany Studios closed. Tiffany had been responsible for persuading rich Americans, who had been buying luxury goods almost exclusively in Europe, to recognize that interior-decoration accouterments and fancy art-glass goods could be designed and produced to the same high standard in the US. By 1946 (even though Tiffany had died more than a decade earlier), the contents of Laurelton Hall were sold at auction by the Tiffany Foundation, which could not afford the upkeep of the estate, to provide for art scholarships. Eventually, the home itself was sold for $10,000, and the parcel of 600 acres (243 hectares) of land around it was subdivided. And further, a 1957 fire gutted the abandoned house, now in ruins. Important exhibitions, from 1950s, have contributed to a revival of an appreciation of Tiffany's work.

Exhibitions/citations Work shown at 1893 *World's Columbian Exposition*, Chicago; 1895, Favrile glass at the opening of Bing's Paris shop; 1885, stained-glass windows at Salon of Société Nationale des Beaux-Arts, Paris; Lily Pod lamp (gold medal) at 1902 *Esposizione Internazionale d'Arte Decorativa Moderna*, Turin; 1904 *Louisiana Purchase Exposition* (pottery), St. Louis; 1915 *Panama-Pacific International Exposition* (pottery), San Francisco; 1975 *The Arts of Louis Comfort Tiffany and His Times*, John and Mable Ringling Museum of Art, Sarasota, Fla., US.

Bibliography Gertrude Speenburgh, *The Arts of the Tiffanys*, Chicago: Lightner, 1956. Robert Koch, 'The Stained-Glass Decades: A Study of Louis Comfort Tiffany (1848–1933) and the Art Nouveau in America,' doctoral thesis, New Haven: Yale University, 1957. Cat., Robert Koch, *Louis Comfort Tiffany, 1848–1933*, New York: Museum of Contemporary Crafts, 1958. Stuart P. Feld, '"Nature in Her Most Seductive Aspects": Louis Comfort Tiffany's Favrile Glass,' *Bulletin of The Metropolitan Museum of Art*, Nov. 1962. Robert Koch, *Louis C. Tiffany: Rebel in Glass*, New York: Crown, 1964. Siegfried Bing, *Artistic America, Tiffany Glass, and Art Nouveau*, Cambridge: MIT, 1970. Cat., Gary A. Reynolds and Robert Littman, *Louis Comfort Tiffany: The Paintings*, New York: Grey Art Gallery and Study Center, 1979. Alastair Duncan, *Tiffany Windows*, New York: Simon & Schuster, 1980 and 1982. Cat., Donald L. Stover, *The Art of Louis Comfort Tiffany*, San Francisco: M.H. de Young Memorial Museum, 1981. William Feldstein Jr. and Alastair Duncan, *The Lamps of Tiffany Studios*, New York: Abrams; London: Thames & Hudson, 1983. Jacob Baal-Teshuva, *Louis Comfort Tiffany*, Cologne: Tashen, 2001. Paola Antonelli (ed.), *Objects of Design: The Museum of Modern Art*, New York: The Museum of Modern Art, 2003: 127.

Tigerman, Stanley (1930–)

American architect; born and active Chicago.

Training Massachusetts Institute of Technology (MIT), Cambridge, Mass.; Institute of Design, Chicago; under Paul Rudolph, 1960, bachelor of architecture degree, and, 1961, master of architecture degree, Yale University, New Haven, Conn.

Biography 1961–62 under Harry M. Weese, Tigerman was the head designer at Skidmore, Owings, and Merrill in Chicago and, from 1962, a partner with Norman Koglin, Chicago; 1964, opened Tigerman and Associates in Chicago; 1965–71, taught, University of Illinois, Chicago Circle; 1960s, was known for designing extremely large structures, including 1968 Instant City; designed 1970–73 vacation house, Burlington, Wis., an example of a refitted old building. His later postmodern buildings included 1977 Daisy House, Porter, Ind., and 1976 Hot Dog House, Harvard, Ill. He and his wife Margaret McCurry (1943–) designed 1980 chair for Knoll, 1983 tableware by Swid Powell, 1983 Tea and Coffee Piazza set by Alessi, 1990 product design by American Standard. Tigerman's later, lighthearted assignments included 1985 Hard Rock Café and 1987 One Pool House, both Chicago. 1988, Tigerman-McCurry participated in the resort site plan and designed buildings at Euro Disney, near Paris. He and McCurry became outspoken voices on contemporary architecture; live in a Mies van der Rohe apartment building, Lake Shore Drive, Chicago. From 1990s, he has been more active in socially conscious projects; wrote the books *Versus: An American Architect's Alternatives* (with Ross Miller and Dorothy Metzger Hobel, New York: Rizzoli, 1982), *The Architect of Exile* (New York: Rizzoli, 1988), and others. 1994 with interior designer Eva Maddox, he established Archeworks (a no-credit one-year internship in urban studies) in Chicago, where a number of buildings and products were created to assist the underprivileged, unemployed, sick, or infirm.

Citations 1985 Alumni Arts Award, Yale University; 1996 Jewish Committee Culture Achievement Award; 2000 Louis Sullivan Award.

Bibliography *Seven Chicago Architects: Beeby, Booth, Cohen, Freed, Nagle, Tigerman, Weese*, Chicago: Richard Gray Gallery, 1976. Muriel Emmanuel, *Contemporary Architects*, New York: St. Martin's, 1980. Stanley Tigerman, *Versus: An American Architect's Alternatives*, New York: Rizzoli, 1982. Officina Alessi, *Tea and Coffee Piazza: 11 Servizi da tè e caffè...*, Milan: Crusinallo, 1983. Robert A.M. Stern, *Modern Classicism*, New York: Rizzoli, 1988. Sarah Mollman Underhill (ed.), *Stanley Tigerman: Buildings and Projects, 1966–1989*, Rizzoli, 1989. Bill Lacy, *100 Contemporary Architects: Drawings and Sketches*, New York: Abrams, 1991. Mel Byars, 'Guerrillas in Our Midst: Stanley Tigerman,' *I.D.*, Jan-Feb. 2001.
> See McCurry, Margaret.

Tihany, Adam D. (1948–)

Interior and furniture/furnishings designer; born Transylvania.

Training Facoltà di Architettura, Politecnico, Milan; apprenticeships in several design studios in Europe.
Biography Tihany was reared in Israel; in Milan, collaborated with Ettore Sottsass on two documentary films about design and architecture; was the art director of design magazine *Rassegna modi abitare oggi*; settled in the US and became the design director of Unigram in New York, where he established his own multidiscliplinary studio in 1978. He has designed commercial and residential interiors, furniture, products, exhibitions, and graphics; conceived and organized 2002 *Grand-HotelSalone* (commissioning ten internationally known designers for individual hotel rooms), Salone del Mobile, Milan. His restaurant interiors have included Le Cirque 2000 and Jean Georges, New York; Gundel, Budapest; Spago, worldwide; Baretto, Paris; 160 Blue, Chicago; numerous others, as well as his own Remi and Regata restaurants worldwide. Other commissions have included Moschino's flagship store in New York, ceramics by Villeroy & Boch, furniture by the Pace Collection and by McGuire, lamps by Baldinger and by Sirmos, linen by Frette, metalware by Christofle, and rugs by M & M Design. He became chairperson, master's-degree program, School of Visual Arts, New York. Tihany wrote the books *Venetian Taste* (cookbook) (with Florence Fabricant, New York: Abbeville, 1994) and *Tihany Design* (with Nina McCarthy, New York: Monacelli, 1999); was the subject of a segment of CNN's *Pinnacle* TV series.

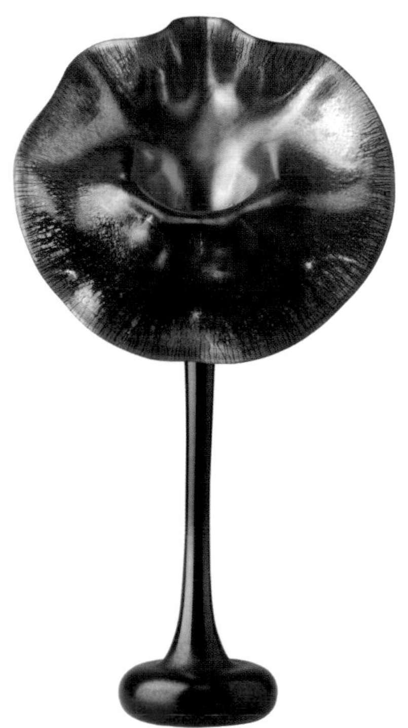

Louis Comfort Tiffany. Vase. 1913. Favrile glass, 20 1/2 x 11 x 4 1/2" (52.1 x 27.9 x 11.4 cm). Mfr.: Tiffany Studios, US. Gift of Joseph H. Heil. MoMA.

Citations 1991 inductee, Hall of Fame, *Interior Design* magazine; member of James Beard's 'Who's Who' in the restaurant industry.

Tilche, Paolo (1925–2000)

Italian architect and designer; born Alexandria; active Milan.

Training To 1949, architecture, Politecnico, Milan.
Biography 1950, Tilche began his career as an architect; was a prolific designer of residences, industrial plants, and offices; became a member, Associazione per il Disegno Industriale (ADI); was known for his inventive shapes and multifunction lighting, glassware, plastic and wooden furniture, domestic kitchenware, and wallpaper for numerous clients such as Arform (furniture), Barbini (blown-glass lighting), Fratelli Guzzini (plastic tabletop accessories), and Ideal Standard (bathroom equipment).
Exhibitions Work included in 1979 and 1983–84 exhibitions, Milan and Philadelphia (catalogs below).
Bibliography *ADI Annual 1976*, Milan: Associazione per il Disegno Industriale, 1976. Cat., *Design & Design*, Milan: Palazzo delle Stelline, 1979. Cat., Kathryn B. Hiesinger and George H. Marcus III (eds.), *Design Since 1945*, Philadelphia: Philadelphia Museum of Art, 1983. Giancarlo Iliprandi and Pierluigi Molinari (eds.), 'Industrial Designers Italiani,' in *Omnibook No. 2*, Udine: Magnus, 1985.

Tillander, Alexander Sr. (1837–1918); Alexander Tillander Jr. (1870–1943)

Finnish jewelers and goldsmiths; active St. Petersburg and Helsinki.

Biography 1860, Tillander the elder established the jewelry firm A. Tillander in St. Petersburg, specializing in diamond jewelry, *objets d'art* in gold and silver, and functional objects such as letter openers, photography frames, and cigarette cases. Tillander was an important supplier of official gifts to the cabinet of Czar Alexander II and to several members of the imperial family. Tillander's customers abroad included the Tiffany store in New York. After the 1917 Russian Revolution, Tillander the younger returned to Helsinki where he continued the jewelry business.
Bibliography A. Kenneth Snowman (ed.), *The Master Jewelers*, London: Thames & Hudson; New York: Abrams, 1990. Géza von Habsburg, *Fabergé, Imperial Craftsman, and His World*, London: Booth-Clibborn, 2000.

Tillett, 'Doris' D.D.

American textile designer.

Biography 1946 with her husband Leslie Tillett (d.1992), who had experience in textile production and color technology, she established a laboratory and studio where printed textiles were designed/produced in New York. The Tilletts created motifs by dyeing directly onto a fabric rather than the traditional procedure of first drawing with watercolors on paper; designed textiles for both custom and mass production. Wholesale clients included Covington, J.C. Penney, and Leacock. Some Tillett designs were adapted from nature, including 1950 Queen Anne's Lace, part of the firm's inventory for more than 30 years. Some of Doris's designs were inspired by Peruvian art, ancient tapestries, and 19th-century sporting prints. 1954, the couple created designs for printed fiberglass by Owens Corning.
Exhibition 1984 *Design Since 1945* (Queen Anne's Lace fabric), Philadelphia Museum of Art (catalog below).
Bibliography 'Pilot Printing Plant,' *Interiors*, vol. 108, June 1949. Don Wallance, *Shaping America's Products*, New York: Reinhold, 1956. Cat., Kathryn B. Hiesinger and George H. Marcus III (eds.), *Design Since 1945*, Philadelphia: Philadelphia Museum of Art, 1983.

Timmermans, Hugo (1967–)

Dutch designer; born Zambia; active Amsterdam.

Biography From 1992, Timmermans has been a professional independent designer; 1995 with Job Smeets (1969–), set up the brand Oval. (Smeets studied at the Hogeschool voor de Kunsten, Utretcht, under Li Edelkoort.) Also with Job Smeets, Timmermans works with Studio Edelkoort and Droog Design. Timmermans's products have included Leaning Mirror (produced by Optic) and 1996 Bumperlights Nana and Rosie floor and ceiling lamps (with Smeets, by Oval). Timmermans separated from Oval, founded Optic in 1997, and designed 1998 Dice lounge chair, 1998 Silver floor lamp, 1999 Milan-O wall cupboard, and 1999 H2O glass-bowl collection. The items in Optic's 1999 O Collection were based on the shape of the letter

Oiva Toikka. Tauperle plates and bowls. 1964. Clear pressed glass, large plate dia. 6 3/4" (17.2 cm), small plate dia. 5 3/8" (13.7 cm), bowl dia. 2" (5 cm). Mfr.: Nuutajärvi Notsjö, Finland. Courtesy Quittenbaum Kunstauktionen, Munich.

'O'—Timmermans discovered that he 'could easily transform virtually any product into an "O" product,' in his words. Willem van der Sluis (1972–) and Timmermans designed 2002 Airco and 2002 Biodomestic lamps by LucePlan. (Van de Sluis is a 1996 graduate of Gerrit Rietveld Academie, Amsterdam.)
Exhibitions/citations First Optic collection included in 1998 *Dutch Individuals*, Mendini Studio parking lot, Milan. Subsequently: Intérieur '98 design biennial, Courtrai; 1999, Designers Block (in *Dutch Individuals* exhibition), London; 1999, Spazio Consolo, Milan. Several Dutch design citations, such as 1992 Prize for Young Designers; 1993 Best Dutch Furniture Design.
Bibliography Philippe Starck (ed.), *International Design Yearbook*, London: Laurence King, 1997.

Timorous Beasties
British design studio; located Glasgow.

History 1990, Timorous Beasties was established by Alistair McAuley (Clydebank, 1967–) and Paul Simmons (Brighton, 1967–), who met while students at the Glasgow School of Art in 1980s. The group both designs and produces contemporary and traditional fabrics and wallpapers for the contract and retail markets. 1999, developed the Strata Bar and the Arches Theatre, both Glasgow (with studio One Foot Taller, a group dubbed 'textile mavericks' by *Blueprint* magazine). The name 'Timorous Beasties' is taken from Robert Burns's poem 'To a Mouse, on Turning Her up in Her Nest with the Plough' (1785): 'Wee, sleekit, cow'rin', tim'rous beastie…'
Exhibition 2001 *Home Alone* (with One Foot Taller), Glasgow Art Fair.

Tinuper, Paola (1967–)
> See Azzolini, Paola.

Tiroler Glashütte
> See Riedel.

Tisdale, David (1956–)
American designer; born San Diego, Cali.

Training University of California, Berkeley; University of California, Davis; art, San Diego State University.
Biography 1981–86, Tisdale was active in David Tisdale Jewelry Design, New York, designing architectonic wearables; 1986, established David Tisdale Design to specialize in tablewares and tabletop items, notably 1985 Picnic anodized aluminum cutlery made by Tisdale himself; recently, jewelry holder and Nurture and Cherish photography frames by Nambé; c. 1995 Mangia! (with Nicole Zeller) by Zelco. Concurrently with Judy Smilow (to 1992), Tisdale a partner in Fresh Design, New York, established 1989. His work has been widely published.
Exhibitions/citations From 1978, work shown in numerous exhibitions, including *Take a Bite: 20th Century Flatware from the Permanent Collection* (Picnic cutlery), Philadelphia Museum of Art. 1985 American Craft Museum Design Award and 1986 Pantone Color Award; both for Picnic; 1996 *Good Design* award for Mangia!), *Chicago Anthenaeum.*

Tisdall, Hans (b. Hans Aufseeser 1910–)
German painter and designer; active Munich, Paris, and London.

Training Akademie der bildenden Künste, Munich.
Biography 1930, Tisdall established a studio on Fitzroy Street, London, and began designing mural paintings, book jackets, and textiles. His 1938 Athene jacquard woven-cotton fabric was produced by Edinburgh Weavers in Carlisle, as well as other 1938–39 patterns. He created large-scale paintings, mosaics, and tapestries for public buildings, including those of English Electric, Manchester University, and Ionian Bank. By 1980s, he was a lecturer in fine art, Central St Martin's School of Art and Design, London; Dartington International Summer School, Dartington Hall, Totnes, Devon; and in Venice.
Exhibitions/citation Work shown at 1937 *Exposition Internationale des Arts et Techniques dans la Vie Moderne* (medal of honor), Paris; 1979 exhibition, London (catalog below). Subject of a 1945 exhibition.
Bibliography Cat., *Thirties: British Art and Design Before the War*, London: Arts Council of Great Britain/Hayward Gallery, 1979.

Tjaarda von Sterkenberg, John (1897–1962)
Dutch automobile engineer, mechanic, designer, race-car driver, pilot.

Training Aeronautical design, the UK.
Biography Tjaarda held patents on the contant-velocity universal joint and unibody construction of automobiles. Studied aerodynamcis under Dr Alexander Klemin; worked for Fokker airplane manufacturer

Kazuhiko Tomita. Morode plates/bowls. c. 1998. Porcelain, salad bowl h. 4 3/8 x dia. 9" (11 x 23 cm). Mfr.: Covo, Italy.

in Germany as an engineer, and in Great Britain; 1923, emigrated to the US and, 1924, to Hollywood, Cal., and worked for custom coachbuilders Locke and Company, for Duesenberg, and others; late 1920s, designed a range of monocoque, streamlined car bodies known as the Sterkenberg series (named for himself and inspired by Paul Jaray's bodies); also designed bodies for Packard, Pierce Arrow, Stutz, and others, including 1932 Briggs Dream Car and 1936 Lincoln Zephyr models; worked under Harley Earl in the Art and Colour Section of General Motors, Detroit, Mich. In World War II, Tjaarda flew in the Dutch airforce and, after the war, he became a pilot for KLM airlines.
Bibliography Penny Sparke, *A Century of Car Design*, London: Mitchell Beazley, 2002.

Toffoloni, Werther (1930–)
Italian designer; born Udine; active Manzano.

Biography Toffoloni designed ceramics, furniture, accessories, and fabrics (in collaboration with Piero Palange to 1975) for various firms in Italy, including the G 54 wooden table and a rocking chair by Germa in Pavia. Other clients included A. Barbini, E. & C. Pecci, Fratelli Montina, Gabbianelli Ceramiche, Gervasoni, Ibisi, Iterby Italiana Mobili, Malobbia, Mobel Italia, Moretuzzo, Schieder Möbel, and Tonon. He became a member, Associazione per il Disegno Industriale (ADI).
Bibliography *ADI Annual 1976*, Milan: Associazione per il Disegno Industriale, 1976.

Toikka, Oiva (1931–)
Finnish ceramicist and glass, stage, and textile designer.

Training 1953–60, ceramics, Taideteollinen korkeakoulu, Helsinki.
Biography 1956–59, Toikka worked at the Arabia pottery and, 1959, at Marimekko textiles. 1960–63, he taught, Taideteollinen korkeakoulu, and, 1959–63, secondary school, Sodankylä; from 1963, was the artistic director of Nuutajärvi Notsjö glassworks; from 1985, visiting designer at Rörstrand Porslinsfabriker, Sweden. From 1960s, Toikka was a costume and scenery designer for Tampere and for theaters and opera houses in Savonlinna, including creating the sets of the ballet *Silkdrum* (1984).
Citations 1970 Lunning Prize; 1975 Valtion Taideteollisuuspalkinto (Finnish state award); 1980 Pro Finlandia prize; Prince Eugen Medal.
Bibliography Jennifer Hawkins Opie, *Scandinavia: Ceramics and Glass in the Twentieth Century*, New York: Rizzoli, 1989.

Tominaga, Kei (1966–)
Japanese designer; born Tokyo.

Training To 1990, Tokyo National University of Fine Arts and Music.
Biography Tominaga's work has included 1998 Warp Pillow in plastic and steel for wall placement, 1999 Stacking Chair for different height variances, 1999 Table Unbalanced in metal weighted at one point with a self-balancing surface, 2001 White Out clock in optical film, 2001 HIMO height-varying stool in wood and rubber. He has designed the Bouzs hanging lamp by Adobe and collaborated with Ross McBride and Takuyuki Miyoshi through design studio Normal.
Exhibitions From 1998, work included in various exhibitions. In Tokyo: subject of venues at Natuka gallery in 1991, Gallery Myu in 1997, Le Doco gallery in 2000, Saatchi and Saatchi gallery in 2001, and various installations.

Tomita, Kazuhiko (1965–)
Japanese designer; born Nagasaki.

Training 1989, bachelor's degree, industrial design, Chiba University, Chiba, Japan; 1990, on Cassina scholarship and British Council grant, furniture design, Royal College of Art, London.
Biography After study in London, Tomita moved to Italy and designed for Rörstrand Porslinsfabriker, Sweden and Italian firms such as Covo ceramics (1998 Morode dinnerware, tea set, cups, and other pieces). 2000, he became the artistic director of Covo and designed its first retail store, in Rome. Designed 2001 Rim dinnerware (with Vico Magistretti) by Rörstrand.
Exhibitions/citations Participated in 1995 *Two Nagasakis*; organized *Two Europeans*, marking 50th anniversary of Nagasaki atomic bomb explosion; others. Subject of *2.5-Dimensional Design*, Ozone Gallery, Tokyo. Prize, Design Eye 89, Nagoya; first prize, 1991 Architectural Future of Stainless Steel competition, British Stainless Steel (BSS); gold medal, 1992 Marchett Award, UK; 1997 Red Dot for high design quality, Design Zentrum Nordrhein Westfalen, Essen; 1998 G-Mark Good Design special prize (for small- and medium-size businesses), Japanese Industrial Design Promotion Organization (JIDPO); 1999, first prize, Nippon Craft Design Exihibition, Tokyo; 2001 Design Plus prize, Ambiente fair, Frankfurt; others.
Bibliography *The International Design Yearbook*, London: Laurence King, 1999, 2000, and 2002.

Tonelli
Italian furniture company; located Montelabbate (PS).

History Founded 1987, Tonelli produces furniture that calls on glass made by Flos and is assembled with acrylic monocomponent resins, sealed via UV rays to eliminate visible joins. Its extensive inventory has included 1988 Albero display unit by Isao Hosoe, 1994 Birillo console by Hermian Sneyders De Vogel, 1994 Camicino side table on rollers and 1994 Comò Alto chest of drawers by Marco Gaudenzi, 1998 Cortesia Carrello trolley and 2002 hanging lamp by D'Urbino/Lomazzi, 2000 Frosty dining table by Dorina Camusso, 2003 Stratos dining table by Denis Santachiara, and a number of products by the inhouse staff. 60% of its production is exported.
> See Flos.

Tonucci, Enrico (1946–)
Italian industrial and graphic designer; born and active Pesaro.

Training In Florence; course in scenographics, Accademia di Belle Arti, Urbino.
Biography From 1970, Tonucci designed furniture, lighting, accessories, and furnishings by Walter Knoll and others in Germany, and by Novalinea and by La Bottega in Italy; became a member, Associazione per il Disegno Industriale (ADI).
Bibliography *ADI Annual 1976*, Milan: Associazione per il Disegno Industriale, 1976. *Modo*, no. 148, Mar.–Apr. 1993: 126–27.

Toraldo di Francia, Cristiano (1941–)
Italian designer; born and active Florence.

Training To 1968, architecture, Florence.
Biography 1966, Toraldo di Francia began his professional career in Florence; from 1966, cofounded Superstudio in Florence with Adolfo Natalini, Roberto Magris, Piero Frassinelli, and Alessandro Magris; has designed furniture systems, furnishings, lighting, and accessories; taught industrial design, Università Internazionale dell'Arte (UIA), Florence; lectured in the US; from 1970, collaborated with Gruppo 9999 and Scuola Separata per l'Architettura Concettuale Espansa (S-Space); 1973–75, cofounded and designed for Global Tools designers' collective; also designed Bazaar seating system and Teso knock-down table by Giovanetti; produced films on architecture and designed post-modern 1987–90 bus station in Florence, and others. He wrote the book *Cultura materiale extraurbana* (with A. Natalini, L. Netti, A. Poli, Florence: Alinea, 1983).
Exhibitions 1972 *Italy: The New Domestic Landscape*, The Museum of Modern Art, New York; 1973 (15th) Triennale di Milano; 1973–75 exhibition of Superstudio's work, touring Europe and the US; 2003 *Superstudio: Life Without Objects*, Design Museum, London.
Bibliography Gianni Patetta, *Cristiano Toraldo di Francia, progetti ed architetture 1980–1988*, Milan: Electa, 1988;
> See Superstudio.

Torck, Emmanuelle (1963–); Emmanuelle Noirot (1961–)
French furniture designers; active Meudon.

Training École Nationale Supérieure des Arts Décoratifs, Paris (Torck to 1963, Noirot to 1961).
Biography 1988, they established a studio for the design of furniture and interiors. Their first work of note has been 1986 Pilo Toic recamier by Christian Farjon, 1990 Lucienne chair range by Idée, 1993 folding table and console by Le Mobilier National, 1994 Feu Follet table lamp by Verre Lumière, 1996 Filo stool and Rapido table by 3 Suisse, 1998 furniture range by Macé, and Arlequin Pyrex oil lamp and 1998 T&N side chair by Cinna. By Ligne Roset: 1992 furniture range, 1993 Cosy Pilo table-lamp combination range, and 1999 club chair. Other furniture/furnishings/objects by these and other firms, as well as Escale range of children's products for the UGAP catalog and custom work for private clients and 1993 interior of Optic Land store.
Citations 1988 Agora grant; 1987, 1993 VIA (French furniture associ-

ation) sponsorship, and 1991 Carte Blanche production support, VIA; 1989 Prix de la Press et de la Critique, Salon du Meuble, Paris.
Bibliography François Mathey, *Au bonheur des formes, design français 1945–1992*, Paris: Regard, 1992: 255. Cat., Sophie Tasma Anargyros et al., *L'école française: les créateurs de meubles du 20ème siècle*, Paris: Industries Françaises de l'Ameublement, 2000. Arlette Barré-Despond (ed.), *Dictionnaire international des arts appliqués et du design*, Paris: Regard, 1996.

Tordarson, Olufur (1963–)

Icelandic architect and designer; born Reykjavik; active New York.

Training 1989, under Robert A.M. Stern and, 1990, master of architecture degree, both Columbia University, New York.
Biography Tordarson was a long-time collaborator of, and designer with, Gaetano Pesce, New York; has taught at a number of institutions, including Rhode Island School of Design, Providence, R.I. Architecture work includes 1984 Beth's house, Washington Island, Wis, US; 1995 Svartsengi power-plant visitors' center, Iceland; 1998 Laugardalur, Olympic-size swimming pool, Reykjavik. In New York: 1999 Gallery 91 and 1999–2000 design store of the New Museum of Contemporary Art. From 1974, he has designed a number of products, lighting, and furniture.
Exhibitions One-person exhibitions include John Elder Gallery, New York, in 2001–02; Museum of Design and Arts, Iceland, in 2002.

Torre, Pierluigi
> See Innocenti, Ferdinado.

Torres Clavé, Josep (1906–1939)

Spanish architect and designer; born Barcelona.

Training 1925–29 under Bona, Azúa, Nebor, and others, Escola Tècnica Superior d'Arquitectura de Barcelona (ETSAB).
Biography 1930, Torres Clavé cofounded Grup d'Arquitectes i Tècnics Catalans per al Progrés de l'Arquitectura Contemporània (GATCPAC), an association that introduced new housing and furniture concepts through Rationalist theories. He designed a number of furniture models, including prototypes for his mother and sister while he was a student; later, for his own home; and examples in production today by Santa & Cole (1931 Gatcpac floor lamp) and Mobles 114 (1934 Butaca armchair, inspired by the traditional *cadirat* of Ibiza). His best-known buildings are 1932–36 Casa Bloc and 1935 Dispensari Antituberculós, both Barcelona, and 1934–35 Garraf houses (with Josep Lluís Sert) in Catalonia. Was a peer of Le Corbusier, Siegfried Giedion, Walter Gropius, Alvar Aalto, and others of the international achitectural congress (CIAM); from 1931, was in practice with Josep Luís Sert—they were joined 1932 by Antonio Bonet; 1935, with Sert and Bonet, formed the firm Muebles y Decoración para la Vivienda Actual (MIDVA, furnishings and decoration for today's living). He died from Italian airplane shrapnel wounds.
Exhibitions Participated in a number of exhibitons and international expositions. Has become known for the chair he designed for the Spanish Republic Pavilion, 1937 *Exposition Internationale des Arts et Techniques dans la Vie Moderne*, Paris. Work subject of 1980 exhibition, Col·legi d'Arquitectes de Catalunya.
Bibliography Raimon Torres (ed.), *Torres Clavé*, Barcelona: Santa & Cole/ETS, 1994.

Torres Tur, Eliás (1944–)

Spanish architect and designer; born Eivissa.

Training To 1968, Escola Tècnica Superior d'Arquitectura de Barcelona (ETSAB), and, 1993, doctoral degree, ETSAB.
Biography 1968 with José Antonio Martínez Lapeña, Torres established an architecture practice; 1973–77, was the architect of the Diocese of Ibiza; from 1969–79, professor, ETSAB; 1977, 1981, and 1984, guest professor, University of California, Los Angeles, and, 1995, Harvard University, Cambridge, Mass.; prepared the manual *Guia de Arquitectura en Ibiza y Formentera (Islas Pitiusas)* (Barcelona: La Gaya Ciencia, 1981). Torres designed 1986 Lampelunas street light (with Martínez and Viader) by Cemusa, 1986 Barcelona and 1986 Hollywood rugs by BVD, and 1987 bus shelter (with José Luís Canosa) by Cemusa. 1990, Torres was a resident, Spanish Academy in Rome.
Citations 1974–5 Premi FAD d'Interiorisme (decorative-arts association); 1986, 1988, 1992 Premi FAD d'Arquitectura; 2000 Premi FAD d'Espais Efimers (ephemeral space) Award, Spain.
Bibliography Juli Capella and Quim Larrea, *Designed by Architects in the 1980s*, New York: Rizzoli, 1988. N. Inagawa, 'Architecture of J.A. Martinez Lapeña + Elias Torres Tur, *Space Design*, no. 4, 1990.
> See Martínez Lapeña, José Antonio.

Torricelli, Eugenio (1948–)

Italian designer; born and active Milan.

Training To 1971, architecture.
Biography 1972, Torricelli began his professional career. Clients have included Sormani (furniture, accessories, and lighting), 1972; Brevetto (mechanical equipment), 1972; Mopoa Milano (clocks), 1974; Velca Legnano (furniture), and Gabbianelli (tableware). 1973, he designed the graphics of magazine *Nuovi orizzonti*, published by the Italian Tourist Bureau; has taught, Liceo Artistico di Brera, Milan; became a member, Associazione per il Disegno Industriale (ADI).
Citation 1973 prize, Concorso Internazionale della Ceramica d'Arte, Faenza.
Bibliography *ADI Annual 1976*, Milan: Associazione per il Disegno Industriale, 1976.

Tosi, Lorenzo (1948–)

Italian designer; born Cortemaggiore; active Milan.

Training To 1974, chemistry; industrial design, Scuola Politecnica di Disegno, Milan.
Biography Tosi was associated with design and communication collaborative Gruppo in Milan, whose members included Giorgio Brambilla, Anna Castelli, and Fabio Stojan; was active in the office of prevention and safety of Montedison in Milan; became a member, Associazione per il Disegno Industriale (ADI).
Bibliography *ADI Annual 1976*, Milan: Associazione per il Disegno Industriale, 1976.

Toso, Aureliano (1894–1979); Gianni Toso (1942–); Renato Toso (1940–)

Italian glass designers; active Murano.

Biographies There have been a large number of Tosos in the glassmaking business (see entry below). 1950s in Murano, Aureliano Toso, an accountant by training, was active as a glass designer in the family glass factory, established in the 19th century. From 1962, Gianni Toso worked there, as did husband and wife Renato Toso and Noti Massari, and Roberto Pamio. (Renato Toso, a graduate, Istituto Universitario di Venezia, and apprentice in the family factory, has designed furniture, furnishings, ceramics, textiles for others, particularly lighting by Artimede and Leucos, through studio of Renato Toso, Noti Massari & Associati, Venice.)
Bibliography *Moderne Klassiker: Möbel, die Geschichte machen*, Hamburg: Gruner + Jahr, 1982. Hans Wichman, *Italien Design 1945 bis heute*, Munich: Die Neue Sammlung, 1988.

Toso, Decio (1901–1988); Luigi Toso (1937–); Mario d'Alpaos (1942–)

Italian glassmakers.

Biography 1923, Decio Toso, Giuseppe d'Alpaos (1899–1980), Guglielmo Barbini (1898–1999), and Gino Francesconi (all former employees of Cristalleria Franchetti) founded Studio Ars Labor Industrie Riunite (S.A.L.I.R), which initially specialized in the engraving and enameling of mirrors and other objects, and used blanks from Ferro Toso & C. and later from others. (Designers working for S.A.L.I.R. included Fulvio Bianconi, Giorgio de Chirico, Riccardo Licata, Gio Ponti, Ettore Sottsass, Agostino Venturini, Vinicio Vianello, and Vittorio Zecchin.) Francesconi resigned in 1932, and Guglielmo Barbini in 1936. Toso and d'Alpaos served as directors to 1976, when management was passed to their children, Luigi Toso and Mario d'Alpaos. In a separate enterprise, after their father Luigi Toso (1871–1933) died, Decio and his brothers Artemio and Mario began managing their father's Società Anonima Industrie Artistiche Riunite Ferro Toso (S.A.I.A.R. Ferro Toso). This merged with Vetreria Artistica Barovier & C. in 1936 and continued production under the name Ferro Toso Barovier Vetreria Artistiche Riunite S.A. and, from 1976, under Barovier & Toso S.r.l.

Tostrup, J.

Norwegian silversmiths; located Christiania (now Oslo).

History 1832, the firm J. [Jacob] Tostrup was founded; became best known for its enamel work, in *champlevé* and *cloisonné* and, from

1890s, specialized in the *plique-à-jour* technique, achieving elegant effects after 1900; also produced cutlery and hollow-ware. 1890–1912, Thorolf Prytz (1858–1938) was the director/designer, creating motifs inspired by local fauna and flora; 1912, was succeeded by his son Jacob Tostrup Prytz (1886–1962). 1920s, Oskar Sørensen designed simple forms suitable for mass production by machinery. 1950s or 1960s, other work included jewelry and vessels by Gine Sommerfeldt. c. 1945, and Grete Prytz Kittelsen (1917–), daughter of Jacob Prytz, who designed for her family's enterprise as well as for other firms.
Exhibitions Work (including standing dishes by Emil Saeter) shown at 1900 *Exposition Universelle*, Paris; Norwegian Pavilion (Tostrup stand designed by Prytz Kittelsen, who received a grand prize) of 1954 (10th) Triennale di Milano; 1952 enamel exhibition (Prytz Kittelsen's new work), Kunstindustrimuseet, Oslo.
Bibliography Annelies Krekel-Aalberse, *Art Nouveau and Art Déco Silver*, New York: Abrams, 1989. L. Opstad, *Tostrup 1832–1982: Seks generasioner i ett museum*, Oslo: Tostrup, 1982.
> See Prytz, Thorolf; Kittelsen, Grete Prytz.

Totem
French design collaborative; located Lyon.

History 1980, Totem was established in Lyon by cabinetmakers Jacques Bonnot (Lyon, 1950–), Frédéric du Chayla (Lyon, 1957–), Vincent Lemarchands (Lyon, 1960–), and Claire Olivès (El-Biar, Algeria, 1958–). Their furniture and furnishings straddled art and utility, often in primary or bright colors. 1980–90 work included about 100 furniture pieces for the town hall of Villeurbanne, near Lyon, and for Musée d'Art Moderne, Saint-Étienne, also signage there. They also designed tableware by Manufacture Nationale de Sèvres; rugs, furniture, and objects for Archimia by Zabro; 1982 Flipper table with a triton leg (perhaps Totem's best-known work); 1983 lamps by Drimmer; 1984 lamps by D'Albret. 1986, Olivès left the group, as did Lemarchands in 1987. 1987–91, only Bonnot and du Chayla were members, and, from 1991, du Chayla alone. (From 1991, Bonnot collaborated with the Ilotopie theater and performance group; from 1999, managed the 'net.labyrinthique et chaotique' Web site.)
Exhibitions Numerous one-group shows: 1981, Galerie Envers, Lyon (Guillotine chair, Tour bookcase, and Bac armchair) and, 1981, Galerie VIA (French furniture association), Paris (Caméléon armchair, Sarcophage secretary, Spaghetti chairs, Armoire de célibataire, Zig Zag table, Lolly Pop chair); others (catalogs below). Since Totem's dissolution, 2000 *Totem, rétrospective*, Musée d'Art Moderne, Saint-Étienne (catalog below).
Bibliography Gilles de Bure, *Le mobilier français 1965–1979*, Paris: Regard, 1983: 130–31. Cat., *Totem, L'île bleue*, Saint-Étienne: Musée de l'Abbaye Sainte-Croix, 1984. Cat., *Martin Szekely, Groupe Totem, exposition de création industrielle*, Vassivière-en-Limousin, 1986. Cat., *Design français 1960–1990: trois décennies,* Paris, Centre George Pompidou, 1988. Cat., *Les années VIA 1980–1990*, Paris: Musée des Arts Décoratifs, 1990. Cat., Claire Fayolle, *Totem 1980–1987*, Saint-Étienne: Musée d'Art Moderne, 2000.
> See du Chayla, Frédéric; Lemarchands, Vincent; Olivès, Claire.

Toulemonde Bochard
French carpet factory; located Wissous.

History 1939, the firm was founded, from 1970s managed by Gérard Toulemonde and began to pursue design research; from early 1980s, has commissioned contemporary designers and artists. 1987, Les Grands Créateurs à Vos Pieds was introduced, Patrick Cambolin created the firm's logo, and a new factory was built. Early on, its rug designers included Andrée Putman (1987 Trasimène, 1988 Come Gris Blanc, 1990 Camille et Sophie), Christian Duc (1987 Minute Passé Chine, 1989 Carré d'as Nuit), Pascal Mourgue (1988 Alhassane Noir), Hilton McConnico (a large number), and others such as Charlotte Derain, Didier Gomez, and Jean-Michel Wilmotte. Contemporary artists' contributions in 1992: Arman (Stain Proof), Pol Bury (Têtes Perdues), Maurice Lemaître (Le Champs d'Orisis), Peter Klasen (K), and others. Prisme was a collection by young designers. 2001, a retail store was opened in Nice, and now throughout France; The firm continues today with designer rugs as well as anonymous examples that incorporate wood, paper, or other non-traditional and traditional materials. The firm is still family owned.
Citation 1992 Design Prize (for the firm's logo), European Community.
Bibliography Arlette Barré-Despond (ed.), *Dictionnaire international des arts appliqués et du design*, Paris: Regard, 1996. www.toulemondebochart.fr.

Karl Trabert. Desk lamp. 1932–34. Metal and chrome-plated tubular stem, h. 17 7/8" (45.4 cm); shade dia. 12 15/16" (32.9 cm), base dia. 7" (17.8 cm). BAG, Switzerland. Philip Johnson Fund. MoMA.

Tourette, Étienne
French enameler; active Paris.

Training Under Louis Houillon, Paris.
Biography Tourette produced jewelry for Georges Fouquet, Lalique, and other jewelers in Paris; from 1900, used *paillons* in his enamel work to lend brilliance to his jewelry, boxes, and vases.
Exhibitions From 1878, showed work jointly with Louis Houillon; independently from 1893, including at 1902 Salon.
Bibliography Léonard Penicaud, 'L'émail aux Salons de 1902,' *Revue de la bijouterie, joaillerie et orfèvrerie*, 1902: 165. Annelies Krekel-Aalberse, *Art Nouveau and Art Déco Silver*, New York: Abrams, 1989.

Towle & Son Company, A.F.; Towle and Jones
> See Lunt Silversmiths.

Toyoda, Hiroyuki (1946–2000)
Japanese designer; born Saitama.

Training To 1973, engineering, architecture faculty, Musashi Institute of Technology, Tokyo; from 1975, Istituto Universitario di Architettura, Venice.
Biography While studying architecture in Venice, Toyoda met Carlo Scarpa, became his disciple, and wrote about him, including the book *Carlo Scarpa, il maestro che incontrai a Venezia* (Carlo Scarpa, the master I met in Venice) (1977) and a 1997 volume on Scarpa with Yutaka Saitō and Nobuaki Furuya (Tokyo: TOTO Shuppan), and organized posthumous Scarpa exhibitions in Europe and Japan. 1970s, he designed for Dino Gavina and then for Gavina's Simón. 1968 work for Simón included Bisanzio table range, Burano floating-glass table, Iseo two-part mirror, and Otero slit-glass mirror, now being reissued by Ultramobile, which has assumed Simon's production. 1985 Pelle chair range remains in production by ICF. 1980s–90s, he designed a number of buildings and renovations in Italy and Japan.

Trabert, Karl
German designer.

Training Bauhaus.
Biography Little is of known of Trabert. However, he designed modern lamps, while he was at the Bauhaus in the late 1920s–early 1930s. A particular model of 1932–34 was produced by G. Schanzenbach of

Frankfurt am Main and, under license, by BAG (Bronzewarenfabrik AG) of Turgi, Switzerland. The Schanzenbach version incorporates a curved translucent glass element into the almost semi-spherical black-painted metal diffuser; the BAG model has no glass element. He also purportedly designed a 1928 floor lamp, whose diffuser was made of Diffuna, a proprietary processed-paper material.

Trabucco, Francesco (1944–)

Italian architect and industrial designer; born Milan.

Training To 1970, Facoltà di Architettura, Politecnico, Milan.
Biography Trabucco began his professional career in the US and Africa; collaborated with Marco Zanuso Sr. on several projects, including IBM offices, Milan; Alitalia headquarters, Rome; Congress Building, Palermo; and Regione Umbria Building, Perugia. From 1974, he has designed furniture and appliances for Alfatec, Elam, Emmegi, Foppa Perdetti, Olivo e Groppo, Rib, and Vortice, partially from 2001, with Mario Faicchia, a partner in studio FT&A. From 1984, Trabucco has been professor of industrial design, Politecnico, Milan, and a visiting professor, Escola Superior de Desenho (ESDI) of the Universidade do Estado, Rio de Janeiro, and ENSCI (les Ateliers), Paris; founded and directed UdR PPI (product-design research unit), Politecnico, Milan. Trabucco's publications: *Dire fare: riflessioni intorno al progettare prodotti industriali* (Bologna: Progetto Leonardo, 1993), *Design: storia e storiografia* (with Vanni Pasca, Bologna: Esculapio, 1995, and *Le case della Triennale: otto progetti di ambienti domestici contemporanei* (with Franco Raggi, Milan: Electa/Triennale di Milano, 1983).
Exhibitions/citations Chief curator, 1983 *Le Case della Triennale*, 17th Triennale di Milano, Milan and Paris; designed Italian section (*La Vita tra Cose e Natura: Il Progetto e la Sfida Ambientale*), 18th Triennale. Design awards have included Premio Compasso d'Oro, Italy; Industrie Forum Design (iF), Hanover; BIO industrial-design biennial, Ljubljana.

Trägårdh, Jan Christer (1931–)

Danish industrial designer.

Training Anders Beckman School of Design, Stockholm; in painting school in southern Europe.
Biography Trägårdh worked for five years in the Bernadotte & Bjørn design firm in Copenhagen; 1957, established his own design studio in Copenhagen for industrial design and product development; became best known for a pot series by Copco (at Bernadotte & Bjørn), possibly Beolit 1000 radio (with Jacob Jensen) by Bang & Olufsen, signage system (with Niels Hartmann) for Modulex, 1979 Concorde turntable arm (with graphics designer Flemming Ljørring) by Ortofon, 1980 Modular rescue kit by Ambu International, 1989 Gourmeta cooking-pot series by Iwachu.
Citations 1982 award, Dansk Designråd (Danish design council); 1991 lifetime grant, Statens Kunstfond (Danish arts foundation).
Bibliography Peter Gyllan, Svend Kindt, and Jens Nielsen, *Design Jan*, Copenhagen: Dansk Design Centre, 1999.

Tram Design

French design workshop; located Charvonnex/Annecy and Limoges.

History 1983, Tram Design was established by Jean-François Mermillot (1951–) to specialize in general consumer products, mechanical equipment, visual-identity programs, and packaging. The multi-disciplinary group's products have included SX91 shoe, 1983 747 ski bindings, and 1984 Profila roller-cutter system by Salomon. And, recently, Pulsar public phone by Landis & Gyr, dental equipment by Anthogyr, automobile tire by Michelin, TV stand by Erard, RP 500 photocopier by Eie, stapler and school-stationery supplies by Maped, Vivial telephone-answering machine by Secom, hiking boot by Lafuma, cycling helmets by Time, and a number of other products.

Tremoleda, Josep Maria (1946–)
> See Massana, Josep Maria.

Tremulus, Alex Sarantos (1914–1994)

American automobile designer.

Biography For a time, Tremulus was active in Beverly Hills, Cal.; 1936, took over the design of 1935–37 Cord 812 from Gordon Guehrig, who was the original designer of the body; from 1937, worked at the Oldsmobile division of General Motors in Detroit, Mich.; subsequently, designed 1941 Chrysler Thunderbolt for Briggs coachbuilders; was adept at futuristic concepts and at working well with engineers to realize his ideas; from 1941, was active with the US airforce on advanced-concept airplanes, a space craft (later called Dyna-Soar), and some so-called flying saucers. Dec. 1946, Preston Thomas Tucker (Capac, Mich., 1903–Chicago 1956), who founded the Tucker Corporation in Chicago in 1946, commissioned Tremulus to create a car for him, giving Tremulus 100 days to accomplish the task. Tremulus built the Tin Goose maquette in tin; clay, traditionally used for maquettes, was not available. And thus Tremulus has essentially become known for this single design —1948 Tucker Torpedo with three headlights (one that moved when the steering wheel was turned) and an interior by Audrey Moore Hodges. 51 examples were built in Chicago in a very large factory, now the site of Ford City Mall on Cicero Avenue. 47 examples have survived. The car was the subject of the film *Tucker: The Man and His Dream* (1948; director, Francis Ford Coppola).
Bibliography Penny Sparke, *A Century of Car Design*, London: Mitchell Beazley, 2002.

Tresoldi, Ambrogio (1933–)

Italian architect, designer, and teacher.

Training From 1960, studied architecture in Milan.
Biography From 1960, Tresoldi collaborated with Alberto Salvati; 1961–62, was an assistant instructor, faculty of architecture, Politecnico, Milan; became active as an architect and an interior and industrial designer.
> See Salvati, Alberto.

Tresserra Clapés, Jaime (1943–)

Spanish architect and interior and furniture designer; born Barcelona.

Biography For 15 years, Tresserra worked as an architect and interior designer; subsequently, pursued furniture, carpet, and lighting design; 1986, set up his own studio; 1989 El Dorado Petit restaurant in New York, designed packaging for the 1992 Olympiad, Barcelona. His furniture has been selected for inclusion in many film sets. His limited-production 1988–89 Carlton House 'Butterfly' articulated desk was widely published.
Exhibitions/citations Participation in a number of exhibitions. Subject of *Jaume Tresserra de la A a la Z*, Feria Internacional del Mueble (FIM), València. Received 1986 Casa Viva award for best design, Mogar Fair, Madrid; best design, 1987 best design stand, FIM, València; 1988, 1989, and 1999 design awards, *Nuevo Estilo* magazine; 1990 Annual Design Review (Butterfly desk), *I.D.* magazine.
Bibliography Albrecht Bangert and Karl Michael Armer, *80s Style: Designs of the Decade*, New York: Abbeville, 1990: 61, 228.

Tribel, Annie (1933–)

French furniture designer; active Paris.

Training 1952–56, École Nationale Supérieure des Arts Décoratifs, Paris.
Biography 1957–60, Tribel traveled in India (and several years later furnished the French embassy in New Delhi). 1962, Tribel joined Atelier d'Urbanisme et d'Architecture, Paris; 1962–68, designed various interiors and furniture for youth clubs, rest homes, theaters (including Le Théâtre de la Ville, Paris), conference rooms, and public institutions, and, 1983, guest rooms in the private apartments, Palais de l'Élysée). She worked for the Théâtre Colline and the new French Ministère des Finances in Bercy; for several years has taught, École Camondo, Paris.
Exhibition Work included in 1988 exhibition, Paris (catalog below).
Bibliography Gilles de Bure, *Le mobilier français 1965–1979*, Paris: Regard/VIA, 1983. Cat., *Design français 1960–1990: trois décennies,* Paris: Centre Georges Pompidou/APCI, 1988. Arlette Barré-Despond (ed.), *Dictionnaire international des arts appliqués et du design*, Paris: Regard, 1996.

Triboy, Maurice (1890–1974)

French cabinetmaker; born Bordeaux.

Biography 1922–54, Triboy worked as a cabinetmaker in Bordeaux where he designed and produced furniture in a highly traditional manner, as illustrated by a rosewood living-room ensemble he created between c. 1930–35 for the woman who founded the Quincaillerie d'Art. Triboy's work was massive in asymmetrical geometric forms, and it also featured distinctively crafted handles in both glass and chromed metal.
Bibliography Pierre Kjellberg, *Art déco: les maîtres du mobilier, le décor des paquebots*, Paris: Amateur, 1986/1990.

Trock, Paula (1889–1979)

Danish textile designer.

Training In Denmark, Sweden, and Finland.
Biography 1928–34, Trock ran a weaving school and workshop in Askov and, 1932–42, in Sønderborg; 1948, established the Spindegården in Askov, where handweaving production made use of lighter, textured yarns, experimental plastic threads, and open weaves; c. 1950, began to design for mass production for Unika-Vaev and others.
Exhibitions/citations Work included in exhibitions at The Metropolitan Museum of Art, New York, in 1960, Kunstindustrimuseet, Copenhagen, in 1963, and 1964 jubilee venue of Den Permanente 1964; 1983–84 exhibition, Philadelphia (catalog below). Gold medals: 1954 (10th), 1957 (11th), and 1960 (12th) editions of Triennale di Milano. Received 1959 Dannebrogordenen (Knights of the Order of Dannebrog) and 1972 lifetime achievement award of Statens Kunstfonds (Danish arts foundation).
Bibliography Bent Salicath and Arne Karlsen (eds.), *Modern Danish Textiles*, Copenhagen: Danish Society of Arts and Crafts and Industrial Design, 1959. Arne Karlsen, *Made in Denmark*, New York: Reinhold, 1960. Cat., Kathryn B. Hiesinger and George H. Marcus III (eds.), *Design Since 1945*, Philadelphia: Philadelphia Museum of Art, 1983.

3 Suisses

French mail-order firm.

History 1938, 3 Suisses was founded; by 1993, was the number two mail-order business in France; from 1977, sold items designed for the firm by Philippe Starck, Andrée Putman, Marc Newson, Christian Ghion, Torck/Noirot, and other established designers. However, much of its goods are standard, inexpensive home furnishings and clothing.

Trondesign

German design studio; located near Kassel.

History 1994, Trondesign was found by engineer Andreas Kraechter (Kassel, 1966–), designer Marcus Heyde (Kassel, 1967–), and modelmaker Achim Reitze (Kassel, 1966–), who design furniture and lighting. They were first commissioned by Holländer Haus in Potsdam. By 2002, the staff had grown to 14 collaborators and consultants. The studio is active in graphic and industrial design, engineering, and model construction, but primarily product/furniture design and branding. Clients have included Audi, Honda, and DaimlerChrysler for work with new materials and experimentation with vaporized fibers and reflective metallic textiles.
Exhibitions/citations Work shown at 2001 Salone del Mobile, Milan; and 2001 *Polarity*, Internationale Möbelmesse, Cologne. Received 1996 Design Plus award (Tik wall clock), Ambiente fair, Frankfurt; 2000 Innovation Prize (enclosed scooter), Cycle and Motorcycle Association.
Bibliography Lucius Spenser, 'Trondesign,' *Modo*, no. 211, Apr. 2001: 57–58. www.trondesign.com.

Truex, Van Day (1904–1979)

American educator, and interior and furnishings designer; born Delphos, Kan.; active New York and Paris.

Training 1922, State Teachers College (now University of Wisconsin-Oshkosh), Oshkosh, Wis.; 1926, bachelor of art degree in advertising, New York School of Fine and Applied Art, New York.
Biography 1925–39, Truex was the chairperson, advertising-illustration department and costume and stage-design department, New York School of Fine and Applied Art, New York; 1934–39, director, New York School of Fine and Applied Arts (known as Paris Ateliers), Paris; 1940–41, vice-president, New York School of Fine and Applied Art, New York (renamed Parsons School of Design in 1941); 1942–52, president, Parsons, where he was the director from 1952–53 and European director and critic-consultant 1954–55. Students under him included Eleanor McMillen, founder of McMillen, and Albert Hadley. He was a design consultant to Edward Fields carpets and Royal Worcester china (White House dinner service). Other work: 1961 neo-Oriental furniture line, Baker Furniture Co., and 1973 Dionysos crystal decanter (in a wine-bottle shape with the sobriquet 'Van ordinaire' and part of the Collection Truex crystal range) by Baccarat. 1955–67, Truex was design director; 1967–78, design consultant; 1978–79, divisional vice-president, Tiffany & Co., New York. When he was hired, Tiffany & Co. chairperson Walter Hoving made the request that nothing should be sold by the store that did not meet with Truex's approval. In addition to his own contributions at Tiffany's, Truex hired freelance designers of crystal and metal wares. As a consultant to Yale & Towne, he designed door pulls and push plates for doors, and persuaded Fernand Léger, Joan Miró, Philip Johnson, Isamu Noguchi, and others to design for the firm as well. 1975, Van Day Truex chair in the history of design was established, Parsons School of Design.
Exhibition/citations Work subject of 2001 *Van Day Truex: Defining 20th-Century Style*, Parsons School of Design, New York. 1942, honorary doctoral degree, Kansas Weslyan University, Salina, Kan.; 1951, Chevalier of the Légion d'Honneur, France; 1966 International Design Award (for Bamboo sterling-silver cutlery by Tiffany), American Institute of Decorators (AID).
Bibliography Van Day Truex, 'Jean-Michel Frank Remembered,' *Architectural Digest*, Sept.–Oct. 1976. *Van Day Truex, Interiors: Character and Color*, Los Angeles: Knapp, 1980. John Esten and Rose Bennett Gilbert, *Manhattan Style*, Boston: Little, Brown, 1990: 7–8. Mark Hampton, *The Legendary Decorators of the Twentieth Century*, New York: Doubleday, 1992. Christopher Petkanas, 'Van Day Truex: Master of Understatement,' *House & Garden*, Jan. 1993: 72–75, 119. Adam Lewis, *Van Day Truex: A Biography*, New York: Henry Holt, 1998. Adam Lewis, *Van Day Truex: The Man Who Defined Twentieth-Century Taste and Style*, New York: Viking Penguin, 2001. Albert Hadley, 'Van's Way,' *Vogue*, Oct. 2001.

Tsé & Tsé Associées; Catherine Lévy (1964–); Sigolène Prébois (1964–)

French studio, marketers, and designers.

Training Both: ENSCI (Les Ateliers), Paris.
History 1992, Lévy and Prébois established Tsé & Tsé Associées design studio and marketers in Paris. Earlier they had designed everyday objects for their own use, which they subsequently began having made and selling; became known for early-1990s Guirlande Cubiste string of lights with bulbs in diminutive Japanese-paper boxes and 1991 Vase d'Avril collection of glass test tubes in a metal cage; have since grown into a studio of about ten; designed/edited

Van Day Truex. Dionysos decanter. 1973. Crystal, decanter h. 12" x dia. 3 1/4" (30.5 x 8.2 cm), stopper l. 3" (7.6 cm). Mfr.: Compagnie des Cristal-leries de Baccarat, France (from 1974). Purchase. MoMA.

Earl Silas Tupper. Tumbler. c. 1945. Polyethylene, h. 4 13/16" x dia. 2 7/8" (12.2 x 7.3 cm). Tupperware Corporation, US. Gift of the manufacturer. MoMA.

other lights such as File Indienne string, Baladeuse sconce, Chignon de Geisha chandelier, and Igloo de Nuit ceramic table lamp, and a number of accessories and guidebooks. Ricard commissioned a bottle motif for its Créations & Saveurs anise collection.
Bibliography Mel Byars, *50 Products: Innovations in Design and Materials*, Hove: RotoVision, 1998. www.tse-tse.com.

Tsukamoto, Kanaé (1968–)

Japanese ceramicist and glass designer.

Training 1991, bachelor of fine arts degree, Kanazawa College of Art; 1997, master of fine arts, Royal College of Art, London.
Biography 1991–92, Tsukamoto was an industrial designer, Mitsubishi Electric Co.; 1992–94, worked at GK Industrial Design Office, Tokyo; 1999, established the studio Kanaé Design Labo in Tokyo with partner and industrial designer Nobu Sugimoto, who studied vehicle design at Royal College of Art. Work has included Contrast drinking glasses and black-and-white dinnerware and Systematic individual dinnerware in a wooden box recycled from Suntory whiskey casks, all for Abode, Kyowa furniture company's retail shop in Tokyo. Also designs products for others.
Exhibition 1997 *Tableware Festival*, Tokyo Dome, Japan; 1997 *Fine and Applied Arts Show*, Royal College of Art, London.

tubular-steel furniture

Technique and material used in furnituremaking.

History The tubular metal chair, associated with quintessential 1920s European avant-garde design, had 19th-century antecedents. Cast-iron furniture arrived with the Industrial Revolution and, from 1825, architect Karl Friedrich Schinkel was one of the first to produce tables, benches, and chairs at an iron foundry in Berlin. Iron tubing was used from c. 1830 for bed frames in Britain, though with awkward solutions to the joining of vertical and horizontal elements. 1827–41, British manufacturer Robert Walter Wingfield patented metal furniture of various designs. Inexpensive iron bedsteads were shown at 1867 *Exposition Universelle*, Paris. Marble-topped cast-iron tables became ubiquitous fixtures in cafés. French manufacturers welded iron tubes with some success; as early as 1844, hollow-tube chairs were produced in Paris, with glue and plaster pumped in for reinforcement. 1911 in Germany, Bernhard Pankok designed a tubular aluminum chair for the Zeppelin. Whereas art historian Sigfried Giedion claims that the bent tubular-steel chairs developed at the Bauhaus were a totally new concept, Marcel Breuer pointed out that his first 1925 Wassily model was suggested by bicycle handlebars and by 19th-century bentwood chairs by Michael Thonet. Although bent steel had been used earlier in furniture, its development as a resilient product by Mannesmann gave it a springy quality, making cantilever construction possible. Even so, Mart Stam in the Netherlands used gas pipes and plumber's elbow joints in an awkward 1924 prototype now regarded as the first steel cantilevered chair. Another Dutchman, J.J.P. Oud, incorporated his own designs for bent tubular-steel furniture in the dining room of his 1926–27 Villa Allegonda, Katwijk. Ludwig Mies van der Rohe brought back sketches of the Stam chair (which had been refined) to Berlin, where he developed his own elegant 1927 version of the cantilever chair (the MR armchair). Like Stam's, it was designed in both side and armchair versions. The US Patent Office refused Mies a patent for his chair, referring him to Harry Nolan's 1922 patent, although the Mies model was produced in tubular steel, unlike Nolan's solid steel rods, and was for indoor use, unlike Nolan's 'lawn chair.' However, when Mies later built a model to American specifications, one was granted. Contemporary attribution to designers in manufacturers' catalogs cannot be relied upon. Tubular-steel furniture resulted in two legendary lawsuits: the 1929 action between Anton Lorenz and manufacturer Thonet, and the lengthy dispute from 1936 between Mies and manufacturer Mauser. The outcome was that only Thonet and Mauser in Germany had rights to the *Freischwinger* (free mover); other manufacturers will have to pay them royalties to 2036, the 50th anniversary of Stam's death. Robert Cromie was the first in Britain to use tubular-steel furniture on a large scale, in the restaurant of 1929 Capital Cinema in Epsom. 1930s, in the US, the bent tubular-metal chairs of Gilbert Rohde and Wolfgang Hoffmann were produced by Lloyd, Troy, and others. Mass production of Marcel Breuer's innovative models has continued since the early 1950s.
Exhibition Oud's, Stam's, and Breuer's bent tubular-steel chairs in apartment interiors at 1927 *Weissenhofsiedlung*, Stuttgart.
Bibliography P.R. d'Yvay, 'Le meuble de l'avenir sera-t-il métallique?,' *Les échos des industries d'art*, no. 33, Apr. 1928: 32–33 (Charlotte Benton translation in *Journal of Design History*, vol. 3, nos. 2 and 3, 1990: 166–67). Ernö Goldfinger and André Szivessy, 'Meubles,' *L'organisation ménagère*, June 1928. Ernö Goldfinger and André Szivessy, 'Meubles: les sièges,' *L'organisation ménagère*, Oct. 1928. Marcel Breuer, 'Metallmöbel,' in Werner Gräff, *Innenräume*, Stuttgart: F. Wedekind, 1928: 133–34. Charlotte Perriand, 'Wood or Metal?,' *The Studio*, vol. 97, 1929. Sigfried Giedion, *Mechanization Takes Command*, Oxford: Oxford University Press, 1948: 490–91. Barbie Campbell-Cole and Tim Benton (eds.), *Tubular Steel Furniture*, London: The Art Book Company, 1979. Cat., *Der Kragstuhl*, Stuhlmusuem Burg Beverungen, Berlin: Alexander, 1986. Sonia Günther (intro.), *Thonet Tubular Steel Furniture Card Catalogue*, Weil am Rhein: Vitra Design, 1989. Otakar Máčel, 'Avant-Garde Design and the Law: Litigation over the Cantilever Chair,' *Journal of Design History*, vol. 3, nos. 2 and 3, 1990: 125–43.

Tucker, Preston Thomas (1903–1956)
> See Tremulus, Alex Sarantos.

Tulusan, Indri (1974–)

German designer; active Berlin and London.

Training 1992–93, medical school, Germany; 1998, bachelor's degree, furniture and product design, Kingston University; 2001, master's degree, product design, Royal College of Art; both London.
Biograply In Berlin: 1997, Tulusan worked at Projectgruppe 7.5; 1998,

BVM; 1999, Vogt+Weizenegger; 1999, freelanced at Die Imaginaire Manufaktur (DIM) on product design and curating exhibitions for the first DIM brush collection. 2000, he was a design assistant at Babylon Design in London on contributions by Claudio Silvestrin, Matthew Hilton, Torsten Neeland, and others; 2001, creative director of Web site 'designproducts.rca.ac.uk'; 2001, interactive designer on the first Noah's Ark project, *Experience Design*, Philips Design, Eindhoven.
Citations 1998 Ray-Ban Award (workdrobe); 1998 Hille Furniture Ltd. Award (overall show and design); 1998, cited for magazine display, *Elle Decoration* Original Design Award; 2000 Kenny Yiip Memorial Award (IntelliSkin project); 2001 Orange Home and Away award (IntelliSkin project); 2001 Lattice Award (sustainability).

Tümpel, Wolfgang (1903–1978)

German metalworker; born Bielefeld; active Halle, Cologne, and Bielefeld.

Training 1921–22, gold- and silversmithing, Kunstgewerbeschule, Bielefeld; 1922–25, metalwork, Bauhaus, Dessau; under Karl Müller, Kunstgewerbeschule Burg Giebichenstein, Halle.
Biography 1927, Tümpel produced a silver and ivory tea set for Dr. Erich Bohn, Breslau (now Wrocław, Poland), on the recommendation of Bauhaus director Walter Gropius. He designed a number of lamps by Goldschmidt und Schwabe, Berlin; was a member of the Gesellschaft für Goldschmiedekunst; 1927, established his own facility Werkstatt für Gefässe, Schmuck, Beleuchtung in Halle and, 1929, moved to Cologne and, 1934, to Bielefeld. From 1951, Tümpel taught, Landeskunstschule, Hamburg, where he managed the metalwork department and was also active as a crafts ceramicist; died in Herdecke/Ruhr.
Exhibition Hand-raised objects shown at 1937 *Exposition Internationale des Arts et Techniques dans la Vie Moderne*, Paris.
Bibliography Heinz Spielmann, *Wolfgang Tümpel und seine Schüler, Goldschmiedekunst und Design*, Hamburg: Museum für Kunst und Gewerbe, 1978. *Sammlung Katalog*, Berlin: Bauhaus Archiv, 1981. Cat., *The Bauhaus: Masters and Students*, New York: Barry Friedman, 1988. Annelies Krekel-Aalberse, *Art Nouveau and Art Déco Silver*, New York: Abrams, 1989. Cat., *Die Metallwerkstatt am Bauhaus*, Berlin: Bauhaus-Archiv, 1992 and 1998. Katja Schneider, *Burg Giebichenstein*, Weinheim: VCH, Acta Humaniora, 1992. Auction cat., *Modernes Design Kunsthandwerk nach 1945*, Munich: Quittenbaun, 1 June 2002: 18–19.

Tupper, Earl Silas (1907–1983); Tupperwear

American inventor, chemist, and engineer; born New Hampshire; son of an inventor. Manufacturer, US and Europe.

Biography By 1917, Tupper began selling the family's farm produce door-to-door; was determined to be a millionaire by age 30; had a number of menial jobs; established the tree-surgery business Tupper Tree Doctors, which failed. From 1936, he worked at a Du Pont plastics factory in Leominster, Mass., where, he later said, 'My education began.' 1938, he established Tupper Plastics, fulfilling a number of governmental contracts and making cigarette cases and tumblers with company logos affixed. By 1940s, plastics had acquired an unsavory reputation for becoming brittle, unstable, and bad smelling. Undeterred, Tupper began to tinker with black polyethylene slag, a waste product from oil refining, and was able to transform it into a durable, non-oily, non-absorbent, hygienic substance. From it, he developed watertight containers with tops derived from the 1946 design of snap-on metal paint cans, patented 1947 as a concept, and produced by the Tupperware Corporation, Farnumsville, Mass. With Brownie Humphrey Wise (1913–92) who had been selling products directly to housewives in their homes, began selling the containers through home parties from 1948; 1951, organized Tupperware Home Parties as a separate entity. 1958, due to Tupper's ego and desire for control, he abruptly dismissed Wise, who had gained national prominence; within months, sold the entire firm to Rexall for $16 million; 1973, moved to Costa Rica, where he pursued humanitarian, utopian, and, some say, crackpot ideas; died there. The firm today is publicly held with headquarters in Orlando, Flor.; 1990, hired Morison Cousins (1935–2001), an industrial designer, who successfully revamped the look of the products and made them museum-quality, as the earliest ones had become. Still sponsoring house parties, the firm has added methods to sell directly through the Internet, at Target stores, TV's Home Shopping Network channel in the US, and other sources.
Citations 1995 Industry Innovation Award, Direct Selling Associations, US; 2003 Red Dot Best of the Best (Garlic Wonder garlic press by Tupperware, Belgium), Design Zentrum Nordrhein Westfalen, Essen.
Bibliography 'Tupperware,' *Time*, Sept. 1947: 90. Elizabeth Gordon, 'Fine Art for 39¢,' *House Beautiful*, vol. 89, Oct. 1947: 130–31. Cat., Kathryn B. Hiesinger and George H. Marcus III (eds.), *Design Since 1945*, Philadelphia: Philadelphia Museum of Art, 1983. Jeremy Myerson and Sylvia Katz, *Conran Design Guides: Tableware*, London: Conran Octopus, 1990. Alison J. Clarke, *Tupperware: The Promise of Plastics in 1950s America*, Washington: Smithsonian, 2001. Mel Byars and Laetitia Wolff, 'Tupperware: Is the Party Over?,' *Graphis*, no 337, Jan.-Feb. 2002: 88–95. Paola Antonelli (ed.), *Objects of Design: The Museum of Modern Art*, New York: The Museum of Modern Art, 2003.

Turk, Marko (1920–1999)

Slovene designer; born Ljubljana, Yugoslavia (now Slovenia).

Training To 1941, Maritime School, Bakar, Croatia; Fakultet za ElektroTehniko, Univerza v Ljubljani.
Biography To 1954, Turk worked at Radio Ljubljana; 1955, established the studio Elektroakusticni Laboratorij (EAL) in Ljubljana, where he was the main designer and manager until his death; became known for his large body of acoustical and electronic products from 1956, including 1963 microphone no. MD9.
Exhibitions/citations Regularly participated in the Electronics Fair, Gospodarsko Razstavišče, Ljubljana. Work subject of 1989–90 exhibition, Ljubljana (catalog below). 1964 (three gold medals and one honorary award), 1966 (gold medal and honorary award), 1988 (gold medal), 1996 (ICSID Excellence Award) BIO industrial-design biennial, Ljubljana; 1965 Prešeren Fund Award, Yugoslavia.
Bibliography Janez Lajovic, *Oblikovalec Marko Turk, Presernova nagrada za leto 1964*, Sinteza, no. 2, 1965: 70–72. Stane Bernik, *Slo venska arhitektura, urbanizem, oblikovanje in fotografija 1945–1978*, Ljubljana, 1979. Cat., Matija Murko, *Marko Turk: Oblikovanje Design 1955–1989*, Ljubljana: Arhitekturni Muzej Ljubljana, 1989.

Turnbull & Stockdale

British textile firm; located Ramsbottom, Lancashire.

History 1881, the firm of textile printing, dyeing, bleaching, and finishing was founded. The same year, Lewis F. Day was appointed the artistic director. The factory produced some of the most interesting printed and hand-blocked fabrics of the late 19th and early 20th centuries. Lindsay Philip Butterfield, C.F.A. Voysey, Silver Studios, and M. Read/H.J. Bull furnished designs to Turnbull & Stockdale. Today, the firm is one of the few hand-block printers in Britain.
Bibliography Valerie Mendes, *The Victoria & Albert Museum's Textile Collection, British Textiles from 1900 to 1937*, London: Victoria and Albert Museum, 1992.

Marko Turk. Microphone no. MD9. 1963. Chrome-plated and enameled metal, h. 8 1/2" x base dia. 4" (21.6 x 10.2 cm). Mfr.: Elektroakusticni Laboratorij, Yugoslavia (now Slovenia). Gift of the mfr. MoMA.

Tusquets Blanca, Óscar (1941–)

Spanish painter, architect, and designer; born and active Barcelona.

Training 1954–60, painting, architecture, and design, Escola d'Arts Aplicades i d'Oficis Artístics (Escola Llotja), Barcelona; 1958–65 under Oriol Bohigas and Frederic Correa, Escola Técnica Superior d'Arquitectura de Barcelona (ETSAB).
Biography 1961–64, Tusquets worked in the studio of architects Frederic Correa and Alfonso Milá and absorbed the principles of the Barcelona School. 1964, Tusquets and his fellow school graduates Pep Bonet, Cristian Cirici, and Lluís Clotet Ballús cofounded Studio PER. 1972, Studio PER members and others (in particular Xavier Carulla) formed Bd Ediciones de Diseño, which has produced much of Tusquets's furniture and product designs and those of others considered too risky by Spanish manufacturers at the time. 1983, Tusquets was one of the 11 architects to design a coffee and tea set by Alessi. To 1983, he collaborated with Clotet on several buildings/restorations/ extensions. Tusquet's controversial 1972 Belvedere Regás building was one of the first postmodern structures—widely published and highly controversial—as was his 1989 restoration/extension Palau de la Música Catalana (by Domènech i Montaner in the early 20th century). Tusquets was strongly influenced by the writings of Robert Venturi. 1975–76, Tusquets was adjunct professor of the design chairmanship in charge of projects at Escola Tècnica Superior d'Arquitectura; a visiting professor, Rhode Island School of Design, Providence; 1980, lecturer, Harvard and Yale Universities; 1984, University of Southern California and University of California at Berkeley; 1981, École Polytechnique Fédérale, Lausanne; 1983, Kunstakademie, Düsseldorf; 1983, Fakultät Architektur, Universität Karlsruhe; 1984, Institut Français d'Architecture; 1982, 1984, and 1985, Universidad Internacional Menéndez Pelayo, Madrid. From 1983, he began to design for Italian firms; was a partner in the publishing firm Tusquets Editores, which issued *Aprendizaje de Las Vegas* (Spanish edition of Venturi's *Learning from Las Vegas* [1972]). 1987, Tusquets founded Tusquets, Diaz & Assoc. with Carlos Díaz and went on to design 1987–90 apartment house for Nexus World Kashil, Fukuoka; 1988–92 public-residential quarters, Barcelona Summer Olympiad Village; 1989–93 Heliopolis building, Montpellier; 1991 pavilion and entrance, Parc de la Villette, Paris; 1991–96 Sant Gervasi residential/shopping complex, Barcelona; 2001 Hotel Miramar (remodeling of restaurant of 1929 Exposición Internacional de Barcelona); 2003 Urbis Badalona home for the aged, Barcelona; 2004 Punta Brava house, Sant Feliu de Guixols, Girona.
Design work Early-1970s Cuc lamp (with Clotet Ballús), 1980 Hypóstila shelving system and 1980 Bourgeois coffee table by Bd Ediciones de Diseño, 1983 Varius armchair by Casas Mobilplast, 1984 Varius chair by Casas, 1985 Talaya shelving by Bd Ediciones de Diseño, 1986 Gaulino chair and stool by Carlos Jané, 1986 Bib-Luz book lamp by Bd Ediciones de Diseño, 1986 jewelry collection by Cleto Munari, 1986 winged table by Casas, 1987 electronic-components cabinet by Artespaña, 1987 Earth and Moon rugs by Bd Ediciones de Diseño, 1987 Suono/Pico/Proto carts (with Clotet) by Zanotta, 1988 Carrito trolley/reading stand by Zanotta, 1988 Vaivén chair-table combination by Casas, 1988 Sofanco public seating for Hijo de E.F. Escofet, 1988 rattan-and-metal Abanica stacking chair by Driade, 1989 Teulada TV cart, 1989 Vortice table by Carlos Jané, 1990 Ali Baba divan by Casas, 1991 Victoria porcelain dinnerware and stainless-steel cutlery range (with wife/chef Victoria Roqué) by Follies, 1996 Oscar armchair by Kettal, 2000 Cúmulus hanging lamp by Leucos, 2001 Tocada table lamp by La Murrina, 2003 Corset chair by Amat-3.
Exhibitions/citations Work shown regularly at the Triennale di Milano and international exhibitions; with Clotet Ballús, participated in 1980 *Design Forum*, Linz. Received 1965, 1970–71, 1983 Premi FAD d'Interiorisme Award (best interiors); 1977–78, 1978–79, 1989 Premi FAD d'Arquitectura Award (best Barcelona building); 1978–79 Premi FAD de Restauració Award (best restoration work); 1984 Crítica and Leon de Oro (for best illustrated book), 7th Biennale di Venezia; 1987 Creu de Sant Jordi, Generalitat de Catalunya; 1986 Delta de Plata and 1987 and 1990 selections, ADI/FAD; 1988 National Design Prize, Spain; 1990 Iberdiseño 90 Award (best 1980s Spanish design); 1995, Chevalier of Ordre des Arts et des Lettres, France; 1996 prize, Feria Internacional del Mueble, Madrid.
Bibliography François Burkhardt, *Oscar Tusquets*, New York: St. Martin's, 1958. Óscar Tusquets Blanca (ed.), *The International Design Yearbook*, 1989. Officina Alessi, *Tea and Coffee Piazza: 11 Servizi da tè e caffè*, Milan: Crusinallo, 1983. Barbara Radice, *Jewelry by Architects*, New York: Rizzoli, 1987. Juli Capella and Quim Larrea, *Designed by Architects in the 1980s*, New York: Rizzoli, 1988. Guy Julier, *New Spanish Design*, New York: Rizzoli, 1991. Marisa Bartolucci, 'Oscar Tusquets,' *Metropolis*, June 1992: 37–42, 56–57. Mel Byars, *50 Chairs: Innovations in Design and Materials*, Hove: RotoVision, 1996.
> See Clotet Ballús, Lluís.

Tuttle, Paul (1918–)

American designer; born Springfield, Mo.

Training Art Center School (today Art Center College of Design), Los Angeles; Taliesen West, Phoenix, Ariz.
Biography Tuttle was associated with Alvin Lustig in Los Angeles, Knoll Associates in New York, Welton Becket and Associates in Los Angeles, architect Thornton Ladd in Pasadena, Cal., and Doetsch und Grether in Basel. From 1956, he lived and worked as a freelance designer in Santa Barbara, Cal. (designing various houses, including renovations and additions) and in Switzerland (where he was employed as an office-furniture designer by Straessle International in Kirchberg). He also designed for Atelier International and numerous others, as well as one-of-a-kind furniture. Work by Straessle: 1970 Anaconda table, 1973 coffee table, 1976 Arco lounge chair and 1987 Jazz 2 PhD chair. By Bud Tullis; 1991 Spring lounge chair, 1994 Super V armchair, 1997 66/97 armchair, 1997 rocking chair. Tullis is a craftsperson active in Solvang, Cal., and from 1982, producing one-of-a-kind chairs by Tuttle.
Exhibitions/citations Work subject of exhibitions in Santa Barbara at the Museum of Art in 1973; University Art Museum in 1987 and 2001–02; 1991 Westmount College, 1991; and also Pasadena (Cal.) Museum of Art, 1966–67; Trudel House Gallery, Baden; Anthony Ralph Gallery, New York, 1992. Work included in numerous international exhibitions from 1951 *Good Design* exhibition/award, The Museum of Modern Art, New York. Citations: 1966 award, Carson, Pirie, Scott department store, Chicago; first prize, 1980 Pacifica Award, Los Angeles; 1980 International Design Products Award, American Society of Interior Designers (ASID); 1980 award, Institute of Business Design (IBD); 1982–93 design grant, US National Endowment for the Arts; 1987 Resource Council Award, New York.
Bibliography 'Young Man on a Mountain,' *House Beautiful*, no. 108, Oct. 1966: 62–63. Cat., Eudorah M. Moore, *The Furniture Designs of Paul Tuttle*, Pasadena: Pasadena Art Museum, 1966. Cat., Eudorah M. Moore, *Paul Tuttle Designer*, Santa Barbara: Museum of Art, 1978. Maeve Slavin, 'Paul Tuttle Out in the Open,' *Interiors*, Aug. 1980: 52-53, 82. David A. Hanks, *Innovative Furniture in America, 1800 to the Present*, New York: Horizon, 1981: 119–20. Kay Wettstein Szakall, 'Architekt und Designer Paul Tuttle,' *Ideales Heim*, Jan. 1986: 18–23.

Tynell, Helena (1918–)

Finnish glassware designer and ceramicist.

Training To 1943, Taideteollinen korkeakoulu, Helsinki.
Biography 1943–46, Tynell designed ceramics by Arabia pottery, Helsinki; 1943–53, lighting by Taito; from c. 1944, glassware by Riihimäki; from 1957, worked for Nord in New York.
Exhibitions Work shown from 1954 (10th) to 1960 (12th) editions of Triennale di Milano; 1955 *H 55*, Hälsingborg; 1961 *Finlandia*, Zürich, Amsterdam, and London; 2004 *Nordic Cool: Hot Women Designers*, National Museum of Women in the Arts, Washington, D.C. Subject of 1998–99 exhibition, Suomen Lasimuseo (catalog below). Received two citations for glass by Glashütte Limburg, (1977 Industrie Forum Design), Hanover.
Bibliography Cat., David Revere McFadden (ed.), *Scandinavian Modern Design 1880–1980*, New York: Abrams, 1982. Cat., Uta Laurén (et al. eds.), *Helena Tynell: Design 1943–1993*, Riihimäki: Suomen Lasimuseo, 1998.

U

Paolo Ulian. Palombella table lamp (detail). c. 2000. MoMA.

UAM (Union des Artistes Modernes)

French organization for the promotion of the arts.

History The 1925 *Exposition Internationale des Arts Décoratifs et Industriels Modernes*, Paris, was realized through the efforts of the Société des Artistes Décorateurs (SAD) and exemplified a sumptuous traditional approach. But it had faded by 1927, when Le Corbusier and others broke with the SAD. Robert Mallet-Stevens proposed a secession and organized a Parisian group equivalent of the Deutscher Werkbund; and thus the Union des Artistes Modernes (UAM) was formed in 1929 by a group of artists, designers, architects, and sculptors, with its first offices in textile designer Hélène Henry's apartment at 7, rue des Grands Augustins, Paris. Mallet-Stevens was its first president, René Herbst its second. Searching for a kind of universality, members called on a stark spareness and an absence of ornamentation, dubbed *la grande nudité* (the great nudity). In addition to Mallet-Stevens, founding members included Pierre Chareau, Eileen Gray, André Lurcat, Jan and Joël Martel, Charlotte Perriand, and Jean Pui forcat. 1930, members showed their work at the UAM's first exhibition, at Musée des Arts Décoratifs, Paris. Through the years, a large number of artists joined the group; by 1932, membership numbered 60. Its first foreign members included Alfred Gelhorn, Emanuel Josef Margold, Josep Nicolas, William Penaat, Gerrit Rietveld, and Bart van der Leck. UAM's first (1934) manifesto—written by Louis Chéronnet and designed by Jean Carlu—was a partial response to Paul Iribe's attacks on modernism. George-Henri Pingusson wrote its second (1949) manifesto, and the UAM gave birth to the movement Formes Utiles, practically realized through exhibitions.

Bibliography René Herbst, *Union des Artistes Modernes*, Paris: Charles Moreau, 1929. Jean-Louis Cohen, 'Mallet-Stevens et l'UAM, comment frapper les masses,' *AMC*, no. 41, Mar. 1977. Arlette Barré-Despond, *UAM*, Paris: Regard, 1986. Cat., *Les années UAM 1929–1958*, Paris: Musée des Arts Décoratifs, 1988.

Ubaldi, Roberto (1940–)

> See Gruppo G14.

Ubertazzi, Alessandro (1944–)

Italian architect, teacher, and industrial designer; born Bibbiena; active Milan.

Training To 1969, architecture, Politecnico, Milan.

Biography 1969, Ubertazzi established his own studio and worked through two further studios in Milan: Intec Architecture Design Consultants (founded, and in the first period inspired, by Tomás Maldonado) and Centro-DA (Centro Studio per il Disegno Ambientale), with Riccardo Nava, Giorgio Romani (1946–1980), and Duccio Soffientini. With the Intec consultancy, Ubertazzi designed a large number of Italian bookshops (including all Feltrinelli stores) and foreign chains. From 1970 with Centro-DA collaborated on the design of clocks and electronic equipment for Italora, consulted on clock design and ergonomics of precision instruments and, from 1975, on sailboat fittings by Nemo and Comar. Other clients have included Azienda Elettrica Milanese (AEM), AEM-Zincar, Alcatel, BMW, the City of Milan, Ente Nazionale Elettricità (ENEL), Giacomini, ICI-Huntsmann, Metra, Sordelli, Superband, Svaba, Whirlpool, and Wind. He wrote numerous essays, articles, and books, including *Muoversi in città* (with Marco Pestalozza, Milan: Touring Club, 1988), *La città diffusa* (Bergamo: Dip. DC, 1990), *Parole al bersaglio* (Bologna: Maggioli, 1998). Ubertazzi has written for magazines *Casabella, Rassegna, Ottagono, and Architettura*, and, 1981, founded the magazine *Habitat ufficio*, which he edited to 1990, and, 1994 also founded magazines *ME—Materiali edili di qualità* and *Recupero & conservazione*, which he edited to 1996. From 1991, he has taught, Facoltà di Architettura, Politecnico, Milan; Facoltà di Architettura, Università degli Studi, Palermo; and Università degli Studi, Florence. 2000, he became a consultant on all the specialized magazines published by Alberto Greco Editore.

Citations 1982 IN/ARCH citation (for a school building, Lombardy).

Bibliography *ADI Annual 1976*, Milan: Associazione per il Disegno Industriale, 1976.

> See Nava, Riccardo; Romani, Giorgio; Soffientini, Duccio.

Uchida, Shigeru (1943–)

Japanese designer; born Yokohama.

Training To 1966, Kuwasawa Design School, Tokyo.

Biography 1970, Uchida established his own eponymous design studio. He has been a lecturer, Kuwasawa Design School from 1973; Tokyo National University of Arts and Music from 1974–78; and, from 1986–87, Washington State University, and Columbia University and Parsons School of Design, both New York; Domus Academy in 1993 and Politecnico in 1996, both Milan; Dutch Design Center Initiative, Utrecht, in 1996; Art Institute of Chicago in 1998; others. 1981 with Ikuyo Mitsuhashi and Toru Nishioka, Uchida established Studio 80. Body of work has included 1969 Free Form chair, 1974 Rattan chair; 1975 Shima Lamp (in the shape of Chichishima, one of the islands of Bonin Archipelago). 1975–80 Seibu department store; 1976–82 boutiques of Issey Miyake; 1977 September and 1981 Nirvana chairs; 1983 Wave Building, Tokyo; 1983–86 boutiques of Yohji Yamamoto (including Y's Superposition); 1984 Charivari store, New York; Japanese

Pavilion at *Expo '85*, Tsukuba; 1986 NY Chair II; 1986 Yohji Yamamoto boutique, Kobe; 1988 Tenderly lamp; 1989 Matsuya department store, Ginza; 1989 Il Palazzo hotel, Fukuoka; 1989 Dear Vera and Dear Morris clocks by Alessi; 1991 Tobu department store, Tokyo; 1993 Kobe Fashion Museum; 1997 Mojiko Hotel, Kitakyushu; 1996 Okazaki chair; 1998 Paper Moon lamp; 2002 Tree lamp.
Exhibitions/citations 1986 *Uchida Furniture*, Gallery 91, New York; 1990 *Shigeru Uchida Kagu*, Chairs, Tokyo; and 1993–98: *Shigeru Uchida Tearoom* of Tobu department store, Spazio Krizia, Milan, Golden Shell Pavilion in Manila, and Asano-EX in Ishikawa. Work included in late-1990s *Japan Today*, traveling to Denmark, Norway, Finland, Sweden, and Austria. 1981 and 1988 Interior Designers Association Award, Japan; 1989 Mainichi Design Award; 1990 grand prize, Shokankyo Design Award; 1995 (1st) Kuwasawa Design Award; 1998 Excellent Member Award, Inter-Design Forum, Japan.
Bibliography *Residential Interiors*, Tokyo: Shincho-sha, 1986. Shigeru Uchida with Toru Nishioka, *Interior Design: Uchida, Mitsuhashi, Nishioka and Studio 80*, New York/Cologne: Taschen, 1987 (vol. 1) and 1996 (vol. 2). *The Era of Chairs*, Tokyo: Kobun-sha, 1988. *Interior Design: Uchida Mitsuhashi Nishioka and Studio 80*, Berlin: Taschen, 1996. Ikuyo Mitsuhashi, *Shigeru Uchida: Interiors, Furniture and Architecture*, Corte Madera: Ginko, 2003.

Udagawa, Masamichi (1964–)

Japanese industrial designer; born Tokyo; active New York.

Training 1983–87, Chiba University, Chiba, Japan; 1989–91, Cranbrook Academy of Art, Bloomfield Hills, Mich.
Biography 1987–89, Udagawa worked at Yamaha Product Design Laboratory, Hamamatsu, Japan; 1991-92, Emilio Ambasz Design Group, New York; 1992–95, as senior designer, Industrial Design Group (IDg), Apple Computer, Cupertino, Cal. While at Apple, taught, California College of Arts and Crafts, San Francisco. 1995–97, Udagawa was active in product development, IDEO design studio, New York; 1997, cofounded Antenna Design, New York, where he and Sigi Moeslinger provide product-design-and-development consulting services. Antenna has been active in industrial, interactive, and environment design, most notably for the Metropolitan Transportation Authority of New York (which included R142 subway cars and automated Metrocard ticket vending machines); also 2000 Executive PDA by Palm, 2000 Aura communicator by Fujitsu, 2003 Bloomberg News airport terminal, and 2003 JetBlue airlines ticket terminals. From 1997, Udagawa has been an associate professor, interactive telecommunications program, New York University.
Exhibitions/citations Work shown widely, including in 2000 *Let's Entertain*, Walker Art Center, Minneapolis; 2001 *Workspheres*, The Museum of Modern Art, New York (catalog below); 2003 National Design Triennial, Cooper-Hewitt National Design Museum, New York. Received 1988 G-Mark Good Design award, Japanese Industrial Design Promotion Organization (JIDPO); 1992 and 1995 Gold IDEA/ *Business Week* magazine awards; 2003 Gold Award, *I.D.* magazine; 2004 Rave Award, *Wired* magazine.
Bibliography Cat., Paolo Antonelli, *Workspheres: Design and Contemporary Work Styles*, New York: The Museum of Modern Art, 2001. Paul Kunkel, *Apple Design: The World of the Apple Industrial Design Group*, New York: Graphis, 1997.

Udal'tsova, Nadezhda Andreevna (1886–1961)

Russian artist and designer; born Orel.

Training 1905–08 Under Konstantin Yuon, Ivan Dudin, and Nikolai Ulianov, Yuon's private art school; 1909–10, K. Kish's studio, Moscow; 1912–13 under Jean Metzinger and Henri Le Fauconnier, principles of Cubism, Académie 'La Palette à Montparnasse,' Paris.
Biography 1912–13, Udal'tsova lived in Paris, where she worked under Metzinger, Le Fauconnier, and André Dunoyer de Segonzac; was fascinated with French art, from Poussin to Picasso. Of all the Russian avant-gardists, her work was the closest to French Cubism, and she worked on the cubed nude. 1913, she returned to Moscow and worked in Vladimir Tatlin's studio The Tower and came into contact with Alexei Grishchenko, Liubov' Popova, and Alekandr Vesnin; 1913–14, was interested in Rayonism, painting some pictures in this style; 1915–17, was briefly attracted to Kasimir Malevich's Suprematism but returned to Cubism and, subsequently, to Naturalism. 1916, she broke with Tatlin and pursued a commission for textile design. 1917–18, assisted Georgii Yakulov, Vladimir Tatlin, and others on the interior design of the Café Pittoresque in Moscow, worked in IZO NKP and was a professor at SVOMAS; from c. 1920, was associated with her husband-artist Aleksandr Drevin. 1921, she and Drevin left INKhUK in protest against the pressure by the Constructivists there. 1920s, she taught textile design at Moscow Textile Institute while turning to painting Cézanne-esque canvases and romantic Russian themes; 1921–34, taught, VKhUTEMAS/VKhUTEIN. She remained active painting and exhibiting until her death in Moscow.
Exhibitions Work included in 1914 exhibition of Bubnovy Valet (Jack of Diamonds), Moscow, and afterward in many exhibitions in the USSR and abroad, including 1915 Tramway; 1915–16 *0–10*; 1916 *The Store of Union of Youth*; 1922 *Erste Russische Kunstausstellung*, Berlin; regularly in 1930s–40s; 2000–01 *Amazons of the Avant-Garde*, Guggenheim Museum, New York (catalog below). Subject of 1928 venue, Leningrad.
Bibliography M. Miasina (ed.), *Stareishie sovetskie khudozhniki o Srednei Azii i Kavkaze*, Moscow, 1973: 220–22. Cat., 'Nadezhda Udaltsova's Cubist Period,' *Women Artists of the Russian Avant-Garde 1910–1930*, Cologne: Galerie Gmurzynska, 1979: 288–308. S.O. Khan-Magomedov, *Vhutemas: Moscou, 1920–1930*, Paris: Regard, 1990: 411–13. Cat., *The Great Utopia: The Russian and Soviet Avant-Garde, 1915–1932*, New York: Guggenheim Museum, 1992. Ekaterina Andreevna Drevina, *Nadezhda Udal'tsova/Ekaterina Drevina*, Moscow: Trilistnik, 1997 Cat., John E. Bowlt and Matthew Drutt (eds.), *Amazons of the Avant-Garde: Alexandra Exter, Natalia Goncharova, Liubov Popova, Olga Rozanova, Varvara Stepanova, and Nadezhda Udaltsova*, New York: Abrams, 2000.

Uehara, Michiko (1949–)

Japanese textile designer; born Okinawa.

Training From 1971 under Yoshihiro Yanagi, began weaving, Tokyo; 1974, returning to Okinawa, under Shizuko Oshiro, traditional textile techniques.
Biography 1979, she established her own studio in Okinawa; has lectured, The Surrey Institute of Art & Design, UK; calls on natural-dyed silk drawn very finely (6.4 derniers) and describes her fabrication process as 'weaving air.'
Exhibitions Work included in numerous venues, including 1999 exhibition, New York and St. Louis (catalog below).
Bibliography Albrecht Bangert and Karl Michael Armer, *80s Style: Designs of the Decade*, New York: Abbeville, 1990. Cat., Cara McCarty and Matilda McQuaid, *Structure and Surface: Contemporary Japanese Textiles*, New York: Abrams/The Museum of Modern Art, 1999.

Ueno, Yukio (1949–)

Japanese glass designer.

Training To 1976, Kuwasawa Design Institute, Tokyo.
Biography From 1977, Ueno worked for Iwata Glass, Tokyo, and became the section chief of design; was a member, Japan Traditional Crafts Association; has worked in painterly style with brush-like patterns, some with the effect of a woven-plaid fabric.
Exhibitions Work included in 1981 and 1990 *Glass in Japan*, Tokyo; 1983 *Japan Traditional Crafts*, Tokyo; 1985 *New Glass in Japan*, Badisches Landesmuseum, Karlsruhe; and 1991 (5th) Triennale of the Japan Glass Art Crafts Association, Heller Gallery, New York (catalog below); 1997–98 *Made in Japan*, The Glasmuseum, Ebeltoft, Denmark.
Bibliography Cat., *Glass Japan*, New York: Heller Gallery and Japan Glass Art Crafts Association, 1991: no. 39.

UFO

Italian radical group of architects; active late 1960s.

History 1967 in Florence, UFO was founded by Carlo Bachi (Pisa 1939–), Lapo Binazzi (Florence 1943–), Patrizia Cammeo (Florence 1943–), Riccardo Foresi (Florence 1941–), Sandro Gioli (who left soon after), and 'Titti' Vittorio Maschietto (Viareggio 1942–) as a radical architecture group. They were graduates of the Facoltà di Architettura, Università degli Studi, Florence. From the beginning, the group collaborated with writer Umberto Eco. Its theme of town 'happenings' was demonstrated in Florence through interior decoration and shop designs. The group used *papier mâché*, polyurethane, blow-ups, literary quotations, and linguistic configurations. Typical examples of the group's work were the design of Sherwood restaurant in Florence and 1969 Bamba Issa discothèque in Forte dei Marmi. From 1972, Binazzi was the director of the group's activities. Three covers of the journal *Domus* featured the ideas of UFO. Members of the group went on to found Global Tools in 1973.
Exhibitions 1968 (14th) Triennale di Milano (urban 'blow-ups'); 1971

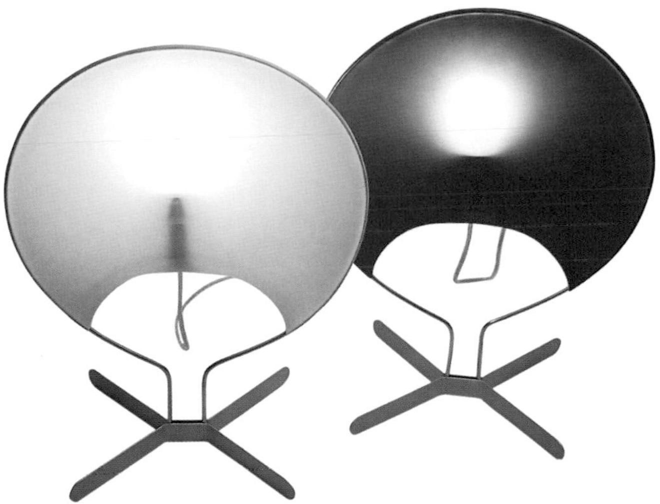

Paolo Ulian. Palombella table lamp. c. 2000. Steel and silicon shower cap, each h. 19 5/8 x w. 13 3/4 x d. 3 1/8" (50 x 35 x 8 cm). Mfr.: the designer, Italy, prototypes.

Salon de la Jeune, Paris; 1976 Biennale Internazionale di Arti Grafiche, Florence; 1978 Biennale di Venezia. Work included in *Radicals: Architettura e Design 1960–75*, 1996 (6th) Mostra Internazionale di Architettura, Venice.
Bibliography Andrea Branzi, *La Casa Calda: Experienze del Nuovo Disegno Italiano*, Milan: Idea, 1982.

UGAP (Union des Groupements d'Achats Publics)

French government design association; located Paris.

History UGAP (formerly Services Généraux d'Achats de Mobilier, SGAM, founded in 1968) was under the direction of the Ministère de l'Economie et des Finances and the Ministère de l'Education Nationale before 1986. The agency publishes an annual catalog of furniture designs for schools, universities, and local institutions. UGAP with Agence pour la Promotion de la Création Industrielle (APCI) has sponsored design com-petitions in which young designers participate. 1975 K2000 school-furniture competition was won by Marc Berthier and Daniel Pigeon, 1982 office-furniture competition by Norbert Scibilla and Serge Guillet, 1984 lighting competition by Sacha Kétoff, 1992 hospital-furniture competition by Sylvain Dubuisson, and others have followed. All citational work is sold through the annual catalog.
Bibliography Arlette Barré-Despond (ed.), *Dictionnaire international des arts appliqués et du design*, Paris: Regard, 1996.

Uhrín, Tibor (1966–)

Slovakian designer; born Martin; active Kremnica.

Training 1984–89, department of industrial design, Slovenská Technická Univerzita, Bratislava.
Biography Uhrín is head, Toy Design Department, Slovenská Technická Univerzita and has thus designed toys, including 1993 Gringo building set by Noris Wood of Kremnica, and a number of tabletop objects, such as 1998 Coatrack for Three Veterans and 2000 Spice Jars for Three Veterans, titled after the Czech children's fairytale/movie *Tři veteráni* (director, Oldřich Lipský, 1983) by AMI Inox Design of Kremnica, and others of his own manufacture.
Exhibitions/citations Work included in 1993 *The Contemporary Slovak Toy*, Bratislava; 1995, 1997–2000 *Design*, Bratislava; 1996 INPEX XII (invention fair), Pittsburgh, Pa., US; 1996 *Trieste Contemporanea*; *Forma 97*, Bratislava; 2000 (2nd) Biennale Internationale du Design, Saint-Étienne, France. Work subject of 1998 exhibition, KFD gallery, Bratislava. 1993 national prize for good design (for Gringo) and first prize, 1995 The Most Beautiful Present competition, both Slovenské Centrum Dizajnu (SDC, Slovak design center), Bratislava.

Ulian, Giuseppe (1959–)

Italian designer; born and active Massa; brother of Paolo Ulian.

Training 1978, Istituto di Arte, Carrara; 1979–84, Accademia di Belle Arte, Carrara; 1991–98, Facoltà di Architettura, Università degli Studi, Florence.
Biography Before enrolling in the Florence university, Giuseppe Ulian worked with several graphic-design studios; from 1990, has collaborated with his brother Paolo Ulian; is a professor of industrial design, Academia di Belle Arti, Venice.
> See Ulian, Paolo (below).

Ulian, Paolo (1961–)

Italian designer; born and active Massa-Carrara; brother of Giuseppe Ulian.

Training 1980–83, painting, Accademia di Belle Arte, Carrara; 1983–87, Istituto Superiore per le Industrie Artistiche (ISIA), Florence (diploma in industrial design in 1990).
Biography 1990–92, Paolo Ulian was an assistant at Enzo Mari e Associati, Milan; from 1990, has collaborated with his brother Giuseppe, as well as working independently; has become known for his ecological concerns and the reprocessing of materials into imaginative solutions, at first one-of-a-kind examples produced by himself and then the first (1995) product in series (Vincastro bookcase by Adelph-Driade). Other work: 2000 pizza knife by Zani & Zani, 2001 Seaside sandals by Sensi, 2001 Cabriolet table/bench by FontanaArte. Other clients have included authentics, Bieffeplast, Opposite, Progetti, Seccosistemi, Segno, Shopenhauer, View, and Wireworks.
Exhibitions/citations 1993 one-person show, Immanenz Gallery, Frankfurt. Work included in *Design for Europe*, Interieur '90 design biennial, Courtrai, Belgium; 1994–96, young-design exhibitions, Opos gallery, Milan; and large number of others, individually and work with his brother. 1990 Design for Europe award, Interieur '90, Courtrai; award, 2000 (1st) *Design Report* magazine, Salone del Mobile, Milan.
Bibliography Paolo Ulian, 'Semiprocessed Waste in the Marble Industry,' *Domus*, no. 745, Jan. 1993: 10-11. Marco Romanelli, 'Paolo Ulian,' *Abitare*, no. 344, Oct. 1995: 194–95; no. 365, Sept. 1997: 163. Arlette Barré-Despond, *Dictionaire international des arts appliqués et du design*, Paris: Regard, 1996: 601. Virginio Briatore, 'Paolo Ulian,' *Interni*, no. 469, Apr. 1997: 155. Enrico Morteo, 'Intelligence of Little,' *L'architettura*, no. 511, May 1998: XII. Mel Byars, *50 Products...*, Hove: RotoVision, 1998. Cristina Morozzi, *Oggetti Risorti*, Genoa: Costa & Nolan, 1998: 115–17. 'Paolo Ulian Portrait', *Design Report*, July-Aug. 2000: 20–35. Emma O'Kelly, 'Paolo Ulian,' *Wallpaper*, July-Aug. 2000: 145. Mel Byars, 'Guerrillas in Our Midst: Paolo and Giuseppe Ulian,' *I.D.*, Jan.–Feb. 2001: 56–57.

Ulrich, Guglielmo (1904–1977)

Italian architect and designer; born Milan.

Training 1923–25, Accademia di Brera; 1926–27, Facoltà di Architettura, Politecnico; both Milan.
Biography Upon graduation from the Politecnico, Ulrich opened his own studio in Milan and became a prolific designer/architect of a range of projects from urban planning to small objects and furniture. 1930, Ulrich, Attilio Scaglia, and Renato Wild founded AR.CA., possibly the first furniture company in Italy to be established for the production of designs by the designer/directors. 1930s, he designed lit-

erally hundreds and hundreds of pieces of furniture, lamps, and utilitarian objects such as door handles, silverware, envelope openers, photography frames, table clocks, and jewelry. He redesigned the interiors in a modern style of the domiciles of the families of the new bourgeoisie (Agnelli, Galtrucco, Mondadori, Pirelli, Toeplitz) as well as those of the old nobility (Calvi di Bergoloi, Cicogna, Viscont). Also during this time, he designed buildings (1934 Sovico, Casa del Fascio, Milan), hotels (1937 in the Lido of Venice with Gio Ponti), headquarters of Banca di Roma, a hospital, shops, country houses, and furnishings for boats. Participated in 1938 town planning (with Cafiero, Guidi, and Valli) of Addis Ababa, Ethiopia. During World War II, he continued to design furniture assiduously, much of which was produced; 1942 for six months, was editor of journal *Domus*; after the war in Milan, designed 1946 building on the via Fatebenefratelli, 1948 building on Corso Buenos Aires (with Piero Bottoni), and 1952 building on Via Vittorio Veneto. Ulrich designed the Galtrucco chain of stores in Picowa, Radaelli, Faraone, Pederzani, and other Italian towns; country and seaside villas; offices; private houses; 1955 retirement home in Robbio di Lomellina. Also furnishings for oceanliners: 1951 *Andrea Doria*, 1953 *Cristoforo Colombo*, 1960 *Leonardo da Vinci*, and 1963 *Raffaello*, as well as for the offices of SIAE (Italian authors' society) and for its 1964 headquarters building on the Grand Canal, Venice. He continued to be quite active in 1950s with the plan for the Atomic Center in Ispra, town plans of Madonna di Campiglio and Punta Ala, restoration of neoclassical Palazzo Tarsis in Milan and Galleria Sassoli De Bianchi in Bologna; 1968–73 large complex of buildings on the Via Ugo Bassi in Milan; worked up to his death on both architecture and paintings, the latter a passion. He wrote the books *Arredamento, mobili e oggetti d'arte decorativa* (with intro. by Gio Ponti, Milan: Görlich, 1942) and *Arredatori contemporanei* (Milan: Görlich, 1949). 1995, the Matteograssi firm, under the Giorgio Pizzitutti brand, began reissuing designs by Ulrich, including sofas, chairs, armchairs, bench, coffee tables, mirrors, bar cabinet, and display cabinets, as well as a collection of table clocks, letter openers, and photography frames.
Exhibitions/citations Work in 1930 (4th) Biennale di Monza, in which he regularly participated thereafter (it became known as Triennale di Milano). Won 1938 national competition for furnishing of Palazzo degli Uffici at *Esposizione Universale di Roma*. 1959 first prize for furniture design (a chair), fair in Trieste. Designed Wanson Pavilion, 1958 *Exposition Universelle et Internationale de Bruxelles (Expo '58)*.
Bibliography Guglielmo Morazzoni, *Mobili di Ulrich*, Milan: Luigi Alfieri, 1945. Ugo La Pietra et al., *Guglielmo Ulrich, gli oggetti fatti ad arte*, Milan: Electa, 1994. Matteo Vercelloni, 'Guglielmo Ulrich,' *Casa Vogue*, Sept. 1994. Daniele Baroni, 'Ulrich: l'elogio del disegno elegante,' *Area*, Dec. 1994. Matteo Vercelloni, 'Il lusso necessario di Guglielmo Ulrich,' *Interni annual*, 1994. Luca Scacchetti, 'Riflessioni sull'eleganza,' *Modo*, Apr. 1996.

Ultramobile

Italian furniture manufacturer; located Calcinelli di Saltara.

History 1996, Ultramobile was established to take over and continue the operations of Simón International, the furniture firm founded 1970 by Gino Gavina, who had also been instrumental in setting up Flos, Gemini, and Gavina (the Simón predecessor). Ultramobile's Simón production includes the 1971 ovoid mirror with Man Ray's words 'les grands transparents' (originally 1938), Matta's 1966 Muro (or Malitte) interlocking sofa units and his 1972 Magritta 'apple/hat' seat, Meret Oppenheim's 1972 Traccia (or Table aux Pieds d'Oiseau, originally of 1936), and others. These items had been out of production, and some, like the Muro, were no longer being marketed by Knoll International, which took over Gavina in 1968. Ultramobile, like few Italian furniture companies, self-manufactures its own products, including new designs by contemporary designers and contract-market components for office installation. Its activities were in full force from 2002.
Bibliography Cat., Vittorio Sgarbi et al., *Dino Gavina, UltraMobile: 50 opere di Dino Gavina*, Begagna: ESG 89, 2000. www.ultramobile.it

Umbert Solá, Nona (1961–)

Spanish fashion and industrial designer; born Barcelona.

Training To 1978, painting, crafts, and pottery, Colegio y Academia ALPE, Barcelona; to 1979, fashion design, Escuela Superior de Diseño y Moda Felicidad Duce (Instituto Feli), Barcelona; from 1983, industrial design, Escola Massana, Barcelona.
Biography 1981–83 with Rodolfo Pastor, Umberto was a painter in a small animation/cartoon-film studio in Barcelona; 1988 with two others, established the studio Haz in Barcelona, designing domestic appliances and work tools. As a scenographer, Umbert is in charge of the set design of the group Agerre Teatroa in San Sebastián, from c. 1980, has been active in fashion design.
Citations 1987 award (for Bridge-Seesaw toboggan); Associazione per il Disegno Industriale (ADI); second prize, 1989 *Italy's Cup*, Milan.
Bibliography Cat., Design Center Stuttgart, *Women in Design: Careers and Life Histories Since 1900*, Stuttgart: Haus der Wirtschaft, 1989: 314–17.

Umeda, Masanori (1941–)

Japanese designer; born Kanagawa; active Italy.

Training 1962, diploma, Kuwazawa Design School, Japan.
Biography 1966, Umeda settled in Italy and worked in the studio of Achille and Pier Giacomo Castiglioni in Milan to 1969; 1970–79, was a consultant designer to Olivetti; 1980, returned to Japan; 1981–83, was active with the Memphis group, which produced his 1983 Orinoco ceramic vase and 1983 Parana ceramic compote. However, it was his 1981 Tawaraya 'boxing-ring' bed, in Memphis's first (1981) collection, that brought attention to him, being widely published as a feature in Karl Lagerfeld's c. 1982 apartment in Monte Carlo. 1986, Umeda established his own studio, U-MetaDesign in Tokyo. Work has included a coffee set by Yamaka, 1988 lamps by Yamagiwa, 1989 toilet fixtures by Inax, interior design of Tomato Bank, office toilet system by Inax, lighting by Yamagiwa and by Iwasaki, 1995 Separa folding screen by Yamakawa, 1990 Getsuen flower-like armchair by Edra, Swatch Art Clock Tower at 1996 Atlanta Summer Olympiad.
Exhibitions/citations Participated in numerous international exhibitions. 1968 BraunPrize, Kronberg, Germany; 1968 Japanese Associated Commercial Designers Prize; 1986 first prize for glass design; 1987 and 1990 awards, Industrie Design Forum (iF), Hanover; 1990 G-Mark Good Design award, Japanese Industrial Design Promotion Organization (JIDPO); 1991 award, Japanese Interior Designers Association; 1997 Good Design award, Chicago Athenaeum.
Bibliography Penny Sparke, *Design in Italy, 1870 to the Present*, New York: Abbeville, 1988. Auction cat., *Memphis: La collection Karl Lagerfeld*, Monaco: Sotheby's, 13 Oct. 1991. www.marutomi.it.

UMS (Utrechtsche Machinale Stoelen Meubelfabriek); UMS Pastoe

Dutch furniture firm; located Utrecht.

History 1908, Fritz Loeb inherited a department store in Utrecht that sold furniture and other items, and began to produce his own-made furniture. From 1913, Loeb's UMS workshop produced furniture for wholesalers. 1915, cabinetmaker D.L. Braakman was hired as the manager of the technical operations. The wide range and high quality of the firm's products made it one of the most important in the Netherlands by 1920s. Its modern furniture models from c. 1923 were not particularly successful, and UMS returned to more popular historicist suites. Modern pieces were shown again at the 1930 Jaarbeurs industries fair, with sober models probably designed by W. Barnasconi. Working with the HOPMI bicycle firm in Utrecht, UMS offered bent tubular-steel furniture designed by H.F. Mertens, which did not sell well and was transferred to HOPMI in 1934. Interior architect A.K. Grimmon of Amsterdam also designed metal furniture by UMS; its stand at the Jaarbeurs fairs included his varnished oak cabinets. c. 1938, the factory began to sell directly to the public. 1955, UMS merged with Pastoe (a manufacturer that based its furniture on geometric forms, founded in 1915) and became UMS Pastoe, producing Cees Braakman's 1954 SM 01 chair with a biomorphic seat and back and spindly bent-iron legs and other serially produced models. (Braakman had earlier replaced his father as the director.) From the end of 1970s, the firm worked with freelance designers, and those of 1970s–90s included Pierre Mazairac, Shigeru Uchida, Pierre Mazairac & Karel Boonzaaijer, Hannes Wettstein, Klaus Vogt, Aldo van den Nieuwelaar, Radboud van Beekhum, in addition to the anonymous Pastoe in-house staff.
Exhibitions From 1917, UMS showed furniture at the Jaarbeurs fairs.
Bibliography Klaus-Jürgen Sembach, *Neue Möbel*, Stuttgart: Hatje, 1982: 226. G. Vreeburg and H. Martens, *UMS Pastoe: Een Nederlandse Meubelfabriek 1913–83*, Utrecht: Centraal Museum, 1983. Cat., *Industry and Design in the Netherlands, 1850/1950*, Amsterdam: Stedelijk Museum, 1985: 276–78. Cat., *Made to Measure: UMS-Pastoe and Cees Braakman, 1948–1968*, New York: R Gallery, n.d. Auction cat., *Modernes Design Kunsthandwerk nach 1945*, Munich: Quittenbaun, 1 June 2002: lots 258–59.
> See Braakman, Cees.

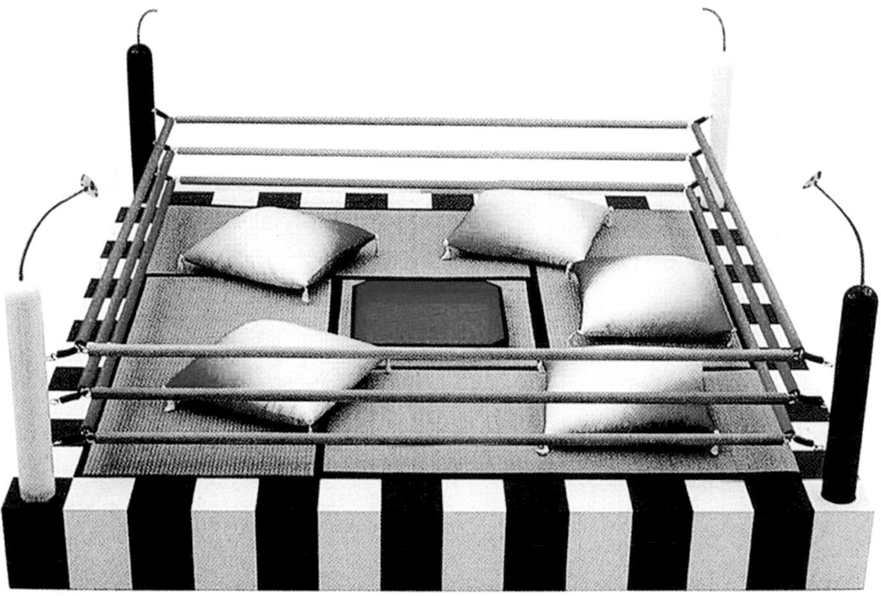

Masanori Umeda. Tawaraya 'boxing-ring' bed. 1981. Wood, plastic veneer, and tatami matting, 177¼ x 177¼" (450 x 450 cm). Mfr.: Memphis, Italy. Courtesy Quittenbaum Kunstauktionen, Munich.

Ungers, Oswald Mathias (1926–)

German architect and designer; born Kaiseresch, Eifel.

Training 1947–50 under Egon Eiermann, architecture, Technische Hochschule, Karlsruhe.
Biography Ungers's designs, based on geometric forms and variations on the square, include furniture by Sawaya & Moroni and 1988 rugs in the Dialog collection by Vorwerk. Beginning in 1951, his architecture has included 1980–84 Polar Research Laboratory, Bremerhaven; 1986 City-West plan for Frankfurt; 1988–94 German Embassy, Washington, D.C.; 1992–94 PTS-Werkstätt, Frankfurt; 2000 Neuer Wallraf-Richartz-Museum, Cologne; 2000 research center, Pottsdam; 2002–05 Rhein Tower, Hammfelddamm. He has taught at a number of institutions in the US, Rome, Moscow, and Vienna, and, 1965–1967, Fakultät für Architektur, Technischen Universität Berlin; from 1971, a member, American Institute of Architects (AIA); from 1992, a member, Moscow branch, International Academy of Architects, Moscow. Like few architects in the second half of the 20th century, Ungers has followed no fashion or school.
Exhibitions Numerous architecture exhibitions including 1957 Bienal Internacional de Arquitetura, São Paulo; 1976 Rationalist architecture exhibition, London; 1976 *Man-trans-Forms*, Cooper-Hewitt National Design Museum, New York; 1978 and 1980 editions of Biennale di Venezia. Cabinet Tower shown at 1985 Triennale di Milano. 1999, honorary doctoral degree, Technische Universität Berlin; 2000, elected to Akademie der Künste, Berlin, and 2002, honorary member, Hochschule für bildende Künste, Hamburg
Bibliography Cat., Carlo Guenzi, *Le affinità elettive*, Milan: Electa, 1985. Auction cat., *Asta di Modernariato 1900–1986, Auction 'Modernariato,'* Milan: Semenzato Nuova Geri, 8 Oct. 1986: lots 99–100. Volker Fischer, *Bodenreform: Teppichboden von Künstlern und Architekten*, Berlin: Ernst und Sohn, 1989. Martin Kieren, *Oswald Mattias Ungers*, Bologna: Zanichelli, 1997.

UNIFA (Union Nationale des Industries Françaises)

French governmental organization.

History 1960s, UNIFA was established to promote the French furniture industry through Salons, including those of Société des Artistes Décorateurs (SAD). 1966, it established Centre de Recherches Esthétiques de l'Ameublement Contemporain (CREAC) to assist young designers and sponsor open competitions such as Premiers Pas at 1965 Salon of SAD and 1967–69 and 1972 Révélation; has organized exhibitions in France and abroad for contemporary French furniture; 1979, participated with the French Ministry of Industry in the formation of Valorisation de l'Innovation dans l'Ameublement (VIA), French furniture association, which sponsors prototypes and assists designers in finding manufacturers as clients.
> See VIA (Valorisation de l'Innovation dans l'Ameublement).

Unifor
> See Molteni.

Unika-Væv; Plus-linje

Danish textile manufacturer.

History 1871, the firm was founded as Hørsholm Klædefabrik. By mid-20th century, the enterprise was being directed by Danish entrepreneur Percy von Halling-Koch. 1959 when he saw Verner Panton's 1958 Cone chairs in a Danish restaurant, he decided to found the division Plus-linje, within Unika-Væv, to market them. The furniture division continued with Panton's c. 1959 Easy Chair C1 (small edition), his subsequent models, and fabrics. 1970, Unika-Væv was acquired by International Contract Furnishings (ICF) of the US. Currently, ICF reproduces Unika-Væv-brand historical designs by Joseph Hoffmann, Marx Benischke, Hans Vollmer, Otto Prutscher, and others to complete the ICF range of Wiener Werkstätte and other reproduction furniture. Contemporary textiles for public and domestic use are also woven. c. 1994, Ruth Adler Schnee's 1940s–50s fabric designs have also been reentered into production.

Unimark International
> See Vignelli, Massimo.

Union des Artistes Modernes
> See UAM.

Union of Soviet Architects
> See VKhUTEMAS.

Union Porcelain Works

American ceramics manufacturer; located Greenpoint, N.Y.

History 1850, William Boch and Brothers founded a factory on Eckford Street, Greenpoint (now the Greenpoint section of Brooklyn), N.Y. where soft-paste porcelain was produced. The firm was also known as the Empire Porcelain Works and Union Porcelain Works. 1861, Thomas Carl Smith, a builder, architect, and native of Bridgehampton, N.Y., on Long Island, acquired a major interest in the firm; 1862, purchased the balance of the firm's shares; 1863, traveled to Europe and visited the ceramics factories of Staffordshire and Sèvres; 1868, began producing hard-paste porcelain (with a kaolinic body). Union Porcelain became the first manufacturer to make true porcelain in the

Up & Up: Michele De Lucchi. Table. c. 1982. Marble and cast stone, 16 3/16 x 39 x 39" (41 x 99 x 99 cm). Mfr.: Up & Up, Italy. Courtesy Quittenbaum Kunstauktionen, Munich.

US, encouraged by high tariffs on imported ceramics, and the first to make vessels with an underglaze decoration on a body of hard porcelain. Smith's quartz and feldspar came from a quarry in Branchfield, Conn., and kaolin from Pennsylvania. 1864–69, the firm was renamed Thomas C. Smith and Co., at 300 Eckford Street, although still known as the Union Porcelain Works. Smith's financial partner was John W. Mersereau. 1869 when his son Charles H.L. Smith joined the firm, it was renamed Thomas C. Smith and Son. Its wares were primarily white hotel china, hardware, electrical insulators, and tiles. Karl L.H. Mueller, who joined the firm as the chief designer in 1874, inaugurated genre-type figure porcelain and portrait medallions of famous Americans, including George Washington, Noah Webster, and Samuel Morse. The firm became best known for its large urn-shaped 1876 Century vase, produced under Mueller's direction;
it was applied with a relief of George Washington and featured panels illustrating events in American history and emblems representing industry. Smith offered studio space at the factory to amateur artists. 1922, the factory was closed.
Exhibitions Century vase shown at 1876 *Centennial Exposition*, Philadelphia; other works in 1878 loan exhibition benefiting New York Society of Decorative Art.
Bibliography Edwin Atlee Barber, *The Pottery and Porcelain of the United States...*, New York: Putnam's, 1901. Doreen Bolger Burke et al., *In Pursuit of Beauty: Americans and the Aesthetic Movement*, New York: Metropolitan Museum of Art/Rizzoli, 1987.

United Glass Bottle Manufacturers (UGBM)
British glassware manufacturer; located Harlow, Essex.

History UGBM was a maker of Ravenhead and Sherdley glass; from 1945, produced new ranges of domestic table glass. A.H. Williamson, a lecturer in the industrial-glass department, Royal College of Art, London, was hired to design certain models. UGBM's products, previous to Williamson's, had been designed by the managers. Williamson advised the technical and production staff and UGBM's distributor, Johnsen & Jorgensen Flint Glass, London.
Bibliography Frederick Cooke, *Glass: Twentieth-Century Design*, New York: Dutton, 1986: 76.

University City Pottery
American ceramics factory; located University City, Mo.

History 1907, the American Women's League established in Missouri to provide members with a program of correspondence courses from the People's University. By 1901, there were 50,000 enrollments. A few of the best students were invited to study at University City, near St. Louis, Missouri, where the faculty was located. Edward G. Lewis, the founder of the League and the People's University, had an interest in art, and the Art Institute in University City was the most developed of the departments. Painting, metal- and leatherwork, handicrafts, and ceramics courses were offered. Lewis, who was familiar with Taxile Doat's technical essay 'Grand Feu Ceramics,' invited Doat to become the director of the School of Ceramic Art in 1909. Doat arrived from France with assistants Eugène Labarrière and Émile Diffloth, who established the first kiln the next year. The distinguished faculty of the school included Kathryn E. Cherry, Edward Dahlquist, Diffloth, Frank J. Fuhrmann, Labarrière, Frederick Rhead, and Adelaide Robineau. They taught about 30 students by correspondence and about ten at University City. Calling on native clays, ceramics were developed there based on designs rendered earlier by Doat at the Manufacture Nationale de Sèvres. The range of glazes included matt, gloss, crystalline, oriental crackle, and alligator skin. 1911, Rhead, Robineau, Diffloth, and Labarrière departed. Concentrating on *flambé*, crystalline, and metallic glazes, Doat stayed on with ceramic chemist William V. Bragdon (subsequently founder of California Faience) until production was discontinued in 1915. And thus Doat returned to France. Lewis sent the pottery equipment of University City to Atascadero, Cal. intending to establish the Art Institute there, but these plans were never realized.
Citation Grand prize (to the school), 1900 *Esposizione Internationale dell'Arte Decorativa Moderna*, Turin.
Bibliography William P. Jervis, 'Taxile Doat,' *Keramic Studio*, no. 4, July 1902: 54–55. M.P. Verneuil, 'Taxile Doat, Céramiste,' *Art et décoration*, no. 16, Sept. 1904: 77–86. Taxile Doat, *Grand Feu Ceramics*, Syracuse: Keramic Studio, 1905. Yvonne Brunhammer et al., *Art Nouveau Belgium, France*, Houston: Rice University, 1976. *American Art Pottery*, New York: Cooper-Hewitt Museum, 1987: 134.

UNOVIS (POSNOVIS; MOLPOSNOVIS)
Russian art institution; founded Vitebsk, Belorussia.

History Active Jan. 1920 to 1923, UNOVIS (Utverditeli NOVogo ISkussetvo, or affirmers of the new art) was the artistic group organized and led by Kazimir Malevich and originally composed of the students and professors at the Free Art Schools in Vitebsk. It was originally called MOLPOSNOVIS (MOLodiye POSledovateli NOVogo ISkusstva, or young followers of the new art) and then was quickly abbreviated to POSNOVIS (POSledovateli NOVogo ISkusstva, or followers of new art). The group espoused new theories and concepts in art that aimed to shape a new Soviet society. Its effects on the Russian avant-garde were quick and wide-reaching. Members included Il'ia Chashnik, Vera Ermolaeva, Anna Kagan, El Lissitzky, Kazimir Malevich, Nikolai Suetin, and Lev Yudin. The group presented the first (1920) Suprematist ballet, choreographed by Nina Kogan, and the first (1913) production of Aleksei Kruchenykh/Mikhail Matiushin's Futurist opera *Pobeda nad solntsem* (victory over the sun) with costumes designed by Vera Ermolaeva under Malevich's direction. The opera was one of the first avant-garde attempts to present abstract art through multiple media simultaneously. Feb. 1920, the institution was renamed UNOVIS, and Vitebsk Art Schools director Marc Chagall was succeeded by Malevich, who drastically changed the school's curricula and made UNOVIS more structured. Ambitiously, one of the first major untakings of UNOVIS was the transformation of the old Russian culture's physical appearance—for example, its buildings and monuments. UNOVIS published two journals, *Aero* (1920) and *UNOVIS* (1920–21), and organized a number of exhibitions. There were branches in Moscow, Perm, Petrograd, Odessa, Orenburg, Samara, Saratov, and Smolensk. After these and other extensive propagandistic activities, most of the artists associated with UNOVIS, signified by Malevich's black square, had moved by 1922 to other schools and cities, and the association was discontinued but not without having had an appreciable impact.

Bibliography Cat., *Kunst und Revolution: Russiche und Sowjetische Kunst 1910–1932*, Vienna: Österreichisches Museum für angewandte Kunst, 1988. S.O. Khan-Magomedov, *Vhutemas: Moscou, 1920–1930*, Paris: Regard, 1990. Cat., *The Great Utopia: The Russian and Soviet Avant-Garde, 1915–1932*, New York: Guggenheim Museum, 1992. Vladimir Kostin and Tamara *ReinKhudozhnik, sudba i velikii perelom: VKhUTEMAS, VKhUTEIN, Poligrafinstitut...*, Moscow: Palmir, 2000.

Up & Up

Italian furniture manufacturer.

History Up & Up was established by Egidio Di Rosa (Tunis, 1942–) and Pier Alessandro Giusti (Massa, 1939–) in Massa (Carrara), near the marble quarries there. Its purpose was to introduce the use of marble into domestic furniture. Special adhesives combine and hold various marble types into a cohesive unit. Its commissioned designers have included Achille Castiglioni, Ugo La Pietra, Alessandro Mendini, David Palterer, Marco Romanelli, Luca Scacchetti, Ettore Sottsass, Andrea Branzi, Michele De Lucchi, Jan Wichers. Up & Up produced Aldo Rossi's 1986 Il Rilievo marble table and Andrea Branzi's 1989 Martina fountain and Quadrio table, also a range for the Ultima Edizione firm for interior and outdoor use.
Exhibitions Work included in numerous venues, including 1991 *Mobili Italiani 1961–1991: le Varie Età dei linguaggi* (Rossi furniture), Milan.

Urban, Josef (1872–1933)

Austrian designer, painter, sculptor, architect, and interior and scenic designer; born Vienna; active Vienna and the US.

Training 1890–93 under Karl von Hasenauer, Akademie der bildenden Künste; subsequently, Polytechnicum; both Vienna.
Biography A member of the Wiener Werkstätte, Urban designed bridges, villas, and the interiors of castles; with his brother-in-law Heinrich Lefler, designed a room at the 1897 winter exhibition at the Österreichisches Museum für Kunst und Industrie, Vienna. Even though he employed Secession motifs, Urban was clearly crafts-oriented. His work in the Austrian pavilion at 1904 *Louisiana Purchase Exposition*, St. Louis, and his talent for stage design brought him many commissions for theaters, from Budapest to Paris. He designed architectural features at the 1908 60th-anniversary pageant in Vienna of Emperor Franz Josef 's coronation. Last decade of 19th century, Urban and Lefler's illustrations adopted an English style, showing the influence of Aubrey Beardsley's work, as in their artwork in *Rolands Knappen* (Vien-na: Gesellschaft für vervielfältigende Kunst, 1898) by Johann Musäus. 1900, Urban and Lefler founded Künstlerbund Hagen (better known as the Hagenbund). 1911, Urban settled in the US; became a scenic designer for the short-lived Boston Opera Company, designing 34 productions; in New York, became the house designer for 12 editions of the *Follies*, produced by Florenz Ziegfeld (1869–1932), for whom Urban created spectacular and somewhat tasteful vaudevillian-type stage shows, which presaged and influenced Hollywood film design and subsequent Ziegfeld productions by others. From 1917, Urban was the artistic director of the Metropolitan Opera, New York, working on 55 productions; designed the interior of nightclub of 1931 Park Avenue Club, New York, and sets for 18 Broadway shows. Urban, the first art director in American films to use modern décors, designed 25 film sets for William Randolph Hearst's Cosmopolitan Productions, including *Photoplay* (1920), *Enchantment* (1921), *The Young Diana* (1922), *Murder at the Vanities* (1934), and *Fashions of 1934* (1934), most of them revealing his Wiener Werkstätte background. Another Hearst/Urban film, *When Knighthood Was in Flower* (1922), cost $1,500,000, an enormous sum at the time. His creations anticipated the best of 1920s design and foretold the 1930s Art Déco style, although immobile cameras and flat direction often undermined his efforts. 1921 or 1922, Urban founded the Wiener Werkstätte of America, New York, which soon closed due to lack of sales. 1925, he returned to architecture and designed Manhattan buildings, including 1927 Ziegfeld Theater (with Thomas W. Lamb), 1927 Hearst International Building at Eighth Avenue and 57th Street (with 2003 superstructure by Foster and Partners), 1929–30 New School for Social Research (the first International Style building in the US) and its Tishman Auditorium (restored in 1993). Urban's 1927 Mar-a-Lago house (118 rooms), Palm Beach, Fla., for Marjorie Merriweather Post was purchased in 1985 by Donald J. Trump and, 1995, changed into a country club by Trump.
Exhibitions Interiors in the Austrian pavilion (gold medal), 1904 *Louisiana Purchase Exposition*, St. Louis; conservatory and man's den settings, 1929 (11th) *The Architect and the Industrial Arts: An Exhibition of Contemporary American Design*, The Metropolitan Museum of Art, New York; color-coded orientation system of 1933–34 *A Century of Progress International Exhibition*, Chicago. Subject of 1987 retrospective, Cooper Hewitt National Design Museum, New York. Theater work subject of 2000 *Architect of Dreams: The Theatrical Vision of Joseph Urban*, Wallach Art Gallery/Columbia University, New York.
Bibliography Howard Mandelbaum and Eric Myers, *Screen Deco: A Celebration of High Style in Hollywood*, New York: St. Martin's, 1985. Robert Waissenberger, *Vienna 1890–1920*, Secaucus, N.J.: Wellfleet, 1984: 136, 148, 149, 191, 270. Suzanne Stephens, 'Eggs to Igloos, at the New School,' *The New York Times*, 1 Oct. 1992: C3. Randolph Carter and Robert Reed Cole, *Joseph Urban: Architecture/Theatre/Opera/Film*, New York: Abbeville, 1992. Cat., Arnold Aronson, *Architect of Dreams: The Theatrical Vision of Joseph Urban*, New York: Columbia University, 2000.

Patricia Urquiola. Fjord armchair. 2002. Steel and polyurethane foam, h. 40 1/8 x w. 37 3/8 x d 31 1/2" (102 x 95 x 80 cm). Mfr.: Moroso, Italy.

Urbinati, Carlo (1949–)

Italian industrial designer; born and active Rome.

Biography 1970, Urbinati began his career; became a member, Associazione per il Disegno Industriale (ADI); has designed lighting, domestic accessories, and sanitary fittings. Clients have included Ellisse, Fratelli Guzzini, Incom Sud, Sis, Teuco Guzzini, and Tulli Zuccari.
Bibliography *ADI Annual 1976*, Milan: Associazione per il Disegno Industriale, 1976.

Urquiola, Patricia (b. Maria Patricia Cristina Blanca Hidalgo Urkiola 1961–)

Spanish designer; born Oviedo; active Milan.

Training To 1989, Escuela Técnica Superior de Arquitectura, Universidad Politécnica, Madrid.
Biography 1990–92, Urquiola lectured within the industrial-design courses by Eugenio Bettinelli and Achille Castiglioni at Politecnico, Milan; ; lectured, ENSCI (Les Ateliers), Paris; 1990–96, was the corporate advisor and managing director, De Padova furniture company, where she and Vico Magistretti designed the Flower chair, Loom sofas, Chaise armchairs, and Chaise Longue. 1993–96, Urquiola, architect Marzia de Renzio, and Emanuela Ramerino established franchises for bars and restaurants in Japan, France, and Spain. Work has included 1999 Chancleta brush by Bosa; 1999 K.U. seating and tables (with Sung Sook Kim) by Faesem; 1998 Step One, Step Two and Step divans, 2000 Lowland and Lowseat, and widely published 2002 Fjord seats by Moroso; 2000 Frozen bookcase and wash basin at *Wonderful World* exhibition, by Kerasan; 2000 Pastilla lamp by Tronconi; 2000 One cabinet (with Piero Lissoni) by Kartell.

Uršič, Branko (1936–)

Slovene designer; born Ljubljana, Yugoslavia (now Slovenia).

Training 1957–62, Faculty of Architecture, Univerza v Ljubljani.
Biography From 1962, Uršič worked at the Stol furniture factory. His best-known chair designs for the firm include 1970 Barbara, 1980 Bambus, and 1991 Iris.
Citations Gold medals and honorary citation at all (except 1964 and 1988) editions of 1964–94 BIO industrial-design biennial, Ljubljana; 1969 Prešeren Fund Award, Yugoslavia; 1985 Plečnik Award.
Bibliography Matija Murko, *Raznovrstnost v preprostosti*, Ljubljana: Sinteza, 1969. Stane Bernik, *Sodobno oblikovanje sedežnega pohištva v Sloveniji*, Ljubljana, 1973. Cat., Peter Krečič and Barbara Rupel, *Stoli Branka Uršiča 1962–1982*, Ljubljana: Arhitekturni Muzej Ljubljana, 1982. Cat., Gregor Košak, *Slovenski povojni stol 1945–91*, Ljubljana, 1992.

Ústav Bytové a Oděvní Kultury (ÚBOK)

Czechoslovak association; located Prague.

History 1947, ÚBOK (institute of housing and clothing culture) was originally founded as the Textilní Tvorba (textile art institute); was later active in interior design and fashion; attempted to improve the aesthetics of industrial design and to involve architects and artists in the process of industrial production and included some of the best glass designers; organized lectures and seminars and published catalogs. Václav Dolejš, Pavel Hlava, Adolf Matura, Václav Šerák, and Jiří Šuhájek worked in the ceramics department. Jarolava Hrušková, Olga Karlíková, Jiří Mrásekz, Zora Smetanová, and Jindřich Vašut designed textiles. However, ÚBOK's involvement with industry was not successful, and its members were unwilling or unable to realize high-quality design in quantity.
Exhibitions 1950s–60s, active in Czechoslovakia's participation in exhibitions, including 1958 *Exposition Universelle et Internationale de Bruxelles* (*Expo '58*) and 1961 (12th) Triennale di Milano

Utility furniture

British program of furniture production; active 1943–52.

History Furniture manufacturing in Britain during World War II was subject to severe restrictions. By 1941, timber shortages were acute, while damage from bombing boosted the demand for furniture and caused prices to rise. Thus, the British government announced the establishment of a program to produce 'Standard Emergency Furniture' and registered the utility mark 'CC41,' which had to appear on every piece of new furniture. A system for rationing furniture was devised, and the president of the Board of Trade appointed a committee headed by Charles Tennyson, vice-president of the Council for Art and Industry and chairperson of the board of governors of the National Register of Art and Design. Members of the Utility Furniture Advisory Committee included Elizabeth Denby, John Gloag, the Rev. Charles Jenkinson, W. Johnstone, Herman Lebus, Gordon Russell, V. Welsford, and E. Winborn. The group was to advise Tennyson 'on specifications for the production of utility furniture of good, sound construction in simple but agreeable designs, for sale at reasonable prices, having due regard to the necessity for the maximum economy of raw materials and labor.' The committee hired designers Edwin Clinch and H.T. Cutler of High Wycombe to design the first series (the Cotswold collection of about 30 pieces), with Gordon Russell's final approval of their designs. The examples were introduced in 1943 through the first Utility catalog and in shops early that year; the collection was manufactured by firms in all sectors of the furniture trade, though too austere for popular taste. The Utility Furniture Advisory Panel dictated the materials used and the nature of the designs. The Chiltern collection, introduced in 1945, was designed to be produced by both hand and machine, because most manufacturers' best tooling had been transferred to the war effort. Chiltern, which combined traditional joinery and contemporary Swedish influence, was produced in more expensive veneered and paneled models in a broader range than the Cotswold. The Cockaigne (later called Cheviot) range was never put into production. This new furniture was available only to newlyweds or people whose furniture had been destroyed by bombing; others had to choose from a restricted range or purchase secondhand. Booth and Ledeboer created other designs that were made by a team of firms. 1944, two radio models were introduced using minimum labor and materials. 1948, Utility Furniture regulations were rescinded, although the price control of the Board of Trade's furniture remained. 1953, the Utility program ended, when there were about 2,500 firms making the tax-free furniture.
Exhibitions 1974 *CC41: Utility Furniture and Fashion*, Geffrye Museum, London (catalog below). Cotswold pieces in 1984 *Design Since 1945* exhibition, Philadelphia Museum of Art.
Bibliography Michael Farr, *Design in British Industry: A Mid-Century Survey*, London: Cambridge, 1955. Cat., *CC41: Utility Furniture and Fashion*, London: Geffrye Museum, 1974. 'Utility CC41,' *Design*, no. 309, Sept. 1974: 62–71. Harriet Dover, *Home Front Furniture: British Utility Design 1941–1951*, Hampshire: Scolar Press, 1991.

Utzon, Jørn (1918–)

Danish architect, urban planner, and industrial designer; born Copenhagen; active variously.

Training 1937–42 under Kay Fisker and Steen Eiler Rasmussen, Det Kongelige Danske Kunstakademi, Copenhagen; 1942–45 under Erik Gunnar Asplund, Stockholm; also in the US.
Biography 1946 for three months, Utzon worked in the office of architect Alvar Aalto in Helsinki; 1947, opened his own offices in Zürich and Ålsgårde and, 1950, in Copenhagen; early on, showed a fondness for the organic architecture of Frank Lloyd Wright and Alvar Aalto; designed late-1960s and early-1970s furniture by Fritz Hansen (including a 1967 furniture line based on a system of arc-shaped components that lock at 45-degree angles). He won competition for what became the controversial Sydney (Australia) Opera House, with drawings in 1957, final plans in 1961, and building competition in 1973. Utzon had moved with his family to Sydney in 1962 but resigned from the project in 1966. He now resides in Haarby. His children are sons Jan (1944–) and Kim (1957–) and daughter Lin (1946–). Jeppe (1970–) is the son and Kickan Utzon (1971–) the daughter of Jan Utzon. All are architects, except Lin, who is an artist, potter, and designer.
Exhibitions/citations Utzon/Hansen furniture collection first shown, 1968 Internationale Möbelmesse, Cologne. Other exhibitions include Paris and London (catalogs below). Subject of 2004 exhibition, Louisiana Museum for Moderne Kunst, Humlebæk, Denmark. Granted major architectural competitions, including the Sydney Opera House (first prize 1956) and Zürich State Theater (1947 gold medal), Royal Academy, Copenhagen; 1947 Bissen prize; 1949 Zacharia Jacobsen Award; 1957 Eckersberg Medal; 1965 medal, Bund Deutscher Architekten (federation of German architects); 1967 C.F. Hansen Medal; 1970 Danish Furniture Prize (for 8108 chair); 1970 recognition, American Institute of Architects (AIA); 1978 gold medal, Royal Institute of British Architects (RIBA); 1985 Order of Australia; Thorvaldsen Medal; 1998 Danish Sonning Award (for cultural accomplishment); 2003 Pritzker Architecture Prize.
Bibliography Cat., *Les assises du siège contemporain*, Paris: Musée des Arts Décoratifs, 1968. Cat., *Modern Chairs 1918–1970*, London: Lund Humphries, 1971. Philip Drew, *The Third Generation: The Changing Meaning of Architecture*, New York: Praeger, 1972. Frederik Sieck, *Nutidig Dansk Møbeldesign–en kortfattet illustreret beskrivelse*, Copenhagen: Bondo Gravesen, 1990. Philip Drew, *The Masterpiece: Jørn Utzon, a Secret Life*, South Yarra, Victoria: Hardie Grant, 1999. Philip Drew, *Utzon and the Sydney Opera House*, Sydney: InSPIRE, 2000.

Utzon, Lin (1946–)

Danish painter, muralist, and textile, ceramics, and glass designer.

Training In crafts and textiles, Sydney, Australia, and Copenhagen.
Biography She has designed porcelain by Royal Copenhagen, ceramics and glass by Rosendahl, sets and costumes for Den Kongelige Ballet (royal Danish ballet); architectural decoration for Bagsværd Community Church (architect, her father Jørn Utzon), for headquarters of Volvo in Göteborg and IBM in Dallas, Tex., and Convention Center in San José, Cal.

Villeroy & Boch: Hans Christiansen (decoration). Covered pot and saucer (no. 2814) (detail). 1902.

V Mire Iskusstv (Mir Ikusstva)
> See World of Art, The

Vaccarone, Alberto (1939–)

Italian architect and designer; born Casale Monferrato; active Turin.

Biography 1970, Vaccarone began his professional career as an architect, town planner, and industrial designer, collaborating with architect Giuseppe Raimondi in the studio A.BA.CO; designed 1973 shelving unit by Tarzia and 1975 glassware by Cristal Art; became a member, Associazione per il Disegno Industriale (ADI).
Bibliography *ADI Annual 1976*, Milan: Associazione per il Disegno Industriale, 1976.

Vaghi, Luigi (1938–)

Italian designer; born Carimate; active Cantù.

Biography 1962, Vaghi began his professional career and designed furniture for clients including Former, Cattadori, Gasparello, and Gilberto Cassina; more recently, designed the Cerasa and Quadro kitchen systems by Polaris. He became a member, Associazione per il Disegno Industriale (ADI).
Bibliography *ADI Annual 1976*, Milan: Associazione per il Disegno Industriale, 1976.

Val Saint Lambert, Verreries et Établissements du

Belgian glass factory; located near Liège.

History 1826, the glassmaking facility was established in a former Cistercian abbey in Val Saint Lambert, near Liège. The founders were chemist M. Kemlin and polytechnic graduate M. Lelièvre, who had worked at the Vonêche crystal works in the Ardennes. The Val Saint-Lambert glassworks rapidly became known for its fine crystal; originally, the workers from the former Vonêche factory were hired. Soon took over the glassworks in Vaux-sous-Chèvremont, Herbatte, and Mariemont; 1861, opened a shop in London. Its most creative period was 1880–1914 in a factory established by Léon Ledru when its large and varied output included the glass designs of Ledru, Dieudonné Masson, Camille Renard-Steinbach, Gustave Serrurier-Bovy, Henry van de velde, and Philippe Wolfers, including pieces with etched decorations by the Desiré brothers and Henri Muller, who had been students of Émile Gallé. Horta's reflecting crystal plates for the chandeliers in 1903 Hôtel Solvay, and possibly the shades on Serrurier-Bovy's lamps, were made by Val Saint Lambert. 1906, the Muller brothers worked at the factory to teach glassmakers the fluogravure technique. From 1980s, the firm has renewed its tradition of working with contemporary designers such as Martin Szekeley, Philippe Starck, and others. The firm has become known for its 'double-colored cut' crystal; also produces one-of-a-kind pieces and trophies; produces the Extase jewelry collection with gold and silver; is the official supplier to the King of Belgium and to 40 kingdoms and heads of states.
Exhibition 1835 *Exposition de l'Industrie*, Brussels.
Bibliography G.P. Woeckel, *Jugendstilsammlung*, Kassel: Staatliche Kunstsammlungen, 1968. H. Hilschenz, *Das Glas des Jugendstils*, Munich: 1973: 69–76. Jacob Philippe, *Le Val Saint-Lambert: ses cristalleries et l'art du verre en Belgique*, Liège: Halbert, 1974. Matine Lempereur, *Les cristalleries du Val Saint-Lambert: la verrerie usuelle à l'époque de l'art nouveau, 1894–1914*, Gembloux: Duculot, 1976. Yvonne Brunhammer et al., *Art Nouveau Belgium, France*, Houston: Rice University, 1976. Alastair Duncan, *Art Nouveau and Art Déco Lighting*, New York: Simon & Schuster, 1978: 52–53.

Valabrega, Vittorio (1861–1952)

Italian furniture manufacturer; active Turin.

History 1884, Vittorio Valabrega and his brother established a furniture manufacturing firm, pursuing historicist styles. When home decoration became popular in 1890s, the firm grew, with more than 50 craftsmen specializing in woodworking and upholstery; by 1898, began to turn toward the prevailing popular *Stile Floreale*, or Italian Art Nouveau, and became known for understated pieces that pointed the way in Italy toward modern furniture design.
Exhibitions/citations Bronze medal, 1884 Turin exhibition; 1898, silver medal, Turin exhibition (small salon with wrought-iron decoration); gold medal, 1900 *Exposition Universelle*, Paris; silver medal, 1902 *Esposizione Internazionale d'Arte Decorativa Moderna*, Turin.
Bibliography Cat., Gabriel P. Weisberg, *Stile Floreale: The Cult of Nature in Italian Design*, Miami: The Wolfsonian Foundation, 1988.

Valentien, Anna Marie (b. Anna Marie Bookprinter 1862–1950); Albert R. Valentien (1847–1925)

American ceramicists; born Cincinnati, Ohio; wife and husband.

Training Anna Marie Bookprinter: Cincinnati Art Academy; under Auguste Rodin, Paris.
Biographies Anna Marie worked in the decorating department of Rookwood Pottery, where her husband-to-be Albert Valentien was in charge. Unable to incorporate sculptural form into Rookwood produc-

tion, the Valentiens left the firm in 1905 but stayed in Cincinnati to 1907, when Albert received a commission from Ellen Scripps to paint California's wild flowers. They settled in San Diego, Cal., where they established the Valentien Pottery, funded by local banker J.W. Sefton Jr., who commissioned Irving Gill to design pottery in 1911. The pottery was probably operational 1911–14.
Bibliography Yvonne Brunhammer et al., *Art Nouveau Belgium, France*, Houston: Rice University, 1976. Paul Evans in Timothy J. Andersen et al., *California Design 1910*, Salt Lake City: Peregrine Smith, 1980: 77.

Valeur, Torben (1920–)

Danish architect and furniture designer.

Training To 1904, architecture, Det Kongelige Danske Kunstakademi, Copenhagen.
Biography 1958–64, Valeur taught, Det Kongelige Danske Kunstakademi; 1960, with Henning Jensen, established a design studio and designed simple, modern furniture by Magnus Olesen, Munch Møbler, and others; also collaborated with Hanne Valeur; from 1963, was associated with Den Permanente.
Exhbitions/citations With Hanne Valeur, participated in 1957 (11th) Triennale di Milano; 1962 *Unga Nordiska Formgivare*, Röhsska Konstslöjdmuseet, Gothenburg; 1962 *Moderne Dänische Wohnkultur*, Vienna. Received 1963 Eckersberg Medal; 1963, became Design Associate, American Institute of Decorators (AID); 1988 Klassikerprisen, Dansk Design Center Prize (M40 furniture system with Valeur by Munch).
Bibliography Frederik Sieck, *Nutidig Dansk Møbeldesign – en kortfattet illustreret beskrivelse*, Copenhagen: Bondo Gravesen, 1990.

Vallauris

French pottery center.

History Vallauris is an area in southeastern France, near Cannes, where pottery has been produced since ancient times, including by Gallo-Romans who made bricks and kitchenware there. Late 19th century, the railroad that extended to the region fostered broader marketing efforts, and some potteries became very active, including those of the Massier and Foucard-Jourdain families. However, with the advent of aluminum and stainless-steel utensils, the 20th century saw a distinct decrease in the demand for ceramic housewares, particularly for cooking. Pablo Picasso's 1948 settling in Vallauris brought the world's attention to the colony. Thus he indirectly encouraged other famous artists to live there, where they drew figurations on a large number of Vallaurisian pots. Contemporary Vallaurisian ware is a lead-glazed earthenware, frequently highly coloured. Table- and cookware are novelties bought by tourists. Having become known as the 'pottery capital of the world,' from 1969, the town has hosted the Biennale de Céramique Contemporain de Vallauris. Recently and annually, the city has invited prominent French designers to participate in a program that results in the production of examples of their work: Olivier Gagnère and Martin Szekely, 1998; François Bauchet and Ronan Bourroulec, 1999; Jasper Morrison (a non-French person) and Pierre Charpin, 2000; Roger Tallon and Radi Designers, 2001; others have followed. Vallaurisian ware designed by Charpin, Gagnère, and others has been the subject of exhibitions in Vallauris.
Bibliography Dominique Forest, *Vallauris: Céramiques de peintres et de sculpteurs*, Paris: Réunion des Musées Nationaux, 1995. Dominique Forest, *17ème Biennale de Ceramique Contemporain de Vallauris*, Paris: Réunion des Musées Nationaux, 2000.

Vallauris. Vase. c. 1951. Glazed pottery, h. 6" (15.2 cm). Mfr.: Vallauris, France. Gift of Greta Daniel. MoMA.

Gino Valle. Cifra 3 clock. 1965. Plastic casing, 3 7/8 x 7 x 3 3/4" (9.8 x 17.8 x 9.5 cm). Mfr.: Solari & C., Italy. Gift of the mfr. MoMA.

Valle, Gino (1923–)

Italian architect, designer, and town planner; born Udine.

Training To 1948, Istituto Universitario di Architettura, Venice; 1951, Graduate School of Design, Harvard University, Cambridge, Mass.
Training In 1948, Valle began working in the architecture office of his father Provino Valle in Udine; for a time in the office of architects Carlo Scarpa and Giuseppe Samonà; subsequently, Valle and his brother Nani Valle took over their father's firm. From 1977, Gino taught, Università degli Studi, Venice. 1959–61, was a consultant to Zanussi; 1978–90, designed for Olivetti. His buildings related to Brutalism and Rationalism, and his 1965–66 double house in Udine reflectes regional styles. He is best known for his automated schedule boards in train stations and airports, by Solari, a system that uses modular flaps, as, on a more modest scale, did his domestic table clocks, including the 1965 Cifra 3 cylindrical model, which has become an icon of 20th-century design. He also designed 1956 Cifra 5 (with Nani Valle) by Solari, and, with others and alone, numerous industrial and commercial buildings in northern Italy, including Udine; 1958–61 Zanussi building, Porcia; 1961 Zanussi administration building, Pordenone; 1966–74 town hall and 1977 tomb of Pier Paolo Pasolini, Casarsa della Delizia; 1980 and 1980–93 IBM buildings, Paris and Milan; 1989 Olivetti building, Ivrea; numerous others.
Exhibitions/citations Work subject of exhibitions, including 1979 *Gino Valle: Architetto 1950–1978*, Padiglione d'Arte Contemporanea di Milano (catalog below). Premio Compasso d'Oro awards: 1956 (Cifra 5 with N. Valle by Solari), 1957 (Emeras electrical clock with Meyer-Provinciali by Solari), 1962 (airport clock/information board by Solari), 1967 (cement panels), 1994 (body of work).
Bibliography 'Fewer Queues, Fewer Questions,' *Design*, no. 215, Nov. 1966: 66. 'Gino Valle,' *Zodiac*, no. 20, 1970: 82–115. Cat., *Gino Valle 1950–1978*, Milan: Padiglione d'Arte Contemporanea di Milano/Idea, 1979. Cat., Kathryn B. Hiesinger and George H. Marcus III (eds.), *Design Since 1945*, Philadelphia: Philadelphia Museum of Art, 1983. Audio cassette, *Gino Valle: An Appropriate Language*, World Microfilms, 1983. Gino Valle, 'Una conversazione con Gino Valle,' *Casabella 49*, no. 519, 1985: 16–17. Vittorio Gregotti, *Il disegno del prodotto industriale*, Milan: Electa, 1986: 342–43. Pierre Alain-Croset, *Gino Valle: progetti e architetture*, Milan: Electa, 1989. Marco Romanelli, *Design Nordest: Carlo Scarpa, Gastone Rinaldi, Fulvio Bianconi, Renata Bonfanti, Gino Valle*, Milan: Abitare Segesta, 1997. Mel Byars with Arlette Barré-Despond, *100 Designs/100 Years: A Celebration of the 20th Century*, Hove: RotoVision, 1999: 144–45.

Vallien, Bertil (1938–)

Swedish designer; born Stockholm; son of a painter and a church minister; husband of Ulrica Hydman.

Training 1957–61, Konstfackskolan, Stockholm; 1961–63, studied and worked in the US and Mexico on a Royal Scholarship.
Biography While in the US, Vallien achieved his first success as a ceramicist, in California; returned to Sweden and settled in the glass-making region of Småland; from 1963, has been designer at Kosta Boda glassworks with a studio in Åfors glassworks; 1963, also active in own workshop, Åfors; from 1967–84, head of glass department, Konstfackskolan, Stockholm; from 1974, lectured and taught at art conferences and art schools internationally and artist-in-residence, Rhode Island School of Design, Providence, R.I.; from 1980, visiting lecturer and, 1984–86, artist-in-residence, Pilchuk Glass Center, Stanwood, Wash.; 1985, artist-in-residence, Rhode Island School of Design; 1992, visiting professor, University of Hawaii; and other teaching positions. He has become known for his sand molds. Recent tableware: 1981 Château series, 12 million glasses sold worldwide; 1992 Satellite; 1993 Domino; 1995 Viewpoints; 1995 Tower; 1996 Chicko; 1998 Brain.
Exhibitions/citations Work shown worldwide, including 1991 (18th) Triennale di Milano. From 1987, subject of numerous exhibitions, including 1998 *Archaeological Archetype* (his first in Stockholm). 1967 Illum Prize, 1984 and 1988 Utmärkt Svensk Form prize (outstanding Swedish design), 1988 Formland prize, 1995 Prince Eugen Medal for Outstanding Achievement in Arts, Sweden; 2001 Visionaries! award (first Swedish recipient), American Craft Museum, New York.
Bibliography Jennifer Hawkins Opie, *Scandinavia: Ceramics and Glass in the Twentieth Century*, New York: Rizzoli, 1989.

Valorisation de l'Innovation dans l'Ameublement
> See VIA.

Valvomo
> See Snowcrash.

Van Alen, William (1883–1954)

American architect; born Brooklyn, N.Y.; active New York.

Training Pratt Institute, Brooklyn; 1908 Lloyd Warren Fellowship allowed for study under Victor-A.-F. Laloux, École des Beaux-Arts, Paris.
Biography 1911, Van Alen returned to New York from Paris; was an office boy in Clarence True's architecture office in Manhattan; worked for architecture firms Copeland & Dole and Clinton & Russell; with H. Craig Severance, established a partnership but dissolved it c. 1925 and henceforward practiced alone. He was eventually known for distinctive multi-storey commercial buildings that eschewed the traditional base, shaft, and capital arrangement. Architecture included 1926 Child's Restaurant Building, 1928 Reynolds Building, and legendary 1928–31 Chrysler Building; all New York. Distinctive features on the latter include the decorative brickwork frieze of automobile wheels and radiator caps, and stainless-steel gargoyles at the 31st-floor level, with other notable work on the 63rd-floor façade. The decoration was derived from the 1929 Chrysler automobile hood ornament. The building's lobby is one of the most striking examples of Art Déco in the US and features dramatic murals, beige and red marble walls, and other walls and elevator doors inlaid with African woods in abstract floral motifs. In his honor, the Van Alen Institute was established to improve public spaces, particularly pertaining to New York.
Exhibition Work included in 1933 *Forward House*, R.H. Macy & Co., New York.
Bibliography F.S. Swales, 'Draftsmanship and Architecture V: Exemplified by the Work of William Van Alen,' *Pencil Points: A Journal for the Drafting Room*, vol. 10, 1929: 514–26. Paul Hollister (foreword; with a commentary by Van Alen on his own house design), 'Forward House,' *Architectural Digest*, 1933. Adolf K. Placzek, *Macmillan Encyclopedia of Architects*, vol. 1, London: Free Press, 1982. Johann N. Schmidt, *William Van Alen: das Chrysler Building, die Inszenierung eines Wolkenkratzers*, Frankfurt: Fischer, 1995.

Bertil Vallien. Vase. c. 1985. Corroded, polished, and unpolished glass, h. 7⅞" (20 cm). Mfr.: Kosta Boda, Sweden. Courtesy Quittenbaum Kunstauktionen, Munich.

Van Briggle, Artus (1869–1904)

American studio potter; born Felicity, Ohio.

Training Painting under Frank Duveneck, Art Academy, Cincinnati, Ohio. In Paris: 1893–96, easel and mural painting, Académie Julian; sculpture and clay modeling, École des Beaux-Arts.
Biography 1887 when the Avon Pottery closed, Maria Storer hired Van Briggle to work at Rookwood Pottery, where he was the senior decorator by 1891. Concurrently, he had his own studio on Mt. Adams. When not at Rookwood, he was an easel painter; 1893, was paid by Rookwood to study in Paris for three years; became interested in Chinese glazes, particularly Ming-dynasty matt glazes which he researched after returning to Rookwood in 1896 and produced a few vases there with these matt glazes. 1899, he suffered from tuberculosis and was forced to live in a more healthful climate, thus establishing his own pottery in Colorado Springs, Colo., with financial support from Storer. Van Briggle began experimenting with local clays in a small kiln at Colorado College, Colorado Springs. From 1902 in less than a year, he produced 300 pieces for exhibition. He accomplished this with thrower Harry Bangs (a young male assistant) and with Van Briggle's fiancée Anne Lawrence Gregory. The pottery became successful; 1903, increased its staff to 14, including German thrower Ambrose Schlegel. 1900–12, the pottery designed at least 904 patterns of art ware. On Van Briggle's 1904 death, his widow Anne took over the pottery and sold it in 1913. It is still in operation, producing early designs.
Exhibitions/citations Work shown at 1893 *World's Columbian Exposition* (a painting), Chicago; 1900 *Exposition Universelle* (some Rookwood matt glazes); 1903 Salon of Société des Artistes Français (two gold, one silver, and 12 bronze medals), Paris; 1904 *Louisiana Purchase Exposition*, St. Louis, Missouri; 1905 *Lewis and Clark Centennial Exposition*, Portland, Oregon.
Bibliography Anne Gregory Van Briggle, 'Chinese Pots and Modern Faience,' *Craftsman*, no. 4, Sept. 1903: 415–25. Dorothy McGraw Bogue, *The Van Briggle Story*, Colorado Springs: Dentan-Berkeland, 1968. Barbara M. Arnest (ed.), *Van Briggle Pottery: The Early Years*, Colorado Springs: Colorado Springs Fine Art Center, 1975. Scot H. Nelson et al., *A Collector's Guide to Van Briggle Pottery*, New Cumberland, Pa.: Halldin, 1986. *American Art Pottery*, New York: Cooper-Hewitt Museum, 1987. Richard Sasicki and Jodie Fania, *The Collector's Encyclopedia of Van Briggle Pottery: An Identification and Value Guide*, Paducah, Ky.: Collector Books, 1993.

van de Groenekan, Gerard A. (1904–1994)

Dutch furniture maker; active Utrecht.

Biography Van de Groenekan was an assistant to architect Gerrit Rietveld; made built-in furniture by Rietveld for the Schröder house in Utrecht from 1924, when Rietveld handed his furniture-making business over to van de Groenekan at age 20. Van de Groenekan handmade Rietveld furniture and lighting to 1971, when he sold the furniture-production license to Cassina. However, the Cassina examples of van de Groenekan's hand-hewing are absent. From 1971 to late 1980s, van de Groenekan restored Rietveld furniture and continued to handmake individual pieces on commission for museums and others. The furniture by him was authentic since he had made Rieveld's furniture/furnishing designs from an early time; even so, no two are exactly alike.
Bibiliography Marijke Küper and Ida van Lijl, *Gerrit Th. Rietveld: The*

Gerad A. van de Groenekan: Gerritt Rietveld. Zig-Zag chair. 1934. Elmwood and brass screws, 29 5/16 x 14 9/16 x 18 1/2" (74.5 x 37 x 47 cm). Mfr.: Gerard A. van de Groenekan, the Netherlands (1950s). Courtesy Quittenbaum Kunstauktionen, Munich.

Complete Works 1888–1964, Utrecht: Centraal Museum, 1992. Peter Vöge, *The Complete Rietveld Furniture*, Rotterdam: 010, 1993.
> See Rietveld, Gerrit Thomas.

van de Velde, Henry Clemens (1863–1957)

Belgian architect, industrial designer, painter, and art critic; born Antwerp; active Belgium, Germany, and the Netherlands.

Training 1881–84, painting, Académie des Beaux-Arts, Antwerp; 1884–85, under Charles Carolus-Duran, in Paris.
Biography Initially a post-Impressionist and Symbolist *pointilliste* painter, van de Velde subsequently became an architect, then an applied artist. His early style was strongly influenced by William Morris and the British Arts and Crafts movement. He returned to Antwerp from Paris; 1886, cofounded the cultural circle Als ik Kan (after Jan van Eyck's motto) and, 1887, L'Art Indépendant, an association of young neo-Impressionist painters; from 1889, took part in the activities of Brussels avant-garde group Les Vingt; 1894, wrote his famous treatise *Déblaiements d'art* (clearing a way in art), opening his campaign to purify the architectural vocabulary of historicist references; with Victor Horta, became known as an avant-garde designer in Belgium; designed his own 1895 Art Nouveau house, Bloemenwerf, in Uccle. The house was an organic *Gesamtkunstwerk* (total work of art)—from architecture to furniture, furnishings, and fittings. Upon seeing the house, Siegfried Bing asked him to design four rooms for Bing's gallery/shop L'Art Nouveau, Paris. 1899, Julius Meier-Graefe also commissioned van de Velde to furnish his shop La Maison Moderne in Paris; that year, van de Velde settled in Germany and remained there to 1917. Meier-Graefe arranged for van de Velde to meet German designers associated with the Art Nouveau magazine *Pan*. In Germany, van de Velde became a prolific designer, with commissions including 1899 Hohenzollern Craftwork Shop, Berlin; 1900–02 Folkwang Museum interior decoration, Hagen; 1900 premises of Habana Tobacco Co.; 1901 Hoby's barber shop, Berlin. 1902, he was appointed artistic director for industry and crafts in the Grand Duchy of Saxe-Weimar-Eisenhach and designed silver for the court jewelers of the Grand Duke and other silver designs by A. Debain, Koch und Bergfeld, Theodor Müller, and his pupil Albert Feinauer. He designed 1906–08 Kunstgewerbeschule building in Weimar, of which he was director from 1908 (its founding having purportedly stemmed from a 1902 seminar of his); 1907, cofounded Deutscher Werkbund but, disagreeing profoundly with Hermann Muthesius's insistence on standardization, left the organization; at the onset of World War I, was forced to give up teaching at the Kunstgewerbeschule due to his Belgian citizenship and recommended Walter Gropius as his replacement as head of the school; continued as artist and author. 1917, moved to Switzerland; 1921–24, lived in the Netherlands and, 1925–47, in Belgium; was commissioned by Helene Kröller-Müller to build the Kröller-Müller Museum (opened in 1935) in Otterlo, the Netherlands; 1926, founded Institut des Arts Décoratifs, Cambrai, where he was the director to 1935; 1926–36, was chairperson of architecture, Universiteit Gent. He died in Zürich.
Exhibitions Work included in 1897 *Exhibition of Applied Arts* (robust and curvilinear furniture), Dresden; 1897 *Exposition Internationale de Bruxelles* (Colonial Museum pavilion with Hanker, Hobé, and Serrurier-Bovy); 1899 *International Art Exhibition of the Munich Secession* (first showing), Munich; 1913 *Exposition Universelle et Industrielle* (a house), Ghent; 1914 Werkbund theater at *Werkbund-Ausstellung*, Cologne; 1937 *Exposition Internationale des Arts et Techniques dans la Vie Moderne* (Belgian pavilion with Eggericx and Verweighen), Paris. Work subject of 1971 exhibition (with Guimard and Horta), Musée des Arts Décoratifs, Paris; 1987 exhibition (paintings), Koninklijk Museum voor Schone Kunsten, Antwerp; 1992–94 exhibition, Karl Ernst Osthaus-Museum, Hagen, and touring.
Bibliography Ernst Karl, *Henry van de Velde: Leben und Schaffen des Künstlers*, Hagen: Folkwang, 1920. Maurice Casteels, *Henry van de Velde*, Brussels: Cahiers de Belgique, 1932. Herman Teirlinck, *Henry van de Velde*, Brussels: Elsevier Ministère de l'Instruction Publique, 1959. A.M. Hammacher, *Die Welt Henry van de Veldes*, Cologne: Dumont Schauberg, Antwerp: Mercator, 1967. K.-H. Hüter, *Henry van de Velde: Sein Werk bis zum Ende seiner Tätigkeit in Deutschland*, East Berlin: Akademie Berlin, 1967. Lieske Tibbe, *Art nouveau en socialisme: Henry van de Velde en de Parti ouvrier belge*, Den Helder: Talsma & Hekking, 1981. Léon Ploegaerts and Pierre Puttemans, *Henry van de Velde*, Brussels: Atelier Vokaer, 1987. Klaus-Jurgen Sembach, *Henry van de Velde*, London: Thames & Hudson, 1989. Klaus Weber, *Henry van de Velde: Das buchkünstlerische Werk*, Freiburg im Breisgau: Rombach, 1994. Sonja Gunter, *Kunstgewerbliche Laienpredigten/Henry van de Velde*, Berlin: Gebr. Mann, 1999.

van den Berg, Gerard (1947–)

Dutch furniture designer.

Biography Gerard van den Berg and his brother Ton founded Montis furniture company for which he also designed; has become known for his seating, particularly the Cheo, the Chaplin and the Longa; does not use the frame as his starting point and claims the hammock

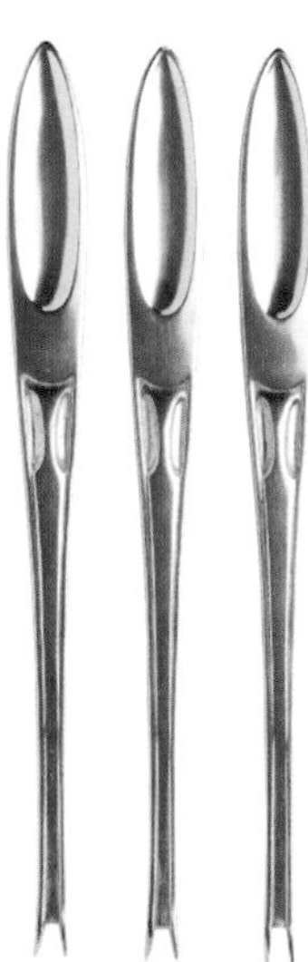

Henry Clemens van de Velde. Lobster forks. 1902–03. Silver, each 7 5/8 x 5/8 x 1/4" (19.4 x 1.6 x 0.6 cm). Mfr.: Theodor Müller, Germany. Marshall Cogan Purchase Fund. MoMA.

provides optimum comfort; 1991, also with his brother, founded seating company Label Produkties in Dorst, which also produces his tables; has designed for other firms, including Molteni, Perobell, and Wittman, under the name Gerard van den Berg Design.
Citations 1984 Kho Liang Ie applied-arts prize of Amsterdam Fonds voor de Kunst; 1984 and 1997 Best Dutch Furniture Design; 1990 Mobilia Prize for Innovation; 1991 Prize for Interior Decoration.

van den Broeke, Floris (1945–)

Dutch furniture designer; active London.

Training 1961–66, painting, Akademie van Kunsten, Arnhem; to 1969, furniture design, Royal College of Art, London.
Biography 1960s, van den Broeke was one of the first British 'designer-makers' of furniture in Britain. Though somewhat inactive, he exerts an appreciable influence on a younger generation of designers in the UK; professor of furniture design, Royal College of Art.
Exhibitions Work subject of 1974 exhibit, Whitechapel Gallery, London; and included in 1980 Crafts Council show, London; 1989 exhibit, Rotterdam; 1990 *Dutch Design*, New York; Design Museum, London, 1991.
Bibliography Frederique Huygen, 'The Britishness of British Design: Een interview met Floris van den Broecke,' *Items*, no. 15, 1985: 21-25. Frederique Huygen, *British Design, Image and Identity*, London: Thames & Hudson, 1989.

van den Nieuwelaar, Aldo (1944–)

Dutch architect and designer; born Tilburg; active Amsterdam.

Training Akademie van Beeldende Kunsten, St. Joost, Breda.
Biography Van den Neuwelaar worked in various architecture and design offices, Amsterdam; 1969, established his own office, Amsterdam; during the 1970s, designed furniture, particularly by Pastoe, and lighting and exhibitions; was a consultant to the Dutch lighting industry. Lighting included: 1974, for the courtyard of Frans Hals Museum, Haarlem; 1978–79 models for De Bijenkorf department store, Amsterdam; and 1980s lamps for ABN Amro bank. His designs were based on pure geometric forms such as 1969 TC2 neon circle and white transformer box by Artimeta, for which he is best known. 1998–99, he was a guest professor, Fakultät für Architektur, Rheinisch-Westfälische Technische Hochschule, Aachen.
Exhibitions/citations Work included in 2004 *MOOI: Licht en Interieur Centraal in Expositie*, Stedelijk Museum, Roermond. 1986 Kho Liang Ie applied-arts prize of Amsterdam Fonds voor de Kunst.
Bibliography *Design from the Netherlands*, Amsterdam: Visual Arts Office for Abroad, 1981: 38–41. Cat., Kathryn B. Hiesinger and George H. Marcus III (eds), *Design Since 1945*, Philadelphia: Philadelphia Museum of Art, 1983.

Van der Hurd, Christine (1951–)

British textile designer; active New York and London.

Training To 1973, Winchester School of Art, Hampshire.
Biography 1976, she settled in the US; designed textiles for clients including Donghia, Kenzo, and Jack Lenor Larsen; wall coverings for Osborne & Little; scarves for Liberty of London; and bedding for J.P. Stevens and Wamsutta. 1980, she began specializing in carpets; 1981 with her husband David Hurd, established Modern Age furniture store (relaunched as Cappellini Modern Age in 1998) and set up her own textile business for rugs; from 1990, designed and produced furnishings and textiles, including rugs, for her own firm; 1991, became a partner of Kate Morrison to design, manufacture and market the first collections of decorative linens; 1993, collaborated with Annie Walwyn Jones on clothing and began de-signing home-furnishing accessories; 1997, returned to the UK and, in addition to a large number of her self-produced carpets, designed 1999 collection by Cappellini. 2000 after years of custom-carpet production, she introduced a retail range, handknotted in Nepal.
Bibliography Michele De Lucchi (ed.), *International Design Yearbook*, London: Laurence King, 2001.

van der Jagt, Peter (1971–)

Dutch designer; active Arnheim, then Rotterdam.

Training Three-dimensional design, Hoge School voor de Kunsten, Arnhem.
Biography Van der Jagt designed 1995 half-scissors letter opener by The Edge/Sample for Industry and, 1996, became an independent designer; designed 1996 Tutti Frutti fruit bowl in recyclable polypropylene by Authentics, 1995 half-scissors letter opener by The Edge/Sample for Industry, and various other products, including floor tiles (with Arnout Visser and Erik Jan Kwakkel), Bottoms Up door chimes (with wine glasses) by Droog Design and 2000 'do break' porcelain/rubber vase (with Frank Tjepkema) by do + Droog Design.
Exhibitions/citation Work widely shown, in Rotterdam, San Francisco, Berlin, Frankfurt, Cologne, Milan, and London. Received 1999

Christine Van der Hurd. Disco (part of the Cuttin' a Rug collection). c. 1997. Wool, 60 x 84" (152 x 213 cm). Mfr.: the designer, UK.

Designprijs, Rotterdam.
Bibliography Mel Byars, *50 Lights...*, Hove: RotoVision, 1997. Mel Byars, *50 Products...*, Hove: RotoVision, 1998. Michele De Lucchi (ed.), *The International Design Yearbook*, London: Laurence King, 2001.

van der Meulen, Jos (1959–)
Dutch designer.

Training Academie van Beeldende Kunsten, Rotterdam.
Biography Van der Meulen is known for his unusual concepts such as 1993 Paper Bags waste baskets by Goods, Amsterdam, the purchasers of which are expected to open up the large envelopes of unused billboard posters (with the addition of gluing) and to fold down the rims for rigidity. Jan Neggers (1956–), an artist and stage designer in Rotterdam, first produced the Paperbag. Subsequently, Van der Meulen designed colorful document files and A4-size blocks of paper to be used as inkjet-printer paper. Also by Goods: Pinch memo holders (clothes pins attached to real twigs).
Bibliography Mel Byars, *50 Products: Innovations in Design and Materials*, Hove: RotoVision, 1998: 142–43.

van der Sluis, Willem (1972–)
> See Timmermans, Hugo.

Van Dissel
Dutch fabrics firm; located Eindhoven.

History 1871–1971, Linenfabrieken E.J.F. van Dissel & Zonen was a fabric manufacturer in Eindhoven; to 1903, wove only domestic linens in simple checks, huckaback patterns, and stripes. W.P.J. van Dissel succeeded his father as the manager of the firm; encouraged the production of high-quality-damask table linens for which three plants were established. The firm was only mechanized in c. 1920, although by then almost no fine linens were being made. Chris Lebeau, who worked there c. 1905–43, was hired to produce up-to-date designs. His first damask designs appeared in a 1906 catalog. 1936–66, Kitty Fischer van der Mijll-Dekker, who had studied at the Bauhaus, designed for van Dissel. Her tea and glass towels of 1935 (orginally by van Dissel) are currently being reissued by the Textielmuseum in Tiburg. Van Dissel's linens were sold to institutions with their names woven into the design, at times combined with Lebeau's borders.
Bibliography Cat., *Industry and Design in the Netherlands, 1850–1950*, Amsterdam: Stedelijk Museum, 1985: 98–101.

van Doesburg, Theo (b. Christiaan Emil Marie Küpper 1883–1931)
Dutch architect, painter, stained-glass artist, and theoretician; born Utrecht.

Biography From 1908, van Doesburg was active as a conventional painter; 1912, became a follower of painter Vasilii Kandinsky; as early as 1915, planned a journal with Piet Mondrian to disseminate neo-Plasticism (intending to transform two-dimensional art into architecture), collaborating with J.J.P. Oud and Jan Wils; 1916 with Oud, founded artists' group Sphinx in Leiden, which was discontinued in 1917, the year of the establishment of the journal *De Stijl*. This gave its name to the now-renowned group of architects and artists seeking a 'radical renewal of art,' for which van Doesburg was the spokesperson. He became known for his use of primary colors and the incorporation of geometric stained-glass windows and tile floors into interiors; designed the distinctive *Composition IV* triptych window (executed by Vennootschap Crabeth of The Hague) in the 1917 townhouse (architect, Jan Wils) in Alkmaar; in the 1917 hallway of Oud's residence in Noordwijkerhout, near Leiden, van Doesburg used wall painting to emphasize the structural elements of the architecture. He traveled to Berlin and in Dessau lectured on De Stijl principles at the Bauhaus; wrote the book *Grundbegriffe der neuen gestaltenden Kunst* in the *Bauhausbücher*, vol. 6, Frankfurt, 1925 (published earlier in Dutch in Amsterdam); was in contact with El Lissitzky and László Moholy-Nagy, resulting in 1922 issue of *De Stijl* on Suprematism and Lissitzky; emphasized the importance of fine art over architecture, which led to his alienation from Oud. From 1920s, he collaborated with Cornelis van Eesteren on models and architectural drawings for the De Stijl architecture exhibition at Léonce Rosenberg's Galerie L'Effort Moderne, Paris, which began the organization's 'international phase,' resulting in Mondrian's final (1925) withdrawal from De Stijl. Van Doesburg organized the 1922 Dada-Constructivist Congress; designed the color scheme for the Little Flower Room in 1924–33 Noailles villa in Hyères and, with Hans Arp and Sophie Taeuber-Arp, 1926–28 interior renovation of Café L'Aubette in Strasbourg, and his own 1929–30 residence in Meudon-Val-Fleury, the antithesis of De Stijl ideas. With van Eesteren, he became active in applying De Stijl principles to town planning; also wrote *De Nieuwe Beweging in de Schilderkunst* (Delft: J. Waltman, 1917), *Drie voordrachten over de nieuwe bildende Kunst* (Amsterdam: Maatschappij voor Goede en Goekoope Lectuur, 1919), and *Klassiek, barok, modern* (Amsterdam: De Sikkel1920). His death marked the end of De Stijl.
Exhibitions Work subject of 1968–69 traveling exhibition, Eindhoven, The Hague, and Basel (catalog below); 1977, Centre Georges Pompidou, Paris.
Bibliography *De Stijl* magazine, complete reprint, Oct. 1917–Jan. 1932, Amsterdam: Athenaeum; The Hague: Bert Bakker; Amsterdam: Van Gennep, 1968. Cat., *Theo van Doesburg 1883–1931*, Eindhoven: Stedelijk van Abbemuseum, 1968. Theo van Doesburg, *Principles of Neo-Plastic Art*, Greenwich, Conn.: New York Graphic Society, 1968. Joost Baljeu, *Theo van Doesburg*, New York: Macmillan, 1974. Allan Doig, *Theo van Doesburg: Painting into Architecture, Theory into Practice*, Cambridge/New York: Cambridge, 1986. Evert van Straaten, *Theo van Doesburg: Painter and Architect*, The Hague: SDU, 1988. Els Hoek (ed.), *Theo van Doesburg: œuvre catalogue*, Utrecht and Otterlo: Centraal Museum/Kröller-Müller Museum, 2000.

Van Doren, Harold L. (1895–1957)
American industrial designer; born Chicago; active Philadelphia.

Training To 1917, Williams College (Phi Beta Kappa), Williamstown, Mass.; 1920–21, painting, Art Students League, New York; 1921–22, first-service fellowship in history, École du Louvre, Paris; 1922–24, Académie de la Grande Chaumière, Paris.
Biography 1917–19, Van Doren served in the army in Italy; returned to New York to study painting and, thence, went on to study in Paris, where he was an artist for the Paris edition of the *Chicago Tribune* newspaper; wrote for *Encyclopedia Britannica*, magazines *Saturday Evening Post* and *House & Garden*, and others; 1925, translated the biographies of Paul Cézanne and Pierre-Auguste Renoir by Ambroise Vollard. 1927–30: he was assistant director, Minneapolis Art Museum, art editor at two Minneapolis newspapers and received his first award in commercial and industrial design, from National Alliance for Art & Industry. 1930, he moved to Toledo, Ohio, at the encouragement of fellow college student Hubert D. Bennett, then president of Toledo Scale, and began designing for the firm. c. 1930, Van Doren and John Gordon Rideout (1898–1951) founded industrial-design office Van Doren & Rideout, where Van Doren designed a 1932 public weighing scale by Toledo Scale, 1933 molded-plastic radio (with Rideout) by Air-King Products Co., 1934 Sno-Plane sled by American

Jos van der Meulen. Paper Bags waste baskets. 1993. Reprocessed printed paper, larger example 34 x 15 x 15" (86.4 x 38.1 x 38.1 cm). Mfr.: Goods, the Netherlands. MoMA.

National of Toledo, 1936 child's scooter (with Rideout, patented), 1936 Magnalite aluminum tea kettle by Wagner Ware. For six months in c. 1935, he was sent by Toledo Scale to Mellon Institute of Industrial Research, Pittsburgh, for research in urea resins, which resulted in new Plaskon (invented by A.M. Howald in 1928). Other clients included Swartzbaugh, DeVilbiss, and Philco. He became well known for his book *Industrial Design: A Practical Guide to Product Design and Development* (New York: McGraw-Hill, 1940); was one of first presidents of Industrial Designers Society of America (IDSA) and a member of the board of directors, Philadelphia Art Alliance, and of Moore Institute of Art, Science and Industry, Philadelphia. Late 1940s, he was a senior partner in Van Doren, Nowland & Schladermundt in New York and Philadelphia; 1950s, left and established Harold Van Doren & Associates in Philadelphia. On his 1957 death from leukemia, the firm's accounts were assumed by Harper Landell (1918–), a Van Doren employee from 1947 and who had formerly worked as a corporate industrial designer at Carrier Corporation in Syracuse, N.Y. 1944–47. Thus Landell changed the name to Harper Landell Design, in Philadelphia.
Exhibitions/citations Work included in exhibitions such as 2000–01 *American Modern...*, The Metropolitan Museum of Art, New York, and touring the US; aluminum-design exhibition, touring the US from 2000; prominent in exhibition, Toledo (Ohio) Museum of Art (catalog below). Late 1940s, received a design award (for work for Philco), Lord & Taylor department store, New York.
Bibliography *Fortune*, Feb. 1934: 88. Jonathan M. Woodham, *Twentieth-Century Ornament*, New York: Rizzoli, 1990: 150–51, 224. Eric Baker, *Great Inventions, Good Intentions*, San Francisco: Chronicle, 1990: 129. J. Stewart Johnson, *American Modern, 1925–1940: Design for a New Age*, New York: Abrams, 2000. Cat., Dennis P. Doordan, *The Alliance of Art and Industry: Toledo Designs for a Modern America*, Toledo: Toledo Museum of Art, 2002.

van Erp, Dirk (1859–1933)
Dutch metalwork designer; born Leeuwarden; active California.

Biography 1886, van Erp emigrated to US after working in his family's hardware business; 1900, was active as a coppersmith in the US Navy shipyards on Mare Island, near San Francisco and transformed used brass gun-shell casings into vases, an avocation that developed into a profitable business. By 1906, Vickery, Atkins, and Torrey in San Francisco, a fashionable shop, was carrying his wares. 1908 with public interest in his work having grown, he opened his own shop in Oakland, Cal., and became a professional art metalworker. His daughter Agatha van Erp and Harry St. John Dixon were two of his apprentices at this time. 1910–11, van Erp was was a partner of designer D'Arcy Gaw in a business (Dirk van Erp Studios) that moved to Sutter Street in San Francisco. Gaw, previously a weaver at Herter Looms in New York, designed several early mica-shade lamps, a type van Erp had initiated and for which he is best known today. By its 1915 zenith, the van Erp enterprise was producing a variety of decorative objects, including vases, planters, bowls, smoking accouterments, and copper electric lamps with mica shades. Some of van Erp and Gaw's work incorporated Grueby tiles. 1916, during World War I, van Erp returned to the shipyards, with the shop managed by his daughter, with assistance from his son William and from Dixon. Dixon later established his own shop. 1929, van Erp retired and left the shop to son William.
Exhibition Work subject of 1989 *The Arts & Crafts Studio of Dirk van Erp*, San Francisco Museum of Craft & Folk Art (catalog below).
Bibliography Bonnie Mattison in Timothy J. Andersen et al., *California Design 1910*, Salt Lake City: Peregrine Smith, 1980: 87. Dorothy Lamoureux, *The Arts and Crafts Studio of Dirk van Erp*, San Francisco: San Francisco Museum of Craft & Folk Art, 1989.

van Hoe, Marc (1945–)
Belgian textil edesigner; born Zulte.

Training Textile weaving and design, Provinciaal Technisch Instituut, Courtrai.
Biography Van Hoe has been motivated by a passion for textiles from the onset of the Industrial Revolution. From 1975, he has been a freelance designer and researcher, specializing in industrial textiles and tapestry; taught, Koninklijke Academie voor Schone Kunsten, Courtrai; lecturer, Academie voor Beeldende Vorming, Tilburg. He has organized several exhibitions such as 1980 *Textielstructuren*, Academie in Courtrai.
Exhibitions Work shown widely, in Belgium, France, Switzerland, the UK, Poland, and Hungary.

van Kempen en Begeer
Dutch silversmiths; located Utrecht and later Voorschoten.

History 1835, J.M. van Kempen (1814–77) established the eponymous silver factory in Utrecht. With quality as its priority, it was operated along traditional lines; 1858, was moved to Voorschoten. English craftspeople were hired to instruct Dutch workers in the new techniques of fork and spoon production. Under manager L.J.S. van Kempen (1838–1910), a separate studio was established to produce both large and small sculptures as well as mechanically made silverwork components. The firm became the largest and oldest manufacturer of silver in the Netherlands. 1845–1903, G.W. van Dokkum worked as a draftsperson and modeler. J.L. Bernhardie, who had become chief draftsperson, worked at the firm 1858–86, succeeded by H.J. Valk 1886–1924. Not until the 20th century did the firm hire non-staff, notably Th. K.L. Sluyterman, who created Art Nouveau ware in c. 1900; even so, the firm still specialized in uninspired classical models. 1919, the C.J. Begeer firm merged with former competitor J.M. van Kempen en Zoon and jeweler J. Vos to become Van Kempen, Begeer en Vos.
Exhibitions Van Kempen displayed silverware designed by van Dokkum at 1851 London *Great Exhibition of the Works of Industry of All Nations*; did not participate in exhibitions after 1900 *Exposition Universelle*, Paris. Subject of c. 1975 exhibition, Rotterdam (catalog below).
Bibliography Cat., *Mensen en zilver: Bijna twee eeuwen werken voor Van Kempen en Begeer, 1975–1976*, Rotterdam: Museum Boymans-van Beuningen, c. 1975. Annelies Krekel-Aalberse, *Art Nouveau and Art Déco Silver*, New York: Abrams, 1989.
> See Begeer.

Van Keppel, Hendrik (1914–); Taylor Green (1914–)
American interior designer; active Los Angeles.

Biography 1938, Van Keppel and Green established an interior-design service in Los Angeles and, 1939, the Van Keppel-Green (VKG) store on Santa Monica Boulevard for the production of their limited or customer-specific furniture. Their modern limited-edition furniture with clean lines included1946 tubular-steel-and-yachting-cord chaise longue and ottoman, one of their first and best-known models, as well as a wider version and side-chair interpretations, and also case goods, tables, and seating. The chaise is currently being produced again by Modernica, Los Angeles. After World War II, they began less-limited-edition furniture that called on industrial raw materials. The gas piping used in their earlier models was replaced with more-refined enameled steel. Sales success led to the expansion of their operation in 1948.

Harold L. Van Doren and John Gordon Rideout. Tea kettle. 1936. Magnalite aluminum with wood handle, h. 8 1/2" x dia. 9 13/16" (21.6 x 25 cm). Mfr.: Wagner Ware, US. Purchase. MoMA.

Hendrik Van Keppel and Taylor Green. Lounge chair and ottoman. 1946. Enameled tubular steel and cotton cord, chair 25 3/4 x 21 x 34 3/8" (65.4 x 53.3 x 87.3 cm), ottoman 12 1/4 x 21 3/8 x 18" (31.1 x 54.3 x 45.7 cm). Mfr.: Van Keppel-Green (VKG), US. Gift of Mr. and Mrs. Gifford Phillips. MoMA.

1950s, they designed for mass-production manufacturers such as Balboa Chrome, Brown-Saltman, and Mueller, and, from 1960s, Brown Jordan, essentially outdoor-furniture firms; and outfitted some Case Study houses, including more traditional upholstered pieces.
Bibliography James J. Cowen, 'Van Keppel-Green... Design Team,' *Furniture Field*, 1951. Cat., K. B. Hiesinger and G. H. Marcus III (eds.), *Design Since 1945*, Philadelphia: Philadelphia Museum of Art, 1983.

van Leersum, Emmy
> See Bakker, Gijs.

van Lieshout, Joep (1963–)

Dutch architect and designer; born Ravenstein.

Training 1980–85, Academie van Beeldende Kunsten, Rotterdam; 1986–87, Ateliers '63, Haarlem; 1987, Villa Arson, Nice, France.
Biography 1995, van Lieshout founded Atelier Van Lieshout (AVL), a multidisciplinary company that operates internationally in art, design, and architecture. The work—ideosyncratic and provocative but practical, uncomplicated, and substantial—has ranged from sculpture, furniture, and bathrooms to mobile-home units and complete architectural refittings. Its large, brightly colored polyester constructions are distinctive, often consisting of large enclosed living spaces. AVL also produces made-to-order furniture for museum collections. The group's initial general focus was on furniture but shifted to so-called artwork in which to live. Its major work is the 2001 AVL-Ville, a 'free state' in the harbor of Rotterdam, which is a collection of AVL's production up to the time of its placement 'where everything is possible within a country over-regulated to an increasingly oppressive degree,' in van Lieshout's words. The self-sufficient AVL-Ville has its own flag, constitution, money, and motto: 'As long as it's art, just about anything's possible.' The group has realized its first AVL-Ville export (the AVL Francise Unit) in Park Middelheim, Antwerp. Lieshout questions the idea of an individual creator/artist, thus AVL is a group effort.
Exhibitions/citations Work included in exhibitions and subject of a large number of venues from 1988. Received 1991 Charlotte Köhler Award; 1992 Prix de Rome; first prize of 1994 Bolidt Floor Concepts competitions; 1997 Anjerfonds-Chabot Award; 1998 Mart Stam Prize; 2000 Wilhelmina-Ring sculpture award; 2002 Stankowski Award.
Bibliography Joep van Lieshout, Udo Kittelmann, Bart Lootsma, and Piet De Jonge, *Joep van Lieshout*, Rotterdam: Boymans-van Beuningen Museum, 1997. Joep van Lieshout and Peter J. Hoefnagels, *The Good, the Bad and the Ugly*, Amsterdam: NAi, 1999. www.ateliervanlieshout.com.

van Onck, Andries (1928–)

Dutch architect and industrial designer; born Amsterdam; active Milan.

Training Under Gerrit Thomas Rietveld; under Tomas Maldonado, Walter Zeischegg, and Max Bill, Hochschule für Gestaltung, Ulm.
Biography 1959, van Onck settled in Italy and, from 1962 under Ettore Sottsass, worked for Olivetti on electronic office equipment (including 1959 Elea 9003 calculator, with Hans von Klier and Sottsass); also a chair by Poltronova (with von Klier); 1972, established his own design studio in Milan and has since collaborated with his wife Hiroko Takeda on products for firms in Italy and abroad. 1970s, van Onck, Antonio Barrese, Peppe Di Giuli, Cees Houtzager, Antonio Locatelli, and Pietro Salmoiraghi founded Studio Pro; designed industrial equipment and electronics for clients including Colussi, Dielectrix, Philips Italiana, and Società Fisica Applicata, and domestic electrical appliances and sound equipment for Flash, La Rinascente, and Varom. Van Onck has also designed (frequently with Takeda) domestic furniture, accessories, and glassware produced by Appiani, Arosio Lissone, Caminda, Cristallerie, Imperatore, Metaltex, Upim, and others. He taught courses in industrial design, Politecnico, Milan; Istituto Superiore per le Industrie Artistiche (ISIA), Florence; ISIA, Rome; and theory and practice in industrial design, Istituto Euro-peo di Design, Milan. He became a member of Società Italiana di Ergonomia; of Kring Industriële Ontwerpers (KIO), Antwerp; from its 1968 founding, juries of Premio SMAU Industrial Design, Salone della Machina e Attrezzature per l'Ufficio, Milan; and of Associazione per il Disegno Industriale (ADI). Others of van Onck and Takeda's products have included 1991 Tiramisù stepladder by Kartell; folding chair, adjustable table, and ashtray by Magis; door handles by Colombo Design and by Olivari; intercom by Amplyvox; lamps by Status. From 1989, van Onck has written a number of articles on design theory.
Citations Premio Compasso d'Oro: 1979 (for switches with Takeda, later in Habitat store range; CS 100 folding table with Giulio Cardelli by Colussi), 1981 (for Tokio door handle/fittings with Tekeda by Olivari), 1987 (for Wing extension table with Takeda by Magis), 1994 (for Tiramisù folding ladder by Kartell).
Bibliography *ADI Annual 1976*, Milan: Associazione per il Disegno Industriale, 1976. *Modo*, no. 148, Mar.–Apr. 1993: 127.

van Severen, Maarten (1956–)

Belgian designer; born Antwerp; son of an abstract painter; active Ghent.

Training Architectuurinstituut Saint-Lucas, Ghent.
Biography After the architecture institute, van Severen worked for

several designers; 1985, began as an independent designer; 1987, established a workshop for limited and semi-industrial furniture, the first of which was a long, slender aluminum table (refined over the years); 1990, turned his attention to chair design. Has designed for firms, including Target Lighting (U-Line lamp), Vitra Obumex (1994 kitchen), and Bulo (Schraag trestle table), and interiors of public and private buildings such as the Villa d'All AVA in Paris and 1995–98 Floirac house, Bordeaux (architect of both, Rem Koolhaas); became known for a highly refined minimalism expressed by 1993 aluminum Low chair (produced from 1999) by his own eponymous firm, founded in 1988. Furniture has included 1998 .03 stacking chair (first project with Vitra and one having become popular), 1992 chair (no. 2), 2000 MVS chaise longue, 2000 LCP chair in PMMA, and other furniture by Vitra; 1998 self-skinned polyurethane Blue bench (available in other colors) by Edra (introduced at Interieur 98 biennial fair); entrances of the Palais Royal in Paris and, in Ghent, those of Museum of Art (1997) and city hall (1998); 2000 LCP chaise longue by Kartell.
Exhibitions/citations Work subject of a 1996 VIA-sponsored venue at Salon du Meuble, Paris; 2004–05 exhibition, Design Museum, Ghent. Included in 1990 *New Furniture*, Museum voor Sierkunst & Vormgeving, Ghent; Interieur 94 and subsequent editions, Courtrai, Belgium; 1996 Triennale di Milano; 1998 *Interior Design*, Cologne; 2000 *Aluminum by Design* touring exhibition, originating at Carnegie Art Museum, Pittsburgh. Received Henry van de Velde Prize at *Interieur 92* fair, Courtrai; 1998, 1999, and 2001 Industrie Forum Design (iF), Hanover; 1998 bi-annual award of design, Cultural Ambassador of Flanders; 1998 award, Design Award of Flemish Government; 1999 Good Design award (with other designers), Chicago Athenaeum; 1999 Design Preis Schweiz; Creator of the Year, 2001 Salon de Meuble, Paris;
Bibliography Mel Byars, *50 Tables...*, Hove: RotoVision, 1997. Jasper Morrison (ed.), *The International Design Yearbook,* London: Laurence King, 1999. Geert Bekaert, *Maarten van Severen*, Ghent: Ludion, 2000. Paola Antonelli (ed.), *Objects of Design: The Museum of Modern Art*, New York: The Museum of Modern Art, 2003: 185.

van Vlissingen

Dutch textile firm; located Helmond.

History 1846, the firm of P. Fentener van Vlissingen was established through the takeover of PA Sutorius in Helmond. 1863, it installed a roller-printing machine; from 1873, began using synthetic dyes; 1905, changed to Indanthren dyes. Having exported worldwide for some time, its cretonne goods (drapery fabrics, cushion covers, and bedspreads) were sold in Britain 1900–12. Some nature-inspired motifs were designed by M. Duco Crop, who designed for the firm 1894–99. 1914–27, van Vlissingen exported goods to Singapore and Bangkok, to 1931 India, and, most importantly, Africa and the Dutch West Indies. The successful Vlisco range of fabrics, based on modern designs and advanced mechanized methods, was introduced in 1927. J.W. Gidding and A. van der Plas designed curtains and table-cloths. With wallpaper manufacturer Rath en Doodeheefver, van Vlissingen established the association Teentoonstelling het Behang en het Gordijn (as a successor to Het Behang en het Gordijn) with the aim of fostering new design work by Dutch artists. This organization led to the formation of Samenwerkende Industrie en Ambacht (an association for the cooperation of industry and crafts), with its journal *Ensemble*. Van Vlissingen's postwar production was, and continues to be, for African markets.
Exhibitions Wares shown at 1927 *Het Behang en het Gordijn* (wallpaper and curtains), Stedelijk Museum, Amsterdam, and touring.
Bibliography Cat., *Industry and Design in the Netherlands, 1850/1950*, Amsterdam: Stedelijk Museum, 1985: 90–93.

Maarten van Severen. Low chair. 1993. Aluminum, 24 3/4 x 19 3/4 x 36 1/4" (62.9 x 50.2 x 92.1 cm). Mfr.: TM, Belgium (2000). Gift of the manufacturer. MoMA.

Andries Van Onck. Tiramisù stepladder. 1991. Epoxy-finished oval steel tube, polycarbonate, and polyurethane, open 35 x 16 1/2 x 24" (88.9 x 41.9 x 61 cm), closed 28 3/4 x 16 1/2 x 2 1/2" (73 x 41.9 x 6.4 cm). Mfr.: Kartell, Italy. Gift of the mfr. MoMA.

Vaněk, Jan (1891–1962)

Czech architect, designer, entrepreneur, and publicist; born Trebitsch (now Třebíč, Czech Republic).

Training School of Woodwork, Chrudim.
Biography Vaněk began working for leading furniture manufacturers in Munich, Stuttgart, and Heilbronn; 1921, organized Spojené Uměleckoprůmyslové Závody (united decorative-arts factories); initiated the production of standard furniture and collaborated with leading foreign architects; 1925, became a founder and, to 1932, director of Standard, a housing association in Brno that produced furniture and furnished standardized family houses; 1933, moved to Prague and founded the Consulting Center for Housing, the House and Garden workshop, and the textile firm Vatex. He published the magazine *Bytová kultura*; organized 1929 *The Civilized Woman* exhibition, publishing the book of same title to advocate women's clothing reform; designed a number of domestic, school, and public interiors.
Bibliography Alena Adlerová, *České užité umění 1918–1938*, Prague: Odeon, 1983.

Vasegaard, Gertrud (b. Gertrud Hjorth 1913–)

Danish ceramicist; born Bornholm, Denmark; wife of Sigurd Steen from 1935 and of Aksel Vilhelm Rode from 1961.

Training 1930–32, Kunsthåndvaerkerskolen, Copenhagen; 1932–33, in the studio of Axel Salto and Bode Willumsen at Saxbo pottery.
Biography From 1933, she was active with her sister Lisbeth Munch-Petersen in their own studio in Gudhjem, Bornholm, and, 1936–48, alone in Holkadalen, Bornholm; became known for her high produc-

Kristian Solmer Vedel. Child's chair. 1957. Beech plywood frame and lacquered seat, 16 x 17 1/2 x 11 1/2" (40.6 x 44.4 x 29.2 cm). Gift of Daniel Morris and Denis Gallion, Historical Design Collection Inc. Mfr.: Torben Ørskov & Co., Denmark. MoMA.

tion standards and designs of handmade stoneware; 1945–59, designed bowls, vases, and the 1957 Chinese-influenced porcelain tea service by Bing & Grøndahl Porcelænsfabrik (working there as a freelance designer and full-time 1948–59); subsequently, designed tea services by Royal Copenhagen, where she was a freelance designer in 1959, particularly Gema porcelain dinnerware, one of three services for the firm. 1959 with her daughter Myre Vasegaard (1936–), she established a studio in Frederiksberg; to 1969, also collaborated with her husband Aksel Rode.
Exhibitions/citations Work included in 1982 *Danish Ceramic Design*, Pennsylvania State University, University Park, Pa., and traveling. Large number of citations include 1948 Theophilus Hansens prize; gold medal at 1957 (11th) Triennale di Milano; 1963 Eckersberg medal; 1964 and 1991 C. L. Davids scholarship; 1976 (two citations for Capella dinnerware by Rosenthal) Industrie Forum Design (iF), Hanover; 1981 Price Eugen medal; 1987 art prize of Skovgaard Museet; 1988 prize, Ole Haslunds Kunstnerfond; 1992 C.F. Hansen medal; 1992 and 1996–98 Dalhof Larsen award; 1993 award, Danmarks Nationalbank's Jubilee Foundation; Thorvald Bindesbøll Medal, Akademirådet, Denmark; 1994 Karl Thyrre award; others.
Bibliography Erik Zahle (ed.), *A Treasury of Scandinavian Design*, New York: Golden Press, 1961. *Danish Ceramic Design*, University Park, Pa.: Pennsylvania State University, 1981. Vibeke Woldbye (ed.): Gertrud Vasegaard, Copenhagen, 1984. Jennifer Hawkins Opie, *Scandinavia: Ceramics and Glass in the Twentieth Century*, New York: Rizzoli, 1989. Cat., Kathryn B. Hiesinger and George H. Marcus III (eds.), *Design Since 1945*, Philadelphia: Philadelphia Museum of Art, 1983.

Vassos, John (1898–1985)

Romanian-Greek illustrator and designer, born Bucharest, Romania; active Boston.

Training Museum of Fine Arts School, Boston; Art Students League, New York.
Biography Vassos produced graphic design for labels, packages, and occasionally small appliances, and illustrated many 1920s-50s publications; was a marketing pioneer and called on applied psychology to analyze buying habits and motivations; for Coca-Cola, designed bottle dispensers with aluminum coils on the bottom of the barrel that sat on the counter to suggest coolness and with red and green bands on the body of the barrel to lend a sense of guarded treasure; 1930s–60s, designed sound equipment for RCA, including the c. 1935 RCA Victor Special (Model N) portable phonograph in aluminum and the first (1939) American TV set (TRK-11), and c. 1932 restyled turnstile by Perey Company of New York. Vassos's version of the turnstile lowered manufacturing costs and increased sales by 25%. Other work: a 1939 patented streamline child's tricycle and a harmonica; 1931 interior of Rismont Tea Room on Broadway and c. 1933 interior of photographer Margaret Bourke-White's studio-office on the 61st floor of Chrysler Building, both New York; wrote and/or illustrated 14 books, published by Dutton, including *Contempo, This American Tempo* (text by his wife Ruth Vassos, 1929) and *Ultimo, An Imaginative Narration of Life Under the Earth* (1930).
Exhibitions Work included in 1939–40 *New York World's Fair: The World of Tomorrow*; 1986 *Machine Age in America 1918–1941*, Brooklyn Museum of Art, Brooklyn, N.Y.; *American Modern, 1925–1940: Design for a New Age*, touring the US (catalogs below); 2000 *Aluminum by Design* touring exhibition, originating at Carnegie Art Museum, Pittsburgh.
Bibliography *Fortune*, Feb. 1934: 88. Cat., Richard Guy Wilson et al., *The Machine Age in America 1918–1941*, New York: Abrams, 1986. Robert A.M. Stern et al., *New York 1930: Architecture and Urbanism Between the Two World Wars*, New York: Rizzoli, 1987. Eric Baker, *Great Inven-tions, Good Intentions*, San Francisco: Chronicle, 1990: 121. Cat., J. Stewart Johnson, *American Modern, 1925–1940...*, New York: Abrams, 2000.

Vchtemas; Vchutein
> See VKhUTEMAS.

Vedel, Kristian Solmer (1923–)

Danish furniture designer.

Training 1944–45 under Kaare Klint, architecture, Det Kongelige Danske Kunstakademi; 1946, furniture design, Kunsthåndværkerskolen; both Copenhagen.
Biography Vedel was strongly influenced by Klint's simple, functional approach to furniture design and production; 1955, established his own design studio in Copenhagen and soon after created two innovative pieces: 1953 melamine stacking dishes (produced from 1960) and 1957 curved-plywood slotted child's chair by Torben Ørskov & Co. He also designed Ørskov's Gourmet range (including black melamine egg cup), turned-oak-birds mini-sculptures by Lassen Tableware, and the popular 1963 Modus range of furniture by Søren Willadsen; 1952–53, taught at Askov Køјskole and, 1953–56, furniture design at Kunsthåndværkerskolen; 1961 with Ane Vedel, established a design studio. 1968, Vedel was head of department of industrial design, The East African University, Nairobi, Kenya, where he was professor of industrial design 1969–71 and in 1975; 1966–68, was chairperson of Industrielle Designere Danmark (IDD).
Exhibitions/citations Work shown at 1958 *Formes Scandinaves*, Musée des Arts Décoratifs, Paris; 1960–61 *The Arts of Denmark*, touring the US; 1969 *Sitzen 69*, Österreichisches Museum für Angewandte Kunst, Vienna; 1984 *Design Since 1945*, Philadelphia Museum of Art (catalogs below). Received 1962 Lunning Prize; silver medal (for child's chair) at 1957 (11th) and gold medal at 1960 (12th) Triennale di Milano.
Bibliography 'Thirty-four Lunning Prize-Winners,' *Mobilia*, no. 146, Sept. 1967. Cat., *Sitzen 69*, Vienna: Österreichisches Museum für Angewandte Kunst, 1969, no. 10. Frederik Sieck, *Nutidig Dansk Møbeldesign–en kortfattet illustreret beskrivelse*, Copenhagen: Bondo Gravesen, 1990. Cat., Kathryn B. Hiesinger and George H. Marcus III (eds.), *Design Since 1945*, Philadelphia: Philadelphia Museum of Art, 1983. Cat., *The Lunning Prize*, Stockholm: Nationalmuseum, 1986. Noritsugu Oda, *Danish Chairs*, San Francisco: Chronicle Books, 1999.

Vedel-Rieper, John (1929–)

Danish industrial designer.

Training To 1949, Skolen for Boligindretning, Copenhagen.
Biography 1954–60, Vedel-Rieper worked with Børge Mogensen; 1960, established his own studio; 1971–75, was associated with Skolen for Brugskunst (formerly Det Tekniske Selskabs Skoler), where he taught 1974–75; from 1972, taught in the furniture laboratory, Det Kongelige Danske Kunstakademi, Copenhagen; has been president, Ornamo (Finnish association of designers), and secretary general in Copenhagen, World Crafts Council. He has designed a range of products, including furniture with Hakon Stephensen by Erhard Rasmussen.
Exhibitions/citation From 1977, work included in exhibitions of the furniture laboratory of the Danske Kunstakademi; in furniture exhibitions in Stockholm, Gothenburg, Malmö, Copenhagen, and Århus. Received 1999 Torsten & Wanja Söderbergs Pris.
Bibliography Frederik Sieck, *Nutidig Dansk Møbeldesign: -en kortfattet illustreret beskrivelse*, Copenhagen: Bondo Gravesen, 1990.

Velcro
> See de Mestral, Georges.

Veneziano, Gianni (1953–)

Italian architect and designer; born and active in Molfetta.

Training 1970–81, architecture degree, Florence; in Chicago.
Biography 1979–81, Veneziano lived in Chicago and became interested in 'designed architecture'; 1987, with Prospero Rasulo, founded Oxido, a gallery for art, architecture, and design in Milan; 1989–98, the collaboration was known as Oxido Zoo. He has served clients, including Demetra, Lumi, Masterly, Partner & Co., Ortolan, RSVP, Sisal, and others; has been supervisor of Spazio S. Orsola Galleria del Progetto in Molfetta. Work has included lighting, furnishings, accessories, and furniture, such as 1989 Dal Giardino degli Incanti leaf chair and 1993 La Luna sconce by Lumi. From late 1990s, he has focused on geometric, minimalist architecture. Exhibition design/organization: *House of Memory*, Phyllis Needelman Gallery, Chicago; *The Sky by Piranesi*, N.A.M.E. gallery, Chicago; *Zucchero*, Underground, Milan; *Marchiño*, La Bottega dei Vasai, Milan; *Icons*, Paris and London; *Italian Icons*, New York; 2003–04 *Uominiluce* (with Alfio Cangiani, which included Veneziano's own lighting), Punto Einaudi, Barletta, and other galleries. He is the coordinator, Spazio S. Orsola design gallery, Molfetta.
Exhibitions Exhibited first in 1975, at the Quadriennale Nazionale d'Arte, Rome, and, subsequently, in large number of gallery, museum, and fair venues in Chicago, Paris, London, and Italy.
Bibliography Fumio Shimizu, *Euro Design*, Tokyo: Graphic-sha 1993. Christina Morozzi and Silvio San Pietro, *Mobili Italiani Contemporanei*, Milan: Archivolto, 1996. Silvia Pecoraro, *Oggetti del Desiderio-Mosaico e Design*, Milan: Electa, 1997. Carrado Maurizio, *La Casa Ecologica*, Bologna: De Vecchi, 1997. Maurizio Vitta, *Gianni Veneziano*, Milan: Archivolto, 1998.

Venini, Paolo (1895–1959); Venini glassworks

Italian glassware designer and maker; active Murano.

Training In the law.
Biography Venini a was a lawyer in Milan before becoming a partner in 1921 with Vittorio Zecchin (1878–1947) and Venetian antiques dealer Giacomo Cappellin (1887–1968) in Vetri Soffiati Muranesi Cappellin-Venini. Their successful quest was to develop a modern style in glass and to bring glassmaking in Murano into the new century. Zecchin—an accomplished painter, decorator, and glass designer, who was opposed to the decoration of glass—became the factory's artistic and technical director. 1925, the factory Cappellin Venini & C. split, and Venini established the V.S.M. Venini glass factory in Murano, where sculptor Napoleone Martinuzzi (1892–1997) was the artistic director. Venini himself designed in a simple, functional style early on; later interpreted modernism (or Novecento) in a livelier and more novel manner than in northern Europe, developing the first modern style in glass, with intense colors. Murano glasswares had traditionally been blown in garish ruby and gold colors and in playful forms of decorative curlicues and filigreed fripperies. Venini commissioned various designers, including Gio Ponti from 1927, Tomoso Buzzi and Carlo Scarpa from 1932, Eugene Berman from 1951, Ken Scott from 1951, Franco Albini from 1954, and Massimo Vignelli from 1956; the practice of hiring freelance designers included Martinuzzi and Fulvio Bianconi; at the 1956 Biennale di Venezia, showed bottles (or decanters) by Ponti and Bianconi called *morandiennes*, made of two-colored cane (an element of extruded glass) and inspired by the paintings of Giorgio Morandi (1890–1964). Other favored techniques were *vetro a fili* (glass with lines) and *zanfirico* (rods of colored glass embedded to create stripes). The firm's 1950 *vetro pezzato* (handkerchief glass) had a patchwork effect of squares in various colors. One of its best-known 1950s forms was the c. 1950 Vaso Fazzoletto (handkerchief vase) by Bianconi, which was simply a square of thin glass melted over a form to make a vase shape. The factory's humorous, if dubiously tasteful, figurines were developed spontaneously through hot-glass experiments. Paolo Venini's own glassware designs achieved a vitality attained through direct contact with glassmaking, an approach not generally employed in northern Europe, where designers' ideas were realized through the factory blowers and handlers. Venini's widow Ginette Venini and his son-in-law Ludovico Diaz de Santillana assumed management of the firm upon his death in Venice and commissioned designers, including Tobia Scarpa, Tapio Wirkkala, and others. 1997, when Royal Copenhagen acquired Orrefors Kosta Boda, BodaNova-Höganäs Keramik, and Venini (which had been sold by the Venini family), the name of the overall group became Royal Scandinavia, with Venini only a brand. However, in 2000, Royal Scandinavia was bought by an investment group and eventually dismantled into various reorganized entities. 2001, Venini was taken over by Italian Luxury Industries Group.
Exhibitions Initial success at 1923 (1st) *Esposizione Internazionale d'Arte Decorativa*, Monza, and 1925 *Exposition Internationale des Arts Décoratifs et Industriels Modernes*, Paris. Work shown at 1923 (1st) Biennale di Monza; 1933 (5th) Triennale di Milano; 1956 Biennale di Venezia; 1983–84 *Design Since 1945* (*vetro pezzato* glassware by Tobia Scarpa and Wirkkala), Philadelphia Museum of Art. Work subject of 1981 *Venini Glass*, Smithsonian Institution, Washington, D.C.; 1996 exhibition, Fondazione Giorgio Cini, Isola di San Giorgio Maggiore (catalogs below); 2001 *Venini: Art and Design in Glass from Venice*, Cooper-Hewitt National Design Museum, New York.
Bibliography Ada Polak, *Modern Glass*, London: Faber & Faber, 1962. Cat., *Venini Glass*, Washington, D.C.: Smithsonian Institution, 1981. Franco Deboni, *Venini Glass*, Turino: Allemandi, 1989. Cat., Alessandro Bettagno, *Gli artisti di Venini: Per una storia del vetro d'arte veneziano*, Milan: Electa, 1996. Anna Venini Diaz de Santillana, *Venini catalogue raisonné 1921–1986*, Milan: Skira, 2000. www.venini.it.
> See Royal Scandinavia.

Paolo Venini. Vase. 1938. Blown glass, h. 7 1/8" (18.1 cm) x dia. 6 3/4" (17.2 cm). Mfr.: Venini & Co., Italy. Gift of the designer. MoMA.

Venosta Fossati-Bellani, Carla (c. 1917–)

Italian architect and designer; born Monza; active Milan.

Training 1950s, Politecnico, Milan.
Biography 1970, Venosta set up her own studio in Milan, designing furniture, accessories, electronic equipment for clients, including Arflex, Argenteria Gabriele De Vecchi, Arti e Mestieri, Bacci, Busnolli, Cinova, Faroana Tiffany, Fasem, Full, Gabbianelli/Voque, Gabrielli, Gallotti e Radice, Ideal Standard, Italidea, Nazzareno, Nicola Trussardi, Ogget, Siv, Tosimobili, and Zanotta; was preoccupied with solving problems of urban living; 1980–81, was vice-president, International Council of Societies of Industrial Design (ISCID); 1980–81, member, promotion committee, 13th ISCID conference, Milan; 1980–83 and 1991–92, member, organizing committee, Associazione per il Disegno Industriale (ADI); from 1983 and 1992, member, board of directors, 17th and 18th editions of Triennale di Milano.
Exhibitions/citations Participated in a number of exhibitions and competitions. Premio Compasso d'Oro: 1979 (Mark 5 medical microprocessor by Amplaid; produced by Ogget), 1981 (for Teknico industrial ceiling fixture by Termisol; Antologia 2 folding bookcase by Tosimobili), and 1989 (for Exalibur organizer by Argenteria Gabriele De Vecchi).
Bibliography *ADI Annual 1976*, Milan: Associazione per il Disegno Industriale, 1976. *Modo*, no.148, Mar.–Apr. 1993: 127.

Venturi, Robert (1925–)

American architect; born and active Philadelphia; husband of Denise Scott Brown.

Training To 1947, bachelor's degree in architecture, and, 1950, master of fine arts degree, Princeton University; 1954–56 on Prix de Rome fellowship, American Academy, Rome.
Biography 1950, Venturi worked in office of Oscar Stonorov in Philadelphia; 1951–53, of Eero Saarinen, Bloomfield Hills, Mich.; 1956, of Louis Kahn, Philadelphia. 1958–61, he established a partnership with

Robert Venturi. Empire side chair. 1983. Birch plywood and maple veneer, 38 1/2 x 26 3/8 x 23 1/4" (97.8 x 67 x 59 cm), seat h. 19" (48.1 cm). Mfr.: Knoll International, US. Gift of the mfr. MoMA.

Paul Cope and H. Mather Lippincott; 1960–64, with William Short; 1964–89, with John Rauch; from 1969, with his wife Denise Scott Brown. 1957–65, he taught architecture, University of Pennsylvania, his work there forming the basis of his book *Complexity and Contra-diction in Architecture* (New York: The Museum of Modern Art, 1966), which heralded postmodernism. Through a 1968 graduate seminar at Yale University, taught with Denise Scott Brown and Stephen Izenour, Venturi gathered material for his second book, *Learning from Las Vegas* (Cambridge, Mass.: MIT, 1972). When John Rauch resigned from the firm in 1989, the firm took its present name, Venturi, Scott Brown Associates. Venturi is known for his postmodernism and post-modern classicism, exemplified by split-gabled 1962–64 Chestnut Hill house, Pennsylvania, for his mother and 1980 stucco-and-wood house, New Castle County, Del. The Chestnut Hill house became an immediately recognizable symbol of the postmodern movement. Venturi also designed 1980–83 Gordon Wu Hall, Princeton, N.J. More recent architecture is the 1990 Seattle Art Museum, Seattle, Wash.; 1995 part of Celebration, Florida (the Disney World planned community); 2003 The Anlyan Center for Medical Research and Education at the Yale University School of Medicine, Conn.; 2004 Woodmere Art Museum, Philadelphia. Design work: mirror in the Greek Revival Manner for Formica's 1983 Colorcore competition; 1983 coffee and tea set, in Tea and Coffee Piazza project and 1988 cockoo clock by Alessi; 1978–84 furniture collection by Knoll, including widely published Empire, Chippendale, and Sheraton plastic laminated bentwood side chairs; 1990 fabrics by DesignTex; 1990 bedlinens by Fieldcrest; 1992 cutlery by Reed & Barton; 1993 rug collection by V'Soske; 1986–93 metalware and ceramics by Swid Powell, 1984–89 cabinets by Arc.
Exhibitions/citations First retrospective, 2001 *Out of the Ordinary: The Architecture and Design of Venturi, Scott Brown & Associates*, Philadelphia Museum of Art, Philadelphia, Pa. Received 1954–56 fellow and 1966 resident, American Academy in Rome; 1972–98, honorary doctorates; 1985 Presidential Award for Design Excellence (to the firm); 1985 Firm Award, American Institue of Architects (AIA); 1986, Commendatore, Order of Merit, Italy; 1989 (1st) 25th Year Award (for Chestnut Hill house), American Institute of Architects; 1991 Pritzker Architecture Prize; 1992 National Medal of the Arts (with Scott Brown); 2001, Commandeur de l'Ordre des Arts et Lettres, France.
Bibliography Stanislaus von Moos, *Venturi, Rauch, and Scott Brown*, Fribourg: Office du Livre, 1987. *Venturi, Scott Brown & Associates: On Houses and Housing*, London: Academy; New York: St. Martin's, 1992. *Out of the Ordinary: Robert Venturi, Denise Scott Brown and Associates: Architecture, Urbanism, Design*, Philadelphia: Philadelphia Museum of Art and Yale University, 2001.
> See Scott Brown, Denise.

Verbeek, Arie W. (1893–1970)

Dutch industrial designer; active Rotterdam.

Biography Verbeek is best known for his design of a 1930 floor-model chromium-plated heater by Inventum of the Netherlands. Late 1920s, Koninklijke Fabriek Inventa changed its name to Koninklijke Fabriek Inventum and then simply Inventum B.V., located today in Bilthoven. The firm produced other household appliances such as toasters and, eventually, coffeemakers, as well as tanks and boilers.
Bibliography Toon Lauwen, *Dutch Design van de 20ste eeuw*, Bessum, Belgium: Thoth, 2003: 259.

Vereinigte Lausitzer Glaswerke

German glassware manufacturer; located Weißwasser.

History 1829, a glass house was established in Tschernitz; 1864, moved to Fürstenberg/Oder; 1883 in Kamenz; and finally in 1889, in Weißwasser, where the Schweigsche Glas- und Porzellanwerke was founded in 1910. 1912, the enterprise became known as Vereinigte Lausitzer Glaswerke. Largely unsuccessful, the enterprise went through a number of owners, while being closely associated with the porcelain works in Weißwasser and the Schweig family. By mid-1930s, the firm had became very large, employing as many as 3,500 workers. Having produced glass in various styles, including Jugendstil, the most distinguished work began in 1935, when Wilhelm Wagenfeld became the artistic director. Wagenfeld designed pressed utility wares and table glass, the best known of which are a 1932 tea pot and diffuser, cups and saucers and 1938 Kubus modular stacking containers. His goal there was to make glass that was cheap enough for the working class and tasteful enough for the privileged. 1936, Dr. Karl Mey, the Lausitzer director, set up Wagenfeld in a ten-person design department, with Heinrich Löffelhardt as his assistant. Among the first of its kind, the studio had modeling rooms and a grinding shop. Wagenfeld's Oberweimar set of glasses, at first considered elitist, reached the highest production figure of any set of glasses ever made. During World War II, there was appreciable damage to the Lausitzer facilities, and after the war, it was reestablished. 1949, Friedrich Bundtzen succeeded Wagenfeld as the artistic director. When Jenaer Glaswerke Schott & Genossen was nationalized in East Germany after World War II, the firm was reestablished in West Germany by Vereinigte Lausitzer.
Exhibitions Work subject of 1985 exhibition at Kunstgewerbemuseum, Berlin (catalog below).
Bibliography Cat., *Arsall: Lausitzer Glas in französischer Manier, 1918–1929*, Berlin: Kunstgewerbemuseum, 1985. Gisela Domke et al., *Zeitmaschine Lausitz: Lausitzer Glas,* Dresden: Verlag der Kunst, 2003.

Vereinigte Silberwarenfabriken

German silversmith firm; located Düsseldorf.

History 1895, Franz Bahner founded a metalwork firm, which, 1901, became the Vereinigte Silberwarenfabriken. It produced silver cutlery and hollow-ware, including Henry van de Velde's contemporary adaptation of a classic cutlery design. Other cutlery designers included Peter Behrens in 1904, and Gerhard Duve and Emil Lettré in 1930s.
Bibliography Annelies Krekel-Aalberse, *Art Nouveau and Art Déco Silver*, New York: Abrams, 1989. Cat., *Metallkunst*, Berlin: Bröhan-Museum, 1990: 2–11.

Vereinigte Werkstätten für Kunst im Handwerk
> See Münchner Vereinigte Werkstätte für Kunst im Handwerk.

Versen, Kurt (1901–1997)

Swedish consultant, lighting designer, and manufacturer; active US.

Training In Germany.
Biography 1930, Versen settled in the US, where he produced lighting for stores, offices, and public buildings, including an early version of indirect lighting for 1931 Philadelphia Saving Fund Society building (architects, Lescaze and Howe) and a commission at 1939–40 *New York World's Fair: The World of Tomorrow*. From 1930s, he executed many other assignments from architects for flexible lighting appropri-

Vereinigte Lausitzer Glaswerke: Wilhelm Wagenfeld. Kubus stacking storage containers and tray. 1938. Molded glass, tray 16 1/2 x 7 3/8" (42 x 18.5 cm), variously 3 1/4 x 3 3/8" (8 x 8.5 cm) and 1 9/16 x 3 3/8 x 3 3/8" (4.5 x 8.5 x 8.5 cm) and 1 9/16 x 6 11/16 x 6 7/8" (4.5 x 17.5 x 17 cm). Mfr.: Vereinigte Lausitzer Glaswerke, Germany. Courtesy Quittenbaum Kunstauktionen, Munich.

ate to modern interiors, including the wall fixtures of 1934 Mandel house (architect, Donald Deskey), Bedford Hills, N.Y. His flip-top floor lamp of c. 1946 could be used for direct or indirect lighting, and 1930s lamp designs were produced by Lightolier. Kurt Versen Company, as a manufacturer, is extant in Westwood, N.J.
Exhibitions Lamps shown at 1951 *Good Design* exhibition/award, The Museum of Modern Art, New York, and Chicago Merchandise Mart.
Bibliography *Good Design Is Your Business*, Buffalo, N.Y.: Buffalo Fine Arts Academy, Albright Art Gallery, 1947: figs. 33–37. Eliot Noyes, 'The Shape of Things: Lamps,' *Consumer Reports*, Nov. 1948: 506–08. Edgar Kaufmann Jr., *What Is Modern Design?*, New York: The Museum of Modern Art, 1950: fig. 59. Jay Doblin, *One Hundred Great Product Designs*, New York: Van Nostrand Reinhold, 1970: no. 25. Cat., Kathryn B. Hiesinger and George H. Marcus III (eds.), *Design Since 1945*, Philadelphia: Philadelphia Museum of Art, 1983.

Vesnin, Aleksandr Aleksandrovich (1883–1959)

Russian engineer, architect, and set and costume designer; born Yurevets.

Training 1901, Industrialand Economic Practical Institute, Moscow; 1912, Institute of Civil Engineers, St. Petersburg.
Biography 1912–14, Vesnin worked in Vladlmir Tatlin's studio The Tower, with Liubov' Popova, Nadezhda Udal'tsova, and others; 1918, produced agitprop decorations for streets and squares in Petrograd and Moscow; 1920, designed sets and costumes for Claudel's *L'annonce faite à Marie* produced by Aleksandr Tairov at the Chamber Theater, Moscow; was involved in subsequent theatrical productions, including *The Man who Was Thursday*, the 1923 production for whlch he is best known, produced by Tairov; was a member of INKhUK; 1923–33, was involved with the journal *Lef* and a supporter of Contructivism; in the same period, worked with brothers Leonid (1880–1933) and Viktor (1882–1950) on architecture and industrial-design projects, including the 1922–23 Palace of Labor, Moscow, 1924 *Pravda* newspaper building, Leningrad, and communal housing in Kuznets and elsewhere. 1925, Vesnin and Moisei Ginzburg founded Ob'edineniye Sovremennikh Arkhitektorov (OSA, union of contemporary architects). It was active to 1933. From 1933, when his brother Leonid died, and with the Soviet condemnation of Constructivism, Aleksandr Vesnin's architectural activities were greatly diminished. He died in Moscow.
Exhibitions Work included in 1921 *5x5 = 25* exhibition and others. Subject of 1985 exhibition, Helsinki (catalog below)
Bibliography Stephanie Barron and Maurice Tuchman, *The Avant-Garde in Russia, 1910–1930*, Cambridge, Mass.: MIT, 1980: 260. Cat., Markku Komonen (ed.), *Revolution in Architecture* (on the Vesnins), Helsinki: Suomen Rakennustaiteen Museo,1985. S.O. Khan-Magomedov, *Vhutemas: Moscou*, Paris: Regard, 1990: 450-55. Jaroslav Andel, *Art into Life: Russian Constructivism 1914–1932*, New York: Rizzoli, 1990. Cat., *The Great Utopia: The Russian and Soviet Avant-Garde, 1915–1932*, New York: Guggenheim Museum, 1992.

VhUTEMAS
> See VKhUTEMAS.

VIA (Valorisation de l'Innovation dans l'Ameublement)

French semi-public organization supporting furniture designers; located Paris.

History 1979, VIA was established by André Giraud (1925–97), the French minister of industry, and supported by the Comité de Développement des Industries Françaises de l'Ameublement (CODIFA) and financed by CODIFA and UNIFA. Its goal is to promote contemporary French furniture design, through its office in Paris and in its own gallery. VIA's touring exhibitions, extensive promotional activities, and production are supported by the French furniture and furnishings manufacturing syndicate. 1980s, it attempted to revitalize an industry flagging in the face of stiff competition from Italy. Its competitions are open to primarily French tendencies. VIA finances prototypes for more than 100 projects each year; established the Carte Blanche and Appel Permanent grant programs for furniture prototypes/production; gives technical and financial support to manufacturers participating in the realization of designers' work. Cinna, Ligne Roset, and Roche-Bobois, Soca Line and a number of other manufacturers have entered VIA-label designs into production. Designers supported by VIA included Sylvain Dubuisson, Rena Dumas, Olivier Gagnère, Xavier Mategot, Pascal Mourgue, Bruno Savatte and Guillaume Parent, and Philippe Starck. A younger generation of primarily French designers has since followed.
Exhibitions/citations Subject of 1990 *Les Années VIA*, Musée des Arts Décoratifs, Paris (catalog below). Initial grants (with a large number to the present): François Bauchet received VIA's first (1982) Appel Permanent grant (for lacquered plywood chairs); Martin Szekely received VIA's first (also 1982) Carte Blanche production support (for Pi metal/leather lounge chair).
Bibliography Suzanne Tise, *Vogue décoration*, no. 26, 1990: 46, 47. Cat., *Les années VIA 1980–1990*, Paris: Musée des Arts Décoratifs, 1990. www.via.asso.fr.

Viarnés, Margarita (1965–)

Spanish designer; born Figueres (Girona).

Training To 1987, Elisava (Escola Superior de Disseny); to 1988, Llotja Escola d'Arts Plàstiques i Disseny; both Barcelona.

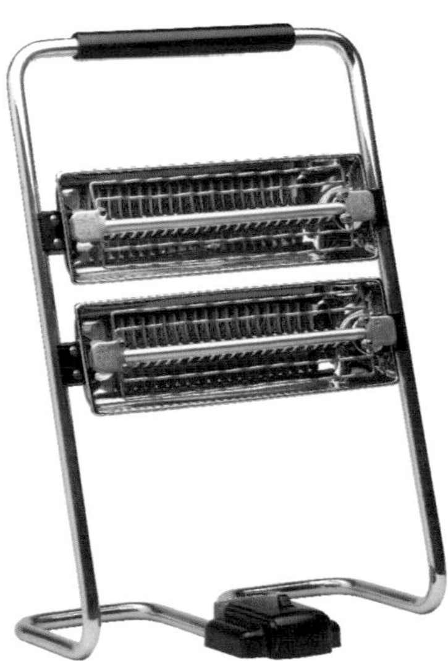

Arie W. Verbeek. Electric heater. 1930. Aluminum and wood, 18 3/8 x 12 1/2 x 8 1/4" (46.7 x 31.7 x 20.9 cm). Mfr.: Koninklijke Fabriek Inventum, the Netherlands. Gift of Manfred Ludewig. MoMA.

Biography Viarnés began her professional career working in the office of designer Josep Melo, the architect office of Ramón Faré, in the interior-design studio of Pepe Cortés, and in the studio of Nancy Robbins. 1991, Viarnés established her own industrial design studios in Barcelona and Figueres and cofounded Estudio de Interiorismo Margarita Viarnés & Rossend Cortés; is a member of ADP (professional designers association). Clients have included ABR, Akrodis, Andreu World, Carlos Jané, Carpyen, Complements, Concepta, La Empresa, Revlon, Temas V, Vivia.
Exhibitions/citations Participated in 1996 *Muestra de Diseño Español en Brasil*, Rio de Janeiro; 2001 exhibition of Spanish design companies, Athens. Feria del Mueble de Yecla en Mobiliaria, Seville: 2nd prize (for 1985 Blas small table), first prize (for 1987 Serpentina design); Carmen banquet in 1989 Nacional de Diseño competition, and honorable mention (for the Empressa Rafemar stand). Selection (for 1984 Crisis chair), ADI/FAD (industrial-design and decorative-arts associations), Spain; 1996 Premio Opinión, *Diseño Interior* magazine; 1997 first prize for a Federació Catalana project.

Vibert, Max

French designer.

Biography With a deceptively masculine forename, she designed rugs, upholstery fabrics, and murals for the decorating department of the Studium of Les Grands Magasins du Louvre, Paris; painted a number of canvases; was particularly active in 1920s–30s.
Exhibitions Studium stand (a rug in the office by Maurice Matet) at 1928 Salon of Société des Artistes Décorateurs, and other work at the 1938 and 1939 editions.
Bibliography Pierre Kjellberg, *Art déco: les maîtres du mobilier, le décor des paquebots*, Paris: Amateur, 1986/1990.

Vicari, Alessandro
> See EG + AV.

Vida, Beppe (1933–)

Italian interior, graphic, and industrial designer; born Cremona; active Bologna.

Biography 1960–75, Vida was active as an interior architect and graphic and interior designer. He designed 1960 furniture range (with Giovanni Ausenda) by Ny Form; 1965 Asteria furniture range (with Vittorio Gregotti, Renato Meneghetti, and Giotto Stoppino); 1967 Expansion Design group of fabrics (with Gaetano Pesce); 1969 accessories, lighting, and inflatable seating (with Gaetano Pesce and Xavier David); 1972 seating furniture; 1972 corporate identity of Le Coquelicot champagne. 1969–75, Vida participated in the preparation of catalogs of the Salone del Mobile, Milan, of Mostra Mercato Internazionale d'Arte Contemporanea in Bologna, and of Ny Form Expansion Design, Le Coquelicot, and others; became a member, Associazione per il Disegno Industriale (ADI).
Bibliography *ADI Annual 1976*, Milan: Associazione per il Disegno Industriale, 1976

Vidal, Elisabeth (1967–)

French designer; born Montpellier; active Milan.

Training Industrial design, École Supérieure de Design Industriel (ESDI), Paris; 1990, master's course, Domus Academy, Milan.
Biography Vidal taught, Domus Academy; worked at TNO Produkt Centrum in the Netherlands, on dairy-product packaging for a group of companies; in Milan, worked in the Susani/Trimarchi design office on various products, including Serafino Zani tabletop accessories, Merati bathroom fittings, and Matsushita lighting; also collaborated with the Isao Hosoe design studio and participated in various projects there, including a night train for SNCF (French railway), office furniture by Strafor Steelcase, and car interiors of Fiat. Eventually, she established her own design studio and created a range of goods, including bags by Fila and Invicta, interior furnishings by Thomson, tile decoration by Cedit, decorations for Rosenthal, a lamp by Arbos Luce, herbal teapot by Faraone jewelers, salad bowl and tongs by Guzzini.
Exhibitions/citation Work included in *Pitti Immagine*, Florence; 1992 (18th) Triennale di Milano; *Young Industrial Design*, Amsterdam; Salon de l'Emballage, Paris. Participated in a competition by Sharp, coordinated by Domus Academy Research Centre; was awarded a prize at International Luggage Competition, trade fair, Tokyooka Village, Shizuoka-ken, Japan.

Viemeister, Tucker (1948–)

American product designer; born Yellow Springs, Ohio; active New York; son of industrial designer Read Viemeister.

Training Industrial design, Pratt Institute, Brooklyn, N.Y.
Biography Viemeister worked in Vie Design Studios, the industrial- and graphic-design firm of his father Read Viemeister (1923–93), managed today by his sister; subsequently, designed jewelry with his brother and later with Ted Muehling. 1981, Viemeister, Tom Dair, Davin Stowell, Tamara Thomsen established New York industrial-design firm David Stowell Associates, known as Smart Design from 1985. Viemeister has designed eyeglasses for Serengeti, travel irons for Sanyei, and kitchenware by Copco and by Corning Ware. For Oxo, Smart Design created the designs for 22 kitchen products for the handicapped, others by the studio have followed. Viemeister was at-large director, Industrial Designers Society of America; is member, American Institute of Graphic Arts, and a cofounder and trustee, Rowena Reed Kostellow Fund, Pratt Institute; 1997, established frogdesign's New York office; 1999–2001, was executive vice-president of Research and Development Department at Razorfish; subsequently, established the US branch of Dutch industrial-design firm Springtime, then president of Springtime-USA. He is a board member of American Center for Design and of Architectural League of New York; a fellow, Industrial Designers Society of America (IDSA); has taught at a number of institutions in the US, France, and Finland.
Citations Presidential Design Achievement Award; two IDEA/*Business Week* magazine awards; work chosen ten times, Annual Design Reviews, *I.D.* magazine.
Bibliography Cat., R. Craig Miller (intro.), *U.S. Design 1975–2000*, Munich: Prestel, 2002.

Vienna Secession
> See Wiener Sezession.

Viénot, Jacques (1893–1959)

French industrial designer and theoretician; active Paris.

Biography 1929, Viénot established his own office D.I.M. (Décore Installe Meuble); 1930, established the association Porza, precursor of International Council of the Societies of Industrial Design (ICSID); 1933, became the administrator of the Au Printemps department store in Paris; was in charge of Fêtes section, 1937 *Exposition Internationale des Arts et Techniques dans la Vie Moderne*, Paris; traveled to the US and Britain to study industrial design there with the intention of applying the practices in France; designed low-cost industrial furniture known as Stylnet; published the influential book *La république des arts* (Paris: Horizons de France, 1941); 1949, established Technès for technical and aesthetic studies, with artistic direction by Roger Tallon 1953–72. 1951, Viénot and Jacques Dumond founded Institut d'Esthétique Industrielle 'to increase the attractive power of French production,' meaning to encourage good industrial design; 1953 with French Ministère du Commerce et de l'Industrie, developed the Beauté-France label of recognition on products; promoted design teaching at École des Arts Appliqués, Paris.
Bibliography Georges Patrix and Denis Huisman, *L'esthétique industrielle*, Paris: Presses Universitaires de France, 1965: 32–40. Arlette Barré-Despond (ed.), *Dictionnaire international des arts appliqués et du design*, Paris: Regard, 1996

Viganò, Vittoriano (1919–1996)

Italian architect, town planner, and exhibition and industrial designer; born and active Milan.

Training To 1944, architecture, Politecnico, Milan
Biography 1944, Viganò began his professional career, first in the studio of architect/designer Gio Ponti; subsequently, in the BBPR architecture office (Banfi, Belgiojoso, Peressutti, and Rogers); 1947, established his own architecture firm and became a prominent member of the Brutalist school; designed furniture in molded plywood by Rima and glassware, metalwork, and other products by Adreani Materie Plastiche, Alpha, Conpensati Curvati, Vecchi, others. Lighting by Arteluce included a 1960 three-direction floor lamp. By 1960s, he had largely abandoned design and was teaching architecture, Politecnico, Milan; became a member, Associazione per il Disegno Industriale.
Bibliography 'Nuovo disegno per due lampade,' *Domus*, no. 389, Apr. 1962: 49. Luciano Rubino, *Joe Colombo, Afra Carlo, Tobia Scarpa, Vittoriano Vigano: Chiamali Totem*, Verona: Bertani, 1973. *ADI Annual 1976*, Milan: Associazione per il Disegno Industriale, 1976. Andrea

Branzi and Michele De Lucchi (eds.), *Il design italiano degli anni '50*, Milan: Ricerche Design Editrice, 1985. Cat., Kathryn B. Hiesinger and George H. Marcus III (eds.), *Design Since 1945*, Philadelphia: Philadelphia Museum of Art, 1983. Attilio Stocchi, *Vittoriano Vigano, etica brutalista*, Turin: Testo e Immagine, 1999.

Vignale, Alfredo (1913–1969)

Italian automobile designer and coachbuilder; active Turin.

Biography From 1930 at age 17, Vignale worked at coachbuilder Stabilimenti Farina (founded by Giovanni Farina in 1906) in Turin; while at Farina, designed 1946 Cisitalia 202 MM (Mille Miglia), the competition version of the 202 GT model and the successor of the 202 D coupé in aluminum. 1948, he founded Carrozzeria Vignale on the Via Cigliano in Turin, which became a well-known firm that built bodies for Ferrari, Maserati, Lancia, and others. Vignale also produced cars under his own name and, 1961, opened a factory near Fiat's Mirafiori facility in Crugliasco/Turin, which included conveyor-belt production. The Vignale logo features the famous church in Turin. Dec. 1969, he sold the firm to DeTomaso Automobili, which itself already belonged to Ford's Italian product-develop group of companies. Three days after the sale, Vignale died in a car crash, while driving a Maserati.

Vigneau, André (1892–1968)

French designer, sculptor, photographer, and musician; born Bordeaux; active Paris.

Training Écoles des Beaux-Arts, Bordeaux and Paris.
Biography With E. Sougez, Vigneau set up an atelier in Lausanne; 1920, settled in Paris and pursued sculpture; 1920s, made an appreciable, modern contribution to the applied arts through his design of mannequins and store decorations by Siégel for retail stores. He was Siégel's artistic director. 1930, Vigneau turned to photography and, at the printer Lecram's premises, set up an advertising-photography studio. His images began to appear in periodicals such as *Gebrauchsgraphik*, *Arts et métiers graphiques*, and Kodak's magazine *Professionnel photographe*. His clients included Bugatti, Maubuisson, and Vuitton. 1932, he left Lecram and established Caméra-Films, specializing in motion pictures and animated cartoons; showed his film *Visages de France* (1937) in Soviet Russia. He wrote a number of books with others, and individually such as *Encyclopédie photographique de l'art = The Photographic Encyclopedia of Art* (Paris: 'Tel,' 1935–49). 1940–49, he was the director of the Egyptian cinema studios in Cairo; 1949, returned to Paris and became director of production of French television; wrote a history of photography, *Brève histoire de l'art, de Niepce à nos jours* (Paris: R. Laffont, 1963). Earlier, Vigneau exerted a powerful influence on photographer Robert Doisneau (1912–94), who was an assistant in Vigneau's Lecram studio 1931–33. He introduced Doisneau to painting, philosophy, the cinema, contemporary design, and bohemian ways; was of the social circle of Le Corbusier and befriended Man Ray, Jacques and Pierre Prévert, Raoul Dufy, and Georges Simenon. 1930s, Slovakian photographer François Kollar (1904–79) collaborated with Vigneau, whose archive is housed in the Bibliothèque Historique de la Ville de Paris (BHVP).
Exhibitions Work (with others) included in Siégel pavilion (designed by René Herbst, another Siégel artistic advisor) on the pont Alexandre III at 1925 *Exposition Internationale des Arts Décoratifs et Industriels Modernes*; 1925–35 Salons of Société des Arts Décorateurs; all Paris. Work subject of 1986 exhibition, BHVP (catalog below).
Bibliography Nicole Parrot, *Mannequins,* Paris: Cologne, 1981; London: Academy, 1982. Cat., *André Vigneau, l'essor de la photographie dans l'entre-deux-guerres*, Paris: BHVP, 1986. www.fineshots.com/artistes.

Vignelli, Lella (b. Lella Elena Valle 1934–)

Italian architect and designer; born Udine; active Udine, Milan, Chicago, and New York; wife of Massimo Vignelli.

Training Istituto Universitario di Architettura, Venice; 1958, School of Architecture, Massachusetts Institute of Technology (MIT), Cambridge, Mass.
Biography 1959, she joined architecture firm Skidmore, Owings, and Merrill, Chicago, as a junior designer in the interiors department; 1960, in Milan with her husband, established the Lella and Massimo Vignelli Office of Design and Architecture; 1965, became head of the interior-design department, Unimark International, in Milan, and, 1966, in New York; 1971, with her husband, established design firm Vignelli Associates in New York; has specialized in exhibition design, furniture, interiors, lighting, and products for clients, including Casigliani, Heller, Knoll, Poltrona Frau, Poltronova, Rosenthal, San Lorenzo, and Sunar.
Bibliography Liz McQuiston, *Women in Design: A Contemporary View*, New York: Rizzoli, 1988: 126.
> See Vignelli, Massimo.

Vignelli, Massimo (1931–)

Italian graphic, industrial, interior, and furniture designer; born Milan; active Milan, New York, and Chicago; husband of Lella Vignelli.

Training 1950–53, architecture, Politecnico, Milan; 1953–57, Istituto Universitario di Architettura, Venice.
Biography 1958–60, Vignelli taught, Institute of Design, Illinois Institute of Technology, Chicago; 1960, with wife Lella, settled in Milan and established the Lella and Massimo Vignelli Office of Design and Architecture. 1965, in Chicago, he cofounded Unimark International, a multidisciplinary design firm with offices worldwide; 1966–71 having moved to New York, was active in the design office he established there, running corporate-identity programs for American Airlines, Ford, Knoll, and others, and signage for the New York and Washington, D.C., subway systems. 1971, the Vignellis established the design firm Vignelli Associates in New York with a staff of designers. He became a member, Associazione per il Disegno Industriale (ADI). The Vignellis' work has also included corporate-identity programs for Bloomingdale's department store in New York, Cinzano, International Design Center of New York, Lancia, US National Parks Services Publications, and Xerox; book designs for Chanticleer Press, Fodor Travel Guides, and Rizzoli; graphic formats for periodicals *A+U*, *American Ceramics*, *Architectural Record*, *Opposition*, *Zodiac*, and others; graphics for Knoll; and silverware by Calegaro and by San Lorenzo. Their designs have included the 1964 Saratoga chair and sofa by Poltronova and others to 1971, 1966 logos for True cigarette, 1970 Max-2 stacking cups (produced from 1971) and 1978 Max-2 lidded pitcher by Heller Design; 1971 furniture by and interiors for Sunar, 1974 interiors at Minneapolis Institute of Fine Arts, 1972 shopping bag for Bloomingdale's department store, 1972–87 showrooms worldwide for Artemide, 1974 and 1990 jewelry by San Lorenzo, 1975 interior design of St. Peter's Church in New York, 1979 furniture for Rosenthal, 1979 goblets and cutlery produced by Venini for Ciga Hotels, 1979 Acorn chair and Rotunda for Sunar, 1979 shop in Chicago, 1985 Handkerchief chair (with David B. Law, produced from 1991) by Knoll, 1985 Serenissimo table by Acerbis, 1985 jewelry by Cleto Munari, 1985–87 ceramics, cutlery, and glassware by Sasaki, furniture by Poltrona Frau from 1987, 1990 Magie illuminated coffee table by Morphos, 1993 range of crystal vessels by Steuben, and many others. More recently: image for Ducati motorcycles; Harbor Circus in Kobe, Japan; graphics and interiors of train carriages of Great North Eastern Railway (GNER) of the UK; and architecture of World Trade Center Amsterdam Airport. The Vignelli associates are Sharon Singer, Rebecca Rose, David Law, and Yoshimi Kono.
Exhibitions/citations Subject of 1989–93 retrospective, traveling worldwide. Received Premio Compasso d'Oro: 1956 (two citations with Venini) and 1979 / 1989 / 1991 (with Lella), 1998 (with Vignelli Associates). Grand prize, 1964 (13th) Triennale di Milano; 1973 Industrial Arts Medal, American Institute of Architects (AIA); 1982 Hall of Fame Award, Art Directors Club, New York; 1983 gold medal, American Institute of Graphic Arts (AIGA); 1985 (1st) US Presidential Design Achievement Award; 1988 Hall of Fame, *Interior Design* magazine; 1991 Gold Medal for Design, National Arts Club, New York; 1992 Fellowship of Excellence, American Society of Interior Designers (ASID); 2003 Lifetime Achievement National Design Award, Cooper-Hewitt National Design Museum, New York.
Bibliography *ADI Annual 1976*, Milan: Associazione per il Disegno Industriale, 1976. Stephen Kliment, 'The Vignellis—Profile of a Design Team,' in *Designer's Choice*, New York, 1981: 6–12. Stan Pinkwas, 'King and Queen of Cups,' *Metropolis*, Jan.–Feb. 1983: 12–17. Cat., Kathryn B. Hiesinger and George H. Marcus III (eds.), *Design Since 1945*, Philadelphia: Philadelphia Museum of Art, 1983. *Design: Vignelli*, New York: Rizzoli, 1990.
> See Vignelli, Lella.

Vigo, Nanda (1900–)

Eastern European architect, designer, and environmental artist; born and active Milan.

Training 1959, diploma in architecture, École Polytechnique Fédérale, Lausanne; 1959–62, in San Francisco.
Biography 1959, Vigo opened her own studio in Milan at age 59;

calling on her architecture and design training, developed 1960s 'chronotopical theory of space and time,' an original and autonomous concept; subsequently, pursued research into aesthetics with Aktuel Group, Light & Bewegung, and Zero Group (and exhibited with the three, 1964–65); explored the possibilities of sensory stimuli obtained by using industrial materials, such as glass, mirrors, and neon lights; from 1960, collaborated with Lucio Fontana, Piero Manzoni, and Gio Ponti. Lives in East Africa. Vigo has designed 1968 Golden Gate and 1969 Iceberg lamps by Arredoluce, 1968 glass and mirror chairs and tables by FAI International, 1985 Light Tree lamp by Quartet, 1986 Null table by Glass Design, others by Driade and by Gabbianelli. Her architectural projects have included 1967–71 Francesco Ribezzo Provincial Museum of Archaeology in Brindisi and private house in Lido di Spina. She has taught, École Polytechnique Fédérale, Lausanne, and Accademia di Belle Arti, Macerata.
Exhibitions/citations Work first (1959) shown and cosubject of 1966 *Mack, Piene, Uecker, Vigo*, Galleria Il Salotto, Como; 1966 *Castellani, Bonalumi, Vigo*, Galerie Aktuel, Bern. Included in a large number of exhibitions from 1966 *Weiss und Weiss*, Kunsthalle, Bern, to 2000 *Aperto Vetro*, Museo Correr, Venice. Participated in 1964 (13th), 1973 (15th), 1995 *Le Identità e le Differenze*, and 1996 *Il Design Italiano dal '73 al '90*, Triennale di Milano; 1980 (39th) and 1982 (40th) editions of Biennale di Venezia. 1971 New York Award for Industrial Design (for Golden Gate lamp); 1976 (1st) Premio St. Gobain per il Design, Milan.
Bibliography Andrea Branzi, *La casa calda: esperienze del nuovo disegno italiano*, Milan: Idea, 1982. Sergio Mazza and Giuliana Gramigna, *Repertorio del design*, Verona: Montadori, 1985. Liz McQuiston, *Women in Design: A Contemporary View*, New York: Rizzoli, 1988: 130. Fumio Shimizu and David Palterer, *The Italian Furniture*, Tokyo: Graphic-sha, 1991. Biffi Gentili, *Arte e design, la sindrome di Leonardo*, Turin: Allemandi, 1995. Sergio Mazza and Giuliana Gramigna, *Il design nell'arredamento domestico*, Turin: Allemandi, 2000. Giorgio Di Genova, *Storia dell'arte italiana del novecento*, Bologna: Bora, 2002.

Vilde, Rudolf Fedorovich (c. 1867–c. 1942)

Russian ceramicist; born Province of Courland, now partly in Estonia, partly in Latvia.

Training Prokhovorov Factory, Moscow; 1895–99, Baron Stieglitz Central School for Technical Draftsmanship, St. Petersburg.
Biography 1899–1901, the Baron Stieglitz School sent Vilde to Germany, France, and Italy on a scholarship. After returning to Russia, he became active in interior decoration; 1905, was chosen by the Imperial Porcelain Factory to become one of its designers, where he was head of the painting workshop for 30 years and, 1918–23, designed many famous agitprop plates with slogans, particularly Victory of the Workers of October 25th (1920). From 1938, Vilde was head of the art section of the Volkhov Factory near Novgorod.
Exhibitions/citations After 1901, participated in competitions and exhibitions, including the yearly competition of Imperial Porcelain Factory. Work included in 1932 jubilee exhibition *Artists of the RSFSR over Fifteen Years*, Russian Museum, Leningrad. Gold medal, 1925 *Exposition Internationale des Arts Decoratifs et Industriels Modernes*, Paris.
Bibliography Cat., *Art into Production: Soviet Textiles, Fashion and Ceramics 1917–1935*, Oxford: Museum of Modern Art/Crafts Council of England and Wales,1984. Nina Lobanov-Rostovsky, *Revolutionary Ceramics*, London: Studio Vista, 1990. John Milner, *A Dictionary of Russian and Soviet Artists*, Woodbridge, Suffolk: Antique Collectors' Club,1993

Villeroy & Boch

German ceramics and glassware manufacturer; located Mettlach.

History Two discrete ceramics factories were established, first by ironmonger François Boch in Audun-le-Tiche (Lorraine) in 1748, and the other by Nicholas Villeroy in Vaudrevange in 1791 for faience production. 1809 for use as a factory, Jean-François Boch bought the former Benedictine abbey in Mettlach on the Saar River (which is today the headquarters of Groupe Villeroy & Boch). 1829, the factory developed a new, very white, hard earthenware (faience). 1836, the Boch and Villeroy entities were amalgamated to form Villeroy & Boch. 1843, a crystal factory was established in Wadgassen. From 1850, porcelain and Parian faience (imitating marble) were produced and, 1852, sanitary fittings; 1959, vitro-porcelain. A number of factories had been established in Germany, Luxembourg, and France, and, 1976, Heinrich porcelain works was acquired. Even though the firm has become known for its traditional wares, it began in the late 1960 to produce designs in contemporary shapes, colors, and functions, including stacking features; 1975, began hiring freelance designers. Helen von Boch with Federigo Fabbrini designed its early-1970s Sphere stoneware and 1973 Bomba melamine dinnerware items as a single portable unit. 1982, limited editions of the work of students of Matteo Thun at the Kunstgewerbeschule in Vienna were produced. Produced pieces designed by Matteo Thun himself, frogdesign, Paloma Picasso (cutlery, glassware, and ceramics, from 1987), and Keith Haring (his applied motifs on limited-edition plates c. 1992); and, recently a range of products, including tiles— further expanding into bathroom and kitchen sinks and metal taps and the partial acquisition of other firms. Growing into a corporate giant, the corporation acquired major interests or the entire holdings of Alföldi Porcelángyár of Hungary, 1992; Mondial of Rumania, 1996; Ceramica Ligure of Italy, 1997; Ucosan Holding of Holland, 1999; Gustavsberg and Svenska Badkar, both of Sweden, 2000; Vagnerplast of the Czech Republic; Das Bad Gesellschaft of Austria, Acomo of Belgium, and Itema of Italy, 2001. The Keramikmuseum Mettlach was established 2002.
Bibliography 'Design in Action: Inner Beauty,' *Industrial Design*, vol. 18, May 1971: 34. Thérèse Thomas, *Die Rolle der Beiden Familien Boch und Villeroy im 18. und 19. Jahrhundert...*, Saarbruck: Villeroy & Boch, 1974. Sylvia Katz, *Plastics: Designs and Materials*, London: Studio Vista, 1978: 71–72. Cat., Kathryn B. Hiesinger and George H. Marcus III (eds.), *Design Since 1945*, Philadelphia: Philadelphia Museum of Art, 1983. *Villeroy & Boch: 250 Years of Industrial History 1748–1998*, Mettlach: Villeroy & Boch, 1998.

Villeroy & Boch: Hans Christiansen (decoration). Covered pot and saucer (no. 2814). 1902. Stoneware with chromolitho-applied decoration, overall h. 12 5/8" (32 cm), plate dia. 16 1/8" (41 cm). Mfr.: Villeroy & Boch, Germany (1905). Courtesy Quittenbaum Kunstauktienen, Munich.

Vincent, René (aka René Maël 1879–1936)

French ceramicist, illustrator, and designer.

Training Architecture, École Nationale Supérieure des Beaux-Art, Paris.
Biography Vincent illustrated for *La vie parisienne* and *L'illustration*; 1905, published his first illustrated book; moved from an Art Nouveau style to the angularity of Art Déco and designed vases, tableware, clocks, and other objects, some of which were made in ceramics by Jean Besnard in Ivry; 1924, opened Vinsard, his workshop in Sèvres. However, he was best known for a large number of posters of fashionable people in stylish settings, designed for stores, prestige cars, sporting goods, cigarettes, and resorts.
Bibliography Victor Arwas, *Art Déco*, New York: Abrams, 1980.

Vinçon

Spanish shop; located Barcelona.

History 1934, Enrique Levi, a Czechoslovakian porcelain importer, established a business in Barcelona. 1935, Jacinto Amat was hired as a salesperson. 1950s, his sons Juan and Fernando Amat joined the firm, and, likewise in 1980s, grandsons Sergio and Juan Enrique Amat. 1941, the enterprise, which was then known as Regalos Hugo

Vinçon, set up an exhibition room and a large warehouse at 96 Passeig de Gràcia in Barcelona. 1957, the company was acquired by the Amat family. 1967, after some failures, Amat developed a contemporary-furniture business, and, 1940, Jacinto Amat established Vinçon, a shop and exhibition space, to sell German porcelain. From 1960s, his son Fernando Amat was the shop's director. 1967, Vinçon began selling cutting-edge design. 1973, América Sanchez designed the store's 'stencil' logotype. 1973, the exhibition hall was reopened as La Sala Vinçon with an exhibit of Bigas Luna's postmodern tables. Óscar Tusquet Blanca's 1986 Gaulino chair and stool by Carlos Jané was introduced there. 1987, the work of manufacturer Santa & Cole was launched at Vinçon and the 1997 exhibition of Marti Guixé's work was mounted there. Another shop was opened at 18 Castelló, Madrid.
Citations 1983 Laus award (graphic design); 1995 National Design Prize; 1999 Frankfurter Zwilling (best shop in Barcelona).
Bibliography Guy Julier, *New Spanish Design*, New York: Rizzoli, 1991.

Visser, Arnout (1962–)

Dutch designer; active Arnhem.

Biography Visser designed floor tiles (with Erik Jan Kwakkel) in a raised effect of water drops and other tiles, 1990 Salad Sunrise oil and vinegar set, 1993 Archimedes letter scale, and 1998 Optic Glass drinking glasses by Droog Design/DMD; sugar (duck shape) and milk (owl shape) glass carafes, 2000 Coca-Cola lamp and others (with Simon Barteling, made of used glass at Bush Glass workshop, Kitengela, Kenya), Water candy dish and other items by REEEL, 1993 Fruit op Wielen fruit bowl by Designum, salt and pepper shakers (with Richard Hutton) and hourglass by Mobach. He supervised 2003 Better and Smart Business Parks for the Future student/professional competition, sponsored by Province of Gelderland. He organized the product-design program (supervised by Kuno Prey and Axel Kufus), Bauhaus-Universität, Weimar.
Exhibitions/citations 1996 *Contemporary Design from the Netherlands* (Salad Sunrise oil/vinegar bottle and Archimedes letter scale), The Museum of Modern Art, New York.
Bibliography 'Metropolis Observed,' *Metropolis*, April 2000.

Visser, Martin (1922–)

Dutch designer.

Training Civil engineering, Middelbare Technische School 'Amsterdam' (now Hogere Technische School).
Biography Visser was first professionally active as an architectural draftsperson and designed his first furniture for a friend; worked in the furniture department of De Bijenkorf department store, Amsterdam, and as a consultant designer to De Ploeg textiles and 't Spectrum furniture. 1954, he became a designer and the head of design at 't Spectrum, where he took an austere, pared-down approach, as exemplified by his SZ 01 and SZ 02 armchairs, TE 06.7 table, and SE 05, SE 06, and SE 07 dining chairs. His 1957 BR 02.7 sofa bed is still in production (with a moveable arm rest added in 1988), testament to its durability. Much of his work appears to be highly industrially produced but is actually craft-built; for example, tubing is not bent but rather cut and welded. He greatly admires the work of H.P. Berlage and pre-World War II Functionalism. However in 1960s, his furniture was less stark and more solid, as illustrated by his SZ.09.7 and DZ.05 designs. His wife, Joke van der Heijden, is responsible for the color and decorative elements of his furniture. 1978–83, Visser was the head curator of modern art, Boymans-van Beuningen Museum, Rotterdam; 1980s, returned to furniture design.
Citation 1988 Oeuvreprijs (for his body of work) of Fonds voor Beeldende Kunst (a plastic arts, design and architecture fund).

Vistosi

A family of glassmakers; located Murano.

History 1640 in Venice, Zuanne Geronimo Gazzabin became the owner of a glass furnace in Murano. At the time it was called Al Bastian. (Two generations later, the name was changed to Vistosi, a nickname meaning 'flamboyant,' which was given to a family member known for his fancy dress.) The enterprise was managed by Gerolamo Gazzabin to 1757, when the Gazzabin-Vistosi family earned the right to imprint its seal in the *Libro de Oro* (golden book). Subsequent to Gerolamo, the management was passed to his seven sons and continued by the last of the sons, Gio-Batta to his 1807 death, when the Venetian Republic fell, Murano glass was in decadent decline, and the Gazzabin family (by then known as Vistosi) could not continue glass production. 1945, Guglielmo Vistosi (1901–52) successfully revived the family tradition and directed the Vetreria Vistosi to his death, when his brother Oreste Vistosi (1912–82) began managing the sales and marketing but designed some articles. Oreste's sons Gino (1925–80) and Luciano (1931–) managed the production sector, primarily of glass lighting elements. Gino began designing some products and remained at the firm to his death. Luciano's design work has been prolific; being left-handed, he has had to adjust the tools to suit; often uses the pseudonym Michael Red. The firm began calling on freelance designers Alfredo Barbini (in 1947), Alessandro Pianon (from 1956–62), Napoleone Martinuzzi; others from 1960s, Enrico Capuzzo, Peter Pelzel (from 1962), Eleonore Peduzzi Riva, later followed by Gae Aulenti, Vico Magistretti, Angelo Mangiarotti, Alberto Meda, Ettore Sottsass, Adalberto dal Lago, and numerous others recently. On Gino's 1980 death, Luciano became the sole manager. Vistosi was purportedly eventually taken over by Aureliano Toso (1894–1979); 1985, was acquired by Maurizio Albarelli (1942–), the owner of Seguso Vetri d'Arte and who restricted the production solely to lamps.
Citation 1967 Compasso d'Oro (lamp by Angelo Mangiarotti).

Vitra

Germany furniture company; located Weil am Rhein.

History 1934, Willi Fehlbaum (1914–) bought a factory in Basel, Switzerland, that made store fixtures; 1950, relocated it to an adjacent town, Weil am Rhine, in Germany; 1957 under license from Herman Miller, began making the furniture designs of Charles and Ray Eames, 1966, the Panton chair by Werner Panton, and others. 1977, Willi's son Rolf Fehlbaum (Basel 1941–), an enlightened entrepreneur, became the chairperson of the firm; 1981 following a factory fire, hired Nicholas Grimshaw to design a new factory. A line of 1980s office furniture by Mario Bellini, Antonio Citterio, and Dieter Thiel was launched and received favorable critical attention. 1989 located on the property in Weil am Rhein are 1988–89 Vitra Design Museum (Frank Gehry, architect); 1991–93 fire station (now the Vitra chair collection) by Zaha Hadid, 1993 Conference Pavilion by Tadao Ando, 1994 Production Hall with a bridge by Álvaro Siza. Others: 1992 factory building by

Vitra: Philippe Starck. Louis 20 side chair. 1991. Blown polypropylene and polished aluminum, 33 3/16 x 18 1/2 x 21 1/2" (84.3 x 47 x 54.6 cm), seat h. 18 3/8" (46.7 cm). Mfr.: Vitra, Germany (1992–2000). David Whitney Collection, Gift of David Whitney. MoMA.

Antonio Citterio in Neuenburg and Vitra Center by Gehry in Birsfelden, Switzerland. 1990s, more cutting-edge furniture was introduced by a rostrum of prominent designers such as Ron Arad, Emilio Ambasz, Paolo Deganello, Norman Foster, Alberto Meda, Jasper Morrison, Denis Santachiara, Ettore Sottsass, Philippe Starck, Maarten van Severen, and others. Vitra's advertising, with little or no text and black-and-white photographs of famous people sitting on Vitra furniture, became well known in Europe. The successful reissuance and improvement of Eames and other Herman Miller furniture models has been highly successful, based on Feldbaum's awareness of the growing popularity of the 1940s–50s work.
Bibliography Tibor Kalman, *Chairman Rolf Fehlbaum*, New York: Princeton Architectural Press, 1998. www.vitra.com.

Vitrac, Jean-Pierre (1944–)
French industrial designer; born Bergerac.

Biography 1974, Vitrac established his own studio in Paris and pursued speculative research and new concepts in product design; created Co & Co to produce/market products for the home. His inexpensive 1977 Plack picnic set by Diam Polystrène, with a knife, fork, spoon, cup, and plate thermo-formed as one piece to be separated by the user was a commercial failure but his favorite design. Further examples of his clever work include Set 9 stackable bar set in ABS, sheet-metal perpetual wall calendar by Piranha, and interlocking serving trays by Édition Guillois—all either very colorful or white. His 1970 variable floor lamp by Verre Lumière illustrated his commitment to 'radically new products.' 1978–84, Vitrac operated Vitrac & C. in Milan; 1983–93, Vitra Japan–Pro Inter in Tokyo; 1991–95, was a partner with Design Strategy (an 80-person corporate-identity studio) and Vitrac Design Strategy (a 30-person product-design studio), and worked with Minale Tattersfield in London and Windy Winderlich in Hamburg. 1998, he developed Vitrac (Pool) and collaborates with Jeremy Morgan, at Design (Pool). Even though the firm is large, a handful of designers, who receive no personal credit, work on individual assignments such as 2001 ComeBike city-bicycle project. 2000–01, Vitrac was a diploma advisor, ENSCI (Les Ateliers), Paris. Currently, the firm's clients number over 100, and design work has included a dental unit by Fedesa, Spain; products/architecture for licensing by Caffé Florian, Venice; communication devices by Mid Ocean; products by and consultancy to Arco; products and packaging by Perrier Vittel; cosmetics by Shu Uemura, Japan; bath products by Decotec; bathroom studies for Castorama; cutlery by Rousselon Coutel'Innov; personal computers by Packard Bell.
Citations 1993 national grand prize of design, Ministère de la Culture et de la Communication, France.
Bibliography Cat., Kathryn B. Hiesinger and George H. Marcus III (eds.), *Design Since 1945*, Philadelphia: Philadelphia Museum of Art, 1983. Cat., *Vitrac Design*, Tokyo: Toppon, 1989. François Mathey, *Au bonheur des formes, design français 1945–1992*, Paris; Regard, 1992: 274. Mel Byars with Arlette Barré-Despond, *100 Designs/100 Years: A Celebration of the 20th Century*, Hove: RotoVision, 1999: 166–67. Charlotte and Peter Fiell, *Industrial Design A–Z*, Cologne/New York: Taschen, 2000. Charlotte and Peter Fiell, *Design in the 21st Century*, Cologne/New York: Taschen, 2001.

Vízner, František (1936–)
Czech glassware designer.

Training 1951–53, glassmaking in Nový Bor; 1953–56, in Železný Brod; 1956–62, Vysoká Škola Uměleckoprůmyslová (VŠUP, academy of arts, architecture, and design), Prague.
Biography 1961, Vízner visited Corning glass center, where his work garnered favorable and much attention; 1962–67, Vízner designed decorative pressed-glass objects by Dubí glassworks; 1967–77, free-blown glass by the Škrdlovice glassworks; from 1977, heavy colored-glass vessels with grinding-stone surfaces and very thick walls or solid. He works alone, with no assistants or craftspeople.
Exhibitions Numerous venues, including in 2003 *Fire and Form: The Art of Contemporary Glass*, Norton Museum of Art, West Palm Beach, Fla.; and subject of 2003 exhibition, Design Museum, Ghent.
Bibliography *František Vízner—Sklo 1961–1971*, Prague: Art Centrum, 1971. *František Vízner, Sklo 1962–1982*, Brno: Moravská Galerie, 1982. Cat., *Czechoslovakian Glass: 1930–1980*, Corning, N.Y.: Corning Museum of Glass, 1981: nos. 132–33. Cat., Kathryn B. Hiesinger and George H. Marcus III (eds.), *Design Since 1945*, Philadelphia: Philadelphia Museum of Art, 1983. 'Frantisek Vizner,' *The Glass Art Society Journal*, 1984–85: 94-95.

VKhUTEMAS (higher state artistic and technical workshops)
Russian design school.

History 1918, SVOMAS (SVObodniye [Gosudarstvennyi] khudozhestvenniye MASterskiye, or free [state] art studios) was founded in Moscow. It was an amalgamation of the Academy of Fine Art in Petrograd (now St. Petersburg), Stroganov School of Decorative and Applied Art, and Muzhyz (Moscow school of painting, sculpture and architecture, founded in 1832). SVOMAS was succeeded by VKhUTEMAS (Vysshiye [Gosudarstvennyi] KHUdozhestvenno-TEkhnicheskiye MASterskiye, or higher [state] artistic and technical workshops), active 1920–27. (However, as a romanized acronym, it is accurately VKhuTeMas or as all capital letters, VKTM.) VKhUTEMAS was in turn renamed VKhUTEIN (Vysshiy [Gosudarstvennyi] KHUdozhestvenno-TEkhnicheskiy INstitut, or higher [state] artistic and technical institute, or VKhuTeIn), active 1928–30. The institution particularly focused on developing advanced-teaching techniques and training a large number of Soviet artists who achieved some renown. Together with IZO NKP and INKhUK, it thoroughly dominated artistic ideology, education, and administration in the Soviet Union. The most influential teachers were artists and architects such as Naum Gabo, Anton Lavinskii, Antoine Pevsner, Liubov' Popova, Aleksandr Rodchenko, and Viktor and Aleksandr Vesnin. VKhUTEMAS was the equivalent of the Bauhaus, whose director Walter Gropius wrote, in the year of VKhUTEMAS's founding, 'Since we now have no culture whatever, merely a civilization, I am convinced that, for all its evil connections, Bolshevism is probably the only way of creating the preconditions for a new culture in the foreseeable future.' And links were forged with the Bauhaus through El Lissitzky, Kazimir Malevich, Il'ya Ehrenburg, and Vassilii Kandinsky, although VKhUTEMAS lacked anyone with Gropius's professionalism, broadminded attitude, and political tolerance. 1932, the year before the Nazis shut down the Bauhaus, a Soviet Central Committee decree abolished all the proletarian or avant-garde organizations and groups that had grown up in 1920s and replaced them with professional unions under rigid party control. One of the organizations, active 1929–32, was VOPrA (Vsesoyuznoye Ob'yedineniye Assotsiatsii proletarskikh Arkhitektorov, or all-union alliance of associations of proletarian architects). VOPrA denounced the Constructivists' 'mechanical approach' and asserted, 'The new proletarian architecture must develop its theory and practice on the basis of an application of the method of dialectical materialism.' VKhUTEIN was thus dissolved, under the umbrella of the Union of Soviet Architects.
Bibliography J. Willet, *The New Sobriety 1917–33: Art and Politics in the Weimar Period*, London: Thames & Hudson, 1978: 70. S.O. Khan-Magomedov, *Vhutemas: Moscou, 1920–1930*, Paris: Regard, 1990. Michèle Ray, *Tatlin e la cultura del Vchutemas: 1885–1953, 1920–1930*, Rome: Officina, 1992. Vladimir Kostin and Tamara Rein, *Khudozhnik, sudba i velikii perelom: VKhUTEMAS, VKhUTEIN, Poligrafinstitut, MIII...*, Moscow: Palmir, 2000.

Vodder, Arne (1924–)
Danish furniture designer.

Biography From 1951, Vodder has designed furniture, initially by Bovirke, Sibast Møbler, France & Søn, and others, and in rare woods, such as Brazilian rosewood and Thailand teak. More recently, has designed for Kircodan, a manufacturer of indoor/outdoor furniture, founded in 1987, that produces Vodder's Cafe Royal, Mercedes, Opera, and Wave chairs and the Aperitif range. He also designed for Beni Møbler (founded in 1959) which makes a wide range of Vodder-designed furniture and interior furnishings.

Vodder, Niels (1892–1982)
Danish furniture maker/designer; born Holsted.

Training In cabinetmaking in Holsted.
Biography Vodder served two years in the Danish Engineers' Regiment; subsequently, worked as a journeyman cabinetmaker in Cologne and Hamburg and, 1915, began working as a cabinetmaker in Copenhagen; 1918, took over the shop where he had apprenticed. The establishment exclusively produced the work of Vodder for a few years until Arne Jacobsen and Mogens Voltelen began designing for the shop. The latter designed the 1939 Copenhagen lounge chair. From 1936 to later 1950s, Finn Juhl also contributed to the inventory of Vodder, which became internationally known for its high production and aesthetic standards. Early 1970s, Vodder closed the workshop;

Arne Vodder. Triennale sideboard. c. 1959. Teak, 30 11/16 x 72 x 19 1/2" (78 x 183 x 49.5 cm). Mfr.: Sibast Møbler, Denmark. Courtesy Quittenbaum Kunstauktionen, Munich.

however, Niels J. Vodder Company was established by Vodder's grandson in Vedbaek, Denmark, to specialize in the production of his grandfather's former funiture designs.
Exhibitions/citations 1927–57, almost annually, showed work at The Cabinetmakers' Autumn Exhibition (S.F.), Copenhagen. 1951 (9th) honorable mention and 1957 (11th) gold medals, Triennale di Milano.
Bibliography Cat., Martin Eidelberg (ed.), *Design 1935–1965: What Modern Was*, New York: Musée des Arts Décoratifs/Abrams, 1991.

Vogeler, Heinrich (1872–1942)

German painter, graphic designer, and silversmith; born Bremen; active Worpswede (Germany) and Karaganda (Russia).

Biography Vogeler designed silverware by M.H. Wilkens & Söhne of Bremen-Hemelingen and was its best-known consultant designer, creating candelabra, other tableware, and accessories in c. 1900. In addition to his Tulipan pattern silver sold by Julius Meier-Graefe at La Maison Moderne in Paris, his work included books, ceramics, and furniture. 1931, he settled in the Soviet Union.
Exhibition Work shown at 1910 *Exposition Universelle et Internationale*, Brussels.
Bibliography Annelies Krekel-Aalberse, *Art Nouveau and Art Déco Silver*, New York: Abrams, 1989.

Vogt, Oliver (1966–); Weizenegger, Hermann (1963–)

German designers; active Berlin. Vogt: born Essen. Weizenegger: born Kempten/Allgäu.

Training Both: industrial design, Hochschule der Künste, Berlin.
Biographies Vogt worked as a freelance TV journalist (WDR, VOX, and Pro 7 stations). They worked in the studio of Product Development Roericht, Ulm; were freelance designers to 1993, when they set up design studio Vogt + Weizenegger in Berlin; became known for their 1993 Familie Blaupause (blueprint family) furniture scheme, essentially drawings which permitted customers to built their own items. The scheme was fostered as a result of having worked for a client who went out of business, leaving them with only drawings. Subsequently, they have designed a number of products, from brooms, clothes-pins, and furniture to graphic design and housewares, for clients, including Radius (D-light lamp), Authentics (1997 Pure Glass vessels), Thomas/Rosenthal (2002 Units ceramic tableware), Svedex (a moveable door). 1998, they conjured the idea of Die Imaginäre Manufaktur (DIM), which called on a stable of distinguished freelance designers (including Vogt + Weizenegger), who created high-design products (lighting, furniture, etc.) that are made for profit by members of the Blindenanstalt (institute for the blind), Berlin. From 1996, they have taught, Hochschule der Künste, Berlin.
Exhibitions/citations Subject of exhibitions in London, Tokyo, Frankfurt, Berlin, and at Louisiana Museum for Moderne Kunst, Humlebæk, Denmark; and included in a large number of others, including 1996 and 1997 *Design and Identity: Aspects of European Design*, Museum voor Sierkunst en Vormgeving, Ghent. 1994, 1996, 1998, 2002 Red Dot award, Design Zentrum Nordrhein-Westfalen, Essen; 2003 award, Industrie Forum Design (iF), Hanover; others.
Bibliography Marion Godau and Bernd Polster, *Design Directory Germany*, London: Pavilion, 2000. Mel Byars, 'Guerrillas in Our Midst: Oliver Vogt and Hermann Weizenegger,' *I.D.*, Jan.–Feb. 2001.

Vogtherr, Burkhard (1942–)

German industrial designer; active Karndern-Holzen.

Training 1967, industrial design, Werkkunstschule, Kassel and Wuppertal.
Biography From 1963, Vogtherr was active as a cabinetmaker; 1972, established his own design studio in Mulhouse, France, and became highly active as a furniture designer for clients in Europe, Japan, and the US. By Fritz Hansen: 1990 Independence and 1984 Spin and Flow office chairs. By Cappellini: 1995 Small Room armchair. By Arflex: 1984 T-Line armchair, 1990 Armilla armchair, 1995 So-Fa sofa, and 2000 Anton side chair. By Rosenthal furniture: 1972 Vario Pillow modular seating, 1973 Hombre chair, 1974 Mecum-Tecum seating unit, 1978 Dondolo chair, and 1979 Consenza sofa. Other clients have included Arco, Bushy, Brunner, Cor, Dietiker, Graffiti, Klöber, Painda, Rolf Benz, Stilwood, Wittmann.
Citations 1969 Bundespreis 'Gute Form,' Rat für Formgebung (German design council), Frankfurt; 1980, 1981, 1982, and 1984 Deutsche Auswahl LGA Stuttgart; 1979, 1980, 1982, 1984, and 1987 awards, Industrie Forum Design (iF), Hanover; 1985, 1987, and 1989 awards, Resources Council, US; 1987 *Schöner Wohnen* Möbel des Jahres, Germany; 1987, 1990 Haus Industrieform, Essen; 1997 Dansk ID Prize.
Bibliography Albrecht Bangert and Karl Michael Armer, *80s Style: Designs of the Decade*, New York: Abbeville, 1990. Marion Godau and Bernd Polster, *Design Directory Germany*, London: Pavilion, 2000. www. vogtherrdesign.com.

Voll, Espen (1965–)
> See Norway Says.

Vollrath Company

American metalware firm.

History 1874, German émigré Jacob Johann Vollrath established his eponymous firm in Sheboygan, Wis., to manufacture farm implements, steam engines, cast-iron stoves, and cooking utensils and emulated the ceramic-coating on cast iron, traditional in Germany but not in the US. Fortunately, the demand for enamelware items greatly increased, particularly by end of 19th century. His customer base expanded from households to restaurants and other food enterprises. Eventually, Vollrath replaced enamel-metalware with stainless-steel, and production expanded. Mid-20th century, the firm became known for simple unadorned forms. Since, Vollrath has expanded, acquired other firms, and today continues to produce wares for the food-service industry, including in stainless steel, aluminum, and molded plastics.
Bibliography http://www.vollrathco.com.

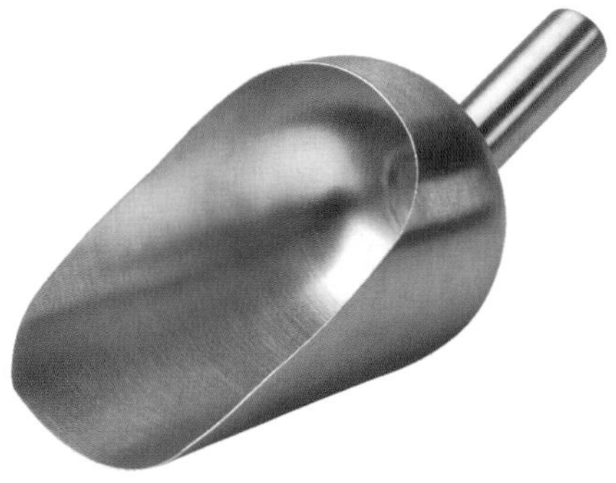

Vollrath Company. Kitchen scoop. Pre-1956. Stainless steel, l. 13" x dia. 5 1/2" (33 x 14 cm). Mfr.: Vollrath Company, US (pre-1956). Purchase. MoMA.

Volonterio, Roberto (1944–)

Italian architect and designer; born Taranto; active Milan.

Training To 1971 under Marco Zanuso and Renzo Piano, Politecnico, Milan.
Biography 1971, Volonterio began his professional career; has designed houses, apartment buildings, and interior architecture for offices and residences; 1990, worked on urban décor for Azienda Energetica Municipale in Milan; became a member, Associazione per il Disegno Industriale (ADI). Clients for furniture, lighting, and industrial design have included Bernini, Elam, Flumen, Ginova, La Linea, Maisa, Quattrifolio, Saporiti, Sormani, and Zanotta.
Citation Award, 1973 (1st) Grandecoro national ceramic competition, Reggio Emilia.
Bibliography *ADI Annual 1976*, Milan: Associazione per il Disegno Industriale, 1976. *Modo*, no. 148, Mar.–Apr. 1993: 127.

Volther, Poul M. (1923–2001)

Danish furniture designer.

Biography After World War II, Volther is best known for 1962 no. EJ-5 lounge chair in chromed spring steel with four elliptical sections (produced to 1992 and then reintroduced into production as the Corona), one of a number of his seating designs by Erik Jørgensen. The separate cross sections of the back and seat supports of the Corona were earlier explored in the wooden cross sections of the back of one of his 1951 wooden side chairs and, particularly 1950s Pyramid chair in oak (with two vertical braces also in wood) by Peder Pedersen. Possibly only four copies of the Pyramid were made. Also, from 1950s, designed other seating by Frem-Røjle.
Bibliography Charlotte and Peter Feill, *Decorative Art 50s*, New York: Taschen, 2000: 158.

von Bohr, Olaf (1927–)

Austrian industrial designer; born Salzburg; active Milan.

Biography 1953–55, Von Bohr worked in the studio of Gio Ponti and, 1954–64, in the studio of Alberto Rosselli; 1955, organized the office development of La Rinascente department store. From 1966, clients have included Velca and Valenti (lighting) and, from 1974, Gedy and Bilumen. He has also designed plastic furniture and accessories, such as 4930-7 modular bookshelves, an articulated table lamp, a record-holder, coat hook, and folding breakfast tray by Kartell, all primarily designed in 1970, and dust bin, seating, and small étagère by Gedy, designed in 1977. He became a member, Associazione per il Disegno Industriale (ADI).
Bibliography *ADI Annual 1976*, Milan: Associazione per il Disegno Industriale, 1976.

von Brauchitsch, Margarethe (1865–1957)

German embroiderer.

Training Under Max Klingerainting, Leipzig; under Koloman Moser, Vienna.
Biography Von Brauchitsch was active late 19th century and early 20th century and may have been associated with the embroidery studio founded in 1895 in Munich by Hermann Obrist, whose influence showed in her work. She became an important Art Nouveau textile designer and cofounder of the Vereinigte Werkstätten für Kunst im Handwerk, Munich. Some of her embroidery designs were published in a 1900 issue of journal *Dekorative Kunst*.
Bibliography Stuart Durant, *Ornament from the Industrial Revolution to Today*, Woodstock, N.Y., 1986: 52. Cat., Kathryn Bloom Hiesinger, *Die Meister des Münchner Jugendstils*, Munich: Stadtmuseum, 1988.

von Brevern, Renate (1942–)
> See Mühlhaus, Heike.

von Klier, Hans (1934–)

Czech industrial designer; born Děčín; active Milan.

Training To 1959, Hochschule für Gestaltung, Ulm.
Biography After working in Sessanta, von Klier settled in Milan, where he was a consultant designer to La Rinascente department store; collaborated with Rodolfo Bonetto; 1960–68, worked in the office of Ettore Sottsass as a designer of furniture and equipment by Olivetti, including 1964 Praxis 48 and 1965 Tekne 3 typewriters, TE 300 teletyper, and 1970 Summa 19 R adding machine; from 1968, was in charge of corporate identity at Olivetti; taught in Britain, Germany, and the US; became known for distinctive lighting such as 1987 Grillo table lamp and 1991 Blob floor/wall lamp (with Hakan Gencol) by Bilumen and 1992–93 products by Zanotta, including clothes rack, ashtray, mirror, and desk. His other Italian and German clients have included Drabert, Foemm, Gavazzi, Planula, Rossi-Arredamenti, Skipper, Valsodo, Viennaline, Wirus. Is a member, Associazione per il Disegno Industriale (ADI).
Exhibitions Educational toys subject of 1962 exhibition, Il Sestante gallery, Milan. Participated in two editons of Triennale di Milano.
Bibliography Cat., Milena Lamarová, *Design a Plastické Hmoty*, Prague: Umĕleckoprůmyslové Muzeum, 1972: 118. *ADI Annual 1976*, Milan: Associazione per il Disegno Industriale, 1976. Alfonso Grassi and Anty Pansera, *Atlante del design italiano 1940–1980*, Milan: Fabbri, 1980: 331. Cat., *Donation Olivetti: Die Neue Sammlung*, Munich, 1986: 39. Fumio Shimizu and Studio Matteo Thun (eds.), *The Italian Design: Descendants of Leonardo da Vinci*, Tokyo: Graphic-sha, 1987: 339. Cat., Hans Wichmann, *Italien Design 1945 bis heute*, Munich: Die Neue Sammlung, 1988.

von Nessen, 'Greta' Margaretta (1900–1978)

Swedish designer; active New York; wife of Walter von Nessen.

Training Kungliga Tekniska Högskolan, Stockholm.
Biography 1925, she settled in the US with her German husband, with whom she cofounded Nessen Studio in New York in 1927, for the design and production of modern lighting. On the 1943 death of her husband, she closed the studio. 1945, she introduced lighting fixtures of her own design and, with her son, revived the Nessen Studio and continued production of her husband's earlier work, including his 1927 swing-arm lighting range, and introduced the work of other designers. Her 1951 Anywhere lamp was economical and popular; its versatility permitted it to be suspended, wall-mounted, or table-set.
Exhibitions 1952 *Good Design* exhibition/award (Anywhere lamp), The Museum of Modern Art, New York, and Chicago Merchandise

Hans von Klier and Ettore Sottsass. Praxis 48 electric typewriter. 1964. Metal and plastics, 5 11/16 x 17 3/4 x 13 3/8" (14.5 x 45 x 34 cm). Mfr.: Ing. C. Olivetti & C., Italy. Courtesy Quittenbaum Kunstauktionen, Munich.

'Greta' Margaretta von Nessen. Anywhere lamp. 1951. Aluminum and enameled metal, h. 14 3/4" x dia. 14 1/4" (37.5 x 36.2 cm). Mfr.: Nessen Studio, US. Architecture and Design Fund. MoMA.

Mart; 1983–84 exhibition, Philadelphia (catalog below).
Bibliography 'Market Spotlight,' *Interior Design*, vol. 42, Mar. 1971: 68. Cat., Kathryn B. Hiesinger and George H. Marcus III (eds.), *Design Since 1945*, Philadelphia: Philadelphia Museum of Art, 1983. *Lighting and Accessories*, Apr. 1988: 22–26. Cat., Pat Kirkham (ed.), *Women Designers in the USA, 1900–2000: Diversity and Difference*, New York: Bard, New Haven: Yale, 2000.
> See von Nessen, Walter.

von Nessen, Walter (1889–1943)

German metalworker; born Iserlohn; active New York; husband of Margaretta von Nessen.

Training Under Bruno Paul, Vereinigte Staatsschulen für freie und angewandte Kunst (Kunstgewerbeschule), Berlin-Charlottenburg.
Biography Paul taught von Nessen the importance of careful workmanship in the tradition of the Deutscher Werkbund and Wiener Sezession. Von Nessen redesigned the interiors of the subway stations in Berlin and taught, Kunstgewerbeschule, Charlottenburg; 1919–23, designed furniture in Stockholm; 1923, settled in New York, where, during his first years, designed/made furniture and furnishings for Manhattan homes and apartments. 1927, he and his wife founded Nessen Studio for design/manufacture in New York and created his now-well-known 1927 swing-arm lamp, which is still in production in various configurations. 1930 when many other businesses were facing bankruptcy, Nessen announced the studio's expansion, attested to by his 1930 catalog of 30 lamps, mirrors, and tables. He designed for architects, designers, and retailers; was a prolific designer for various American firms, including Chase Brass & Copper Co., from which his most prolific commissions came and for which he created a 1930 ten-item collection. For his Chase metalware, he used pre-existing extruded industrial metal parts for ashtrays, bowls, and other items such as 1933 Diplomat and 1934 Continental coffee services that are among his finest work. From mid-1930s, his approach was more Functionalist (such as a 1935 table lamp by Pattyn Products, Detroit, Mich.) than his late-1920s revival styles in luxury materials. He did much of his work in metal, although he also designed some wooden furniture. Despite a fondness for torchère lamps, he did not mimic the forms of pre-electric lighting but borrowed techniques of indirect illumination from theater designers. Eliel Saarinen; Skidmore, Owings, and Merrill; and Florence Knoll included von Nessen lamps in their interiors, thus making them ubiquitous in tasteful 1950s–60s settings. Von Nessen innovatively incorporated brass with satin chrome, spun aluminum, Bakelite, fiberglass, and natural cherry and rosewood into his work. 1952, the Nessen Studio was bought from the von Nessen family by Stanley Wolf and thus named Nessen Lamps in 1985. The firm was purchased by J.J.I. Lighting Group in 1987. The firm was named Nessen Lighting in c. 1990.
Exhibitions Work shown at 1929 *Modern American Design in Metal*, Newark Museum, Newark, N.J., where von Nessen's chair appeared alongside Mies van der Rohe's; 1930 *Modern Age Furniture* (torchère lamp), W. & J. Sloane store; 1930 *Third International Exhibition of Contemporary Industrial Design* (adjustable ball-bearing lamp), New York, sponsored by the American Federation of Arts; 1931 exhibition (torchère lamp), American Union of Decorative Arts and Craftsmen (AUDAC), New York; 1932 *Design and Industry Exhibition* (wall sconces, glassware, tables, and other accessories), New York; 1937 *Exposition Internationale des Arts et Techniques dans la Vie Moderne*, Paris (granted a gold medal); 1935 *Contemporary American Industrial Art, 1934* (metal, ceramic, and glass objects) and *Contemporary American Industrial Art: 1940, 15th Exhibition*, both Metropolitan Museum of Art, New York; and numerous others.
Bibliography 'Von Nessen, Walter,' in *Who's Who in American Art*, 1936–37, Washington, D.C.: American Federation of the Arts, 1937. Obituary, *The New York Times*, 5 Sept. 1943: 28. Kimberly Sichel, *Industrial Design*, May–June 1984: 38–42. *Home Lighting and Accessories*, Apr. 1988: 22–26. Cat., J. Stewart Johnson, *American Modern, 1925–1940....*, New York: Abrams, 2000.

von Savigny, Christiane (1958–)

German furniture designer; born Frankfurt am Main.

Training In law, Bayerische Julius-Maximilian-Universität, Würzburg; 1977–82, in product design, Germany; 1977–79, in woodworking, Germany, France, and England.
Biography 1980, von Savigny worked at home-decorating firm House and Garden in Munich; 1981, at the Rodolfo Bonetto design studio in Milan; briefly, Freie Kunstschule in Zürich; 1983, at a cabinetmaking workshop in Schauenburg, near Kassel; 1983–88, was a furniture and interior designer at Thonet, designing its Programme 400 stacking chair; from 1988, has been an independent consultant designer in Stuttgart.
Bibliography Cat., Design Center Stuttgart, *Women in Design: Careers and Life Histories Since 1900*, Stuttgart: Haus der Wirtschaft, 1989.

von Wersin, Wolfgang (1882–1976)

Czech designer; born Prague; active Germany.

Training In architecure, Munich; under Hermann Obrist, Lehrund Versuchs-Ateliers für angewandte und freie Kunst (Debschitz-Schule), Munich.
Biography 1882 appears to be the correct year of von Wersin's birth. From 1912, von Wersin designed for the Deutsche Werkstätten; 1913, became a member of the Deutsche Werkbund; from 1929, was the director, Die Neue Sammlung museum in Munich; subsequently, designed ceramics and glassware by Augarten, Erhard & Söhne, Meissen, Nymphenburg, Rosenthal, and Vereinigte Lausitzer Glaswerke. He died in Bad Ischl.
Exhibitions Subject of 1984 *Wolfgang von Wersin (1881–1976): Gestaltung und Produktentwicklung*, Die Neue Sammlung, Munich; 1991–92 *Wolfgang von Wersin 1882–1972: Vom Kunstgewerbe*

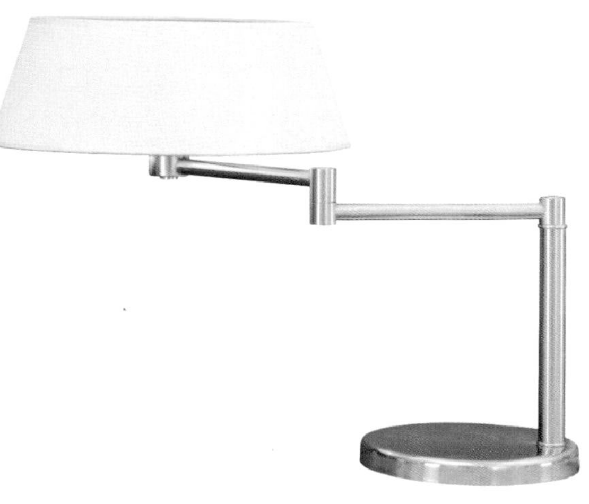

Walter von Nessen. Desk lamp. 1927. Chrome-plated brass, h. 16" (40.6 cm). Mfr.: Nessen Studio, US. Gift of the mfr. MoMA.

Wolfgang von Wersin. Tea caddy. c. 1954. Brass, overall 4 1/8 x 2 7/8 x 2 1/8" (10.5 x 7.3 x 5.4 cm). Mfr.: Ehrhard & Söhne, Germany. Gift of Philip Johnson. MoMA.

zur Industrieform, Münchner Stadtmseum.
Bibliography Alfred Ziffer, *Wolfgang von Wersin 1882–1976*, Munich: Klinkhardt & Biermann, 1991. Alfred Ziffer, *Nymphenburger Moderne*, Munich: Münchener Stadtmuseum, 1997.

von Zülow, Franz (1883–1963)

Austrian painter, graphic and product designer; born Vienna.

Training 1901–02 under Joseph Eugen Hörwarther and Hubert Landa, graphics workshop and laboratory; for a short time as a guest student of Christian Griepenkerls, Akademie der bildenden Künste; 1903–04 under Felician von Myrbach and 1904–06 under Carl Czeschka, Kunstgewerbeschule; all Vienna.
Biography 1903–15, von Zülow was active in his own publishing house and invented a kind of paper stencil for screen printing (patented in 1907); from 1908, illustrated and sketched for the Wiener Werkstätte and designed porcelain, textiles, and furniture; from 1925, was active as a canvas and fresco painter and, from 1945, received a number of commissions for public mural paintings and mosaics; from 1955, was president of the artists' guild in the Mühlviertel area of Austria. 1920–21, he taught, Keramischen Lehrwerkstätte Schleiß (ceramic-art training workshop), Gmunden, Austria, and remained there as artistic advisor to 1961; from 1949, taught, Kunstgewerbeschule, Linz. He died in Vienna.

Vondráčková, Jaroslava (1894–1989)

Czech textile designer, producer, and publicist; born Prague.

Training In painting, Prague, Paris, and Berlin.
Biography 1923, Vondráčková established her own workshop; 1929, set up a studio with Božena Pošepná; 1926, became a member of the Czechoslovakian Werkbund (SČSD) and belonged to the Devětsil group; visited the Bauhaus several times and befriended Otti Berger. Vondráčková experimented with artificial fibers; worked at Rodier in Paris; traveled to Scotland to study Harris-tweed production; 1930s, collaborated with some leading modern Czech architects and designed simple textiles in a Functionalist style.
Bibliography Alena Adlerová, *České užité umění 1918–1938*, Prague: Odeon, 1983.

Votteler, Arno (1929–)

German designer; born Freudenstadt.

Training 1948–50, interior architecture, Kunsthandwerkschule, Bonndorf/Schwarzwald; 1954–55 under Herbert Hirche, Staatliche Akademie der bildenden Künste, Stuttgart.
Biography From 1953, Votteler worked for Walter Knoll furniture firm and designed one of his best-known works, 1952 upholstered armchair in bent tubular steel; was a freelance designer, collaborating with Robert Gutmann in London; 1961, established his own studio in Brunswick; from 1961, taught industrial design, Hochschule für bildende Künste, Brunswick; from 1967, Staatliche Akademie der bildenden Künste, Stuttgart, where he is the director of Weißenhof-Institut (forum of interior architecture and furniture design), which he founded in 1980. He has lectured in institutions in Rio de Janeiro; Columbus, Ohio; Ahmedabad; Taiwan; and Beijing; is a member, Deutsches Werkbund, and cofounder, Verband Deutscher Industriedesigner (VDID, German industrial designers' association). Design work includes 1969 TV casing by Blaupunkt-Bosch, 1969 Design 90 office system by Planmöbel Eggersmann, and 1978 office chair by Martin Stoll. He has written the books *Wege zum modernen Möbel* (Dva, 1989); *125 Jahr Knoll...* (a history of Walter Knoll, with Herbert Eilmann, 1990); *Ideen für eine neue Bürowelt* (1992); and others; and on his pedagogy: *Innenarchitektur und Möbeldesign-Klasse Prof. Votteler* (with Ulrike Förschler, 1991) and *Der Marktplatz rund um die Themen: 3D-Architektur-Visualisierung-Bildbearbeitung* (on the Weißenhof-Institut, with Eilmann, 1991).
Bibliography Cat., *Design Made in Germany*, Cologne, 2001: 56.

Voulkos, Peter (1924–2002)

American ceramicist and glassware designer; born Bozeman, Mont.; active Oakland, California.

Training To 1951, Montana State University, Bozeman; 1952, master's degree, California College of Arts and Crafts, Oakland; under Maija Grotell, Cranbrook Academy of Art, Bloomfield, Mich.
Biography Voulkos was head of ceramics at University of California, Berkeley. He and Rudy Autio directed the prestigious Archie Bray Foundation in Montana, a ceramics residency program founded in 1951 and a launching point for many artists over half a century. Summer 1953, Voulkos was appreciably influenced by his association with potters, painters, and performing artists at Black Mountain College, Asheville, N.C.; 1979–84, concentrated on plates, then vessel-shaped 'stacks' in an *anagama* (a Japanese wood-burning kiln); 1989, returned to ceramic sculpture and is today considered as having been a pioneer in post-World War II ceramics.
Exhibitions/citations Subject of 1958–59 exhibition, Pasadena Art Museum (now Norton Simon Museum), California; 1960, The Museum of Modern Art, New York; 1978, Museum of Contemporary Crafts (now American Craft Museum), New York; 1995–96 touring exhibitions; 1999, Frank Lloyd Gallery, Santa Monica, Cal. Work shown at 1959 (20th) *Ceramic International Exhibition*, The Metropolitan Museum of Art; one of six artists in 1981–82 ceramic-sculpture exhibition, Whitney Museum of American Art; both New York. Citations at 1950 National Ceramic Exhibition, Syracuse Museum of Fine Arts (now Everson Museum of Art), N.Y.
Bibliography Rose Slivka, *Peter Voulkos: A Dialogue with Clay*,

Peter Voulkos. Jar. c. 1956. Stoneware, h. 21 5/8" x dia. 14 13/16" (55.5 x 37.6 cm). Mfr.: the designer, US. Gift of Mrs. Gifford Phillips. MoMA.

Boston and New York: New York Graphic Society, 1978. Jim Leedy, *Voulkos*, Goffstown, N.H.: Studio Potter, 1993. Rose Slivka and Karen Tsujimoto, *The Art of Peter Voulkos*, Tokyo: Kodansha/Oakland Museum, 1995.

Voysey, Charles Francis Annesley (1857–1941)

British architect and designer; born Hessle, Yorkshire.

Training Apprenticeship under several prominent architects, including John Pollard Seddon 1874–78.
Biography 1879, Voysey began working in the office of architect Saxon Snell, a specialist in the design of charitable institutions and hospitals; 1880–82, worked in the office of architect George Devey in London, who was a designer of country houses for the wealthy, including Lord Lytton, the Marquis of Lorne, Lord Granville, the Rothschilds, the Duke of Westminster, and Henrietta Montefiore. 1882, Voysey established his own architectural practice in Queen Anne's Gate, London, and pursued a strong original style infused with an original interpretation of traditional vernacular details. 1888, he began to design furniture, wallpaper, and textiles, influenced by the Arts and Crafts movement. Art Nouveau characteristics were expressed in his metalware. His textiles and wallpapers reflected the influence of A.H. Mackmurdo, with whom he worked. An 1895 clock in cast aluminum and copper illustrates Voysey's restrained, unadorned approach. He was a skilful self-publicist and arranged the exposure of his work in international venues and frequently in *The Studio* journal. His Sept. 1893 interview in the journal may have been the earliest of its type with a designer. 1890s, he designed wallpapers by Essex, and its magazine advertisements. Voysey, some of whose patterns may have inspired the images of Walter Crane, was in turn influenced by Japanese art. Like many contemporaries, such as Frank Lloyd Wright, he believed that furniture and furnishings should be site-specific to each architectural commission. However, some of his designs were intended for mass production and were among the most commercially successful of their time. He designed numerous small and medium-sized houses in England, including 1891 Forster house, Bedford Park, London; 1899 Julian Sturgis house, Surrey; 1899 H.G. Wells's Spade House, Sandgate, Kent; 1905–06 Burke house, Hollymount; and Broadleys in the Lake District. Most of his furniture was in oak, often unstained and unpolished with an emphasis on the joints and pegs. He can be linked to the modern movement through his concern for function and the reduction of ornamental details. He was unwilling to alter his Arts and Crafts allegiance and was rather inactive after World War I.
Exhibitions/citations Architecture represented in 1894, 1895 (with the Glasgow School), and 1897 editions, Salon de la Libre Esthétique, Liège; 1902 *Esposizione Internazionale d'Arte Decorativa Moderna*, Turin. Subject of 1970 *Charles F.A. Voysey*, Santa Barbara, Cal.; 1978 *C.F.A. Voysey: Architect and Designer, 1857–1941*, Brighton (catalog below); included in 1959 *Art Nouveau: Art and Design at the Turn of the Century*, The Museum of Modern Art, New York; 1981 *Architect-Designers, Pugin to Mackintosh,* The Fine Art Society, London. 1936, elected Honorary Royal Designer for Industry, UK; 1940 gold medal, Royal Institute of British Architects (RIBA).
Bibliography John Brandon-Jones, *C.F.A. Voysey: A Memoir*, London, 1957. David Gebhard, *Charles F. A. Voysey*, Los Angeles: Hennessey & Ingalls, 1957. Cat., John Brandon-Jones et al., *C.F.A. Voysey: Architect and Designer, 1857–1941*, Brighton: Lund Humphries/Brighton Pavilion, 1978. Duncan Simpson, C.F.A. Voysey: *An Architect of Individuality*, New York: Whitney, 1981. Cat., *Architect-Designers, Pugin to Mackintosh*, London: Fine Arts Society, 1981. Stuart Durant, *The Decorative Designs of C.F.A. Voysey*, London: Lutterworth, 1990. Stuart Durant, *C.F.A. Voysey*, London: Academy, New York: St. Martin's, 1992. Cat., *C.F.A. Voysey: Decorative Design*, Glasgow: Hunterian Art Gallery, 1992. W. Hitchmough, *The Homestead: C.F.A. Voysey*, London: Phaidon, 1994. W. Hitchmough, *C F A Voysey*, London: Phaidon, 1995.

Vretzaki, Helen (1960–)

Greek industrial designer; born Edessa.

Training 1977–83 under Lavas George, architecture, Aristotelian University of Thessalonica.
Bibliography From 1983, she has been an interior designer of homes and shops and the designer of stands in, and the hall of, the HELEXPO international fair conference center, Thessalonica; 1984, became a member of the Tetras group; 1986, began designing objects for various domestic uses and for industry and business such as stoves, bathroom fixtures, and furniture, including 1986 Ktenion clothes stand by Studio Epsilon of Thessalonica.
Exhibitions/citations Work included in 1986 (8th) Biennial of Young Artists of Europe and the Mediterranean, Thessalonica; 1987 (3rd) *European Exhibition of Creation–SAD '87*, Grand Palais, Paris; 1987 (5th) (third prize for Pyramis furniture system) and 1988 (6th) (first prize for Nautilus furniture group) editions, Panhellenic Competition of Furniture Design—FURNIDEC, Thessalonica; 1988 Biennale de la Création, Namur; 1989 *Design Objects II*, Gallery Popi K, Athens.
Bibliography Cat., Design Center Stuttgart, *Women in Design: Careers and Life Histories Since 1900*, Stuttgart: Haus der Wirtschaft, 1989: 260–63.

Vroom, Marcel (1956–)

Dutch industrial designer; born Leiden.

Training 1974–81, industrial-design engineering, Technische Universiteit, Delft.
Biography Vroom has been active in design research, new-product development, and investigations into intelligent buildings and products, including for communication, interface, laboratory and medical work, cooking, and computing, and office and laboratory furniture; also in interior and exterior design. 1981–83, he was graphic and industrial designer in Amsterdam. In Rotterdam: 1983–87 as a cofounder, he was the director of Landmark Design & Consulting (known as Landmark Design & Technology 1987–89); 1993–97, worked at Global Design Network; 1997, established his own research-and-design firm in Rotterdam. Vroom has taught, lectured, and mentored, Faculteit Bouwkunde (faculty of architecture), Technische Universiteit, Eindhoven; Faculteit Bouwkunde and Delft School of Design, Technische Universiteit, Delft; Hogeschool voor de Kunsten, Arnhem; Akademie voor Industriële Vormgeving, Eindhoven. Clients have included Ahrend, Allied Data Technologies, Alphatron, Antec Leyden, ATAG Kitchen Group, De Ster, Dutch KPN Research, Dutch KPN Telecom, Eco Chemie, Haier, Hitron, Holec Holland, Honeywell, Kembo, KLM Royal Dutch Airlines, NS Dutch Railways, Novem, NUON, Philips Design, Spark Holland, Sysmax, ThermoQuest. Vroom has served on several juries and is a member of numerous professional Dutch design associations.
Exhibitions/citations Work included in 1987 *Holland in Vorm*, Stedelijk Museum, Amsterdam; 1989 *Dutch Design Expo*, Nagoya, Japan; 1996 *Kast me inhoud*, Techniek Museum, Delft; 1996 *Contemporary Design from the Netherlands*, The Museum of Modern Art, New York; 1998 *Design and Identity*, Louisiana Museum for Moderne Kunst, Humlebæk, Denmark. Received 1987, 1996, 1997, 1998, 2000 prizes, Good Industrial Design Foundation, Netherlands; 1989 Encouragement Award, Amsterdam Fonds voor de Kunst; 1992 and 1995 Aluminum Award, Netherlands; 1993 Designprijs, Rotterdam; 1995 Kho Liang Ie applied-arts prize of Amsterdam Fonds voor de Kunst (for complete body of work and certain products; 1997 award, Industrie Forum Design (iF), Hanover.

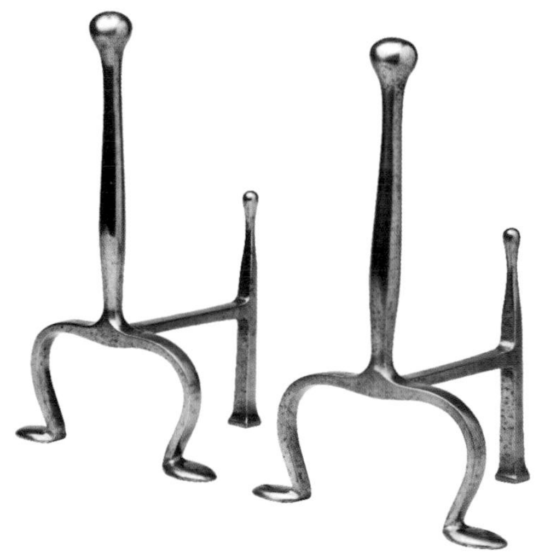

Charles Francis Annesley Voysey. Andirons. c. 1900. Wrought iron, each overall 12 x 7 x 6 7/8" (30.5 x 17.8 x 17.5 cm). Mfr.: Thomas Elsey and Co., UK. Mr. and Mrs. Walter Hochschild Purchase Fund. MoMA.

Vrubel, Mikhail (1856–1910)

Russian painter, graphic and theater artist, ceramicist, and sculptor; born Omsk.

Training 1864, 1868–69, Drawing School of OPKh (society for the encouragement of the arts), St. Petersburg; 1874–79, law, St. Petersburg University; 1880–84, art, St. Petersburg Academy.
Biography Vrubel was highly accomplished in all fine-art media and theater and furniture design; was intimate with the Abramstevo circle and, thus, painted scenery for Savva Mamontov's Moscow Private Opera (founded in 1885) and was invited to work in the pottery facility on Mamontov's estate Abramstevo (acquired in 1870), near Moscow, in the house of which Vrubel painted panels. Vrubel restored frescoes in the Church of St. Cyril, Kiev, 1884–89, and executed original frescoes there, and organized the project for murals in the Cathedral of St. Vladimir; designed stage sets for Diaghilev's Les Ballets Russes; became known as the most inspired Russian symbolist, nearing Abstract Expressionism. Vrubel was an obsessive and, 1902, went mad, though in moments of lucidity continued to work. He became blind in 1906 and died in an insane asylum in St. Petersburg.
Exhibitions Showed fine art with the V Mir Iskusstva (the world of art) group in venues from 1900; with the Moscow Society of Artists from 1899; with other groups; and as the subject of numerous international exhibitions.

V'Soske, Stanislav (1900–1983)

Polish textile designer and manufacturer; active the US.

Biography V'Soske and his brother established a factory in Grand Rapids, Mich. and, from 1924, designed and wove the first hand-tufted rugs in the US; late 1930s, opened a second manufacturing facility in Puerto Rico; in addition to producing hand-finished, fine-quality, rugs of his own designs in vibrant colors, occasionally with figurative motifs, commissioned other designers and artists over the years, including Stuart Davis, George Nelson, and Michael Graves; 1950s, wove the rug for the Green Room of The White House in Washington, D.C.; has become best known for high-pile, sculpted, molded rugs. Stanislav V'Soske's own designs had titles such as Riders in the Spring.
Bibliography 'V'Soske 1959 Exhibition of Rugs,' *Interiors*, vol. 118, Apr. 1959: 134–35. 'The V'Soske Rugmakers,' *American Fabrics*, no. 51, fall 1960: 83–86. Cat., Kathryn B. Hiesinger and George H. Marcus III (eds.), *Design Since 1945*, Philadelphia: Philadelphia Museum of Art, 1983.

Vuitton, Louis

French luggage and fashion firm; from 1860, located Asnières.

Biography 1835 at age 14, Louis Vuitton (Cons-le-Sannier 1821–Paris 1892) left his home village of Anchay in the Jura mountain range of France for Paris. He travelled there by foot, being very poor and, ironically, carrying only one piece of luggage. Vuitton worked briefly as a stable boy and a kitchen helper, aspiring to be a woodworker; 1837, became an apprentice to a luggage, or packing-case, maker named Maréchal; 1854, set up his own shop on the rue Neuve-des-Capucines (now rue des Capucines) and became the first (1854) to make trunks with flat tops which made them stackable in the holds of oceanliners and in the baggage compartments of trains. He covered them in elegant gray Trianon canvas. So successful was his enterprise that he became in the service of the Empress Eugénie and thus her favorite 'wrinkle-free packer.' 1872, he introduced the striped red and beige colour scheme; 1876, invented the wardrobe trunk; 1888, created the Daumier canvas (square pattern). Explorer Savorgnan de Brazza ordered a special trunk-bed from Vuitton for his 1876 trip to the Congo. 1890, Louis Vuitton's son Georges (1857–1936) created a special lock featuring five pick-proof tumblers; 1892, began a study of the evolution of transportation and luggage that led to the book *Le voyage: dépuis les temps les plus reculés jusqu'à nos jours* (Paris: E. Dentu, 1894). To discourage counterfeiters of the luggage, the 'LV' symbol, imprinted on paint-impregnated canvas, was introduced in 1896. 1901, introduced the Steamer bag, precursor of today's soft luggage, originally a laundry bag for inside a wardrobe trunk. Georges's son Gaston (1883–1970) began the establishment of branches worldwide and designed 1924 Keepall bag, forerunner of the duffel bag, and 1932 Noé for vintners to transport champagne bottles. Gaston assembled a rather large collection of antique traveling cases displayed in 1926 in the London, Boston, New York, and Paris shops. The company added dressing tables, manicure sets, glass scent bottles, silver accessories, and, today, jewelry and clothing to its range. 1936 Stokowski writing desk/trunk, first made for conductor Leopold Stokowski, is still available today. The firm remained small and family owned to 1943, when French businessman Henry Racamier (1913–2003) married Odile Vuitton, granddaughter of the founder. 1977, Racamier thus took over the firm, when it had only two shops, in France, and rapidly expanded and diversified the enterprise to eventually grow 50 fold. 1985 Epi non-monogrammed-leather series in six brightly colored leathers was among the newer introductions. 1983, the Louis Vuitton Cup, a citation for sailboat racing, was established. 1991, Christian Liaigre designed a leather and sycamore travel-furniture set. The directors of design have been Françoise Jollant Kneebone 1987–94 and Xavier Dixsaut hence. 1987, the firm was merged to form LVMH Moët Hennessy–Louis Vuitton, an unhappy consortium. 1990 after much rancor, Bernard Arnault, having acquired a major interest in the consortium, became the chief executive officer; Henry Racamier was forced to leave, and the Vuitton family sold its 27% stake. 1998, American fashion designer Marc Jacobs, who had become known for his Grunge look, was appointed the artistic director and introduced the firm's first ready-to-wear clothing and footwear and his first bag by Vuitton. 1997 line of pens designed by Anouska Hempel, 2001 jewelry, and 2002 Tambour watches were introduced. More recent bags have included 2000 range with Daumier Savage historical square pattern, 2001 Grafitti by Jacobs and Stephen Sprouse, 2002 Patchwork by Jacobs and illustrator Julie Verhoven, 2003 interpretations of the 'LV'/flower by Japanese artist Takashi Murakami, 2003 Suhali goatskin, 2004 Sac de Nuit, and 2004 Boulogne Multi-Color shoulder model.
Exhibition/citations Work subject of 1987 *L'invitation au voyage: autour de la donation Louis Vuitton*, Musée des Arts Décoratifs, Paris. First awards, at 1867 *Exposition Universelle*, Paris.
Bibliography Georges Vuitton, *Objets de voyage et de campement: industries du caoutchouc et de la gutta-percha*, Paris, 1910 (a report on the French Section, class 99, group XV, 1910 *Exposition Universelle et Internationale*, Brussels). Henry L. Vuitton, *La malle aux souvenirs*, Paris: Mengès, 1984. Cat., *L'invitation au voyage: autour de la donation Louis Vuitton*, Paris: Musée des Arts Décoratifs, 1987. S. Bonvicini, *Louis Vuitton: une saga francaise*, Paris: Fayard, 2004.

Vuokko
> See Nurmesniemi, Vuokko.

Vyse, Charles (1882–1971)

British ceramicist; born Staffordshire.

Training At age 14, apprenticeship as a modeler and designer, Doulton, Staffordshire; Hanley Art School; 1905–10, sculpture, Royal College of Art, and, 1910, Camberwell School of Art; both London.
Biography 1919, Charles Vyse and his wife Nell began the production of ceramic figures based on people in the street, in a studio on Cheyne Row, Chelsea, London; were members of a colony of various types of potters, including Reginald Wells and Gwendolen Parnell; created figurines—a specialty of Chelsea—and attractive pots with sophisticated glazes, including those produced by wood-ash-glaze experiments, and ceramics based on celadon and other wares. Charles developed an interest in Chinese Sung pottery and used the extensive collection of his neighbor George Eumorfopoulos as a reference for the Sung style; 1930s, experimented with drawn-on brushwork; after the extensive war damage of the studio in 1940, became a modeler and instructor in pottery, Farnham School of Art, Surrey; was elected a member, Royal Society of Sculptors. Nell became an expert in ceramic chemistry; offered the technical foundation for Charles's production of chun, celadon, tenmoku and t'zu chou glazes on stoneware pots.
Exhibitions From 1922, his work regularly at British Institute of Industrial Art (BIIA) exhibitions, Victoria and Albert Museum; annually to 1963, at Walker's Gallery, Bond Street; both London.
Bibliography Cat., *Thirties: British Art and Design Before the War*, London: Arts Council of Great Britain/Hayward Gallery, 1979. *British Art and Design, 1900–1960*, London: Victoria and Albert Museum, 1983.

W

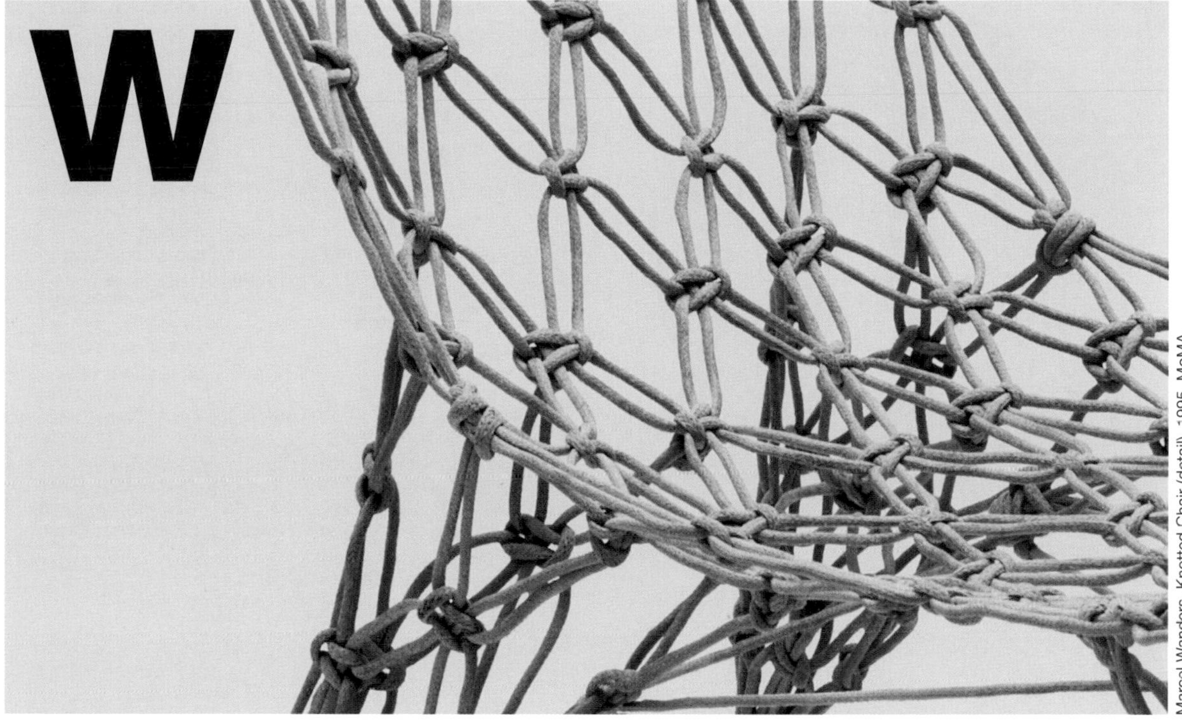

Marcel Wanders. Knotted Chair (detail). 1995. MoMA.

Waals, Peter van der (1870–1937)

Dutch furniture designer and maker; active Britain.

Training In The Hague, Brussels, Berlin, and Vienna; from 1899, London.
Biography 1901, Waals became the foreperson and cabinetmaker in the workshop of cabinetmakers Ernest Barnsley and Ernest Gimson at Daneway House, near Sapperton, Gloucestershire; subsequently, as an important member of the group, supervised the production of the Gimsons' designs and trained the craftspeople in the workshop. On Sidney Gimson's 1926 death, Waals moved the workshop facility to Chalford, Gloucestershire, and continued his furniture production there in the manner of the Gimsons.
Bibliography Cat., *Thirties: British Art and Design Before the War*, London: Arts Council of Great Britain/Hayward Gallery, 1979.

Wächtersbacher Steingutfabrik

German ceramics factory; located in Schlierbach.

History From 1760 in England, Josiah Wedgwood's successful development of stoneware, known then as 'English porcelain,' became favored over faienceware. The introduction of the new type porcelain to Continental Europe in c. 1806–10 resulted in the establishment of a number of stoneware factories whose produce achieved a popularity greater than fairence's or porcelain's. Unfortunately, fine cracks eventually and unfortunately appeared due to firing techniques, as seen in antique examples. In the area of Schlierbach—Wächtersbach/Hessen—a white-clay deposit fostered the founding of a stoneware factory on 8 June 1832, eventually to be known as Wächtersbacher Steingutfabrik. 1956, it became the property of the principality Ysenburg/Büdingen. Under the direction of Max Roesler (active at the plant 1874–90), certain social conditions were put into place; a school was established, and freelance designers were commissioned. An aesthetic high point occurred during the tenure of Christian Neureuther, when Art Nouveau-style wares were being produced and when the plant cooperated with the Darmstadt artists' cololony. Those at Darmstadt, who designed for the plant, included Josef Maria Olbrich and Hans Christiansen. Neureuther was the director of the art department from 1903–21 and also a designer. At the end of World War II, the Wächtersbach Steingutfabrik achieved a level of prominence, if only in size, by becoming the second largest ceramics factory in Germany. (Villeroy & Boch was the largest.) The operation is still active today.
Bibliography Heinz and Lilo Frensch, *Wächtersbacher Steingut*, Königstein im Taunus: K. R. Langewiesche Nachfolger, H. Köster, 1978.

Waddell, Theodore (1928–)

American designer.

Biography Waddell is best known for his 1970 innovative lighting device by Toscano Manetti in Florence, Italy. Appropriately titled Lamp Sticks and conceived with Italian designer Dante Bandini (1940–), it features small ampule-type bulbs on metal rods with positive and negative electrical-wire poles at each end that can be randomly and loosely arranged within a glass bowl. The lamp is more an intriguing novelty than one providing a utilitarian light source. Also with Bandini, Waddell designed a 1969 version with the ampule arranged horizontally, extending on positive/negative poles from a center-placed transformer in ABS. It was purportedly by or for Zanotta.

Wagenfeld, Wilhelm (1900–1990)

German architect and industrial designer; born Bremen.

Training 1915–18, apprenticeship, Koch und Bergfeld metalsmithy, Bremen, and, concurrently, Kunstgewerbeschule, Bremen; 1919–21, Staatliche Zeichenakademie, Hanau; 1921–22, privately in Bremen and Worpswede; 1923–24, under László Moholy-Nagy, Bauhaus, Weimar.
Biography 1925–29, Wagenfeld was an assistant instructor at the Bauhaus in Weimar, where he designed primarily lighting fixtures, including 1923–24 MT8 table lamp in nickel-plated brass with a disk base resting on three small hemispherical feet and a cylindrical column surmounted by a metal ring on which rests a somewhat hemispherical glass diffuser. The lamp (reflective of Adolf Loos's 1910 table lamp for the Villa Steiner, today made by Woka) was one of the earliest examples of the Bauhaus design philosophy. It was produced in two versions: one with a glass disk base, and one with a metal one. To 1928, it was produced in both versions by Schwintzer und Gräff, Berlin; by 1930, made in a variant model by Bünter und Remmeler in Frankfurt; 1931, further adapted by Wagenfeld in the model by Architekturbedarf in Dresden; is still in production today in a Wagenfeld-approved version by Tecnolumen in Bremen. (Former Bauhaus student Carl Jacob Junker later claimed that he was involved in the design of the MT8 lamp. Some authorities dispute this.) In the Bauhaus metalworking department, Wagenfeld pursued glasswork, metalwork, and woodcutting for graphics. Subsequently his pedagogy included: director of the metal workshop, Staatliche Hochschule für Baukunst und Handwerk, Weimar; and, 1931–35, Kunstgewerbeschule, Berlin. 1930–34, he worked for Jenaer Glaswerke Schott & Genossen, designing mass-produced heat-resistant glass kitchenware, including the 1932 tea pot and diffuser, cups and saucers, 1934 coffee percolator, and

Wächtersbacher Steingutfabrik: Christian Neureuther. Platter. 1906. Stoneware and copper, dia. 12 3/16" (31 cm). Mfr.: Wächtersbacher Steingutfabrik, Germany (copper element by WMF). Courtesy Quittenbaum Kunstauktienen, Munich.

1935 kitchenware, some models still being produced; designed pressed-glass utility wares and table glass by Vereinigte Lausitzer Glaswerke, of which he was artistic director 1935–49, and moved from Weißwasser to Berlin. His best-known designs include 1938 Kubus-Geschirr (cube-formed dishes) modular stacking containers (nine pressed-glass sections forming a cube shape when assembled) and 1938 zigzag-shaped ink bottle by the Pelikan ink company, both by Lausitzer. His stated goal at Lausitzer was to make glasswares that were cheap enough for the working class and tasteful enough for the privileged. 1936, Dr. Mey, co-chairperson of Lausitzer, set up Wagenfeld in a ten-person design department. Wagenfeld's Oberweimar set of glasses, at outset considered elitist, actually outsold every set of glasses ever made worldwide. From 1942, he was forced to serve in the German army and, due to his reluctance to support the Nazi regime, was sent to the Eastern front, where he was taken prisoner by the Russians. Returning to Germany in the autumn of 1947, he became a professor of design, Hochschule für Bildende Künste, Berlin, and continued at Lausitzer to 1949; from 1950, was a freelance designer; 1954, established his own studio in Stuttgart; became a consultant designer to Württembergische Metallwarenfabrik (WMF) for a number of products, including lighting, as well as inflight hospitality packs for Lufthansa airlines, porcelain by Rosenthal, and electrical appliances by Braun. 1958, he founded and was the publisher of magazine *form* (now owned by Birkhaüser). Wagenfeld's early work was widely published, including through journals *Die Form* and *Kunst und Handwerk*. He wrote articles on industrial design theory, which stressed a Functionalist approach as a prerequisite to good design. He died in Stuttgart. 1998, the Wilhelm Wagenfeld Haus was established at the Design Zentrum, Bremen.

Exhibitions/citations Work subject of 1960 *Industrieware von Wilhelm Wagenfeld*, Kunstgewerbemuseum, Zürich; *Wilhelm Wagenfeld: 50 Jahre Mitarbeit in Fabriken*, Kunstgewerbemuseum, Cologne, in 1973 and Die Neue Sammlung, Munich, in 1974; 1980 *Wilhelm Wagenfeld: Schöne Form, Gute Ware*, Württembergisches Landesmuseum, Stuttgart; 2000 *100 Years of Wilhelm Wagenfeld*, Wilhelm Wagenfeld Haus, Bremen. Received 1936 (6th) (bronze medal), 1940 (7th) (grand prize), and 1957 (11th) (grand prize) editions of Triennale di Milano; two grand prizes, 1937 *Exposition Internationale des Arts et Techniques dans la Vie Moderne* (Jenaer and Lausitzer designs), Paris; 1968 Berliner Kunstpreis, Bonn; 1969 Heinrich Tessenow Medal, Technische Universität, Hanover; 1969 Bundespreis 'Gute Form,' Rat für Formgebung (German design council), Frankfurt.

Bibliography Cat., *Industrieware von Wilhelm Wagenfeld*, Zürich: Kunstgewerbemuseum, 1960. Cat., *Wilhelm Wagenfeld: 50 Jahre Mitarbeit in Fabriken*, Cologne: Kunstgewerbemuseum; Munich: Die Neue Sammlung, 1973. Carl-Wolfgang Schümann, *Wilhelm Wagenfeld: Du Bauhaus à l'industrie*, Cologne: Kunstgewerbemuseum der Stadt Köln, 1973–75. Cat., *Wilhelm Wagenfeld: Schöne Form, Gute Ware*, Stuttgart: Württembergisches Landesmuseum, 1980. *Sammlung Katalog*, Berlin: Bauhaus Archiv, Museum für Gestaltung, 1981. Magdalena Droste in Ann Morgan (ed.), *Contemporary Designers*, London: Macmillan, 1981. Beate Manske and Gudrun Scholz (eds.), *Taglich in der Hand: Industrieformen von Wilhelm Wagenfeld aus sechs Jahrzehnten*, Bremen: Worpsweder, 1987. Torsten Bröhan, *Glaskunst der Moderne: von Josef Hoffmann bis Wilhelm Wagenfeld*, Munich: Klinkhardt & Biermann, 1992. Walter Scheiffele et al., *Wilhelm Wagenfeld und die moderne Glasindustrie: Eine Geschichte der deutschen Glasgestaltung von Bruno Mauder, Richard Süssmuth, Heinrich Fuchs und Wilhelm Wagenfeld bis Heinrich Löffelhardt*, Stuttgart: Hatje Cantz, 1994. *Zeitgemäß und zeitbeständig: Industrieformen von Wilhelm Wagenfeld*, Bremen: Hauschild, 1999. Magdalena Droste, *The Bauhaus Light by Carl Jacob Jucker and Wilhelm Wagenfeld*, Frankfurt: form, 1998. Mel Byars with Arlette Barré-Despond, *100 Designs/100 Years: A Celebration of the 20th Century*, Hove: RotoVision, 1999: 60–61. Wilhelm Wagenfeld: *Gestern, heute, morgen: Lebenskultur im Alltag*, Bremen: Hauschild, 2000. Cat., Beate Manske (ed.), *Wilhelm Wagenfeld (1900–1990)*, Ostifildern-Ruit: Hatje Cantz, 2000. Wilhelm Wagenfeld (Günther Beyer, ed.), *Die Form muß wie ein Diener sein* (compact disk), Hamburg: Hörbuch Hamburg, 2000. Christiane Weber-Stöber, *Wilhelm Wagenfeld: Schmuck*, Bremen: Hauschild, 2001. Paola Antonelli (ed.), *Objects of Design: The Museum of Modern Art*, New York: The Museum of Modern Art, 2003: 72–73, 76.

Wagner, Otto (1841–1918)

Austrian architect and designer; born and active Vienna.

Training 1857, Technische Hochschule, Vienna; 1860, Bauakademie, Berlin; 1861–63 under Eduard von der Nüll and August Sicard von Sicardsburg, Akademie der bildenden Künste, Vienna.

Biography Wagner's historicist early work was mainly confined to the design of apartment houses. 1890s, he worked on the periphery of the Art Nouveau style, showing more classical tendencies by the turn of the century. He wrote the book *Moderne Architektur: seinen Schülern ein Führer auf diesem Kunstgebiete/von Otto Wagner.* (Vienna: A. Schroll, 1896, and emendations in various subsequent editions). Its publication, marking a turning-point in his career, argues that modern life should be the starting point for the creative artist. 1894, Wagner became head of and an influential professor at Akademie der bildenden Künste, Vienna, with Josef Hoffmann and Josef Maria Olbrich among his pupils. He was responsible for the design of the Vienna city railway project in the last decade of 19th century and thus established a large drawing office with about 70 collaborators, including Hoffmann, Leopold Bauer, Max Fabiani, Jožef Plečník, and the office's chief draftsperson and manager, Olbrich. Wagner's early object-design work included 1902 silver by J.C. Klinkosch. He was a member, Deutscher Werkbund, as were his pupils Adolf Loos and Olbrich. Examples of his architecture: 1894 Der Anker aluminum shop facade, Vienna, 1898 train station, Karlsplatz, Vienna; 1898 Majolika house, Vienna;

Theodore Waddell and Dante Bandini. Light Sticks lamp (bowl model no. B 7). 1970. Glass, chrome, and injection-molded plastic, h. 7 1/2" x dia. 8 1/4" (19 x 21 cm). Mfr.: Toscano Manetti, Italy. Gift of the designer. MoMA.

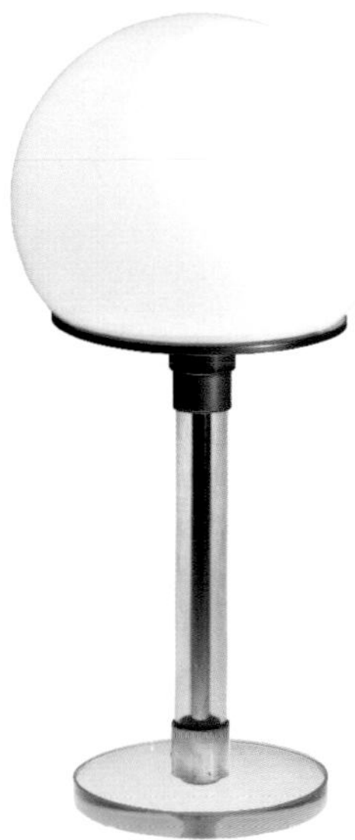

Wilhelm Wagenfeld. Table lamp (no. MT8). 1923–24. Glass and chrome-plated metal, h. 18" (45.7 cm) x dia. 8" (45.7 x 20.3 cm), base dia. 5 1/2" (14 cm). Mfr.: Bau-haus Metal Workshop, Germany. Gift of Philip Johnson. MoMA.

1906–07 Kaiserbad sluice-house, Danube Canal; and 1908–13 Lupus Hospital, Vienna. One of the buildings for which he is best known and for which he designed distinctive furniture, especially with the incorporation of aluminum elements, is 1904–06 Österreichische Postparkasse (Austrian postal savings bank, extant today), Vienna. His furniture for the Postparkasse continues to be produced, as do a number of his lamps, by Woka of Vienna.
Exhibitions Work shown at Austrian stand, 1902 *Esposizione Internazionale d'Arte Decorativa Moderna* (including silver designs for Klinkosch), Turin, and 1902 winter exhibition, Österreichisches Museum für Kunst und Industrie, Vienna. Work was subject of 1963 *Otto Wagner: Das Werk des Architekten*, Vienna; included in 2000 *Aluminum by Design* touring exhibition, originating at Carnegie Art Museum, Pittsburgh.
Bibliography Otto Wagner, *Modern Architecture: A Guidebook for his Students to this Field of Art*, Santa Monica: Getty Center for the History of Art and the Humanities, 1988 (reprint of 1902 ed., with emendations to 1896, 1898, 1914 eds. of *Moderne Architektur*, Vienna). Joseph August Lux, *Otto Wagner eine monographie*, Munich: Delphin, 1914. Hans Tietze, *Otto Wagner*, Vienna: Rikola, 1922. Cat., Otto Antonia Graf, *Otto Wagner: Das Werk des Architekten*, Vienna: Hessisches Landesmuseum, 1964. Heinz Geretsegger and Max Peintner, *Otto Wagner, 1841–1918: The Expanding City: The Beginning of Modern Architecture*, New York: Rizzoli, 1979. Dorothee Müller, *Klassiker des modernen Möbeldesign: Otto Wagner—Adolf Loos—Josef Hoffmann—Koloman Moser*, Munich: Keyser, 1980. Robert Waissenberger et al., *Vienna 1890–1920*, Secaucus, N.J.: Wellfleet, 1984: 172–83. Paul Asenbaum, *Otto Wagner: Möbel und Innenräume*, Saltzburg/Vienna: Residenz, 1984. Cat., *Otto Wagner, Vienna 1841–1918: Designs for Architecture*, Oxford: Museum of Modern Art, 1985. Robert Trevisiol, *Otto Wagner*, Bari: Laterza, 1990. Mel Byars with Arlette Barré-Despond, *100 Designs/100 Years: A Celebration of the 20th Century*, Hove: RotoVision, 1999. Paola Antonelli (ed.), *Objects of Design: The Museum of Modern Art*, New York: The Museum of Modern Art, 2003: 38–39.

Wakefield Rattan

American furniture manufacturer; located Wakefield, Mass.

History Cyrus Wakefield Sr. (1811–73), a Boston grocer, began experimenting in c. 1844 with discarded bundles of raffia and wrapping ordinary chairs in cane strips. He imported split rattan from China and became a major supplier of cane to furniture manufacturers; 1855, moved his facility to Mill River, South Reading, near Boston, and established Wakefield Rattan there. 1856 when the Opium War disrupted his supplies, he turned to a by-product of the reeds that were being used to make skirt hoops and baskets, devising furniture made from the inner part of the reeds that could be stained and painted. (Whereas, natural rattan could only be varnished.) His early models from rattan cane and domestic willow were in the fancy, tendrilled forms popular at the time. 1868, the town of South Reading was renamed Wakefield, and, by 1870s, the plant covered 10 acres (4 ha.). 1870, Wakefield's assistant William Houston invented a process for weaving cane for use as the upholstery of railroad and streetcar seats. c. 1875, his nephew and successor Cyrus Wakefield purchased several small competitors, including American Rattan. 1883, a branch on the West Coast and an additional factory in Chicago were established. 1889, the firm was bought by a Wakefield competitor, Heywood Brothers of Gardner, Mass., and became known as Heywood Brothers and Wakefield.
Citation Award for design and workmanship, 1876 *Centennial Exposition*, Philadelphia.
Bibliography Constance Cary Harrison, *Woman's Handiwork in Modern Homes*, New York: Scribner's, 1881: 191, 193–94. Esther Gilman Moore, *History of Gardner, Massachusetts, 1785–1967*, Gardner, Mass: Hatton Print, 1967: 222–28. Ruth A. Woodbury, *Wakefield's Century of Progress*, Wakefield, Mass., 1968: 3–7. Doreen Bolger Burke et al., *In Pursuit of Beauty: Americans and the Aesthetic Movement*, New York: Metropolitan Museum of Art/Rizzoli, 1987.
> See Heywood Brothers.

Wakely and Wheeler

British silversmiths; located London.

History 1891, the firm was founded by Arthur Wakely and partner Wheeler. 1920s–30s, its artisans included W.E. King and F.S. Beck, chaser B.J. Colson, and designers James Warwick, Leslie Auld, R.M.Y. Gleadowe, Reginald Hill, Harold Stabler, Kenneth Mosley, Cyril Shiner, and Arthur Wakely himself. Early on, the workshop produced silver in Art Nouveau and Arts and Crafts styles, although most of its production was in historicist forms. The firm is still active today in London.
Bibliography Annelies Krekel-Aalberse, *Art Nouveau and Art Déco Silver*, New York: Abrams, 1989.

Otto Wagner. Armchair. 1902. Beech wood and aluminum, 30 7/8 x 22 1/4 x 20 1/4" (78.5 x 56.5 x 51.5 cm), seat h. 18 5/8" (47.3 cm). Mfr.: Gebrüder Thonet, Austria (1904). Estée and Joseph Lauder Design Fund. MoMA.

Don Wallance. Design 1 cutlery. 1952. Stainless steel, longest (knife) l. 7 3/4 x w. 3/4" (19.7 x 1.9 cm), shortest (spoon) l. 6 x w. 1 1/8" (15.2 x 2.9 cm). Mfr.: C. Hugo Pott, Germany. Gift of H.E. Lauffer Co. MoMA.

Wakisaka, Katsuji (1944–)

Japanese textile designer.

Training 1960–63, in textile design, Kyoto.
Biography 1963–65, Wakisaka worked for Itoh in Osaka; 1965–68, for Samejima in Kyoto; 1968–76, designed printed fabrics for Marimekko in Helsinki (including a number of motifs for children); from 1976, created patterns for printed and woven fabrications by Jack Larsen of New York and by Wacoal of Tokyo. Wakisaka has returned to designing for Marimekko, with numerous early playful patterns still in production, and recently designed *jikatabi* (traditional Japanese split-toe shoes) by Sou-Sou in Kyoto.
Exhibition Wacoal fabric was subject of a 1980 exhibition sponsored by the Japan Design Committee.
Bibliography 'Bright Spell Forecast,' *Design*, no. 289, Oct. 1973: 58–61. Cat., Kathryn B. Hiesinger and George H. Marcus III (eds.), *Design Since 1945*, Philadelphia: Philadelphia Museum of Art, 1983.

Wall, James (1877–1952); Gertrude Wall (1881–1971)

British ceramists; active US; husband and wife.

Biographies James Wall worked for Royal Doulton ceramics works before settling in the US; 1922 with his wife Gertrude, established the Walrich Pottery in California. It was named after their son, RICHard WALl. The spirit of their work was akin to that of their pottery neighbor California Faience and of Marblehead Pottery in Massachusetts. Furniture designer/producer Gustav Stickley expressed a fondness for the simplicity of their wares, which featured monochromatic glazes applied to simple forms, with one color complementing the other. Many of the glazes were developed by James Wall. 1930s, its production ended. Subsequently, Gertrude Wall was an instructor in various arts-and-crafts programs. Richard Wall worked for Westinghouse in Emeryville, Cal., where high-voltage porcelain insulators were produced, and later taught firing techniques to art students in some schools in San Francisco.
Bibliography Paul Evans in Timothy J. Andersen et al., *California Design 1910*, Salt Lake City: Peregrine Smith, 1980: 74, 77.

Wallance, Donald A. (1909–1990)

American metalworker and furniture designer; born New York; active Croton-on-Hudson, N.Y.

Training To 1930, New York University; 1936–40, Design Laboratory, New York.
Biography 1940–41, Wallance was the design and technical director of the National Youth Administration in Louisiana; during World War II, was active in the Office of the Quartermaster General, Washington, D.C., participating in a variety of design projects; subsequently, became a consultant on the design of mass-produced furniture for soldiers' families living abroad; 1944, was discharged but continued to work for the Quartermaster Corps to 1948; 1949, established a small studio in Croton-on-Hudson, N.Y. (near New York City), where he worked alone and occasionally collaborated on graphic-design projects with his wife Shula. Influenced by the Arts and Crafts movement, he labeled himself an 'industrial craftsman'; became well known, but not today, for his book *Shaping America's Products* (New York: Reinhold, 1956). 1951, he began designing tableware, cutlery, and accessories by H.E. Lauffer. His 1952 Design 1 brushed stainless-steel cutlery was designed for Lauffer and produced by Pott in Germany. Other work: 1958–64 hospital furniture by Hard Manufacturing of Buffalo, N.Y., and a 1959 range of cooking and serving pieces by Kensington (Aluminum Company of America). c. 1960, he was a consultant and designer on Philharmonic Hall, Lincoln Center, New York, where his 1964 auditorium seating was installed. Subsequent designs: 1978–79 Design 10 plastic cutlery by Lauffer (so named because it was his 10th design by Lauffer), for which the obsessive Wallance made wooden models first and plastic next, conducted extensive tests with various types of plastics, and developed a special mold that effected a finish to diminish scratching. His archive is housed in the Cooper-Hewitt National Design Museum, New York.
Citations Golden Form award (for Bedford stainless-steel cutlery), fair in Jaarbeurs, Utrecht, Netherlands.
Bibliography Donald A. Wallance, 'Design in Plastics,' *Everyday Art Quarterly*, vol. 6, 1947: 3–4, 15. Ada Louise Huxtable, 'Stainless Comes to Dinner,' *Industrial Design*, vol. 1, Aug. 1954: 30–38. Cat., Kathryn B. Hiesinger and George H. Marcus III (eds.), *Design Since 1945*, Philadelphia: Philadelphia Museum of Art, 1983. Mel Byars with Arlette Barré-Despond, *100 Designs/100 Years: A Celebration of the 20th Century*, Hove: RotoVision, 1999: 168–69.

Wallander, Alf (1862–1914)

Swedish painter, ceramicist, metalworker, and glassware, furniture, and textile designer.

Training 1879–85, Kungliga Tekniska Högskolan, Stockholm; 1885–89, Academie Morot & Constant, Paris.
Biography 1895–1910, Wallander worked at Rörstrand in Lidköping, where, from 1900, he was its artistic director; designed furniture and textiles by Svensk Konstslöjdsutställning Selma Giöbel, where, from 1899, he was director; 1908–09, designed glassware by Kosta glassworks and, 1908–14, by Reijmyre glassworks; from 1908, was a senior tutor, Kungliga Tekniska Högskolan, Stockholm.
Exhibitions Work shown at 1897 *Konstoch Industriutställningen* (work by Rörstrand), Stockholm; 1900 *Exposition Universelle*, Paris.
Bibliography Cat., David Revere McFadden (ed.), *Scandinavian Modern Design 1880–1980*, New York: Abrams, 1982. Jennifer Hawkins Opie, *Scandinavia: Ceramics and Glass in the Twentieth Century*, New York: Rizzoli, 1989.

Wallén, Pia (1957–)

Swedish designer; born Umeå.

Training 1980–83, fashion design, Anders Beckman School of Design, Stockholm.
Biography Based on her fashion studies, Wallén has used felt and wood fabric in unexpected and new ways for a variety of domestic products and clothes, describing her work in felt as 'one of the world's oldest textile techniques.' She designed the pleated felt curtains for the cinema of the Moderna Museet and auditorium of Arkitekturmuseet, both Sweden and both 1997. Her 1992 three-piece felt slippers with her distinctive contrasting stitching were widely published. Primarily a fashion designer, Wallén has also designed interiors and felt furnishings and tabletop objects, including products by David Design; 1993 Crux (cross) blankets and 1998 Crux rug and other rugs by Asplund in felt and bowls, jewelry with colored felt, clothes, and bags, based on the construction of the tennis ball, in Asplund's 2000 Dot Collection; also products in 1992 Progretto Ogetto collection by Cappellini.
Exhibitions/citations From 1986, work included in large number of exhibitions, including at the House of Culture, Stockholm, and Victoria and Albert Museum, London, and in *French and Scandinavian Design*, Copenhagen; *Swedish Style*, Tokyo; *Design World 2000*, Konstindustrimuseet, Helsinki. Awards include Swedish Fashion Council designer prize (felt garments); 1989 Designer of the '90s, *Sköna Hem* interior-design magazine; 1993 Swedish Artists' Board citation (for ten-year work grant); two Utmärkt Svensk Form citations (for outstanding Swedish design for carpets, and felt garments).

Walrich Pottery
> See Wall, James.

Walsh Walsh, John
British glassware manufacturer; located Birmingham.

History 1850, John Walsh Walsh bought a glassworks in Birmingham, England, which had been in operation for a century before. The factory developed 'opaline brocade' glass in c. 1897; made a large amount of glassware in styles popular at the turn of the century, with historicist deeply cut crystal its specialty. Early 20th century, the factory continued historicist and also Victorian types, popular with the British. 1923, the firm became publicly held and managed by John's grandsons Philip and Sydney Walker; became known as the Soho and Vesta Glass Works. 1928, John's great-grandson W.G. Riley was director of the firm, which made the popular 1929 Pompeiian glassware with random bubbles, a departure for the firm, and introduced blown glass with an iridescence; 1930s, made glass in modern forms. Designer/sculptor Walter Gilbert designed 1930–31 lighting panels. 'Clyne' Farquharson, the John Walsh Walsh head designer from 1935–51, designed, pressed, and engraved vases and bowls by the firm. Due to World War II, production stopped in 1942 but, after the war, continued only to 1951.
Exhibitions Pompeiian ware shown at 1929 British Industries Fair. Work by Farquharson in 2004 *English Glass Between the Wars: Cut glass from 1930–1939 by Keith Murray & Clyne Farquharson*, Hamilton Art Gallery, Victoria, Australia.
Bibliography Frederick Cooke, *Glass: Twentieth-Century Design*, New York: Dutton, 1986: 60, 67–68. Charles R. Hajdamach, Broadfield House Glass Museum, *British Glass, 1800–1914*; Woodbridge, Suffolk: Antique Collectors' Club, 1991. Victor Arwas, *The Art of Glass*, New York: Rizzoli, 1997. Eric Reynolds, *The Glass of John Walsh Walsh, 1850–1951*, Shepton Beauchamp: Richard Dennis, 1999.
> See Farquharson, 'Clyne' William.

Walter, Almaric (1859–1942)
French glassmaker and ceramicist; born Sèvres.

Training École Nationale de la Manufacture de Sèvres.
Biography 1902, Almaric began working with *pâte-de-verre* and, 1908–14, executed glass sculptures in the material at Daum in Nancy, based on models by Henri Bergé, the factory's artistic director. 1919, Walter established his own workshop, where he continued with *pâte-de-verre* objects; by 1925, had ten employees; produced windows and objects based on models such as the Tanagra figurines in the Musée du Louvre in Paris and 18th-century reliefs.
Bibliography Yvonne Brunhammer et al., *Art Nouveau Belgium, France*, Houston: Rice University, 1976.

Walters, Carl (1883–1955)
American ceramicist; active Woodstock, N.Y.

Training 1905–07, Minneapolis School of Art; 1908–11 under Robert Henri, New York School of Fine Arts, New York.
Biography 1919, Walters established a workshop in Cornish, N. H.; 1920, moved to Woodstock, N.Y., where he first produced ceramic candlesticks, bowls, plates, and vases with applied calligraphic motifs inspired by Persian pottery and, subsequently, made whimsical ceramic animals based on hollow clay forms.
Bibliography 'Carl Walters—Sculptor of Ceramics,' *Index of Twentieth-Century Artists*, June 1936: 305. Garth Clark, *A Century of Ceramics in the United States, 1878–1978*, New York: Dutton/Everson Museum of Art, 1979: 338.

Walton, Allan (1891–1948)
British painter, decorator, architect, and textile designer and manufacturer; active London.

Training Under an architect, apprenticeship, London; painting, Slade School of Art, London; under W.R. Sickert, Westminster School of Art; Académie de la Grande Chaumière, Paris.
Biography Walton was a member of the 'London Group' of artists; 1925 with his brother, established Allan Walton Textiles in London and commissioned some of the most enterprising screen prints of 1930s, designed by Vanessa Bell and Duncan Grant. He designed carpets, embroideries, and printed fabrics and, late 1920s, became the head of the decorating department, Fortnum and Mason department store, London, for whose clients he decorated fashionable and stylish décors, occasionally with wall decorations painted by John Armstrong; decorated 1925 Restaurant Français, Leicester Square, London, and 1927 Restaurant Boulestin, Covent Garden, London, both with Clough Williams-Ellis and overseen by X. Marcel Boulestin. Their design for Restaurant Français was innovative, attracting a clientele who came there as much for the décor as the food. He was an influential propagandist of so-called good design and a member of most of the British industrial-design and art-education organizations; 1943– 45, was director, Glasgow School of Art.
Exhibitions Frequently showed paintings and watercolors.
Bibliography Cat., *Thirties: British Art and Design Before the War*, London: Arts Council of Great Britain/Hayward Gallery, 1979. Stephen Calloway, *Twentieth-Century Decoration*, New York: Rizzoli, 1988: 167, 235. Valerie Meads, The *Victoria & Albert Museum's Textile Collection, British Textiles from 1900 to 1937*, London: Victoria and Albert Museum, 1992.

Walton, George Henry (1867–1933)
British architect and designer; born and active Glasgow.

Training Evening classes, Glasgow School of Art.
Biography Walton spent the first ten years of his career in Glasgow; 1888, established a retail shop and a decorating workshop there. His commissions included 1897–98 designs for Clutha glass by James Couper & Sons, stained-glass panels by William Burrell, furniture by and interiors for Liberty's, and the refurbishment of Miss Cranston's tea rooms (previously designed by Charles Rennie Mackintosh) on Argyle and Buchanan Streets, Glasgow. 1898, he settled in London; designed interiors for Kodak in Glasgow, Brussels, Vienna, Milan, London, Moscow, and St. Petersburg. Even though closely associated with the Arts and Crafts movement, Walton's designs were more subdued than those of Mackintosh and Christopher Dresser. Working in a rectilinear manner, his exaggeratedly vertical interiors incorporated white-painted full-length wall panels. His furniture was influenced by Sheraton and Chippendale, and his interiors featured inglenooks with built-in settles, and sideboards at the ends of rooms, Arts and Crafts predilections. Later in his career he designed and built houses in London, Oxfordshire, Wales, and France. 1901 'The Leys' house near Elstree, Hertfordshire, exemplifies his mature style.
Bibliography Elizabeth Aslin, *The Journal of The Decorative Arts Society 1890–1940*, Decorative Arts Society, 1980. Stephen Calloway, *Twentieth-Century Decoration*, New York: Rizzoli, 1988: 66. K. Moon, *George Walton: Designer and Architect*, Oxford: White Cockade, 1993.

Wanders, Marcel (1963–)
Dutch designer; active Amsterdam.

Training 1981–82, Academie voor Industriele Vormgeving, Eindhoven; 1982–85, Academie voor Toegepaste Kunsten, Maastricht 1983–85, Academie voor Schone Kunsten, Hasselt, Belgium; 1985–88, Hogeschool voor de Kunsten, Arnhem.
Biography Wanders began his professional career working in Dutch

Carl Walters. Plate. 1937. Glazed ceramic, h. 1 3/4" (4.4 cm) x dia. 11 1/4" (28.6 cm). Mfr.: the designer, US. Gift of Abby Aldrich Rockefeller. MoMA.

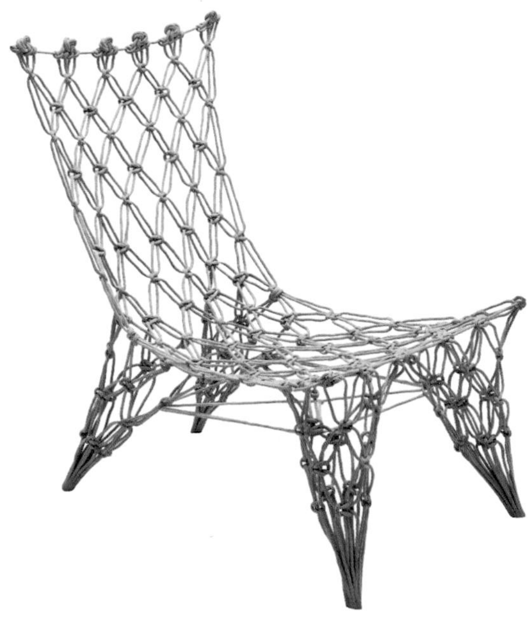

Marcel Wanders. Knotted Chair. 1995. Carbon fibers and epoxy-coated aramid fibers, 28 x 19 3/4 x 24 1/2" (71.1 x 50.2 x 62.2 cm). Mfr.: the designer, the Netherlands. Gift of the Peter Norton Family Foundation. MoMA.

firms and studios (1986, Artifort, Maastricht; 1987, BRS Premsela Vonk–Gijs Bakker, Amsterdam); 1988, became an independent industrial designer; 1992 with four other former fellow students, founded WAA design consultancy, serving clients such as KLM. Subsequently, he designed for Apple, Auping, KPN, Swatch, and Droog Design (including a CD with 'ambient dance music' and about a dozen more products). 1995, he established his own studio, Wanders Wonders, now with a staff of seven women; developed his own consumer label. Recent clients for furniture, lighting, and accessories: Auping, Authentics, British Airways, Boffi, Flos, Habitat, KLM, Magis, Mandarina Duck, Rosenthal, Salviati, Virgin Atlantic, and WMF. His best-known design is 1995 aramid-and-carbon-fiber Knotted Chair, marketed by Droog Design, later by Cappellini. Other work: Royal Wing (VIP lounge) in the Dutch Pavilion, *Expo 2000*, Hanover; 1997, participated in the high-tech experimental program, Technische Universiteit, Delft (from which the Knotted Chair stemmed). From 1987, has taught and been a guest lecturer at a number of schools; 2001, established Moooi as a manufacturing/editing entity for designs by himself and others.
Exhibitions/citations Work included in *Design World 2000*, Konstindustrimuseet, Helsinki; numerous others. Subject of 2003 *The Wonderful Marcel Wanders*, Vessel Gallery, London. Received 1986 first prize, Café Modern design competition, Nescafé; 1996 Kho Liang Ie applied-arts consolation prize, Amsterdam Fonds voor de Kunst; 1997 Designprijs Rotterdam (for Knotted Chair); 1993 and 2000 (two citations) Designprijs, Rotterdam; 2000 George Nelson Award, *Interiors* magazine; 2001 Designer of the Year category, Rave Awards, *Wired* magazine; 2002 invitational competition (with 23 others), Museum Het Kruithuis, 's-Hertogenbosch, for the design of a crown (his entry in ProtoFunctional WaterClear plastic by DSM Somos) for the wedding of Prince Willem-Alexander and Maxima Zorreguita.
Bibliography Mel Byars, *50 Chairs...*, Hove: RotoVision, 1966. Mel Byars, *50 Products: Innovations in Design and Materials*, Hove: RotoVision, 1999. Mel Byars, *Design in Steel*, London: Laurence King, 1999. Mel Byars with Arlette Barré-Despond, *100 Designs/100 Years: A Celebration of the 20th Century*, Hove: RotoVision, 1999: 202–03. Y. Joris (ed.), *Wander's Wonders: Design for a New Age*, Rotterdam: 010, 1999.
> See Moooi.

Wanscher, Ole (1903–1985)

Danish architect, furniture designer, and writer; son of art historian and sculptor Vilhelm Wanscher.

Training Bygningsteknisk Skole; to 1929, School of Cabinetmaking, Det Kongelige Danske Kunstakademi, Copenhagen.
Biography 1924–27 while under Kaare Klint at the Copenhagen academy, Wanscher worked for him, having become a follower; 1928, established his own office in Copenhagen and designed furniture that called on high standards of woodworking and cabinetmaking. He cofounded the Cabinetmakers' Autumn Exhibition (S.E.), Copenhagen; 1955–73, filled the position held by Klint, who died 1954, as professor of architecture, Det Kongelige Danske Kunstakademi. His furniture—heavily influenced by historical Egyptian, English, Greek and Chinese furniture—included models by A.J. Iversen; 1951 easy chair in oak and wickerwork by Rud Rasmussen Snedkerier Aps; 1951 rocking chair by France & Søn. Models by P. Jeppesen Møbelfabrik (now P.J. Furniture): 1949 armchair (no. 149), 1953 Benedikte reclining and 1963 Benedikte dining chairs, 1960 folding Egyptian stool, 1962 rosewood armchair (reminiscent of his 1959 rosewood-and-leather chair/ottoman, with or without arms). Wanscher considered construction to be primary and treated furniture as if it were architecture; wrote books including *Furniture Types* (1932), *Outline History of Furniture* (1941), *English Furniture 1680–1800* (1944), *Møbelkunsten* (the art of furnituremaking), and *Studier i Møbeltypernes Æstetik og Historie* (studies in the aesthetics and history of furniture types) (1946–56) (new edition: *Møbelkunsten, Typer og Interiører fra fem Aartusinder*, or the art of furnituremaking, types and interiors from five millennia, Copenhagen: Thaning og Appels, 1966).
Exhibitions/citations Work included in 1937 *Exposition Internationale des Arts et Techniques dans la Vie Moderne*, Paris; 1942 *Dansk Kunsthåndværk*, Nationalmuseet, Stockholm; 1956–59 *Neue Form aus Dänemark*, touring Germany; 1958 *Formes Scandinaves*, Musée des Arts Décoratifs, Paris; 1960–61 *The Arts of Denmark*, touring the US; 1964–65 *Formes Danoises*, France; 1964–67 *Design in Scandinavia*, touring the US. Gold medal, 1960 (11th) Triennale di Milano; 1966 Georg Jensen Sølvsmedie design competition (silver cutlery). 1963–68, he was a fellow, Det Kongelige Danske Kunstakademi (from 1968, a member).
Bibliography Cat., *Georg Jensen Silversmithy: 77 Artists, 75 Years*, Washington, D.C.: Smithsonian, 1980. Cat., David Revere McFadden (ed.), *Scandinavian Modern Design 1880–1980*, New York: Abrams, 1982: 272, no. 219. Frederik Sieck, *Nutidig Dansk Møbeldesign – en kortfattet illustreret beskrivelse*, Copenhagen: Bondo Gravesen, 1990.

Ward, Neville (1922–1989)

British interior designer.

Training Architecture, Liverpool University; Edinburgh College of Art.
Biography 1948, Ward established the practice Ward and Austin, now called Ward Associates. He designed the original façade of the Design Centre in the Haymarket, London; a Thames-side restaurant adjunct to 1951 *Festival of Britain*; interiors of Sealink ferries' 1960 oceanliner *Oriana*, and other ships; numerous exhibitions; products, ranging from pianos to decorative laminates.

Wardle, Thomas (1831–1909)

British fabric designer; born Macclesfield, Cheshire.

Biography Wardle became knowledgeable about old and new dyeing techniques through his father, a well-established silk dyer; 1870, met William Morris through his brother-in-law George Wardle, the general manager of Morris and Co. Thomas Wardle and Morris shared an interest in traditional silk-dyeing techniques. Mid-1870s, Wardle printed 14 designs for Morris and Co. However, by 1881, Morris had become dissatisfied with Wardle's work and began his own production in Merton Abbey. 1881, Wardle established Wardle & Co. in Leek to dye silk embroidery threads and yarns for woven textiles and velvets; also imported silk from India, which he dyed or overprinted; commissioned Walter Crane, Lewis F. Day, C.F.A. Voysey, and Léon Solon to design for his firm; was a cofounder of the Silk Association. 1879, his wife Elizabeth established the Leek Embroidery Society. He wrote the books *On the Present Development of Power-Loom Weaving of Silk Fabrics at Lyon* (Manchester: Wm. Harris, 1893) and *Kashmir: Its New Silk Industry...* (London: Simkin, Marshall..., 1904).

Ware, Alice Hathaway Cunningham (b. Alice Hathaway Cunningham 1851–1937)

American amateur ceramicist and woodcarver; born Cambridge, Mass.; active Boston and Milton, Mass.

Training From 1905 under Philip Hale, drawing, Museum of Fine Arts, Boston.

Biography 1870s, she became a ceramicist. Her work was compared to that of Hannah Barlow of Doulton in the UK and Laura Fry in Cincinnati, Ohio, US. Her interest in Japanese motifs was fostered by her father's involvement in the China trade. She became in charge of porcelain-painting classes at Museum of Fine Arts, Boston; painted oils, watercolors, and pastels; also painted tiles to be applied to fireplaces, still seen today in some homes in Milton, Mass.
Exhibitions Work included in Women's Pavilion, 1876 *Centennial Exhibition*, Philadelphia; 1899 Boston Society of Arts and Crafts exhibition (wood carvings).
Bibliography Emma Forbes Ware, *Genealogy: Robert Ware of Dedham, Massachusetts, (1642–1699), and His Lineal Descendants*, Boston: C.H. Pope, 1901: 286. Obituary, 'Mrs. William R. Ware', *The New York Times*, 2 Apr. 1937: 23. Doreen Bolger Burke et al., *In Pursuit of Beauty: Americans and the Aesthetic Movement*, New York: Metropolitan Museum of Art/Rizzoli, 1987: 479.

Warkuß, Harmut (1940–)
German automobile designer; born Wroclaw.

Biography 1964–68, Warkuß designed for Audio and then for Ford; 1968–76, was a designer at Audio, where he was responsible for design from 1976–94, designing the 1994 Avus (with 'J.' Mays). 1994, Warkuß was replaced by Peter Schreyer and, thence from 1994–2004, was in charge of the overall design program of VAG, or the Audi group (Audi, Seat, Audi, and Lamborghini). Schreyer was active in the Wolfsburg facility; Warkuß in Martorell, Spain. Warkuß designed 1999 Bugatti EB 16/4 Veyron (with Fabrizio Giugiaro) and 1999 Bugatti EB 18/3 Chiron.
Bibliography Penny Sparke, *A Century of Car Design*, London: Mitchell Beazley, 2002. Marco Degl'innocenti, *Harmut Warkuß: Volkswagen Design*, Milan: Automobilia, 2002

Wärff, Ann
> See Wolff, Ann.

Warner and Sons
British textile manufacturer; located Braintree, Essex.

History 1870, Warner, Sillet and Ramm was founded by Benjamin Warner (1828–1908) to take advantage of the thwarting of the French silk industry caused by the Franco-Prussian War. Warner's became the leading 19th- and 20th-century silk weavers and cotton printers; was known as Warner and Ramm 1875–92 and Warner and Sons after 1892. The firm was noted for its high-quality technical achievements and designs; hired leading designers of the day. Warner himself was interested in improving contemporary and early commissioned designer Owen Jones. Others designing for Warner's included B.J. Talbert, Walter Crane, E.W. Godwin, G.C. Haité and the Silver Studio. The firm supplied Liberty's, Collinson & Lock and Debenham & Freebody. Its 1930s designers included Alec Hunter, Eileen Hunter, and Theo Moorman. Moorman and Alec Hunter were responsible for handwoven prototypes intended for power-loom production. As production manager 1932–58, Alec Hunter oversaw style and design and worked with the freelance designers, who were often not weavers, to translate their motifs into machine-woven goods. Warner's fabrications included those in natural yarns, sometimes with trial rayon, metallic strips, and cellophane.
Bibliography Cat., *A Century of Warner Fabrics, 1870 to 1970*, London: Victoria and Albert Museum, 1973. Cat., *Thirties: British Art and Design Before the War*, London: Arts Council of Great Britain/Hayward Gallery, 1979. Cat., Hester Bury, *A Choice of Design 1850–1980: Fabrics by Warner and Sons Ltd*, Braintree: Warner, 1981. Mary Schoeser, *Owen Jones Silks*, Braintree: Warner, 1987.

Warren and Fuller
American wallpaper manufacturer; located New York.

History 1855, the firm of J.S. Warren was founded; subsequently, produced patterned paper in the style of the Aesthetic Movement. 1882, John H. Lange became a partner of J.S. Warren and William H. Fuller. Clarence Cook was engaged to write the history of the firm and describe its papers, in the small book *What Shall We Do Without Walls?* (New York, 1880; reprinted 1881). In it, Louis Comfort Tiffany's and Samuel Colman's designs for the firm were illustrated. In the firm's 1881 design competition, Warren and Fuller received entries from Britain, France, Germany, and the US; the judges were furniture maker Christian Herter, metalworker Edward C. Moore, and painter Francis Lathrop. The four prizes went to Americans, including Candace Wheeler (first prize for a bee-motif paper) and her daughter Dora Wheeler (fourth prize). The firm produced a full range of papers, including plain and embossed, bronzed and iridescent, washable 'tile' motif, fireproof asbestos, and flocked.
Exhibition Work shown at 1893 *World's Columbia Exposition*, Chicago.
Bibliography Catherine Lynn, *Wallpaper in America: From the Seventeenth Century to World War I*, New York: Norton, 1980. Charles C. Oman and Jean Hamilton, *Wallpapers: A History and Illustrated Catalogue of the Collection of the Victoria and Albert Museum*, London: Victoria & Albert Museum; New York: Abrams, 1982: 73, 77. Doreen Bolger Burke et al., *In Pursuit of Beauty: Americans and the Aesthetic Movement*, New York: Metropolitan Museum of Art/Rizzoli, 1987.

Watanabe, Riki (1911–)
Japanese designer; born Tokyo.

Training To 1936, industrial woodworking, Industrial Academy, Tokyo.
Biography After the Academy, Riki Watanabe worked for the Industrial Laboratory in the Gunma Prefecture, where Bruno Taut was teaching woodworking and bamboo craft; 1949, established an eponymous firm; designed furniture by Kiyoshi Seike and, with Isamu Kenmochi, a public bar. 1952, Riki Watanabe, Sōri Yanagi, Isamu Kenmochi founded the Japan Industrial Designer Association, of which Watanabe was the first chairperson; 1956, reinterpreted traditional rattan furniture; after 1980, designed interiors of the Prince Hotel chain, Japan. Work has included 1952 Rope chair, 1957 Torii stool, 1967 Center table, 1966 Riki stool, 1999 Uni tray range, and a recent collection of wristwatches by Alba.
Bibliography 'Riki Watanabe Collection,' *Living Design*, no. 18.

Waterer, John William (1892–1977)
British leather-goods designer.

Biography Waterer was managing director of S. Clark, for which he designed and produced luggage and other leather goods; was the instigator of the use of the zipper on luggage and inventor of the lightweight suitcase; wrote numerous books (see below) in an arcane style of lengthy sentences; was a specialist on a number of subjects, including Islamic-Spanish córdovan leather of the Middle Ages. He and Claude Spiers founded the collection at the Museum of Leathercraft, Northampton (one of three worldwide dedicated to leather).
Bibliography John W. Waterer, *Leather in Life, Art and Industry...*, London: Faber & Faber, 1946. John W. Waterer, *Leather and Craftsmanship*, London: Faber & Faber, 1950. John W. Waterer, *Leather*, Oxford: Clarendon, c. 1956. John William Waterer, 'Birth and Growth of a New Museum—The Museum of Leathercraft,' *Museum Journal*, no. 66, Dec 1966: 203–12. John W. Waterer, *Leather Craftsmanship*, London: G. Bell & Sons, 1968. Cat., Neil MacGregor, *A Catalogue of Leather in Life, Art and Industry: John W. Waterer, 1892–1977, A Centenary Exhibition*, Northampton: Museum of Leathercraft, 1992.

Waterford Crystal; Penrose Glass House
Irish glass manufacturer.

History 1783, George and William Penrose, who were brothers and Quakers, established crystal-making factory Penrose Glass House, located beside Merchants' Quay at the port of Waterford in Ireland. The business was costly to set up, with the intention to make fine, clear crystal equal to the highest standards of Continental Europe. John Hill, also a Quaker, managed the 50 to 70 employees. Exportation was highly active, to Spain, the America colonies, the West Indies, and Newfoundland, and the enterprise became successful. Its production was favored by some wealthy people such as King George III, who ordered a set of Waterford crystal for use at his resort. However, new owner George Gatchell closed the factory in 1851, primarily due to exorbitant British excise taxes. The enterprise was thus dormant for 103 years, until the mood of an anticipated independent Irish republic (made official in 1948) was fomenting the Irish people's interest in the value of the Irish arts. And based on this tenor of the time, a small factory to be known as Waterford Crystal was founded quite near the original site in 1947. Today some of the early cutting motifs are again being produced, including Lismore. Recently, the product range has been expanded to include china, linens, stainless-steel cutlery, pens, jewelry, and specialty items. 1991, Waterford introduced Marquis, the first new pattern since the company's demise. 1986, Waterford Crystal bought Wedgwood to form the conglomer-

ate Waterford Wedgwood plc., which in turn acquired a major share of Rosenthal porcelain/glass in 1998 (with the share increased to 90% in 2001). The entity acquired Stuart & Sons glass in 1998, All-Clad cookware in 1999, Hutschenreuther ceramics in 2000, and W-C Designs textiles in 2001. The Waterford Wedgwood headquarters are in Kilbarry, Ireland. (As a separate and unrelated entity, engraver/designer John Coughlan re-formed the Penrose business in 1974 as Penrose Crystal at 32a John Street in the city of Waterford.)
Citation Gold medal (to Penrose Crystal), 1851 *Great Exposition*, London.
> See Wedgwood.

Watrous, Gilbert A. (1919–)
American industrial designer; active San Diego, Cal.

Training Industrial design, Illinois Institute of Technology, Chicago.
Biography 1957–c. 1962, Watrous was a partner in the studio Visual and Industrial Design in San Diego, where he designed products for various clients, including air conditioning units by Convair and audio equipment by Stromberg-Carlson.
Citations Special prize (1950 floor lamp with a fully-articulated adjustable arm on a low tripod base, by Heifetz Mfg. Co.), 1950 international competition for lamp design, The Museum of Modern Art, New York.
Bibliography William J. Hennessey, *Modern Furnishing for the Home*, vol. 1, New York: Rheinhold, 1952: 245; New York: Acanthus, 1997 reprinted ed. Cat., Kathryn B. Hiesinger and George H. Marcus III (eds.), *Design Since 1945*, Philadelphia: Philadelphia Museum of Art, 1983.

Waugh, Sidney (1904–1963)
American sculptor and glassware designer; born Amherst, Mass.

Training Amherst (Massachusetts) College; School of Architecture, Massachusetts Institute of Technology (MIT), Cambridge, Mass.; École des Beaux-Arts, Paris; apprenticeship under and assistant to Henri Bouchard

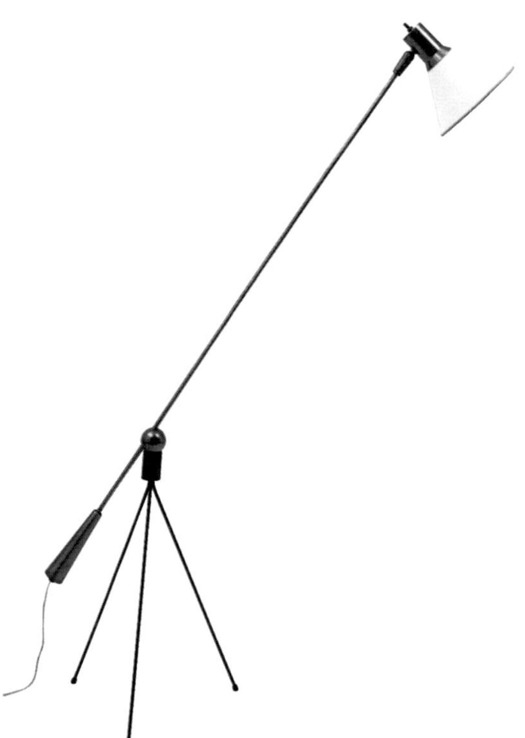

Gilbert A. Watrous. Floor lamp. 1950. Enameled steel, steel, lead, brass, and linen, articulable stand h. 19 to 55" (48.3 to 139.7 cm). Mfr.: Heifetz Mfg. Co., US. MoMA.

Biography Waugh created a number of international monuments, including *Andrew Mellon* (1952), Washington, D.C.; 1942–57, was director, Rhinehart School of Sculpture, Baltimore. 1933, Waugh and Arthur Houghton reorganized Steuben Glass, where he was the chief associate designer and the artistic advisor to his death. Waugh designed both the form and the engraved motifs for Steuben glass pieces, particularly one-of-a-kind examples such as The Devil and Daniel Webster bowl, based on Stephen Vincent Benét's poem, and the widely published 1935 Gazelle bowl, still in production by Steuben for an extemely high price. His large body of glass work also included 'The Arts' trophy for the Henry Johnson Fisher Lifetime Achievement Award, Magazine Publishers Association, US. He wrote the books *The Art of Glass Making* (New York: Dodd, Mead, 1937) and *The Making of Fine Glass* (New York: Dodd, Mead, 1947).
Citations Received 1929 Prix de Rome; Herbert Adams Memorial Award (for sculpture).
Bibliography *Sidney Waugh*, New York: Norton/National Sculpture Society, 1948. Mary Jean Madigan, *Steuben Glass; An American Tradition in Crystal*, New York: Abrams, 1982.

Weaver, Paul
> See Taylor, Michael.

Webb, Philip (1831–1915)
British architect and designer; born Oxford.

Training 1849–52 under architect John Billing, apprenticeship, Reading.
Biography Webb became the principal assistant in the office of architect G.E. Street in Oxford; while there in 1856, met William Morris and became greatly influenced by the writings of John Ruskin; 1858, established his own office and began to design Morris's 1859 Red House in Bexley Heath. With its asymmetrical and free ground plan and symbiotic interior and exterior, the unpretentious red-brick house became an influential early example of a new type of domestic architecture in the Gothic Revival, or neo-Gothic, style and the first to fully manifest the Arts and Crafts movement. 1861, Webb became a partner in Morris, Marshall, Faulkner and Co., for which he designed solid furniture in oak in a simplified and austere Gothic Revival style, stained glass, book covers, simple small glass items, and metalwork with medieval references. His town and country houses combined medieval and 19th-century elements in an unconventional manner, one of the best known being the 1891 house in Standen, East Grinstead.
Bibliography W.R. Lethaby, *Philip Webb and His Work*, London: Oxford University/Milford, 1935; reprinted, London: Raven Oak, 1979. John Brandon-Jones, 'Philip Webb,' in Peter Ferriday (ed.), *Victorian Architecture*, London: J. Cape, 1963. Robert Macleod, *Style and Society: Architectural Ideology in Britain, 1835–1914*, London: RIBA, 1971. Edward Hollamby, *Red House, Bexleyheath 1859, Architect, Philip Webb*, London: Architecture and Design Technology; New York: Van Nostrand Reinhold, 1991.

Webb and Corbett, Thomas; Webb Corbett
British glassware manufacturer; located Stourbridge, Worcestershire.

History 1897, Thomas Webb and Corbett was established by Thomas and Herbert Webb (connected with Thomas Webb and Sons of the Dennis glassworks) and George Harry Corbett at the White House Glass Works in Wordsley. White House had been previously operated by W.H., B. & J. Richardson. At various times, it operated in two sites in Stourbridge. 1903, Thomas Webb retired due to ill health. 1906, the firm acquired the Tutbury Glass Works in Burton-upon-Trent; by 1914, made glassware in Coalbournhill, Amblecote, with decorating, cutting, and a showroom at White House Glassworks in Wordsley. But after a 1914 fire, all operations were located at Coalbournhill. 1946, Herbert Webb died, and Irene Stevens became a designer at the firm but left in 1957 to teach in the glass department of Stourbridge College. 1953, the name was changed to Webb Corbett Ltd. L. Green designed its 1958 Bouquet range of cut glass, and David, Marquess of Queensberry, its 1963 Queensberry—Harlequin range (centerpieces, bowls, vases, tumblers, etc. in a stark geometrical pattern of clear cut glass). 1965, David Smith became the chief designer for both Stourbridge and Tutbury factories. 1969, the factories were acquired by Royal Doulton, and, 1980, the glassware became only a brand, known as 'Royal Doulton Crystal by Webb Corbett,' and Tutbury factory was closed. 1986, the Webb Corbett brand was discontinued to become known only as 'Royal Doulton Crystal.'

Exhibition/citation Subject of 1997 centenary exhibition, Broadfield House, Kingswinford, West Midlands, England. 1964 Duke of Edinburgh's Prize for Elegant Design (Queensberry—Harlequin range).
Bibliography Frederick Cooke, *Glass: Twentieth-Century Design*, New York: Dutton, 1986: 77, 78–79.

Webb and Sons, Thomas

British glassware manufacturer.

History 1829, Thomas Webb (1804–69) entered the glassmaking industry and, subsequently, became a partner of Webb and Richardsons in Wordsley, taking over the Wordsley Flint Glassworks from the Wainwright Brothers. 1833, Webb's father John Webb also entered the glass industry and became a partner of John Shepherd at the neighboring White House glassworks. On John's 1835 death, Thomas succeeded to his share in the Shepherd and Webb enterprise. 1840, Thomas moved to the Platts in Amblecote and established 'Thomas Webb's Glassworks.' On his 1869 death, his son Thomas Wilkes Webb took over. 1876, John Northwood produced Webb's Denis or Pegasus vase. Webb's famous craftspeople were brothers Thomas (1849–1926) and George Woodall (1850–1925); soon after 1878, it began cameo-glass production. 1877, a patent was taken out by Thomas Webb for the Iris range. Noted Bohemian engraver William Fritsche (c. 1853–1924) was at Webb's for 50 years. The firm was known for its bronze glass from 1873, Peach Bloom glass from 1885, Old Roman from 1888, and Tricolour from 1889. 1919, the Dennis Glassworks association ended. David Hammond designed its 1960s Bodiam cut-glass range. c. 1993, Thomas Webb closed. The trademark was assumed by Edinburgh Crystal, which makes glass in Edinburgh under the Thomas Webb brand.
Exhibitions/citations Grand prizes (to the associated Dennis Glassworks), 1878 and 1889 *Exposition Universelle*, Paris. Thomas Wilkes Webb (son of the founder) elected Chevalier of Légion d'Honneur, France.
Bibliography Victor Arwas, *Glass: Art Nouveau to Art Deco*, New York: Rizzoli, 1977. H.W. Woodward, *Art, Fear and Mystery: The Story of Thomas Webb & Sons Glassmakers*, Stourbridge: Mark & Moody, 1978.

Weber, 'Kem' Karl Emanuel Martin (1889–1963)

German designer; born Berlin; active Hollywood, Cal.

Training 1904, apprenticeship under Eduard Schultz, the royal cabinetmaker in Potsdam; 1908–10, under Bruno Paul, Vereinigte Staatsschulen für freie und angewandte Kunst (Kunstgewerbeschule), Berlin-Charlottenburg, Germany.
Biography While still a student, Weber was involved with the supervision of the German Pavilion construction at 1910 *Exposition Internationale et Universelle de Bruxelles*; 1914, traveled to California to design the German segment of 1915 *Panama-Pacific International Exposition*, San Francisco, and became trapped there by the events of World War I; after the war's end, was refused permission to return to his homeland. Thus, Weber taught and opened a studio in Santa Barbara and thence settled in Los Angeles in 1921, where he worked as a draftsperson from 1922–27 in the design studio of furniture/decorating store Barker Brothers. 1924, he became a naturalized US citizen and, from about this time, was the artistic director at Barker Brothers, responsible for furniture, store interiors, and packaging, and established the Modes and Manner shop/department within the store. 1927, he opened his own studio in Hollywood, dubbing himself an 'industrial designer'; was unable to work in a modern idiom due to postwar anti-German prejudice, although he continued to find some commissions. By 1926, the cultural climate became more sympathetic to modernism, and Weber was virtually the only decorative-arts designer to carry the modern movement to the West Coast, though his style was nevertheless his own. He designed 1927 Today vase and 1928–29 cocktail shakers by Friedman Silver, 1934–35 clocks (including the Zephyr) by Lawson Time Company, and 1929 silver cocktail shaker by Porter Blanchard. Some tea sets after Weber designs have been recently made. His designs for various silver vessels were simple and undecorated and, like all of his work, were intended for industrial production. Though Weber lived in California through 1920s, his effect on design in New York was as great as if he had been a resident of Manhattan. He was an innovator of multifunctional furniture, and his pieces often mimicked the soaring skyscraper silhouette with which Paul Frankl has been likewise identified. The 1929 interiors of Sommer & Kaufman shoe store in San Francisco and 1928–29 Friedman residence in Banning exemplified his more decorative approach. His c. 1934–35 Airline chair featured sweeping arms, was flat-packed for shipping, and was again reproduced in 1993. At first the chair was issued in limited numbers by Weber's own Airline Chair Co.; even so the Walt Disney Studio purchased hundreds. Weber wrote numerous articles on the new streamline aesthetic; 1931–1941, taught, Art Center School (today Art Center College of Design), Pasadena; 1945, returned to Santa Barbara, where he established a studio in his home and designed private homes for the next decade or so.
Exhibitions Work included in 1928 *Exposition of Art in Industry at Macy's*, Macy's department store, New York; 1991 *What Modern Was* (Airline chair), Montréal, and touring the US. Work subject of 1969 *Kem Weber: The Moderne in Southern California 1920 through 1941* (catalog below), and 2000–01 *Designing the Moderne: Kem Weber's Bixby House*; both University of California, Santa Barbara, Cal.
Bibliography Kem Weber, 'What About Modern Art?,' *Retailing*, 23 Nov. 1929: 20. Cat., David Gebhard and Harriette von Breton, *Kem Weber: The Moderne in Southern California 1920 Through 1941*, Santa Barbara: University of California, 1969. Karen Davies, *At Home in Manhattan: Modern Decorative Arts, 1925 to the Depression*, New Haven: Yale, 1983: 72–73. Annelies Krekel-Aalberse, *Art Nouveau and Art Déco Silver*, New York: Abrams, 1989. Cat., Martin Eidelberg (ed.), *Design 1935–1965: What Modern Was*, New York: Musée des Arts Décoratifs/Abrams, 1991.

Philip Webb. Finger bowls. c. 1880. Vaseline glass, each variably 3 x 5 3/4" (7.6 x 14.6 cm). Mfr.: J. Powell & Sons. Dorothy Cullman Purchase Fund. MoMA.

Weckström, Björn (1935–)

Finnish metalworker and jewelry and glassware designer.

Training To 1956, Kultaseppäkoulu, Helsinki.
Biography 1956–63, Weckström was a freelance designer; 1957, a designer at Hopeakontu; from 1963, at Lapponia Jewelry, Helsinki; from 1964, at Kruunukoru. He designed furniture and was a sculptor in various media; 1981, settled in Italy and turned to sculpture exclusively.
Exhibitions/citations Subject of exhibitions in Finland and abroad. Awards at 1960 (12th) Triennale di Milano; 1962 second prize and 1967 medal of merit, Finnish Jewelry Society event; 1968 Lunning Prize; 1971 Pro Finlandia prize; 1972 Illum Prize.
Bibliography Cat., David Revere McFadden (ed.), *Scandinavian Modern Design 1880–1980*, New York: Abrams, 1982. Cat., *The Lunning Prize*, Stockholm: Nationalmuseum, 1986: 184–89.

Wedgwood

British ceramics manufacturer; factory located Burslem and Barlaston.

Training From a young age, an apprentice in various factories.
Biography/history By 1754, Josiah Wedgwood (1730–95) was experimenting with clay bodies and glazes; 1759, founded the ceramics firm that is extant today. In the beginning, he produced ordinary

Josiah Wedgwood. Coffee pot. 1768. Black basalt with glazed interior, 6 5/8 x 7 1/4" x dia. 4 1/4" (16.8 x 18.4 x 10.8 cm). Gift of Josiah Wedgwood & Sons, Inc., of America. Mfr.: Josiah Wedgwood & Sons, US (1952). MoMA.

tableware; by 1764, included ornamental wares, among them classical vases and portrait busts. The firm became one of the first to use artists to design its range of goods and to call on industrial-production techniques. By late 18th century, consultant designers John Flaxman and George Stubbs had been commissioned to design for the firm. Success was achieved through the 1765 creation of an inexpensive, lightweight earthenware known as cream ware or Queen's ware. Production also included fine-grained matt earthenware in black, blue, and other colors, known as jasper ware (from 1774) or, in black, known as basalt ware (from 1768). 1840s–c. 1860, it produced copies of classical antique pottery, and its 1860–c. 1910 range included brightly colored majolica, realized through relief molds (revived earlier by Minton). 1859, Josiah Wedgwood III's grandson Godfrey Wedgwood (1833–1905) joined the firm and became the director at turn of the century. The firm's freelance designers included French painter Émile-Aubert Lessore, who began in 1858 and continued to paint Wedgwood pieces after 1863, even though he returned to France. Others were Walter Crane in 1867–c. 1888 and Christopher Dresser in c. 1866–68. One of Dresser's best-known designs is an 1867 two-handled vase, transfer-printed on unglazed earthenware (illustrated in Dresser's book *Principles of Decorative Design*, 1873). 1880, Thomas Allen, previously at Minton for 27 years, became Wedgwood's artistic director. Under Allen, Wedgwood set up a design department, where Allen instigated a range of *japonisant* ivory-bodied porcelain (like Royal Worcester's) and less expensive transfer-printed 1870s–80s earthenware. 1940, the Wedgwood firm moved to Barlaston, Staffordshire. Its 20th-century designers, who were actively promoted by the firm, included Walter Crane, Susie Cooper, Keith Murray, Eric Ravilious, John Skeaping, and C.F.A. Voysey. The Wedgwood Museum contains the world's largest collection of Wedgwood ceramics, ranging from a unique group of Josiah Wedgwood's original trials of Queen's ware (later delivered in 1774 as a 900-plus-piece dinner service to Czarina Catherine of Russia) to the five-foot (1.52 m) Exhibition Vase by Lessore. 1986, Waterford Crystal bought Wedgwood to form the holding company Waterford Wedgwood.
Bibliography William Burton, *Josiah Wedgwood and His Pottery*, London and New York: Cassell, 1922. Alison Kelly, *Decorative Wedgwood in Architecture and Furniture*, London: Country Life, 1965. Alison Kelly, *The Story of Wedgwood*, London: Faber & Faber, 1962. David Buten and Patricia Pelehach, *Émile Lessore, 1805–1876: His Life*, Merion, Pa.: Buten Museum of Wedgwood, 1979. Robin Reilly and George Savage, *The Dictionary of Wedgwood*, Woodbridge: Antique Collectors' Club, 1980. Maureen Batkin, *Wedgwood Ceramics, 1846–1959: A New Appraisal*, London: Richard Dennis, 1982. Doreen Bolger Burke et al., *In Pursuit of Beauty: Americans and the Aesthetic Movement*, New York: Metropolitan Museum of Art/Rizzoli, 1987: 480–81.

Weedon, Harry W. (1887–1970)

British architect.

Training 1904, in architecture, Birmingham; 1907–12, Royal Academy School, London; 1908–12 under architect R.F. Atkinson, apprenticeship.
Biography 1912, Weedon established his own architecture practice, where he designed cinemas at first, including the 1912–13 example in Perry Barr, Birmingham; 1920s, designed industrial and public buildings, housing developments in Birmingham, and houses in Warwickshire and, subsequently, the renovation of the Deutsch and Brenner factory in Hockley; was an interior-design consultant to Oscar Deutsch's Odeon Theatres, serving as the architecture consultant from c. 1934. His Odeon designs included cinemas 1935 (with J.C. Clavering) in Kingstanding, Birmingham; 1936 (with Clavering and R. Bullivant) in Scarborough; 1936 (with Clavering) in Sutton Coldfield; 1937 (with Bullivant) in Burnley; 1937 (with Budge Reid) in Crewe; 1937 (with Andrew Mather) in Leicester Square, London; and 1938 (with P.J. Price) in Chorley. Weedon developed a design program for the theater chain and oversaw its other architects; 1934–39, was involved in commissions for over 250 cinemas. After World War II, Weedon's firm's architecture included schools and industrial buildings, such as those for carmaker Austin in Longbridge, Birmingham.
Bibliography Cat., *Thirties: British Art and Design Before the War*, London: Arts Council of Great Britain/Hayward Gallery, 1979.

Weese, 'Harry' Harold Mohr (1915–1998)

American architect; born Evanston, Ill.; active Chicago.

Training 1938, bachelor's degree in architecture, Massachusetts Institute of Technology (MIT), Cambridge, Mass.; urban-planning fellowship, Cranbrook Academy, Bloomfield Hills, Mich.
Biography At Cranbrook, Weese worked with Eero Saarinen; from 1940, was employed by Skidmore, Owings & Merrill (SOM) in Chicago; from 1941 during World War II, US Army Corps of Engineers; 1946–47, returned to SOM; 1947, set up Harry Weese Associates in Chicago; throughout his career, was a high-profile advocate of urban planning and architecture concerning contemporary economic, political, and social issues. Best-known work is the metropolitan rail system in Washington, D.C.; U.S. embassy in Accra, Ghana; Arena Stage complex near Washington, D.C. Late 1980s, he headed the restoration of Louis Sullivan's 1887–89 Auditorium Building in Chicago; is possibly unknown for having designed products, such as lighting. He died in Manteno, Ill.
Citations Numerous awards and honors; 1961, elelcted a fellow, American Institute of Architects (AIA).

Wegner, Hans Jørgen (1914–)

Danish designer; son of master cobbler Peter M. Wegner; born Tønder, Jutland.

Training 1931 under a cabinetmaker, apprenticeship in Tønder, and at Teknologisk Institut; 1936–38, Akademiets Arkitektskole, Copen-

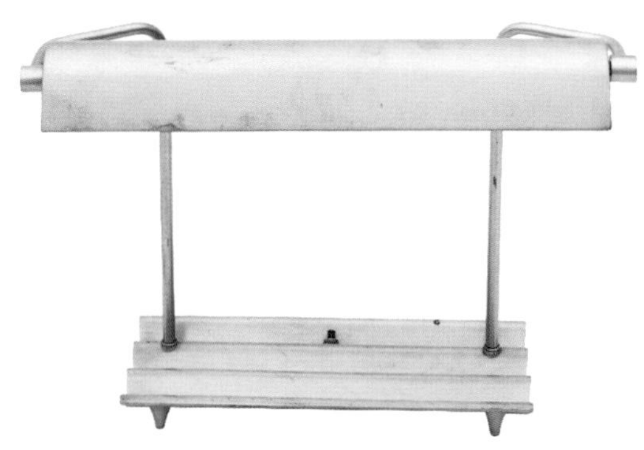

'Harry' Harold Mohr Weese and Benjamin Baldwin. Desk lamp. c. 1940. Metal, 12 1/2 x 17 x 7" (31.8 x 43.2 x 17.8 cm). Mfr.: Mutual Sunset Lamp Mfg. Co., US. Purchase Fund. MoMA.

Hans Wegner. Cowhorn chair (no. PP 505). 1952. Walnut and cane, 29 x 21 3/4 x 16 3/4" (73.7 x 55.3 x 45.1 cm). Mfr.: Johannes Hansen Møbelsnedkeri, Denmark (1958). Phyllis B. Lambert Fund. MoMA.

hagen; 1938, Kunsthåndværkerskolen, Copenhagen.
Biography 1938–43, Wegner was an assistant to Arne Jacobsen and Erik Møller; 1943, opened his own office in Gentofte; 1946–53, was a lecturer, Kunsthåndværkerskolen, Copenhagen. Meeting Johannes Hansens in 1940 or 1941 resulted in his numerous designs for Hansen's Copenhagen furniture workshop, including 1949 Round Chair (or simply 'The Chair' in the US). Following, Wegner designed for AP-Stolen, Carl Hansen, CM Furniture, Danish CWS, FDB, Fritz Hansen, Getama, Planmøbel, P.P. Møbler, and Ry-møbler, creating more than 500 models; also designed the interiors of headquarters of major companies. However, he is best known for his early wood pieces, many of them still in production today. Even so, his subsequent tubular-steel furniture and 1960 Bull leather chair/ottoman are no less distinguished. His historically referenced 1947 Påfuglestolen (peacock) chair by Johannes Hansen features a dramatic bentwood back. Some discontinued furniture models have been reentered into production by others; they include 1960 Ox lounge chair/stool originally by AP-Stolen and now by Erik Jørgensen. In addition to furniture, his work included silverware, lighting, and wallpaper.
Exhibitions/citations Showed work regularly at Cabinetmakers' Autumn Exhibitions (S.E.), Copenhagen; included in a large number of venues worldwide. Received 1951 (1st) Lunning Prize; awards at 1951 (9th) (grand prize), 1954 (10th) (diploma of honor and gold medal), and 1957 (11th) (silver medal) editions of Triennale di Milano; 1956 Eckersberg Medal; 1959 and 1965 Cabinetmakers' Guild prize, Copenhagen; 1959 Citation of Merit, Pratt Institute, Brooklyn, N.Y.; 1961 Prince Eugen Medal; 1961, 1967, and 1968 awards, American Institute of Decorators (AID); 1997 (8th) International Design Award, Osaka. Was elected Honorary Royal Designer for Industry, UK, 1959, and honorary member, Royal Danish Academy of Fine Arts, 1995. Granted an honorary doctoral degree, Royal College of Art, London, 1997.
Bibliography Arne Karlsen, *Made in Denmark*, New York: Rheinhold, 1960. Erik Zahle, *A Treasury of Scandinavian Design*, New York: Golden Press, 1961. Johan Møller-Nielsen, *Wegner: En Dansk Møbelkunstner = Wegner: Sitting Pretty*, Copenhagen: Gyldendal-Johannes Hansen, 1965. Cat., *Modern Chairs 1918–1970*, London: Lund Humphries, 1971. Henrik Sten Møller, *Tema med Variationer: Hans J. Wegner's Møbler,* Tønder: Sønderjyllands Kunstmuseum, 1979. Irving Sloane, 'Hans Wegner: A Modern Master of Furniture Design,' *Fine Woodworking*, no. 20, Jan.–Feb. 1980: 36–42. Cat., David Revere McFadden (ed.), *Scandinavian Modern Design 1880–1980*, New York: Abrams, 1982. Cat., *The Lunning Prize*, Stockholm: Nationalmuseum, 1986. Frederik Sieck, *Nutidig Dansk Møbeldesign – en kortfattet illustreret beskrivelse*, Copenhagen: Bondo Gravesen, 1990. Noritsugu Oda, *Danish Chairs*, San Francisco: Chronicle Books, 1999. Jens Bernsen, *Hans J. Wegner om design = Hans J. Wegner on Design*, Copenhagen: Dansk Design Centre, 1994–95.
> See Hansen, Johannes.

Weihrauch, Svend (1899–1962)

Danish silversmith; active Århus.

Biography For a number of years, Weihrauch worked at the Georg Jensen Sølvesmedie in Copenhagen; from 1928, was the artistic director and shop manager of the firm Frantz Hingelberg in Århus and created about 4,500 designs for hollow-ware, cutlery, and jewelery, some in an Art Déco manner. He developed a new method for attaching insulation materials to metal pots containing hot liquids, primarily for wooden handles and bases. 1931–35, his work was geometric and, from 1935, more organic. From 1940, he called on the use of silver wire in jewelry, thus influencing the design.
Exhibitions Weihrauch's Hingelberg silverware first shown abroad at 1935 *Exposition Universelle et Internationale de Bruxelles*, and, subsequently, 1937 *Exposition Internationale des Arts et Techniques dans la Vie Moderne*, Paris and 1939 *New York World's Fair: The World of Tomorrow.*
Bibliography Jacob Thage, *Danske smykker = Danish Jewelry*, Copenhagen: Komma & Clausen, 1990. Cat., Jörg Schwandt, *Svend Weihrauch: sløv, 1928–1956, en dansk funktionalist = Svend Weihrauch: silber, 1928–1956, ein dänischer Funktionalist*, Kolding: Museet på Koldinghus, 1998. Annelies Krekel-Aalberse, *Art Nouveau and Art Déco Silver*, New York: Abrams, 1989.

Weil, Daniel (1953–)

Argentine architect and designer; born Buenos Aires; active London.

Training To 1977, architecture, University of Buenos Aires; 1978–81, industrial design, Royal College of Art, London.
Biography From 1981, Weil has designed digital clocks, radios, and lighting by his own firm Parenthesis. Viewed both as art and utilitarian objects, his various radio designs—screen-printed in colorful motifs and featuring exposed wiring and electronic parts—were offered both as inexpensive production pieces and as limited-edition items in galleries. Weil believes that design should be not only technical and stylish but also intellectual; has explored the relationship among design, art, and function; uses irony and counter-irony in realizing highly individual pieces that have attained cult status. 1985. Weil and Gerald Taylor founded the design/production firm Parenthesis, where his work included 1981 Bag radio, 1982 Walking radio, 1982 Cambalache radio, 1982 China Wall radio, and 1984 Walter flower vase, Small Door radio, and Claire fruit bowl. His 1981 Bag radio renamed as

Svend Weihrauch. Pitcher. 1946. Silver and ivory, h. 7 1/2" (19.1 cm). Mfr.: Frantz Hingelberg, Denmark. Gift of Franklin Field. MoMA.

Daniel Weil. Bag radio. 1981. Flexible PVC casing, 11 1/2 x 8 5/16" (29.2 x 21.1 cm). Mfr.: Parenthesis, UK. Skidmore, Owings & Merrill Design Collection Purchase Fund. MoMA.

1984 Andante, a deconstructed assemblage of colorful separated parts in a clear plastic bag to be wall-hung, to become part of the Anthologie Quartett collection. 1980s, Weil designed unrealized products (1985 trays and baskets) for Alessi. His 1985 Light Box publication contains a sketchbook and a collection of objects, including a silkscreen print on fabric, six color plates, and two printed circuit boards. From 1991, Weil has taught industrial design, Royal College of Art.
Exhibitions Work shown worldwide. Anthologie Quartett radio introduced at 1984 Internationale Möbelmesse, Cologne.
Bibliography Cat., Kathryn B. Hiesinger and George H. Marcus III (eds.), *Design Since 1945*, Philadelphia: Philadelphia Museum of Art, 1983. Terry Ilott, 'Martian Crafts,' *Crafts*, no. 62, May–June 1983: 30–33. Juli Capella and Quim Larrea, *Designed by Architects in the 1980s*, New York: Rizzoli, 1988. Albrecht Bangert and Karl Michael Armer, *80s Style: Designs of the Decade*, New York: Abbeville, 1990.

Weill, Bruno (aka Béwé)
> See Thonet Frères.

Weinand, Herbert Jakob (1953–)
German designer; born Wittlich, Eifel; active Berlin.

Training Under a cabinetmaker, apprenticeship; 1973, studies in interior, furniture, and product design in Germany and Italy.
Biography 1980, Weinand became active as an interior architect, furniture designer, and film maker; from 1984, designed numerous interiors of shops, restaurants, and establishments (including Bleibtreu hotel) in Berlin, Luxembourg, and Mainz; 1985, opened his own Galerie Weinand; was a participant in 1980s German avant-garde movement, particularly with design group Berliner Zimmer; designed 1986 Kubus I + II table with oversized industrial casters, and also 1988 Karajan I desk and Karajan II typewriter table, shaped as grand pianos in black lacquer with white silkscreened keys, by Designwerkstatt. He has taught furniture design, Fachhochschule Lippe und Höxter, Detmold.
Exhibitions Work shown in Austria, Germany, and Italy.
Bibliography Albrecht Bangert and Karl Michael Armer, *80s Style: Designs of the Decade*, New York: Abbeville, 1990. Petra Eisele, 'Deutsches Design als Experiment: Theoretische Neuansätze und ästhetische Manifestationen seit den sechziger Jahren,' doctorale dissertation, Berlin: University of the Arts, 2001.

Weininger, Andor (1899–1986)
Hungarian designer; born Pécs.

Training In architecture, Budapest; 1921–28, Bauhaus, Weimar and Dessau.
Biography While at the Bauhaus, Weininger's stage designs made an appreciable contribution to the theater there, and he founded the Bauhaus Jazz Band, beloved for its lively party music. From 1928, he was active as a decorator in Berlin and, with his wife Eva Fernbach, designed innovative lamps and furniture; moved to the Netherlands in 1939, to Canada in 1951, and to New York in 1958. Weininger was the only major Bauhaus figure to have lived in Canada.
Exhibitions Showed paintings, ranging from abstraction to Surrealism, in numerous venues. Represented Canada at Bienal de São Paulo, Brazil. Subject of a 2000 exhibition (catalog below).
Bibliography Lionel Richard, *Encyclopédie du Bauhaus*, Paris: Somogy, 1985: 212. Cat., Peter Nisbet (ed.), *Andor Weininger: Works in the Busch-Reisinger Museum*, Cambridge, Mass.: Harvard University Art Museums, 2000.

Weishaupt, Carl
German firm of silversmiths; located Munich.

History l802, Anton Weishaupt (1774–1832) founded the firm. Carl Weishaupt (1802–64) continued the business, which went on to become one of the oldest German silversmithies. The firm produced the 1911 cutlery designed by Richard Riemerschmid, who created very few silver designs, and also silverware based on Carl Weishaupt's own and others' ornamental sources. A box made in the workshops featured an angular, spiral motif borrowed from designs by Patriz Huber, of the Darmstadt artists' colony.
Exhibitions Wares shown at 1914 *Werkbund-Ausstellung*, Cologne; 1922 *Deutsche Gewerbeschau*, Munich.
Bibliography Annelies Krekel-Aalberse, *Art Nouveau and Art Déco Silver*, New York: Abrams, 1989. Cat., *Metallkunst*, Berlin: Bröhan-Museum, 1990: 500–01.

Weiss, Ivan (1946–)
Danish ceramicist.

Training 1962–66, in overglaze painting, Royal Copenhagen Porcelain Manufactory; 1970–72, in Japan.
Biography 1966–70, Weiss collaborated with ceramicist/painter Nils Thorsson at Royal Copenhagen Porcelain Manufactory; from 1972, worked by Royal Copenhagen Porcelain Manufactory (later a part of Royal Scandinavia). He has taught, College of Arts and Crafts, Kolding.
Exhibitions/citations Work subject of recent exhibitions: 1995, Yamaguchi-shi, Japan; 1997 Skålen (bowl) and 1999 Lågkrukker, Galleri Nørby, Copenhagen; 1998, Mitsukoshi, Japan; 1999 *Stentøj og Porcelain* (stoneware and porcelain), Royal Copenhagen; 1999, Keramikmuseet Grimmerhus, Denmark. Work shown in exhibitions, including 1981 *Danish Ceramic Design*, Pennsylvania State University. Received 1974 Ravenna Prize, Concorso Internazionale della Ceramica d'Arte, Faenza, Italy; 1978 Kunsthåndværkerpris, Teknisk Selskabs Skolers, Denmark.

Reinhold Weiss. Desk fan (no. HL 1). 1961. Plastic and steel casing, 5 1/2 x 5 1/2 x 2 3/4" (14 x 14 x 7 cm). Mfr.: Braun, Germany. Gift of the mfr. MoMA.

Bibliography Cat., David Revere McFadden (ed.), *Scandinavian Modern Design 1880–1980*, New York: Abrams, 1982.

Weiss, Reinhold (1934–)

German industrial designer; active the US.

Training To 1959, Hochschule für Gestaltung, Ulm.
Biography While at the Ulm school, Weiss worked with Hans Gugelot; also became the associate director of the product-design department and executive designer of the appliance division. His austerely Functionalist products epitomize the post-World War II aesthetics of the manufacturer Braun and the Ulm design school such as 1961 HL 1 desk fan (and 1971 HL 70 desk fan, with Jürgen Greubel), 1961 HE 1/12 electric kettle, 1961 HT 1 and 1963 HT 2 toasters, H 7 fan/heater, 1967 KSM 1 coffee grinder (and 1975 KMM 1/121 coffee grinder, with Hartwig Kahlcke). 1967, Weiss settled in Chicago and joined the staff of Unimark; 1970, established his own office in Chicago for the design of graphics and products.
Citations 1970 Bundespreis Produktdesign (for HL 1 fan), Rat für Formgebung (German design council), Frankfurt; 1972 award (for package design), American Institute of Graphic Arts (AIGA); gold medal, 1982 Industry Fair, Brno.
Bibliography Tomás Maldonado and Gui Bonsiepe, 'Science and Design,' *Ulm*, vols. 10–11, May 1964: 16–18. Cat., Kathryn B. Hiesinger and George H. Marcus III (eds.), *Design Since 1945*, Philadelphia: Philadelphia Museum of Art, 1983: 235, 1–50. Paola Antonelli (ed.), *Objects of Design: The Museum of Modern Art*, New York: The Museum of Modern Art, 2003: 230–31.

Weitling, Otto (1930–)

Danish architect and designer.

Training To 1953, Bygmesterskole, Kolding; to 1956, Kunstakademiet, Copenhagen.
Biography Weitling worked in the architecture/design office of Arne Jacobsen alongside Hans Dissing and, 1988, with Dissing, established architecture/design firm Dissing + Weitling in Copenhagen; designed a number of important buildings but, in the design community, became best known for 1989 Air Titanium highly flexible eyeglass frames by Linberg Optic Design.
Exhibitions 1995 *Mutant Materials in Contemporary Design*, The Museum of Modern Art, New York, and traveling.
Citations For the Air Titanium: 1989 Dansk ID Prize; 1992 grand prize, G-Mark Good Design award, Japanese Industrial Design Promotion Organization (JIDPO); 1993 The Baden-Württemberg International Design Prize; 1993 award, Industrie Forum Design (iF), Hanover.
Bibliography Cat., Paola Antonelli, *Mutant Materials in Contemporary Design*, New York: The Museum of Modern Art/ Abrams, 1995.
> See Dissing, Hans.

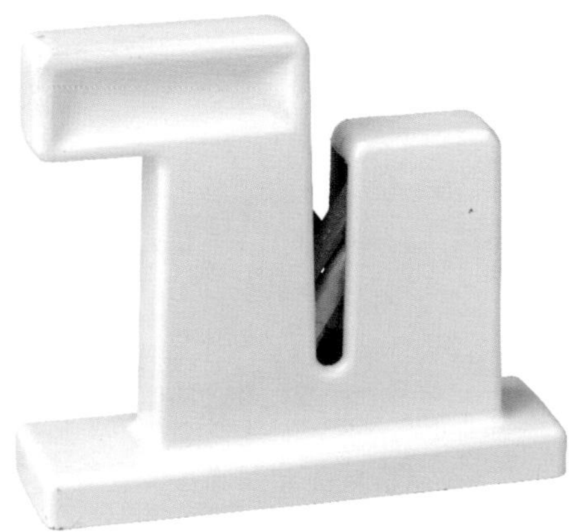

Robert Radford Welch. Nutcracker. 1958. Stainless steel, l. 6 x w. 1 7/8" (l. 15.3 x w. 4.8 cm). Mfr.: J. & J. Wiggin/Old Hall Works, UK. Gift of the mfr. MoMA.

William Archibald Welden. Covered saucepan. 1938. Copper-clad stainless steel, overall h. 5 1/2" x dia. 7 1/2" (14 x 19 cm). Mfr.: Revere Copper and Brass Co., US. Gift of the Education Department. MoMA.

Welburn, Edward (1950–)

Automobile designer; born Philadephia.

Training 1972, bachelor's degree, product design and sculpture, College of Fine Arts, Howard University, Washington, D.C.
Biography 1972, Welburn began as an associate designer of automobiles in the advanced-design studios of General Motors (GM) on the Oldsmobile, Saturn, and Opel marks and designed 1986 Oldsmobile Aerotech that acheived two world records of more than 257 m.p.h. (414 k.p.h.), driven by A.J. Foyt; worked at GM facilities in Europe and, 1998, was appointed director of GM's new Corporate Brand Center in Detroit, Mich.; 2001, became director of three body-on-frame studios at GM, overseeing the 2002 Cadillac Escalade SUV, 2003 Chevy SSR, 2003 Hummer H2, and others; 2003, was appointed vice-president and the sixth design chief of GM, succeeding Wayne Cherry, who retired.

Welch, Robert Radford (1929–2000)

British product designer and silversmith; born Hereford.

Training 1946–47 and 1949–50 under Victor Moody, painting, Malvern School of Art; 1950–52 under C.J. Shiner and R. Baxendale, silversmithing, Birmingham College of Art; 1952–55 under Robert Gooden, silversmithing, Royal College of Art, London.
Biography 1955, Welch established his own workshop in Chipping Campden, where he pursued the tradition of the Arts and Crafts designers, who had worked there at C.R. Ashbee's Guild of Handicrafts at the beginning of the 20th century. From 1955, he was a consultant designer to Old Hall Tableware, creating various products such as a toast rack in stainless steel, a material in which he specialized. Other products: cutlery, enamel-steel objects, lighting, door furniture, alarm clocks, and bathroom fixtures. After a 1953–54 visit to Sweden and Norway, he became influenced by Scandinavian design and, soon after, taught, Central School of Arts and Crafts from 1956–59, and Royal College of Art from 1960–71, both London. Products for private commissions and manufacturers: cast-iron and enamel cookware by Prinz in 1966 and by Lauffer in 1970, stoneware by Brixham Pottery in 1970, clocks by Westclox in 1964, lamps by Lumitron from 1966–68, and a professional-knife range by Kitchen Devel in 1979. 1969, he set up a retail shops, now in Chipping Campden and Warwick. More recently, Virgin Atlantic airlines' Upper Class section employed his dinnerware as did, in 2000, the Burj Al Arab, Dubai, the world's first seven-star hotel. He wrote the self-published autobiography *Hand & Machine* (Mill Chipping Campden, 1986). His son William Welch (a student at University of Central England, Birmingham, and Royal College of Art) is the design director of the firm, which continues to produce metal dinnerware, crystal, kitchenware, and lighting.
Exhibitions/citations Work included in 1956 exhibition, Foyles Art Gallery, London; 1964 exhibition, Heal's, London; 1967 exhibition, Skjalm Petersen Shop, Copenhagen; 1969 exhibition, Leeds Art Gallery; 1974 exhibition, Crafts Advisory Council, London; 1983–84 *Design Since 1945*, Philadelphia Museum of Art. Silver medal (with David Mellor), 1957 (9th) Triennale di Milano; British Design Centre Awards (stainless-steel toast rack by Old Hall Tableware, 1958; electric alarm clock for Westclox, 1964; Alveston cutlery, 1965); silver

medal, 1974, Biennial International Art Book Prize (for *Robert Welch: Design in a Cotswold Workshop*); 1975 Jerusalem Book Fair. 1965, elected Honorary Royal Designer for Industry, UK; 1972, elected a fellow of Royal College of Art, London; 2001 Snowdon Award for Disability Projects and 2002 Oxo/Peugeot Design Award (both for cutlery for the handicapped, to William Welch).
Bibliography Graham Hughes, *Modern Silver Throughout the World*, London: Studio Vista, 1967. Colin Forbes (ed.), *Robert Welch: Design in a Cotswold Workshop*, London: Lund Humphries, 1973. Fiona MacCarthy, *British Design Since 1880*, London: Lund Humphries, 1982. Cat., Kathryn B. Hiesinger and George H. Marcus III (eds.), *Design Since 1945*, Philadelphia: Philadelphia Museum of Art, 1983. Fiona MacCarthy and Patrick Nuttgens, *An Eye for Industry*, London: Lund Humphries/Royal Society for Arts, 1986.

Welden, William Archibald (1900–1970)
American metalworker.

Biography By 1933, Welden was a consultant designer to Revere Copper and Brass in Rome, N.Y., where he created wares in close association with its technicians. Later as head of design there, he designed a 1937 cookware collection (with Helen Dryden) and 1938 Revere Ware range of copper-bottomed cookware in stainless steel. These cooking pots and pans featured the absence of rivets to the handles. And the copper was derived from traditional French copper cooking pots; the Welden solution featured a thick plating of copper to the stainless-steel body to offer highly effective heat-absorption. However, more élitist but a reflection of inexpensive American modernism was his c. 1938–41 Sheridan serving set (with the adjunct Empire cocktail shaker and Hercules tray in chrome over brass with a Catalin plastic trim), similar but different from his Park serving set of the same period. Welden's 1954 cookware by Revere with heat-resistant metal (rather than plastic) handles for the institutional market has remained in continuous production. Welden also designed architectural ornaments and decorative metalwork for others.
Bibliography Don Wallance, *Shaping America's Products*, New York: Reinhold, 1956: 41–45. Cat., Kathryn B. Hiesinger and George H. Marcus III (eds.), *Design Since 1945*, Philadelphia: Philadelphia Museum of Art, 1983. Jim Linz, *Art Deco Chrome*, Atglen, Pa.: Schiffer, 1999.
> See Revere Copper and Brass.

Weller, Samuel A. (1851–1925); Weller Pottery
American commercial art potter; potteries located Ohio.

Biography/history c. 1872, Samuel A. Weller established a small pottery in Fultonham, near Zanesville, Ohio, to produce plain and decorated crocks and flowerpots, using local common red clay; relocated the works to Putnam (now part of Zanesville), Ohio; 1888, had established another pottery in Zanesville itself; 1891, occupied the plant previously housing American Encaustic Tiling to produce ornamental pottery, having been encouraged by a visit to the stand of William A. Long's Lonhuda Pottery of Steubenville, Ohio, at 1892 *World's Columbian Exposition*, Chicago. 1894, Weller became a partner with Long, moving the latter's pottery to Zanesville and began producing Lonhuda faience. 1896, Long left and began working for the pottery J.B. Owens in Zanesville. Weller continued with brown-shaded, high-glazed ware, renamed Louwelsa (after his new-born daughter Louise and himself), in production to 1918; produced the Aurelian, Samantha, and Tourada wares with solid brushed grounds. 1895, Charles B. Upjohn became the head designer, whose major contribution was 1900 Dickensware II in sgraffito. Weller's 1898 blue-gray and pale-green Eocean ware imitated Rookwood's Iris ware. By 1902, Weller was able to offer a wide range of art ware. 1902–04, Frederick H. Rhead developed Weller's Jap Birdimal, using the squeeze-bag technique, and L'Art Nouveau ranges. From 1901, Jacques Sicard worked at the pottery and produced its Sicardo line with metal lusters on iridescent grounds. Weller became one of the largest producers of art pottery in the US. By 1906, it ran 25 kilns and used the most modern machinery; after World War I, production of art ware ended, although artistic director John Lessell produced several new early-1920s art ranges, including Lamar ware and the lustrous LaSa decorated with landscapes and trees. After Weller's 1925 death, the pottery became known as S.A. Weller. With much reduced production, the firm survived to 1948.
Bibliography Kenneth H. Markham, 'Weller Sicardo Art Pottery,' *Antiques Journal*, no. 19, Sept. 1964: 18. Louise Purviance et al., *Weller Art Pottery in Color*, Des Moines: Wallace-Homestead, 1971. Sharon Huxford and Bob Huxford, *The Collector's Encyclopedia of Weller Pottery*, Paducah, Ky.: Collector's Books, 1979. Betty Purviance Ward and Nancy Schiffer, *Weller, Roseville, and Zanesville Art Pottery and Tile*, Atglen, Pa.: Schiffer, 2000. *American Art Pottery*, New York: Cooper-Hewitt Museum, 1987: 104–05.

Welles, Clara Barck (1868–1965)
American metalworker and entrepreneur; born Oregon; active Chicago.

Training School of the Art Institute of Chicago.
Biography 1900, Welles was primarily responsible for establishing the Kalo Shop, the largest Chicago producer of hand-wrought silverware, at 175 Dearborn Street. (*Kalo* is Greek for 'beautiful.') It was the first of a series of Arts and Crafts shops to be established in Chicago. At first, all designs were by Welles, who produced classic round and curving forms. Later designs were created by Yngve Olsson, who emigrated to Chicago before World War I and was an engraver and chaser of most of Kalo's wares as the chief designer and co-owner. After 1905, Welles employed up to 25 silversmiths, whom she trained herself and who also produced copper pieces. The smiths included Bjorne O. Axness, Robert P. Bower, Einar Johansen, Arne Myhre, Daniel P. Pederson, and Julius Randahl. Kalo continued to be the most important producer of handmade silver in Chicago after the end of 1910s, rendering rounded forms and hammered surfaces. Welles was active in the Cordon Club, a group of professional women in the arts, and was known for offering women opportunities in the metalsmithing trade; frequently lectured on silversmithing to labor groups. By 1940, Welles retired and turned over Kalo to employees Bower, Myhre, Olsson, and Pederson. 31 July 1970, Kalo closed, after the deaths of Pederson and Olsson.
Bibliography Sharon S. Darling with Gail Farr Casterline, *Chicago Metalsmiths*, Chicago: Chicago Historical Society, 1977. A. Krekel-Aalberse, *Art Nouveau and Art Déco Silver*, New York: Abrams, 1989.

Wells, Reginald (1877–1951)
British ceramicist.

Training Sculpture, Royal College of Art, London.
Biography 1909, Wells learned to pot at the Coldrum Pottery near Wrotham, Kent, and was one of the first to revive traditional slipware techniques. He also worked with Chinese-style glazes on what he called 'soon' (for Sung) pottery and made stoneware figures.
Bibliography *British Art and Design, 1900–1960*, London: Victoria & Albert Museum, 1983.

Wende, Theodor (1883–1968)
German silversmith; active Berlin, Darmstadt, and Pforzheim.

Training At jewelry firms, Berlin and Dresden; Königlich Preussische Zeichenakademie, Hanau; under Bruno Paul, Vereinigte Staatsschulen für freie und angewandte Kunst (Kunstgewerbeschule), Berlin-Charlottenburg.
Biography 1913, Wende became a member of the Darmstadt artists' colony of Grand Duke Louis IV of Hesse-Darmstadt. Of the 23 artists who worked at Darmstadt during its 15 years of activity, Ernst Riegel and his successor Wende were the only goldsmiths. Wende had a preference for large hammered surfaces with Cubism-influenced abstract ornamentation; 1921, became professor, Badische Kunstgewerbeschule, Pforzheim.
Bibliography Annelies Krekel-Aalberse, *Art Nouveau and Art Déco Silver*, New York: Abrams, 1989. Cat., *Metallkunst*, Berlin: Bröhan-Museum, 1990: 512-13.

Wendingen
> See Wijdeveld, Hendricus Theodorus.

Wennerberg, Gunnar Gison (1863–1914)
Swedish painter, ceramicist, and textile and glassware designer.

Training In Uppsala; 1886–1908, in painting, Paris; and at Sèvres.
Biography 1895–1908, Wennerberg was the artistic director of Gustavsberg ceramics factory, bringing a new style to its wares and incorporating motifs from nature; was at Gustavsberg when imitation Wedgwood jasper ware was being made there. 1908, he left the firm but had concurrently, worked for the Kosta glassworks 1898–1909 and, c. 1900, he designed carved cameo-glass vessels by Kosta and blown glass by Orrefors. 1902–08, he taught painting, Kungliga

Konsthögskolan, Stockholm; from 1908, worked at Manufacture Nationale de Sèvres in France and drew cartoons for woven textiles by Handarbetets Vänner.
Exhibitions Work shown in numerous exhibitions; subject of 1981 retrospective at Waldemarsudde, Stockholm (catalog below).
Bibliography Cat., *Gunnar Gison Wennerberg*, Stockholm: Prins Eugens Waldemarsudde, 1981. Cat., David Revere McFadden (ed.), *Scandinavian Modern Design 1880–1980*, New York: Abrams, 1982. Jennifer Hawkins Opie, *Scandinavia: Ceramics and Glass in the Twentieth Century*, New York: Rizzoli, 1989.

Werner, Sidse (1931–1989)
Scandinavian cabinetmaker, weaver, industrial designer, and architect.

Biography Werner was a weaver of carpets and textiles and designed lamps, tabletop products, and furniture, including 1972 Series 9 (or 9999) umbrella stand/ashtray and coat rack by Fritz Hansen, and Apoteker lamp range and other glass items by Holmegård Glasværks 1979–89.

West, Franz (1947–)
Austrian artist and designer; born and active Vienna.

Training 1980s under Bruno Gironcali, Akademie der bildenden Künste, Vienna; in Frankfurt and in New York.
Biography Primarily an artist, West designed lighting and furniture by Meta-Memphis, including 1989 Schöne Aussicht welded-iron chair, 1989 Privatlampe des Künstlers floor lamp, and 1991 Haus Lange ceiling lamp.
Exhibitions Fine art subject of exhibitions in Frankfurt, Krefeld, Milan, and New York. Work shown at 1990 Biennale di Venezia; 1992 and 1997 Documenta, Kassel; internationally in fine-art and applied-art venues.
Bibliography Albrecht Bangert and Karl Michael Armer, *80s Style: Designs of the Decade*, New York: Abbeville, 1990: 123, 236. Auction cat., *Modernes Design Kunsthandwerk nach 1945*, Munich: Quittenbaum, 4 Dec. 2001: lot 137.

Westman, Ernst Carl (1866–1936)
Swedish architect and furniture and interior designer.

Training IASPIS (royal academy of free arts), Stockholm; 1900, in England.
Biography Westman practiced in Stockholm and Umeå; based on his feeling that the Swedish were prejudiced and short-sighted, left for America; 1895, returned to Sweden; was greatly influenced by C.F.A. Voysey, Hugh Baillie Scott, and the Arts and Crafts movement; designed primarily simple furniture, expressive in form, and decidedly Swedish. Having broken his leg and ankle, Westman met Dr. Rissner, and, through the doctor, he was thus introduced to Julia von Bahr who commissioned Westman to design the 1906 Romanäs Nursing Institution for tuberculosis patients. He also built the doctor's residence there, and his own home and 1905 Medical Association building, both Stockholm; 1916 Rohsska Konstslöjdmuseet Gothenburg. Also in Stockholm, plans for the Palace of Justice.
Bibliography Hofberg, Herman (et al), *Svenskt Biografiskt* Handlexikon, Stockholm: Bonnier, 1906 2nd ed., vol. 2: 713. Cat., David Revere McFadden (ed.), *Scandinavian Modern Design 1880–1980*, New York: Abrams, 1982.

Wettstein, Hannes (1958–)
Swiss designer; born Ascona.

Biography 1982, Wettstein began as a freelance designer in Zürich. Work has include 1982 Metro, the first low-voltage lighting system on contact wires, and 1994 Cyos lighting system, both by Belux from 1985 seating and tables by Baleri Italia, 1991 redesign of audio sets by Revox, 1992 Intro and Soirée lighting by O luce, 1996 Xen bed system and 2000 sofa by Cassina, 1989 Z and 1995 V-Matic watches by Ventura, 1996 interior design and furnishings of Grand Hyatt Hotel (architect, Rafael Moneo) in Berlin, 1996 Spy table lamp by Artemide, 1996 Duke and Ever chairs by Wittmann, 1997 Roots sofa and chair, 1999 Travé table by Pastoe, 2000 Master sofa by Arflex, 2000 Alfa fiberglass chair by Molteni. 1991–96, he was a lecturer, Eidgenössische Technische Hochschule (ETH), Zürich; from 1994, has taught, Hochschule für Gestaltung, Karlsruhe; 1993, cofounded studio 9D Design, Zürich.
Exhibition Work included in *Design World 2000*, Konstindustrimuseet, Helsinki.
Bibliography Rafael Moneo and Hannes Wettstein, *Grand Hyatt Berlin*, Basel: Birkhäuser, 2000. Michele De Lucchi (ed.), *The International Design Yearbook*, London: Laurence King, 2001.

Wettstein, Robert Adrian (1960–)
Swiss designer; born Zürich.

Training In orthopedic technology.
Biography 1985, Wettstein opened his own practice and workshop, serving clients including Anthologie Quartett, Authentics, Die Imaginäre Manufaktur (DIM), and Noto/Zeus. 1986, he established the Structure Design and 'change.to/comfort (ctc)' trademarks. Work under Structure Design has included Herz clothes stand, Spunk lamp, 1986

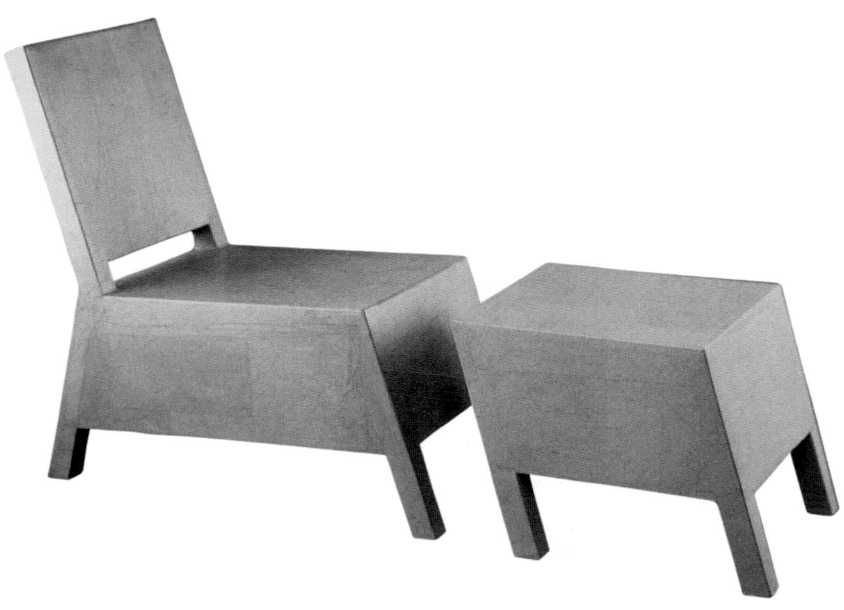

Robert Wettstein. Bastian chair and stool. 1991. Paper and wood, h. 31 1/4 x w. 17 1/8 x l. 47 5/8" (80 x 44 x 141 cm). Mfr.: Structure Design, Switzerland.

Echo chair, Twinset egg cup, 1990 Alberto carbon-fiber lamp and chair, and 1991 Bastian paper and wood lounge chair/ottoman. Also Europalette eating-utensils program (with others, presented at Swiss Design Center, Milan, in 2000).
Exhibitions/citations Work included in large number of exhibitions. Received 1993 Swiss Design Prize (for 1992 Airos chair).
Bibliography *The International Design Yearbook*, New York: Abbeville, 1994, 1996, 2002. Charlotte and Peter Fiell (eds.), *1000 Chairs*, Cologne: Taschen, 2000.

Wewerka, Stefan (1928–)

German architect and designer; born Magdeburg; active Cologne and Berlin.

Training To 1947, architecture and town planning; to 1954, earth architecture; to 1961, sculpture and painting.
Biography Wewerka became known in 1960s for his idiosyncratic chairs and other everyday objects, which he cut up or distorted. 1970s, he also started to design furniture within the former, but industrially produced, approach. This has included 1974 Classroom chair by Tecta, where he worked from 1977; from 1975, developed the 'sitting tool' with multiple seating positions; 1979, began designing clothing; 1981, executed jewelry designs by Cleto Munari in Vicenza, Italy. His other Tecta work included 1971 B1 three-leg chair, 1979 M1 table, 1982 B5 one-piece bent-steel tube chair, 1982 D2 armchair, 1982 L30 lamp, 1983 L6 table, and 1984 kitchen pole—some still in production.
Exhibition Work subject of 1998 exhibition, Museum für Kunsthandwerk, Frankfurt am Main (catalog below).
Bibliography Cat., *Der Kragstuhl*, Stuhlmuseum Burg Beverungen, Berlin: Alexander, 1986. Juli Capella and Quim Larrea, *Designed by Architects in the 1980s*, New York: Rizzoli, 1988. Cat., V. Fischer and A. Gleiniger, *Stefan Wewerka: Architect, Designer, Object Artist = Architekt, Designer, Objektkünstler*, Stuttgart: Axel Menges, 1998.

Wharton, Edith Newbold (1862–1937)

American writer and interior designer; active New York.

Biography Wharton collaborated with Ogden Codman Jr. on interiors and on the influential book *The Decoration of Houses* (New York: Scribner's, 1897), observing, 'We have passed from the golden age of architecture to the gilded age of decoration.' They began working together within a distinctly historicist style, when Codman designed her house 'Land's End' in Newport, R.I. After an extensive collaboration, Wharton, not known for her fidelity, hired another architect to build her most important house. She was a prolific fiction writer, including the books *Ethan Frome* (New York: Scribner's, 1911) and *The Age of Innocence* (New York/London: D. Appleton, 1920).
Exhibitions Paintings, drawings, sculpture, and books in 1994 *Glancing Backward: Edith Wharton*, National Academy of Design, New York.
Bibliography John Esten and Rose Bennett Gilbert, *Manhattan Style*, Boston: Little, Brown, 1990: 2. Eleanor Dwight, *Edith Wharton: An Extraordinary Life*, New York: Abrams, 1994. Shari Benstock, *No Gifts from Chance: A Biography of Edith Wharton*, New York: Scribner's Sons, 1994. Diane de Margerie, *Edith Wharton: lecture d'une vie*, Paris: Flammarion, 1999–2000.
> See Codman Jr., Ogden.

Wheeler, Candace (b. Candace Thurber 1827–1923)

American textile and wallpaper designer; born Delhi, N.Y.; active New York.

Biography She was an amateur artist who painted china and rendered needlework, greatly influenced by the embroideries of the Royal School of Art Needlework in London that she saw at 1876 *Centennial Exposition*, Philadelphia. From 1877, she was the vice-president and corresponding secretary of the New York Society of Decorative Art, where classes were taught by Samuel Colman, Lockwood de Forest, John La Farge, Louis Comfort Tiffany, and others. 1878, she founded the Women's Exchange, which sold goods, crafts, and foodstuffs to 1980s on Madison Avenue, New York. 1879, she was hired by Louis Comfort Tiffany as a textile specialist in his new decorating firm Associated Artists, where she designed wallpaper to its 1883 close. To 1907, she was assisted by her daughter Dora to continue designing textiles for a firm managed by her son. She invented new techniques in textile production; designed fabrics by the silk mill Cheney Brothers in Connecticut; was appointed director of the Bureau of Applied Arts for New York State stand at 1893 *World's Columbian Exposition*, Chicago, and the interior decorator of Women's Building there. She wrote the books *Household Art* (New York: Harper, 1893), *Principles of Home Decoration, with Practical Examples* (New York: Doubleday, Page, 1903), *The Development of Embroidery in America* (New York/London: Harper, 1921), and the autobiography *Yesterdays in a Busy Life* (New York/London: Harper, 1918).
Exhibitions/citations First prize (for a portière design), 1879 New York Society of Decorative Art exhibition; 1881 design competition (first prize to Candace; fourth prize to daughter Dora) sponsored by wallpaper manufacturer Warren and Fuller. Work subject of 2001–02 exhibition, The Metropolitan Museum of Art, New York (catalog below).
Bibliography 'Candace Wheeler, Textile Designer,' *Antiques 112*, Aug. 1977: 258–61. Karal Ann Marling, 'Portrait of the Artist as a Young Woman: Miss Dora Wheeler,' *Bulletin of the Cleveland Museum of Art 65*, Feb. 1978: 47–57. Virginia Williams, 'Candace Wheeler, Textile Designer for Associated Artists,' *Nineteenth Century* 6, summer 1980: 60–61. Cat., Amelia Peck and Carol Irish, *Candace Wheeler: The Art and Enterprise of American Design, 1875–1900*, New York: Metropolitan Museum of Art/Yale, 2001.

Whipple, Richard (1916–1964)
> See Philco.

Whistler, James Abbott McNeill (1834–1903)

American painter; born Lowell, Mass.; active Europe.

Training Drawing, Imperial Academy of Science, St. Petersburg; from 1851, West Point Military Academy, New York; 1855 or 1856, École Impériale et Spéciale du Dessin, Paris; 1856, under Swiss painter Charles Gleyre.
Biography Expelled from West Point, Whistler worked briefly in Baltimore as an etcher in the drawings division of the US Coast and Geodetic Survey before deciding to become an artist and moving to Paris; 1858, produced his first set of etchings. 1860s–70s, his prolific activity in printmaking encouraged pursuit of the medium in Britain, France, and the US. 1858–59, he produced his first major painting, *At the Piano*, and settled in Wapping, London. His early work was influenced by the Pre-Raphaelites, and Oriental influences showed up in his work of 1860s, when he produced the first of his purely decorative compositions. 1870s, he became interested in furniture, picture-frame, and exhibition design, and interior decoration and thus decorated 1876–77 Peacock Room (dining room) of Frederick Richards Leyland (designed by Thomas Jeckyll; installed today at Freer Gallery, Washington, D.C.). A widely publicized altercation between Leyland and Whistler overshadowed the room's ambitious decoration. He declared bankruptcy in 1879 and went to Venice but returned to London, producing the *Set of Twenty-Six Etchings* (1886) of Venice and *Notes* (1887) lithographs. 1880s–90s, Whistler's influence began to show in work of artists William Merritt Chase, Thomas Wilmer Dewing, and John H. Twachtman. 1890, Whistler met Charles Lang Freer of Detroit, who became his chief patron in the US. From 1898, Whistler's own

Jan Wichers and Alexander Blomberg. Domino table. 1979. Acrylic on building board, 17¾ x 35⅝ x 35⅝" (45.1 x 90.5 x 90.5 cm). Mfr.: Rosen-thal Einrichtung, Germany. Gift of the mfr. and Aram Designs Ltd. MoMA.

'Company of the Butterfly' sold his works. 1898, he became president, International Society of Sculptors, Painters, and Gravers.
Exhibitions *At the Piano* painting (rejected by 1859 Paris Salon) shown at Royal Academy of Arts, London. *The White Girl, No. 1 (Symphony in White)* (1862) (rejected by 1862 Royal Academy of Arts exhibition and 1863 Paris Salon) shown with Édouard Manet's *Le Déjeuner sur l'Herbe* at 1863 Salon des Refusés, Paris. Furniture suite by E.W. Godwin and Whistler, made by William Watt, shown at 1878 *Exposition Universelle*, Paris. First solo exhibitions included 1889, Wunderlich Gallery, New York; 1904 memorial exhibition, Boston; International Society, London, 1905; École Nationale des Beaux-Arts, Paris, 1905.
Bibliography Denys Sutton, *Nocturne: The Art of James McNeill Whistler*, London: Country Life, 1963. Cat., Allen Staley, *From Realism to Symbolism: Whistler and His World*, New York: Wildenstein, 1971. Cat., David Park Curry, *James McNeill Whistler at the Freer Gallery of Art*, Washington, D.C.: Freer Gallery of Art, 1984. Doreen Bolger Burke et al., *In Pursuit of Beauty: Americans and the Aesthetic Movement*, New York: The Metropolitan Museum of Art/Rizzoli, 1987. Linda Merrill, *The Peacock Room*, New Haven: Yale, 1998.

Whistler, Laurence (1912–2000)

British glass engraver, glassware designer, and writer; brother of Rex Whistler.

Training Oxford University.
Biography Initially, Whistler considered becoming an architect, then a poet; c. 1935, he was encouraged by architect Edwin Lutyens and by his brother Rex Whistler to take up glass engraving. However, only once did he execute an engraving to a design by Rex, who informally taught Laurence drawing. Lutyens and his daughter Lady Ridley became important contacts and patrons to Whistler. After engraving glass, which he called 'window writing,' Whistler made bottles, decanters, panels, goblets, and, commissioned by clients, caskets and windows; designed some historicist (mostly neo-Georgian) glass tableware, blown by others, including workers at Whitefriars Glassworks. Whistler, along with John Hutton, revived stipple engraving; became the first of numerous British artists to have glassware designs produced by Steuben. Other work: 1947–48 King George's Casket and windows in Sherborne Abbey, Eastbury, Bedfordshire, and in the Guards' Chapel, St. Hugh's College, Oxford. Wrote a number of books (see below), including one on his brother's work (see bibliography of 'Whistler, Rex' below) and a number of volumes of poetry; 1939, married actress Jill Furse, who died 1944, same year as his brother.
Exhibitions/citations Work shown at Agnew's, London, 1969; Marble Hill, 1972; Corning Museum, Corning, N.Y., 1974; Ashmolean Museum, Oxford, 1976; Fine Art Society, London, 1977; and included in 1979–80 *Thirties* exhibition, Hayward Gallery, London (catalog below). 1934 (1st) King's Gold Medal for Poetry (now Queen's Gold Medal for Poetry), UK; appointed Companion of the British Empire (CBE).
Bibliography John Hadfield (ed.), 'Artist in Glass: The Engravings of Laurence Whistler,' *The Saturday Book: 15*, London: Hutchinson, 1955. Laurence Whistler, *Engraved Glass 1952–58*, London: Rupert Hart-Davis, 1959. Laurence Whistler, *The Image on the Glass*, London: John Murray/Cupid, 1975. Cat., *Thirties: British Art and Design Before the War*, London: Arts Council of Great Britain/Hayward Gallery, 1979. John Jacob and Nicholas Penny, *Fifty Years on Glass: Engraved Glasses by Laurence Whistler and by His Sons and Daughter, Simon, Daniel, and Frances Whistler*, Oxford: Ashmolean Museum; London: Greater London Council, 1985. Laurence Whistler, *Scenes and Signs on Glass*, Woodbridge: Cupid, 1985. Laurence Whistler (illustrator), *St. Nicholas, Moreton: The Engraved-Glass Windows*, Suffolk: Baron, 1986. Laurence Whistler, *Point Engraving on Glass*, New York: Walker, 1992. Laurence Whistler, *The Initials in the Heart* (memoir), Boston: Houghton, Mifflin, 1994.

Whistler, Rex John (1905–1944)

British painter, theater designer, and book illustrator; brother of Laurence Whistler.

Training 1922–25 under Henry Tonks, Slade School of Art, London; and in Rome.
Biography Whistler was probably best known for the 1926–27 decorations in the refreshment room of Tate Gallery, London. His many private commissions included 1932 *Nine Samuels* pair of carved-wood urns, 160 in. (400 cm) tall, for Samuel Courtauld to commemorate Courtauld and eight other 'Samuels': Butler, Coleridge, Johnson, Pepys, the Prophet, Richards, Rogers, Scott). Whistler also designed costumes for the 1934 production of Shakespeare's *The Tempest* at Stratford-upon-Avon; 1936–38 decorations for Sir Philip Sassoon's stately home at Plas Newydd. Other work: 1934 scenery for *Fidelio* at Covent Garden; 1934 scenery and costumes for Mozart's *Le Nozze di Figaro* at Sadler's Wells; 1936 poster, program, scenery, and costumes for the adaptation of Jane Austen's *Pride and Prejudice* at St. James's Theatre, and, 1937, for Laurence Housman's *Victoria Regina* at Lyric Theatre; all in London. He illustrated Jonathan Swift's *Gulliver's Travels* (Cresset Press, 1930), Edward James's *The Next Volume* (The James Press, 1932), Walter de la Mare's *The Lord Fish* (Faber and Faber, 1933), *Fairy Tales and Legends* (Cobden-Sanderson, 1935) by Hans Christian Andersen; designed stamps, bookplates, and ephemera, including 1930 envelope for the National Trust, 1932 earthenware by Wedgwood, 1932–36 Christmas catalogs (with witty drawings) by Fortnum and Mason store, London, 1935 Valentine's Day greeting telegram, 1935 carpet for Edward James woven by Wilton Royal Carpet Factory, and monuments. He died in action in World War II.
Bibliography Laurence Whistler, *Rex Whistler: His Life and Drawings*, London: Art and Technics, 1948. Rex Whistler, *Designs for the Theatre*, London: Batsford for Curtain Press, 1950. Cat., *Thirties: British Art and Design Before the War*, London: Arts Council of Great Britain/Hayward Gallery Gallery, 1979.

Whitefriars Glass

British glassware manufacturer.

History 1680, Whitefriars was built on a former Carmelite monastery site in London; 1834, was taken over by James Powell to become James Powell & Sons, remaining in the family to 1919, when it became James Powell & Sons (Whitefriars) Ltd. From c. 1840, the factory produced glass by Charles Winston, who returned its wares to a purer ancient style but, from 1850s, produced Venetian-style glassware. It employed leading craftsperson Joseph Leicester; 1880–1920, was directed by Harry J. Powell (1835–1922) and became long associated with the Aesthetic Reform and active in raising design standards. Late 19th century, Philip Webb's designs for the Powell glasshouse of Whitefriars prefigured 20th-century forms. William Wilson played a significant role in the revival of diamond-point engraving as the managing director from 1950–73. He hired George Baxter as a staff designer. Whitefriars Glass, known as such from 1963, engaged the services of John Hutton, one of the most accomplished postwar engravers and etchers of glass and a reviver of stipple engraving along with Laurence Whistler, for whom Whitefriars also created forms.
Exhibition Work subject of 1996 exhibition, Manchester City Art Galleries (catalog below).
Bibliography Wendy Evans et al., *Whitefriars Glass: James Powell & Sons of London*, London: Museum of London, 1995. Cat., Lesley Jackson (ed.), *Whitefriars Glass: The Art of James Powell & Sons*, Shepton Beauchamp: Richard Dennis, 1996.
> See Powell, Edmund Barnaby; Powell, James.

Wichers, Jan (1944–)

German interior architect and furniture designer.

Biography Wichers established an interior-architecture studio in Hamburg with about a dozen interior designers on staff; works on a number of homes, offices, and public spaces, such as Sheikh Al Maktoum's villa, Dubai; Son Severin hotel, Majorca; Municon conference center, Munich airport; restaurants in Kempinski Airport Hotel, Munich; board of directors offices of Bertelsmann, Gütersloh; furniture by de Sede (including its shop in Paris), Hans Kaufeld, Rosenthal Einrichtung, Status, and Up & Up.
Bibliography www.studio-wichers.de.

wicker

Vegetable fiber used in furniture and utility-goods manufacture.

History Woven furniture has been produced since ancient times. The term derives from *vikker* (Scandinavian for 'willow,' and denotes woven furniture rather than a specific material. Wicker furniture has been produced from swamp reed, raffia, willow, thin bamboo, thin wooden strips, or even twisted paper. Yet strictly, most wicker furniture is made of a flexible and water-resistant rattan of the palm-vine variety that grows in Malaysia and elsewhere in the Far East. Cane (a rattan bark by-product) is woven for the seats and backs of chairs. Lightweight and weather-resistant furniture in wicker was popular

from 1850s, peaking first in America 1865–80, then in the Orient and Europe. From c. 1880, reed furniture was used indoors and usually painted gold, brown, green, and white. Rectilinear in form, it reflected Oriental furniture designs. 1917, Marshall Burns Lloyd patented a method of producing wicker-like material from paper twisted into strands, used for furniture manufactured by Lloyd Looms.
Bibliography Richard Saunders, *Collecting and Restoring Wicker Furniture*, New York: Crown, 1976. Richard Saunders, *Collector's Guide to American Wicker Furniture*, New York: Hearst, 1983. Doreen Bolger Burke et al., *In Pursuit of Beauty: Americans and the Aesthetic Movement*, New York: The Metropolitan Museum of Art/Rizzoli, 1986. Lee J. Curtis, *Lloyd Loom...*, New York: Rizzoli, 1991.
> See Lloyd, Marshall Burns.

Wiener Sezession (Vienna Secession)

Group of Austrian artists and architects.

History 1897, a number of artists in Vienna, led by Gustav Klimt (with Joseph Maria Olbrich, Josef Hoffmann, and Koloman Moser), founded the Vereinigung bildender Künstler Österreichs, generally known as the Wiener Sezession. It was born from a dissatisfaction with the traditional practices of the Kunstlerhausgenossenschaf (essentially the 'Vienna Academy'). Many of its proponents taught at the Akademie der bildenden Künste in Vienna. Emulating the Münchner Sezession (founded in 1982) and Berliner Sezession (founded in 1893), members partially sought an alternative to Art Nouveau, believing it to be decadent, but, like Gustav Klimt, were primarily against the Kunstlerhaus's commercial motivations that appeared to diverge from the way most Austrians lived. Group members presented their ideas from the first (1898) issue of the Sezession's journal *Ver Sacrum* (sacred spring). The Sezession also built 1897–98 Kunsthalle (exhibition hall) on the Karlsplatz in Vienna, after a design by Olbrich and Klimt, with stained-glass and interior decorations by Moser. The inscription by Ludwig Hevesi placed over the door reads: *Der Zeit ihre Kunst, der Kunst ihre Freiheit* (To each age its art, to art its freedom). The organization sought to introduce the Viennese public to the best of modern European decorative art. At the Kunsthalle, members showed their works and those of foreign honorary members—fine and the applied artists together—several times a year. At 1900 (8th) Wiener Sezession exhibition, Hoffmann invited foreigners to include their work: C.R. Ashbee, Charles Rennie Mackintosh, Henry van de Velde, those of the stable of Julius Meier-Graefe's La Maison Moderne shop in Paris, and others. Ashbee's jewelry and silver objects were shown in the 1906 (27th) exhibition. The invitations to foreigners expresed the Secessionists' interest in non-Austrian art, and this interest was one of the ways in which they were appreciably different from the Kunstlerhaus, whose member felt that foreign art subverted Austrian traditions. The Wiener Werkstätte—the effort by Sezession members to enter into commerce—was based on Ashbee's Guild of Handicraft.
Bibliography Robert Waissenberger, *Die Wiener Secession: Eine Dokumentation*, Vienna/Munich: Jugend & Volk, 1971. Nicolas Powell, *The Sacred Spring: The Arts in Vienna 1898–1918*, London: Studio Vista, 1974. Werner Fenz, *Kolo Moser: Internationaler Jugendstil und Wiener Secession* (Österreichisches Museum für Kunst und Industrie), Salzburg: Residenz, 1976. James Shedel, *Art and Society: The New Art Movement in Vienna*, 1897–1914, Palo Alto, Cal.: SPOSS, 1981. Jaroslava Bubnová, *Vienna Secession: 1898–1998: The Century of Artistic Freedom*, Munich/New York: Prestel, 1998.
> See Wiener Werkstätte (below).

Wiener Werkstätte

Austrian art and crafts studio; located Vienna.

History 1903, the Produktivgenossenschaft von Kunsthandwerkern in Wien (art-craft workshop cooperative in Vienna) was founded by Wiener Sezession members Josef Hoffmann and Koloman Moser, financially backed by Fritz Wärndorfer, later joined by Carl Otto Czeschka. As much a movement as a financial enterprise, the Wiener Werkstätte (as it was generally called) had support from artist Gustav Klimt and architect Otto Wagner. The workshop was founded around the work of Charles Rennie Mackintosh, E.W. Godwin, and the principles of C.R. Ashbee's Guild of Handicraft, all of which Hoffmann admired. The exponents of the British counterpart organizations were not required to have formal training, whereas Werkstätte employees had to show their *Befähigungsnachweis* (the evidence of their apprenticeship and journeymanship and the acquisition of a master's certificate). The Werkstätte's goals: (1) the fulfillment of the ideals of the guild system; (2) the establishment of a direct relationship among designers, craftspeople, and the public by producing well-designed furniture, metalwork, graphics, bookbinding, and textiles; and (3) the realization of all the plastic arts and interiors as a *Gesamtkunstwerke* (total work of art). Additional goals: (4) the revitalization and revalidation of middle-class taste, turning it against historicism and an imitation of the past, and (5) the reversal of the decline in the quality of handmade objects. Also in contrast to the British Arts and Crafts movement, exponents of the Wiener Werkstätte acknowledged that their rejection of the machine would in fact result in expensive goods but, nevertheless, considered the prices to be somehow linked to the group's redemptive role through art, a *fin-de-siècle* notion. Aesthetic features of the work included a reduction of ornamentation, honed down and clean surfaces, and repetitive geometric, linear patterns. Its silver designers included Czeschka, Dagobert Peche, Hoffmann, Moser, Otto Prutscher, and Eduard Josef Wimmer-Wisgrill. Its silversmiths included Arthur Berger, Josef Czech, Adolf Erbrich, Augustin Grötzbach, Josef Hossfeld, Josef Husnik, Karl Kallert, Alfred Mayer, Eugen Pflaumer, Karl Ponocny, Anton Pribit, J. Sedlicky, and Josef Wagner. Within ten years, as many as 100 production workers were being employed. Since the Werkstätte had no facilities of its own for manufacturing glass, the work was hired out to the Bohemian glass houses E. Bakalowitz, Johann Loetz Witwe, Johann Oertl, Karl Schappel, Ludwig Moser, and Meyrs Neffe. Bakalowitz was effective in promotion and distribution. J. & L. Lobmeyr joined the forces of the Werkstätte once its products had been established in European markets. The group's success prompted the formation of other *Werkstätten* (workshops), which were organized along similar lines in other cities, notably Munich and Dresden. By 1932, the year of the Wiener Werkstätte's closing, its 212 members included 139 students and 20 professors from the Kunstgewerbeschule of Vienna.
Bibliography Werner J. Schweiger, *Wiener Werkstätte: Kunst und Handwerk 1903–1932*, Vienna: Brandstätter, 1982. Werner J. Schweiger, *Wiener Werkstätte: Design in Vienna, 1903–1932*, New York: Abbeville, 1984. W. Neuwirth, *Wiener Werkstätte: Avantgarde, Art déco, Industrial Design*, Vienna: W. Neuwirth, 1984. Waltraud Neuwirth, *Wiener Werkstätte: Die Schutmarken = The Registered Trade Marks*, Vienna: W. Neuwirth, 1985. Wanda Quoika-Stanka, *The Wiener Werkstatte*, Monticello, Ill.: Vance Bibliographies, 1987. *Wiener Werkstätte: Glas, Keramik, Holz, Leder, Metall: Aus den beständen des Österreichischen Museums für angewandte Kunst*, Vienna: Österreichisches Museum für angewandte Kunst, 1990. Cat., *Expressive Keramik der Wiener Werkstätte 1917–1930*, Munich: Bayerische Vereinsbank, 1992: 126–27.

Wieselthier, 'Vally' Valerie (1895–1945)

Austrian designer; born Vienna.

Training 1914–18 under Michael Powolny, Koloman Moser, Josef Hoffmann, and others, Kunstgewerbeschule, Vienna.
Biography Wieselthier was head of the ceramic workshop at the Wiener Werkstätte and worked in a highly idiosyncratic style with coarse modeling and drip-glass effects; 1922, established her own workshop in Vienna; 1924 designed for ceramics and fabrics, when the Augarten porcelain factory reopened; with Gudrun Baudisch, designed the three-dimensional binding on the book that celebrated the 25th anniversary of the workshop: *Die Wiener Werkstätte, 1903–1928: Modernes Kunstgewerbe und sein Weg* (Vienna: Krystall-Verlag, 1929). 1929, she settled in New York and designed ceramics by Contempora there and by Sebring Pottery in Ohio; taught, Tulane University, New Orleans, La.; also designed glassware, jewelry, textiles, *papier-mâché* mannequins, furniture, and the metal elevator doors of 1929–30 Squibb building (architect, Ely Jacques Kahn), New York.
Exhibitions/citations Work first (1922) shown in Germany and at 1925 *Exposition Internationale des Arts Décoratifs et Industriels Modernes* (gold and silver medals), Paris; 1928 *International Exhibition of Ceramic Art*, The Metropolitan Museum of Art, New York. Work subject of exhibitions at Art Center, 1928, and Weyhe Galleries, 1930, both New York.
Bibliography Ruth Canfield, 'The Pottery of Vally Wieselthier,' *Design*, Nov. 1929: 104. Obituary, *The New York Times*, 3 Sept. 1945: 23. Günther Feuerstein, *Vienna–Present and Past: Arts and Crafts–Applied Art–Design*, Vienna: Jugend und Volk, 1976. Garth Clark, A *Century of Ceramics in the United States, 1878–1978*, New York: Dutton, 1979. Waltraud Neuwirth, *Die Keramik der Wiener Werkstätte*, Vienna: Selbstverlag, 1981. Karen Davies, *At Home in Manhattan: Modern Decorative Arts, 1925 to the Depression*, New Haven: Yale, 1983. *Wiener Werkstätte: Glas, Keramik, Holz, Leder, Metall: Aus den beständen des Österreichischen Museums für angewandte Kunst*,

Vienna: Österreichisches Museum für angewandte Kunst, 1990. Cat., *Expressive Keramik der Wiener Werkstätte 1817–1930*, Munich: Bayerische Vereinsbank, 1992.

Wight, Don (1924–)

American artist, photographer, and textile designer; active San Francisco and New York.

Training 1942–43, Alfred (N.Y.) University; 1945–47 under Josef and Anni Albers, Black Mountain College, N.C.
Biography 1947, Wight was an apprentice weaver in the studio of Dorothy Liebes in San Francisco; 1948–66, was active in New York and, from 1977, abroad. He designed patterns for printed textiles by numerous firms, including Bates, Brunschwig et Fils, Jack Lenor Larsen, Liebes's enterprise, and Schumacher.
Exhibitions Work included in 1951 (Garden of Glass printed fabric) and 1954 *Good Design* exhibitions/awards, The Museum of Modern Art, New York, and Chicago Merchandise Mart; 1983–84 exhibition (a fabric by Larsen), Philadelphia (catalog below).
Bibliography Cat., Kathryn B. Hiesinger and George H. Marcus III (eds.), *Design Since 1945*, Philadelphia: Philadelphia Museum of Art, 1983.

Wiherheimo, Yrjö (1941–)

Finnish furniture and industrial designer.

Training Interior architecture and design, Taideteollinen korkeakoulu, Helsinki.
Biography From 1967, Wiherheimo became active as a professional designer; 1969, began working independently; 1969–73, was vice-chairperson, Sisustusarkkitehdit (SIO, Finnish association of interior architects); 1974–79, taught in the department of architecture and, from 1981, taught furniture design, both Teknillinen korkeakoulu, Helsinki. He has also taught furniture design abroad, including Statens Hogskole for Konsthandverk og Design, Bergen, Norway, from 1987 - 93, and at institutions in Chile, Argentina, and India. From 1980, he was the chief designer and artistic director of Vivero and designed for others in Finland, Sweden, and Italy, as well as furniture by Asko and by Haimi, both of Helsinki, and plastics by Nokia. 1981, he established his own studio, K & Y Wiherheimo, with Pekka Kojo (Lahti, 1956–) from 1984; designed a number of chairs and tables (with Simo Heikkilä) by Klaessons; 1985–86, was a board member, Suomen Taideteollisuusyhdistys (Finnish society of crafts and design).
Exhibitions/citations Work included in several domestic and foreign exhibitions. Received numerous prizes and awards.
Bibliography Cat., David Revere McFadden (ed.), *Scandinavian Modern Design 1880–1980*, New York: Abrams, 1982.

Wiener Werkstätte: Josef Hoffmann. Vase. c. 1905. Painted perforated metal. 4 1/4 x 3 1/8 x 3 1/8" (10.8 x 8 x 8 cm). Mfr.: Wiener Werkstätte, Metall-Arbeit, Vienna, Austria (c. 1903–32). Estée and Joseph Lauder Design Fund. MoMA.

Wiinblad, Bjørn (1918–)

Danish ceramicist, glassware and textile designer, and graphic artist; active Copenhagen.

Training 1936–39, Teknisk Skole, Copenhagen; 1940–43, illustration, Det Kongelige Danske Kunstakademi, Copenhagen; 1943–46 under Lars Syberg, in ceramics at Taastrup.
Biography 1946–56, Wiinblad was a designer for the Nymølle faïence factory; from 1952, was active in his own studio in Kongens Lyngby; from 1957, worked for Rosenthal, and for decorations and designs for various commissions, including hotels and restaurants, in the US, the UK, Japan, and Europe. 1965, he was a theater designer for the Dallas Theater Center and subsequently the Pantomime Theater in Tivoli Gardens, Copenhagen; designed sculpture in silver by Hans Hansen Sølvsmedie in Kolding, and metalwork and furniture by others.
Bibliography *Björn Wiinblad*, Copenhagen: Det Danske Kunstindustrimuseum, 1981. Cat., David Revere McFadden (ed.), *Scandinavian Modern Design 1880–1980*, New York: Abrams, 1982. Jennifer Hawkins Opie, *Scandinavia: Ceramics and Glass in the Twentieth Century*, New York: Rizzoli, 1989.

Wijdeveld, Hendricus Theodorus (aka Henrik Theodor Wijdeveld 1885–1987)

Dutch architect and publisher; active Amsterdam.

Training Architecture and decoration, London.
Biography Wijdeveld was editor of *Wendigen* (turnings, or changes), the sophisticated avant-garde art and architecture journal that explored innovative typographic design (eventually known as *Wendingentypografie*) in a large format (13 x 13 in./33 x 33 cm) and with the use of sans-serif typefaces in an often illegible layout. It was published as an organ of the Architectura et Amicitia group in Amsterdam. Wijdeveld designed the typography and covers but sometimes commissioned others to design the graphics, such as El Lissitsky. *Wendigen*, published from 1918–31, was in many ways remarkable; played an important role in promoting the ideas of the Amsterdam School; also included articles on African sculpture, Far Eastern art, and Native American basketwork. 1924, Wijdeveld designed the exhibition stand for Philips at the fair in Jaarbeurs, Utrecht; as an architect, was interested in utopian design and known for his contact with Frank Lloyd Wright and expressionist architects including Hermann Finsterlin, Erich Mendelsohn, and Bruno Taut. The 1925–26 *Wendigen* issues on Wright's work, reprinted numerous times since by others, was a landmark. 1926, Wijdeveld left the journal.
Exhibitions 2001 *Wendingen*, Ubu Gallery, New York.
Bibliography H. Oldewarris, 'Wijdeveld Typografie,' *Forum voor architectuur en daarmee verwante kunsten 25*, no. 1, 1975. Giovanni Fanelli et al., *Wendigen 1918–1931: documenti dell'arte olandese del Novecento*, Florence: Centro Di, 1982. Cat., Giovanni Fanelli and Ezio Godoli (text), Paolo Portoghesi (intro.), *Wendingen: Art and Design in the Nineteenth Century Dutch Magazine = Grafica e cultura in una rivista olandese del Novecento*, Milan: F.M. Ricci, 1986. *Wendingen 1918-1931: Amsterdamer Expressionismus*, Darmstadt: Darmstädter Galerie 19. Jahrhundert / Haus Deiters, 1992. Martijn F. Le Coultre et al., *Wendingen: A Journal for the Arts, 1918–1932*, New York: Princeton Architectural Press, 2001.

Wikkelsø, Illum (1919–1999)

Danish furniture designer.

Training To 1941, Kunsthåndværkerskolen, Copenhagen; 1938 under a cabinetmaker, apprenticeship.
Biography Wikkelsø worked with architects Jacob Kjær, Peter Hvidt, and Orla Mølgård-Nielsen; 1954, established his own design studio; designed furniture by P. Schultz, A. Mikael Laursen, Silkeborg Møbelfabrik (under C.F. Christensen), Holger Christensen, Søren Willadsen, and, N. Eilersen.
Bibliography Frederik Sieck, *Nutidig Dansk Møbeldesign – en kortfattet illustreret beskrivelse*, Copenhagen: Bondo Gravesen, 1990.

Wilde, Fred H.

British ceramicist.

Biography 1885, Wilde settled in the US, where he was associated with several tile firms, including Robertson Art Tile in Morrisville, Pa., and Pacific Art Tile (later Western Art Tile) in Tropico, Cal.; 1916–18,

was the third successive artistic director at the Arequipa Art Pottery, succeeding Frederick H. Rhead and Albert L. Solon; became the ceramics engineer of Pomona Tile Los Angeles, when it was established in 1923, remaining there to 1940.
Bibliography Paul Evans in Timothy J. Andersen et al., *California Design 1910*, Salt Lake City: Peregrine Smith, 1980: 71, 77. 'Fred H. Wilde: His Life and Work,' *Flash Point Journal*, vol. 1, nos. 1–4, part 1–3; vol. 2, no. 1, part 4.

Wildenhain, Franz (or Frans) Rudolf (1905–80)

German ceramicist; born Leipzig; husband of Marguerite Wildenhain.

Training In lithography; 1924–25, ceramics, Bauhaus, Dornburg; from 1925, Burg Giebichenstein (later Kunstgewerbeschule), Halle.
Biography 1933 with his wife, he established the workshop Pottenbakkerij Het Kruikje in the Netherlands; 1947, joined his wife in the US, who had emigrated there in 1940; 1950–56, taught pottery in Rochester, N.Y.
Exhibitions/citation Work subject of retrospectives at State University of New York, Binghamton, 1974–75; Bevier Gallery, Rochester, 1975 (catalogs below). 1958 Guggenheim Fellowship.
Bibliography Cat., *Frans Wildenhain Retrospective*, Binghamton, N.Y.: State University of New York at Binghamton, 1974. Cat., *Frans Wildenhain: A Chronology of a Master Potter*, Rochester, N.Y.: Rochester Institute of Technology, 1975. Barbara Cowles (compiler), 'Frans Remembered,' 1980 (unpaginated manuscript in American Art / Portrait Gallery Library, Washington, D.C.). Lionel Richard, *Encyclopédie du Bauhaus*, Paris: Somogy, 1985. Cat., *Keramik und Bauhaus*, Berlin: Bauhaus-Archiv, 1989: 154–200, 264.
> See Wildenhain, Marguerite (below).

Wildenhain, Marguerite (b. Marguerite Friedländer 1896–1985)

French ceramicist; born Lyon, France; wife of Franz Wildenhain.

Training 1914, sculpture, Hochschule für Angewandte Kunst, Berlin; 1919–25 under Gerhard Marcks and Max Krehan, ceramics, Bauhaus, Dornburg; from 1925, Burg Giebichenstein (later Kunstgewerbeschule), Halle.
Biography 1916–17, she worked as a designer in a porcelain factory in Rudolfstadt, before entering the Bauhaus, and already a pottery journeyperson. She became active in the Bauhaus Pottery Workshop (established in 1920 by Gerhard Marcks and Max Krehan) and focused on non-ornamental ceramics, like fellow Bauhaus student Trude Petri. From 1926, she was the director of the ceramics workshop at Burg Giebichenstein; from 1929, began designing for Staatliche Porzellan-Manufaktur (now and formerly known as Königliche Porzellan-Manufaktur or KPM), Berlin. She designed KPM's now-well-known 1930 Halle service (or Hallische Form tea set), to which Petri contributed concentric gilt bands in 1931, and 1930 Burg-Giebichenstein dinner service. The latter showed an attempt to infuse craft-like elements into mass-produced wares. 1930, she married Franz Wildenhain and, 1933, they settled in Putten, the Netherlands, where they established the workshop Pottenbakkerij Het Kruikje, which was active 1933–40 and where they designed earthenware for firms including De Sphinx in Maastricht, in 1936. 1940, she emigrated to the US and settled at Pond Farm in Guerneville, Cal.; 1940–42, taught, College of Arts and Crafts, Oakland, Cal.; briefly, was the director of the pottery division, Appalachian Institute of Arts and Crafts, Banner Elk, N.C. She returned to Guerneville and began working in her own workshop; 1947, was joined by her husband. A notable ceramicist, she helped establish the school and workshop in 1949 at the Pond Farm Pottery, where she was a teacher and potter-in-residence. Even though the pottery closed 1953, she still directed a popular summer school there. She wrote the books *The Invisible Core: A Potter's Lfe and Thoughts* (Palo Alto, Cal., Pacific Books, 1973), *Pottery: Form and Expression* (New York: American Craftsmen's Council, 1959), and *That We Look and See: An Admirer Looks at the Indians* (1979). She died in Guerneville.
Exhibitions Work shown at 1947 (11th) *Ceramic National Exhibition* touring exhibition, organized by Syracuse Museum of Fine Art, Syracuse, N.Y.; 1959 (20th) *Ceramic International Exhibition*, The Metropolitan Museum of Art, New York. Work subject of 1980–81 *Marguerite*, Oakland (California) Museum, and Mint Museum of Art, Atlanta, Ga. (catalog below).
Bibliography Cat., Lynn M. Colvin (ed.), *Marguerite: A Retrospective Exhibition of the Work of Master Potter Marguerite Wildenhain*, Ithaca, N.Y.: Cornell University, 1980. Lionel Richard, *Encyclopédie du Bauhaus*, Paris: Somogy, 1985: 212. Cat., *Keramik und Bauhaus*, Berlin: Bauhaus-Archiv, 1989: 154–200, 268. R. Craig, Miller, *Modern Design 1890–1990*, New York: Abrams, 1990. Gerhard Marcks, *The Letters of Gerhard Marcks and Marguerite Wildenhain, 1970–1981: A Mingling of Souls*, Ames: Iowa State University; Decorah, Iowa: Luther College, 1991.

Marguerite Wildenhain. Bowl. c. 1945. Glazed pottery, h. 3 5/8" (9.2 cm) x dia. 8" (20.3 cm). Mfr.: the designer, US. Gift of Gump's. MoMA.

Wilkens und Söhne, M.H.

German silversmiths; located Bremen-Hemelingen.

History 1810, M.H. Wilkens und Söhne was founded by Martin Heinrich Wilkens (1782–1869), who was infatuated with the malleable, soft, and versatile characteristics of metal. By the beginning of 20th century, was the leading silverware producer in Germany, along with Bruckmann & Söhne; hired designers, including Peter Behrens, Albin Müller, and Heinrich Vogeler, and, 1910–40, H. Bulling, Alfred Donant, C. Krauss, and Karl Müller. Even so, modern-design silver remained a sideline. Vogeler was the smithy's best-known freelancer; c. 1900, designed candelabra, table ornaments, and cutlery for the firm. His Tulip pattern by Wilkens was sold at Julius Meier-Graefe's La Maison Moderne, Paris. Some of Wilkens's wares, like those at 1922 Munich exhibition (see below), showed a Viennese influence; others had Art Déco characteristics.
Exhibitions Silverware designed by Bulling and Müller shown at 1922 *Deutsche Gewerbeschau*, Munich.
Bibliography Annelies Krekel-Aalberse, *Art Nouveau and Art Déco Silver*, New York: Abrams, 1989. Cat., *Metallkunst*, Berlin: Bröhan, 1990: 534–42.

Wilkes & Ashmore

British industrial-design studio; located Horsham.

History 1961–65, Richard Beeching (Kent, 1913–85) was the chairperson of the British Railways Board (BRB). During his tenure, he worked in conjunction with the BRB Design Panel and design consultants Wilkes & Ashmore to develop a plan for a new corporate image, which materialized as the famous blue/gray passenger-train stock of British Rail (formerly British Railways). Wilkes & Ashmore's designs for British Rail train included 1958 5200 (Type 2/Class 24), D5085 Derby / D5058 (Type 2/Class 24), *5300 – 5346* (Class 25) diesels with the yellow front-and-rear panels (built by British Rail in Derby, Crewe, and Darlington), and other particularly stylish examples, at least through 1966. The Class 24 are now being produced as toy models in the OO-gauge scale (1:76) by Backmann Industries of Altdorf bei Nürnberg, Germany. Wilkes & Ashmore also designed domestic products; from 1959, David Lawrence Higgins worked in the studio for a time. Documentation on the firm's activities in the train sector is housed in National Railway Museum Library and Archives, York.
Bibliography R.H.N. Hardy, *Beeching: Champion of the Railway*, London: Ian Allan, 1989.

Wilkes & Ashmore. Flashlight (no. 9222), c. 1966. Plastic, overall 4 x 2 5/8 x 1" (10.2 x 6.6 x 2.5 cm). Mfr.: British Ever Ready Export Company (BEREC), UK. Gift of the manufacturer. MoMA.

Willers, Margarete (1883–1977)

German textile designer; born Oldenburg.

Training From 1905, painting and drawing, Düsseldorf and Munich; under Maurice Denis, Paris; 1921–22, weaving, Bauhaus, Weimar.
Biography 1927–28, she had her own workshop at the Bauhaus; 1928–43, was director of the handweaving and embroidery studio, Folkwangschule, Essen; 1943–55, taught in the handweaving studio in Bückeburg; 1955–60, ran an independent studio.
Bibliography Cat., Gunta Stölzl, *Weberei am Bauhaus und ams eigener Werkstätt*, Berlin: Bauhaus-Archiv, 1987: 167. Cat., *The Bauhaus: Masters and Students*, New York: Barry Friedman, 1988. Sigrid Wortmann Weltge, *Women's Work: Textile Art from The Bauhaus*, San Francisco: Chronicle, 1993.

Williams, Petr (1902–1947)

Russian painter and graphic and theater artist; born Moscow.

Training From 1909, V.N. V.N. Meshkov's school of painting, drawing and sculpture, Moscow, Moscow; 1918–24 under Konstantin Korovin, Vasillii Kandinsky, and Petr Konchalovskii, SVOMAS (free state art studios); 1922-23, VKhUTEMAS (formerly SVOMAS).
Biography 1913 with his father, Williams traveled in Italy and Germany; while studying at VKhUTEMAS, 1922-23, was head, Museum of Artistic Culture; was a founder, Society of Easel Artists; 1928, traveled in France, Italy, and Germany and became interested in theater productions; from 1929, worked as a theater artist for significant Moscow theatres. 1941–47, he was the chief artist of the Bolshoi Theater, where he designed lush sets and sumptuous costumes, including for the 1940 production of Sergei Prokofiev's *Romeo and Juliet* (choreographer, Leonid Lavrovsky) by the Bolshoi Ballet at Kirov Theater; died in Moscow.
Exhibitions Work included in all four exhibitions of Society of Easel Artists from 1925-30.

Williams, Theo (1967–)

British designer; born Oxford.

Training In Bristol and Manchester; 1990, industrial-design degree.
Biography Williams designed playground equipment for a firm in Skelmersdale, near Liverpool; 1991, settled in Milan, Italy, and worked for Marco Zanuso Jr. on furniture, lighting, and accessories; subsequently for six months, with Aldo Cibic on furniture, Fiat 500 interior, and others; 1992, first became a staff designer, at Nava Design to 1997 (subsequently at Nava Press) and, concurrently (1993) established an independent practice; and has worked as a freelance designer for Armani, Calvin Klein, Nava Design, Prada, Pyrex Europe, Technolgym Italia, Tronconi, and a 1994 honey pot and sugar bowl by Alessi and bathroom stands by Dornbracht. He has also designed a range of products by Lexon, France, where he was the art director from 2000–02; for Ritzenhoff, decorated 1995 Milk! goblet, 1998 ashtrays, and 1999 pilsner goblet. From 2004, he developed branding for Mexxsport.
Citations Through Nava Design: 1995 and 1996 (two citations) Design Plus, Ambiente fair, Frankfurt; 1996 Premio SMAU Industrial Design (two selections), Salone della Machina e Attrezzature per l'Uffizio, Milan.
Bibliography *International Design Yearbook*, London: Laurence King, 2002 and 2003.

Williamson, Alexander Hardie (1907–1994)

British painter and industrial designer.

Biography Early 1950s, Williamson designed machine-pressed utility glass by United Glass Bottle Manufacturers (UGBM), makers of Ravenhead and Sherdley brands. Williamson being hired as the UGBM consultant designer signaled a major and progressive change in the firm's approach. He also designed a half dozen mid-1930s vessels by The Crystal Glass Company (formerly Bagley's Glass); was a teacher of industrial glass design, Royal College of Art, London.
Bibliography Michael Farr, *Design in British Industry: A Mid-Century Survey*, London: Cambridge, 1955: 145. Cat. leaflet, 'Slim Jims and Tubbies; The Life and Work of Designer Alexander Hardie Williamson,' Kingswinford: Broadfield House Glass Museum, 1996.

Willumsen, Jens Ferdinand (1863–1958)

Danish artist, architect, photographer, and ceramicist; born Copenhagen.

Training Technical school; 1881–85, architecture, Det Kongelige Danske Kunstakademi, Copenhagen.
Biography In 1890 in Brittany, Willumsen met Paul Gauguin, from whom he learned various techniques of painting methods and decorating in polychrome; also associated with various members of Gauguin's Symbolist movement and thus the Nabis group; also 1890, met Odilon Redon and was likewise influenced by him. Willumsen designed the 1897–1913 independent art exhibitions building in Copenhagen; 1897–1900, was the artistic director of Bing & Grøndahl, Copenhagen. He died in Cannes, France. 1957, J.F. Willumsens Museum (architect, Tyge Hvass) was opened in Frederikssund, Denmark.
Exhibitions/citations Paintings shown at 1891 Salon des Indépendants and the Impressionist and Symbolist exhibition (with the Nabis Group), LeBarc de Boutteville's gallery, Paris. Ceramics shown at 1889 *Exposition Universelle* (honorable mention award); 1900 *Exposition Universelle*; both Paris. 1947 Thorvaldsens Medal.
Bibliography Cat., David Revere McFadden (ed.), *Scandinavian Modern Design 1880–1980*, New York: Abrams, 1982.

Willys-Overland Motors
> See Probst, Karl K.

Theo Williams. Handy Light torch (flashlight). c. 2002. ABS plastic, aluminum, and xenon bulb, l. 5 3/4 x dia. 5/8" (14.8 x 1.6 cm). Mfr.: Lexon, France.

Wilm, Ferdinand Richard (1880–1972)

German silversmith; born and active Berlin.

Training Königlich Preussische Zeichenakademie, Hanau.
Biography From 1911, Ferdinand Wilm worked for his family's firm (founded in 1767; see entry below); called on sterling silver in the production of handmade silverware. 1932, Wilm, Peter Behrens, Ludwig Roselius, and Wilhelm Wätzoldt (director of the Staatliche Museen zu Berlin) founded the Deutsche Gesellschaft für Goldschmiedekunst, of which almost all the independent silversmiths in Germany became members; 1920s, made Peter Behrens's silver designs in the Wilm workshop.
Bibliography *Ferdinand Richard Wilm: Ein Goldschmiedehaus*, Berlin: Ohne Ort und Verlag, 1930. Annelies Krekel-Aalberse, *Art Nouveau and Art Déco Silver*, New York: Abrams, 1989. Cat., *Metallkunst*, Berlin: Bröhan-Museum, 1990: 543–45.

Wilm, H.J.

German silversmiths.

History 1767, the firm was founded in Berlin by Gottfried Ludwig Wilm (1746–1829) and takes its name from his nephew Hermann Julius Wilm. From 1911, family member Ferdinand Richard Wilm worked at the firm, furthering the development and improvement of silversmithing. From 1924, it was directed by Ludwig Riffelmacher, who encouraged massive, carefully detailed hand-raised work. Early 1930s, Erna Zarges-Dürr worked there. From 1945, the firm, directed by Johann Renatus Wilm, was located in Hamburg.
Bibliography Annelies Krekel-Aalberse, *Art Nouveau and Art Déco Silver*, New York: Abrams, 1989. Cat., *Metallkunst*, Berlin: Bröhan-Museum, 1990: 543–45.

Wilmotte, Jean-Michel (1948–)

French interior architect and designer of furniture, lighting, and accessories; born Soissons; active Paris.

Training From 1968, interior architecture, École Camondo, Paris.
Biography 1975, Wilmotte established the office Governor in Paris which employed a large staff by late 1980s; 1977, opened furniture showroom Academy in Paris, to show his own work; undertook interior design projects, including 1982–83 bedroom of President François Mitterrand in the Palais de l'Élysée, Paris, and 1984 office of the French ambassador in Washington, D.C. 1986, Wilmotte established an office and showroom in Tokyo and, 1987, offices in Nîmes and Cannes; late 1980s, designed the Musée des Beaux-Arts and Hôtel de Ville in Nîmes, a reception-conference room and projection facilities for the Canal + TV network, and the Bunka Mura cultural center in Tokyo. Architecture and interior-architecture work has included Palais des Congrès, Grasse and Lyon; offices and apartments, Tokyo; 1989 interiors beneath the Pyramid (I.M. Pei, architect) of the Musée du Louvre, Paris; 1990–98 renovation, Musée des Beaux-Arts, Lyon; 1993–97 Institut Universitaire de Technologie, Auxerre; 1994 Musée du Chiado (coordinating architect, IPPAR, Joao Herdad), Lisbon; 1994 urban furniture/lighting on avenue des Champs Élysées, Paris; 1996 reconstruction of Musée les Quais 'Hennessy,' Cognac; 1998 Gana contemporary art gallery, Seoul; 1999 reconstruction, Collège de France, Paris; 1999 construction/reconstruction, Pôle Européen de Gestion et d'Economie, Strasbourg; 2003 Palais des Congrés, Bordeaux; 2000 École Alsacienne, Paris; 2001 Musée d'Art et d'Industrie, Saint-Étienne; a number of others. Designed furniture by Mobilier International and by Nobilis; fabrics by Casal, Nobilis, and Suzanne Fontan; carpets by Flipo, Tisca, and Toulemonde Bochart; a faïence dinner service by Gien. Some furniture projects were sponsored by VIA (French furniture association), of which he was a founding member. Other furniture/furnishings: 1983 Washington lamp (still in production; originally for French ambassador's offices) by Lumen Center; 1983 Cylindre chair, 1984 Élysée stool, 1986 outdoor chair for the park of the Palais-Royal, Paris; 1987 Etalon table base, 1988 La Fontaine chair, 1988 Palmer chest (sponsored by VIA) in various models, Auriga cast-aluminum outdoor bench by Hess Form + Licht, tables/seating by SIF for Banque du Luxembourg.
Exhibitions/citations Work shown at 1989 *L'Art de Vivre*, Cooper-Hewitt National Design Museum, New York; 1990 *Les années VIA*, Musée des Art Décoratifs, Paris. Creator of the Year, 1989 Salon du Meuble, Paris; 1989 Carte Blanche production support, VIA.
Bibliography Jean-Louis Pradel, *Wilmotte*, Paris: Electa Moniteur, 1988. Cat., Garth Hall and Margo Rouard Snowman, *Avant-Première: Contemporary French Furniture*, London: Eprouvé, 1988. François Mathey, *Au bonheur des formes, design français 1945–1992*, Paris: Regard, 1992. Francis Rambert et al, *Jean-Michel Wilmotte*, Paris: Regard, 1996. Jean-Louis Pradel, *Mémoire d'empire*, Arles: Actes Sud, 1999. Jean-Louis Pradel, *Wilmotte*, Paris: Le Moniteur/Electa, 1999.

Wilsgaard, Jan (1930–)

Swedish automobile designer.

Biography 1960s–80s, Wilsgaard designed the sturdy, rational automobile bodies for which Volvo Car Corporation (founded in 1927) has become known and which exemplified for his prediliction for square shapes. Typical designs of Wilsgaard, as Volvo's chief designer, ranged from the first, 1966 Volvo 144, to 1991 Volvo 850, the latter typical of Wilsgaard's approach. When introduced, the 144 model was dubbed 'the safest car in the world' (as was likewise the 1998 S70). He redesigned 1963–69 P1800/P1800S/P1800E (not his design originally) as the 1971 1800 model. It was popular due to more rear headroom and luggage space and was sent to custom-auto-body-workshop Coggiola in Italy to be transformed into Wilsgaard's Beachcar. Some auto historians have claimed his 1982 760 model to be one of the most important cars in history. Early 1990s, Peter Horbury, a former Volvo designer and subsequent partner of MGA in Coventry, succeeded Wilsgaard in Volvo's design studio in Gothenberg, Sweden, as the corporate design director. (The firm also has a design studio in Helmond, the Netherlands.) 1999, Ford bought the Volvo Car Corporation, regarded as one of Sweden's 'crown jewels.'
Citations Gold medal (for model 144's braking system), Swedish Automobile Association; 1966 Car of the Year (model 144) in Scandinavia.
Bibliography K.K. Beck, *The Body in the Volvo*, New York: Walker, 1987. Christer Olsson, *Volvo Gothenburg Sweden*, St. Paul, Minn.: Motorbooks International, 1995. Christer Olsson, *Volvo Cars: A Rhapsody 1927–2000*, Oslo/Copenhagen: Norden Media, 2000. Jean Christer Olsson, *Volvo 75 Years: 1927–2002*, Oslo/Copenhagen: Norden Media, 2002.

Wilson, Elsie Cobb (1877–1949)

American interior decorator; born Washington, D.C.

Training Parsons School of Design, New York.
Biography Before World War I, she first worked for a decorator and, by 1919, had decorated her own clients' offices in New York and Washington, and eventually Palm Beach, Fla. She employed Eleanor McMillen (Brown), which was McMillen's first professional position as a decorator, and Dorothy Marckwald. If Elsie de Wolfe were the first American interior designer, then Wilson was the second. Wilson decorated great houses and apartments along America's Eastern seaboard as well as US embassies in Paris, Peking, and Tokyo; helped to restore the Marine Commandant's house in Washington for the parents of Lady Brooke Astor. Wilson's taste expressed the new refinement and restraint of post-Victorian décor. She arranged furniture for conversation rather than for style; worked in a narrow, strict range of austere taste, blending European tradition with American discipline. In a conservative style, she decorated the apartment of her sister Mrs. Cornelius Bliss on Fifth Avenue in New York and Bliss's house on Long Island. Wilson was active to 1936, when her firm was reorganized as Smyth, Urquhart Marckwald, which had individual and corporate clients and designed the interiors of 1940 oceanliner *America*.
Bibliography Mark Hampton, *Legendary Decorators of the Twentieth Century*, New York: Doubleday, 1992.

Wilson, Henry (1864–1934)

British architect, sculptor, and silversmith.

Training Kidderminster School of Art.
Biography Wilson became chief assistant to architect J.D. Sedding. On Sedding's 1891 death, Wilson took over the firm and completed Sedding's unfinished work; after 1890, became interested in metalworking and, c. 1895, established a workshop; joined the Art-Workers' Guild; from 1896 under W.R. Lethaby, taught metalworking, Central School of Arts and Crafts, London; having met Alexander Fisher at the Central School, collaborated with him for a short time; taught, Royal College of Art, London; from c. 1902, taught, Victoria Street School of Jewellers and Silversmiths, Birmingham; wrote the design and technique manual *Silverwork and Jewellery: A Text-Book for Students and Workers in Metal* (London: J. Hogg, 1903), still considered one of the best handbooks on the subject; the 2nd edition (1912) includes a chapter on Japanese metalworking techniques, which is based on lectures and demonstrations of instructors Unno Bisei of Tokyo Fine Art College and R. Kobayashi. 1915, Wilson succeeded Walter Crane as presi-

dent of Arts and Crafts Exhibition Society; 1917, became master of Art-Workers' Guild. J. Paul Cooper, who later established his own workshop, worked with Wilson. 1898, H.G. Murphy was apprenticed to Wilson and, subsequently, became his assistant.
Exhibitions From 1889, work shown regularly at Arts and Crafts Exhibition Society, and included in the British pavilion, 1925 *Exposition Internationale des Arts Décoratifs et Industriels Modernes*, Paris.
Bibliography Charlotte Gere, *American and European Jewelry 1830–1914*, New York: Crown, 1975. Annelies Krekel-Aalberse, *Art Nouveau and Art Déco Silver*, New York: Abrams, 1989.

Wilson, Lynne (1952–)
British furniture and textile designer; born Epsom, Surrey; active Milan.

Training To 1975, Kingston Polytechnic (now Kingston University); to 1979, Royal College of Art, London.
Biography For three months, Wilson was a design apprentice in the Centro Design Prototipo of Cassina in Meda, Italy; 1979–80 with Mario Bellini, worked on projects for Rosenthal and Cleto Munari; 1982, began as a freelance designer, for Italian furniture clients and created her first commercial product, the Lotto knock-down chair by Mobilia Italia. From 1984, she designed other textiles for Centro Design e Comunicazione, Milan, 1985 Felice metal-tube and polyurethane divan (prototype), 1985 Oltre il Giardino and 1986 Il Risveglio textile collections by Assia, 1985 Toba knock-down table by Gemini (designed in 1979 while at Royal College of Art), 1987 Paradiso Ritrovato curtains by Fanair, and others since.
Bibliography Liz McQuiston, *Women in Design: A Contemporary View*, New York: Rizzoli, 1988: 136.

Wilson, Norman (1902–)
British ceramicist.

Training North Staffordshire Technical College.
Biography Wilson began working for Wedgwood in Etruria, where he was the works manager from 1927; 1928, developed the gas-fired china glost tunnel kiln; 1928–62, produced NW Unique Pieces, usually turned and thrown, with three or four glazes; 1931, developed the oil-fired earthenware glost tunnel kiln; 1933, introduced the two-color bodies and the Moonstone matt glaze applied to 1932–33 Annular dinner service by John Goodwin, Tom Wedgwood, and others; 1934, introduced Alpine Pink glaze. His 1933–35 Matt Green and Matt Straw glazes were applied to Keith Murray's wares and John Skeaping's animal figurines. 1932–39, Wilson produced numerous decorative shapes in the Veronese glaze, in other glazes, and with silver luster. He designed 1935 Globe shape, decorated by artists including Victor Skellern; 1946, became the production manager of Wedgwood in Barlaston, where he created the 1955 Barlaston shape and, 1961, became the joint managing director.
Bibliography Cat., *Thirties: British Art and Design Before the War*, London: Arts Council of Great Britain/Hayward Gallery, 1979.

Wilson, William (1914–)
British glassware designer; active Wealdstone, Middlesex.

Training 1930–33, St. Martin's School of Art; subsequently, Central School of Arts and Crafts, both London.
Biography At the age of 14, Wilson joined the stained-glass department of James Powell & Sons (Whitefriars) on Wigmore Street in London, as an errand boy. He studied at nights and during some days while at Powell; 1933, transferred to the works in Wealdstone, where he designed domestic glassware and played a significant role in the revival of diamond-point engraving. He encouraged fashionable modern glass in the Scandinavian style; 1940, became the works manager and, subsequently, the general manager, then director and, 1950–73, was the managing director, working as a designer throughout. He hired George Baxter as a staff designer.
Bibliography Cat., *Thirties: British Art and Design Before the War*, London: Arts Council of Great Britain/Hayward Gallery, 1979. Frederick Cooke, *Glass: Twentieth-Century Design*, New York: Dutton, 1986: 73-75.

Wimmer-Wisgrill, Eduard Josef (aka Eduard Josef Wimmer 1882–1961)
Austrian fashion, costume, theater-set, and furniture designer and metalworker; born Vienna.

Training 1901–07, School of Commerce; and Akademie für angewandte Kunst (Kunstgewerbeschule); both Vienna.
Biography Wimmer-Wisgrill was an assistant to Koloman Moser at the Wiener Werkstätte in Vienna, where he was the director of its fashion department 1910–22. He designed silverware and jewelry there. Partially due to his influence, the geometric forms of the Wiener Werkstätte became less austere, and bell-flowers, heart-shaped leaves, and spiraling tendrils appeared. 1912–13, 1918–21, and 1925–53, he was a professor, Akademie für angewandte Kunst (Kunstgewerbeschule), Vienna; remained at the Wiener Werkstätte to its 1932 closure. A ziggurat-shaped wooden chest with mother-of-pearl inlay in the Österreichisches Museum für angewandte Kunst, Vienna, is particularly dramatic.
Bibliography Charlotte Gere, *American and European Jewelry 1830–1914*, New York: Crown, 1975. Werner J. Schweiger, *Wiener Werkstätte*, Vienna: Christian Brandstaetter, 1982: 269. Annelies Krekel-Aalberse, *Art Nouveau and Art Déco Silver*, New York: Abrams, 1989. *Wiener Werkstätte: Glas, Keramik, Holz, Leder, Metall: Aus den beständen des Österreichischen Museums für angewandte Kunst, Wien*, Vienna: Österreichisches Museum für angewandte Kunst, 1990.

Windingstad, Sigbjørn (1965–)
Norwegian industrial designer; born Fana; active Oslo.

Training 1989–93, Department of Industrial Design, Statens Håndverks- og Kunstindustriskole, Oslo; 1991–92, visiting student, ENSCI (Les Ateliers), Paris; 1994–95, CAD studies in Microstation, Cimtec engineering firm; 1995, Euclid and 3D-CAD studies, Nestor firm.
Biography 1984–86, 1987, 1988–92, Windingstad worked at Det Norske Veritas on FEM software documentation. 1994, he established an industrial-design consultancy in Oslo; 1996, moved to Stryn, Norway, for the development/design of new range of autobus bodies by Vest-Karosseri; 1997, re-established a design studio in Oslo, specializing in vehicle design. With a Texas group of designers, he developed vehicle bodies (a new line of autobuses by Vest-Karosseri and low-floor minibus by Bewa Bil og Inredning of Sweden). He also designed an autobus computer and was active in interface and product design in Thoreb, Sweden. While at various firms, other assignments have included electric-vehicle prototype at Peter Opsvik design firm, cabinet and interface of mobile induction-heater by Elva Induksjon (EFD Group from 1996), radio studio and VIP lounge in a semitrailer interior for Radio P4, ice-cube machine by Blue Ice & Co., grocery box by Dynoplast, 1992–93 guide for French autobus tourists, 2000 Bagman plastic-bag holder. 1995–96, Windingstad was a board member of Norska Industridesignere (NID, Norwegian industrial design association).
Exhibitions/citations Work included in Les Ateliers school (participant) entry, 1992 Triennale di Milano; 1994–95 *Varde* (Nordic design exhibition), traveling to London, Rome, Berlin, Vienna, Budapest; *Generation X: Young Nordic Design*, traveling the world from 2000. Winner, 2001 crutches competition of Norwegian national handicap association; prize (for Mamout bicycle), 1995 Unge Talenter, NID and Norska Designrådet (ND, Norwegian design council); 1997 Young Designer of the Year, Norsk Form.

Wines, James (1932–)
American building, landscape, and product designer; born Oak Park, Ill.; active New York.

Training 1955, bachelor of arts degree in art history and visual arts, Syracuse (N.Y.) University.
Biography 1969, Wines founded Sculpture in the Environment (SITE) in New York to explore socially and environmentally responsible solutions to the design of buildings, interiors, public spaces, and commercial products (including 1998 Binary Code wristwatch) and became known for his and SITE's unorthodox approach. Projects, drawings, and essays have been extensively published in the professional, popular, and academic journals of 25 countries. He has taught courses and held workshops at numerous schools and universities worldwide, including 1984–90, chairperson, Environmental Design, Parsons School of Design; from 1991, Distinguished Professor of Architecture, New School for Social Research; both New York. He wrote *De-Architecture* (New York: Rizzoli, 1985), *Polemics: Aesthetics of Green Architecture* (New York: Wiley-Academy, 1997), *SITE: Sculpture in the Environment* (with Herbert Muschamp, New York: Rizzoli, 1989), *Green Architecture: The Art of Architecture in the Age of Ecology* (Cologne: Taschen, 2000), and others, including numerous journal articles.
Exhibitions/citations Architectural works included in more than 100 museums and galleries in North America, Europe, and Asia. SITE buildings and interiors granted major design awards. Wines assigned fellowships by the Pulitzer Foundation, Guggenheim Foundation, Ameri-

Tapio Wirkkala. Platter. 1951. Hand-carved laminated plywood. 1 1/2 x 10 x 8 3/4" (3.8 x 25.4 x 22.2 cm). Mfr.: the designer, Finland. Gift of the designer. MoMA.

can Academy in Rome, Ford Foundation, Graham Foundation, Kress Foundation, New York State Council on the Arts, and National Endowment for the Arts; 1995 Chrysler Award for Design Innovation.
> See SITE.

Winkler, Catherine (1906–1989)
> See Philco.

Wirkkala, Tapio Veli Ilmari (1915–1985)

Finnish glassware, wood, graphic and exhibition designer and metalworker; born Hanko; husband of ceramicist Rut Bryk (1916–1999).

Training 1933–36, sculpture, Taideteollinen korkeakoulu, Helsinki.
Biography Wirkkala was one of the most fecund and celebrated postwar Finnish designers; 1947–85, was the chief designer of Iittala glassworks, and concurrently active as a freelance designer. His 1947 Kantarelli vase and 1951 laminated wooden dishes by Soinne gained him initial recognition. He also designed 1970 Coreano dish and 1970 Bolla bottles by Venini; from 1950s, became a highly influential designer of glass; designed the Finnish pavilions at 1952 (9th) and 1954 (10th) editions of Triennale di Milano and 1958 *Exposition Universelle et Internationale de Bruxelles* (*Expo '58*); 1951–54, was the artistic director of Taideteollinen korkeakoulu; 1955, established his own workshop in Helsinki; 1955–56, worked in the studio of Raymond Loewy in New York; and, as clients, for Rosenthal from 1956–85, Venini glassworks from 1959–85, Orfèvrerie Christofle, and Airam. Designed mid-1960s stacking glasses, which set a trend; 1963 Puukko knife and 1965 Karelia suite of drinking glasses by Hackman, which became an instant success. He died in Helsinki.
Exhibitions/citations Work included in a large number of exhibitions. Subject of 1976 exhibition, Stedelijk Museum, Amsterdam; 1981–82 worldwide traveling exhibition; 1983, Musée des Arts Décoratifs, Paris; 1987–88 *Tapio Wirkkala, Venini*, Suomen Lasimuseo, Riihimäki; 2000 *Tapio Wirkkala: Eye, Hand, Thought*, Taideteollisuusmuseo, Helsinki (catalogs below). Received first prize, 1946 Iittala glass competition. Triennale di Milano (with Kaj Franck): 1947 (8th) three gold medals and a grand prize. Triennale (alone): 1951 (9th) three grand prizes (design, glass, carving), 1954 (10th) three grand prizes (design, glass, sculpture), 1960 (12th) grand prize and gold medal, 1964 (13th) silver medal. 1951 (1st) Lunning Prize; 1961, elected honorary member, Royal Society of Arts, London, and 1972, academician there; 1963, 1966, 1967, 1969, and 1973 gold medals, Concorso Internazionale della Ceramica d'Arte, Faenza; honorary doctoral degree, Royal College of Art, London; 1964, elected Honorary Royal Designer for Industry, UK; 1975, honorary member, Diseñadores Industriales, Instituto Politécnico Nacional, Mexico City; honorary academician, Académie de l'Architecture, France, and 1983 silver medal; 1980 Prince Eugen Medal.
Bibliography Cat., Tapio Wirkkala, *Contemporary Finnish Design*, Washington, D.C.: Smithsonian Institution, 1972. Cat., Wil Bertheux and Ada Stroeve, *Tapio Wirkkala*, Amsterdam: Stadsdrukkerij van Amsterdam, 1976. Cat., *Tapio Wirkkala*, Helsinki: Société des Arts Décoratifs de Finlande, 1983. 'Interview with Tapio Wirkkala,' *Domus* 619, July-Aug. 1981: 6–7. Pekka Suhonen, 'Counterpoints in Tapio Wirkkala's Output,' *Form Function Finland*, no. 2, 1981: 38–43. Cat., *The Lunning Prize*, Stockholm: Nationalmuseum, 1986: 36–41. Jennifer Hawkins Opie, *Scandinavia: Ceramics and Glass in the Twentieth Century*, New York: Rizzoli, 1989. Cat., Marianne Aav, *Tapio Wirkkala 1915–1985: Eye, Hand, Thought*, Helsinki: Taideteollisuusmuseo/WSOY, 2000.

Witzmann, Carl (1883–1952)

Austrian architect and designer; born Vienna.

Training Apprenticeship as joiner; under Josef Hoffmann, Kunstgewerbeschule, Vienna.
Biography Witzmann worked at the Wiener Werkstätte; from 1908, taught, Kunstgewerbeschule, Vienna, where he was a professor of furniture design from 1910; was active as an architecture, furniture, and exhibition designer. In Vienna, Witzmann designed 1907 Igler house, 1923–24 refurbishment of the theater on the Josefstadt, 1929 Apollo cinema, 1930 presentation area of Rathaus (city hall), 1931 Theater Scala Wien, 1931 Moulin Rouge, and 1931 Café Fenstergucker. 1929 sconces and a ceiling fixture are being reproduced by Woka of Vienna. He died in Vienna.

Wlach, Oskar (1881–1863)

Austrian architect and furniture and interior designer; born Vienna.

Training Architecture, Technische Hochschule (TH), Vienna.
Biography Wlach contributed to Viennese architecture/design during the Sezession period but his output was modest. Josef Frank, after studying at the TH in Vienna, first colllaborated with Oskar Strnad and then with Wlach and Strnad. Wlach's distinctive modern architecture, in marked constrast to the prevailing Jugendstil style, includes a number of single-family dwellings and residences in Vienna, such as 1912 Hoch house (with Strnad and Frank), 1914 Wasserman house (with Strnad and Frank), and 1929–31 Julius and Margarete Beer house in Poetzleinsdorf (with Frank, and located next to Adolf Loos's 1928 Möller house). 1910, Wlach and Frank founded the interior-design firm and modern-furniture store Haus und Garten in Vienna, which produced furniture, textiles, and utensils. Wlach, Frank, and Strnad also designed the interiors for a number of clients. The simple, light furnishings that they created became the basis of the Wiener Wohnstil (Viennese living style), popular in 1920s and early 1930s. Wlach died in New York.

Wogg: Benny Mosimann. Wogg 18 stacking sideboard. c. 1998. Polycarbonate and melamine, each unit h. 17 3/8 x 58 1/4 x d. 14 5/8" (44 x 148 x 37 cm). Mfr.: Wogg, Switzerland.

Wohnbedarf: Marcel Breuer. Couch. 1930–31. Tubular steel, flat chrome-plated steel bars, and upholstered cushions, 53 1/4 x 55 1/8 x 28 1/2" (135.3 x 140 x 72.4 cm). Mfr.: EMBRU-Werke, Switzerland (attribution). Gift of Lily Auchincloss. MoMA.

Exhibition Work included in 1998 *Die Wiener Werkbundsiedlung 1930–1932*, Architekturzentrum, Vienna.
Bibliography Günther Feuerstein, *Vienna—Present and Past: Arts and Crafts—Applied Art—Design*, Vienna: Jugend und Volk, 1976.

WMF
> See Württembergische Metallwarenfabrik.

Wogg; Gebrüder Gläser
Swiss furniture manufactuer.

History 1972, Willi Gläser reorganized his family's furniture manufacturer Gebrüder Gläser to diversify the firm's activities; it was at the time directed by his father Willi (of the same first name) and his uncle Otto Gläser. 1981 in Baden-Dättwil, Willi and his cousin Otto established what is today a respected high-design brand: Wogg (Willi und Otto, Gebrüder Gläser). Wogg cabinets, tables, shelves, and accessories—first (1983) on sale in Switzerland and worldwide from 1984—are manufactured by the corporate entity Gläser AG. Wogg's consultant designers have included Atelier Oï, Hans Eichenberger, Ginbande Design, Trix and Robert Haussmann, Masayuki Kurokawa, Christophe Marchand, Adrian Meyer, Benny Mosimann, Johann Munz, Ludwig Roner, Richard Wassmann, and Hannes Wettstein.
Exhibitions From 1983, a large number of venues.
Bibliography *The International Design Yearbook*, London: Laurence King, 1988, 1997, and 2001.

Wohlert, Vilhelm (1920–)
Danish architect and furniture designer.

Training To 1944, architecture, Det Kongelige Danske Kunstakademi, Copenhagen.
Biography 1948, Wohlert established his own architecture office; 1951–53, taught, University of California and, 1944–46 and 1953–59, Det Kongelige Danske Kunstakademi. From 1950, he designed furniture and worked on some architecture commissions with architect Jørgen Bo. Architecture includes supervision (from 1958, with Bo) of alterations on the Louisiana Museum for Moderne Kunst, Humlebæk; 1979–83 Museum Bochum, Bochum; 1988–92 restoration of 1840–42 Saint Ansgar Cathedral, Copenhagen. Early 1960s, Andreas Hansen worked in Wohlert's office, and Alfred Homann there from 1972–79.
Exhibitions/citations Work shown in Danish architecture and design venues in London, New York, and Stockholm. Received 1958 Eckersberg Medal; Bundespreis Produktdesign, Rat für Formgebung (German design council), Frankfurt.
Bibliography Nikolaus Pevsner, *A History of Building Types*, Princeton, N.J.: Princeton University, 1979. Frederik Sieck, *Nutidig Dansk Møbeldesign – en kortfattet illustreret beskrivelse*, Copenhagen: Bondo Gravesen, 1990. T. Kappel, *Arkitektur DK*, July 1991: 337–39, 426–33; Aug. 1992: 305–21.

Wohnbedarf
Swiss furniture and furnishings store and makers; initially located Zürich.

History 1931, Wohnbedarf (German for household requirements) was founded by Sigfried Giedion, Rudolf Graber, and Werner Max Moser to sell modern design to middle-class customers. Its first store was at Claridenstrasse 47 in Zürich, and its interior was designed by architect/designer Ernst F. Burckhardt. It arranged for the mass production, or batch production, of its-own-commissioned designs of standardized, basic models of furniture, including cabinets, chairs, and modular configurations. Early 1930s while working on the Neubühl settlement near Zürich, Max Bill designed the firm's letterhead, advertisements, flyers, invitation cards, and the first (1931) Wohnbedarf logo. From 1934 and a number of years hence, Herbert Bayer designed most of the store's printed advertising and promotion. Alvar Aalto's bentwood furniture was sold at Wohnbedarf before the 1935 founding of his Artek firm in Helsinki. An active and important designer for Wohnbedarf, Aalto's entire collection of bentwood furniture was included in the catalog *New Wooden Furniture: Aalto, Wohnbedarf* (1934) designed by Bayer. Marcel Breuer's convertible sofa was produced by EMBRU-Werke and sold through Wohnbedarf. 1935, the enterprise became wholly owned by Graber and his mother. The firm began to sell furniture and furnishings from other enterprises and is still in business today with branch stores in various Swiss cities.
Bibliography Stanislaus von Moos, 'Wohnbedarf und Lebensform,' *Archithese*, no. 2, 1980. Friederike Mehlau-Wiebking et al., *Schweizer Typenmöbel 1925–35, Sigfried Giedion und die Wohnbedarf AG*, Zürich: gta, 1989.

Wolcott, Frank E. (d. 1944); Silex; Proctor-Silex; Hamilton Beach
Wilcott: American inventor; manufacturers.

Biography 1909, the two sisters Mrs. Ann Birdges and Mrs. Sutton of Salem, Mass., acquired the rights to the design of a vacuum-type coffee maker to be produced in clear high-heat-resistant Pyrex (or borosilicate) clear glass, a Corning Glass Work's proprietary material. It was

Frank E. Wolcott: Coffee maker. c. 1928. Borosilicate glass and metal, overall: h. 15 1/4" (28.8 cm). Mfr.: Frank E. Wolcott Manufacturing Company, US. Gift of Mrs. M. Rawson. MoMA.

sold under the name Silex (Sanitary and Interesting method of making Luscious coffee, and Easy to operate due to its X-ray-like transparency). 1915, the sisters had their coffee-brewing device made by Frank E. Wolcott Manufacturing Company in New England. The invention was special in that examples such as French models were made in a glass not resistant to high temperatures. The sales of a number of the Wolcott-made pots, sold to hotels and short-order cafés, brought the product to the public's attention and, thus, popularity. 1929, Frank E. Wolcott Manufacturing Company became a part of The Silex Company of Hartford, Conn. 1930–43, Wolcott himself was granted a number of patents for coffee- and/or tea-brewing designs, which called on the incorporation of Pyrex glass. Some other Silex designers (also with patents) included Anne M. Boever in late 1920s–30s and Ludwig Reichold in 1940s. So popular were the Silex coffee syphons that they became generically known as 'silex pots.' 1920s for a short time, H.C. Fry Glass Company made the glass for Silex. The history of Silex to today weaves an intricate, but typical, 20th-century corporate web: 1920, Philadelphia Textile Machinery Company (founded in 1885) formed Proctor & Schwartz. For the acquisition of new thermostat technology, Proctor & Schwartz formed Proctor & Schwartz Electric Company. 1960, Proctor & Schwartz and Silex merged to form Proctor-Silex, which was purchased by SCM Corporation in 1966. In another arena, 1904, the founders of U.S. Standard Electrical Works of Racine, Wis., hired young farm boy Chester Beach and former cashier L.H. Hamilton. Beach made inprovements to the first lightweight high-speed motor (one running on AC or DC power). This motor revolutionized the small-appliance industry and became the basis for a new range—including the first Hamilton Beach product, a 1910 electric hand-held body massager. The firm went on to make a number of now-legendary wares, including a stand-held food mixer. 1990, NACCO Industries bought 80% of Hamilton Beach and already owned Proctor-Silex. Thus, 1990, NACCO married the two entities into Hamilton Beach/Proctor-Silex to become the largest U.S. manufacturer of small kitchen appliances.
Exhibitions 84" (213 cm) replica of a glass coffee maker simulating its operation, at the Silex stand, 1939–40 *New York World's Fair: The World of Tomorrow*.
Bibliography Edward and Joan Bramah, *Coffee Makers: 300 Years of Art & Design*, London: Quiller, 1995. www.baharris.org/coffee. www.idsa.org/whatis/100yr/pyrex.htm.

Wolff, Ann (b. Anneliese Schaefer 1937–)

German glassware designer; born Lübeck; active Sweden.

Training In graphic design, Hamburg; 1958–60, Hochschule für Gestaltung, Ulm; and in Zürich.
Biography 1960–64, she was a designer at Pukeberg Glasbruk and, 1964–78, at Kosta Boda glassworks; 1978, established her own studio in Transjö, Sweden; has lectured in Europe, the US, Japan; 1977, 1978, 1983, and 1985, was a guest lecturer, Pilchuck School of Glass, Standwood, Washington; 1982–85, taught, Sunderland Polytechnic, UK; 1985, changed her name to Wolff. Work has included 1983 My Red Thread bowl.

Terence Woodgate. Paulina table, chair, and stool. c. 1998. Maple and fabric, table h. 14 5/8 x w. 24 x d. 20 1/2" (37 x 61 x 52 cm), chair h. 27 1/2 x w. 24 x d. 23 5/8" (70 x 61 x 60 cm), stool h. 14 5/8 x w. 24 x d. 20 1/2" (37 x 61 x 52 cm). Mfr.: Montina, Italy.

Edward Wormley. Table. c. 1951. Walnut and cherry, w. 39 x d. 30" (99.1 x 76.2 cm). Mfr.: Dunbar Furniture Manufacturing Corp., US. Gift of the mfr. MoMA.

Exhibitions/citations 1967 Swedish state traveling scholarship; 1968 Lunning Prize (with Göran Wärff).
Bibliography Cat., *The Lunning Prize*, Stockholm: Nationalmuseum, 1986: 190–93.

Wolff Olins
British design studio.

History 1965, Wolff Olins was established in London. Its work has ranged from graphics to interiors, with a specialization in corporate-identity programs, such as for British Telecom. Wally Olins and Michael Wolff (b. 1933) were the original principals; although Wolff left the partnership in mid-1980s, the name was retained by the design consultancy. The services they offer today mainly concern branding.
Bibliography Penny Sparke, *Introduction to Design and Culture in the Twentieth Century*, London: Allen & Unwin, 1986.

Wollenweber, Eduard
German silversmiths; located Munich.

History Prior to the second half of 19th century, Wollenweber established his workshop; became a silversmith to the Bavarian court. Adolf von Mayrhofer, after an apprenticeship in the workshop of F. Harrach, Munich, worked c. 1891–1903 as assistant to Wollenweber, whose workshop produced c. 1900 silver designs of A. Strobl and c. 1912 of Adelbert Niemeyer. During World War II, the smithy was permanently closed.
Exhibition 1922 *Deutsche Gewerbeschau* (silverwares), Munich.
Bibliography Annelies Krekel-Aalberse, *Art Nouveau and Art Déco Silver*, New York: Abrams, 1989: 131, 143, 261.

Wood, Beatrice (1893–1998)
American ceramicist; born San Francisco.

Training Under Glen Lukens, Gertrud and Otto Natzler, Viveka, and Otto Heino; and 1938, University of Southern California, Los Angeles.
Exhibition Work included in 1947 (11th) *Ceramic National Exhibition*.
Bibliography Lindsay Smith (ed.), *I Shock Myself: The Autobiography of Beatrice Wood*, Ojai, Cal.: Dillingham Press; San Francisco: Chronicle, 1985. Beatrice Wood, *Playing Chess with the Heart: Beatrice Wood at 100*, San Francisco: Chronicle, 1994. Francis M. Naumann, ed., *Beatrice Wood: A Centennial Tribute*, New York: American Craft Museum, 1997.

Wood, Kenneth
> See Kenwood.

Wood, Ruby Ross Goodnough (b. Ruby Ross Pope 1880–1950)
American interior decorator; born Monticello, Ga.

Biography She settled in New York; first worked as a reporter for a Georgia newspaper and then edited a farm journal published by William Randolph Hearst; as a freelance writer, wrote Sunday features for other newspapers and personal stories for *The Delineator*, edited by Theodore Dreiser (1911). She ghost-wrote articles for *Ladies' Home Journal* (1912) and the book *The House in Good Taste* (New York: The Century, 1913), both credited to interior decorator Elsie de Wolfe, and, under Wood's own name, the book *The Honest Home* (1914). 1914, she began working at Au Quatrième decorating studio of the Wanamaker's department store, New York, and became the studio's director when Nancy Vincent McClelland left in 1918. Wood was known briefly as Ruby Rose Goodnough but soon after married Chalmers Wood; opened her own shop and, by 1920s, was a leading society decorator in a distinctively American style that was less formal and luxurious than that of her predecessors, and less grandiose than its European counterpart. She persuaded decorator Billy Baldwin, a fellow Southerner, to move to New York to work with her, 1935–50. Wood's c. 1936 interiors for Mr. and Mrs. Wolcott Blair's house (architect, David Adler) in Palm Beach, Fla., were typical of her style; it was decorated in cream leather, Elsie de Wolfe's leopard chintz, and Swedish off-white textured cotton for curtains recessed into monumental romanesque windows. The floor was paved with diamond-shaped slabs of old, parchment-colored Cuban marble. The furniture in Wood's own house (architect, William Delano) on Long Island, N.Y., was eclectic, diffident, and unselfconsciously combined with no particular concern for the value of individual items.
Bibliography Robert L. Green, 'The Legendary Ruby Ross Wood,' *Architectural Digest*, Oct. 1979. John Esten and Rose Bennett Gilbert, *Manhattan Style*, Boston: Little, Brown, 1990: 4. M. Hampton, *Legendary Decorators of the Twentieth Century*, New York: Doubleday, 1992.

Woodgate, Terence (1953–)
British designer; born London.

Training Westminster College and Middlesex College; mid-1980s for two years, furniture, lighting, and product design, City of London Polytechnic (now London Guildhall University).
Biography Woodgate has designed for Cappellini, Casas, Concord Lighting, Montina, Punt Mobles, SCP, Teunen & Teunen, and Victoria Design; 1994, set up a studio in Portugal, and 1996, in the UK (Sussex).
Citations British Design Award; The Best of the Best award, Design Zentrum Nordrhein-Westfalen, Essen; both 1992.
Bibliography Jasper Morrison (ed.), *The International Design Yearbook*, London: Laurence King, 1999.

Woodnotes
> See Puotila, Ritva.

World Kitchen
> See Corning Glass Works.

world of art, the
> See Mir Iskusstvs, V.

Wormley, Edward (1907–1995)

American furniture designer; active Chicago and New York.

Training 1926–27, School of the Art Institute of Chicago.
Biography 1928–31, Wormley worked in the design studio of Marshall Field's department store in Chicago and Berkey & Gay in Grand Rapids, Mich.; 1931–70, was the chief designer, director of design, and consultant, Dunbar Furniture of Berne, Ind., for which he conservatively and prolifically designed modern wood and upholstered furniture to appeal to a wide range of tastes. 1945, he opened his own office in New York, continuing to design furniture by Dunbar and also designed furniture by Drexel, carpets by Alexander Smith, cabinets for audio/visual equipment by RCA, textiles by Schiffer Prints, and lighting by Lightolier. His postwar work showed Scandinavian and Italian influences but, earlier on, called on wood and fabric in what he called 'transitional forms' for potential American customers not ready, or never ready, for stark modernism. One of his most highly regarded designs is 1947 Listen to Me chaise longue by Dunbar. 1967, he closed his New York office, moved to Weston, Conn., and continued to consult to Dunbar.
Exhibitions/citations Work included in 1951 and 1952 (six pieces of furniture) Good Design exhibitions/awards, The Museum of Modern Art, New York, and Chicago Merchandise Mart. 1962 Elsie De Wolfe Award (with Terence Robsjohn-Gibbings); 1979 (1st) Designer of Distinction, American Society of Interior Designers (ASID).
Bibliography George Nelson (ed.), *Chairs*, New York: Whitney, 1953. W.J. Hennessey and E.D. Hennessey, *Modern Furnishings for the Home*, vol. 2, New York: Reinhold, 1956; New York: Acanthus, reprint 1997. Edgar Kaufmann Jr., 'Edward Wormley: 30 Years of Design,' *Interior Design*, vol. 32, Mar. 1961: 190. Cat., Kathryn B. Hiesinger and George H. Marcus III (eds.), *Design Since 1945*, Philadelphia: Philadelphia Museum of Art, 1983. Cherie Fehrman and Kenneth Fehrman, *Postwar Interior Design, 1945–1960*, New York: Van Nostrand Reinhold, 1987. Judith Gura et al. (eds.), *Edward Wormley: The Other Face of Modernism*, Northampton, Mass.: Designbase/New York: Lin-Weinberg Gallery, 1997.

Wortmann, Constantin (1970–)
> See büro für form.

Wright, Frank Lloyd (b. Frank Lincoln Wright 1867–1959)

American architect, designer, and theorist; born Richland Center, Wis.; active Chicago; Spring Green, Wis.; Chandler and Paradise, Ariz.; and Tokyo.

Training 1885–87 (no diploma), engineering, University of Wisconsin, Madison, Wis.
Biography In Chicago: from 1887, Wright (whose birth year is sometimes reported as 1869, contrary to reliable research) worked for architect Lyman Silsbee (1848–1913); 1889–92, in the architecture firm of Dankmar Adler and Louis Sullivan; 1893–96, in partnership with architect Cecil Corwin (formerly of Silsbee's office). 1896–97, he was in private practice in Oak Park, a suburb of Chicago and, 1897–1909, in Chicago. 1909–11, Wright traveled in Europe; 1911, built his first house and studio, named Taliesin ('shining brow' in Gaelic) and resumed his private practice in Spring Green, Wis.; 1912, once again opened an office again in Chicago. 1914, Taliesin was partially destroyed by fire, and Wright built Taliesin II; 1915–20, was active in an office in Tokyo, while supervising his Imperial Hotel (destroyed in 1978); 1921–24, created the world's first concrete 'texture-block' (cinder-block) houses. 1925, Taliesin II was partially destroyed by another fire, resulting in Taliesin III. 1928, he worked in La Jolla, Cal.; 1928–29, was active in an office (a temporary desert camp he called Ocatillo) in Chandler, Ariz.; 1932, founded the Wright Foundation Fellowship at Taliesin, where students paid to be his employees; 1938, built Taliesin West in Paradise (near Scottsdale), Ariz.; was active in both Wisconsin and Arizona for the rest of his life. Wright exerted a profound influence on architecture and the decorative arts in the US and Europe, especially the Netherlands, and became America's greatest architect. Wright's first (1889) furniture was designed for his Oak Park residence; its most characteristic feature was its angularity and exaggerated verticality, with long, narrow spindles on his now-famous tall chairs. (Influenced by Victorian design, Wright's first spindles were round, replaced soon after by square ones.) Wright's work was not only crucial to architectural development in the 20th century but also an important source of Arts and Crafts design, from 1898–1915. Much of his furniture/furnishings showed a kinship with the Mission furniture designed and made by the Stickley brothers, Elbert Hubbard, and others, and their philosophies of incorporating art into everyday life were also compatible with Wright's. (Some early clients installed Stickley furniture in Wright houses.) 1900–14 as a leader of the so-called Prairie School of architecture, Wright espoused that the furniture of a house should reflect the entire structure as a *Gesamtkunstwerk* (total work of art). He designed furniture for a third of all his structures; regarded built-in furniture as the link between the interior space and moveable furniture. Even though he never insisted on handcrafted objects, he maintained a close relationship with the firms and people who produced his designs, such as with George Niedecken of Niedecken-Walbridge, a firm specializing in interior design that supervised the interiors of some of Wright's most important Prairie houses in Oak Park. 1901, Wright delivered his seminal lecture 'The Art and Craft of the Machine' at Jane Addams's Hull House, Chicago. His 1902–06 Larkin office building, Buffalo, N.Y., is considered by many to be his most important contribution to design—it was fitted with the first metal office chairs and desks that did not imitate wood (some historians claim), although they may have had an applied fake-wood pattern. 1904 wooden chairs with slab-like seats and backs (also designed for his own house) were created for the Larkin building and others; they had a great influence on furniture design through Gerrit Rietveld and his famous 1918 Tood Blauuwe Stoel (red blue chair), in the Netherlands. Wright designed 1908–10 Robie house, Chicago, with many notable geometric light-hearted stained-glass windows. His essay 'In the Cause of Architecture' (in journal *Architectural Record*, 1908) was influential on architecture and industrial design in Europe and often quoted by C.R. Ashbee, a major British proponent of the Arts and Crafts movement. A two-volume 1910 portfolio of Wright's work, prepared by him in Europe and published in Berlin as *Ausgeführte Bauten und Entwürfe von Frank Lloyd Wright* (buildings and projects of Frank Lloyd Wright), also had a powerful impact on European architecture and design. Jan Kotěra's 1906–12 municipal museum in Königgrätz (now Hradec Králové, Czech Republic) was the first structure in Europe clearly influenced by Wright. Walter Gropius's work at 1914 *Werkbund-Ausstellung*, Cologne, was indebted to Wright's 1909–10 Park Inn Hotel in Mason City, Iowa. Ludwig Mies van der Rohe's 1923–24 brick country house project paraphrased the Wright Prairie-house type.

Frank Lloyd Wright. Office armchair. 1904-06. Painted steel and oak, 36 1/2 x 21 x 25" (92.7 x 53.3 x 63.5 cm), seat h. 19" (48.2 cm). Mfr.: The Van Dorn Iron Works Co., US. Gift of Edgar Kaufmann, Jr. MoMA.

Wright's heavily embellished 1912–23 Imperial Hotel, Tokyo, exemplifies his fondness at the time for sharp-angled polygonal forms, expressed also in the furniture that, along with china dinnerware, textiles, and other furnishings, was designed and made for the hotel. (The structure withstood the 1923 earthquake of the time) The architecture and furniture of Ailene Barnstall's 1916–21 house in Los Angeles ideocyncratically illustrates his interest in Pre-Columbian Mesoamerican structures and forms. He wrote *An Autobiography* in 1932 (London/New York: Longman's, Green). His 1934–37 Liliane S. and Edgar J. Kaufmann Sr. country home 'Fallingwater' in Mill Run, Pa., was designated a National Historic Landmark in 2000. The plywood furniture for his 1950s Usonian houses was designed to be made by the houses' on-site carpenters, local craftspeople, or their owners. His 1930–50s domestic furnishings, such as wallpaper and textiles, were mass-produced, but the furniture by Henredon-Heritage was commercially unsuccessful. From 1986, reproductions of Wright's earlier furniture designs began to be manufactured under Frank Lloyd Wright Foundation licenses by Cassina, silver and crystal by Tiffany, textiles by Schumacher, and stained-glass windows by Oakbrook Esser Studios. Most of the reissued textile designs were not original but rather interpretations and new colorings of Wright's recurring motifs; 1950s originals were not by Wright either but by students at Taliesin West. The number of published books and essays about Wright's work and life, including intimate details, is enormous, and his own-design buildings exceed 1,000 and built structure exceed 430. He died in Phoenix, Ariz.

Architecture Partially, in addition to the above: 1893–94 Winslow house, River Forest, Ill.; 1902–04 Dana house, Springfield, Ill.; 1900 'A Home in a Prairie Town' project in *Ladies' Home Journal*, Feb. 1901; 1902–03 Willits house, Highland Park, Ill.; 1902–04 Darwin Martin house, Buffalo, N.Y.; 1905–08 Unity Temple, Oak Park; 1913–14 Midway Gardens, Chicago; 1923 Milard House, Pasadena, Cal.; 1935 – 37 Hanna House, Palo Alto, Ill.; 1936–37 Jacobs House I, Madison, Wis.; 1936–50 S.C. Johnson & Son Administration Building and Research Tower, Racine, Wis.; 1943–59 Solomon R. Guggenheim Museum, New York; 1952–56 H.C. Price Tower, Bartlesville, Okla.; 1953–59 Beth Shalom Synagogue, Elkins Park, Pa.; 1957–62 Marin County Civic Center, San Rafael, Cali.

Exhibitions Major venues have included 1910 exhibit, Berlin (one of the earliest); 1991–92 *Frank Lloyd Wright: Preserving an Architectural Heritage*, touring the US; 1993 retrospective, The Museum of Modern Art, New York; 1996–97, Whitney Museum of American Art, New York; 1996–97, traveling from Centre Canadien d'Architecture (CCA), Montréal; 1999 *Merchant Prince and Master Builder: Edgar J. Kaufmann and Frank Lloyd Wright*, Carnegie Museum of Art, Pittsburgh, Pa.; *Light Screens: The Leaded Glass of Frank Lloyd Wright*, traveling from 2001; 2001 *Frank Lloyd Wright: Die lebendige Stadt*, traveling from Vitra Design Museum, Berlin. Permanent Wright installations/homes: 1889–95 Frank Lloyd Wright Home and Studio, Oak Park; 1911, 1914, 1925–59 Taliesin, Spring Green, Wis.; living room of 1912–14 Francis W. Little house (Northome), Wayzata, Minn., in The Metropolitan Museum of Art, New York (acquired 1972), and library of the Little house in Allentown Art Museum, Allentown, Pa.; 1935–37 department-store office of Edgar J. Kaufmann Sr., Pittsburgh, in Victoria & Albert Museum, London, installed in 1993; 1937–56 Taliesin West, Scottsdale, Ariz.; and others as well as a number of individual houses.

Bibliography Frederich Gutheim (ed.), *Frank Lloyd Wright on Architecture: Selected Writings 1894–1940*, New York: Duell, Sloan, and Pearce, 1941. Frank Lloyd Wright, *The Future of Architecture*, New York: Horizon, 1953. Arthur Drexler, *The Drawings of Frank Lloyd Wright*, New York: The Museum of Modern Art, 1962. William Allin Storrer, *The Architecture of Frank Lloyd Wright: A Complete Catalogue*, Chicago: University of Chicago, 2002 3rd ed. H. Allen Brooks, *The Prairie School: Frank Lloyd Wright and His Midwest Contemporaries*, New York: Norton, 1976. Robert L. Sweeney, *Frank Lloyd Wright: An Annotated Bibliography*, Los Angeles: Hennessey & Ingalls, 1978. Filippo Alison, *Frank Lloyd Wright: Designer of Furniture*, Naples: Fratelli Fiorentino, 1997. Robert C. Twombly, *Frank Lloyd Wright: His Life and Architecture*, New York: Wiley, 1979. David A. Hanks, *The Decorative Designs of Frank Lloyd Wright*, New York: Dutton, 1979; Mineola, N.Y.: Dover, 1999 2nd ed. Peter Reed and Terence Riley (eds.), *Frank Lloyd Wright: Architect*, New York: The Museum of Modern Art, 1994. Paola Antonelli (ed.), *Objects of Design: The Museum of Modern Art*, New York: The Museum of Modern Art, 2003: 42–43.

Wright, John (1940–)

British interior and furniture designer.

Training Late 1970s, Royal College of Art, London.

Biography 1966, Wright, Jean Schofield, and Jill Walker opened a design office in London. Wright's range of objects has included domestic and office furniture, lighting, and accessories. He and Schofield designed 1964 C1 knock-down chair by Anderson Manson Decorations of London. He taught, School of Interior Design, London. He and Hugh Casson were members of a team of designers who designed the first-class and tourist-class 1960 furniture and interiors of 1961 cruiseliner *Canberra*, the largest postwar British passenger ship, but dwarfed by superliners since the 1990s.

Exhibitions Work subject of 1986 exhibition, *One Off*, London; 1988, Yves Gastou, Paris; 1988, *Themes and Variations*, London; 1988, Dilmos, Milan; 1989, *Art to Use*, Frankfurt; 1990, Galerie Margine, Zürich; 1990, *Crucial*, London; 1993, Ateliers im Museum Kunsterkolonie, Darmstadt; 1994, Rohsska Museet, Gothenburg. Wright and Schofield's chairs included in 1966 *Vijftig Jaar Zitten*, Stedelijk Museum, Amsterdam, and 1970 *Modern Chairs 1918–1970*, Whitechapel Gallery, London (catalog below).

Bibliography Mary Gilliat, *English Style*, London: Sydney Bodley Head, 1966. Cat., *Modern Chairs 1918–1970*, London: Lund Humphries, 1971. Auction cat., *British Design*, London: Phillips, 25 Sept. 2001: various lots.

Wright, John Lloyd (1892–1972)

American designer and architect; son of Frank Lloyd Wright.

Biography John Lloyd Wright was Frank Lloyd Wright's second son; became an architect and writer; invented toys such as Wright Blocks and Timber Toys sets. He also invented the better-known Lincoln Logs (introduced to the public in 1918, patented on 31 Aug. 1920), and marketed by his own eponymous firm in Chicago. The construction set was a simple one, claiming an affinity to the log cabin occupied by US president Abraham Lincoln as a child and becoming more elaborate in later versions; during World War II, its patriotic associations made it appropriate as a wartime toy for a boy. Purportedly, the idea came to John Lloyd in 1916 in Tokyo, while visiting his father's earthquake-proof 1915–22 Imperial Hotel, which was being built using interlocking elements. 1999, Hasbro sold a license to K'Nex, a specialist in construction toys, to make/market the Log series. 100,000 or so sets of the original design had been sold from its introduction to 2000. In other activities, John Lloyd wrote about his famous parent in the book *My Father Who Is on Earth* (New York: Putnam's, 1946). The Frank Lloyd Wright Preservation Trust, Oak Park, Illinois, houses articles on his father, several manuscripts, and papers and literature, including The Toy Collection, an archive of drawings, correspondence, brochures, photographs, and other documentation relating to John Lloyd's own toy activities.

Wright, Russel (1904–1976)

American designer of domestic goods; born Lebanon, Ohio; active New York.

Training Painting, Cincinnati Art Academy, under Frank Duveneck; 1920, Art Students League, New York; 1922, law, Princeton University; from 1923, architecture, Columbia University, New York.

Biography Wright was the first designer of home products to have his name mentioned in the manufacturer's advertising. In a peculiar manner, he managed to balance Functionalism, Art Déco, and vernacular Mission style. He was raised as a Quaker, and his puritanism and Midwest practicality informed his work, which reflected a change in lifestyles in America after the Depression. He was drawn to the theater through his friendship with playwright Thornton Wilder, and, 1924, Norman Bel Geddes offered him a job designing theater sets. 1927, Wright became involved in the decorative arts by casting miniature versions of his papier-mâché stage props; under the influence of his wife Mary (b. Mary Einstein, 1905–52), moved away from theater design to design and produce household accessories in spun aluminum that sold well and launched his career. 1930, he established Russel Wright Incorporated (called Russel Wright Accessories from 1935, later Russel Wright Associates, to be closed in 1957) and a workshop in his hometown, Lebanon, Ohio. He began designing other metalware, including 1930 cutlery in sterling silver that echoed the designs of Jean Puiforcat and Josef Hoffmann, though the pieces have a style of their own; 1933–34, executed designs for chromium-plated accessories by Chase Brass and Copper. His enormously successful Modern Living furniture line by Conant-Ball was introduced at R. H. Macy department store in New York in 1935. Mary Wright, his sales representative, coined the word 'blonde' for the bleached finish of maple wood used in his furniture. He patented a wooden chair with an adjustable back. 1937, Wright concentrated on ceramics, resulting in American Modern by Steubenville Pottery, a highly successful line of

Russel Wright. Casual China dinnerware (part of a service). 1946. Glazed vitreous china casserole dish h. 3" x dia. 8 1/4" (7.6 x 21 cm), casserole lid dia. 8 1/4" (21 cm). Mfr.: Iroquois China Co., US. Gift of Garrison Products. MoMA.

dinnerware produced 1939–59. At one time, there was hardly a household in America which did not have a piece of Wright's china. Curvaceous and witty, the pieces have become classics of popular design. 1955 as a consultant to US State Department, he developed ideas for cottage industries in Southeast Asia; 1965, designed over 100 products for manufacture in Japan; 1967, abandoned most of his design activities and became a consultant to US National Parks Service on programming and planning. He became disappointed by the failure of his American Way home furnishings venture; his wife died at the peak of his fame, and Wright retreated to Manitoga, his country home near Garrison, N.Y., and worked only occasionally thereafter. Other design work: 1932 radio cabinet by Wurlitzer; 1934 60-piece furniture range by Heywood-Wakefield; 1943–46 freeform art ceramics by Bauer Pottery; 1945 Melmac dinnerware by Northern Industrial Chemical; 1946 Casual China by Iroquois; glassware from 1945 by Century Metalcraft and, subsequently, by numerous other firms; 1951 Highlight glassware and pottery by Paden City Pottery; 1949 Flair glassware by Imperial Glass; 1950 Easier Living 50-piece furniture range by Stratton; 1950 range of metal furniture by Samsonite.
Exhibitions c. 1931 cocktail shaker included in 1931 exhibition of American Union of Decorative Arts and Craftsmen; other work in 1934 *Machine Art*, The Museum of Modern Art, New York; 1983–84 exhibition, Philadelphia Museum of Art (catalog below); 1985 *High Styles*, Whitney Museum of American Art, New York. Subject of 2001–02 *Russel Wright: Creating American Lifestyle*, Cooper-Hewitt National Design Museum, New York (catalog below).
Bibliography Mary Wright, *Mary and Russel Wright's Guide to Easier Living*, New York: Simon & Schuster, 1951. William J. Hennessey, *Russel Wright: American Designer*, Cambridge: MIT, 1983. Cat., Kathryn B. Hiesinger and George H. Marcus III (eds.), *Design Since 1945*, Philadelphia: Philadelphia Museum of Art, 1983. *Russel Wright: Good Design Is for Everyone—In His Own Words*, New York: Universe, 2001. Cat., Donald Albrecht, *Russel Wright: Creating American Lifestyle*, New York: Cooper-Hewitt, 2001.

Württembergische Metallwarenfabrik (WMF)
German manufacturer; located Geislingen.

History 1853, Straub & Schweizer was founded by Daniel Straub, a miller from Geislingen, and the Schweizer brothers. 1880, it was amalgamated with competitor A. Ritter in Esslingen to form Württembergische Metallwarenfabrik (WMF). 1894–1931, Albert Mayer directed the design studio. By c. 1900 with a staff of 3,500, it specialized in domestic metalware, including silverplating on cutlery and hollow-ware, pewter, copper, and brass. Its products were sold in sales outlets in Berlin, Cologne, Vienna, Warsaw, and elsewhere. To 1900, its styles were neo-Renaissance and rococo. After 1900, it concentrated on Jugendstil forms. 1905, WMF took over Orivit, manufacturers of hollow-ware and cutlery in machine-pressed pewter. 1920s, WMF developed the new glass techniques Myra, Lavauna, and Ikora; c. 1928, began producing silverware, some of which was designed by Fritz August Breuhaus, Paul Haustein, and Richard Riemerschmid. 1920s–50s, NKA (its contemporary decorative-products department) was called on for WMF's designs. 1920s, the firm acquired sole rights to V2A steel, developed by Krupp, for household goods, patented by WMF as Cromargan. The firm grew into a diversified industrial giant. 1950, Wilhelm Wagenfeld was hired as a consultant designer and, throughout 1950s, designed a large number of products for the firm; his glass for the firm was precisely developed with models and measured drawings, even though the models were mouth-blown. He also created some WMF lamps. Active today, WMF has facilities which produce glass and crystal works in Göppingen and metalware for the hotel/catering industry; has commissioned contemporary designers such as Sebastian Bergne, Pierre Cardin, Garouste and Bonetti, James Irvine, Josep Lluscà, Ole Palsby, Matteo Thun, and Marcel Wander.
Citations Award, *London International Exhibition on Industry and Art, 1862*; 1969 citations (29 products), Industrie Forum Design (iF), Hanover.
Bibliography *Objekte des Jugendstils*, Bern: Beneli, 1975: 261. Alastair Duncan, *Art Nouveau and Art Déco Lighting*, New York: Simon & Schuster, 1978: 126. Cat., *WMF Glas, Keramik, Metall, 1925–50*, Berlin: Kunstgewerbemuseum, 1980. Annelies Krekel-Aalberse, *Art Nouveau and Art Déco Silver*, New York: Abrams, 1989. Cat., *Metallkunst*, Berlin: Bröhan-Museum, 1990: 546–79.

Wyld, Evelyn (1882–1973)
American designer; active Paris.

Training Royal College of Music, London.
Biography c. 1907, Wyld settled in Paris. She and Eileen Gray traveled to North Africa, where they learned weaving and natural-color wool dyeing from native women. 1909, Wyld returned to Britain, where she studied weaving and rug knotting, and again settled in Paris, taking along looms and a teacher from the National School of Weavers. Eyre de Lanux worked in Wyld's business, Atelier du Tissage, on the rue Visconti, Paris. 1927, Wyld and Eyre de Lanux began living together in a relationship to 1933. Wyld also supervised the rugs designed by Gray, woven by apprentices in the atelier. At one point, eight women worked in the three rooms of the atelier on the top floor of the building where Honoré de Balzac had earlier operated a print shop. The wool came from the Auvergne region of France, was dyed in Paris, and, for Gray's designs, had labels attached that read 'Designed by Eileen Gray at the workshop of Evelyn Wyld.' Gray's rugs were given names such as Ulysse, Hannibal, Macédoine, Pénélope, Fidèle, Casimir, Biribi, Héliogabale (the Roman emperor), D (for 'Damia,' the stage name of singer/actress Marie-Louise Damien), and E (for 'Eileen'). The best seller was Footit (for one of the clowns in the team of Chocolat et Footit). Gray's rugs were rigidly geometric; Wyld's tended to be flowery. 1929, Wyld and de Lanux moved to Saint-Tropez, then to La Roquette-sur-Siagne, and, 1932, opened the shop Décor in Cannes, which closed the next year due to the world financial crisis. They designed interiors and lacquered furniture, some with the assistance of Seizo Sugawara, the lacquer specialist.
Exhibitions Wyld and de Lanux showed furniture and rugs at 1927, 1929, and 1932 Salons of Société des Artistes Décorateurs and 1930 (1st) Union des Artistes Modernes (UAM), both Paris; 1931 rug exhibition, Curtis Moffat Gallery, London.
Bibliography Peter Adam, *Eileen Gray, Architect/Designer*, New York: Abrams, 1987. Philippe Garner, *Eileen Gray: Design and Architecture, 1878–1976*, Cologne: Taschen, 1993.
> See de Lanux, Eyre; Gray, Eileen Moray.

Württembergische Metallwarenfabrik (WMF): Wilhelm Wagenfeld. Salt and pepper shakers. 1953. Glass and stainless steel, each h. 2" (5.1 cm) x dia. 1 1/2" (3.8 cm). Mfr.: Württembergische Metallwarenfabrik (WMF). Gift of Walter Schnepel. MoMA.

X–Y

Sōri Yanagi. Butterfly stool (detail). 1954. MoMA.

XO

French design firm; located Servan, near Paris.

History 1985, XO was established by Gérard Mialet to market products of a high aesthetic, particularly in seating with Philippe Starck's Dr. Sonderbar armchair (designed in 1983) and Shiro Kuramata's Sing Sing chair (designed in 1986). XO has been from the onset under the art direction of Starck, who oversees the product line as well as advertising and also designs for the firm. 1993, Yann Cuacaud became an associate of the firm. The core of the business has stemed from the use of polypropylene to make stools and chairs for residential and contract use; however, other materials, such as wood and metals, have been called on. Its stable of international designers has included Pierangelo Caramia, Christian Ghion, Matthew Hilton, Patrick Jouin, Martijn Prins, and Bob Wilson. Starck's work for the firm: 1981 Dole Melipone folding-base table, 1986 Ray Hollis ashtray, 1986 Théâtre du Monde cabinet, 1991 Bubu stool, 1997 Cheap Chic chair, 1988 Royalton bar stool in polished aluminium, 1998 Os Library shelving, 1999 Poaa handweights, 1999 Slick-Slick chair in gas-injected polypropylene, 2000 Slik-Slik chair, 2001 The Club wooden armchair, and 2002 Bubu stool. Other products: 1987 Hamlet Machine by Wilson, 2000 Link shelving by Prins, 2001 Fold chair by Jouin, and 2002 Insideout Murano glass vase by Ghion. The firm, with nine office employees, is successful. As examples and all by Starck, Cheap Chic annual sales are 20,000; Slik-Slik are 50,000, and Bubu stool are 50,000.
Bibliography www.xo-design.com.

Yakulov (or Iakulov), Georgii Bogdanovich (1884–1928)

Russian set designer and decorator; born Tiflis (now Tbilisi, Georgia).

Training 1901–03, Institute of Painting, Sculpture, and Architecture, Moscow.
Biography From 1905, Yakulov developed his theory of light; after 1907, became involved with the Moscow Association of Artists; 1910 – 11, was active as the decorator of galas, spectacles, and other public events; 1913, was among a group of Russian artists, including Natan Al'tman, Marc Chagall, Aleksandra Exter, Liubov' Popova, Ivan Puni, and Nadezhda Udal'tsova, who traveled to Paris. There he met Robert and Sonya Delaunay, whose theories of simultaneous contrasts of color corresponded to his own ideas. With Aleksandr Rodchenko, Vladimir Tatlin, and others, he participated in the design of the interior of 1917 Café Pittoresque, Moscow; from 1918, became active in set design; 1919, co-signed the *Imagist Manifesto*; became a professor, VKhUTEMAS, Moscow; joined the Obmokhu (society of young artists); early 1920s, primarily designed sets but also 1923–26 Baku Commissars monument; 1925, traveled to Paris again, where he designed the set for *Le pas d'acier* of Les Ballets Russes (whose performance was realized in 1927, when he returned to Moscow).
Exhibitions Work first shown at 1907 edition of Moscow Association of Artists; subsequently, included in exhibitions in USSR and abroad. Work subject of a 1975 exhibition, Moscow (catalog below).
Bibliography *Notes et documents édités par la Société des Amis de Georges Yakoulov*, Paris: Société des Amis de Georges Yakoulov, 1967–75. S. Aladzhalov, *Georgii Yakulov*, Yerevan: Armenian Theatrical Society, 1971. Cat., M. Sarkisian et al., *Georgii Iakulov: katalog vystavki*, Moscow: Sovetskii Khudozhnik, 1975. E. Kostina, *Georgii Yakulov*, Moscow: Sovetskii Khudozhnik, 1979. Stephanie Barron and Maurice Tuchman, *The Avant-Garde in Russia, 1910–1930*, Cambridge: MIT, 1980: 264. Lesley-Anne Sayers, 'Rediscovering Diaghilev's *Pas d'acier*,' doctoral thesis, UK: Bristol University, 1999.

Yalos

Italian accessories and dinnerware company.

History 1996, Yalos Casa Murano, a division of Effetre Industriale S.p.A., was founded in Murano; pursued technological research and experimentation toward realizing unusual, uncommon glassware. Its artistic director is Giorgio Cugliari, who designs for the firm, as do Aldo Cibic, Toso-Massari & Associati, Almerico de Angelis, and the Sÿn designers. The examples in its 2001 collection were contributed to by designers Ronen Joseph, Claudio Marturano, and Renato Montagner. Yalos plates include Fior di Loto by de Angelis, Bikini by Cugliari, and Marmara by Cibic. 50% of its production is exported.

Yamaguchi, Kazuma (1946–)

Japanese industrial designer; born Osaka; active Milan.

Biography 1970, Yamaguchi began his professional career and settled in Milan; became known for lighting and vehicle-body designs; became a member, Associazione per il Disegno Industriale (ADI). Clients have included Bon Marché, Leonardo Auto, and Stilnovo. He participated in 1973 bicycle competion of ICSID, Kyoto.
Bibliography *ADI Annual 1976*, Milan: Associazione per il Disegno Industriale, 1976.

Yamakado, Hiroyuki (1946–); Agnès Yamakado (1953–)

Japanese and French designers; husband and wife.

Training Agnès: in mathematics, Japan.
Biography 1981, they settled in France, where they established their

XO: Philippe Starck. Royalton bar stool. 1988. Cast aluminum and velvet, h. 30 1/4" x dia. 14 1/2" (76.8 x 36.8 cm). Mfr.: XO, France. David Whitney Collection, Gift of David Whitney. MoMA.

eponymous company in Meudon in 1986 for the production and marketing of their own furniture designs. Products include 1986 Etretat table, 1987 Cinderella folding side chair, 1987 Météo coat rack, 1987 Arima modular folding table, 1992 Cocotte stacking chair, 1993 Bancoq modular bench, 1999 Serafine screen/lamp, 1999 4X4 office chair (with or without arms), 1999 BT computer desk, 2000 Dalya B club chair, 1999 chairs for Potel & Chabot delicatessen in Paris, 2000 Milarepa and Angelo Milarepa wood-and-resin tables, 2000 Coq bar stool, 2000 Tomo stacking side chair, trolley, and storage rack, 2002 Milarepa TV table, and a number of others. 1997, opened a showroom in the Viaduc des Arts, Paris. Designed 1990–2000 Scenario range of furniture for La Redoute mail-order catalog; 2002, began manufacture of their furniture in a facility in Anjou.
Exhibitions/citations All Paris: Yam rocking chair shown at 1985 Salon of Sociéte des Arts Décorateurs; 1992 Grand Prix de la Critique (for Cocotte chair) and 1996 Nombre d'Or du Mobilier Contemporain, Salon du Meuble. Work subject of 1996 *Hommage à Yamakado*, Printemps department store; 1996 *Connivance with Design*, Galerie VIA (French furniture association). Coordinated 2000 *La Chaise dans Tous ses États*, Art du Viaduc des Arts. Received 1997 Le Nombre d'Or prize, Mobilier Contemporain; 1997 Viaduc de Bronze (with Sophie Jacqmin) during the Geste d'Art for their creation of Imaginary Garden, Viaduc des Arts.
Bibliography www.via.asso.fr. www.yamakado.com.

Yamanaka, Kazuhiro (1971–)

Japanese designer; active London.

Training 1992–95, bachelor's degree in interior design, Musashino Art University, Tokyo; 1995–97, master's degree in furniture design, Royal College of Art, London.
Biography The 1997 Beyond the Moon aluminium/halogen lamp (self-produced, sponsored by Aram Designs, London) was one of Yamanaka's earliest products. He has designed furniture, including office models, and 2001 chairs and lighting of white polypropylene sheets. Clients have included Boffi. His stated goal is 'the achievement of the maximum impact with the minimum use of materials.'
Exhibitions/citations Work included in 1994 and 1995 *Future Office Design*, Tokyo Design Center; 1995 *Interior Design*, Ozone, Tokyo; 1997 *New Designers*, Design Business Centre, London; 1998 *Bare*, O-porto, London. Cited in 1994 and 1995 Office Furniture Competition, Interoffice, Japan. Received 1999 100% Design/Crafts Council scholarship; 1999 and 2000 finalist, 100% Design/*Blueprint* magazine award; 2000 finalist, Salone Satellite/*Design Week* magazine, Milan.
Bibliography 'Experts Choice: The Best of Milan,' *Frame*, July–Aug. 2000.

Yamaoka, Kazuhiko (1961–)

Japanese product designer and planner.

Training To 1984, engineering department, Chiba University,
Biography Yamaoka began his professional career in charge of non-Japanese-market TV design at NEC's Central Research Laboratories in Kawasaki (Kanagawa); 1988, was in charge of design at the newly established Home Media Research Institute of NEC Home Electronics; worked for a time in the corporate planning division and, from 1997, in Sound Design Business Promotion and, subsequently, as design director in NEC's product-planning division. He has been active in the development of, for example, the ThiN project, which calls on advanced, easy-to-use, playful human-interface technology. He is the director of SADECO (design council of Saitama Prefecture, Japan).

Yamashita, Kasumasa (1937–)

Japanese architect and designer; born Tokyo.

Biography Yamashita taught, Institute of Art and Design, Tokyo; working as a designer, one of 11 who created a service for Alessi's 1983 Tea and Coffee Piazza project.
Citation 1977 prize, Annual Design Award, Architectural Institute of Japan.
Bibliography Officina Alessi, *Tea and Coffee Piazza: 11 Servizi da tè e caffè*, Milan: Crusinallo, 1983. *Les carnets du design*, Paris: Mad-Cap Productions/APCI, 1986: 71.

Yamo (b. Mohamed Yahiaoui 1958–)

Algerian designer and interior architect; born Bou-Ismaïl; active Champigny-sur-Marne, France.

Training To 1982, École Nationale des Beaux-Arts, Algiers; 1986–88 under Jean-Claude Maugirard et Daniel Pigeon, École Nationale Supérieure des Arts Décoratifs, Paris.
Biography From a base in France from mid-1980s, Yamo has been particularly interested in Japan, where he worked on a lighting project, illustrating kites in glass, for a palace in Osaka; designed the interior architecture of the apartment of Gladys Fabre, sofa for Anne de Lierville, a metal and glass collection (with Sabrina), numerous glass designs (with Bernard Pictet), jewelry, and paintings; established the Atelier Prototype Métal workshop in the furniture department at École Nationale Supérieure des Arts Décoratifs, Paris. Other designs have included 1988 La Flèche lighting fixture by Drimmer, 1989 Wacapou furniture collection by Roche-Bobois, objects by Techniland, 1990 table service by Christofle, furniture by Cecotti, and others more recently. Other clients: KL Artistes et Modèles, Luminaires, and Pictet. From 1990, he has collaborated with interior architect Corinne Metrah.
Exhibitions/citations All Paris: work first shown at Galerie VIA (French furniture association), Paris, 1988. Winner, 1987 Drimmer-sponsored competition (Le Fourmilier and Teyla lighting fixtures, prototype realized through an Appel Permanent grant from VIA); 1989 gold award, Salon du Meuble; 1989 Palme d'Or award for young designers; Lampe d'Argent award, 1992 Salon International du Luminaire; Oscar (for Ouage oil lamp), Syndicat National des Architectes d'Intérieur (SNAI).
Bibliography Cat., *Les années VIA 1980–1990*, Paris: Musée des Arts Décoratifs, 1990: 182–83. 'Les designers du soleil,' *Maison française décoration internationale*, June 1992.

Yanagi, Sōri (1915–)

Japanese industrial designer; active Tokyo.

Training To 1940, Western painting, Tokyo National University of Fine Arts and Music.
Biography Yanagi first worked in the office of architect Junzo Sakakura, through whom he met Charlotte Perriand and thus was an assistant to her in Japan in 1942; 1950, established his own industrial-design studio; has retained a traditional Japanese sensibility toward materials and forms while concentrating on efficiency, structure, and logic; has been credited with laying the foundations of postwar industrial design. 1952, Yanagi, Riki Watanabe, and Isamu Kenmochi found-

ed the Japan Industrial Designers Association; designed wooden furniture, including his legendary 1954 Butterfly two-part bent-plywood stool, produced from 1956 to today by Tendo Mokko. His prolific design work has also included automobiles, optical instruments, highways, bridges, 1948–50 tea pot by Matsumura Iron Stone China Co., 1954 plastic stacking stool (now by Habitat), 1960 handcrafted casserole by Shussai-kiln, some wares by other potteries, 1967 glassware by Sasaki, a number of pieces by Yamaya Glass Co., 1970 can opener by Kosaka-Hamono, 1973 aluminum cigarette container by Aoki, 1974 public seating for the new subway in Yokohama, maps/signage of the public zoo in Nogeyama, 1998 T3035 dining chair by Tendo Mokko. Yanagi has said: 'I prefer gentle and rounded forms [because] they radiate human warmth.' Currently, he heads his own design office and is manager of Nippon Mingei-Kan.
Exhibitions/citations Wooden furniture included in 1982 *Contemporary Vessels: How to Pour*, National Museum of Modern Art, Tokyo, and traveling (catalog below). Gold medal (for (porcelain tea pot by Tajimi Ceramic Institute), 1956 (11th) Triennale di Milano; first prize, 1951 (1st) Japanese Competition for Industrial Design; 2001 Long-Selling Good Design award (for stainless-steel bowl and cutlery by Sato-Shoji Corp.); G-Mark award, Japanese Industrial Design Promotion Organization (JIDPO).
Bibliography 'Produzione recente di Sori Yanagi,' *Stile Industria*, no. 28, Aug. 1960: 42–45. Bruno Munari, 'Design According to Yanagi,' *Domus*, no. 609, Sept. 1980: 40–41. Cat., Toyojirō Hida, *Contemporary Vessels: How to Pour*, Tokyo: National Museum of Modern Art, 1982: nos. 192–99. Cat., Kathryn B. Hiesinger and George H. Marcus III (eds.), *Design Since 1945*, Philadelphia: Philadelphia Museum of Art, 1983. Paola Antonelli (ed.), *Objects of Design: The Museum of Modern Art*, New York: The Museum of Modern Art, 2003: 138. www.japon.net/yanagi.

Ybargüengoitia, Manel (1954–)
Spanish industrial and graphic designer; born Barcelona.

Training Interior design, Lotja Escola Superior d'Arts Plàstiques i Disseny; interior architecture, Federación Internacional de Arquitectos de Interior, artistic drawing studio, Escola Massana; industrial-design studio, Escuela Industrial; all Barcelona. Master's degree in industrial design, Escuela Politécnica Superior, Universidad de Girona.
Biography 1985–95, Ybargüengoitia was the director of the magazine *Y-N S.L.*; from 1996, director of the magazine *Eklipta*; organizing member of the first Premios ECIA 96 de Arquitectura Interior; taught, LAI Escola de Disseny (Universitat Internacional de Catalunya), and Elisava (Escola Superior de Disseny), both Barcelona. He has been highly active as an interior-architect and industrial and ID-program designer for clients, including B.Lux (lighting from 1991), Vanlux (lighting from 1991), Hugo Boss (1995 showroom, Barcelona), Renfe, Audi (stand at 1996 Salon de l'Automobile, Paris), Carlos Jané (furniture; stands, furniture fairs in València in 1996, Cologne in 1998, Japan in 1998, Milan, in 2002), Transport Ciutat Comtal (ID program and interior of the autobus line in 1997 and of Tomb autobus in 2001), Gobierno de La Rioja (1997 autobus terminal, Logroño), Fontdor (1998 ID program and packaging), Honda (1999 Greens-Honda offices, Barcelona), Coca-Cola (1999 bottle and image of Santolín water), Park-Mobel Industrias (2000 ID program), Pincolor (ID program and point-of-purchase materials), Grupo Sarbus (2001 autobus image and interior), TramVia Metropolità (2001 ID program and interior of Tramvía de Barcelona), Noge (2002 redesign of Touring vehicles), Castrosua (2002 redesign of vehicles).
Bibliography *Industrial Design—European Masters/3*, Barcelona: Atrium, 1992. Juliet Pomés Leiz and Ricardo Feriche, *Barcelona Design Guide = Barcelona guía de diseño*, Barcelona: Gili, 1999 (and subsequent eds).

Sōri Yanagi. Butterfly stool. 1954. Maple-veneer plywood and metal, 15 1/2 x 17 3/8 x 12 1/8" (39.4 x 44.1 x 30.8 cm). Mfr.: Tendo Mokko, Japan (from 1956). Gift of the designer. MoMA.

Yellin, Samuel (1885–1940)
Polish metalworker; active Philadelphia, Pa.

Training Metalsmithing in Germany, Belgium, and Britain.
Biography 1906, Yellin settled in Philadelphia, where he opened a shop in 1909; became successful by designing for architects, particularly the partnership McKim, Mead, and White. In expanded facilities, his studio (completed in 1915) on Arch Street was designed by Walter Mellor and Arthur Meigs; it included a showroom, drafting room, museum, library, and a very large work area with 60 forges and more than 200 workers. Yellin's workers specialized in chisel decoration, *repoussé*, and polishing. He believed in traditional forging with hammer and anvil, although he used standard rods, bars, and plates, and employed electronically controlled blowers for even temperatures during forging. He lectured on the history of metalworking.
Bibliography Anne Yaffe Phillips, *From Architecture to Object*, New York: Hirschl and Adler, 1989: 66.

Yli-Viikari, Tapio (1948–)
Finnish ceramicist; born Polvijärvi.

Training To 1974 under Kyllikki Salmenhaara, Taideteollinen korkeakoulu, Helsinki.
Biography 1974–76 under Kyllikki Salmenhaara, Yli-Viikari was a teaching assistant at Taideteollinen korkeakoulu; 1976–87, a designer and head of the department of art and design at Arabia pottery, Helsinki, and, 1980–87, responsible for the firm's exhibition activities, organizing more than 80 venues in Finland and abroad on ceramic art and design. He was responsible for 1984 renovation of Arabia Museum and Gallery; from 1987, has been a freelance exhibition designer; also from 1987, head of the ceramics department, Taideteollinen korkeakoulu, where he has established a glass program and research laboratory. He is a member of Ornamo (Finnish association of designers), from 1974; National Council for Ceramic Art, US, from 1985; Suomen Taideteollisuusyhdistys (Finnish society of crafts and design), from 1987 (and a design juror 1988–92); board member of Arabia Foundation, from 1989; founding member, Keramos Society, 1990; Society of Glass Technology, Sheffield, UK, from 1990; Southern California section, American Ceramic Society, from 1992.
Citation 1978 Finnish State Design Prize (for Kokki ovenware by Arabia).

Yoshida-Katz, Satomi (b. Satomi Yoshida 1968–)
Japanese designer; active the US and Japan.

Training Degree in interior design, Iowa State University, Ames, Iowa.
Biography 1987, Yoshida moved to the US for university study; has designed interiors for corporate, retail, governmental, and entertainment clients, and also furniture, furnishings, and lighting; was active in Seattle and San Francisco before settling in Walnut Creek, Cal. has worked in both the US and Japan. One of her best-known designs is the Urchin resin container (with Roberto Zanon) by Benza.

Yoshino, Toshiyuki (1959–)
Japanese designer; born Yokohama; active Japan and Italy.

Training 1980–84, metalworking and, 1984–87, master's degree in industrial design (machinery design), Tokyo National University of Fine Arts and Music.

Biography 1987–88, Yoshino worked as an interior designer at Tanseisha, Tokyo; 1988–89, was a freelance designer in Tokyo; 1989–90, was a scholar at Deutscher Akademischer Austausch Dienst (DAAD; German academic exchange service) in Germany; 1990–92, worked at Industrial Design Centre of Pioneer, Tokyo; from 1994, has been a freelance designer in Milan; 1999, established own furniture brand Eremus. Work has included furniture by Cattelan Italia (from 1994), by Datalogic (2000), and by Sami (from 2001).

Yoshioka, Tokujin (1967–)

Japanese designer.

Training To 1986, Kuwasawa Design School, Tokyo.
Biography 1987–88, Yoshioka worked in the office of Shiro Kuramata, Tokyo; from 1988, has been in charge of Issey Miyake's shop design; from 1992, has been a freelance designer and, 2000, established Tokujin Yorhioka Design, Tokyo. His first chair design, 2000 Honey-Pop armchair in honeycomb-structured paper, became highly successful. Other designs: 2001 Tofu light fixture by Yamagiwa; and 2002 Tokyo-pop lounge chair, 2003 Tokyo-pop 2 stool, and three other products, all by Driade. 2003 Clouds environment was installed in the Driade showroom, Milan, for its 35th anniversary. Interiors, displays, exhibitions, and architecture for various clients.
Citations 1994 and 1996 Award of Gold, CS Design; 1997 Award of Excellence, JDC Design; 2000 and 2002 Award of Excellence, Annual Design Review, *I.D.* magazine; 2001 A&W Award, Coming Designer of the Future; 2001 Mainchi Design Award.
Bibliography Karim Rashid (ed.), *The International Design Yearbook*, London: Laurence King, 2003. Paola Antonelli (ed.), *Objects of Design: The Museum of Modern Art*, New York: The Museum of Modern Art, 2003: 280.

Young, Dennis (1917–)

British furniture, interior, and industrial designer.

Training Royal College of Art, London.
Biography 1946, Young opened his own design office in London; became chief designer at the Isotype Institute of Visual Education and a consultant designer to Baume, to Natural Rubber Bureau, and to British Vita; designed fiberglass furniture by Gaeltarra Eireann; lectured on furniture and interior design at Camberwell School of Art. His 1947–48 Shell chair for Design London was an early manifestation of ergonomic furniture; during its conception, he used a 'sitting box,' with modeling clay, to record the body shapes of 67 people.
Exhibitions Work included in 1951 *Festival of Britain*, London; 1965 *International Exhibition*, Moscow; 1966 *Europlastic Exhibition*, Paris; 1967 *Furniture Exhibition*, Ireland; 1971 *Modern Chairs* (catalog below)
Bibliography Ernö Goldfinger, *British Furniture Today*, London: Alec Tiranti, 1951. S.H. Glenister, *Contemporary Design in Woodwork*, London: Murray, 1955. Roberto Aloi and Agnoldomenico Pica, *Mobili Tipo*, Milan: Ulrico Hoepli, 1956. Dennis and Barbara Young, *Furniture in Britain Today*, London: Alec Tiranti, 1964. Cat., *Modern Chairs 1918–1970*, London: Lund Humphries, 1971. Robert Elwall, *Ernö Goldfinger*, London: Academy, 1996.

Young, Michael (1966–)

British designer; born Sunderland.

Training To 1992, furniture and product design, Kingston Polytechnic (now Kingston University).
Biography 1992–94 while a student, Young worked with Tom Dixon at Space Studio, London; 1994, introduced his first collection of woven-steel and Smarty furniture, in Paris and Tokyo; 1995–99, was active in his own studio MY 022 UK Ltd., London, and designed 1995 collection by E&Y, Tokyo; 1998, relocated to Iceland and began designing for Rosenthal and Cappellini and developed the S.M.A.K. Iceland jewelry company. Other clients have included Christopher Farr Carpets, Eurolounge, Idée, Laurent Perrier champagne, Magis, Ritzenhof, Sawaya & Moroni, and SOM architects. 2000, Young and his wife Katrín Pétursdóttir established 2000 MY Studio Ehf., in Reykjavic, Iceland; taught at college of design, Reykjavic; 2002, settled in Paris.
Exhibitions/citations Work included in exhibits at Design Museum, London; Musée des Arts Décoratifs, Paris; *Die Neue Sammlung*, Munich; Portuguese Museum, Lisbon; shown at fairs: Salone del Mobile (introduced Fly furniture), Milan, 1997; 1999 100% Design (introduced 1999 Stick Light by Eurolounge); 2001 *100% Design* (c. 1996 Magazine furniture, reintroduced by Twentytwentyone), London. 1994 grant, Crafts Council, London; Talente 95 citation, Germany.
Bibliography Alexander Payne, *We Like This: Michael Young*, London: Black Dog, 2000.
> See Pétursdóttir, Katrín.

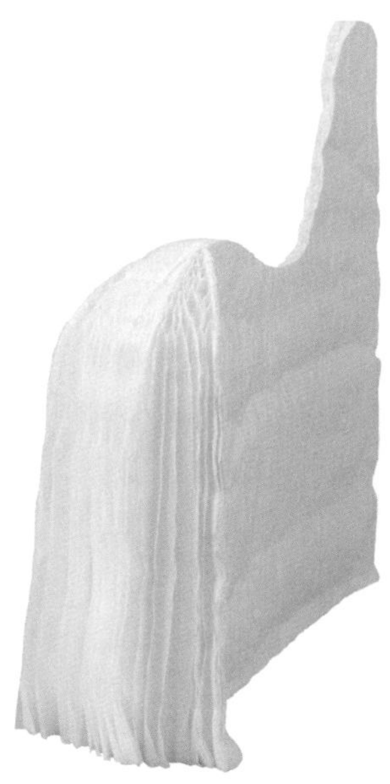

Tokujin Yoshioka. Honey-Pop armchair. 2000. Paper, unfolded: 31 1/4 x 32 x 32" (79.4 x 81.3 x 81.3 cm), folded: 31 1/4 x 36 1/2 x 3/4" (79.4 x 92.7 x 1.9 cm). Mfr.: the designer, Japan. Gift of the designer. MoMA.

Michael Young. MY 68 side chair. c. 1998. Beech or beech-stained wenge, h. 30 1/2 x w. 15 x d. 15" (80 x 38 x 38 cm). Mfr.: Sawaya & Moroni, Italy.

Yuon, Konstantin (1875–1958)

Russian painter and graphic and theater artist; born Moscow.

Training 1893–98, Moscow College; 1898–1900, in the studio of Valentin Serov.
Biography While in Serov's studio, Yuon visited Europe; 1900, was active in Moscow and a full member of the Academy of Fine Arts and, 1925–29, of AKhRR (association of artists of revolutionary Russia). Activities in the theater from 1911 included designs for Serge Diaghilev's 1913 production of Mussorgskii's *Boris Godunov* at the Theatre des Champs-Elysées, Paris. Subjects of Yuon's paintings were old churches, monasteries, and Russian nature and the countryside. In the Soviet period, he retained his fondness for Russia; became known for his cheerful Russian folk scenes; died in Moscow.
Exhibitions Showed work with Circle of the Itinerants, 1900; World of Art, from 1903; Union of Russian Artists, from 1903; work also included in Diaghilev's Russian section, 1906 Salon d'Automne show, Paris.

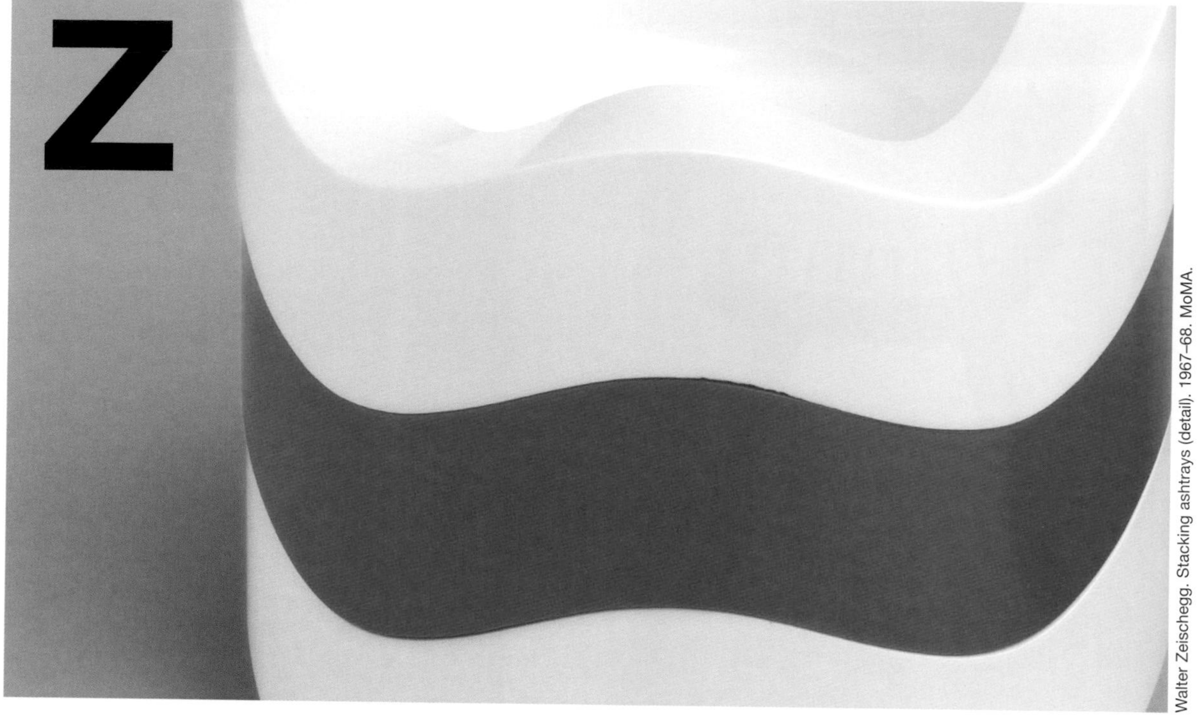

Walter Zeischegg. Stacking ashtrays (detail). 1967–68. MoMA.

Zaccai, Gianfranco (1947–)

Italian-American designer; born Trieste.

Training 1970, bachelor of industrial design degree, Syracuse (N.Y.) University, US; 1978, bachelor of architecture degree, Boston (Mass.) Architectural Center, US.
Biography 1983, Zaccai founded Design Continuum, with today's offices in Milan, Seoul, and near Boston. Staff design work has included 1991 Pump athletic shoe by Reebok, 1993 Bio water purifier by Samsung, 1994 Specialist 2 knee-surgery instrument by Johnson & Johnson, 1995 corner shelving unit by Desalto, 1998 Arctis Expe mountaineering boot by Koflach, 2000 titanium padlock by Master Lock, 2001 pass and collateral system for US National Parks Service, 2002 TT-X1 professional disk-jockey turntable by Numark. Design Continuum's staff in West Newton near Boston, Mass., has included John Costello, Roy Thompson, Stephanie Schwartz, Gregg Flender, David Malina.
Exhibition/citation 2000 Mind'Space project (with Haworth and others) included in 2001 *Workspheres*, The Museum of Modern Art, New York (catalog below). 2002 Red Dot award (for Mio instant-film camera, Continuum's US staff, by Polaroid), Design Zentrum Nordrhein-Westfalen, Essen.
Bibliography Gianfranco Zaccai, 'Designing the What,' *Design DK* (journal of Danish Design Center), 1998. Andrew Hargadon and Robert I. Sutton, 'Building an Innovation Factory,' *Harvard Business Review*, May–June, 2000. Mel Byars, *50 Sports Wares: Innovations in Design and Materials*, Hove: Roto Vision, 1999. Cat., Paolo Antonelli, *Workspheres: Design and Contemporary Work Styles*, New York: The Museum of Modern Art, 2001.

Zadikian, Zadik (1948–)

Armenian sculptor and furniture designer.

Training In sculpture, Yerevan, Armenia; Academy in Rome.
Biography 1967, Zadikian escaped from the USSR by swimming the Araks River and lived for a time in Istanbul and Beirut. 1974, he settled in New York and began working in a technique that suggests the sculptural clay fragments found in archeological digs. His 1975 installation *1,000 Bricks Gilded in 22-Carat Gold Leaf* at P.S. 1 on Long Island, N.Y., showed an interest in gold leaf, later used on his furniture pieces. c. 1987, he began to design utilitarian objects, including the massive Nina sofa and Regina chairs in voluptuous rounded forms. The furniture was made in cast plaster from a clay original and finished in a marbleized gilding.
Bibliography Alice Feiring, 'Casting Chrones,' *Metropolis*, Oct. 1991: 45.

Žák, Ladislav (1900–1973)

Czech architect, designer, painter, and writer.

Training 1919–24, painting under Karel Krattner, Akademie Výtvarných Umení (academy of fine arts); and, 1924–27 under Josef Gočár, architecture, Vysoká Škola Uměleckoprůmyslová (VŠUP, school of applied arts); both Prague.
Biography 1927, Žák became a member of SVU Aleš (association of fine arts), Brno; 1928, joined the Czechoslovakian Werkbund (SČSD); from 1933, was a member of Svaz Socialistických Architektů (union of Socialist architects); to 1930, taught at secondary schools in Prague, Brno, and Plzeň; 1946–73, was an associate professor of landscape architecture and town planning, Akademie Výtvarných Umení, Prague; specialized in the interior design of housing, particularly small flats, based on functional flexibility; designed 1931 Malý Byt (small flat) collection of tubular-steel furniture and 1937 Lidový Byt (popular flat) collection of furniture. One of his metal easy chairs, made by Gottwald, is comparable to the best of European models of the time and of a similar aesthetic. Žák incorporated this tubular-metal furniture into his 1930s family houses in Prague Vysočany and in Prague Hodkovičky, and in three villas in Prague Baba—all exemplary of his interest in social and collective housing. He wrote for various periodicals, supporting the ideas of functional housing, and the book *Obytná krajina* (a living landscape); after World War II, was active primarily as a landscape architect.
Bibliography Alena Adlerová, *České užité umění 1918–1938*, Prague: Odeon, 1983. Vladimír Šlapeta et al., *Czech Functionalism*, London: Architectural Association, 1987: 84.

Zane, Michael S. (1948–)

American designer and inventor.

Training In history.
Biography Zane lived for a brief time in Florence, Italy; returned to Boston, Mass., US, where his father operated a sheet-metal shop and lighting company; 1973, bought the rights to a bicycle lock from, and paid royalties to, the patent-holder, mechanic Stan Kaplan. The original design, of which 50 examples were produced, was crude. However, Zane asked for the advice of potential users, retailers, and college professors in a quest for refinement, eventually calling on assistance from his father's shop facilities. The final design, with his brother Peter L. Zane (1950–), was much lighter and included Zane's patented vinyl-coated 'bent foot,' a tubular steel cross bar, and an Ace II tubular key-lock cylinder. Thus the tamper-proof Kryptonite 4 lock was completed in 1976 and named for the fictitious substance,

Michael S. Zane and Peter L. Zane. Kryptonite 4 bicycle lock. 1976. Vinyl-coated zinc and nickel-plated steel, h. 10 5/8 x w. 7 1/2" (27 x 19.1 cm). Mfr.: KBL Corporation, US. Gift of the mfr. MoMA.

kryptonite, the only material that will make comic-strip character Superman weak. The lock has become ubiquitous worldwide, including a large number of exploitative imitations.
Bibliography Mel Byars with Arlette Barré-Despond, *100 Designs/100 Years: A Celebration of the 20th Century*, Hove: RotoVision, 1999.

Zanello, Gastone (1931–)

Italian industrial designer; born Tarcento; active Pordenone.

Biography 1958, Zanello began his career working as a design consultant, like Gino Valle, for Industrie Zanussi in Pordenone on the design of some of its domestic electrical appliances, including 1967 Coordinata kitchen project (with the Zanussi staff), 1967 Rex 700 kitchen, P5 Rex washing machine, and Naonis range of kitchen appliances. He became a member, Associazione per il Disegno Industriale (ADI).
Bibliography *ADI Annual 1976*, Milan: Associazione per il Disegno Industriale, 1976.

Zani & C., Serafino; Zani & Zani

Italian silver- and metalsmiths; located Lumezzane Gazzolo.

History In Lumezzane (the area the Romans called 'the land of metals'), Serafino Zani (1918–81) worked in the kitchen-utensils factory of his father Bernardo Lorenzo Zani; 1936, set up an enterprise of his own. From 1979, the firm concentrated on the use of metals and, 1984, established a department for research. The firm's designers—commissioned today by the Zani family, which continues to manage the firm—have included Isao Hosoe, Fabio Marinai, Marco Ricci, Ettore Sottsass, Andries van Onck, and Tapio and Sami Wirkkala. The firm has also commissioned a new generation of designers such as Silvana Angeletti, Massimo Mandelli, Paolo Romiti, Daniele Ruzza, and Elisabeth Vidal. Even though the firm has remained small and been conservatively managed, its inventory of sophisticated tabletop objects and accessories in metal, plastics, and other materials has been varied and imaginative, with high aesthetic values. From 1954, Enzo Mari has also designed for the firm. More recent products have included 1992–96 Piuma cutlery and hanging rack, 1984 Manu fruit bowl and Smith & Smith cutting board by Mari; 1999 Cuffietta Collection placemats/napkins by Franca Zani; Morbidi welded-PVC vase and Legaccio Metallico placemat by Claudio La Viola; 1998 La Zaniezani coffee percolator by Sottsass; 1999 pizza knife and salami knife (produced from 2001) by Paolo Ulian. Bruno Munari's 1955 TMT ashtray still in production, has become a classic. The design supervisors are Marco Susani and Mario Trimarchi. Serafino Zani's son Roberto manages the firm today.
Bibliography Cat., Hans Wichmann, *Italien Design 1945 bis heute*, Munich: Die neue Sammlung, 1988. Arlette Barré-Despond (ed.), *Dictionnaire international des arts appliqués et du design*, Paris: Regard, 1996. www.serafinozani.it.

Zanine, Caldas, José (1919–2001)

Brazilian architect; born Belmonte, Bahia.

Training Autodidactic.
Biography As a child, Zanine made his own toys; 1929, worked as a draftsperson and became inspired by 16th- and 17th-century Brazilian colonial architecture; began as an architectural model maker and designed a variety of chairs, tables, and units by Fábrica de Móveis Z, one of the first firms in Brazil to make modern furniture. His furniture consisted of solid hewn-wood chairs and chaises and tribal-drum-like wooden tables. Because the country was poor at the time, he recycled used materials in his furniture and architecture and, despite his contact with modernists, perhaps incongruently combined wood (not concrete) with rocks and large glass windows. He was inventive and creative, and continuously sought simplicity. Zanine became known as the *'papa da construção em madeira no Brasil'* (Brazilian pope of wooden construction). From c. 1965, he designed/built houses for private clients—including composer Antonio Carlos Jobim, pianist Nelson Freire, and actor Florinda Bolkan—and a number of public buildings. His structures expressed a harmony between living and the environment, featured visible solid timber framing elements, and were placed on stilts to encourage air circulation. As a result of his service as an advisor on the new city of Brasília, anthropologist Darcy Ribeiro invited him to lecture at the Universidade de Brasília (UnB). He founded DAM (foundation for the development and application of Brazilian woods) to foster sound forestry and logging methods and encourage the use of wood for low-cost public housing. Subsisting on a small pension from the UnB, he subsequently died poor, without a proper house of his own.
Exhibition/citation Subject of 1989 exhibit, Musée du Louvre, Paris. 1989 silver medal, Académie des Beaux-Arts, Paris.
Bibliography Elisabeth de Portzamparc, 'Brazil's Maverick Architect Zanine's Rich Woodwork,' *Elle Decor*, Aug. 1991: 64–67.

Zanini, Marco (1954–)

Italian architect; born Trento.

Training To 1978 under Adolfo Natalini, architecture, Università degli Studi, Florence.
Biography 1975–77, Zanini worked for the Argonaut Company in Los Angeles; was active as a freelance designer in San Francisco; 1977, returned to Milan and worked in Ettore Sottsass's studio, initially as an assistant, later as a partner; 1980, cofounded Sottsass Associati in Milan, where he designed for its first two collections, as well as 1981–88 furniture, lighting, and glass designs by Memphis, the group that he, Sottsass, and others established. His Memphis work included 1981 Dublin sofa; 1982 Rigel glass container, Arturo and Vega glass goblets, Alpha Centauri glass vase, Cassiopea glass goblet, and Victoria and Baykal ceramic vases; 1983 Colorado ceramic tea pot and Beltegeuse glass goblet; 1984 Lucrezia armchair; 1985 Amazon cabinet, Rossella hanging light, and Broccoli compote; 1986 Roma iridescent fiberglass armchair; and 1987 Juan chaise longue. At Sottsass Associati, Milan, he has designed graphics, jewelry, industrial machinery and products, furniture by Knoll, Esprit retail stores, glassware by Ritzenhoff, domestic interiors, showrooms, exhibitions, 2000 redesign of 1950s Interaction Design House (original architect, Eduardo Vittoria) in Ivrea, and urban furniture for a variety of clients worldwide, in addition to the Fascia pen and jewelry pieces by Acme Studios and 1995 Domaniblu wall clock. He cofounded the ABC cultural group in Milan.
Exhibitions Work included in a number of shows. Among his private endeavors, 1988 *49 Drawings and Some Short Stories*, Galleria Antonia Jannone, Milan.
Bibliography Marco Zanini, 'A Well Traveled Man,' in *Design ist unsichtbar*, Vienna, 1981: 464–74. Barbara Radice (ed.), *Memphis: The New International Style*, Milan: Electa, 1981: 65–66. Christine Colin, 'Memphis a encore frappé,' *Décoration Internationale*, no. 51, Dec. 1982–Jan. 1983: 54–57, 206. Cat., Kathryn B. Hiesinger and George H. Marcus III (eds.), *Design Since 1945*, Philadelphia: Philadelphia Museum of Art, 1983. Fumio Shimizu and Studio Matteo Thun (eds.), *The Italian Design: Descendants of Leonardo da Vinci*, Tokyo: Graphic-sha, 1987: 329.

Zanon, Roberto (1963–)

Italian designer; Camposampiero.

Training To 1989, degree in architecture, Università degli Studi, Venice.

Biography Zanon is active in architecture and restoration; from 1986, designed a number of widely published consumer products, including ceramics, furniture, glassware, tabletop accessories, and textiles; from 1995, has taught/lectured in Bangalore, Hong Kong, Lisbon, Oporto, Padova, and Venice; 1995, cofounded Y&Z Design Atrium, an international, multidisciplinary design studio with offices in Italy, Japan, and the US; 1997, became an associate of Mobas, a consortium of international product designers to design/develop consumer products; 1998, cofounded Gruppo di Ricerca e Design (gRiD), which is active in furniture research and experimentation; 2000, became a member of Wagner Associati interior- and industrial-design agency; has written a large number of articles for journals, including *Arch'it*, *Art Leader*, *Contemporart*, and *Modo*, and, from 1999, has been a correspondent for Korean magazine *Design Net*.
Exhibitions/citations From 1986, work included in a number of exhibitions, primarily in Italy. Large number of awards for industrial and product designs.

Zanotta
Italian furniture manufacturer; located Nova Milanese.

History Established in 1932 by Aurelio Zanotta (1925–97), the firm was particularly innovative and daring in Italy after World War II and supportive of Anti-Design groups. Its early work, some still in production and some as reproductions of early work by other manufacturers, includes 1929 Lira armchair and 1930 Comacina desk (originally produced by Thonet as B36) by Piero Bottoni; 1934 Follia side chair, 1936 Sant'Elia armchair, and 1936 Lariana side chair by Giuseppe Terragni; 1935 Susanna and Genni armchairs (reissued by Zanotta from 1982) by Gabriele Mucchi; 1947 Pontina side chair by Gio Ponti; 1937 Milo mirror, 1946 Reale table, and 1959 Fennis side chair by Carlo Molino; 1938 Spartana chair (production from the 1970s of a version of the original Landi aluminum chair) by Hans Coray; 1940 Leonardo table base by Achille Castiglioni; 1947 Maggiolina armchair by Marco Zanuso; 1950 Bramante table base by the Castiglionis; 1950 Sgabillo stool by Max Bill; and various other models by unidentified designers. Its landmark Anti-Design models include 1967 Blow clear plastic inflatable chair by De Pas, D'Urbino, and Lomazzi; the Castiglionis' 1970 Messandro tractor seat stool (designed in 1957); Superstudio's 1970 Quaderna laminate table range; and 1970 Sacco bean bag chair by Gatti, Paolini, and Teodora. By 1990, its stable of almost 60 international designers included Liisi Beckmann, Finland; Max Bill, Switzerland; Gilles Derain, France; Willie Landels, the UK; and Oscar Blanca Tusquets and Lluís Clotet Ballus, Spain; and numerous others more recently. Italian designers have been Gae Aulenti, Riccardo Dalisi, Ugo La Pietra, Alessandro Mendini, Gio Ponti, Ettore Sottsass/Sottsass Associati, and Giotto Stoppino. Founder Aurelio Zanotta's daughter Eleonora Zanotta manages the firm today. 2002, Zanotta introduced Living Food consumables, such as pasta and water, and opened a retail store, Milan.
Exhibitions/citations Work included in 1972 *Italy: The New Domestic Landscape*, The Museum of Modern Art, New York, and a number of other venues; subject of 1985 *1932–1985 Histoire du Design Zanotta*, Istituto Italiano di Cultura, Paris, Strasbourg 1986, Cologne 1987. Gold medals, 1948 (7th) and 1951 (9th) Triennali di Milano; 1968 (Guscio shelter by Roberto Menghi), 1979 (Sciangai clothes stand by De Pas, D'Urbino, and Lomazzi), and 1987 (Tonietta chair by Enzo Mari) Premio Compasso d'Oro; prizes at 1973 'BIO 5,' 1977 'BIO 7,' and 1988 'BIO 12' industrial-design biennials, Ljubljana; first prize, 1986 5-Star citation, ADI/Tecnhotel Hospitality, Fiera di Genova.
Bibliography Stefano Cascani, *Mobile come architettura il disegno della produzione Zanotta*, Milan: Arcadia, 1984. www.zanotta.it.

Zanotto, Paolo (1954–)
Italian designer; born Milan.

Training 1969–73, Liceo Artistico della Scuola Beato Angelico; 1973–79, faculty of architecture, Politecnico; both Milan.
Biography All activities in Milan: 1980–81, Zanotto was active in research at UNICITE-CNR; 1982–88, was a consultant to Studio G14 Progettaione-Sezione Design; 1987, collaborated with Nautilus on AFX mountain-climbing gear by Asolo; 1988, with Fusi Renata and Mollica Silvana, established Fusi Mollica Zanotto Architetti Associati.
> See Fusi, Renata; Mollica, Silvana.

Zanuso Jr., Marco (1954–)
Italian architect and designer; active Milan.

Training 1978 under Adolfo Natalini, architecture, Università degli Studi, Florence.
Biography Zanuso worked with his father and Adolfo Natalini; taught, Politecnico, Milan; from 1980, has specialized in architecture and industrial design in his own studio; 1983, with Luigi Greppi, Pietro Greppi, and Bepi Maggiori, founded lighting firm Oceano Oltreluce; 1980s, collaborated with Alessandro Mendini's studio; from 1999, designed tables, seating, beds, and the 2000 Ito glass-and-steel table by Driade.

Zanotta: De Pas, Gionatan, Donato D'Urbino, and Paolo Lomazzi. Blow inflatable armchair. 1967. Pneumatic structure and PVC plastic, 33 x 47 1/8 x 40 1/2" (83.8 x 119.7 x 102.9 cm). Mfr.: Zanotta, Italy. Gift of the mfr. MoMA.

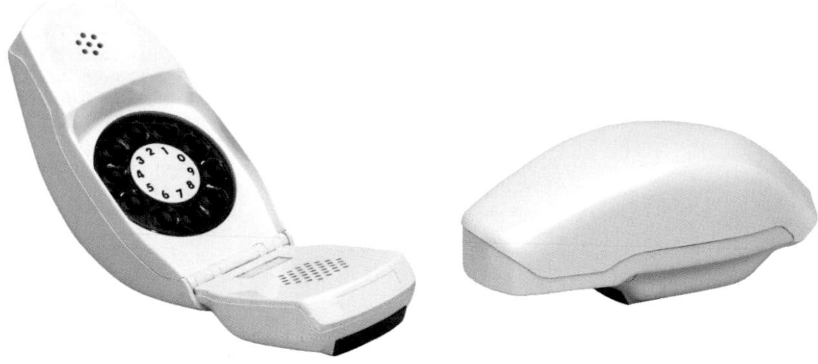

Marco Zanuso Sr. and Richard Sapper. Grillo folding telephone. 1965. ABS polymer, 2 3/4 x 6 1/2 x 3 1/4" (7 x 16.5 x 8.3 cm). Gift of the mfr. Mfr.: Societa Italiana Telecomunicazioni Siemens, Italy. MoMA.

Other work includes furniture by De Padova, 1993 seating in the Metrica collection by Arte, 1997 Pilsner goblet by Ritzenhoff.
Bibliography Fumio Shimizu and Studio Matteo Thun (eds.), *The Italian Design: Descendants of Leonardo da Vinci*, Tokyo: Graphic-sha, 1987: 330. Cristina Morozzi and Silvio Sanpietro, *Mobili italiani contemporanei*, Milan: Archivolto, 1996. Mel Byars, *Design in Steel*, London: Laurence King, 2003.

Zanuso Sr., Marco (1916–2001)

Italian architect and designer; born Milan.

Training To 1939, architecture, Politecnico, Milan.
Biography After World War II, he practiced as a member of the Italian modern movement; 1945–86, was a professor of architecture, design, and town planning, Politecnico, Milan; from 1949, was professor, Istituto di Tecnologia, faculty of architecture, Politecnico, Milan, where he became the director in 1970. 1945, he established his own design office in Milan after serving in the Italian navy; was an editor of architecture and design journals *Domus* and *Casabella*; in early 1950s, began designing furniture in bent-metal tubing, organized theoretical debates, and designed several editions of Triennale di Milano. His chair design for 1948 low-cost furniture competition sponsored by The Museum of Modern Art, New York, included a new joining mechanism for the fabric seat to be suspended from the tubular-steel frame. Serving as Olivetti's architect, he designed its 1956–58 factory and office in São Paulo with honeycomb cells covered with a thin-shell vault roof, and in Buenos Aires. Other architecture included IBM's headquarters in Milan and its factory in Rome; 1983 renovation of Teatro Fossati (now Teatro Studio del Piccolo) and the 1995 neo-Brutalist Piccolo Teatro, both Milan. The pioneering 1951 Lady armchair for Arflex featured the innovative application of latex-foam upholstery and Nostrocord (a synthetic rubber to replace traditional metal springs); 1962 Lambda chair was of a sheet-metal construction; and 1964 4999 child's stacking chair was the first to call on polyethylene for a piece of furniture and the first chair made entirely of injection-molded plastic. These projects brought highly favorable attention to Zanuso. His 1955 sofa-bed for Arflex incorporated an innovative mechanism for converting a sofa to a bed. 1958–77, he and Richard Sapper collaborated on numerous pieces that have subsequently become cult objects: 1962 Doney 14 TV and 1964 TS 502 radio by Brionvega, 1965 Grillo folding telephone by Siemens, and early-1970s scales and timer by Terraillon. Working for Brionvega from 1962, their other work was noted for its elegant visual solutions. 1956–58, Zanuso was a member of the Congrès Internationaux d'Architecture Moderne (CIAM), and Istituto Nazionale Urbanistica; 1956, cofounded Associazione per il Disegno Industriale (ADI) and its Premio Compasso d'Oro; served on international juries; was one of the guiding forces behind the formation of the Triennale di Milano and of Milan's urban-planning program. Other design work: 1987 Cleopatra and Antonio side tables by Memphis, 1989 I Buoni Sentimenti table by Galerie Néotù, 1983 Caraffa tea pot by Cleto Munari, 1985 Due Z hardware fittings by Fusital, and 1986 Laveno table by Zanotta. Zanuso belonged to a generation of designers committed to the exploration of new technology/materials developed during World War II, and exemplified the elegant but irreverent approach for which Italian design is now known. He died in Milan.
Exhibitions/citations Chair shown at 1948 *International Competition for Low Cost Furniture Design*, The Museum of Modern Art, New York; sewing machine by Borletti shown at 1957 (11th) Triennale di Milano; Lady armchair, Grillo telephone, and Doney 14 and Black 201 TV sets at 1983–84 *Design Since 1945* exhibition, Philadelphia Museum of Art (catalog below). Editions of Triennale di Milano: grand prizes and two gold medals at 1948 (8th), grand prize and two gold medals at 1951 (9th), grand prize and gold medal at 1954 (10th), gold medal at 1957 (11th), silver medal at 1960 (12th), and gold medal at 1964 (13th). Premio Compasso d'Oro. 1954, 1956, with Sapper, 1962, 1964, 1967, 1970 (six citations), 1979 (five citations), individually and with Alberto. Gold seal prize (for Lambda chair), 1965 *La Casa Abitata* exhibition, Florence; Interplas prize (for a chair by Kartell); gold medal (for Necchi knife sharpener), 1966 BIO 2 industrial-design biennial, Ljubljana; 1966 gold medal, Italian Ministry of Trade and Industry; 1971 prize, Salone dell'Industrializzazione Edilizia (SAIE); 1972 Bolaffi prize.
Bibliography Gillo Dorfles, *Marco Zanuso: Designer*, Rome: Editalia, 1971. Cat., Milena Lamarová, *Design a Plastické Hmoty*, Prague: Uměleckoprůmyslové Muzeum, 1972: 160. Paolo Fossati, *Il design in Italia*, Turin: Einaudi, 1972. *ADI Annual 1976*, Milan: Associazione per il Disegno Industriale, 1976. Andrea Branzi and Michele De Lucchi (eds.), *Il design italiano degli anni '50*, Milan: Ricerche Design Editrice, 1985. Cat., Kathryn B. Hiesinger and George H. Marcus III (eds.), *Design Since 1945*, Philadelphia: Philadelphia Museum of Art, 1983. S. Brandolin and G. Polin, 'Studio Associato Marco Zanuso e Pietro Crescini: Un nuovo complesso teatrale a Milano,' *Casabella* 48, no. 508, 1984: 4–15. Fumio Shimizu and Studio Matteo Thun (eds.), *The Italian Design: Descendants of Leonardo da Vinci*, Tokyo: Graphic-sha, 1987. Giuliana Gramigna and Paola Biondi, *Il design in Italia dell'arredamento domestico*, Turin: Allemandi, 1999. Paola Antonelli (ed.), *Objects of Design: The Museum of Modern Art*, New York: The Museum of Modern Art, 2003: 161, 236–37, 238.
> See Sapper, Richard; Drion, Giuseppe.

Zanussi

Italian manufacturer; located Pordenone.

History 1916, Antonio Zanussi (1890–1946), son of a blacksmith, established a workshop to produce and repair domestic woodburning ovens in Pordenone. Its pre-World War II cookers, and vacuum cleaners had streamline styling. 1933, Rex (after 1931 oceanliner *Rex*) was established as a trademark; 1954, refrigerators joined the line of products; 1954, the first Zanussi washing machine; 1965, its first dishwasher. 1950s, the firm established a design department. Its innovative designs have included an 18-in. (45-cm) wide dishwasher. Gino Valle designed its 1958 cooker and 1950s kitchen appliances which he grouped together into units with refined casings and controls. Other designers have included Gastone Zanello and Andries van Onck. 1984, Zanussi was bought by Electrolux to be-come Electrolux Zannusi (Electrolux Group). The firm's designs up to mid-1980s

sought to be unobtrusive; its 1980s Wizard collection included more visually assertive objects for the kitchen. 1987 Wizard refrigerator by Zanussi's design director Roberto Pezzetta has joined a more successful inventory such as 1996 Zoe washing machine and Oz and Teo advanced domestic appliances. 1993, Pezzetta became design director of Electrolux European Management Design.
Citations Premio Compasso d'Oro: 1962 (for Mod. 700 Rex gas stove), 1967 (for P5 washing machine), 1979 (for temperature-controlled bath), 1981 (for body of work; corporate-image program), 1987 (for Wizard refrigerator by Pezzetta), 1989 (four citations), and 1991 nomination (for Michelangelo/Deco System by Valboni; Matura 9140 by Pezzetta and Zanussi design staff), and 1998 selection (Soft Tech electric oven). 1991 (for Manhattan refrigerator) and 1999 (for Oz refrigerator), Goed Industrieel Ontwerp, the Netherlands; 1997 Design Prestige (for Oz and Zoe concept design products), Brno, Czech Repub-lic; 1998 Premio de Diseño (for Oz refrigerator), Feria Internacional de La Habana, Cuba. Good Design awards, Chicago Athenaeum, Chicago: 1999 (for Oz refrigerator, Soft Tech electric oven, Input washing machine), 2000 (for Iz washing machine and Aluminium built-in set of appliances), and 2002 (for Izzi dishwasher).
Bibliography *Issue 2*, London: Design Museum, 1989. Mel Byars, *On/Off: New Electronic Products*, New York: Universe, 2001.
> See Pezzetta, Roberto.

Zapf, Otto (1931–)
German furniture designer.

Training Mathematics, Universität Johann Wolfgang Goethe, Frankfurt.
Biography From 1956, Zapf designed his first furniture with Dieter Rams and, subsequently has designed important modular systems furniture. 1959, Zapf and Niels Wiese-Vitsoe founded Vitsoe & Zapf, which Zapf left in 1972, the same year he designed the Zapf Office System by Knoll. He also designed 1976 Office Chair Collection by Knoll and Management Office by Vitra, also 7500 workstations for Pacific Telesis.
Bibliography Arlette Barré-Despond (ed.), *Dictionnaire international des arts appliqués et du design*, Paris: Regard, 1996.

Zapp, Walter (b. Valters Caps 1905–2003); Minox
Latvian inventor and designer; born Riga.

Training Apprenticeship, engraving in Tallinn, Estonia; 1921, apprenticeship, lithography, printing house in Riga; 1922, apprentice, photo studio in Tallinn.
Biography By 1922, Zapp had already begun thinking about making a very small camera (eventually to be the Minox and known as the 'spy camera' due to its use as such in films). 1932, he established a joint venture with Richard Jürgen, who provided financial support, and called on the expertise of optician Karl Indus and mechanic Hans Epner. 1932–36 in Tallinn, Zapp began work on a miniature-camera prototype. 1936–40 having been rejected by German firms such as AGFA, Jürgen turned to the governmental enterprise Valsts Electro-Techniska Fabrika (VEF) in Riga for support in the production of the 1936 VEF Riga Minox camera (patented on 22 Dec. 1936 by VEF).

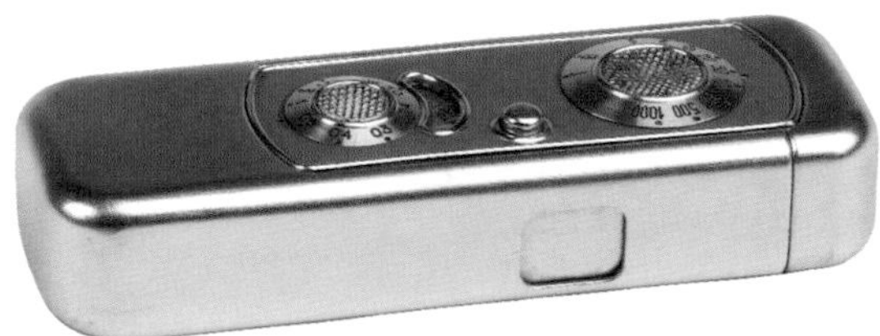

Walter Zapp (b. Valters Caps). VEF Riga Minox camera. 1936. Stainless steel, closed 5/8 x 3 1/8 x 1 1/16" (1.6 x 8 x 2.7 cm), expanded 5/8 x 3 3/4 x1 1/16" (1.6 x 9.5 x 2.7 cm). Mfr.: Valsts Electro-Techniska Fabrika (VEF), Latvia (1937–42). Marshall Cogan Purchase Fund. MoMA.

Possibly 17,000 examples were made. In the beginning, one of Zapp's many challenges was the development of appropriately small film, which was solved by slicking 35-mm motion-picture film. 1941 due to the Soviet army's occupation of the Baltic region, where Riga and Tallinn are located, Zapp settled in Germany; 1941–45, worked at Electron Microscopy Department of AEG, Berlin. First half of 1940s, Minox cameras were stamped with Nazi swastikas. 1945, the end of World War II, Zapp and Jürgen renewed their relationship, and, after a two-year hiatus, they founded and managed Minox GmbH in Wetzlar to make the cameras. From 1950, the firm continued without Zapp, who settled in Switzerland and continued to work in the field of miniature photography. Several Minox models have been produced in the post-World War II years, including the II (1948–49), II/IIIS (1950–69), B (1958–72), C (1969–78), BL (1972–77), LX (1978–96), EC (1995–96), AX Gold II (1994–95), and others through to today, as well as Minox-appropriate stands, flash attachments, projectors, and other accessories. 1996, Minox GmbH was taken over by Leica Camera, and Zapp became associated with the new, young management at Minox, acted as an advisor, and helped the division to develop new technologies. The 1998 special edition CLX, similar to the original model, commemorates the 60th birthday of the VEF Minox. By the end of 1990s, about one million Minox cameras had been sold, since its introduction. Zapp died in Binningen, Switzerland.
Citations To Zapp: 2001, honorary doctoral degree, Latvian Business Academy, Riga; 2001, Cross of Honor of the Latvian Republic.
Bibliography N. Upenieks, 'Technikas Apskats,' *Technical Review*, no. 111, 1988: 7–9. Hubert E. Heckmann, *Minox—Variationen in 8x11*, Hamburg: Friederich Wittig, 1992 1st ed., 1995 2nd ed., 1995 English ed. Joseph David Cooper, *The Minox Manual*, New York: Universal Photo Books, 1961. Morris G. Moses, *The Spy Camera: The Minox Story*, Hove, UK: Hove Foto Books, 1990 2nd ed.. Michael Pritchard and Douglas St. Denny, *Spy Camera: A Century of Detective and Subminiature Cameras*, London: Classic Collections, 1993.

Zarges-Dürr, Erna (1907–)
German silversmith; active Pforzheim, Leipzig, Berlin, and Stuttgart.

Training 1924–27, in Bruckmann & Söhne, Heilbronn, as the first woman in the silversmiths' department; from 1927 under Theodor Wende and others, Kunstgewerbeschule, Pforzheim.
Biography 1930–33, she worked in the workshops of Ernst Treusch in Leipzig, and of H.J. Wilm in Berlin; 1933, established her own workshop in Heilbronn; 1936–39, relocated to Stuttgart. Her work showed carefully studied proportions with original, modern ornamentation.
Citations Numerous awards, including a gold medal (for 1932 silver wine jug), 1937 *Exposition Internationale des Arts et Techniques dans la Vie Moderne*, Paris. Also included in other international exhibitions.
Bibliography Annelies Krekel-Aalberse, *Art Nouveau and Art Déco Silver*, New York: Abrams, 1989.

Zbryk, Burgess (1964–)
> Egawa, Rie.

Zecchin, Francesco (1894–1986)
Italian glassmaker; born Murano.

Training Engineering, Università degli Studi, Padova.
Biography Zecchin was a glass technician and, from 1925, was an owner of Vetri Soffiati Muranesi Venini & C., which closed in 1932 due to the Great Depression. Subsequently, Zecchin and Vetri Soffiati's former artistic director Napoleone Martinuzzi cofounded Zecchin-Martinuzzi Vetri Artistici e Mosaici, also in Murano, which closed in 1938. After World War II, Zecchin built glass ovens for glassmakers; died in Murano. That Francesco Zecchin was related to Vittorio Zecchin is not known for certain but assumed.
> See Zecchin, Vittorio (below).

Zecchin, Vittorio (1878–1947)
Italian painter and decorator; born Murano.

Training To 1901, Accademia di Belle Arti, Venice.
Biography Zecchin became a major figure of 20th-century Murano glass design. c. 1913, was a freelance designer to Artisti Barovier. 1921 when antiques dealer Giacomo Cappellin and lawyer Paolo Venini founded Vetri Soffiati Muranesi Cappellin Venini & C., Zecchin became the firm's first artistic director. However, after disagreements in 1925, he withdrew, and he and Cappellin founded Maestri Vetrai Muranesi Cappellin & C. and installed the master glassblowers of the

Walter Zeischegg. Stacking ashtrays. 1967. Melamine, each h. 2" x dia. 5 1/4" (5.1 x 13.4 cm). Mfr.: Helit, Germany. Gift of Bonniers, Inc. MoMA.

former firm in their new enterprise, which closed in 1932 due to the Great Depression. 1933–34, Zecchin was the first artistic director of Artistica Vetreria e Soffieria Barovier Seguso e Ferro; produced free-lance designs for Studio Ars et Labor Industrie Riunite (S.A.L.I.R.) 1931–42, Arte Vetraria Muranese (AVEM) from 1932, and others. He died in Murano.
Exhibitions 1924, 1926, 1932, 1934, 1938, 1942, 1952 Biennali di Venezia. 2002 *Vittorio Zecchin 1878-1947, pittura, vetro, arti decorative*, Museo Correr, Venice (catalog below).
Bibliography F. Deboni, *Venini Glass*, Basel: Wiese, 1990: 34. Cat., Marino Barovier, Marco Mondi and Carla Sonego (eds), *Vittorio Zecchin 1878–1947, pittura, vetro, arti decorative*, Venice: Marsilio, 2002.
> See Zecchin, Francesco.

Zeischegg, Walter (1917–1983)

Austrian designer; born Vienna.

Biography 1951–68, Zeischegg taught at Hochschule für Gestaltung, Ulm, Germany; designed various products, including undulating stackable ashtray no. 84009, fruit dish no. 84047, tabletop magazine rack no. 63527, bookends no. 63616, most of them in melamine, by Helit Presswerk, Westfalen. He died in Ulm.
Bibliography Cat., *Plastics + Design*, Munich: Die Neue Sammlung, Munich, 1997.

Zeisel, Eva (1906–)

Hungarian designer and ceramicist; born Budapest; active Germany, Russia, Austria, and the US.

Training 1923–24 under Vaszari, painting, Képzömüvészeti Akadémia (Academy of Art), Budapest; subsequently, apprenticeship in pottery.
Biography 1927–32, she worked first for the Kispest earthenware factory in Budapest, and for various ceramics factories in Germany, including as a ceramics designer at Schramberg Majolika Fabrik and at the Carsten ceramics factory. She was familiar with the Deutscher Werkbund and Bauhaus forms and, 1932, went to the Soviet Union, where she worked in various ceramics factories, including a sanitary ceramics plant and, under Nikolai Suetin, the Lomonosov Porcelain Factory in Leningrad (now St. Petersburg). Suetin applied motifs to some of her forms. From 1934, she worked for the Deulevo ceramics factory in Moscow; became artistic director, Central Administration of the Glass and China Industry of the USSR, Moscow; 1936–37, during the Stalin Purges, was imprisoned, released, and deported. She married sociologist/lawyer Hans Zeisel in England and, 1938 through Vienna and London, settled in US, where one of her first commissions came from Sears, Roebuck & Co., Chicago. 1939–52, she taught at Pratt Institute, Brooklyn, N.Y., and, 1959–60, Rhode Island School of Design, Providence, while also designing for clients. Her 1940s ceramic designs reflect an organic orientation of the time. Her 1942–45 Museum White dinnerware, designed in collaboration with The Museum of Modern Art, New York, and produced by Castleton China Co. in New Castle, Pa., reflected Functionalist ceramics produced by major factories in Europe, especially those in Arzberg and Berlin. 1946 Town and Coun-try dinner service was produced by Red Wing Pottery, US. She designed a 1950 knock-down chair with a zippered plastic cover by Richards-Morgenthau, wooden pieces by Salisbury Artisans from 1951, and 1952 dinnerware for Hall China. Her late 1990s–early 2000s work included designs for the Zsolnay factory, Pecs, Hungary; Kiespester-Granit, Budapest; and Klein-Reid, US;

Eva Zeisel. Museum White bowl, hot-water pot, creamer, and cup and saucer (examples from an extensive service). c. 1942-1945, bowl h. 2 1/2" (6.4 cm) x dia. 4 3/4" (12.1 cm), cover h. 1 3/8" (3.5 cm) x dia. 4" (10.2 cm), hot-water pot 8 3/4 x 6 x 4 1/4" (22.2 x 15.2 x 10.8 cm), creamer 4 1/2 x 4 1/2 x 3 3/4" (11.4 x 11.4 x 9.5 cm), tea cup 2 x 5 3/8 x 4 1/2" (5.1 x 13.7 x 11.4 cm) and saucer h. 1" (2.5 cm) x diam. 6 5/8" (16.8 cm). Glazed porcelain. Mfr.: Castleton China Co., US. Gift of the mfr. MoMA.

Carlo Zen. Side chair. c. 1905. Rosewood, mother-of-pearl, metal, and silk-and gold-thread, 36 15/16 x 14 3/8 x 13 1/4" (93.8 x 36.5 x 33.7 cm), seat h. 16 7/8" (42.9 cm). Gift of John Goodwin. MoMA.

including an aluminum range of vases by Nambé. Also from late 1990s, with the assistance of her son-in-law as entrepreneur, The Museum of Modern Art and The Metropolitan Museum of Art, both New York, reproduced earlier works with new glazes and in new colors, designed and supervised by Zeisel, who lives in New York.
Exhibitions/citation Museum White china dinnerware subject of 1946 *Modern China by Eva Zeisel*, The Museum of Modern Art, New York. Work subject of 1984 traveling exhibition, organized by Musée des Arts Décoratifs, Montrèal (catalog below). Work included in numerous venues. Received 1982 Senior Fellowship, National Endowment for the Arts.
Bibliography 'In the Showrooms: Furniture,' *Interiors*, vol. 109, Mar. 1950: 122. 'Merchandise Cues,' *Interiors*, vol. 111, Feb. 1952: 114. Jay Doblin, *One Hundred Great Product Designs*, New York: Whitney, 1970: 62. Cat., Kathryn B. Hiesinger and George H. Marcus III (eds.), *Design Since 1945*, Philadelphia: Philadelphia Museum of Art, 1983. Cat., *Eva Zeisel: Designer to Industry*, Montrèal: Musée des Arts Décoratifs; Chicago: University of Chicago, 1984. Cat., Martin Eidelberg (ed.), *Design 1935–1965: What Modern Was*, New York: Musée des Arts Décoratifs/Abrams, 1991. Lucie Young et al., *Eva Zeisel*, San Francisco: Chronicle, 2003.
> See Hall China Company, The.

Zeitner, Herbert (1900–1988)

German silversmith; born Coburg; active Berlin.

Training Königlich Preussische Zeichenakademie, Hanau.
Biography 1924, Zeitner established his own workshop in Berlin; taught, Vereinigte Staatsschulen für freie und angewandte Kunst (Kunstgewerbeschule), Berlin-Charlottenburg; 1939, became director of the goldsmiths' master workshop, Preußische Akademie der Künste.
Bibliography Annelies Krekel-Aalberse, *Art Nouveau and Art Déco Silver*, New York: Abrams, 1989. Cat., *Metallkunst*, Berlin Bröhan-Museum, 1990: 580–81, 600.

Zelco

American design firm/manufacturer; located Mt. Vernon, N.Y.

History 1976, Noel and Adele Zeller founded the firm whose products were originally designed, manufactured, marketed, and sold from the basement and garage of their house. The company grew appreciably to include facilities in the US, Italy, Hong Kong, Korea, and China; produces a range of products sold in more than 30 countries. The Zeller family continues to research, design, develop, market, and distribute a line of goods that has included Double Plus calculator, Mangia! picnic cutlery, and fluorescent pocket light. The Itty Bitty book light may have been its first successful item. The Computer Accessories range was designed by the Zellers, Seth Greenwald, and Lukie Bernstein.
Exhibition/citations Noce nutcracker included in 1995 *Mutant Materials in Contemporary Design*, The Museum of Modern Art, New York, and traveling (catalog below). Zelco received Accent on Design award, International Gift Fair, New York; Roscoe award, Resource Council, US; Premio SMAU Industrial Design, Salone della Machina e Attrezzature per l'Ufficio, Milan; G-Mark Good Design award, Japanese Industrial Design Promotion Organization (JIDPO); Design Achievement Award, Industrial Designers Society of America (IDSA); gold medal, IDSA/*Business Week* magazine; honor for highest design quality, Design Innovationen 92, Design Zentrum Nordrhein-Westfalen, Essen; Good Design awards, Chicago Antheneaum; three Andy awards, Advertising Club of New York.
Bibliography Cat., Paola Antonelli, *Mutant Materials in Contemporary Design*, New York: The Museum of Modern Art/Abrams, 1995. www.zelco.com.

Zelenka, František (1896–1942)

Czech architect and stage and graphic designer; born Prague.

Training České Vysoké Učení Technické (Czech technical university), Prague.
Biography 1930, Zelenka became a member of Czechoslovakian Werkbund (SČSD); designed a number of interiors, among them the flat (with its Blue Room) for composer Jaroslav Ježek; wrote for various magazines; 1929–32, was active as a stage designer at Osvobozené Divadlo (the liberated theater) and, subsequently, for the Národní Divadlo (national theater) and Stavovské theater, both Prague; 1926–37, designed a number of posters for theaters and films. During World War II, he died in the Auschwitz-Birkenau extermination camp.
Bibliography Alena Adlerová, *České užité umění 1918–1938*, Prague: Odeon, 1983.

Zemp, Werner (1940–)

Swiss designer; active Cabiate (Italy).

Biography 1967, Zemp began his professional career in Germany; 1973, settled in Italy, becoming active as an environmental designer for department stores, sports stadia, and playgrounds; became a member, Associazione per il Disegno Industriale (ADI). Clients have included the Institut für Räumlichen Städtebau, Bern; Instituto de Investigaciones Tecnológicas (Intec), Corfo; Karl Steiner, Limbiate; and La Rinascente department store, Milan.
Bibliography *ADI Annual 1976*, Milan: Associazione per il Disegno Industriale, 1976.

Zen, Carlo (1851–1918)

Italian cabinetmaker; active Milan; father of Piero Zen.

Biography From c. 1880 Carlo Zen directed the most important furniture workshop in Milan; was active in the *stile floreale* and, after 1902 *Esposizione Internazionale d'Arte Decorativa Moderna*, Turin, continued to be known for his Art Nouveau and symbolist motifs. He was not a designer himself but rather factory owner and manager. From 1898, his firm was associated with Haas of Vienna, whose designers included Otto Eckmann. Zen's artisans called on inlays of mother-of-pearl, and their elegant, asymmetrical patterns became more geometric c. 1910 and showed the simplification typical of German and Austrian aesthetics. 1906, Zen's son Piero (1879–1950) joined the family firm as a designer.
Bibliography Cat., Eleanora Bairati et al., *L'Italia Liberty: arredamento e*

arti decorativi, Milan: Görlich, 1973. Cat., Gabriel P. Weisberg, *Stile Floreale: The Cult of Nature in Italian Design*, Miami: The Wolfsonian Foundation, 1988.

Zena
Swiss manufacturer; located Affoltern.

History Zena was founded by Alfred Neweczerzal, inventor of 1947 Rex (no. 11002) vegetable peeler. By 1990, was selling for one-fifth of its 1947 price and continues to be made, the same as the original aluminum model. Its moveable blade portion is a patented invention. The newer Star model is made of stainless steel; the Rapid and Model 2000 are in colored ABS. With still a relatively small inventory of models, Zena also makes a thong-type aparagus peeler, Rex slicer, MagicOne vegetable peeler, and blades.
Exhibition Work included in 1991 *Schweizer Erfindungen*, Globus department store, Basel.
Bibliography Cat., *Unbekannt-Vertraut: 'Anonymes' Design im Schweizer Gebrauchsgerät seit 1920*, Zürich: Museum für Gestaltung, 1987.

Zenith
> See Budlong, Robert Davol; McDonald Jr., Eugene F.

Zenith Industriell Design
Swedish design studio; located Malmö.

History The group specializes in industrial design; is led by Mårten Rittfeldt, also the chairperson of Föreningen Svenska Industridesigner (SID, Swedish industrial-design association) in c. 2002. Work has included Aqueduct conference-table system by Offecct and products for other clients such as Alfa Laval Automation, Cagiva Motor Italia, FOA, LEGO, Mölnlycke, and Volvo.
Citations 1997 Utmärkt Svensk Form (for 1997 LCD monitors); 1998 CeBit Oscar of *Chip* computer magazine (for 1998 Multi Q panel computer).

Zeppelin
German airship.

History The Zeppelin airship was named after Graf (count) Ferdinand von Zeppelin (1838–1917), the head of the Luftschiffbau-Zeppelin and who was succeeded by Hugo Eckener. Most notable among the German Zeppelins was 1936–37 *Hindenburg* (LZ 129). Its predecessor was 1928 *Graf Zeppelin* (LZ 127); others included *Bodensee* (LZ 120) and *Nordstern* (LZ 121). Interior architect Fritz Breuhaus de Groot designed, laid out, and decorated the *Hindenburg* (with artist Otto Arpke (1886–1943) and chief constructor Ludwig Dürr at Luftschiffbau-Zeppelin). Breuhaus made innovatory use of aluminum in the brown fabric-upholstered furniture and for the casing of the Blüthner grand piano. 1911, Bernhard Pankok also designed an aluminum chair for a Zeppelin. A reconstructed *Hindberg* (LZ 129) is kept in the Zeppelin Museum in Friedrichshafen, Germany, where the LZ-Archiv of the Luftschiffbau-Zeppelin firm is also housed.
Bibliography J. Gordon Vaeth, 'Zeppelin Decor: The Graf Zeppelin and the Hindenburg,' *Journal of Decorative and Propaganda Art*, no. 15, winter/spring 1990: 53. Lutz Tittel, *Zeppelin Collection Heinz Urban* ('Writings on the History of the Zeppelin-Luftschiffahrt,' no. 4), Friedrichshafen: Zeppelin Museum, 1986. Lutz Tittel, *Graf Zeppelin: Leben und Werk* (Writings on the History of the Zeppelin-Luftschiffahrt, no. 4), Friedrichshafen: Zeppelin Museum, 1992. Cat., *Zeppelin Museum Friedrichshafen: Technik und Kunst*, Friedrichshafen: Zeppelin Museum, 1997. www.zeppelin-museum.de.

Nicos Zographos. Zographos side chair. 1966. Chrome-plated tubular steel with leather, 31 x 20 x 22" (78.7 x 50.8 x 55.9 cm). Mfr.: The General Fireproofing Co. (1969). Gift of the mfr. MoMA.

Zernova, Ekaterina (1900–1995)
Russian decorative, mural, graphic, and theater artist, and painter; born Simferopol.

Training In the F. Roerberg studio; physics and mathematics department, Moscow University; 1919–24, VKhUTEMAS.
Biography Zernova settled in Moscow; 1921–31, was active in book illustration, journal graphics, placard art, stage-set design for several theater performances; became a member, Society of Easel Artists; is best known for her monumental and decorative art work, murals, mosaics, reliefs, and appliqués; painted renowned *The Handover of Tanks*; died in Moscow.

Zeus
Italian design group; located Milan.

History 1984, Zeus was founded by Sergio Calatroni, Roberto Marcatti, Ruben Mochi, and Maurizio Peregalli. Peregalli designed a chair and table collection for Zeus; was the artistic director and partner of Noto, which designed Zeus's collections and interiors. Peregalli is now the director of Zeus and Noto.
Bibliography Fumio Shimizu and Studio Matteo Thun (eds.), *The Italian Design: Descendants of Leonardo da Vinci*, Tokyo: Graphic-sha, 1987. *The International Design Yearbook*, London: Thames & Hudson, 1986, 1987, 1989, 1990. Andrea Branzi (ed.), *Il design italiano 1964-1990*, Milan: Electa, 1996. Nelly Bellati, *New Italian Design*, New York: Rizzoli
> See Peregalli, Maurizio.

Ziba Design
American design studio.

History 1984, Ziba Design was founded by Schrab Voussoughi, with headquarters in Portland, Ore., and offices in San Jose, Cal.; Tokyo; and Taipei; employs a large, highly productive staff, serving multinational clients, including Black and Decker, Coleman, Estée Lauder, Federal Express, Kenwood, Fugitsu, Intel, Microsoft, Nike, Sanyo, Sprint, Sunbeam, and Whirlpool.
Exhibitions/citations Work included in 2000 National Design Triennial, Cooper-Hewitt National Design Museum, New York; 2002 *U.S. Design*, touring the US. Number of citations, including awards from Industrial Designers Society of America (IDSA) than any other US design firm.
Bibliography Cat., Donald Albrecht et al., *Design Culture Now: The National Design Triennial*, New York: Princeton Architectural Press,. 2000. Mel Byars, *On/Off: New Electronic Products*, New York: Universe, 2001. Cat., R. Craig Miller (intro.), *U.S. Design 1975–2000*, Munich: Prestel, 2002.

Zimpel, Julius (1896–1925)
Austrian silversmith; active Vienna.

Training Under Koloman Moser, Kunstgewerbeschule, Vienna.
Biography Zimbel was a designer, including of silverware, at Wiener Werkstätte, and follower of Dagobert Peche, its artistic director.
Bibliography Günther Feurstein, *Vienna—Present and Past: Arts and Crafts—Applied Art—Design*, Vienna: Jugend und Volk, 1976. Werner J. Schweiger, *Wiener Werkstätte*, Vienna: Brandstaeter, 1982: 269.

Annelies Krekel-Aalberse, *Art Nouveau and Art Déco Silver*, New York: Abrams, 1989.

Zographos, Nicos (1931–)
American interior and furniture designer.

Biography Zographos has designed interiors and products for a number of clients, including architects Philip Johnson, Gordon Bunshaft, Walter Gropius, and I.M. Pei. Many of his products are self-manufactured; however, 1966 Zographos side chair was produced by The General Fireproofing Co.
Bibliography Peter Bradford, *The Design Art of Nicos Zographos*, New York: Monacelli, 2000.

Zoritchak, Yan (1944–)
Slovakian industrial designer; born Zdiar; active Paris.

Training 1959, advanced school of glassmaking, Zelezny Brod; 1963–69, under Stanislas Libensky, Vysoká Škola Umĕleckoprůmyslová (VŠUP, academy of arts, architecture, and design), Prague.
Biography Zoritchak was the director of Centre International de Recherche sur le Verre et les Arts Plastiques. He and his wife Catherine Zoritchak (1947–) designed 1984 Espace 2000 dinner plate in a geometric motif in Corning industrial glass. Zoritchak has become known primarily for glass sculpture and is considered one of the major precursors of French contemporary glass art. When he settled in France in 1970, French glass art was practically unknown.
Exhibitions/citation Sculpture subject of 1995 exhibition, Glasmuseet, Ebeltoft, Denmark; 1999 *L'Homme et l'Univers*, Palais de la Découverte, Paris. 1987 Chevalier of the Ordre des Arts et Lettres, France.
Bibliography *Les carnets du design*, Paris: Mad-Cap Productions/APCI, 1986: 49. Ashai Shimbun, 'Yan Zoritchak,' *Stained Glass Art*, vol. 1, no. 7, 1986. Janine Bloch-Dermant, *Le verre en France: d'Emile Gallé à nos jours*, Paris: Éditions de l'Amateur, 1986: 377–81. A. Dolez, 'Le Monumental de Zoritchak,' *Revue de la Céramique et du Verre*, no. 48, 1989: 17–21. Cat., *Yan Zoritchak*, Paris: Galerie l'Eclat du Verre, 2000.

Zsolnay Porcelánmanufaktúra (aka Pécs Pottery)
Hungarian pottery; located Pécs.

History 1851, Miklós Zsolnay (1857–1922) established a pottery in Pécs. 1853–65, Ignác Zsolnay (1826–90) managed the operation, the first Hungarian ceramics factory. 1865, his brother Vilmos Zsolnay (1828–1900) took over as the director and eventually brought international fame to the manufacturing complex and developed it into a worldwide exporter. Initial production was a limited amount of utilitarian wares for local customers, such as decorative architectural terracotta and simple dishes. By 1883, the pottery had grown to 450 employees and, by 1900, to 1,000. Its early work was primarily stoneware decorated in Hungarian folk styles. 1870s, the factory began producing lusterware in a neo-Renaissance style and imitation Iznik, known as *ivoir-fayence* (applied with a colored porcelain glaze and cured at high temperatures). 1890s, József Rippl-Rónai designed numerous Art Nouveau-style pieces. Even so, by this time, much of the factory's production continued to be for architectural and industrial uses. Miklós Zsolnay (1857–1925) succeeded his father as the director, and the enterprise is still active today. Through the 20th century, its range expanded to include the prevailing styles of Western Europe—historicist, Art Nouveau, Art Déco, modern, and postmodern—on urns and fountains, mirrors and small sculptures, tiles for furniture, and a large number of other decorative and utilitarian objects. Miklós Zsolnay, the namesake of his grandfather who founded the firm, amassed a famed collection of ceramics, collected during his 1887–88 travels in Turkey. Zsolnay archives are housed in the Janus Pannonius Museum, Pécs.
Exhibitions Work subject of 1986 exhibition, Museum of Arts and Crafts, Budapest, and Österreichisches Museum für angewandte Kunst, Vienna (catalog below); 2002 *Hungarian Ceramics from the Zsolnay Manufactory, 1853–2001*, Bard Graduate Center, New York.
Bibliography Karl Csányi, *Geschichte der Ungarischen Keramik, des Porzellane und ihre Marken*, Budapest: Fonds für bildende Künste, 1954. Margit Mattyasovszky Zsolnay and Eva Hárs, *A Zsolnay keramia, vesetö a JPM állandó kiállításához*, Pécs: A Janus Pannonius Múzeum, 1966. *Zsolnay*, Budapest: Corvina, 1975. Cat., Éva Hárs, *The Zsolnay Ceramics*, Pécs: Pécsi Szikra Nyomada, 1982. Cat., *Zsolnay: Ungarische Jugendstilkeramik*, Budapest/Vienna: Österreichisches Museum für angewandte Kunst, 1986.

Toni Zuccheri. Flacon. c. 1964. Mouth-blown glass with *giada* effect, h. 5 7/8" (15 cm). Mfr.: Venini & C., Italy. Courtesy Quittenbaum Kunstauktionen, Munich.

Zuber
French wallpaper firm; located Rixheim.

History Jean Zuber was a salesperson for textile and wallpaper printer Hartmann Risler in Mulhouse; 1802, became the director and controller of the firm. He went on to establish his own firm, Jean Zuber et Cie., as the first producer of scenic wallpaper and, with J. Dufor, the best; 1804, introduced his first dated scenic paper *Vues de Suisse*. At this time, he specialized in Empire-style textured papers and hired accomplished designers. 1850, the firm adopted mechanical printing. Individual designs were kept in active production during many years, in some cases into the 20th century. Zuber's papers were exported worldwide, including to the US in the mid-19th century, even installed in The White House, Washington, D.C., when it was initially constructed and decorated and in its diplomatic reception rooms in the 20th century. Zuber's scenic papers depicting horse racing and views of Boston and Niagara Falls were widely published. André Marty painted scenes for the firm in c. 1925, and his image of the updated *Déjeuner sur l'Herbe* motif was used by Louis Süe and André Mare in their interiors for clients. Zuber is still active today.
Bibliography Jean Zuber, *Réminiscences et souvenirs de Jean Zuber, Père*, Mulhouse: V. Bader, 1895. E.A. Entwistle, *French Scenic Wallpaper 1800–1860*, Leigh-on-Sea: F. Lewis, 1972. Odile Nouvel et al., *Wallpapers of France, 1800–1850*, London: A. Zwemmer, 1981. Patricia Bayer, *Art Deco Interiors*, London: Thames & Hudson, 1990: 51.

Zuccheri, Toni (1936–)
Italian glass designer.

Training To 1960, architecture, Venice.
Biography 1963–84, Zuccheri worked at Venini glassworks in Murano, developing techniques, shapes, and colors; worked with Lucio Fontana, Gaetano Pesce, and Gio Ponti; designed for VeArt (1972 Sextant lamp) and V-Linea from 1971–79, Barovier & Toso from 1982–84, de Majo from 1988–90. Also, from 1996–98, he designed for Cristallerie Imperatore, Sardinia Crystal, and Seguso Viro and developed processes for fusing and mixing metals to and with glass. From 1970, Zuccheri with partner Franco Buzzi Ceriani has been active as an architect; lives/works in San Vito al Tagliamento, Murano, and Milan.
Exhibitions/citations Work shown in the US and Europe and at editions of Biennale di Venezia, from 1964. Campiello prize (for sculpture); 1981 Fenice d'Oro (for the Cinema Exhibition), Venice.
Bibliography Marc Heiremans, *20th-Century Murano Glass*, Stuttgart: Arnoldsche, 1996. www.sanvito.net/tonizuccheri.

Zuid-Holland, Koninklijke Plateelbakkerij
Dutch ceramics factory; located Gouda.

History E. Estié and others founded the firm Weduwe Brantjes Pur-

merend; 1898, Estié established his own company in Gouda in former earthenware factory Het Hert owned by A. Jonker Krjnszoon, with whom Estié became a partner. Both Delft-blue ware and colored pottery in figurative designs were produced there, and some items were decorated with linear floral designs similar to eggshell porcelain by Rozenburg. The limited-edition Gouda pattern may have been designed by W.G.F. Jansen, at the firm 1898–99. 1903, the firm was incorporated as Koninklijke Plateelbakkerij Zuid-Holland. Its utility ware, commissioned by the firm De Woning and known as Duizendjes Motif (a thousand motifs), was designed by C.J. van der Hoef and decorated from 1904 with geometric designs. W.P. Hartgring designed new decorations for the New-P range. As new techniques were introduced, industrial artists were hired to produce new decorations, including Thomas A.C. Colenbrander, at Zuid-Holland from 1912–13, and H.L.A. Breetvelt from 1916–23. Painters executed their motifs. By its 1965 closure, it had become Gouda's largest and best-known ceramics factory.
Bibliography Cat., *Industry and Design in the Netherlands, 1850/1950*, Amsterdam: Stedelijk Museum, 1985.

Zwart, Piet (1885–1977)
Dutch architect and designer; born Zaandijk.

Training 1902–07, architecture and drawing courses, Rijksacademie van Beeldende Kunsten, Amsterdam; 1913–14, Technische Hogeschool, Delft.
Biography 1919, Zwart became acquainted with De Stijl principles through Vilmos Huszár and Jan Wils; 1920–21 with Huszár, collaborated on furniture designs; 1920–22 with Wils and Huszár, collaborated on architecture; from 1921, worked in the architecture firm of H.P. Berlage, becoming chief assistant there in 1925; from 1923, designed publicity for NKF (Dutch cable works); 1923, met El Lissitzky and Kurt Schwitters; designed 1925–26 interiors of restaurant Leo Faust in Paris and some 1922–29 glassware by Leerdam. However, the form of Leerdam's 1924 hexagonal yellow-glass egg set/breakfast plate (elements of which were only partially manufactured due to problems with heat-resistant glass production) was Berlage's idea, adapted by Zwart (and originally for Helene Kröller-Müller). 1927–29, Zwart designed glass by P. Kristalunie in Maastricht; 1927, left Berlage's firm and joined design group Ring Neuer Werbegestalter; 1929, became a high-profile designer for the PPT (Dutch postal, telegraph, and telephone service) and thus is primarily now known for his graphic design for the PPT and for numerous other firms.
Exhibitions/citation Work subject of 1961, 1964, 1973, and 1983, exhibitions in the Netherlands (catalogs below). 1966, elected Honorary Royal Designer for Industry, UK.
Bibliography Cat., Otto Treumann en Wim Crouwel, *Piet Zwart, typotekt*, Amsterdam: Stedelijk Museum, 1961. Cat., *Piet Zwart en PPT*, Gemeentemuseum, The Hague: Kassel, 1964. Herbert Spencer, *Pioneers of Modern Typography*, New York: Hastings House, 1969: 110–21. Cat., Kees Broos, *Piet Zwart*, The Hague: Gemeentemuseum, 1973. 'Piet Zwart,' *Studio International*, Apr. 1973: 176–80. Arthur Allen Cohen, *Piet Zwart, typotekt*, New York: Ex Libris, 1980. Cat., *Piet Zwart en het gezicht van Bruynzeel's potloden industrie*, Rotterdam: Museum Boymans-van Beuningen, 1983.

'Toots' Mary Ann Zynsky. Bowl. 1984. Lead crystal (*filet-de-verre*), 3 3/4 x 10 3/4 x 8 1/4" (9.5 x 27.3 x 21 cm). Mfr.: the designer, US. Emilio Ambasz Fund. MoMA.

Zwerger, Reinhold (1924–)
Austrian industrial designer; born Kirchberg.

Biography Zwerger was a designer at Eumig in Austria, which produced his 1957 C16 16 mm-film camera (developed by Georg Malek), 1974 Mark S O&M film projector, and other models.
Bibliography Günther Feuerstein, *Vienna—Present and Past: Arts and Crafts—Applied Art—Design*, Vienna: Jugend und Volk, 1976.

Zwicky, Stefan (1952–)
Swiss interior and furniture designer; born and active Zürich.

Biography Zwicky worked at Peter D. Bernoulli interior design studio in Zürich and the design studio of Olivetti in Milan; 1983, established his own studio in Zürich. His 1980 Grand Confort, sans Confort—Hommage à Corbu furniture-sculpture (a parody of Le Corbusier's 1927 Grand Confort armchair) featured solid-concrete 'cushions' and a reinforcing-iron-rod frame.
Exhibitions Work included in 1989 *Mobilier Suisse*, Galerie des Brèves du CCI, Centre Georges Pompidou, Paris.
Bibliography Albrecht Bangert and Karl Michael Armer, *80s Style: Designs of the Decade*, New York: Abbeville, 1990: 83, 236.

Zwollo Jr., Frans (1896–)
Dutch silversmith; active Oosterbeek; son of Frans Zwollo Sr.

Training Under his father.
Biography 1931, Zwollo established a workshop in Oosterbeek.
Bibliography Annelies Krekel-Aalberse, *Art Nouveau and Art Déco Silver*, New York: Abrams, 1989.

Zwollo Sr., Frans (1872–1945)
Dutch silversmith; active Amsterdam, The Hague, and Hagen (Germany); father of Frans Zwollo Jr.

Training At Bonebakker, Amsterdam; Delheid, Brussels.
Biography 1897–1907, Zwollo was the first teacher of metalworking, Haarlemsche School voor Kunstnijverheid; 1910–14, was recommended by architect J.L.M. Lauweriks as director, Hagener Silverschmiede, where he intended 'to execute chasing and embossing perfectly after designs by our best artists and in this way to create an institute capable of equaling the Wiener Werkstätte.' However, most of the silver designs created under Zwollo at Hagener Silverschmiede and made by Lauweriks attracted little interest. Karl Ernst Osthaus, who managed the workshop, was unable to obtain commissions despite publicity and exhibitions. 1914, Zwollo returned to the Netherlands, where, to 1932, he taught metalworking at the Akademie voor Beeldende Kunst, The Hague. 1931, Frans Zwollo Jr. (1896–) established his own, separate workshop in Oosterbeek.
Exhibitions Work subject of 1982 *Franz Zwollo en zihn tijd* in Rotterdam, Arnhem, and The Hague (catalog below).
Bibliography Cat., *Franz Zwollo en zijn tijd*, Rotterdam: Museum Boijmans-van Beuningen, 1982: 53. Annelies Krekel-Aalberse, *Art Nouveau and Art Déco Silver*, New York: Abrams, 1989.

Zynsky, 'Toots' Mary Ann (1951–)
American glass designer; born Boston, Mass.; active in Paris, France.

Training Bachelor of fine arts degree, Rhode Island School of Design, Providence, R.I.; under Dale Chihuly, Pilchuck Glass School, Stanwood, Wash.
Biography Mid-1980s, she spent six months in Ghana on a special research project, recording Ghanaian music. In the beginning of her work with glass, she stretched canes by hand but later used a machine especially for the purpose. She arranges the cane-pulled glass threads on a plaster foundation, heats them in a kiln to melt them downward into a mold, and trims the still-hot edges by hand. Her work is colorful and playful. Has taught, Pilchuck Glass School.
Exhibitions From 1973, in a number of one-person and group venues.

Zziggurat
Italian design group.

History 1969, Zziggurat was created, with members including Alberto Breschi, Giuliano Fiorenzuoli, Gigi Gavini, and Roberto Pecchioli; ex-

plored architectural semiotics with its references to myth, history, and the subconscious; organized 1971 *Vita, Morte e Miracoli dell'Architettura* seminar/exhibition, Space Electric, Florence. Its members participated in the 1973 formation of Global Tools.
Exhibition Work included in *Radicals: Architettura e Design 1960–75* at 1996 (6th) Mostra Internazionale di Archittettura, Venice.
Bibliography Andrea Branzi, *La casa calda: esperienze del nuovo disegno italiano*, Milan: Idea, 1982.
> See Global Tools.